The **Rough Guide** to

Europe

ON A BUDGET

this edition written and researched by

Sophie Barling, Tim Burford, Lucy Cowan, Ella Davies, Donald Eastwood, Chris Fitzgerald, Natasha Foges, Hannah Forbes Black, Anya Goldstein, Alex Gladwell, Victoria Hall, Olivia Humphreys, Mike Kielty, Anna Khmelnitski, Sophie Middlemiss, Victoria Noble, Jane Orton, Alex Larman, Emily Paine, Mark Rogers, Mark Rushmore, Rmishka Singh, Kate Tolley, Andy Turner, Kate Turner, Ann-Marie Weaver and Matt Willis

NEW YORK • LONDON • DELHI

www.roughguides.com

INTERNATIONAL
BUDGET YOUTH HOSTEL
HOSTEL
76
THE GALLERY

Contents

Colour section 1

Introduction 6
When to go 8
Ideas 10

Itineraries 17

Basics 27

Getting there 29
Getting around 34
Accommodation 39
The media 41
Festivals and annual events 42
Culture and etiquette 44
Work and study 44
Travel essentials 46

Guide 57

1 Andorra 57
2 Austria 73
3 Belgium & Luxembourg 103
4 Britain 131
5 Bulgaria 217
6 Croatia 243
7 Czech Republic 273
8 Denmark 301
9 Estonia 329
10 Finland 349
11 France 369
12 Germany 453
13 Greece 527
14 Hungary 585
15 Ireland 613
16 Italy 657
17 Latvia 751
18 Lithuania 769
19 Morocco 791
20 The Netherlands 829
21 Norway 857
22 Poland 887
23 Portugal 919
24 Romania 955
25 Russia 979
26 Serbia 1003
27 Slovakia 1021
28 Slovenia 1041
29 Spain 1063
30 Sweden 1149
31 Switzerland and Liechtenstein 1179
32 Turkey 1215

Travel store 1263

Small print & Index 1265

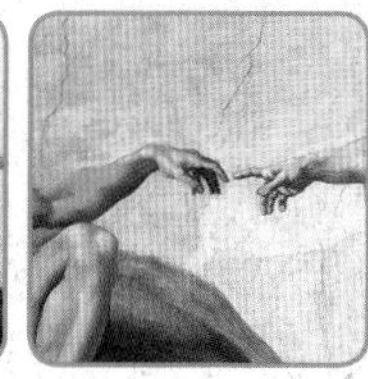

◄◄ ASSISI, ITALY ◄ HOSTEL, AMSTERDAM

0
500 km
Metres
4000
2000
1000
400
200
0
below sea level
Arctic Circle
REYKJAVÍK
ICELAND
Faroes
Shetland
Bergen
ATLANTIC OCEAN
NORTH SEA
Edinburgh
Belfast
IRELAND
DUBLIN
York
UNITED KINGDOM
Cardiff
LONDON
Århus
DENMARK
Hamburg
NETHERLANDS
AMSTERDAM
BRUSSELS
BELGIUM
Cologne
GERMANY
LUX.
Frankfurt
PARIS
LUXEMBOURG
FRANCE
Munich
BERN
Zürich
SWITZERLAND
Bordeaux
Lyon
Milan
Venice
Santiago de Compostela
Bilbao
Porto
PORTUGAL
ANDORRA
Marseille
MONACO
SAN MARINO
Florence
MADRID
LISBON
SPAIN
Barcelona
Corsica (Fr.)
ROME
Valencia
Ibiza
Mallorca
Sardinia
Seville
MEDITERRANEAN
Tangier
Casablanca
RABAT
Fes
ALGIERS
TUNIS
MOROCCO
Essaouira
Marrakesh
ALGERIA
TUNISIA

NORWAY
SWEDEN
FINLAND
OSLO
HELSINKI
St Petersburg
RUSSIA
STOCKHOLM
TALLINN
ESTONIA
BALTIC SEA
Gothenburg
RĪGA
LATVIA
MOSCOW
COPENHAGEN
LITHUANIA
KALININGRAD (RUSSIA)
VILNIUS
MINSK
BELARUS
BERLIN
WARSAW
POLAND
KIEV
PRAGUE
CZECH REPUBLIC
Kraków
UKRAINE
SLOVAKIA
BRATISLAVA
VIENNA
AUSTRIA
BUDAPEST
HUNGARY
MOLDOVA
CHIŞINĂU
ROMANIA
LJUBLJANA
SLOVENIA
ZAGREB
CROATIA
BELGRADE
GEORGIA
BOSNIA-HERZEGOVINA
BUCHAREST
BLACK SEA
T'BILISI
SARAJEVO
SERBIA & MONTENEGRO
BULGARIA
Adriatic Sea
SOFIA
SKOPJE
ALBANIA
MACEDONIA
İstanbul
ITALY
Naples
TIRANA
Thessaloníki
ANKARA
TURKEY
GREECE
Aegean Sea
İzmir
ATHENS
Sicily
SYRIA
SEA
MALTA
Crete
CYPRUS
LEBANON
IRAQ

Introduction to

Europe

Every year thousands of travellers pack their backpacks and set off on a European adventure. It's easy to see why – the "Old World" has an amazingly rich variety of cultures, languages, and classic must-see sights all squeezed into a user-friendly continent. In the same day you can ski down a black run, grab lunch in a sun-drenched piazza, admire world-class art, before winding down at a beachside bar. Add to this hassle-free transport, open borders and a widely used single currency and you have the proverbial travel playground.

FJORD, NORWAY

With some of the highest living costs on earth, "Europe" and "budget travel" may seem a tricky combination. But behind the glossy surface of haute couture, royal palaces and €6 cappuccinos you'll find a **low-cost destination** waiting to be discovered. Europe has the best hostel network on the planet, delicious street food and a huge student population catered for by affordable bars, clubs and restaurants. The key is knowing where to look and we've included budget tips throughout this guide from fishing for your supper in Istanbul to finding a cheap pint in central London.

Where Europe begins and ends is a little hazy and its boundaries with Russia, the Middle East and North Africa have seen plenty of two-way traffic over the centuries. This book covers all the quintessential European **sights** and cities from Paris to Warsaw, Athens to Helsinki as well as destinations as diverse as Moscow and Marrakesh. Off the beaten track, a huge range of **landscapes** open up from Arctic Lapland to the Saharan desert, Atlantic surf beaches to Alpine peaks. In fact, you'll probably find deciding where to go the hardest part of your trip.

For a shot of inspiration, flip to our **Ideas** section where you'll find the best that Europe has to offer, from heavyweight art and architecture to the coolest festivals and activities. We then follow up with **Itineraries** offering the greatest journeys across the region. The **Basics** section will help plan your trip further with all the nitty gritty on hostels and camping to rail passes and a year planner of the best events. And each chapter within the **Guide** itself begins with a country profile covering the key places not to miss and rough costs from dorm beds to bus tickets.

LEANING TOWER, PISA

The new age of the train

As travellers agonize over their carbon footprint and budget flights become a guilty pleasure, the humble **train** is firmly back in the spotlight. High-speed lines and spectacular stations are popping up across Europe and there's never been a better time to travel by rail. Simply looking at an arrivals board whirring its way through destinations can quicken the pulse – Paris, Rome, Warsaw, Moscow and Berlin are just a platform away. What's more, a range of cheap, convenient **rail passes** have long made the train the first choice of the budget traveller. Launched back in 1973, the InterRail pass has proved so popular that the verb "to InterRail" has come to describe the whole experience of backpacking across Europe while its sister Eurail pass for non-Europeans has made this adventure available to all. Both passes can be tailored to your trip, whether you're crossing the entire continent or staying in one country (see p.34 for more).

ST PANCRAS INTERNATIONAL, LONDON

When to go

Europe is a year-round destination and you'll always find somewhere it's the perfect time to visit. In terms of your wallet, travelling in the **off season** (basically October through to May) makes a lot of sense with hotels dropping rates and prices becoming more negotiable. This is especially true of tourist hotspots such as Paris, Rome and Barcelona where during the height of summer you'll find yourself queuing for hours to get into the key sights and struggling to locate a hostel bed.

If you are travelling during the **peak summer months**, try heading east – the Balkan coastline, the Slovenian mountains and Baltic cities are all fantastic places to make the most of your money. As the tourist traffic begins to die down, **autumn** is the ideal time to explore the Mediterranean coastline and islands as well as the cities of Spain and Italy which begin to look their best at this time of year. The European **winter** brings world-class skiing and snowboarding, atmospheric Christmas markets and legendary New Years' parties and there's still the option of blue skies and sun in Morocco and Turkey. While it's no secret that **spring** is the time to hit the French capital, it's also worth heading north to the Netherlands, Scandinavia and the British Isles where you'll find beautifully long days and relatively affordable prices before the summer season kicks in around July.

PARC GÜELL, BARCELONA

You and the EU

After a tricky birth in the aftermath of World War II, the **EU** (European Union) is now reaching maturity. A recent growth spurt has increased the number of member states to 27 and it now stretches from the beaches of Portugal in the west, across the former Iron Curtain, to the shores of the Black Sea in Bulgaria. So what does this self-styled "family of democratic nations" mean to the average traveller? Well, a key part of it is likely to be in your pocket – the **euro** (€) is the currency of fifteen EU countries and the remainder (apart from the notable exceptions of Britain, Denmark and Sweden) are likely to adopt it once their economies are ready. You'll also find your passport gathering dust as there are no internal **border controls** among the countries using the euro (although you should carry ID for random checks), and if you run into trouble dial ☎**112** – the universal EU emergency number. If you're lucky enough to hold an EU passport, the continent really begins to open up: you can work, study, shop, receive free healthcare and even take your pet wherever you like across the member states.

While **weather extremes** are not the issue they are in say, Asia or Africa, you should still bear them in mind when planning your trip. The Arctic winter experienced in Scandinavia and Russia can bring temperatures as low as -35°C (-31°F) while the sun barely rises above the horizon for months. In these regions you'll find opening times are severely restricted and even road and rail lines closed outside of May to September. At the opposite end of the scale, the central and eastern continental regions of Europe often have swelteringly hot summers while recent heat waves have seen even London sweating it out at 38°C (100°F).

Ideas Art and culture

THE MONA LISA, THE LOUVRE Follow the Da Vinci trail to the world's most famous painting. **See p.377**

SISTINE CHAPEL, THE VATICAN Michelangelo's magnum opus is worth craning your neck for. **See p.672**

THE PARTHENON, ATHENS A key image of Western Civilization and the blueprint for grand civic buildings the world over. **See p.538**

THE HERMITAGE, ST PETERSBURG Catch a glimpse of Russia's imperial past at this fabulously rich collection of art. **See p.997**

AYA SOFYA, ISTANBUL Christianity and Islam meet at this sixth century architectural marvel. **See p.1223**

SHAKESPEARE'S GLOBE THEATRE, LONDON See a Shakespeare play the way it was meant to be seen at this recreation of an Elizabethan theatre. **See p.143**

MUSEO GUGGENHEIM, BILBAO An American import perhaps but you can't deny this is Europe's most spectacular museum. **See p.1093**

OLD TOWN, KRAKÓW Soak up the atmosphere at this beautifully preserved medieval old town. **See p.906**

Ideas Outdoor activities

TAKING A SAUNA, FINLAND A traditional cure for weeks spent in hostels and trains – finish up with a bone-chilling plunge if you're brave enough. **See p.365**

HIKING THE TATRA MOUNTAINS, POLAND The gradiose Tatras range offer world-class hiking in summer and some of Europe's best-value skiing in winter. **See p.913**

ISLAND-HOPPING, GREECE Sail your way across the Aegean aboard a yacht or traditional *kaïkia*. **See p.558**

HOT AIR BALLOONING CAPPADOCIA, TURKEY Cruise over these bizarre rock formations from the best vantage point possible. **See p.1259**

SURFING, PORTUGAL Join the surf bums riding the Atlantic breakers off Portugal's coast. **See p.949**

SKIING AND SNOW-BOARDING, CHAMONIX, FRANCE The valleys around Mt Blanc offer the gnarliest and liveliest skiing and boarding on the continent. **See p.437**

WHITE-WATER RAFTING, SLOVENIA Slovenia is a magnet for adrenaline junkies and its foaming mountain rivers are perfect for rafting and kayaking. **See p.1057**

RIDING THE GREAT PLAIN, HUNGARY Experience the big skies and wild expanse of Hungary's Great Plain on horseback. **See p.609**

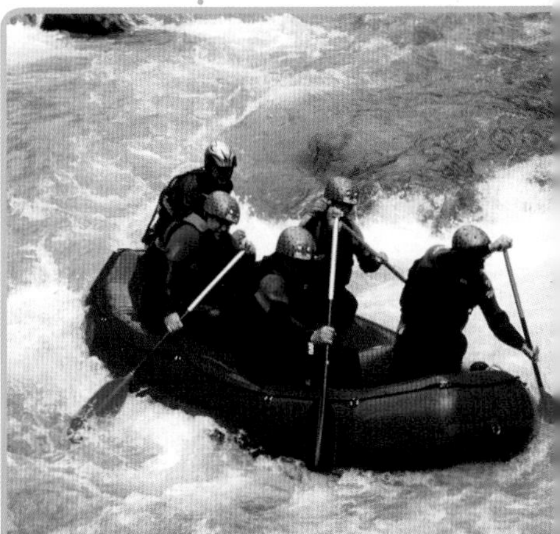

Ideas Festivals and events

SUMMER IN IBIZA, SPAIN The white island offers hard-core clubbing, mega *discotecas* and plenty of beaches on which to sleep it all off. **See p.1120**

ST PATRICK'S DAY, IRELAND Ireland's national holiday is the time to dress up and drink up especially on the home turf of Dublin. **See p.42**

CARNIVAL, VENICE Venetians let their hair down with ten days of masks, costumes and frenetic partying in the run-up to Lent. **See p.702**

OKTOBERFEST, MUNICH Two weeks of unadulterated beer guzzling at the world's largest public festival. **See p.522**

EXIT FESTIVAL, SERBIA A beautiful fortress setting, a thumping sound system and top-name acts – what's not to like? **See p.1017**

FIESTA DE SAN FERMÍN, SPAIN Try your luck outrunning a bovine freight train or just stand back and enjoy the fun at this week-long Pamplona Fiesta. **See p.1103**

LOVE PARADE, GERMANY Berlin's free love and techno fest is Europe's wildest festival and now on tour across Germany. **See p.43**

GLASTONBURY FESTIVAL, ENGLAND "Glasto" is the one music festival where it doesn't matter who's playing, you'll have a great time anyway. **See p.165**

Ultimate experiences

Our team of intrepid travel writers scoured the continent for the best places to eat, sleep and party on a budget. Here they pick out the highlight of their trip.

ANN-MARIE, TURKEY
Paragliding, Kas. See p.1248

ALEX, BRITAIN
Edinburgh festival. See p.198

ANNA, BALTIC STATES
Cycling the Curonian Spit, Lithuania. See p.788

SOPHIE, IRELAND
A night out in rural Galway. See p.639

DONALD, FRANCE
The CAPC musée, Bordeaux. See p.410

ANYA, GERMANY
Brunch in Berlin's Prenzlauer Berg. See p.469

CHRIS, MORROCO
Haggling in Marrakesh. See p.824

ELLA, AUSTRIA & SWITZERLAND
Hiking the Jungfrau. See p.1199

KATE, PORTUGAL
The Quinta da Regaleira, Sintra. See p.935

EMILY, ITALY
A walk between the Cinque Terre. See p.690

SOPHIE, RUSSIA
Twilight in St Petersburg. See p.995

KATE, GREECE
Clubbing on Íos. See p.563

NATASHA, ITALY
Pizza in Naples. See p.734

RMISHKA, CROATIA & HUNGARY
Motovun Film Festival. See p.257

MIKE, POLAND
Malbork Castle. See p.905

VICTORIA, SPAIN
Lazing in Retiro Park, Madrid. See p.1075

MARK, SERBIA & SLOVENIA
Rafting the Soca Valley. See p.1057

ITINERARIES

ITINERARIES

Britain and Ireland ... 19
France and the low countries ... 20
Germany and central Europe ... 20
Spain, Portugal and Morocco ... 21
Italy, Greece and Turkey ... 22
Eastern Europe ... 23
Scandinavia ... 23
Russia and the Baltic States ... 24
The Grand Tour ... 25

Europe itineraries

You can't expect to fit everything Europe has to offer into one trip and we don't suggest you try. On the following pages are a selection of itineraries that guide you through the different regions of the continent, taking you from Moorish palaces in Spain to Santa's village in the Arctic Circle. We've also included our own Grand Tour for those wanting to see the highlights on a tighter schedule. Each itinerary could be done in two to three weeks if followed to the letter but don't knock yourself out – with so much to see and do you're going to get waylaid somewhere you love or head off the suggested route.

BRITAIN AND IRELAND

❶ **LONDON** One of the world's greatest cities, London requires lots of energy and even more money but for culture, nightlife and history there are few places to match it. **See p.138**

❷ **CAMBRIDGE** The famous university town offers the chance to punt along the river, admire the university architecture or down a few in a student pub. **See p.174**

❸ **YORK** From a Viking museum and medieval streets to a Gothic minster and national rail collection, if you want to soak up some British history, York is the place to do it. **See p.184**

❹ **EDINBURGH** With its stunning cityscape, lively bars and – if you time it right – international festival, the Scottish capital has something for everyone. **See p.198**

❺ **THE HIGHLANDS** For getting away from it all, Britain's most remote region and highest mountains are the perfect destination for some R and R. **See p.214**

❻ **THE LAKE DISTRICT** With its millions of visitors don't expect to wander lonely as a cloud, but this area of lakes and mountains is still a captivating spot. **See p.181**

❼ **CAERNARFON CASTLE** Of all North Wales's splendid castles, this is the most impressive. **See p.197**

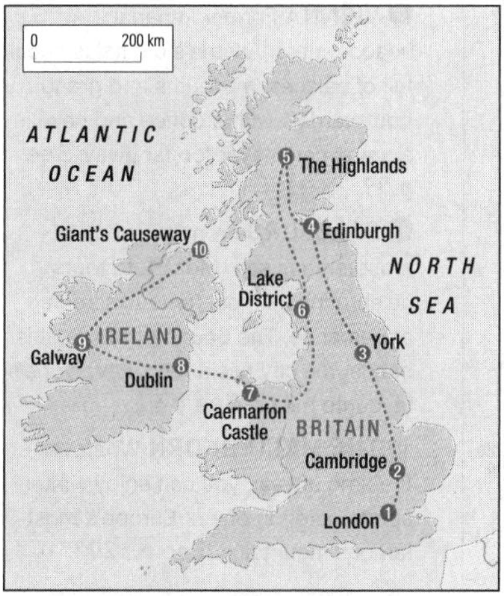

❽ **DUBLIN** Convivial pubs, the best Guinness, Georgian architecture and a fascinating literary heritage make Ireland's capital a great introduction to the country. **See p.620**

❾ **GALWAY** If you're looking for the legendary Irish craic, head for this West Coast town with its festivals, live music and friendly atmosphere. **See p.639**

❿ **THE GIANT'S CAUSEWAY** Long one of Ireland's top attractions, this geological wonder still amazes – 37,000 polygonal basalt columns can't be wrong. **See p.651**

FRANCE AND THE LOW COUNTRIES

1 **AMSTERDAM** Whether you're looking for culture, cannabis, clubs or cuisine, the Netherlands' largest city has it all. **See p.835**

2 **BRUGES** It may be busy and touristy but this gem of Flemish architecture is still worth a visit for its atmospheric canals and beautiful buildings. **See p.123**

3 **PARIS** Laze over a coffee in a Left Bank café, arrange a romantic rendezvous with your new Gallic friend or tick off the many museums in Europe's most enticing capital. **See p.376**

4 **THE LOIRE VALLEY** Bucolic valley that's filled with some of the most impressive chateaux you'll see in the country. **See p.397**

5 **BORDEAUX** Elegant bustling city and world-famous wine-growing region combine to make this a great destination. **See p.409**

6 **THE PYRENEES** Clear your head after all that wine with the fresh air and fine walks of this mountain range bordering Spain. **See p.414**

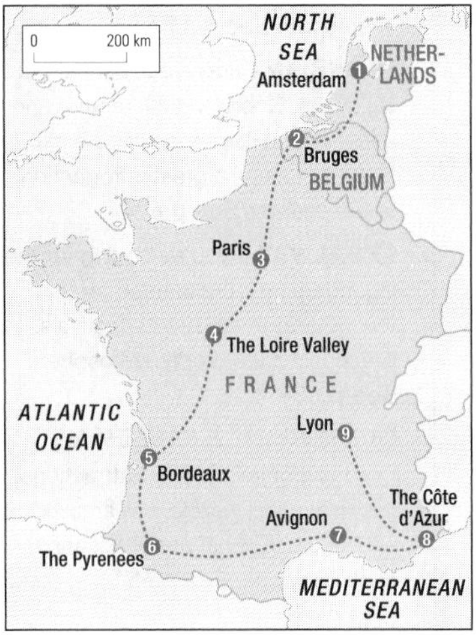

7 **AVIGNON** A former papal residence with a suitably impressive legacy of buildings and monuments, Avignon also draws the crowds with its July drama festival. **See p.431**

8 **THE CÔTE D'AZUR** Nice, Cannes, St Tropez, Monaco – the names alone ooze glamour so get your glad rags on and show the world your fabulous side. **See p.438**

9 **LYON** If the Côte d'Azur hasn't broken the bank, then there's no better city in which to indulge your passion for French cuisine than here in the country's gastronomic capital. **See p.428**

GERMANY AND CENTRAL EUROPE

1 **BERLIN** Warfare, destruction, division and reunification have shaped this fascinating city, while the modern architecture and frantic nightlife give it an über contemporary feel. **See p.461**

2 **DRESDEN** Utterly destroyed in World War II, this Baroque city was carefully rebuilt and is once again Germany's most attractive. **See p.477**

3 **PRAGUE** Whether it's beautiful architecture, great eating and drinking, or buzzing nightlife you're after, Prague has it all. **See p.280**

4 **VIENNA** Former imperial headquarters, Austria's capital is chock full of palaces, museums and grand boulevards – with a coffee and cake in a grand café never too far away. **See p.79**

5 **SALZBURG** From music by its most famous son, Mozart, to tours celebrating its most famous screen appearance, The Sound of Music, this handsome city has a few of everyone's favourite things. **See p.92**

6 **THE MATTERHORN** Whatever the time of year, you can enjoy winter sports here, on one of Europe's most famous mountains. **See p.1203**

❼ **ZÜRICH** Archetypal clean and efficient Swiss city worth a detour thanks to its delightful old town, wonderful lake setting and great café culture. **See p.1205**

❽ **MUNICH** Oktoberfest (actually in late September) or not, the Bavarian capital has a lively nightlife scene and enough parks, museums and churches to occupy you till it's time for the next beer. **See p.518**

❾ **THE RHINE GORGE** Taking a cruise on this stretch of Germany's best-known river allows you to see the region's beautiful countryside and clifftop castles. **See p.498**

SPAIN, PORTUGAL AND MOROCCO

❶ **BARCELONA** Innovative architecture, city beaches, late-night bars and atmospheric old town – the Catalan capital has more than enough to have you staying longer than you planned. **See p.1109**

❷ **MADRID** Some of Europe's best museums to fill your days, some of Europe's best bars and clubs to fill your nights. If you're eating before 9pm, dancing before midnight and asleep before dawn, you haven't experienced a truly Madrileño evening. **See p.1070**

❸ **LISBON** Portugal's immediately likeable capital has a great setting, delicious food and a huge amount of historic interest. **See p.926**

❹ **THE ALGARVE** Southern Portugal's beaches, especially on Ilha de Tavira, are second to none – and the nightlife isn't bad either. **See p.947**

❺ **SEVILLE** Learn to flamenco, knock back some fine wine or get lost in the Jewish Quarter – for many, Seville encapsulates Spain. **See p.1137**

❻ **GRANADA** For a taster of what's to come in Morocco, take a detour to

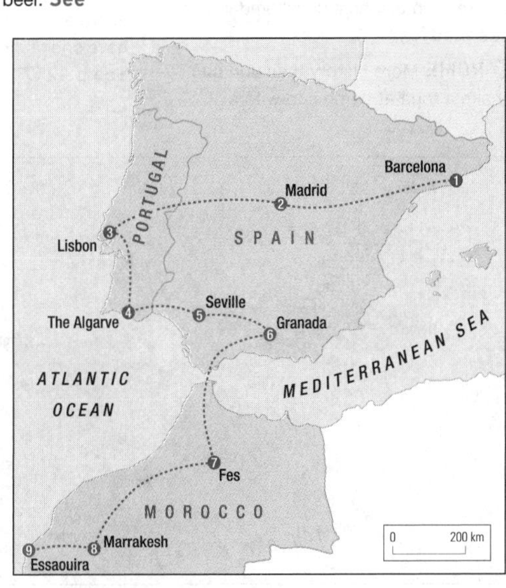

Granada and its beautiful Alhambra Palace, an extraordinary reminder of Moorish architectural skill. See p.1130

❼ **FES** Once across the Straits of Gibraltar, dive head first into Morocco with a stay in this medieval city of labyrinthine alleys, souks and mosques. See p.808

❽ **MARRAKESH** Stunning, atmospheric city with the Atlas Mountains as a backdrop and the live circus that is the Djemaa el Fna square at its heart. See p.820

❾ **ESSAOUIRA** Lovely seaside and surfing resort that was once a hippie favourite and still retains a laid-back, arty feel. See p.825

ITALY, GREECE AND TURKEY

❶ **VENICE** Packed with visitors throughout the year, this unique, stunning city still has plenty of quieter corners where you can enjoy the beauty all by yourself. See p.694

❷ **FLORENCE** Birthplace of the Renaissance and a beautiful city in its own right, Florence's artistic treasures will inspire even the most uncultured visitor. See p.707

❸ **ROME** More history than you can shake a toga at combined with a modern vibe make the Italian capital unmissable. See p.665

❹ **NAPLES** The home of pizza – and best place to eat it – Naples is also a frenetic, crumblingly attractive city, while for actual ruins nearby Pompeii gives you an insight into how the ancient Romans used to live. See p.730

❺ **ATHENS** Crowded, noisy and polluted the Greek capital may be, but its influence on Western culture and the buildings that provide tangible evidence of its former greatness are worth a few days of anyone's time. See p.535

❻ **THE GREEK ISLANDS** You say Cyclades, I say Dodecanese. Whatever your persuasion, island-hopping Greek style allows you to sunbathe, dine and party on a different island each day. See p.558

❼ **EPHESUS** Turkey's best-preserved archeological site is a treasure trove of ruined temples, public toilets, mosaics and baths. See p.1243

❽ **CAPPADOCIA** A long trip east through Anatolia but Cappadocia's rock-hewn buildings and volcanic landscape have an irresistible allure – and if you can afford a balloon trip over the area, you'll have one of the highlights of your trip. See p.1257

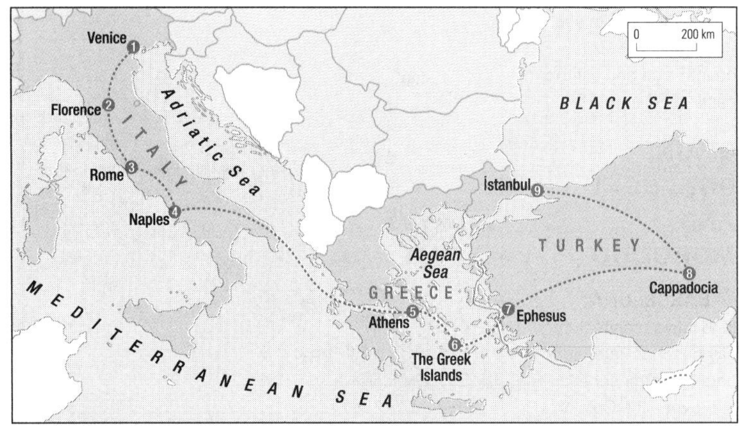

❾ **İSTANBUL** Gaze in awe at the Blue Mosque, shop your way through the covered bazaar and reward your sightseeing endeavours with a genuine Turkish bath. **See p.1223**

EASTERN EUROPE

❶ **WARSAW** Don't be put off by the mishmash of architecture, the Polish capital has a reconstructed old town, beautiful parks and a energetic bar, club and restaurant scene. **See p.894**

❷ **KRAKÓW** You won't be the only one enjoying this historic city's sights but it's still a must-visit place. **See p.906**

❸ **BUDAPEST** Visit the museums and admire the views from hilly Buda, then cross the not-so-blue Danube for the restaurants and nightspots of Pest. **See p.592**

❹ **TRANSYLVANIA** You probably won't see any vampires but the mountain-hiking and quaint villages in this corner of Romania easily reward a visit. **See p.970**

❺ **RILA** South of Sofia lies Bulgaria's biggest and most revered monastery, known for its wonderful architecture and fine mountain setting. **See p.230**

❻ **BELGRADE** Not the most obvious of destinations, but the Serbian capital is fast attracting a hip crowd thanks to its cool nightlife. **See p.1010**

❼ **DUBROVNIK** Dramatic views and a well-preserved medieval centre make this Adriatic port a highly recommended stop on any trip. **See p.268**

❽ **LJUBLJANA** Small but perfectly formed, Slovenia's capital is a thoroughly enjoyable, easily manageable city in which to unwind. **See p.1047**

SCANDINAVIA

❶ **COPENHAGEN** Relatively inexpensive by Scandinavian standards, and highly user-friendly, the Danish capital is a lively, welcoming introduction to the region. **See p.308**

❷ **OSLO** Uncrowded city, close to equally uncrowded woodland and beaches, make Oslo a hugely enjoyable capital in which to stay. **See p.864**

❸ **THE FJORDS** No trip to Norway would be complete without a visit to the country's western coastline and its magnificent fjords. **See p.874**

❹ **LOFOTEN ISLANDS** Try your hand at fishing, gawp at the awe-inspiring mountain scenery, or simply relax in the friendly villages. **See p.883**

❺ **JOKKMOKK** Enjoy the extremely long summer nights, local Sámi culture and traditional handicrafts in this Arctic Circle town. **See p.1175**

❻ **STOCKHOLM** The handsome island setting of Sweden's capital complements the wealth of museums and nightlife on offer. **See p.1156**

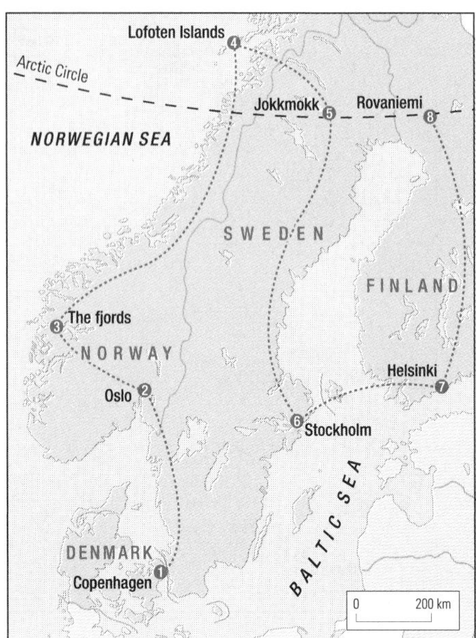

❷ **ST PETERSBURG** In a wonderful location, with jaw-dropping architecture and priceless art collections, Russia's second city is at its best during the midsummer White Nights festival. **See p.994**

❸ **TALLINN** From obscure Soviet backwater to booming party town, it's been a long time since Estonia's capital has had it so good. **See p.335**

❹ **RĪGA** The Baltic States' one true metropolis, Latvia's capital is full of architectural treasures and is the gateway to some wonderful coastal scenery. **See p.757**

❺ **VILNIUS** Most beautiful of the Baltic capitals, cosmopolitan and atmospheric Vilnius's largely undiscovered status means you can get a break from the crowds. **See p.775**

❻ **CURONIAN SPIT** This narrow strip of land consisting of mountainous sand dunes is the place to get your hiking boots on and strike out on the numerous walking trails. **See p.781**

❼ **HELSINKI** Distinctly Russian in atmosphere, Helsinki has a grand feel to it, tempered by the locals' enthusiasm in summer for outdoor eating, drinking and concerts. **See p.356**

❽ **ROVANIEMI** Back to the Arctic Circle, but this time for traditions of a very different kind – namely a visit to Santa Claus Village and the chance to prove you've been good. **See p.366**

RUSSIA AND THE BALTIC STATES

❶ **MOSCOW** From Red Square and the Kremlin to the Stalinist skyscrapers of the 1950s, the Russian capital is chaotic, beautiful in parts and always fascinating. **See p.987**

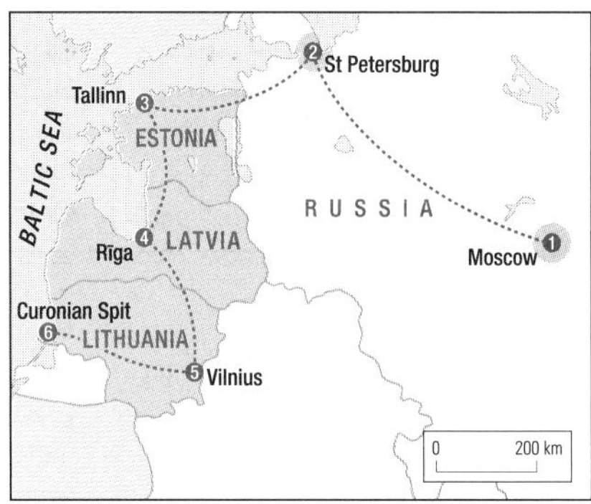

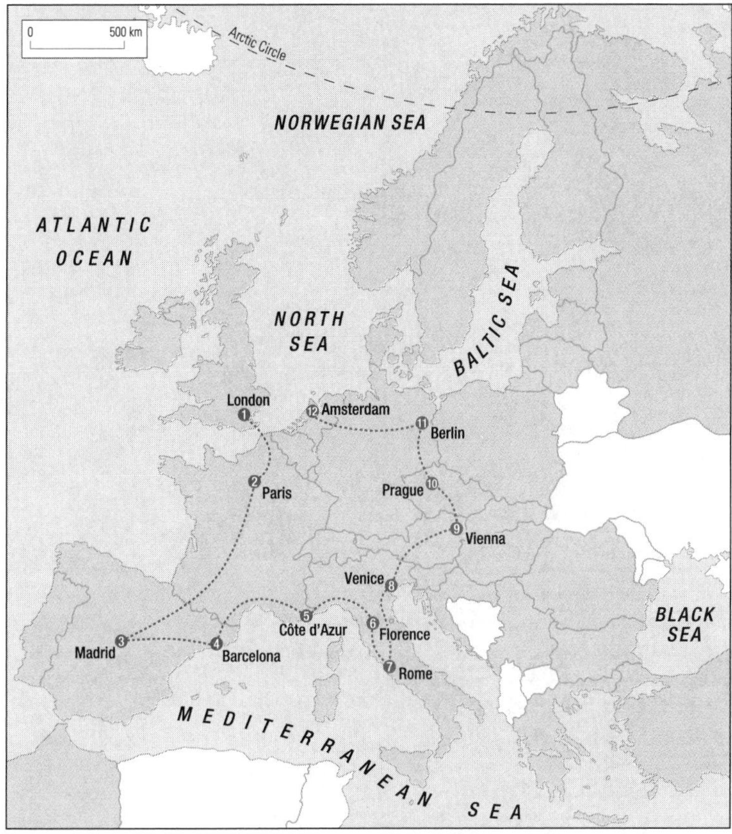

THE GRAND TOUR

Follow in the footsteps of the nineteenth-century Grand Tourists with this classic itinerary. For more information on all these see the relevant separate itinerary.

❶ **LONDON** p.138

❷ **PARIS** p.376

❸ **MADRID** p.1070

❹ **BARCELONA** p.1109

❺ **THE CÔTE D'AZUR** p.438

❻ **FLORENCE** See p.707

❼ **ROME** See p.665

❽ **VENICE** See p.694

❾ **VIENNA** See p.79

❿ **PRAGUE** See p.280

⓫ **BERLIN** See p.461

⓬ **AMSTERDAM** See p.835

BASICS

Basics

Getting there ... 29
Getting around ... 34
Accommodation ... 39
The media ... 41
Festivals and annual events ... 42
Culture and etiquette ... 44
Work and study ... 44
Travel essentials ... 46

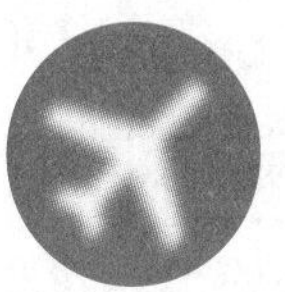

Getting there

Airfares always depend on the season with the highest being roughly mid-June to early September and over the Christmas period. Note also that flying on weekends sometimes adds quite a bit to the round-trip fare; price ranges quoted below assume midweek travel.

Barring special offers, the cheapest of the **airlines' published fares** usually require advance purchase of two to three weeks, and impose certain restrictions, such as heavy penalties if you change your schedule. Many airlines offer youth or student fares to **under-26s**; a passport or driving licence is sufficient proof of age, though these tickets are subject to availability and can have eccentric booking conditions. Most cheap return fares will only give a percentage refund, if any, should you need to cancel or alter your journey, so check the restrictions carefully before buying.

You can often cut costs by going through a **discount agent**, who in addition to dealing with discounted flights may also offer special student and youth fares and a range of other travel-related services such as travel insurance, rail passes and tours.

If Europe is only one stop on a longer journey, and especially if you are based in Australia or New Zealand, you might want to consider buying a **Round-the-World (RTW) ticket**. Figure on US$1500–2000/Aus$2500 for a RTW ticket including one or two European stopovers.

FROM THE US AND CANADA

From the **US** the best deals are generally out of New York and Chicago to London. Fixed-date advance-purchase tickets for midweek travel to London cost around US$500 in low season (roughly speaking, winter), US$700 in high season (summer, Christmas and Easter) from New York, US$550/800 from Chicago. A more flexible ticket will set you back around US$1600 out of New York, US$1750 out of Chicago. Fixed-date advance-purchase alternatives include New York to Paris for US$500/900, US$400/900 to Frankfurt, US$450/900 to Madrid, or US$600/1100 to Athens; flying from Chicago, discounted tickets can be had at US$500/1000 to Paris, US$500/1000 to Frankfurt, US$600/1000 to Madrid, or US$700/1150 to Athens. There are promotional offers from time to time, especially in the off-peak seasons; Virgin Atlantic, for example, sometimes has very cheap New York–London fares in late winter with no advance purchase necessary. It's worth noting that budget airline Zoom (Ⓦwww.flyzoom.com) has recently started flying from New York JFK and Bermuda to Paris, London and other UK destinations at greatly reduced prices.

From the **west coast** the major airlines fly at least three times a week (sometimes daily) from Los Angeles, San Francisco and Seattle to the main European cities, with flexible economy-class tickets from LA to London at around US$2300. If you don't mind buying your tickets a couple of weeks in advance and having fixed dates, you can get to London for US$550/900 (low/high season), to Paris for US$650/1000, to Frankfurt for US$600/1000, to Madrid for US$650/1100, or to Athens for US$700/1300.

From Canada

Most of the big airlines fly to the major European hubs from **Montreal** and **Toronto** at least once daily (three times a week for smaller airlines). From Toronto, London is your cheapest option, with the lowest direct round-trip fare around Can$650/870. For a flexible economy-class ticket on the same

FLY LESS – STAY LONGER! TRAVEL AND CLIMATE CHANGE

Climate change is the single biggest issue facing our planet. It is caused by a build-up in the atmosphere of carbon dioxide and other greenhouse gases, which are emitted by many sources – including planes. Already, flights account for around 3–4% of human-induced global warming: that figure may sound small, but it is rising year on year and threatens to counteract the progress made by reducing greenhouse emissions in other areas.

Rough Guides regard travel, overall, as a global benefit, and feel strongly that the advantages to developing economies are important, as are the opportunities for greater contact and awareness among peoples. But we all have a responsibility to limit our personal "carbon footprint". That means giving thought to how often we fly and what we can do to redress the harm that our trips create.

Flying and climate change

Pretty much every form of motorized travel generates CO_2, but planes are particularly bad offenders, releasing large volumes of greenhouse gases at altitudes where their impact is far more harmful. Flying also allows us to travel much further than we would contemplate doing by road or rail, so the emissions attributable to each passenger are greater. For example, one person taking a return flight between Europe and California produces the equivalent impact of 2.5 tonnes of CO_2 – similar to the yearly output of the average UK car.

Less harmful planes may evolve but it will be decades before they replace the current fleet – which could be too late for avoiding climate chaos. In the meantime, there are limited options for concerned travellers: to reduce the amount we travel by air (take fewer trips, stay longer!), to avoid night flights (when plane contrails trap heat from Earth but can't reflect sunlight back to space), and to make the trips we do take "climate neutral" via a carbon-offset scheme.

Carbon-offset schemes

Offset schemes run by **climatecare.org**, **carbonneutral.com** and others allow you to "neutralize" the greenhouse gases that you are responsible for releasing. Their websites have simple calculators that let you work out the impact of any flight. Once that's done, you can pay to fund projects that will reduce future carbon emissions by an equivalent amount (such the distribution of low-energy lightbulbs and cooking stoves in developing countries). Please take the time to visit our website and make your trip climate neutral.

www.roughguides.com/climatechange

route, you're looking at around Can$3300. Fares from Montreal to Paris start at Can$900/1080. Vancouver has daily flights to several European cities, with round-trip fares to London from around Can$780/1115, depending on the season. Canadian budget airline Zoom (Ⓦwww.flyzoom.com) has recently started flying from several airports in Canada to Paris, London and other UK destinations at greatly reduced prices.

FROM THE UK

Heading **from Britain** to destinations in northwestern Europe, it's best value to go by train, long-distance bus and ferry. However the further you go the less expensive air travel becomes, and it's normally cheaper to fly than take the train to most parts of southern Europe.

By plane

London is predictably Britain's main hub for air travel, offering the highest frequency of flights and widest choice of destinations from its five airports (Heathrow, Gatwick, Stansted, Luton and City). **Manchester** also has flights to most parts of Europe, and there are also regular services to the Continent from Birmingham, Bristol, Cardiff, Glasgow, Edinburgh, Leeds/Bradford and Newcastle.

Budget airlines such as easyJet, bmibaby

and Ryanair (see Getting around, p.38 for a full list) offer low-cost tickets to airports around Europe (though not always the most convenient ones), and they often have some seriously cheap special offers in winter. They also have by far the least expensive flights if you only want to go one-way, as they charge for each leg of the journey separately. It's also worth checking with flight agents who specialize in low-cost, discounted flights (charter and scheduled), some of them – like STA Travel or Trailfinders – concentrating on deals for young people and students. In addition, there are agents specializing in offers to a specific country or group of countries on both charters and regular scheduled departures.

To give a rough idea of **prices** booked through agents on midweek return scheduled flights in high season reckon on paying £75–120 to Paris, Brussels or Amsterdam; £85–150 to Scandinavia; £70–150 to the major cities of Spain or Italy; £170–250 to Athens; £135–250 to Istanbul; or £80–250 to the major cities of eastern Europe.

By train

Direct **trains** through the Channel Tunnel from London to Paris (15 daily, 2hr 15min) and Brussels (9 daily, 1hr 51min) are operated by **Eurostar**. Tickets for under-26s start at £40 one-way, £59 return. For over-26s, the cheapest return ticket, at £59, costs less than a single fare, which is £154.50 – in theory, the cheaper ticket involves a "compulsory return". Through-ticket combinations with onward connections from Brussels and Paris can be booked through Trainseurope, International Rail and Rail Europe.

Other rail journeys from Britain involve some kind of **sea crossing**, by ferry or, sometimes, catamaran. Tickets can be bought from International Rail, and from some major rail stations (in London, at Charing Cross if routed via France or Belgium, or at Liverpool Street or from Ⓦwww.amsterdamexpress.co.uk if routed via the Hook of Holland). For some destinations, there are cheaper Super-Apex fares requiring advance booking and subject to greater restrictions. Otherwise, international tickets are valid for two months and allow for stopovers on the way, providing you stick to the prescribed route (there may be a choice, with different fares applicable). One-way fares are generally around two-thirds the price of a return fare. If you're **under 26** you're entitled to all sorts of special deals, not least cut-price youth fares.

For **rail passes**, contacts and other types of discounted rail travel, see "Getting around", p.34.

By bus

A long-distance **bus**, although much less comfortable than the train, is at least a little cheaper. The main operator is **Eurolines** (Ⓦwww.eurolines.co.uk), which has a network of routes spanning the continent. **Prices** can be up to a third less than the equivalent train fare, and there are marginally cheaper fares on most services for those under 26, which undercut youth rail rates for the same journey. As an example, current Eurolines fares from London's Victoria Coach Station to Paris or Amsterdam start at £25 for a one-way ticket booked four days in advance or a return booked fifteen days in advance (with special offer £17 one-way fares on some services). There's usually a discount of £4–10 if you buy your ticket at least four days in advance, and bigger discounts for return journeys booked two weeks or a month in advance. Connecting services from elsewhere in Great Britain add around £15–20 each way to the price of the ticket.

Eurolines also has **Minipass** return tickets from London to two or more European cities, valid for ninety days. Alternatively, you might consider Eurolines' fifteen-, thirty- and forty-day passes, or one of the various passes offered by **Busabout** for their services around the continent (see "Getting around", p.38)

By ferry

There are numerous **ferry services** between Britain and Ireland, and between the British Isles and the European mainland. Ferries from the southeast of Ireland and the south coast of England connect with northern France and Spain; those from Kent in southeast England reach northern France and Belgium; those from Scotland and the east coast and northeast of England cross the North Sea to Belgium, the Netherlands, Germany and Scandinavia.

Ferry operators

Brittany Ferries ⓣ0870/243 5140, ⓦwww.brittanyferries.co.uk. Portsmouth to Caen, Cherbourg and St Malo; Poole to Cherbourg; Plymouth to Roscoff and Santander.
Condor Ferries ⓣ0845/641 0240, ⓦwww.condorferries.co.uk. Poole to Cherbourg; Portsmouth, Poole, and Weymouth to St Malo via Jersey and Guernsey.
DFDS Seaways ⓣ0870/533 3111, ⓦwww.dfdsseaways.co.uk. Harwich to Cuxhaven (Germany), Esbjerg (Denmark); Newcastle to Amsterdam, and seasonally to Gothenburg (Sweden) and Kristiansand (Norway).
Fjord Line ⓣ 0870/143 9669, ⓦwww.fjordline.co.uk. Newcastle to Stavanger, Haugesund and Bergen.
Norfolk Line ⓣ0870/870 1020, ⓦwww.norfolkline.com. Dover to Dunkerque.
P&O Ferries ⓣ0870/520 2020, ⓦwww.poferries.com. Hull to Zeebrugge and Rotterdam; Dover to Calais; Portsmouth to Bilbao and Le Havre.
SeaFrance ⓣ0870/571 1711, ⓦwww.seafrance.com. Dover to Calais.
Smyril Line ⓣ01595/690 845, ⓦwww.smyril-line.com. Lerwick (Shetland) to Bergen, with connecting P&O Scottish service from Aberdeen.
Superfast Ferries ⓣ**0870/234 0870**, ⓦwww.superfast.com. Rosyth (near Edinburgh) to Zeebrugge (Belgium).
Stena Line ⓣ0870/400 6798, ⓦwww.stenaline.co.uk. Harwich to Hook of Holland.
Transmanche Ferries ⓣ0800/917 1201, ⓦwww.transmancheferries.com. Newhaven to Dieppe.

FROM IRELAND

There are direct flights **from Dublin** to most major cities in mainland Europe, and connections from those or from London to practically any airport you want to fly to. There are also direct flights to the Continent **from Shannon** and **from Cork**. **Bus or train/ferry** combination tickets provide a slower though slightly less expensive alternative.

By plane

No-frills airlines, such as Ryanair, are usually the cheapest, especially in winter, and especially if you only want a one-way journey. You may save a little money travelling by land, sea or even air to London and buying your flight there, but the difference isn't much, and if you're going to London by surface routes, you may as well carry on that way into Europe. **From Belfast**, there are direct flights with easyJet to Amsterdam, Paris, Nice, Malaga and Alicante. For other destinations, you'll have to change at one of those, or at London (served by easyJet, BMI, BA and Flybe) or Manchester (served by BA and bmibaby).

By bus and train

From Ireland, direct **rail** tickets to Europe via Britain generally include both boat connections, and are available from Iarnród Éireann's Continental Rail Desk in the Republic, or Northern Ireland Railways in the North, with discounted under-26 tickets available from these and from USIT. Eurolines **bus services** connect in London for onward travel to the Continent.

Bus and train contacts

Eurolines ⓣ01/836 6111, ⓦwww.eurolines.ie.
Iarnród Éireann ⓣ01/703 1885, ⓦwww.irishrail.ie.
Northern Ireland Railways ⓣ028/9066 6630, ⓦwww.translink.co.uk.

Ferry operators

Brittany Ferries ⓣ021/427 7801, ⓦwww.brittanyferries.ie. Cork to Roscoff (March–early Nov).
Irish Ferries Republic ⓣ0818/300 400, UK ⓣ0870/517 1717, ⓦwww.irishferries.com. Dublin to Holyhead; Rosslare to Pembroke, Cherbourg (March–Dec) and Roscoff (March–Dec).
Norfolk Line Republic ⓣ01/819 2999, UK ⓣ0870/600 4321, ⓦwww.norfolkline-ferries.co.uk. Belfast and Dublin to Birkenhead.
P&O Irish Sea Republic ⓣ1800/409 049, UK ⓣ0870/242 4777, ⓦwww.poirishsea.com. Larne to Cairnryan and Troon (March–Sept); Dublin to Liverpool.
Stena Line Republic ⓣ01/204 7777, ⓦwww.stenaline.ie, UK ⓣ028/9074 7747, ⓦwww.stenaline.co.uk. Rosslare to Fishguard; Dun Laoghaire and Dublin to Holyhead; Belfast to Stranraer; Larne to Fleetwood.
Swansea–Cork Ferries Republic ⓣ021/427 1166, UK ⓣ01792/456116, ⓦwww.swansea-cork.ie. Cork to Swansea (March–early Jan).

FROM AUSTRALIA AND NEW ZEALAND

There are **flights** from Melbourne, Sydney, Adelaide, Brisbane and Perth to most European capitals, and there's not a great deal of difference in the fares to the busiest destinations: a scheduled return from Sydney to London, Paris, Rome, Madrid, Athens or Frankfurt should be available through travel agents for around A$1900 in low season (Australia's summer, Europe's winter). A one-way ticket costs slightly more than half that, while a return flight from Auckland to Europe is approximately NZ$2000 in low season. Asian airlines often work out cheapest, and may throw in a stopover, while there are often bargain deals to be had from Melbourne to Athens on Olympic Airways. Some agents may also offer "open jaw" tickets, flying you into one city and out from another, not necessarily even in the same country. For RTW deals and other **low-price tickets**, the most reliable operator is STA Travel, who also supply packages with companies such as Contiki and Busabout, can issue rail passes, and advise on visa regulations – for a fee they'll even do all the paperwork for you.

FROM SOUTH AFRICA

There are flights from Johannesburg and Cape Town to most European capitals and you can fly with many major airlines, sometimes via a hub airport. Air France flies direct to Paris from Johannesburg for around R6000, from Cape Town for slightly more; British Airways flies direct to London from Johannesburg or Cape Town for around R8000. Flying to Frankfurt with Lufthansa is slightly more at about R9000 from Johannesberg. You might also try flying with Emirates via Dubai.

ONLINE BOOKING SITES

www.expedia.co.uk (in UK), **www.expedia.com** (in US),
www.expedia.ca (in Canada)
www.flightcentre.com
www.lastminute.com (in UK)
www.opodo.co.uk (in UK)
www.orbitz.com (in US)
www.travelocity.co.uk (in UK), **www.travelocity.com** (in US), **www.travelocity.ca** (in Canada) **www.zuji.com.au** (in Australia), **www.zuji.co.nz** (in New Zealand)

AGENTS AND OPERATORS

ebookers UK 0800/082 3000, Republic of Ireland 01/488 3507, www.ebookers.com. www.ebookers.ie Low fares on an extensive selection of scheduled flights to Europe.

North South Travel UK 01245/608 291, www.northsouthtravel.co.uk. Discounted fares worldwide. Profits are used to support projects in the developing world, especially the promotion of sustainable tourism.

STA Travel US 1-800/781-4040, UK 0871/2300 040, Australia 134 STA, New Zealand 0800/474 400, SA 0861/781 781; www.statravel.com. Worldwide specialists in independent travel; also student IDs, travel insurance, car rental, rail passes, and more.

Trailfinders UK 0845/058 5858, Republic of Ireland 01/677 7888, Australia 1300/780 212, www.trailfinders.com. One of the best-informed and most efficient agents for independent travellers.

USIT 01/602 1904, Northern Ireland 028/9032 7111, www.usitnow.ie. Ireland's main student and youth travel specialists.

Getting around

It's easy enough to travel in Europe, and a number of special deals and passes can make it fairly economical too. Air links are extensive and, thanks to the growing number of budget airlines, flights are often cheaper than taking the train, but you'll appreciate the diversity of Europe best at ground level, by way of its enormous and generally efficient web of rail, road and ferry connections.

BY TRAIN

Trains are generally the best way to make a tour of Europe. The rail network in most countries is comprehensive and the continent boasts some of the most scenic rail journeys you could make anywhere in the world. **Costs** are relatively low, too, even in the richer parts of northwest Europe, where – apart from Britain – trains are heavily subsidized, and prices are brought down further by passes and discount cards. We've covered the various passes here, as well as the most important international routes and most useful addresses; frequencies and journey times are given throughout the guide.

During the summer, especially if you're travelling at night or a long distance, it's best to make **reservations** whenever you can; on some trains (most French TGV services, for example) it's compulsory. See our "extra charges" box for more on supplements.

If you intend to do a lot of rail travel, the **Thomas Cook European Timetable** (Ⓦwww.thomascookpublishing.com) is an essential investment, detailing the main lines throughout Europe, as well as ferry connections, and is updated monthly.

Finally, whenever you board an international train in Europe, check the route of the car you are in, since trains frequently split, with different carriages going to different destinations.

Europe-wide rail passes

InterRail

Lauched back in 1972, InterRail passes have long been synonymous with young European backpackers travelling across the continent on the cheap. There are two types of pass available: the Global Pass and One Country Pass. Both can be bought direct from Ⓦwww.interailnet.com and from main stations and international rail agents in all thirty countries covered by the scheme. To qualify, you need to have been **resident** in one of the participating countries for six months or more. The only countries in this book which are not covered by the scheme are Andorra, Estonia, Latvia, Lithuania, Morocco and Russia.

InterRail Global Pass The daddy of all rail passes, offering access to almost the entire European rail network. You can choose between four different time periods: continuous blocks of 22 days or one month, or set amounts of travel – either five days within ten days or ten days within 22 days. Youth

EXTRA RAIL CHARGES

Note that even if you've bought an InterRail or Eurail pass, you will still need to pay **extra charges** or **supplements** to travel on most express trains (such as Eurostar, TGV and ICE), night trains and those on special scenic routes. Even where there is in theory no supplement, there's often a compulsory reservation fee, which may cost you double if you only find out about it once you're on the train. For details of charges check the InterRail website under "special trains". You can often avoid these charges if you plan your journey within domestic networks.

(under-26) passes valid for second-class travel start from €159/£107 for five days up to €399/£270 for a month. Note that you cannot use the pass in the country in which you bought it although discounts of up to fifty percent are usually available.

InterRail One Country Pass Same principle as the Global Pass but valid for just one country (or the Benelux zone of Belgium, the Netherlands and Luxembourg). Time periods and prices vary depending on the country. A three-day youth pass will set you back €32/£21 in Bulgaria, €71/£48 in Spain and €125/£85 in France.

Eurail

Non-European residents aren't eligible for InterRail passes. For them the **Eurail** scheme (Ⓦwww.eurail.com) offers a range of passes giving unlimited travel in over twenty European countries. There are **four types** of pass – the Global Pass, Select Pass, Regional Pass and One Country Pass, all of which should be bought outside of Europe. Apart from some One Country Passes, all are available at discounted youth (under-27) rates for second-class travel and saver rates for adults travelling in groups.

Eurail Global Pass A single pass valid for travel in twenty countries: Austria, Belgium, Croatia, Denmark, Finland, France, Germany, Greece, Hungary, Ireland, Italy, Luxembourg, the Netherlands, Norway, Portugal, Romania, Slovenia, Spain, Sweden and Switzerland. There are seven different time periods available from ten days travel within two months, up to three months continuous travel. Prices start at €330/US$435 for a youth pass valid for fifteen days.

Eurail Select Pass Allows you to select a pass covering three, four or five bordering countries out of the eighteen countries above plus five "bonus" countries. Prices start at €202/US$275 for a three-country youth pass valid for five days travel within two months.

Eurail Regional Pass Similar to the Select Pass but offering pre-determined combinations of countries. Prices depend on the country combination; for example an Austria-Czech Republic youth pass valid for five days travel in two months will cost you €135/US$185 whereas the same period for Germany–Switzerland costs €203/US$275.

Eurail One Country Pass Offers travel within one of the following seventeen countries (or the Benelux zone of Belgium, the Netherlands and Luxembourg): Austria, Croatia, Czech Republic, Denmark, Finland, Greece, Hungary, Ireland, Italy, the Netherlands, Norway, Poland, Portugal, Romania, Slovenia, Spain and Sweden. Prices vary depending on the size of the country and whether youth passes are available: for example a youth pass in Denmark valid for three days travel costs €39/US$55; the same time period in Spain costs €143/US$195 in Spain where special youth passes are not available.

Regional rail passes

In addition to the InterRail and Eurail schemes there are a few **regional rail passes** which can be good value if you're doing a lot of travelling within one area; we've listed some of the main ones below. **National rail passes** (apart from InterRail and Eurail, see opposite) are covered in the relevant chapter of the Guide.

Balkan Flexipass Offers unlimited first-class-only travel through Bulgaria, Greece, Macedonia, Romania, and Turkey including Serbia and Montenegro. Prices start at US$240 for five days travel in one month.

Britrail pass + Ireland Ⓦwww.britrail.com. Allows unlimited travel in Britain, Northern Ireland and the Republic of Ireland. The pass also includes a round-trip crossing of the Irish Sea via ferry. Prices start from US$462 for five days standard-class travel in one month.

European East Pass Gives five days' travel in a month in Austria, the Czech Republic, Hungary, Poland and Slovakia for US$199, plus up to five additional days at US$26 each.

ScanRail pass Ⓦwww.scanrail.com. Valid on the rail networks of Denmark, Norway, Sweden and Finland, and costs US$203 (US$291 for over-26s) for five days' travel in two months, US$273 (US$390) for ten days in two months, and US$316 (US$453) for 21 days unlimited.

Rail contacts

UK

European Rail Ⓣ020/7387 0444, Ⓦwww.europeanrail.com.

Eurostar Ⓣ0870/518 6186, Ⓦwww.eurostar.com.

Ffestiniog Travel Ⓣ01766/512400, Ⓦwww.festtravel.co.uk,

International Rail Ⓣ0870/751 5000, Ⓦwww.international-rail.com.

InterRail Ⓦwww.interrailnet.com

The Man in Seat 61 Ⓦwww.seat61.com.

Rail Europe Ⓣ0870/837 1371, Ⓦwww.raileurope.co.uk.

Trainseurope Ⓣ0871/700 7722, Ⓦwww.trainseurope.co.uk.

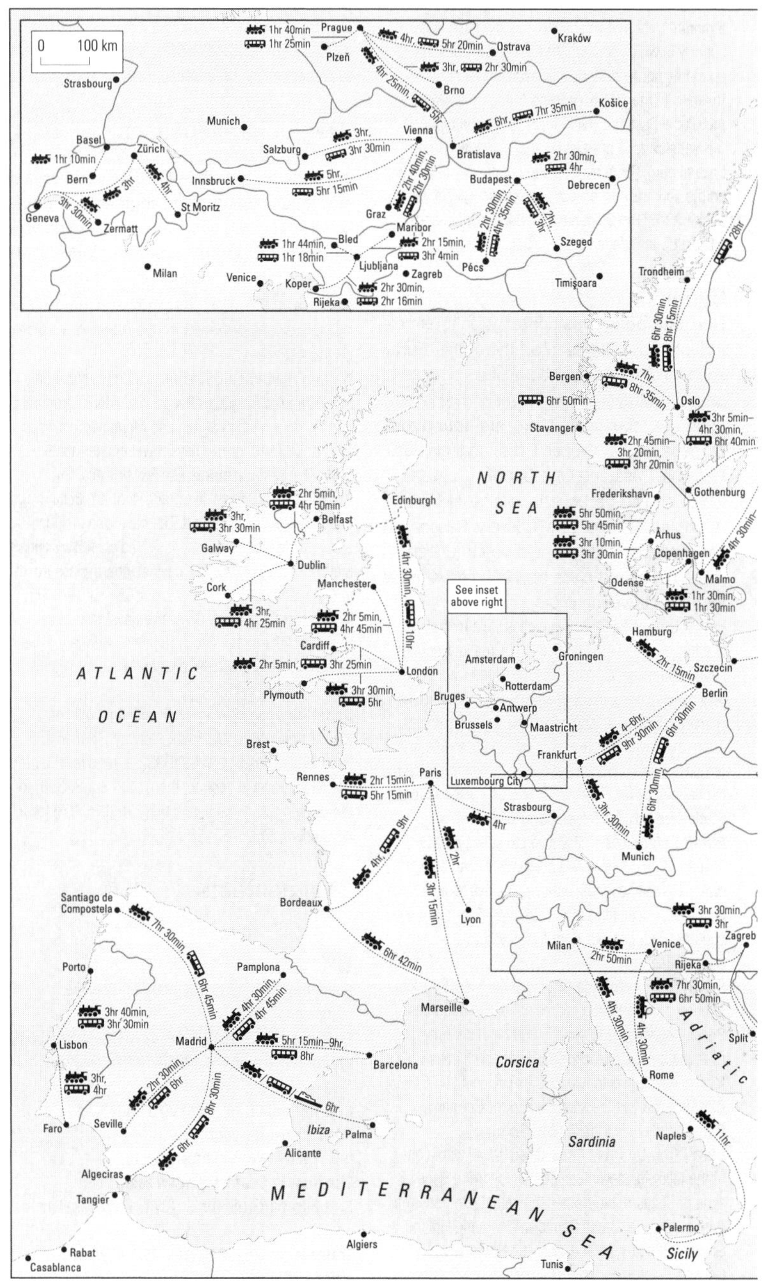
0 100 km
Prague
Plzeň
1hr 40min
1hr 25min
4hr, 5hr 20min
Ostrava
Kraków
3hr, 2hr 30min
Brno
4hr 25min, 5hr
Strasbourg
Munich
Košice
6hr, 7hr 35min
Vienna
Bratislava
Basel
Zürich
1hr 10min
Salzburg
3hr, 3hr 30min
Bern
Innsbruck
5hr, 5hr 15min
2hr 40min, 2hr 30min
Budapest
2hr 30min, 4hr
Debrecen
3hr
4hr
Geneva
3hr 30min
Zermatt
St Moritz
Graz
Maribor
2hr 30min, 4hr 35min
2hr, 3hr
1hr 44min, 1hr 18min
Bled
2hr 15min, 3hr 4min
Szeged
Ljubljana
Zagreb
Pécs
Milan
Venice
Koper
2hr 30min, 2hr 16min
Rijeka
Timişoara
Trondheim
28hr
6hr 30min, 8hr 15min
Bergen
7hr, 8hr 35min
Oslo
6hr 50min
Stavanger
3hr 5min–4hr 30min, 6hr 40min
2hr 45min–3hr 20min, 3hr 20min
NORTH SEA
Frederikshavn
Gothenburg
5hr 50min, 5hr 45min
Århus
3hr 10min, 3hr 30min
Copenhagen
4hr 30min
Malmo
Odense
1hr 30min, 1hr 30min
2hr 5min, 4hr 50min
Edinburgh
3hr, 3hr 30min
Belfast
Galway
Dublin
4hr 30min
10hr
Manchester
Cork
3hr, 4hr 25min
2hr 5min, 4hr 45min
See inset above right
Hamburg
Cardiff
2hr 5min, 3hr 25min
Groningen
2hr 15min
Szczecin
ATLANTIC OCEAN
London
Amsterdam
Rotterdam
Berlin
Plymouth
3hr 30min, 5hr
Bruges
Antwerp
Brussels
Maastricht
4–6hr, 9hr 30min
6hr 30min
Brest
Frankfurt
Rennes
2hr 15min, 5hr 15min
Paris
Luxembourg City
Strasbourg
4hr
3hr 30min
6hr 30min
9hr
4hr
2hr
3hr 15min
Munich
Bordeaux
Lyon
Santiago de Compostela
7hr 30min, 6hr 45min
3hr 30min, 3hr
Zagreb
Milan
2hr 50min
Venice
6hr 42min
Rijeka
Porto
Pamplona
4hr 30min, 4hr 45min
7hr 30min, 6hr 50min
Marseille
4hr 30min
4hr 30min
Adriatic
3hr 40min, 3hr 30min
Split
Lisbon
Madrid
5hr 15min–9hr, 8hr
Barcelona
Corsica
Rome
2hr 30min, 6hr
3hr, 4hr
8hr 30min
6hr
Faro
Seville
Ibiza
Palma
Naples
11hr
6hr
Alicante
Sardinia
Algeciras
Tangier
MEDITERRANEAN SEA
Palermo
Algiers
Rabat
Sicily
Casablanca
Tunis

JOURNEY TIMES BY TRAIN & BUS
HIGH-SPEED TRAIN TIMES
Rome–Naples 1hr 30min
Paris–Brest 2hr 15min
Paris–London 2hr 35min
London–Brussels 1hr 25min
Paris–Bordeaux 3hr
Paris–Brussels 1hr 25min
Brussels–Amsterdam 2hr 40min
Amsterdam–Frankfurt 3hr 45 min
Copenhagen–Stockholm 5hr
Barcelona–Alicante 4hr 40min
Berlin–Hamburg 1hr 30min
Geneva–Zürich 2hr 43min
Milan–Zürich 3hr 40min
0 100 km
Groningen
1hr, 2–3hr
Amsterdam
Rotterdam
2hr 20min, 4hr 12min
2hr 35min
Bruges
Antwerp
45min
1hr
Brussels
Maastricht
3hr
Luxembourg City
Tromsø
Rovaniemi
12hr, 13hr 25min
Joensuu
5hr 30min, 7hr 10min
1hr 55min, 2hr 30min
7hr, 9hr
Turku
Helsinki
St Petersburg
Stockholm
Tallinn
10hr
4hr 35min–8hr 50min
8hr 30min, 8hr
BALTIC SEA
15hr
15hr 30min
5hr 30min
17hr, 19hr
Riga
Moscow
10hr 30min
5hr 30min, 5hr
Vilnius
Minsk
Gdańsk
5hr
4hr, 6hr
Warsaw
2hr 30min, 7hr 30min
Kiev
Kraków
See inset above left
Suceava
6hr 30min, 6hr 30min
Timişoara
6hr 30min, 7hr 30min
3hr, 2hr 50min
Belgrade
Bucharest
Constanţa
BLACK SEA
T'bilisi
11hr
Sarajevo
8hr, 7hr 30min
Varna
Yerevan
Sofia
7hr 30min, 5hr 30min
Burgas
Dubrovnik
2hr 30min, 2hr
Plovdiv
Sea
İstanbul
5hr–9hr, 5hr 30min
Thessaloníki
Ankara
0 500 km
7hr 40min, 6hr
6hr 30min (+ 2hr), 5hr
Corfu
Aegean Sea
7hr
10hr
İzmir
Athens
7hr
Antalya

US

ACP Rail International ⓣ1-866-9-EURAIL, ⓦwww.eurail-acprail.com. Eurailagent.
BritRail Travel ⓣ1-866/BRITRAIL, ⓦwww.britrail.com. British passes.
Europrail International Canada ⓣ1-888/667-9734, ⓦwww.europrail.net. European and many individual country passes.
Eurail ⓦwww.eurail.com
Rail Europe US ⓣ1-877/257-2887, Canada ⓣ1-800/361-RAIL, ⓦwww.raileurope.com. Official Eurail agent, with the widest range of regional and one-country passes.
ScanTours ⓣ1-800/223-7226 or 310/636-4656, ⓦwww.scantours.com. Eurail, Scandinavian and other European country passes.

Australia and New Zealand

CIT World Travel Australia ⓣ02/9267 1255 or 03/9650 5510, ⓦwww.cittravel.com.au. Eurail and Italian rail passes.
Octopus Travel ⓣ1300/727 072, ⓦwww.octopustravel.com.au.
Rail Plus Australia ⓣ03/9642 8644, ⓦwww.railplus.com.au; NZ ⓣ09/377 5415, ⓦwww.railplus.co.nz. Eurail and BritRail passes.

BY BUS

Long-distance journeys between major European cities are generally slow, uncomfortable and not particularly cheap, especially if you have a rail pass. With a limited itinerary, however, a **bus pass** or **circular bus ticket** can undercut a rail pass, especially for over-26s. There's also the option of a bus tour if you're on a tight schedule or simply want everything planned for you.

Eurolines ⓦwww.eurolines-pass.com. Offers the Eurolines pass valid for travel between forty cities in sixteen countries . It costs £189 (£225 for over-26s) for fifteen days in high season (23 June–10 Sept as well as Chrismas/New Year) and £245 (£299) for 30 days. Prices are around a third lower in low season.
Busabout ⓦwww.busabout.com. Offers a hop-on, hop-off service throughout western Europe operating May–Oct. There are three "loops" on offer (Northern, Southern and Western) as well as Flexitrip Pass where you design your own trip. Prices start from £289 for a one loop pass or £239 for the Flexitrip Pass for which extra days cost £29.
Contiki ⓦwww.contiki.com. Long-established operator offering bus tours throughout Europe from eleven to 46 days. An eleven-day tour from Amsterdam to Barcelona costs £819 including hotel accommodation and meals.

BY FERRY

Travelling by **ferry** is often the most practical way to get from one part of Europe to another, the obvious routes being from the mainland to the Mediterranean islands, as well as moving between the countries bordering the Baltic and Adriatic seas. There are countless routes serving a huge range of destinations, too numerous to outline here; where possible we've given the details of ferries to other countries within each chapter. For further details of schedules and operators, see the *Thomas Cook European Timetable*.

BY PLANE

Most European countries now have at least one budget airline selling **low-cost flights** online, and invariably undercutting train and bus fares on longer international routes. Apart from its environmental impact (see p.30), travelling by air means you miss the scenery and "feel" for a country that ground-level transport can provide, and there's also the inconvenience of getting between airports and the cities they serve, often quite a haul in itself. But, if you're pressed for time, and especially if you want to get from one end of Europe to another, taking the plane is definitely an option.

At the time of writing there were forty five budget airlines serving 319 airports in Europe. We've listed the more established operators below but for full details of routes visit ⓦwww.flycheapo.com.

European budget arilines

Air Berlin ⓦwww.airberlin.com
bmibaby ⓦwww.bmibaby.com
easyJet ⓦwww.easyjet.com.
Ryanair ⓦwww.ryanair.com.
FlyGlobespan ⓦwww.flyglobespan.com.
Germanwings ⓦwww.germanwings.com
Jet2 ⓦwww.jet2.com
MyAir ⓦwww.myair.com
Norwegian Air Shuttle ⓦwww.norwegian.no
Sky Europe ⓦwww.skyeurope.com
Sterling ⓦwww.sterling.dk
Thomsonfly ⓦwww.thomsonfly.com
Transavia ⓦwww.transavia.com
TUIfly ⓦwww.tuifly.com
Vueling ⓦwww.vueling.com
Wizzair ⓦwww.wizzair.com

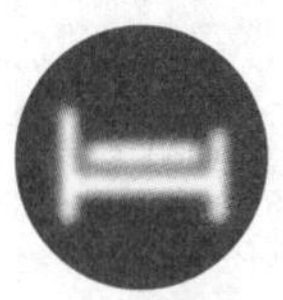

Accommodation

Although accommodation is one of the more crucial costs to consider when planning your trip, it needn't be a stumbling block to a budget-conscious tour of Europe. Indeed, even in Europe's pricier destinations the hostel system means there is always an affordable place to stay. If you're prepared to camp you can get by on very little while staying at some excellently equipped sites.

The one thing you should bear in mind is that in the more popular cities and resorts – Florence, Venice, Amsterdam, Prague, Barcelona, the Algarve, and so on – things can get very busy during the peak summer months, and even if you've got plenty of money to throw around you should book in advance.

HOSTELS

The cheapest places to stay around Europe are the innumerable **hostels** that cover the continent. Some of these are private places, but by far the majority are official hostels, members of **Hostelling International** (HI), which incorporates the national youth hostel associations of every country in the world. Youth hostelling isn't the hearty, up-at-the-crack-of-dawn and early-to-bed business it once was; indeed, hostels have been keen to shed this image of late and now appeal to a wider public. In many countries they simply represent the best-value overnight accommodation available. Most are clean, well-run places, always offering dormitory accommodation, and often a range of private single and double rooms, or rooms with four to six beds. Many hostels also either have self-catering facilities or provide low-cost meals, and the larger ones have a range of other facilities – a swimming pool and a games room for example. There is usually no age limit but where there is limited space, priority is given to those under 26.

Strictly speaking, to use an HI hostel you have to have **membership**, although if there's room you can stay at most hostels by simply paying a bit extra. If you do intend to do a lot of hostelling, however, it's certainly worth joining, which you can do through your home country's hostelling association. We've given the name and address of the relevant national hostelling organization in each chapter if you want further information. HI hostels can usually be booked through their country's hostelling association website, almost always over-the-counter at other hostels in the same country, and often through the international HI website, ⓦwww.hihostels.com. Alternatively try ⓦwww.hostels.com or ⓦwww.hostelz.com who also offer non HI-affiliated hostels.

Youth hostel associations

US and Canada

Hostelling International-American Youth Hostels US ⓣ1-301/495-1240, ⓦwww.hiayh.org.
Hostelling International Canada ⓣ1-800/663-5777, ⓦwww.hihostels.ca.

UK and Ireland

Youth Hostels Association (YHA) England and Wales ⓣ0870/770 8868, ⓦwww.yha.org.uk.
Scottish Youth Hostels Association ⓣ01786/891 400, ⓦwww.syha.org.uk.
Irish Youth Hostel Association Republic of Ireland ⓣ01/830 4555, ⓦwww.irelandyha.org.
Hostelling International Northern Ireland ⓣ028/9031 5435, ⓦwww.hini.org.uk.

Australia, New Zealand and South Africa

Australia Youth Hostels Association Australia ⓣ02/9565 1699, ⓦwww.yha.com.au.
Youth Hostelling Association New Zealand ⓣ0800/278 299 or 03/379 9970, ⓦwww.yha.co.nz.
Hostelling International South Africa ⓣ21/424 2511, ⓦwww.hihostels.com.

ACCOMMODATION PRICE CODES

Throughout this guide, accommodation is coded on a scale of ❶ to ❾ outlined below. For hostels the code indicates the cost of a dorm bed, for hotels, the cheapest double room and for campsites the costs of a night's stay per person. All codes represent high-season prices.

❶ up to €10	❹ €31–40	❼ €61–75
❷ €11–20	❺ €41–50	❽ €76–90
❸ €21–30	❻ €51–60	❾ over €90

HOTELS AND PENSIONS

With **hotels** you can really spend as much or as little as you like. Most hotels in Europe are graded on some kind of star system. One- and two-star category hotels are plain and simple on the whole, usually family-run, with a number of rooms without private facilities; sometimes breakfast won't be included. In three-star hotels all the rooms will have private facilities, prices will normally include breakfast and there may well be a phone or TV in the room; while four- and five-star places will certainly have all these, plus swimming pool, and other such facilities. In the really top-level places breakfast, oddly enough, isn't always included. When it is, in the Netherlands, Britain or Germany, it's fairly sumptuous; in France it won't amount to much anyway and it's no hardship to grab a croissant and coffee in the nearest café.

Obviously prices vary greatly, but you're rarely going to be paying less than £25/US$50 for a basic double room even in southern Europe, while in the Netherlands the average price is around £50/US$100, and in Scandinavia and the British Isles somewhat higher than that. In some countries a **pension** or B&B (variously known as a guesthouse, *pensão*, *gasthaus* or numerous other names) is a cheaper alternative, offering smaller, simpler accommodation, usually with just a few rooms. In some countries these advertise with a sign in the window; in others they can be booked through the tourist office, which may demand a small fee. There are various other kinds of accommodation – apartments, farmhouses, cottages, *paradores* in Spain, *gîtes* in France, and more – but most are geared to longer-term stays and we have detailed them only where relevant.

CAMPING

The cheapest form of accommodation is, of course, a **campsite**, either pitching your own tent or parking your caravan or camper van. Most sites make a charge per person, plus a charge per plot and/or another per vehicle. Bear in mind, especially in countries such as France where camping is very popular, that facilities can be excellent (though the better the facilities, the pricier the site). If you're on foot you should add in the cost and inconvenience of getting to the site, since most are on the outskirts of towns, sometimes further. Some sites have **cabins**, which you can stay in for a little extra, although these are usually fairly basic affairs, only really worth considering in regions like Scandinavia where budget options are thin on the ground. In Britain, the AA issues *Camping and Caravanning Europe* (£10.99), which provides a **list of campsites** in eleven West European countries. Alternatively, **tourist offices** can recommend well-equipped and conveniently located sites.

As for **camping rough**, it's a fine idea if you

COUCHSURFING

Couchsurfing (Ⓦwww.couchsurfing.com) is a free Internet-based hospitality service offering travellers the chance to stay with local people. Hosts are verified through references and a vouching system but you should obviously think carefully about who you are prepared to stay with and have a back-up plan if things don't work out (there are plenty of **safety tips** detailed on their website). There are more than 300,000 couchsurfer members in 216 countries worldwide.

can get away with it – though perhaps an entire trip of rough camping is in reality too gruelling to be truly enjoyable. In some countries it's easy – in parts of Scandinavia it's a legal right, and in Greece and other southern European countries you can usually find a bit of beach to pitch down on – but in others it can get you into trouble with the law.

Camping carnets

If you're planning to do a lot of camping, an **international camping carnet** is a good investment. The carnet gives discounts at member sites, serves as useful identification, and is obligatory on some sites in Portugal and some Scandinavian countries. Many campsites will take it instead of making you surrender your passport during your stay, and it covers you for third-party insurance when camping. However, the carnet is not recognized in Sweden, where you may have to join their own scheme. In **the US and Canada**, the carnet is available from home motoring organizations, or from Family Campers and RVers (FCRV; ⓣ1-800/245-9755, ⓦwww.fcrv.org). FCRV annual membership costs US$25 per family, and the carnet an additional US$20. In **the UK and Ireland**, the carnet costs £4.50, and is available to members of the AA in Ireland or the RAC in the UK, or for members only from either of the following: the Camping and Caravanning Club (ⓣ024/7669 4995, ⓦwww.campingandcaravanningclub.co.uk; annual membership £33. The club's foreign touring arm, Carefree Travel Service (ⓣ024/7642 2024), provides the camping carnet free if you take out insurance with them; they also book ferry crossings and inspect camping sites in Europe.

The media

British and American newspapers and magazines are widely available in Europe, sometimes on the day of publication, more often the day after. They do, however, cost around three times as much as they do at home.

Exceptions to this rule are the *Guardian* and *Financial Times*, which print European editions that are cheaper and available on the day of issue. The *International Herald Tribune* and *USA Today* can be found just about everywhere. If you're lucky you may come across the odd *New York Times* or *Washington Post*, while *Time*, *Newsweek* and *The Economist* are all widely available.

In addition to these there are often locally produced **English-language papers** available in major European capitals, usually on a weekly or monthly basis. These are often a much more engaging way to get your news fix and learn more about local issues. Some national papers also provide English-language content **online**. For example, the Italian daily *Corriere della Sera* (ⓦwww.corriere.it/english) and the French newspaper *Le Figaro* (ⓦwww.lefigaro.fr/english)

You can listen to the **BBC World Service** on medium wave, at 648kHz (western Europe) or 1323kHz (southeastern Europe); short wave frequencies include 6195, 9410, 12,095, 15,565 and 17,640kHz. In addition, FM stations in cities from Gibraltar to Helsinki slot the BBC news and/or some programming into their schedules; ⓦwww.bbc.co.uk/worldservica has details, and, of course, ⓦwww.bbc.co.uk/news from around the world. **Voice of America** (ⓦwww.voa.gov) can be found on 9825, 15,195 or 15,495kHz short wave, among other frequencies. As for **television**, CNN, Eurosport and MTV Europe are all popular and normally available in pricier hotels. In many parts of Europe there is, in any case, a reasonable choice of terrestrial channels, since a border is never far away and you can often pick up at least one other country's TV stations.

Festivals and annual events

There's always some event or other happening in Europe, and the bigger shindigs can be reason enough for visiting a place – some are even worth planning your entire trip around. Be warned, though, that if you're intending to visit a place during its annual festival you need to plan well in advance, since accommodation can be booked up months beforehand, especially for the larger, more internationally known events. For a complete guide to world festivals check out Ⓦworldparty.roughguides.com.

FESTIVAL CALENDAR

Many of the **festivals** and **annual events** you'll come across in Europe were – and in many cases still are – religious affairs, commemorating a local miracle or saint's day. Others are decidedly more secular – from film and music festivals to street carnivals – but just as much fun. The following are some of the biggest celebrations, further information on which can be found online or at local tourist offices.

January

Twelfth Night (Jan 6) Rather than Christmas Day, this is the time for present-giving in Spain, while in Orthodox Eastern Europe, the sixth of January is Christmas Day.
La Tamborrada, San Sebastián, Spain (Jan 20) Probably the loudest festival you will encounter as scores of drummers take to the streets of San Sebastián.

February

Berlin Film Festival, Germany (Feb 7–17, 2008) Home of the Golden Bear award, this film bash is more geared towards the general public than the more famous one in Cannes.
Carnival/Mardi Gras (Feb 5, 2008) Celebrated most famously in Venice, there are smaller events across Europe, notably in Viareggio (Italy), Luzern and Basel (Switzerland), Cologne (Germany), Maastricht (Netherlands) and tiny Binche (Belgium); Ⓦwww.mardigrasday.com.

March

St Patrick's Day (March 17) Celebrated wherever there's an Irish community, in Dublin it's a five-day festival with music, parades and a lot of drinking.
Las Fallas, Valencia, Spain (March 15–19) The passing of winter is celebrated in explosive fashion with enormous bonfires, burning effigies and plenty of all-night partying.

April

Easter (March 23, 2008) Celebrated with most verve and ceremony in Catholic and Orthodox Europe, where Easter Sunday or Monday is usually marked with some sort of procession; note that the Orthodox Church's Easter can fall a week or two either side of the Western festival.
Feria de Abril, Seville, Spain (April 8–13, 2008) A week of flamenco music and dancing, parades and bullfights, in a frenzied and enthusiastic atmosphere.
Queens Day, Amsterdam (April 30) Queen Beatrix's official birthday is the excuse for this anarchic 24-hour drinking and dressing-up binge.
Maggio Musicale, Florence, Italy (late April until early July) Festival of opera and classical music.

May

Cannes Film Festival, France The world's most famous cinema festival is really more of an industry affair than anything else; Ⓦwww.festival-cannes.fr.
Cooper's Hill Cheese-Rolling, Gloucestershire, England (May 26, 2008) One of Europe's most eccentric annual events where a bunch of daredevils throw themselves down a hill in pursuit of a circular cheese. Ⓦwww.cheese-rolling.co.uk.

PinkPop Festival, Landgraaf, Netherlands Holland's biggest pop music festival; ⓦ www.pinkpop.nl.

June

Festa do São João, Porto, Portugal (June 23–24) Portugal's second city puts on the mother of all street parties culminating in revellers hitting each other with plastic hammers.
Glastonbury Festival, England Despite being one of Europe's largest (and most expensive) music festivals, Glastonbury is a surprisingly intimate affair thanks to its beautiful setting and hippie vibe; ⓦ www.glastonburyfestivals.co.uk.

July

Love Parade, Germany The world's biggest street rave hits Dortmund in 2008; see ⓦ www.loveparade.de for dates and details.
Roskilde Festival, Denmark (July 3–6, 2008) An eclectic range of music (rock, dance, folk) and performance arts, with profits going to worthy causes; ⓦ www.roskilde-festival.dk.
Fiesta de San Fermín, Pamplona, Spain Anarchic fun, centred on the running of the bulls through the streets of the city, plus music, dancing and of course a lot of drinking.
The Palio, Siena, Italy Italy's most spectacular annual event, a bareback horse race between representatives of the different quarters of the city around the main square.
Montreux Jazz Festival, Switzerland These days only loosely committed to jazz, this festival takes in everything from folk to breakbeats.
The Proms, London (July–Sept) World-famous concert series that maintains high standards of classical music at egalitarian prices; ⓦ www.bbc.co.uk/proms.
Exit Festival, Novi Sad, Serbia Europe's hippest music festival held in a beautiful fortress and attacting the likes of the Prodigy and White Stripes. ⓦ www.exitfest.org.
Avignon Festival, France Slanted towards drama but hosts plenty of other events too and is a great time to be in town.
Dubrovnik Summer Festival, Croatia (July and August) A host of musical events and theatre performances against the backdrop of the town's beautiful Renaissance centre.

August

Edinburgh Festival, Scotland A mass of top-notch and fringe events in every performing medium, from rock to cabaret to modern experimental music, dance and drama; ⓦ www.eif.co.uk.
Notting Hill Carnival, London Predominantly Black British and Caribbean celebration that's become the world's second biggest street carnival after Rio.
Locarno Film Festival, Switzerland Movies from around the world compete on the banks of Lake Maggiore; ⓦ www.pardo.ch.
La Tomatina, Buñol, Spain The last Wednesday of August sees the streets of Buñol packed for a one-hour food fight disposing of 130,000 kilos of tomatoes.

September

Venice Film Festival, Italy First held in 1932, this is the world's oldest film festival.
Regata Storica, Venice, Italy A trial of skill for the city's gondoliers.
Galway International Oyster Festival, Ireland The arrival of the oyster season is celebrated with a three-day seafood, Guinness and dancing shindig; ⓦ www.galwayoysterfest.com.
Ibiza Closing Parties, Spain The summer dance music mecca goes out with a bang in September with all the main clubs holding closing parties.
Oktoberfest, Munich, Germany A huge beer festival and fair (held in the last two weeks of September, despite the name), attracting vast numbers of people to consume gluttonous quantities of beer and food.
Ramadan Commemorating the revelation of the Koran to the Prophet Muhammad, this month of fasting from sunrise until sunset ends with a huge celebration called Eid el-Fitr (on or around 2 Oct 2008). Morocco, Turkey and Muslim areas of Bulgaria and Greece.

October

Combat des Reines, Switzerland Quirky cow-fighting contest held to decide the queen of the herd in the Valais region of Switzerland. The main event is the copious drinking and betting on the sidelines (and no, the cows don't get hurt).
Mondial du Snowboard, Les Deux Alpes, France World-class boarders and plenty of hangers kick off the snow season at this beautiful alpine resort.

November

Bonfire Night, Lewes, England Huge processions and tremendous fireworks light up this sleepy town on Nov 5 every year.
Madonna della Salute Festival, Venice, Italy Annual candle-lit procession across the Grand Canal to the church of the Santa Maria della Salute.

December

Christmas Festive markets sprout up across the continent in the run-up to Christmas. One of the best is found in Cologne, Germany.

New Year's Eve Celebrated with fireworks and parties across Europe, it's probably best experienced in Edinburgh where over a hundred thousand cram the streets for "Hogmanay".

Culture and etiquette

Europe has an exciting mix of cultures varying greatly from country to country. While it is impossible to generalize, there are some broad themes worth noting. For country specific information, see the "Culture and etiquette" section at the beginning of each chapter.

Although it varies from one country to the next, **tipping** is not really the serious business it is in North America. In many countries it's customary to leave at least something in most restaurants and cafés, if only rounding the bill up to the next major denomination. Even in swankier establishments, a ten percent tip is sufficient, and you shouldn't feel obliged to tip at all if the service was bad, especially if service has been included in the bill. In smarter hotels you should tip hall porters, and cab drivers expect a tip in Britain and Ireland, but not necessarily on the Continent.

While **cigarette smoking** is fast going out of fashion in northwestern Europe, it remains pretty uninhibited in Eastern Europe and parts of the Mediterranean, where it's considered quite normal to smoke in a restaurant without asking permission. However there is move to change all that with Europe-wide smoking bans on the cards. In a few countries, smoking is now illegal in all enclosed workplace environments including pubs, restaurants and even a company car: Denmark, Italy Ireland, Sweden and the UK are now smokefree and France and the Netherlands plan to impose a ban in 2008.

Work and study

The best way of getting to know a country properly is to work there and learn the language. Study opportunities are also a good way of absorbing yourself in the local culture, but they invariably need to be fixed up in advance; check newspapers for ads or contact one of the organizations listed opposite.

WORKING IN EUROPE

There are any number of jobs you can pick up on the road to supplement your spending money. It's normally not hard to find **bar** or **restaurant work**, especially in large resort areas during the summer, and your chances will be greater if you speak the local language

– although being able to speak English may be your greatest asset in more touristy areas. Cleaning jobs, nannying and **au pair** work are also common, if not spectacularly well paid, often just providing room and board plus pocket money. Some of them can be fixed up on the spot, while others need to be organized before you leave home.

The other big casual earner is **farm work**, particularly grape-picking, an option from August to October when the vines are being harvested. The best country for this is France, but there's sometimes work in Germany too, and you're unlikely to be asked for documentation. Also in France, along the Côte d'Azur, and in other yacht-havens in Greece and parts of southern Spain, there is sometimes **crewing work** available, though you'll obviously need some sailing experience.

Rather better paid, and equally widespread, if only during the September to June period, is **teaching English** as a foreign language (TEFL), though it's becoming harder to find English-teaching jobs without a TEFL qualification. You'll normally be paid a liveable local salary, sometimes with somewhere to live thrown in, and you can often supplement your income with more lucrative private lessons. The TEFL teaching season is reversed in Britain and to a lesser extent Ireland, with plenty of work available during the summer in London and on the English south coast (but again, some kind of TEFL qualification is pretty well indispensable).

Another tip for working abroad, whether teaching English or otherwise, is to get hold of one of the books on summer jobs abroad and how to work your way around the world published in the UK by Vacation Work; call ⓣ01865/241 978 or visit ⓦwww.vacationwork.co.uk for their catalogue. Travel magazines like *Wanderlust* (ⓦwww.wanderlust.co.uk) have a Job Shop section which often advertises job opportunities with tour companies. ⓦwww.studyabroad.com is a useful website with listings and links to study and work programmes worldwide.

STUDYING IN EUROPE

Studying abroad invariably means learning a language, doing an intensive course that lasts between two weeks and three months and staying with a local family. There are plenty of places you can do this, and you should reckon on paying around £200/US$380 a week including room and board. If you know a language well, you could also apply to do a short course in another subject at a local university; scan the classified sections of the newspapers back home, and keep an eye out when you're on the spot. The EU runs a programme called **Erasmus** in which university students from Britain and Ireland can obtain mobility grants to study in one of 26 European countries (including other EU countries, plus Bulgaria, Iceland, Liechtenstein, Norway, Romania and Turkey) for three months to a full academic year if their university participates in the programme. Check with your university's international relations office, or see ⓦeuropa.eu.int/comm/education/programmes/mundus/index_en.html.

Work and study contacts

AFS Intercultural Programs ⓦ**www.afs.org, UK** ⓣ**0113/242 6136, US** ⓣ**1-800/AFS-INFO, international enquiries** ⓣ**+1-212/807-8686.** Global UN-recognized organization running summer programmes to foster international understanding.

American Institute for Foreign Study ⓦ**www.aifs.com. UK** ⓣ**020/7581 7300, US** ⓣ**1-800/727-2437.** Language study and cultural immersion for the summer or school year, as well as au pair programmes.

ASSE International ⓦ**www.asse.com. Australia** ⓣ**03/9775 4711, Canada** ⓣ**1-800/361-3214, UK** ⓣ**01952/460 733, US** ⓣ**1-800/333-3802.** International student exchanges and summer language programmes across most of Europe.

Association for International Practical Training ⓦ**www.aipt.org. US** ⓣ**410/997-2200.** Summer internships in various European countries for students who have completed at least two years of college in science, agriculture, engineering or architecture.

British Council ⓦ**www.britishcouncil.org. UK** ⓣ**0161/957 7775.** The Council's Recruitment Group (ⓣ020/7389 4931) recruits TEFL teachers with degrees and TEFL qualifications for posts worldwide (check the website for a list of current vacancies), and its Education and Training Group (ⓣ020/7389 4169) runs teacher exchange programmes and enables those who already work as educators to find out about teacher development programmes abroad.

Council on International Educational Exchange (CIEE) ⓦ**www.ciee.org/study. US** ⓣ**1-800/40-**

STUDY. An international organization worth contacting for advice on studying, working and volunteering in Europe. They run summer-semester and one-year study programmes, and volunteer projects.

International House Ⓦ www.ihlondon.com. UK Ⓣ 020/7518 6999. Head office for reputable English-teaching organization that offers TEFL training leading to the award of a Certificate in English Language Teaching to Adults (CELTA), and recruits for teaching positions in Britain and abroad.

World Learning Ⓦ www.worldlearning.org. US Ⓣ 1-800/257-7751. The Experiment in International Living (Ⓦ www.usexperiment.org) has summer programmes for high-school students, while the **School for International Training** (Ⓦ www.sit.edu/studyabroad) offers accredited college semesters abroad, with language and cultural studies, homestay and other academic work, in Croatia, the Czech Republic, France, Germany, Ireland, Morocco, the Netherlands, Russia, Spain and Switzerland.

Travel essentials

COSTS

It's hard to generalize about what you're likely to spend travelling around Europe. Some countries – Norway, Switzerland, the UK – are among the most expensive in the world, while in others (Turkey, for example) you can live like a lord on next to nothing. In general, countries in the north and west of Europe are more expensive than those in the south and east. See our "rough costs" entries at the start of each chapter for example costs.

Accommodation will be your largest single expense, and can really determine where you decide to travel. **Food and drink** costs also vary wildly, although again in most parts of Europe you can assume that a cheap restaurant meal will cost £5–10/US$9–18 a head, with prices nearer the top end of the scale in Scandinavia, at the bottom end in eastern and southern Europe, and below that in Turkey and Morocco. **Transport** costs are something you can pin down more exactly if you have a rail pass. Nowhere, though, are transport costs a major burden, except perhaps in Britain where public transport is less heavily subsidized than elsewhere.

The bottom line for an **average daily budget** touring the continent – camping, self-catering, hitching, etc – might be around £15/US$30 a day per person. Adding on a rail pass, staying in hostels and eating out occasionally would bring this up to perhaps £25/US$50 a day, while staying in private rooms or hotels and eating out once a day would mean a personal daily budget of at least £45/US$90.

> **PRICES**
>
> At the beginning of each chapter you'll find a guide to "rough costs" including food, accommodation and travel. Prices are quoted in euros for ease of comparison. Within the chapter itself prices are quoted in local currency.

As for ways of **cutting costs**, there are plenty. It makes sense, obviously, to spend less on transport by investing in some kind of rail pass. The most obvious way to save on accommodation is to use hostels; you can also save by planning to make some of your longer trips at night, if you're able to sleep easily on trains or buses. Regarding eating, self-catering – especially at lunchtime when it's just as easy to have a picnic lunch rather than eat in a restaurant or café – will save money.

CRIME AND PERSONAL SAFETY

Travelling around Europe should be relatively trouble-free, but, as in any part of the world, there is always the chance of petty theft. However, conditions do vary greatly from, say, Scandinavia, where you're unlikely to encounter much trouble of any kind, to the inner-city areas of metropolises such as London, Paris or Barcelona, where the crime-rate is higher, and poorer regions such as Morocco, Turkey and southern Italy, where street crime is low but tourists are an obvious target.

Safety tips

In order to minimize the risks, you should take some basic **precautions**. First and perhaps most important, you should try not to look too much like a tourist. Appearing lost, even if you are, is to be avoided, and it's not a good idea – especially in southern Europe – to walk around flashing an obviously expensive camera: the professional bag-snatchers who tour train stations can have your valuables off you in seconds.

Be discreet about using a **mobile phone**, and be sure to put it back into a secure pocket as soon as you've finished. If you're waiting for a train, keep your eyes (and hands if necessary) on your bags at all times; if you want to sleep, put everything valuable under your head as a pillow. You should be cautious when choosing a train compartment and avoid any situation that makes you feel uncomfortable. **Padlocking** your bags to the luggage rack if you're on an overnight train means that they're more likely to still be there in the morning.

If you're staying in a hostel, take your valuables out with you unless there's a very secure store for them on the premises; having **photocopies** of your passport and ID is a good idea. Storing a copy of your address book with friends or family can be worthwhile too. If you're driving, don't leave anything valuable in your parked car.

If the worst happens and you do have something stolen, inform the **police** immediately (we've included details of the main city police stations in the text); the priority is to get a statement from them detailing exactly what has been lost, which you'll need for your insurance claim back home. Generally you'll find the police sympathetic enough, sometimes able to speak English, but often unwilling to do much more than make out a report for you.

Drugs

It's hardly necessary to state that **drugs** such as amphetamines, cocaine, heroin, LSD and ecstasy are illegal all over Europe, and although use of cannabis is widespread in most countries, and legally tolerated in some (famously in the Netherlands, for example), you are never allowed to possess more than a tiny amount for personal use, and unlicensed sale remains illegal. Penalties for possession can be severe (in certain countries, such as Turkey, even possession of cannabis can result in a hefty prison sentence) and your consulate is unlikely to be sympathetic.

ELECTRICITY

The supply in Europe is 220v (240v in the British Isles), which means that anything on North American voltage (110v) normally needs a transformer. However, one or two countries (notably Spain and Morocco) still have a few places on 110v or 120v, so check before plugging in. Continental, Moroccan and Turkish sockets take two round pins, British and Irish ones take three square pins. A travel plug which adapts to all these systems is useful to carry. See Ⓦwww.kropla.com for more.

ENTRY REQUIREMENTS

Citizens of the UK (but not other British passport holders), Ireland, Australia, New Zealand, Canada and the US do not need a visa to enter most European countries (current exceptions are listed in the box below), and can usually stay for one to three months, depending on nationality; for some countries, passports must be valid at least six months beyond the end of stay. EU countries never require visas from British or Irish citizens. Always check **visa requirements** before

VISA ALERT!

Everyone needs a **visa** to visit **Russia**. American, Australian, British, Canadian and Irish citizens need a visa for **Turkey** (available at the border). You will need a **transit visa** if passing through **Ukraine** or **Belarus** (when travelling, for example, from Poland, Slovakia, Hungary or Romania to Moscow).

travelling, as they can and do change; this especially applies to Canadian, Australian and New Zealand citizens intending to visit Eastern European countries. We have listed embassy contacts below.

Fifteen countries (Austria, Belgium, Denmark, Finland, France, Germany, Greece, Iceland, Italy, Luxembourg, the Netherlands, Norway, Portugal, Spain and Sweden), known as the **Schengen Group**, now have joint visas which are valid for travel in all of them; in theory, there are also no immigration controls between these countries, but, in practice, there are often more ID spot-checks within their borders. A further nine countries – Czech Republic, Estonia, Hungary, Latvia, Lithuania, Malta, Poland, Slovakia and Slovenia – are set to join the group in 2008.

European embassies

Andorran UK ⓣ020/8874 4806; US ⓣ212/750 8064.

Austrian US ⓣ202/895-6700; Canada ⓣ613/789-1444; UK ⓣ020/7235 3731; Ireland ⓣ01/269 4577; Australia ⓣ02/6295 1533, ⓦwww.aussenministerium.at/canberra; NZ ⓣ04/499 6393, ⓔsimanke@woosh.co.nz; South Africa ⓣ12/452-9155.

Belgian Australia ⓣ02/6273 2501, ⓔcanberra@diplobel.be; Canada ⓣ613/236-7267 ⓔottawa@diplobel.org; Ireland ⓣ01/205 7100, ⓔDublin@diplobel.org; NZ ⓣ09/915 9146, ⓔimackenzie@farrowjamieson.co.nz; South Africa ⓣ21/419-4690, ⓔconsucap@iafrica.com; UK ⓣ020/7470 3700, ⓔlondon@diplobel.be; US ⓣ202/333-6900, ⓔwashington@diplobel.org.

British Australia ⓣ02/6270 6666; Canada ⓣ613/237-1530, ⓔgeneralenquiries@britainincanada.org; Ireland ⓣ01/205 3700 ⓔmanagement.dubli@fco.gov.uk; NZ ⓣ04/924 2888, ⓔppa.mailbox@fco.gov.uk; South Africa ⓣ12/421-7500, ⓔmedia.pretoria@fco.gov.uk; US ⓣ202/588-7800.

Bulgarian Australia ⓣ02/6286 9600, ⓔbulgem@bigpond.net.au; Canada ⓣ613/789-3215; Ireland ⓣ01/660 3293 ⓔbulgarianembassydublin@eircom.net; UK ⓣ020/7584 9400; US ⓣ202/387-0174. ⓔoffice@bulgaria-embassy.org; South Africa ⓣ12/342-.3720, ⓔembulgsa@iafrica.com.

Croatian Australia ⓣ02/6286 6988; Canada ⓣ613/562-7820; Ireland: ⓣ01/476 7181; NZ ⓣ09/836 5581; South Africa ⓣ12/342-1206; UK ⓣ020/7387 2022; US ⓣ202/588-5899.

Czech Australia ⓣ02/9371 0860, ⓔsydney@embassy.mzv.cz; Canada ⓣ613/562-3875, ⓔottawa@embassy.mzv.cz; Ireland ⓣ01/668 1135, ⓔdublin@embassy.mzv.cz; NZ ⓣ09/522 8736, ⓔauckland@honorary.mzv.cz; South Africa ⓣ12/431 2380, ⓔpretoria@embassy.mzv.cz; UK ⓣ020/7243 1115, US ⓣ202/274-9100, ⓔwashington@embassy.mzv.cz.

Danish Australia ⓣ02/6273 2196, ⓔdkembact@dynamite.com.au; Canada ⓣ613/562-1811; Ireland ⓣ01/475 6404; NZ ⓣ09/537 3099, ⓔdanish.nz@xtra.co.nz; South Africa ⓣ12/430-9340, ⓦwww.ambpretoria.um.dk; UK ⓣ020/7333 0200, ⓔlonamb@um.dk; US ⓣ202/234-4300.

Estonian Australia ⓣ02/9810 7468; Canada ⓣ613/789-4222, ⓔembassy.ottawa@mfa.ee; Ireland ⓣ01/219 6730 ⓔembassy.dublin@mfa.ee; South Africa ⓣ21/913-3850; UK ⓣ020/7589 3428, ⓔembassy.london@estonia.gov.uk; US ⓣ202/588-0101, ⓔinfo@estemb.org.

Finnish Australia ⓣ02/6273 3800, ⓔsanomat.can@formin.fi; Canada ⓣ613/288 2233, ⓔembassy@finland.ca; Ireland ⓣ01/478 1344, ⓔsanomat.dub@formin.fi; NZ ⓣ04/499 4599; South Africa ⓣ12/343-0275, ⓔsanomat.pre@formin.fi; UK ⓣ020/7838 6200, ⓔsanomat.lon@formin.fi; US ⓣ202/298-5800 ⓔsanomat.was@formin.fi.

French Australia ⓣ02/6216 0100. ⓔembassy@ambafrance-au.org; Canada ⓣ613/789-1795; Ireland ⓣ01/277 5000; NZ ⓣ04/384 2555; South Africa ⓣ12/425-1600, ⓔfrance@ambafrance-rsa.org; UK ⓣ020/7073 1000; US ⓣ202/944-6166.

German Australia ⓣ02/6270 1911; Canada ⓣ613/232-1101; Ireland ⓣ01/269 3011; NZ ⓣ04/473 6063; South Africa ⓦwww.pretoria.diplo.de; UK ⓣ020/7824 1300; US ⓣ202/ 944-6195.

Greek Australia ⓣ02/6273 3011; Canada ⓣ613/238-6271, ⓔembassy@greekembassy.ca; Ireland ⓣ01/676 7254, NZ ⓣ04/473 7775, ⓔinfo@greece.org.nz; South Africa ⓣ11/645-6000, ⓦwww.grconsulatejhb.co.za; UK ⓣ020/7229 3850, ⓔconsulategeneral@greekembassy.org.uk; US ⓣ202/939-1300.

Hungarian Australia ⓣ02/6282 3226, ⓔhungcbr@ozemail.com.au; Canada ⓣ613/230-2717, ⓔconsulate.ott@kum.hu; Ireland ⓣ01/661 2902, ⓔhungarian.embassy@eircom.net; NZ ⓣ04/973 7507, ⓔinfo@hungarianconsulate.co.nz; UK ⓣ020/7235 5218, US ⓣ202/362-6730.

Irish Australia ⓣ02/6273 3022, ⓔirishemb@cyberone.com.au; Canada ⓣ613/233-6281; South Africa ⓣ12/342-5062, ⓔpretoria@dfa.ie; NZ ⓣ09/977 2252; UK ⓣ020/7235 2171; US ⓣ202/462-3939.

Italian Australia ⓣ02/6273 3333, ambasciata.

canberra@esteri.it; Canada ⓣ613/232-2401, ⓔambasciata.ottawa@esteri.it; Ireland ⓣ01/660 1744, ⓔambasciata.dublino@esteri.it; NZ ⓣ04/473 5339, ⓔambasciata.wellington@esteri.it; South Africa ⓣ12/423-0000, ⓔegreteria.pretoria@esteri.it; UK ⓣ020/7312 2200, ⓔambasciata.londra@esteri.it; US ⓣ202/612-4400, ⓔaffariconsolari.washington@esteri.it.

Latvian Australia ⓣ61/2974 45981, ⓔdalins@optusnet.com.au; Canada ⓣ613/238-6014, ⓔembassy.canada@mfa.gov.lv; Ireland ⓣ01/428 3320; South Africa ⓣ11/505-9100, ⓔneishlos@icon.co.za; UK ⓣ020/7312 0040; US ⓣ202/328-2840, ⓔembassy@latvia-usa.org.

Lithuanian Australia ⓣ02/9498 2571, ⓔviktoras@astron.net.au; Canada ⓣ613/567-5458, ⓔamb.ca@urm.lt; NZ ⓣ09/571 1822, ⓔsaul@f1rst.co.nz; South Africa ⓣ12/328-3550, ⓔlietuvosior@pluto.co.za; UK ⓣ020/7486 6401; US ⓣ202/234-5860, ⓔinfo@ltembassyus.org

Luxembourg Australia ⓣ02/9253 4708, ⓔconsul@trafalgarcorporate.com; South Africa ⓣ02/285-4400, ⓔwebmaster@southafrica.be; UK (and Ireland) ⓣ020/7235 6961, ⓔemb@luxembourg.co.uk; US ⓣ202/265-4171.

Moroccan Australia ⓣ02/6290 0755; Canada ⓣ613/236 7301; Ireland ⓣ01/660 9449; NZ ⓣ09/520-3626; South Africa; ⓣ12/343-0230; UK ⓣ020/7581 5001; US ⓣ202/462-7980.

Netherlands Australia ⓣ02/6220 9400, ⓔan@minbuza.nl; Canada ⓣ613/237-5030, ⓔinfo@goholland.com; Ireland ⓣ01/269 3444, ⓔdub-info@minbuza.nl; NZ ⓣ04/471 6390, ⓔwel@minbuza.nl; South Africa ⓣ12/425-4500, ⓔpre@minbuza.nl; UK ⓣ020/7590 3200; US ⓣ202/244-5300.

Norwegian Australia ⓣ02/6273 3444, ⓔemb.canberra@mfa.no; Canada ⓣ613/238-6571, ⓔemb.ottawa@mfa.no; Ireland ⓣ01/662 1800, ⓔemb.dublin@mfa.no; NZ ⓣ04/471 2503; South Africa ⓦwww.norway.org.za; UK ⓣ020/7591 5500, ⓔemb.london@mfa.no; US ⓣ202/333-6000, ⓔemb.washington@mfa.no.

Polish Australia ⓣ02/6273 1208; Canada ⓣ613/789-0468; Ireland ⓣ01/283 0855; NZ ⓣ04/475 9453; South Africa: ⓣ12/430-2631; UK ⓣ0870/774 2700, US ⓣ202/234-3800.

Portuguese Australia ⓣ02/6290 1733; Canada ⓣ613/729-0883; Ireland ⓣ01/289 4416; NZ ⓣ04/382 7655; South Africa ⓣ12/341-2340; UK ⓣ020/7235 5331; US ⓣ202/328-8610.

Romanian Australia ⓣ02/6286 2343, ⓔroembassy@roembau.org; Canada ⓣ613/789-3709, ⓔromania@cyberus.ca; Ireland ⓣ01/668 1275, ⓔambrom@eircom.net; NZ ⓣ04/476 6883; South Africa ⓣ12/460-6940, ⓔromembsa@global.co.za; UK ⓣ020/7937 9666, ⓔroemb@roemb.co.uk; US ⓣ202/232-4846, ⓔoffice@roembus.org.

Russian Australia ⓣ02/6295 9033, ⓔrusembassy.australia@rambler.ru; Canada ⓣ613/235-4341, ⓔrusemb@rogers.com; Ireland ⓣ01/492 3492, ⓔduconsul@indigo.ie; NZ ⓣ04/476 6113, ⓔinfo@rus.co.nz; South Africa ⓣ12/362-1337, ⓔruspospr@mweb.co.za; UK ⓣ020/7229 3628, ⓔoffice@rusemblon.org; US ⓣ202/298-5700.

Serbian Australia ⓣ02/6290 2630, ⓔyuembau@ozemali.com.au; Canada ⓣ613/233-6289; NZ ⓣ02/6290 2630; South Africa ⓣ12/460-5626; UK ⓣ020/7235 7092; US ⓣ202/332-0333.

Slovakian Australia ⓣ02/6290 1516, consul@slovakemb-aust.org; Canada ⓣ613/749-4442, ⓔottawa@slovakembassy.ca; Ireland ⓣ01/660 0012, ⓔslovak@iol.ie; NZ ⓣ09/366 5111, ⓔslovakconsulate@kiely.co.nz; South Africa ⓣ12/342-2051 ⓔslovakem@telkomsa.net; UK ⓣ020/7313 6470, ⓔmail@slovakembassy.co.uk; US ⓣ202/237-1054, ⓔinfo@slovakembassy-us.org.

Slovenian Australia ⓣ02/6243 4830; Canada ⓣ613/565-5781, ⓔvot@gov.si; New Zealand ⓣ02/6243 4830, ⓔvca@gov.si; South Africa ⓣ61/478-2000, ⓔinfo.mzz@gov.si; UK ⓣ020/7222 5700, ⓔvlo@gov.si; US ⓣ202/667-5363, ⓔvwa@gov.si.

Spanish Australia ⓣ02/6273 3555, ⓔembespau@mail.mae.es; Canada ⓣ613/747-2252; Ireland ⓣ01/269 1640; NZ ⓣ03/366 0244, ⓔembespau@mail.mae.es; South Africa ⓣ12/460-0123; UK ⓣ020/7589 8989, ⓔconspalon@mail.mae.es; US ⓣ202/452-0100.

Swedish Australia ⓣ02/6270 2700, ⓔsweden@iimetro.com.au; Canada ⓣ613/241-8200, ⓔsweden.ottawa@foreign.ministry.se; Ireland ⓣ01/474 4400, ⓔambassaden.dublin@foreign.ministry.se; NZ ⓣ02/6270 2700, ⓔsweden@iimetro.com.au; South Africa ⓣ12/426-6400, ⓔsweden@iafrica.com; UK ⓣ020/7917 6400, ⓔambassaden.london@foreign.ministry.se; US ⓣ202/467-2600, ⓔambassaden.washington@foreign.ministry.se.

Swiss Australia ⓣ02/6162 8400, ⓔvertretung@can.rep.admin.ch; Canada ⓣ613/235-1837; Ireland ⓣ01/218 6382, ⓔvertretung@dub.rep.admin.ch; NZ ⓣ04/472 1593, UK ⓣ020/7616 6000, ⓔswissembassy@lon.rep.admin.ch; US ⓣ202/745-7900, ⓦwww.swissemb.org.

Turkish Australia ⓣ02/6234 0000, ⓔturkembs@bigpond.net.au; Canada ⓣ613/789-4044; Ireland ⓣ01/668 5240, NZ ⓣ04/472 1292, ⓔturkem@xtra.co.nz; South Africa ⓣ12/342-6051, ⓔpretbe@global.co.za; UK ⓣ020/7393 0202, ⓔturkish.emb@btclick.com; US ⓣ202/612-6700, ⓔcontact@turkishembassy.org.

Customs

Customs and duty-free restrictions vary throughout Europe, but are standard for travellers arriving in the EU at one litre of spirits, plus two litres of table wine, plus 200 cigarettes (or 250g tobacco, or fifty cigars). There is no duty-free allowance for travel within the EU; in principle you can carry as much in the way of duty-paid goods as you want, so long as it is for personal use. Note that Andorra, Gibraltar, the Channel Islands, the Canary Islands, Ceuta, Melilla and northern Cyprus are outside the EU for customs purposes. Remember that if you are carrying prescribed drugs of any kind, it might be a good idea to have a copy of the prescription to show to suspicious customs officers. Note also that for health reasons, many countries, including all EU members, restrict the importation of meat, fish, eggs, vegetables and honey, even for personal consumption.

GAY AND LESBIAN TRAVELLERS

Gay men and lesbians will find most of Europe a tolerant part of the world in which to travel, the west rather more so than the east. Gay sex is no longer a criminal offence in any country covered by this book except Morocco, but some still have measures that discriminate against gay men (a higher age of consent for example). Lesbianism would seem not to officially exist, so it is not generally subject to such laws. For further information, check the International Lesbian and Gay Association's European region website at Ⓦwww.ilga-europe.org.

HEALTH

There aren't many particular health problems you'll encounter travelling in Europe. You don't need to have any **inoculations** for any of the countries covered in this book, although for Morocco and Turkey typhoid jabs are advised, and in southeastern Turkey malaria pills are a good idea for much of the year – check Ⓦwww.cdc.gov/travel/regionalmalaria for full details. When travelling, remember to be up-to-date with your polio and tetanus boosters.

EU citizens resident in the UK or Ireland are covered by reciprocal health agreements for free or reduced-cost emergency treatment in many of the countries in this book (main exceptions are Morocco and Turkey). To claim this, you will often need only your passport, but you may also be asked for your European Health Insurance Card (EHIC) or proof of residence. In EU countries plus Norway, Switzerland and Liechtenstein you'll definitely need an EHIC which you can apply for in Britain at Ⓦwww.dh.gov.uk, in Ireland at Ⓦwww.ehic.ie.

Without a Health Insurance card, you won't be turned away from hospitals but you will almost certainly have to pay for any treatment or medicines. Also, in practice, some countries' doctors and hospitals charge anyway and it's up to you to claim reimbursement when you return home. Make sure you are insured for potential medical expenses, and keep copies of receipts and prescriptions.

Contraceptives

Condoms are available everywhere, and are normally reliable international brands such as Durex, at least in northwestern Europe; the condoms in eastern European countries, Morocco and Turkey are of uncertain quality, however, so it's best to stock up in advance.

AIDS is of course as much of a problem in Europe as in the rest of the world, and it hardly needs saying that unprotected casual sex is extremely dangerous; members of both sexes should carry condoms.

The pill is available everywhere, too, though often only on prescription; again, bring a sufficient supply with you. In case of emergency, the morning-after pill is available from pharmacies without a prescription in Belgium, Denmark, Finland, France, Morocco, Norway, Portugal, Sweden, Switzerland and the UK.

Drinking water

Tap water in most countries is drinkable, and only needs to be avoided in southern Morocco and parts of Turkey. **Unfamiliar food** may well give you a small dose of the runs, but this is usually nothing to worry

ROUGH GUIDES TRAVEL INSURANCE

Rough Guides has teamed up with Columbus Direct to offer you travel insurance that can be tailored to suit your needs.

Readers can choose from many different travel insurance products, including a low-cost backpacker option for long stays; a short-break option for city getaways; a typical holiday package option; and many others. There are also annual multi-trip policies for those who travel regularly, with variable levels of cover available. Different sports and activities (trekking, skiing, etc) can be covered if required on most policies.

Rough Guides travel insurance is available to the residents of 36 different countries with different language options to choose from via our website – www.roughguidesinsurance.com – where you can also purchase the insurance.

Alternatively, UK residents should call 0800/083 9507; US citizens should call 1-800/749-4922; Australians should call 1/300/669 999. All other nationalities should call +44 870/890 2843.

about, and is normally over in a couple of days; you shouldn't go plugging yourself up with anti-diarrhoea pills in the meantime.

Pharmacies

For minor health problems it's easiest to go to the local **pharmacy** which you'll find pretty much everywhere. In more serious cases contact your nearest consulate, which will have a list of English-speaking doctors, as will the local tourist office. In the accounts of larger cities we've listed the most convenient hospital casualty units/emergency rooms.

INSURANCE

Wherever you're travelling from, it's a very good idea to have some kind of **travel insurance**. Before paying for a new policy, however, it's worth checking whether you're already covered: students will often find that their student health coverage extends during the vacations and for one term beyond the date of last enrolment.

Otherwise you should contact a specialist **travel insurance company**, or consider Rough Guides' own travel insurance deal (see box). A typical policy usually provides cover for the loss of baggage, tickets and – up to a certain limit – cash or cheques, as well as cancellation or curtailment of your journey. Most of them exclude so-called **dangerous sports** unless an extra premium is paid: in Europe this can mean anything from scuba-diving to mountaineering, skiing and even bungee-jumping. With **medical coverage**, you should ascertain whether benefits will be paid as treatment proceeds or only after you return home, and whether there is a 24-hour medical emergency number. When securing baggage cover, make sure that the per-article limit will cover your most valuable possession. If you need to make a claim, you should keep receipts for medicines and medical treatment, and in the event you have anything stolen, you must obtain an official statement from the police.

INTERNET AND EMAIL

More and more **Internet cafés** are opening up across Europe and in major capitals you're likely to find many hotels and cafés offer **wireless access** (Wi-Fi) for those with their own laptops. Obviously the further you get off the beaten track, connection speeds are likely to diminish and you may have to resort to somewhat expensive dial-up access.

LEFT LUGGAGE

Almost every train station of any size has facilities for depositing **luggage**, either lockers or a desk that's open long hours every day. We've given details in the accounts of the major capitals.

MAIL

We've listed the **central post offices** in major cities and given an idea of opening hours. Bear in mind, though, that throughout much of Europe you can avoid the queues in post offices by buying stamps from newsagents, tobacconists and street kiosks. If you know in advance where you're going to be and when, it is possible to receive mail through the **poste restante** system, whereby letters addressed to you, marked "poste restante" and sent to the main post office in any town or city will be kept under your name – for at least two weeks and usually for a month. When collecting mail, make sure you take your passport for identification, and be aware that there's a possibility of letters being misfiled by someone unfamiliar with your language; try looking under your first name as well as your surname.

MAPS

Whether you're doing a grand tour or confining yourself to one or two countries, you will need a decent **map**. Though you can often buy maps on the spot, you may want to get them in advance to plan your trip – if you know what you want, the best advice is to contact a firm such as Stanfords in the UK (Ⓦwww.stanfords.co.uk) or Rand McNally in the US (Ⓦwww.randmcnally.com); both sell maps online or by mail order. In addition, Rough Guides produce a range of regional and country maps printed on rip-proof, waterproof paper (see Ⓦwww.roughguides.com for the full range).

We've recommended the best maps of individual countries throughout the book Other detailed maps covering Europe include Kümmerley & Frey (1:2,750,000), Michelin (1:3,000,000), Hallwag (1:3,600,000), Freytag & Berndt (1:3,500,000), and Philip's (1:3,500,000). Of those, only the first three show railways, and all of them omit large parts of Turkey and Morocco. If you intend to travel mainly by rail, it might be worth getting the Thomas Cook Rail Map of Europe. For extensive motoring, it's better to get a large-page road atlas such as Michelin's Tourist and Motoring Atlas.

THE EURO (€)

The euro (seep.9) is the currency of fifteen EU countries. Coins come as 1c, 2c, 5c, 10c, 20c, 50c, €1 and €2. One side of the coin states the denomination while the other side has a design unique to the issuing country. Euro notes come as €5, €10, €20, €50, €100, €200 and €500. At the time of writing, £1 was worth €1.40, US$1 got you 69c, Can$1 was 68c, Aus$1 equalled 60c and NZ$1 was 53c.

MONEY

The easiest way to carry your money is in the form of plastic. Hotels, shops and restaurants across the continent accept major **credit and debit cards**, although cheaper places may not. More importantly, you can use them 24/7 to get cash out of ATMs throughout Europe, including Morocco and Turkey, as long as they are affiliated to an international network (such as Visa, MasterCard or Cirrus). As well as carrying a **cash back-up**, you may also want to consider **travellers' cheques**, in either US dollars, euros or UK pounds.

In some countries **banks** are the only places where you can legally change money, and they often offer the best exchange rates and lowest commission. Local banking hours are given throughout this book. Outside normal hours you can normally resort to **bureaux de change**, often located at train stations and airports, though their rates and/or commissions may well be less favourable.

PHONES

It is nearly always possible, especially in western Europe, to make **international calls** from a public call box; this can often be more trouble than it's worth from a coin phone due to the constant need to feed in change, although most countries now have phone cards, making the whole process much easier. Otherwise, you can go to a **post office**, or a special **phone bureau**, where you can make a call from a private booth and pay afterwards. Most countries have these in one form or another, and the local tourist office will point you in the right direction. Avoid using the phone in your **hotel room** – unless you have money to burn.

To **call any country** in this book from Britain, Ireland or New Zealand, dial ⓣ00, then the country code (see box), then the city/area code (if there is one) without the initial zero – except for Russia, Latvia and Lithuania, where an initial 8 is omitted, Italy, where the initial zero must be dialled, and Spain, where the initial 9 must be dialled – then the local number. From the US and most of Canada, the international access code is ⓣ011, from Australia it's ⓣ0011; otherwise the procedure is the same.

To **call home** from almost all European countries, including Morocco and Turkey, dial ⓣ00, then the country code, then the city/area code (without the initial zero if there is one), then the local number. The exception is Russia, where you dial ⓣ8, wait for a continuous dialling tone and then dial ⓣ10, followed by the country code, area code and number.

For **collect calls**, "Home Country Direct" services are available in most of the places covered in this book. In the UK and some other countries, international calling cards available from newsagents enable you to call North America, Australia and New Zealand very cheaply. Most North American, British, Irish and Australasian phone companies either allow you to call home from abroad on a credit card, or billed to your home number (contact your company's customer services before you leave to find out their toll-free access codes from the countries you'll be visiting), or else will issue an international calling card which can be used worldwide, and for which you will be billed on your return. If you want a calling card and do not already have one, leave yourself a few weeks to arrange it before leaving.

Mobile/cellphones

Cellphones from the US and Canada may not work in Europe – for details contact your provider. **Mobiles** from the UK, Ireland, Australia and New Zealand can be used in most parts of Europe, and a lot of coun-

CLOTHING AND SHOE SIZES

Women's dresses and skirts									
American	4	6	8	10	12	14	16	18	
British	8	10	12	14	16	18	20	22	
Continental	38	40	42	44	46	48	50	52	
Women's blouses and sweaters									
American	6	8	10	12	14	16	18		
British	30	32	34	36	38	40	42		
Continental	40	42	44	46	48	50	52		
Women's shoes									
American	5	6	7	8	9	10	11		
British	3	4	5	6	7	8	9		
Continental	36	37	38	39	40	41	42		
Men's suits									
American	34	36	38	40	42	44	46	48	
British	34	36	38	40	42	44	46	48	
Continental	44	46	48	50	52	54	56	58	
Men's shirts									
American	14	15	15.5	16	16.5	17	17.5	18	
British	14	15	15.5	16	16.5	17	17.5	18	
Continental	36	38	39	41	42	43	44	45	
Men's shoes									
American	7	7.5	8	8.5	9.5	10	10.5	11	11.5
British	6	7	7.5	8	9	9.5	10	11	12
Continental	39	40	41	42	43	44	44	45	46

tries – certainly in Western Europe – have nearly universal coverage, but you may have to inform your provider before leaving home to get international access switched on, and you will be charged for receiving calls and even voicemail. Also note that it will not always be possible to charge up or replace your pre-paid cards, so again check beforehand and, if necessary, top up your credit before you leave. A standard two-pin socket is used on the Continent so you may also need an adaptor for charging your phone.

The most useful resource for information on phone codes and electrical systems around the world is the encyclopedic website Ⓦwww.kropla.com.

SHOPPING

Europe is a great place to **shop** – with outlets running the gamut from high fashion houses in Paris and Milan to the souks of Morocco you'll be spoilt for choice. We've included country-specific information on shopping in each individual chapter, especially in capital cities. See the chart on p.53 for size conversions.

TIME

This book covers four **time zones** (see map, opposite) Note that GMT (Greenwich Mean Time aka UTC, or Universal Time), is five hours ahead of Eastern Standard Time, eight hours ahead of Pacific Standard Time, eight hours behind Western Australia, ten hours behind eastern Australia, and twelve hours behind New Zealand. Note that all countries in this book (except Morocco) have daylight saving time from March to October; thankfully, they usually manage to all change over at the same time, but this change, along with daylight saving in North America, Australia and New Zealand, can affect the time difference by an hour either way.

TOURIST INFORMATION

Before you leave, it's worth contacting the **tourist offices** of the countries you're intending to visit for free leaflets, maps and brochures. This is especially true in parts of central and eastern Europe, where up-to-date maps can be harder to find within the country. Bulgaria does not have an official tourist office, and neither does Russia except in the US; their embassies will have some information, but it will be about rules and regulations rather than transport and sightseeing.

Once you're in Europe, on-the-spot information is easy enough to pick up. Most countries have a network of **tourist offices** that answer queries, dole out a range of (sometimes free) maps and brochures, and can often book accommodation, or at least advise you on it. They're better organized in northern Europe – Scandinavia, the Netherlands, France, Switzerland – with branches in all but the smallest village, and mounds of information; in Greece, Turkey and eastern Europe you'll find fewer tourist offices and they'll be less helpful on the whole, sometimes offering no more than a couple of dog-eared brochures and a photocopied map. We've given further details, including a broad idea of opening hours, in the introduction for each country.

Tourist information websites and offices

If there is no office in your home country, apply to the embassy instead.

Andorra Ⓦwww.turisme.ad; UK Ⓣ020/8874 4806.
Austria Ⓦwww.austria.info. Australia Ⓣ02/9299 3621; Canada Ⓣ416/967-3381; Ireland Ⓣ189/093 0118; UK Ⓣ0845/101 1818; US Ⓣ212/944-6880.
Belgium Ⓦwww.visitbelgium.com. Canada Ⓣ514/457-2888; UK Ⓣ0800/954 5245; US Ⓣ212/758-8130;.
Britain Ⓦwww.visitbritain.com. Australia Ⓣ02/9021 4400 or 1300/858 589; Canada Ⓣ1-888/VISIT-UK; Ireland Ⓣ01/670 8000; New Zealand Ⓣ0800/700 741; US Ⓣ1-800/462-2748.
Bulgaria Ⓦwww.bulgariatravel.org.
Croatia Ⓦwww.croatia.hr. UK Ⓣ020/8563 7979; US Ⓣ1-800/829 4416.
Czech Republic Ⓦwww.czechtourism.com. Canada Ⓣ416/363-9928; UK Ⓣ020/7631 0427; US Ⓣ212/288-0830.
Denmark Ⓦwww.visitdenmark.com. UK Ⓣ020/7259 5959; US Ⓣ212/885-9700.
Estonia Ⓦwww.visitestonia.com.
Finland Ⓦwww.visitfinland.com. Canada & US Ⓣ1-800/FIN-INFO; Ireland Ⓣ01/407 3362; UK Ⓣ020/7365 2512.
France Ⓦwww.franceguide.com. Australia Ⓣ02/9231 5244; Canada Ⓣ514/288-2026; Ireland Ⓣ1560/235 235 (premium rate); UK Ⓣ0906/824

4123 (premium rate); US ⓣ410/286-8310.
Germany ⓦwww.germany-tourism.de. Australia ⓣ02/8296 0488; Canada & US ⓣ1-800/651-7010; Ireland ⓣ1800/484 480; UK ⓣ020/7317 0908.
Greece ⓦwww.gnto.gr. Australia ⓣ02/9241 1663; Canada ⓣ416/968-2220; UK ⓣ020/7495 9300; US ⓣ212/421-5777.
Hungary ⓦwww.hungary.com. UK & Ireland ⓣ00800/3600 0000; US ⓣ212/355-0240.
Ireland ⓦwww.tourismireland.com. Australia ⓣ02/9299 6177; Canada & US ⓣ1-800/223-6470; New Zealand ⓣ09/977 2255; UK ⓣ0800/039 7000.
Italy ⓦwww.enit.it. Australia ⓣ02/9262 1666; Canada ⓣ416/925-4882; UK ⓣ020/7399 3562; US ⓣ212/245-4822.
Latvia ⓦwww.latviatourism.lv.
Lithuania ⓦwww.tourism.lt. US ⓣ718/423-6161.
Luxembourg ⓦwww.ont.lu. UK ⓣ020/7434 2800; US ⓣ212/935-8888.
Morocco ⓦwww.visitmorocco.org. Australia ⓣ02/9299 6177; Canada ⓣ514/842-8111; UK ⓣ020/7437 0073; US ⓣ212/557-2520.
Netherlands ⓦwww.holland.com.
Norway ⓦwww.visitnorway.com. UK ⓣ020/7389 8800; US ⓣ212/885-9700.
Poland ⓦwww.polandtour.org. UK ⓣ0870/067 5010; US ⓣ201/420-9910.
Portugal ⓦwww.visitportugal.com. Canada ⓣ416/921-7376; Ireland ⓣ1800/943 131; UK ⓣ0845/355 1212; US ⓣ646/723-0200.
Romania ⓦwww.romaniatourism.com. UK ⓣ020/7224 3692; US ⓣ212/545-8484.
Russia ⓦwww.russia-travel.com. US ⓣ1-877/221-7120; UK ⓣ020/7495 7570, ⓦwww.visitrussia.org.uk
Serbia ⓦwww.serbia-tourism.org. UK ⓣ020/7629 2007.
Slovenia ⓦwww.slovenia.info. US ⓣ954/491-0112; UK ⓣ0870/225 5305.
Spain ⓦwww.tourspain.es. US ⓣ212/265-8822; Canada ⓣ416/961-3131; UK ⓣ020/7486 8077.
Sweden ⓦwww.visit-sweden.com. Worldwide toll-free ⓣ800/3080 3080; Ireland ⓣ01/247 5440; UK ⓣ020/7108 6168; US ⓣ212/885-9700.
Switzerland ⓦwww.myswitzerland.com. Canada ⓣ011-800/1002 0030; UK ⓣ00800/1002 0030; US ⓣ1-877/794-8037.
Turkey ⓦwww.tourismturkey.org. UK ⓣ020/7629 7771; US ⓣ212/687-2194.

TRAVELLERS WITH DISABILITIES

Prosperous northern Europe is easier for **disabled travellers** than the south and east, but the gradual enforcement of EU accessibility regulations is making life easier throughout the European Union at least. **Wheelchair access** to public buildings nonetheless remains far from common in many countries, as is wheelchair accessibility to public transport. Most buses are still inaccessible to wheelchair users, but airport facilities are improving, as are those on cross-Channel ferries. As for rail services, these vary greatly: France, for example, has very good facilities for disabled passengers, as have Belgium, Denmark, Switzerland and Austria, but many other countries make little if any provision.

WOMEN TRAVELLERS

One of the major irritants for women travelling through Europe is **sexual harassment**, which in Italy, Greece, Turkey, Spain and Morocco especially can be almost constant for women travelling alone. By far the most common kind of harassment you'll come across simply consists of street whistles and cat-calls; occasionally it's more sinister and very occasionally it can be dangerous. Indifference is often the best policy, avoiding eye contact with men and at the same time appearing as confident and purposeful as possible. If this doesn't make you feel any more comfortable, shouting a few choice phrases in the local language is a good idea; don't, however, shout in English, which often seems to encourage them. You may also come across gropers on crowded buses and trains, in which case you should complain as loudly as possible in any language – the ensuing scene should be enough to deter your assailant.

YOUTH AND STUDENT DISCOUNTS

It's worth flashing whichever discount card you've got at every opportunity – you never know what you might get. If you're a student, an **International Student Identity Card** (ISIC for short) is well worth investing in. It can get you reduced (usually half-price, sometimes free) entry to museums and other sights – costs which can eat their way into your budget alarmingly if you're doing a lot of sightseeing – as well as qualifying you for other discounts in certain cities. It can also save you money on some transport costs, notably ferries, and especially if you are over 26. For Americans there's also a health benefit, providing up to US$3000 in emergency medical coverage and US$100 a day for up to sixty days in hospital, plus a 24-hour hotline to call in the event of a medical, legal or financial emergency. The card costs US$22 in the US, Can$16 in Canada, £7 in the UK, €13 in Ireland, Aus$18 in Australia, and NZ$20 in New Zealand. If you're not a student but under 26, get an **International Youth Travel Card**, which costs the same and can in some countries give much the same sort of reductions. Both cards are available direct from Ⓦwww.isiccard.com or from youth travel specialists such as STA and Travel Cuts.

As well as the above options, the **EURO<26 youth card** (Ⓦwww.euro26.org) entitles anyone under 26 to a wide range of discounts on transport services, tourist attractions, activities and accommodation for up to a year. It is available online for people living outside Europe and at designated outlets throughout the continent (apart from England and France) for residents – you'll need proof of age and a passport-sized photo. Although the card is valid across the region, prices vary in individual countries (from around €5 to €14), as do the relevant discounts (see website for full details).

Andorra

HIGHLIGHTS

GRANVALIRA: the best skiing and mountain-biking in the Pyrenees
THE GR7: hike along an old smugglers' route
SHOPPING: from electronics to alcohol, prices are much cheaper than in France and Spain
CALDEA: the largest natural thermal springs in Europe
CASA DE LA VALL: Andorra's new parliament meets several times a year in this sixteenth-century edifice

ROUGH COSTS

DAILY BUDGET Basic €30/with the occasional treat €50–60

DRINK €2 for a beer/wine.

FOOD You can easily dine out for €10.

HOSTEL/BUDGET HOTEL Free if staying in a refuge/€30–40

TRAVEL Buses cost about €1.40 per journey

FACT FILE

POPULATION 76,900

AREA 468 sq km

LANGUAGE Catalan

CURRENCY Euro (€)

CAPITAL Andorra la Vella (population 22,000)

INTERNATIONAL PHONE CODE ⓣ376

Basics

Often falling off the itineraries of most European travellers, Andorra is a tiny country nestled in the Pyrenees. One of the oldest nations in Europe, it was one of the buffer territories set up by Charlemagne in the eighth century to keep the Islamic Moors at bay. It remained an anachronistic feudal state until 1993, when Andorrans voted for an independent, democratic principality – although, technically, the country's "princes" are the president of France and the Spanish Bishop of Urgell.

Andorra's forty-odd hamlets are scattered across the valleys, with several dozen Romanesque churches and chapels, and trails that wend their way to mountains and alpine lakes beyond. The capital, **Andorra la Vella**, offers a few sights and most of the shopping, while next-door **Escaldes-Engordany** lays claim to the biggest thermal spa in Europe. To the northwest, the remote town of **Pal** remains virtually untouched by modernity, while **Arinsal** makes a great stop for an après-ski drink. Ordino's hills have access to excellent alpine paths, while sleepy towns such as **Serrat** offer breathtaking views. East of Ordino, a road weaves through jaw-dropping mountainscapes to **Canillo**, which boasts a captivating Romanesque chapel, and further north, **Soldeu**, a sleepy place just a stone's throw from France.

CHRONOLOGY

219 BC The Romans explore the Pyrenees.
803 AD Emperor Charlemagne captures the area that is known as present-day Andorra from the Islamic Moors.
843 Charlemagne's grandson grants the Valley of Andorra to the Count of Urgell from the Spanish town of La Seu d'Urgell.
1133 The Count of Urgell gives Andorra to the Catholic Bishop of Urgell.
1278 Andorra's sovereignty is divided between the Bishop of Urgell and the Count of Foix in France.
1607 King Henry IV of France declares that the Head of the French State will become a co-prince of Andorra, alongside the Bishop of Urgell.
1799 French revolutionaries end France's rule of Andorra.
1806 Napoleon reinstates France's interest in Andorra, to prevent a Spanish invasion.
1866 First steps towards democracy in the "Nova Reforma".
1914 Andorra declares war on Germany in World War I but does not fight.
1934 Russian adventurer Boris Skossyreff proclaims himself King of Andorra. The Spanish arrest him a few days later.
1939 Andorra remains neutral during World War II.
1958 Andorra finally declares peace with Germany, having been forgotten at the Treaty of Versailles after World War II.
1970 Women given the vote.
1993 First constitution is established, reducing the influence of the princes and placing more power in the hands of the Andorran people.
1999 Andorra adopts the euro.
2005 The Liberal Party win elections.

ARRIVAL

Getting to Andorra isn't the easiest of tasks. There is no airport in the country itself, but several companies operate **buses** from Spain and France: Alsina Graells (Ⓣ826 567. Ⓦwww.alsinagraells.com) arrives daily from Barcelona (€20) and Lleida in Spain (€14); Novatel (Ⓣ803 789, Ⓦwww.andorrabybus.com) does airport transfers from Barcelona and Toulouse (€25–28); and Eurolines (Ⓣ805 151, Ⓦwww.eurolines.es) runs daily services from Madrid and Barcelona (€20) and several buses weekly from other Spanish cities. Hispano Andorra (Ⓣ821 372) has a few daily buses to all the main towns from La Seu d'Urgell in Spain (€2.40) and l'Hospitalet in France (€7.70), where you can hop on SNCF trains.

GETTING AROUND

Once in the country, getting around is fairly straightforward, mainly because Andorra's small size enables you to visit most places on day-trips. The finest way to tour Andorra is on **foot** – the gorgeous scenery and well-marked paths make for wonderful hiking – though public transport is also a reliable and cost-effective option. A good **bus** network covers the main towns, with each line connected to the capital, Andorra La Vella; the most you'll pay for a ticket is around €4.60, which would take you from Andorra la Vella to Pas de la Casa on the French border. With limited time or energy, however, a **car** is your best choice. Fuel is a lot cheaper than in the rest of Europe, and you can rent a car in the capital for around €60 per day. **Taxis** are fairly cost-effective and, if you're in a group, are a viable option – a trip from Andorra la Vella to Arinsal, nearly halfway across the country, costs €13.

ACCOMMODATION

Good **budget accommodation** is hard to come by, and most of the cheaper options, located in the capital of Andorra la Vella, have zero charm. Prices run sky-high in high season – July to August (when reservations are a must) and December to March – expect to pay at least €40 for a double room. On the other end of the scale, there are many well-equipped **campsites** throughout the country that are very cheap. Another popular option in the summer is staying for free in one of Andorra's 26 state-run **refugis**, simple mountain cabins – information is available at tourist offices around the country. Camping in the wild is illegal except around these cabins.

FOOD AND DRINK

Andorran **food** is generally characterized by rich meat and cheese dishes, though there are influences from French and Spanish cuisines. Breakfasts consist of an espresso and a croissant or tartine du pain. Lunch at many restaurants is an inexpensive plat du jour, while dinner is usually a full-on Catalan affair of chargrilled fish, fowl or steak alongside fresh aubergine, tomatoes and garlic.

Typical Andorran **dishes** include *trinchat* (cabbage, potatoes and bacon), *estofat d'isard* (goat stew), *truite de ríu* (river trout), *coques* (clam-filled cakes), *xai* (roast lamb), *escudella* (chicken, sausage and meatball stew) and *crema catalana* (dessert custard with a caramel crust). Buying alcohol in supermarkets will be absurdly cheap, but prices can run high in some bars and restaurants. Spanish *vino* is generally the local drink of choice, and house wines are a safe and inexpensive choice, though for the more discerning, the medium-bodied Buzet or exotic and fruity Penedès are both good bets.

CULTURE AND ETIQUETTE

As the only country in the world to have **Catalan** as its official language, you'll find small signs in shop/café windows across Andorra indicating that staff prefer to use Catalan. Hostels and tourist offices are also keen to hand out pocket-sized cards with basic Catalan phrases. However, if you get stuck, Spanish is spoken almost everywhere and basic English is used in the more touristy establishments.

Another thing that stands out is the courteous **driving style** on Andorran roads – something that neighbouring countries don't seem to share. Here, you won't have to dodge traffic to cross the road, and cars will generally stop at crossings.

SHOPPING

Andorra offers **duty-free shopping** on most goods. In some smaller shops, you can ask for *el descuento*, an extra ten-percent discount for foreigners, though this is at the discretion of the establishment. The official duty-free allowances for alcohol and tobacco are currently 5 litres of wine, 1.5 litres of spirits and 300 cigarettes. You'll probably slip past the French border with an extra bottle or two, but the Spanish guards are known to be much more strict.

SPORTS AND OUTDOOR ACTIVITIES

Skiing is the main attraction during winter; however, the ski resorts (Grandvalira, Vall Nord and La Rabassa) are still open from June/July to September for alternative outdoor adventures, ranging from rafting to quad biking. All year round, **hiking** is a popular option – even if you're an inexperienced hiker, there are several easy routes that lead through some of the Pyrenees' most spectacular features.

COMMUNICATIONS

Phonecards (€3 or €6) are sold in shops and tourist offices. Phoning outside the country can be very expensive, however, local calls cost minimum €0.10 from payphones. The local operator is ⓣ111; international operator is ⓣ119. **Post offices** around the country are either Spanish or French – the latter is more efficient. You'll need to buy special Andorran stamps to post anything. **Internet** access is available in all the main towns.

ANDORRA ON THE NET

- www.andorra.ad Tourist board site.
- www.andorramania.com Lots of information, largely geared towards skiers.
- www.alltravelandorra.com Details on getting to Andorra and accommodation.
- www.andorraportal.com Directory of restaurants and shopping establishments.
- www.skiandorra.ad Site covering Andorra's ski resorts.

EMERGENCIES

The biggest danger in Andorra is the risk of spending too much money in the ubiquitous duty-free shops. Otherwise, be careful on the mountain roads that have some very sharp curves. Each commune has its own *Centre de Salud*, where you can find on-duty doctors for non-urgent health issues. For **emergencies**, call an ambulance or get to the hospital in Escaldes-Engordany. Twenty-four-hour **pharmacies** rotate on a daily basis – just check in the window of any pharmacy for a full timetable complete with addresses and telephone numbers.

EMERGENCY NUMBERS

Police ⓣ110; Ambulance and Fire ⓣ118; Medical ⓣ116; Mountain Rescue ⓣ112.

ENTRY REQUIREMENTS

In theory, **passports** are required to cross the Andorran border, so make sure you have yours ready. If entering by bus, you may not be inspected, but you'll probably have to present your passport when buying your bus ticket.

INFORMATION & MAPS

The Ministeri de Presidència i Turisme operates **tourist offices** in the capital and most large towns. Be sure to ask for their brochures *Cultural Itineraries* and *Mountain Activities*, which detail dozens of good hiking, biking and rock-climbing routes. For general walking around the country, the best **map** is Rando Édition's *Andorra-Cadi 21*. The more detailed (1:50.000) *Muntanys d'Andorra* charts are best for greater exploration and are available at tourist offices.

MONEY AND BANKS

Andorra uses the **euro** (€). You'll find **exchange facilities** at most post offices and banks (Mon–Fri 9am–1pm & 3–5pm, Sat 9am–noon), there are **ATMs** throughout the country, and credit cards can be used just about everywhere.

OPENING HOURS, HOLIDAYS AND FESTIVALS

Most shops open from 9am to 8pm, with a near-obligatory siesta between 1 and 4pm and reduced hours on Sundays. Shops and banks are closed on the following **public holidays**: Jan 1; Jan 6; March 14; Holy Thurs–Easter Mon; May 1; Ascension, Pentecost and Whit Mon; June 24; Aug 15; Sept 8; Nov 1; Nov 4; Dec 8; Dec 24–26; Dec 31. **Churches** open daily in July and August from 10am to 7pm. The summer months also see local **festivals** in many of Andorra's townships. The main ones are in Canillo (third Sun & Mon in July); Sant Julià de Lòria (last Sun, Mon & Tues in July); Escaldes-Engordany (July 25–27); Andorra la Vella (first Sat, Sun & Mon in Aug); La Massana and Encamp (Aug 15–17); and Ordino (Sept 16–17).

Catalan (Català)

	Catalan	Pronunciation
Yes	*Sí*	See
No	*Noh*	Noh
Please	*Si us plau*	See-uus-plow
Thank you	*Graciés*	Gra-see-ess
Hello/Good day	*Hola*	Oh-lah
Goodbye	*Adéu*	A-day-uu
Excuse me	*Perdoni*	Perdoni
Where?	*On?*	On?
Good	*Bon/Bona*	Bo
Bad	*Mal*	Mal
Near	*Aprop*	Aprop
Far	*Lluny*	Yoon
Cheap	*Barat*	Barat
Expensive	*Car*	Car
Open	*Obert*	Obert
Closed	*Tancat*	Ton-cot
Today	*Avui*	A-body
Yesterday	*Ahir*	Uh-ear
Tomorrow	*Demà*	De-mah
How much?	*Quant val?*	Kwant val?
What time is it?	*Quina hora és?*	Kwina ora es?
I don't understand	*No ho entenc*	No hoe entayn
Do you speak English?	*Parles anglès?*	Parles ang-lays?
One	*Un/Una*	Oon/Oona
Two	*Dos/Dues*	Dohs/Doo-es
Three	*Tres*	Trrhes
Four	*Quatre*	Kwa-trer
Five	*Cinc*	Seenk
Six	*Sis*	Sees
Seven	*Set*	Set
Eight	*Vuit*	Vweet
Nine	*Nou*	No
Ten	*Deu*	Deoo

Andorra la Vella

Lying at the confluence of three mountain rivers, the national capital of **ANDORRA LA VELLA** is a bit of a misnomer. "Old Andorra" is for the most part a collection of neon-lit windows to soulless tourist restaurants and ageing storefronts – all placed against the stunning backdrop of towering mountains. Where once the streets bustled with shepherds and their livestock – most of the capital was farmland until a few decades ago – today it exists more or less as a base for shoppers and wealthier skiers. Since most buses arrive here, you'll probably end up passing through once or twice during your stay, and while it's not the best introduction to Andorra, the city holds a few sights to while away an afternoon – and enough bargain hunting to while away a few lifetimes.

What to see and do

The capital is bisected by the Avinguda del Príncep Benlloch, which further east becomes the shop-filled Avinguda de Meritxell and then, on towards neighboring Escaldes-Engordany, Avinguda de Carlemany. The old quarter lies just south of Príncep Benlloch.

Barri Antic and the Casa de la Vall

Towards the western end of town, **Barri Antic** is the capital's old quarter and, with its cobbled streets and quiet plaças, a great escape from the shopping mall that is the rest of the city. In the centre is one of the oldest parliaments in Europe – and certainly the smallest – the **Casa de la Vall** (Mon–Sat 9.30am–1.30pm & 3–7pm, Sun 10am–2pm; Nov–April closed Sun; free guided tours; bookings required on ⓣ829 129). Built in 1580 and complete with towers, battlements and steel-barred windows, it provides an appropriately historical base for the courts and the Sindic, Andorra's representative house. Among the rocks below, the government is busily constructing a modern parliament building, due to open in 2008. East of the Casa de la Vall, Plaça Príncep Benlloch is presided over by the town's main church, **Església de Sant Esteve**. Originally an eleventh-century construction, it's now been mostly modernized throughout, though it does retain two lovely altarpieces. South of here, Plaça del Poble makes a great hangout in the evenings and houses the **Centre de Congresos**, one of the country's only theatre and music venues, though performance season runs in winter only.

Grans Magatzems Pyrénées and the Museu del Parfum

Avinguda Meritxell and the streets around have the highest concentration of shops including Andorra's largest department store, the **Grans Magatzems Pyrénées**, at no.11 (Mon–Fri 9.30am–8pm, Sat 9.30am–9pm, Sun 9.30am–7pm; Aug weeknights until 9pm), which also houses several cafeteria-style restaurants on the top floor. At the other end of the pungency spectrum, a fifteen-minute stroll east along Avinguda Meritxell brings you to the **Museu del Perfum**, av Carlemany 115 (Tues–Fri 10am–1pm & 4–8pm, Sat 10am–2pm & 3.30–8pm, Sun 10am–1.30pm; ⓣ801 926, ⓦwww.julia.ad; €5, free to customers of Júlia Perfumería on ground floor). The small museum displays hundreds of bottles dating from 700BC to the present and has an ingenious contraption that allows visitors to mix the essences of several dozen plants, herbs and spices, and waft the resulting bouquet.

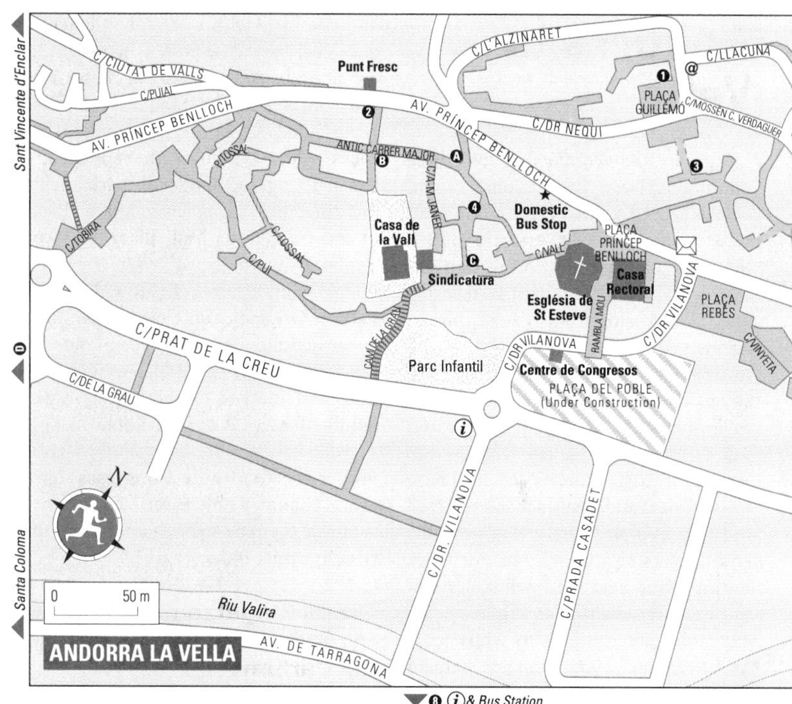

Santa Coloma

Two kilometres south of the capital, **Santa Coloma** is the most famous church in Andorra, frequently represented on postcards and tourist bureau walls. It was built in several stages over a few hundred years beginning in the ninth century, and the entire interior was once literally plastered with beautiful iconography, though most of the murals now reside in museums in Berlin and Massachusetts. All that remains of note is a small geometric Agnus Dei, just at the triumphal arch.

Sant Vicenç d'Enclar

A thirty-minute walk west up the rocky hillside via Santa Coloma brings you to **Sant Vicenç d'Enclar**, Andorra's oldest church, and the remains of a pre-medieval fortification where the Counts of Urgell – the original rulers of Andorra – once played fort. The church itself was rebuilt in 1979 and is in quite good nick, but the remains of the embrasured walls behind it, rumoured to date from the sixth century, have all but succumbed to the passage of time.

Arrival and information

Buses International buses arrive at the Central d'Autobusos, located just southeast of the small Parc Central, five minutes south of the city centre. Domestic buses leave from just west of pl Benlloch.

National tourist office Prat de la Creu, on the corner with c/Dr Vilanova (Mon–Sat 9am–1pm & 3–7pm, Sun 10am–1pm; Sept–June closed Sun; ⓣ820 214).

Commune tourist office Pl de la Rotonda (July & Aug Mon–Sat 9am–9pm, Sun 9am–7pm; Sept–June 9.30am–1.30pm & 3.30–7.30pm; ⓣ827 117). They should be able to help with finding a place to stay but are otherwise not overly useful or friendly – the maps aren't very detailed and the staff speak basic English.

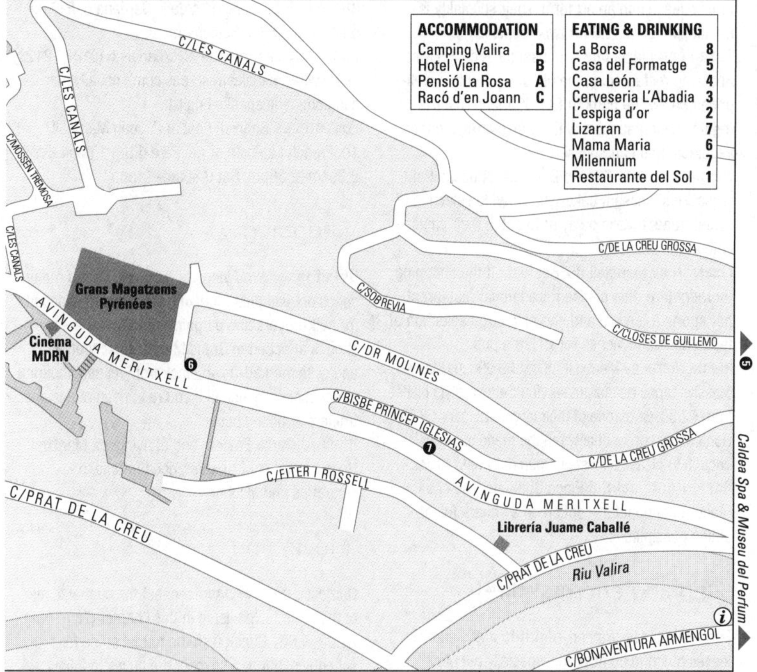

Accommodation

Camping Valira av de Salou ⓣ722 384, ⓦwww.campvalira.com. The not-quite-in-the-wild camping facilities are good, and there is a pool and restaurant. ❶, bungalows ❹

Hotel Viena c/de la Vall 32 ⓣ829 233, ⓕ829 915. Comfortable rooms in the old quarter, all with bathroom and TV. Downstairs is a large café-bar with pool table and Internet. ❹

Pensió La Rosa Antic Carrer Major 18 ⓣ&ⓕ821 810. Just inside the gates of the old quarter, the 24 simply styled rooms are excellent value. ❸

Racó d'en Joan c/de la Vall 20 ⓣ820 811. Well located in the old town next to the parliament, with friendly staff and tidy rooms. The attached restaurant serves inexpensive meals. ❹

Eating

The cheapest eats in town are to be had from Punta Fresc, a budget **supermarket** with large range of products, at Príncep Benlloch 22 – it's a great place to stock up before a day's hike.

Casa del Formatge Passatge Antònia Font Caminal 1, Escaldes-Engordany. Located just off of av Carlemany, this unique shop-cum-restaurant

TREAT YOURSELF

The **Caldea Spa** (daily 9am–midnight; closed most of Nov and 3 weeks in May; €30.50 for 3hr, €23 for 2hr evening session; ⓣ800 999, ⓦwww.caldea.com), 1km east of Casa de la Vall, in Escaldes-Engordany, is the largest health centre on the continent, pumping in water from the nearby thermal springs to offer everything from Turkish baths to exfoliating hydromassages. Particularly spectacular are the mountain views from the outdoor lagoon. The thermal water is rich in sodium, silica and sulphur and is reputed to have considerable antalgic effects for skin and respiratory ailments. Even if the spa is not your cup of tea, the eleventh-floor bar offers some nice views.

turns cheese into an art form. Their speciality is fondue, priced at €26 for two people.
Casa Léon Placeta de la Consòrcia. A cosy, Franco-Andorran restaurant in the old quarter with a well-priced *carte*. The bargain €11.30 *menu rustic* is a regal four-course meal with soup, starter, meat or vegetable main and dessert.
L'Espiga d'Or av Príncep Benlloch, opposite Punt Fresc. This pleasant bakery has a wide selection of sweet treats to take away or to eat in their small café at the back.
Lizarran av Meritxell 86. Set just off the shopping thoroughfare, this pleasant traditional restaurant-bar sports a terrace and serves a large selection of tapas and sandwiches for €1.20 a pop.
Mama Maria av Meritxell 25 ⓣ869 996, ⓕ829 998. Massive tapas restaurant serving Catalan-style dishes from €2.30. Or try one of their large pizzas for €9.50. Don't expect great quality but the menu is extensive enough to please all tastes. Open daily until 11pm.
Restaurante del Sol Plaça Guillemó. The cheapest – and most popular – option on a square full of dining possibilities.

Drinking and nightlife

Party animals be warned, **nightlife** in the capital leaves much to be desired, especially out of ski season.
La Borsa av Tarragona 36. Just around the corner from the bus station, a happening club in-season, but social rigor mortis otherwise.
Cerveseria L'Abadia Cap del Carrer 2. Up the stairs from the Pl Guillemó, this popular local pub has Leffe and Hoegaarden on draught. Open daily til 3am.
Milennium av Dr Mitjavila 13. A loud disco-bar with a dartboard, table football and €2 beer.

Directory

Bookstore Librería Jaume Caballé, av Fiter Rossell 31.
Car Rental Hertz ⓣ880 000; Avis ⓣ871 855; Europcar ⓣ874 290.
Cinema MDRN Cinemes av Meritxell 26. Offers good discounts weekday afternoons with tickets at €3.30 (daily 3.30–10.30pm). All films in Spanish.
Embassies The UK embassy is in La Massana, 5km north of town, at av Sant Antoni 32 (ⓣ839 840). The closest US, Canadian, Australian and New Zealand representatives are in Barcelona.
First Aid Centre c/La Lacuna on the corner with c/Mossè Enric Marfany (Mon–Fri 8.30am–8.30pm, Sat, Sun and public holidays 9–11am & 6–7pm).
Hospital Hospital Nostra Senyora de Meritxell, just next to Caldea spa (ⓣ871 000).
Internet Future@point, c/de la Sardana 6; E-Café c/l'Alziranet 5 (pl. Guillemó).
Pharmacy Les Tres Creus, c/Canals 5 (ⓣ820 212, ⓦwww.farmacialestrescreus.com), usually has someone who speaks English.
Post offices Spanish Post at C. Joan Maragall 10; French La Poste at rue Pere d'Urg 1 (Mon–Fri 8.30am–2.30pm, Sat 9.30am–1pm).

Shopping

Outlet Pyrenees Avinguda Meritxell. One of many shops on Avinguda Meritxell, the prime destination for bulk-buyers and bargain-hunters, this small shop is attached to Grans Magatzems Pyrénées and sells marked-down stock from its neighbouring store. Especially useful if you're in need of designer trainers or hiking boots.
Hiper Andorra Eastern end of Avinguda Meritxell. Huge budget supermarket, good for cheap cigarettes and alcohol.

Moving on

Domestic **bus services** connect the capital to all of the main towns listed in this chapter (7am–9pm; €1.20–4.60). Check with the tourist office for schedules, but don't expect the buses to follow them.
Buses Barcelona (9–12 daily; 3hr 30min–4hr 30min); l'Hospitalet (twice daily; 1hr 15min); La Seu d'Urgell (hourly Mon–Sat, 5 daily Sun; 30–45min); Madrid (daily; 9hr); Málaga (twice weekly; 18hr 15min); Toulouse (2–6 daily Mon, Wed, Fri & Sun; 2hr 30min); Valencia (3 weekly; 8hr 30min).

Northern and western Andorra

Perching above the narrow western valleys, the 2942-metre Coma Pedrosa is Andorra's largest mountain, and the snowy peaks here are drained by the Riu Valira del Nord. The main towns of **La Massana** and **Ordino** have a few sights to hold your interest, but the real joy is in the hiking. The roads that meander out to the Spanish border give access to tranquil, unspoilt towns such as **Pal** and **El Serrat**, not to mention some of the most pristine countryside you'll find in the Pyrenees.

LA MASSANA

Ascending northwest out of Escaldes-Engordany, the CG3 follows the Valira del Nord through a verdant valley, arriving at **LA MASSANA** five or so kilometres on. The town itself, presided over by a modern church clock tower, has little to detain you, though the trails in this area make for some excellent hiking - check with the tourist office for specifics. You're best off pressing on and up 3km southwest to Sispony, and the interesting **Casa Rull** (Tues–Sat 9.30am–1.30pm & 3–6.30pm, Sun 10am–2pm; last entrance 45min before closing; €2.40), an ethnographic museum built around a borda, a typical pre-twentieth-century Andorran household. Halfway between La Massana and Ordino, you can book a scenic **helicopter tour** of the northern mountains and valleys through Heliand (☎837 929); a ten-minute ride costs €65 (min 4 people).

Information

Tourist Office c/Major ☎835 693 (Mon–Sat 9am–1pm & 3–7pm, closed Sun pm). The book *36 Interesting Itineraries of Ordino and La Massana*, which covers all the walks in great detail is available at the tourist office (€2).

Internet El Siurell, av. San Antón 33. Also does snacks.

Accommodation

Borda Jovell Hostel av Jovell 18 ☎836 520, Ⓦwww.andornet.ad/bordajovell. Up the steep hill in Sispony, this basic hostel has 100 bunks for low prices. Get even cheaper rates by bringing your own sleeping bag. Dorms ❷

Camping Xixerella Carretera de Pal ☎836 613, Ⓦwww.campingxixerella.com. Campsite with great facilities, and activities from mini-golf to volleyball. ❶

Hostal Palanques c/Vaillant-Chevance ☎835 007. An excellent B&B option in the centre of town, with its own bar-restaurant. ❹

Rifugi de Compadrosa ☎327 955. Far off in the northwestern hills and accessible on foot from Erts, this cabin is open June–Oct and is the only refuge that serves meals. Free.

Eating

Versio Original Carrer Josep Rossell. This trendy establishment has great pop-art decor and comfortable seats. The menu comprises fresh, modern cuisine, from salads to risottos. Set lunches available.

Vesuvio av. San Antón 45. Nicely laid out Italian restaurant serving tasty pizzas for about €8. Set menus €9.90.

PAL AND ARINSAL

At the western end of the La Massana commune lies **PAL**, one of the best-preserved villages in Andorra, hugging the slopes that veer up to the popular ski resort of Pal-Arinsal. The town's medium-sized **Sant Climent** church has a large porch that looks onto the cemetery as well as some older houses, now much dilapidated. Head back down to La Massana to take the road up to **ARINSAL**, 2km northwest, known for its lively **nightlife**: try the pub *Rocky Mountain* (on Ctra. General d'Arinsal, at the top of the Arinsal valley) for live music on Saturday nights plus other themed events throughout the week, or, for night owls, the club *El Surf* (next to the cable-car station), which stays open until 4am during the ski season. If you have a car - or strong legs - continue west up the windy road to the **Vallnord** ski area some great views over to the mountains that are staggered to the east.

ORDINO

The quiet town of **ORDINO** makes a great base for getting out to explore Andorra's northern peaks and valleys. On the town's pedestrian walkway, the peatonal, **Casa Areny-Plandolit** (Tues–Sat 9.30am–1.30pm & 3–6.30pm,

AMBLING ABOUT ANDORRA

Though cars are helpful for moving between towns, by far the best way to see Andorra is **on foot**, and you don't have to be an experienced hiker to do so. Three primary **long-distance trails** run across much of the country, and offer varying levels of trekking. They comprise the **GR7**, which crosses all the way from the French border to Spain via the capital; the **GR11**, a jagged, mountainous route across the heart of the country; and the **GRP1**, a perimeter trail that hugs much of the northern national frontier. Off these main routes, smaller *camins* connect them to the towns below and the rugged hills above. You can easily do a few day or overnight hikes, making full use of any of Andorra's several dozen *refugis*, all but two of which are free, and most have room for at least ten people, so even in the busy summer months you're likely to get one. A number of ski centres also rent out mountain bikes (around €15–20 per day) and sell lift passes during the summer: you can either bike straight up the steep slopes or ascend in a relaxing funicular, then ride leisurely down. Whatever you decide, your first stop should be one of the local tourist offices to grab a copy of *Andorra Mountain Activities*, an excellent handbook that maps out dozens of alpine paths for hiking and biking all over the country. The *Rough Guide to the Pyrenees* is also packed with helpful, detailed information on outdoor activities in the region.

Sun 10am–2pm; €2.40) is a luxurious mansion dating from 1633 and was the residence of the eponymous Don Guillem d'Areny-Plandolit, a wealthy and powerful nineteenth-century baron who served as president of Andorra. A mandatory guided tour explains everything you could want to know in halting English. Just next door is the **Museu Postal** (same hours and price), walking you through the history of postal Andorra. Back down the hill right at the entrance to town on c/ Ordino, Nicolai Sidristyi's **Museu de la Miniatura** is a must. This artist's work is mind-boggling - be sure to squint at the palm tree, pyramid and camels, which all sit in the eye of a needle (Tues–Sat 9.30am–1.30pm & 3.30–7pm, Sun 9.30am–1.30pm; €4).

Information

Tourist office Located next to the sports centre on Travessia d'Ordino in Ordino (July & Aug Mon–Sat 8.30am–6pm, Sun 8am–5pm; Sept–June Mon–Sat 9am–1pm & 3–7pm, Sun 9am–1pm; ⓣ737 080) and offers a free information service for Bluetooth phones.

Accommodation

Borda Ansalonga 2km north along CG3 ⓣ850 374, ⓦwww.campingansalonga.com. Spectacular riverside camping with great facilities including a pool, restaurant and bar. Open mid-May to Sept & Nov–April. ❶

Hotel Ordino Ctra. General d'Ordino ⓣ747 847, ⓦwww.hotelordino.com. Very welcoming staff, and log cabin-esque bedrooms with good views. Washing service provided, and guests share the swimming pool with the more expensive *Hotel Prats* along the road. ❼

Santa Barbara Plaça d'Ordino ⓣ738 100, ⓕ837 092. An attractive building in the village centre, located on the main pedestrianized street. Many of the nicely done-up and spacious rooms have views onto the main *plaça*. ❻

Eating

Most restaurants are on the **peatonal**, and there's enough variety for to suits most tastes:

Armengol Come here for cheap pasta dishes and pizzas.

Bar Quim This restaurant fills up around lunchtime, when the clientele tucks into the €10 set menu.

Vertical Limit Café Interesting decor – snowboarding equipment pinned to the walls, alongside a dartboard and TV screens. A good spot for sandwiches, crepes and snacks.

5 Sentits Just outside of town at Ctra General 3. Quite out of the way but very trendy compared to other Ordino eating establishments. Relax on a comfy leather sofa, leaf through a magazine and enjoy a wide range of beverages. There is also a shop area selling interesting-shaped teapots.

EL SERRAT

Push on north along the CG3 past a waterfall a few kilometres on, to **EL SERRAT**, and the near-empty rough country around it - about the only virgin terrain Andorra has left. From here, a few seldom-beaten paths run up out of the valley, east to the lush **Parc Nacional Sorteny** and west to the **Llacs de Tristaina (Tristaina Lakes)** that border Spain.

Eastern Andorra

The road running east of Andorra la Vella all the way to the French border, passes through 30km of mountain scenery, dominated to the east by the expansive **Grandvalira ski resort**. The town of **Encamp** offers a few points of interest, while **Canillo** is a great base for exploring the countryside. **Prats** and **Soldeu**, meanwhile, are smaller, less developed and much more serene.

ENCAMP

Northeast of Escaldes-Engordany, the mountains ascend above the sloping road, while across the Riu Valira d'Orient, the hills hold a few settlements. Of these, Villa is the largest and retains some well-maintained traditional architecture. Continuing up the CG2 you arrive at **ENCAMP**, with a few museums and Andorra's largest church, the modern **Sant Eulàlia**, with its leaning bell tower. **Cal Cristo** on Carrer dels Cavallers (July–Aug Tues–Sat 10am–1pm & 4–7pm; Sept–June Tues–Fri 3–6.30pm; €2.50) is a humble mountain home that's been turned into a museum of farming life. There's little particularly Andorran about the **Museu de les Dues Rodes** (National Automobile Museum), av Coríncep Episcopal 64 (Tues–Sat 9.30am–1.30pm & 3–6.30pm, Sun 10am–2pm; €2.40), but the collection will interest motor fanatics. In summer, it's worth catching the funicular into the mountains (daily 10am-6pm, €7 return, buy tickets at the tourist office in front of the Funicamp) where a free minibus takes tourist groups around the lakes.

Information

Tourist office Plaça del Consell 1 (Mon–Sat 9am–1pm & 3–7pm, Sun 9am–4pm; ⓣ731 000, ⓦwww.encamp.ad).

Accommodation

Caliu d'en Josep av Coprínçep Francès 4, ⓣ831 210, ⓔres.caliu.josep@andorra.ad. This is an excellent bet, right in the centre of Encamp. The family-run business has spotless rooms and its downstairs eatery serves cheap cafeteria-style food.

Càmping Internacional Ctra. de Vila, ⓣ831 609. Very central site with swimming pool, ❶, bungalow ❼

Residència Relax Ctra. Bellavista 14, ⓣ834 777. Local homeowner who rents out a few rooms. The house is right next to the Funicamp, so a useful location for skiers. ❸

MERITXELL

Just north of Encamp (about halfway to Canillo) is **MERITXELL**, the spiritual core of Andorra. Built in the shape of a Greek cross, the **Santuari de Meritxell** (daily except Tues 9.15am–1pm & 3–6pm; free) is today the most important church in the country. Destroyed by fire in 1972, all that remains is the apse and western wall, and the uninspiring replacement is a bizarre mix of Romanesque, Florentine and Islamic art influences. Inside, the wide-eyed statue of the Virgin on the eastern wall is a reproduction of the one lost in the blaze.

CANILLO

The countryside around **CANILLO** offers some great opportunities for hiking, biking and canyoning – the tourist office can provide full details. Dominating the town is the Palau de Gel, a massive aluminium-sided ice rink (general entry €8.70), though a half-hearted attempt has been made to make it look somewhat "Andorran". Atop the old quarter is the **Sant Serni** church, whose small graveyard makes for a pleasant stroll, and provides some nice views over the town below. On Thursdays in summer, the small *plaça* outside the tourist office holds an **artisan market**.

From the town centre, follow the pebbly road towards the tiny village of **PRATS**, passing the stubby **Cross of the Seven Arms**. Erected in 1477, the Gothic stone bears depictions of Christ and the Virgin on two of the weather-beaten limbs; amputation of the seventh is said to be the work of the devil.

Information

Tourist office Canillo's tourist office, in the centre on the main avinguda Sant Joan de Caselles (Mon–Sat 9am–1pm & 3–7pm, Sun 8am-4pm; ⓣ753 600, ⓦwww.vdc.ad), hands out Valls de Canillo, an excellent pocket-sized brochure offering details on local walks in the hills.

Accommodation

Camping Casal Ctra. General ⓣ851 451, ⓦwww.campingcasal. Given the lack of budget accommodation in Canillo, your best bet is probably camping. Casal is just a few hundred metres west from the tourist office and open all year round. ❶

Camping Pla Prat de l'Areny de Moixa ⓣ851 333, ⓦwww.campingpla.cyberandorra.com. Not far from *Camping Casal*, *Pla* also offers standard campsite facilities. ❶, bungalows ❾

Pensió Comerç Ctra. General ⓣ851 020. Central but basic accommodation. ❸

Eating

Burger Roc Further up from *Taberna de l'Iguana*, this takeaway place does great burgers and fries for those after a junk-food fix.

La Roda Opposite the police station on Carrer Perdut. Specializes in barbecued meats and has a pool table.

Taberna de l'Iguana Opposite the tourist office. Serves filling crepes that are highly recommended. Internet access also available.

EN ROUTE TO FRANCE: SOLDEU AND PAS DE LA CASA

Past Canillo, the landscape is one of rolling hills, the odd petrol station and many more examples of the country's stone architecture. Considered the best in the Pyrenees, the slopes of the **Grandvalira ski resort** loom east, blanketed by plenty of snowfall in the winter and verdant green after May. Grandvalira is the largest ski resort in Andorra, stretching from Canillo to Pas de La Casa, and, as such, can accommodate a range of abilities, from beginners to experts, with five black (very difficult) runs; for more information, see ⓦwww.grandvalira.com. In summer, walkers can **hike** across sixteen trails of varying difficulty, while the resort also converts into a **mountain-bike park** (July 6–Sept 9 daily 10am–5pm), accessed by the cable car from Canillo or Soldeu. A €20 day-pass gives unlimited use of a freestyle bike park, eleven freeride and cross-country tracks (covering a total of 70km), plus the cable-car ride. Bikes can be hired from shops in both towns. Just past, a river slices into the mountains in front of the Vall d'Incles, opening up at **SOLDEU**, a tiny, quiet place that has the vague air of a Seventies' ski village. There's little going on, but check with the tourist office in Canillo for tips on hiking routes from here.

Accommodation

Hotel Bruxelles c/General ⓣ851 010, ⓕ852 099. Right in the centre of Soldeu, the *Bruxelles* has some nice rooms and also serves good, cheap meals. ❺

Eating and drinking

Slim Jim's Just up from Soldeu's church. Serves inexpensive deli-style sandwiches and jacket potatoes with hot fillings. Internet access available until late.
Fat Albert's Also along from the town church. *Slim Jim's* bigger brother, this watering hole stays open later in the evenings and is also a great live-music venue.

Pas de la Casa

The most enjoyable way to reach **PAS DE LA CASA** is the road over the Bord d'Envalira, the Pyrenees' highest pass, proffering dazzling views, but a tunnel (€5.20) now affords quicker access. "Pas" borders both on France and on the downright offensive: its chintzy dwellings evoke a high-rise dystopia. It's earned the moniker "Ibiza on ice" thanks to a rocking, spring break-style nightlife, with no fewer than twenty up-all-night bars frequented by British tourists in the winter months. Outside ski season, however, Pas calms down somewhat.

Information

Internet CyberPas Cafè, just above the *plaça*.
Tourist office A small office is on Placa de l'Església (Ⓣ855 292).

Accommodation

Hotel Almeria Plaça Coprínceps 22, Ⓣ755 655. One of the cheaper central options, located above a supermarket. Rooms are en suite and come with TV. Breakfast included. ❻
Hotel L'Edelweiss c/Major 20, Ⓣ855 192, Ⓕ856 292. More centrally located en-suite rooms. The hotel also has a restaurant and bar. ❺

Eating and drinking

La Borrufa Co-Princeps 24. Central restaurant serving good Portuguese dishes.
Havana Club Plaza dels Vaquers. Not far from *Underground*, this spot lives up to its name by playing Cuban music and serving *lots* of rum.
Underground Plaça Sant Josep. Right in the hub of Pas de la Casa's nightlife, this joint is famous for its killer shots and rowdy Dutch DJs. If this doesn't appeal, try bar-hopping to other popular night-spots on the plaça, such as *KYU* and *West End*.

Austria

HIGHLIGHTS

COFFEE AND CAKE, VIENNA: indulge in mouthwatering treats in one of Vienna's ornate coffeehouses

THE SOUND OF MUSIC TOUR, SALZBURG: cheesy, but a firm favourite

VIENNESE ART: feast your eyes on stunning paintings by Gustav Klimt and Egon Schiele

HALLSTATT: visit this picture-postcard village in the lovely Salzkammergut region

ADVENTURE SPORTS, INNSBRUCK: hiking, mountain-biking, canyoning and more, in the stunning setting of the Austrian Alps

ROUGH COSTS

DAILY BUDGET basic €50/ with occasional treat €70

DRINK Beer, wine or coffee €2.50

FOOD Schnitzel €8.50

HOSTEL/BUDGET HOTEL Dorm €16/ double room €58

TRAVEL Graz–Vienna (2hr 40min) €30; Vienna–Salzburg (3hr) €43

FACT FILE

POPULATION 8.3 million

AREA 83,860 sq km

LANGUAGE German

CURRENCY Euro (€)

CAPITAL Vienna (population: 1.7 million)

INTERNATIONAL PHONE CODE ⓣ43

Basics

Glorious Alpine scenery, monumental Habsburg architecture, and the world's favourite musical movie – Austria's tourist industry certainly plays up to the clichés. However, it's not all bewigged Mozart ensembles and schnitzel; modern Austria boasts some of Europe's most varied museums and contemporary architecture, not to mention a plethora of trendy bars and clubs.

Long the powerhouse of the Habsburg Empire, Austria underwent decades of change and uncertainty in the early twentieth century. Shorn of her empire and racked by economic difficulties, the state fell prey to the promises of Nazi Germany. Only with the end of the Cold War did Austria return to the heart of Europe, joining the EU in 1995.

Politics aside, Austria is primarily known for two contrasting attractions – the fading imperial glories of the capital, and the stunning beauty of its Alpine hinterland. **Vienna** is the gateway to much of central Europe and a good place to soak up the culture of *Mitteleuropa*. Less renowned provincial capitals such as **Graz** and **Linz** provide a similar level of culture and vitality. The most dramatic of Austria's Alpine scenery is west of here, in and around the **Tyrol**, whose capital, **Innsbruck**, provides the best base for exploration. **Salzburg**, between Innsbruck and Vienna, represents urban Austria at its most picturesque, an intoxicating Baroque city within easy striking distance of the mountains and lakes of the **Salzkammergut**.

CHRONOLOGY

1st century BC Romans take over Celtic settlements in present-day Austria
788 AD Charlemagne conquers Austrian land.
1156 The "Privilegium Minus" gives Austria the status of Duchy.
1278 The Habsburgs seize control of the area, and retain it until WWI.
1773 Wolfgang Amadeus Mozart becomes Court Musician in Salzburg.
1797 Napoleon defeats Austria forces, taking Austrian land.
1814 An Austrian coalition force defeats Napoleon.
1866 Austrian territory is lost as a result of the Austro-Prussian war.
1899 Sigmund Freud publishes *The Interpretation of Dreams*. introducing the concept of the ego.
1914 The assassination of the Austrian Archduke, Franz Ferdinand, begins the events that lead to WWI.
1920 A new constitution creates the Republic of Austria.
1938 Hitler incorporates Austria into Germany through "Anschluss".
1945 Austria is occupied by Allied forces as WWII ends.
1965 *The Sound of Music* draws attention to Austria on the big screen.
1967 Austrian Arnold Schwarzenegger becomes the youngest ever Mr Universe at the age of 20.
1980s Protests at election of President Kurt Waldheim, due to rumours implicating him in Nazi war crimes.
1995 Austria joins the EU.
1999 The far-right Freedom Party led by Joerg Haider wins 27 percent of vote in national elections.
2004 Social Democrat Heinz Fischer is announced as President.
2007 Rioting teenagers in Krems, Lower Austria are played music by Mozart and Beethoven in an attempt to calm them down.

ARRIVAL

Austria's major international **airport** lies less than thirty minutes outside of Vienna by S-Bahn or the City Airport Train. You can also fly to Salzburg, Innsbruck, Graz and Linz; all of which are served by low-cost airlines from the UK. The capital is one of central Europe's major rail-hubs. **Trains** from

Budapest and the west terminate at the Westbahnhof; whilst those from Bratislava, Prague and occasionally Berlin arrive into the Südbahnhof. Trains from Croatia and Slovenia stop in the south of Austria at Graz, before also terminating here. Both stations are short, easy hops from central Vienna by tram or U-Bahn. Arriving from northern Italy (Verona and Venice, for example), it's likely you'll arrive in Innsbruck, which also has good rail connections with Munich and southern Germany. Regular services also cross the Swiss border to Bregenz and Feldkirch.

GETTING AROUND

Austria's **public transport** system is fast, efficient and comprehensive. Austrian Federal Railways, or **ÖBB** (Ⓦwww.oebb.at), runs a punctual, clean and comfortable network, which includes most towns of any size. **Trains** marked EC or EN (*EuroCity* and *EuroNight* international expresses), ICE or IC (Austrian InterCity expresses) are the fastest. Those designated D (*Schnellzug*) or E (*Eilzug*) are next, stopping at most intermediate points, while the *Regionalzug* is the slowest service, stopping at all stations. InterRail and Eurail passes are valid.

The **Bahnbus** and **Postbus** system serves remoter villages and Alpine valleys; fares are around €10 per 100km. As a general rule, Bahnbus services, operated by ÖBB, depart from outside train stations; the Postbus tends to stop outside the post office. Daily and weekly regional travelcards (*Netzkarte*), covering both trains and buses, are available in many regions.

Austria is bike-friendly, with **cycle lanes** in all major towns. Many train stations rent **bikes** for around €15 per day (€10 with a valid rail ticket). You can return them to any station for an extra fee of €10/€5.

ACCOMMODATION

Outside popular tourist spots such as Vienna and Salzburg, **accommodation** need not be too expensive. Outside Vienna, expect to pay a minimum of €50 for a double with bathroom. Good-value **B&B** is usually available in the many small family-run hotels known as *Gasthöfe* and *Gasthaüser*, with prices starting at €50 for a double. In the larger towns and cities a **pension** or *Frühstuckspension* will offer similar prices. Most tourist offices also have a stock of **private rooms** or *Privatzimmer*, although in well-travelled rural areas, roadside signs offering *Zimmer Frei* are fairly ubiquitous anyway (double room €30–45).

There are around 100 **HI hostels** (*Jugendherberge* or *Jugendgästehaus*), run by either the ÖJHV (☎01/533 5353, Ⓦwww.oejhv.or.at) or the ÖJHW (☎01/533 1833, Ⓦwww.oejhw.or.at). Rates are €13–20, normally including a nominal breakfast. Sheet sleeping bags are obligatory, although the cost of renting one is often included in the charge. Many hostels also serve lunch and dinner for an additional €3.50–5.50. There are also a number of excellent **independent hostels**.

Austria's high standards are reflected in the country's **campsites**, most of which have laundry facilities, shops and snack bars. Most are open May–Sept, although in the winter-sports resorts many open year-round. In general, you can expect to pay €5–8 per person, €3–9 per pitch.

FOOD AND DRINK

Eating out in Austria is often cheaper than self-catering, but both will take a large chunk out of your daily expenses. For ready-made snacks, try a bakery (*Bäckerei*) or confectioner's (*Konditorei*). **Fast food** centres on the *Würstelstand*, which sells hot dogs, *Bratwurst* (grilled sausage), *Käsekrainer* (spicy sausage with cheese), *Bosna* (spicy, thin Balkan sausage) and *Currywurst*. In town-centre *Kaffeehäuser* or cafés and bars you can get light meals and snacks starting at about €5; most restaurant and café menus have filling stand-bys for less than €6. Main dishes (*Hauptspeisen*) are dominated by schnitzel (tenderized veal) often accompanied by potatoes and a vegetable or salad: Wienerschnitzel is fried in breadcrumbs, *Pariser* in batter, *Natur* served on its own or with a creamy sauce. In general you can expect to pay €6–10 for a standard main course.

Drink

For urban Austrians, daytime drinking traditionally centres on the **Kaffeehaus**, relaxed places serving alcoholic and soft drinks, snacks and cakes, alongside a wide range of different coffees: a *Schwarzer* is small and black, a *Brauner* comes with a little milk, while a *Melange* is half-coffee and half-milk; a *Kurzer* is a small espresso; an *Einspänner* a glass of black coffee topped with *Schlag*, the ubiquitous whipped cream. A cup of coffee in one of these places is pricey (€2.50–3) and numerous stand-up coffee bars are a much cheaper alternative at €1.50 a cup. Most cafés also offer a tempting array of freshly baked **cakes and pastries**.

Night-time drinking centres on **bars** and cafés, although more traditional *Bierstuben* and *Weinstuben* are still thick on the ground. Austrian **beers** are good quality. Most places serve the local brew on tap, either by the *Krügerl* (half-litre, €3), *Seidel* (third-litre, €1.80) or *Pfiff* (fifth-litre, €0.80–1.30). The local **wine**, drunk by the *Viertel* (25cl mug) or the *Achterl* (12.5cl glass), is widely consumed. The *Weinkeller* is the place to go for this or, in the wine-producing areas, a *Heuriger* or *Buschenshenk* – a traditional tavern, customarily serving cold food as well.

CULTURE AND ETIQUETTE

Austrian culture and etiquette is much like the rest of Western Europe, with leisurely café culture a central fixture. In restaurants, bars and cafés tipping is expected; it's customary to round up to the nearest euro.

SPORTS AND ACTIVITIES

With stunning mountain scenery and beautiful lakes, Austria is an ideal destination for skiing, snowboarding, hiking, rafting and adventure sports.

Skiing and snowboarding are major national pastimes and Austria boasts a number of top-rate resorts; **St Anton** is renowned both for its nightlife and gruelling moguls; whilst charming **Kitzbühel** is a better bet for intermediates. **Innsbruck** makes an excellent base for summer and winter sports; the nearby **Stubai Glacier** has snow all year long and is a popular spot for summer skiing (lift pass €28.70/ day). **Hiking** trails in the Tyrol are clearly marked according to a colour scheme; black routes are only for the intrepid – the casual hiker should stick to blue and red. Tourist offices can generally provide details of routes in the area.

COMMUNICATIONS

Most **post offices** are open Mon–Fri 8am–noon & 2–6pm; in larger cities they do without the lunch break and also open Sat 8–10am; a few are open 24hr. **Stamps** can also be bought at tobacconists (*Tabak-Trafik*). The smallest coin accepted in **public phones** is €0.20; two should suffice for a local call. Insert €0.50 and upwards if calling long distance, or buy a phone card (*Telefonkarte*), available from tobacconists. You can make international calls from all public phones, but it's easier to do so from larger post offices, which have booths. The operator and directory enquiries number is ⓣ118 11. **Internet access** is widespread in the big cities, less so in rural areas; expect to pay around €5/hr.

EMERGENCIES

Austria is law-abiding and reasonably safe. **Police** (*Polizei*) are armed, and are not renowned for their friendliness. As for **health**, city hospital casualty departments will treat you and ask questions later. For prescriptions, **pharmacies** (*Apotheke*) tend to follow normal shopping hours. A rota system covers night-time and weekend opening; each pharmacy has details posted in the window.

EMERGENCY NUMBERS

Police ⓣ133; Ambulance ⓣ144; Fire ⓣ122.

INFORMATION & MAPS

Tourist offices (usually *Information*, *Tourismusverband*, *Verkehrsamt*, *Fremdenverkehrsverein*) are plentiful, often hand out free maps and almost always book accommodation. A good general **map** is the 1:500,000 Freytag & Berndt. The 1:200,000 Generalkarte series of regional maps is useful for lengthier touring, as are the 1:50,000 Freytag & Berndt Wanderkarten and rival Kompass Wanderkarten.

MONEY AND BANKS

Austria's currency is the **euro** (€). Banking hours tend to be Mon–Fri 8am–12.30pm & 1.30 or 2–3 or 4pm; in Vienna they're mostly Mon–Fri 8am–3pm, Thurs until 5.30pm. Post offices charge slightly less commission

AUSTRIA ON THE NET

ⓦ**www.austria.info** Austrian Tourist Board website.
ⓦ**www.wien.info** Vienna's Tourist Board website.
ⓦ**www.oebb.at** Train site, including excellent English-language journey planner.
ⓦ**www.austrosearch.at** Search engine, news and chat for all things Austrian.
ⓦ**www.tiscover.com** Detailed information on all regions of the country.
ⓦ**www.wienerzeitung.at** Website of the official Vienna city authorities' newspaper, with an English version packed with news and tourist information.

STUDENT AND YOUTH DISCOUNTS

It is definitely worth carrying an **ISIC card** in Austria; entry to museums and art galleries is costly, particularly in Vienna, and proving your student status will reap substantial savings (often up to fifty percent).

on exchange than banks, and in larger cities are open longer hours.

OPENING HOURS AND PUBLIC HOLIDAYS

Traditionally, **opening hours** for **shops** are Mon–Fri 9am–noon & 2–6pm, with late opening on Thurs till 7 or 8pm & Sat 8am–noon. It's increasingly common for shops to open all day Sat and in big cities most also stay open at lunchtimes. Many **cafés and restaurants** also have a weekly *Ruhetag* (closing day). Shops and **banks** close, and most museums have reduced hours, on **public holidays**: Jan 1, Jan 6, Easter Mon, May 1, Ascension Day, Whit Mon, Corpus Christi, Aug 15, Oct 26, Nov 1, Dec 8, Dec 25 & 26.

GERMAN LANGUAGE AND PHRASES

A high proportion of Austrians speak English, though any attempt at learning a few phrases of **German** will be heartily appreciated – the standard greeting throughout Austria is *Grüss Gott*.

Vienna

Most people visit **VIENNA** (Wien in German) with a vivid image in their minds: a romantic place, full of imperial nostalgia, opera houses and plates of exquisite cake. If anything, the city is even more visually overwhelming than you'd expect: an eclectic feast of architectural styles, from High Baroque, through the monumental imperial projects of the late nineteenth century, to Modernist experiments and enlightened municipal planning.

Vienna became an important centre with the rise of the Babenberg dynasty in the tenth century. In 1278 the city fell to **Rudolf of Habsburg**, but didn't become the imperial residence until 1683 due to threats from the Turks. The great aristocratic families, grown fat on the profits of the Turkish wars, flooded in to build palaces and summer residences in a frenzy of construction that gave Vienna its **Baroque character**. By the end of the Habsburg era the city had become a breeding-ground for the ideological passions of the age: nationalism, socialism, Zionism and anti-Semitism. This turbulence was reflected in the **cultural sphere**, and the ghosts of Freud, Klimt, Schiele, Mahler and Schönberg are nowadays bigger tourist draws than old stand-bys such as the Lipizzaner horses and the Vienna Boys' Choir.

What to see and do

Central Vienna may well bowl you over with its grandiosity, but for all that, it's surprisingly compact: the historical centre, or **Innere Stadt**, is just 1km wide at its broadest point. Most of the important sights are concentrated in the central district and along the Ringstrasse. The best way to grasp its grand sweep is to board tram #1 or #2 from outside the Staatsoper (opera house), both of which circle the boulevard. Judicious use of public transport enables you to travel from one side of the city to the other in less than thirty minutes, meaning that even more peripheral sights, such as the monumental imperial palace at **Schönbrunn**, are easily accessible.

Stephansdom

The obvious place to begin a tour of the city is **Stephansplatz**, the lively pedestrianized central square dominated by the hoary Gothic bulk of the **Stephansdom** (Mon–Sat 6am–10pm, Sun 7am–10pm; free). The highlight in the nave is the early-sixteenth-century carved stone. To get a good look at the Wiener Neustädter Altar, a masterpiece of late Gothic art, and, to its right, the tomb of the Holy Roman Emperor Friedrich III, you must sign up for a guided tour (English tours April–Oct daily 3.45pm; €4). The **catacombs** (Mon–Sat 10–11.30am & 1.30–4.30pm, Sun 1.30–4.30pm; €4) contain the entrails of illustrious Habsburgs housed in bronze caskets. Best views are to be gained from a strenuous climb up to the 137m-high spire, nicknamed Steffl or "Little Stephen" (daily 9am–5.30pm; €3).

East and north of Stephansplatz

The warren of alleyways north and east of the cathedral preserve something of the medieval character of the city, although the architecture reflects centuries of continuous rebuilding. The seventeenth-century **Jesuitenkirche** on Dr.-Ignaz-Seipel-Platz is by far the most awesome High Baroque church in Vienna. Inside, the most striking features are the red and green barley-sugar spiral columns, the exquisitely carved pews and the clever trompe-l'oeil dome. Nearby, on the far side of Stubenring, is Vienna's most enjoyable museum, known as the **MAK** (Tues

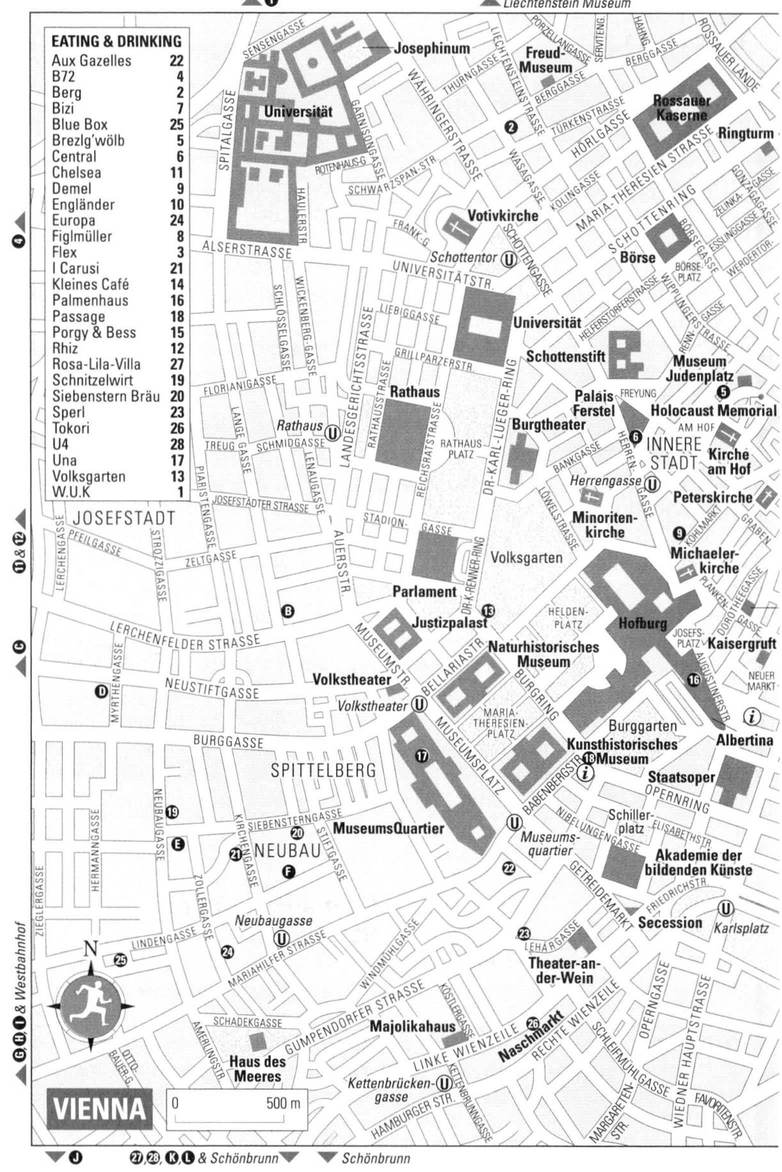

10am–midnight, Wed–Sun 10am–6pm; €7.90, free on Sat; Ⓦwww.mak.at). The highlights of its superlative, eclectic collection, dating from the Romanesque period to the twentieth century, are Klimt's *Stoclet Frieze* and the unrivalled collection of Wiener Werkstätte products.

Judenplatz

North of Stephansdom, **Judenplatz**, one of the prettiest little squares in

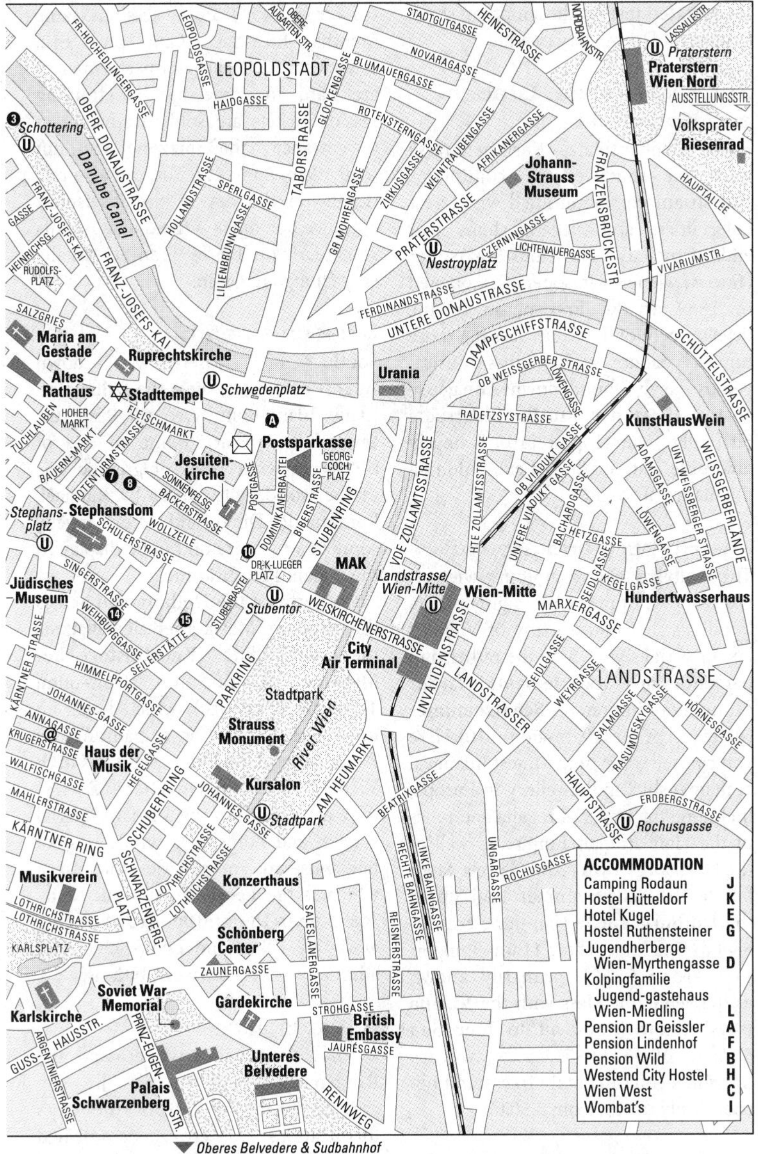

Vienna, is dominated by the bleak concrete **Holocaust Memorial**, designed by British sculptor Rachel Whiteread. Judenplatz stands on the site of the medieval Jewish ghetto and you can view the foundations of an old synagogue at the excellent **Museum Judenplatz** at no. 8 (Sun–Thurs 10am–6pm, Friday 10am–2pm; €3). Buy a joint ticket for €7 if you also plan to visit the intriguing **Jüdisches Museum** (daily except Sat 10am–6pm; €5; Ⓦwww.jmw.

at), **situated** just off the shopping street Graben, at Dorotheergasse 11.

Kärntnerstrasse, Graben and Kohlmarkt

From Stephansplatz, Kärntnerstrasse leads off southwest, a continuous pedestrianized ribbon lined with street entertainers and elegant shops that ends at the city's illustrious **Staatsoper** (ⓦwww.wiener-staatsoper.at), opened in 1869 as the first phase of the development of the Ringstrasse. A more unusual tribute to the city's musical genius can be found down Annagasse at the **Haus der Musik**, Seilerstätte 30 (daily 10am–10pm; €10), a hugely enjoyable, state-of-the-art exhibition on the nature of sound.

The Hofburg and around

The **Hofburg** (ⓦwww.hofburg-wien.at) is a complex of immense, highly ornate buildings that house many of Vienna's key imperial sights. Skip the rather dull parade of **Kaiserappartements** in favour of the more impressive **Schatzkammer** (daily except Tues 10am–6pm; €10). Here you can see some of the finest medieval craftsmanship and jewellery in Europe, including the imperial regalia and relics of the Holy Roman Empire as well as the Habsburgs' own crown jewels. Steps beside the Schatzkammer lead up to the **Hofburgkapelle** (Jan–June & mid-Sept to Dec Mon–Thurs 11am–3pm, Fri 11am–1pm; €1.50), primarily known as the venue for Mass with the **Vienna Boys' Choir** (mid-Sept to June Sun 8.15am; ⓣ01/533 9971, ⓦwww.wsk.at), for which you can obtain free, standing-room-only tickets from 8.30am.

Spanish Riding School and Lipizzaner Museum

On the other side of Josefsplatz, a door leads to the imperial stables, home to the white horses of the **Spanish Riding School** (performances: March–June & Sept, Oct & Dec; standing from €22, seats from €45. Training sessions: same months Tues–Sat 10am–1pm; €12; ⓦwww.srs.at). Tickets for performances are hard to come by, but training session tickets are sold in advance at the entrance to the **Lipizzaner Museum** (daily 9am–6pm; €5). You can also buy tickets on the day at the Josefsplatz entrance box office – the queue is at its worst early on, but by 11am it's usually easy enough to get in.

Museums nearby

South of Josefsplatz, down Augustinerstrasse, lies the **Albertina** (daily 10am–6pm, Wed till 9pm; €9; ⓦwww.albertina.at), home to one of the largest collections of graphic arts in the world, with works by Raphael, Rembrandt, Dürer and Michelangelo, some of which are on public display in the elegant **Prunkräume**.

Southwest of the Hofburg and across the Ring in Maria-Theresien-Platz is the outstanding **Kunsthistorisches Museum** (Tues–Sun 10am–6pm, Thurs till 9pm; €10), which holds an unparalleled collection of paintings by Pieter Bruegel the Elder. Nearby is **MQ**, Vienna's **MuseumsQuartier** (ⓦwww.mqw.at), housed in the former imperial stables, and home to a whole host of new museums and galleries, the best of which is the **Leopold Museum** (daily 10am–6pm, Thurs till 9pm; €9), boasting works by Klimt and Egon Schiele, in addition to temporary exhibitions.

Rathausplatz

By now you will have crossed the **Ringstrasse**, built to fill the gap created when the last of the city's fortifications were demolished in 1857 and subsequently lined with monumental civic buildings. **Rathausplatz**, northwest of the Hofburg, is the Ringstrasse's showpiece square, framed by four monumental public buildings: the Rathaus (City Hall), the Burgtheater, Parlament and

VIENNA'S HEURIGEN

If you fancy sampling some Austrian wines and a scenic excursion out of the city, take a trip to one of the rustic wine-producing villages situated on Vienna's outskirts. To the north of the Danube, Stammersdorf (tram #31 from Schottentor; 40 min) is surrounded by vineyards and filled with traditional, family-run *heurigen* (wine-taverns). A great place to start is **Wienhof Wieninger**, 21, Stammersdorfstrasse 78 (Mon–Fri 3pm–midnight, weekends noon–midnight), which has a pleasant garden, an excellent, inexpensive buffet and a good selection of own-label whites available by the glass.

the Universität – all completed in the 1880s.

The Belvedere

South of the ring, the **Belvedere** (tram #D from the opera house) is one of Vienna's finest palace complexes. Two magnificent Baroque mansions face each other across a sloping formal garden. The loftier of the two palaces, the **Oberes Belvedere** (Tues–Sun 10am–6pm; €9.50; Ⓦwww.belvedere.at), has the best concentration of paintings by Klimt in the city, including *The Kiss*.

St Marxer Friedhof

The **St Marxer Friedhof**, on Leberstrasse (daily 7am–dusk) was Vienna's principal cemetery from 1784 to 1874. It was here in 1791 that **Mozart** was given a pauper's burial in an unmarked mass grave. A column erected in 1859 marking the area in which the composer was interred now stands in Vienna's greatest necropolis, the **Zentralfriedhof** (daily 7/8am–5/7pm; tram #6 or #71) on Simmeringer Hauptstrasse. Eminent musicians, principally Beethoven, Schubert, Brahms and the Strauss family, lie a short way beyond Gate 2, to the left of the central avenue.

Schönbrunn

The biggest attraction in the west of the city is the imperial summer palace of **Schönbrunn** (Ⓦwww.schoenbrunn.at; U4 to Schönbrunn), a palace designed by Fischer von Erlach on the model of residences like Versailles. To visit the palace rooms or **Prunkräume** (daily 8.30am–4.30/5pm; July & Aug till 6pm) there's a choice of two tours: the "Imperial Tour" (€9.50), which takes in 22 state rooms; and the "Grand Tour" (€12.90 with an audioguide or €15.40 with a tour guide), which includes all forty rooms. However, the shorter tour misses out the best rooms – such as the Millions Room, a rosewood-panelled chamber covered from floor to ceiling with wildly irregular Rococo cartouches, each holding a Persian miniature watercolour. Be warned, the palace can become unbearably overcrowded at the height of summer, with lengthy queues and time delays of one hour or more on entrance. There are also coaches and carriages in the **Wagenburg** (April–Oct daily 9am–6pm; 7pm July and August; €4.50), a **Maze and Labyrinth in the Schlosspark** (daily: April–Oct 9am–5/6pm; Nov 10am–3.30pm; €2.90) and the **Gloriette** – a hilltop colonnaded monument, now a café (daily 9am–dusk), from which you can enjoy splendid views back towards the city. The park is also home to Vienna's excellent **Tiergarten** or Zoo (daily 9am–5/6.30pm; €12).

Arrival and information

Air Vienna airport Flughafen Wien-Schwechat (Ⓦenglish.viennaairport.com) is located around 20km southeast of the city. The cheapest way to reach central Vienna is to take S-Bahn line S7 to Wien-Mitte station (every 30min; 30min; €3.40 single). The City Airport Train (CAT; every 30min; 15min; €9 single) also runs to Wien-Mitte and

VIENNA'S ADDRESSES

The city is divided into **numbered districts** (Bezirke). District 1 is the Innere Stadt, the area enclosed by the Ringstrasse (a sweeping boulevard-cum-ring road); districts 2–9 are arranged clockwise around it; beyond here, districts 10–23 are a fair way out. All Viennese addresses begin with the number of the district, followed by the name of the street, and then the number of the house or building followed, where relevant, by the number of the apartment separated by a forward slash.

is faster, with a check-service for Air Berlin and Austrian Airlines. Buses (every 20–30min; €6 single) run to U-Bahn Schwedenplatz (20min) in the centre and to the Südbahnhof (25min) and Westbahnhof (40min).

Train International trains from the west and from Hungary terminate at the Westbahnhof, five metro stops from the city centre; services from eastern Europe, Italy and the Balkans arrive at the Südbahnhof, south of the city centre (U-Bahn Südtiroler Platz and a five-minute walk or tram #D); services from Lower Austria and the odd train from Prague arrive at Franz-Josefs-Bahnhof, north of the centre (tram #D).

Bus Long-distance buses arrive at Vienna's main bus terminal, the City Air Terminal beside Wien-Mitte, on the eastern edge of the city centre (U-Bahn Landstrasse).

Boat DDSG (Ⓦwww.ddsg-blue-danube.at) from further up the Danube, or from Bratislava or Budapest, dock at the Schiffahrtszentrum by the Reichsbrücke, some way northeast of the city centre – the nearest station (U-Bahn Vorgartenstrasse) is five minutes' walk away, one block west of Mexicoplatz.

Tourist office Vienna's main tourist office (daily 9am–7pm; Ⓣ24555, Ⓦwww.wien.info) is behind the opera house on Albertinaplatz. It has multilingual staff and can help arrange accommodation. The excellent wien info website (in English) has links to many of the key museums and sights. All points of arrival have tourist kiosks which can help with accommodation.

Information centre for young people Wienxtra-Youthinfo, at Babenbergerstr. 1 (Mon–Sat noon–7pm; Ⓣ17 79, Ⓦwww.wienxtra.at), near the Kunsthistorisches Museum is geared towards providing information for backpackers and students. It also sells tickets for various gigs and club nights.

City transport

So many attractions are in or around the Innere Stadt that you can do and see a great deal on foot.

Public transport runs 5am–midnight (outside these times night buses called NightLine run from Schwedenplatz). The network consists of trams (Strassenbahn or Bim), buses, the U-Bahn (metro) and the S-Bahn (fast commuter trains).

Tickets Buy your ticket from the ticket booths or machines at U-Bahn stations and from tobacconists, and punch it on-board buses and trams or before entering the U- or S-Bahn. Fares are calculated on a zonal basis: tickets for the central zone (covering all of Vienna) cost €1.70 and allow unlimited changes on any mode of transport. Much better value is a travel pass (Netzkarte; €5.70/13.60 for 24/72hr) and the much-touted Wien-Karte or Vienna Card (€18.50). This acts as a 72-hour travel pass and also gives minor (sometimes only ten percent) discounts at attractions. If you already possess an ISIC card, the best-value option is to simply buy a travel pass.

Bike rental City Bike (Ⓦwww.citybikewien.at) offers self-service bike rental from Stephansplatz and other locations around the city. Pedal Power, 2, Ausstellungstr. 3 (Ⓣ01/729 7234, Ⓦwww.pedalpower.at; €24 for 5 hours).

Taxis run from the ranks around town; to book, call Ⓣ31300, 40100 or 60160.

Accommodation

There's no shortage of expensive **accommodation**, but extreme pressure on the cheaper end of the market means booking ahead is essential in summer and advisable during the rest of the year.

Hostels

Hostel Hütteldorf 13, Schlossberggasse 8 Ⓣ01/877 1501, Ⓦwww.hostel.at. A 300-bed hostel, with dorms plus some double and triple rooms. Out in the sticks, but convenient if you want to explore the wilds of the Lainzer Tiergarten and Schönbrunn. S- and U-Bahn Hütteldorf. Dorms ❷, rooms ❹

Kolpingfamilie Jugend-gastehaus Wien-Miedling 12, Bendlgasse 10–12 Ⓣ01/813 5487, Ⓦwww.kolpinghaus-wien12.at. Large, institutional hostel with singles and doubles as well as dorm beds. Easily reached from the city centre. U-Bahn Niederhofstr. Dorms ❷, rooms ❺

Hostel Ruthensteiner 15, Robert Hamerlinggasse 24 ☎01/893 4202, www.hostelruthensteiner.com. Excellent hostel within easy walking distance of the Westbahnhof. One of Austria's first independent hostels, Ruthensteiner is friendly, relaxed and international. There's a spacious leafy courtyard (complete with giant chess set), plus a bar, musical instruments, kitchen, bbq, internet and laundry facilities. Breakfast not included. U-Bahn Westbahnhof. Dorm beds ❷, doubles ❺

Westend City Hostel 6, Fügergasse 3 ☎01/597 6729, www.westendhostel.at. A few minutes' walk from the Westbahnhof, this refurbished 211-bed former hotel has dorms and en-suite doubles. Friendly staff, a patio, left-luggage and laundry services. Dorms ❷, rooms ❻

Jugendherberge Wien-Myrthengasse 7, Myrthengasse 7 & Neustiftgasse 85 ☎01/523 6316, www.oejhv.or.at. A short walk up Neustiftgasse from U-Bahn Volkstheater is this most central of the HI hostels, with 270 beds (some doubles) divided between two nearby addresses. Book well in advance and go to the Myrthengasse reception on arrival. Dorms ❷, rooms ❹

Wombat's 15, Grangasse 6 and Mariahilferstr. 137 ☎01/897 2336, www.wombats.at. With hostels at two different locations near the Westbahnhof, Wombats is an excellent option, particularly if you're looking to party. The hostel on Mariahilferstrasse opened in 2007 and like the Grangasse 'base', boasts a stylish bar (you even get a free welcome drink), plus internet and laundry. Breakfast not included. Dorm beds ❸, doubles ❺

Hotels and pensions

Pension Dr Geissler 1, Postgasse 14 ☎01/533 2803, www.hotelpension.at. Anonymous modern pension; all rooms have cable/satellite TV, and those with shared facilities are among the cheapest in the Innere Stadt. U-Bahn Schwedenplatz. ❺

Hotel Kugel 7, Siebensterngasse 43 ☎01/523 3355, www.hotelkugel.com. Bright, four-poster en-suite rooms in a good Neubau location; with rather dingy budget rooms available for students. U-Bahn Neubaugasse. ❺

Pension Lindenhof 7, Lindengasse 4 ☎01/523 0498, pensionlindenhof@yahoo.com. Quirky pension in a great location just off Mariahilferstrassse. The hallway is filled with plants and rooms have creaky parquet flooring. Breakfast is included, but you pay €2 extra per shower in rooms with shared facilities. U-Bahn Neubaugasse. Doubles ❺ or ❼ en suite.

Pension Wild 8, Lange Gasse 10 ☎01/406 5174, www.pension-wild.com. Friendly, laid-back pension, a short walk from the Ring in a student district behind the university. Especially popular with backpackers and gay travellers; booking is essential. U-Bahn Rathaus/Volkstheater. Doubles with shared facilities ❺, en-suite rooms ❽

Campsites

Camping Rodaun 23 An der Au 2 ☎01/888 4154. Nice location by a stream on the southwestern outskirts of Vienna, near the Wienerwald (Vienna Woods). Tram #60 from U-Bahn Hietzing to its terminus, then 5-min walk. April–Oct. ❷

Wien West 14 Hüttelbergstr. 80 ☎01/914 2314, www.wiencamping.at. In the plush far-western suburbs of Vienna, close to the Wienerwald, with two- and four-bed bungalows to rent. Bus #151 from U-Bahn Hütteldorf or a 15-min walk from tram #49 terminus. Tents ❷, Bungalows ❸

Eating

Cafés

Berg 9, Berggasse 8. Adjoined to a gay bookshop, Berg is trendy, modern and relaxed, attracting a mixed gay/straight clientele. Good food, often with an Asian twist. Mains €10. Open till 1am. U-Bahn Schottentor.

Central 1, Herrengasse 14. Traditional meeting place of Vienna's intelligentsia, and Trotsky's favourite *Kaffeehaus* – of all Vienna's cafés, perhaps the most ornate. Snacks and mains for under €10. Closes 8pm. U-Bahn Herrengasse.

Demel 1, Kohlmarkt 14. Elaborately displayed, Demel's patisseries and cakes are highly prestigious and correspondingly pricey. Closes 7pm. U-Bahn Herrengasse.

Engländer 1, Postgasse 2; U-Bahn Stubentor. Great *Kaffeehaus* with a long pedigree that went under for a few years but has come back with a vengeance. Snacks €3–7, mains €9–15. Open till 1am.

Europa 7, Zollergasse 8. Lively, modern café attracting a young trendy crowd. Good breakfast menu. Open till 5am. U-Bahn Neubaugasse.

Kleines Café 1, Franziskanerplatz 3. Tiny café with outside seating, tucked away in a tranquil cobbled square, serving delicious open sandwiches (€3.50). U-Bahn Stephansplatz.

Palmenhaus 1, Burggarten. Beautiful, stylish café, housed in a lofty greenhouse in the Burggarten behind the Hofburg, filled with lush palms and foliage. Salads €5–10, mains €12.50–22. Open till 2am. U-Bahn Karlsplatz.

Sperl 6, Gumpendorferstr. 11. The fin-de-siècle interior is one of the finest of the city's coffee-house scene, with reasonably priced food (€6.50). July & Aug closed Sun. Open till 11pm. U-Bahn Karlsplatz/Babenbergerstr.

AUSTRIA VIENNA

Una 7, Museumsplatz 1; U-Bahn Museumsquartier. Best of the MuseumsQuartier cafés, *Una* boasts a vaulted floral ceramic ceiling, an imaginative menu and a friendly vibe. Open till midnight; closed Sun eve.

Restaurants

Aux Gazelles 6, Rahlgasse 5. The full over-the-top North African monty, this vast enterprise includes a café, brasserie, oyster bar, *salon de thé* and even a small hammam. *Tagines* €16.50. Closed Sunday. U-Bahn Museumsquartier.

Bizi 1, Rotenturmstrasse 4 and other locations. Cheap, central, self-service stomach-filler chain serving pizzas for €7 (€2.50 per slice). U-Bahn Stephansplatz.

Brezlg'wölb 1, Ledererhof 9, off Drahtgasse. Cosy, candle-lit, cavern-like place serving Austrian favourites. Mains €10. Open till 1am. U-Bahn Schwedenplatz.

Figlmüller 1, Wollzeile 5. In a little side alley, this very popular place is famous for its Wienerschnitzel (€12). Closed Aug. U-Bahn Stephansplatz.

I Carusi 7, Kirchengasse 21. Modern, stylish trattoria with high ceilings, serving excellent thin-crust pizzas (€9.50). U-Bahn Neubaugasse.

Schnitzelwirt 7, Neubaugasse 52. Another great place to eat Wienerschnitzel – and half the price of Figlmüller at €6. Closed Sun. Tram #49.

Siebenstern Bräu 7, Siebensterngasse 19. Popular modern Bierkeller that brews its own beer and serves solid Viennese food from €6. U-Bahn Volkstheater/Neubaugasse.

Tokori Naschmarkt stand, 177–178. Simple Japanese place in the market, serving up generous portions of sushi and noodles for €7. U-Bahn Karlsplatz.

Markets

Naschmarkt the city's main fruit and veg market is held off Karlsplatz (Mon–Fri 6am–7.30pm, Sat 6am–5pm). It's a great place to assemble a picnic or grab a quick lunch: there's a plethora of stalls and snack joints, serving everything from falafel to sushi.

Drinking and nightlife

B72 8, Stadtbahnbögen 72, Hernalser Gürtel Ⓦwww.b72.at. Dark, designer club featuring a mixture of DJs and live indie bands; one of several beneath the U-Bahn arches. Open till 4am. U-Bahn Alserstr.

Blue Box 7, Richtergasse 8 Ⓦwww.bluebox.at. Musikcafé with resident DJs and a good snack menu. Open till 2am or later. U-Bahn Neubaugasse.

Flex 1, Donaukanal Ⓦwww.flex.at. Vienna's most serious dance-music club by the canal, attracting some of the city's best DJs. Open till 4am. U-Bahn Schottenring.

Passage 1, Babenberger Passage, Burgring/Babenbergerstrasse Ⓦwww.sunshine.at. Funky futuristic DJ club, in a converted pedestrian underpass. Open till 4am. U-Bahn Museumsquartier/Volkstheater.

rhiz 8, Gürtelbögen 37–38, Lerchenfelder Gürtel Ⓦwww.rhiz.org. Bar/café/club under the U-Bahn arches, with several DJs spinning everything from dance to trance. Open till 4am. U-Bahn Josefstädterstr.

Rosa-Lila-Villa 6, Linke Wienzeile 102 Ⓦwww.villa.at. Gay and lesbian centre housing a café/restaurant with a nice leafy courtyard. A good place to pick up information about events. Open till 2am. U-Bahn Pilgramgasse.

U4 12, Schönbrunnerstr. 222 Ⓦwww.u-4.at. A dark, cavernous disco, playing mostly break beats and house, plus frequent gigs. Popular with the alternative crowd; gay and lesbian night on Thurs. Open till 5am. U-Bahn Meidling-Hauptstr.

Volksgarten 1, Burgring 1 Ⓦwww.volksgarten.at. Situated in the park of the same name, Volksgarten is Vienna's longest-running club. Open till 5am. The retro Volksgarten pavilion bar next door also has resident DJs and is open till 2am. U-Bahn Volkstheater.

w.u.k. 9, Währingerstr. 59 Ⓦwww.wuk.at. Big old school turned arts venue with a relaxed café and a wide programme of events, including live music and DJ nights. Open till 2am. Tram #40, #41 or #42.

Entertainment

The local **listings magazine** *Falter* (Ⓦwww.falter.at) has comprehensive details of the week's cultural programme and is pretty easy to decipher. The tourist office also publishes the free monthly *Programm*. Bookings for classical venues can usually be made at Bundestheaterkassen, 1, Hanuschgasse 3 (Ⓦwww.bundestheater.at). Cheap standing-room tickets are often available by queuing up an hour before a performance.

Chelsea 8, Gürtelbögen 29–31, Lerchenfelder Gürtel. Popular, grungy rock venue with up-and-coming Brit guitar bands. Situated underneath the railway arches. U-Bahn Thaliastr.

Konzerthaus 3, Lothringerstr. 20 (Ⓦwww.konzerthaus.at). Major classical venue, which also has performances of jazz and world.

Musikverein 1, Karlsplatz 6 (Ⓦwww.musikverein-wien.at). Ornate concert hall, home of the Vienna Philharmonic.

TREAT YOURSELF

As befits its musical pedigree, Vienna is home to one of Europe's most prestigious opera houses, the **Staatsoper** (1, Opernring 2 (Ⓣ01/513 1513, Ⓦwww.wiener-staatsoper.at). The season runs from September to June and ticket prices run the gamut from a mere €7 to over €250. They often sell out weeks in advance, but it can be worth asking at the ticket office. If you want to see a performance without breaking the budget, hundreds of standing place tickets (*Stehplätze*) go on sale each night eighty minutes before a performance from just €2/3.50. Ask at the ticket office under the arcades at the opera house for details. Opera and operetta are also staged at the **Volksoper**, 9, Währingerstr. 78 (Ⓦwww.volksoper.at).

Porgy & Bess 1, Riemergasse 11, Ⓣ01/512 8812, Ⓦwww.porgy.at. A converted porn cinema, now the home for Vienna's top jazz venue, attracting acts from all over the world. U-Bahn Stubentor.

Shopping

Mariahilferstrasse is one of the most popular shopping streets in the city, and certainly the best for high-street clothes shops and the big chains. **Neubaugasse**, nearby, has a more eclectic range of boutiques. On Saturday mornings a **flea market** extends south of the Naschmarkt (U-Bahn Kettenbrückengasse).

Aida 1, Stock-im-Eisen-Platz 2. Look out for Aida's distinctive pink neon signs; this ubiquitous Viennese coffee chain also sells great cakes and sweets to take home. U-Bahn Stephansplatz.

Shakespeare & Co 1, Sterngasse 2, Ⓦwww.shakespeare.co.at. Friendly English-language bookshop; also sells translations of Austrian authors. U-Bahn Schwedenplatz.

Wein & co 6, Getreidmark 1. Wine shop with a number of branches around the city, selling a wide selection of Austrian and international wines. U-Bahn Karlsplatz.

Directory

Embassies Australia, 4, Mattiellistr. 2–4 Ⓣ01/50674, Ⓦwww.australian-embassy.at; Canada, 1, Laurenzerbergg. 2 Ⓣ01/531 383 000, Ⓦwww.kanada.at; Ireland, 1, Rotenturmstr. 16–18 Ⓣ01/715 4246; UK (consular and passports), 3, Jaurèsgasse 10 Ⓣ01/716 135 333, Ⓦwww.britishembassy.at; US, 9, Boltzmanngasse 16 Ⓣ01/31339, Ⓦwww.usembassy.at.

Hospital Allegemeines Krankenhaus, 9, Währinger Gürtel 18–20; U-Bahn Michelbeuern-AKH.

Internet *Surfland Internet Café*, 1, Krugerstrasse 10; *World Net Café*, Bürohaus, Mariahilferstr. 103.

Laundry Waschsalon 7, corner of Urban Loritz-Platz and Westbahnstr. Closes 11pm.

Pharmacy Alte Feldapotheke, opposite the Stephansdom and at the Westbahnhof.

Post offices 1, Fleischmarkt 19; Westbahnhof; Südbahnhof (all 24hr).

Exchange Outside banking hours try the offices at the Westbahnhof (daily 7am–10pm) or the Südbahnhof (Mon–Fri 7am–7pm; July & Aug also Sat & Sun 6.15am–9pm), or the 24hr automatic exchange machines around Stephansplatz.

Moving on

Trains Bratislava (2 hourly; 1 hr); Bregenz (5 daily; 7hr 30 min); Budapest (7 daily; 3hr); Graz (hourly; 2hr 40min); Innsbruck (every 2hr; 5hr); Krems (every 25min; 1hr 15min); Linz (2 hourly; 2hr); Melk (hourly; 1hr 10min); Prague (4 daily; 4 hr 15min) Salzburg (1–2 hourly; 3hr–3hr 20min).

Boats DDSG (Ⓦwww.ddsg-blue-danube.at) operates boats at weekends between Vienna, Linz and Passau during the summer, with year-round services on the most scenic stretch between the historic towns of Krems and Melk. The journey takes about three hours upstream, two downstream, and costs around €17.50 each way.

The Danube Valley

MELK

For real High Baroque excess, head for the early eighteenth-century **Benedictine monastery** at **MELK** – a pilgrimage centre associated with the Irish missionary St Coloman. The monumental coffee-cake monastery, perched on a bluff over the river, dominates the town. Highlights of the interior (Easter–Oct daily 9am–5/6pm; rest of year guided tours only: 11am & 2pm; €7, €8.80 with guided tour; Ⓦwww.stiftmelk.at) are the exquisite library, with a cherub-infested ceiling by Troger, and the rather lavish monastery church, with similarly impressive work by Rottmayr.

Melk's river station is about ten minutes' walk north of town; the train station is at the head of Bahnhofstrasse, which leads directly into the old quarter. The tourist office Babenbergstr. 1 (April–Oct Mon–Sat 9/10am–5/6/7pm, Sun 10am–2pm, July–Aug also Sun 5–7pm; Ⓣ02752/52307), has a substantial stock of private rooms, though most are out of the centre. The **HI hostel** is ten minutes' walk from the tourist office, at Abt Karl-Str. 42 (Ⓣ02752/52681, Ⓦwww.oejhv.or.at; March to mid-Dec; dorms ❷, doubles ❺, breakfast included). The town **campsite** is a similar distance in the opposite direction, *Melker Camping* (Ⓣ02752/53291, Ⓔfaehrhaus-jensch@melker.net; March–Nov), by the river station ❶.

LINZ

Away from its industrial suburbs, **LINZ** is a pleasant Baroque city straddling the Danube, even though its greatest claim to fame is as the childhood home of Adolf Hitler, something about which the local tourist board is understandably coy. The heart of the city is the rectangular expanse of the main square, **Hauptplatz**, with its pastel-coloured facades and central Trinity Column, crowned by a gilded sunburst. In the nearby **Pfarrkirche**, a gargantuan marble slab contains Emperor Friedrich III's heart (the rest of him is in Vienna's Stephansdom). A modern addition to the city's cultural scene nestles beside the Danube: the shimmering, hangar-like steel and glass **Lentos** (daily except Tues 10am–6pm, Thurs till 9pm; €6.50; Ⓦwww.lentos.at) shows contemporary and modern art, including Klimt, Kokoschka, and Schiele. Linz's other major attraction is the unusual **Ars Electronica Center** (Wed–Sun 9/10am–5/6pm, Fri till 9pm; €6; Ⓦwww.aec.at). This "museum of the future" is dedicated to new technology and contains a range of interactive high-tech exhibits (including some rather less cutting-edge computer games, such as Sim City). The main highlight is the "CAVE", a virtual-reality room with 3D projections on the walls and floor – get there early to book for it. At the time of writing, the museum was housed **at Graben 5; it is due to return to its permanent home across the river at** Hauptstrasse 2 (with new exhibits), when refurbishment work is completed towards the end of 2008.

ORIENTATION

Linz straddles the **Danube**. To the north of the river lies the suburb of **Urfahr**; to the south is located the city's compact **old town**, the hub of which is the **Hauptplatz**. Many of the city's liveliest bars are clustered just a short walk to the west of here, around the triangle formed by **Hoffgasse**, **Altstadt** and **Hahnengasse**. Heading south from the Hauptplatz, the busy shopping street **Landstrasse** leads south towards the train station, whilst parallel **Herrengasse** brings you to the cathedral.

Arrival and information

Train station Linz's train station is 2km south of the centre, at the end of the city's main artery, Landstrasse; tram #3 runs to Hauptplatz.
Tourist office Alte Rathaus, Hauptplatz 1 (Mon–Fri 8am–6/7pm, Sat & Sun 10am–6/7pm; Ⓣ0732/7070 1777, Ⓦwww.linz.at).

Accommodation

Campsite Seeweg 11 Ⓣ0732/24 78 70, Ⓔkolmer@ione.at; mid-March to Oct; bus #33 or #33a from Rudolfstrasse in Urfahr. On the Pleschinger See, 3km northeast of the centre on the Danube. Tents only. ❷

Jugendherberge Kapuzinerstr. 14 ⓣ0732/78 27 20; March–Sept. Friendly and central youth hostel five minutes' walk from Hauptplatz, with 4- and 6-bed dorms. ❷

Goldenes Dachl Hafnerstr. 27 ⓣ0732/77 58 97, ⓔgoldenesdachl@gmx.at. Pleasant family-run guesthouse with spacious rooms one block south of the cathedral. Rooms available with shared or private facilities ❻

Wilder Mann Goethestr. 14 ⓣ0732/65 60 78, ⓦmembers.aon.at/wilder-mann. Family-run place, down near the station; rooms available with shared facilities or with en-suite showers but hallway WCs. ❺

Eating

Alte Welt Hauptplatz 4 (closed Sun). Unpretentious bar and wine-cellar in a cosy courtyard just off the Hauptplatz. Austrian/Italian-influenced mains; €6.50–12. Open till 2am.

Da Ignazio Altstaat 7. Cavernous and intimate, this *trattoria* serves excellent Sicilian food, with an emphasis on fish. Pasta €8.50, lunch menu €6.50/8.50.

Klosterhof Landstr. 30. Former monastery with large beer garden serving solid Austrian fare. Schnitzel €9.60.

Traxlmayr Promenade 16. Traditional coffee house; a good place to treat yourself to a slice of Linzer Torte, the town's ubiquitous almond and jam *torte* (€2.60). Closed Sun.

Drinking and nightlife

Entremundo Harrachstrasse 1. Vinothek, with modern interior, selling Austrian and international wines by the glass.

Posthof Posthofgasse 43 (bus #46) ⓦwww.posthof.at. Organizes regular gigs and club nights.

Smaragd Altstadt 2. One of several bar-clubs lining Altstadt, with cocktails and a dance floor. Open till 6am. Live music Tues–Thurs, including a popular latino night (Thurs).

Strom Kirchengasse. Grungy café-bar just across the river, with regular alternative acts performing in the upstairs club, *Stadtwerkstatt*. Closed Mon.

Moving on

Bus St Florian (Mon–Fri 15 daily, Sat 8 daily, Sun 2 daily; 35min).

GRAZ

Austria's second-largest city, **GRAZ**, owes its importance to the defence of central Europe against the Turks. From the fifteenth century, it was constantly under arms, rendering it more secure than Vienna and leading to a modest seventeenth-century flowering of the arts (the Baroque style appeared first in Graz). The city's former reputation as a conservative place full of pensioners has been superseded, thanks to a clutch of modern, glass and steel architectural adventures and a large student population; Graz's recent UNESCO World Heritage status has also given the city a flush of confidence. It's a relaxing place in which to spend a few days without the tourist traffic of Innsbruck or Salzburg.

What to see and do

Graz is compact and easy to explore, most sights being within striking distance of the broad **Hauptplatz** square.

Schlossberg

The easiest way to get your bearings is to take a trip up this wooded hill overlooking the town: either walk up a balustraded stone staircase which zigzags from Schlossbergplatz to the summit or take the hi-tech lift (Oct–April daily 8am–12.30pm, May–Sept daily 8am–1.30pm; €0.60 each way) or funicular (daily: April–Sept 9am–11pm; Oct–March 10am–10pm; €1.70), which lies a little further along Sackstrasse. The **Schloss**, or fortress, was destroyed by Napoleon in 1809; only a few prominent features survive – most noticeably the huge sixteenth-century **Uhrturm** (clock tower), and more distant **Glockenturm** (bell tower), whose bell, "Liesl", is said to be cast from 101 Turkish cannonballs.

Around the Hauptplatz

From Hauptplatz, it's a few steps to the River Mur and two examples of Graz's architectural renaissance: **Kunsthaus**

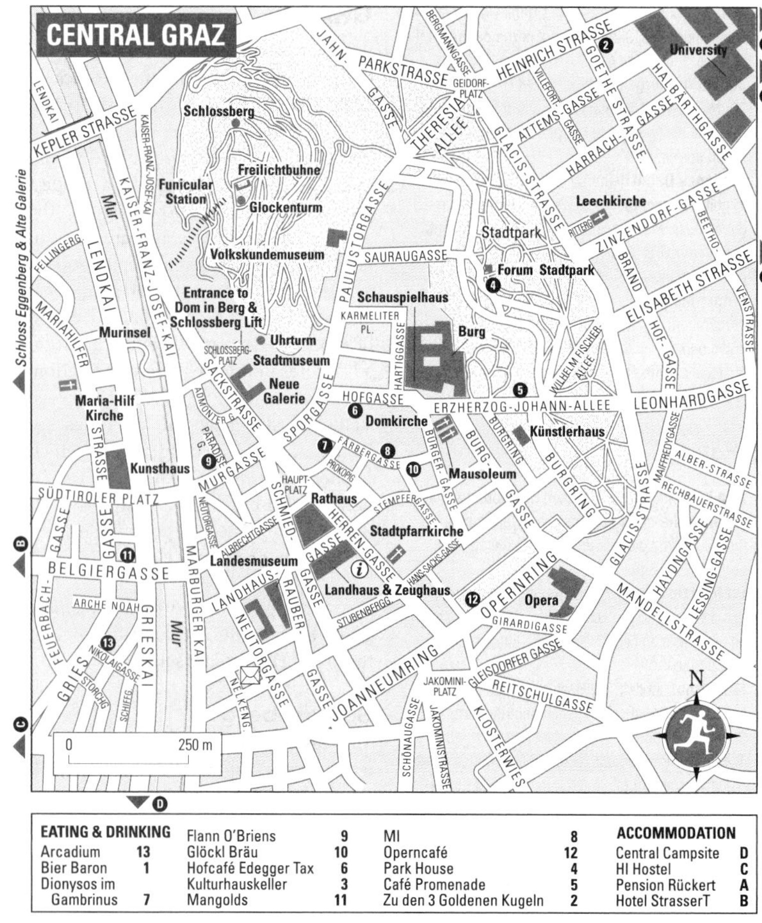

Graz (Tues–Sun 10am–6pm, Thurs till 8pm; €7; ⓦwww.kunsthausgraz.at), resembling a giant submarine, exhibits programmes of contemporary design, video-installation and photography, while the **Murinsel** is an ultra-modern floating bridge-cum-meeting place linking the two banks, inspired by an opened mussel shell.

From the southern end of Hauptplatz, Herrengasse leads towards the sixteenth-century **Landhaus**, and the adjacent **Zeughaus** (April–Oct Mon–Sun 10am–6pm, Thurs till 8pm; Nov–March Mon–Sat 10am–3pm; Sunday 10am–4pm; €7), which bristles with weapons used to keep the Turks at bay.

Mausoleum of Ferdinand II

On the other side of Herrengasse, Stempfergasse leads into a neighbourhood of narrow alleyways that dog-leg their way up the hill towards the **Mausoleum of Ferdinand II** (daily 10.30am–noon & 1.30–3/4pm; €4.50). It's a fine example of the early Baroque style, begun in 1614 when its intended incumbent was a healthy 36-year-old.

Landesmuseum Joanneum

Both the Zeughaus and the Kunsthaus fall under the umbrella of the Landesmuseum Joanneum (ⓦwww.museum-joanneum.at), a vast institution, incorporating a number of collections housed in different museums across the city. A €7 entry ticket functions as a day-pass, granting free access to all branches. Schloss Eggenberg (daily 8am–5/7pm), 4 km west of the city centre, is worth a visit (tram #1 from the Hauptplatz). This baroque palace was designed in imitation of the Escorial for the newly enobled Hans Ulrich von Eggenberg (1568–1634), chief minister to Ferdinand II. The Schloss is home to the Alte Galerie (Tues–Sun 10am–5/6pm, Thurs till 8pm; €7), which contains Gothic devotional paintings including a macabre *Triumph of Death* by Jan Bruegel. Tours of the Prunkräume or state rooms are conducted in English and German on the hour (Tues–Sun 10am–4pm, except 1pm). The house was designed by Pietro de Pomis as an allegory of the universe (there are 24 rooms, 365 windows, four towers and so on); the highlight is the 'room of the planets', a great hall with an elaborate ceiling depicting signs of the zodiac.

Arrival and information

Trains Graz's train station is on the western edge of town, a fifteen-minute walk or short tram ride (#1, #3, #6 or #7) from Hauptplatz.
Tourist office at the station (Mon–Fri 9am–6pm, Sat 9am–3pm; ⓣ0316/80750, ⓦwww.graztourismus.at) and a bigger one at Herrengasse 16 (Mon–Fri 10am–7pm, Sat & Sun 10am–6pm).
City transport Central Graz has an effective bus and tram network. Both branches of the tourist office can sell you a 24hr transport pass for €3.70 (valid on both), which is worthwhile if you plan on making more than a couple of journeys (singles cost €1.70). Simply validate the pass the first time you travel.
Internet Sit 'n' Surf, Hans-Sachs-Gasse 10 (Mon–Sat 8am–midnight).

Accommodation

HI Hostel Idlhofgasse 74 ⓣ0316/70 83 50, ⓦwww.jgh.at. Friendly, modern hostel within easy walking distance of both the train station and centre. Booking is advisable. In addition to dorms and budget doubles, the complex offers more expensive hotel-style rooms with TV and en-suite. Dorms ❷, doubles ❻
Pension Rückert Rückertgasse 4 ⓣ0316/32 30 31. Friendly pension in a leafy suburb, 2km from the centre, close to the University district. Some rooms due to be renovated in 2008. Take tram #1 to Teggethofplatz. ❼
Hotel Strasser Eggenburger Gürtel 11 ⓣ0316/71 39 77, ⓦwww.hotel-strasser.at. Despite its rather shabby exterior, *Strasser* has comfortable, if garish, doubles with TV and massage shower. Close to the station and 15 minutes' walk from the centre. ❻
Central Campsite Martinhofstr. 3 ⓣ0316/378 5102, ⓦwww.tiscover.at/campingcentral; April–Oct; bus #32 from Jakominiplatz. Well-equipped campsite south of Graz, with a large swimming pool. ❸

Eating

Cafés

Hofcafé Edegger Tax Hofgasse 8. Sedate, genteel little café, adjoined to long-established city-centre cake shop. Closed Sun.
Operncafé Opernring 22. Traditional coffeehouse near the Opera house. Popular in the evenings.
Café Promenade Erzherzog-Johann-Allee 1. Attractive neo-classical pavilion, with stylish modern décor and a terrace overlooking the Stadtpark. Open till midnight, serving soups (€3.20), salads and mains (€6–12.50).

Restaurants

Bier Baron Heinrichstrasse 56. Student favourite; a friendly pub serving vast portions of hearty Austrian standards. Schnitzel €9.
Dionysos im Gambrinuskeller Farbergasse 6–8. Central Greek restaurant serving up souvlaki, *mezze* and grills. Mains from €7.
Glöckl Bräu Glockenspielplatz 2–3. Traditional place, with busy beer terrace serving hearty Austrian fare for under €10.
Mangolds Griesgasse 11. Popular self-service place, with fresh juices and a large salad bar (you pay according to the weight of your plate); a great veggie option. Mon–Fri 11am–7pm, Sat 11am–4pm.

Zu den 3 Goldenen Kugeln corner of Goethestrasse and Heinrichstrasse. Legendary chain, doling out cheap schnitzel-and-chips (€6.50); take bus #31 from Jakominiplatz to the Geidorfplatz stop.

Drinking and nightlife

Bars

Flann O'Brien's Paradiesgasse. Lively Irish pub, with plenty of outside seating.
MI Färberplatz. Stylish, split level third-floor café-bar, with a designer interior and an attractive roof-terrace. 9am–2am; closed Sun.
Park House Stadtpark. Buzzing pavilion, tucked away in park, with regular DJ nights. Open till 4am.

Clubs

Arcadium Griesgasse 25 ⓦwww.arcadium.at. Regular guest DJs and live music nights; everything ranging from latin to hip hop and trance. Wed–Sat, open till 4am.
Kulturhauskeller Elisabethstrasse 31. A popular student dive, open till 5am. Closed Sun and Mon.

Moving on

Train Innsbruck (4 daily; 6hr); Linz (3 daily; 3hr 10min); Salzburg (every 2–3hr; 4hr 10min).

SALZBURG

For many visitors, **SALZBURG** represents the quintessential Austria, offering ornate architecture, mountain air, and a musical heritage provided by the city's most famous son, Wolfgang Amadeus **Mozart**, whose bright-eyed visage peers from every box of the city's ubiquitous chocolate delicacy, the *Mozartkugeln*.

What to see and do

Salzburg's compact centre straddles the River Salzach. The city and surrounding area used to be ruled by a series of prince-archbishops and the resulting collection of episcopal buildings on the **west bank** forms a tight-knit network of alleys and squares, overlooked by the medieval **Hohensalzburg fortress**. From here it's a short hop over the river to a narrow ribbon of essential sights on the **east bank**.

Mozartplatz and around

From the Staatsbrücke, the main bridge, tourists are funneled along Judengasse and up into **Mozartplatz**, home to a statue of the composer and overlooked by the **Glockenspiel**, a seventeenth-century musical clock whose chimes attract crowds at 7am, 11am and 6pm. The complex of Baroque buildings on the right exudes the ecclesiastical and temporal power wielded by Salzburg's archbishops, whose erstwhile living quarters – the **Residenz** – dominate the west side of Residenzplatz. You can make a self-guided audio-tour of the lavish **state rooms** (daily 10am–5pm; combined ticket with Residenzgalerie €8.20), and then visit the **Residenzgalerie** (closed Mon), one floor above, which includes works by Rembrandt and Caravaggio.

Domplatz and Franziskanerkirche

From here arches lead through to **Domplatz**, dominated by the pale marble facade of the **Dom**, an impressively cavernous Renaissance structure with dazzling ceiling frescoes. Across Domplatz, an archway leads through to the Gothic **Franziskanerkirche**, which houses a fine Baroque altar around an earlier *Madonna and Child*. The altar is enclosed by an arc of nine chapels, adorned in a frenzy of stucco ornamentation. Look out also for the twelfth-century marble lion that guards the stairway to the pulpit.

Mozarts Geburtshaus and Mozarts Wohnhaus

Getreidegasse leads back to the centre, lined with opulent boutiques, painted facades and wrought-iron shop signs. At no. 9 is the canary yellow **Mozarts Geburtshaus** (daily 9am–6/7pm, ⓦwww.mozarteum.at; €6.50; joint ticket with Wohnhaus €10), where the musical prodigy was born (in 1756) and lived till the age of 17. Between the waves

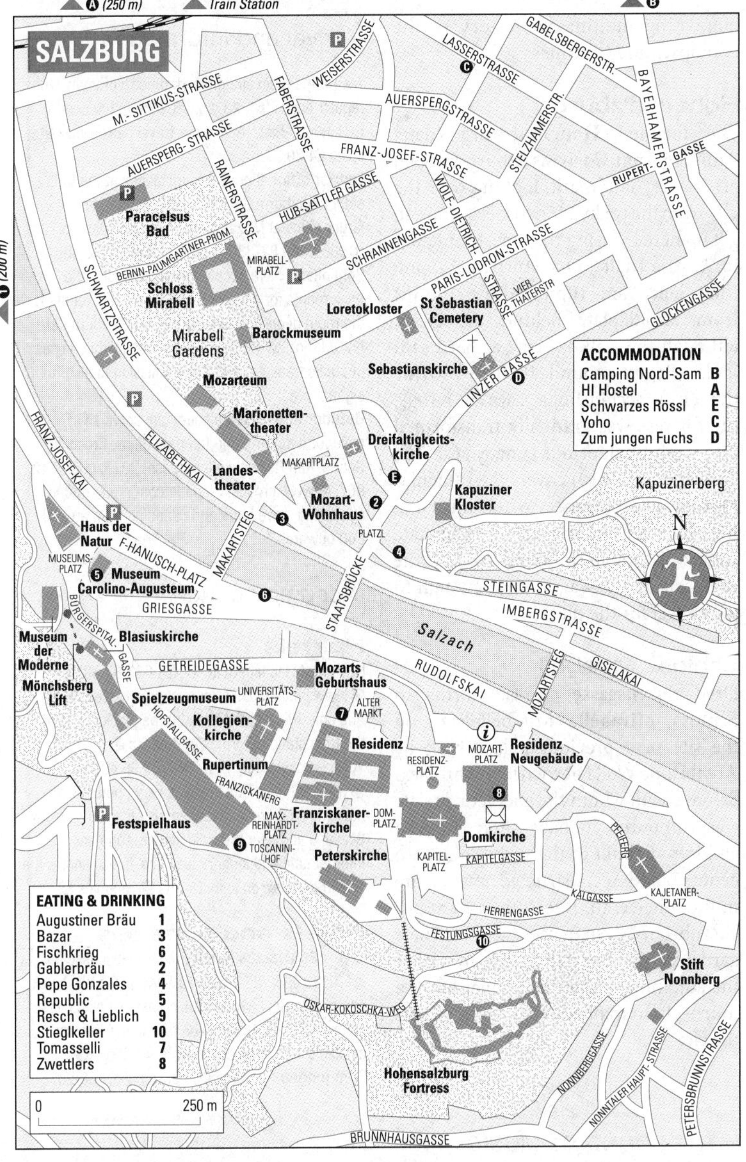

of tour parties it can be an evocative place, housing some fascinating period instruments, including a baby-sized violin used by Wolfgang Amadeus as a child.

Two blocks northwest of Platzl, on Makartplatz, is **Mozarts Wohnhaus**, the family home from 1773 to 1787 (daily 9am–6/7pm; €6.50; joint ticket with Geburtshaus €10), containing an engrossing multimedia history of the composer and his times.

Hohensalzburg

The fortified **Hohensalzburg** (daily 9am–5/6/7pm; Ⓦ www.salzburg-burgen.at) is a key landmark, looking over the city from the rocky Mönchsberg. You can get up here by using the oldest funicular in Austria (daily: Oct–April 9am–5pm, May–Sept 9am–10pm; every 10min) from Kapitelplatz behind the Dom, although the walk up isn't as hard as it looks. Begun around 1070 to provide the city's archbishops with a refuge, the fortress was gradually transformed into a more salubrious courtly seat. The 'fortress card' (€10) covers the funicular journey and entrance to the museum, including an audio-guide for the state rooms, although a roam around the ramparts and passageways is enough to gain a feel for the place.

Schloss Mirabell

Dreifaltigkeitsgasse leads north to **Schloss Mirabell**, Mirabellplatz, on the site of a previous palace built by Archbishop Wolf Dietrich for his mistress Salome, with whom the energetic prelate was rumoured to have sired a dozen children. Rebuilt in the early eighteenth century, and reconstructed after a fire in the nineteenth, it features a Baroque, cherub-lined staircase and ornate gardens – the rose-filled high ground of the adjoining Kurgarten, which offers a much-photographed view back across the city.

Arrival and information

Trains the main station is 1km north of town, with regular buses (#1, #3, #5, #6, #25) to the central F.-Hanusch-Platz. A 24-hour travel pass (Netzkarte) costs €4.20.

Tourist office there's a tourist kiosk at the train station (platform 2a; daily 9am–7/8pm), and a larger office at Mozartplatz 5 (daily 9/10am–6/7pm; Ⓣ 0662/889 87-330, Ⓦ www.salzburginfo.at). Both offices have accommodation details and book rooms for a fee of €2.20 plus ten percent of the room deposit; they also sell the Salzburg Card (€23/31 for 24/48hr), which grants unlimited use of public transport and free admission to all of the sights.

Outdoor activities Salzburg can serve as a base for a day-trip into the mountains: Crocodile Sports, Karl Reisenbichlerstrasse, 20 (Ⓣ 0662/642 907, Ⓦ www.crocodile-sports.com), runs rafting, canyoning, cave tours and canoeing from around €40 upwards.

Accommodation

Hostels

HI Hostel Haunspergstr. 27 Ⓣ 0662/87 50 30, Ⓦ www.jungehotels.at/haunspergstrasse July & Aug only. HI-affiliated hostel three blocks west of the train station. Dorms ❷, doubles ❺

Yoho Paracelsusstr. 9 Ⓣ 0662/87 96 49, Ⓦ www.yoho.at. This hostel is very popular with backpackers (book ahead) and it's easy to see why. Sociable and near the train station, Yoho has a bar, internet café and laundry facilities. It also shows the *Sound of Music* on loop. Dorms ❷, doubles ❺

Hotels and pensions

Schwarzes Rössl Priesterhausgasse 6 Ⓣ 0662/87 44 26, Ⓦ www.academia-hotels.co.at; July–Sept. Wonderful, creaky old place, in a central location. Great value for money. Rooms available with shared or private facilities. ❻

Zum jungen Fuchs Linzergasse 54 Ⓣ 0662/875

THE SOUND OF MUSIC

Salzburg certainly wastes no time cashing in on its connection with the legendary singing Von Trapp family, immortalized in the movie **The Sound of Music**. From its kiosk on Mirabellplatz, Panorama Tours (Ⓣ 0662/874 029, Ⓦ www.panoramatours.com) runs what they dub **"The Original Sound of Music Tour"** (daily 9.30am & 2pm; 4 hours; €35) on which you're bussed to the key locations from the film, such as Hellsbrun Palace and Mondsee Cathedral, played the soundtrack and sent away with a free edelweiss souvenir.

496. Spartan, but clean pension, hidden up a dingy stairwell. Given the location, something of a bargain. Doubles ❺

Camping

Camping Nord-Sam Samstr. 22a ☎0662/64 04 94, ⓦwww.camping-nord-sam.com. The most convenient campsite; April–Oct; bus #23. Tents ❸

Eating

Cafes

Bazar Schwarzstr. 3. Popular coffeehouse – primarily because it boasts a pleasant river-view terrace. Breakfast €4.50–11.
Tomasselli Alter Markt 9. Elegant, rather up-market coffeehouse.

Restaurants

Fischkrieg F.-Hanusch-Platz 4, This riverside place serves up everything from fishburgers to grilled squid, from €6.60. Closes at 6.30pm and Sun.
Gablerbräu Linzergasse 9, ⓦwww.gablerbrau.com. Cheerful Austrian restaurant (mains from €7), also serving sandwiches and smaller eats. Fantastic salad and *antipasti* buffet for €4/7.
Resch & Lieblich Toscaninihof 1. Tucked away near the Festspielhaus, this restaurant offers good-value Austrian cuisine in dining rooms carved out of the Hohensalzburg cliffs. Mains under €10.
Stieglkeller Festungsgasse 10. Enormous brewery with a beer terrace overlooking the town. Solid traditional fare for around €7.

Drinking and nightlife

Augustiner Bräu Augustinerstr. 4–6. Fifteen minutes northwest of the centre, this vast beer hall has a raucous open-air terrace. Own-brewed beer is served in huge glasses. Open from 2.30/3pm daily.
Pepe Gonzales Steingasse 3. Intimate cocktail bar near the river. Open till 3am.
Republic Anton-Neumayr-Platz 2. Trendy restaurant-club, serving food until 11pm. The wide-ranging DJ and live music programme (anything from salsa to blues or electro) attracts a young, hip crowd. Open till 4am Friday and Saturday.
Zwettlers Kaigasse 3. A relaxing pub with good food (Schnitzel €10) and blues music.

Entertainment

The city hosts dozens of **concerts** – many of them Mozart-related – all year round; check with Salzburg Ticket Service (ⓦwww.salzburgticket.com), inside the tourist office on Mozartplatz. **Salzburg Festival** (end-July to end-Aug; ⓦwww.salzburgfestival.at) is one of Europe's premier festivals of classical music, opera and theatre. Call ☎0662/8045 500 for tickets or visit the ticket office next to the Festspielhaus. The city is at its most vibrant during the festival; concerts are also projected outside on an open-air cinema screen.

Directory

Consulates UK, Alter Markt 4 ☎0662/84 81 33; US, Alter Markt 1 ☎0662/84 87 76.
Exchange Outside banking hours try at the main station (Mon–Fri 8.30am–8pm, Sat 8.30am–4pm).
Hospital Sankt Johann's Spital/Laneskrankenhaus, Müllner Hauptstr. 48 ☎0662/4482.
Internet Prabkahar, opposite the train station is €1 for 30min.
Laundry Bubble Point, Karl-Wurmb-Str. 3 (daily 7am-11pm).
Left luggage 24hr lockers at the main station.
Pharmacy Elisabeth Apotheke, Elisabethstr. 1. Closed Saturday afternoon and Sunday.
Post office Postamt 1010, Residenzplatz 9.

Moving on

Trains Innsbruck (11 daily; 2hr); Linz (hourly; 1hr 20min).
Bus Strobl (for St. Wolfgang) (hourly; 1hr 15min); Hallstatt (9 daily; 2hr 30min).

THE SALZKAMMERGUT

The peaks of the **Salzkammergut** may not be as lofty as those further south, but the lakes that fill the glacier-carved troughs separating them make for some spectacular scenery. Most of the settlements here are modest, quiet until the annual summer influx of visitors.

St Wolfgang

Hourly buses between Salzburg and Bad Ischl run east along the southern shores of the Wolfgangersee, though they bypass the lake's main attraction, the village of **ST WOLFGANG**, on the opposite shore: get off at Strobl, at the lake's eastern end, and pick up a connecting bus from there. St Wolfgang can be crowded in summer, but is worth visiting, if only to see the **Pfarrkirche**, just above the lake shore; its high altar, an extravagantly pinnacled structure 12m high, was completed between 1471 and 1481, and features brightly gilded scenes of the *Coronation of the Virgin* in the centrepiece flanked by scenes from the life of St Wolfgang. Little trains climb the local **Schafberg** peak (May–Oct; €24 return; to avoid queuing, reserve a seat on ☎06138/2232, Ⓦwww.schafbergbahn.at; InterRail/Eurail discounts) from a station on the western edge of town. The **tourist office** (May–Oct Mon–Fri 9am–8pm, Sat 9am–noon & 2–6pm, Sunday 2–6pm; Nov–April Mon–Fri 9am–5pm, Sat 9am–noon; ☎06138/8003, Ⓦwww.wolfgangsee.at) is at the eastern entrance to the road tunnel, and can help arrange accommodation.

Bad Ischl

It was the soothing properties of the waters and tranquil ambience that still permeates the town of **BAD ISCHL** today that prompted the penultimate Habsburg emperor, Franz Josef, to summer in the **Kaiservilla** (Nov, Feb & March Wed 10am–4pm, April daily 10am–4pm; May to mid-Oct daily 9.30am—4.45pm; €9.50, park only €3.50) across the River Ischl from the centre. Beyond the villa (which is crammed with the victims of the emperor's hunting expeditions), stretches a park containing the **Marmorschlössel** (April–Oct daily 9.30am–5pm; €2), a neo-Gothic teahouse built for the Empress Elizabeth in 1861. The interior is atmospheric and now houses a small, yet absorbing museum of photography.

Both the **bus** and **train stations** are on the eastern fringe of the centre, a few steps from the **tourist office**, Bahnhofstr. 6 (Mon–Fri 8am–6pm, Sat 9am–noon; July & Aug Sat till 3pm and also Sun 10am–1pm; ☎06132/27757, Ⓦwww.badischl.at). For **accommodation**, there's a modern, functional HI hostel conveniently located near the swimming pool at Am Rechensteg 5 (☎06132/26577, Ⓦwww.oejhv.or.at; beds in three and four person en-suite rooms ❷), and the clean and comfy ivy-clad *Eglmoos*, at Eglmoosgasse, 14 (☎06132/23154; July–Sept; ❺). Another choice is the friendly *Steininger*, with rooms above a café on Leitenbergerstr (☎06132/25260, Ⓦwww.gh-steininger.at; closed mid-Jan–Feb, ❻). There are plenty of restaurants along the river and in town offering Austrian standards. If you've had enough schnitzel, *Venezia* on Schulgasse serves cheap pizza and pasta dishes.

Moving on

Train Hallstatt (12 daily; 30min).
Bus Hallstatt (5–7 daily; 40min); Salzburg (hourly; 1hr 40min); St Wolfgang (2 hourly; 45min).

HALLSTATT

The jewel of the Salzkammergut is the UNESCO World Heritage Site of **HALLSTATT**, which clings to the base of precipitous cliffs on the shores of the Hallstättersee, 20km south of Bad Ischl. With towering peaks and a pristine lake, this is a stunning setting in which to hike, swim or rent a boat. Arriving by train is an atmospheric and evocative experience; the station is on the opposite side of the lake, and the ferry, which meets all incoming trains, gives truly dramatic views. (Note that after 6.30pm, trains don't stop here and instead continue to Obertraun, 5km away on the lakeshore.) **Buses** stop in the suburb of Lahn, a ten-minute lakeside walk away.

What to see and do

Hallstatt gave its name to a distinct period of Iron Age culture after Celtic remains were discovered in the salt mines above the town. Many of the finds date back to the ninth century BC, and can now be seen in the **Museum Hallstatt** (April–Oct daily 10am–4/6pm; Nov–March

Tues–Sun 11am–3pm; €7.50; Ⓦwww.museum-hallstatt.at).

The **Pfarrkirche** has a south portal adorned with sixteenth-century Calvary scenes and, inside, a Gothic winged altar on the right with heavily gilded statuettes of the Madonna and Child flanked by St Catherine (the patron of woodcutters, on the left) and St Barbara (the patron of miners). In the graveyard outside is a small stone structure known as the **Beinhaus** (daily 10am–4.30/6pm; €1), traditionally the repository for the skulls of villagers. The skulls, some of them quite recent, are inscribed with the names of the deceased and dates of their death, and are often decorated.

Steep paths behind the graveyard lead up to a highland valley, the **Salzachtal** (1hr 30min of hard hiking), where the **salt mines** that provided the area's prosperity can be viewed (guided tour only: May–Oct daily 9.30am–3/4.30pm; €15.50). You can also take the **funicular** (May–Oct daily 9am–4.30pm/6pm; every 15 minutes; €8.50 return) from the nearby suburb of Lahn. A combined ticket for tour and funicular is €21.

Arrival and information

Tourist office Located in the centre of town (Mon–Fri 9am–noon & 2–5pm; July & Aug no lunch break and also Sat 10am–2pm; Ⓣ06134/8208, Ⓦwww.hallstatt.net).

Accommodation

Campsite Klausner-Höll Lahnstrasse Ⓣ06134/8322, Ⓦwww.campingwelt.com/klausner-hoell. A short walk from the landing stage at Lahn, on the outskirts of the village. Quiet and well-equipped. Open mid-April to mid-Oct. ❷

Gasthaus zur Mühle Kirchenweg 36 Ⓣ06134/8318. Cosy guesthouse set back from the landing stage with dorms and doubles. ❷

Seethaler Mortonweg 22 Ⓣ06134/8421, Ⓔpension.seethaler@kronline.at. A great place to stay – each room in this labyrinthine house has a balcony with a stunning lake view. ❺

Eating and drinking

Bräugasthof Seestr. 120. Excellent Austrian food, with a popular lakeside terrace and competitively priced fresh fish, from €13.50.

Gasthaus zur Mühle Welcoming, small bar in the friendly guesthouse.

Outdoor activities

Canoes and other boats can be rented from the boatshed beside the landing stage (€8 for 30min). The tourist office can advise on a route for the four-hour **hike** up to the Wiesberghaus mountain hut (Ⓣ06134/20620; Jan–Oct; ❷), and also sell you guides detailing other hiking trails in the area.

Western Austria

West towards the mountain province of the **Tyrol**, the grandiose scenery of Austria's Alpine heartland begins to develop. Most trains from Vienna and Salzburg travel through a corner of Bavaria in Germany before joining the Inn valley and climbing back into Austria to the Tyrolean capital, **Innsbruck**. A less direct but more scenic route (more likely if you're coming from Graz) cuts by the majestic **Hoher Tauern** – site of Austria's highest peak, the Grossglockner – before joining the Inn valley at Wörgl. The exclusive resort-town of **Kitzbühel** provides a potential stop-off, although Innsbruck offers the most convenient mix of urban sights and Alpine splendour. Further west, **Bregenz**, on the shores of Lake Constance, makes for a tranquil stop before pressing on into Germany or Switzerland.

INNSBRUCK

High in the Alps, with ski resorts within easy reach, **INNSBRUCK** is a compact city hemmed in by towering mountains.

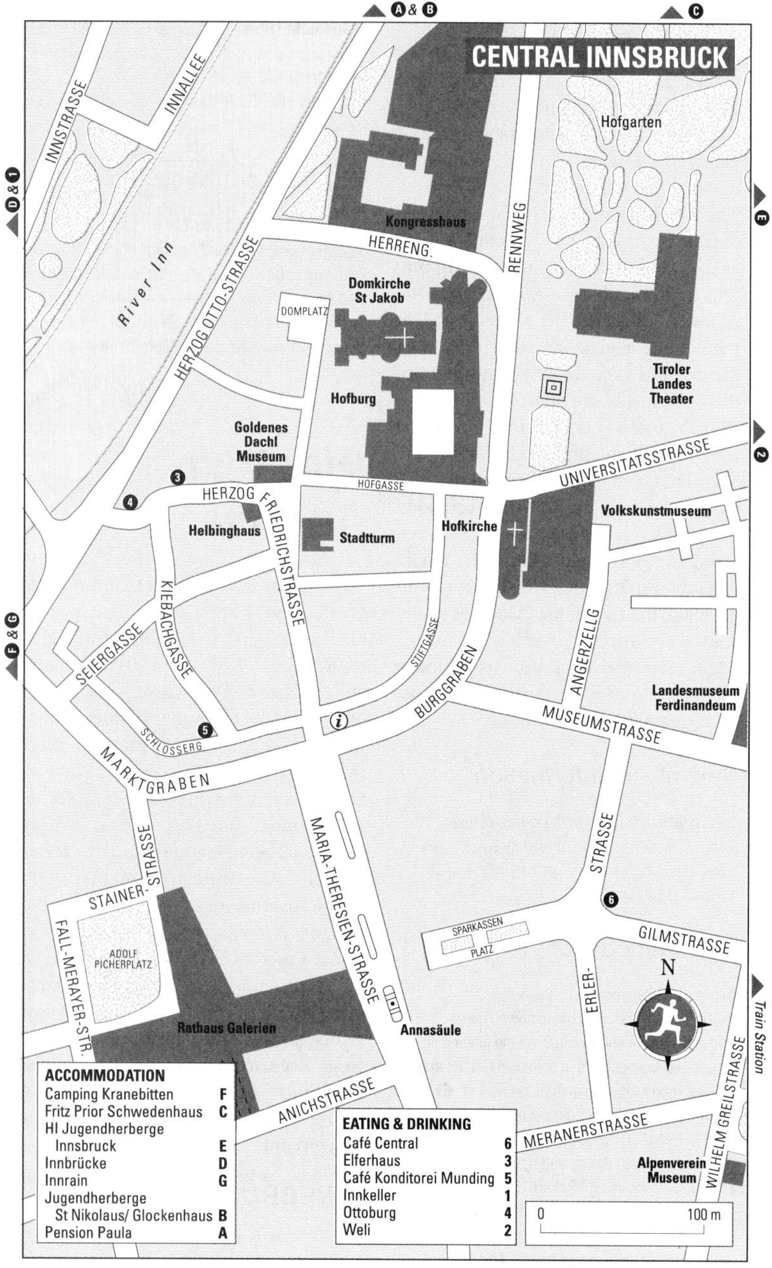
CENTRAL INNSBRUCK
A & B
C
D & 1
E
2
F & G
Train Station
Hofgarten
Kongresshaus
Domkirche St Jakob
DOMPLATZ
Hofburg
Tiroler Landes Theater
Goldenes Dachl Museum
Helbinghaus
Stadtturm
Hofkirche
Volkskunstmuseum
Landesmuseum Ferdinandeum
Rathaus Galerien
Annasäule
Alpenverein Museum
ADOLF PICHERPLATZ
SPARKASSEN PLATZ
River Inn
INNSTRASSE
INNALLEE
HERZOG OTTO-STRASSE
HERRENG.
RENNWEG
HOFGASSE
HERZOG FRIEDRICHSTRASSE
UNIVERSITATSSTRASSE
KIEBACHGASSE
SEIERGASSE
SCHLOSSERG
STIFTGASSE
BURGGRABEN
ANGERZELLG
MUSEUMSTRASSE
MARKTGRABEN
MARIA-THERESIEN-STRASSE
STAINER-STRASSE
FALL-MERAYER-STR.
STRASSE
GILMSTRASSE
ERLER-
ANICHSTRASSE
MERANERSTRASSE
WILHELM GREILSTRASSE
N
0
100 m
ACCOMMODATION
Camping Kranebitten F
Fritz Prior Schwedenhaus C
HI Jugendherberge Innsbruck E
Innbrücke D
Innrain G
Jugendherberge St Nikolaus/ Glockenhaus B
Pension Paula A
EATING & DRINKING
Café Central 6
Elferhaus 3
Café Konditorei Munding 5
Innkeller 1
Ottoburg 4
Weli 2

It has a rich history: Maximilian I based the imperial court here in the 1490s, placing this provincial Alpine town at the heart of European politics and culture for a century and a half. This combination of historical pedigree and proximity to the mountains has placed Innsbruck firmly on the tourist trail.

What to see and do

Most attractions are confined to the central Altstadt, bounded by the river and the Graben, following the course of the moat which used to surround the medieval town.

Maria-Theresien-Strasse

Innsbruck's main artery is **Maria-Theresien-Strasse**, famed for the view north towards the great rock wall of the Nordkette, the mountain range that dominates the city. At its southern end the triumphal arch, **Triumphpforte**, was built for the marriage of Maria Theresa's son Leopold in 1756. Halfway along, the **Annasäule**, a column supporting a statue of the Virgin, was erected to commemorate the retreat of the Bavarians, who had been menacing the Tyrol, on St Anne's Day (July 26), 1703. Herzog-Friedrich-Strasse leads on into the centre, opening out into a plaza lined with arcaded medieval buildings. At the plaza's southern end is the **Goldenes Dachl**, or "Golden Roof" (though the tiles are actually copper), built in the 1490s to cover an oriel window from which the court of Emperor Maximilian could observe the square below. The **Goldenes Dachl Museum** (May–Sept daily 10am–5pm; Oct–April Tues–Sun 10am–5pm; €4; Ⓦwww.tiroler-landesmuseum.at), though flashy, is something of a disappointment. Aside from a brief glimpse of the balcony, the main attraction is an entertaining video-style documentary about the emperor Maximilian.

Domplatz

An alley to the right leads down to Domplatz and the ostentatious **Domkirche St Jakob**, home to a valuable *Madonna and Child* by German master Lucas Cranach the Elder, although it's buried in the fussy Baroque detail of the altar. The adjacent **Hofburg**, entered around the corner, has late-medieval roots but was remodelled in the eighteenth century, its Rococo state apartments crammed with opulent furniture (daily 9am–5pm; €5.50). At the head of Rennweg, entered through the **Tiroler Volkskunstmuseum** (see below), is the **Hofkirche** (Ⓦwww.hofkirche.at), which contains the imposing **Cenotaph of Emperor Maximilian** (Mon–Sat 9am–5/5.30pm; €3, free on Sun). This extraordinary project was originally envisaged as a series of 40 larger-than-life statues, 100 statuettes and 32 busts of Roman emperors, representing both the real and the spiritual ancestors of Maximilian, but in the end only 32 of the statuettes and 20 of the busts were completed. Upstairs is the Silberkapelle or silver chapel, named after the silver Madonna that adorns the far wall.

Museums and galleries

The same complex houses the **Tiroler Volkskunstmuseum** (hours as for Hofkirche, but closed Sunday; €5; combined ticket with Hofkirche €6.50), which features recreations of traditional wood-panelled Tyrolean peasant interiors. The **Tiroler Landesmuseum Ferdinandeum**, a short walk south at Museumstr. 15 (June–Sept daily 10am–6pm, Thurs till 9pm; Oct–May Tues–Sun 10am–6pm; €8), contains one of the best collections of Gothic paintings in Austria; most originate from the churches of the South Tyrol (now the Italian region of AltoAdige). Also worth a visit is **Schloss Ambras** (daily 10am–5/7pm; closed Nov; €8), 2km southeast on tram #6. Alternatively take tram #3 to Amras and then walk for ten minutes on the path leading beneath the motorway and up the hill. Set in attractive grounds, this was the home of Archduke Ferdinand of Tyrol and still houses a collection of Habsburg portraits and an intriguing selection of curios amassed from around the globe, including giant playing cards, fossils and musical instruments.

Hungerburg plateau

A good starting point for hikes is the Hungerburg plateau; the quickest route up to higher altitudes is the new **Hungerburgbahn cable railway**, which runs from the Innsbruck Congress Centre. Alternatively, Bus #J runs directly to the Hungerburg cable-car station, from where a two-stage sequence of cable-cars continues to just below the summit of the Nordkette range (€19.10 return), where you can enjoy stupendous views of the high Alps.

Arrival and information

Train Trains arrive at Innsbruck's main station on the Südtirolerplatz, just to the east of the old town. It's an easy walk from here into the centre.
Bus Buses arrive immediately to the south of the train station.
Tourist office Innsbruck's train station has a tourist kiosk (daily 9am–7pm), while the main office is at Burggraben 3 (daily 9am–6pm; Ⓣ0512/59850, Ⓦwww.innsbruck.info).
City transport Both tourist offices sell the "Innsbruck Card" (€24/29/34 for 24/48/72hr), which allows free travel in the centre and admission to all the sights. A 24-hour transport pass costs €3.80. An Innsbruck Club Card (given free on hotel check-in) gives free, guided hikes, reduced cable-car fares and free lake bathing.

Accommodation

Hostels

Fritz Prior Schwedenhaus Rennweg 17b Ⓣ0512/585 814; July and Aug only). Excellent hostel ten minutes' walk from the centre (or bus #4). Four-bed dorms come with en-suite bathrooms and there are also laundry facilities and internet access. Dorms ❷, doubles ❹
HI Jugendherberge Innsbruck Reichenauerstr. 147 Ⓣ0512/346 179, Ⓦwww.youth-hostel-innsbruck.at. Large, functional HI hostel on the outskirts of the city. Bus #0 stops outside and runs every 5–10min during the day. Dorms ❷, doubles ❺
Jugendherberge St Nikolaus/ Glockenhaus Weiherburggasse 3, Ⓣ0512/286 515, Ⓦwww.hostelnikolaus.at. This homely pension and hostel is ten minutes' walk from town, in an old house full of character. Breakfast not included. Take Bus D or E from the station to St Nikolas Church. Dorms ❷, doubles ❺

Hotels and pensions

Innbrücke Innstr 1 Ⓣ0512/281 934, Ⓔinnbruecke@nextra.at. Guesthouse located in a convenient spot, just over the bridge from the old town; doubles available with bathroom ❼ or without bathroom ❻
Innrain Innrain 38 Ⓣ0512/588 981, Ⓦwww.gasthof-innrain.com. Pleasant family-run place, above a café near the old town. ❺
Pension Paula Weiherburggasse 15 Ⓣ0512/292 262, Ⓦwww.pensionpaula.at. Friendly, good-value pension in a chalet on a hillside north of the river – ask for a room with balcony and mountain views. ❻

Camping

Camping Kranebitten Kranebittner Allee 214 Ⓣ0512/28 41 80, Ⓦwww.campinginnsbruck.com; well-equipped campsite 5km west of town. Bus #LK from Boznerplatz, a block west of the station, to Klammstrasse. ❷

Eating and drinking

Cafés and restaurants

Café Central Gilmstr. 5 Venerable coffeehouse serving up excellent cakes and decent breakfasts (from €6). Good spot to linger over a coffee.
Café-Konditorei Munding corner of Kiebachgasse and Schlossergasse. Renowned for its sweets and pastries.
Ottoburg Herzog-Friedrich-Str. 1. More up-market restaurant with solid Austrian fare. Mains €13–18. Closed Mon.

Bars

Elferhaus Herzog-Friedrich-Strasse 11. Popular old-town beer bar, with a lively atmosphere, serving good food for under €10.

Innkeller Innstr. 1. Popular, friendly late-night bar just across the river from the old town.
Weli Ing-Etzelstr. 26. Informal, unpretentious café/bar with snacks. Good starting point for exploring the various bars under the railway arches. Open from 7pm.

Outdoor activities

The Innsbruck Alpine School (Ⓦwww.asi.at) runs a programme of guided **hikes** (June–Sept; free with a Club Innsbruck Card), including sunrise and lantern-lit ones; the tourist office has details. **Bikes** can be rented from Sport Neuner (Ⓣ0512/561 501; from €20/day). As befits such a stunning setting, there's a range of **adventure sports** – ask the tourist office for their activities brochure. Snow stays on the nearby Stubai Glacier (Ⓦwww.stubaier-gletscher.com) all year, making summer **skiing** possible. There's 110km of downhill runs in total; lift passes cost €28.70 per day (summer) or €36 (winter). Adrenaline junkies can shoot down the 1000-metre **bobsleigh run** in just over a minute (Aug–Oct Wed–Fri 4pm & 6pm; Ⓣ05275/5386, Ⓦwww.knauseder-event.at; €25). Flugschule Parafly (Ⓣ05226/3344, Ⓦwww.parafly.at), are one of several operators able to arrange tandem **paraglides** (from €100).

Directory

Consulates UK, Kaiserjägerstr. 1 Ⓣ0512/588 320.
Exchange Western Union, in the train station (Mon–Fri 9am–12.30pm & 1.30pm–4/6pm).
Hospital Universitätklinik, Anichstr. 35 Ⓣ0512/504.
Internet access International Telephone Discount, Südtirolerplatz 1; open till 11pm.
Laundry Bubble Point, Andreas-Hoferstr. 37 & Brixnerstr. 1 (Mon–Fri 8am–10pm, Sat & Sun 8am–8pm).
Left luggage At the station; 24hr lockers.
Pharmacy Apotheke Bahnhof, by the train station (Mon–Fri 8am–6pm, Sat 8am–noon).
Post office Maximilianstr. 2 (24hr).

Moving on

Trains Bregenz (8 daily; 2hr 40min)
International trains Munich (2 hourly; 2hr 30min); Venice (2 daily; 5hr 55min); Florence (3 daily; 6hr 30min).

BREGENZ

On the eastern tip of the Bodensee (Lake Constance), **BREGENZ** is an obvious staging post on journeys into neighbouring Germany, Liechtenstein or Switzerland. The Vorarlbergers who live here speak a dialect close to Swiss German, and have always considered themselves separate from the rest of Austria. At first sight Bregenz is curiously disjointed, the tranquil lakeside parks cut off from town by the main road and rail links along the lakeshore.

What to see and do

Most points of interest are in the old town, up the hill from the lake, around **St Martinsturm**, an early seventeenth-century tower crowned by a bulbous wooden dome. Up the street from here is the seventeenth-century **town hall**, an immense half-timbered construction with a steeply inclined roof. Down in the modern town near the lake on Kornmarkt, the **Kunsthaus Bregenz** (Tues–Sun 10am–6pm/8pm, Thurs till 9pm; €10; Ⓦwww.kunsthaus-bregenz.at), known as the KUB, is a cool green cube that hosts high-profile modern art exhibitions. The **Vorarlberger Landesmuseum**, Kornmarkt 1 (Tues–Sun 10am–5pm; Thurs till 8pm; €6; Ⓦwww.vlm.at), has some outstanding paintings by Angelika Kauffmann, a local painter who achieved success in eighteenth-century London. Beyond here, leafy parks line the lake to the **Festspielhaus**, a modern concert hall built to accommodate the **Bregenz Festival** (mid-July to mid-Aug; Ⓦwww.bregenzerfestspiele.com; tickets from €26), which draws thousands of opera lovers every year. A cable car rises from a station at the eastern end of town to the **Pfänder** (daily 8am–7pm; €10.20), a wooded hill with excellent views; you can also follow the worthwhile Pfänderweg on foot to the top (1hr 30min).

Arrival and information

Tourist office Bahnhofstr. 14 (July–Sept Mon–Sat 8.30am–7pm; Oct–June Mon–Fri 8.30am–6pm, Sat 9am–noon; Ⓣ05574/49590, Ⓦwww.bregenz.at).

Accommodation

Pension Gunz Anton-Schneiderstr.38 ⓣ05574/43657, ⓔpension_rest_gunz@aon.at. Friendly, centrally-located pension above the café of the same name. ❻

HI Hostel Mehrerauerstr. 5 ⓣ05574/42867, ⓦwww.jfgh.at. HI-affiliated hostel west of the train station, popular with families. Near to the lake, with laundry and internet facilities. Dorms have communal showers. ❷

Pension Sonne Kaiserstr. 8 ⓣ05574/42572, ⓦwww.bbn.at/sonne. Extremely central place on one of Bregenz's main shopping streets; hikes its rates steeply during the festival, though. ❼

Seecamping Bodengasse 7, mid-May to mid-Sept ⓣ05574/71895, ⓦwww.seecamping.at. Bregenz's largest campsite, along the lakeshore, 2km west. Tents ❷

Eating and drinking

Cuba Bahnhofstr. Popular and centrally located café-bar, split over two floors, with occasional live music.

Goldener Hirschen Kirchstr 8. Atmospheric, beamed tavern with hearty Austrian fare from €2.50–13 and local wines.

Gunz Anton-Schneider-Str. 38. Small café serving traditional Austrian food at low prices (from €5). Closed Tues.

Café Sito Maurachgasse, 6. Tiny, backstreet café, with an extensive selection of magazines, serving coffee, smoothies and bagels to a studenty clientele.

Moving on

Trains Innsbruck (8 daily; 2hr 40min); Vienna (5 daily; 7hr 30min).

Belgium and Luxembourg

HIGHLIGHTS

BRUGES: see why everyone raves about this perfect medieval town
GHENT: marvel at the town's castle and lively bars
BRUSSELS: see the most well-preserved square in the country, the Grand-Place
ARDENNES: cycle, kayak or hike through the Ardennes woods
LUXEMBOURG CITY: visit Europe's most dramatically sited capital

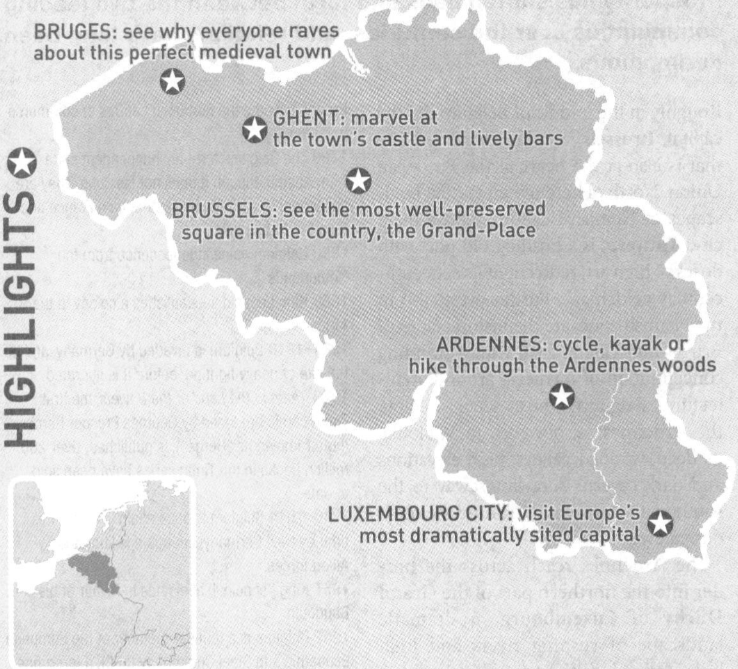

ROUGH COSTS

DAILY BUDGET basic €35/ occasional treat €50

DRINK Jupiler beer €1.60

FOOD Mussels with chips €10–15

HOSTEL/BUDGET HOTEL €15–20/€55–65

TRAVEL Train: Brussels–Antwerp (40min) €6; Brussels–Namur (1hr 20min) €4

CURRENCY Euro (€)

FACT FILE

POPULATION Belgium: 10.5 million; Luxembourg: 480,000

AREA Belgium: 30,582 sq km; Luxembourg: 2,586 sq km

LANGUAGE Belgium: Flemish, French, German; Luxembourg: Letzebuergesch, French, German

CAPITAL Belgium: Brussels; Luxembourg: Luxembourg City

INTERNATIONAL PHONE CODE Belgium: ⓣ32; Luxembourg: ⓣ352

Basics

A federal country, with three official languages and an intense regional rivalry, Belgium has a cultural diversity that belies its rather dull reputation. Its population of around ten million is divided between Flemish-speakers in the north (about sixty percent) and French-speaking Walloons to the south (forty percent), with a few pockets of German-speakers in the east. Prosperity has shifted back and forth between the two leading communities over the centuries, and relations have long been acrimonious.

Roughly in the middle of Belgium lies the capital, **Brussels**, a culturally varied city that is also at the heart of the European Union. North of here stretch the flat landscapes of Flemish Belgium, whose main city, **Antwerp**, is a bustling old port with doses of high art, redolent of its sixteenth-century golden age. Further west, also in the Flemish zone, are the historic cities of Bruges and Ghent, each with a stunning concentration of medieval art and architecture. Belgium's most scenic region, the **Ardennes**, is, however, in Wallonia, its deep, wooded valleys, high elevations and dark caverns sprawling away to the south, with the town of **Namur** the obvious gateway.

The Ardennes reach across the border into the northern part of the **Grand Duchy of Luxembourg**, a dramatic landscape of rushing rivers and high hills topped with crumbling castles. The best base for rural expeditions is **Luxembourg City**, an exceptionally picturesque town with a rugged setting. The city has a population of around eighty thousand, making it one of Europe's smallest capitals.

CHRONOLOGY

Belgium

54 BC Julius Caesar defeats the Belgae tribes.
496 AD The King of the Franks, Clovis, founds a kingdom which includes Belgium.
1400–1500 Belgian cities of Antwerp, Brussels and Bruges become the European centres of commerce and industry.
1790 The Belgians form an independent state from Austria, though it does not last long. They are subsequently invaded by Austria, then France and then the Netherlands.
1830 Belgium gains independence from the Netherlands.
1885 King Leopold II establishes a colony in the African Congo.
1914–1918 Belgium is invaded by Germany, and is the site of heavy fighting, before it is liberated.
1929 *Tintin in the Land of the Soviets*, the first Tintin comic produced by Georges Prosper Remi (better known as "Hergé"), is published. Over 200 million books in the Tintin series have been sold to date.
1940–1944 Belgium is once again invaded, this time by Nazi Germany, but again is liberated by Allied forces.
1951 King Leopold III abdicates in favour of his son, Baudouin.
1957 Belgium is a founder member of the European Economic and Steel Community (EEC), a forerunner to the European Union.
1960 Belgium grants independence to the Congo.
1967 René Magritte, one of the great Surrealist artists, dies.
1992 Belgium ratifies the Maastricht Treaty on the European Union.
2005 Nationwide strike action against proposed government reform of pension schemes.

Luxembourg

963 AD Count Siegfried of Ardenne founds the capital of Luxembourg.
1354 Luxembourg's status is raised from fief to duchy by Emperor Charles IV.
1477 The Habsburgs take control of Luxembourg.

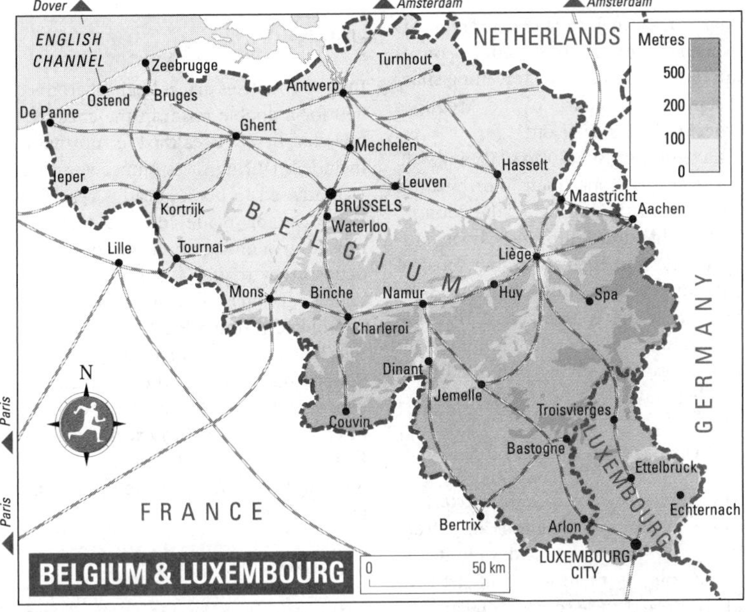

1867 Second Treaty of London ensures Luxembourg's independence and neutrality.
1890 Luxembourg announces its own ruling monarchy, relinquishing its ties to the Netherlands.
1939–1945 Luxembourg is invaded by Nazi Germany.
1957 Luxembourg is the founder member of the European Economic Community (EEC).
1964 The Grand Duchess Charlotte abdicates; her son becomes Grand Duke Jean.
2000 Grand Duke Jean abdicates, handing responsibility over to his son Henri.

ARRIVAL

Brussels has two **airports**: the closer one is Zaventem, while Charleroi (where the budget airlines including Flybe and Ryanair fly to) lies about 55km from the centre. There are frequent **rail** connections from Paris, London, Amsterdam and Luxembourg, with almost all international trains getting in to Bruxelles-Midi (Brussel-Zuid), and frequently also stopping in Ghent or Antwerp. Eurolines **buses** from Paris, Amsterdam, London and other destinations get into Gare du Nord.

GETTING AROUND

Travelling around Belgium is rarely a problem. Distances are short, and an efficient, reasonably priced train network links all the major and many minor towns and villages. Luxembourg, on the other hand, can be a tad more problematic: the train network is not extensive and bus timetables can demand careful study for longer journeys.

By train

Belgium's railway system (Ⓦwww.b-rail.be) – SNCB in French, NMBS in Flemish – is comprehensive and efficient, and fares are comparatively low. InterRail and Eurail passes are valid throughout the network. If you are under 26 and spending some time in Belgium, ask for the Go-Pass, which gets you ten journeys between any Belgian stations for €45. SNCB/NMBS also publishes information on offers and services in their comprehensive timetable book, which has an English-language section and is available at major train stations. **Buses** are only really used for travelling short distances, or in parts of the Ardennes where rail lines fizzle out.

Luxembourg's railways (Ⓦwww.cfl.lu) comprise one main north–south route down the middle of the country, with a handful of branch lines fanning out from the capital, but most of the country can only be reached by bus. **Fares** are comparable with those in Belgium, and there are a number of passes available, giving unlimited train and bus travel.

By bike

The modest distances and flat terrain make **cycling** in Belgium an attractive proposition. That said, only in the countryside is there a decent network of signposted cycle routes. You can take your own bike on a train for a small fee or rent one from any of around thirty train stations during the summer at about €10 per day; note also that some train excursion tickets include the cost of bike rental. Full details, with a list of stations offering bike rental, are on the SNCB/NMBS website and in the *Train & Vélo* leaflet (available at stations). In Luxembourg you can rent bikes for around €10 a day, and take your own bike on trains (not buses) for a minimal fee per journey. The Luxembourg Tourist Office has leaflets showing cycle routes and also sells cycling guides.

ACCOMMODATION

Hotel accommodation is one of the major expenses on a trip to Belgium or Luxembourg – indeed, if you're after a degree of comfort, it's going to be the costliest item by far. There are, however, **budget alternatives**, principally the no-frills end of the hotel market, private rooms – effectively B&Bs – arranged via the local tourist office and hostels.

Hotels

In both countries **prices** begin at around €60 for a double room in the cheapest one-star hotel. **Breakfast** is normally included. During the summer you'd be well advised to book ahead – **reservations** can be made for free through most tourist offices on the day itself; the deposit they require is subtracted from your final hotel bill. Private rooms can be booked through local tourist offices too. Expect to pay €40–60 a night for a double, but note that they're often inconveniently situated on the outskirts of cities and towns. An exception is in Bruges, where private rooms can be booked direct and many are in the centre.

Hostels

Belgium has around thirty well-run **HI hostels**, run by two separate organizations. In Flanders (northern Belgium), this is Vlaamse Jeugdherbergcentrale (Ⓣ032 32 72 18, Ⓦwww.vjh.be); in Wallonia (southern Belgium) it's Les Auberges de Jeunesse de Wallonie (Ⓣ022 19 56 76, Ⓦwww.laj.be). Most charge a flat rate per person of €14–20 for a bed in a dormitory or €42–48 for a double room, with breakfast included. Many also offer meals for €5–15. During the summer you should book ahead wherever possible. Some of the more touristy cities such as Bruges, Antwerp and Brussels also have **privately run hostels**. These normally charge about €20 for a dorm bed.

There are ten HI hostels in **Luxembourg**, all of which are members of the Centrale des Auberges de Jeunesse Luxembourgeoises (Ⓣ26 27 66 40, Ⓦwww.youthhostels.lu). Dorm-bed rates for HI members are €15.30–16.30, with non-members paying an extra €3. Breakfast is always included; lunch or dinner is €6–8.

Camping

In **Belgium**, there are literally hundreds of campsites, anything from a field with a few tent pitches through to extensive complexes. All, however, apply the same one- to five-star Benelux grading system. The vast majority are one- and two-star establishments, for which two adults with a car and a tent can **expect to pay** €10–20 per night. Surprisingly, most four-star sites don't cost much more – add about €5 – though the occasional five-star campsite can reach €50. All of **Luxembourg**'s campsites are detailed in the Duchy's free tourist office booklet. They are classified into three broad bands: the majority are in Category 1, the best-equipped and most expensive classification. Prices vary considerably, but are usually €3–5 per person, plus €3–5 for a pitch. In both countries, it's a good idea to **reserve** ahead during peak season; individual campsite phone numbers are listed in the free **camping booklets**, and in Luxembourg the national tourist board (Ⓣ42 82 82 10, Ⓦwww.ont.lu) will make a reservation on your behalf.

FOOD AND DRINK

One of the great pleasures of a trip to Belgium is the cuisine, which goes well beyond mussels and fries. If you stay away from tourist spots, it's hard to go wrong. Luxembourg's food is less varied and more Germanic, but you can still eat out extremely well. As for drink, **beer** is one of the real delights of Belgium, and Luxembourg produces some very drinkable white **wines**.

Southern Belgian (or Wallonian) cuisine is similar to traditional French, retaining its neighbour's fondness for rich sauces and ingredients. In **Flanders** to the north the food is more akin to that of the Netherlands, with mussels and French fries the most common dish. Throughout the country, pork, beef, game, fish and seafood are staple items, often cooked with butter, cream and herbs, or sometimes in beer; hearty soups are also common. There are plenty of good vegetarian options too, such as quiche and salad. The Ardennes is renowned for its smoked ham and pâté.

In both countries, many **bars** offer inexpensive meals, at least at lunchtimes, and in addition a host of cafés serve simple dishes – omelettes, steak or mussels with chips for instance. **Cafés** are often also the most fashionable places to be, especially in the cities. Most serve a dish of the day for around €10. Restaurants are usually more expensive, but the food is generally excellent.

Belgium is also renowned for its **chocolate**. The big chocolatiers, Godiva and Leonidas, have shops in all the main towns and cities, but very good quality chocolate is also available in supermarkets at a much lower price – try Jacques or Côte d'Or.

Drink

Drinking **beer in Belgium** is a real treat. The most common brands are Stella Artois, Jupiler and Maes, but this merely scratches the surface. In total, there are about seven hundred speciality beers from dark stouts to fruit beers, wheat beers and brown ales – something to suit any palate and enough to overwhelm the hardiest of livers. The most famous are the strong ales brewed by the country's six **Trappist monasteries**, of which the most widely available is Chimay. **Luxembourg** doesn't really compete, but its three most popular brews – Diekirch, Mousel and Bofferding – are pleasant enough lagers. French **wines** are the most commonly available, although Luxembourg's wines, produced along the north bank of the Moselle, are very drinkable. You'll find Dutch-style **jenever** (a local gin) in most bars in the north of Belgium, and in Luxembourg home-produced, super-strong **eau-de-vie**, distilled from various fruits.

STUDENT AND YOUTH DISCOUNTS

Most museums and galleries offer substantial discounts to those under 26, even if you don't have an ISIC card. Train travel is also cheaper for travellers aged under 26 if you buy a Go-Pass (see "Getting around", p.105). HI hostels charge an extra €3 per night if you're not a member.

CULTURE AND ETIQUETTE

The Belgians' relaxed attitude extends to the service – it's not unusual to be left waiting at the bar while the barman methodically polishes all the glasses. Don't worry about politely drawing some attention to yourself, as they're usually very helpful once they've noticed you. It's normal to give a 10% tip in restaurants and cafés.

SPORTS AND OUTDOOR ACTIVITIES

The Ardennes woods are ideal for hiking, kayaking, cycling and horseriding (see p.128 for operators); cross-country skiing is also an option. La Roche-en-Ardenne and Bouillon make excellent bases in Belgium, while in Luxembourg the towns of Vianden and Echternach (each about an hour from Luxembourg City) are popular destinations for hikers and cyclists. See "Getting Around" on p.106 for more information on cycling in Belgium and Luxembourg.

COMMUNICATIONS

Post offices are usually open Mon–Fri 9am–noon & 2–5pm. Some urban post offices also open on Saturday mornings. Many public phones take only phonecards, which are available from newsagents and post offices. There are no area codes in either country. **Mobile phone** coverage is good. **Internet** access is widespread, with at least one or two cybercafés in all the larger cities; libraries are often a good bet where all else fails.

BELGIUM AND LUXEMBOURG ON THE NET

ⓦ **www.artsite.be** Details of Belgium's best-known art galleries and museums.
ⓦ **www.belgiumtheplaceto.be** or ⓦ **www.belgique-tourisme.net** Information on Brussels and southern Belgium.
ⓦ **www.luxembourg.co.uk** The Luxembourg tourist board in London.
ⓦ **www.visitbelgium.com** Belgium's tourist office in North America.
ⓦ **www.visitflanders.com** Information on Brussels and the Flanders region.

EMERGENCIES

You shouldn't have much cause to come into contact with the **police** in either country. If you're unlucky enough to have something **stolen**, report it immediately to the nearest police station and get a report number, or better still a copy of the statement itself, for your insurance claim when you get home. With regard to **medical emergencies**, if you're reliant on free treatment within the EU health scheme, try to remember to make this clear to the ambulance staff and any medics you subsequently encounter. Outside working hours, all **pharmacies** should display a list of open alternatives. Weekend rotas are also listed in local newspapers.

EMERGENCY NUMBERS

Belgium Police ⓣ101; fire & ambulance ⓣ100.
Luxembourg Police ⓣ113; fire & ambulance ⓣ112.

LANGUAGES

There are three official languages in **Belgium** (Flemish, which is effectively Dutch, plus French and German), but you will be able to get by in English easily in the Flemish north and just about in the French south too. Natives of **Luxembourg** speak Letzebuergesch, a dialect of German, but most people also speak French and German and many speak English too. See p.373, p.460 and p.834 for some basic French, German and Dutch language tips.

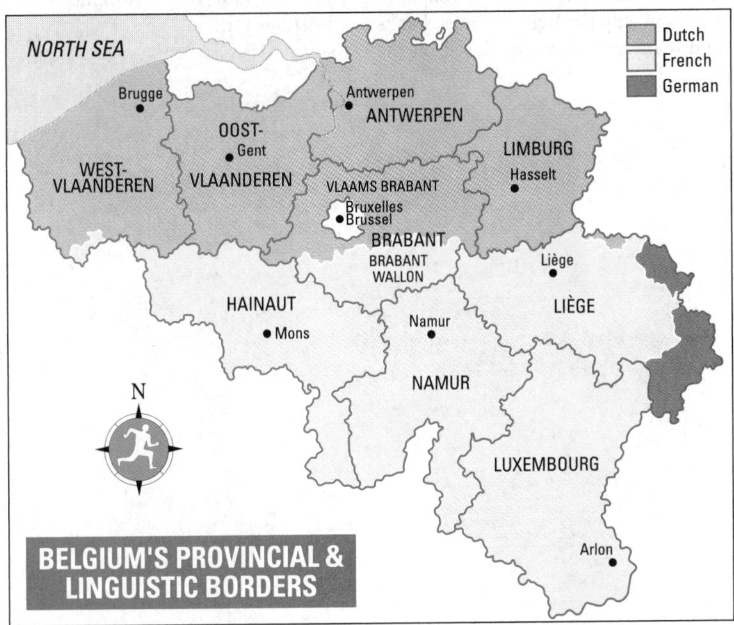

BELGIUM'S PROVINCIAL & LINGUISTIC BORDERS

INFORMATION & MAPS

In both Belgium and Luxembourg, there are **tourist offices** in all but the smallest of villages. They usually provide free local maps, and in the larger towns offer a free accommodation-booking service too. The best general road **map** is the easy-to-use Baedeker & AA Belgium and Luxembourg (1:250,000) map.

MONEY AND BANKS

Belgium and Luxembourg both use the **euro** (€). **Banks** are the best places to change money and are generally open Mon–Fri 9am–4/4.30pm in both countries, though some have a one-hour lunch break between noon and 2pm. **ATMs** are commonplace.

OPENING HOURS AND HOLIDAYS

In both countries, the weekend fades painlessly into the week with some shops staying closed on Monday morning, even in major cities. Nonetheless, normal **shopping hours** are Mon–Sat 9/10am–6/7pm with many urban supermarkets staying open until 8/9pm on Fridays and smaller places shutting early on Saturday. In the big cities, a smattering of convenience stores (*magasins de nuit/avondwinkels*) stay open either all night or until around 1/2am daily, and some souvenir shops open late and on Sundays too. Most museums are closed on Mondays. Many bars have relaxed closing times, claiming to stay open until the last customer leaves. Less usefully, many restaurants and bars close for at least a couple of weeks in July or August. Shops, banks and many museums are closed on the following **public holidays**: New Year's Day, Easter Sunday, Easter Monday, Labour Day (May 1), Ascension Day (forty days after Easter), Whit Sunday, Whit Monday, Luxembourg National Day (Luxembourg only; June 23), Belgian National Day (Belgium only; July 21), Assumption (mid-August), All Saints' Day (November 1), Armistice Day (Belgium only; November 11), Christmas Day.

Brussels

Wherever else you go in Belgium, it's hard to avoid **BRUSSELS** (Bruxelles, Brussel), a capital boasting architecture and museums to rank with the best in Europe, a well-preserved medieval centre and an energetic nightlife. It's also very much an international city, with European civil servants and business folk, plus immigrants from Africa, Turkey and the Mediterranean, making up a quarter of the population.

The city takes its name from Broekzele, or "village of the marsh", which grew up in the sixth century on the trade route between Cologne and the towns of Bruges and Ghent. In the nineteenth century it became the capital of the newly independent Belgium, and was kitted out with all the attributes of a modern European capital. Since World War II, the city's appointment as headquarters of both NATO and the EU has brought major developments, including a metro.

What to see and do

Central Brussels is enclosed within a rough pentagon of boulevards – the **petit ring** – which follows the course of the medieval city walls. The centre is also divided between the Upper and Lower Towns, the former being the traditional home of the city's upper classes who kept a beady eye on the workers down below.

The Grand-Place

The obvious place to begin any tour of the **Lower Town** is the **Grand-Place**, the commercial hub of the city since the Middle Ages. With its stupendous spired tower, the **Hôtel de Ville** (tours in English: April–Sept Tues & Wed 3.15pm, Sun 10.45am & 12.15pm; Oct–March Tues & Wed only 3.15pm; €3) dominates the square, and inside you can view various official rooms. But the real glory of the Grand-Place lies in its **guildhouses**, mostly built in the early eighteenth century, their slender facades swirling with exuberant carving and sculpture. Check out the **Roi d'Espagne** on the west side of the square, at no. 1. Once the headquarters of the guild of bakers and named after its bust of Charles II, the last of the Spanish Habsburgs. Moorish and Native American prisoners flank Charles, symbolizing his mastery of a vast empire. At no. 5, the **Maison de la Louve** was once the home of the influential archers' guild and its elegant pilastered facade is studded with pious representations of concepts like Peace and Discord. Adjoining it, at no. 6, the **Maison du Cornet** was the headquarters of the boatsmen's guild, a fanciful creation of 1697 whose top storey resembles the stern of a ship.

Musée de la Ville de Bruxelles

Most of the northern side of the Grand-Place is taken up by the sturdy neo-Gothic **Maison du Roi**, a reconstruction of a sixteenth-century Habsburg building that now holds the **Musée de la Ville de Bruxelles** (Tues–Sun 10am–5pm; €3). Here you'll find an eclectic mix of locally manufactured tapestries, ceramics, pewter, carved altar pieces and porcelain.

The Manneken Pis

Rue de l'Etuve leads south from the Grand-Place down to the **Manneken Pis**, a diminutive statue of a little boy pissing that's supposed to embody the "irreverent spirit" of the city and is today one of Brussels' biggest tourist draws. Jérome Duquesnoy cast the original statue in the 1600s, but – much to the horror of the locals – it was stolen several times and the current one is a copy.

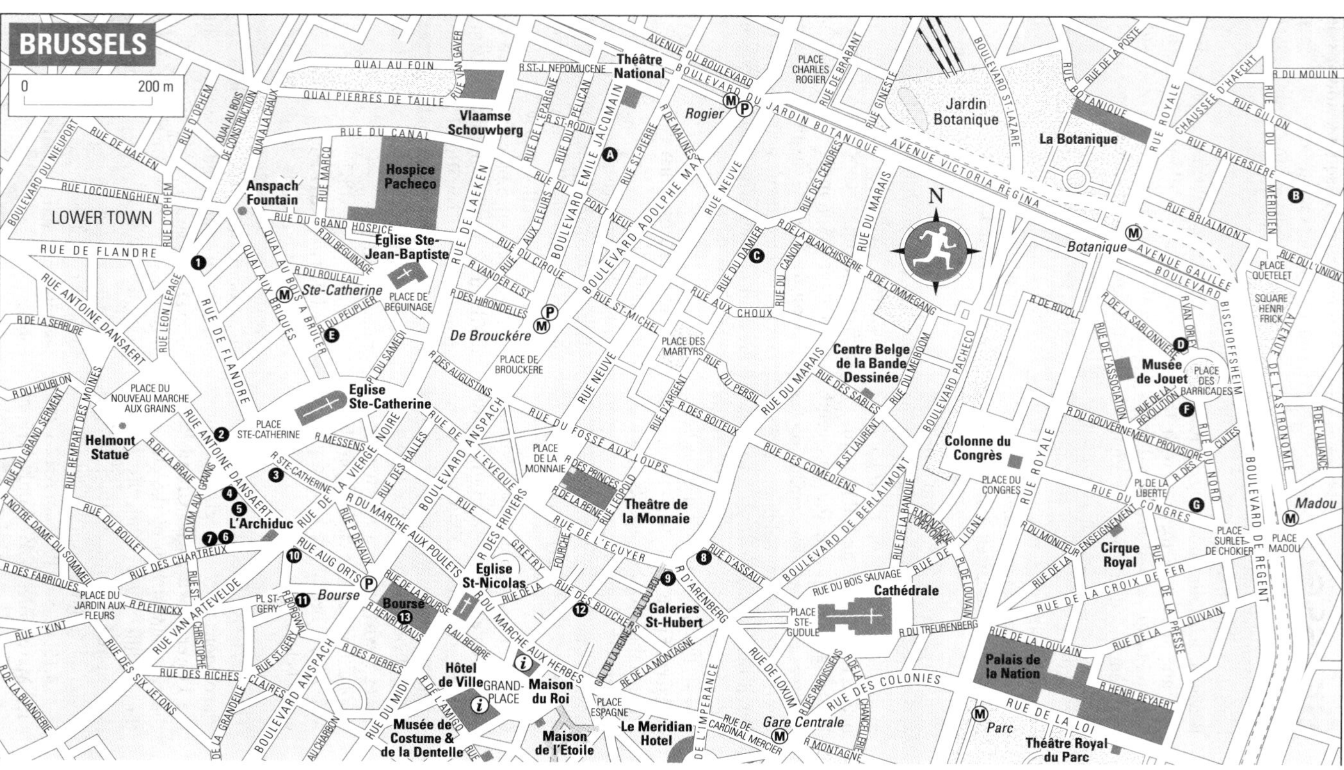
BRUSSELS
0
200 m
LOWER TOWN
Jardin Botanique
La Botanique
Botanique
Rogier
Théâtre National
Vlaamse Schouwberg
Hospice Pacheco
Eglise Ste-Jean-Baptiste
Ste-Catherine
Eglise Ste-Catherine
Anspach Fountain
Helmont Statue
L'Archiduc
De Brouckère
Centre Belge de la Bande Dessinée
Musée de Jouet
Colonne du Congrès
Cirque Royal
Palais de la Nation
Théâtre Royal du Parc
Parc
Cathédrale
Théâtre de la Monnaie
Galeries St-Hubert
Eglise St-Nicolas
Bourse
Hôtel de Ville
Maison du Roi
Maison de l'Etoile
Musée de Costume & de la Dentelle
Le Meridian Hotel
Gare Centrale
Madou
BOULEVARD DE REGENT
AVENUE DE L'ASTRONOMIE
BOULEVARD BISCHOFFSHEIM
AVENUE GALILEE
RUE ROYALE
BOULEVARD ST-LAZARE
AVENUE VICTORIA REGINA
BOULEVARD DU JARDIN BOTANIQUE
BOULEVARD PACHECO
BOULEVARD DE BERLAIMONT
BOULEVARD ADOLPHE MAX
BOULEVARD EMILE JACQMAIN
BOULEVARD ANSPACH
RUE NEUVE
RUE DU MARAIS
RUE DE LAEKEN
RUE DE FLANDRE
RUE ANTOINE DANSAERT
QUAI AUX BRIQUES
QUAI AU BOIS A BRULER
RUE DU MARCHE AUX POULETS
R DU MARCHE AUX HERBES
RUE DE LOXUM
RUE DES COLONIES
RUE DE LA LOI
RUE DU FOSSE AUX LOUPS
RUE DU MIDI
R DE LA MONTAGNE
PLACE DE BROUCKERE
PLACE DE LA MONNAIE
PLACE STE-CATHERINE
PLACE DES MARTYRS
PLACE CHARLES ROGIER
PLACE STE-GUDULE
PLACE DU CONGRES
GRAND-PLACE
PLACE SURLET-DE CHOKIER
PLACE MADOU
PLACE DU NOUVEAU MARCHE AUX GRAINS
PLACE DU JARDIN AUX FLEURS

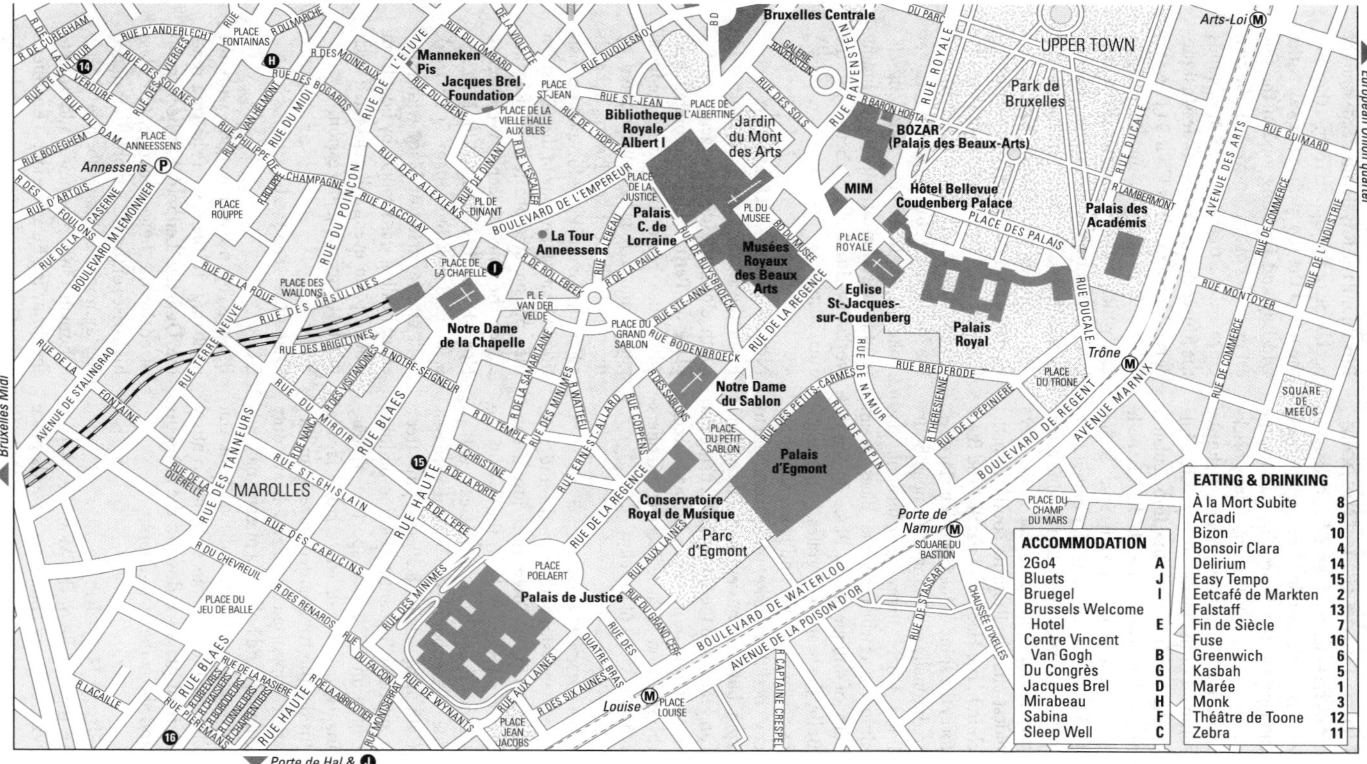
European Union quarter
Bruxelles Midi
Porte de Hal & J
ACCOMMODATION
2Go4 A
Bluets J
Bruegel I
Brussels Welcome Hotel E
Centre Vincent Van Gogh B
Du Congrès G
Jacques Brel D
Mirabeau H
Sabina F
Sleep Well C
EATING & DRINKING
À la Mort Subite 8
Arcadi 9
Bizon 10
Bonsoir Clara 4
Delirium 14
Easy Tempo 15
Eetcafé de Markten 2
Falstaff 13
Fin de Siècle 7
Fuse 16
Greenwich 6
Kasbah 5
Marée 1
Monk 3
Théâtre de Toone 12
Zebra 11
UPPER TOWN
MAROLLES
Bruxelles Centrale
Arts-Loi
Trône
Porte de Namur
Louise
Annessens
Manneken Pis
Jacques Brel Foundation
Bibliotheque Royale Albert I
Jardin du Mont des Arts
BOZAR (Palais des Beaux-Arts)
Park de Bruxelles
MIM
Hôtel Bellevue Coudenberg Palace
Palais des Académis
Palais C. de Lorraine
Musées Royaux des Beaux Arts
Eglise St-Jacques-sur-Coudenberg
Palais Royal
La Tour Anneessens
Notre Dame de la Chapelle
Notre Dame du Sablon
Palais d'Egmont
Conservatoire Royal de Musique
Parc d'Egmont
Palais de Justice
PLACE FONTAINAS
PLACE ST-JEAN
PLACE DE L'ALBERTINE
PLACE DE LA VIELLE HALLE AUX BLES
PLACE ANNEESSENS
PLACE ROUPPE
PL DE DINANT
PLACE DE LA JUSTICE
PL DU MUSEE
PLACE ROYALE
PLACE DE LA CHAPELLE
PLACE DES WALLONS
PL E VAN DER VELDE
PLACE DU GRAND SABLON
PLACE DU PETIT SABLON
PLACE DU TRONE
PLACE DU CHAMP DU MARS
SQUARE DU BASTION
SQUARE DE MEEÛS
PLACE POELAERT
PLACE DU JEU DE BALLE
PLACE LOUISE
PLACE JEAN JACOBS
BOULEVARD M LEMONNIER
BOULEVARD DE L'EMPEREUR
BOULEVARD DE WATERLOO
BOULEVARD DE REGENT
AVENUE MARNIX
AVENUE DE LA POISON D'OR
AVENUE DE STALINGRAD
AVENUE DES ARTS
CHAUSSÉE D'IXELLES
RUE ROYALE
RUE DUCALE
RUE DE LA REGENCE
RUE HAUTE
RUE BLAES
RUE DES TANNEURS
RUE TERRE NEUVE
RUE DU MIDI
RUE DES URSULINES
RUE DU POINCON
RUE DE NAMUR
RUE BREDERODE
RUE MONTOYER
RUE DE COMMERCE
RUE DE L'INDUSTRIE
RUE GUIMARD
RUE RAVENSTEIN
PLACE DES PALAIS

Notre Dame de la Chapelle and the Quartier Marolles

Across boulevard de l'Empereur, a busy carriageway that scars this part of the centre, you'll spy the crumbling brickwork of **La Tour Anneessens**, a chunky remnant of the medieval city wall, while to the south gleams the immaculately restored **Notre Dame de la Chapelle** (June–Sept Mon–Sat 9am–5pm & Sun 11.30am–4.30pm; Oct–May daily 12.30–4.30pm; free), a sprawling Gothic structure founded in 1134 that is the city's oldest church. Running south from the church, rue Haute and parallel rue Blaes form the spine of the **Quartier Marolles**, traditionally a working-class neighbourhood where today gentrification has almost overwhelmed rue Blaes in an eddy of antique shops. **Place du Jeu de Balle**, the heart of Marolles, has retained its earthy character and is the site of the city's best **flea market** (daily from 7am to 2pm, but at its busiest on Sundays). You can get back to the Upper Town using the free lift from nearby Place Breugel, which drops you off in Place Poelaert and offers fantastic views of the city.

The Upper Town

The steep slope that marks the start of the **Upper Town** rises just a couple of minutes' walk to the east of the Grand-Place. Here, at the east end of rue d'Arenberg, you'll find Brussels **Cathedral** (daily 8.30am–6pm; free), a splendid Brabantine-Gothic building begun in 1220 and sporting a striking twin-towered, white stone facade. Inside, the triple-aisled nave is an airy affair supported by plain, heavy-duty columns and holding a massive oak pulpit featuring Adam and Eve. Look out also for the gorgeous sixteenth-century **stained-glass windows** in the transepts and above the main doors.

Place Royale

In the middle of the Mont des Arts, a wide stairway climbs up towards **place Royale** and **rue Royale**, the dead-straight backbone of the Upper Town. Ahead to the left of the top of the stairway is the **Old England Building**, one of the finest examples of Art Nouveau in the city. Once a department store, it now holds the **Musée des Instruments de Musique**, at rue Montagne de la Cour 2 (Tues–Fri 9.30am–5pm, Sat & Sun 10am–5pm; €5), which contains an impressive collection of antique musical instruments. Back on place Royale, at the start of rue de la Régence, the **Musées Royaux des Beaux Arts** (Tues–Sun 10am–5pm; €5 for both museums) comprises two museums: the Musée d'Art Moderne and the Musée d'Art Ancien, which together make up Belgium's most satisfying all-round collection of fine art, including works by Breugels, Rubens and the Surrealists.

Notre Dame du Sablon

From the Beaux Arts it's a short stroll south along rue de la Régence to the **place du Petit Sablon**, decorated with 48 statues representing the medieval guilds, and a fountain surmounted by the counts Egmont and Hoorn, beheaded on the Grand-Place for their opposition to Spanish tyranny in the 1500s. On the opposite side of rue de la Régence stands the fifteenth-century church of **Notre Dame du Sablon** (Mon–Fri 9am–6.30pm, Sat & Sun 10am–7pm; free), built after a statue of Mary with powers of healing was brought by boat from Antwerp, an event still celebrated each July by Ommegang procession.

Outside the petit ring: the EU

Brussels by no means ends with the petit ring. To the east of the ring road, the **Quartier Leopold** has been colonized by the huge concrete and glass high-rises of the **EU**, notably the winged **Berlaymont** building beside Métro Schuman. One of the newer additions to the sprawling EU is the lavish **European**

COMICS IN BRUSSELS

Belgium is a city made for comic book fans. The Comic Strip Museum (Centre Belge de la Bande Dessinée) at 20 rue des Sables (Tues-Sun 10am-6pm; €7.50) focuses on Belgian comics (Tintin, Smurfs, etc) but also contains an interesting permanent exhibition about the creation of a comic strip. Boulevard Lemonnier, between La Bourse and Place Anneessens, boasts ten comic book shops. Rather endearingly, various walls around the city have been decorated with building-sized scenes from comic strips, and tourist information can supply you with a trail following the major ones. If you're around in early October, you might be able to catch the city's annual Comics Festival (Ⓦwww.comicsfestivalbelgium.com).

Union Parliament building (free guided tours: usually Mon–Thurs 10am & 3pm, Fri 10am; Ⓣ02 284 34 57, Ⓦwww.europarl.eu.int), an imposing structure topped off by a spectacular curved glass roof. It's a couple of minutes' walk from place du Luxembourg, behind the Quartier Léopold train station.

Arrival and information

Air The main airport is in Zaventem, 13km northeast of the centre, served by regular trains to the city's three main stations (30min; €2.80). No-frills airlines fly into Charleroi, 55km south of Brussels, and a shuttle bus leaves for the city every hour or so (1 hr; €11).
Train Brussels has three main train stations – Bruxelles-Nord, Bruxelles-Centrale and Bruxelles-Midi, each a few minutes apart. The majority of international trains, including expresses from London, Amsterdam, Paris and Cologne, stop only at Bruxelles-Midi (Brussel-Zuid). Bruxelles-Centrale is a five-minute walk from Grand-Place; Bruxelles-Nord lies in the business area just north of the main ring road; and Bruxelles-Midi is south of the city centre. To transfer from one of the three main stations to another, simply jump on the next available mainline train.
Bus Eurolines buses arrive at the Gare du Nord complex.
Tourist office BIT (Bruxelles International Tourisme), in the Hôtel de Ville on the Grand-Place (May–Sept daily 9am–6pm; Oct–Dec & Easter to end-April Mon–Sat 9am–6pm, Sun 10am–2pm; Jan until Easter Mon–Sat 9am–6pm; Ⓣ02 513 89 40, Ⓦwww.brusselsinternational.be). They also have a smaller office (May–Sept Mon–Thurs, Sat & Sun 8am–8pm, Fri 8am–9pm; Oct–April Mon–Thurs 8am–5pm, Fri 8am–8pm, Sat 9am–6pm & Sun 9am–2pm) on the main concourse of the Bruxelles–Midi train station. There's also a Belgian tourist information centre near the Grand-Place at rue du Marché aux Herbes 63 (Mon–Fri 9am–6pm, Sat–Sun 9am–1pm, 2–6pm; Ⓣ02 504 03 90). All three offices and some museums also sell the Brussels Card, which gets you free entry into 23 museums, free public transport, as well as selected reductions in bars and shops. It costs €20/28/33 for 1/2/3 days. You can also pick up maps for an Art Nouveau or comic strip trail around the city.

City transport

Public transport The easiest way to get around central Brussels is to walk, but to reach some of the more outlying attractions you'll need to use public transport. The system, called STIB (Ⓦwww.stib.be), runs on a mixture of bus, tram, prémétro (underground tram) and metro lines. Services run from 6am until midnight, after which night buses take over; route maps are available free from the tourist office and from STIB kiosks.
Tickets A single flat-fare ticket costs €1.50, a five-journey ticket costs €6.70, and ten costs €11 – all available from tram and bus drivers, metro kiosks and ticket machines. A day-pass (*carte de jour/dagpas*), available at metro and prémétro stations, allows unlimited travel for 24hr and costs €4.
Taxis can be picked up from ranks around the city – notably on Bourse and place de Brouckère; to book, phone Taxis Verts (Ⓣ02 349 49 49) or Taxis Orange (Ⓣ02 349 43 43).

Accommodation

Belgium's central reservation agency, Resotel Ⓣ02 779 39 39, Ⓦwww.belgium-hospitality.com), operates an efficient hotel reservation service, seeking out the best deals and discounts. Alternatively, if you arrive in the city with nowhere to stay, both BIT offices (see above) operate a same-night hotel booking service. The service is provided free – you just pay a percentage of the room rate as a deposit and this is then subtracted from your final hotel bill.

Hostels

2Go4 Boulevard Emile Jacmain-laan 99 ⓣ02 219 30 19 ⓦwww.2go4.be. Excellent hostel with designer lounge and extremely helpful staff. Large groups (of over six) aren't admitted, which gives the place a cosy atmosphere, as does the fireplace in the lounge. Some rooms have baths – ask for the penthouse (which is the same price as the other rooms). Wi-Fi access and free city map; breakfast not included. Dorms ❸; double room ❼

Bruegel rue du Saint-Esprit 2 ⓣ02 511 04 36, ⓦwww.vjh.be. Huge official IYHF hostel in a fun area towards the Marolles. A basic breakfast – as well as the hire of sheets – is included in the overnight fee, and dinner costs €9.10. Check-in 10am–1pm & 2–4pm; curfew at 1am. Métro Gare Centrale; dorms ❷; double ❻

Le Centre Vincent Van Gogh rue Traversière 8 ⓣ02 217 01 58, ⓦwww.chab.be. A rambling, spacious, 228-bed hostel with a good reputation and friendly staff, though it can all seem a bit chaotic. Laundry and kitchen facilities available and no curfew; bedsheets and breakfast included. Located just out of the Petit Ring. Métro Botanique. 18–35 year olds only. Dorms ❷; double ❻

Jacques Brel rue de la Sablonnière 30 ⓣ02 218 01 87, ⓦwww.laj.be. This official IYHF hostel is modern and comfortable. Breakfast and bedding are included in the price, there's no curfew (you get a key) and cheap meals can be bought on the premises. Check-in 7.30am–1am. Métro Madou; dorms ❷; double ❺

Sleep Well rue du Damier 23 ⓣ02 218 50 50, ⓦwww.sleepwell.be. Bright but bland hostel beloved of school groups and situated close to the city centre, with (often empty) bar, restaurant and lounge areas. Métro Rogier; dorms ❷; double ❻

Hotels

Les Bluets rue Berckmans 124, Saint Gilles ⓣ02 534 39 83,ⓦwww.bluets.be. Charming, family-run hotel with just ten en-suite rooms in a large, handsome old stone terrace house. Immaculate decor in rich fin-de-siècle style. No lift. One block south of the "petit ring" and métro station Hôtel des Monnaies. ❼

Brussels Welcome Hotel quai au Bois à Brûler 23, ⓣ02 219 95 46, ⓦwww.hotelwelcome.com. Friendly, family-run three-star in the heart of the Ste Catherine district. Each of the seventeen colourful themed rooms is decorated in the style of a particular country or region, and it's well located near plenty of good bars and restaurants. Métro Ste Catherine. ❾

Mirabeau place Fontainas 18 ⓣ02 511 19 72, ⓦwww.hotelmirabeau.be. Friendly, medium-sized hotel with thirty small en-suite rooms, plainly decorated. Windows are not soundproofed, so interior rooms are quieter than those on the square. Large, modern breakfast room at the front with a small bar. Prémétro Anneessens. ❾

Sabina rue du Nord 78 ⓣ02 218 26 37 ⓦwww.hotelsabina.be. Basic pension in an attractive late nineteenth-century townhouse with 24 workaday, en-suite rooms. Triples and quads available. Discounts and cheaper weekend rates. A five- to ten-minute walk from Métro Madou. ❾

Eating

Brussels has an international reputation for the quality of its **cuisine**, and even at the dowdiest snack bar you'll find well-prepared Bruxellois dishes featuring amalgamations of Walloon and Flemish ingredients and cooking styles. In addition, the city is among Europe's best for sampling a wide range of different cuisines – from the Turkish restaurants of St Josse to Spanish, Vietnamese and Japanese places. You can keep costs down by sticking to the city's **cafés** and **bars**, some of which provide food to rival that of many a restaurant.

Cafés

Arcadi rue d'Arenberg 18. A good spot for lunch, tea or an early evening meal. The menu offers a lot of choice, but the salads, quiches and fruit tarts are particularly delicious. Mains €7. Daily 7/8am–11pm. Métro De Brouckère or Gare Centrale.

Eetcafé de Markten place du Vieux Marché aux Grains. Vibrant café offering no–nonsense, good quality salads (€8), lasagnes and quiches at very reasonable prices. Mon–Sat 11am–11pm, Sun 11am–7pm. Métro Ste Catherine.

Le Fin de Siècle rue de Chartreux 32. Delicious Belgian food in buzzing street full of cafés and art galleries. Prémetro Bourse. Mains around €12.

Restaurants

Easy Tempo Rue Haute 146. Deservedly popular pizza place with a great interior. Closed Sun eve and Mon. Métro Louise. Margharita pizza €8.

Kasbah rue Antoine Dansaert 20 ⓣ02 502 40 26. Popular with a youthful, groovy crowd, this Moroccan eatery is as famous for its cool décor as for its delicious North African specialities.

TREAT YOURSELF

Bonsoir Clara rue Antoine Dansaert 22 ⓣ02 502 09 90. Moody, atmospheric lighting, geometrically mirrored walls and smooth jazz-meets-house background music make this one of the city's most chic restaurants. The menu is full of Mediterranean, French and Belgian classics rendered in full *nouvelle* style. Reservations recommended. Mon–Fri noon–2.30pm & daily 7–11.30pm. Prémétro Bourse. Main courses €20.

Reservations necessary at the weekend. Daily noon–3pm & 6.30pm–midnight. Prémétro Bourse. Mains €15.

La Marée rue de Flandre 99 ⓣ02 511 00 40. There's another La Marée on rue au Beurre, so don't get confused – this one (the better of the two) is a pocket-sized bistro specializing in fish and mussels. The décor is pretty basic, but the food is always creative. Wed–Sat noon–2pm & 6.30–10pm. Closed Mon & Tues. Métro Ste Catherine. Mains €12.

Drinking and nightlife

If you're after a drink, the enormous variety of bars is one of the city's real joys.

Bars

À la Mort Subite rue Montagne aux Herbes Potagères 7. Infamous 1920s bar that loaned its name to a popular bottled beer. It occupies a long, narrow room with nicotine-stained walls, long tables and lots of mirrors, and on a good night is inhabited by a dissolute arty clientele. Mon–Fri 10am–1am, Sat 11am–1am, Sun 1pm–1am. Métro Gare Centrale.

Delirium Impasse de la Fidelité 87. Home of Delirium Tremens ("the best beer in the world"), this place has long been a backpacker favourite and boasts over two thousand types of beer. Floris, its sister café opposite, serves fifty kinds of Absinthe. Métro Gare Centrale. Open Mon–Sat until 4am, Sun until 1am.

Le Falstaff rue Henri Maus 17–23. Long-established café-cum-restaurant much lauded for its charming Art Nouveau decoration. Attracts a mixed bag of tourists, Eurocrats and bourgeois Bruxellois. Daily 10am–1am. Prémétro Bourse.

Le Greenwich rue des Chartreux 7. Smoky, quiet bar patronised by chess and backgammon enthusiasts and selling beer at rock-bottom prices. Daily 11am–1am. Prémétro Bourse.

Monk rue Ste Catherine 42. Large and popular bar named after the jazz musician Thelonious Monk – appropriately a grand piano has pride of place. Unusually for Brussels, the service is at the bar. Mon–Sat 11am–1am, Sun and hols 4pm–1am. Métro Ste Catherine.

Théâtre de Toone Impasse Schuddeveld 6. Ancient bar belonging to the Toone puppet theatre. Daily noon–11pm. Métro Gare Centrale.

Zebra place St Géry 33–35. This small bar attracts a young crowd who come for the upbeat atmosphere on this lively square. Sun–Thurs noon–midnight, Fri & Sat noon–2am. Prémétro Bourse.

Clubs

De Bizon rue du Pont de la Carpe 7. Fun bar with free blues jam sessions every Monday. Prémétro Bourse.

Fuse rue Blaes 208 ⓦwww.fuse.be. Techno club usually open Wednesday to Saturday with monthly gay nights. Métro Porte de Hal. Entry €5 before midnight, €10 after.

Shopping

Aside from the Marolles flea market (see "What to see and do", p.114), Rue Antoine Dansaert is a good, if pricey, spot for fashion – check out Stijl at number 74. If you're looking for some chocolate to take home, try Planète Chocolat (rue du Lombard 24), which holds demonstrations every Saturday at 4pm (€7).

Directory

Embassies Australia, rue Guimard 6 (ⓣ02 286 05 00); Canada, avenue de Tervuren 2 (ⓣ02 741 06 11); Great Britain, rue d'Arlon 85 (ⓣ02 287 62 11); Ireland, rue Wiertz 89–93 (ⓣ02 235 66 76); New Zealand, 7th Floor, square de Meeus 1 (ⓣ02 512 10 40); South Africa, rue de la Loi 26 (ⓣ02 285 44 00); USA, boulevard du Régent 27 (ⓣ02 508 21 11).

Hospital Hôpital St Pierre, Rue Haute 322 ⓣ322 535 3111.

Internet BXL, Place de la Vieille Halle aux Blés 46.

Laundry Was-Salon Lavoir, rue de Laeken 145, 7am–10pm.

Left luggage At all three main train stations.

Listings *Agenda* is a useful English-language listings magazine, available free in many hostels, hotels and shops. *Use-It* guides, free in hostels, are also extremely helpful.

Pharmacies Agora, rue du Marché aux Herbes 109; Multipharma, rue du Marché aux Poulets 37.
Post office First floor, Centre Monnaie, pl de la Monnaie.

Moving on

Train to: Antwerp (every 30min; 40min); Bruges (every 30min; 1hr); Ghent (every 30min; 40min); Luxembourg City (every 2hr; 2hr 30min); Namur (hourly; 50min); Ostend (hourly; 1hr 20min).

Cross-border train routes

Brussels Luxembourg City (3hr; hourly); Arlon (2hr 40min; hourly); Paris (1hr 30min; hourly); Amsterdam (2hr 40min; hourly); London (2hr; every 2hr).

Northern Belgium

The region to the north of Brussels is almost entirely **Flemish-speaking** and possesses a distinctive and vibrant cultural identity, its pancake-flat landscapes punctuated by a string of fine historic cities. These begin with **Antwerp**, a large old port dotted with many reminders of its sixteenth-century golden age. To the west, in Flanders, lie two more fascinating cities – **Ghent** and **Bruges** – which became prosperous during the Middle Ages on the back of the cloth trade. All three cities have great bars and restaurants too.

Belgium's main international **ferry port** is **Zeebrugge**, with ferries from Hull and Rosyth in Britain. Ferries dock out on a mole 2km from the train station, so check with the ferry company to make sure they provide onward bus connections.

ANTWERP

ANTWERP, Belgium's second city, fans out from the east bank of the Scheldt about 50km north of Brussels. Many people prefer it to the capital and indeed it does have a denser concentration of things to see, including some fine churches and distinguished museums – reminders of its auspicious past as centre of a wide trading empire. In recent years, the city has also become the effective capital of Flemish Belgium, acting as a lively cultural centre with a spirited nightlife.

What to see and do

At the centre of Antwerp is the spacious **Grote Markt**, where the conspicuous **Brabo fountain** comprises a haphazard pile of rocks surmounted by a bronze of Silvius Brabo, the city's first hero, depicted flinging the hand of the giant Antigonus – who terrorized passing ships – into the Scheldt. The north side of Grote Markt is lined with daintily restored sixteenth-century guildhouses, while the west is hogged by the **Stadhuis** (tours Mon–Thurs at 2pm; €1), a handsome structure completed in 1566 and one of the most important buildings of the Northern Renaissance.

Onze Lieve Vrouwe Cathedral

Southeast of Grote Markt, the **Onze Lieve Vrouwe Cathedral** (Mon–Fri 10am–5pm, Sat 10am–3pm, Sun 1–4pm; €2) is one of the finest Gothic churches in Europe, dating from the middle of the fifteenth century. Inside, the seven-aisled nave is breathtaking. Four early paintings by **Rubens** are displayed here.

Plantin-Moretus Museum

It takes about five minutes to walk southwest from the cathedral to the **Plantin-Moretus Museum**, on Vrijdagmarkt (Tues–Sun 10am–5pm; €6), which occupies the grand old mansion of Rubens' father-in-law, the printer Christopher Plantin. One of Antwerp's most interesting museums, it provides a marvellous

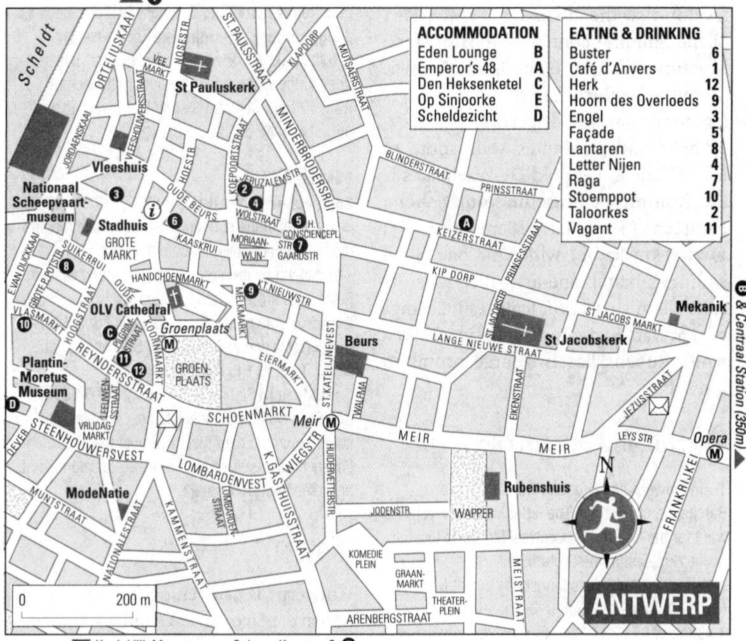

insight into how Plantin and his family conducted their printing business.

The Nationaal Scheepvaartmuseum and around

The **Nationaal Scheepvaartmuseum** at Steenplein 1 (Tues–Sun 10am–5pm; €4), a maritime museum that occupies the Steen, is the remaining gatehouse of what was once an impressive medieval fortress. It's a short walk east to the impressively gabled **Vleeshuis** (Tues–Sun 10am–5pm; €5), built for the guild of butchers in 1503 and distinguished by its striped brickwork. Just north of here, along Vleeshouwersstraat, **St Pauluskerk** (May–Sept daily 2–5pm; free) is a dignified late Gothic church built for the Dominicans in the early sixteenth century. Inside, the airy and elegant nave is decorated by a series of paintings depicting the Fifteen Mysteries of the Rosary, including Rubens' exquisite *Scourging at the Pillar* of 1617.

Rubenshuis and St Jacobskerk

Ten minutes' walk east of the Grote Markt is the **Rubenshuis**, at Wapper 9 (Tues–Sun 10am–5pm; €6), the former home and studio of Rubens, now restored as a very popular museum. Rubens died in 1640 and was buried in **St Jacobskerk**, just to the north at Lange Nieuwstraat 73 (April–Oct daily except Tues 2–5pm; €3). The artist and his immediate family are buried in the chapel behind the high altar, where, in one of his last works, *Our Lady Surrounded by Saints*, he painted himself as St George, his two wives as Martha and Mary, and his father as St Jerome.

ModeNatie and Museum voor Schone Kunsten

South from the Groenplaats along Nationalestraat, the **ModeNatie** (Ⓦwww.modenatie.com) is an ambitious complex spread over several floors that showcases some of the avant-garde fashion that the city is famous for. Part of the building contains **MoMu** (Mode Museum; daily 10am–6pm; Ⓦwww.momu.be), which has some great contemporary fashion displays.

About fifteen minutes' walk south of ModeNatie at Leopold De Waelplaats is the **Koninklijk Museum voor Schone Kunsten** (Tues–Sun 10am–5pm, €6; Ⓦwww.kmska.be), which has one of the country's better fine art collections. Its early Flemish section features paintings by Jan van Eyck and Quentin Matsys, while Rubens has two large rooms to himself.

Arrival and information

Train Antwerp has two mainline train stations, Berchem and Centraal. The latter is the one you want for the city centre. Centraal Station is located about 2km east of the Grote Markt.

Information Antwerp's tourist office is at Grote Markt 13 (Mon–Sat 9am–5.45pm, Sun 9am–4.45pm; Ⓣ03 232 01 03, Ⓦwww.visitantwerpen.be).

City transport

Trams #2 and #15 (direction Linkeroever) run from the Diamant underground tram station beside Centraal Station to the centre; get off at Groenplaats.

Tickets A flat–rate single fare ticket on any part of the city's transport system costs €1; a 24-hour pass (*dagpas*) €3.80.

Accommodation

Finding **accommodation** is rarely difficult, although there are surprisingly few places in the centre. Many mid-priced and budget establishments are around Centraal Station, where you should exercise caution at night. The tourist office has a comprehensive list of places and will make bookings for you.

Hostels

Den Heksenketel Pelgrimstraat 22 Ⓣ03 226 71 64, Ⓦwww.heksenketel.org/hostel. Your best bet for cheap, central accommodation. Downstairs there's a folk-music bar with regular jam sessions. Take tram #2 or #15 to Groenplaats. Dorm beds ❷

Jeugdherberg Op Sinjoorke Eric Sasselaan 2 Ⓣ03 238 02 73, Ⓦwww.vjh.be. Decent HI hostel close to the ring road, 5km south of the centre. Tram #2 from Centraal Station to Antwerp Expo. Dorm beds ❷, double rooms ❺

Hotels

Eden Lange Herentalsestraat 25 Ⓣ03 233 06 08. Chain hotel in the diamond district, whose modern rooms are perfectly adequate but quite plain – and stand by for attack in the mosquito season. Breakfasts are very good though. ❻

Emperor's 48 Keizerstraat 48 Ⓣ04 8603 3397. Comfortable and well-designed B&B on a quiet street. Tram #11 to Kipdorp. ❼

Scheldezicht Sint Jansvliet 10-12 Ⓣ03 231 66 02, Ⓦwww.hotelscheldezicht.be. On a pleasant square near the river just outside of the centre. Lovely breakfast area compensates for rooms that have seen better days. ❼

Eating

Antwerp is an enjoyable and inexpensive place to **eat**, full of informal café-restaurants. Several of the best are clustered on Suikerrui and Grote Pieter Potstraat near the Grote Markt, and there's another concentration in the vicinity of Hendrik Conscienceplein. For **fast food**, try the kebab and falafel places on Oude Koornmarkt.

Cafés

Lantaren Haarstraat 16. Café famous for its delicious coffee-based concoction called "chocolaccinos". Open noon–10pm; closed Mon.

Letter Nijen Wolstraat 11. Like sitting in a neighbour's cosy kitchen and being plied with their delicious homemade food. Salads go for around €10, quiches for €7. Try the cakes. Tues–Fri 8am–6pm, Sat 10am–6pm; closed Sun.

Restaurants

Facade H. Conscienceplein 18 Ⓣ03 233 59 31. Excellent restaurant on a lively square, serving traditional Belgian fare (mains €12) with an imaginative twist. Daily 11am–11pm.

Hoorn des Overvloeds Melkmarkt 1 Ⓣ03 232 83 99. Excellent, unpretentious fish restaurant, good for lunch and dinner; look out for the daily specials. Daily noon–10pm. Mains €14.

De Stoemppot Vlasmarkt 12 Ⓣ03 231 36 86. *Stoemp* is a traditional Flemish dish consisting of puréed meat and vegetables – and this cosy little restaurant is the best place to eat it. Closed Wed. Mains €10.

De Taloorkes Lange Koepoorstraat 61 ⓣ03 234 39 98. Five minutes' walk from Grote Markt but a world away from its touristy offerings, this lively yet laidback locals' restaurant serves mouthwatering stews and mussels dishes. Daily noon–10pm. Mains €15.

Drinking and nightlife

Antwerp is an excellent place to drink, the narrow lanes of its centre dotted with small and atmospheric bars.

Bars

Buster Kaasrui 1 ⓣ03 232 51 53. Straightforward bar featuring a wide range of live music most nights. Closed Sun & Mon.

Den Engel Grote Markt 3. Handily located, traditional bar with an easygoing atmosphere in a guildhouse on the main square. It attracts a mixture of businesspeople and locals from the residential enclave round the Vleeshuis.

De Herk Reyndersstraat 33. Tiny bar in ancient premises set around a courtyard, offering a good range of beers and ales – including an excellent Lindemans gueuze – to a twentysomething, modish clientele.

Raga H. Conscienceplein 18. Wine bar with friendly owner and great jazz soundtrack – good for the lone traveller, with lots of books to read.

De Vagant Reyndersstraat 21. Specialist gin bar serving an extravagant range of Belgian and Dutch *jenevers* in comfortable, laid-back surroundings.

Clubs

Café d'Anvers Verversrui 15 ⓣ03 226 38 70, ⓦwww.cafe-d-anvers.com. Popular house club in a converted church. Open Thurs–Sat.

Shopping

Kammenstraat is good for vintage clothes shops, while Lange Koepoortstraat has plenty of secondhand record shops including FatKat at 57 and Record Collector at 70. There's a flea market every Friday at Vrijdagmarkt where everything from old computers to antique furniture is noisily auctioned off. Mekanik at Sint Jacobsmarkt 73 is the biggest comic book shop in Belgium, stocking everything from underground graphic novels to the famous Belgian publications such as Tintin and The Smurfs.

Moving on

Train Bruges (hourly; 1hr 20min); Brussels (every 30min; 40min); Ghent (every 30min; 50min); Ostend (hourly; 1hr 40min).

GHENT

The largest town in western Europe during the thirteenth and fourteenth centuries, **GHENT (Gent)** was once at the heart of the medieval Flemish cloth trade, with thousands of city folk producing cloth for the rest of Europe. The trade, however, began to decline in the early sixteenth century and Ghent decayed, until better times finally returned in the nineteenth century when the city was industrialized. It's now the third largest city in Belgium, an appealing place with bags of character, great restaurants and a clutch of first-rate historic sights; the relatively tourist-free streets come as a relief after a trip to Brussels or Bruges.

What to see and do

The best place to start exploring is at the mainly Gothic St Baaf's Cathedral, squeezed into the corner of St Baafsplein (Mon–Sat 8.30am–5.30pm, Sun noon–

BOAT TRIPS

Throughout the year, boat trips explore Ghent's inner waterways, departing from various sites around the city, including the Graslei and Korenlei (April–Oct daily 10am–6pm; Nov–March Sat & Sun 11am–4pm). Trips last forty minutes, cost €5, and leave roughly once every fifteen minutes, though the wait can be longer as boats often only depart when reasonably full.

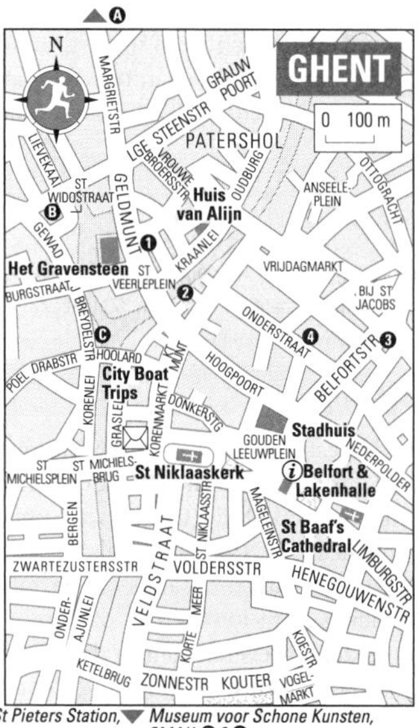

St Pieters Station, Museum voor Schone Kunsten, SMAK, 5&6

ACCOMMODATION		EATING & DRINKING	
Annex	A	Avalon	1
Brooderie	C	Charlatan	3
Jeugdherberg		Make-Up Club	5
De Draecke		Pane e Vino	6
HI Hostel	B	Pink Flamingos	4
		't Dreupelkot	2

5pm; free). Inside, a small chapel (daily: April–Oct Mon–Sat 9.30am–5pm, Sun 1–4.30pm; Nov–March Mon–Sat 10.30am–4pm, Sun 1–4pm; €3) holds Ghent's greatest treasure, the altarpiece of the *Adoration of the Mystic Lamb*, a wonderful early fifteenth-century painting by Jan van Eyck.

The Belfort and Stadhuis

On the west side of St Baafsplein lurks the medieval Lakenhalle (Cloth Hall), a gloomy hunk of a building one of whose entrances leads to the adjoining **Belfort** (Belfry; mid-March to mid-Nov daily 10am–6pm; €3), a much-amended edifice dating from the fourteenth century. A lift climbs up to the roof for excellent views over the city centre.

The Graslei and Patershol

Located a short walk west of the Stadhuis, the Graslei forms the eastern side of the old city harbour and is home to a splendid series of medieval guildhouses. On warm days it's packed with students sunning themselves. Nearby, just to the east, are the narrow cobbled lanes and alleys of the **Patershol**, a pocket-sized district that was formerly home to the city's weavers, but is now Ghent's main restaurant quarter. To the west, on Sint Veerleplein, stands Het Gravensteen (Oct–Mar 9am–5pm, April–Sept 9am–6pm; €6), a spectacular twelfth-century castle, complete with a chilling torture museum.

SMAK and the Museum voor Schone Kunsten

Strolling south from the centre along Ghent's main shopping street, Veldstraat, it takes about twenty minutes to reach the old casino, parts of which have been turned into SMAK (Citadelpark; Tues–Sun 10am–6pm; €5; Ⓦwww.smak.be), a museum of contemporary art that is well known for its adventurous programme of temporary exhibitions.

Arrival, information and city transport

Arrival Of Ghent's two train stations, St Pieters is the handiest one for town, about 2km to the

GHENT FESTIVAL

Every year in the second half of July, Ghent pulsates with the *Gentse Feesten*: stages are set up in all the city's main squares and for ten days blast out every kind of music from reggae to folk and jazz. Accommodation can get booked up months before the festival, so be sure to make a reservation. Try to avoid arriving in Ghent just afterwards – everything is shut for the next two weeks or so as the city takes a rest.

south of the city centre, from where you can get a connecting tram (see below).

Information The tourist office (daily: April–Oct 9.30am–6.30pm; Nov–March 9.30am–4.30pm; ⓣ09 266 52 32, ⓦwww.visitgent.be) is in the centre, in the crypt of the Lakenhalle, on the Botermarkt.

City transport From the covered stops beside St Pieters, trams run up to the Korenmarkt, plumb in the centre of town, every few minutes. All trams have destination signs and numbers at the front, but if in doubt check with the driver. The flat-rate fare per journey is €1.20.

Accommodation

Ghent has several especially enticing **places to stay** and the tourist office publishes a free and comprehensive brochure detailing local accommodation. They also operate a free **hotel booking service**, which is especially useful in July and August, when vacant rooms are thin on the ground.

The Annex Molenaarsstraat 43 ⓣ09 233 20 80, ⓦwww.bedandbreakfast-gent.be. Quirky, laidback place with just two rooms, as well as a garden and artist's studio. Take trams #1, 10 or 11 to Gravensteen to get here. ❺

Brooderie Jan Breydelstraat 8 ⓣ09 225 06 23. Three neat and trim little rooms above an appealing little café, handily located in the city centre. The included breakfast is excellent. Trams #1, 10 or 11 to Gravensteen. ❼

Jeugdherberg De Draecke HI Hostel St Widostraat 11 ⓣ09 233 70 50, ⓦwww.vjh.be. Excellent, well-equipped HI hostel in the city centre. There are over a hundred beds, and facilities include lockers, bike rental and a bar. Advance reservations advised. Trams #1, 10 or 11 to Gravensteen. Dorms ❷; double rooms ❺

Eating

Ghent's numerous cafés and restaurants offer the very best of Flemish and French cuisine. The fancier restaurants are concentrated in and around the Patershol, while less expensive spots, including a rash of fast-food joints, cluster the Korenmarkt.

Avalon Geldmunt 32. This café and tearoom offers a wide range of well-prepared vegetarian food, all served in a tranquil environment. Café: Mon–Sat noon–2pm; tearoom: Mon–Fri 2–6pm. Daily special €7.50.

Pane e Vino Savaanstraat 5. Cheap and delicious pizzas in a simple setting. Closed Sun. Margharita pizza €4.50.

Drinking and nightlife

Bars

The Charlatan Vlasmarkt 6. Studenty bar with at least three concerts a week. Free gigs every Thursday. Closed Mon.

't Dreupelkot Groentenmarkt 12. Cosy bar specializing in *jenever*, of which it stocks more than 215 brands, all kept at icy temperatures.

Pink Flamingos Onderstraat 55. Weird and wacky little place stuffed with everything kitsch, from plastic statues to tacky religious icons. Attracts a groovy crowd, and is a great place for an aperitif or cocktails. Mon–Wed noon–midnight, Thurs & Fri noon–3am, Sat 2pm–3am, Sun 2pm–midnight. Food served until 11pm.

Clubs

Make-Up Club Ketelvest 51b, ⓦwww.make-up-club.be. The only club in central Ghent; take tram #1 to Ketelvest. Entry €5. Open Fri–Sat.

Moving on

Train Antwerp (every 30min; 50min); Bruges (every 20min; 25min); Brussels (every 30min; 40min); Ostend (every 30min; 50min).

BRUGES

The reputation of **BRUGES (Brugge)** as one of the most perfectly preserved medieval cities in Europe has made it the most popular tourist destination in Belgium. Inevitably, the crowds tend to overwhelm the city's charms, but you would be mad to come to Belgium and miss the place. Bruges boomed throughout the Middle Ages, sharing control of the Flemish cloth trade with its two great rivals, Ghent and Ieper (Ypres), its weavers turning English wool into items of clothing that were exported all over the world. By the end of the fifteenth century, however, Bruges was in decline, partly because of a recession in the cloth trade and partly because the Zwin river – the city's vital link to the North Sea – was silting up. By the 1530s its sea trade had collapsed completely, and Bruges simply withered away. Frozen in time, the city escaped damage in both world wars to emerge as the perfect tourist attraction.

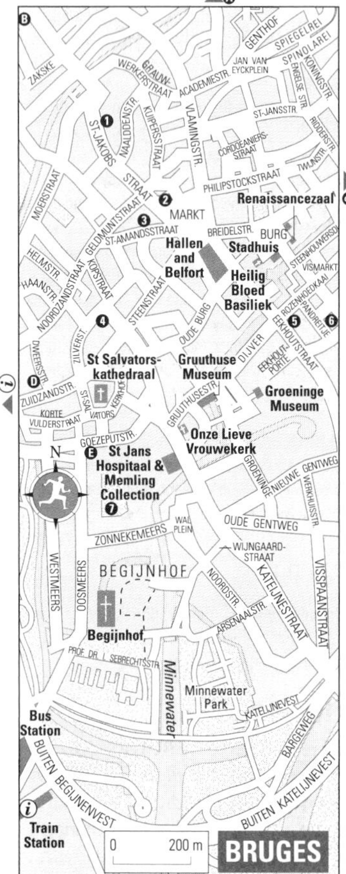

ACCOMMODATION		EATING & DRINKING	
Bauhaus Budget Hotel	C	B-in	7
De Goezeput	E	Het Brugs Beertje	4
Jacobs	A	L'Estaminet	6
Passage Hostel/Hotel	D	Médard	3
Snuffel Backpacker Hostel	B	Pickles	2
		De Republiek	1
		't Eekhoetje	5

What to see and do

The older sections of Bruges fan out from two central squares, Markt and Burg. Markt, edged on three sides by nineteenth-century gabled buildings, is the larger of the two, an impressive open space flanked on its south side by the mighty **Belfort** (Belfry; daily 9.30am–5pm; €5), built in the thirteenth century when the town was at its richest and most extravagant. The belfry is attached to the rectangular **Hallen**, a much-restored edifice dating from the thirteenth century. Entry to the Belfry is via the Hallen; inside, a tapering staircase leads up to the roof from where there are wonderful views over the city centre.

The Burg and the Heilig Bloed Basilek

From the Markt, Breidelstraat leads through to the Burg, whose southern half is fringed by the city's finest group of buildings. One of the best is the Heilig Bloed Basiliek (Basilica of the Holy Blood; daily: April–Sept 9.30am–noon & 2–6pm; Oct–March Mon, Tues & Thurs–Sun 10am–noon & 2–4pm, Wed 10am–noon; free), named after a phial of the blood of Christ brought back here from Jerusalem by the Crusaders, and one of the holiest relics in medieval Christendom. The basilica divides into a shadowy Lower Chapel, built to house another relic, that of St Basil, and an Upper Chapel where the phial is stored in a grandiose silver tabernacle. The Holy Blood is still venerated on Ascension Day, when it is carried through the town in a colourful but solemn procession.

The Stadhuis

To the left of the basilica, the **Stadhuis** has a beautiful, turreted sandstone facade dating from 1376. Inside, the magnificent **Gothic Hall** (daily 9.30am–5pm; €2.50) boasts fancy vault-keys depicting New Testament scenes and romantic paintings commissioned in 1895 to illustrate the history of the town. The price of admission covers entry to the former alderman's mansion, the nearby **Renaissancezaal 't Brugse Vrije** (Tues–Sun 9.30am–12.30pm & 1.30–5pm), also on the square. It has just one exhibit: an enormous sixteenth-century marble and oak chimneypiece carved in honour of the ruling Habsburgs, who are flattered by their enormous codpieces.

The Groeninge and Gruuthuse Museums

From the arch beside the Stadhuis, Blinde Ezelstraat ("Blind Donkey Street") leads south across the canal to the huddle of picturesque houses crimping the **Huidenvettersplein**, the old tanners' quarter that now holds some of the busiest drinking and eating places in town. Nearby, the Dijver follows the canal to the **Groeninge Museum**, at Dijver 12 (Tues–Sun 9.30am–5pm; €8), which houses a superb sample of Flemish paintings from the fourteenth to twentieth centuries. The best section is the early Flemish work, including several canvases by Jan van Eyck. Further along the Dijver, at no. 17, the **Gruuthuse Museum** (Tues–Sun 9.30am–5pm; €6) is sited in a rambling fifteenth-century mansion and holds a varied collection of fine and applied art, including intricately carved altar pieces, locally made tapestries and many different types of antique furniture.

Onze Lieve Vrouwekerk

The **Onze Lieve Vrouwekerk** (Tues–Sat 9.30am–5pm, Sun 1.30–5pm; €2.50), on Mariastraat, is a rambling shambles of a building, but among its assorted treasures is a delicate marble *Madonna and Child* by Michelangelo and, in the **chancel** (same opening hours; €2.50) the exquisite Renaissance **mausoleums** of Charles the Bold and his daughter Mary of Burgundy. Plastered with lime mortar, the inside walls of all the vaults sport brightly coloured **grave frescoes**, a specific art that flourished hereabouts from the late thirteenth to the middle of the fifteenth century.

St Jans Hospitaal and Begijnhof

Opposite the church, the large medieval ward of **St Jans Hospitaal** (Tues–Sun 9.30am–5pm; €8) has been turned into a lavish museum celebrating the city's history in general and St John's hospital in particular. In addition, the old Hospital chapel displays a small but exquisite collection of paintings by **Hans Memling**. Born near Frankfurt in 1433, Memling spent most of his working life in Bruges, producing serene but warmly coloured and stunningly beautiful paintings. From St Jans, it's a quick stroll down to the **Begijnhof** (daily 9am–6pm or sunset if earlier; free), a circle of whitewashed houses around a tidy green. Nearby, the picturesque **Minnewater** is billed in much publicity hype as the "Lake of Love". The tag certainly gets the canoodlers going, but in fact the lake – more a large pond – started life as a city harbour.

Arrival and information

Arrival Bruges's train station adjoins the bus station about 2km southwest of the centre. Local buses leave from outside the train station for the main square, the Markt; tickets cost €1.20.

Information The main tourist office is in the city concert hall, the Concertgebouw, a ten-minute walk west of the Markt at 't Zand 34 (daily 10am–6pm, Thurs till 8pm; ⓣ050 44 86 86, ⓦwww.brugge.be). There is a smaller branch inside the train station (April–Sept Tues–Sat 10am–1pm & 2–6pm; Oct–March Tues–Sat 9.30am–12.30pm & 1–5pm; ⓣ050 44 86 86).

Accommodation

Hostels

Passage Hostel Dweersstraat 26 ⓣ050 34 02 32, ⓦwww.passagebruges.com. The most agreeable hostel in Bruges, accommodating fifty people in ten comparatively comfortable dormitories. Breakfast is €5 extra. Run by the same people, the **Passage Hotel** next door offers simple but well-maintained doubles, some with shared facilities. Advance reservations advised. Dorms in hostel ❷; double rooms in hotel ❺

Snuffel Backpacker Hostel Ezelstraat 47–49 ⓣ050 33 31 33, ⓦwww.snuffel.be. Well-run hostel to the west of the centre with four- to twelve-bed dorms and a cosy, laid-back bar which stays open till late. The only downside is having to walk

BATTLE THROUGH THE AGES

Throughout its history, Belgium has frequently found itself a crossroads in conflicts, and these days many of its former battlegrounds make popular day-trips for tourists. An hour from Ghent, the town of **Ieper (Ypres)** has a moving museum and memorial to those who died during WWI. **Bastogne**, deep in the Ardennes woods, was the site of the Battle of the Bulge, one of WWII's bloodiest battles. The town's historical centre has displays on local life at the time and shows a film commemorating the events. **Waterloo** is an easy day-trip from Brussels, just forty minutes on the bus – you can visit both the battleground itself and the Musée Wellington.

through the usually busy bar to get to the showers. Rooms are decorated in lively contemporary style by local artists and art students. Bikes are available for rent, and there are regular BBQs in summer. Reservations recommended April–Sept. Dorms ❷

Hotels

Bauhaus Budget Hotel Langestraat 133 ⓣ050 34 10 93, ⓦwww.bauhaus.be. Cheap and cheerful hotel/hostel comprising twenty private rooms, dorms and apartments. An excellent bar lends the place some atmosphere. Dorms ❷; double rooms ❹

De Goezeput Goezeputstraat 29 ⓣ050 34 26 94. Set in a charming location on a quiet street near the cathedral, this outstanding two-star hotel occupies an immaculately refurbished eighteenth-century convent complete with wooden beams and hundreds of antiques. ❽

Jacobs Baliestraat 1 ⓣ050 33 98 31, ⓦwww.hoteljacobs.be. Creatively modernized old brick building, a ten-minute walk to the northeast of the Markt. The 23 rooms are decorated in brisk modern style, though some are a tad small. Take bus #4 or 8 to Langerei/Carmerbrug. ❼

Eating

Most of the city's **restaurants and cafés** are geared up for tourists, churning out some pretty mediocre stuff. Exceptions, including the places we recommend below, are well worth seeking out.

't Eekhoetje Eekhoutstraat 3 ⓣ050 34 89 79. Bright and airy tearoom with a small courtyard, whose efficient and friendly staff serve a good selection of tasty snacks and light meals such as omelettes, pasta and toasties. Daily except Wed 7.30am–7.30pm. Salads €8.

L'Estaminet Park 5. Groovy neighbourhood café-bar with a relaxed feel and a diverse and cosmopolitan clientele. First-rate beer menu and good pasta dishes. Daily except Thurs 11.30am–1am or later. Mains €8.

Médard Sint-Amandsstraat 18. Family-run Italian restaurant with generous portions of pasta – just €3 for a huge bowl. Very close to the main square. Open 11am–8pm, closed Thurs.

Pickles Just off the Markt; one of the best options for fries. Open till 4am on the weekend.

Drinking and nightlife

B-in Mariastraat 38 ⓦwww.b-in.be. The coolest place in town, this recently opened bar-club is kitted out with eye-catching coloured fluorescent tubes. Guest DJs play house on the weekends, and there are reasonably priced drinks and cocktails. Gets going about 11pm. Free entry. Tues–Sat 11am till late.

Het Brugs Beertje Kemelstraat 5. This small and friendly speciality beer bar claims a stock of three hundred beers, which aficionados reckon is one of the best selections in Belgium, and there are tasty snacks too, such as cheeses and salad. Popular with backpackers. Daily except Wed 4pm–1am.

De Republiek St Jakobsstraat 36. Trendy bar with a lovely terrace and DJs at weekends.

Moving on

Train Antwerp (hourly; 1hr 20min); Brussels (every 30min; 1hr); Ostend (every 20min; 15min); Zeebrugge (hourly; 15min).

Southern Belgium

South of Brussels lies **Wallonia**, French-speaking Belgium, where a belt of heavy industry interrupts the rolling farmland that itself precedes the high wooded hills of the **Ardennes**. The latter spreads over three provinces – Namur in the west, Luxembourg in the south and Liège in the east – and is a great place for hiking and canoeing. The best gateway town for the Ardennes is the provincial centre of **Namur**, an hour from Brussels by train.

NAMUR

NAMUR is a pleasant, medium-sized town, whose antique centre is dotted with elegant, eighteenth-century mansions. It also possesses a number of first-rate restaurants and a lively bar scene, lent vigour by its university students; however you wouldn't know it during late July and August, when many of its best cafés and bars are shut.

What to see and do

Namur occupies an important strategic location, straddling the confluence of the rivers Sambre and Meuse, the main result being the massive, rambling **Citadel** (open 24hr; free), which rolls along the top of the steep bluff overlooking the south bank of the Sambre. Its nooks and crannies can take a couple of days to explore, though you can speed things up by using the tourist mini-train (April–Oct; €5), which runs every half-hour.

Cutting through the old town centre is **rue de l'Ange** and its continuation **rue de Fer**, which together comprise the main shopping street. A few metres east of here, the **Trésor du Prieuré d'Oignies**, at rue Julie Billiart 17 (Treasury of the Oignies Priory; Tues–Sat 10am–noon & 2–5pm, Sun 2–5pm; €2), is Namur's best – and smallest – museum. Located in a nunnery, it holds a spellbinding collection of reliquaries and devotional pieces created by local craftsman Hugo d'Oignies in the first half of the thirteenth century; the nuns give the guided tour in English.

Arrival and information

Arrival Namur's train and bus stations are on the northern edge of the city centre on Place de la Station.

Information The tourist office is just a few steps away on square Léopold, at the north end of rue de Fer (daily 9.30am–6pm; ⓣ081 24 64 49, ⓦwww.ville.namur.be). They give advice on cycling, walking and canoeing in the Ardennes and will also arrange accommodation. There's also a seasonal tourist information chalet (April–Oct daily 9.30am–6pm), ten minutes' walk away, over the Sambre bridge on the other side of the centre.

Accommodation

Auberge de Jeunesse ave Félicien Rops 8 ⓣ081 22 36 88, ⓦwww.laj.be. This hundred-bed hostel occupies a big old house on the southern edge of town on the banks of the Meuse past the casino, a fair way out of town; its friendliness makes up for the inconvenient location. There's no lock-out and the hostel has a kitchen, laundry and self-service restaurant. It's 3km from the train station; buses #3 or #4 run here from the centre. Dorms ❷; double rooms ❺

Beauregard ave Baron de Moreau 1 ⓣ081 23 00 28. Part of Namur's casino complex, this hotel has large and modern rooms, some with a river view and balcony. It's a ten-minute walk south of the centre, on the banks of the Meuse below the citadel. ❼

Eating and drinking

Namur has an excellent selection of **restaurants** and **bars**, many of them clustered in the quaint, pedestrianized squares just west of rue de l'Ange, on and around place Marché-aux-Légumes and neighbouring place Chanoine Descamps.

Restaurants

Le Moulin à Poivre rue Bas de la Place 19 ⓣ081 23 11 20. Cosy little restaurant offering tasty French food from premises just off place d'Armes. Main courses around €18.

TREAT YOURSELF

Les Tanneurs rue des Tanneries 13 ⓣ081 24 00 24, ⓦwww.tanneurs.com. Comfortable four-star hotel in a lavishly and imaginatively renovated old brick mansion, located down a quiet alley close to the town centre. The cheap rooms are fine, but if you're prepared to pay a lot more you can get a room with its own sauna, Jacuzzi or hammam. Highly recommended. Rooms ❻–❾

Le Temps des Cerises rue des Brasseurs 22 ⓣ081 22 53 26. Intimate restaurant offering a quality menu. Main courses €20.

Bars

Le Chapitre rue du Séminaire 4. Unassuming, sedate little bar behind the cathedral, with an extensive beer list.
Henry's Bar pl St Aubain 3. Right by the cathedral, this is a big loud brasserie in the best tradition.
Le Monde à L'Envers rue Lelièvre 28. Lively, fashionable bar just up from the cathedral. A favourite spot for university students.
Piano Bar pl Marché-aux-Légumes. One of Namur's most popular bars. Live jazz Fri & Sat from 10pm.

Moving on

Train to: Brussels (every 30min; 50min); Luxembourg City (hourly; 1hr 40min).

LA ROCHE-EN-ARDENNE

If you've had enough of Belgian cities or flatness, head to the Ardennes for a change of scene. **La Roche-en-Ardenne** is one of the area's best bases for outdoor activities; it's a small town and gets packed in the summer, but it's easy to escape into the gorgeous woods that surround it. The only downside is that, aside from the town's fairly impressive castle ruins (daily 10/11am–4/5pm; €4), there's not too much to amuse you if the weather's bad.

Hiking maps are available for a few euros in the tourist information office. There's no shortage of companies offering excursions or bike rental (see below). A day of kayaking costs about €18, and you can rent a mountain bike for about €20 a day.

Arrival and information

Train and bus The nearest trains get to La Roche is Marloie or Melreux. Both are about half an hour from La Roche and buses leave every two hours or so. Catch bus #3 from Melreux or #15 from Marloie. Buses drop passengers off in the centre of town.
Tourist Information Place du Marche 15 ⓣ084 36 77 36, ⓦwww.la-roche-tourisme.com. Offers Internet access. Daily 9.30am–5pm, 9.30am–6pm Jul–Aug.

Activities

All of the operators below offer hiking, cycling, rafting and horseriding. Also check out ⓦwww.larochailes.be for paragliding information.
Ardenne Aventures rue du Hadja 1 (Pont du Gravier) ⓣ084 41 19 00, ⓦwww.ardenne-aventures.be.
Brandsport Auberge La Laiterie, Mierchamps 15 ⓣ04 41 10 84, ⓦwww.brandsport.be.
Les Kayaks de L'Ourthe rue de l'Eglise 35 ⓣ084 36 87 12.

Accommodation

Domaine des Olivettes Chemin de Soeret 12 ⓣ084 41 16 52, ⓦwww.lesolivettes.be. Just out of town, this place combines a hostel, hotel, restaurant and equestrian centre. It's a relaxed place with a pleasant restaurant and bar. Dorms ❶; double rooms ❼
Camping Le Vieux Moulin Petite Strument 62 ⓣ084 41 15 07, ⓦwww.strument.com. About 800m to the south of the town centre, along the Val du Bronze. A huge campsite with a pleasant setting beside a stream. Open Easter–Oct. ❶

Eating and drinking

La Roche's restaurants are generally overpriced and underwhelming: **Le Clos René** (rue Chamont 30) is virtually the only exception, a delightful pancake house that also serves delicious pear cider (*cidre de poire*). Pancakes start at €6. Aside from this, your best bet is to buy delicious local ham and pâté or an *assiette* of local produce from the butchers. **Maison Bouillon et Fils** (Place du Marché 9).

Luxembourg

The **Grand Duchy of Luxembourg** is one of Europe's smallest sovereign states, a tiny principality with a population of around 450,000. Many travellers write it off as a dull and expensive financial centre, but this is a mistake. **Luxembourg City**, the country's agreeable and dramatically sited capital, is well worth one or two nights' stay, and from here it's a short hop – by road, rail or bus – to the forested **hills** of the Ardennes that fill out the northern part of the country. Every native speaks the indigenous language, Letzebuergesch – a dialect of German that sounds a bit like Dutch – but most also speak French and German and many speak English too.

LUXEMBOURG CITY

LUXEMBOURG CITY is one of the most spectacularly sited capitals in Europe. The valleys of the rivers Alzette and Pétrusse, which meet here, cut a green swath through the city, their deep canyons once key to the city's defences, but now providing a beautiful setting.

What to see and do

Luxembourg City divides into three distinct sections. The **old town**, on the northern side of the Pétrusse valley, is very appealing and its tight grid of streets holds most of the city's sights. On the opposite side of the Pétrusse is the **modern city** – less attractive and of interest only for its train station and cheap hotels. Don't miss the **valleys** too, accessible by lift from Place St Esprit or by foot; here the atmospheric Grund area and the parkland provide another great panorama, this time up at the massive bastions that secure the old town.

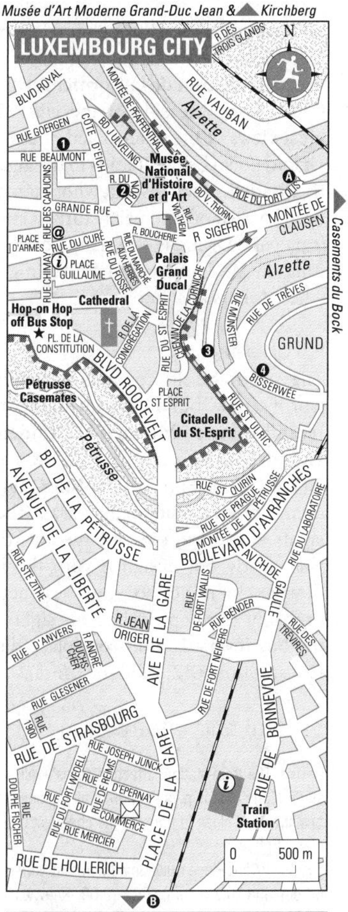

The old town

The old town focuses on two squares, the more important of which is **place d'Armes**, fringed with cafés and restaurants. To the north lie the city's principal shops, mainly along **Grande Rue**, while on the southern side a small alley cuts through to the larger **place Guillaume**, the venue of Luxembourg's main general market (Wed & Sat am). Nearby, on Marché aux Poissons, a group of patrician mansions holds the city's largest and choicest museum, the **Musée National d'Histoire et d'Art** (Tues–Sun 10am–5pm, Thurs 10am–8pm; €5), where there's an enjoyable sample of fifteenth- and sixteenth-century Dutch and Flemish paintings. East of the museum lie the **Casements du Bock** (daily March–Oct 10am–5pm; €1.75), underground fortifications built by the Spaniards in the eighteenth century. The city occupies an ideal defensive position and its defences were reinforced on many occasions – hence the massive bastions and subterranean artillery galleries that survive today. These particular casements are the most diverting to visit – though several

LUXEMBOURG CITY

ACCOMMODATION		EATING & DRINKING	
Auberge de Jeunesse	A	Art Café	1
Kockelscheuer	B	Brasserie Bonaparte	4
		Café' des Artistes	3
		Chiggeri	2

others are also open throughout the summer – and afterwards you can follow the dramatic **chemin de la Corniche**, which tracks along the side of the cliff with great views of the slate-roofed houses of **Grund** down below. It leads to the gigantic **Citadelle du St-Esprit**, whose top has been levelled off and partly turned into a leafy park. Grund is especially worth visiting on Wednesday and Friday nights, when its bars kick into action.

Kirchberg

The east of the city contains some noteworthy new buildings, including the recently opened **Musée d'Art Moderne Grand-Duc Jean** at Park Dräi Eechelen 3 (Wed 11am–8pm, Thurs–Mon 11am–6pm, ⓦwww.mudam.lu; €5). These sights are spread over a large area that was clearly not designed with the pedestrian in mind, so your best bet is probably the hop-on hop-off sightseeing bus (every 20min from place de la Constitution; €12; valid for 24hrs).

Arrival and information

Arrival The train station, fifteen minutes' walk south of the old town, is the hub of all the city's bus lines and close to many of the cheapest (but plainest) hotels.
Tourist office Place Guillaume (Mon–Sat 9am–6/7pm, Sun 10am–6pm; ⓣ22 28 09, ⓦwww.lcto.lu). There is a branch of the national tourist office inside the train station (June to mid-Sept Mon–Sat 9am–6.30pm, Sun 9am–12.30pm & 2–6pm; mid-Sept to May daily 9am–12.30pm & 1.45–6pm; ⓣ42 82 82 20; ⓣwww.ont.lu). It sells the Luxembourg Card, which entitles you to unlimited use of public transport throughout the Grand Duchy and admission to selected museums and attractions from Easter to October (1/2/3 days for €10/17/24).

Accommodation

Most **hotels** are clustered near the train station, which is the least interesting part of town. You're much better off staying in the old town and won't necessarily pay much more to do so, though you're limited to just a handful of places.
Auberge de Jeunesse rue du Fort Olisy 2 ⓣ22 68 89, ⓦwww.youthhostels.lu. Excellent, hotel-style HI hostel 3km northeast of the station on the edge of the old town in the Alzette Valley. It has a laundry and cooking facilities and breakfast is included. Dorms ❷
Campsite Kockelscheuer route de Bettembourg 22 ⓣ47 18 15, ⓦwww.camp-kockelscheuer.lu. Take bus #5 from the station to get to this agreeably located campsite three miles out of the city. Closed Nov–April. ❶

Eating

The old town is crowded with inexpensive **cafés** and **restaurants**. French cuisine is popular here, but traditional Luxembourg dishes are found on many menus too, mostly meaty affairs such as neck of pork with broad beans (*judd mat gaardebounen*) or black sausage (*blutwurst*). Keep an eye out also for *gromperenkichelchen* (potato cakes usually served with apple sauce) and, in winter, stalls and cafés selling *glühwein* (mulled wine).
Art Café rue Beaumont 1a. Beautiful café decorated like a plush theatre. Mains €10.
Brasserie Bonaparte rue Bisserwee 7. In the Grund part of town, this pizza place has a lovely terrace. Mains around €8.

Drinking and nightlife

As for **drinking**, there's a lively bar scene in the old town and Grund.
Café des Artistes Montée du Grund 22. Very atmospheric little piano bar Édith Piaf would feel at home in. Closed Mon.
Chiggeri rue du Nord 15. Groovy bar-cum-café in the old town that has a great atmosphere, funky décor and a mixed straight and gay clientele.

Directory

Bike rental rue Bisserwee 8, Grund ⓣ496 23 83. Easter to Oct daily 10am–noon & 1–8pm; advance booking advised.
Internet Cyber-Beach, rue du Curé 3 ⓣ47 80 70.
Laundry Quick-Wash, rue de Strasbourg 31 ⓣ48 78 33.
Left luggage At the train station.
Pharmacies Goedert, pl d'Armes 5; Mortier, ave de la Gare 11.
Post office rue Aldringen 25 (Mon–Fri 7am–7pm, Sat 7am–5pm).

Moving on

Train to: Brussels (hourly; 2hr 30min); Namur (hourly; 1hr 40min).

Britain

HIGHLIGHTS

OVER THE SEA TO SKYE: craggy peaks, sparkling water and Celtic mystery in the Scottish islands

EDINBURGH FESTIVAL: the world's biggest arts festival

STRATFORD-UPON-AVON: Shakespeare's home town and host to the world-renowned Royal Shakespeare Company

THE BRITISH MUSEUM: an unrivalled collection of arts and antiquities in the centre of London

SURFING, NEWQUAY: test the Atlantic rollers

ROUGH COSTS

DAILY BUDGET basic €45 / the occasional treat €95

DRINK Lager €4 per pint

FOOD Fish and chips €6

HOSTEL/BUDGET HOTEL €22/€60–90

TRAVEL train: London-Brighton €30; bus London-Manchester €30

FACT FILE

POPULATION 60 million (includes Northern Ireland)

AREA 244,820 sq km

LANGUAGE English

CURRENCY British Pound (£)

CAPITAL London (population: 8 million)

INTERNATIONAL PHONE CODE ⓣ44

Basics

The single most important thing to remember when travelling around Britain is that you're visiting not one country, but three: England, Wales and Scotland. That means contending with three capital cities (London, Cardiff and Edinburgh) and three sets of national identity – not to mention the myriad of accent shifts as you move between them.

London is a ceaselessly entertaining city, and is the one place that features on everyone's itinerary. **Brighton** and **Canterbury** offer contrasting diversions – the former an appealing seaside resort, the latter one of Britain's finest medieval cities. The southwest of England has the rugged moorlands of **Devon** and the rocky coastline of **Cornwall**, and the historic spa city of **Bath**. The chief attractions of central England are the university cities of **Oxford** and **Cambridge**, and Shakespeare's hometown, **Stratford-upon-Avon**. Further north, the former industrial cities of **Manchester**, **Liverpool** and **Newcastle** are lively, rejuvenated places, and **York** has splendid historical treasures, but the landscape is again the real magnet, especially the uplands of the **Lake District**. For true wilderness, head to the **Welsh mountains** or **Scottish Highlands**. The finest of Scotland's lochs, glens and peaks, and the magnificent scenery of the west coast islands, can be reached easily from the contrasting cities of **Glasgow** and **Edinburgh** – the latter perhaps Britain's most attractive urban landscape.

CHRONOLOGY

54 BC The Romans attack "Britannia" but are forced back until a successful invasion in AD 43.

1066 AD Norman duke William the Conqueror wins the Battle of Hastings, defeating the last Anglo-Saxon ruler, King Harold II.

1215 The Magna Carta forms the basis upon which English law is built.

1301 Edward I conquers Wales, giving his heir the title Prince of Wales.

1603 King James VI of Scotland also becomes James I of England in the Union of the Crowns.

1603 William Shakespeare writes *Macbeth*.

1653 Republican Oliver Cromwell made Lord Protector of Britain, after victory in the English Civil War.

1707 The Act of Union unites the parliaments of Scotland and England, with the addition of Ireland in 1800.

1800s The Industrial Revolution helps Britain to expand her Empire and become a dominant world force.

1914 Britain enters the First World War.

1928 Women get the vote after a hard-fought campaign.

1939 Britain declares war on Germany.

1945 Prime Minister Winston Churchill officially announces the end of the war in Europe on 8 May.

1947 Indian Independence from British rule.

1960s The Beatles sing their way through the swinging sixties.

1979 Margaret Thatcher becomes Britain's first female Prime Minister.

1997 Public mourning as "people's Princess" Diana, dies in an accident.

1998 Devolution in Scotland and Wales.

2005 On 7 July, London is rocked by terrorist bombings, leaving 52 dead.

"**Great Britain**", or more usually just "Britain", is a geographical term, referring to the largest of the British Isles. However, it can also be used politically, referring to central government, "British" nationals and to denote a united British team at sporting events such as the Olympics. "**United Kingdom**" is a political term, referring to the sovereign state of England, Scotland, Wales and Northern Ireland. Northern Ireland is covered with the rest of the island of Ireland in Chapter 15.

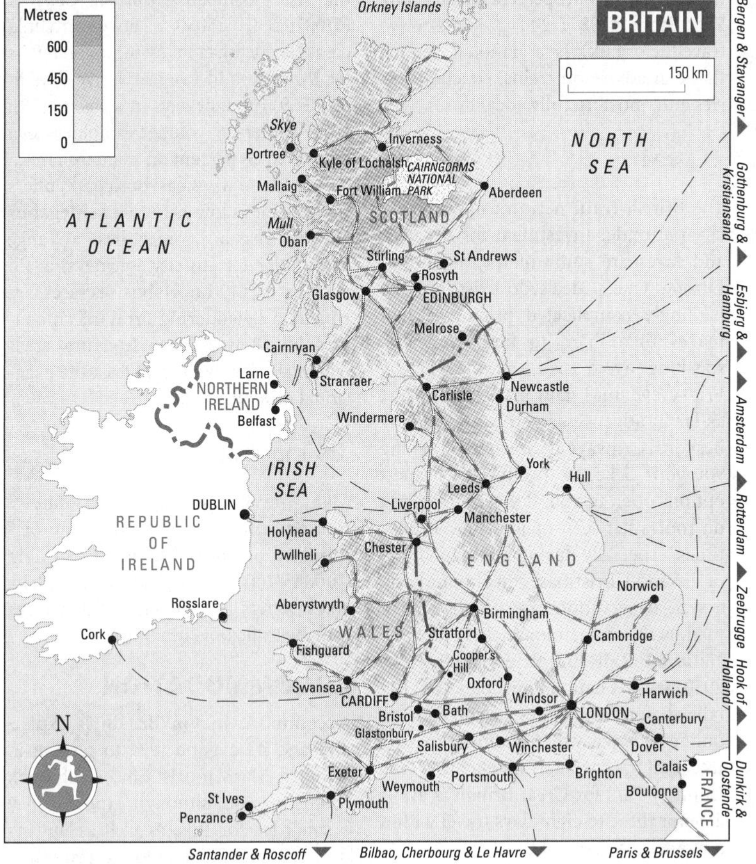

ARRIVAL

If you're travelling from outside mainland Europe, clearly, the only direct route to the islands of Britain is by **air**. Long-haul flights now land at a range of destinations throughout the UK, including Birmingham, Manchester and Edinburgh, though most international passengers still find themselves passing through London's Gatwick or Heathrow at some stage. Budget airlines serve destinations throughout Europe and prices can be amazingly cheap if you book far enough in advance. No-frills carriers like Ryanair ⓦwww.ryanair.com and easyJet www.easyjet.com operate out of Luton and Stansted near London and smaller regional airports around the country. Other options from Europe include one of the most pleasant; the **Eurostar** (ⓦwww.eurostar.com) high speed train from Paris or Brussels to St Pancras International in London. Another alternative is by **sea**: ferries from Belgium, Denmark, France, Holland, Norway, Ireland and Spain docking at a variety of ports around the UK.

GETTING AROUND

Most places are still accessible by train and/or coach (as long-distance buses are known), though costs are among the highest in Europe. **Traveline** (daily 7am–9pm; ⓣ0871/200 2233, ⓦwww.traveline.org.uk) is a national service that can advise on trains, coaches, ferries and, most usefully, local buses.

By train

The British **train** network has suffered chronic under-investment for decades, and **fares** are some of the highest in Europe. Cheap deals do exist, but the bafflingly complicated pricing system makes them hard to find. Generally speaking, avoid rush hours (especially Friday evening), and book your ticket as far in advance as you can to get the best deals. Always ask the person selling you your ticket to specify the cheapest options open to you. If you're travelling on routes between major cities at busy times, especially during public holidays or around Christmas, you should book a seat. Reservations are usually free if made at the same time as ticket purchase. **National Rail Enquiries** (ⓣ0845/748 4950, ⓦwww.nationalrail.co.uk) has details of all train services; or you can buy online at ⓦwww.thetrainline.com. The InterRail (www.interrailnet.com) One Country Pass for Great Britain is available for three to eight days travel within a month and starts at £136.

By bus

The **bus** services run by National Express (ⓣ0870/580 8080, ⓦwww.nationalexpress.com) duplicate many intercity rail routes, very often at half the price or less. If you're a student, or under 26 you can buy a National Express Coachcard (£10), which gives up to thirty percent off standard fares. Their BritXplorer Pass offers unlimited travel for visitors at £79 for seven days, £139 for two weeks and £219 for a month. Both the Coachcard and Pass are valid on National Express through-routes to Scotland, but not on services within Scotland itself. These are provided by the sister company **Scottish Citylink** (ⓣ0870/550 5050, ⓦwww.citylink.co.uk), which has its own Explorer Pass for three days in five (£35), five days in ten (£59) or eight days in sixteen (£79); **Euro under-26** youth cardholders can save up to 20 percent on standard fares.

EasyBus (ⓦwww.easybus.co.uk) offers services for as low as £1, while **Megabus** (ⓦwww.megabus.com/) has a range of popular city-to-city journeys, again starting at £1. **Local bus services** are run by a bewildering array of companies, but there are very few rural areas which aren't served by at least the occasional minibus.

By tour bus

Many travellers prefer the flexibility of touring Britain on "jump-on-jump-off" **minibus** or **special tours**. Road Trip (ⓣ0845/200 6791, ⓦwww.roadtrip.co.uk) offers fully inclusive budget bus tours with flexible itineraries.

ACCOMMODATION

Accommodation in Britain is expensive and it's a good idea to reserve in advance. Many tourist offices will book rooms for you, although expect to pay a small fee for this, as well as putting down a ten-percent deposit on your first night's stay.

In tourist cities it's hard to find a double in a **hotel** for less than £50 a night but budget accommodation in the form of **guesthouses** and **B&Bs** – often a comfortable room in a family home, plus a substantial breakfast – starts at around £25 a head, more in London.

Britain has an extensive network of **HI hostels** operated by the Youth Hostel Association (ⓦwww.yha.org.uk). In Scotland (ⓦwww.syha.org.uk), a bed for the night can cost as little as £5, except in the cities, where you might pay more than twice that. In England and Wales charges start at around £12. **Privately run hostels** are generally of a comparable standard and can be several pounds cheaper. There are more than 750 official **campsites** in Britain, charging from around £5 per person per night and it is often preferable to stay at a well appointed site over a hostel of inferior quality and inflated price. In the countryside, farmers will often let you camp in a field if you ask, sometimes charging a couple of pounds. Camping rough is illegal in designated parkland and nature reserves.

FOOD AND DRINK

Long reviled as a culinary wasteland, Britain has seen a transformation in both the quality and variety of its restaurants. If you're on a tight budget, the temptation is still to head for the nearest fast-food joint, but with a little effort, alternatives can easily be found and higher-end establishments will often offer good lunchtime or early evening deals. "Modern British" cuisine – in effect anything inventive – has been at the core of this change, though wherever you go you'll find places serving Indian, Italian and Chinese food.

Food

In many B&Bs you'll be offered an **"English breakfast"** – basically sausage, bacon and fried eggs – although most places will give you the option of cereal, toast and fruit as well. Every major town will have upmarket restaurants, but the quintessential British meal is **fish and chips**. However, the once ubiquitous fish-and-chip shop ("chippy") is now outnumbered on Britain's high streets by kebab and burger joints. Less threatened is the so-called "greasy spoon", generally a down-at-heel diner where the average menu will include variations on sausages, fried eggs, bacon and chips.

Many **pubs** also serve food including steak-and-kidney pie, shepherd's pie (minced lamb topped with potato), chops or steaks, accompanied by potatoes and veg. **Gastro-pubs** can offer menus to rival any restaurant. There's also an increasing number of **vegetarian** restaurants, especially in the larger towns, but most places – including pubs – will make some attempt to cater for vegetarians.

Drink

Drinking traditionally takes place in the **pub**, where a standard range of draught beers – sold by the pint or half-pint – generates most of the business, although imported bottled beers are also popular. Beers fall into two distinct groups: cold, blond, fizzy **lager** and the very different darker ale, or **bitter**. In England, pubs are generally open Mon–Sat 11am–11pm, Sun noon–10.30pm (though some close daily 3–5.30pm); hours are often longer in Scotland, while Sunday closing is common in Wales.

In Scotland, the national drink is of course **whisky**. The best are the single malts, produced by small distilleries using local spring water.

CULTURE AND ETIQUETTE

Famed for their "stiff upper lip" and polite reticence, the British do tend to be more reserved than their continental counterparts, though the difference is hardly noticeable in the pub, where most socialising still happens. Possibly the most cosmopolitan place in Europe – in the larger cities anyway – Britain has developed a reputation for liberal tolerance and benefits from a diverse range of faiths, creeds and colours. The official religion remains the Protestant Church of England, though society and government are now essentially secular.

Tipping is expected, though not mandatory, when paying the bill in restaurants, and a sum of between ten and twelve percent of the total is the norm. It's also customary to tip taxi drivers and hairdressers a small sum, though it is not necessary to tip bartenders when buying drinks at a bar or pub.

SPORTS AND OUTDOOR ACTIVITIES

Football (soccer) is a British obsession, –"the beautiful game" was codified here in 1863, and seeing a match is a must for any sports fan. Unfortunately it can be extremely difficult and costly to acquire tickets. The best option to guarantee seeing a Premier League match is to choose a lesser known club; in London, Fulham (Ⓦwww.fulhamfc.com) are a good bet as are Middlesbrough (Ⓦwww.mfc.co.uk) in the northeast, but check the Premier League website in England (Ⓦwww.premierleague.com) or in Scotland (Ⓦwww.scotprem.co.uk) for detailed information. **Rugby** and **cricket**, though popular, do not generally inspire the same fervent tribalism as football.

Britain's diverse geography and geology, and access to large bodies of fresh and salt water, mean that venues for **outdoor pursuits** are easily accessible. The uplands of Wales (Ⓦwww.adventure.visitwales.com) Scotland (Ⓦwww.adventure.visitscotland.com) and the English Lake District (Ⓦwww.lakedistrictoutdoors.co.uk) are particularly good for hiking, climbing and rafting, while Devon and Cornwall (Ⓦwww.southwestsurf.info) have the best **surfing** in the UK. **Walking** is also one of the finest ways to see the country, and an excellent infrastructure of long-distance footpaths crisscrosses Britain (Ⓦwww.walkingbritain.co.uk).

COMMUNICATIONS

Post offices open Mon–Fri 9am–5.30pm, and some open on Sat 9am–12.30/1pm. Most **public phones** are operated by BT – though the ubiquity of mobile phones has seen a significant decline in their numbers –and take all coins from 10p upwards (minimum charge 20p), as well as £5, £10 or £20 phonecards, available from post offices and newsagents. An increasing number accept credit cards too. Newsagents can sell you good-value cards from other phone companies for making international calls. Domestic calls are cheapest from 6pm to 8am and at weekends. For the operator, call Ⓣ100 (domestic) or Ⓣ155 (international); of several directory enquiry lines, BT's is Ⓣ118500. **Internet cafés** are common, and you'll also find access at some hostels and some public phones. Prices vary, but £1 should be enough for you to reply to your email.

EMERGENCIES

Police remain approachable and helpful. Tourists aren't a particular target for criminals except in the crowds of the big cities, where you should be on your guard against **pickpockets**. Britain's bigger conurbations all contain inner-city areas where you may feel uneasy after dark, but these are usually away from tourist sights. **Pharmacists** dispense only a limited range of drugs without a doctor's prescription. Most are open standard shop hours, though in large towns some may stay open as late as 10pm. Local newspapers carry lists of late-opening pharmacies. For complaints that require immediate attention, go to the **accident and emergency** (A&E) department of the local hospital.

EMERGENCY NUMBERS

Police, fire & ambulance Ⓣ999 or 112.

INFORMATION & MAPS

Tourist information centres (TICs) exist in virtually every British town, offering a basic range of maps and information. **National Parks** (Ⓦwww.anpa.gov.uk) also have their own information centres,

BRITAIN ON THE NET

www.visitbritain.com Tourist board site with links to regional sites.
www.rail.co.uk Information on public transport.
www.backpackers.co.uk The low-down on independent hostels.
www.knowhere.co.uk Irreverent local knowledge.
www.streetmap.co.uk Town plans and area maps.

which are better for guidance on outdoor pursuits. The most comprehensive series of maps is produced by the **Ordnance Survey** (www.ordnancesurvey.co.uk) – essential if you're planning more serious hiking or you're walking.

MONEY AND BANKS

The **pound** (£) sterling, divided into 100 pence, remains the national currency. There are coins of 1p, 2p, 5p, 10p, 20p, 50p, £1 and £2; and notes of £5, £10, £20 and £50; notes issued by Scottish banks are legal tender but often not accepted south of the border. At the time of writing, £1 was worth €1.47 and $2.00. Normal **banking hours** are Mon–Fri 9.30am–5pm, but some branches open on Saturday. **ATMs** accept a wide range of debit and credit cards. Shops, hotels, restaurants and most other places readily accept **credit cards** for payment.

MUSEUMS AND MONUMENTS

Many of Britain's national **museums** are free, but stately homes and monuments are often administered by the state-run **English Heritage** (given as EH in opening times through this chapter; www.english-heritage.org.uk) and **Historic Scotland** (HS; www.historic-scotland.gov.uk); while in Wales **CADW** (www.cadw.wales.gov.uk) owns several dramatic ruins. The annual fee for EH is £40 (£25 if you're under 19 or a student), for HS £37 (£28 if you're a full-time student) or you can get an Explorer pass for access to 75 sites over a three, seven, or ten day period (from £19). Membership of CADW is £37 (£18 if you're between 16 and 20) and their Explorer Pass is £10.50 for 3 days or £17.00 for 7 days. The privately run **National Trust** (NT; www.nationaltrust.org.uk) and **National Trust for Scotland** (NTS; www.nts.org.uk) also run a large number of gardens and stately homes nationwide; annual membership of NT/NTS costs £43.50/£40 (£19.50/£15 for under-26s), and each pass is recognized by the other. The **Great British Heritage Pass**, which covers sites administered by all the organizations above and many others too, is available from the British Visitor Centre, Lower Regent St, London, and selected tourist information centres (£28/39/52/70 for 4/7/15/30 days; www.visitbritain.com for details), as well as worldwide agents.

OPENING HOURS AND HOLIDAYS

General **shop hours** are Mon–Sat 9am–5.30/6pm, although an increasing number of places in big towns are also open Sun (usually 10am–4pm) and till 7/8pm at least once a week. In England and Wales, **public holidays** ("bank holidays") are: Jan 1, Good Fri, Easter Mon, first Mon and last Mon in May, last Mon in Aug, Christmas Day and Boxing Day (Dec 25 & 26). In Scotland, Jan 1, Jan 2 & Dec 25 are the only fixed public holidays, otherwise towns are left to pick their own.

England

The largest and most populous of the component parts of the United Kingdom, **ENGLAND** has historically enjoyed political and financial dominance over its smaller neighbours, and this may in part explain its less developed sense of national identity, imbued as it is with an inherent sense of superiority.

Blessed with a more temperate climate than Wales and Scotland, evidence of human settlement in this part of Britain dates from as early as 5000BC. From 43AD, Roman colonization, followed by the ascendance of Germanic peoples – the Anglo-Saxons – and later the Christianisation of their disparate, pagan kingdoms, had bought a degree of unification that pushed the indigenous Celts further into the north and west. By 886, after a victory over marauding Vikings, King Alfred the Great was proclaimed as the first king of the English. This line of Anglo-Saxon kings was to end in 1066 when William of Normandy, a duchy in what is now northern France, defeated Harold II at the Battle of Hastings. It was this event, and the subsequent Norman linguistic and legislative imperatives, that sculpted much of what is considered to be English today.

The English **landscape**, though romanticised in pastoral literature as flat, green and pleasant, varies enormously, changing dramatically over relatively short distances; the populous, industrialised areas such as Manchester or London giving way to the glacially scoured Lake District or the hidden coves and precipitous cliffs of Cornwall.

LONDON

With a population of just under eight million, **LONDON** is Europe's biggest city, spreading over an area of more than 600 square miles from its core on the River Thames. This is where the country's news, art and money are made, and there's an undeniable aura of excitement and success. However, all this comes at a price; with high accommodation and transport costs, this is one of the most expensive cities in the world.

London's world-class museums and **galleries** – from the British Museum to Tate Modern – have been reinvented in recent years and the vast majority are free of charge. You could spend days just shopping in the city's famous department stores and the offbeat weekend **markets**. The music, **clubs** and gay scene too are second to none, while **pubs** and restaurants offer an array of world cuisine suited to any pocket. For a little respite, the city's "green lungs" are some of the best in the country. Central **parks** including Hyde Park and St James's Park are worth a stroll, as are the wilds of Hampstead Heath, Greenwich and Kew.

What to see and do

The majority of sights are north of the **River Thames**, but there's no single focus of interest. Most people head, at one time or another, to the area around Whitehall, with **Trafalgar Square** at one end and Parliament Square at the other. All are just a ten-minute stroll east of **Buckingham Palace**. The busiest, most popular area for visitors and Londoners alike is the **West End**, centred on Leicester Square and Piccadilly Circus, and home to the majority of the city's theatres and cinemas. The financial district lies a mile or so to the east, and is known, confusingly, as the **City of London**, at once the most ancient and most modern part of London. Over on the other side of the river, the **South Bank** has become a prime destination thanks to the London Eye, Tate Modern and Shakespeare's Globe. Further afield, **Greenwich** makes for a great day out, as do the Royal Botanic Gardens at

Kew, and the outlying royal palaces of **Hampton Court** and **Windsor Castle**.

Trafalgar Square and the National Gallery

Trafalgar Square's focal point is **Nelson's Column**, featuring the one-eyed admiral who died whilst defeating the French at the 1805 Battle of Trafalgar. Four lions guard the column's base, while two adjacent fountains are a magnet for overheating sightseers during the summer.

Extending across the north side of the square is the bulk of the **National Gallery** (daily 10am–6pm, Wed till 9pm; free; ⓦwww.nationalgallery.org.uk), one of the world's great art collections. A quick tally of the National's masterpieces includes works by Raphael, Michelangelo, Leonardo da Vinci and Velázquez, some of Rembrandt's most searching portraits, and several famous Impressionist and Post-Impressionist works by the likes of Van Gogh and Monet. Tickets for the major exhibitions cost around £10 and should be booked in advance. Round the side of the National Gallery, in St Martin's Place, is the **National Portrait Gallery** (daily 10am–6pm, Thurs & Fri till 9pm; free; ⓦwww.npg.org.uk), which houses portraits of the great and good from Hans Holbein's larger-than-life drawing of Henry VIII to photographs of the latest pop stars.

The Mall and Buckingham Palace

The tree-lined sweep of **The Mall** runs from Trafalgar Square through the imposing Admiralty Arch, and on to **Buckingham Palace** (Aug & Sept daily 9.45am–6.00pm; £15.00; ⓦwww.royal.gov.uk). The palace has served as the monarch's permanent residence only since the accession of Queen Victoria in 1837. The building's exterior, last remodelled in 1913, is as bland as could be, but inside it's suitably lavish. There's more high-class art on display in the **Queen's Gallery** (daily 10am–5.30pm; £8.00), on the south side of the palace. When Buckingham Palace is closed, most folk simply mill about outside the gates, with the largest crowds assembling for the **Changing of the Guard** (May–July daily 11.30am; August–March alternate days; no ceremony if it rains). However, you're better off heading for the **Horse Guards** building on Whitehall (see below), where a more elaborate equestrian ceremony takes place (Mon–Sat 11am, Sun 10am). Wherever you watch the Changing of the Guard, you can relax afterwards in the immaculately laid out **St James's Park.**

Whitehall

Heading south from Trafalgar Square is the broad sweep of **Whitehall**, lined with government buildings. The original Whitehall was a palace built for King Henry VIII and subsequently extended, but virtually the only bit to survive a fire in 1698 is the supremely elegant **Banqueting House** (Mon–Sat 10am–5pm; £4.50; ⓦwww.hrp.org.uk), home to some vast ceiling paintings by Rubens, glorifying the Stuart dynasty. Further down the west side of Whitehall is **10 Downing St**, residence of the Prime Minister since 1732. During World War II, the Cabinet was forced to vacate Downing Street in favour of a bunker in nearby King Charles Street. The **Churchill Museum and Cabinet War Rooms** (daily 9.30am–6pm; £11; ⓣ020/7930 6961, ⓦwww.iwm.org.uk) – left more or less as they were in 1945 – provide a glimpse of the claustrophobic suites from which Winston Churchill directed wartime operations and a fascinating insight to the life of the man himself.

The Houses of Parliament

Clearly visible at the south end of Whitehall is one of London's best-known buildings, the Palace of Westminster, better known as the

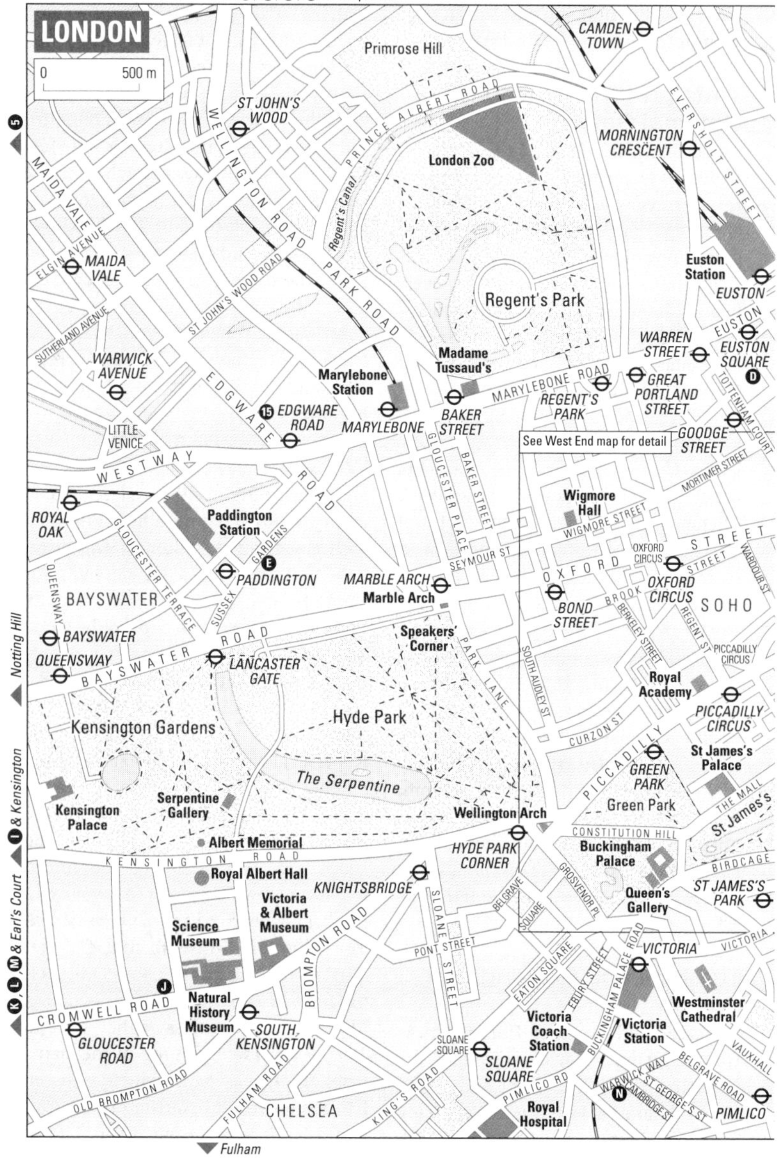

Houses of Parliament. The city's finest Gothic Revival building and symbol of a nation once confident of its place at the centre of the world, it's distinguished above all by the ornate, gilded clock tower popularly known as **Big Ben**, after the thirteen-ton bell that it houses. The original royal palace, built by Edward the Confessor in the eleventh century, burnt down in 1834. The only part to

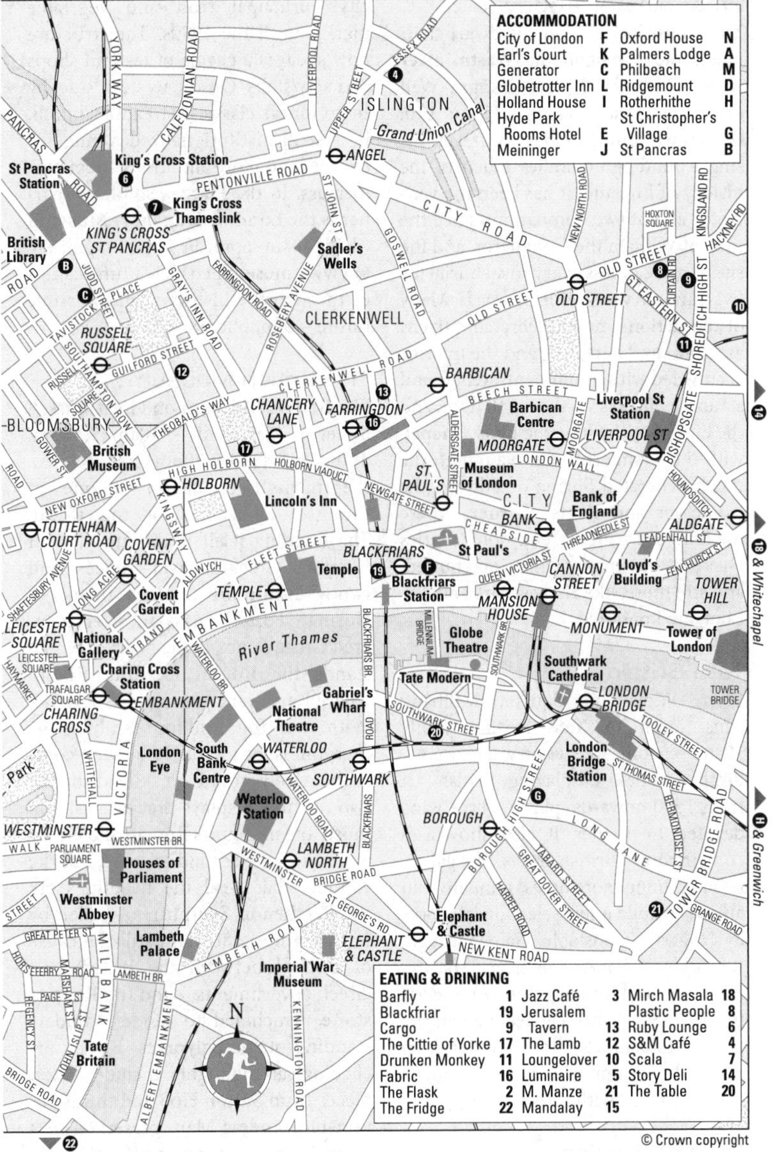

survive is the magnificent Westminster Hall, which can be glimpsed en route to the **public galleries** from which you can watch parliament's proceedings – Friday is the easiest day to get tickets (free; ⓦwww.parliament.uk), when sittings commence at 9.30am: turn up early to avoid queues.

Westminster Abbey

The Houses of Parliament dwarf their much older neighbour, **Westminster Abbey** (Mon–Fri 9.30am–3.45pm, Wed until 7pm, Sat 9.30am–1.45pm; £10; Ⓦwww.westminster-abbey.org), yet this single building embodies much of the history of England: it has been the venue for all but two coronations since the time of William the Conqueror, and the site of more or less every royal burial for five hundred years until George II. Many of the nation's most celebrated citizens are honoured here, too, and the interior is crowded with monuments, reliefs and statuary. Entry is via the north door, and the highlights include the **Lady Chapel**, with its wonderful fan vaulting, the much venerated Shrine of Edward the Confessor and **Poets' Corner**, where the likes of Chaucer, Tennyson, Charles Dickens and many others are buried, and still more, like Shakespeare and T.S. Eliot, are honoured.

Tate Britain

From Parliament Square, Millbank runs south to **Tate Britain** (daily 10am–5.50pm; free; Ⓦwww.tate.org.uk; Pimlico tube). Displaying British art from 1500 onwards, plus a whole wing devoted to Turner, it also showcases contemporary British artists. The galleries are rehung more or less annually, but always include a fair selection of works by Hogarth, Constable, Gainsborough, Reynolds, Blake, Spencer, Bacon, Hockney and others. The **Tate Boat** (Ⓣ020/7887 8888) carries passengers from Millbank to Tate Modern on Bankside (see opposite; every 40min; £4 single or £2.60 with a Travelcard).

Covent Garden

Northeast of Trafalgar Square lies the attractive area of **Covent Garden**, centred on the Piazza, London's oldest planned square, laid out in the 1630s, and now centred on the nineteenth-century market hall that housed the city's principal fruit and vegetable market until the 1970s. The structure now shelters a gaggle of tasteful shops and arty stalls. On the western side, by Inigo Jones's classical St Paul's Church, is a semi-institutionalized venue for buskers and more ambitious street performers. In the Piazza's southeast corner is the **London Transport Museum** (daily 10am–6pm, Fr 11am–9pm; £8; Ⓦwww.ltmuseum.co.uk), a fun scamper through the history – and possible future – of public transport.

The British Museum

The **British Museum** on Great Russell Street (Sat–Wed 10am–5.30pm, Thurs & Fri till 8.30pm; free; Ⓦwww.thebritishmuseum.ac.uk) is one of the great museums of the world. The building itself is the grandest of London's Greek Revival edifices, and is now even more amazing, thanks to Norman Foster's glass-and-steel covered Great Court, at the heart of which stands the **Round Reading Room**, where Karl Marx penned *Das Kapital*. With over four million exhibits, the museum is far too big to be seen comprehensively in one go – head for the two or three displays that interest you most. The museum's Roman and Greek antiquities are second to none, but the exhibits that steal the headlines are the **Parthenon Sculptures** – taken by Lord Elgin in 1801 and still the cause of discord between the British and Greek governments – and the **Rosetta stone**, which led to modern understanding of hieroglyphics. British archeological highlights include Saxon pieces from Sutton Hoo and the 2000-year-old Lindow Man, preserved in a Cheshire bog after his sacrificial death. One collection everyone heads for is the vast Egyptian mummy display upstairs, while high-profile exhibitions take place throughout the year (ticket prices vary).

The London Eye and South Bank

The South Bank of the Thames is home to one of London's most prominent landmarks, the **London Eye** (daily: Oct–May 10am–8pm, June–Sept 10am–9pm; £15; Ⓣ0800/500 0600, Ⓦwww.londoneye.com), a 135m-tall observation wheel that revolves above the Thames. From the Eye, a riverside footpath heads east past the strikingly ugly concrete edifices of the **South Bank Centre** (Ⓦwww.sbc.org.uk) and **National Theatre** (Ⓦwww.nationaltheatre.org.uk), taking in the craft shops and restaurants in Gabriel's Wharf and the OXO tower, for a mile or so before reaching Bankside, the old entertainment district of Tudor and Stuart London.

Tate Modern

Contemporary Bankside is dominated by the austere former power station, which has been transformed into **Tate Modern** (daily 10am–6pm, Fri & Sat till 10pm; free; Ⓦwww.tate.org.uk). The collection is arranged thematically, and revisions take place every six months or so, but you're pretty much guaranteed to see works by Monet, Bonnard, Matisse, Picasso, Dalí, Mondrian, Warhol and Rothko. For information on the Tate boat service see Tate Britain above. Major exhibitions run for about three months and tend to be very popular, so it's worth booking ahead.

Directly outside Tate Modern is Norman Foster's **Millennium Bridge**, London's famous bouncing bridge, which wobbled so worryingly when it first opened in 2000 that it was closed for repairs for almost two years. The crossing, with spectacular views, will take you effortlessly over to St Paul's Cathedral (see below).

Globe Theatre

Dwarfed by Tate Modern is **Shakespeare's Globe Theatre** (Ⓦwww.shakespeares-globe.org), a reconstruction of the polygonal playhouse where most of the Bard's later works were first performed. The Globe's pricey but stylish exhibition (daily: May–Sept 9am–5pm; Oct–April 10am–5pm; £9) is well worth a visit, and includes a guided tour of the theatre, except in the afternoons during the summer – when you're better off watching a show.

St Paul's Cathedral

The finest building in the area of London now known as the City is St Paul's Cathedral (Mon–Sat 8.30am–4pm; £9.50; Ⓦwww.stpauls.co.uk; St Paul's tube), designed by Christopher Wren. The most distinctive feature of this Baroque edifice is the dome, second in size only to St Peter's in Rome, and still a dominating presence on the London skyline. The interior of the church, recently cleaned and restored to its former glory, is filled with dull imperialist funerary monuments, for the most part, but a staircase in the south transept leads up to a series of galleries in the dome. The internal **Whispering Gallery** is the first, so called because of its acoustic properties – words whispered to the wall on one side are clearly audible on the other. The broad exterior Stone Gallery and the uppermost Golden Gallery both offer good panoramas over London. The **crypt** is the resting place of Wren himself, along with Turner, Reynolds and other artists, but the most imposing sarcophagi are the twin black monstrosities occupied by the Duke of Wellington and Lord Nelson.

Tower of London

The **Tower of London** (March–Oct Tues–Sat 9am–6pm, Sun & Mon 10am–6pm; Nov–Feb Tues–Sat 9am–5pm, Sun & Mon 10am–5pm; £16; Ⓦwww.hrp.org.uk), is on the river a mile southeast of St Paul's. Despite all the hype, it remains one of London's most remarkable buildings, and is somewhere all visitors should explore. For a start, the Tower is the most perfectly preserved (albeit heavily restored) medieval fortress in the country, begun by William the Conqueror, and pretty much completed by the end of the thirteenth century. Before you set off exploring, take one of the free tours given by the "Beefeaters", ex-servicemen in Tudor costume. The central White Tower holds part of the **Royal Armouries** collection (the rest resides in Leeds), and, on the second floor, the Norman Chapel of St John, London's oldest church. Close by is Tower Green, where the likes of Lady Jane Grey, Anne Boleyn and Catherine Howard were beheaded. The Waterloo Barracks house the **Crown Jewels**, among which are the three largest cut diamonds in the world.

Tower Bridge

River views from the Tower of London are dominated by the twin towers of **Tower Bridge**, completed in 1894 and now one of London's most famous landmarks. The raising of the bridge to allow tall ships through remains an impressive sight. Sadly, though, you can only visit the walkways linking the summits of the towers by joining a guided tour dubbed the "Tower Bridge Experience" (April–Sep 10am–6.30pm; Oct–March 9.30am–6pm; £6; Ⓦwww.towerbridge.org.uk).

Hyde Park

The best way to approach **Hyde Park**, London's largest central green space, is from the southeastern corner known as Hyde Park Corner. Here, in the middle of the traffic interchange, stands the **Wellington Arch** (Wed–Sun 10am–4/5pm; £3.20; EH), placed here to commemorate Wellington's victories in the Napoleonic Wars and now housing a small museum. In the middle of Hyde Park is the **Serpentine Lake**, with a popular lido towards its centre; the nearby **Serpentine Gallery** (daily 10am–6pm; free; Ⓦwww.serpentinegallery.org) hosts excellent contemporary art exhibitions. Nearby stands the **Albert Memorial**, an over-decorated Gothic canopy covering a gilded statue of Queen Victoria's much-mourned consort, who died in 1861.

Kensington Palace

To the west of Hyde Park are Kensington Gardens, leading to **Kensington Palace** (daily 10am–5/6pm; £12; Ⓦwww.hrp.org.uk), a modestly proportioned Jacobean brick mansion that was Princess Diana's London residence following her separation from Prince Charles. The highlights of the sparsely furnished state apartments are the *trompe-l'oeil* ceiling paintings by William Kent, and the oil paintings in the King's Gallery.

Victoria and Albert Museum

London's richest concentration of free museums lies to the south of Hyde Park. In terms of sheer variety and scale, the **Victoria and Albert Museum** (daily 10am–5.45pm; Fri until 10pm; free; Ⓦwww.vam.ac.uk), on Cromwell Road, is the greatest museum of applied arts in the world. The most celebrated of the V&A's numerous exhibits are the Raphael Cartoons, seven vast biblical paintings that served as templates for a set of tapestries destined for the Sistine Chapel. Other highlights include the refurbished Jameel gallery housing the enormous Ardabil carpet, the oldest in the world; fascinating displays of fashion through the ages, more Constable paintings than the Tate and a decent collection of Rodin sculptures.

Science Museum and the Natural History Museum

Established as a technological counterpart to the V&A, the **Science Museum** on Exhibition Road (daily 10am–6pm; free; Ⓦwww.sciencemuseum.org.uk) is undeniably impressive. First off, visit the Making of the Modern World, a display of inventions such as Puffing

Billy, the world's oldest surviving steam train, and a Ford Model T, the world's first mass-produced car. From here, the darkened, ultra-purple Wellcome Wing beckons you in, its ground floor dominated by the floating, sloping underbelly of the museum's IMAX cinema. The four floors of the Wellcome Wing are filled with hi-tech hands-on gadgetry. Back on Cromwell Road, the nearby **Natural History Museum** (Mon–Sat 10am–5.50pm; free; Ⓦwww.nhm.ac.uk) is London's most handsome museum. Most folk come here with the kids to see the Dinosaur gallery, and wince at the creepy-crawlies. Even more stunning, however, is the Red Zone, a visually exciting romp through the earth's evolution. The most popular sections are the slightly tasteless Kobe earthquake simulator, and the spectacular display of gems and crystals in the Earth's Treasury.

Madame Tussaud's

A short stroll southwest of Regent's Park, on busy Marylebone Road, is one of London's most enduring tourist traps, **Madame Tussaud's** (daily 9/9.30am–5.30/6.00pm; £25); Ⓦwww.madame-tussauds.co.uk), which has been pulling in the crowds since the good lady arrived in 1802 with the sculpted heads of guillotined aristocrats. The entrance fee might be extortionate, the likenesses risible, but you can still rely on finding some of London's biggest queues here.

London Zoo

As with almost all of London's royal parks, Londoners have Henry VIII to thank for Regent's Park, which he confiscated from the Church for yet more hunting grounds. Flanked by some of the city's most elegant residential buildings, the park is best known for **London Zoo** (daily 10am–4/5.30pm; £14.50; Ⓦwww.londonzoo.co.uk), one of the world's oldest and most varied collections of animals, which hides in the northeastern corner.

Hampstead Heath and Highgate Cemetery

North of Regent's Park is the affluent suburb of Hampstead, which gives access to **Hampstead Heath**, one of the few genuinely wild areas left within reach of central London. One major attraction east of Hampstead is **Highgate Cemetery**, ranged on both sides of Swains Lane (Highgate or Archway tube). Highgate's most famous corpse is Karl Marx, who lies in the East Cemetery (daily 10/11am–4/5pm; £2; Ⓦwww.highgate-cemetery.org); more atmospheric is the overgrown West Cemetery (guided tours only: March–Nov Mon–Fri 2pm, Sat & Sun hourly 11am–4pm; Dec–Feb Sat & Sun hourly 11am–3pm; £5), with its spooky Egyptian Avenue and terraced catacombs.

Greenwich

Some seven miles southeast of central London, **Greenwich** (pronounced "gren-itch") is one of London's most beguiling spots, a haven of water and sky looking northwards to the virile skyscrapers of Canary Wharf. Transport links are good: boats run regularly from Westminster Pier, trains run from Charing Cross, and the Docklands Light Railway scoots east from Bank or Tower Gateway in the City via the redeveloped Docklands, south to the Cutty Sark, the famous tea clipper, sadly closed for restoration after a devastating fire in 2007. Hugging the riverfront to the east is Christopher Wren's beautifully symmetrical Baroque ensemble of the **Old Royal Naval College** (daily 10am–5pm; free; Ⓦwww.greenwich-foundation.org.uk). Across the road the **National Maritime Museum** (daily 10am–5pm; free; Ⓦwww.nmm.ac.uk) exhibits model ships, charts and globes, and has been wonderfully rejuvenated with some inventive new galleries under an enormous glazed roof. From here Greenwich Park stretches up the hill, crowned by the Wren-inspired

Royal Observatory (daily 10am–5pm; free), home of Greenwich Mean Time and Zero Longitude and the suitably alien-looking Peter Harrison Planetarium (shows Mon–Fri hourly 1-4pm, Sat & Sun hourly 11am–4pm; £6), a bronze-clad cone embedded amid the original buildings, offering a mesmerising and informative journey through space.

Kew Gardens and Hampton Court

Boats ply westwards from Westminster Pier upstream to **Kew** where you'll find the **Royal Botanic Gardens** (daily 9.30am–dusk; £12.25; Kew Gardens tube; Ⓦwww.kew.org), established in 1759, and now home to over forty thousand species. Further upstream, thirteen miles southwest of the centre and also served by riverboat, is the finest of England's royal mansions, **Hampton Court Palace** (April–Oct daily 10am–6pm; Nov–March closes 4.30pm; £13; Ⓦwww.hrp.org.uk). Built in 1516 by the upwardly mobile Cardinal Wolsey, it was enlarged and improved by Henry VIII, and later rebuilt by William III who hired Wren to remodel the buildings. If your energy is lacking, the most rewarding sections are Henry VIII's State Apartments, which feature the glorious double hammerbeamed Great Hall, the King's Apartments, and the Tudor Kitchens. In the grounds, seek out the Great Vine, the Lower Orangery Exotics Garden, and, of course, the famous **Maze**, laid out in 1714, which lies just north of the palace.

Arrival

Air Flying into London, you'll arrive at one of the capital's five international airports: Heathrow, Gatwick or Stansted (Ⓦwww.baa.com), Luton (Ⓦwww.london-luton.co.uk) or City (Ⓦwww.londoncityairport.com). From **Heathrow**, fifteen miles west, the Piccadilly Line underground runs to central London in about an hour (£4), or there are Heathrow Express trains to Paddington Station (every 15min; £14.50). National Express also runs coach services to Victoria Coach Station (every 30min; 55min; from £4). After midnight, night bus #N9 runs to Trafalgar Square (every 20min; 1hr; £2). **Gatwick**, thirty miles south, is connected by several train companies: the Gatwick Express speeds to Victoria Station (every 15min; 30min; £14.90), although Southern trains on the same route are cheaper (every 15min; 45min; £8.90), and Thameslink trains run to Blackfriars and King's Cross (every 15min; 45min; around £10). **Stansted**, 34 miles northeast, is served by Stansted Express trains to Liverpool Street Station (every 15min; 45min; £14.50 single); hop off at Tottenham Hale to join the Victoria line. National Express services run to Victoria Coach Station (every 20/30min; 1hr 30min; £10), as does the Terravision Express Shuttle (Ⓦwww.lowcostcoach.com; every 30min; £8). From **Luton**, 37 miles north, free buses shuttle to Luton Airport Parkway station, from where there are Thameslink trains to King's Cross and Blackfriars stations and Midland Mainline trains to St Pancras Station (every 15min; 30min; £11). Green Line bus #757 runs from the airport terminal into central London (every 15/20min; 1hr 15min; £9). From **London City**, ten miles east, the best route into London is via the DLR (regular services; Bank 22min; £4).

Train Eurostar services from Paris or Brussels terminate at St Pancras International. Trains from the English Channel ports arrive at Victoria, Waterloo or Charing Cross stations, while those from elsewhere in Britain come into one of London's numerous mainline termini (most important are Paddington or Waterloo from the west, Euston or King's Cross from the north, and Liverpool Street from the east), all of which have tube stations.

Bus Buses from around Britain and continental Europe arrive at Victoria Coach Station, 500m walk south of Victoria train station.

Information

Tourist information London's flagship centre is the Britain and London Visitor Centre, near Piccadilly Circus at 1 Regent St (Mon 9.30am–6.30pm, Tues–Fri 9am–6.30pm, Sat 9am–5pm, Sun 10am–4pm; Ⓦwww.visitlondon.com), which has multi-lingual staff and Internet facilities, and also acts as a ticket and travel agency. There are other branches including: Greenwich (daily 10am–5pm), and Tate Modern (daily 10am–6pm). The City Information Centre (Mon–Sat 9.30am–5pm, Sun 10am–4.30pm; Ⓣ020/7332 1456, Ⓦwww.cityoflondon.gov.uk), opposite St Paul's Cathedral, is another well-run option.

OYSTER CARDS

The cheapest way to pay for single journeys in London is to use an **Oyster** swipe Card (ⓦtfl.gov.uk/oyster), valid on the Underground, buses and the DLR. You can store cash on the card as well as Travelcards and bus passes, and top it up at most stations when you need to. When using an Oyster, single bus fares are halved and tube fares in Zone 1 are reduced to £1.50. You can buy pre-loaded cards before you come to the UK from overseas agents, or order them from the Visit London website (ⓦwww.visitlondonoffers.com/oyster-card).

City transport

The **Transport for London (TfL) information** office at Piccadilly Circus tube station (Mon–Sat 7.15am–9pm, Sun 8.15am–8pm; ⓦwww.tfl.gov.uk) will provide free transport maps, with other desks at Heathrow Terminals 1, 2 and 3, and Euston, King's Cross, Liverpool Street and Victoria stations. There's also a 24-hour phone line for information on all bus, tube and river-boat services (ⓣ020/7222 1234).

Underground (metro) The quickest way to get around London is via the London Underground network (daily 5.30/7.30am–12.30am). Tickets must be bought in advance from the machines or booths in station entrance halls and need to be kept until the end of your journey so that you can leave the station; if you cannot produce a valid ticket on demand, you'll be charged an on-the-spot penalty fare of £20. A one-way journey in central Zone 1 costs a whopping £4, so it's worth getting an Oyster card (see above). To find your way around get a free tube map from a station – the various lines are colour coded and the beautifully designed map is simple to use.

Buses are a good way to see the city especially from the top of London's famous double deckers. In most of central London – and anywhere indicated with a yellow panel on the bus stop – you need to buy a single ticket (£2) from the machine at the bus stop before boarding. Show the ticket to the driver on entering. After midnight, night buses prefixed with the letter "N" take over; fares remain the same. Note that the majority of bus stops outside the centre are request stops.

Boats River-boat trips on the Thames are a great way to see the city. Westminster Pier, beside Westminster Bridge, Embankment Pier and Waterloo Pier, near the London Eye, are the main central embarkation points and there are regular sailings to Tower Bridge, Greenwich, Kew and Hampton Court. Timings and services alter frequently so pick up the Thames River Services Booklet from a TfL travel information office, phone ⓣ020/7222 1234 or visit ⓦwww.thamesclippers.com. Tickets are pricey but Travelcards get you a third off your fare.

Taxis If you're in a group, London's metered black cabs (taxis) can be a viable way of riding across the centre; there's a minimum £2.20 fare and a two mile journey costs around £5. However, after 8pm fares go sky high and you're best off using the tube. A yellow light in the roof above the windscreen tells you if the cab is available – just wave to hail it. To book in advance, call ⓣ020/7272 0272. Minicabs look just like regular cars and are considerably cheaper than black cabs, but you need to book by phone as you can't hail them in the street.

Bikes Cycling, although not for the faint-hearted, is popular in London. A good central option for bike hire is London Bicycle Tour Co (£3/hr, £18/day; ⓣ020/7928 6838, ⓦwww.londonbicycle.com) in Gabriel's Wharf on the South Bank, otherwise you can find hire shops through the London cycling campaign website (ⓦwww.lcc.org.uk). You can pick out cycle-friendly routes using the free London cycle guides available from transport information offices.

Accommodation

The Visit London hotel booking service (ⓣ0845/644 3010, ⓦwww.visitlondon.com) will get you the best available prices with no additional charge. Student rooms are also available over Easter and from July to September; try Imperial College (ⓣ020/7594 9507, ⓦwww.imperial.ac.uk) or the LSE (ⓣ020/7955 7370, ⓦwww.lse.ac.uk)

Hostels

To book a hostel bed, contact the individual hostels, or for HI hostels, the YHA (ⓣ0870 770 8868, ⓦwww.yha.org.uk). A good website for booking independent hostels is ⓦwww.hostellondon.com.

City of London 36 Carter Lane ⓣ0870 770 5764, ⓦwww.yha.org.uk. 200-bed hostel right by St Paul's Cathedral with crowded dorms or private rooms. The area is very quiet at night but it's close to the centre. St Paul's or Blackfriars tube. Dorms ❸, doubles ❾

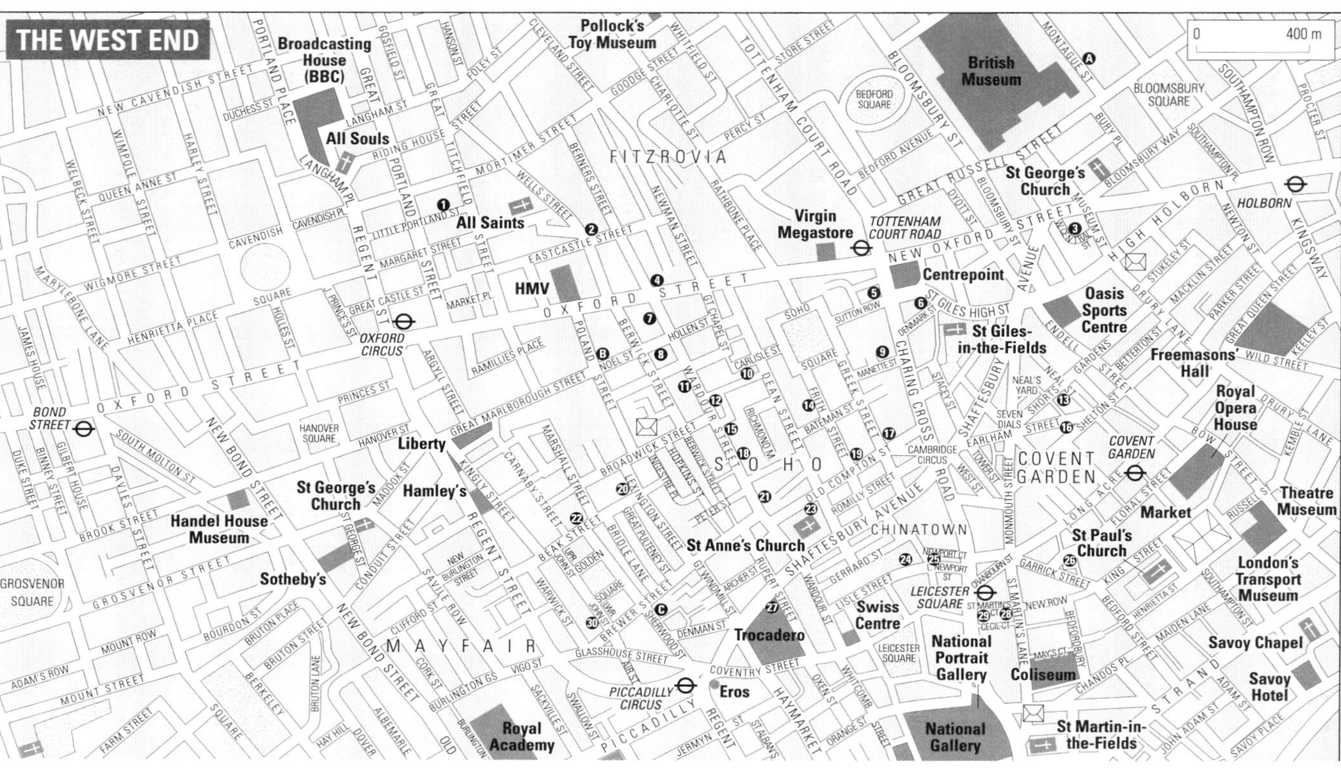
THE WEST END
0
400 m
Broadcasting House (BBC)
Pollock's Toy Museum
British Museum
All Souls
All Saints
FITZROVIA
St George's Church
Virgin Megastore
TOTTENHAM COURT ROAD
HOLBORN
Centrepoint
HMV
Oasis Sports Centre
St Giles-in-the-Fields
Freemasons' Hall
OXFORD CIRCUS
Royal Opera House
BOND STREET
Liberty
COVENT GARDEN
SOHO
COVENT GARDEN
St George's Church
Hamley's
Theatre Museum
Market
Handel House Museum
St Anne's Church
CHINATOWN
St Paul's Church
London's Transport Museum
GROSVENOR SQUARE
Sotheby's
LEICESTER SQUARE
Swiss Centre
Trocadero
National Portrait Gallery
Savoy Chapel
MAYFAIR
Coliseum
Savoy Hotel
PICCADILLY CIRCUS
Eros
Royal Academy
National Gallery
St Martin-in-the-Fields
BEDFORD SQUARE
BLOOMSBURY SQUARE
SOHO SQUARE
HANOVER SQUARE
LEICESTER SQUARE
PORTLAND PLACE
NEW CAVENDISH STREET
TOTTENHAM COURT ROAD
BLOOMSBURY ST
GREAT RUSSELL STREET
SOUTHAMPTON ROW
KINGSWAY
HIGH HOLBORN
NEW OXFORD STREET
OXFORD STREET
REGENT STREET
CHARING CROSS ROAD
SHAFTESBURY AVENUE
NEW BOND STREET
WARDOUR STREET
DEAN STREET
GREEK STREET
OLD COMPTON ST
CARNABY STREET
BERWICK STREET
DRURY LANE
LONG ACRE
BOW STREET
ST MARTIN'S LANE
STRAND
PICCADILLY
HAYMARKET
COVENTRY STREET
GLASSHOUSE STREET
SAVILE ROW
CONDUIT STREET
BROOK STREET
GROSVENOR STREET
WIGMORE STREET
HARLEY STREET
WIMPOLE STREET
MARYLEBONE LANE
BERKELEY SQUARE

EATING & DRINKING

100 Club	4	Gaby's	29
Aperitivo	22	Heaven	31
Bar Italia	19	Hummous Bros	18
Bar Rumba	27	Imli	11
Belgo Centraal	16	Imperial China	24
Borderline	9	Kulu Kulu	30
Busaba Eathai	15	The Lamb & Flag	26
Candy Bar	10	Malletti	8
The Champion	2	Maoz Vegetarian	23
Dog and Duck	14	Mildred's	20
The End	3	Mr. Jerk	7
First Out	6	Papaya	12
Food for Thought	13	Salisbury	28
Fook Sing	25	The Social	1
Freedom	21	Stockpot	17
G.A.Y.	5	The Wolseley	32

ACCOMMODATION

Museum Inn	A
Oxford Street	B
Piccadilly Hotel	C

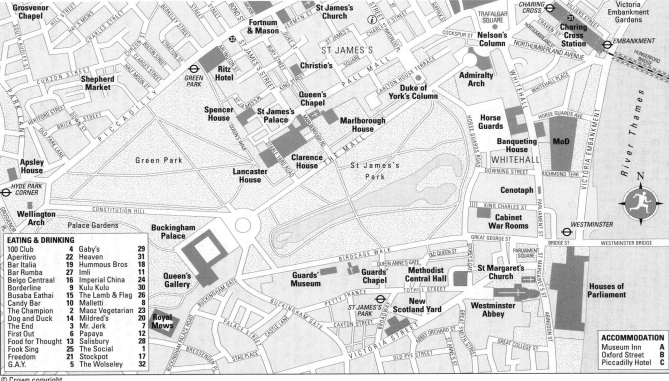

Earl's Court 38 Bolton Gardens ⓣ020/7373 7083, ⓦwww.yha.org.uk. Newly refurbished and comfortable with good-value meals. Earl's Court tube. Dorms ❹, doubles ❾
Generator Compton Place ⓣ020/7388 7666, ⓦwww.generatorhostels.com. Raucous, 837-bed hostel with neon-lit post-industrial decor and a youthful clientele. No doubles, twin rooms have bunks. Russell Sq or Euston tube. Dorms ❷, twins ❹
Holland Park Holland Walk ⓣ020/7937 0748, ⓦwww.yha.org.uk. Fairly convenient for the centre, with a nice location overlooking parkland. Dorms only. Holland Park or High St Kensington tube. Dorms ❹
Meininger 65-67 Queen's Gate ⓣ020/3051 8173, ⓦwww.meininger-hostels.com. Efficient operation within sight of the Natural History Museum. South Kensington or Gloucester Road tube. Dorms ❷, twin ❼
Oxford Street 14 Noel St ⓣ020/7734 1618, ⓦwww.yha.org.uk. In the heart of the West End, but with only 75 beds, it fills up fast. Discounts for weekly stays. Oxford Circus or Tottenham Court Rd tube. Dorms ❹, doubles ❽
Palmers Lodge 40 College Crescent ⓣ020/7483 8470, ⓦwww.palmerslodge.co.uk. Superb new hostel in a converted Victorian mansion. Mixed dorms include double beds for couples. Swiss Cottage tube. Dorms ❸, doubles ❺
Piccadilly Hotel 12 Sherwood Street ⓣ020/7434 9009, ⓦwww.piccadillybackpackers.com. A lively and friendly hostel situated in the heart of the West End. Private "Pod" beds available in some dorms. Piccadilly Circus tube. Dorms ❷, doubles ❽
St Christopher's Village 121 Borough High St ⓣ020/7407 1856, ⓦwww.st-christophers.co.uk. Upbeat and cheerful hostel in a series of buildings near London Bridge, with a café and late bar on site. London Bridge tube. Dorm ❷, twins ❺
St Pancras 79 Euston Rd ⓣ020/7388 9998, ⓦwww.yha.org.uk. Modern hostel in a good location opposite St Pancras station and within walking distance of both the West End and Camden Town. King's Cross tube. Dorms ❹, doubles ❾

Hotels and B&Bs

Hyde Park Rooms Hotel 136 Sussex Gardens ⓣ020/7723 0225, ⓦwww.hydeparkrooms.com. Welcoming, family-run B&B near Paddington station. Paddington tube. ❼
Oxford House 92–94 Cambridge St ⓣ020/7834 6467. Friendly B&B with pristine rooms and shared facilities; booking essential. Victoria tube. ❼
Philbeach 30–31 Philbeach Gardens ⓣ020/7373 1244, ⓦwww.philbeachhotel.co.uk. London's busiest gay hotel with a popular restaurant attached. Excellent student rates available. Earl's Court tube. ❾
Ridgemount 65–67 Gower St ⓣ020/7636 1141, ⓦwww.ridgemounthotel.co.uk. Old-fashioned, family-run Bloomsbury hotel with a garden and a laundry service. Goodge St tube. ❽

Campsites

Abbey Wood Federation Rd ⓣ020/8311 7708, ⓦwww.caravanclub.co.uk. Leafy, well-equipped Caravan Club site, east of Greenwich. Open all year. Train from Charing Cross to Abbey Wood. ❸
Crystal Palace Crystal Palace Parade ⓣ020/8778 7155, ⓦwww.caravanclub.co.uk. All-year Caravan Club site, maximum two weeks' stay in summer, three in winter. #3 bus from Piccadilly. ❷

Eating

London is a great place in which to **eat out** with the chance to sample more or less any kind of cuisine. The only drawback is that it can be very pricey, but for those on a budget, there are still plenty of options: Asian food, especially Indian and Bangladeshi curry, is the cheapest.

Snacks and quick meals

Bar Italia 22 Frith St. Open 24hr except Sun 7am–4am. Tiny, buzzing café serving coffee and snacks that's a Soho institution. Mains from £3.20. Leicester Sq tube.
Food For Thought 31 Neal St. Subterranean vegetarian restaurant serving delicious inexpensive food. Mains from £3. Covent Garden tube.
Fook Sing 25 Newport Court. No frills and not many tables at this Chinatown café, but the cooking which hails from China's Fujian province excites, as do the bargain prices. Mains from £4. Leicester Sq tube.
Gaby's 30 Charing Cross Rd. Jewish café serving a wide range of home-cooked veggie and Mediterranean specialities. Hard to beat for value, choice and location. Mains £3.80–£9.00. Leicester Sq tube.
Hummus Bros 88 Wardour St. The prices at this slick café are as attractive as their bowls of filling, sloppy houmous served with tasty extras. Mains £2.50–£5. Tottenham Court Rd tube.
Maoz Vegetarian 43 Old Compton St. Vegetarian fast-food falafel shop – open late, providing a healthy option for drunken revellers at under a fiver. Tottenham Court Rd tube
M. Manze 87 Tower Bridge Rd. Beautiful old pie shop selling authentic Cockney fare – a taste of old London at reliably low prices. Try pie & mash (£2.30) or the jellied eels (£2.35). Borough tube.
Mr Jerk 189 Wardour St. Excellent place to escape

TREAT YOURSELF

Tea at the Wolseley Traditional British afternoon tea doesn't come much more special than this. Exquisite cream teas from £9.50 in the Art Deco surroundings of the opulent *Wolseley* restaurant at 160 Piccadilly. Don't worry about dressing up though; the experience is surprisingly inclusive and relaxed.

the hordes of Oxford Street shoppers, this lively, compact place dishes up generous portions of Caribbean staples for under £10. Tottenham Court Rd tube.

Papaya 14 St Anne's Court. The limited menu, fresh flavours and no-nonsense decor make this Thai café a must, though not at weekends when it's closed. Mains £3.50. Tottenham Court Rd tube.

Story Deli 3 Dray Walk. A bit of a departure in this area known for its curry houses, but the pizzas here are among the best in town, veggie options are plentiful and all ingredients are organic. Mains under £10. Liverpool St tube.

Restaurants

Aperitivo 41 Beak St. Bustling, Italian tapas restaurant serving inventive dishes to share. Mains from £5.50. Oxford Circus tube.

Belgo Centraal 50 Earlham St. Hugely popular Belgian restaurant, famed for its mussels and dizzying selection of beers. Set lunch £5.95. Covent Garden tube.

Busaba Eathai 8–13 Bird St (other branches at Wardour St and Store St). Stylish surroundings complement stylish food in this sleek Thai restaurant. Mains £5.50–£9. Bond St tube.

Imli 167–169 Wardour St. A contemporary take on Indian food, serving curry tapas-style. Dishes start at around £4. Tottenham Court Rd tube.

Imperial China White Bear Yard, 25 Lisle St. Large restaurant with excellent *dim sum*, and service that is Chinatown brusque. Dishes from £2.30. Leicester Sq tube.

Kulu Kulu 76 Brewer St (other branches on Shelton St and Thurloe Place). Fine sushi at this authentic Japanese diner. No-frills but excellent value. Dishes £1.20–£3.60. Piccadilly Circus tube.

Mandalay 444 Edgware Rd. A real gem, serving pure, freshly cooked, unreconstructed Burmese cuisine. Closed Sun. Mains £3.90–£6.90. Edgware Rd tube.

Mildred's 45 Lexington St. Generous portions of tasty vegetarian fare served in a lively setting. Prices are good value and the food ranges from burgers to stir-fries. Light meals under £5. Closed Sun. Oxford Circus or Piccadilly Circus tube.

Mirch Masala 111–113 Commercial Road (other branches London Rd and Upper Tooting Rd). Close to, but not on, Brick Lane – home to pushy curry touts – this no-frills Punjabi keeps regulars happy with mains from £3. Bring your own bottle. Aldgate East or Whitechapel tube.

S&M Café 4–6 Essex Rd (other branches on Brushfield St and Portobello Rd, Ⓦwww.sandmcafe.co.uk). Evocative 1950s café with user-friendly menu comprising excellent sausage, mash and gravy. Mains £6. Angel tube.

Stockpot 18 Old Compton St. There's a touch of the school dinners about the menu here, but the *Stockpot* won't be beaten on price. Honest, reliable dishes from £3.50. Leicester Sq or Tottenham Court Rd tube.

Drinking and nightlife

From Victorian **pubs** serving ale to old gents, to hip **bars** and **clubs** frequented by an eternally young, hip clientele, London has it all. For a break from the West End head out east to the trendy Shoreditch and Old Street areas. That said, the places dubbed most fashionable seem to change as often as their patrons' haircuts, so it's worth buying a copy of *Time Out*, the weekly listings magazine.

Pubs and bars

Blackfriar 174 Queen Victoria St. One of the capital's most lovely and most unusual pubs, with marble walls, stained-glass windows and carved or illustrated monks in every nook and cranny. Blackfriars tube.

Dog & Duck 18 Bateman St. Tiny pub that's retained its old character and a loyal clientele. Leicester Sq tube.

Drunken Monkey 222 Shoreditch High Street. A warm, but lively ambience waits in this haven for cocktail and *dim sum* lovers. Old Street or Liverpool Street tube.

Flask 14 Flask Walk. Convivial local, close to the station and serving good food and real ale. Hampstead tube.

Jerusalem Tavern 55 Britton St. Cool Clerkenwell's the setting for this popular pub serving some of the best ales in London.

Lamb 94 Lamb's Conduit St. You can feel the history in this atmospheric boozer decorated with portraits of music hall stars. Holborn tube.

Lamb & Flag Rose St. A respite from hectic Covent Garden, this compact pub was once known as the

LONDON DRINKING ON A BUDGET

For a break from London's sky-high drink prices check out the sensitively restored Victorian pubs owned by the **Samuel Smith's** brewery. Prices are kept staggeringly low by the omission of large-corporation spirits and soft drinks, and a pint of lager will cost around £2. Try the *Cittie of York*, 22 High Holborn, the *Champion*, 12-13 Wells St or the *Fitzroy Tavern*, on Charlotte St, W1.

Bucket of Blood – after the prizefights held here. Covent Garden tube.

Loungelover 1 Whitby St. Lavish, bejewelled cocktail bar – you'll need to dress well if you don't want to feel intimidated. Exquisite cocktails don't come cheap – but even if you only have one, it's worth it for the fabulously camp decor. Liverpool St tube.

Ruby Lounge 33 Caledonian Road. Great pre-club bar with deep red walls and boudoir-like lighting. DJs spin some decent groove and funk tunes. Kings Cross tube.

Salisbury 90 St Martin's Lane. One of the most beautifully preserved Victorian pubs in the centre. Leicester Sq tube.

The Social 5 Little Portland St. Buzzing, industrial club/bar, with great DJs playing everything from rock to rap for a truly hedonistic crowd. Oxford Circus tube. Closed Sun.

Clubs

Bar Rumba 36 Shaftesbury Ave. Small West End venue with a programme of Latin, drum and bass and funk. Piccadilly Circus tube.

Cargo 83 Rivington Street. Live music bar/club with globally influenced music, trendy crowds and a laid back vibe. Old Street tube.

The End 16a West Central St. A club designed by clubbers for clubbers – large and spacious with chrome minimalist decor. Tottenham Court Rd tube.

Fabric 77a Charterhouse St. If you're seriously into dance music, head for Fabric at the weekends and get there early. Farringdon tube.

The Fridge 1 Town Hall Parade. A haven for hardcore fans of trance in this South London institution. Brixton tube.

Plastic People 147 Curtain Road. An intimate venue playing a mix of house, hip-hop, funk and jazz. Old Street or Liverpool St tube.

The Scala 278 Pentonville Rd. An eclectic club holding unusual and multi-faceted nights that take in film, live bands and music from hip-hop to deep house. King's Cross tube.

Gay and lesbian nightlife

Candy Bar 4 Carlisle St. Britain's first seven-day all-girl bar offers a retro-style cocktail bar-cum-pool room upstairs; a noisy, beery ground level cruising area. Tottenham Court Rd tube.

First Out 52 St Giles High St. The West End's original gay café/bar, and still permanently packed, serving good veggie food at reasonable prices. Mains from £6.25. Tottenham Court Rd tube.

Freedom 66 Wardour St, Soho. Hip, busy café/bar attracting a gay and straight crowd. Leicester Sq tube.

G.A.Y. The Astoria, 157 Charing Cross Rd. Huge, unpretentious and fun-loving dance nights for a young crowd on Fri & Sat. Tottenham Court Rd tube.

Heaven under the Arches, Villiers St. Britain's most popular gay club, this legendary, 2000-capacity club continues to reign supreme. Charing Cross or Embankment tube.

Entertainment

Cinemas

Prince Charles 2–7 Leicester Place Ⓦwww.princecharlescinema.com. The bargain basement of London's cinemas, with a programme of newish movies and cult favourites. Leicester Sq tube.

Curzon Cinemas Various locations including Soho, Mayfair and Chelsea. Arthouse chain specialising in European cinema.

National Film Theatre South Bank. Serious arts cinema showing up to ten different films each day. Waterloo tube.

Live music venues

100 Club 100 Oxford St. Historically important venue – the Sex Pistols played here – in a very central location hosting quality new talent. Tottenham Court Rd tube.

Barfly 49 Chalk Farm Road. Where a large array of punk, rock and indie bands make their debut. Camden Town or Chalk Farm tube.

Borderline Orange Yard, Manette St. Intimate venue best known for Indie and ska. Good place to catch new bands. Also has club nights. Tottenham Court Rd tube.

Jazz Café 5 Parkway. Futuristic, white-walled venue with an adventurous booking policy including Latin, rap, funk, hip-hop and musical fusions. Camden Town tube.

Luminaire 211 High Road. Fantastic recent addition to the indie scene, showcasing a diverse range of up-and-comers. Kilburn tube.

Theatres

London's West End **theatre** scene is dominated by big musicals, but there's plenty of other stuff on offer, too. Cut-price stand-by tickets can sometimes be had on the day, otherwise head for the large booth in Leicester Square selling half-price tickets (Mon–Sat 10am–7pm, Sun noon–3pm) for that day's performances at all West End theatres (they specialize in the top end of the price range). An even better bargain are the standing tickets for around £5 for the **Proms** (July–Sept), the annual classical music festival held at the Royal Albert Hall, or the free classical concerts that take place during weekday lunchtimes in the City's churches.

Donmar Warehouse Earlham St Ⓦwww.donmar-warehouse.com. Formerly the spiritual home of Sam Mendes, and the best bet for a central off-West End show. Covent Garden tube.

English National Opera Coliseum St Martin's Lane Ⓦwww.eno.org. More radical and democratic than the ROH, with opera (in English) and ballet. Leicester Sq tube.

ICA Nash House, The Mall Ⓦwww.ica.org.uk. Theatre, dance, films and art at London's enduringly cutting-edge HQ. Charing Cross tube.

National Theatre South Bank Centre, South Bank Ⓦwww.nationaltheatre.org.uk. The NT has three separate theatres, and consistently good productions – some sell out months in advance, but discounted day seats are available. Waterloo tube.

Sadler's Wells Rosebery Avenue Ⓦwww.sadlerswells.com. London's biggest dance venue puts on a mix of the best contemporary dance, kids' shows and ballet. Angel tube.

Shakespeare's Globe New Globe Walk Ⓦwww.shakespeares-globe.org.uk. Replica open-air Elizabethan theatre that puts on shows from mid-May to mid-Sept, with standing tickets for £5. London Bridge, Blackfriars or Southwark tube.

Shopping

London's up there with Paris and New York for sheer **shopping** variety and there are many stores you won't find anywhere else. If you're on a budget and can't afford to splurge, window shopping is still a great way of spending time; better still: visit one of the capital's famous markets (see below).

Shopping streets

Covent Garden (Ⓦwww.coventgardenlife.com) is a tourist destination in itself (see p.150) and host to designer stores and independent fashion outlets that line the Neal Street area, Floral Street and Long Acre.

Oxford Street Though dominated by tacky souvenir stores, this remains London's most famous and frequented shopping strip. It's home to gargantuan branches of high street shops including Top Shop, H&M and Nike Town.

Soho and Carnaby Street London's famously seedy red light district, with quirky fashion shops, independent record stores and erotica to suit the broadest of tastes. The western boundary of Soho is marked by Carnaby Street (Ⓦwww.carnaby.co.uk), which, although still trading heavily on its association with the swinging London of the sixties, is still a good bet for cool trainers and young fashion.

Markets

Borough Market Off Borough High St (Thurs 11am–5pm, Fri noon–6pm, Sat 9am–4pm). Atmospheric food market selling gourmet foods from game to English wine. If you haven't the money to spare, don't worry: a whole range of free tasters are on offer. London Bridge tube.

QUINTESSENTIAL LONDON SHOPS

Everyone heads to Harrods (Mon-Sat 10am-9pm, Sun noon-6pm; Ⓦwww.harrods.com) on Brompton Road. It's huge, sells just about anything and has an incredible food hall decked out in Arts and Crafts tiling. On Oxford Street, **Selfridges** (Mon-Fri 9.30am-8/9pm, Sun 11.30am-6.30pm; Ⓦwww.selfridges.com) is a juggernaut of a department store. Famous for its creative window displays, it sells everything from clothes and accessories to books and electronics. **Hamleys** (Mon-Sat 9/10am-8pm Sun noon-6pm; Ⓦwww.hamleys.com) on Regent Street is reputedly the world's largest toy shop and, if you can bear the children, it's worth having a play yourself or shopping for gifts. Just off Regent Street is Great Marlborough St and the elegant mock-Tudor department store **Liberty** (Mon–Sat 10am-7/9pm Sun noon-6pm; Ⓦwww.liberty.co.uk), with jewellery, scarves, bags and fabrics in rich, and peculiarly calming, surroundings.

Columbia Road market Columbia Rd (Sun 8am–1pm). Quite literally, London's most colourful market – a riot of fabulous flowers and plants surrounded by quirky jewellery and craft shops. Shoreditch or Liverpool St tube.
Portobello Road market Portobello and Golborne Rds (antique market Sat 4am–6pm; general market Mon–Wed 8am–6pm, Thurs 9am–1pm, Fri & Sat 7am–7pm). The antiques, bric-à-brac and assorted paraphernalia are still a draw, but the local fashionistas come for the vintage clothes and young designers' stalls under the Westway. Take time to explore well-heeled Notting Hill's funky shops and cafés. Ladbroke Grove or Notting Hill Gate tube.
Spitalfields Market Commercial St (Sun 10 am–5pm). Arty heart of the East End selling delicious ethnic food, crafts and fashionable clothes. Liverpool St tube.

Directory

Embassies Australia, Australia House, Strand ⓣ020/7379 4334 (Holborn tube); Canada, 38 Grosvenor Street ⓣ020/7258 6600 (Bond St tube); Ireland, 17 Grosvenor Place ⓣ020/7235 2171 (Hyde Park Corner tube); New Zealand, 80 Haymarket ⓣ020/7930 8422 (Piccadilly Circus tube); United States, 24 Grosvenor Square ⓣ020/7499 9000 (Bond St tube).
Exchange Shopping areas such as Oxford St and Covent Garden are littered with private exchange offices, but their rates are usually worse than the banks. You'll find branches of major banks all around the centre.
Hospitals St Mary's Hospital, Praed St ⓣ020/7886 6666 (Paddington tube); University College Hospital, Grafton Way ⓣ0845/1555 000 (Euston Square tube).
Internet easyEverything: 9 Tottenham Court Rd (Tottenham Court Rd tube), 358 Oxford St (Bond St tube), 456 Strand (Charing Cross tube) and across the city.
Left luggage At all airport terminals and major train stations.
Pharmacy Bliss, 5 Marble Arch, W1 (daily 9am–midnight). Marble Arch tube.
Post office 24–28 William IV St (Leicester Sq or Charing Cross tube). Mon–Fri 8.30am–6.30pm, Sat 9am–5.30pm.

Moving on

Train Aberdeen (12 daily; 7hr 30min); Bath (1–2 hourly; 1hr 30min); Brighton (every 15min; 1hr–1hr 20min); Bristol (every 30min; 1hr 45min); Cambridge (every 15min; 45min); Cardiff (hourly; 2hr–2hr 20min); Dover (every 30min; 1hr 45min); Durham (hourly; 2hr 45min); Glasgow (hourly; 5hr 30min); Liverpool (hourly; 2hr 45min); Manchester (every 30min; 2hr 20min); Newcastle (every 30min; 3hr); Oxford (every 20–30min; 1hr); Penzance (9 daily; 5hr 15min–7hr); Stratford-upon-Avon (5 daily; 2hr 15min); York (every 30min; 2hr).
International Eurostar services direct to Paris (13 daily; 2hr 15min); Lille (9 daily; 1hr 45 min); Brussels (6-9 daily; 2hr 5min).
Bus Aberdeen (5 daily; 12hr); Bath (hourly; 2hr 30min–4hr 20min); Brighton (hourly; 1hr 15min); Bristol (hourly; 2hr 30min); Cambridge (1–2 hourly; 2hr–3hrs); Cardiff (hourly; 3hr–4hr); Dover (1–2 hourly; 2hr 30min–3hr); Durham (6 daily; 6hr 20min–8hr 15 min); Edinburgh (6 daily; 8hr 40min–12hr 30min); Glasgow (9 daily; 7hr 50min–9hr 20min); Inverness (5 daily; 12hr 35min–13hr 30min); Liverpool (1–2 hourly; 4hr 50min–7hr 10min); Manchester (1–2 hourly; 4hr 15min–6 hr 35min); Newcastle (5 daily; 6hr 30min); Oxford (every 15min; 1hr 40min); Penzance (9 daily; 8hr 20min–9hr 55min); Stratford (5 daily; 3hr 15min–5hr 35min); York (hourly; 4hr 30min–6 20min).
International Amsterdam (3-5 daily; 12hrs); Berlin (1 daily; 19hrs); Dublin (3–5 daily; 12–16hrs); Paris (6 daily; 10–hrs).

Southeast England

Nestling in self-satisfied prosperity, **southeast England** is the richest part of Britain. Swift, frequent rail and coach services make it ideal for **day-trips** from London. Medieval ecclesiastical power-bases such as **Canterbury** and **Winchester** offer an introduction to the nation's history; while on the coast is the upbeat, hedonistic resort of **Brighton**, London's playground by the sea.

DOVER

DOVER is the main port of entry along this stretch of coast, and the country's busiest. It's not a particularly inspiring town, and its famous White Cliffs are best enjoyed from a boat several miles out. **Ferries** sail to Calais from the Eastern Docks, which is also the starting point for SpeedFerries' catamaran service to Boulogne. The main **train station**, for services to Canterbury and London (last one around 10pm), is Dover Priory, ten minutes' walk west of the centre and served by shuttle buses (£1) from the Eastern Docks. **Coaches** to London (last one around 8.20pm) pick up from both docks and the town-centre bus station on Pencester Road. The **tourist office** is on Biggin Street (daily 9/10am–4/5.30pm; Oct–March closed Sun; ⓣ01304/205108, ⓦwww.whitecliffscountry.org.uk).

CANTERBURY

CANTERBURY, one of England's oldest centres of Christianity, was home to the country's most famous martyr, Archbishop Thomas à Becket, who fell victim to Church–State rivalry in 1170. It became one of northern Europe's great pilgrimage sites, as Chaucer's *Canterbury Tales* attest, until Henry VIII had the martyr's shrine demolished in 1538. The cathedral remains the focal point of a compact centre, which is enclosed on three sides by medieval walls. Today, as well as hosting a sizeable student population, it's thronged with visitors, but remains relatively unspoilt.

What to see and do

Built in stages from 1070 onwards, the vast **Cathedral** (Mon–Sat 9am–5/6.30pm, Sun 12.30–2.30pm & 4.30–5.30pm; £6.50; ⓦwww.canterbury-cathedral.org) derives its distinctive presence from the perpendicular thrust of the late Gothic towers, dominated by the central, sixteenth-century Bell Harry tower. In the northwest transept, a modern sculpture, portraying ragged swords, is suspended over the place where Becket met his violent end. You'll also want to see the Romanesque arches of the crypt, one of the few remaining visible relics of the Norman Cathedral. East of the cathedral, across the ring road, are the evocative ruins of **St Augustine's Abbey** (April–June Wed–Sun 10am–5pm, July–Sep daily 10am–6pm, Sep–March Sun 11am–5pm; £4.00; EH), on the site of a church founded by St Augustine, who began the conversion of the English in 597. The best exposition of local history is provided by the interactive **Museum of Canterbury**, on Stour St (Mon–Sat 10.30am–5pm & June–Sept Sun 1.30–5pm; £3.40; ⓦwww.canterbury-museums.co.uk).

Arrival and Information

Train Canterbury has two train stations: Canterbury East for most services from London Victoria and Dover Priory, and Canterbury West for services from London Charing Cross – the stations are ten minutes south and northwest of the centre respectively.

Bus The bus station is on St George's Lane, below High Street.

Tourist Information The tourist office is opposite the entrance to the cathedral at 13 Sun St (Sep–Nov daily 9.30/10am–4/5pm; Dec–Feb closed Sun; March–August daily 10am–5/6pm, Sun 10am-4pm; ⓣ01227/378 100, ⓦwww.canterbury.co.uk).

Accommodation

Ann's House 63 London Rd ⓣ01227/768767. Traditional Victorian villa, a short walk from West Station, offering comfortable rooms, most en suite. ❼

KiPPS hostel 40 Nunnery Fields ⓣ01227/786121, ⓦwww.kipps-hostel.com. A short walk south of the centre, this friendly place has free Internet access and a garden with space for a couple of tents. Dorms ❸, doubles ❺

St Stephen's Guest House 100 St Stephen's Rd ⓣ01227/767644, ⓦwww.st-stephens.fsnet.co.uk. Ten minutes' walk north along the river Stour, this place has attractive gardens. ❼

YHA 54 New Dover Rd ⓣ0870/770 5744, ⓦwww.yha.org.uk. Victorian villa a mile southeast of the centre. There's a self-catering kitchen and Internet access. No doubles. Dorms ❹

Canterbury Camping & Caravanning Bekesbourne Lane ⓣ01227/463216, ⓦwww.campingandcaravanningclub.co.uk. A mile outside the city and served by regular buses. There's an attractive wooded area for backpackers. ❷

Eating and drinking

Bell & Crown 10 Palace St. A friendly medieval pub with excellent home-cooked food.

Café des Amis 95 St Dunstan's St. This popular place has been around for years and still has a loyal following for its authentic Mexican fare. Mains from £7.95.

Casey's 5 Butchery Lane. Irish pub serving Irish stew and soda bread, with occasional live folk music.

Coffee & Corks 13 Palace St. Serving delicious coffee in a bohemian sanctuary away from the crowds, this charming establishment has books, board games and an almost horizontally relaxed vibe.

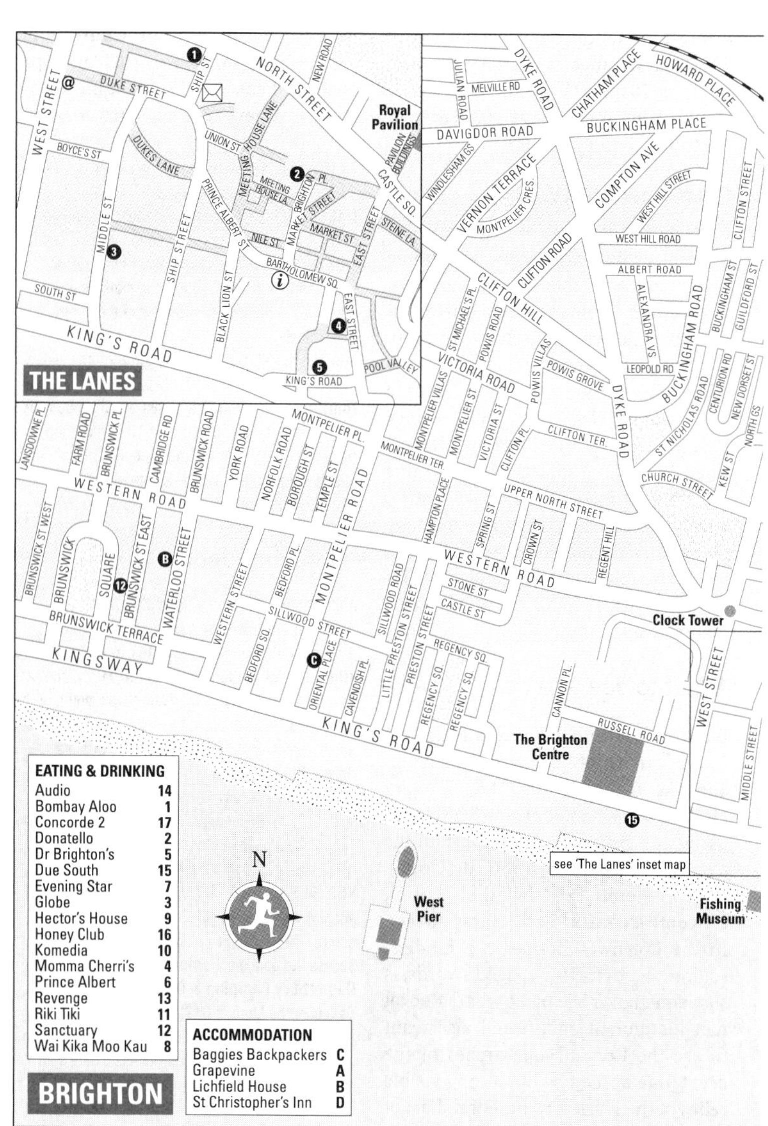

Lanna Thai 2 Dover St. Good Thai food at affordable prices. The special express lunch costs £8.50 for two courses and a drink.

Simple Simon's 3 Church Lane. Old hostelry, wedged down an impossibly narrow lane, popular with students, with live music almost nightly.

BRIGHTON

BRIGHTON has been a prime target for day-tripping Londoners since the Prince Regent (later George IV) started holidaying here in the 1770s with his mistress, launching a trend for the "dirty weekend".

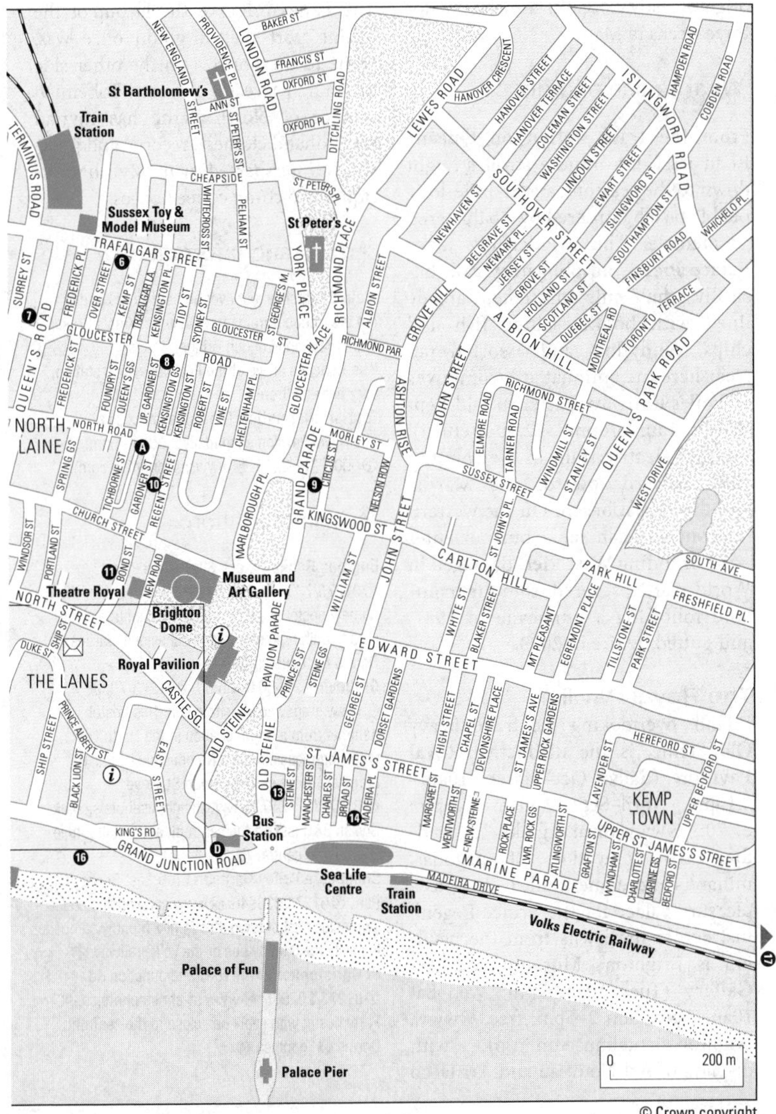

One of Britain's most entertaining seaside resorts, the city has emerged from seediness to embrace a new, fashionable hedonism, in the process becoming one of the country's premier gay centres. This factor – along with a large student presence – has endowed Brighton with a buzzing nightlife scene, and there's a colourful music and arts festival (Ⓦwww.brightonfestival.org.uk), which runs for three weeks in May.

What to see and do

From the train station on Queen's Road it's a ten-minute stroll straight down to the seafront, a four-mile-long pebble beach bordered by a balustered promenade. The wonderfully tacky **Palace Pier** is an obligatory call, basically a half-mile amusement arcade lined with booths selling fish and chips, candyfloss and assorted tat. Near here the antiquated locomotives of **Volk's Railway** (Easter to mid-Sept daily 11am–5/6pm; £2.50 return), the first electric train in the country, run eastward towards the Marina and the nudist beach. On the western seafront you can see – but not enter – the brooding **West Pier**, damaged in World War II, severed from the mainland following a hurricane in 1987, and gutted by fire in 2003.

The Royal Pavilion

Inland, overlooking the traffic-heavy Old Steine, is the distinctive **Royal Pavilion** (daily: Oct–March 10am–5.15pm, April–Sept 9.30am–5.45pm; £7.70; Ⓦwww.royal.org.uk), a wedding-cake confection of pagodas, minarets and domes built in 1817 as a pleasure palace for the Prince Regent. Just across the lawns from the pavilion is Brighton's **Museum and Art Gallery** (Tues 10am–7pm, Wed–Sat 10am–5pm, Sun 2–5pm; free; Ⓦwww.brighton.virtualmuseum.info), with displays of Art Nouveau and Art Deco furniture and a pair of the corpulent Prince Regent's enormous trousers.

The Lanes and North Laine

Lying to the south and north of the Pavilion and museum are two areas of shops and cafés that are among Brighton's main draws: a block back from the seafront, the narrow alleys of **The Lanes** preserve the layout of the fishing port that Brighton once was, while to the north – on the other side of Church Street – the arty, bohemian quarter of **North Laine** has myriad secondhand clothes-, record- and junkshops interspersed with stylish boutiques and co-op coffee houses.

Arrival and information

Train Brighton is just over an hour from London (on the frequent trains from Victoria, King's Cross, Blackfriars and London Bridge).

Bus Coaches arrive at the Pool Valley bus station, very near the front.

Tourist Information The tourist office is at The Royal Pavilion shop (daily 9.30am–5pm; Ⓣ0906/711 2255, Ⓦwww.visitbrighton.com).

Accommodation

Baggies Backpackers 33 Oriental Place Ⓣ01273/733740. Just beyond the West Pier this homely hostel has spacious rooms, a huge video library, guitars to strum, and occasional parties. Dorms ❷, doubles ❻

Grapevine 29–30 North Rd Ⓣ01273/703985, Ⓦwww.grapevinewebsite.co.uk. This hostel benefits from a great location in the North Laine, with clean, basic rooms. No doubles. Dorms ❸

Lichfield House 30 Waterloo St, Hove Ⓣ01273/777740, Ⓦwww.fieldhousehotels.co.uk. Stylish B&B just off the seafront, about half a mile west of the centre. ❽

Sheepcote Valley Caravan Club East Brighton Park Ⓣ01273/626546, Ⓦwww.caravanclub.co.uk. Two miles east of town, this family-friendly campsite is easily reached by bus or the Volks railway. ❷

St Christopher's Inn 10 Grand Junction Rd Ⓣ01273/202035, Ⓦwww.st-christophers.co.uk. Party hostel with lively bar, close to the seafront. Dorms ❸, doubles ❻

Eating

Bombay Aloo 39 Ship St. Indian place in the Lanes; check out the £5 all-you-can-eat veggie buffet.
Donatello 1–3 Brighton Place. Lively Italian in the Lanes serving Italian staples to a stream of hungry punters. Pizzas start from under £5.
Momma Cherri's 11 Little East St. Jambalaya, pig's feet and Southern-fried catfish are just some of the soul-food delicacies on offer at this fun American diner. Enormous mains for £11.
The Sanctuary 51 Brunswick St. Fresh fish, veggie treats and strumming musicians make this lovely café a local favourite. Mains from £6.
Wai Kika Moo Kau 11 Kensington Gardens. Funky global veggie café-restaurant in North Laine, with low prices. Mains from £6.

TREAT YOURSELF

For superior, yet relaxed, seafood head to **Due South** at 139 Kings Road Arches. Opened in 2003, it brings a classier touch to the sometimes tatty seafront. With an uninterrupted sea view, seasonal produce and scrumptious food, it's worth missing breakfast and lunch for. Mains from £12.50.

Drinking and nightlife

Brighton has a frenetic **nightlife** that can compete with that of many larger English cities and it's certainly the best on the south coast. We've listed a few of the most highly rated places below, but for full listings, pick up a copy of *The Brighton* magazine or check out ⓦwww.brighton.co.uk. Brighton also has a lively **gay scene**; for full details check out the free listings magazine *3Sixty* or ⓦwww.gay.brighton.co.uk.

Pubs

Dr Brighton's 16 Kings Rd. Popular gay haunt on the seafront.
Evening Star 55–56 Surrey St. This convivial pub near the station serves exemplary ales to a diverse crowd, managing to please both Brighton hipsters and ale-loving old timers. Live music in the evenings.
Globe 78 Middle Street. Recently refurbished pub, with a warm, wine-red interior, comfy armchairs and a growing reputation for good food.
Hector's House Grand Parade. A favourite student hangout with pre-club music and cheap drinks.
Prince Albert 48 Trafalgar St. Near the station, this pub has live rock and real ales, though the grubby interior might deter some.
Riki Tik 18a Bond St. Stylish, leather-clad cocktail bar that reverberates to the sounds of some of Brighton's top DJs. Open until 3am at weekends.

Clubs and live music

Audio 10 Marine Parade, ⓦwww.audiobrighton.com. This is Brighton's trendiest club, specializing in funk and house.
Concorde 2 Madeira Drive, ⓦwww.concorde2.co.uk. Live music venue with club nights at weekends.
Honeyclub 214 Kings Rd Arches, ⓦwww.thehoneyclub.co.uk. By the seafront near the bottom of Ship St, this attracts a youngish crowd, dancing to garage, house and hip-hop.
Komedia 44 Gardner St, ⓦwww.komedia.co.uk. Cool venue offering everything from cabaret to rock gigs.
Revenge 32 Old Steine, ⓦwww.revenge.co.uk. Predominantly gay venue. Cabaret on Mon night.

WINCHESTER

WINCHESTER's rural tranquillity betrays little of its former role as the political and ecclesiastical power base of southern England. A town of Roman foundation fifty miles southwest of London, Winchester rose to prominence in the ninth century as King Alfred the Great's capital, and remained influential well into the Middle Ages. The shrine of St Swithun, Alfred's tutor and Bishop of Winchester, made the town an important destination for pilgrims.

What to see and do

Alfred's statue stands at the eastern end of the Broadway, the town's main thoroughfare, which becomes High Street as it progresses west towards the train station. To the south of here is the **Cathedral** (daily 8.30am–6pm; £5 donation; ⓦwww.winchester-cathedral.org.uk); much of its exterior is twelfth-century, although there's some Norman stonework visible in the south transept. Above the high altar are mortuary chests holding the remains of the pre-Conquest kings of England. The Angel chapel contains sixteenth-century wall paintings of the miracles of the Virgin Mary, although a modern protective replica now covers the originals. Jane Austen is buried on the north side of the nave; the inscription on the floor slab remembers her merely as the daughter of a local clergyman, ignoring her renown as a novelist. Be sure to see Anthony Gormley's pensive statue in the periodically flooded crypt. Immediately outside are traces of the original Saxon cathedral, built by Cenwalh, king of Wessex, in the mid-seventh century. The true grandeur of this structure is shown by a model in the **City Museum** (April–Oct Mon–Sat 10am–5pm; Nov–March Tues–Sat 10am–4pm, Sun noon–4pm; free) on the western side of the cathedral close; other exhibits include mosaics and pottery from Roman Winchester.

The Great Hall

Further west along High Street is the thirteenth-century **Great Hall** (daily 10am–5pm; free), a banqueting chamber used by successive kings of England and renowned for what is alleged to be King Arthur's Round Table. South of the cathedral is the fourteenth-century Pilgrims Hall, from where a signposted route leads through a medieval quarter to **Winchester College**, the oldest of Britain's public schools. It's then a half-hour stroll across the Water Meadow to the hospital of **St Cross** (Mon–Sat 9.30/10.30am–3.30/5pm; £2.50), founded in 1132. Continuing a medieval tradition, needy wayfarers may still apply for the "dole" here – a tiny portion of bread and beer.

Arrival and information

Train Winchester's train station is about a mile northwest of the cathedral on Stockbridge Road.
Bus The bus terminal is on Broadway, just opposite the Guildhall.
Tourist Information The tourist office is situated in the Guildhall (Mon–Sat 9.30/10am–5/5.30pm, Sun 11am–4pm; Oct–April closed Sun; ⓣ01962/840500, ⓦwww.visitwinchester.co.uk).

Accommodation

Winchester is a pricey place to stay the night. There are no **hostels**, though the Morn Hill campsite is a decent option, two miles out (ⓣ01962/869877, ⓦwww.caravanclub.co.uk; ❷). Ask at the tourist office for B&B options (❻).

Eating and drinking

Alcatraz Rosso 24–26 Jewry St. Cool, modern restaurant serving pizza and pasta for around £7.
Blues 1A Southgate St. A good bet for lunch, this café offers snacks, filling meals and a buzzy atmosphere.
Wykeham Arms 75 Kingsgate Street. Just outside the cathedral precinct to the south, this traditional pub has cosy nooks and crannies and tasty, though not cheap, food.

The West Country

England's **West Country** has never been a precise geographical term, but as a broad generalization, the cosmopolitan feel of the southeast begins to fade into a slower, rural pace of life from **Salisbury** onwards, becoming more pronounced the further west you travel. In Neolithic times a rich and powerful culture evolved here, as shown by monuments such as **Stonehenge** and **Avebury**, and the isolated moorland sites of inland **Cornwall**. Urban attractions of western England include **Bristol** and the well-preserved Regency spa town of **Bath**; those in search of rural peace and quiet should head for the compelling bleakness of **Dartmoor**. The southwestern extremities of Britain include some of the most beautiful stretches of coastline, its rugged, rocky shores battered by the Atlantic, although the excellent sandy beaches make **Cornwall** one of the country's busiest corners over the summer. All of the region's major centres can be reached fairly easily by train or coach from London. Local bus services cover most areas, although in the rural depths of Dartmoor they can be very sparse indeed. Check the tourist office website Ⓦwww.westcountrynow.com.

SALISBURY

SALISBURY's central feature is the elegant spire of its **Cathedral** (daily 7.15am–6.15/7.15pm; £5.00 donation; Ⓦwww.salisburycathedral.org.uk), the tallest in the country, rising over 400ft. With the exception of the spire, the cathedral was almost entirely completed in the thirteenth century, and is one of the few great English churches that is not a hotch-potch of different styles. An octagonal **chapter house**, approached via the extensive **cloisters** (Mon–Sat 9.30/10am–5.15/6.45pm, Sun noon–5.30pm; free), holds a collection of precious manuscripts, among which is one of the four extant copies of the Magna Carta. Most of Salisbury's remaining sights are grouped in a sequence of historic houses around The Close, the old walled inner town around the cathedral. The **Salisbury and South Wiltshire Museum**, opposite the main portal of the cathedral on West Walk (Mon–Sat 10am–5pm; July & Aug also Sun 2–5pm; Ⓦwww.salisburymuseum.org.uk), is a good place to bone up on the Neolithic history of the region before heading out to Stonehenge and Avebury. **Mompesson House** on The Close's North Walk (April–Oct Sat–Wed 11am–5pm; £4.70) is a fine eighteenth-century house complete with Georgian furniture and fittings.

Arrival and information

Train It's a short walk east from Salisbury's train station (services from London Waterloo) across the River Avon into town.
Bus Buses from nearby Winchester and elsewhere terminate behind Endless St.
Tourist office A block south of the bus station, the tourist office is just off Market Square (daily 9.30/10.30am–4.30/6pm; closed Sun in winter; Ⓣ01722/334956, Ⓦwww.visitsalisbury.com).

Accommodation

Highveld 44 Hulse Rd Ⓣ01772/338172, Ⓦwww.salisburybedandbreakfast.com. B&B with a sweet cottage garden; not far from Salisbury centre. ⑦
94 Milford Hill 94 Milford Hill Ⓣ01722/322454. Small, comfortable B&B close to the youth hostel. ⑦
Salisbury Caravan Club Castle Rd Ⓣ01722/320713, Ⓦwww.campingandcaravanningclub.co.uk. A peaceful, family site a mile north of town. ②
YHA Milford Hill House, Milford Hill Ⓣ01722/327572, Ⓦwww.yha.org.uk. Excellent, secluded hostel five minutes' walk east of the city centre. Dorms ③, doubles ⑦

Eating and drinking

Haunch of Venison 1 Minster St. Tiny, atmospheric, old pub supposedly home to two ghosts, the "Grey Lady" and the "Demented Whist Player". The food's good, but expensive. Mains from £10.
Michael Snell's Tea Rooms St Thomas's Square. Patisserie and café, serving snacks and delicious buns.
The Mill 7 The Maltings. Popular pub offering bar meals and outdoor seating. Mains from £6.
Moloko 5 Bridge St. Cool café and vodka bar, open till late.

STONEHENGE

The uplands northwest of Salisbury were a thriving centre of Neolithic civilization, the greatest legacy of which is **STONEHENGE** (daily 9/9.30am–4/7pm; £6.30; EH). It's served by buses from Salisbury. You can also take a tour – ask at the bus station for details – or get an Explorer (£6.99) or Wiltshire Day Rover (£6.50) pass, which are valid all day and include travel to Avebury and Bath. The monument was built in several distinct stages and adapted to the needs of successive cultures, the first stones being raised within earthworks about 3500 BC. During the next six hundred years, the incomplete bluestone circle was transformed into the familiar formation observed today. At its centre are the five local Wiltshire sarsen stones up to 21ft in height and topped by horizontal slabs. The way in which the sun's rays penetrate the central enclosure at dawn on midsummer's day has led to speculation about Stonehenge's role as either an astronomical observatory or a place of sun worship. The only way to enter the circle itself is take a **guided tour outside visiting hours** (apply on ⓣ01722/343834 or at ⓦwww.english-heritage.org.uk; £12).

AVEBURY

Salisbury also serves as a base for visiting the more atmospheric Neolithic site at **AVEBURY**. Bus #5 runs here daily from Salisbury. The Avebury monoliths were probably erected soon after 2500 BC, and the main circle – with a diameter of some 1300ft – easily beats Stonehenge in terms of scale, though it's not as impressive in its architectural sophistication. The atmosphere here is far more relaxed, however, and you can contemplate the grassy site armed with a pint or two from the *Red Lion* village pub, set right beside the main stone circle. Avebury's **Alexander Keiller Museum** (daily 10am–4/6pm; £4.20) has displays on the monoliths, while the **Barn Gallery** (same times, same ticket) favours a more interactive approach. Both are worth visiting before or after exploring the cluster of archeological sites to the south of Avebury, best approached along the (signposted) **West Kennet Avenue**. The enormous conical mound of **Silbury Hill** just west of here, Europe's largest Neolithic construction, dating from around 2600 BC is the most impressive. Signposted up a track on the other side of the A4, **West Kennet Long Barrow** is a stone passage grave in use for over fifteen hundred years from about 3700 BC. Get details from Avebury's **tourist office** on Green Street (daily 9.30/10am–4.30/5.30pm; ⓣ01672/539425, ⓦwww.visitkennet.co.uk).

BATH

BATH is an ancient Roman spa revived in the eighteenth century as a retreat for the wealthy upper classes. Extensive reconstruction put into effect by Neoclassicist architects John Wood and his son, John Wood the Younger, gives the town its appearance, with terraces of honeyed sandstone fringed by spindly black railings.

What to see and do

The Roman Baths and Abbey

The hot spring that gave the city its name was dedicated to Sulis, the Celtic goddess of the waters, and provided the centrepiece of an extensive **Roman Baths** complex, now restored and holding a fascinating museum (daily 9/9.30am–5.30/6pm; July–Aug till 9pm; ⓦwww.romanbaths.co.uk; £10.25). The pools, pipes and underfloor heating are remarkable demonstrations of the ingenuity of Roman engineering. The **Pump Room** (free), built above the Roman site in the eighteenth century, is now a restaurant and tea room where you can sample the waters while listening to genteel tunes from the resident chamber ensemble. Next to the Roman Baths, **Bath Abbey** (Mon–Sat 9am–4.30/6pm, Sun 1–2.30pm & 4.30–5.30pm; £2.50 donation; ⓦwww.bathabbey.org) is renowned for the lofty fifteenth-century vault of its choir and the dense carpet of gravestones and memorials that cover the floor. The Abbey's **Heritage Vaults** (Mon–Sat 10am–4pm; free with Abbey donation) house Saxon and Norman objects and a reconstruction of the original building.

The Royal Crescent and Assembly Rooms

The best of Bath's eighteenth-century architecture is on the high ground to the north of the town centre, where the well-proportioned urban plan-

TREAT YOURSELF

Follow in the footsteps of Roman bathers and pamper yourself in stylish, contemporary surroundings at **Thermae Bath Spa** (daily 9am–8pm; ⓦwww.thermaebathspa.com), Britain's only natural hot spa. A two-hour session, with access to the spectacular open-air rooftop pool, costs £20.

ning of the Woods is showcased by the elegant **Circus** and the adjacent **Royal Crescent**. The house at **1 Royal Crescent** is now a museum (Tues–Sun 10.30am–5pm; closed Jan to early-Feb; £5), showing how the Crescent's houses would have looked in the Regency period. The social calendar of Bath's elite centred on John Wood the Younger's **Assembly Rooms** (daily 11am–5/6pm; £6.75), just east of the Circus; it includes the fascinating **Fashion Museum** (daily 11am–4pm; ⓦwww.fashionmuseum.co.uk; joint ticket with Roman Baths £13.50).

Arrival and information

Train and bus The train and bus stations are both on Manvers Street, five minutes south of the centre.
Tourist office The tourist office is just off the Abbey churchyard (Mon–Sat 9.30am–5/6pm, Sun 10am–4pm; ⓣ0906/711 2000, ⓦwww.visitbath.co.uk). Bath hosts the eclectic **International Music Festival** (ⓦwww.bathmusicfest.org.uk) in May and June. Accommodation at this time can be hard to find – indeed, you should book early if staying in Bath at any time.
Internet try the *Green Park Brasserie* at Old Green Park Station, off James St (ⓣ01225/338565; £3/hr).

Accommodation

Backpackers' Hostel 13 Pierrepoint St ⓣ01225/446787, ⓦwww.hostels.co.uk. Relaxed and centrally located hostel, just five minutes' walk north of the train and bus stations. No doubles. Dorms ❷.
Belmont 7 Belmont, Lansdowne Rd ⓣ01225/423082, ⓦwww.belmontbath.co.uk. Fairly large rooms in a house designed by John Wood near the Assembly Rooms and Circus. ❼
YHA Bathwick Hill ⓣ0870/770 5688, ⓦwww.yha.org.uk. A hillside villa a mile east of town; bus #18 or #418. Dorms £12.50.
YMCA Broad Street Place ⓣ01255/325900, ⓦwww.ymca.org.uk. Large, 67-room hostel in the centre of town. Dorms ❷, doubles ❻

Eating and drinking

Cafés and restaurants

Café Retro 18 York St. Popular café and bistro with an inventive international menu and a relaxed atmosphere. Great breakfasts too. Evening mains £3.50–£10. Closed Sun & Mon.
Walrus and Carpenter 28 Barton St. Friendly place behind the theatre, serving steaks and burgers as well as veggie dishes. Mains from £7.50.
Yum Yum 17 Kingsmead Sq. An antidote to countless genteel tea rooms, this Thai place serves fresh, inventive food. Try the £5.95 lunch special.

Pubs

The Bell 103 Walcot St. Everything you could want from a neighbourhood pub with a great range of beers, a mixed and lively crowd, garden and live music Mon and Wed eve, plus Sun lunch.
The Porter 15 George St. Something of a Bath institution, with decent vegetarian food at lunchtime, live music during the week and DJ sets at weekends. Next door is *Moles* club, the best, and only place to see decent live music in Bath.
The Salamander 3 John St. This small, characterful pub can get uncomfortably crowded with knowledgeable drinkers lapping up the locally brewed ales. The upstairs restaurant does exceptionally fine food, though it doesn't come cheap.

BRISTOL

Situated on a succession of lumpy hills twelve miles west of Bath and just inland from the mouth of the Avon, the city of **BRISTOL** grew rich on transatlantic trade – slaving, in particular – in the early part of the nineteenth century. It has moved on since then, while remaining a wealthy, commercial centre, and is home to a major university and a thriving cultural scene that produced some of the most significant bands (see entertainment and nightlife) of the nineties; and Banksy – guerrilla artist and agent provocateur whose subversive stencils adorn neglected city walls throughout the country. More ethnically diverse than other cities in the Southwest, in part because of its dubious heritage, Bristol manages to combine clued-up urban culture with enticing green spaces and striking industrial and domestic architecture.

What to see and do

The city centre – in so much as there is one – is an elongated traffic interchange. Its southern end gives onto the **Floating Harbour**, an area of waterways that formed the hub of the old port and is now the location of numerous bars and restaurants as well as two of Bristol's best contemporary arts venues, housed in converted warehouses on either side of the water: the **Arnolfini** (Ⓦwww.arnolfini.org.uk), a cool, white gallery space, and the **Watershed Arts Centre** (Ⓦwww.watershed.co.uk), which has a pleasant, reasonably priced café serving food until late. Behind the Watershed lies at-Bristol (Ⓦwww.at-bristol.org.uk), a hands-on science centre with all the usual interactive displays and hi-tech gadgetry.

From the Arnolfini, on Prince's Wharf, a swing bridge leads to the quayside **Bristol Industrial Museum,** which, at the time of writing, was closed for refurbishment (Ⓦwww.bristol-city.gov.uk/museums). Just east of here rises the **Church of St Mary Redcliffe** (Mon–Sat 8/8.30am–4/5pm, Sundays 8am–7pm), a glorious Gothic confection begun in the thirteenth century. A brief walk further east along busy Redcliffe Way brings you to the excellent **British Empire and Commonwealth Museum**, attached to the main train station (daily 10am–5pm; £7.95; Ⓦwww.empiremuseum.co.uk), which reviews Britain's colonial empire and the trading network that succeeded it.

SS Great Britain

A short walk west along the southern side of the harbour, or a brief ride on the ferry, brings you to Isambard Kingdom Brunel's **SS Great Britain** (daily 10am–4.30/6pm; £10.50) the world's first propeller-driven iron ship, launched from this dock in 1843, and to a replica of the *Matthew*, which carried John Cabot to North America in 1497. The former is a beautifully restored ship sitting on a wonderful "glass sea", allowing for exploration above and below the water line.

Clifton

The suburb of **CLIFTON** is a great place to wander with airy terraces reminiscent of the Georgian splendours of nearby Bath. It's a somewhat genteel quarter, but full of enticing pubs and with a spectacular focus in the **Clifton Suspension Bridge** (Ⓦwww.clifton-suspension-bridge.org.uk), another creation of the indefatigable engineer and railway builder Brunel, spanning the limestone abyss of the Avon Gorge. On a height above the bridge, the diminutive **Observatory** (daily 11am/noon–4/5pm; closed when cloudy; £2) holds a Victorian camera obscura which encompasses views of the gorge and bridge, and provides access to a steep tunnel ending at Giant's Cave, a ledge on the side of the gorge (same hours; £2).

Arrival and information

Air Bristol's airport is eight miles south of town. Regular buses run from the stations and the city centre.

Train Bristol's main Temple Meads train station is a five-minute bus ride southeast of the centre, or a fifteen-minute walk.

Bus The bus station is close to the Broadmead shopping centre on Marlborough Street.

Tourist office There's a tourist office in the at-Bristol complex on Harbourside (daily 10am–5/6pm; Ⓣ0906/711 2191, Ⓦwww.visitbristol.co.uk).

Accommodation

Bristol Backpackers 17 St Stephen's St ⓣ0117/925 7900, ⓦwww.bristolbackpackers.co.uk. Loud, friendly place in the heart of the pub district, with late bar and Internet access. Dorms ❸, twin ❻

Full Moon 1 North St ⓣ0117/924 5007, ⓦwww.fmbristol.co.uk. Slick new hostel, near the bus station, with a late bar and good food. Dorms ❸, twin ❻

YHA 14 Narrow Quay ⓣ0870/770 5726, ⓦwww.yha.org.uk. Splendidly situated hostel in an old wharfside building next to the Arnolfini. Dorms ❸, Twin ❼ (prices include breakfast).

Eating and drinking

Coronation Tap 8 Sion Place. Clifton institution, student favourite, and the home of Exhibition Cider, a lethal brew restricted to half pint measures. A must if you want to sample the West Country's regional tipple.

Cosies 34 Portland Sq. An unassuming wine bar by day, *Cosies* attracts a cool night-time crowd with dubstep, drum'n'bass and reggae.

Highbury Vaults 164 St Michael's Hill. Loved by locals and students alike, this homely establishment has a snug interior and a heated garden.

Olive Shed Floating Harbour, Princes Wharf. Located at the waterside amid ramshackle wharfs, this relaxed hangout serves delicious Mediterranean-style cuisine in charming surroundings. Tapas dishes from £2.50.

Planet Pizza 83 Whiteladies Rd. Good-value pizzeria with a mellow feel and some outside tables. Buy-one-get-one-free Sun–Wed. A quarter pizza £3.95.

Entertainment and nightlife

For **nightlife** listings galore check out the magazine *Venue* (ⓦwww.venue.co.uk; £1.50) available at any newsagent. Arnolfini and Watershed both have arts **cinemas**, and there's a renowned **theatre** company at the Old Vic on King St. In recent decades Bristol's vibrant music scene has produced a host of influential names (Tricky, Massive Attack, Portishead); top **clubs** are listed below.

Academy Frogmore St. Central and capacious club home to live bands and big-name DJs.

Blue Mountain Stokes Croft. Non-mainstream club spinning funk, hip-hop and drum'n'bass.

Thekla The Grove. Great riverboat venue staging eclectic events until 2am or later.

Moving on

Train Bath (every 20min; 11min–20min); Birmingham (every 30min; 1hr 30min); Cardiff (every 20 min; 40min); Salisbury (hourly; 1hr 10min); York (hourly; 4hr).

Bus Bath (3 daily; 50min); Birmingham (9–10 daily; 2hr–4hr 50min); Cardiff (every 1–2 hours; 1hr 10min); Oxford (1 daily; 2hr 50min); Salisbury (1 daily; 2hr 10 min).

GLASTONBURY

GLASTONBURY is a small rural town whose associations with the Holy Grail and King Arthur have made it a magnet for those with a taste for the mystical – the **Tor**, a natural mound overlooking the town, is identified with the Isle of Avalon and the young Jesus Christ was a supposed visitor.

The impressive ruins of the **Abbey** are approached from nearby Magdalene St (daily 9/10am–4.30/6pm; £4.50; ⓦwww.glastonburyabbey.com); the choir is alleged to hold the tomb of King Arthur and Guinevere. A mile to the east is the Tor, at the base of which stands the natural spring known as **Chalice Well** (Nov–Feb daily 10am–4pm, Mar–Oct daily 10am–

GLASTONBURY FESTIVAL

Glastonbury is synonymous with the world-famous **Glastonbury Festival** held at Worthy Farm over the last weekend in June. First hosted in 1970 by avuncular farmer, Michael Eavis, this small-scale event cost £1 including free milk from the farm. Nowadays, it draws 150,000-plus people to its binge of music, cabaret and all-round hedonism and the £150 tickets sell out in hours. Old-hands complain about the erection of the impenetrable security fence that now rings the site and the exorbitant cost of tickets, but there's still nothing else quite like it (ⓦwww.glastonburyfestivals.co.uk).

5.30pm; £3; ⓦwww.chalicewell.org.uk). The ferrous waters that flow from the hillside here were popularly thought to have gained their colour from the blood of Christ, supposedly flowing from the Holy Grail, buried here by Joseph of Arimathea.

The **tourist office** is housed in the Tribunal on the High Street (daily 10am–4/5.30pm; ⓣ01458/832954, ⓦwww.glastonburytic.co.uk). There's a friendly crowd at the Glastonbury Backpackers **hostel** on Market Place (ⓣ01458/833353, ⓦwww.glastonbury-backpackers.com; dorms ❸, rooms ❻), while the Isle of Avalon **campsite** is a short walk up Northload Street from the centre (ⓣ01458/833618; ❷). For **food and drink**, the *Backpackers* has cheap, filling meals and a lively bar with events.

DARTMOOR

Dartmoor (ⓦwww.dartmoor-npa.gov.uk) is one of England's most beautiful wilderness areas, an expanse of wild uplands some 75 miles southwest of Bristol. It's home to an indigenous breed of **wild pony** and dotted with **tors**, characteristic wind-eroded pillars of granite. One focus for visitors in the middle of the park is **POSTBRIDGE**, reached by local bus from Exeter and Plymouth on the #82 Transmoor service (twice daily in summer, weekends only in winter). Famous for its medieval bridge over the East Dart river, this is a good starting point for walks in the woodlands surrounding **Bellever Tor** to the south. Postbridge's **tourist office** is on the main road through the village (daily Easter–Oct daily 10am–5pm, Nov–Dec weekends 10am–4pm, closed Jan–Easter; ⓣ01822/880272, ⓦwww.dartmoor-npa.gov.uk). The nearest **hostel** is at Bellever, one mile south (ⓣ0870/770 5692, ⓦwww.yha.org.uk; dorms ❸, small discount for arrival on foot/bike).

> **Camping** wild on Dartmoor for one or two nights is permissible, though you shouldn't pitch on farmland, within 100m of a road or on an archaeological site.

Okehampton

The wildest parts of the moor, around its highest points of High Willhays and Yes Tor, are south of the market town of **OKEHAMPTON** – served by regular buses from Plymouth and Exeter. Despite the stark beauty of the terrain, this part of the moor is used by the Ministry of Defence as a firing range: details of times when it's safe to walk the moor are available from the **tourist office** on Fore Street (Mon–Sat 10am–5pm; ⓣ01837/53020, ⓦwww.okehampton.co.uk). Surrounded by woods one mile southwest of town is the now crumbling Norman keep of Okehampton Castle (April–Sept daily 10am–5/6pm; £3; EH). There's a YHA **hostel/activity centre** in a converted goods shed at the station (ⓣ0870/770 5978, ⓦwww.yha.org.uk; dorms ❸). Bike hire available.

THE EDEN PROJECT

In the heart of Cornwall, England's most southwesterly county, the **Eden Project** (April–Oct daily 10am–6pm, Nov–March daily 10am–4pm; £14; ⓦwww.edenproject.com) lies four miles northeast of St Austell (bus #T11 from St Austell train station or #T10 from Newquay). Occupying a 160-foot-deep disused clay pit, the centre showcases the diversity of the planet's plant-life in a stunningly landscaped site. The centrepiece is two vast geodesic "biomes", or conservatories, one holding plants more usually found in warm, temperate zones, and the larger of the two recreating a tropical environment, with teak and mahogany trees, and even a waterfall and river gushing through. Equally impressive are the external grounds, where the various plantations are interspersed with brilliant swathes of flowers. There are timed story-telling sessions, a lawn-carpeted arena where Celtic and other music is played, and good food on hand. Allow at least half a day for a full exploration, but arrive early to avoid congestion.

PENZANCE AND AROUND

The busy port of **PENZANCE** forms the natural gateway to the westernmost extremity of Cornwall – and, indeed, England – the Penwith Peninsula, and all the major sights of the region can be reached on day-trips from here. From the **train station**, at the northern end of town, Market Jew Street threads its way through the town centre, culminating in the Neoclassical facade of Market House, fronted by a statue of local-born chemist and inventor Humphry Davy. The centre's not particularly inspiring, though west of here, a series of pleasant parks and gardens punctuate the quiet residential streets overlooking the promenade. The **Penlee House Gallery and Museum**, off Morrab Road (Mon–Sat 10/10.30am–4.30/5pm; £3, free on Sat; Ⓦwww.penleehouse.org.uk), features works by members of the Newlyn school, late nineteenth-century painters of local land- and seascapes.

St Michael's Mount

The view east across the bay is dominated by **St Michael's Mount**, site of a fortified medieval monastery perched on an offshore pinnacle of rock. At low tide, the Mount is joined by a cobbled causeway to the mainland village of Marazion (regular buses from Penzance); at high tide, a boat can ferry you over (£1.50). You can amble around part of the Mount's shoreline, but most of the rock lies within the grounds of the **castle**, now a stately home belonging to Lord St Aubyn (April–Oct 10.30am–5.30pm, closed Sat; £6.40).

Land's End

The other obvious excursion is to **LAND'S END**, the extremity of the Penwith Peninsula, accessible on frequent buses from Penzance. Despite the hold it exerts over the popular imagination, the site may fail to live up to expectations – especially now that a particularly grim theme park has been built here – so it's worthwhile using the coastal path to explore some of the less frequented spots of the peninsula. A mile and a half south of Land's End you'll find rugged beauty at **Mill Bay**, while there are acres of beaches the same distance north at **Whitesand Bay**, and more spectacular headlands around **Cape Cornwall**, four miles north of Land's End.

Arrival and information

Train and bus Penzance train and bus stations are at the northeastern end of town, a step away from Market Jew Street.

Tourist office The tourist office (Easter–Sep daily 9am–5pm; October–Easter Mon–Fri 9am-5pm, Sat 10am–1pm; Ⓣ01736/362207, Ⓦwww.go-cornwall.com) is by the bus station.

Accommodation

Penzance Backpackers Alexandra Road Ⓣ01736/363836, Ⓦwww.pzbackpack.com. Friendly independent hostel on a quiet tree-lined road. dorms ❸, doubles ❺

Whitesands Hotel Sennen, near Whitesand Bay Ⓣ01736/871776. Excellent hotel with a cheaper surf lodge and tipis for groups. Tipis accommodate six (£80).

YHA Castle Horneck, Alverton Ⓣ0870/770 5992, Ⓦwww.yha.org.uk. Converted Georgian manor house about a mile from the centre off the Land's End Road. Closed Jan. dorms ❸, doubles ❼

Eating and drinking

The Admiral Benbow 46 Chapel Street. Seventeenth-century pub adorned with maritime fittings.

Archie Browns Bread Street. Veggie café and healthfood shop using locally sourced ingredients.

Cocos 12 Chapel Street. Colourful restaurant serving snacks, cakes, coffee as well as heartier fare. Mains from £9.00.

The Turk's Head Chapel Street. Ancient inn with a piratical heritage that includes a smugglers' tunnel. Touristy but fun.

CORNISH INDEPENDENCE

Though very few still speak the Cornish language fluently, many residents consider themselves as having Celtic ancestry and there is a small but vocal **Cornish independence** movement. The ultimate aim of greater autonomy from Westminster is likely to remain unfulfilled, but the cause received an unexpected boost, in 2004, when, during a Christmas episode of *The Simpsons*, Lisa Simpson was spied waving the black and white Cornish flag and shouting Cornish political slogans.

ST IVES AND THE NORTH CORNWALL COAST

Across the peninsula from Penzance, the fishing village of **ST IVES** is the quintessential Cornish resort, featuring a maze of narrow streets lined with whitewashed cottages, sandy beaches and lush subtropical flora. The village's erstwhile tranquillity attracted several major artists throughout the twentieth century – Ben Nicholson and Barbara Hepworth among them. You can see examples of the work of these and others at **Tate St Ives**, overlooking Porthmeor Beach (daily 10am–4.20/5.20pm; Nov–Feb closed Mon; £5.75; ⓦwww.tate.org.uk/stives). A combined ticket (£8.75) admits you to the much more charming **Barbara Hepworth Museum and Garden** on Barnoon Hill (same hours), which preserves the studio of the modernist sculptor. Of the town's three beaches, the north-facing Porthmeor occasionally has good surf, and boards can be rented at the beach.

The **train station** is at Porthminster Beach, just north of the **bus station** on Station Hill. The **tourist office** in the Guildhall, Street an Pol (June to Sep Mon–Sat 9am–5/5.30pm, Sun 10am–4pm; Oct to May Mon–Fri 9am–5pm, Sat 10am–1pm; ⓣ01736/796297, ⓦwww.go-cornwall.com), is a couple of minutes from both stations. Nearby is the *St Ives Backpackers* **hostel**, in a restored Wesleyan chapel on The Stennack, opposite the cinema (ⓣ01736/799444, ⓦwww.backpackers.co.uk/st-ives; dorms ❸, doubles ❻).

Newquay

Buffeted by Atlantic currents, Cornwall's north coast has a harsh grandeur, and is the area of the West Country most favoured by the **surfing** set. King of the surf resorts is **NEWQUAY**, whose somewhat tacky centre is surrounded by seven miles of golden sands, including Fistral Beach, the venue for surfing championships. There's a **tourist office** at Marcus Hill (mid-May to mid-Sept Mon–Sat 9.30am–5.30pm, Sun 9.30am–1pm; mid-Sept to mid-May Mon–Fri 9.30am–4.30pm, Sat 9.30am–12.30pm; ⓣ01637/854020, ⓦwww.newquay.co.uk), and numerous campsites and hostels, including *Newquay International Backpackers*, 69 Tower Rd (ⓣ01637/879366, ⓦwww.backpackers.co.uk/newquay; dorms ❸, doubles ❼), and *Matt's Surf Lodge*, 110 Mount Wise (ⓣ01637/874651, ⓦwww.matts-surf-lodge.co.uk; dorms ❸, doubles ❻).

Padstow

Ten miles north, **PADSTOW** makes a more appealing base for some first-class beaches, such as Constantine Bay, four miles west, and Polzeath, on the eastern side of the Camel estuary. Primarily a fishing port, Padstow is renowned for its fish restaurants, not least those belonging to celebrity chef Rick Stein; dodge the expensive *Seafood Restaurant* and *St Petroc's Bistro* in favour of the more casual *Rick Stein's Café*, 10 Middle St, which serves lunchtime snacks and moderately priced evening meals, his *Seafood Deli* on South Quay for take-aways, and *Stein's Fish & Chips* (from £5.96), also on South Quay. There's a YHA **hostel** just off the beach at Treyarnon Bay (Ⓣ0870/770 6076, Ⓦwww.yha.org.uk; call for winter opening; dorms ❸, doubles ❼).

Central England

Central England was the powerhouse of the Industrial Revolution and its once gritty towns and cities are gradually reinventing themselves. Birmingham, at the hub of this sprawl, boasts one of the best concert halls and orchestras in the country, but is still unlikely to feature on a whistlestop national tour. The university town of **Oxford**, and **Stratford-upon-Avon**, the birthplace of William Shakespeare, are the main draws here – and, in the east of the region, the other major university town of **Cambridge**.

OXFORD

Think of **OXFORD** and inevitably you think of its university, revered as one of the world's great academic institutions, inhabiting honeystone buildings set around ivy-clad quadrangles. The **university,** which dominates the town centre, has long operated a collegiate system in which many students and tutors live, work and take their meals together in the same complex of buildings – usually a couple of quadrangles ("quads") with a chapel, library and dining hall. Taken together, the colleges form a dense maze of historic buildings in the heart of the city. Note that access may be restricted during examinations – especially in May and June – conferences and functions.

What to see and do

The main point of reference is **Carfax**, a central crossroads overlooked by the chunky **Carfax Tower** (daily 10am–4/5pm; £2), one of many opportunities to enjoy a panorama of Oxford's "dreaming spires".

Christ Church, Merton and Magdalen colleges

From here, head south down St Aldates to the biggest of Oxford's colleges, **Christ Church** (Mon–Sat 9am–5pm, Sun 1–5pm; £4.90). The main entrance – though visitors are usually ushered in further south – is overlooked by the imposing Tom Tower, built in 1681 by Wren, and opens onto the vast expanse of Tom Quad, mostly dating from the college's foundation in the sixteenth century. An indication of the prestige and wealth of the college is that the city's late Norman **cathedral** also serves as the college chapel.

South of Christ Church, **Christ Church Meadow** offers gentle walks – either east along Broad Walk to the River Cherwell or south along New Walk to the Thames (referred to hereabouts as the Isis). From the Broad Walk, paths lead to **Merton** (Mon–Fri 2–4pm, Sat & Sun 10am–4pm; free), perhaps the prettiest of the city's colleges, and Rose Lane, which emerges at the eastern

PUNTING OXBRIDGE

Hiring a **punt** – essentially a flat-bottomed Venetian-style gondola powered by a brave soul brandishing a pole – is one of the finest ways to experience both Oxford and Cambridge. In Oxford, Cherwell boathouse (Ⓦwww.cherwellboathouse.co.uk) rents punts for £12 an hour for exploration of the less touristy upstream stretch of the River Cherwell or, for a more central option, try the Magdalen Bridge Boathouse. In Cambridge, Scudamore's punts (Ⓦwww.scudamores.co.uk) can be hired from £14 an hour for a cruise downstream past the architectural splendours of the college Backs or, for the adventurous, a trip upstream to rural Grantchester.

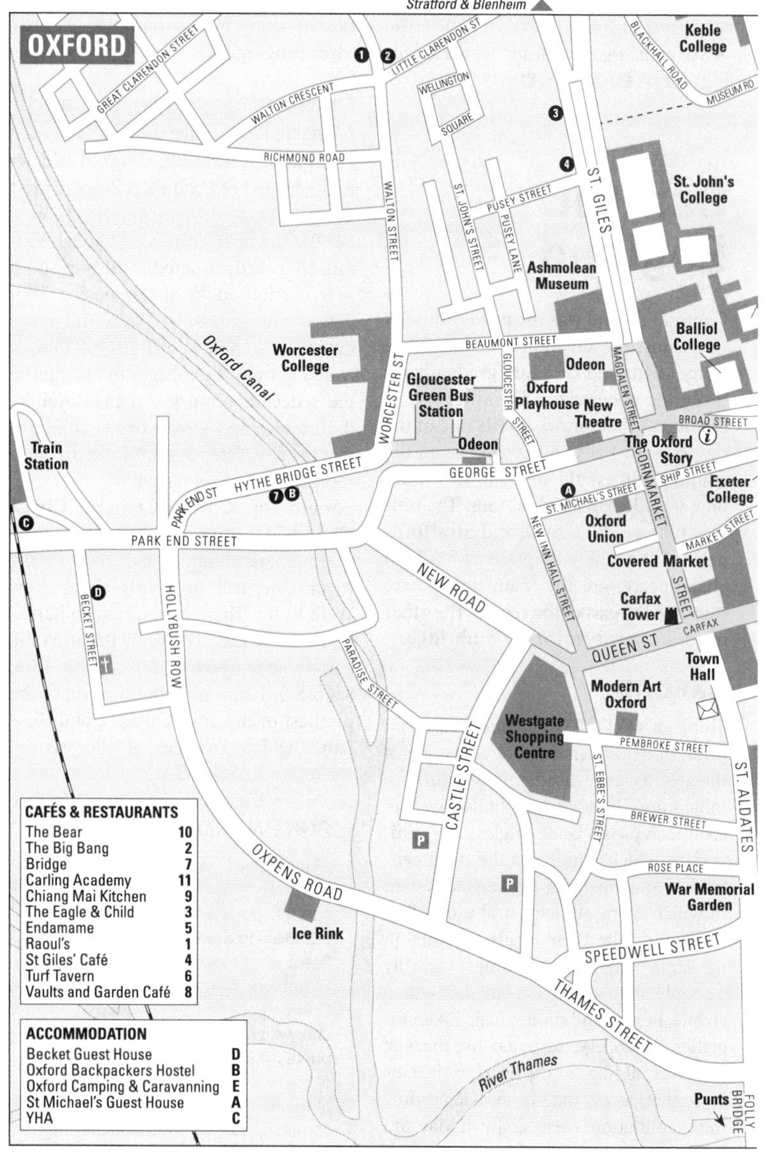

end of the High St opposite **Magdalen College** (pronounced "maudlin"; daily noon/1–6pm; £3). From here, it's a brief stroll to the bridge over the River Cherwell, where you can rent **punts** in summer. (See box, p.169)

The Radcliffe Camera, Bodleian Library and the Sheldonian

Many of the university's most important and imposing buildings lie just north of the High Street. The most dramatic

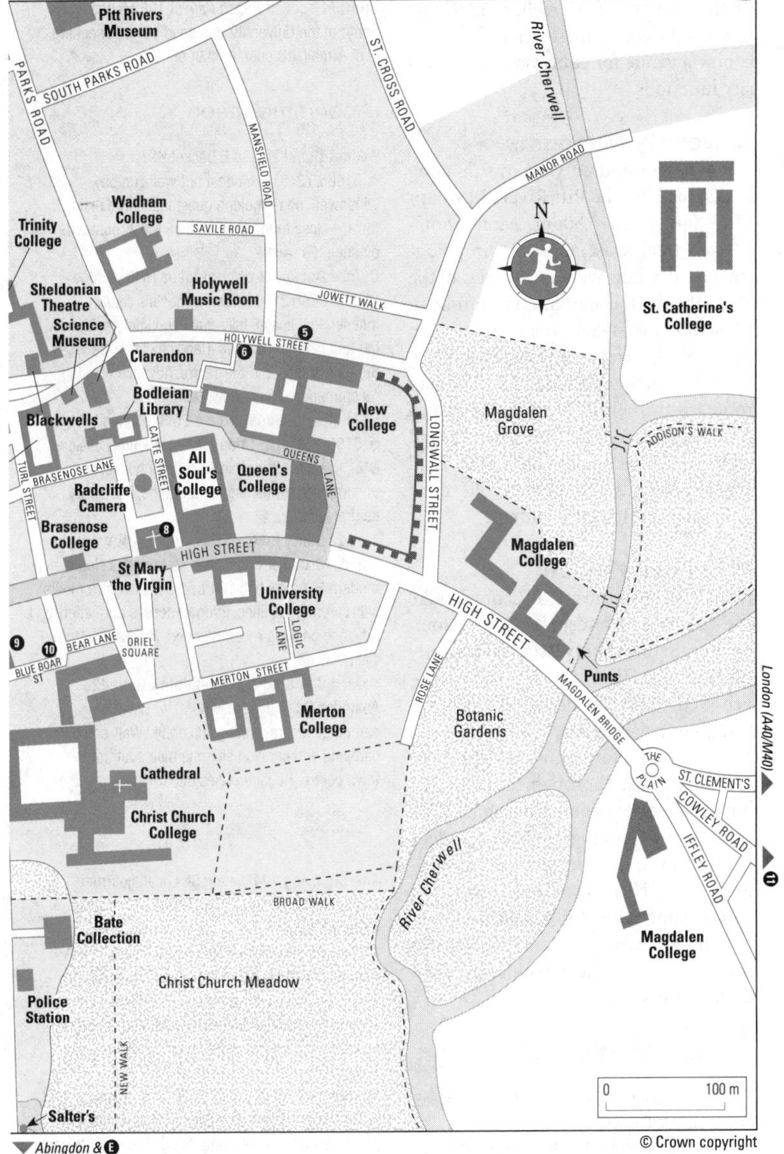

is the Italianate **Radcliffe Camera**. Built in the 1730s by James Gibbs, it is now used as a reading room for the **Bodleian Library**, whose main building is immediately to the north in the Old Schools Quadrangle. Most of the library is closed to the general public, but you can see several parts of it on an hour-long guided tour (Mon–Sat 10.30 & 11.30am & 2 & 4pm; £6). The adjacent **Sheldonian Theatre** (Mon–Sat 10am–12.30pm & 2–3.30/4.30pm; £2), a copy of the Theatre of Marcellus in Rome, was designed by Christopher Wren and is now a venue for concerts and university functions.

University Museums

A couple of hundred yards north along Parks Road lies the **Pitt Rivers Museum** (Tue–Sun 10am–4.30pm, Mon noon–4.30pm; free), a fascinating anthropological hoard, while five minutes west of the Sheldonian is the mammoth **Ashmolean Museum** (Tues–Sat 10am–5pm, Sun noon–5pm; free; Ⓦwww.ashmolean.org). Highlights include the Egyptian rooms with their well-preserved mummies and sarcophagi; the Islamic and Chinese art sections, which both hold superb ceramics; and the rich collections of French and Italian paintings.

Bleinheim Palace

Eight miles northwest of Oxford (take the #20 bus to Woodstock) sprawls John Vanburgh's **Blenheim Palace** (Feb–early Dec daily 10.30am–5.30pm; early Dec–Feb Wed–Sun same hours; £16; Ⓦwww.bleinheimpalace.com), conceived in 1705 as a gift for John Churchill, the 1st Duke of Marlborough, and later the birthplace of Winston Churchill. With carvings by Grinling Gibbons, gardens laid out by Capability Brown and ceilings from Nicholas Hawksmoor, the palace showcases top eighteenth-century British creative talent and benefits from a colourful new exhibition elucidating its history.

Arrival and information

Train From Oxford's train station, it's a five- to ten-minute walk to the centre.
Bus Long-distance buses terminate at the central Gloucester Green bus station.
Tourist office The tourist office is at 15 Broad St (Mon–Sat 9.30am–5pm, Easter–Oct also Sun 10am–3.30pm; Ⓣ01865/726871, Ⓦwww.visitoxford.org).
Bike rental Bike Zone at 6 Lincoln House, Market St, off Cornmarket (Ⓣ01865/728877), is the best place for rental.
Internet access *Reach Café* at 138 Magdalen Rd, South of the University, is a good bet for checking your e-mail. It's open until 9pm.

Accommodation

Becket Guest House 5 Becket St Ⓣ01865/724675. Modest but well-run bay-windowed, non-smoking guesthouse in a plain terrace close to the train station. Most rooms are en suite. ❼
Oxford Backpackers Hostel 9a Hythe Bridge St Ⓣ01865/721761, Ⓦwww.hostels.co.uk. Independent hostel, fully-equipped kitchen, laundry, bar and internet facilities. Handy location, between the train station and the centre. Advance booking recommended. No curfew. Dorms ❸
St Michael's Guest House 26 St Michael's St Ⓣ01865/242101. Often full, this friendly, basic B&B, in a cosy three-storey terrace house, has unsurprising furnishings and fittings, but a very central location. ❼
YHA 2a Botley Rd Ⓣ0870/770 5970, Ⓦwww.yha.org.uk. Next door to the train station, this clean, modern HI hostel has 184 beds, inexpensive meals, self-catering facilities, internet access and laundry. Advance booking recommended. No curfew. Dorms ❹, twins ❼
Oxford Camping & Caravanning Club 426 Abingdon Rd Ⓣ01865/244088, Ⓦwww.campingandcaravanningclub.co.uk. Well-equipped camping and caravan site one mile south of the town centre. Regular buses into town. ❷

Eating

The Big Bang 124 Walton St. Local, gourmet sausages and quality mash. The £4.50 lunch menu's a bargain.
Chiang Mai Kitchen Kemp Hall Passage, 130A High St Ⓣ01865/202233. Superb Thai food – including a vegetarian menu – and excellent service, in a timber-framed seventeenth-century building off the west end of High St. Mains from £7.50.
Endamame 15 Holywell St. Terrific Japanese food and modest prices have quickly secured this tiny restaurant a loyal following. Mains from £6. Closed Tues, Wed & Sun eves and all day Mon.
St Giles' Café 52 St Giles. Modern furnishings, but the food is unreconstructed greasy spoon; enormous cooked breakfasts for £5.
Vaults and Garden Café University Church, High Street. Organic café on Radcliffe Square, open for breakfast and lunch, serving tasty salads, soups and main meals for under £5.

Drinking and nightlife

For listings of gigs and other events, consult *Daily Info*, a poster put up in colleges and all around town (daily term-time, otherwise weekly; Ⓦwww.dailyinfo.co.uk).

The Bear 6 Alfred St. Ancient inn with low ceilings, real ales and snippets from interesting neck ties – proffered by their owners in exchange for a pint.

The Bridge 6 Hythe Bridge St. Mainstream club plying drunken punters with commercial dance, RnB and pop.

Carling Academy 190 Cowley Rd Ⓣ01865/420042, Ⓦwww.oxford-academy.co.uk. Oxford's most respected live music and dance venue, with bands and club nights throughout the week.

The Eagle & Child 49 St Giles. This pub was once the haunt of J.R.R. Tolkien, C.S. Lewis and other literary types, and still attracts an engaging mix of professionals and academics.

Raoul's 32 Walton St. The place to head if you can't stomach another historical tavern. Clean lines, fun, retro decor and great cocktails.

Turf Tavern Off Holywell St. This atmospheric pub, tucked down a winding alleyway (which also connects with New College Lane), offers good food, fine ales and outdoor seating.

STRATFORD-UPON-AVON

STRATFORD-UPON-AVON makes the most of its association with William Shakespeare, who was born here on April 23, 1564. There are five restored properties recalling the Bard, three in the town itself and two on the outskirts. If you've time to visit them all, it's worth considering a **combined ticket** on sale at all five sites (£9/three town properties, £13/all five); otherwise save your money and go and watch the excellent Royal Shakespeare Company instead (see below).

What to see and do

Top of everyone's Bardic itinerary is **Shakespeare's Birthplace Museum** (Nov–March Mon–Sat 10am–4pm, Sun 10.30am–4pm; April–May & Sept–Oct Mon–Sat 10am–5pm, Sun 10.30am–5pm; Jun–Aug Mon–Sat 9am–5pm, Sun 9.30am–5pm; £6.50), on Henley Street, comprising an ugly modern visitor centre attached to the heavily restored half-timbered building where the great man was born. A short walk away is the engaging **Nash's House**, Chapel Street (Nov–March daily 11am–4pm; Apr–May & Sept–Oct daily 11am–5pm; June–Aug Mon–Sat 9.30am–5pm, Sun 10am–5pm; £3.50), once the property of Thomas Nash, first husband of Shakespeare's granddaughter, Elizabeth Hall. The house is kitted out with period furnishings and has a display on the history of Stratford.

Old Town Street is home to the impressive medieval **Hall's Croft** (opening hours as Nash's House; £3.50), former home of Shakespeare's elder daughter, Susanna, and her doctor husband, John Hall. Immaculately maintained, it holds a fascinating display on Elizabethan medicine. Beyond, Old Town Street steers right to reach the handsome **Holy Trinity Church** (Mon–Sat 8.30/9am–4/5/6pm, Sun 12.30–5pm; free), whose mellow, honey-coloured stonework is enhanced by its riverside setting. Shakespeare lies buried here in the chancel (£1.50).

About a mile west of the town centre in Shottery is **Anne Hathaway's Cottage** (daily 9/9.30/10/10.30am–4/5pm; £5),

THE ROYAL SHAKESPEARE COMPANY

The **Royal Shakespeare Company**, or RSC (Ⓦwww.rsc.org.uk), works on a repertory system, which means you could see four or five different plays in a visit of a few days. Tickets start at around £5 for standing room and a restricted view, rising to £30 for the best seats in the house, though note that the most popular shows get booked up months in advance. At the time of writing, the main RSC performance space is the Courtyard Theatre, a temporary building accommodating productions whilst the other theatres are overhauled in an ambitious plan due for completion in 2010. Box office (Mon–Sat 9am–8pm; Ⓣ0870/609 1110).

whose wooden beams and thatching were home to Anne before she married Shakespeare.

Arrival and information

Train Stratford's train station is on the northwestern edge of town, ten minutes' walk from the centre; it's served by hourly shuttles from Birmingham and frequent trains from London Paddington and Marylebone.
Bus Long-distance buses pull into the Riverside Station on the east side of the town centre, off Bridgeway.
Tourist office The tourist office (Mon–Sat 9.30am–5pm, Sun 10.30am–4.30pm; ⓣ0870/160 7930, ⓦwww.shakespeare-country.co.uk) is a couple of minutes' walk from the bus station by the bridge at the junction of Bridgeway and Bridgefoot; it operates an efficient accommodation booking hotline.
Bike rental Bike hire is available at Clarke's Cycles, 3 Guild St (ⓣ01789/205057).
Internet The *Java Café* at 28 Greenhill St is nice and central.

Accommodation

Parkfield Guest House 3 Broad Walk ⓣ01789/293313, ⓦwww.parkfieldbandb.co.uk. Very pleasant B&B in a rambling Victorian house down a residential street off Evesham Place. Most of the rooms are en suite. Less than 10mins walk from the centre. ❽
Stratford Racecourse Campsite Luddington Rd ⓣ01789/201063, ⓦwww.stratfordracecourse.net. Well-equipped camping and caravan site one mile southwest of the town centre. Regular buses into town (not Sun). Closed Oct–March. ❷
YHA Hemmingford House, Alveston ⓣ0870/770 6052, ⓦwww.yha.org.uk. HI hostel occupying a rambling Georgian mansion on the edge of the pretty village of Alveston, two miles east of the town centre on the B4086. Dorms and some en-suite rooms, plus laundry, internet access, cafeteria and kitchen. Regular buses from Stratford's Riverside bus station. Dorms ❸, doubles ❼

Eating and drinking

Deli Cafe 13–14 Meer St. Small café with an eclectic menu offering traditional English fare alongside more exotic dishes. Mains from £4. Licensed.
The Dirty Duck (aka *The Black Swan*) 53 Waterside. The archetypal actors' pub, stuffed to the gunwales every night with a vocal entourage of RSC employees and hangers-on. Essential viewing, plus good food.
The Garrick Inn 25 High St. Arguably the town's most photogenic and best-preserved old ale house: exposed beams, real ales and decent food.
Russons 8 Church St ⓣ01789/268822. Excellent, good-value cuisine, featuring interesting meat and vegetarian dishes on the main menu and an extensive blackboard of seafood reflecting the catch of the day; cheaper lunch and pre-theatre menus. Mains from £6.95. Closed Sun & Mon.

CAMBRIDGE

Tradition has it that the University of **CAMBRIDGE** was founded by refugees from Oxford, who fled that town after one of their number was lynched by hostile townsfolk in the 1220s; there's been rivalry between the two institutions ever since. What distinguishes Cambridge is "**the Backs**", the green swath of land straddling the River Cam, which overlooks the backs of the old colleges, and provides the town's most enduring image of grand academic architecture. Note that, as in Oxford, access to the colleges may be restricted during examinations – especially in May and June – conferences and functions.

What to see and do

A logical place to begin a tour is **King's College**, whose much celebrated **chapel** (term time Mon–Fri 9.30am–3.30pm, Sat 9.30am–3.15pm, Sun 1.15–2.15pm; rest of year Mon–Sat 9.30am–4.30pm, Sun 10am–5pm; £4.50) is an extraordinarily beautiful building, home to an almost equally vaunted choir (term-time evensong Tues–Sat 5.30pm). King's flanks King's Parade, originally the medieval High Street, at the northern end of which is the **Senate House**, the scene of graduation ceremonies on the last Saturday in June, when champagne corks fly. Adjacent Trinity Street holds the main entrance to **Gonville and Caius College**, known simply as Caius (pronounced "keys"), whose two adjoining courts boast three fancy gates representing different stages on the path to academic enlightenment. On the south side, the "Gate of Honour" leads into Senate House Passage, which itself heads west to **Clare College** (daily 10am–5pm; £2). One of seven colleges founded by women, Clare's plain period-piece courtyard leads to one of the most picturesque of all the bridges over the Cam, **Clare Bridge**. Beyond lies the Fellows' Garden, one of the loveliest college gardens open to the public (times as college).

Trinity College

Just north of Caius, **Trinity College** (daily 10am–5pm; £2.20) is the largest of the Cambridge colleges. A statue of Henry VIII, who founded it in 1546, sits in majesty over Trinity's Great Gate, his sceptre replaced with a chair leg by a student wit. Beyond lies the vast asymmetrical expanse of Great Court, which displays a fine range of Tudor buildings, the oldest of which is the fifteenth-century clock tower – the annual race against its midnight chimes is now common currency thanks to the film *Chariots of Fire*. To get through to Nevile's Court – where Newton first calculated the speed of sound – you must pass through "the screens", a passage separating the Hall from the kitchens, a common feature of Oxbridge colleges. The west end of Nevile's Court is enclosed by the beautiful Wren Library (term time Mon–Fri

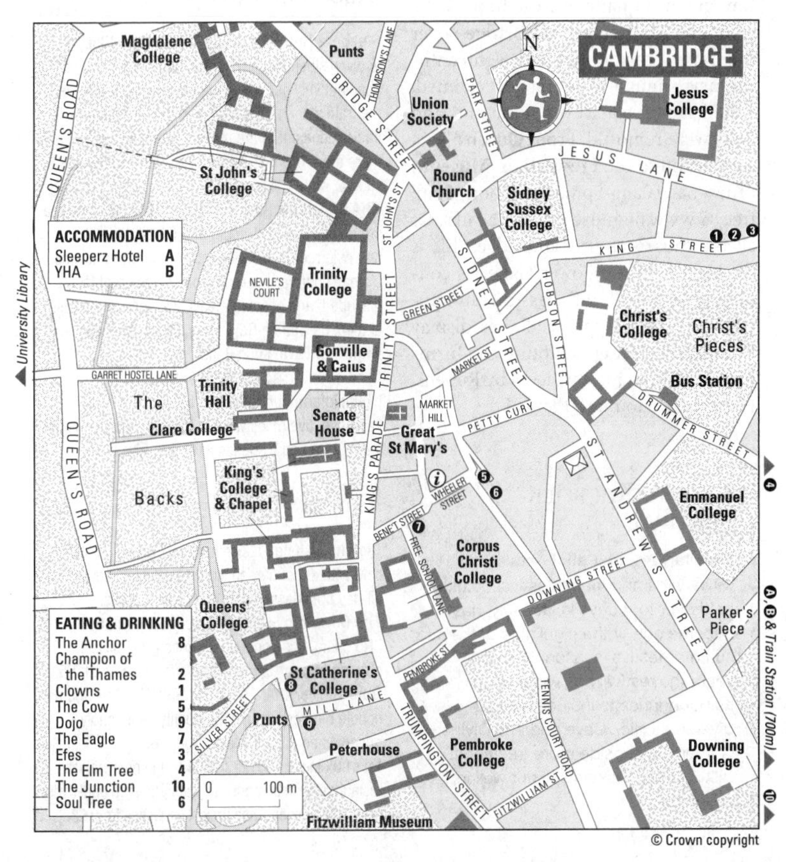

noon–2pm, Sat 10.30am–12.30pm; rest of year Mon–Fri only; free). Back outside Trinity, it's a short hop to the River Cam, where you can go **punting** – the quintessential Cambridge activity (see p.169) .

Queen's College and the Fitzwilliam Museum

Doubling back along King's Parade, it takes about five minutes to reach **Queens' College** (daily 10am–3/4.30pm; £1.50), accessed through the gate on Queen's Lane, just off Silver Street. Here, the Old Court and the Cloister Court are twin fairytale Tudor courtyards, with the first the perfect illustration of the original collegiate ideal with kitchens, library, chapel, hall and rooms all set around a tiny green. Equally eye-catching is the wooden **Mathematical Bridge** over the Cam, a copy of the mid-eighteenth-century original which, it was claimed, would stay in place even if the nuts and bolts were removed. From Queens', it's a short stroll to the **Fitzwilliam Museum** (Tues–Sat 10am–5pm, Sun noon–5pm; free; Ⓦwww.fitzmuseum.cam.ac.uk). Of all the museums in Cambridge, this is the best, with the Lower Galleries containing a wealth of classical antiquities, while the Upper Galleries display European painting, sculpture and furniture, including masterpieces by Rubens, Hogarth, Renoir and Picasso.

CAMBRIDGE FOLK FESTIVAL

The **Cambridge Folk Festival** (Ⓦwww.cambridgefolkfestival.co.uk), held over four days in late July, has become one of the highlights of the summer festival season. In recent years the festival has widened its boundaries to include acts as diverse as Nick Cave and The Divine Comedy, alongside more traditional folk sounds. Tickets sell out well in advance.

Arrival and information

Trains Cambridge train station is a mile or so southeast of the city centre, off Hills Road. It's a twenty-minute walk into the centre, or take shuttle bus #3.
Bus The bus station is centrally located on Drummer Street.
Tourist office The tourist office is on Wheeler Street, off King's Parade (Mon–Sat 10am–5/5.30pm, plus Easter–Oct Sun 11am–3pm; Ⓣ0871/226 8006, Ⓦwww.visitcambridge.org), and operates a useful accommodation booking service (Ⓣ01223/457581).
Bike rental There are several bike hire outlets, including Station Cycles outside the train station (Ⓣ01223/307125).
Internet *Budget Internet Café* at 30 Hills Rd is a good option at under a pound for an hour.

Accommodation

Sleeperz Hotel Station Rd Ⓣ01223/304050, Ⓦwww.sleeperz.com. This popular hotel is in an imaginatively converted warehouse, right outside the train station. Most of the rooms are bunk-style affairs done out in the manner of a ship's cabin, and there are a few doubles too. All are en suite, with shower and TV. ❽
YHA 97 Tenison Rd Ⓣ0870/770 5742, Ⓦwww.yha.org.co.uk. This well-equipped HI hostel has dorms and twin rooms, laundry and self-catering facilities, a small courtyard garden, and serves breakfast (included) and evening meals. It's close to the train station, off Station Rd. Dorms ❸, doubles ❼
Highfield Farm Long Road, Comberton Ⓣ01223/262308, Ⓦwww.highfieldfarmtouringpark.co.uk. Quiet, rural campsite, five miles west of the city, twenty-minute journey, served by buses #18/18A. ❷

Eating

Clowns 54 King St. Licensed, day-and-night Italian café with a roof garden, serving cakes, sandwiches, all-day breakfasts, pasta and daily specials.
The Cow Corn Exchange Street. Now run by the BRB chain, this popular pub does great pizzas, offering two-for-one on Tuesdays. Pizzas from £5.
Dojo 1 Miller's Yard Ⓣ01223/363471. Pan-Oriental noodle bar serving up high quality, reasonably priced Asian dishes. Mains from £6.
Efes 80 King St Ⓣ01223/350491. Intimate Turkish restaurant, with chargrilled meats prepared under your nose and a decent *meze* selection. Mains from £8.

Drinking and nightlife

The Anchor Silver St. The pick of the riverside pubs, with outside seating, though it can be very crowded in summer.

Champion of the Thames 68 King St. Gratifyingly old–fashioned central pub with decent beer and a student/academic clientele.

The Eagle Benet St. An ancient inn with a cobbled courtyard where Crick and Watson sought inspiration in the 1950s, at the time of their discovery of DNA. It's succumbed recently to a certain chain pub mediocrity, but is still worth it for the history.

The Elm Tree Orchard Street. Tiny, comfortable pub that's worth seeking out for its programme of live jazz.

The Junction Clifton Rd ⓣ01223/511511, ⓦwww.junction.co.uk. Live bands, club nights, comedy, drama, dance, performance and digital art at this popular and eclectic venue.

Soul Tree 106 Guildhall St, ⓦwww.soultree.co.uk. Welcome addition to Cambridge's sometimes turgid nightlife, with soon-to-be-big live acts and soul, funk and disco club nights.

Northern England

The main draw of **northern England** is the **Lake District**, a scenic region just thirty miles across, taking in stone-built villages, sixteen major lakes and the steeply pitched faces of England's highest mountains. However, to restrict yourself purely to the outdoors would be to do a disservice to cities such as **Manchester** and **Liverpool** in the northwest, and **Newcastle** in the northeast, whose centres are alive with the ostentatious civic architecture of nineteenth-century capitalism and twenty-first-century renewal. An entirely different angle on northern history is provided by the great ecclesiastical centres of **Durham** and **York**, where famous cathedrals provide a focus for extensive medieval remains.

MANCHESTER

Few cities in the world have embraced social change so heartily as **MANCHESTER**. From engine of the Industrial Revolution to cutting–edge metropolis, the city has no real rival in England outside of London. With a huge student population, a lively **Gay Village**, and a strong history of churning out talent for the twin glories of British culture – music and football – Manchester hosts one of the country's most vibrant social and cultural scenes.

What to see and do

From the main Piccadilly train station, it's a few minutes' walk northwest to **Piccadilly Gardens** (hub of the local tram and bus network), from where the principal city sights can all be explored on foot.

A quarter of mile from here is the **Manchester Art Gallery** on Mosley St (Tues–Sun 10am–5pm; free; ⓦwww.manchestergalleries.org), which includes a fine collection of pre-Raphaelite paintings, impressionistic pictures of Manchester by Adolphe Valette and an excellent interactive gallery.

Royal Exchange Theatre and Urbis

A short walk west of Piccadilly Gardens is St Ann's Square, home to the wonderful Royal Exchange Theatre (ⓦwww.royalexchange.co.uk). If you don't have time to see a show, pop in and have a look at the building, the Classical cotton exchange with florid, pink marble columns and lofty cupolas housing the stage, an egg-like module that squats in the centre forming a spherical performance space. New Cathedral Street runs through a landscaped expanse to **Urbis** in Cathedral Gardens (daily 10am–6pm; free; wwww.urbis.org.uk), a spectacular, wedge-shaped glass building with displays exploring life in different world cities and a stylish café bar.

Museum of Science and Industry

South down Deansgate and right into Liverpool Road is a celebration of the triumphs of industrialization at the superb **Museum of Science and Industry** (daily 10am–5pm; free; wwww.msim.org.uk), where exhibits include working steam engines, textile machinery, a hands-on science centre, atmospheric recreations of period rooms, and a glimpse of the Manchester sewer system complete with realistic smells.

Salford Quays and Old Trafford

Metrolink trams run from Mosley Street to **Salford Quays**, scene of a massive urban renewal scheme in the old dock area. Centrepiece is the spectacular waterfront **Lowry Centre** (daily 10/11am–5pm; free; ⓦwww.thelowry.com), where, as well as theatres and galleries, room is always made for the work of the artist L.S. Lowry, best known for his "matchstick men" scenes. To get here, take the tram to Harbour City, or walk down the docks from the Salford Quays stop. A footbridge runs across the docks to the **Imperial War Museum North** (daily 10am–6pm March–Oct, 10am–5pm Nov–Feb; free; ⓦwww.iwm.org.uk/north), a striking aluminium-clad building designed by Daniel Libeskind, where imaginative exhibits explore the effects of war since 1900. It's as resonant in its way as the other great building that looms in the near distance, Old Trafford, home of **Manchester United Football Club**, whose museum is sited in the North Stand (daily 9.30am–5.30pm; museum & tour £10, museum only £6.50; Metrolink to Old Trafford; advance booking essential for tours, ⓣ0870/442 1994, ⓦwww.manutd.com).

Arrival and information

Air The airport is ten miles south, with a fast and frequent train service to Piccadilly.

Train Most trains arrive at Piccadilly station, on the city's east side.

Bus Long–distance buses stop at Chorlton Street, just west of Piccadilly station.

Tourist office The Manchester Visitor Centre is in the town hall extension on Lloyd Street, facing St Peter's Square (Mon–Sat 10am–5.30pm, Sun 10.30am–4.30pm; ⓣ0871/222 8223, ⓦwww.visitmanchester.com.), with branches at the airport and the Lowry too.

Accommodation

The Hatters 50 Newton St ⓣ0161/236 9500, ⓦwww.hattersgroup.com. A converted listed building in the fashionable Northern Quarter is home to this bright and modern hostel. A good range of facilities is available and staff will provide tourist information and book tours. No curfew. Dorms ❸, doubles ❼

Hilton Chambers 15 Hilton St ⓣ0161/236 4414, ⓦwww.hattersgroup.com. Another option from the Hatters Group, this large, fun hostel has internet access, space for barbecues and a travel information desk. No curfew. Dorms ❸, doubles ❽

The Ox 71 Liverpool Rd ⓣ0161/839 7740, ⓦwww.theox.co.uk. Nine rooms above a classy bar-restaurant opposite the Science and Industry Museum. ❽

YHA Potato Wharf, Castlefield ⓣ0870/770 5950, ⓦwww.yhamanchester.org.uk. Opposite the Science and Industry Museum, this well-designed HI hostel (all dorm rooms have private bathrooms), has a great canalside location. Dorms ❹, twin ❼

Eating

For **budget eating**, head a couple of blocks east of the visitor centre to Chinatown. Alternatively, the scores of restaurants along Wilmslow Road in Rusholme (buses #40–49), otherwise known as "Curry Mile", feature some of Britain's best (and least expensive) Asian cooking.

Dimitri's 1 Campfield Arcade, Deansgate. Pick and mix from the Greek/Spanish/Italian menu, or grab an arcade table and sip a drink. Mains from £5.50.

Earth 16–20 Turner St. Veggie food – curries, pies, salads and juices – in a stylish Northern Quarter café in the Manchester Buddhist Centre. Mains from £2.60. Closed Mon & Sun.

East 52 Faulkner St. Popular dim sum restaurant in Chinatown. The £3.50 lunch menu is superb value.

Gogi's IFCO Centre, Wimslow Rd. Top-rated curry house on the curry mile. Mains for under £5.

Oklahoma 74 High Street. A café/record store/art gallery/novelty shop that defies

MANCHESTER MUSIC

In 1978, local TV personality Tony Wilson started **Factory Records** and gave voice to a musical movement that came to define both Manchester and Britain's post-punk musical soundscape. Bands like Joy Division, New Order and the Happy Mondays emerged and embraced the new electronic music that was played at Factory's club, The **Hacienda**, the prototype for the industrial, warehouse spaces ubiquitous in club design today. Crippled by debt and hounded for its ambiguous stance on ecstasy use, the Hacienda closed in 1997, but its legacy lives on in Manchester's self-assured urban cool and reputation for great music.

categorization and epitomizes the creative energies of the Northern Quarter. It has to be seen to be believed.

Drinking and nightlife

The grooviest places to **drink** are in the Castlefield area around Liverpool Road; under the railway arches along Deansgate Locks (Whitworth Street West); in the Northern Quarter around Oldham Street; and the Gay Village around Canal Street. For details of **nightlife**, consult Friday's *Manchester Evening News*.

Britons Protection 50 Great Bridgewater St. Elegantly decorated traditional pub, with good home-made food, comedy nights and other events, and a beer garden.

Dry Bar 28–30 Oldham St. A "Madchester" institution – it was owned by Factory Records – and catalyst for much of what goes on in the Northern Quarter, this cool bar has banned the likes of Liam Gallagher for bad behaviour.

Dukes '92 Castle St, Castlefield. Former stableblock for canal horses, now a large, sociable pub with terrace seating, a woodfire pizza oven and a great-value range of pâtés and cheeses.

Mr Thomas' Chop House 52 Cross St. Long, narrow Victorian pub with a Dickensian feel and beautiful tiling, serving Lancashire hotpot and other traditional dishes.

Music Box, 65 Oxford St (ⓣ0161/236 9971, ⓦwww.themusicbox.info). Respected underground club hosting several popular nights and live bands during the week.

Sankeys Beehive Mill, Radium St, Ancoats (ⓣ0161/236 5444, ⓦwww.sankeys.info). Serious clubbers get sweaty at Tribal Sessions and Bugged Out at weekends. On Thursdays, Indie night, The Aftershow showcases hotly tipped bands.

The Temple 100 Great Bridgewater St. A tiny, converted public toilet – yes that's right – stocking a wide selection of Belgian beers.

Moving on

Train Newcastle (every 30mins; 3hr); Windermere (hourly; 1hr 45min); York (every 30min; 1hr 30min).
Bus Durham (6 daily; 4hr 30min); Glasgow (10 daily; 4hr 55min–7hr); Newcastle (10 daily; 5hr); York (hourly; 3hr 20min).

LIVERPOOL

Once Britain's main transatlantic port and the empire's second city, **LIVERPOOL** spent too many of the twentieth-century postwar years struggling against adversity. Things are looking up at last, as regeneration projects brighten the centre and the old docks on the River Mersey, while the successful bid to be European Capital of Culture for 2008 promises to transform the way outsiders see the city. Acerbic wit and loyalty to one of the city's two great football teams are the linchpins of Liverpudlian or "Scouse" culture, along with an underlying pride in the local musical heritage – fair enough from the city that produced The Beatles.

What to see and do

Trains deposit visitors at Lime Street station on the eastern edge of the city, from where it's a short walk to William Brown Street and the renowned **Walker Art Gallery** (daily 10am–5pm; free; ⓦwww.thewalker.org.uk), including a representative jaunt through British art history, with Hogarth, Gainsborough, Stubbs and Hockney all well represented.

The Waterfront

From here it's a fifteen-minute walk west to the **Pier Head** and Liverpool's waterfront, where it's worth taking a "Ferry 'cross the Mersey" (as sung by Gerry and the Pacemakers) to Birkenhead for the views back towards the city; ferries serve commuters during morning and evening rush hours (£2.20 return), but in between operate hourly cruises with commentary (Ⓦwww.merseyferries.co.uk; £5.10). Just behind the ferry terminal, but best seen from the river itself, stands the Liver Building, with its enormous clock faces and perched, local mascots – two Liver birds on each clock tower. A short stroll south is the **Albert Dock**, showpiece of the renovated docks area, whose main focus is **Tate Liverpool** (Tues–Sun 10am–6pm; free; Ⓦwww.tate.org.uk/liverpool), northern home of the national collection of modern art. Occupying the other side of the dock is the **Maritime Museum** (daily 10am–5pm; free; Ⓦwww.merseysidemaritimemuseum.org.uk), now joined with the International Slavery Museum, a sobering exploration of the transatlantic slave trade and its legacy. The Albert Dock is also home to **The Beatles Story** (daily 10am–6pm; £9.99; Ⓦwww.beatlesstory.com), a multimedia attempt to capture the essence of the Fab Four's rise.

The Cavern Quarter

The city centre area around **Mathew Street** has been designated the **Cavern Quarter**, its pubs and shops providing an excuse to wallow in Beatles nostalgia, especially at the rebuilt version of the *Cavern Club* (hosting live bands Wed–Sun), where The Beatles played in the 1960s. You can take a two-hour "Magical Mystery Tour" of other sites associated with the band, such as Penny Lane and Strawberry Fields, on a bus that departs from The Beatles Story and ends up at the *Cavern Club* (daily tours; book at The Beatles Story or tourist offices; £12.95; Ⓦwww.cavernclub.co.uk). Real fans also won't want to miss touring **20 Forthlin Rd**, home of the McCartney family from 1955 to 1964, and **Mendips**, the house where John Lennon lived between 1945 and 1963. Both are preserved by the National Trust and only accessible on a pre-booked minibus tour (Easter–Oct Wed–Sun; Ⓣ0870/900 0256; £13), departing twice daily from Albert Dock.

The cathedrals

To the east, at either end of Hope Street, stand the city's two very different but equally powerful twentieth-century cathedrals: the Roman Catholic **Metropolitan Cathedral** (daily 8am–5/6pm; donation requested), ten minutes' walk up Mount Pleasant, is a vast inverted funnel of a building, while the pale red, neo-Gothic Anglican **Liverpool Cathedral** (daily 8am–6pm; donation requested) is the largest in the country, a muscular, neo-Gothic creation, designed by Sir Giles Gilbert Scott in 1903, but not completed until 1978.

Arrival and information

Air Liverpool John Lennon airport is eight miles south, with buses heading into town every twenty minutes.
Train Trains arrive at Lime Street Station, on the eastern edge of the city centre; coaches stop on Norton Street, northeast of the station.
Boat Ferry arrivals – including from Dublin and Belfast – dock just north of Pier Head.
Tourist office The tourist office is (Ⓣ0151/233 2008, Ⓦwww.visitliverpool.com) on Whitechapel (Mon–Sat 9am–5.30pm, Sun 10.30am–4.30pm).

Accommodation

From mid-June to early September there is **budget accommodation** (❻) at the self-catering student halls at John Moores University (Ⓣ0151/231 3093, Ⓦwww.livjm.ac.uk) and the University of Liverpool (Ⓣ0151/794 4726, Ⓦwww.liv.ac.uk).
Aachen 89–91 Mount Pleasant Ⓣ0151/709 3477, Ⓦwww.aachenhotel.co.uk. The most popular and central budget hotel, with value-for-money rooms and big "eat-as-much-as-you-like" breakfasts. ❼

International Inn 4 South Hunter St, off Hardman St ⓣ0151/709 8135, ⓦwww.internationalinn.co.uk. Converted Victorian warehouse with en-suite dorms for two to ten people, helpful staff, plus kitchen, laundry and no curfew. Adjacent café has Internet access. Dorms ❸, twin ❻
YHA Wapping ⓣ0870/770 5924, ⓦwww.yha.org.uk. One of the best HI hostels, just south of Albert Dock. Smart three-, four- or six-bed rooms, all with private bathroom, plus licensed café, laundry and 24hr reception. Dorms ❹, triple ❾

Eating and drinking

Inexpensive **food** can be found around Mount Pleasant and Hardman and Bold streets, while Berry and Nelson streets to the south form the heart of **Chinatown**. As for **pubs** and **bars**, Fleet, Slater and Wood streets and Concert Square (off Bold Street) are where all the action is.
The Baltic Fleet 33a Wapping. Restored maritime pub with real ales and a great period feel.
Korova 39–41 Fleet St. Chic bar/club/diner opened by Scouse electronica outfit Ladytron. The focus is, most definitely, on the music, with live bands and DJs playing to a very cool crowd.
The Magnet 45 Hardman St. Blood-red decor and a bit of Barry White – it's groovy, plus there's a funky club downstairs and a diner that stays open until 2am. Also showcases quality live talent.
May Sum 180-181 Elliot St. There are some fifty-plus dishes to choose from at this hugely popular eat-all-you-can Chinese buffet. It's not the place for haute cuisine, but the food's not bad and can't be faulted for value. Before 5.30pm Mon–Thurs it's £5.90.
The Philharmonic 36 Hope St. Fabulous, ornate pub boasting mosaic floors, gilded wrought-iron gates and marble decor in the gents.
Tabac 126 Bold St. Contemporary café-bar, serving a wide-ranging menu to Liverpool creatives.
Yuet Ben 1 Upper Duke St. The celebrated, yet reasonably priced Peking cuisine here is authentic and, refreshingly, vegetarians are not given the cold shoulder – try the set menu for £9.50. Mains from £6.50.

Nightlife and entertainment

The evening paper, the *Liverpool Echo*, has what's-on listings, while annual festivals like the Summer Pops (July) and International Beatles Festival (August) are when the city lets its hair down.
Everyman Theatre and Playhouse Hope Street ⓣ0151/709 4776, ⓦwww.everymanplayhouse.com. Multi-purpose venue presenting drama, dance, poetry and music – not to mention cheap food and a great bar.
FACT 88 Wood St ⓣ0151/707 4450, ⓦwww.fact.co.uk. The Foundation for Art and Creative Technology shelters two galleries showing film, video and new media projects, as well as an arthouse cinema, café and bar.
Liverpool Academy 11–13 Hotham St ⓣ0151/707 3200, ⓦwww.liverpoolacademy.co.uk. The best medium-sized live music venue in town with good club nights.
Nation Wolstenholme Sq ⓣ0151/707 1309, ⓦwww.cream.co.uk. Nightclub hosting Liverpool's most infamous nights – Cream and Chibuku.
Royal Court Theatre 1 Roe St ⓣ0870/787 1866, ⓦwww.royalcourtliverpool.co.uk. Good for touring plays and stand-up comedians.

Moving on

Train Cardiff (some change at Crewe; every 45 min–1 hr; 4hr); Manchester (every 15 min; 50min); York (2 hourly; 2hr 20min).
Bus Cardiff (4 daily; 6hr 20min); Manchester (hourly; 1hr); Newcastle (hourly; 6hr 15min–7hr 50min); Oxford (9 daily; 5hr 30min); York (hourly; 3hr 50min–5hr).

THE LAKE DISTRICT

The site of England's highest peaks and its biggest concentration of lakes, the glacier-carved **Lake District National Park** is the nation's most popular walking area. The weather here in Cumbria changes quickly, but the sudden shifts of light on the bracken and moorland grasses, and on the slate of the local buildings, are part of the area's appeal.

Arrival and local transport

The most direct access is via the main-line **train** route from London Euston towards Glasgow, disembarking at Lancaster, from where bus #555 runs to Kendal, Windermere, Ambleside, Grasmere, Keswick and Carlisle – the open-top #599 bus is a summer alternative between Windermere and Grasmere. Alternatively, you could get off the train at **Oxenholme**, connecting with a branch line service to Kendal and Windermere; or take a direct train

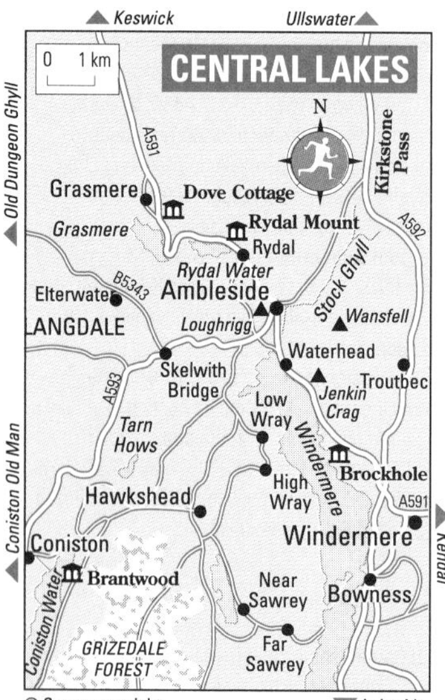

from Manchester to Windermere. A National Express **coach** service runs daily from London Victoria and Manchester to the Lake District, while local **Stagecoach buses** go everywhere in the region – an **Explorer Ticket** £9/day, valid on their entire network and available on the bus, is just one of many local passes, including bus-and-boat tickets. The region boasts 27 youth hostels and dozens of campsites, covering all the destinations described below. For more **information** visit Ⓦwww.lake-district.gov.uk; the official site of the Cumbria Tourist Board is Ⓦwww.golakes.co.uk.

Windermere

Windermere is the largest of the lakes, with its main town of **WINDERMERE** (where the train from Oxenholme/Kendal stops) set a mile or so back from the water. Other than the short climb up to the viewpoint of **Orrest Head** (30min), it offers little to do, though it is the region's main service centre. The **tourist office** is just outside the train station (daily 9am–6/7.30pm; Ⓣ015394/46499). **Bikes** can be rented from Country Lanes at the train station (Ⓣ01539/444544, Ⓦwww.countrylanes.co.uk).

Accommodation

Brendan Chase 1 College Rd Ⓣ01539/445638, Ⓦwww.placetostaywindermere.co.uk. Friendly B&B, particularly toward backpackers and hikers, with en-suite rooms. ❼

Lake District Backpackers' Lodge High St Ⓣ01539/446374, Ⓦwww.lakedistrictbackpackers.co.uk. Cosy dorm accommodation, close to the station. Dorms ❷

YHA Bridge Lane Ⓣ01539/443543, Ⓦwww.yha.org.uk. Located at Troutbeck, two miles northwest of Windermere town, with great views over the lake. A shuttle-bus (£2) meets trains at the station. Dorms ❸, doubles ❺

Bowness

For the lake itself, catch the bus from outside Windermere station to the prettier, but often more crowded, lake-shore town of **BOWNESS**, where you can rent a rowboat or take a longer trip by ferry. Lake **ferries** (Ⓣ01539/43360, Ⓦwww.windermere-lakecruises.co.uk) run to Lakeside at the southern tip (£8 return) or to Waterhead (for Ambleside) at the northern end (£7.70 return). A 24-hour Freedom-of-the-Lake ticket costs £14. There are also boats (£5.80 return) to the excellent **Lake District National Park Visitor Centre** at Brockhole (April–Oct daily 10am–5pm; free; Ⓣ01539/446601; bus #555 or #599). A mile and a half south of Bowness on foot, there's the rare chance to visit a house designed by one of the major exponents of the Arts and Crafts Movement, Mackay Hugh Baillie Scott's **Blackwell** (early-Feb to Dec daily 10.30am–4/5pm; £5.45; Ⓦwww.blackwell.org.uk). Accommodation in Bowness tends to be more expensive, but don't miss a drink or a bar meal in *The Hole in't Wall* **pub**, behind the church, the town's oldest hostelry.

Ambleside

Take bus #555 or #599 from Windermere or touristy Bowness. In town, the **tourist office** is in the Central Buildings by the Market Cross (daily 9am–5.30pm; ⓣ01539/432582) and the tiny **Ambleside Museum** (daily 10am–5pm; £2.50) has the lowdown on lakeland writers and artists. *Zeffirelli's*, a cinema on Compston Road, specializes in inexpensive vegetarian food, either in the daytime café or upstairs in the dinner-only pizza **restaurant** and the Novel Café and bookshop, 101 Lake Rd, provides a haven away from the hubbub of the town.

Accommodation

Ambleside Backpackers Old Lake Rd ⓣ01539 432340, ⓦwww.englishlakesbackpackers.co.uk. Independent, family-run hostel, with immaculate rooms, located in a quiet part of town. Dorms ❸
Ambleside Football Club Seasonal campsite on the pitch next to Rothay Park on the west side of town. Showers, WC and self-catering facilities. Summer only. ❷
Linda's Shirland, Compston Rd ⓣ01539/432999. A lovely, little B&B run by the eponymous, indefatigable Linda. Cheaper rates for self-caterers. ❻
YHA Waterhead ⓣ0870/770 5672, ⓦwww.yha.org.uk. One of the Lake District's best-sited HI hostels fronting the lake at Waterhead. Breakfast included. Dorms ❹, doubles ❽

Elterwater and Langdale

The #516 bus (April–Oct only) from Ambleside runs four miles west to the charming hamlet of **ELTERWATER**, centred on a tiny green and boasting another HI hostel, *Elterwater* (ⓣ0870/770 5816; dorms ❸, bunk twin ❻), as well as the *Britannia Inn* (ⓣ015394/37210), an old lakeland pub with tasty food. The dramatic peaks of **Langdale**, three miles further up the valley (end of the #516 bus route), can be scaled from the equally venerable *Old Dungeon Ghyll*, a pricey hotel with terrific hikers' bar. Next door is the cheaper *Sticklebarn* pub and Bunkhouse with basic dorm beds (ⓣ015394/37356; dorms ❷). Canny campers stay nearby at the ✪ *Great Langdale* **campsite** (ⓣ01539/437668 ❷), a spotless site, at the foot of the brooding Langdale Pikes, owned by the National Trust.

Keswick and Derwent Water

Principal hiking and tourist centre for the northern lakes, **KESWICK** (pro-

LAKE DISTRICT LUMINARIES

The sublime lakeland landscape has been an inspiration to some of England's most revered literary figures. **William Wordsworth** lived at Rydal Mount (daily 9.30/10am–4/5pm; Nov–Feb closed Tues; £5, gardens only £2.50; ⓦwww.rydalmount.co.uk), three miles northwest of Ambleside on the #555 bus, and the more interesting Dove Cottage (daily 9.30am–5.30pm; closed Jan; £6.50; ⓦwww.wordsworth.org.uk) at Grasmere. Wordsworth and his sister Dorothy lie in simple graves in the churchyard of St Oswald's, in the village.

Beatrix Potter, author, illustrator and botanist, lived at Hill Top (April–Oct Mon–Wed, Sat & Sun same hours; £5.40; NT), a lovely seventeenth-century house in the hamlet of Near Sawrey. You can take a ferry from Bowness and cover the steep two miles to the house on foot or by minibus. Get there early to beat the crowds.
From Coniston, reached by bus #505, you can take the wooden *Coniston Launch* (£5.40 & £7.80 return, ⓣ01539/436216, ⓦwww.conistonlaunch.co.uk) or the Steam Yacht *Gondola* (April–Oct; £6 return, ⓣ01539/41288, ⓦwww.nationaltrust.org.uk/gondola) to the elegant lakeside villa, **Brantwood** (mid-March to mid-Nov daily 11am–5.30pm; mid-Nov to mid-March Wed–Sun 11am–4.30pm; £5.95, gardens only £4; ⓦwww.brantwood.org.uk), once home of artist and critic **John Ruskin**. The house is full of Ruskin's own drawings and sketches, as well as items relating to the pre-Raphaelite painters he inspired.

nounced "kez-ick") lies on the shores of **Derwent Water**. The **Keswick Launch** (mid-March to Nov daily; Dec to mid-March Sat & Sun; £7.90 round trip; ⓣ01768/772263, ⓦwww.keswick-launch.co.uk) runs right around the lake and you can get off at Hawes End for the climb up **Cat Bells** (1481ft), best of the lakeside vantage points. The trek up **Skiddaw** (3050ft; 5hr), north of town, is more demanding, but the easiest of the many true mountain hikes around and about. Otherwise, stroll a mile and a half eastwards to **Castlerigg Stone Circle**, a Neolithic monument commanding a spectacular view, or take the #77/77A/79 bus ride down into **Borrowdale**, south of town, perhaps the most beautiful valley in England. **Buses** use the terminal behind Booths Foodstore, off Main Street. Keswick's **tourist office** is in the Moot Hall, Market Square (daily 9.30am–4.30/5.30pm; ⓣ01768/772645), and there's **bike rental** from Keswick Mountain Bikes on Southey Hill (ⓣ01768/775202, ⓦwww.keswickmountainbikes.co.uk). Keswick's most agreeable **café** is the *Lakeland Pedlar*, Henderson's Yard, off Main Street, and there are fine **pub** meals and good beer at the *Lake Road Inn* and the *Four In Hand*, both on Lake Rd. **Theatre by the Lake** (ⓣ01768/774411, ⓦwww.theatrebythelake.com) hosts drama, dance and music.

Accommodation

Bluestones 7 Southey St ⓣ01768/774237, ⓦwww.bluestonesguesthouse.co.uk. A welcoming guest house that offers big buffet breakfasts. ❼

Keswick Camping Crow Park Rd ⓣ01768/772392, ⓦwww.campingandcaravanningclub.co.uk. Very convenient location west of town, five minutes from the bus station, this well-appointed site can be crowded. Booking advised. ❷

YHA Station Road ⓣ0870/770 5894, ⓦwww.yha.org.uk. The local HI hostel has a pleasant riverside location and a modern interior. Licensed restaurant. Bike hire available. Dorms ❸, Twin ❼

YORK

It's the spectacular Gothic Minster, cobbled alleyways and ancient walls that draw tourists to **YORK**, but the city's character-forming experiences go back a lot further than that. It was the principal northern headquarters of the Romans, while the city's position as the north's spiritual capital dates from 627, when Edwin of Northumbria adopted Christianity. Northumbrian power crumbled in the face of a Danish invasion that swept through York in 866, and by 876 the Vikings were firmly entrenched in "Jorvik", beginning a century of Scandinavian rule.

What to see and do

Best introduction to York is a stroll around the **city walls** (daily till dusk), a three-mile circuit – two miles of it on the walls themselves – that takes in the various medieval "bars", or gates, and grants fine views of the Minster. A free two-hour **guided walk** (daily at 10.15am, plus additional tours over summer at 2.15pm & 6.45pm), led by the York Association of Voluntary Guides, departs from outside the art gallery in Exhibition Square; just turn up.

York Minster

Ever since Edwin built a wooden chapel on the site, **York Minster** (Mon–Sat 9/9.30am–5pm, Sun noon–3.45pm; £5.50; ⓦwww.yorkminster.org) has been the centre of religious authority for the north of England. Most of what's visible now was built in stages between the 1220s and the 1470s, and today it ranks as the country's largest Gothic building. Inside, the scenes of the East Window, completed in 1405, and the abstract thirteenth-century Five Sisters window represent the finest collection of stained glass in Britain. Various parts of the Minster have separate admission charges, though the full £9 ticket covers all the attractions – don't miss climbing

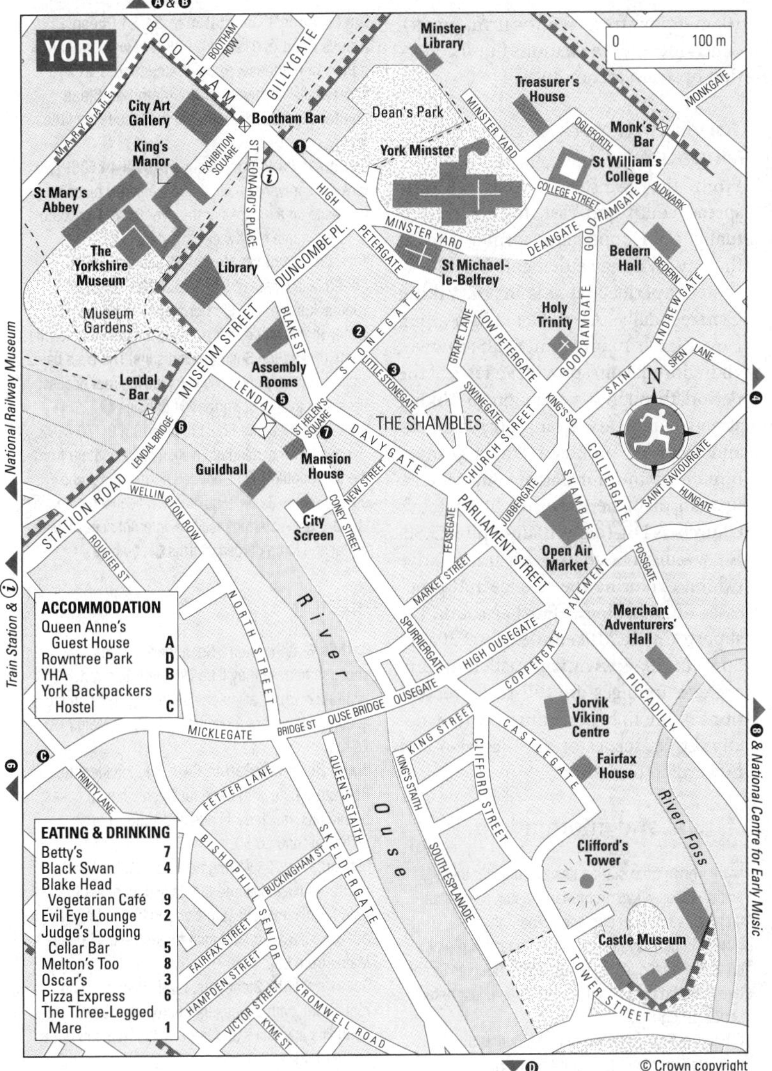

the central tower, which gives views over the medieval pattern of narrow streets to the south, known as the **Shambles**.

Yorkshire Museum and National Railway Museum

Southwest of the Minster, just outside the city walls, Museum Gardens leads to the ruins of the Benedictine abbey of St Mary and the **Yorkshire Museum** (daily 10am–5pm; £4; Ⓦwww.yorkshiremuseum.org.uk), which contains much of the abbey's medieval sculpture, and a selection of Roman, Saxon and Viking finds. Another museum worth a call is the excellent **National Railway Museum**, ten minutes' walk from the station on Leeman Rd (daily

10am–6pm; free; Ⓦwww.nrm.org.uk), which includes the nation's finest collection of steam locomotives.

Jorvik and York Castle Museum

From the Minster shopping streets spread south and east, focusing eventually on Coppergate, former site of the city's Viking settlement. The blockbuster experience that is **Jorvik Viking Centre** (daily April–Oct 10am–5pm, Nov–March 10am–4pm; £7.95; Ⓦwww.vikingjorvik.com) provides a taste of the period through a recreation of Viking streets, complete with appropriate smells and recorded sounds, to the accompaniment of an informative commentary. Just north of here, within St Saviour's Church, is **Dig** (daily 10am–5pm; £5.50; Ⓦwww.digyork.co.uk), an informative exhibit exploring the science and processes of archeology. Further south, the superb **Castle Museum** (daily 9.30am–5pm; £6.50; Ⓦwww.yorkcastlemuseum.org.uk) indulges in full-scale recreations of life in bygone times, with evocative street scenes of the Victorian and Edwardian periods.

Arrival and information

Train York's train station lies just outside the city walls, with services from Manchester, as well as fast trains from London and Edinburgh.
Buses Long-distance coaches drop off and pick up at the train station, as well as on Rougier Street, two hundred yards north of the station, just before Lendal Bridge.
Tourist office There's a tourist office at the train station (Mon–Sat 9am–5/6pm, Sun 9.30/10am–4/5pm), though the main one is over Lendal Bridge, in the De Grey Rooms on Exhibition Square (Mon–Sat 9am–5/6pm, Sun 10am–4/5pm; Ⓣ01904/550099, Ⓦwww.visityork.org).

Accommodation

The University of York offers good-value rooms and self-catering flats during Easter and summer holidays (Ⓣ01904/432037, Ⓦwww.york.ac.uk; ❽).

Queen Anne's Guest House 24/26 Queen Anne's Road Ⓣ01904/629389, Ⓦwww.queen-annes-guesthouse.co.uk. Welcoming B&B a short walk northwest of Bootham Bar. Clean, comfortable rooms, most with en-suite facilities. ❼
Rowntree Park Terry Avenue Ⓣ01904/658997, Ⓦwww.caravanclub.co.uk. Conveniently placed campsite on the banks of the river Ouse, just south of town, within easy walking distance. ❷
York Backpackers Hostel Micklegate House, 88–90 Micklegate Ⓣ01904/627720, Ⓦwww.yorkbackpackers.co.uk. Dorm space, doubles and family rooms in a rather grand listed building, former home of the High Sheriff of Yorkshire. There's a café, kitchen, laundry and cosy bar, plus Internet access. Breakfast included. Dorms ❸, doubles ❻
York YHA 42 Water End, Clifton Ⓣ0870/770 6102. HI hostel twenty minutes' walk along Bootham from the tourist office. Four-bedded dorms and some private rooms (book in advance), a licensed café, laundry, self-catering facilities, internet access, bike rental and large garden. Dorms ❸, twin ❼

Eating

Betty's 6–8 St Helen's Sq. If there are tea shops in heaven they'll be like *Betty's*, a York institution which also serves main courses, to the accompaniment of a pianist, until 9pm. Mains £5–11.
Blake Head Vegetarian Café 104 Micklegate. Bookstore/café with patio for freshly baked cakes, breakfasts, quiches, salads and soups. Lunch dishes around £6.50.
Melton's Too 25 Walmgate. Exposed brickwork, scattered cushions and the daily papers set the tone for this relaxed café-bar and bistro. Delicious, but expensive – go at lunch to get the best deals. Mains from £6.
Oscar's 8 Little Stonegate. Lively wine bar and restaurant, with a pleasant courtyard, that does a good line in snacks and larger bites. You can get a baguette for £3.30.
Pizza Express River House, 17 Museum St. Grand old riverside club rooms with sought-after balcony, the venue for this chain's usual menu of underwhelming pizzas. It's the location that's memorable here. Pizzas for around £7.

Drinking and nightlife

Black Swan Peasholme Green. York's oldest (sixteenth-century) pub with some superb stone flagging and wood panelling, and regular singer-songwriter and folk nights.

Evil Eye Lounge 42 Stonegate. Inviting bar with comfy sofas, an encyclopaedic range of spirits, quaffable cocktails and great Thai food. The kind of place where "a quick pint" turns into a big night out. Open until 1am at weekends.

Judge's Lodging Cellar Bar 9 Lendal. Lively drinking hole in the eighteenth-century cellars of a smart hotel, with a large outdoor terrace and regular DJ nights.

The Three-Legged Mare 15 High Petergate. York Brewery's cosy outlet for its own quality beer and definitely a pub for grown-ups – no jukebox, no video games and no kids.

Entertainment

Cultural entertainment is wide and varied, with the National Centre for Early Music in St Margaret's Church, Walmgate (Ⓣ01904/658338, Ⓦwww.ncem.co.uk), hosting a prestigious **early music festival** in July, plus world, jazz and folk gigs. Indie and guitar-pop bands play most nights of the week at *Fibbers*, Stonebow House, Stonebow (Ⓣ01904/651250, Ⓦwww.fibbers.co.uk), while there's an art-house **cinema**, City Screen, 13 Coney St (Ⓣ0871/704 2054, Ⓦwww.picturehouses.co.uk), with riverside café-bar and live music and DJ nights.

DURHAM

Seen from the train, **DURHAM** presents a magnificent sight, with cathedral and castle perched atop a bluff enclosed by a loop of the River Wear (pronounced "weer"), and linked to the suburbs by a series of sturdy bridges. Nowadays a quiet provincial town with a strong student presence, Durham was once one of northern England's power bases: the Bishops of Durham were virtual royal agents in the north for much of the medieval era, responsible for defending a crucial border province frequently menaced by the Scots.

What to see and do

The town initially owed its reputation to the possession of the remains of St Cuthbert, which were evacuated to Durham in the ninth century because of Viking raids. Since then, his shrine has dominated the eastern end of the spectacular **Cathedral** (Mon–Sat 9.30am–5pm, Sun 12.30–5pm; £4 donation requested; Ⓦwww.durhamcathedral.co.uk). The cathedral itself is the finest example of Norman architecture in England, and also contains the tomb of the Venerable Bede, the country's first historian. The **Treasures of St Cuthbert** exhibition is in the undercroft (Mon–Sat 10am–4.30pm, Sun 2–4.30pm; £2.50), while the **tower** gives breathtaking views (Mon–Sat 9.30/10am–3/4pm; £3). On the opposite side of Palace Green is the **castle** (guided tours only; daily; £5; Ⓦwww.durhamcastle.com), a much-refurbished Norman edifice that's now a university hall of residence. A half-hour stroll follows a pathway on the wooded river bank below the cathedral and castle, all the way around the peninsula, passing a succession of elegant bridges.

Arrival and information

Train Durham train station is ten minutes' walk from the centre, via either of two river bridges.

Bus The bus station is just south on North Road.

Tourist office The tourist office is at Millennium Place (Mon–Sat 9.30am–5.30pm, Sun 11am–4pm; Ⓣ0191/384 3720, Ⓦwww.durhamtourism.co.uk), where there's also a theatre, library, café and bar.

Accommodation

There's no hostel, but Durham University has **rooms** available – including within the castle – at Easter and from July to September (Ⓣ0800/289970, Ⓦwww.dur.ac.uk/conference_tourism; ❼), while good-value **B&Bs** include *12 The Avenue* (Ⓣ0191/384 1020; ❻), west of the city centre.

Eating and drinking

Durham's no clubbers paradise, but there are some nice **pubs** and The Gala Theatre and Cinema at Millennium Place hosts drama, music, comedy and film nights (Ⓣ0191/332 4041, Ⓦwww.galadurham.co.uk).

The Almshouse Palace Green. Restaurant, in a fine location next to the cathedral, conjuring up tasty dishes for around £7 (till 8pm in summer).

Court Inn Court Lane. The best dining pub in town as well as a mobile free zone. Perfect for a quiet pint.

Pancake Café Crossgate. Student favourite serving up enticing sweet and savoury pancakes.
Vennel's Café Saddler's Yard. Café serving everything from cakes to pasta in a lovely little hidden courtyard off Saddler St – the upstairs bar here kicks into action after 7pm.

NEWCASTLE UPON TYNE

Once a tough, industrial city with a proud shipbuilding heritage, **NEWCASTLE** has retained its undeniable raw vigour, most conspicuously in its famously high-spirited nightlife. These days, it's streets ahead of its rivals in the northeast, and has a slew of fine galleries and arts venues, as well as a handsome Neoclassical downtown area fanning out from the lofty Grecian column of **Grey's Monument**, the city's central landmark.

What to see and do

Arriving by train, your first view is of the **River Tyne** and its redeveloped quaysides, along with the Norman keep of the castle itself. A famous series of bridges spans the Tyne, linking Newcastle to the Gateshead side of the river – the single steel arch form of the **Tyne Bridge**, built in 1929, both echoed and revitalised by the hi-tech "winking" **Millennium Bridge**, a wonderful sweeping arc of sparkling steel channelling pedestrians over the river.

Laing Gallery and BALTIC

The northeast's main art collection is housed in the **Laing Gallery** on New Bridge Street (Mon–Sat 10am–5pm, Sun 2–5pm; free; ⓦwww.twmuseums.org.uk), but it has been overshadowed by the opening of **BALTIC**, the excellent Centre for Contemporary Art (daily 10am–6pm, Thurs until 8pm; free; ⓦwww.balticmill.com), on the Gateshead side of the Tyne next to the Millennium Bridge. Second only in scale to London's Tate Modern, this con-

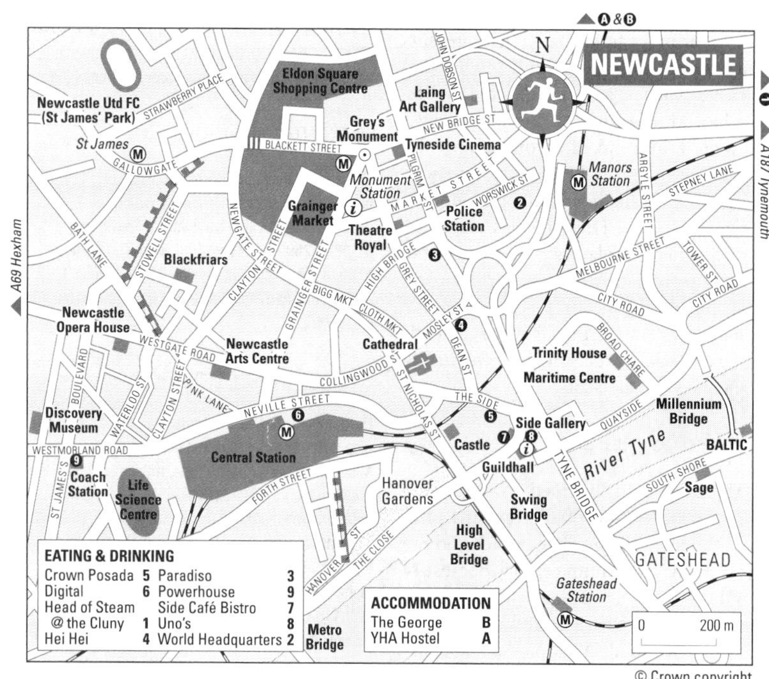

© Crown copyright

verted former flour mill accommodates exhibition galleries, artists' studios, a café-bar and two restaurants.

The Sage

The Baltic has been joined by the similarly ambitious **The Sage Gateshead** (Ⓦwww.thesagegateshead.org), a billowing steel, aluminium and glass structure by Norman Foster that's home to the Northern Sinfonia, one of Europe's most acclaimed chamber orchestras. The building has its detractors – it looks like a decapitated slug – but the full programme of concerts, classical and contemporary, and activities running throughout the year have transformed this side of the river. A free monthly guide to events at The Sage can be obtained here or at the tourist office.

Day-trips

Easy out-of-town trips on the Metro can take you to **Bede's World** (Mon–Sat 10am–4.30/5.30pm, Sun noon–4.30/5.30pm; £4.50; Ⓦwww.bedesworld.co.uk; Bede station), five miles east in Jarrow, which imaginatively evokes the life and times of the great early Christian scholar, alongside the remains of Bede's monastery; and to the excavations at **Segedunum** (daily April–Oct 10am–5pm, Nov–March 10am–3pm; £3.95; Ⓦwww.twmuseums.org.uk/segedunum), the "strong fort" four miles east of Newcastle that was the last outpost of Hadrian's great border defence.

Arrival and information

Air The airport is six miles north, served by the local Metro system (Day Saver for unlimited rides, £3.50 after 9am depending on the day).
Train Newcastle's Central Station is five minutes' walk south of Grey's Monument.
Bus The coach station, on St James's Boulevard, is a few minutes' walk west of the station.
Ferry A ferry port (for crossings from Amsterdam and Scandinavia) is in North Shields, seven miles east, with connecting buses running to the centre.
Tourist office There are tourist offices on Market Street (Mon–Sat 9/9.30am–5.30pm, Ⓣ0191/277 8000, Ⓦwww.visitnewcastlegateshead.com) and at Guildhall, Quayside (Mon–Fri 10am–5pm, Sat 9am–5pm, Sun 9am–4pm; same number).

Accommodation

The University of Northumbria (Ⓣ0191/227 3215) and Newcastle University (Ⓣ0191/222 6296) offer good-value, summertime B&B (mostly single rooms) in their halls of residence (❼). Upmarket Jesmond – a mile north of the centre and on the Metro – is the main location for budget hotels and **B&Bs**, with the family-run *George*, 88 Osborne Rd (Ⓣ0191/281 4442; ❼) offering decent, en-suite rooms at reasonable prices. The HI **hostel** at 107 Jesmond Rd (Ⓣ0191/281 2570; dorm ❸, twin ❼) in a converted townhouse has a common room, a kitchen, a dining room and clean, basic rooms.

Eating

Hei Hei 46 Dean St. Chic, modern Chinese that delivers on taste too. Mains from £5.95.
Paradiso 1 Market Lane. A bustling café-bar with great Italian food and live jazz on Sundays. The two-course lunch menu is £8.95.
Side Café Bistro 1–3 The Side. Arty café, gallery and cinema near the quayside serving simple food in relaxed surroundings.
Uno's 18 Sandhill. Popular pizza place that can't be faulted for value. Happy hour pizzas (noon–5/7pm) are £4.50.

Drinking and nightlife

City-centre **pubs** and **bars** are clustered around the notorious **Bigg Market**, a block west of Grey Street, and down on the slightly more sophisticated **Quayside**. The free monthly listings magazine, *The Crack*, is the best way to find out about gigs, clubs and other entertainment.
Crown Posada 31 The Side. A traditional drinking den with a beautifully preserved Victorian interior and good ales.
Digital Times Square. The new home of Shindig, Newcastle's legendary house night, and proud owner of the best sound system in the city.
Head of Steam @ the Cluny 36 Lime St. Outstanding pub attracting discerning Geordies who go for the, not incompatible, blend of real ales and cutting-edge music. It has another branch on Neville St.
Powerhouse 7–19 Westmoreland Rd. The Northeast's only exclusively gay club, playing something for everyone over its three floors. It closes at 4am.

World Headquarters Carliol Square, Ⓦwww.trenthouse.com. Six-floor (including a skatepark and an art gallery) club that's relaxed, inclusive and very cool. The fun lasts until 3am.

HADRIAN'S WALL

HADRIAN'S WALL (Ⓦwww.hadrianswall.org), separating Roman England from barbarian Scotland can be a wonderfully atmospheric place, especially on a rainy day, when it's not difficult to imagine Roman soldiers gloomily contemplating their bleak northern posting from atop the wall. Nowadays **Hadrian's Wall Path**, an 84-mile waymarked trail (5–7 days), runs from coast to coast, linking the substantial remains – the start is at Segedunum fort at Wallsend (see p.189), where you get your "walk passport" stamped. Otherwise, the best jumping-off point and base for longer exploration is the abbey town of **HEXHAM**, 45 minutes west of Newcastle by train or bus. Some of the finest preserved sections of wall include **Housesteads** (daily 10am–4/6pm; £4.10), the most complete Roman fort in Britain, set in spectacular countryside, and the partly recreated fort and lively museum at **Vindolanda** (daily: April–Sept 10am–6pm; Oct/Nov & Feb/March 10am–5pm; Dec/Jan Wed–Sun 10am–4pm; £4.95; Ⓦwww.vindolanda.com). A decent walk, covering around 7.5 miles and taking in both Housesteads and Vindolanda, as well as some dramatic scenery, is the circular route starting and finishing at Once Brewed.

Arrival and information

Bus The Hadrian's Wall #AD122 bus (Easter–Oct: up to 5 daily in summer, restricted services at other times; 1-day ticket £7, 3-days £14, 7-days £28) runs between Hexham, Carlisle via all the main sites; at least once a day it links through to Newcastle and Wallsend. The year-round #685 bus runs from Carlisle to Housesteads via Haltwhistle (on the Newcastle–Carlisle train line).

Tourist office Hexham has a tourist office, in the main town car park (daily 9am–5/6pm; Nov–Easter closed Sun; Ⓣ01434/652200, Ⓦwww.hexhamnet.co.uk). There's also a National Park Centre at Once Brewed (daily 9.30am–5pm; Nov–Easter Sat & Sun 10am–3pm).

Accommodation and eating

There's plenty of **accommodation** including at the *Once Brewed* HI hostel, 15 miles west of Hexham (Ⓣ0870/770 5980; dorm ❸) and the nearby *Twice Brewed Inn* (Ⓣ01434/344534, Ⓦwww.twicebrewedinn.co.uk; ❼ closed Jan), a friendly **pub** with simple rooms, food served until 8.30pm, local beers and internet access.

Wales

The relationship between England and **Wales** (Cymru in Welsh) has never been entirely easy. Impatient with constant demarcation disputes, the eighth-century Mercian king Offa constructed a dyke to separate the two countries: the 177-mile **Offa's Dyke Path** that still marks the border to this day. In the late thirteenth century, the last of the Welsh native princes, Llewelyn ap Gruffudd, was killed, and Wales passed uneasily under English rule. The arrival of the 1999 National Assembly for Wales, the first all-Wales tier of government for nearly six hundred years, may well indicate that power is shifting back, though so far it's a slow trickle.

Much of the country, particularly the **Brecon Beacons** in the south and **Snowdonia** in the north, is relentlessly mountainous and offers wonderful walking and climbing terrain. **Pembrokeshire** to the west boasts a spectacular rugged coastline, dotted with offshore island nature reserves. The biggest towns, including the capital **Cardiff** in the south, **Aberystwyth** in the west, and **Caernarfon** in the north, all cling to the coastal lowlands, but even then the mountains are no more than a bus-ride away. **Holyhead**, on the island of **Anglesey**, is the main British port for ferry sailings to the Irish capital, Dublin.

WELSH CULTURE AND LANGUAGE

Indigenous **Welsh culture** survives largely through language and song. The Eisteddfod festivals of Welsh music, poetry and dance still take place throughout the country in summer – the annual Royal National Eisteddfod (Ⓦwww.eisteddfod.org.uk), a very Welsh affair that breaks out in a different location during the first week of August, and the Llangollen International Musical Eisteddfod (Ⓦwww.internationaleisteddfod.co.uk), held on the first full week in July, being the best-known examples.

The **Welsh language** is undergoing a revival and you'll see it on bilingual road signs all over the country, although you're most likely to hear it spoken in the north, west and mid-Wales, where for many, it's their first language. Some **Welsh place-names** have never been anglicized, but where alternative names do exist, we've given them in the text.

Some basics
Hello *Helo*
Goodbye *Hwyl*
Please *Os gwelwch chi'n da*
Thank you *Diolch*

CARDIFF

Though once shackled to the fortunes of the coal-mining industry, Wales's largest city, **CARDIFF** (Caerdydd), 150 miles west of London, has made its mark as the vibrant Welsh capital, and since 1999 has been the home of the Welsh Assembly. The city's narrow Victorian arcades are interspersed with new shopping centres and wide pedestrian precincts.

What to see and do

The geographical and historical heart of the city is **Cardiff Castle** (tours daily 9.30am–5pm; £7.50 full tour, grounds only £3.75). Standing on a Roman site developed by the Normans, the castle was embellished by William Burges in the 1860s, and each room is now a wonderful example of Victorian "medieval" decoration; best of all are the Chaucer Room, the Banqueting Hall, the Arab Room and the Fairy-tale Nursery. Five minutes' walk northeast, the **National Museum and Gallery** in Cathays Park (Tues–Sun 10am–5pm; free; Ⓦwww.nmgw.ac.uk) houses a fine collection of Impressionist paintings, and natural history and archaeological exhibits.

Cardiff Bay

A half-hour walk south of the centre is the **Cardiff Bay** area, also reached by bus #7 from Central Station, or a train from Queen Street. Once known as Tiger Bay, the long-derelict area (birthplace of singer Shirley Bassey) has seen massive redevelopment since the opening of the Welsh Assembly. The area is now dominated by the imposing **Wales Millennium Centre** (Ⓣ0870/040 2000, Ⓦwww.wmc.org.uk), which houses a huge theatre for the performing arts. Nearby is the **Visitor Centre** (daily 9.30/10.30am–5/6pm, Ⓣ029/2046 3833), known popularly as "The Tube" for its unique, award-winning design. Pleasant waterfront walks, glittering architecture and an old Norwegian seamen's chapel converted into a cosy café add to the new air of refinement.

Around Cardiff

The **Museum of Welsh Life** is at St Fagans, four miles west of the centre on buses #32/320. This 100-acre open-air museum is packed with reconstructed rural and industrial heritage buildings (daily 10am–5pm; free; wwww.nmgw.ac.uk). Fans of William Burges' elaborate interiors shouldn't miss the fairy-

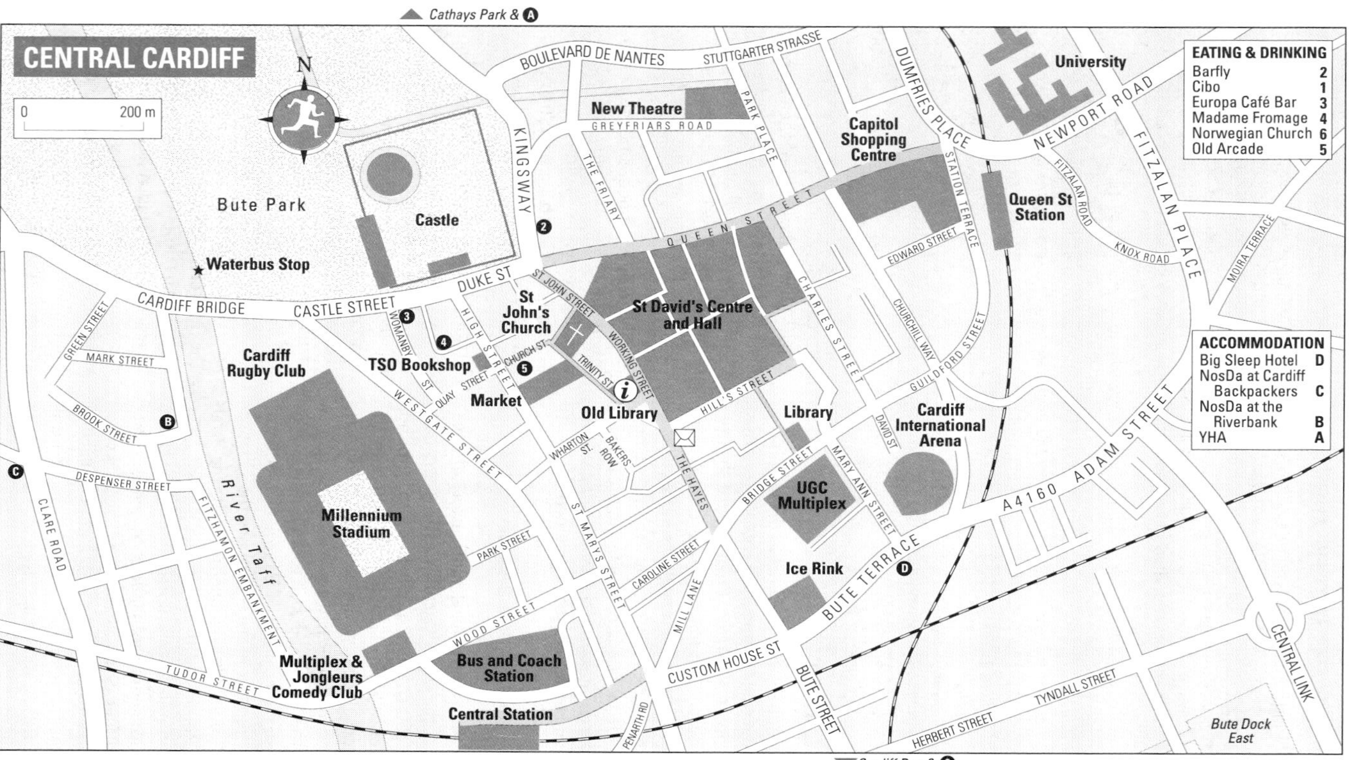
CENTRAL CARDIFF
0 200 m
N
EATING & DRINKING
Barfly 2
Cibo 1
Europa Café Bar 3
Madame Fromage 4
Norwegian Church 6
Old Arcade 5
ACCOMMODATION
Big Sleep Hotel D
NosDa at Cardiff Backpackers C
NosDa at the Riverbank B
YHA A
Cathays Park & A
Cathedral Road, Llandaff & 1
Cardiff Bay & 6
Bute Park
Waterbus Stop
Castle
Kingsway
Boulevard de Nantes
Stuttgarter Strasse
New Theatre
Greyfriars Road
Park Place
Capitol Shopping Centre
Dumfries Place
University
Newport Road
Fitzalan Place
Fitzalan Road
Knox Road
Moira Terrace
Queen St Station
Station Terrace
Queen Street
The Friary
Edward Street
Duke St
St John Street
St John's Church
St David's Centre and Hall
Charles Street
Churchill Way
Guildford Street
Cardiff Bridge
Castle Street
Womanby St
High Street
Church St
Trinity St
Working Street
Cardiff Rugby Club
TSO Bookshop
Quay Street
Market
Old Library
Hill's Street
Library
David St
Cardiff International Arena
Adam Street
A4160
Green Street
Mark Street
Brook Street
Westgate Street
Wharton St.
Bakers Row
The Hayes
Bridge Street
UGC Multiplex
Mary Ann Street
Despenser Street
Clare Road
River Taff
Millennium Stadium
Fitzhamon Embankment
Park Street
St Marys Street
Caroline Street
Mill Lane
Ice Rink
Bute Terrace
Wood Street
Bus and Coach Station
Multiplex & Jongleurs Comedy Club
Tudor Street
Central Station
Penarth Rd
Custom House St
Bute Street
Tyndall Street
Herbert Street
Central Link
Bute Dock East

tale **Castell Coch** at Tongwynlais, five miles north of town on bus #26 (April–Oct daily 9.30am–5/6pm; Nov–March Mon–Sat 9.30am–4pm, Sun 11am–4pm; £3.50; closed for six weeks every Jan & Feb). Perched dramatically on a steep, forested hillside, Burges' lavish Victorian showpiece was commissioned by the third Lord Bute as a country retreat, complete with turrets.

Arrival and information

Train/bus Long-distance coaches, and buses from the airport, arrive at the bus terminal, right beside Cardiff Central train station, south of the city centre off Penarth Road (local trains use Queen Street station instead, east of the centre).

Tourist office The Visitor Centre is at The Old Library (Mon–Sat 9.30am–6pm, Sun 10am–4pm; ⓣ0870/1211 258, ⓦwww.visitcardiff.info).

Accommodation

Big Sleep Hotel Bute Terrace ⓣ029/2063 6363, ⓦwww.thebigsleephotel.com. Trendy, budget hotel with clean lines and a modern interior. ❽

NosDa at Cardiff Backpackers 98 Neville St ⓣ029/2034 5577, ⓦwww.nosda.co.uk. Excellent hostel with a young crowd, barbecues and a bar. No curfew at weekends. Dorms ❸, doubles ❼

NosDa at the Riverbank 53–59 Despenser St ⓣ029/2037 8866, ⓦwww.nosda.co.uk. Sister hostel to Nosda on Neville St, this new riverside place offers excellent facilities at budget prices. There's a bar, terrace, internet access, nightclub and 24hr reception. Facilities are open to residents at their other hostel. Dorm ❸, doubles ❽

YHA 2 Wedal Rd ⓣ0870/770 5750, ⓦwww.yha.org.uk. Cardiff's HI hostel is a couple of miles north of the centre at 2 Wedal Rd. No doubles or twins. Dorms ❷

Eating and drinking

Barfly Kingsway. The best place to go for live indie music.

Cibo 83 Pontcanna St. Small Italian trattoria serving sandwiches and more substantial fare. Mains from £6.

Europa Café Bar 25 Castle St. Bohemian hangout that attracts an arty/student crowd with nice coffee by day and an alcohol licence by night. They've recently expanded their range with live music and DJs.

Madame Fromage 18 Castle Arcade. Cheese experts, serving up delicious soups, cold platters and larger bites in a pretty Victorian arcade opposite the castle.

Norwegian Church Cardiff Bay. The café in this sweet old sailor's church is great for salads and snacks.

Old Arcade 14 Church St. One of the few old pubs in the centre to have retained some character, despite a recent refurbishment.

CHEPSTOW AND TINTERN ABBEY

South Wales' most spectacular historic monument is accessible from the market town of **CHEPSTOW** (Cas-Gwent), a sleepy spot boasting stunning views of cliff-faces soaring above the river and of the first stone **castle** in Britain, built by the Normans in 1067 (April–Oct daily 9.30am–5/6pm; Nov–March Mon–Sat 9.30am–4pm, Sun 11am–4pm; £3.50). Nothing within the town can match the six-mile stroll north along the Wye to the romantic ruins of **Tintern Abbey**, built in 1131 and now in a state of majestic disrepair (same hours as castle; £3.50). If you don't fancy walking, catch bus #69 (every 2hr), which runs from Chepstow to Tintern and on to Monmouth, eight miles north. The fourteenth-century *Moon and Sixpence* pub – almost a mile north of the Abbey by the river – does excellent food. For information on Chepstow and the popular **Offa's Dyke Path** contact the **tourist office** on Bridge St (daily 10am–5.30pm; ⓣ01291/623772). If you want to stay, try *The Coach and Horses Inn* on Welsh Street (ⓣ01291/622626; doubles ❽). The cheapest option is some way out of town: the spooky St Briavels Castle HI **hostel** (ⓣ0870/770 6040, ⓦwww.yha.org.uk; dorms ❷) is set in a moated Norman castle seven miles northeast of Chepstow, reached by bus #69.

THE BRECON BEACONS

The **Brecon Beacons National Park** (ⓦwww.breconbeacons.org) occupies a vast area of rocky uplands that are perfect walking territory. The Beacons themselves, a pair of hills 2900ft high accessed from Brecon town, share the limelight with the **Black Mountains** north of Crickhowell. Dedicated Beacons buses (ⓦwww.visitbreconbeacons.com) run from Cardiff and Newport to Brecon, passing through Merthyr Tydfil or Abergavenny and Crickhowell, but trains from Newport veer off into England after Abergavenny.

What to see and do

The market town of **ABERGAVENNY** (Y Fenni) sits in a fold between seven green hills at the eastern edge of the park, about fifteen miles north of Newport. Before setting out for the mountains, pick up maps from the combined **tourist office** and **national park information office** (daily 9.30/10am–4.30/6pm; ⓣ01873/857588) on Cross Street beside the bus station – and check what sort of weather you can expect, as conditions change rapidly. The most accessible walking areas are the **Sugar Loaf** (1955ft), four miles northwest, and **Holy Mountain** (Skirrid Fawr; 1595ft), three miles north. Serious hikers can attempt the 100-mile Beacon Way, traversing the entire national park from Abergavenny to Llangadog, that should take around eight days. If you want to stay in Abergavenny, The *Black Sheep* **hostel** in the *Great Western Hotel* opposite the train station is a good option (ⓣ01873/859125, ⓦwww.blacksheepbackpackers.com; dorm ❷, twin ❸).

Crickhowell and Hay-on-Wye

CRICKHOWELL (Crughywel), a friendly village with a fine seventeenth-century bridge five miles west of Abergavenny, is more picturesque. A great six-mile hike into the Black Mountains from here takes you through remote countryside to tiny **Partrishow Church**; inside, you'll find a rare carved fifteenth-century rood screen complete with dragon, and an ancient mural of the grim reaper. For more dramatic scenery, you could try the six-and-a-half mile round-trip to Table Mountain, the summit of which offers great views of the Black Mountains. Beaufort Street in Crickhowell holds the **tourist office** (April–Oct daily 9.30am–5pm; ⓣ01873/812105, ⓦwww.crickhowell.org.uk), and the best value accommodation in town is at the excellent *Riverside Campsite* (ⓣ01873/810397; ❶) by the bridge. To the north of the Black Mountains, on the border with England, is the small town of **Hay-on-Wye**, famous as the secondhand book capital of the world. As well as being piled high with bargain books, the charming town hosts an important literature festival in June every year and has more than its fair share of great pubs and places to eat.

Brecon

The largest of the central Brecon Beacons rise just south of **BRECON** (Aberhonddu), a lively little town eight miles west of Crickhowell that springs to life in mid-August for the huge international Brecon Jazz Festival (ⓦwww.breconjazz.co.uk). For details of the numerous trekking routes and an extensive programme of guided walks, call in at the **tourist office** in the Cattle Market car park beside Morrisons (daily 9.30am–4/5/5.30pm; ⓣ01874/622485). The Brynich Caravan Park, half-an-hour from town, is a good option for camping (ⓣ 01874/623325 ❷) and there's an HI **hostel** two miles east of Brecon at Groesfford (ⓣ0870/770 5718, ⓦwww.yha.org.uk; dorms ❸, twin ❻), a mile off the Abergavenny bus route, while the *Held Bunkhouse* hostel is in Cantref (ⓣ01874/624646, ⓦwww.heldbunkhouse.co.uk; group bookings only; ❷), a mile southwest of town.

PEMBROKESHIRE COAST NATIONAL PARK

PEMBROKE (Penfro), birthplace of Henry VII, is a sleepy town, easily ac-

FERRIES TO IRELAND

Two **ferries** to Rosslare in Ireland (4hr) leave from **Pembroke Dock**, two miles north of Pembroke, every day. About 17 miles further north on bus #411 – at the end of the main train line from Cardiff and London - is **Fishguard** (Abergwaun), another embarkation point for Rosslare, with ferries and catamarans departing daily. **Holyhead (Caergybi)**, on Anglesey, is the busiest Welsh ferry-port, with several daily ferry and catamaran sailings leaving for Dublin.

cessible by train from Cardiff. From here you can explore the UK's only coastal **National Park** that sweeps around this edge of the southwestern peninsula of Wales; its coastal path includes some of the country's most stunning and remote scenery. From Pembroke, bus #349 runs north to Haverfordwest where you can catch bus #411 sixteen miles west to **ST DAVID'S** (Tyddewi), one of the most enchanting spots in Britain, with a beautiful **cathedral** (Ⓦwww.stdavidscathedral.org.uk; £3 donation requested), delicately tinted purple, green and yellow by a combination of lichen and geology. Constructed between 1180 and 1522, it hosts a prestigious classical music festival in late May or early June. Across a thin trickle of river the remains of the magnificent fourteenth-century **Bishop's Palace** (Easter–Oct daily 9.30am–5/6pm; Nov–Easter Mon–Sat 9.30am–4pm, Sun 11am–4pm; £2.90), add to the wonderful setting. St David's HI **hostel** is at Llaethdy, close to Whitesands Beach (Ⓣ0870/770 6042; dorms ❷, twin ❺) and *Pen Albro*, 18 Goat St (Ⓣ01437/720865; ❻), is a central **B&B**. The **visitor centre** is at the Grove (Easter–Oct daily 9.30am–5.30pm; Nov–Easter Mon–Sat 10am–4pm; Ⓣ01437/720392, Ⓦwww.stdavids.co.uk).

ABERYSTWYTH

ABERYSTWYTH, a lively, thoroughly Welsh seaside resort of neat Victorian terraces, has a thriving student culture. The train station is ten minutes south of the seafront, reached by walking up Terrace Rd past the **tourist office** (July & Aug daily 10am–6pm, Sept–June Mon–Sat 10am–5pm; Ⓣ01970/612125). Upstairs, the eclectic **Ceredigion Museum** (free) contains coracles once used by local fishermen as well as a reconstructed cottage interior. The flavour of the town is best appreciated on the seafront, where one of Edward I's castles bestrides a windy headland to the south. There's also a Victorian **camera obscura** further north, which can be reached via the clanking **cliff railway** (April–Oct daily 10am–5/6pm; Nov–March Wed–Sun 10am–4pm; £2.75 return). For a more extended rail trip, you could take the very popular **Vale of Rheidol** narrow-gauge steam train to **Devil's Bridge**, a canyon where three bridges span a dramatic waterfall (April–Oct; 3hr return trip, 1hr to Devil's Bridge; £13). The town seafront is lined with genteel **guest houses**; try *Yr Hafod*, 1 South Marine Terrace (Ⓣ01970/617579; ❽). Out of term-time, contact the University of Wales about beds in **student halls** (Ⓣ01970/621960; ❼). *The Treehouse*, on Eastgate, is a great daytime vegetarian café with mains from £6.50. Check out the university's Arts Centre on Penglais Hill for films, plays, exhibitions and other events.

Harlech

North of Aberystwyth the train passes through a succession of seaside resorts before reaching **HARLECH**, where one of the best of Edward I's great castles, later Owen Glyndwr's residence, grows from a rocky crag overlooking the sea (April–Oct daily 9.30am–5/6pm; Nov–March Mon–Sat 9.30am–4pm, Sun 11am–4pm;

£3.50); the ramparts offer panoramic views over the mountains of Snowdonia on one side and Tremadog Bay on the other. Below the town, over undulating sand dunes, is Harlech beach, four miles of pristine sand - though you'll have to pass through the rather snooty Royal St. David's Golf Club to get there. There's not much to do in town, but if you want **to stay**, try the *Arundel B&B*, High Street (ⓣ01766/780637; ❺).

SNOWDONIA AND THE NORTH COAST

Snowdonia National Park is an enormous area stretching from Aberdyfi in the south to Conwy on the north coast. What most people mean when they refer to Snowdonia, though, is the glory of **North Wales** – Mount Snowdon (3560ft), and the blue-grey, slate towns and villages that surround the peak. With some of the most dramatic mountain scenery Britain has to offer – jagged peaks, towering waterfalls and glacial lakes decorating every roadside – it's not surprising that walkers congregate here in large numbers, and there's a steady stream of tourist traffic even in the bleakest months of the year.

What to see and do

Whatever season you're here, make sure you're equipped with suitable shoes, warm clothing, and food and drink to see you through any unexpected hitches. There are two main access routes. From Porthmadog, a few miles north of Harlech, **buses** skirt the base of Snowdon west to Caernarfon and Llanberis, and east to Blaenau Ffestiniog; while mainline **trains** from Crewe and Chester hug the north coast through Bangor to Holyhead, with a branch line heading south to Betws-y-Coed and Blaenau Ffestiniog.

Llanberis and Snowdon

Regular buses run the seven miles east from Caernarfon to **LLANBERIS**, a lakeside village in the shadow of **Snowdon**, at 3560ft the highest mountain in England and Wales. With the biggest concentration of guest houses, hostels and restaurants close to the mountains, Llanberis offers the perfect base for even the most tentative Snowdonian exploration. The longest but easiest ascent of the mountain is the Llanberis Path, a signposted five-mile hike (3hr) that is manageable by anyone reasonably fit. Alternatively, you can cop out and take the generally steam-hauled **Snowdon Mountain Railway** (daily mid-March to October; £20; ⓦwww.snowdonrailway.co.uk), which operates from Llanberis to the summit café, pub and post office, weather permitting (note that at time of writing trains terminate at Clogwyn, three-quarters of the way up the mountain, due to rebuilding of the summit centre). The slate quarries that seared Llanberis's surroundings now lie idle, with the **Welsh Slate Museum** (Easter–Oct daily 10am–5pm; Nov–Easter daily except Sat 10am–4pm; free; ⓦwww.nmgw.ac.uk) remaining as a memorial to the workers' tough lives. Nearby, the Dinorwig Pumped Storage Hydro Station is carved out of the mountain and can be visited on underground tours (£7) starting at the **Electric Mountain Museum** (daily 9.30/10am–4.30/5.30pm, which has a good café.

Buses stop near the **tourist office**, 41 High St (Easter–Oct daily 10am–6pm; Nov–Easter Wed & Fri–Sun 11am–4pm; ⓣ01286/870765, ⓔllanberis.tic@gwynedd.gov.uk). The enduringly popular *Pete's Eats*, 40 High St, satisfies walkers' appetites.

Accommodation

Walkers have a good choice of **accommodation**. The Sherpa Bus services (£4 all-day) collectively encircle Snowdon providing access to several **HI hostels** (ⓦwww.yha.org.uk), each at the base of a footpath up the mountain.

Bryn Gwynant Nantgwynant ⓣ0870/770 5732. Victorian mansion with a kitchen, restaurant and lounge. Dorms ❷, twin ❺

Llanberis Llyn Celyn ⓣ0870/770 5928. A short walk from Llanberis high street, this popular option is close to the fastest path up Snowdon. Dorms ❸, twin ❻

Pen-y-Pass Nantgwynant ⓣ0870/770 5990. An atmospheric old climbers' lodge and another good place from which to ascend Snowdon, with a games room and bar. Dorms ❷, twin ❺.

Snowdon Ranger Rhyd Ddu ⓣ0870/770 6038. Old inn at the foot of the mountain. There's a lake to swim in, a games room, restaurant and kitchen. Dorms ❷, twin ❹

Conwy

A couple of miles west of Llandudno Junction is **CONWY**, where Edward I's magnificent **castle** (April–Oct daily 9.30am–5/6pm; Nov–March Mon–Sat 9.30am–4pm, Sun 11am–4pm; £4.50) and the town walls are a UNESCO World Heritage Site. The entrance contains the **tourist office** (same hours; ⓣ01492/592248). The ramparts offer fine views of Thomas Telford's recently restored 1826 suspension bridge (April–Oct daily; £1) over the River Conwy. For camping you could try *Conwy Touring Park*, Trefriw Rd (ⓣ01492/592856, ⓦwww.conwytouringpark.com; ❷), about a mile-and-a-half out of town. Otherwise, there's Conwy **HI hostel**, Lark Hill, just west of the centre (ⓣ0870/770 5774, ⓦwww.yha.org.uk; dorm ❸, twin ❻).

Caernarfon

West of Conwy, trains pass through **Bangor** on the way to Holyhead. To get to **CAERNARFON** – the springboard for trips into Snowdonia from the north – you'll need bus #1/5 from the bus station off Bangor High St. **Caernarfon Castle** (daily: April–Oct 9.30am–5/6pm; Nov–March 9.30/11am–4pm; £4.90), built in 1283, is arguably the most splendid castle in Britain. Little of the interior has survived, however, and the three-acre space is largely grassed over; it's here that the Princes of Wales are invested. Buses stop on Penllyn, just across Castle Square from the **tourist office**, Castle Street (daily 10am–4.30/6pm; Nov–Easter closed Wed; ⓣ01286/672232, ⓦwww.visitcaernarfon.com). In town, the cheapest place to stay is *Totters*, an excellent backpacker hostel at 2 High St (ⓣ01286/672963; dorms ❸, doubles ❻); *Tegfan Guesthouse*, 4 Church St (ⓣ01286/673703; ❼), is another good bet.

Anglesey

The Menai Bridge was built by Thomas Telford in 1826 to connect North Wales with the island of **Anglesey** (Ynys Môn) across the Menai Straits, and it's one of the two chief sights on the little island, even though it's been superseded by a newer rival alongside. The other draw is the last of Edward I's masterpieces, **Beaumaris Castle** (April–Oct daily 9.30am–5/6pm; Nov–March Mon–Sat 9.30am–4pm, Sun 11am–4pm; £3.50), reached by bus #53, #57 or #58 from Bangor. The giant castle was built in 1295 to guard the straits and has a fairy-tale moat enclosing its twelve sturdy towers. From Holyhead, at the island's western tip, you can take a ferry to Ireland (see box, p.195).

Scotland

Scotland is a model example of how a small nation can retain its identity within the confines of a larger one. Down the centuries the Scots, unlike the Welsh, successfully repulsed the expansionist designs of England, and when the "old enemies" formed a union in 1603, it was because King James VI of Scotland inherited the English throne, rather than the other way around. Although the two countries' parliaments merged one hundred years later, Scotland retained many of its own institutions, notably distinctive legal and educational systems. However, the most significant reawakening of Scottish political nationalism since then has been in the last few years, with a separate parliament looking after most of Scotland's day-to-day affairs being re-established in Edinburgh in 1999.

Most of the population clusters between the two principal cities: stately **Edinburgh**, the national capital, with its magnificent architecture and imperious natural setting, and earthy **Glasgow**, a powerhouse of the Industrial Revolution but now as well known for its cultural core as its rough edges. Although the third city, Aberdeen, perched on the North Sea coast, has grown wealthy through offshore oil, Scotland is overwhelmingly rural outside the Central Belt. In the **Highlands and Islands**, the harsh, mountainous landscape is spectacularly beautiful, its rugged landscapes enhanced by the volatile climate, producing an extraordinary variety of moods and colours. It's a terrific place for those keen on outdoor activities, and much of the scenery – such as the famous **Loch Lomond** and **Loch Ness** – is easily accessible.

EDINBURGH

EDINBURGH, the showcase capital of Scotland, is a historic, cosmopolitan and cultured city. Its stone-built houses, historic buildings and fairytale castle, perched on a rocky crag right in the heart of the city, make it visually stunning and it is little surprise that this city is the most popular draw for tourists in Scotland. The 440,000 population swells massively in high season, peaking in mid-August during the **Edinburgh Festival**, by far the biggest arts event in Europe. Yet despite this annual invasion, the city is still emphatically Scottish in character and atmosphere, mixing rich history with fast-moving current affairs that have seen the re-establishment of a Scottish parliament and the consequent reaffirmation of Edinburgh as a dynamic European capital.

What to see and do

The centre has two distinct parts. The castle rock is the core of the medieval city, where nobles and servants lived side by side for centuries within tight defensive walls. Edinburgh earned the nickname "Auld Reekie" for the smog and smell generated by the cramped inhabitants of this **Old Town**, where the streets flowed with sewage tipped out of tenement windows and disease was rife. The **New Town** was begun in the late 1700s on farmland lying to the north of the Castle. Edinburgh's wealthier residents speculated profitably on tracts of this land and engaged the services of eminent architects in their development. The result is an outstanding example of Georgian town planning, still largely intact.

THE EDINBURGH FESTIVAL

The city's essential cultural event is the **Edinburgh Festival** (Ⓦwww.edinburgh-festivals.com), by far the world's largest arts jamboree, which was founded in 1947 and now attracts thousands of artistes from August to early September. The event is, in fact, several different festivals taking place at around the same time: the Edinburgh International Festival traditionally presents highbrow fare; but it's the frenetic Fringe (Ⓦwww.edfringe.com) that gives the city its unique buzz during August, with all sorts of unlikely venues turned into performance spaces for a bewildering array of artistes. In addition, there's a Film Festival, a Jazz Festival, and a Book Festival. Tickets are available at the venues and from the International Festival Office, The Hub, Castlehill (Ⓣ0131/473 2015), or the Fringe Office, 180 High St (Ⓣ0131/226 0026).

HAUNTED EDINBURGH

From serial killing, corpse dealers Burke and Hare, to the malevolent Mackenzie Poltergeist, the winding streets and underground vaults of the Old Town shelter a multitude of spooks, and several entertaining **ghost tours** operate around the High Street. Some favour a historical approach while others lean firmly toward the high-theatrical, using "jumper-ooters" - usually costumed students - to scare unsuspecting tour-goers. **The Real Mary King's Close** (Ⓣ0870/243 0160, Ⓦwww.realmarykingsclose.com) on Warriston Close, offers a fine balance between the informative and the chilling.

The Old Town and castle

The cobbled **Royal Mile** – composed of Castlehill, Lawnmarket, High Street and Canongate – is the central thoroughfare of the **Old Town**, running down a prominent ridge to the Palace of Holyroodhouse from the **Castle** (daily 9.30am–5/6pm; £11), a formidable edifice perched on sheer volcanic rock. Within its precincts are St Margaret's Chapel, containing the ancient crown jewels of Scotland and the even older Stone of Destiny, coronation stone of the kings of Scotland. There's a large military museum here, too, and the castle esplanade provides a dramatic setting for the Military Tattoo, an unashamed display of martial pomp staged during the Festival. Year round, at 1pm (not Sun) a cannon shot is fired from the battlements.

Museum of Scotland

Further down at the southern end of Lawnmarket, George IV Bridge leads south from the Royal Mile to Chambers Street; here the **Museum of Scotland** (daily 10am–5pm; Ⓦwww.nms.ac.uk), housed in an imaginatively designed modern sandstone building, is home to many of the nation's historical treasures, ranging from Celtic pieces to twentieth-century icons.

The High Kirk of St Giles and Parliament House

Back on the Royal Mile, High Street starts at Parliament Square, dominated by the **High Kirk of St Giles** (Mon–Sat 9am–5/7pm Sun 1–5pm; donation £3), whose beautiful crown-shaped spire is an Edinburgh landmark. Inside, the Thistle Chapel is an amazing display of mock-Gothic woodcarving. On the south side of Parliament Square are the Neoclassical law courts, incorporating the seventeenth-century **Parliament House**, under whose spectacular hammerbeam roof the Scottish parliament met until the 1707 Union.

John Knox's House and the Scottish Parliament

The final section of the Royal Mile, Canongate, starts just beyond medieval **John Knox's House** (Mon–Sat 10am–6pm; plus Sun noon–6pm during July & August; £3.50), the atmospheric home of the city's fierce Calvinist cleric, and is dominated by the new **Scottish Parliament** (daily 9/10am–4/6pm; free) a costly and controversial but undoubtedly striking piece of contemporary architecture.

The Palace of Holyroodhouse

Next door is the contrasting **Palace of Holyroodhouse** (daily April–Oct 9.30am–6pm, Nov–March 9.30am–4.30pm; £9.50), the Royal Family's official Scottish residence, which principally dates from the seventeenth century. The public are admitted to the sumptuous state rooms unless the royals are in residence. The **Queen's Gallery** (same opening hours; £5) displays works of art from the royal collection. The pal-

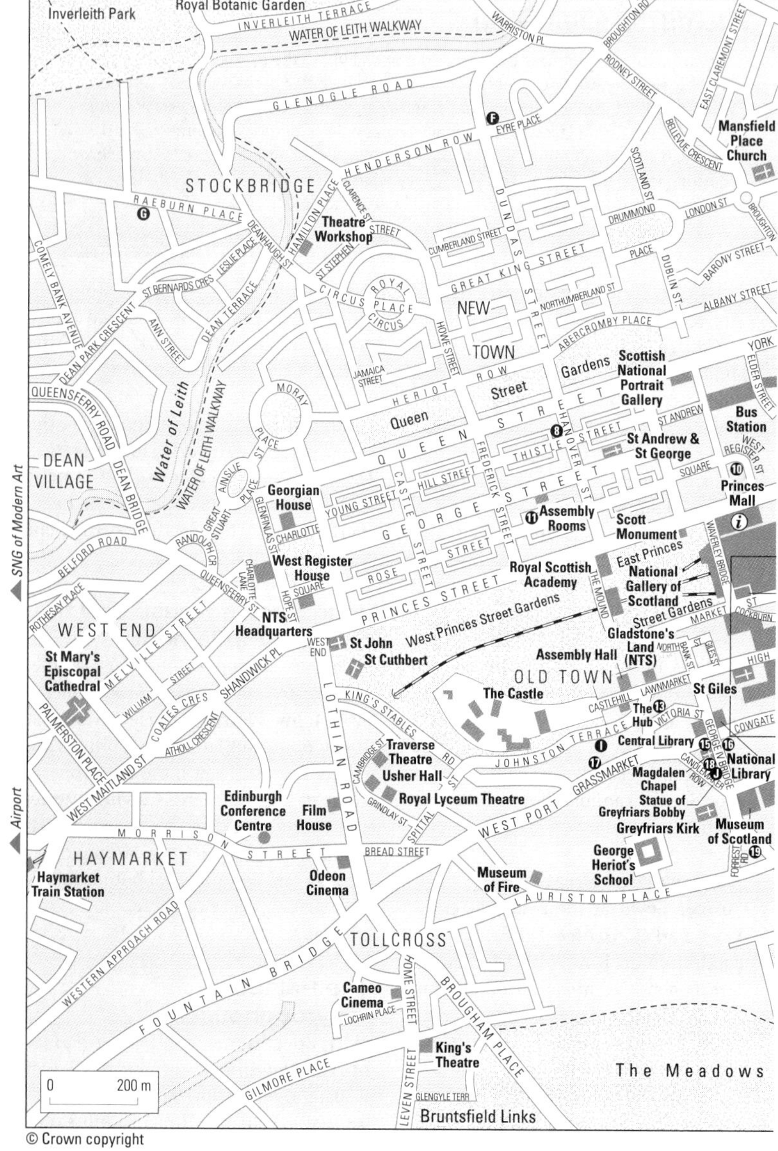

ace looks out over Holyrood Park, from where fine walks lead along the **Salisbury Crags** and up **Arthur's Seat** beyond; a fairly stiff climb is rewarded by magnificent views over the city and out to the Firth of Forth.

The New Town

The clear divide between the Old and **New Town** is the wide grassy valley of Princes Street Gardens, along the north side of which runs **Princes St**, the main shopping area. Splitting the gardens

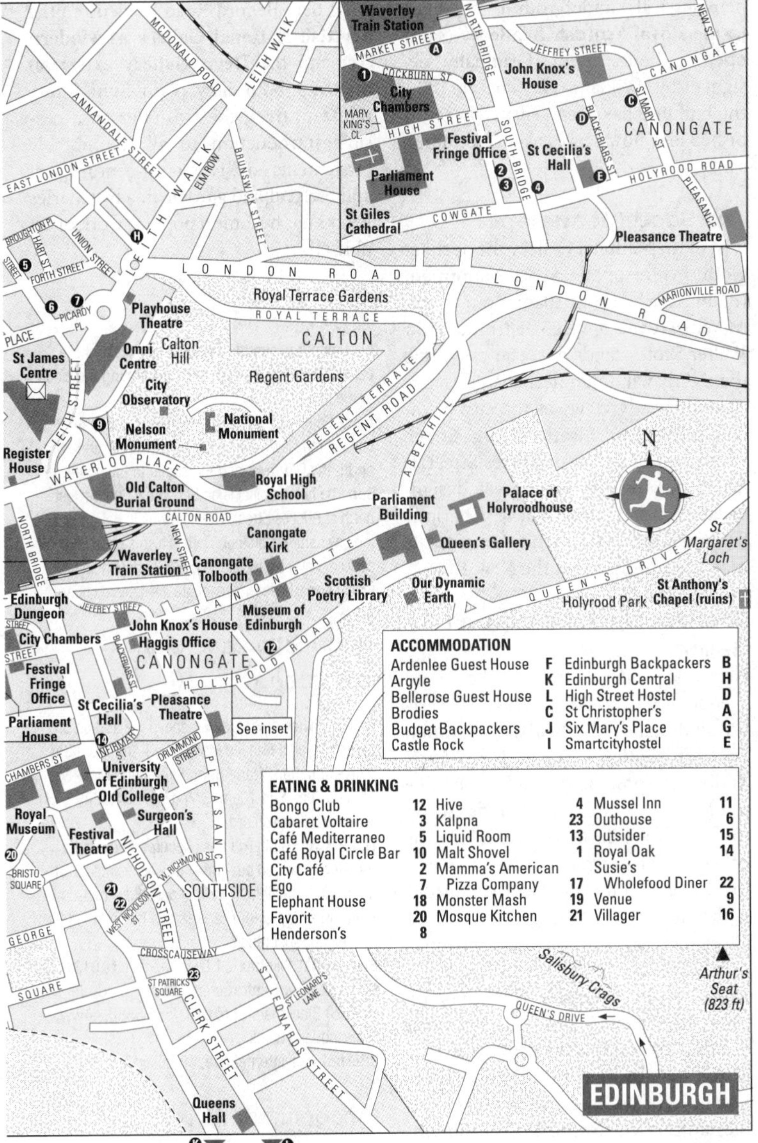

halfway along is the **National Gallery of Scotland** (daily 10am–5pm, Thurs till 7pm; free), an Athenian-style sandstone building. One of the best small collections of pre-twentieth-century art in Europe, it includes works by major European artists including Botticelli, Titian, Rembrandt, Degas, Gauguin and Van Gogh. Look out for the charming *Reverend Robert Walker Skating* by Henry Raeburn – a postcard favourite. The National is linked, via a splendid neo-classical underground chamber, to the **Royal Scottish Academy** (same opening hours; free). Originally designed by William Playfair in 1826, the building has been sensitively refurbished and now serves as an exhibition space.

The Scott Monument

East of the National Gallery the peculiar Gothic spire of the **Scott Monument** (daily April–Sep 9/10am–6pm, Oct–March 9/10am–3pm; £3), a tribute to Sir Walter Scott, stands out. You can climb the tightly winding internal spiral staircase for heady views of the city below and hills beyond. Nearby George Street, which runs parallel to Princes Street, is fast becoming the domain of designer-label shops, while suave Charlotte Square, at its western end, remains the most elegant square in the New Town.

Scottish National Portrait Gallery

North of George Street is the broad avenue of Queen Street, at whose eastern end stands the **Scottish National Portrait Gallery** (daily 10am–5pm, Thurs till 7pm; free). The remarkable red sandstone building is modelled on the Doge's Palace in Venice; inside the collection of portraits offers an engaging procession through Scottish history with famous Scots such as Bonnie Prince Charlie on display alongside contemporary heroes like Sean Connery.

East of here, **Calton Hill** rises up above the New Town and is worth heading up both for the views you'll get across the city, and for an odd collection of Neoclassical buildings including the unfinished **National Monument**, perched on the very top of the hill.

Scottish National Gallery of Modern Art

In the northwest corner of the New Town lies **Stockbridge**, a smart residential suburb with bohemian pretensions; from here Belford Road leads up to the **Scottish National Gallery of Modern Art** and the **Dean Gallery** extension opposite (both daily 10am–5pm, Thurs till 7pm; free); the two offer an accessible introduction to all the notable movements of twentieth-century art and the sculpted garden area by Charles Jencks has become a popular work of art in itself.

Arrival

Air Edinburgh airport is seven miles west of the centre; there are bus connections around the clock to the city.
Train Edinburgh's Waverley Station is bang in the centre; the New Town and Princes Street lie to the north, the Old Town and the castle to the south.
Bus The bus terminal is on St Andrew Square, just north of Princes Street. The best way to get around the city centre is on foot. There's also a good local bus service; day-passes (£2.50 or £2.30 depending on which firm's buses you use) are available on board.

Information and city transport

Tourist office 3 Princes St, above the station on the top level of Princes Mall (July & Aug Mon–Sat 9am–8pm, Sun 10am–8pm; Sept–June Mon–Sat 9am–5/7pm, Sun 10am–5/7pm; ⓣ0845/225 5121, ⓦwww.edinburgh.org).
Tickets An Edinburgh Pass secures free airport transfer, unlimited bus travel and access to 27 of the city's attractions (one-day pass £24, two-day £36, three-day £48). The pass can be obtained from the main tourist office.
Bike rental Biketrax, 11 Lochrin Place ⓣ0131/228 6333, ⓦwww.biketrax.co.uk; Edinburgh Cycle Hire, 29 Blackfriars St ⓣ0131/556 5560, ⓦwww.cyclescotland.co.uk.
Internet easyInternetcafe, 58 Rose St.

Accommodation

In addition to the places listed below, you can get **student rooms** (ⓢ) over the summer, though they're not cheap; try Napier University (ⓣ0845/260 6040) or Pollock Hall, Edinburgh University (ⓣ0131/651 2007). If you want to stay during the Festival (early Aug to early Sept), you'll need to book months in advance and be prepared to pay more than the usual high season prices.

Hostels

Argyle 14 Argyle Place, Marchmont ⓣ0131/667 9991, ⓦwww.argyle-backpackers.co.uk. Quieter hostel, with small dorms and a dozen double/twin rooms. Pleasant location in studenty Marchmont. Dorms ❷, doubles ❻

Brodies 93 High St, Old Town ⓣ0131/556 2223, ⓦwww.brodieshostels.co.uk. Tucked down a typical Old Town close, it's cosier than many others, but with limited communal areas. Dorms ❷, doubles ❼

Budget Backpackers 37–39 Cowgate ⓣ0131/226 6351, ⓦwww.budgetbackers.com. Welcoming and relaxed hostel, in a great location in the Grassmarket, with a great chill-out room, friendly staff and decent rooms. Dorms ❷, doubles ❻

Castle Rock 15 Johnston Terrace, Old Town ⓣ0131/225 9666, ⓦwww.scotlands-top-hostels.com. Friendly 200-bed hostel tucked below the castle ramparts. It comes with a comfortable lounge, 'period' features and a ghost. Dorms ❸, doubles ❼

Edinburgh Backpackers 65 Cockburn St, Old Town ⓣ0131/220 1717, ⓦwww.hoppo.com. Big hostel with a great central location in a side street off the Royal Mile. Rooms are of a good standard and clean. Dorms ❸, doubles ❼

Edinburgh Central 9 Haddington Place ⓣ0131/524 2090, ⓦwww.edinburghcentral.org. Excellent, new HI hostel off Leith Walk, proving the SYHA can keep up with the pace, with airy, clean rooms and a café/bistro. Dorms ❸, doubles ❼

High Street Hostel 8 Blackfriars St, Old Town ⓣ0131/557 3984, ⓦwww.scotlands-top-hostels.com. Large, lively well-known hostel, in a sixteenth-century building just off the Royal Mile, with basic rooms. Dorms ❸, doubles ❻

Smartcityhostel 50 Blackfriars St, Old Town ⓣ0131/524 1989, ⓦwww.smartcityhostels.com. Superb, new hotel-standard accommodation, with a stylish bar, terrace and restaurant. The spotless rooms are all en-suite. Dorms ❸, doubles ❽

St Christopher's Inn 9–13 Market St, Old Town ⓣ0131/226 1446, ⓦwww.st-christophers.co.uk. 110 beds (all bunks) with smaller rooms as well as dorms and a bar downstairs. The bunks are a tad rickety. Dorms ❸, doubles ❼

Hotels and B&Bs

Ardenlee Guest House 9 Eyre Place ⓣ0131/556 2838, ⓦwww.ardenlee.co.uk. Welcoming guest house, near the Royal Botanic Garden, with comfortable rooms. ❽

Bellerose Guest House 36 Minto St ⓣ0131/554 3700, ⓦwww.belleroseguesthouse.co.uk. Chintzy, but good-value, guest house a few miles south of town. ❼

Six Mary's Place Raeburn Place ⓣ0131/332 8965, ⓦwww.sixmarysplace.co.uk. Collectively run "alternative" guest house; has a no-smoking policy and offers excellent home-cooked vegetarian meals. ❽

Campsites

Edinburgh Caravan Club Marine Drive, Silverknowes ⓣ0131/312 6874. Pleasantly located close to the shore in the northwestern suburbs, 30min from the centre on bus #28. ❷

38 Mortonhall Gate Frogston Rd ⓣ0131/664 1533. A good site, five miles south of the centre, near the Braid Hills; take bus #11 (marked Captain's Rd) or #31 from the centre of town. Closed Jan–March. ❷

Eating

Cafés

Café Mediterraneo 73 Broughton St ⓣ0131/557 6900. Deceptively large dining space serving good-quality Italian food at great prices. Mains from under £5.

Elephant House 21 George IV Bridge. Popular café near the university, with a cavernous back room, made famous by JK Rowling's pre-Potter patronage. Mains from £4.

Favorit Teviot Pl. Modern café/diner open till the wee small hours.

Mosque Kitchen 19a West Nicholson St. Authentic, delicious curries served from the back of the Edinburgh Central Mosque. The food's on plastic plates, but the outdoor tables and basic setting can't detract from the taste or value. £3.

Restaurants

Henderson's 94 Hanover St. Self-service restaurant with a lively atmosphere, good-value vegetarian food and occasional live music. Mains from around £5.

Kalpna 2 St Patrick Sq ⓣ0131/667 9890. Prize-winning vegetarian Indian; great prices for superb food. Try the £6 lunch menu.

Mamma's American Pizza Company 30 Grassmarket. Good pizzas and a lively atmosphere that often spills out onto the Grassmarket cobbles. Pizzas for around £5.

Monster Mash 4a Forrest Rd ⓣ0131/225 7069. Hugely popular diner, serving quality renditions of British standards at small cost. £4.95 set lunch.

Mussel Inn 61–65 Rose St ⓣ0131/225 5979. Owned by two Scottish shellfish farmers; you can feast here on a kilo of mussels and a basket of chips for under £10.
The Outsider 15–16 George IV Bridge ⓣ0131/226 3131. Stylish, vibrant restaurant in the Old Town serving modern, filling food. It's not cheap, but there's an £11 set lunch.
Susie's Wholefood Diner 51 West Nicolson St. Popular student veggie/vegan café. Bring your own bottle. Mains for under £5.

Drinking and nightlife

The city has a lively **nightlife**, and venues change name and location with such speed that the only way to keep up with what's going on is to get hold of *The List*, a comprehensive listings magazine published fortnightly. **Gay nightlife** is centred on the top of Leith Walk, notably at *C.C. Bloom's* and *Planet Out*, next to the Playhouse on Greenside Place.

Pubs and bars

Café Royal Circle Bar 19 West Register Street. Make a point of visiting this Grade A listed pub, arguably Edinburgh's most beautiful watering-hole.
City Café 19 Blair St. A bar, club and internet café rolled into one. The food's good too.
Malt Shovel 11 Cockburn St. Good beer, plenty of local colour and a wide choice of single malt whiskies; live jazz some evenings.
The Outhouse 12a Broughton St Lane. A heated outdoor area makes this the venue for year-round alfresco drinking.
Villager 49–50 George IV Bridge. Busy bar-cum-diner in the Old Town.

Live music and clubs

Bongo Club 37 Holyrood Rd, ⓦwww.thebongoclub.co.uk. Top club, playing reggae, funk, soul, drum and bass and electro. The big nights go on until 3am.
Cabaret Voltaire 36–38 Blair St, ⓦwww.thecabaretvoltaire.com. Eclectic beats and the occasional live band. You can party until 3am.
Ego 14 Picardy Pl, ⓦwww.clubego.co.uk. Popular club playing anything from house to swing to a mixed crowd. Doors close at 3am.
Liquid Room 9c Victoria St, ⓦwww.liquidroom.com. Holds house and indie nights; also a popular live venue. Doors close at 3am.
Royal Oak Infirmary St. Venue for Scottish folk music.
The Hive 15–17 Niddrie St, ⓦwww.myspace.com/clubhive. Cool, subterranean club spinning everything from drum and bass to metal.
Venue 17–21 Calton Rd. Features up-and-coming indie bands as well as a range of club nights.

Directory

Embassies and consulates Australia, 21–23 Hill St ⓣ0131/226 8161; Canada, 50 Lothian Rd ⓣ0131/473 6320; USA, 3 Regent Terrace ⓣ0131/556 8315; New Zealand, 5 Rutland Sq ⓣ0131/222 8109.
Exchange Several big bank branches on and around Andrew, Hanover and George squares.
Hospital Royal Infirmary, Old Dalkieth Rd ⓣ0131/536 1000.
Laundry Sundial, 7 East London St; Tarvit Launderette, 7 Tarvit St.
Left luggage At Waverley Station and in lockers by St Andrew Square bus station.
Pharmacy Boots, 11 Princes St.
Post office St James' Shopping Centre, near the east end of Princes St.

Moving on

Train Aberdeen (hourly; 2hr 30min); Durham (every 30 min; 2hr); Glasgow (every 15min; 50min); Inverness (10 daily; 3hr 50min); Newcastle (every 30 min; 1hr 30min); Leuchars for St Andrews (hourly; 1hr 10min); Stirling (every 30min; 50min); York (every 30 mins; 2hr 30min).
Bus Aberdeen (hourly; 3hr); Durham (3 daily; 4hr 30min); Glasgow (every 15min; 1hr 20min); Inverness (8 daily; 4hr 30 min); Kyle of Lochalsh for Skye (5 daily; 7hr); Manchester (9 daily; 6hr 25min); Newcastle (3 daily; 3hr); St Andrews (every 30min; 2hr–3hr); Stirling (hourly; 1hr).

GLASGOW

GLASGOW is the largest city in Scotland, home to 750,000 people. It once thrived on the tobacco and cotton trade and, most famously, on the shipbuilding on the River Clyde. Despite the subsequent, and catastrophic, decline of the shipping industry, the Victorian-coined "second city of the Empire" tag lingers in the solid civic buildings of George Square and the Merchant City, and in the elegant mansions of the South Side and West End. It's less immediately physically appealing than gentrified Edinburgh, but is favoured by many for its garrulous locals and more down-to-earth ambience. Having shrugged off its post-industrial malaise, rejuvenated Glasgow has undergone a change of image, symbolized recently by winning the competition to host the 2014 Commonwealth Games. It's also home to the world's best art schools and a live music scene to rival that of London or Manchester.

What to see and do

Glasgow's centre lies on the north bank of the Clyde, around the grandiose **George Square**, a little way east of Central Station. Just south of the square, down Queen Street, is the **Gallery of Modern Art** (Mon–Wed & Sat 10am–5pm, Thurs 10am–8pm, Fri & Sun 11am–5pm; free). Formerly a "temple of commerce" built by one of the eighteenth-century tobacco lords, it now houses an exciting collection of contemporary Scots art, notably works by Toby Paterson and John Byrne. A short way west on Mitchell Lane, just off Buchanan Street, **The Lighthouse** (Mon–Sat 10.30am–5pm, Tues from 11am, Sun noon–5pm; £3; ⓦwww.thelighthouse.co.uk) was the first commission of Glasgow's famous architect Charles Rennie Mackintosh, whose distinctively streamlined Art Nouveau designs appear in shops all over the city; inside is an exhibition devoted to the man and a panoramic view over the city.

Glasgow School of Art

Just off Sauchiehall Street (pronounced "socky-hall"), is the **Glasgow School of Art**, 167 Renfrew St, a remarkable building designed by Mackintosh that is a fusion of Scottish manor house solidity and modernist refinement. The interior, making maximum use of natural light, was also furnished and fitted entirely by the architect, and can be seen on a guided tour (daily between 10.30am and 4pm; Oct–March closed Sun; £6.50; ⓣ0141/353 4526, ⓦwww.gsa.ac.uk).

Cathedral and Necropolis

Northeast of George Square is the **cathedral** on Castle Street (Mon–Sat 9.30am–4/5.30pm, Sun 1–4/5.30pm). Built in 1136, destroyed in 1192 and rebuilt soon after, it's the only Scottish mainland cathedral to have escaped the hands of the country's sixteenth-century religious reformers, whose hatred of anything that smacked of idolatry wrecked many of Scotland's ancient churches. Just as interesting as the cathedral is the adjacent **Necropolis**, a hilltop cemetery for the magnates who made Glasgow rich; there are great views across the city from here.

Kelvingrove Art Gallery

The boundaries of the leafy West End are marked by the magnificent, baroque crenellations of **Kelvingrove Art Gallery** (daily 10/11am–5pm; free; ⓦwww.glasgowmuseums.com), which boasts pieces by Rembrandt, Degas, Millet, Van Gogh and Monet, as well as an impressive body of Scottish painting. Don't miss Dali's *Christ of St John of the Cross* – an arresting vision of the crucifixion painted as if from above. Sitting on the banks of the River Kelvin, the museum regards the sober gothic tower of The University of Glasgow, which peers down from its hilltop across the river. The two engage in a dialogue of educated refinement that typifies much of the thoroughly green and pleasant West End, a district worth exploring for its fine domestic architecture and enticing cafés and shops.

The Burrell Colection

About four miles south of the centre, in **Pollok Country Park** (bus #45, #48 or #57 from Union St, or train to Pollokshaws West), is the astonishing **Burrell Collection**, housed in a custom-built gallery (Mon–Thurs & Sat 10am–

BRITAIN

SCOTLAND

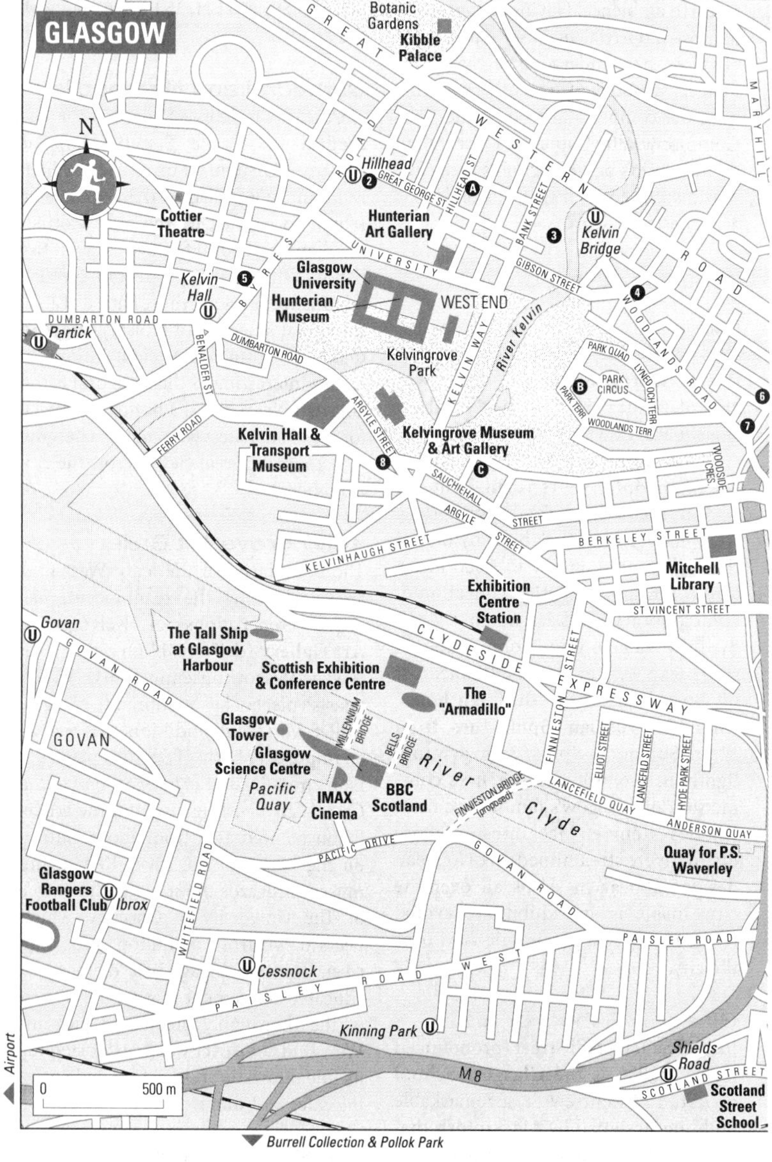

5pm, Fri & Sun 11am–5pm; free). Sir William Burrell began collecting at the age of 15 and kept going until his death at 96, buying an average of two pieces a week. Works by Memling, Cézanne, Degas, Bellini and Géricault feature among the paintings, while in adjoining galleries there are pieces from ancient Rome and Greece, medieval European arts and crafts, and a massive selection of Chinese artefacts, with outstanding ceramics, jades and bronzes.

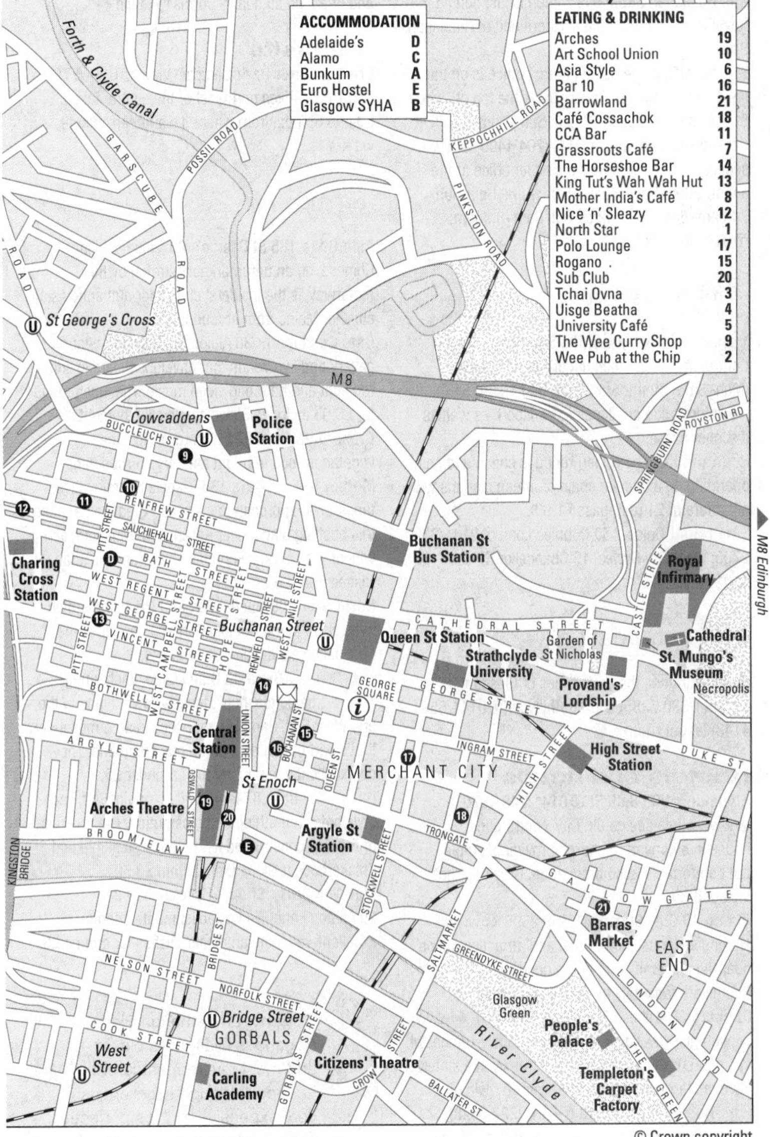

Arrival and information

Air Glasgow International airport (Ⓣ0141/887 1111) is eight miles west of the city, with regular buses shuttling to Buchanan Street Bus Station; Glasgow Prestwick airport (Ⓣ0871/223 0700), thirty miles south, is connected to the city centre by train.

Train Glasgow has two main train stations: Central serves all points south and west, Queen Street serves Edinburgh and the north. It's an easy city to explore on foot – the grid pattern of the centre makes navigation relatively simple.

Bus Buchanan Street bus station is just behind the Royal Concert Hall at the northern end of Buchanan Street.
Tourist office The helpful tourist office is on the south side of George Square, near the top of Queen Street (Mon–Sat 9am–6/8pm, Sun 10am–6pm; Oct–April closed Sun; ⓣ0141/204 4400, ⓦwww.seeglasgow.com); there's a smaller office at the airport (Mon–Sat 7.30am–5pm; April–Sept Sun 7.30am–5pm, Oct–March Sun 8am–3.30pm; ⓣ0141/848 4440).

City transport

Transport information The Strathclyde Travel Centre, above St Enoch underground station (Mon–Sat 8.30am–5/5.30pm, Sun 10am–5pm), has information on all public transport, as well as discount passes.
Underground The Underground is cheap and easy, operating on a circular chain of fifteen stations with a flat fare of £1 (day-pass £1.90).
Bike rental Dales, 150 Dobbies Loan ⓣ0141/332 2705; West End Cycles, 16 Chancellor St ⓣ0141/357 1344.

Accommodation

During summer, the universities of Glasgow (ⓣ0141/330 5385) and Strathclyde (ⓣ0141/553 4148) let out **rooms**. ❼

Hostels and hotels

Adelaide's 209 Bath St ⓣ0141/248 4970, ⓦwww.adelaides.co.uk. City-centre guest house in a converted church providing simple but comfortable accommodation. Breakfast not included. ❼
Alamo 46 Gray St ⓣ0141/339 2395, ⓦwww.alamoguesthouse.com. Quiet and attractive option near the university that offers good value for money. Rooms are tastefully furnished and comfy. ❼
Bunkum 26 Hillhead St ⓣ0141/581 4481, ⓦwww.bunkumglasgow.co.uk. Welcoming, family-run hostel in a great position close to the university in a stately Victorian terrace. No curfew. Dorms ❷, twin ❺
Euro Hostel 318 Clyde St ⓣ0141/222 2828, ⓦwww.euro-hostels.co.uk. Huge 360-bed hostel on the banks of the River Clyde. A convenient if somewhat soulless option. There's a bar, chill-out room and a 24hr alcohol licence. Dorms ❸, doubles ❼
Glasgow SYHA 8 Park Terrace ⓣ0870/155 3255, ⓦwww.syha.org.uk. Refurbished hostel in a listed building beside Kelvingrove Park. Good position for going out in the West End. All rooms are en-suite and of a high standard. Dorms ❸, twin ❼

Campsite

Craigendmuir Park Campsie View ⓣ0141/779 4159. Four miles northeast of the centre; take a train to Stepps, from where it's a fifteen-minute walk. ❷

Eating

Asia Style 185 St George's Rd. This no-frills Chinese, on an unremarkable stretch by the motorway, is the insiders' choice for authentic Asian cuisine. Mains from around £5.
Café Cossachok 38 Albion St. Russian restaurant, gallery and live venue that envelops diners in soft red light and haunting violin music. The lunch menu for £6.95 includes Slavic staples like borscht.
Grassroots Café 97 St George's Rd. Fine vegetarian food in bright and airy surroundings.
Mother India's Café 1355 Argyle St. Innovative, tapas-style approach to curry and great value make this bustling place, near Kelvingrove Museum, a winner. Alex "Franz Ferdinand" Kapranos is a fan. Dishes from £5.
North Star 108 Queen Margaret Drive. Bohemian café, close to the Botanic Gardens, that does the best bacon sandwiches in Glasgow.
Tchai Ovna 42 Otago Lane. Enchanting "magic teashop", tucked down a lane in the arty West End. Sample exotic teas in an atmosphere that's part opium den, part hippy commune. They do excellent vegetarian food for under £5.
University Café 87 Byres Rd. An original Art Deco-style café, something of an institution. The menu is of the unreconstructed kind – think steak pie and Knickerbocker Glory. Dishes from £3.50.
The Wee Curry Shop 7 Buccleuch St and 29 Ashton Lane. Tiny establishments offering excellent-value Indian meals. Dishes for around £6.

TREAT YOURSELF

Rogano 11 Exchange Place. *Rogano* is Glasgow's oldest and most revered restaurant. The food, though excellent, is very expensive, but it's perfectly acceptable to join the well-heeled locals at the bar for a glass of champagne and an oyster (six will cost £9). The 1930s Art Deco interior, which mirrors the same style as the luxury liners built on the Clyde at that time, is a must-see.

Drinking and nightlife

Pubs and nightspots cluster around the city centre, the suave Merchant City to the east of Queen Street, and the West End around Byres Rd and Ashton Lane; a charming cobbled street lined with bars and eateries.

Pubs and bars

Bar 10 10 Mitchell Lane. A great pre-club bar with DJs. Its industrial interior is the work of Ben Kelly, designer of Manchester's fabled, but now demolished, *Hacienda*.

CCA Bar 350 Sauchiehall St. Arty hangout within the Centre for Contemporary Arts serving continental beers to a good-looking crowd.

The Horseshoe Bar 17 Drury St. Rarely a quiet moment at this city-centre pub which features the longest bar in the UK and almost perpetual karaoke.

Uisge Beatha 232–246 Woodlands Rd. Warm, candle-lit pub with kilted bar staff, stuffed animals and a friendly blend of locals and students supping a vast array of whiskies.

Wee Pub at the Chip 12 Ashton Lane. Tiny, convivial pub attached to the *Ubiquitous Chip* restaurant. Get there early if you want one of the few seats.

Clubs

The Arches 253 Argyle St, Ⓦwww.thearches.co.uk. Cavernous club and live venue, under Central Station, that pulls off gigs, theatre and lysergic club nights with equal aplomb. The bigger nights can go on past 4am.

Art School Union 15 Union St. Cheap drinks, and anything from drum and bass to cabaret, make this a favourite for students and serious clubbers alike.

Polo Lounge 84 Wilson St. Popular gay club that mixes refined drinking upstairs with a packed, cruisey dance floor in the basement.

Sub Club 22 Jamaica St, Ⓦwww.subclub.co.uk. Underground club and purveyor of the finest techno and electro.

Entertainment

Cinema and theatre

Centre for Contemporary Arts (CCA) 350 Sauchiehall St, Ⓦwww.cca-glasgow.com. Cultural centre that has a reputation for a programme of controversial performances and exhibitions.

Citizens' Theatre 119 Gorbals St Ⓣ0141/429 0022, Ⓦwww.citz.co.uk. Southside theatre famous for sourcing top Scottish talent and producing innovative and thought-provoking work.

Glasgow Film Theatre Rose Street Ⓣ0141/332 8128, Ⓦwww.gft.org.uk. Wonderful cinema showing art films and old favourites.

Tramway Theatre 25 Albert Drive Ⓣ0845/330 3501, Ⓦwww.tramway.org. Intimate performance spaces, showing challenging theatre, in a complex that includes the tranquil Hidden Gardens.

Live music

Barrowland 244 Gallowgate, Ⓦwww.glasgow-barrowland.com. Acclaimed live venue, voted the best in Britain, with a medium-size capacity for soon-to-be-big bands and more established acts.

King Tut's Wah Wah Hut 272a Vincent St, Ⓦwww.kingtuts.co.uk. Famous as the place where Oasis were discovered, and still hosts excellent gigs.

Nice 'n' Sleazy 421 Sauchiehall St, Ⓦwww.nicensleazy.com. Late-night bar, with the best jukebox in town and great gigs in its sweaty basement.

Directory

Hospital Royal Infirmary, 84 Castle St Ⓣ0141/211 4000.

Laundry Bank Street Laundry, 39–41 Bank St; Majestic Launderette, 1110 Argyle St.

Pharmacy Boots, Buchanan Galleries.

Police Pitt St Ⓣ0141/532 2000.

Post office 47 St Vincent St.

Moving on

Train Aberdeen (hourly; 2hr 35min); Inverness (10 daily; 3hr 15min); Mallaig for Skye (Mon–Sat 3 daily; Sun 1 daily; 5hr 15min); Oban for Mull (3 daily; 3hr); Wigan or Preston for Liverpool & Manchester (13 daily; 2hr 30min); Newcastle (every 15–30 min; 2hr 40min); Stirling (every 30 min; 30min).

Bus Aberdeen (7 daily; 3hr 15min); Inverness (8 daily; 4hr); Liverpool (8 daily; 5hr 20min–8hr 20min); Manchester (6 daily; 5hr 30min); Newcastle (2 daily; 4hr); Oban for Mull (7 daily; 3hr); St Andrews (12 daily; 2hr 20min); Stirling (hourly; 45min).

STIRLING

Occupying a key strategic position between the Highlands and Lowlands at the easiest crossing of the River Forth, **STIRLING** has played a major role throughout Scottish history. With its castle and steep, cobbled streets, it can appear like a smaller version of Edinburgh.

What to see and do

Imperiously set on a rocky crag, the atmospheric and explorable **castle** (daily 9.30am–5/6pm; £8.50) combined the functions of a fortress with those of a royal palace. Highlights within the complex are the **Royal Palace**, dating from the late Renaissance, and the earlier **Great Hall**, where recent restoration, including a complete rebuilding of the vast hammerbeam roof, has revealed the original form and scale. The oldest part of Stirling is grouped around the streets leading up to the castle. Look out for the Gothic **Church of the Holy Rude** (daily 10am–5pm), with its fine timber roof, where the infant James VI – later James I of the United Kingdom – was crowned King of Scotland in 1567. From here, Broad Street slopes down to the lower town, passing the **Tolbooth**, the city's newly restored arts and cultural centre. Stirling is famous as the scene of Sir William Wallace's victory over the English in 1297, a crucial episode in the Wars of Independence. The Scottish hero was commemorated in the Victorian era with the **Wallace Monument** (daily 9.30am–6.00pm, shorter hours in winter; £6.50) a bizarre Tolkienesque tower that seems ugly close up, though compensation comes in the stupendous views – finer even than those from the castle.

Arrival and information

Train and bus The train and bus stations are both just east of the centre in the lower part of town.
Tourist office The tourist office at 41 Dumbarton Rd is in the lower part of town (July & Aug daily 9am–7pm; Sept–June Mon–Sat 9/10am–5/6pm; ⓣ08707/200 620, ⓦwww.visitscottishheartlands.com).

Accommodation

10 Gladstone Place ⓣ01786/472681, ⓦwww.cameron-10.co.uk. Friendly guest house in a pretty Victorian property. ❼
Willy Wallace Hostel 77 Murray Place ⓣ01786/446773, ⓦwww.willywallacehostel.com. Lively, welcoming backpacker hostel with a comfortable common room. Dorms ❸, doubles ❻
Witches Craig Campsite Off St Andrew's Rd ⓣ01786/474947, ⓦwww.witchescraig.co.uk; closed Nov–March. Picturesque site, three miles east of town off the A91. Take bus #23 or #62. ❸
YHA St John St ⓣ0870/004 1149, ⓦwww.syha.org.uk. The *HI* hostel is a little characterless but occupies a great setting at the top of town in a converted church. Dorms ❸, twin ❻

Eating

Barton Bar and Bistro Barnton St. Licensed café serving staples from £5.
Cisco's 70 Port St. Bustling Italian café that does coffee and snacks.
La Ciociara 41 Friars St. Good-value Italian in the heart of Stirling.

ST ANDREWS

Well-groomed **ST ANDREWS**, on the coast 56 miles northeast of Edinburgh and reachable as a day-trip from the capital, has the air of a place of importance. Retaining memories of its days as medieval Scotland's metropolis, it is the country's oldest university town, the Scottish answer to Oxford or Cambridge, with a snob-appeal to match – Prince William is a recent alumnus – and in term time, the town can feel overawed by the large numbers of well-to-do students. St Andrews has an exalted place in Scottish sporting history too, having six golf courses including the oldest in the world.

What to see and do

Entering the town from the Edinburgh road, you pass no fewer than four golf links, the last of which is the **Old Course**, the most famous and – in the opinion of Jack Nicklaus – the best in the world. At the southern end of the Old Course, down towards the waterfront, is the **British Golf Museum** (April–Oct Mon–Sat 9.30am–5.30pm, Sun 10am–5pm; Nov–March daily 10am–4pm; £5.25; ⓦwww.britishgolfmuseum.co.uk); if you want to step onto the famous fairways, head to the **Himalayas** putting green, located right by the first hole and only £1 per round. Sweeping north from the Old Course is a wonderful crescent of sandy beach; immediately south of the Old Course begins North Street, one of St Andrews' two main arteries. Much of it is taken up by university buildings, with the tower of **St Salvator's College** rising proudly above all else. Together with the adjoining chapel, this dates from 1450 and is the earliest surviving part of the university.

The castle and cathedral

Further east, you can reach the ruined **castle** on North Castle Street (April–Sept daily 9.30am–5.30pm; Oct–March daily 9.30am–4.30pm; £5, or combined ticket with cathedral £7). A short distance further along the coast is the equally ruined Gothic **cathedral** (same hours; £4), the mother church of medieval Scotland and the largest and grandest ever built in the country. With the cathedral entrance ticket you can get a token to ascend the austere Romanesque **St Rule's Tower** – part of the priory that the cathedral replaced – for superb views over the sea and town.

Arrival and information

Train There are no direct trains, though frequent buses connect with the train station five miles away in Leuchars.

Bus The bus station is west of town on City Road.

Tourist office St Andrews' tourist office, 70 Market St (Mon–Sat 9.30am–7pm, Sun 10.30am–5pm; shorter hours and closed Sun in winter; ⓣ01334/472021, ⓦwww.standrews.com/fife), will book rooms for a ten percent deposit – worth paying in the summer and during big golf tournaments, when accommodation is in short supply.

Accommodation

Cairnsmill Caravan Park ⓣ01334/473604. A large, family campsite a mile from town with a swimming pool and games room. Bunk house accommodation available. ❷

St Andrews Tourist Hostel ⓣ01334/479911, ⓦwww.standrewshostel.com. Nicely decorated hostel with clean, basic dorm rooms, a well-equipped kitchen and comfy lounge. dorms ❷

Eating and drinking

Byre Theatre Café Abbey St. By day, the bistro at the Byre theatre does tea and coffee in pleasant contemporary surroundings.

Criterion 99 South St. Pleasantly refurbished pub that has good ales and company.

Grillhouse Inchcape House, St Mary's Place. Informal, Mexican restaurant with a fun atmosphere and good food for reasonable prices. At lunch you can get a filling main for less than £5.

Ma Bell's Though part of a hotel, this relaxed drinking den's a student favourite. Cocktails and pop music are the order of the day.

LOCH LOMOND AND THE TROSSACHS

Loch Lomond – the largest stretch of fresh water in Britain – is the epitome of Scottish scenic splendour, thanks in large part to the ballad that fondly recalls its "bonnie, bonnie banks". The easiest way to get to the loch is to take one of the frequent trains from Glasgow Queen Street Station to **BALLOCH** at its southwestern tip, from where you can take a cruise around the 33 islands nearby. The **western shore** is very developed, with the upgraded A82 zipping along its banks. The only place to find any peace and quiet now is on the **eastern shore**, large sections of which are only accessible via the footpath which forms part of the West Highland Way. The easiest access to the graceful peak of **Ben Lomond** (3192ft) is from Rowardennan, from where it's a straightforward three-hour hike to the summit; in summer you can reach Rowardennan by ferry from Inverbeg on the western shore.

Trossachs National Park

Loch Lomond is at the heart of the **Trossachs National Park**, Scotland's first national park, opened in 2002. A huge

MIDGE ALERT

During the summer months, particularly in wetter areas, the highlands and islands are blighted by **midges**; tiny biting insects that appear in swarms during the mornings and evenings. If you're camping or hiking, make sure you have insect repellent – old-hands swear by Avon's Skin So Soft range of moisturizers – or a midge hood; a net fitting over a wide-brimmed hat that, while making no concessions to fashion, should protect the face.

development called Lomond Shores incorporating shops, information points and cafés has been built at Balloch; the Gateway Centre here is the best place for information (daily 9/10.30am–4.30/7pm; ⓣ0845/345 4978, ⓦwww.lochlomond-trossachs.org) and a taste of the park if you're not able to explore further. A couple of miles northwest of Balloch is Scotland's most beautiful **HI hostel**, complete with resident ghost (ⓣ0870/004 1136; March–Oct; dorms ❸); and there's another alluringly sited HI hostel at Rowardennan (ⓣ0870/004 1148; March–Oct; dorms ❷, twin ❺). The tourist office has details of the wide choice of **campsites** and **B&Bs** in all the villages.

THE ISLE OF MULL

The **ISLE OF MULL** is the most accessible of all the Hebridean islands off the west coast of Scotland: just forty minutes by ferry from **Oban**, which is linked by train to Glasgow. The chief appeal of the island is its remarkably undulating coastline – three hundred miles of it in total. Despite its proximity to the mainland, the slower pace of life is clearly apparent: most roads are single lane, with only a handful of buses linking the main settlements. **CRAIGNURE**, the ferry terminal for boats from Oban (4–6 daily; 45min; £4.15 single), is little more than a smattering of cottages. It does, however, have the island's main **tourist office** (daily 8.30/10.30am–5/7pm; ⓣ0870/720 0610), a decent pub, bike rental and a campsite. On its way into Craignure, the ferry passes the dramatic **Duart Castle** (April Sun–Thurs 11am–4pm; May to mid-Oct daily 10.30am–5.30pm; £5; ⓦwww.duartcastle.com), two miles' walk along the bay. The stronghold of the MacLean clan from the thirteenth century, it was restored earlier last century – you can peek in the dungeons and ascend to the rooftops.

Tobermory

Mull's "capital", 22 miles northwest of Craignure, is easily the most attractive fishing port on the west coast of Scotland, its clusters of brightly coloured houses and boats sheltering in a bay backed by a steep bluff. For a list of the local **B&Bs** head for the **tourist office** (April–Oct daily 9/10am–5/6pm; ⓣ0870/720 0625), in the Mac ferry ticket office at the northern end of the harbour. The **HI hostel** (ⓣ0870/004 1151; dorms ❷, closed Nov–Feb) is on Main Street, or you could try the *Tobermory Campsite* (ⓣ01688/302624; ❷, closed Nov–Feb) twenty minutes' walk from town on the Dervaig road. Also on Main Street is the *Mishnish Hotel* pub, popular for live folk music at the weekends.

THE ISLE OF IONA

At the opposite end of Mull, 35 miles west of Craignure, is the **ISLE OF IONA**. This tiny island has been a place of pilgrimage for several centuries: it was here that St Columba fled from Ireland in 563 and established a monastery that was responsible for the conversion of more or less all of pagan Scotland. The present **Abbey** (daily 9.30am–4/6pm; £3.30) dates from around 1200, though it's been restored since, and Iona's oldest building, **St Oran's Chapel**, lies just south. It stands at the centre of the burial ground, Reilig Odhrain, which is said to contain the graves of sixty kings, including the two immortalized by Shakespeare – Duncan and Macbeth. In front stand three carved crosses from the eighth and ninth centuries, among the masterpieces of early European sculpture. Iona is a popular day-trip in summer, reached in a few minutes by ferry from **Fionnphort** at the western tip of Mull. Camping's not permitted, but the excellent *Iona Hostel* (ⓣ01681/700781, ⓦwww.ionahostel.co.uk; dorms ❸), a mile or so from the ferry, has comfortable beds and superb views.

THE ISLE OF STAFFA

A basaltic mass rising direct from the sea, the **Isle of Staffa** is the northern end of the Giant's Causeway (see p.651), and is the most romantic of Scotland's many uninhabited islands. On one side, its rockface has been cut into caverns of cathedral-like dimensions, notably **Fingal's Cave**, whose haunting noises inspired Mendelssohn's *Hebrides Overture*. To get to Staffa, jump aboard the *Iolaire* (ⓣ01681/700358; £20), which sails out of Fionnphort and Iona.

THE ISLE OF SKYE

The bare and bony promontories of the **ISLE OF SKYE** fringe a deeply indented coastline and its spectacular summits, azure water and bright, clear light, make it one of the most captivating spots in Britain. The most popular destination on the island is the **Cuillin ridge**, whose jagged peaks dominate the island during clear weather; equally dramatic are the rock formations of the Trotternish peninsula in the north.

Elgol and the Cuillin

The best approach to the Cuillin is via **ELGOL**, fourteen miles southwest of Broadford at the end of the most dramatic road in Skye and served by bus #49. From here there are boat trips on the *Bella Jane* (ⓣ0800/731 3089, ⓦwww.bellajane.co.uk; one-way £13.50, return trip £18) to Loch Coruisk. Serious hikers head for **GLENBRITTLE**, west of the Cuillin, where there's an HI hostel (ⓣ0870/004 1121; dorms ❷, closed Oct–Feb) and a campsite not far away by the sandy beach (ⓣ01478/640404; ❷, closed Nov–March).

Portree

The only real town on Skye is **PORTREE**, an attractive fishing port in the north of the island. The town has several hostels, smartest of which is the *Bayfield Backpackers* (ⓣ01478/612231; dorm ❷), Bayfield, though the *Portree Independent Hostel* in the old post office is larger (ⓣ01478/613737; dorms ❷). Food in Portree can be pricey, but the fish and chips down by the harbour are excellent. If you can dip further into your pocket, the welcoming *Isles Inn* serves traditional Scottish fare, including haggis.

The Old Man of Storr and Uig

From Portree, head north up the east coast of the **Trotternish** peninsula. Some nine miles from Portree, at the edge of the Storr ridge, is a distinctive 165-foot obelisk known as the **Old Man of Storr**, while a further ten miles north, rising above Staffin Bay, are the **Quiraing** – a spectacular forest of rock formations. The straggling village of **UIG**, on the west coast, has ferries to the islands of the Outer Hebrides, including Harris and North Uist, as well as an HI hostel (ⓣ0870/004 1155; dorms ❷, closed Oct–March).

Arrival and information

However you arrive on the island, you'll end up in the southeastern corner, where there's a concentration of hostels.

Bus From the train terminus of Kyle of Lochalsh, buses head over the Skye Bridge to Kyleakin.

Ferry Trains terminate at Mallaig, from where you can take the ferry to Armadale in the southeast corner of the island. There's also a restricted summer service from Glenelg to Kylerhea.
Tourist Information In the South, Broadford, an unremarkable village, has a small tourist office (April–June & Oct Mon–Sat 9.30am–5.30pm; July & Aug 9am–7pm, also Sun 10am–5pm; ⓣ01471/822361). Portree has the island's main tourist office just off Bridge Road (Mon–Sat 9am–5.30/7pm; April–Oct also Sun 10am–4pm; ⓣ01478/612137).

INVERNESS

Capital of the Highlands, **INVERNESS** is 160 miles north of Edinburgh, the train line between the two traversing the gentle countryside of Perthshire before skirting the stark Cairngorm mountains. Approaching from Skye in the west, there's the magnificent eighty-mile train journey from Kyle of Lochalsh. The town has a fine setting astride the River Ness at the head of the Beauly Firth, but despite having been a place of importance for a millennium – it was probably the capital of the Pictish kingdom and the site of Macbeth's castle – there's nothing remarkable to see, nor any particularly strong sense of character. The chief attractions of historical interest lie some six miles east of town, reached by regular buses. **Culloden Moor** was the scene in 1746 of the last pitched battle on British soil, when the troops of "Butcher" Cumberland crushed Bonnie Prince Charlie's Jacobite army in just forty minutes. This ended forever Stuart ambitions of regaining the monarchy, and marked the beginning of the break-up of the clan system which had ruled Highland society for centuries. At the time of writing, the Culloden visitor centre was undergoing major renovations.

Arrival and information

Inverness airport (ⓣ01667/464000) is seven miles northeast of town.
Tourist office on Castle Wynd (March–Sept Mon–Fri 9am–7pm, Sat 9am–6pm, Sun 9.30am-5pm; Oct–Feb Mon–Fri 9am–5pm, Sat 10am–4pm; ⓣ01463/234353, ⓦwww.visithighlands.com) charges £3 to find a room.
Bike Hire *Barney's*, 35 Castle St (ⓣ01463/232249).

Accommodation

Bazpackers 4 Culduthel Rd ⓣ01463/717663. The smallest hostel in town with an open fire, friendly staff and views over the River Ness. Dorms ❷, doubles ❺
Eastgate Backpackers 38 Eastgate ⓣ01463/718756, ⓦwww.eastgatebackpackers.com. There's a young crowd at this well-run hostel in the centre of town, though its position on the main shopping thoroughfare's uninspiring. Dorms ❷, doubles ❺
Inverness Student Hotel 8 Culduthel Rd ⓣ01463/236556. Cosy, welcoming hostel that's the pick of the budget accommodation in town, with great views and a quiet location by the castle. Dorms ❷
YHA Victoria Rd ⓣ0870/0041127, ⓦwww.syha.org.uk. Large, modern HI hostel with excellent facilities, though it's not the most central option. Dorms ❸

Eating and drinking

Hootananny's 67 Church St. Inverness isn't famous for its nightlife, but you could do much worse than come here, a lively pub that has live gigs and good Thai food.
Pivo 38-40 Academy St. Popular bar specialising in European beers and spirits.

Moving on

Train Aberdeen (10 daily; 2hr 15min); Kyle of Lochalsh for Skye (Mon–Sat 4 daily; Sun 3 daily; 2hr 30min); Stirling (some change at Perth; 9 daily; 2hr 45min).
Bus Aberdeen (change at Perth; 7 daily; 5hr 45min); Stirling (4 daily; 3hr 50min).

LOCH NESS

Loch Ness forms part of the natural fault line known as the Great Glen, which slices across the Highlands between Inverness and Fort William. In the early 1800s, Thomas Telford linked the glen's lochs by means of the **Caledonian Canal**, enabling ships to pass between the North Sea and the Atlantic without having to navigate Scotland's treacherous northern coast. Today, pleasure-craft galore ply the route, with cruises from Inverness (summer only; book at tourist office) providing the most straightforward way of seeing the terrain. Most visitors are eager to catch a glimpse of the elusive **Loch Ness Monster**: to find out the whole story, take a bus to **DRUMNADROCHIT**, fourteen miles southwest of Inverness, where the **Loch Ness 2000 Exhibition** (daily: July & Aug 9am–8pm; shorter hours at other times; £5.95; ⓦwww.loch-ness-scotland.com) attempts to breathe life into the old myth. Most photographs allegedly showing the monster have been taken around the ruined **Castle Urquhart** (daily April–Sept 9.30am–6.30pm, Oct–March until 4.30pm; £6.50, includes entry to the visitor centre), one of Scotland's most beautifully sited fortresses, a couple of miles further south.

THE HIGHLANDS

With its beguiling mix of bare hills, green glens and silvery lochs and rivers, the spectacular scenery of the **Highlands** (which covers most of Scotland north of the Central Belt and west of Aberdeen) is a major draw. The distances involved, however, as well as poor public transport, mean that you really need a few days to explore any one part of it properly. Coachloads of sightseers take in what they can from carefully positioned viewpoints on the main roads, but **outdoor activities** are a major reason to visit: most tourist information centres and backpacker hostels carry information on good local hiking routes, bike rental and adventure sports.

While you can get a taste of the Highlands as far south as Loch Lomond and the Trossachs National Park, barely an hour from Edinburgh or Glasgow, any trip to Inverness, Mull or Skye will take you through some magnificent upland country. Obvious stopping-points for further exploration include **AVIEMORE**, at the foot of the looming Cairngorm range, which offers challenging hiking, ancient pine forests, and skiing and other winter sports in season. On the west coast, the town of **FORT WILLIAM** is a great base for draws such as **Ben Nevis** (the UK's highest peak), the **West Highland Way** long-distance footpath and **Glen Coe**, where soaring scenery and poignant history combine like nowhere else in the country. If you want to climb 'The Ben', the easiest route up begins just outside Fort William, but make sure you plan well and wear suitable clothing, as capricious weather conditions and poor visibility can combine to make the ill-prepared hiker extremely miserable. Using the easiest, tourist path to make the ascent and come back down again takes around seven hours.

Highlands transport

Public transport Getting around the Highlands without a car does require patience, although good-value travel passes are available on First ScotRail's train network (ⓦwww.firstscotrail.com), which

THE LOCH NESS MONSTER

Tales of "**Nessie**" date back at least as far as the seventh century, when the monster came out second best in an altercation with St Columba. However, the possibility that a mysterious prehistoric creature might be living in the loch only attracted worldwide attention in the 1930s, when sightings were reported during the construction of the road along its western shore. Numerous appearances have been reported since, but even the most hi-tech surveys of the loch have failed to come up with conclusive evidence.

has some superbly scenic stretches including the famous West Highland Line from Glasgow to Oban, Fort William and Mallaig.

Tours A couple of rival companies offer lively minibus tours designed specifically for backpackers: Haggis (Ⓣ0131/557 9393, Ⓦwww.haggisadventures.com) and Macbackpackers (Ⓣ0131/558 9900, Ⓦwww.macbackpackers.com) depart from Edinburgh on trips lasting between one and seven days; you can also buy a jump-on/jump-off ticket allowing you to cover their circuits (which generally take in Inverness, Skye, Oban and Stirling) at your own pace.

ABERDEEN

On the east coast 120 miles north of Edinburgh, **ABERDEEN** is the third city of Scotland. Solid and hard-wearing like the distinctive silver-grey granite used for so many of its buildings, it has been nicknamed the "Silver City", although its wealth is built on black gold – North Sea oil.

What to see and do

Best of the sights is down Shiprow, near the eastern end, where Provost Ross's House, a sixteenth-century mansion, now abuts the award-winning **Maritime Museum** (Mon–Sat 10am–5pm, Sun noon–3pm; free). The collection here describes Aberdeen's relationship with the sea through imaginative displays, films and models, including a thirty-foot oil rig. A further short walk downhill is the bustling **harbour** area, seen at its best in the early morning, before the daily fish market winds down at 8am. Across Union Street from Shiprow is Broad Street, dominated by **Marischal College**, the younger half of Aberdeen University. Its facade, a century-old historicist extravaganza, is probably the most spectacular piece of granite architecture in existence. Less than a mile east of Union Street is the best **beach** to be found in any British city, a great two-mile sweep of clean sand, very popular in summer.

Arrival and information

Bus and train The bus and train stations are on Guild Street, 200m south of Union Street.

Tourist office The tourist office, 23 Union St (June–Sept Mon–Sat 9am–7pm, Sun 10am–4pm; Oct–May Mon–Sat 9.30am–5.30pm; Ⓣ01224/288828), can help with finding B&B accommodation for a small fee (£4).

Accommodation

Aberdeen HI Hostel 8 Queen's Rd Ⓣ0870/004 1100, Ⓦwww.syha.co.uk. Take buses #14 or #15 from the Union Street or #27 from the station. This comfortable, converted Victorian mansion, in a good-looking part of town, has 114 beds, a lounge and internet access.

Eating and drinking

The Ashvale 46 Great Western Rd Ⓣ01224/596 981. Long rated as one of Britain's best fish-and-chip shops.

Café 52 on The Green near Union Street Ⓣ01224/590 094. Hip restaurant serving up inventive dishes which tend towards the expensive. The lunch menu offers sandwiches from £4.50 and mains from around £7.

Lemon Tree Arts Centre Café 5 West North St Ⓣ01224/642 230, Ⓦwww.lemontree.org. Good place for lunch (open Thursday-Sunday) serving solid staples for around £6, often to the sounds of live jazz and blues.

Ma Cameron's 6 Little Beaumont St. Popular pub with a great atmosphere, weekly live music and comfy snug.

Prince of Wales St Nicholas Lane. Aberdeen's most colourful real ale pub with traditional decor and a sensitively preserved long bar.

Moving on

Train Edinburgh (every 30min; 1hr 15min); Glasgow (hourly; 2hr 35min); London (5 daily; 7hr)

Ferry Lerwick, Shetland (8 weekly; 12hr 30min); Kirkwall, Orkney (5 weekly; 6hr).

Bulgaria

HIGHLIGHTS

ALEXSANDAR NEVSKI CHURCH, SOFIA: the capital's most striking building

RILA MONASTERY: fabulous frescoes deep in the mountains

BANSKO: skiiing and snowboarding on the cheap

THE BLACK SEA COAST: white sand and beach bars

PLOVDIV'S OLD QUARTER: get lost among the ornate houses and Roman remains

ROUGH COSTS

DAILY BUDGET Basic €20/occasional treat €35

DRINK Beer (0.5l/€0.35)

FOOD *Shopska* salad (€1)

HOSTEL/BUDGET HOTEL €10

TRAVEL Train: Sofia–Plovdiv (150km) €5; Bus: €5

FACT FILE

POPULATION 7.3 million

AREA 110,910 sq km

LANGUAGE Bulgarian

CURRENCY Lev (Lv)

CAPITAL Sofia (Population: 1.1 million)

INTERNATIONAL PHONE CODE ☎359

Basics

If the Western image of Bulgaria has altered dramatically in recent years, it is largely thanks to the modernization of the country's tourist infrastructure coupled with soaring foreign interest in inexpensive rural and coastal properties. Several dramatic mountain ranges, superb beaches, numerous historic towns and a web of working villages with traditions straight out of the nineteenth century are crammed into a relatively compact country.

Independent travel is increasingly common: costs are low, and for the committed there is much to take in. Foremost among the towns featuring romantic National Revival era architecture are Koprivshtitsa, Bansko and Plovdiv. The monasteries are stunning, too – the finest, Rila, should be on every itinerary. For city life aim for **Sofia**, Plovdiv, and the cosmopolitan coastal resorts of **Varna** and Burgas. More than anything else, this is a land of adventures: once you step off the beaten track, road signs and bus timetables often disappear or are only in the Cyrillic alphabet, and few people speak a foreign language, but almost everyone you meet will be determined to help you on your way.

CHRONOLOGY

4000s BC Thracian tribes settle in the area of present-day Bulgaria.
600s BC Greeks settle in the area known as present-day Bulgaria.
100s AD Romans invade the Balkan Peninsula.
200 A popular Roman amphitheatre draws people to Serdica (Sofia).
681 The Kingdom of the Bulgars is formed.
864 Bulgaria accepts the Orthodox Church.
1396 The Ottomans conquer Bulgaria, ushering in almost five hundred years of Turkish rule.
1886 The Treaty of Bucharest ends the Serbo-Bulgarian war begun the previous year, and Bulgaria gains territory.
1908 Bulgaria declares itself an independent kingdom.
1912 First Balkan War; Bulgaria sustains heavy losses in victory over the Ottomans.
1913 Second Balkan War; previous allies Serbia and Greece defeat Bulgaria.
1914–1918 Bulgaria sides with the Central Powers during World War I.
1945 Soviet army invades German-occupied areas of Bulgaria.
1954 Todor Zhivkov becomes head of the Bulgarian Communist Party in power.
1989 Zhivkov ousted among calls for democratisation.
1991 New constitution proclaims Bulgaria a Parliamentary Republic.
2001 Former King Simeon II is elected Prime Minister.
2004 Bulgaria joins NATO.
2007 Bulgaria joins the EU.

ARRIVAL

The majority of tourists arrive at Sofia airport, although in summer many fly directly to the coastal cities of Varna and Burgas on charter flights. Frequent **low-cost flights** from London and other European cities to Sofia are provided by Wizzair (Ⓦwww.wizzair.com) and easyJet (Ⓦwww.easyjet.com). The national carrier Bulgaria Air (Ⓦwww.air.bg) runs regular flights to most of Europe as well as Tel Aviv, Beirut and Dubai, but there are no direct flights to or from North America or Australasia. Bulgaria has land borders with five countries and a reliable **rail network**. A couple of popular routes are from Bucharest to Veliko Tûrnovo (5–6hr) or to Sofia (11hr), and from Thessaloniki to Sofia (10hr), while trains from Istanbul traverse the country, stopping at Plovdiv (11hr) and Sofia (14hr) before continuing to Belgrade. Eurolines (Ⓦwww.eurolines.bg) has offices in most major Bulgarian cities and runs frequent **bus** services to destinations throughout Europe. At the north of the Black Sea coast it's possible to travel

from Romania to Durankulak by foot or **car**; the closest crossing to the south coast from Turkey is at Malko Tûrnovo, which is best crossed by car.

GETTING AROUND

Public transport in Bulgaria is inexpensive but often slow and not always clean or comfortable. Travelling by **bus** (*avtobus*) is usually the quickest way of getting between major towns and cities, with a growing number of faster and more comfortable privately run services. Generally, you can buy **tickets** at the bus station (*avtogara*) at least an hour in advance when travelling between towns, but on some routes they're only sold when the bus arrives. On rural routes, tickets are often sold by the driver.

By train

Bulgarian State Railways (BDZh; ⓦwww.bdz.bg) can get you to most towns; trains are punctual and fares low. Express services (*ekspresen*) are restricted to main routes, but on all except the humblest branch lines you'll find so-called Rapid (*barz vlak*) trains. Where possible, use these rather than the snail-like *patnicheski* services. Long-distance or overnight trains have reasonably priced couchettes (*kushet*) and/or sleepers (*spalen vagon*). For these, on all expresses and many rapids, you need seat **reservations** (*zapazeni mesta*) as well as **tickets** (*bileti*). To ensure a seat in a non-smoking carriage (*myasto nepooshachi*), you will have to specify this when booking. In large towns, it's usually easier to obtain tickets and reservations from **railway booking offices** (*byuro za bileti*) rather than at the station, and it's wise to book a day in advance at weekends and in summer. Tickets can only be bought on the day of travel at the station. Advance bookings are required for **international tickets** and are bought through the Rila Agency (ⓦwww.bdz-rila.com);

branches can be found in all major cities. Most stations have **left-luggage** offices (*garderob*). InterRail, EuroDomino, Balkan Flexipass and Bulgarian Flexipass are valid, although it can easily work out cheaper to buy your rail tickets as you go.

ACCOMMODATION

Most one- and two-star **hotels** (for the most part uninspiring high-rise blocks) rent double rooms from around 50Lv, a little more in Sofia and Plovdiv. Cosier family-run hotels are common on the coast and in village resorts such as Koprivshtitsa and Bansko. **Private rooms** (*chastni kvartiri*) are available in most large towns, and are usually administered by accommodation agencies, although in the smaller resorts you can usually find a room by asking around; expect to pay around 25–50Lv for a double, more in Sofia and Plovdiv. As a rule, private rooms in big cities will be in large residential blocks, while those in village resorts can often be in atmospheric, traditional houses.

The number of good quality private **hostels** (*turisticheska spalnya*) is growing, and they now exist in most places of interest. Some towns have a **campsite** (*kamping*; usually summer only) on the outskirts, although these are few and far between, and can be unkempt affairs with poor connections to the town centre. Many also feature two-person chalets (20–30Lv per night).

Camping rough is technically illegal and punishable with a fine, though authorities usually turn a blind eye.

FOOD AND DRINK

Sit-down meals are eaten in either a **restorant** (restaurant) or a **mehana** (tavern). There's little difference between the two, save that a *mehana* is likely to offer folksy décor and a wider range of traditional Bulgarian dishes. Wherever you go, you're unlikely to spend more than 20Lv for a main course, salad and drink. The best-known traditional dish is *gyuvech* (which literally means "earthenware dish"), a rich stew comprising peppers, aubergines and beans, to which is added either meat or meat stock. *Kavarma*, a spicy meat stew (either pork or chicken), is prepared in a similar fashion. **Vegetarian meals** (*yastia bez meso*) are hard to obtain, although *gyuveche* (a variety of *gyuvech* featuring baked vegetables) and *kachkaval pane* (cheese fried in breadcrumbs) are worth trying.

Foremost among **snacks** are *kebapcheta* (grilled sausages), or variations such as *shishche* (shish kebab) or *kiofteta* (meatballs). Another favourite is the *banitsa*, a flaky-pastry envelope with a filling – usually cheese – sold by street vendors in the morning and evening. Elsewhere, *sandvichi* (sandwiches) and *pitsi* (pizzas) dominate the fast-food repertoire. Bulgarians consider their **yoghurt** (*kiselo mlyako*) the world's finest, and hardly miss a day without consuming it.

Drink

The quality of Bulgarian **wines** is constantly improving, and the industry now exports worldwide. Among the best reds are the heavy, mellow Melnik, and rich, dark Mavrud. Dimyat is a good dry white. If you prefer the sweeter variety, try Karlovski Misket (Muscatel) or Tramminer. Cheap native **spirits** are highly potent, and should be drunk diluted with water in the case of *mastika* (like ouzo in Greece) or downed in one, Balkan-style, in the case of *rakiya* – brandy made from either plums (*slivova*) or grapes (*grozdova*). Bulgarian **beer** is as good as any, and brands such as Kamenitza, Zagorka, and Shumensko are preferable to pricey imported alternatives, although Staropramen, brewed locally under licence, offers some healthy competition.

Coffee (*kafe*) usually comes *espresso* style. **Tea** (*chai*) is nearly always herbal – ask for *cheren chai* (literally "black tea") if you want the real stuff, normally served with lemon.

> **BODY LANGUAGE**
>
> Bulgarians shake their heads when they mean "yes" and nod when they mean "no". Sometimes they reverse these gestures if they know they're speaking to foreigners, thereby complicating the issue further. Emphatic use of the words *da* (yes) and *ne* (no) should help to avoid misunderstandings.

CULTURE AND ETIQUETTE

Social etiquette in Bulgaria is still rather formal. Shaking someone's hand is the most common form of **greeting** and you should address someone with their title and surname unless you know them well. Only close friends and family members address each other by their first names and are more tactile with each other, exchanging hugs and maybe kisses. It is appropriate to wait for the Bulgarian person to decide when to become less formal with you. When invited to someone's home it is polite to bring a small gift, and something from your own country will be particularly appreciated by your host.

In restaurants the attitude towards **tipping** is much the same as throughout the rest of Europe, and leaving a tip will definitely be well received, although it is not obligatory.

SPORTS AND OUTDOOR ACTIVITIES

Bulgaria's mountainous terrain offers plenty of adventurous options. The **ski season** lasts from December to March, and the country has several well-known **resorts**. Perhaps the most famous is Bansko, in the spectacular Pirin mountain range in the southwest, with alpine peaks and challenging runs perfect for experienced skiers and snowboarders. Other large resorts include Pamporovo in the Rhodope mountains, which is the best for beginners, and Borovets and Malyovitsa in the Rila range.

Of all Bulgaria's ranges, the **Rila mountains** (Ⓦwww.rilanationalpark.org) provide some of the country's most attractive **hiking** destinations, including the highest peak – Mount Musala (2925m) – from where a two–three-day trail leads to Rila Monastery (see p.230). For the best maps, advice and organised hikes visit Odysseia-In in Sofia (see p.226).

Despite the popularity of team sports such as basketball, handball and volleyball, none can compete with **football** in terms of the passions involved. Teams in the premier division ("A" Grupa) play on Saturday or Sunday afternoons. **Tickets** are generally cheap and sold at booths outside the grounds on the day of the match. The Bulgarian Football Association maintains an informative website with English-language content (Ⓦwww.bulgarian-football.com).

COMMUNICATIONS

Post offices (*poshta*) are usually open Mon–Sat 8.30am–5.30pm, longer in big towns. The main office will have a poste restante facility, but postal officers tend to return mail to sender if it's not claimed immediately.

Card-operated **public phones** are on the whole reliable and can be used to make international calls. **Phonecards** (*fonkarta*) for both Bulfon's orange phones and Betcom's blue phones are available from post offices and many street kiosks and shops. The operator number for domestic calls is Ⓣ121, for international calls Ⓣ0123.

You'll find **Internet cafés** in most towns and cities, where you'll rarely pay more than 1.50Lv per hour.

EMERGENCIES

Petty theft is a danger on the coast, and the Bulgarian **police** can be slow in filling out insurance reports unless you're insistent. Foreign tourists are no longer a novelty in much of the country, but **women** travelling alone can expect to encounter stares, comments and some-

BULGARIA ON THE NET

Ⓦ **www.bulgaria.com** Comprehensive travel information.
Ⓦ **www.discover-bulgaria.com** Travel information and hotel booking.
Ⓦ **www.sofiaecho.com** News site.
Ⓦ **www.travel-bulgaria.com** Information on history and culture, as well as travel.

times worse from macho types, and clubs on the coast are pretty much seen as meat markets. A firm rebuff should be enough to cope with most situations. Note that everyone is required to carry some form of **ID** at all times.

If you need a **doctor** (*lekar*) or dentist (*zabolekar*), go to the nearest *poliklinika* (health centre), whose staff might speak English or German. Emergency treatment is free of charge although you must pay for **medicines** – larger towns will have at least one 24-hour pharmacy.

INFORMATION AND MAPS

There are few publicly funded **tourist offices** in Bulgaria, and those that do exist are fairly basic. Most main towns have agencies, working on commission, who will book accommodation and transport for you, but are of little use for other information. The best general **maps** of Bulgaria and Sofia are published by Kartografiya and Domino; both are available in Latin alphabet versions and sold at street stalls, petrol stations and bookshops.

EMERGENCY NUMBERS

Police ⓣ166; ambulance ⓣ150; fire ⓣ160.

MONEY AND BANKS

Until Bulgaria joins the Eurozone (target date: Jan 1, 2010) the currency remains the **lev** (Lv), which is divided into 100 stotinki (st) and pegged to the euro. There are notes of 1Lv, 2Lv, 5Lv, 10Lv, 20Lv and 50Lv, and coins of 1st, 2st, 5st, 10st, 20st and 50st, and 1Lv. Since it was revalued in 1999, the lev has been stable, although hotels and travel agencies frequently quote prices in euros. Nonetheless, you can always pay in the local currency, and many places prefer it. At the time of writing, €1 was equal to around 2Lv, $1 to 1.50Lv, and £1 to 2.90Lv. Museums and galleries charge in leva; producing a **student ID card** will often get you a discount. Be sure to keep a ready supply of coins for small purchases, as shops are often unable to change larger denomination notes.

Banks are open Mon–Fri 9am–4pm, and there are ATMs in every town. Private exchange bureaux, offering variable rates, are widespread – but beware of hidden commission charges. Also watch out for black market moneychangers who approach unwary foreigners with offers of better rates; if they sound too good to be true, they are. Many smaller banks and offices won't take travellers' cheques, and while Visa and MasterCard are gaining greater acceptance, credit cards are generally acceptable only at the more expensive shops, hotels, and restaurants.

OPENING HOURS AND HOLIDAYS

Big-city **shops** and **supermarkets** are generally open Mon–Fri 8.30am–6pm or later; on Sat they close at 2pm. In rural areas and small towns, an unofficial siesta may prevail between noon and 3pm. Many shops, offices, banks and museums are closed on the following **public holidays**: Jan 1, March 3, Easter Sun, Easter Mon, May 1, May 24, Sept 6, Sept 22, Dec 25 & Dec 31. Additional public holidays may occasionally be called by the government.

Bulgarian

Hotel and travel agency staff in Sofia and the larger towns and coastal resorts generally speak some **English**, but knowledge of foreign languages elsewhere in the country is patchy; younger people are more likely to know a few words of English. Most street signs, menus and so on are written in the **Cyrillic** alphabet, but an increasing number have English transliterations.

	Bulgarian	**Pronunciation**
Yes	Да	Da
No	Не	Ne
Please	Моля	**Mol**ya
Thank you	Благодаря	Blago**dar**ya
Hello/Good day	Добър ден	**Do**bur den
Goodbye	Довиждане	Do**vizh**danye
Excuse me	Извинявайте	Izvin**yav**itye
Where	Къде	Ku**de**
Good	Добро	**Dob**ro
Bad	Лошо	**Losh**o
Near	Близо	**Bliz**o
Far	Далече	Dal**eych**e
Cheap	Евтино	**Ef**tino
Expensive	Скъпо	S**kup**o
Open	Отворено	Ot**vor**eno
Closed	Затворено	Zat**vor**eno
Today	Днес	Dnes
Yesterday	Вчера	Ve**che**ra
Tomorrow	Утре	**U**tre
How much is...?	Колко струва?	Kolko str**oo**va?
What time is it?	Колко е часът?	Kolko ai cha**su**?
I don't understand	Не разбирам	Ne raz**bir**am
Do you speak English?	Говорите ли английски?	Gov**or**ite li Ang**lis**ki?
One	Един/Една	Ed**in**/ed**na**
Two	Две	Dve
Three	Три	Tree
Four	Четри	**Che**tiri
Five	Пет	Pyet
Six	Шест	Shest
Seven	Седем	**Sed**em
Eight	Осем	**Os**em
Nine	Девет	**Dev**yet
Ten	Десет	**Des**yet

Useful phrases

Do you have any vegetarian dishes?	Имате ли вегетерианска храна?	Imate li vegitarianska hrana?
Cheers	Наздраве	Nazdrave
The bill, please	Може ли сметката	Mozhe li smetkata
Is this the bus for.....?	Това ли е автобусът за....?	Tova li avtobusat za…?
Is this the train to....?	Това ли е влакът за......?	Tova li e vlakut za…?
Have you got a single/double room?	Имате ли единична двойна стая?	/Imate li edinichna/ dvoyna staya?
How much for the night?	Колко струва нощувката?	Kolko struva noshtuvkata?

BULGARIA BASICS

Sofia

With its drab suburbs and crumbling old buildings **SOFIA** (СОФИЯ) can appear an uninspiring place to first-time visitors,. However, much has been done in recent years to revitalize the heart of the city, and once you've settled in and begun to explore, you'll find it a surprisingly laid-back place, especially on fine spring days, when its lush public gardens and pavement cafés buzz with life. Urban pursuits can be combined with the outdoor possibilities offered by verdant **Mount Vitosha**, just 12km to the south.

Sofia was founded by a Thracian tribe some three thousand years ago, and various **Roman ruins** attest to its zenith as the regional imperial capital of Serdica in the fourth century AD. The Bulgars didn't arrive on the scene until the ninth century, and with the notable exception of the thirteenth-century Boyana Church, their cultural monuments largely disappeared during the Turkish occupation (1396–1878), of which the sole visible legacy is a couple of stately **mosques**. The finest architecture postdates Bulgaria's liberation from the Turks: handsome public buildings and parks, and the magnificent **Aleksandûr Nevsky Cathedral**.

What to see and do

Most of Sofia's **sights** are centrally located and within easy walking distance of each other. Bulevard Vitosha forms the heart of the shopping district and leads north to the Church of Sveta Nedelya, from where Bulevard Tsar Osvoboditel passes the major public buildings culminating with the grand Aleksandûr Nevski Church.

Sveta Nedelya Church

At the heart of Sofia is **Ploshtad Sveta Nedelya**, a pedestrianized square dominated by the distinctive **Sveta Nedelya Church** (daily 7am–7pm), whose broad dome dominates the vast interior chamber. Colourful modern frescoes adorn every square inch of its walls.

The Largo, Party House and Council of Ministers

Heading north, you'll come to the **Largo**, an elongated plaza flanked on three sides by severe monumental buildings, including the towering monolith of the former **Party House**, originally the home of the Communist hierarchy, and now serving as government offices. The plaza extends westwards to the Serdika metro station, watched over by the city's symbol, the **Sofia Monument**, representing the eponymous Goddess of Wisdom. On the northern side of the Largo is the **Council of Ministers** (Bulgaria's cabinet).

The Banya Bashi Mosque and the mineral baths

Just beyond, on bulevard Knyaginya Mariya Luiza, you'll find the **Banya Bashi Mosque**, built in 1576 by Hadzhi Mimar Sonah, who also designed the great mosque at Edirne in Turkey. The mosque is not officially open to tourists but modestly dressed visitors may visit outside of prayer times. Behind stand Sofia's **mineral baths**, housed in a yellow and red-striped fin-de-siècle building, closed since 1986 and still being restored. Locals gather daily to bottle the hot, sulphurous water that gushes from public taps into long stone troughs outside, opposite ul. Ekzarh Yosif.

The Rotunda of St George and the Presidency

Sofia's oldest church is the fourth-century **Rotunda of St George**, which houses frescoes from the eighth century onwards. Next to the church is the **Presidency**, guarded by soldiers in colourful nineteenth-century garb (Changing of the Guard hourly).

The Archeological Museum

Immediately to the east of the Rotunda of St George, a fifteenth-century mosque now holds the **Archeological Museum** (Tues–Sun 10am–6pm; 10Lv), whose prize exhibit is a magnificent gold cauldron and cups of the Thracian Valchitran treasure. Also on show is a collection of Thracian armour, medieval church wall paintings and numerous Roman tombstones.

The City Art Gallery

The **City Art Gallery** (Tues–Sat 10am–6pm, Sun 11am–5pm; free) in the City Garden, immediately to the south of Ploshtad Aleksandûr Battenberg, stages monthly exhibitions of contemporary Bulgarian art.

The Russian Church and Aleksandûr Nevsky Cathedral

Follow bulevard Tsar Osvoboditel east, and you'll see the **Russian Church**, a stunning golden-domed building, with an emerald spire and an exuberant mosaic-tiled exterior, concealing a dark, candle-scented interior. Just beyond is a particularly busy road junction; turn left, up ul Rakovski, and you'll see **Aleksandûr Nevsky Cathedral** (daily 7am–7pm, daily liturgy at 8am and 5pm; free), one of the finest pieces of architecture in the Balkans. Financed by public subscription and built between 1882 and 1924 to honour the 200,000 Russian casualties of the 1877–78 War of Liberation, it's a magnificent structure, bulging with domes and semi-domes and glittering with gold leaf. Within the gloomy interior, a beardless Christ sits enthroned above the altar, and numerous scenes from his life, painted in a humanistic style, adorn the walls. The crypt, entered from outside (Tues–Sun 10am–5.30pm; 4Lv), contains a superb collection of icons from all over the country.

The National Gallery for Foreign Art

On the northeastern edge of the cathedral square, an imposing white building houses the **National Gallery for Foreign Art** (Wed–Mon 11am–6pm; 10Lv, free Mon), which devotes a lot of space to Indian wood-carvings and second-division French and Russian artists, though there are a few minor works by the likes of Rodin, Chagall and Kandinsky. Heading west across the square, you'll pass two recumbent lions flanking the Tomb of the Unknown Soldier, set beside the wall of the plain, brown-brick **Church of Sveta Sofia**.

Borisova Gradina

Down bul Tsar Osvoboditel, past Sofia University, is **Borisova Gradina**, named after Bulgaria's interwar monarch, Boris III. The park – the largest in Sofia – has a rich variety of flowers and trees, outdoor bars, two football stadiums and two huge Communist monuments, still impressive despite the graffiti and rubbish scattered around them.

Mount Vitosha

A wooded granite mass 20km long and 16km wide, **Mount Vitosha**, 12km south of the city, is where Sofians come for picnics and skiing. The ascent of its highest peak, the 2290-metre **Cherni Vrah**, has become a traditional test of stamina. Getting here on public transport is straightforward, although there are fewer buses on weekdays than at weekends. Take tram #5 from behind the Law Courts to Ovcha Kupel bus station, then change to bus #61, which climbs through the forests towards **Zlatni Mostove**, a beauty spot on the western shoulder of Mount Vitosha beside the so-called **Stone River**. Beneath the large boulders running down the mountainside is a rivulet which once attracted gold-panners. Trails lead up beside the rivulet towards the moun-

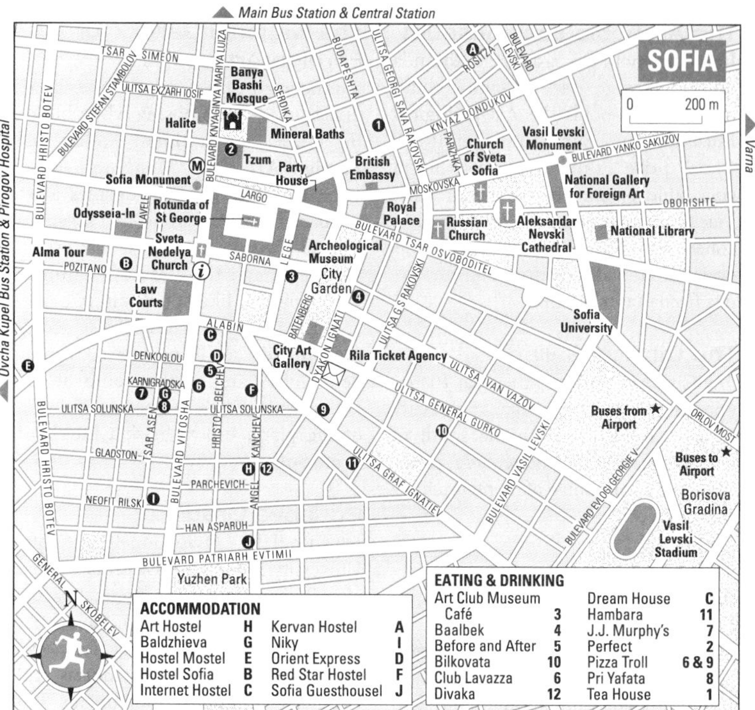

tain's upper reaches: Cherni Vrah is about two to three hours' walk from here.

Arrival and information

Air The best way to get into town from Sofia airport is to catch minibus #30, which runs until around 10pm (every 15–30min), and operates like a shared taxi; it will take you to the city centre for 1.50Lv. Waiting taxis might well try to charge you an exorbitant 40Lv or more, so it's wise to book one at the booth in the arrivals hall (8–12Lv).

Train Trains arrive at Central Station (Tsentralna Gara), a concrete hangar harbouring a number of exchange bureaux and snack bars, but little else to welcome the visitor. Five minutes' ride along bul Knyaginya Mariya Luiza (tram #1 or #7) is pl Sveta Nedelya, within walking distance of several hotels and the main accommodation agencies.

Bus Most buses arrive in the new bus station, just next to the train station, although some Bansko services and Blagoevgrad buses (for connections to Rila Monastery) use the Ovcha Kupel terminal, 5km southwest of the centre along bul Tsar Boris III (tram #5 from behind the Law Courts).

Tourist office The National Information and Advertising Centre on Sveta Nedelya (Mon–Fri 9am–5.30pm; ⓣ02/987-9778, ⓦwww.bulgariatravel.org), is the official tourist office, but a better bet is the friendly travel agent Odysseia-In, at bul Stamboliiski 20 (entrance on ul Lavele; Mon–Fri 9am–7.30pm, daily in summer; ⓣ02/980-5102, ⓦwww.odysseia-in.com), which charges a 5Lv consultation fee, although not for accommodation booking. In addition, the free quarterly *Sofia In Your Pocket* guide (ⓦwww.inyourpocket.com), distributed in bars, hotels and restaurants, is a great source of information.

City transport

Tickets There's a flat fare of 70st on all urban routes, whether by bus (*avtobus*), trolleybus (*troleibus*), the one-line metro system, or tram (*tramvai*). Tickets (*bileti*) are sold from street kiosks and occasionally on board, and must be punched as you enter the vehicle (inspections are frequent and there are spot fines of 7Lv for fare-dodgers). Note that if you're travelling with luggage, you should buy and punch two tickets. Kiosks at the main tram stops sell one-day tickets (*karta za edin den;* 3Lv) and strip (*talon*) of ten tickets for 6Lv. Metro tickets must be bought from the station; a "combination ticket" (*kombiniran bilet*) costs 1Lv and is valid for one metro and one bus or tram journey.

Taxis The most reliable taxis are the yellow OK taxis, charging about 59st per kilometre until nightfall, and 70st afterwards, and 60st initial fare; make sure the driver has his meter running. Additionally, there's a fleet of private **minibuses** (*marshrutka*), acting like shared taxis and covering around forty different routes across the city for a flat fare of 1.50Lv. Destinations and routes are displayed on the front of the vehicles – in the Cyrillic alphabet – and passengers flag them down like normal taxis, calling out when they want them to stop.

Accommodation

Sofia has a number of small, reasonably priced **hotels** and a growing number of good **hostels**. **Private rooms** (3) can be booked by agencies such as Odysseia-In (see opposite) and Alma Tour, at bul Stamboliiski 27 (Mon–Fri 9am–6.30pm, Sat 10.30am–4pm; ⓣ02/987-7233, ⓦwww.almatour.net).

Hostels

Art Hostel Angel Kanchev 21a ⓣ02/987-0545, ⓦwww.art-hostel.com. Sofia's trendiest hostel, hosting art exhibitions, live music and drama performances. Resident DJs, an extensive travel library and varied events and activities add to the mix. Guests have access to a kitchen and tea room, as well as free Internet and Wi-Fi. Breakfast included. Dorm 1; private apartment 4

Hostel Mostel 2A Makedonia Blvd ⓣ 08/8922-3296, ⓦwww.hostelmostel.com. Modern, very welcoming hostel with free 24-hour Internet access and satisfying all-you-can-eat breakfast. The new location has a large, comfortable lounge space, with flat screen TV, DVDs, and a very sociable atmosphere. You also get a free bowl of pasta and a beer for every night of your stay. Dorm 1, private room 3

Hostel Sofia Pozitano 16 ⓣ02/989-8582, ⓦwww.hostelsofia.com. Clean and well-run two-dorm, fourteen-bed hostel, just behind the Law Courts, with shared kitchen, bathroom and cable TV. Breakfast, dinner, Internet and drinks included. 1

Internet Hostel Alabin 50a ⓣ02/989-9419, ⓔinterhostel@yahoo.co.uk. Friendly hostel with doubles, triples and quads, as well as apartments. Located inside a shopping arcade on the second floor, above the *Dream House* restaurant. Kitchen and free Internet access. Breakfast included, with a number of different options to choose from. Dorm 1, double room 3

Kervan Hostel Rositza 3 ⓣ02/983-9428, ⓦwww.kervanhostel.com. Three-dorm Bohemian-style hostel in a quiet area of central Sofia, minutes from Nevsky Cathedral. Bike rental is available, and there's also a kitchen plus free Internet and Wi-Fi access. The hostel also offers a range of day trips and even bungee jumping. Breakfast included. Dorm 1, double room 3

Orient Express Hostel 8A Hristo Botev Blvd. Small and homely new hostel, with modern fittings and flat-screen TVs in every room combined with traditional antique and salvaged furniture. Dormitories, doubles and triples available – one room has an impressive balcony overlooking the old buildings of the city centre. Very friendly and helpful staff. Breakfast and free Internet access included. Dorm 1, double room 3

Red Star Hostel Angel Kanchev 6 ⓣ02/986-3341, ⓔredstarhostel@yahoo.com. Modern hostel with clean and cosy doubles, triples and dorms. Breakfast included, along with free Internet access. Dorm 1, double room 3

Sofia Guesthouse 27 Patriarch Evtimiy Blvd ⓣ02/981-3656 or 02/400-3097, ⓦwww.sofiaguest.com. Large new hostel in the city centre with clean, bright rooms and TV lounge. Free breakfast, laundry and pick up/ drop off service from the train/bus station or Sofia airport. Dorm 1, private room 3

Hotels

Baldzhieva Tsar Asen 23 ⓣ02/981-1257, ⓔbaldjievahotel@yahoo.com. Small hotel in a smart townhouse one block west of bul Vitosha. Rooms are clean and cosy, all with phone, fridge, TV and bathroom. Breakfast included 5

Niky ul. Neofit Rilski 16 ⓣ02/952 3058, ⓦwww.hotel-niky.com. Excellent-value accommodation in a converted apartment block just off the main bul. Vitosha. Basic doubles are small but neat and tidy with modern showers and a/c; bigger apartment-style rooms have a kitchenette and en-suite bath. 5

Eating

The cheapest places to grab a beer or a coffee are the many **cafés** and kiosks around bul Vitosha or in the city's public gardens, In addition, there are plenty of pricier restaurants offering a range of international cuisine.

BULGARIA SOFIA

Cafés

Art Club Museum Café Corner of Saborna & Lege. Chic café with a pleasant patio, set amid Thracian tombstones next to the Archeological Museum. Live DJs in the basement Thurs, Fri & Sat nights. Serves variety of light meals, desserts and drinks, such as cappuccino with coconut and banana (2.70Lv). Open 24hr.
Club Lavazza Vitosha 13. Smart place for coffee and cakes, which also offers light meals and an excellent-value English breakfast.
Tea House (Chai vuv fabrikata) Georgi Benkovski 11. Atmospheric traditional tea house with a formidable array of teas including 'monks' tea', Kashmir tchai and rose, all for around 2Lv.

Restaurants

Baalbek Dyakon Ignati 4. Highly regarded Lebanese establishment, with sit-down restaurant upstairs and fast-food counter offering kebabs, *shawarma* and falafel on the ground floor.
Before & After Hristo Botev Blvd 12. An elegant and popular restaurant near the *Orient Express Hostel*, with a range of Bulgarian, Turkish and Continental dishes, including some fantastic traditional desserts. Also great for vegetarian options, including grilled vegetables in yoghurt and dill (5.30Lv). The restaurant also hosts tango dances on Sundays.
Divaka Gladston 54. Bright and busy restaurant, just west of Graf Ignatiev, behind the *Art Hostel*, serving excellent, meat-heavy Bulgarian dishes. Chicken kebab 8Lv, vegetarian shish kebab 6Lv. Open 24hr.
Dream House Alabin 50a ⓣ02/980-81 63. The only fully vegetarian restaurant in Sofia, with a good choice of meals and snacks using seasonally available produce. Example dishes include grilled bean croquettes with salsa (3.50Lv) and tofu and algae soup (1.80Lv). On the first floor above the shopping mall, in an intimate setting with friendly staff. They also deliver within the city centre area.
Perfect In the sunken plaza beneath Tzum. Spacious, modern place, offering reasonably priced Bulgarian and international dishes, including grills, salads and pizzas.
Pizza Troll Vitosha 27. One of the better pizza and pasta restaurants in the centre, with vaguely Art Nouveau décor. There's another branch on Graf Ignatiev.
Pri Yafata Solunska 28. Brash but fun take on a traditional *mehana*, complete with live music, costumed staff and a great Bulgarian menu.

Drinking and nightlife

For evening entertainment, there's an ever-growing number of **clubs**, most playing a mix of pop and the ubiquitous local "folk pop"(*chalga*). Jazz and Latino music are also popular.

Bars

Bilkovata ul. Tsar Shishman 22. A buzzing, smoky cellar with decent music and a young crowd, Bilkovata is something of a legend in Sofia, fondly remembered by successive generations of students, arty types and young professionals, and still going strong. Packed beer garden in summer. Daily 10am–2am.
Hambara ul. 6-ti septemvri 22. Hidden behind an unmarked doorway just off the street, this dark, candle-lit, stone-floored bar is one of the most atmospheric places in the centre for a long night of drink-fuelled conversation. Live jazz several nights a week. Daily 7pm–2am.
J.J. Murphy's Karnigradska 6. Sofia's top Irish bar, offering filling pub grub, big-screen sports and live music at the weekends.

Clubs

Clubs can fill up on Fridays and Saturdays, when you may be kept waiting outside. Entrance fees range from 5Lv to 20Lv depending on the venue, more if a major DJ is manning the decks.
Bibliotekata Vasil Levski 88. Glitzy nightclub beneath the National Library building, drawing in a moneyed young crowd.
Blaze Slavyanska 36. Lively bar and club near the university, with a good sound system and trendy clientele. Daily 9pm–3am.
Caramba Tsar Osvoboditel 4. Sofia's premier Latino club, featuring different Latin rhythms nightly.
Exit ul. Lavele 16 ⓦwww.exit-club.com. This popular gay club also serves food in the daytime and early evening.
My Mojito Ivan Vazov 12. One of Sofia's trendiest clubs, with regular DJ slots and a laid-back crowd.

Entertainment

Cinema

Cineplex bul. Arsenalski 2 ⓣ02/964-3007, ⓦwww.cineplex.bg. Multi-screen cinema in the City Center Sofia shopping mall, with various snack possibilities in the vicinity.
Odeon bul. Patriarh Evtimiy 1 ⓣ02/969-2469. Shows oldies and prize-winning art films past and present. Small café in the lobby.

Live music

Alcohol ul Rakovski. Underground nightspot that looks like a huge subterranean barn and has an eclectic something-for-everybody music policy. An Oriental-style chillout room boasts cushions and hubble-bubble pipes.

Chervilo bul. Tsar Osvoboditel 8. Stylish city-centre club offering the latest in house, techno, Latin and lounge music on two floors. The action spreads out onto the terrace in summer, when it's more like an elite, pay-to-enter pavement café than a club.

Swingin' Hall Dragan Tsankov 8. Cheap, cheerful and crowded bar, with live music (usually pop/rock or jazz) on two stages.

Shopping

The city's main shopping street, **bulevard Vitosha**, is the place where you are most likely to come across familiar high-street shops and brands.

Malls For upmarket and luxury goods you can also head to Sofia's premier shopping mall, Tzum, or to the Halite building, which is found on bulevard Knyaginy Mariya Luiza, opposite the Banya Bashi Mosque. The Halite building is an elegant example of the city's early twentieth-century architecture and houses Sofia's central food hall, with three floors of shops and restaurants.

Markets One of the best is the Zhenski pazar market on ulitsa Stefan Stambolov, which has trinkets, fresh fruit, vegetables and other foodstuffs on sale. Another market worth trying is found at the apex of the three central churches, the Aleksandûr Nevski Church, the Russian Church and the Church of Sveta Sofia, on pl. Aleksandûr Nevski. There's an odd mix of religious paintings, Turkish-influenced silver jewellery, traditional Bulgarian peasant clothing, lace and textiles, and antique and replica Communist items on the long line of open-air stalls. Some may find the large array of Nazi memorabilia on some of the tables in rather bad taste.

Directory

Embassies and consulates Australia, Trakia 37 ⓣ02/946-1334; Canada, Moskovska 9 ⓣ02/969-9717; UK, Moskovska 9 ⓣ02/933-9222; US, Kozyak 16 ⓣ02/937-5100.

Gay Sofia Bulgarian Gay Organization, bul Vasil Levski 3 (ⓣ02/987-6872, ⓦwww.bgogemini.org).

Hospital Pirogov hospital, bul General Totleben 21 ⓣ02/51531. For an ambulance call ⓣ150.

Internet access Site, at 45 Vitosha Blvd (ⓣ02/986-0896, ⓦwww.siteout.net). Colour scanning and printing, CD/DVD burning and web cameras all available. Internet 3Lv per hour; open 24hr.

Pharmacy No. 7, pl Sveta Nedelya 5. Open 24hr.

Post office Ul General Gurko 6 (daily 7am–8.30pm).

Moving on

Bus Bansko (8 daily; 3hr); Burgas (8 daily; 7hr); Koprivshtitsa (2 daily; 2hr); Plovdiv (hourly; 2hr); Rila village (2 daily; 2hr); Varna (5 daily; 7hr); Veliko Tûrnovo (8 daily; 4hr).

Train Blagoevgrad (6 daily; 2hr 30min–3hr 30min); Burgas (3 daily; 6hr 30min); Gorna Oryahovitsa (10 daily; 4hr 30min); Koprivshtitsa (5 daily; 1hr 40min); Plovdiv (20 daily; 2hr–3hr 30min); Septemvri (16 daily; 1hr 30min–2hr 15min); Varna (5 daily; 8hr 30min).

Southern Bulgaria

The route south from Sofia skirts the Rila and Pirin mountain ranges, swathed in forests and dotted with alpine lakes, and home to Bulgaria's highest peaks. If time is short, the place to head for is the most revered of Bulgarian monasteries, **Rila**, around 30km east of the main southbound route. **Bansko**, on the eastern side of the Pirin range, boasts a wealth of traditional architecture, as well as being a major ski resort and a good base for hiking. Another much-travelled route heads southeast from Sofia towards Istanbul. The main road and rail lines now linking Istanbul and Sofia essentially follow the course of the Roman Serdica–Constantinople road, past towns ruled by the Ottomans for so long that foreigners used to call this part of Bulgaria "European Turkey". Of these, the most important is **Plovdiv**, Bulgaria's second city, whose old quarter is a wonderful mixture of National Revival mansions and classical remains. Some 30km south of Plovdiv is **Bachkovo Monastery**, containing Bulgaria's most vivid frescoes.

RILA MONASTERY

As the most celebrated of Bulgaria's religious sites, famed for its fine architecture and mountainous setting – and declared a World Heritage site by UNESCO – the **Rila Monastery** receives a steady stream of visitors, many of them day-trippers from Sofia. Joining one of these one-day tours from the capital is the simplest way of getting here, but can work out expensive (most tours cost around €70). It's much more economical to get there by public transport, though realistically you'll have to stay the night.

What to see and do

Ringed by mighty walls, the monastery has the outward appearance of a fortress, but this impression is negated by the beauty of the interior, which even the crowds can't mar. Graceful arches above the flagstoned courtyard support tiers of monastic cells, and stairways ascend to wooden balconies. Bold red stripes and black-and-white check patterns enliven the facade, contrasting with the sombre mountains behind and creating a harmony between the cloisters and the **church**. Richly coloured frescoes shelter beneath the church porch and cover much of its interior. The iconostasis is splendid, almost 10m wide and covered by a mass of intricate carvings and gold leaf. Beside the church is **Hrelyo's Tower**, the sole remaining building from the fourteenth century. Cauldrons, which were once used to prepare food for pilgrims, occupy the soot-encrusted kitchen on the ground floor of the north wing, while on the floors above you can inspect the spartan refectory and panelled guest rooms. Beneath the east wing is the **treasury** (daily 8.30am–4.30pm; 7Lv), where, among other things, you can view a wooden cross carved with more than 1500 miniature human figures by the monk Raphael during the 1790s.

Arrival and information

Bus There are three daily buses from Sofia's Ovcha Kupel terminal to Rila village, from where four buses a day make the 27km run up to the monastery. Otherwise, you'll need to catch the bus or train to Dupnitsa or Blagoevgrad in the Struma Valley, and then change to a local bus for Rila village.

Accommodation

It's possible to stay in the monastery's reasonably comfortable **rooms** (gates close at 11pm; ❸). The pleasant *Zodiac* campsite (follow the signs; ⓣ048/772 657; 30Lv double bungalow, 10Lv per person camping) has smart double bungalows, a good restaurant, and occupies an attractive riverside spot.

Eating and drinking

The **restaurants** outside the east gate are decent, but sometimes overcharge stray foreigners; the *Drushliavitsa* is preferable to the *Rila* and both serve fresh trout. For cheap snacks, delicious bread and doughnuts, you should head for the bakery opposite the east gate.

BANSKO

Lying some 40km east of the main Struma Valley route, **BANSKO** (БАНСКО) is the primary centre for walking and skiing on the eastern slopes of the Pirin mountains. It's a traditional agricultural centre that has witnessed massive investment in ski tourism in recent years, resulting in the current eyesore of half-built apartment blocks and hotels squeezed into the backyards of stone-built nineteenth-century farmhouses. Despite this overdevelopment, the central old town, with its numerous traditional pubs hidden away down labyrinthine cobbled streets, is as attractive as ever and the perfect place to wind down after a hard day on the slopes.

Though connected to Sofia and other towns by bus, Bansko can also be reached by a **narrow-gauge railway**, which leaves the main Sofia–Plovdiv line at Septemvri and forges its way across the highlands. It's one of the most scenic trips in the Balkans, but also one of the slowest, taking five hours to cover just over 100km.

What to see and do

Bansko centres on the modern pedestrianized pl Nikola Vaptsarov, where the **Nikola Vaptsarov Museum** (daily 8am–noon and 2–5.30pm; 3Lv) contains a display relating to the local-born poet and socialist martyr. Immediately north of here, pl Vazrazhdane is watched over by the solid stone tower of the **Church of Sveta Troitsa**, whose interior contains exquisite nineteenth-century frescoes and icons. On the opposite side of the square, the **Rilski Convent** contains an icon museum (Mon–Fri 9am–noon and 2–5pm, closed weekends; 3Lv) devoted to the achievements of Bansko's nineteenth-century icon painters. From the main square, ul Pirin leads north towards the **cable car,** along with its buzzing collection of ski-hire shops, bars and restaurants. The cable car (daily 8.30am–5pm, 16Lv) operates during the ski season so the numerous **hiking trails** are only accessible by foot or car out of season. Ski passes start at 50Lv per day to 300Lv for six days (half-price for children), with ski and snowboard hire at around 30Lv per day. In the summer months, the other option for reaching the summit is to head west - on foot or by taxi - via a steep fourteen-kilometre uphill climb to the Vihren hut, where cheap dorm accommodation (❶) is available. This is the main trailhead for hikes towards the 2914-metre summit of **Mount Vihren** (Bulgaria's second-highest peak), or gentler rambles around the meadows and lakes nearby.

Arrival and information

Bus There are eight buses a day to Bansko from Sofia, although if you're approaching the area from Rila, it's far easier to head for Blagoevgrad and change buses there. At Bansko, the bus and train stations are on the northern fringes of town, ten minutes' walk from pl Vaptsarov.

Tourist information The main tourist office (irregular hours; ⓣ07443/4611) is by the bus and train stations. In addition, the winter edition of the *Bansko In Your Pocket* guide (ⓦwww.inyourpocket.com), distributed in bars, hotels and restaurants, is a useful source of information.

Accommodation

Durchova Kushta 5 P R Slavejkov St ⓣ07443/8223, ⓦwww.durchova-kashta.com. En-suite rooms with TV, phone and minibar. Also has a sauna and can arrange car rental. ❻

Kadiyata ul. Yane Sandanski 8 ⓣ0749/88555 or 0899 969 370, ⓦwww.kadiata.bansko.bg. Family-run place in the heart of the old town, offering smart en-suites with modern furnishings and TV. ❸

Sharkova kashta ul. 5-ti Oktomvri 26 ⓣ07443/85024 or 0899 447 952. Seven neat and tidy doubles featuring en-suite shower and TV, either on the second floor of a typical Bansko house or in an adjoining bungalow in the garden. There's no breakfast and the ground-floor *mehana* doesn't open til noon, but it's comfy and central nevertheless. ❷

Eating and drinking

Dedo pene ul. Aleksandŭr Buynov 1, just south of pl. Vazrazhdane. The whole range of traditional Bulgarian food and Bansko specialities, in a characterful dining room crammed with folksy decorations – and you can sit in the vine-shaded courtyard in summer.

Molerite ul. Glazne 41, just north of pl. Nikola Vaptsarov.Two floors of wooden benches and ethnic textiles, and superb local specialities such as roast lamb and sword-grilled shish kebabs. Turns into a folk-pop disco after about 11pm.

Oxygen ul. Stefan Karadzha 27. Basement bar in the town centre with mixed programme of DJ-driven sounds, potent cocktails and good vibes.

Moving on

Train Dobrinishte (4 daily; 15min); Razlog (4 daily; 20min); Septemvri (4 daily; 5hr 20min); Velingrad (4 daily; 4hr 30min).

Bus Blagoevgrad (12 daily; 1hr); Gotse Delchev (12 daily; 1hr); Plovdiv (2 daily; 4hr); Razlog (10 daily; 30min); Sofia (12 daily; 3hr).

PLOVDIV

Bulgaria's second largest city, **PLOVDIV** (ПЛОВДИВ), has more obvious charms than Sofia, which locals tend to look down on. The old town embodies Plovdiv's long history – Thracian fortifications subsumed by Macedonian masonry, overlaid with Roman and Byzantine walls. Great timber-framed mansions, erected during the Bulgarian renaissance, symbolically look down upon the derelict Ottoman mosques and artisans' dwellings of the lower town. But this isn't just another museum town: the city's arts festivals and trade fairs are the biggest in the country, and its restaurants and bars are equal to those of the capital.

What to see and do

Plovdiv centres on the large **Ploshtad Tsentralen**, dominated by the monolithic *Hotel Trimontium Princess*. Heading north from here, the pedestrianized ul Knyaz Aleksandûr I Battenberg, lined with shops, cafés and bars, leads onto the attractive **Ploshtad Dzhumaya**, where stallholders gather to sell a range of touristy knick-knacks, including paintings, jewellery and icons. The ruins of a **roman stadium**, visible in a pit beneath the square, are just a fragment of the arena where up to thirty thousand spectators watched gladiatorial spectacles. Among the variously styled buildings here, the **Dzhumaya Mosque**, with its diamond-patterned minaret and lead-sheathed domes, steals the show; it's believed that the mosque, sadly now looking a little dilapidated, dates back to the reign of Sultan Murad II (1359–85).

The Old Quarter

With its cobbled streets and colourful mansions covering one of Plovdiv's three hills, the **Old Quarter** is a painter's dream and a cartographer's nightmare. As good a route as any is to start from pl Dzhumaya and head east up ul Saborna. Blackened fortress walls dating from Byzantine times can be seen around Saborna and other streets, sometimes incorporated into the dozens of timber-framed National Revival houses that are Plovdiv's speciality. Outside and within, the walls are frequently decorated with niches, floral motifs or false columns, painted in the style known as *alafranga*. Turn right, up the steps beside the Church of Sveta Bogoroditsa, and continue, along twisting cobbled lanes, to the **Roman Theatre** (daily 8am–6pm; 3Lv), the best preserved in the country, and still an impressive venue for regular concerts and plays (advertised around the town and in the local press).

The State Gallery of Fine Arts and around

Back on Saborna, the **State Gallery of Fine Arts** (Mon–Sat 9am–5.30pm; 3Lv, free Thurs) holds an extensive collection of nineteenth- and twentieth-century Bulgarian paintings, including some fine portraits by Stanislav Dospevski. Further along, the **Church of SS Constantine and Elena** contains a fine gilt iconostasis, partly decorated by the prolific nineteenth-century artist Zahari Zograf, whose work also appears in the adjacent **Museum of Icons** (Mon–Sat 9am–5.30pm; 3Lv, free Thurs). A little further uphill is the richly decorated **Kuyumdzhioglu House**, now home to the **Ethnographic Museum** (Tues–Sun 9am–noon & 2–5pm; 4Lv). Folk costumes and crafts are on display on the ground floor, while upstairs, the elegantly furnished rooms reflect the former owner's taste for Viennese and French Baroque.

Arrival and information

Bus Two of Plovdiv's three **bus stations** are near the train station: Rodopi, serving the mountain resorts to the south, is just on the other side of the tracks; while Yug, serving Sofia and the rest of the country, is one block east. The third bus station,

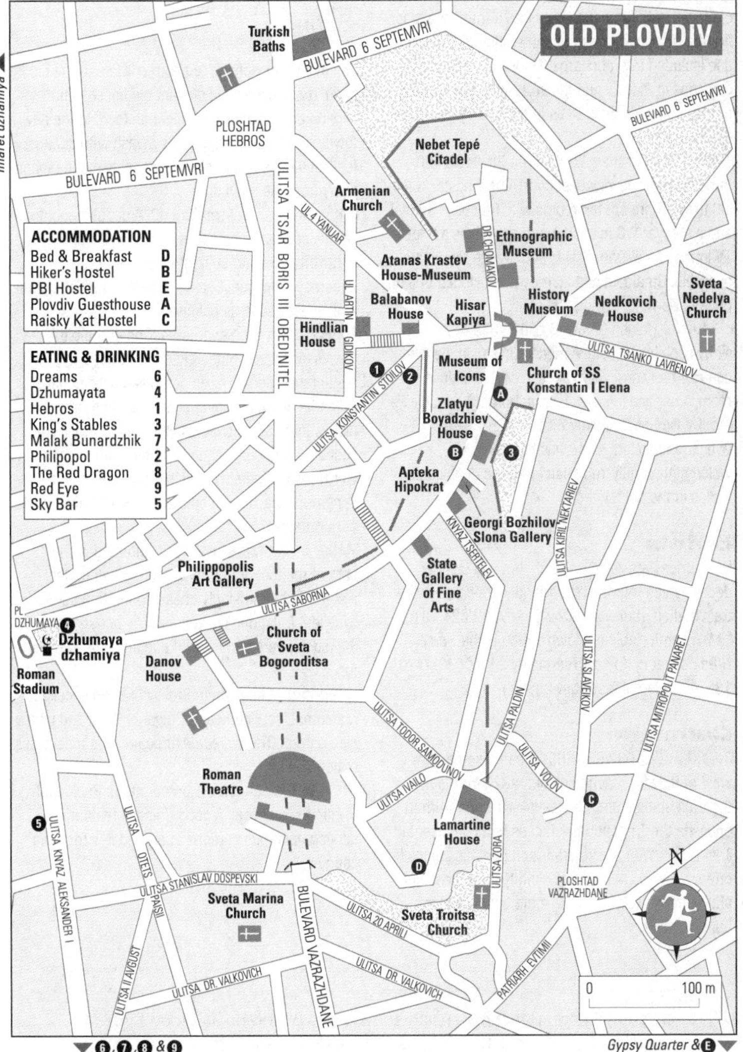

Sever, is north of the river and serves destinations such as Koprivshtitsa and Veliko Tûrnovo.

Rail Plovdiv's train station is on the southern fringe of the centre, on bul Hristo Botev.

Tourist Information Centre Located behind the post office at Ploshtad Tsentralen 1, the centre (ⓣ032/656 794, ⓦwww.plovdiv.bg) can reserve hotel rooms, arrange excursions, and book car rental.

Accommodation

Private rooms (③) can be booked through Esperansa, at Ivan Vazov 14 (daily 24hrs; ⓣ032/260 653, ⓦwww.esperansa.hit.bg).

Hostels

Hiker's Hostel 53 Saborna Str, ⓣ0885/194 553, ⓦwww.hikers-hostel.org. Comfortable and friendly hostel in the middle of the old town, with fantastic views and a traditional open fire during winter. Breakfast and unlimited Internet use included free of charge. They also organize day-trips in Plovdiv and the surrounding area. Guests can even pitch tents in the back yard. Dorm ❶ ; twin room ❷

Plovdiv Guesthouse 20 Saborna Str, ⓣ02/400-3098 ⓦwww.plovdivguest.com. A new hostel in the old town. There are ten rooms with fifty beds in total and a shower/WC in each room, as well as a large TV lounge area. Dormitories and private rooms are available. Breakfast and laundry are included free of charge. Dorm ❶ ; twin room ❸

PBI Hostel Naiden Gerov 13 ⓣ032/638 467, ⓦwww.pbihostel.com. A modern hostel in the town centre with twenty dorm beds, a double ensuite room, a bar and Internet access. Dorm ❶; double ❸

Raisky Kat ul Slaveikov 6 ⓣ032/268 849, ⓔacommodacion_svetla@yahoo.com. A welcoming, family-run hostel offering doubles and triples in the old town. ❶

Hotels

Hotel prices are relatively high, but you can get decent-value rooms at the friendly *Trakia*, near the train station at ul Ivan Vazov 84 (ⓣ032/624 101; ❼). A comfortable old town option is the *Bed & Breakfast* at ul Knyazh Tseretelev 24 (ⓣ0887/420 185, ⓔbedbreakfast@abv.bg; ❺).

Campsite

Gorski Kat ⓣ032/951 360. Located some 4km west of Plovdiv, reached by bus #222 from outside the train station, or on buses #4, #18 or #44 from opposite the Trimontium Princess hotel on ploshtad Tsentralen. With a restaurant and bar, this campsite offers a self-contained and slightly more peaceful alternative to staying in the main town. Double bungalows ❷

Eating

The most atmospheric **restaurants** are in the old town, many occupying elegant old houses and serving good, traditional Bulgarian food. In the new town, ul Knyaz Aleksandûr I is awash with cheaper fast-food outlets, though better quality can be found away from the main drag.

Dreams Knyaz Aleksandûr I 42. A popular spot for coffee, cocktails and cakes.

Dzhumayata Café built into the side of the Dzhumaya mosque. Serves authentic Turkish coffee and sweets, such as baklava.

King Stables Str. Saborna 9a. One of the old town's nicest and most reasonably priced restaurants. Serves large portions of traditional Bulgarian food, including some excellent grilled dishes that cost between 1.80Lv and 7.40Lv. The yoghurt with home-made blueberry jam is definitely worth trying. There's also a bar that offers equally generous measures of spirits and weekly live music performances.

Malak Bunardzhik ul Volga 1. Situated in the park at the foot of the Hill of the Liberators, this is a smart but surprisingly cheap option that serves excellent Bulgarian cuisine such as *chushki byurek* (baked peppers stuffed with egg and white cheese) for 3Lv.

Philipopol ul Konstantin Stoilov 56b. An excellent restaurant, serving hearty Bulgarian food and with a nice garden. The *shkembe* (tripe soup) is a delicious option (2Lv).

The Red Dragon On the corner of bul Ruski and ul Filip Makedonski. A good Chinese restaurant, serving generous portions at around 6Lv for main courses.

TREAT YOURSELF

If you really feel like experiencing some of the best wine and food that southern Bulgaria has to offer, head to the restaurant of the **Hebros Hotel** at 51 A. K. Stoilov Str (ⓣ032/260 180 or 032/625 929, ⓦwww.hebros-hotel.com), in the historic old town. The traditional Bulgarian menu usually changes depending on what the chef has found in the market that day, although there are always vegetarian options and an array of desserts. Main courses are around 18Lv and appetizers, such as hot foie gras with apples, around 6Lv. Tempting as the food is, it is the wine that really gives Hebros its reputation (it was voted Bulgaria's best restaurant by *Bacchus* wine magazine in 2003). There are recommended wines for every dish, as well as an extensive cellar with wines from all over Bulgaria, including regional varieties from the Rose Valley, the Thracian Lowlands, the Black Sea and the Danube Plain. Prices run the full gamut between 9 and 199Lv.

TAKE THE NIGHT TRAIN TO ISTANBUL

There's a nightly **train** to Istanbul, which leaves Plovdiv at 9.50pm; tickets should be bought in advance from the BDZh/Rila office opposite the train station at bul. Hristo Botev 31A (Mon–Fri 8am–6pm, Sat 8am–2pm).

Turkish visas can be bought at the Kapikule frontier (UK citizens £10; US citizens US$20; Canadian citizens US$45; Australian and New Zealand citizens US$20) – you can use pounds or dollars, but have the exact sum ready in cash, as they don't always have change and won't let you in without the visa. Other nationals should contact the Turkish consulate at ul Filip Makedonski 10 in Plovdiv (☎032/632 309) for current visa prices.

Drinking and nightlife

The best drinking holes are the pavement cafés of ul Knyaz Aleksandûr I. The Kapana area just north of the Dzhumaya mosque is the best place to head for late-night drinks and dancing.

Gepi ul. Lady Strangford 5. A vibrant bar-cum-club with frequent live music as well as retro, dance, jazz, and Latino nights. Located up a side street just west of ploshtad Dzhumaya. Open 9pm–4am.

Morris A trendy nightclub with regular live music, north of the river at bul Maritsa 122. Open 9pm–4am.

Red Eye ul. Gladston 8. Just off ploshtad Tsentralen, this tiny, but incredibly popular bar is crammed into the first floor of a rickety old building. Features a staple diet of rock and retro.

Sky Bar ul. Knyaz Alexandur 32. Sleek, outdoor cocktail bar with white leather sofas and plasma video screens.

Directory

Hospital Sonel Farma Medical Centre. Bul. Hristo Botev 47A. ☎032/632 094.

Internet Try Elite at ul Patriarch Evtimi 24, or Fantasy, at ul Knyaz Aleksandûr I 31.

Post Office pl. Tsentralen 1 (Mon-Sat 7am–7pm & Sun 7am–11am).

Pharmacy Kamea, next to Union Bank at bul. 6 Septemvri 76. Open 24hr.

Travel agents Several agencies at the Yug bus station sell tickets for international buses. Hebros Bus (daily 7.30am–7pm; ☎032/626 916), a Eurolines agent, can book seats on buses to Greece, Turkey and Western Europe.

Moving on

Train Burgas (6 daily; 4–5hr); Istanbul (1 nightly; 10hr 30min); Sofia (14 daily; 2hr–3hr 30min); Varna (3 daily; 5hr).

Bus Avtogara Rodopi: Smolyan (via Bachkovo monastery) (hourly; 40min); Avtogara Sever: Koprivshtitsa (1 daily; 2hr 30min); Veliko Tûrnovo (2 daily; 4hr); Avtogara Yug: Burgas (2 daily; 4hr); Sofia (hourly; 2hr); Varna 2 daily; 5hr).

DAY-TRIPS FROM PLOVDIV

The most attractive destination south of Plovdiv is **Bachkovo Monastery** (daily 7am–8pm; free), around 30km away and an easy day-trip from the city (hourly buses from Rodopi station to Smolyan). Founded in 1038 by two Georgians in the service of the Byzantine Empire, this is Bulgaria's second-largest monastery and is placed on the tentative list for UNESCO World Heritage status.

A great iron-studded door admits visitors to the cobbled courtyard, surrounded by wooden galleries and adorned with colourful frescoes. Along one wall is a pictorial narrative of the monastery's history, showing Bachkovo roughly as it appears today, and watched over by the Madonna and Child. Beneath the vaulted porch of Bachkovo's principal church, **Sveta Bogoroditsa**, are frescoes depicting the horrors in store for sinners; the entrance itself is more cheery, overseen by the Holy Trinity.

Just outside the main gate is the recently restored **ossuary**, which dates from the eleventh century and contains a number of early medieval frescoes, but sadly it's rarely open to visitors. It's possible to **stay** in recently refurbished rooms in the monastery (☎03327/277; 14Lv per person with shared bathroom and cold water, 34Lv per person with hot water and ensuite), and there are three **restaurants** just outside; *Vodopada*, with its mini-waterfall, is the best.

Central Bulgaria

For over a thousand years, Stara Planina – known to foreigners as the **Balkan range** – has been the cradle of the Bulgarian nation. It was here that the Khans established the First Kingdom, and here, too, after a period of Byzantine control, that the Boyars proclaimed the Second Kingdom and created a magnificent capital at **Veliko Tûrnovo**. Closer by, the **Sredna Gora** (Central Mountains) was inhabited as early as the fifth millennium BC, but for Bulgarians this forested region is best known as the Land of the April Rising, the nineteenth-century rebellion for which the picturesque town of **Koprivshtitsa** will always be remembered.

Although they lie a little way off the main rail lines from Sofia, neither Veliko Tûrnovo nor Koprivshtitsa is difficult to reach. The former lies just south of Gorna Oryahovitsa, a major rail junction midway between Varna and Sofia, from where you can pick up a local train or bus; the latter is served by a stop on the Sofia–Burgas line, where four daily trains in each direction are met by local buses to ferry you the 12km to the village itself.

KOPRIVSHTITSA

Seen from a distance, **KOPRIVSHTITSA** (КОПРИВЩИЦА) looks almost too lovely to be real, its half-timbered houses lying in a valley amid wooded hills. It would be an oasis of rural calm if not for the tourists drawn by the superb architecture and Bulgarians paying homage to a landmark in their nation's history. From the Bridge of the First Shot to the Place of the Scimitar Charge, there's hardly a part of Koprivshtitsa that isn't named after an episode or participant in the **April Rising of 1876**. As neighbouring towns were burned by the *Bashibazouks* – the irregular troops recruited by the Turks to put the rebels in their place – refugees flooded into Koprivshtitsa, spreading panic. The rebels eventually took to the hills while local traders bribed the *Bashibazouks* to spare the village – and so Koprivshtitsa survived unscathed, to be admired by subsequent generations as a symbol of heroism.

What to see and do

All of the town's museums are open 9.30am–5.30pm, with half of them closing on Mondays, and the other half on Tuesdays. You can buy a combined ticket for all six for 5Lv at the tourist office and at any of the museums; individual houses are priced at 2Lv each. It's also possible to hire an English-speaking guide for a two-hour tour (20Lv).

HORSERIDING IN THE RILA MOUNTAINS

A unique way to experience the spectacular terrain of the Rila mountains is by **horseback**. Some of the trails pass through virtually untouched forest areas and alongside staggering glacial lakes; there are also some seriously rocky options for experienced or adventurous riders. The tour operator Horseriding Bulgaria (20 Saborna Str, Plovdiv, ⓣ02/400-3095, ⓦwww.horseridingbulgaria.com) offers a number of tour options, including individual tours with a guide, out of their Iskar Ranch at the foot of the Rila mountains. They can organise tours of different difficulty grades and can also offer riding instruction if you need it.

A street running off to the west of the main square leads to the **Oslekov House** (closed Mon). Its summer guest room is particularly impressive, with a vast wooden ceiling carved with geometric motifs. Near the Surlya Bridge is the birthplace of the poet **Dimcho Debelyanov** (closed Mon), who is buried in the grounds of the hilltop **Church of the Holy Virgin**.

A gate at the rear of the churchyard leads to the birthplace of **Todor Kableshkov** (closed Mon), leader of the local rebels. Kableshkov's house now displays weapons used in the Rising and features a wonderful circular vestibule. Continuing south, cross the **Bridge of the First Shot**, which spans the Byala Reka stream, and head up ul Nikola Belodezhdov, and you'll come to the **Lyutov House** (closed Tues), once home to a wealthy yoghurt merchant and today housing some of Koprivshtitsa's most sumptuous interiors. On the opposite side of the River Topolnitsa, steps lead up to the birthplace of another major figure in the Rising, **Georgi Benkovski** (closed Tues). A tailor by profession, he made the famous silk banner embroidered with the Bulgarian Lion and "Liberty or Death!".

Arrival and information

Bus Buses arrive at a small station 200m south of the main square.

Tourist information The tourist office on the main square (Ⓣ07184/2191; Ⓔkoprivshtitsa@hotmail.com; daily 9am–5pm) and a museum centre (Ⓣ07184/2191; Wed–Sun 9.30am–5.30pm) both sell tickets for Koprivshtitsa's six house museums. The tourist office can also book private rooms (❸) in charming village houses. Advance reservations are recommended in summer.

Accommodation

Bolyarka Ⓣ07184/2043. Four-room B&B just uphill from the centre, offering bright, pine-furnished rooms and a lovely garden. ❷

Panorama Ⓣ07184/2035, Ⓦwww.panoramata.com. A well-run complex south of the centre with smart modern rooms on the ground floor and traditional-style rooms above; most have sweeping views of the town. ❸

Trayanova Kashta Ⓣ07184/3057. Just up the street from the Oslekov House, this has delightful rooms in the National Revival style. ❸

Eating and drinking

Dyado Liben Inn A fine nineteenth-century mansion opposite the main square serving traditional dishes such as *gyuvech* (meat stew) for 4.50Lv.

Lomeva Kashta A folk-style restaurant just north of the square, serving grills and salads from 3.50Lv.

Moving on

Bus Plovdiv (1 daily; 2hr 30min); Istanbul (1 nightly; 8hr 30min); Sofia (4 daily; 2hr).

VELIKO TÛRNOVO

With its dramatic medieval fortifications and huddles of antique houses teetering over the lovely River Yantra, **VELIKO TÛRNOVO** (ВЕЛИКО ТЪРНОВО) holds a uniquely important place in the minds of Bulgarians. When the National Assembly met here to draft Bulgaria's first constitution in 1879, it did so in the former capital of the Second Kingdom (1185–1396), whose civilization was snuffed out by the Turks. It was here, too, that the Communists chose to proclaim the People's Republic in 1944.

What to see and do

Modern Tûrnovo centres on **Ploshtad Mayka Balgariya**: from here bul Nezavisimost (which becomes ul Stefan Stambolov after a few hundred metres) heads northeast into a network of narrow streets that curve above the River Yantra and mark out the old town, with its photogenic houses. Continuing along Stefan Stambolov, you'll notice steps leading downhill to ul General Gurko; don't miss the **Sarafina House** at no. 88 (Mon–Fri 9am–5.30pm; 4Lv), whose elegant restored interior is notable for its splendid octagonal vestibule and a panelled rosette ceiling.

Museum of the Bulgarian Renaissance and Constituent Assembly

Rejoining Stefan Stambolov and continuing downhill, you'll find the blue-and-white building where the first Bulgarian parliament assembled in 1879. It's now home to the **Museum of the Bulgarian Renaissance and Constituent Assembly** (Mon & Wed–Sun 9am–6pm; 4Lv), where you can see a reconstruction of the original assembly hall, and a collection of icons.

Tsarevets

Ivan Vazov leads directly to the medieval fortress, **Tsarevets** (daily: April–Oct 8am–7pm, Nov–March 9am–5pm; 4Lv). The boyars Petar and Asen led a successful rebellion against Byzantium from this citadel in 1185, and Tsarevets remained the centre of Bulgarian power until 1393, when, after a three-month siege, it fell to the Turks. The partially restored fortress is entered via the **Asenova Gate** halfway along the western ramparts. To the right, paths lead round to **Baldwin's Tower**, where Baldwin of Flanders, the so-called Latin Emperor of Byzantium, was incarcerated by Tsar Kaloyan. Above lie the ruins of the royal palace and a reconstruction of the thirteenth-century Church of the Blessed Saviour.

Arrival and information

Train All trains between Sofia and Varna stop at Gorna Oryahovitsa, from where local trains and frequent buses cover the remaining 13km to Veliko Tûrnovo. From Tûrnovo train station, 2km south of the city centre, buses #4 and #13 run to pl Mayka Balgariya.

Bus The main bus terminal (Avtogara Zapad) is southwest of town; bus #10 and trolley buses #1 and #21 go to the centre. Private buses to Sofia and the coast pick up and drop off just behind the tourist office.

Tourist office There's a tourist office at pl Mayka Balgariya (Mon–Fri 8am–6pm, summer also Sat 8am–6pm; ⓣ062/600 768) and 24-hour Internet access nearby at Nezavisimost 32.

Accommodation

Comfort ul Paneyot Tipografov 5 ⓣ062/628 728. A spotless, family-run place, with splendid views of the Tsarevets. Located just above the Varosh Quarter's bazaar. ❻

Hikers Hostel Rezervoarska 91 ⓣ088/96 1661, ⓦwww.hikers-hostel.org. A friendly hostel tucked away in a narrow street above the Varosh Quarter which offers yet more striking views, along with excellent dorm accommodation, free Internet access and kitchen. Dorm ❶, twin room ❷

Hostel Mostel 10 Iordan Indjeto Str ⓣ0897/859 359, ⓦwww.hostelmostel.com. Located in a beautifully restored 140-year-old Turkish building south of the road leading to Tsarevets. The hostel offers a free all-you-can-eat breakfast, plus a free dinner and a beer for every night of your stay, laundry and free Internet. There is a barbecue and tent space in the garden and the dormitories and private rooms are comfortable. Dorm ❶, private room ❸

Eating and drinking

Café Aqua ul. Stefan Stambolov. A relaxed café overlooking the gorge, with good coffee and cakes.

Mecha Dupka Serves authentic Bulgarian fare (main courses 5–6Lv) in a cellar below ul Rakovski in the Varosh Quarter, often with accompanying music and dancing.

Rich A good cheap option – with a great view – down some steps off Stefan Stambolov at ul Yantra 1.

Shastlivetsa Stambolov 79. Restaurant on the main road towards Tsarevets offering local dishes, as well as a large range of pizzas and pastas. Main courses around 4Lv.

Yasna pl Slaveykov. A good spot for coffee or cocktails.

Moving on

Bus Burgas (5 daily; 4hr 30min); Plovdiv (4 daily; 4hr 30min); Sofia (hourly; 4hr); Varna (hourly; 5hr).

Train Veliko Tûrnovo to Gorna Oryahovitsa (8 daily; 30min). Gorna Oryahovitsa to Sofia (8 daily; 4hr 30min).

International trains Must be booked in advance through the Rila/BDZh office behind the tourist offica at ul. Kaloyan 2 (Mon–Fri 8am–noon & 1–4.30pm, Sat 8am–noon). Bucharest (2 daily; 5–6hr); Budapest (1 daily; 18hr); Istanbul (1 daily; 13hr); Moscow (1 daily; 48hr); Thessaloniki (1 daily; 13hr).

The Black Sea coast

Bulgaria's **Black Sea** resorts have been popular holiday haunts for more than a century, though it wasn't until the 1960s that the coastline was developed for mass tourism, with Communist party officials from across the former Eastern Bloc descending on the beaches each year for a spot of socialist fun in the sun. Since then, the **resorts** have mushroomed, growing increasingly sophisticated as the prototype mega-complexes have been followed by holiday villages. With fine weather practically guaranteed, the selling of the coast has been a success in economic terms, but with the exception of ancient **Sozopol** and touristy **Nesebar**, there's little to please the eye. Of the coast's two cities – **Varna** and **Burgas** – the former is by far preferable as a base for getting to the less-developed spots.

VARNA

VARNA (ВАРНА) as a settlement dates back almost five millennia, but it wasn't until seafaring Greeks founded a colony here in 585 BC that the town became a port. The modern city is used by both commercial freighters and the navy, as well as being a popular tourist resort in its own right. It's a cosmopolitan place, and nice to stroll through: Baroque, nineteenth-century and contemporary architecture are pleasantly blended with shady promenades and a handsome seaside park.

What to see and do

Social life revolves around **Ploshtad Nezavisimost**, where the opera house and theatre provide a backdrop for restaurants and cafés. The square is the starting point of Varna's evening promenade, which flows eastward from here along bul Knyaz Boris I and towards bul Slivnitsa and the seaside gardens. Beyond the opera house, Varna's main lateral boulevard cuts through pl Mitropolit Simeon to the domed **Cathedral of the Assumption**. Constructed in 1886, it contains a splendid iconostasis and bishop's throne, with armrests carved in the form of magnificent winged panthers. The **Archeology Museum** on the corner of Mariya Luiza and Slivnitsa (Tues–Sun 10am–5pm; Nov–March closed Sun; 4Lv) houses one of Bulgaria's finest collections of antiquities. Most impressive are the skeletons and gold jewellery, some dating back almost six thousand years.

South of the centre, on ul Han Krum, are the extensive remains of the third-century **Roman baths** (April–Oct Tues–Sun 10am–5pm, Nov–March Mon–Fri 10am–5pm; 3Lv). It's still possible to discern the various bathing areas and the once huge exercise hall. At the southern edge of the Sea Gardens, the **Navy Museum** (Mon–Fri 10am–6pm; 2Lv) is worth a trip to see the boat responsible for the Bulgarian Navy's only victory; it sank the Turkish cruiser *Hamidie* off Cape Kaliakra in 1912.

Arrival and information

Air Varna airport is about a 50-minute ride (take bus #409) northwest of the city.

Train The train station is ten minutes' walk south of the centre along ul Tsar Simeon.

Bus The bus terminal is a ten-minute journey (bus #1, #22 or #41) northwest of the centre on bul Vladislav Varnenchik.

Tourist Office Located on ploshtad Musala (summer daily 9am–6pm; ⓣ052/654 519). The staff sell city maps, reserve hotel rooms, organize excursions and arrange car rental. In addition, the summer edition of the *Varna In Your Pocket* guide (Ⓦwww.inyourpocket.com), distributed in bars, hotels and restaurants, is a useful source of information.

Internet access Try Doom, at ul 27 July 13, or Cyber X, at Knyaz Boris I 53, both open 24hr.

Accommodation

Private rooms (❷–❹) can be arranged by Astra Tour in the railway station (daily; summer 7am–10pm; winter 9am–6pm; Ⓣ052/605 861, Ⓔastratur@yahoo.com) who also sell useful city maps.

Hostels

Flag Hostel ul. Sheinovo 2, first floor Ⓣ0897/408 115, Ⓦwww.varnahostel.com. Very central but hard to find; phone ahead for directions. It offers three dormitories, kitchen access, 24hr check-in and free breakfast. Friendly staff. ❶

Gregory's Backpackers Hostel 82 ul. Fenix 82, Zvezditsa. Very friendly and busy hostel, with a tent area as well as dormitories and double rooms. The licensed bar, Internet café area and barbecue in the garden only add to the sociable atmosphere. Located just outside the city, they offer a free daytime pick-up and drop-off service from Varna train and bus stations, as well as a free beach shuttle. Dorms ❶, double rooms ❸

Yo Ho Ho Hostel bul. Saborni 44. A fun, welcoming hostel, centrally located just behind the cathedral, with a nautical theme including staff in pirate costume. Breakfast is included and there are Internet and laundry facilities. ❶

Eating and drinking

Restaurants

Arkitekt ul Musala 10. A traditionally furnished wooden townhouse west of the centre serving authentic Bulgarian dishes and plenty of grilled meat (3–6Lv), with a pleasant courtyard garden.

Happy Bar and Grill Ploshtad Nezavisimost. American-style eatery with a picture menu offering a mixture of Bulgarian and international food. The *kashkaval pane* (battered cheese) is particularly good (3Lv).

Morske vulk ul. Odrin. Just south of ploshtad Exarch Yosef, this is one of the friendliest and cheapest restaurants in town, with a vibrant, alternative crowd and brilliant Bulgarian dishes, including vegetarian options such as pizza for 5Lv.

Bars

There are plenty of **bars** to choose from along bul Knyaz Boris I, while in summer, the **beach**, reached by steps from the Sea Gardens, is lined with open-air bars, fish restaurants and a seemingly unending strip of nightclubs. Outside high season, though, it's pretty dismal.

Moving on

Bus Burgas (hourly; 3hr); Dobrich (every 30min; 50min); Golden Sands (every 20–30min; 20min); Sunny Beach (hourly; 2hr 10min); Veliko Tûrnovo (7 daily; 4hr).

Train Dobrich (1 daily; 2hr 45min); Plovdiv (3 daily; 6–7 hr); Sofia (6 daily; 8–9hr).

BURGAS

The south coast's prime urban centre and transport hub, **BURGAS** (БУРГАС) can be reached by train from Sofia and Plovdiv, or by bus from Varna, and provides easy access to the picture-postcard town of Nesebar to the north and Sozopol to the south. Burgas's train and bus stations are both located at the southern edge of town, near the port. Bypassed by most tourists, the pedestrianized city centre, lined with smart boutiques, bars and cafés, is pleasant enough, though Burgas's best features are the well-manicured **Sea Gardens**, overlooking the beach and its rusting pier at the eastern end of town. If you want to stay, contact Dimant, at ul Tsar Simeon 15 (street sign reads Republikanska; Mon–Sat: summer 8.30am–8.30pm; winter 8.30am–6.30pm; Ⓣ056/840 779, Ⓔdimant91@abv.bg), which can book **private rooms** (❷). The city's **hotels** tend to be pricey; *Hotel Elite*, at ul. Morska 35 (Ⓣ056/845780; ❻) is the only reasonable hotel in the town centre, while the ageing *Primorets* in the Sea Gardens at ploshtad Alexander Batenberg 2 (Ⓣ056/843 137; ❸) offers good value and is close to the beach.

NESEBAR

Founded by Greek colonists from Megara, **NESEBAR** (НЕСЕБЪР) – 35km northeast of Burgas and served by buses every forty minutes – grew into a thriving port during the Byzantine era, and ownership alternated between Bulgaria and Byzantium until the Ottomans captured it in 1453. The town remained an important centre of Greek culture and the seat of a bishop under Turkish rule, which left Nesebar's **Byzantine churches** reasonably intact. Nowadays the town depends on them for its tourist appeal, demonstrated by the often overwhelming stream of summer visitors crossing the man-made isthmus that connects the old town with the mainland. Outside the hectic summer season, the place seems eerily deserted, with little open other than a few sleepy cafés.

What to see and do

The **Archeological Museum** (Mon–Fri 9am–7pm, Sat & Sun 9am–1pm & 2–6pm; 4Lv) stands just inside the city gates and has an array of Greek tombstones and medieval icons on display. Immediately beyond the museum is **Christ Pantokrator**, the first of Nesebar's churches, currently in use as an upmarket art gallery. It features an unusual frieze of swastikas – an ancient symbol of the sun and continual change. Downhill on ul Mitropolitska is the eleventh-century church of **St John the Baptist** (now also an art gallery), only one of whose frescoes still survives. Overhung by half-timbered houses, ul Aheloi branches off from ul Mitropolitska towards the **Church of Sveti Spas** (summer only: Mon–Fri 10am–5pm, Sat & Sun 10am–1.30pm; 2Lv), outwardly unremarkable but filled with seventeenth-century frescoes.

A few steps to the east lies the ruined **Old Metropolitan Church**, dominating a plaza filled with pavement cafés and street traders. The church itself dates back to the sixth century, and it was here that bishops officiated during the city's heyday. Standing in splendid isolation beside the shore, the ruined **Church of St John Aliturgetos** represents the zenith of Byzantine architecture in Bulgaria. Its exterior employs limestone, red bricks, crosses, mussel shells and ceramic plaques for decoration.

Arrival

Bus Buses arrive at either the harbour at the western end of town, or further up Han Krum before turning around to head for the nearby Sunny Beach resort.

Accommodation

Private rooms (❶–❸), many in fine old houses, can be booked through Messemvria, at Messembria 10 (Ⓣ0554/45880, Ⓦwww.messemvria.com), near the St John Baptist church.

Rai ul Sadala 7 Ⓣ0554/46094. A small and comfortable family-run pension on the northern side of the peninsula. Open summer only. ❸

Tony ul Kraybrezhna 20 Ⓣ0554/42403. Nearby the Rai in the old town, this hotel's pleasant, a/c rooms have balconies with sea views. ❹

Eating and drinking

There are plenty of **places to eat**, although most restaurants are aimed at the passing tourist crowd, serving predictably mediocre food. Two of the better options are the *Kapetanska Sreshta*, overlooking the harbour, and the sea-facing *Neptun*, towards the far end of town. **Snacks** are available from summertime kiosks along the waterfront.

Moving on

Bus Burgas (every 40 min; 50min); Sofia (7 daily; 6hr 30min).

SOZOPOL

SOZOPOL (СОЗОПОЛ), the oldest settlement in Bulgaria, was founded in the seventh century BC by Greek colonists from Miletus, who called the town Apollonia and prospered by trading textiles and wine for honey and corn. The town's charm owes much to its **architecture**, the old wooden houses jostling for space, their upper storeys almost meeting across the town's narrow cobbled streets. Today it's a busy fishing port and holiday resort, especially popular with East European tourists.

What to see and do

The **Archeological Museum** (summer Mon–Fri 10am–5pm; winter Mon–Fri 8am–noon; 2Lv) behind the library holds a worthwhile collection of ancient ceramics, as well as a number of artefacts uncovered in the local area. Further into the town, follow the signs to the **Southern Fortress Wall and Tower Complex** (summer only, 9.30am–7.30pm; 4Lv), which gives access to a beautifully restored tower dating from the 4th century BC.

Arrival and information

Bus Half-hourly buses from Burgas arrive at ploshtad Han Krum on the southern edge of the old town, while buses from other Bulgarian cities usually arrive and depart from the new town at ploshtad Cherno More.
Tourist Office In the absence of a municipal tourist office, the best source of information is Lotos tourist agency located high in the new town at ul. Musala 7 (summer daily 8am–8pm; ⓣ0550/23925, ⓦwww.aiatour.com).

Accommodation

Accommodation in Sozopol can be even harder to find during summer than in Nesebar, and most places shut down for the rest of the year. The Lotos tourist agency (see below) can arrange private rooms (❶–❷ per person). Of the few official old town hotels, *Rusalka*, on the south of the peninsula at ul. Milet 36 (ⓣ0550/23047, ❹) is the best value and has great sea views. **Campers** can head for *Zlatna Ribka* (ⓣ0550/22427; 4Lv per person, 5Lv per tent, double bungalow 20Lv), a popular seaside campsite 3km north of town on the Burgas bus route.

Eating and drinking

The *Chuchura* at ul. Ribarska 10 on the west side of the old town, and the *Vyatarna Melnitsa*, at ul Morski Skali 27 on the northern tip of the peninsula, are a couple of good, if touristy **restaurants** offering traditional Bulgarian cuisine as well as a good range of fish (around 20Lv per person).

Moving on

Bus Old town bus stop: Burgas (every 30 min; 50min).
New town bus stop: Plovdiv (5 daily; 5 hrs); Sofia (7 daily; 7hr 15min).

Croatia

HIGHLIGHTS

AMPHITHEATRE, PULA: visit the sixth largest amphitheatre in the world

ZADAR: visit this buzzing town and discover its unique Sea Organ

DIOCLETIAN'S PALACE, SPLIT: be amazed by this extraordinary 1700-year-old palace

VIS ISLAND: relax on the coast's lushest island

BOL: go windsurfing at one of the Adriatic's most attractive beaches

DUBROVNIK SUMMER FESTIVAL: enjoy world-class classical music at Croatia's prestigious festival

ROUGH COSTS

DAILY BUDGET Basic €27/occasional treat €34

DRINK Litre of local wine €7

FOOD Čevapčići (mini kebabs) €5

PRIVATE ACCOMMODATION/ HOSTEL/PENSION €14–27

TRAVEL Ferry travel within Dalmatian islands €3–5; Bus: Zagreb–Split €20

FACT FILE

POPULATION 4.4 million

AREA 56,542 sq km

LANGUAGE Croatian (Hrvatski)

CURRENCY Kuna (kn)

CAPITAL Zagreb (Population: 800,000)

INTERNATIONAL PHONE CODE ⓣ385

CROATIA BASICS

Basics

An independent kingdom in the tenth century, Croatia (Hrvatska) was subsequently absorbed by the Austro-Hungarian Empire before becoming part of the new state of Yugoslavia in 1918. Under Communist rule (from 1945), it declared its independence in 1991. War raged until 1995, when a return to stability saw tourists flooding back to a country that boasts one of Europe's finest stretches of coastline, and an array of impressive architecture dating back to Roman times.

The capital, **Zagreb**, is a lively central European metropolis, combining elegant nineteenth-century architecture with plenty of cultural diversions and a vibrant café scene. The peninsula of **Istria** contains many of the country's most developed resorts, with old Venetian towns like **Rovinj** rubbing shoulders with the raffish port of **Pula**. Further south lies **Dalmatia**, a dramatic, mountain-fringed stretch of coastline studded with islands. Dalmatia's main towns are **Zadar**, an Italianate peninsula town, and **Split**, an ancient Roman settlement and modern port which provides a jumping-off point to a series of enchanting **islands**. South of Split lies the medieval walled city of **Dubrovnik**, site of an important festival in the summer and a magical place to be, whatever the season.

CHRONOLOGY

168 BC The Romans conquer the Illyrians in the area known as present-day Croatia.
600s AD Early Croatian Slavic forefathers settle in the region.
799 Charlemagne invades the Dalmatian area of Croatia, establishing Frankish interest in the area.
925 Tomislav is crowned the first King of Croatia.
1102 Croats are forced to accept Hungarian rule.
1214 The Statute of the Island of Korcula is the first document in Europe to abolish the slave trade.
1526 Habsburg dynasty takes control of Croatia after the Battle of Mohacs.
1918 After defeat of Habsburgs in WWI, Croatia joins the Kingdom of the Serbs, Croats and Slovenes.
1929 The kingdom becomes known as Yugoslavia.
1945 General Tito leads successful resistance campaigns against the Nazis.
1980 Tito dies, leading to calls by Balkan countries for independence from Yugoslavia.
1989 The collapse of Communism heightens the call for political and national autonomy.
1990 Conservative Franjo Tudjman is elected President.
1991 Croatia declares its independence, leading to military campaigns by the Serbs against the Croats.
1995 Croat forces take control of large areas, forcing Croatian Serbs to flee Croatia. The Dayton Peace Accords end the war.
2005 Fugitive General Ante Gotovina, wanted for war crimes, is captured in the Canary Islands. Croatia beat Slovakia to win the tennis Davis Cup.

ARRIVAL

The principal international **airports** for flights from Europe are Dubrovnik, Pula, Split, Zadar and Zagreb. Generally, bus transfers into town are available through Croatia Airlines, although other companies also organise transfers into the centre.

Ferry routes to Croatia run frequently from Italy – Ancona, Pescara and Bari to Split, Hvar and Dubrovnik. Detailed information can be found on Ⓦwww.jadrolinija.hr.

Croatia is linked by **rail** with Austria, Bosnia-Herzegovina, Hungary, Italy, Serbia and Montenegro, Slovenia and Switzerland and is part of the **Eurolines** network, partnered with AutoTrans in Croatia. Visit Ⓦwww.eurolines.com or Ⓦwww.autotrans.hr for details.

GETTING AROUND

Croatian Railways *(Hrvatske željeznice;* Ⓦwww.*hznet.hr)* runs a smooth and ef-

ficient service. Trains (*vlak*, plural *vlakovi*) are divided into *putnički* (slow ones, which stop at every halt) and IC (intercity trains that are faster and more expensive). Tilting trains operate on the Zagreb–Split line, which take half the usual journey time. Timetables (*vozni red*) are usually displayed on boards in stations – *odlazak* means departure, *dolazak* arrival. You may travel on all trains with an **InterRail** pass, and must pay a small reservation fee for longer journeys.

By bus

The **bus** network is run by an array of small local companies, the leading one is AutoTrans (ⓦwww.autotrans.hr): services are well integrated and bus stations tend to be well-organized affairs. If you're at a big city bus station, tickets (*karta*) must be obtained from ticket windows before boarding the bus. Elsewhere, they can be bought from the driver. You'll be charged around 7kn for items of baggage to be stored in the hold.

By ferry

Jadrolinija (ⓦwww.jadrolinija.hr) operates **ferry** services down the coast on the Rijeka–Split–Korčula–Dubrovnik route at least once a day in both directions between June and August, and two or three times weekly for the rest of the year. Rijeka to Dubrovnik is a 22-hour journey, involving one night on the boat. In addition, ferries and faster catamarans link Split with the islands of Brač, Hvar, Vis and Korčula. **Fares** are reasonable for short trips: Split to Hvar costs around €4. For longer journeys, prices vary greatly according to the level of comfort you require. **Book** in advance for longer journeys, wherever possible.

Ferries are a good means of **moving on** from Croatia, with connections to Italy (Split and Zadar to Ancona, Pula and Rovinj to Trieste, Dubrovnik to Bari, Rovinj to Venice).

ACCOMMODATION

Private rooms (*privatne sobe*) have long been the mainstay of Croatian tourism. Bookings are made through the local tourist office or private travel agencies (usually open daily 8am–8/9pm in summer). Prices are around €20/150kn per person for a simple double sharing a toilet and bathroom, €28/200kn for a double with en-suite facilities; stays of less than three nights are often subject to a surcharge of thirty percent or over. Places fill up quickly in July and August: it's a good idea to arrive early or book ahead. Single travellers will sometimes find it difficult to get accommodation at all at this time, unless they're prepared to pay the price of a double room; at other times, you could expect to get a thirty percent discount. It's very likely you'll be offered a place to stay by elderly ladies waiting outside train, bus and ferry stations, particularly in southern Dalmatia. Don't be afraid to take a room offered in this manner, but be sure to establish the location and agree a price before setting off: expect to pay around twenty percent less than you would with an agency. However you find a room, you can usually examine it before committing to paying for it.

Hostels are cropping up more and more – especially in the larger towns – as Croatia becomes increasingly incorporated into backpackers' itineraries. The Croatian Youth Hostel website (Ⓦwww.hfhs.hr) has details and prices of HI-affiliated hostels in the country.

One-star **hotels** are in short supply; in most places, the cheapest are two-star, where you should expect to pay €50–70/400–550kn for a double room. In addition to hotels, there's a growing number of family run **pensions**, offering 2- or 3-star comforts at a slightly cheaper price – €40–60/300–450kn a double being the average.

FOOD AND DRINK

Croatia has a varied and distinctive range of **cuisine**, largely because it straddles two culinary cultures: the fish- and seafood-dominated cuisine of the Mediterranean and the hearty meat-oriented fare of central Europe.

For breakfasts and fast food, look out for street stalls or snack-food outlets selling *burek* (about 8kn), a flaky pastry filled with cheese; or grilled meats such as *čevapčići* (rissoles of minced beef, pork or lamb sold in a bun with relish; 30kn for a dozen in street-stalls). Bread (*kruh*) is bought from either a supermarket or a *pekarna* (bakery).

A **restaurant** menu (*jelovnik*) will usually include speciality starters such as *pršut* (home-cured ham) and *paški sir* (piquant hard cheese). Typical main courses include *punjene paprike* (peppers stuffed with rice and meat), *gulaš* (goulash) or some kind of *odrezak* (fillet of meat, often pan-fried), usually either *svinjski* (pork) or *teleški* (veal). On the coast, you'll be regaled with every kind of seafood. *Riba* (fish) can come either *na žaru* (grilled) or *pečnici* (baked). *Brodet* is a hot peppery fish stew. Other main menu items on the coast are *lignje* (squid), *škampi* (unpeeled prawns eaten with the fingers), *rakovica* (crab), *oštrige* (oysters), *kalamari* (squid), *školjke* (mussels) and *jastog* (lobster); *crni rizoto* is risotto with squid.

No town is without at least one pizzeria, serving good stone-baked pizzas from 30kn, making them the cheapest places to eat and also the easiest, especially for vegetarians. Typical **desserts** include *palačinke* (pancakes), *voćna salata* (fruit salad) and *sladoled* (ice cream).

Drink

Croatia is laden with relaxing cafés (*kavanas*) for daytime drinking. Coffee (*kava*) is usually served black unless specified otherwise – ask for *mlijeko* (milk) or *šlag* (cream). Tea (*čaj*) is widely available, but is drunk without milk.

Croatian **beer** (*pivo*) is of the light lager variety; Karlovačko and Ožujsko are two good local brands to look out for. The local **wine** (*vino*) is consistently good and reasonably cheap: in Dalmatia there are some pleasant, crisp whites wines such as *Kastelet*, *Grk* and *Posip*, as well as reds including the dark heady *Dingač* and *Babić*; in Istria, *Semion* is a bone-dry white, and *Teran* a light fresh red. Local spirits include *medenica*, a honey-based slow-burning nectar; *loza*, a clear grape-based spirit; and *Maraskino*, a cherry liqueur from Dalmatia.

CULTURE AND ETIQUETTE

With an almost ninety percent Roman Catholic population, religious holidays in Croatia are celebrated with gusto – not least because outward displays of religion were discouraged by Tito, leading to a what seems like "making up for lost time" attitude. A fun-loving people generally, especially among the younger generation, Croatians are welcoming and will happily engage you in conversations about food, wine and politics over a *raki* or two.

A service charge is not usually added to restaurant bills and it is the norm to leave a **tip** at your discretion (ten percent is quite acceptable).

SPORTS AND OUTDOOR ACTIVITIES

The Dalmatian coast is great for **watersports**, including windsurfing, kitesurfing, wake-boarding and some less hardcore pursuits, such as banana-boating and renting a motorboat. If you're a serious watersports fan, head to Brač: in July, the week-long Vanka Regule extreme sports event takes over Sutivan, near Supetar; there's free diving and windsurfing – and some more land-based sports, such as climbing and biking. See Ⓦwww.sutivan.hr for more.

Croatia's latest tennis hero, Ivan Ljubičić, along with other international successes, have ensured Croatia's status as a fertile ground for rising **tennis**-stars, with the ATP tournaments in Umag making the sport ever more popular in the country. **Football** remains the nation's favourite diversion, Dinamo Zagreb being the best-known team internationally. The Maksimir stadium is situated in the northeast borough of the capital and is set to be refurbished by 2010.

COMMUNICATIONS

Post offices (*pošta* or HPT) are discernible by their bright yellow signs and open Mon–Fri 7/8am–8pm, Sat 8am–1pm. In big towns and resorts, some are open daily and until 10pm. Stamps (*marke*) can also be bought at newsstands, and letter-boxes are painted the same bright yellow as post office signs.

Public **phones** use cards (*telekarta*), which come in denominations of 15kn,

CROATIA ON THE NET

Ⓦwww.adriatica.net General info about the Adriatic resorts, and an online booking service with a wide range of apartments, villas and hotels.
Ⓦwww.croatia.hr Croatia's tourist board site.
Ⓦwww.istra.com Covers the Istrian peninsula.
Ⓦwww.dalmacija.net Comprehensive coverage of the Dalmatian islands.
Ⓦwww.dubrovnik-online.com Excellent city site, including message board.

25kn, 50kn and 100kn; you can buy these from post offices or newspaper kiosks. When making long-distance and international calls, you can also go to the post office, where you're assigned a cabin and given the bill afterwards.

Internet is available in the capital and most towns and cities; expect to pay around 25kn per hour.

EMERGENCIES

The crime rate is low by European standards. Police (*policija*) are generally helpful when dealing with holiday-makers, although they can be slow when filling out reports. They also often make routine checks on identity cards and other documents; always carry your passport. Hospital treatment is free for EU members. Travel insurance comes highly recommended though, as public facilities are not always available. **Pharmacies** (*ljekarna*) tend to follow normal shopping hours (see below) and a rota system covers night-time and weekend opening; details are posted in the window of each pharmacy.

EMERGENCY NUMBERS

Police ⓣ92; fire ⓣ93; ambulance ⓣ94; sea rescue and diving alert ⓣ9155.

INFORMATION & MAPS

Most towns of any size have a **tourist office** (*turističke informacije*), which will give out brochures and local maps. Few offices book private rooms, but they will at least direct you to an agency that does. Freytag & Berndt produce a good 1:600,000 **map** of Croatia, Slovenia and Bosnia-Herzegovina, as well as 1:100,000 regional maps of Istria and the Dalmatian coast.

STUDENT AND YOUTH DISCOUNTS

The majority of museums and attractions offer concessionary prices on the presentation of a valid **ISIC card**.

MONEY AND BANKS

The local currency is the **kuna** (kn), which is divided into 100 lipa. There are coins of 1, 2, 5, 10, 20 and 50 lipa, and 1kn, 2kn and 5kn; and notes of 5kn, 10kn, 20kn, 50kn, 100kn, 200kn, 500kn and 1000kn. Accommodation and ferry prices are often quoted in euros, but you still pay in kuna. **Banks** (*banka*) are open Mon–Fri 9am–5pm (sometimes with longer hours in the summer), Sat 7.30am–1pm. Money can also be changed in post offices, travel agencies and **exchange bureaux** (*mjenjačnica*). Credit cards are accepted in a large number of hotels and restaurants, and you can use them to get cash from ATMs. At the time of writing, €1 was equal to around 7kn, $1 to 6kn, and £1 to 11kn.

OPENING HOURS AND HOLIDAYS

Most **shops** open Mon–Fri 8am–8pm, Sat 8am–1pm, although many supermarkets, outdoor markets and the like are open daily 7am–7pm. **Museum and gallery** times vary from place to place, although most are closed Mon. All shops and banks are closed on the following **public holidays**: Jan 1, Jan 6, Easter Mon, May 1, Corpus Christi, June 22, June 24, Aug 5, Aug 15, Oct 8, Nov 1, and Dec 25 & 26.

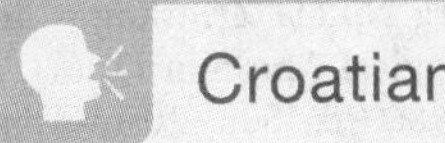

Croatian

	Croatian	Pronunciation
Basics		
Yes	*Da*	Dah
No	*Ne*	Neh
Please	*Molim*	Mo-leem
Thank you	*Hvala*	Hvahlah
Hello/Good day	*Bog/Dobar dan*	Dobahr dan
Goodbye	*Bog/Dovidjenja*	Doh veedehnyah
Excuse me	*Izvinite*	Izvineet
Sorry	*Oprostite*	Auprausteete
Today	*Danas*	Danass
Good	*Dobro*	Dobroh
Bad	*Loše*	Losheh
How much is....?	*Koliko stoji...?*	Koleekoh sto-yee?
What time is it?	*Koliko je sati?*	Koleekoh yeh satee?
I don't understand	*Ne razumijem*	Neh rahzoomeeyehm
Do you speak English?	*Govorite li engleski?*	Govoreeteh lee ehngleskee?
One	*Jedan*	Yehdan
Two	*Dva*	Dvah
Three	*Tri*	Tree
Four	*Četiri*	Cheteeree
Five	*Pet*	Pet
Six	*Šest*	Shest
Seven	*Sedam*	Sedam
Eight	*Osam*	Osam
Nine	*Devet*	Devet
Ten	*Deset*	Deset
Getting around		
Where is?	*Gdje je?*	Gdyeh ye?
Where are?	*Gdje su?*	Gdyeh soo?
entrance	*ulaz*	oolaz
exit	*izlaz*	eezlaz
Tourist Office	*Turistički Ured*	Tooristichkee oored
toilet	*zahod*	zah-haud
hotel	*hotel*	hautel
private rooms	*sobe*	saubey
museum	*muzeja*	moozeya
church	*crkva*	tsrkvah
Accommodation		
I'd like to book	*Ja bih revervirala*	Ya bee reserveerahla
Single room	*Jednokrevetnu sobu*	Yednau-krevetnoo sauboo
Double room	*Dvokrevetnu sobu*	Dvoau-krevetnoo sauboo
I'd like to see the room	*Mogu li vidjeti sobu*	Maugoo lee vidyetlee sauboo
Cheap	*Jeftino*	Yeftinoh
Expensive	*Skupo*	Skoopoh
Open	*Otvoreno*	Otvoreenoh
Closed	*Zatvoreno*	Zatvoreenoh

Zagreb

Capital of Croatia since 1991, **ZAGREB** has served as the cultural and political focus of the state since the Middle Ages. The city grew out of two medieval communities, Kaptol, to the east, and Gradec, to the west, each sited on a hill and divided by a river long since dried up but nowadays marked by a street known as Tkalčićeva. Zagreb grew rapidly in the nineteenth century, and the majority of its buildings are relatively well-preserved, grand, peach-coloured monuments to the self-esteem of the Austro-Hungarian Empire. Nowadays, with a population reaching almost one million, Zagreb is the trendy, boisterous capital of a newly self-confident nation. A number of good museums and a varied and vibrant nightlife ensure that a few days here will be well spent.

What to see and do

Zagreb falls neatly into three parts. **Donji Grad** or "Lower Town", which extends north from the train station to the main square, Trg bana Jelačića – the bustling centre of the modern city. Uphill from here, to the northeast and the northwest, are the older quarters of **Kaptol** (the "Cathedral Chapter") and **Gradec** (the "Upper Town"), both peaceful districts of ancient mansions, quiet squares and leafy parks.

The Art Pavilion and Archeological Museum

Tomislavov Trg, opposite the train station, is the first in a series of three shaded, green squares that form the backbone of the lower town. Its main attraction is the **Art Pavilion** (Mon–Sat 11am–7pm, Sun 10am–1pm; 20kn, free Mon; ⓦwww.umjetnicki-paviljon.hr), built in 1898 and now hosting art exhibitions in its gilded stucco and mock-marble interior. In the last of the three squares – **Trg Nikole Zrinskog** – lies the **Archeological Museum** (Tues–Fri 10am–5pm, Sat & Sun 10am–1pm; 20kn; ⓦwww.amz.hr), which houses interesting pieces from prehistoric times to the Middle Ages.

Ilica and the National Theatre

Flanked by cafés, hotels and department stores, **Trg bana Jelačića** is hectic with the whizz of trams and hurrying pedestrians; the statue in the centre is of the nineteenth-century governor of Croatia, Josip Jelačića. Running west from the square, below Gradec hill, is **Ilica**, the city's main shopping street. A little way along it and off to the right, you can take a **funicular** (daily 6.30am–9pm, every 10min; 3kn) up to the Kula Lotrščak; alternatively, head south via **Preradovićev Trg**, a small lively square where there's a flower market, to **Trg maršala Tita**. This is a grandiose open space, centred on the late nineteenth-century **National Theatre**, a solid ochre-coloured pile behind a water sculpture by Ivan Meštrović, the strangely erotic *Well of Life*.

The Museum of Arts and Crafts and the Ethnographic Museum

The impressive **Museum of Arts and Crafts** (Tues–Sat 10am–7pm, Sun 10am–2pm; 20kn; ⓦwww.muo.hr) holds a display of pieces dating from the Renaissance to the present day, while on Mažuranićev Trg, the **Ethnographic Museum** (Tues–Thurs 10am–6pm, Fri–Sun 10am–1pm; 15kn, free Thurs) has a collection of costumes from every corner of the country, as well as an array of curious items brought back by Croatian explorers from all over the world.

Mimara Museum

One of Zagreb's most prized art collections is housed at the **Mimara Museum** (Tues–Wed & Fri–Sat 10am–5pm, Thurs 10am–7pm, Sun 10am–2pm; 20kn):

Novi Zagreb & Museum of Contemporary Art

the art and archeological collection of Zagreb-born Ante Topić Mimara. Highlights include Chinese art from the Shang through to the Song dynasty as well as a fine collection of European paintings, including works by Rembrandt, Rubens, Renoir and Velázquez.

The cathedral and Kaptol

The filigree spires of Zagreb's **cathedral** mark the edge of the district (and street) known as **Kaptol**, ringed by the ivy-cloaked turrets of the eighteenth-century **Archbishop's Palace.** Destroyed by an earthquake in 1880, it was rebuilt in neo-Gothic style, with a high, bare structure interior. Behind the altar lies a shrine to Archbishop Stepinac, head of the Croat church in the 1940s, imprisoned by the Communists after World War II, and beatified by the Pope in 1998.

Gradec

Gradec is the most ancient and atmospheric part of Zagreb, a leafy, tranquil backwater of tiny streets, small squares and Baroque palaces. From Trg bana Jelačića, make your way to the **Dolac market**, which occupies several tiers immediately beyond the square; this is the city's main food-market, held every morning. From the far side of Dolac market, the long since dried-up river **Tkalčićeva** spears north, dividing Kaptol and Gradec. Entry to Gradec proper from here is by way of **Krvavi Most,** which connects the street with Radićeva. On the far side of Radićeva, the **Kamenita Vrata** is a gloomy tunnel with a small shrine that formed part of Gradec's original fortifications. Close by, the **Kula Lotršćak** (May–Oct Tues–Sun 11am–8pm; 10kn) marks the top station

MUSEUM OF CONTEMPORARY ART

Plans to expand Zagreb southward are set to kick off with the opening of the **Museum of Contemporary Art** (Ⓦwww.msu.hr), over the river Sava, in spring 2008. The Croatian architect, Igor Franić, won first place in a national competition to design the museum, which is set to become Zagreb's largest and most prestigious, housing nine thousand works by Picasso, Dali and Miro. The building will have exhibition space on five floors, a library, auditorium, multimedia halls and lively outdoor exhibitions and promises to breathe new life into the south bank.

of the funicular (see p.250) and provides fantastic views over the rest of the city and the plains beyond.

Church of St Mark and Meštrović Atelier

Focus of **Markov Trg** is the squat **Church of St Mark,** a hugely renovated place, whose tiled roof displays the coats-of-arms of the constituent parts of Croatia. Just north of Markov Trg, at Mletačka 8, is the **Meštrović Atelier** (Tues–Fri 10am–6pm, Sat & Sun 10am–2pm; 20kn), a wonderful exhibition dedicated to Croatia's most famous twentieth-century artist in the sculptor's former home and studio.

The Historical Museum of Croatia and Museum of Zagreb

The **Historical Museum of Croatia**, at Matoševa 9 (Mon–Fri 10am–6pm, Sat & Sun 10am–1pm; 10kn; Ⓦwww.hismus.hr), is the venue for prestigious temporary exhibitions. The superb **Museum of Zagreb**, at Opatička 20 (Tues–Fri 10am–6pm, Sat & Sun 10am–1pm; 20kn) tells the tale of Zagreb's development, from medieval times to the early twentieth century, with the help of a host of donations from the city's wealthier households, as well as displaying political and religious propaganda posters.

Arrival and information

Train Zagreb's central train station is on Tomislavov Trg, on the southern edge of the city centre, a ten-minute walk from Trg bana Jelačića, the main square.
Bus The main bus station is a fifteen-minute walk east of the train station, at the junction of Branimirova and Držićeva – trams #2, #3 and #6 run between the two stations, with #6 continuing to the main square.
Air Zagreb airport is 10km southeast of the city; Croatia Airlines buses run to the main bus station (7am–8pm, every 30min; 25kn).
Tourist office There are two tourist offices in central Zagreb; the main one is at Trg bana Jelačića 11 (Mon–Fri 8.30am–9pm, Sat 9am–5pm, Sun 10am–2pm; Ⓣ01/48-14-051, Ⓦwww.zagreb-touristinfo.hr), the other is at Trg N. Zrinskog 14 (Mon, Wed & Fri 9am–5pm; Tues & Thurs 9am–6pm, Sat & Sun 9am–6pm; Ⓣ01/49-21-645).
Discount cards Both tourist offices sell the Zagreb Card (72hr, 90kn), which gives unlimited city transport and good discounts in museums and restaurants. The superb, free *Zagreb In Your Pocket* (Ⓦwww.inyourpocket.com), available from the tourist offices, hotels and shops, is by far the best source of information on the city.
Listings The free monthly pamphlet *Events and Performances*, available from the Zagreb tourist office, contains listings in English of all forthcoming events.

City transport

Tickets Flat-fare tram and bus tickets (*karte*) are sold from cigarette and newspaper kiosks (6.50kn) or from the driver (8kn). Day tickets (*dnevne karte*) cost 18kn. Validate your ticket by punching it in the machines on board the trams.
Bus The bus network serves the capital's peripheries, setting off from the suburban side of the train station.
Trams The easiest way to get about, with sixteen routes altogether. Buses #2 and #6 run between the bus and train stations, #6 taking you into Jelčić, the main crossing point in the city. There is a four-line network of night services. Tickets are valid for 90mins if traveling in one direction.
Taxis There are ranks at the station and Jelačić,

as well as other points around town. The standard rate is 25kn plus 7kn per kilometre, which goes up by 20 percent 10am–5pm, Sundays and holidays. Luggage costs 5kn per item.

Accommodation

In addition to the **hostels** and **private rooms** listed below, some student rooms are available (mid-July to late Sept only; ❹). The two main locations are at Cvijetno naselje, Odranska 8 (Ⓣ01/61-91-245; tram #14 or #17 from Trg bana Jelačića), and Stjepan Radić, Jarunska 2 (Ⓣ01/36-34-255; tram #17 from Trg bana Jelačića).

Hostels and pensions

Private rooms Arranged through the Evistas agency at Šenoe 28, midway between the train and bus stations (Mon–Fri 9am–8pm, Sat 9.30am–5pm; Ⓣ01/48-39-546, Ⓔeevistas@zg.htnet.hr). ❸

Hostel Lika Pasmanska 17 Ⓣ098/561-041, Ⓦwww.hostel-lika.com. Incredibly friendly management, reasonable dorms with clean facilities and nightly barbeques in a shady garden. *Lika* is trying hard to be Zagreb's best hostel and staff go out of their way to help. Take tram #6 to Slovonska, then follow the yellow feet painted on the ground. ❷

Nokturno Skalinska 4A Ⓣ01/48-13-325, Ⓦwww.nokturno.hr. Situated in a good location off Tkalčićeva, Nokturno offers basic, clean single, 2-, 3- or 4-bed rooms. ❷

Omladinski Hostel Petrinjska 77 Ⓣ01/48-41-261. Large, run-down hostel near the train station. A little better than sleeping in the station itself. ❷

Ravnice Hostel 1. Ravnice 38b Ⓣ01/233-23-25, Ⓦwww.ravnice-youth-hostel.hr. Fabulous, welcoming hostel 20min east of the centre. Tram #4, #11, #12 or #7 to the Ravnice stop, by the Kraš chocolate factory, then 5min walk south along 1. Ravnice. ❷

Campsites

The nearest **campsite** (Ⓣ01/65-30-444, Ⓦwww.motel-plitvice.hr) is 10km southwest of town at the *Plitvice Motel* beside the main Zagreb–Ljubljana motorway; there's no public transport to it.

Eating

Zagreb has a wealth of cafés and bars offering outdoor seating in the pedestrian area around Gajeva and Bogovićeva – particularly along trendy Tkalčićeva, just north of Trg bana Jelačića. For **picnic food**, head to the area around Dolac market.

Cafés

K.&.K Jurišićeva 3. Intimate split-level café, whose every spare inch of wall space is covered in old pictures of Zagreb.

Princess Gajeva 4. Enticing cakes, fabulous ice cream. Good for gossip and people-watching.

Vincek Ilica 18. The very best place in town to stop for ice cream (8kn), cakes and hot chocolate.

Restaurants

Boban Gajeva 9. Popular and central pasta place in the vaulted basement of the stylish café of the same name. 40–60kn per dish.

Cantinetta Teslina 14. A chic restaurant serving good-quality Croatian and Italian food, just south of the main square. Closed Sun. Mains around 75kn.

Club Havana Perkovčeva 2. This great Cuban restaurant, located under the Press Club on a side street behind the Ethnographic Museum, has high-class food, sophisticated decor and attentive waiting staff, making It the most engaging place in town to eat. Closed Sun.

Kerempuh Kaptol 3, Dolac. Hidden away behind the main fruit-and-veg market (which is where fresh ingredients are sourced for the daily-changing menu); this is one of the best places in town to fill up on traditional Croatian favourites. Lunchtime special 50kn.

Makronova Ilica 72. Friendly, stylish and compact vegetarian restaurant serving imaginative and tasty fare, including macrobiotic cakes. Shares its first-floor location with Zagreb's premier health food shop. Open Mon–Fri from noon. Between 30–55kn.

Nokturno Skalinska 4. One of the best budget eateries in the area, dishing out lovely pizza, pasta and salads. In a sloping, cobbled street off the enchanting Tkalčićeva, adjacent to the hostel of the same name. Salads 25kn.

Rubelj Frankopanska 2 & Dolac market. Cheapest central place for simple but tasty grilled meat standards. Roughly 30kn/dish.

TREAT YOURSELF

Pod Grickim Topom on the steps leading down from Strossmayerovo Šetalište to Trg bana Jelačića. Enjoy superb Croatian food in this pretty, popular restaurant. Indulge in Croatian paté, monkfish carpaccio or Zagreb steak. From 65–125kn.

Drinking and nightlife

Bars

Bulldog Bogovićeva 6. A typically elegant Zagreb bar and pavement café, this is one of the most popular meeting places in the town centre. *Millenium*, next door, is good for an evening ice cream.

Dobar Zvuk Gajeva 18. Popular café-bar with cheap drinks and a moderately bohemian clientele.

Hemingway Dežmanova and Trg Maršala Tita. Funky chain cocktail bar, popular with Zagreb's smart set.

Melin Monroe Košarska 19. This energetic, grungy pub is a terrific alternative to the posier establishments nearby on Tkalčičeva.

Sedmica Kačićeva 7A. A bar so hidden away you imagine having to whisper "open sesame" at random keyholes – look out for the circular beer sign above the doorway. *Sedmica* is patronized by Zagreb's artists and bohemians, and has flyers for cultural events pinned to the entrance-hall walls. No entry after 11pm.

Clubs

Aquarius Aleja Mira bb. At the eastern end of Lake Jarun, 4km southwest of the centre, this place specializes in techno and drum 'n' bass. Occasional live bands too. Thurs–Sun.

Global Hatzova 14. Laid-back gay club with a good mix of people. Operates as a sex shop and café in the daytime, giving way to strippers, movie-nights and dancing later on.

Močvara Tvornica Jedinstvo building, Trnjanski nasip. The "Swamp" is an unpretentious cultural centre in an old factory on the banks of the River Sava. Live gigs, film shows and DJ nights – something happens every night. Take any bus heading for Novi Zagreb and alight just before the bridge – the club is on your right.

Saloon Tuškanac 1a. In a leafy corner of town, 500m west of the centre, *Saloon* was established in 1960 and is still going strong. Music is an enjoyable mish-mash of commercial disco. Tues–Sat with weekend after-parties.

Sax Palmotićeva 22. Large, comfortable basement club, two blocks east of Trg N. Zrinskog, with live music (with a jazz bias) most nights.

Entertainment

Live music

Croatian Musical Institute Gundulićeva 6 ⓣ01/48-30-922. Intimate chamber-music concerts.

Lisinski Concert Hall south of the train station at Trg Stjepana Radića 4 ⓣ01/61-21-166, ⓦwww.lisinski.hr. The city's main orchestral music venue. Ticket office Mon–Fri 9am–8pm, Sat 9am–2pm.

Theatre

National Theatre Trg maršala Tita 15 ⓣ01/48-28-532, ⓦwww.hnk.hr. Provides the focus for serious, Croatian-language drama, as well as opera and ballet. Ticket office Mon–Fri 10am–1pm & 5–7.30pm, Sat 10am–1pm and 90min before each performance, Sun 30min before each performance.

Shopping and markets

High street shopping The principal area for shopping is along Ilica, off Trg Bana Jelačića, which has several independent stores as well as familiar high-street names such as Mango and Lush, punctuated by handsome coffee-shops and a few tempting bakeries.

Designer shopping Frankopanska, off Ilica, features upmarket brands and designers such as Diesel, Galliano, Moschino and Lacoste. Sheriff and Cherry at Medvegradska 3 (closed Sun) and Prostor on Mesnička 5 (at the end of a small courtyard) are very popular boutiques.

Markets The bric-à-brac market in Britanski Trg on a Sunday is a magpie's dream – jewellery, traditional Croatian embroidery, farming implements, binoculars… you name it, it's there. Worth going to even just to have a coffee on the sidelines and watch bargain-hunters pick up extraordinary curios. Get there before 2pm for a piece of the action.

Directory

Embassies Australia, Nova Ves 11 ⓣ01/48-91-200; Canada, Prilaz Gjure Deželića 4 ⓣ01/48-81-200; UK, Ivana Lučića 4 ⓣ01/60-09-100; US, Thomasa Jeffersona 2 ⓣ01/66-12-200.

Exchange In the main post office on Branimirova.

Hospital Draskovićeva 19 ⓣ01/46-10-011.

Internet Aquarius, Kralja Držislavova 4; Art Net Club, Preradovićeva 25; Charlie's, Gajeva 4a; Sublink, Teslina 12.

Laundry Predom, Draškovićeva 31 (Mon–Fri 7am–7pm, Sat 8am–noon).

Left luggage At the train and bus stations (both 24hr).

Pharmacy Ilica 43 (24hr).

Post offices Branimirova 4 (24hr); Jurišićeva 13 (Mon–Fri 7am–9pm, Sat 7am–7pm, Sun 8am–2pm).

Moving on

Train Pula (2 changes; 2 daily; 6hr 40min); Rijeka (4 daily; 5hr); Split (3 daily; 5hr 30mins).
Bus Dubrovnik (7 daily; 9–11hr); Pula (12 daily; 4–6hr); Rijeka (hourly; 3hr); Rovinj (5 daily; 7hr); Split (hourly; 8hr).

Istria

A large peninsula jutting into the northern Adriatic, **Istria** is Croatian tourism at its most developed. Many of the towns here were resorts in the nineteenth century, and in recent years their proximity to northern Europe has ensured an annual influx of sun-seekers from Germany, Austria and the Netherlands. Yet the growth of modern hotel complexes, sprawling campsites and (mainly concrete) beaches has done little to detract from the essential charm of the region. This stretch of the coast was under Venetian rule for four hundred years and there's still a fair-sized Italian community, with Italian very much the second language. Istria's largest centre is the port city of **Pula**, which, with its Roman amphitheatre and other relics of Roman occupation, is a rewarding place to spend a couple of days. On the western side of the peninsula, the resort town of **Rovinj**, with its cobbled piazzas and shuttered houses, is almost overwhelmingly pretty.

PULA

Once the chief port of the Austro-Hungarian Empire, **PULA** is an engaging combination of working port, naval base and brash riviera town. The Romans put the city squarely on the map when they arrived in 177 BC, transforming it into an important commercial centre.

What to see and do

The first-century-BC **Roman Amphitheatre** (daily: June–Sept 8am–7pm; Oct–May 9am–5pm; 20kn) is the sixth largest in the world, and once had space for over 23,000 spectators. The outer shell is fairly complete, as is one of the towers, up which a slightly hair-raising climb gives a good sense of the enormity of the structure and a view of Pula's industrious harbour. The cavernous rooms underneath, which would have been used for keeping wild animals and Christians before they met their death, are now given over to piles of crusty amphorae and reconstructed olive presses. The amphitheatre houses the annual **Pula Film Festival** at the end of July, established in 1953 to promote Croatian cinema. See ⓦwww.pulafilmfestival.hr for information.

The Triumphal Arch and the Temple of Augustus

South of the amphitheatre, central Pula circles a pyramidal hill, scaled by secluded streets and topped with a star-shaped

MOVING ON FROM ISTRIA: RIJEKA

Travelling on from Istria towards Zagreb or Dalmatia, most routes lead through the port city of **RIJEKA**, hardly worth a stop-off in its own right but an important transport hub for onward travel: regular **buses** run from here to Zagreb, Zadar, Split and Dubrovnik, and it's the starting point for the Jadrolinija coastal **ferry**, which calls in at Zadar, Split and Dubrovnik on its way south. Rijeka's train and bus stations are about 400m apart; the former at the western end of Trpimirova, the latter at the eastern end of the same street on Trg Žabica. The Jadrolinija ferry office (daily 7am–6/9pm; ⓣ051/211-444) is along the waterfront from the bus station at Riva 16.

Venetian fortress. On the eastern side of the hill, Istarska – which later becomes Giardini – leads down to the first-century-BC **Triumphal Arch of the Sergians**, through which ul Sergijevaca, a lively pedestrianized thoroughfare, leads in turn to a square known as **Forum** – site of the ancient Roman forum and now the centre of Pula's old quarter. On the far side of here, the slim form of the **Temple of Augustus** was built between 2 BC and 14 AD to celebrate the cult of the emperor; its imposing Corinthian columns, still intact, make it one of the best examples of a Roman temple outside Italy.

The cathedral and Archeological Museum

Heading north from Forum along Kandlerova leads to Pula's **cathedral** (June–Aug daily 10am–1pm & 5–8pm; 5kn), a broad, simple and very spacious structure that purports another mixture of periods and styles: a fifteenth-century renovation of a Romanesque basilica built on the foundations of a Roman temple. From the cathedral, you can follow streets up to the top of the hill, the site of the original Roman Capitol and now the home of a mossy seventeenth-century **fortress**, built by the Venetians and housing a pretty uninspiring local museum. You're better off following tracks to the far side of the fortress where there are the remains of a small **Roman Theatre** (free) and the **Archeological Museum** (May–Sept Mon–Sat 9am–8pm, Sun 10am–3pm; Oct–April Mon–Fri 9am–2pm; 12kn), which has pillars and toga-clad statues mingling haphazardly with ceramics, jewellery and trinkets from all over Istria, some dating back to prehistoric times.

Arrival and information

Train Pula's train station is a ten-minute walk north of the centre, at the far end of Kolodvorska.
Bus The bus station is a similar distance northeast of the centre, along Istarska Divizije.
Tourist office Located in the Forum (June–Sept Mon–Sat 8am–10pm, Sun 9am–10pm; Oct–May daily 8am–4pm; ⓣ052/219-197, ⓦwww.pulainfo.hr), the office can provide information for all of Istria.

Accommodation

Private rooms Book through Arenatours, Splitska Ulica 1 ⓣ052/529-400, ⓦwww.arenaturist.hr, or Atlas, Ulica Starih Statuta 1 ⓣ052/393-040. ❷
Pula Youth Hostel Valsaline bay, 4km south of the centre ⓣ052/391-133; 90kn; take bus #2 or #3 from Giardini to Vila Idola and then bear right towards the bay. HI-affiliated hostel. ❷

Campsite

Stoja (ⓣ052/387-144) on a rocky wooded peninsula 3km southeast of town; take bus #1 from Giardini.

Eating and drinking

The vast market on Narodni Trg will yield all the provisions you'll need. Most eating-out options are around the amphitheatre.
Augustov Hram Kapitolinski Trg 9. Cheap and good Croatian fayre in a pavement café offering *čevapi* (mince kebabs), stuffed paprikas, cabbage salad and much more. Dishes from 15kn.
Jupiter Castropola 38. A pretty and tranquil pizzeria perched on a hill just near the fortress. Splendid pizzas from 30kn.
Scaletta Flavijevska 26. Opposite the hotel of the same name is a great Italian in a quaint setting. Try the "Scaletta risotto", flavoured with saffron. From 75kn.
Uliks Trg Portarata 1. An elegant bar next to the triumphal arch, with a special Irish cocktail dedicated to James Joyce, who taught at a school in the building.
Zen Cesta Prekomorski Brigada. A lively late-night drinking spot on the ring road, about 10 minutes' walk west from the bus station.
Uljanik Dobrilina 2. Counter-cultural club of many years' standing that has DJ nights at weekends and live music in summer. Otherwise, during the summer, the liveliest party venues are in Verudela, 3km south of town.

Moving on

Bus Dubrovnik (1 daily; 14hr); Rijeka (every 30min; 2hr 30min); Rovinj (20 daily; 1hr); Split (3 daily; 10hr); Zagreb (16 daily; 4–6hr).

ROVINJ

ROVINJ lies 40km north of Pula, its harbour an attractive mix of fishing boats and swanky yachts, its quaysides a blend of sun-shaded café tables, and the thick orange of fishermen's nets.

What to see and do

From the main square, **Trg maršala Tita**, the Baroque **Vrata svetog Križa** leads up to Grisia Ulica, lined with galleries selling local art. It climbs steeply through the heart of the old town to **St Euphemia's Church** (June–Sept daily 10am–2pm & 3–6pm), dominating Rovinj from the top of its peninsula. This eighteenth-century church, Baroque in style, has the sixth-century sarcophagus of the saint inside; and you can climb its 58-metre-high tower (same times; 10kn).

Trg Valdibora is home to a small fruit and vegetable market. Paths on the south side of Rovinj's busy harbour lead south towards **Zlatni rt**, a densely forested cape, crisscrossed by tracks and fringed by rocky **beaches**. Other spots for bathing can be found on the two islands just offshore from Rovinj – **Sveta Katarina**, the nearer of the two, and **Crveni otok**, just outside Rovinj's bay; both are linked by boats from the harbour (every 30min).

Arrival and information

Bus Rovinj's bus station is five minutes' walk southeast of its centre, just off Trg na lokvi, at the junction of Carrera and Carducci.

Tourist office Located just back from the waterfront at Obula Pina Budicin 12 (June–Sept daily 8am–10pm; Oct–May Mon–Fri 8am–3pm, Sat 8am–1pm, Sun 9am–1pm; ⓣ052/811-566, ⓦwww.tzgrovinj.hr.).

Accommodation

Private rooms Organized from Natale, opposite the bus station at Carducci 4 ⓣ052/813-365. ❷

Campsite

Porton Biondi (Aleja Porton Biondi 1 ⓣ052/813-557, ⓦwww.portonbiondi.hr), occupies a pine-shaded site right by the sea, 1km north of town. Open mid-March to Nov. ❷

Eating and drinking

Da Sergio Grisia 11. One of the best places for pizzas at around 45kn.

Monte Carlo Svetoga Križa. A more rough and ready alternative to Valentino (beer, rather than cocktails) where you can intersperse afternoon drinks with refreshing dips in the sea.

TREAT YOURSELF

Puntalina Sv Križa 43. Staff at the family-run *Puntalina* are very welcoming and will happily advise you on the best Istrian, French or Italian wine to suit your meal (and your budget). Oven-baked catch of the day (for two or three to share) is absolutely exquisite (300kn/kg) and pasta dishes (70–90kn) are fantastically generous. It's essential to reserve a table – preferably overlooking the sea – because this is one dining experience you won't want to miss out on.

MOTOVUN FILM FESTIVAL

Watching a silent film with live piano accompaniment as the legendary Motovun mist creeps over the hillside beside you is one of the most perfect cinematic experiences. Motovun's five-day **Film Festival** draws hordes of film- and party-lovers alike to this mysterious medieval village perched atop a hill. The festival adopts a **theme**, which in past years has included Erotica and Japanese Horror.

When the curtain falls the fun doesn't stop, with DJs pumping out the music each night in makeshift clubs along the city walls. The festival is **free**, as is the campsite at the bottom of the hill – for other accommodation it's wise to book well in advance. During the festival, buses from Rijeka run to Motovun or nearby, with local buses running to the bottom of the hill. See ⓦwww.motovunfilmfestival.com for more.

Valentino Svetoga Križa. An outdoor cocktail bar perched on the rocks over the Adriatic. Perfect for a sunset cocktail, albeit slightly pricey.
Konoba Veli Jože Svetog Križa 1. Top-notch seafood in a bustling pavement bistro. Mains 70kn.

Moving on

Bus Pula (hourly; 1hr); Rijeka (8 daily; 5hr).

The Dalmatian Coast

Stretching from Zadar in the north to the Montenegrin border in the south, the **Dalmatian Coast** is one of Europe's most dramatic shorelines. All along, well-preserved medieval towns sit on tiny islands or just above the sea on slim peninsulas, beneath a grizzled karst landscape that drops precipitously into some of the clearest – and cleanest – water in the Mediterranean. For centuries, the region was ruled by Venice, spawning towns, churches and architecture that wouldn't look out of place on the other side of the water. The busy northern port city of **Zadar** provides a vivacious introduction to the region. Otherwise, the main attractions are in the south: the provincial capital **Split** is served by trains from Zagreb and provides onward bus connections with the walled city of **Dubrovnik**. Ferry and catamaran connections to the best of the islands – **Brač, Hvar, Vis** and **Korčula** – are also from Split.

ZADAR

A bustling town of around 100,000 people, **ZADAR** boasts a compact historic centre crowded onto a tapered peninsula jutting northwest into the Adriatic. It displays a pleasant muddle of architectural styles, with Romanesque churches competing for space with modern café-bars.

What to see and do

Zadar's main square – or **Forum** – is dominated by the ninth-century **St Donat's Church** (summer only: daily 9am–10pm; 10kn), a hulking cylinder of stone with a bare interior built– according to tradition – by St Donat himself, an Irishman who was bishop here for a time. Opposite, the **Archeological Museum** (summer Mon–Sat 9am–noon & 5–8pm, Sun 9am–noon; winter Mon–Sat 9am–2pm; 20kn; ⓦwww.amzd.hr) has an absorbing collection of Neolithic, Roman and medieval Croatian artefacts. The adjacent **Permanent Exhibition of Church Art** (Mon–Sat 10am–1pm & 6–8pm, Sun 10am–1pm; 20kn) is a storehouse of Zadar's finest church treasures. On the northwestern side of the Forum, the twelfth- and thirteenth-century **Cathedral of St Anastasia** has an arcaded west front reminiscent of Tuscan churches. Around the door frame stretches a frieze of twisting acanthus leaves, from which various beasts emerge – look for the rodent and bird fighting over a bunch of grapes.

South of the Forum

Southeast of the Forum lies **Narodni Trg**, an attractive Renaissance square overlooked by the clock tower of the sixteenth-century **Guard House**. A little further southeast, on Trg Petra Zoranića, the Baroque **St Simeon's Church** houses the exuberantly decorated reliquary of St Simeon, ordered by Queen Elizabeth of Hungary in 1377 and fashioned from 250kg of silver by local artisans.

Arrival and information

Train and bus Zadar's train and bus stations are about 1km east of the town centre, a fifteen-minute walk or a quick hop on municipal bus #5 – tickets cost 8kn from the driver or 10kn (valid for two journeys) from kiosks.
Boat Ferries arrive on Liburnska obala, from where the town centre is a five-minute walk uphill.
Tourist office Narodni Trg (May–Sept daily 8am–

THE SEA ORGAN

Zadar's quirkiest feature, the **Sea Organ** was part of a millennium project to redesign the old city's coast. It consists of wide marble steps leading into the sea, with a crafty set of polyethylene tubes and cavities carved underneath, which enable the sea and wind to orchestrate a constant harmony. A strange sound a bit like pan-pipes crossed with whale-sounds, the Organ has to be seen – and heard – to be believed. Jump into the inviting sapphire water from the marble steps and appreciate the Organ from the element that creates it.

midnight; Oct–April Mon–Fri 8am–8.30pm, Sat & Sun 8am–2.30pm; ⓣ023/316-166, ⓦwww.zadar.hr) has maps and information on the city.

Accommodation

Private rooms Organised by Aquarius Nova Vrata bb (ⓣ023/212-919, ⓦwww.jureskoaquarius.com and Miatours, Vrata sv. Krševana (ⓣ023/254-300, ⓦwww.miatours.hr) both found under the arches in the town wall near the ferry quays. Miatours also sell ferry tickets to Pula (one-way 100kn). ❷ ❸
Venera, Šime Ljubića 4a ⓣ023/214-098 ⓦwww.hotel-venera-zd.hr. An old-town pension offering minuscule but neat en suites. ❸
Zadar Youth Hostel Obala kneza Trpimira 76 ⓣ023/331-145, ⓔzadar@hfhs.hr. Big, friendly hostel about 4km northwest at the beach resort of Borik (bus #5 or #8 from the bus and train stations). ❷

Campsite

Borik campsite (ⓣ023/332-074). Well-equipped campsite near Zadar Youth Hostel.

Eating

Arsenal Trg Tri Bunara ⓦwww.arsenalzadar.com. *Arsenal* opened its doors as an arts centre, lounge-bar, restaurant and event venue in 2005, and now houses one of the coolest spots in Zadar, if not Croatia. Pop in for a reasonably priced breakfast, lunch or dinner, peruse the boutiques framing the warehouse (that sell exquisite coral jewellery) or catch a concert or film (ask at Information for details). Also has a helpful tourist information centre and Internet until 4am.
Dva Ribara Borelli 7. Tasty pizzas and salads in a cool, modern restaurant. 50kn.
Kornat Liburnska Obala 6. A vast yet cozy restaurant right on the harbour with lovely fish, and hearty steak dishes. Reasonably priced, given its fairly posh décor (mains from 80kn), with good house wine. A hit with the locals too.
Pet Bunara Trg Pet Bunara ⓦwww.petbunara.hr. One of the oldest pizzerias in Zadar with good food and an ambient terrace. Excellent service and an entertaining karaoke bar next door. From 35kn.

Drinking and nightlife

Barbarella's in the grounds of Hotel Pinija, Petrčane (12km north of Zadar). Named after the club in Birmingham frequented by the founders of *The Garden* (see below) in their youth, *Barbarella's* has been done up to resemble a retro seventies cocoon with a banging dance-floor to boot.
Dina Varoška 2. One of several atmospheric café-bars tucked into the alleys off Narodni Trg – head down Klaiča and its continuation Varoška to find them. *Dina* is a tiny gallery and café with palette-shaped tables perfectly poised for watching the world stroll by.
Gotham City Marka Oreškovića. A popular *Batman*-themed summer nightclub north of the city.

Moving on

Bus Dubrovnik (10 daily; 8hr 30min); Pula (2 daily; 6hr 30min); Rijeka (11 daily; 4hr 30min); Split

TREAT YOURSELF

A kind of tree-house for grown-ups, **The Garden** (Bedemi zadarskih pobuna; ⓦwww.thegardenzadar.com) lounge-bar sits high up in the city walls: there are big beds to relax on, cocktail in hand, as well as a dance-floor that regularly boasts big-name DJs. The founders have also been running the Garden Festival since 2006 in Petrčane. One of the rising stars in Croatia's calendar of summer festivals, the festival pulls in DJs from across Europe and throws in hotel accommodation as well.

(every 30min; 3hr 30min); Zagreb (18 daily; 4hr 30min).

SPLIT

The largest city in the region, and its major transit hub, **SPLIT** is a hectic place, but one of the most enticing spots on the Dalmatian coast. At its heart lies a crumbling old town built within the precincts of Diocletian's Palace, one of the most outstanding classical remains in Europe.

What to see and do

Built as a retirement home by Dalmatian-born Roman Emperor Diocletian in 305 AD, **Diocletian's Palace** has been modified over the centuries, but has remained the core of Split. The best place to start a tour of the palace area is on the seaward side, through the **Bronze Gate**, a functional gateway giving access to the sea that once came right up to the palace itself. Inside, you find yourself in a vaulted hall, from which imposing steps lead through the now domeless vestibule to the **Peristyle**. These days the Peristyle serves as the main town square, crowded with cafés. At the southern end, steps lead up to the **vestibule**, a round, formerly domed building that's the only part of the imperial apartments to be left anything like intact. You can get some idea of the grandeur of the old apartments by visiting the **subterranean halls** (daily: July & Aug 8am–8pm; Sept–June 8am–noon and 4–7pm; 10kn) beneath the houses that now stand on the site; the entrance is to the left of the Bronze Gate.

The cathedral

On the east side of the Peristyle stands one of two black granite Egyptian sphinxes, dating from around 15 BC, which flanked the entrance to Diocletian's mausoleum; the octagonal building, surrounded by an arcade of Corinthian columns, has since been converted into Split's **cathedral** (Mon–Sat 7am–7pm). On the right of the entrance is the **campanile** (Mon–Sat 7am–7pm; 10kn), a restored Romanesque structure – from the top, the views across the city are splendid. The walnut and oak main **doorway** to the cathedral is one of its most impressive features – carved in 1214 and showing scenes from the life of Christ. Inside, the dome is ringed by two series of decorative Corinthian columns and a frieze that contains portraits of Diocletian and his wife. The beautiful Romanesque **pulpit** sits on capitals tangled with snakes, strange beasts and foliage. The church's finest feature is a cruelly realistic *Flagellation of Christ* depicted on the Altar of St Anastasius, completed by local artist Juraj Dalmatinac in 1448.

The Golden Gate and Archeological Museum

North of the cathedral and reached by following Dioklecijanova is the grandest and best preserved of the palace gates, the **Golden Gate**. Just outside there's a piece by Meštrović, a gigantic statue of the fourth-century Bishop **Grgur Ninski**. Fifteen minutes' walk northwest of here, the **Archeological Museum** at Zrinsko Frankopanska 25 (June–Sept Tues–Sat 9am–1pm & 4–7pm, Sun 10am–noon; Oct–May Tues–Fri 9am–2pm, Sat & Sun 10am–noon, although check at tourist office as times are erratic; 20kn) contains comprehensive displays of Illyrian, Greek, medieval and Roman artefacts. Outside, the arcaded courtyard is crammed with a wonderful array of Greek, Roman and early Christian gravestones, sarcophagi and decorative sculpture.

The Marjan Peninsula

If you want some peace and quiet, head for the woods of the **Marjan peninsula** west of the old town. It's accessible from the long road, Obala hrvatskog narodnog preporoda, via Sperun and then Senjska, which cuts up through the slopes of the **Varoš** district. Most of Marjan's visitors stick to the road around the edge of the promontory with its scattering of tiny rocky **beaches**; the Bene beach, on the far northern side, is especially popular. From the road, tracks lead up into the heart of the Marjan Park, which is thickly wooded with pines. The main historical highlight of the area lies some fifteen minutes west of the centre (bus #12 from the seafront).

Meštrović Gallery

The **Meštrović Gallery**, Ivana Meštrovića 46 (May–Sept Tues–Sun 9am–9pm, closed Mon; Oct–April Tues–Sat 9am–4pm, Sun 10am–3pm; 15kn, includes entrance to Kaštelet), is housed in the ostentatious Neoclassical building that was built – and lived in – by Croatia's most famous twentieth-century artist, the sculptor Ivan Meštrović (1883–1962). This fabulous collection consists largely of boldly fashioned bodies curled into elegant poses. Meštrović's former workshop, **Kaštelet** (same times; 20kn, free with gallery ticket), is 300m up the same road, and contains a chapel decorated with one of his most important set-piece works: a series of wood-carved reliefs showing scenes from the Stations of the Cross.

Arrival and information

Air Split airport is 16km west of town; Croatia Airlines buses connect with scheduled flights and run to the waterfront Riva (30kn); alternatively the #37 Split–Trogir bus runs from the main road outside the airport to the suburban bus station (15kn).
Train and bus Split's main bus and train stations are next to each other on Obala Kneza Domagoja, five minutes' walk round the harbour from the centre.
Boat The ferry terminal for both domestic and international ferries – and the Jadrolinija booking office – is a few hundred metres south of here.
Tourist office The Peristyle of the Palace (June–Sept Mon–Sat 8am–9pm, Sun 8am–1pm; Oct–May Mon–Fri 8am–8pm, Sat 8am–1pm, closed Sun; ⓣ021/345-606, ⓦwww.visitsplit.com).
Internet Head to *Backpacker's Caffe* near the bus station, which also sells secondhand books in English.
Listings Find flyers for gigs and festivals in *Planet Jazz* and the *Ghetto Club*.

Accommodation

Private rooms Booked through the helpful Turist Biro Obala narodnog preporoda 12, on the waterfront ⓣ021/347-100. ❸
Omladinski Hostel, Velebitska 27 ⓣ021/538-025; ⓔinfo@hoteldujam.com. Hostel in a college dorm, a fifteen-minute walk out of town along Slobode (or bus #9 from the harbour). Clean and convenient with laundry and basic kitchen facilities. ❷
Split Hostel Narodni trg 8, ⓣ021/342-787 ⓦwww.splithostel.com. Very central hostel run by helpful Australians who like boozing with their guests. ❷

Eating

The daily market at the eastern edge of the old town is the place to shop for fruit, veg and local cheeses.
Dioklecijan Dosud 9. A stone's throw from the *Ghetto Club* (see below) and the perfect lunchtime eatery, set in a homely terrace. Locals and visitors alike come to take in the view through three stone arches overlooking the sea. A compact menu offers tasty *čevapi* (baby kebabs) and mouth-watering stuffed paprika at 30–40kn a dish.
Konoba kod Jože Sredmanuška 4. Ten minutes' northeast of the old town. An atmospheric place with rustic charm specializing in seafood. Go for catch of the day at 330kn/kilo. Other mains from 60kn.
Šperun Šperun 3. An inventive menu with dinky pavement seating. The oven-baked seabass with almonds (80kn) is especially juicy.
Konoba Varoš ban Mladenova 7. A traditional Dalmatian restaurant, which will appeal to carnivores. Mains from 70kn.

Drinking and nightlife

The beach at Bačvice, a few minutes' walk south past the railway station, is a popular party place in summer.
Ghetto Club Posud 10. A great spot to have a beer, the bohemian *Ghetto Club* is a bar, café and gallery and there's a little bookshop in the courtyard selling "The Split Mind" – a publication in English and

Croatian that showcases young Croatian literary talent.

Planet Jazz Grgura Ninskog. A popular little place, and rightly so. *Planet Jazz* will lift your spirits and pave the way for a night of dancing.

Puls Buvinina 1. A bohemian café-bar sprawled across wide steps decorated with cushions, mini-sofas and tables and chairs.

Shook Mihovilova Širina. An upbeat café and the gateway of the *Shook-Puls-Ghetto Club* crawl – effortlessly taking you from coffee hour to cocktail hour.

Teak just off Majstora Jurja. A pleasant, popular joint which is good for a coffee or a cocktail. The same goes for the nearby *Porta* and *Kala café-bars*.

Moving on

Bus Dubrovnik (17 daily; 4hr 30min); Pula (3 daily; 10hr); Rijeka (11 daily; 8hr); Zadar (hourly; 3hr 30min); Zagreb (every 30min; 7–9hr).

Ferries Dubrovnik (2 weekly; 8hr); Hvar (Stari Grad) (5 daily; 2hr); Korčula (Vela Luka) (2 daily; 3hr); Rijeka (2 weekly; 10hr); Supetar (10 daily; 1hr); Vis (3 daily; 2hr 30min).

BRAČ

BRAČ is famous for its milk-white marble, which has been used in places as diverse as Berlin's Reichstag, the high altar of Liverpool's Metropolitan Cathedral, the White House in Washington – and, of course, Diocletian's Palace. In addition to the marble, a great many islanders were once dependent on the grape harvest, though the phylloxera (vine lice) epidemics of the late nineteenth century and early twentieth century forced many of them to emigrate. Even today, as you cross Brač's interior, the signs of this depopulation are all around in the tumbledown walls and overgrown fields. The easiest way to reach Brač is by **ferry** from Split to **Supetar**, an engaging, laid-back fishing port on the north side of the island, from where it's a straightforward hour's bus journey to **Bol**, a major windsurfing centre on the island's south coast and site of one of the Adriatic's most beautiful beaches, the **Zlatni Rat** (Golden Horn).

Supetar

Though the largest town on the island, **SUPETAR** is a rather sleepy village onto which package tourism has been painlessly grafted. There's little of specific interest, save for several attractive shingle **beaches** which stretch west from the harbour, and the **Petrinović Mausoleum**, a neo-Byzantine construction on a wooded promontory 1km west of town, built by sculptor Toma Rosandić to honour a local businessman.

Arrival and information

Tourist office Beside the ferry dock at Porat 1 (July & Aug daily 8am–10pm; June & Sept daily 8am–4pm; Oct–May Mon–Fri 8am–4pm; ⓣ021/630-551, ⓦwww.supetar.hr).

Accommodation

Private rooms Available from Atlas (ⓣ021/631-105) on the harbourfront at Porat 10. ❷

Hostel Villa Sunce on Zdenko Akmadzic ⓦwww.zdenkoo.tk. Friendly staff offer a warm welcome, and will collect you from the ferry. ❷

Pansion Palute 1.5km west of the harbour at Put pašike 16 ⓣ021/631-541, ⓔpalute@st.t-com.hr. A friendly pension, but soon fills up. ❸

Campsite

Supetar campsite (ⓣ021/631-066) is1.5km east of the ferry dock. SItuated in pine woods, it has easy access to beautiful, rocky parts of the coast.

Eating and drinking

Palute Porat 4. The best of the places to eat on the harbourfront: serves good grilled fish (mains from 70kn).

Vinotoka Dobova 6. Serves a wide range of traditional Croatian food and an extensive choice of local wines (mains about 90kn).

Activities

Scuba diving The Numitor Central in the Iberostar Supetrus Hotel complex at Put Vela Luke 4 (ⓣ021/630-421; closed Nov–March) rents out gear and arranges scuba and snorkelling courses (from 220kn),

Mountain biking The Numitor Central (see above) rents out mountain bikes (120kn/day).

Bol

Stranded on the far side of the Vidova Gora mountains, you cannot help but be overwhelmed by the beauty of **BOL's** setting, or the charm of its old stone houses. However, the main attraction of the village is its beach, **Zlatni rat**, which lies to the west of the centre along the wooded shoreline. The pebbly cape juts into the sea like an extended finger, changing shape from season to season as the wind plays across it. Unsurprisingly, it does get very crowded during summer. While you're here, look in at the late-fifteenth-century **Dominican Monastery** (daily 10am–noon and 5–9pm, though times vary so ask at the tourist office; 10kn), dramatically perched on a bluff just east of central Bol.

Arrival and information

Buses From Supetar, buses stop just west of Bol's harbour.

Tourist office Situated near the *Big Blue Cafe* (June–Aug daily 8am–10pm; Sept–May Mon–Fri 8.30am–2pm; ⓣ021/635-638, ⓦwww.bol.hr).

Accommodation

Private rooms Adria 100m west of the bus stop at Vladimira Nazora 28 (ⓣ021/635-966, ⓦwww.adria-bol.hr) book private accommodation on the island. Likewise, the nearby Boltours Vladimira Nazora 18 ⓣ021/635-693, ⓦwww.boltours.com arrange private rooms and apartments. ❷

Campsites

Kito Camping Karmelić Srećko, Ante Radića 1, ⓣ021/635-551 ⓔkamp_kito@inet.hr. Large, friendly campsite close to the beach and centre of Bol, with kitchens and a nearby supermarket. ❶

Tenis Camping Potočine bb ⓣ021/635-943. A good campsite in between the centre of town and Zlatni rat. ❶

Eating and drinking

Cocktail Bar Bolero Put Zlatnog rata. A shady spot right on the waterfront; relax in capacious wicker sofas set around the bar. Becomes crowded later on, with booming latino music and windsurfers unwinding after a day's exertions.

Gust Above the harbour at F. Radića 14. Has one of the widest ranges of traditional Dalmatian food of the many waterfront restaurants. The cozy, rustic interior feels like the inside of a barrel of wine, although outdoor seating is perhaps more refreshing. 70kn for mains.

Konoba Mlin Ante Starčevića 11. A lovely al fresco restaurant in an old stone-mill, with live music and an outdoor grill where freshly caught fish are cooked to taste. Mains 60–90kn.

Maza, Starčevića 10. Perfect pizzas in a romantic seaside setting away from the crowded tourist spots. Watch as paper-thin pizza-bases are flung into the air before your eyes and cooked in an outdoor oven. The devilishly hot "picante" is great – certainly not one for the faint-hearted. From 45kn.

Activities

Windsurfing Big Blue (ⓣ021/635-614, ⓦwww.big-blue-sport.hr), on the path leading to Zlatni rat, is the best of several windsurfing centres; as well as board rental (€15/hr) and a range of courses for beginners, they also rent out sea kayaks (€3.75/hr).

Mountain biking Bikes are available from *Big Blue Cafe* (see above) (€15/day). Free cycling maps are found in the tourist office.

HVAR

One of the most hyped of all the Croatian islands, **HVAR** is undeniably beautiful – a slim, green slice of land punctured by jagged inlets and cloaked with hills of spongy lavender. Tourist development hasn't been too crass, and the island's main centre, Hvar Town, retains much of its old Venetian charm. At least one daily hydrofoil from Split arrives at Hvar Town itself; numerous ferries head for Stari Grad, 4km east, from where buses run into Hvar Town.

What to see and do

The best view of **HVAR TOWN** is from the sea: a tiny town hugging the bay, grainy-white and brown with green splashes of palms and pines. At the centre, the main square is flanked to the south by the arcaded bulk of the **Venetian arsenal**, the upper storey of which was added in 1612 to house a

theatre (closed for refurbishment at the time of writing, otherwise daily: June–Aug 9am–1pm and 5–11pm; Sept–May 11am–noon; 10kn), the oldest in Croatia – and now converted into a cinema. At the eastern end of the square is Hvar's **cathedral** (usually open mornings), a sixteenth-century construction with an eighteenth-century facade – a characteristic mixture of Gothic and Renaissance styles. Inside is routine enough, but the **Bishop's Treasury** (daily: June–Aug 9am–noon and 5–7pm; Sept–May 10am–noon; 10kn) is worth the entry fee for its small but fine selection of chalices and reliquaries. The rest of the old town stretches back from the piazza in an elegant confusion of twisting lanes and alleys. Up above, the **fortress** (April–Sept daily 8am–dusk; 10kn) is a telling example of sixteenth-century military architecture. From the fort, you can pick out the fifteenth-century **Franciscan Monastery** (Mon–Fri 10am–noon and 5–7pm; 15kn), to the left of the harbour; next door, the monastic church is pleasingly simple, with beautifully carved choir stalls.

Beaches

The **beaches** nearest to town are rocky and crowded, so it's best to make your way towards the **Pakleni otoci**, just to the west. Easily reached by water taxi from the harbour (about 20kn each way), the Pakleni are a chain of eleven wooded islands, three of which cater for tourists with simple bars and restaurants: Jerolim, a naturist island, is the nearest; next is Marinkovac; then Sv Klement, the largest of the islands. Bear in mind that camping is forbidden throughout Pakleni, and that naturism is popular.

Arrival and information

Tourist office On the waterfront below the theatre at Trg sv. Stjepana bb (July & Aug daily 8am–2pm & 3–10pm; June & Sept Mon–Sat 8am–1.30pm & 4–9pm, Sun 10am–noon & 6–8pm; Oct–May Mon–Sat 8am–1pm; ⓣ021/741-059, ⓦwww.tzhvar.hr).

Accommodation

Private rooms Contact Atlas on the harbour at Obala bb (ⓣ021/741-911, ⓔatlas-hvar@st.htnet.hr) or Pelegrini, by the ferry dock at Riva bb (ⓣ021/742-743). ❸

The Green Lizard Lucica (residential area) ⓣ0981/718-729, ⓦwww.greenlizard.hr. A clean, family-run hostel 10 mins' walk from the ferry port, which has a choice of inexpensive shared dorms and private rooms, some with beautiful sea views. Staff will come and pick you up from the ferry or bus. ❷

Jagoda & Ante Bracanovič House Poviše Škole 21 ⓣ021/741-416, ⓔvirgilye@yahoo.com. Free pickup from bus station. A great budget choice with apartments, balconies and shared kitchen. ❷

Campsite

Milna campsite ⓣ021/745-027, ⓦwww.hvar.hr/mala-milna. About 3km southeast of town on Milna Bay – most Hvar Town–Stari Grad buses drop off nearby. ❶

Eating and drinking

Carpe Diem On the Riva (harbourfront). The epitome of jet-set; said to be the best cocktail bar in Croatia, it attracts glamorous partygoers to its vase-sized cocktail pitchers and thumping speakers like moths to a flame.

Junior Pučkog ustanka 4. Go to *Junior* for a mean shrimp pasta and other reasonably priced seafood dishes. Situated in a narrow street that runs parallel to the ferry dock. 60kn.

Hanibal Trg sv Stjepana 12. Slightly flashy, *Hanibal* is located in the main square, so offers up good people-watching opportunities. Mains cost around 85kn.

Macondo Petra Hektorovića. Signposted in a backstreet two blocks uphill from the main square in Groda (Hvar's oldest neighbourhood) this restaurant is the best place for meat and fish. The cozy stone walls with an open-fire provide a great setting to try the owner's potent home-made wine. Mains start at 70kn.

Veneranda Šumica bb, Hvar Town, east of harbour. Look out for the luxury *Hotel Delfin* from which there are stairs leading up to the club. A monastery-turned-nightclub shows films in the early evening before the crowds from *Carpe Diem* come to rip up the dancefloor later on.

Moving on

Bus Stari grad (7 daily; 35min).
Ferry Korčula (Vela Luka) (1 catamaran daily; 45min); Split (catamaran: 2 daily, 1hr 30min); Vis (1 weekly; 1hr).

VIS

Compact, humpy, and at first glance a little forbidding, **VIS** is situated further offshore than any other of Croatia's inhabited Adriatic islands. Closed to foreigners for military reasons until 1989, the island has never been overrun by tourists, and even now depends much more heavily on independent tourism than its package-oriented neighbours. Croatia's bohemian youth have fallen in love with the place over the last decade, drawn by its wild mountainous scenery, two good-looking towns, **Vis Town** and **Komiža**, and a brace of fine wines, including the white *Vugava* and the red *Viški plavac*. Ferries and, in summer, catamarans from Split arrive at Vis Town, from where buses depart for Komiža on the western side of the island.

Vis Town

VIS TOWN is a sedate arc of grey-brown houses on a deeply indented bay, above which looms a steep escarpment covered with the remains of abandoned agricultural terraces. The nicest parts of town are east of the ferry landing in the suburb of **Kut**, a largely sixteenth-century tangle of narrow cobbled streets overlooked by the summer houses built by nobles from Hvar. A kilometre further on lies a small British war cemetery, and just behind it, a wonderful pebbly **beach**. Heading west around the bay soon brings you to a small peninsula, from which the campanile of the Franciscan **monastery of St Hieronymous** rises gracefully alongside a huddle of cypresses.

Arrival and information

Tourist office Just to the right of the ferry dock (May–Sept daily 8am–2pm & 5–8pm; Oct–April Mon–Fri 8am–2pm; ⓣ021/717-017, ⓦwww.tz-vis.hr). The website has extensive accommodation information.

Accommodation

Private rooms Ionios (Obala Sv Jurja 37 ⓣ021/711-532, ⓔionios@st.hinet.hr) book private rooms on the island (❷) and also rent out scooters and cars, and organize trips to Biševo.
Paula Petra Hektorovića 2 ⓣ021/711-362, in Kut. Small pension-like hotel with rooms split between two 200-year old stone houses. ❹

Eating and drinking

Doručak kod Tihane Obala Sv Jurja 5. "Breakfast at Tihana" occupies the ground floor and patio of Vis's first hotel, built in 1911, in the Art Nouveau or "Tiffany" style, hence its name. If the "Beefsteak of Love" was a person, you'd want to marry it, and the orange soup is worth a go. Mains from 60kn.
Kantun Biskupa Mihe Pusića. A wine bar, restaurant and art gallery, *Kantun* is worth a visit

BEETLING AROUND VIS

Venturing inland by scooter or in an open-top VW Beetle is an exhilarating way to explore the island's rugged landscape. Vis can be traversed in half a day and there are enticing wine-buying opportunities along the way, as friendly elderly women set up roadside stalls, with unbeatable prices.

For **secluded beaches**, take local roads off the main road (turnings for beaches are marked) – it's quite an adventure scrambling your way down to the sea on steep, rocky paths but you'll be rewarded with some of the best coves for swimming.

There are many car/scooter rental agencies on the island – ask at the tourist office for maps and advice on which beaches to head for.

if only for a drink in their relaxing shady garden. Mains from 70kn.

Kod Paveta Dinko I Anka Tomić. One of the cutest joints in Croatia, opposite Vis's open-air cinema. Excellent service and food – try the home-made gnocchi from 45kn.

Pizzeria Katerina IvaniŠević Marinko, near the ferry dock. Good for a quick bite (around 50kn), with cheap beers. Next door's bar plays an eclectic mix of music until the early hours, beneath a bamboo roof.

Pojoda Don Cvijetka Maraovića (in Kut). Worth splashing out a little bit extra to sample fantastic seafood, surrounded by orange and lemon trees in *Pojoda's* lovely garden. Mains around 100kn.

Moving on

Bus Komiža (5 daily; 25min).

Ferry Hvar (1 weekly; 1hr); Split (3 ferries daily; 2hr 30min; 1 catamaran daily; 1hr).

Komiža

KOMIŽA, 10km from Vis Town, is the island's main fishing port – a compact town with a palm-fringed seafront on one side and a ring of mountains on the other. Dominating the southern end of the harbour is the **Kaštel**, a stubby sixteenth-century fortress which now holds a charming **Fishing Museum** (June–Sept Mon–Sat 10am–noon and 7–10pm, Sun 7–10pm; 10kn). Komiža's nicest **beaches** are ten minutes south of the museum, where you'll find a sequence of pebbly coves. Each morning, small boats leave Komiža harbour for the nearby island of Biševo in order to visit the so-called **Blue Cave**: a grotto filled with eerie shimmering light, it's well worth seeing – expect to pay around 120kn for the trip.

Buses from Vis Town terminate about 100m behind the harbour, from where it's a short walk southwards to the **tourist office** (on the Riva just beyond the Kaštel; July & Aug Mon–Sat 8am–1pm & 6–10pm; Sept–June Mon–Fri 8am–1pm; ⓣ021/713-455). Private rooms (❷) can be booked at Darlić, on the harbourfront ⓣ021/713-760, ⓦwww.darlic-travel.hr on the island. Srebrnatours Ribarska 4 (ⓣ021/713 668, ⓦwww.srebrnatours.hr) also organizes private rooms, as well as trips to the caves and other diving excursions. There are a couple of nice pizzerias on the harbour, and one very good seafood **restaurant**, *Bako*, just off Ribarska at Gundulićeva 1 offering mains from 60kn. For **drinking,** head for the tiny main square, Škor, which is ringed by lively café-bars, the liveliest of which is *Škor*.

KORČULA

Like so many islands along this coast, **KORČULA** was first settled by the Greeks, who gave it the name Korkyra Melaina or "Black Corfu" for its dark and densely wooded appearance. Even now, it's one of the greenest of the Adriatic islands, and one of the most popular. The island's main settlement is **Korčula Town**, and the rest of the island, although beautifully wild, lacks any real centres.

What to see and do

KORČULA TOWN sits on a beetle-shaped hump of land, a medieval walled city ribbed with a series of narrow streets that branch off the spine of the main street. The Venetians first arrived here in the eleventh century, and stayed, on and off, for nearly eight centuries. Their influence is particularly evident in Korčula's old town, which huddles around the **Cathedral of St Mark** whose facade is decorated with a gorgeous fluted rose window and a bizarre cornice frilled with strange gargoyles. The interior is one of the loveliest in the region – a curious mixture of styles, ranging from the Gothic forms of the nave to the Renaissance northern aisle, tacked on in the sixteenth century.

The Bishop's Treasury

The best of the church's treasures have been removed to the **Bishop's Treasury** (July & Aug: daily 10am–noon and 5–

7pm; at other times enquire at the tourist office; 10kn), a couple of doors down. This small collection of fine and sacral art is one of the best in the country, with an exquisite set of paintings, including a striking *Portrait of a Man* by Carpaccio and a Leonardo da Vinci sketch of a soldier wearing a costume bearing a striking resemblance to that of the Moreška dancers (see p.268).

Town Museum and the House of Marco Polo

A former Venetian palace holds the **Town Museum** (July & August daily 9am–1pm and 5–7pm; rest of year Mon–Sat 9am–1pm; 10kn), whose more modest display contains a plaster cast of a fourth-century-BC Greek tablet from Lumbarda – the earliest evidence of civilization on Korčula. Close by the main square, down a turning to the right, is another remnant from Venetian times, the so-called **House of Marco Polo** (July & Aug daily 10am–1pm and 5–7pm; Sept–June Mon–Sat 10am–1pm; 10kn). Korčula claims to be the birthplace of Marco Polo, although it seems unlikely that he had any connection with this seventeenth-century house, which these days is little more than an empty shell with some terrible twentieth-century prints.

Beaches

Your best bet for **beaches** is to head off by water taxi from the old harbour to one of the **Skoji islands** just offshore. The largest and nearest of these is **Badija**, where there are some secluded rocky beaches, a couple of snack bars and a naturist section. There's also a sandy **beach** just beyond the village of **Lumbarda**, 8km south of Korčula (reached by hourly bus in the summer).

Arrival and information

Bus Korčula's bus station is 400m southeast of the old town. There's also a bus service from Dubrovnik, which crosses the narrow stretch of water dividing the island from the mainland by ferry from Orebić.

Boat The main coastal ferry docks at Korčula Town harbour. In addition, local ferries travel daily between Split and Vela Luka at the western end of Korčula island, from where there's a connecting bus service to Korčula Town.

Tourist office On the northwestern side of the peninsula from the ferry port at Obala dr. Franje Tudmana 4 (June–Sept Mon–Sat 8am–3pm & 5pm–8.30pm, Sun 9am–1.30pm; Oct–May Mon–Sat 8am–noon; ⓣ020/715-701, ⓦwww.korcula.net).

Accommodation

Private rooms Check out Marko Polo Biline 5 ⓣ020/715-400 ⓦwww.korcula.com. The office is situated between the bus station and the entrance to the old town. ❸

Onelove Hvratske Zajednice 6 ⓣ020/716-755 ⓦwww.korculabackpacker.com. The place to stay if you want to party with other travellers. The hostel has 4-, 6- and 15-bed dorms and is not far from the ferry port and bus terminal, where staff come to meet you. You can rent boats, scooters and bikes here too. ❷

Eating and drinking

For a dazzling array of fresh fruit, head to the small market situated to the right of the main steps by the harbour leading up to the Old Town. Wherever you eat, do try some of the excellent **local wines**: the delicious dry white *Grk* from Lumbarda, Posip from Smokvica, or the headache-inducing red Dingač from Postup on Peljesac.

Adio Mare Sv. Roka 2 (Old Town) ⓣ020/711-253. Popular and atmospheric restaurant near Marco Polo's House with an open-plan kitchen, so you can watch as chefs prepare Dalmatian specialities; book ahead or arrive early to get a table. 70kn.

Gradski Podrum Put Sventi Antuna bb (just inside the main gate of the old town). Good "Korcula-style" dishes from 50kn.

Mareta Ulica Sv. Roka 4. A welcoming place, which serves up succulent seafood (including a robust shark steak) and great local wines. Tables are placed on steps leading up from the seafront into the Old Town, so there's a steady stream of people to watch as you enjoy your food. Mains from 80kn.

Massimo Setaliste Petra Kanavelic. This cocktail bar esconced in a medieval turret is one of the prime spots for admiring a Korčula sunset. You

MOREŠKA

Performances of Korčula's famous folk dance, the **Moreška**, take place outside the main gate to the old town, throughout the summer, every Monday and Thursday evening (tickets from Marko Polo Agency on Biline 5; 50kn). This frantic, sword-based dance is the story of a conflict between the Christians (in red) and the Moors (in black): the heroine, Bula, is kidnapped by the evil foreign king and his army, and her betrothed tries to win her back in a ritualized sword fight which takes place within a shifting circle of dancers.

have to go up (and eventually come down) by ladder – worth keeping in mind after a couple of *Massimo's* ultra-strong brews.

Planjak Plokata 21. Cheap and functional, with grilled meat dished from 40kn.

Moving on

Ferries (from Vela Luka) Hvar (1 catamaran daily; 45min); Split (2 ferries daily; 3hr; 1 catamaran daily; 1hr 30min).

DUBROVNIK

DUBROVNIK is a beautifully preserved medieval fortified city, situated at the southern tip of Croatia. First settled by Roman refugees in the early seventh century and given the name Ragusa, the town soon exploited its favourable position on the Adriatic with maritime and commercial genius. By the mid-fourteenth century, having shaken off the yoke of first the Byzantines and then the Venetians, it had become a successful and self-contained city-state, its merchants trading far and wide. Dubrovnik fended off the attentions of the Ottoman Empire and continued to prosper until 1667, when an earthquake devastated the city. Though the city-state survived, it fell into decline and, in 1808, was formally dissolved by Napoleon. An eight-month siege by Yugoslav forces in the early 1990s caused much destruction, but the city swiftly recovered.

What to see and do

The Old Town and Pile Gate

The **Pile Gate**, main entrance to the old town, is a fifteenth-century construction complete with a statue of St Blaise, the city's protector, set in a niche above the arch. The best way to get your bearings is by making a tour of the fabulous **city walls** (daily: May–Sept 8am–7.30pm; Oct–April 10am–3pm; 50kn), 25m high and with all five towers intact. Of the various towers and bastions that punctuate the walls, the 1455 **Minčeta fortress**, which marks the northeastern side, is by far the most imposing.

Within the walls, Dubrovnik is a sea of roofs faded into a pastel patchwork, punctured now and then by a sculpted dome or tower. At ground level, just inside the Pile Gate, **Onofrio's Large Fountain**, built in 1444, is a domed affair at which visitors to this hygiene-conscious city had to wash themselves before they were allowed any further.

DUBROVNIK SUMMER FESTIVAL

The prestigious **Summer Festival** is held July 10 to August 25 and is a good time to be around, with classical concerts and theatre performances in most of the city's courtyards, squares and bastions. Book tickets well in advance – you can try your luck with booking on the day, although you may end up without a proper seat, having to stand or sit on stairs for the performance. Contact ⓣ020/326-100, ⓦwww.dubrovnik-festival.hr for more.

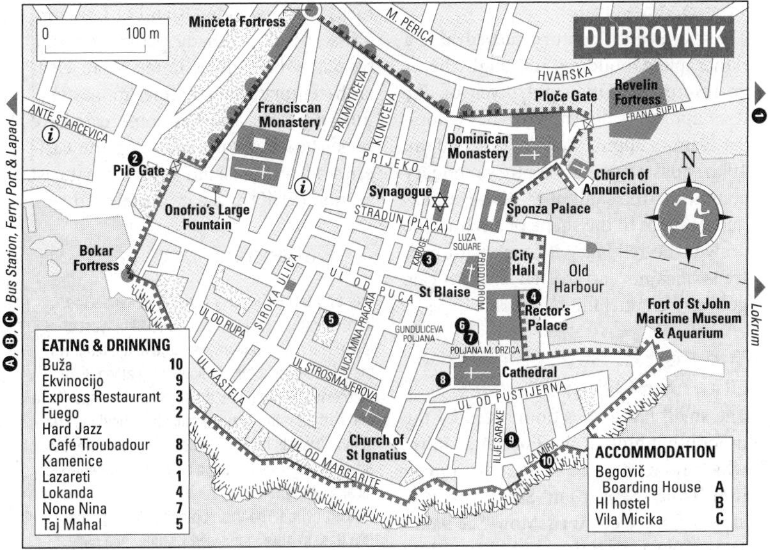

The Franciscan Monastery and Stradun

The treasury (daily 9am–6pm; 20kn) of the fourteenth-century **Franciscan Monastery** complex (free access) holds some fine Gothic reliquaries and manuscripts tracing the development of musical scoring, together with relics from the apothecary's shop, dating from 1317 and claiming to be the oldest in Europe. From outside the monastery church, **Stradun** (also known as Placa), the city's main street, runs dead straight across the old town, its limestone surface polished to a slippery shine by the tramping of thousands of feet. Its far end broadens into the airy **Luža Square**, the centre of the medieval town and even today the hub of much of its activity, especially during the Summer Festival. On the left, the **Sponza Palace** was once the customs house and mint, with a facade showing off an elegant weld of florid Venetian Gothic and more sedate Renaissance forms; its majestic courtyard is given over to contemporary art exhibitions.

Church of St Blaise

Built in 1714, the Baroque-style **Church of St Blaise** serves as a graceful counterpoint to the palace. Outside the church stands the carved figure of an armoured knight, known as **Orlando's Column** and once the focal point of the city-state.

The Dominican Monastery and Rector's Palace

The arcaded courtyard of the **Dominican monastery,** filled with palms and orange trees, leads to a small **museum** (daily 9am–6pm; 15kn), with outstanding examples of local sixteenth-century religious art. Back on Luža, a street leads round the back of St Blaise towards the fifteenth-century **Rector's Palace**, the seat of the Ragusan government, in which the incumbent Rector sat out his month's term of office. Today it's given over to the **City Museum** (May–Sept daily 9am–6pm; Oct–April Tues–Sun 9am–2pm; 35kn), though for the most part it's a rather paltry collection, with mediocre sixteenth-century paintings and dull furniture.

The cathedral

The seventeenth-century **cathedral** is a rather plain building, although there's an impressive Titian polyptych of *The Assumption* inside. The **Treasury** (Mon–Sat 9am–5.30pm, Sun 11am–5.30pm; 10kn) boasts a twelfth-century reliquary containing the skull of St Blaise; an exquisite piece in the shape of a Byzantine crown, the reliquary is stuck with portraits of saints and frosted with delicate gold and enamel filigree work.

The Fort of St John and the Church of St Ignatius

The small harbour is dominated by the monolithic hulk of the **Fort of St John**, which now houses a downstairs **aquarium** (May–Sept Mon–Sat 9am–8pm, closed Sun; Oct–April Mon–Sat 9am–1pm; 30kn); upstairs is the **maritime museum** (May–Sept daily 9am–6pm; Oct–April Tues–Sun 9am–2pm; 35kn), which traces the history of Ragusan sea power through a display of naval artefacts and model boats. Walking back east from here, you skirt one of the city's oldest quarters, **Pustijerna**, much of which predates the seventeenth-century earthquake. On the far side, the **Church of St Ignatius**, Dubrovnik's largest, is a Jesuit confection, modelled, like most Jesuit places of worship, on the enormous church of Gesù in Rome. The steps that lead down from here also had a Roman model – the Spanish Steps – and they sweep down to **Gundulićeva Poljana**, the square behind the cathedral which is the site of the city's morning fruit and vegetable market.

Beaches

The noisy and crowded main city beach is a short walk east of the old town; a better bet is to head for the less crowded, and somewhat cleaner, beach on the Lapad peninsula, 5km to the west, or to catch one of the taxi boats from the old city jetty (April–Oct 8am–5pm, every 30min, journey time 10min; 25kn return) to the wooded island of **Lokrum**. Crisscrossed by shady paths overhung by pines, Lokrum is home to an eleventh-century Benedictine monastery-turned-palace and has some extensive rocky beaches running along the eastern end of the island – with a naturist section (FKK) at the far eastern tip.

Arrival and information

Bus and boat The ferry and bus terminals are located in the port suburb of Gruž, 3km west of town. The main western entrance to the old town, the Pile Gate, is a thirty-minute slog along ul Ante Starčevića; you'd be better off catching a bus – #1a and #1b from the ferry terminal or behind the bus station. Tickets for local buses are bought from the driver (12kn; exact change only) or from newspaper kiosks (10kn).

Tourist office The main branch is just up from Pile Gate at Ante Starčevića 7 (June–Aug daily 8am–8pm, Nov–April Mon–Sat 9am–3pm, closed Sun ⓣ020/427-591 ⓦwww.tzdubrovnik.hr). Another one is opposite the ferry terminal in Gruž (same hours).

Listings The free monthly *Dubrovnik Riviera Guide*, available from hotels and the tourist office, lists bus and ferry timetables as well as forthcoming events.

Accommodation

Private rooms Booked through Gulliver, opposite the ferry terminal at Obala Stjepana Radića 32 (ⓣ020/410-888, ⓦwww.gulliver.hr), and Dubrovnikturist, at put Republike 7 (ⓣ020/356-969, ⓦwww.dubrovnikturist.hr). ❷ ❸

Begovič Boarding House Primorska 17 ⓣ020/435-191, ⓕ020/453-752. Clean, hostel-style accommodation in the beachy Lapad area with friendly staff. ❷

HI Dubrovnik Vinka Sagrestana 3; steps lead up from Bana Jelačića 15–17 ⓣ020/423-241, ⓔdubrovnik@hfhs. Connected to the Old Town and bus and ferry terminals by buses #1, #1A, #1B and #7. Alternatively, head up Ante Starčevića from the ferry port and turn uphill to the right after five minutes. Basic, well-run hostel with good showers, a leafy breakfast courtyard and friendly staff. ❷

Vila Micika Mata Vodopica 10, Lapad ⓣ020/437-332, ⓦwww.vilamicika.hr. A family-run pension offering hostel-style arrangements (a bed in a clean and comfortable 1-, 2- or 3-person room) as well as bright en-suite doubles. Take bus #6 to Lapad post office. ❸–❹

Eating

Ekvinocijo Ilije Sarake 10. Family-run seafood eatery near the Cathedral. Ask for their famous home-made brandy to kick off your meal. Mains from 45kn, fish 150kn.
Express Restaurant Kaboge 1. A decent self-service canteen with vegetarian options. Soup 9kn, risotto 30kn.
Kamenice Gundulićeva Poljana 8. A simple place serving up cheap portions of *girice* (tiny deep-fried fish) and *kamenice* (oysters). About 50kn/portion.
Lokanda Right on the old harbour, this restaurant serves up a small but fantastic seafood menu including a sinister-looking but tasty black cuttlefish risotto. 50kn.
Taj Mahal Nikole Gučetića 2. Don't be fooled by its name – *Taj Mahal* offers traditional Bosnian fare and is tucked away off the main drag. A welcome respite from the standard fish restaurants.

Drinking and nightlife

The pavement cafés at the eastern end of Stradun are popular spots for daytime and evening **drinking**, but for something with a bit more character, head for the smaller café-bars in the backstreets. For harder drinking late into the night head to ulica bana Jelačića outside the Old Town.
Buža Iza Mira (near St Stephen's tower). A beautiful spot for a dip in the sea and a drink, *Buža* is perched on the rocks and accessed via a hole in the city walls.
Fuego outside the Pile Gate. Mainstream Latino club just outside old town with cheap drinks offers all night.
Hard Jazz Café Troubadour Bunićeva Poljana. A buzzing hotspot with live music most nights.
Lazareti just beyond Pile Gate, Frana Supila 8. A former quarantine house which plays host to live music, themed disco nights and a bit of techno thrown is for good measure. The cutting-edge *Močvara* club in Zagreb has held a festival here, cementing *Lazareti's* cool status.
None Nina Pred Dvoram. A perfect place for refreshment in comfy wicker chairs arranged stadium-style facing the Rector's Palace. Look up to see people scrambling around the City Walls.

Shopping

Markets The market in Gundulićeva Poljana is the best for local produce, but get there early to snag some good picnic items (except Sun).
Boutiques Most of the standard souvenir shops in Dubrovnik are along Stradun, and tend to be overpriced. The heavenly Kraš Bonbonniere on Zamanjina 2, has gorgeous chocolates and bon-bons. For uber-cool fashion, check out the Sheriff and Cherry store on Djordićeva 4, and for Croatian designers head to Kadena on Celestina Medovića 2, which has unique pieces at affordable prices.
Consulates UK, Petilovrijenci 2 ☎311-466.
Exchange Nova Banka, Stradun (Mon–Fri 7.30am–8pm, Sat 7.30am–1pm).
Hospital Roka Mišetića bb ☎020/431-777.
Internet access Dubrovnik Internet Centar, Brsalje 1 (daily 9am–9pm); *Netcafe*, Prijeko 21 (daily 9am–11pm).
Left luggage At the bus station (daily 6am–9.30pm).
Pharmacy Kod Zvonika, Stradun (Mon–Fri 7am–8pm, Sat 7.30am–3pm).
Post office A. Starčevića 2 (Mon–Fri 7am–9pm, Sat 7am–7pm, Sun 9am–2pm).

Moving on

Bus Korčula (1 daily; 3hr 30min); Rijeka (6 daily; 11hr 30min); Split (18 daily; 4hr 30min – make sure you take your passport, as you pass through Bosnia on the way); Zadar (9 daily; 8hr 30min); Zagreb (8 daily; 11hr).
Ferry Korčula (5 weekly; 3hr); Rijeka (2 weekly; 22hr); Split (3 weekly; 8hr).

Czech Republic

PRAGUE: lose yourself in the streets of Staré Město

KUTNÁ HORA: see the human bones in the subterranean ossuary at Sedlec

PLZEŇ: visit the home of Pilsner Urquell, the original lager

OLOMOUC: discover a more laid-back side to the Czech Republic in this lovely university town

ČESKÝ KRUMLOV: a trip along the Vltava River is the best way to see this fairytale town

ROUGH COSTS

DAILY BUDGET Basic €30/occasional treat €37

DRINK Pilsner Urquell €1.50

FOOD Pizza €3–4

HOSTEL/BUDGET HOTEL €15/€30

TRAVEL Train: Prague – Karlovy Vary (236km) €10; Bus: 2hrs 15 min (€5)

FACT FILE

POPULATION 10.3 million

AREA 78,866 sq km

LANGUAGE Czech

CURRENCY Czech koruna (Kč)

CAPITAL Prague

INTERNATIONAL PHONE CODE ⓣ420

Basics

Czechoslovakia's "Velvet Revolution" of 1989 was the most unequivocally positive of Eastern Europe's anti-Communist upheavals, as the Czechs and Slovaks shrugged off 41 years of Communist rule without a shot being fired. Just four years on, however, the country split into two separate states: the Czech Republic and Slovakia. The Czechs – always the most urbane, agnostic and liberal of the Slav nations – have fared well, joining the European Union in 2004, although they have had to contend with rising crime and an increasing cost of living. For coverage of Slovakia, see Chapter 27.

Almost untouched by the wars of the twentieth century, the Czech capital **Prague** is justifiably one of the most popular destinations in Europe. Not only an incredibly beautiful city with a wealth of Art Nouveau, Baroque and Renaissance architecture layered on Gothic foundations, it's also a lively meeting place for young people from all over Europe.

The rolling countryside of **Bohemia** is swathed in forests and studded with well-preserved medieval towns and castles, especially in the south around **České Budějovice**. In the west, you'll find the spa towns of **Karlovy Vary** and **Mariánské Lázně**. The country's eastern province, **Moravia**, is every bit as beautiful, but less touristed. **Olomouc** is the most attractive town here, but **Brno**, the regional capital, has its own pleasures and lies within easy reach of Moravia's spectacular **karst region**.

CHRONOLOGY

4th Century BC The Celtic "Boii" tribe inhabit the area now known as Bohemia (from the Latin Boiohaemum)

500s AD Slavic tribes arrive

830 AD The Great Moravian Empire is established along the Morava River.

907 Hungarians take over the Moravian empire.

1355 Charles IV, "the father of the Czech nation", is crowned Holy Roman Emperor, as Prague enjoys economic prosperity.

1458 After years of fighting between Protestants and Catholics, George of Podebrady is pronounced King, and maintains a peaceful rule.

1526 King Ferdinand I of the Habsburg dynasty takes the Czech throne, reintroducing Catholicism as the main religion.

1800s Rapid growth in nationalism and industrialisation.

1843 The sugar cube is invented in the Czech town of Dačice.

1916 Franz Kafka completes his famous work *The Metamorphosis*.

1918 The independent Republic of Czechoslovakia is declared at the end of WWI.

1938 German troops enter the Sudetenland area of western Czechoslovakia.

1945 German occupation ends as the Allies move in.

1948 The Communist Party seizes control.

1968 The "Prague Spring" sees a period of political liberalisation, before Soviet invasion is sent to repress it.

1972 Martina Navratilova wins the Czech National Tennis Championships at the age of 15.

1989 The "Velvet Revolution" returns democracy to Czechoslovakia.

1993 The Czech Republic and Slovakia divide peacefully into two countries.

2004 The Czech Republic joins the EU.

2007 Protests at US plans to build a radar base near Prague.

ARRIVAL

Prague's **airport**, Ruzyně, served by low-cost airlines and local carriers, is a 20-minute taxi ride northwest of the city. There are direct flights from more

than a dozen UK airports and from New York's JFK airport. Ryanair has recently opened a direct flight to Brno from London Stansted.

Arriving by **train** from the west, you're most likely to end up at Praha hlavní nádraží, Prague's main station, a 15-minute walk from Wenceslas Square. This is where most international trains terminate; there are direct services from major European cities, including Berlin, Vienna and Budapest.

Prague's main **bus station**, with international and domestic services, is Praha-Florenc on the eastern edge of Staré Město (metro Florenc).

GETTING AROUND

The Czech Republic has one of the most comprehensive **rail** networks in Europe. Czech Railways (České dráhy or ČD; ⓦwww.cd.cz) runs two main types of trains: *rychlík* (R) or *spěšný* (Sp) trains are the faster ones which stop only at major towns, while *osobní* trains stop at just about every station, averaging as little as 30kph. Fast trains are further divided into SuperCity (SC), which are first class only, EuroCity (EC) or InterCity (IC), for which you need to pay a supplement, and Expres (Ex), for which you don't. **Tickets** (*jízdenky*) for domestic journeys can be bought at the station (*nádraží*) before or on the day of departure. ČD runs reasonably priced **sleepers** to and from a number of cities in neighbouring countries, for which you must book as far in advance as possible. **InterRail** and Eurail passes are valid in the Czech Republic.

Regional buses – mostly run by the state bus company, Česká státní automobilová doprava (ČSAD; ⓦwww.csadbus.cz) – travel to most destinations, with private companies such as ČEBUS providing an alternative on popular intercity routes. **Bus stations** are usually next to the train station, and though some have ticket offices you can usually buy your ticket from the driver. For long-distance journeys it's a good idea to book your ticket at least a day in advance. A useful website for train and bus times is ⓦwww.vlak.cz.

ACCOMMODATION

Accommodation can be the most expensive aspect of travelling in the Czech Republic. There is no organized hostel system as such, though some places are now affiliated with Hostelling International (HI). To book accommodation **online**, try Ⓦwww.avetravel.cz (particularly good for private rooms) or Ⓦwww.marys.cz.

The capital has a number of **hostels**, many of which are very centrally located. Dorm beds range from €10–15. The student travel organization CKM at Mánesova 77 in Prague (Ⓣ222 721 595, Ⓦwww.ckm.cz) can arrange cheap **student accommodation** in the big university towns during July and August and rates are usually from 250Kč per person for dorm beds. The KMC (Young Travellers Club), at Karolíny Světlé 31 in Prague (Ⓣ222 220 347, Ⓦwww.kmc.cz), is an umbrella organization for youth hostels throughout the Republic which can also help organize accommodation.

Most old state **hotels** have been refurbished by their new owners, and many new ones have opened, particularly in the more heavily touristed areas. In the newer places, continental or buffet-style breakfast is normally included. Ignore the star system as it's no guarantee of quality, service or atmosphere.

Private rooms are available in Prague, Brno and many of the towns on the tourist trail, and are a good bet – keep your eyes peeled for signs saying *Zimmer Frei* or book through the local tourist office. Prices start at around 300Kč per person per night, more in Prague.

Campsites, known as *autokemp*, are plentiful throughout the Republic; the facilities are often basic and the ones known as *tábořiště* are even more rudimentary; pitch prices range from about 60–80Kč. Most sites have simple **chalets** (*chaty* or *bungalovy*) for anything upwards of 500Kč for two people. The Shocart map *Kempy a chatové osady ČR* lists Czech campsites and is sold in many bookshops.

FOOD AND DRINK

The good news is that you can eat and drink very cheaply in the Czech Republic. The bad news is that forty years of culinary isolation and centralization under the Communists allowed few innovations in Czech cuisine. Still, washed down with the divine Czech beer, anything tastes good.

The whole concept of **breakfast** (*snidaně*) is alien to the Czechs. Popular street snacks include *bramborák*, a potato pancake with flecks of bacon, *párek*, a frankfurter dipped in mustard or ketchup and shoved in a white roll, and *smažený sýr* – a slab of melted cheese fried in breadcrumbs and served in a roll with tartare sauce. The better Czech cafés have proper espresso machines serving decent **coffee** (*káva*); elsewhere, the Czechs drink Turkish-style coffee or *turecká*, with grains at the bottom of the cup. The **cake shop** (*cukrárna*) is an important part of the country's social life, particularly on Sundays when it's often the only place that's open.

Restaurants (*restaurace*) always display their menus and prices outside. They serve hot meals from about 11am until 9pm. Most **pubs** (*pivnice*) also serve basic hot dishes, as do **wine bars** (*vinárna*) – often the most stylish places around. Lunchtime menus start with soup (*polévka*), one of the country's culinary strong points. **Main courses** are overwhelmingly based on pork (*vepřový*) or beef (*hovězí*), but one treat is carp (*kapr*), traditional at Christmas and cheaply and widely offered just about everywhere, along with trout (*pstruh*). Goose (*husa*), duck (*kachna*) and wild boar (*kanci maso*) dishes are also generally delicious. Main courses are served with **dumplings** (*knedlíky*) or vegetables, most commonly potatoes (*brambory*) and cabbage (*zelí*). With the exception of pancakes (*palačinky*), filled with chocolate or fruit and cream, fruit dumplings (*ovocné knedlíky*) and ice cream (*zmrzlina*), desserts can be pretty uninspiring.

Drink

Even the simplest *bufet* (self-service cafeteria) in the Czech Republic almost invariably has beer (*pivo*) on draught. **Pubs**, most of which close around 11pm, are still a predominantly male affair, with heavy drinking the norm; **wine bars** are more upmarket, and **cocktail bars** have opened up in larger towns.

The Czech Republic tops the world league table of **beer** consumption – hardly surprising since its beer ranks among the best in the world. The most natural starting point for any beer tour is the Bohemian city of **Plzeň** (Pilsen), whose local lager is the original Pils. The other big brewing town is **České Budějovice** (Budweis), home to Budvar, a mild beer by Bohemian standards but still leagues ahead of the American Budweiser. There's also a modest selection of medium-quality **wines**; the largest wine-producing region is southern Moravia. The home-production of firewater is a national pastime, resulting in some almost terminally strong concoctions, most famously a plum brandy called *slivovice*. The best-known Czech **spirit** is Becherovka, a medicinal herbal tipple from Karlovy Vary, known as a *beton* when ordered with ice and tonic.

CULTURE AND ETIQUETTE

Generally, **tips** are handed over directly, rather than left on the table, although this is changing. Ten percent is usual, depending on the establishment: give fifteen percent for more upmarket places.

If you travel on **trains**, you will find that there is a distinct etiquette for sharing a carriage. At the very least, people usually say *Dobry den* (hello) when they enter a carriage, and *Na shledanou* (goodbye) when they leave.

SPORTS AND ACTIVITIES

Football is a national obsession. The most successful team in the country is Sparta (Ⓦwww.sparta.cz), who play at Prague's 20,000-seat AXA Arena by the Letná plain (five minutes' walk from Metro Hradčanská). Matches are usually on Saturdays Aug–Nov and Mar–May.

Ice hockey is a national craze: you can see live matches in bars in most towns in the Czech Republic, or arrange to see games in stadiums during the season. Prague has two teams: Sparta, for whose matches you can reserve tickets by emailing Ⓔskala@hcsparta.cz; and Slavia, for whom you can book tickets through Ⓦwww.sazkaticket.cz.

Otherwise, there are plenty of **wilderness activities** such as cycling, hiking and rock climbing to be enjoyed in Bohemia, as well as **caving** in the Moravian karst.

COMMUNICATIONS

Most **post offices** (*pošta*) are open Mon–Fri 8am–5pm, Sat 8am–noon. Look for the right sign to avoid queuing: *známky* (stamps), *dopisy* (letters) or *balky* (parcels). You can also buy

THE CZECH REPUBLIC ON THE NET

Ⓦ**www.czech.cz** Basic information on the whole country.
Ⓦ**www.pis.cz** Prague's tourist office site.
Ⓦ**www.praguepost.com** Online version of the capital's own English-language paper.
Ⓦ**www.radio.cz/english** Updated news and cultural features.
Ⓦ**www.ticketpro.cz**, Ⓦ**www.ticketstream.cz**, Ⓦ**www.ticketsbti.cz** Three good sites for finding out what's on in Prague and booking tickets online.

stamps from newsagents, tobacconists and kiosks. The majority of **public phones** only take phonecards (*telefonní karty*), available from post offices, kiosks and some shops. You can make local and international calls from all card phones, all of which have instructions in English. You'll find **Internet cafés** in almost every Czech town; charges are usually 60–100Kč/hr.

EMERGENCIES

Pickpockets are as rife in the centre of Prague as in any European capital, particularly in the Old Town Square, on the #22 tram, in the metro and in the main railway stations. **Theft** from cars is also a problem. By law, you should carry your **passport** with you at all times, though you're unlikely to get stopped.

Minor ailments can be easily dealt with at a **pharmacy** (*lékárna*), but language is likely to be a problem outside the capital. If it's a repeat prescription you want, take any empty bottles or remaining pills along with you. If the pharmacist can't help, they'll be able to direct you to a **hospital** (*nemocnice*).

EMERGENCY NUMBERS

Police ☎158; fire ☎150; ambulance ☎155.

INFORMATION & MAPS

Most cities and towns have their own **tourist office** (*informační centrum*), where you should find at least one English-speaker. A comprehensive range of **maps** is usually available, often very cheaply, either from the tourist office or from bookshops, petrol stations and some hotels. Ask for a *plán města* (town plan) or *mapa okoli* (regional map). For hiking, Klub českých turistů produces a 1:50,000 *turistická mapa* series detailing the country's complex network of marked footpaths.

STUDENT AND YOUTH DISCOUNTS

Discounts can be quite substantial – often students pay just half or two-thirds of adult prices – but you must make sure you get an ISIC card, as many places will not accept regular university cards. Worth considering is the **Praguecard** (Ⓦwww.praguecard.biz): it costs €30, is valid for a year and includes three days' free city transport and coupons for free entry to some – though not all – major attractions. It can be bought at tourist offices, the airport and some hotels.

MONEY AND BANKS

The local **currency** is the Czech *crown*, or *koruna česká* (Kč), which is divided into one hundred hellers or *haléěě* (h). Crowns come in coins of 1Kč, 2Kč, 5Kč, 10Kč and 20Kč; notes are in denominations of 20Kč, 50Kč, 100Kč, 200Kč, 500Kč, 1000Kč and 2000Kč (less frequently 5000Kč). **Banks** are the best places to change money and normally open Mon–Fri 8am–5pm. Given the abundance of **ATMs**, credit and debit cards are a cheaper and more convenient way of carrying funds than travellers' cheques, though it's a good idea to keep some hard currency in cash for emergencies. At the time of writing, €1 was equal to 27Kč, $1 to 19Kč, and £1 to 40Kč.

OPENING HOURS AND HOLIDAYS

Shops are open Mon–Fri 9am–5pm, with some, especially in Prague, and most supermarkets, staying open till 6pm or later. Smaller shops close for lunch between noon and 2pm, while others stay open late on Thursdays. In larger towns, some shops stay open all day at weekends, and the corner shop (*večerka*) stays open daily till 11pm. Museums, galleries and churches are

Czech

	Czech	Pronunciation
Yes	*Ano*	UH-no
No	*Ne*	Neh
Please	*Prosím*	RO-seem
Thank you	*Děkuji vam*	DYE-koo-yi vam
Good day/Hello	*Dobry den/Ahoj*	DOB-rie den/A-hoy
Goodbye	*Na shledanou*	Nu SHLE-dan-uh
Excuse me	*Promiňte*	PROM-in-teh
Where?	*Kde*	Gde
Good	*Dobrý*	DOB-rie
Bad	*Špatný*	SHPUT-nie
Near	*Blízko*	Blee-sko
Far	*Daleko*	DUH-lek-o
Cheap	*Levný*	LEV-nie
Expensive	*Drahý*	DRU-hie
Open	*Otevřeno*	OT-evrsh-en-o
Closed	*Zavřeno*	ZAVRSH-en-o
Today	*Dnes*	Dnes
Yesterday	*Včera*	FTCH-er-a
Tomorrow	*Zítra*	ZEET-ra
How much is...?	*Kolík stojí...?*	KOL-ik STO-yee
What time is it?	*Kolík je hodin?*	KOL-ik ye HOD-in
I don't understand	*Nerozumím*	NE-ro-zoom-eem
Do you speak English?	*Mluvíte Anglicky?*	Myuv-ee-te ANG-lits-ky
One	*Jeden*	YED-en
Two	*Dva*	DVA
Three	*Tři*	Trshi
Four	*Čtyři*	CHTIRSH-i
Five	*Pět*	Pyet
Six	*Šest*	Shest
Seven	*Sedm*	SED-um
Eight	*Osum*	OSS-um
Nine	*Devět*	DEV-yet
Ten	*Deset*	DESS-et
Getting around		
Where...?	*Kde...?*	Gudeh
Tourist Information Office	*Turistická Informační Kancelář*	Tooritskah informuchnyee kuntselar
Toilet	*Toaleta*	Tu-uleta
Square	*Náměstí*	Nahmnyestyee
Station	*Nádraží*	Nahdrujee
Platform	*Nástupíště*	Nahstoopish-tyeh

generally open daily; synagogues are closed on Saturdays and Jewish holidays. Many attractions are closed on Mondays.

Public holidays include Jan 1, Easter Mon, May 1, May 8, July 5 & 6, Sept 28, Oct 28, Nov 17, Dec 24–26.

Prague

Architecturally, Prague is a revelation: few other cities anywhere in Europe look so good, and no other European capital can present six hundred years of architecture so untouched by war; even the severe floods of 2002 have left little trace. Alongside its heritage, Prague has a lively atmosphere, and is a great place to enjoy a variety of nightlife – from traditional pubs to funky bars – or just relax and soak up the view in one of the city parks and gardens.

Prince Bořivoj, the first Christian ruler, founded the Přemyslid dynasty and his grandson, Prince Václav, became the **Good King Wenceslas** of the Christmas carol and the country's

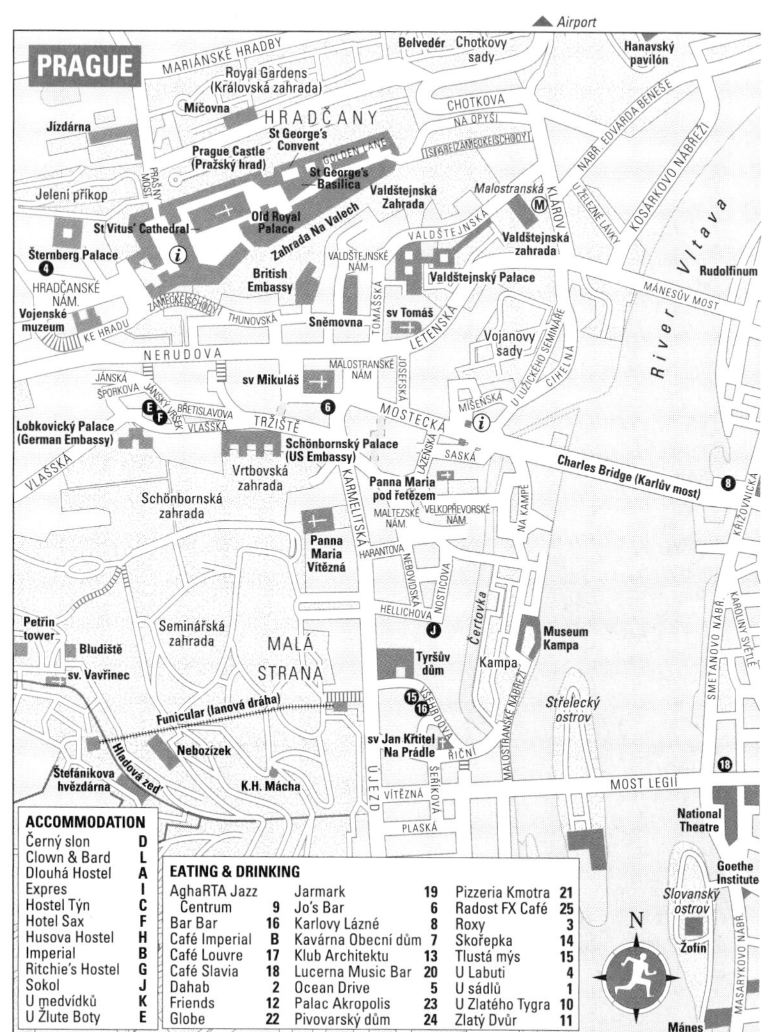

patron saint. Prague enjoyed its golden age under Holy Roman Emperor **Charles IV**, who transformed it into one of the most important cities in fourteenth-century Europe. He founded the university and an entire new town, Nové Město, along with iconic gothic structures such as the Charles Bridge and St Vitus' Cathedral.

What to see and do

The River Vltava divides the capital into two unequal portions. The castle district of Hradčany and Malá Strana are on the left bank, and Staré Město, Josefov and Nové Město are on the right.

Hradčany, on the hill, contains the most obvious sights – the castle, the cathedral and the old royal palace. Below

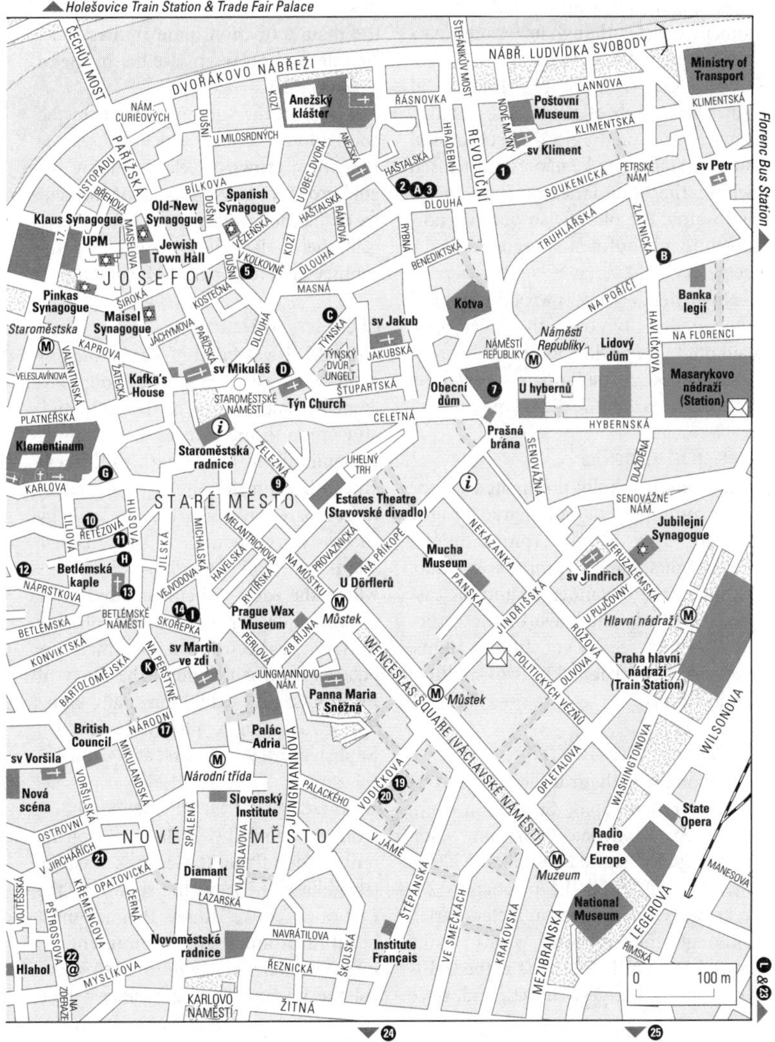

MUSEUM AND BUILDING ENTRY

If you want to see the interior of historic buildings in Prague, such as castles and some churches, often the only way is to go on a **guided tour** that will last at least 45 minutes; the last tour usually leaves an hour before the advertised closing time. Ask for an *anglický* text, an often unintentionally hilarious English résumé. **Entrance tickets** to most sights of interest throughout the Czech Republic rarely cost more than 50–100Kč, so prices are only quoted in this chapter where the admission fee is prohibitively high.

Hradčany, **Malá Strana** (Little Quarter), with its narrow eighteenth-century streets, is the city's ministerial and diplomatic quarter, though its Baroque gardens are here for all to enjoy.

Over the river, **Staré Město** (Old Town) is a web of alleys and passageways centred on the city's most beautiful square, Staroměstské náměstí. Enclosed within the boundaries of Staré Město is **Josefov**, the old Jewish quarter, now down to a handful of synagogues and a cemetery.

Nové Město (New Town), the focus of the modern city, covers the largest area, laid out in long wide boulevards – most famously Wenceslas Square – stretching south and east of the old town.

Prague Castle

Hradčany is wholly dominated by the city's omnipresent landmark, **Prague Castle** (daily 5/6am–11pm/midnight; most sights 9am–4/5pm; Ⓦwww.hrad.cz). It is free to wander around the castle courtyards and nave of the cathedral, but to see its constituent sights, you can buy various kinds of multiple entry tickets.

St Vitus' Cathedral

Work on the **cathedral** (daily; Mar–Oct Mon–Sat 9am–5pm, Sun noon–5pm; Nov–Feb Mon–Sat 9am–4pm, Sun noon–4pm) started under Charles IV, who employed the precocious 23-year-old German mason Peter Parler, although the cathedral wasn't finally completed until 1929. The cathedral is the country's largest church, and, once inside, it's difficult not to be impressed by its sheer height. The grand **Chapel of sv Václav**, by the south door, is easily the main attraction. Built by Parler, its rich decoration resembles the inside of a jewel casket.

A door in the south wall leads to the coronation chamber, which houses the Bohemian **crown jewels**, including the gold crown of St Wenceslas. At the centre of the choir, within a fine Renaissance grill, cherubs lark about on the sixteenth-century marble **Imperial Mausoleum**.

Old Royal Palace

The **Old Royal Palace** (*Starý královský palác*) is just across the courtyard from the south door of the cathedral, and home to the princes and kings of Bohemia from the eleventh to the seventeenth centuries. It's a sandwich of rather bare royal apartments built by successive generations. The massive **Vladislav Hall** (*Vladislavský sál*) is where the early Bohemian kings were elected, and where every president since Masaryk has been sworn into office. The palace's basement holds "**The story of Prague Castle**" exhibition (daily 9am–5pm), including a 40-minute film (in English every 90min; first at 9.45am).

St George's Basilica

Don't be fooled by the uninspiring red facade of the **St George's Basilica** (Bazilika sv Jiří), on the square to the east of St Vitus – this is Prague's most beautiful **Romanesque monument**. Its inside is meticulously restored to recreate the honey-coloured basilica which replaced the original tenth-century church in 1173.

Convent of St George

The **Convent of St George** (Jiřský klášter), was founded in 973, and now houses the National Gallery's **Rudolfine and Baroque art collection** (Tues–Sun 10am–6pm; ⓦwww.ngprague.cz). It is mostly of specialist interest only, though it includes a brief taste of the overtly sensual and erotic Mannerist paintings from the reign of Rudolf II (1576–1612).

Golden Lane

Golden Lane (Zlatá ulička) is a blind and crowded alley of miniature sixteenth-century cottages in dolly-mixture colours. A plaque at no. 22 commemorates Franz Kafka's brief sojourn here during World War I.

The Royal Gardens

North of the castle walls, across the **Powder Bridge** (Prasný most), is the entrance to the **Royal Gardens** (Královská zahrada; April–Oct daily 10am–6pm), founded in the early sixteenth century and still the best-kept gardens in the country, with fountains and immaculately cropped lawns. At the end of the gardens is Prague's most celebrated Renaissance legacy, the **Belvedér**, a delicately arcaded summerhouse.

Šternberg Palace

Hradčanské náměstí fans out from the castle's main gates, surrounded by the oversized palaces of the old nobility. A passage down the side of the Archbishop's Palace leads to the early eighteenth-century **Šternberg Palace** (Tues–Sun 10am–6pm; ⓦwww.ngprague.cz), housing the National Gallery's relatively modest **Old European art collection** (ie non-Czech), which primarily consists of works from the fifteenth to eighteenth centuries, the most significant of which is the **Festival of the Rosary** by Dürer.

Sv Mikuláš

Malostranské náměstí is the main square in Malá Strana. Here, you will find the former Jesuit seminary and church of **sv Mikuláš** (daily 9am–4/5pm; tower: April–Oct daily 10am–6pm; Nov–March Sat & Sun 10am–5pm; free), possibly the most magnificent Baroque building in the city. Nothing of the plain west facade prepares you for the overwhelming High Baroque interior – the **fresco** in the nave alone covers over 1500 square metres, and portrays some of the more fanciful feats of St Nicholas.

Petřín tower

South of the main square, a continuation of Karmelitská brings you to the **funicular railway** up Petřín hill (daily 9am–11.20/11.30pm; every 10–15min; 50Kč), a more pleasant green space than most in Prague, and a good place for a picnic and views from the **Petřín tower** (April, Sept & Oct daily 10am–6/7pm; May–Aug daily 10am–10pm; Nov–March Sat & Sun 10am–5pm).

Charles Bridge

Linking Staré Město to Malá Strana is the **Charles Bridge** (*Karlův most*), the city's most famous monument, begun in 1357. The **statues** that line it – brilliant pieces of Jesuit propaganda added during the Counter-Reformation – have made it renowned throughout Europe and choked with tourists throughout the year.

Klementinum

On the north side of the Charles bridge is the massive **Klementinum** (March–Oct Mon–Fri 2–6/7pm, Sat & Sun 10/11am– 6/7pm; Nov–Feb Sat & Sun 11am–6pm), the former Jesuit College, completed just before the order was turfed out of the country in 1773. The Klementinum is now home to the collections of the **national library**. You can take a tour of the spectacular Baroque

Library and the **astronomical tower**, the views from which are the most stunning in Prague.

Staroměstské náměstí

A few blocks east is **Staroměstské náměstí**, the most spectacular square in Prague and the city's main marketplace from the eleventh century until the beginning of the twentieth. At its centre is the dramatic Art Nouveau **Jan Hus Monument**, featuring the great fifteenth-century religious reformer. The best-known sight on the square, however, is the **Astronomical Clock** (chimes hourly 9am–9pm), which features a mechanical performance by Christ and the Apostles. The clock is an integral part of Staroměstská radnice, the **town hall**, inside which you can view a few chambers (Mon 11am–5/6pm, Tues–Sun 9am–5/6pm), climb the tower and get a close-up view of the mechanical figures.

Týn Church and Týnský dvur

Towering over Staroměstské náměstí, Staré Město's most impressive Gothic structure is the mighty **Týn Church**, whose towers rise above the two arcaded houses which otherwise obscure its facade. Behind, at the end of Týnská, lies the **Týnský dvur**, a stunning fortified courtyard where customs duties used to be collected; it houses the Renaissance Granovský Palace plus some upmarket shops and cafés.

Josefov

Within Staré Město lies **Josefov**, the Jewish quarter of the city until the end of the nineteenth century, when this ghetto area was demolished in order to create a beautiful bourgeois district on Parisian lines.

Most synagogues and sights of Josefov are covered by one ticket, available from the synagogues themselves (daily except Sat & Jewish holidays 9am–4.30/6pm; 300Kč, plus another 200Kč for the Old-New Synagogue; Ⓦwww.jewishmuseum.cz). Perhaps the most moving place to visit in Prague is the **Pinkas Synagogue**'s walls, which have been transformed into an epitaph to the 77,297 Czechoslovak Jews who were killed during the Holocaust. Upstairs, children's drawings from the Theresienstadt (Terezín) camp are displayed.

The **Old Jewish Cemetery** can be entered from Pinkasova. The jumble of Gothic, Renaissance and Baroque tombstones are a poignant reminder of the ghetto, its inhabitants subjected to overcrowding even in death.

The **Old-New Synagogue** is the religious centre of Prague's Jewish community. Opposite the synagogue is the Židovská radnice, the old Jewish town hall, which has a distinctive anticlockwise clock with Hebrew characters. East of Pařížská, at Věženská 1, is the highly ornate neo-Byzantine **Spanish Synagogue**.

The National Theatre

In Nové Město, at the river end of Národní is the gold-crested **National Theatre**, completed in 1881, a proud symbol of the Czech nation. Refused money by the Austrian state, Czechs of all classes dug deep into their pockets to raise funds for the venture themselves.

FRANZ KAFKA

The writer **Franz Kafka** spent most of his life in and around Josefov, and the destruction of the Jewish quarter, which continued throughout his childhood, had a profound effect on his psyche; a small exhibition (Tues–Fri 10am–6pm, Sat 10am–5pm) on the site of his birthplace, at náměstí Franze Kafky 5, tells the story of his life.

The Mucha Museum

A turning halfway along Na příkopě leads to the **Mucha Museum**, at Panská 7 (daily 10am–4/6pm; 120Kč; ⓦwww.mucha.cz), dedicated to the most famous Czech practitioner of Art Nouveau, Alfons Mucha.

Obecní dům

On náměstí Republiky stands the **Obecní dům**, the Municipal House. Begun in 1903, it was decorated inside and out with the help of almost every artist connected with the Czech Art Nouveau, or Secession, movement. You can take a guided **tour** of the interior (also in English); tickets are available from the information centre inside (daily 10am–6pm; 150Kč; ⓦwww.obecnidum.cz).

TREAT YOURSELF

The easiest way of soaking up the Obecní dům's dramatic **interior**, brimming with mosaics and pendulous chandeliers, is to have a pricey but perfectly brewed coffee, and marvel at the extravagant cake trolley, in its dazzling Art Nouveau café, **Kavárna Obecní dům** (7.30am–11pm), to the left of the entrance.

Wenceslas Square

The pivot of modern Prague and the political focus of the events of 1989 is the wide, gently sloping **Wenceslas Square** (Václavské náměstí). The square's history of protest goes back to the Prague Spring of 1968: towards the top end, there's a small **memorial** to the victims of Communism, the most famous of whom, the 21-year-old student **Jan Palach**, set himself alight on this very spot in 1969 in protest against the Soviet occupation.

The National Museum

The **National Museum** (daily 9/10am–5/6pm; 100Kč), one of the great symbols of the nineteenth-century Czech national revival, boasts a monumental glass cupola, sculptural decoration and frescoes telling the story of the regions of the Czech Republic through the ages. The museum is heavily focused on zoological and geological exhibits.

Trade Fair Palace: The Museum of Modern Art

One excellent reason to hop on a tram is to visit the city's modern art museum, housed in a stylish 1920s functionalist building, known as the Trade Fair Palace (Veletržní palác; Tues–Sun 10am–6pm; 100Kč for each floor visited or 250Kč for all four; ⓦwww.ngprague.cz;), on Dukelských hrdinů 47 (tram #5 from nám. Republiky). The museum's raison d'être is its unrivalled collection of nineteenth- and twentieth-century **Czech art**, but it also houses the National Gallery's modest collection of nineteenth- and twentieth-century **European art**, including works by Klimt, Schiele, Picasso and the French Impressionists, as well as temporary exhibitions of contemporary Czech and foreign art.

Arrival and information

Air Prague's airport, Ruzyně, is 10km northwest of the city. The cheapest way of getting into town is to take local bus #119 (4am–midnight; every 7–15min; 20min) to Dejvická metro station, the start of line A, which will take you directly to the centre of town. Alternatively, there's the ČEDAZ express minibus (5.30am–9.30pm; every 30min; 20min to Dejvická, 40min–1hr to city centre), which stops first at Dejvická metro station, and terminates at náměstí Republiky (90Kč). This service will also take you straight to your accommodation for around 480Kč per drop-off – a bargain if there's a few of you (960Kč for 5–8 people). "Fixed-price" taxis are expensive, at around 700Kč per taxi to the centre.

Train Arriving from the west, you're most likely to end up at Praha hlavní nádraží, the main station. It's only a short walk to Wenceslas Square from here (inadvisable at night), and the station has its own metro stop on line C, a direct line to Museum on Wenceslas Square, and with connections to the main sights. International expresses passing through

Prague usually stop only at Praha Holešovice station, north of the city centre (metro Nádraží Holešovice). Some trains from Moravia and Slovakia wind up at the central Praha Masarykovo station (metro Náměstí Republiky), and trains from the south at Praha Smíchov station (metro Smíchovské nádraží).

Bus The main bus station is Praha-Florenc on the eastern edge of Staré Město (metro Florenc).

Tourist office The best place to go for information is the Prague Information Service, or PIS (Pražská informačni služba), which has several branches around town; the main office is at Na příkopě 20 (Mon–Fri 9am–6/7pm, Sat 9am–3/5pm; April–Oct also Sun 9am–5pm; ⓦwww.pis.cz). The staff speak English, but their helpfulness varies; they can usually answer most enquiries, and organize accommodation, sell maps, guides and theatre tickets. As for events, it's worth getting hold of the English-language monthly *Prague Events* or *Heart of Europe*, both with good listings sections.

Internet *Globe* (see opposite; daily 10am–midnight; 1.50 Kč/min) has several fast terminals.

City transport

Tickets There are two main tickets: the 12Kč *přestupní jízdenka* is valid for an hour (1hr 30min off-peak), and allows you to change metro lines, trams and buses as often as you like; the 8Kč *nepřestupní jízdenka* allows you to travel for up to fifteen minutes on a single tram or bus, or up to four stops on the metro. Buy tickets from a tobacconist, kiosk or the ticket machines inside metro stations and at some tram stops, then validate them on board or at the metro entrance. To take a large backpack on public transport you'll need an extra half-fare ticket.

Travel passes If you're going to be using the system a lot, it's worth getting hold of a travel pass (*Časová jízdenka*; 70Kč/24hr, 200Kč/72hr, 250Kč/week); remember to validate it when you first use it. Plain-clothes inspectors check tickets – it's a fine of 400Kč on the spot if it's not valid.

Metro The metro (daily 5am–midnight) is the fastest and most useful form of city transport. **Trams** Running every 10–15min, trams navigate Prague's hills and cobbles with remarkable dexterity. Tram #22, whose run includes Vinohrady and Hradčany, is a good way to sightsee, but beware of pickpockets. Night trams #51–59 (midnight–4.30am; every 30min) all pass by Lazarská in Nové Město.

Taxis The horror stories about Prague taxi drivers ripping off tourists are too numerous to mention, so your best bet is to call the English-speaking AAA (ⓣ140 14; 34Kč plus 25Kč per 1km), rather than go to the mafia-controlled taxi ranks.

Accommodation

Prague's hotels are exorbitant for what you get; as a result, most tourists on a budget now stay in private rooms or hostels, both of which are easy to organize on arrival. The main international train stations and the airport have accommodation agencies dealing with hotels, pensions and occasionally private rooms too. Prague's university, the Karolinum, rents out over a thousand **student rooms** in summer; contact the booking office at Voršilská 1, Nové Město (Mon–Fri only; ⓣ224 930 010; beds available July to mid-Sept; from around 350Kč.

Hostels

Clown and Bard Borivojova 102 ⓣ222 716 453, ⓦwww.clownandbard.com. If you don't mind being a little way out of the city, this lively hostel is a good bet. Tram #5, #9 or #26 from the main train station. Dorms ❷, doubles ❹

Hostel Týn Týnská 19, Staré Město ⓣ224 828 519, ⓦwww.hostel-tyn.web2001.cz. Excellent location; offers four- and five-bed dorms and simple doubles. Metro Náměstí Republiky. Dorms ❷ doubles ❺.

Husova Hostel Husova 3, Staré Město ⓣ222 220 078, ⓦwww.travellers.cz. Cosy hostel tucked away in the lively side streets of Staré Město. Metro Můstek. Dorms ❷, doubles ❺

Ritchie's Hostel Karlova 9, Staré Město ⓣ222 221 229, ⓦwww.ritchieshostel.cz. A hostel-cum-hotel wonderfully located between the Staroměstské náměstí and the Charles Bridge. Dorms and rooms with or without en-suite bathrooms. Internet access. Metro Staroměstská. Dorms ❶, doubles ❼

Sokol Nosticova 2, Malá Strana ⓣ257 007 397, ⓦwww.sokol-cos.cz/hostel.html. Student hostel in a great location near the river and castle. Tram #12, #20 or #22 from metro Malostranská. Dorms ❷, doubles ❸

Travellers' Hostel Dlouhá 33, Staré Město ⓣ224 826 662, ⓦwww.travellers.cz. Centrally located hostel, with dorms and one- to six-bed rooms. There's also a bar, laundry and Internet access. Metro Náměstí Republiky. Dorms ❷, doubles ❺

Hotels and pensions

Černý slon Týnská 1, Staré Město ⓣ222 321 521, ⓦwww.hotelcernyslon.cz. A four-star hotel with beautifully refurbished rooms and a wine cellar, in a medieval house near the Staroměstské náměstí. Metro Náměstí Republiky. ❾

Expres Skořepka 5, Staré Město ⓣ224 211 801, ⓦwww.hotel-expres.com. Friendly staff, modern

TREAT YOURSELF

Reopened in August 2007, the lovely **Imperial Hotel** (Na Poříčí 15, Nové Město ⓣ246 011 661, ⓦwww.hotel-imperial.cz; Metro Náměstí Republiky; ⑨) has been painstakingly refurbished and is now a mixture of Cubist and neo-Renaissance styles. Pure luxury.

rooms and a reasonable price. The cheapest rooms come without en-suite facilities. Metro Národní třída. ⑨

Hotel Sax Jánský Vršek 328/3, Malá Strana, ⓣ257 531 268, ⓦwww.sax.cz. Modern rooms and a lovely location. Metro Malostranská. ⑨

U medvídků Na Perštýně 7 ⓣ224 211 916, ⓦwww.umedvidku.cz. Friendly, central place with fresh, airy rooms rooms above a famous Prague pub. Metro Národní třída. ⑨

U Žlute Boty Jánský Vršek 11, Malá Strana, ⓣ257 534 134, ⓦwww.zlutabota.cz. With a lovely location in a quiet backstreet, beautifully furnished rooms and warm staff, this hotel exudes character. ⑨

Eating

While traditional Czech food still predominates in the city's pubs, Prague now has a wide range of **restaurants** offering anything from French to Japanese cuisine. Steer clear of places in the main tourist areas, such as either side of the Charles Bridge, which tend to be overpriced and of indifferent quality. The city's **cafés** are pretty varied – from Art Nouveau relics, which also do food, and swish espresso bars (both of which are called *kavárna* and are licensed), to simple cafés offering coffee and cakes (*cukrárna*).

Cafés

Café Imperial Na poříčí 15, Staré Město. Newly refurbished to its Habsburg-era splendour, this Kaffeehaus has a new lease of life.

Café Louvre Národní 20, Nové Město. Resurrected Habsburg-era Kaffeehaus with high ceiling, mirrors, daily papers and a billiard hall, this was once the haunt of Franz Kafka and Max Brod.

Café Slavia Národní 1, Nové Město. Famous café opposite the National Theatre, with great riverside views, decent meals and Manet's *Absinthe Drinker* on the wall.

Dahab Dlouhá 33, Staré Město. Offers tasty Middle Eastern snacks and hookahs to a background of funky world music.

Globe Pštrossova 6, Nové Město. Large, buzzing café, at the back of the English-language bookstore of the same name. A serious expat hangout, but enjoyable nevertheless.

Restaurants

Bar Bar Všehrdova 17, Malá Strana. Arty crêperie with generous, cheap salads and sweet and savoury pancakes. Mains 90–275Kč.

Jarmark Vodičkova 30, Nové Město. Popular, inexpensive self-service steak and salad buffet where the chef prepares your food in front of you; a few veggie dishes on offer too. Mains 105–399Kč.

Klub Architektů Betlémské nám. 5, Staré Město ⓣ224 401 214. Attractive, lively cellar restaurant serving tasty Czech and vegetarian cuisine. Booking recommended. Mains 120–160Kč.

Pizzeria Kmotra V Jirchářích 12, Nové Město. Hugely popular basement pizza place in the backstreets behind Národní. Mains 95–150Kč.

Radost FX Café Bělehradská 120, Vinohrady. Superb veggie food attracts an ultra-fashionable crowd. Open till very late; brunch at weekends. Mains 145–285Kč.

Skořepka Skořepka 1, Staré Město. Czech and international dishes served in this pleasant, folk-style restaurant with vaulted ceiling, hidden in the backstreets of Staré Město. Mains 129–649Kč.

Tlustá mýs Všehrdova 19, Malá Strana. Cosy cellar bar, restaurant and gallery, offering reasonably priced, hearty Czech food washed down with Pilsner Urquell. Mains 60–250Kč.

U sádlů Klimentská 2, Staré Město. Deliberately over-the-top themed medieval banqueting hall serving inexpensive hearty fare and lashings of frothing ale. Mains 145–285Kč.

U Labuti Hradčanské Náměstí, Hradčany. Reasonably-priced restaurant in a location handy for the castle. Mains 140–200Kč.

Zlaty* Dvůr Husova 9, Staré Město. Live Jazz, goulash and beer in this stylish private courtyard and intimate cellar in Staré Město. Mains 99–299Kč.

Drinking and nightlife

For no-nonsense boozing you need to head for a **pub** (*pivnice*), which invariably serves excellent beer by the half-litre, but many of which close around 11pm. For late-night drinking, head for one of the **clubs** or all-night bars.

Bars and Pubs

Friends Náprstkova 1, Staré Město. A friendly, laid-back gay/lesbian cellar bar in the old town.

Jo's Bar Malostranské náměstí 7, Malá Strana. A narrow bar in Malá Strana that is the original expat/backpacker hangout. Tex-Mex food served all day, bottled beer only and a heaving crowd guaranteed most evenings. Downstairs is Jo's Garáž disco.

Ocean Drive V Kolkovně 7, Josefov. Stylish, brightly decorated cocktail bar, drawing a young, buzzy crowd.

Pivovarskýdům Lipova 15, Nové Město. In-house brewery offering everything from wheat beer to a banana variety, along with excellent Czech pub grub and good service.

U Zlatého Tygra
Husova 17, Staré Město. "The Golden Tiger" is a traditional, atmospheric pub offering Pilsner and hearty Czech food.

Clubs

Karlovy lázně Novotného lávka 1, Staré Město Ⓦwww.karlovylazne.cz. A staple of the Prague club scene, this is a high-tech megaclub by the Charles Bridge; techno on the top floor, progressively more retro as you descend to the Internet café on the ground floor.

Lucerna Music Bar Vodičkova 36, Nové Město Ⓦwww.musicbar.cz. Central, small dance space, with live, mainly indie, music. A staple of Prague nightlife.

Radost FX Bělehradská 120, Vinohrady Ⓦwww.radostfx.cz. Still the slickest (and latest-opening – till 5am) all-round dance club venue in Prague, with a great veggie café-restaurant attached. The "Lollypop" gay house parties held here always draw the crowds.

Entertainment

Theatre

Theatre in Prague is thriving; unless you know the language your scope is limited, but there's also a tradition of innovative mime and puppetry in the city. Tickets are cheap and available from various agencies around town, including Ticketpro (Ⓦwww.ticketpro.cz) as well as from tourist offices and the venues themselves.

Pop and rock music

As far as **live music** is concerned, the classical scene still has the edge in Prague, though there are also some good **jazz clubs**.

AghaRTA Jazz Centrum Železná 16, Staré Město Ⓦwww.agharta.cz. Prague's best jazz club, with a good mix of top international names and local bands.

Palác Akropolis Kubelíkova 27, Vinohrady Ⓦwww.palacakropolis.cz. Decent live arts/world music venue in the backstreets of Žížkov, renowned for Romany and other ethnic music festivals. Tram #5, #9 or #26.

Roxy Dlouhá 33, Staré Město Ⓦwww.roxy.cz. Once a cinema, now a live music venue with a gallery and theatre, as well as club nights.

Classical music

Throughout the year, concert halls, churches and palaces host **classical concerts**, which also take place in the main venues (listed below). In the summer open-air concerts and plays are organised at Hradčany.

Estates Theatre (Stavovské divadlo) Ovocný trh 1, Staré Město Ⓦwww.narodni-divadlo.cz. Theatre, ballet and opera in the venue that premiered Mozart's *Don Giovanni*.

Národní Divadlo Národní 2, Nové Město Ⓦwww.narodni-divadlo.cz. Grand nineteenth-century theatre with a highly ornate interior showing theatre, ballet and opera.

Rudolfinum Alsovo nábřeží 12, Staré Město Ⓦwww.rudolfinum.cz. Stunning Neo-Renaissance concert hall and home to the Czech Philharmonic.

Prague State Opera Wilsonova 4, Nové Město Ⓦwww.opera.cz. The former German opera house and the city's second-choice venue for opera and ballet.

Smetana Hall Obecní dům, náměstí Republiky 5, Nové Město. Fantastically ornate and recently renovated Art Nouveau concert hall, which is home to the excellent Prague Symphony Orchestra.

Shopping

Wenceslas Square and its surrounding streets are the best places to buy souvenirs and jewellery; you will also find book and department stores here.

Havelske Trziste Havelska. Main open-air market in the city centre, just a couple of minutes' walk from Wenceslas Square. Sells crafts, fruit and vegetables.

THE PRAGUE SPRING

The **Prague Spring** international music festival (Ⓦwww.festival.cz), traditionally begins on May 12, the day of Smetana's death, with a performance of *Má vlast*, and finishes on June 2 with a rendition of Beethoven's Ninth. Atmospheric venues include Obecní dům, Týn Church and the Rudolfinum.

Nový Smíchov Mall Plzenksa 8. A huge shopping mall with high-street names and a supermarket.

Directory

Embassies and consulates Australia (honorary), Klimentská 10, Nové Město ⓣ296 578 350; Canada, Muchova 6, Hradčany ⓣ272 101 800; New Zealand, Dykova 19, Vinohrady ⓣ222 514 672; Ireland, Tržiště 13, Malá Strana ⓣ257 530 061; UK, Thunovská 14, Malá Strana ⓣ257 402 111; US, Tržiště 15, Malá Strana ⓣ257 530 663.
Hospital Na Františku Hospital, Na Františku 847 ⓣ222 801 111, ⓣ248 102 80/69 emergencies (English spoken).
Laundry Laundryland, Londýnska 71, Nové Město (daily 8am–10pm) has a basement bar. Several other locations around town.
Left luggage There are lockers or left-luggage offices at all of the train stations.
Pharmacies Palackého 5, Nové Město ⓣ224 946 982 (Mon–Fri 7am–7pm, Sat & Sun 8am–noon); Štefánikova 6, Malá Strana ⓣ257 320 918 (24hr).
Post office Jindřišská 14, Nové Město (daily 2am–midnight).

Moving on

Train Domestic: Brno (every 1–2hr; 2hr 40min–3hr 40min); České Budějovice (up to 14 daily; 2hr 15min–3hr); Karlovy Vary (3 daily; 4hr 5min–5hr 10min); Mariánské Lázně (10 daily; 2hr 55min); Olomouc (1–2 hourly; 3hr 10min–3hr 30min); Plzeň (hourly; 1hr 40min).
International: Dresden (daily; 2hrs 30min); Bratislava (daily; 5hrs 20min).
Bus Domestic: Brno (every 30min–1hr; 2hr 20min–3hr 30min); České Budějovice (up to 8 daily; 2hr 30min–3hr 25min); Český Krumlov (2–6 daily; 2hr 40min–3hr 25min); Karlovy Vary (hourly; 2hr 10min–2hr 20min); Kutná Hora (hourly on weekdays; 1hr 15min); Mariánské Lázně (2–5 daily; 2hr 45min–3hr 15min); Olomouc (up to 8 daily; 3hr 50min–5hr).
International: Berlin (daily; 6hr 30min); Bratislava (up to six daily; 3–6hr).

Bohemia

Prague is the natural centre and capital of Bohemia; the rest divides easily into four geographical districts. **South Bohemia**, bordered by the Šumava Mountains, is the least spoilt; its largest town by far is the brewing centre of **České Budějovice**, and its chief attraction, aside from the thickly forested hills, is a series of well-preserved medieval towns, whose undisputed gem is **Český Krumlov**.

Neighbouring **West Bohemia** has a similar mix of rolling woods and hills, despite the industrial nature of its capital **Plzeň**, home of Pilsen beer and the Škoda empire. Beyond here, as you approach the German border, Bohemia's famous **spa region** unfolds, with magnificent resorts such as **Mariánské Lázně** and **Karlovy Vary** enjoying sparkling reputations.

There's some great walking and climbing country in East Bohemia, but the only essential stop on a quick tour is the silver-mining centre of **Kutná Hora**.

ČESKÉ BUDĚJOVICE

Since its foundation in 1265, **České Budějovice** has been a self-assured town, convinced of its own importance. In medieval times the town made its money from silver mining and taxing salt as it passed through from Linz to Prague. In the seventeenth century war and fire pretty much destroyed the place but it was rebuilt by the Habsburgs in lavish style. If you're travelling on to Český Krumlov you'll almost certainly have to change train or bus here – České Budějovice is a great place to stretch your legs and try the tasty local Budvar **beer**.

What to see and do

The compact Old Town is only a five-minute walk from the **train** and **bus** stations, both to the east of the city centre: head along the pedestrianized Lannova třída. The medieval grid plan leads inevitably to the magnificent central **náměstí Přemysla Otakara II**, one of Europe's largest market squares. Its buildings are elegant enough, but it's the arcades and the octagonal **Samson's Fountain** – once the only tap in town – that make the greatest impression.

The 72-metre status symbol, the **Black Tower** (Černá věž), one of the few survivors of the 1641 fire, leans gently to one side of the square; its roof gallery (10am–6pm: April–Oct Tues–Sun; July & Aug Mon–Sat) provides superb views.

The **Budvar brewery** is 2.5km up the road to Prague, on Karolíny Světlé (bus #2), and has a modern *pivnice* inside the nasty titanium-blue headquarters. You'll need to book ahead for tours (Ⓣ387 705 341, Ⓦwww.budweiser.cz).

Arrival and information

Arrival The town's train and bus stations are just a five-minute walk from the old town. There are several daily direct trains and buses from Prague; it's possible to make your visit a day-trip, but if you want to visit the brewery, you should consider staying overnight.
Tourist office Namáměstí Premysla Otakara 2 (May–Sept Mon–Fri 8.30am–6pm, Sat 8.30am–5pm, Sun 10am–noon & 12.30–4pm; Oct–April Mon–Fri 9am–4pm, Sat 9am–noon & 1–3pm; Ⓣ386 801 413, Ⓦwww.c-budejovice.cz).

Accommodation

Hotel Klika, Hroznova 25 Ⓣ387 318 171, Ⓦwww.hotelklika.cz. Riverside location with light, modern rooms and genuine but not necessarily English-speaking staff. ❾
Hotel Malý Pivovar Karla IV Ⓣ386 360 471, Ⓦwww.malypivovar.cz. Ideally placed for beer-sampling; wooden-beamed rooms in a sixteenth-century burgher house. ❾
Stromovká Autocamp Ⓣ387 203 597. April–October. Ample room for tents; 2km southwest of the town. Bus #16 from Lidická třída. ❶
U solné brány, Radniční 11 Ⓣ386 354 121, Ⓦwww.hotelusolnebrany.cz. Helpful staff and pleasant, but unremarkable rooms. ❼

Eating and drinking

C K Solnice, Česka. A rough-around-the-edges bar with occasional live jazz.
Malý pivovar, Karla IV. Run by Budvar, this serves great pub food and predictably good beer. Mains 56–318 Kč.

Moving on

Train Brno (4–5 daily; 4hr 20min); Český Krumlov (8 daily; 1hr); Plzeň (12–13 daily; 2hr–3hr 25min).
Bus Brno (3–6 daily; 3hr 30min–4hr 30min); Český Krumlov (every 15–30min; 25–50min).

ČESKÝ KRUMLOV

Český Krumlov is a tiny, near-perfect medieval town with a fantastically over-the-top Renaissance castle and beautiful houses on its narrow cobbled streets. Despite the crowds of trippers in high summer it's still a relaxing place to spend a couple of days and by rented bike or canoe, or on foot, you can easily venture out into the surrounding countryside.

What to see and do

The twisting River Vltava divides the town into two: the circular Staré Město on the right bank and the Latrán quarter on the hillier left.

Latrán Chateau

For centuries, the focal point of the town has been the **castle** in Latrán (Tues–Sun: April–May & Sept–Oct 9am–5pm; June–Aug 9am–6pm). There's a choice of two tours: Tour 1 (160Kč) concentrates on the stunning Renaissance parts of the castle and Tour 2 (140Kč) will take you into the slightly less remarkable eighteenth- and nineteenth-century quarters. From the castle, a covered walkway puts you high above the town in the unexpectedly expansive terraced gardens.

The town hall and museums

The main square, náměstí Svornosti, boasts a long, white Renaissance arcade,

ACTIVITIES ON THE VLTAVA

In the summer, trips along the river offer lovely views of the city. Sit back and enjoy a lazy riverboat cruise, or navigate the weirs by canoe or kayak. Ask at the tourist office for details, or try the agencies Vltava Ⓦwww.ckvltava.cz or Maleček Ⓦwww.malecek.cz.

connecting two-and-a-half Gothic houses to create the **town hall.**

On the other side, the high lancet windows of the **church of sv Vitus** rise above the red rooftops.

Along Horní street, just off the square, the Regional **Museum** (March–April & Oct–Dec Tues–Fri 9am–4pm, Sat & Sun 1–4pm; May, June & Sept daily 10am–5pm; July & Aug daily 10am–6pm) has a room-sized model of the town.

West of the square, on Široká, is the **Egon Schiele Art Centrum** (daily 10am–6pm; 180Kč; Ⓦwww.schieleartcentrum.cz). The museum is devoted in part to the Austrian painter Egon Schiele, who lived here briefly in 1911. It also houses temporary exhibitions by contemporary artists.

Arrival and information

Arrival The town's bus station is a five-minute walk northeast of the inner town; the train station is further out, 1km from the chateau. In both cases, you will have to change at České Budějovice if coming from Prague.

Tourist office Náměstí Svornosti 2 (daily: April, May & Oct 9am–6pm; June & Sept 9am–7pm; July–Aug 9am–8pm; Nov–March 9am–5pm; Ⓣ380 704 622, Ⓦwww.ckrumlov.cz); Internet access; situated on the main square.

Accommodation

There are several **campsites** south of town along the road to Rožmberk but you'll need your own transport to get there.

Na louži Kájovská 66 Ⓣ380 711 280, Ⓦwww.nalouzi.cz. Small, popular hotel-pub with a welcoming atmosphere. Advance booking advisable. ❺

TREAT YOURSELF

Medieval-style *Hotel Růže* (Horni 154, Ⓣ380 772 100, Ⓦwww.hotelruze.cz; ❾) in the old Jesuit college is the plushest place in town. If you're going to splash out, there's no better place to do it: the breakfasts are fabulous and the rooms sheer indulgence.

Travellers Hostel Soukenická 43 Ⓣ380 711 345, Ⓦwww.travellers.cz. Popular HI-affiliated hostel. ❷

Eating and drinking

Eggenberg Latrán 27. Drinking is best done here at the lively "brewery tap."

Papa's Living Restaurant Latrán 13. Funky Mexican, Italian and veggie dishes. Mains 145–409Kč.

U písaře Jana Horní 151. A vast menu, including an extensive range of fish options. Worth eating here for the view of the chateau and the river alone. Mains 135–430Kč.

PLZEŇ

Plzeň is Bohemia's second city, with a population of around 175,000. Despite its industrial character, there are compensations – eclectic architecture and an unending supply of (probably) the best beer in the world.

What to see and do

The main square, náměstí Republiky, presents a full range of architectural styles, starting with the exalted heights of the Gothic **cathedral of sv Bartoloměj,** its green spire (daily 10am–6pm) reaching up almost 103m. Over the way rises the sgraffitoed Renaissance Old Town Hall, self-importantly one storey higher than the rest of the square. Here and there other old structures survive, but the vast majority of Plzeň's buildings hail from the city's heyday during the industrial expansion around the beginning of the twentieth century.

The Pilsner Urquell brewery

The reason most people come to Plzeň is to sample its famous 12° Plzeňský Prazdroj, better known as **Pilsner Urquell** abroad. The degree is an indication of the strength of malt extract, not alcohol content: most Czech beers are 3–6% alcohol. Beer has been brewed in the town since it was founded in 1295, but it wasn't until 1842 that the famous Bürgerliches Brauhaus was built, after a near-riot by the townsfolk over the declining quality of their brew. For a guided tour of the **brewery** (Ⓣ377 062 888, Ⓦwww.beerworld.cz; 120Kč), you can either book in advance or simply show up at 12.30pm or 2pm for tours in English. You could, of course, just settle for a half-litre or two at the vast **Na Spílce** pub (daily 11am–10pm), just inside the brewery's triumphal arch.

Arrival and information

Train and bus Plzeň's **train stations** are works of art in themselves: your likeliest point of arrival is Hlavní nádraží, just a little east of the city centre. The **bus terminal** is on the west side of town. From both stations, the city centre is only a short walk away. There are direct buses from Prague.

Tourist office Nám. Republiky 41 Ⓣ378 035 330, Ⓦwww.plzen-city.cz (April–Sept daily 9am–6pm; Oct–March Mon–Fri 10am–5pm, Sat & Sun 10am–3.30pm). Plzeň is not an easy day-trip from Prague, so if you're visiting from the capital, you can ask the tourist office to help you to arrange **private rooms**, which cost 250–600Kč.

Accommodation

Pension K Bezručova 156/13 Ⓣ377 329 683, Ⓦwww.pilsenhotel.eu. Centrally located with accommodating, though not necessarily English-speaking staff. ❺

Pension V Solní Solní 8 Ⓣ377 236 652, Ⓦwww.volny.cz/pensolni. Small, intimate pension in a central location. ❹

U Salzmannů Pražská 8 Ⓣ377 235 855, Ⓦwww.usalzmannu.cz. Cute en-suite rooms with kitchenette above a friendly pub. ❾

Ostender campsite 6km north of the city. Take tram #1 (direction Boleveke), then bus #30. ❶

Eating and drinking

Na Parkánu Veleslavínova 4. Formerly a prison and a malt-house, this is now an atmospheric ale-house/restaurant near the brewery museum. Mains 59–299Kč.

Na Spílce U Prazdroje 7. The pub-restaurant of the Pilsner brewery is the largest pub in the Republic, with traditional Czech fare to enjoy with your beer. Mains 199Kč.

U Salzmannů Pražská 8. Traditional Czech fare in a cosy setting. Mains 79–499Kč.

MARIÁNSKÉ LÁZNĚ

Once one of the most fashionable European spas, Mariánské Lázně is not quite so exclusive today. Visitors expecting the bling of Karlovy Vary will be disappointed; the clientele is largely made up of elderly Germans. However, the riotous fin-de-siècle architecture is gradually being restored, and sumptuous, regal buildings rise up from the pine-clad hills. Add to this the stunning, unspoilt surrounding countryside and increasingly lively local scene, and the town has a curative feel of its own.

What to see and do

The focal point of the spa is the Kolonáda. This beautiful wrought-iron colonnade gently curves like a whale-ribbed railway station, the atmosphere relentlessly genteel and sober, although the view has been marred by a functionless concrete splat left by Communist planners. The spa's first and foremost spring, Křížový pramen, has its own adjoining Neoclassical colonnade (daily 6am–6pm). Mariánské Lázně's altitude lends an almost subalpine freshness to the air, and walking is as important to "the cure" as the various specialized treatments; maps showing marked walks in the area are available in hotels and shops.

Arrival and information

Bus and train Buses and trains from all directions stop 3km from the spa, from where trolleybus #5 runs up Hlavní třída to the centre. This is not an easy day-trip from Prague, although it is possible to travel direct by train or bus, so you might want to consider staying overnight.

Tourist office Hlavní 47 (daily 10am–noon & 1–6pm; ⓣ354 622 474, ⓦwww.marienbad.cz). Has Internet access and can help to arrange cheap accommodation. Local agency Informservis (Hlavní 222, ⓣ603 242 564) provide information about the area and organize a range of wilderness and sporting activities.

Accommodation

The spa hotels are extremely pricey, but there are a few cheaper options.

Oradour, Hlavní třída 43 ⓣ354 624 304, ⓦwww.penzionoradour.wz.cz. Good location, offering rooms with shared facilities. ❷

Pension Edinburgh Ruská 310/56 ⓣ354 620 804, ⓦwww.pensionedinburgh.com. Friendly pension with pleasant rooms, conveniently located above the Scottish pub. ❺

Polonia Hlavní třída 50 ⓣ354 622 451 ⓦwww.hotelpolonia.cz. Adequate rooms in a leafy setting overlooking the spa gardens. ❾

Eating and drinking

Art Café Ruská 315. Recently opened café with live jazz every Friday attracting a young crowd.

Café Polonia Hlavní třída 50. Bubblegum pop music in an opulent setting that's as rich as its cakes.

Na Rampe Kollárova 707. Close to the railway station, behind the supermarket, this club has live – mostly rock – music on Fridays, and attracts mainly a young crowd.

Scottish Pub Ruská 310/56. Weather-dependent live music in the garden draws a young, local crowd.

Moving on

Train Karlovy Vary (6–7 daily; 1hr 40min–2hr 20min); Plzeň (hourly; 1hr 10min–1hr 35min).

Bus Plzeň (up to 7 daily; 1hr25min).

KARLOVY VARY

Karlovy Vary, undisputed king of the Bohemian spas, is one of the most cosmopolitan Czech towns. Its international clientele – largely Russians – annually doubles the local population, which is further supplemented by thousands of able-bodied tourists in summer, mostly German.

What to see and do

The best way to take in Karlovy Vary is to wander up the river stopping to sip the medicinal water at the **springs** along the way. You can buy kitsch teapot-like drinking cups at souvenir kiosks. The water is hot and surprisingly salty – the sweet wafers you'll see people munching are designed to take away the taste. Start at the **Thermal**, a Communist-era construction that has an open-air, spring-water **swimming pool** (Mon–Sat 8am–9.30pm, Sun 9am–9.30pm). The valley narrows in front of the graceful **Mlýnská kolonáda**, each of whose four springs is more scalding than the last. Most powerful of the town's twelve springs is the **Vřídlo**, which belches out over 2500 gallons every hour. The smooth marble floor of the modern **Vřídelní kolonáda** (the old fountain was melted down for armaments by the Nazis) allows patients to shuffle up and down contentedly, while inside the glass rotunda the geyser shoots hot water forty feet upwards.

Also worth checking out are Dientzenhofer's Baroque masterpiece, the **church of sv Maria Magdaléna**, and Karlovy Vary's most famous shopping street, the **Stará louka**.

Arrival and information

Train and bus Trains from Prague arrive at Horní Nádraží to the north of town while trains from Mariánské Lázně come in at Dolní nádraží close to the main **bus station** and the town centre. Buses run to the spa area from all stations. If you're bussing it from Prague get off one stop early at Tržnice, even closer to the spa area.

Tourist office next to the Mlýnská kolonáda at Lázeňská 1 ⓣ353 224 097, ⓦwww.karlovyvary.cz (Mon–Fri 8am–5pm, Sat & Sun 10am–4pm).

Accommodation

It's best to start looking for accommodation early in the day. Karlovy Vary is very fashionable, so nothing comes cheap.

Hotel Kavalerie František Nosek TGM 43 ⓣ353 229 613, ⓦwww.kavalerie.cz. Conveniently

TREAT YOURSELF

The stellar **Grand Hotel Pupp** (Mírové Náměstí 2 ⓣ353 109 111, ⓦwww.pupp.cz; ⑨) hosts the annual Karlovy Vary International Film Festival, has starred in *Last Holiday*, starring Queen Latifah, and was cast as "Hotel Splendide" in the James Bond film *Casino Royale*. Boasting two excellent restaurants, a nightclub and casino, this is spa glamour at its most decadent.

close to the bus and railway stations, this hotel offers comfortable, quiet rooms. ⑤

Hotel Kučera Stará louka 2 ⓣ353 235 053, ⓦwww.hotelkucera.com. Uninspiring but adequate rooms in a good location. ⑦

Eating and drinking

Caffee Pizzeria Venezia Zahradní 43. Reliable pizza place serving a large range of pizza and pasta, as well as meat and fish dishes. Pizza 69–120Kč.

Elefant Stará louka. Karlovy Vary's swishest café with exquisite ice-cream concoctions (try the Nut Temptation), 70–145Kč.

Grand Restaurant *Grand Hotel Pupp*, Mírové Náměstí 2. If you can't afford to stay in the hotel, you could try the excellent but pricey restaurant. Very attentive service and beautifully prepared food. Mains 280–590Kč.

KUTNÁ HORA

The sleepy town of **Kutná Hora**, an easy day-trip from Prague, was once one of the most important centres in Bohemia. The medieval lanes are dominated by the massive towers of sv Jakub and sv Barbora, while the ground beneath the town is riddled with old silver workings. From 1308 Bohemia's royal mint at Kutná Hora converted the silver into coins called Groschen which were used all over Central Europe.

The most straightforward way to get here is to take a bus from Florenc in Prague; otherwise the train is cheap and takes less than an hour.

What to see and do

The ossuary at Sedlec

If you have taken the train from Prague, you will arrive at the main station, near the suburb of Sedlec; from here it's an easy walk to the ossuary or *kostnice*. Otherwise, take bus #1 or #4 from town to the giant tobacco factory 3km northeast of the centre; you'll find the **ossuary** (daily: April–Sept 8am–6pm; Oct–March 9am–noon & 1–4/5pm) behind the Baroque church of the Assumption Of Our Lady. The ancient gothic chapel was scattered with holy earth from Golgotha in the twelfth century. The ensuing vogue for being buried here ensured that the piles of bones mounted up until the nineteenth century, when František Rint was given leave to get creative with them. The resulting decorations are an arresting sight: the ossuary is embellished with over forty thousand sets of human bones.

Cathedral of sv Barbora

The hill that leads to the imposing **Cathedral of sv Barbora** (daily: 9am–5.30pm) is lined with Baroque sculptures of saints similar to those on the Charles Bridge in Prague. Not to be outdone by Prague's St Vitus' Cathedral, the miners of Kutná Hora financed the construction of this great cathedral, dedicated to Barbara, the patron saint of miners and gunners. From the outside it's an incredible sight, bristling with pinnacles, finials and flying buttresses in an overt gothic statement. Inside, streams of light through the plain glass illuminate the vaulted nave.

The Italian Court

From the pretty but unassuming main square Palackého naměstí, head down 28 října to the Italian Court where Florentine craftsmen minted coins. Entrance is by guided tour only. In English, they take around thirty minutes (daily: April–Sept 9am–6pm; March & Oct 10am–5pm; Nov–Feb 10am–4pm) and cost 130Kč. The **park** next door runs down to the river and is a pleasant picnic spot.

The Mining Museum

In a tiny medieval fort, the Mining Museum (April–Oct Tues–Sun 9/10am–5/6pm; 130Kč) has a collection of silver; visitors can descend into the mines.

Arrival and information

Arrival Trains from Prague arrive at the main train station, near Sedlec. Take the #1 or #4 bus into the town centre (where buses from Prague arrive), or one stop further to sv Barbora.

Tourist office Palackeho náměstí 377 (April–Sept daily 9am–6pm; Oct–March Mon–Fri 9am–5pm, Sat & Sun 10am–4pm; ⓣ327 512 378, ⓦwww.kh.cz). Can book **private rooms** and has **Internet access**.

Accommodation

Hotel Anna Vladislavova 372 ⓣ327 516 315, Wsweb.cz/hotel.anna. With clean, modern rooms, the hotel has its own restaurant and pub under a Renaissance vaulting. ❺

Penzion Centrum Jakubská 57 ⓣ327 514 218 ⓦwww.centrum.penzion.com. Rooms on a pleasant courtyard right by sv Jakub. Friendly staff. ❼

Santa Barbara Campsite Česká ⓣ327 512 051. April–October. Northwest of the town centre, this campsite has hot showers and a restaurant. ❶

Moravia

Wedged between Bohemia and Slovakia, **Moravia** is the smallest of the three provinces that once made up Czechoslovakia, but perhaps the prettiest, friendliest and most bucolic. Although the North Moravian corridor is heavily industrialized – and towns and cities here suffer more from unemployment than any other region in the Czech Republic – much of Moravia is rural, and folk roots, traditions and religion are strongly felt. The Moravian capital, **Brno**, a once-grand nineteenth-century city, is within easy striking distance of Moravia's spectacular **karst region**. In the northern half of the province, the Baroque riches of the Moravian prince-bishopric have left their mark on the old capital, **Olomouc**, now a thriving university town and one of the region's main attractions.

BRNO

BRNO is the Czech Republic's second-largest city after Prague and is enlivened by a large student population. After the milling tourist crowds of Prague, Brno can feel like a refreshing dose of real life. In the nineteenth century it was a major textile centre and known as "rakousky Manchestr" (Austrian Manchester). Between the wars the city enjoyed a cultural boom, heralded by the 1928 Exhibition of Contemporary Culture, which provided an impetus for much of the city's pioneering functionalist architecture. After the war, Brno's German-speakers (one quarter of the population) were sent packing on foot to Vienna. Capital fled with the capitalists and centralized state funds were diverted to Prague and Bratislava.

What to see and do

Zelný trh

Though it's known as the "cabbage market", you'll find a notable lack of cabbages here. A wonderfully evocative vegetable market on a sloping cobbled square, with a huge fountain at its centre, this is a colourful place for an amble.

The Moravian Museum

The **Moravian Museum** (Tues–Sat 9am–5pm) contains a worthy collection of ancient and medieval artefacts.

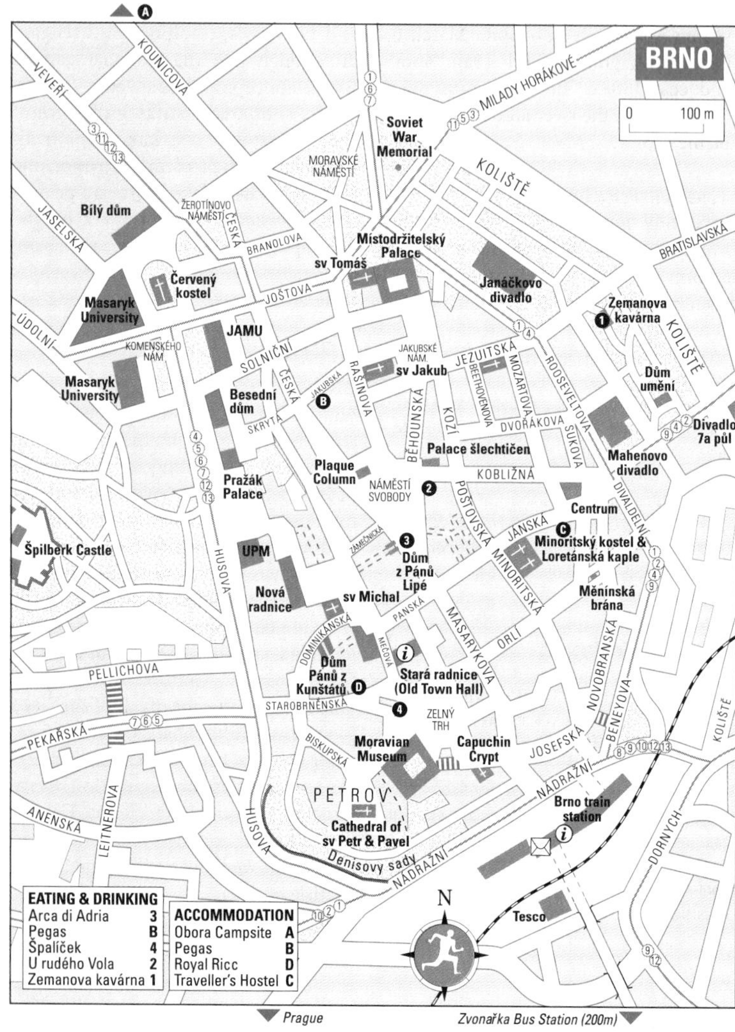

Capuchin Crypt

This eerie **crypt** (March–Sept Mon–Sat 9am–noon & 2–4.30pm, Sun 11–11.45am & 2–4.30pm; Oct–Feb closed Mon), in the Capuchin church, houses a gruesome collection of mummified dead monks and dignitaries.

The Old Town Hall

Clearly visible from Zelný trh is the **Old Town Hall**. Anton Pilgram's Gothic doorway is its best feature: the thistly pinnacle above the statue of Justice is symbolically twisted – Pilgram's revenge on the town aldermen who short-changed him for his work. Inside, the courtyards and passageways are jam-packed with tour groups, most of them here to see the so-called **Brno dragon** (actually a stuffed crocodile) and the *Brno Wheel*, made in 1636 by a cartwright from nearby Lednice. The **tower**

MUTĚNICE WINE REGION

Famous for its award-winning wines, a product of the fertile Moravian soil, this region makes an unusual day-trip from Brno. You'll need to a willingness to stray from the beaten track and a Czech dictionary, but the rewards are a real insight into the largely tourist-free Moravian countryside. The best way to taste the best of the region's wines is to visit Vinařská, a wine "settlement" in the village of Mutěnice (Ⓦwww.mutenice.cz/welcome-in-mutenice/). From Prague, take the bus towards Hodoní from Zvonařka main station (about a ten-minute walk south of the train station).

(April–Sept daily 9am–5pm) is worth the climb for the panorama across the red-tiled rooftops.

Cathedral of SS Peter and Paul

Southwest of the square, the Petrov hill – on which the **Cathedral of SS Peter and Paul** stands – is one of the best places to escape from the streets below. The cathedral's needle-sharp Gothic spires dominate the skyline for miles around, but close up, the crude nineteenth-century rebuilding has made it a lukewarm affair.

UPM

On the western edge of the city centre, the **UPM** Museum of Applied Arts at Husova 14 (Wed–Sun 10am–6/7pm) contains one of the country's best collections of applied art, displaying everything from medieval textiles to swirling Art Nouveau vases; it also hosts excellent temporary shows.

Pražák Palace

Pražák Palace (Wed–Sun 10am–6/7pm) offers an impressive cross-section of twentieth-century Czech art.

Špilberk Castle

Špilberk Castle was one of the worst prisons in the Habsburg Empire, and later a Gestapo jail; the dungeons (daily 9am–5/6pm; Ⓦwww.spilberk.cz) are open to the public, while the city museum (May–Sept Tues–Sun 9am–6pm; April & Oct Tues–Sun 9am–5pm; Nov–March Wed–Sun 10am–5pm) occupies the upper floors.

Arrival and information

Air Brno airport, served by budget carrier Ryanair, is 220km southeast of Prague; from the airport, take bus #76 to the main bus station.

Train and bus Brno's main train and bus stations sit close together, on the edge of the city centre; the train station has lockers and a 24-hour left-luggage office.

Tourist office Old Town Hall at Radnická 8 (April–Sept Mon–Fri 8.30am–6pm, Sat & Sun 9am–5.30pm; Oct–March Mon–Fri 9am–6pm, Sat 9am–5.30pm, Sun 9am–3pm; Ⓣ542 211 089, Ⓦwww.ticbrno.cz).

City transport

It's an easy walk to all the sights but if you do want to take a tram it's 8Kč for a 10-minute ticket (plenty of time to get anywhere in the city centre) and 13Kč for a 40-minute ticket. You'll need to pay a half-fare for your bag, too, if it's bulky. Buy your ticket from one of the yellow machines or kiosks near the stop and validate it on board.

Accommodation

Obora Campsite Ⓦwww.autocampobora.cz. A fifteen-minute bus ride (#103) from Brno, in a valley near the lake. ❶

Pegas Jakubská 4 Ⓣ542 210 104, Ⓦwww.hotelpegas.cz. Central hotel with clean, comfortable rooms and its own microbrewery. ❾

Royal Ricc Starobrněská 10 Ⓣ542 219 262, Ⓦwww.romantichotels.cz. Especially welcoming and ideally located with comfortable rooms. ❾

Traveller's Hostel Jánská 22 Ⓣ542 213 573, Ⓦwww.travellers.cz. Centrally located, clean, modern hostel. ❷

Eating and drinking

Arca di Adria Náměstí Svobody 17. A popular Italian-run café serving great pizzas and ice cream. Mains 150–200Kč.
Pegas see p.297. Moravia's first microbrewery, now one of the biggest in the Czech Republic.
Špalíček Zelný trh. Tables outside in summer and lashings of the local Starobrno beer. Mains from 69Kč.
U rudého vola Kobližná 2. Elegant restaurant with a peaceful arcaded patio under a glass roof. Service can be slow. Mains 100–225Kč.
Zemanova kavárna Park Koliště. An exact replica of Fuchs' functionalist café of 1923: a place to see and be seen. Coffee and cakes 123Kč.

Moving on

Train Blansko (3 daily, 30min); Olomouc (up to 7 daily; 1hr 25min).
Bus Blansko (3 daily, 30min); Olomouc (hourly; 1hr 20min–1hr 50min).

OLOMOUC

Once capital of Moravia and seat of the bishopric, **Olomouc** (pronounced "olla-moats") has a lot going for it: a fine old town, spacious cobbled squares and a plethora of Baroque fountains, not to mention a healthy quota of university students and a few interesting festivals. The Staré Město is a strange contorted shape, squeezed in the middle by an arm of the Morava.

What to see and do

In the western half of the old town, all roads lead to the city's two central squares, which are hinged to one another at right angles. The irregular Horní náměstí has an astronomical clock – a modern reconstruction of the original, which was destroyed in World War II.

Olomouc is justly proud of its **fountains**. Hercules, in Horní náměstí, is the symbolic protector of the town, holding the Olomouc eagle in his hand. Also in this square is Julius Caesar, accompanied by a sitting dog and the river gods Moravus and Danubius, emblems of loyalty, and the modern Arion fountain, representing justice. The Neptune Fountain in Dolní náměstí stands for the fertility of Moravian soil.

The Holy Trinity Column and the Moravian Theatre

Big enough to house a (usually locked) chapel at its base, the **Holy Trinity Column** to the west of the town hall is the country's largest plague column. Plague columns are found all over the Czech Republic; monuments in honour of the Virgin Mary, their purpose is to give thanks for sparing the patrons from the plague – as in this case – or some other catastrophe.

Set into the west facade of Horní náměstí is the **Moravian Theatre**, where Mahler spent a brief spell as Kapellmeister.

Sv Michál

Two of the city's best-looking backstreets, Školní and Michalská, lead southeast from Horní náměstí up to the church of **sv Michál**, plain on the outside but inside clad in a masterly excess of Baroque.

Panna Maria Sněžná

Firmly wedged between the two sections of the old town is the Jesuit church of **Panna Maria Sněžná**, deemed particularly necessary in a city where Protestantism had spread like wildfire in the sixteenth century.

Cathedral of sv Václav

Three blocks east of náměstí Republiky, the **Cathedral of sv Václav** started life as a Romanesque basilica, though the current structure is mostly nineteenth-century neo-Gothic. However, the walls and pillars of the nave are prettily painted in Romanesque style. The **crypt** (Tues & Thurs–Sat 9am–5pm, Wed 9am–4pm, Sun 11am–5pm) holds a macabre display of gory reliquaries.

THE MORAVIAN KARST REGION

Lying 25km northeast of Brno, the **Moravian karst** is a region of rolling fields, forests and limestone hills. Over thousands of years the limestone has eroded, creating deep and dramatic caves: you can take guided tours of some at **Skalnū Mlżn** – catch an early morning train from Brno to Blansko and then hop on a connecting bus. If you don't make the bus it's a beautiful 8km hike through the beech woods: follow the green and white waymarkers from outside the train station. Tickets for the caves are sold at the Skalní Mlýn ticket office. Following the stream for another kilometre (or taking the Eko-train), you'll come to **Punkevnū** (Mon 10am–3.50pm, Tues–Sun 8.20am–5pm; closed Mon in winter; closes 2–3hr earlier in winter; ⓦwww.cavemk.cz), the most dramatic cave, with an underground boat ride. Back at the ticket office there's a **hotel**, **café** and **bike rental**.

Arrival and information

Train The station is 1.5km east of the Staré Město; on arrival take any tram heading west up Masarykova and get off after three or four stops; **Bus** The bus station is further out, and connected to the centre by tram #4.
Tourist office In the town hall (daily 9am–7pm; ⓣ585 513 385, ⓦwww.olomouc-tourism.cz); can book private rooms.

Accommodation

Hotel Arigone Univerzitní 20 ⓣ585 232 351, ⓦwww.arigone.cz. Pleasant rooms in a gorgeous little backstreet leading to Horní Náměstí. ❺
Na hradě Michalskská 4 ⓣ585 203 231, ⓦwww.penzionnahrade.cz. Welcoming staff and a central but quiet location with pleasant, modern rooms. ❼

Eating and drinking

Caesar Horní náměstí. In the cobbled vaults under the town hall, this is a popular, atmospheric pizzeria. Mains 56–156Kč.
Café Mahler Horní náměstí 11. Wonderful location by the Caesar Fountain on Horní náměstí, where you can people-watch and try a tantalizing range of ice cream.
Maruška Horní náměstí. Vast menu of Czech/International fare, including vegetarian options. Mains 130–460Kč.
U červeného volka Dolní Náměstí. Reasonably priced Czech/Italian dishes, plus a wide range of veggie dishes. Mains 79–105Kč.

Moving on

Train Brno (5 daily; 1hr 30min); Ostrava (daily; 1hr 30min.
Bus Brno (up to 15 daily; 1hr 30min); Ostrava (daily, 2hr).

Denmark

HIGHLIGHTS

SKAGEN: sample fantastic seafood and world-class art at this lovely seaside resort

ÅRHUS NIGHTLIFE: Denmark's second city buzzes with a mixture of live music and trendy riverside bars

NY CARLSBERG GLYPTOTEK: Copenhagen's finest gallery houses a jaw-dropping collection of art

VIKING SHIP MUSEUM, ROSKILDE: take to the seas on board a Viking longboat

ODENSE: quaint, cobbled and home to Denmark's biggest literary export – Hans Christian Andersen

ROUGH COSTS

DAILY BUDGET Basic €30/ with occasional treat €50

DRINK Carlsberg (pint) €4.75

FOOD *Pølser* (Danish hot dog) €3

HOSTEL/BUDGET HOTEL €17/€40

TRAVEL train: Copenhagen–Århus (210km) €42; bus: €33

FACT FILE

POPULATION 5.4 million

AREA 43,094 sq km

LANGUAGE Danish

CURRENCY Danish krone (kr)

CAPITAL Copenhagen (population 1.7million)

INTERNATIONAL PHONE CODE ⓣ45

Basics

According to a 2006 survey, Denmark is the happiest place to live on the planet. It certainly seems that way when you meet the locals – Danes are some of the most gregarious people you are likely to meet, with an instinctive sense of fun and even a special word (*hygge*) to describe the art of creating a cosy, convivial atmosphere. Add to that an efficient transport infrastructure, pristine environment and the fact that everything you find, from a chair to an office block, seems to be designed to perfection, and the survey begins to make perfect sense (in case you were wondering, the US came 23rd and Britain 41st).

Wedged between mainland Europe and Scandinavia, Denmark has preserved a distinct national identity, exemplified by the universally cherished royal family and the reluctance to fully integrate with the EU (the Danish rejection of the euro was more about sovereignty than economics). There's also a sense of a small country that has long punched above its weight; it once controlled much of northern Europe and still maintains close ties with Greenland, its former colony.

Geographically, three main landmasses make up the country – the islands of **Zealand** and Funen and the peninsula of Jutland, which extends northwards from Germany. Most visitors make for Zealand (Sjælland), and, more specifically, **Copenhagen**, an exciting focal point with a beautiful old centre, a good array of museums and a boisterous nightlife. **Funen** (Fyn) has only one real urban draw, **Odense**, once home to Hans Christian Andersen; otherwise, it's renowned for cute villages and sandy beaches. **Jutland** (Jylland) has, as well as some varied scenery, ranging from soft green hills to desolate heathlands, **Århus** and **Aalborg**, two of the liveliest Danish cities.

CHRONOLOGY

400 BC "Tollund Man", a body found preserved in a bog in 1950, provides evidence of habitation during the Iron Age.
500 AD First mention of the "Dani" tribe is made by foreign sources.
695 First Christian mission to Denmark.
825 First Danish coinage introduced.
1397 The Union of Kalmar unites Denmark, Sweden and Norway under a single Danish monarch.
1523 Sweden leaves the Kalmar Union.
1536 Religious Reformation leads to the establishment of the Danish Lutheran Church.
1629 Sweden heavily defeats Charles IV's Denmark in the Thirty Years' War, resulting in losses of Danish territory.
1814 Denmark cedes Norway to Sweden.
1836 Hans Christian Andersen writes "The Little Mermaid".
1849 Constitutional monarchy is established.
1864 Defeat by Prussia results in the loss of much territory.
1914 Neutrality is adopted during WWI.
1918 The vote is granted to all Danes.
1934 Children's playtime is transformed by the invention of Lego by Ole Kirk Christiansen.
1940 Nazi invasion meets minimal resistance.
1945 Denmark is liberated by Allied forces.
1979 Greenland is given greater autonomy by the Danish.
1989 First European country to legalise same-sex marriages.
2004 Crown Prince Frederick marries Australian Mary Donaldson in a lavish ceremony.
2006 Cartoon depictions of the Prophet Mohammed in Danish newpapers spark mass protests in the Muslim world.

ARRIVAL

The vast majority of visitors arrive in Copenhagen, either flying in to its gleaming **Kastrup Airport** or pulling in to the city's **Central Station**, connected with the European rail network via Germany

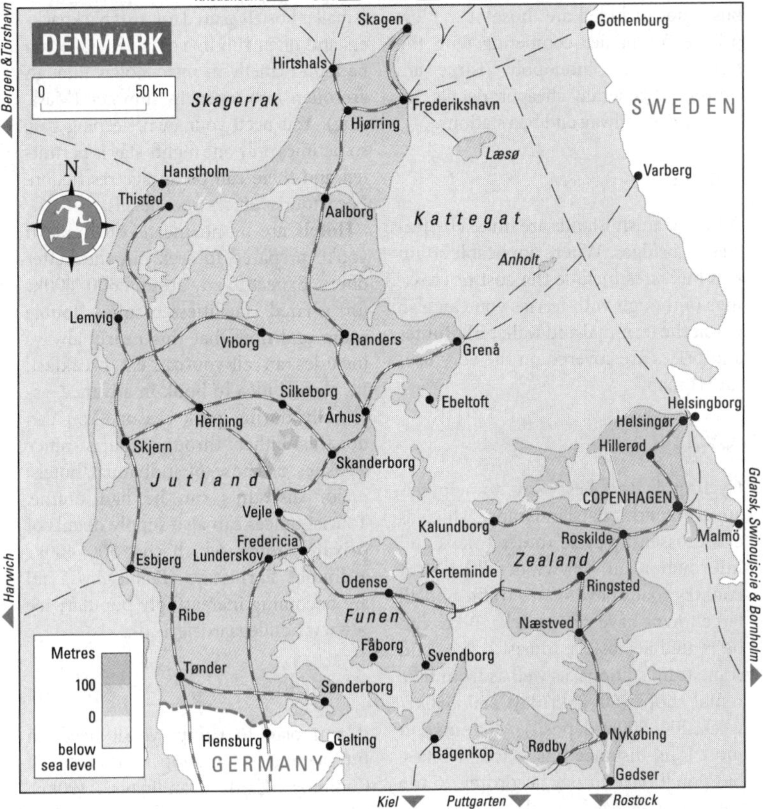

and, across the spectacular Oresund bridge, to Sweden. Most international bus routes also arrive at Central Station. In addition, Denmark's four **regional airports** – Aalborg, Århus, Billund and Esbjerg – handle a growing number of budget flights mostly operated by Ryanair or Sterling. There are regular **ferry services** to and from the UK (via Esbjerg) and Sweden and Norway (both via Frederikshavn or Hirtshals).

GETTING AROUND

Denmark has swift and easy-to-use **public transport.** Danish State Railways (Danske Statsbaner or DSB; Ⓦwww.dsb.dk) runs an exhaustive and reliable **rail** network co-run on some stretches by private companies and supplemented by a few privately owned rail lines. Train types range from the large intercity expresses *(Lyntog)* to smaller local trains *(regionaltog).* **InterRail**, Eurail and **Scanrail** passes are valid on all DSB trains, with reduced rates on most privately owned lines. Ticket prices are worked out according to a countrywide zonal system and travel by local transport within the zone of departure and arrival is included in the price. Everywhere not served by train can be easily reached via the bus network, which often supplements the train timetable. Some are operated privately, some by DSB itself and railcards are valid. DSB **timetables** or *Køreplan* (free) detail train, bus and ferry services, including the S-train and Metro systems in Copenhagen. The only buses not included are those of the few private companies competing with the state-controlled monopoly. These are slower but generally cheaper; details can be found at railway and bus stations.

Ferries

All the Danish islands are linked by **ferries** or bridges. Where applicable, train and bus fares include the cost of crossings (although with ferries you can also pay at the terminal and walk on). Routes and prices are covered on the very useful HI map.

Cycling

Cycling is the best way to appreciate Denmark's flat landscape, which is crisscrossed by cycle routes (maps and information at Ⓦwww.dcf.dk). Most country roads have sparse traffic and all large towns have cycle tracks. Bikes can be rented at hostels, tourist offices and some train stations, as well as from bike rental shops (50–75kr/day, 250–350kr/week; 200–500kr deposit). All trains and most long-distance buses accept bikes, but you'll have to pay according to the zonal system used to calculate passenger tickets – 50kr to take your bike from Copenhagen to Århus by train with 20kr on top if you want to reserve a space in advance; 80kr by bus.

ACCOMMODATION

Accommodation is a major expense when travelling in Denmark, although there is a wide network of good-quality **hostels**. Most have a choice of private rooms, often with en-suite toilets and showers, as well as dorm accommodation; nearly all have cooking facilities. Rates are around 130kr per person for a dorm bed; non-HI members pay an extra 35kr a night (160kr for a one-year HI membership). Danhostel Danmarks Vandrerhjem (Ⓦwww.danhostel.dk) produces a free hostel guide. For a similar price, **sleep-ins** (smaller hostels geared towards backpackers and often run by volunteer staff) can be found chiefly in major towns though are often only open in summer (May–Aug). You need your own sleeping bag, sometimes only one night's stay is permitted and there can be an age restriction. Local tourist offices have details.

Hotels are by no means off-limits if you're prepared to seek out the better offers. Expect to pay around 500–600kr for shared facilities/en-suite double room and note that this nearly always includes an all-you-can-eat breakfast. It's a good idea to book in advance, especially during peak season. You can do this either through tourist-office websites or those of individual hotels; major discounts can be had online. Tourist offices can also supply details of **private rooms**, which cost 300–400kr a double. **Farmstays** *(Bondegårdsferie)* are becoming increasingly popular; see Ⓦwww.bondegaardsferie.dk.

Camping

If you plan to **camp**, you'll need an International Camping Card, or a Camping Card Scandinavia (90kr), which is available at official campsites. A Transit Pass (25kr) can be used for a single overnight stay. Most campsites are open April to September, while a few stay open all year. There's a rigid **grading system**: one-star sites have toilets and at least one shower; two-stars also have basic cooking facilities and a food shop within 2km; three-stars include a laundry and a TV-room, four-stars also have a shop, while five-stars include a cafeteria. Prices are around 55–65kr per person. Many campsites also have **cabins** to rent, usually with cooking facilities, for 2000kr–4000kr per week for a six-berth place, although they are often fully booked in summer. Tourist offices offer a free leaflet listing all sites. **Camping rough** without permission is illegal, and an on-the-spot fine may be imposed.

FOOD AND DRINK

Traditional **Danish food** is characterised by rather stodgy meat/fish and two veg combos, although the quality of ingredients is usually excellent. Specialities worth seeking out include *stegt flæsk med persille sovs* (thinly sliced fried pork with boiled potatoes and a creamy parsley sauce) and the classic *røget skild* (smoked herring). **Breakfast** (*morgenmad*) is usually a treat, with almost all hotels and hostels offering a sumptuous spread of cereals, freshly made bread, cheese, ham, fruit juice, milk, coffee and tea, for around 40–60kr (if not included in the price of the room). **Brunch**, served in most cafés from 11am until mid-afternoon, is a popular and filling option for late starters and costs 60–120kr. A traditional **lunch** (*frokost*) is *smørrebrød* – slices of rye bread heaped with meat, fish or cheese, and assorted trimmings – sold for 15–35kr a piece and very filling. An excellent-value set lunch can usually be found at restaurants and *bodegas* (bars that sell no-frills food). *Tilbud* is the "special", *dagens ret* the "dish of the day", and you can expect to pay around 60kr for these, or 80–120kr for a three-course set lunch.

For daytime **snacks**, there are hot dog stands (*pølsevogn*) on all main streets and at train stations, serving hot dogs (*pølser*), toasted ham and cheese sandwiches (*parisertoast*) and chips (*pommes frites*). Bakeries and cafés sell Danish pastries (*wienerbrød*), tastier and much less sweet than the imitations sold abroad. Restaurants are pretty expensive for dinner (reckon on 120–150kr) but you can usually find a Middle Eastern or Thai place offering **buffets** for around 80–100kr. Kebab shops are also very common and often serve pizza slices for around 30kr. If you plan to save money by **self-catering**, head for Netto or Fakta supermarkets, where the food and drink are good value.

Drinking

The most sociable places to **drink** are pubs (variously known as a *værtshus*, *bar* or *bodega*) and cafés, where the emphasis is on lager. The cheapest is bottled – the so-called gold **beer** (Guldøl or Elefantøl; 25–35kr/bottle) is the strongest. Draught lager (Fadøl) is more expensive and a touch weaker, but tastes fresher. The most common brands are Carlsberg and Tuborg although small independent breweries are beginning to make their mark. Most international **wines** (from 40kr) and **spirits** (20–40kr) are widely available. There are many varieties of **schnapps** including the potent Aalborg-made Aquavit.

CULTURE AND ETIQUETTE

Denmark is one of the most liberal and tolerant countries on earth, despite a recent political swing to the right, and you are unlikely to run into cultural problems. One thing to bear in mind is that the Danish language doesn't have a specific word for "please" so don't be upset if Danes leave it out when conversing with you in English (which most Danes speak almost perfectly). When wandering about make sure you don't stray into the cycle lanes alongside most roads and note that locals will wait for the green "walk" light at pedestrian crossings even when there isn't a car in sight.

Tipping is not expected as service charges are included in hotel, restaurant and bar bills; however, if you think you've had particularly good service it's not unheard of to leave a few kroner. Note that smoking was banned in public places including most bars, cafés and restaurants in August 2007.

SPORTS AND OUTDOOR ACTIVITIES

With over 1,600 registered clubs, football (soccer) is far and away the most popular sport in Denmark. The biggest teams are FC Copenhagen and Brøndby (both from the capital) who play in the twelve-team Superliga (Ⓦwww.dbu.dk). As for outdoor activities, things are pretty low-key although there is a series of cycle routes and hiking paths (Ⓦwww.dvl.dk) and watersports are always an option thanks to Denmark's spotlessly clean beaches and waterways; ask at tourist offices for details of safe places to swim.

COMMUNICATIONS

Post offices are open Mon–Fri 9.30/10am–5/6pm and Sat 9.30/10am–noon/2pm, with reduced hours in smaller communities. You can also buy stamps from most newsagents. Coin-operated **phones** are white and require a minimum of 3kr for a local call (they swallow one of the coins if the number is engaged), and 5kr for international calls; **phonecards** for the blue phones (which are a little cheaper) come as 30kr, 50kr and 100kr. The operator number is Ⓣ118 (domestic), Ⓣ113 (international) – both 8kr/min. **Internet access** is free at most libraries and some tourist offices, and most towns have cybercafés.

EMERGENCIES

You're unlikely to have much contact with **police**, as street crime and hassle are minimal; however you'll find them helpful and most speak English. For **prescriptions**, doctors' consultations and dental work – but not hospital visits – you have to pay on the spot.

INFORMATION & MAPS

Most places have a **tourist office** that can help with accommodation. They're open daily, with long hours, in the most popular spots, but have reduced hours from October to March. All airports and many train stations also offer a hotel booking service. A good general **map** is by *Hallwag*, but the HI Association map is also excellent and available free at Ⓦwww.danhostel.dk.

> **EMERGENCY NUMBERS**
>
> All emergencies Ⓣ112.

MONEY AND BANKS

Currency is the **krone** (plural *kroner*), made up of 100 øre. It comes in notes of 50kr, 100kr, 200kr, 500kr and 1000kr, and coins of 25øre, 50øre, 1kr, 2kr, 5kr, 10kr and 20kr. **Banking hours** are Mon–Fri 9.30/10am–4pm, Thurs till 5.30/6pm. Banks are plentiful and are the easiest place to **exchange cash** and travellers' cheques although they charge 30kr per transaction. Forex bureaux charge only 20kr to exchange cash and 10kr per travellers' cheque but are scarce. Most airports and ferry terminals have late-opening exchange facilities, and ATMs are widespread. At the time of writing, €1 was equal to 7.5kr, $1 to 5.5kr and £1 to 11kr.

OPENING HOURS AND HOLIDAYS

Standard **shop hours** are Mon–Fri 9.30/10am–5.30/7pm, Sat 9/9.30am–2/5pm. All shops and banks are closed, and public transport and many museums run to Sunday schedules on **public holidays**: Jan 1; Maundy Thurs to Easter Mon; Prayer Day (4th Fri after Easter);

> **DENMARK ON THE NET**
>
> Ⓦ**www.visitdenmark.com** Excellent Danish tourist board site.
> Ⓦ**www.useit.dk** For budget travellers; focuses mainly on Copenhagen.
> Ⓦ**www.cphpost.dk** News and reviews from the *Copenhagen Post*, the capital's English-language weekly.
> Ⓦ**www.aok.dk** Listings for most of Zealand.
> Ⓦ**www.visitcopenhagen.com** Official Copenhagen tourist site.
> Ⓦ**www.rejseplanen.dk** Public transport journey planner (with English-language option).

STUDENT AND YOUTH DISCOUNTS

Your ISIC card will get you between thirty and fifty percent off most museum and gallery admission prices, although bear in mind free entry is often available on Wednesdays and Sundays. If you're staying long-term a DSB Wildcard (175kr) offers 50 percent off train fares for a year (Ⓦ www.dsb.dk).

Ascension (40th day after Easter); Whit Sun & Mon; Constitution Day (June 5); Dec 24 (pm only); Dec 25 & 26. On **International Workers' Day**, May 1, many offices and shops close at noon.

Danish

	Danish	Pronunciation
Yes	*Ja*	Ya
No	*Nej*	Nye
Please	*Vær så venlig*	Verso venly
Thank you	*Tak*	Tagg
Hello/Good day	*Goddag*	Go-dah
Goodbye	*Farvel*	Fah-vell
Excuse me	*Undskyld*	Unsgul
Good	*God*	Gouth
Bad	*Dårlig*	Dohli
Near	*Nær*	Neh-a
Far	*Fjern*	Fee-ann
Cheap	*Billig*	Billie
Expensive	*Dyr*	Duy-a
Open	*Åben*	Oh-ben
Closed	*Lukket*	Lohggeth
Ticket	*billet*	bill-led
Today	*Idag*	Ee-dah
Yesterday	*Igår*	Ee-goh...
Tomorrow	*Imorgen*	Ee-mon
How much is....?	*Hvad koster....?*	Vath kosta....?
I'd like...	*Jeg vil gerne ha...*	yai vay gerna ha
What time is it?	*Hvad er klokken?*	Vath ea cloggen?
Where is....?	*Hvor er.....?*	Voa ea...?
A table for...	*et bord till*	et boa te...
I don't understand	*Jeg forstår ikke*	Yai fusto igge
Do you speak English?	*Taler de engelsk?*	Tayla dee engellsgg?
One	*En*	Ehn
Two	*To*	Toh
Three	*Tre*	Tray
Four	*Fire*	Fee-a
Five	*Fem*	Fem
Six	*Sex*	Segs
Seven	*Syv*	Syu
Eight	*Otte*	Oddeh
Nine	*Ni*	Nee
Ten	*Ti*	Tee

Copenhagen

COPENHAGEN (København) is one of Europe's most user-friendly capitals: welcoming and compact, with a centre largely given over to pedestrians. First-rate galleries, museums and summertime street entertainers fill your days, while by night the live music and intimate bar and club scene are rivalled only by those on offer in Århus.

Until the twelfth century, when **Bishop Absalon** built a castle on Christiansborg's present site there was little more than a tiny fishing settlement to be found here. Trade and prosperity flourished with the introduction of the Sound Toll on vessels in the Øresund, and the city became the Baltic's principal harbour, earning the name **København** ("merchant's port"). By 1443 it had become the Danish capital. A century later, Christian IV created Rosenborg Slot, Rundetårn and the districts of Nyboder and Christianshavn, and in 1669 Frederik III graced the city with its first royal palace, Amalienborg.

What to see and do

The historic core of the city is **Slotsholmen**, originally the site of the twelfth-century castle and now home to the huge Christiansborg complex. Just over the Slotsholmen Kanal to the north is the medieval maze of **Indre By** ("inner city"), while to the south the island of **Christianshaven** is dotted with cutting-edge architecture as well as the alternative enclave of **Christiania**. Northeast of Indre By are the royal quarters of Kongens Have and **Frederiksstaden**, while to the west the expansive Radhuspladsen leads via the Tivoli Gardens to Central Station and the hotspots of **Vesterbro** and **Nørrebro**.

Tivoli Gardens

Just off hectic Vesterbrogade outside the station is Copenhagen's most famous attraction, the elegant **Tivoli Gardens** (mid-April to mid-Sept Sun–Thurs 11am–11pm, Fri–Sat 11am–midnight; mid-Nov to end Dec closes one hour earlier; Ⓦwww.tivoli.dk; 79kr), an entertaining mixture of landscaped grounds, outdoor concerts (every Fri) and white-knuckle thrills. You'll probably hear it before you see it thanks to its high perimeter walls and the constant screams from the roller coasters (multi-ride tickets 200kr).

Ny Carlsberg Glyptotek

Founded by Carslberg tycoon Carl Jacobsen, the **Ny Carlsberg Glyptotek** (Tues–Sun 10am–4pm; 50kr, Sun free; Ⓦwww.glyptoteket.dk) is Copenhagen's finest gallery. There's a knockout selection of Greek and Roman sculpture on the first floor as well as some excellent examples of modern European art, including Degas casts, Monet's *The Lemon Grove* and works by Gauguin, Toulouse-Lautrec and Van Gogh upstairs. Wind up your visit with a slice of delicious cake in the gallery café facing the delightful winter garden.

Vesterbro

Directly behind the train station begins **Vesterbro**, Copenhagen's red-light district and one of the hippest areas in the city. It's home to a great selection of shops, bars and restaurants as well as the diverting **Københavns Bymuseum** at Vesterbrogade 59 (City Museum; 10am–4pm; closed Tues, late opening Wed; Ⓦwww.bymuseum.dk), which covers the history of the city. While the area is perfectly safe to walk around, day and night, male travellers may want to give Istegade a wide berth later in the evening to avoid being propositioned.

The Carlsberg Visitors Centre

"Probably the best beer in the world" goes the ad slogan. Well, you can decide for yourself at the **Carslberg Visitors**

Centre (Tues–Sun 10am–4pm; 40kr, students 25kr; ⓦwww.visitcarlsberg.dk) along Gamle Carlsberg Vej (buses #6a and #26). As well as learning how to create the perfect pint at the Jacobsen Brewhouse, you also get to sample two beers from a choice of Carlsberg, Tuborg and Jacobsen brews.

Strøget and Indre By

Beyond Rådhuspladsen and its impressive town hall, pedestrianized **Strøget** leads into the heart of **Indre By**. This is Denmark's premier shopping area, with the likes of Prada and Hermes jostling for space with the ubiquitous H&M and local giant, Illums Bolighus. There are plenty of affordable independent boutiques running off the arterial streets. About halfway along Strøget and hard to miss thanks to its pink neon lights, the **Museum Erotica** at Købmagergade 24 (May–Sept 10am–11pm; Oct–April Sun–Thurs 11am–8pm, Fri & Sat 10am–10pm; 89kr), is worth a peek for its suprisingly studious account of the history of sex from the kama sutra to Paris Hilton DVDs. Strøget ends at **Kongens Nytorv**, the city's largest square, where you'll find an equestrian statue of Copenhagen's founder, Christian V, in the centre and some of the best hotdog stalls in town.

The Rundetaarn

One of the capital's quirkiest sights, the 42-metre-high **Rundetaarn** (Round Tower; Sept–May Mon–Sat 10am–5pm, Sun noon–5pm; June–Aug Mon–Sat 10am–8pm, Sun noon–8pm; 25kr; ⓦwww.rundetaarn.dk) dominates the skyline northwest of Strøget in the city's university or latin quarter. Built as an observatory under the auspices of Christian IV and finished in 1642, the main attraction is the view from the top reached via a 209-metre spiral walkway. It's still a functioning observatory and you can view the night sky through its astronomical telescope during winter (Tues & Wed 7–10pm).

Nørrebro

Formerly a rather edgy area like Vesterbro, **Nørrebro**, northwest across the canal from Indre By, has undergone something of a renaissance in recent years and is now crammed with cafés, bars and clubs centred around the Sankt Hans Torv square. It's also worth wandering around by day, particularly for the **Assistens Kirkegård**, a cemetery which locals use as a park in summer. Among its famous permanent residents are Hans Christian Andersen and the philosopher Søren Kirkegaard.

Nyhavn

Running from Kongens Nytorv, a slender canal divides the two sides of **Nyhavn** ("new harbour"), picturesquely lined by colourful eighteenth-century houses – now bars and cafés – and thronged with tourists in summer.

Frederiksstaden

Just north of Nyhavn, the royal district of **Frederiksstaden** centres on cobbled

COPENHAGEN ON A BUDGET

Copenhagen can be a tricky place to get by on a budget but with a bit of planning you can make the most of your wallet. Museums with **free admission** include the National Museum, the Museum of the Danish Resistance and the Statens Museum for Kunst (National Gallery) while many others offer free entry one day per week. You should also consider buying a CPHCARD (see p.313) for free entry to many attractions. As for getting around, you can walk or cycle to most places of interest and there are also **cheap boat tours** available with Netto boats (regular departures from Heibergsgade, Nyhavn; 10am–5pm; 30kr; ⓦwww.havnerundfart.dk) taking in the same sights as the more expensive tours.

Amalienborg Slotsplads, home to the four identical **Amalienborg** royal palaces. Two remain as royal residences, and there's a changing of the guard at noon, if the monarch is at home. In the opposite direction is the great marble dome of **Frederikskirken**, also known as "Marmorkirken" or marble church (Mon–Thurs 10am–5pm, Fri–Sun noon–5pm; free), which was modelled on St Peter's in Rome. Further along Bredgade, a German armoured car commandeered by the Danes to bring news of the Nazi surrender marks the entrance to the **Frihedsmuseet** (Museum of the Danish Resistance Movement; Tues–Sat 10am–4pm, Sun 10am–5pm; free).

The Little Mermaid

Just north of the Kastellet fortress, on a corner overlooking the harbour, sits the diminutive **Little Mermaid**, a magnet for tourists since her unveiling in 1913. A bronze statue of a Hans Christian Andersen character, it was sculpted by Edvard Eriksen and paid for by the

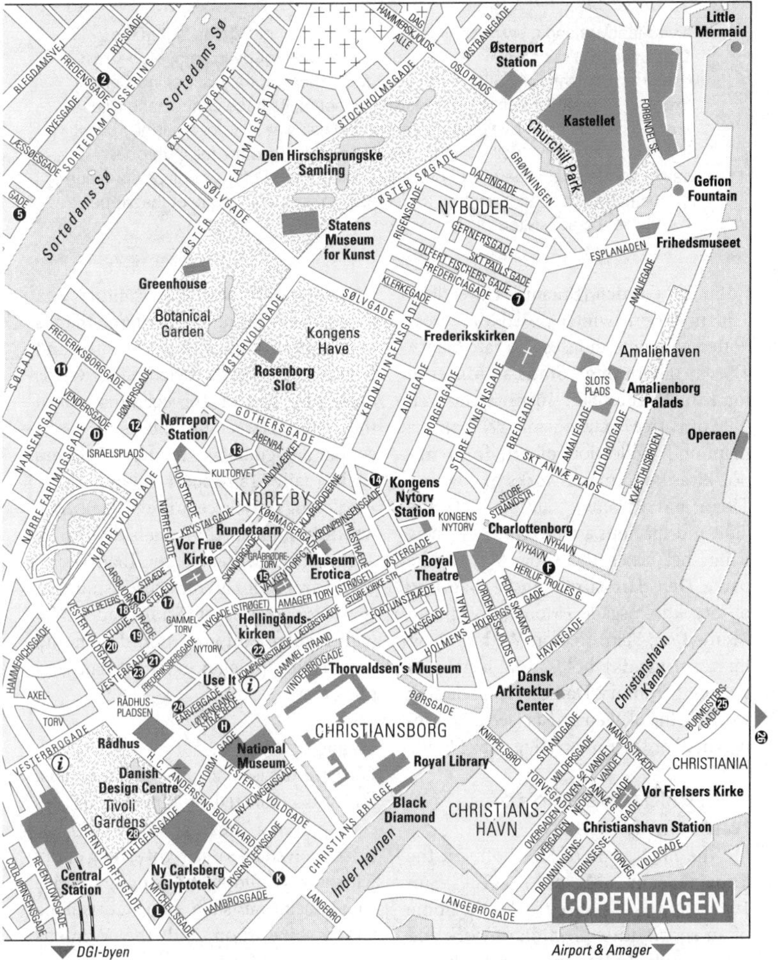

founder of the Carlsberg brewery. Over the years she's been the victim of several attacks, having her head and arms chopped off and even blown up by a bomb in 2003, but she remains the most enduring symbol of the city.

Kongens Have and Rosenborg Slot

Kongens Have is the city's oldeset public park and a popular spot for picnics. Within the park at 4a Østre Voldgade is the fairytale **Rosenborg Slot** (May–Oct daily 10/11am–3/5pm; Nov–April Tues–Sun 11am–2pm; 60kr) which served as the main residence of Christian IV. The main building includes the furnished rooms used by the regal occupants, although the highlight is the downstairs treasury, where the **crown jewels** and rich accessories worn by Christian IV are on display.

The Botanical Garden and art galleries

On the west side of Kongens Have is the

TREAT YOURSELF

If you fancy taking a swim or simply unwinding after hitting the sights the **DGI-byen** leisure complex (Ⓣ33.29.81.40, Ⓦwww.dgi-byen.com; Mon–Thurs 6.30am–midnight, Fri 6.30am–7pm, Sat & Sun 9am–5pm), just behind Central Station is a great spot in which to kill a few hours. Its huge centrepiece ellipse-shaped pool is rarely overcrowded and good value at 52kr for a full-day pass. If you want to really spoil yourself, the spa centre offers the full bathrobe, sauna and jacuzzi experience for 245kr (including use of the pool) plus a range of treatments from acupuncture to full-body massages. If none of that appeals then have a crack at ten-pin bowling (from 125kr for an hour).

Botanical Garden (Botanisk Have; daily 8.30am–4/6pm; winter closed Mon; free) dotted with greenhouses and rare plants. The neighbouring **Statens Museum for Kunst** (Tues–Sun 10am–5pm, Wed till 8pm; free; Ⓦwww.smk.dk) holds a mammoth collection of art, from minor Picassos to major works by Matisse, Titian and Rubens – although it's the light and spacious architecture of its new wing that steals the show. Across the park, **Den Hirschsprungske Samling** on Stockholmsgade (Mon & Wed–Sun 11am–4pm; 50kr, free on Wed; Ⓦwww.hirschsprung.dk) holds a collection of twentieth-century Danish art, including work by the Skagen artists (see p.27), renowned for their interesting use of light.

Thorvaldsens and the National Museum

On the north side of Slotsholmen, the **Thorvaldsens Museum** (Tues–Sun 10am–5pm; 20kr, Wed free) is the home of an enormous collection of work and memorabilia (not to mention the body) of Denmark's most famous sculptor, Bertel Thorvaldsen, who lived from 1770 to 1844. A short walk away over the Slotsholmen moat is the **National Museum** (same hours; 50kr, free on Wed; Ⓦwww.natmus.dk), which has excellent displays on Denmark's history from the Ice Age to the present day – including an eye-watering selection of Viking swords and daggers.

Christianshavn

From Christiansborg, a bridge crosses to **Christianshavn**, built by Christian IV in the early sixteenth century and nicknamed "Little Amsterdam" thanks to its small canals, cute bridges and Dutch-style houses. Reaching skywards on the far side of Torvegade is one of the city's most recognizable features, the copper and golden spire of **Vor Frelsers Kirke** (daily 11am/noon–3.30pm; tower April–Aug only; free, tower 20kr). Also worth a look is the canalside **Dansk Arkitektur Center** (daily 10am–5pm; 40kr; free for architecture students, Ⓦwww.dac.dk.), at Strandgade 27B, with regular exhibitions on design and architecture plus an excellent café and bookshop.

Christiania

Christiania is a former barracks area that was colonized by hippies after declaring itself a "free city" in 1971. It has since evolved into a self-governing entity with quirky buildings housing alternative small businesses such as the Christiania Cykler bike shop and the Women's Smithy, as well as shops, cafés, restaurants, music venues, and – famously – an open hash market on Pusherstreet. There are guided tours of the area (July & Aug daily 3pm, rest of the year Sat & Sun only; 30kr; Ⓣ32.95.65.07, Ⓦwww.christiania.org), starting at the main gate by Prinsessegade, but it's just as fun to wander around on your own. Note that no photos are allowed on Pusherstreet.

Arrival

Air Kastrup airport is 11km southeast of the centre, and is served by a mainline train to Central Station (5am–midnight every 10min; midnight–5am hourly;

12min; 28.50kr). It is also linked by metro along the yellow M2 line (useful if you are staying outside the centre).

Train Trains pull into Central Station (Københavns Hovedbanegård or Københavns H on tickets) near Vesterbrogade.

Bus Long-distance buses from elsewhere in Denmark stop either at various points round Central Station or a short bus or S-train ride from the centre.

Boat Ferries dock an S-train ride away north of the centre at Nordhavn.

Information

Tourist office Vesterbrogade 4a, across from Central Station ⓣ70.22.24.42, ⓦwww.visitcopenhagen.com (May–June Mon–Sat 9am–6pm; July & Aug Mon–Sat 9am–8pm, Sun 10am–6pm; Sept–April Mon–Fri 9am–4pm, Sat 9am–2pm. They will book accommodation (including private rooms) for a 100kr fee. Alternatively you can book yourself for free via their website.

Use-It Rådhusstræde 13 ⓣ33.73.06.20, ⓦwww.useit.dk (mid-June to mid-Sept daily 9am–7pm; mid-Sept to mid-June Mon–Wed 11am–4pm, Thurs 11am–6pm, Fri 11am–2pm). Centrally located in the Huset complex this is far better for youth and budget-oriented information. The friendly staff provide poste restante and free Internet access, luggage storage and a useful free magazine, *Playtime*.

Discount cards If you're sightseeing on a tight schedule, consider the CPHCARD (199/429kr for 24/72hr), which is valid for the entire public transport network (including much of eastern Zealand) and gives entry to most museums and attractions in the area. It's available at tourist offices, hotels, travel agents and the train station.

City transport

Metro, S-tog and bus An integrated network of buses, electric S-trains (S-tog) and an expanding metro covers the city (5am–1am); night buses (*natbus*) take over after 1am, and there's a less frequent metro service on Thursday, Friday and Saturday nights. Night fares are double daytime fares. You can get a free route map from stations.

Tickets The cheapest ticket is the *billet* (19kr for two zones), valid for an hour's unlimited travel. You can also buy a *Klippekort* containing ten *billets* (120kr for two zones). Other options include the CPHCARD (see above); the *24-hour billet* (110kr), which covers the same area for 24 hours, but doesn't include admission to museums; and the *Flexicard 7 days* (195kr for two zones). Make sure you stamp *billets* when boarding buses or in machines on station platforms. Single *billets* can be bought on board buses; all other tickets are available at train stations and newsagents. Travelling without a ticket can get you an instant 500kr fine.

Cycling The City Bike scheme (April–Nov; ⓦwww.bycyklen.dk) allows you to borrow bikes from racks across the city for a deposit of 20kr, which is returned when the bike is locked back into any other rack.

Accommodation

Copenhagen has a good selection of **hostels** although most are a little way out from the centre; space is only likely to be a problem in the peak summer months, when you'll have to book in advance or turn up as early as possible to be sure of a place. **Hotels** can be pricey but there are often online deals available and a few cheaper options in the centre. Note that **private rooms** (❸) booked through the tourist office are usually an S-train ride away from the centre. Breakfast is not included in the prices given, unless otherwise stated.

Hostels and sleep-ins

City Public Hostel Absalonsgade 8, Vesterbro ⓣ33.31.20.70, ⓦwww.city-public-hostel.dk. Noisy sixty-bed dorm on the lower floor, less crowded conditions on other levels. Just ten minutes' walk from the train station. Buses #6a and #26 stop close by. May to mid-Aug only ❸; breakfast 20kr.

Danhostel Copenhagen City H C Andersens Boulevard 50 ⓣ33.11.85.85, ⓦwww.dgi-byen.dk/hostel. Priding itself as Europe's largest "designer" youth hostel, this thousand-bed monster is housed in a multi-storey building overlooking the harbour. Rooms come in four-to eight-bed versions. A short walk from Central Station. ❸

Hotel Jørgensen Rømersgade 11 ⓣ33.13.81.86, ⓦwww.hoteljoergensen.dk. Gay-friendly hotel offering good-value dorm accommodation with a buffet breakfast included. A stone's throw from Nørreport station on Israels Plads. ❷

Sleep in Green Ravnsborggade 18, Nørrebro ⓣ35.37.77.77, ⓦwww.sleep-in-green.dk. Eco-friendly hostel (solar power, organic breakfasts etc) with eight-, twenty- and thirty-eight bed dorms (breakfast 40kr). Age limit 35. Ten minutes from the centre by bus #5a or #16, nightbus #81N and #84N. Mid June–end Oct only ❷

Sleep in Heaven Struensegade 7, Nørrebro ⓣ35.35.46.48, ⓦwww.sleepinheaven.com. Popular hostel in a quiet spot next to Assistens

Kirkegård. The two large halls are divided into four- and eight-bed compartments. Pleasant atmosphere, with youthful staff; age limit 35; breakfast 40kr. Ten minutes from the centre by bus #12 or #69, nightbus #92N. ❷

Hotels

Absalon Helgolandsgade 15 ⓣ33.24.22.11, ⓦwww.absalon-hotel.dk. Decent three-star (en-suite rooms) with a one-star annexe (shared bathroom). Price includes delicious breakfast buffet with freshly baked bread. ❼–❾

Cab Inn City Mitchellsgade 14 ⓣ33.46.16.16, ⓦwww.cabinn.com. Good value, clean cabin-style rooms close to Tivoli and the station. All come with en-suite bathrooms and free tea and coffee. Two other branches in Frederiksberg (see map and website). ❽

Sømandshjemmet Bethel Nyhavn 22 ⓣ33.13.03.70, ⓦwww.hotel-bethel.dk. Friendly former seamen's hostel in a fantastic location on Nyhavn. Good-sized clean rooms. Breakfast included. Bus #19 or Kongens Nytorv metro station. ❾

Campsites

Camping Absalon Korsdalsvej 132, Rødovre ⓣ36.41.06.00, ⓦwww.camping-absalon.dk. Reasonable site, with basic facilities, 9km southwest of the city. S-train line B to Brøndbyøster, then ten minutes' walk or bus #550S. Open all year. ❷

Bellahøj Camping Hvidkildevej 66 ⓣ38.10.11.50, ⓦwww.bellahoj-camping.dk. The most central site but rather grim, with long queues for the showers. Bus #2a, nightbus #82N. June–Aug. ❶

Charlottenlund Strandpark Strandvejen 144, Charlottenlund ⓣ39.62.36.88, ⓦwww.campingcopenhagen.dk. Beautifully situated 6km from Copenhagen at Charlottenlund Beach and with good, clean facilities. Very busy in summer. S-train line A, B or C to Svanemøllen then bus #14. Mid-May to mid-Sept.

Eating

Copenhagen has more Michelin-starred restaurants than the rest of Scandinavia put together but there is also a range of budget options where you can eat out for less than 100kr. Heading out of the centre, towards Nørrebro and Vesterbro, is your best bet for saving a few kroner. If you're **self-catering**, numerous bakeries sell freshly made *rundstykker* (crispy rolls) and flaky Danish pastries. Rhein van Hauen on Mikkelbryggersgade 8 near Rådhuspladsen are celebrated pastry masters, and Emerys, with bakeries at Vesterbrogade 34, Nørrebrogade 8, and Østerbrogade 51 do outstanding organic bread and rolls. For take-away *smørrebrød* try the outlets at Domhusets Smørrebrød, Kattesundet 18, Centrum Smørrebrød, Vesterbrogade 6C, and Klemmen at Central Station. There's also a Netto supermarket at Nørre Voldgade 94, Nørrebrogade 43, Landemærket 11 and Store Kongensgade 47. Fakta is on Nørrebrogade 14–16 and on Borgergade 27.

Cafés

Bang & Jensen Istedgade 130. Popular café at the quieter end of Istedgade, offering a filling brunch until 4pm, and sandwiches and light meals all day. Turns into a busy bar at night. Brunch 75kr.

Café Bjørgs Vestervoldgade 19. Bright, central café serving excellent coffee and good-value sandwiches, salads and brunch. Brunch 89kr.

Det Gule Hus Istedgade 48. Trendy bright-yellow café/bar offering three types of brunch (85kr) and a range of evening meals including filling salads. Mains 70kr.

Floras Kaffebar Blågårdsgade 27. A temple to coffee with outdoor seating in summer, this place also does a good chilli con carne and homemade burgers. Mains 69kr

Front Page Sortedams Dosseringen 21. With its lakeside setting, this is a perfect spot for a quiet coffee or a cool beer and tapas sundowner. Tapas for two 95kr.

La Galette Larsbjørnstræde 9. Authentic Breton pancakes made with organic buckwheat and an array of fillings – from ham and eggs to smoked salmon and caviar. Pancakes 35–100kr

Paradis Vesterbro Torv. Italian-style ice-cream outlet with a huge range of flavours. Also branches at Sankt Hans Torv and Løngangstræde, Indre By. Two scoops 20kr.

Restaurants

Addis Mesob Fredensgade 11. You may not have come to Copenhagen to try Ethiopian food but this place isn't to be missed. Try their spicy stews eaten by hand with flatbread. Mains 69kr.

Atlas Bar Larsbjørnsstræde 18. Busy basement bar/restaurant with an imaginative range of world food from Indonesian chicken to Mexican vegetarian stew (kitchen closes 10pm). Mains from 80kr.

Ida Davidson Store Kongensgade 70. With 220 types of *smørrebrød*, you're going to find at least one you like at this Copenhagen institution. *Smørrebrød* from 50kr.

La Rocca Vendersgade 23-25. Elegant candlelit Italian restaurant, worth stretching the budget for. Try the marinated smoked salmon with peppers at 85kr.

> **TREAT YOURSELF**
>
> For the "coolest" experience in town head to the new **Absolut Ice Bar** at Løngangstræde 27 (Mon–Tues 5pm–midnight, Wed–Fri 5pm–1am, Sat 10am–1am, Sun 10am–8pm; ⓦwww.absoluticebarcopenhagen.com). You'll be kitted out with a fur coat and gloves to brave the -5C temperature and served a tasty vodka cocktail in an ice glass, all for a slightly steep 150kr. The bar is part of the ultra-hip *Hotel 27*, ❾ also home to the decadent *Honey Ryder* cocktail bar and *Wine Room* restaurant.

Pasta Basta Valkendorfgade 22. Popular with drinkers, this late-night spot offers a wide range of Italian dishes and a great-value buffet. Mon–Thurs & Sun open till 3am, Fri & Sat till 5am. Pasta buffet 79kr.

Ranee's Blagards Plads 10. A little slice of Bangkok in this lovely Nørrebro square. Authentic Thai food cooked to perfection with quality ingredients. Mains 145kr.

RizRaz Kompagnistræde 20. Stylish Mediterranean chain with a wide selection of *mezze* and an excellent vegetarian lunch buffet for 69kr. Another branch at Store Kannikestræde. Mains 69–110kr.

Tasty Burmeistersgade 34. Aptly named Indian hidden away between Prinsessegade and Christianshavn's canal. Good selection of fish curries including a fantastic prawn biryani. Mains from 69kr.

Thai Esan Lille Istedgade 7. Good value and perennially popular Thai fare. If it's full, try Thai Esan 2 around the corner at Halmtorvet 44. Mains 80kr.

Wagamama Tietgensgade 20. Copenhagen branch of the London-based noodle chain. The Japanese-inspired mains are served quickly and you needn't worry about getting a table as diners are sat along benches. Mains from 85kr.

Drinking and nightlife

Bars

Andy's Bar Gothersgade 33B. Packed late-night bar with a very jovial vibe – you'll end up leaving the place with lots of new friends. Daily 11pm to 6am.

Brew Pub Vestergarde 29. Popular micobrewery with a great beer garden bang in the centre of town. Try the Cole Porter Ale (35kr).

Caféen Blågårds Apotek Blågårds Plads 20. Unpretentious bar with mixed crowd of students attracted by the cheap beer and an older crowd here for the regular live blues and jazz.

Cosy Bar Studiestræde 24. One of the oldest gay bars in Copenhagen. Cosy pub atmosphere with dance floor downstairs – rarely gets going before 4am.

Ideal Bar Enghavevej 40. Part of the Vega music complex, this bar has a cool 1950s interior and a buzzing pre-club vibe.

Musen og Elefanten Vestergade 21. Cosy little bar serving the potent Elephant Beer from a carved trunk upstairs while downstairs punters chat in a relaxed, candlelit setting.

Nemoland Christiania. Run by Christiania residents, this is one of the city's most popular open-air bars with picnic tables and decent café food. In winter, the crowd moves indoors to the pool tables and backgammon boards.

Oscar Rådhuspladsen 77. Café-bar in a perfect location off Rådhuspladsen attracting gay and straight customers alike. DJs hit the decks on Fri and Sat nights.

Our Bar Studiestræde 7. Current hangout for Copenhagen's beautiful people. Probably the best cocktails in town (from 65kr) made with top-quality ingredients.

Pussy Galore's Flying Circus Sankt Hans Torv 30. Popular café-bar that comes into its own in the evening when the locals sip cocktails outside with warm blankets over their laps.

Sebastopol Sankt Hans Torv 2. Trendy café-bar on the Sankt Hans Torv square that catches the last rays of sun and gathers large crowds in summer. Good brunches too.

Clubs

Apparatet Nørrebrogade 184 ⓦwww.myspace/apparatet. Worth the trip out from the centre (hop on a #5A bus), this is Copenhagen's coolest club with a hip-yet-friendly crowd and good-value cocktails (50kr). Wed 9pm–1am, Thurs–Sat 8pm–4am.

Klub Tease 34 Hausergade ⓦwww.klubtease.dk. The capital's best gay club with a riotous mix of disco, house and electro tunes. Free admission for transvestites and drag queens (everyone else 50kr after 1am). Sat 11pm–5am.

Stengade 30 Stengade 18 ⓦwww.stengade30.dk. Alternative hangout with a mix of live hip hop, techno and indie club nights Tues 9pm–2am, Wed–Sat 10pm–5am. 50kr.

> **GAY COPENHAGEN**
>
> The Danish capital has a small but lively **gay scene** and hosts regular gay festivals and events including an annual Pride march. Check out ⓦwww.visitcopenhagen.com/gay for more information.

Stereo Bar Linnésgade 16A. Intimate club/bar playing mostly latin, house and drum'n'bass. Free entry. Wed–Sat 8pm–3am.
Vega Natklub Enghavevej 40 ⓦwww.vega.dk. Part of the Vega live music complex in trendy Vesterbro, this club offers a good mix of underground and mainstream house and electro. Fri– Sat 11pm–5am. Free until 1am, then 60kr.

Shopping

Clothes Istegade and the parallel Vesterbrogade have the best selection of boutiques including vintage and little-known designer wear. Check out Donn Ya Doll, Istedgade 55 for a great range of gadgets and Scandinavian designer labels. Among the clothes shops off Strøget you'll find Lust, Mikkel Bryggersgade 3A, a sleaze-free erotic gift shop aimed at women and couples.
Danish design ILLUM, hard to miss halfway down Strøget at Østergade 52, is Copenhagen's premier department store and sells a range of Danish homeware. Even if you can only afford a teaspoon, It's worth visiting just to marvel at the interior. Nearby is Bang & Olufsen's flagship store at Kongens Nytorv 26, selling top-end hi-fi at slightly cheaper prices than you'll find outside Denmark. At the more affordable end of the spectrum, the Bodum store at Østergade 10 offers a range of imaginative kitchenware including their classic cafetiere.
Markets The most central market is the celebrated but pricey Gammel Strand flea market (every Fri & Sat 8am–5pm) which mainly focuses on antiques. It's better to head out a bit further to Nørrebro's Assistens Cemetery for cheaper deals on everything from porcelain to clothes (every Sat May–mid Oct 7am–2pm).

Entertainment

Cinema

Cinemateket at Filmhuset Gothersgade 55, Indre By ⓦwww.dfi.dk. Modern cinema, home to the Danish film institute. Booking advisable.
Gloria Biografen ⓦwww.gloria.dk Stylish little cinema, with a good mix of mainstream and arhouse films.

Live music

As well as the below options check out the live music programme at clubs Stengade 30 and Vega.
Drop Inn Kompagnistræde 34. Laid-back, unpretentious jazz café. Cheap beer and late opening hours.
Mojo Løngangsstræde 21C, Indre By ⓦwww.mojo.dk. Atmospheric, divey blues venue with live acts every night. Happy hour 8–10pm. Entrance free or 60/120kr depending on act.

Opera and theatre

Royal Theatre Kongens Nytorv ⓦwww.kgl-teater.dk. Denmark's main arts venue hosts ballet, opera and drama. If you're under 30 a 65 percent discount is available for some performances while unsold tickets go for half-price.
Operaen Christianshavns Torv ⓦwww.operaen.dk. The city's spectacular opera house is as much an architectural as a musical attraction. A cheap way to see a performance is to buy a standing stalls ticket on the day of performance (from 60kr).

Directory

Bike rental Københavns Cykelbørs, Gothersgade 157; Københavns Cykler, Reventlowsgade 11; Østerport Cykler, Oslo Plads 9.
Bike tours City Safari ⓣ33.23.94.90, ⓦwww.citysafari.dk. Cycle tours with knowledgeable guides starting from the Danish Architecture Centre; daily summer 1.30pm, 250kr for three hours including bike rental.
Embassies Australia, Dampfærgevej 26 ⓣ70.26.36.76; Canada, Kristen Bernikowsgade 1 ⓣ33.48.32.00; Ireland, Østbanegade 21 ⓣ35.42.32.33; Netherlands, Toldbodgade 33 ⓣ33.70.72.02; New Zealand, use UK; UK, Kastelsvej 40 ⓣ35.44.52.00; US, Dag Hammerskjölds Allé 24 ⓣ35.55.31.44.
Exchange Den Danske Bank at the Airport (daily 6am–8.30pm); Forex and X-Change at the Central Station (daily 7/8am–9pm).
Hospital Rigshospitalet, Blegdamsvej 9 ⓣ35.45.35.45.
Internet Use-It Rådhusstroede 13 ⓦwww.useit.dk (free); Moomtown Axeltorv 1–3, oppoite Tivoli main entrance (30kr per hour)
Left luggage Free for a day at Use-It, Rådhusstræde 13. Otherwise, lockers at Central Station, from 25kr for 24hr.
Pharmacies Steno Apotek, Vesterbrogade 6C;

Sønderbro Apotek, Amagerbrogade 158. Both 24hr.
Post office Købmagergade 33, and at Central Station.

Moving on

Trains Aalborg (hourly; 4hr 40min); Frederikshavn (hourly; 6hr); Hamburg (hourly; 5hr); Helsingør (every 20min; 50min); Malmö (every 30min; 22min); Odense (56 daily; 1hr 30min); Roskilde (8 hourly; 25min).
Buses Aalborg (3–5 daily; 4hr 45min); Århus (6–7 daily; 3hr); Malmö (hourly; 55min)

Day trips from Copenhagen

When the weather's good, you can top up your tan at the **Amager Strandpark beach** just 5km from the centre (bus #12 or take the Metro to Lergravsparken then a 15min walk along Øresundsvej; www.amager-strand.dk). If you're in the mood for an amusement park but don't fancy the neatness of Tivoli, venture out to **BAKKEN** (April to early Sept daily noon/2pm–10pm/midnight; 199kr; ⓦwww.bakken.dk), close to the Klampenborg stop at the end of lines C and F+ on the S-train. Besides slightly sinister clowns and some vintage rollecoasters it offers pleasant woods to wander around.

Two more excellent attractions are on Zealand's northeastern coast. Fifteen minutes' walk from Rungsted Kyst train station, the peaceful **Karen Blixen Museum** (May–Sept Tues–Sun 10am–5pm; Oct–April Wed–Sun 11am/1pm–4pm; 45kr; ⓦwww.isak-dinesen.dk) presents a moving testament to this remarkable woman, best known as the author of *Out of Africa*. In **HUMLEBÆK**, 10km further north and a short walk from its train station, is **Louisiana**, an outstanding modern art gallery, at Gammel Strandvej 13 (daily 10am–5pm, Wed till 10pm; 90kr; ⓦwww.louisiana.dk). The gallery's setting is worth the journey alone, a harmonious blend of art, architecture and the natural landscape.

The rest of Zealand

As home to Copenhagen, **Zealand** is Denmark's most important and most visited region, and, with a swift metropolitan transport network covering almost half of the island, you can always make it back to the capital in time for an evening drink. North of Copenhagen, **Helsingør** (Elsinore) the departure point for ferries to Sweden, is the site of the legendary Kronborg Slot. To the west, and on the main train route to Funen, is **Roskilde**, its extravagant cathedral the resting place for Danish monarchs, and with a gorgeous location on the Roskilde fjord, from where five Viking boats were salvaged and are now restored and displayed in a specially built museum.

HELSINGØR

First impressions of **HELSINGØR** are none too enticing, but away from the bustle of its train and ferry terminals it's a quiet and likeable town. Its position on the narrow strip of water linking the North Sea and the Baltic brought the town prosperity when, in 1429, the Sound Toll was imposed on passing vessels. Today, it's once again an important waterway, with ferries to Swedish Helsingborg accounting for most of Helsingør's through-traffic and innumerable cheap booze shops.

What to see and do

The town's great tourist draw is **Kronborg Slot** (May–Sept daily 10.30am–5pm; Oct–April Tues–Sun 11am–3/4pm; 60kr, 85kr joint ticket with the Maritime Museum; Copenhagen Card not valid), principally because of its literary associations as Elsinore Castle, where Shakespeare's Hamlet strode the famous ramparts. There's no evidence that

Shakespeare ever visited Helsingør, and the tenth-century character Amleth on whom his hero was based long predates the castle. Nevertheless, the Hamlet souvenir business continues to thrive here. The present castle dates from the sixteenth century when it stood out like a raised fist into the sound, a warning to passing ships not to consider dodging the toll. Though various parts have been destroyed and rebuilt since, it remains a grand affair, enhanced immeasurably by its setting; the interior, particularly the royal chapel, is spectacularly ornate.

The castle also houses the surprisingly captivating **National Maritime Museum** (40kr, 85kr joint ticket with the castle), which, apart from a motley collection of model ships and nautical knick-knacks, contains relics from Denmark's conquests in Greenland, India, the West Indies and West Africa, as well as the world's oldest surviving ship's biscuit (1852).

The medieval quarter

Helsingør's well-preserved medieval quarter is dominated by **Stengade**, the main pedestrianized street, linked by a number of narrow alleyways to Axeltorv, the town's small market square and a nice place to enjoy a beer. Near the corner of Stengade and Skt. Annagade is Helsingør's cathedral, **Skt. Olai's Kirke** (daily 10am–2pm), with its renovated spire. Just beyond is Skt. Mariæ Kirke, whose **Karmeliterklostret**, built circa 1400, is now the best-preserved medieval monastery in Scandinavia (guided tours only Mon–Fri 2pm; 20kr). Its former hospital now contains the **Town Museum** (daily noon–4pm; 20kr), which displays an unnerving selection of surgical tools used in early brain operations.

Arrival and information

Train and tourist office The train station is on Jernbanevej, a 2min walk south of the centre. The tourist office is just opposite at Havnepladsen 3 ⓣ49.21.13.33, ⓦwww.visithelsingor.dk. Mon–Fri 10am–4/5/6pm, Sat 10am–1/2pm,

Accommodation

Danhostel Helsingør Nordre Strandvej 24 ⓣ49.21.16.40, ⓦwww.helsingorhostel.dk. Beautifully located hostel in a restored villa right on the beach (suitable for swimming) 2km north of town; bus #340 from the station. Dorms ❸ doubles ❼

Eating and drinking

Café Manhattan Jernbanevej 6, opposite station. Good spot to shoot some pool and meet the locals. Happy hour Thurs–Sat 8–10pm.

Phonoteket Stengade 36. Grab a coffee and a cake in this hip music store cafe. Coffee 24kr.

Pizzeria Pakhuset Strengade 26. Great value pizza and pasta in a trattoria-style restaurant. Pizza 52kr.

Moving on

Train Copenhagen (every 20min; 50min).

FERRIES TO SWEDEN

Three **ferry** companies (ⓦwww.acelink.dk, ⓦwww.hhferries.dk and ⓦwww.scandlines.dk) make the twenty-minute crossing from Helsingør to Helsingborg in Sweden every 20-30min (around 40kr return). All services leave from the main terminal by the train station. Eurail and Scanrail passes are valid on Scandlines and InterRail and the Copenhagen Card gives a fifty percent discount.

ROSKILDE

Once the capital of Denmark, **ROSKILDE** is worth a visit even if you can't make it to its famous rock festival (see opposite). Its Viking Ship museum is a world-class attraction while the cathedral and old centre are lovely to wander around.

What to see and do

The fabulous **Roskilde Domkirke** (April–Sept Mon–Sat 9am–5pm, Sun 12.30–5pm; Oct–March Tues–Sat

ROSKILDE FESTIVAL

Book well in advance if you wish to stay during the **Roskilde Festival** (Ⓦwww.roskilde-festival.dk), one of the largest open-air music festivals in Europe, attracting almost 100,000 people annually. Note that tickets go on sale in December and tend to sell out quickly. The festival takes place late June/early July (3-6 July, 2008) and there's a special free camping ground beside the festival site, to which shuttle buses run from the train station every few minutes.

10am–3.45pm, Sun 12.30–3.45pm; 25kr), was founded by Bishop Absalon in 1170 and largely completed by the fourteenth century, although bits have been added since. It's stuffed full of dead Danish monarchs including twenty-one kings and eighteen queens. The most impressive chapel is that of Christian IV, full of bronze statues, frescoes and vast paintings of scenes from his reign. Upstairs in the Great Hall, a small **Cathedral Museum** (April–Sept Mon–Fri 11am, 1pm & 3pm, Sat 10am, Sun 1pm & 2pm; Oct–March Tues–Fri noon & 1pm, Sat noon, Sun 1pm & 2pm; access only with Cathedral staff) provides an engrossing introduction to the Cathedral's colourful history.

A roofed passageway, the Arch of Absalon (not open to the public), runs from the Cathedral into the **Roskilde Palace** next door, housing the diverting **Museum of Contemporary Art** (Tues–Fri 11am–5pm, Sat & Sun noon–4pm when there are exhibitions on; 30kr, Wed free) which hosts temporary exhibitions and includes a charming sculpture garden.

The Viking Ship Museum

Fifteen minutes' walk north of the centre on the banks of the fjord is the modern **Viking Ship Museum** (daily 10am–5pm; 80kr; Ⓦwww.vikingeskibsmuseet.dk). Inside, five superb specimens of Viking shipbuilding are displayed: a deep-sea trader, a merchant ship, a warship, a ferry and a longship, each one retrieved from the fjord where they had been sunk to block invading forces. Outside, you can watch boat-building and sail-making using only tools and materials available during the Viking era; when the weather allows you can also experience the ship's seaworthiness on the fjord – you'll be handed an oar when you board and be expected to pull your weight as a crew member (50min; 55kr on top of the museum ticket), a humbling experience when you consider similar ships made it all the way to Greenland.

Arrival and information

Train and bus The train station is at the southern edge of town. The bus station is within the same complex

Tourist office Gullandsstræde 15 Ⓣ46.31.65.65, Ⓦwww.visitroskilde.dk. A short walk from the main square. Mon–Fri 9am–5pm, Sat 10am–1/2pm.

Accommodation

Roskilde Vandrerhjem Vindeboder 7 Ⓣ46.31.65.65 Ⓦwww.rova.dk. Beautifully situated modern hostel in the harbour area near the Viking museum. Dorms ③, doubles ⑥

Eating and drinking

Gimle Helligkorvej 2 Ⓣ46.37.19.82 (10min walk east of the tourist office). Live music venue with a café serving burgers (49kr) and the like noon-midnight. Turns into a club Fri & Sat nights (midnight-5am).

Snekken Vindeboder 16 Ⓣ46.35.21.84. Stylish harbourside restaurant with good range of salads and sandwiches. Nachos 64kr.

Moving on

Train Copenhagen (every 30min; 30min); Odense (every 30min; 1hr 10min).

Funen

Funen is the smaller of the two main Danish islands. The pastoral outlook of the place and the laid-back fishing villages along the coast draw many visitors, but the main attraction is Odense, Denmark's third city and the birthplace of writer Hans Christian Andersen and composer Carl Nielsen.

ODENSE

Named after Odin, chief of the pagan gods, **ODENSE** (pronounced Own-suh) is over a thousand years old. It's one of Denmark's most attractive cities with cobbled streets set around the Odense Å river. The inner core of the city is pedestrianized with a range of good museums to visit; the nightlife is surprisingly energetic, with a focus on live music.

What to see and do

The city's major attraction is the ✪ **Hans Christian Andersen Hus** at Bangs Boder 29 (June–Aug daily 9am–6pm; Sept–May Tues–Sun 10am–4pm; Ⓦwww.museum.odense.dk; 60kr), where the writer was born in 1805. The museum includes a library of Andersen's works and headphones for listening to some of his best-known fairy tales read by the likes of Sir Lawrence Olivier. There's also plenty of intriguing paraphernalia on the man, including school reports, manuscripts, paper cuttings and drawings from his travels. Check out the telling quotes on Andersen's unconventional looks and talent: "he is the most hideous man you could find but has a poetic childish mind," commented a female contemporary.

Hans Christian Andersens Barndomshjem and Skt Knuds Kirke

There's more about Andersen at Munkemøllestræde 3–5, between Skt. Knud Kirkestræde and Horsetorvet, in the tiny **Hans Christian Andersens Barndomshjem** (Childhood Home; daily 10/11am–3/4pm; 25kr), where the writer lived between the ages of two and fourteen. Nearby, the crypt of **Skt. Knuds Kirke** (Mon–Sat 9/10am–4/5pm, Sun noon–5pm; free) holds the remains of King Knud II and his brother Benedikt, both murdered in 1086 at the altar of nearby Skt. Albani Kirke. The cathedral's Gothic exterior is complemented by an elegant white interior while its main draw is the rather overwhelming wooden altarpiece, coated in twenty-three carat gold leaf; one of the greatest works of the Lübeck master, Claus Berg.

The Fyns Kunstmuseum

At Jernbanegade 13, the **Fyns Kunstmuseum** (Funen Art Gallery; Tues–Sun 10am–4pm; Ⓦwww.museum.odense.dk; 40kr), just a few minutes' walk from Skt. Knuds, gives a good introduction to the Danish art world during the late nineteenth century; the collection contains some stirring works by Vilhelm Hammershøi, P.S. Krøyer, Michael and Anne Ancher, and H.A. Brendekilde's emotive *Udslidt ("Exhaustion")*. A short walk east, at Claus Bergs Gade 11, in a wing of Odense's Concert Hall, is the **Carl Nielsen Museet** (Thurs & Fri 4–8pm, Sun noon–4pm; 25kr; Ⓦwww.museum.odense.dk). Born in a village just outside Odense, Nielsen is best remembered in Denmark for his popular songs, though it was his operas, choral pieces and symphonies that established him as a major international composer.

Brandts

West of the centre is the **Brandts arts complex** on Brandts Passage just off Vestergade. Once a large textile mill, the area has been beautifully converted and now features an art school, cinema, music library, and three museums (July & Aug daily 10am–5pm; Sept–June closed Mon; 40kr combined ticket; Ⓦwww.brandts.dk). In the large hall that once housed the huge machinery is the **Kunsthallen** which displays works by the cream of new talent in art and design, and the **Museet for Fotokunst**, featuring changing exhibitions of photography. On the third floor the **Danmarks Mediemuseum** chronicles the development of printing, bookbinding and illustrating from the Middle Ages to the present. Further down Brandts Passage, upstairs at no. 29, the tiny **Tidens Samling** (daily 10am–5pm; ⓦwww.tidenssamling.dk; 30kr) gives an intimate insight into the changing fashions of sitting-rooms and clothing since the beginning of the twentieth century.

Den Fynske Landsby

South of the centre at Sejerskovvej 20 is **Den Fynske Landsby** (Funen Village; April–Oct Tues–Sun 10am–5pm/7pm; 60kr; Nov–March Sun 11–5pm; 40kr; ⓦwww.museum.odense.dk), a living, breathing nineteenth-century village made up of buildings from all over Funen. In summer free shows are staged at the open-air theatre. Bus #42 runs to the village from the city centre.

Arrival and information

Train and bus Odense train station is part of a large shopping mall five minutes' walk north of the centre. Long-distance buses also terminate here.
Tourist office The tourist office (July & Aug Mon–Fri 9.30am–6pm, Sat & Sun 10am–3pm; rest of year Mon–Fri 9.30am–4.30pm, Sat 10am–1pm; ⓣ66.12.75.20, ⓦwww.visitodense.com) is on the Vestergade side of the Rådhus – follow the signs.
Internet There's free Internet access in the library at the train station.

Accommodation

Hostels

Danhostel Odense City Østre Stationsvej 31 ⓣ66.11.04.25, ⓦwww.cityhostel.dk. Conveniently located in a former hotel next to the train station, this five-star hostel has clean dorms and a good café. Dorms ❸, doubles ❼ (inc buffet breakfast)
Odense Danhostel Kragsbjerggaard Kragsbjergvej 121 ⓦwww.odense-danhostel.dk. Sister hostel to the city branch, this one is set in a manor house surrounded by woodland 2km south of the centre (bus #61 & 63 from the station). Dorms ❸ doubles ❼ (inc buffet breakfast).

Hotels

City Hotel Odense Hans Mules Gade 5 ⓣ66.12.12.58, ⓦwww.city-hotel-odense.dk. Reliable, modern hotel with bright, clean en-suite rooms and huge buffet breakfast. Discounts often available. ❾
Det Lille Hotel Dronningensgade 5 ⓣ66.12.28.21, ⓦwww.lillehotel.dk. Friendly, inexpensive little hotel a short walk east of the station. Shared bathrooms. ❻

Campsite

DCU Camping Odensevej 102 ⓣ66.11.47.02 ⓦwww.camping-odense.dk. Located near Den Fynske Landsby on the outskirts of Odense, this campsite has decent facilities including a heated pool. Take bus #21, #22 or #23 from the train station towards Højby. ❶

Eating and drinking

Australian Bar Brandts Passage 10 ⓣ66.11.83.90. Aussie-themed sports bar by day switching to a popular nightclub after 10pm (40kr entrance).
Baker's Café Fisketorvet 2 (near the tourist office). Reliable spot for freshly made pastries and sandwiches (45kr).
Café Biografen Brandts Passage 39-41. Trendy bar attached to an artsy cinema. Club sandwich 62kr.
Café Cuckoo's Nest Vestergade 73 ⓣ65.91.57.87. Classy option for brunch (94kr; served till 3pm) or a drink in the evening thanks to its wide selection of bottled beers. Mains from 74kr.
Froggys Café Vestergade 68 ⓣ65.90.74.47. Cosy café/bar bang in the centre serving delicious salads and the legendary Froggy's burger (83kr). DJs at weekends.
Mosaik Asylgade 7-9 ⓣ66.11.83.90. Best place in town for a dance and a cocktail. 5kr shots every Thursday. Thurs–Sat 11pm–5am.
Ryan's of Odense Fisketorvet 12. The local Irish bar doesn't disappoint with a friendly atmosphere and half-decent Guinness. Afternoon happy hour 11am–5pm.

Moving on

Train Århus (2-3 hourly; 1hr 40min); Copenhagen (every 30min; 1hr 30min); Esbjerg (8 daily; 1hr 20min).

Jutland

Long ago, the Jutes, the people of **Jutland**, were a separate tribe from the more warlike Danes who occupied the eastern islands. In pagan times, the peninsula had its own rulers and it was here that the ninth-century monarch Harald Bluetooth began the process that would eventually bond the two tribes into a unified Christian nation. By the Viking era, however, the battling Danes had spread west, absorbing the Jutes, and real power gradually shifted towards Zealand, where it has largely stayed ever since. Unhurried lifestyles and rural calm are the overriding impressions of Jutland for most visitors; indeed, its distance from Copenhagen makes it the most distinct and interesting area in the country. **Århus**, halfway up the eastern coast, is Jutland's main urban centre and Denmark's second city. Further inland, the landscape is the most dramatic in the country– all stark heather-clad moors, dense forests and swooping gorges. North of vibrant **Aalborg**, sited on the bank of the Limfjord, the landscape reaches a crescendo of storm-lashed savagery around **Skagen**, on the very tip of the peninsula.

THE FERRY PORTS: ESBJERG AND FREDERIKSHAVN

There are two main international ferry ports in Jutland. **ESBJERG** has overnight ferries to and from Britain (Ⓦwww.dfdsseaways.com); bus #5 connects the passenger harbour with the centre (fifteen minutes' walk). The aiport (used by Ryanair and bmi) is 10km east of the city and connected by bus #8, 44 and 48. The train station, with trains to and from Copenhagen (3hr 11min), is at the end of Skolegade, and, at no. 33, you'll find the tourist office (Mon–Fri 9/10am–5pm, Sat 9.30/10am–1/3.30pm; Ⓣ75.12.55.99, Ⓦwww.visitesbjerg.dk). **FREDERIKSHAVN**, in the far north of the region (2hr 40min by train from Århus), has express ferries to Sweden and Norway (Ⓦwww.stenaline.dk). Its ferry terminal is near Havnepladsen, not far from the centre. All buses and most trains terminate at the central train station, a short walk from the town centre; some trains continue to the ferry terminal itself. The tourist office is close by at Skandiatorv 1 (mid-June to Aug daily 8.30am–5/7pm; Sept to mid-June Mon–Fri 9am–4pm, Sat 11am–2pm; Ⓣ98.42.32.66, Ⓦwww.frederikshavn-tourist.dk).

ÅRHUS

Denmark's second-largest city, **ÅRHUS** (pronounced OW-hus) is an instantly likeable assortment of intimate cobbled streets, sleek modern architecture, brightly painted houses and laid-back students. It's small enough to get to grips with in a few hours, but lively enough to make you linger for days – an excellent music scene, interesting art, pavement cafés and energetic nightlife all earn it the unofficial title of Denmark's capital of culture.

What to see and do

Arhus's main street, the pedestrianized Søndergade leads down from the train station, across the river and into the main town square, Bispetorvet. The square is dominated by the fifteenth-century **Domkirke** (Mon–Sat 9.30/10am–3/4pm) a massive Gothic church with some exquisite frescoes decorating the whitewashed interior as well as a miniature Danish warship hanging from the ceiling. Just around the corner at Domkirkeplads 5, you'll find the **Kvindemuseet** or Women's Museum (Mon-Fri 10am-5pm; 40kr; Ⓦwww.womensmuseum.dk) with an intriguing set of exhibitions on wom-

DENMARK'S OLDEST CITY?

Until recently it was thought that **Vikings** first settled in Arhus or *Aros* ("river mouth" in old Nordic) around the year 900. However, new excavations have revealed that they arrived as early as the mid-eighth century, causing no end of excitement for the local tourist board who are cheekily claiming Arhus is "arguably" **Denmark's oldest city**. This is unlikely to go down well in Ribe, Southern Jutland, the current holder of the title with evidence of Viking settlement from the beginning of the eighth century. The rivalry is set to increase as archaeologists continue to dig deeper.

en's changing roles in Danish society as well as an excellent cafe. The area to the north, known as the Latin Quarter, is crammed with browsable shops, galleries and enticing cafés.

The Viking Museum

Across the road from the cathedral, hidden away in the basement of the Nordea bank, is the **Viking Museum** (Mon–Fri 10am–4pm, Thurs till 5.30pm; free),

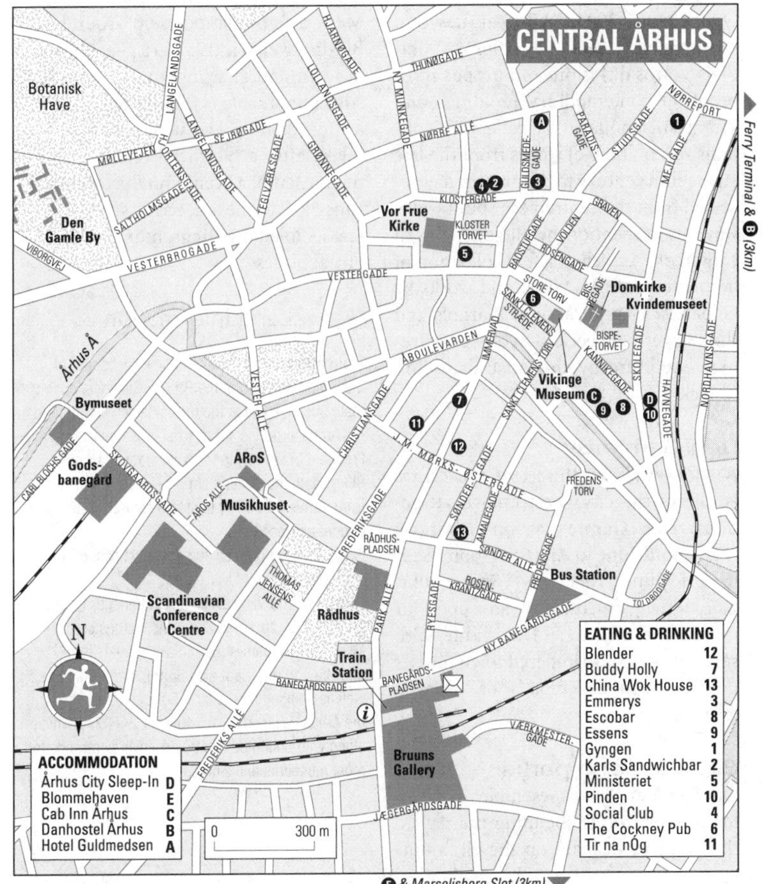

which will fill you in on Århus's early development.

The Rådhus

One of Denmark's most divisive buildings, Arhus's 1941 **Rådhus** was designed by Arne Jacobsen and Eric Moller in a modern functionalist style. Above the entrance hangs Hagedorn Olsen's huge mural, *A Human Society*, symbolically depicting the city emerging from World War II. You can wander in and investigate this for yourself, but to enjoy a view over the city and bay from the bell tower, you'll need to take a guided tour (mid-June to Aug Mon–Fri 11am; 10kr).

ARoS

Opened in 2004, **ARoS** (Tues–Sun 10am–5pm, Wed till 10pm; 90kr; Ⓦwww.aros.dk) is one of Europe's most beautiful contemporary buildings and a fantastic modern art gallery. It contains seven floors of works from the late eighteenth century to the present day accessed from the centrepiece spiral walkway reminiscent of the Guggenheim in New York. As well as a fine collection of homegrown artists you'll find works by Gilbert & George, several Warhols and the staggeringly eerie *Boy*, a five-metre-high sculpture by the Australian Ron Mueck.

Den Gamle By

A short walk northwest of the centre is one of the city's best-known attractions, **Den Gamle By**, on Viborgvej (daily: mid-June to Aug 9am–6pm; Sept to mid-June 10/11am–3/5pm; 90kr; Ⓦwww.dengamleby.dk), an open-air museum of traditional Danish life, with seventy-odd half-timbered town houses popular with coachloads of geriatric tourists.

Beaches and parks

On Sundays Århus resembles a ghost town, most locals spending the day in the parks or beaches on the city's outskirts. The closest **beaches** are north of the city at Riis Skov, easily reached by bus #6 or #16. Otherwise, Marselisborg Skov, south of the centre, is the city's largest park, and home to the **Marselisborg Slot**, summer residence of the Danish royals: its landscaped grounds can be visited when the monarch isn't staying.

Moesgård Prehistoric Museum

Ten kilometres south of Århus, the **Moesgård Prehistoric Museum** (daily 10am–4/5pm; Oct–March closed Mon; 45kr; Ⓦwww.moesmus.dk), reached direct by bus #6, details Danish civilizations from the Stone Age onwards. Its most notable exhibit is the "Grauballe Man", a body dating from around 100 BC discovered in 1952 in a peat bog west of town and amazingly well preserved. Also remarkable is the Illerup Ådal collection of Iron Age weapons, found in a lake after a sacrificial offering. From the museum, a scenic "prehistoric trail" runs 3km to the sea, past a scattering of reassembled dwellings, monuments and burial places.

Arrival and information

Train and bus The train station is just south of the centre and part of the Bruuns Gallery shopping mall. Buses pull in at the terminus across the road.
Air Århus airport is 44km west of the centre. Frequent buses run to the train station (45min; 85kr). Note that Billund airport is also reachable from Århus (80min by bus) and served by many budget carriers.
Ferry Ferries from Zealand dock just east of the centre at the end of Nørreport.
Tourist office VisitAarhus are at Banegardspladsen 20 (Ⓣ87.31.50.10, Ⓦwww.visitaarhus.com; Mon–Fri 9/9.30am–4/6pm, Sat 10am–1/3pm; mid-June to mid-Sept also Sun 9.30am–1pm). As well as booking rooms for a 50kr fee, they offer the Århus Passport (119/149kr for 24/48hr), which, along with unlimited bus travel, covers entrance to most museums and sights.

City tranport

Buses You'll need buses only to reach the Moesgård Museum, the beaches and woods on the outskirts. A basic ticket costs 18kr from machines in the back of the bus and is valid for any number of journeys for two hours from the time stamped on it.
Cycle hire From May to October you can borrow one of the 400 free city bikes (Ⓦwww.aarhusbycykel.dk) dotted around the city centre (20kr coin deposit).

Accommodation

The tourist office can arrange private rooms (❻) for a 50kr booking fee.

Hostels

Århus City Sleep-In Havnegade 20 Ⓣ86.19.20.55, Ⓦwww.citysleep-in.dk. The most central hostel. Facilities include a breakfast café, guest kitchen, pool/TV rooms and a courtyard for summer barbecues. Dorms ❷, doubles ❻
Danhostel Århus Marienlundsvej 10 Ⓣ86.16.72.98, Ⓦwww.aarhus-danhostel.dk. Peaceful hostel set in woods, 3km northwest of the centre and close to the popular Den Permanente beach. Regular bus connections include #1, #6, #8, #9, #16, #56 and #58. Dorms ❷, doubles ❼

Hotels

Cab Inn Århus Kannikegade 14 Ⓣ86.75.70.00, Ⓦwww.cab-inn.dk. Good-value cabin-style rooms in a central location by the river. Buffet breakfast included.

TREAT YOURSELF

With only one budget hotel in Århus you might want to consider a splurge. **Hotel Guldmedsen** (Ⓣ86.13.45.50, Ⓦwww.hotelguldsmeden.dk; ❾) is a characterful place to stay with 27 stylish rooms and a lovely courtyard garden. They also offer a fantastic organic breakfast buffet.

Campsite

Blommehaven Ørneredevej 35 Ⓣ86.27.02.07, Ⓦwww.blommehaven.dk.Overlooking a bay, 3km south of the city centre, this site has access to a beautiful beach. Closed mid-Oct to mid-March (bus #6 or #19). ❶

Eating

There is no shortage of trendy restaurants in Århus, especially along the river at Åboulevarden. If you can't afford the somewhat inflated prices, it's a lovely spot for a picnic. For **self-catering**, there's a late-opening supermarket (8am–midnight) at the train station and another close to the City Sleep-In.

Cafés

Emmerys Guldsmedgade 24–26. Superb organic Danish bread and pastries; the coffee is freshly ground and the cakes (35kr) are to die for.
Ministeriet Kloster Torvet 5 Ⓣ86.17.11.88. Sit outside and enjoy the delicious brunch at this stylish café-restaurant. Brunch 80kr.

Restaurants

China Wok House Sønder Alle 9 Ⓣ86.17.11.88. Chinese staples all around 45kr plus a good range of takeaway bento boxes (60kr).
Gyngen Mejlgade 53. Great veggie burgers (80kr) and a mean chilli con carne with crème fraîche. Closed Sun; mains from 59kr.
Karls Sandwichbar Klostergade 32. Huge homemade burgers (55kr) and twenty types of delicious pizza (30kr at lunchtime).
Pinden Skolegade 29 Ⓣ86.12.11.02. The best place in town for traditional Danish food including a knockout *stegt flæsk med persille sovs* (84kr). Closed Sun.

Drinking and nightlife

Thanks to its large student population, Århus nightlife almost matches that of Copenhagen.

Bars

The Cockney Pub Maren Smeds Gyde 8. Cosy little bar with an excellent range of real ales and a sociable clientele.
Escobar Skolegade 32. Popular student hangout with cheap beer (25kr draft), loud music and friendly bar staff. Open till 3am.
Essens Åboulevarden 30. The best bar along Åboulevarden: über cool interior and awesome cocktails. Mojitos start at 50kr.
Tir na nÓg Frederiksgade 40. Large, lively Irish bar with big-screen football and live folk/rock music at weekends. Open till 3am.

Clubs

Blender Telefonsmogen 6 Ⓦwww.blender-aarhus.dk. The "club for everyone" with four floors of bars and dancefloors. Occasionally hosts gay/lesbian only nights but usually a mixed crowd. Fri-Sat 10.30pm-6am. Entrance 75kr.

Buddy Holly Frederiksgade 29 Ⓦ www.buddy-aarhus.dk. Cheap and cheerful club that soaks up the late-night crowd. Plenty of drinks deals and a ladies night on Thurs. Mon–Thurs & Sat 11pm-6am, Fri 9pm-6am.

Social Club Klostergade 34 Ⓦwww.socialclub.dk. Large warehouse-style club with a huge dancefloor and free entrance for students. Thurs-Sat 11pm-5am.

Moving on

Train Aalborg (34 daily; 1hr 15min–1hr 30min); Copenhagen (38 daily; 3hr–3hr 15min); Odense (40 daily; 1hr 30min–1hr 45min).

AALBORG

The main city of north Jutland, **AALBORG** is renowned for its raucous nightlife and nearby Viking burial ground. It's also the main transport terminus for the region, and will be a likely stop on your way north to the beaches of Skagen.

What to see and do

Aalborg's well-preserved **old town** is worth a wander, with pleasant cobbled streets and a small but elegant Gothic cathedral, the **Budolfi Domkirke** (Mon–Fri 9am–3/4pm, Sat 9am–noon/2pm) housing a collection of religious paintings. On the other side of Østerågade, the sixteenth-century **Aalborghus Slot** is notable for its **dungeon** (May–Oct Mon–Fri 8am–3pm; free) and underground passages (till 9pm). Those after a further culture fix should head to the **Nordjyllands Kunstmuseum** (Tues–Sun 10am–5pm; 40kr, free in December; Ⓦwww.nordjyllandskunstmuseum.dk), a stunning modern art gallery surrounded by a sculpture park (take bus #15 or walk ten minutes east of the train station).

Apart from the above, the city's main attractions are bacchanalian in nature. Leading down to the waterfront, **Jomfru Ane Gade** is Denmark's booziest street, boasting over three hundred bars and packed most evenings. Aalborg is also the home of Aquavit, the potent Scandinavian spirit, and you can sample some on a guided tour of the **V&S Distillery** at Olensens Gade 1, a ten-minute walk northwest of the centre (Ⓣ98.12.42.00, Ⓦwww.vsdistillers.dk; tours Mon & Sat 10am and 2pm; 40kr; other times by appointment).

Lindholm Høje

A few kilometres north of Aalborg, the atmospheric **Lindholm Høje** (Lindholm Hills; free) is Scandinavia's largest Viking burial site with more than seven hundred graves. It's best to visit early or late in the day as the slanting sunlight glints off the burial stones set in the outline of a Viking ship. You can learn more about the lives of those buried beneath your feet at the site's **museum** (Ⓣ99.31.74.40; April–Oct daily 10am–5pm; Nov–March Tues & Sun 11am–4pm; 30kr). To get to Lindholm take metro bus #2 (every 15–30min).

Arrival and information

Air Aalborg airport (served by budget airline Sterling) is 7km northwest and connected to the centre by metro bus #2.

Train and bus Both terminals are on J.F. Kennedys Plads, ten minutes' walk southwest of the centre.

Tourist office Centrally located in the old town at Østerågade 8 (Mon–Fri 9am–4.30/5.30pm, Sat 10am–1/4pm; Ⓣ98.12.60.22, Ⓦwww.visitaalborg.com).

Accommodation

Danhostel Aalborg Ⓣ98.11.60.44, Ⓦwww.danhostelnord.dk/aalborg. Large, well-equipped hostel 3km west of the town on the Limfjord bank beside the marina – take bus #13 to the Egholm ferry junction and continue on foot for five minutes following the signs. ❸

Prinsen Hotel Prinsensgade 14 Ⓣ98.13.37.33, Ⓦwww.prinsen-hotel.dk. Across from the train station, this is the best-value hotel in the centre (although note that the cheap CAB INN chain are set to hit Aalborg in April 2008). ❽

Strandparken Skydebanevej 20 Ⓣ89.12.76.29, Ⓦwww.strandparken.dk. Pleasant site with access to an open-air swimming pool and beach. Closed mid-Sept to March. ❶

Eating and drinking

Packed with late-opening bars, clubs and restaurants, **Jomfru Ane Gade** dominates Aalborg's nightlife and keeps prices competitive with plenty of food and drink deals luring the punters in.

Café Vesterå Vesterå 4 Ⓦwww.cafevesteraa.dk. Loungey bar-café offering decent burgers (74kr) during the day and cocktails in the evening. The upstairs club attracts big-name house DJs.

Fyrtøjet Jomfru Ane Gade 7. Ancient-looking restaurant serving up delicious Danish classics – the two-course lunch is good value at 80kr.

Studenterhuset Gammeltorv 11 Ⓣ98.11.43.12 Ⓦwww.studenterhuset.dk. Student-run music venue and café – the place to catch local Danish bands. Mon–Sat 11.30am–late.

Moving on

Train Århus (2 hourly; 1hr 20min); Copenhagen (2 hourly; 4hr 30min); Frederikshavn (hourly; 1hr 10min).

Bus Copenhagen (3 daily; 4hr 45min); other bus connections via Hobro include Århus (1–2 daily; 4hr) and Odense (4 weekly; 4hr).

SKAGEN

About 100km north of Aalborg, **SKAGEN** perches at the very top of Denmark amid a breathtaking landscape of heather-topped sand dunes. Now a popular resort, it attracts thousands of visitors every year thanks to its artistic connections and wonderful seafood restaurants.

What to see and do

Much of Skagen's appeal lies in aimlessly wandering its marina, watching the comings and goings of the yachtie set, or cycling out to the beaches along its coastal bike paths. There is one star sight however, the **Skagen Museum** (follow the signs from the train station; May–Sept daily 10am–5pm; Nov–March Wed–Sun 10am–3pm; 70kr; Ⓦwww.skagensmuseum.dk), displaying much of the work of the influential Skagen artists. Nearby, at Markvej 2–4, is the home of one of the group's leading lights and his wife, herself a skilful painter: the **Michael and Anna Anchers Hus** (April–Oct daily 10/11am–3/6pm; Nov–March Sat 11am–3pm; 50kr). The exhibition evokes the atmosphere of the time through an assortment of used tubes of paint, piles of canvases, paintings, sketches, books and ornaments.

THE SKAGEN ARTISTS

Skagen has long been popular with artists thanks to the warm, golden sunlight that illuminates its coastal scenery. During the 1870s a group of painters inspired by naturalism settled here and began to paint the local fishermen working on the beaches as well as each other. The **Skagen artists**, among them Michael and Anna Ancher and PS Krøyer, stayed until the turn of the century and achieved international recognition for their work, now on display at the Skagen Museum.

Grenen

The forces of nature can be appreciated at **Grenen**, 3km north of Skagen (hourly bus #79 in summer), along Sct. Laurentii Vej, Fyrvej and the beach, where two seas – the Kattegat and Skagerrak – meet, often with a powerful clashing of waves. You can get to the tip by a tractor-drawn bus (mid-April to mid-Oct; 20kr return) – although it's an enjoyable walk through some beautiful scenery.

Arrival and information

Train and bus The train station is on Sct. Laurentii Vej, the town's main thoroughfare. It is served by privately operated trains from Frederikshavn (50 percent discount with Eurail, ScanRail and InterRail) roughly once an hour.

Tourist office Vestre Strandvej 10 close to the marina Ⓣ98.44.13.77, Ⓦwww.skagen-tourist.dk (June–Aug Mon–Sat 9am–6pm & Sun 10am–4pm; rest of year Mon–Fri 10am–4pm, Sat 10am–4pm). Can arrange private rooms for 75kr.

Cycle hire Skagen Cykeludlegning next door to the tourist office (75kr per day).

Accommodation

Danhostel Skagen Rolighedsvej 2 ⓣ98.44.22.00, ⓦwww.danhostelnord.dk/skagen. A little way out of the centre, but the five- to twelve-bed dorms are clean and good value. If you're arriving by train it's closest to the Frederikshavnsvej stop. Closed Dec–mid Feb. ❷

Grenen Camping Fyrvej ⓣ98.44.25.46, ⓦwww.grenencamping.dk. By the beach 1.5km along the road to Grenen. Closed mid-Sept to early May). ❶

Eating and drinking

Skagen has fantastic "fresh-off-the-boat" **seafood** and you should treat yourself to a blowout meal at one of the marina restaurants. Eating on a budget can be tricky but there are plenty of pizza and kebab joints at the Sct Laurentii Vej/Havnevej crossroads.

Buddy Holly Havnevej 16 ⓦwww.buddy-skagen.dk. Pretty cheesy but this is Skagen's liveliest club with plenty of drinks deals and friendly bar staff. 11pm–5am in summer.

Guldbagaren Skagen Sct Laurentii Vej 104. Bakery/café serving a great range of pastries and sandwiches, plus excellent coffee.

Pakhuset Rødspættevej 6 by the marina. Grab an outside table and settle in for delicious seafood with a Danish twist – try the *Rødspættefileter* (fillet of plaice) with curry sauce and rye bread (78kr).

Moving on

Train Frederikshavn (hourly; 40min).

Estonia

HIGHLIGHTS

TALLINN'S OLD TOWN: wander this beautifully preserved corner of the city

LAHEMAA NATIONAL PARK: pristine wilderness teeming with wildlife on Estonia's north coast

SAAREMAA: a perfect island getaway with a beautiful castle and relaxing spa hotels

TARTU: party the night away with the student population of Tartu

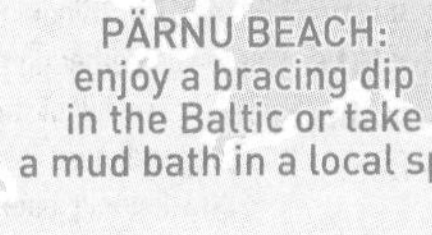

PÄRNU BEACH: enjoy a bracing dip in the Baltic or take a mud bath in a local spa

ROUGH COSTS

DAILY BUDGET basic €45/occasional treat €60

DRINK A. Le Coq beer €2

FOOD Blood sausage and sauerkraut €2.50

HOSTEL/BUDGET HOTEL €20/€40

TRAVEL Bus: Tallinn–Saaremaa (5hr) €13; Tartu–Tallinn (2hr) €9

FACT FILE

POPULATION 1.4 million

AREA 45,227 sq km

LANGUAGE Estonian; Russian, German and Finnish widely spoken

CURRENCY Kroon (EEK)

CAPITAL Tallinn (population: 411,000)

INTERNATIONAL PHONE CODE ⓣ372

Basics

It's a tribute to the resilience of the people of Estonia that, since independence in 1991, they've transformed their country from a dour outpost of the Soviet Union into a confident and technologically advanced EU member. The Estonians have had the misfortune to be surrounded by powerful, warlike neighbours. Conquered by the Danes in the thirteenth century, then German crusading knights, then Swedes and Russians, the country snatched independence at the end of World War I. This brief freedom was extinguished by the Soviets in 1940 and the country disappeared from view again only to emerge from the Soviet shadow in 1991.

Estonia's capital, **Tallinn**, is an atmospheric city with a magnificent **medieval centre** and lively nightlife. Two other major cities – **Tartu**, a historic university town, and **Pärnu**, a popular seaside resort – are worth a day or so each. To get a feel for the unspoilt countryside head for the island of **Saaremaa**: the island capital **Kuressaare** is home to one of the finest castles in the Baltics. **Lahemaa National Park**, outside Tallinn, offers a taste of pristine wilderness.

CHRONOLOGY

100s AD Tacitus refers to the Aestii people – the forebears of the Estonians.
1154 Estonia depicted on a map of the world for the first time.
1219 Danish conquer North Estonia, ushering in over a century of Danish rule.
1227 German crusaders invade the rest of Estonia.
1346 Danish territories in Estonia sold to the German Livonian Order.
1525 First book printed in the Estonian language.
1561 Livonian Order surrender their Estonian territory to Sweden.
1625 Sweden takes control over all Estonia.
1632 Estonia's first university opens in Tartu.
1721 Russia defeats Sweden in the Northern War and takes over Estonia.
1816 Serfdom is abolished in Estonia.
Late 1800s The spread of the Estonian language in schools is instrumental in increasing Estonian nationalism.
1918 Estonia states its claim to independence but is invaded by the Red Army starting the Estonian War of Independence.
1920 The Russians are defeated giving Estonia full independence.
1934 Authoritarian rule is established by Prime Minister Konstantin Pats.
1940 Soviets invade Estonia.
1944 Soviets maintain control by end of WWII, ushering in Communist rule.
1988 The "Singing Revolution" begins with huge crowds gathering to sing national songs.
1991 The fall of the Soviet Union leads to Estonian independence.
2004 Estonia joins NATO and EU.
2007 Estonia is the first country to introduce Internet voting for national elections.

ARRIVAL

The compact and ultra-modern **Tallinn Airport** (Ⓦwww.tallinn-airport.ee) is served by fifteen European airlines, including easyJet. Estonian Air (Ⓣ372 640 1101, Ⓦwww.estonian-air.ee), the national carrier, has direct flights from many major capitals including London, Dublin, Frankfurt, Barcelona and Stockholm. International **bus lines**, such as Eurolines (Ⓦwww.eurolines.ee), Ecolines (Ⓦwww.ecolines.net) and Hansabuss (Ⓦwww.hasabuss.ee) connect Tallinn via Tartu or Pärnu to Russia (Kaliningrad, St Petersburg), Latvia (Riga), Lithuania (Vilnius, Kaunas), Poland (Krakow, Warsaw), and Germany (Berlin, Bonn, Cologne, Hamburg, Munich, Stuttgart), among

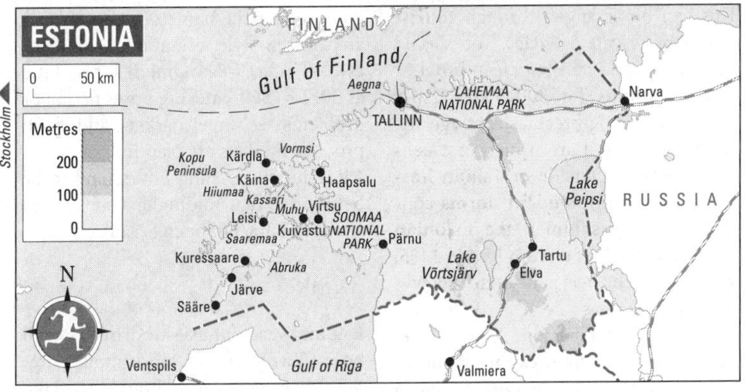

others. The only two international **rail services** from Estonia are the daily overnight trains from Tallinn to Moscow and St Petersburg – book seats for this in advance. Tallinn can also be reached by **ferry** from Helsinki, Finland and from Stockholm, Sweden; there are departures at least once hourly between 7am and 9pm daily, and one overnight departure daily, respectively (Ⓣ372 631 8550, Ⓦwww.portoftallinn.com), and in the summer there are also daily services between the island of Saaremaa and Ventslips, Latvia (Ⓦwww.sklferries.ee).

GETTING AROUND

Places covered in this chapter are all reached easily by **bus**, and **schedules** are posted on-line with an English version (Ⓦwww.bussireisid.ee). **Tickets** can be bought either from the bus station ticket office or direct from the driver. Buy tickets in advance if you're travelling in the height of summer or at weekends and opt for an express (*ekspress*) bus if possible. **Buses** are also the best method for travelling to neighbouring Baltic countries, with numerous daily services linking Tallinn, Vilnius and Riga via Pärnu.

The **rail network** is limited, but the domestic routes in operation are as fast as buses and slightly cheaper. Ticket windows at stations are marked *linnalähedanel* for suburban lines, *piletite müük* for national services and *rahvusvaheline* for international. Both train and bus **information** is available from station timetable boards – departure is *väljub*, arrival is *saabub*.

The bigger cities have efficient **public transport** systems, while smaller places, such as Saaremaa, are best explored by **bike**; inexpensive rentals are available. Due to the scarcity of public transport on the islands, many locals hitchhike, but the usual precautions apply.

ACCOMMODATION

Though cheaper than in Western Europe, **accommodation** in Estonia will still take a large chunk out of most budgets. **Youth hostels** aside, booking a **private room** is often the cheapest option (usually 250–400EEK per person).

ESTONIA ON THE NET

Ⓦ**www.visitestonia.com** Tourist board site.
Ⓦ**www.weekend.ee** Entertainment listings.
Ⓦ**www.balticsworldwide.com** News, listings and links from the bimonthly Baltic *City Paper*.
Ⓦ**www.baltictimes.com** English-language weekly newspaper.

This can be arranged through **tourist offices** or private agencies. You should be able to find plain but clean **hotel** or **pension rooms** for 300–500EEK per person including breakfast, though the cheapest of these are usually not centrally located. Outside of Tallinn **hostels** are often just **student dorms** converted for the summer; the **Estonian Youth Hostel Association** (☎646 1455, ⓦwww.baltichostels.net and ⓦwww.hostels.com) has details. Beds cost 100–200EEK per person. An ex-Soviet phenomenon is the **cabin campsite** (*kämping*), offering accommodation in three- to four-bed cabins (shared facilities) for 180–260EEK per person; many of them will also let you pitch a tent.

FOOD AND DRINK

Mainstays of Estonian cuisine include soup (*supp*), dark bread (*leib*), sour cream (*hapukoor*) and herring (*heeringas*), a culinary legacy of the country's largely peasant past. A typical **national dish** is *verevorst* and *mulgikapsad* (blood sausage and sauerkraut); various kinds of smoked fish, particularly eel (*angerjas*), perch (*ahven*) and pike (*haug*), are popular, as are **Russian dishes** such as *pelmeenid* (ravioli with meat or cabbage and mushrooms). You'd have to be invited into a local home to enjoy Estonian food at its best; there are, however, a few good places to try Estonian food in Tallinn, and both the capital and Tartu boast an impressive choice of ethnic **restaurants**. Outside these two cities, **vegetarians** will find little to choose from.

When eating out, it's cheaper to head for bars and cafés, many of which serve **snacks** like pancakes (*pannkoogid*) and salads (*salatid*). In a café you should be able to have a modest meal for 60–90EEK, while in a typical restaurant two courses and a drink would come to around 160EEK. If you really want to keep costs down then try one of the various **fast-food options**. Some places going under the name of **café** (*kohvik*) are canteen-style restaurants with dishes-of-the-day (*päevapraad*) for as little as 30EEK. **Self-catering** poses no major problems, as supermarkets and fresh produce markets are plentiful.

Restaurant opening hours tend to be between 11am-midnight; cafes keep similar hours, but open 8/9am.

Drink

Estonians are enthusiastic drinkers, with **beer (õlu)** being the most popular tipple. The principal local brands are **Saku** and **A. Le Coq**, both of which are rather tame light lager-style brews, although both companies also produce stronger, dark beers – the most potent are found on the islands (Saaremaa õlu is the best known). In bars a lot of people favour **vodka** (*viin*) with mixers which, thanks to generous measures, is a more cost-effective route to oblivion. Local alcoholic specialities include **hõõgvein** (mulled wine) and **Vana Tallinn**, a pungent dark liqueur which some suicidal souls mix with vodka. **Pubs and bars** – most of which imitate Irish or American models – are beginning to take over, especially in Tallinn; if you're not boozing, head for a *kohvik* (café), where alcohol is still served but getting drunk is not a priority. **Coffee** (*kohvi*) is usually of the filter variety, and **tea** (*teed*) is served without milk (*piima*) or sugar (*suhkur*) – ask for both if necessary. Bars are usually open from noon until 2/4am on weekends.

CULTURE AND ETIQUETTE

Estonia has fully embraced the digital age and there is a proliferation of free wi-fi hot spots all over the country, in the capital and rural areas alike, and computer literacy per capita is among the highest in Europe. Estonians themselves tend to be reserved when you first meet them, though if you are lucky enough to be invited to a local home, you will see their warm and generous side. Unused to loud displays of emotion, they are scandalized by the loutish behaviour of foreign stag parties, although they themselves enjoy sociable drinking. **Tipping** is relatively new here and ten percent is sufficient in restaurants to reward good service; otherwise just round up the bill.

SPORTS AND OUTDOOR ACTIVITIES

Football and **basketball** are the national sports; for the former, go to the **A. Le Coq Arena** (Asula 4c, ⓣ627 9940) whereas Tallinn's **Kalev Stadium** (Juhkentali 12, ⓣ644 5171) is the best place to see a basketball game. In the summertime, Estonia becomes a haven for **watersports** enthusiasts; windsurfing, kayaking, canoeing or simply hitting the beach. **Hiking**, **biking** and **horse-riding** are popular both on the Estonian mainland and on the islands off its coast, such as Saaremaa and Hiimaa. Estonia is also home to an unusual sport – **kiiking** (ⓦwww.kiiking.ee), involving a swing and extreme manoeuvring. Almost twenty percent of Estonia is protected land, divided between four **national parks** and numerous **nature reserves**, which are home to many species of wild animals and birds. National parks are best visited between May and September; **RMK** (ⓦwww.rmk.ee) manages the protected areas and camp sites.

COMMUNICATIONS

Post offices (*postkontor*) are open Mon–Fri 9am–6pm & Sat 9am–3pm. **Poste restante** is generally held for a month. You can buy **stamps** here and at some shops, hotels and kiosks. Most **public phones** take phonecards (of 30, 50 and 100EEK; available at kiosks and post offices) for local and long-distance calls. You'll find **Internet cafés** in most towns; expect to pay 25–60EEK/hr. There is a proliferation of free **wi-fi** all over Estonia with most cafes, restaurants and hostels offering the service.

EMERGENCY NUMBERS

Police ⓣ110; fire & ambulance ⓣ112.

EMERGENCIES

Theft and **street crime** are at relatively low levels, and if you keep your wits about you, you should come to no harm. The **police** (*politsei*) are mostly very young and some speak English. **Emergency health care** is free and, at least in Tallinn, emergency operators speak English.

INFORMATION & MAPS

Tourist offices can be useful for booking B&Bs and hotel rooms, as well as good-quality free **maps**; most bookstores also have good map sections. **Addresses** often include *mantee* (mnt.), meaning road; *puistee* (pst.), avenue; *tänav* (tn.), street; and *väljak*, square. The *In Your Pocket* guides (ⓦwww.inyourpocket.com) are invaluable listings guides, available from tourist offices and kiosks for 25EEK.

MONEY AND BANKS

Currency is the **Eesti kroon** (Estonian Crown, abbreviated EEK), pegged to the euro at €1 to 15.65EEK, and divided into 100 sents. Notes come as 2, 5, 10, 25, 50, 100 and 500 EEK and **coins** as 0.10, 0.20, 0.50, 1 and 5 EEK. Bank

STUDENT AND YOUTH DISCOUNTS

Many places to stay give a ten percent discount to ISIC card holders, as do some eateries. Other perks include half-price entry to most museums and sights, and it's even worth enquiring about reduced-price long-distance bus tickets.

Estonian

	Estonian	Pronunciation
Yes	*Jah*	Yah
No	*Ei*	Ey
Please	*Palun*	Palun
Thank you	*Aitäh/tänan*	Ayteh, tanan
Hello/Good day	*Tere*	Tere
Goodbye	*Head aega*	Heyad ayga
Excuse me	*Vabandage*	Vabandage
Where?	*Kus*	Kus
Student ticket	*Õpilase pilet*	Ypilahse pilet
Toilet	*Tualett*	Tualet
I'd like	*Ma sooviksin*	Mah sawviksin
I don't eat meat	*Ma ei söö*	Mah ay serr
The bill, please	*Palun arve*	Pahlun ahrrve
Good	*Hea*	Heya
Bad	*Halb*	Holb
Near	*Lähedal*	Lahedal
Far	*Kaugel*	Cowgal
Cheap	*Odav*	Odav
Expensive	*Kallis*	Kallis
Open	*Avatud*	Avatud
Closed	*Suletud*	Suletud
Today	*Täna*	Tana
Yesterday	*Eile*	Eyle
Tomorrow	*Homme*	Homme
How much is....?	*Kui palju maksab...?*	Kuy palyo maksab…?
What time is it?	*Mis kell praegu on?*	Mis kell prego on?
I don't understand	*Ma ei saa aru*	May saaru
Do you speak English?	*Kas te räägite inglise keelt?*	Kas te raagite inglise kelt?
One	*Uks*	Uks
Two	*Kaks*	Koks
Three	*Kolm*	Kolm
Four	*Neli*	Neli
Five	*Viis*	Vees
Six	*Kuus*	Koos
Seven	*Seitse*	Seytse
Eight	*Kaheksa*	Koheksa
Nine	*Üheksa*	Ooheksa
Ten	*Kümme*	Koome

(*pank*) opening hours are Mon–Fri 9am–4pm, many staying open in larger towns till 6pm and most also open Sat 9am–2/4pm. **ATMs** are widely available. **Credit cards** can be used in most hotels, restaurants and stores, but outside urban areas cash is preferred.

OPENING HOURS AND HOLIDAYS

Most **shops** open Mon–Fri 9/10am–6/7pm & Sat 10am–2/3pm, but many larger ones stay open later and are also open Sun. **Public holidays**, when most shops and all banks are closed, are: Jan 1, Feb 24, Good Fri, Easter Mon, May 1, June 23 & 24, Aug 20, Dec 25 & 26.

Tallinn

The port city of **TALLINN**, Estonia's compact capital, has been shaped by nearly a millennium of outside influence. Its name, derived from the Estonian for "Danish Fort" (*taani linnus*), recalls that the city was founded by the Danes at the beginning of the thirteenth century, and since then political control has nearly always been in the hands of foreigners. Tallinn was one of the leading cities of the **Hanseatic League**, the German-dominated association of Baltic trading cities, and for centuries it was known to the outside world by its German name, **Reval**. Even when Estonia was ruled by Sweden and Russia, the city's public life was controlled by the German nobility and its commerce run by German merchants. Today reminders of foreign rule abound in the streets, where each of the city's one-time rulers has left their mark. Once the staple crumbling backdrop for Soviet fairy-tale films, Tallinn has now reinvented itself as a weekend getaway for Europeans, and these days its buzzing cafés, pubs and clubs can offer a variety of hedonistic pursuits on a night out, though, be warned: the cobbled streets of Old Town make it the worst place in the world to wear high heels.

What to see and do

The heart of Tallinn is the **Old Town**, still largely enclosed by the city's medieval walls. At its centre is the **Raekoja plats**, the historic marketplace, above which looms **Toompea**, the hilltop stronghold of the German knights who controlled the city during the Middle Ages. West of the city centre there are several places worth a visit including: **Kadriorg Park**, a peaceful wooded area to the east with a cluster of historic buildings and a view of the sea, the forested island of **Aegna** and the **TV Tower**, which offers the best panoramic view of Tallinn and the surrounding area; on a clear day, you can see the coast of Finland.

Raekoja plats

Raekoja plats, the cobbled, gently sloping market square at the heart of the Old Town, is as old as the city itself. On its southern side stands the fifteenth-century **Town Hall** (*Tallinna Raekoda*), boasting an elegant arcade of Gothic arches at ground level, and a delicate steeple at its northern end. Near the summit of the steeple, **Vana Toomas**, a sixteenth-century weather vane depicting a medieval town guard, is Tallinn's city emblem. The well-labelled and informative **museum** inside the cellar hall (July–Aug Mon–Sat 10am–4pm; Sept–Oct 15; 40EEK) depicts Tallinn town life through the ages, and there is a good view from the belfry. For an even better view, climb the spiral staircase of the **Town Hall Tower** (*Raekoja Torn*; Jun–Aug daily 11am–6pm; 30EEK). The **Town Council Pharmacy**, in the north-eastern corner, with a white seventeenth-century façade, is known to have existed in 1422 and may be much older.

Church of the Holy Ghost and St Nicholas Church

Close to Raekoja plats are a couple of churches that neatly underline the social divisions of medieval Tallinn. The fourteenth-century **Church of the Holy Ghost** (May–Sept Mon–Sat 10am–5pm; Oct–April Mon–Sat 10am–4pm; 10EEK) on Pühavaimu near to the Town Council Pharmacy, is the city's most appealing church, a small Gothic building with stuccoed limestone walls, stepped gables and a tall, verdigris-coated spire. In 1535 priests here compiled an Estonian-language Lutheran catechism, an important affirmation of identity at a time when most Estonians had been reduced to serf status. The ornate clock set in the wall above the entrance dates from 1680 and is the oldest in Tallinn.

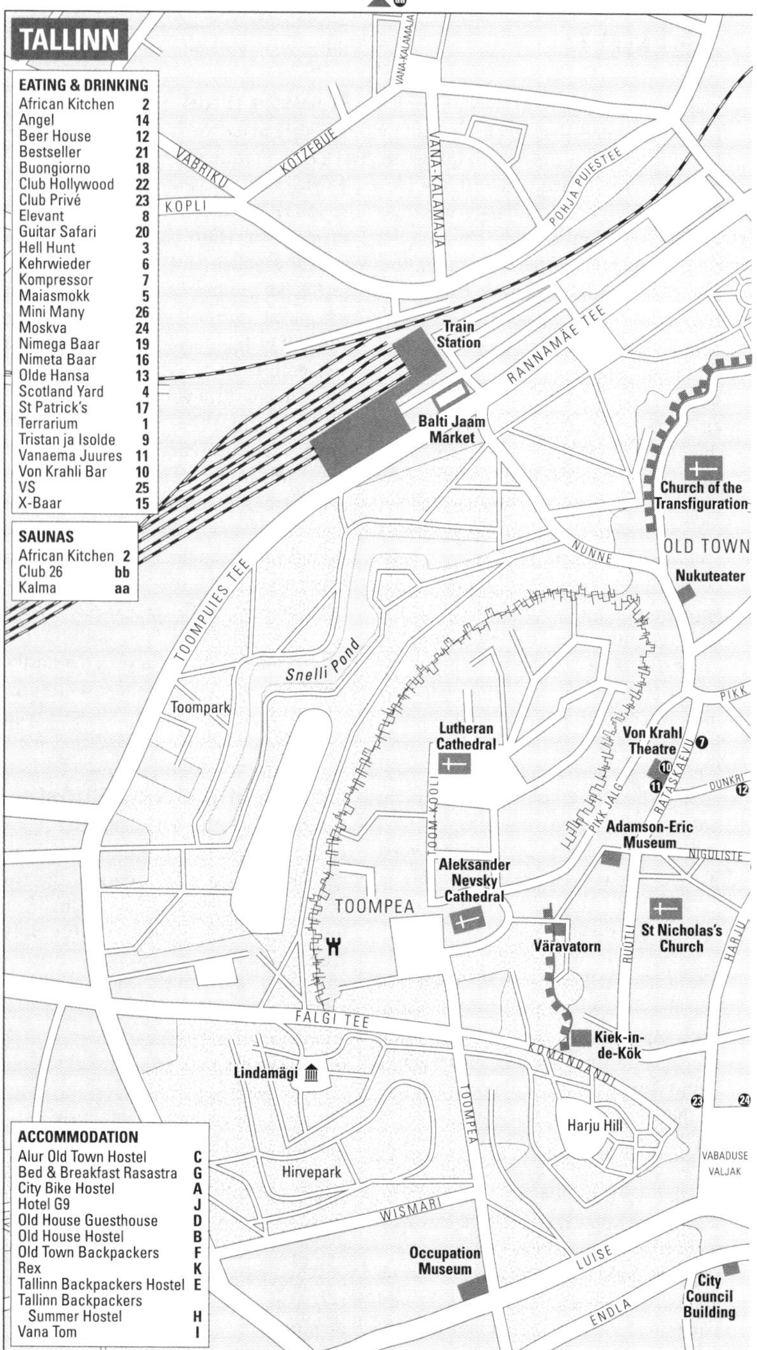
TALLINN
EATING & DRINKING
African Kitchen 2
Angel 14
Beer House 12
Bestseller 21
Buongiorno 18
Club Hollywood 22
Club Privé 23
Elevant 8
Guitar Safari 20
Hell Hunt 3
Kehrwieder 6
Kompressor 7
Maiasmokk 5
Mini Many 26
Moskva 24
Nimega Baar 19
Nimeta Baar 16
Olde Hansa 13
Scotland Yard 4
St Patrick's 17
Terrarium 1
Tristan ja Isolde 9
Vanaema Juures 11
Von Krahli Bar 10
VS 25
X-Baar 15
SAUNAS
African Kitchen 2
Club 26 bb
Kalma aa
ACCOMMODATION
Alur Old Town Hostel C
Bed & Breakfast Rasastra G
City Bike Hostel A
Hotel G9 J
Old House Guesthouse D
Old House Hostel B
Old Town Backpackers F
Rex K
Tallinn Backpackers Hostel E
Tallinn Backpackers Summer Hostel H
Vana Tom I
VANA-KALAMAJA
KOTZEBUE
VABRIKU
KOPLI
POHJA PUIESTEE
Train Station
RANNAMÄE TEE
Balti Jaam Market
Church of the Transfiguration
OLD TOWN
NUNNE
Nukuteater
TOOMPUIESTEE
Snelli Pond
Toompark
PIKK
Lutheran Cathedral
Von Krahl Theatre
DUNKRI
RATASKAEVU
PIKK JALG
TOOM-KOOLI
Adamson-Eric Museum
NIGULISTE
Aleksander Nevsky Cathedral
TOOMPEA
St Nicholas's Church
Väravatorn
RUUTLI
HARJU
FALGI TEE
Kiek-in-de-Kök
KOMANDANDI
Lindamägi
TOOMPEA
Harju Hill
VABADUSE VALJAK
Hirvepark
WISMARI
Occupation Museum
LUISE
City Council Building
ENDLA

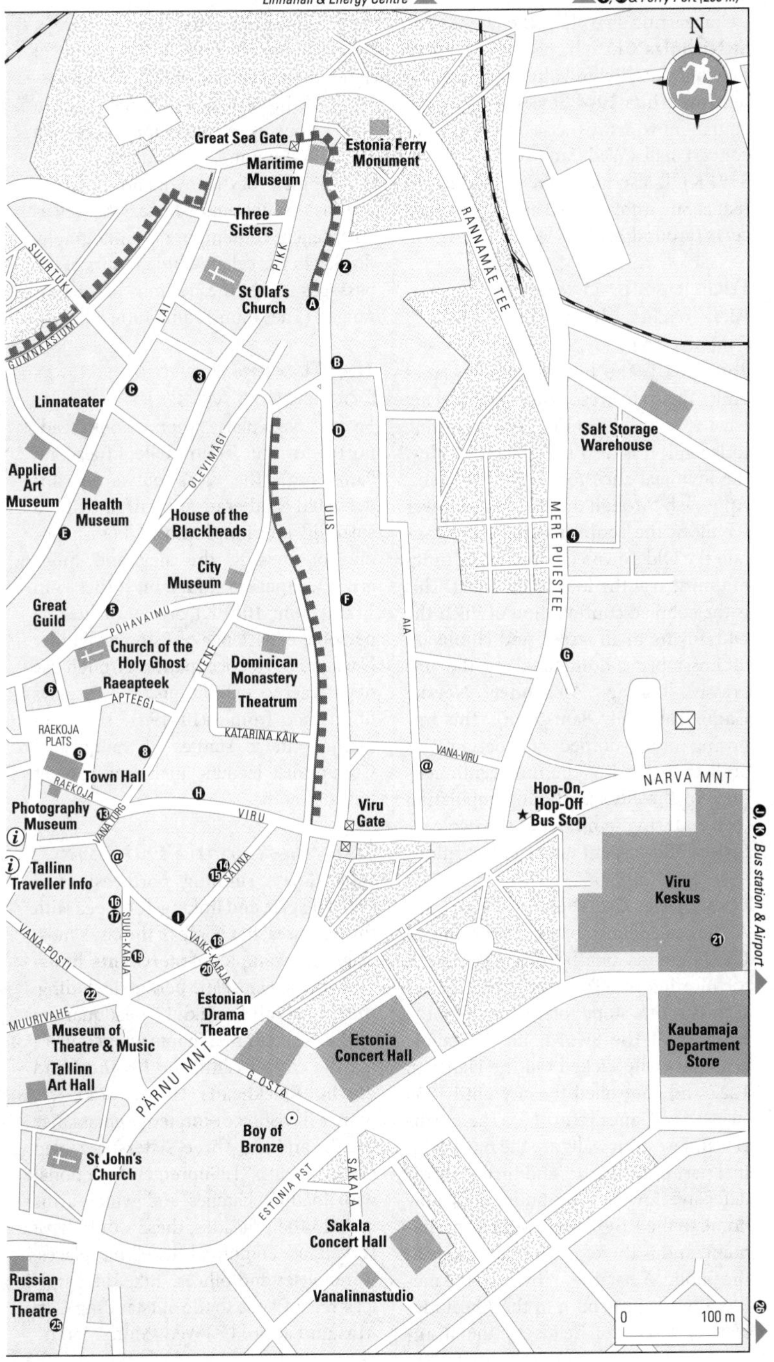
Linnahall & Energy Centre
1, bb & Ferry Port (200 m)
N
Great Sea Gate
Estonia Ferry Monument
Maritime Museum
Three Sisters
St Olaf's Church
SUURTÜKI
GÜMNAASIUMI
PIKK
LAI
RANNAMÄE TEE
Linnateater
Applied Art Museum
Health Museum
OLEVIMÄGI
House of the Blackheads
City Museum
UUS
Salt Storage Warehouse
MERE PUIESTEE
Great Guild
PÜHAVAIMU
Church of the Holy Ghost
VENE
Dominican Monastery
Theatrum
AIA
Raeapteek
APTEEGI
RAEKOJA PLATS
KATARINA KÄIK
VANA-VIRU
Town Hall
RAEKOJA
NARVA MNT
Hop-On, Hop-Off Bus Stop
Photography Museum
VANATURG
VIRU
Viru Gate
J, K, Bus station & Airport
Tallinn Traveller Info
SAUNA
Viru Keskus
SUUR-KARJA
VAIKE-KARJA
VANA-POSTI
MUURIVAHE
Museum of Theatre & Music
Estonian Drama Theatre
Estonia Concert Hall
Kaubamaja Department Store
Tallinn Art Hall
PÄRNU MNT
G. OSTA
Boy of Bronze
St John's Church
ESTONIA PST
SAKALA
Sakala Concert Hall
Russian Drama Theatre
Vanalinnastudio
0
100 m

Contrasting sharply is the late Gothic **St Nicholas Church**, just southwest of Raekoja plats. Rebuilt after being mostly destroyed in a 1944 Soviet air raid, the church now serves as a museum and concert hall (Wed–Sun 10am–4.30pm; 35EEK). It also hosts free organ recitals (Sat & Sun 4pm) as well as evening **concerts** (around 100EEK).

Toompea and the Alexander Nevsky Cathedral

Toompea is the hill where the Danes built their fortress after conquering what is now Tallinn in 1219. According to legend, it is also the grave of **Kalev**, the mythical ancestor of the Estonians. Approach through the sturdy gate tower – built by the **Teutonic Knights** to contain the Old Town's inhabitants in times of unrest – at the foot of Pikk jalg. This is the cobbled continuation of Pikk, the Old Town's main street, and climbs up to Lossi plats, dominated by the impressive-looking **Alexander Nevsky Cathedral** (daily 8am–7pm). This imposing onion-domed concoction was built at the end of the nineteenth century for the city's Orthodox population – an enduring reminder of the two centuries Tallinn spent under tsarist rule.

Toompea Castle

At the head of Lossi plats, pink **Toompea Castle** stands on the original Danish fortification site. Today's castle is the descendant of a stone fortress built by the **Knights of the Sword**, the Germanic crusaders who kicked out the Danes in 1227 and controlled the city until 1238 (when the Danes returned). The northern and western walls are the most original part of the castle, and include three defensive towers. The building is now home to the **Riigikogu**, Estonia's parliament, and is therefore out of bounds to the public. A narrow archway in the medieval walls just south of the Alexander Nevsky Cathedral leads to the ironically named **Virgins' Tower**, once a prison for prostitutes. A little south of here on Komandandi tee is the imposing **Kiek-in-de-Kök tower** dating from 1475, housing a **museum** (Tues–Sun 10.30am–5/6pm; 25EEK) displaying the development of the town and its fortifications throughout its history, as well as an excellent contemporary photography display in the cellar. Guided tours of the passages under the bastions can be arranged (Tues–Sun 11am–4pm; 50EEK).

The Toomkirik and Occupation Museum

From Lossi plats, Toom Kooli leads north to the **Toomkirik** (Tues–Sun 9am–6pm), the city's outwardly understated Lutheran cathedral, with a splendid interior. South of Lossi plats, on Toompea 8, the airy and modern **Occupation Museum** (Tues–Sun 11am–6pm; 10EEK) brings to life the personal experience of Estonians under Nazi and Soviet occupation through use of interactive exhibitions, and displays of artefacts from 1940–1991. The basement contains statues of vanquished Communist leaders, including a giant bust of Lenin.

Elsewhere in the Old Town

Pikk tänav, running northeast from Pikk jalg gate and linking Toompea with the port area, has some of the city's most elaborate examples of **merchants' houses** from the Hanseatic period, including: the **Great Guild** at Pikk 17, headquarters of the German merchants who controlled the city's wealth; the **Brotherhood of the Blackheads House**, Pikk 26, with a lavishly decorated Renaissance façade; and the **Three Sisters**, a gabled group at Pikk 71. Supremely functional with loading hatches and winch-arms set into their facades, these would have served as combined dwelling places, warehouses and offices. Take the parallel street of Vene to the outstanding **City Museum** at no. 17 (Wed–Mon: March–

Oct 10.30am–6pm, Nov–Feb 10.30am–5pm; 35EEK), which recounts the history of Tallinn from the thirteenth century through to Soviet and Nazi occupation and beyond in imaginative multimedia style, with helpful staff at hand.

St Olaf's Church

Continuing north along Pikk brings you to the enormous, Gothic **St Olaf's Church**, first mentioned in 1267 and named in honour of King Olaf II of Norway, who was canonized for battling against pagans in Scandinavia. The church is chiefly famous for its 124-metre **spire**, which you can climb for a spectacular view of the city (daily 10am–5pm; 25EEK).

The Maritime Museum and city wall

At its far end Pikk is straddled by the sixteenth-century **Great Coast Gate**, flanked by two towers. The larger of these, the aptly named **Fat Margaret Tower**, has walls four metres thick and now houses the **Estonian Maritime Museum** (Wed–Sun 10am–6pm; 35EEK; some English captioning), a surprisingly entertaining four floors of nautical instruments and scale models of ships. Down Suur-Kloostri, west of Lai street, is one of the longest extant sections of Tallinn's medieval **city wall**. The 4km of walls that surrounded the Old Town were mostly constructed during the fourteenth century, and enhanced over succeeding centuries. Today, 2km are still standing, along with twenty-six of the original forty-six towers.

Kadriorg Park

Kadriorg Park, a heavily wooded area 2km east of the Old Town, was laid out according to the instructions of Russian tsar **Peter the Great**, who first visited Tallinn in 1711, the year after the Russian conquest. The main entrance to the park is at the junction of Weizenbergi tänav and J. Poska (tram #1 or #3 from Viru väljak). Weizenbergi cuts through the park, running straight past **Kadriorg Palace**, a Baroque residence designed by the Italian architect **Niccolò Michetti**, which Peter had built for his wife Catherine. The palace houses the **Museum of Foreign Art** (May–Sept Tues–Sun 10am–5pm; Oct–April Wed–Sun 10am–5pm; 50EEK), with a fine collection of Dutch and Russian paintings. A short walk up Weizenbergi, the excellent futuristic-looking **KUMU** building houses the largest collection of Estonian art (daily 11am–6pm; 75EEK all exhibitions), featuring paintings from the eighteenth to the twentieth centuries influenced by contemporary artistic trends, as well as innovative modern exhibitions; don't miss the room with talking heads.

Lauluväljak

Walk down Mäekalda for around fifteen minutes to Narva mnt. On the other side of this busy road is the **Lauluväljak**, a vast amphitheatre that's the venue for **Estonia's Song Festivals.** These gatherings, featuring massed choirs thousands strong, have been an important form of national expression since the first all-Estonia Song Festival was held in Tartu in 1869, and are held every two years. The present structure, which can accommodate 15,000 singers (with room for a further 30,000 or so on the platform in front of the stage), went up in 1960. The grounds were filled to capacity for the 1988 festival when 30,000 people joined their voices in song as a significant public expression of longing for independence from Soviet rule, in what became known as the **"Singing Revolution"**. A tree-lined avenue heads downhill from the amphitheatre to Pirita tee, which runs along the seashore.

Pirita Beach and Aegna Island

To reach Tallinn's popular **Pirita Beach** and the large wooded park stretching behind it, take bus # 1, 34, or 38 from the underground stop at the Viru Centre. An hour's ride on the boat from the nearby **Pirita harbour** (100EEK return), tiny peaceful **Aegna** is an excellent day-trip destination (Mon & Wed–Fri two ferries daily; Sat & Sun four ferries daily; tourist office has updated timetable). Its forest-covered interior and clean beaches attract locals who come here for a few days' camping in the summer.

Arrival and information

Air The airport is 3km southeast of the city centre and linked to Viru väljak by bus #2 (every 20min between 6am and midnight). It stops behind the Viru shopping mall, five minutes' walk from Old Town's Viru Gate, one of several entrances to the historic part of the city.

Train and bus Tallinn's train station is at Toompuiestee 35, just northwest of the Old Town, ten minutes' walk to the Town Square (Raekoja plats), while the city's bus terminal is at Lastekodu 46, 2km southeast of the centre – trams #2 and #4 run from nearby Tartu mnt. to Viru väljak at the eastern entrance to the Old Town; alternatively, take any bus heading west along Juhkentali.

Boat Arriving by sea, the passenger port is just northeast of the centre at Sadama 25.

Tourist office The tourist office, in the Old Town at Kullasseppa 4 (April–Oct Mon–Fri 9am–6pm, Sat & Sun 10am–5pm; Nov–March Mon–Fri 9am–5pm, Sat 10am–3pm; ⓣ645 7777, ⓦwww.tourism.tallinn.ee), sells various maps and city guides. You can also buy a Tallinn Card here (90/250/300/350EEK for 6/24/48/72hr), which gives free entry to all museums and churches, unlimited use of public transport and other discounts. The widely available free paper *Tallinn This Week* (ⓦwww.ttw.ee), the excellent *City Paper* (ⓦwww.balticsworldwide.com; 33EEK) and the informative *Tallinn In Your Pocket* (ⓦwww.inyourpocket.com; 35EEK) city guide have what's on listings.

City transport

Public transport Though most sights can be covered on foot, Tallinn has an extensive tram, bus and trolleybus network. Tickets (*talongid*) common to all three systems are available from kiosks near stops for 10EEK or from the driver for 15EEK. Validate your ticket using the on-board punches.

Taxis Taxis are reasonably cheap (around 10EEK/km, slightly more after 10pm) though as a foreigner you may occasionally find your meter running faster than it should. Most companies have a minimum charge of 35EEK, but a taxi from one point in the city centre to another rarely exceeds 50EEK.

HOP-ON, HOP-OFF BUS TOUR.

For easy access to attractions outside Old Town, such as Kadriorg, complete with running commentary, hop on one of the tour buses just outside Viru Gate; there are three routes, and you can buy travel passes of varied lengths by the bus station. 24hr/160EEK.

Accommodation

Though the range of hostel and budget **accommodation** in central Tallinn is improving, demand still outstrips supply in summer, and if arriving without a reservation you may be forced to stay in a distant suburb. You can book central and excellent-value **private rooms** with *Bed & Breakfast Rasastra*, just north of Viru väljak at Mere 4 (daily 9.30am–6pm; ⓣ661 6291, ⓦwww.bedbreakfast.ee), an agency offering rooms (❷–❸) in family homes throughout the Baltics, and private **apartments** (❹–❺) for longer stays.

TALLINN TRAVELLER INFO

Opposite the tourist office Is an information tent (daily 10am–10pm) run by students; join the excellent **nightlife tour** (180 EEK/person; price includes four drinks and entry to one nightclub) and discover Tallinn's hottest spots, led by young, knowledgeable, multi-lingual guides. During the day they also offer the Tallinn Walking Tour, covering the main historical sites In Old Town, and the Funky Bike Tour, featuring Old Town and beyond. Cool free map of Tallinn available.

Hostels

Alur Rannamäe 3 ⓣ631 1531, ⓦwww.alurhostel.com. Friendly and well-run place in an old wooden house near the train station. Quiet, with clean and cozy doubles. Dorms ❷; rooms ❸

City Bike Hostel Uus 33 ⓣ511 1819, ⓦwww.citybike.ee. Small hostel with 9 beds, wi-fi, lounge and kitchenette. Bicycles for rent; bike tours around Tallinn offered, plus transfers to/from Lahemaa National Park. Bed linen 30EEK, towels 15EEK. Dorms ❷; doubles ❷

Old House Hostel Uus 26 ⓣ641 1281, ⓦwww.oldhouse.ee. Rambling Old Town house with a small dorm and a handful of cozy doubles with shared bath. Dorms ❷; rooms ❸

Old Town Backpackers Uus 14 ⓣ517 1337, ⓦwww.balticbackpackers.com. Two large rooms with bunk beds and additional pull-out couches. Breakfast and free use of sauna included. ❷

Rex Tartu mnt 62 ⓣ633 2181, ⓦwww.hot.ee/allarp3. Functional hostel around the corner from the bus station, with basic but adequate dorms as well as a few doubles and singles with shared bath. Dorms ❷; rooms ❸

Tallinn Backpackers Lai 10 ⓣ644 0298, ⓦwww.tallinnbackpackers.com. Lively 2-dorm hostel with cellar bar, wi-fi, video room and sauna. Day trip to Lahemaa National Park offered. Dorms ❷. Affordable singles, doubles and triples are found at **Tallinn Backpackers Summer Hostel**, its quiet sister, ideally located on Viru 5, with clean rooms, kitchen, internet, wi-fi and cheap laundry service. It also gives you access to Tallinn Backpackers facilities. Rooms ❸–❹

Vana Tom Väike-Karja 1 ⓣ631 3252, ⓦwww.hostel.ee. Large Old Town hostel with dorms and doubles. Friendly and with a very central (if somewhat noisy) location, but it could be a bit cleaner. Breakfast included. Dorms ❷; rooms ❸

Guesthouses and B&Bs

Hotell G9 Gonsiori 9 ⓣ626 7100, ⓦwww.hotelg9.ee. Sparsely-furnished but comfy en suites on the third floor of an apartment building, nicely poised between the Old Town and the bus station. Breakfast costs 50EEK extra. ❹

Old House Guest House Uus 22 ⓣ641 1464, ⓦwww.oldhouse.ee. Second branch of the Old House has five small but clean rooms with shared facilities (❸) and a comfortable seven-bed dorm ❷

Eating

The variety and quality of **restaurants** in Tallinn keeps getting better, and though traditional fare figures prominently on many menus, the choice of international cuisines you'll find around the Old Town would be impressive anywhere. These are the best places for vegetarians, though conventional restaurants usually offer one or two meat-free options. Most of the **cafés** and **bars** listed below also offer inexpensive snacks and meals.

Cafés

Bestseller Viru väljak 4/6. Popular café on the top floor of the Viru Centre mall, inside the Rahva Raamat bookstore. Great juices, wraps and salads. 30-40EEK.

Kehrwieder Saiakang 1. Comfy sofas ideal for curling up with a top-quality coffee in this dimly lit cellar café, with big windows looking out on Raekoja plats. Coffee 35EEK.

Kompressor Rataskaevu 3. Roomy café-bar popular with a youngish crowd, and famous for its wonderfully stodgy and filling Estonian pancakes (45EEK).

Maiasmokk Pikk 16. Tallinn's most venerable café – founded in 1864 – with a beautiful wood-panelled interior. Queue up for your coffee and pastry, then take your used dishes back when you're done. Coffee 30EEK.

Miny Many Maakri 26, behind the Radisson Hotel. Cheap, old-fashioned lunch spot in the new town, with filling meat-and-potatoes dishes at around 35EEK. Mon–Fri till 7pm, Sat till 5pm.

Tristan ja Isolde Raekoja plats 1. Dark, atmospheric café in the Town Hall with a full range of drinks and tasty salads and cakes. Cappuccino 35EEK.

Restaurants

African Kitchen Uus 34. Good selection of peanut, coconut and rice dishes, some spicy and many vegetarian, prepared by a Nigerian chef and served in a jungle-themed lounge. Tasty smoothies (40EEK) and prawn dishes (170EEK).

Beer House Dunkri 5. Busy, roomy beer cellar which brews its own ales and serves up generous portions of grilled meat (160EEK) and pizza (150EEK). Live music most nights.

Buon Giorno Müürivahe 17. Genial atmosphere and affordable pizza and pasta; popular with Tallinn's resident Italians. Mains 90EEK.

Elevant Vene 5. Chic Indian restaurant with affordable range of dishes, including plenty of vegetarian choices.

Olde Hansa Vana turg 1. Extremely popular yet affordable medieval-style restaurant. Ask your serving wench for a starter plate to share and some elk/boar/bear sausages (250 EEK).

Vanaema Juures Rataskaevu 10/12. A cozy cellar restaurant in Old Town, "Grandma's Place" serves quality traditional Estonian food in an unpretentious setting. Try Grandma's Roast or lamb in blue cheese sauce (250EEK). Closes 6pm Sundays.

Drinking and nightlife

Most of Tallinn's highly popular clubs cater for a mainstream crowd. More underground, cutting-edge dance music events change location frequently and are advertised by flyposters, or try asking around in the city's hipper bars; expect to pay 50–150EEK admission.

Bars

Hell Hunt Pikk 39. Lively pub packed with expats and locals most nights; it is spacious, friendly and serves its own excellent dark Hunt beer.
Nimeta Baar (Pub Without a Name) Suur-Karja 4/6. Along with its sister venture the **Nimega Baar (Pub With a Name)** across the street at Suur-Karja 13, this lively bar draws in an expat crowd. DJs and live music at weekends, international football matches screened live.
Scotland Yard Mere pst. 6e. Large and lively pub with nightly live music, large dance floor, and toilets shaped like electric chairs.
St. Patrick's Suur-Karja 8. The pick of Tallinn's Irish pubs, set in a beautifully restored medieval house and popular with expats, tourists and locals alike. Your fourth beer comes free. Happy hour 4–6pm daily.
Von Krahli Bar Rataskaevu 10/12. Large hip hangout that's always packed with a bohemian crowd. Frequent live music – from alternative to reggae to hip-hop. Good, cheap food: huge daily specials 45EEK.
VS Pärnu mnt. 28. Purple/silver industrial decor, chilled beats, late-night DJs, hip clientele and great Indian food all make this one of the top spots in Tallinn. Bring a friend if you order the tikka biriyani (185EEK).
X-Baar Sauna 1. Extremely popular gay bar with bright pink décor and Estonian karaoke most nights.

Clubs

Angel Sauna 3 Ⓦwww.clubangel.ee. Frequented by a mixed gay and straight crowd for great music and free vodka, Tallinn's premier gay club can be difficult to get into on weekends; put your name on the list online. Lively bar upstairs. Wed–Sat 10pm–4am. Entry 75EEK
Club Hollywood Vana-Posti 8 Ⓦwww.clubhollywood.ee. Large Old Town dance club playing techno, R'n'B and hip hop. Very popular with a younger crowd. Wed–Sat 10pm–4am; 50–100EEK.
Club Privé Harju 6 Ⓦwww.clubprive.ee. Style-conscious temple to cutting-edge dance culture, attracting big-name DJs and live bands. Free entry for ladies before midnight. Casual/club wear, but no jogging bottoms or trainers. Thurs–Sat 10pm–4am
Moskva Vabaduse väljak 10. Polished, bright and popular club/café/restaurant that buzzes with a hip crowd. Extensive cocktail list and good cakes; modest portions. DJs on weekends. Closes 2am Fri & Sat.
Terrarium Sadama 6 Ⓦwww.terrarium.ee. Visiting international DJs, Russian men and beautiful young things frequent this minimalist club by the port. Free drinks for girls before midnight. Occasional male stripper. Wed–Sat 10pm–4am; 50–100EEK

Entertainment

Cinemas

Coca-Cola Plaza Hobujaama 5. Ⓦwww.forumcinemas.ee. High-tech 11-screen cinema showing the latest blockbusters. 120EEK.
Sõprus Vana-Posti 8 Ⓦwww.kino.ee. Shows a full range of indepedent films. 40–80EEK.

Live music

Estonia Concert Hall Estonia pst. 4 Ⓣ614 7760, Ⓦwww.concert.ee. Tallinn's premier venue for classical music.
Estonian National Opera Estonia pst. 4 Ⓣ683 1201, Ⓦwww.opera.ee. Frequent opera and ballet performances; book in advance.
Linnahall Mere pst. 20 Ⓣ641 1500, Ⓦwww.linnahall.ee. Live pop concert venue by the harbour.
Song Festival Grounds Narva mnt. 95 Ⓣ611 21 00, Ⓦwww.lauluvaljak.ee. This indoor concert hall hosts international stars as well as musicals.

Saunas

Saunas are a quintessential part of Estonian life, and private saunas are common in most guesthouses and hotels, as well as a number of restaurants. While, traditionally, saunas started out as an important part of health and cleanliness rituals, for many Estonians they are now places to socialise with family and friends and to warm up during the long winter months. Estonian saunas tend to be wooden, specialising in dry heat, as opposed to its Latvian and Lithuanian neighbours' steam saunas.
African Kitchen Uus 34 Ⓣ644 2555, Ⓦwww.africankitchen.ee. The funky private sauna in this popular restaurant has its own sound system. You can hire it for 250EEK/hr; ask at the bar. Noon–1am; Fri & Sat noon–2am.

SAUNA ETIQUETTE

The first thing to do when you go to an Estonian **sauna** is get naked. Being completely naked is the norm, while in mixed saunas, wrapping a towel around you is up to your discretion. Once you get used to the heat, try scooping some water onto the hot stones; it evaporates instantaneously, raising the temperature. Once everyone is sweating profusely, you might notice others gently swatting themselves or their friends with birch branches; this increases circulation and rids the body of toxins. Make sure you don't overdo it – ten minutes should be long enough, but get out immediately if you start to feel dizzy. Locals normally follow up with a plunge into a cold lake, although a cold shower suffices.

Club 26 (in Reval Hotel Olümpia) Liivalaia 33 ⓣ631 5585, ⓦwww.revalhotels.com. The ultimate sauna experience – complete with a wonderful bird's-eye view of Tallinn – at the health club on the 26th floor of the Olümpia hotel. Private saunas hold up to 10 people. 300EEK/hr until 3pm, 600EEK/hr after. Mon–Fri 6:30am–11pm; Sat & Sun 7.30am–11pm.

Kalma Vana-Kalamaja 9a ⓣ627 1811, ⓦwww.bma.ee/kalma. Kalma is Tallinn's oldest public bath (built in 1928), containing private saunas for rent as well as men's and women's general baths (complete with swimming pool). Men 100–120EEK, women 80–100EEK. Daily 10am–11pm

Shopping

Antiik Lai Come here for all your Soviet kitsch, including a number of Lenin busts varying in size.
Knit market Müürivahe & Viru. All manner of hand-made knitwear and linens at this small outdoor market, open daily in the summer during the day.
Natural Style Pikk, near Hobusepea. Linen, amber, wool and ceramic goods in tiny artisan's workshops. near Nunne.
Viru Keskus Viru Väljak 4. Modern mall just outside Old Town's Viru Gate.

Directory

Embassies Canada, Toom-Kooli 13 ⓣ27 3311; Ireland, 2nd floor, Vene 2 ⓣ681 1888; UK, Wismari 6 ⓣ667 4700; US, Kentmanni 20 ⓣ668 8100.
Exchange Outside banking hours, try the Monex exchange offices in the ferry dock, or the Kaubamaja or Stockmann department stores (all daily 9am–8pm).
Hospital Ravi 18 ⓣ620 7015. English-speaking doctors available.
Internet access *Kohvik@Grill*, Aia 3 (daily 9am–9pm; 30EEK/hr); *Neo*, Väike-Karja 12 (24hr; 35EEK/hr).
Laundry Sauberland, Maakri 23; *Seebimull*, Liivalaia 7.
Left luggage At the bus station (Mon–Sat 6.30am–10.20pm, Sun 7.45am–8.20pm).
Pharmacies Aia Apteek, Aia 10 (8:30am-midnight); Tõnismäe Apteek, Tõnismägi 5 (24hr).
Police Pärnu mnt. 11 ⓣ612 3523.
Post office Narva mnt. 1, opposite the Viru Hotel. Mon-Fri 7:30am–8pm; Sat 8am–6pm.

Moving on

Train Pärnu (2 daily; 3hr); Tartu (3 daily; 3hr 20min); Moscow (1 daily; 16 hr); St Petersburg (1 daily, 9hr)
Bus Kuressaare (6 daily; 4hr 30min); Pärnu (every 30min; 2hr); Tartu (every 30min; 2hr 30min).
Ferry Helsinki, Finland (15–25 daily; 1hr 40min–4hr).

LAHEMAA NATIONAL PARK

The largest of Estonia's **national parks**, **Lahemaa** stretches along the north coast, comprising lush forests with ample wildlife, pristine lakes, ruggedly beautiful coves and wetlands, dotted with tiny villages throughout. Public transport is infrequent, although it is possible to catch a bus to various parts of the park, but cycling is the best way to get around. Hitchhiking is practised among locals, but usual precautions apply.

The **Lahemaa National Park Visitor Centre** (ⓣ329 5555, ⓦwww.lahemaa.ee May–Aug 9am–7pm; Sept 9am–5pm) is located in tiny **Palmse**, 8km north of **Viitna**, a village on Route 1; you can take a bus from Tallinn to Viitna in the

Narva direction (every half-hour; 1hr) and then cycle up to Palmse (it may be possible to stow the bike on the bus for an additional charge). The helpful staff at the visitor centre can advise on camping and other **accommodation**, biking and hiking trails, nature tours (book guides well in advance in summer), and provide a detailed map of the area; contact them before leaving.

Whether you want to visit the fishing villages along the coast and walk to Hara island during low tide, hike the interior or visit the restored old German manors in the villages of Vihula, **Sagadi** and Kolga, the park warrants several days' exploration. There are **bicycles for rent** at the Sagadi manor (160EEK/day); alternatively, make arrangements at Tallinn's *City Bike Hostel* (see p.341), which arranges transfers and day-trips to Lahemaa.

Western Estonia

SAAREMAA

The island of **SAAREMAA**, off the west coast of Estonia, is yet under-exploited, leaving its forests and coastline ripe for exploration. It was the last part of Estonia to come under foreign control (when the Knights of the Sword captured it in 1227) and the locals have always maintained a strong-minded indifference to the influence of foreign occupiers, leading many to claim that the island is one of the most authentically Estonian parts of the country. Its main town, **Kuressaare**, remains much as it was before World War II and is home to one of the finest **castles** in the Baltic region. Buses from Tallinn, Tartu and Pärnu come here via a ferry running from the mainland village of **Virtsu** to **Muhu island**, which is linked to Saaremaa by a causeway.

What to see and do

Kuressaare

In Kurressaare's **Kesk väljak** (main square) you'll find the yellow-painted **Town Hall**, dating from 1670, its door guarded by stone lions. From the square, Lossi runs south past a **monument** commemorating the 1918–20 **War of Independence**, the eighteenth-century white Orthodox **Nikolai church**, and on to the magnificent **Kuressaare Castle**. Surrounded by a deep moat, it was founded during the 1260s as a stronghold for the bishop of Ösel-Wiek. The formidable structure you see today dates largely from the fourteenth century and is protected by huge, seventeenth-century ramparts. The labyrinthine keep houses the **Saaremaa Regional Museum** (May–Sept daily 11am–7pm; Oct–April Wed–Sun 11am–7pm; 40EEK); you can reach the interesting collection of displays by going up and down spiral staircases and peering into numerous cellars. These cover Saaremaa's history and culture and wildlife; it's also possible to climb the watchtowers, one of which houses stunning contemporary art and photography exhibitions. Play Robin Hood at the **archery range** by the handicraft workshops to the right of the castle (4 arrows/15EEK or 60EEK/15 minutes, 10:30am–5:30pm).

Around the island

Saaremaa is mostly flat, and cycling the 40km route from Kuressaare to **LEISI**, on the opposite side of the island, is a wonderful way of seeing rural Estonia, with alternating landscapes of pine forest, tiny villages and vast fields. Rent a bike from Bivarix Rattapood (Tallinna 26, Mon–Sat 10am–6pm; 80EEK/4hrs, 150EEK/day). Follow Route 10 out of town and turn left onto Route 79; the traffic is very light. **KAALI** village makes a worthy detour halfway along – it is home to a giant **meteorite crater**, a round, murky green pool about 100m in diameter, thought to be at least four thousand years old. Try the delicious *solyanka* (Russian meat soup) at the *Kaali Tavern* across the road.

Just short of Leisi lies **ANGLA**, with five much-photographed wooden windmills by the roadside. Take the bus back to Kuressaare (29EEK, plus 15EEK for the bicycle); the Leisi bus 'station' is a brightly-graffitied shelter to the right of the main road; get a bus timetable printout in Kuressaare.

Alternatively, cycle to **JARVE**, 10km southwest of Kuressaare along Route 77, the local beach hangout. A long narrow strip of sand, hidden behind the dunes, it's just a short walk through the pine forest; the crystal-clear and cold water is a welcome respite in the summer. Route 77 carries on down to the tip of the Torgu peninsula, ending 47km from Kuressaare in an amazing view from the jagged cliffs.

Arrival and information

Bus From the bus station on Pihtla turn left onto Tallinna in order to reach the main square.
Tourist office The tourist office in the town hall (Tallinna 2; June–Aug daily 9am–7pm, Sept–May Mon–Fri 9am–5pm; ⓣ45/33120, ⓦwww.saaremaa.ee) can book private rooms across the island for around 200EEK per person (but only if you require accommodation on the day of arrival), and provide information on cycling trails around Saaremaa, outdoor pursuits, numerous hiking trails and camping facilities.
Internet access is at the public library, Raekoja 1 (Mon–Fri 9am–6pm, Sat 10am–4pm).

Accommodation

Piibelehe Holiday Home Piibelehe 4 ⓣ45/36206, ⓦwww.piibelehe.ee. On the outskirts of town, this place has several guest rooms with shared facilities; it also offers camping. Tents ❶; rooms ❷
Kraavi Holiday Cottage 500m southeast of the castle at Kraavi 1 ⓣ45/55242, ⓦwww.kraavi.ee. Cosy and tidy modest doubles, with a hearty breakfast included. Use of sauna and bicycle rent cost extra. ❷
Ovelia Majutus Suve 8 ⓣ45/55732. Friendly and clean guest house with shared facilities 10 minutes' walk from bus station. ❷

TREAT YOURSELF

Spa Hotel Ruutli Pargi 12 ⓣ45/48100, ⓦwww.sanatoorium.ee. Luxurious hotel with airy rooms, cable TV, wi-fi and buffet breakfast included. Numerous spa treatments on offer, such as: "Charcot's Shower" – strip naked and be pummelled with strong jets of water (135 EEK); and "Neo-Qi energy cocoon" – undergo infrared sauna, steam room, vibration massage and Vichy shower, followed by water massage (290EEK). Book treatments in advance. ❾

Eating and drinking

Classic Lossi 9. Bustling café with an excellent selection of pasta, salads (20–75EEK), omelettes and pancakes (35EEK). ISIC discounts.
La Perla Lossi 3. Good-sized portions of well-cooked, inexpensive pasta. Mains 75–95EEK.
Vaekoja Tallinna mnt 3. Restaurant on the main square serving delicious savoury pancakes (50EEK).
Vana Konn Kauba 6. Youth-oriented drinking spot with Czech and German beers on tap, a pool table and Estonian pub grub. Pelmeni 35EEK.
Veski Pärnu 19. Popular pub in an old windmill. Meat dishes stand out. Mains 90–160EEK.

Moving on

Bus Leisi (8 daily; 55min); Tallinn (6 daily; 4hr 30min); Parnu (3 daily; 3hr); Tartu (2 daily; 5hr 30min)

PÄRNU

PÄRNU, Estonia's main seaside resort, comes into its own in summer, when it fills with local and foreign visitors and plays host to daily cultural and musical events. The wide sandy beach is popular with everyone, while the festivals cater to a more alternative crowd.

What to see and do

Rüütli, cutting east-west through the centre, is the Old Town's main pedestrianised thoroughfare, lined with shops and eateries. Near the junction with Aia is the worthwhile **Pärnu Museum**, Rüütli 53 (daily 10am–6pm; 20EEK), tracing local history up until World War II. The oldest building in town is the **Red Tower** (Mon–Sat 10am–5pm), a fifteenth-century remnant of the medieval city walls on Hommiku, a block north from Rüütli, past the **artisan stalls**. At the western end of Uus is the Orthodox green-domed **Catherine Church**, dating from 1760 and named after the Russian empress **Catherine the Great**. Follow Nikolai south from the centre and you'll reach the **Chaplin Centre** (daily 9am–9pm; Ⓦwww.chaplin.ee; 25EEK;) set in the Communist party HQ at Esplanaadi 10. It holds regular shows, film festivals and changing exhibitions of contemporary Estonian art. South of here Nikolai joins Supeluse, which leads to the beach, passing beneath the trees of the shady **Rannapark**. At the southern end of Supeluse is the grand, colonnaded Mudravilla, the former public mud baths, built in 1926. Beyond the sand dunes is Pärnu's main attraction – the wide clean sandy **beach**, busy only during the summer months. Lined with ice-cream kiosks and beer tents, the beach is packed with sun worshippers playing volleyball, splashing in the shallow waves and even kite-surfing.

Arrival and information

Train the train station is about 5km east of the centre at Riia mnt. 116.
Bus The bus station is on Pikk at the northeastern edge of the Old Town (information & ticket office round the corner at Ringi 3; daily 6.15am–7.30pm). Luggage storage by Platform 8 (Mon–Fri 8am–7:30pm, Sat–Sun 9am–5pm; 20EEK/day).
Tourist office The tourist office at Rüütli 16 (June–Aug Mon–Sat 9am–6pm, Sun 10am–3pm; Sept–May Mon–Fri 9am–5pm; Ⓣ447 3000, Ⓦwww.parnu.ee) can book accommodation for 25EEK; extensive information available on Pärnu.
Internet head to the Chaplin Centre (see above; 30EEK/hr).

TREAT YOURSELF

Tervise Paradiis Side 14 Ⓦwww.terviseparadiis.ee. You don't have to stay in this hotel to make use of its extensive spa treatments, including the famous mud bath. There is also a popular water park onsite. 10am–10pm. 290EEK/adult for a day ticket to the water park; 250EEK/person/day for outpatient spa therapy; 3100EEK/adult luxurious body care 2-day package.

Accommodation

Hostel Lõuna Lõuna 2 Ⓣ443 0943, Ⓦwww.hot.ee/hostellouna. Centrally located, with comfortable, spacious dorms (❷) and doubles (❷–❸).
Konse Holiday Village 2km east at Suur-Jõe 44a Ⓣ534 35092, Ⓦwww.konse.ee. Has spotless rooms (❸) and tent pitches (❶).
Terve Hostel Ringi 50, Ⓣ507 7332, Ⓦwww.terve.ee. Guesthouse run by an effusive hostess offers airy, clean doubles with shared facilities. ❹

Eating and drinking

Club Tallinn Narva mnt. 27. The most popular club in Pärnu caters to the 20-something crowd. Varied music; open June–Aug Wed–Sat 11pm–6am.
Kuursaal Mere pst. 22. Popular 1890s tavern by the beach with tasty "Big Bellyful of Meat" dishes. Mains 75–160EEK. Closes 4am Fri & Sat.
Onu Sam Suvituse 11. Serves inexpensive burgers, hot dogs and pizza (20–35EEK) to beach-bound revelers. Open 24 hours.
Ruutlihoov Ruutli 29. This lively pub has friendly service and live music on weekends. Beer 30EEK
Steffani Nikolai 24. Extremely popular restaurant with a wide choice of tasty pizza and pasta dishes. Huge *calzones* 85EEK. Closes 2am Fri & Sat.
Sunset Club Ranna pst. 3. Hosts beach-side music events popular with a young crowd, with retro *Star Café* upstairs featuring DJs. Fri & Sat 10pm–4am.

Moving on

Bus to: Kuressaare (4 daily; 3hr); Tallinn (every 30min; 2hr); Tartu (20 daily; 2hr 30min).

Eastern Estonia

TARTU

The main sights of **TARTU**, less than three hours from Tallinn by bus, lie between **Cathedral Hill**, right in the centre, and the **River Emajõgi**.

What to see and do

Tartu is a lively town with events all year round (ⓦwww.visittartu.com). The city's centre is its cobbled **Town Hall Square**, fronted by the Neoclassical **Town Hall,** a pink-and-white edifice with the Kissing Students statue in front of it. The northeast corner features the **Leaning House** housing the **Tartu Art Museum**. The Neoclassical theme continues in the cool white facade of the main **Tartu University** building at Ülikooli 18, just north of the square. About 100m beyond the university is the red-brick Gothic **St John's Church**, founded in 1330, and most famous for the pint-sized terracotta sculptures set in niches around the main entrance.

Behind the Town Hall, Lossi climbs **Cathedral Hill**, a pleasant park with the remains of the red-brick Cathedral at the top. Built by the Knights of the Sword in the thirteenth century, it boasts the best view of Tartu from the rooftop terrace (June–Aug 10am–5pm; Sept Wed–Sun 11am–5pm; Oct–Nov Sat–Sun 11am–5pm; 15EEK). Nearby is the **sacrificial stone** left over from Estonia's pagan past; students now burn their exam notes on it.

The former **KGB headquarters** on Riia house a cellar **museum** with exhibits on deportations and life in the gulags, summarised in English (Tues–Sat 11am–4pm; 5EEK). Just north of the centre, a walk through the historic **Soupilin** (Soup Town) district, with streets named after fruit and vegetables, old wooden houses and a colourful bohemian population of musicians, artists and students, offers a glimpse into pre-war Tartu.

Arrival and information

Train and bus The train station is about 500m southwest of the centre at Vaksali 6, and the bus station is just east of the centre at Turu 2. There's luggage storage at the bus station (5–20EEK/bag; weekdays 7:30am-9pm, Sat 7:30am–5pm, closed Sun).
Tourist office Tartu's tourist office at Raekoja plats 14 (Mon–Fri 9am–5pm, Sat 10am–3pm; May–Sept also Sun 10am–3pm; ⓣ7/442 111, ⓦwww.tartu.ee) can assist with accommodation. *Tartu in Your Pocket* is sold here (25EEK).
Internet *Zum Zum*, Küüni 2 (daily 9am–11pm; 35EEK/hr).

Accommodation

Hostel Narva Narva mnt. 27 ⓣ740 9955, ⓦwww.kyla.ee. Five spotless, self-contained apartments 5mins walk from Old Town Square. Book in advance. ❷–❸
Hostel Pepleri Pepleri 14 ⓣ740 9955, ⓦwww.kyla.ee. 40 tidy rooms, all en-suite, just ten minutes' walk from the centre. ❷–❸
Hostel Raatuse Raatuse 22 ⓣ740 9955, ⓦwww.kyla.ee. 21 spacious rooms, sharing kitchen and bathroom facilities. ❶–❸
Hotel Tartu Soola 3 ⓣ731 4300, ⓦwww.tartuhotell.ee. Clean hotel with helpful staff offering budget "youth room" triples, doubles and 4-person family rooms. Fifteen percent ISIC discount on regular rooms. ❶–❺
Uppsala Maja Jaani 7 ⓣ736 1535, ⓦwww.uppsalamaja.ee. Friendly central guesthouse with 5 immaculate rooms, a large kitchen, dining room and wi-fi. ❸–❺

Eating

Crepp Ruutli 16. Chic café with delicious warm salads and filling crepes (30EEK).
Gruusia Saatkond Rüütli 8. Georgian restaurant specializing in excellent grilled meat dishes. Shashliks 120–160EEK.
Tsink Plekk Pang Küütri 6. Serves Chinese and Indian food, including numerous vegetarian options, in an arty café ambiance. Mains 80EEK.

University Café Ulikooli 20. Bargain buffet serving a selection of salads and hot dishes; pay by weight. 11.90EEK/100g

Drinking and nightlife

Atlantis Narva mnt. 2. Large and lively mainstream disco across the river. Tues–Sat 10pm–4am; admission 50–125EEK.

Place Beer Colours Kuuni 2. Lounge café with moving ceiling and interesting beer cocktails; press a button on your table to order.

Who Wouldn't Like Johnny Depp? Kompanii St. 2. DJs, varied music mix, lively young crowd. Wed–Sat 10pm–4am; admission 75EEK.

Wilde Pub Vallikraavi 4. This vast, literary-themed pub offers tea, coffee, alcohol and Irish/Estonian pub grub amidst grand furniture and sepia photographs. Live music. Happy hour 5–7pm. Closes 2am Fri & Sat.

Zavood Lai 30. Funky-coloured dive bar with an alternative clientele, just north of the centre. Closes 4am.

Moving on

Bus Kuressaare (6 daily; 6hr); Pärnu (20 daily; 2hr 30min); Tallinn (every 30min; 2hr 30min); Elva (every 30min; 30 min).

ELVA

25 km south of Tartu, the little resort of **Elva** sits between two pretty lakes, **Verevi** and **Arbi**, and is surrounded by ancient forest, some of it over one thousand years old. Lake Arbi is opposite the bus station, just behind the friendly and helpful **tourist office** on Pikk 2 (Tues–Fri 10am–5pm, Sat 10am–3pm; ⓣ7/45 6141, ⓦwww.elva.ee); the staff can provide detailed information on hiking and biking trails in the **Elva Vitipalu nature reserve**, 2km southeast of town. To reach the reserve, cross the **train tracks** behind the bus station and turn right on Vaikne. Carry on until the signposted turning on the left, just before the cemetery. The trails pass by pristine lakes, along the Elva River and through pine forests. Lake Verevi lies a short walk along Tartu mnt. to your right if you walk up the embankment behind the outdoor amphitheatre on the shore of Lake Arbi.

For **accommodation** there are numerous rest stops and camping grounds in the reserve. Alternatively, *Guesthouse Elva*, Karneri 6, to the left of Vaikne (ⓣ7/300 139, ⓦwww.elvakylalistemaja.ee; ❸-❹), has several airy rooms with wooden floors, breakfast included. There's also *Verevi Motel*, H. Raudsepa 2, by Lake Verevi (ⓣ7/45 7084, ⓦwww.verevi.ee; ❹), which has clean rooms and bikes to rent.

Out of several **eateries** on Kesk, *Tomi Pubi*, a popular pub, serves up decent helpings of meat-and-potato dishes (80EEK) and *Café Kuldrannake* has a good selection of coffees (30EEK) and light meals.

Moving on

Bus Tartu (every 30min; 30min).

Finland

HIGHLIGHTS ✪

KUOPIO SAUNA: warm your bones at the world's biggest woodsmoke sauna

LENIN MUSEUM, TAMPERE: fascinating museum delving into the relationship between Lenin and Finland

OLAVINLINNA CASTLE, SAVONLINNA: the best-preserved medieval castle in Finland

DESIGN DISTRICT, HELSINKI: sample the shops, cafés and nightlife of this vibrant area of the capital

ROUGH COSTS

DAILY BUDGET Basic €30/with the occasional treat €40

DRINK *Salmiakki* (liquorice-flavoured vodka) €4–6 a shot

FOOD Reindeer stew with potatoes €9

HOSTEL/BUDGET HOTEL €20

TRAVEL Helsinki–Tampere €31

FACT FILE

POPULATION 5.2 million

LAND AREA 338,145 sq km

LANGUAGE Finnish and Swedish

CURRENCY Euro (€)

CAPITAL Helsinki (population 560,000)

INTERNATIONAL PHONE CODE ⓣ358

Basics

One of Europe's most culturally isolated and least understood countries, Finland has been independent only since 1917, having been ruled for hundreds of years first by the Swedes and then by Tsarist Russia. Its position on the cusp of Europe means that Finland draws influences from Russia as much as the west, and has preserved a distinct identity still present under the increasingly glossy and Europeanized surface. Non-Finnish-speakers will find even the language disorientating – it has nothing in common with other European tongues. But Finland's strangeness is also part of its charm. Much of the country's history has involved a struggle for recognition and survival, and so modern-day Finns have a well-developed sense of their own culture.

The country is mostly flat and punctuated by huge forests and lakes, but has wide regional variations. The south contains the least dramatic scenery, but the capital, **Helsinki**, more than compensates, with its brilliant architecture and superb collections of national history and art. Stretching from the Russian border in the east to the industrial city of **Tampere**, the vast waters of the **Lake Region** provide a natural means of transport for the timber industry – indeed, water here is a more common sight than land with towns lying on narrow ridges between lakes. North of here, Finland ranges from the flat western coast of **Ostrobothnia** to the thickly forested heartland of **Kainuu** and gradually rising fells of **Lapland**, Finland's most alluring terrain and home to the Saami, semi-nomadic reindeer herders.

CHRONOLOGY

1800 BC Tribes from Russia settle in Lapland.

98 AD Roman historian Tacitus writes first recorded reference of the "Fenni".

1150s Sweden invades southwestern Finland.

1293 Sweden defeats Finland again, establishing dividing lines between the Catholic West and Orthodox East.

1642 First complete Finnish translation of the bible produced.

1721 In the Treaty of Uusikaupunki, Sweden cedes Finnish land to Russia.

1809 Russians take Finland after military victory over Sweden.

1812 Helsinki is declared capital of Finland.

1858 Confusion caused as Russia forces Finns to drive on the right-hand side of the road.

1860 Finland acquires its own currency, the markka.

1906 Finland gains its own national parliament. Finnish women are the first in the world to receive full political rights.

1917 Finland declares independence from Russia.

1939–40 Soviet troops invade Finland but meet fierce resistance during the "Winter War".

1941 Under the Moscow Peace Treaty, the southeast territory of Karelia is ceded to the Russians.

1952 Helsinki holds the Olympic Games.

1987 Finnish company Nokia begins to make hand-held mobile phones.

1995 Finland joins the EU.

2000 Tarja Halonen becomes the first female president.

2002 Finland adopts the euro.

2006 National celebrations as Finnish death metal group Lordi win Eurovision song contest.

2006 Finnish parliament votes in favour of the EU constitution.

ARRIVAL

There are over twenty airports dotted around the country, but you're most likely to arrive at Helsinki Vantaa or

Tampere Pirkkala, which are the main hubs for **international flights**. Ryanair (www.ryanair.com) flies into Tampere from the UK, Latvia and Germany, but the biggest low-cost airline in Finland is Blue1 (www.blue1.com), which offers routes to and from most major European cities. Finnair (www.finnair.com) is also a good bet for cheap flights. If you're combining a trip to Finland with travel in the rest of Scandinavia, you might well arrive by **ferry** from Stockholm at either Helsinki or Turku (known as Åbo in Swedish). The trip takes up to 15 hours – contact Silja Line for tickets and timetables (www.tallinksilja.com/en/).

GETTING AROUND

For the most part trains and buses integrate well, and you'll only need to plan with care when travelling through the remoter areas of the far north and east. **Trains** are operated by Finnish State Railways (VR; www.vr.fi). Comfortable Express and InterCity trains, plus tilting Pendolino trains, serve the principal cities several times a day. If you're travelling by night train, it's better to go for the more expensive sleeper cars if you want to get any rest, as no provision is made for sleeping in the ordinary seated carriages. Elsewhere, especially on east–west hauls through sparsely populated regions, trains are often tiny or replaced by buses on which rail passes are still valid. **InterRail** and **ScanRail** passes are valid on all trains. The best timetable is the *Rail Pocket Guide* published by VR and available from all train stations and tourist offices. **Buses** – privately run, but with a common ticket system – cover the whole country, but are most useful in the north. Tickets can be purchased at bus stations and most travel agents; only ordinary one-way tickets can be bought on board. The timetable (*Pikavuoroaikataulut*), available at all main bus stations, lists all bus routes.

Domestic flights can be comparatively cheap as well as time-saving, especially if you're planning to visit Lapland and the far north. Finnair (Ⓦwww.finnair.com) and Blue1 (Ⓦwww.blue1.com) are the main operators, though, generally, cheaper tickets are only available if booked well in advance. One-way tickets with Blue1 can be especially good value.

ACCOMMODATION

There's a good network of official **HI hostels** as well as a few independents. Most charge €5–6 for breakfast and bed linen is often extra, too, so if you're on a tight budget it's worth bringing your own sheets. Dorms are usually single-sex.

Hotels are expensive. Special offers in summer mean that you'll be able to sleep well on a budget in high season, but may have difficulty finding anything affordable out of season – the reverse of the norm. You can **book** through Hotel Booking Centre (Ⓣ 09/2288 1400), inside the train station in Helsinki. The free *Finland: Budget Accommodation* booklet, available from any tourist office, contains a comprehensive list of hostels and campsites.

Taking advantage of discount schemes and summer reductions, such as the **Finncheque**, must be arranged through the Finnish Tourist Board or a specialist travel agent before arriving in Finland; each cheque entitles the holder to one night's accommodation with breakfast in participating chains, for use daily between June and Sept all year (Fri–Sun.) More information can be obtained from Ⓦwww.finncheque.fi. In many towns you'll also find **tourist hotels** (*matkustajakoti*) offering fewer frills for €35–50 per person, and **summer hotels** (*kesähotelli*; June–Aug only), which offer decent accommodation in student blocks for €25–45 per person.

Official **campsites** (*leirintäalue*) are plentiful. Most open from May or June until August or September, although some stay open longer and a few all year round. Many three-star sites also have cottages, often with TV, sauna and kitchen. Invest in a Camping Card (€6), available at all sites, valid for a year and usable everywhere in Scandinavia.

FOOD

Finnish food is a mix of Western and Eastern influences, with Scandinavian-style fish specialities and exotic meats such as reindeer and elk alongside dishes that bear a Russian stamp – pastries, and casseroles strong on cabbage and pork. **Breakfasts** (*aamiainen*) are buffets of herring, eggs, cereals, cheese, salami and bread. You can lunch on the economical **snacks** sold in market halls (*kauppahalli*) or adjoining cafés. Most train stations and some bus stations and supermarkets also have cafeterias offering a selection of snacks and light meals, and street stands turn out burgers and hot dogs for around €3. Otherwise, campus **mensas** are the cheapest places to get a hot dish (around €4). Theoretically, you have to be a student, but you're unlikely to be asked for ID. In regular restaurants or *ravintola*, **lunch** (*lounas*) deals are good value, with many places offering a lunchtime buffet table (*voileipäpöytä* or *seisovapöytä*) stacked with a choice of traditional goodies for a set price of €8.50–13. Pizzerias are another good bet, serving lunch specials for €6–9. For **evening meals**, a cheap pizzeria or *ravintola* will serve up standard plates of meat and two veg. In Helsinki and the big towns there's usually a good range of options, including Chinese and Thai. Prices run from €6 for a cheap pizza to €50 for a substantial meal plus drinks in a smart restaurant.

Drink

Most restaurants are fully licensed, and many are frequented more for drinking than eating. **Bars** are usually open till midnight or 1am and service stops half an hour before closing. You have to be 18 to buy beer and wine, 20 to buy spirits, and some places have an age limit of 24. The main – and cheapest – outlets for take-out alcohol are the ubiquitous government-run **ALKO** shops (Mon–Thurs 10am–5pm, Fri 10am–6pm; Oct–April also Sat 9am–2pm).

Beer (*olut*) falls into three categories: "light beer" (I-Olut), like a soft drink; "medium strength beer" (*keskiolut*, III-Olut), perceptibly alcoholic, sold in supermarkets and cafés; and "strong beer" (A-Olut or IV-Olut), on a par with the stronger European beers, and only available at licensed restaurants, clubs and ALKO shops. Strong beers, such as Lapin Kulta and Koff, cost about €2.50 per 500ml can. Imported beers go for €2.50–3 per can. Finlandia **vodka** is €16 for a 700ml bottle; Koskenkorva, a rougher vodka, is €15. You'll also find Finns knocking back salmiakki, a premixed vodka/liquorice cocktail which looks and tastes like cough medicine.

CULTURE AND ETIQUETTE

To an outsider, Finns can seem almost alarmingly withdrawn: little value is put on exuberance, and you can have an entire conversation with a Finn without them making any discernible facial expression. Showing off is frowned upon and social gaffes like interrupting someone halfway through a sentence, bragging or talking too loudly show up awkwardly against the general background of social calm. Underneath this reserve, of course, Finnish people are as full of enthusiasm and affection as any other nation, and if you strike up a conversation you'll find that Finns can be friendly and welcoming once you get past the national code of restraint. This is all the more true when there's drink around, but alcohol abuse really is a noticeable problem here, and it's wise to avoid trying to keep up with the Finnish capacity for drinking.

Tipping is rare in Finland. Service is usually included in restaurant bills although it's common to round the bill up to the nearest convenient figure when paying in cash (the same applies for taxi fares).

SPORTS AND OUTDOOR ACTIVITIES

The winter landscape lends itself to **cross-country skiing**, and the season lasts from December until January in the south and April in northern and central Finland. There are ski slopes, too – try Ruka or Pyhä – and several operators offering off-piste skiing. Watery pursuits like **kayaking** are a worthwhile option in the lake regions, especially around Lake Inari and Saimaa. Popular national sports include the distinctively Finnish *päsepallo*, similar to baseball, and ice hockey.

COMMUNICATIONS

Communications are dependable and quick. **Post offices** are generally open 9am–6pm, with later hours in Helsinki. Public **phones** are ubiquitous; you'll need a phone card (*puhelinkortti*), available at post offices and tourist offices; some phones also accept credit cards. International calls are cheapest between 10pm and 8am. Directory enquiries are ⓣ118 (domestic) and ⓣ020208 (international). Free **internet access** is readily

FINLAND ON THE NET

Ⓦ**www.visitfinland.com** The Finnish tourist board site.
Ⓦ**www.sauna.fi** The Finnish Sauna Society.
Ⓦ**www.srmnet.org** Finnish Youth Hostel Association.

available, even in the most out-of-the-way places – most likely at the local library (though you may need to book a few hours in advance) or the tourist office.

EMERGENCIES

You won't have much cause to come into contact with the Finnish **police**, though if you do they are likely to speak English. As for **health problems**, if you're insured, you'll save time by seeing a doctor at a private health centre (*lääkäriasema*) rather than waiting at a national health centre (*terveyskeskus*). Medicines must be paid for at a **pharmacy** (*apteekki*), generally open daily 9am–6pm; outside these times, a phone number for emergency help is displayed on every pharmacy's front door.

Finnish

Stress on all Finnish words always falls on the first syllable.

	Finnish	Pronunciation
Yes	*Kyllä*	Koo-leh
No	*Ei*	Ay
Thank you	*Kiitos*	Keetos
Hello/Good day	*Hyvää päivää*	Hoo-veh pai-veh
Goodbye	*Näkemiin*	Nek-er-meen
Excuse me	*Anteeksi*	Anteksi
Where?	*Missä?*	Miss-eh
Good	*Hyvä*	Hoo-veh
Bad	*Paha*	Paha
Near	*Lähellä*	Le-hell-eh
Far	*Kaukana*	Kau-kanna
Cheap	*Halpa*	Halpa
Expensive	*Kallis*	Kallis
Open	*Avoinna*	Avoyn-na
Closed	*Suljettu*	Sul-yet-oo
Today	*Tänään*	Ten-ern
Yesterday	*Eilen*	Aylen
Tomorrow	*Huomenna*	Hoo-oh-menna
How much is....?	*Kuinka paljon maksaa?*	Koo-inka pal-yon maksaa
What time is it?	*Paljonko kello on?*	Palyonko kello on
I don't understand	*En ymmärrä*	Enn oomerreh
Do you speak English?	*Puhutteko englantia?*	Poohut-tuko englantia
One	*Yksi*	Uxi
Two	*Kaksi*	Caksi
Three	*Kolme*	Col-meh
Four	*Neljä*	Nel-yeh
Five	*Viisi*	Veesi
Six	*Kuusi*	Coosi
Seven	*Seitsemän*	Sayt-se-men
Eight	*Kahdeksan*	Car-deksan
Nine	*Yhdeksän*	Oo-deksan
Ten	*Kymmenen*	Kummenen

INFORMATION AND MAPS

Most towns have a **tourist office**, some of which will book accommodation for you. In summer they are open daily 9am–7pm in more popular centres; in winter, hours are much reduced and some don't open at all. The best general **map** is by *Freytag & Berndt*; there's also an excellent publication, *Finland Facts and Map*, available from tourist offices.

EMERGENCY NUMBERS

☎112 for all emergency services

MONEY AND BANKS

Finland's currency is the **euro** (€). Banks are open Mon–Fri 9.30am–4.15pm. Some **banks** have exchange desks at transport terminals, and **ATMs** are widely available. You can also change money at hotels, but the rates are generally poor. **Credit cards** are widely accepted right across the country.

OPENING HOURS AND HOLIDAYS

Shops generally open Mon–Fri 9am–6pm, Sat 9am–4pm. Along with banks, they close on **public holidays**, when most public transport and museums run to a Sunday schedule. These are: Jan 1, Jan 6 (Epiphany), Good Fri and Easter Mon, May 1, Ascension (mid-May), Whitsun (late May), Midsummer (late June), All Saint's Day (early Nov), Dec 6, Dec 24, 25 and 26.

Helsinki

An instantly loveable city of 560,000 people, **HELSINKI** is quite different from the other Scandinavian capitals, closer both in mood and appearance to the major cities of eastern Europe. For a century an outpost of the Russian Empire, Helsinki's very shape and form has been derived from its more powerful neighbour. Yet during the twentieth century it became a showcase for independent Finland, much of its impressive architecture reflects the dawning of Finnish nationalism and the rise of the republic. Today, visitors will find a youthful buzz, on the streets, where the boulevards, outdoor cafés and restaurants are crowded with Finns taking advantage of the short summer. At night the pace picks up in Helsinki's great selection of pubs and clubs and free rock concerts in the numerous parks.

What to see and do

Following a devastating fire in 1808, and the city's designation as Finland's capital in 1812, Helsinki was totally rebuilt in a style befitting its new status: a grid of wide streets and neoclassical brick buildings modelled on the then Russian capital, St Petersburg. **Esplanadi**, a wide tree-lined boulevard across a mishmash of tramlines from the harbour, is Helsinki at its most charming. To the north is Senate Square, dominated by the exquisite form of the recently renovated **Tuomiokirkko** (cathedral; Mon–Sat 9am–6pm, Sun noon–6pm; free), designed by Engel and completed after his death in 1852. After the elegance of the exterior, the spartan Lutheran interior comes as a disappointment; more impressive is the gloomily atmospheric **crypt** (same times as cathedral; entrance on Kirkkokatu), now often used for exhibitions.

Uspenski Cathedral

Walking east, the square at the end of Aleksanterinkatu is overlooked by the onion domes of the Russian Orthodox **Uspenski Cathedral** (Mon–Sat 9.30am–4pm, Sun noon–3pm, Oct–April closed Mon; tram #3). Inside, there's a glitzy display of icons. Beyond is Katajanokka, a wedge of land extending between the harbours, where a dockland development programme is under way, converting the old warehouses into pricey new restaurants and apartments.

City Museum

Just a block south of Senate Square, the **City Museum** at Sofiankatu 4 (Mon–Fri 9am–5pm, Sat & Sun 11am–5pm; €4, free entry on Thurs) offers a record of 450 years of Helsinki life in an impressive permanent exhibition called "Helsinki Horizons".

Atheneum Art Museum

Directly opposite the bus station is the **Atheneum Art Museum**, Kaivokatu 2 (Tues–Fri 9am–6/8pm, Sat & Sun 11am–5pm; €6/ €8 during special exhibitions). Its stirring selection of artworks spans the period 1710 to 1980, including Akseli Gallén-Kallela and Albert Edelfelt's scenes from the Finnish epic, the *Kalevala*, and Juho Rissanen's moody studies of peasant life, recalling a time when the spirit of nationalism was surging through the country.

Kiasma and Lasipalatsi

Kiasma is Helsinki's museum of contemporary art (Tues 9am–5pm, Wed–Sun 10am–8.30pm; €5.50). Its gleaming steel-clad exterior and hi-tech interior make it well worth a visit, and temporary exhibitions are drawn from a vast collection, including everything from paintings to video installations. Opposite is the **Lasipalatsi**, a multimedia complex situated in a recently renovated 1930s classic Functionalist building, now home to a number of trendy shops and cafés.

Parliament and National Museum

Further along on the left, the multi-columned and rather solemn **Parliament**

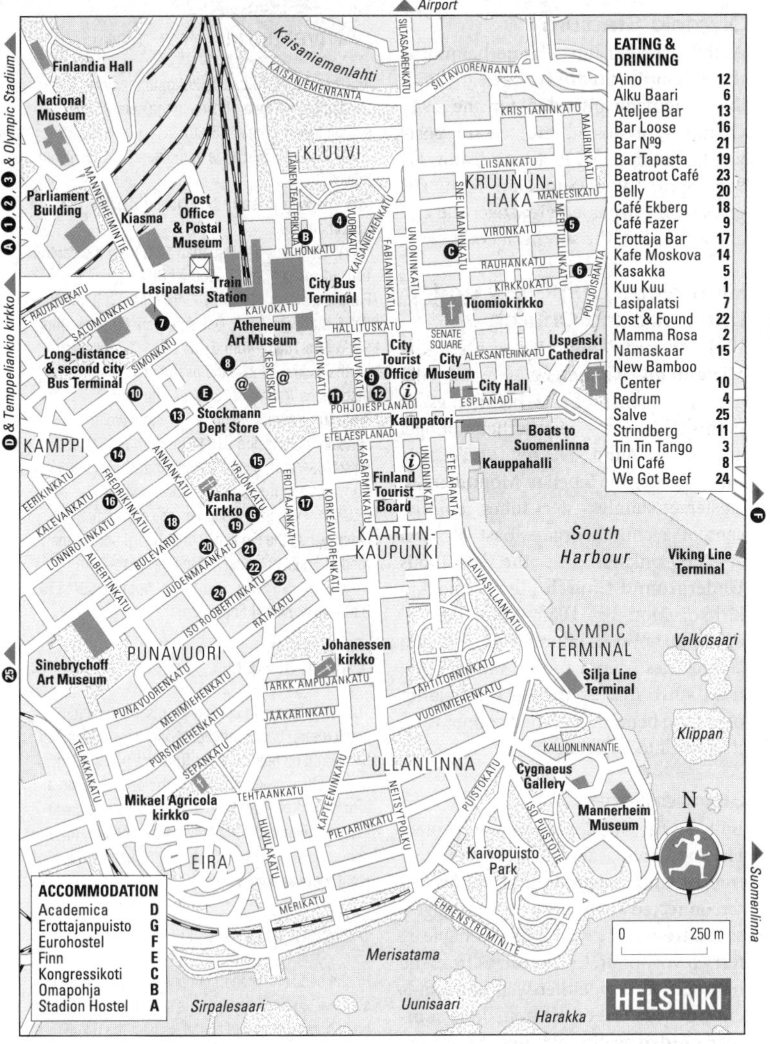

Building (guided tours Sat 11am & 12.30pm, Sun noon & 1.30pm; July & Aug also Mon–Fri 11am & 1pm; free) was completed in 1931. There's more information on the parliament from the attached visitor centre, Arkadiankatu 3 (July & Aug Mon-Fri 10am-4pm; rest of year Mon–Thurs 10am–6pm, Fri till 4pm; free). North of here is the **National Museum** (Tues–Sun 11am–6/8pm; €5.50), its design drawing on the country's medieval churches and granite castles. The exhibits, from prehistory to the present, are exhaustive; it's best to concentrate on a few specific sections, such as the fascinating medieval church art and the ethnographic displays from the nation's varied regions. Look out for the world's oldest fishing net.

Olympic Stadium

A little further up Mannerheimintie, the **Olympic Stadium** is clearly visible; originally intended for the 1940 Olympics, it hosted the second post-war games in 1952. Its **tower** (Mon–Fri 9am–8pm, Sat & Sun 9am–6pm; €2) gives an unsurpassed view over the city and a chunk of the southern coast.

Hietaniemi Cemetery and Underground Church

Back towards the city centre, the **Hietaniemi Cemetery** houses the graves of some of the big names of Finnish history – Mannerheim, Engel and Alvar Aalto. Nearby, you'll find the very elegant Sibelius Monument, a cluster of stainless steel tubes reminiscent of a church organ. East of here, at Lutherinkatu 3, is the late-1960s **Underground Church** (Temppeliaukio kirkko; Mon–Fri 10am–8pm, Sat till 6pm, Sun noon–1.45pm & 3.15–5.45pm; closed Tues 1–2pm and during services; tram #3B). Blasted from a single lump of granite beneath a domed copper roof, it's a thrill to be inside.

Suomenlinna

Built by the Swedes in 1748 to protect Helsinki from seaborne attack, the fortress of **Suomenlinna** stands on five interconnected islands and is the biggest sea fortress in the world. It's reachable by ferry (every hour; €3.60 return) from the harbour: you can either visit independently or take one of the hour-long summer **guided walking tours**, beginning close to the ferry stage and conducted in English (June–Aug daily 10.30am, 1pm & 3pm; €5). Suomenlinna has a few museums, none particularly riveting. The best of the lot is **Suomenlinna Museum** (daily 10am–4/6pm; €5) which contains a permanent exhibition on the island, but it's the views back across the water towards the capital that are truly superb.

Arrival and information

Air The airport, Vantaa, is 20km to the north, connected by Finnair buses to the central train station (every 20min; €5.20).

Train The train station is in the heart of the city on Kaivokatu.

Bus The long-distance bus station is a short way up Simonkatu.

Ferry Terminals are less than 1km from the centre.

Tourist office The City Tourist Office at Pohjoisesplanadi 19 (May–Sept Mon–Fri 9am–8pm, Sat & Sun 9am–6pm; Oct–Apr Mon–Fri 9am–8pm, Sat & Sun 10am–4pm ⓣ09/169 3757, ⓦwww.visithelsinki.fi) stocks the useful, free listings magazines *Helsinki This Week* and *City*.

Museum passes If you're staying a while, consider purchasing a Helsinki Card (€33/43/53 for 24/48/72hr), giving unlimited travel on public transport and free entry to more than forty museums. For information on the rest of the country, use the Finnish Tourist Board across the road at Eteläesplanadi 4 (Mon–Fri 9am–5pm; May–Sept also Sat & Sun 11am–3pm; ⓣ09/4176 9300, ⓦwww.visitfinland.com).

City transport

The city's transport system (trams, buses and a small metro) is very efficient. One-way tickets can be bought on board (€2) or from the bus station, tourist office or kiosks around the centre, while a **tourist ticket** (€6/12/18 for one/three/five days) permits unlimited use of the whole network for the period covered. Tram #3T follows a useful figure-of-eight route around the centre.

Accommodation

Hostel beds are in short supply, especially during summer, so booking ahead is sensible. You can book hotel rooms and hostel beds at the **Hotel Booking Centre** at the train station for a fee of €5 in person or for free by email or phone (June–Aug Mon–Fri 9am–7pm, Sat 9am–6pm, Sun 10am–6pm; Sept–May Mon–Fri 9am–6pm, Sat 9am–5pm; ⓣ09/2288 1400, ⓔhotel@helsinkiexpert.fi).

Hostels and tourist hotels

Academica Hietaniemenkatu 14 ⓣ09/1311 4334 ⓦwww.hostelacademica.fi On the fringes of the city centre with single-sex dorms and double rooms. HI and student card discounts. Breakfast and bed linen included in price. June–Aug only. Dorms ❸, rooms ❻

Erottajanpuisto Uudenmaankatu 9 ⓣ09/642 169. Atmospheric and sociable hostel in a grand but shabby old building close to Mannerheimintie. Dorms ❸, rooms ❼

Eurohostel Linnankatu 9 ⓣ09/622 0470, ⓦwww.eurohostel.fi. The biggest hostel in Finland, close to the ferry terminals and with a free sauna. Dorms, ❸ rooms ❻

Omapohja Itäinen teatterikuja 3 ⓣ09/666 211, ⓦwww.gasthausomapohja.com. No dorms here, just plain, slightly fusty rooms. The cheapest have shared bathrooms. ❼

Stadion Hostel Olympic Stadium ⓣ09/477 8480. Some 2km out of the centre and often crowded, but cheap and open all year. Trams #3T, #4, #7 and #10 to stadium, then follow the signs. Dorms ❷

Hotels

Finn Kalevankatu 3b ⓣ09/684 4360, ⓦwww.hotellifinn.fi. A peaceful, modern option on the top floor of an office block, virtually in the city centre. ❼

Kongressikoti Snellmaninkatu 15a ⓣ09/135 6839, ⓦwww.kongressikoti.com. Appealing, cosy place close to Senate Square. Negotiable discounts for longer stays. ❼

Campsite

Rastila Karavaanikatu 4 ⓣ09/3107 8517. Located 13km east of the city centre, near the end of the metro line and served by night buses #90N till 1.30am during the week and 4.15am Fri & Sat. ❷

Eating

Many places offer good-value **lunchtime** deals, and there are plenty of affordable ethnic **restaurants** and fast-food *grillis* for the evenings. At the end of Eteläesplanadi the old market hall, Kauppahalli (Mon–Fri 8am–7pm, Sat 8am–4pm), is good for snacks and reindeer kebabs.

Cafés

Alku-Baari Kirkkokatu 1. Tiny, unassuming café with a devoted local following, where you'll find fresh, authentic Finnish food. Thursday is pea soup and pancakes day. Open 7am–3pm.

Café Ekberg Bulevardi 9. Nineteenth-century fixtures and a *fin-de-siècle* atmosphere, with starched waitresses bringing expensive sandwiches and pastries to marble tables. Lunch €8.40

Café Fazer Kluuvikatu 3. Owned by Finland's biggest chocolate company, with celebrated pastries.

Uni Café Mannerheimintie 3. Cheap, filling meals at this university cafeteria right in the centre of town.

Restaurants

Aino Pohjoisesplanadi 21. Justifiably popular place in the centre of town, serving up delicious and hearty Finnish food. Closed Sun. Mains from €12.

Bar Tapasta Uudenmaankatu 13. Bustling tapas joint with Spanish beers and wine to accompany the fairly authentic food. Open from 4.30pm, closed on Sun. Tapas from €4.60.

Kasakka Meritullinkatu 13. Great atmosphere and food in this old-style Russian restaurant. Mains from €18.

Lasipalatsi Mannerheimintie 22–24. Decent modern Finnish food served in a classic Functionalist-style building with great views of the street life below. Mains from €8.

Mamma Rosa Runeberginkatu 55. A classic pizzeria also serving fish steaks and pasta. Mains €13–23.

Namaskaar Mannerheimintie 100. Indian restaurant with a popular evening buffet and plenty of vegetarian options. Mains from €10.

New Bamboo Center Annankatu 29. Authentic Malay food at very low prices. Decor is basic but the service is cheerful and fast. Mains €6.

Salve Hietalahdenranta 11. Unselfconsciously old-school sailors' restaurant that has been serving up the same heavy Finnish fare for over a century. Well worth a visit. Mains €6–11.

Strindberg Pohjoisesplanadi 33. The upstairs restaurant serves contemporary Scandinavian cuisine, while the street level café is one of the places in town to see and be seen. Mains from €15.

Drinking and nightlife

Drinking can be enjoyed in the city's many pub-like restaurants; on Fridays and Saturdays it's best to arrive as early as possible to get a seat. Helsinki has a vibrant night scene, with several venues putting on a steady diet of **live music** and occasional free gigs on summer Sundays in Kaivopuisto park. There's also a wide range of **clubs and discos**, which charge a small admission fee (€5–8). For details of **what's on**, read free fortnightly paper *City*, found in record shops, bookshops, department stores and tourist offices.

Bars

Ateljee Bar Roof of *Hotel Torni*, Yrjönkatu 26. The best views of Helsinki in a stylish atmosphere.

Bar Nº9 Uudenmaankatu 9. A popular hang-out for professionals at lunchtime and bohos in the evening, it has a beer list and menu as cosmopolitan as its staff. Food is reasonably cheap and filling and there is always a vegetarian option.

Bar Loose Fredrikinkatu 34. Hip, Detroit-inspired rock'n'roll bar, open till 2am every night.
Beatroot Iso Roobertinkatu 10. Intimate, beatniky bar. At weekends the downstairs club, the Rose Garden, is open till late.
Café Tin Tin Tango Töölöntorinkatu 7. Oddball café/bar with laundry machines and a sauna (book a day in advance). Slough off the travel dirt and have a beer at the same time.
Erottaja Bar Erottajankatu 15–17. Stripped-down underground bar. Busy at weekends, when DJs play electro and the like until 3am.
Kafe Moskova Eerikinkatu 11. Like the Cold War never happened. Intimate, cool Russian-themed bar.
Kuu Kuu Museokatu 17. Appealingly arty neighbourhood pub with an easygoing air and a good selection of beers and whiskys.

Clubs

Belly Uudenmanakatu 16–20. Genuinely eclectic schedule of club nights and live music.
Lost & Found Annankatu 6. Straight-friendly gay club with the latest opening hours on the block. Two bars on two floors, with a small dance-floor downstairs. Very popular at weekends.
Redrum Vuorikatu 2. Some excellent, inventive club nights and an unbeatable sound system. Central and open till the wee small hours.
We Got Beef Iso Roobertinkatu 21. Reggae, ska and funk are the turntable mainstays at this hipster favourite.

Gay Helsinki

Finland decriminalized homosexuality in 1971 and introduced partnership laws in 2001. In recent years the **gay scene** in Helsinki has flourished and there's an impressive number of exclusively gay and gay-friendly establishments. For the latest details, pick up a copy of the monthly **Z magazine** – in Finnish only but with a useful listings section – widely available in larger newsagents, or drop into the state-supported gay organization SETA, Hietalahdenkatu 2b 16 (Ⓣ09/681 2580, Ⓦwww.seta.fi).
dtm (Don't Tell Mamma) Annankatu 32 The capital's legendary gay night club, with occasional drag shows and house music most nights.
Hercules Lönnrotinkatu 4b. Not quite as trendy as dtm, this club plays varied music, including some of Finland's best offerings.
Nalle Pub Kaarlenkatu 3–5. The heart of Helsinki's lesbian scene. Worth the trip a little way out of the city centre.
Room Albert Kalevankatu 36. One of Helsinki's better neighbourhood bars; attracts the young and beautiful.

Shopping

On the corner of Aleksanterinkatu and Mannerheimintie is the Constructivist brick exterior of the sprawling **Stockmann Department Store**, which sells everything from bubble gum to Persian rugs. Further along Mannerheimintie, steps head down to the **Tunneli** shopping complex. Elsewhere, look out for Design District stickers, marking the city's most interesting boutiques and designer shops.
Design Forum Finland Erottajankatu 7. Comprehensive shop, café and studio space devoted to Finnish design: clothes, homeware, ceramics, jewellery, you name it.
Helsinki 10 Eerinkinkatu 3. Some great clothing brands from Finland and further afield at this lovingly stocked boutique.
Limbo Annankatu 13. Finnish clothing brand established in 1994. Also stocks work by other Finnish designers. Some men's clothes, but mostly quirky, colourful womenswear and accessories.
Lux Uudenmankatu 26. Clothes, books, comics and records, with a focus on up-and-coming young designers.
Stupido Iso Roobertinkatu 23. Independent record shop with a dedicated Finnish section featuring a lot of heavy metal and Europop. A good place to pick up flyers and listings.

Directory

Embassies Australia, Museokatu 25b Ⓣ09/477 6640; Canada, Pohjoisesplanadi 25b Ⓣ09/228 530; Ireland, Erottajankatu 7A Ⓣ09/646 006; UK, Itäinen Puistotie 17 Ⓣ09/2286 5100; US, Itäinen Puistotie 14a Ⓣ09/616 250.
Exchange Apart from the banks, try Travelex at the airport (5.30am–11.30pm) or Forex at the train station (daily 8am–9pm).
Hospital Marian Hospital, Lapinlahdenkatu 16 Ⓣ09/4716 3339.
Internet Akateeminen Kirjakauppa (Micronia department), Keskuskatu 2; Netcup, Aleksanterinkatu 52; *mbar* in the Lasipalatsi, Mannerheimintie 22–24.
Laundry Rööperin pesulapalvelut, Punavuorenkatu 3.
Left luggage At the train station.
Pharmacy Yliopiston Apteekki, Mannerheimintie 5 & 96 (24hr).
Post office Mannerheiminaukio 1.

Moving on

Air Ivalo for Inari (2–3 daily; 1hr 40min); Oulu (10–15 daily; 1hr); Rovaniemi (5–7 daily; 1hr 20min).

Train Oulu (8 daily; 7hr); Rovaniemi (5 daily; 9hr 45min); Tampere (hourly; 2hr); Turku (12 daily; 2hr).
Bus Porvoo (15 daily; 1hr).
Ferry Rostock, Germany (June to early Sept 3 weekly; 24hr); Stockholm, Sweden (2 daily; 17hr); Tallinn, Estonia (15–25 daily; 1hr 40min–4hr).

AROUND HELSINKI: PORVOO

About 50km east of Helsinki, **PORVOO** is one of the oldest towns on the south coast and one of Finland's most charming. Its narrow cobbled streets, lined by small wooden buildings, give a sense of the Finnish life that pre-dated the capital's bold squares and Neoclassical geometry. Close to the station, the **Johan Ludwig Runeberg House**, Aleksanterinkatu 3 (Mon–Sat 10am–4pm, Sun 11am–5pm; Sept–April closed Mon & Tues; €5), is where the famed Finnish poet lived from 1852; one of his poems provided the lyrics for the Finnish national anthem. The old town is built around the hill on the other side of Mannerheimkatu, crowned by the fifteenth-century **Tuomiokirkko**, where Alexander I proclaimed Finland a Russian Grand Duchy and convened the first Finnish Diet. The cathedral survived a serious arson attack in 2006 and is undergoing repair work; it's expected to reopen in 2009. The town's past can be explored in the **Porvoo Museum** (daily 10am/noon–4pm; Sept–April closed Mon & Tues; €5) at the foot of the hill in the main square.

Buses run daily from Helsinki to Porvoo (€8.70 one-way; 1hr), arriving opposite the **tourist office**, which is at Rihkamakatu 4 (Mon–Fri 9am–4.30/6pm, Sat & Sun 10am–2/4pm; Sept to early June closed Sun; ⓣ019/520 2316, ⓦwww.porvoo.fi). There's a **hostel** at Linnankoskenkatu 1–3 (ⓣ019/523 0012; ❸) and a **campsite** (ⓣ019/581 967; June–Aug; ❶) 1.5km from the town centre. The cheapest place to eat is *Rosso* at Piispankatu 21. €9–16.

Southwest Finland

The area west of Helsinki is probably the blandest section of the country – endless forests interrupted only by modest-sized patches of water and virtually identical villages and small towns. The far **southwestern** corner is more interesting, with islands and inlets around a jagged shoreline and some of the country's distinctive Finnish-Swedish coastal communities.

TURKU

TURKU was once the national capital, but lost its status in 1812 and most of its buildings in a ferocious fire in 1827. These days it's a small and sociable city, bristling with history and culture and with a sparkling nightlife, thanks to the students from its two universities.

What to see and do

To get to grips with Turku and its pivotal place in Finnish history, cut through the centre to the Aura river which splits the city. This tree-framed space was, before the great fire of 1827, the bustling heart of the community, and is overlooked by Turku's **Tuomiokirkko** (daily 9am–7/8pm except during services), erected in the thirteenth century and still the centre of the Finnish Lutheran Church. Despite repeated fires, a number of features survive. There's a small museum in the south gallery exhibiting the religious knick-knacks collected by the church over the course of its history.

Turku Art Museum

The **Turku Art Museum** (Tues–Fri 11am–7pm, Sat & Sun 11am–5pm; €6/7.50 during special exhibitions) is housed in a lovely dedicated building constructed in 1904. It contains one of the better collections of Finnish art, with works by all the great names of the country's golden age plus a commendable stock of modern pieces.

Aboa Vetus and Ars Nova

Retrace your steps to the riverbank to find Turku's newest and most splendid museum, the combined **Aboa Vetus and Ars Nova** (daily 11am–7pm; €8). Digging the foundations of the modern art gallery revealed a warren of medieval lanes, now on show as part of an exhibition exploring Turku's past. The gallery comprises 350 striking works plus temporary exhibits, and there's a great café too.

Turku Castle

Crossing back over Aurajoki and down Linnankatu and then heading towards the mouth of the river will bring you to **Turku Castle** (daily 10am–3/6pm; mid-Sept to mid-April closed Mon; €7). If you don't fancy the walk, hop on bus #1 from the market square. The featureless exterior conceals a maze of cobbled courtyards, corridors and staircases, with a bewildering array of finds and displays, comprising a 37-room historical museum. The castle probably went up around 1280; its gradual expansion accounts for the patchwork architecture.

Arrival and information

Tourist office Aurakatu 4 (Mon–Fri 8.30am–6pm; also Sat & Sun, April–Sept 9am–4pm, rest of year 10am–3pm; ⓣ02/262 7444, ⓦwww.turkutouring.fi).
Train and bus Both the stations are within easy walking distance of the river, just north of the centre.
Ferry For the Stockholm ferry, stay on the train for the terminal, 2km west, or catch bus #1 on Linnankatu.

Accommodation

Campsite Ruissalo ⓣ02/262 5100; June–Aug; bus #8. On the island of Ruissalo, which has two sandy beaches and overlooks Turku harbour.
Linnasmaki Lustokatu 7. ⓣ02/4123 500 ⓦwww.linnasmaki.fi 56-room summer hostel in the Christian Institute. Basic, but good value. Mid-May to mid-Sept only. ❸
Omena Hotelli Humalistonkatu 7 ⓣ020/424 4034. Alvar Aalto fans should stay in this building designed by Finland's most famous architect. The hotel is self-service, with an automated reception area. ❻
Hostel Turku Linnankatu 39 ⓣ02/262 7680, ⓔhostel@turku.fi. Take bus #1 or #30. Excellent hostel by the river. ❷
Tuure Bed and Breakfast ⓣ02/233 0230 Clean, pleasant little guesthouse in the centre of town. ❺

Eating and drinking

Near the tourist office, **Market Square** (*Kauppatori*) sells fresh produce, and in summer is full of open-air cafés; nearby, the effervescent market hall or **Kauppahalli** (Mon–Fri 8am–5pm, Sat 8am–2pm) offers a slightly more upmarket choice of delis and other eateries. Floating bar-restaurants change each summer, but look out for **Papa Joe**, **Svarte Rudolph** and **Donna**.

Cafés and restaurants

Baan Thai Kauppiaskatu 17. Great Thai food at respectable prices. Mains €7
Blanko Aurakatu 1. Popular bar/restaurant just opposite the tourist office. Good lunches, and house and electro DJs till 3am at weekends. Mains from €8.
Herman Läntinen Rantakatu 37. A bright, airy storehouse dating from 1849, with excellent lunches from €12.
Hot Wings Humalistonkatu 16. Finnish chain. Forget the misleading name – this is more about cheap, sensible lunches and chatting over coffee than greasy chicken.

Bars and clubs

Alvar Humalistonkatu 7. Affable, vaguely trendy bar whose wide range of beers and ciders attracts a diverse crowd.
Klubi Humalistonkatu 8. Cavernously, studenty venue featuring live bands and DJ nights – for listings, check the posters liberally applied to lampposts all over town.
Kuka Linnankatu 17. Furnished with an eclectic mix of classic Finnish design pieces and retro madness, this cool, arty bar attracts Turku's creative types. Live music or DJs several nights a week.
Monk Humalistonkatu 3. Excellent and rather lovely looking jazz venue. Open till 4am Wed–Sat.
Puutorin Vessa Puutori. Turku's oddest bar – the building was a public toilet before being

converted into a fun, pubby venue with daytime coffee and live music and singalongs in the evenings.

Moving on

Train Tampere (8 daily; 2hr).
Ferry Stockholm (4 daily; 10–11hr).

Finland's Lake Region

About a third of Finland is covered by the **Lake Region**, a huge area of bays, inlets and islands interspersed with dense forests. Despite holding much of Finland's industry, it's a tranquil, verdant area, and even **Tampere**, the major industrial city, enjoys a peaceful lakeside setting. The eastern part of the region is the most atmospheric: slender ridges furred with conifers linking the few sizeable landmasses. The regional centre, **Savonlinna**, stretches delectably across several islands and boasts a superb medieval castle.

TAMPERE

TAMPERE, a leafy place of parks and lakes, is Scandinavia's largest inland city. Its rapid growth began just over a century ago, when the Scot James Finlayson opened a textile factory, drawing labour from rural areas where traditional crafts were in decline. Metalwork and shoe factories soon followed, their owners paternally promoting a vigorous local arts scene for the workforce. Free outdoor concerts, lavish theatrical productions and one of the best modern art collections in Finland maintain such traditions to this day.

What to see and do

The main streets run off either side of Hämeenkatu. To the left, up slender Hämeenpuisto, the **Lenin Museum** at no. 28 (Mon–Fri 9am–6pm, Sat & Sun 11am–4pm; €4) commemorates Lenin's ties with Finland and his life in general; the absorbing exhibition has a devoted, train-spotter feel. Moomin fans shouldn't miss the adorable Moomin Museum (Tues–Fri 9am–5pm, Sat & Sun 10am–6pm, Jun–Aug open Mon 9am–5pm; €4) in the basement of the city library at Hämeenpuisto 20, a respectful and exhaustive overview of Tove Jansson's creations. Nearby, at Puutarhakatu 34, the **Art Museum of Tampere** (Tues–Sun 10am–6pm; €5) holds temporary art exhibitions, but if you're looking for Finnish art you might be better off visiting the **Hiekka Art Gallery**, a few minutes' walk away at Pirkankatu 6 (Tues–Thurs 3–6pm, Sun noon–3pm; €5). Better still is the tremendous **Sara Hildén Art Museum** (daily 11am–6pm, closed Mon Oct–April; €4), built on the shores of Näsijärvi, a quirky collection of Finnish and foreign modern works; take bus #16 from the centre.

Arrival and information

Train The train station is at Rautatienkatu 25, at the end of Hämeenkatu.
Bus The long-distance bus station is in the town centre, off Hämeenkatu.
Tourist office By the river, Verkatehtaankatu 2 (June–Sept Mon–Fri 9am–8pm; Sat & Sun 10am–5pm; rest of year Mon–Fri 9am–5pm, Sat & Sun 10am–5pm; ⓣ 03/5656 6800, ⓦ www.gotampere.fi).

Accommodation

Hostel Sofia Tuomiokirkonkatu 12a ⓣ 03/254 4020, ⓦ www.tnnky.fi/hostel. Bright, attractive hostel just opposite the cathedral. ❸
Härmälä Campsite ⓣ 03/265 1355. 4km south of the city centre; bus #1. Mid-May to late Aug only. ❷

Eating and drinking

Café Europa Aleksanterinkatu 29. Busy, arty bar tucked away on a side street off the main drag. Pricey drinks. Open late at weekends.

Kahvila Pulo Ojakatu 3. This bookish, high-ceilinged space is the best café in town. Try the cakes and admire the beautiful furniture.
Kahvila Taikapapu Tuoniokirkonkatu 26. Tiny one-room café off the main street, with great coffee, muffins and sandwiches.
Tullikammari Itsenäisyydenkatu. Busy nightclub in an old customs house behind the train station.
Valo Puutarhakatu 11. Relaxed bar with battered old sofas, popular with students. Live music once a month.

Moving on

Train Helsinki (hourly; 2hr); Oulu (7 daily; 5hr); Savonlinna (2 daily; 5hr); Turku (8 daily; 2hr).

SAVONLINNA

SAVONLINNA is one of the most relaxed towns in Finland, a woodworking centre that also makes a decent living from tourism and its renowned **opera festival** (ⓣ015/476 750, ⓦwww.operafestival.fi) in July. It's packed throughout summer, so book well ahead if you're visiting at this time. Out of peak season, its streets and beaches are uncluttered, and the town's easy-going mood makes it a pleasant place to linger.

What to see and do

The best locations for soaking up the atmosphere are the **harbour** and **market square** at the end of Olavinkatu, where you can cast an eye over the grand *Seurahuone* hotel, with its Art Nouveau fripperies. Follow the harbour around picturesque Linnankatu, or better still around the sandy edge of Pihlajavesi, which brings you to atmospheric and surprisingly well-preserved **Olavinlinna Castle** (guided tours daily 10am–3/5pm; €5), perched on a small island. Founded in 1475, the castle witnessed a series of bloody conflicts until the Russians claimed possession of it in 1743 and relegated it to the status of town jail. Nearby is the **Savonlinna Regional Museum** in Riihisaari (July to August daily 11am–5pm; rest of the year closed Mon; €4), which occupies an old granary and displays an intriguing account of the evolution of local life, with rock paintings and ancient amber carved with human figures.

Arrival and information

Train There are two train stations: be sure to get off at Savonlinna-Kauppatori, just across the main bridge from the tourist office.
Bus The bus station is off the main island, but within easy walking distance of the town centre.
Tourist office Puistokatu 1 (June–Aug daily 9am–6/8pm, Sept–May Mon–Fri 9am–5pm; ⓣ015/517 510, ⓦwww.savonlinnatravel.com).

Accommodation

Malakias Pihlajavedenkatu 6 ⓣ015/533 283. Summer hotel 2km west of the centre along Tulliportinkatu and then Savontie. ❻
Perhehotelli Hospitz Linnankatu 20 ⓣ015/515 661, ⓦwww.hospitz.com Attractive, central hotel. Prices go up during the opera festival. ❽
Savonlinna SKO Hostel Opistokatu 1 ⓣ015/72 910. Likeable summer hostel (Jun–Aug only) in the town's Christian Institute. Dorms ❸, rooms ❻
Savonlinna Camping Vuohimäki Vuohimäentie 60 ⓣ015/537 353. The nearest campsite, though still a good 7km from the centre. June–Aug; bus #4. ❸

Eating and drinking

Good, cheap **food** is available at the pizza joints along Olavinkatu and Tulliportinkatu. *Majakka*, Satamakatu 11, offers tasty Finnish nosh at lunchtime.

Moving on

Train Parikkala for Helsinki (2 daily; 50min).

Around Savonlinna

Savonlinna boasts beautiful scenery all around, and the place to sample it is **Punkaharju Ridge**, a narrow strip of land between the Puruvesi and Pihlajavesi lakes, 28km from town. Locals say it has the healthiest air in the world, super-oxygenated by abundant conifers. This is the Lake Region at its most breathtakingly beautiful. The ridge is traversable by road and rail, both running into the town of Punkaharju and passing the incredible **Retretti Arts Centre** (June–Aug daily 10am–5pm/6pm; €15), set in caves and with a large sculpture park. Trains and buses make the short journey between Savonlinna and Retretti.

KUOPIO

The pleasant lakeside town of **KUOPIO** is best known for its enormous smoke sauna, the biggest in the world, and makes for a worthwhile pitstop on your way north to Lapland. One of the best times to visit is during the annual Kuopio Dance Festival (Ⓦwww.kuopiodancefestival.fi) in mid-June.

What to see and do

Built on a grid system, the centre is easy to navigate. Just south of the train station is the main square, Kauppatori. From here Kuauppakatu leads east to the **Kuopio Museum** (Tues–Fri 10am–5pm, Sat & Sun 11am–4pm; €2.50) at number 23 with two floors of natural and cultural history. Further up the road, at number 35, the **Kuopio Art Museum** (Tues-Fri 10am-5pm, open till 7pm on Weds, Sat & Sun 11am–5pm; €3) is housed in a converted bank. The thoughtfully curated temporary exhibitions focus mainly on modern Finnish art. Around the corner on Kuninkaankatu, the **Victor Barsokevitsch Photographic Centre** (Jun–Aug Mon–Fri 10am–7pm, Sat & Sun 11am–4pm; Sept–May Tues–Fri 11am–5pm, Sat & Sun 11am–3pm; summer €5, winter €3) is a real find – one of the best photography galleries in the country, with changing exhibitions featuring the gallery's founder and other photographers.

The smoke sauna

Kuoipio's **woodsmoke sauna** (Tuesdays year-round, plus Thursdays mid-May–mid-Sept; €10; Ⓦwww.rauhalahti.fi) is the main draw in town, and about as quintessentially Finnish an experience as you'll find. It's located 4km south of the centre at the *Rauhalahti* spa hotel which also runs a traditional Finnish evening each night the sauna is open – ask at the tourist office for details.

Arrival and information

Train and bus Kuopio's train and bus stations are located opposite each other just north of Kauppatori square.

Tourist office Within the City Hall at Haapaniemenkatu 17 Ⓣ017/182 584, Ⓦwww.kuopioinfo.fi (June–Aug Mon–Fri 9.30am–5pm, July also Sat 9.30am–3pm, rest of year Mon–Fri 9.30am–4.30pm). You may want to buy the **Kuopio Card** (€12) on sale here; it offers free entry to the town's museums as well as admission to the smoke sauna.

Accommodation

Camping Atrain Pelonniementie 50 Ⓣ017/723 038. Attractive lakeside campsite, with cottages and space for tents. ❷

Hostelli Hermanni Hermanninaukio 3e Ⓣ040/910 9083. Comfortable if basic hostel 1.5km out of town. Dorms ❷, rooms ❻

Youth Hostel Virkkula Asemakatu 3 Ⓣ040/418 2178. Summer hostel in a converted school just by the train station. Mid-June–early Aug. ❷

Eating and drinking

Atlantis Puijonkatu 27b. Looks unpromising from the outside, but the pizza is good and it's open well into the small hours.

Café Kaneli Pohjolankatu 2a. Charming little café cluttered with knick-knacks and pictures, with great coffee and cake.

Coffeehouse Haapaniemanikatu 24–26. Drab chain café on the main square, but good for cheap food or a coffee stop between galleries.

Sampo Kauppakatu 13. Proudly traditional fish restaurant that has been serving Finnish dishes since 1931. Mains around €10.

Moving on

Train Tampere for Helsinki (4–5 daily; 3hr 30min).

Northern Finland

The northern regions take up a vast portion of Finland: one third of the country lies north of the Arctic Circle. It's sparsely populated, with small communities often separated by long distances. The coast of **Ostrobothnia** is affluent due to the adjacent flat and fertile farmland; busy and expanding **Oulu** is the region's major city as well as a centre of high-tech expertise, though it maintains a pleasing small-town atmosphere. Further north, **Lapland** is a remote and wild territory whose wide open spaces are home to several thousand Saami, who have lived in harmony with this harsh environment for millennia. There is an extensive bus service and regular flights from Helsinki. Make sure you try Lappish cuisine, too – fresh cloudberries, smoked reindeer and wild salmon are highlights.

OULU

OULU, with its renowned university, is a leading light in Finland's burgeoning computing industry. During the nineteenth century it was the centre of the world's tar production, and the city's affluence and vibrant cultural scene date from that time. On Kirkkokatu, the copper-domed and stuccoed **Tuomiokirkko** (daily June–Aug 11am–8/9pm; Sept–May Mon–Fri noon–1pm) seems anachronistic amid the bulky blocks of modern Oulu. Across the small canal just to the north, the **North Ostrobothnia Museum** (daily 10/11am–6/7pm; closed Mon; €3) has a large regional collection with a good Saami section.

Arrival and information

Bus and train The stations are connected, linked to the city centre by several parallel streets feeding down to the *kauppatori* and *kauppahalli* (markets) by the water beyond.
Tourist office Uusikatu 26 (Mon–Fri 9am–4pm; mid-June to Aug until 6pm also Sat & Sun 10am–3pm; ⓣ08/5584 1330, ⓦwww.visitoulu.fi). Due to move early 2009, probably to Torikatu 10.
Internet Try the library at Kaarenväylä 3.

Accommodation

Hotel Turisti Rautatienkatu 9 ⓣ08/563 6100, ⓦwww.hotelturisti.fi. Central hotel opposite the train station with good deals for singles and at weekends. ⑨
Camping There's a campsite (ⓣ08/5586 1350) with cabins on Hietasaari Island, 4km from town; take bus #17 from Isokatu in the town centre.

Eating and drinking

Café Saara, Kirkkokatu 2. A rather grown-up café serving sandwiches and light meals.
Finlandia Hallituskatu 31. No-nonsense pizzeria.
Jumpru Pub Kappurienkatu 6. Popular bar and nightclub sporting opulent leather armchairs.
Katri Antell Rotuaari Kirkkokatu 17. Traditional bakery/café justly famed for its cakes (closed Sun).
Never Grow Old Hallituskatu 13–17. Quirky reggae bar perfect for late-night dancing.

Moving on

Train Rovaniemi (5 daily; 3hr).

ROVANIEMI

Easily reached by train, **ROVANIEMI** is touted as the capital of Lapland, though its mundane shopping streets are a far cry from the surrounding rural hinterland. The elegant wooden houses of old Rovaniemi were razed by departing Nazis at the close of World War II, and the town was completely rebuilt during the late 1940s. Though generally architecturally uninspiring, an exception is to be found on the south side of town near the bus and train stations, where pristine Aalto-designed civic buildings line Hallituskatu.

What to see and do

The best way to prepare yourself for what lies further north is to visit the 172m-long glass tunnel of **Arktikum**, Pohjoisranta 4 (daily 9/10am–5/7pm; Sept to mid-May closed Mon; €11; ⓦwww.arktikum.fi). Subterranean galleries along one side house the **Provincial Museum of Lapland** with genuine Saami crafts and costumes alongside the imitations sold in souvenir shops to emphasize the romanticization of their culture. Across the corridor is the **Arctic Centre**, which gives a thorough treatment of all things circumpolar. For a couple of weeks either side of midsummer, the **midnight sun** is visible from Rovaniemi, the best vantage points being either the striking bridge over the Ounaskoski or atop the forested and mosquito-infested hill, Ounasvaara, across the bridge. Most other things of interest are outside town, not least the **Arctic Circle**, 8km north and connected by the hourly bus #8 from the railway station (€5.80 return). On the circle is the **Santa Claus Village** (daily 9/10am–5/7pm; free), a large log cabin where you can meet Father Christmas all year round and leave your name for a Christmas card from Santa himself.

Arrival and information

Bus The bus station is just west of the centre, off Postikatu, a few minutes' walk east from the train station.

Tourist office Rovakatu 21 (Mon–Fri 8am–5pm; June–Aug also Sat & Sun 10am–4pm; ⓣ016/346 270, ⓦwww.rovaniemi.fi).

Train The station is just outside the town centre, at Ratukatu 3.

Accommodation

Hostel Rudolf Koskikatu 41. Modern hostel ten-minutes' walk from the centre at the junction of Koskikatu and Tukkipojantie. There are no staff on site; check-in and reservations are handled by the *Clarion Hotel Santa Claus*, Korkalonkatu 29 (ⓣ016/321 321, ⓦwww.hotelsantaclaus.fi). June–Aug ❸, Sept–May ❹

Ounaskoksi Camping ⓣ0400/692 421. Campsite on the far bank of Ounaskoski, facing town. A twenty-minute walk from the station. ❶

Eating and drinking

Arnold's Bakery US-style coffee-and-doughnuts place inside the drab Sampo Keskus shopping centre.

Kauppayhtiö Vallakatu 24. Unexpectedly fantastic café/bar with a mishmash of retro furniture. DJs at the weekend and a gallery at the back. Free Wi-Fi.

Mia Maria Rovakatu 14. A decent, low-priced pizzeria with a proper wood-fired oven.

Zoomit Korkalonkatu 29. Uninspiring but popular bar on the ground floor of the *Clarion Hotel*.

Moving on

Train Helsinki (5 daily; 9hr 45min); Oulu (5 daily; 3hr).

Bus Inari (4 daily; 5hr 30min); North Cape (June to late Aug 1 daily; 10hr 30min).

INARI

A half-day bus ride north of Rovaniemi, **INARI** lies along the fringes of Inarijärvi, one of Finland's largest lakes, and makes an attractive base from which to further explore this part of Lapland. In the town itself, the excellent **Siida** (Saami Museum; daily 9/10am–5/8pm; Oct–May closed Mon; €8; ⓦwww.siida.fi) has an outstanding outdoor section giving you an idea of how the Saami survived in Arctic conditions in their tepees, or *kota*, while the indoor section has a well-laid-out exhibition on all aspects of life in the Arctic. Towards the northern end of the village, summer boat tours (€12) depart from under the bridge to the ancient Saami holy site on the island of **Ukonkivi**. If walking's your thing then check out the pretty **Pielpajärvi Wilderness Church**, a two-hour well-signposted 7km hike from the village.

The **bus** stops outside the **tourist office** (Mon–Fri 9/10am–5/6/7pm; June–

Sept also Sat & Sun; ⓣ016/661 666, ⓦwww.inarilapland.org), on the main street, Inarintie, before continuing to Karasjok in Norway and – from June to late August only – the North Cape. Staff here have information on guided snow-scooter trips in winter and fishing trips around the lake in summer.

Finding **accommodation** should not be too problematic, though Inari does get very busy during the summer. The *Inarin Kultahovi* (ⓣ016/671 221; ⓦwww.hotelkultahovi.fi; ❽) at Saarikoskentie 2 is a basic hotel with a decent **restaurant**. The Uruniemi **campsite** (ⓣ016/671 331, ⓔwww.uruniemi.com; Oct–April advanced booking obligatory; ❷) is about 2km south of the village in a lovely location right by the lake.

France

HIGHLIGHTS

MUSÉE D'ORSAY, PARIS: the capital's most enjoyable and surprising museum, with an unparalleled collection of Impressionist art

REIMS: taste your way around the heart of the Champagne region

AVIGNON: stunning architecture, great cafés and a lively summer festival

BIARRITZ: big waves and massive nights out at Europe's lively surf capital

CORSICA: explore the rugged mountains and fine sand beaches of the "island of beauty"

ROUGH COSTS

DAILY BUDGET Basic €30/ occasional treat €45 (add €10 for Paris).

DRINK Glass of wine €2.50, beer €3

FOOD Baguette/sandwich €2-4

CAMPING/HOSTEL/BUDGET HOTEL €8/€12–25/€25-35

TRAVEL Paris–Nice by train (921km) 6 hr, €100.

FACT FILE

POPULATION 64.2 million

AREA 674, 843km (including Corsica)

LANGUAGE French

CURRENCY Euro (€)

CAPITAL Paris (population: 12 million)

INTERNATIONAL PHONE CODE ⓣ33

Basics

France is one of Europe's most stylish and dynamic countries. The largest in the continent, it offers a variety of different cultural and geographical experiences unmatched in any other European country.

If you arrive from the north, you may pass through the Channel ports or **Normandy**, with its considerable allure, to **Paris**, one of Europe's most elegant and compelling capitals. To the west lie the rocky coasts of **Brittany** and, just south, the grand **Loire Valley**, though most people push on further south to the limestone hills of **Provence**, the canyons of the **Pyrenees** mountains on the Spanish border, or the glamorous Riviera coastline of the **Côte d'Azur**. There are good reasons, however, for taking things more slowly, not least the Germanic towns of **Alsace** in the east, the gorgeous hills and valleys of the **Lot** and the **Dordogne**, and, more adventurously, the high and rugged heartland of the **Massif Central**.

CHRONOLOGY

51 BC Julius Caesar conquers Gaul.
486 AD Clovis I, leader of the Franks, establishes his rule over Gaul.
800 Charlemagne rules as King of the Franks.
1066 William, the Duke of Normandy, invades England and is crowned King of England.
1337 The Hundred Years War with England begins.
1431 After leading the French army to victory, Joan of Arc is burnt at the stake for heresy, at the age of 19.
1589 Henry IV is the first of the Bourbon dynasty to become King of France. Enforces Catholicism over the country.
1789 The French Revolution ends the rule of the monarchy and establishes the First Republic.
1804 Napoleon I declares himself Emperor of the French Empire.
1815 Napoleon I is defeated at the battle of Waterloo; the monarchy is restored.
1848 Louis-Napoleon, Napoleon I's nephew, is made President of the Second Republic before declaring himself Emperor a few years later.
1871 Defeat in the Franco-Prussian War leads to the creation of the Third Republic.
1872 Monet starts the Impressionist Movement.
1889 Eiffel Tower is built, making it the tallest building in the world.
1905 Church and State are legally separated.
1914–1918 WWI – over 1.5 million killed.
1939–1944 Nazi Germany occupies France leading to four years of fascist rule under the Vichy regime. France is liberated by Allied forces in August, 1944.
1962 Algeria gains independence from French colonial rule.
1995 Jacques Chirac elected President.
2002 French pay a little more for their croissants as the Euro replaces the Franc.
2007 Nicolas Sarkozy is elected President, narrowly beating Ségolène Royal, France's first female presidential candidate.

ARRIVAL

The main hub for arrivals by air is Paris Charles de Gaulle, which is served by both major and budget airlines. In addition, around 34 other airports are served by budget airlines, including Lille, La Rochelle and Marseille. France has excellent, often high-speed, train connections to the rest of continental Europe. The main point of entry from most countries is Paris: Gare du Nord links to Amsterdam, Brussels, Germany and the UK; Gare de Lyon to Italy; and Gare d'Austerlitz to Spain. There are also excellent connections from the south of France to Italy and Spain.

The Eurolines coach service (ⓦwww.eurolines.com) connects most European countries to France; again, the main arrival point in Paris is the Gare Routière in the suburb of Bagnolet.

GETTING AROUND

France has the most extensive **rail** network in Western Europe, run by the government-owned SNCF (ⓦwww.

sncf.com). The only areas not well served are the Alps and the Pyrenees, where rail routes are replaced by SNCF buses. Private bus services tend to be uncoordinated and are best used only as a last resort.

Train fares are reasonable, especially if booked well in advance; Paris to Lyon, for example, can cost as little as €40, but twice that if booked on the same day as travel. InterRail and Eurail passes are valid on normal trains at all times. The high-speed and very efficient TGVs (*Trains à Grande Vitesse*) require reservations (€5), and there is a supplement to travel at peak times. All tickets (not passes) must be stamped in the orange machines in front of the platform of the train station (*gare*) on penalty of a steep fine. All but the smallest stations have an information desk and most have *consignes automatiques* – coin-operated left-luggage lockers.

The word *autocar* on a timetable column indicates that it's an **SNCF bus service**, on which rail tickets and passes are valid.

Should you wish to **cycle** in France, you'll find it easier to cope outside of the big cities, where traffic can be overwhelming. Bikes go free on some SNCF trains, though the standard charge is €10. The main SNCF stations and larger tourist offices also rent bikes for around €10–15 per day.

ACCOMMODATION

Outside mid-July to the end of August, it's generally possible to turn up in any town and find **accommodation**.

All **hotels** are officially graded and are required to post their tariffs inside the entrance. A pleasant alternative are **chambres d'hôtes** – B&B in a house or on a farm. These vary in standard and usually cost the equivalent of a two-star hotel.

There's a wide network of official **hostels** (*auberges de jeunesse*) and two national associations: Federation of Youth Hostels (Ⓦwww.fuaj.org) and French Hostels League (Ⓦwww.auberges-de-jeunesse.com) as well as several other unofficial ones.

In rural areas, **gîtes d'étape** provide bunkbeds and simple kitchen facilities: they are listed, along with mountain refuges, on Ⓦwww.gites-refuge.com.

Local campsites can be a good budget alternative as they are generally clean, well-equipped and in a prime location. Ask tourist offices for lists of sites or consult Ⓦwww.campingfrance.com.

FOOD AND DRINK

Eating out in France isn't particularly cheap, but if sensible, you should be able to get decent **plats du jour** with wine for less than €15.

Generally the best place to eat **breakfast** is in a bar or café. Most serve *tartines* (baguette with butter), croissants and sweet favourites like *pain au chocolat* or *pain au raisin*. **Coffee** (*un café*) is invariably served black and strong; *un crème* is served with milk. **Tea** (*thé*) is less popular, though most cafés and restaurants serve it, and hot chocolate (*chocolat chaud*) is delicious and widely available.

Cafés are often the best option for a light **lunch**, serving omelettes, sandwiches (generally half-baguettes filled with cheese or meat) and *croque-monsieur* (toasted ham and cheese sandwich). On street stalls you'll also find *frites* (chips/french fries), *crêpes*, *galettes* (wholewheat pancakes) and *gaufres* (waffles).

A **brasserie** is an inexpensive, all-day alternative to restaurants, and both generally serve food from noon to 2pm & 7 to 9/9.30pm, with city-centre brasseries often serving until late. The best offers are normally the *formule* (set menu, often including a drink) or the *plat du jour* (daily special).

If you're a vegetarian, you may find eating in France difficult as meat tends to be the major component of most meals. Nevertheless, as long as you make it clear that you're *un végétarien*, something can normally be arranged in all but the most basic of places.

DRINK

Drinking in France is a fine art, though while people might seem to put away Herculean quantities, public drunkenness is heavily frowned upon.

Wine (*vin*) is the national drink, and drunk at just about every meal or social occasion. *Vin de table* or *vin ordinaire* (table wine) is cheap and generally drinkable. In a café, a glass of wine is simply *un rouge* (red) or *un blanc* (white). A carafe (*le pichet*), normally two-thirds of a bottle, is usually best value.

Beer can often be very expensive. However, beer on tap (*à la pression*) often cheap – just ask for *une pression*, or *un demi* for a half. Spirits such as **cognac** and **armagnac**, and of course the notorious **absinthe**, are widely drunk but not cheap. A pleasant, inexpensive pre-dinner drink is *un kir*, a mix of white wine and crème de cassis.

CULTURE AND ETIQUETTE

The French might seem rather brusque on first acquaintance, but are in fact some of Europe's most open-minded, interesting and pleasant people. Making

French

	French	Pronunciation
Basics		
Yes	*Oui*	Whee
No	*Non*	No(n)
Please	*S'il vous plaît*	Seel voo play
Thank you	*Merci*	Mersee
Hello/Good day	*Bonjour*	Bo(n)joor
Goodbye	*Au revoir/à bientôt*	Orvoir/abyantoe
Excuse me	*Pardon*	pardo(n)
Today	*Aujourd'hui*	Ojoordwee
Yesterday	*Hier*	Eeyair
Tomorrow	*Demain*	Duhma(n)
What time is it?	*Quelle heure est-il?*	Kel ur et eel
I don't understand	*Je ne comprends pas*	Je nuh compron pah
How much?	*Combien?*	combyen
Do you speak English?	*Parlez-vous anglais?*	Parlay voo onglay
One	*Un*	Uh(n)
Two	*Deux*	Duh
Three	*Trois*	Trwah
Four	*Quatre*	Kattre
Five	*Cinq*	Sank
Six	*Six*	Seess
Seven	*Sept*	Set
Eight	*Huit*	Wheat
Nine	*Neuf*	Nurf
Ten	*Dix*	Deess
Getting around		
Where's the...?	*Où est...?*	Oo ay...?
Entrance	*Entrée*	Ontray
Exit	*Sortie*	Sortee
Tourist office	*Office de tourisme*	Ofees der tooreesmer
Toilet	*Toilettes*	Twalet
Hotel	*Hôtel*	Otel
Youth hostel	*Auberge de jeunesse*	obairzh der zhernes
Main square	*Place central*	Plas sontral
Church	*Église*	Ay-gleez
Museum	*Musée*	Mewzay
What time does the...leave?	*À quel heure part...?*	A kel er par...?
Boat	*Le bateau*	Ler bato
Bus	*Le bus*	Ler bews
Plane	*L'avion*	Lavyon
Train	*Le train*	Ler trun
Accommodation		
Do you have a... room?	*Avez-vous une chambre...?*	avay voo ewn shombrer...?
Double	*Avec un grand lit*	avek un grand lee
Single	*À un lit*	A un lee
Cheap	*Bon marché*	Bo(n) marchay
Expensive	*Cher*	Share
Open	*Ouvert*	Oovair
Closed	*Fermé*	Fermay

an effort to speak the language, however dreadful your accent, is always highly appreciated, and a few basic words of everyday French will get you a lot further than any amount of grimacing and pointing.

It's customary to **tip** porters, tour guides, taxi drivers and hairdressers, usually one to two euros. Restaurant prices almost always include a service charge, so there's no need to leave an additional cash tip unless you feel you've received service out of the ordinary.

SPORTS AND OUTDOOR ACTIVITIES

The main sport in France is undoubtedly **football**, which is held in high esteem on all levels. Victory in the 1998 World Cup led to immense national pride; defeat in 2006's World Cup Final to Italy however was less welcome. The French football league (Ⓦwww.lfp.fr) is divided into Ligue 1 (the highest), Ligue 2 and National; teams playing in the first category include Saint-Étienne, Lyon and Nantes. Match tickets are available from specific club websites, or in the town they are playing – ask at the local tourist office.

Rugby is another major pursuit, especially in Southern France, and the country often puts up a good showing in the Six Nations Tournament in March and April. Further details of rugby fixtures can be found at the French-language website Ⓦwww.francerugby.fr. **Cycling** is also popular, especially the annual Tour de France, an epic 3000km race across the country every July.

COMMUNICATIONS

Post offices (*la Poste*) are widespread and generally open from 8.30am to 6.30pm Monday to Friday, and 8.30am to noon on Saturday. **Stamps** (*timbres*) are also sold in *tabacs* (tobacconist shops). International **phone calls** can be made from any phone box (*cabine*), using phonecards (*télécartes*), which are available from post offices, *tabacs* and train station ticket counters. For all calls within France you must dial the entire ten digit number, including area code. The number for directory enquiries is Ⓣ12. **Internet access** is widespread, if not especially cheap; prices begin at around €4/hr and can go up to €10/hr in major cities.

FRANCE ON THE NET

Ⓦ**www.tourisme.fr** French Tourist Board.
Ⓦ**www.franceguide.com** Excellent resource, with links to many tourist offices.
Ⓦ**www.france.com** Indispensable guide on traveling around the country and places to stay, with the opportunity to interact with other travellers.
Ⓦ**www.discoverfrance.net** Useful tourist information, with links to other sites.
Ⓦ**www.viafrance.com** Information on festivals, expos, events and concerts.

EMERGENCIES

There are two main types of **police**, the Police Nationale and the Gendarmerie Nationale, and you can report a theft, or any other incident, to either.

To find a **doctor**, ask for an address at any *pharmacie* (chemist) or tourist information office. Consultation fees for a visit will be €20–25 and you'll be given a *Feuille de Soins* (Statement of Treatment) for any insurance claims.

EMERGENCY NUMBERS

Police Ⓣ17; Ambulance Ⓣ15; Fire Ⓣ18.

INFORMATION & MAPS

Most towns and villages have a *Syndicat d'Initiative* (SI) or *Office de Tourisme*, giving out local **information** and free maps. The larger ones can book accommodation anywhere in France, and most can find you a local room for the night, albeit with an added service charge.

The best overall nationwide **map** is the red Michelin no. 721/989 (1:1,000,000); the Michelin yellow series (scale 1:200,000) is better for regional detail. The IGN green (1:100,000 and 1:50,000) and blue (1:25,000) maps are good if you're planning to walk or cycle.

MONEY AND BANKS

The currency of France is the **euro** (€). Standard **banking hours** are Mon–Fri 9am–noon & 2–4.30pm; some also open on Saturday. The Banque Nationale de Paris often gives the best rates and the lowest commissions. **ATMs** can now be found all over France and most accept foreign cards. Credit cards are generally accepted by larger shops, and most restaurants and hotels.

OPENING HOURS AND HOLIDAYS

Basic **working hours** are 9am–noon/1pm and 2/3–6.30pm. The traditional **closing days** are Sunday and Monday, though you'll always find at least one *boulangerie* (bakery) open. **Museums** are usually closed on Monday and Tuesday, with reduced opening hours outside of summer. All shops, museums and offices are closed on the following **national holidays**: Jan 1, Easter Sun & Mon, Ascension Day, Pentecost, May 1, May 8, July 14, Aug 15, Nov 1, Nov 11, Dec 25.

STUDENT AND YOUTH DISCOUNTS

Most of the museums and attractions listed here offer a student or under-26 discount, which can be anything up to a third off. To make the most of these, buy an **ISIC** (International Student) or **IYTC** (International Youth) card. For more information see Ⓦwww.isiccard.com.

Paris

PARIS is one of the greatest cities in the world. Breathtakingly romantic, endlessly stylish and entirely compelling, experiencing life here is to become readjusted to beauty and pleasure. Undoubtedly France's jewel in the crown, it is an essential stop on any visit.

It is a surprisingly manageable city, with much pleasure to be derived from the different **quartiers** that comprise it, each with its own unique style and atmosphere; from the cosmopolitan **St-Germain** to the cobbled streets and village atmosphere of **Montmartre**. In addition, there are countless bars, clubs, restaurants and cafés that compete with the best of anything on offer elsewhere in Europe, and some of the most beautiful architecture to be found anywhere in the world.

What to see and do

Paris is split into two halves by the Seine, each with its own distinct identity. On the north of the river, the **Right Bank** *(Rive Droite)* is home to the grands boulevards and most monumental buildings, many dating from the civic planner Baron Haussmann's nineteenth-century redevelopment. Most of the major museums are here, as well as the city's widest range of shops around rue de Rivoli and Les Halles.

The **Left Bank** *(Rive Gauche)* has a noticeably different feel. A legendary Bohemian hang-out since the nineteenth century, the city's best range of bars and restaurants are based here, as well as some of its most evocative streets, such as the areas around St-Germain and St-Michel. These days much of the area has given in to commerce, with increasingly expensive and chic shops opening up, though it's not hard to discover some of its old spirit if you wander off the main roads.

PARISIAN ARRONDISSEMENTS

Paris is divided into twenty postal districts, known as *arrondissements*, which are used to denote addresses. The first, or *premier* (abbreviated as 1er), is centred on the Louvre and the Tuileries, with the rest (abbreviated as 2e, 3e, 4e etc) spiralling outwards in a clockwise direction.

Parts of Paris, of course, don't sit so easily within such definitions. **Montmartre**, rising up to the north of the centre and dominated by the great white dome of Sacré Coeur, has managed to retain a village-like atmosphere despite tourist saturation, and some of the beautiful *îles* in the middle of the Seine are essential stops.

The Arc de Triomphe, Champs-Élysées and around

The imposing **Arc de Triomphe** (daily 10am–10.30/11pm; €6; ⓣ01.55.37.73.77; M° Charles-de-Gaulle-Étoile), at the head of the Champs-Élysées, is a striking Parisian landmark, matched only by the Eiffel Tower, though it's probably not worth the admission fee. The celebrated **avenue des Champs-Élysées** contains many of the city's most impressive shops and restaurants. It leads to the vast **place de la Concorde**, a traffic nightmare, whose centrepiece, a gold-tipped obelisk from the temple of Luxor, was presented to the city by the viceroy of Egypt in 1829. Beyond lies the formal **Jardin des Tuileries** (daily 8/9am–7/8pm; M° Concorde), the perfect place for a stroll with its grand vistas and symmetrical flowerbeds. Towards the river, the **Orangerie** (daily 12.30–7pm, until 10pm Friday; €4.50; M°Concorde; ⓦwww.musee-orangerie.fr) displays Monet's largest water-lily paintings in a specially designed room, as well as works by Cézanne, Matisse, Utrillo and Modigliani.

The Louvre

On the east side of the Jardin des Tuileries is arguably the world's most famous museum, the **Louvre** (daily except Tues 9am–6pm; Wed & Fri till 9.45pm; €8.50, €6 after 6pm; M° Palais Royal-Musée du Louvre/Louvre-Rivoli; ⓦwww.louvre.fr). The building was first opened to the public in 1793, during the Revolution, and within a decade Napoleon had made it the largest art collection on earth with the takings from his empire, which explains the remarkably eclectic collection.

The main entrance is via I.M. Pei's iconic glass pyramid, but to avoid the (lengthy) queues, enter through the Louvre Rivoli Metro station or through the Louvre carousel. You can't see it all in one day – instead, pick just a few of the collections to concentrate on. Most people head straight for Da Vinci's *Mona Lisa*, but the crowds are rather off-putting. Instead, it's worth exploring some of the other sections such as **Egyptian Antiquities**, which includes the pink granite *Mastaba Sphinx* and **Sculpture**, which covers the entire development of the art in France from Romanesque to Rodin, as well as Italian and northern European sculpture.

> **MUSEUM ENTRY**
>
> Many museums offer **discounted entry** to under-26s (with ID) with reduced fees for all on Sundays. They're also often free on the first Sunday of every month, but they do get very busy because of it.

The Pompidou Centre

From the Louvre, it's a short walk to the **Pompidou Centre** (place Georges Pompidou; daily 11am–10pm; M° Rambuteau; ⓦwww.centrepompidou.fr), famous for its striking design. Masterminded by Renzo Piano and Richard Rogers, who had the innovative idea of turning its insides out to allow for maximum space inside. However it's undeniably showing its age, despite an expensive refit in the late 1990s. The main reason to visit is the hugely popular **Musée National d'Art Moderne** (daily except Tues 11am–9pm; €8–10), one of the world's great collections of modern art, spanning from 1905 to the present day, taking in Cubism, Surrealism and much more along the way.

The Marais

Just east of the Pompidou Centre lies the **Marais**, one of Paris's more striking quartiers. This very chic area is defined by its designer clothes shops, trendy cafés and bars, and cool nightlife; perhaps unsurprisingly, it's one of the city's main gay hotspots. The **Musée d'Art et d'Histoire du Judaïsme**, 71 rue du Temple (daily except Sat 10/11am–6pm; €6.80; M° Rambuteau; ⓦwww.mahj.org), pays homage to the area's Jewish roots, with a major display of Jewish artefacts and historical documents as well as paintings by Chagall and Soutine. A short walk east brings you to the seventeenth-century Hôtel Juigné Salé, which is home to the **Musée Picasso**, 5 rue de Thorigny (daily except Tues 9.30am–5.30/6pm; €6.70; M° St-Paul; ⓦwww.musee-picasso.fr), housing a substantial collection of the artist's personal property – a must-visit for all Picasso fans.

The Bastille and Île St-Louis

A short walk southeast of the museum, past the famous Colonne de Juillet, which is topped by a green bronze figure of Liberty, is **place de la Bastille**, the site of the Bastille prison that was famously stormed in 1789, beginning the French Revolution. Just south of here, across Henri IV bridge is the **Île St-Louis**, one of the centre's swankier quarters. From here, it's a peaceful and atmospheric walk through to the Île de la Cité, with some lovely pavement cafés worth stopping at along the way.

Île de la Cité

The **Île de la Cité** is where the city first started in the third century BC, when a tribe of Gauls known as the Parisii settled here. The most obvious attraction is the astounding Gothic **Cathédrale de Notre-Dame** (daily 7.45am–6.45pm, closed Sat 12.30–2pm; free; M° Cité), which dates from the mid-fourteenth century and was extensively renovated in the nineteenth. Immortalized by Victor Hugo's *The Hunchback Of Notre*

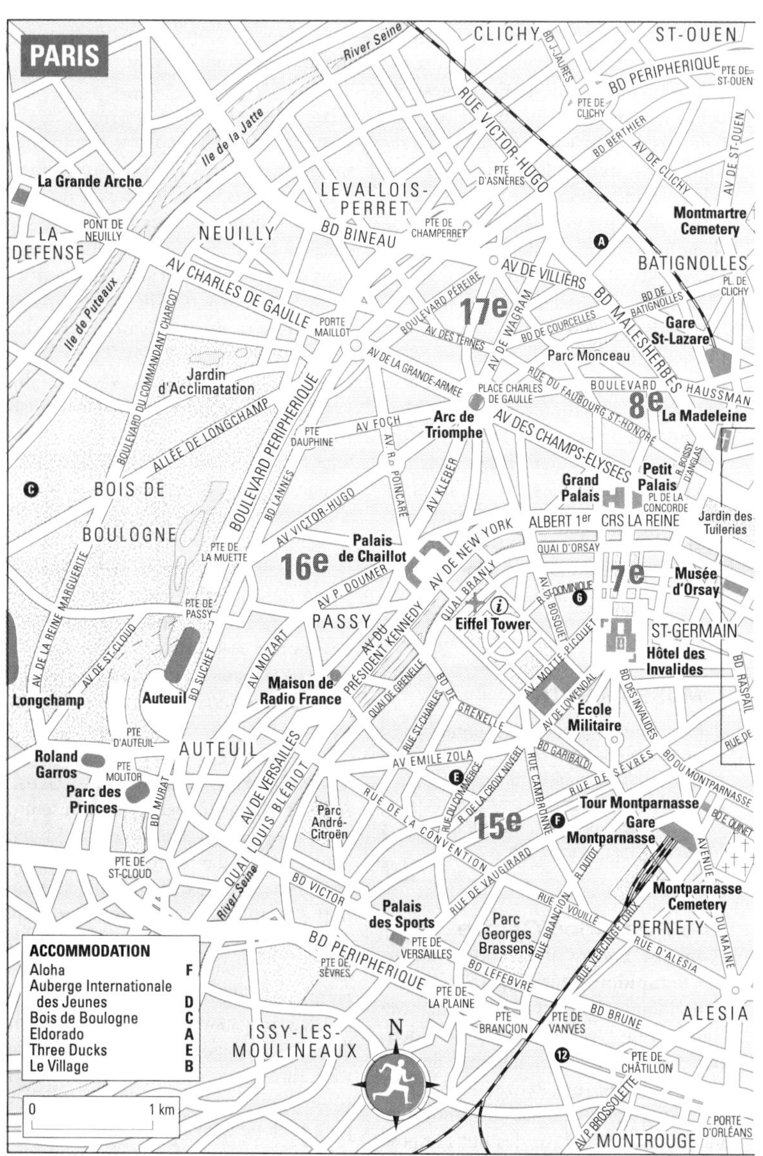

Dame, it's worth a guided tour (daily 9/10am–5/9pm; €7.50; Ⓦwww.monum.fr) to see the stunning sculptures of the towers close-up.

At the western end of the island lies **Sainte-Chapelle**, 4 bd du Palais (daily 9.30/10am–5/6.30pm; €6.50; M° Cité; Ⓦwww.monum.fr). One of the finest achievements of French Gothic style, it is lent a fragility by its height and huge expanses of glorious stained glass.

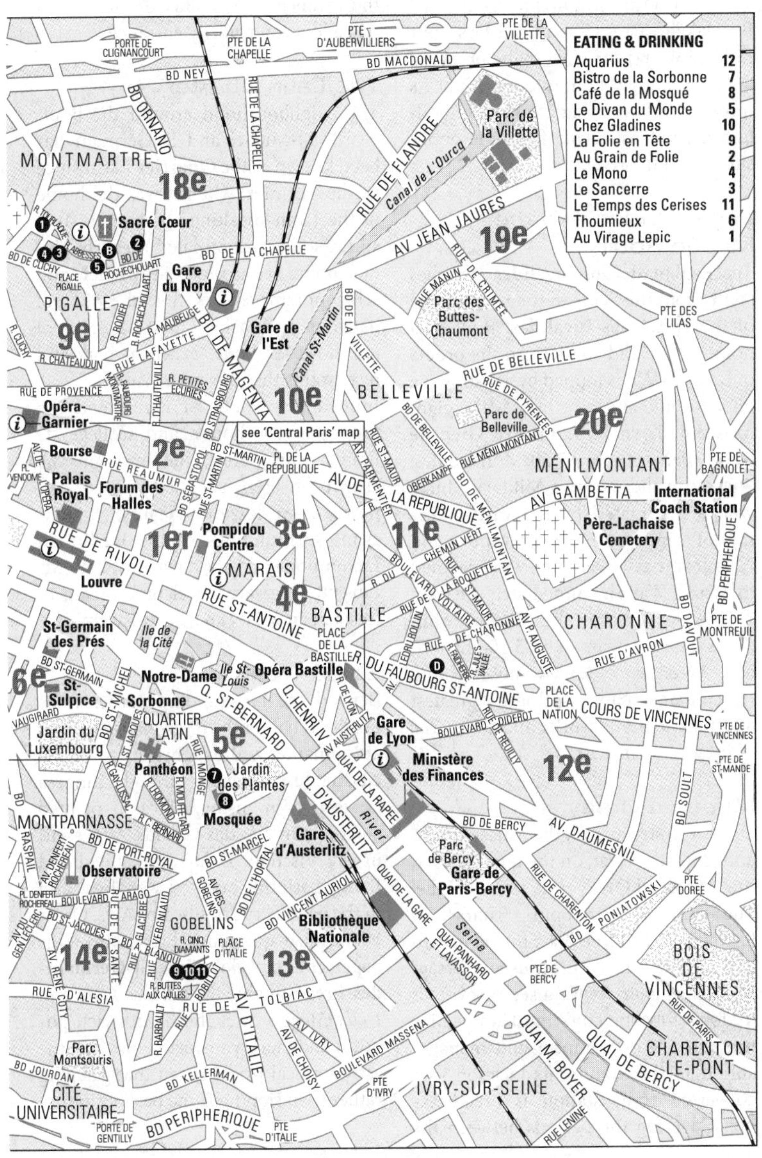

The Eiffel Tower

Gustave Eiffel's iconic tower is, rightly or wrongly, the defining image of Paris for most tourists. Hugely controversial on its 1889 debut, it has come to be recognized as one of the city's leading sights. If you wish to pay it a visit (daily 9/9.30am–11pm/midnight; €4.20; M° Bir Hakeim/RER Champ de Mars-Tour Eiffel; Ⓦwww.tour-eiffel.fr) be prepared for frustratingly long queues. It's at its most impressive at night, when fully illuminated – especially from the opposite side of the river.

Les Invalides and the Musée Rodin

The **Esplanade des Invalides** stretches south from the Seine to the wide facade of the **Hôtel des Invalides**. Built as a home for invalid soldiers on the orders of Louis XIV, it is topped by a distinctive gilded dome and now houses the giant **Musée de l'Armée,** 129 rue de Grenelle (daily 10am–5/6pm; €7.50; M° Invalides; Ⓦwww.invalides.org). Military buffs will be fascinated by the vast collection of armour, uniforms, weapons and Napoleonic relics, and the wing devoted to World War II. Immediately east, on 77 rue de Varenne, the **Musée Rodin** (Tues–Sun 9.30am–4.45/5.45pm; €7; M° Varenne; Ⓦwww.musee-rodin.fr) contains many of Rodin's greatest and most famous works, including *The Thinker* and *The Kiss.*

Musée d'Orsay

Down the street from the Musée Rodin and along the river, on the quai d'Orsay, the **Musée d'Orsay** (62 rue de Lille; Tues–Sun 9/10am–6pm, Thurs till 9.45pm; €7.50, free 1st Sun of month and to under-18s; RER Musée d'Orsay/M° Solférino; Ⓦwww.musee-orsay.fr) is undoubtedly the city's most innovative museum. More compact and manageable than the Louvre, its location in a converted train station is breathtaking. Covering the periods between the 1840s and 1914, its collection features legendary artists like Renoir, Van Gogh and Monet, and famous works such as Manet's *Le Déjeuner Sur L'Herbe* and Courbet's striking *The Origin Of The World.* The queues are always long, so it makes sense to book the day before at the advanced ticket office on site, which will allow you priority entrance.

The Latin Quarter

The neighbourhood around the boulevards St-Michel and St-Germain has been known as the **Quartier Latin** since medieval times, when it was the home of the Latin-speaking universities. It is still a student-dominated area, its pivotal point being **place St-Michel**, and schizophrenic in its mixture of cool hangouts and tacky tourist traps. There are, however, some excellent bars and restaurants that reward a visit.

Immediately south of here stand the prestigious Sorbonne and Collège de France universities, the jewel in the crown of French education and renowned worldwide. Nearby, the elegant surroundings of the **Jardin du Luxembourg** (daily dawn to dusk; M° Luxembourg) are a welcome breath of fresh air in what can be a noisy city.

St-Germain

Beyond the Luxembourg gardens, the northern half of the 6^{e} *arrondissement* is an upmarket and expensive part of the city, but fun to wander through. The area is steeped in history: Picasso painted *Guernica* in rue des Grands-Augustins; in rue Visconti, Delacroix painted and Balzac's printing business went bust; and in the parallel rue des Beaux-Arts, Oscar Wilde died quipping "Either the wallpaper goes or I do". **Place St-Germain-des-Prés** contains the famous *Flore* and *Deux Magots* cafés, both with rich political and literary histories; however the astronomical prices mean that gawping rather than sipping is the best option.

GÉRALD DE NERVAL

In a city full of eccentrics and madmen, the surrealist poet and writer Gérald de Nerval (1808–1855) was first among equals. His best-documented insanity was keeping a lobster as a pet; he named it Thibault and would take it for walks around St-Germain on a blue ribbon, scandalizing the city. He eventually killed himself by hanging himself from a window grating, and is buried in the Père Lachaise cemetery (see below).

Montparnasse

On the southern side of the Luxembourg gardens is the former bohemian quarter of Montparnasse. It has somewhat lost its lustre since the erection of the hideous 59-storey skyscraper **Tour Montparnasse**, which has rightly become one of the city's most hated landmarks since its construction in 1973. Its sole redeeming feature is the view it offers if you take the lift to the top floor (daily 9.30am–10.30/11.30pm; €8.50; Ⓦ www.tourmontparnasse56.com; M° Montparnasse-Bienvenue). The nearby **Montparnasse cemetery** (blvd Edgar Quinet; daily 8/9am–5.30/6pm; free; M° Raspail) has plenty of illustrious names, including Baudelaire and Serge Gainsbourg.

Montmartre

In the far opposite side of the city, in the middle of the 18ᵉ *arrondissement*, is the glorious district of **Montmartre**. It can get rather horribly touristy around place du Tertre and Sacré-Cœur – the best way to enjoy the area is to wander through the village-like streets which still suggest a bygone age. Crowning the **Butte Montmartre** is the nineteenth-century neo-Byzantine **Sacré-Cœur** (daily 6am–10.30pm; free; M° Anvers/Abbesses; Ⓦ www.sacre-coeur-montmartre.com). It's worth noting that the views from the top of the dome (daily 9am–6/7pm; admission €5) can be rather disappointing, except on the clearest of days. To get to the top of the Butte, take the funicular from place Suzanne-Valadon (ordinary métro tickets and passes are valid) or climb the (very) steep stairs via place des Abbesses. Off nearby rue Lepic is the **Moulin de la Galette**, the last remaining windmill in Montmartre. Down the hill on boulevard de Clichy, the Moulin Rouge and Pigalle should be avoided except by the curious; petty crime is rife and it's incredibly seedy, even in the middle of the day.

AMÉLIE

The 2001 film *Amélie* contributed greatly to the city's tourist industry, presenting as it did a romanticized, cleaner and brighter version of Montmartre. Unsurprisingly, the location has capitalized on the tourist trade, and *Amélie*-related merchandise can be seen everywhere. The café in which Amélie works in the film is the real-life *Café des Deux Moulins*, at 15 rue de Lepic, south of rue des Abbesses. The *crème brulee* is, fittingly, named after her.

Père Lachaise

The world's most famous graveyard, the **Père-Lachaise cemetery**, boulevard de Ménilmontant, 20ᵉ (daily 8/9am–5.30/6pm; M° Père-Lachaise), attracts pilgrims to the graves of Oscar Wilde (in division 89) and Jim Morrison (in division 6). There are countless other famous people buried here, among them Chopin and Edith Piaf.

Arrival and information

Air Paris has two main airports: Charles de Gaulle and Orly. A much smaller one, Beauvais, is used primarily by the low-cost airlines Ryanair and Wizzair. Charles de Gaulle (CDG) is 23km northeast and connected to Gare du Nord train station by

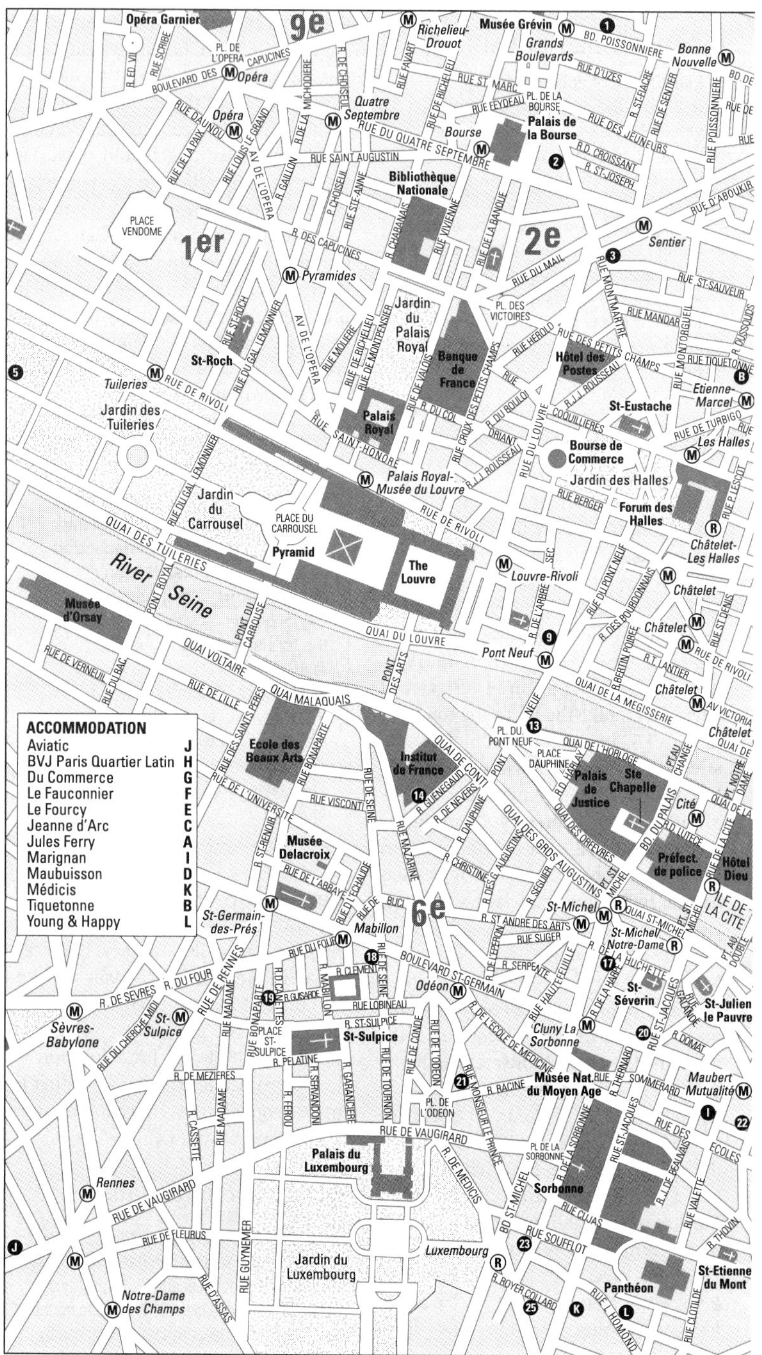
ACCOMMODATION
Aviatic J
BVJ Paris Quartier Latin H
Du Commerce G
Le Fauconnier F
Le Fourcy E
Jeanne d'Arc C
Jules Ferry A
Marignan I
Maubuisson D
Médicis K
Tiquetonne B
Young & Happy L
Opéra Garnier
9e
1er
2e
6e
Musée Grévin
Richelieu-Drouot
Grands Boulevards
Bonne Nouvelle
Opéra
Quatre Septembre
Bourse
Palais de la Bourse
Bibliothèque Nationale
PLACE VENDOME
Pyramides
Sentier
Jardin du Palais Royal
Banque de France
Hôtel des Postes
St-Roch
Tuileries
Jardin des Tuileries
Palais Royal
St-Eustache
Etienne-Marcel
Les Halles
Bourse de Commerce
Palais Royal-Musée du Louvre
Jardin des Halles
Forum des Halles
Châtelet-Les Halles
Jardin du Carrousel
PLACE DU CARROUSEL
Pyramid
The Louvre
Louvre-Rivoli
River Seine
Musée d'Orsay
Châtelet
Pont Neuf
Ecole des Beaux Arts
Institut de France
PLACE DAUPHINE
Palais de Justice
Ste Chapelle
Cité
Musée Delacroix
Préfect. de police
Hôtel Dieu
ILE DE LA CITE
St-Germain-des-Prés
Mabillon
St-Michel
St-Michel Notre-Dame
St-Séverin
St-Julien le Pauvre
Odéon
Sèvres-Babylone
St-Sulpice
Cluny La Sorbonne
Musée Nat. du Moyen Age
Maubert Mutualité
Palais du Luxembourg
Sorbonne
Rennes
Jardin du Luxembourg
Luxembourg
Panthéon
St-Etienne du Mont
Notre-Dame des Champs

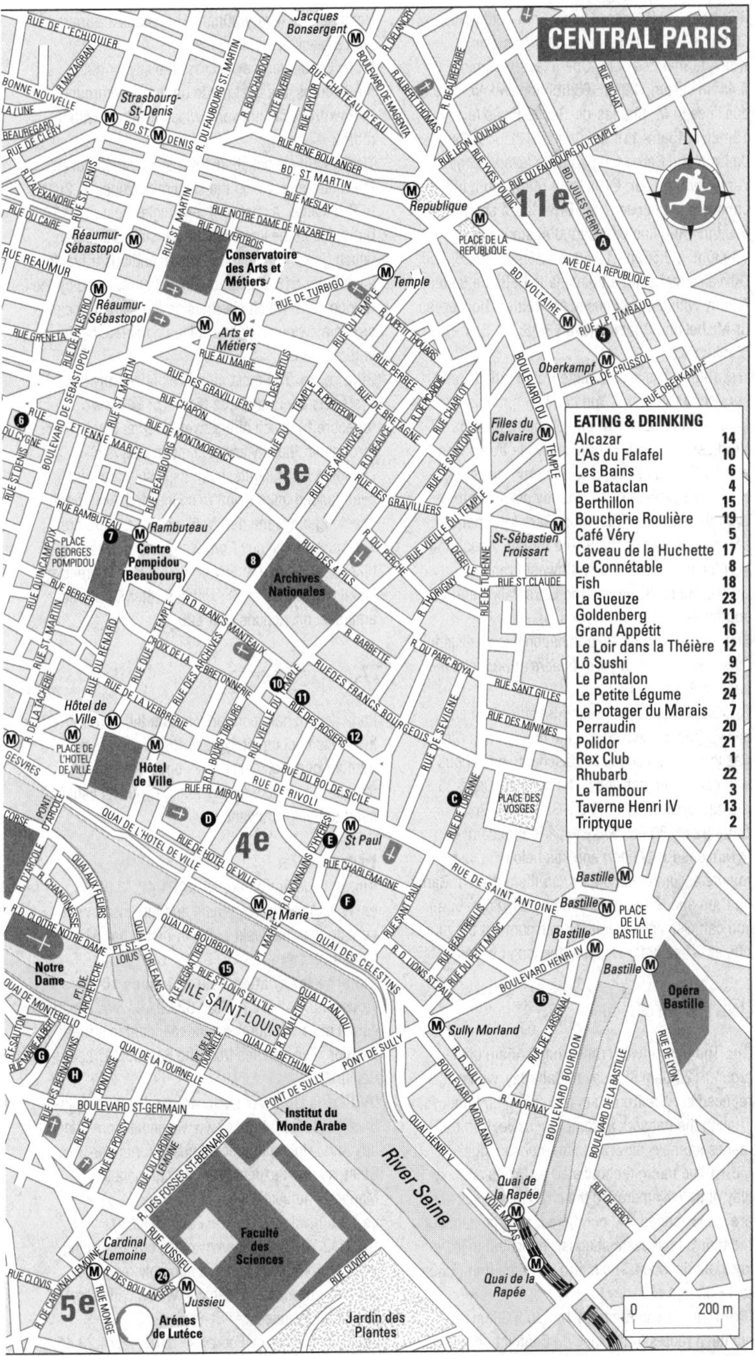

FRANCE

PARIS

RER train line B (every 15min, 5am–midnight; 30min; €7.85). There's also the Roissybus, which terminates at M° Opéra (every 15min, 5.45am–11pm; 45min; €8.60) and two Air France bus lines to M° Charles-de-Gaulle-Étoile (every 15min, 5.45am–11pm; 50min; €12), or to Gare de Lyon and Gare Montparnasse (every 30min, 7am–9pm; 1 hour; €12). Orly, 14km south of Paris, connects to the centre via Orly-Rail, a shuttle bus then RER line C to Gare d'Austerlitz (every 15–30min, 5.50am–10.50pm; 35min; €5.25) and Orlyval, a fast shuttle train line to RER line B station Antony with connections to M° Dénfert-Rochereau, St-Michel and Châtelet (every 4–8min, 6am–11pm; 35min; €8.85).

Train Paris has six mainline train stations, all served by the métro. You can buy national and international tickets at any of them. Gare du Nord serves northern France, while trains from nearby Gare de l'Est go to eastern France. Gare St-Lazare serves the Normandy coast; Gare de Lyon the south and the Alps; Gare Montparnasse serves Chartres, Brittany, the Atlantic coast and TGV lines to Tours and southwest France; and Gare d'Austerlitz serves the Loire Valley and the southwest.

Bus Most international and national long-distance buses use the main *gare routière* at Bagnolet in eastern Paris (M° Gallieni).

Tourist office There are tourist office branches all over the city, which sell the handy *Paris City Passport* (€5), a booklet of discounts on various attractions and activities. The main one is at 25 rue des Pyramides 1er (Mon–Sat 10am–7pm; Ⓣ08.92.68.30.00, Ⓦwww.paris-info.com; M° Pyramides/RER Auber) and can help with last-minute accommodation, as can the offices at Gare de Lyon and Gare du Nord (both daily 8am–6pm). You can also book tickets to museums at the tourist offices – handy for skipping the long queues.

City transport

Bus The bus network runs from 5.45am until around 12.30am Monday to Saturday, with a reduced service from 7am to 8.30pm on Sundays. Though the network is comprehensive, traffic makes journeys slow and time-consuming.

Métro The métro (abbreviated as M°) is an easy way of travelling around the city. The various lines are colour-coded and numbered, and the name of the train's final destination is signposted to let you know its direction. The métro operates from 5.30am to 12.30am.

Night bus These run from 1am to 5.30am on eighteen routes from place du Châtelet near the Hôtel de Ville (every 30min–1hr); stops are marked with a black and yellow owl.

Train Longer journeys across the city, or out to the suburbs, are best made on the underground RER express rail network, which overlaps with the metro.

Tickets Single tickets (€1.40) are valid on buses, the métro and, within the city limits (zones 1–2), the RER rail lines. A carnet of ten singles costs €10.50, but those in the know will buy a carte d'orange, which gives you unlimited metro and bus travel for a week for €16. It is gradually being replaced by the Navigo card, which operates on the same principle but as a swipe card; this will be complete by the end of 2008.

Bike rental The most effective and worthwhile system is the Roue Libre (€10–15; Ⓦwww.rouelibre.fr) which offers twenty rental points throughout the city and a complete service including locks, lights, helmets, insurance, and even guided tours if you're so inclined. Also worth checking out is the new Velib scheme: there are 750 racks in the city from which you can rent a bike (depositing it at any of the others). There is an initial deposit fee of €1, with a further €1 per hour; annual subscriptions cost €29.

Accommodation

Paris accommodation ranges from the ultra-luxurious to completely basic, but there are a number of good, inexpensive options for budget travellers – to take full advantage you will usually need to book in advance.

Hostels

Aloha 1 rue Borromée, 15e Ⓣ01.42.73.03.03, Ⓦwww.aloha.fr. Welcoming and fun hostel with very good drink deals at the in-house bar. M° Volontaires. ❷

Auberge Internationale des Jeunes 10 rue Trousseau, 11e Ⓣ01.47.00.62.00, Ⓦwww.aijparis.com. Laid-back but noisy independent in a great location, five minutes from the Bastille. M° Ledru-Rollin. ❷

BVJ Paris Quartier Latin 44 rue des Bernardins, 5e Ⓣ01.43.29.34.80, Ⓦwww.bvjhotel.com. Clean, tidy and rather institutional hostel for under-35s. Quiet, so don't expect all-night partying. M° Maubert-Mutualité. ❸

Le Fauconnier 11 rue du Fauconnier, 4e Ⓣ01.42.74.23.45, Ⓦwww.mije.com. Charming and comfortable hostel in a superbly renovated seventeenth-century mansion with a courtyard. Breakfast included. M° St-Paul. ❸

Le Fourcy 6 rue de Fourcy, 4e Ⓣ01.42.74.23.45,

Ⓦ www.mije.com. Large, friendly hostel in a stunning mansion with small, four- to eight-bed dorms. Breakfast included and there's a decent, budget restaurant on site. M° St-Paul. ❸

Jules Ferry 8 bd Jules-Ferry, 11e Ⓣ 01.43.57.55.60, Ⓦ www.fuaj.org. Small and easily accessible hostel, in a lively, gay-friendly area along the Canal St-Martin. Perennially popular – get there early in the day. M° République. ❸

Maubuisson 12 rue des Barres, 4e Ⓣ 01.42.74.23.45, Ⓦ www.mije.com. One of the best hostels in the city, thanks to its striking architecture and comfortable rooms, situated in a magnificent medieval building on a quiet street. Breakfast included. M° Pont-Marie. ❸

Three Ducks 6 place Étienne-Pernet, 15e Ⓣ 01.48.42.04.05, Ⓦ www.3ducks.fr. Lively hostel with an inexpensive bar and use of kitchen. Very busy in summer. M° Félix Faure; ❷

Le Village 20 rue d'Orsel, 18e Ⓣ 01.42.64.22.02, Ⓦ www.villagehostel.fr. Attractive Montmartre hostel with good facilities and a terrace that has views of Sacré-Coeur. 2am curfew. M° Anvers. ❸

Young and Happy 80 rue Mouffetard, 5e Ⓣ 01.45.35.09.53, Ⓦ www.youngandhappy.fr. The name says it all; the clientele in this vibrant, up-for-it establishment tend to enjoy partying, and this is the place to hang out with like-minded souls. 2am curfew. M° Monge/Censier-Daubenton; ❸

Hotels

Aviatic 105 rue de Vaugirard, 6e Ⓣ 01.53.63.25.50, Ⓦ www.aviatic.fr. Charming, beautifully kept small hotel near Montparnasse. The rooms are comfortable and well decorated; breakfast is included. M° Montparnasse. ❻

Du Commerce 14 rue de la Montagne-Ste-Geneviève, 5e Ⓣ 01.43.54.89.69, Ⓦ www.commerce-paris-hotel.com. Welcoming budget hotel in the heart of the Latin Quarter, with bright, if rather garish, rooms. M° Maubert-Mutualité. ❹

Eldorado 18 rue des Dames, 17 e Ⓣ 01.45.22.35.21, Ⓦ www.eldoradohotel.fr. Very popular budget hotel near the Gare St-Lazare, with a bohemian, laid-back atmosphere, comfortable and spacious rooms and a private garden. Book well in advance. M° Place de Clichy. ❸

Jeanne d'Arc 3 rue de Jarente, 4 e Ⓣ 01.48.87.62.11, Ⓦ www.hoteljeannedarc.com. Lovely, laid-back hotel in the Marais, with friendly staff and lovely rooms. Due to its great reputation, it fills up quickly, so book in advance. M° St Paul. ❻

Marignan 13 rue du Sommerard, 5e Ⓣ 01.43.54.63.81, Ⓦ www.hotel-marignan.com. Excellent backpacker-oriented hotel, with free laundry and self-catering facilities; good choice of triples and singles. Special offers available if you book well ahead. M° Maubert-Mutualité. ❺

Médicis 214 rue St-Jacques, 5e Ⓣ 01.43.54.14.66, Ⓔ hotelmedicis@aol.com. Famous for having been one of Jim Morrison's hangouts, this friendly small hotel attracts plenty of Doors fans, as well as anyone with an eye for a bargain. RER Luxembourg. ❸

Tiquetonne 6 rue Tiquetonne, 2e Ⓣ 01.42.36.94.58. Good-value place that appears not to have been changed for about fifty years and with great hospitality, set on a small, attractive street. Closed Aug. M° Étienne-Marcel. ❸

Camping

Bois de Boulogne Allée du Bord de l'eau Ⓣ 01.45.24.30.00, Ⓦ www.campingparis.fr. The city's major campsite is situated in the Bois de Boulogne, the city's largest open space, and offers a range of facilities including showers and a canteen. A very cheap option, but there's a €13 booking fee for first-time visitors. To get here, take bus #244 from M° Porte Maillot. ❷

Eating

Eating out in Paris need not be an extravagant affair. It's a good idea to make lunch your main meal, when many places offer reasonable *prix-fixe* (fixed price) menus, which often include a beer or glass of wine. Even at dinner, it's possible to have a meal for less than €15 in many places. Anyone in possession of an ISIC card is eligible to apply for tickets for the university restaurants run by CROUS – see Ⓦ www.crous-paris.fr for a list of addresses, and buy your ticket from the restaurants themselves.

Cafés

Berthillon 31 rue St-Louis-en-l'Île, 4e. Expect long queues for the best ice creams and sorbets in the city; the divine flavours include salted caramel and apricot. Single scoop €3. Closed Mon & Tues. M° Pont Marie.

Café de la Mosquée 39 rue Geoffroy-St-Hilaire, 5e. This oasis of calm offers great mint tea and Middle Eastern cakes (€2). Daily 10am–midnight. M° Jussieu.

Café Véry Jardin des Tuileries, 1er. The best of a number of café-restaurants in the gardens, this place is popular with artsy types and serves toasted sandwiches (€3–5) and more substantial snacks. Daily noon–7pm. M° Concorde.

Le Loir dans la Théière 3 rue des Rosiers, 4e. Peaceful, quirky retreat with leather armchairs and a laid-back atmosphere. Midday *tartines* and omelettes, fruit teas and cakes (€2–4) served all

VEGETARIAN PARIS

Vegetarian food in Paris doesn't have the greatest of reputations – unsurprisingly where the term *viande* (meat) and food are often interchangeable – but an increasing number of places are now offering vegetarian options, with a number of inexpensive places completely dedicated to it. The restaurants below are some of the best places to head to.

Aquarius 40 rue de Gergovie, 14^{e}. Fashionable, stylish and inexpensive veggie hangout with a good wine list and a menu that includes salads, risotto and curry. M° Plaisance. Lunch menu €11.

Au Grain de Folie 24 rue de la Vieuville, 18^{e}. One for the uncompromising vegetarian, thanks to the heavily vegan-based menu, this homely Montmartre restaurant specializes in unpretentious and basic fare. Prix fixe €12–16. M° Abbesses.

Le Potager du Marais 22 rue Rambuteau, 3^{e}. Chic and lively vegetarian restaurant with some great daily specials, such as a brilliant aubergine curry. Prix fixe €20. M° Rambuteau.

day, and a great Sunday brunch. M° St-Paul.

Le Sancerre 35 rue des Abbesses, 18e. Hangout for the young and trendy in the Abbesses area of Montmartre, serving mouthwatering quiche (€6). Daily 7am–2am. M° Abbesses.

Taverne Henri IV 13 pl du Pont-Neuf, Île de la Cité, 1er. Old-style wine bar serving generous plates of meats and cheeses (€8); glass of wine €3. Closed Sun & Aug. M° Pont-Neuf.

Restaurants

L'As du Falafel 34 rue des Rosiers, 4e. Known for serving the city's best falafel, amongst other things; try their pitta special – cabbage, aubergine, hummus and Tabasco sauce (€6.50). Sun–Thurs M° St-Paul.

Bistro de la Sorbonne 4 rue Toullier, 5e. Large portions of traditional French and North African dishes at good prices and a buzzing ambience. Main courses from €7. M° Place Monge.

Boucherie Roulière 24 Rue des Canettes, 6e. Carnivores everywhere will get a kick out of this splendid, narrow restaurant, where some of the best steaks (from €12) in Paris are served. They come beautifully rare, with shallots and garlic, and the chips are cooked to perfection. M° Mabillon.

Chez Gladines 30 rue des Cinq-Diamants, 13^{e}. Tiny, welcoming corner bistro serving hearty Basque dishes. Close to the cool bars of the Butte-aux-Cailles. Lunch menu €10. M° Corvisart.

Foyer du Vietnam 80 rue Monge, 5^{e}. Very popular student place where you can enjoy Vietnamese curries and noodle dishes for under €10, including wine. M° Monge.

Goldenberg 7 rue des Rosiers, 4e. Paris's best known Jewish restaurant serves borscht, blinis, strudels and other central European dishes. Try the beef goulash (€10). M° St-Paul.

Grand Appétit 9 rue de la Cerisaie, 4e. Vegetarian and macrobiotic meals for around €15 in this dedicated eco-vegetarian restaurant. M° Bastille.

Lô Sushi 1 rue du Pont-Neuf, 8e. Good sushi (€2–7) and great soups. You can talk to fellow diners via the Internet, if you so desire. Daily until midnight. M° Pont-Neuf.

Le Mono 40 rue Véron, 18e. Togolese restaurant serving delicious grilled fish and meats (from €15) in a boisterous, noisy atmosphere. Save space for the divine banana desserts. Closed Wed. M° Abbesses.

Perraudin 157 rue St-Jacques, 5e. Well-known traditional bistro in the Latin Quarter with menus that are especially strong on game and fish. Lunch menu €18. M° Cluny-La Sorbonne.

La Petite Légume 36 rue des Boulangers, 5e. Tiny, homely vegetarian café with an organic approach, including delicious home-made bread. Set menu €14. Closed Sun. M° Jussieu.

Polidor 41 rue Monsieur-le-Prince, 6e. Historic bistro that was a favourite of James Joyce; short-

TREAT YOURSELF

Alcazar 62 rue Mazarine, 6e. True Parisian style in this famous, hip bar & brasserie, with great cooking – especially the *escargots* and *huîtres* (oysters) – and legendary atmosphere, thanks to the great, unfailingly pleasant service. It's also historically famous; it used to be one of the major music halls, rivalled only by the Moulin Rouge. A must-visit. Set menu from €20. M° Odeon.

TREAT YOURSELF

Thoumieux 79 rue St-Dominique, 7e. Stylish, old-fashioned brasserie in an upmarket location, with good, solid bistro meals such as *cassoulet de poulet* (chicken casserole) and calves' liver. Set lunch from €20. M° Invalides.

tempered service but an excellent budget menu (lunch €10) – try the great leg of lamb. M° Odéon.

Le Temps des Cerises 18–20 rue de la Butte-aux-Cailles, 13e. Homely, good-value neighbourhood bistro with reassuringly traditional dishes such as steak-frites and a decent wine list. Lunch menu €13.50. M° Corvisart.

Au Virage Lepic 61 rue Lepic, 18e. Simple, good-quality food, focusing on meat and game, served in a noisy, friendly, old-fashioned bistro. Set menu €10. M° Abbesses.

Drinking & nightlife

Drinks are charged in bars according to where you sit, with standing at the bar the cheapest option. The university quarter near St-Germain-des-Prés has some great spots, as does the Marais with its small, crowded café-bars and trendy gay bars. Most places are open all day until around 2am, and many offer an early evening "happy hour" until around 8pm. Be warned that beer is much more expensive than wine and can cost up to €8 for a pint. For **listings**, the best weekly guides are *Pariscope* (€0.40), with a small section in English, or *L'Officiel des Spectacles* (€0.35).

Bars

Le Connétable 55 rue des Archives, 3e. This lively, cosmopolitan bar attracts a mixed crowd of all ages, especially after midnight. Wine from €4. Daily 11am–3pm, 7pm–3am. M° Rambuteau.

Le Divan du Monde 75 rue des Martyrs, 18e Ⓦwww.divandumonde.com. Café-bar with an eclectic selection of live music and occasional big-name DJs. Drinks from €5. M° Pigalle.

Fish 69 rue de Seine, 6e. Great wine bar in a hip location, with a fantastic range of drinks, friendly English-speaking staff and even a proper counter bar where you can sit, drink and chat. Wine from €4. Tues–Sun noon-2pm, 7–10.45pm. M° Mabillon.

La Folie en Tête 33 rue de la Butte-aux-Cailles, 13e. Down to earth, fun place, decorated with old musical instruments; happy-hour drinks from €1.50. Mon–Sat 5pm–2am. M° Place-d'Italie.

La Gueuze 19 rue Soufflot, 5e. Belgian beers aplenty in this monastic-looking bar near the Jardin du Luxembourg. Great happy-hour from 4–7pm, and also 11pm–2am Fri–Sun. 9am–2am daily. M° St-Michel.

Le Pantalon 7 rue Royer-Collard, 5e. Eccentrically decorated but entertaining bar with cheaper-than-average drinks and an absurd daily happy hour from 5.30–7.30pm, when pints cost from €2.50. Mon–Sat 11am–2am. M° St-Michel.

Rhubarb 18 rue Laplace, 5e. Boisterous student pub with excellent cocktails (from €6), and €2 shots all day Mon–Thurs. 5/7pm–2am. M° Maubert-Mutualité.

Le Tambour 41 rue Montmartre, 2e. Lovely bar on a quiet side street which has a great range of wines at reasonable prices, beginning at around €3 a glass. Tues–Sat noon–3am, Sun & Mon 6pm–3am. M° Sentier.

Clubs

Les Bains 7 rue du Bourg-l'Abbé, 3e. This hip-hop and garage club is located in an old Turkish bath, which makes for an unusual, subterranean atmosphere. Entrance free–€8. Daily midnight–dawn. M° Étienne-Marcel.

Le Bataclan 50 bd Voltaire, 11e Ⓦwww.bataclan.fr. This old theatre has one of the best line-ups of any venue, covering everything from international and local dance, to rock, opera, comedy and techno nights. M° Oberkampf.

Caveau de la Huchette 5 rue de la Huchette, 5e. Very popular basement jazz club featuring excellent bebop and big-band groups. Entrance €10. M° St-Michel.

Rex Club 5 bd Poissonnière, 2e. Big-name DJs flock to this club. Entrance €12. 10pm–4am. M° Grands-Boulevards.

Triptyque 142 rue Montmartre, 2e Ⓦwww.letriptyque.com. Acid jazz, trip hop and electronica spun every day of the week. Entrance €10. M° Bourse/Grands Boulevards.

Gay and lesbian Paris

Paris has a well-established **gay scene** concentrated mainly in the Halles, Marais and Bastille areas. For information, check out *Têtu* (Ⓦwww.tetu.com), France's main gay monthly magazine, or visit the main information centre, Centre Gai et Lesbien de Paris, 3 rue Keller, 11e (Ⓣ01.43.57.21.47, Ⓦwww.cglparis.org; M° Ledru-Rollin/Bastille).

Banana Café 13 rue de la Ferronnerie, 1er. Seriously hedonistic club-bar, packing in the punters with up-tempo clubby tunes. Entry €8; happy hour 6.30–9.30pm. M° Châtelet.

Bar Central 33 rue Vieille-du-Temple, 4e. An old, dimly lit hangout in the Marais, attracting a quieter, more laid-back clientele. Paris's sole gay-only hotel is just above. Mon–Fri 4pm–2am, Sat & Sun 2pm–2am. M° St-Paul.

Le Mixer 23 rue Ste-Croix-de-la-Bretonnerie, 4e ⓣ01.48.87.55.44. Popular gay, lesbian and straight-friendly bar with futuristic decor, a good atmosphere and a tiny dance-floor. M° Hôtel-de-Ville. Entrance free before 10pm, €5 after.

Le Pulp 25 bd Poissonnière, 2e ⓦwww.pulpeclub.com. Done up in the style of a nineteenth-century music hall, this popular lesbian bar is well known for the antics of its uninhibited clientele. Cover around €10; open till dawn. M° Grands-Boulevards.

Redlight 34 rue du Départ, 15e ⓣ01.42.79.94.53, ⓦwww.enfer.fr. Popular club with huge weekend house nights that kick off from 1am or so. M° Montparnasse-Bienvenüe.

Entertainment

Cinema tickets cost around €8 in Paris and discounted tickets are offered across the city on Wednesdays. Films are identified as either **v.o.**, which means they're shown in their original language, or **v.f.**, which means they're dubbed into French. If you're a film buff, visit the **Cinémathèque Française**, 51 rue Bercy, 12e – a fantastic state-sponsored cinema that specializes in talks, presentations and screenings.

Many theatres and concert venues offer standby tickets at a reduced rate, which are generally only released around twenty minutes before the performance. The **Cité de la Musique**, 221 av Jean-Jaurès, 19e (M° Porte-de-Pantin; standby €5; ⓦwww.cite-musique.fr) has an eclectic programme that covers Baroque, contemporary works, jazz, *chansons* and world music, while the city's original opera house, **Palais Garnier**, place de l'Opéra, 9e (M° Opéra; standby €15; ⓦwww.opera-de-paris.fr) stages operas and ballets within its lavish interior.

Shopping

Galeries Lafayette 40 blvd Haussmann, 9e ⓦwww.galerieslafayette.com. This massive department store sells everything from lingerie and designer fashion to books and DVDs. Worth a visit just to gawp at the astonishing architecture. M° Auber.

Marché aux Puces de St-Ouen rue des Rosiers, 18e ⓦwww.les-puces.com. Bargain hunters from all over France congregate on this massive flea market (Europe's largest), with over 2500 stalls – be prepared to haggle. M° Porte de Clignancourt.

Réciproque 88 & 95 rue de la Pompe, 16e. Heavily reduced (up to half-price) dépôt-vente selling seconds and old stocks of clothing. Great for accessories and last season's hits.

TREAT YOURSELF

Hédiard 21 place de la Madeleine, 8e, M° Madeleine ⓦwww.hediard.fr. Gastronomes will be in seventh heaven here, where the finest foods have been sold since its foundation in 1854. The likes of fine chocolates, great wines and some amazing delicacies are all readily available – and the budget-conscious will be able to find a few less expensive treats too.

Directory

Embassies and consulates Australia, 4 rue Jean-Rey, 15e ⓣ01.40.59.33.00; Canada, 35 av Montaigne, 8e ⓣ01.44.43.29.00; Ireland, 4 rue Rude, 16e ⓣ01.44.17.67.00; New Zealand, 7 rue Léonard-de-Vinci, 16e ⓣ01.45.01.43.43; UK, 35 rue du Faubourg-St-Honoré, 8e ⓣ01.44.51.31.00; US, 2 rue St Florentin, 1er ⓣ01.43.12.22.22.

Exchange A good *bureau de change* is the Comptoir des Tuileries, near the Louvre at 27 rue de l'Arbre Sec, 1er ⓣ01.42.60.17.16.

Hospital Contact SOS-Médecins ⓣ01.43.37.77.77 for 24-hour medical help, or dial ⓣ15 for emergencies.

Internet *Cybercafe de Paris*, 15 rue des Halles, 1€ (20¢/5min); *Café Orbital*, 3 rue de Médicis (€3/15min, €7/hr).

Left luggage Lockers (€3.50–9.50) are available at all train stations.

Pharmacy Dérhy, 84 av des Champs-Élysées is open 24hr.

Post office 52 rue du Louvre, 1er.

Moving on

Train to: Avignon (13 daily; 2hr 40min–3hr 30min); Bayonne (7–10 daily; 4hr 45min); Bordeaux (hourly; 3hr); Boulogne (4–6 daily; 2hr 10min); Carcassonne (hourly; 5hr 10min–8hr); Clermont-Ferrand (5–7 daily; 3hr 30min); Dijon (hourly; 1hr 40min); Grenoble (hourly; 3hr); Le Havre (10–14 daily; 2hr); Lille (hourly; 1hr); London St Pancras (hourly; 2hr 15min); Lyon (hourly; 2hr); Marseille (hourly; 3hr); Montpellier (10 daily; 3hr 25min); Nancy (12 daily; 3hr); Nantes (2 hourly; 2hr); Nice (2 hourly; 5hr 30min–6hr); Nîmes (10 daily; 3hr); Poitiers (2 hourly; 1hr 40min); Reims (frequent; 45 minutes–1 hr 40 min); Rennes (hourly; 2hr 15min); Rouen (hourly; 1hr 15min); Strasbourg (12–13 daily; 2hr 15 min); Toulouse (10 daily; 5hr–6hr 30min); Tours (hourly; 1hr–2hr 30min).

DAY-TRIPS FROM PARIS

Around 32km east of the city is **Disneyland Paris** (daily 9/10am–8/11pm; €40; RER line A to Marne-la-Vallée; Ⓦwww.disneylandparis.com), a 5000-acre slice of the fantastical. You know what you're going to get here: chirpy cartoon characters, plenty of schmaltz and too many queues. Anyone over the age of twelve might find its incessant, forced geniality (as well as the highly commercialized nature of it all) very off-putting; instead, head out to stately **Versailles**, the cathedral of **Chartres** or Monet's beautiful garden at **Giverny** for a far more enjoyable day.

Versailles

The **Palace of Versailles** (Tues–Sun 9am–5.30/6.30pm; €7.50, €5.30 after 3.30pm; Ⓦwww.chateauversailles.fr) is the epitome of decadence and luxury, with its staggeringly lavish architectural splendour that is a homage to its founder, the "Sun King" Louis XIV. There's too much to see here in a single visit, so it's best to concentrate on the famous **Grands Appartements**, which contain the Galerie des Glaces (Hall of Mirrors) where the peace treaty at the end of WW1 was signed, as well as countless great works of art. The **ornamental gardens** are particularly splendid and ostentatious, complete with canals, boating lakes and fountains. The easiest way to get to Versailles is on the half-hourly RER line C5 from Gare d'Austerlitz to Versailles-Rive Gauche (40min; €5.10 return).

Chartres

About 35km southwest of Versailles, an hour by frequent train (€12.50) from Paris-Montparnasse, is the modest market town of **CHARTRES**. It's well worth visiting to see the **Cathédrale Notre-Dame** (daily 8am–7.15/8pm; Ⓦwww.cathedral-chartres.com), one of Europe's most impressive architectural achievements. A magnificent Gothic structure , it was built in the thirteenth century and has a number of fascinating features, including the tallest Romanesque steeple in existence and the *Ste-Voile,* reputedly the Holy Veil worn by the Virgin Mary. English-language tours take place twice a day (€10; Mon–Sat April–Nov at midday & 2.45pm).

Giverny

Less than an hour west of Paris, **GIVERNY** is famous for **Monet's house and gardens,** complete with water-lily pond (April–Oct Tues–Sun 9.30am–6pm; €5.50, €4 gardens only; Ⓦwww.fondation-monet.com). Monet lived here from 1883 until his death in 1926 and the gardens that he laid out were considered by many – including Monet himself – to be his "greatest masterpiece"; the best months to visit are May and June, when the rhododendrons flower around the lily pond and the wisteria hangs over the Japanese bridge, but it's overwhelmingly beautiful at any time of year. To get here, take a train to nearby **Vernon** from Paris-St-Lazare (4–5 daily; 45min), then either rent a bike or take the Gisors bus from the station (not Mon). The nearby **Musée d'Art Américain**, 99 rue Claude Monet

(€5.50) is also worth a visit, focusing as it does on the work of American impressionist painters in France in the late nineteenth century.

Northern France

Northern France includes some of the most industrial and densely populated parts of the country. However, there are curiosities within easy reach of the Channel ports – of which **Boulogne** is the prettiest. Further south, the *maisons* and vineyards of **Champagne** are the main draw, for which the best base is **Reims,** with its fine cathedral.

BOULOGNE

BOULOGNE is the one notable northern Channel port, due to its pleasant architecture and good food and drink. Its **Ville Basse** (Lower Town), centring on place Dalton, is home to some of the best butchers and *pâtisseries* in the north, as well as an impressive array of fish restaurants. Rising above, the **Ville Haute** (Upper Town) is one of the gems of the northeast coast, flanked by grassy ramparts that give impressive views over the town and port. The **tourist office**, 24 Quai Gambetta (July & Aug daily 9am–7pm; Sept–June Mon–Sat 9am–12.30pm & 2–6pm, April–June also Sun 10am–1pm; Ⓦwww.tourisme-boulognesurmer.com), beside the fish market and ferry terminal, can advise on availability of rooms. Your best bet is the friendly **hostel** in front of the train station, 56 place Rouget de Lisle (Ⓣ03.21.99.15.30; Ⓔboulogne-sur-mer@fuaj.org; ❷). Most of the budget **hotels** are around the port area: try *Alexandra,* 93 rue Thiers (Ⓣ03.21.30.52.22, Ⓦwww.hotel-alexandra.fr; ❹), or *Hôtel des Arts,* 102 bvd Gambetta (Ⓣ03.21.31.53.31; ❹). For **eating**, try *Chez Jules,* 8 place Dalton, which serves good, unpretentious local food. Opposite the cathedral on rue de Lille, *Estaminet du Château* offers inexpensive menus in a pleasant setting, and *La Cave* at 24 rue du Port d'Étain serves magnificent *escargots* (snails). *La Houblonnière,* 8 rue Monsigny, is the best place to head for a beer or glass of wine.

LILLE

LILLE has historically suffered from some of the country's worst poverty, crime and racial conflict. However, in recent years it has shaken off most of its negative image, aided by being made European City of Culture in 2004. Though still a little rough around the edges, its lively atmosphere and some good cultural activities make it worth a visit. Marking the southern boundary of the old quarter, the **Grand Place**, also known as place du Général de Gaulle, is a busy square dominated by the old exchange building, the lavishly ornate **Vieille Bourse**, which now houses an afternoon book market (Mon–Sat). South of the old quarter lies the modern place Rihour, beyond which is the **Musée des Beaux-Arts**, place de la République (Mon 2–6pm, Wed–Sun 10am–6pm, Fri till 7pm; €4.60), a notable fine arts museum that's well worth a visit to see its excellent collection of Renaissance art.

Arrival and information

Train The train station is only a few minutes' walk from the old town, down Av le Courbier.
Tourist office In the old Palais Rihour on place Rihour (Mon–Sat 9.30am–6.30pm, Sun 10am–noon & 2–5pm; Ⓦwww.lilletourism.com).
Internet Net-K, 13 rue de la Clef (€3/hr).

Accommodation

Auberge de Jeunesse 12 rue Malpart Ⓣ03.20.57.08.94. A basic, good-value youth hostel, centrally located near the Hôtel de Ville. Breakfast included. ❷

Hôtel Faidherbe 42 place de la Gare ⓣ03.20.06.27.93. This pleasant and well-equipped hotel is clean, welcoming and just opposite the station. ❸

Hôtel de France 10 rue de Béthune ⓣ03.20.57.14.78, ⓔhotel.de.france.lille@wanadoo.fr. This small hotel may lack atmosphere, but it's quiet and comfortable, in a very central location. ❹

Eating and drinking

Les Brasseurs, 18–22 place de la Gare. A fun microbrewery (part of a small chain) with good local beers from €4.

L'Envie 34 rue des Bouchers. Stylish, sophisticated hangout that isn't at all pricey; a dish of mussels costs €8.50.

Aux Moules, 34 rue de Béthune. A fine little restaurant that specializes in the excellent regional speciality *carbonnade* (beef braised in sugar and beer).

T'Rijsel, 25 rue de Gand. A welcoming and hip atmosphere in this stylish bar; beer from €3.50 a pint.

Moving on

Train Calais (hourly; 1hr 10min); London St Pancras (hourly; 1hr 30min); Paris (twice hourly; 1hr).

REIMS

REIMS is a nondescript mid-sized city in the heart of the Champagne region, worth a stop for both the champagne and its wonderful cathedral.

What to see and do

The west front of the **Cathédrale Notre Dame** (daily 8am–7pm), battered by fire and artillery during WWI, is striking, even if the restoration job leaves something to be desired. Inside, the stained glass includes stunning designs by Marc Chagall in the east chapel and glorifications of the champagne-making process in the south transept.

If you're in town for the **Champagne**, head to place des Droits-de-l'Homme and place St-Niçaise, around which most of the champagne *maisons* are congregated; the majority charge a small fee for their cellar tours, which invariably include a tasting at the end, and many require prior appointment. Of those that don't, **Mumm**, 34 rue du Champ-de-Mars (March–Oct daily 9.30–11am & 2–4.30pm; Nov–Feb Sat & Sun 2–5pm; €7), is informative but informal, while **Piper-Heidsieck**, 51 bd Henry Vasnier (daily 9.30–11.45am & 2.30–6pm; closed Jan & Feb; €7.50), is rather glitzy and ostentatious. Of those you have to book, **Veuve Clicquot**, 1 place des Droits-de-l'Homme (April–Oct Mon–Sat; Nov–March Mon–Fri; €7; ⓣ03.26.89.53.90, ⓦwww.veuve-clicquot.fr), is the least pompous. All have English language tours.

Arrival and information

Train Reims train station is on the northwest edge of the town centre, on Square Colbert.

Tourist office 2 rue Guillaume de Machault (daily: Easter to mid-Oct 9/10am–6/7pm; mid-Oct to Easter Mon–Sat 10/11am–4/5pm; ⓦwww.reims-tourisme.fr).

Internet *Clique et Croque*, 27 rue de Vesle.

Accommodation and eating

Alsace, 6 rue Général Sarrail ⓣ03.26.47.44.08. The cheapest and least pretentious of the hotels in the centre of town, offering a no-frills but comfortable night's sleep. ❹

Bristol 76 place Drouet d'Erlon ⓣ03.26.40.25.52, ⓦwww.Bristol-reims.com. Comfortable rooms and a great central location make up for the mediocre breakfast. ❹

Centre International de Séjour Parc Léo Lagrange ⓣ03.26.40.52.60, ⓦwww.cis-reims.com. Functional and rather institutional youth hostel that nevertheless offers adequate accommodation. Fifteen minutes' walk from the station or take buses B, K, H and N. ❷

Eating and drinking

L'Apostrophe, 59 place Drouet d'Erlon. Stylish surroundings and a good range of café-brasserie fare, such as very good rabbit. Menus from €12.

Le Continental 95 place Drouet d'Erlon. Near the station, this civilized restaurant is great for a glass of champagne (€7).

Les Trois Brasseurs, 73 place Drouet d'Erlon.

Great little microbrewery that serves excellent beer (from €2.50).

Moving on

Train to: Paris (hourly; 1hr 45min); Strasbourg (8 daily; 2hr)

Normandy

To the French, the essence of **Normandy** is in its food and drink. A gourmand's paradise, this is the land of butter and cream, cheese and seafood, cider and calvados. Pleasures also lie in the feel of the landscape – lush meadows and orchards, half-timbered houses – and such architectural highlights as the legendary Mont St-Michel. **Rouen,** the Norman capital, is by far the most compelling of the region's urban centres, while **Bayeux** is rightly celebrated for its eponymous tapestry, as well as being a good starting point for the famous Normandy D-Day beaches.

The main ports of entry along this stretch of coast are Le Havre, Cherbourg and Dieppe, of which **DIEPPE** is worth at least a brief stop, with a good market, a castle and some decent restaurants. Its **tourist office** is beside the ferry terminal on Pont Ango (Mon–Sat 9am–noon/1pm & 2–6/8pm; summer also Sun 10am–1pm & 3–6pm; ⓦwww.dieppetourisme.com) and the **train station** is about 800m southwest of the ferry terminal and tourist office.

BAYEUX

BAYEUX's magnificent cathedral and world-famous tapestry depicting the 1066 invasion of England by William the Conqueror make it one of the highlights of a visit to Normandy. The famous **Bayeux Tapestry** is housed in the **Centre Guillaume le Conquérant**, rue de Nesmond (daily 9/9.30am–6/6.30/7pm; Nov to mid-March closed 12.30–2pm; €7.40). A 70m strip of linen gorgeously embroidered over nine centuries ago, it records scenes from the Norman Conquest, along with more banal accounts of everyday life. The **cathedral**, place de la Liberté (8.30am–6/7pm), is a spectacular thirteenth century edifice, though some parts stretch back to the eleventh century.

Bayeux's **train station** is on the southern side of town, on boulevard Sadi Carnot and the **tourist office** is at Pont St Jean (Mon–Sat 9am–7pm, Sun 9am–12.30pm & 2–6.30pm; Oct–June closed Mon–Sat 12.30–2pm & all day Sun; ⓦwww.bayeux-tourism.com). Most affordable of the **hotels** are the *Mogador*, 20 rue Alain Chartier (ⓣ02.31.92.24.58, ⓔhotel.mogadoo@wanadoo.fr; ❹), and *La Gare*, 26 pl de la Gare (ⓦwww.Normandy-tours-hotel.com, ⓣ02.31.92.10.70; ❸), which is also the home for Normandy Tours (see box, opposite). The *Family Home*, 39 rue du Général de Dais (ⓣ02.31.92.15.22; ❸), north of the cathedral, is a friendly and decent **hostel**, and good food too. The nearest **campsite** is on boulevard d'Eindhoven, a fifteen-minute walk from the centre or you can catch bus #3 (ⓣ02.31.92.08.43; closed Oct–April; ❶). Most of the **restaurants** are on pedestrianized rue St-Jean, of which the best is probably *La Table du Terroir* at no 42, a carnivorous paradise with menus from €12.

MONT ST-MICHEL

On the far western edge of Normandy, the island of **Mont St-Michel** is the site of the strikingly picturesque **Gothic abbey** (tours daily 9/9.30am–6/7pm; €8). The abbey church, long known as the Merveille, is visible from all around the bay; it's especially striking at night, when bathed in white and amber light. The granite structure was sculpted to match the contours of the hill, and the overall impression is striking, although there have been murmurings about the need for a restoration soon. It's also important to remember to keep an eye

D-DAY BEACHES

On June 6, 1944, 135,000 Allied troops stormed the beaches of Normandy in an operation known as "Overlord", the largest in history. After heavy fighting, which saw thousands of casualties on both sides, the Allied forces took command of all the beaches, which was a major turning point of World War II. The 80km stretch of beaches north of Bayeux that saw the D-Day landings include Omaha, now home to the **Musée Mémorial d'Omaha Beach** (Ⓦwww.musee-memorial-omaha.com; 9.30/10am–6/6.30pm), where exhibits include uniforms and a tank. Arromanches, 10km northwest of Bayeux, was the main unloading point for cargo (some four million tonnes of it) and the interesting museum here, **Musée du Débarquement**, place du 6 juin (Ⓦwww.normandy1944.com), has further information on France's liberation. One of the best ways to see the beaches is on a tour: contact either D-Day Tours (Ⓣ02.31.51.70.52; €35–45) or Normandy Tours (Ⓣ02.31.92.10.70; €34–39.)

on the tide; the Mont can become entirely surrounded by the sea remarkably quickly, making leaving it difficult. The best way of getting there is to take the train to Pontorson, and then take one of the regular buses. A good place for lunch is *Crêperie La Sirène*, serving hearty, unpretentious food from €6.

ROUEN

ROUEN represents a triumph of ingenuity over history. More or less destroyed during WWII, a lavish restoration project has seen the city's impressive churches and half-timbered houses returned to their former glory, making this a lovely place to stroll round. Joan of Arc was burned at the stake in 1431 at the place du Vieux-Marché, the town's focal point, facing the cathedral and the Gros-Horloge, a colourful one-handed clock that spans the street named after it. Just off here is the **Cathédrale de Notre-Dame** (Mon 2–6pm, Tues–Sun 8am–6pm), a Gothic masterpiece built in the twelfth and thirteenth centuries, and now best known for Monet's series of paintings of it that explore the interaction between light and shadow. Also worth a visit is the **Musée des Beaux-Arts**, Esplanade Marchel-Duchamp (Ⓣ02.35.71.28.40; €3), with a fine collection of art including, naturally, a Monet painting of the cathedral.

Arrival and information

Train The main train station, Rouen Rive-Droite, is a ten-minute walk or one métro stop from the centre.
Bus The bus station is just off the southern end of the main rue Jeanne d'Arc.
Tourist office Opposite the cathedral at 25 pl de la Cathédrale (Mon–Sat 9am–12.30pm & 1.30–6/7pm, Sun 9.15/10am–12.30/1pm & 2–6pm; Oct–April closed Sun afternoon; Ⓦwww.rouentourisme.com).
Internet *Cyber Net*, 47 pl du Vieux-Marché (€4/hr).

Accommodation

Campsite Municipal rue Jules-Ferry, in Déville-lès-Rouen Ⓣ02.35.74.07.59. Situated 5km out of town, this campsite provides all the usual amenities such as a shop, café and showers. To get here, take bus #2 from Théâtre des Arts. ❶
Le Palais 12 rue du Tambour Ⓣ02.35.71.41.40. Extremely central hotel, though the spacious and comfortable rooms could be a little cleaner. ❹
Sphinx 130 rue Beauvoisine Ⓣ02.35.71.35.86. Run by a jolly, singing couple, this clean, friendly little budget hotel is a good choice. ❸

Eating and drinking

La Boîte à Bières 35 rue Cauchoise. The town's most fun bar, with a great atmosphere and good (sometimes live) music.
Brasserie Paul 1 place de la Cathédrale. An old-fashioned and very French brasserie where you can have a good meal of calves' liver and *escargots* from €10.
Pascaline 5 rue de la Poterne. A great place to try Rouen's most famous dish, duckling (*caneton*), which can be enjoyed as part of the €12 set menu.

Le P'tit Bec 182 rue Eau de Robec. A good range of basic, filling meals, with particular emphasis on local cheeses and bread; set menus from €12.

Moving on

Trains Caen (hourly; 2 hr); Dieppe (12–15 daily; 45min); Le Havre (12–15 daily; 1hr); Paris (6–8 daily; 1hr 10min).

Brittany

The striking coastline, sandy beaches and lush countryside of Brittany seem to belong to a very different part of France; it seems almost unbelievable that the verdant pastures are within easy reach of Paris and Normandy. It comes as no surprise that people here are both fiercely proud and defiantly isolationist; you might be forgiven for thinking at times that you had left France altogether.

BRETON CULTURE

Reluctantly unified with France in 1532 for political reasons, it would be wrong to see Brittany as quintessentially French. While the Bretons have seen their language steadily eradicated and local customs phased out, a strong sense of community is still alive and well here. The region's recent economic resurgence, helped partly by summer tourism, has largely been due to local initiatives, such as the promotion of Celtic artistic identity through local festivals of traditional Breton music, poetry and dance, and today 700,000 people speak Breton as a first or second language.

ST-MALO

ST-MALO, walled and built with the same grey granite as Mont St-Michel, looks best from the River Rance and the sea. Day-tripping tourists are an ever-present curse, and treated as such, but the beautiful old walled city is a lovely place to wander about aimlessly for at least a day or so. The **town museum**, in the castle to the right as you enter the main city gate, Porte St-Vincent (daily 10am–noon/12.30pm & 2–6pm; winter closed Mon; €5), covers the city's eventful history, which has encompassed colonialism, slave-trading and privateers, amongst other initiatives. The much-damaged **Cathédrale St-Vincent** on place Jean de Châtillon is also worth a look, although it's a shadow of its former glory.

Arrival and information

Train The station is on the other side of the docks from the town centre, a ten-minute walk.
Bus Buses from out of town stop at Porte St-Vincent.
Tourist office Esplanade St-Vincent (Mon–Sat 9/10am–12.30pm & 1.30/2.30–6/7.30pm; winter closed Sun; ⓦwww.saint-malo-tourisme.com).
Internet Cop Imprime, 39 bd des Talards (€4/hr).

Accommodation

Auberge de Jeunesse Éthic Étapes 37 av du Père Umbricht ⓣ02.99.40.29.80, ⓦwww.centrevarangot.com. Clean and relatively comfortable hostel a short bus ride (#2 or #5) from the centre. Book well in advance. ❷
Camping Aleth Cité d'Aleth, Gaston Buy ⓣ02.99.81.60.91, ⓦcamping-saint-malo.fr. Gorgeously located campsite on a peninsula by the beach that's also well located for nightlife. The amenities include a café/shop and showers. ❷
Le Louvre, 2 rue des Marins ⓣ02.99.40.86.62. Comfortable, smartly decorated hotel with friendly bilingual staff in the heart of the old city. ❻
Le Nautilus, 9 rue de la Corne de Cerf ⓣ02.99.40.42.27, ⓦwww.lenautilus.com. Popular and welcoming small hotel with a private honesty bar; the perfect place for a late-night glass of Calvados. ❹
Hôtel San Pedro 1 rue Ste-Anne's ⓣ02.99.40.88.57, ⓦwww.sanpedro-hotel.com. Pleasant, unassuming hotel with sea views and good facilities. Much cheaper if four are sharing a quad room. ❺

Eating & Drinking

Coquille d'Oeuf 20 rue de la Corne de Cerfs. Pizzas, baguettes and quiches are on offer here (from €5).
La Biniou 3 place de la Croix. Traditional Brittany *crêperie*, serving over one hundred different varieties, from €2; the best is the one flambéed in Calvados.
Le Brick 5 rue Jacques-Cartier. Filling, hearty meals of seafood and crêpes that start from around €7.
L'Alchimiste 7 rue St-Thomas. The best bet in town for a drink, this funky, cool bar has theatrical touches (wine €3).

Moving on

Train Dinan (8 daily; 1hr); Paris (3 daily; 3hr); St-Malo (hourly; 1hr).

QUIMPER AND AROUND

QUIMPER is the oldest Breton city and, like many in the region, it's a lovely place to wander around, with its cobbled streets, timber-framed buildings, overlooked by the beautiful woods of Mont Frugy. The city is justly proud of its enormously striking Gothic **Cathédrale St-Corentin** (9/9.30–noon & 1.30–6.30pm), while the adjacent **Musée des Beaux-Arts**, 40 pl St-Corentin (July & Aug daily 10am–7pm; Sept–June closed noon–2pm & Tues; Nov–March also closed Sun 10am–noon; €4), has an important collection of drawings by Cocteau, Max Jacob and Gustave Doré (shown in rotation) and nineteenth- and twentieth-century paintings of the famed Pont-Aven school. Avoid coming in the last week of July, when the **Festival de Cornouaille** is held, which celebrates Breton music, costume and dance; though charming, it makes it impossible to find accommodation.

Arrival and information

Train and Bus The train and bus stations are situated next to each other, a short walk east along the river from the town centre.
Tourist office 7 rue de la Déesse, place de la Résistance (July & Aug Mon–Sat 9am–7pm, Sun 10am–12.45pm & 3–5.45pm; June & Sept closed Sun afternoon; Oct–May closed all Sun & Mon–Sat 12.30–1.30pm; ⓣ02.98.53.04.05, ⓦwww.quimper-tourisme.com).

Accommodation

Auberge de Jeunesse 6 av des Oiseaux ⓣ02.98.64.97.97, ⓔquimper@fuaj.org. Clean, efficient and soulless, but it does offer self-catering facilities. Take bus #1 from place de la Résistance. ❷
Camping Municipal avenue des Oiseaux, Bois du Séminaire ⓣ02.98.55.61.09. Located in a wooded park, this campsite has showers, a small shop and a café. To get here, take bus #1 from place de la Résistance. ❶
Hôtel le Derby 13 av de la Gare ⓣ02.98.52.06.91. Rather bland business accommodation, though reasonably priced and handy for the station. ❸
TGV 4 rue de Concarneau ⓣ02.98.90.54.00, ⓦwww.hoteltgv.com. Smart, bright hotel that's handy for the old city; all of the small rooms are en suite. ❹

Eating and drinking

La Krampouzerie 9 rue du Sallé. Run by a jolly husband and wife, who serve regional specialities with unusual ingredients, such as *galettes* with seaweed and ginger caramel (from €5).
Crêperie du Sallé 6 rue du Sallé. The wide range of crêpes (from €3) served in this lovely half-timbered building include ingredients such as sausage, bacon and cheese.
Café le XXI 38 place Saint-Corentin. Probably the most stylish bar in the old town, this fun place is a good choice for a glass of wine or beer.

Moving On

Train to: Paris (8 daily, 4hr 45min); Rennes (5 daily, 2hr 30min).

CARNAC

About 30km southeast along the coast from the functional port of Lorient, **CARNAC** is home to one of the most important prehistoric sites in Europe, a congregation of some two thousand or so semi-megalithic **menhirs** stretching for more than 4km to the north of the village, long predating the Pyramids or

Stonehenge. While this is fascinating to archaeologists, non-enthusiasts might be less enthralled, despite the undeniable historical importance of the stones; it doesn't help that little context or information is provided for English speakers. For more information, visit the **Musée de la Préhistoire**, 10 pl de la Chapelle, near rue du Tumulus in Carnac-Ville (daily 10am–12.30pm & 1.30–6/7pm, closed Wed am; €5) and the **Maison des Mégalithes**, rte des Alignements (daily: May & Jun 9am–7pm; July & Aug 9am–8pm; Sept–April 9am–5.15pm). Carnac itself, made up of Carnac-Ville and the newer seaside resort of Carnac-Plage, is popular in summer but otherwise it's a bit of a ghost town. The best of the many **beaches** is the smallest, the Men Dû, just off the road towards La Trinité. **Buses** arrive outside the main **tourist office**, 74 av des Druides in Carnac-Plage (July & Aug Mon–Sat 9am–7pm, Sun 3–7pm; Sept–June Mon–Sat 9am–1pm & 2pm–7pm; ⓣ02.97.52.13.52, ⓦwww.ot-carnac.fr). A good option for **accommodation** is the *Auberge Le Ratelier*, 4 Chemin du Drouet (ⓣ02.97.52.05.04; ❹), which has a lovely restaurant. For **camping** by the sea, head towards Mon Dû (ⓣ02.97.52.04.23, ⓦwww.camping-du-mendu.com; closed Oct–Easter; ❷), which offers showers, a basic shop and a small café. For good-value food, head to the *Crêperie St-George*, 8 allée du Parc, which also serves *moules* and *carbonnade* (from €9).

QUIBERON

South of Carnac is the lively port town of **QUIBERON**, a jumping-off point for boats out to the nearby islands or a good base for exploring the peninsula. The ocean-facing shore, known as the **Côte Sauvage**, is a wild and unswimmable stretch, but the sheltered eastern side has safe and calm sandy beaches. **Port Maria**, the fishing harbour, is the most active part of town, with a good variety of bars and restaurants.

The **train station**, which operates in July and August only (a SNCF bus service provides a link to nearby Auray station the rest of the year), is a couple of minutes north of the centre on place de la Gare, and the **buses** also arrive in front of here. The **tourist office** is at 14 rue de Verdun (July & Aug Mon–Sat 9am–7.30pm, Sun 9.30am–12.30pm & 2.30–7pm; Sept–June Mon–Sat 10am–noon & 2–6pm; ⓣ02.97.50.45.12, ⓦwww.quiberon.com). Of the **hotels**, the best choice is *l'Océan*, 7 quai de l'Océan (ⓣ02.97.50.07.58, ⓦwww.hotel-de-locean.com; closed Oct–March; ❹), which offers fabulous harbour views from the more expensive rooms. Alternatively the local **hostel**, 45 rue du Roch Priol (ⓣ02.97.50.15.45; ❷), is a relatively comfortable option with large, though impersonal rooms, 500m from the beach. The seafront is lined with fish **restaurants**: try *Le Port Maria* for fresh, tangy *moules* or oysters and scallops (set lunch €15). The **cafés** by the long bathing beach are also enjoyable, such as the *Bar de la Marine*, 20 quai de l'Océan, which has excellent views overlooking the quay.

NANTES

Though **NANTES** is no longer officially part of Brittany, it remains closely affiliated to the region, with the vibrant, lively atmosphere reminiscent of other Breton towns. Crucial to its self-image is the **Château des Ducs** (9am/10am–6pm/7pm; €8), subjected to a certain amount of damage over the centuries but still preserving the form in which it was built by two of the last rulers of independent Brittany, François II and his daughter Duchess Anne, who was born here in 1477. In 1800 the castle's arsenal exploded, shattering the stained glass of **Cathédrale de St-Pierre et St-Paul** (9am–6pm/7pm), 200m away, just one of many disasters that have befallen the church. Back past the château is the Île Feydeau, which was once an island before the channels of the Loire that surrounded it were dried up after World War II. Nearby the **Musée Jules Verne** (daily 10am–noon & 2pm–6pm, Sun afternoon only; €3.20) is an interesting museum, dedicated to Jules Verne, who was born here.

The **train station** is a short way east of the castle on the rue de Richebourg. The **tourist office** is in the FNAC book and music store on place du Commerce (Mon–Sat 10am–6pm; ⓣ02.40.20.60.00, ⓦwww.nantes-tourisme.com). For **accommodation**, try the charming, atmospheric and extremely central *Hôtel Rénova*, 11 rue Beauregard (ⓣ02.40.47.57.03, ⓦwww.hotel-renova.com; ❹) or *St Daniel*, 4 rue du Bouffay (ⓣ02.40.47.41.25; ⓦwww.hotel-stdaniel.com; ❹), overlooking the St-Croix church courtyard. The city's **hostel**, at 2 pl de la Manu (ⓣ02.40.29.29.20; ❷), is a ten-minute walk east of the train station along the tram tracks, or take tram #1 to Beaujoire; price includes breakfast. The place du Commerce is a largely pedestrianized area thronged with decent, inexpensive **bars** and **restaurants**. Try *Ma Saison Préférée*, 10 rue du Château, for delicious savoury tarts and quiches (from €6) and *Café Cult*, place du Change, for a cool, bohemian atmosphere and some great cheese and cured ham dishes (from €12).

The Loire Valley

With countless châteaux overlooking the stunning river and panoramic views over the vineyards that serve some of France's most delicious wine, the Loire Valley is deservedly one of France's most celebrated regions. Alongside the luxurious châteaux and the Loire, the last "wild" river in France, there are also numerous lovely towns to be visited, including dependably enjoyable **Tours** and laid-back **Saumur** and **Chinon**.

TOURS

The elegant and compact regional capital **TOURS** makes a good base for travelling around the Loire. The city has two main areas, situated on either side of the central rue Nationale. To the east looms the extravagant towers and stained-glass windows of the **Cathédrale St-Gatien** (9am–7pm), with some handsome old streets behind. Adjacent, the **Musée des Beaux-Arts** (9am–12.45pm & 2–6pm, closed Tues; €4), on place François Sicard, has some beautiful paintings in its collection, notably Mantegna's *Christ in the Garden of Olives* and *Resurrection*, and a delightful formal garden. The **old town** crowds around medieval place Plumereau, on the west side of the city, with half-timbered houses that are so imposing and neatly ordered they appear to have come off a Hollywood set.

Arrival and information

Train station is located to the south of the city, on Rue Édouard Vaillant.

Tourist office is in front of the train station at 78–82 rue Bernard-Palissy (8.30/9am–6/7pm, Sun 10am–12.30/1pm & 2.30–5pm; mid-Oct to mid-April closed lunch and Sun afternoon; ⓣ02.47.70.37.37, ⓦwww.ligeris.com).

Accommodation

Auberge de Jeunesse de Vieux Tours 5 rue Bretonneau ⓣ02.47 37 81 58, ⓦwww.ajtours.org. Inexpensive, friendly hostel, with nice optional extras such as individual fridges in your room (50¢/day) and bike rental (€10/day); breakfast is included. ❷

Hôtel du Cygne 6 rue du Cygne ⓣ02.47.66.66.41, ⓦperso.wanadoo.fr/hotelcygne.tours. Charming little hotel located on a picturesque side street, just ten minutes' walk from the station. ❺

Regina 2 rue Pimbert ⓣ02.47.05.25.36. Decent little one-star place, clean and unpretentious, with a 1am curfew. ❸

Hôtel Val de Loire 33 blvd Heurteloup ⓣ02.47.05.67.53, ⓔhotel.val.de.loire@club-internet.fr. A pleasant and good-value hotel in a very central location. All fourteen rooms are nicely decorated. ❸

Eating and drinking

Comme Autre Fouée 11 rue de la Monnaie. This charmingly old-fashioned place specializes in the miniature filled sweet and savoury snacks *fouée* – dough filled with things like goats' cheese or honey.

La Palais, 15 place Jean Jaurès. The best spot to hang out; around €3 for a beer.

Moving on

Train Chenonceaux (5–7 daily; 30min); Chinon (5–10 daily; 45min); Orléans (frequent; 1hr–1hr 30min); Saumur (frequent; 45min).

CHATEAUX NEAR TOURS

Villandry

One of Northern France's major attractions is the château of **VILLANDRY** (daily 9am–5/6.30pm; gardens till 5.30/7.30pm; €8, €5.50 gardens only), about 13km west, with its extraordinary ornamental Renaissance **gardens** – the largest in France – set out on several terraces with marvellous views over the river. The handsome château – one of the last in the area – dates from 1536 and has a collection of Spanish paintings and a Moorish ceiling from Toledo. There's no public transport here, but you can rent a bike in Tours and enjoy a wonderful ride along the banks of the Cher. Alternatively a shuttle bus runs from the château to Savonnières, 4km northeast of Villandry, six to nine times a day in both directions.

Chenonceaux

Perhaps the finest Loire château is that straddling the river at **CHENONCEAUX** (daily 9am–4.30/7pm; €9), about 15km from Villandry and accessible by train from Tours. As with Villandry, the stunning formal gardens are likely to be the highlight for most visitors, with their river views, although the beautiful interior has many charms as well. The château served as a demarcation point during WWII between Nazi-occupied northern France and the Vichy-run south; thus, countless refugees fleeing the Nazis sought shelter here.

Chinon

The ruined château at **CHINON** (daily 9/9.30am–5/7pm; €6) is a fascinating relic of France's historic past, with parts of it dating from the twelfth and thirteenth century. It is even possible to see, in the western **Tour Coudray,** thirteenth-century graffiti carved by imprisoned and doomed Templar knights. The Fort St-Georges section of the château will be closed until at least the end of 2008 for excavations. Wedged between the castle and the River Vienne, the ancient town of Chinon is an attractive place to stop; the tiny *Hôtel de la Treille*, 4 pl Jeanne d'Arc (Ⓣ02.47.93.07.71; ❸) is a pleasant place to stay. Across the river on Île-Auger, there is a **campsite** (Ⓣ02.47.93.08.35; ❷) that rents out kayaks in summer to both guests and visitors. The **tourist office** is on place Hofheim (May–Nov daily 10am–7pm; Oct–April closed 1pm–2pm & Sun; Ⓣ02.47.93.17.85, Ⓦwww.chinon.com). *La Treille* is a wonderfully old-fashioned **restaurant** that serves excellent game and meat; lunch menu €12, while *La Lycorne*, 15 rue Rabelais, has rather eccentric décor, including a British red phone box, and a cheap €10 lunch menu.

SAUMUR

SAUMUR is a peaceful, pretty riverside town, and a good place to base yourself, within easy reach of Tours and Chinon. The town is a major centre of absinthe distillation; the **Distillerie Combier**, 48 rue Beaurepaire (€3), offers bilingual tours and tastings. On a more cultural note, the immense **Abbaye de Fontevraud** (daily 9/10am–5.30/6.30pm; €8), 13km on bus #16 from the town centre (4–6 daily;

35min), was founded in 1099 as both a nunnery and a monastery with an abbess in charge. Its chief significance is as the burial ground of the Plantagenet kings and queens, notably Henry II, Eleanor of Aquitaine and Richard the Lionheart; some of the tombs are extraordinarily elaborate.

Arrival and information

Train Saumur's train station is on the north bank of the river; head over two bridges to get to the south bank and the main part of the town.
Tourist office place de la Bilange (Mon–Sat 9.15am–7pm, Sun 10/10.30am–noon/12.30pm & 2.30–5.30pm; mid-Oct to mid-May closed 1pm–2pm and Sun afternoon; ⓣ02.41.40.20.60, ⓦwww.ot-saumur.fr); bikes are available for hire here.

Accommodation

Camping l'Île d'Offard rue de Verden ⓣ02.41.40.30.00, ⓦwww.cvtloisirs.com. Nicely located campsite on an island, ten minutes' walk from the town centre. ❷
Centre International de Séjour Île d'Offard Île d'Offard ⓣ02.41.40.30.00. An unpretentious and clean hostel that offers quiet and central accommodation. ❸
Le Cristal 10 place de la République ⓣ02.41.51.09.54, ⓔcrystal@saumur.net. A two-star delight with river views from most rooms and Internet access in all, as well as a good breakfast. ❹
Le Volney 1 rue Volney ⓣ02.41.51.25.41, ⓦwww.levolney.com. Small hotel on the south side of town, with exceptionally friendly and helpful staff. ❹

Eating

Auberge St-Pierre 6 place St-Pierre. This trendy, laid-back restaurant has a fairly inexpensive menu, including good steak (€10).
Les Forges de St-Pierre 1 place St-Pierre. A stylish establishment that nevertheless serves excellent lamb and chicken; lunch €12.

Moving on

Train to: Angers (5–9 daily, 20min); Tours (frequent; 40min).

ORLÉANS

Due south of Paris, **ORLÉANS** became legendary when Joan of Arc delivered the city from the English in 1429. Stained-glass windows in the nave of the enormous, Gothic **Cathédrale Sainte-Croix** (daily 9.15am–noon & 2.15–5pm; free) tell the story of her life, from her childhood through to her heroic military career and her eventual martyrdom. Immediately opposite, the **Musée des Beaux-Arts** (Tues–Sat 9.30am–12.15pm & 1.30–5.45pm, Sun 2–6.30pm; €3) has an excellent collection of French paintings.

Arrival and information

Train The train station is on the busy place d'Arc, north of the town centre, connected by rue de la République to the central place du Martroi.
Tourist office Place d'Arc (April–Aug daily 9.30am–6.30pm; Sept–March closed lunch & Sun; ⓣ02.38.24.05.05, ⓦwww.ville-orleans.fr).

Accommodation

Hôtel de l'Abeille 64 rue Alsace-Lorraine ⓣ02.38.53.54.87. This pleasant little hotel is stuffed full of memorabilia of Joan of Arc. Rooms are clean, comfortable and en suite. ❺
Auberge de Jeunesse 7 av de Beaumarchais ⓣ02.38.53.60.06, ⓔauberge.crjs45@wanadoo.fr. Ten kilometres south of the city centre, best reached by the tram to the Université L'Indien, this basic hostel is slightly sterile but very cheap indeed. ❶
Hôtel Le Bannier 13 rue du Faubourg-Bannier ⓣ02.38.53.25.86. A no-frills place, with basic but serviceable beds and communal bathrooms. ❸
Camping Municipal rue de la Roche, St-Jean-de-la-Ruelle ⓣ02.38.88.39.39. This campsite, 3km out of town, has showers, a café/bar and shop. To get here, take bus #26. Open July–Aug. ❷
Hôtel de Paris 29 rue du Faubourg-Bannier ⓣ02.38.53.39.58. Clean budget hotel handily located near the train station; the more expensive rooms have en-suite bathrooms. ❸

Eating

La Petite Marmite 178 rue de Bourgogne. A lovely timber-framed building houses this restaurant, which serves traditional dishes such as *carbonnade* and *escargots* (from €8).

Le Metalic 119 rue de Bourgogne. The hippest bar in town, with great DJs. Open till 3am.

Moving on

Train Blois (frequent; 45min); Paris (hourly; 1hr); Tours (frequent; 1hr 30min).

Burgundy

Although its unassuming nature and general lack of set-piece sights means that it's unlikely to be top of anyone's "must-see" list in France, Burgundy nevertheless has some charming towns and villages, as well as some of the country's finest food and drink. **Dijon**, the capital, is a slick and affluent town with many remnants of old Burgundy. South, there are the famous **vineyards**, which have an international reputation and are a major moneymaker. **Beaune** is a good place to sample the best of the wine, and be sure to try local specialities such as *escargots à la bourguignonne, bœuf bourguignon* and *coq au vin*.

DIJON

DIJON, famous for its mustard, grew out of its strategic position on the merchant route from Britain up the Seine and across the Alps to the Adriatic. But it was as capital of the dukes of Burgundy from 1000 until the late 1400s that it knew its finest hour. The dukes used their tremendous wealth and power to make Dijon one of Europe's greatest centres of art, learning and science. Though it lost some of this status when it was incorporated into the French kingdom in 1477, it has remained one of the pre-eminent provincial cities, especially since the industrial boom of the mid-nineteenth century.

What to see and do

Although it has undeniably seen finer days, the Palais des Ducs, in the heart of the city, is notable both for the fifteenth-century **Tour Philippe le Bon** (April–Nov daily 9am–noon & 1.45–5.30pm; Dec–March Sat & Sun 9am–3.30pm, Wed 1.30–3.30pm; tours every 15min; €2.30), from whose terrace you can allegedly see Mont Blanc on a clear day, and the fourteenth-century **Tour de Bar**, which houses the magnificent **Musée des Beaux-Arts** (daily except Tues 9.30/10am–5/6pm; €3.90), with its collection of paintings ranging from Titian and Rubens to Monet and Manet. The museum ticket also allows you to visit the vast kitchen and recently restored **Salle des Gardes**, richly appointed with panelling, tapestries and a minstrels' gallery. The palace looks onto the impressive **place de la Libération**, a gracious semicircular space designed in the late seventeenth century and bordered by houses of honey-coloured stone.

Behind it is the tiny, enclosed **place des Ducs** and a maze of lanes flanked by beautiful old houses, most notably on **rue des Forges**. Parallel to this, **rue de la Chouette** passes the north side of the impressive thirteenth-century Gothic church of **Notre-Dame**, the north wall of which holds a small sculpted owl (*chouette*), which people touch for luck. Just to the south, the **Musée Archéologique**, 5 rue Docteur-Maret (daily except Tues 9am–6pm; Oct to mid-May also closed 12.30–1.30pm; free), has a number of rather amusing Celtic and Roman artefacts celebrating wine.

Arrival and information

Train and Bus Dijon train and bus stations sit next to each other at the end of avenue Maréchal-Foch, five minutes from place Darcy.

Tourist office Place Darcy (daily: May to mid-Oct 9am–7pm; mid-Oct to April 10am–6pm; Ⓣ03.80.44.11.44, Ⓦwww.dijon-tourism.com); also at 34 rue des Forges (Mon–Sat 9am–noon & 2–6pm).

Internet *Cyberisey*, 53 rue Berbisey (€3/hr).

Accommodation

Camping du Lac Off boulevard Chanoine Kir, about 3km from the centre. ⓣ03.80.43.54.72. This pleasant campsite has the usual amenities, such as hot showers, a small café and a shop. To get here, take bus #12. Closed Nov–March. ❷

Hôtel Chateaubriand 3 av Maréchal Foch ⓣ03.80.41.42.18, ⓦwww.hotelchateaubriand.fr. This inexpensive budget hotel at least has the advantage of being close to the station, and the stylish public décor befits somewhere far grander. The rooms themselves are small but quite comfortable. ❹

CRISD, 1 blvd Champollion ⓣ03.80.72.95.20, ⓦwww.auberge-cri-dijon.com. This very comfortable budget option has excellent self-catering facilities and is 2.5km from the centre – take bus #5 from place Grangier. ❷

Hostellerie Le Sauvage 64 rue Monge ⓣ03.80.41.31.21, ⓔhoteldusauvage@free.fr. Beautifully restored fifteenth-century hotel in a great central location, with lovely staff and a good restaurant. ❺

Le Jacquemart, 32 rue Verrerie ⓣ03.80.60.09.60, ⓦwww.hotel-lejacquemart.fr. A basic but adequate small hotel handily located in the centre. ❸

Eating

Au Bon Pantagruel 20 rue Quentin. Near the covered market, this inexpensive bistro serves fine meals from €14.

Le Chabrot 36 rue Monge. Stylish and pleasant bistro – the snails (€8) are particularly good.

Clos des Capucines, 3 rue Jeannin. Fantastic Burgundian cuisine at competitive prices – mains from €10, and lunch from €7.

La Dame d'Aquitaine 23 place Bossuet. History lovers will be in heaven at this studiously old-fashioned place, located in a thirteenth-century cellar; highlights include duck's breast in blackberry sauce and *coq au vin*. Lunch from €15.

Drinking and nightlife

Au Vieux Léon, 52 rue Jeannin.
This friendly, unpretentious youth-orientated place often has some great, cheap offers on drinks (beer €3).

Le Cappuccino 132 rue Berbisey. One of Dijon's best bars, this fun dive serves over one hundred beers (€3) and nearly as many wines.

Le Cintra 13 av Foch. For a quieter, more relaxed evening, this mix of piano bar and low-key disco is a great option.

Café de l'Univers 47 rue Berbisey. If you want a serious club night, this is the one for you; on Saturdays and Sunday mornings, things go on until 9am.

Moving on

Train Beaune (frequent; 20min); Lyon (frequent; 1hr 30min–2hr 15min).

BEAUNE AND THE BURGUNDY VINEYARDS

BEAUNE is the major producer of the region's best wine, and one of the best places in France for tasting it. Its other major attraction is the fifteenth-century hospital, the **Hôtel-Dieu** on the corner of place de la Halle (daily 9am–6.30pm; €5.80). The vast stone-flagged hall has a quite staggeringly terrifying painting of the *Last Judgement* by Roger van der Weyden, the major reason for visiting. On nearby rue d'Enfer is the **Musée du Vin** (daily 9.30am–5/6pm; Dec–March closed Tues; €5.40), which does an excellent job of contextualising and ex-

BURGUNDY VINEYARDS

The Burgundy vineyards are justly famous for their produce. The best way to explore them is on the **Route des Grand Crus** ⓦwww.route-des-grands-crus-de-bourgogne.com), which takes in such places as **Montrachet** and **Chassagne**, both famous for their high-calibre wines. It should be noted that the wines are cheaper (If not exactly cheap) if bought from source - expect to pay around €10 for a good bottle and €20 and upwards for an excellent one. If you fancy learning more about the wines, the **École des Vins de Bourgogne** in Beaune, 6 rue du 16e Chasseurs (ⓣ03.80.26.35.10), offers reasonably priced (from €15) crash courses in wine appreciation, some in English.

plaining the region's wine history. The **Marché aux Vins** (daily 9.30–11.30am & 2–5.30pm; €10), the town's main wine-tasting establishment, is a rather more taster-friendly experience, allowing you to sample numerous delectable vintages. Other places where you can taste wine include **Patriarche Père et Fils**, 5 rue du Collège (ⓣ03.80.24.53.78; €10), where you sample thirteen wines on an hour-long guided tour of the cellar, and the **Reine Pédauque**, rue de Lorraine (ⓣ03.08.22.23.11; €7.50), an eighteenth-century cellar where you can sample at least four wines.

Arrival and information

Train From Beaune train station, the town centre is 500m up avenue du 8 Septembre, across the boulevard and left onto rue des Tonneliers.
Bus Buses leave from rue Maufoux, beyond the walls.
Tourist Office Opposite the Hôtel-Dieu (Mon–Sat 9/10am–5/7pm, Sun 10am–1pm & 2–5/6pm; ⓣ03.80.26.21.30, ⓦwww.ot-beaune.fr), with useful information on wine tours.

Accommodation

Arcantis Hôtel au Grand St Jean 18 rue du Faubourg Madeleine ⓣ03.80.24.12.22, ⓦwww.hotel-au-grand-st-jean.com. Though it doesn't quite live up to its name, the hotel has a comforting, pleasant feel about it and has spotlessly clean rooms. ❹
Les Cent Vignes rue Auguste Dubois ⓣ03.80.22.03.91. One kilometre out of Beaune, this good-value campsite has showers and a shop. Walk or take bus #2 from the tourist office. ❶
Hôtel Foch 24 bd Maréchal Foch ⓣ03.80.24.05.65. This is a pleasant little hotel, run by a charming (if deaf) old lady; shared bathrooms. ❸

Eating and Drinking

Bistrot Bouguignon 8 rue Monge. Tiny but charming restaurant that does a good-value lunch (€13), with wine from €3 a glass.
Pickwick's Pub & Wine Bar 2 rue Notre Dame. This hilariously tacky would-be English pub is worth a look if you're a whisky connoisseur – they have an excellent range, starting at €5.
Piqu' Boeuf Grill 2 rue Faubourg Madeleine. Carnivores will love this place, with some lovely wines (from €4), and rich, bloody steaks (€12).

Alsace and Lorraine

Dominated by the remarkable city of Strasbourg, the Eastern region of France often appears to be more like parts of Germany or Switzerland than the rest of the country. Despite this, the Alsatian people remain fiercely and proudly French. The *mélange* of cultures is at its most vivid in the string of little wine towns that punctuate the *Route du Vin* along the eastern margin of the wet and woody **Vosges** mountains. By comparison, the province of **Lorraine**, though it has suffered much the same vicissitudes, is rather dull, the elegant eighteenth-century provincial capital of **Nancy** being the main exception. Food and drink in this region are excellent; from the Kronenbourg and Heineken breweries of Strasbourg to delicious white Rieslings and Gewürztraminers, the alcohol is excellent (and relatively inexpensive), and the *winstubs* (or wine rooms) that dominate towns offer inexpensive, unpretentious food based around pork, veal and beef, often in stews or casseroles.

NANCY

NANCY, capital of Lorraine, is unexpectedly refined and beautiful, dominated by opulent squares and splendid boulevards. The centre of this is **place Stanislas**, a supremely elegant, partially enclosed square at the far end of rue Stanislas, dominated by the **Hôtel de Ville**. The roofline of this UNESCO World Heritage Site is topped by florid urns and lozenge-shaped lanterns dangling from the beaks of gilded cockerels. On the west side of the square, the excellent **Musée des Beaux-Arts** (daily except Tues 10am–6pm; €6) boasts work by Caravaggio, Dufy, Modigliani and Matisse. A little to the north is the **Musée Lorrain**, 64 Grande-Rue (daily except Tues 10am–12.30pm & 2–6pm; €3.10), devoted to Lorraine's history and with a room of etchings by the seventeenth-century artist, Jacques Callot, whose concern with social issues presaged much nineteenth- and twentieth-century art. It's housed in the splendid Palais Ducal, which is worth a look on its own merits. From here it's a twenty-minute walk to the **Musée de l'École de Nancy**, 36–38 rue du Sergent Blandan (Wed–Sun 10.30am–6pm; €4.60), which has a collection of Art Nouveau furniture and furnishings, arranged as if in a private house.

Arrival and information

Train Nancy train station is at the end of rue Stanislas, a five-minute walk from place Stanislas.
Tourist office rue Pierre Fourier (Mon–Sat 9am–6/7pm, Sun 10am–1/5pm; ⓣ 03.83.35.22 41, ⓦ www.ot-nancy.fr). Buy *Le Pass Nancy* (€14) – this gets you reduced museum entry, a cinema ticket, guided city tour and other goodies.
Internet *e-café*, 11 rue des Quatre Églises.

Accommodation

Hôtel de l'Académie 7bis rue des Michottes ⓣ 03.83.35.52.31. Cheap, clean and cheerful hotel in the town centre. ❸
Camping de Brabois ⓣ 03.83.27.18.28, ⓔ campeoles.brabois@wanadoo.fr. The nearest campsite to town, with showers, shop and a café on-site. Around 2km out of the city; take bus #3 or #5 from the train station. Closed mid-Oct to March. ❶
Centre d'Accueil Château de Rémicourt, Villers-lès-Nancy ⓣ 03.83.27.73.67. The local hostel is a 10-minute bus ride, but is a respectable and friendly option for a night's stay. To get here, take bus #126 to St-Fiacre. ❷

Eating

Chez Bagot 45 Grande-Rue. This stylish family-run restaurant is rightly proud of its good fish dishes; try the hake (from €10).
L'Excelsior 50 rue Henri Poincaré. This stylish Art Deco place is a great stop for a hearty meal; the *sauerkraut* is an especially good option (from €12). The wine list is good too, with some nice glasses from €4.

Moving on

Train Paris (10 daily; 1hr 30min); Strasbourg (8–13 daily; 1hr 30min).

STRASBOURG

STRASBOURG is a major capital city with the feel of a charmingly provincial town. It has one of the loveliest cathedrals in France, an ancient but active university and is the current seat of the Council of Europe and the European Court of Human Rights, as well as part-time base of the European Parliament. Even if you're not planning to spend much time in eastern France, Strasbourg is a genuine highlight and well worth a detour.

What to see and do

Strasbourg focuses on two main squares, the busy **place Kléber** and, to the south, **place Gutenberg**, named after the fifteenth-century pioneer of printing type.

Cathédrale de Notre-Dame

The major landmark is the nearby **Cathédrale de Notre-Dame** (daily 7–11.30am & 12.40–7pm; free), which beautifully combines ostentatious grandeur with what seems almost like chocolate-box fragility. Climb to the top platform for stunning views to the Black Forest, and don't miss the tremendously complicated **astrological clock** (open only noon–12.20pm; €1), built in 1842. Visitors arrive in droves to witness its crowning performance – striking the hour of noon with unerring accuracy at 12.30pm.

South of the Cathedral

The **Musée de l'Oeuvre Notre-Dame,** 3 pl du Château (Tues–Sun 10am–6pm; €4), houses the original sculptures from the cathedral exterior, as well as some of Europe's finest collected stained glass. A

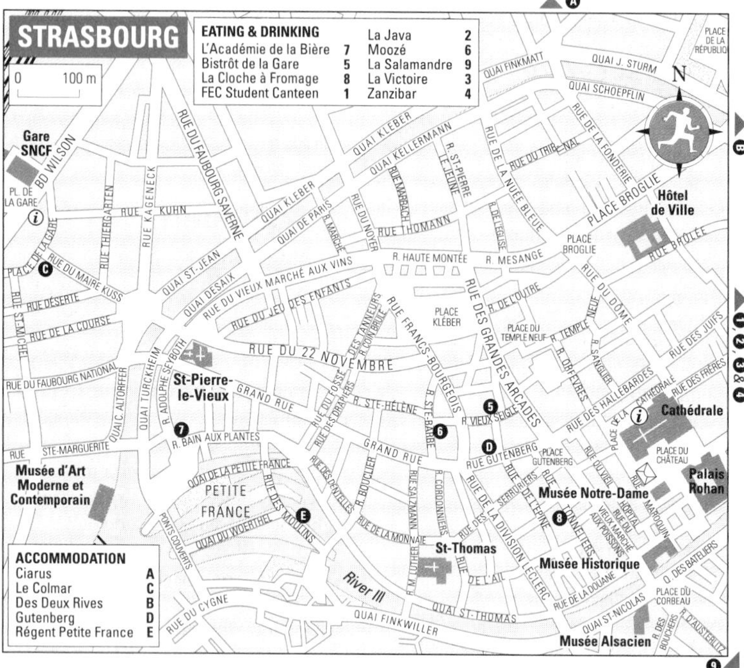

particular highlight is the *Les Amants Trépassés* in room 23, which makes the average Hollywood "torture porn" film look mild in comparison.

Grand Île & Petite France

There's little reason to look round the European parliament unless you're a political junkie; instead, the beautiful **Grand Île** section of the city is the most striking, featuring the beautiful Petite France area. This has winding streets bordered by sixteenth- and seventeenth-century houses with carved woodwork and decked with flowers. It's especially pleasant on summer evenings when it is illuminated. The name "Petite France" was given to the area by the Alsatians in the seventeenth century, having been a quarantine for patients of a devastating sixteenth-century venereal disease, attributed to the French. The **Musée d'Art Moderne et Contemporain**, 1 pl Jean-Hans Arp (Tues, Wed, Fri & Sat 11am–7pm, Thurs noon–10pm, Sun 10am–6pm; €5), stands on the west bank of the river and houses an impressive collection featuring Monet, Klimt, Ernst and Klee. If your tastes are more alcoholic, pop into **Kronenbourg**, a short way from the centre on 68 route d'Oberhausbergen (Tues–Sat 10am–4pm; €5), which runs daily **brewery** tours.

Arrival and information

Train The train station is ten minutes by foot from place Kléber.

Tourist office 17 place de la Cathédrale (daily 9am–6/7pm; ⓣ 03.88.52.28.28, ⓦ www.ot-strasbourg.fr); there are also branches in the underground shopping centre in front of the train station and at the Pont de l'Europe, at the German border.

Internet *Midi Minuit*, 5 pl du Corbeau (€3/hr).

Accommodation

It's worth bearing in mind that hotels – never cheap at the best of times – get booked up early when the European Parliament is in session, which takes place one week a month; visit Ⓦwww.europarl.eu.int for up-to-date information.

CIARUS 7 rue de Finkmatt Ⓣ03.88.15.27.88, Ⓦwww.ciarus.com. Pleasant and comfortable hostel, with regular social events. In the north of the city, around 25 minutes by foot, or take bus #2, #4 or #10 from place Gutenberg. ❸

Le Colmar 1 rue du Maire Kuss Ⓣ03.88.32.16.89, Ⓔhotel.le.colmar@wanadoo.fr. One of the best budget options near the train station, with en-suite rooms and a good buffet breakfast. ❸

Des Deux Rives rue des Cavaliers by the Pont de l'Europe Ⓣ03.88.45.54.20. Quiet hostel with a 2am curfew; ideal for those seeking a quiet night's sleep; ❷

Gutenberg 31 rue des Serruriers Ⓣ03.88.32.17.15, Ⓦwww.hotel-gutenberg.com. Good-value option based near the cathedral, with all the sights on the doorstep. ❼

Eating

Bistrôt de la Gare 18 rue du Vieux-Marché-aux-Grains. This homely little place serves good pasta and salads, with meals from €10.

La Cloche à Fromage 27 rue des Tonneliers. If you're into cheese, this is heaven. €20 will buy you a wide selection of different cheeses.

FEC Student Canteen place St-Étienne. Good, unpretentious meals at rock-bottom prices, such as beef stew and fish. Expect to pay no more than €4 for a main course.

Moozé 1 rue de la Demi-Lune. A lovely Japanese place where a plate of sushi will cost you around €3.

La Victoire 24 quai des Pêcheurs. Pleasant, inexpensive *winstub* (wine room) food, from around €8 for a filling meal.

TREAT YOURSELF

Régent Petite France 5 rue des Moulins Ⓣ03.88.76.43.43, Ⓦwww.regent-hotels.com. Fabulous, if expensive, option right in the heart of Petite France – however there are occasional special offers that take this (just) into the realms of the affordable if you allow for a special treat. The rooms have great views overlooking the river. ❾

Drinking and nightlife

L'Académie de la Bière 17 rue Adolphe-Seyboth Frequented by locals and tourists alike, who come to appreciate the fine beer served here; pints from €3.

La Java 6 rue du Faisan. Funky, cool little club with low admission prices (€2) and a good student crowd. Beers from €4.

La Salamandre 3 rue Paul-Janet. Great for live music and dancing; House and R 'n' B dominate when DJs are playing. Admission €3–5

Zanzibar 1 place St-Étienne. Cellar bar with a hip crowd of young people thronging the sweaty dance floor; admission from €4.

Moving On

Train: Basel (frequent; 1hr 15min); Frankfurt (8–9 daily; 2 hr 30min); Nancy (frequent; 1hr 15min); Paris (hourly; 2hr 20min)

Poitou-Charente

Vast horizons punctuated by fields of sunflowers, rich pastures and groves of poplars typify **Poitou-Charente**. The coast – distinctly Atlantic, with dunes, pine forests and misty mud flats – has copious charm, and lacks the busy glitz of the Côte d'Azur. The principal port, **La Rochelle**, is one of the prettiest and most distinctive towns in France, while the nearby islands of **Ré** and, farther south, **Oléron**, out of season at least, are lovely, with kilometres of sandy beaches and ancient oyster beds. **Poitiers** has a clutch of good churches in a pleasant, if sleepy, old centre. South of here, the valley of the slow, green Charente river, epitomizes *paysanne* France, accessible on boat trips from **Cognac**, made famous by its brandy.

POITIERS

POITIERS is a charming country town with eclectic noble architecture that derives from its enduring and often influential history as seat of the dukes of Aquitaine.

What to see and do

Communal life takes place between the tree-lined **place Leclerc** beneath the attractive Hotel de Ville, and the stalls and cafés of **place Charles de Gaulle**, a few streets north. Upon the latter sits the intricate **Notre-Dame-la-Grande** (Mon–Sat 9am–7pm, Sun 2–7pm; free), whose elaborate, almost fussy, Romanesque facade describes scenes from the Bible in high relief, though the heads were defaced in the Wars of Religion. Around the corner on place Lepetit, the nineteenth-century columns of the **Palais de Justice** (Mon–Fri 8.45am–noon & 1.45–5.30pm; free) hide the Tolkenesque, twelfth-century great Gothic hall of the powerful dukes of Aquitaine. In one corner, a flight of stairs give access to the old castle keep and lead out onto the roof for a memorable view over the town. From here, head east to find, literally in the middle of rue Jean-Jaurès, the fourth-century **Baptistère St-Jean** (daily Jun–Sept 10.30am–12.30pm & 3–6pm; Oct–May 10.30am–noon & 2.30–4.30pm , closed Tues; €), reputedly the oldest Christian building in France. Inside, the sunken octagonal font was – until the seventeenth century – the only place in town to conduct a proper baptism, and it still sits among ancient and faded frescoes. Next door, the **Musée de Sainte-Croix** (June–Sept Tues–Fri 10am–noon & 1.15–5/6pm; Sat–Mon 1.15–5/6pm; €3.60) houses a diverse collection that includes works by Rodin and Max Ernst; the highlight is *Grande Goule*, Jean Gargot's sculpture of the mythical beast who is said to have roamed the city's sewers in the seventeenth century.

Arrival and information

Rail The train station is on Bd du Grand Cerf; a ten-minute walk from place Leclerc.

Tourist office 45 pl Charles de Gaulle (mid-June to mid-Sept Mon–Sat 10am–10pm, Sun 10am–6pm & 7–10pm; mid-Sept to mid-June Mon–Sat 10am–6pm; ⓣ05.49.41.21.24, ⓦwww.ot-poitiers.fr). The friendly team will book accommodation, and there are cultural films and exhibits displayed on the first floor.

Accommodation

Auberge de Jeunesse 1 allée Roger Tagault ⓣ05.49.30.09.70. In a wooded park 3km from the town centre, this hostel has clean four-bed dorms (sheets provided); facilities include pool, table tennis and Internet access. Take bus #3 from the station to Cap Sud. ❷

Bistrot de la Gare 131 bd du Grand-Cerf ⓣ05.49.58.56.30. This friendly, welcoming hotel is the cheapest choice near the station; the bar here is good value. ❸

Camping Le Porteau rue du Porteau ⓣ05.49.41.44.88. Characterless municipal site ten minutes north of town on bus #7. Closed mid-Sept–May. ❶

Plat d'Étain 7–9 rue du Plat d'Étain ⓣ05.49.41.04.80, ⓦwww.hotelduplatdetain.com. Tucked away in the centre, this little hotel offers clean en suites, some with great views across the town. ❺

Eating and drinking

La Serrurerie 28 rue des Grandes Écoles ⓣ05.49.41.05.14, ⓦwww.laserrurerie.com. A bustling café-bistrot that exhibits art. Excellent if slightly pricey food, and great drinks. Cocktails €5.30, try their "French coffee" – a cognac variant of an Irish coffee.

Fruity Club 31 rue du Marché ⓣ05.49.61.39.14. Sandwiches and cocktails in fruit-themed surroundings; try their home-made yoghurt breakfasts (€4).

La Tarterie 14 pl Charles VII ⓣ05.49.47.56.93, ⓦwww.latarterie.fr. Nothing but tarts here – take your pick of sweet or savoury – all are delicious, especially the banana-chocolate (€4.60). Open 8am–9.30pm.

Petit Cabaret 188 Grand-rue ⓣ05.49.46.79.71. Great venue for music, exhibitions and late drinking; pizzas are served in the non-smoking restaurant at the back (€8).

Moving on

Train Bordeaux (15 daily; 1hr 45min); La Rochelle (10–12 daily; 1hr 15min–1hr 45min); Paris (17 daily; 1hr 30min–1hr 45min); Tours (18 daily; 50min–1hr 20min).

LA ROCHELLE

LA ROCHELLE has an exceptionally beautiful seventeenth- and eighteenth-century centre and waterfront, and a lively, busy air. Granted a charter by Eleanor of Aquitaine in 1199, it rapidly became a port of major importance, trading in salt and wine. Following a makeover in the 1990s which established a university, pedestrianized the centre and moved out the fishing operation, La Rochelle has become the largest Atlantic yachting port in Europe, without the glitzy exclusivity of some of its Mediterranean counterparts.

What to see and do

The heavy Gothic gateway of the **Porte de la Grosse Horloge** straddles the entrance to the old town, dominating the pleasure-boat-filled inner harbour, which is guarded by two sturdy towers, Tour de la Chaîne and Tour St Nicholas (10am–1pm & 2–7pm; €5). Behind the Grosse Horloge, the main shopping street, **rue du Palais** is lined with eighteenth-century houses and arcaded shop fronts, while to the east, rue du Temple leads to the Franco-Italian-style **Hôtel de Ville**, commissioned by Henri IV, whose initials, intertwined with those of Marie de Medici, are carved on the ground-floor gallery (guided tours: June–Sept daily 3pm; July & Aug daily 3 & 4pm; Oct–May Sat & Sun 3pm; €4). Further riches lie inside the **Musée du Nouveau Monde**, 10 rue Fleuriau (Mon & Wed–Sat 10am–12.30pm & 2–6pm, Sun 2.30–6pm; €3.50), a commemorative to the town's dubious fortunes from slavery, sugar, spices and coffee. For **beaches** – and bicycle paths – you're best off crossing over to the **Île de Ré**, a narrow, sand-rimmed island immediately west of La Rochelle (take the Rébus buses from place de Verdun). Out of season it has a slow, misty charm, centred around the cultivation of oysters and mussels; in summer it's packed to the gills. **Île d'Oléron**, just south of La Rochelle, is less crowded and more wooded, but also has a number of excellent beaches as well as a lovely bird sanctuary, the Marais aux Oiseaux (April, May & Sept 10am–12am, 2pm–7pm; June–Aug 10am-8pm; €3.80).

Arrival and information

Train From the train station, it's a seven-minute walk down avenue du Général de Gaulle to the town centre.
Tourist office By the harbour on place de la Petite Sirène, (July & Aug Mon–Sat 9am–8pm; Sept, April–June Mon–Sat 9am–6/7pm, Sun 10.30am–5.30pm; Oct–March Mon–Sat 10am–12.30pm & 1.30pm–6pm, Sun 10am–1pm; ⓣ 05.46.41.14.68, ⓦ www.larochelle-tourisme.fr).
Internet *Squat*, 63 rue St-Nicolas.

Accommodation

Atlantic 23 rue Verdière ⓣ 05.46.41.16.68. A friendly and informal hotel, with the cheapest double room in the old town (4). The rest of the rooms are en suite. 5
FUAJ La Rochelle 17 av des Minimes ⓣ 05.46.44.43.11, ⓦ www.fuaj.org. Well-situated hostel twenty minutes from the centre. Dorms are roomy and regular barbecues and sea activities are organized. Take bus #10 from the train station to "La Sole". 2
Le Soleil av Crépeau ⓣ 05.46.44.42.53. This municipal campsite has ping-pong, pétanque and hot showers, and allows barbecues. Its best asset is its location; just 800m from the town centre, right by the sea, next to an amusingly creepy mechanical puppet museum. 1
Le Bordeaux 45 rue St-Nicolas ⓣ 05.46.41.31.22, ⓦ www.hotel-bordeaux-fr.com. Freshly renovated and clean en suites, thankfully double glazed as it's on a street with a plethora of good bars and restaurants. Free wireless in all rooms. 7
Henri-IV 31 rue des Gentilshommes ⓣ 05.46.41.25.79, ⓔ henri-iv@wanadoo.fr. A tastefully decorated sixteenth-century building in the centre of town that has charming, clean rooms and helpful hosts. 7

Eating

Café de la Paix pl de Verdun ⓣ 05.46.41.39.79. The old mirror-lined variety show hall exudes excess, though thankfully not through its prices. Try the excellent *coquilles Saint-Jacques* (scallops; €12) or simply sip a coffee on the square.

COGNAC DAY TRIP

On the La Rochelle to Bordeaux line, the little town of **COGNAC** is shrouded in the heady scent of its famous brandy. Of the various *cognac chais* (distilleries) huddled around the end of the Grande-Rue, Hennessy, 1 rue de la Richonne (March–Dec daily 10am–5/6pm; ⓣ05.45.35.72.68; €6), offers the best tours, which include tastings, a short boat trip and a rousing video. This seventh-generation Irish family firm holds 180,000 barrels of various blends, made under the guidance of the *maître du chai*'s expert eye, nose and palate. A good restaurant choice in town is *La Bonne Goule*, 42 allées de la Corderie, for their local Charentais plates, such as *cagouilles* (snails cooked in white wine) or *daube de boeuf* (hearty beef stew). If you get carried away with the brandy and need to stay the night, head for the grand *Hotel d'Orléans*, 25 rue d'Angoulême (ⓣ05.45.82.01.26; ④).
ⓦwww.tourism-cognac.com
ⓦwww.hennessey.com

Quai 22 22 quai Duperré ⓣ05.46.50.66.08, ⓦwww.quai22.com. Popular with students and the best value on the port, serving steak, fish and pizzas. Three-course menu with wine €14.
Original Pasta 19 rue des Templiers. Fast-food pasta in big, filling boxes and small, but adequate, boxes with a choice of sauces. Big box & drink €5.80.
À Côté de Chez Fred 34 rue St-Nicolas ⓣ05.46.41.21.35. Next to a fishmonger, this is the best place in town to enjoy fresh fish; head here at lunchtime for their more affordable menus (2 courses, €10).

Drinking and nightlife

Cave de la Guignette 8 rue St Nicolas ⓣ05.46.41.05.75. Hugely popular bar serving flavoured white wine identified by colour. The "rouge" is the nicest (€8 a bottle).
Les Têtes Brûlées 20 rue Verdière, ⓦwww.barlestetesbrulees.com. A roguish old pilot runs this amusingly decorated bar, decked out with naval goodies. *Demi-pression* €2.60.
Le Piano 12 cours du Temple. With a lovely courtyard setting and live Indie bands, this bar is where *Rochelais* in the know go to drink; *demi* €2.50, open 7pm–2am.
L'Oxford Prom de la Concurrence ⓣ05.46.41.51.81, ⓦwww.club-oxford.com. This fun nightclub plays techno, ragga and house, with a second room for 1980s tunes. Entry €10 including one alcoholic or two non-alcoholic drinks.

Moving on

Trains Cognac (6 daily; 1hr 20min–3hr 15min); Bordeaux (6 daily; 2hr 10min–2hr 30min); Poitiers (12 daily; 1hr 15min–1hr 45min); Nantes (4 daily; 1hr 50min–2hr)

Aquitaine and the Dordogne

Lush, steamy and green, the southwest of France can feel like a lower-latitude England. Although undoubtedly beautiful, the most famous spots in the **Dordogne** heartlands can become oppressively crowded in summer. **Bordeaux**, the first city of Aquitaine and the global wine community, boasts a freshly polished centre and has class by the glass. A rugged, unspoiled coast and famous surf spots lie to the west, and east out of **Gironde** is the undulating and fertile **Périgord Blanc**, named after the white of its rocky outcrops. The regional capital is **Périgueux**, whose central position and regular transport connections make it a good base, especially for the cave paintings at **Les Eyzies** and around.

BORDEAUX

After a decade-long makeover, **BORDEAUX** has shaken off its stuffy image, sorted out its transport and cleaned its grand eighteenth-century centre, which last year became France's second UNESCO urban heritage site. If you're a fan of the area's world-famous wines, you won't want to miss a wine tour or the **Fête du Vin**, a four-day celebration held on even years at the end of June. Although

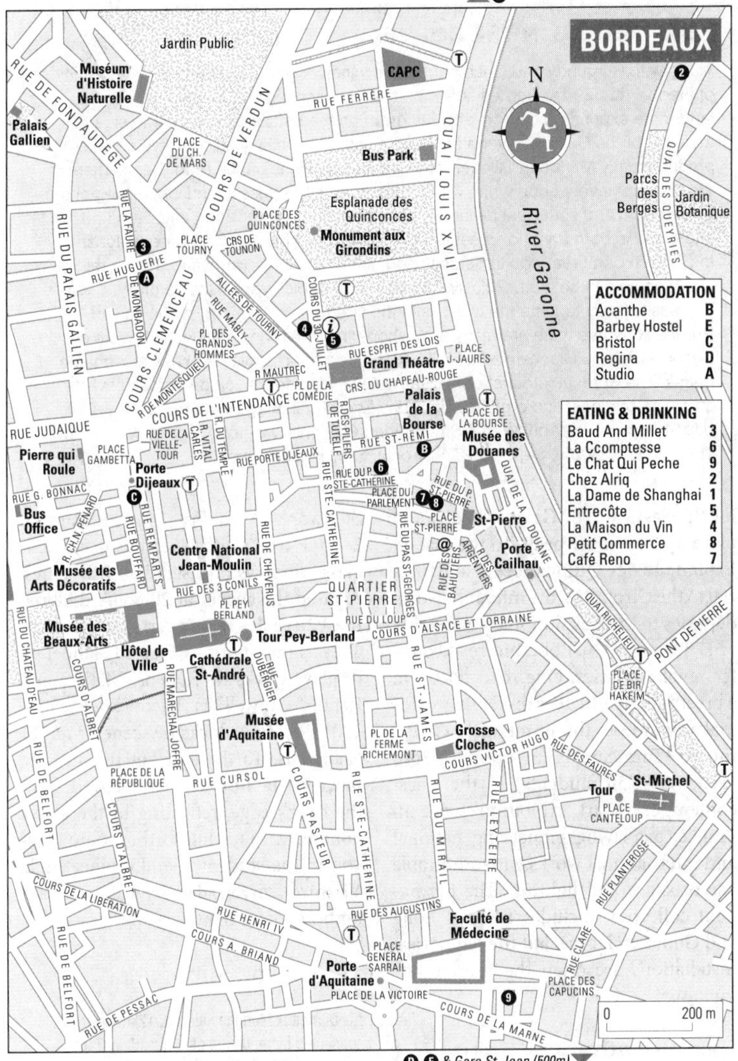

the surrounding landscape is nothing special, the pine-covered expanses of Les Landes and the wild, unfettered Atlantic **coast**, home to surf mecca Lacanau-Océan, are just a stone's throw away.

What to see and do

The centre of Bordeaux bends around the east bank of the Garonne river in the shape of *un croissant de lune* (a crescent moon) – and is colloquially known as *Porte de la Lune*.

Le Triangle d'Or and Quinconces

The "golden triangle", full of chic Parisian boutiques, runs between **place Gambetta**, with its eighteenth-century Porte Dijeaux, place de la Comédie hold-

WINE TASTING IN THE BORDEAUX REGION

Along with Burgundy and Champagne, the wines of Bordeaux form the Holy Trinity of French **viticulture**. Bordeaux is mostly a red-wine region, growing high-class (and more expensive) **Cabernet Sauvignon** on the Left Bank (the countryside to the west of the Garonne river and Gironde estuary), while smaller growers make predominantly Merlot and Cabernet-Franc based wines on the Right Bank. There are also some very good white wines, largely from the Pessac and Graves regions to the south and south-east – largely based on **Sauvignon Blanc** and **Semillon**, and come in both dry and sweet forms. Unlike a lot of New World wine regions, the French don't really do large-scale tourism on their vineyards and the overall atmosphere can be a bit exclusive, so you have to pick your visits carefully.
The easiest way to taste the wines is in the village of **St Emilion**, to the east of Bordeaux, where there are many wine shops that hold wine tastings. L'Envers du Decor, 11 rue du Clocher (☎05.57.74.48.31), is a good choice and has reasonable prices. The Bordeaux tourist office (see below) has information on châteaux visits and wine-tastings, and organizes half-day English-language wine tours (May–Oct daily 1.30pm; Nov–April Wed & Sat 1.30pm; €26) and two-hour *dégustations* (Aug Thurs & Sat 4.30pm; Sept–July Thurs only; €20, including meal).

ing the classical 1780 **Grand Théâtre** and place Tourny at the peak. To the east on **Esplanade des Quinconces** is a memorial to the Girondins, the influential local deputies to the Revolutionary Assembly of 1789, purged by Robespierre as counter-revolutionaries. One road north, in a breathtaking nineteenth-century colonial warehouse, the unmissable **CAPC musée** (Tues–Sun 11am–6pm, till 8pm Wed; €5/€2.50 students) is the finest contemporary art exhibition space in France, displaying pioneering national and international works with admirable use of space and lighting. The permanent collection includes Richard Long and Gilbert&George, but the temporary installations are often the most exciting.

Sainte-Catherine, Saint Pierre and Place de la Victoire

The central pedestrian artery, **rue Ste-Catherine**, leads down from place de la Comédie to the city's best historical museum, the **Musée d'Aquitaine**, 20 cours Pasteur (Tues–Sun 11am–6pm; free), which illustrates the history of the region from prehistoric times through to the 1800s. To the east stands the **Cathédrale St-André** (Mon–Fri 7.30–11.30am & 2–6pm; free), with its exquisite stained-glass windows and slender twin spires. Around the corner at 20 cours d'Albret, the **Musée des Beaux-Arts** (daily except Tues 11am–6pm; €5/€2.50 students) displays works by Rubens, Matisse and Renoir, as well as Lacour's evocative 1804 Bordeaux dockside scene, *Quai des Chartrons*. To the east lies the striking **place de la Bourse**, best viewed from the river's edge, reflecting in the glassy Font du Miroir, while farther south takes you to the student-friendly **place de la Victoire**, surrounded by cafés, restaurants and late-night bars.

Arrival and information

Air Bordeaux Mérignac airport, 12km west, is connected by regular shuttle bus (daily 7am–10.45pm; 30–45min; €6) to place Gambetta, cours du 30-Juillet and Gare St Jean.

Train The station, Gare St Jean, lies 2km south-east of central Bordeaux, easily accessed by tram C from Esplanade des Quinconces (10min; €1.30).

Tourist office The main **tourist office** at 12 cours du 30-Juillet (daily 9am–7.30pm, Sun till 6.30pm; ☎05.56.00.66.00, Ⓦwww.bordeaux-tourisme.com) organises a plethora of wine and city tours and there is also a small booth outside the station.

Internet *Artobas*, 7 rue Maucoudinat.

Getting Around

Tram/bus The hubs of the comprehensive transport networds are pl Gambetta for buses and Esplanade des Quinconces for trams. Buy tickets at coin dispensers before boarding; one hour's travel €1.30, day pass €4.80.
Bike/skates Pierre qui roule, 32 pl Gambetta (☎05.57.85.80.87; bikes €9/day, skates €6/day).

Accommodation

Acanthe 12–14 rue St-Rémi ☎05.56.81.66.58 Ⓦwww.acanthe-hotel-bordeaux.com. This is a tasteful treat, with en-suite rooms that have been individually decorated; some have balconies. ❻
Barbey Hostel 22 cours Barbey ☎05.56.33.00.70, Ⓦwww.auberge-jeunesse-bordeaux.eu. New, spotless dorms and Internet access, but pricey for what it is and lacking a little in atmosphere. ❷
Bristol 4 rue Bouffard ☎05.56.52.88.24, Ⓦwww.hotel-bordeaux.com. A sister hotel to the *Studio* (see below) but with nicer rooms, some of which have cooking facilities. ❹
Regina 34 rue Charles Dominique ☎05.56.91.32.88, Ⓦwww.hotelreginabordeaux.com. A nineteenth-century building opposite the station presided over by friendly owners and a sleepy guard dog. Rooms are clean and all have showers; those on the first floor are the best. ❹
Studio 26 rue Huguerie ☎05.56.48.00.14 Ⓦwww.hotel-bordeaux.com. A big backpacker's haunt with forty clean, white rooms in three buildings along a lively, central street, and cheap Internet access. ❸

Eating

Chez Alriq ZA du quai de Queyries ☎05.56.86.58.49. Fabulously unique gypsy restaurant-theatre-venue where hearty dishes such as lamb couscous (€12) are followed by indescribably eclectic performance (circus, theatre, bands). To get there, follow the right bank north of Pont de Pierre, forking left past the Jardin Botanique into the old shipyard.
Café Reno 34 rue du Parlement St-Pierre. One of the most fun places to eat, where you can enjoy make-your-own salads (€7), big breakfasts (€6) and excellent hot chocolates. They also teach knitting and provide wool and needles.
L'Entrecôte 4 cours du 30 Juillet. Simplicity at its tastiest: a lovingly tender steak, served in a fabulous sauce, with a green salad and all the thin chips you can eat (€16). The dessert menu is extensive – try the profiteroles (€5.50). Expect to queue.
Le Petit Commerce 22 rue du Parlement ☎05.56.79.76.58. This effortlessly cool little restaurant, one of many around pl du Parlement, is much lauded for its fish menus; two-course lunch menu with a glass of wine €12.

TREAT YOURSELF

Baud & Millet, 19 rue Huguerie (☎06.70.79.24.93, Ⓦwww.baudetmillet.fr) For a cheese lover, there is no better way to spend a day than sitting in this incredible eighteenth-century wine *cave*, where for €22 you can have unfettered access to their well-stocked wet cheese celler (*fruitière*). Enjoy it with their freshly cooked bread and one of 950 wines from around the world (from €4 a glass). The characterful M. Baud speaks excellent English and delights in helping with the choice.

Drinking and nightlife

La Comptesse 25 rue du Parlement-Ste-Catherine ☎05.56.51.03.07. Eclectic, bumping music, often samba or electro, to shake your *derrière* to late night; demi €3. Open 8pm-2am.

SURFING IN LACANAU

Bordeaux's nearest beach, **Lacanau-Océan**, is well-known for its beautiful lake and famous for its world-class **surfing**. If you fancy catching some waves, take bus #702 from opposite gare St Jean (3 daily; 1hr 15min; €6.50) – once there, you can rent boards and learn to surf at Lacanau Sports Club (☎05.56.26.38.84), located on the corner of bd Plage and bd Liberty. *Hostel Villa Zénith*, 16 av Adjudant-Gultrd (☎05.56.26.36.49; ❷) is 200m from the beach and has comfy four- and six-bed dorms, cooking facilities and equipment lockers.
Ⓦwww.lacanau.com
Ⓦwww.lacanausurfclub.com

Le Chat qui Pêche 16 rue Garat ⓣ05.56.31.11.39. There's a lot of good places to head to around pl Victoire and this live music joint (mostly jazz) is one of the best; demi €2.50.
La Dame de Shanghaï 1 Quai Lalande ⓣ05.57.10.20.50. A Chinese-themed nightclub on a boat, which also serves good Chinese food at lunchtime. A twenty-minute walk from the centre along the left bank, then turn left at Hanger 20 up rue Faure, and take the first right.
La Maison à Vin 1 cours du 30-Juillet ⓣ05.56.00.22.88. Promoters for Bordeaux wine growers and home to a wine-tasting school, the bar here is a good place to start for a taster of the region's excellent wines.

Moving on

Train Bayonne and Biarritz (8 daily; 1hr 45min–3hr 30min); Marseille (6 daily; 5hr 45min–7hr 15min); Nice (3 daily; 8hr 30min–10hr 10min); Paris (19 daily; 3hr–3hr 30min); Périgueux (13 daily; 1hr 10min–1hr 30min); Toulouse (16 daily; 2hr–2hr 45min)

PÉRIGUEUX

The bustling market town of **PÉRIGUEUX**, with its beautiful Renaissance and medieval centre, makes a fine base for visiting the Dordogne's prehistoric caves.

What to see and do

The centre of town focuses on **place Bugeaud**, west of which is the **Cathédrale St-Front** – its square, pineapple-capped belfry surging above the roofs of the surrounding medieval houses. During a nineteenth-century restoration, the architect Paul Abadie added five Byzantine domes to the roof, which served as a prototype to his more famous Sacré Coeur in Paris. North along rue St-Front leads to the **Musée du Périgord**, at 22 cours Tourny (Mon & Wed–Fri 10am–5.30pm, Sat & Sun 1–6pm;€), boasting some beautiful Gallo-Roman mosaics found locally. East of here, the old town has a number of fine Renaissance palaces, particularly along rue Limogeanne and on place St-Louis.

Arrival and information

Train The train station is a ten-minute walk to the west of pl Bugeaud.
Tourist Office 26 pl Francheville (daily 9/10am–1pm & 2–6pm; ⓣ05.53.53.10.63, ⓦwww.perigueux.fr).
Internet *L'Avant Première*, 28 cours Montaigne.

Accommodation

Hôtel des Barris 2 rue Pierre Magne ⓣ05.53.53.04.05. This small riverside hotel is the cheapest in town; try to get one of the four rooms that overlook the cathedral. ❹
Barnabé 80 rue des Bains ⓣ05.53.53.41.45, ⓦwww.barnabé-perigord.com. This campsite, on the banks of the river Isle, offers shaded pitches, table tennis and occasional live music at the bar. To get there cross pont des Barris and follow the south river bank for 2km. ❶
Comfort Hôtel Régina 14 rue Denis-Papin ⓣ05.53.08.40.44, ⓔcomfort.perigueux@wanadoo.fr. This lovely 1930s hotel is handy for the station and has newly renovated, bright green ensuite rooms. ❻

Eating and Drinking

Au Bien Bon 15 rue des Places. Its good menus feature meaty local specialities including tender duck *magrets*; 2-course lunch menu, €14.
Gouter de Charlotte 9 rue Voltaire. Healthy but filling crêpes and galettes (€8) are served in this charming old café overlooking the square.
La Vertu, 11 rue Notre-Dame ⓣ05.53.53.20.75. A friendly, local inn with a flowery terrace serving cheap beers, cocktails and sturdy dinners (€13). Also has a cosy double room (❸).

Moving on

Train Bordeaux (13 daily; 1hr 10min–1hr 30min); Clermont-Ferrand (4 daily; 5hr 10min–7hr 30min); Les Eyzies (5 daily; 30min); Paris (12 daily; via Libourne or Limoges; 4–5hr).

THE VÉZÈRE VALLEY CAVES

This lavish cliff-cut region, riddled with **caves** and subterranean streams, is half-an-hour or so by train from Périgueux. Cro-Magnon skeletons were unearthed here in 1868 and since then an incredible wealth of archeological evidence of the life of late Stone Age people has been found. The paintings that adorn the caves are remarkable not only for their age, but also for their exquisite colouring and the skill with which they were drawn.

What to see and do

The centre of the region is **LES EYZIES**, a rambling, somewhat unattractive village dominated by tourism. Worth a glance before or after visiting the caves is the **Musée National de la Préhistoire** (July & Aug daily 9.30am–6.30pm; Sept–June daily except Tues 9am–12.30pm & 2.30–5.30pm; €4.50). Les Eyzies' **tourist office**, 19 rue de la Préhistoire (June–Sept Mon–Sat 9am–7pm, Sun 9/10am–noon & 2–5/6pm; Oct–May Mon–Sat 9am–noon & 2–6pm, closed Sun, except Apr & May 10am–noon & 2–5pm; Ⓣ05.53.06.97.05, Ⓦwww.leseyzies.com) has information on private rooms in the area, internet and rents out bikes for €14 per day. The Périgueux **tourist office** has a factsheet detailing how to get to the caves and back in a day

Font de Gaume caves

Just outside Les Eyzies, off the road to Sarlat, the **Grotte de Font de Gaume** (daily except Sat: mid-May to mid-Sept 9.30am–5.30pm; mid-Sept to mid-May 9.30am–12.30pm & 2–5.30pm; Ⓣ05.53.06.86.00; €6.10) contains dozens of polychrome paintings, the colour remarkably preserved by a protective layer of calcite. The tours last forty minutes but only two hundred people are admitted each day, so to be sure of a place you should reserve in advance by phone or arrive before 9.30am.

The Cap Blanc frieze

The **Abri du Cap Blanc** (daily: April–June, Sept & Oct 10am–noon & 2–6pm; July & Aug 10am–7pm; Ⓣ05.53.59.21.74; €5.90) is a steep 7km bike ride from Les Eyzies. This is not a cave but a rock shelter, containing a 15,000-year-old frieze of horses and bison, the only exhibited prehistoric sculpture in the world.

Grotte des Combarelles

The road continues to the **Grotte des Combarelles** (daily: June–Sept daily 9.30am–5.30pm; Oct–May daily 9am–12.30pm & 2–5.30pm; Jan–April closed Mon & Tues; €6.10), whose engravings of humans, reindeer and mammoths from the Magdalanian period (about twenty thousand years ago) are the oldest in the region.

Montignac

Up the valley of the Vézère river to the northeast, **MONTIGNAC** is more attractive than Les Eyzies. Its prime interest is the cave paintings at nearby **Lascaux** – or, rather, the tantalizing replica at Lascaux II (April–Sept daily 9.30am–7pm; July & Aug daily 9am–8pm; Oct–March daily 10am–12.30pm & 2–5.30pm; mid-Nov to March closed Mon; forty-minute guided tour €8); the original has been closed since 1963 due to deterioration caused by the breath and body heat of visitors. Executed seventeen thousand years ago, the paintings are known as the finest prehistoric works in existence. The **tourist office** is at place Bertran-de-Born (Mon–Sat 10am–1pm & 3–6pm; Ⓣ05.53.51.82.60, Ⓦwww.bienvenue-montignac.com). Montignac is short on moderately priced **accommodation**; the best option is the *Hôtel de la Grotte*, 63 rue du 4 Septembre (Ⓣ05.53.51.80.48, Ⓦwww.hoteldelagrotte.fr; ❸), which has a nice restaurant (two-course dinner menu €15). There's also a **campsite**, *Le Moulin du Bleufond* (closed mid-Oct to March; Ⓣ05.53.51.83.95, Ⓦwww.bleufond.com; ❷), on the riverbank.

The Pyrenees

Basque-speaking and damp in the west, snowy and Occitan-speaking in the middle, dry and Catalan in the east, **the Pyrenees** are physically beautiful, culturally varied and decidedly less developed than the Alps. The entire range is marvellous walking country, especially the central **Parc National des Pyrénées**, with its 3000-metre-high peaks, streams, forests, flowers and wildlife. In the foothills, **Lourdes** is a monster of kitsch that has to be seen to be believed, while **Toulouse**, the capital of the Midi-Pyrenees, has youthful energy bouncing off its red-bricked walls.

TOULOUSE

TOULOUSE is one of the most vibrant provincial cities in France, a result of a policy to make it the country's centre of hi-tech industry. Always an aviation centre – St-Exupéry and Mermoz flew out from here on their pioneering flights over Africa in the 1920s – Toulouse is now home to Aérospatiale, the driving force behind Airbus and the Ariane space rocket. Added zest comes from its large student population, second only to that of Paris.

What to see and do

The centre of **Toulouse** is a rough hexagon clamped around a bend in the wide, brown Garonne river.

Place du Capitol and the old city

The **place du Capitole** is the site of Toulouse's town hall and a prime meeting-place, with numerous cafés and a weekday market. South of the square, and east of rue Alsace-Lorraine, lies the old town – a lovely place for a stroll. Its cobbled streets are lined with the ornate *hôtels* of the merchants who grew rich on the woad trade, which formed the city's economic staple until the sixteenth century. The predominant building material here is the flat Toulousain brick, whose cheerful rosy colour gives the city its nickname of *ville rose*. Best known of these palaces is the **Hôtel d' Assézat**, towards the river end of rue de Metz, which houses the marvellous private art collection of the **Fondation Bemberg** (Tues–Sun 10am–12.30pm & 1.30–6pm, Thurs till 9pm; €4.60), including excellent works by Bonnard. A short walk east on the rue de Metz, the **Musée des Augustins**, (Mon & Thurs–Sun 10am–6pm, Wed 10am–9pm; €3), incorporates the two cloisters of an Augustinian priory and houses collections of outstanding Romanesque and Gothic sculpture.

Around place St-Sernin

Rue du Taur leads northwards from place du Capitole to place St-Sernin and the largest Romanesque church in France, **Basilique de St-Sernin** (daily: July–Sept 8.30am–6.15pm, Sun till 7.30pm; Oct–Jun 8.30–11.45am & 2–5.45pm, Sun till 7pm). Dating back to 1080, it was built to accommodate passing hordes of Santiago pilgrims and is one of the loveliest examples of its kind. Inside, the ambulatory is well worth a visit for its succession of richly housed relics and exceptional eleventh-century marble bas-reliefs. Opposite the church, the **Musée St-Raymond** (daily 10am–6pm, till 7pm July & Aug; €3) houses exhibits charting the history of the Roman town of Tolosa, as Toulouse was then known.

Les Jacobins

West of place du Capitole, on rue Lakanal, the church of **Les Jacobins** (daily, 9am–7pm) is another unmissable ecclesiastical building. This is a huge fortress-like rectangle of unadorned brick, with an interior divided by a central row of slender pillars from whose capitals spring a colourful splay of vaulting ribs. Beneath the altar lie the bones of the

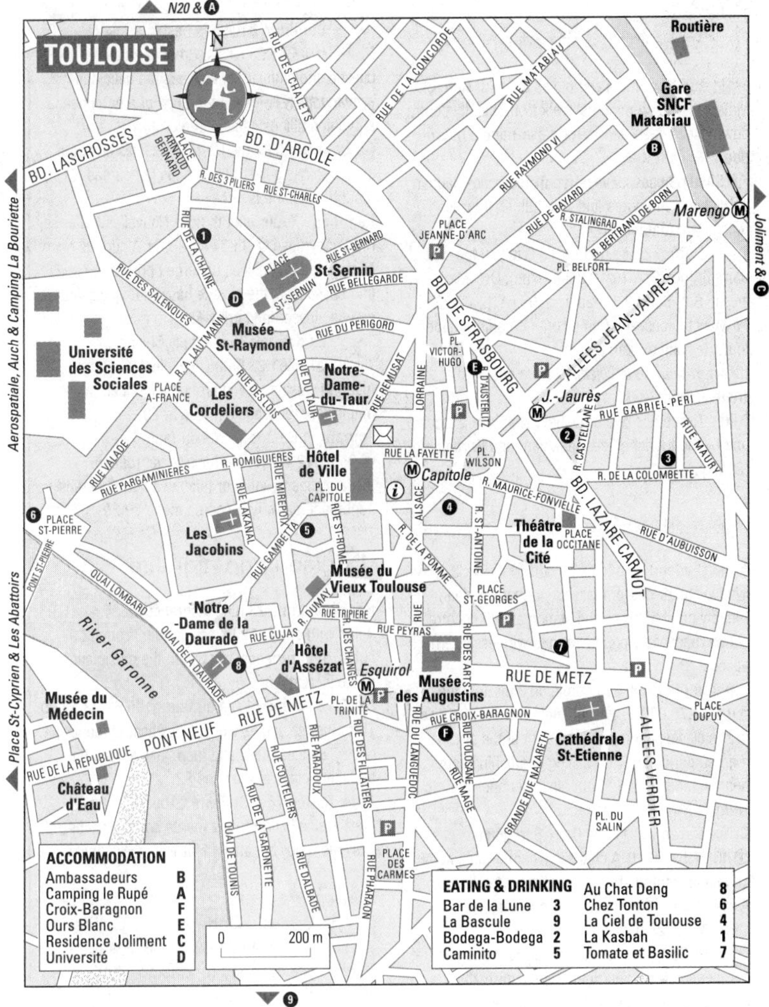

philosopher St Thomas Aquinas, while the north side reveals a tranquil cloister (daily 10am–7pm; €3).

St-Cyprien on the Left Bank

Across the Pont-Neuf on the west bank of the Garonne stands the brick tower of the inspirational **Chateaux d'eau**, (Tues-Sun 1-7pm; €2.50) the first public gallery dedicated to photography in France and holding over four thousand pieces, along with antique equipment. Continue west from the river, then north up Allées de Fitte to the vaulted nineteenth-century slaughterhouse, **Les Abattoirs**, (Tues–Sun 11am–7pm; €6/free first Sun of every month), whose comprehensive modern and contemporary art collections include an awestriking eight-metre-high Picasso theatre screen.

Arrival and information

Train and bus Trains and buses arrive at Gare Matabiau, fifteen minutes' walk from the city centre down allées Jean-Jaurès, or a five-minute métro ride.

Air Shuttle buses leave Aéroport Toulouse-Blagnac every twenty minutes and take half an hour to reach Gare Matabiau (€4).

Tourist office place Charles de Gaulle (Mon–Sat 9am–6/7pm, Sun 10/10.30am–7pm; Oct–May closed Sat–Sun 12.30–2pm; ⓣ05.61.11.02.22, ⓦwww.toulouse-tourisme.com); organises good tours, leaving at 3pm (€9).

Internet *Chat de la Voisine*, 25 rue des Sept Troubadours.

Bikes Tisseo has two branches – by Gare Matabiau and by the tourist office; bank card and ID required (€2/day).

Accommodation

Ambassadeurs 68 rue de Bayard ⓣ05.61.62.65.84, ⓦwww.hotel-des-ambassadeurs.com. A clean, friendly hotel between the station and the centre with a reasonably priced bar and wireless Internet access. ❹

Camping le Rupé 21 chemin du Pont de Rupé ⓣ05.61.70.07.35, ⓔcampinglerupe31@wanadoo.fr. The closest campsite, just north of the city in a green park with waterskiiing and fishing spots nearby. Take bus #59 from place Jeanne-d'Arc to "Rupé". ❶

Croix-Baragnon 17 rue Croix-Baragnon ⓣ05.61.52.60.10. A charming, comfortable hotel on an old, central street full of little art galleries. Also has a good breakfast selection. ❹

Ours Blanc 25 pl de Victor-Hugo ⓣ05.61.23.14.55, ⓦwww.hotel-ours-blanc.fr. Set in a beautiful building right in the centre, this very romantic hotel has cosy rooms, including one with a great roof terrace. ❼

Residence Jolimont 2 av Yves Brunaud ⓣ05.34.30.42.80. ⓔfoyerjolimont@wanadoo.fr. Standard *auberge de jeunesse*, friendly and clean. ❷

Hôtel de l'Université 26 rue Émile-Cartailhac ⓣ05.61.21.35.69. You cannot beat this central hotel for price, though it is a little ageing and basic. ❸

Eating

La Bascule 14 av Maurice-Hauriou ⓣ05.61.52.09.51. An old establishment serving classical regional cuisine, including *cassoulet*, as well as tasty fish dishes. Three-course menu €22.

Caminito 3 rue des Gestes ⓣ05.61.23.51.74. Great Argentinian cuisine, the highlight of which is the delicious *empanadas* (€2.90), with a range of meat, cheese and onion fillings. Closed Sun.

Au Chat Deng 37 rue Peyrolières. This tiny blue brasserie has good-value menus (2 courses, €13), though à la carte is pricey.

Le Ciel de Toulouse 6th floor, Nouvelles Galleries, rue Lapeyrouse ⓣ05.34.45.98.98. A curious neon-lit cafeteria that dishes up large portions of stews and *cassoulets;* the terrace has great views. Main course, dessert and drink €9.

La Kasbah 30 rue de la Chaîne ⓣ05.61.23.55.06. Excellent, authentic Algerian cuisine served around a fountain, with mains very reasonable priced at €9.

Tomate et Basilic 10 rue du Taur ⓣ05.61.12.48.21. Inexpensive yet refined pasta dishes to eat in or take away. The pasta is handmade daily. Two-course menu €9.20.

Drinking and nightlife

Bar de la Lune 22 rue Palaprat ⓣ05.34.41.16.96. Relax with one of 120 types of beer (from €2 a bottle) in this friendly bar where the music allows for conversation.

La Cave Poésie 71 rue du Taur ⓣ05.61.23.62.00. This intimate venue, which plays host to theatre, poetry, dance, music and more, has a good bar attached; glass of red wine €2.

Chez Tonton 16 pl St-Pierre ⓣ05.61.21.89.54. Specializing in France's favourite *apéro – pastis* (€2), this little rugby bar often holds live music nights.

TREAT YOURSELF

Bodega-Bodega 1 rue Gabriel Péri ⓣ05.61.63.03.63. Swap your money for casino-style chips as you enter this high-quality cocktail bar (sangria €7), which also serves tapas until 11pm. It's always a fun, energetic place that's great for a dance. Daily 7pm–2am, Sat 8pm–4am; €6.50 entry after 10.30pm, redeemable at the bar.

Moving on

Train Domestic: Bayonne-Biarritz (8 daily; 3hr–4hr 30min); Bordeaux (16 daily; 2hr–2hr 45min); Carcassonne (18 daily; 45min–1hr 15min); Lourdes (9–10 daily; 2hr); Lyon (10 daily via Montpellier;

2 direct daily; 4hr–4hr 40min); Marseille (9 daily; 4hr); Paris (8 daily; 5hr–8hr 20min).
International: Barcelona (3 daily, via Narbonne; 4hr 50min–5hr 45min).
Bus Andorra (2 daily; 3hr 30min) from Matabiau station.

LOURDES

In 1858 Bernadette Soubirous, 14-year-old daughter of a poor local miller in **LOURDES**, had eighteen visions of the Virgin Mary in a spot called the Grotte de Massabielle. Miraculous cures at the grotto soon followed and Lourdes grew exponentially; it now sees six million Catholic pilgrims a year and whole streets are devoted to the sale of religious kitsch. At the **grotto** itself – a moisture-blackened overhang by the riverside with a statue of the Virgin inside – long queues of the faithful process through. Above looms the first, neo-Gothic church built here, in 1871, and nearby the massive subterranean **basilica** has a capacity of twenty thousand. Lourdes **train station** is on the northeastern edge of town. At avenue Francis Lagardère a **funicular** makes the 1000m ascent through the pines up to the Pic du Jer, where the Pyrenees begin. For the **tourist office** on place Peyramale turn right outside the station, then left down Chaussée Maransin (Mon–Sat 9am–noon & 2–6/7pm; Easter–Oct also Sun 11am–6pm; ⓣ05.62.42.77.40, ⓦwww.lourdes-france.com). There's an abundance of inexpensive **hotels** on avenue de la Gare, and more en route to the grotto and around the castle. **Hostel** accommodation is at *Pension Familiale*, 44 rue de l'Égalité (ⓣ05.62.94.26.75; ❷ including meals). Closest of several **campsites** is *La Poste*, 26 rue de Langelle (closed mid-Oct to Easter; ⓣ05.62.94.40.35; ❶), between the train station and post office.

GAVERNIE AND BARÈGES

From Lourdes train station, several SNCF buses run daily to **GAVERNIE** and **BARÈGES**, two resorts near the heart of the **Parc National des Pyrénées Occidentales**. From either, a few hours on the Pyrenees-spanning hiking trail, GR10 or the harder HRP (*Haute Randonnée Pyrénéenne*), brings you to staffed alpine refuges (rough camping is not generally allowed in the park). In summer, serious and properly equipped hikers may wish to continue on the trails, which continue to be well-served with refuge houses, though the weather and terrain make them highly dangerous in winter. The Lourdes and Bayonne tourist offices have information, or check ⓦwww.lespyrenees.net. **Gavernie** is smaller and pricier than Barèges, but has an incomparable cirque towering above, forming the border with Spain. You can **stay** in dorms at *Le Gypaëte* (ⓣ05.62.92.40.61; ❸), or **camp** at the primitive but superbly set *La Bergerie* (ⓣ05.62.92.48.41; ❶), towards the cirque. **BARÈGES** has more of a real village feel, with a good streamside **campsite** – *La Ribère* (ⓣ05.62.92.69.01) – and two high-quality **gîtes** next to each other: *L'Oasis* (ⓣ05.62.92.69.47, ⓦwww.gite-oasis.com; ❹) and *L'Hospitalet* (ⓣ05.62.92.68.08; ❸). The Tour de France often passes through in mid-July, while in winter, Barèges offers some of the best downhill skiing in the Pyrenees.

Côte Basque

With a defined cultural identity, the young and energetic **Basque coast** has fast become the antidote to the characterless glitz of the Riviera. Lively **Biarritz** has become the country's surf capital, while **Bayonne**, the capital of French Basque country, has a great *fête* at the start of August and an excellent cultural museum and art gallery.

BIARRITZ

A former Viking whaling settlement, **BIARRITZ** became famous in the

PELOTE BASQUE

The fastest ball game in the world, *pelote* (or *pilota* in Basque) consists, in essence, of propelling a ball (*pelote*) against a wall (*fronton*) so that your opponent cannot return it. There are over twenty modalities with different courts, rackets and balls, but the three main ways to play are: bare-handed *(main nue)*, with a wooden bat *(paleta)* and, in the fastest version, slung from a wicker claw *(cesta-punta or jai alai)*, in which the pelote has reached speeds of over 300km/hr. The biggest tournaments in Biarritz – the Open in July and the Gant d'Or in August, played in the parc Mazon, on av Joffre and the Plaza Berri on av Foch – are great spectacles, often with the crowd singing the score after every point. If you fancy trying it out yourself, head to the centre sportif El Hogar d'Anglet (ⓣ05.59.57.10.90; bus #72 to El Hogar from Hotel de Ville in Bayonne), which runs free introductory classes.

nineteenth century when Empress Eugénie started coming here with the last French Emperor, Napoleon III. He built her a seaside palace in 1855 and an impressive list of kings, queens and tsars followed, bringing *belle époque* and Art Deco grandeur to the resort. Surfing arrived here fifty years ago and today Biarritz is the undisputed surf capital of Europe, hosting the prestigious week-long Surf Festival in July, which includes a longboard competition and nightly parties on the Côte des Basques beach.

What to see and do

The town's beaches are the main attraction. The best surfing is found on the long competition beach, **Plage de la Côte des Basques**, to the south, though the busy, central Grande Plage offers better scope for showing off on a surf board and is more comfortable for relaxing on. Those less interested in surfing should try the intimate **Port-Vieux** beach for a calmer swim. On a rainy day, the **Musée de la Mer** (July & Aug daily 9.30am–midnight; Sept–June daily 9.30am–7pm; Nov–March Tues–Sun 9.30am–12.30pm & 2–6pm; €7.50), opposite Rocher de la Vierge, has an interesting aquarium taken from the Bay of Biscay, and a rooftop seal pool. **Asiatica**, at 1 rue Guy Petit (Mon–Fri 10.30am–7pm, Sat & Sun 2–8pm; €7), uphill and left off avenue Foch, houses one of Europe's most important collections of oriental art.

Arrival and information

Train The station lies 3km from the centre in La Négresse. Buses #2 and the "navette des plages" (see opposite) connect it to square d'Ixelles.
Air Aérodrome Biarritz-Bayonne-Anglet is ten minutes from av Foch in the town centre by bus #6.
Tourist office Square d'Ixelles (July & Aug daily 9am–7pm; Sept–June Mon–Sat 9–6pm, Sun 10am–2pm; ⓣ05.59.22.37.10, ⓦwww.biarritz.fr); accommodation booking service and Internet access.
Scooter Sobilo, 24 rue Peyroloubilh (ⓣ05.59.24.94.47) rents scooters and beach buggies; ID and credit card required.

Accommodation

Le Baron de Biarritz 13 av du Maréchal Joffre ⓣ05.59.22.08.22. Small but reasonable rooms, and rather eccentric service at this hotel just south of the centre, which also has an affordable Vietnamese restaurant. ❺
Camping de Parme rte de l'Aviation ⓣ05.59.23.00.23 ⓦwww.campingdeparme.com. Near to Anglet train station, this bustling campsite has well-spaced pitches (though not always shaded), good swimming and sports facilities, plenty of showers and a fun bar. ❷
FUAJ Biarritz 8 rue Chiquito de Cambo ⓣ05.59.41.76.00, ⓦwww.fuaj.org. Just 1.5km from the beach and close to the station and the lake, this comfortable, award-winning hostel has two- to four-bed dorms, rents out bicycles and has some good deals on surf lessons. ❷
Maïtagaria 34 av Carnot ⓣ05.59.24.26.65,

Ⓦ www.hotel-maitagaria.com. Central, family-run hotel with clean, tasteful en-suite rooms and free wireless. Unlike most places in town, its prices don't go up drastically during the summer, and there is a great open fire in winter. ❼

Le Petit Hotel 11 rue Gardères Ⓣ 05.59.24.87.00, Ⓦ www.petithotel-biarritz.com. Bright, colourful rooms literally a stone's throw from the beach, with discounts for those aged under 26 (except July–Aug). ❼

Eating and drinking

Blue Cargo av d'Ilbarritz, Bidart Ⓣ 05.59.23.54.87. This open-air beach café is a great place to watch the sunset. At night, the terrace and the beach become the dance floor, popular with young surfers. Open April–Sept daily 11am–2am; to get here take the beach bus to Boulogne.

Le Caveau 4 rue Gambetta Ⓣ 05.59.24.16.17. This fun gay-friendly club is the best in town. Get there before midnight to avoid the €10 cover charge.

Les Halles Pl Sobradiel Ⓣ 05.59.34.52.02. Most towns have a good *halles* (covered food market) but this one is excellent. Go for breakfast, a picnic lunch or to indulge in a *gateau Basque* (jam or custard filled cake).

Bar Jean 5 rue des Halles Ⓣ 05.59.24.41.00. Don't miss out on this local tapas favourite, which also does a well priced set menu for €17; tapas €6, sangria €3.

Sideria Hernani 29 av Maréchal Joffre Ⓣ 05.59.23.01.01. Heavy wooden tables, barrels and local warmth accompany excellent Basque cuisine and cider. The *Côte de Boeuf* (€17) is huge but well worth it.

Le Surfing 9 bld du Prince-de-Galles Ⓣ 05.59.24.78.72. Grills and seafood for under €10 in this laid-back restaurant, which is decorated with antique surf boards.

Moving on

Train Bayonne for connections to Spain(14 daily; 15–30min); Paris (5 daily, connect in Bayonne; 5hr–6hr 15min).

Bus Bus #1 from square d'Ixelles and #2 from outside the casino both go to Bayonne; in July and August, the "navette des plages" (beach bus) covers all the beaches from Anglet to Ilbarritz, departing from outside the casino, where the "bus de nuit" (night bus) departs every fifty minutes between 10pm and 5am going to station and the Hotel de Ville in Bayonne. See Ⓦ www.bus-stab.com for further information.

BAYONNE

Capital of the French Basque country and home of the bayonet, **BAYONNE** lies 6km inland at the junction of the Nive and Adour rivers. Having escaped the worst effects of mass tourism, it remains a cheerful and pretty town, with the shutters on the older half-timbered houses painted in the distinctive Basque tones of green and rust-red.

What to see and do

The town's two medieval quarters line the banks of the Nive, whose quays here are home to many bars and restaurants. Grand Bayonne on the west bank is the administrative and commercial centre, while Petit Bayonne, to the east, has a more bohemian feel and is full of places to eat and drink.

Petit Bayonne

On **Quai des Corsaires,** along the Nive's east bank, stands the **Musée Basque** (Tues–Sun: April–Oct 10am–6.30pm; Nov–March 10am–12.30pm & 2–6pm; €5.50/€3 students), which provides a comprehensive overview of modern Basque culture. The city's second museum, **Musée Bonnat**, rue Jacques Laffitte (daily except Tues: May–Oct 10am–6.30pm; Nov–April 10am–12.30pm & 2–6pm; €5.50, €9 joint ticket with

FÉRIA

Wear red, green and white for the *Fête de Bayonne* in the first week of August, a smaller, less tourist-dominated version of Pamplona's San Fermin (see p.1103). You can't run with the bulls at this festival but try to catch the waking of King Léon daily at midday, when drunken crowds gather outside the Hôtel de Ville and sing a song imploring him to get out of bed ("debout, debout, debout Léon!") until the giant puppet king comes out onto the balcony. Ⓦ www.fetes.bayonne.fr

Musée Basque), is an unexpected treasury of art, including works by Goya, El Greco, Rubens and Degas.

Grand Bayonne

The **Cathédrale Ste-Marie**, across the Nive, looks best from a distance, its twin spires rising with airy grace above the houses; the **cloister** (Sun–Fri 9.30am–12.30pm & 2–5pm; free) rewards a visit with a good view of the stained glass and buttresses. Near here are a number of chocolateries and the small but interesting **Choco-musée de Puyodebat** on rue d'Espagne (daily 10.30am–noon & 4.30–6pm; free), which introduces the local relevance and techniques of chocolate-making. Jewish chocolatiers fled the Spanish Inquisition and came to Bayonne carrying a devilish brew, hot chocolate. Frowned on by the church for its aphrodisiac qualities, it nonetheless spread throughout France. Cazenave (below) is the only place to try it.

Arrival and information

Train Bayonne's train station is in the St-Esprit quarter on the opposite bank of the Adour from the centre, ten minutes' walk over the Pont St-Esprit.
Tourist office Take rue Bernède from the Hôtel de Ville, to place des Basques (Mon–Sat 7/9am–6/7pm; July & Aug also Sun 10am–1pm; Ⓣ 05.59.46.01.46, Ⓦ www.bayonne-tourisme.com); they have an excellent scheme that lends bikes for free.
Internet *CyberNetCafé*, place de la République.

Accommodation

Hôtel des Basques 4 rue des Lisses Ⓣ 05.59.59.08.02. Charmingly dilapidated hotel with basic rooms and clean facilities, right in the thick of Petit Bayonne. ❸
Monbar 24 rue Pannecau, Petit Bayonne Ⓣ 05.59.59.26.80. Though lacking a little in character, this quiet family-run hotel has clean and bright en-suite rooms. ❸
Paris Madrid Pl de la Gare Ⓣ 05.59.55.13.98. Peaceful, clean and comfortable en-suite rooms. The owner Patrick speaks fluent English and can provide good advice on the area; there's also an English-language book collection in the TV room. Get in quick before it's demolished in 2010. ❸

Eating and drinking

Cazenave 19 Arceaux du Pont-Neuf. The pick of the chocolatiers; try its famous hot chocolate (known here as *chocolat mousseux*) flavoured with vanilla or cinnamon, or the artisan chocolate bars all made from raw South American cacao.
Café Victor Hugo 1 rue Victor Hugo Ⓣ 05.59.25.62.26. Basque beef and fish and a good vegetarian selection in an ideal location overlooking the Nive and the Adour, although the service isn't great. Two-course menu €12.
Bistrot Ste-Cluque 9 rue Hugues, St-Esprit Ⓣ 05.59.55.82.43. Make sure you try the local cured ham (€7), flavoured with salt from nearby mines, at this jolly bistrot by the station; three-course dinner menu €17.
Salud 63 rue Pannecau Ⓣ 05.59.59.14.49. Family-owned café that does good lunches and cocktails (from €4). At night, the son spins Latino music on the decks.

Moving on

Train Domestic: Bordeaux (8 daily; 3hr–4hr 30min); Hendaye (14 daily; 35min) on the border with Spain, where the Euskotren makes the crossing to St Sébastien (every 30min; 45min); Lourdes (6 daily; 1hr 30min–1hr 50min); Paris (6 daily; 4hr 45min–5hr 15min); Toulouse (6 daily; 3hr 10–4hr 40mins).

Languedoc and Roussillon

Languedoc is more an idea than a geographical entity. The modern region only covers a mere fraction of the lands that once stretched south from Bordeaux and **Lyon** into **Spain** and northwest **Italy**, where, until the middle ages, the *langue d'Oc* was spoken. The influence of the Cathars, a heretical religious sect, can be seen in castles and fortified towns throughout the region, including at **Carcassonne**. The old Roman town of **Nîmes** is a good place to start exploring, as is young, partying **Montpellier**. The

PONT DU GARD

This stunning vestige of the 50km aqueduct built in the first century AD to carry spring water from Uzès to Nîmes is a poignant memorial to the hubris of Roman civilization. It nestles peacefully in the valley of the Gardon river; children play in the fresh water beneath and couples disappear up the shady banks. Tours are run from the informative museum on the left side of the valley; to get there, take a bus from Nîmes to Uzès, where six *navettes* run to the Pont each day; bring a swimsuit, walking shoes and a picnic. ⓦwww.ot-pontdugard.com

nearby beaches are largely windswept and cut off from their hinterland by marshy lakes. To the south, **Roussillon**, or French Catalonia, maintains much of its former Catalan identity, though there is little support nowadays for reunification with Spanish Catalunya, to which it was joined until the seventeenth century. The hills and valleys here provide opportunities for some fine walking, and the coast improves along the colourful and largely unspoiled **Côte Vermeille**, below the region's likeable main town, **Perpignan**.

NÎMES

NÎMES is intrinsically linked to two things: ancient Rome – whose influence is manifest in some of the most extensive **Roman remains** in Europe – and denim, a word corrupted from *de Nîmes*. First manufactured as *serge* in the city's textile mills, **denim** was exported to the USA to clothe workers, where a certain Mr Levi-Strauss made it world famous.

What to see and do

The old centre of Nîmes spreads northwards from place des Arènes, site of the magnificent first-century **Les Arènes** (daily: March–Oct 9am–5/6/7pm; Nov–Feb 9.30am–4.30pm; €7.70), the best-preserved Roman arena in the world. Turned into a fortress by the Visigoths while the Roman Empire crumbled, it went on to became a huge medieval slum before it was fully restored. Now, with a retractable roof, it hosts opera, an international summer jazz festival and the high-spirited *Ferías* on Pentecost and the third weekend of September, with bullfights galore. Another Roman survivor can be found northeast along boulevard Victor Hugo – the **Maison Carrée** (daily: March–Oct 9am–6/7/8pm; Nov–Feb 10am–5pm; free), a compact temple built in 5 AD and celebrated for its harmony of proportion. Northeast of Les Arènes along boulevard Amiral-Courbet are the **Musée Archéologique** and the **Musée d'Histoire Naturelle** (Tues–Sun 10am–6pm; free) both of which hold a sizeable collection of Roman artefacts. Further south, the **Musée des Beaux-Arts** on rue Cité Foulc (Tues–Sun 10am–6pm; €4.90) prides itself on a huge Gallo-Roman mosaic showing the *Marriage of Admetus*.

Arrival and information

Train and Bus Nîmes bus and train station is at the end of avenue Feuchères, a five-minute walk southeast from the amphitheatre. Regional buses leave from bays situated out the back.
Air The airport is 8km to the south, accessible by shuttle buses leaving from avenue Feuchères.
Tourist office 6 rue Auguste, by the Maison Carrée (Mon–Sat 8.30/9am–7/9pm, Sun 10am–5/6pm; ⓣ04.66.58.38.00, ⓦwww.ot-nimes.fr); buy the monument and museum pass (€10.20) here, which gives access to the town's attractions for three days.
Internet *Netgames*, place de la Maison Carrée.

Accommodation

Cat 22 bd Amiral-Courbet ⓣ04.66.67.22.85. Well positioned off pl du Grand Temple, this charming little hotel's well-decorated and clean rooms with fans are the best value in town; ❸
Central 2 place du Château ⓣ04.66.67.22.85,

Ⓦ www.hotel-central.org. The clean blue and white décor of this comfortable hotel is a little nautical. Rooms have fans and wifi. ❹
Domaine de la Bastide route de Générac Ⓣ 04.66.62.05.82. 5km south of the centre this passable, shady campsite has a bar, restaurant and rents out barbecues. Be warned, only one of the three shower blocks is heated. Take bus D from outside the station to stade de la Bastide. ❷
FUAJ Nimes 257 chemin de l'Auberge de Jeunesse, Cigale Ⓣ 04.66.68.03.20. Set in a beautiful arboretum, in the hills 2km west of Nîmes, this friendly hostel offers well kept two-, four- or six-bed dorms and camping. Good cooking facilities and inexpensive bicycle and scooter rental. Take bus I from the station to "Stade". Dorms ❷, camping ❶

Eating and drinking

L'Ancient Théatre 4 rue Racine Ⓣ 04.66.21.30.75. An intimate and romantic spot for tasty Mediterranean dishes (mainly fish) with three-course set menus from €16.
Mogador 2 place du Marché. A cheap and friendly café, with a terrace on the square that catches the afternoon sun, serving tasty savoury tarts and other French dishes; *plat du jour* €9.
O'Flaherty's 21 bd de l'Admiral-Courbet. Irish pub, serving *boeuf à la Guinness*, beautiful home-smoked salmon (€6) and a wide selection of whiskey to live country and rock music.
La Truye qui Filhe 9 rue Fresque. Food has been served at this address since the fourteenth century – the beautiful building is now home to a dirt cheap self-service canteen providing different hearty hot dishes every day. Two-course menu and wine €8.30.
Les 3 Maures 10 bd des Arènes. Tapas is served from lunch until midnight in this bull and rugby obsessed bar that really livens up in the evening with good DJs. Open until 2am, no lunch Sun.

Moving on

Train Arles (6 daily; 25min); Avignon (16 daily; 30min); Clermont-Ferrand (3 daily; 5hr); Lyon (9 daily; 1hr 20min); Marseille (14 daily; 50min–1hr 20min); Montpellier (frequent; 30min); Nice (6 daily, via Marseille; 4–5hr); Paris (11 daily; 3hr); Perpignan (13 daily; 2hr 10min–2hr 40min).

MONTPELLIER

MONTPELLIER is a vibrant city, renowned for its ancient university, once attended by such luminaries as Petrarch and Rabelais. Ruled over by the **Kings of Mallorca** for almost a hundred and fifty years during the Middle Ages, today it's the regional capital of Languedoc-Roussillon and a cosmopolitan, youthful place.

What to see and do

At the town's hub is **place de la Comédie**, a grand oval square paved with cream-coloured marble and surrounded by cafés. The **Opéra**, an ornate nineteenth-century theatre, presides over one end, while the other end leads onto the pleasant Champs de Mars park. Nearby, the much-vaunted **Musée Fabre** (Tues, Thurs, Fri & Sun 10am–6pm, Wed 1pm–9pm, Sat 11am–6pm; €6) has finally reopened its art collection. Behind the Opéra lie the tangled, hilly lanes of Montpellier's **old quarter**, full of seventeenth- and eighteenth-century mansions and small museums. One of the more interesting is the **Musée Languedocien**, 7 rue Jacques-Coeur (Mon–Sat: July–August 3-6pm; Sept–June 2.30–5.30pm; €6), which houses an eclectic display spanning prehistory to the eighteenth century, from China to Rome, including some stunning Ming vases. At the end of rue Foch, on the western edge of town, are the formal gardens of the Promenade de Peyrou. The **Jardin des Plantes** (Tues–Sun noon–6/8pm; free), just north of here, with its alleys of exotic trees, is France's oldest botanical garden, founded in 1593.

Arrival and information

Train and Bus The train and bus stations are on the southern edge of town, a short walk down rue de Maguelone from the centre.
Air The airport is 8km to the west of Montpellier, by the beaches, connected to the city by *navettes* (€4.80, including one bus or tram connection in town).
Tourist office The main branch, by place de la Comédie (Mon–Fri 9am–6.30pm, Sat 10am–6.30pm, Sun 10am–1pm & 2–5.30pm; Ⓣ 04.67.60.60.60, Ⓦ www.ot-montpellier.fr) books accomodation and sells tickets for events; there's

MONTPELLIER MARKETS

"*Allez-allez-allez*!" is the call of Montpellier's stall holders in the many markets around the town. Here's three of the best: **Les Halles Jacques-Coeur** (daily 8am–8pm/2pm Sun) opposite the tram on bd Antigone has quality home-made food; across the *place*, the **Marché Paysan** (Sun 9.30am–1.30pm) sells all local produce; **Plan-Cabanes**, at Faubourg du Courreau and Gambetta (daily 7.30am–1.30pm) is the most fun – here you can eat Arab and African cuisine for peanuts.

also a desk in the train station during July and August.

Internet *Hall the net*, 6 rue des clos René.

Accommodation

Les Étuves 24 rue des Étuves ⓣ04.67.60.78.19, ⓦwww.hoteldesetuves.fr. A small family run hotel, full of belle époque touches. The spotless, white rooms have en-suite showers or baths. ❹

Les Fauvettes 8 rue Bonnard ⓣ04.67.65.73.30. The cheapest hotel in town offers clean doubles with toilets in a peaceful little house beyond the park, five minutes' walk from the centre. ❸

FUAJ Montpellier rue des Écoles-Laïques ⓣ04.67.60.32.22. Housed in an characterful building in the old town, this welcoming hostel has comfy bunks and provides breakfast, table football and pool, but no cooking facilities. ❷

TREAT YOURSELF

Hôtel du Parc 8 rue Achille-Bégé ⓣ04.67.41.16.49, ⓦwww.hotelduparc-Montpellier.com. Tasteful and individually decorated rooms in luxurious eighteenth-century manors don't often come this cheap. All rooms equipped with minibars, free wifi and en-suite bathrooms with hair-dryers; those on the ground floor have little terraces. ❺

Eating and drinking

Barberousse 6 rue Boussaires. A small and packed *taverne* that offers fifty potent, flavoured rums (€4). Great for pre-club drinking.

Bistrot d'Alco 4 rue Bonnier-d'Alco ⓣ04.67.63.12.89. Gorgeous Provençal cuisine is served in this friendly bistro, including roast camembert with sliced apple to dip in it; two courses €14, three courses €16.

Chez Doumé 5 rue des Teissiers ⓣ04.67.60.48.76. A friendly place where you can gorge on the rich delights of *andouillette* (sausage made from the colon and stomach of a pig; €8). Simple, meat-filled three-course menus cost €11 for lunch or €14 for dinner.

La Dune allée de la Plage ⓣ04.67.56.43.43. A beachside club that might have washed up from Ibiza: big screens, concrete casing and heaving with young people.

Sens 2 rue de l'Herberie ⓣ04.67.54.31.79. Brilliant sandwiches, *carpaccio*, salads, soups and other home-made food served up in this stylish café; meal deals (sandwich, soup, dessert and drink) for €10.

Moving on

Train Domestic: Avignon (12 daily; 1hr); Barcelona (4 daily, 2 via Port-Bou; 4hr 20min–7hr); Carcassonne (9 daily; 1hr 25min–1hr 45min); Marseille (10 daily; 1hr 30min–2hr 20min); Nîmes (frequent; 30min); Paris (12 daily; 3hr 30min); Perpignan (16 daily; 1hr 30min–2hr).

CARCASSONNE

The fairy-tale aspect of **CARCASSONNE'S** old town (*la Cité*), was the inspiration for the castle in Walt Disney's *Sleeping Beauty*. It was rescued from ruin in 1844 by Viollet-le-Duc, and his rather romantic restoration has been furiously debated ever since. Unsurprisingly, it's become a real tourist trap, with its narrow lanes lined with innumerable souvenir shops and regularly crammed with hordes of day-trippers.

What to see and do

There's no charge for admission to the main part of the Cité, or the grassy *lices* (moat) between the walls. However, to see the inner fortress of the **Château Comtal** (daily 9.30am–5/6.30pm; €7.50), with its small **museum** of medieval sculpture, and to walk along the walls, you have to join one of the half-hourly guided tours from the ticket office. Opposite the Château on chemin des Anglais, the **Musée Memoires du Moyen Âge** (mid-Jan to mid-Dec daily 10am–7pm; €5) provides an informative and accessible history of the medieval town, conveyed through videos and detailed models. In addition to wandering the town's narrow streets, don't miss the beautiful, thirteenth century church of **St-Nazaire** (daily 9–11.45am & 1.45–5/6pm; free) at the end of rue St-Louis.

Arrival and information

Train The station is on the northern edge of the new town, at the end of ave du Maréchal Joffre – take bus #2 to get to la Cité.

Tourist office Located in the turret of the eastern entrance to *la Cité,* the Porte Narbonnaise (July–Aug daily 9am–7pm; Sept–June daily 9am–5pm; Ⓣ04.68.10.24.30, Ⓦwww.carcassonne-tourisme.com); well stocked with leaflets and tour information.

Accommodation

Astoria 53 rue Jean Bringer Ⓣ04.68.25.31.38, Ⓦwww.astoriacarcassonne.com. Proximity to the station and price are the main selling points of this clean, basic hotel. ❹

Campéole la Cité rte St-Hilaire Ⓣ04.68.25.11.77. This campsite has a well-shaded riverside location and good sporting facilities, less than ten minutes' walk from the Cité. ❷

FUAJ Carcassone rue du Vicomte-Trencavel Ⓣ04.68.25.23.16, Ⓦwww.fuaj.org. A great budget place with a real community feel in the middle of the old town. The price includes breakfast, and there's also table tennis, themed nights in the bar, bike rental and daily trips to the surrounding countryside. ❷

Le Pont-Vieux 32 rue Trivalle Ⓣ04.68.25.24.99, Ⓦwww.hoteldupontvieux.com. Pleasant hotel with comfortable, air-conditioned rooms. There are great views of the old town from the roof terrace, and rooms 6 and 11 open onto the garden. Buffet breakfast included. ❼

Eating and drinking

Blanche de Castille 21 rue Cros Mayrevieille. This outstanding patisserie has a peaceful patio at the back, where you can enjoy omelettes, salads and tarts. Don't leave without a jar of their delicious home-made jam (€4)

La Courtine 4 pl Marcou. The best choice in this bar-lined square serves refreshingly different dishes, such as half-lobster in tomato salsa, and local wine (the young owner's family run a vineyard) for only €10.

Jardin de la Tour 11 rue porte de l'Aude Ⓣ04.68.25.71.24. Hidden up against the walls of the cité, this restaurant has a charming terrace on which to enjoy *cassoulet* to live Jazz and enjoy views across the old town; book ahead in summer. Three-course menu €22.

Bar à Vins 6 rue du Plô, Ⓦwww.myspace.com/lebarvins. This unconventional wine bar has a largely regional cellar, but also good cocktails and tapas (€4), and hosts a good mix of live music and DJs. Glass of house red (€2.30); they do great breakfasts too – waffle & *vin chaud* €5.

Moving on

Train Domestic: Montpellier (9 daily 1hr 25min–1hr 45min); Nice (6 daily, via Marseille; 4–5hr); Paris (11 daily; 3hr); Perpignan (13 daily, via Narbonne; 1hr 30min–2hr); Toulouse (18 daily; 45min–1hr 15min)

International: Barcelona (4 daily, 2 via Narbonne; 4hr–6hr 30min)

MEDIEVAL STYLE

The jostling crowds in *la Cité* can bring out the warrior in anyone. If you fancy a duel, **Saint Louis** on rue Cros Mayrevieille, sells €2 plastic swords, or €5 wooden ones for the discerning swordfighter. Next door, in **L'Éperon Medieval**, you can even pick up a replica broadsword for a hefty €80, while high-quality tunics can be found in the shop of the amusing but undeniably tacky **Musée Medieval**, by porte de l'Aude.

PERPIGNAN

This far south, climate and geography alone ensure a palpable Spanish influence, but **PERPIGNAN** is actually Spanish in origin and home to the descendants of refugees from the Spanish Civil War. This southern atmosphere is intensified by its sizeable North African community, including Arabs and French settlers repatriated after Algerian independence in 1962. It's a cheerful city, with Roussillon's red and yellow striped flag atop many a building, and makes an ideal stop-off en route to Spain or Andorra.

What to see and do

The centre of **Perpignan** is marked by the palm trees and smart cafés of **place Arago.** From here rue d'Alsace-Lorraine and rue de la Loge lead past the massive iron gates of the classical **Hôtel de Ville** to the tiny **place de la Loge**, the focus of the renovated old heart of the city. Just north up rue Louis-Blanc is one of the city's few remaining fortifications, the crenellated fourteenth-century gate of **Le Castillet**, now home to the **Casa Païral**, a fascinating museum of Roussillon's Catalan folk culture (daily except Tues 10/11am–6.30pm; €4). South past place Rigaud and place des Esplanades, which crowns the hill that dominates the southern part of the old town, is the **Palais des Rois de Majorque** (June–Sept, 10am–6pm, rest of the year 9am-5pm; €4), a two-storey palace with a great, arcaded courtyard dating from the late thirteenth century.

Arrival and information

Train The station is a ten-minute walk from the city centre.
Bus The bus station is by Pont Arago, on avenue Général-Leclerc.
Tourist office In the Palais des Congrès at the end of boulevard Wilson (Mon–Sat 9am–6/7pm, Sun 9/10–noon/4pm; ⓣ04.68.66.30.30, ⓦwww.perpignantourisme.com).

COLLIOURE AND THE CÔTE VERMEILLE

The Vermilion Coast is named for its richly coloured rocks, which attracted artists such as Picasso, Dali and Matisse. The latter's 1905-6 paintings of Collioure saw the birth of Fauvism, the forerunner to Cubism. Aside from these colourful rocks, the coast is also home to some lovely beaches and charming fishing towns. Over ten trains a day run between Perpignan and Collioure (25mins). ⓦwww.collioure.com

Accommodation

Avenir 11 rue de l'Avenir ⓣ04.68.34.20.30, ⓦwww.avenirhotel.fr. There's plenty of cheap options by the station but this one is the best; the clean rooms have comfortable beds and some lead onto a large balcony. ❸
Le Catalan rte de Bompas ⓣ04.68.63.16.92, ⓦwww.camping-catalan.com. A lively campsite 5km from the centre, with washing machines, a swimming pool and frequent pétanque competitions. Ask for shade as not all pitches have it. ❶
FUAJ Perpignon Parc de la Pépinière ⓣ04.68.34.63.32. This old hostel, situated by the river has dorms with four to eight beds and cooking facilities. Light sleepers be warned – it's right next to the railway tracks. ❷
Hotel de la Loge 1 rue Fabriques-Nabot ⓣ04.68.34.41.02; ⓦwww.hoteldelaloge.fr. A beautiful sixteenth-century house just off the lively place de la Loge whose charming rooms all have en-suite showers and toilets. ❺

Eating and drinking

Bodega du Castillet 13 rue Fabriques-Couberts. Traditional Catalan seafood including anchovies in vinegar and grilled octopus, just around the corner from pl de la Loge. Mains €5–€11.
Espi 43 quai Vauban. Delicious breakfasts, home-made ice cream (€2) and soft macaroons (€1) are amougst the many treats in this large and famous café-patisserie overlooking the Basse river.
Trois Soeurs 2 rue Fontfroide. A scenic spot opposite the cathedral for sangria (€3); the inventive, tapas-based food is quite steep but the

pear and saffron gratin (€6.50) is excellent.
Républic Café pl de la République. There is a relaxed, low-key, house vibe in this reasonably priced bar (also known as the Rep), with outdoor seating in sunny weather. Open from 3 to 10.30pm in summer and 5pm to 2am in winter; *demi pression* €2.80.

Moving on

Train Domestic: Carcassonne (13 daily, via Narbonne 1hr 30min–2hr); Montpellier (16 daily; 1hr 30min–2hr); Paris (5 daily; 5 hr–9hr 20min); Toulouse (16 daily; 1hr 30min–2hr).
International**:** Barcelona (5 daily, 3 via Port Bou; 2hr 50min–5hr).

The Massif Central

Thickly forested and cut into by numerous rivers and lakes, the **Massif Central** occupies a huge part of central France and is geologically the oldest part of the country, and culturally one of the most firmly rooted in the past. The heart of the region is the **Auvergne**, a wild, inaccessible, almost lunar, landscape dotted with extinct volcanic peaks known as *puys*. To the southeast are the gentler wooded hills of the **Cévennes** that form part of the **Parc National des Cévennes**. Only a handful of towns have gained a foothold in this rugged terrain: **Le Puy**, spiked with jagged pinnacles of lava, is the most compelling with its majestic cathedral, while the youthful provincial capital, **Clermont-Ferrand** at its best out of the summer season, when its large student population is in town.

CLERMONT-FERRAND

CLERMONT-FERRAND is an incongruous capital for rustic Auvergne. The lively, youthful city houses a major university and is best known as a manufacturing city, long home to Michelin and the French umbrella industry. However, it has a pretty, well-preserved historic centre and makes a good base for exploring the Massif and the nearby **Puy de Dôme.**

What to see and do

Clermont's most immediate feature is its *ville-noire* aspect – so-called for the local black volcanic rock used in many of its buildings. The dark and soaring **Cathédrale Notre-Dame de L'Assomption**, on place Victoire, was begun in 1248 and completed in the nineteenth century by Carcassonne's restoration architect Viollet-le-Duc. Inside you can wonder at the slenderness of its high pillars and at its pink stained-glass windows before climbing the spiral stairscase of the **Tour de la Bayette** (daily 9–11.15am & 2–6pm; €1.50) for fine city panoramas. On the southwestern edge of old Clermont, the huge and soulless **place de Jaude** is the hub of the city and the main shopping area. In the centre, a rousing statue of the mythologised Gallic chieftain Vercingétorix, who in 52 BC led his people to their only victory over Julius Caesar, looks fatefully over his shoulder as he charges towards the shopping complex. East of place de Jaude, the **Musée Bargoin**, 45 rue Ballainvilliers (Tues–Sat 10am–noon & 1–5pm, Sun 2–7pm; closed Nov–Dec; free), has some especially good Gallo-Roman collections, alongside detailed Asian textiles.

Arrival and information

Train The station is on avenue de l'URSS, fifteen minutes' walk east of the centre and connected by frequent buses to place de Jaude.
Tourist office place de la Victoire (May–Sept Mon–Fri 9am–7pm, Sat & Sun 10am–7pm; Oct–April Mon–Fri 9am–6pm, Sat 10am–1pm & 2–6pm, Sun 9.30am–12.30pm & 2–6pm; Ⓣ 04.73.98.65.00, Ⓦ www.clermont-fd.com); particularly good for advice on hiking and mountain biking in the region.
Internet *Cyberfrag*, 3 rue de la Boucherie.

Accommodation

Foch 22 rue Maréchal-Foch ⓣ04.73.93.48.40, ⓔregina.foch@wanadoo.fr. Central option with a lovely conservatory for breakfast (€6) and clean, no-frills rooms. ❹

Grand Hôtel du Midi 39 av de l'URSS ⓣ04.73.92.44.98, ⓦwww.grandhoteldumidi.com. A good-value hotel by the station with large rooms, all with satellite television and Internet access in the lobby. ❸

Camping Indigo Royat rte de Gravenoire ⓣ04.73.35.97.05, ⓦwww.camping-indigo.com. Excellent campsite with over two hundred pitches well spread across a wooded terrain. The wide range of facilities includes a heated pool, Jacuzzi, tennis courts and a mini-cinema. Closed Nov–March; to get here take bus #41 from central Clermont. ❶

Eating and drinking

Les Augustes 5 rue Sous-les-Augustins ⓦwww.cafe-lecture.org. This superb café serves sandwiches, soups and simple hot food (€8) and has events every night ranging from music to poetry and debate. Daily except Sun 9am–1pm.

15-13 3 rue des Chaussetiers. This *crêperie* has a bewitching setting in the vaulted rooms and secluded courtyard of a sixteenth-century mansion. Try the prawn and rice "crêpe indienne" (€8).

Marché St-Pierre ⓣ04.73.31.27.88. The market is full of great local artisan produce, such as *truffade* (potato pancake), Auvergne blue cheese and sparkling chardonnay. Open daily except Sun 7am–7.30pm, liveliest on Saturdays.

Café Pascal place de la Victoire. Offers excellent-value meat and vegetable *plats du jour* and cheap drinks (cocktails €4). An English-language quiz is held on Wednesdays during term time.

Pyros 3 bld Trudaine. This cocktail place (from €1.50) is the best choice on the boulevard full of bars, boasting a dart board and a wide range of music. Daily 5pm–2am.

Moving on

Train to: Lyon (8 daily; 2hr 20 min); Marseille (6 daily, 5 via Lyon; 4hr 40min–8hr 30min); Nîmes (3 daily; 5hr); Paris (8 daily; 3hr 10 min–3hr 45min); Le Puy (4 daily; 2hr 20 min–2hr 45min); Toulouse (4 daily; 6hr–8hr 20min).

LE PUY-EN-VELAY

LE PUY sprawls across a broad basin in the mountains, a muddle of red roofs and poles of volcanic rock; both landscape and architecture are completely theatrical. The **Cathedral**, at the top of Mount Corneille, with its small, almost Byzantine cupolas and Romanesque façade, dominates the old town. The Black Virgin inside is a copy of the revered original that was burned during the Revolution; it is paraded through the town on August 15. Other lesser treasures are on display in the sacristy, beyond which is the entrance to the beautiful twelfth-century **cloister** (daily: July & Aug 9am–6.30pm; Sept–June 9am–noon & 2–5/6.30pm; €4.60). The nearby **church of St-Michel** (daily: May–Sept 9am–6.30pm; Oct–April 9.30am–noon & 2–5.30pm; €2.75), at the top of **Rocher d'Aiguilhe**, is an eleventh-century construction that appears to grow out of the rock.

The main bus stop and train station are on place du Maréchal-Leclerc, a fifteen-minute walk from the **Tourist office** on place du Breuil (Sept–June Mon–Sat 8.30am–noon & 1.30–6.15pm, Sun 10am–noon; July & Aug daily 8.30am–7.30pm; ⓣ04.71.09.38.41, ⓦwww.ot-lepuyenvelay.fr). The *Régional*, 36 bd Maréchal Fayolle, (ⓣ04.71.09.37.74; ❸) is a basic hotel attached to a friendly bar, with cheap and comfortable doubles; even cheaper are the old but clean dorms in *Centre Pierre Cardinal*, 9 rue Jules Vallès (ⓣ04.71.05.52.40; closed weekends Oct–March; ❶) which has basic breakfasts (€3) and cooking facilities. The municipal **campsite**, *Bouthézard* (ⓣ04.71.09.55.09; closed Nov to mid-March; ❶), is half an hour's walk north from the station, or take bus #6 from chemin de Roderie. For inexpensive regional **food** and a good cheeseboard, sit out on the beautiful terrace of the *Âme des Poètes*, by the cathedral on rue Séguret, or *La Main à la Pâte*, a *crêperie* at 59 rue Chaussade. There are three **trains** to Lyon daily (2hr 25min) and four to Clermont Ferrand (2hr 20min–2hr 40min).

Rhône Valley and Provence

Provence is held by many as the most irresistible region in France, with attractions that range from the high mountains of the southern **Alps** to the wild plains of the **Camargue**. Yet, apart from the coast, large areas remain remarkably unscathed by development. Its complete integration into France dates only from the nineteenth century and, although the Provençal language is rarely heard, the accent is distinctive even to a foreign ear. The main problem is choosing where to go. Except for the big city delights of **Lyon** – not strictly in Provence but the main gateway for the region – there's not much to detain you before the old papal stronghold of **Avignon**, which also hosts a wonderful summer festival. Deeper into Provence, on the edge of the flamingo-filled lagoons of the **Camargue**, the ancient settlement of **Arles** boasts an impressive Roman legacy.

LYON

LYON, France's third-largest city, became a UNESCO **World Heritage Site** in 1998, one of only six urban sites in the world thus honoured. With a population of more than two million, including over 100,000 university students, the city has a vibrant nightlife and cultural scene, the highlight of which is the summer-long **festival** *Les Nuits de Fourvière*, celebrating theatre, music and dance. Other festivals include the excellent *Nuits Sonores* (May), an intimate music festival, and in winter, *les Nuits Lumière* – named after the Lyonnais fathers of motion pictures, the Lumière brothers.

What to see and do

The city's charms are manifold, not least its gastronomy: there are more restaurants per square metre here than anywhere else on earth. It also has a beautifully preserved old Renaissance quarter and an elegant town centre of grand boulevards and public squares.

Le Presqu'Île

North from Gare de Perrache, the pedestrian rue Victor-Hugo opens out onto the vast **place Bellecour**, which dwarfs even the statue of Louis XIV on horseback. On rue de la Charité, the **Musée des Tissus et Arts Decoratifs** (Tues–Sun 10am–5.30pm; €5; M° Bellecour), has an interesting collection of fabrics, clothes and tapestries dating from ancient Egypt to the present, alongside a collection of period furnishings. Northwest of place Bellecour, on the right bank of the Saône, the quai St-Antoine is lined every morning with a colourful food market; a Sunday book market lies just upriver. Heading north and inland from the river, the centrepiece of **Place des Terreaux** is an imposing nineteenth-century fountain sculpted by Bartholdi, more famously responsible for New York's Statue of Liberty. The square also features the splendidly ornate **Hôtel de Ville**, as well as the **Musée des Beaux-Arts** (daily except Tues 10/10.30am–6pm; €6; M° Hôtel de Ville). This absorbing collection includes ancient Egyptian, Greek and Roman artefacts as well as works by Rubens, Renoir and Picasso.

La Croix Rousse

North of Place des Terreaux, the old silk weavers' district of **La Croix Rousse** has an authentic, creative feel to it. It is still a **working-class** area, but today only twenty or so people work on the computerized looms that are kept in business by the restoration and maintenance of France's palaces and châteaux. You can watch traditional looms in action at **La Maison des Canuts**, 10 rue d'Ivry (Tues–Sat 10am–6.30pm; free; M° Croix Rousse), one block north of place de la Croix Rousse; printed and handpainted

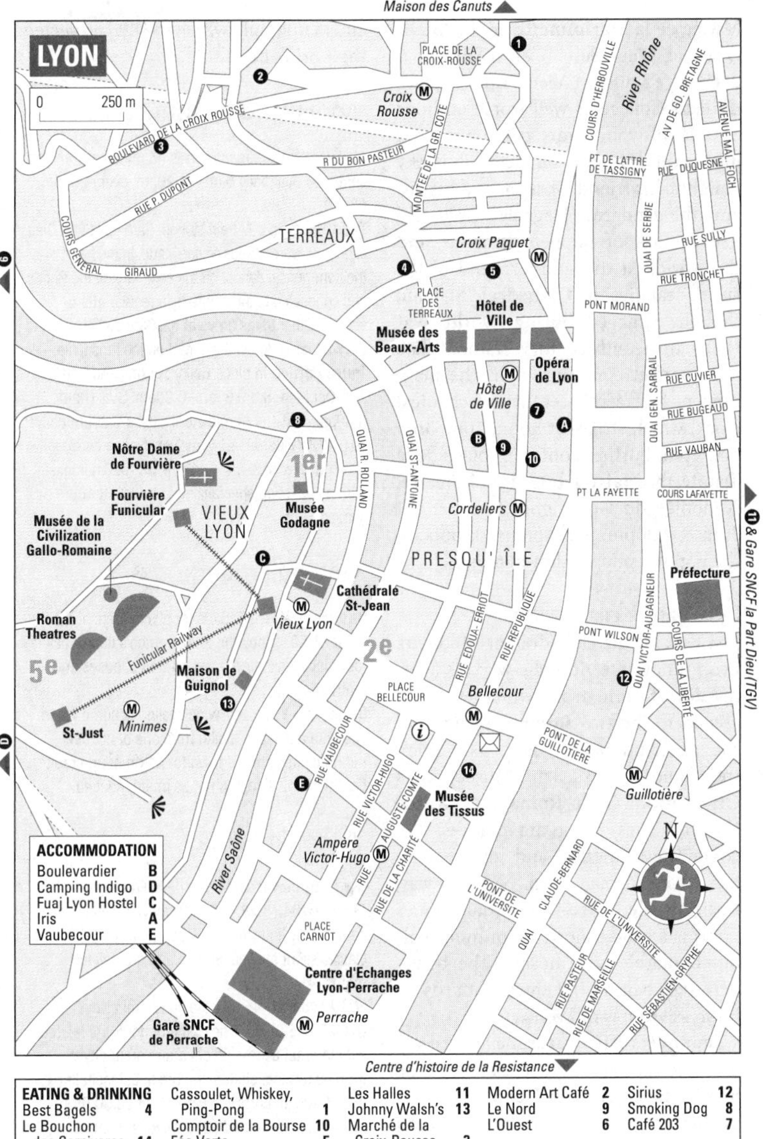

EATING & DRINKING					
Best Bagels 4	Cassoulet, Whiskey, Ping-Pong 1	Les Halles 11	Modern Art Café 2	Sirius 12
Le Bouchon des Carnivores 14	Comptoir de la Bourse 10	Johnny Walsh's 13	Le Nord 9	Smoking Dog 8
	Fée Verte 5	Marché de la Croix-Rousse 3	L'Ouest 6	Café 203 7

silk scarfs and ties are sold in the boutique shop (from €30).

Vieux Lyon

The tangled streets on the left bank of the **Saône** form an attractive muddle of cobbled lanes and Renaissance facades. The famous *traboulés*, or covered alleyways, that run between streets were originally used to transport silk safely through town, later serving as wartime escape routes and hideouts for *la Résistance*. The

Musée de la Marionnette, in the Musée Gadagne (Tues–Sun 10am–12.30pm & 2–6pm; €3.80; M°Vieux-Lyon), place du Petit Collège, is well worth an hour or two of your time, containing not just Lyon's famous puppets – cheeky Guignol, his friend Gnafron and his enemy the gendarme Flageolet – but also a collection of puppets from around the world. At the southern end of the rue St-Jean lies the **Cathédrale St-Jean;** though damaged during World War II, its thirteenth-century stained glass is in perfect condition, as is the magnificent fourteenth-century mechanical clock, which strikes at noon, 2pm, 3pm and 4pm. Further south, off place de la Trinité, the **Maison de Guignol theatre,** 2 montée du Gourgignol (Wed & Sat 3pm & 4.30pm; Sun 3pm; €9), puts on the popular puppet shows in French.

Lyon Romain

Just beyond the cathedral, at M° Vieux Lyon on avenue Adolphe-Max, is a **funicular station**, from which you can ascend to the two **Roman theatres** on rue de l'Antiquaille (daily 9am–7pm; free), and the excellent **Musée de la Civilisation Gallo-Romaine**, 17 rue Cléberg (Tues–Sun 10am–6pm; €3.80), containing mosaics and other artefacts from Roman Lyon. Not far away, **Basilique de Notre-Dame** (daily 8am–7pm) is a gaudy showcase of multi-coloured marble and mosaic. The belvedere (€4) behind the church affords an impressive view of Lyon's rivers.

Reminders of the war are never far away in France and the **Centre d'Histoire de la Résistance et de la Déportation**, 14 av Berthelot (Wed–Sun 9am–5.30pm; €4), tells of the immense courage and ingenuity of the French resistance. It also serves as a poignant memorial to the city's deported Jews. To the southeast of town, the new **Musée Lumière**, 25 rue du Premier-Film (Tues–Sun 11am–6.30pm; €6; M° Monplaisir-Lumière), houses the Lumière brothers' cinematograph, which in 1895 projected the world's first film.

Arrival and information

Air Lyon-St-Exupéry airport is 45 minutes from the centre by bus (daily 6am–11.20pm, every 20min; €8.50).
Train The main TGV train station, Gare de la Part Dieu, is on boulevard Marius-Vivier-Merle, in the heart of the commercial district on the east bank of the Rhône, and connected to the centre by a regular métro service. Other trains arrive at the Gare de Perrache, to the southern edge of the centre on the Presqu'île.
Tourist office In place Bellecour (mid-April to mid-Oct Mon–Sat 9.30am–6.30pm, Sun 10am–5.30pm; mid-Oct to mid-April closes 5.30pm daily; ⓣ04.72.77.69.69, ⓦwww.lyon-france.com).
Internet *Raconte-moi La Terre*, 38 rue Thomassin, with a bookshop specializing in travel literature (closed Sun).

Getting around

Bus-train-Metro Tickets for all city transport cost a flat €1.50, or buy the tourist office's liberté ticket for a day's unlimited travel on trams, buses and métro (€4.20).
Bikes Velo-V is a city-wide cycling scheme where you take and leave a bike from one of about a hundred sites around town for €1 an hour; credit card authorization, but not payment, needed.

Accommodation

Boulevardier 5 rue de la Fromagerie ⓣ04.78.28.48.22, ⓦwww.leboulevardier.com. A new hotel with a pleasant bar that screens classic silent movies. Simple and great value rooms. ❺
FUAJ Lyon 41–45 montée du Chemin Neuf ⓣ04.78.15.05.50. One of the better FUAJ hostels, with Internet access, kitchen and great city views from its terrace; sheets and breakfast included. ❷
Iris 36 rue de l'Arbre Sec ⓣ04.78.28.00.95. Individually decorated and spacious rooms at this hotel, which is the best choice for location. ❹
Camping Indigo Lyon Porte de Lyon ⓣ04.78.35.64.55, ⓦwww.camping-lyon.com. The closest campsite, with a bar and restaurant with Internet terminals, and a summer swimming pool. Ten minutes by bus #89 from the bus station in Gare de Vaise, north of the city. ❶
Vaubecour 28 rue Vaubecour ⓣ04.78.37.44.91. An old hotel with simple but clean rooms and an

TREAT YOURSELF

Paul Bocuse is arguably the greatest French chef alive today. One of the pioneers of *nouvelle cuisine* and the architect behind Lyon's rise in culinary status, he was awarded the Legion of Honour on the back of his truffle soup. His four *brasseries* in Lyon – named after compass points – serve food that will delight your senses, at surprisingly accessible prices. The pick are **Rotisserie "le Nord"**, 18 rue Neuve (ⓣ04.72.10.69.69), which serves traditional French cuisine such as onion soup (€6.90) and steak *tartare* (€14.50); and the newest addition, **Brasserie "l'Ouest"**, 1 quai du Commerce (ⓣ04.37.64.64.64), specializing in coastal cuisine – try the delicious crab and saffron soup (€11.80), followed by the Norwegian fish stew (€18.10). ⓦwww.bocuse.fr

enthusiastic welcome. Very handy for Gare de Perrache and going out in the old town. ❹

Eating

Best Bagels pl Robatel ⓣ04.78.27.65.61. This café lives up to its name – try the pepper-filled "spicy Louisiana". The attached shop sells a good range of American food brands, from Oreos to Dr Pepper. Bagel, crisps, donut and drink €8.

Le Bouchon des Carnivores 8 rue des Marroniers ⓣ04.78.42.97.69. Decorated with paintings, photos and models of bulls, this is one of the best places to try Lyon's meaty cuisine. The speciality is *Boeuf Charolais* – tender steaks from cows reared near the local village of Charolles. Three-course menu €16.

Cassoulet, Whiskey, Ping-pong 4ter rue de Belfont ⓣ04.78.27.19.79. Apart from offering what it says on the sign – the owner's three favourite things – this little bar has good jazz, cheap beer and wine and a great atmosphere. *Cassoulet* €9, whiskey from €2.

Les Halles 102 cours Lafayette. Lyon's covered market is full of high quality treats, including a number of *bars à huîtres* (oyster bars; six oysters €5). Tues–Sat 7am–noon & 3–7pm, Sun 7am–noon.

Marché de la Croix Rousse bld de la Croix Rousse. A huge and busy market where you can get great-value rotisserie chicken and roast potato lunches (€4); open Tues–Sun 7am–1pm.

Café 203 9 rue du Garet. This delightful café and deli attracts a young crowd and offers outstanding hot *tagines*, savoury tarts and stews for very reasonable prices (two-course menu and glass of wine €9). Free Internet also available.

Drinking and nightlife

Comptoir de la Bourse 33 rue de la Bourse. Over one hundred costly but award-winning cocktails (€8.50) served up in this lavish little bar in the centre; try the excellent White Russian.

La Fée Verte 4 rue Pizay. A small dedicated absinthe bar where DJs play accessible hip-hop and electro. Absinthe €2.70.

Johnny Walsh's 56 rue St Georges ⓣ04.78.42.98.76. This brilliant Irish pub in the old town (Guinness €4.50) never fails to draw a young and fun English and French clientele. Live music on Monday and Tuesdays. Open daily 7pm–3am.

Modern Art Café 65 Bd de la Croix Rousse ⓦwww.modernartcafé.net. Recline on a deckchair or retro leather sofa in this unpretentious bar where the friendly owner organizes art exhibitions and brilliant and original DJs and art exhibitions.

Sirius Berges du Rhône ⓣ04.78.71.78.71. ⓦwww.lesirius.com. Club on an ironclad pirate-style boat that has good live bands and DJs in two rooms. Good rum punch (€3) to swig while you jig.

The Smoking Dog 16 rue Lainière ⓣ04.78.28.38.27. There's always lots going on in this friendly English pub (pint of ale €4), from poker nights to karaoke. Daily 2pm–1am.

Moving on

Train Domestic: Annecy (13 daily; 1hr 50min–2hr 15min); Avignon (frequent; 1hr 5min–2hr 45min); Chamonix (5 daily, via St Gervais; 3hr 50min–5hr); Dijon (17 daily; 1hr 40min–2hr 45min); Geneva (13 daily; 1hr 45min–2hr 30min); Grenoble (frequent; 1hr–2hr 10min); Marseille (frequent; 1hr 45min–3hr 45min); Paris (frequent; 1hr 50min–2hr 10min). International: Turin (via Porto Susa; 2 daily, 4–5hr).

AVIGNON

AVIGNON, great city of the popes and for centuries one of the major artistic centres of France, is today one of the country's biggest tourist attractions and is always crowded in summer. It's an immaculately preserved medieval town, and it's worth putting up with

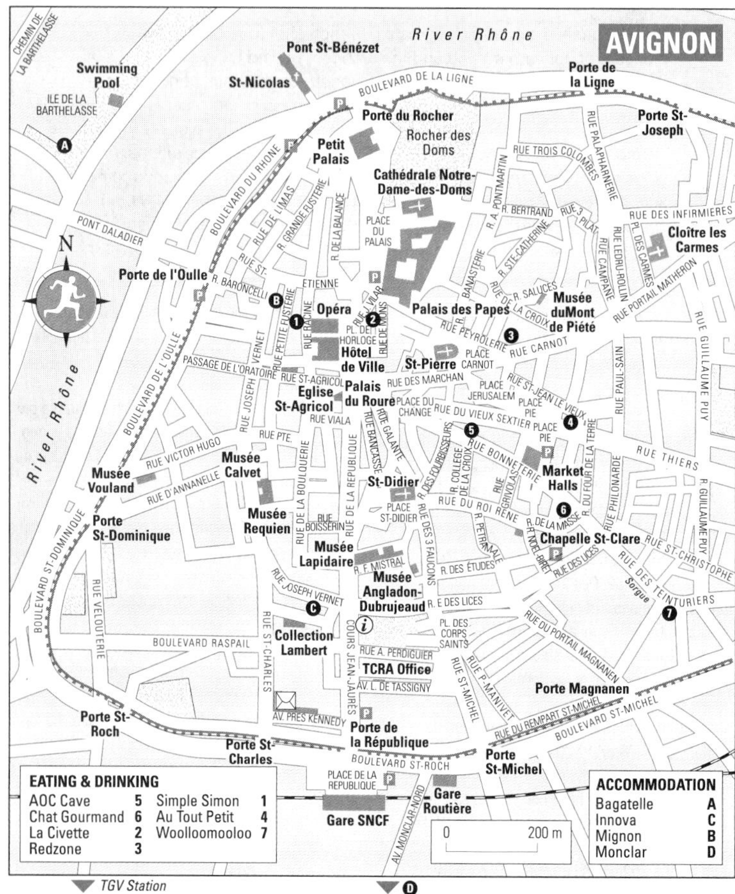

the inevitable queues and camcorder-wielding hordes to enjoy its unique stock of monuments, churches and museums. During the **Avignon festival** in July, it's the only place to be, though as around 200,000 spectators come here for the show, doing any normal sightseeing becomes virtually impossible.

What to see and do

Central **Avignon** is enclosed by thick medieval walls, built by one of the nine popes who based themselves here in the fourteenth century, away from the anarchic feuding and rival popes of Rome. **Place de l'Horloge** is lined with cafés and market stalls on summer evenings, above which towers the enormous **Palais des Papes** (daily: April–June 9am–7pm; July to mid-Sep 9am–8pm; mid-Sep & Oct 9am–7pm; Nov–March 9.30am–5.45pm; €9.50, joint ticket with Pont St-Bénézet €11.50). Save your money though: the denuded interior gives little indication of the richness of the papal court, although the building is impressive for sheer size alone. The nearby **Musée du Petit Palais** (daily except Tues 9.30/10am–1pm & 2–5.30/6pm; €6) houses a collection of religious art from the thirteenth to sixteenth centuries, while more modern works are on show at the **Musée Calvet**, 65 rue Joseph-Vernet (daily except Tues 10am–1pm & 2–6pm; €6) and in the **Collection Lambert**, 5 rue Violette (Tues–Sun 11am–6/7pm; €5.50). Jutting out halfway across the river is the famous **Pont St-Bénézet** (same hours as Palais des Papes; €4). The struggle to keep the bridge in good repair against the ravages of the Rhône was finally abandoned in 1660, three-and-a-half centuries after it was built, and today just four of the original 22 arches survive.

Arrival and information

Train Avignon's main train station is opposite the porte de la République on boulevard St-Roch, on the southern edge of the city centre. A regular shuttle bus runs to the separate TGV station, 3km to the southeast, from just inside porte de la Republique.

Tourist office 41 cours Jean-Jaurès (April–Oct, Mon–Sat 9am–6pm/7pm, Sun 10am–5pm; Nov–March, Mon–Fri 9am–6pm, Sat 9am–5pm, Sun 10am–noon; Ⓣ04.32.74.32.74, Ⓦwww.avignon-tourisme.com); accommodation booking service and English language tours.

Internet *Chez Wam*, 34 rue de la Bonneterie.

Accommodation

Bagatelle 25 allée Antoine-Pinay Ⓣ04.90.86.30.39 (camping), Ⓣ04.90.86.71.31 (hostel). The nearest of several campsites, well-located on Île de la Barthelasse, just ten minutes' walk from the centre. It also has a busy hostel with clean, spacious dorms and ten private rooms. Both give access to washing machines, a shop and a bar with free Internet access. Hostel ❷, campsite ❶

Innova 100 rue Joseph-Vernet Ⓣ04.90.82.54.10, Ⓔhotel.innova@wanadoo.fr. Small, clean and sound-proofed en-suite rooms. A good price for the centre. ❸

Mignon 12 rue Joseph Vernet Ⓣ04.90.82.17.30, Ⓦwww.hotel-mignon.com. This little hotel is the best value inside the city walls; with satellite TV, air conditioning and WiFi in all of the individually and tastefully decorated rooms; breakfast, taken downstairs or in bed, is included in the price. ❺

Monclar 13-15 av Monclar Ⓣ04.90.86.20.14, Ⓦwww.hotel-monclar.com. An attractive eighteenth-century house with a pleasant garden, situated close to the train station. Rooms are clean and bright and there is free Internet access. ❺

AVIGNON FESTIVAL

During Avignon's three-week July **festival** (Ⓣ04.90.27.66.50, Ⓦwww.festival-avignon.com, Ⓦwww.avignon-off.org), over one hundred venues show multiple plays every day, alongside opera, classical music and film. The most popular aspect of the festival is probably the **street performers** – musicians, magicians, dancers, jugglers, clowns, artists and mime acts – which bring great colour and noise to the city. Make sure you book your hotel early.

Eating and drinking

Le Chat Gourmand 84 rue Bonneterie Ⓣ04.90.14.02.25. A sweet little café that serves large and tasty salads (€12) and is decorated with cats floor to ceiling.

Simple Simon 26 rue de la Petite-Fusterie Ⓣ04.90.86.62.70. The tongue-in-cheek chintz is one of the many pleasures of this English teahouse serving up large portions of cheddar scones and salads. Save room for dessert (apple crumble €7).

Au Tout Petit 4 rue d'Amphoux Ⓣ04.90.82.38.86, Ⓦwww.autoutpetit.fr. This little hidden gem is so small that the chef is also the waiter. The truly creative fusion cuisine includes crab and lemongrass ravioli (€9) and melon and orange flower soup (€4)

Wooloomooloo 16bis rue des Teintures Ⓣ04.90.85.28.44. World food and drink, from Caribbean rum & lime punch (€4) to Moroccan chicken and prune *tagine* (€13), served in perhaps the most idyllic spot in town. Midday two-course menu €14.

Drinking and nightlife

AOC Cave & Bar à vins 5 rue Trémoulet Ⓣ04.90.25.21.04. Friendly, English-speaking Christophe will guide you through his selection of over 150 types of wine, much of which is the local Côtes du Rhône. Prices start from €2 a glass.

La Civette place de l'Horloge. There are many touristy brasseries on the square; this one, facing the opera, is one of the best and a great place for a snack or an early evening meal.

Redzone 25 rue Carnot, Ⓦwww.redzonebar.com. The most popular club in town plays salsa on Tuesday, electro on Sunday, and an approachable blend of house, r'n'b and hip-hop on all other nights. Open Mon–Sat 7pm–3am, Sun 9pm–3am; free entry.

Moving on

Train Arles (frequent; 20–40min); Lyon (13 daily; 1hr 10min); Nice (6 daily; 3hr–4hr 10min); Nîmes (15 daily; 20–40min); Paris (15 daily; 2hr 40min–3hr 30min); Toulouse (11 daily, 8 via Nîmes or Montpellier; 3hr 10min–4hr 30min).

ARLES

Further down the Rhône sits the last capital of the Western Roman Empire, and showpiece for two millennia of culture, **ARLES**. In 1888 Vincent Van Gogh was drawn in by the picturesque town, where he painted *Starry Night* and *Night Café*, but also got into a drunken argument with Gauguin and cut off the lower part of his left ear. Today, Arles has identified itself as the centre of French photography as home to the École National de Photographie and host to the summer photographic festival, Les Rencontres (June to mid-Sept; Ⓦwww.rencontres-arles.com).

What to see and do

Around the Amphitheatre

No original Van Gogh paintings remain in Arles, but the **Fondation Van Gogh** (April–Oct daily 10.30am-8pm; Nov–March Tues–Sun 11am–5pm; €7) in the Palais de Luppé, 24 Rond-Point des Arènes exhibits works based on his masterpieces by well-known contemporary artists, such as Hockney and Bacon. The main streets of Arles are **Boulevard des Lices**, and the right-angled rue Jean-Jaurès, continuing into rue Hôtel-de-Ville. Between these last two thoroughfares lies **Cathédrale St-Trophime,** whose doorway is one of the most famous examples of twelfth-century Provençal carving, depicting a *Last Judgement* trumpeted by rather enthusiastic angels. The **cloister** (daily 9/10am–4.30/6pm; €3.50), with its mix of Romanesque and Gothic architecture, is also worth a look.

Cirque Romain

The best insight into Roman Arles can be found at the **Musée de l'Arles Antique** (daily April–Oct 9am–7pm, Nov–March 10am–5pm; €5.50), west of the town centre, by the river. The fabulous mosaics, sarcophagi and sculpture illuminate Arles' early history; alongside the museum you can see the impression of the **Cirque Romain**, built in the first century AD and originally seating twenty thousand.

Place Constantin

Housed in a splendid medieval building once used by the Knights of the Order of Malta, the **Musée Réattu** (daily: March–Oct 10am–noon & 2–5pm; Nov–Feb 1–5pm; €4) hosts a fine collection of modern art, including sketches and sculptures by Picasso. Opposite are the remains of the fourth-century **Roman baths** (daily: March & April 9am–midday & 2–6pm; May–Sept 9am–7pm; Oct–Feb 9–11.30am & 2–4.30pm; €3).

Arrival and information

Train The train station is a few blocks north of the Amphitheatre, close to the Porte de la Cavalerie.
Tourist office Opposite rue Jean Jaurès on boulevard des Lices (April–Sept daily 9am–5.45/6.45pm; Oct–March Mon–Sat 9am–4.45/5.45pm, Sun 10am–2.15pm; Ⓣ04.90.18.41.20, Ⓦwww.tourisme.ville-arles.fr) provides a hotel booking service.
Internet *Hexaworld*, rue du 4 Septembre, by the train station.

Accommodation

La Bienheureuse Ⓣ04.90.98.48.06. Seven kilometres from the centre on RN453 at Raphèle-lès-Arles, this is the most pleasant of the five campsites within easy reach of the city. It has a restaurant, swimming pool and regular bus connections. ❶

Hostel 20 av Maréchal-Foch ⓣ04.90.96.18.25. Clean dorm rooms and helpful staff, and well placed for nightlife, just five minutes from bd des Lices. Cooking facilities and Internet on site; closed Jan. ❷

Mirador 3 rue Voltaire ⓣ04.90.96.28.05, ⓦwww.hotel-mirador.com. Cosy en-suite rooms at this modest hotel, conveniently situated between the station and the centre. ❹

Le Voltaire 1 pl Voltaire ⓣ04.90.96.49.18, ⓔlevoltaire13@aol.com. Good rooms with balconies and fans in this friendly, family-run hotel, although the thin walls may bother some. ❸

Eating and Drinking

Cargo de Nuit 7 av Sadi Carnot ⓦwww.cargodenuit.com. A popular live venue that hosts established bands and DJs of all genres from salsa and Cuban to rock and techno; admission €10–15.

La Fuente 20 rue de la Calade ⓣ04.90.93.40.78. A delicious marriage of French and Iberian cuisine, including lobster in a madeira sauce, in a romantic plant-filled courtyard. Three-course dinner from €19.

La Gueule du Loup 39 rue des Arènes, ⓣ04.90.96.96.69. A charming, stone-walled inn where you can sample traditional Provençal cuisine; two-course lunch €12.

La Pagode 1 rue Augustin ⓣ04.90.96.23.09. Ignore the clichéd decor and muzak – the Chinese and Vietnamese food here is filling and tasty, especially for the price; egg soup €4.

Walla'beer 7 rue Molière. The terrace of this good-value Australian bar is a good place to start the night; pint of Fosters €4.

THE CAMARGUE

The flat, marshy delta immediately south of Arles – the **Camargue** – is a beautiful area, used as a breeding-ground for the bulls that participate in local *corridas* (bullfights), and the white horses ridden by their herdsmen. The wildlife of the area is also made up of flamingos, marsh- and seabirds, and a rich flora of reeds, wild flowers and juniper trees. The only town is **SAINTES-MARIES-DE-LA-MER**, best known for the annual **Gypsy Festival** held each May, and which is linked by a regular bus service to Arles. It's a pleasant, if touristy place, with some fine sandy beaches; if you're interested in bird-watching or touring the lagoons, your first port of call should be the **tourist office** on 5 av Van Gogh (daily: July & Aug 9am–8pm; Sept–June 9am–5/7pm; ⓣ04.90.97.82.55, ⓦwww.saintesmaries.com), which has information on a number of organized cycle, horse and boat tours of the area and can tell you where to **rent bicycles**, **horses** or **4x4s**, if you prefer to explore the delta alone. For **hotels**, try the excellent waterside *Camille* on avenue de la Plage (ⓣ04.90.97.80.26, ⓦwww.hotel-camille.camargue.fr; ❺) or the cool and quiet rooms of the rustic *Mirage*, 14 rue Camille-Pelletan (ⓣ04.90.97.80.43, ⓦwww.lemirage.camargue.fr; ❺).

The French Alps

Rousseau wrote in his *Confessions*, "I need torrents, rocks, pine trees, dark forests, mountains, rugged paths to go up and down, precipices at my elbow to give me a good fright." And these are, in essence, the principal joys of the **French Alps**. Along the mountains' western edge, **Grenoble** is a good starting point, but also an interesting old university town in its own right. Head to **Chamonix**, the principal base for accessing **Mont Blanc** and revered by extreme sports enthusiasts.

GRENOBLE

The economic and intellectual capital of the French Alps, **GRENOBLE** is a thriving city, beautifully situated on the **Drac** and **Isère** rivers. The old centre, south of the Isère, focuses on **place Grenette** and place **Notre Dame**, both popular with local students, who lounge around in the many outdoor cafés, but the best social spot is the Jardin de Ville. For a good introduction to the region, visit the **Musée**

HIKING IN THE ALPS

There are six national and regional parks in the Alps – Vanoise, Écrins, Bauges, Chartreuse, Queyras (the least busy) and Vercors (the gentlest) – each of which covers ideal walking country, as does the Route des Grandes Alpes, which crosses all the major massifs from Lake Geneva to Menton and should only be attempted by seasoned hikers. All walking routes are clearly marked and equipped with refuge huts, known as *gîtes d'étape* (Ⓦwww.gites-refuges.com). The Maison de la Montagne in Grenoble and Chamonix provides detailed information on GR paths (an abbreviation of *Grande Randonnée* meaning "long ramble"), and local tourist offices often have maps of walks in their areas. Bear in mind that anywhere above 2000m will only be free of snow from early July until mid-September.

Dauphinois, 30 rue Maurice-Gignoux (daily except Tues 10am–6/7pm; free), which occupies the former convent of Ste-Marie-d'en-Haut on rue Maurice-Gignoux. The **Musée de Grenoble**, 5 pl Lavalette (daily except Tues 10am–6pm; €5) just by Notre-Dame, is considered, by dint of its twentieth-century masterpieces, to be one of the best in Europe. Grenoble's highlight, however, especially in good weather, is the trip by *téléphérique* from the riverside quai Stéphane Jay up to **Fort de la Bastille** on the steep slopes above the north bank of the Isère (daily 9.15/11am–6.30pm/12.15am; €5.70 one-way). It's a hair-raising ride to an otherwise uninteresting fort, but the views over the mountains and down onto the town are stunning.

Arrival and information

Train and bus The train and bus stations are on the western edge of the centre, at the end of avenue Félix Viallet.

Tourist office 14 rue de la République, near place Grenette (Mon–Sat 9am–noon & 2–6pm, Sun 10am–1pm; April–Sept also Sun 2–5pm; Ⓣ04.76.42.41.41, Ⓦwww.grenoble-isere.info).

Hiking information Cross rue Raoul Blanchard to the Maison de la Montagne desk, where you can pick up detailed information on hiking and climbing.

Internet *Neptune*, 2 rue de la Paix.

Accommodation

Alizé 1 pl de la Gare Ⓣ04.76.43.12.91, Ⓦwww.hotelalize.com. The best-value hotel of many by the station, with clean, simple and quiet rooms, some with en-suite showers. ❹

FUAJ Grenoble 10 av du Gesivaudan Ⓣ04.76.09.33.52. This new and eco-friendly hostel has ultra-clean dorms and a good atmosphere. Although a little way from the town centre, it organizes great-value skiing packages in the winter. Take bus #1 to *la quinzaine* or tram A to *la rampe*. ❷

Du Moucherotte 1 rue Auguste Gâché Ⓣ04.76.54.61.40. The huge, quiet rooms are testament to the address's former glory: high ceilings, marble fire-places and antique bedsteads. Clean but a little dusty. ❹

Les Trois Pucelles Ⓣ04.76.96.45.73, Ⓦwww.camping-trois-pucelles.com. Four kilometres from Grenoble, in Seyssins, this campsite has sixty pitches in an arboretum by the Drac river, with two swimming pools and a restaurant. Open all year; to get here take tram A to *La Poya* then change onto bus #51 to *Mas des Îles*, from here it's 400m south at the river's edge. ❶

Eating and drinking

Bukana 1 quai Créqui. The flags across the ceiling reflect the diversity of the exchange student clientele in this little bar, which has cheap deals, televised sport (in English) and table football.

Café des Arts 36 rue St Laurent. Eat and drink in this intimate venue to live music, usually jazz, from 8pm to midnight. Three-course menu €17.

La Fondue 5 rue Broderie Ⓣ04.76.15.20.72. An urban log cabin serving up a great fondue (€11.50) and the local dish *tartiflette* (potato gratin with bacon and cheese).

Mark XIII 8 rue Lakanal Ⓣ04.76.86.26.94, Ⓦwww.marcxiii.eu. A two-floor bar and venue that draws in an exciting depth and variety of underground electronic DJ talent (progressive house, drum'n'bass, techno, ambient). A real treat.

Pivano 33 av Alsace-Lorraine. This rather

unremarkable looking café serves fresh juice, a good range of hot drinks and the best chocolate orange *fondant* south of Lyon (€2.50).

Tonneau de Diogène 6n pl Notre Dame. Cheap and hearty food and a genuine bohemian atmosphere, amongst books and chess boards, make this a favourite with students. Steak-frites €8.50.

Vieux Manoir 50 rue Saint Laurent. A maze of passages leads through this vaulted dungeon club, to three areas playing music from three different decades. Daily 10.30pm–5am; entry €10.

Moving on

Train Domestic: Annecy (12 daily; 1hr 20min–1hr 50min); Chamonix (6 daily via St Gervais; 4hr–6hr 15min); Lyon (frequent; 1–2hr); Turin (3 daily, via Chambery; 3hr 45min–4hr 30min).

Bus to: Valence TGV, for connections to the south coast (frequent; 55min–1hr 20min)

CHAMONIX AND MONT BLANC

At 4810m, **MONT BLANC** is both Europe's highest mountain and the Alps' biggest draw. Nestled at its base, the village of **CHAMONIX**, unlike many Alpine resorts that become largely uninhabited out of season, is lively year-round; in summer it's popular for rock climbing and hiking, while in winter its draw is the vast skiing possibilities of the area. If you're only here for a day, consider taking the **téléphérique** (daily: April to mid-June & Sept 8.10am–4/4.30pm; mid-June to Aug 6.10/7.10am–4.30pm; early Nov & mid-Dec to March 8.30am–3.30pm; ⓣ08.92.68.00.67; €35 return), which soars to the **Aiguille du Midi** (3842m), a terrifying granite pinnacle on which the cablecar station and a restaurant are precariously balanced. Here, the view of **Mont Blanc**, coupled with the altitude, will literally leave you breathless. At your feet is the snowy plateau of the **Col du Midi**, with the glaciers of the **Vallée Blanche** and **Géant** advancing at their millennial pace. To the right, a steep snowfield leads to the "easy" ridge route to the summit with its cap of ice. Book the *téléphérique* ahead to avoid the queues and get there early, before the clouds and the crowds close up.

Arrival and information

Train Chamonix station is three minutes' walk from the centre, down Avenue Michel Croz. Behind it, at Montvers station, a mountain train serves only the glaciers.

Bus Buses leave from in front of the train station.

Tourist office 85 pl du Triangle-de-l'Amitié (daily 8.30am–12.30pm & 2–7pm; ⓣ04.50.53.00.24, ⓦwww.chamonix.com); able to book accommodation and provides good information on local activities and advises on weather and snow conditions.

Mountain information The Maison de la Montagne (daily 9am–noon & 3–6pm; ⓣ04.50.53.22.08, ⓦwww.ohm-chamonix.com) on pl de L'Église is the place for organizing climbing, trekking, mountain biking and parapenting.

Accommodation

Camping Marmottes 147 rte du Nants ⓣ04.50.53.61.24, ⓦwww.camping-lesmarmottes.com. Situated off the main road, south of Chamonix, this campsite offers a free bus connection to town, fresh croissants in the morning and free barbecues. Closed Oct to mid-June. ❷

Gîtes de Montaigne ⓣ 04.50.53.16.03, ⓦwww.clubalpin-chamonix.com. The more adventurous can stay up the mountain in these catered bunk houses along the major trails. Contact the Maison de la Montaigne (see above) for more information. ❸

Gîte Vagabond 365 av Ravanel-le-Rouge, ⓣ04.50.53.15.43 ⓦwww.levagabond.co.uk. This lively and friendly hostel is a good choice year-round and invaluably cheap for the ski-season (book ahead). People mingle every evening in the bar and it's well known for its monthly barbeques. ❷

TREAT YOURSELF

La Boule de Neige 362 rue Joseph Vallot, ⓣ04.50.91.84.07, ⓔtracktion2@hotmail.com. An effortlessly cool hotel just five minutes from the town centre. The cosy, clean rooms come with showers, wireless and beautiful views. There's a great bar and a hot tub in the beer garden. ❼

Eating and drinking

Alan Peru 199 av. de l'Aiguille du Midi ⓣ04.50.53.16.04. Clever fusion cooking combining regional and Asian influences. Blankets are provided for those sitting outside. Malaysian *laksa* with chilli, tofu, noodles €12, lemon grass crème brûlé €5.
Chambre 9 272 av. Michel Croz ⓣ 04.50.53.00.31. A renowned, loud and lively bar on the ground floor of the *Gustavia* hotel, full of young, dancing tourists; cocktails €6.50.
Micro Brasserie de Chamonix (MBC) 350 route du Bouchet ⓣ04.50.53.61.59, ⓔmbc-info@wanadoo.fr. A great Canadian-owned bar that brews its own beer, serves massive burgers, and has live music in winter. 2.5 litre pitcher of lager €21.50.
Tigre, Tigre 239 av. Michel Croz ⓣ 04.50.55.53.42. Warm up with this likeable Indian restaurant's large curries (€11–€13) after coming down the mountain.

Moving on

Train Le Fayet (11 daily; 40min) where you can connect to Annecy (5 daily; 1hr 30min) and Lyon (6 daily; 3hr 10min–4hr).
International: Martigny (at least 5 daily; 1hr 40min), where you can connect to Milan.
Bus Geneva (2–5 daily; 2hr; €35); Courmayeur in Italy (2–6 daily; 45min; €9.50).

Marseille and the Côte d'Azur

The **Côte d'Azur**, synonymous with glamour, wealth and luxury, is one of the prettiest but most built-up stretches of coast in the world. While its reputation as a pricey playground for the super-rich still holds, holidaying here need not be much more expensive than elsewhere in France, providing you avoid the more obvious tourist traps. The coast's eastern reaches are its most spectacular, the mountains breaking their fall just a few metres before levelling off to the shore. **St-Tropez** is a charming high spot, though very expensive and hard to get to. **Nice**, however, is more reasonably priced and great fun, and is situated at the heart of the Riviéra. At the opposite end of the coast, the vast, cosmopolitan sprawl of **Marseille** is quite different, with its big-city buzz and down-to-earth charm. July and August are the busiest months of the year, when accommodation can be hard to come by; and May can be equally hectic, with both **Monaco**'s Grand Prix and **Cannes**' Film Festival pulling in the crowds.

MARSEILLE

France's second most populous city, **MARSEILLE** has been a major centre of international maritime trade ever since it was founded by Greek colonists 2600 years ago. Like the capital, the city has suffered plagues, religious bigotry, republican and royalist terror, had its own Commune and Bastille-storming, and it was the presence of so many revolutionaries from this city marching to Paris in 1792 that gave the name *Marseillaise* to the national anthem. A working city with little of the glamour of its ritzy Riviera neighbours, it is nevertheless a vibrant, exciting place, with a cosmopolitan population including many Italians and North Africans. It's also a world-class diving and sailing centre, and, surprisingly, France's second fashion capital.

What to see and do

The old harbour, or **Vieux Port**, is the hub of the town and a good place to indulge in the sedentary pleasure of observing the city's streetlife over a *pastis*. Two **fortresses** guard the entrance to the harbour and the town extends outwards from its three quais.

Le Panier

On the northern side of the harbour is the original site and former old town of Marseille, known as **le Panier**. During

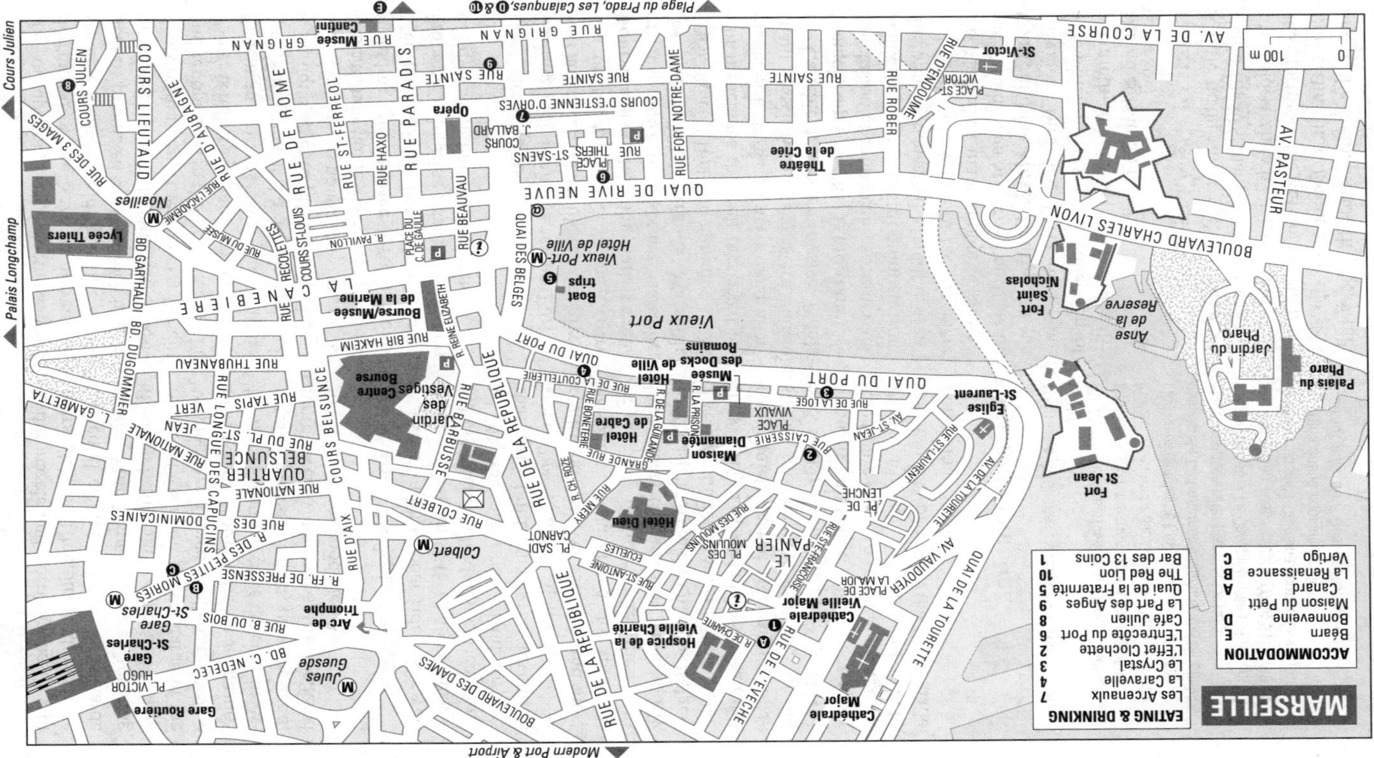
MARSEILLE
ACCOMMODATION
Béarn E
Bonneveine D
Maison du Petit Canard A
La Renaissance B
Vertigo C
EATING & DRINKING
Les Arcenaulx 7
La Caravelle 4
Le Crystal 3
L'Effet Clochette 2
L'Entrecôte du Port 6
Café Julien 8
La Part des Anges 9
Quai de la Fraternité 5
The Red Lion 10
Bar des 13 Coins 1
Palais Longchamp
Cours Julien
Modern Port & Airport
Plage du Prado, Les Calanques, D & 10
E
Vieux Port
Gare St-Charles
Gare Routière
Arc de Triomphe
Centre Bourse
Jardin des Vestiges
Bourse/Musée de la Marine
Opéra
Lycée Thiers
Hôtel Dieu
Hospice de la Vieille Charité
Cathédrale Major
Cathédrale Vieille Major
Maison Diamantée
Hôtel de Cabre
Musée des Docks Romains
Hôtel de Ville
Eglise St-Laurent
Fort St Jean
Fort Saint Nicholas
Anse de la Reserve
Palais du Pharo
Jardin du Pharo
Théâtre de la Criée
St-Victor
Musée Cantini
Boat trips
Vieux Port-Hôtel de Ville
Noailles
Colbert
Jules Guesde
QUARTIER BELSUNCE
LE PANIER
LA CANEBIERE
QUAI DU PORT
QUAI DE RIVE NEUVE
QUAI DES BELGES
BOULEVARD CHARLES LIVON
QUAI DE LA TOURETTE
RUE DE LA REPUBLIQUE
RUE DE ROME
RUE PARADIS
RUE ST-FERREOL
COURS BELSUNCE
BD. DUGOMMIER
100 m

the occupation, large sections were dynamited by the Nazis to prevent resistance members hiding in the small, densely populated streets, which in turn prompted a mass deportation of residents from the northern docks. Rebuilt and repopulated in the 1950s, today's Le Panier is full of a young, fashionable and bohemian working-class. The quarter's main attraction is **La Vieille Charité**, a Baroque seventeenth-century church and hospice complex, on rue de la Charité, now home to several museums, including the **Musée d'Archéologie Méditerranéenne** (Tues–Sun 10/11am–5/6pm; €2), housing a superb collection of Egyptian mummified animals.

La Canebière

Leading east from the Vieux Port is **La Canebière**, Marseille's main street. Just off the lower end, in the **Centre Bourse,** a giant shopping mall, is a museum of finds from Roman Marseille, the **Musée d'Histoire de Marseille** (Tues–Sun 10/11am–5/6pm; €2), which includes the well-preserved remains of a third-century Roman merchant vessel. At the far eastern end of La Canebière, the impressive **Palais Longchamp** (bus #81) is the grandiose conclusion of a nineteenth-century aqueduct and water is still pumped from the fountain beneath the building's central colonnade. South of La Canebière are Marseille's main shopping streets, rue Paradis, rue St-Ferréol and rue de Rome, and the **Musée Cantini**, 19 rue Grignan (Tues–Sun 10/11am–5/6pm; €2), which houses a fine collection of twentieth-century art with works by Dufy, Léger and Picasso.

South of the Vieux Port

A little further west is the **Abbaye St-Victor** (daily 8.30am–6.30pm; free), the city's oldest church. It looks and feels like a fortress – the walls of the choir are almost 3m thick. Dominating the skyline to the south, astride the rocky hill, is the marble and porphyry basilica of Marseille's most famous landmark, the cathedral of Notre-Dame de la Garde (daily 7am–7/8pm; free). Crowning the high belfry, and visible across most of the city is a 9m gilded statue of the Virgin Mary, known locally as the *Bonne Mère* (Good Mother). Inside are beautiful mosaics and shrines covered in *ex-votos* – trinkets, plaques, paintings and, more recently, football shirts – offered to the Saints for good luck.

Chateau d'If et la Plage

A twenty-minute boat ride takes you to the **Château d'If** (daily 9.30am–5.30/6.30pm; Oct–March closed Mon; €4.70), the notorious island fortress that figured in Dumas' great adventure story, *The Count of Monte Cristo*. In reality, no one ever escaped, and most prisoners, incarcerated for political or religious reasons, ended their days here. Boats (€10 return) leave hourly for the island from the **Quai des Belges**. Twenty minutes southeast of Marseille (bus #21), **Les Calanques**, beautiful rocky inlets carved from white limestone, provide fine bathing, diving and walking, though they are closed annually mid-June until September due to fire risks. To reach the **Plage du Prado**, Marseille's main sand **beach**, take bus #83 or #19 to the Promenade Pompidou (20min).

Arrival and information

Train Gare St-Charles a 15min walk from the city centre.
Air Marseilles Airport is 25km away, connected by shuttle buses to the train station (20–30min).
Public transport Buses and the métro cover the city: *solos* (singles) €1.40, *cartes journée* (day passes) €4.80 from métro stations and on buses. The bus station is on place Victor Hugo.
Tourist office 4 La Canebière (Mon–Sat 9am–7/7.30pm, Sun 10am–5/6pm; Ⓣ04.91.13.89.00, Ⓦwww.marseille-tourisme.com); offers a free accommodation booking service.
Internet *Infocafé*, 1 Quai de Rive Neuve.

Accommodation

Béarn 63 rue Sylvabelle ⓣ04.91.37.75.83. A few blocks south of the harbour, this cheerful hotel has simple, clean rooms and serves breakfast in bed until midday. ❹

Bonneveine impasse Dr Bonfils, off av Joseph Vidal ⓣ04.91.17.63.30. Near Les Calanques, just 200m from the beach, this is a fun hostel, with clean dorms of between two and nine beds, all with reading lights. Organizes tours, bike rental and horse riding. Take bus #44 to the Bonnefon stop. ❷

Maison du Petit Canard 2 impasse Ste-Françoise ⓣ04.91.91.40.31, ⓦmaison.petit.canard.free.fr. A small, friendly place with colourful rooms, in the middle of the Panier district. There are also great value en-suite studios with kitchenettes. ❺

La Renaissance 80 rue Longue-des-Capucins ⓣ04.91.90.25.17. Big, soft beds in these spacious and newly done-up rooms, organized around a beautiful, old spiral staircase. ❸

Vertigo 42 rue Petits Mariés ⓣ04.91.91.07.11, ⓦwww.hotelvertigo.fr. Clean hostel with original local art on the walls and friendly hosts. Faciltiies include a bar, kitchen and cheap Internet (free wireless). ❷

Eating

Les Arcenaulx 25 cours d'Estienne-d'Orves ⓣ04.91.59.80.30. A wonderfully decorated tearoom, stuffed with books, that serves cheap pâtisseries with a great selection of teas (€2). The Provençal dinner menus are quite pricey for their quality (€22).

L'Effet Clochette 2 pl des Augustins ⓣ04.91.90.15.75. A charming café, whose prices (*pastis* €1.80), quality and friendly service put the more flashy cafés around the nearby port to shame. The innumerable highlights include roast chicken (€7.50) and peach & mint ice cream (€3.80).

L'Entrecôte du Port 6 Quai de Rive Neuve ⓣ04.91.33.84.84. Renowned for its steak and mussels, this is also a great place to try Marseille's culinary speciality, *bouillabaisse*; two-course menu €16.

La Part des Anges 33 rue Sainte ⓣ08.26.10.09.72. A fun restaurant/wine bar with a very good cellar (glass of wine €2), a generous and well-picked organic cheese board (€5–8), and large meat dishes (from €10.50).

Quai de la Fraternité In the morning, fishermen sell fish straight from their nets at open-air stalls at the bottom of the port; in the afternoon they are often grilled here (€4).

Drinking and nightlife

La Caravelle 34 quai du Port ⓣ04.91.90.36.64. Pleasant first floor setting for a classy quayside *pastis* (€4) – get here early to sit on the small balcony.

Le Crystal 148 quai du Port ⓣ04.91.91.57.96. Expensive (cocktails €7) but decadent, this is the best choice of Quai du Port's many bars.

Café-Espace Julian 39 cours Julian, ⓦwww.espace-julien.com. A popular bar and the town's best music venue, orientated towards Reggae, world music and Hip-Hop – it's where France's foremost rapper IAM started out.

Red Lion 231 av Pierre Mendès. If you're out by the beach then this bustling and jovial British pub, with hearty lunches under €8 and a good choice of whiskies, is the best place to go.

Bar des 13 coins 42 rue St François. Inside the muralled walls of this cheerful bar, guest bands play soul, funk and much more from Thursday to Saturday. They serve good, cheap food (under €7) and drinks cost around €2.30.

Moving on

Train Arles (frequent; 40min–1hr); Cannes (15 daily; 2hr); Lyon (frequent; 1hr 40–2hr); Montpellier (9 daily; 1hr 30min–2hr); Nice (15 daily; 2hr 20min–2hr 45min).

Ferry Corsica; Porto Torres, Sardinia (2–8 fortnightly; 27hrs); Tunis, Tunisia (2–8 weekly; 21–23hr).

CANNES

Fishing village turned millionaires' playground, **CANNES** is best known for the **International Film Festival**, held in May, during which time it is overrun by the denizens of Movieland, their hangers-on, and a small army of paparazzi. The seafront promenade, **La Croisette**, and the **Vieux Port** form the focus of Cannes' eye-candy life, while the old town, **Le Suquet**, on the steep hill overlooking the bay from the west, with its quaint winding streets and eleventh-century castle, is a pleasant place to wander. Meanwhile, the attractive **Îles des Lérins**, composed of touristy Ste Marguerite and the quieter St Honorat, home to a Cistercian monastery, are just a ten-minute ferry ride from the Vieux Port (€10).

Arrival and information

Train The train station is on rue Jean Jaurès, a short walk north of the centre along rue des Serbes.
Tourist office The main office is in the Palais des Festivals on the waterfront and there is also a booth at the station (both Mon–Sat 9am–7pm; ⓣ04.93.39.24.53, ⓦwww.cannes.fr).
Internet *Dream Cybercafé*, 6 rue du Commt. Vidal.

Accommodation

Albe 31 rue Bivouac Napoléon ⓣ04.97.06.21.21, ⓦwww.albe-hotel.com; A great-value two-star with bright and clean rooms with air con, just one street from the Palais and the beach. ❹
Le Chalit 27 av Galliéni ⓣ04.93.99.22.11, ⓦwww.le-chalit.com. A couple of minutes uphill from the station, this independent hostel has a great location and clean and comfortable rooms; book ahead in summer. ❷
Iris 77 bd Carnot ⓣ04.93.68.30.20. This decent hostel has double rooms as well as six-bed dorms, and a good atmosphere on its outdoor terrace in the evenings; frustratingly, there's just one shower for up to 30 people. ❸
Parc Bellevue 67 av Maurice Chevalier ⓣ04.93.47.28.97, ⓦwww.parcbellevue.com; The nearest campsite is in the suburb of La Bocca, 3km to the west of Cannes; most plots are shaded and there is a 40m pool. Take bus #2 from the train station. ❷

Eating and drinking

Au Bec Fin 12 rue du 24 Août. Good traditional cooking, including a superb *soupe au pistou* (€6) and good *plats du jour*. Three-course set menu €18; closed Sun & Mon evening.
Le Bouchon d'Objectif 10 rue de Constantine. An excellent, reasonably priced bistro serving local food with a twist of sophistication, such as truffle ravioli (€9).
Palais Club ⓦwww.palais-club.com. The grand venue for the film awards becomes a huge indoor and outdoor club in July and Aug, with an impressive international DJ line up. Out of season it plays venue to a variety of live bands. Entry from €10.
Le Petit Majestic 6 rue Tony Allard. This is the best place in town for breakfast, lunch (omelette €7.50) and afternoon drinks; a real and reasonably priced locals' bar, it also draws film industry types during the festival.
Le Sevrina 3 rue Félix-Faure. This small and comfortable inn serves good-sized pizza, pasta and fondue; two-courses and glass of wine €15.
Zanzibar 85 rue Félix-Faure. One of the oldest gay bars in France, this wood-panelled bar is fun and also hetero-friendly.

Moving on

Train to: Marseille (16 daily; 2hr–2hr 20min); Monaco (frequent; 1hr–1hr 10min); Nice (frequent; 25–40min); St Raphael (frequent; 20–40min).

NICE

NICE, capital of the French Riviera and France's fifth-largest city, grew into a **major tourist resort** in the nineteenth century, when large numbers of foreign visitors – many of them **British** – were drawn here by the mild Mediterranean climate. The most obvious legacy of these early holidaymakers is the famous **promenade des Anglais** stretching along the pebble beach, which was laid out by nineteenth-century English residents to facilitate their afternoon stroll by the sea. These days, Nice is a busy, bustling traffic-jammed city, but it's still a lovely place, with a beautiful location and attractive historical centre. **Carnival** (Feb/early March) packs out the town, with parades and music culminating at Mardi Gras, a city-wide party that takes up every street.

What to see and do

Vieux Nice and La Plage

The old town, **Vieux Nice**, nestles around the hill of Nice's former château, a rambling collection of narrow alleys lined with tall, rust-and-ochre houses, and centring on **place Rossetti** and the **Baroque Cathédrale Ste-Réparate**. Nearby is the entrance to the **Parc du Château** (there's an elevator and stairway by the Tour Bellanda), decked out in a mock-Grecian style that harks back to the original Greek settlement of Nikea. The point of climbing the stairs, apart from enjoying the perfumed greenery,

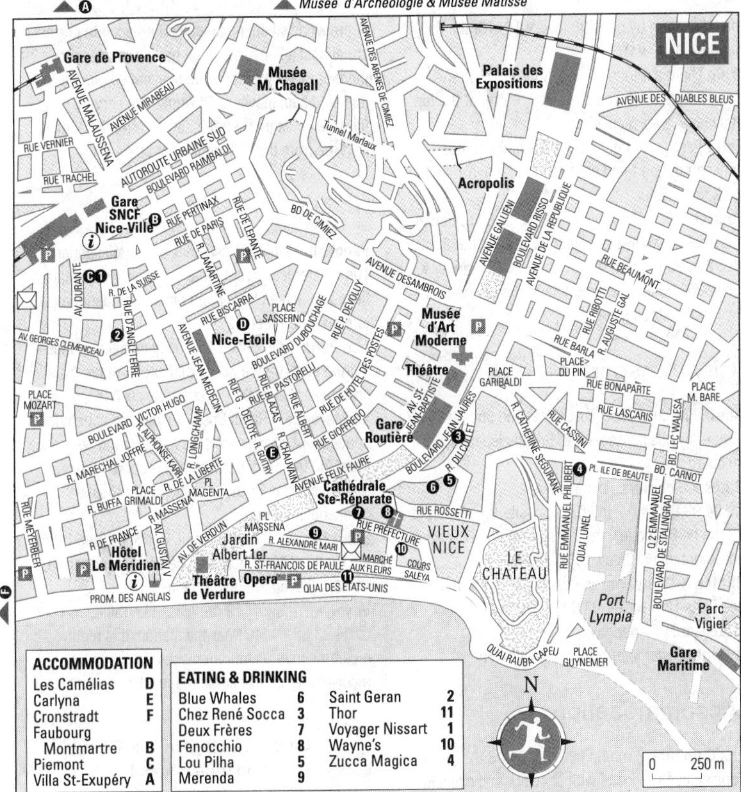

is to admire the view stretching west over the bay. Nearby, on promenade des Arts, is the **Musée d'Art Moderne et d'Art Contemporain** (Tues–Sun 10am–6pm; €4), with a collection of Pop Art and neo-Realist work, including pieces by Andy Warhol and Roy Lichtenstein.

Cimiez

Up above the city centre is **Cimiez**, a posh suburb that was the social centre of the town's elite some seventeen centuries ago, when the city was capital of the Roman province of Alpes-Maritimae. To get here, take bus #15 from in front of the train station. The **Musée d'Archéologie**, 160 av des Arènes (daily except Tues 10am–6pm; €4) houses excavations of the Roman baths, along with accompanying archeological finds. Overlooking the museum is the wonderful **Musée Matisse** (daily except Tues 10am–6pm; €4): Nice was the artist's home for much of his life and the collection covers every period. Nearby, the beautiful **Musée Chagall**, 16 av du Docteur Ménard (daily except Tues 10am–5/6pm; €5.50), exhibits dazzlingly colourful Biblical paintings, stained glass and book illustrations. The lovely gardens at both museums are accessible as part of their entrance charge.

Arrival and information

Air Nice airport is 6km southwest of the city, connected to the train station by buses #99 and #23 (every 30min; daily 8am–9pm; €4) and to the city centre by bus #98 (every 10–15min; daily 6am–9.30pm; €4).

Train The main train station, Nice-Ville, is ten-minute walk northwest from the centre, at the top of avenue Jean-Médecin.

Ferry Passenger boats arrive at Quai Infernet, between the port and old town, and a five-minute walk from either.

Tourist office The main branch is at 5 promenade des Anglais (Mon–Sat 8/9am–6/8pm; June–Sept also Sun 9am–6pm; ⓣ08.92.70.74.07, ⓦwww.nicetourism.com), with outlets at the airport and next to the station.

City transport

Bus Single bus tickets cost €1.30 and one- and seven-day bus passes (€4/€15) can also be bought on board.

Bikes & Scooters Holiday Bikes (ⓣ04.93.85.84.04) in ADA, opposite the station at 23 rue de Belgique, hire bikes (€14/day, €65/week) and scooters (€32/day, €160/week).

Skates & Skateboards Rollerstation, 49 Quai des États-Unis (ⓣ04.93.62.99.05; skates €6/skateboards €9 per day).

Internet *Cyberpoint*, 10 avenue Félix-Faure.

Accommodation

Les Camélias 3 rue Spitalieri ⓣ04.93.62.15.54. Popular, central hostel with showers and sinks in the dorm rooms and shared toilets. ❷

Carlyna 2 rue Sacha Guitry ⓣ04.93.80.77.21, ⓦwww.int1.com/carlyna. Spic-and-span hotel just paces from the Promenade des Anglais. All 24 rooms have TV, phone and air con. ❻

Faubourg Montmartre 32 rue Pertinax ⓣ04.93.62.55.03. A fun, friendly and atmospheric hostel where mingling and regular room parties are statutory, but tidiness and privacy are not so prized; cooking facilities and fridges are available. ❷

Cronstadt 3 rue Cronstadt ⓣ04.93.82.00.30, ⓦwww.hotelcronstadt.com. A block from the sea, this exquisite courtyard hotel is run by a friendly Swedish couple and has ten charmingly decorated rooms and delicious breakfasts. ❾

Hôtel du Piemont 21 rue Alsace Lorraine ⓣ04.93.88.25.15. The clean and cheap double rooms and cheerful owners make this hotel a good pick, despite somewhat tasteless decoration and showers that are literally in the rooms. ❸

Villa St-Éxupéry 22 Av Gravier ⓣ0800.307.409 (free in France) or ⓣ04.93.84.42.83, ⓦwww.vsaint.com. Housed in an beautiful old monastery above town, this is one of the world's best hostels; the immaculate dorms are almost all ensuite, some have terraces, and there are free Internet terminals and wifi in the bar (the old chapel), where €1 drinks are served. Call for a free pick up from the station after 9.10pm, or anytime from the Gravier stop of bus #1. ❸

Eating

Fenocchio 2 place Rossetti & 6 rue Poissonnerie. The master ice-cream maker of Nice, with fantastic flavours such as honey and pinenut or jasmine and tomato. One scoop €2.

Lou Pilha 3 rue Collet. This busy canteen makes a great stop, try the *socca* (flat-bread made from chickpeas; €2) or the *moules-frites* (€7).

La Merenda 4 Raoul Bosio. Tucked away behind a nondescript door, an ex-chef of the grand *Negresco Hotel* (on the prom des Anglais) prepares fautless Niçoise cuisine for those in the know. Closed weekends; menu €25.

Saint Geran 12 rue Paganini. Delicious food from the island of Mauritius, with seafood menus from €11.50. Closed Sun eve & Mon.

Voyageur Nissart 19 rue Alsace Lorraine, ⓣ04.93.82.19.60. Near the station, this highly recommended restaurant dishes up good value Niçoise fare; three-course menu €13, closed Mon.

TREAT YOURSELF

La Zucca Magica 4bis Quai Papacino ⓣ04.93.56.25.27. Multiple cuisine awards blot up the windows, adding to the twilight inside owner Marco's magical, candle-lit grotto. Five courses of sensational vegetarian cooking (€29) leave you as pleasantly full as their delicious stuffed tomatoes.

Drinking and nightlife

Blue Whales 1 rue Mascoïnat ⓣ04.93.62.90.94. A relaxed place, fitted out with a pool table and frequented by friendly young locals. Happy hour 6pm–midnight (€3.50).

Chez René Socca 2 rue Miralhéti. A brilliant spot – big wooden tables dominating the little street – to drink while gobbling down socca from their cantine; *Socca* €2, *demi* of lager €2, Closed Mon.

Les Deux Frères 1 rue du Moulin ⓣ04.93.80.77.61, ⓦwww.myspace.com/barles2freres. A very cool bar with neon lighting and park benches. They have a varied, nightly

DAY-TRIP TO VENCE

If you're looking for something a bit different in what can often be an overcrowded and touristy area in the Cote d'Azur, head up to the small towns of **St-Paul de Vence** and **Vence**, both around twenty miles from Nice. The unspoilt medieval atmosphere of the towns attracted painters such as Chagall and Matisse, and St-Paul de Vence features a staggering 64 separate art galleries. As well as spending some time in the city, it's well worth visiting the **Chapelle du Rosaire** in Vence, av Henri Matisse (Mon, Wed & Sat 2–5pm, Tues & Thurs 10–11.30am & 2–5.30pm, closed November; €2.80), decorated by Matisse and a hallmark to the evolution of twentieth-century religious art.

line-up, but principally electro and drum'n bass; demi €2.60.

Thor 32 cours Saleya. The fifty different European beers and cheap menus on offer attract both locals and tourists in droves. At ladies night (Tues), women get free wine top-ups.

Wayne's 15 rue de la Préfecture. Live music every night at this bar, which heaves with backpackers. Dancing on the table is a nightly ritual. Daily 2.30pm–12.30am, happy hour 7–9pm.

Moving on

Train Genoa (12 daily, 7 via Ventimiglia; 3–4hr); Marseille (16 daily; 2hr 30min–2hr 45min); Milan (6 daily, 3 via Ventimiglia; 4hr 45min).
Monaco (12 daily; 40mins); Paris (6 daily; 5hr 30min–11hr); Lyon (5 daily; 4hr 20min–4hr 40min); Avignon (9 daily; 3hr–4hr 15min).

MONACO

The tiny independent principality of **MONACO** rears up over the rocky Riviera coast like a Mediterranean Hong Kong. The ruling family, the **Grimaldis**, have held power here for more than seven centuries. **Prince Rainier III** famously put **Monaco** on the map when he married American actress **Grace Kelly**, and firmly held on to the throne for 56 years. The three-kilometre-long state consists of the old town of **Monaco-Ville**; **Fontvieille**; **La Condamine** by the harbour; **Larvotto**, with its artificial beaches of imported sand; and, in the middle, **MONTE CARLO**. There are relatively few conventional sights; best is the superb aquarium at the **Musée Océanographique** on avenue St-Martin (daily 9.30/10am–6/7.30pm; €11), which displays a living coral reef, transplanted from the Red Sea into a 40,000-litre tank. Lovers of ceremony may also enjoy the formal changing of the guard on the **place du Palais** at 11.55am. The most fun to be had is dressing up to the nines and trying to persuade the doormen at the **Casino Barrière** (open daily noon to dawn; €15; over-18s only) to let you in. You will need trousers, leather shoes, a shirt, preferably striped, and a decent swagger, at least.

Arrival and information

Train Monaco train station is underground, reached from av Prince-Pierre. Bus #4 (direction Larvotto) takes you from the train station to the Casino-Tourism stop, near the tourist office.

Bus The bus station is on place d'Armes.

Tourist office 2a bd des Moulins (Mon–Sat 9am–7pm, Sun 10am–noon; Ⓣ92.16.61.16, Ⓦwww.monaco-tourisme.com).

Accommodation

Hôtel de France 6 rue de la Turbie Ⓣ93.30.24.64, Ⓦwww.monte-carlo.mc/france. Comfortable and clean, this is as cheap as they get for a double room in the centre. ❽

RIJ Villa Thalassa Ⓣ04.93.78.18.58. This clean and welcoming hostel is a great choice, being so cheap and just 3km away from Monte Carlo along the coast near a good beach at Cap d'Ail. You can walk here in 25 minutes from the city. ❷

Eating and drinking

Karément 10 av Princess Grace. If you are too scruffy, poor or drunk to get into the famous, neighbouring nightclub *Jimmyz*, go here. At €10 entry plus two drinks (free for girls Thurs), you can tell yourself it's much better anyway.

McCarthy's 7 rue Portier. A friendly late-night boozer that will serve you your cheapest pint in town; Guinness (€6/€4 during happy hour 6–8pm)

Pulcinella rue Portier. Generally over-priced Mexican food, but the *plat de la semaine* (€12) is a good and tasty deal and the staff are friendly.

Stars 'n' Bars 1er, 6 quai Antoine Ⓦwww.starsnbars.com. The feisty, well-known bar on the quai serves up good-value food (for Monaco). Pizza €12; catch the 5.30–7.30pm happy hour.

Corsica

Despite nearly two-and-a-half centuries of French rule, the island of **CORSICA** has more in common culturally with **Italy** than with its governing country, with which it has been locked in a grim – and often bloody – struggle for autonomy since 1974. A history of repeated invasion has strengthened the cultural identity of this island whose reputation for violence and xenophobia has overshadowed the more hospitable nature of its inhabitants. One third **national park** and known to the French as the "île de beauté" – island of beauty – there is an amazing diversity of natural landscape in Corsica. Its magnificent rocky coastline is interspersed with **outstanding beaches**, while the mountains soar to 2706m at **Monte Cinto** – one of a string of Pyrenean-scale peaks lining the island's granite spine. The extensive forests and sparkling rivers provide the locals with a rich supply of game and fresh fish: **regional specialities** include wild boar, chestnut-flour dishes, a soft ewe's cheese called *brocciu* and some of France's most **prized** *charcuterie* (cured meats).

Two French *départements* divide Corsica, each with its own capital: Napoleon's birthplace, **Ajaccio** on the southwest coast, and **Bastia**, which faces Italy in the north. The old capital of **Corte** dominates the interior, backed by a formidable wall of mountains. Of the coastal resorts, **Calvi** draws tourists with its massive citadel and long sandy beach; while **Bonifacio**'s Genoan houses perch atop limestone cliffs, overseeing the clearest water in the Mediterranean, on the island's southernmost point. Still more dramatic landscapes lie around the **Golfe de Porto** in the far northwest, where the famous red cliffs of the **Calanches de Piana** rise over 400m.

AJACCIO

Set in a magnificent bay, **AJACCIO** combines all the ingredients of a Riviera-style town with its palm trees, spacious squares, glamorous marina and street cafés. **Napoleon** was born here in 1769, but did little for the place except to make it the island's capital for the brief period

ISLAND TRANSPORT

Train Corsica's narrow-gauge train crosses the mountains to connect the island's main towns along the most scenic of lines. InterRail and other cards reduce the fare to half for all services, or you could buy a **Carte Zoom**, which gives one week's unlimited train travel for €47. The cards are available from any station.

Bus Buses are regular if a little infrequent between the larger towns but they rarely reach the interior villages, and often leave extremely early in the morning. Services are scaled back drastically between November and May.

Scooter With little public transport, many secluded beaches and roads that undulate and meander Corsica is a great place to rent a scooter. Try Agence Corse Location, 51 cours Napoléon in Ajaccio (€50/day), Corse Moto Services on quai Nord in Bonifacio (€40/day) or Garage d'Angeli at 4 rue Villa St-Antoine in Calvi (€40–50/day).

of his empire. It is, however, a pleasant place to spend time, particularly around the harbour and narrow streets inland from the fifteenth-century **Genoese** citadel. Halfway down rue Cardinal-Fesch, the **Musée Fesch** (Mon 1.30–5.15/6pm, Tues–Sun 9.15am–12.15pm & 2.15–5.15/6.30pm; €5.35) is home to the country's most important collection of Renaissance paintings outside Paris, including works by Botticelli, Titian and Poussin. As for **beaches**, avoid the Plage St-François, below the citadel, in favour of the cleaner **Plage Trottel**, ten minutes further southwest from the centre along the promenade.

Arrival and information

Air The airport, Campo dell'Oro, is 8km southeast and connected to the town by shuttle bus (*navette* €5); taxis cost around €25.

BASTIA: COMING AND GOING

Bastia is the island's main transport hub – while there's little of particular interest here, it's likely that you'll pass through the town at least once during your visit.
Air Bastia's airport, Poretta, is 16km south of town. Shuttle buses (35min; €8) meet all flights and stop outside the train station.
Bus Buses to and from Bonifacio (2 daily; 4hr) stop opposite the post office on av Mal-Sébastiani; for Calvi (2 daily; 3hr) wait outside the train station; Corte (3 daily; 1hr 25min–1hr 45min) and Ajaccio (2 daily; 3hr) buses go from opposite the tourist office.
Ferry The port is in the north of town, a five-minute walk from the centre.
Train The station, west of place St-Nicolas serves: Ajaccio (4–5 daily; 3hr 15min); Calvi (2 daily; 3hr); Corte (2–4 daily; 1hr 30min).

Train The train station is a ten-minute walk north along the seafront.
Bus and ferry The ferry port and bus station occupy the same building off quai L'Herminier.
Tourist office On the Place du Marché (April–June, Sept & Oct Mon–Sat 8am–7pm, Sun 9am–1pm; July & Aug Mon–Sat 8am–8.30pm, Sun 9am–1pm & 3–7pm; Nov–March, Mon–Fri 8am–12.30pm & 2–6pm, Sat 8am–midday & 2–5pm; Ⓣ04.95.51.53.03, Ⓦwww.tourisme.fr/ajaccio).
Internet *Game.net* on the corner of cours Napoléon and place de Gaulle.

Accommodation

Marengo 2 rue Marengo Ⓣ04.95.21.43.66, Ⓦwww.hotel-marengo.com. A sweet little hotel with spacious, clean rooms that boast air-con and double glazing, some leading onto a floral courtyard. ❻
Kallisté 51 cours Napoléon Ⓣ04.95.51.34.45, Ⓦwww.hotel-kalliste-ajaccio.com. The best hotel in Ajaccio, with attractive, air conditioned rooms in a tastefully renovated nineteenth-century building. Extras include a currency exchange, scooter rental and free Internet. ❻
Le Barbicaja Ⓣ04.95.52.01.17 The most convenient campsite has some shade, a bar and hot showers, though little else, but then it is 300m from the beach and just 3km from place Général de Gaulle on bus #5. Closed Oct to mid-April.

Eating and drinking

Ariadne rte des Sanguinaires Ⓣ04.95.52.09.63. Thai and Moroccan meat and fish dishes (two-course menu €15) or pizzas (€10–11) to the slow beat of salsa or reggae, live most nights, and a terrace on the beach.
Grand Café Napoléon 10 cours Napoléon. Well-known place in the city centre to sip a cocktail (€8), or a coffee (€1) while nibbling olives and people-watching on the terrace.
Marché Campinchi Opposite the tourist office, this market is open every day, and is a great place to try local cheese and some of Corsica's famed *charcuterie* at its cheapest.
Le Trou dans le Mur 1 bd du Roi-Jérôme Ⓣ04.95.21.49.22. A busy restaurant near the market, serving great lasagne (€14) and good Italian desserts. Open lunchtime and Friday evenings.
U Cinnaronu 3 rue Mal Ornano Ⓣ04.95.21.49.37. A small restaurant with a great range; grilled seafood, pizzas and Corsican specialities such as delicious *figatellu* (flame grilled liver sausage, €11).

Moving on

Train to: Bastia (4 daily; 3hr 15min); Calvi (2 daily; 4hr 30min); Corte (2–4 daily; 2hr).
Bus to: Bastia (2 daily; 3hr); Bonifacio (2 daily; 4hr); Corte (2 daily; 2hr).

LE GOLFE DE PORTO

Corsica's most startling landscapes surround the **GOLFE DE PORTO**, on the west coast. A deep blue bay enfolded by outlandish red cliffs, among them the famous **Calanches de Piana** rock formations, the gulf is framed by snow-topped mountains and a vast laricio pine forest. The entire area holds endless possibilities for outdoor enthusiasts, with a superb network of marked trails (free maps available from the **Ajaccio** tourist office, see above) and **canyoning** routes, perfect bays for **kayaking** and some of the

FERRIES

The three principal ferry companies serving the island are Corsica Ferries (Ⓦwww.corsicaferries.com), Mobylines (Ⓦwww.mobylines.it) and SNCM (Ⓦwww.sncm.fr). Prices are between €20 and €40, with the cheapest from the Italian ports. From October to March routes are scaled back to several journeys a week, check websites for details:

From mainland France

Nice to: Ajaccio* (5 daily; 4hr–5hr 20min); Bastia* (1 daily; 5hr); Calvi* (3 daily; 3–6hr). Marseille to: Ajaccio* (6 weekly; 8hr 45min–12hr); Bastia (1 daily; 12hr 30min–13hr); Calvi (1 weekly; 11hr 30min).

From mainland Italy

Livorno to Bastia* (April–Oct 9 weekly; 4hr); Genoa to Bastia* (1 daily; 4hr 45min); Savona to: Bastia (1 weekly 3hr 30min); Calvi (1 weekly; 3hr)

From Sardinia

Santa-Teresa-di-Gallura to Bonifacio (2–8 daily; 1hr); Porto Torres to Ajaccio (1 weekly; 4hr 30min)
Routes marked * are covered by superfast NGV hydrofoils.

FLIGHTS

Air France and its partner company **Air Corsica** (CCM) have regular flights to Corsica's four airports at Ajaccio, Bastia, Calvi and Figari (near Bonifacio). Prices are generally cheaper the earlier you book them, and it's often possible to get discounts if you are under 25.
Air France Ⓣ08.20.82.08.20, Ⓦwww.airfrance.fr
Air Corsica Ⓣ04.95.29.05.09, Ⓦwww.aircorsica.com.

To/from France

Paris direct: Ajaccio (3–4 daily; 1hr 35min); Bastia (3–4 daily; 1hr 35min); Calvi (4–19 weekly; 1hr 35min); Figari (5 weekly; 1hr 45min;).
Paris via Marseilles/Nice: Ajaccio (3–4 daily; 2hr 45min–3hr 45min); Bastia (4–5 daily; 2hr 50min–3hr 55min); Calvi (2–3 daily; 2hr–2hr 25min); Figari (3–4 daily; 2hr 55min–3hr 20min).
Nice: Ajaccio (4–5 daily; 50min); Bastia (4 daily; 50min); Calvi (2–5 daily; 45min); Figari (1–3 daily; 55min)
Marseille to: Ajaccio (3–5 daily; 55min–1hr 10min); Bastia (4–5 daily; 55min); Calvi (3–4 daily; 1hr); Figari (2–4 daily; 1hr 15min).

finest **diving** sites in the Mediterranean. Less adventurous visitors can explore the coast on one of the excursion boats from the village of **PORTO**, the gulf's main tourist hub, where there's a **tourist office** (Ⓣ04.95.26.10.55, Ⓦwww.porto-tourisme.com) and a huge range of **accommodation**. Best value among the cheap **hotels** is *Le Golfe*, 1km from the sea opposite the Genoese watchtower (Ⓣ04.95.26.13.33; ❺). *Camping Oliviers*, situated just along from the supermarket on the main road east from the village (Ⓣ04.95.26.14.49, Ⓦwww.camping-oliviers-porto.com; ❷) is lovely, with its pitches under the shade of olive trees, a bar and swimming pool, gym, hot-tub, massages and hammam. For an inexpensive **restaurant** meal, try one of the pizzerias lining the roadside above the marina.

CALVI

Seen from the water, the great citadel of **CALVI** resembles a floating island, defined by a hazy backdrop of snowcapped mountains. The island's third port, the town draws thousands of tourists for its

6km of sandy beach. The **Haute Ville**, a labyrinth of cobbled lanes and stairways encased by a citadel, rises from **place Christophe Colomb**, which links it to the town and marina of the Basse Ville. The square's name derives from the local belief that the discoverer of the New World was born here, in a now ruined house on the edge of the citadel. Though disputed by historians, you'll come across his image in many of the shops, restaurants and hotels scattered around the **Basse Ville**, which backs onto the marina. To reach the public **beach**, keep walking south, past the boats in the marina, and – unless you want to pay for a lounger and waited service – past the private beach bars.

Arrival and information

Air Calvi's Ste-Catherine airport is 8km southeast of the town, connected by only taxis (€16–18).
Train The train station, on av de la République, is just off the marina to the south of the town centre.
Bus Buses to and from Bastia and Calenzana stop in pl Porteuse d'Eau, next to the station, Porto buses stop outside the supermarket 200m south of the train station.
Ferry The ferry port is on the opposite side of the marina, below the citadel.
Tourist office Tucked away behind the station on the beach side at the end of rue Joffre (April–Oct daily 9am–5/7pm; Nov–March Mon–Sat 9am–midday & 2–5pm; ⓣ04.95.65.16.67, ⓦwww.tourisme.fr/calvi).

Accommodation

Hôtel du Centre 14 rue Alsace-Lorraine ⓣ04.95.65.02.01. The most convenient budget accommodation, hidden away in the Basse Ville, with modest and well-kept rooms. ❸
U Carabellu rte de Pietra-Maggiore, 04.95.65.14.16. Hostels are a rare breed in Corsica, so book ahead for this one, whose generally spacy and tidy dorms are better in the main building. It has a great out-of-town spot overlooking the bay; from the station, turn left down av de la République, then right at the Total garage after 500m and keep walking for 3.5km. ❸
La Pinède ⓣ04.95.65.17.80, ⓦwww.camping-calvi.com. One of the smartest of several campsites that are sheltered in the pine forest behind the public beach, with tennis, a bar and a good shop. It's a 2km walk along av de la Republique or take the hourly beach train (*ferrovière*) towards Île Rousse for two stops; open Apr–Oct. ❷

Eating and drinking

Club 24 quai Landry. This club on the quay is a draw for local party-goers as well as beach tourists; cocktails €8.
Pizzeria Cappuccino quai Landry. This restaurant has a busy atmosphere and serves up good value *calzones* (€10–12) and pasta.
La Santa Maria 14 rue Clemenceau. Lively but touristy, and thus a little pricey, this restaurant serves Corsican specialities such as *stifatu*, a tasty blend of stuffed meats (€13.50).

TREAT YOURSELF

Chez Tao Palais des Éveques ⓣ04.95.65.00.73. A famous, beautiful and expensive piano bar, set in a vaulted sixteenth-century interior. If the delicious food is a little too pricey, get a drink on the terrace and enjoy impressive views of the bay.

Moving on

Train Ajaccio (2 daily; 4hr 30min); Bastia (2 daily; 3hr); Corte (2 daily; 2hr 30min).
Bus Bastia (daily except Sun; 2hr 15min); Porto: (2 daily; 3hr)

CORTE

Perching on the rocky crags of the island's spine, **CORTE**, the island's only interior town, is regarded as the spiritual capital of Corsica, as this is where **Pasquale Paoli** had his seat of government during the brief period of independence in the eighteenth century. Paoli founded a university here and its student population adds a much-needed bit of life. For outdoor enthusiasts, this is also an ideal base for **trekking** into the island's steep valleys, with two superb gorges stretching west into the heart of the mountains.

THE GR20

Popularly regarded as the greatest and most stunning of the **Grandes Randonnées** (trekking routes roaming across Europe) the GR20 runs from Calenzana in the north to Conza in the south along the dramatic granite spine of the island. Despite such a reputation, the route is manageable for anyone in reasonable shape with basic trekking common sense. It takes around two weeks to complete, walking 2–6hr per day; red and white waymarks show the route, which is well serviced with bunked **mountain refuges**. Although the refuges cook and sell food, several days' supplies and a good stock of water are recommended, and proper hiking equipment (boots, warm clothing, purification tablets) are essential. Do not attempt the route outside of the summer months; even then there is some residual snow in parts. Buses go from Calvi to Calenzana (July & Aug, 2 daily; June & Sept, 4 weekly; 30min; €6), where the walk begins.
Ⓦwww.calinzana.corsica-isula.com.
Ⓦwww.parc-naturel-corse.com/randos.

What to see and do

The main street, **cours Paoli**, runs the length of town, culminating in **place Paoli**, a pleasant market square lined with cafés. A cobbled ramp leads from here up to the **Ville Haute**, where you can still see the bullet marks made by Genoese soldiers during the War of Independence in tiny **place Gaffori**. Continuing north you'll soon come to the gates of the **Citadel**, whose well-preserved ramparts enclose the **Museu di a Corsica** (Tues–Sun 10am–6/8pm; June–Sept daily; Nov & Dec closed Sun; €5.30), hosting a collection of old farming implements that's far less compelling than the building itself. Best views of the citadel, the town and its valley are from the **Belvédère**, a man-made look-out post on the southern end of the ramparts.

Arrival and information

Train Corte's train station is 1km east of town at the foot of the hill near the university.
Bus Buses stop at the south end of cours Paoli.
Tourist office In the *citadelle* (Mon–Fri 9am–1pm & 2–6/8pm; Ⓣ04.95.46.26.70, Ⓦwww.corte-tourisme.com); it also houses the Parc Naturel Régional Corse office, the best information source on the island for walkers.

Accommodation

Hôtel HR allée du 9 Septembre Ⓣ04.95.45.11.11, Ⓦwww.hotel-hr.com. A cheap and cheerful place, if a little bare and functional, in a converted police station near the station, ten minutes from the centre. ❸
De la Poste 2 place Padoue Ⓣ04.95.46.01.37. This small central hotel on a tree-lined square has quiet and comfortable en-suites. ❺
Hotel du Nord 22 cours Paoli Ⓣ04.95.46.00.68, Ⓦwww.hoteldunord-corte.com. The oldest hotel in town is well-maintained and pleasantly decorated; it's a friendly place with a busy bar and Internet access. ❼
Ferme Équestre l'Albadu Ⓣ04.95.46.24.55. The nicest of the seven local campsites, located fifteen minutes' walk from the town – follow the main road south down the hill from place Paoli and take the second right after the second bridge. It opens onto superb scenery and organizes horse riding. ❷

Eating and drinking

A Merenda 3 rue Paoli. Popular café, frequented by students who come for the cheap meals, such as *steak-frites* (€7.50), paninis (€3.50) and *bruschetta* (€4).
Café du cours 22 rue Paoli. Student nights and well-priced drinks at this busy, local bar which also has Internet, some live Corsican bands and daytime left-luggage facilities; *demi* €3.20.
U Museu 1 rampe Ribanelle, Ⓣ04.95.61.08.36. Huddled beneath the citadel walls, this place serves a superb goat's cheese salad and tasty wild boar stew; three-course menu €15.

Moving on

Train Ajaccio (2–4 daily; 2hr); Bastia (2–4 daily; 1hr 30min); Calvi (2 daily; 2hr 30min).
Bus Ajaccio (2 daily; 2hr); Bastia (2 daily; 1hr 15min); Calvi (daily except Sun; 2hr 15min).

BONIFACIO

The port of **BONIFACIO** has a superb, isolated position on a narrow peninsula of dazzling white limestone at Corsica's southernmost point, only minutes by boat from Sardinia. For hundreds of years the town held the most powerful **fortress** in the Mediterranean and was a virtually independent republic; today, a sense of detachment from the rest of Corsica persists, and many Bonifaciens still speak their own dialect. It has become a chic holiday spot and sailing centre, and can be unbearably overcrowded in midsummer.

What to see and do

The **Haute Ville** is connected to the marina by a steep flight of steps at the west end of the quay, at the head of which you can enjoy glorious views across the straits to Sardinia. Within the massive fortifications of the citadel is an alluring maze of cobbled streets. Heading west you emerge from the houses at the **Cimetière Marin**, a walled cemetery at the far end of the promontory filled with elaborate mausoleums. Down in the marina, a **boat excursion** (around €14) round the base of the cliffs gives a fantastic view of the town and the **sea caves**, grottoes where the rock glitters with rainbow colours and the turquoise sea is deeply translucent. Some outstanding beaches lie near Bonifacio, most notably the shell-shaped **plage de la Rondinara**, 10km north; further north still, off the main Porto-Vecchio road, the **plages de Santa Giulia** and **Palombaggia** wouldn't look out of place in the Maldives. Buses to Rondinara leave 2-4 times daily, from the back of the quay.

Arrival and information

Bus Buses stop in the car park at the base of the harbour.
Ferry Boats from Santa-Teresa-di-Gallura on Sardinia dock at the far end of the quay.
Tourist office In the Haute Ville, at the bottom of rue Fredi-Scamaroni (May–Sept daily 9am–8pm; Oct–April Mon–Fri 9am–noon & 2–6pm; ⓣ04.95.73.11.88, ⓦwww.bonifacio.fr).
Internet *Boni Boom* on quai Comparetti.

Accommodation

L'Araguina av Sylver Bohn. ⓣ04.95.73.02.96. The only campsite close to the town has lumpy and sandy pitches but loans out tents for those unprepared. It's north from the marina, 1km out of town. ❶
Étrangers av Sylver Bohn ⓣ04.95.73.01.09. Located opposite the campsite, this hotel is the most satisfying in the area, boasting air con in the more expensive rooms. ❹
Royal pl Bonaparte ⓣ04.95.73.00.51. Although great value in winter, with views of the port from the dearer rooms, alongside air con, soft beds and good service, this hotel in the old town is pretty steep in season. ❾

Eating and drinking

Archivolto 2 rue Archivolto ⓣ04.95.73.17.58. Under fairy lights hanging from the trees that line this little old square, a friendly family serve their father's delicious innovations on Corsican cuisine. Mains €12 to €14 – try the excellent terrines.
B52 quai Camparetti. A laid-back and tasteful late-night bar, with tapas bites to accompany their house cocktails.
Cantina Doria rue Doria ⓣ04.95.73.40.59. Another family offers up carefully prepared and satisfying southern specialities; Corsican soup, *lasagne aux fromages de cru* and Bonifacian-style *aubergine à la bonifacienne*; three-course menu for €15.
Café del Mar 25 quai Camparetti. An Ibiza-style club, with music you can hear across the dock and a beach hut bar; great for a late dance.

Moving on

Bus Ajaccio (July–Sep; 3 daily Mon–Sat, 1 daily Sun; 3hr 30min); Porto Vecchio, for connections to Bastia (2 daily, 4 daily in July and Aug; 30min).
Ferry Santa-Teresa-di-Gallura in Sardinia (2–8 daily; 1hr).

Germany

HIGHLIGHTS

BERLIN: dramatic history and gritty modernity combine in this most untamed of European capitals

DOM, COLOGNE: Cologne's cathedral is Gothic grandeur on a massive scale

ZWINGER, DRESDEN: stunning Baroque palace housing several excellent museums

FREIBURG: mosaic streets, a majestic setting and one of Germany's most beautiful churches

OKTOBERFEST, MUNICH: the world's most famous beer festival

ROUGH COSTS

DAILY BUDGET Basic €40/with the occasional treat €55

DRINK Beer (half-litre €3.50)

FOOD Schnitzel €8

HOSTEL/BUDGET HOTEL €18/€40–70

TRAVEL Munich–Berlin (500km) €105 by ICE train, €45 by bus

FACT FILE

POPULATION 82.3 million

AREA 357,090 sq km

LANGUAGE German

CURRENCY Euro (€)

CAPITAL Berlin (population: 3.4 million)

INTERNATIONAL PHONE CODE ⓣ49

Basics

With its quaint medieval villages, dynamic urban centres and beautiful landscapes, from the tranquil Baltic coast in the north to the forests and mountains of the south, Germany's got something for everyone. It also has a rich cultural diversity, a hangover from the days when the country was a patchwork of independent states. This regionalism is one of the most fascinating aspects of the country, allowing extremes of tradition and modernity to coexist – as well as scores of dialects, brewing traditions and cuisines.

Another advantage of this regionalism is the number of cities in Germany with the cosmopolitan air – and world-class museum collections – of national capitals. **Berlin** itself is electrifying – an old city bursting with youth, art and energy. **Munich** is a star attraction, with great museums and a thriving nightlife. **Cologne**'s skyline is still dominated by a spectacular cathedral begun in 1248, while its decidedly impious Carnival celebration is the biggest in Europe. **Hamburg**, burned to the ground in 1943, is now a bustling harbour city with a rollicking nightlife to boot. In the east, as well as Berlin, there's the Baroque splendour and thriving counterculture of **Dresden**. Then there are the smaller towns, offering another side of Germany: the pastoral, the quaint, the romantic. There's nowhere as well loved as the university town of **Heidelberg**, while smaller stars such as **Trier**, **Regensburg** and **Potsdam** all reward exploration.

Among the scenic highlights are the **Bavarian Alps** on Munich's doorstep, the **Bodensee** (Lake Constance) marking the Swiss border, the **Black Forest** and the **Rhine Valley**, whose majestic sweep has spawned a rich fund of legends and folklore.

CHRONOLOGY

57 BC Julius Caesar invades and conquers "Germania Inferior".

800 AD Charlemagne, the Frankish ruler over territory including Germany, is crowned Holy Roman Emperor.

1438 Habsburg dynasty rules over Germany with election of Albert I.

1517 Dissatisfied with Catholicism, Martin Luther starts the Protestant Reformation.

1648 End of the Thirty Years War between European Catholic and Protestant powers leads to the division of Germany into princely states.

1801 Beethoven premiers the "Moonlight Sonata".

1848 Karl Marx writes the "Communist Manifesto".

1871 Unification of Germany under Otto von Bismarck, after German success in the Franco-Prussian War.

1880s Bismarck establishes German colonies in Africa.

1918 Germany defeated in WWI.

1919 Treaty of Versailles enforces heavy reparation payments upon Germany.

1923 Hyper-inflation creates massive economic problems.

1933 Hitler becomes Chancellor of Germany

1939 WWII begins as Germany invades Poland.

1939–1945 Millions die at the hands of the Nazis in concentration camps during the Holocaust.

1945 Germany is defeated, as the Allies occupy the country.

1949 Germany is divided between the Communist East and Democratic West.

1989 The Berlin Wall is torn down.

1990 Collapse of Soviet Union leads to the reunification of Germany.

2002 The European Central Bank in Frankfurt issues the first euro banknotes.

2005 Angela Merkel becomes first female Chancellor.

ARRIVAL

Flying is, predictably, the cheapest and most convenient way to get to Germany

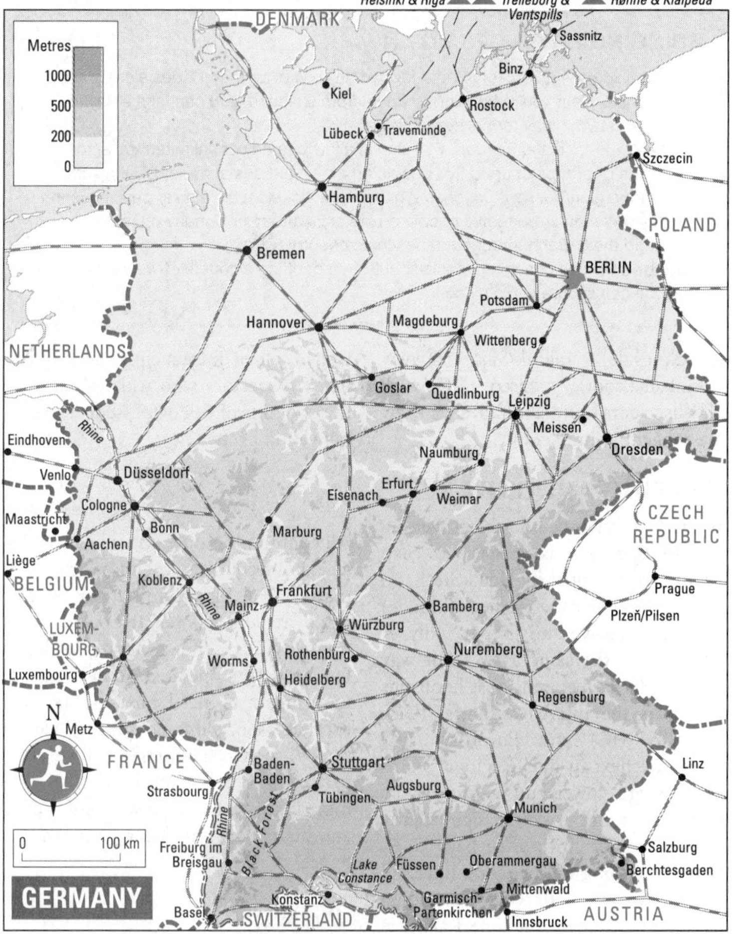

from overseas, as well as from many other European countries thanks to the proliferation of discount airlines. Germany's largest airport is Frankfurt Airport (FRA), and there are over forty others to choose from.

By train and bus

Rail and bus lines connect Germany with destinations throughout continental Europe and the UK. **Train** connections can be found at the Deutsche Bahn website (Ⓦwww.bahn.de), while several private **bus** companies, such as BerlinLinienBus (Ⓦwww.berlinlinienbus.de), Gulliver's (Ⓦwww.gulliver.de), Eurolines (Ⓦwww.eurolines.com) and Touring (Ⓦwww.touring.de) run international routes from as far afield as Barcelona and Bucharest.

By boat

Ferries operate services between the German Baltic ports of Lübeck, Rostock and Sassnitz-Mukran and Denmark, Finland, Latvia, Lithuania and Sweden. The major carriers are Scandlines (Ⓦwww.

BRINGING DB PRICES DOWN

Hop on hop off A DB ticket is valid for two days, with as many stops along the way as you'd like. So if you're heading to Berlin from Cologne, you can take a day in Hannover on your way for no extra charge.

Länder-Tickets (€24–29 group, €18 single) allow one day of unlimited travel for individuals or groups of up to five people on regional trains and the S-Bahn within any Land (region/county). Schönes Wochenende tickets are a similar deal, covering one day of travel for up to five people on either Saturday or Sunday on regional trains and the S-Bahn throughout the whole country (€33).

Early bird DB has changing specials, but often booking a couple of weeks in advance can secure you a discount price.

scandlines.de), Tallink/Silja (Ⓦwww.tallinksilja.com), Lisco (Ⓦwww.dfdslisco.com) and Finnlines (Ⓦwww.passenger.finnlines.com).

GETTING AROUND

While it's certainly not cheap, getting around Germany is quick and easy. **Trains** are operated by Deutsche Bahn (DB), whose website (Ⓦwww.bahn.de) is comprehensive and user-friendly. A return costs the same as two one-way tickets. The fastest and most luxurious service is the InterCityExpress (ICE). InterCity (IC) and EuroCity (EC) trains are next in line. Regional trains (RE/RB) are slower, run on less heavily used routes and are often significantly cheaper. Major cities often have an **S-Bahn** commuter rail network. InterRail and Eurail are both valid (including on S-Bahn trains). The InterRail One Country Pass (Ⓦwww.InterRailnet.com) is available for Germany, providing 3, 4, 6, or 8 days of travel in one month (€189/209/260/299).

Supplements apply on sleepers, and for InterRailers on ICE, Thalys (a service between Cologne and Brussels), and Berlin–Warszawa Express trains as well. Buy your ticket before getting on the train: online, from a ticket machine, or at the station.

Some cities have a **U-Bahn**, or metro/tram system. Usually, you'll need to buy and validate your ticket before boarding, although some trams have ticket machines on board. U-Bahns are patrolled, albeit infrequently, by ruthless ticket inspectors who will levy an on-the-spot fine of €40 on passengers without valid tickets.

By bus

All communities in Germany have reliable, if infrequent, local buses; stops are marked "H". Most inter-city **buses** are run by regional cooperatives in association with DB, although there are also a few privately operated routes. You're most likely to need buses in remote rural areas, or along designated "scenic routes", such as the Romantic Road (see p.513), where scheduled services are more luxurious than on standard routes and buses pause at major points of interest.

By bicycle

Cyclists are well catered for: many smaller roads have cycle paths, and bike-only lanes are a common sight in cities. If you want to take your bike on a train, it'll need its own ticket: €4.50 on regional trains and €9 on IC/EC trains. Bikes are not allowed on ICE services.

ACCOMMODATION

It's advisable to reserve ahead for **accommodation** in Germany, especially in the cities, where trade fairs and heavy seasonal tourism cause beds to book out in a hurry. Most hostels and hotels now take bookings online, and nearly all tourist offices can reserve accommodation for a fee.

Hostels

You're never far away from a large, functional **HI hostel** (*Jugendherberge*) run by DJH (Ⓣ05231/74010, Ⓦwww.djh.de) – but at any time of the year they're liable to be block-booked by school groups, so reserve as far in advance as possible. Unfortunately, these official hostels are often pricey (around €22), sterile and far from the action. HI members aged 27 and over, "seniors", pay around €3 extra per night; non-members, if admitted at all, also pay an extra €3 per night. Breakfast and sheets are always included; there are usually no curfews or lockouts, but reception hours may be limited. In larger cities, you'll find **independent hostels**, which tend to have a lot more personality, less-stringent rules and more in the way of customer service. Expect to pay €16–22. Breakfast and sheets are not always included. For more on backpackers' hostels, check out Backpacker Network Germany (Ⓦwww.backpackernetwork.de).

Hotels

Hotels are graded, clean and comfortable. In country areas, prices start at about €30 for a double room; in cities, about €40. **Pensions** are plentiful, either in the form of rooms above a bar or restaurant or in a private house. An increasingly popular budget option is **B&B**; rates start around €20 for a double. Check with the tourist office or look for signs saying *Fremdenzimmer* or *Zimmer frei*.

Even the most basic **campsites** have toilets, washing facilities and a shop, while the grandest have swimming pools and supermarkets. Prices usually comprise a fee per person and per tent (each €3–7), plus extra for vehicles. Many sites are full from June to September, so check in early in the afternoon. Aside from those in popular skiing areas, most close for winter.

FOOD AND DRINK

German **food** is both good value and high quality, but it helps if you share the national penchant for solid, meat-heavy fare and fresh salads. The majority of hotels and guesthouses include **breakfast** in the price of the room – typically, a small platter of cold meats and cheeses, with a selection of breads, marmalades, jams and honey, and sometimes muesli and yoghurt. Elegant cafés are a popular institution, serving *Kaffee und Kuchen*, a choice of coffee and cakes. The easiest option for a snacks however, is to head for the ubiquitous **Imbiss** stands and shops, which serve döner kebap, sausages, meatballs and fries, plus sometimes soup, schnitzels, chops, spit-roasted chicken and salads.

Lunch tends to be treated as the main meal, with good-value menus on offer. A *Gaststätte*, *Gasthaus*, *Gasthof*, *Brauhaus* or *Wirtschaft* functions as a *gemütlich* (cosy) meeting-point, drinking haven and restaurant. Their cuisine resembles hearty home-cooking, and portions are usually generous. Main courses are overwhelmingly based on pork, served with a variety of sauces. Sausages feature regularly, with distinct regional varieties. **Vegetarians** will find Germany fairly difficult – traditional menus are almost exclusively for carnivores – though student towns and the larger cities are quickly becoming veggie-friendly. Germany's multicultural society is mirrored in its wide variety of **ethnic eateries**: Italian restaurants are the most reliable, but there are also plenty offering Balkan, Greek, Turkish and Chinese cooking. University-run *Mensas* are the cheapest places to eat, and though you're supposed to have a valid student card, no one seems to check.

Drink

For **beer** drinkers, Germany is paradise; around forty percent of the world's breweries are found here, with over six hundred in Bavaria alone. Munich's beer gardens and beer halls are the most famous drinking dens in the country, offering a wide variety of premier products, from dark lagers through tart *Weizens* to powerful *Bocks*. Cologne holds the world record for the number of city breweries, all of which produce the beer called *Kölsch*, but wherever you go you can be fairly sure of getting a locally brewed beer. There are many high-quality German wines, especially those made from the Riesling grape. **Apfelwein** is a variant of cider beloved in and around Frankfurt. The most popular **spirits** are the fiery *Korn* and after-dinner *Schnapps*, which are usually fruit-based.

CULTURE AND ETIQUETTE

Most Germans are friendly, hospitable and helpful, and if you stand at a corner long enough with a map in your hand, someone's bound to volunteer to help you out. There are, however, a couple of faux-pas that can get you in trouble. **Jaywalking** is illegal in Germany; you could be fined if caught, but are most likely to get off with disapproving looks from passers-by. Wandering into bike lanes, which usually occupy the street-side half of the footpath and are marked in red, could get you killed in Berlin and cursed at elsewhere.

Paying at a restaurant is also a little different. If you're in a group, you'll be asked if you want to pay individually (*getrennt*) or all together (*zusammen*). To **tip**, round your bill up to the next €0.50 or €1 and give the total directly to the waiter.

SPORTS AND OUTDOOR ACTIVITIES

Bundesliga Football is the major spectator sport in Germany, with world-class clubs playing in top-notch stadiums (revamped for the 2006 World Cup) before die-hard fans. Important matches sell out well in advance; tickets can be purchased online at the clubs' websites. For more information on teams, schedules and ticketing, check out ⓦwww.bundesliga.de/en.

Germany's great outdoors has a lot to offer, with **hiking** and **cycling** featuring high on the list. The most popular regions for hiking are in the Black Forest and the Bavarian Alps, but there are well-maintained, colour-coded hiking routes all over Germany. The country is crisscrossed with long-distance cycling routes, though most travellers choose to do only small segments. The cycling page on Germany's tourism website (ⓦwww.germany-tourism.de/cycling) has a useful route-finding feature and English-language brochures (available for download) on all the major routes.

The best places in Germany for **winter sports** are in the south. For cross-country skiing, head to the Black Forest region around Triberg (see p.507). For downhill, the Bavarian Alps, especially around Garmisch-Partenkirchen (see p.524) are your best bet.

COMMUNICATIONS

Post offices are open Mon–Fri 8am–6pm & Sat 8am–1pm. Call shops are the cheapest way to phone abroad, though you can also **phone** abroad from all payphones except those marked "National"; phonecards are widely available. The operator is on ⓣ03. Internet access is easy to find in larger towns and cities. Expect to pay €2–4/hr.

GERMANY ON THE NET

ⓦ**www.germany-tourism.de** Official tourist board site.
ⓦ**www.stadtplandienst.de** City maps.
ⓦ**www.webmuseen.de** Information on the country's museums.
ⓦ**www.galerie.de** Digest of the country's galleries and artists.
ⓦ**www.party.de** Nightlife and events listings.

EMERGENCIES

The **police** (*Polizei*) usually treat foreigners with courtesy. Reporting thefts at local police stations is straightforward, but inevitably there'll be a great deal of bureaucracy to wade through. The level of theft in eastern Germany has increased dramatically, but provided you take the normal precautions, there's no real risk. Doctors generally speak English. **Pharmacies** (*Apotheken*) can deal with many minor complaints and staff will often speak English. All display a rota of local pharmacies open 24hr. In western Germany you'll find international *Apotheken* in most large towns who'll be able to fill a prescription in English.

EMERGENCY NUMBERS

Police ⓣ110; Fire & Ambulance ⓣ112

INFORMATION & MAPS

You'll find a **tourist office** in virtually every town. Staff are invariably friendly and efficient, providing large amounts of literature and maps. The best general **map** is Kümmerly and Frey's 1:500,000. Specialist cycling or hiking maps can be bought in the relevant regions. **Altstadt**, widely used in this chapter and on street signs, means "Old Town".

MONEY AND BANKS

German currency is the **euro** (€). **Exchange facilities** are available in most banks, post offices and commercial exchange shops called *Wechselstuben*. The Reisebank has branches in the train stations of most main cities (generally open daily, often till 10/11pm). Basic **banking hours** are Mon–Fri 9am–noon & 1.30–3.30pm, Thurs till 6pm. **Credit cards** are accepted relatively infrequently; never assume that an establishment will take plastic. **ATMs** are widespread.

STUDENT DISCOUNTS

A **student ID card** in Germany is invaluable: almost all sights and museums, and even some cinemas, give generous student discounts – up to fifty percent. Note that foreigners are ineligible for almost all local public transport discounts.

OPENING HOURS AND HOLIDAYS

Shops open at 8am and close around 6–8pm weekdays and 2–4pm Saturdays, and are closed all day Sunday (except for bakers, who may open for a couple of hours between 11am and 3pm). Smaller shops also close noon–2pm. Exceptions are pharmacies, petrol stations and shops in and around train stations, which stay open late and at weekends. **Museums** and **historic monuments** are, with few exceptions (mainly in Bavaria), closed on Monday. **Public holidays** are: January 1, January 6 (regional), Good Friday, Easter Monday, May 1, Ascension Day, Whit Monday, Corpus Christi (regional), August 15 (regional), October 3, November 1 (regional) and December 25 and 26.

German

Mini-pronunciation guide Consonants: “w” is pronounced like the English “v”; “sch” is pronounced “sh”; “z” is “ts”. The German letter “ß” is basically a double “s”. Vowels: “ei” is “eye”, “ie” is “ee”, “eu” is “oy”.

	German	Pronunciation
Yes	*Ja*	Yah
No	*Nein*	Nine
Please	*Bitte*	Bitteh
Thank you	*Danke*	Duhnkeh
Hello/Good day	*Güten Tag*	Gooten Tahg
Goodbye	*Tschüss, ciao,* or *auf Wiedersehen*	Chuss, chow, or owf veederzain
Excuse me	*Entschuldigen Sie, bitte*	Entshooldigen zee bittuh
Today	*heute*	Hoyteh
Yesterday	*gestern*	Gestern
Tomorrow	*morgen*	Morgan
What time is it?	*Wie spät ist es?*	Vee shpate ist es?
I don't understand	*Ich verstehe nicht*	Ik vershtayeh nikt
How much is....?	*Wieviel kostet...?*	Vee feel costet...?
Do you speak English?	*Sprechen Sie Englisch?*	Sprecken zee aing-lish?
I'd like a beer	*Ich hätte gern ein Bier*	Ik hetteh gairn ein beer
Where is...?	*Wo liegt…?*	Vo leegt
entrance	*der Eingang (on foot)/ die Einfahrt (by car)*	dare aingahng/dee ainfart
Exit	*der Ausgang (on foot)/ die Ausfahrt (by car)*	dare owsgahng/dee owsfart
Toilet	*das WC/die Toilette*	dahs vay-tsay/dee toyletteh
Hotel	*das Hotel*	das hotel
HI hostel	*die Jugendherberge*	dee yoogendhairbairgeh
Hostel	*das Hostel*	das hostel
Main train station	der *Hauptbahnhof*	howptbahnhof
What time does the… leave/arrive?	*Um wieviel Uhr fährt... ab/kommt… an?*	oom veefeel oor fairt… ahb/komt… ahn?
Boat/ferry	*das Boot/die Fähre*	das boat/dee faireh
Bus	*der Bus*	dare boos
Plane	*das Flugzeug*	das Floog-tsoyg
Train	*der Zug*	dare tsoog
bed	*ein Bett*	ein Bett
Cheap	*billig*	billig
Expensive	*teuer*	toy-er
Open	*offen/auf*	uhffen/owf
Closed	*geschlossen/zu*	gehshlossen/tsoo
One	*Eins*	Einz
Two	*Zwei*	Tsvi
Three	*Drei*	Dry
Four	*Vier*	Fear
Five	*Fünf*	Foonf
Six	*Sechs*	Zex
Seven	*Sieben*	Zeeben
Eight	*Acht*	Ahkt
Nine	*Neun*	Noyn
Ten	*Zehn*	Tsain

Berlin

Energetic and irreverent, **BERLIN** is a welcoming, exciting city where the speed of change in the past few years has been astounding. With a long history of decadence and cultural dynamism, the revived national capital has become a magnet for artists and musicians, who were quick to see the opportunities that the cheap properties of the former East provided. Culturally, it has some of the most important archeological collections in Europe. Its nightlife is an exuberant, cutting-edge mix that could keep you occupied for weeks. And in 2006, the city's Olympiastadion staged the finals of the football World Cup, affirming Berlin's role as a world city.

The city reeks of modern European history, having played a dominant role in Imperial Germany, during the Weimar Republic after 1914, and in the Nazis' Third Reich. After 1945, the city was partitioned by the victorious Allies, and as a result was the frontline of the Cold War. In 1961, its division into two hostile sectors was given a very visible expression by the construction of the notorious Berlin Wall. After the Wall fell in 1989, Berlin became the national capital once again. These days, parliament (Bundestag) sits in the renovated Reichstag building, and the city's excellent museum collections have been put back together again, housed in buildings at the forefront of architectural design. The central district of **Mitte** (extending either side of the main Unter den Linden boulevard, in what was formerly the Communist East), **Kreuzberg**, bohemian **Prenzlauer Berg** and **Friedrichshain** are where things are liveliest.

What to see and do

Most of Berlin's main sights are in the central district of **Mitte**, clustered on Unter den Linden boulevard between the Brandenburg Gate and Museuminsel. To the south lies Potsdamer Platz and the museums of the Kulturforum, while to the west you'll find the central shopping area, the Ku'damm, and the famous Bahnhof Zoo.

The Brandenburg Gate

The most atmospheric place to start a tour of Berlin is the **Brandenburg Gate**, built as a city gate-cum-triumphal arch in 1791 and now – since it stands at the fulcrum between the city's eastern and western halves – the much-photographed symbol of German reunification. Immediately behind, it's just possible to make out the marked course of the **Berlin Wall**, which divided the city for 28 years until November 9, 1989.

The Reichstag

The **Reichstag** building is the nineteenth-century home of the German parliament, remodelled by Norman Foster for the resumption of its historic role in 1999. Its glass cupola has become a landmark, and the popular trip to the top (daily 8am–midnight; free) affords a stunning view. The queue tends to be shorter in the late afternoon.

The Holocaust Memorial

To the south of the Brandenburg Gate lies the bold, newly built Holocaust Memorial (also known as the **Memorial to the Murdered Jews of Europe**), a monument consisting of nearly three thousand upright concrete slabs of varying height arranged in a dizzying grid. The underground information centre (Ort der Information; Tues–Sun: April–Sept 10am–8pm; Oct–March 10am–7pm; free; Ⓦ www.stiftung-denkmal.de) offers a sophisticated exhibition on the Holocaust.

Unter den Linden

East of the Brandenburg Gate stretches broad and stately **Unter den Linden**,

once Berlin's most important thoroughfare. Post-unification renewal, including over-sized embassies, museums and swank stores flanking the boulevard, only hint at its former grandeur.

At nos. 13–15, the **Deutsche Guggenheim Berlin** (daily 11am–8pm, Thurs till 10pm; €4/3; Ⓦwww.deutsche-guggenheim-berlin.de) hosts three to four major exhibitions of modern and contemporary art per year. Nearby **Bebelplatz** was the site of the infamous Nazi book-burning of May 10, 1933; an unusual, but poignant, memorial – an underground room housing empty bookshelves visible through a glass panel set in the centre of the square – marks the event.

More than anyone, it was architect Karl Friedrich Schinkel who shaped nineteenth-century Berlin and one of his most famous creations can be found opposite the Staatsoper further along Unter den Linden: the **Neue Wache**, a

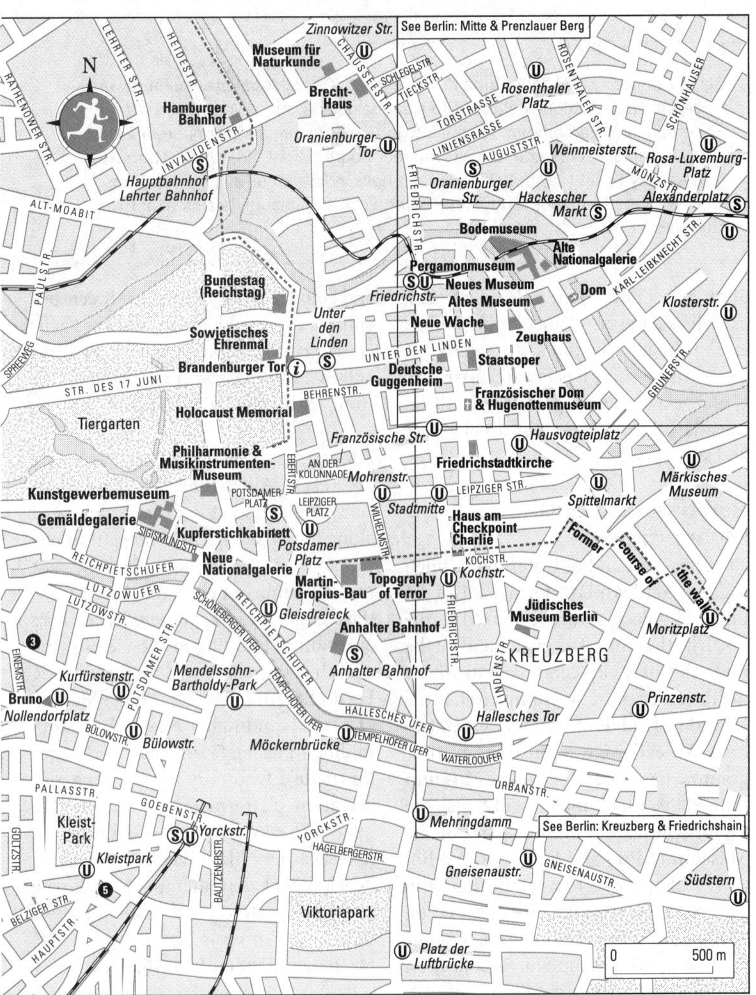

former royal guardhouse resembling a Roman temple and now a memorial to victims of war and tyranny. Next door is Berlin's finest Baroque building, the old Prussian **Zeughaus** (Arsenal). Newly renovated, it houses the excellent **Deutsches Historisches Museum** (daily 10am–6pm; €5; ⓦwww.dhm.de), with comprehensive exhibitions covering two thousand years of German history.

The Gendarmenmarkt

Following Charlottenstrasse south from Unter den Linden, you come to the **Gendarmenmarkt**, whose appeal is derived from the **Französischer Dom** and the lookalike Friedrichstadtkirche on either side of the square. The latter was built as a church for Berlin's influential Huguenot community at the beginning of the eighteenth century, while the former now contains the **Hugenottenmuseum** (Tues–Sat noon–

MUSEUM ENTRY

Berlin's superb **state museums and galleries** (Gemäldegalerie, Kunstgewerbemuseum, Neue Nationalgalerie, Alte Nationalgalerie, Altes Museum, Bodemuseum, Pergamonmuseum, Berggruen Museum and Hamburger Bahnhof; ⓦwww.smb.spk-berlin.de) are all **free** four hours before closing on **Thursdays**. A three-day ticket (**SchauLUST Pass**) for all Berlin's state-owned museums, as well as the Deutsche Guggenheim and Jewish Museum, is a steal at €15/students €7.50.

5pm, Sun 11am–5pm; €2/students €1), as well as a tower whose platform offers extraordinary views of the centre. A block west of here lies **Friedrichstrasse**, a high-class shopping district with an eclectic mix of modernist architecture and swank cafés.

Schlossplatz and Museuminsel

At the eastern end of Unter den Linden is grassy **Schlossplatz**, former site of the imperial palace, now overlooked to the north by the Dom. The *Platz* stands at the midpoint of a city-centre island whose northwestern part, **Museuminsel**, is the location of some of Berlin's best museums. An extensive reconstruction programme has closed the **Neues Museum** until 2009, after which it will house the Ägyptisches Museum and parts of the Museum of Pre- and Early History. But there's plenty else to see, starting with the **Alte Nationalgalerie** (Tues–Sun 10am–6pm, Thurs till 10pm; €8/students €4), which contains a collection of nineteenth-century European art. At the island's northern tip is the newly reopened **Bode-Museum** (daily 10am–6pm, Thurs till 10pm; same prices), presenting Byzantine art and medieval to eighteenth-century sculpture. In the **Altes Museum** (same hours and prices) are Greek and Roman antiquities; the Egyptian collection is also being temporarily housed here until 2009. It's the **Pergamonmuseum** (same hours; €10/students €5), however, that boasts the real treasure-trove of the ancient world: two must-sees unearthed by German archeologists in the nineteenth century and reassembled here are the spectacular Pergamon Altar, which dates from 160 BC, and the huge Processional Way from sixth-century BC Babylon.

Alexanderplatz

To reach **Alexanderplatz**, the stark commercial hub of eastern Berlin, head along Karl-Liebknecht-Strasse (the continuation of Unter den Linden), past the Neptunbrunnen fountain and the thirteenth-century Marienkirche. Like every other building in the vicinity, the church is overshadowed by the gigantic **Fernsehturm** (TV tower; daily: March–Oct 9am–midnight; Nov–Feb 10am–midnight; €8.50; ⓦwww.berlinerfernsehturm.de), whose 203-metre-high observation platform and revolving café offer unbeatable views. Southwest of here lies the **Nikolaiviertel**, a modern development that attempts to re-create the winding streets and small houses of this part of prewar Berlin, which was razed overnight on June 16, 1944.

Potsdamer Platz

The heart of prewar Berlin used to be to the south of the Brandenburg Gate, its core formed by **Potsdamer Platz**. A huge commercial project here, involving various eateries, theatres and a shopping mall built within the impressive Sony Centre, attempts to re-create the area's former liveliness. Just to the east, in a parking lot near the corner of Wilhelmstrasse and An der Kolonnade, lies the unmarked site of **Hitler's bunker**, where the Führer spent his last days.

The Kulturforum and its museums

West of Potsdamer Platz lies the Kulturforum, a series of museums centred on the unmissable **Gemäldegalerie** (Tues–Sun 10am–6pm, Thurs till 10pm; €8/students €4). Inside is a world-class collection of old masters, covering all the main European schools from the Middle Ages to the late eighteenth century. One highlight of the German section is Cranach's tongue-in-cheek *The Fountain of Youth*. The interconnected building to the north houses the **Kunstgewerbemuseum** (Tues–Fri 10am–6pm, Sat & Sun 11am–6pm; same ticket), a sparkling collection of European arts and crafts. A couple of minutes' walk to the south, the **Neue Nationalgalerie** (Tues, Wed & Sun 10am–6pm, Thurs–Sat 10am–10pm; same ticket) hosts temporary modern art exhibitions and has a good permanent collection of twentieth-century German paintings, best of which are the Berlin portraits and cityscapes by George Grosz and Otto Dix.

Gropius-Bau and Topography of Terror

Southeast of here, the **Martin-Gropius-Bau** at Niederkirchnerstr. 7 (Mon & Wed–Sun 10am–8pm; admission varies; Ⓦwww.gropiusbau.de), a Renaissance-style building built in the late nineteenth century, hosts prestigious temporary art exhibitions. Next door, the captivating open-air exhibition, **Topography of Terror** (daily: May–Sept 10am–8pm; Oct–April 10am–6pm; free; Ⓦwww.topographie.de), occupies the former site of the Gestapo and SS headquarters and documents their chilling histories.

Checkpoint Charlie

From here it's a ten-minute walk on Wilhelmstrasse and Kochstrasse to the site of the notorious Checkpoint Charlie, the most infamous crossing-point between East and West Berlin in the old days; evidence of the trauma the Wall caused is still on hand in the popular **Haus am Checkpoint Charlie** at Friedrichstr. 43–45 (daily 9am–10pm; €9.50/students €5.50; Ⓦwww.mauer-museum.com), a private museum that tells a slightly one-sided history of the Wall and the desperate stories of those who tried to cross it.

The Jewish Museum

The checkpoint area marks the northern limit of **Kreuzberg**, famed for its large immigrant community and its self-styled "alternative" inhabitants and nightlife. Daniel Libeskind's striking zinc-skinned **Jewish Museum Berlin**, at Lindenstr. 9–14 (Mon 10am–10pm, Tues–Sun 10am–8pm, last entry 1hr before closing; €5/students €2.50; Ⓦwww.jmberlin.de), documents the culture, notable achievements and history of Berlin's Jewish community using a plethora of multimedia exhibits, art installations, religious artefacts and historic manuscripts.

Bahnhof Zoo and Ku'damm

Bahnhof Zoo (Zoo Station) is at the centre of the city's western side – a short walk south and you're at the eastern end of the Kurfürstendamm, or **Ku'damm**, a 3.5-kilometre strip of ritzy shops, cinemas, bars and cafés. A landmark here is the memorable **Kaiser-Wilhelm-Gedächtniskirche** church (Mon–Sat 10am–4/6pm), destroyed by British bombing in 1943 and left as a reminder of the horrors of war. There's little to do on the Ku'damm other than stroll, window-shop and spend money; the main attraction nearby is the seriously kitsch **Erotikmuseum** at Joachimstaler Str. 4 (daily 9am–midnight), devoted to two thousand years of erotic art, sex toys and aphrodisiacs. Unfortunately, its seediness and disorganization make it less fun than it sounds.

Tiergarten

The zoo itself, beside Zoo Station, forms the beginning of the giant **Tiergarten**, a restful expanse of woodland and a good place to wander along the banks of the Landwehrkanal. Strasse des 17 Juni heads all the way through the Tiergarten to the Brandenburg Gate.

Schloss Charlottenburg

Four kilometres northwest of the Tiergarten is the sumptuously restored **Schloss Charlottenburg** at Spandauer Damm 10–22 (Tues–Sun 9am–5pm; Old Palace €10/students €7; New Wing €6/students €5; Ⓦwww.spsg.de). Commissioned by the future Queen Sophie Charlotte in 1695, it was added to throughout the eighteenth and early nineteenth centuries. The resulting complex provides an idea of life at the Hohenzoller court over the centuries. Admission to the Old Palace includes a tour of the main state apartments and self-guided visits to the private chambers (where the Prussian crown jewels can be seen), while the New Wing includes a wonderful array of paintings by Watteau and other eighteenth-century French artists. Just south of the Schloss complex, the **Museum Berggruen** at Schlossstr. 1 (Tues–Sun 10am–6pm; €6/students €3) presents a large Picasso collection, as well as works by Matisse, Klee and Giacometti.

The East Side Gallery

Stretching along the River Spree, the open-air **East Side Gallery** is a 1.3-kilometre-long section of the Berlin Wall that has been preserved as a memorial in its original location. Covered with paintings by international artists, including one of a Trabi, the famous GDR car, breaking through the Wall, this unprepossessing memorial provides an interesting opportunity to reflect on the trauma of division and the regime that came to rule the GDR.

The Olympiastadion

Located at the extreme west of the city is the site of the 2006 Football World Cup final, the **Olympiastadion.** If you can't make it to a Hertha BSC (Ⓦwww.herthabsc.de) match to marvel at the stadium's architecture, you can take a tour (€4/students €3; Ⓣ030/25 00 23 22, Ⓦwww.olympiastadion-berlin.de). Though it's theoretically open daily, times vary considerably depending on matches and events; be sure to check online or at the tourist office. To get here take U- or S-Bahn to Olympiastadion.

Arrival

Air From Berlin's Tegel airport (TXL; Ⓦwww.berlin-airport.de) the frequent #TXL express bus (€2.10) runs to the Hauptbahnhof as well as to Alexanderplatz, while #X9 express or local #109 buses (€2.10) run to Bahnhof Zoologischer Garten (usually referred to as Bahnhof Zoo). From Berlin's Schönefeld airport (SXF) S-Bahn trains run to Alexanderplatz, the Hauptbahnhof and Bahnhof Zoo (every 30min; 20–30min; €2.10); bus #X7 runs to nearby U-Bahn Rudow. From Berlin's Tempelhof Airport the U-Bahn #6 runs to the centre.

Train The new Hauptbahnhof is located slightly northeast from the Brandenburg Gate, and is well connected to the rest of the city by S- and U-Bahn. Some trains from Poland and the East terminate at Bahnhof Lichtenberg, easily accessible on the S-Bahn.

Bus Most international buses stop at the bus station (ZOB), linked to the centre by express buses #X34 and #X49, as well as regular buses #104, #139, #218, #349 and #M49; U-Bahn #2, from Kaiserdamm station; S-Bahn from Messe-Nord/ICC.

Information

Tourist office The most convenient tourist office is at the main train station (daily 8am–10pm; Ⓣ030/25 00 25, Ⓦwww.visitberlin.de). Additional offices are at Brandenburger Tor (daily 9.30/10am–8pm) and at Ku'damm, Kurfürstendamm 21 (Mon–Sat 9.30am–8pm, Sun 9.30am–6pm). They offer a room-booking service (rooms from ❹); €3 in person or free online or over the phone.

Discount passes The 48/72-hour Welcome Card (Ⓦwww.berlin-welcomecard.de; Berlin AB 48/72hr €16/21; Berlin and Potsdam ABC 48/72hr

€17.50/24) provides free travel and up to fifty percent off at many of the major tourist sights. Better value though if you intend to visit lots of museums is the SchauLUST Museumpass (see p.464).

City transport

Metro The U-Bahn metro system is efficient and extensive; trains run daily 4am–12.30am (Fri & Sat all night). The S-Bahn, whose stops are further apart, travels to the outer suburbs (such as Wannsee) and out of the city boundaries (eg Potsdam).
Bus and tram The city bus network – and the tram system in eastern Berlin – covers most of the gaps left by the U-Bahn: night buses run at intervals of around twenty minutes, although the routes often differ from daytime ones; free maps are available at most stations.
Tickets can be bought from machines at U-Bahn station entrances, on trams, or from bus drivers; good for any mode of transport, they cost €2.10, allow you to travel in two of the three tariff zones (AB), and are valid for a single trip once validated (*entwertet*) in the yellow machines on platforms. Longer trips across three tariff zones (ABC), from central Berlin to Potsdam for example, cost €2.70. A Kurzstreckentarif (short-trip ticket; €1.20) allows you to travel up to three train or six bus/tram stops. A day ticket is €6.10 for two tariff zones, a seven-day card €25.40.
Taxi If you hail a taxi on the street – rather than at a stand or by phone – you'll pay €3.50 for a two-kilometre ride. You must clearly say you want a short-trip price (Kurzstreckentarif) before the trip starts. Otherwise, a taxi costs €3 at flag fall and €1.55–1.20/km. Taxis can be ordered on ⓣ030/44 33 22.

Accommodation

Berlin has tons of great **hostels**, primarily in the happening districts of Mitte, Prenzlauer Berg, Kreuzberg and Friedrichshain; most of the hotels, on the other hand, are near the Ku'damm – in the less exciting west. Accommodation in **high season** can be hard to find – especially if there's a festival or major event taking place – and it's best to call at least a couple of weeks in advance. Most of the accommodation listed can be booked online.

Hostels

BaxPax ⓦwww.baxpax.de. Trio of backpacker outfits with clean, bright-as-a-button rooms. *Kreuzberg* (Skalitzer Str. 104 ⓣ030/695 183 22; U-Bahn Görlitzer Bahnhof) and *Mittes Backpacker* (Chausseestr. 102 ⓣ030/283 909 65; U-Bahn Zinnowitzer Str.) are laid-back, offering cooking facilities, bike rental and (in Kreuzberg only) a rare chance to sleep in a VW Beetle. The *Downtown BaxPax* (Ziegelstrasse 28 ⓣ030/278 748 80; S- & U-Bahn Friedrichstr.) is in the best location, but lacks flair. Sheets €2.50. Dorms ❷, rooms ❺–❻
The Circus Weinbergsweg 1a, Mitte ⓣ030/28 39 14 33, ⓦwww.circus-berlin.de. Welcoming, clean, fun and deservedly popular base near the action in the east, with helpful staff. U-Bahn Rosenthaler Platz. Sheets €2. Dorms ❷, rooms ❺
City Stay Hotel Rosenstr. 16, Mitte ⓣ030/23 62 40 31, ⓦwww.citystay.de. Bright and airy hostel in the bustling heart of Mitte which, thanks to its off-street location, is a peaceful and safe base for travellers. Hackescher Markt S-Bahn. Dorms ❷, rooms ❺
EastSeven Schwedter Str. 7 ⓣ030/936 222 40, ⓦwww.eastseven.de. Cosy backpackers' place with kitchen and garden, between Mitte and Prenzlauer Berg. U-Bahn Senefelderplatz. Sheets €3. Dorms ❷, rooms ❺
Heart of Gold Hostel Johannisstr. 11, Mitte ⓣ030/29 00 33 00, ⓦwww.heartofgold-hostel.de. Fantastic location in the heart of downtown Mitte, this *Hitchhiker's Guide*/starship-themed place has a relaxing bar, spotless rooms and friendly pilots. Sheets included. U-Bahn Oranienburger Tor. Dorms ❷, rooms ❺
Helter Skelter Kalkscheunenstr. 4–5, Mitte ⓣ030/280 44 997, ⓦwww.helterskelterhostel.com. Lively and central backpackers' with kitchen and sheets included. U-Bahn Oranienburger Tor. Dorms ❷, rooms ❺.
Lette'm Sleep Lettestr. 7, Prenzlauer Berg ⓣ030/44 73 36 23, ⓦwww.backpackers.de. Chilled-out and comfortable hostel with free Internet, a kitchen and an ideal Prenzlauer Berg location. U-Bahn Eberswalder Str. Dorms ❷, rooms ❺
Meininger ⓣ030/66 63 61 00, ⓦwww.meininger-hostels.de. Although not directly in the centre, all these places are modern, friendly, and include breakfast and sheets. Prenzlauer Berg: Schönhauser Allee 19 (U-Bahn Senefelderplatz); Schöneberg: Meininger Str. 10 (U-Bahn Rathaus Schöneberg); Kreuzberg: Hallesches Ufer 30 & Tempelhofer Ufer 10 (U-Bahn Möckernbrücke). Dorms ❷, rooms ❺–❼
Odyssee Globetrotter Hostel Grünberger Str. 23, Friedrichshain ⓣ030/29 00 00 81, ⓦwww.globetrotterhostel.de. Young, well-organized hostel with individually designed rooms, ideally situated

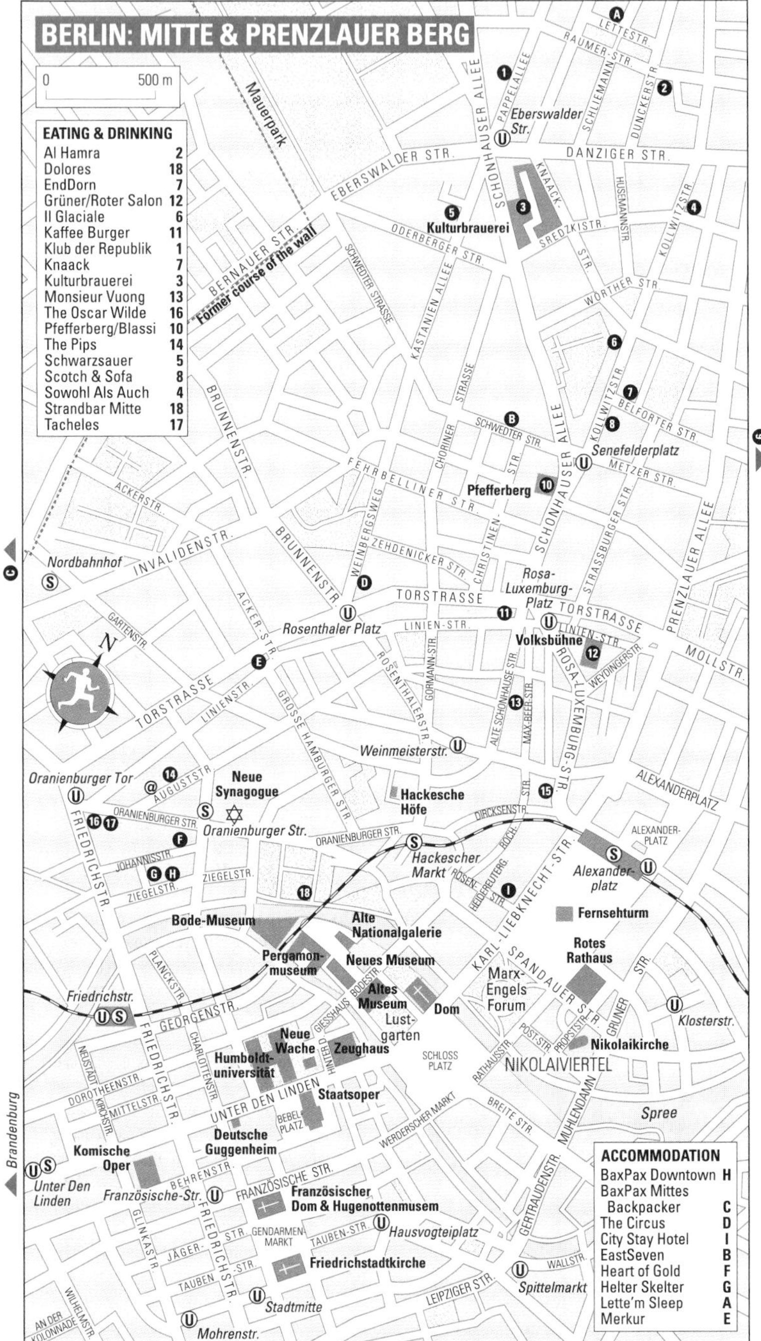
BERLIN: MITTE & PRENZLAUER BERG
0 500 m
EATING & DRINKING
Al Hamra 2
Dolores 18
EndDorn 7
Grüner/Roter Salon 12
Il Glaciale 6
Kaffee Burger 11
Klub der Republik 1
Knaack 7
Kulturbrauerei 3
Monsieur Vuong 13
The Oscar Wilde 16
Pfefferberg/Blassi 10
The Pips 14
Schwarzsauer 5
Scotch & Sofa 8
Sowohl Als Auch 4
Strandbar Mitte 18
Tacheles 17
ACCOMMODATION
BaxPax Downtown H
BaxPax Mittes Backpacker C
The Circus D
City Stay Hotel I
EastSeven B
Heart of Gold F
Helter Skelter G
Lette'm Sleep A
Merkur E
Mauerpark
Former course of the wall
Eberswalder Str.
Kulturbrauerei
Senefelderplatz
Pfefferberg
Nordbahnhof
Rosenthaler Platz
Rosa-Luxemburg-Platz
Volksbühne
Weinmeisterstr.
Oranienburger Tor
Neue Synagogue
Oranienburger Str.
Hackesche Höfe
Hackescher Markt
Alexanderplatz
Fernsehturm
Rotes Rathaus
Bode-Museum
Alte Nationalgalerie
Pergamon-museum
Neues Museum
Altes Museum
Dom
Lust-garten
Marx-Engels Forum
Friedrichstr.
Klosterstr.
Neue Wache
Zeughaus
Humboldt-universität
Nikolaikirche
NIKOLAIVIERTEL
Staatsoper
Spree
Deutsche Guggenheim
Komische Oper
Brandenburg
Unter Den Linden
Französische-Str.
Französischer Dom & Hugenottenmusem
Hausvogteiplatz
Friedrichstadtkirche
Spittelmarkt
Stadtmitte
Mohrenstr.
GERMANY
BERLIN

for the Friedrichshain nightlife scene – though a touch far from the sights. U-Bahn Frankfurter Tor. Dorms ❷, rooms ❺

Hotels

Berolina Stuttgarter Platz 17 ⓣ030/32 70 90 72, ⓦwww.hotel-berolina.de. Friendly, functional place, with five-bed rooms (€65). Breakfast not included. Right next to S-Bahn Charlottenburg. ❺

Bogota Schlüterstr. 45 ⓣ030/881 50 01, ⓦwww.hotelbogota.de. Traditional-style place, with plentiful doubles and a dozen four-bed rooms (€134), in a stuffy but comfortable 1911 building – ask about the history. S-Bahn Savignyplatz. ❼

Bregenz Bregenzer Str. 5 ⓣ030/88 14 307, ⓦwww.hotelbregenz-berlin.de. Very quiet and cosy family-run set-up with bright one- to four-bed rooms. Only a 5min walk from the Ku'damm. U-Bahn Adenauer-Platz. ❻

Korfu 11 Rankestr. 35 ⓣ030/21 24 790, ⓦwww.hp-korfu.de. Unexciting but clean and simple rooms in a central location. Breakfast not included but free Internet access provided. U-Bahn Kurfürstendamm. Shared bathroom ❻, en suite ❽

Merkur Torstr. 156 ⓣ030/28 29 523, ⓦwww.hotel-merkur-berlin.de. Comfortable rooms, including one with five beds, within easy walking distance of city-centre attractions and local nightlife. Most rooms have showers. U-Bahn Rosenthaler Platz. ❽

Eating

The range and quality of **restaurants** in Berlin is unmatched in any other German city. The cheapest way of warding off hunger is to hit the *Imbiss* snack stands, or one of the *Mensas*, officially for German students but usually open to anyone who looks the part. One of the most fun ways to feed yourself in Berlin is to head to the bustling Kreuzberg/Neukölln market (Tues & Fri noon–6pm) on the Maybach Ufer (U-Bahn to Schönleinstr. or Kottbusser Tor), where cheap breads, veggies, meat and Turkish sweets are in ample supply.

Cafés

Al Hamra Raumerstr. 16, Prenzlauer Berg. Relaxed, extremely popular Arabian-style café/bar. Good food and cheap drinks every day – Sunday's "Orientale Brunch" until 5pm is especially tasty (€8). U-Bahn Eberswalder Str. or S-Bahn Prenzlauer Allee.

Café Einstein Kurfürstenstr. 58, Charlottenburg. Housed in a seemingly ancient mansion, this place exudes the formal ambience of the prewar Berlin *Kaffeehaus*, with international newspapers, breakfast served daily till 2pm and delicious *Kuchen* (€5). U-Bahn Nollendorfplatz.

Curry 36 Mehringdamm 36, Kreuzberg. One of the best places to try Berlin *Currywurst* (€3) – a traditional fast-food combination of grilled sausage, hot tomato sauce and curry powder. Open until 4am every day. U-Bahn Mehringdamm.

Il Glaciale Kollwitzstrasse 59, Prenzlauer Berg. This tiny gelateria makes all its ice cream in-house, with delectable, exciting results. Open April–Nov. Grape-tahini scoop €.70. U-Bahn Senefelderplatz.

Neues Ufer Hauptstr. 157, Schöneberg. Cramped, cool yet casual and kitschy gay café. Cappuccino €3. U-Bahn Kleistpark.

Schwarzsauer Kastanienallee 13–14, Prenzlauer Berg. Large, trendy bar/café, serving scrumptious breakfasts at €3–5. U-Bahn Eberswalder Str.

Sowohl Als Auch Kollwitzstr. 88, Prenzlauer Berg. Hands-down the best cakes in the land, with an extensive coffee and tea menu to boot. Black Forest gateau €4. U-Bahn Eberswalder or Senefelderplatz.

Restaurants

Carib Motzstr. 30, Schöneberg. Caribbean cuisine, friendly service, a mixed, relaxed crowd and lethal rum cocktails. Jamaican jerk chicken €8. U-Bahn Nollendorfplatz or Viktoria-Luise-Platz.

Il Casolare Grimmstr. 30, Kreuzberg. A wonderful, always-packed Italian restaurant offering great pizzas and a unique line in punk poster interior decor. Pizzas from €7. U-Bahn Schönleinstr.

Dolores Rosa-Luxemburg-Str. 7, Mitte.

TREAT YOURSELF

Dinner Delicious Vietnamese cuisine at *Monsieur Vuong* (see p.471), a fixture on the Mitte dining circuit.

Dessert & Drinks Amble north on Alte Schönhauser Strasse to *Scotch & Sofa* for cocktails (see p.471) or to *Sowohl Als Auch* for heavenly cakes (see above).

Live Music & Dancing Splurge on a concert at a small venue like the *Knaack* (see p.472), then head to an all-night club or relaxed lounge such as *Klub der Republik* (see p.471) till the sun rises.

Morning-After Brunch Sleep it off, then head to *Schwarzsauer* (p.469) or one of the myriad breakfast spots around Helmholtzplatz (U-Bahn Eberswalder Str.) for an irresistible brunch buffet.

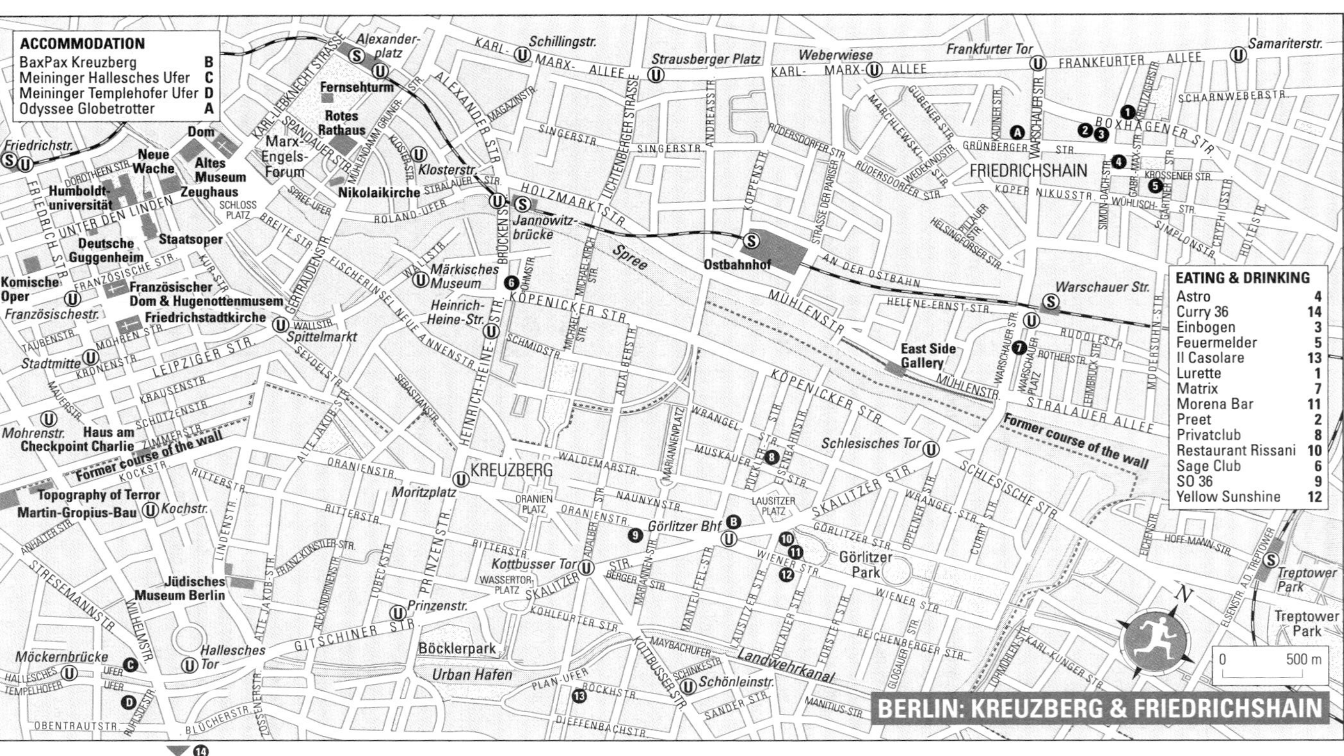
BERLIN: KREUZBERG & FRIEDRICHSHAIN
ACCOMMODATION
BaxPax Kreuzberg B
Meininger Hallesches Ufer C
Meininger Templehofer Ufer D
Odyssee Globetrotter A
EATING & DRINKING
Astro 4
Curry 36 14
Einbogen 3
Feuermelder 5
Il Casolare 13
Lurette 1
Matrix 7
Morena Bar 11
Preet 2
Privatclub 8
Restaurant Rissani 10
Sage Club 6
SO 36 9
Yellow Sunshine 12
FRIEDRICHSHAIN
KREUZBERG
Spree
Landwehrkanal
Former course of the wall
Alexanderplatz
Fernsehturm
Rotes Rathaus
Marx-Engels-Forum
Nikolaikirche
Dom
Neue Wache
Altes Museum
Zeughaus
Humboldt-universität
Deutsche Guggenheim
Staatsoper
Komische Oper
Französischer Dom & Hugenottenmusem
Friedrichstadtkirche
Märkisches Museum
Ostbahnhof
East Side Gallery
Haus am Checkpoint Charlie
Topography of Terror
Martin-Gropius-Bau
Jüdisches Museum Berlin
Görlitzer Park
Böcklerpark
Urban Hafen
Treptower Park
0 500 m

Mouthwatering California-style Mexican food, complete with full-on San Francisco decor and the predictable concentration of expats. Chicken mole burrito €4.25. S-/U-Bahn Alexanderplatz or Hackescher Markt.
Einbogen Simon Dach Str. 1, Friedrichshain. Stylish bar/restaurant serving decent German cuisine, with outdoor seating and all-you-can-eat deals on Sundays for €7. U-Bahn Boxhagener Str.
EndDorn Belforter Str. 27, Prenzlauer Berg. Brick-walled eatery/bar where every dish (pasta, chilli con carne, baguettes, breakfast etc) costs less than €5. Closed Sun, drinks only Sat. U-Bahn Senefelderplatz.
Jules Verne Schlüterstr. 61, Charlottenburg. Meals here are international, unusual and delicious, ranging from chicken saté to cannelloni. Sunday brunch is divine. Lunch €5.50, dinner €10. S-Bahn Savignyplatz.
Monsieur Vuong Alte Schönhauser Str. 46, Mitte. Small, hip and popular Vietnamese place with a high-quality, low-price menu that changes daily. Meals €7. U-Bahn Weinmeisterstrasse.
Preet Boxhagener Str. 17, Friedrichshain. Popular, pukka and cheap Punjabi restaurant in the thick of the bars and clubs. Mattar Paneer €3.90. Open till midnight. U-Bahn Boxhagener Str.
Restaurant Rissani Spreewaldplatz 4, Kreuzberg. Next to the park off Wiener Strasse, this place has a relaxed atmosphere and platefuls of mouthwatering Moroccan food at low prices (from €6). U-Bahn Görlitzer Bhf.
Yellow Sunshine Wiener Str. 19, Kreuzberg. Low-key yet delicious organic vegetarian diner with a huge menu. "Vegaburger" €3.39. U-Bahn Görlitzer Bhf.

Drinking and nightlife

Berlin **nightlife** in the city outstrips many other European capitals, and it's centred on several different neighbourhoods. Most of the action is in **Eastern Berlin**: Oranienburger Strasse and Rosenthaler Strasse in Mitte host dozens of new bars and clubs that attract a young professional crowd as well as tourists, while the streets further north in Prenzlauer Berg, such as Kastanienallee, and to the east around Boxhagener Strasse in Friedrichshain, and a little further south, in Kreuzberg, range from slightly alternative to solidly hipster. Berlin's diverse **gay scene** is spread across the city, but with a focus of sorts in Schöneberg, around Nollendorfplatz. The magazine *Siegessäule* (www.siegessaeule.de) has current listings and can be picked up in many cafés, libraries and shops.

Bars

Astro Simon-Dach-Str. 40, Friedrichshain. Always packed pre-club kitsch bar with different DJs nightly. U-Bahn Frankfurter Tor.
Feuermelder Krossenerstr. 24, Friedrichshain. Lively corner bar popular with scruffy artsy types on Boxhagener Platz. U-Bahn Samariterstr.
Klub der Republik Pappelallee 81, Prenzlauer Berg. You'll find cheap drinks and frequent live DJs in this fabulous chilled-out lounge/bar with comfy sofas. Fire-escape steps up to the entrance. U-Bahn Eberswalder Str.
Lurette Boxhagener Str. 105, Friedrichshain. Retro bar/club, complete with Sixties wall projections, dishing up cheap cocktails to an upbeat lounge crowd. U-Bahn Samariterstr.
Morena Bar Wiener Str. 60, Kreuzberg. Studenty, blue-tiled bar that opens early for good breakfasts. U-Bahn Görlitzer Bhf.
The Oscar Wilde Friedrichstr. 112, Mitte. A large pub near Oranienburger Tor U-Bahn, for those who prefer their pints black and with a creamy white head. Live music and TV sports coverage most weekends. U-Bahn Oranienburger Tor.
The Pips Auguststr. 84, Mitte. Packed, welcoming and friendly bar with vibrant designer furnishings and different cocktail offers every day. Closed Sun & Mon. U-Bahn Oranienburger Str.
Schwarzes Café Kantstr. 148, Charlottenburg. Kantstrasse's best hang-out for the young and chic, with a bohemian atmosphere, good music and Kölsch on tap. Great 24-hour breakfasts, too (€7). Open 24/7 except Tues 3–11am. S-/U-Bahn Savignyplatz or Zoologischer Garten.
Scotch & Sofa Kollwitzstr. 18, Prenzlauer Berg. Trendy, relaxed pre-club bar with free Internet and a loyal crowd. U-Bahn Senefelderplatz.
Strandbar Mitte Monbijoustr. 3, Mitte. Seasonal (April–Oct), popular beach-themed bar with sand and deck chairs overlooking the River Spree. S-Bahn Hackescher Markt or Oranienburger Str.
Tacheles Oranienburger Str. 54–56, Mitte. Unintimidating squatters' alternative arts centre that's something of an institution. It includes a cinema, three bars and beer garden. U-Bahn Oranienburger Tor.

Clubs

Don't bother turning up before midnight to clubs in Berlin. The ones below are open nightly unless otherwise indicated. To find out what's on, pick up one of the listings magazines, *Zitty* (www.zitty.de), *Tip* (www.berlinonline.de/tip), or the English-language *Exberliner* (www.exberliner.com).
Grüner Salon & Roter Salon Rosa-Luxemburg-Platz 2, Mitte www.gruener-salon.de, www.

roter-salon.de. Two clubs in one; 1920s ballroom ambience with live music, DJs and various musical styles depending on the day of week. U-Bahn Rosa-Luxemburg-Platz.

Kaffee Burger Torstr. 60, Mitte. Small, meandering former GDR bar decorated in deep flushed red, with an attached live music venue and infamously funky Russian disco twice monthly. U-Bahn Rosenthaler Platz/Rosa-Luxemburg-Platz.

Knaack Greifswalder Str. 224, Prenzlauer Berg Ⓦwww.knaack-berlin.de. Indie, rock and pop club, as well as live music venue. Tram to Am Friedrichshain.

Matrix Warschauer Platz 18, Friedrichshain Ⓦwww.matrix-berlin.de. Famous disco that aims to satisfy all tastes across three dance floors. House, soul, rock and more. U-Bahn Warschauer Str.

Pfefferberg/Blassi Schönhauser Allee 176, Prenzlauer Berg. Bars, dance floors, basement club (Ⓦwww.pfefferbank.de) and wonderful beer garden in summer with live music. U-Bahn Senefelder Platz.

Privatclub Pücklerstr. 34, Kreuzberg Ⓦwww.privatclub-berlin.de. Highly intimate basement club (under Markthalle) with an eclectic and unpredictable lightshow, drawing in a dance-oriented crowd of all ages. Open Fri & Sat. U-Bahn Görlitzer Bhf.

Sage Club Köpenicker Str. 78 Ⓦwww.sage-club.de. Very popular club with three dance floors and a swimming pool. Strict door policy but worth persevering. U-Bahn Heinrich-Heine-Str.

SO 36 Oranienstr. 190, Kreuzberg. Dark, punky cult club with a large gay and lesbian following. Live music and techno–outbreaks of belly dancing are not unknown. U-Bahn Görlitzer Bhf.

Entertainment

CineStar Potsdamerstr. 4 Ⓦwww.cinestar.de. Cinema in the Sony Centre on Potsdamer Platz that screens films in English; €8/students €6. S-/U-Bahn Potsdamer Platz.

Deutsche Oper Bismarckstr. 35 Ⓣ030/34 10 249, Ⓦwww.deutscheoperberlin.de. Opera and ballet in a large, modern venue, plus good classical concerts too. U-Bahn Deutsche Oper.

Junction Bar Gneisenaustr. 18, Kreuzberg Ⓦwww.junction-bar.de. A fixture on the local jazz circuit, with nightly live music and DJs at the weekends. U-Bahn Gneisenaustr.

Komische Oper Behrenstr. 55–57 Ⓣ030/47 99 74 00, Ⓦwww.komische-oper-berlin.de. Some very good opera productions are staged here and the house orchestra performs classical and contemporary music. U-Bahn Französische Str.

Philharmonie Herbert-von-Karajan-Str. 1 Ⓣ030/25 48 80, Ⓦwww.berliner-philharmoniker.de. Custom-built home of the world's most celebrated orchestra, the Berlin Philharmonic. U-/S-Bahn Potsdamer Platz.

Staatsoper Unter den Linden 7 Ⓣ030/20 35 40, Ⓦwww.staatsoper-berlin.org. Excellent operatic productions in one of central Berlin's most beautiful buildings.. S-/U-Bahn Friedrichstr.

Shopping

Clothes Boutiques and local designers are in good supply in Berlin, though bargains can be hard to find. The part of Mitte just northeast from S-Bahn Hackescher Markt is the best place for shoe boutiques. Head to Prenzlauer Berg (from Kastanienallee to Helmholzplatz) for high-quality, high-priced local designers, and to the Boxhagener Platz area in Friedrichshain for the latest hipster apparel.

Markets Flea markets (*Flohmärkte*) abound in Berlin; head to the Mauerpark in Prenzlauer Berg on Sunday from 8am to 6pm (tram M10 to Bernauer Str./Wolliner Str.) for the best bargains.

Directory

Bike rental and tours Fat Tire, beneath the TV tower at Alexanderplatz; €12/day. Their bike tours are a handy way to see the city with a friendly guide showing you all the Berlin unmissables on a ten-kilometre, four-hour tour with beer-garden pit stop (Ⓣ030/24 04 79 91, Ⓦwww.berlinbikerental.com; €20/students €18).

Embassies and consulates Australia, Wallstr. 76–79 Ⓣ030/88 00 880; Canada, Leipziger Platz 17 Ⓣ030/20 31 20; Ireland, Friedrichstr. 200 Ⓣ030/22 07 20; New Zealand, Friedrichstr. 60 Ⓣ030/20 62 10; South Africa, Tiergartenstr.18 Ⓣ030/22073 202; UK, Wilhelmstr. 70–71 Ⓣ030/20 45 70; US, Neustädtische Kirchstr. 4–5 Ⓣ030/2385 174.

Exchange Reisebank, at the Hauptbahnhof (daily 8am–10pm), Zoo Station (daily 7.30am–10pm), Friedrichstrasse station (daily 8am–8pm) and Ostbahnhof (daily 8am–8/10pm).

Hospitals Charité University Clinic, Schumannstr. 20/21 Ⓣ030/2802 2; Krankenhaus Prenzlauer Berg, Fröbelstr. 15 Ⓣ030/42 420; Vivantes Klinikum Spandau, Neue Bergstr. 6 Ⓣ030/338 70.

Internet easyEverything, Kurfürstendamm 224, and NetLounge, Auguststr. 89.

Laundry Hermannstr. 74–75.

Left luggage At major stations.

Pharmacy Apotheke Haupbahnhof, at the Hauptbahnhof. Open 24/7.

Post office Joachimsthaler Str. 7 (Mon–Sat 8am–midnight, Sun 10am–6pm).

Moving on

Train Dresden (hourly; 2hr); Frankfurt (hourly; 4hr); Hamburg (hourly; 2hr 30min); Hannover (hourly; 1hr 30min); Leipzig (hourly; 2hr); Munich (frequent; 6hr 30 min); Prague (every 2hr; 4hr 30min); Warsaw (8 daily; 6hr); Weimar (every 2hr; 3hr).

DAY-TRIPS FROM BERLIN

Thirty-five kilometres north of the city lies **Sachsenhausen concentration camp** (daily: mid-March to mid-Oct 8.30am–6pm; mid-Oct to mid-March 8.30am–4.30pm; free; Ⓦwww.gedenkstaette-sachsenhausen.de), a sobering place where roughly 100,000 people died at the hands of the Nazis. The original buildings have been turned into a decentralized museum on and memorial to the events that took place at the camp. Take S-Bahn #1 to Oranienburg (every 10min; 50min; Zone C), and then bus #804 (hourly) or a twenty-minute signposted walk.

Potsdam

POTSDAM makes an excellent day-trip from Berlin; take S-Bahn 7 (every 10min; 40min; zone C) or a regional train. The city's main draw is Park Sanssouci (2km east from main station; bus #695 or bus #X15 on weekends; joint ticket covering entry to all sights below €15/students €10; Ⓦwww.spsg.de), a dazzling collection of eighteenth- and nineteenth-century Baroque and Rococo palaces and ornamental gardens that were the fabled retreat of the Prussian kings. To avoid the crowds, visit on a weekday. **Schloss Sanssouci** (Tues–Sun: April–Oct 9am–5pm; Nov–March 9am–4pm; €12/students €8), the star attraction, was a pleasure palace completed in 1747 where Frederick the Great could escape the stresses of Berlin and his wife. You should head here first, as tickets are timed and sell out fast. West of the palace is the **Bildergalerie** (May–Oct only: Tues–Sun 10am–5pm; €3/students €2.50), a restrained Baroque creation with paintings by Rubens, Van Dyck and Caravaggio. On the opposite side of the Schloss, steps lead down to the **Neue Kammern** (April Sat & Sun 10am–5pm; May–Oct Tues–Sun; €3/students €2.50), originally used as an orangery and later converted into a guest palace. Walking west through 1.5km of stylized gardens, you'll see the massive Rococo **Neues Palais** (Mon–Thurs, Sat & Sun: April–Oct 9am–5pm; Nov–March 9am–4pm; €5/students €4). The interior is exquisitely opulent – the ground-floor Grotto Hall alone, decorated from floor to ceiling with shells and semiprecious stones to form images of sea monsters and dragons, merits a trip from Berlin.

Eastern Germany

By the time the Communist GDR (German Democratic Republic, or East Germany) was fully incorporated into the Federal Republic (West Germany), one year after the peaceful revolution (or Wende) of 1989, most vestiges of the old political system had been swept away. Yet there remains a long way to go before the two parts of the country achieve parity, and the cities of **eastern Germany** are still in the process of social and economic change. Berlin stands apart from the rest of the East, but its sense of excitement finds an echo in the two other main cities – **Leipzig**, which provided the vanguard of the revolution, and **Dresden**, the beautiful Saxon capital so ruthlessly destroyed in 1945. Equally enticing are some of the smaller places, notably **Weimar**, the fountainhead of much of European art and culture. The small towns of **Meissen** and **Quedlinburg** retain more of the appearance and atmosphere of prewar Germany than anywhere in the West.

LEIPZIG

LEIPZIG has always been among the most dynamic of German cities. With its influential and respected university, and a tradition of trade fairs dating back to the Middle Ages, there was never the degree of isolation from outside influences experienced by so many cities behind the Iron Curtain. Leipzigers have embraced the challenges of reunification, and the city's imposing monuments, narrow cobbled backstreets and wide-ranging nightlife make for an inviting visit.

What to see and do

Most points of interest lie within the old centre. Following Nikolaistrasse due south from the train station brings you to the **Nikolaikirche**, a rallying point during the Wende. Although a sombre medieval structure outside, inside the church is a real eye-grabber thanks to rich decoration, works of art and pink columns designed to resemble palms. A couple of blocks west is the Markt, whose eastern side is entirely occupied by the **Altes Rathaus**, built in the grandest German Renaissance style with elaborate gables, an asymmetrical tower and the longest inscription to be found on any building in the world. On the north side of the square is the handsome **Alte Waage**, or weigh house.

Haus der Geschichte

Just southwest of the Markt, at Grimmaische Str. 6, is the **Haus der Geschichte** (Tues–Fri 9am–6pm, Sat & Sun 10am–6pm; free; Ⓦwww.hdg.de), a fascinating multimedia museum on the history of the GDR and the people's resistance to dictatorship.

The Alte Handelsbörse and Museum der Bildenden Künste

To the rear of the Altes Rathaus, approached by a graceful double flight of steps, is the **Alte Handelsbörse**, a Baroque gem that was formerly the trade exchange headquarters. Two minutes' walk further north, at 10 Katharinenstrasse, is the immense new building of the **Museum der Bildenden Künste** (Tues & Thurs–Sun 10am–6pm, Wed noon–8pm; €7/students €5, free admittance second Mon every month; Ⓦwww.mdbk.de), a distinguished collection of old masters, including Cranach and Rubens.

The Thomaskirche and Bach-Museum

Klostergasse leads southwards to the **Thomaskirche**, where Johann Sebastian Bach served as cantor for the last 27 years of his life. Predominantly Gothic, the church has been altered down the centuries. The most remarkable feature is its musical tradition: the Thomanerchor choir, which Bach once directed, can usually be heard on Fridays (6pm), Saturdays (3pm) and during the Sunday service (9.30am). Directly across from the church is the **Bach-Museum** (daily 10am–5pm; €4/students €2; Ⓦwww.bach-leipzig.de), with an extensive show of mementos of the great composer.

Close by, at Dittrichring 24 and Käthe-Kollwitz-Strasse, is another historically important museum, the Round Corner or **Runde Ecke** (daily 10am–6pm; free), a fascinating trawl through the methods and machinery of the Stasi, East Germany's secret police.

Arrival and information

Air The Leipzig-Halle Airport is connected with the main train station by the Airport Express train (every 30min; 15min).

Train Leipzig's enormous Hauptbahnhof is at the northeastern end of the Ring, which encircles the old part of the city.

Tourist office The tourist office is located opposite the station's Osthalle (East Hall) at Richard-Wagner-Str. 1 (Mon–Fri 9.30am–6pm, Sat 9.30am–4pm, Sun 9.30am–3pm; Nov–Feb opens Mon–Fri at

10am; ⓣ0341/71 04 260, ⓦwww.leipzig.de); it can book private rooms (service free, ⑤).

Discount pass The Leipzig Card (€8.90/18.50 for one/three days) covers unlimited use of public transport and provides discounted admission to museums. A day-ticket for the city transport system costs €5.20, a single trip €1.80.

Accommodation

Auensee Gustav-Esche-Str. 5 ⓣ0341/46 51 600, ⓦwww.camping-auensee.de. This campsite is open year-round, with bungalow rooms available (⑤). Reception April–Oct 2–9.30pm; Nov–March 2–7.30pm; tram #10 or #11 to Annaberger Str., then bus #80 to Auensee. ❶

Central Globetrotter Kurt-Schumacher-Str. 41 ⓣ0341/14 98 960, ⓦwww.globetrotter-leipzig.de. Popular backpacker spot three minutes' walk west of the station. Sheets €2.50, sleeping bags not allowed. Dorms ❷, rooms ❹

Sleepy Lion Käthe-Kollwitz-Str. 3 ⓣ0341/99 39 480, ⓦwww.hostel-leipzig.de. Well-run hostel just west of the centre. Tram to Gottschedstr. Sheets €2.50, sleeping bags not allowed. Dorms ❷, rooms ❺

Zur City Karl-Liebknechtstr. 40 ⓣ0341/2 11 33 05, ⓦwww.pension-leipzig.de. Excellent pension between the hip Südvorstadt neighbourhood and the centre. Quads available, breakfast not included. ❺

Eating and drinking

Leipzig is refreshingly affordable: meals are around €5, entry to clubs or shows around €4.

Ilses Erika Bernhard-Göring-Str. 152, Südvorstadt. ⓦwww.ilseserika.de. Indie bar, club and music venue Thurs–Sat; beer garden all summer long. Tram to Connewitz Kreuz.

Maga Pon Gottschedstr. 11. The trendiest spot in town may just be this well-located and eccentrically decorated *Waschcafé* – scrambled eggs and a load of laundry, €3 each.

Moritzbastei Universitätsstr. 9 ⓦwww.moritzbastei.de. A tightly packed collection of bars and clubs, including one of the biggest student clubs in Europe. Housed beneath the medieval city fortifications. Tram to Leuschner-, Ross-, or Augustusplatz.

naTo Karl-Liebknecht-Str. 46, Südvorstadt ⓦwww.nato-leipzig.de. Popular studenty bar, live music venue and cinema with films in their original language – though that's more likely to be Spanish than English. Tram to Südplatz.

Zur Pleissenburg Ratsfreichulstr. 2. Great-value bar/restaurant in the centre serving hearty German food daily until 4am. They still accept the old German Mark. Ribs for €5.50.

Moving on

Train Berlin (hourly; 1hr); Dresden (hourly; 1hr 40min); Meissen (hourly; 2hr); Weimar (frequent; 50min–1hr 20min).

WEIMAR

Despite its modest size, **WEIMAR** has played an unmatched role in the development of German culture: Goethe, Schiller and Nietzsche all made it their home, as did the Cranachs and Bach, and the architects and designers of the Bauhaus school. The town was also chosen as the drafting place for the constitution of the democratic republic established after World War I, a regime whose failure ended with the Nazi accession. Birthplace of the Hitler Youth movement, Weimar is also where Buchenwald, one of the most notorious concentration camps, was built, and its preservation here is a shocking reminder of the Nazi era. Add to all this the town's cobbled streets and laid-back, quietly highbrow atmosphere and Weimar is worth a day's detour.

What to see and do

Weimar's main sights are concentrated in the city's walkable centre, south of the main train station and on the west side of the River Ilm. The Park an der Ilm stretches 2km southwards, while the former concentration camp at Buchenwald is a bus ride to the northwest.

The Schloss and Markt

Weimar's former seat of power was the **Schloss**, set by the River Ilm at the eastern edge of the town centre, a Neoclassical complex of a size more appropriate for ruling a mighty empire. On the ground floor of the **museum** now housed within (Tues–Sun: April–Oct 10am–6pm; Nov–May 10am–4pm; €5/

students €4; ⓦwww.swkk.de) is a collection of old masters, including pieces by both Cranachs, and Dürer's portraits of the Nuremberg patrician couple Hans and Elspeth Tucher. South of nearby Herderplatz is the spacious **Markt**, lined with an unusually disparate jumble of buildings, of which the most eye-catching is the green and white gabled Stadthaus on the eastern side, opposite the neo-Gothic Rathaus.

The Schillerhaus and around

Schillerstrasse snakes away from the southwest corner of the Markt to the **Schillerhaus** (Mon & Wed–Sun: April–Sept 9am–6pm, Sat till 7pm; Oct 9am–6pm; Nov–March 9am–4pm; €4/students €3; ⓦwww.swkk.de), the home of the poet and dramatist for the last three years of his life. Beyond lies Theaterplatz, in the centre of which is a large monument to Goethe and Schiller. The **Nationaltheater** on the west side of the square was founded and directed by Goethe, though the present building, for all its stern Neoclassical appearance, is a modern pastiche.

The Goethewohnhaus und Nationalmuseum

On Frauenplan, south of the Markt is the **Goethewohnhaus und Nationalmuseum** (Tues–Sun: April–Sept 9am–6pm, Sat till 7pm; Oct 9am–6pm; Nov–March 9am–4pm; Wohnhaus €6.50/students €5; Nationalmuseum €3/students €2.50; combined €8.50/students €6.50), where Goethe lived for some fifty years until his death in 1832.

The Park an der Ilm and Schloss Belvedere

The **Park an der Ilm** stretches from the Schloss to the southern edge of town on both sides of the river; aim for the southern suburb of Oberweimar, where stands the full-blown summer palace of **Schloss Belvedere** (April–Oct Tues–Sun 10am–6pm; €4/students €3; ⓦwww.swkk.de), whose light and airy Rococo style forms a refreshing contrast to the Neoclassical solemnity of so much of the town.

Konzentrationslager Buchenwald

The **Konzentrationslager Buchenwald** (Tues–Sun: April–Oct 10am–6pm; Nov–March 10am–4pm; free; ⓦwww.buchenwald.de) is situated north of Weimar on the Ettersberg heights, and can be reached by bus #6 (hourly from Goetheplatz and the train station). Over 240,000 prisoners were incarcerated in this concentration camp, with 65,000 dying here. Very few original buildings remain, but an audioguide (€3) and the historical exhibition paint a vivid picture of life and death in the camp.

Arrival and information

Train Weimar's train station, on the Leipzig line, is a twenty-minute walk north of the main sights.
Tourist office One of the tourist offices (Mon–Sat 10am–6pm) is at the Welcome Centre at Friedenstr. 1; another, larger one is at Markt 10 (Mon–Sat 9.30am–7pm, Sun 9.30am–3pm; ⓣ03643/74 50, ⓦwww.weimar.de).

Accommodation

DJH Germania Carl-August-Allee 13 ⓣ03643/85 04 90, ⓦwww.djh-thueringen.de. Neat and tidy HI hostel between the station and the centre. There's another DJH on the other side of the centre at Humboldt Str. 17 (ⓣ03643/85 07 92). ❸
Hababusch Geleitstr. 4 ⓣ03643/850737, ⓦwww.hababusch.de. The cheapest and most central hostel, environmentally minded and idiosyncratic, with a kitchen. Most rooms are tiny and packed. Sheets €2.50. Dorms ❶, rooms ❷
Savina Meyerstr. 60 ⓣ03643/8 66 90, ⓦwww.pension-savina.de. Recently refurbished pension where all rooms have en-suite bathrooms. ❼

Eating and drinking

Weimar's range of eating and drinking spots comes as a surprise, given its relatively small size. There's also a market on the Markt daily except Sunday from 9am to 4.30pm.

ACC Burgplatz 1. A relaxed bar and restaurant with quiet candlelit tables lining a cobbled side street, free Internet and an upstairs gallery. Specials €5.

Residenz-Café Grüner Markt 4. Plush, candlelit old-fashioned coffee house and restaurant, with mains at €6–11.

Zum Zwiebel Teichgasse 6. Deservedly popular, cosy and lively restaurant serving local specialities and veggie options. Closed weekdays 3–5pm. Mains around €9.

Moving on

Train Dresden (hourly; 2hr); Eisenach (every 30min; 1hr); Leipzig (frequent; 50min–1hr 20min).

EISENACH

A small town on the edge of the Thuringian Forest, **EISENACH** is home to the best-loved medieval castle in Germany, the **Wartburg**. The castle complex, first mentioned in 1080, includes one of the best-preserved **Romanesque palaces** this side of the Alps, as well as newer additions, including the Festsaal, a nineteenth-century Historicist interpretation of medieval grandeur so splendid that Ludwig II of Bavaria had it copied for his fairy-tale palace Neuschwanstein. Also on view is the **Lutherstube**, the room in which Martin Luther translated the New Testament into the German vernacular while in hiding in 1521–2. The Palas can only be viewed on **guided tours** (daily: March–Oct 8.30am–5pm; Nov–Feb 9am–3.30pm; €6.50/students €3.50; ⓦwww.wartburg.de); there's usually a half-hour English tour at 1.30pm; otherwise, join any tour (every 15min) and ask for a translation of the guide's script.

The Wartburg is a good hour's walk from the **train station** (take the footpath Haintal from the Reuter Villa); alternatively, from April to October bus #10 runs hourly from the train station to Eselstation, from where it's a thirty-minute climb to the castle.

The DJH at Mariental 24 (ⓣ03691/74 3259, ⓦwww.djh-thueringen.de; ❷) is clean and friendly; it's a thirty-minute walk from the station or take bus #3 or #10. The **tourist office** at Markt 9 (Mon–Fri 10am–6pm, Sat 10am–4pm; ⓣ03691/79 230, ⓦwww.eisenach.de) can point you to ample private **accommodation**.

DRESDEN

Once generally regarded as Germany's most beautiful city, **DRESDEN** survived World War II largely unscathed until the night of February 13, 1945. Then, in a matter of hours, it was reduced to ruins in saturation bombing – according to official figures at least 35,000 civilians died, though the total was probably considerably higher, as the city was packed with people fleeing the advancing Red Army. With this background, it's all the more remarkable that Dresden is the one city in the former East Germany that has slotted easily into the economic framework of the reunited Germany, and the post-Communist authorities have now brilliantly restored most of the historic buildings.

What to see and do

The city's main sights are in the picturesque **Altstadt**, which lies on the southern bank of the River Elbe. In the bohemian **Neustadt**, north of the river and most easily accessed from the Neustadt Bahnhof, you'll find the backpackers' hostels as well as a thriving alternative scene.

The Hauptbahnhof and around

If you arrive at the Hauptbahnhof, you see the worst of modern Dresden first: the **Prager Strasse**, a vast Stalinist pedestrian precinct with a few fountains and statues thrown in for relief, though undergoing something of a facelift at the moment. Beyond the inner ring road at the far end is the **Altmarkt**, much extended after its wartime destruction; the only building of note

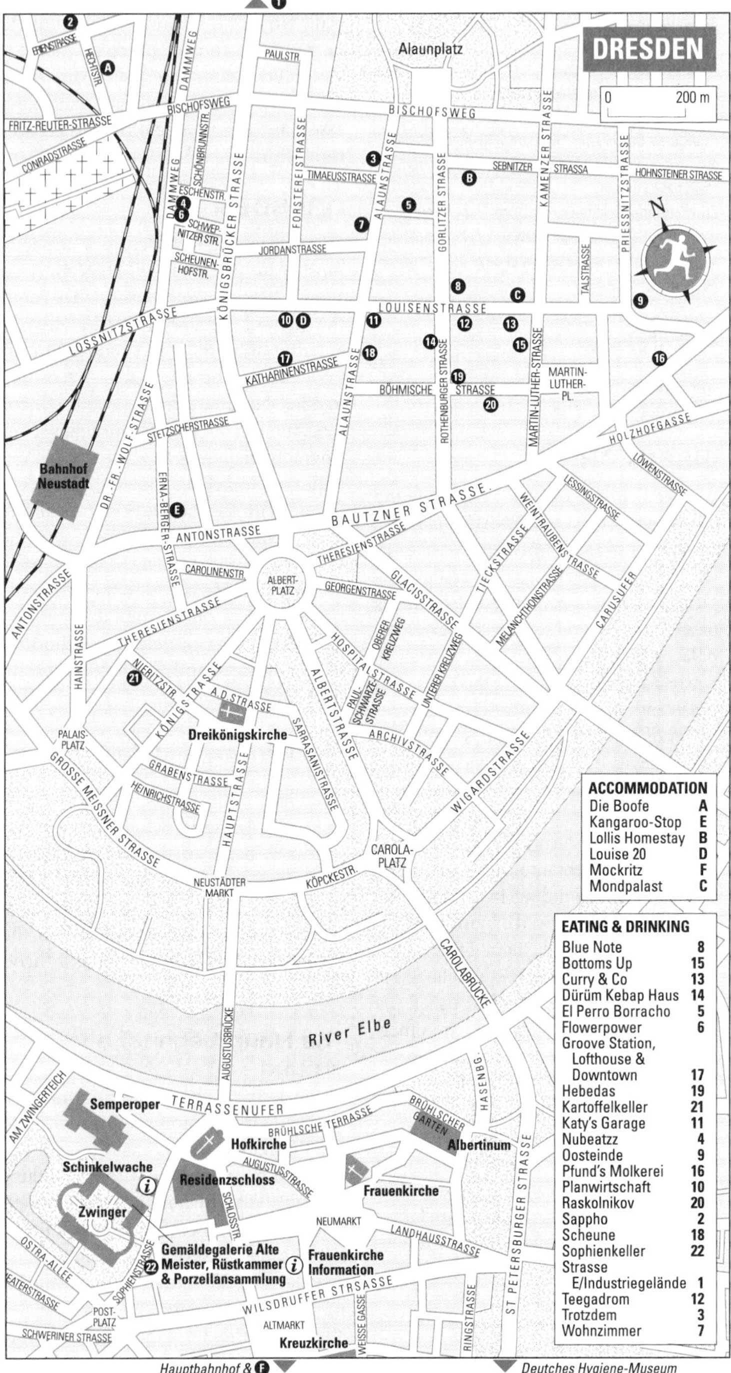
DRESDEN
0
200 m
N
Alaunplatz
PAULSTR.
DAMMWEG
BISCHOFSWEG
ERIENSTRASSE
HECHTSTR.
FRITZ-REUTER-STRASSE
CONRADSTRASSE
SCHÖNBRUNNSTR.
ESCHENSTR.
SCHWEP-NITZER STR.
SCHEUNEN-HOFSTR.
KÖNIGSBRÜCKER STRASSE
FÖRSTEREISTRASSE
TIMAEUSSTRASSE
ALAUNSTRASSE
JORDANSTRASSE
GÖRLITZER STRASSE
SEBNITZER STRASSA
KAMENZER STRASSE
HOHNSTEINER STRASSE
PRIESSNITZSTRASSE
TALSTRASSE
LOUISENSTRASSE
LOSSNITZSTRASSE
KATHARINENSTRASSE
BÖHMISCHE STRASSE
ROTHENBURGER STRASSE
MARTIN-LUTHER-STRASSE
MARTIN-LUTHER-PL.
HOLZHOFGASSE
LÖWENSTRASSE
STETZSCHERSTRASSE
DR.-FR.-WOLF-STRASSE
Bahnhof Neustadt
ERNA-BERGER-STRASSE
ANTONSTRASSE
BAUTZNER STRASSE
LESSINGSTRASSE
WEINTRAUBENSTRASSE
TIECKSTRASSE
THERESIENSTRASSE
CAROLINENSTR.
ALBERT-PLATZ
GEORGENSTRASSE
GLACISSTRASSE
MELANCHTHONSTRASSE
CARUSUFER
HAINSTRASSE
OBERER KREUZWEG
HOSPITALSTRASSE
UNTERER KREUZWEG
NIERITZSTR.
KÖNIGSTRASSE
A.D.STRASSE
PAUL-SCHWARZE-STRASSE
ALBERTSTRASSE
Dreikönigskirche
SARRASANISTRASSE
ARCHIVSTRASSE
WIGARDSTRASSE
PALAIS-PLATZ
GROSSE MEISSNER STRASSE
GRABENSTRASSE
HEINRICHSTRASSE
HAUPTSTRASSE
CAROLA-PLATZ
NEUSTÄDTER MARKT
KÖPCKESTR.
CAROLABRÜCKE
AUGUSTUSBRÜCKE
River Elbe
AM ZWINGERTEICH
Semperoper
TERRASSENUFER
BRÜHLSCHE TERRASSE
BRÜHLSCHER GARTEN
HASENBG.
Hofkirche
Albertinum
Schinkelwache
AUGUSTUSSTRASSE
Residenzschloss
Frauenkirche
SCHLOSSSTR.
Zwinger
NEUMARKT
LANDHAUSSTRASSE
ST PETERSBURGER STRASSE
OSTRA-ALLEE
Gemäldegalerie Alte Meister, Rüstkammer & Porzellansammlung
Frauenkirche Information
SOPHIENSTRASSE
THEATERSTRASSE
WILSDRUFFER STRSASSE
POST-PLATZ
ALTMARKT
WEISSE GASSE
RINGSTRASSE
SCHWERINER STRASSE
Kreuzkirche
Hauptbahnhof & F
Deutches Hygiene-Museum
ACCOMMODATION
Die Boofe A
Kangaroo-Stop E
Lollis Homestay B
Louise 20 D
Mockritz F
Mondpalast C
EATING & DRINKING
Blue Note 8
Bottoms Up 15
Curry & Co 13
Dürüm Kebap Haus 14
El Perro Borracho 5
Flowerpower 6
Groove Station, Lofthouse & Downtown 17
Hebedas 19
Kartoffelkeller 21
Katy's Garage 11
Nubeatzz 4
Oosteinde 9
Pfund's Molkerei 16
Planwirtschaft 10
Raskolnikov 20
Sappho 2
Scheune 18
Sophienkeller 22
Strasse E/Industriegelände 1
Teegadrom 12
Trotzdem 3
Wohnzimmer 7

that remains is the **Kreuzkirche**, a church that mixes a Baroque body with a Neoclassical tower. On Saturdays at 6pm, and at the 9.30am Sunday service, it usually features the Kreuzchor, one of the world's leading church choirs.

The Albertinum and Frauenkirche

North of here, the **Albertinum** (ⓦwww.skd-dresden.de), which is closed until late 2009 for renovation, houses the outstanding New Masters Gallery and, in it, one of the greatest of Romantic paintings, Friedrich's *Cross in the Mountains*. West of the Albertinum is the **Neumarkt**, dominated by the Baroque, domed **Frauenkirche**. Only a fragment of wall was left standing after the war, and after fierce controversy, the decision was taken in 1991 to rebuild the church completely, using many of the same stones, with much of the funding coming from the UK and US. Unfortunately, opportunities to view the ornate interior are limited as the opening times are short and inconsistent owing to frequent special events. It's a good idea to head here first and check the opening times on site to plan your visit.

The Residenzschloss

The colossal **Residenzschloss** (Wed–Mon 10am–6pm; Historisches Grünes Gewölbe €10 timed ticket, can also be purchased online in advance; Neues Grünes Gewölbe €6/students €3.50; ⓦwww.skd-dresden.de), recently reopened, houses the **Grünes Gewölbe** or Green Vault collection, a dazzling array of Wettin treasury items named after the green walls of the original treasury. The three thousand items of the Historisches Grünes Gewölbe, assembled by August the Strong between 1723 and 1730, can once again be admired in the stunning Baroque mirrored rooms of their historic setting, while the Neues Grünes Gewölbe, containing decorative items from the Renaissance to the Classical period, is on view upstairs.

MUSEUM ENTRY

A day ticket to all of the outstanding Staatliche Kunstsammlungen Dresden museums (except the Historisches Grünes Gewölbe and special exhibitions) costs €12/students €7 (ⓦwww.skd-dresden.de).

The Zwinger and Rüstkammer

Baroque Dresden's great glory was the palace known as the **Zwinger** (Tues–Sun 10am–6pm; ⓦwww.skd-dresden.de), which faces the Residenzschloss and now contains several museums. Beautifully displayed in the southeastern pavilion, entered from Sophienstrasse, is the **Porzellansammlung** (€6/students €3.50), featuring porcelain items from the famous Meissen factory, as well as from China and Japan. The southwestern pavilion, closed until 2009, is known as the **Mathematisch-Physikalischer Salon**, and offers a fascinating array of globes, clocks and scientific instruments. In the nineteenth-century extension is the **Gemäldegalerie Alte Meister** (€6/students €3.50), whose collection of old masters ranks among the dozen best in the world: you'll find Raphael's *Sistine Madonna*, Titian's *Christ and the Pharisees* and Veronese's *Marriage at Cana* in the Italian section while the German section includes Dürer's *Dresden Altarpiece*, Holbein's *Le Sieur de Morette* and Cranach's *Duke Henry the Pious*. On the north side of the Zwinger stands the **Rüstkammer** (€3/students €2), a wonderful collection of weaponry that includes a magnificent Renaissance suit of armour for man and horse, depicting scenes from the Hercules saga. This collection is due to move to the Residenzschloss in the near future.

Deutsches Hygiene-Museum

Ten minutes' walk south of the Frauenkirche, the **Deutsches Hygiene-Museum** (Tues–Sun 10am–6pm; €6/ students €3; Ⓦwww.dhmd.de) is a fascinating museum of the physical and social human being. The permanent collection focuses on the body and its functions, while temporary exhibits explore the interface of politics, culture, science and medicine.

The Neustadt

Across the River Elbe, the **Neustadt** was a planned Baroque town and its layout is still obvious, even if few of the original buildings survive. Today it's the focus of the city's gentrification, with a burgeoning art scene; you can get a feel for it by taking a wander through the bohemian **Kunsthofpassage** with its courtyards, houses and arty shops.

Arrival

Air Dresden Airport (Ⓦwww.dresden-airport.de) is connected to the Hauptbahnhof and the Neustadt Bahnhof by S-Bahn #1 (every 30min; 13–23min; €1.80).
Train Dresden has two main train stations – the Hauptbahnhof, south of the Altstadt, and Neustadt Bahnhof, at the northwestern corner of the Neustadt, convenient for the backpacker hostels and nightlife.

Information

Tourist office There's a tourist office at Prager Str. 10 (Mon–Sat 10am–6pm; Ⓣ0351/4919 2100, Ⓦwww.dresden-tourist.de), a short walk from the Hauptbahnhof; and another in the heart of the Altstadt, in the Schinkelwache on Theaterplatz (Mon–Fri 10am–6pm, Sat & Sun 10am–4pm). Both can book private rooms and pensions (from ❸).
Discount passes The Dresden-City-Card (€21/24hr) and the Dresden Regio-Card (€32/72hr) cover public transport, SKD museum admission and sundry discounts.

City transport

Trams, buses and S-Bahn Public transport is frequent and reliable, though you are unlikely to need it much, as the main sights are easily walkable. A single ticket for zone one, which is all you need for the city, costs €1.80; a day ticket costs €4.50 and a week ticket €17.
Taxi Taxis can be booked on Ⓣ0351/211211.

Accommodation

Die Boofe Hechtstr. 10, Neustadt Ⓣ0351/801 3361, Ⓦwww.boofe.de. Tidy hostel with its own sauna (€4.50/hr) and garden, ten minutes north of Neustadt Bahnhof in the Hechtviertel artists' ghetto. Sheets included. Dorms ❷, rooms ❺
Kangaroo-Stop Erna-Berger-Str. 8–10, Neustadt Ⓣ0351/314 34 55, Ⓦwww.kangaroo-stop.de. New, cheap hostel with a kitchen on a quiet street 3min from the Neustadt Bahnhof. Dorms ❷, rooms ❹
Lollis Homestay Görlitzer Str. 34, Neustadt Ⓣ0351/81 08 458, Ⓦwww.lollishome.de. This wonderfully cosy backpackers' is right in the centre of the lively Neustadt, with friendly staff, a kitchen and free bikes – though the central location means it can be loud at night. Tram to Alaunplatz or 20min from Neustadt Bahnhof. Sheets €2. Dorms ❷, rooms ❺
Louise 20 Louisenstr. 20, Neustadt Ⓣ0351/8894 894, Ⓦwww.louise20.de. Bright, quiet, hotel-quality hostel – unfortunately, slightly soulless. Dorms ❷, rooms ❹
Mockritz Boderitzer Str. 30 Ⓣ0351/47 15 250, Ⓦwww.camping-dresden.de. This campsite is open year-round; take bus #76 from the Hauptbahnhof. Reception 4–9pm. ❶
Mondpalast Louisenstr. 77, Neustadt Ⓣ0351/56 34 050, Ⓦwww.mondpalast.de. Another great backpackers' with a kitchen, on one of the Neustadt's main thoroughfares. Bike rentals €7/day. Tram to Louisenstr., Pulsnitzerstr. or a 20min walk from the Neustadt Bahnhof. Sheets €2. Dorms ❷, rooms ❺

Eating

Cafés

Pfund's Molkerei Bautzner Str. 79, Neustadt. Touristy café/restaurant attached to a dairy shop, with immaculately restored Jugendstil decor. Fresh buttermilk €1.
Planwirtschaft Louisenstr. 20, Neustadt. Café-bar-restaurant and *biergarten* serving breakfast all day (€7).
Sappho Hechtstr. 23, Neustadt. Relaxed lesbian café-bar with a young crowd. Breakfast buffet €6. Evenings only during the week; closed Mon.
Teegadrom Louisenstr. 48, Neustadt. An alternative

to the Neustadt hipster scene: calm and candlelit, with board games. 7pm–1/2am.

Restaurants

Curry & Co Louisenstr. 62, Neustadt. Ultra-hip, minimalist Currywurst joint. Currywurst & fries €3.50.

Dürüm Kebap Haus Rothenburger Str. 41, Neustadt. A rock-bottom-priced favourite, serving as a cheap takeaway, quick restaurant and general meeting place. Dürüm Döner €4.

El Perro Borracho Kunsthof alleyway, Alaunstr. 70, Neustadt. A highly regarded, lively Spanish eatery. Tapas from €3.

Kartoffelkeller Nieritzstr. 11, Neustadt. Potato served in a myriad different ways, in a beautiful cellar space, at good rates. Roast potatoes with herring fillets €8.

Oosteinde Preissnitzstr. 18, Neustadt. Delicious, good-value food served under a low vaulted roof or outside in a peaceful beer garden. Meals from €6.

Raskolnikov Böhmische Str. 34, Neustadt. A large, rambling, bohemian Russian bar/café and restaurant. Great food and atmospheric beer garden. Borscht €4.

Sophienkeller Taschenberg 3, Altstadt. Super-touristy, terrifically kitschy eighteenth-century themed vault restaurant, with excellent meals from €7.

Drinking and nightlife

With over 130 **bars and clubs** clustered around a handful of cobbled, narrow streets, the Neustadt provides something for everyone. For up-to-date nightlife **listings**, pick up a copy of *Sax*, or *Dresdner* from kiosks or backpacker hostels.

Bars

Blue Note Görlitzer Str. 2b, Neustadt Ⓦwww.bluenote-dresden.de. Dark, cavernous, smoke-filled jazz bar that gets packed to the gills every night for its live music; daily 8pm–5am.

Bottoms Up Martin-Luther-Str. 31, Neustadt. Down a quiet backstreet away from the main action, this large easy-going bar and beer garden is an unpretentious favourite.

Hebedas Rothenburger Str. 30, Neustadt. A large, crumbling and basic pub that epitomizes the Neustadt alternative scene.

Scheune Alaunstr. 36–40, Neustadt Ⓦwww.scheune.org. Neustadt arts centre with a welcoming bar, large beer garden, live music, theatre, and gay and lesbian nights.

Trotzdem Alaunstr. 81, Neustadt. Chilled, funky bar with intimate corners and a good choice of beer.

Wohnzimmer Alaunstr. 27/Jordanstr. 19, Neustadt. Two levels of living-room-themed bar, with comfy couches and good cocktails.

Clubs

Groove Station, Lofthouse & Downtown Katherinenstr. 11–13, Neustadt Ⓦwww.groovestation.de, Ⓦwww.lofthouse-dresden.de & Ⓦwww.downtown-dresden.de. Set around a courtyard, this rough-and-ready rock, hip-hop and dance bar and live music complex has been a Neustadt cornerstone for years.

Flowerpower Eschenstr. 11, Neustadt Ⓦwww.flower-power.de. It's always the summer of love at this rock and oldies student club.

Strasse E/Industriegelände Werner-Hartmann-Straße 2 Ⓦwww.strasse-e.de. Industrial area turned club/venue mini-city north of the Neustadt, where there's guaranteed to be something on. Tram #7 or #8 to Industriegelände.

Katy's Garage Alaunstr. 48, Neustadt Ⓦwww.katysgarage.de. Another Neustadt institution – you'll recognize this disco by the car on its roof.

Nubeatzz Eschenstr. 11, Neustadt Ⓦwww.nubeatzz.de. Packed club next to *Flowerpower* hosting regular student, pop and hip-hop nights. Mon, Fri & Sat; entry free.

Moving on

Train Berlin (every 2hr; 2hr); Leipzig (every 30min; 1hr–1hr 40min); Meissen (every 30min; 45min); Munich (hourly; 6hr); Prague (every 2hr; 2hr 30min); Weimar (hourly; 2hr); Wroclaw (5 daily; 4hr 30min).

DAY-TRIPS FROM DRESDEN

The **Sächsische Schweiz** (Saxon Switzerland) region southeast of Dresden is a natural wonderland, offering ample opportunities for hiking, cycling and climbing. The majestic sandstone mountains here, along the Elbe, are featured prominently in the work of the famous Romantic painter Caspar David Friedrich; you can trace his steps along the 115-kilometre Malerweg (Painter Route), overnighting in the tourist-friendly villages along the way. There are countless day hikes if you're looking for a shorter route; one of the best loved runs from Königstein to

Rathen via Lilienstein (7km), through woods and open vistas.

It's easy to visit this region from Dresden; just take S-Bahn #1 (every 30min; 3-zone ticket €5.10) to Kurort Rathen, Königstein or Bad Schandau and follow trailheads from there; local buses also connect these towns. The tourist office in Dresden (see p.480) sells maps and gives information on the Sächsische Schweiz, or you could check out the region's own tourist information at Ⓦwww.saechsische-schweiz.de.

Meissen

The cobbled square and photogenic rooftop vistas are reason enough to visit the porcelain-producing town of **MEISSEN,** which, unlike its neighbour Dresden, survived World War II almost unscathed.

What to see and do

Walking towards the centre from the train station, you see Meissen's commandingly sited castle almost immediately, rising just back from the Elbe's edge. The present building, the **Albrechtsburg** (daily: March–Oct 10am–6pm; Nov–Feb 10am–5pm; Jan 15–31 weekends only; €3.50/students €2; Ⓦwww.albrechtsburg-meissen.de), is a late fifteenth-century combination of military fortress and residential palace. Cocooned within the castle precinct is the Gothic **Dom** (daily: April–Oct 9am–6pm; Nov–March 10am–4pm; €2.50/students €1.50; combined ticket €5.50/students €3.50); inside, look out for the superb brass tomb-plates of the Saxon dukes and the rood screen with its colourful altarpiece.

The **Staatliche Porzellan-Manufaktur Meissen** is at Talstr. 9 (daily: May–Oct 9am–6pm; Nov–April 9am–5pm; €8.50/students €4.50; Ⓦwww.meissen.de), about 1.5km south of the central Markt. This is the latest factory to manufacture Dresden china, whose invention came about when Augustus the Strong imprisoned the alchemist Johann Friedrich Böttger, ordering him to produce gold. Instead, he invented the first true European porcelain, according to a formula that remains secret. In addition to seeing the works, you can also view the **museum**, which displays many of the factories' finest creations.

Arrival and information

Train The train station is on the opposite side of the River Elbe from the centre. It's a 20min walk over the railroad bridge or the Altstadtbrücke; both are signposted.

Tourist office Meissen's tourist office is at Markt 3 (April–Oct Mon–Fri 10am–6pm, Sat & Sun 10am–4pm; Nov–March Mon–Fri 10am–5pm, Sat 10am–3pm, Jan closed weekends; Ⓣ03521/41 940, Ⓦwww.touristinfo-meissen.de).

Northern Germany

Hamburg, Germany's second city, is infamous for the sleaze and hectic nightlife of the Reeperbahn strip – yet it also has a more sophisticated cultural scene. In this unprepossessing region, another maritime city, **Lübeck**, has a strong pull, with a similar appeal to the mercantile towns of the Low Countries. To the east, Stralsund and Rügen Island on the Baltic offer medieval architecture and serene coastlines. To the south lies **Hannover**, worth a visit for its museums and gardens. The province's smaller towns present a fascinating contrast – the former silver-mining town of **Goslar**, in particular, is unusually beautiful.

HAMBURG

Stylish media centre and second-largest port in Europe, **HAMBURG** is undeniably cool – more laid back than Berlin or Frankfurt, more sophisticated than Munich or Cologne, and with nightlife to rival the lot. Its skyline is dominated by the pale green of its copper spires and domes, but a few houses and the churches are all that's left from older times. Much of the subsequent rebuilding might not be especially beautiful, but the result is an intriguing mix of old and new, coupled with an appealing sense of open space – two-thirds of Hamburg is occupied by parks, lakes or tree-lined canals, adding some much-needed leafiness to this major industrial metropolis.

What to see and do

A good place to begin your exploration is the oldest area, the **harbour**, dominated by the clock tower and green dome of the St Pauli Landungsbrücken. The main tourist draw is a one-hour **boat tour** of the harbour (many companies operate these; prices start at €10), but they are best avoided unless you have a fascination for industrial containers. More interesting is the late nineteenth-century **Speicherstadt** lying a little to the east, filled with tall, ornate warehouses and the smell of spices and coffee wafting on the breeze. Here, you can wander and crisscross the bridges at will – Hamburg has more of them than Venice or Amsterdam.

The Fischmarkt and Altona

The main road along the waterfront west of Landungsbrücken is Hafenstrasse. On the waterfront here, one of the city's main weekly events takes place: the **Fischmarkt**. Come early on Sunday and you'll find yourself in an amazing trading frenzy; everything is in full swing by 5am and by 10am it's all over. Hafenstrasse runs west to the trendy suburb of **Altona**, where tons of cafés and bars cluster just west of the Altona S-Bahn stop.

St Pauli

Just to the north of the Landungsbrücken is the red-light district and nightlife centre of **St Pauli**. Its main artery is the notorious **Reeperbahn** – ugly and unassuming by day, blazing with neon at night. Running off here is Grosse Freiheit, the street that famously hosted The Beatles' first gigs.

The Rathaus

The commercial and shopping district centres on **Binnenalster** lake and the neo-Renaissance **Rathaus** (guided tours hourly in English: Mon–Thurs 10.15am–3.15pm, Fri 10.15am–1.15pm, Sat 10.15am–5.15pm, Sun 10.15am–4.15pm; €3), a magnificently pompous demonstration of the city's power and wealth in the nineteenth century.

The Kunsthalle

Away to the east, north of the Hauptbahnhof is the **Kunsthalle**, Hamburg's unmissable art collection (Tues–Sun 10am–6pm, Thurs till 9pm; €8.50/€5, during the last hour before closing €3; Ⓦwww.hamburger-kunsthalle.de). The two-building collection, ranging from Old Masters to contemporary artists, includes works by Master Bertram, Rembrandt, Caspar David Friedrich, Ernst Ludwig Kirchner, Gerhard Richter and Jenny Holzer, among countless others. Nearby is the **Museum für Kunst und Gewerbe** (Museum of Arts and Crafts; same hours and prices, €5 from 4pm Tues and from 5pm Thurs; Ⓦwww.mkg-hamburg.de), which hosts exciting exhibitions from graphic design to the latest in furniture.

Arrival

Air An Airport Express connects Hamburg Airport to the main train station (every 15min; 25min; €5), or take bus #110 (every 10min; €2.60) to Ohlsdorf stop and then the U- or S-Bahn into the centre. The Lübeck-Blankensee Airport (served by Ryanair and

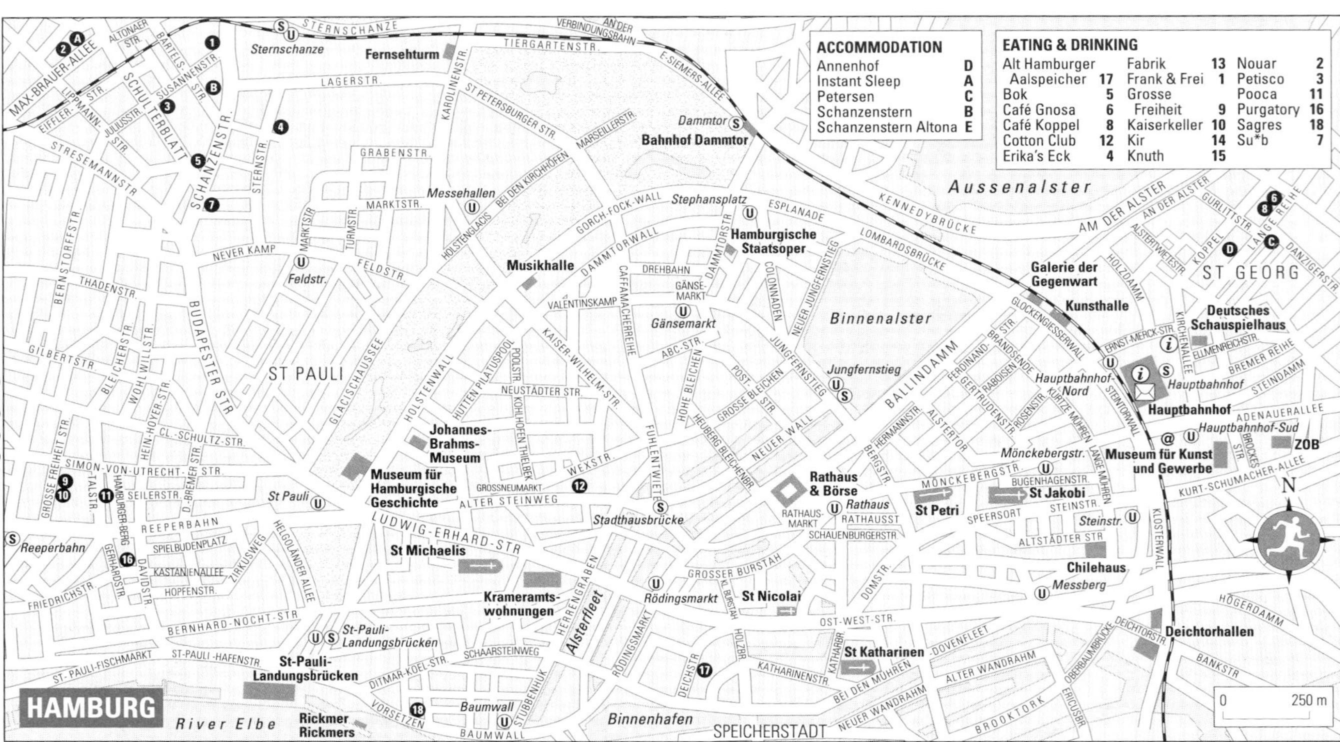
HAMBURG
ACCOMMODATION
Annenhof D
Instant Sleep A
Petersen C
Schanzenstern B
Schanzenstern Altona E
EATING & DRINKING
Alt Hamburger Aalspeicher 17
Bok 5
Café Gnosa 6
Café Koppel 8
Cotton Club 12
Erika's Eck 4
Fabrik 13
Frank & Frei 1
Grosse Freiheit 9
Kaiserkeller 10
Kir 14
Knuth 15
Nouar 2
Petisco 3
Pooca 11
Purgatory 16
Sagres 18
Su*b 7
Aussenalster
Binnenalster
ST GEORG
ST PAULI
River Elbe
Binnenhafen
SPEICHERSTADT
Alsterfleet
Sternschanze
Fernsehturm
Bahnhof Dammtor
Dammtor
Messehallen
Stephansplatz
Hamburgische Staatsoper
Musikhalle
Gänsemarkt
Feldstr.
Jungfernstieg
Galerie der Gegenwart
Kunsthalle
Deutsches Schauspielhaus
Hauptbahnhof
Hauptbahnhof-Nord
Hauptbahnhof-Sud
ZOB
Museum für Kunst und Gewerbe
Mönckebergstr.
St Jakobi
St Petri
Rathaus & Börse
Rathaus
Steinstr.
Chilehaus
Messberg
Deichtorhallen
Johannes-Brahms-Museum
Museum für Hamburgische Geschichte
St Pauli
Stadthausbrücke
St Michaelis
Krameramtswohnungen
Rödingsmarkt
St Nicolai
St Katharinen
St-Pauli-Landungsbrücken
Baumwall
Rickmer Rickmers
Reeperbahn
Altona, E, 13, 14 & 15
N
0 250 m

Wizzair) is connected to Hamburg by shuttle bus #A20 (timed to flights; 1hr 15min; €8).
Train The Hauptbahnhof is at the eastern end of the city centre.

Information

Tourist office The helpful tourist office in the Hauptbahnhof (Mon–Sat 8am–9pm, Sun 10am–6pm; ⓣ040/30 05 13 00, ⓦwww.hamburg-tourismus.de) has a room-finding service (€4, from ❺). There's also a branch in the airport (daily 6am–11pm).
Discount pass The Hamburg Card (single: €8/18/33, group up to five people: €11.80/29.80/51 for 1/3/5 days) gives reduced admission to some of the city's museums as well as free use of public transport.

City transport

Hamburg is big, so its extensive public transport network, made up of U-Bahn, S-Bahn and buses, can come in handy. A short trip costs €1.30, a single trip €2.60, a day ticket €5.10, a day ticket for up to five people €8.60, and a three-day ticket €15.

Accommodation

Annenhof Lange Reihe 23 ⓣ040/24 34 26, ⓦwww.hotelannenhof.de. Friendly, renovated hotel on a café-lined street near the train station. Reception closes at 8pm weekdays, at 6pm weekends; no breakfast. Shared bathroom ❻
Bed and breakfast ⓣ040/491 56 66, ⓦwww.bed-and-breakfast.de. Call in advance Mon–Fri to book private rooms. From ❺
Instant Sleep Max-Brauer-Allee 277 ⓣ040/43 18 23 10, ⓦwww.instantsleep.de. Located in the lively Schanze area, this friendly backpackers' has the cheapest beds in town, and a kitchen and Internet access. S-/U-Bahn Sternschanze. Sheets €2, no breakfast. Dorms ❷, rooms ❺
Petersen Lange Reihe 50 ⓣ040/24 98 26, ⓦwww.ghsp.de. Stylish hotel-cum-gallery hung with paintings by owner Sarah Petersen, in a fully restored eighteenth-century house complete with impeccably furnished rooms. 10min from the station. From ❼
Schanzenstern Bartelsstr. 12 ⓣ040/439 84 41, ⓦwww.schanzenstern.de. Eco-hostel in the Schanze area, with an attached organic restaurant. Sheets included. S-/U-Bahn Sternschanze. Dorms ❷, rooms ❻
Schanzenstern Altona Kleine Rainstr. 24–26 ⓣ040/3991 9191, ⓦwww.schanzenstern.de. This Schanzenstern annexe is located in hip Altona, though is very functional and seriously lacking in personality. S-Bahn Altona. Dorms ❷, rooms ❼

Eating

Alt Hamburger Aalspeicher Deichstr. 43. One of the best-known addresses in the city centre for traditional German cuisine and fish dishes. Pricey but worth it. From €13. U-Bahn Baumwall.
Bok Schulterblatt 3. A very popular outlet of the excellent local Asian fusion eatery. Panang Gai €9. U-/S-Bahn Sternschanze.
Café Koppel Koppel 66, northeast of the train station in St Georg district. Best known for its delicious wholemeal chocolate cake (€3), this place also serves a good range of vegetarian dishes and has a summer garden.
Erika's Eck Sternstr. 98. This is a firm student favourite, serving the best breakfast in the city and hot meals almost round the clock. Mon–Fri 6pm–2pm, Sat & Sun 6pm–9am. Snacks from €1. U-/S-Bahn Sternschanze.
Frank & Frei Schanzenstr. 93. Enormous salads, pasta and pizza-like *Flammkuchen* for €7. U-/S-Bahn Sternschanze.
Petisco Schulterblatt 78. A popular Portuguese restaurant, serving authentic, inexpensive fare. Mixed fish plate €6. U-/S-Bahn Sternschanze.
Sagres Vorsetzen 42. Portuguese restaurant near the harbour, with generous portions. Mon–Fri 3pm–midnight, Sat & Sun noon–midnight. Grilled shark fillet €11. U-/S-Bahn Landungsbrücken or Baumwall.

Drinking and nightlife

Hamburg's **nightlife** is outstanding, including an animated bar scene and a wide range of excellent clubs. St Pauli is the city's main venue for clubbing and live music, with big-name DJs and bands playing at weekends. Admission is generally about €10. The student bar scene is in Schanzenviertel, while Altona attracts young professionals. The best way to find out what's on in the lively **gay scene** is through *Hinnerk* magazine, available from the tourist office.

Bars

Café Gnosa Lange Reihe 93. Well-known gay bar/café northeast of the train station. Packed at weekends. Marvellous cakes €3.

Knuth Grosse Rainstr. 21. Relaxed café-bar catering to hip twenty- and thirtysomethings. S-Bahn Altona.
Nouar Max-Brauer-Allee 275. Hip bar with retro decor, right next to *Hostel Instant Sleep*. Closed Mon. S-/U-Bahn Sternschanze.
Purgatory Friedrichstr. 8. Tiny gay and lesbian bar/club with an even tinier dance floor. U-/S-Bahn St Pauli or Reeperbahn.
Su*b Schanzenstr. 18. Packed shabby-chic bar blasting indie rock. U-Bahn Feldstr.

Clubs

Fabrik Barnerstr. 36 Ⓦwww.fabrik.de. Major live music and club venue in Altona, with a huge range of music and occasional mixed gay nights. Usually open nightly; entry from €7 (club nights) to €40 (major live acts). S-Bahn Altona.
Kaiserkeller Grosse Freiheit 36 Ⓦwww.grossefreiheit36.de. Massive subterranean club below Grosse Freiheit playing mostly alternative music; famous for hosting The Beatles in the early 1960s. Closed Tues & Sun. U-/S-Bahn St Pauli or Reeperbahn.
Kir Barnerstr. 16 Ⓦwww.kir-hamburg.de. Dance club spinning indie and electro with occasional mixed gay and lesbian nights. Closed Tues and Sun. S-Bahn Altona.
Pooca Hamburger Berg 12. Reggae, hip-hop and indie-rock are always on at this chill micro-club on one of St Pauli's less intense streets. Nightly; no cover. U-/S-Bahn St Pauli or Reeperbahn.

Entertainment

Cotton Club Alter Steinweg 10 Ⓦwww.cotton-club.de. Traditional jazz and blues club, with live music Mon–Sat 8pm. €5–10. S-Bahn Stadthausbrücke or U-Bahn Rödingsmarkt.
Grosse Freiheit Grosse Freiheit 36 Ⓦwww.grossefreiheit36.de. A tourist attraction in itself, Hamburg's leading live venue books major acts most weekends. Emphasis on goth and rock. U-/S-Bahn St Pauli or Reeperbahn.

Directory

Bike rental At left luggage in the train station for €10/day. Also at Fahrradstation, Schlüterstr. 11, €3–6/day, depending on the bike; Mon–Fri 9am–6pm; S-Bahn Dammtor.
Consulates Canada, Ballindamm 35 Ⓣ040/4600 270; New Zealand, Domstr. 19 Ⓣ040/4425 550; US, Alsterufer 28 Ⓣ040/411 71 100.
Exchange Reisebank, at the train station.
Hospital Krankenhaus Bethesda, Glindersweg 80 Ⓣ040/725 540. Bus #135 or #235.
Internet In the southern building of the main train station (Hauptbahnhof-Süd).
Laundry Schnell & Sauber Schanzenstr. 27, 6am–11pm, €3.50.
Left luggage At the train station.
Pharmacy At the train station.
Post office At the train station.

Shopping

Hamburg is a shopper's paradise. Mönckebergstrasse, running from the train station to the Rathaus, is department store central, while Poststrasse and Neuer Wall (just east of the Rathaus) is the place to window-shop exclusive designers. For the young unknowns, however, you'll have to abandon the centre for the chic boutiques of the Schanze and Karolinen districts. The areas around the Sternschanze station and around Marktstrasse (U-Bahn Feldstr.) are good places to start.

Moving on

Train Århus (2 daily; 5hr); Berlin (hourly; 1hr 30min); Copenhagen (4 daily; 4hr 40min); Frankfurt (hourly; 3hr 30min); Hannover (every 30min; 1hr 25min); Lübeck (every 30min; 50min); Munich (hourly; 6hr); Rostock (hourly; 2hr–2hr 30min).

LÜBECK

Just an hour from Hamburg, **LÜBECK** makes a great day-trip. Set on an egg-shaped island surrounded by the water defences of the River Trave and the city moat, the pretty Altstadt is a five-minute walk from the train station, past the twin-towered and leaning **Holstentor** (daily: Jan–March 11am–5pm; April–Dec 10am–6pm; €5/students €2.50), the city's emblem.

What to see and do

On the waterfront to the right of the Holstentor is a row of lovely gabled buildings – the **Salzspeicher** (salt storehouses). Straight ahead, over the bridge and up Holstenstrasse, the first church on the right is the Gothic **Petrikirche**; an elevator goes to the top of its spire (daily

9am–9pm; €3/students €2) for city-wide views. Back across Holstenstrasse is the Markt and the elaborate **Rathaus**. Just behind, you'll find **Konditorei-café Niederegger**, renowned for its vast marzipan display; its old-style first-floor café is surprisingly affordable and crammed with marzipan products, while the top floor is a free museum dedicated to the sugary substance.

Behind the north wing of the town hall stands the **Marienkirche**, Germany's oldest brick-built Gothic church. The interior makes a light and lofty backdrop for the church's treasures: a magnificent 1518 carved altar, a life-sized figure of John the Evangelist dating from 1505, a beautiful Gothic gilded tabernacle and an ornate astronomical clock. The church's huge bells remain embedded in the floor where they fell when the church was bombed in 1942.

Katharinenkirche, to the east, on the corner of Königstrasse and Glockengiesserstrasse, boasts three sculptures on its west facade by Ernst Barlach; he was commissioned to make a series of nine in the early 1930s, but had completed only these when his work was banned by the Nazis. To the north at Königstr. 9–11 are the **Behnhaus** and the **Drägerhaus**, two patricians' houses now converted into a museum (Tues–Sun: Jan–March 11am–5pm; April–Dec 10am–5pm; €5/students €2.50; Ⓦwww.behnhaus-draegerhaus.de), housing a good collection of modern and nineteenth-century paintings, including works by Kirchner, Munch and Caspar David Friedrich, as well as furniture and porcelain.

Arrival and information

Train Lübeck train station is just west of the Altstadt; walk down Konrad-Adenauer-Strasse 5min until you reach the Holstentor.

Tourist office The main tourist office is at Holstentorplatz 1 (June–Sept Mon–Fri 9.30am–7pm, Sat 10am–3pm, Sun 10am–2pm; Oct–May Mon–Fri 9.30am–6pm, Sat 10am–3pm; Dec also Sun 10am–2pm; Ⓣ01805/88 22 33, Ⓦwww.luebeck-tourismus.de).

Discount passes The Happy Day Card (€5/10 24/72hr) covers public transport and up to a fifty percent discount at museums. A variety of combined tickets for the city's museums are available: two museums in three days costs €7/students €4, three in three days €10/5, all museums in one week €15/8.

Moving on

Train Copenhagen (4 daily; 4hr); Hamburg (hourly; 50min); Rostock (hourly; 2–3hr).

Ferry Lisco Baltic Service (Ⓣ04502/88 66 90, Ⓦwww.dfdslisco.com): Lübeck-Travemünde to Riga (4 times a week; 33hr; €74). Finnlines (Ⓣ04502/80543, Ⓦwww.ferrycenter.fi): Lübeck to Helsinki (9 weekly; 28hr; €206).

ROSTOCK

A former ship-building centre and member of the Hanseatic League, **ROSTOCK** is Germany's main Baltic port, with passenger ferries heading for Denmark, Sweden, Finland and Latvia several times daily.

Arrival and information

Air A special shuttlebus (#127, timed departures, €8.40) links Rostock-Laage Airport, served by AirBerlin, with the Rostock train station.

Train The Hauptbahnhof is a 20min walk south of the centre.

Ferry From the harbour (Seehafen), take bus #45 or #49 to Lütten Klein (every 30min), then the S-Bahn to the station; or take bus #49 to Dierkower Kreuz (every 30min) and transfer to a U-Bahn to the station; or walk 20min to the S-Bahn stop "Seehafen" and take the S-Bahn to the station (hourly from 5.03am–22.03pm).

Tourist office The tourist office is at Neuer Markt 3 (May & Sept Mon–Fri 10am–6pm, Sat & Sun 10am–4pm; June–Aug Mon–Fri 10am–7pm, Sat & Sun 10am–4pm; Oct–April Mon–Fri 10am–6pm, Sat 10am–3pm; Ⓣ0381/381 2222, Ⓦwww.rostock.de).

Accommodation

Bräckföst Beginenberg 25 ⓣ0381/444 3858, ⓦwww.braeckfoest.de. New, basic hostel in the centre; breakfast is, ironically, not included. Reception till 8pm, sheets €2. Tram to Steintor or 15min walk from the station. Dorms ❷, rooms ❺
Hanse Doberaner Str. 136 ⓣ0381/128 6006, ⓦwww.hanse-hostel.de. Backpackers' with kitchen and Internet, near the happening part of town – though out of the centre. Tram to Volkstheater. Sheets €2, no breakfast. Dorms ❷, rooms ❺.

Moving on

Train Berlin (every 2hr; 3hr); Hamburg (hourly; 2hr 30min); Stralsund (every 2hr; 1hr).
Ferry Scandlines, Am Warnowkai 8 ⓣ0381/20 73 317 ⓦwww.scandlines.de, to: Gedser (Denmark; 10 daily; 1hr 45min; June–Aug €10, Sept–May €5); Trelleborg (Sweden; 3 daily; 6hr–7hr 30min; June–Aug €24, Sept–May €20); Ventspils (Latvia; 4 weekly; 26hr; €55–75); Silja line ⓦwww.silja.com to: Helsinki (daily; 25hr; €72–97).

RÜGEN

Boasting beaches, forests and the chalk cliffs that inspired Caspar David Friedrich, the Baltic island of **RÜGEN** has a long history as a holiday destination. These days, the visitors here are mainly families and pensioners, but there's plenty to see and do even if you don't fit into either category.

The best **place to stay** is the youth hostel, right on the beach in the resort town of **BINZ** (DJH, Strandpromenade 35 ⓣ038393/325 97, ⓦwww.jh-binz.de; ❸, rooms ❺). From there, local buses and trains can take you to the island's highlights: the chalk cliffs of **Nationalpark Jasmund** (bus #23 to Königsstuhl) and the countless hiking and cycling trails through Rügen's varied landscape. **Sassnitz-Mukran**, in the northeast, is a port with services to Denmark, Sweden and Lithuania.

Arrival and information

Train The train station is at Binz's edge; it's a signposted 10min walk to the centre.
Ferry The Fährhafen Sassnitz/Mukran (ⓦwww.faehrhafen-sassnitz.de) is a 2km walk from the Dubnitz bus stop, which is connected to Binz by bus #20 (every 30min; 24min). Bus #18 runs four times daily directly from the port to the Sassnitz train station. From there, you can catch trains to mainland Germany.
Tourist office Binz's tourist office is located in the Kurverwaltung, just inland from the Promenade at Heinrich-Heine-Strasse 7 (April–Oct Mon–Fri 9am–6pm, Sat & Sun 10am–6pm; Nov–March Mon–Fri 9am–4pm, Sat & Sun 11am–4pm; ⓣ038393/148 148, ⓦwww.ostseebad-binz.de).

Moving on

Train Binz to: Berlin (hourly; 4hr 30min); Rostock (hourly; 2hr); Stralsund (hourly; 1hr).
Ferry Scandlines (ⓣ038392/644 20, ⓦwww.scandlines.de) Sassnitz/Mukran to: Rønne (Denmark; 1–2 daily; 3hr 30min; June–Aug €22, Sept–May €15); Trelleborg (Sweden; 5 daily; 4hr; June–Aug €15, Sept–May €12).
Lisco Baltic Service (ⓣ038392/646 814, ⓦwww.dfdslisco.com) to Klaipeda (Lithuania; 3 weekly; 19hr; €64).

HANNOVER

HANNOVER is a major transport hub and trade-fair city and, unfortunately, that's primarily what it looks like. The city's showpiece – refreshingly – is not a great cathedral, palace or town hall, but a series of **gardens** and first-class museums. Hannover's location at the intersection of many major cross-country rail lines and its lack of budget accommodation make it a perfect candidate for a pit stop – on your way somewhere else.

What to see and do

Hannover's commercial centre is a short walk southwest of the train station. The best museums are further south, on the other side of Friedrichswall, while the splendid royal gardens are northwest of the centre.

The Altes Rathaus and Marktkirche

A short distance southwest of the train station, a few streets of rebuilt half-timbered buildings convey some impression of the medieval town. The elaborate brickwork of the high-gabled fifteenth-century **Altes Rathaus** is impressive, despite the shop-filled, modern interior. Alongside is the fourteenth-century red-brick Gothic **Marktkirche**, with some miraculously preserved stained glass.

Niedersächsisches Landesmuseum and Sprengel Museum

Southeast of the Marktkirche, across Friedrichswall on Willy-Brandt-Allee, is the **Niedersächsisches Landesmuseum** (Tues–Sun 10am–5pm, Thurs till 7pm; €4/students €3, Fri 2–5pm free; U-Bahn Aegidientorplatz; ⓦwww.nlmh.de), housing an excellent collection of paintings from the Middle Ages to the early twentieth century. A bit further down the road lies the **Sprengel Museum** (Tues 10am–8pm, Wed–Sun 10am–6pm; €7/students €4; ⓦwww.sprengel-museum.de), with a first-rate collection of twentieth- and twenty-first century painting and sculpture.

The gardens

The royal gardens of **Herrenhausen**, featuring Europe's biggest fountain, can be reached by U-Bahn #4 or #5. Proceeding north from town along Nienburger Strasse, head past the Welfengarten on the right. To the left, the dead-straight Herrenhäuser Allee cuts through the **Georgengarten**, an English-style landscaped garden with an artificial lake, created as a foil to the magnificent formal **Grosser Garten** (daily 9am till dusk; €3, free mid-Oct to early April), the city's pride and joy. If possible, time your visit to coincide with the playing of the fountains (April–Sept daily 11am–noon & 2/3–5pm).

Arrival and information

Airport S-Bahn #5 (every 30min; 20min; €2.70) runs between Hannover Airport and the main train station.

Train and bus The train station is in the centre of town; behind is the bus station.

Tourist office The tourist office is across from the train station, at Ernst-August-Platz 8 (Mon–Fri 9am–6pm, Sat 9am–2pm; May–Sept also Sun 9am–2pm; ⓣ0511/12345 111, ⓦwww.hannover-tourism.de); they'll book you into a hotel (from ❼) for a €2 fee.

Discount pass The Hannover Card (single: €9/15, up to 5 people €17/29 for 1/3 days), covers public transport and provides discounts to the main museums and sights.

Internet Tele Klick, Schillerstr. 23. Daily 9am–midnight; €2.50/hr.

Bike rental Fahrradstation, next to the station. Mon–Fri 6am–11pm, Sat & Sun 8am–11pm. Bikes €7.50/day.

Accommodation

Hannover charges fancy business prices for accommodation, which can double during trade fairs.

Am Thielenplatz Thielenplatz 2 ⓣ0511/32 76 91, ⓦwww.smartcityhotels.com. The lowest rates in the centre are at this swank new hotel; they'll cut €7 per person off the price if you don't want breakfast. ❻–❾

DJH Ferdinand-Wilhelm-Fricke-Weg 1 ⓣ0511/1317 674, ⓦwww.jugendherberge.de. Modern HI hostel, with two- and four-bed dorms. Take U-Bahn #3 or #7 to Fischerhof, double back north, then turn right on Lodemannweg; it's a signposted 10min walk from there. ❸

Flora Heinrichstr. 36 ⓣ0511/38 39 10, ⓦwww.hotel-flora-hannover.de. Spotless hotel behind the train station, offering an excellent breakfast. ❼

Eating and drinking

There are lots of cafés and bars around Goetheplatz, just west of the centre; for nightlife, head to the Lister Meile, behind the station.

Fire Knochenhauerstr. 30. A trendy gay bar serving food, near Markthalle. Sandwiches €3.33.

Markthalle Karmaschstr. 49. For snacks, head for this joint, where German, Italian, Spanish and Turkish stalls sell good-value meals. Mon–Wed 7am–8pm, Thurs–Fri 7am–10pm, Sat 7am–4pm.

Zaza Hamburger Allee 4a ⓦwww.zaza-club.de. Popular club offering house, funk and soul. Behind the train station, off Lister Meile.

Moving on

Hannover Berlin (hourly; 1hr 30min); Cologne (hourly; 2hr 40min); Goslar (every 30 min; 1hr 30min); Frankfurt (hourly; 2hr 20min); Hamburg (every 20min; 1hr 20min).

GOSLAR

GOSLAR is an absurdly picturesque mining town located at the northern edge of the gentle wooded Harz mountains. Silver was discovered in the nearby Rammelsberg in the tenth century, and Goslar soon became the "treasure chest of the Holy Roman Empire". The presence of a POW hospital during World War II spared the town's attractive medieval architecture from bombing; it's now a UNESCO World Heritage site.

What to see and do

The town's geographic and cultural centre is the **Marktplatz**, with an elegantly Gothic **Rathaus** and buildings with roofs of bright-red tiles and contrasting grey slate. The **Huldigungssaal** in the Rathaus (April–Oct daily 11.30am–3pm; €3.50) contains a dazzling array of medieval wall and ceiling paintings. Just behind the Rathaus is the **Marktkirche**, facing the sixteenth-century **Brusttuch** house, whose top storey is crammed with satirical carvings. Look out for the famous "Butterhanne", a milkmaid churning butter with one hand and clutching her bare bottom with the other. Goslar's half-timbered beauty begins in earnest in the streets behind the church – the Frankenberg Quarter – with the oldest houses lying in the Bergstrasse and Schreiberstrasse areas.

Kaiserpfalz

On the southern edge of the centre is the **Kaiserpfalz**, built in the early eleventh century. Much of the interior (daily 10am–5pm, Nov–March till 4pm; €4.50) is occupied by the vast Kaisersaal, decorated with Romantic depictions of the German emperors.

Mönchehaus Museum and churches

Northwest of Marktplatz is the **Mönchehaus Museum** (Tues–Sat 10am–5pm, Sun 10am–1pm; €3; Ⓦwww.moenchehaus.de). A black-and-white half-timbered building over 450 years old, it's the curious home to Goslar's modern art collection, which includes a Joseph Beuys room. East of here, the **Jakobikirche** contains a moving *Pietà* by the great sixteenth-century sculptor Hans Witten, while to the north, the early thirteenth-century **Neuwerkkirche** (April–Oct Mon–Fri 10am–noon & 2.30–4.30pm, Sat & Sun 2.30–4.30pm; free) is dominated by its two striking polygonal towers.

Arrival and information

Train Head left out of the train station; it's a 5min walk into the centre.

Tourist office Goslar's tourist office is at Markt 7 (May–Oct Mon–Fri 9.15am–6pm, Sat 9.30am–4pm, Sun 9.30am–2pm; Nov–April Mon–Fri 9.15am–5pm, Sat 9.30am–2pm; Ⓣ05321/78 060, Ⓦwww.goslar.de).

Accommodation

DJH Rammelsberger Str. 25 Ⓣ05321/22 240, Ⓦwww.jugendherberge.de/jh/goslar. The quaint HI hostel is a 30min walk southwest from the centre (or bus #808 to Theresienhof). ❸

Gästehaus Möller Schieferweg 6 Ⓣ05321/23 098. An excellent guesthouse a few minutes' walk west from the train station. Generous breakfast. ❺

Zur Börse Bergstr. 53 Ⓣ05321/34 510, Ⓦwww.hotel-boerse-goslar.de. This is one of the prettiest hotels, right in the centre. ❺

Eating and drinking

The market on Fischemäkerstrasse (Tues & Fri mornings) is a great place to pick up snacks of sausages and fish rolls.

Butterhanne Marktkirchhof 3. Serving coffee and cakes as well as full meals. Breakfast from €2.

Köpi am Markt Worthstr. 10. Restaurant and bar that does salads and steaks (€7.50). 5pm–1am.

Worthmühle Worthstr. 4. Charming establishment serving mouthwatering local specialities – try the game dishes such as venison €12.

Moving on

Train Berlin (hourly; 3hr); Hamburg (hourly; 2hr 30min); Hannover (every 40min; 1hr 10min).

Central Germany

Central Germany is the most populous region of the country and home to the zone of heaviest industrialization – the Ruhrgebiet. Within this conurbation, **Cologne** stands out, managing to preserve many of the splendours of its long centuries as a free state. Neighbouring **Bonn** is another historic city, renowned for being the birthplace of Beethoven. The other city of historical interest is **Aachen**, the original capital of the Holy Roman Empire. To the south the Rhineland-Palatinate is the land of the national epic, of the alluring Lorelei, of robber barons and of the traders who used the river routes to make the country rich. Nowadays pleasure cruisers – and the Koblenz–Mainz rail line – run through the **Rhine Gorge**, past a wonderful landscape of rocks, vines, white-painted towns and ruined castles. Industry exists only in isolated pockets, and **Mainz**, the state capital, only just ranks among the forty largest cities in Germany. Its monuments, though, merit more than a passing glance, while **Trier** preserves the finest buildings of classical antiquity this side of the Alps. In the province of Hesse, dynamic **Frankfurt** dominates, with its banking and communications industries providing the region's real economic base.

COLOGNE (KÖLN)

COLOGNE (Köln) has a population of just over a million, and its huge Gothic Dom is the country's most visited monument. The Dom is about all that was spared in World War II, putting the city at the mercy of a botched 1950s rebuild. The people here do more than enough to compensate for their city's unremarkable architecture: Cologne is undeniably the friendliest and most fun-loving city in the country. Try and coincide your visit with the annual **Carnival** in early spring – Cologne boasts the largest street parties in Germany and the entire city does nothing but celebrate for a full five days.

Cologne has a long and glorious history – as a Roman colony (*Colonia*), then a pilgrimage centre, later a major trading city, and finally as the marketer of toilet water eau de Cologne.

What to see and do

Cologne's sights are all within walking distance of the train station, in the dense centre hugging the west bank of the Rhine.

The Dom

One of the largest Gothic buildings ever constructed, Cologne's gigantic **Dom** (daily 6am–7.30pm; free) is built on a scale that reflects its power – the archbishop was one of the seven Electors of the Holy Roman Empire, and the Dom remains the seat of the Primate of Germany. Begun in 1248, the extravagant project was abandoned in 1560, to be resumed only in the nineteenth century. The centrepiece of this cathedral is the spectacular golden shrine to the Magi, made in 1181. Other masterpieces include the ninth-century Gero crucifix, the most important monumental sculpture of its period, and Stefan Lochner's *Adoration of the Magi*, the greatest achievement of the fifteenth-century Cologne school of painters. Climb the 509 steps to the top of the south tower for a breathtaking panorama over the city and the Rhine (daily: May–Sept 9am–6pm; March, April & Oct 9am–5pm; Nov–Feb 9am–4pm; €2). The **Domschatzkammer**

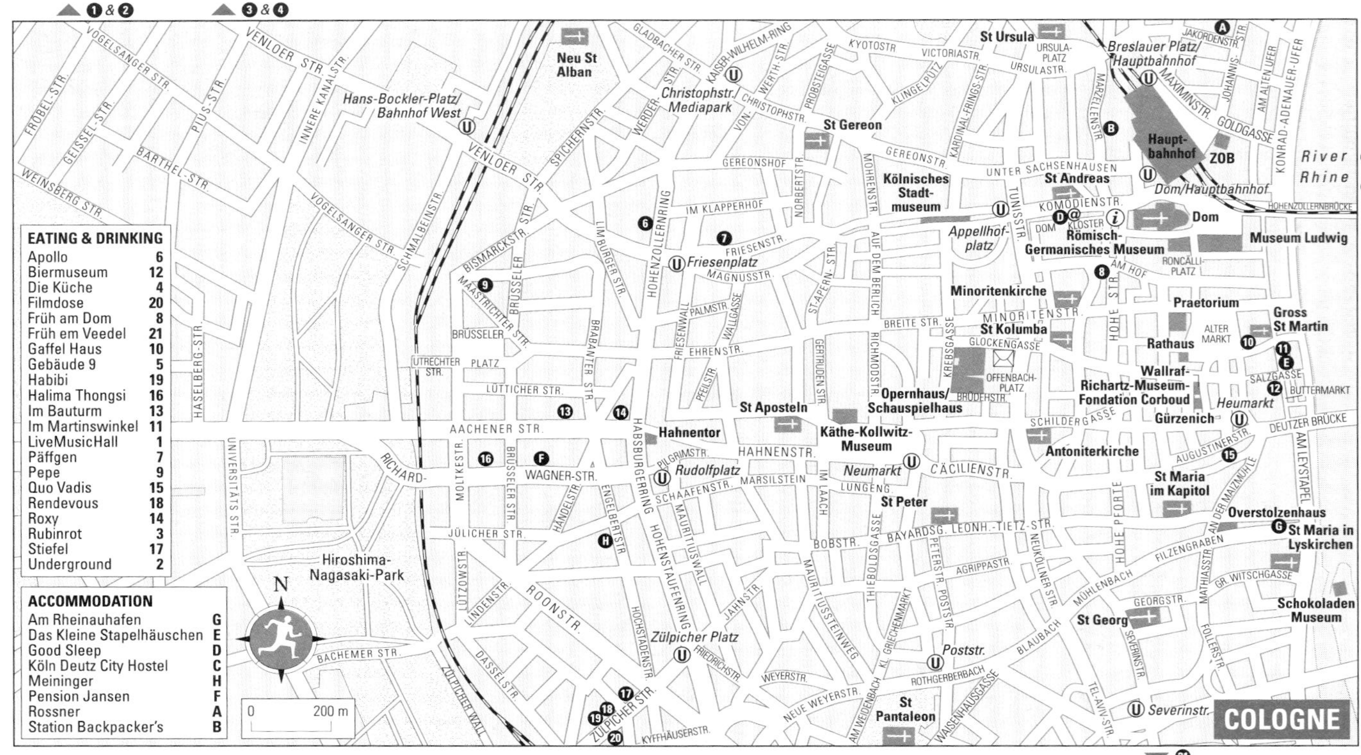
COLOGNE
1 & 2
3 & 4
C & 5
21
EATING & DRINKING
Apollo 6
Biermuseum 12
Die Küche 4
Filmdose 20
Früh am Dom 8
Früh em Veedel 21
Gaffel Haus 10
Gebäude 9 5
Habibi 19
Halima Thongsi 16
Im Bauturm 13
Im Martinswinkel 11
LiveMusicHall 1
Päffgen 7
Pepe 9
Quo Vadis 15
Rendevous 18
Roxy 14
Rubinrot 3
Stiefel 17
Underground 2
ACCOMMODATION
Am Rheinauhafen G
Das Kleine Stapelhäuschen E
Good Sleep D
Köln Deutz City Hostel C
Meininger H
Pension Jansen F
Rossner A
Station Backpacker's B
N
0 200 m
River Rhine
Hauptbahnhof
ZOB
Dom
Dom/Hauptbahnhof
Breslauer Platz/ Hauptbahnhof
Museum Ludwig
Römisch-Germanisches Museum
St Ursula
St Andreas
St Gereon
Neu St Alban
Kölnisches Stadtmuseum
Appellhofplatz
Minoritenkirche
St Kolumba
Praetorium
Rathaus
Alter Markt
Gross St Martin
Wallraf-Richartz-Museum-Fondation Corboud
Heumarkt
Gürzenich
Antoniterkirche
St Maria im Kapitol
Overstolzenhaus
St Maria in Lyskirchen
Schokoladen Museum
St Georg
Severinstr.
St Pantaleon
Poststr.
St Peter
Neumarkt
Käthe-Kollwitz-Museum
Opernhaus/ Schauspielhaus
St Aposteln
Hahnentor
Rudolfplatz
Zülpicher Platz
Friesenplatz
Christophstr./ Mediapark
Hans-Bockler-Platz/ Bahnhof West
Hiroshima-Nagasaki-Park
Venloer Str.
Aachener Str.
Hohenzollernring
Habsburgerring
Hohenstaufenring
Hohenzollernbrücke
Deutzer Brücke
Konrad-Adenauer-Ufer
Am Leystapel
Hohe Str.
Hohe Pforte
Cäcilienstr.
Schildergasse
Breite Str.
Ehrenstr.
Richmodstr.
Mauritiussteinweg
Universitäts Str.
Zülpicher Str.
Roonstr.

(daily 10am–6pm; €4, joint ticket with tower €5) in the cellars, entered from the north side of the building, contains a stunning array of treasury items, the original sculptures from the medieval south portal and items excavated from Merovingian royal graves.

Museum Ludwig and the Römisch-Germanisches Museum

In a modern building next to the Dom, the outstanding **Museum Ludwig** (Tues–Sun 10am–6pm, till 10pm first Fri every month; €7.50; ⓦwww.museenkoeln.de) is huge, and one of Germany's premier collections of modern art, particularly strong on American Pop Art and German Expressionism. The neighbouring **Römisch-Germanisches Museum** (Tues–Sun 10am–5pm, Wed till 8pm; €5; ⓦwww.museenkoeln.de) was built directly over its star exhibit, the Dionysus Mosaic, which can be viewed *in situ*. The finest work of its kind in northern Europe, it was created for a patrician villa in about 200 AD. The museum has a collection of Roman glass reckoned to be the world's finest, but of more general appeal is the dazzling array of jewellery on the first floor, mostly dating from the Dark Ages.

Gross St Martin and the Rhine

For nearly six hundred years, the tower of **Gross St Martin**, one of Cologne's twelve Romanesque churches, was the dominant feature of the city's skyline. Just behind it is the best spot to enjoy the Rhine, in the grassy park before Buttermarkt. For the best view of the Altstadt, cross the bridge and walk along the other side of the Rhine.

Wallraf-Richartz-Museum

Southwest of Gross St Martin is the strikingly angular **Wallraf-Richartz-Museum** (Tues 10am–8pm, Mon–Fri 10am–6pm, Sat & Sun 11am–6pm; €5.80; ⓦwww.museenkoeln.de), whose holdings centre on the fifteenth-century Cologne school as well as a fine Impressionist collection.

Schokoladenmuseum

Further south, on the banks of the Rhine, is the **Schokoladenmuseum** (Tues–Fri 10am–6pm, Sat & Sun 11am–7pm, last entry 1hr before closing; €6.50; ⓦwww.schokoladenmuseum.de), a thoroughly enjoyable museum focusing on the history and production of chocolate. The highlight is the chocolate fountain where white-clad attendants hand out freshly created samples.

Arrival

Air Cologne/Bonn Airport is connected to the train station by S-Bahn line S13 (every 20min; 12min; €2.30). Düsseldorf Airport has its own train station, with frequent connections to Cologne main station (every 30min; 40min; €12). Bohr Omnibus (ⓦwww.bohr-omnibusse.de) operates a shuttle bus between Cologne main station and Airport Weeze (called Düsseldorf-Weeze by Ryanair; 6 daily; 2hr 30min; €18), as well as the Frankfurt-Hahn Airport (hourly 5pm–midnight; 1hr 45min; €12).
Train The Hauptbahnhof is immediately below the Dom in the centre of the city.
Bus The bus station (ZOB) is directly behind the train station – take exit Breslauer Platz.

Information

Tourist office The main tourist office (Mon–Sat 9am–8pm, Sun 10am–5pm; ⓣ0221/221 304 00, ⓦwww.koelntourismus.de), directly in front of the Dom, can book hotel rooms for €3 (from ❻). They publish a monthly bilingual guide to what's on, *Köln im*, but far better is *Stadt Revue* (€3), available at newsagents. There's also a tourist office at the airport, in Terminal 2 (Mon–Fri 7am–8pm, Sat 8am–8pm, Sun 9.30am–6pm).
Discount passes The WelcomeCard (single: €9/14/19, up to three people: €18/28/38 for 24hr/48hr/72hr) provides free transport and around twenty percent off most sights.

City transport

The public transport network is a mixture of buses and trams/U-Bahn. A short trip costs €1.40, a single trip €2.30, a day-pass €6.40 (€9.50 for five people) and a strip of four single trips €7.80.

Accommodation

Hostels

Am Rheinauhafen Rheingasse 34–36 ⓣ0221/230247, ⓦwww.am-rheinauhafen.de. Basic hostel, with no extras or hang-out feel, in the southern Altstadt. U-Bahn Heumarkt. Dorms ❸, rooms ❼

Köln Deutz City Hostel Siegesstr. 5 ⓣ0221/814711, ⓦwww.jugendherberge.de/jh/koeln-deutz. Large and functional HI hostel close to Deutz station, directly across the Rhine from the Altstadt. Dorms ❸, rooms ❼

Meininger Engelbertstr. 33–35 ⓣ0221/92 40 90, ⓦwww.meininger-hostels.com. This branch of the hostel chain has a great location, roughly between the student area and downtown. Breakfast included. U-Bahn Rudolphplatz or Zülpicher Platz. Dorms ❷, rooms ❹

Station Backpacker's Marzellenstr. 40–48 ⓣ0221/912 53 01, ⓦwww.hostel-cologne.de. Large, privately run hostel just north of the station, with kitchen and free Internet. Dorms ❷, rooms ❺

Hotels and pensions

Das Kleine Stapelhäuschen Fischmarkt 1–3 ⓣ0221/272 7777, ⓦwww.koeln-altstadt.de/stapelhaeuschen. Characterful Altstadt hotel/restaurant rebuilt to resemble its seventeenth-century appearance, very near Gross St Martin. Rooms overlooking the river are the nicest. ❽

Good Sleep Komödienstr. 19–21 ⓣ0221/25 72 257, ⓦwww.goodsleep.de. Bare-bones but clean hotel, with good central location. ❼

Pension Jansen Richard-Wagner-Str. 18 ⓣ0221/251 875, ⓦwww.pensionjansen.de. Friendly, simple six-room pension; all rooms have TV. Rudolfplatz U-Bahn. ❼

Rossner Jakordenstr. 19 ⓣ0221/12 27 03. Homely and clean, and looking exactly as it must have in the 1950s, this is the pick of the cluster of hotels behind the station. ❺

Eating

Cafés

Die Küche Simrockstr. 2, Ehrenfeld. Café-bar that looks like your grandmother's kitchen, though the clientele is definitely hip. Meals €6, cocktail specials €3. U-Bahn Körnerstr.

Im Bauturm Aachener Str. 24. Build your own breakfast at this lovely bohemian café-by-day, bar-by-night, open daily until 3am. Breakfasts from €3. U-Bahn Rudolphplatz.

Pepe Antwerpener Str. 63. Chic café-restaurant-bar serving enormous and excellent salads. Salad Pepe €9. U-Bahn Friesenplatz.

Quo Vadis Vor St Martin 8–10. Cosy gay café/bar between Neumarkt and Heumarkt serving light meals. Hosts popular Eighties nights. Breakfast €5.

Restaurants

Habibi Zülpicher Str. 28. Serving arguably the best falafel in Germany, this Lebanese restaurant in the student neighbourhood stays open late for the night-out munchies. Eat in/take out. Falafel €2. U-Bahn Zülpicher Platz.

Halima Thongsi Brüsseler Str. 24. Delicious Thai food, a little off the beaten track. Red chicken curry €6. U-Bahn Rudolphplatz.

Im Martinswinkel Fischmarkt 9. The cheapest and least touristy of the riverfront restaurants, serving salads and sausages, coffee and cake. Bratwürst plate €10.

Rendevous Zülpicher Str. 11a. One of a handful of good-value Italian restaurants in the student area. Big portions and a young, friendly crowd. Pizza €4.50. U-Bahn Zülpicher Platz.

Beer halls

Früh am Dom Am Hof 12–14. Located opposite the Dom, this heavily touristed Brauhaus serves excellent food. Ribs €9.

Gaffel Haus Alter Markt 20–22. One of the most genuine old-style restaurants, serving huge portions; much cosier than most beer halls. Schnitzel €12.

Päffgen Friesenstr. 64–66, just off Friesenplatz. Less touristy than the places near the Dom with

KÖLSCH

Cologne's unique beer, **Kölsch** is a light and aromatically bitter brew served in a small, thin glass (hence its rather effete image among German beer-drinkers). The best places to try it are the *Brauhäuser*, brewery-owned beer halls, which, although staffed by horribly matey waiters called *Köbes*, are definitely worth sampling, not least because they serve some of the tastiest food in the city.

a younger clientele, and Kölsch brewed on the premises. Mains €9.

Drinking and nightlife

Nightlife is concentrated in several distinct quarters. In the city centre, Gross St Martin in the Altstadt catches the tourists and businessmen, while the area south of Heumarkt has a handful of popular **gay and lesbian** bars. Ehrenfeld's hip, alternative scene centres on Venloer Str., between Venloer Str. and Körnerstr. U-Bahn stations. The dense Zülpicher Strasse area (in the southwest of the city) is the student quarter, packed with cheap restaurants and lively bars. Most mainstream clubs are on the Ring between Zülpicher Platz and Christophstr. U-Bahn stations.

Bars

Biermuseum Buttermarkt 39, Altstadt. Small bar tucked away near the river serving eighteen types of beer on tap and over fifty types of bottled beer.

Filmdose Zülpicher Str. 39 Ⓦwww.filmdose-koeln.de. Fun pub that's packed with students enjoying a post-lecture Kölsch; it has a tiny cabaret stage and also shows films in English. All-day breakfasts €5. U-Bahn Dasselstr./Bhf Süd.

Früh em Veedel Chlodwigplatz 28. This neighbourhood pub serves to-die-for potato pancakes (Reibekuchen €5). U-Bahn Chlodwigplatz.

Rubinrot Sömmeringstr. 9, Ehrenfeld. Red-tinted and always packed, this bar serves excellent and creative cocktails. U-Bahn Venloer Str.

Stiefel Zülpicher Str. 18. This dilapidated and chill punk-rock bar in the student quarter is a great place to nurse a beer or play some pool. U-Bahn Zülpicher Platz.

Clubs

Apollo Hohenzollernring 79–83 Ⓦwww.apolloclub.de. Two bumping floors of R&B, techno and disco. Fri & Sat; €10. U-Bahn Friesenplatz.

Gebäude 9 Deutz-Mühlheimer-Str. 127–129 Ⓦwww.gebaeude9.de. Intimate bar, club and theatre hall where events and exhibitions take place, as well as drum 'n' bass/live gigs. U-Bahn Messe/Deutz.

LiveMusicHall Lischtstr. 30 Ⓦwww.livemusichall.de. Don't let the name fool you: this is primarily a DJ'd club, with regular pop, rock, and 80s nights. Fri, Sat & some Wed. U-Bahn Venloer Str.

Roxy Aachener Str. 2. Open midnight until 7am, this is the place to hit at the end of the night. Two bars, one packed dance floor and an eclectic music mix. U-Bahn Rudolphplatz.

COLOGNE'S CARNIVAL

Though Cologne's **carnival** (the "fifth season") actually begins as early as November 11, the real business starts with Weiberfastnacht on the Thursday prior to Lent. The city goes wild for the next five days until Ash Wednesday; prepare yourself for drunken dancing in the streets and taverns and some wild costumes. The best of the numerous parades are the alternative Geisterzug Saturday night, complete with fire-juggling and drumming, and the spectacular Rose Monday Parade, which features music, floats and caricatures of politicians.

Underground Vogelsanger Str. 200 Ⓦwww.underground-cologne.de. Great for live gigs, especially rock and punk, the *Underground* has a big indie and alternative following. Free entry mid-week, and beer garden. U-Bahn Venloer Str.

Directory

Bike rental Rent-a-Bike, Markmannsgasse, on the banks of the Rhine before the Deutzer Brücke Ⓣ0171/629 8796. Three-hour tour (May–Oct daily 1.30pm, €15), bike rental (€10/day).

Cinema Metropolis, Ebertplatz 19 Ⓦwww.metropolis-koeln.de. Small cinema showing English-language films. U-Bahn Ebertplatz.

Consulates Canada, Benrather Strasse 8, Düsseldorf Ⓣ0211/172 170; UK, Yorckstr. 19, Düsseldorf Ⓣ0211/94480.

Hospital St Marien, Kunibertskloster 11 Ⓣ0221/77120.

Internet TelePost, Komödienstr. 19. €1.50/hr.

Laundry Pantaleonsmühlengasse 42, southwest of the centre, near Barbarossaplatz; €3.50.

Left luggage At the train station.

Pharmacy At the train station.

Post office Breite Str. 6 & branch at the station.

Moving on

Train Aachen (every 30min; 1hr); Amsterdam (hourly; 2hr 30min); Berlin (hourly; 4hr 20min); Bonn (every 20min; 30min); Brussels (hourly; 2hr 30min–4hr); Frankfurt (every 30min; 1hr 10min); Heidelberg (hourly; 2–3hr); Luxemburg (hourly; 3hr

30min); Mainz (hourly; 1hr 45min); Paris (every 2hr; 4hr); Stuttgart (hourly; 2hr 15min).
River cruise K-D Ⓦwww.k-d.com to: Bonn (March–Oct daily; 3hr).

DAY-TRIPS FROM COLOGNE: BONN

A great day-trip from Cologne, **BONN** served as West Germany's unlikely capital from 1949 until the unification of 1990, when Berlin was restored to its former status. Although Bonn's administrative role has diminished, it still remains a surprisingly interesting place to visit, not least for its superb museums – and for being the birthplace of Beethoven.

What to see and do

The small **Altstadt** is now a pedestrianized shopping area centred on two spacious squares. The square to the east is named after the huge **Münster**, whose central octagonal tower with its soaring spire is the city's most prominent landmark. Head around the back to check out the gigantic decapitated heads of the church's patrons, the martyrs SS Cassius and Florentius. The Markt square is dominated by a very different monument, the pink Rococo **Rathaus**, and hosts a market every day except Sunday.

The Beethoven-Haus and the Schloss

A couple of minutes' walk north of here, at Bonngasse 20, is the **Beethoven-Haus** (April–Oct Mon–Sat 10am–6pm, Sun 11am–6pm; Nov–March Mon–Sat 10am–5pm, Sun 11am–5pm; €5; Ⓦwww.beethoven-haus-bonn.de), one of the few old buildings in the centre to have escaped wartime devastation. Beethoven left the city for good at the age of 22, but this hasn't deterred Bonn from building up the best collection of memorabilia of its favourite son. To the east is the Baroque **Schloss**, an enormously long construction that was formerly the seat of the Archbishop-Electors of Cologne and is now used by the university.

The Museumsmeile

The **Museumsmeile** (U-Bahn Heussallee) is home to the **Kunstmuseum** (Tues–Sun 11am–6pm, Wed till 9pm; €5; Ⓦkunstmuseum.bonn.de), with a fine Expressionism collection. Next door is the **Kunst- und Ausstellungshalle** (Tues & Wed 10am–9pm, Thurs–Sun 10am–7pm; €12, combined ticket with Kunstmuseum €15.50; Ⓦwww.bundeskunsthalle.de), a monumental post-modern arts centre for important temporary exhibitions. On the other side of the Kunstmuseum is the **Haus der Geschichte** (Tues–Sun 9am–7pm; free; Ⓦwww.hdg.de), a fascinating museum exploring German contemporary history from the end of World War II to the present.

Arrival and information

Train and bus Bonn train station lies in the middle of the city; just to the east is the bus station, whose local services, along with the trams (which become the U-Bahn in the city centre), form part of a system integrated with Cologne's (though the cities are in different zones). A short trip costs €1.40, a single trip €2.30, a day-pass €6.40 (€9.50 for five people) and a strip of four single trips €7.80.
Tourist office The tourist office (Mon–Fri 9am–6.30pm, Sat 9am–4pm, Sun 10am–2pm; Ⓣ0228/77 50 00, Ⓦwww.bonn-region.de) is near Münsterplatz, at Windeckstr. 1.
Discount pass The WelcomeCard (single: €9/14/19, up to three people: €18/28/38 for 24hr/48hr/72hr) is a great deal in Bonn, providing free travel and free admission to almost all museums and sights.

Eating

Alter Zoll Brassertufer 1, at Konviktstr. Best *Biergarten* in town, with a great Rhine view and yummy snacks. There's a discount on pizza from noon to 3pm (€2.60). Summer only.
Cassius Garten Maximilianstr. 28d, across from the station. Offers mouthwatering veggie choices, buffet

style. Open Mon–Sat 11am–8pm. €1.50/100g, twenty percent off between 7 and 8pm.
Zebulon Stockenstr. 19. This Altstadt bar is a big favourite with students, especially of the American-study-abroad variety. Light meals €3.20.

Moving on

Train Cologne (every 10min; 30min); Koblenz (every 15min; 40min–1hr).
River cruise Cologne (March–Oct: 1–2 daily; 2hr); Koblenz (June–Sept daily; 5hr).

AACHEN

AACHEN – bordering both Belgium and the Netherlands – was the hub in the eighth century of the great empire of Charlemagne, a choice made partly for strategic reasons but also because of the presence of hot springs. Exercising in these waters was one of the emperor's favourite pastimes and the health-enriching properties of these waters is still a major draw. Aachen has a laid-back atmosphere that reflects its large student population, making it a good day-trip from Cologne or stop-off point between countries.

What to see and do

Although the surviving architectural legacy of Charlemagne is small, Aachen retains its crowning jewel, the former **Palace chapel**. Now the heart of the **Dom** (daily 7am–6/7pm; Ⓦwww.aachendom.de), the original octagon had to be enlarged by adding the Gothic chancel to accommodate the number of pilgrims that poured in. At the end of the chancel, the gilded shrine of Charlemagne, finished in 1215 after fifty years' work, contains the remains of the emperor, while in the gallery is the imperial throne, which you can only see on a tour (Sat & Sun 2pm; €2.50). Next to the Dom, the **Schatzkammer** (Mon 10am–1pm, Tues–Sun 10am–6pm, Thurs till 9pm; €4/students €3; entrance on Johannes-Paul-II-Str.) is a dazzling treasury and UNESCO World Heritage site. Highlights among its collections are the tenth-century Lothar Cross and a Roman sarcophagus once used as Charlemagne's coffin. The emperor's palace once extended across the Katschhof to the site of the fourteenth-century **Rathaus**, which incorporates two of the palace's towers and has a facade lined with the figures of fifty Holy Roman Emperors, 31 of whom were crowned in Aachen. The glory of the interior (daily 10am–1pm & 2–5pm; €2/students €1) is the much-restored Kaisersaal, repository of the crown jewels – in reproduction. The Rathaus fronts the expansive **Markt**, which boasts the finest medieval houses left in the city.

TREAT YOURSELF

If you can't make it to Baden-Baden, you could settle for the healing waters Charlemagne once enjoyed. A luxurious spa treatment at the **Carolus Thermen** (daily 9am–11pm, last entry at 9.30pm; Ⓦwww.carolus-thermen.de), northeast of the centre, will soak away the accumulated grunge of weeks on the road. Take bus #34 or #51. Two and a half hours costs €10, a full day €14.50.

Arrival and information

Air Maastricht Aachen Airport. From there, board any train to Aachen (hourly; 1hr; €9).
Train The centre is ten minutes' walk from the train station – down Bahnhofstrasse, then left into Theaterstrasse.
Tourist office The tourist office occupies the Atrium Elisenbrunnen on Friedrich-Wilhelm-Platz (Mon–Fri 9am–6pm, Sat 9am–2pm; April–Dec also Sun 10am–2pm; Ⓣ0241/18 02 960, Ⓦwww.aachen.de).

Eating and drinking

The student quarter centres on Pontstrasse, which is lined with bars and cheap eateries.
Egmont Pontstr. 1. This classy, wood-panelled bistro is a popular haunt. Snacks from €1.50.

Kittel Pontstr. 37. Relaxed café with good-size portions of great food, €5–7. Open until 3am.
Labyrinth Pontstr. 156. Large pub serving Greek-style food. Grills €6.
Leo van den Daele Büchel 18. The best place to try spiced gingerbread *Printen*, the main local speciality. Printen €2.
Postwagen Markt 40. The most celebrated bar/restaurant in town with a cheerful Baroque exterior and wonderful cosy rooms inside. Mains €8.

Moving on

Trains Brussels (hourly; 1hr 30min–2hr); Cologne (every 30min; 35min–1hr); Liège (every 40min; 50min); Maastricht (hourly; 1hr); Paris (every 2hr; 3hr).

MAINZ

At the confluence of the Rhine and Main rivers, **MAINZ** is an agreeable mixture of old and new, with an attractive restored centre and a jovial populace – it's second only to Cologne in the carnival stakes. Ecclesiastical power aside, prestige came through Johannes Gutenberg, who revolutionized the art of printing here.

What to see and do

Rearing high above the centre of Mainz is the **Dom** (March–Oct Mon–Fri 9am–6.30pm, Sat 9am–4pm, Sun 1–2.45pm & 4–6.30pm; Nov–Feb Mon–Fri & Sun till 5pm), crowded in by eighteenth-century houses. Choirs at both ends of the building indicate its status as an imperial cathedral, with one area for the emperor and one for the clergy. Visit the spacious **Markt** when it's packed with market stalls (Tues, Fri & Sat mornings). Dominating the adjoining Liebfrauenplatz is the **Gutenberg Museum** (Tues–Sat 9am–5pm, Sun 11am–3pm; €5/students €3; Ⓦwww.gutenberg.de). This fascinating museum of printing is a fitting tribute to one of the greatest inventors of all time, whose pioneering development of movable type led to the mass-scale production of books.

Arrival and information

Train The train station is a 15min walk northwest of the city centre; head down Bahnhofstrasse or take a tram or bus to Höffchen.
Tourist office The tourist office (Mon–Fri 9am–6pm, Sat 10am–4pm, Sun 11am–3pm; Ⓣ06131/28 6210, Ⓦwww.info-mainz.de) is in the Brückenturm am Rathaus, by the pedestrian street Am Brand and offers a free room-booking service, from ❻.

Accommodation

DJH Otto-Brunfels-Schneise 4 Ⓣ06131/85 332, Ⓦwww.jugendherberge.de. Your basic HI hostel, with single, double (two beds) and four-bed rooms, in the wooded heights of Weisenau. Buses #62, #63 & #92 will take you within 400m. Juniors ❷, seniors ❸
Stadt Coblenz Rheinstr. 49 Ⓣ06131/629 0444, Ⓦwww.stadtcoblenz.de. Conveniently located and comfy hotel near the Dom, though some of the rooms suffer from street noise. ❻–❼
Terminus Alicenstr. 4 Ⓣ06131/22 98 76, Ⓦwww.hotel-terminus-mainz.de. Surly-staffed but nicely outfitted hotel near the station with en-suite rooms. ❽

Eating and drinking

Mainz boasts more vineyards on its outskirts than any other German city; the many lovely wine bars are the best places to sample their product.
Alt Deutsche Weinstube Liebfrauenplatz 7. The oldest wine bar in town, offering cheap daily dishes. Evenings only; local wine from €2.60.
Havana Rheinstr. 49, below the *Stadt Coblenz*. A Cuban/Mexican bar and restaurant, which gets packed out at weekends.
Weinhaus Schreiner Rheinstr. 38. The best restaurant in town, open weekday evenings and Sat lunch. Salad with duck and rabbit €12.

Moving on

Train Cologne (every 20min; 2hr); Frankfurt (every 20 min; 30min); Heidelberg (hourly; 1hr); Koblenz (every 30min; 1hr); Stuttgart (hourly; 1hr 30min); Trier (hourly; 2hr 30min).
River cruises K-D Ⓦwww.k-d.com to: Bacharach/Kaub (March–Oct 1–2 daily; 2hr 30min); Koblenz (May–Sept 2 daily; 5hr 30min).

THE RHINE GORGE

North of Mainz, the Rhine bends westwards and continues undramatically until **BINGEN**, where it widens and swings north into the breathtaking eighty-kilometre **Rhine Gorge** – a UNESCO World Heritage region. The most famous point along the Rhine is the **Lorelei**, a much-photographed rocky projection between Oberwesel and St Goar, where, legend has it, a blonde woman would lure passing mariners to their doom with her siren song. The best way to visit this region is by boat or by bike, spending a night in Bacharach or Koblenz, but if you're pressed for time, the train will do just fine. The rail line between Koblenz and Mainz runs right along the river's banks, allowing for wonderful views of the Gorge from the windows on the train's eastern side. Some **river cruises** (mainly April–Oct) depart from Mainz, although more regular through-services start from Bingen. The full one-way boat fare from Bingen to Koblenz is €26/students €13 (6hr; return €28/students €14). Eurail and InterRail are valid on the train line; two cyclists travel for the price of one on Tuesdays.

Bacharach

At **BACHARACH**, 10km downstream from Bingen, the twelfth-century castle of Burg Stahleck houses an HI **hostel** (☎06743/12 66, Ⓦwww.djh.de; dorms ❷, rooms ❸) – hands down the best DJH in Germany. It's a steep climb up the hill to get there, but the views of the Rhine valley are worth it. The best hotel is the lovely half-timbered *Im Malerwinkel* (☎06743/1239, Ⓦwww.im-malerwinkel.de; all rooms en suite ❻), built into the old town wall. There's also a **campsite** at Strandbadweg 9 (☎06743/1752, Ⓦwww.camping-sonnenstrand.de; ❶), 5min south of the station.

Koblenz

Quiet **KOBLENZ** stands where the Rhine and Mosel meet at the **Deutsches Eck** (German corner). Across the Rhine in the district of **Ehrenbreitstein** is the imposing **Festung**. One of the largest fortresses in the world, it's now home to an HI **hostel** (☎0261/97 28 70, Ⓦwww.jugendherberge.de; dorms ❷, rooms ❸). The Festung and hostel can be reached by chairlift in the summer, a five-kilometre walk from the station, or buses #7, #8, and #9 to Ehrenbreitstein Berg Str. The central *Jan van Werth*, Van-Werth-Str. 9 (☎0261/3 65 00; Ⓦwww.hoteljanvanwerth.de; ❺, singles for ❸), is also a good option. The **campsite** (☎0261/82 719, Ⓦwww.camping-rhein-mosel.de; April to mid-Oct; ❶) is opposite Deutsches Eck.

Moving on

Train Koblenz to: Bacharach (hourly; 40min–1hr); Bingen (every 30min; 30–55min); Cologne (every 30min; 1hr); Frankfurt (hourly; 1hr 30min); Heidelberg (hourly; 2hr); Mainz (every 30min; 50min); Stuttgart (hourly; 2hr 20min); Trier (hourly; 1hr 30min).
River cruises K-D Ⓦwww.k-d.com Koblenz to: Bacharach/Kaub (March–Oct 2–3 daily; 4hr 30min); Bingen (March–Oct 1–2 daily; 6hr); Bonn (May–Sept daily; 4hr); Cologne (May–Sept daily; 6hr); Mainz (May–Sept daily; 7hr).

TRIER

Birthplace of Karl Marx and the oldest city in Germany, **TRIER** was once the capital of the Western Roman Empire. Nowadays, it has the less-exalted role of regional centre for the upper Mosel valley, its relaxed air a world away from the status it formerly held. Despite a turbulent history, an amazing amount of the city's past has been preserved, in particular the most impressive group of Roman monuments north of the Alps and several UNESCO World Heritage sites.

What to see and do

The centre corresponds roughly to the Roman city and can easily be covered on foot. From the train station, it's a few minutes' walk down Theodor-Heuss-Allee to the **Porta Nigra**, northern gateway to Roman Trier. From here, Simeonstrasse runs down to the **Hauptmarkt**, a busy pedestrian shopping area, with stalls selling fruit and flowers. At the southern end of the Hauptmarkt, an almost-hidden Baroque portal leads to the exquisite Gothic **St Gangolf**, built by the burghers of Trier in an attempt to aggravate the archbishops, whose political power they resented.

The Dom and Konstantinbasilika

Up Sternstrasse from the Hauptmarkt is the magnificent Romanesque **Dom** (daily 6.30am–5.30/6pm) on the site of an original built in the fourth century for Emperor Constantine. The present building dates from 1030, and the facade has not changed significantly since then. From here, take Liebfrauenstrasse past the ritzy **Palais Kesselstadt** and turn left on An der Meerkatz, to the **Konstantinbasilika** (April–Oct Mon–Sat 10am–6pm, Sun noon–6pm; Nov–March Mon–Sat 11am–noon & 3–4pm, Sun noon–1pm). Built as Constantine's throne hall, its dimensions are awe-inspiring: 30m high and 67m long, it is completely self-supporting. It became a church for the local Protestant community in the nineteenth century.

The Rheinisches Landesmuseum

The **Rheinisches Landesmuseum** (usually open daily, but enquire at the tourist office for latest opening hours and admission fee; Ⓦwww.landesmuseum-trier.de) is southwest of here, at Weimarer Allee 1. Easily the best of Trier's museums, its collection brings to life the sophistication and complexity of Roman civilization; prize exhibit is the *Neumagener Weinschiff*, a Roman sculpture of a wine ship. A few minutes' walk further south, the **Kaiserthermen** (daily 9am–4/5/6pm; €2.10/students €1.60) was once one of the largest bath complexes in the Roman world. The extensive underground heating system has survived, and you can walk around the service channels and passages.

The Karl-Marx-Haus

Southwest of the Hauptmarkt is the **Karl-Marx-Haus** at Brückenstrasse 10 (April–Oct Mon 1–6pm, Tues–Sun 10am–6pm; Nov–March Mon 2–5pm, Tues–Sun 10am–1pm & 2–5pm; €3/students €2; Ⓦwww.museum-karl-marx-haus.de), the house where Karl Marx was born. It now houses a modern three-storey museum on his life and work, as well as a general history of Communism up to the present.

Arrival and information

Tourist office Trier's tourist office, An der Porta Nigra (Jan & Feb Mon–Sat 10am–5pm, Sun 10am–1pm; March, April, Nov & Dec Mon–Sat 9am–6pm, Sun 10am–3pm; May–Oct Mon–Thurs 9am–6pm, Fri & Sat 9am–7pm, Sun 10am–5pm; Ⓣ0651/97 8080, Ⓦwww.trier.de), sells the Trier-Card (€9/3 days), which covers transport and provides discounts at the museums.

Bike rental At the train station, by platform 11. Mid-April to Oct daily 9am–7pm; Nov to mid-April Mon–Fri 10am–6pm. €8/day.

Accommodation

DJH An der Jugendherberge 4 Ⓣ0651/14 6620, Ⓦwww.djh.de. Brand-new HI hostel, with games rooms and sports facilities. Bus #12. ❷, rooms ❺

Camping Treviris Luxemburger Str. 81 Ⓣ0651/820 09 11, Ⓦwww.camping-treviris.de. Campsite on the western bank of the Mosel, over the Konrad-Adenauer bridge. Open April–Oct. ❶

Hille's Gartenfeldstr. 7 Ⓣ0651/710 27 85, Ⓦwww.hilles-hostel-trier.de. This homely independent hostel provides a clean and sociable base for travellers. Sheets included. Located 10min south of the station; reception 4–6pm, July–Oct till 8pm. Dorms ❷, rooms ❺

Eating and drinking

Alt Zurlauben Zurlaubener Ufer 79, north of the Kaiser-Wilhelm-Brücke. This traditional tavern, complete with ample outdoor seating overlooking the Mosel, makes an excellent place to try out the local cider, Viez. Meat platter €5. Daily from 3pm.

AstArix Karl-Marx-Str. 11. This relaxed student bar is your best bet for good and inexpensive food, and there's always something on at night. Pizza €3.50–5.

Forum Hindenburgstr. 4 Ⓦwww.forum-trier.com. An invariably packed café/bar/club spinning Latin, house and hip-hop to a younger crowd. Occasional live shows. Open Wed–Sat.

Weinstube Palais Kesselstatt Liebfrauenstr. 10. Late-opening, well-known wine bar – the pick among the many possibilities for tasting the local wines. Wine from €4.

Moving on

Train Cologne (hourly; 2hr 30min); Frankfurt (hourly; 3hr); Koblenz (every 30min; 1hr 30min–2hr); Luxembourg (hourly; 50min).

FRANKFURT

Straddling the River Main just before it meets the Rhine, **FRANKFURT AM MAIN** is a city with two faces. The cut-throat financial capital of Germany, with its fulcrum in the Westend district, it's also a civilized place that spends more per year on the arts than any other city in Europe. It has one of the best ranges of museums in the country, and some excellent (if expensive) nightlife. Over half of the city, including almost all the centre, was destroyed during the war and the rebuilders opted for innovation rather than restoration, resulting in an architecturally mixed skyline – half intimidating skyscrapers, half sweetly Germanic red-brick buildings.

What to see and do

The city centre is defined by the old city walls, now transformed into a semicircular stretch of public gardens. **Römerberg** is the historical and geographical centre. Charlemagne built his fort on this low hill to protect the original *frankonovurd* (Ford of the Franks), but the whole quarter was flattened by bombing in 1944. The most significant survivor was the thirteenth-century St Bartholomäus or **Dom**, and even that emerged with only its main walls intact. To the right of the choir is the restored Wahlkapelle, where the seven Electors used to make their final choice of Holy Roman Emperor.

Museum für Moderne Kunst and Imperial Hall

To the north, in Domstrasse, is the **Museum für Moderne Kunst** (Tues–Sun 10am–5pm, Wed till 8pm; €6/students €3, free last Sat of the month; Ⓦwww.mmk-frankfurt.de), a three-storey affair featuring major modern artists (Lichtenstein, Warhol, Flavin, Beuys) and innovative temporary exhibitions. At the opposite end of the Römerberg is the **Römer**, formerly the Rathaus. The **Imperial Hall** (Kaisersaal; daily 10am–1pm & 2–5pm; €2), with its distinctive facade of triple-stepped gables, has recently been restored and fronts the Römerplatz market square, home to a twinkling **Christmas Market** in December.

Jewish Museum

A short distance to the west, on Untermainkai, is the **Jewish Museum** (Jüdisches Museum; Tues–Sun 10am–5pm, Wed till 8pm; €4/students €2; Ⓦwww.juedischesmuseum.de), providing an interesting look at the city's Jewish community, which lost 10,000 people to the Nazis.

Sachsenhausen and Museumsufer

For a laid-back evening out, head for **Sachsenhausen**, the city-within-a-city on the south bank of the Main. The network of streets around Affentorplatz is home to the famous apple-wine (*Ebbelwei*) houses, while on Schaumainkai – also known as **Museumsufer** – the Saturday **flea market** is worth a

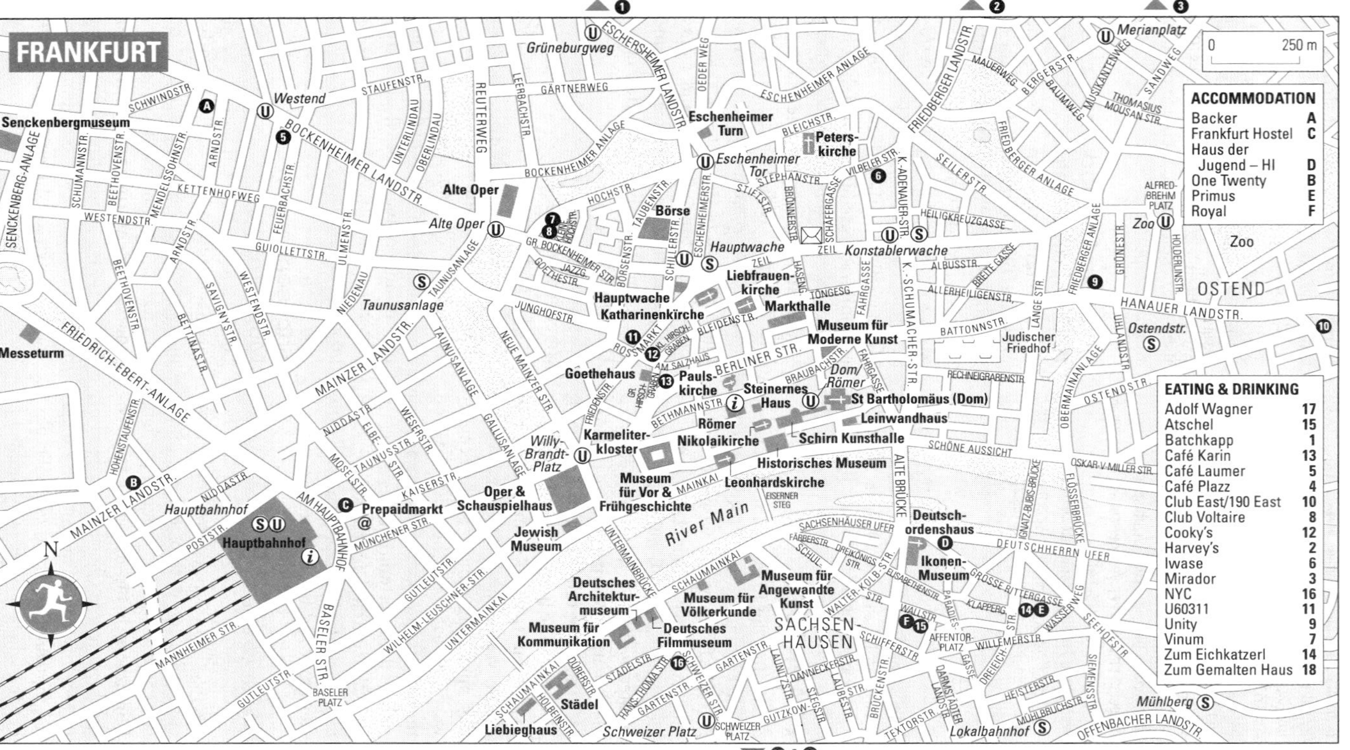
FRANKFURT
0 250 m
ACCOMMODATION
Backer A
Frankfurt Hostel C
Haus der Jugend – HI D
One Twenty B
Primus E
Royal F
EATING & DRINKING
Adolf Wagner 17
Atschel 15
Batchkapp 1
Café Karin 13
Café Laumer 5
Café Plazz 4
Club East/190 East 10
Club Voltaire 8
Cooky's 12
Harvey's 2
Iwase 6
Mirador 3
NYC 16
U60311 11
Unity 9
Vinum 7
Zum Eichkatzerl 14
Zum Gemalten Haus 18
Senckenbergmuseum
Messeturm
Westend
Alte Oper
Börse
Eschenheimer Turm
Eschenheimer Tor
Peterskirche
Hauptwache
Konstablerwache
Liebfrauenkirche
Markthalle
Katharinenkirche
Museum für Moderne Kunst
Goethehaus
Paulskirche
Steinernes Haus
Dom/Römer
St Bartholomäus (Dom)
Leinwandhaus
Römer
Nikolaikirche
Schirn Kunsthalle
Historisches Museum
Leonhardskirche
Karmeliterkloster
Willy-Brandt-Platz
Museum für Vor & Frühgeschichte
Oper & Schauspielhaus
Jewish Museum
Prepaidmarkt
Hauptbahnhof
Taunusanlage
Judischer Friedhof
Zoo
OSTEND
Ostendstr.
Merianplatz
River Main
Deutschordenshaus
Ikonen-Museum
Museum für Angewandte Kunst
Museum für Völkerkunde
Deutsches Architekturmuseum
Deutsches Filmmuseum
Museum für Kommunikation
Städel
Liebieghaus
SACHSENHAUSEN
Schweizer Platz
Lokalbahnhof
Mühlberg
Alte Brücke
Eiserner Steg
N
17 & 18

browse. Museumsufer is also lined with excellent museums, pick of the bunch being the **Städel**, located at no. 63 (Tues–Sun 10am–6pm, Wed & Thurs till 9pm; €10/students €8; ⓦwww.staedelmuseum.de), one of the most comprehensive art galleries in Europe. All the big names in German art are represented, including Dürer, Holbein and Cranach – as well as other European masters from Rembrandt to Picasso. The **Deutsches Filmmuseum**, at no. 41 (Tues–Fri 10am–5pm, Wed till 7pm, Sat 2–7pm, Sun 10am–7pm; €2.50/students €1.30; screenings €6/€5; ⓦwww.deutsches-filmmuseum.de), has its own cinema and is a popular spot for foreign films and art-house screenings. If you're into architecture, check out the **Deutsches Architekturmuseum**, no. 43 (Tues & Thurs–Sun 11am–6pm, Wed till 8pm; €6/students €3; ⓦwww.dam-online.de), installed in an avant-garde conversion of a nineteenth-century villa. The museum's highpoint is the "house within a house" which dominates the museum like an oversized dolls' house.

Arrival

Air Frankfurt Airport has its own long-distance train station, Frankfurt Flughafen Fernbahnhof, with regular rail links to most German cities and a frequent service (every 15min; 11min; €2.20) to the main train station (Frankfurt Hauptbahnhof). The airport is also linked to the train station by two S-Bahn lines. The deceptively named **Frankfurt Hahn Airport** (ⓦwww.hahn-airport.de), served by Ryanair and Wizzair, is actually a 2-hour bus ride from the Frankfurt Hauptbahnhof (hourly from 3am–10pm; 2hr; €12).
Train From the Hauptbahnhof it's a 15min walk to the centre, or take U-Bahn line #4 or #5, or tram #11.

Information

Tourist office There are two main tourist offices: in the train station (Mon–Fri 8am–9pm, Sat & Sun 9am–6pm; ⓣ069/21 23 8800, ⓦwww.frankfurt-tourismus.de), and at Römerberg 27 (Mon–Fri 9.30am–5.30pm; Sat & Son till 4pm). Free listings magazines, *Frizz* and *Strandgut*, are available at both.
Discount passes The Frankfurt Card (€8/12 for 1/2 days) can be bought from tourist offices and allows travel throughout the city, plus fifty percent off entry charges to most museums. The Museumsufer Ticket (€12/students €6) provides free entrance to 26 museums for two days.

City transport

Frankfurt has an integrated public transport system made up of S-Bahn, U-Bahn and trams. A short trip is €1.65, a single trip €2.20 and a day ticket €5.40.

Accommodation

Accommodation is pricey, thanks to the expense-account clientele – and rates can double during trade fairs. For a €3 fee the tourist office will book a room.

Hostels

Frankfurt Hostel Kaiserstr. 74 ⓣ069/24 75 130, ⓦwww.frankfurt-hostel.com. Right in front of the station with Internet and common room/kitchen. Sheets and breakfast included. Dorms ❸, rooms ❼.
Haus der Jugend–HI Deutschherrnufer 12, Sachsenhausen ⓣ069/6100 150, ⓦwww.jugendherberge-frankfurt.de. Around 470 places in dorms of up to twelve beds each. 2am curfew. Bus #46 to Frankensteiner Platz – in the evenings and at weekends take tram #16 to Lokalbahnhof. Juniors ❷, seniors ❸; rooms ❺–❼

Hotels

Backer Mendelssohnstr. 92 ⓣ069/74 79 92. Clean and close to the university, although use of the showers costs €2 a time. U-Bahn #6 or #7 to Westend. ❹
One Twenty Mainzer Landstr. 120 ⓣ069/74 2628, ⓦwww.hotelonetwenty.de. Pleasant budget hotel just north of the train station, away from the sleazier streets. Shared bathroom ❹, en suite ❺
Primus Grosse Rittergasse 19–21 ⓣ069/62 3020 ⓦwww.royal-primus-hotels.de. Basic, good-value hotel in Sachsenhausen. All rooms en suite. ❻
Royal Wallstr. 17 ⓣ069/62 3026 ⓦwww.royal-primus-hotels.de. Slightly more upscale big sister of *Hotel Primus*. In the heart of Sachsenhausen, close to some of the well-known apple-wine taverns. ❼

Eating

Café Karin Grosser Hirschgraben 28. Frankfurt institution that's friendly, unpretentious and well worth a visit. Breakfast all day and bistro/bar in the evenings. Pasta €8, Apfelwein €1.55.
Café Laumer Bockenheimer Landstr. 67. One of Frankfurt's oldest cafés, halfway up the Westend's main thoroughfare. The all-day breakfasts are a true indulgence (€7).
Café Plazz Kirchplatz 8. Stupendous selection of dishes served in generous portions, including delicious home-made cakes (€2.20). U-Bahn #6 or #7 to Kirchplatz.
Iwase Vilbeler Str. 31. Tiny Japanese place, with seating at the counter and a few tables. Closed Sun. Maki from €6.
Mirador Bergerstr. 65. Trendy, gold-dusted café-bar on a street lined with such places. Drink specials €5, U-Bahn #4 to Merianplatz.
Vinum Kleine Hochstr. 9. Rustic wine cellar with local range of wines to try (from €3). Slightly pricey food (€10) but in the heart of Frankfurt.

Drinking and nightlife

Apfelwein (cider) is Frankfurt's speciality. Although you'll find it everywhere, the apple-wine taverns of Haidhausen are the most atmospheric places to try it. The trendiest **bars** and **clubs** can be found around the Salzhaus in the centre and in the Ostend district, around Hanauer Landstrasse.

Apple-wine taverns

Adolf Wagner Schweizer Str. 71, Sachsenhausen. One of the best of the taverns, with a lively clientele of all ages and a cosy garden terrace. Meals €12, Apfelwein €1.60.
Atschel Wallstr. 7. This place offers a more extensive menu than many of its counterparts, and has bargain set lunches. Closed Mon. "Frankfurt slaughter platter" (consisting of almost every part of the slaughtered pig) €7.20.
Zum Eichkatzerl Dreieichstr. 29, Sachsenhausen. An excellent, traditional tavern with a large courtyard and some veggie options from €7. 2pm–midnight, closed Mon.
Zum Gemalten Haus Schweizer Str. 67, Sachsenhausen. A bit kitsch with its oil-painted facade and stained-glass windows, but quite intimate and lively, with long rows of tables outside. Closed Mon & Tues. Schnitzel €10.

Bars

Club Voltaire Kleine Hochstr. 5. Tasty, good food with a Spanish bias, and an eclectic clientele. Frequent events include musical improvisation evenings and political debates. Open 6pm–1am. Sheep's cheese with tomatoes €6.
Harvey's Bornheimer Landstr. 64. Slick, high-ceilinged colonnaded bar in an appealing end-of-terrace building, in the northeast of the city, which in the evening hosts a mainly gay and lesbian crowd. Tram #12 to Friedberger Platz.
NYC Hans-Thoma-Str. 1, at Schweizerstr., Sachsenhausen. Funky café/bar with tasty pancakes (€4), a young crowd and outside tables. S-/U-Bahn to Schweizer Platz.

Clubs

Batschkapp Maybachstr. 24 Ⓦ www.batschkapp.de. Grimy, sweaty venue for top-rank indie bands – avoid the school-age club nights though. S-Bahn #6 to Eschersheim or U-Bahn #1, #2, #3 to Weisser Stein.
Club East/190 East Hanauer Landstr. 190. Top disco in Frankfurt's hippest area. Packed out at weekends, with excellent house, techno and funk nights. Tram #11 to Schwedlerstr.
Cooky's Am Salzhaus 4 Ⓦ www.cookys.de. Hip-hop, house and soul club north of Berliner Strasse, hosting popular DJ nights plus occasional live acts.
U60311 Rossmarkt 6, at Am Salzhaus Ⓦ www.u60311.net. Long-standing favourite and one of the best techno clubs in town, in a former pedestrian underpass. It would be hard to find if it weren't for the queue. Hauptwache U-Bahn.
Unity Hanauer Landstr. 2 Ⓦ www.unity1.de. Intimate, crowded and fun club, playing house music until 5am. Closed Mon. U-Bahn Zoo or Ostendstr.

Directory

Consulates Australia, Neue Mainzer Str. 52–58 (Main Tower) Ⓣ 069/90558 0; US, Giessener Str. 30 Ⓣ 069/75 350.
Exchange Reisebank, at the train station.
Hospital Bürgerhospital, Nibelungenallee 37–41 Ⓣ 069/15 000.
Internet PrePaidMarkt, Kaiserstr. 81. In front of the train station, €2/hr.
Laundry Wash World, Moselstr. 17. East of the station. Closed Sun; €4.
Left luggage At the train station.
Pharmacy At the train station.
Post office At the train station and at Goetheplatz 6.

Moving on

Train Berlin (every 30min; 4–5hr); Cologne (every 30min; 1hr 10min); Hamburg (every 30min; 3hr

45min); Heidelberg (every 30min; 1hr); Munich (hourly; 3hr); Nuremberg (every 30min; 2hr); Würzburg (every 30min; 1hr 10min).

Baden-Württemberg

The southwestern province of **Baden-Württemberg** is the most prosperous part of the country. The motor car was invented here in the late nineteenth century, and the region has stayed at the forefront of world technology ever since, with **Stuttgart** still the home of Daimler-Chrysler and Porsche. Germany's most famous university city, **Heidelberg**, is here, as is the spa resort of **Baden-Baden**, which remains wonderfully evocative of its nineteenth-century heyday as the playground of Europe's aristocracy. The scenery is wonderful too: its western and southern boundaries are defined by the Rhine and its bulge into Germany's largest lake, the **Bodensee** (Lake Constance). Within the curve of the river lies the **Black Forest**, source of another of the continent's principal waterways, the Danube.

HEIDELBERG

Home to Germany's oldest university, **HEIDELBERG** is majestically set on the banks of the swift-flowing Neckar, 70km south of Frankfurt. For two centuries, it has seduced travellers like no other German city. Centrepiece is the Schloss, a compendium of magnificent buildings, somehow increased in stature by their ruined condition. The rest of the city has some good museums, but the main appeal is its picturesque cobbled streets, crammed with old-style eateries and student pubs. In spring and early summer, the streets hum with activity and late-night parties – by July and August, most students have left, only to be replaced by swarms of tourists.

What to see and do

The dominating **Schloss** can be reached from the Kornmarkt by the *Bergbahn* funicular (€5 return), which continues to the Königstuhl viewpoint (€8 return); you can also walk up in ten minutes via the Burgweg. At the southeastern corner is the most romantic of the ruins, the Gesprengter Turm; a collapsed section lies intact in the moat, leaving a clear view into the interior. The **Schlosshof** (daily 8am–5.30pm; €3.50/students €1.70; Ⓦwww.schloss-heidelberg.de) is a group of Renaissance palaces that now contain the diverting Pharmacy Museum and the Grosses Fass, an eighteenth-century wine-barrel capable of holding 220,000 litres.

The Altstadt

The **Altstadt**'s finest surviving buildings are grouped around the sandstone **Heiliggeistkirche** on Marktplatz. Note the tiny shopping booths between its buttresses, a feature ever since the church was built. The striking Baroque **Alte Brücke** is reached from the Marktplatz down Steingasse; dating from the 1780s, it was painstakingly rebuilt after being blown up during World War II. The **Palais Rischer** on Untere Strasse was the most famous venue for the university's *Mensur*, or fencing match; wounds were frequent and prized as badges of courage – for optimum prestige, salt was rubbed into them, leaving scars that remained for life. Universitätsplatz, the heart of the old town, is flanked by the eighteenth-century **Alte Universität** (April–Sept Tues–Sun 10am–6pm; Oct Tues–Sun 10am–4pm; Nov–March Tues–Sat 10am–4pm; €3/students €2.50) and the **Neue Universität**, erected with US funds in 1931. The oddest of Heidelberg's traditions was that its students used not to

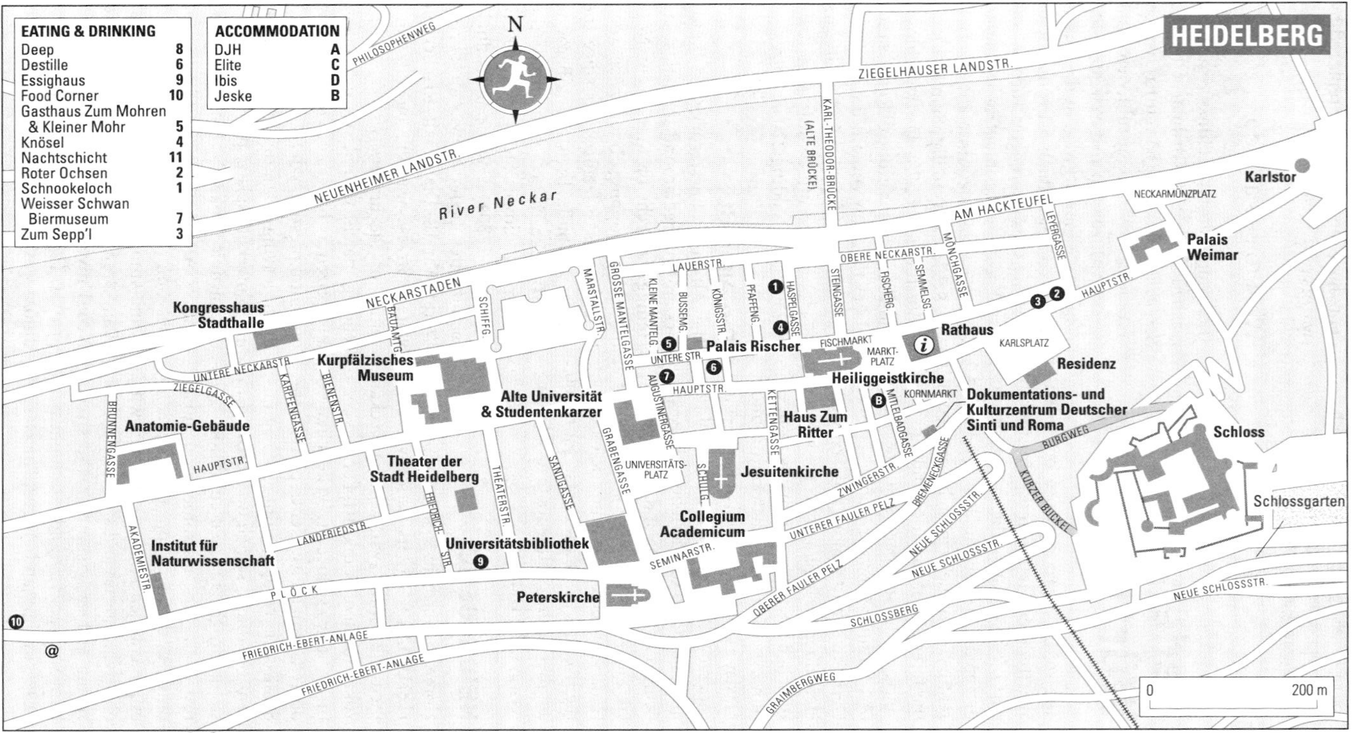
HEIDELBERG
EATING & DRINKING
Deep 8
Destille 6
Essighaus 9
Food Corner 10
Gasthaus Zum Mohren & Kleiner Mohr 5
Knösel 4
Nachtschicht 11
Roter Ochsen 2
Schnookeloch 1
Weisser Schwan Biermuseum 7
Zum Sepp'l 3
ACCOMMODATION
DJH A
Elite C
Ibis D
Jeske B
N
River Neckar
Karlstor
Palais Weimar
Rathaus
Residenz
Palais Rischer
Heiliggeistkirche
Dokumentations- und Kulturzentrum Deutscher Sinti und Roma
Schloss
Schlossgarten
Haus Zum Ritter
Jesuitenkirche
Collegium Academicum
Alte Universität & Studentenkarzer
Kurpfälzisches Museum
Kongresshaus Stadthalle
Anatomie-Gebäude
Theater der Stadt Heidelberg
Universitätsbibliothek
Institut für Naturwissenschaft
Peterskirche
ZIEGELHAUSER LANDSTR.
NEUENHEIMER LANDSTR.
PHILOSOPHENWEG
KARL-THEODOR-BRÜCKE
(ALTE BRÜCKE)
AM HACKTEUFEL
NECKARMÜNZPLATZ
LEYERGASSE
HAUPTSTR.
OBERE NECKARSTR.
MÖNCHGASSE
SEMMELSG.
FISCHERG.
STEINGASSE
HASPELGASSE
PFAFFENG.
KÖNIGSSTR.
BUSSEMG.
KLEINE MANTELG.
LAUERSTR.
GROSSE MANTELGASSE
MARSTALLSTR.
SCHIFFG.
NECKARSTADEN
BAUAMTG.
UNTERE NECKARSTR.
ZIEGELGASSE
KARPFENGASSE
BIENENSTR.
BRUNNENGASSE
AKADEMIESTR.
PLÖCK
FRIEDRICH-EBERT-ANLAGE
LANDFRIEDSTR.
FRIEDRICH-STR.
THEATERSTR.
SANDGASSE
GRABENGASSE
UNIVERSITÄTS-PLATZ
AUGUSTINERGASSE
UNTERE STR.
SCHULG.
SEMINARSTR.
KETTENGASSE
FISCHMARKT
MARKT-PLATZ
KORNMARKT
KARLSPLATZ
MITTELBADGASSE
ZWINGERSTR.
UNTERER FAULER PELZ
OBERER FAULER PELZ
BREMENECKGASSE
NEUE SCHLOSSSTR.
BURGWEG
KURZER BUCKEL
SCHLOSSBERG
GRAIMBERGWEG
0
200 m
Bismarckplatz & 8
Hauptbahnhof, Post Office, C, D & 11

be subject to civil jurisdiction: offenders were dealt with by the university authorities, and could serve their punishment at leisure. The **Students' Prison** around the corner at Augustinergasse 2 (Studentenkarzer; same hours and ticket as Alte Universität) was used from 1778 to 1914; its spartan cells are covered with graffiti.

Arrival and information

Air The Baden-Airpark (or Karlsruhe/Baden-Baden Airport; Ⓦwww.badenairpark.com), which Ryanair and AirBerlin use, is connected to the Heidelberg train station by the Baden-Airpark-Express (bus #140; 1hr 30min).

Train and bus Heidelberg's train and bus stations are in an anonymous quarter west of the centre. Tram #5 and buses #32, #33 and #34 run to Bismarckplatz at the western end of the Altstadt; from there, head down Hauptstrasse into the centre.

Tourist office The main tourist office is on the square outside the station (April–Oct Mon–Sat 9am–7pm, Sun 10am–6pm; Nov–March Mon–Sat 9am-6pm; Ⓣ06221/19 433, Ⓦwww.cvb-heidelberg.de); another well-run office is in the Rathaus on Marktplatz (Mon–Fri 10am–6pm, Sat 10am–5pm).

Discount pass The Heidelberg Card (1 day/2 day/4 day €10/14/20) provides free entrance to some sights but no transport.

City transport Heidelberg is small, but the bus and tram system can come in handy. Single trip €2.10, 24hr ticket €5, 24hr ticket for up to five people €8.50.

Internet Heidelberger Internet Café, Plöck. 8. Daily 10am–10pm, €1/hr.

Accommodation

Hotels are often booked solid; the chart outside the tourist office lists any vacancies.

DJH Tiergartenstr. 5 Ⓣ06221/651 190, Ⓦwww.jugendherberge-heidelberg.de. This hostel is on the north bank of the Neckar, about 4km from the centre. Take bus #32 from Hauptbahnhof or Bismarkplatz to "Jugendherberge". ❸

Elite Bunsenstr. 15 Ⓣ06221/257 34, Ⓦwww.hotel-elite-heidelberg.de. Lovely, friendly hotel ten minutes from the centre. ❼

Ibis Willy-Brandt-Platz 3 Ⓣ06221/9130, Ⓦwww.ibishotel.com. Comfortable hotel chain right next to the train station. All rooms en suite, free Internet. Breakfast not included. ❼

Jeske Mittelbadgasse 2 Ⓣ06221/23 733, Ⓦwww.pension-jeske-heidelberg.de. This is a good, central option, a few steps off Marktplatz. Breakfast not included. ❻

Eating and drinking

Some of the best places to eat are the city's atmospheric **student taverns**, known for their basic dishes at reasonable prices.

Deep Hauptstr. 1, Bismarckplatz Ⓦwww.deep-club.de. Heidelberg's premier club for house. Dress up. Fri & Sat.

Destille Untere Strasse 16. The best of the buzzing drinking spots along this alley and always packed.

Essighaus Plöck 97. A traditional restaurant serving large set menus at low prices (€6–15). Mon dinner only.

Food Corner Neugasse 21, at Plöck. A nice, sit-down döner and pizza joint, between Bismarckplatz and the centre. Pizza €4.50.

Gasthaus Zum Mohren & Kleiner Mohr Untere Str. 5. Young, hip restaurant-bar, with mains from €7.

Knösel Haspelgasse 16. Try the famous Heidelberger Studentenkuss, a dark chocolate filled with praline and nougat (€2), at this chic café or at the shop next door.

Nachtschicht Bergheimer Strasse 147 Ⓦwww.nachtschicht.com. Popular club in a former factory with hip-hop, disco and house nights. Just north of the train station. Wed–Sat.

Roter Ochsen Hauptstr. 217. This is one of the city's most famous student taverns, so prices here are slightly above average. Mains €10.

Schnookeloch Haspelgasse 8. The oldest tavern in town and still cosy. Swabian ravioli (*Maultaschen*) €8.

Weisser Schwan Biermuseum Hauptstr. 143. Spacious establishment offering 24 types of beer with its meals. Mains €6.50.

Zum Sepp'l Hauptstr. 213. Next to *Roter Ochsen* – the other famous student tavern – and plastered with stolen street signs. Schnitzel €7.50.

Moving on

Train Frankfurt (every 30min; 1hr); Freiburg (every 30min; 2hr); Mainz (every 30min; 1hr 20min); Stuttgart (every 30 min; 40min).

THE BLACK FOREST REGION

Home of the cuckoo clock and source of the celebrated Danube River, the

TREAT YOURSELF

Above the Römerbad, just east on Römerplatz, is the famous **Friedrichsbad** (daily 9am–10pm, last entry 2hr before closing; women and men bathe separately; Ⓦwww.roemisch-irisches-bad.de); begun in 1869, it's as grand as a Renaissance palace. Speciality of the house is a three-hour "Roman-Irish Bath", a series of baths, showers and steam of varying temperatures, that will set you back €21 (€29 for soap-brush massage). At the **Caracalla Therme** (daily 8am–10pm, last entry 2hr before closing; 2/3/4hr €13/15/17; same website), a little further east in a modern complex, you're allowed to wear a swimsuit, can decide for yourself when to switch baths, and men and women can bathe together.

Black Forest, stretching 170km north to south, and up to 60km east to west, is Germany's largest and most beautiful forest. Its name reflects the mountainous landscape darkened by endless pine trees and, as late as the 1920s, much of this area was an eerie wilderness, a refuge for boars and bandits. Nowadays, many of its villages are geared toward the tourist trade, brimming with shops selling tacky souvenirs; the old forest trails have become gravel paths smoothed down for easier walking. Most of the Black Forest is associated with the Margravate of Baden, whose old capital, **Baden-Baden**, is at the northern fringe of the forest, in a fertile orchard and vine-growing area. **Freiburg im Breisgau**, one of the most enticing cities in the country, is surrounded by the forest.

Baden-Baden

The therapeutic value of the town's hot springs, first discovered by the Romans, is still the main draw in **BADEN-BADEN** – hardly the recipe for a party atmosphere. Nevertheless, it's a pretty town for an afternoon's stroll.

What to see and do

Along the west bank of the tiny River Oos runs Baden-Baden's most famous thoroughfare, Lichtentaler Allee, landscaped with exotic trees and shrubs. It's flanked by the **Kunsthalle** (no. 8a; Tues–Sun 11am–6pm, Wed till 8pm; €5/students €4; Ⓦwww.kunsthalle-baden-baden.de), an exhibition venue for international modern and contemporary art, and the **Museum Frieder Burda** (no. 8b; same hours; €9/students €7, combined ticket with Kunsthalle €12/students €10; Ⓦwww.museum-frieder-burda.de), which contains an excellent collection including several works by Beckmann, Kirchner, Picasso and de Kooning, to name just a few. Just north at Kaiserallee 1 is the famously opulent **Casino**, the oldest in Europe, whose gilded frescoes and chandeliers are well worth a peek (Kurhaus; daily tours, German only April–Oct 9.30am–12.30pm; Nov–March 10–11.30am; €4 or visit in the evening for a flutter, €3; Ⓦwww.casino-baden-baden.de). Smart clothes and passports are obligatory in the evening.

Arrival and information

Air The Baden-Airpark (or Karlsruhe/Baden-Baden Airport; Ⓦwww.badenairpark.com), served by Ryanair and AirBerlin, is connected to the Baden-Baden train station by bus #205 and the Baden-Airpark-Express (bus #140). The latter also travels to Karlsruhe and Heidelberg main train stations.

Train The train station is 4km northwest in the suburb of Oos; buses #201, #205 or #216 all go to the centre, "Leopoldplatz/Stadtmitte".

Tourist office The main tourist office is in the Trinkhalle on Kaiserallee (Mon–Sat 10am–5pm, Sun 2–5pm; Ⓣ07221/275 200, Ⓦwww.baden-baden.de), and can book rooms (from ❼).

Accommodation

DJH Hardbergstr. 34 Ⓣ07221/52 223, Ⓦwww.jugendherberge-baden-baden.de. A particularly uninspiring HI hostel between the train station and the centre. Curfew at 11.30pm, reception 5–11pm. Take bus #201, #205, or #216 to "Grosse-Dollen-Strasse"; from there it's a signposted 10min climb. Juniors ❷, seniors ❸

Deutscher Kaiser Hauptstr. 35 ⓣ07221/72 152, ⓦwww.hoteldk.de. This pleasant, family-run hotel is 2km from the centre in the lovely suburb of Lichtental; four-bed rooms available (❼). Take bus #201 to "Eckerlestr." ❺

Eating and drinking

The centre is full of cheap snack joints.

Leo's Luisenstr. 10. A trendy café-bar serving huge, delicious salads (€11). Open until 2am.

Löwenbräu Gernsbacher Str. 9. If you're sick of Swabian fare, head to Löwenbräu and eat like a Bavarian. Boisterous summer beer garden. Traditional breakfast (*Weisswurst*, *brezn* & beer) €6.

Moving on

Train Freiburg (hourly; 40min); Heidelberg (every 30min; 1hr 20min); Strasbourg (hourly; 1hr 30min); Triberg (hourly; 1hr 10min).

Triberg

The natural wonders of the Black Forest are at your feet in **TRIBERG**, a tiny resort town in the middle of the region. While the town itself feels like one big monument to the cuckoo clock, the surrounding area offers two hundred kilometres of the best cross-country skiing in Germany, as well as excellent hiking and mountain-biking trails for outdoor enthusiasts of all levels.

With a total drop of 163m over seven stages, the **Triberg Waterfalls** (daily 9am–10pm; €2.50/students €2) are some of Germany's highest; enter on Hauptstrasse, in the centre of town. Across the street is the kitschy Schwarzwaldmuseum at Wallfahrtstrasse 4 (daily: April–Oct 10am–6pm; Nov–March 10am–5pm; ⓦwww.schwarzwaldmuseum.de; €4.50). The tourist office (same hours; ⓣ07722/86 64 90, ⓦwww.dasferienland.de), in the same building, provides maps of the region and a free room-booking service (from ❷). The youth hostel is an almost vertical three-kilometre walk from the train station at Rohrbacher Strasse 35 (ⓣ07722/41 10, ⓦwww.jugendherberge-triberg.de; juniors ❷, seniors ❸), while family-run *Zum Bären* at Haupstr. 10 (ⓣ07722/44 93; ❻) is central and a good deal for single travellers, as well.

Moving on

Train From the train station it's a signposted 15min walk uphill to the centre. Baden-Baden (hourly; 1hr 15min); Freiburg (hourly; 1hr 40min); Heidelberg (hourly; 2hr 30min); Konstanz (hourly; 1hr 30min); Stuttgart (every 30min; 3hr).

Freiburg im Breisgau

FREIBURG IM BREISGAU – midway between Strasbourg (France) and Basel (Switzerland) – basks in the laid-back atmosphere you'd expect from Germany's sunniest city. It's been a university town since 1457 and its youthful presence is maintained all year round with the help of a varied programme of festivals. It's a thoroughly enjoyable place to visit, and makes the perfect urban base for exploring the surrounding Black Forest – if you can bring yourself to leave.

What to see and do

The city's highlight is the dark-red sandstone **Münster**, whose openwork spire makes it one of the most dazzling churches in the country. Begun in about 1200, the church has a masterly Gothic nave, resplendent with flying buttresses, gargoyles and statues – the magnificent sculptures of the west porch are the most important German works of their time. From the tower (April–Oct Mon–Sat 9.30am–5pm, Sun 1–5pm; Nov–March Tues–Sat 10am–4.30pm; €1.50/students €1) there's a fine panorama of the city and the surrounding forest-blanketed hills. Walking south from here on Kaiser-Josef-Strasse, Freiburg's central axis, you come to the Martinstor, one of two surviving towers of the medieval fortifications. Just southeast of here is the main channel of the Bächle; follow it along Fischerau (the old fishermen's street) and Gerberau, to the **Schwaben Tor**, the other thirteenth-century tower.

Arrival and information

Train and bus The train station, with the bus station on its southern side, is about a 10min walk west from the city centre. *Shake'n Surf*, Bismarckallee 5, is a cheap Internet café near the station (daily 10am–10pm).
Tourist office Following Eisenbahnstrasse, you come to the tourist office in the Altes Rathaus at Rathausplatz 2–4 (June–Sept Mon–Fri 8am–8pm, Sat 9.30am–5pm, Sun 10am–noon; Oct–May Mon–Fri 8am–6pm, Sat 9.30am–2.30pm, Sun 10am–noon; ⓣ0761/38 81 880, ⓦwww.freiburg.de). For €3, they'll find you a room (from ❷). They also have hiking and biking maps, as well as suggestions for numerous trailheads accessible by public transport.

Accommodation

Black Forest Hostel Kartäuserstr. 33 ⓣ0761/881 78 70, ⓦwww.blackforest-hostel.de. Built in an old factory, this buzzing backpackers' is by far the best place to stay in town. Well-equipped kitchen, Internet, and bikes for €5/day. Sheets €3. Tram to Schwabentorbrücke or 30min walk east from the station. Dorms ❷, rooms ❺
Hirzberg Kartäuserstr. 99 ⓣ0761/35 054, ⓦwww.freiburg-camping.de. The most convenient of Freiburg's three campsites, between the two hostels to the east of the centre. Open year-round. Tram to Stadthalle, then head north across the Dreisam. ❶
Schemmer Eschholzstr. 63 ⓣ0761/20 74 90, ⓦwww.hotel-schemmer.de. West of the train station, this is the cheapest central hotel. Tram to Eschholzstr. or a 10min walk. ❻

Eating and drinking

Nightlife revolves around the junction of Universitätstrasse and Niemenstrasse; pick up a free *Frizz* magazine to see what's on.
Art Café Niemensstr. 4. At the hub of Freiburg's nightlife scene, offering the pizza-like *Flammenkuchen* (€4.50).
Karma Bertoldstr. 51–53 ⓦwww.karma-freiburg.de. The *Karma* complex has everything you need: a café-bar daily till 3am, a restaurant (closed Sun) with weekday lunch specials (€7.50) and a club in the cellar bumping funk and house Fri & Sat.
Oberkirchs Weinstube Münsterplatz 22. Pricey but excellent restaurant, serving local specialities. Ox with Späztle €14.
Reis-Garten Kartäuserstr. 3–7. Lip-smacking good Thai food near the *Black Forest Hostel*; lunch specials €4, dinner from €5.

Moving on

Train Basel (hourly; 45min); Frankfurt (hourly; 2hr); Heidelberg (hourly; 1hr 45); Strasbourg (hourly; 1hr 30min); Stuttgart (hourly; 2hr); Zürich (hourly; 2hr).

STUTTGART

In the centre of Baden-Württemberg, 85km southeast of Heidelberg, **STUTTGART** is home to the German success stories of Bosch, Porsche and Daimler-Chrysler. Founded around 950 as a stud farm (Stutengarten), it became a town only in the fourteenth century. Though certainly not the comeliest of cities, it has a range of superb museums and a sophisticated cultural scene and nightlife.

What to see and do

From the train station, Königstrasse passes the dull modern Dom and enters Schlossplatz, on the south of which is the **Altes Schloss**, home to the **Württembergisches Landesmuseum** (Tues–Sun 10am–5pm; €2; ⓦwww.landesmuseum-stuttgart.de). This large and richly varied museum explores the history of the region from the Stone Age to the present through archeological exhibitions as well as arts and crafts. Northeast of Schlossplatz at Konrad-Adenauer-Strasse 30–32 is the **Staatsgalerie** (Tues–Sun 10am–6pm, Thurs till 9pm, first Sat in month till midnight; €4.50/students €3, free on Wed; ⓦwww.staatsgalerie.de). The most startling work in the Old Masters section is the violently expressive *Herrenberg Altar* by Jörg Ratgeb; the New Gallery focuses on various schools within twentieth-century art movements.

The Mercedes-Benz-Museum and the Porsche Museum

Two of Stuttgart's most famous names put corporate propaganda to work with outstanding results. The new **Mercedes-Benz-Museum** (Tues–Sun 9am–6pm; €8/students €4; S-Bahn #1 to Gottlieb-Daimler-Stadion ⓦwww.mercedes-benz.com/museum) is an absolute must. Following one of two routes through the spiralling, modern museum constitutes a multimedia crash-course in modern German history. There are tons of vehicles on display, from the first-ever motorbike on, but it's the luxury cars and the machines specially designed for world-record attempts that steal the show. In late 2008, **Porsche** will open its new, flashy museum – in the meantime, the "old" museum is still open (Mon–Fri 9am–4pm; weekends till 5pm; free). The rotating display of twenty classic vehicles illustrate the company's cars from the 356 Roadster of 1948 to current models. The museums are beside the Neuwirtshaus station on S-Bahn line #6.

Arrival and information

Air Stuttgart Airport is linked to the train station by S-Bahn #2 and #3 (every 10/20min; 30min).
Train and bus Stuttgart's train and bus stations are in the centre of town. A day ticket for the extensive integrated public transport network costs €5.40, a single trip €1.80.
Tourist office The main tourist office is opposite the train station at Königstr. 1a (Mon–Fri 9am–8pm, Sat 9am–6pm, Sun 11am/1pm–6pm; ⓣ0711/22 280, ⓦwww.stuttgart-tourist.de). There's also a branch at the airport, in Terminal 3 (Mon–Fri 8am–7pm, Sat & Sun 9am–noon & 1–6pm).
Discount passes The StuttCard Plus (€17.50/three days) covers public transport, admission to most museums and numerous freebies; the basic StuttCard (€12/three days) gives the same benefits without public transport.
Internet, youth information and bike rental You'll find Internet access, bike rental, information for young people and helpful staff at the youth centre Tips'n'Trips, Lautenschlagerstr. 22 (Mon–Fri noon–7pm, Sat 10am–2pm), 200m southwest of the station. Internet €2/hr; bikes for 24hr: €15/students €11.

Accommodation

Alex 30 Alexanderstr. 30 ⓣ0711/83 88 950, ⓦwww.alex30-hostel.de. Convenient independent hostel near the Bohnenviertel. U-Bahn to Olgaeck or 20min walk southeast from the station. Sheets are included. Dorm ❸, rooms ❻
DJH Haussmannstr. 27 ⓣ0711/24 1583 or 0711/66 4747 0, ⓦwww.jugendherberge-stuttgart.de. New, standard DJH. Take tram #15 or bus #42 to Eugensplatz and then continue 5min uphill. ❸
Jugendgästehaus Richard-Wagner-Str. 2. ⓣ0711/24 1132 or 0711/248 9730, ⓦwww.hostel-stuttgart.de. Independent hostel without much personality, but breakfast and sheets are included. Tram #15 to Bubenbad. Dorms ❷, rooms ❺
Museumstube Hospitalstr. 9 ⓣ0711/29 6810, ⓦwww.museumstube.de. This is the city's cheapest hotel, family-owned, clean and central. No breakfast. Shared bathroom ❺, en suite ❼

Eating and drinking

Stuttgart is surrounded by vineyards, and the numerous Weinstuben are excellent places to try good-quality, traditional noodle-based dishes and local wines at low cost. *Lift* and *Prinz Stuttgart*, available from newsagents, have complete **nightlife** listings.
Bett Friedrichstr. 23 ⓦwww.bett-lounge.de. Laid-back, popular lounge that's open every night, with occasional live gigs.
Calwer-Eck-Bräu Calwerstr. 31. Microbrewery with good beer and food. Mains €8, beer €2.70. S-Bahn Stadtmitte.
M1 Breitscheidstr 12 ⓦwww.m1-theclub.com. House and electro-pop reign supreme at this hotspot below the ultramodern Bosch-Areal complex. Closed Mon & Tues. U-Bahn Berliner Platz.
Palast der Republik Friedrichstr. 27. A tiny circular funk shack on the square where Bolzstrasse meets Lautenschlagerstrasse, with outdoor seating in the summer.
Weinhaus Stetter Rosenstr. 32. A lovely atmosphere, excellent service and the widest choice of wines in town await you at this family-run Weinstube. The lentil soup with sausages (€6) is outstanding. Wine from €3.

Moving on

Train Freiburg (hourly; 2hr); Heidelberg (every 30min; 40min–1hr 15min); Konstanz (every 2hr; 2hr 10min); Munich (hourly; 2hr 20min); Zurich (every 2hr; 2hr 45min).

KONSTANZ AND THE BODENSEE

In the far south, hard up against the Swiss border, **KONSTANZ** lies at the tip of a tongue of land sticking out into the **Bodensee** (Lake Constance). The town itself is split by the water; the **Altstadt** is an enclave on the southern shore. The huge, tranquil lake is unexpected, and lends Konstanz the otherwise northern air of a harbour town. The town's convivial atmosphere is best experienced in the summer, when street cafés invite long pauses and the water is a bustle of sails.

What to see and do

The most prominent building is the **Münster** church, dating from the Romanesque period and located in the heart of the Altstadt. The regional highlights are two small Bodensee islands. The nearby **Insel Mainau** (daily: April–Oct 7am–8pm; Nov–March 9am–6pm; bus #4 from the train station; €13/students €6.60, half-price after 5pm; Ⓦwww.mainau.de) has a royal park featuring magnificent floral displays, formal gardens, greenhouses, forests, a butterfly house and a handful of well-placed restaurants. The other island, the UNESCO World Heritage site **Reichenau**, preserves three stunning Romanesque churches. You can reach this tranquil island 8km west of Konstanz by bike, ferry (summer only) or with public transport: take a regional train to Reichenau station, then change to bus #7372 to "Mittelzell" (Mon–Fri only; 14 daily; 50min).

Arrival and information

Konstanz's **tourist office** is beside the **train station** at Bahnhofplatz 13 (April–Oct Mon–Fri 9am–6.30pm, Sat 9am–4pm & Sun 10am–1pm; Nov–March Mon–Fri 9.30am–12.30pm & 2–6.30pm; Ⓣ1805/13 30 30, Ⓦwww.konstanz.de); they can book accommodation in private rooms (❺).

Accommodation

The **hostel** is *Jugendwohnheim Don Bosco* at Salesianerweg 5 (Ⓣ07531/622 52, Ⓦwww.donbosco-kn.de; Reception 4–8pm; ❷; bus #1 or #4 to Tannenhof). The best **private rooms** are at *Diegruber's*, Bärlappweg 19 (Ⓣ07531/77278; ❺). Kultur-Rädle, Bahnhofplatz 29 (Mon–Fri 9am–12.30pm & 2.30–6pm, Sat 10am–4pm; April–Oct also Sun 10am–12.30pm; Ⓦwww.kultur-raedle.de; €10/day) rents bicycles.

Lake cruises

You can get information on **cruises** and **ferries** from the Bodensee-Schiffsbetriebe at Hafenstr. 6 (Ⓣ07531/36 40 389, Ⓦwww.bsb-online.com). Ferries run regularly around the lake, as well as on a scenic trip to the impressive Rhine falls in Switzerland (€30), covered in Chapter 00.

Moving on

Train Basel (every 30min; 2hr 30min); Freiburg (hourly; 2hr 15min–3hr 15min); Munich (every 30min; 4hr); Stuttgart (hourly; 2hr 15min–3hr); Zürich (every 30min; 1hr 15min).

Bavaria

Bavaria (Bayern), which occupies the whole southeastern chunk of the country out to the Austrian and Czech frontiers, is the home of all the German clichés: beer-swilling men in *Lederhosen*, sauerkraut and *Wurst*. But that's only a small part of the picture, and almost entirely restricted to the Alpine region south of the magnificent state capital, **Munich**. In the western parts, around pristine Swabian **Augsburg**, the food is less pork and sausage and more pasta and sauce, and the landscape gentle farming country ideal for camping and cycling holidays. To the north lie Nuremberg and Würzburg in Protestant **Franconia** (Franken), a region within a region, known for its vineyards and nature parks. Eastern Bavaria – apart from its capital **Regensburg** – is relatively

THE ROMANTIC ROAD

The **ROMANTIC ROAD** (Romantische Strasse) is the most famous and well-loved tourist route in Germany, running from the vineyards of Würzburg in northern Bavaria over 366km of pastoral scenery and quaint medieval villages to the fairy-tale castles of Füssen in the south. Taking the Romantic Road is as cheesy as it sounds – but it will show you the charming, picturesque Germany the brochures promise.

The Road can be travelled in either direction, and most visitors only do a part of the route or a couple points on it. Check out the official website, ⓦwww.romantischestrasse.de.

Bus From April to October, Touring (ⓣ069/7903 230, ⓦwww.romanticroadcoach.de) runs buses once daily in each direction between Frankfurt and Munich, up and down the Road, with short stops in many of the towns. The whole trip takes thirteen hours (€99) each way, from Würzburg to Füssen nine hours (€59). You could also take the bus from Würzburg to Rothenburg, for instance, which gets in at noon, and then catch the northerly bus at 6pm back to Würzburg (return €19).

Train Not all points on the Road are served by the Deutsche Bahn, but going by train to one or two towns (like Würzburg, Rothenburg, Augsburg, or Füssen) is a great way to avoid the bus crowds and get a feel for the route.

Bicycle Touring by bike is the most scenic way to explore the region. The well-maintained cycling route stretches 424km from the Main to Bavarian Alps – order a route map online (ⓦwww.romantischestrasse.de) or pick one up from any of the tourist offices along the way.

poor; life in its highland forests revolves around logging and workshop industries such as glass production.

WÜRZBURG

The Franconian city of **WÜRZBURG** nestles idyllically between sloping vineyards and city parks on both sides of the River Main. The Residenz and the Festung, as well as numerous churches, are monumental reminders of the town's glory days as a prince-bishopric; otherwise, Würzburg's appeal today lies in its abundant green spaces and the lively, down-to-earth atmosphere provided by its huge student population. It's a worthwhile and relaxing place to spend a day or two.

What to see and do

The splendid Baroque **Residenz** (daily: April–Oct 9am–6pm; Nov–March 10am–4.30pm; €5/students €4; ⓦwww.schloesser.bayern.de) was built in the eighteenth century by the Würzburg prince-bishops to demonstrate their wealth and power. The highlights of this palace, designed by then-unknown Balthasar Neumann, include his grandiose staircase and a fresco by G.B. Tiepolo, one of the world's largest, showing the four continents deferring to the then prince-bishop. Over forty palace rooms are open to visitors, though some can only be seen on a guided tour (English tours at 11am & 3pm, included in the price of admission). The **court gardens** are lovely, free and open daily until dusk.

The Festung Marienberg

The **Festung Marienberg** (April–Oct only, Tues–Sun 9am–6pm; €4/students €3; ⓦwww.schloesser.bayern.de), on the left bank of the Main, was the prince-bishops' fortress for almost five hundred years, until they moved into the Residenz in 1719. A fascinating building in itself, it now contains a museum on the city's history.

Arrival and information

Train The station is 10min north of the centre; head down Kaiserstr.

Tourist office The tourist office, in the Falkenhaus on Marktplatz ⓣ0931/37 23 98, ⓦwww.wuerzburg.de), sells the Welcome Card (€3), which entitles the bearer to reduced prices at most sights. They also organize city walking tours (in English: May–Oct Sat 1pm; mid-June to mid-Sept daily except Sat 6.30pm; €5).
Internet N@tcity Sanderstr. 27. Daily 11am–10pm; €1/hr.

Accommodation

Babelfish Prymstrasse 3 ⓣ0931/3040 430 ⓦwww.babelfish-hostel.de. This small, welcoming backpackers' 5min east of the station has helpful staff, a kitchen and bikes for €5/day. Sheets €2.50. Dorms ❷, rooms ❺
DJH Burkarderstr. 44 ⓣ0931/425 90, ⓦwww.wuerzburg.jugendherberge.de. Standard HI hostel, below the Festung Marienberg on the left bank of the Main. Tram #3 or #5 to Ludwigsbrücke. Reception 3–6pm & 7–10pm. ❸
Siegel Reisgrubengasse 7 ⓣ0931/529 41. Quirky pension in a great location between the station and the centre; head down the stairs from Kaiserstr. Shared bathrooms. ❼
Spehnkuch Röngenring 7 ⓣ0931/547 52, ⓦwww.pension-spehnkuch.de. Nice, modern pension with shared bathrooms just west of the station. ❻

Eating and drinking

Bürgerspital Weinstuben Theaterstraße 19. This historic wine cellar makes a wonderful setting in which to sample Frankish cuisine and wines. Tripe €6, wine from €3.60.
Kult Landwehrstr. 10. *Kult* is an understated bar-café serving delicious, filling food at low prices. The atmosphere's laid-back until nighttime, when the tattoed twentysomethings pack on in. Veggie burger €3.20.
Time Out Frankfurter Str. 1. Local boy/NBA star Dirk Nowitzki supposedly painted the ceiling of this laid-back lounge, a former hang-out of his. Excellent *biergarten* as well.

Moving on

Train Frankfurt (every 30min; 1hr 10min); Munich (every 30min; 2hr); Nuremberg (every 30min; 1hr); Rothenburg (hourly; 1hr).

ROTHENBURG OB DER TAUBER

The **Romantic Road** (see p.513) winds its way along the length of western Bavaria, running through the most visited – and most beautiful – medieval town in Germany: **ROTHENBURG OB DER TAUBER.** This fairy-tale place is besieged with tour groups during the day, so make a point of spending a night – or at least an evening – so as to appreciate it in relative peace.

What to see and do

The views of the surrounding countryside from the fourteenth-century town walls are magnificent, but Rothenburg's true charms lie amongst its medieval half-timbered houses and cobbled streets. The sloping **Marktplatz** is dominated by the arcaded front of the Renaissance Rathaus; the sixty-metre tower of the older **Gotisches Rathaus** behind (daily: April–Oct 9.30am–12.30pm & 1–5pm; Dec noon–3pm; Nov & Jan–March weekends only noon–3pm; €1) provides the best views.

The Ratsherrntrinkstube clocks

The other main attractions on the Marktplatz are the figures on each side of the three clocks of the **Ratsherrntrinkstube**, which seven times daily undramatically re-enact an episode that allegedly occurred during the Thirty Years War. The fearsome Catholic General Tilly agreed that Protestant Rothenburg would be spared if one of the councillors could drain in one draught a tankard holding over three litres of wine. Former mayor Nusch duly sank the contents of the so-called *Meistertrunk* (master draught), then took three days to sleep off the effects. Northeast of the Marktplatz is the Gothic **St Jakob-Kirche** (daily: April–Oct 9am–5.15pm; Nov & Jan–

March 10am–noon & 2–4pm; Dec 10am–5pm; €2/students €0.50), with its massive towers (currently undergoing massive restoration) and exquisitely carved altars.

The Kriminalmuseum

Of the local museums, the most interesting is the **Kriminalmuseum** at Burggasse 3 (daily: April–Oct 9.30am–6pm; Nov, Jan & Feb 2–4pm; Dec & March 10am–4pm; last entry 45min before closing; €3.80/students €2.60; ⓦ www.kriminalmuseum.rothenburg.de), containing collections of medieval torture instruments and related objects such as the beer barrels that drunks were forced to walk around in.

Arrival and information

Train The train station is a 10min, unsignposted walk east of the city walls. Out of the station, head left on Bahnhofstr., and then right on Ansbacherstr., which will take you straight through Röder gate into the city.

Tourist office Rothenburg's tourist office, in the Ratstrinkstube on Marktplatz (May–Oct Mon–Fri 9am–6pm, Sat & Sun 10am–3pm; Nov–April Mon–Fri 9am–noon & 1–5pm, Sat 10am–1pm, Dec also Sun 10am–3pm; ⓣ 09861/404 800, ⓦ www.rothenburg.de), provides free Internet access and room-booking (from ❹).

Accommodation

DJH Mühlacker 1 ⓣ 09861/94 160, ⓦ www.rothenburg.jugendherberge.de. Housed in two beautifully restored houses and a modern annexe off the bottom of Spitalgasse. Reception from 3pm. ❷

Pöschel Wenggasse 22 ⓣ 09861/34 30, ⓦ www.pensionpoeschel.de. Charming family-run pension, with an excellent breakfast. ❹

Raidel Wenggasse 3 ⓣ 09861/31 15, ⓦ www.romanticroad.com/raidel. Wonderfully creaky and housed in a 600-year-old house, this guesthouse oozes atmosphere. ❺

Zur Goldenen Rose Spitalgasse 28 ⓣ 09861/46 38, ⓦ www.zur-goldenen-rose.de. This Gasthof has pleasant rooms and serves great home-cooked food in one of the town's many fine restaurants. Closed Jan & Feb. Shared bathroom ❹, en suite ❻

Moving on

Train Augsburg (hourly; 2hr 20min); Nuremberg (hourly; 1hr 15min); Würzburg (hourly; 1hr 10min).

NUREMBERG

In many minds, the medieval town of **NUREMBERG** (Nürnberg) conjures up images of the Nazi rallies and war-crimes trials. The "Nuremberg Laws" of 1935, which deprived Jews of their citizenship and forbade relations between Jews and Gentiles, were the device by which the Nazis justified their extermination of six million Jews, 10,000 of whom came from Nuremberg. However, the Nazis' choice of Nuremberg had less to do with local support of Nazi ideology than with what medieval Nuremberg represented in German history: Adolf Hitler considered it to be the "most German of all German cities". Yet the infamy caused by the city's recent past seems a world away from the friendly, bustling town that greets visitors today. Nuremberg has a relaxed air that makes whiling away a day amongst its half-timbered houses, fine museums and beer halls an altogether enjoyable experience.

What to see and do

On January 2, 1945, a storm of bombs reduced ninety percent of Nuremberg's centre to ash and rubble, but you'd never guess it from the meticulous postwar rebuilding. The reconstructed medieval core is compact, surrounded by its ancient city walls and neatly bisected by the River Pegnitz. The **Kaiserburg**, whose **Sinwellturm** can be ascended for great views (daily: April–Sept 9am–6pm; Oct–March 10am–4pm; €3/students €2), forms the northwest corner of the city walls.

St Sebaldus and the Hauptmarkt

Heading south, you'll find the city's oldest church, the thirteenth-century **St**

ACCOMMODATION			
DJH	A	Falafel	4
Lette'm Sleep	C	Lebkuchen Schmidt	1
Pfälzer Hof	B	Mach 1	2
Vater Jahn	D	Mohr	5
EATING & DRINKING		Souptopia	6
Barfüsser	8	Stereo Deluxe	9
Bratwürst Herzle	7	Treibhaus	3

Sebaldus. Highlights include the impressive bronze shrine of St Sebald. The **Hauptmarkt**, further south, hosts daily markets and the famous Christmas market. At noon, a clockwork mechanism tinkles away on the facade of the **Frauenkirche**.

St Lorenz

On the south side of the river rises **St Lorenz**, home to a graceful, late fifteenth-century sandstone tabernacle, some 20m high. Across the plaza is the oldest house in the city, the thirteenth-century **Nassauer Haus**, now a T-Mobile shop.

The Germanisches Nationalmuseum

The **Germanisches Nationalmuseum** (Kartäusergasse 1; Tues–Sun 10am–6pm, Wed till 9pm; €6/students €4, free after 6pm on Wed; Ⓦwww.gnm.de) presents the country's cultural history through the largest and most important collection of the artefacts and art of German central Europe from the Bronze Age to the present. Look out for the first globe of the earth, made by Martin Behaim in 1491 – just before Columbus "discovered" America.

The Neues Museum

The **Neues Museum** (Tues–Fri 10am–8pm, Sat & Sun 10am–6pm; €4/students €3, Sun €1; Ⓦwww.nmn.de) offers a cross-section of contemporary art and design, including works by Gerhard Richter and Verner Panton.

The Fascination and Terror exhibition

The Nazi Party rallies were held on the Zeppelin and March fields in the suburb of Luitpoldhain. Nearby, in the gargantuan but never-completed Congress Hall, the **Dokuzentrum's Fascination and Terror** is an unmissable multimedia exhibition documenting the history of the rally grounds and the ruthless misuse of power under National Socialism (Mon–Fri 9am–6pm, Sat & Sun 10am–6pm; €5/students €2.50; tram #6 or #9 to Dokuzentrum; Ⓦwww.museen.nuernberg.de).

Arrival and information

Air The U2 connects the Nürnberg airport with the train station (every 15min; 12min).

Train The Hauptbahnhof is just outside the southern edge of the city walls; follow Königstr. into the centre.

Tourist office The main tourist office (Mon–Sat 9am–7pm; Ⓣ0911/23 36 132, Ⓦwww.nuernberg.de) is at the entrance to the Altstadt opposite the

train station. There's a smaller office at Hauptmarkt 18, in the Altstadt (Mon–Sat 9am–6pm; May–Oct also Sun 10am–4pm; ⓣ0911/23 155 55).
Discount pass The Nürnberg Card (€19/two days) covers public transport plus entrance to museums.
City transport There is an U-Bahn and bus system; a single trip costs €1.80, a day ticket (or both Sat & Sun) €3.60.
Internet *Flat-S*, top floor of the train station's middle hall; open 24hr; €4/hr.

Accommodation

DJH Burg 2 ⓣ0911/23 09 360, ⓦwww.nuernberg.jugendherberge.de. The HI hostel has a wonderful location within the Kaiserburg, overlooking the Altstadt. U-Bahn 2 to Rathenauplatz, then bus #36 to Burgstr. or 25min walk from the station. ❸
Lette'm Sleep Frauentormauer 42 ⓣ0911/9928 128, ⓦwww.backpackers.de. This friendly and popular hostel offers free Internet access. Sheets €3. Dorms ❷, rooms ❺
Pfälzer Hof Am Gräslein 10 ⓣ0911/221 411. This little hotel is in a calm corner of central Nuremberg, off Kornmarkt. ❹–❻
Vater Jahn Jahnstr. 13 ⓣ0911/44 45 07. Friendly pension just south of the Opernhaus on the other side of the railway tracks. ❺–❼

Eating and drinking

There are plenty of *Imbiss*-type snack-joints in the pedestrian zone around St Lorenz, while the area around Rathenauplatz U-Bahn is packed with student café-bars. To find out what's on, pick up the monthly *Dopplepunkt* magazine from the tourist office, or *Plärrer* magazine (€2) from any kiosk.
Barfüsser Hallplatz 2. This popular beer hall in cavernous cellars brews its own beer and serves good food. Schnitzel €8.
Bratwurst Herzle Brunnengasse 11. More down-to-earth than some options, *Herzle* is a great place for sampling Nuremberg's mini-sausages. Four Bratwürstl €4.70.
Falafel *Imbiss* next to St Lorenz serving delicious Egyptian fare and, improbably, pizza. Falafel €2.80.
Lebkuchen Schmidt Hauptmarkt. Taste Christmas year-round at this shop selling the Nuremberg specialty: a spicy gingerbread cookie called *Lebkuchen* (€2).
Mach 1 Kaiserstr. 1–9 ⓦwww.mach1-club.de. This trendy club is has four different bars and a plethora of DJs. Thurs–Sat 10pm–5am.
Mohr Färberstr. 3. Fashionable café-bar in the Altstadt, open late. Pasta specials €4.
Souptopia Lorenzerstr. 27. If you're sick of sausage, head for this little wonder, where five types of soup are on offer daily, including at least one vegan option. Bowl €5.
Stereo Deluxe Klaragasse 8. This lounge-like club is chiller than most and hosts indie and pop nights. Thurs–Sat 9pm–3am.
Treibhaus Karl-Grillenberger-Str. 28. Refreshingly out-of-the-way yet still in the Altstadt, this hip café-bar offers everything you need from 8am to 2am. South of Maxbrücke. Huge, delicious salads €5.50, cocktails €5.

Moving on

Nuremberg Augsburg (every 30min; 1–2hr); Berlin (hourly; 4hr 30min); Frankfurt (hourly; 2hr); Leipzig (hourly; 3hr); Munich (hourly; 1hr 40min); Regensburg (hourly; 1hr); Vienna (every 2hr; 5hr); Würzburg (every 30min; 1hr).

REGENSBURG

The undisturbed medieval ensemble of central **REGENSBURG**, stunningly located on the banks of the Danube midway between Nuremberg and Munich, can easily be visited as a day-trip. Getting lost in the web of cobbled medieval lanes, nursing a drink in one of the wide, sunny squares or cycling along the Danube are the main draws here.

What to see and do

A good place to start is the twelfth-century **Steinerne Brücke**, the only secured crossing along the entire length of the Danube at the time it was built. To the left, the **Historische Wurstküche** (daily 9am–7pm) originally functioned as the bridge-workers' kitchen. This local institution, run by the same family for generations, serves little else but delicious Regensburg sausages (plate €6). Just south, the Gothic **Dom**, begun around 1250, has some beautiful fourteenth-century stained-glass windows. The cathedral's Domspatzen boys' choir is famous throughout Germany; catch them performing during Sunday services at 10am. A short way south, the Neupfarrkirche occupies the site of the old synagogue, wrecked during the

1519 Jewish expulsion. **Schloss Thurn und Taxis** (visit only possible with tour, July–Sept daily at 1.30pm; €11.50/ students €9; ⓦwww.thurnundtaxis.de), one of the largest inhabited palaces in Europe, is in the converted monastic buildings of the abbey of St Emmeram in the city's southern quarter.

Arrival and information

Train Maximilianstrasse leads straight from the train station north to the centre.
Tourist office The tourist office is at Rathausplatz 3 (Mon–Fri 9am–6pm, Sat 9am–4pm, Sun 9.30am–4pm; Nov–March Sun until 2.30pm; ⓣ0941/507 4410, ⓦwww.regensburg.de).
Bike rental Rent a Bike ⓣ0800/460 2460. Branches next to and opposite the station. €9.50/ day.
Internet *Internet Café*, train station first floor. Expensive but convenient access; daily: 6am–11pm; €4/hr.

Eating and drinking

Brauereigaststätte Kneitinger Arnulfsplatz 3. For a real Gaststätte experience, head for this honourable establishment to the east of the centre, whose delicious Bavarian fare precipitates heart attacks throughout the region. Roast ox €8.
Dicker Mann Krebsgasse 6. Vine-covered and candlelit café-restaurant on a tiny side street off Haidplatz serving delicious, good-value meals. Breakfast for €3, dinner specials from €5.
Goldene Ente Badstr. 32. A lovely beer garden popular with students, across the Eisener Steg (iron bridge) from the Altstadt. Head cheese €7.
Oma Plüsch Rote-Stern-Gasse 6. Cosy and friendly with huge portions and cheap beer. Roast pork €6.

Moving on

Train Munich (hourly; 1hr 30min); Nuremburg (hourly; 1hr); Pilsen/Plzen (twice daily; 2hr 40min); Vienna (every two hours; 4hr).

MUNICH

Founded in 1158, **MUNICH** (München) has been the capital of Bavaria since 1503, and as far as the locals are concerned it may as well be the centre of the universe. The city is impossibly energetic, bursting with a good-humoured self-importance that is difficult to dislike. After Berlin, Munich is Germany's most popular city – with its compact and attractive old centre, it is certainly much easier to digest. It also has a great setting, with the mountains and Alpine lakes just an hour's drive away. The best time of year to come here is from June to early October, when the beer gardens, street cafés and bars are in full swing – not least for the world-famous **Oktoberfest** beer festival.

What to see and do

Just ten minutes' walk east of the train station, the twin onion-domed towers of the red-brick Gothic Frauenkirche **(Dom)** form the focus of the city's skyline. The pedestrian shopping street **Kaufingerstrasse**, just below, heads east to the centre and the main square, the Marienplatz.

Marienplatz

The **Marienplatz** is the bustling heart of Munich, thronged with crowds being entertained by street musicians and artists. At 11am and noon (and 5pm March–October), the square fills with tourists as the tuneless carillon in the **Rathaus** tower jingles into action. To the right is the plain Gothic tower of the Altes Rathaus, which now houses a vast toy collection in the **Spielzeugmuseum** (daily 10am–5.30pm; €3).

Alter Peter and the Viktualienmarkt

Close by, the **Peterskirche** tower (Alter Peter; Mon–Fri 9am–6.30pm, Sat & Sun 10am–6.30pm; €1.50) offers the best views of the Altstadt. Directly below, you'll find the **Viktualienmarkt**, a huge open-air food market selling everything from *Weisswurst* and beer to fruit and veg. West of here, at Sendlinger Str. 62, stands the pint-sized **Asamkirche**, one of the most splendid Rococo churches in Bavaria.

MUNICH

ACCOMMODATION

4 You München	E
A&0	D
Am Kaiserplatz	A
Am Siegestor	B
Easy Palace	K
Easy Palace Station	F
Eder	I
Euro Youth Hostel	J
Jedermann	H
Steinberg	C
Wombat's	G

EATING & DRINKING

Al Mercato	23
Alter Simpl	2
Andechser Am Dom	11
Atomic Café	12
Augustiner Bräustuben	9
Backstage	10
Bella Italia	14
Café Glockenspiel	16
Café Kreutzkamm	8
Chinesischer Turm	3
Dalí	1
Der Kleine Chinese	22
Haxnbauer	15
Hofbräuhaus	13
Inges Karotte	25
Kultfabrik	24
Mensa	4
Münchner Bier Brotzeitstüberl	21
Mylord	26
Opatija	18
Pfälzer Weinprobierstuben	7
Prinz Myshkin	19
Soul City	6
Tumult	5
Vorraum	20
Weisses Bräuhaus	17

Schloss Nymphenburg (3km)
Alte Pinakothek, Neue Pinakothek & Pinakothek der Moderne
2 & Maxvorstadt
3, 4, 5, A, B, C & Schwabing (1km)
Unterfahrt
Haidhausen & 24

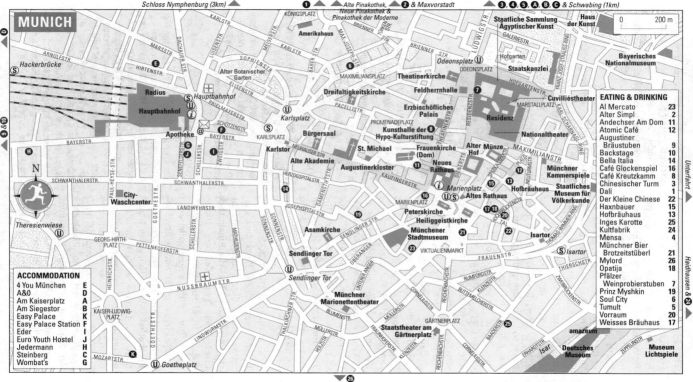

The Hofbräuhaus and the Residenz

Northeast of Marienplatz is the **Hofbräuhaus**, Munich's largest and most famous drinking hall (see p.522). North of here, on Residenzstrasse, is the entrance to the palace of the Wittelsbachs, the immense **Residenz** (daily: April to mid-Oct 9am–6pm; mid-Oct to March 10am–4pm; €6; Ⓦwww.residenz-muenchen.de). One of Europe's finest Renaissance buildings, it was so badly damaged in the last war that it had to be almost totally rebuilt. At 1.30pm, the selection of chambers open to the public changes, so arrive before the switch if you want to see both selections. The splendid Antiquarium, the oldest part of the palace, is open all day long. A separate ticket is necessary to see the fabulous treasures of the **Schatzkammer** (same hours; €6, €9 combined ticket); the star piece is the dazzling stone-encrusted statuette of St George, made around 1590. Across Odeonsplatz from the Residenz is one of the city's most regal churches, the **Theatinerkirche**, whose golden-yellow towers and green copper dome add a splash of colour to the roofscape.

The Pinakothek museums

For art lovers, it's the Pinakothek museums around Barerstrasse that are the city's main draw. The **Alte Pinakothek** (Tues 10am–8pm, Wed–Sun 10am–6pm; €5.50, €1 Sun; Ⓦwww.pinakothek.de) is one of the largest galleries in Europe, housing the world's finest assembly of German art. The **Neue Pinakothek** (Mon & Thurs–Sun 10am–6pm, Wed 10am–8pm; permanent collection/special exhibition/combined €4/9/12, €1/9/10 Sun; Ⓦwww.pinakothek.de) holds a fine collection of nineteenth-century art. The **Pinakothek der Moderne** (Tues–Sun 10am–6pm, Thurs till 8pm; €9.50, €1 Sun; Ⓦwww.pinakothek.de) would be worth visiting for its stunning architecture alone. The stark glass-and-concrete structure presents an impressive collection, from Dalí and Picasso to German greats such as Beckmann and Polke, and features exhibitions of design, architecture and graphics.

The Deutsches Museum

Munich's most overwhelming museum – the **Deutsches Museum** (daily 9am–5pm; €8.50; Ⓦwww.deutsches-museum.de) – occupies a mid-stream island in the Isar, southwest of the centre. Covering every conceivable aspect of technical endeavour, from the first flint tools to the research labs of modern industry, this is the most compendious collection of its type in Germany.

Arrival

Air Munich's airport, Franz Josef Strauss Flughafen, is connected to the Hauptbahnhof by S-Bahn #1 or #8.

Train The Hauptbahnhof is in the centre, 2km west of Marienplatz.

Bus The ZOB is on Arnulfstrasse, behind the station.

Information

Tourist office There are tourist offices (Ⓣ089/233 96 500, Ⓦwww.muenchen.de) at Bahnhofplatz 2 (April–Oct Mon–Sat 9am–8pm, Sun 10am–6pm; Nov–March Mon–Sat 9.30am–6.30pm, Sun 10am–6pm) and in the Rathaus on Marienplatz (Mon–Fri 10am–8pm, Sat 10am–4pm; Dec also Sun 2–6pm), either of which can book rooms (from ❼).

City transport

Metro, trams & buses Short trips (up to two S- or U-Bahn stops, or up to four bus or tram stops) cost €1.10, single trips €2.20. One-day/three-day passes, valid for all public transport in the central city area, are a good investment at €5/12 (single) and €9/21 (two people). Also available are strip cards (€10.50 for 10); stamp two strips for every zone crossed – the zones are shown on maps at stations and tram and bus stops. For short trips, only one strip needs to be cancelled.

Taxis Taxizentrale München Ⓣ089/21 610. There's a charge for ordering a taxi by phone and for luggage. Base charge €2.70, €1.60/km.

BREAKFAST OF CHAMPIONS

Weisswurst (white veal sausage), *Brezen* (bready pretzels eaten with sweet mustard) and *Weissbier* (wheat beer) make up a typical **Bavarian breakfast**. While touristy restaurants in Munich will serve them from dawn till dusk, traditionally the highly perishable *Weisswurst* aren't to be eaten past noon. How the traditionalists function with a half-litre of beer in them before noon is anyone's guess.

Accommodation

Cheap accommodation can be hard to find, especially in summer. If you're going to be in town during Oktoberfest, it's essential to book well in advance; be warned that prices can double during this period.

Hostels

4 you München Hirtenstr. 18 ⓣ089/55 21 660, ⓦwww.the4you.de. Scruffy but lively eco-friendly outfit very close to the main station, with some singles and doubles, as well as standard dorms. Linen and breakfast included. Dorms ❷, rooms ❻

A&O Arnulfstr. 102 ⓣ089/452 359 5800, ⓦwww.aohostels.com. This site of the rather bland A&O chain is a 15min walk west from the station or S-Bahn Hackerbrücke. Dorms ❷, rooms ❼

Easy Palace Mozartstr. 4 ⓣ089/558 7970, ⓦwww.easypalace.de. Welcoming hostel within spitting distance of the Oktoberfest grounds; 15min walk south from the train station or U-Bahn to Goetheplatz. Sheets included. Dorms ❷, rooms ❽

Euro Youth Hotel Senefelderstr. 5 ⓣ089/59 908 8011, ⓦwww.euro-youth-hotel.de. Good atmosphere and location with late-closing bar and helpful staff. Dorms ❷, rooms ❼

Wombat's Senefelderstr. 1 ⓣ089/59 98 91 80, ⓦwww.wombats-hostels.com. The pick of the backpackers' bunch. Modern, lively and central with a great bar, winter garden and friendly staff. Sheets included. Dorms ❷, rooms ❼

Hotels and pensions

Am Kaiserplatz Kaiserplatz 12 ⓣ089/34 91 90. Very friendly place in a good location with big rooms, each done out in a different style – from red satin to Bavarian rustic. Four-bed rooms can be arranged. U-Bahn Münchener Freiheit. Shared bathroom ❺

Am Siegestor Akademiestr. 5 ⓣ089/39 95 50, ⓦwww.hotel-siegestor.de. Friendly place and good location in the lively area of Schwabing, north of the centre. Some rooms are more modern than others. U-Bahn Universität. ❼–❾

Easy Palace Station Schützenstr. 7 ⓣ089/55 25 210, ⓦwww.easypalace.de. Between the station and the centre; what this clean, basic hotel lacks in charm it makes up for in convenience. ❺–❽

Eder Zweigstr. 8 ⓣ089/55 46 60, ⓦwww.hotel-eder.de. Cosy hotel in a quiet road near the train station, offering nicely appointed rooms. ❻–❽

Jedermann Bayerstr. 95 ⓣ089/54 32 40, ⓦwww.hotel-jedermann.de. Classy, family-run hotel just 5min walk from the train station. The buffet breakfast is especially good and free Internet is available. ❻–❽

Steinberg Ohmstr. 9 ⓣ089/33 10 11, ⓦwww.pension-steinberg.de. Friendly and in a good location near the Englischer Garten. U-Bahn Giselastr. ❼–❽

Eating

Gaststätten offer filling soups, salads and sandwich-type dishes. An excellent place to stock up on fresh bread, sausages and fruit is the bustling Viktualienmarkt, which offers an array of outdoor eateries in summer.

Cafés

Alter Simpl Türkenstr. 57. Famous literary café-bar and favoured student haunt named after the satirical magazine *Simplicissimus*. Lunch €5.

Café Glockenspiel Marienplatz 28 (5th floor). Classy café-bar with a fusion menu and surprisingly few tourists; it has a direct view across to its namesake. The entrance is in the passageway behind the shops. Cappuccino €4.

Café Kreutzkamm Maffeistr. 4. Airy and elegant; one of the best (and most expensive) *Kaffee-und-Kuchen* establishments. Closed Sun. Cake €6.

Mensa Leopoldstr. 13. The main *Uni-Mensa*, open for lunch Mon–Fri. Meals €3. U-Bahn Giselastr.

Restaurants

Al Mercato Prälat-Zistl-Str. 12. No-frills Italian serving cheap pizzas and pasta dishes, just south of the Viktualienmarkt. Closed Sun. Pizza €6.

Andechser am Dom Weinstr. 7a, behind the Dom. Traditional place serving beer from the Andechs monastic brewery and solid Bavarian fare to a cheerful crowd. Mains €11.

Bella Italia Herzog-Wilhelm-Str. 8. One of a small chain of inexpensive Italian restaurants, south of Karlsplatz. Open late. Pasta €6.20.

OKTOBERFEST

The huge **Oktoberfest**, held on the Theresienwiese fairground for sixteen days following the penultimate Saturday in September, is an orgy of beer drinking, spiced up by fairground rides that are so hairy they're banned in the US. The fairgrounds are divided along four main avenues, creating a boisterous city within a city, heaving from morning till night. The event began when a fair held to celebrate a Bavarian royal wedding in October 1810 proved so popular that it's been repeated ever since. For more information, check out Ⓦwww.oktoberfest.de.

Der Kleine Chinese Im Tal 28. Cheap, filling Chinese dishes served all day in this tiny eatery near Marienplatz. Mains €4.60.
Haxnbauer Corner of Sparkassenstr. and Ledererstr. Specializes in Germany's famous roasted pork knuckles; the lamb version is no less tasty. Knuckles €15.
Opatija Hochbrückenstr. 3. Excellent, cosy Croatian restaurant with good prices, despite its proximity to Marienplatz. Ground lamb €6.
Prinz Myshkin Hackenstr. 2. Best vegetarian in the city, with international dishes served beneath a high, vaulted ceiling. Mains €11.

Drinking and nightlife

Drinking is central to social life in Munich and, apart from the *Gaststätten* and beer gardens, the city has a lively café-bar culture. North of the centre, hip student bar/cafés in the Maxvorstadt fade into the glitz of Schwabing. For a good alternative head for Haidhausen, across the river to the southeast of the centre; it has a nice mix of bars, cafés and restaurants. For listings check out the English-language *MunichFound* (Ⓦwww.munichfound.de).

Bars and beer halls/gardens

Augustiner Bräustuben Landsbergerstr. 19. Off the tourist track, this was once the house of Augustinian monks and now serves marvellous food in an atmospheric setting. Roast pork €6.
Chinesischer Turm Englischer Garten 3. One of several beer gardens in the lovely Englischer Garten. Frequent live Bavarian brass band appearances. Lunch from €6.50.
Dalí Tengstr. 6, Schwabing. Chic Spanish bodega serving delicious tapas. Open 5pm–1am. Jamón serrano €5. U-Bahn Josephsplatz.
Hofbräuhaus Platzl 9. The most famous and touristy of the beer halls, but beer and food prices are reasonable. Mass (1L beer) €6.60.
Münchner Bier Brotzeitstüberl Viktualienmarkt. Popular beer garden in the centre of the market, with wooden trestles set under oak trees. Bratwurst €3.
Pfälzer Weinprobierstuben Residenzstr. 1. Despite the splendid chandeliers, this has an unpretentious buzz, serving excellent wines from western Germany. Wine from €3.50.
Tumult Blütenstr. 4 Ⓦwww.tumult-in-muenchen.de. Packed classic-tattoo/Fifties-burlesque themed bar in the Maxvorstadt catering to a friendly and hip rockabilly-punk crowd. Closed Sun. U-Bahn Universität.
Weisses Bräuhaus Im Tal 7. Famous for its *Weissbier* (€3.30) and a little cosier than the Hofbräuhaus.

Clubs

Most of Munich's **clubs** are either east or west of the centre; expect to pay €5–15.
Atomic Café Neuturmstr. 5 Ⓦwww.atomic.de. Retro-style bar, club and live music venue near the Hofbräuhaus catering to a fashionable, rock-loving crowd.
Backstage Friedenheimer Brücke 7 Ⓦwww.backstage089.de. One of the best clubs in town, with nightly DJs spinning everything from hip-hop and electro to rock. Plenty of live shows as well. Tram to Steubenplatz or Lautensackstr.
Kultfabrik Grafinger Str. 6, Haidhausen Ⓦwww.kultfabrik.de. Along with adjacent *Optimolwerke* at Friedenstr. 10 (Ⓦwww.optimolwerke.de), this mini-city of clubs and bars housed in a network of old factory buildings attracts upwards of 30,000 on any given weekend. A mix of musical genres and locales makes this Munich's premier nightspot. S- or U-Bahn Ostbahnhof.
Vorraum Im Tal 15, entrance on Hochbrückenstr. Tiny chilled-out lounge across from *Opatija* that stays open late and has DJs Fri & Sat; closed Sun.

Gay Munich

Despite Bavaria's deep conservatism, Munich has an active and visible **gay scene**, centred primarily on Gärtnerplatz. *OurMunich* is a free gay listings mag, unfortunately in German only.

Inges Karotte Baaderstr. 13 ⓦwww.inges-karotte.de. Café-bar predominantly for lesbians, open daily from 6pm. U-Bahn Fraunhoferstr.
Mylord Ickstattstr. 2a. Nostalgic, comfy bar with an older crowd, 5min southwest from Gärtnerplatz. U-Bahn Fraunhoferstr.
Soul City Maximilianplatz 5. Popular gay disco in the heart of the city; Thursday nights heteros welcome. S-/U-Bahn Karlsplatz.

Entertainment

Munich has three first-rate symphony **orchestras** – the Münchener Philharmoniker, the Bayrisches Rundfunk Sinfonie Orchester and the Staatsorchester – as well as eleven major and numerous fringe **theatres**. Advance tickets for plays and concerts can be bought at the box offices or at the tourist office at Marienplatz (ⓦwww.muenchenticket.de).
Museum-Lichtspiele Lilienstr. 2, Haidhausen. ⓦwww.museum-lichtspiele.de. Small cinema showing English-language films.
Olympiapark ⓦwww.olympiapark-muenchen.de. Free concerts by the lake in summer, daily in August. U-Bahn Olympiazentrum.
Unterfahrt Einsteinstr. 42, Haidhausen ⓦwww.unterfahrt.de. Showcase for avant-garde jazz, with many big names gracing the stage. U-Bahn Max-Weber-Platz.

Directory

Bike rental Radius (daily: April to mid-Oct 9.30am–6pm; mid-Oct to March weather dependent; ⓦwww.radiusmunich.com; €15/day), at the train station near platform 32. They also offer bike and walking tours.
Consulates Canada, Tal 29 ⓣ089/2199 570; Ireland, Denningerstr. 15 ⓣ089/2080 5990; South Africa, Sendlinger-Tor-Platz 5 ⓣ089/231 1630; UK, Möhlstr. 5 ⓣ089/211 090; US, Königinstr. 5 ⓣ089/2888 623.
Exchange Reisebank, at the train station and airport.
Hospital Chirugische Klinik und Poliklinik Innenstadt, Nussbaumstr. 20 ⓣ089/5160 2611; Bereitschaftsdienst der Münchener Ärtze, Elisenstr. 3 (ⓣ01805/19 1212), is a late-night clinic near the train station.
Internet easyInternetcafé, Bahnhofplatz 1. Open 24hr. €2–3/hr.
Laundry City-Waschcenter, Paul-Heyse Str. 21. Open daily 7am–10pm, €4/load.
Left luggage At the train station.
Pharmacy Bahnhof-Apotheke, Bahnhofplatz 2.
Post office Bahnhofplatz 1.

Moving on

Munich Augsburg (every 20min; 40min); Berchtesgaden (hourly; 3hr); Berlin (hourly; 6hr); Garmisch-Partenkirchen (hourly; 1hr 30min); Innsbruck (every 30min; 2–3hr); Nuremberg (every 20min; 1hr–2hr); Regensburg (every 20min; 1hr 30min); Salzburg (every 30min; 1hr 30min–2hr); Vienna (hourly; 4–6hr).

DAY-TRIPS FROM MUNICH

Schloss Nymphenburg (daily: April to mid-Oct 9am–6pm; mid-Oct to March 10am–4pm; €5, €10 combined ticket with pavilions and Marstall), the summer residence of the Wittelsbachs, is reached by tram #17 from the train station. Its kernel is a small Italianate palace begun in 1664 for the Electress Adelaide, who dedicated it to the goddess Flora and her nymphs – hence the name. More enticing than the palace itself are the wonderful park and its four distinct pavilions (individual pavilions €2). Don't miss the stunning **Amalienburg**, the hunting lodge built behind the south wing of the Schloss by court architect François Cuvilliés. This supreme expression of the Rococo style marries a cunning design – which makes the little building seem like a full-scale palace – with the most extravagant decoration imaginable.

Dachau

On the northern edge of Munich, the town of **Dachau** was the site of Germany's first **concentration camp** (Tues–Sun 9am–5pm; free; ⓦwww.kz-gedenkstaette-dachau.de), and the motto that greeted arrivals at the gates has taken its chilling place in the history of Third Reich brutality: *Arbeit Macht Frei*, "Work Sets You Free". There are many original buildings still standing, and a replica hut gives an idea of the conditions under which prisoners were forced to live. There's also a thorough exhibition of photographs and text in

English detailing the history of the Third Reich. Turn up at 11.30am or 3.30pm and you can view the short, disturbing documentary *KZ-Dachau* in English. There are also weekend **tours** in English at 1.30pm. Take the S2 to Dachau, then bus #726 to "KZ-Gedenkstätte".

THE BAVARIAN ALPS

It's among the picture-book scenery of the **Alps** that you'll find the Bavarian folklore and customs that are the subjects of so many tourist brochures. The region also encompasses some of the most famous places in the province, such as the Olympic ski resort of **Garmisch-Partenkirchen** and the fantasy castle of **Neuschwanstein**, just one of the lunatic palaces built for mad King Ludwig II of Bavaria. The western reaches are generally cheaper and less touristy, partly because they're not so easily accessible to Munich's weekend crowds. Much of the eastern region to **Berchtesgaden** is heavily geared to the tourist trade, but outside July and August, it's considerably quieter.

King Ludwig II's fairy-tale palaces

Lying between the Forggensee reservoir and the Ammer mountains, around 100km by rail from Munich, **FÜSSEN** and the adjacent town of **SCHWANGAU** are the bases for visiting Bavaria's two most popular castles. **Schloss Hohenschwangau** (daily: April–Sept 9am–6pm; Oct–March 10am–4pm; ⓦwww.hohenschwangau.de; €9), originally built in the twelfth century but heavily restored in the nineteenth, was where Ludwig II spent his youth. A mark of his individualism is left in the bedroom, where he had the ceiling painted with stars that were spotlit in the evenings. **Schloss Neuschwanstein** (same hours; €9, €17 combination ticket for both castles), the ultimate storybook turreted castle and the inspiration for Disneyland's Sleeping Beauty Castle, was built by Ludwig a little higher up the mountain. The architectural hotchpotch includes a Byzantine throne hall and an artificial grotto. Left incomplete at Ludwig's death, it's a monument to a very sad and lonely man. The interiors of these castles can only be visited with timed tickets on guided tours; tickets can be purchased online or at the **Ticket-Service** (Alpseestr. 12, Hohenschwangau ⓣ08362/93 08 30, ⓦwww.hohenschwangau.de; daily: April–Sept 8am–5pm; Oct–March 9am–3pm). Take the train to Füssen (hourly from Munich; 2hr) and then bus #73 to Hohenschwangau. The nearest HI **hostel** is in Füssen, a ten-minute walk from the train station at Mariahilferstr. 5 (ⓣ08362/77 54, ⓦwww.fuessen.jugendherberge.de; juniors ❷, seniors ❸), otherwise the **tourist office** at Kaiser-Maximilian-Platz 1 in Füssen (April–Oct Mon–Fri 9am–6/6.30pm, Sat 10am–2pm, Sun 10am–noon; Nov–March Mon–Fri 9am–5pm, Sat 10am–2pm; ⓣ08362/93 850, ⓦwww.fuessen.de) can book accommodation. Füssen is also the end of the much-publicized **Romantic Road** from Würzburg via Augsburg (see p.513), served by special tour buses in season.

Garmisch-Partenkirchen

GARMISCH-PARTENKIRCHEN is the most famous town in the German Alps, partly because it's at the foot of the highest mountain – the **Zugspitze** (2962m) – and partly because it hosted the 1936 Winter Olympics. It has excellent facilities for skiing, skating and other winter sports, as well as for hiking in the summer; the **tourist office** at Richard-Strauss-Platz 1 (Mon–Sat 8am–6pm, Sun 10am–noon; ⓣ08821/180 700, ⓦwww.garmisch-partenkirchen.de) has maps and full accommodation lists. The ascent of Zugspitze by **rack-railway** or **cable car** (both €47 return, €38 in winter) is the most memorable local excursion.

DJH Jochstr. 10 ⓣ08821/967 050, ⓦwww.djh.de. In the northern suburb of Burgrain; take bus #3 or #4. Closed mid-Nov to Dec 26. ❸
Eierschmalz Promenadestr. 4 ⓣ08821/2434. Homey B&B in central Garmisch. ❺
Geyer-Ostler Mohrenplatz 5 ⓣ08821/2847. Friendly B&B with an excellent location just north of Marienplatz. ❺
Zur Schranne Griessstr. 4. Hearty food in a traditional Wirtshaus, off Marienplatz. Ox €8.
Zum Wildschütz Bankgasse 9. Sample wild game at this kitschy restaurant southwest of Marienplatz. Lovely summer terrace. Venison €8.

Mittenwald

Cuddled up against the Austrian border and just 15km from Garmisch-Partenkirchen, tiny **MITTENWALD**, makes a lovely base for hiking and cycling. The **Karwendel mountain** towering above is a popular climb, and the view from the top is exhilarating; a cable car goes there (€22 return). The **tourist office**, at Dammkarstr. 3 (Mon–Fri 8.30am–5/6pm, Sat 9am–noon, plus Sun 10am–noon in May–Sept & Dec; ⓣ08823/33 981, ⓦwww.mittenwald.de), provides free maps of the area. The youth hostel, Buckelwiesen 7 (ⓣ08823/1701, ⓦwww.mittenwald.jugendherberge.de; juniors ❷, seniors ❸) is 4km north of the town. There are plenty of good **guesthouses**, such as the outdoorsy *Bergzauber*, Klausnerweg 26 (ⓣ08823/939 60, ⓦwww.bergzauber.de; ❺), with bike-repair facilities on the premises, and the central *Simon*, Soiernstr. 6 (ⓣ08823/1363, ⓦwww.simon-mittenwald.de; ❻). The nearest **campsite** (ⓣ08823/5216 ⓦwww.camping-isarhorn.de; closed Nov to mid-Dec; ❶) is 3km north, on the road to Garmisch.

> **TREAT YOURSELF**
>
> **Paraglide** in the Bavarian Alps and treat yourself to a truly awesome adventure. Many different kinds of trips are available, and no experience is necessary. Try Aerotaxi, Beim Gerber 2, Mittenwald (ⓣ08823/32 91 40 or 0171/2819 199, ⓦwww.aerotaxi.de; €75–110).

Berchtesgaden

Almost entirely surrounded by mountains at Bavaria's southeastern extremity – but easily reached by rail from Munich – the area around **BERCHTESGADEN** has a magical atmosphere, especially in the mornings, when mists rise from the lakes and swirl around lush valleys and rocky mountainsides.

What to see and do

A star attraction is the stunning emerald **Königssee**, Germany's highest lake, which bends around the foot of the towering **Watzmann** (2713m), 5km south of town – regular buses run out here – and has year-round **cruises** (every 30min; €15 return). You can also take a cable car up the **Jenner**, immediately above the lake (€20 return), used mostly by skiers in the winter months. Berchtesgaden is still indelibly associated with **Adolf Hitler**, who rented a house in the nearby village of Obersalzberg, which he later enlarged into the **Berghof**, a stately retreat where he could meet foreign dignitaries. High above the village, Hitler's Kehlsteinhaus, or **"Eagle's Nest"**, survives as a restaurant, and can be reached by special bus and lift from Obersalzberg once the snow has melted (April to mid-Oct; €14.50 return). In addition to downhill skiing facilities for the winter months, Berchtesgaden has some great **mountain walks** to take you away from the crowds in summer – maps of suggested walking routes can be found at the **tourist office** (mid-May to mid-Oct Mon–Fri 8.30am–6pm, Sat 9am–5pm, Sun 9am–3pm; mid-Oct to mid-May Mon–Fri 8.30am–5pm & Sat 9am–noon; ⓣ01805/86 5200, ⓦwww.berchtesgadener-land.info), opposite the train station. Berchtesgaden is also home to an unexpected diversion, the **Salzbergwerk** (daily: May–Oct 9am–5pm; Nov–April 11.30am–3pm; Ⓦ www.salzbergwerk-berchtesgaden.de; €14), a historic salt mine that's been refurbished with an hour-long amusement-park-like ride/tour through its massive underground caverns.

Accommodation

Guest house options include the friendly *Haus am Hang*, Göllsteinbichl 3 (Ⓣ 08652/43 59, Ⓦ www.hausamhang.de; ④), and *Haus Achental*, Ramsauer Str. 4 (Ⓣ 08652/4549; ⑤), where all rooms have bathrooms. The tourist office can direct you to any of the five **campsites** in the valley.

Greece

HIGHLIGHTS

METEORA: awe-inspiring Byzantine monasteries in a magical setting

ATHENS: roam the Acropolis and hit the capital's clubs

OLYMPIA: discover where the games were born

SANTORÍNI: take in the sunset from this spectacular island

KNOSSOS: visit the home of the Minotaur

ROUGH COSTS

DAILY BUDGET BASIC €30/with the occasional treat €40

DRINK Oúzo €3

FOOD Souvláki (shish kebab) €8

HOSTEL/BUDGET HOTEL €10/€30

TRAVEL Bus: Athens–Delphi €13; ferry: Athens–Crete €32

FACT FILE

POPULATION 11.2 million

AREA 131,900 sq km (including 6000 islands)

LANGUAGE Greek

CURRENCY Euro (€)

CAPITAL Athens (population: 4 million)

INTERNATIONAL PHONE CODE ⓣ30

Basics

With 166 inhabited islands and a landscape that ranges from Mediterranean to Balkan, Greece has enough appeal to fill months of travel. Its historic sites span four millennia of civilization and even today, a visit can still seem like a personal discovery. The beaches are distributed along a long, convoluted coastline, and include cosmopolitan resorts as well as remote islands where boats may call only once or twice a week. In many respects what makes Greece special are the simple pleasures of its natural environment, climate and food.

The country is the sum of an extraordinary diversity of influences. Romans, Arabs, Frankish Crusaders, Venetians, Slavs, Albanians, Turks, Italians, as well as the thousand-year Byzantine Empire, have all been and gone since the time of Alexander the Great. Each has left its mark: the **Byzantines** through countless churches and monasteries, particularly at the ghost town of Mystra; the **Venetians** in impregnable fortifications such as Monemvasiá in the Peloponnese; the **Franks** with crag-top castles, again in the Peloponnese but also in the Dodecanese and east Aegean. Most obvious, perhaps, is the heritage of four hundred years of **Ottoman Turkish** rule which exercised an inestimable influence on music, cuisine, language and way of life.

Even before the fall of Byzantium in the fifteenth century, the Greek country people – peasants, fishermen, shepherds – had created one of the most vigorous and truly **popular cultures** in Europe, which endured until quite recently in songs and dances, costumes, embroidery, furniture and the whitewashed houses of popular image. But Greek architectural and musical heritage in particular has undergone a recent renaissance.

CHRONOLOGY

c.800 BC Homer writes *The Iliad* and *The Odyssey*.
776 BC First Olympic Games are held in Olympia.
486 BC The building of the Parthenon is completed.
399 BC The trial and execution of Socrates, the founding father of philosophy, takes place.
380 BC Plato establishes the Athens Academy.
323 BC Alexander the Great dies heralding the beginning of the Hellenistic period.
88 BC Romans attack Athens.
330 AD Byzantine empire established at Constantinople. Christianity becomes dominant religion.
1387 The Ionian Islands fall under Venetian rule.
1456 Ottoman Turks invade Athens and occupy the city.
1829 Greeks win their independence from Ottoman rule.
1833 Athens becomes the capital of Greece.
1924 Monarchy is abolished in favour of a Republic.
1935 The monarchy is restored.
1941 Greece is invaded and occupied by German, Italian and Bulgarian forces. Liberation comes three years later with the help of heavy resistance fighting.
1952 A new constitution is passed which retains the monarchy as head of state whilst introducing parliamentary democracy.
1967 Military coup led by Colonel George Papadopoulos.
1973 Monarchy is abolished and Papadopoulos is overthrown in a bloodless coup.
1974 Turkish invasion of Greek-held northern Cyprus.
2002 Greece adopts the single European currency.
2004 The Olympic games are held in Athens.
2007 Forest fires claim the lives of 61 Greeks.

ARRIVAL

By **air**, there are international airports on the mainland at Athens and Thessaloníki, both of which are well-connected with their respective city cen-

tres. Other destinations served by budget flights include Crete, Corfu and Rhodes, as well as numerous other mainland and island destinations. By **boat**, there are regular ferries from Ancona, Bari, Brindisi, Trieste and Venice in Italy, arriving at Corfu, Igoumenítsa and Pátra. Eurail and InterRail pass holders may travel with Superfast Ferries (Ⓦwww.superfast.com/adriatic) at **discounted fares** from Ancona and Bari. From Turkey, you can travel by boat to the Dodecanese and the northern Aegean islands (Rhodes, Kós, Sámos, Híos and Lésvos). By **land**, crossing into Greece is possible from Albania, Macedonia, Bulgaria and Turkey either by bus or by train, arriving in Thessaloníki. There are two trains daily from Belgrade via Skopje. Three trains daily connect Sofia to Thessaloníki, one of which starts its journey in Budapest. From Istanbul, two trains leave daily, one of which is an intercity service (IC91). Buses connect mainland Greece with departure points in Albania, Bulgaria and Turkey. If you arrive overland from the north at Thessaloníki, onward travel to the rest of the country is straightforward.

GETTING AROUND

The **rail** network (Ⓦwww.osenet.gr) is limited, and trains are slower than the equivalent buses – except on the showcase IC (intercity) lines. However, most trains are cheaper than buses, and some of the routes are highlights in their own right. **Eurail** and **InterRail** are valid, though passholders must reserve like everyone else, and there's a small supplement on the intercity services. It is essential to validate your train

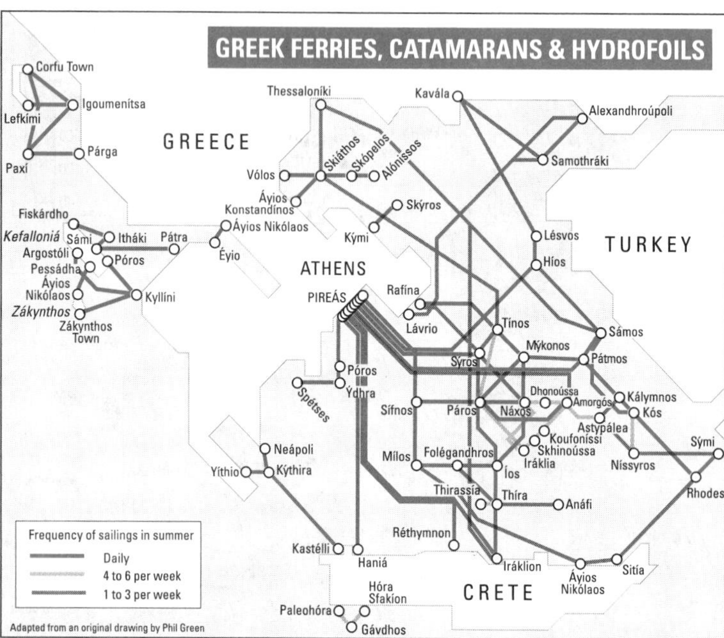

ticket on the platform before you board the train.

Buses form the bulk of public land transport, and service on the major routes is efficient, with companies organized nationally into a syndicate called **KTEL**. If starting a journey from a bus station, you will be issued with a one-way ticket which has a seat number. Return tickets are rarely found.

Schedules for **sea transport** are notoriously erratic. Regular ferry tickets are best bought on the day of departure, unless you need to reserve a cabin – although from March 23 to 25, the weeks before and after Orthodox Easter and during August it's best to book several days in advance. The cheapest ticket is "deck class". Leave plenty of time for your journey as ferries are often late, or take longer to reach their destinations than scheduled. Hydrofoils and high-speed catamarans are roughly twice as fast and twice as expensive as ordinary ferries. In season, *kaïkia* (caiques) sail to more obscure islets.

Once on the islands, almost everybody rents a **scooter** or a **bike**. Scooters cost from €12 a day, mountain bikes a bit less. To rent a motorbike (anything over 50cc) you usually need to show an appropriate licence.

ACCOMMODATION

Most of the year you can turn up pretty much anywhere and find a **room**. Only around Easter (Orthodox, see p.534) and during July and August are you likely to experience problems; at these times, it's worth booking well in advance. If it's not possible to book ahead, head off the standard tourist routes, or arrive at each new place early in the day.

Hotels are categorized from "Luxury" down to "E-class", but these ratings have more to do with amenities and number of rooms than pricing. Throughout Greece, you have the additional option of **privately let rooms** (*dhomátia*). These are divided into three classes (A–C), and are usually cheaper than hotels. As often as not, rooms find you: owners descend on ferry and bus arrivals to fill any space they have. On the islands, minibuses from campsites and hotels meet new arrivals for free transfers. Increasingly, rooms are being eclipsed by **self-catering facilities**, which can be equally good value; if signs or touts are not apparent, ask for studios at travel agencies which usually cluster around arrival points. There are a handful of **hostels** outside Athens, which charge around €8-12 a night. Note that hotels and hostels do not normally include breakfast in their prices; an extra charge of €5 is standard.

Official **campsites** range from basic island compounds to highly organized complexes, mostly closed in winter (Nov–April). Rough camping is forbidden, and the regulations do get enforced occasionally.

FOOD AND DRINK

Eating out in Greece is popular and reasonably priced: €10–15 per person for a meal with beer or cheap wine. Greeks generally don't eat breakfast. **Snacks**, however, can be one of the distinctive pleasures of Greek eating. *Tyrópites* and *spanakópites* (cheese and spinach pies respectively) are on sale everywhere, as are *souvlákia* (small kebabs) and *yíros* (doner kebabs), served in *píta* bread with garnish. In choosing a **taverna**, the best strategy is to go where the locals go. Typical dishes to try include *moussakás* (aubergine and meat pie), *yígandes* (white haricot beans in red sauce), *tzatzíki* (yoghurt, garlic and cucumber dip), *melitzanosaláta* (aubergine dip), *khtapódhi* (octopus) and *kalamarákia* (fried baby squid). Note that people eat late: 2.30–4pm for lunch & 9–11.30pm for dinner, although plenty of eateries serve food all day long.

Drink

The traditional coffee shop *or* **kafenío** is the central pivot of life in rural villages; like tavernas, these range from the sophisticated to the old-fashioned. Their main business is sweet Greek coffee, but they also serve spirits such as aniseed-flavoured *oúzo* and brandy, as well as beer and soft drinks. Islanders take pre-dinner *oúzo* an hour or two before sunset: you'll be served a glass of water alongside, to be tipped into your *oúzo* until it turns milky white. **Bars**, often housed in buildings of historic interest, are now ubiquitous in the largest towns and resorts. Drinks, at €5.50–10, are invariably more expensive than at a *kafenío*.

CULTURE AND ETIQUETTE

It is important to be respectful when visiting one of Greece's many **churches** or **monasteries**, and appropriate clothing should be worn – covered arms and legs for both sexes. The more popular sites often provide such clothing, should you be without it. Photography is also banned in sacred places. Another important part of Greek life is the afternoon **siesta**, when peace and quiet are valued. In restaurants, **tipping** is not expected but usually customers round up the bill, or leave a little more for exceptional service. **Topless bathing** is now legal on virtually all Greek beaches but, especially in smaller places, be aware of local sensitivities before stripping off (and full nudity is tolerated only at designated or isolated beaches).

SPORTS AND OUTDOOR ACTIVITIES

Greece has a wide range of outdoor activities to suit all budgets. The larger islands and larger seaside resorts on the mainland have countless opportunities for **watersports** – including waterskiing,

GREECE ON THE NET

www.culture.gr Ministry of Culture site; info on ruins and museums, including opening hours and prices.
www.athensnews.gr Useful and literate English-language weekly.
www.gnto.gr Greek National Tourist Organization site.
www.poseidon.ncmr.gr Sophisticated oceanographer's site that's the best window on current Greek weather.
www.gtp.gr Information on all ferry and hydrofoil schedules except some minor local lines.

windsurfing, diving and snorkelling. The best way to gather information is to head to the nearest beach, where there are usually information kiosks offering bookings and advice. The country's mountainous landscape provides plenty of **walking** and **climbing** options. The most rewarding areas are in northern Greece, concentrating around Mount Olympus to the east and the Epirus region to the northwest. Always wear sturdy walking boots for long treks, and carry plenty of water. If you want to do some serious hiking, it is worth buying a specialist hiking map (see below).

COMMUNICATIONS

Most **post offices** operate Mon–Fri 7.30am–2pm, and into the evening and even weekends in the largest cities and major resorts. **Stamps** can also be bought at designated postal agencies inside newsstands or stationers. **Poste restante** is reasonably efficient. **Public phones** are mainly card-operated, though many cafés and kiosks have counter-top coin-op models. Buy phone cards from newsagents and kiosks. It's possible to make collect (reverse-charge) or charge-card calls from these phones, but you need credit on a Greek phone-card to begin. There are no area codes per se; you merely dial all ten digits of every phone number. The operator is on ☎132 (domestic) or ☎139 (international). All big towns have several places with **Internet** access, and there's usually at least one place on the more visited islands. Expect to pay around €1.50–5 per hour.

EMERGENCIES

The most common causes of a run-in with the **police** are drunken loutishness and camping outside an authorized site. For minor medical complaints go to the local **pharmacy**, usually open Mon–Fri 8am–2pm. Details of pharmacies open out-of-hours are posted in all pharmacy windows. For serious medical attention you'll find English-speaking doctors in all bigger towns and resorts; consult the tourist police for names. Emergency treatment is free in state hospitals, though you'll only get the most basic level of nursing care.

EMERGENCY NUMBERS

Police ☎110; Ambulance ☎166; Fire ☎199.

INFORMATION AND MAPS

The **National Tourist Organization (EOT)** publishes an array of free regional pamphlets and maps. There are EOT offices in most larger towns and resorts; in other places, try equally good municipal tourist offices which often have longer opening hours. The **tourist police** often have lists of rooms to let, but are mostly there to assist if you have a serious complaint about a hotel or restaurant. The most reliable **maps** are published in Athens. Road Editions (www.road.gr) has the best range for mainland regions and islands; maps by Emvelia Editions (www.em-

Greek

	Greek	Pronunciation
Yes	*Néh*	Ne
No	*Óhi*	Ohi
Please	*Parakaló*	Parakalo
Thank you	*Efharistó*	Efharisto
Hello/Good day	*Yás sas/Hérete*	Yas sas/Herete
Goodbye	*Adío*	Adio
Excuse me	*Signómi*	Siynomi
Sorry	*Lupámai*	Lipame
When?	*Póte?*	Pote?
Where?	*Pou?*	Poo?
Good	*Kaló*	Kalo
Bad	*Kakó*	Kako
Near	*Kondá*	Konda
Far	*Makriá*	Makria
Cheap	*Fthinó*	Fthino
Expensive	*Akrivó*	Akrivo
Open	*Aniktó*	Anikto
Closed	*Klistó*	Klisto
Today	*Símera*	Simera
Yesterday	*Khthés*	Khthes
Tomorrow	*Ávrio*	Avrio
How much is....?	*Póso káni...?*	Poso kani…?
What time is it?	*Ti óra íneh...?*	Ti ora ine…?
I don't understand	*Dhen katalavéno*	en katalaveno
Do you speak English?	*Xérete angliká?*	Xherete anglika?
Do you have a room?	*Éhete éna eléfthero domátio?*	Ehete ena elefthero domatyo?
Where does this bus go to?	*Pou piyaínei autó to leoforeío?*	Poo piyeni afto to leoforio?
What time does it leave?	*Ti óra févyi?*	Ti ora fevyi?
A ticket to...	*Éna isitírio yiá…*	Ena isitirio yia…
I'm going to...	*Páo stó…*	Pao sto…
Can I have the bill please?	*To logariasmó, parakaló?*	To loghariazmo, parakalo?
One	*Éna/mía*	Ena/mia
Two	*Dhýo*	Thio
Three	*Trís/tría*	Tris/tria
Four	*Tésseres/Tesseris*	téssera/tessera
Five	*Pénde*	Pende
Six	*Éxi*	Exhi
Seven	*Eftá*	Efta
Eight	*Októ*	Okto
Nine	*Enéa*	Enea
Ten	*Dhéka*	Theka

velia.gr) include useful town plans; and Anavasi (Ⓦwww.anavasi.gr) produce the best mountaineering maps, plus excellent coverage of the Sporades and Cyclades.

MONEY AND BANKS

Greece's currency is the **euro** (€). **Banks** are normally open Mon–Thurs 8am–2.30pm, Fri 8am–2pm. They charge a flat fee (€2–3) to change money, the

National Bank usually being the cheapest; travel agencies and designated money-exchange booths give a poorer rate, but often levy a sliding two-percent commission, which makes them better than banks for changing small amounts. Plenty of **ATMs** accept foreign cards; in isolated areas without ATMs, a small quantity of US dollar/sterling notes – not travellers' cheques – will prove useful. **Credit cards** are generally accepted in more upmarket hotels, restaurants and shops.

OPENING HOURS AND HOLIDAYS

Shops generally open at 8.30–9am, then take a long break at 2–2.30pm before reopening in the late afternoon (5.30/6pm–8.30/9pm) on Tuesday, Thursday and Friday only. However, tourist areas have shops and offices often staying open right through the day. On Sundays many shops remain closed and **public transport** reduces dramatically or ceases completely, so be careful not to get stranded. Opening hours for **museums** and **ancient sites** change with exasperating frequency, although many are closed on Mondays. Smaller sites generally close for a long siesta (even when they're not supposed to), as do monasteries. Many state-owned museums and sites are free for students from EU countries (a valid card is required, but not necessarily an ISIC). Non-EU students, and all over-65s, generally pay half-price. Most museums and archeological sites are free on the following days: every Sunday Nov to end of March; 1st Sunday of April, May, June & Oct; 2nd Sunday of July–Sept; all national holidays. There's a vast range of **public holidays** and **festivals**. The most important, when almost everything will be closed, are: Jan 1 and 6, 1st Mon of Lent, March 25, May 1, Orthodox Easter Sun and Mon (April 27 in 2008, April 19 in 2009), Pentecost/Whit Mon, Aug 15, Oct 28, Dec 24–27.

Athens

ATHENS has been inhabited continuously for over seven thousand years. Its acropolis, protected by a ring of mountains and commanding views of all seagoing approaches, was a natural choice for prehistoric settlement. Its development as a city-state reached its zenith in the fifth century BC with a flourish of art, architecture, literature and philosophy that has pervaded Western culture ever since. Following World War II, the city's population has risen from 700,000 to four million – around a third of the country's population. The speed of this process is reflected in Athens' chaotic mix of retro and contemporary: cutting-edge clothes shops and designer bars stand by the remnants of the Ottoman bazaar, while brutalist 1960s apartment blocks dwarf crumbling Neoclassical mansions. The **ancient sites** are the most obvious of Athens' attractions, but the attractive cafés, landscaped stair-streets, and markets, the startling views from the hills of Lykavitós and Filopáppou, and, around the foot of the Acropolis, the scattered monuments of the Byzantine, medieval and nineteenth-century town all have their appeal.

What to see and do

Pláka is the best place to begin exploring the city. One of the few parts of Athens with charm and architectural merit, its narrow streets and stepped lanes are flanked by nineteenth-century Neoclassical houses. The interlocking streets provide countless opportunities for watching the world – or at least, the tourists – go by. Whilst the Acropolis complex is an essential sight, there is much pleasure to be found in stumbling across smaller and more modest relics, such as the fourth-century Monument of Lysikratos, or the first-century Tower of the Winds. Or take a walk through the pleasant National Gardens, away from the chaos of Athens' traffic-choked streets. Save some energy for the balmy evenings, however – with gastronomic delights and funky bars, Athens knows how to juxtapose the ancient with the modern, leaving the visitor full of the wonders of both.

The Acropolis

A rugged limestone outcrop, watered by springs and rising abruptly from the plain of Attica, the **Acropolis** (daily 8am–2.30/7pm) was one of the earliest settlements in Greece, supporting a Neolithic community around 5000 BC. During the ninth century BC, it became the heart of the first Greek city-state, and in the fifth century BC, Pericles had the complex reconstructed under the direction of architect and sculptor Pheidias, producing most of the monuments visible today, including the Parthenon. Having survived more or less intact for over two millennia, the Acropolis finally fell victim to the vagaries of war. In 1801 Lord Elgin removed the frieze (the "Elgin Marbles"), which he later sold to the British Museum and which has

> **FERRY PORTS**
>
> The port of **PIREÁS**, effectively an extension of Athens, is the main terminus for international and inter-island ferries. Get there from Athens by metro: Pireás is the last stop on Line #1 heading southwest from Monastiráki. Once there, blue and white buses shuttle passengers around the port for free. The other ports on the east coast of the Attic peninsula, Rafína and Lávrio, are alternative departure points for many of the Cycladic and northeastern Aegean islands. Frequent buses connect them with central Athens.

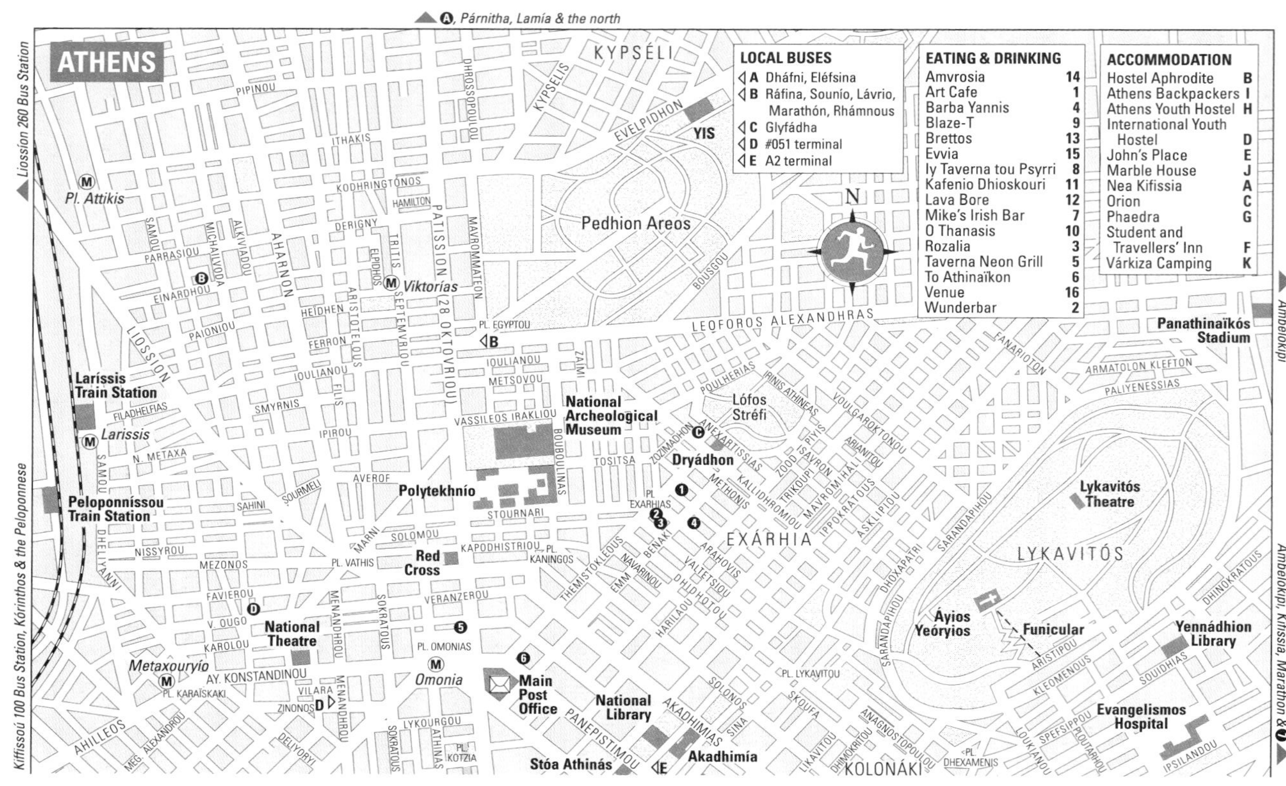
ATHENS
LOCAL BUSES
A Dháfni, Eléfsina
B Ráfina, Sounío, Lávrio, Marathón, Rhámnous
C Glyfádha
D #051 terminal
E A2 terminal
EATING & DRINKING
Amvrosia 14
Art Cafe 1
Barba Yannis 4
Blaze-T 9
Brettos 13
Evvia 15
Iy Taverna tou Psyrri 8
Kafenio Dhioskouri 11
Lava Bore 12
Mike's Irish Bar 7
O Thanasis 10
Rozalia 3
Taverna Neon Grill 5
To Athinaïkon 6
Venue 16
Wunderbar 2
ACCOMMODATION
Hostel Aphrodite B
Athens Backpackers I
Athens Youth Hostel H
International Youth Hostel D
John's Place E
Marble House J
Nea Kifissia A
Orion C
Phaedra G
Student and Travellers' Inn F
Várkiza Camping K
A, Párnitha, Lamía & the north
Liossion 260 Bus Station
Kiffissoú 100 Bus Station, Kórinthos & the Peloponnese
Ambelókipi
Ambelókipi, Kifissiá, Marathon & 7
KYPSÉLI
Pedhion Areos
YIS
Pl. Attikis
Viktorías
Larissis
Laríssis Train Station
Peloponníssou Train Station
National Archeological Museum
Polytekhnío
Lófos Stréfi
Dryádhon
EXÁRHIA
LYKAVITÓS
Lykavitós Theatre
Áyios Yeóryios
Funicular
Panathinaïkós Stadium
Yennádhion Library
Evangelismos Hospital
KOLONÁKI
Red Cross
National Theatre
Metaxouryío
Omonia
Main Post Office
National Library
Stóa Athinás
Akadhimía
LEOFOROS ALEXANDHRAS
PATISSION (28 OKTOVRIOU)
PANEPISTIMOU
AKADHIMIAS
N

ATHENS

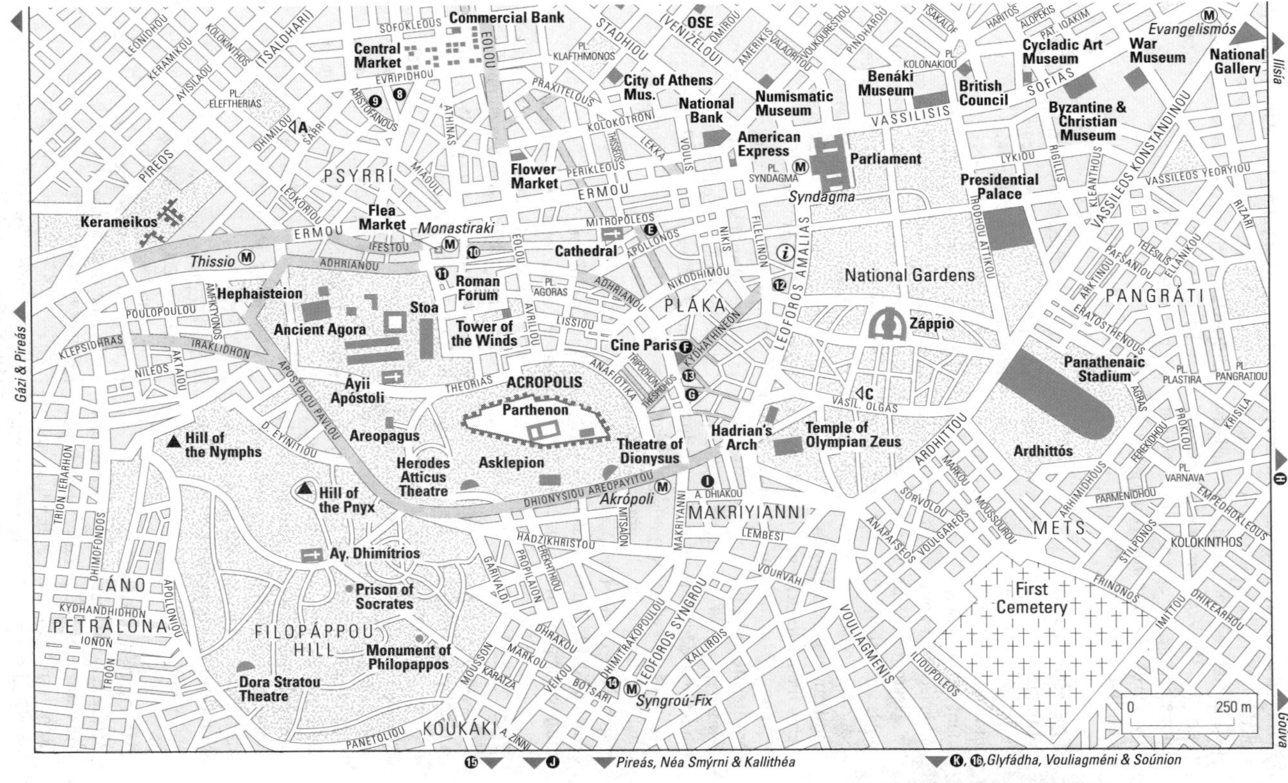
Commercial Bank
Central Market
OSE
City of Athens Mus.
National Bank
Numismatic Museum
American Express
Benáki Museum
British Council
Cycladic Art Museum
War Museum
National Gallery
Evangelismós
Byzantine & Christian Museum
Parliament
Presidential Palace
Syndagma
PSYRRÍ
Flower Market
Flea Market
Monastiraki
Keramеikos
Thissio
Cathedral
National Gardens
Záppio
Roman Forum
Hephaisteion
Stoa
Ancient Agora
Tower of the Winds
PLÁKA
Cine Paris
ACROPOLIS
Parthenon
Áyii Apóstoli
Areopagus
Hill of the Nymphs
Herodes Atticus Theatre
Asklepion
Theatre of Dionysus
Hadrian's Arch
Temple of Olympian Zeus
Akrópoli
MAKRIYIANNI
Hill of the Pnyx
Ay. Dhimítrios
Prison of Socrates
FILOPÁPPOU HILL
Monument of Philopappos
Dora Stratou Theatre
ÁNO PETRÁLONA
KOUKÁKI
Syngroú-Fix
PANGRÁTI
Panathenaic Stadium
Ardhittós
METS
First Cemetery
Ilísia
Goúva
Gázi & Pireás
Pireás, Néa Smýrni & Kallithéa
Glyfádha, Vouliagméni & Soúnion
0 250 m

caused much controversy ever since. Whilst the original religious significance of the Acropolis is now non-existent, it is still imbued with a sense of majesty and awe. The vistas are worth the climb alone, as the Acropolis' natural height gives visitors a rare opportunity to gain a bird's-eye view over the capital.

The Parthenon

With the construction of the **Parthenon**, fifth-century Athens reached an artistic and cultural zenith. No other monument in the ancient Greek world had achieved such fame, and it stood proud as a symbol of the greatness and the power of Athens. The first and largest building constructed by Pericles' men, the temple is stunning and maximizes refinements to achieve an unequalled harmony in temple architecture. Built on the site of earlier temples, it was intended as a new sanctuary for Athena and a house for her cult image, a colossal statue decked in ivory and gold plate that was designed by Pheidias and considered one of the Seven Wonders of the Ancient World; unfortunately the sculpture was lost in ancient times.

The Erechtheion

To the north of the Parthenon stands the **Erechtheion**, the last of the great works of Pericles. The building is intentionally unlike anything else found among the remnants of ancient sites. The most bizarre and memorable feature is the Porch of the Caryatids, as the columns are replaced by six maidens (caryatids) holding the entablature gracefully on their heads. The significance of this design continues to puzzle both historians and visitors.

Acropolis Museum

At the time of research, the **Acropolis Museum** was temporarily closed, but is set to reopen in 2008. It will contain nearly all the portable objects removed from the Acropolis since 1834. Prize exhibits will include the *Moschophoros*, a painted marble statue of a young man carrying a sacrificial calf; the graceful sculpture of Athena Nike adjusting one sandal, known as *Iy Sandalízoussa*; and four caryatids from the Erechtheion.

Herodes Atticus Theatre and Theatre of Dionysus

Dominating the southern slope of the Acropolis hill is the second-century Roman **Odeion of Herodes Atticus**, restored for performances of music and classical drama during the summer festival (the only time it's open). The main interest hereabouts lies in earlier Greek sites to the east, pre-eminent among them the **Theatre of Dionysos**. Masterpieces of Aeschylus, Sophocles, Euripides and Aristophanes were first performed here, at one of the most evocative locations in the city. The ruins are impressive; the theatre, rebuilt in the fourth century BC, could hold some seventeen thousand spectators.

The Agora

Northwest of the Acropolis, the **agora** was the nexus of ancient Athenian city life, where acts of administration, commerce and public assembly competed for space. The site is a confused jumble of ruins, dating from various stages between the sixth century BC and the fifth century AD. For some idea of what you are surveying, head for the **museum** in the rebuilt Stoa of Attalos. At

ANCIENT MONUMENTS ENTRY

The entry ticket to the Acropolis (€12, non-EU students €6, EU students free) is valid for four days and allows free access to all the other ancient sites in Athens. Otherwise, minor sites charge a separate €2 admission fee if you haven't visited the Acropolis, and open daily 8am–2.30/7pm.

the far corner of the agora precinct sits the nearly intact but distinctly clunky Doric **Temple of Hephaistos**, otherwise known as the Thissíon from the exploits of Theseus depicted on its friezes.

The Roman Forum

The **Roman Forum**, or Roman agora, was built as an extension of the Hellenistic agora by Julius Caesar and Augustus. The best-preserved and most intriguing of the ruins, though, is the graceful, octagonal structure known as the **Tower of the Winds**. It was designed in the first century BC by a Syrian astronomer, and served as a compass, sundial, weather vane and water-clock powered by a stream from one of the Acropolis springs. Each face of the tower is adorned with a relief of a figure floating through the air, personifying the eight winds.

Sýndagma Square and the National Gardens

All roads lead to Platía Syndágmatos – **Sýndagma Square** – with its pivotal metro station. Geared to tourism, with a main post office, banks, luxury hotels and travel agents grouped around, it has little to recommend it. Behind the parliament buildings on the square, the **National Gardens** provide the most refreshing spot in the city, a shady oasis of trees, shrubs and creepers. South of the gardens stands **Hadrian's Arch**, erected by the Roman emperor to mark the edge of the classical city and the beginning of his own. Directly behind are sixteen surviving columns of the 104 that originally comprised the **Temple of Olympian Zeus** – the largest in Greece, dedicated by Hadrian in 131 AD.

Museums

At the northeastern corner of the National Gardens is the fascinating and much-overlooked **Benáki Museum**, Koumbári 1 (Mon, Wed, Fri & Sat 9am–7pm, Thurs 9am–midnight, Sun 9am–3pm; €6, students €3), with a well-organized collection that features Mycenaean jewellery, Greek costumes, memorabilia of the Greek War of Independence and historical documents, engravings and paintings.

Taking the second left off Vassilísis Sofías after the Benáki Museum will bring you to the **Museum of Cycladic and Ancient Greek Art**, Neofýtou Dhouká 4 (Mon & Wed–Fri 10am–4pm, Sat 10am–3pm; €5, students €2.50), impressive for both its subject and the quality of its displays.

To the northwest, beyond Omónia, the fabulous **National Archeological Museum**, Patissíon 44 (Mon 1–7.30pm, Tues–Sun 8am–7.30pm; €7, students €3), contains gold finds from the grave circle at Mycenae, including the so-called Mask of Agamemnon, along with an impressive classical art collection and findings from the island of Thíra, dating from around 1450 BC, contemporary with the Minoan civilization on Crete.

Arrival and information

Air The Suburban Rail line whisks you from Elefthería Venizélos airport to Laríssis train station (hourly; 7am–midnight; €6), involving a change at Nerantziotissa, where you can also transfer to the Line #1 metro. Although this is the quickest mode of transport, the airport is also directly connected to the Line #3 metro (every 30min; 5am–midnight; €6). The X95 express bus (every 10–15min; 24hr) from outside Arrivals goes direct to Sýndagma Square, the X94 express bus (every 15–20min; 7.30am–10pm) heads for Ethnikí Ámyna metro station, whilst the X96 express bus (every 15–20min; 24hr) heads to Pireás port; these cost €3.20 single.

Train International trains arrive at the Laríssis train station to the northwest of the city centre, with its own metro station on Line #2. From here, there are trains to all parts of Greece, although for some destinations in the Peloponnese you may need to take the Suburban Rail to Corinth and change there.

Bus Buses from northern Greece and the Peloponnese arrive at Kifissoú 100 bus station, ten minutes from the centre by bus #051 (5am–midnight). Buses from central Greece arrive closer to the centre at Liossíon 260, north of the train station. From here bus #024 goes to Sýndagma (5am–midnight). Most international buses drop off at the train station or Kifissoú 100; a few will drop you right in the city centre.

Boat If you arrive by boat at Pireás, the easiest way to get to the centre is by metro on Line #1, with the station being a few steps from the quay.

Tourist office The city's main EOT tourist office is at Leofóros Amálias 26 (Mon–Fri 9am–7pm, Sat–Sun 10am–6pm; ⓣ2103 310 392, ⓔinfo_desk@gnto.gr).

City transport

Tickets For €3 you can buy a ticket valid on all public transport for 24hr. All public transport operates daily from 5am–midnight. At the weekend (Fri–Sun) the trams operate for 24hr.

Bus and trolley Athens' bus and trolley network is extensive but very crowded at peak times. Tickets for buses must be bought in advance from kiosks and validated once on board.

Tram A tram line built for the Olympiad runs from Sýndagma to the seaside resorts of Glyfádha and Faliro.

Metro Line #1 of the metro runs from Pireás to Kifissiá, with central stops at Thissío, Monastiráki and Omónia; Line #2 runs from Áyios Andónios to Áyios Dhimítrios via Sýndagma and a station at the foot of the Acropolis; Line #3 heads east from Monastiráki to Dhoukíssis Plakendías (with special metro cars continuing direct to the airport). Tickets (€0.80) are available at all stations from automatic coin-op dispensers or staffed windows. They must be validated before boarding the metro.

Taxis can be surprisingly difficult to hail and fairly expensive. Taxi drivers will often pick up a whole string of passengers along the way, each passenger paying the full fare for their journey – so if you're picked up by an already occupied taxi, memorize the meter reading; you'll pay from then on, including a €1.50 minimum charge.

Accommodation

Accommodation can be packed to the gills in July and August but for much of the rest of the year there is good availability.

Hostels

Hostel Aphrodite Inárdhou 12, Omónia ⓣ2108 810 589, ⓦwww.hostelaphrodite.com. Friendly and helpful hostel with clean rooms, a travel service, lively bar and free 24hr Internet access; dorms ❷; doubles ❸

Athens Backpackers Makri 12, Makriyiánni ⓣ2109 224 044, ⓦwww.backpackers.gr. Laid-back hostel with clean, spacious dorms, Internet access, free breakfast and rooftop bar with Acropolis views. ❸

Athens Youth Hostel Dhamáreos 75, Pangráti ⓣ2107 519 530, ⓦwww.athens-yhostel.com. In a congenial (if remote) neighbourhood – trolleys #2 or #11 stop nearby – with cooking and laundry facilities. ❷

International Youth Hostel Víktoros Ougó 16, Omónia ⓣ2105 232 540, ⓔinfo@aiyh-victorhugo.com. Central Athens' cheapest option, an official HI hostel with a cheerful atmosphere, well-kept facilities and helpful staff, though the location isn't wonderful; dorms ❷; doubles ❸

Student and Travellers' Inn Kydhathinéon 16, Pláka ⓣ2103 244 808, ⓦwww.studenttravellersinn.com. Popular, clean and well-run hotel-cum-hostel in a prime location. Cheerful rooms, as well as luggage storage, free Internet access and garden bar with a big screen; dorms ❷; doubles ❼

Hotels

John's Place Patróöu 5, Pláka ⓣ2103 229 719. Dark rooms with baths in the hall, but neat and well kept. Centrally located, it is in a peaceful backstreet off Mitropóleos, with a cheap restaurant on the ground floor; ❺

Marble House Cul-de-sac off Anastasíou Zínni 35, Koukáki ⓣ2109 228 294, ⓦwww.marblehouse.gr. Peaceful, welcoming pension south of the Acropolis. Most rooms en suite and with balcony; all rooms have fans and fridge. Closed in Jan and Feb. ❺

Orion Emm. Benáki 105, corner Anexartisías, Exárhia ⓣ2103 302 387, ⓔorion-dryades@mail.com. Quiet, well-run budget hotel across from the Lófos Stréfi park – a steep final walk to get there, yet close to many attractions. Rooftop kitchen and common area with an amazing view. ❺

Phaedra Adhriánou & Herefóndos 16, Pláka ⓣ2103 238 461, ⓔinfo@hotelphaedra.com. Cheerful and clean rooms with a/c, just over half en suite. Excellent location on a pedestrian street overlooking a Byzantine church and the Acropolis. ❻

Campsites

Nea Kifissia Potamoú 60, Néa Kifissiá ⓣ2106 205 646, ⓔcamping@hol.gr. In a leafy suburb, this year-round place has its own swimming pool. Metro to Kifissiá then bus #522 or #523 behind the station. ❷

Várkiza Camping Km27 on the Athens–Sounion road ⓣ2108 973 615. Large year-round site by the beach, 20km south of the centre. Bus A3 from Amalías Avenue to Glyfáda, then #115 to Várkiza. ❷

Eating

Despite the touts and tourist hype, Pláka provides a pleasant evening's setting for a meal, but for good-value, good-quality fare, outlying neighbourhoods such as Psyrrí, Omónia and Exárhia are better bets. Quintessentially Greek **ouzerí** and **mezedhopolía** serve filling *mezédhes* (the Greek version of tapas) along with drinks, adding up to a substantial meal. Note that Athens sells some of Europe's most expensive coffee at €3 for an espresso even at an ordinary café: developing a taste for Greek coffee (*ellinikós*) will prove slightly cheaper.

Cafés and ouzerí

Evvia Yeoryíou Olymbíou 8, Koukáki. Fresh dips and seafood titbits, plus good bulk wine or *oúzo*; sidewalk seating on this pedestrian street. Daily except Aug.

Kafenio Dhioskouri Dhioskoúron 13, Pláka ⓣ2103 253 333. Popular, shady bar/café with an unbeatable view of the ancient agora, where cold drinks and coffees take precedence over slightly pricey snacks. *Mezédhes* €5–9.

To Athinaïkon Themistokléous 2, cnr Panepistimíou, Omónia ⓣ2103 838 485. Long-established sophisticated *ouzerí* with marble tables and old posters, popular with local workers at lunch; strong on fresh seafood. Closed Sun.

Restaurants

Amvrosia Dhrákou 3-5, right by Syngroú-Fix metro, Veïkoú ⓣ2109 220 281. The best grill on this pedestrian street, always packed. Good takeaway *ghýros* (Greek kebabs), or enjoy a whole roast chicken at outdoor tables. Kebabs €6–9.

Barba Yannis Emmanouíl Benáki 94, Exárhia ⓣ2103 824 138. Vast menu of inexpensive oven-cooked food, served indoors and out. The restaurant's interior has an old-fashioned charm. Food is best at lunch, but it's open until 1am Mon–Fri, 6pm Sat. Mains €5–8.

Iy Taverna tou Psyrri Eskhýlou 12, Psyrrí ⓣ2103 214 923. Straightforward taverna that excels in grilled/fried seafood, vegetable starters and wine from basement barrels. Arrive early (supper only) or wait for a table. Mains €5–8.

O Thanasis Mitropóleos 69, Monastiráki ⓣ2103 244 705. Reckoned the best *souvláki* and Middle Eastern kebab in this district. Always packed with locals at lunchtime, but worth the wait. Take out or eat in. Kebabs €8.

Rozalia Valtetsíou 58, Exárhia ⓣ2103 302 933. The best all-round *mezédhes*-and-grills taverna with an extensive menu. There's a garden open in summer. *Mezédhes* €4.

Taverna Neon Grill Dorou 5, Omónia ⓣ2105 200 577. The blue skies and birds painted onto the ceiling set the tone for this relaxed restaurant. It is airy and spacious, serving all the Greek favourites. Souvláki €6.

Drinking and nightlife

Many **bars** are open as cafés during the day, serving snacks and coffees, but transform themselves in the evenings, often with live music. The bars in Exárhia are popular with local students and are relaxed and more affordable, whilst those in Kolonáki are cool and hip, although more expensive. All **clubs** charge admission fees, sometimes as much as €15–20, although this usually includes a free drink. Clubs do not start filling up until after midnight but stay open until dawn. In summer much of Athens' nightlife moves to larger outdoor venues on the southern coast, easily accessible by tram which operates round the clock at weekends.

Bars

Art Cafe Themistokléous & Dervenion 60, Exárhia ⓣ2103 300 837. A small and intimate bar serving everything from *Mythos* (Greek beer) and traditional oúzo to fruity cocktails. Sit at the cosy downstairs bar or at outdoor tables. Open until 2am. Oúzo €3; cocktails €7.

Brettos Kydathinéon 41, Pláka ⓣ2103 232 110. With colourful bottles and wooden barrels lining the walls, this is a sophisticated spot which oozes reminders of its hundred-year history. Open until 3am. Oúzo €3; cocktails €7.

Mike's Irish Bar Sinópis 6, Ambelókipi ⓣ2107 776 797. A lively watering hole which has something to suit everyone, including karaoke, live music, and big screens for sporting matches. Guinness drinkers will be especially well catered for. Open from 8pm.

Wunderbar Themistokléous 80, Exárhia ⓣ2103 818 577. Handy Exárhia meeting place that's open all day – first café, then bar, and finally club with electro and techno-pop sounds.

Clubs

Blaze-T Aristofánous 30, Psyrrí ⓣ2103 234 823. Freestyle disco, long-established by Psyrrí standards, with sounds ranging from hip-hop to techno.

Lava Bore Filellínon 25, Pláka. Athens' most central option, which is also one of the cheapest. Admission is €7 which includes a free shot. Open 10pm–5am.

Venue Km30 on the Athens–Sounion road, Várkiza ⓣ2108 970 333. Lush setting and eclectic

TREAT YOURSELF

The Athens Festival (☎2109 282 900, ⓦwww.greekfestival.gr) from late May to late Sept encompasses classical Greek theatre, contemporary dance, classical music, big-name jazz, traditional Greek music and a smattering of rock shows. Most performances take place at the Herodes Atticus Theatre, which is memorable in itself on a warm summer's evening. There are also special bus excursions to the great ancient theatre at Epidaurus. Tickets from €15. The main festival box office is at Hatzikhrístou 23.

selection of dance music, including some Greek, attracts a young crowd.

Entertainment

For up-to-the-minute **listings**, get yourself a copy of the English-language weekly *Athens News* (ⓦwww.athensnews.gr), which has details for clubs, galleries, concerts and films.

Cine Paris Kydhathinéon 22, Pláka ☎2103 220 721. Spend an evening under the stars and watch a film at one of the city's outdoor cinemas. The centrally located Cine Paris has evening performances for €7, accompanied by views of the Acropolis.

Dora Stratou Dance Theatre Filopáppou Hill ☎2103 244 395, ⓦwww.grdance.org. May–Sept: Tues–Sat 9.30pm, Sun 8.15pm. Dancers, singers and folk musicians unite to give spectators an insight into continuing local Greek traditions. Classes are also available.

Shopping

Books and maps Compendium (Níkis 28 off Sýndagma) has books on Greece, travel guides (including Rough Guides), magazines and a secondhand section. Eleftheroudhakis (Panepistimíou 17 plus other branches) has the largest foreign-language stock in town, plus maps.

Clothes If you're looking for high-street shopping, then you'll find a wide variety of shops and stores along Ermoú, much of which is pedestrianized.

Markets The Monastiráki flea market is open daily and has an interesting selection of weird and wonderful goods for sale. Sunday is the best time for a visit, however, as the market expands into the surrounding streets. The nearby bustling Central Market sells local foods.

Souvenirs Tourists head to Pláka where souvenir shops follow one after the other, and where leather goods, such as sandals and bags, and jewellery take precedence. For gifts check out **Lesvos Shop**, Athinás 33, for its reasonably priced oúzo, wines, olive oil, baklava, and honey as well as toiletries such as olive-oil soap.

Directory

Embassies and consulates Australia, Dhimitríou Soútsou 37 ☎2108 704 000; Canada, Ioánni Yennadhíou 4 ☎2107 273 400; Ireland, Vassiléos Konstandínou 7 ☎2107 232 771; New Zealand, Kifissiás 268 ☎2106 874 700; UK, Ploutárhou 1, Kolonáki ☎2107 272 600; US, Vassilísis Sofías 91 ☎2107 212 951.

Hospitals Evangelismós, with its own metro stop, is the most central, but KAT, way out in Maroússi, is the designated Greater Athens emergency ward.

Internet Easy Internet Café, main branch over *Everest* at Pl. Syndágmatos; Museum Internet Café, Patissíon 46; Sofokleous.com Internet Café, Stadhíou 5.

Laundry Angélou Yerónda 10, off Platía Filomoússou Eterías, Pláka.

Left luggage Many hotels store luggage for free. If not, try Pacific Ltd, Níkis 26, Syndágma ☎2103 241 007.

Pharmacies These are numerous, but unlike other shops open only Mon–Fri 8am–2pm. Outside these hours, check any pharmacy window for the nearest duty pharmacy.

Post offices Main branch Eólou 100, just off Omónia; more convenient one on Mitropóleos, corner Sýndagma.

Moving on

Train Corinth (18 daily; 1hr 20min); Kalamáta (4 daily; 7–8hr); Pátra (9 daily; 3hr 20min–4hr); Pýrgos (5 daily; 5–6hr); Thessaloníki (11 daily; 4hr 15min–8hr); Vólos (1 daily; 4hr 30min).

Bus Corfu (4 daily; 11hr); Corinth (hourly; 1hr 30min); Delphi (6 daily; 3hr); Ioánnina (9 daily; 7hr 30min); Kalamáta (13 daily; 4hr 30min); Kefalloniá (3 daily; 7hr); Kými, for Skýros ferries (2 daily; 3hr 30min); Mycenae-Fíkhti (hourly; 2hr); Náfplio (hourly; 2hr 50min); Pátra (every 30min; 3hr); Pýrgos (15 daily; 6hr); Rafína (every 30min; 1hr 30min); Sounion (hourly; 2hr); Spárti (10 daily; 3hr 30min); Thessaloníki (6 daily; 7hr 30min); Tríkala (8 daily; 4hr 30min); Vólos (12 daily; 5hr 20min); Zákynthos (5 daily; 6hr).

Ferry (from Pireás) to: Crete (5–7 daily; 12hr); Híos (1–2 daily; 6–9hr); Íos (2–3 daily; 3hr 30min–10hr); Kós (1–2 daily; 7–12hr); Lésvos (2 daily; 8hr 30min–12hr); Mýkonos (3 daily; 3hr 30min–5hr 30min); Náxos (3–4 daily; 4–8hr); Páros (3–4 daily; 3hr 30min–7hr); Pátmos (daily; 11hr); Rhodes (10 weekly; 11–23hr); Sámos (4–5 daily; 7hr 30min–14hr); Santoríni (3–5 daily; 4–8hr); Sífnos (4–5 daily; 2–7hr); Sýros (3 daily; 2–4hr).

DAY-TRIPS FROM ATHENS

The 70km of shoreline south of Athens has good but highly developed beaches. At weekends the sands fill fast, as do innumerable bars, restaurants and clubs. But for most visitors, this coast's attraction is at the end of the road. **Cape Sounion** is among the most imposing spots in Greece, and on it stands the fifth-century BC Temple of Poseidon (daily 9.30am–sunset; €4, students free), built in the time of Pericles as part of a sanctuary to the sea god. In summer you've faint hope of solitude unless you arrive before the tours do, but the temple is as evocative a ruin as Greece can offer. Doric in style, it preserves sixteen of its thirty-four columns, and the view is stunning. Below the promontory lie several coves, the most sheltered of which is a five-minute walk east from the car park and site entrance. The main Sounion **beach** is more crowded, but has a group of tavernas at the far end, which – considering the location – are reasonably priced. There's a single **campsite** about 5km short of the cape, the *Bacchus* (Ⓣ2292 039 572; Ⓦwww.tggr.com/camping-bacchus; ❷). Buses to Sounion leave every hour from the KTEL terminal on Mavromatéon at the southwest corner of the Pédhion Áreos park in central Athens. They alternate between coastal and inland services, the latter slightly longer and more expensive (the coastal route takes around 2hr).

The Peloponnese

The appeal of the **Peloponnese** is hard to overstate. This southern peninsula seems to have the best of almost everything Greek. Its **beaches** are among the finest and least developed in the country. Its ancient sites include the Homeric palace of Agamemnon at **Mycenae**, the Greek theatre at **Epidaurus** and the sanctuary of **Olympia**, host to the Olympic Games for a millennium. Medieval remains run from the fabulous castle at **Acrocorinth** and the strange tower-houses and frescoed churches of the **Máni**, to the extraordinary Byzantine towns of **Mystra** and **Monemvasiá**. The Peloponnese also boasts Greece's most spectacular train route, an hour-long journey on the **rack-and-pinion rail line** from Dhiakoftó to Kalávryta that follows the Vouraikós River through a narrow and vertiginous gorge.

PÁTRA

The city of **PÁTRA** is one of the largest in the country, and connects the mainland to Italy and the Ionian Islands. Unlike many other destinations in the Peloponnese, Pátra is a thriving working city and has a life of its own which extends far beyond tourism, despite the number of travellers passing through. In 2006 the city was named the European Capital of Culture, and unsurprisingly there are enough sites and museums to

GETTING TO THE PELOPONNESE

The usual approach from Athens is on the frequent buses and trains that run via modern **Kórinthos** (Corinth). From Italy and the Adriatic, **PÁTRA** is the main port of the Peloponnese, although some ferries from the Ionian Islands arrive at Kyllíni.

fill a day's sightseeing. However the city is best enjoyed in the evening, when thousands of party-going university students transform the streets. At the heart of the drinking scene is Agíou Nikoláou, a pedestrian street which is crammed with popular bars.

Arrival and information

Train The train station is located by the port on Óthonos Amalías.
Bus Buses arrive at the KTEL Achaia bus station 200m north of the train station.
Ferry Ferries from all departure points arrive at the port close to the bus and train stations.
Tourist office Óthonos Amalías 6 (daily 8am–10pm; ⓣ2610 461 740, ⓦwww.infocenterpatras.gr). A friendly and well-stocked information centre, which also has free bikes for hire.
Tourist police Pátra's tourist police (ⓣ2610 452 512) is at the Italian ferry terminal.

Accommodation

Pension Nicos Patréos 3 and Agíou Andhréou 121 ⓣ2610 623 757. Rooms (some en suite) are a little small but this hotel is convenient for the port, train and bus stations and there's a rooftop bar. ❸
Youth Hostel Iróön Polytekhníou 62 ⓣ2610 427 278. Crumbling and shabby hostel located 1.5km north of the centre. However it does have the cheapest beds in town. ❶

Moving on

Train Athens (10 daily; 3hr 30min–4hr); Corinth (7 daily; 2hr–2hr 30min); Kalamáta (5 daily; 4–5hr); Pýrgos (8 daily; 1hr 40min–2hr).
Bus Ámfissa (4 daily; 3hr); Athens (33 daily; 3hr); Ioánnina (2 daily; 4hr 30min); Kalamáta (2 daily; 4hr); Pýrgos (7 daily; 2hr).
Ferry Corfu (1 daily; 7hr); Igoumenítsa (1 daily; 8–10hr); Itháki (2 daily; 3–4hr); Kefalloniá (3 daily; 2hr 30min–3hr).

ANCIENT CORINTH

Whoever possessed **CORINTH** – the ancient city that displaced Athens as capital of the Greek province in Roman times – controlled both the trade between northern Greece and the Peloponnese, and the short-cut between the Ionian and Aegean seas. It's unsurprising, therefore, that the city's history is a catalogue of invasions and power struggles, until it was razed by the Romans in 146 BC. The site lay in ruins for a century before being rebuilt, on a majestic scale, by Julius Caesar in 44 BC. Nowadays, the remains of the city occupy a rambling site below the acropolis hill of Acrocorinth, itself littered with medieval ruins. To explore both you need a full day, or better still, to stay close by. The modern village of **ARHÉA KÓRINTHOS** spreads around the main archeological zone, where you'll find plenty of places to eat and sleep, including a scattering of **rooms** to rent in the backstreets.

What to see and do

The main excavated site (daily 8am–5/7.30pm; €6) is dominated by the remains of the Roman city. You enter from the south side, which leads straight into the **Roman agora**. The real focus, however, is a survival from the classical Greek era: the fifth-century BC **Temple of Apollo**, whose seven austere Doric columns stand slightly above the level of the forum. Towering 575m above the lower town, **Acrocorinth** (summer: daily 8.30am–7pm; winter: Tues–Sun 8.30am–3pm; free) is an amazing mass of rock still largely encircled by 2km of wall. During the Middle Ages this ancient acropolis of Corinth became one of Greece's most powerful fortresses. It's a 4km climb up (about 1hr), but well worth it. Amid the sixty-acre site, you wander through a jumble of semi-ruined chapels, mosques, houses and battlements, erected in turn by Greeks, Romans, Byzantines, Franks, Venetians and Ottomans.

Arrival

Bus and train Frequent bus and train services run from Athens and Pátra to modern Kórinthos, from where you can catch a local bus from KTEL

Kórinthos or the main square to Arhéa Kórinthos and the adjacent site (hourly; 20min; €1.20).

Accommodation

Shadow Rooms Arhéa Kórinthos ⓣ2741 031 481. Located along the Kórinthos road heading out of the village, these en-suite rooms open out onto a veranda with beautiful views across the village. Prices include breakfast. ❺

Tasos Rooms ⓣ2741 031 225. A good choice, these are clean rooms with a/c and shared bathrooms. There's a popular restaurant downstairs, too, run by the owners. ❸

Moving on

Train Athens (hourly; 1hr 20min); Dhiakoftó (9 daily; 1hr 15min–1hr 30min); Kalamáta (4 daily; 6hr–7hr 30min); Pátra (9 daily; 2hr–2hr 30min).

Bus (KTEL bus station) Ancient Corinth (hourly; 20min); Árgos (hourly; 1hr); Kalamáta (7 daily; 3–4hr); Mycenae-Fíkhti (hourly; 30min); Náfplio (hourly; 1hr 20min); Spárti (8 daily; 3–4hr).

MYKÍNES (MYCENAE)

Southwest of Corinth, the ancient site of **MYCENAE** is tucked into a fold of the hills just 2km northeast of the modern village of **Mykínes**. Agamemnon's citadel, "well-built Mycenae, rich in gold", as Homer wrote, was uncovered in 1874 by the German archeologist Heinrich Schliemann, who was convinced of a factual basis to Homer's epics. Brilliantly crafted gold and sophisticated architecture bore out the accuracy of Homer's epithets. The buildings unearthed by Schliemann show signs of having been occupied from around 1950 BC until 1100 BC, when the town, though still prosperous, was abandoned. No coherent explanation has been found for this event, but war between rival kingdoms was probably a major factor.

What to see and do

You enter the **Citadel of Mycenae** (daily 8am–3/7.30pm; €8, EU students free) through the mighty **Lion Gate**. Inside the walls to the right is **Grave Circle A**, the cemetery which Schliemann believed contained the bodies of Agamemnon and his followers, murdered on their triumphant return from Troy. In fact the burials date from about three centuries before the Trojan war, but they were certainly royal, and the finds are among the richest yet unearthed. Schliemann took the extensive **South House**, beyond the grave circle, to be the Palace of Agamemnon. But a much grander building was later discovered on the summit of the acropolis. Rebuilt in the thirteenth century BC, it is, like all Mycenaean palaces, centred on a **Great Court**. The small rooms to the north are believed to have been royal apartments and in one of them the remains of a red stuccoed bath have led to its fanciful identification as the place of Agamemnon's murder. Outside the walls of the citadel lay the main part of the town and extensive remains of **merchants' houses** have been uncovered near to the road. A few minutes' walk down the road is the astonishing **Treasury of Atreus**, a royal burial vault entered through a majestic fifteen-metre corridor.

Arrival

Orientation The village of Mykínes is one main street, where all accommodation and eateries are located. You will need to travel onward from Fíkhti or the ancient site to get there.

Train There's a train station at Fíkhti, 2km west of Mykínes.

Bus Most long-distance KTEL buses will drop you off at Fíkhti, whilst three daily buses from Náfplio stop at the site entrance.

Tours There are numerous bus tours from Athens, making this a popular day-trip destination.

Accommodation

Hotel Belle Hélène ⓣ2751 076 225. Once the home of Schliemann, these rooms are spacious and the shared bathrooms are clean. Prices include breakfast. ❹

Rooms Dassis ⓣ2751 076 123, ⓔdassisrooms@yahoo.com. Although a little shabby, the en-suite rooms are equipped with a/c, TV and balconies. There's Internet access too. Price includes breakfast. ❺

Camping Atreus ☎2751 076 221. This shady campsite comes equipped with clean facilities, a swimming pool, and a restaurant on site. Open late Feb to early Oct. ❶

Camping Mycenae ☎2751 076 121. This basic campsite is smaller with less facilities than the town's other camping option, but is open all year round. ❶

Eating

Taverna O Spiros ☎2751 076 115, ⓦwww.spiros-mikines.com. Surrounded by flowers and foliage, enjoy traditional Greek dishes at this friendly local taverna. Mains €6.

Moving on

Bus Argos (3 daily; 30min); Náfplio (3 daily; 50min).

NÁFPLIO

NÁFPLIO, a lively, beautifully sited town with a faded elegance, inherited from when it was briefly modern Greece's first capital, makes an attractive base for exploring the area or for resting up by the sea.

What to see and do

The main fort, the **Palamídhi** (daily 8am–3/7pm; €4), is most directly approached by 899 stone-hewn steps up from Polyzoïdhou Street. Within its walls are three self-contained castles, all built by the Venetians in the 1710s. To the west, the **Acronafplía** fortress occupies the ancient acropolis, whose walls were adapted by successive medieval occupants. The third fort, the photogenic **Boúrtzi**, occupies the islet offshore from the harbour and allowed the Venetians to close the shallow shipping channel with a chain. In the town itself, Platía Syndágmatos, the main square, is a great place to relax over a coffee. There's also a thriving nightlife, with a string of bars along the waterfront at Bouboulínas.

Arrival and information

Train The train station is on the waterfront, 600m north of the bus station.

Bus Buses arrive on Syngroú, just south of the interlocking squares Platía Trión Navárhon and Platía Kapodhístria.

Tourist office The unreliable EOT tourist office is at 25-Martíou 2 (daily 9am–1pm & 4–8pm; ☎2752 024 444).

Accommodation

Dimitris Bekas Rooms Efthimiopoúlou 26 ☎2752 024 594. Don't be disheartened by the stone steps leading up to this welcoming pension – the views from the roof terrace are stunning. It is located close to the centre of the old town. ❸

Hotel Economou Argonaftón 22 ☎2752 023 955. A 15min walk out of town and in need of renovation, but this hotel is one of only a few budget options. Even when full, you will be squeezed in somewhere. ❸

Pension Atheaton Aggélou Terzáki 31 & Papaníkolaou 1 ☎2752 021 557, ⓦwww.atheaton.com. A welcoming, family-run pension with tastefully decorated rooms. Room rates are negotiable, so it's worth bargaining. ❺

Eating

Old Mansion Siokóu 7 ☎2752 022 449. Bustling taverna serving up Greek favourites to the accompaniment of live traditional music (Fri–Sun). Mains €7–12.

Omorfi Tavernaki Vassilísis Ólgas 16. Greek cuisine is served at reasonable prices at this taverna, which has a cosy interior and plenty of outdoor seating. Mains €6–10.

Moving on

Bus Argos (hourly; 20min); Athens (hourly; 3hr); Epidaurus (4 daily; 45min); Mycenae (3 daily; 50min); Trípoli (4 daily; 1hr).

EPIDAURUS

From the sixth century BC to Roman times, **EPIDAURUS**, 30km east of Náfplio, was a major spa and religious centre; its **Sanctuary of Asclepius** was the most famous of all shrines dedicated to the god of healing. The magnificently preserved 14,000-seat theatre (daily 8am–5/7pm; €6, Sun free), built in the fourth century BC, merged so well into the landscape that it was rediscovered only in the nineteenth century. Constructed with mathematical precision, it has near-perfect acoustics: from the highest of the 54 tiers of seats you can hear coins dropped in the orchestra. Close by is a small **museum** (Mon noon–5/7pm, Tues–Sun 8am–5/7pm; same ticket as theatre) containing various statuary and frieze fragments. The sanctuary itself encompasses hospitals, dwellings for the priest-physicians, and hotels and amusements for the fashionable visitors. Most people take in Epidaurus as a day-trip from Náfplio, but a memorable experience is to catch an evening classical theatre **performance** (June–Aug Fri & Sat; ⓦwww.greekfestival.gr). You can sometimes camp near the car park, or **stay** in **LYGOURIÓ**, 5km north, at *Hotel Alkyon*, Asklipíou 195 (ⓣ2753 022 002; ❺). There are four campsites on the beach at Paléa Epídhavros; *Verdelis* (ⓣ2753 041 425, ⓦwww.campingverdelis.gr; ❷) is the best bet. The nearest **restaurant** to the theatre is *Oasis* on the Lygourió road, though *Leonides* in the village proper is better.

MYSTRA

A glorious, airy place, hugging a steep flank of Taïyetos, **MYSTRA** is an astonishingly complete Byzantine city that once sheltered a population of some twenty thousand. The castle on its summit was built in 1249 by Guillaume II de Villehardouin, fourth Frankish Prince of the Morea (as the Peloponnese was then known), and together with the fortresses of Monemvasiá and the Máni it guarded his territory. In 1262 the Byzantines drove out the Franks and established the Despotate of Mystra. This isolated triangle of land in the southeastern Peloponnese enjoyed considerable autonomy from Constantinople, flowering as a brilliant cultural centre in the fourteenth and early fifteenth centuries and only falling to the Ottomans in 1460, seven years after the Byzantine capital was conquered.

What to see and do

To explore the site of the **Byzantine city** (daily 8am–3/7.30pm; €5), it makes sense to take the bus from Spárti (see below) to the top entrance, then explore a leisurely downhill route. Following this course, the first identifiable building that you come to is the fourteenth-century church of **Ayía Sofía**. The **Kástro**, reached by a path that climbs directly from the upper gate, maintains the Frankish design of its thirteenth-century construction, though modified by successive occupants. Heading down from Ayía Sofía, there are two possible routes. The right fork winds past the ruins of a Byzantine mansion, while the left fork passes the massively fortified **Náfplio Gate** and the vast, multi-storeyed complex of the **Despots' Palace**. At the **Monemvasiá Gate**, linking the upper and lower towns, turn right for the **Pandánassa convent**, which is perhaps the finest that survives in the town. Further down on this side of the lower town make sure you see the diminutive **Perívleptos monastery**, whose single-domed church, partly carved out of the rock, contains Mystra's most complete cycle of frescoes. The **Mitrópolis**, or cathedral, immediately beyond the gateway, ranks as the oldest of Mystra's churches, built from 1270 onward.

Arrival

Bus Ten daily buses ply the route from Spárti to Néos Mystrás (€1.20), and then continue up the hill to the site.

SPÁRTI

SPÁRTI (ancient Sparta, though there's little left to see) is a good alternative base to Mystra, with cheaper accommodation. Spárti has everything you would expect from a town of its size, including vibrant bars and cafés. If you want to see Mystra without sacrificing an evening's worth of entertainment, then make it a day trip from Spárti.

Arrival

Bus The KTEL bus station is at the far eastern end of Lykoúrgou, a 10min walk from the centre. Buses for Mystra leave from here.
Internet Ladas Lykoúrgou 130 ⓣ2731 083 016, ⓦwww.cafe-ladas.gr. Price per hour is €2.

Accommodation

Apollon Thermopýlon 84 ⓣ2731 022 491. This friendly hotel has plenty of clean and comfortable en-suite rooms. ❹
Castle View Néos Mystrás ⓣ2731 083 303, ⓦwww.castleview.gr. Shady and quiet, this campsite is within walking distance of the village. Buses to Néos Mystrás stop at the entrance. Open early April to late Oct. ❷
Hotel Cecil Paleológou 125 ⓣ2731 024 980. A warm welcome awaits at this small hotel, with clean en-suite rooms equipped with a/c and TV. ❺
Paleologio Mystras 2.5km from Spárti ⓣ2731 022 724. Well-run campsite with good facilities. Buses to Néos Mystrás stop at the entrance. Open all year. ❶

Eating and drinking

Diethenes Paleológou 105 ⓣ2731 028 636. The garden is an oasis of calm, especially atmospheric in the evenings. Hearty Greek favourites are dished up to the sound of birdsong. Mains €6.
Event Café Kleomvrótou ⓣ2731 081 115. The red and black decor makes a statement at this popular bar, serving coffees by day and cocktails by night. Open until late. Oúzo €2.70; cocktails €6.50.

Moving on

Bus Areópoli (2 daily; 2hr); Athens (10 daily; 3hr); Corinth (10 daily; 1hr 30min); Kalamáta (2 daily; 1hr 30min); Monemvasiá (3 daily; 2hr 30min); Yíthio (5 daily; 50min).

MONEMVASIÁ

Set impregnably on a great eruption of rock connected to the mainland by a causeway, the Byzantine seaport of **MONEMVASIÁ** is a place of grand, haunted atmosphere. At the start of the thirteenth century it was the Byzantines' sole possession in the Morea, eventually being taken by the Franks in 1249 after three years of siege. Regained by the Byzantines as part of the ransom for the captured Guillaume de Villehardouin, it served as the chief commercial port of the Despotate of the Morea. At its peak in the Byzantine era, Monemvasiá had a population of almost sixty thousand.

What to see and do

A causeway connects mainland **Yéfira** to Monemvasiá. The twenty-minute walk provides some wonderful views, but there is also a free shuttle bus in season. The **Lower Town** once sheltered forty churches and over 800 homes, though today a single main street harbours most of the restored houses, plus cafés, tavernas and a scattering of shops. The foremost monument is the **Mitrópolis**, the cathedral built by Emperor Andronikos II Komnenos in 1293, and the largest medieval church in southern Greece. Across the square, the tenth-century domed church of **Áyios Pétros** was transformed by the Ottomans into a mosque and is now a small **museum** of local finds (Mon noon–7.30pm, Tues–Sun 8am–7.30pm; admission free). Towards the sea is a third church, the **Khrysafítissa**, with its bell hanging from an old acacia tree in the courtyard. The climb to the **Upper Town** is highly worthwhile, not least for the solitude. Its fortifications, like those of the lower town, are substantially intact; within, the site is a ruin, though infinitely larger than you could imagine from below.

Arrival and information

Bus Buses arrive in the village of Yéfira on the mainland, where most accommodation is located. The bus stop is outside Malvasia Travel.

TREAT YOURSELF

Malvasia Monemvasiá ⓣ2732 061 323, ⓔmalvazia@otenet.gr. If Monemvasiá has cast its enchanting spell over you, then splash out to stay on the rock itself. Malvasia is a peaceful hotel full of character and charm, and retains many traditional features. The views are breathtaking. ❼

Information There is no official tourist information office, but Malvasia Travel is helpful. It also sells bus tickets.

Accommodation

Akrogiali Yéfira ⓣ2732 061 360. The best budget option: nine spotless rooms in the centre of the town. ❺

Camping Paradise 3.5km south of Yéfira ⓣ2732 061 123, ⓦwww.camping-monemvasia.gr. The nearest campsite is near a decent beach, and has plenty of facilities including Internet access. Open late March to late Nov. ❶

Eating

Matoula Monemvasiá ⓣ2732 061 660. This restaurant has plenty of fresh fish on offer, and a shady terrace on which to enjoy the food and the views. Mains €8–12.

To Kanoni Monemvasiá ⓣ2732 061 169. A small and friendly place with split-level seating, offering a variety of vistas. Also open for breakfast. Mains €7–10.

Moving on

Bus Athens (3 daily; 6hr); Corinth (3 daily; 4hr 30min); Spárti (2hr 30min); Trípoli (3hr 30min).

YÍTHIO

YÍTHIO, Sparta's ancient port, is the gateway to the dramatic Máni peninsula and one of the south's most attractive seaside towns. Its somewhat low-key harbour, with occasional ferries, has a graceful nineteenth-century waterside, while out to sea, tethered by a long narrow causeway, is the islet of **Marathoníssi** (ancient Kranae), where Paris and Helen of Troy spent their first night after her abduction from Sparta.

Arrival

Bus Buses from Athens and Spárti drop you close to the centre of town, at the bus station which is located on Vassiléos Pávlou.

Accommodation

Rooms Matina Vassiléos Pávlou 19 ⓣ2733 022 518. Little English is spoken but a warm welcome awaits. Rooms are spacious and airy, and there's a small terrace too. ❹

Meltemi On the Yíthio–Areópoli road ⓣ2733 022 833, ⓦwww.campingmeltemi.gr. A recently redecorated campsite with good facilities. Also hires out bungalows. Open early April to late Oct. ❶

Saga Pension Tzanetáki ⓣ2733 023 220, ⓦwww.sagapension.gr. Spacious and comfortable rooms, most with balconies towards the sea. There's also a popular restaurant downstairs. ❺

Eating

En Plo Vassiléos Pávlou 27 ⓣ2733 021 444. Tiled floors, wooden beams and stone walls decorate the interior, or there's outdoor seating right on the waterfront. Open all day. Mains €5–7.

To Korali Plateia Yíthio ⓣ2733 023 452. This is the place to do as the locals do – order some oúzo and watch the world go by from its position in the corner of the square.

Moving on

Bus to: Areópoli (4 daily; 30min); Athens (6 daily; 4hr 15min); Corinth (6 daily; 2hr 45min); Spárti (6 daily; 50min); Trípoli (6 daily; 1hr 45min).

THE MÁNI PENINSULA

The southernmost peninsula of Greece, the **Máni peninsula**, stretches from Yíthio in the east and Kalamáta in the west down to Cape Ténaro, mythical entrance to the underworld. It's a wild and arid landscape with an idiosyncratic culture and history: nowhere in Greece seems so close to its medieval past. There are numerous opportunities for a variety of outdoor activities. The quickest way into it is to take a bus from Yíthio to **AREÓPOLI**, gateway to the so-called Inner Máni. For onward travel to Outer Máni, a change at Ítylo is involved.

Arrival

Bus Buses from Yíthio drop you in the centre of town, alongside the main square. The bus station is close by behind the small church – look for the KTEL sign outside.

Accommodation

Hotel Kouris Main Square ☎2733 051 340. All rooms are en suite and have balconies, and it's the cheapest option in town. ❸

Pyrgos Tsimova Behind the Church of Taxiárhes ☎2733 051 301. A renovated tower-house in the old lower town, full of character and charm. ❺

Moving on

Bus Ítylo (4 daily; 20min); Yíthio (4 daily; 30min).

Outer Máni

More attractions lie to the north of Areópoli, along the eighty-kilometre road to Kalamáta, which has views as dramatic and beautiful as any in Greece. There are numerous cobbled paths for hiking and a series of **small beaches**, beginning at **ÁYIOS NIKÓLAOS**, which has fish tavernas and rooms, and extending more or less through to Kardhamýli. **STOÚPA**, which has possibly the best sands, is now geared very much to British tourism, with several small hotels, two **campsites**, supermarkets and tavernas. **KARDHAMÝLI**, 8km north, remains a beautiful place despite its commercialization and busy road, with a long pebble beach and a restored tower-house quarter.

Arrival

Bus Buses stop in Kardhamýli next to the main square. There is no bus station, but the travel agent has bus timetables and other information.

Accommodation

Iphigenia Rooms Kardhamýli ☎2721 073 648. A wonderful base for exploring the area. Rooms have small kitchenettes and balconies. A warm familial welcome awaits. ❹

Lela's Kardhamýli ☎2721 073 541, or ☎6977 71 6017 in winter. Tucked away (look for signs from the main road), these rooms occupy prime position beside the sea. There's also a good taverna (see below). ❺

Eating and drinking

Aman Café Kardhamýli ☎2721 073 266. Next to Lela's, this lively bar is the perfect place to watch the sunset from the leafy terrace. Open all day. Cocktails €7.50.

Lela's Kardhamýli ☎2721 073 541. With an ever-changing menu, *Lela's* is ideal for a delicious, home-cooked meal. Go early to grab a table with the best views. Mains €8.

Moving on

Bus Kalamáta (3 daily; 1hr).

OLYMPIA

The historic resonance of **OLYMPIA**, which for over a millennium hosted the Panhellenic Games, is rivalled only by Delphi or Mycenae. Its site, too, ranks with this company, for although the ruins are confusing, the setting is as perfect as could be imagined: a luxuriant valley of wild olive and plane trees beside the twin rivers of Alfiós and Kladhéos, overlooked by the pine-covered hill of Krónos. The contests at Olympia probably began around the eleventh century BC, slowly developing over the next two centuries from a local festival to a major quadrennial celebration attended by states from throughout the Greek world. The games eventually fell victim to the Christian Emperor Theodosius's crackdown on pagan festivities in 391–2 AD, and his successor ordered the destruction of the temples, a process completed by invasion, earthquakes and, finally, by the River Alfiós changing its course to cover the sanctuary site. There it remained, covered by seven metres of silt and sand, until the 1870s.

What to see and do

The entrance to the **ancient site** (daily 8am–3/7.30pm; €6, or €9 with museum) leads along the west side of the sacred precinct wall, past a group of public and official buildings. Here the fifth-century BC sculptor Pheidias was responsible for creating the great gold and ivory cult statue in the focus of the precinct, the great Doric **Temple of Zeus.** The smaller **Temple of Hera**, behind, was the first built here; prior to its completion in the seventh century BC, the sanctuary had only open-air altars. Rebuilt in the Doric style in the sixth century BC, it's the most complete structure on the site. However, it's the 200-metre track of the **Stadium** itself that makes sense of Olympia: the start and finish lines are still there, as are the judges' thrones in the middle and seating banked to each side, which once accommodated up to thirty thousand spectators. Finally, in the **archeological museum** (Mon 11am/12.30pm–5/7.30pm, Tues–Sun 8am–5/7.30pm; €6, or €9 with site), the centrepiece is the statuary from the Temple of Zeus, displayed in the vast main hall. Most famous of the individual sculptures is the **Hermes of Praxiteles**, dating from the fourth century BC; one of the best-preserved of all classical sculptures, it retains traces of its original paint.

Arrival and information

Train and bus Most people arrive at Olympia via Pýrgos, which has frequent buses and trains to the site. The train station is close to the town's centre. The bus stop is at one end of Praxitéles Kondhýli.
Tourist office On Praxitéles Kondhýli (daily 8am–3pm; ⓣ2624 023 100), with useful travel information displayed in the window.

Accommodation

Camping Diana ⓣ2624 022 314. The closest campsite, 1km from the site, has a pool and good facilities. Open early March to late Dec. ❷
Hotel Hermes Praxitéles Kondhýli ⓣ2624 022 577. The rooms are faded and dated, and the plumbing and electrical sockets are to be treated with caution, but it's the cheapest hotel in town. ❸
Youth Hostel Praxitéles Kondhýli 18 ⓣ2624 022 580. This dingy hostel is in the centre of town but this is its only selling point. There's hot water only in the mornings and evenings, and an 11pm curfew. ❶

Eating

Symposio Karamanli ⓣ2624 023 620. This taverna is located away from the neon lights of those on the main drag, and this is reflected in the prices. Good food, welcoming atmosphere. Grills €6–8.

Moving on

Bus Pýrgos (hourly; 45min); Trípoli (3 daily; 3hr 30min).

Central and northern Greece

Central and northern Greece has an indeterminate character, encompassing both ancient and modern, from the mythical home of the gods on **Mount Olympus** to the urban splendour of **Thessaloníki**, and a plethora of landscapes. The highlights lie at the fringes: **Delphi** and **Ósios Loukás** above all, and further northwest at the otherworldly rock-monasteries of **Metéora**. Access to these monasteries is through **Kalambáka**, beyond which the **Katára pass** over the Píndhos Mountains provides a stunning backdrop. En route lies **Métsovo**, perhaps the easiest location for a taste of mountain life, though blatantly commercialized. Nearby **Ioánnina**, once the stronghold of the notorious Ali Pasha, retains some character, and serves as the main transport hub for trips into the relatively unspoilt villages of **Zagóri**, around the **Víkos gorge**.

ONWARD TRAVEL

IGOUMENÍTSA is Greece's third passenger port after Pireás and Pátra, with almost hourly ferries to Corfu; several daily to and from Italy make it a likely arrival point. The tourist office is next to the customs house on the old quay (daily 8am–2pm; ⓣ2665 022 227), whilst the bus station, with connections to Athens, Thessaloníki and Pátra sits two blocks back from here in the town centre, on Kyprou. There are frequent bus and train services from Thessaloníki on to Bulgaria, Romania or Turkey, though you should get any necessary visas in Athens.

DELPHI

Access to the extraordinary site of **DELPHI**, 150km northwest of Athens, is simple: six buses arrive from the capital daily, passing through **Livádhia**, the nearest rail terminus, on their way. With its position on a high terrace overlooking a great gorge, in turn dwarfed by the ominous crags of Parnassós, it's easy to see why the ancients believed Delphi to be the centre of the Earth. But what confirmed this status was the discovery of a chasm that exuded strange vapours and reduced all comers to frenzied, incoherent and obviously prophetic mutterings. For over a thousand years a steady stream of pilgrims toiled their way up the dangerous mountain paths to seek divine direction, until the oracle eventually expired with the demise of paganism in the fourth century AD.

What to see and do

You enter the **Sacred Precinct of Apollo** (daily 7.30am–3/7.30pm; €6, or €9 with museum) by way of a small agora, enclosed by ruins of Roman porticoes and shops for the sale of votive offerings. The paved **Sacred Way** begins after a few stairs, zigzagging uphill between the foundations of memorials and treasuries to the **Temple of Apollo**. The theatre and stadium used for the main events of the Pythian games are on terraces above the temple. The **theatre**, built in the fourth century BC, was closely connected with Dionysos, god of drama and wine. A steep path leads up through pine groves to the stadium, which was banked with stone seats in Roman times. The **museum** (Mon noon–6.30pm, Tues–Sun 7.30am–7.15pm) contains a collection of Archaic sculpture matched only by finds on the Acropolis in Athens; the most famous exhibit is *The Charioteer*, one of the few surviving bronzes of the fifth century BC. Following the road east of the sanctuary towards Aráhova, you reach a sharp bend. To the left, the celebrated **Castalian spring** still flows from a cleft in the cliffs, where visitors to Delphi were obliged to purify themselves in its waters. Across and below the road from the spring is the **Marmaria** or Sanctuary of Athena Pronoia (same hours as main site; free), the "Guardian of the Temple". The precinct's most conspicuous building is the **Tholos**, a fourth-century BC rotunda whose purpose remains a mystery. Above the Marmaria, a **gymnasium** also dates from the fourth century BC though it was later enlarged by the Romans.

Arrival and information

Bus The small bus station is on Pávlou & Fredheríkis, at the opposite end of the town to the archeological site.

Tourist office The helpful tourist office, above the town hall on Pávlou & Fredheríkis (Mon–Fri 7.20am–2.30pm; ⓣ2265 082 900), has up-to-date transport schedules.

Accommodation

Apollon 1.5km west towards Ámfissa ⓣ2265 082 750, ⓦwww.apolloncamping.gr. A good camping option, and the closest to Delphi. Open all year. ❷

Athina Pávlou & Fredheríkis 55 ⓣ2265 082 239. Most rooms at this guesthouse face the valley for spectacular views, and all have fans. Prices include breakfast. ❸

Sibylla Pávlou & Fredheríkis 9 ⓣ 2265 082 335, ⓦ www.sibylla-hotel.gr. The recently renovated rooms are clean and comfortable, with helpful staff. Close to the site. ❸

Eating

Iy Skala On the stair-street opposite the *Sibylla* ⓣ 2265 082 442. A small taverna serving a good selection of reasonably priced set menus (€8–10).

Taverna Vakchos Apóllonos Street ⓣ 2265 083 186, ⓦ www.vakchos.com. This taverna combines a wonderful setting and mouthwatering food. The menu includes plenty of home-made dishes, including wine and baklava. Mains €6–8.

Moving on

Bus Athens (6 daily; 3hr); Pátra (2 daily; 4hr); Thessaloníki (2 daily; 5hr).

KALAMBÁKA AND METÉORA

Few places are more exciting to arrive at than **KALAMBÁKA** and the neighbouring village of Kastráki. Your eye is immediately drawn to the weird grey cylinders of rock overhead – these are the outlying monoliths of the extraordinary valley of **Metéora**. To the right you can make out the monastery of Ayíou Stefánou, firmly planted on a massive pedestal; beyond stretches a chaos of spikes, cones and stubbier, rounded cliffs. The earliest religious communities in the valley emerged during the late tenth century, when hermits made their homes in the caves that score many of the rocks. In 1336 they were joined by two monks from Mount Áthos, one of whom established the first monastery here. Today, put firmly on the map by films such as the James Bond *For Your Eyes Only*, the four most visited monasteries are essentially museums. Only two others, Ayías Triádhos and Ayíou Stefánou, continue to function with a primarily religious purpose. Each monastery levies an **admission charge** of €2 and operates a strict **dress code**: skirts for women (supplied at the monasteries), long trousers for men and covered arms for both sexes.

What to see and do

Visiting the monasteries demands a full day, which means staying two nights nearby. From Kastráki, the fourteenth-century **Ayíou Nikoláou Anápavsa** (9am–3.30pm, closed Fri) is reached first. Some 250m past the car park and stairs to Ayíou Nikoláou, a clear path leads up a ravine between assorted monoliths; soon, at a fork, you've the option of bearing left for Megálou Meteórou or right to Varlaám. **Varlaám** (9am–5pm, closed Thurs) ranks as one of the oldest and most beautiful monasteries in the valley. From the fork below Varlaám the path also takes you northwest to **Megálou Meteórou** (9am–5pm, closed Tues), the grandest of the monasteries and also the highest. Next you follow trails until you reach the signed access path for the tiny, compact convent of **Roussánou** (daily 9am–6pm). It's less than a half-hour from Roussánou to the vividly frescoed **Ayías Triádhos** (9am–6pm, closed Thurs), approached up 130 steps carved through a tunnel in the rock. **Ayíou Stefánou** (9.30am–2pm & 3.30–6pm, closed Mon), the last of the monasteries, lies a further fifteen minutes' walk east of Ayías Triádhos; bombed in World War II, it's the one to omit if you've run out of time.

Arrival

Train The train station in Kalambáka is 100m south of the bus staion.

Bus Buses arrive at the bus station in Kalambáka on Ikonomou. All long-distance buses from Thessaloníki or the south involve a change at Tríkala. To get to Kastráki you can either walk for 20min along the sign-posted road, or take one of the hourly buses (in season only) from Platía Dhimarhíou, at the fountain, two of which continue to Metéora (Mon–Fri 9am & 12.30pm, Sat & Sun 8.30am & 1pm).

Internet *All Time Café* Kastráki ⓣ 2432 023 930 (8pm–3am).

Accommodation

Plakias ⓣ2432 022 504. A homely feel accompanies these clean and crisp en-suite rooms, although the ground floor rooms sacrifice their views of Metéora. ❸

Hotel Sydney ⓣ2432 023 079, ⓕ2432 077861. One of the first hotels as you arrive in Kastráki. Rooms have balconies and a/c, and there's Internet access in the lobby. ❹

Hotel Tsikeli ⓣ2432 022 438, ⓦwww.tsikelihotel.gr. A wonderful, relaxing guesthouse, with simple rooms and stunning views. Breakfast is served in the lush garden. ❹

Vrachos ⓣ2432 022 293, ⓦwww.campingmeteora.gr. A well-equipped campsite with a large swimming pool. Also offers rock-climbing lessons and bike hire. ❷

Eating

Bakalarkaia ⓣ2432 023 170. Eat at this traditional taverna below the square and church, for cheap fried hake and house wine. Mains €5–7.

Paradhissos ⓣ2432 022 723. This taverna offers a spacious terrace with beautiful views and a variety of Greek cuisine. Mains €5–8.

Moving on

Train Athens (2 daily; 5hr).

Bus Ioánnina (3 daily; 3hr); Métsovo (3 daily; 1hr 30min); Tríkala (hourly; 30min).

MÉTSOVO

MÉTSOVO spreads just west of the Katára pass, which cuts across the dramatic Píndhos Mountains. This spectacular setting is home to a high mountain town built on two sides of a ravine and encircled by a mighty range of peaks. From below the main road, eighteenth- and nineteenth-century stone houses, with their wooden balconies and modern tile roofs, spill down the hillside to the main *platía*, where a few old men, magnificent in full traditional dress, still loiter after Sunday Mass. Métsovo boasts quite a range of **accommodation** and apart from around July 26, date of the main local **festival**, and during skiing season, you'll have little difficulty getting a room.

What to see and do

The town **museum** occupies the Arhondikó Tosítsa (tours only 9am–1.30pm & 4–6pm, closed Thurs; €3), an eighteenth-century mansion restored to former glory, with a fine collection of crafts and costumes. The **Museum of Modern Greek Art** (10–4/6.30pm, closed Tues), also known as the E. Averoff Gallery, houses a permanent exhibition of paintings and sculptures created by the greatest Greek artists of the nineteenth and twentieth centuries.

Arrival

Bus There is no bus station, but buses arrive at the central square. Buses from Thessaloníki will drop you on the main road above the village, 2km away.

Accommodation

Filoxenia ⓣ2656 041 021. Tucked away behind the *platía* with picturesque ravine views from some rooms, this is a great budget option. ❹

Hotel Flokas ⓣ2656 041 309, ⓦwww.metsovo.biz/hotelflokas. Adorned with wooden furniture and colourful fabrics, this is another cosy option. Signposted from the *platía*. ❺

Eating

To Koutouki tou Nikola Beneath the post office, ⓣ2656 041 732. A family-run restaurant offering hearty meals. Expect to be served by each family member at least once. Mains €6–8.

Moving on

Bus Ioánnina (6 daily; 1hr 30min); Kalambáka (3 daily; 1hr 30min); Tríkala (3 daily; 2hr).

IOÁNNINA

IOÁNNINA, with its peaceful lakeside setting, is best, and most often, approached from the direction of Métsovo, through more spectacular folds of the Píndhos Mountains. The fortifications of the old town, former capital of the Albanian Muslim chieftain Ali Pasha, are punctuated by towers and minarets. From this base Ali, "the Lion of Ioánnina", prised from the Ottoman Empire a fiefdom encompassing much of western Greece. Disappointingly, most of the city is modern and undistinguished; however, the fortifications of Ali's citadel, the **Kástro**, survive more or less intact. Apart from this, the most enjoyable quarter is the old **bazaar** area, outside the citadel's main gate.

On the far side of the lake from Ioánnina, the island of **Nissí** is served by water-buses (every 30min; €1.70) from the quay northwest of the Froúrio. Its village, founded during the sixteenth century, is flanked by several beautiful, diminutive monasteries, with the best thirteenth-century frescoes in **Filanthropinón**.

Arrival and information

Bus The main bus station is at Zozimádhon 4, serving most points north and west; a smaller terminal at Bizaníou 19 connects villages south and east.
Tourist office Dhodhónis 39 (Mon–Fri 7.30am–2.30pm, also open evenings and Sat am in summer), south of the centre, can provide information on the whole Epirus region.
Internet Try *The Web* at Pyrsinélla 21 ⓣ2651 026 813. Open 24hr. Price per hour €2.50.

Accommodation

Dellas Rooms Nissí ⓣ2651 081 494. If you want to stay on the island, try these basic rooms kept by the Dellas family. ❸
Filyra Andhroníkou Paleológou 18 ⓣ2651 083 560. Modern, bright studios with individual touches located in the historic Kástro. Small kitchenettes are ideal for self-catering. ❼
Limnpoula Kanari 10 ⓣ2651 025 265. The pleasant lakeshore Limnopoula campsite is 2km out of town on the Pérama/airport road. ❶

Eating

Fysa Roufa Avéroff 55 ⓣ2651 026 262. Open 24 hours a day, a real bonus, this popular restaurant serves oven dishes. Mains €5–8.
To Rembetiko Platía Georgíou 14 ⓣ2651 075 535. This friendly taverna serves traditional fare at reasonable prices, with *rembétika* music playing in the background. Mains €4–6.

Moving on

Bus Athens (9 daily; 7hr 30min); Igoumenítsa (8 daily; 2hr); Métsovo (4 daily; 1hr 30min); Pátra (2 daily; 4hr 30min); Thessaloníki (6 daily; 5hr); Tríkala (2 daily; 4hr).

THESSALONÍKI

Second city of Greece, **THESSALONÍKI** feels more Balkan-European and modern than Athens. The city's **nightlife** is buzzing, with many bars and clubs concentrated in the regenerated warehouse area of Ladhádhika around the port. During the Byzantine era, it was the second city after Constantinople, reaching a cultural "Golden Age" until the Ottoman conquest in 1430. As recently as the 1920s, the city's population was as mixed as any in the Balkans: besides the Ottoman Turks, who had been in occupation for close on five centuries, there were Slavs, Albanians and the largest European **Jewish** community of the period – eighty thousand at its peak. Today, however, there is little to detain you aside from the excellent archeological museum, and a couple of frescoed Byzantine churches full of mosaics.

What to see and do

The renovated **Archeological Museum** (Mon 1–7.30pm, Tues–Sun 8am–7.30pm; €4) is a few paces from the White Tower, the last surviving bastion of the city's medieval walls. The museum contains finds from the tombs of Philip II of Macedon and others at the ancient Macedonian capital of Aegae (Vergina). They include startling amounts of gold and silver – masks, crowns, necklaces, earrings, bracelets – all of extraordinary craftsmanship, although the exhibits are now depleted following the transfer of the star items back to a purpose-built subterranean gallery at Vergína itself (see p.557). Among the city's many **churches**,

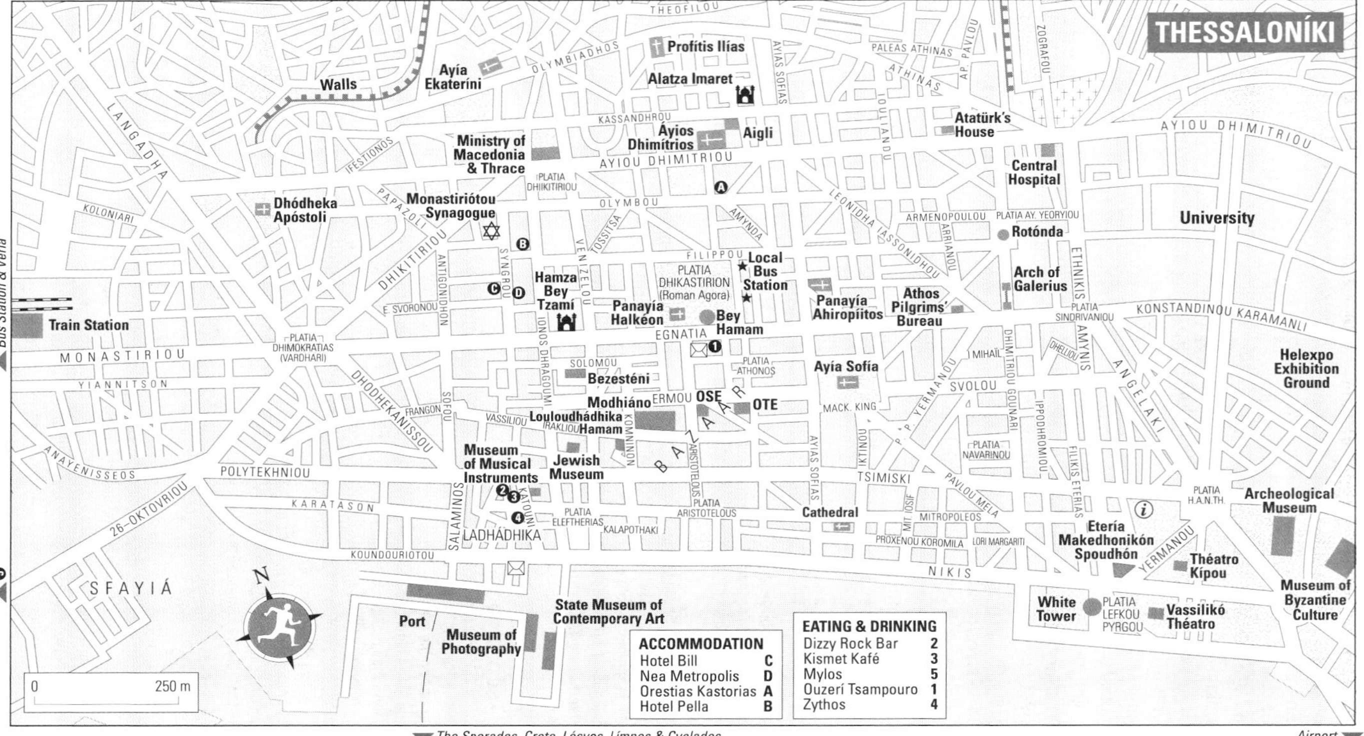
THESSALONÍKI
Walls
Ayía Ekateríni
Profítis Ilías
Alatza Imaret
Áyios Dhimítrios
Aigli
Atatürk's House
Central Hospital
University
Ministry of Macedonia & Thrace
Dhódheka Apóstoli
Monastiriótou Synagogue
Rotónda
Arch of Galerius
Local Bus Station
PLATIA DHIKASTIRION (Roman Agora)
Hamza Bey Tzami
Panayía Halkéon
Bey Hamam
Panayía Ahiropiítos
Athos Pilgrims' Bureau
Train Station
Helexpo Exhibition Ground
Ayía Sofía
Bezesténi
Modhiáno
OSE
OTE
Louloudhádhika Hamam
Museum of Musical Instruments
Jewish Museum
BAZAAR
LADHÁDHIKA
Cathedral
Archeological Museum
Eteria Makedhonikón Spoudhón
Théatro Kípou
Museum of Byzantine Culture
White Tower
PLATIA LEFKOU PYRGOU
Vassilikó Théatro
State Museum of Contemporary Art
Port
Museum of Photography
SFAYIÁ
THEOFILOU
OLYMBIADHOS
KASSANDHROU
AYIAS SOFIAS
PALEAS ATHINAS
ATHINAS
AP. PAVLOU
ZOGRAFOU
IOULIANDU
AYIOU DHIMITRIOU
LANGADHA
IFESTIONOS
PLATIA DHIIKITIRIOU
OLYMBOU
KOLONIARI
PAPAZOLI
AMYNDA
LEONIDHA IASSONIDHOU
ARMENOPOULOU
PLATIA AY. YEORYIOU
ARRIANOU
DHIKITIRIOU
ANTIGONIDHON
SYNGROU
VENIZELOU
TOSSITSA
FILIPPOU
ETHNIKIS
PLATIA SINDRIVANIOU
KONSTANDINOU KARAMANLI
E. SVORONOU
IONOS DHRAGOUMI
EGNATIA
PLATIA DHIMOKRATIAS (VARDHARI)
MONASTIRIOU
YIANNITSON
SOLOMOU
PLATIA ATHONOS
MIHAÏL
DHIMITRIOU GOUNARI
DHELIOU
AMYNIS
ANGELAKI
DHODHEKANISSOU
FRANGON
SOFOU
VASSILIOU
IRAKLIOU
ERMOU
MACK. KING
P.P. YERMANOU
SVOLOU
IPPODHROMIOU
KOMNINON
ARISTOTELOUS
AYIAS SOFIAS
IKTINOU
PLATIA NAVARINOU
FILIKIS ETERIAS
ANAYENISSEOS
POLYTEKHNIOU
TSIMISKI
PAVLOU MELA
26-OKTOVRIOU
KARATASON
SALAMINOS
KATOUNI
PLATIA ELEFTHERIAS
KALAPOTHAKI
PLATIA ARISTOTELOUS
MIT. IOSIF
MITROPOLEOS
PROXENOU KOROMILA
LORI MARGARITI
PLATIA H.A.N.TH.
YERMANOU
KOUNDOURIOTOU
NIKIS
N
0
250 m
ACCOMMODATION
Hotel Bill C
Nea Metropolis D
Orestias Kastorias A
Hotel Pella B
EATING & DRINKING
Dizzy Rock Bar 2
Kismet Kafé 3
Mylos 5
Ouzerí Tsampouro 1
Zythos 4
Bus Station & Véria
5
The Sporades, Crete, Lésvos, Límnos & Cyclades
Airport

the best three are Áyios Yeóryios, originally a Roman rotunda, decorated with superb mosaics emerging from long restoration; Áyios Dhimítrios, with more seventh-century mosaics of the patron saint in various guises; and still-later Ayía Sofía, with mosaics of the *Ascension* and the *Virgin Enthroned*.

Arrival and information

Air From the airport, 16km out at Mikrá, buses #78 (every 15–20min; 5.30am–11pm) and #78N (every 30min, 11pm–5.30am) run to the train station and KTEL terminal.
Train The train station on the west side of town is a short walk from the central grid of streets and the waterfront.
Bus Buses use a KTEL terminal 3km southwest of the centre; city buses #8 & #31 go there from Egnatía (€0.60).
Ferry The port is at the southern edge of the city, close to Ladhádhika.
Tourist office A helpful tourist office is located at Tsimiskí 136 (Mon–Sat 9am–9pm & Sun 9am–3pm; ⓣ2310 221 100).

Accommodation

Hotel Bill Syngroú 29, corner Amvrossíou ⓣ2310 537 666. Rooms (some with private bathroom) are dated and drab but are the cheapest in town. ❸
Nea Mitropolis Syngroú 22 ⓣ2310 530 363, ⓦwww.neametropolis.gr. Elegant hallways, big and bright rooms, and a central location make this hotel a pleasing option. ❺
Orestias Kastorias Agnóstou Stratiótou 14 ⓣ2310 276 517, ⓦwww.okhotel.gr. Housed in a recently renovated neoclassical building, the simple rooms have balconies with views towards the Roman Forum or Áyios Dhimítrios. ❺
Hotel Pella Íonos Dhragoúmi 63 ⓣ2310 524 221. A friendly and accommodating hotel with small but well-equipped, spotless rooms. ❺

Eating

Ouzerí Tsampouro Alley off Platía Áthonos ⓣ2310 281 435. There are plenty of *ouzerís* in this area, and this is one of the most popular. Striking black and white photos decorate the outside walls. Souvláki €5.
Zythos Platía Katoúni 5 ⓣ2310 540 284, ⓦwww.zithos.gr. A hip bar-restaurant, with dozens of well-kept foreign beers and an innovative menu. Mains €6–8.

Drinking and nightlife

Dizzy Rock Bar Egiptou 5. It may look closed from the outside, but this edgy bar keeps on rocking until the early hours.
Kismet Kafé Platía Katoúni 11 ⓣ2310 548 490. Intimate and cosy, with mellow sounds. Outside there are candlelit tables, perfect for a relaxed drink. Closed Sun.
Mylos Andhréou Yeoryíou 56 ⓣ2310 525 968. The main indoor music venue is the multidisciplinary complex *Mylos,* out in an old flour mill, where you'll find more bars, a summer cinema and exhibition galleries.

Directory

Consulates Canada, Tsimiskí 17 ⓣ2310 256 350; UK, Aristotélous 21 ⓣ2310 278 006; US, Tsimiskí 43 ⓣ2310 242 905. If you need a visa for onward Balkan travel, best get it in Athens.
Hospital Yenikó Kendrikó, Ethnikís Amýnis 41 ⓣ2310 211 211.
Internet Atlantic City, Venizelou; IQ Station, Ágiou Dhimítriou.
Laundry Bianca, Antoniádhou 3; Freskadha, Filíppou 105.
Post office Aristotélous 26; open all day Mon–Fri, Sat & Sun am.

Moving on

Train Athens (11 daily; 4–7hr); Kateríni (13 daily; 40min–1hr); Litóhoro (4 daily; 1hr); Vólos (2 daily; 3hr).
Bus Athens (6 daily; 7hr 30min); Delphi (2 daily; 6hr); Ioánnina (6 daily; 5hr); Kalambáka (6 daily; 3hr 30min); Litóchoro (hourly; 1hr 30min); Métsovo (6 daily; 3hr 30min); Tríkala (6 daily; 3hr); Véria (hourly; 1hr 15min); Vólos (8 daily; 4hr).
Ferry Híos (3 weekly; 18–20hr); Íos (1 weekly; 26hr); Iráklion (2 weekly; 30–33hr); Lésvos (4 weekly; 15hr); Mýkonos (1 weekly; 19hr 30min); Náxos (1 weekly; 24hr); Páros (1 weekly; 22hr); Santoríni (1 weekly; 28hr); Skópelos (3 weekly; 7–9hr).

VERGÍNA (ANCIENT AEGAE)

In 1977, archeologists discovered the burial sanctuary of the ancient

Macedonian dynasty which culminated in Alexander the Great at the hitherto insignificant village of **VERGÍNA**. The four **Royal Tombs** (Mon noon–3/7.30pm, Tues–Sun 8am–3/7.30pm; €8) constitute the focus of an unmissable underground museum, featuring delicate gold and silver funerary artefacts, the facades of the tombs, and the bones of the deceased in ornate ossuaries. It's easy to make this a day-trip from Thessaloníki: hourly buses ply to Véria, from where eleven onward buses per day cover the final 20 minutes to modern Vergína village.

MOUNT OLYMPUS

Highest, most magical and most dramatic of all Greek mountains, **Mount Olympus** – the mythical seat of the gods – rears straight up nearly 3000m from the shores of the Thermaïkos gulf. Dense forests cover its lower slopes and its wild flowers are gorgeous. If you're well equipped, no special expertise is necessary to reach the top between mid-June and October, though it's a long hard pull, and its weather is notoriously fickle. You'd do well to buy a proper **map** of the range in Athens or Thessaloníki (#31 Road Editions 1:50,000 is adequate).

Litóhoro and the climb

The usual approach to Mount Olympus is via **LITÓHORO** on the eastern slopes, a pleasant village with a magnificent mountain setting. The easiest way to reach the village is to travel by bus or train to Katerini, from where hourly buses make the 25-minute journey. There is a train station at Litóhoro, but it is inconveniently located. Best-value **accommodation** is the hotel *Enipeas*, with balconied rooms and a central location (☎2352 084 328; ❺). Best **eats** are at *To Pazari*, uphill on 25 Martou, or *Taverna Zeus*, at the start of the road up the mountain. There's a small tourist information office (summer only: Mon–Fri 9am–2pm & 3–9pm, Sat & Sun 10am–2pm & 5–9pm) opposite the bus stop, which can provide information on the region.

Four to five hours' walking along the well-marked, scenic E4 long-distance path up the Mavrólongos canyon brings you to **Priónia**, from where there's a sharper three-hour trail-climb to the *Spilios Agapitos* **refuge** (☎2352 081 800; €10 per person; closed mid-Oct to mid-May). It's best to stay overnight here, as you need to make an early start for the three-hour ascent to **Mýtikas**, the highest peak (2917m), as the summit frequently clouds over towards midday. The path continues behind the refuge, reaching a signposted fork above the tree line in about an hour; straight on, then right, takes you to Mýtikas via the ridge known as Kakí Skála, while the abrupt right reaches the *Yiosos Apostolidhis* **hut** in one hour (no phone; €10 per person; closed mid-Sept to mid-June). From the hut there's an enjoyable loop down to the **Gortsiá** trailhead and from there back down into the Mavrólongos canyon, via the medieval monastery of Ayíou Dhionysíou.

The Cyclades

The **Cyclades** is the most satisfying Greek archipelago for island-hopping, with its vibrant capital on **Sýros**. The majority of the islands are arid and rocky, with brilliant-white, cubist architecture, making them enormously popular with tourists. **Íos**, the original hippie island, is still a backpackers' paradise, while **Mýkonos** – with its teeming old town, nude beaches and highly sophisticated clubs and bars (many of them gay) – is by far the most visited of the group. Arriving by ferry at the partially submerged volcanic caldera of **Santoríni**, meanwhile, is one of the world's great travel adventures. **Páros**,

Náxos and **Sífnos** are nearly as popular, while the one major ancient site worth making time for is **Delos**, the commercial and religious centre of the classical Greek world. Almost all of the Cyclades are served by boats from Pireás, but there are also ferries from Rafína.

SÝROS

Home to the capital of the Cyclades, **Sýros** is the most populous island in the archipelago. The main town and port of **ERMOÚPOLI** is a lively spot, bustling with a commercial life that extends far beyond tourism. Crowned by two imposing churches, the Catholic Capuchin **Monastery of St Jean** in the medieval quarter of Ano Sýros and the Orthodox **Anástasis**, the city is one of the most religiously and culturally diverse places in the whole of Greece.

Accommodation

Dream Off Naxou ⓣ2281 084 356, ⓕ2281 086 452. Decent, basic rooms, some with balconies, run by a charming family and situated just back from the waterfront. ❺

Kastro Rooms Kalomenopoúlo 12 ⓣ2281 088 064. Spacious rooms in a beautiful old mansion house near the main square, with access to a communal kitchen. ❺

Eating

Stin Ithaki Toy Ai Kyp. Stefanou 1 ⓣ2281 082 060. Tucked down a side street, this welcoming taverna has all the Greek classics and vibrant bougainvillea overhead. Mains €6–8.

Yiannena Estiatorio Platía Kanári ⓣ2281 082 994. Popular, friendly spot by the water with a French bistro feel. Serves great seafood and other Greek standards. Mains €6–9.

Moving on

Ferry Íos (5 weekly; 5–8hr 30min); Mýkonos (3–4 daily; 30min–1hr 15min); Náxos (2–3 daily; 1hr 15min–2hr); Pireás (3–4 daily; 1hr 30min–5hr 30min); Santoríni (1 daily; 4–10hr); Sífnos (1 daily; 3hr 30min–6hr 30min).

SÍFNOS

Although **Sífnos** – notable for its classic Cycladic architecture and pottery – often gets crowded, its modest size makes exploring the picturesque island a pleasure, whether by the excellent in-season bus service or on foot over a network of old stone pathways.

KAMÁRES, the port, is tucked at the base of high bare cliffs in the west. A steep twenty-minute bus ride takes you up to **APOLLONÍA**, a rambling collage of flagstones, belfries and flowered courtyards. The island bank, post office and tourist police are all here, while the Aegean Thesaurus agency (ⓣ2284 033 151, ⓦwww.thesaurus.gr) should be able to help with rooms. As an alternative base, head for **KÁSTRO**, a forty-minute walk or regular bus ride below Apollonía on the east coast; built on a rocky outcrop with an almost sheer drop to the sea on three sides, this medieval capital of the island retains much of its character. The island's finest walk is through the hills to **VATHÝ**, a fishing village around three hours from Apollonía's Katavatí "suburb".

Accommodation

Makis Camping Kamáres ⓣ2284 032 366, ⓦwww.makiscamping.gr. This campsite has good facilities, as well as five en-suite rooms with sea views. Open early April to late Oct; camping ❶; doubles ❺

Hotel Stavros Kamáres ⓣ2284 033 383, ⓦwww.sifnostravel.com. These crisp en-suite rooms have balconies with sea views. There's also a decent book exchange in the reception. ❻

Moving on

Boat Íos (2 weekly; 6hr); Mýkonos (1 weekly; 5hr); Náxos (6 weekly; 4hr 15min); Pireás (3 daily; 2hr 15min–5hr 30min); Santoríni (10 weekly; 1hr 40min–10hr); Sýros (1 daily; 3hr 30min–6hr 30min).

MÝKONOS

Mýkonos has become the most popular and expensive of the Cyclades, visited

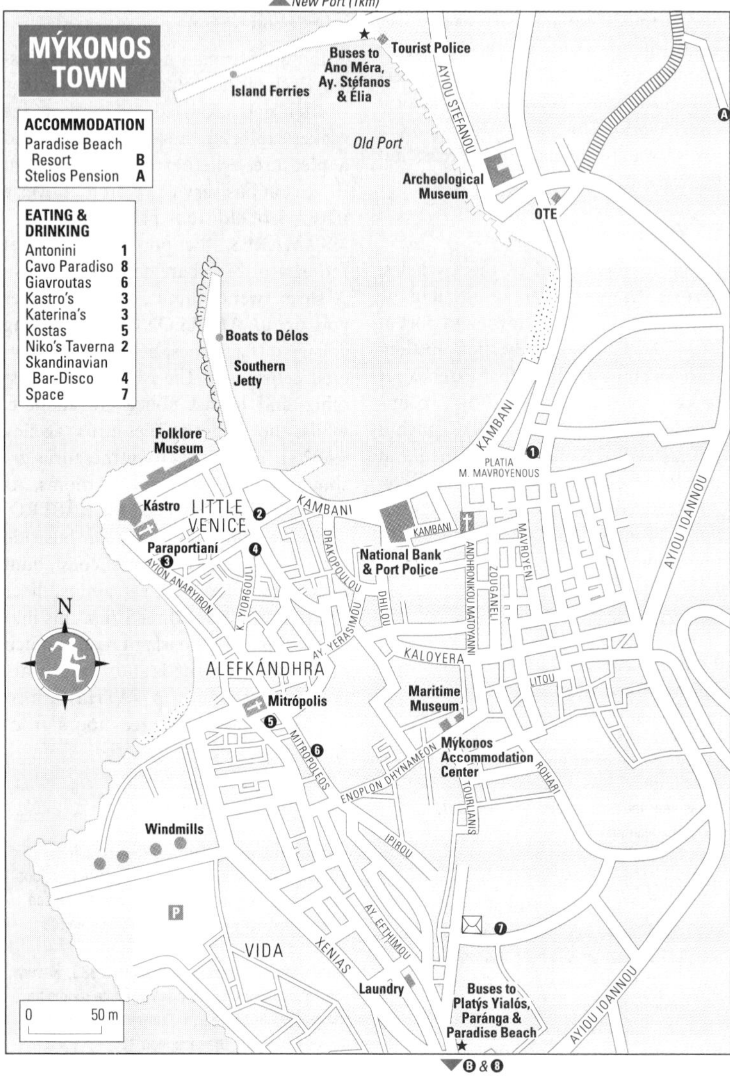

by nearly a million tourists a year. If you don't mind the crowds, the upmarket capital, **MÝKONOS TOWN** (also known as **HÓRA**), is one of the most beautiful and vibrant of all island towns. Dazzlingly white, it's the archetypal island-postcard image, with sugar-cube buildings stacked around a cluster of seafront fishermen's dwellings.

The closest decent **beach** is **Áyios Stéfanos**, 4km north and connected by a very regular bus service, though **Platýs Yialós**, 4km south, is marginally less crowded. A *kaïki* service from Mýkonos town connects almost all the beaches east of Platýs Yialós: gorgeous, pale-sand **Paránga** beach, popular with campers; **Paradise**, well sheltered by its headland

and predominantly nudist; and **Super Paradise**, which has a friendly atmosphere and two bars. Probably the island's best beach is **Eliá** on the southeast coast: a broad sandy stretch with a verdant backdrop, split in two by a rocky area. Less busy, but harder to get to, is **Pánormos Bay** on the island's windswept northern coast, with its relatively sheltered Pánormos and Áyios Sostis beaches.

Arrival and information

Air The airport is about 3km out of town, a short taxi ride away.
Ferry Boats dock at either the "new" port. (2km out of town) or the more central "old" port. Frequent local buses connect the two. *Kaïkia* to Delos leave from the southern jetty.
Information Ferries are met by a horde of hotel and room touts; you'd do better to proceed to the helpful Mýkonos Accommodation Centre in town (Mon–Sat 9am–9pm & Sun 10am–9pm; ⓣ2289 023 160, ⓦwww.mykonos-accommodation.com). They also have information about activities around the island.
Island buses The harbour curves around past the dull, central beach, behind which is the bus station for Áyios Stéfanos. A second bus terminus, for beaches to the south of town, is right at the other end of Hóra, beyond the windmills.
Police Continue along the seafront to the southern jetty for the tourist and port police.

Accommodation

Paradise Beach Resort ⓣ2289 022 129, ⓦwww.paradisemykonos.com. A lively campsite, also with beach cabins and rooms. Open early April to end Oct. ❷
Stelios Pension ⓣ2289 024 641, ⓕ2289 026 779. A white-washed Mykonian-style building, with comfortable rooms which have balconies. On steps leading up from behind the OTE. ❾

Eating

Antonini Platía M. Mavroyénous ⓣ2289 022 319. A reliable choice on the main square, serving Greek dishes at reasonable prices. Mains €7–9.
Giavroutas Mitropóleos 11 ⓣ2289 023 063. Open until 6am, this restaurant has a pleasant beachy feel, with whitewashed walls and wooden furniture. Mains €7–10.
Kostas Mitropóleos 5 ⓣ2289 023 326. Buried deep in the town's labyrinthine centre, this restaurant serves everything from seafood to grills. Mains €8–10.
Niko's Taverna near the port at Little Venice ⓣ2289 024 320. Another popular option, strong on fresh fish but also serving traditional Greek cuisine. Mains €7–9.

Drinking and nightlife

Cavo Paradiso Paradise Beach ⓦwww.cavoparadiso.gr. Close to the *Paradise Beach Resort*, this usually packed after-hours club is one of the stops on the international DJ circuit.
Kastro's Little Venice. Enjoy an early-evening drink in this intimate bar on the waterfront, serving fruity and "special" cocktails. Opens at 6.30pm.
Katerina's Little Venice ⓣ2289 023 084. Low-key decor combined with sea views from the terrace make this a relaxing place for a drink. Cocktails €10. Open all day.
Skandinavian Bar-Disco A good choice for the backpacker set, the buzzing bars are numerous and housed around a small square. Plenty of room for dancing, too.
Space Lákka Square ⓣ2289 024 100 for table reservations. The largest dance club in town, home to a host of resident and guest DJs. Get ready to party.

Moving on

Ferry Íos (1–2 daily; 1hr 30min–7hr); Náxos (3–4 daily; 30min–1hr); Páros (5 daily; 40min–1hr 40min); Pireás (3–4 daily; 3hr 30min–5hr 30min); Santoríni (1–2 daily; 2hr 15min–9hr); Sífnos (1 weekly; 5hr); Sýros (3 daily; 30min–2hr).

DELOS

The skeletal remains of ancient **DELOS** (Tues–Sun 8.30am–3pm; €5) give some idea of the past grandeur of this sacred isle a few sea-miles west of Mýkonos. Accessible only as a day-trip by *kaïki* (€12.50 return, including a guided tour) from the southern jetty in Mýkonos Town, this tiny island can be thoroughly explored in a few hours. Delos's ancient claim to fame is as the place where Leto gave birth to the divine twins Artemis and Apollo; one of the first things you see on arrival is the **Sanctuary of Apollo**, while three Temples of Apollo stand in a row along the Sacred Way. To the east towards the museum you pass the **Sanctuary of Dionysos** with its marble phalluses on tall pillars. To the north is the **Sacred Lake** where Leto gave birth: guarding it is a group of lions, masterfully executed in the seventh century BC. Set out in the other direction from the agora and you enter the residential area, known as the **Theatre Quarter**. There are some nice mosaics to be seen: one in the **House of the Trident** – better ones in the **House of the Masks** – including a vigorous portrayal of Dionysos riding on a panther's back. A steep path from here leads up **Mount Kýnthos** for spectacular views back down over the ruins and out to the surrounding Cyclades.

PÁROS

With its old villages, monasteries, fishing harbour and labyrinthine capital, **Páros** has everything one expects from a Greek island, including boat connections to virtually the entire Aegean.

All ferries dock at **PARIKÍA**, the main town, with its ranks of white houses punctuated by the occasional Venetian-style building and church domes. Just outside the centre, the town also has one of the most interesting churches in the Aegean – the sixth-century **Ekatondapylianí**, or "Church of One Hundred Gates". The town culminates in a seaward Venetian **kástro**, whose surviving east wall incorporates a fifth-century-BC round tower. The second village of Páros, **NÁOUSSA** retains much of its original character as a fishing village with winding, narrow alleys and simple Cycladic houses. Though very busy in summer, it makes a good base for exploring nearby beaches.

Arrival and information

Tourist information Located in the windmill in the centre of the roundabout opposite the quay (Mon–Fri 9am–4pm).

Island buses The bus stop is centrally located in Parikía next to the quay. There are buses to Náoussa (every 30min).

Accommodation

Hotel Captain Manolis Market Street, Parikía ⓣ2284 021 244, ⓦwww.paroswelcome.com. Centrally located yet quiet, the rooms are clustered around a peaceful garden. ❻

Krios Camping 2km from Parikía ⓣ2284 021 705, ⓦwww.krios-camping.gr. Has good facilities, including Internet and a pool. Open early May to late Sept. ❶

Rena Rooms Parikía ⓣ2284 022 220, ⓦwww.cycladesnet.gr/rena. Close to the port and the beach, this excellent pension has good-value rooms, and sea views from the top floor. ❹

Stella Náoussa ⓣ2284 051 317, ⓦwww.hotelstella.gr. A small and peaceful guesthouse, with a leafy courtyard and old town location. ❼

Young Inn Náoussa ⓣ6976 415 232, ⓦwww.young-inn.com. Comfortable en-suite bedrooms, some with kitchenettes, with free transfers to the port. A sociable place, as there are all kinds of organized activities; dorms ❶; doubles ❸

Eating

Argonautica Platía M. Mavroyénous, Parikía ⓣ2284 023 303. A friendly restaurant on the main square, a good spot for watching the town spring to life in the evening. Mains €7–9.

Trata Parikía ⓣ2284 024 651. Found down a side street off the road heading east out of town, this popular taverna specializes in seafood. Mains €6–8.

Moving on

Ferry Íos (1–2 daily; 1hr–3hr 30min); Mýkonos (4–5 daily; 40min–1hr 40min); Náxos (6–7 daily; 30min–1hr); Pireás (4 daily; 3–5hr); Santoríni (3–4 daily; 1hr 45min–3hr); Sífnos (1–2 daily; 3hr 30min–4hr 30min); Sýros (1–2 daily; 30min–1hr 30min).

NÁXOS

Náxos is the largest and most fertile of the Cyclades with high mountains, intriguing central valleys, a spectacular north coast, sandy beaches in the south-west and Venetian towers and fortified mansions scattered throughout.

What to see and do

A long causeway protecting the harbour connects **NÁXOS TOWN** with the islet of Palátia, where the huge stone portal of an unfinished sixth-century-BC **Temple of Apollo** still stands. Most of the town's life goes on down by the port or in the streets just behind it; the quaint Old Market Street has narrow, stone paths leading to small shops and a handful of restaurants and cafés. From here, stepped lanes lead up past crumbling balconies and through low arches to the fortified medieval **kástro**, near the **Archeological Museum** (Tues–Sun 8am–7.30pm; €3), with its important early sculpture collection and a Hellenistic mosaic on the roof terrace. The town has a laid-back feel, with unashamedly long happy hours which last for most of the day. There's a thriving nightlife, with plenty of bars scattered along the waterfront and the bigger clubs dominating either end.

The beaches

The island's best **beaches** are regularly served by buses in season. Within walking distance of Náxos Town is **Áyios Yeóryios**, a long sandy bay south of the hotel quarter, with several tavernas and the *Soula Hotel*. An hour's walk further south, however, you'll find the more inviting **Áyios Prokópios** and **Ayía Ánna** beaches, with plenty of rooms to let and a few modest tavernas. Beyond the headland stretches **Pláka** beach, a 5km-long vegetation-fringed expanse of white sand, which comfortably holds the summer crowds of nudists and campers from its two friendly campsites: *Maragas* (Ⓣ2285 024 552; ❶), which also has double rooms, and the newer *Plaka* (Ⓣ2285 042 700; Ⓦwww.plakacamping.gr; open early April to late Oct; ❷).

Arrival and information

Ferry Boats dock at the ferry quay at the northern end of Náxos Town.

Tourist information Located opposite the quay, you can pick up leaflets or leave your luggage here (daily 8.30am–midnight; Ⓣ22850 25 201).

Island buses The bus stop in Náxos Town is between the quay and the tourist information office. There are buses to Ayía Ánna (every 30min), Áyios Prokópios (every 30min) and Pláka (every 30min).

Accommodation

Despina's Rooms Náxos Town Ⓣ2285 022 356. Hidden beneath the castle, the rooms are small but clean and airy, with shared bathroom and balconies with sea views. ❹

Hotel Panorama Náxos Town Ⓣ2285 022 330, Ⓔpanoramanaxos@in.gr. A comfortable hotel in the old town whose name gives a clue to its main attraction – a large roof terrace with stunning views. ❺

Soula Hotel Áyios Yeóryios beach Ⓣ2285 023 196, Ⓔhotel-soula@nax.forthnet.gr. A family-run budget hotel close to both the beach and the town, with free Internet access; dorms ❷; doubles ❹

Eating and drinking

Elia Old Market Street, Náxos Town Ⓣ2285 024 884. Housed in a beautiful stone building, this smart bar has live music and an enticing atmosphere. Also serves breakfast and lunch. Open 9am–3pm & 7pm–late. Cocktails €5.

Manolis Garden Taverna Old Market Street, Náxos Town Ⓣ2285 025 168. A peaceful spot for an evening meal, where you will find traditional Greek dishes at good prices. Open from 6pm. Mains €6–8.

Popi's Grill Paralia, Náxos Town. On the seafront, serving traditional Greek fare. It also has its own wine and cheese shop. Mains €6–8.

Moving on

Ferry Íos (1–2 daily; 30min–4hr); Mýkonos (3 daily; 30–45min); Páros (6–7 daily; 30min–1hr); Pireás (5 daily; 4hr–5hr 30min); Santoríni (2–3 daily; 1hr 30min–2hr 15min); Sífnos (6 weekly; 4hr); Sýros (1–2 daily; 1hr 15min–5hr).

ÍOS

Once a hippie hang-out, the island remains popular with a younger crowd seeking fun and sun, which **Íos,** party capital of the Aegean, provides in abundance. However, although no other island attracts more under-25s, Íos has miraculously maintained much of its traditional Cycladic charm, with picture-perfect whitewashed houses and churches. Íos's lively nights compel lazy days, perfect for exploring the island.

What to see and do

Don't expect a quiet stay in the town of **HÓRA**, as every evening the streets throb to music with the larger **clubs** clustered near the bus stop. To get the most out of the nightlife, start around 11pm with the bars and clubs around the central square, which tend to close at 3am. Around this time the larger clubs on the main street begin to liven up, and the party continues (even if you don't) until 8am. For up-to-date listings see Ⓦwww.iospartyisland.com.

The most popular stop on the island's bus routes is **MYLOPÓTAS**, site of a magnificent beach and mini-resort. There are plenty of activities on offer, including quad biking (Far Out Moto Club; Ⓣ2286 092 345), water sports and diving (Ⓣ2286 091 622, Ⓦwww.ios-sports.gr). It gets very crowded, so for a bit more space, head away from the terminus where there are dunes behind the beach. From Yialós, boats depart daily at around 10am to **MANGANÁRI** on the south coast, the beach to go to for a serious tan. You can also reach Manganári by bus, as there are two daily buses from Hóra and Mylopótas.

Arrival

Ferry Boats dock at the quay in Yialós. Regular buses connect the port to Hóra and Mylopótas (every 15min; 8am–12.30am).

Accommodation

Camping Ios Yialós Ⓣ2286 091 329. The nearest campsite to the port, and quieter than those on Mylopótas beach. ❶
Drakos Pension Mylopótas Ⓣ2286 091 626. Pleasant rooms in a Cycladic-style building next to a popular Greek restaurant. ❼
Far Out Camping Mylopótas Ⓣ2285 091 468, Ⓦwww.faroutclub.com. By far the most popular campsite, thanks to its facilities and fun factor. Also has bungalows to hire. Open early April to late Sept. ❷
Francesco's Hóra Ⓣ2286 091 223, Ⓦwww.francescos.net. A favourite option with the backpacker set, here you will find the only dorm beds in town as well as private rooms. Lively bar and terrace with sea views; dorms ❷; doubles ❻
Marko's Village Hóra Ⓣ2286 091 059, Ⓦwww.markosvillage.com. Tastefully decorated rooms set around a pool and noisy bar, a short stumble from the nightlife. Free Internet access. ❽

Eating

Ali Baba's Hóra Ⓣ2286 091 558. Thai chefs dish up generous portions of authentic Thai food, served in a relaxed atmosphere. Open from 6pm. Stir-fries €9.
Harmony Mylopótas Ⓣ2286 091 613, Ⓦwww.come2gether.no. A laid-back Mexican restaurant overlooking the beach, with hammocks and cushioned sofas. Open from noon. Enchiladas €10.
Old Byron Hóra Ⓣ6978 192 212. An intimate restaurant with funky decor, serving generous meze plates to share. A restaurant for those with an appetite. Open from 6pm. Plates €5–7.
Pomodoro Hóra Ⓣ2286 091 387. A wonderful roof garden with vistas over Íos invites you to sample the Italian and Mediterranean cuisine on offer. There's a selection of unusual fusion main courses too. Open from 6.30pm. Pasta €7–11.

Drinking and nightlife

Astra Main square. This small bar with hippy decor serves fruity cocktails and is a good place to start.
Kandi Main street. The most popular place to wind up, Kandi's dance floor throbs until dawn (and beyond). Entry €5 including a free cocktail.
Orange Bar Main square. A small but lively bar famous for its delicious chocolatey shots and rock music.
Slammer Bar Main square Ⓦwww.slammerbar.com. Legendary bar, although beware of saying the word "slammer" too loudly. Plays popular music from the eighties to current hits. Entry €5 including a free drink.
Sweet Irish Dream Main street. Satisfy your cravings for a pint of the black gold here. Entry €5 including a free drink.

Moving on

Ferry Mýkonos (1–2 daily; 2–6hr); Náxos (1–2 daily; 50min–4hr); Páros (1–2 daily; 1hr–3hr

30min); Pireás (2–3 daily; 1hr 30min–10hr); Santoríni (3–4 daily; 30min–4hr); Sífnos (2 weekly; 6hr); Sýros (6 weekly; 4hr–8hr 30min).

SANTORÍNI (THÍRA)

Santoríni is the epitome of relaxation, with its sun-drenched beaches and ambling white-washed stone paths. The island (a partially submerged volcanic caldera poking above the ocean's surface in five places) is a welcome destination to those who have spent too many nights partying on Íos. As the ferry manoeuvres into the great bay, gaunt, sheer cliffs loom hundreds of feet above. Nothing grows to soften the view, and the only colours are the reddish-brown, black and grey pumice strata layering the cliff face of **THÍRA**, Santoríni's largest island. Despite a past every bit as turbulent as the geological conditions that formed it, the island is now best known for its spectacular views, dark-sand beaches and light, dry white wines.

What to see and do

Regular buses meeting the ferries at **Órmos Athiniós** make their way to the island's capital **FIRÁ;** half-rebuilt after a devastating earthquake in 1956 and lurching dementedly at the cliff's edge. Besieged by day-trippers from cruise-ships, it's somewhat tacky and commercialized, though watching the sunset from a cliff-hugging terrace of any of the overpriced restaurants you'll understand why. There's no shortage of **rooms** in the area, though most are expensive. The town boasts a couple of **museums** (Tues–Sun 8.30am–3pm; €3 for both): the Archeological Museum, near the cable car to the north of town, and the Museum of Prehistoric Thíra, between the cathedral and the bus station.

Around the island

Near the northwest tip of the island is one of the most dramatic towns of the Cyclades, **ÍA**, a curious mix of pristine white reconstruction and tumbledown ruins clinging to the cliff face. With a post office, travel agencies and an excellent **youth hostel** (see overleaf), it makes a good base from which to explore the island. Santoríni's **beaches** are bizarre: long black stretches of volcanic sand which get blisteringly hot in the afternoon sun. There's little to choose between **KAMÁRI** and **PERÍSSA**, the two main resorts: both have long beaches and a mass of restaurants, rooms and apartments, although Períssa gets more backpackers. At the southwest tip of the island, evidence of a Minoan colony was found at **Akrotíri** (summer Tues–Sun 8.30am–3pm; €5; bus from Firá or Períssa), a town buried under banks of volcanic ash. Nearby is the spectacular, red sand **Kókkini Ámmos** beach.

BOAT TRIPS TO THE VOLCANO

Daily **boat trips** run from either Firá or Ía (€10–30) to the charred volcanic islets of Paleá Kaméni and Néa Kaméni, and on to the relatively unspoiled islet of Thirassía, which was once part of Thíra until shorn off by an eruption in the third century BC.

Arrival

Ferry Most boats arrive at the somewhat grim port of Órmos Athiniós from where buses meeting the ferries make their way to the island's capital.
Island buses Bus services are plentiful enough between Firá and other destinations around the island.

Accommodation

Anna Períssa ⓣ2286 082 182, ⓔannayh@otenet.gr. A basic and noisy youth hostel on the main road, with large dormitories and helpful staff. Free transfers from the port. ❶
Caldera View Camping Akrotíri ⓣ2286 082 010, ⓦwww.calderaview-santorini.com. The newest and best campsite on the island, with good facilities. Open late April to early Oct. ❶

Santorini Camping Firá ⓣ2286 022 944, ⓦwww.santorinicamping.gr. A shady campsite with a pool, restaurant and Internet access among other facilities. Also has wooden tents for hire. ❷

Youth Hostel Ía ⓣ2286 071 465. An excellent hostel with a terrace and shady courtyard, a bar, and clean dormitories. Prices include breakfast. ❷

Moving on

Ferry Crete (1–2 daily; 1hr 45min–7hr 30min); Íos (4–5 daily; 30min–4hr); Mýkonos (2–3 daily; 2hr 30min–8hr); Náxos (2–3 daily; 1hr 30min–4hr); Páros (2–3 daily; 1hr 45min–5hr 30min); Pireás (4–5 daily; 4–9hr); Sífnos (1–2 daily; 1hr 30min–8hr); Sýros (1–2 daily; 4–10hr).

The Dodecanese

The **Dodecanese** islands lie so close to the Turkish coast that some are almost within hailing distance of the shore. They were only included in the modern Greek state in 1948 after centuries of occupation by Crusaders, Ottomans and Italians. Medieval **Rhodes** is the most famous, but almost every one has its classical remains, its Crusaders' castle, its traditional villages and grandiose, Italian-built Art Deco public buildings. The main islands of Rhodes, **Kós** and **Pátmos** are connected almost daily with each other, and none is hard to reach. Rhodes is the principal transport hub, with ferry services to Turkey and Cyprus, as well as connections with Crete, the northeastern Aegean islands, the Cyclades and the mainland (Kavála, Alexandhroúpoli and Pireás).

RHODES

It's no surprise that **Rhodes** is among the most visited of Greek islands. Not only is its east coast lined with sandy beaches, but the core of the capital is a beautiful and remarkably preserved medieval city.

What to see and do

RHODES TOWN divides into two unequal parts: the compact old walled city and the new town sprawling around it in three directions. First thing to meet the eye, and dominating the northeast sector of the city's fortifications, is the **Palace of the Grand Masters** (summer Mon 12.30–7pm, Tues–Sun 8am–7.30pm; winter Mon 12.30–3pm, Tues–Sun 8am–3pm; €6, or €10 combo ticket with other museums). Two excellent **museums** occupy the ground floor: one devoted to medieval Rhodes, the other to ancient Rhodes. The heavily-restored **Street of the Knights** (Odhós Ippotón) leads due east from the front of the palace. The "Inns" lining it housed the Knights of St John for two centuries, and at the bottom of the slope the Knights' Hospital now houses the **Archeological Museum** (Tues–Sun 8.30am–7pm; €3, or €10 combo ticket), where the star exhibits are two statues of Aphrodite. Across the way is the **Byzantine Museum** (Tues–Sun 8.30am–2.40pm; €2 or €10 combo ticket), housed in the Knights' chapel and highlighting the island's icons and frescoes. Heading south, it's hard to miss the most conspicuous Ottoman monument in Rhodes, the candy-striped **Süleymaniye Mosque** (ask at the tourist office for opening hrs; free).

Haráki and Líndhos

Heading down the east coast from Rhodes Town, the giant promontory of **Tsambíka**, 26km south, is the first place to seriously consider stopping – there's an excellent eponymous beach just south of the headland. The best overnight base on this stretch of coast is probably **HARÁKI**, a tiny port with rooms and tavernas overlooked by a ruinous castle. **LÍNDHOS**, Rhodes' number-two tourist attraction, erupts 12km south of Haráki. Its charm is undermined by commercialism and crowds, and there are relatively few self-catering units that

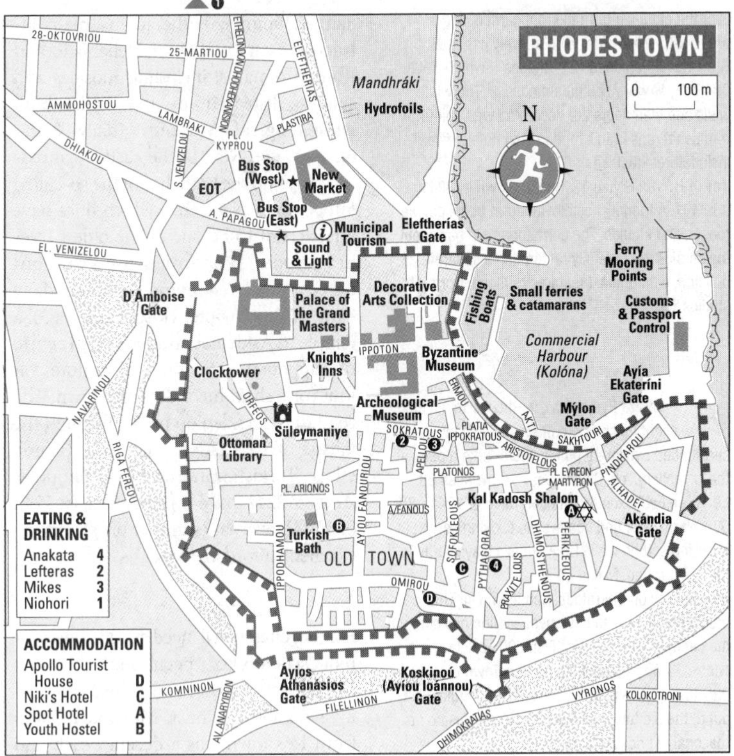

aren't block-booked through package companies – find vacancies through Pallas Travel (ⓣ2244 031 494, ⓦwww.pallastravel.gr). On the hill above the town, the Doric **Temple of Athena** and Hellenistic stoa (porch-like building used for meetings and commerce) stand inside the inevitable knights' castle (summer Mon 12.30–7pm, Tues–Sun 8am–7pm; winter Tues–Sun 8am–3pm; €6). Líndhos's beaches are crowded and overrated, but you'll find better ones heading south past Lárdhos, the start of 15km of intermittent coarse-sand beach up to and beyond the growing resort of **Yennádhi**. Inland near here, the late Byzantine frescoes in the village church of **Asklipió** are among the best on Rhodes.

Arrival and information

Ferry Boats dock at the harbour in Rhodes Town outside the walls of the Old Town, south of the New Town.

Tourist office The EOT tourist office (Mon–Fri 8am–2.45pm; ⓣ2241 023 255) and the municipal tourist office (June–Sept daily 7.30am–11pm) are arrayed around the Italian-built New Market.

Island buses Buses for the rest of the island leave from two terminals within sight of the market.

Internet *Rock Style* at Dhimokratías 7, just southwest of the old town, and *Cosmonet*, at Platía Evreon Martyon 45.

Accommodation

Apollo Tourist House Omírou 28C, Rhodes Town ⓣ2241 032 003, ⓦwww.apollo-touristhouse.com. Six individual en-suite rooms with large double beds. Simple yet elegant. ❻

Niki's Hotel Sofokléous 39, Rhodes Town ⓣ2241 025 115, ⓦwww.nikishotel.gr. Wonderful views over the old town from the roof garden, and breakfast served outside on a lovely patio. ❺

Spot Hotel Perikléous 21, Rhodes Town ⓣ 2241 034 737, ⓦ www.spothotelrhodes.gr. The white walls and tiled floors are decorated with colourful traditional rugs in this modernized hotel. Prices include breakfast. ❻

Youth Hostel Eryíou 12, Rhodes Town ⓔ 2241 030 491. A friendly hostel with dorm beds, double rooms, and studios. The dormitories are basic, but the studios are carefully restored in a separate building, with original features retained. Dorm ❶; studios ❹

Eating

Anakata Pythagora 79, Rhodes Town. Enjoy a light lunch or a coffee in this shady garden surrounded by vibrant pink flowers. Take a peek at the art gallery, too. Closed Sun. Sandwiches €3.

Lefteras Evdhóxou 49, Rhodes Town ⓣ 2241 038 597. Here you'll find home-style cooking served in a garden setting while Greek music plays softly in the background. Mains €6–8.

Mikes Alley off Sokrátous, Rhodes Town. This modest taverna with pavement seating has some of the cheapest fish in town. Fish €20 per kilo.

Niohori Ioánni Kazoúli 29, Rhodes Town ⓣ 2241 035 116. This restaurant is worth the 10min walk out of the old town, as it serves Greek cuisine at reasonable prices. Mains €5–7.

Moving on

Ferry Crete (4 weekly; 10–12hr); Kós (2–3 daily; 2hr 30min–3hr 30min); Pátmos (2 daily; 4–5hr); Pireás (9 weekly; 12–15hr).

KÓS

Kós is the largest and most popular island in the Dodecanese after Rhodes, and there are superficial similarities between the two. Like its rival, the harbour here is also guarded by a castle of the Knights of St John, the streets are lined with ambitious Italian public buildings, and minarets and palm trees punctuate extensive Greek and Roman remains.

What to see and do

Mostly modern **KÓS TOWN**, levelled by a 1933 earthquake, fans out from the harbour. Apart from the **castle** (daily 8am–6.30pm; €3), the town's main attraction is its wealth of Hellenistic and Roman remains, including mosaics and statues displayed in the Italian-built **Archeological Museum** (daily 8am–6.30pm; €3). Next to the castle, scaffolding props up the branches of the so-called Hippocrates plane tree, which does have a fair claim to be one of the oldest trees in Europe. Hippocrates is also honoured by the **Asklepion** (summer daily 8am–6.30pm; winter closes earlier; €3), a temple to Asklepios and renowned centre of Hippocratic teaching, 45 minutes on foot (or a short bus ride) from town. The road to the Asklepion passes through the village of **PLATÁNI**, where the island's ethnic Turkish minority run the popular *Arap* (ⓣ 2242 028 442) and *Sherif* (ⓣ 2242 023 784) tavernas (summer only), serving excellent, affordable food.

The beaches

For **beaches** you'll need to use buses or rent scooters or pedal-bikes. Around 12km west of Kós Town, **Tingáki** is easily accessible but busy. **Mastihári**, 30km from Kós town, has a decent beach and private rooms for hire. Continuing west, buses run as far as **Kéfalos**, which covers a bluff looking back along the length of Kós. Well before Kéfalos are **Áyios Stéfanos**, where the exquisite remains of a mosaic-floored fifth-century basilica overlook tiny Kastrí islet, and **Kamári**, the package resort just below Kéfalos. Beaches begin at Kamári and extend east past Áyios Stéfanos for 7km, almost without interruption; "Paradise" has the most facilities, but "Magic" (officially Polémi) and Langádhes are calmer and more scenic.

Arrival and information

Ferry Boats arrive at the harbour, to the north of the centre in Kós Town.

Tourist office The helpful municipal tourist office (Mon–Fri: May–Oct 7.30am–3pm; Nov–April 8.30am–2.30pm; ⓣ 2242 024 460), 500m south of the ferry dock on the shore road, offers maps and ferry schedules.

Island buses Buses arrive 500m west of the tourist office. From the centre there are buses to Plataáni (15 daily), Tingáki (12 daily), Mastihári (7 daily) and Paradise (6 daily).

Accommodation

Hotel Afendoulis Evripýlou 1, Kós Town ⓣ2242 025 321, ⓦwww.afendoulishotel.com. Homely en-suite rooms with balconies are set around a mezzanine floor, and there's a warm family welcome. ❹

Pension Alexis Irodhótou 9, Kós Town ⓣ2242 028 798, ⓦwww.pensionalexis.com. The accommodating Sonia will welcome late arrivals and provide a never-ending supply of information about Kós. A popular budget option set around a shady garden with a sociable veranda. ❹

Eating

Ambavris 1.5km inland in the eponymous hamlet. This taverna may be some distance out of town, but it has an excellent selection of *mezédhes* and is popular with the locals. Dinner only. Mains €6–8.
Koakon Artemisías 56 ⓣ2242 025 645. Located in a residential area, this restaurant has a varied menu offering good-quality Greek cuisine including fish dishes. Mains €6–8.

Moving on

Ferry Pátmos (3 daily; 1hr 30min–2hr 30min); Pireás (7 weekly; 9–12hr); Rhodes (2–3 daily; 2–4hr).

PÁTMOS

St John the Divine reputedly wrote the Book of Revelation in a cave on **Pátmos**, and the monastery which commemorates him, founded here in 1088, dominates the island both physically and politically. While the monks no longer run Pátmos as they did for more than six centuries, their influence has stopped most of the island going the way of Rhodes or Kós.

What to see and do

SKÁLA, the port and main town, is the only busy part of the island, crowded with day-trippers from Kós and Rhodes. The **Monastery of St John** (daily 8am–1.30pm; Tues, Thurs & Sun also 4–6pm; monastery free, treasury €5) shelters behind massive defences in the hilltop capital of **HÓRA**. Buses go up, but the thirty-minute walk along a beautiful old cobbled path puts you in a more appropriate frame of mind. Just over halfway is the **Monastery of the Apocalypse**, built around the cave where St John heard the voice of God issuing from a cleft in the rock. This is merely a foretaste, however, of the main monastery, whose fortifications guard a dazzling array of religious treasures dating back to medieval times. Hóra itself is a beautiful little town whose antiquated alleys conceal over forty churches and monasteries, plus dozens of shipowners' mansions dating from the island's heyday in the seventeenth and eighteenth centuries.

The beaches

The next bay north of the main harbour in Skála shelters **Méloï Beach**, with a well-run campsite. For swimming, the second beach north, **Agriolivádhi**, is usually less crowded. From Hóra a good road runs above the package resort of Gríkou to the isthmus of **Stavrós**, from where a thirty-minute trail leads to the excellent beach, with one seasonal taverna, at **Psilí Ámmos** (summer *kaïki* from Skála). There are more good beaches in the north of the island, particularly **Livádhi Yeránou**, shaded by tamarisk groves and with a decent taverna, and **Lámbi** with volcanic pebbles and another quality taverna, *Leonidas*.

Arrival and information

Ferry Boats arrive at the harbour, in the middle of Skála.
Tourist office Close to the police station opposite the harbour, the helpful municipal tourist office (daily 9am–3pm & 4–10pm Mon–Fri & 5–8pm Sat & Sun) can assist with accommodation.
Island buses The bus stop is next to the harbour. There are buses to Hóra (11 daily) and Gríkou (8 daily).

Accommodation

Pension Maria Pascalidis In Skála on the road to Hóra ☎2247 032 152. A homely feel pervades this pension, with its fragrant front garden and basic rooms. ❸

Stefanos Camping Méloï ☎2247 031 821. A basic campsite, but with clean facilities and a restaurant. Open May–Oct. ❶

Villa Knossos Netiá district of Hóra ☎2247 032 189. Tasteful blue and white decor adorns these good-sized, smart en-suite rooms with balcony. Free transportation to the port in Skála. Open April–Oct. ❻

Yeoryia Triandafyllou Hóra ☎2247 031 963. Four-poster beds are one of many luxuries, alongside a peaceful terrace with sea views and the use of a kitchen. Advance reservations are required. Open April–Oct. ❺

Eating

Grigoris Skála ☎2247 031 515. Bustling taverna with pavement seating; head upstairs to the terrace for a better atmosphere. House specials are found alongside the usual favourites. Souvláki €5.

Ouzerí To Hiliomodhi Skála ☎2247 034 080. As the decor encompassing the terrace suggests, this is the place for fish and seafood dishes. Open from 5pm. Mains €5–7.

Moving on

Ferry Kós (3 daily; 2hr–2hr 30min); Pireás (2 weekly; 7–12hr); Sámos (1–2 daily; 1–3hr).

The northeastern Aegean islands

The seven scattered islands of the **northeastern Aegean** form a rather arbitrary archipelago. Local tour operators do a thriving business shuttling passengers for absurdly high tariffs between the easternmost islands and the Turkish coast. **Sámos** is the most visited, and was – until a week-long forest fire devastated a fifth of the island in 2000 – perhaps the most verdant and beautiful while **Lésvos** is more of an acquired taste, though once smitten you may find it hard to leave.

SÁMOS

Sámos was the wealthiest island in the Aegean during the seventh century BC, but fell on hard times thereafter; today its economy is heavily dependent on package tourism. All ferries to and from Pireás and the Cyclades call at both Karlóvassi in the west and Vathý in the east; additionally there are services to the Dodecanese out of Pythagório in the south.

What to see and do

VATHÝ, the capital, also known as Sámos, lines the steep-sided shore of its namesake bay and is of minimal interest except for its hill quarter of tottering, tile-roofed houses, Áno Vathý, and an excellent **Archeological Museum** (Tues–Sun 8.30am–3pm; €3, students €2), containing a wealth of peculiar votive offerings and a huge, five-metre statue of an idealized youth. West of Vathý, the busy resort of **Kokkári** is enchantingly set between twin headlands at the base of still partly forested mountains. Nearby beaches are pebbly and exposed, prompting its role as a major windsurfers' resort.

Around the island

Some 13km west of Vathý, untouristed **ÁYIOS KONSTANDÍNOS** has several modest pensions and hotels, plus three excellent **tavernas**. Less than an hour's walk west from the functional port town of Karlóvassi, **Potámi** is a popular beach ringed by forest and weird rock formations; for more solitude you can continue another hour or so on foot to the two bays of **Mikró Seïtáni** (pebbles) and **Megálo Seïtáni** (sand). But for an amenitied beach resort in the west of the island, shift south to **ÓRMOS**

MARATHAKÁMBOU, adjacent to 2km of sand and pebbles at Votsalákia package resort.

Arrival and information

Boat Boats from the Dodecanese arrive at the southern port of Pythagório – buses (13 daily) travel from here to Vathý. Boats from elsewhere call at both Karlóvassi and Vathý.
Tourist office Located at Themistoklí Sofoúli 107 in Vathý (Mon–Sat).
Island buses The bus stop in Vathý is located to the south of the centre, 100m from the tourist office. There are buses to Áyios Konstandínos (14 daily), Kokkári (10 daily) and Órmos Marathakámbou (2 daily).

Accommodation

Pension Dreams Áreos 9, Vathý ⓣ2273 024 350, ⓦwww.samosdreams.tk. This small pension has seven comfortable rooms of different shapes and sizes, but all have balconies. There's a rooftop studio, too. Multilingual and helpful management. ❹
Pension Trova Manóli Kalomíri 26, Vathý ⓣ2273 027 759. A guesthouse with a real family feel, some rooms with private bathroom, some without, but all clean. ❸

Eating

Garden Manóli Kalomíri, Vathý ⓣ2273 024 033. This colourful garden restaurant has a fun atmosphere with quirky features, and it serves meat and fish dishes. Souvláki €6.
To Kyma Áyios Konstandínos ⓣ2273 094 251. Signposted from the main road, this taverna has a selection of ready-cooked meals and a great seafront location. Mains €6–8.
T'Ostrako Themistoklí Sofoúli 141, Vathý ⓣ2273 027 070. On the waterfront, this ouzerí serves affordable seafood. Mains €4–6.

Moving on

Ferry Kós (1 daily; 3hr 30min–4hr); Pátmos (1–2 daily; 1–3hr); Pireás (1–3 daily; 7–12hr); Rhodes (2 weekly; 10hr).

LÉSVOS

Lésvos, birthplace of Sappho, the ancient world's foremost woman poet, may not at first seem particularly beautiful, but the craggy volcanic landscape of pine and olive groves grows on you. Despite the inroads of tourism, this is still essentially a working island, with few large hotels outside the capital, Mytilíni, and the resorts of Skála Kallonís and Mólyvos.

What to see and do

Few people stay in **MYTILÍNI**, but do pause long enough to peek at the **Archeological Museum**, with its superb Roman mosaics (Tues–Sun 8.30am–3pm; €3). Sleepy **MÓLYVOS**, also known as Mithymna, on the northwestern coast, is easily the most attractive spot on Lésvos, and much more appealing than its neighbour Petra. Tiers of sturdy, red-tiled houses mount the slopes between the picturesque harbour and the Genoese castle. Wandering through the cobbled streets is a pleasure, since the town's hillside location provides plenty of stunning vistas across the sweeping bay. If the exploration has worn you out, reward yourself with a visit to the **hot springs** of Eftaloú (private tubs 9am–6pm; €5). The main lower road, past the tourist office, heads towards the picturesque harbour, where there are some good-quality seafood tavernas. Lésvos's best beach is at **SKÁLA ERESSOÚ** in the far southwest, with rooms far outnumbering hotels. Tavernas with wooden terraces line the beach – try *Eressos Palace* or *Blue Sardine*. **PLOMÁRI** in the southeast, long the *oúzo* capital of Greece, is another good base, though beaches lie some distance either side.

Arrival and information

Ferry Boats arrive at the quay in Mytilíni. On arrival, turn left to reach the town centre.
Tourist office The office in Mytilíni is located at Aristárhou 6 near the quay (Mon–Fri 9am–1pm, ⓣ2251 042 511). The office in Mólyvos is close to the bus stop (summer only: Mon–Sat

10am–8.30pm, Sun 10.30am–2pm & 5–8.30pm; ⓣ2253 071 347; ⓦwww.mithymna.gr) and can help with accommodation.

Island buses The bus station in Mytilíni is located at the southwestern end of the waterfront, slightly inland near Platía Konstandinopóleos. There are buses to Mólyvos (5 daily), Plomári (5 daily), and Skála Eressoú (3 daily).

Accommodation

Pension Lida Plomári ⓣ2252 032 507. A fine restoration inn occupying adjacent old mansions, with seaview balconies for most units. ❹

Molivos Camping Mólyvos ⓣ2253 071 169, ⓦwww.molivos-camping.com. A shady campsite with good facilities, 800m from town. Open early May to late Oct. ❶

Nassos Guest House Mólyvos ⓣ2253 071 432, ⓦwww.nassosguesthouse.com. A charming converted Turkish house built around 1900. There are fine views of the town from the rooms and the terrace. ❸

Eating

The Captain's Table Mólyvos ⓣ2253 071 241. Set among the fishing boats in the picturesque harbour, here you will find good fish dishes as well as traditional fare. Open from 5.30pm. Fish dishes €7–8.

To Hani Mólyvos ⓣ2253 071 618. Near the market, this friendly restaurant serves delicious meals, complemented by a wonderful terrace with views over the town towards the sea. Mains €6–8.

Moving on

Ferry Pireás (1–2 daily; 9–13hr); Thessaloníki (4 weekly; 14hr).

The Sporades

The **Sporades**, scattered across the northwestern Aegean, are an easy group to island-hop. The three northern islands – package-tourist haven Skiáthos, Alónissos and **Skópelos**, the pick of the trio – have good beaches, transparent waters and thick pine forests. **Skýros**, the fourth Sporade, is isolated from the others and less scenic, but with perhaps the most character; for a relatively uncommercialized island within a day's travel of Athens it's unbeatable.

GETTING TO THE SPORADES

The **Sporades** are well connected to Athens by bus and ferry via Áyios Konstandínos (for Skópelos) or Kými (for Skýros), and to Vólos (for Skópelos). Be aware that the only way to get to Skýros is from the mainland port of Kými.

SKÓPELOS

More rugged yet better cultivated than neighbouring Skiáthos, **Skópelos** is also very much more attractive. **SKÓPELOS TOWN** slopes down one corner of a huge, almost circular bay. There are dozens of rooms to let – take up one of the offers when you land or visit the Roomowners Association for vacancies. Within the town, spread below the oddly whitewashed ruins of a Venetian *kástro*, are an enormous number of churches – 123 reputedly, though some are small enough to be mistaken for houses.

Buses run along the island's one asphalt road to Loutráki about seven times daily, stopping at the turn-offs to all the main beaches and villages. **Stáfylos** beach, 4km out of town, is the closest, but it's small, rocky and increasingly crowded; the overflow, much of it nudist, flees to **Valanió**, just east. Much more promising, if you're after relative isolation, is sandy **Limnonári**, a fifteen-minute road-walk or short *kaïki* ride from **AGNÓNDAS** (tavernas and rooms). The large resort of **Pánormos** has become overdeveloped, but slightly further on, **Miliá** offers a tremendous 1500m sweep of tiny pebbles beneath a bank of pines.

Arrival and information

Ferry Boats arrive at the quay in the middle of Skópelos Town. The island also has another port at Loutráki.
Roomowners Association Found opposite the quay (daily 9.30am–2pm; ⓣ2424 024 576), they have lists of the island's accommodation.
Island buses The bus stop is located next to the quay, near the taxi rank. There are buses to Agnóndas (20 daily), Loutráki (8 daily), Miliá (17 daily), Pánormos (17 daily) and Stáfylos (20 daily).

Accommodation

Arhontiko Skópelos Town ⓣ2424 022 765. This welcoming guesthouse has traditional decor and a homely atmosphere, situated on a quiet, cobbled street. ❹
Hotel Regina Skópelos Town ⓣ2424 022 138. Close to the waterfront, these spacious en-suite rooms have large double beds and balconies. Prices include breakfast. ❻

Eating

Alexander Skópelos Town ⓣ2424 022 324. A delightful garden restaurant, serving traditional Greek food alongside more unusual local specials, such as pork with plums. Open from 7pm. Mains €7–12.
O Molos Old Harbour, Skópelos Town ⓣ2424 022 551. A reliable taverna along the waterfront, serving typical Greek cuisine at reasonable prices. Mains €7–8.

Moving on

Ferry Áyios Konstandínos (3–4 daily; 2hr 15min–3hr); Skiáthos (12–15 daily; 30min–1hr); Vólos (7–8 daily; 2hr 30min–3hr 30min).

SKÝROS

Skýros remained until the 1980s a very traditional and idiosyncratic island. The older men still wear the vaguely Cretan costume of cap, vest, baggy trousers, leggings and clogs, while the women favour yellow scarves and long embroidered skirts. Skýros also has a particularly lively *Apokriátika* or pre-Lenten **carnival**, featuring the "Goat Dance", performed by masked revellers in the village streets.

What to see and do

A **bus** connects Linariá – a functional little port with a few tourist facilities – to **SKÝROS TOWN**, spread below a high rock rising precipitously from the coast. Traces of classical walls can still be made out among the ruins of the Venetian *kástro*; within the walls is the crumbling, tenth-century monastery of **Áyios Yeóryios**. Despite the town's peaceful afternoons, the narrow streets come alive in the evening, as the sun sets behind the hills, bathing the white buildings in a soft light. There are several hotels and plenty of **rooms** to let in private houses; you'll be met with offers as you descend from the bus. The campsite is down the hill at the fishing village of **MAGAZIÁ**, with rooms and tavernas fronting the island's best beach.

Arrival and information

Ferry Boats arrive at the functional port of Linariá. Buses meet the boats and connect the port to Skýros Town.
Information There is no tourist office, but Skyros Travel on the main street (ⓣ2222 091 123, ⓦwww.skyrostravel.com) can help with accommodation.

Accommodation

Hotel Elena Skýros Town ⓣ2222 091 738. These rooms, with tiled floors, white walls and wooden furniture, are clean and comfortable, and centrally located. ❺

Eating

Liakos Skýros Town ⓣ2222 093 509. Tasty local dishes are served on a rooftop terrace which has a panoramic view over the town. Open Mon from 6pm, Tues–Sun from 1pm. Mains €6–11.
Nostos Café Skýros Town ⓣ2222 091 797. On the central square above the bank, this is the perfect place for a pre-dinner drink as you watch the sunset from the terrace.
O Pappous k'Ego Skýros Town ⓣ2222 093 200. This popular eatery opens for dinner only and serves Skyrian specialities with a smile. Tables spill out onto the cobbled pavement. Mains €5–9.

Moving on

Ferry Kými (2 daily; 2hr).

The Ionian islands

The six **Ionian islands** are, both geographically and culturally, a mixture of Greece and Italy. Floating on the haze of the Adriatic, their green silhouettes come as a surprise to those more used to the stark outlines of the Aegean. The islands were the Homeric realm of Odysseus and here alone of all modern Greek territory the Ottomans never held sway. After the fall of Byzantium, possession passed to the Venetians, and the islands became a keystone in that city-state's maritime empire from 1386 until its collapse in 1797. Tourism has hit **Corfu** in a big way but none of the other islands has endured anything like the same scale of development, although the process seems well advanced on parts of **Zákynthos**. For a less sullied experience, head for **Kefalloniá** or **Itháki**.

CORFU (KÉRKYRA)

Corfu's natural appeal remains an intense experience, if sometimes a beleaguered one, for it has more package hotels and holiday villas than any other Greek island. The commercialism is apparent the moment you step ashore at the ferry dock, or cover the 2km from the airport.

What to see and do

KÉRKYRA TOWN, the capital, has a lot more going for it than first exposure to the summer crowds might indicate. The cafés on the Esplanade and in the arcaded Listón have a civilized air, and become lively bars when the sun sets. The Palace of SS Michael and George at the north end of the Spianádha is worth visiting for its **Asiatic Museum** (Tues–Sun 8.30am–7.30pm; €3) and **Municipal Art Gallery** (daily 9am–5pm; €1.50). The **Byzantine Museum** (Tues–Sun 8am–7pm; €2) and the cathedral are both interesting, as is the **Archeological Museum**, Vraíla 3 (Tues–Sun 8.30am–3pm; €3), where the small but intriguing collection features a 2500-year-old Medusa pediment. The island's patron saint, Spyrídhon, is entombed in a silver-covered coffin in his own church on Vouthrótou, and four times a year, to the accompaniment of much celebration and feasting, the relics are paraded through the streets. Some 5km south of town lies the picturesque convent of **Vlahérna**, which is joined to the plush mainland suburb of Kanóni by a short causeway; the tiny islet of **Pondikoníssi** in the bay can also be visited by a frequent *kaïki* service (€1.50 return).

Around the island

Much of the island's coastline has been remorselessly developed; the tiny village of **VÁTOS**, just inland from west-coast Érmones, is the one place within easy reach of Kérkyra Town that has an easy, relaxed feel to it and reasonable rooms and tavernas. Nearby **PÉLEKAS** is rather busy, but it's a good alternative base. The best option for independent travellers is to stay in the village, which has a free bus service to the beaches of Pélekas and Glyfada. Thanks to the village's hilltop location, there are some fine views over the surrounding countryside towards the coast. Further south, **ÁYIOS GÓRDHIS** beach is more remote but that hasn't spared it from the crowds who come to admire the cliff-girt setting. Beyond Messongí stretches the flat, sandy southern tip of Corfu. **Áyios Yeóryios**, on the southwest coast, consists of a developed area just before its beautiful beach, which extends north alongside the peaceful Korissíon lagoon. **Kávos**, near the cape itself, rates with its many clubs and discos as the nightlife capital of the island; for daytime solitude and swimming, you can walk to beaches beyond the nearby hamlets of Sparterá and Dhragotiná.

Arrival and information

Air The airport is 2km from the town. There is no direct bus, but local buses #2 and #3 leave from 500m north of the terminal gates. A taxi should cost €10.
Ferry Boats arrive at the new port, which is 1km west of town.
Tourist office There's a municipal information booth at Platía Saróko (summer only: Mon–Sat 8am–11pm, Sun 8am–4pm).
Roomowners Association The best source of independent accommodation in Kérkyra Town and around the island is located at D. Theotóki 2A near the Archeological Museum (daily 9am–1.30pm) ⓣ2261 026 133, ⓔoitkcrf@otenet.gr).

Island transport

Local buses The bus stop is at Platía Saróko, where there's also a helpful kiosk with timetable information. Bus #11 goes to Pélekas (7 daily).
Long-distance buses The bus station is on Avramiou, near the new fortress and the new port.

Accommodation

Kérkyra

Dionysus Camping Village Dhassiá, 8km north of Kérkyra town ⓣ2661 091 417, ⓦwww.dionysuscamping.gr. Campsite with good facilities and sporting activities. Also has bungalows to hire for an extra €10 per person. Take local bus #7. Open early April to late Oct. ❶
Europa Yitsiáli 10, ⓣ2661 039 304. Situated close to the new port, these are the cheapest rooms in town, although hot water and cleanliness are not guaranteed. ❸

Around the island

Corfu Traveler's Inn Áyios Górdhis ⓣ2661 053 935, ⓔcorfutravelersinn@hotmail.com. Beachside accommodation with plenty of activities on offer. Prices include breakfast and dinner; dorms ❸; doubles ❻
Pension Paradise Pélekas 2261 094 530. Good value en-suite rooms, located in the village. All have private kitchens with fridges for self-caterers. ❸
The Pink Palace Áyios Górdhis ⓣ2661 053 103, ⓦwww.thepinkpalace.com. A youth-orientated holiday village that has everything you could imagine. Prices include breakfast and dinner; dorms ❸; doubles ❻
Vatos Camping Vatos ⓣ2661 094 505. A small and simple campsite but close to the picturesque Myrtiótissa Beach. ❶

Eating and drinking

Kérkyra

Aleko's Beach On the jetty below the Palace of SS Michael and George, serving typical Greek cuisine and seafood. Go later in the evening to get the best atmosphere. Mains €7–9.
Mikro Café Theotóki & Kotárdou 42 ⓣ2661 031 009. A delightful café-bar, tucked away with an inviting garden. Perfect for an evening drink. Beers €3, cocktails €6.50.
To Paradosiakon Solomoú 20 ⓣ2661 037 578. This colourful restaurant with pavement seating serves a good range of traditional dishes. Open from 10am. Mains €7–9.

Pélekas

Jimmy's Pélekas ⓣ2661 094 284. Opposite a tiny, yellow church, this friendly taverna serves excellent food all day, including a selection of vegetarian dishes and local specials. Mains €7–9.
Zanzibar Pélekas. Small, popular café-bar with an extensive cocktail menu and live music in the evenings. Beers €2, cocktails €4.50.

Moving on

Ferry Brindisi (2 daily; 8hr); Igoumenítsa (hourly; 1hr 30min); Pátra (daily; 7–8hr).

KEFALLONIÁ

Kefalloniá is the largest, and, at first glance, least glamorous, of the Ionian islands; the 1953 earthquake that rocked the archipelago was especially devastating here, with almost every town and village levelled. Couple that with the islanders' legendary eccentricity, and with poor infrastructure, it's no wonder tourism didn't take off until the late 1980s. Already popular with Italians, the island has, more recently, been attracting large numbers of British tourists, in no small part thanks to Louis de Bernières' novel, *Captain Corelli's Mandolin*, which was set here. There's plenty of interest: beaches to compare with the best on Corfu or Zákynthos, good local wine and the partly forested mass of Mount Énos (1628m). The island's size, skeletal bus service and shortage of summer accommodation make renting a motorbike or car a must for extensive exploration.

What to see and do

ARGOSTÓLI, with daily ferries to Kyllíni on the mainland, is the bustling, concrete island capital. The town's **Archeological Museum** (Tues–Sun 8.30am–3pm; free) is second only to Corfu's in the archipelago. Heading north, you come to the beach of **Mýrtos**, considered the best on the island, although lacking in facilities; the closest places to **stay** are nearby Dhivaráta and almost bus-less **Ássos**, a beautiful fishing port perched on a narrow isthmus linking it to a castellated headland. At the end of the line, **Fiskárdho**, with its eighteenth-century houses, is the most expensive place on the island; the main reason to come would be for the daily **ferry** to Lefkádha island, and crossings to Itháki. Heading further south along the eastern coast, **SÁMI**, set against a natural backdrop of verdant, undulating hills, nestles itself into a sweeping bay. The town is the second port on the island, with boats to Itháki and Pátra. For film fanatics Sámi has an added appeal, since the region was the setting for the 2001 film *Captain Corelli's Mandolin*. However, **AYÍA EFIMÍA**, 10km north, makes a far more attractive base. Between the two towns, 3km from Sámi, the **Melissáni cave** (daily 9am–sunset; €6), a partly submerged Capri-type "blue grotto", is well worth a stop. Southeast from Sámi are the resorts of **PÓROS**, with regular ferries to Kyllíni.

Arrival and information

Ferry Ferries from Kyllíni mostly dock at Póros, although a daily ferry docks at Argostóli. Ferries from Pátra dock at Sámi.

Tourist offices The waterfront tourist office in Argostóli (Mon–Fri 7.30am–2.30pm; in summer also Mon–Fri 6–10pm & Sat–Sun 9am–2pm & 6–10pm; ⓣ 26710 22 248) keeps comprehensive lists of accommodation. There's also a small but helpful tourist office in Sámi near the quay (ⓣ 2674 022 019).

Island buses The bus station in Argostóli is just past the causeway, on I. Metaxa. There are buses to Ayía Efimía (4 daily), Fiskárdho (2 daily), Póros (2 daily) and Sámi (4 daily). There is no bus service on Sundays.

Accommodation

Karavomilos Beach Sámi ⓣ 2674 022 480, ⓦ www.camping-karavomilos.gr. A shady campsite near the beach, 1km from town. Open early May to late Sept. ❷

Hotel Melissani Sámi ⓣ 2674 022. An interesting, if wacky, choice of decor adorns this colourful hotel. The fifteen en-suite rooms have balconies or verandas. Open May to Oct. ❺

Moustakis Hotel Ayía Efimía ⓣ 2674 061 030, ⓦ www.moustakishotel.com. Small but smart, this family-run hotel offers clean rooms with balconies. ❼

St Gerassimos Agíou Gerassímou 6, Argostóli ⓣ 2671 028 697. A warm welcome greets you at this centrally located hotel. Rooms are slightly dated but are well-equipped. ❺

Eating and drinking

Captain's Table Cnr I. Metaxa & 21 Maïou, Argostóli ⓣ 2671 027 170. A waterfront restaurant with a nautical theme serving everything from home-made pizza to fresh fish. Mains €6–9.

Mermaid Restaurant Sámi ⓣ 2674 022 202. Occupying a wonderful location along the seafront, this friendly restaurant uses local produce to create hearty dishes. Mains €6–9.

Phoenix Vergoti 2, Argostóli. Just off the central square, this enclosed garden is a peaceful spot for a coffee by day, and a popular bar by night.

Moving on

Ferry Itháki (5 daily; 30–45min); Kyllíni (11–12 daily; 1hr 15min–3hr); Pátra (3 daily; 2hr 30min).

ZÁKYNTHOS

Only an hour from Kyllíni on the mainland, **Zákynthos** now gets close to half a million visitors a year. Most tourists, though, are conveniently housed in one place, Laganás, on the south coast; if you avoid July and August, and steer clear of Laganás and the developing villages of Argási and Tsiliví, there's still a peaceful Zákynthos to be found in the thick vineyards, orchards and olive groves of the interior, and some excellent beaches.

What to see and do

The most tangible hints of the former glory of **ZÁKYNTHOS TOWN** are in **Platía Solomoú**, the grand and spacious main square. At its waterside corner stands the beautiful fifteenth-century sandstone church of **Áyios Nikólaos**, whose paintings and icons are displayed in the imposing **Byzantine Museum** (Tues–Sun 8am–7.30pm; €3, students free), by the town hall. The large church [illegible]**s Dhionýsios** was one of the few buildings left standing after the earthquake, and newly painted murals cover the interior. If you've a couple of hours to fill, walk up the cobbled path to the town's massive Venetian fortress (daily 8am–2/7.30pm; €3) for great views across the town and sea.

To get to the **beaches**, buses depart from the station on Filitá (one block back from the seafront), but since the island is fairly flat, apart from the north and west, it's an ideal place to rent a **bike** – available from Moto-Saki, opposite the phone office. In the summer a number of boats depart from the quay for day-trips around the island.

Arrival and information

Ferry Ferries from Kyllíni dock at the harbour at the southern end of the town.
Tourist office The tourist police on waterfront Lombárdhou have information about accommodation and bus services.
Roomowners Association The Roomowners Association (☎2695 049 498) also has vacancies all over the island.

Accommodation

Hotel Egli Cnr Loútzi & Lombárdhou ☎2695 028 317. A waterfront hotel which has a lacklustre welcome but clean and comfortable rooms. ❼

Eating

Arekia ☎2695 026 346. A twenty-minute walk out of town brings you to this taverna offering a succulent range of dishes and the best nightly *kantádhes* (traditional song and dance) to be heard anywhere. Mains €7–9.
Corner Platía Agíou Márkou 10 ☎2695 042 654. With a menu offering both Italian and Greek cuisine, this restaurant has delicious home-made pizzas in a good setting. Pizzas €6–9.

Moving on

Boat Kyllíni (5–7 daily; 1hr).

Crete

CRETE is distinguished as the home of the **Minoan** civilization, Europe's earliest, which made the island the centre of a maritime trading empire as early as 2000 BC and produced artworks unsurpassed in the ancient world. It's one of the few islands that could probably support itself without tourists, yet mass tourism is all too evident. Much of the north coast, in particular, is overdeveloped and, though there are coastal areas that have not been spoiled, they are getting harder and harder to find. The capital, **Iráklion**, is not the prettiest town on the island, although visits to its superb Archeological Museum and the Minoan palace at nearby **Knossos** are all but compulsory. There are other great Minoan sites at **Mália** on the north coast and at **Phaestos** in the south. Near the latter are the remains of the Roman capital at **Gortys**. Historical

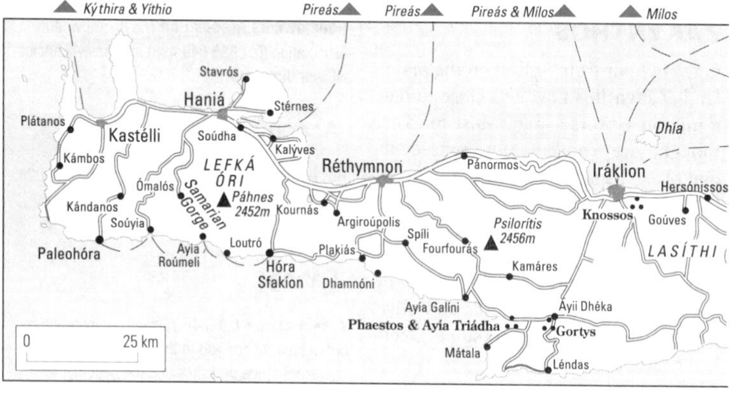

heritage apart, the main attractions are that inland this is still a place where traditional rural life continues, and that the island is big enough to ensure that, with a little effort, you can still get away from it all. If you want it, there's also a surprisingly sophisticated club scene in the north-coast cities, and plenty of manic, beer-soaked tourist fun in the resorts in between.

IRÁKLION

The best way to approach **IRÁKLION** is by sea; that way you see the city as it should be seen, with Mount Ioúktas rising behind and the Psiloritis range to the west. As you get closer, it's the fifteenth-century city walls which first stand out, still dominating and fully encircling the oldest part of town, and finally you sail in past the great Venetian fort defending the harbour entrance. Unfortunately, big ships no longer dock in this old port but at great modern concrete wharves alongside. One thing Iráklion does have going for it is a great **café** life: the pedestrianized alleys off Dedhálou, especially Koráï, are crammed with tables and packed evenings and weekends. The only real sight of interest is the **Archeological Museum**, just off the north side of the main square, Platía Eleftherías (Mon 1–7.30pm, Tues–Sun 8am–7.30pm; €6). It hosts a collection that includes almost every important prehistoric and Minoan find on Crete (go early or late in the day to avoid tour groups).

Arrival and information

Ferry Boats dock at the quay which is at the eastern end of town. As you arrive, turn right to reach the centre.

Buses For all points along the north-coast highway and Knossos use Bus Station A close to the ferry

TRANSPORT AND ORIENTATION

Crete's **transport connections** are excellent. There are regular ferries from Pireás to Iráklion, Réthymnon, Haniá and Áyios Nikólaos, as well as regular connections to Kastélli and Sitía (all on the north coast), a constant stream of buses plying between these places, and onward bus connections from these main centres to much of the rest of the island. Thanks to the tourists, there are also plenty of **day-trips** available in season, and small boats linking villages on the south coast. Rather than head for Iráklion, you're better off basing yourself initially in the beautiful city of Haniá (for the west, the mountains and the famous Samarian Gorge), in Réthymnon (only marginally less attractive, and handy for Iráklion, the major Minoan sites and the south), or Sitía to explore the far east.

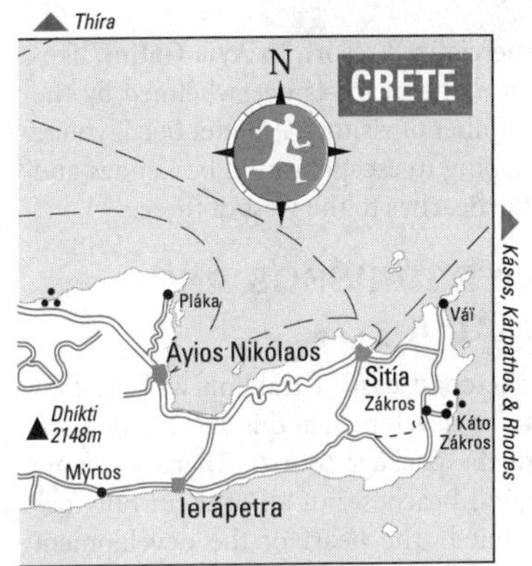

dock; services on inland routes to the south and west (for Phaestos, for example) leave from a terminal outside the city walls at Haniá Gate.

Tourist office Close to the museum is the EOT tourist office (Mon–Sat 8.30am–8.30pm; ⓣ2810 246 106, ⓦwww.heraklion-city.gr).

Internet Gallery Games, Koráï 14, is open daily until 4am. Price per hour is €1.50.

Accommodation

Creta Camping Káto Goúves ⓣ2897 041 400. The nearest campsite to Iráklion, which lies 16km east; Hersónissos-bound buses will drop you there. Open all year. ❶

Hellas Rent Rooms Hándhakos 24 ⓣ2810 288 851. A popular option, with a roof garden at the top with cheap breakfasts, a snack bar and panoramic views. Dorms ❷; doubles ❸

Rea Kalimeráki 1 ⓣ2810 223 638, ⓦwww.hotelrea.gr. A clean and comfortable pension in a quiet location, with friendly staff. Open April to Oct. ❹

Youth Hostel Víronos 5 ⓣ2810 286 281, ⓔheraklioyouthhostel@yahoo.gr. An airy building with dormitories of varying sizes. Cheap and organic meals are served in the restaurant, with home-grown ingredients. ❶

Eating

Galini Títou 20 ⓣ2810 224 457. Behind the church of Áyios Títos, tuck into the cheapest lunches in town alongside the locals. Pitta €2.

Peri Orexeos Koráï 10 ⓣ2810 222 679. A good choice for typical Cretan cuisine. A pleasant terrace is also good for lazy breakfasts and snacks. Mains €6–9.

TREAT YOURSELF

Utopia Handakos 51 ⓣ2810 341 321. A chocolate-lover's paradise. This café might serve Iráklion's most expensive coffee (prices from €5), but the generous serving of cakes and biscuits on the side makes for a guilt-free splurge. Guilt-free only if you manage to resist the chocolate fondues and other sweet treats on the menu, of course.

Moving on

Island buses Áyios Nikólaos (every 30min; 1hr 30min); Haniá (hourly; 2hr 30min); Hersónissos (every 30min; 45min); Knossos (every 10min; 20min); Mália (every 30min; 45min); Phaestos (8 daily; 1hr 30min); Réthymnon (hourly; 1hr 30min); Sitía (6 daily; 3hr).

Ferry Mýkonos (1–2 daily; 5–9hr); Iráklion to Páros & Cyclades (1–2 daily; 4–12hr); Iráklion to Pireás (2–3 daily; 6–12hr); Iráklion to Rhodes (2 weekly; 12–13hr); Kastélli to Yíthio (2 weekly; 7–8hr); Áyios Nikólaos and Sitía to Rhodes (3 weekly; 10hr).

KNOSSOS

The largest of the Minoan palaces, **KNOSSOS** (daily: April–Sept 8am–7.30pm, Oct–Mar 8.30am–5pm; €6; frequent buses from Iráklion) reached its cultural peak over 3500 years ago. As soon as you enter the palace of King Minos through the West Court, it is clear how the legend of the Labyrinth of the Minotaur grew up around it. Evidence of a luxurious lifestyle is plainest in the **Queen's Suite**, off the grand **Hall of the Colonnades** at the bottom of the stunningly impressive **Grand Staircase** (which visitors are no longer allowed to use but which can be viewed from above). On the floor above the Queen's domain, you can glimpse a set of rooms in a sterner vein, generally regarded as the **King's Quarters**. The staircase opens into a grandiose reception chamber known as the **Hall of the Royal Guard**, its walls decorated in repeated shield patterns. At the top of the staircase (visitors ascend by timber steps) you emerge onto the broad **Central Court**, which would once have been enclosed by the walls of the buildings all around. On the far side, in the northwestern corner of the courtyard, is the entrance to one of Knossos' most atmospheric survivals, the **Throne Room**, in all probability the seat of a priestess rather than a ruler.

GORTYS

About 1km west of the village of Áyii Dhéka, where the bus drops you off, **GORTYS** (daily 8am–7.30pm; €4) is the ruined capital of the Roman province of Cyrenaica, which included not only Crete but also much of North Africa. If you walk here from Áyii Dhéka you'll get an idea of the huge scale of the place at its height in the third century AD. An enormous variety of remains, including an impressive **theatre**, is scattered across the fields south of the main road. At the main entrance to the fenced site, north of the road, is the ruinous but still impressive basilica of **Áyios Títos**, the island's first Christian church and burial place of the saint (Titus) who converted Crete and was also its first bishop. Beyond this is the **Odeion**, which houses the most important discovery on the site, the **Law Code** – ancient laws inscribed on stones measuring about 10m by 3m.

PHAESTOS AND THE SOUTH

Some 17km west of Gortys, the **Palace of Phaestos** (daily 8am–7.30pm; €4) is another of the island's key Minoan sites. Unlike Knossos, the palace was not substantially reconstructed and requires a little more imagination, but the location is stunning, a hillside position giving a commanding view over the Messará plain.

From here you could continue towards the **south coast**. The easiest destination – some buses from Phaestos continue there – is **Mátala**, formerly a 1960s hippie hang-out, and now a pretty commercialized resort. In **Ayía Galíni**, likewise, the beach is overwhelmed by the number of visitors. A better bet, if you're hoping to escape, would be Léndas and the beaches to the west of there.

HERSÓNISSOS AND MÁLIA

The coast east of Iráklion was the first to be developed, and is still the domain of the package tourist. There are some good beaches, but all of them fully occupied. The heart of the development lies around **HERSÓNISSOS** and **MÁLIA**, which these days form virtually a single resort. If it's the party-holiday spirit you're after, this is the place to come. Hersónissos is perhaps slightly classier, but Mália was a bigger place to start with, which means there's a real town on the south side of the main road, with more chance of reasonably priced food and accommodation. Wherever you go, you'll have no problem finding bars, clubs and English (or Irish or even Dutch) pubs. Some of the better beaches stretch east from Mália, where the atmospheric ruins of the **Palace of Mália** (Tues–Sun 8am–7pm; €4), much less visited than Knossos or Phaestos, boast a virtually intact ground plan.

SITÍA

Sleepy **SITÍA**, the port and main town of the relatively unexploited eastern edge of Crete, may be about to wake up. For the moment, though, it still offers a plethora of waterside restaurants, a long sandy beach and a lazy lifestyle little affected by the thousands of visitors in peak season. To find cheap accommodation, there are several **rooms** in places around Kondhiláki, a few streets back from the harbour. At the eastern end of the island, **VÁÏ BEACH** is the most famous on Crete thanks to its ancient grove of palm trees. In season, though, its undoubted charms, now fenced off, are diluted by crowds of day-trippers.

Other beaches at nearby **Ítanos** or **Pálekastro** – Crete's main windsurfing centre – are less exotic but emptier. Or head further south – at **Káto Zákros** the pebbly beach is right by another important Minoan palace.

Arrival and information

Bus The bus station is found on the southern edge of town, a short walk from the town's centre.
Ferry The harbour is centrally located, close to all amenities.
Tourist offices The tourist office is on the seafront (Mon–Fri 9.30am–2.30pm & 5–9pm, Sat 9.30am–2.30pm; ⓣ2843 028 300).

Accommodation and eating

Hotel Arhontiko Kondhiláki 16, Sitía ⓣ2843 028 172. This welcoming family-run guesthouse has clean and simple rooms, and a leafy garden at the front. ❸
Taverna Mihos Kornárou 117, Sitía ⓣ2843 022 416. A traditional taverna with seating along the waterfront as well. There's a varied menu, including seafood and Cretan specials. Mains €5–9.

Island transport

Bus Áyios Nikólaos (7 daily; 1hr 30min); Iráklion (7 daily; 3hr); Mália (7 daily; 2hr 15min).

RÉTHYMNON

West of Iráklion, the old town of **RÉTHYMNON** is a labyrinthine tangle of Venetian and Turkish houses set around an enclosed sixteenth-century harbour and wide sandy beach. Medieval minarets lend an exotic air to the skyline, while dominating everything from the west is the superbly preserved outline of the **Venetian fortress** (daily 8am–8pm; €3.10). Much of the pleasure is in wandering the streets of the old town once the sun has set; there's an unbroken line of tavernas, cafés and cocktail bars right around the waterside and into the area around the old port. Better-value eateries are found around the seventeenth-century Venetian **Rimóndi Fountain**, an easily located landmark. The heart of Réthymnon's nightlife – which, although abundant, doesn't warm up until midnight – centres on the Venetian port.

Arrival and information

Bus From the bus station, head around the inland side of the fortress to reach the beach and the centre.
Tourist office Located right on the beach (Mon–Fri 8am–2.30pm, Sat 10am–4pm; ⓣ2831 029 148).

Accommodation

Barbara Dokimaki Rooms Dambérgi 14 ⓣ2831 024 581. Pleasant en-suite rooms with kitchenettes, set around a small courtyard or terrace area. ❹
Camping Elizabeth Missiria, 4km east of Réthymnon ⓣ2831 028 694, ⓦwww.camping-elizabeth.com. This campsite is in the hotel strip along the beach, served by frequent buses from the main bus station. Open April–Oct. ❷
Olga's Pension Soulíou 57 ⓣ2831 053 206. Small but attractive rooms are individually decorated, and there's a flower-filled roof garden. A real gem. ❹
Youth Hostel Tombázi 41 ⓣ2831 022 848, ⓦwww.yhrethymno.com. This friendly and relaxed hostel has clean facilities, cheap breakfasts and Internet access. The best bargain in town. ❶

Eating

Stella's Kitchen Soulíou 55 ⓣ2831 028 665. Popular with the locals, this café is good for breakfasts and great-value daily specials, a couple of which are always vegetarian. Open 8am–9pm. Mains €5–6.
To Pigandi Xanthoúdhidhou 31 ⓣ2831 027 522. Despite the well-dressed clientele, this unpretentious restaurant is great value. Theres's an atmospheric garden and excellent food with attentive service. Mains €7–12.

Drinking and nightlife

Metropolis Nearchou 15. A funky bar with a scattering of themed events, karaoke and live music. Free entry. Check out ⓦwww.metropolis-crete.com for listings.
Rock Club Cafe I. Petichaki 6. A long-standing favourite near the harbour, this club kicks off around midnight and plays mainstream sounds.

HIKING THE SAMARIAN GORGE

The **Samarian Gorge** – Europe's longest – is an easy day-trip from Haniá (May–Oct only), as there are regular buses. If you do it, though, be warned that you will not be alone: dozens of coachloads set off before dawn from all over Crete for the dramatic climb into the White Mountains and the long (at least 4hr) walk down. At the bottom of the gorge is the village of Ayía Roúmeli from where boats will take you east to Hóra Sfakíon and your bus home, or west towards the pleasant resorts of Soúyia and Paleohóra. The mountains offer endless other **hiking challenges** to help you escape the crowds. Soúyia and Paleohóra are both good starting points, as is Loutró, a tiny place halfway to Hóra Sfakíon, accessible only by boat. These places also have decent beaches, and from Paleohóra you can reach more at the far west of the island where only Elafoníssi, an isolated beach with an almost tropical-lagoon feel, ever sees crowds.

Moving on

Bus Haniá (hourly; 1hr); Iráklion (hourly; 1hr 30min).

Plakiás

Réthymnon lies at one of the narrower parts of Crete, so it's relatively quick to cut across from here to the south coast. The obvious place to head is **PLAKIÁS**, a growing resort which has managed to retain a small-town atmosphere. There are numerous **rooms**, very busy in August, as well as a relaxed and friendly youth **hostel** (Ⓣ2832 032 118, Ⓦwww.yhplakias.com; ❶) at the back of the town, and *Camping Appollonia* (Ⓣ2832 031 507; ❶) on the road in from Réthymnon. Locals can point you in the direction of quieter beaches all around, with boat trips to many of them.

HANIÁ

HANIÁ is the spiritual capital of Crete; for many, it is also the island's most attractive city – especially in spring, when the snowcapped peaks of the Lefká Óri (White Mountains) seem to hover above the roofs.

What to see and do

The **port area** is the oldest and the most interesting part of town. The little hill that rises behind the landmark domes of the quayside Mosque of the Janissaries is called **Kastélli**, site of the earliest Minoan habitation and core of the Venetian and Turkish towns. Beneath the hill, on the inner harbour, the arches of sixteenth-century Venetian arsenals survive alongside remains of the outer walls. Behind the harbour lie the less picturesque but more lively sections of the old city. Around the cathedral on Halídhon are some of the more animated shopping areas, particularly leather-dominated **Odhós Skrídhlof**. Haniá's **beaches** all lie to the west: the packed city beach is a ten-minute walk beyond the Maritime Museum, but for good sand you're better off taking the local bus from the east side of Platía 1866 along the coast road to Kalamáki. In between you'll find emptier stretches if you're prepared to walk some of the way.

Arrival and information

Bus The bus station is on Odhós Kydhonías, within easy walking distance of the centre: turn right, then left down the side of Platía 1866, and you'll emerge at a major road junction opposite the top of Halídhon, the main street of the old quarter.
Ferry Ferries dock about 10km away at the port of Soúdha: there are frequent city buses which will drop you by the market on the fringes of the old town.
Tourist office The very helpful municipal tourist office (summer only: Mon–Fri 8am–2.30pm; Ⓣ2821 036 155) is in the *Dhimarhío* (town hall) at Kydhonías 29, four blocks east of the bus station. They will provide a free town map plus help with accommodation.

Internet *Triple W*, on the corner of Balantinou & Halídhon, is open 24 hours a day.

Accommodation

Camping Hania 4km west of town ⓣ2821 031 138. A small site, but it has a pool and is close to the beaches. Get there by city bus from Platía 1866. Open early March to late Oct. ❶

Earini Rooms Halídhon 27 ⓣ2821 057 666. A hospitable welcome and decent rooms are found at this well-situated guesthouse. There's also a large apartment. ❺

Mme Bassia Betólo 45–51 ⓣ2821 055 087, ⓦwww.mmebassia.gr. A charming pension with a homely atmosphere. Traditionally decorated rooms are a good size, and there's a tiny roof garden at the top. ❻

Pension Nora Theotokopoúlou 60 ⓣ2821 072 265, ⓔpensionnora@yahoo.co.uk. Charming a/c en-suite rooms in an old wooden Turkish house, all with access to a shared kitchen. ❹

Eating and drinking

Ellotia 1 Párodos Pórtou 6 ⓣ2821 087 146. Tucked away, this cosy garden taverna serves delicious traditional fare in a leafy setting. Grills €6–9.

Metropolitan Betólo 28 ⓣ2821 040 920. Food is pricey, but come to this American-style bar in the evenings for live music from 10pm. Cover charge €1.50.

Ouzúdoino Aktí Papanikolí 6 ⓣ2821 073 315. A 10min walk out of town, but worth it for a quiet waterfront location and a good selection of seafood. Open from 9.30am for breakfast. Seafood €5–8.

Tamam Zambelíou 49 ⓣ2821 058 639. A converted Turkish bathhouse houses this restaurant which has an adventurous menu. Especially popular with vegetarians and wine-lovers. Mains €5–9.

Moving on

Bus Iráklion (hourly; 2hr 30min); Omalos (for the Samarian Gorge; 4 daily when the gorge is open; 1hr); Réthymnon (hourly; 1hr).

Hungary

HIGHLIGHTS ✪

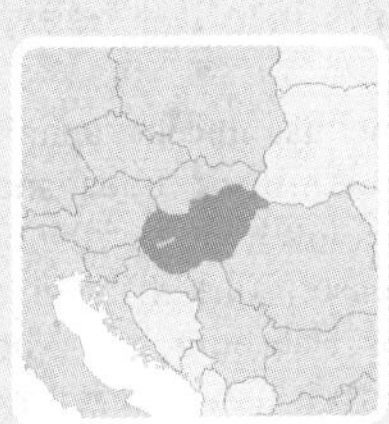

SZÉPASSZONY VALLEY: sup some outstanding wines at the valley's various cellars

SZÉCHENYI BATHS, BUDAPEST: take a plunge into the steamy, healing waters

COMMUNIST STATUE PARK, BUDAPEST: visit the fascinating graveyard for statues of old dictators

KECSKEMÉT: enjoy fabulous horse-riding, followed by dinner at one of Hungary's best restaurants

PÉCS: chill out in this young, lively city packed with brightly coloured buildings and great cafés

ROUGH COSTS

DAILY BUDGET €25

DRINK Beer (large) €1.10

FOOD Goulash €3.50

HOSTEL/BUDGET HOTEL €10–30

TRAVEL Budapest–Szeged by train (175km) €12; bus Pécs–Keszthely (150km) €10

FACT FILE

POPULATION 10 million

AREA 93,000 sq km

LANGUAGE Hungarian

CURRENCY Forint (Ft)

CAPITAL Budapest (population 2.4 million)

INTERNATIONAL PHONE CODE ⓣ36

Basics

Visitors who refer to Hungary as a Balkan country risk getting a lecture on how this small, landlocked nation of ten million people differs from "all those Slavs": locals fiercely identify themselves as Magyar – a race that transplanted itself from Central Asia into the heart of Europe over a thousand years ago.

The magnificent capital **Budapest** (split into historic Buda and vibrant Pest), is a lovely mix of the old – with coffee houses, Turkish baths and a penchant for Habsburg bric-á-brac – and the new: it has an eager modern feel, with international fashions snapped up and adapted to local tastes. Outside the capital, there's much to explore: a short way north of Budapest, on a beautiful stretch of the River Danube, is **Szentendre**, while to the west lies **Lake Balaton**, the "nation's playground", encircled with a string of brash resorts, such as **Siófok** and **Keszthely**, and the lush volcanic **Badacsony** region. The Great Plain stretches south, covering half of the country with some stunning National Parks and the culture-rich cities of Szeged and Kecskemét. Other highlights include the delightful city of **Sopron**, on the border with Austria, and Turkish-flavoured Pécs, in the south. The forested Northern Uplands in the far northeast towards Ukraine envelop the beautiful Baroque town of **Eger**, also famed for its wine.

CHRONOLOGY

9 BC Area around the Danube is conquered by the Romans.
453 AD Attila the Hun's empire is based in Hungary.
896 Country of the Magyars founded.
1000 Kingdom of Hungary established by Saint Stephen.
1242 The Mongols attack Hungary, wreaking havoc across the country.
1526 The Hungarian army is defeated by the Ottomans in the Battle of the Mohacs and the country is split into three areas.
1699 The Turks are defeated and expelled from Hungary by the Austrian Habsburgs.
1867 In order to quell separatist calls, Austria accepts greater Hungarian autonomy and officially becomes Austria-Hungary.
1918 After WWI, Austria-Hungary is split into two countries.
1938 Hungarian journalist Lasislao Jose Biro invents the ballpoint pen.
1939 Hungary opts for neutrality at the beginning of WWII.
1945 Soviets invade Hungary, causing devastation.
1947 Soviets consolidate their post-war power in Hungary.
1956 National uprising against Soviet occupation is brutally repressed.
1989 Collapse of Soviet Communism.
1990 Hungary's first free elections held.
2004 Hungary joins the EU.
2006 Mass protests as it transpires the government had lied about its election promises.
2007 Hungary regains world record for largest number of people kissing simultaneously with 6400 couples joining lips.

ARRIVAL

Flights to Budapest arrive at Ferihegy airport, 20km from the centre; bus and metro connect into Budapest or alternatively, there's an airport bus that will take you straight to your accommodation. Several budget airlines now fly to Balaton airport – the closest town is Keszthely, with a regular bus service between the two.

Most international **trains** arrive to Keleti pu in Budapest, although Nyugati pu and Déli pu also handle international arrivals (see "Arrivals" section in Budapest). Global or "One Country" Interrail passes are valid on all trains; seats must be reserved at the station however, costing a roughly 350-480Ft per journey.

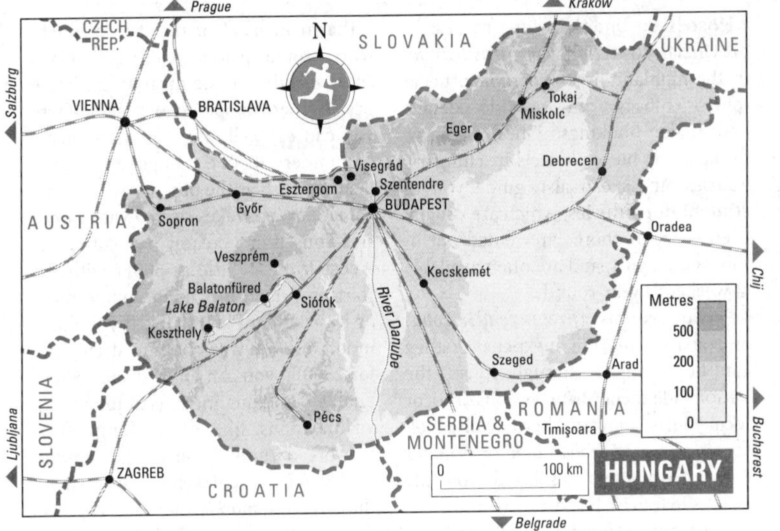

International **buses** are generally operated by Eurolines, or Volánbusz, its Hungarian associate, with their two main terminals in Budapest.

GETTING AROUND

Public transport in Hungary is cheap, clean and fairly reliable. The only problem is getting information – staff rarely speak anything but Hungarian.

Intercity **trains** are the fastest way of getting to the major towns, though seat reservations, made at any MÁV office, are compulsory and cost an extra 350–480Ft; *személyvonat* trains, which stop at every hamlet en route, do not incur the reservation fee. You can buy **tickets** *(jegy)* for domestic services at the station *(pályaudvar* or *vasútállomás)* on the day of departure, but it's best to buy tickets for international trains *(nemzetközi gyorsvonat)* at least 36hr in advance. You're permitted to break your journey once. When buying your ticket, specify whether you want a one-way ticket *(egy útra)*, or a return *(retur* or *oda-vissza)*. For a journey of 100km, travelling second-class on an express train, expect to pay around 2000Ft.

Volán runs the bulk of Hungary's **buses**, which are often the quickest way to travel between the smaller towns. Arrive early to confirm times and get a seat. For **long-distance services** from Budapest and the major towns, you can book a seat up to 30min before departure; after that, you get them from the driver (and risk standing). For a journey of 100km, expect to pay around 1500Ft.

ACCOMMODATION

Accommodation tends to fill up during high season, so it's wise to **book ahead**. Outside Budapest and Lake Balaton (where prices are thirty percent higher), a three-star **hotel** *(szálló* or *szálloda)* will charge from around 12,000Ft for a double room with bath and TV; solo travellers often have to pay this too, since singles are rare. **Inns** *(fogadó)* and **pensions** *(panzió)* tend to be more charismatic than hotels – and charge a little les – as they are usually run by families, who pride themselves on offering a typically hearty Hungarian breakfast to set you on your way.

Hostels go under various names: in provincial towns they're *turistaszálló*, in the highland areas *turistaház.* Local tourist offices can provide details and make bookings. Check Ⓦwww.backpackers.hu for hostels in Hungary. Tourist offices can also guide you to **student dormitories**, which are usually even cheaper: rooms are rented out in July and August, and are often available at weekends year-round.

Private rooms *(fizeţo vendégszoba)* and apartments are inexpensive; they can be arranged through Ibusz, the nationwide agency (Ⓦwww.ibusz.hu), or local tourist offices. Alternatively, look for signs saying *szoba kiadó* or *Zimmer Frei,* frequently displayed outside houses in tourist-heavy towns, and often outside homes recommended by Ibusz as well. Doubles range from 4000Ft in provincial towns to around 6000Ft in Budapest and around Balaton.

Bungalows *(faház)* proliferate around resorts and on the larger campsites. First-class bungalows come with kitchens, hot water and a sitting room or terrace, and will cost a few thousand forints, while the most primitive at least have clean bedding and don't leak. **Campsites** (usually signposted *Kemping*) range from de luxe to third class. In high season, expect to pay anything up to 3500Ft, more around Lake Balaton.

FOOD AND DRINK

For foreigners, the archetypal **Hungarian dish** is goulash *(gulyásleves)* – historically a soup made of potatoes and meat, which was later flavoured with paprika. Hungarians like a calorific **breakfast** *(reggeli)* that includes cheese, eggs and salami, plus bread and jam. **Coffee houses** *(kávéház)* are increasingly trendy and you'll find many serving breakfast and a coffee with milk *(tejeskávé)* or whipped cream *(tejszínhabbal).* Most Hungarians take their coffee short and strong *(eszpresszó).*

The main meal of the day is **lunch**, when some places offer set menus *(napi menű)*, a basic meal at moderate prices. There are plenty of places where you can eat well and sink a few beers for under 2000Ft. Soups and small dishes – such as the popular *Hortobágyi palacsinta* (pancakes stuffed with mince and doused in a creamy paprika sauce) – cost from as little as 600Ft with the starting price for a main course more or less standard at 1200Ft. If you fancy indulging, you won't have to stretch far: for 2500Ft, you can enjoy dishes whose quality – and quantity – is fit for a king.

Hungarians like most things fried in breadcrumbs, such as *rántott csirkecomb* (chicken drumstick), though *marhapörkölt* (beef stew) is also popular. In traditional places, the only choice for **vegetarians** will be breaded and fried cheese, mushrooms or cauliflower (*rántott sajt/gomba/karfiol*). A whole range of places sell **snacks:** pancakes *(palacsinta, from 1000Ft)* with fillings are very popular, as are strudels *(rétes, about 350Ft).* On the streets you can buy, in summer, corn-on-the-cob *(kukorica)* and in winter, roasted chestnuts *(gesztenye)*; while stalls selling fried fish *(sült hal)* are common in towns near rivers or lakes.

Drink

Hungary's mild climate and diversity of soils is perfect for **wine** *(bor)*, which is perennially cheap, whether you buy it by the bottle *(üveg)* or the glass *(pohár).* Perhaps the most famous region is the Tokaj-Hegyalja, known predominantly for dessert wine. *Bikavér*, produced in Eger and known as "Bull's Blood", is well-known, robust red, while the rich, sweet Médoc Noir, from the same vineyard, is worth a try. The best whites are found in the Balaton region, especially around the Badacsony.

Wine bars *(borozó)* are ubiquitous, while true grape devotees make pilgrimages to the wine cellars *(borpince)* around Pécs and Eger. The best-known types of **brandy** *(pálinka)* are distilled from apricots *(barack)* and plums *(szilva)*, the latter often available in private homes in a mouth-scorching, home-distilled version. **Beer** *(sör)* of the lager type *(világos)* predominates, although you can also find **brown ale** *(barna)*: these come in draught form *(csapolt sör)* or in bottles *(üveges sör)*. Local brands to look out for are Pécsi Szalon sör and Soproni Ászok.

CULTURE AND ETIQUETTE

Hungarians are not generally a reserved bunch, and almost always go out of their way to help if you need directions or assistance. The younger generation are especially welcoming and approachable, eager to show visitors a good time and share their views on their country and its history.

The expected rules apply regarding sensible clothing in churches and places of worship. **Tipping** waiters and taxi-drivers roughly 10 percent is more or less expected; in restaurants it is more common to do so as part of paying the bill, rather than leaving it on the table.

SPORTS AND OUTDOOR ACTIVITIES

Hungary offers some of the best **horseriding** in Europe, as well as fantastic horse-shows during the summer. Head for the Great Plain, especially Kecskemét and areas around the Kiskunság National Park. There are a number of tour operators but it's cheapest to go for independent ones – local tourist offices have relevant details. Visit Ⓦwww.hiddentrails.com/hungary.htm for details.

The flatness of the Great Plain and beautiful landscape is great for **cycling**. Tourinform can provide cycling maps with recommended routes, and bikes can be hired in almost every town at reasonable prices. There are scores of **hiking** opportunities all over the country; the Badacsony in Balaton, in particular, is very accessible, and has stunning views over the lake to reward you at the end of your trek. Head to Tourinform for maps and information.

COMMUNICATIONS

Larger **post offices** *(posta)* are usually open Mon–Fri 8am–6pm, Sat 8am–1pm. Smaller branches close at 3pm and don't always open on Saturday. You can make local calls from **public phones**, where 40Ft is the minimum charge, or, better, from cardphones; cards come in 50 and 120 units and can be bought from post offices and newsstands. To make national calls, dial Ⓣ06, wait for the buzzing tone, then dial the area code and number. You can make international calls from most public phones: dial t00, wait for the buzzing tone, then dial the country code as usual. **Internet access** is widely available (usually 500–800Ft/hr) in most towns.

HUNGARY ON THE NET

Ⓦ**www.hungarytourism.hu** National tourist office.
Ⓦ**www.travelport.hu** Excellent general site.
Ⓦ**www.budapestinfo.hu** Comprehensive site with up-to-the-minute listings.
Ⓦ**www.elvira.hu** Train timetables and information.
Ⓦ**www.pecs.hu** A young, fun site with loads of info.

EMERGENCIES

Tourists are treated with respect by the police *(rendörség)* – unless they're suspected of black-marketeering, drug smuggling or driving under the influence of alcohol. Most have a smattering of

Hungarian

Basics	Hungarian	Pronunciation
Yes	*Igen*	I-gen
No	*Nem*	Nem
Please	*Kérem*	Kay-rem
Thank you	*Köszönöm*	Kur-sur-nurm
Hello/Good day	*Jó napot*	Yo nopot
Goodbye	*Viszontlátásra*	Vee-sont-lar-tarsh-rar
Excuse me	*Bocsánat*	Botch-ah-not
Good	*Jó*	Yo
Bad	*Rossz*	Ross
Today	*Ma*	Ma
Yesterday	*Tegnap*	Teg-nop
Tomorrow	*Holnap*	Hall-nop
How much is....?	*Mennyibe kerül...?*	Men-yi-beh keh-rool...?
What time is it?	*Hány óra van?*	Hine-ora von
I don't understand	*Nem értem*	Nem ear-tem
Do you speak English?	Beszél Angolul?	Beh-sail ong-olool?
One	*Egy*	Edge
Two	*Kettö*	Ket-tur
Three	*Három*	Hah-rom
Four	*Négy*	Naidge
Five	*Öt*	Urt
Six	*Hat*	Hot
Seven	*Hét*	Hait
Eight	*Nyolc*	Nyolts
Nine	*Kilenc*	Kee-lents
Ten	*Tíz*	Teez
Getting around		
Where is/are?	*Hol van/vannak?*	Hawl- von/von-nok?
Entrance	*bejárat*	beyah-ro
Exit	*kijárat*	kiyah-rot
Women's toilet	*női*	nuy
Men's Toilet	*férfi mosdó*	fayr-fi maws-daw
Toilet	*WC*	vait-say
hotel	*szálloda*	sahlaw-da
Railway station	*vasútállomás*	voh-sootal-law-mass
Bus/train stop	*megalló*	meh-gall-o
Plane	*repülőgép*	repoo-lur-gepp
Near	*közel*	kur-zel
Far	*távol*	tav-oll
Accommodation		
Single room	*egyágyas szoba*	edg-yahg-yos saw-ba
Double room	*kétágyas szoba*	kay-tadg-yas soba
Cheap	*Olcsó*	Ol-cho
Expensive	*Drága*	Drah-ga
Open	*Nyitva*	Nyeet-va
Closed	*Zárva*	Zah-rva

EMERGENCY NUMBERS

Police ☎107; Ambulance ☎104; Fire ☎105.

German, but rarely any other foreign language. Be sure to always carry your passport or a photocopy.

All towns and some villages have a **pharmacy** *(gyógyszertár* or *patika)*, with staff – often German-speaking – authorized to issue a wide range of drugs. Opening hours are generally Mon–Fri 9am–6pm, Sat 9am–noon or 1pm; signs in the window give the location of all-night pharmacies *(ügyeletes gyógyszertár)*. Tourist offices can direct you to local medical centres or doctors' surgeries *(orvosi rendelő)*; these will probably be in private *(magán)* practice, so be sure to carry health insurance. EU citizens have reciprocal arrangements for emergency treatment, but only at state hospitals.

INFORMATION & MAPS

You'll find branches of **Tourinform**, Hungary's national Tourist Office, in the capital and in just about every other town across the country; branches are open Mon–Fri 9am–5/8pm; summer also open Sat & Sun. They don't book accommodation, but do have information on where rooms and beds are available, including the booklets *Hungarian Hotel* and *Camping Guide*. There are also **local tourist offices** in larger towns (such as Balatontourist around Lake Balaton), where you can **book rooms**; opening hours are Mon–Fri 9am–4/6pm; summer also Sat 8am–1pm. It's cheapest to buy your **maps** in Hungary: the best is Cartographia's full-country fold-out sheet (1:450,000).

MONEY AND BANKS

Currency is the **forint** (Ft), which comes in notes of 200Ft, 500Ft, 1000Ft, 2000Ft, 5000Ft, 10,000Ft and 20,000Ft, and in coins of 1Ft, 2Ft, 5Ft, 10Ft, 20Ft, 50Ft and 100Ft (the 50Ft coin is easily confused with the 10Ft coin). At the time of writing, €1=250Ft, US$1=190Ft, and £1=380Ft. Standard **banking hours** are Mon–Thurs 8am–4pm, Fri 8am–3pm. **ATMs** are widespread throughout the country, and you can use a **credit card** to pay in many hotels, restaurants and shops.

OPENING HOURS AND HOLIDAYS

Shops are generally open Mon–Fri 10am–6pm, Sat 10am–1pm, except on the following public holidays: Jan 1, March 15, Easter Mon, May 1, Whit Mon, Aug 20, Oct 23, Nov 1, Dec 25 & 26.

Budapest

The importance of **BUDAPEST** to Hungary is difficult to overestimate. Around two million people – one-fifth of the population – live in the city, and everything converges here: wealth, political power, cultural life and transport. Surveying the city from Castle Hill, it's obvious why Budapest was dubbed the "Pearl of the Danube" – its grand buildings and sweeping bridges look magnificent, especially when floodlit.

The **River Danube** (Duna) determines basic orientation, with **Pest** sprawled across the eastern plain and **Buda** reclining on the hilly west bank.

Each of Budapest's 23 districts (*kerületek*) is designated on maps, street signs and at the beginning of addresses by a Roman numeral; "V" is Belváros (inner city), on the Pest side; "I" is the Castle district in Buda.

What to see and do

Castle Hill (Várhegy) is the most prominent feature of the **Buda** district, a plateau one mile long, laden with old mansions and the huge Buda Palace. **Pest**, across the river, is busy, happening and brimming with youthful enthusiasm – quite the opposite of its fairytale "other half".

Buda: Castle Hill

Castle Hill is easily reached via the **Chain Bridge**, opened in 1849 and the first permanent bridge between Buda and Pest. From the busy Clark Ádám tér on the western side of the bridge, you can ride up Castle Hill on the nineteenth-century funicular or **Sikló** (daily 7.30am–10pm; 700Ft up or 1300Ft return), or else make the view even more satisfying by walking up the leafy path from Clark Ádám tér. Alternatively, take the red metro to Moszkva tér and the *Várbusz* from there.

Szentháromság tér

By midday, **Szentháromság tér**, the square at the heart of the district, is crammed with tourists, buskers, handicraft vendors and other entrepreneurs, a multilingual spectacle played out against the backdrop of the wildly asymmetrical **Mátyás Church** (Mon–Sat 9am–5pm, Sun 1–5pm; 650Ft). The church is a riotous nineteenth-century recreation grafted onto those portions of the thirteenth-century structure that survived one hundred and fifty years of Ottoman rule, during which time it became a mosque, to be turned back into a church after the siege of 1686. An equestrian statue of **King Stephen** stands just outside the church, commemorating the ruler who forced Catholicism onto his subjects, thus aligning Hungary with the culture of Western Europe. Behind the church is the **Fishermen's Bastion** or Halászbástya (daily mid March to Oct 8.30am–11pm; 100–200Ft), which offers a splendid view of Parliament across the river.

Buda Palace

To the south of Szentháromság tér the street widens as it approaches the **Buda Palace**. The fortifications and dwellings have undergone relentless invasions and reconstructions since the thirteenth century, each time rebuilt in the architectural style of the age. Today's neo-Classical style was taken on following destruction during the Second World War. The **National Gallery** (Tues–Sun 10am–6pm; free, 800Ft for visiting shows), occupying the central wings B, C and D, contains Hungarian art spanning the Middle Ages to the present day. On the far side of the Lion Courtyard, the fascinating and comprehensive **Budapest History Museum** in Wing E (Wed–Mon 10am–4/6pm, closed Tues; 1100Ft) gives the turbulent history of the city, with reproductions of what it would have looked like in medieval times.

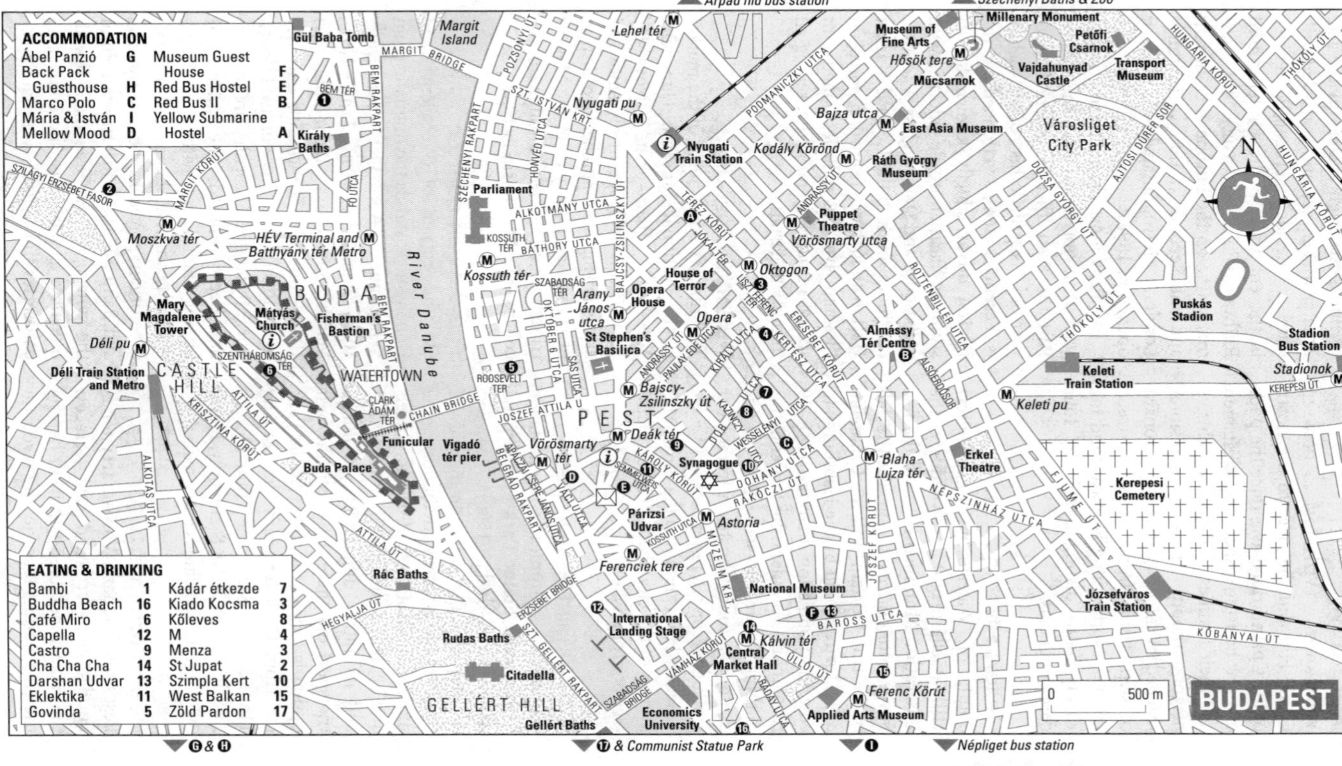
BUDAPEST
ACCOMMODATION
Ábel Panzió G
Back Pack Guesthouse H
Marco Polo C
Mária & István I
Mellow Mood D
Museum Guest House F
Red Bus Hostel E
Red Bus II B
Yellow Submarine Hostel A
EATING & DRINKING
Bambi 1
Buddha Beach 16
Café Miro 6
Capella 12
Castro 9
Cha Cha Cha 14
Darshan Udvar 13
Eklektika 11
Govinda 5
Kádár étkezde 7
Kiado Kocsma 3
Kőleves 8
M 4
Menza 3
St Jupat 2
Szimpla Kert 10
West Balkan 15
Zöld Pardon 17
Árpád híd bus station
Széchenyi Baths & Zoo
Népliget bus station
& Communist Statue Park
Gül Baba Tomb
Margit Island
Király Baths
Moszkva tér
HÉV Terminal and Batthyány tér Metro
Mary Magdalene Tower
Mátyás Church
Fisherman's Bastion
Déli pu
Déli Train Station and Metro
CASTLE HILL
BUDA
WATERTOWN
River Danube
Funicular
Buda Palace
Vigadó tér pier
Rác Baths
Rudas Baths
Citadella
GELLÉRT HILL
Gellért Baths
Parliament
Kossuth tér
Arany János utca
St Stephen's Basilica
Opera House
House of Terror
Oktogon
Opera
Bajcsy-Zsilinszky út
Deák tér
Vörösmarty tér
PEST
Synagogue
Párizsi Udvar
Astoria
Ferenciek tere
International Landing Stage
Central Market Hall
Kálvin tér
National Museum
Economics University
Applied Arts Museum
Ferenc Körút
Nyugati pu
Nyugati Train Station
Lehel tér
Kodály Körönd
Puppet Theatre
Vörösmarty utca
Ráth György Museum
East Asia Museum
Bajza utca
Museum of Fine Arts
Hősök tere
Műcsarnok
Millenary Monument
Vajdahunyad Castle
Petőfi Csarnok
Transport Museum
Városliget City Park
Puskás Stadion
Stadion Bus Station
Stadionok
Keleti Train Station
Keleti pu
Almássy Tér Centre
Blaha Lujza tér
Erkel Theatre
Kerepesi Cemetery
Józsefváros Train Station
MARGIT BRIDGE
CHAIN BRIDGE
ERZSÉBET BRIDGE
SZABADSÁG BRIDGE
0 500 m
N

Watertown

Watertown (Víziváros), between Castle Hill and the river to the north of the Chain Bridge, was once the poor quarter housing fishermen, craftsmen and their families. Today it's a reclusive neighbourhood of old mansions, reached by alleys which mostly consist of steps rising from the main street, Fő utca. North along Fő utca stand the **Király baths** distinguishable by four copper cupolas.

Gellért Hill

South of Watertown rises **Gellért Hill** (Gellérthegy), crowned by the **Liberation Monument**, one of the few Soviet monuments to survive the fall of the Iron Curtain, and the **Citadella**, a low fortress built by the Habsburgs to cow the population after the 1848–49 revolution. Nowadays the fort contains nothing more sinister than a few exhibits, a tourist hostel, a terrace bar and an overpriced restaurant.

Gellert Hill is home to the most well-known of the city's baths, Gellert Baths (see box, opposite).

Communist Statue Park

Budapest's ironically nostalgic **Communist Statue Park** (Szoborpark; daily 10am–dusk; 1500Ft; Ⓦwww.szoborpark.hu) also lies on this side of the river and is worth a detour to see the monumental statues of Marx, Engels and Lenin. It's stuck out in district XXII and it's rather difficult to get public transport out there. However, the best option is to take the direct Statue Park bus from Deák tér (daily: July & Aug 11am & 3pm; Sept–June 11am; Dec 3–21 & Jan 7–Feb 29 Sat & Sun only, 11am; 3950Ft return, includes entry fee).

Pest: Vörösmarty tér

Pest's main square, **Vörösmarty tér** is flooded with crowded café terraces; the most venerable institution here is the **Gerbeaud** patisserie, the favourite of Budapest's high society in the late nineteenth century, and now filled with tourists. Beside Gerbeaud's terrace is the entrance to the Underground Railway (Földatti Vasút), the first metro line on the European continent and the second in the world (after London's Metropolitan line), when it opened in 1896.

The city's most chic shopping street, **Váci utca**, runs south from the square. Past the Pesti Theatre, where twelve-year-old Liszt made his concert debut, is **Ferenciek tere**, overlooked by the **Párizsi udvar**, chiefly known for its stunning "Parisian arcade", adorned with arabesques and stained glass. Váci utca continues south to the **Central Market Hall**, with its fancy ironwork, porcelain tiles and vivacious stalls festooned with strings of paprika and garlic, selling all things Hungarian.

National Museum

Ten minutes' stroll north of the market is the **National Museum** (June–Oct Tues–Sun 10am–6pm, Nov–May 10am–5pm; free), sensitively renovated and showing a comprehensive display of Hungarian history from the Magyar tribes' arrival in 896 through to the collapse of communism in 1989.

The Jewish quarter

On the corner of Wesselényi and Dohány utca, stands the dramatic main **Synagogue** (April–Oct Sun–Thurs 10am–6pm, Fri 10am–3pm, Nov–March Sun–Thurs 10am–3pm, Fri 10am–2pm; 1900Ft including entrance to National Jewish Museum next door). The Byzantine-Moorish architecture has been restored; the interior is utterly magnificent with shimmering golden geometric shapes and a 5000-tube organ, played in the past by Liszt and Saint Saëns. In the streets behind the synagogue lies Pest's main **Jewish quarter**, a favourite spot for cute patisseries and stylish new restaurants.

TAKING A BATH IN BUDAPEST

Budapest has some of the grandest **baths** in Europe, and a visit to one of them is an essential part of any trip to the city. A basic ticket covers three hours in the pools, sauna and steamrooms (*gözfürdo*), with a money-back scheme operating in the Széchenyi and Gellért baths; for example, if you stay just an hour, you get 200Ft back. Supplementary tickets are available for such delights as the mud baths (*iszapfürdo*) and massages (*masszázs*).

Built in 1913, the magnificent **Gellért baths**, with original Art Nouveau furnishings, awesome mosaics, sculptures and stained glass attracts the most visitors (Mon–Fri 6am–7pm, Sat & Sun 6am–5/7pm; 2800Ft pool and locker, 3100Ft pool and cabin). You can get cheaper tickets just for the stunning thermal baths (which close earlier at weekends; separate baths for men and women).

The Turkish **Király baths** date back to 1565; men and women must visit separately (men only Tues, Thurs & Sat 9am–8pm; women only Mon, Wed & Fri 7am–6pm; 1200Ft). The atmospheric **Rudas baths** (men only) house a charming octagonal pool under a characteristic Turkish dome (Mon–Fri 6am–8pm, Sat 6am–5pm, Sun 8am–5pm; 1400Ft).

The lovely **Széchenyi Spa Baths** in Pest are the hottest in the capital (May–Sept daily 6am–7pm, open late in July & Aug, ask in baths for details; Oct–April 6am–5pm; 2400Ft).

St Stephen's Basilica

Peering over the rooftops to the north of Vörösmarty tér is the dome of **St Stephen's Basilica**, from the top of which there's a fine view over the city (dome: April–Oct daily 9am–5pm; 600Ft). On his name day, August 20, St Stephen's mummified hand – Hungary's most famous reliquary – is paraded round the building; the rest of the year, the hand is on show in a side chapel.

Parliament

Dominating the banks of the Danube is the large dome of the **Parliament,** a stupendous nineteenth-century creation whose impressive interior is replete with sweeping staircases and a gilded 96m-high central dome. It houses the old **Coronation Regalia,** the most prized treasure in Hungary. There are daily **tours** of the building – in English – if parliamentary business allows (10am, noon, 2pm; free for EU citizens, 2400Ft for others; tickets from Gate X, half-way along the east front).

Andrássy út

To the east of St Stephen's basilica, **Andrássy út** runs dead straight for 2.5km, a parade of grand buildings laden with gold leafing, including the magnificent Opera House at no. 22. A little further along, at no. 60, is the **House of Terror** (Tues–Fri 10am–6pm, Sat & Sun 10am–8pm; 1500Ft). Once the headquarters of the dreaded secret police, the building now houses a collection of sobering exhibits pertaining to Stalin, the Nazis and the Holocaust, as well as the Soviet "liberation" and the 1956 uprising.

Hosök tere

Hosök tere was built to mark the 1000th anniversary of the Magyar conquest; its centrepiece is the **Millenary Monument**, portraying the great Magyar leader Prince Árpád, as well as statues of Hungary's most illustrious leaders, from King Stephen to Kossuth. Also on the square is the **Museum of Fine Arts** (Tues–Sun 10am–6pm; free), the jewel of which is a collection of paintings by El Greco. Behind the museum lies **Budapest**

Zoo (daily 10am–6pm; 1700Ft), worth a visit for the architecture alone – the Palm House, the Elephant House and the Aviary in particular. Opposite the zoo are the yellow neo-Baroque walls of the **Széchenyi baths**. Watch locals play chess on floating boards while wallowing in the steam.

The Városliget and Petőfi Csarnok

The **Városliget** (City Park) starts just behind the Hosők tere and holds the romantic Vajdahunyad Castle, an imitation of a Transylvanian castle of the same name. Originally constructed in wood and cardboard in 1896, the castle was made a permanent fixture eight years later, and rebuilt in stone and brick. The mysterious statue of the hooded monk Anonymus in the castle court is worth a look – it depicts the first historian to chronicle Hungarian history in a twelfth-century court.

An artificial lake stretches out at the foot of the castle, popular with rowers in the summer and a spectacular spot for ice-skating in the winter. Heading behind Vajdahunyad will lead you to **Petőfi Csarnok**, a youth leisure centre that hosts big-name concerts (check out Ⓦwww.petoficsarnok.hu) and a fine flea market (see "Shopping", p.599, for details)

Arrival and information

Air From Ferihegy airport, an airport minibus will deliver to specific hotels (2300Ft; book it in the terminal building). By public transport, take the Reptérbusz (airport bus) to the final stop Kobánya-Kispest and from there, the metro ten stops to the centre, Deák tér. The airport taxi-drivers are notorious sharks and best avoided.

Train There are three main train stations, all of which are directly connected by metro with the central Deák tér metro station in the Belváros, in the district of Pest. Keleti station handles most international trains, including those from Vienna (Westbahnhof), Belgrade, Bucharest, Zagreb and Bratislava, as well as domestic arrivals from Sopron and Eger; Nyugati station receives trains from Prague and Bratislava, some from Bucharest, and domestic ones from the Danube Bend; and Déli station has one train a day from Vienna (Südbahnhof), the occasional train from Zagreb, and domestic services from Pécs and Lake Balaton.

Bus The central bus station is at Népliget (blue metro 3), serving international destinations and routes to Transdanubia. Also in Pest, Stadion bus station (red metro) serves areas east of the Danube; and Árpád híd bus station (blue metro) serves the Danube Bend.

Boat Hydrofoils from Vienna dock alongside the Danube embankment on the Pest side.

Tourist office Tourinform (daily 8am–8pm; Ⓣ1/438-8080, Ⓦwww.tourinform.hu) is just around the corner from Deák tér metro at Süţo utca 2, behind the big yellow Lutheran church; other branches are on Liszt Ferenc tér (Mon–Fri 10am–6pm) and in the Castle District on Szentháromság tér (daily 9am–9pm). Other offices include the Vista Tourist Center, Paulay Ede utca 7 (Mon–Fri 9am–8pm, Sat & Sun 10am–6pm; Ⓣ1/267-8603, Ⓦwww.vista.hu) and Budapest Tourist, in the subway in front of Nyugati train station (Mon–Fri 9am–4pm; Ⓣ1/342-6521).

Discount passes A Budapest Card (6450/7950Ft for two/three days), available at the airport and town centre tourist offices, hotels and major metro stations, gives unlimited travel on public transport, free museum admission, reductions on the airport minibus and other discounts.

City transport

Metro The metro (daily 4.30am–11.15pm) has three lines intersecting at Deák tér and is fairly easy to navigate. A basic 230Ft ticket is valid for a journey along one line, and also for a single journey on buses, trolleybuses, trams and the HÉV suburban train as far as the city limits. You can also buy 180Ft tickets for metro journeys of up to three stops.

Buy tickets from metro stations or (quicker) from street stands or newsagents, and punch them in the machines at the station entrance (or on board buses, trolleybuses and trams): inspectors often wait at the bottom of the escalators to check tickets and hand out fines.

Bus and tram Buses (*busz)* with red numbers make limited stops, while those with the red suffix "E" go nonstop between termini; all run frequently during the day – as do trams (*villamos*) and trolleybuses (*trolibusz*) – and every thirty to sixty minutes between 11pm and dawn along routes with a night service (denoted with the black suffix "E"). Get a pass (1350/3100Ft for one/three days), or buy a book of tickets (ten 2050Ft, twenty 3900Ft)

– don't tear them out, as they are only valid if kept in the book.

Taxi Taxis are a common rip-off, unless booked through a company. Go for Főtaxi (☎1/222-2222) or the English-speaking Citytaxi (☎1/211-1111): both charge a basic fee of around 300Ft plus up to 240Ft per kilometre.

Accommodation

The best places to stay are districts V, VI and VII in Pest, and the parts of Buda nearest Castle Hill. **Hotels** are generally expensive, and many of the better places expect payment in euros. For bookings, contact the Vista Visitor Center, VI, Paulay Ede utca 7 (☎1/429-9950, ⓦwww.vista.hu). **Hostels** can be booked through the Hungarian Youth Hostel Association near Keleti Station (☎1/413-2065, ⓦwww.youthhostels.hu). **Private rooms** downtown cost from 4500Ft a night, rising to 10,000Ft or more in high season.

Hostels

Back Pack Guesthouse XI, Takács Menyhért utca 33 ☎1/385-8946, ⓦwww.backpackbudapest.hu. Charming, clean place, with a shaded garden, and only 20min from the centre. Lots of city information, plus rock climbing and cave trips. Tram #49 or bus #7 to Tétényi út stop in Buda. Dorms ❷, one double ❷

Marco Polo VII, Nyár utca 6 ☎1/413-2555 ⓦwww.marcopolohostel.com. Clean, well-located hostel in the Jewish quarter. ❷

Mellow Mood V, Bécsi utca 2 ☎1/411-1310, ⓦwww.mellowmoodhostel.com. Friendly, well-run and very centrally located hotel with 270 beds in doubles and rooms of four, six and eight beds, all overlooking the street. Book in Keleti Station and you get a lift in the Mellow Mood van. Dorm beds from ❷, doubles ❷

Museum Guest House VIII, Mikszáth Kálmán tér 4, 1st floor ☎1/318-9508, ⓦwww.budapesthostel.com. Behind the National Museum and handy for central bars and cafés, there are three clean dorms here, each with seven or eight mattresses on the floor. Free Internet. Dorms ❷

Red Bus Hostel V, Semmelweis utca 14 ☎1/266-0136, and **Red Bus II** VII, Szövetség utca 35 ☎1/321-7100, both ⓦwww.redbusbudapest.hu. Clean, quiet hostels with basic facilities but great, central locations. Red Bus Books next door to *Red Bus Hostel* will swap all your dog-eared paperbacks. Dorms ❷, rooms ❷

Yellow Submarine Hostel VI, Teréz körút 56 ☎1/331-9896, ⓦwww.yellowsubmarinehostel.com. Compact, warm and friendly, with cheap dorms and a bustling common-room kitchen. Ten minutes from Nyugati. Dorms 2800Ft (with breakfast), rooms ❸

Hotels and pensions

Ábel Panzió XI, Ábel Jenő utca 9 ☎1/381-0553, ⓦwww.hotels.hu/abelpanzio. Fantastic 1913 villa with beautiful Art Nouveau fittings in a quiet street a 30min walk from the Belváros. Take tram #6 to Móricz Zsigmund Körter then #61 to Szúret utca. Just ten rooms, so it's essential to book in advance. Discount for cash payments. ❺

Mária & István IX, Ferenc körút 39 ☎1/216-0768, ⓔmariaistvan@axelero.hu. Friendly couple who rent out rooms in their flat, each with own fridge, shower and WC. ❸

Campsites

Csillebérc Camping XII, Konkoly Thege M. út 21 ☎1/395-6537, ⓦwww.datanet.hu/csill. Large, well-equipped site also offering a range of bungalows. A short walk from the last stop of bus #21 from Moszkva tér. Open all year. ❷

Római Camping III, Szentendrei út 189 ☎1/368-6260, ⓔromai@matavnet.hu. Another huge site beside the road to Szentendre in Rómaifürdő (25min by HEV). Rates include use of the nearby swimming pool. Open all year. ❶

Eating

Magyar cooking has been overtaken in Budapest's restaurants by scores of places devoted to international cuisine. Prices by Western European standards are very reasonable, and your budget should stretch to at least one binge in a top-flight place.

Patisseries

Centrál V, Károlyi Mihály utca 9. Grand old coffee house, three minutes' walk south from Ferenciek tere, restored to its former glory, with a broad menu ranging from cheap to very expensive.

Müvész VI, 29. Classic old coffee house that's less touristy and cheaper than *Gerbeaud*.

TREAT YOURSELF

Gerbeaud (V, Vörösmarty tér 7) is a popular, extremely grand patisserie in central Pest. A coffee and a *torte* will set you back around 1500Ft. The same rich pastries are cheaper in *Kis Gerbeaud* around the corner.

Ruszwurm I, Szentháromság utca 7. Excellent cakes, served production-line fashion to those taking a break from sightseeing on Castle Hill.

Snacks

Bombay Express Andrássy út 44. Fun Indian fast-food on Oktogon with tasty wraps (650Ft) and refreshing mango lassi.

Duran Sandwich Bar V, Október 6 utca 15. A quirky joint with a wide selection of fresh mini-sandwiches for you to pick and mix. From 149Ft apiece. Closed Sun.

Falafel Faloda VI, Paulay Ede utca 53. Best of the city's falafel joints. From 400Ft. Closed Sat & Sun

Karma Café VI, Liszt Ferenc tér 11. Beautifully decorated café with excellent tapas, situated on Pest's trendiest square for eateries. Dinner will set you back about 1900Ft.

Restaurants

Govinda V, Vigyázó Ferenc utca 4. An oasis of spiritual calm in a little side street, just north of Roosevelt tér, serving a good range of Indian vegetarian dishes (600Ft each) and salads.

Kádár étkezde VII, Klauzál tér 9. Jewish home-cooking in the old quarter, where friendly staff serve lunches of boiled beef in fruit sauces. Closed Sun & Mon. From 900Ft.

Kiado Kocsma VI, Jókai tér 3. Gorgeous interior, heavenly tapas (try the aubergine paté), Moroccan teas and exhibitions to aid chilling out in style. From 900Ft.

Kőleves Dob utca/Kazinczy utca (next to Klauzal Ter). Marvellous restaurant at the heart of the Jewish quarter. Fresh, colourful, high-quality ingredients in a wide range of inventive dishes, including first-class almond-coated chicken (1350Ft). Lovely staff, funky music and vegetarian-friendly as well.

M Kersetz ut (off Liszt Ferenc tér). *M*'s shoebox-sized restaurant is a delightful place; the plain walls have had all the accoutrements of a café drawn onto them – books, a hat-stand, a fish tank – with a highly animated chef to boot (he's real). The food completes the picture – fresh, beautifully prepared Franco-Hungarian delights. Weekly changing menu, from 1190Ft.

Menza VI, Liszt Ferenc tér. Stylish, retro-looking place offering excellent and moderately priced Hungarian dishes to be enjoyed al fresco. Try stuffed paprika for 1400Ft.

St Jupat Retek ut 16. Good Hungarian food in a peaceful garden near the bustling Mammut Malls. From 1690Ft.

Drinking and nightlife

Look out for "Kerts" – fun, makeshift bars set up for short periods of time in buildings awaiting demolition (although *Szimpla Kert* has become a permanent fixture). They are often advertised in the local press, or else ask in other bars for them.

Bambi I, Bem tér. Atmospheric old bar from the socialist era with a typical crew of old locals playing chess. Serves breakfast, snack lunches, cakes and alcohol.

Café Miro I, Úri utca 30. A trendy bar in the Castle district, which often has live music. Its sister bar in Mammut serves good food.

Castro V, Madách ter 3. A lively, hip place which also has internet access.

Darshan Udvar VIII, Krúdy Gyula utca 7. The largest bar in a growing complex of bars, cafés and shops. Set at the back of the courtyard, with oriental/hippie decorations, good food, world music and leisurely service.

Eklektika V, Semmelweis utca 21. Arty, gay-friendly bar with 1960s furniture, art exhibitions, a pasta/salad menu and women-only evenings on the second Saturday of the month.

Szimpla Kert VII, Kazinczy utca 14. The original "kert" promotes "an alternative culture" from an abandoned warehouse, with film-screenings, food and a great outdoor bar open til 2am.

Zöld Pardon XI, by the Buda end of Petőfi Bridge. Giant outdoor bar, with live music, sprawling across the grass near the university quarter. May–Oct. Tram #4 or #6 to Petőfi Bridge.

Clubs

The floating party scene (held on river boats) is growing constantly: check flyers and posters around town, or look in the "Könnyű" section of *Pesti Est*, the free listings magazine in cinema foyers. There's also a variety of cheap **student clubs**. Entry costs anything from 800–4000Ft.

Buddha Beach IX, Közraktár utca 9–11 ☎1/476-0433. Outside bar attracting a wealthy young crowd, that's one of the few places you can dance outside until the early hours with an awesome view of the capital. Good bar food so it's worth booking a table if you're eating. March–Oct.

Capella V, Belgrád rakpart 23. Drag queens, jungle music and lots of kitsch: just the place for a night on the town.

Cha Cha Cha IX, Kálvin tér subway. Despite its strange location – or maybe because of it – this place attracts a big crowd that spills out into the concourse, and has DJs at weekends. Closed Sun.

West Balkan IX, Kisfaludy utca 16. Superb, giant and very upbeat club with both indoor and outdoor dance areas. May–Sept.

Entertainment

Tickets for most events can be bought through Ticket Express (VI, Andrássy út 18; ⓣ1/312-0000, ⓦwww.tex.hu) for classical and pop music; or Publika for rock and jazz, VII, Károly körút 9 (ⓣ1/322-2010). **Almássy tér Cultural Centre** VII, Almássy tér 6. Popular venue for folk music.
Petofi Csarnok Városliget; ⓦwww.petoficsarnok.hu. Folk music, dance events and big acts in the City Park.
Trafó IX, Liliom utca 41; ⓦwww.trafo.hu. A revamped transformer station in Pest with its finger on the capital's cultural pulse and a café-bar that frequently hosts local young jazz giants.
Fonó in Buda at XI, Sztregova utca 3; ⓦwww.fono.hu. Happening music hall and CD store, specialising in Central/East European folk, ethno jazz, recently branching out into theatre and art as well.

Festivals

Budapest Spring Festival 2 weeks in March or April; ⓦwww.festivalcity.hu. An eclectic mix of jazz, folk, opera, chamber music, exhibitions, flamenco shows and theatre. The festival pulls in world-class artists and takes place in various venues over the capital. The Budapest Fringe Festival runs at the same time, usually offering fresh, underground talent (same website).
Summer on the Chain Bridge every weekend July–Aug. Scores of classical and popular concerts; the famous bridge is jam-packed with market stalls, food and live music.
Sziget Festival Aug 8–15; ⓦwww.sziget.hu. Bigger every year, Sziget (meaning "island") attracts some of the biggest rock and pop acts to the headiest party on the Danube.
St Stephen's Day Aug 20. The area around the Royal Palace becomes one big folk and crafts fair, and in the evening people line the embankments to watch the fireworks.
Autumn Music Weeks late Sept to late Oct. Features top international acts.

Shopping

Shops There are several malls with standard high-street names, notably the Mammut and Mammut II by Moskvá tér (ⓦwww.mammut.hu). Most shops open Monday to Friday 10am to 6pm, and on Saturday until 1pm, although many are staying open later at the weekend, including Sundays. The main shopping area within the capital is south of Vörösmarty tér in central Pest, with glamorous designer places located on Váci utca and Petőfi Sándor utca.
Markets The Central Market Hall in Pest is a great place for presents, and a better alternative to the pricey tourist-oriented places by the Vár. There are three flea markets in Budapest, but the best one is Petőfi Csarnok (Sat & Sun 7am–2pm) in the Városliget.

Directory

Embassies and consulates Australia, XII, Királyhágó tér 8–9 ⓣ1/457-9777; Canada, XII, Budakeszi út 32 ⓣ1/392-3360; Ireland, V, Szabadság tér 7, 7th floor, Bank Center ⓣ1/302-9600; New Zealand, VI, Teréz körút 38, ⓣ1/428-2208; UK, V, Harmincad utca 6 ⓣ1/266-2888; US, V, Szabadság tér 12 ⓣ1/475-4400.
Exchange Gönc Szövetkezeti Takarékpénztár at V, Rákóczi út 5; Magyar Külkereskedelmi Bank at Türr István utca at the top of Váci utca, Pest; Tribus tourist office V, Apáczai Csere János utca 1.
Hospitals V, Hold utca 19, behind the US embassy ⓣ1/311-6816; II, Ganz utca 13–15 ⓣ1/202-1370.
Internet CEU Net, V, Október 6 utca 14 (daily 11am–10pm); Electric Café, VII, Dohány utca 37 (daily 9am–midnight); Millenarium Park C Building (free for one hour); Matávpont, V, Petőfi utca 17–19 and all large shopping malls (daily 9am–8pm).
Listings *Budapest In Your Pocket* is available from hotel foyers and bookshops. *Key to Budapest* is excellent, targeted at a young, hip audience. Also see ⓦwww.pestiside.hu.
Maps Tourist offices supply free maps, but far better is the wirebound 1:25,000 Budapest Atlas (1700Ft), from newsstands, bookshops and Tourinform offices.
Pharmacies Alkotás utca 1B, opposite Déli station, and Teréz körút 41, near Oktogon, are both open 24hr.
Police Tourists can report a crime at V, Kecskeméti út (ⓣ1/317-0711) or V, Szalay utca (ⓣ1/373-1000) police stations.
Post office V, Petőfi utca 13.
Tours The Discover Hungary agency (ⓣ1/266-8777, ⓦwww.discoverhungary.com), Süţo utca 2, offers a varied programme of citywide excursions, bike rides and pub crawls.

Moving on

Train Balatonfüred (every 1–2hr; 2hr 30min); Pécs (11 daily; 3hr); Kecskemét (12 daily; 1hr 30min);

Siófok (14 daily; 2hr); Sopron (7 daily; 3hr); Szeged (12 daily; 2hr 30min); Szentendre (every 10–20min; 40min); Eger (8 daily; 1hr 50min–2hr 20min).
Bus Balatonfüred (5 daily; 2hr 15min–3hr); Eger (hourly; 2hr–3hr 20min); Hévíz (4 daily; 3hr 20min- 4hr); Keszthely (4 daily 3hr 15min–4hr 15min); Pécs (5 daily; 4hr); Siófok (7 daily; 1hr 35min–2hr 10min); Sopron (3-5 daily; 3hr 45min); Szentendre (every 30min, 30–45min).
Ferry/Hydrofoil (Usually operating April–Oct/Nov, weather permitting) Szentendre (1–3 daily; 1hr 40min); Vienna (1–2 daily; 6hr 20min).

SZENTENDRE

To escape Budapest's humid summers, many people flock north of the city to the **Danube Bend**, one of the grandest stretches of the river. The historic town of **SZENTENDRE** on the west bank is the most popular day-trip from the capital (40min by HÉV train from Batthyány tér; 1hr 30min by boat from Vigadó tér pier), a friendly maze of houses painted in autumn colours, secret gardens, and alleys leading to hilltop churches.

What to see and do

Szentendre's original character was largely shaped by Serbs seeking refuge from the Ottomans. Their townhouses – now converted into galleries, shops and cafés – form a set piece around **Fő tér**, the main square. On the north side of the square is **Blagovestenska Church** (Tues–Sun 10am–5pm; winter open for worship only; 200Ft), with a striking iconostasis painted by Mikhail Zivkovic (1776–1824). Just around the corner at Vastagh György utca 1 stands the wonderful **Margit Kovács Museum** (June–Aug Tues–Sun 9am–7pm; Sept–May 9am–5pm; 600Ft), displaying the lifetime work of Hungary's greatest ceramicist and sculptor, born in 1902. Above Fő tér there's a fine view over Szentendre's steeply banked rooftops and gardens from the hilltop **Templom tér**, from which the spire of the **Serbian Orthodox Cathedral** pokes above a walled garden; tourists are generally not admitted, but you can see the cathedral iconostasis and treasury in the adjacent **museum** (April–Oct Wed–Sun 10am–5pm; 400Ft). Beyond the square at Bogdányi út 32 is the impressive contemporary arts centre, **ArtMill**, so-called because it is housed in a large disused sawmill (daily 10am–8pm free Mon, 500Ft otherwise). It's an exciting new development covering 700 square metres, displaying the works of local and visiting international artists.

Hourly buses run from the HÉV terminal out along Szabadságforrás út to Szentendre's fascinating **Village Museum** (Tues–Sun 9am–5pm; 1000Ft; Ⓦwww.skanzen.hu), which has reconstructed villages from six regions of Hungary.

Arrival and information

Bus and train stations The bus and train stations are located ten minutes' walk south of town. Local buses run in along Dunakanyar körut. The ferry port is 100m north of the town centre – a five-minute walk away.
Tourist office Tourinform, Dumtsa Jenő utca 22 (June–Aug Mon–Fri 9am–7pm, Sat & Sun 9am–6pm; Sept–May Mon–Sat 9.30am–4.30pm, Sun 10am–2pm; Ⓣ26/317-965, Ⓔszentendre@tourinform.hu).
Listings There are regular pop and rock concerts in the centre of town: see Tourinform for the lowdown.

Accommodation

For accommodation, the cheapest option is a private room, advertised widely throughout town, though there are a handful of good-value pensions.
Horváth Panzió North of the centre at Daru piac 2. Ⓣ26/313-950, Ⓦwww.option.hu/Horvath. Small, quiet pension decorated with Hungarian folk crafts. ❸
Ilona Panzió Rákóczi utca 11 Ⓣ26/313-599. Pleasant location in the heart of the old quarter. ❸
Zita Panzió Őrtorony utc 16 Ⓣ26/313-886. Modest six-room pension a stone's thrown from the bus and train stations. ❷

Campsite

On Pap Island (Ⓣ26/310-697, Ⓦwww.pap-sziget.hu; May–Sept), 1.5km north of town – take any bus heading towards Visegrád or Esztergom and get off by the *Danubius Hotel*. Also has a small hostel ❷

Eating and drinking

Café Adria Kossuth utca 4. Sweet café in a graceful, shady courtyard. Perfect for refreshment to or from the station.

Avakum Alkotmány 4. Cooling café in a cellar near the Belgrade church.

Café Dorothea Jankó Janos 4. The sloping patio is a perfect spot for a glass of excellent local wine and lunch, serving up wonderful salads and homemade pasta from 980Ft.

Palapa Dumtsa Jenő utca 22. Super Mexican with good food, handsome cocktails and sterling service. From 1300Ft for mains.

Rab Ráby Kucsera Ferenc utca 1. Traditional, filling, Magyar cuisine from 1500Ft for a hearty dish.

Western Hungary

The major tourist attraction to the west of the capital is **Lake Balaton**, over-romantically labelled the "Hungarian sea", but very much the nation's playground, with vacation resorts lining both shores. The more built-up southern shore has the livelier resorts, chief amongst which is **Siófok** – the lake's popular party place – while, on the western tip, lies the appealing university town of **Keszthely** and Europe's largest thermal lake at **Hévíz**. Worth a trip to the northern shore is the seductive Badacsony village, located beneath a hulk of volcanic rock next to three other small villages.

More than other regions in Hungary, the western region of **Transdanubia** is a patchwork land, an ethnic and social hybrid. Its valleys and hills, forests and mud flats have been a melting pot since Roman times: settled by Magyars, Serbs, Slovaks and Germans; torn asunder and occupied by Ottomans and Habsburgs; transformed from a state of near-feudalism into brutal collectives; and now operating under modern capitalism. All the main towns display evidence of this evolution, especially **Sopron**, with its gorgeous, and well-preserved, medieval centre, and **Pécs**, which boasts an Ottoman mosque and minaret.

SIÓFOK

The largest, busiest and trashiest resort on Balaton, **SIÓFOK** is *the* place to come for bathing, boozing and dancing. The two main waterfront resort areas are Aranypart (Gold Shore) to the east of the Sió Canal, and Ezüstpart (Silver Shore) to the west. Though the central stretch of shoreline consists of paying **beaches** (daily mid-May to mid-Sept 7am–7pm; 1000Ft), there are free *strand* beaches 1km further along at both resort areas. You can rent **windsurfing** and wakeboards from 1700Ft/hour and small **sailing** boats at most beaches. Sailing boats cost from €120 (excluding tax) for up to six people for one day.

Arrival and information

Bus and train The bus and train stations are next to each other in the centre of town on Fő utca.

Tourist office Tourinform office in the water tower (Víztorony) on Szabadság tér (mid-June to mid-Sept Mon–Fri 8am–8pm, Sat & Sun 10am–12pm; mid-Sept to mid-June Mon–Fri 9am–4pm; Ⓣ84/315-355, Ⓦwww.siofok.com). They book private rooms, as can Ibusz, inside the atrium at Fő utca 174/6 (June–Aug Mon–Fri 8am–6pm, Sat 9am–6pm, Sun 9am–1pm; Sept–May Mon–Fri 8am–4pm; Ⓣ84/510-720, Ⓔi081@ibusz.hu).

Accommodation

Touring Hotel Cseresznye utca 1/0 Ⓣ84/310-551, Ⓔtouring@siofok-hostel.com. Large hostel open May–Sept. ❸

Város Kollégiuma Petőfi Sétány 1 Ⓣ84/312-244, Ⓦwww.siofokvaroskollegiuma.sulinet.hu. Large student residence accommodating visitors in summertime. On the shore of Golden Beach 5 min from Siófók. ❶

Campsites

Aranypart Camping Szent László utca 183–185 ☎84/352-801. 5km east of the centre (bus #2) is a large, well-equipped campsite. Mid-April to mid-Sept. Tent ❷, chalets ❹

Ezüstpart Camping Liszt Ferenc sétány 5 ☎84/350-374. 4km west of the centre (bus #1 from the Baross Bridge). May–Sept. Tents ❷, chalets ❸

Eating and drinking

Amigo Fő utca 99. Varied menu including a fantastic range of pizzas for around 1800Ft.

Café Roxy Szabadság tér 1. Offers a good selection of salads, stews and grills, as well as decent breakfasts. From 1200Ft.

Flört (🌐www.flort.hu). Just off Fő utca on the east bank of the canal. High-energy techno and club anthems keep the party people occupied until it's time to hit the beach again in the morning.

Palace Dance Club west of town at Deák Ferenc utca 2. Buses leave every hour from 9pm outside the Víztorony (water tower). The most famous club in Siófok is two floors of house, dance, techno and a steady stream of foam parties until dawn.

Moving on

Ferry Badacsony (July–Aug 2 daily; 4hr 20min).

Bus Kesthely (2 daily) 1hr 40mins.

KESZTHELY

Gracefully absorbing thousands of visitors, **KESZTHELY** possesses charm to suit everyone's taste, with some good eating and drinking options, several beaches, and a university to give it a life of its own.

Keszthely's waterfront has two bays (one for swimming, the other for ferries) formed by man-made piers, a slew of parkland backed by plush hotels and miniature golf courses, and dozens of fast-food joints. In the evenings, action shifts from the water to the centre, where the bars and restaurants work at full steam.

What to see and do

Walking up from the train station along Martírok útja, you'll pass the **Balaton Museum** at the junction with Kossuth Lajos utca (Tues–Sun 9am–5pm; 340Ft), holding exhibits on the region's history and wildlife. Kossuth utca is given over to cafés, vendors, buskers and strollers and leads up towards the **Festetics Palace.** Founded in 1745 by Count György Festetics (Tues–Sun July & Aug 10am–6pm, rest of year 10am–5pm; 1500Ft), the palace attracted the leading lights of Magyar literature from the nineteenth century onwards. Highlights are the gilt, mirrored ballroom and the Helikon Library, a masterpiece of joinery and carving built in 1801. The palace stages regular summer concerts – check with Tourinform (see below) or the Palace Ticket Office.

Arrival and information

Train and bus The train and bus stations are five minutes' walk southwest of the cluster of lakeside hotels along Kazinczy utca. Some buses, however, drop off on Fő tér, halfway along Kossuth utca, the main drag.

Boat The dock is roughly ten minutes' walk south of the centre, along Erzsébet királyné útja.

Tourist office The Tourinform office is at Kossuth utca 28 (June to mid-Sept Mon–Fri 9am–10pm, Sat & Sun 9am–6pm; mid-Sept to May Mon–Fri 9am–5pm, Sat 9am–1pm; ☎83/314-144, 🌐www.keszthely.hu).

Accommodation

For budget accommodation, private rooms are your best bet, advertised widely throughout town or bookable through Keszthely Tourist, Kossuth utca 25 (June–Aug daily 9am–8/9pm, Sept–May Mon–Sat 8am–5pm; ☎83/312-031, 🌐www.keszthelytourist.hu). For information on rooms in college dorms (July & Aug daily; rest of year weekends only), check with Tourinform (see above).

Forras Panzió Római ut 1 ☎83/311-418 Ⓕ314-617. Big hostel-style pension west of the station. ❸

Műzeum Panzió Műzeum utca 3 ☎ & Ⓕ83/313-182. Friendly management in this cute pension near the station. ❸

Campsites

Castrum Camping Móra Ferenc ut 48 ☎83/312-120. April–Oct. 1km north of the train station and the best place to go with a car.
Sport Camping Csárda utca ☎83/313-777. Mid-May to Sept. A big, friendly campsite just south of the train station.
Zalatour Camping Entz Géza Sétány ☎83/312-782 ⓔzala@balatontourist.hu.Mid-April to mid-Oct. Large, family friendly and well-equipped. ❷

Eating and drinking

Close to Kossuth Lajos ut is the daily **Piac Market** (off Bem József utca) that sells fresh fruit, as well as traditional Hungarian foodstuffs – paprika, honey and jars of pickles.
Béke Vendéglő Kossuth utca 50, Homemade Hungarian food for around 1700Ft.
Café Pelso next to the Gothic parish church on Fő tér. Dynamic café, ideal for a break from sightseeing and a cheeky cocktail.
Di Marcello Pizzeria Városház utca 4. Rustic pizzeria in a tranquil courtyard. Pasta 900Ft, pizzas from 1200Ft.
Easy Music House Kossuth Lajos ut 79. Good student bar with live music. There's also the *Kolibri* bar next door if you fancy a change of scene.
Oázis Rákóczi tér 3, down Szalasztó utca from the palace. Superb healthy all-vegetarian option with a packed salad bar and friendly service. A filling plate of salad costs about 700Ft. Mon–Fri 11am–4pm.

Moving on

Bus Hévíz (every 15min; 10–20min). Badacsony (8 daily; 1hr)
Ferry Badacsony (July–Aug 4 daily; 2hr).

HÉVÍZ

Half-hourly buses from Keszthely train station run to **HÉVÍZ**, a spa based around Europe's largest thermal lake, **Hévízi Gyógy-tó**. The wooden terraces surrounding the **Tófürdo** ("lake bath"; daily 8.30/9am–5/6pm; entry tickets: 3hr 1300Ft, all day 2800Ft) have a vaguely fin-de-siècle appearance, but the ambience is contemporary, with people sipping beer while bobbing on the murky, egg-scented lake in rented inner-tubes. Having had a soak, there's no real reason to hang around, but if you do want to **stay**, then Hévíz Tourist, Rákóczi utca 2 (Mon–Fri 8.30am–5.30pm, Sat 9am–1pm; ☎83/340-479 & 341-348, ⓔheviztour@axelero.hu), can book **private rooms** (❷). The best central **restaurant** is the *Rózsakert* opposite the baths, and there's a late-night **bar** and **casino** in the *Hotel Thermál.*

BADACSONY

The **BADACSONY** – a hefty hunk of cooled molten magma and volcanic rock with four villages nestled at its feet – is one of Hungary's most striking features. **Badacsony village** is the most visitor-friendly of the four, with some of the best hiking opportunities in the country.

What to see and do

The main attractions of Badacsony – the **Rósa Szegedy House** and **Rose Rock** – lie nestled among the vineyards, between the glassy lake south of the railway track and the tip of the village.

Róza Szegedy House and Rose Rock

For a novel way to avoid a steep walk, take one of the open-top jeep taxis (600Ft per person) from Park utca – the main street – up through the vineyards to the **Róza Szegedy House** (Szegedy Róza Ház; May–Sept Tues–Sun 10am–6pm; 300Ft). Róza Szegedy met her future husband, the poet Sándor Kisfaludy, on the rugged slopes of Badacsony in 1795, and he wrote some of his most beautiful works from the house. Now a museum, the house contains some of his literature and Szegedy's original furniture.

Up a path a little further from **Róza** Szegedy House is **Rose Rock** (Rókzako), where romance lingers on; according to legend, if a man and woman sit together with their backs facing Lake Balaton and think about each other, they shall marry within a year.

Kisfaludy and the Stone Gate

The Rose Rock is a great starting point for an invigorating hike to the **Kisfaludy** lookout tower (437m) and, twenty minutes further north, the **Stone Gate** formed from two great basalt towers. Both points offer splendid views of the lake and the green patchwork of Badacsony's vineyards. For a longer hike buy a 1:80,000 scale map and ask at Tourinform for suggested routes. After a hike you'll want to jump straight into the lake – Badacsony has clean, paying beaches (700Ft), accessible just by the ferry pier.

Arrival and information

Train station The train station is right in the village, just up from the ferry pier.
Bus stop Buses stop on the main street, Park utca.
Tourist information Tourinform is on Park utca 6 (mid-June to mid-Sept Mon–Fri 9am–7pm, Sat & Sun 9am–6pm; mid-Sept to Oct & May to mid-June Mon–Fri 9am–5pm & Sat 9am–1pm; Nov–April 9am–3.30pm; ⓣ 87/431-046, ⓦ www.badacsony.com).

Accommodation

Balatontourist (next door to Tourinform, see above) can book **private rooms** (May–June & Sept Mon–Fri 8.30am–3.30pm, Sat 8am–noon; July & Aug Mon–Sat 8am–9pm, Sun 8am–noon; ⓣ 87-531-021, ⓔ badacsony@balatontourist.hu; ❷–❸), as will Miditourist, at Egri Sétany 3 (daily: July & Aug 8am–9am; May, June & Sept to mid-Oct 9am–6pm; ⓣ 87/431-117, ⓦ www.miditourist.hu).
Hotel Neptun Római ut 170 ⓣ 87/431-293 ⓦ www.borbaratok.hu. an excellent budget choice with huge, yet cheap, rooms. ❷

Campsite

Campsite 8261 Badacsony, a fifteen-minute walk west of the ferry pier (mid-May to Sept; ⓣ 97/531-041). ❶

Eating and drinking

Bacchus Kossuth utca 1. Gorgeous views over the lake from *Bacchus's* terrace and very nice local wines (hence the name). Exceptionally friendly service. From 1100Ft.
Kisfaludy Ház Szegedy Róza utca 87, by the Róza Szegedy museum. The restaurant offers a fabulous panorama of Balaton and delicious food at a reasonable price.
Neptun (part of the *Hotel Neptun*), Római ut 170. Nice salads and soups make *Neptun* a good stop-off point for lunch. From 900Ft.

SOPRON

SOPRON – the nearest big Hungarian town to Vienna and consequently a popular destination – has 240 listed buildings, which allow it to claim to be "the most historic town in Hungary".

What to see and do

The horseshoe-shaped **Belváros** (inner town) is north of Széchenyi tér and the main train station. At the southern end, **Orsolya tér** features Renaissance edifices dripping with loggias and carved protrusions, and a Gothic church. Heading north towards the main square, **Új utca** (New Street – one of the town's oldest thoroughfares) is a gentle curve of arched dwellings painted in red, yellow and pink, with chunky cobblestones and pavements. At no. 22 stands one of the **synagogues** (May–Oct Tues–Sun 10am–6pm; 600Ft) that flourished when the street was known as Zsidó utca (Jewish Street); Sopron's Jewish community survived the expulsion of 1526 only to be almost annihilated during World War II.

Goat Church

The main source of interest is on Fő tér – a parade of Gothic and Baroque architecture partly overshadowed by the **Goat Church** – so called, as legend has it, because its construction was financed by a goatherd whose flock unearthed a cache of loot.

Storno House and Firewatch Tower

The Renaissance **Storno House**, also on the square, exhibits an enjoyable collection of Roman, Celtic and Avar relics, plus mementoes of Liszt (Tues–Sun: April–Sept 10am–6pm; Oct–March 2pm–6pm; 1000Ft). North of here rises Sopron's symbol, the **Firewatch Tower** (May–Sept daily 10am–8pm; April, Sept & Oct Tues–Sun 10am–6pm; 700Ft), founded upon the stones of a fortress originally laid out by the Romans. From the top there's a stunning view of the town's narrow streets and weathered rooftops. The **"Gate of Loyalty"** at the base of the tower commemorates the townfolk's decision, when offered the choice of Austrian citizenship in 1921, to remain Magyar subjects. Walk through it and you'll emerge onto Elő kapu, a short street where the houses are laid out in a saw-toothed pattern.

Arrival and information

Train The train station is on Mátyás Király utca, 500m south of Széchenyi tér and the old town; Sopron is linked to Vienna by a fast intercity service, though it's not on the main Budapest–Vienna route.
Bus The bus station is to the northwest of the old town, five minutes' walk along Lackner Kristóf utca from Ógabona tér.
Tourist office Tourinform is inside the Liszt Cultural Centre at Liszt utca 1 (mid-June to mid-Sept Mon–Fri 9am–5pm, Sat & Sun 9am–2pm; mid-Sept to mid-June Mon–Fri 9am–5pm, Sat 9am–3pm; ⓣ99/517-560, ⓦwww.tourinform.sopron.hu).
Internet Új utca 3 (Mon–Wed 1–7pm, Thurs & Fri 11am–7pm).

Accommodation

Ciklámen Tourist, Ógabona tér 8 (Mon–Fri 8am–4.30pm, Sat 8am–noon; ⓣ99/312-040) can organise private accommodation in and around town.
Bástya Panzió Patak utca 40 ⓣ99/325-325, ⓦwww.bastya-panzio.ehc.hu Good pension just across the Ikva stream to the northeast of town. ❹
Brennbergi Youth Hostel Brennbergi utca 82 ⓣ99/313-166 ⓔtabor@sopron.hu. 4km west of town and reached by buses #3 and #10 from the bus station ❶
Jégverem Panzió Jégverem utca 1 ⓣ99/510-113, ⓦwww.jegverem.hu. Not far from *Bastya*, a quaint inn atmosphere, with lovely restaurant attached. ❹

Eating and drinking

Cézár cellar Hátsókapu utca 2. Good wine and light bites in a candlelit medieval cellar. A favourite with the locals.
Dömötöri Kavehaz, Széchenyi tér 13. Picturesque spot for coffee and delicious strudels. *Teaház* opposite is also lovely and has a cosy interior that smells enticingly of cakes.
Fórum Pizzeria Szent György utca 3. Decent pizzas, a pleasant setting and happy staff. Also does a good line in pastas and salads. From 1000Ft.
Jégverem Fogadó Jégverem utca 1. A wide-ranging menu with tantalizing Hungarian dishes from 1400Ft. A rustic garden setting adds to its appeal.
Liszt Szalon Café (and chocolate shop). Szent György utca 12. Daily 10am–10pm. Delicate cakes served in a pretty courtyard.
Rókalyukhoz opposite *Várkerület Söröző*. An extensive and eclectic international menu in a relaxed setting. Pizzas start at 699Ft, mains 1500Ft.

Esterházy Palace

Some 27km east of Sopron (hourly buses), in the village of Ferțod, lies a monument to one of the country's most famous dynasties: the **Esterházy Palace**. Originally minor nobility, the Esterházy family began its rise thanks to Miklós Esterházy I (1583–1645), who married two rich widows, sided with the Habsburgs, and got himself elevated to count. The palace itself was started by his grandson, Miklós the Ostentatious. Fronted by a vast horseshoe courtyard where Hussars once pranced to the music of Haydn – Esterházy's resident maestro for many years – the palace was intended to rival Versailles. **Guided tours** (every 40min; March–Oct Tues–Sun 10am–6pm; Nov–Feb Fri–Sun 10am–4pm; 1350Ft) cover 23 of the 126 rooms in the palace, including several blue-and-white chinoiserie salons, the Banqueting Hall with its superb ceiling fresco, and one room displaying **Haydn memorabilia**. There's a Tourinform office opposite the palace gates (April–Oct Mon–Sat 9am–5pm; Nov–March Tues–Sat 10am–4pm; ⓣ99/370-544, ⓔfertod@tourinform.hu), and should you wish to **stay**, try the

*Újvári Panzi*o*, about 500m from the palace at Kossuth utca 57a (Ⓣ99/537-097, Ⓔinfo@ujvaripanzio.hu; 4), or the *Kata Vendégház*, 1km down Vasút utca at Mikes Kelemen utca 2 (Ⓣ99/370-857, Ⓦwww.hotels.hu/kata_fertod; ❸).

PÉCS

PÉCS is one of Transdanubia's largest and most attractive towns; indeed, it lays claim to being the finest in the country, with its tiled rooftops climbing the vine-laden slopes of the Mecsek range. Besides some good museums, the fifth-oldest university in Europe (founded in 1367) and a great market, Pécs contains Hungary's best examples of **Islamic architecture**, a legacy of the long Ottoman occupation.

What to see and do

The majority of Pécs's main sites are concentrated in the **Belváros** (Old Town), radiating outwards from Széchenyi tér in the centre: it's easy to take them in, starting with the synagogue by Kossuth tér, then heading through the centre towards the leafier western side, where you'll find the magnificent cathedral.

Synagogue and Mosque of Gázi Kászim Pasha

Heading up Bajcsy-Zsilinszky út from the bus terminal, or by bus #30 from the train station towards the centre, you'll pass the **synagogue** (May–Oct Mon–Fri & Sun 10am–5pm; 300Ft). The beautiful nineteenth-century interior is hauntingly impressive, with romantic frescoes swirling around a space emptied by the murder of almost 3500 Jews – ten times the number that live in Pécs today. During the Ottoman occupation (1543–1686), a similar fate befell the Christian population, whose principal church was converted into the **Mosque of Gázi Kászim Pasha** (mid-April to mid-Oct Mon–Sat 10am–4pm, Sun 11.30am–4pm, mid-Oct to mid-April Mon–Sat 10am–noon, Sun 11.30am–2pm; donations) to the north on Széchenyi tér. In a twist of history, the mosque has changed sides again and operates as the City Centre Catholic Parish Church.

Archeological Museum and Cathedral

Behind the mosque, the **Archeological Museum** (Tues–Sun 10am–4pm; 300Ft) displays items testifying to a Roman presence between the first and fifth centuries. From here you can follow either Káptalan or Janus Pannonius utca towards the **cathedral** (April–Oct Mon–Sat 9am–5pm, Sun 1–5pm, Nov–March Mon–Sat 10am–4pm, Sun 1pm–4pm; 700Ft, which includes a glass of wine at the Bishop's Wine Cellar just around the corner from the main entrance). Though its architects have incorporated a crypt and side-chapels from eleventh- to fourteenth-century churches, the cathedral is predominantly nineteenth-century neo-Romanesque.

Pécs Fair

Pécs Fair, held on the morning of the first Sunday of each month – and the Friday and Saturday immediately before – sees some hard bargaining and hard drinking, and there are smaller markets on the same site every Sunday. Bus #50 carries local shoppers from outside the Konzum store in Rákóczi utca (get a ticket from a newsstand or the train station before boarding), but taxis are reasonable and easily available from Széchenyi tér. Pécs is also an excellent starting-point for heading to the nearby **wine region** of Villány to the south – ask at Tourinform for further information.

Arrival and information

Train The train station is a 20min walk south of the centre on Indoház tér.

Bus The bus station is a short walk northeast of the train station on Zsolyom utca.

Tourist office Tourinform is at Széchenyi tér 9 (June–Sept Mon–Fri 8am–5.30pm, Sat 9am–2pm, closed Sun; Oct–May Mon–Fri 8am–4pm; ⓣ72/213-315, ⓔbaranya-m@tourinform.hu), adjoining office offers
Internet Next to Tourinform (see above; same hours)

Accommodation

For inexpensive, central accommodation, you can book a private room or student hostel bed through Mecsek Tours, Ferencesek utca 41 (ⓣ72/513-307, ⓔutir@mecsektours.hu), or Ibusz, Király utca 11 (Mon–Fri 9am–5pm; ⓣ72/212-157, ⓔi077@ibusz.hu)
Főnix Hotel Hunyádi út 2 ⓣ72/311-680, ⓦwww.fonixhotel.hu. Just north of Széchenyi tér, an eccentric building with rooms like treehouse cabins. Lovely staff. ❸
Laterum Hotel/Youth Hostel Hajnóczi utca 37 ⓣ72/252-113; ⓦwww.laterum.hu. 3km west of the centre near the University campus, take bus #2 or #4. ❷

Campsite

Familia Privát Camping 3km east at Gyöngyösi I. utca ⓣ72/327-034. Take bus #31. Reasonable campsite that's open all year. ❶

Eating and drinking

Az Elefántos Jokai tér 6. Simple but tasty and filling pizza and pasta dishes with occasional live music to accompany your meal. From 1000Ft
Cellárium next to the *Főnix Hotel*. A cavernous cellar restaurant serving up high quality Hungarian cuisine. Closed Sun.
Coffeein Café Széchenyi tér 9. Popular daytime and evening, for coffee or cocktails in a lounge-style setting. Daily 8am–midnight, Fri & Sat till 2am.
Dóm Étterem Király utca 3. Very old-world interior with good house specialities. A better summer option is the outside terrace, although for only pizzas and pasta. From 1400Ft.
Kioszk Szent Istvan tér. Sweet café next to the cathedral with friendly staff and a range of liqueurs.
Replay Café and Bar Király utca 4. High-octane atmosphere in this restaurant and bar with Mexican and American-style dishes for about 1400Ft. Daily 10am–2am.

Eastern Hungary

The hilly and forested northern region of **eastern Hungary** will not feature prominently in any hurried tour of the country, but nobody should overlook the gorgeous wine-producing town of **Eger**, and the nearby "Valley of the Beautiful Woman", famed for its wine cellars.

EGER

Its colourful architecture suffused by sunshine, **EGER** seems a fitting place of origin for *Egri Bikavér*, the famous red wine marketed abroad as "Bull's Blood", which brings hordes of visitors to the town. Despite occasional problems with accommodation, it's a fine place to hang out and wander around, not to mention all the opportunities for drinking.

What to see and do

The principal attractions in Eger stretch either side of the main square, **Dobó István tér**, with the compact, cobbled streets around the castle situated northwest of the centre. The square itself is a vast, bustling affair, surrounded by little boutiques; nearby, on Knézich utca, is the elegant fourteen-sided minaret that has become Eger's most photographed structure.

Cathedral

The Neoclassical **cathedral**, designed by József Hild and constructed between 1831 and 1836, is five minutes' walk southwest from the main square. The florid **Lyceum** directly opposite the cathedral is worth visiting for its library (April–Sept Tues–Sun 9.30am–3pm, Oct–March Sat & Sun only 9.30am–12pm; 450Ft), whose beautiful floor and fittings are made of polished oak. While in the building, check out the

observatory, at the top of the tower in the east wing (same hours; 450Ft), where a nineteenth-century *camera obscura* projects a view of the entire town.

Archbishop's Palace

Close by stands the **Archbishop's Palace** (10am–4/5pm; 250Ft), a U-shaped Baroque pile with fancy wrought-iron gates; in its right wing you'll find the treasury and a history of the bishopric of Eger. Cross the bridge and head to the left where a slender minaret extends skyward (April–Oct 10am–6pm; 140Ft), looking rather lonely without its mosque, which was demolished during a nineteenth-century building boom.

Castle

Uphill from Dobó István tér are the gates of the **castle** (exhibition times: daily March–Oct 9am–5pm, Nov–Feb 10am–4pm; 1000Ft, castle times vary so check with Tourinform). From the bastion overlooking the main gate, a path leads up to the ticket office and the fifteenth-century **Bishop's Palace**: tapestries, ceramics, Turkish handicrafts and weaponry fill the museum upstairs, while downstairs are temporary exhibits and a Hall of Heroes, where a life-size marble István Dobó lies amid a bodyguard of heroes of the 1552 siege in which two thousand soldiers and Eger's women repulsed a Turkish force six times their number.

Arrival and information

Trains from Budapest arrive at the station on Állomás tér; to reach the centre, walk up the road to Deák Ferenc út, catch bus #10 or #12, and get off when you see the cupola of the cathedral.

Tourist office Tourinform office at Bajcsy-Zsilinszky utca 9 (mid-June to Aug Mon–Fri 9am–6pm, Sat & Sun 9am–1pm; Sept to mid-June Mon–Fri 9am–5pm, Sat 9am–1pm; ⓣ36/517-715, ⓦwww.eger.hu).

Accommodation

For student hostels and private rooms contact Ibusz, Széchenyi utca 9 (ⓣ36/311-451, ⓔi047@ibusz.hu), or Express, Széchenyi utca 28 (ⓣ36/427-757).

Hotel Minaret Knézich K. utca 4 5 ⓣ36/410-233, ⓔinfo@hotelminaret.hu. Big, welcoming hotel in the centre of Eger. includes breakfast. ❹

Tourist Motel Mekcsey utca 2 ⓣ36/429-014. Basic place just along from the castle. ❷

Tulipán Szépasszonyvölgy 71, Heves County ⓣ36/410-580. Campsite in the Szépasszony Valley; open all year. ❶

Eating and drinking

Efendi Kossuth utca 19. Large portions of traditional Hungarian specialities from 1600Ft.

Egri Est Café Széchenyi utca 16. A good drinking spot that occasionally has live music.

Palacsintavár Dobó utca 9. Terrific range of sweet and savoury pancakes and an amusing interior festooned with all manner of things: postcards, exotic cigarette packs and magazine covers.

Várkert Étterem Dózsa György ter 8. Atmospheric eatery with a convivial terrace serving brilliant Hungarian specialities. The vampish blackcurrant deer stew with blood orange is beautifully rich. From1200Ft.

TASTING IN THE VALLEY OF THE BEAUTIFUL WOMAN

Just west of town, in the Szépasszonyvölgy- translated as "Valley of the Beautiful Woman" - local **vineyards** produce four types of wine: *Muskotály* (discreet, semi-sweet Muscatel), *Bikavér* (Bull's Blood - smooth, spicy and ruby red), *Leányka* (medium-dry white with a hint of herbs) and *Medoc Noir* (rich, dark and sweet red) – and it's possible to sample all of them in the cellars here. Finding the best cellar is a matter of luck and taste, but you could try Auntie Anci's Olaszrizling at no. 28 or the Medoc Noir in Sándor Arvai's at no. 31. Cellars tend to close by 8pm. Take a taxi (around 800Ft; ⓣ36/411-222) or tackle the 20min walk back uphill to town.

The Great Plain

Encompassing half of Hungary, the **Great Plain** is romantically wild and liberating in its expansive flatness; yet punishing winters and the trammeling monotony of its landscape make for harsh living conditions in its more remote villages. Between the Danube and the Tisza are two lively, culturally rich cities, **Kecskemét** and **Széged**, as well as protected National Parks for superb horse-riding.

KECSKEMÉT

Easily accessible as a day trip from Budapest, **KECSKEMÉT** is the ideal place to escape the hustle and bustle of the capital and explore the countryside. With its eclectic architecture and a pedestrianized centre, the town has a self-assured feel about it – due, in part, to Kecskemét's comparatively harmonious history: unlike neighbouring towns it was spared devastation by the Turks, who took a shining to the place instead. Not only is the town itself charming, it is also the gateway to the lovely **Kiskunság National Park**.

What to see and do

The main attraction in Kecskemét is the marvellous **Cifra Palace** – an exemplary Art Nouveau creation designed by Géza Markus in 1902, which now houses the **Kecskemét Art Gallery** (Tues–Sat 10am–5pm, Sun 1.30pm–5pm; 500Ft). The collection includes work by the Jewish painter, István Farkas, who died in Auschwitz. Upstairs is the magnificent peacock ballroom, once a casino, and further up a terrace offers a close-up view of the Art Nouveau chimneys and gables.

South of Szabadság tér is the **Town Hall** – its elaborate decoration and musical clock seemingly fit for a toy town. The building, constructed in 1893 is well worth a look around, especially the Grand Hall, which contains murals by Bertalan Székely, who decorated the Matyás Church in Budapest. The Town Hall operates under somewhat irregular opening hours, however you should be able to have a look around if you ask at reception. In the summer, films are projected in the courtyard – ask at Tourinform for details.

One of the best museums in Kecskemét is the **Hungarian Photography Museum** at Katona József tér 12 (Wed–Sun 10am–5pm; 200Ft) in a former dance-hall, with excellent rotating exhibitions of mostly Hungarian, and some international, photographers.

Arrival and information

Bus and train stations The bus and train stations are next to one another north of the centre. Head down Nagykőrösi utca or Rákóczi utca from the station towards the main square, Szabadság tér.

Tourist information Tourinform is situated in the corner of the Town Hall (Mon–Fri 8am–5pm, May–June & Sept also open Sat 9am–1pm, July & Aug also Sun 9am–1pm; ⓣ76/481-065, ⓦwww.kecskemet.hu). They can give detailed information on horse-riding operators and trips to the Kiskunság National Park.

Accommodation

Private apartments can be booked with Ibusz at Korona utca 2 in the Malom shopping centre (daily Mon–Sat 10am–7pm, Sun 10–2pm). During the summer rooms in colleges (❷) are available from Jókai tér 4 (ⓣ76/481-529) and Izsáki utca 10 (ⓣ76/506-526).

Fábián Panzió at Kápolna utca 14 ⓣ76/477-677 ⓦwww.hotels.hu/Fabian. Run by a super-friendly family and the best place to stay by far in Kecskemét. Smart, spacious rooms and the wonderful breakfast includes home-made apricot jam. Doubles ❸–❹

Eating and drinking

Geniusz Kisfaludy utca 5. Plainly decorated convivial place with some quite adventurous dishes

TREAT YOURSELF

An unforgettable dining experience, **Kecskeméti Csárda** serves Hungarian food at its richest, tastiest, and most calorific: "colossal" is probably the best way to describe the portions. Anything with bacon is worth going for – Mangalica pigs, reared in the region, are said to make the finest bacon. There are also lots of goose dishes to choose from, and the pork is succulent (and cheaper). Good dishes are around 2500Ft, but you could easily share one. Excellent wines too. Kölcsey ut 7, ⓣ76/488686.

from a Hungarian and international menu. Great duck and red cabbage for 1800Ft.

Liberté Sazbadság tér 2. Attractive spot for a drink or light bite under an outsized awning, where you can hear the chimes of the Town Hall clock and watch people amble by. Salads under 1200Ft.

Teatrum Szabadság tér 4. Glorious tea- and coffee-house where you can easily while away an hour or so – there are two cabinets packed with second-hand English books upstairs.

Activities

Horse-riding Somodi Tanya farm (ⓣ76/377-095 ⓦwww.somoditanya.hu) in Fülöpháza has wonderful horses and accommodates all levels of riding ability (2500Ft/hr) for fantastic hacks in the countryside bordering the Kiskunság National Park. Call to arrange in advance and someone will pick you up from the bus. There are a handful of buses per day, so check the schedule first. Also has lodging – if you want to wake up to an early morning ride – and a restaurant. For other horse-riding operators, ask Tourinform.

Moving on

Train Budapest (10 daily; 1hr 30min); Szeged (12 daily; 1–2hr).

Bus Budapest (every 60–90min; 1hr 45min); Szeged (10 daily; 1hr 30min).

SZEGED

Szeged, the most sophisticated city in the Great Plain, straddles the River Tisza before it enters Serbia. The present layout of the city dates from after the great flood of 1879, when the Tisza swelled and destroyed most of the city, forcing its inhabitants to start again. Thanks to help from foreign capital, it was rebuilt using every architectural style possible, with strapping new buildings and squares that seem to laugh in the face of the flood with their enormous size. The place is now vibrant with music festivals and has a thriving university atmosphere.

What to see and do

The centre of activity in Szeged is **Dom tér square**, surrounded by impressive arcades and busts of celebrated Hungarians. It was created in 1920 to accommodate the enormous **Votive Church** (Mon–Sat 9am–6pm, Sun 9.30am–10am, 11–11.30am & 1–6pm; 400Ft), which the townsfolk pledged to erect after the great flood At 12.15pm, 5.45pm and, in summer, 8.45pm, the charming **Musical Clock** on the south side of the square comes alive, as figurines from inside the clock pop out and move to the chiming of bells.

Móra Ferenc Museum

The **Móra Ferenc Museum** (daily 10am–5pm; 400Ft) contains a huge painting of the great flood by Pál Vágó and an interesting section on the Avars, the people displaced by the arriving Magyars at the beginning of the eighth century.

From the museum, it's a short walk to the grassy Széchenyi tér, and to the Baroque **Town Hall** – scene of countless weddings; look out for the pretty "Bridge of Sighs", modelled on the Venetian original, which links the hall to a neighbouring house. The Klauzál tér, a charming piazza south of the hall, has some tantalizing ice-cream parlours – perfect for a cooling refreshment.

Great Synagogue

The **Great Synagogue** (Új Zsinagóga) is one of the largest synagogues in Europe; the entrance is on Jósika utca, not far from Klauzál tér (April–Sept Mon–Fri & Sun 10am–noon & 1–5pm; Oct–March same days 10am–2pm; 400Ft). Built between 1900 and 1903 by Lipót Baumhorn, who designed twenty two synagogues throughout the country, it is purported to be the finest example of his work, with a spectacular dome in blue stained glass.

Thermal baths

For rest and relaxation, head to the **thermal baths** on Tisza Lajos körút (8am–8pm; 700Ft), which has indoor steam baths, ten pools and a water-park with some retro flumes.

Arrival and information

Bus station Mars tér, a five-minute walk to the heart of the Belváros.
Train station South of the Belváros (old city), a short tram ride on the #1.
Tourist information Tourinform, Dugonics tér 2 (mid-May to mid-Sept Mon–Fri 9am–6pm, Sat 9am–1pm; mid-Sept to mid-May Mon–Fri 9am–4pm; ⓣ63/488-690; ⓔszeged@tourinform.hu). They also have an info-point in Széchenyi tér (8am–8pm).
Festivals As host of the famous Szeged Open Air Festival (wⓦww.szegediszabadteri.hu) in July and August, Szeged attracts swarms of culture-hungry Hungarians and tourists to a steady stream of opera, theatre and classical music concerts.

Accommodation

Private rooms (❷) can be booked through Szeged Tourist located at Klauzál tér 7 (Mon–Fri 9am–5pm; ⓣ62/420-428, ⓔszegedtourist@mail.tiszanet.hu) and Ibusz on Oroszlán utca 3 (Mon–Fri 9am–6pm, Sat 9am–1pm; ⓣ62/471-177, ⓔi085@ibusz.hu). College dorms are available in the summer – ask at Tourinform.
Familia Panzió Szentharomság utca 71 ⓣ62/441-122, ⓦⓦww.familiapanzio.hu Large, friendly place south of the centre and a ten-minute walk west of the train station. ❸ ❹

Campsite

Partfürdő Camping Középkikötő sor ⓣ62/430-843. On the river bank in Újszeged with wooden chalets (❷) and near to the relaxing thermal baths.

Eating and drinking

The fruit and veg **market** is just behind Mars tér, and abounds in tumbling piles of paprika and aromatic seasonal fruits.
Botond Étterem Széchenyi tér. A simple, reasonably priced choice in the centre of town with mains at around 1700Ft.
Chaplin Bar & Grill Arany János utca 5. Fun, budget option that has student-fayre at student fares (350Ft for a bagel or falafel, 450Ft for spaghetti).
Halászcsárda Roosevelt tér 14. Welcoming restaurant with a lively band of staff, folk music and tasty fish goulash.
Kiskörössy Halászcárda at Felzo-Tizsa-part 336. Take bus #73 or #73Y from Mars tér and ask the driver to tell you the stop. The restaurant is on the riverbank and any fish you order will be so fresh it seems to have jumped straight from the water onto your plate – delicious.

Moving on

Train Budapest (11 daily; 2hr).
Bus Budapest (7 daily; 3hr); Kecskemét (10 daily; 1hr 30min).

FIERY FISH GOULASH

Szeged is known for its **halászlé** (fish goulash), served up in convivial tureens to share – dozens of people often crouch over the spicy cauldron in the busier restaurants, ladling it generously between bowls. The more varieties of fish in the soup, the better it is, according to the generations-old recipes that are still followed to this day. The other vital ingredient is **paprika**, more of which is produced in Szeged than anywhere else in Hungary. It's the sizzling paprika-glow that makes halászlé impossible to recreate – so get your fill while you can.

Ireland

HIGHLIGHTS

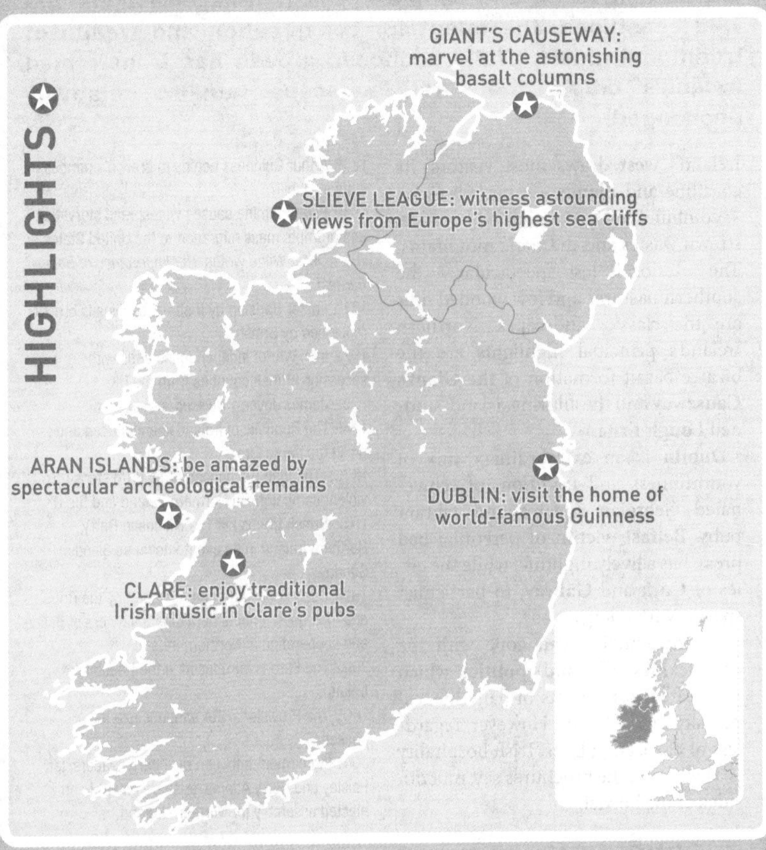
GIANT'S CAUSEWAY: marvel at the astonishing basalt columns
SLIEVE LEAGUE: witness astounding views from Europe's highest sea cliffs
ARAN ISLANDS: be amazed by spectacular archeological remains
DUBLIN: visit the home of world-famous Guinness
CLARE: enjoy traditional Irish music in Clare's pubs

ROUGH COSTS

DAILY BUDGET Basic €40/occasional treat €60–70

DRINK Guinness €4.50/pint

FOOD Irish stew €10

HOSTEL/BUDGET HOTEL €15/€35–45

TRAVEL Bus: Kilkenny–Dublin €10.80

FACT FILE

POPULATION 6.1 million

AREA 70,300 sq km

LANGUAGE English; Gaelic

CURRENCY Euro € (Republic); pound sterling £ (Northern Ireland)

CAPITAL Dublin (Republic: 1.1 million); Belfast (Northern Ireland: 300,000)

INTERNATIONAL PHONE CODE ☎353 (Republic); ☎44 (Northern Ireland)

Basics

In both Northern Ireland and the Republic, Ireland's lures are its landscape and people – the rain-hazed loughs and wild coastlines, the talent for conversation and wealth of traditional music. While economic growth has transformed Ireland's cities, the rural landscape remains relatively unchanged.

Ireland's **west** draws most visitors; its coastline and islands – especially Aran – combine vertiginous cliffs, boulder-strewn wastes and dramatic mountains. The interior is less spectacular – the southern pastures and low wooded hills are the classic landscapes. Northern Ireland's principal highlights are the bizarre basalt formation of the **Giant's Causeway** and the alluring, island-studded **Lough Erne**.

Dublin is an extraordinary mix of youthfulness and tradition, of rejuvenated Georgian squares and vibrant pubs. **Belfast**, victim of perennial bad press, has a lively nightlife, while the cities of **Cork** and **Galway**, in particular, sparkle with energy.

No introduction can cope with the complexities of Ireland's **politics**, which permeate most aspects of daily life, especially in the North. However, regardless of partisan politics, Irish hospitality is as warm as the brochures say, on both sides of the border.

CHRONOLOGY

1st Century BC Romans refer to Ireland as "Hibernia".

432 AD Saint Patrick arrives in Ireland, converting pagans to Christianity.

795 Viking raids on Ireland.

1167 Arrival of Anglo-Norman invaders, ushering in eight hundred years of English rule.

1532 Irish Catholics are persecuted after the English Reformation.

1690 Battle of the Boyne marks decisive victory by Protestant William of Orange over Catholic King James II of England.

1759 Arthur Guinness begins to brew his famous stout in Dublin.

1845 Potato famine causes widespread starvation and prompts mass migration to the United States.

1895 Oscar Wilde writes *The Importance of Being Earnest*.

1916 Easter Uprising by Irish nationalists is brutally repressed by British.

1922 Irish War of Independence ends with secession of Irish counties from the UK.

1922 James Joyce's *Ulysses* is published.

1949 The Republic of Ireland is announced and given the name Eire.

1970s The Irish Republican Army (IRA) steps up violent campaigns in Northern Ireland and the UK.

1972 British troops kill 13 civilians in Derry, Northern Ireland in an event known as Bloody Sunday.

1998 Good Friday Agreement signed by the British and Irish governments heralding a new era of peace and cooperation in Northern Ireland.

2002 The Euro is introduced in the Republic of Ireland.

2005 The Provisional IRA announces a full ceasefire.

2007 Agreement between rival party leaders, Ian Paisley and Gerry Adams, to share power in an elected assembly for Northern Ireland.

ARRIVAL

Ireland has four international **airports**: Dublin, Cork, Shannon and Belfast International. Regional airports, which also serve the UK, are Belfast City, Derry, Donegal, Galway, Kerry, Knock, and Sligo.

Ferry routes from the UK comprise Cairnryan–Larne, Fishguard–Rosslare, Fleetwood–Larne, Holyhead–Dublin, Holyhead–Dun Laoghaire, Isle of Man–Belfast, Isle of Man–Dublin, Liverpool–Belfast, Liverpool–Dublin,

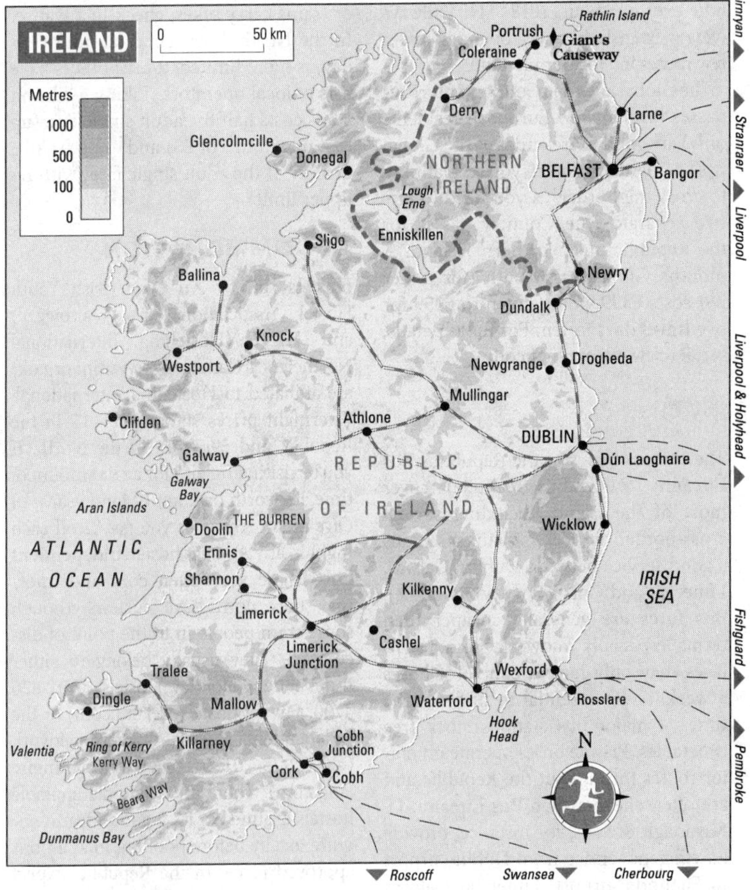

Pembroke–Rosslare, Stranraer–Belfast and Troon–Larne. Travelling by ferry without a vehicle is not expensive (about £46 return), and departure times are generally more civilised than most low-cost flights. Taking a car on the ferry is pricey (£200–300 in high season), but if you're travelling in a group and can share the cost, it's a very convenient option.

GETTING AROUND

You can **save money** on rail and bus services by buying multi-journey tickets in advance; the **Emerald Card/Irish Rover** tickets give you unlimited bus/rail travel for 3, 5, or 15 days. See Ⓦwww.buseireann.ie/asp/ExplorerList.asp for more information.

By train

In the Republic, Iarnród Éireann (Ⓦwww.irishrail.ie) operates **trains** to most major towns and cities. Few routes run north–south across the country, so, although you can easily get to the west coast by train, you can't use the railways to explore. The **Dublin–Belfast line** is the only cross-border service, and very frequent stops north of Dublin means it's not a particularly fast route, the full journey taking a little over two hours (€18). NI Railways (Ⓦwww.translink.co.uk) operates just a few routes in Northern Ireland.

The Global and One Country **InterRail** passes (available to European residents only) are valid in Ireland, but the Global pass is better value if you're planning to cross the border, as you need to buy two separate One Country passes for the Republic and Northern Ireland. A month's Global Pass Youth (for under 26) costs €399, going down to €159 for five travel days in ten. For more details, see Ⓦwww.interrailnet.com.

By bus

The express **buses** of the Republic's Bus Éireann (Ⓦwww.buseireann.ie) cover most of the island, including several cross-border services. Citylink also runs a good service between Dublin, Galway, Limerick and Cork (Ⓦwww.citylink.ie). Bus **fares** are generally cheaper than trains, especially midweek. Remote villages may only have a couple of buses a week, so it's essential to find out the times – major bus stations stock free timetables. Private buses operate on major routes throughout the Republic and are often cheaper than Bus Éireann: J.J. Kavanagh & Sons, for instance, provide an efficient service from Dublin airport to Shannon airport, Limerick, Galway, Kilkenny and Waterford (Ⓦwww.jjkavanagh.ie, Ⓣ056/883 1106). In the North, Ulsterbus (Ⓦwww.translink.co.uk) runs regular and reliable services.

By bike

Cycling is an enjoyable and reasonably safe way of seeing Ireland. In the Republic, bikes can be rented in most towns and Raleigh is the main operator (€20/day, €80/week; from €100 deposit, depending on the dealer; Ⓣ01/465 9659, Ⓦwww.raleigh.ie); local dealers (including some hostels) are cheaper. It costs an extra €10 to carry a bike on a bus, and €3–10 on a train, though not all buses or trains carry bikes; check in advance. In the North, bike rental (around £15/day) is more limited; tourist offices have lists of local operators. Taking a bike on a bus costs half the adult single fare (up to a maximum of £5) and, on a train, a quarter of the adult single fare (with no upper limit).

ACCOMMODATION

Hostels run by **An Óige** (Irish Youth Hostel Association; Ⓦwww.anoige.ie) and **HINI** (Hostelling International Northern Ireland; Ⓦwww.hini.org.uk) are affiliated to Hostelling International. Overnight prices start at €11–17 in the Republic and £9.50–13 in the North. If you're visiting Ireland for a fair amount of time, it's worth paying €10 for a year's *An Oige* membership, as you get €2 off each night in any *An Oige* hostel. **Independent hostels** are very often cozy and informal; they don't have curfews, though some cram people in to the point of discomfort. They usually belong to either Independent Holiday Hostels (Ⓣ01/836 4700, Ⓦwww.hostels-ireland.com) or the Independent Hostels Owners network (Ⓣ074/973 0130, Ⓦwww.hostellingireland.com). There are a few disreputable hostels around, so it's a good idea to enquire locally before booking in at a non-approved place. In the Republic, expect to pay €10–18 for a dorm bed (more in Galway, Cork and Dublin), €17–32 (rising to €46 in some Dublin hostels) per person for private rooms where available; in the North, it's £7–12/£14–25.

B&Bs vary enormously, but most are welcoming, warm and clean. Expect to pay from around €32/£20 per person; en-suite facilities are usually a little more and most **hotels** are generally pricier. For an extra €4 (Republic) or £2 (Northern Ireland), you can book through tourist offices. Booking ahead is always advisable during high season and major festivals, and reserving via the Internet generally gets you cheaper rates; it's increasingly preferred by hostel and B&B owners.

Camping usually costs around €10 a night in the Republic, £7 in the North. In out-of-the-way places nobody minds where you pitch. Farmers in popular tourist areas may ask for a small fee to use their land. Some hostels also let you camp on their land for around €8/£5 per person.

FOOD AND DRINK

Irish **food** is meat-orientated. B&Bs usually provide a "traditional" **Irish breakfast** of sausages, bacon and eggs (although many offer vegetarian alternatives). **Pub lunch** staples are usually meat or fish and two veg, with a few veggie options, while specifically vegetarian places are sparse outside major cities and popular tourist areas. All towns have fast-food outlets, but traditional fish-and-chips is a better bet, especially on the coast. For the occasional treat, there are some very good seafood restaurants, particularly along the southwest and west coasts. Most towns have daytime cafés serving a selection of affordable hot dishes, salads, soups, sandwiches and cakes.

Drink

Especially in rural areas, the **pub** is the social heart of the community and the focus for the proverbial **craic** (pronounced "crack"), a particular blend of Irish fun involving good company, witty conversation and laughter, frequently against a backdrop of music. The classic Irish drink is **Guinness**, best in Dublin, home of the brewery, while the Cork stouts, Beamish and Murphy's have their devotees. For English-style keg **bitter**, try Smithwicks, while **lager** brands include Carlsberg, Harp and Budweiser. Irish **whiskeys** may seem expensive, but the measures are large: try Paddy, Jameson's or Bushmills.

CULTURE AND ETIQUETTE

With the huge influx of visitors to Ireland in recent years, the country has acquired an increasingly **cosmopolitan** feel, particularly in the big cities. Ironically, this outside influence has also encouraged an increased sense of national identity and heritage, one symptom of which is the prevalence of traditional music sessions in pubs.

Despite the decreasing influence of Catholicism in Ireland, old-school manners and family values still reign here. It's hard to miss the hospitality and friendliness that most clearly define the Irish.

Smoking is now banned in all indoor public places, including pubs, cafés and restaurants. Most pubs, however, have installed outdoor smoking areas of some description. In restaurants and cafés, a ten percent **tip** is generally expected for good service.

SPORTS AND OUTDOOR ACTIVITIES

Walking and **cycling** in Ireland are great ways of enjoying some of the country's fantastic landscapes, and is in some very rural places unavoidable, even if you're not keen (see Ⓦwww.walking.ireland.ie for suggested routes). There are great opportunities for **horseriding** (see Ⓦwww.discoverireland.ie); a lovely ride is along the white sands of Connemara. **Watersports** are popular: Ireland is increasingly praised for its surfing spots, such as Portrush in the north, Bundoran in Donegal, and Lahinch in Clare (see Ⓦwww.isasurf.ie).

The two great Gaelic sports, **hurling** (the oldest field game in Europe, and similar to hockey, though arguably more exciting) and **Gaelic football** (a mixture of soccer and rugby, but predating both these games), are very popular spectator sports. Croke Park Stadium in Dublin is home to the big fixtures (see Ⓦwww.gaa.ie and Ⓦwww.crokepark.ie for information and tickets).

Horseracing (Ⓦwww.goracing.ie) looms large on the sporting agenda: you'll never be far from a race in Ireland, whether it's a big racecourse like Galway or a soggy village affair in the middle of nowhere.

COMMUNICATIONS

Main **post offices** are open Mon–Fri 9am–5.30pm, Sat 9am–1pm. Stamps and phonecards are often available in newsagents. **Public phones** are everywhere, and usually take **phonecards** (available at post offices and many newsagents); coin-operated phones are rare in rural areas. **International calls** are cheaper at weekends or after 6pm (Mon–Fri). For the **operator** in the Republic call ⓣ10 (domestic) or ⓣ114 (international); in Northern Ireland ⓣ100 or ⓣ155. To call the Republic from Northern Ireland dial ⓣ00353 followed by the area code (without the initial 0) and the local number (note cross-border calls are charged at the international rate). To call the North from the Republic use the code ⓣ048, followed by the eight-digit local number. **Internet access** is widely available and costs about €1.50 per hour; it's generally cheaper in big towns and cities.

IRELAND ON THE NET

ⓦwww.tourismireland.com Information on getting to Ireland from all over the world.

ⓦwww.discoverireland.ie Bord Fáilte.

ⓦwww.discovernorthernireland.com Northern Ireland Tourist Board.

ⓦwww.ireland.com *Irish Times* site with up-to-date info on Dublin.

ⓦwww.browseireland.com Useful site with a massive number of Irish links.

ⓦwww.ntni.org.uk Details of the National Trust's properties in Northern Ireland.

EMERGENCIES

The Republic's police are known as the **Gardaí** (pronounced "gar-dee"), while the **PSNI** (Police Service of Northern Ireland) operates in the North. **Hospitals** and medical facilities are high quality; you'll rarely be far from a hospital, and both Northern Ireland and the Republic are within the European Health Insurance Card scheme (formerly E111). Most **pharmacies** open standard shop hours, though in large towns some may stay open as late as 10pm; they dispense only a limited range of drugs without a doctor's prescription.

EMERGENCY NUMBERS

In the Republic ⓣ112 or ⓣ999; in Northern Ireland ⓣ999.

INFORMATION & MAPS

Tourist offices are abundant in Ireland, in the smaller as well as larger towns on the tourist trail. **Bord Fáilte** provides tourist information in the Republic and it's the **Northern Ireland Tourist Board** in the North. They provide free maps of the city/town and immediate vicinity, and sell a selection of more extensive and specialised maps. The best **maps** are the Michelin 1:400,000 (#405) and the AA 1:350,000. The Ordnance Survey's four 1:250,000 regional Holiday Maps are useful; its 1:50,000 Discovery series is the best option for walkers.

MONEY AND BANKS

Currency in the Republic is the **euro** (€), in Northern Ireland the **pound sterling** (£). Standard **bank hours** are Mon–Fri 9.30am–4.30pm (Republic and Northern Ireland). However, hours vary from branch to branch; most have a later closing time on Thurs (5pm) and some are open Saturday morning. There are **ATMs** throughout Ireland – though not in all villages – and most accept a variety of cards. The exchange rate at the time of writing was €1.47/£1.

OPENING HOURS AND HOLIDAYS

Opening hours are roughly Mon–Sat 9am–6pm, with some late evenings (usually Thurs or Fri), half-days and Sunday opening. In rural areas, hours are often more flexible, with later closing times. The main **museums and attractions** will normally be open regular shop hours, though outside the cities, many only open during the summer. A **student card** often gives reduced entrance charges and, if you're visiting sites run by the Heritage Service in the Republic (ⓦwww.heritageireland.ie), it's worth buying a **Heritage Card** (€21, students €8), which provides a year's unlimited admission.

Public holidays in the Republic are: Jan 1, St Patrick's Day (March 17), Good Friday (bank holiday), Easter Monday, May Day (first Mon in May), June Bank Holiday (first Mon in June), August Bank Holiday (first Mon in Aug), October Bank Holiday (Halloween, last Mon in Oct), Dec 25 & 26. In the North: Jan 1, St Patrick's Day (March 17), Good Friday, Easter Monday, May Day (first Mon in May), Spring Bank Holiday (last Mon in May), July 12, August Bank Holiday (last Mon in Aug), Dec 25 & 26.

THE IRISH LANGUAGE

Though **Irish** is the first language of the Republic, you'll rarely hear it spoken outside the areas officially designated as *Gaeltacht* ("Irish-speaking"), namely West Cork, West Kerry, Connemara, some of Mayo and Donegal, and a tiny part of Meath. However, two important words you may encounter sometimes appear on the doors of pub toilets *Fir* (for men) and *Mná* (for women). You'll also find the word *Fáilte* (welcome) popping up frequently as you enter towns and tourist spots. A few other words to get your tongue round:

Sláinte	cheers, good health
Gardai	police
An lár	city centre
Dia dhuit	hello
Slán	goodbye

More information on the Gaeltacht areas is available at ⓦwww.gaelsaoire.ie.

Dublin

Set on the banks of the River Liffey, **DUBLIN** is a splendidly monumental city – yet it is also youthful, with a lively nightlife. Ireland's booming economy has brought extensive urban regeneration, but sadly there's still much deprivation. Ironically, though, it's this very collision of the old and the new, the slick and the shabby, that gives Dublin such an exciting vibe.

Dublin began as the Viking trading post **Dubh Linn** (Dark Pool), which soon amalgamated with the Celtic settlement of **Baile Átha Cliath** (Town of the Hurdle Ford) – still the Irish name for the city. The city's fabric is essentially **Georgian**, hailing from when the Anglo-Irish gentry invested their income in new townhouses. After the 1801 Act of Union, Dublin entered a long economic decline, but remained the focus of much of the agitation that eventually led to independence.

What to see and do

Dublin's fashionable **Southside** is home to the city's trendy bars, restaurants and shops – especially in the cobbled alleys of buzzing **Temple Bar** leading down to the **River Liffey** – and most of its historic monuments, centred on **Trinity College**, **Grafton Street** and **St Stephen's Green**. But the **Northside**, with its long-standing working-class neighbourhoods and inner-city communities, vaunts itself as the real heart of the city. Across the bridges from Temple Bar are the shopping districts around **O'Connell Street**, where you'll find a flavour of the old Dublin. Here, you'll also find a fair amount of graceful – if slightly shabby – residential streets and squares, with plenty of interest in the museums and cultural hotspots around elegant **Parnell Square.**

The Vikings sited their assembly and burial ground near what is now **College Green**, a three-sided square where **Trinity College** is the most famous landmark.

Trinity College

Founded in 1592, Trinity College played a major role in the development of a Protestant Anglo-Irish tradition: right up to 1966, Catholics had to obtain a special dispensation to study here, though now they make up the majority of the students. The stern grey- and mellow red-brick buildings are ranged around cobbled quadrangles in a larger version of the quads at Oxford and Cambridge. **The Old Library** (Mon–Sat 9.30am–5pm, Sun 9.30am/noon–4.30pm; €8, students €7; Ⓦwww.tcd.ie/library) owns numerous Irish manuscripts. Pride of place goes to the ninth-century **Book of Kells**, adorned with patterns and fantastic animals intertwined with the capitals. The **Book of Durrow** is equally interesting, being the first of the great Irish illuminated manuscripts, dating from between 650 and 680. If you are interested in beautiful antique artefacts, the books are well worth a visit.

Grafton Street and around

Just south of College Green, the streets around pedestrianized **Grafton Street** frame Dublin's quality shopping area – High Street chains, boutiques, department stores, designer clothes, as well as some secondhand, more alternative shops. At the south end of Grafton St lies **St Stephen's Green**, whose pleasant gardens and pools are the focus of Georgian city planning. Running parallel to Grafton Street, Kildare Street harbours the imposing Leinster House, built in 1745 as the Duke of Leinster's townhouse, and now the seat of the Irish parliament, the **Dáil** (pronounced "doyle"). You can visit the house by prior arrangement only, Ⓣ01/618 3000.

National Museum

Alongside is the **National Museum** (Tues–Sat 10am–5pm, Sun 2–5pm; free; Ⓦwww.museum.ie), the repository of the treasures of ancient Ireland. Much of its prehistoric gold was found in peat bogs, along with a sacrificed human and the Lurgan Longboat. The Treasury and the Viking exhibition, which give you a great feel for Ireland's history, display such masterpieces as the Ardagh Chalice and Tara Brooch – perhaps the greatest piece of Irish metalwork – and St Patrick's Bell.

Merrion Square and the National Gallery

Around the block, the other side of Leinster House overlooks **Merrion Square**, the finest Georgian plaza in Dublin. No. 1 was once the home of Oscar Wilde, and a flamboyant statue on the green opposite shows the writer draped insouciantly over a rock; on Sundays the square's railings are used by artists selling their works. Here, the **National Gallery** (Mon–Sat 9.30am–5.30pm, Thurs until 8.30pm, Sun noon–5.30pm; free; Ⓦwww.nationalgallery.ie) owns a fair spread of European old masters and French Impressionists, but the real draw is the trove of Irish paintings, best of which is the permanent exhibition devoted to Ireland's best-known painter, Jack B. Yeats.

Temple bar

Dame Street, leading west from College Green, marks the southern edge of the **Temple Bar** quarter, where you'll find a mass of lively restaurants, pubs, boutiques and arts centres. At night the area tends to play host to tourists out looking for a good time, as well as to Stag and Hen parties – so expect a particularly raucous, and messy, kind of fun.

Dublin Castle

Uphill, tucked away behind City Hall, **Dublin Castle** (Mon–Fri 10am–4.45pm, Sat & Sun 2–4.45pm; €4.50, Ⓦwww.dublincastle.ie) was founded by the Normans, and symbolized British power over Ireland for seven hundred years. Though parts date back to 1207, it was largely rebuilt in the eighteenth century following fire damage. Tours of the State Apartments reveal much about the extravagant tastes and foibles of the viceroys and the real highlight is the excavations in the Undercroft, where elements of Norman and Viking Dublin are still visible. The Clock Tower building now houses the **Chester Beatty Library** (Mon–Fri 10am–5pm, Sat 11am–5pm, Sun 1–5pm; Oct–April closed Mon; free; Ⓦwww.cbl.ie), a sumptuous and massive collection of books, objects and paintings amassed in the twentieth century by the American collector, Sir Arthur Chester Beatty, on his travels around Europe and Asia.

Christ Church Cathedral

Over the brow of Dublin Hill, **Christ Church Cathedral** (daily 9/9.45am–6/5pm summer/winter; €5; Ⓦwww.cccdub.ie) is a resonant monument built between 1172 and 1240 and heavily restored in the 1870s. The crypt museum now houses a small selection of the Cathedral's treasures, the least serious of which include a mummified cat and rat, found trapped in an organ pipe in the 1860s.

St Patrick's Cathedral

Five minutes' walk south from Christ Church is Dublin's other great Norman edifice, **St Patrick's Cathedral** (daily 9am–5/6pm; Nov–Feb Sun closes 3pm; €5.50; Ⓦwww.stpatrickscathedral.ie) founded in 1191, and replete with relics of Jonathan Swift, its dean from 1713 to 1747. Handel's *Messiah* received its first performance here in 1742.

Guinness Brewery

A mile west of Christ Church, the **Guinness Brewery** covers 64 acres on either side of James's Street. Guinness is the world's largest single beer-exporting company, dispatching some 300 million pints a year. Set in the centre of the brewery, the **Guinness Storehouse** (daily 9.30am–5pm; July and August until 7pm; €14; 10% discount if you book online; Ⓦwww.guinness-store

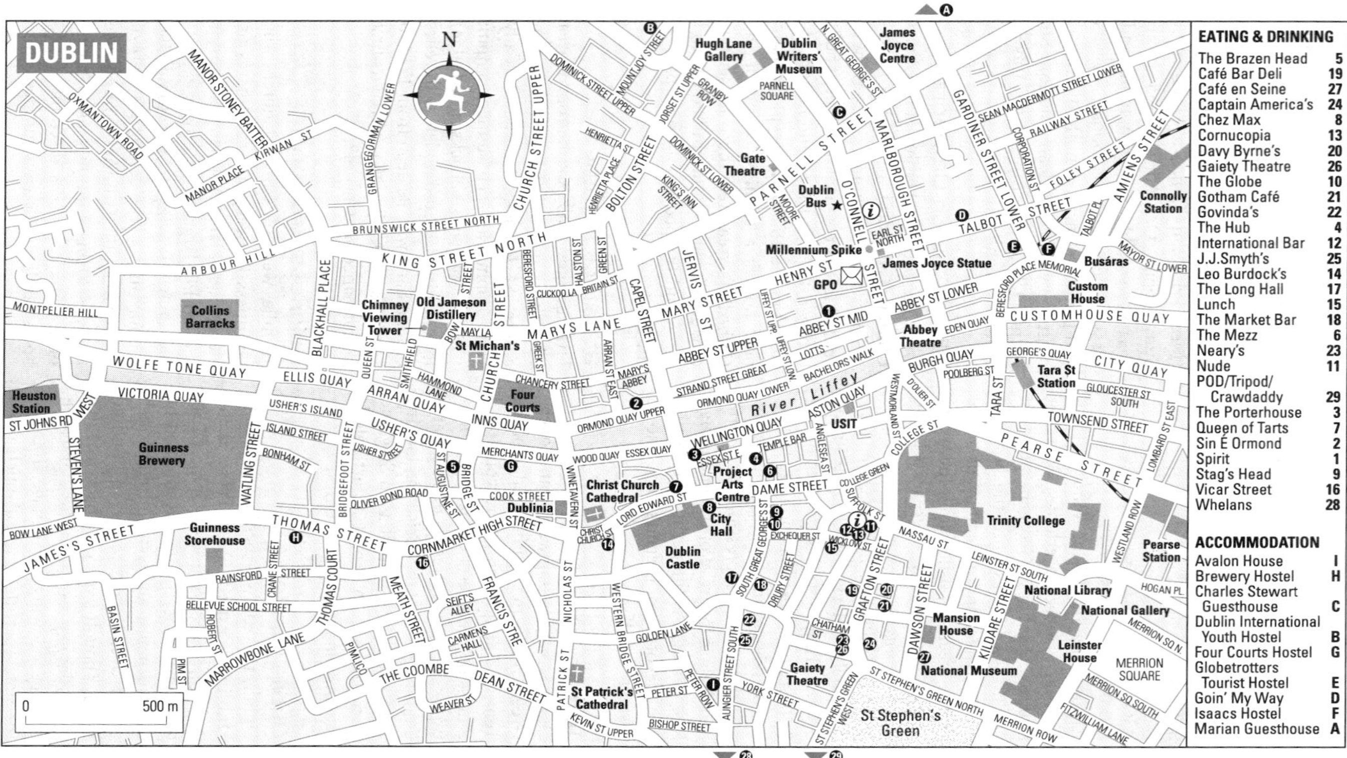
DUBLIN
EATING & DRINKING
The Brazen Head 5
Café Bar Deli 19
Café en Seine 27
Captain America's 24
Chez Max 8
Cornucopia 13
Davy Byrne's 20
Gaiety Theatre 26
The Globe 10
Gotham Café 21
Govinda's 22
The Hub 4
International Bar 12
J.J.Smyth's 25
Leo Burdock's 14
The Long Hall 17
Lunch 15
The Market Bar 18
The Mezz 6
Neary's 23
Nude 11
POD/Tripod/Crawdaddy 29
The Porterhouse 3
Queen of Tarts 7
Sin É Ormond 2
Spirit 1
Stag's Head 9
Vicar Street 16
Whelans 28
ACCOMMODATION
Avalon House I
Brewery Hostel H
Charles Stewart Guesthouse C
Dublin International Youth Hostel B
Four Courts Hostel G
Globetrotters Tourist Hostel E
Goin' My Way D
Isaacs Hostel F
Marian Guesthouse A
Phoenix Park
Irish Museum of Modern Art
Kilmainham Gaol
0 500 m
Hugh Lane Gallery
Dublin Writers' Museum
James Joyce Centre
Gate Theatre
Dublin Bus
Millennium Spike
James Joyce Statue
GPO
Busáras
Custom House
Connolly Station
Abbey Theatre
Tara St Station
USIT
Trinity College
Pearse Station
National Library
National Gallery
Leinster House
Mansion House
National Museum
Merrion Square
St Stephen's Green
Gaiety Theatre
St Patrick's Cathedral
Dublin Castle
City Hall
Project Arts Centre
Christ Church Cathedral
Dublinia
Four Courts
St Michan's
Old Jameson Distillery
Chimney Viewing Tower
Collins Barracks
Heuston Station
Guinness Brewery
Guinness Storehouse
River Liffey
O'Connell Street
Parnell Street
Gardiner Street Lower
Talbot Street
Amiens Street
Henry St
Mary Street
Capel Street
Dame Street
Grafton Street
Dawson Street
Kildare Street
Nassau St
Pearse Street
Townsend Street
Custom House Quay
City Quay
Burgh Quay
Wellington Quay
Ormond Quay Lower
Ormond Quay Upper
Inns Quay
Arran Quay
Ellis Quay
Wolfe Tone Quay
Victoria Quay
Usher's Quay
Merchants Quay
Wood Quay
Essex Quay
Thomas Street
James's Street
Cornmarket High Street
Patrick St
Dean Street
The Coombe
Meath Street
Francis Stre
Church Street
King Street North
Arbour Hill
Manor Stoney Batter
Oxmantown Road
Montpelier Hill
St Johns Rd West
Steven's Lane
Bow Lane West
Marrowbone Lane
Thomas Court
Bridgefoot Street
Bridge St
Watling Street
Church Street Upper
Grangegorman Lower
Brunswick Street North
Blackhall Place
Bolton Street
Dominick Street Upper
Dominick St Lower
Marlborough Street
Abbey St Lower
Abbey St Mid
Abbey St Upper
Westmoreland St
College St
Tara St
Westland Row
St Stephen's Green North
Merrion Row
Aungier Street South
York Street
South Great George's St
Western Bridge Street
Kevin St Upper
Bishop Street
Winetavern St
Nicholas St

house.com) serves as a kind of theme park for Guinness-lovers – and even if you're not a fan of Guinness, you can't fail to be entertained by the interactive displays and activities, which include learning how to pour the perfect pint and watching some of those great Guinness TV ads again. Visits to the Storehouse end with reputedly the best pint of Guinness in Dublin, in the panoramic *Gravity Bar* at the top of the building (the head of the pint), which has truly amazing views over the city.

Irish Museum of Modern Art

Regular buses (#26, #51, #79 and #90) run along The Quays to Heuston Station from where it's a five-minute walk to the **Royal Hospital Kilmainham**, Ireland's first Neoclassical building, dating from 1680, which now houses the **Irish Museum of Modern Art** (Tues–Sat 10am–5.30pm, Sun noon–5.30pm, Wed 10.30am–5.30pm; free; Ⓦwww.modernart.ie). Its permanent collection of Irish and international art includes lens-based work by Gilbert and George, sculpture by Damien Hirst, and paintings by Sean Scully, Francesco Clemente and Peter Doig.

General Post Office and the Monument of Light

Halfway up O'Connell Street looms the **General Post Office** (Mon–Sat 8am–8pm, Sun 10.30am–6.30pm; free), the insurgents' headquarters in the 1916 Easter Rising; only the frontage survived the fighting, and you can still see where bullets were embedded in the pillars. Across the road on the corner of Essex Street North is a **statue of James Joyce**. At the same junction, where the city's most famous landmark, Nelson's Pillar, once stood (it was blown up by the IRA on the fiftieth anniversary of the Easter Rising in 1966), stands a huge, illuminated stainless-steel spike – the **Monument of Light** – representing the city's hopes for the new millennium.

Parnell Square

At the northern end of O'Connell Street lies Parnell Square, one of the first of Dublin's Georgian squares. Its plain red-brick houses are broken by the grey-stone **Hugh Lane Gallery** (Tues–Sat 10am–6pm, Fri & Sat until 5pm, Sun 11am–5pm; Ⓦwww.hughlane.ie), once the Earl of Charlemont's townhouse and the focus of fashionable Dublin. The gallery exhibits work by Irish and international masters, and features a reconstruction of Francis Bacon's working studio. Almost next door, the **Dublin Writers Museum** (Mon–Sat 10am–5/6pm, Sun 11am–5pm; €7; Ⓦwww.writersmuseum.com) whisks you through Irish literary history from early Christian writings up to Samuel Beckett. Two blocks east of Parnell Square, at 35 North Great George's St, the **James Joyce Centre** (Tues–Sat 10am–5pm; €5; Ⓔinfo@jamesjoyce.ie) runs intriguing walking tours of the novelist's haunts (€10; Ⓣ01/878 8547); combined tickets with the Dublin Writers Museum are available.

Old Jameson Distillery

Fifteen minutes west of O'Connell Street, on Bow Street, is the **Old Jameson Distillery** (daily 9am–6pm, last tour 5.30pm; €9.75; Ⓦwww.jamesonwhiskey.com). Tours cover the history and method of distilling what the Irish called *uisce beatha* (anglicized to whiskey and meaning "water of life") – which differs from Scotch whisky by being thrice-distilled and lacking a peaty undertone – and end with a tasting session involving different types of whiskey, Scotch and bourbon. The Distillery also has two **bars**, which pride themselves on their Jameson cocktails, and a **restaurant** which serves breakfast and lunch (9am–4.45pm; light lunch €7). Outside, a lift chugs you to the top of the old distillery **chimney** (Mon–Sat 10am–5.30pm, Sun 11am–5.30pm; €5), where an observation platform provides panoramic views of the city.

Phoenix Park

Phoenix Park is one of the world's largest urban parks, and great if you want to escape the hustle and bustle of the centre (bus #10 from O'Connell Street or #25 from Wellington Quay); originally priory land, it's now home to the Presidential Lodge and attractions such as **Dublin Zoo** (Mon–Sat 9.30am–4/6pm, Sun 10.30am–4/6pm; €14; Ⓦwww.dublinzoo.ie).

Arrival and information

Air The airport is six miles north of the city; Airlink buses #747 and #748 run to Busáras bus station (every 10–20 min; €6 single, €10 return; 30min), and the AerDart service #A1 (every 15min; €5.50 single) connects with the DART railway at Howth Junction, or there are regular Citybus services #16A, #41, #41B & #41C (every 10–20min; €1.75). A taxi to the centre of Dublin should cost €15–20.
Train Trains terminate at either Connolly Station on the Northside, or Heuston Station on the Southside.
Bus Bus Éireann coaches arrive at Busáras bus station, off Beresford Place, just behind The Custom House; private buses use a variety of central locations.
Boat Ferries dock at either Dún Laoghaire, six miles south of the city centre, from where DART railway connects to the city (every 20min; €1.90; 20min), or at the closer Dublin Port, where an unnumbered Citybus service (€2.50; 15min) – or the local bus #53 – meets arriving ferries; through-coaches from Britain usually drop you at Busáras.
Listings For what's-on listings, see the free *Event Guide*, *In Dublin* and *Totally Dublin* or, for music events, *Hot* (€3.50).
Tourist office Suffolk St, off College Green (Mon–Sat 9am–5.30/7pm; June/July & Aug also Sun 10.30am–3pm/5pm; Ⓦwww.visitdublin.com), with branches at 14 Upper O'Connell St, the Dún Laoghaire ferry terminal and the airport.
Travel agency USIT on Aston Quay, by O'Connell Bridge (Mon–Fri 9.30am–6.30pm, Thurs till 7pm, Sat 9.30am–5pm; Ⓣ01/602 1904, Ⓦwww.usit.ie) books B&Bs during the summer and includes a travel agency offering student discounts.

City transport

Bus Dublin has an extensive route network and all buses are exact fare only. Fares are €0.90–1.85, a one-day bus pass is €6, with a pack of five one-day passes costing only €17.30, or there are bus and rail passes (including DART) for one day/three days (€8.80/€17.30). Free bus timetables are available from Dublin Bus, 59 Upper O'Connell St. Nitelink night buses cost €4–6, depending on your destination.
Tram The LUAS tram service operates along two routes: from Connolly Station to Tallaght via Abbey Street to Heuston Station, and from St Stephen's Green to Sandyford. Tickets cost €1.50–2.10 single, €2.70–4 return. A one-day pass is €4.50 and a combined bus/LUAS one-day pass €6.50.
Train The DART railway links Howth and Malahide to the north of the city with Bray to the south via Pearse, Tara St and Connolly stations in the city centre (maximum fare €4).
Bike rental Cycle Ways, 185 Parnell St Ⓣ01/873 4748.

Accommodation

Although Dublin has stacks of accommodation, anywhere central will probably be full at weekends, around St Patrick's Day (March 17), at Easter and in high summer so it's always wise to book ahead (preferably online). The cheaper places to stay are generally north of the river, especially around the bus and train stations northeast of the centre. All hostels listed provide free breakfast, unless stated.

Hostels

Avalon House 55 Aungier St Ⓣ01/475 0001, Ⓦwww.avalon-house.ie. Friendly, if sometimes noisy, hostel with cramped dorms but plenty of twin or four-bedded rooms, and a good café. Dorms ❷, rooms ❹
Brewery Hostel 22–23 Thomas St Ⓣ01/435 8600, Ⓦwww.irish-hostel.com. Housed in a fine converted library, this small hostel often has space when others are full. Regular BBQs when the weather's good. Breakfast not provided. Dorms ❷, rooms ❹
Dublin International Youth Hostel 61 Mountjoy St Ⓣ01/830 1766. An Óige's Dublin flagship, occupying a former convent. It's a massive, well-equipped hostel, holding 293 beds, including a few private rooms (early booking necessary), in a rather dreary location. Dorms ❸, rooms ❺
Four Courts Hostel 15–17 Merchants Quay, Ⓣ01/672 5839, Ⓦwww.fourcourtshostel.com. In a very central location, this hostel is housed in Georgian buildings overlooking the River Liffey. Excellent facilities and helpful staff. Dorms ❷, rooms ❹
Globetrotters Tourist Hotel 46 Gardiner St Lower Ⓣ01/873 5893, Ⓦwww.globetrottersdublin.com. Upmarket hostel where security-locked dorms and individual bed lights make for a peaceful night's sleep. Also some spacious private rooms. Dorms ❸, rooms ❻
Goin' My Way 15 Talbot St Ⓣ01/878 8484,

ⓔ goinmyway@esatclear.ie. Small, family-run place near O'Connell Street. Its midnight curfew makes this one of Dublin's quieter hostels and it's good value. Dorms ❷, rooms ❸

Isaacs Hostel 2–5 Frenchman's Lane ⓣ 01/855 6215, ⓦ www.isaacs.ie. Housed in an eighteenth-century wine warehouse with its own restaurant on site, offering eight- and ten-bed dorms and a few cozy twins. Conveniently close to the bus station. Dorms ❷, rooms ❹

Guesthouses and B&Bs

Charles Stewart Guesthouse 5/6 Parnell Square, ⓣ 01/878 0350, ⓦ www.charlesstewart.ie. Very reasonably priced accommodation in elegant Georgian surroundings and with friendly staff. Virtually opposite the Gate Theatre. ❹

Marian Guesthouse 21 Upper Gardiner St ⓣ 01/874 4129, ⓦ www.marianguesthouse.ie. Welcoming, good-value, family-run guest house about a mile north of the city centre. ❹

Camping

Camac Valley Tourist Caravan and Camping Park Naas Rd, Clondalkin ⓣ 01/464 0644, ⓦ www.camacvalley.com. The most convenient campsite, located on the N7, a 35min drive from the centre. This site has excellent facilities, including an Internet café. The #69 bus goes to and from the centre (Aston Quay, near O'Connell Bridge – make sure you ask the driver for Camac Valley), stopping right outside the campsite. The last bus back from the centre is at 11.15pm, so if you're any later, a taxi (around €25) is your only option. ❶

Eating

Café Bar Deli *Bewley's Café*, Grafton St. Great pasta, pizza and salads in a room that sports some fabulous wallpaper and stained-glass windows. Mains from €10.50. You can also catch a lunchtime performance in its theatre upstairs.

Captain America's 44 Grafton St. Reasonably priced burgers, steaks and seafood served amidst a host of rock'n'roll memorabilia. Student nights Mon–Wed with discounts on drinks.

Chez Max 1 Palace St, off Dame St. Small, French restaurant hidden away in a little corner next to the castle. Food is relatively pricey (€14.50, *moules frites*), so go for a drink or coffee.

Cornucopia 21 Wicklow St. One of the city's few vegetarian cafés and highly popular too. Mains €12.

Gotham Café 8 South Anne St. Lively place offering an extensive and reasonably priced global menu.

Govinda's 4 Aungier St. Huge helpings of dhal and rice and tasty vegetarian curries, plus daily veggie specials, served by very friendly staff.

Leo Burdock's 2 Werburgh St. Dublin's best fish-and-chips – takeaway only. Fresh cod is €5.75. There's another branch on Liffey Street Lower. Closed Sun.

Lunch 63 South William St. Vibrant Italian café serving good-value pizza, pasta and panini. Mains €6–10.

The Market Bar Fade St. Dublin's first gastro-bar serving classy tapas and Mediterranean food in a converted abattoir. Mains €11.

Nude 21 Suffolk St. Canteen-style café serving hot and cold wraps, panini, pasta, soups, salads and smoothies. Sizeable dish of pasta €6.50.

Queen of Tarts Dame St. Tiny café offering irresistible cakes and pastries as well as savoury food.

Drinking and nightlife

Most of Dublin's eight hundred pubs serve food as well as drink. The **music** scene – much of which is pub-based – is volatile, so it's always best to check the listings magazines (see opposite). The best clubs can be found around Temple Bar and on Harcourt Street, off St Stephen's Green.

Bars

Davy Byrne's 21 Duke St. An object of pilgrimage for *Ulysses* fans, since Leopold Bloom stopped here for a snack. Attracts a sophisticated crowd and also serves good food (traditional Irish stew €11.50).

The Globe South Great George's St. Trendy, dimly lit hangout with loud music and lots of space. Backs onto *RíRá*, an intimate but very lively club.

The Long Hall South Great George's St. Victorian pub encrusted with mirrors and antique clocks.

Neary's 1 Chatham St. Plenty of bevelled glass and shiny wood, plus Liberty print curtains to show some style appropriate for its theatrical clientele.

Sin É Ormond Quay Upper. Cool and popular Northside bar with a great range of beers and splendid soundtracks.

Stag's Head Dame Court, Dame St, almost opposite the Central Bank. Wonderfully intimate pub, full of mahogany, stained glass and mirrors. Very popular with local Dubliners. It does good lunches, too.

Clubs

Gaiety Theatre South King St. The theatre transforms itself into one of Dublin's major clubs on Friday and Saturday nights, with DJs on three levels and the city's latest-serving bar.

The Hub 23–24 Eustace St. Plenty of indie-inspired rock bands in the evening, plus punk to funk club

TREAT YOURSELF

Sip on a cocktail or two at Dublin's classiest establishment – **Café en Seine** (40 Dawson St; ⓣ01/677 4567; 11am–3am, Mon–Sun) is an art nouveau-style café bar with three floors and five bars, and an experience in itself. It's hugely popular on Friday and Saturday nights with a lively, sophisticated crowd, so expect to queue after 11pm.

nights into the small hours, with a big reggae night on Wednesdays.

POD/Tripod/Crawdaddy 35 Harcourt St. If you're looking for a very big night out, this is the place. Multiple venues housed in an old railway station, famously photographed in 1900 with a train crashed through its walls. Great local House DJs are a regular feature at the *POD*, with occasional international guests. Itself a three-in-one venue space, *Tripod* offers something for everyone, and its Saturday club night claims to be "the biggest thing to hit Harcourt St. since the 9.55 from Bray".

Spirit Middle Abbey St. Its club-night on Friday, *Revelation*, with three local DJs plus international guests, is one of Dublin's hottest nights out.

Entertainment

Dublin's **theatres** are among the finest in Europe, offering a good mix of classical and more avant-garde performances. Ticket prices start from around €20, with concessions offered on Mon–Thurs nights and for matinees.

Cinemas

Irish Film Institute 6 Eustace St, Temple Bar ⓣ01/679 5744, ⓦwww.irishfilm.ie. Shows both classics and newly released independent films, and has a shop and educational programme with a strong Irish emphasis. There's also a good bar and restaurant.

Savoy 17 Upper O'Connell St ⓣ0818/776 776, ⓦwww.savoy.ie. Mainstream films and blockbusters at this six-screen cinema.

Screen D'Olier St ⓣ0818/300 301, ⓦwww.screencinema.ie. Art-house and independent films.

Live music

The Brazen Head 20 Lower Bridge St. The oldest pub in Dublin, with traditional music nightly from 9.30pm.

International Bar 23 Wicklow St. Large saloon with rock bands and a comedy club upstairs or in the cellar.

J.J. Smyth's 12 Aungier St. One of the few places to catch local jazz and blues talent.

The Mezz 23–24 Eustace St. Rock café-bar with live music every night (and not just rock – also jazz, blues, funk, soul, reggae). Bar food served 2.30–9.30pm. Mains from €6.50.

The Porterhouse 16–18 Parliament St. There are live gigs every night at this popular bar, which brews its own beer. Also has a great supper menu – mains €7.50–18.50.

Vicar Street 58–59 Thomas St. One of the city's finest music venues, offering a varied programme of major music and comedy acts, plus assorted club nights.

Whelans 25 Wexford St. Notorious music pub attracting a host of up-and-coming international stars as well as local talent. Recently renovated to include more facilities for musicians and another bar.

Shopping

Charity, vintage, and secondhand Campden St has some good charity shops, while Harlequin, Castle Market, and Wild Child, Great George's St. South, sell good quality vintage gear.

SLANE CASTLE

Every year since 1981, **Slane Castle**, which overlooks the River Boyne and is 45km northwest of Dublin, has played host to one of the largest **outdoor concerts** in Ireland. Past performers at the concert – which is held on a Saturday in August – have included The Rolling Stones, U2, Madonna, Oasis, and REM, and you couldn't find a more spectacular setting for a great music event. Needless to say, tickets sell out within minutes. Details of the next concert can be found at ⓦwww.slanecastle.ie. There's a great hostel, Slane Farm Hostel (ⓣ041/988 4985, ⓦwww.slanefarmhostel.ie; dorms ❷, rooms ❸), just outside the town, which also allows camping at €8 per night. Book well in advance for August.

High Street chains and department stores Try Grafton St, Henry St and O'Connell St for a spattering of high street shops, including Topshop (top of Grafton St) and Penny's (37 O'Connell St), which sells ridiculously cheap clothes, footwear, and accessories. If you can't find what you're looking for here, head out to Dundrum ((Mon–Fri 9am–9pm, Sat 9am–7pm & Sun 10am–7pm; Ⓦwww.dundrum.ie), home to the biggest shopping centre in Europe; you can get there in about 12 minutes by taking the LUAS from St. Stephen's Green to Balally, or get bus #44A or 48A.
Markets You can pick up some great bargains on retro clothes and accessories or fake designer T-shirts at Cow's Lane Market on Saturdays. George's St Arcade (Mon–Sat) also has some interesting buys – books, vinyl and artwork, as well as clothes.

Directory

Embassies Australia, Fitzwilliam House, Wilton Terrace ⓣ01/664 5300; Canada, 64–65 St Stephen's Green ⓣ01/417 5000; UK, 31–33 Merrion Rd ⓣ01/205 3700; US, 42 Elgin Rd, Ballsbridge ⓣ01/668 8777.
Exchange Thomas Cook, 118 Grafton St; General Post Office; most city centre banks.
Hospitals Southside: St James's, James St ⓣ01/410 3000; Northside: Mater Misericordiae, Eccles St ⓣ01/885 8888.
Internet Central Cybercafé, 6 Grafton St; Global Internet Café, 8 Lower O'Connell St; Oz Cyber Café, 39 Abbey St Upper; Planet Cyber Café, 13 St Andrew's St.
Laundry All American Launderette, Wicklow Court, South Great George's St.
Left luggage Busáras, Heuston and Connolly stations.
Pharmacy Dame Street Pharmacy, 16 Dame St; O'Connell's, 55 O'Connell St.
Post office O'Connell St; St Andrew's St.

Moving on

Train (Connolly) Belfast (7 daily, Mon–Sat; 5 on Sun; 2hr 10min); Drogheda (33 daily; 30min–1hr); Rosslare (3 daily; 3hrs); Sligo (4–5 daily; 3hr 10min–3hr 30min).
Train (Heuston) Cork (15 daily, Mon–Sat; 10 on Sun; 2hr 50min); Ennis (4 daily, via Limerick; 2hr 55min–3hr 40min); Galway (6–7 daily; 2hr 20min–2hr 50min); Kilkenny (6 daily Mon–Sat, 4 on Sun; 1hr 40min–1hr 50min); Killarney (7 daily; 3hr 30min–3hr 50min); Westport (2–3 daily; 3hr 20min–3hr 40min).
Bus Belfast (20 daily; 2hr 55min); Cashel (6 daily; 2hr 50min); Cork (6 daily; 4hr 25min); Derry (9 daily; 4hr); Donegal town (6 daily; 3hr 45min–4hr 10min); Doolin (2 daily; 6hr 15 min); Drogheda (35 daily; 1hr 20min); Ennis (12 daily; 4hr 20min–6hr 50min); Enniskillen (6 daily; 2hr 20min–3hr); Galway (15 daily; 3hr 30min); Kilkenny (6 daily; 2hr 10min–2hr 30min); Killarney (5 daily; 6hr 10min); Newgrange (3 daily; 1hr 40min–1hr 55min); Portrush (1–2 daily; 5hr 40min); Rosslare Harbour (13 daily; 3hr 20min); Sligo (6 daily; 4hr); Westport (3 daily; 5hr–5hr 40min).

From Wexford to Cork

The southeast is Ireland's sunniest and driest corner. The region's medieval and Anglo-Norman history is richly concentrated in **Kilkenny**, a bustling, quaint inland town, while to the west, at the heart of County Tipperary is the **Rock of Cashel**, a spectacular natural formation topped with Christian buildings from virtually every period. In the southwest, **Cork** is both relaxed and spirited, the perfect place to ease you into the exhilarations of the west coast.

WEXFORD

WEXFORD is a convenient stop-off point if you're coming into Ireland from Rosslare. It's a fairly bustling town during the day, with the main concentration of shops and businesses on the long stretch, North and South Main Street. Its early Celtic and Nordic heritage is apparent in the town's narrow streets and old town walls.

Wexford can seem like a ghost town on weekday nights, but scratch the surface and you'll find there's a fair amount of *craic* to be had in the town's lively pubs and bars. October brings an injection of energy with the Wexford Opera Festival (Ⓦwww.wexfordopera.com).

For nature and history lovers, the **Irish National Heritage Park** at Ferrycarrig (3 miles west of town off the N11, ⓣ053/912 0733, Ⓦwww.inhp.com; €7.50) is a worthwhile trip, taking you through nine

FERRIES

Ferries from Wales (Fishguard and Pembroke) and France (Cherbourg and Roscoff) arrive at **ROSSLARE HARBOUR**, on the southeastern corner of Ireland. Daily trains leave here for Wexford, Waterford and Dublin, and there are also daily bus services to Dublin and the west. The nearest **tourist information centre** is in Wexford (Crescent Quay ⓣ053/912 3111; ⓔwexfordtouristoffice@failteireland.ie; all year round 9.30am–5pm Mon–Fri, 10am–5pm Sat; call the office for additional times).

thousand years of Irish history in the appropriate settings. The **John F Kennedy Arboretum** at New Ross, 37km west of Wexford on the N25, (ⓣ051/388 171, ⓦwww.heritageireland.ie; €3) comprises 252 hectares of flora and fauna in stunning landscape, as well as a maze and a lake.

The only **hostel** in Wexford is *Kirwan House Hostel*, 3 Mary St (ⓣ053/21208, ⓦwww.hostelwexford.com; dorms ❷, rooms ❸). The hostel is in a pretty Georgian building and has clean, bright rooms; staff are very friendly. Just up the road on George Street is *St. George's Guesthouse*, which has fresh, pleasant décor, and can accommodate small groups at a discount (ⓣ05/914 3474, ⓦwww.stgeorgeguesthouse.com; bed and breakfast ❹).

For **food** and **drink** try *The Centenary Stores* on Charlotte Street, which has a live band on Monday and Thursday nights. There's also a BBQ every Monday night in the summer. Food is served noon–6pm, with mains from €10. The *Sky and the Ground* pub on South Main Street hosts music nearly every night (both traditional and non-traditional bands), and also serves food.

LIMERICK

LIMERICK, which lies on the river Shannon, is at the heart of the region of Ireland known as the Midwest, and is equidistant between Galway to the north and Cork to the south. As such it is an important **transport hub**, with major roads from Dublin, Galway, Killarney, and Cork converging here.

Limerick is steeped in history: its origins are Viking, and the impressive buildings of King John's Castle and St. Mary's Cathedral bear witness to the city's Norman heritage.

The only **hostel** in Limerick is *Courtbrack Accommodation* on Courtbrack Avenue, South Circular Road, (ⓣ061/302 500, June 9–Sept 2; dorm ❸, room ❸), which has good facilities, and is around ten minutes' walk from the centre.

For reasonable **food** in a pleasant setting, try *The Locke Bar and Bistro* (3 George's Quay; food served from 3pm; mains €5–12), where you can sit outside overlooking the river. For lunch or supper, there's *The Green Onion* (Old Town Hall, Rutland St; Tues–Sat), a snazzy café-restaurant that serves good quality sandwiches, salads and pasta.

Good **bars** include *Charlie Chaplin's*, on Chapel Street, which has a great

WEXFORD AND HOLLYWOOD

An unlikely coupling, perhaps, but one of which Wexford is very proud. The dramatic opening scene of the 1998 Spielberg film *Saving Private Ryan*, starring Tom Hanks and Matt Damon, was filmed at Curracloe Beach, 9km northeast of town. And Duncannon Fort, southwest of town on the Hook Head peninsula, was a location for the 2002 film *The Count of Monte Cristo*, starring James Caviezel and Guy Pearce. The fort has a visitors' centre (ⓣ051/389 454, ⓦwww.duncannonfort.com; daily 10am–5.30pm summer, Mon–Fri 10am–5pm winter; €5) where you can see the sword used in the final scene of the film.

atmosphere and a DJ every night; and *South's* on Quinlan Street, decked out in smart, Parisian-style décor, and which serves delicious toasted sandwiches.

From Limerick, **Shannon airport** is only 24km northwest. Bus Éireann run direct services from Limerick to Dublin, Cork, Killarney, Tralee, Waterford, Ennis, Galway, Westport, Sligo, and Derry. Irish Rail operate direct trains to Dublin, Cork, and Ennis.

KILKENNY

KILKENNY is Ireland's finest medieval city, its castle set above the broad sweep of the River Nore and its narrow streets laced with carefully maintained buildings. In 1641, the city became the virtual capital of Ireland, with the founding of a parliament known as the Confederation of Kilkenny. The power of this short-lived attempt to unite resistance to English persecution of Catholics had greatly diminished by the time Cromwell's wreckers arrived in 1650. Kilkenny never recovered its prosperity, but enough remains to indicate its former importance.

What to see and do

Left at the top of Rose Inn Street is the broad **Parade**, which leads up to the castle. To the right, the High Street passes the eighteenth-century **Tholsel**, once the city's financial centre and now the town hall. Beyond is **Parliament Street**, the main thoroughfare, where the **Rothe House** (April–Oct Mon–Sat 10.30am–5pm, Sun 3–5pm; Nov–March 10.30am–4.30pm, closed Sun; ⓦwww.rothehouse.com; €4) provides a unique example of an Irish Tudor merchant's home, comprising three separate houses linked by cobbled courtyards. This end of town's highlight is the thirteenth-century **St Canice's Cathedral** (ⓣ056/776 4971; ⓦwww.stcanicescathedral.ie; Mon–Sat 9/10am–1pm & 2–4/6pm, Sun 2–4/6pm; €4), which has a fine array of sixteenth-century monuments, many in black Kilkenny limestone. The **round tower** next to the church (same hours; €3; combined ticket with cathedral €6) is the only remnant of a monastic settlement reputedly founded by St Canice in the sixth century; there are superb views from the top. It's the imposing twelfth-century **Castle**, though, which defines Kilkenny (ⓣ056/772 1450; tours daily: April–Sept 10/10.30am–5/7pm; Oct–March Tues-Sun 10.30am–12.45pm and 2–5pm; €5.30 ⓦwww.heritageireland.ie). Its library, drawing room, bedrooms and Long Gallery of family portraits are open for viewing, as is the **Butler Gallery** (ⓣ056/776 1106, ⓦwww.butlergallery.com; April–Sept 9.30/10am–6/5pm; Oct–March 10.30am–12.45pm & 2–5pm), housing exhibitions of modern art.

Arrival and information

Train and bus The bus and train stations are just north of the centre, off John St.
Tourist office Follow John St over the river and climb Rose Inn St; based in the sixteenth-century Shee Alms House (ⓣ056/775 1500; Mon–Fri 9/9.30am–6/5.30pm, Sat 10am–6pm, July & Aug also Sun 11am–1pm & 2–5pm).
Listings The weekly *Kilkenny People* (€1.80) and *Whazon?* has listings information. See also ⓦwww.kilkenny.ie and ⓦwww.southeastireland.com for more details on what to do in the area.
Festivals The town is renowned for The Cat Laughs comedy festival in June (ⓦwww.thecatlaughs.com) and its Arts Festival in August (ⓦwww.kilkennyarts.ie).

Accommodation

Advance booking is advisable in summer, especially during festival weeks in June and August. The tourist office runs a booking service to find available rooms if you haven't booked ahead; there's a €4 charge.
Banville's 49 Walkin St ⓣ056/777 0182, ⓔmbanville@eircom.net. Very pleasant and friendly B&B, a 5min walk from town centre. ❹
Kilkenny Tourist Hostel 35 Parliament St ⓣ056/776 3541, ⓔkilkennyhostel@eircom.net. An excellent budget option in a rambling Georgian building. Dorms ❷, rooms ❸
MacGabhainn's Backpacker Hostel 24 Vicar St ⓣ056/777 0970, ⓦwww.hostelworld.

com, Ⓔhostel-vicarstreet@hotmail.com. Great little hostel with good facilities. Dorms ❷, rooms ❹

Camping

Tree Grove camping Danville House, New Ross Rd Ⓣ056/777 0302, Ⓔtreecc@iol.ie. March–Nov 15. One mile south of the city on the R700. Bike hire available. ❶

Eating

Billy Byrne's 39 John St Ⓣ056/772 1783. Fine bar lunches.

Café Sol William St Ⓣ056/776 4987 Ⓦwww.cafesolkilkenny.com. Mon–Sat 11.30am–10pm, Sun noon–9pm. Great for lazy breakfasts and wholesome lunches; light mains €8.

Kyteler's Inn St Kieran St. Food in medieval surroundings; get there early.

Sandwich Espresso 23 Rose Inn St. Good sandwiches made to order; they can even deliver free of charge (minimum 6 sandwiches).

Drinking and nightlife

Edward Langton's 69 John St. Huge, swanky bar; the very popular club is alive and kicking on Tuesdays, Thursdays and Saturdays from 10pm.

Kilkenny River Court Hotel The Bridge, John St. Treat yourself to an early drink on the terrace overlooking the river and castle.

The Pumphouse Parliament St. Popular with young and old, locals and travellers alike. Music most nights, and there's also a pool table.

Tynan's 2 Horseleap Slip, St. John's Bridge. Worth visiting for its cozy Victorian interior; there are still relics from its days as a pharmacy and grocery store.

Moving on

Train Dublin (6 daily; 1hr 40min–2hr).

Bus Cork (8 daily; 2hr 50min–5hr 20min); Dublin (7 daily; 2hr 15min–2hr 45min).

THE ROCK OF CASHEL

Approached from north or west, the extraordinary **ROCK OF CASHEL** (daily 9am–4.30/7.30pm, last admission 45min before closing; €5.30; Ⓦwww.heritageireland.ie) appears as a mirage of crenellations rising bolt upright from the vast encircling plain and is where St Patrick reputedly used a shamrock to explain the doctrine of the Trinity. Walking from **Cashel** town, ten minutes to the east, the first sight you'll encounter on the Rock is the fifteenth-century **Hall of the Vicars**, whose vaulted undercroft contains the original **St Patrick's Cross**. **Cormac's Chapel**, built in the 1130s, is the earliest and most beautiful of Ireland's Romanesque churches; both north and south doors feature intricate carving, while inside, the alleged sarcophagus of King Cormac has an exquisite design of interlacing serpents and ribbon decoration. The graceful limestone **Cathedral**, begun in the thirteenth century, is Anglo-Norman in conception, with its Gothic arches and lancet windows. The tapering **round tower** is the earliest building on the Rock, dating from the early twelfth century. The **Cashel Heritage Centre** (Ⓣ062/62511, Ⓦwww.cashelheritagecentre.com; March–Oct 9.30am–5.30pm; Nov–Feb 9.30am–5.30pm, closed Sat & Sun; free) on Main Street has a small exhibition that covers the history of the town, as well as tourist information.

Arrival and information

Bus Buses going towards Cork drop off and pick up outside the *Bakehouse Bakery* on Main St, those towards Dublin on the other side of the street.

Tourist office Main St (Ⓣ062/61333; opening times as for Cashel Heritage Centre, see opposite).

Accommodation

Hostels

Cashel Holiday Hostel 6 John St Ⓣ062/62330, Ⓦwww.cashelhostel.com. Very central, just off Main St. Dorms ❷, rooms ❸

Cashel Lodge Dundrum Rd (R505) Ⓣ062/61003 Ⓦwww.cashel-lodge.com. Five minutes' walk out of town, this newly renovated coach house is blessed with spectacular views. Camping is also permitted. Dorms ❷, rooms ❹

B&Bs

Cashel Town B&B 5 John St Ⓣ062/62330 Ⓦwww.cashelbandb.com. Next door to, and run by the same people as *Cashel Holiday Hostel*, this is a comfortable, friendly place on a lovely street.

Rockside House Rock Villas Ⓣ062/63813

Ⓦwww.joyrockside.com. Friendly and cozy, on a pretty, quiet street very close to the rock.

Eating and drinking

Chiefs Main St. There's a DJ Thurs–Sun night, and traditional music prior to the DJ on Sunday evenings.
Daverns 20 Main St. Traditional music Mondays and Wednesdays from 9pm.
Feehan's Main St. Lively old bar in the evenings, also recommended for a lunchtime visit.
Henry's Main St. All-day breakfast, and cheap, hearty food (bangers n' mash €6).
Ryan's Daughter Ladyswell St Ⓣ062/62688. Traditional Irish fare in rustic surroundings. Mains €10.

Moving on

Bus Cork (6 daily; 1hr 35min); Dublin (6 daily; 2hr 50min).

CORK

Everywhere in **CORK** there's evidence of its history as a great mercantile centre, with grey stone quaysides, old warehouses, and elegant, quirky bridges spanning the River Lee to each side of the city's island core – but the lively atmosphere and large student population, combined with a vibrant social and cultural scene, are equally powerful draws. Massive stone walls built by invading Normans in the twelfth century were destroyed by William III's forces during the **Siege of Cork** in 1690, after which waterborne trade brought increasing prosperity, as witnessed by the city's fine eighteenth-century bow-fronted houses and ostentatious nineteenth-century churches.

What to see and do

The graceful arc of **St Patrick's Street** – which with **Grand Parade,** forms the commercial heart of the centre – is crammed with major chain stores and, just off here on Princes Street, the sumptuous **English Market** (Mon–Sat 9am–5.30pm) offers the chance to sample local delicacies like drisheen (a peppered sausage made from a sheep's stomach lining and blood). On the far side of St Patrick's Street, chic Paul Street is a gateway to the bijou environs of French Church Street and Carey's Lane. In the west the island is predominantly residential, though Fitzgerald Park is home to the **Cork Public Museum** (Mon–Sat 11am–1pm & 2.15–5/6pm, Sun 3–5pm; free), which focuses on Republican history.

Shandon area

North of the River Lee is the historic **Shandon area,** a reminder of Cork's eighteenth-century status as the most important port in Europe for dairy products. The striking **Cork Butter Exchange survives,** stout nineteenth-century Neoclassical buildings given over to craft workshops. At one corner of the old butter market is the **Cork Butter Museum** (O'Connell Square Ⓣ021/430 0600, Ⓦwww.corkbutter.museum; July–Aug 10am–6pm; March–Oct 10am–5pm), which exhibits, amongst other items, a keg of thousand-year-old butter. Behind the square is the pleasant Georgian church of **St Anne Shandon** (Ⓣ021/450 5906, Ⓦwww.shandonbells.org; Mon–Sat 10am–5/4pm, last entry 45min before closing; €6), easily recognizable from all over the city by its weather vane – an eleven-foot salmon. The church tower gives excellent views over the city and an opportunity to ring the famous bells: a good stock of sheet tunes is provided. Around two miles west of here, in Sunday's Well, is the nineteenth-century **Cork City Gaol** (Ⓣ021/430 5022, Ⓦwww.corkcitygaol.com; daily 9.30/10am–6/5pm, last admission 1hr before closing; €7), with an excellent taped tour focusing on social history.

Arrival and information

Train Cork's train station is about one mile east of the city centre on Lower Glanmire Rd.
Bus The bus station is on Parnell Place alongside Merchant's Quay.
Ferry Boats from Swansea and Roscoff arrive at Ringaskiddy, some ten miles out, from where there's a bus into the centre.

Tourist office Grand Parade (Mon–Sat 9/9.30am–6/4.45pm; July & Aug also Sun 10am–5pm; ⓣ021/425 5100, ⓦwww.corkkerry.ie)
Internet Internet Exchange, Wood St.
Listings Pick up the free *Whazon?* (ⓦwww.whazon.com) or the *Evening Echo. Totally Cork* also has listings, plus good reviews and articles.
Festival There's an international jazz festival in late October (ⓦwww.corkjazzfestival.com).

Accommodation

Hostels

Aaran House Tourist Hostel Lower Glanmire Rd ⓣ021/455 1566, ⓔtracy_flynn3@hotmail.com. Clean and friendly, very convenient for train and bus stations. Dorms and triples ❷
Bru Hostel 57 McCurtain St ⓣ021/450 1074, ⓦwww.bruhostel.com. An excellent budget option, this trendy hostel also has a bar attached, where guests can claim a free pint. Dorms ❷, rooms ❸
Cork International Hostel 1–2 Redclyffe, Western Road ⓣ021/454 3289, ⓔcorkyh@gofree.indigo.ie. Part of the An Óige group, this hostel has a big front garden, and is fifteen minutes' walk from the centre or bus #8 to the University. Dorms ❷, rooms ❸
Kinlay House Bob & Joan's Walk, Shandon ⓣ021/450 8966, ⓦwww.kinlayhousecork.ie. With great facilities, this friendly hostel is in a lovely part of town near St. Anne's Shandon; dorms ❷, rooms ❸
Sheila's 4 Belgrave Place, Wellington Rd ⓣ021/450 5562 ⓦwww.sheilashostel.ie. A comfortable hostel set back from the hustle and bustle of town. Dorms ❷, rooms ❸

B&Bs

Oaklands Glanmire Rd Lower ⓣ021/450 0578. Reasonably priced, near the train station. ❹
Tara House 52 Glanmire Rd Lower ⓣ021/450 0294. Next door to *Oaklands*. ❹

Eating

Café-Bar-Deli Academy St. This ever-popular restaurant serves delicious pasta dishes (€13) and pizza from €9.
Farmgate Café English Market. Enjoy wholesome, fresh food sourced from the surrounding market in a bustling atmosphere. Mains €10–14.
Four Liars Bistro Shandon. A quiet spot up by St. Anne's. The sirloin steak here is renowned, and you can bring your own wine.
Liberty Grill 32 Washington St. Brunch (served till 5pm Mon–Sat) and burgers are this restaurant's speciality. Mains from €10.
Peppercorns Café 8 Pembroke St. All-day breakfast and cheap lunches, plus smoothies and coffee.
Tony's Bistro North Main St. Cork's ultimate greasy spoon. The all-day breakfast is €6.
Uncle Pete's Pizzeria Pope's Quay. Good quality takeaway (with limited seating outside) offering pizza, pasta, wine, coffee, and ice cream. Open late.

Nightlife

Bodega Nights Coal Quay. Popular late café-bar with regular DJs. Open Wed–Sun.
Crane Lane Phoenix St. Theatre with a late bar, open daily. Arty and sophisticated, with regular gigs and shows.
Fred Zepellins Parliament St. Rock bar with a mix of live gigs and DJs. Cheap pints from 4–8pm Mon–Thurs.
The Roundy 1 Castle St. Trendy café-bar with DJs and live gigs upstairs.
The Savoy Patrick St. Cork's premier club, open Thurs–Sat, with DJs and live music.
Scotts Caroline St. A restaurant by day, this glitzy venue has a big bar and club nights on Friday and Saturday.
The Thirsty Scholar Western Rd. As its name suggests, this great pub is close to the university and accordingly popular with students in term time.

Entertainment

Live music

An Spailpín Fánach South Main St. Traditional music every night, except Saturday, in this cozy bar.
Sin É Coburg St. Traditional music on Tuesday from 9.30pm; other live music is on Thursday from 9.30pm, Friday and Sunday 6.30pm.
Sláinte Market Lane. Traditional music Wednesday and Thursday nights, while on Friday local jazz, rock or funk sessions take place. On Sundays there's a BBQ from 6pm.

Theatre and cinemas

The Kino Cinema Washington Street ⓣ021/427 1571 ⓦwww.kinocinema.net. Screens independent films and co-hosts the excellent film festival in mid-October (ⓦwww.corkfilmfest.org).
Triskel Arts Centre Tobin Street ⓣ021/427 2022 ⓦwww.triskelart.com. A lively spot with cinema, exhibitions, readings and concerts.

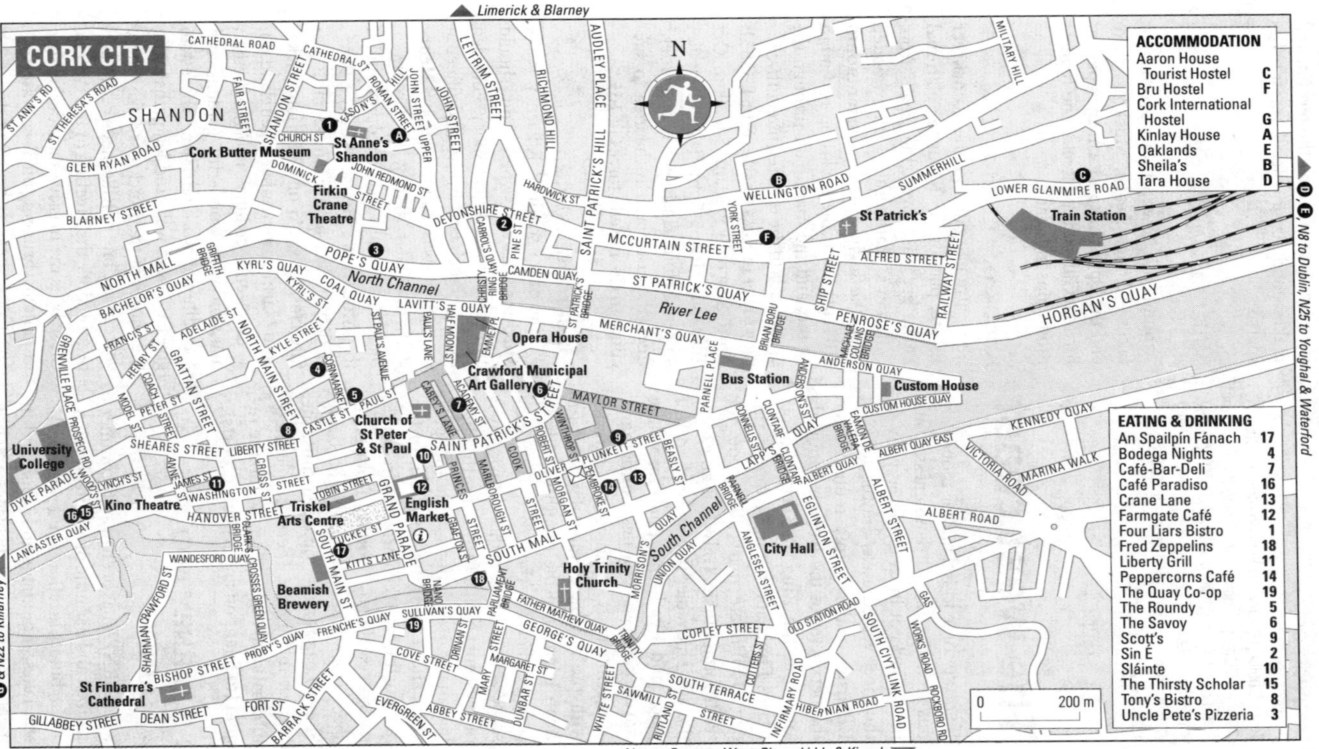
CORK CITY
Limerick & Blarney
D, E, N8 to Dublin, N25 to Youghal & Waterford
Airport, Passage West, Ringaskiddy & Kinsale
G & N22 to Killarney
ACCOMMODATION
Aaron House Tourist Hostel C
Bru Hostel F
Cork International Hostel G
Kinlay House A
Oaklands E
Sheila's B
Tara House D
EATING & DRINKING
An Spailpín Fánach 17
Bodega Nights 4
Café-Bar-Deli 7
Café Paradiso 16
Crane Lane 13
Farmgate Café 12
Four Liars Bistro 1
Fred Zeppelins 18
Liberty Grill 11
Peppercorns Café 14
The Quay Co-op 19
The Roundy 5
The Savoy 6
Scott's 9
Sin É 2
Sláinte 10
The Thirsty Scholar 15
Tony's Bistro 8
Uncle Pete's Pizzeria 3
0
200 m
N
SHANDON
Cork Butter Museum
St Anne's Shandon
Firkin Crane Theatre
Train Station
St Patrick's
North Channel
River Lee
South Channel
Opera House
Crawford Municipal Art Gallery
Bus Station
Custom House
Church of St Peter & St Paul
English Market
University College
Kino Theatre
Triskel Arts Centre
Beamish Brewery
Holy Trinity Church
City Hall
St Finbarre's Cathedral
CATHEDRAL ROAD
FAIR STREET
SHANDON STREET
GLEN RYAN ROAD
BLARNEY STREET
NORTH MALL
POPE'S QUAY
LEITRIM STREET
RICHMOND HILL
AUDLEY PLACE
SAINT PATRICK'S HILL
MCCURTAIN STREET
WELLINGTON ROAD
SUMMERHILL
LOWER GLANMIRE ROAD
ST PATRICK'S QUAY
MERCHANT'S QUAY
PENROSE'S QUAY
HORGAN'S QUAY
NORTH MAIN STREET
GRATTAN STREET
SHEARES STREET
SAINT PATRICK'S STREET
GRAND PARADE
SOUTH MALL
SOUTH MAIN ST
MAYLOR STREET
OLIVER PLUNKETT STREET
ALBERT QUAY
EGLINTON STREET
ALBERT STREET
ALBERT ROAD
KENNEDY QUAY
VICTORIA ROAD
MARINA WALK
SOUTH CIYT LINK ROAD
GEORGE'S QUAY
SOUTH TERRACE
BISHOP STREET
GILLABBEY STREET
DEAN STREET
BARRACK STREET
ABBEY STREET
EVERGREEN ST

Moving on

Train Dublin (15 daily (10 Sun); 2hr 35min–3hr 35min); Killarney (9 daily; 1hr 30min–2hr).
Bus Cashel (8 daily; 1hr 35-50min); Dublin (6 daily; 4hr 25min); Galway (12 daily; 4hr 25min); Kilkenny (7 daily (only 2 direct); 3hr 10min–4hr 15min); Killarney (13 daily; 2hr).

The west coast

If you've come to Ireland for mountainous scenery, sea and remoteness, you'll hit the jackpot in County Kerry. By far the most visited areas are the town of **Killarney** and a scenic route around the perimeter of the Iveragh Peninsula known as the **Ring of Kerry**. County Clare's **Ennis** and the more tourist-ridden **Doolin** are marvellous spots for **traditional music**. **Galway** is an exceptionally enjoyable, free-spirited sort of place, and a gathering point for young travellers. To its west lies **Connemara**, a magnificently wild coastal terrain, with the nearby, elementally beautiful **Aran Islands**, in the mouth of Galway Bay. Further up the coast, the landscape softens around the historic town of **Westport**, while further north, **Sligo** has many associations with the poet Yeats and a lively, bustling feel. In the far northwest, the two-hundred-mile folded coastline of **County Donegal** is spectacular, with the highlight being **Slieve League**'s awesome sea cliffs, the highest in Europe. There are plenty of international flights directly into the region (to Shannon and Knock airports).

KILLARNEY AND AROUND

KILLARNEY has been heavily commercialized and has little of architectural interest, but its location amid some of the best lakes, mountains and woodland in Ireland definitely compensates. **Cycling** is a great way of seeing the terrain, and makes good sense – local transport is sparse.

What to see and do

Around the town, three spectacular **lakes** – Lough Leane, Muckross Lake and the Upper Lake – form an appetizer for MacGillycuddy's Reeks, the highest mountains in Ireland.

Knockreer Estate

The entrance gates to the **Knockreer Estate**, part of the **Killarney National Park**, are just over the road from Killarney's cathedral. Tall wooded hills, the highest being **Carrantuohill** (1041m), form the backdrop to **Lough Leane**, and the main path through the estate leads to the restored fifteenth-century tower of **Ross Castle** (Ⓣ064/35851; April–Sept daily 9/10am–5/6.30pm; Oct Tues–Sun 10am–5pm; last admission 45min before closing; €5.30; gardens free), the last place in the area to succumb to Cromwell's forces in 1652.

Muckross Estate

A mile or so south of Killarney is the **Muckross Estate**, where you should aim first for Muckross Abbey. Founded by the Franciscans in the mid-fifteenth century, it was suppressed by Henry VIII, and later, finally, by Cromwell. Back at the main road, signposts point to **Muckross House** (daily 9am–5.30/7pm, last admission 45 mins before closing; €5.75 or €8.65 joint ticket with farm; Ⓦwww.heritageireland.ie), a nineteenth-century neo-Elizabethan mansion with wonderful gardens and a traditional working farm. The estate gives access to well-trodden paths along the shores of the Muckross Lake where you can see one of Killarney's celebrated beauty spots, the **Meeting of the Waters**. Close by is the massive shoulder of Torc Mountain, shrugging off **Torc Waterfall**. The Upper Lake is beautiful, too, with the main road running along one side up to Ladies' View, from where the view is truly spectacular.

Gap of Dunloe and the Black Valley

West of Killarney lies the **Gap of Dunloe**, a natural defile formed by glacial overflow that cuts the mountains in two. **Kate Kearney's Cottage**, a pub located six miles from Killarney at the foot of the track leading up to the Gap, is the last fuelling stop before **Lord Brandon's Cottage**, a summer tearoom (June–Aug), seven miles away on the other side of the valley. The track winds its way up the desolate valley between high rock cliffs and waterfalls, past a chain of icy loughs and tarns, to the top, where you find yourself in what feels like one of the most remote places in the world: the **Black Valley**, named after its entire population perished during the famine (1845–49). There's a wonderfully isolated An Óige **hostel** here too (March–Nov; ⓣ064/34712, dorms €13). The quickest way to Killarney from here is to carry on down to Lord Brandon's Cottage and take the boat back across the Upper Lake.

Arrival and information

Train and bus The bus and train stations are next to each other on Park Road, a short walk east of the centre.
Tourist office Beech Road off New St (Mon–Sun 9am–6pm; June & Sept 9am–8pm; July & Aug Mon–Sat 9.15am–5pm; ⓣ064/31633, ⓦwww.corkkerry.ie).
Internet Leaders, 9 Beech Rd; Web-Talk, 53 High St.
Listings Check out *The Kerryman* (€1.80, from all newsagents).

Accommodation

Hostels

Killarney Railway Hostel Fair Hill ⓣ064/35299 ⓦwww.hoztel.com. Clean and friendly and opposite the station. Dorms ❷, rooms ❸
Neptune's Town Hostel New St ⓣ064/35255 ⓦwww.neptuneshostel.com. Good facilities, including free WiFi. Breakfast not included. Dorms ❷, rooms ❷
Paddy's Palace Hostel 31 New St ⓦwww.paddyspalace.com. Very close to National Park entrance; dorms ❷, rooms ❷
The Súgan Hostel Lewis Rd ⓣ064/33104 ⓦwww.killarneysuganhostel.com. Lovely, family-run hostel with colourful décor. There's also bike hire here, cheaper if you're a guest. It's right next to a good bar, too. Dorms ❷, rooms ❷

Camping

Flesk Caravan and Camping Muckross Rd ⓣ064/31704 ⓦwww.campingkillarney.com. A mile south of the centre on the N71 Kenmare road. ❶

Eating and drinking

The Country Kitchen New St. Cheap, hearty food, including all-day breakfast.
McSorley's College St. There's traditional music in the main bar here every night in summer, followed by a live band. Upstairs its club is the biggest in Killarney, open nightly.
Mustang Sally's Main St. Decent bar food, and its popular club *The Venue* is open Thursday, Friday and Saturday nights.
O'Connor's Bar High St. Great little pub with local Irish musicians Thursday and Friday. You can also book Gap of Dunloe tours here (see above).
Salvador's 9 High St. Pizza, seafood and steak in candle-lit surroundings.

Moving on

Train Cork (9 daily; 1hr 20min–1hr 40min); Dublin (7 daily; 3hr 15–30min).
Bus Cork (13 daily; 1hr 35–50min); Dingle (2–5 daily; 2hr–2hr 40min); Dublin (10 daily; 6hr 10min–7hr 30min); Waterville (1 daily; 1hr 55min).

THE RING OF KERRY

Most tourists view the spectacular scenery of the 110-mile **Ring of Kerry**, west of Killarney, without ever leaving their tour coach or car; therefore, anyone straying from the road or waiting until the afternoon, when the buses stop running, will experience the slow twilights of the Atlantic seaboard in perfect seclusion. **Cycling** the Ring takes three days, and a bike provides access to mountain roads. **Buses** from Killarney circle the

Ring in summer (May–Sept 2 daily; from €20 return). The public bus departs from the bus station and private tour operators from their respective offices in town; you can book the private buses through the tourist office. For the rest of the year, buses travel only the largely deserted mountain roads, as far as Cahersiveen.

VALENTIA ISLAND

At **Kells Bay** (heading anticlockwise on the main N70 around the Ring of Kerry), the road veers inland towards **CAHERSIVEEN**, the main shopping centre for the western part of the peninsula. It has an independent **hostel**, *Sive*, 15 East End (Ⓣ066/947 2717, Ⓔinfo@sivehostel.ie; dorms ❷, rooms ❸). From the town, lanes lead out to **VALENTIA ISLAND**, Europe's most westerly harbour, its position on the Gulf Stream providing a mild, balmy climate. A **ferry** (April–Sept; single €1.50, return €2) crosses from Reenard Point (2.5 miles from Cahersiveen) to **Knightstown** whose main street has a few shops, a post office and a couple of bars.

As the island is a mere 11km by 3km, the best way to see the island is to **walk**. The much-touted **Grotto**, tucked away inside the entrance to a gaping slate quarry (which used to provide slates to roof the House of Commons), holds a crude statue of the Virgin perched two hundred feet up amid dripping icy water. More exciting is the spectacular cliff scenery to the northwest. Valentia Island's **accommodation** options are *Spring Acre* (March–Nov; Ⓣ066/947 6141, Ⓔ springacre@eircom.net; bed and breakfast ❹) opposite the pier where the ferry docks, while *The Ring Lyne* (Ⓣ066/947 6103, Ⓔtheringlyne@hotmail.com; dorms ❷, rooms ❸) provides **hostel** accommodation in Chapeltown, four miles west.

BALLINSKELLIGS

The stretch of coast south of Valentia is wild and almost deserted, apart from a scattering of farms and fishing villages. Sweet-smelling, tussocky grass dotted with wild flowers is raked by Atlantic winds, ending in abrupt cliffs or sandy beaches. In **BALLINSKELLIGS** the *Skellig* (Ⓣ066/947 9942, Ⓦwww.skellighostel.com; dorms ❷, rooms ❸) provides good quality **hostel** accommodation. The village is a focus of the Kerry Gaeltacht (Irish-speaking area), busy in summer with schoolchildren and students learning Irish. It's an ideal place to visit if you're in need of some isolated tranquillity, but there's not a lot to do or see – save beautiful scenery.

WATERVILLE

Formerly a favourite holiday spot of Charlie Chaplin and his family, **WATERVILLE**, across the bay from Ballinskelligs, is the best base on the Ring for exploring the coast and the mountainous country inland. For **accommodation** try *The Old Cable House* in the former transatlantic Cable Station (Ⓣ066/947 4233, Ⓦwww.oldcablehouse.com; ❺), or *Klondyke House*, New Line Road (Ⓣ066/947 4119, Ⓦhomepage.eircom.net/~klondykehouse; ❹). Alternatively, there's the *Bru na Domoda* hostel at Maistir Gaoithe, seven miles up the Inny Valley (May–Oct; Ⓣ066/947 4782, Ⓦwww.dromid.ie; dorms ❷, rooms ❸).

DINGLE

DINGLE, little more than a few streets by the side of Dingle Bay, is the best base for exploring the stunning **Dingle Peninsula** (see opposite).

What to see and do

Formerly Kerry's leading port in medieval times, then later a centre for smuggling, the town's main attractions nowadays are aquatic: the star of the show is undoubtedly **Fungi** the dolphin who's been visiting the town's natural harbour for some twenty years (a number of boats offer trips out to see him from around €15). Alternatively, there's **Oceanworld** on the waterfront (daily 10am–5pm; €11; ⓦwww.dingle-oceanworld.ie), whose numerous aquaria include a touch pool and shark tank as well as a turtle exhibition.

Arrival and information

Arrival info The nearest train stations are Killarney and Tralee. Via car or bus, take the N86 from Tralee, or the R561 from Castlemaine to reach Dingle. Bus Éireann provides a bus service between Dingle and Killarney and Tralee. The bus stop is at the back of Supervalu on Strand St.
Tourist office The Quay (Mon–Fri 9/10am–7/5pm; July & Aug also Sat 9am–7pm, Sun 10am–5pm; ⓣ066/915 1188) can book accommodation.
Internet *Dingle Internet Café*, Main St.

Accommodation

Ballintaggart House ⓣ066/915 1454, ⓔinfo@dingleaccommodation.com. Lovely old hunting lodge, one mile east of Dingle town; it also has a campsite. Open Easter–Oct; dorms ❷, rooms ❹
Begley's Lower Main Street ⓣ066/915 0993. Informal and friendly, this is one of the few budget B&Bs in Dingle. ❹
The Goat Street Café Goat Street ⓣ066/915 2770, ⓔinfo@thegoatstreetcafe.com. Budget accommodation above a pleasant café. Limited rooms, so book ahead. ❷

Eating and drinking

An Café Liteartha Dykegate Lane, ⓣ066/915 2204. Tea, coffee and cake in the cozy back-room of a bookshop.
An Droichead Beag Main St. Nightly traditional music sessions in this brilliantly atmospheric pub.
Dick Mack's Green St. Many a celebrity has stopped for a drink here; check out the names on the pavement outside.
O'Flaherty's Bridge St. There're traditional music sessions most nights in this big, colourful bar.
The Oven Doors Holyground. Serves everything from tea and scones to inexpensive pizzas. Open all day till 9pm.

TREAT YOURSELF

Doyle's John Street, ⓣ066/915 1174, ⓦwww.doylesofdingle.com. Dinner at this renowned seafood restaurant is a gastronomic experience not easily topped. Reservations essential. Mains €20–30.

DINGLE PENINSULA

The **Dingle Peninsula** is a place of intense, shifting beauty: spectacular mountains, long sandy beaches and splinter-slatted rocks. It defines the extraordinary coast at **Slea Head** and ensures that, remote though it is, it's firmly on the tourist trail. Here is one of the greatest concentrations of Celtic ruins in Ireland, and the now uninhabited Blasket Islands once generated a wealth of Irish literature.

Public transport in the west of the peninsula amounts to a **bus** from Dingle to Dunquin, making **cycling** the best way to explore; bikes are available at Foxy John's on Main Street (€10/50 per day/week).

The Irish-speaking area west of Dingle is rich in relics of the ancient Gaelic and early Christian cultures: there's the spectacular **Dún Beag** (daily 9am–6/7pm; €3), about four miles west of Ventry. A promontory fort, its defences include four earthen rings, with an underground escape route by the main entrance. West of the fort, the hillside above the road is studded with stone **beehive huts**, cave dwellings, forts, churches, standing stones and crosses – over five hundred in all. The beehive huts were built and used for storage up until the late nineteenth century, but standing among ancient buildings – for example, the **Fahan group** – you're looking over a landscape that's remained essentially unchanged for centuries.

Slea Head

At **Slea Head** the view encompasses the desolate, splintered masses of the **Blasket Islands** (uninhabited since 1953, though there are some summer residents). In the summer, boats bound for **Great Blasket** depart daily from the pier just south of Dunquin (June–Aug every 30min, Easter–May & Sept to mid-Oct hourly; ⓣ066/915 6422; €25 return). Great Blasket's delights are simple ones: tramping the footpaths that criss-cross the island, sitting on the beaches watching the seals and dolphins, or savouring the stunning sunsets. Camping is free, and there's a café serving good, cheap vegetarian meals. At **DUNQUIN**, there's an **An Óige hostel** (Feb–Nov; ⓣ066/915 6121, ⓔmailbox@anoige.ie; dorms ❷).

ENNIS

In daytime hours there's little of interest in County Clare's main town, **ENNIS**, and the town's lack of a hostel means that budget travellers don't tend to stay long. At night, however, you'll find a town buzzing with traditional music, so if you're a fan, a visit here won't be wasted. Nightly pub sessions are the local music scene's lifeblood and safe bets for high-standard sessions include: *Cruise's*, Abbey Street (nightly); *Kelly's*, Carmody Street (Sat & Sun); *Brogan's*, O'Connell St (Tues & Thurs); and *The Copper Jug*, Court View (Fri). Custy's Music Store on O'Connell Street is a fantastic source of information. The town hosts a couple of traditional music **festivals**: Fleadh Nua (ⓦwww.fleadhnua.com) in the last week of May, and the Ennis Trad Festival (ⓦwww.ennistradfestival.com) in mid-November.

Arrival and information

Train and bus The bus and train stations sit alongside one another, a ten-minute walk southeast of the town centre down Station Road.
Tourist office Same building as the Clare Museum on Arthur's Row (June–Sept Mon–Sun 9.30am–5.30pm; Oct–May Tues–Sat 9.30am–1pm & 2–5pm; ⓣ065/682 8366, ⓦwww.shannonregiontourism.ie) with the same opening hours.
Bike rental Bikes can be rented from Tierney's Cycles, 17 Abbey St.

Accommodation

The tourist office (see above) can also organise accommodation.
The Barge Rooms 1 Newbridge Rd ⓣ065/682 4888. Reasonable accommodation attached to a bar, restaurant and club, so you're never far from late-night entertainment. Breakfast not included. ❸
Newpark House Roslevan Tulla Rd ⓣ065/682 1233. Certainly not a budget option, but if you feel like something different, this seventeenth-century country house provides it. Breakfast at this quiet refuge, 2km north of town, is a real treat. ❺

Eating and drinking

Ennis Gourmet Store 1 Barrack St ⓣ065/684 3314. Great for tasty salads and tapas, or a spoiling hamper of food.
Numero Uno 3 Barrack St ⓣ065/684 1740. Cheery pizza place, to eat in or take away.

Moving on

Trains Dublin (8 daily; 3hr 5min–4hr 25min).
Bus Doolin (3 daily; 1hr 25min); Dublin (18 daily; 4hr 45min–6hr 15min)

DOOLIN

Some twenty-five miles northwest of Ennis is the seaside village of **DOOLIN**, famed for a steady, year-round supply of **traditional music** in its three pubs, though these can often be crowded with tourists. There's plenty of accommodation including four **hostels**, all charging from around €15 for a dorm bed: *Paddy's Doolin Hostel* (ⓣ065/707 4421, ⓦwww.doolinhostel.com; ❷); *Rainbow Hostel* (ⓣ065/707 4415, ⓦhomepage.eircom.net/~rainbowhostel; ❷); *Flanagan's Village Hostel* (ⓣ065/707 4564; ❷); and *Aille River Hostel* (ⓣ065/707 4260, ⓦwww.esatclear.ie/~ailleriver; ❷).

All Doolin's pubs serve excellent **food**; the *Lazy Lobster,* Roadford and *Doolin Café,* Roadford are two of the best restaurants. A **ferry** (April–Sept) runs from Doolin pier to the **Aran Islands** (see p.638). **The Cliffs of Moher**, four miles south of Doolin, are the area's most famous tourist spot, their great bands of shale and sandstone rising 660 feet above the waves.

GALWAY

The city of **GALWAY** began as a crossing point on the River Corrib, and developed as a strong Anglo-Norman colony. Granted city status in 1484, it developed a flourishing trade with the Continent, especially Spain. When Cromwell's forces arrived in 1652, however, the city was besieged for ninety days and went into a decline from which it has only recently recovered.

Today, the town has a justified reputation as party capital of Ireland. University College guarantees a high number of young people in term-time, but the energy is most evident during Galway's **festivals**, especially the **Arts Festival** in the last two weeks of July (Ⓦwww.galwayartsfestival.com).

What to see and do

The prosperity of maritime Galway was expressed in the distinctive townhouses of the merchant class, remnants of which are littered around the city, even though development has destroyed some of its character. Just about the finest medieval townhouse in Ireland is fifteenth-century **Lynch's Castle**, on Shop Street – along with Quay Street, the social hub of Galway. Now housing the Allied Irish Bank, it has a stone facade decorated with carved panels, gargoyles and a lion devouring its prey. Down by the River Corrib stands the **Spanish Arch**; more evocative in name than in reality, it's a sixteenth-century structure that was used to protect galleons unloading wine and rum. Across the river lies the **Claddagh** district, the old fishing village that once stood outside the city walls and gave the world the Claddagh ring as a symbol of love and fidelity. Past the Claddagh the river widens out into **Galway Bay**; for a pleasant sea walk follow the road until it reaches **Salthill**, the city's seaside resort. There are several beaches along the prom, though for the best head two miles from Salthill to **Silverstrand** on the Barna road.

GALWAY RACES

For locals, the **Galway Races** is the most important event in the social and sporting calendar, and renowned worldwide. Held in the last week of July, the Summer Festival Race Meeting sees seven days of hardcore betting and socializing by day, and partying by night – with the Guinness flowing freely throughout. Admission is €20–30, and there's a good student discount with valid ID. A shuttle bus runs during race week from Eyre Square to the racecourse, 5km out of town (€7 return). See Ⓦwww.galwayraces.com for further information. Booking accommodation in advance during this week is essential.

Arrival and information

Train and bus The bus and train stations are off Eyre Square, on the northeast edge of the city centre.
Tourist office Forster St (May–Sept daily 9am–5.45/7pm; Oct–April Mon–Sat 9am–5.45pm; kiosk in Eyre Square high summer Ⓣ091/537 700, Ⓦwww.irelandwest.ie). Books B&B accommodation.
Internet *Café 4*, High St; Netaccess, Olde Malte Arcade, High Street; E-2008, Forster St.
Listings See the weekly *Galway Advertiser* (free) or *Galway City Tribune* (€1.60).

Accommodation

Barnacles Quay Street House 10 Quay St Ⓣ091/568 644, Ⓦwww.barnacles.ie. Very convenient for the plethora of good pubs and cafés on Quay Street. Dorms ❷, rooms ❸
Kinlay House Merchant's Rd Ⓣ091/565 244, Ⓦwww.kinlaygalway.ie. Newly refurbished, centrally located hostel just off Eyre Square. Day tours to the Aran Islands, the Cliffs of Moher and Connemara depart right outside the door. Dorms ❷, rooms ❸

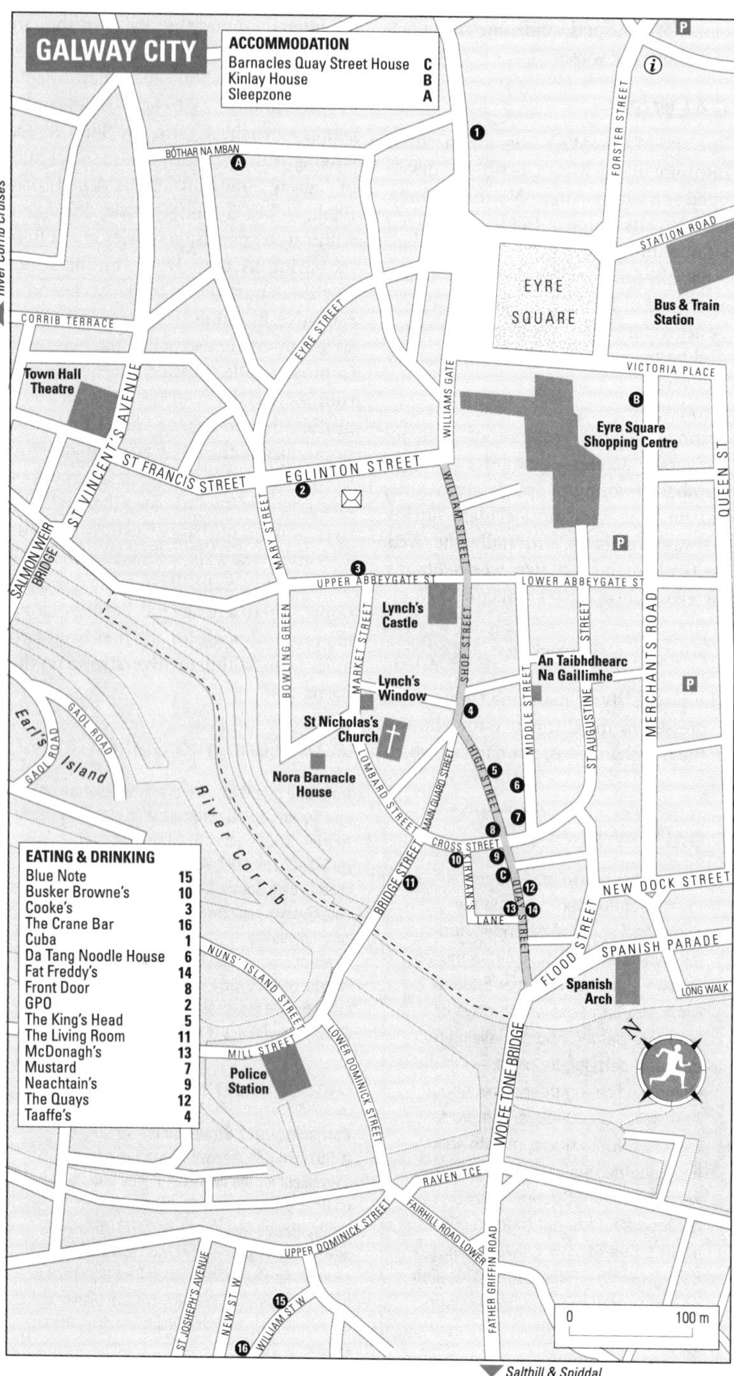
GALWAY CITY
ACCOMMODATION
Barnacles Quay Street House C
Kinlay House B
Sleepzone A
EATING & DRINKING
Blue Note 15
Busker Browne's 10
Cooke's 3
The Crane Bar 16
Cuba 1
Da Tang Noodle House 6
Fat Freddy's 14
Front Door 8
GPO 2
The King's Head 5
The Living Room 11
McDonagh's 13
Mustard 7
Neachtain's 9
The Quays 12
Taaffe's 4
River Corrib Cruises
Salthill & Spiddal
BÓTHAR NA MBAN
CORRIB TERRACE
EYRE STREET
EYRE SQUARE
FORSTER STREET
STATION ROAD
Bus & Train Station
Town Hall Theatre
ST VINCENT'S AVENUE
WILLIAMS GATE
VICTORIA PLACE
Eyre Square Shopping Centre
QUEEN ST
ST FRANCIS STREET
EGLINTON STREET
WILLIAM STREET
MARY STREET
SALMON WEIR BRIDGE
UPPER ABBEYGATE ST
LOWER ABBEYGATE ST
Lynch's Castle
SHOP STREET
BOWLING GREEN
MARKET STREET
Lynch's Window
An Taibhdhearc Na Gaillimhe
MERCHANTS ROAD
MIDDLE STREET
ST AUGUSTINE STREET
St Nicholas's Church
Earl's Island
GAOL ROAD
Nora Barnacle House
LOMBARD STREET
MAIN GUARD STREET
HIGH STREET
River Corrib
CROSS STREET
BRIDGE STREET
KIRWAN'S LANE
QUAY STREET
NEW DOCK STREET
FLOOD STREET
SPANISH PARADE
Spanish Arch
LONG WALK
NUNS' ISLAND STREET
MILL STREET
Police Station
LOWER DOMINICK STREET
WOLFE TONE BRIDGE
RAVEN TCE
FAIRHILL ROAD LOWER
UPPER DOMINICK STREET
FATHER GRIFFIN ROAD
ST JOSHEPH'S AVENUE
NEW ST W
WILLIAM ST W
0
100 m

Sleepzone Bóthar na mBan, Wood Quay ⓣ091/566 999, ⓦwww.sleepzone.ie. There's a free Internet café at this excellent hostel. Breakfast not included. Dorms ❷, rooms ❹

Camping

Ballyloughnane Caravan Park Ballyloughlane, Renmore (April–Sept; ⓣ091/752 029). Family-run park three miles east of the centre, overlooking Galway Bay.

Eating

Busker Browne's Kirwans Lane. Reasonably priced food is served at this trendy bar-restaurant. Mains from €10.

Cooke's 28 Abbeygate St Upper. Go for filling seafood chowder in smart surroundings.

Da Tang Noodle House 2 Middle St. Excellent noodle dishes at reasonable prices. €8–9.50.

Fat Freddy's Quay St. Good pizzas, salads, and antipasti at this fun, colourful bistro. Mains €10–15.

McDonagh's 22 Quay St. A must for the freshest seafood at any time of day, especially the renowned fish and chips. Mains €8–34.

Mustard 1 Middle St. Gourmet pizza and burger bar. Mains €7–14.

Drinking and nightlife

The Quay Street area leading down to the river is known as the "Left Bank" due to the proliferation of popular pubs, restaurants and cafés.

Bars

The Crane Bar 2 Sea Rd. Holds revered traditional music sessions nightly from 9pm.

Front Door Cross St. Big, light bar with great décor and DJs every weekend.

The King's Head 15 High St. Reputedly serves the best Guinness in town. Live music most nights.

The Living Room Bridge St. Popular late night bar on three levels with retro décor. DJ Thurs–Sun.

The Quays Quay St. One of the city's best-loved pubs, whose atmospheric interior was taken from a medieval French church. Serves good-value food around midday.

Neachtain's 17 Cross St. Old-fashioned pub that attracts an eccentric, arty crowd.

Taaffe's 19 Shop St. One of the best places to hear traditional music, where there are nightly sessions.

Clubs

Blue Note 3 West William St. Popular with students and an alternative crowd. Check out their "Hangover Brunch" on Sundays.

Cuba Eyre Square. Very popular club, on three floors.

GPO Eglinton St. Different club nights every night of the week. Free entry for students with ID cards.

Moving on

Train Dublin (6 daily; 2hr 30min–3hr).

Bus Cork (12 daily; 4hr 25min); Doolin (4 daily; 1hr 40min–2hr 50min); Dublin (16 daily; 3hr 30–45min); Killarney (7 daily; 4hr 40min); Westport (8 daily; 1hr 35min–3hr 45min).

THE ARAN ISLANDS

The **ARAN ISLANDS** – **Inishmore, Inishmaan** and **Inisheer**, lying thirty miles out across the mouth of Galway Bay – make spectacular settings for a wealth of early remains and some of the finest archeological sites in Europe. The isolation of the Irish-speaking islands prolonged the continuation of a unique, ancient culture into the early twentieth century.

GETTING TO THE ISLANDS

There are daily **ferries** to Inishmore year-round (less frequently to the other islands), departing from Galway city, Rossaveal (20 miles west by bus) and Doolin in County Clare – the cost of a return trip starts at around €25, depending on the season, with some student reductions and good-value accommodation packages – contact the below offices for information. Book tickets in Galway city through Aran Island Ferries, 4 Forster St (ⓣ091/568 903, ⓦwww.aranislandferries.com); Inismór Ferries, 29 Forster St (ⓣ091/566 535, ⓦwww.arandirect.com); or O'Brien Shipping (ⓣ065/707 4455 or ⓣ091/567 283, ⓦwww.doolinferries.com) – all three companies have desks in Galway tourist office.

You can also **fly** with Aer Árann Islands (ⓣ091/593 034, ⓦwww.aerarannislands.ie) for around €45 return; book at Galway tourist office.

Inishmore

Although **INISHMORE** is very tourist-orientated, its wealth of dramatic ancient sites overrides such considerations. It's a long strip of an island, a great tilted plateau of limestone with a scattering of villages along the sheltered northerly coast, and land that slants up to the southern edge, where tremendous cliffs rip along the entire shoreline. As far as the eye can see is a tremendous patterning of stone, some of it the bare pavements of grey rock split into bold diagonal grooves, latticed by dry-stone walls.

What to see and do

Most of Inishmore's sights are to the northwest of Kilronan, the island's principal town. The first hamlet in this direction is Mainistir, from where it's a short signposted walk to the twelfth-century **Teampall Chiaráin (Church of St Kieran)**, one of several ecclesiastical sites on Inishmore. Three miles or so down the main road is Kilmurvey, a fifteen-minute walk from the most spectacular of Aran's prehistoric sites, **Dún Aonghasa**: it's accessed via the **visitor centre** (daily 10am–4/6pm; €2.10; Ⓦwww.heritageireland.ie). Nearby **Dún Eoghanachta** is a huge drum of a stone fort, set in a lonely field with the Connemara mountains as a backdrop. It's accessible by tiny lanes from Dún Aonghasa with a detailed map (the visitor centre sells ordnance survey maps); otherwise retrace your steps to Kilmurvey and follow the road west for just over a mile. At the **seven churches**, just east of Eoghannacht, there are ancient slabs commemorating seven Romans who died here, testifying to the far-reaching influence of Aran's monasteries. The site is, in fact, that of two churches and several domestic buildings, dating from the eighth to the thirteenth centuries, and includes St Brendan's grave, adorned by an early cross with interlaced patterns.

Arrival and information

Bus The seasonal minibus (€10) runs up through the island's villages; you can walk back to the ferry dock from any point.
Ferry Boats dock at Kilronan.
Tourist office Just west of where the ferry docks at Kilronan; daily 10/11am–7/5pm; Ⓣ099/61263.
Bike rental Mullin's and Burke's near the pier.

Accommodation

Accommodation can be booked through the Kilronan tourist office, or when you buy your ferry ticket.
Kilronan Hostel Kilronan Village Ⓣ099/61255, Ⓦwww.kilronanhostel.com. Cheery hostel with great facilities, including free Internet and WiFi. Very convenient for the ferry. Dorms ❷
Mainistir House Hostel Ⓣ099/61318, Ⓦwww.mainistirhousearan.com. Twenty minutes' walk west from the pier, this peaceful, nicely decorated hostel offers a renowned "all you can eat" buffet every night for €15. Dorms ❷, rooms ❸

Eating and drinking

Seafood is the island's great speciality, with most of the popular restaurants located in Kilronan.
Dún Aonghasa/Aran Fisherman Restaurant Very varied menu to suit all tastes, including vegetarian, but not cheap. Mains €17–35.
Pier House Restaurant Spectacular setting with panoramic views and great food, but pricey, so go for light food (from €7.50).
Joe Watty's Bar A great pub with traditional music most nights; serves good soups and stews, from €6.

Inishmaan

In comparison with Inishmore, **INISHMAAN** is lush, with stone walls forming a maze that chequers off tiny fields of grass and clover. The island's main sight is **Dún Chonchubhair**: built some time between the first and seventh centuries, its massive oval wall is almost intact and commands great views. Inishmaan's indifference to tourism means that amenities for visitors are minimal; if you arrive on spec, ask at the pub for information (Ⓣ099/73003)

– it's a warm and friendly place that also serves snacks in summer. For **accommodation,** try the B&B *Ard Álainn* (April–Sept; ⓣ099/73027, ⓦwww.galway.net/pages/ard-alainn; ④) or *An Dún* (ⓣ099/73047, ⓦwww.inismeainaccommodation.com; ④), both near Dún Chonchubhair.

Inisheer

INISHEER, less than two miles across, is the smallest of the Aran Islands, and tourism plays a key role here. A great plug of rock dominates the island, its rough, pale-grey stone dripping with greenery, topped by the fifteenth-century **O'Brien's Castle**, standing inside an ancient ring fort. Set around it are low fields, a small community of pubs and houses, and windswept sand dunes. The **Inisheer Island Cooperative** hut by the pier (Mon–Thurs 9am–5pm, Fri 9am–4pm; ⓣ099/75008) will give you a map and a list of **B&Bs**; *Radharc an Chláir*, by the castle (ⓣ099/75019; ④), is a good bet. There's also a **hostel,** *Brú Radharc na Mara* (mid-March to Oct; ⓣ099/75024, ⓔmaire.searraigh@oceanfree.net; dorms ②, rooms ③), and a **campsite** near the pier. Meals are available at the *Óstán Inis Oírr* hotel. For **music,** head for *Tigh Ned's* bar.

WESTPORT

Set on the shores of Clew Bay, **WESTPORT** is one of the west's liveliest spots. Planned by the eighteenth-century architect James Wyatt, its formal layout comes as quite a surprise in the midst of its rural surrounds. The craggy **Croagh Patrick** makes an imposing background to the town, standing at 2510 feet above the bay – the climb is a strenuous one, but rewarded by spectacular views. St Patrick reputedly prayed on the mountain for forty days for the conversion of the Irish to Christianity, and on the last Sunday of July, known as "Reek Day" which coincides with the Celtic festival of Lughnasa, many tackle the pilgrimage to the summit barefoot.

Another attraction is **Westport House** (April–Sept 11.30am–5.30pm; March & Oct Sat & Sun only; ⓣ098/27766; €11.50–20; ⓦwww.westporthouse.ie), a mile or so out of town towards the bay. The beautifully designed house dates from 1730 and is privately owned: the present family are direct descendants of legendary pirate Grace O'Malley of Clew Bay. Inside the house is a *Holy Family* by Rubens and an upstairs room with intricate Chinese wallpaper dating from 1780 – outside there's a giant water flume, train rides, boating and a bird and animal park.

Arrival and information

Bus The bus stop is on Mill St in the centre.
Train The station is on Altamount St, ten minutes north of the centre.
Tourist office James St (Mon–Sat 9am–1pm and 2–5.45pm; June–Aug also Sun; ⓣ098/25711, ⓦwww.irelandwest.travel.ie).
Internet *Dunnings Cyberpub*, The Octagon, James St.

Accommodation

For more B&Bs check for availability at the tourist office, which charges a €4 booking fee.
The Old Mill James St ⓣ098/27045, ⓦwww.oldmillhostel.com. Westport's only hostel is situated in an old stone courtyard and is extremely central. Dorms ②, rooms ③
Radharc Na Mara Deer Park East, Newport Rd, ⓣ098/28166. Good value, friendly B&B a short walk from town. ④

Eating

Antica Rome Bridge St. Offers a good selection of pizzas and does tasty fish and chips. Pizzas from €8.
The Quay Cottage The Quay ⓣ098/26412. By the entrance to Westport House, this restaurant prides itself on its seafood dishes and serves plenty of vegetarian food. Mains €12–25.
Sol Rio Bridge St ⓣ098/28944. This relaxed, Mediterranean-style restaurant serves a mix of continental and Irish food, and is a good lunch option. Lunch mains €5–10.

The Stuffed Sandwich Bridge St ⓣ098/27611. Makes every kind of sandwich you could think of, as well as smoothies and salads. €4.50–7.

Drinking and nightlife

Cozy Joe's Bridge St. Has a late bar with a DJ till 2am Thurs–Mon.
Matt Molloy's Bridge St. This bar is owned by the eponymous Chieftains' flute player, and occasionally features visiting celebrities.
Oscar's Club Mill St. Part of the *Westport Inn Hotel*, and open Thurs–Sun nights from midnight; don't expect a wild night, although it gets a reasonable crowd in on a Saturday.
Toby's Bar The Fairgreen. Small, cozy bar high above the river, perfect for a quiet drink or a chat with local old-timers.

Moving on

Train Dublin (3 daily; 3hr 30min–3hr 40min).
Bus Dublin (5 daily; 5hr); Galway (3 daily; 1hr 50min).

SLIGO

SLIGO is, after Derry, the biggest town in the northwest of Ireland. The legacy of **W.B. Yeats** – perhaps Ireland's best-loved poet – is still strongly felt here: the **Yeats Memorial Building** on Hyde Bridge (Mon–Fri 10am–5pm; free; ⓦwww.yeats-sligo.com) features a photographic exhibition and film on his life, while the poet's Nobel Prize for Literature and other memorabilia are on show in the **Sligo County Museum** on Stephen Street (Tues–Sat 10am–5pm; €2.10). **The Model Arts Centre** on The Mall (Tues–Sat 10am–5.30pm, Sun 11am–4pm; free; ⓦwww.modelart.ie) houses works by the poet's brother, **Jack B. Yeats**, and also displays a broad representation of modern Irish art. Across the River Garavogue on Abbey Street stands the thirteenth-century **Dominican Friary.** See the visitor centre (mid-March to end of Oct daily 10am–6pm; Nov & Dec Fri–Sun 9.30am–4.30pm; €2.10; ⓦwww.heritageireland.ie) for more introduction.

Arrival and information

Train The station is on Union Street, five minutes west of the centre.
Bus The station is near the train station, on Lord Edward St.
Tourist office Temple Street (June–Aug daily 9/10am–6/7pm; Sept–May Mon–Fri 9am–5pm; ⓣ071/916 1201, ⓦwww.sligotourism.ie).
Bike rental Flanagan's, Market Yard.
Internet *Cygo Internet Café*, 19 O'Connell St.
Listings Check the weekly *Sligo Champion* (€1.60).

Accommodation

Hostels

Harbour House Finisklin Rd ⓣ071/917 1547, ⓦwww.harbourhousehostel.com. Comfortable hostel ten minutes' walk from the centre. Breakfast not included. Dorms ❷, rooms ❸
White House Hostel Markievicz Rd ⓣ071/914 5160. By the river north of Hyde Bridge, this place is central and popular, if a little shabby. Dorms ❷

B&Bs

Tree Tops Cleveragh Rd ⓣ071/916 0160, ⓦwww.sligobandb.com. A mile southeast along Pearse Rd; very pleasant rooms and friendly hosts. ❹

Camping

Greenlands Caravan Park Rosses Point ⓣ071/917 7113. Open April–Sept 14, this park is 8km west of town (bus #473) on the seafront. ❷
Strandhill Caravan and Camping Park Strandhill ⓣ071/916 8111. Open April–Oct and located 5km from town (bus #472), the beach here, while unsafe for swimming, attracts plenty of surfers. ❶

Eating

Bistro Bianconni O'Connell St. Hugely popular, this smart place does great pizza. Get there early on weekend nights. Pizzas from €15.
Café Bar Deli Rear Stephen's St. Large choice of very tasty dishes. Wed–Sun from 6pm. Mains €6.50–13.
The Left Bank Rear Stephen's St. Below *Café Bar Deli*, this music bar and restaurant, very popular with young professionals, serves a good range of food and snacks in the day. Mains €9.50.
The Loft 17–19 Lord Edward St. Extensive menu of world cuisine. The adjoining *Gateway Bar* does less expensive bar food. Mains €10–18.

Drinking and nightlife

Earley's Bridge St. One of the best pubs for traditional music (Thurs).
Envy Teeling St. Open Thurs and Sat night from 9.30pm, this popular club attracts a young crowd.
Toff's Kennedy Parade. Next to the *Embassy Bar*, this lively club is open from 11pm.
Velvet Bridge St. Large, swanky club housed in an old brewery. Dress up.

Moving on

Train Dublin (5 daily; 3hr 5min).
Bus Derry (6 daily; 2hr 30min); Dublin (9 daily; 3hr 15–50min); Enniskillen (6 daily; 1hr 25–55min); Galway (5 daily; 2hr 35min).

DONEGAL TOWN

DONEGAL town is a busy place focused around its old marketplace – The Diamond – and a fine base for exploring the stunning coastal countryside and inland hills and loughs. Just about the only sight in the town itself is the well-preserved shell of **O'Donnell's Castle** on Tírchonaill Street by The Diamond (mid-March to end of Oct daily 10am–6pm, last admission 45 mins before closing; €3.70; ⓦwww.heritageireland.ie), a fine example of Jacobean architecture. On the left bank of the River Eske stand the few ruined remains of **Donegal Friary**, while on the opposite bank a woodland path known as Bank Walk offers wonderful views of **Donegal Bay** and towards the **Blue Stack Mountains**.

Arrival and information

Bus The bus stop for Bus Eireann departures and arrivals is outside the *Abbey Hotel* in the centre of town; private company Feda O'Donnell buses from Galway arrive outside the tourist office.
Tourist office The Quay (Easter–Sept Mon–Sat 9am–5/8pm, July & Aug also Sun 9am–8pm; ⓣ074/972 1148, ⓦwww.irelandnorthwest.ie).

Accommodation

There are dozens of B&Bs in Donegal, but to avoid a lot of walking, it's simplest to call in at the tourist office, see above.

Donegal Town Independent Hostel ⓣ074/972 2805, ⓔlincunn8@eircom.net. Just past the roundabout on the Killybegs road, a five-minute walk from town, this peaceful hostel also has camping. Dorms ❷, rooms ❷
Atlantic Guesthouse, Main St ⓣ074/972 1187. Family-run establishment in the centre of town with bright and cheery rooms. ❹

Eating and drinking

The Blueberry Tea Room Castle St. Good-quality, reasonably priced food served in a very cozy atmosphere. It has an Internet café upstairs. Mains up to €9.50.
Dunnion's Bar Bridge St. This is a lively bar packed with local old-timers, even at midday. Traditional music every night.
Simple Simon The Diamond. Get a healthy, take-away lunch from this organic food store. €2–5.
The Harbour Quay St. Opposite the tourist office, this restaurant serves excellent burgers and pizzas. Daily from 3pm. Mains €10–25.

Moving on

Bus Derry (3–7 daily; 1hr 30min); Dublin (9–10 daily; 3hr 30min–5hr 55min); Glencolmcille (2 daily; 1hr 25min); Sligo (8 daily; 1hr 5–55min).

TEELIN BAY AND SLIEVE LEAGUE

To the west of Donegal town lies one of the most stupendous landscapes in Ireland – the stark and beautiful **Teelin Bay** and the majestic **Slieve League cliffs**. An ideal **base** for exploring the region is the busy, but always welcoming, *Derrylahan Independent Hostel* (ⓣ074/973 8079, ⓔderrylahan@eircom.net; dorms ❷, rooms ❸), a two-mile walk from Kilcar along the coastal road to Carrick.

There are two routes up to the ridge of **SLIEVE LEAGUE**: a back way following the signpost to Baile Mór just before Teelin, and the road route from Teelin to Bunglass, a thousand sheer feet above the sea. The former path has you looking up continually at the ridge known as One Man's Pass (see overleaf), on which walkers seem the size of pins, while the frontal approach swings you up to one of the most thrilling cliff scenes in the world, the **Amharc Mór**. On a good day you can see a third of Ireland from the summit.

GLENCOLMCILLE

Dangerous in windy weather, **One Man's Pass** is only a few feet wide in places and leads via Malinbeg – where there's the excellent *Malinbeg Hostel* (Ⓣ074/9730006, Ⓦwww.malinbeghostel.com; dorms ❷, rooms ❷) – and Malinmore to **GLENCOLMCILLE** (the Glen of St Columbcille), the name by which Columba was known after his conversion. Since the seventh century, following Columba's stay in the valley, it has been a place of pilgrimage: every June 9 at midnight the locals commence a three-hour barefoot itinerary of the cross-inscribed slabs that stud the valley basin, finishing up with Mass at 3am in the small church. If you want to attempt Turas Cholmcille ("Columba's Journey") yourself, get a map of the route from the **Folk Village Museum** (Easter–Sept Mon–Sat 10am–6pm, Sun noon–6pm; €3; Ⓦwww.glenfolkvillage.com), a cluster of replica, period-furnished thatched cottages. A path up to the left from here leads to the wonderfully positioned *Dooey Hostel* (Ⓣ074/973 0130, Ⓦwww.dooeyhostel.com; dorms ❷, rooms ❷), while **B&Bs** include *Corner House* (April–Sept; Ⓣ074/973 0021; ❹), four hundred yards down the Ardara road from *Biddy's Bar* in the village centre. *Roarty's* bar, at the other end of the village, is good for lively, traditional music sessions, particularly on a Friday. The best **food** on offer in Glencolmcille is at *An Cistín*, part of the Foras Cultúir Uladh complex.

Northern Ireland

Both the pace of political change and the uncertainty of its future continue to characterize Northern Ireland. In 1998, after thirty years of "The Troubles", its people overwhelmingly voted in support of a political settlement and, it was hoped, an end to political and sectarian violence. For a time the political process gradually inched forwards, hampered by deep mistrust and suspicion on both sides, and inter-community tensions still rife in parts of Belfast. Recently, however, considerable headway has been made in the peace process, with the resumption of devolved government in Northern Ireland. The North is an increasingly safe place for tourists. **Belfast** and **Derry** are two lively and attractive cities, and the northern coastline – especially the weird geometry of the **Giant's Causeway** – is as spectacular as anything in Ireland, while to the southwest is the huge lake complex **Lough Erne**, and **Enniskillen**, a town resonant with history.

BELFAST

A quarter of Northern Ireland's population lives in the capital, **BELFAST**. While the legacy of "**The Troubles**" is clearly visible in the landscape of areas like West Belfast – the peace walls, derelict buildings and political murals – security measures have been considerably eased, though there are certain flashpoints such as the Short Strand and the Ardoyne, which are inadvisable to visit.

There's no doubt that the city is going from strength to strength: fashionable shops are reinvigorating the streets, the arts scene is flourishing, and new restaurants and clubs are opening up all the time. Despite its turbulent history, the city is imbued with a new zest for life.

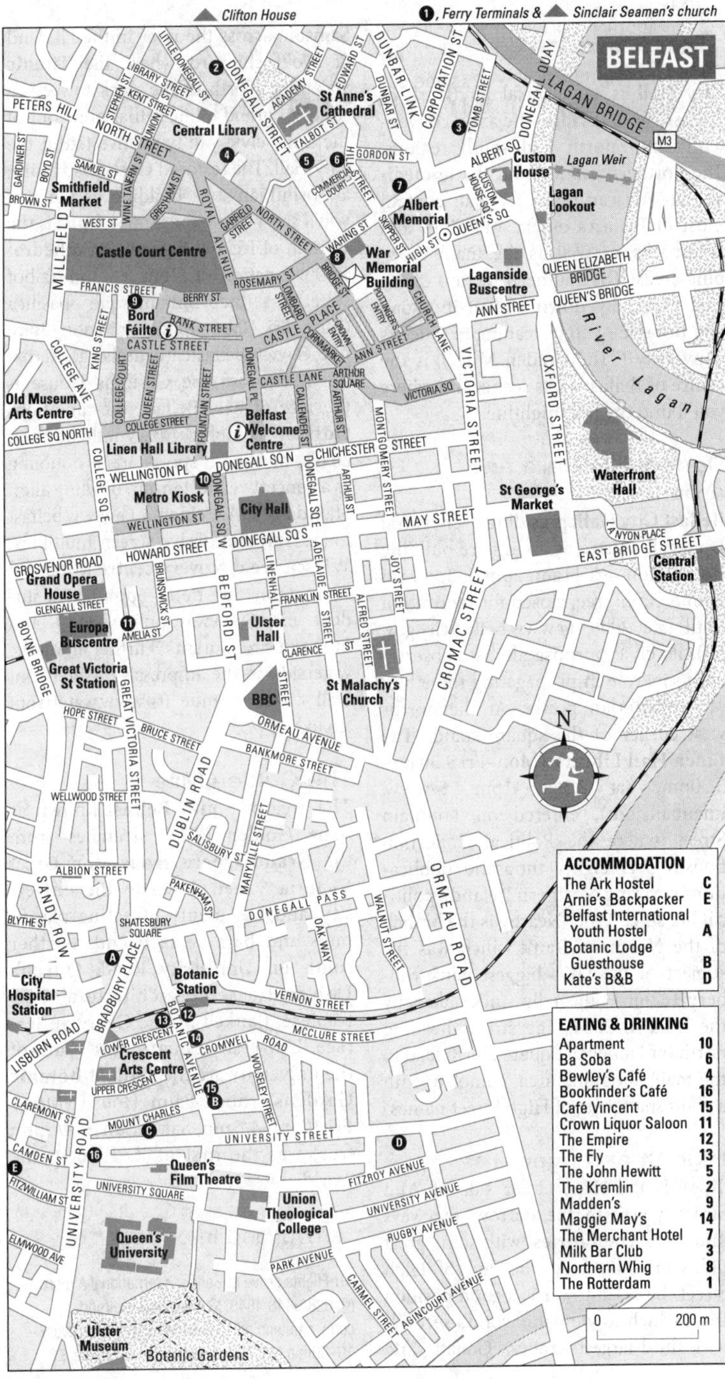

IRELAND

NORTHERN IRELAND

What to see and do

City Hall is the central landmark of Belfast, and divides the city conveniently into north and south regions. The northern section and the immediate environs around City Hall contain most of Belfast's official buildings and landmarks, as well as the main shopping areas. The southern section of the city, especially down University Road and Botanic Avenue, leading to Queen's University ("The Golden Mile"), is the centre of Belfast's arts scene, and where you'll find the best nightlife.

Donegall Square and around

Belfast City Hall, presiding over central Donegall Square, is an austere building (tours Mon–Fri 11am, 2pm & 3pm, Sat 2pm & 3pm; free; closed for renovation until late 2009; Ⓦwww.belfastcity.gov.uk), its civic purpose almost subservient to its role in propagating the ethics of Presbyterian power. At the northwest corner of the square stands **The Linen Hall Library** (Mon–Fri 9.30am–5.30pm, Sat 9.30am–1pm; Ⓦwww.linenhall.com), entered on Fountain Street, where the Political Collection houses over eighty thousand publications covering Northern Ireland's political life since 1966. Nearby is the branch of the **Northern Bank** which was the subject of the UK's biggest bank robbery (£26m), allegedly undertaken by the IRA, in 2004. The streets heading north off Donegall Square North lead to the main shopping area, complete with a good spattering of High Street names.

High St and river area

Towards the river, either side of Ann Street, you're in the narrow alleyways known as **The Entries**, with some great old saloon bars. At the end of High Street the clock tower is a good position from which to view the world's second- and third-largest cranes, Goliath and Samson, across the river in the Harland & Wolff shipyard where the **Titanic** was built. North of the clock tower is a series of grand edifices that grew out of the same civic vanity as invested in the City Hall. The restored **Customs House**, a Corinthian-style building, is the first you'll see, but the most monolithic is the Church of Ireland **St Anne's Cathedral** at the junction of Donegall and Talbot streets, a neo-Romanesque basilica (Mon–Fri 10am–4pm, Sun noon–3pm; free; Ⓦwww.belfastcathedral.org). Across the river from the Customs House is the face of new Belfast, the ambitious **Odyssey** complex (Ⓦwww.theodyssey.co.uk) housing a sports arena doubling as a concert venue, ten-pin bowling alley, Sheridan IMAX cinema (Ⓦwww.belfastimax.com) and twelve-screen multiplex, **W5 science discovery centre** (Mon–Sat 10am–6pm, Sun noon–6pm; £6.50, student £5; Ⓦwww.w5online.co.uk) and numerous restaurants. Further along the waterside is the impressive Waterfront Hall concert venue (Ⓦwww.waterfront.co.uk).

The Golden Mile

The area of **South Belfast** known as "The Golden Mile" stretches from the **Grand Opera House,** on Great Victoria Street, down to the university, and has plenty of eating-places, pubs and bars at each end. Further south on University Road, **Queen's University** is the architectural centrepiece, flanked by the Georgian terrace, University Square. Just south of the university are the verdant **Botanic Gardens** whose Palm House (Mon–Fri 10am–4/5pm, Sat & Sun 2–4/5pm; free) was the first of its kind in the world.

Arrival and information

Air Flights arrive at Belfast International Airport (Ⓣ028/9448 4848, Ⓦwww.belfastairport.com), nineteen miles west of town (buses every 10–30min to Europa bus station; £6 single, £9

SECTARIAN MURALS

The Republican and Loyalist **murals** on the Falls and Shankill Roads in West Belfast are a must-see feature of a trip to the city: the government is gradually replacing this political artwork, mostly painted during the height of the "Troubles" to represent the political and religious loyalties of the respective communities. The open-topped Belfast City Sightseeing buses include the murals in their tour of Belfast, departing every 30min from Castle Place (£11). Taxi Trax (Castle Junction on King St, near City Hall, ⓣ028/9031 5777; £8) offer bespoke taxi tours including West Belfast, and the drivers are usually very good guides. The most interesting way of viewing the murals, however, is to take a walking tour with political ex-prisoners, who present both Republican and Loyalist viewpoints. Tours (2hrs; 11am Mon–Sat & Sun 2pm; ⓣ028/9020 0770, ⓦwww.coiste.ie/politicaltours; £8; assemble at the bottom of Divis Towers, Falls Rd).

return), or Belfast City Airport, three miles northeast (ⓣ028/9093 9093, ⓦwww.belfastcityairport.com; bus #600 every 20min to city centre 6am–9.50pm; £2.20 return).

Train Most trains call at the central Great Victoria Street Station, though those from Dublin and Larne terminate at Central Station on East Bridge Street.

Bus Buses from Derry, the Republic, the airports and ferry terminals arrive at Europa bus station beside Great Victoria Street train station; buses from the north coast use Laganside Buscentre in Queen's Square. A regular Centrelink bus connects all bus and train stations.

Boat Ferries from Stranraer dock at Corry Road (taxi £7); and those from Liverpool further north on West Bank Road (taxi £8); while ferries from Cairnryan dock twenty miles north at Larne (bus or train into centre).

Tourist office The Belfast Welcome Centre, 47 Donegall Place (Mon–Sat 9am–5.30/7pm, summer Sun noon–5pm; ⓣ028/9024 6609, ⓦwww.gotobelfast.com). Bord Fáilte, for information about the Republic, is at 53 Castle St (Mon–Fri 9am–5pm; ⓣ028/9026 5500).

Listings *The Big List* (ⓦwww.thebiglist.co.uk; free), available in pubs and record shops, the web-based *wheretonight.com* (ⓦwww.wheretotonight.com) and the *Belfast Evening Telegraph*.

City Transport

Information on all buses and trains is available at ⓣ028/9066 6630 or ⓦwww.translink.co.uk.

Bus The city is served by Metro bus service. Passes allowing travel anywhere on the network cost £3.50 for all day Mon–Sat (£2.50 after 10am Mon–Sat, or all day Sun). Otherwise, journeys range from £1–£1.60. The Metro kiosk in Donegall Square West provides free bus maps. Ulsterbus serves the outlying areas.

Night Bus Saturday late-night buses from Donegall Square West (1–2am; £3.50).

Bike Rental Lifecycles, Unit 35, Smithfield Market.

Accommodation

Hostels

The Ark Hostel 44 University St ⓣ028/9032 9626, ⓦwww.arkhostel.com. Friendly, comfortable hostel close to the university, with a 2am curfew. Dorms ❷

Arnie's Backpackers 63 Fitzwilliam St ⓣ028/9024 2867, ⓦwww.arniesbackpackers.co.uk. Cheerful and relaxed independent hostel, near the university. Dorms ❷, rooms ❸

Belfast International Youth Hostel 22–32 Donegall Rd ⓣ028/9031 5435. Large, well-equipped but characterless modern HINI hostel, just west of Shaftesbury Square. Dorms ❷, rooms ❷

B&Bs

Botanic Lodge Guesthouse 87 Botanic Ave ⓣ028/9032 7682. Nicely positioned in the vibrant university area of town. ❹

Kate's B&B 127 University St ⓣ028/9028 2091, ⓔkatesbb127@hotmail.com. Popular B&B, off University Road, offering an "all you can eat" breakfast. ❹

Eating

Many of the best places to **eat** and the liveliest **pubs** can be found around Great Victoria Street and in the university area.

Restaurants and cafés

Ba Soba 38 Hill St. Belfast's first and most popular noodle bar, packed even at lunchtime. Closed Mon.

TREAT YOURSELF

Afternoon tea at *The Merchant Hotel* (Waring St ⓣ028/9023 4888, ⓦwww.themerchanthotel.com) in Belfast's Cathedral Quarter is an extremely spoiling affair. You'll feel distinctly regal sipping your Earl Grey in the splendour of the Great Room of the hotel, which used to be the headquarters of the Ulster Bank. On offer are freshly baked scones, assorted sandwiches and delicious pastries – and even champagne, if you're feeling really decadent.

Bewley's Café Donegall Arcade. Excellent coffee house serving good-value breakfasts, lunches and snacks. £5–12.

Bookfinders Café 47 University Rd. Bohemian café at the back of a charmingly messy bookshop. From £3.

Café Vincent 78 Botanic Ave. Fine breakfasts, value-for-money high teas and plenty of pizzas.

Maggie May's 45 Botanic Ave. Huge, economically priced portions in this cozy café with lots of veggie choices.

Drinking and nightlife

Belfast's best entertainment is pub music. There's also a vibrant club scene and plenty of DJ bars.

Pubs

Crown Liquor Saloon 46 Great Victoria St. The city's most famous pub, decked out like a spa bath, with a good range of Ulster food, such as champ and colcannon (both potato dishes) and Strangford oysters in season.

The Empire 42 Botanic Ave. Music hall and cellar bar in a converted church, with nightly live music or comedy.

The John Hewitt Donegall St. Owned by Belfast Unemployed Resource Centre, this popular bar has some of Belfast's best traditional music sessions (Tues 9.30pm, Wed 9pm, Sat 6pm).

Madden's Smithfield. Unpretentious and atmospheric pub, with regular traditional music sessions (Fri & Sat).

The Rotterdam 54 Pilot St. Names big and small play in this docklands venue, plus traditional music on Thurs (9.30pm).

Clubs and DJ bars

Apartment 2 Donegall Square. Swish bar where the bright young Belfast crowd goes to be seen; DJs most nights.

The Fly 5–6 Lower Crescent. About as hip as Belfast gets – three floors of music and occasional mayhem.

The Kremlin 90 Donegall St. Ireland's biggest gay venue with a host of events throughout the week.

Milk Bar Club 10–14 Tomb St. Ever-popular and ever-packed club playing dance music for all tastes every night of the week.

Northern Whig 2–10 Bridge St. Massive bar in the premises of the old newspaper, featuring pre-club DJs most nights.

Shopping

High Street and department stores The main shopping area in Belfast is the long stretch of Donegall Place and Royal Avenue, where you'll find big fashion and retail names. The big shopping centre CastleCourt is on Royal Avenue.

Arcades and Markets Wander off the main thoroughfare of Royal Avenue and you'll find both more alternative and more locally inspired outlets. Haymarket Arcade has some great film and music stores. East of City Hall off Oxford Street you'll find the Belfast institution that is St. George's Market, which on Fridays and Saturdays displays all sorts of delicacies.

Vintage/Alternative Unsurprisingly, things get even more alternative in the university area: The Rusty Zip, 28 Botanic Avenue, is full of vintage gems, and No Alibis, 83 Botanic Avenue is a great bookstore which specializes in crime and often holds music events in the evening.

Directory

Exchange Thomas Cook, 11 Donegall Place (ⓣ028/9055 0030); and the Belfast Welcome Centre (see below).

Hospitals Belfast City Hospital, Lisburn Rd (ⓣ028/9032 9241); Royal Victoria, Grosvenor Rd (ⓣ028/9024 0503).

Internet Belfast Welcome Centre, 47 Donegall Place; *Friends Café*, 109–113 Royal Ave; ITXP, 175–177 Ormeau Rd; Revelations, 27 Shaftesbury Square.

Left luggage Belfast Welcome Centre, 47 Donegall Place.

Police North Queen St ⓣ028/9065 0222.

Post office Castle Place.

Moving on

Train Coleraine (9–10 daily; 1hr 30–45min); Derry (5–9 daily; 2hr 30min); Dublin (5–8 daily; 2hr 20min); Larne Harbour (9–15 daily; 1hr 10min). **Bus** Derry (11–32 daily; 1hr 50min); Dublin (20 daily; 3hr); Enniskillen (5-16 daily; 2hr–2hr 20min).

THE GIANT'S CAUSEWAY

Since 1693, when the Royal Society publicized it as one of the great wonders of the natural world, the **Giant's Causeway**, 65 miles northwest of Belfast on the coast, has been a major tourist attraction. Consisting of an estimated thirty-seven thousand polygonal basalt columns, it's the result of a massive subterranean explosion some sixty million years ago which spewed out a huge mass of molten basalt onto the surface and, as it cooled, solidified into massive polygonal crystals.

Taking the path down the cliffs from the **visitor centre** (daily 10am–4.30/5/6pm; ⓣ028/2073 1855 ⓦwww.giantscausewaycentre.com; free; car parking £5), or the shuttle bus (every 15min; £1.60 return) brings you to the most spectacular of the blocks where many people linger, but if you push on, you'll be rewarded with relative solitude and views of some of the more impressive formations high in the cliffs. One of these, **Chimney Point**, has an appearance so bizarre that the ships of the Spanish Armada opened fire on it, believing that they were attacking Dunluce Castle, a few miles further west. An alternative two-mile circuit follows the spectacular cliff-top path from the visitor centre, with views across to Scotland, to a flight of 162 steps leading down the cliff to a set of basalt columns known as the **Organ Pipes**, from where paths lead round to the shuttle-bus stop alongside the Causeway proper.

GETTING TO THE GIANT'S CAUSEWAY

Trains from Belfast go to Coleraine, where there's a regular connection to Portrush; from either, you can catch the "open-topper" bus (July & Aug 4 daily; £3.30 single, £5.90 return) to the Causeway, or from Portrush there's bus #172, both running via Bushmills. A restored **narrow-gauge railway** runs between Bushmills and the Causeway (July–Aug 3–5 daily, plus some days in other months; 20min; ⓣ028/2073 2844; single £2.50, return £4.50). The **Antrim Coaster coach** (Goldline Express #252) runs from Larne direct to the Causeway (2 daily; Oct–June not Sun; 2hr 30min) and on to Coleraine via Bushmills, Portrush and Portstewart, Antrim Glens and stunning seascapes en route.

THE MOURNE MOUNTAINS

If you're based in Belfast but fancy a day-trip out of the metropolis, the beautiful **Mourne Mountains** provide the perfect escape. The mountain range comprises twelve peaks, of which Slieve Donard, at 850m, is the highest in Northern Ireland. From Belfast, buses #20, 720, and 237 run from the Europa bus station to Newcastle (up to 15 daily; 1hr); from Newcastle, the Mourne Rambler sevice runs from July 2–Aug 2, tracking a loop through the area (£4.50 day ticket; ⓦwww.discovernorthernireland.com).

Carrick-a-Rede

If you've developed an appetite for the stunning scenery and walks on this coast, a visit to the **Carrick-a-Rede Rope Bridge**, 13km east of the Causeway, is a must (March–Oct daily 10am–6/7pm, weather permitting; £3). For the last two hundred years, fishermen have reputedly erected a bridge from the mainland cliffs to Carrick-a-Rede island over a vast chasm, so as to check their salmon nets. Now, the National Trust is responsible. Bear in mind that venturing across the swaying rope bridge high above the water is an exhilarating experience, but not for the faint-hearted. Ulsterbus #402 runs between Bushmills and the rope bridge via the Causeway in summer months.

PORTSTEWART

PORTSTEWART, a pleasant coastal resort 10 miles west of the Giant's Causeway, makes a good base: there's an IHH **hostel**, *Rick's Causeway Coast Independent Hostel*, at 4 Victoria Terrace (ⓣ028/7083 3789, ⓔrick@causewaycoasthostel.fsnet.co.uk; dorms ❷, rooms ❷) and several **B&B** options. The bus stop for the Giant's Causeway is 100m from the hostel.

There are some reasonable **bars**, including *Shenanigans* on the Promenade, which is open till 1am. If you're after a big night out, *Kelly's* (1 Bushmills Rd, ⓦwww.kellysportrush.co.uk) is a short taxi-ride away, and its **club** night, *Lush!*, on Wednesdays and Saturdays is renowned. **Surfing** can be organized at Ocean Warriors on the Promenade, ⓣ028/7083 6500.

DERRY

DERRY lies at the foot of Lough Foyle, less than three miles from the border with the Republic. The city presents a beguiling picture, its two hillsides terraced with pastel-shaded houses punctuated by stone spires, and, being seventy per cent Catholic, has a very different atmosphere from Belfast. However, from Partition in 1921 until the late 1980s Derry's Catholic majority was denied its civil rights by gerrymandering, which ensured that the Protestant minority maintained control of all important local institutions. The situation came to a head after the Protestant Apprentice Boys' March in August 1969, when the police attempted to storm the Catholic estates of the Bogside. In the ensuing tension, British troops were widely deployed for the first time in Northern Ireland. On January 31, 1972, the crisis deepened when British paratroopers opened fire on civilians, killing thirteen unarmed demonstrators in what became known as **Bloody Sunday**. Derry is now greatly changed: tensions eased considerably here long before Belfast, thanks in part to a determinedly even-handed local council, although defiant murals remain and marching is still a contentious issue. The city centre has undergone much regeneration too, and Derry has a justifiable reputation for innovation in the arts.

What to see and do

You can walk the entire mile-long circuit of Derry's seventeenth-century **city walls** – some of the best-preserved defences left standing in Europe. Reinforced by bulwarks, bastions and a parapetted earth rampart, the walls encircle the original medieval street pattern with four gateways – Shipquay, Butcher, Bishop and Ferryquay – surviving from the first construction, in slightly revised form.

Guildhall Square and around

The best starting point is the **Guildhall Square**, once the old quay, where most of the city's cannons are lined up, between Shipquay and Magazine gates, their noses peering out above the ramparts. A reconstruction of the medieval **O'Doherty Tower** houses splendid displays on the city's turbulent political history and a new exhibition on the Spanish Armada (check with the tourist office for opening times – see below). Turning left at **Shipquay Gate**, the promenade doglegs at Water Bastion where the River Foyle once lapped the walls at high tide. Continue on to Newgate Bastion and **Ferryquay Gate**, where you can look out across the river to the Waterside area, once primarily Protestant, now almost half Catholic – further evidence of the lessening of the city's political tensions.

St. Columb's Cathedral

Between Ferryquay and Bishop's Gate the major sight is the Protestant **St Columb's Cathedral** (Mon–Sat 9am–4/5pm; £2; ⓦwww.stcolumbscathedral.org), just within the southern section of the walls; it overlooks **The Fountain**, the Protestant enclave immediately outside the same stretch of walls, and offers one of the best views of the city. In 1688/89 Derry played a key part in the Williamite victory over the Catholic King James II by holding out against a fifteen-week siege that cost the lives of one-quarter of the city's population. The cathedral was used as a battery during the siege, and in the entrance porch you'll find the cannonball shot into the grounds by the besieging army with proposals for the city's surrender.

South wall sights and the Bogside

Back on the walls, pass the white sandstone **courthouse** next to Bishop's Gate and you'll see, downhill to the left, the only remaining tower of the old Derry jail. At the **Double Bastion** sits the Roaring Meg cannon, used during the siege, while down in the valley below are the streets of the Bogside. These were once the undisputed preserve of the IRA, and **Free Derry Corner** marks the site of the original barricades erected against the British army at the height of the Troubles. Nearby are the Bloody Sunday and Hunger Strikers' memorials. Further along the city wall is the **Royal Bastion**, former site of the Rev. George Walker statue which was blown up in 1973. It is in Walker's and their predecessors' memory that the Protestant Apprentice Boys march around the walls every August 12.

Arrival and information

Air City of Derry airport (ⓣ028/7181 0784, ⓦwww.cityofderryairport.com) is seven miles northeast, connected to the centre by bus.
Train Trains from Belfast arrive on the east bank of the Foyle with a free connecting bus to the bus station.
Bus The station is on Foyle Street beside Guildhall Square.
Tourist office 44 Foyle Street (July–Sept daily 9/10am–5/7pm; Oct–June Mon–Fri 9am–5pm, mid-March to June also Sat 10am–5pm; ⓣ028/7126 7284, ⓦwww.derryvisitor.com).
Internet *Webcrawler Cyber Café*, 52 Strand Rd.
Listings Check the bi-weekly *Derry Journal* (£0.90).

Accommodation

Derry City Independent Hostel 44 Great James St ⓣ028/7137 7989, ⓦwww.derry-hostel.co.uk. North of the city walls, half-a-mile down Strand Road, a very friendly hostel which has regular BBQs in the summer. Dorms ❷, rooms ❸
Dolce Vita 12 Princes St ⓣ028/7137 7989. Run by the people at *Derry City*, this is a very smart budget option. Dorms ❷, rooms ❸
The Saddler's House 36 Great James St ⓣ028/7126 9691, ⓦwww.thesaddlershouse.com. Beautifully decorated Georgian townhouse. This, together with its sister B&B *The Merchant House*, is a real treat. Late-night revellers not welcome. ❹

Eating

Badger's Bar 16 Orchard St. Good-value pub lunches.
Boston Tea Party 15 The Craft Village. With a large assortment of sandwiches, cakes and other goodies, this place will make for a good Derry tea party, at least.
Cafe Calm 4 Shipquay Place. Good selection of sandwiches, soups, and bagels.
The Exchange Exchange House, Queen's Quay. Upmarket restaurant and wine bar serving a variety of tasty dishes.

Drinking and nightlife

Bound for Boston 27–31 Waterloo St. This live music venue has a great beer-garden and seven pool tables.
Downey's Shipquay St. Claims to be "Ireland's largest R&B club" and has music most nights.

Earth Niteclub Above *Café Roc* and hugely popular with the same sort of crowd, only a bigger one.
Peadar O'Donnell's/The Gweedore Bar 59–63 Waterloo St. Traditional and contemporary music every night.
Pepe's Strand Rd. Gay pub and club (Fri & Sat) which plays a lot of cheese.

Moving on

Train Belfast (4–9 daily; 2hr 30min); Coleraine (5–9 daily; 1hr).
Bus Donegal (3–7 daily; 1hr 25–45min); Dublin (7 daily; 4hr); Enniskillen (5–15 daily; 2hr–4hr 20min); Sligo (3–5 daily; 2hr 30min).

ENNISKILLEN

An attractive, conservative small town, **ENNISKILLEN** sits on a lake island, a narrow ribbon of water passing each side of the town between Lower and Upper **Lough Erne**. The water loops its way around the core of the town, its glassy surface lending Enniskillen a sense of calm and reflecting the mini-turrets of **Enniskillen Castle**. Rebuilt by William Cole, to whom the British gave Enniskillen in 1609, the castle houses the **Fermanagh County Museum** and the **Regimental Museum of the Royal Inniskilling Fusiliers** in the keep (July & Aug Tues–Fri 10am–5pm, Sat–Mon 2–5pm; May, June & Sept closed Sun; Oct–April closed Sat & Sun; £2.95; Ⓦwww.enniskillencastle.co.uk), a proud, polished display of paraphernalia of the town's historic regiments. A mile along the Belfast road stands **Castle Coole** (1–6pm: May–Aug daily except Thurs; April & Sept, Sun & bank holidays; £5; Ⓦwww.enniskillen.com/castle-coole). A perfect Palladian building of Portland stone, with an interior of fine plasterwork and superb furnishings, it sits in a beautiful landscaped garden (daily 10am–4/8pm; free).

Lough Erne

The earliest people to settle in this region lived on and around the two lakes of **Lough Erne**, which features many crannogs (artificial islands). The maze of waterways protected the settlers from invaders and created an enduring cultural isolation. Stone carvings suggest that Christianity was accepted far more slowly here than elsewhere: several pagan idols have been found on Christian sites, and the early Christian remains on the islands reveal the influence of pagan culture.

The easiest place to visit is **Devenish Island**, two miles northwest of Enniskillen. St Molaise founded a monastic settlement here in the sixth century and it remained an important religious centre up until the early seventeenth century. It's a delightful setting and the considerable ruins span the entire medieval period. There are regular ferries (April–Sept daily 10am–6pm; £2.25) from Trory Point, three miles north of Enniskillen on the A32 road. Four miles further north along the Kesh road lies **Castle Archdale** forest park from whose marina ferries (Oct–March Sat & Sun 2–6pm; April–Sept Sat & Sun 10am–6pm; July & Aug daily 10am–6pm; £3) depart to **White Island**. The island's ruined abbey is known for its early Christian carvings that look eerily pagan: the most disconcerting is the lewd female figure known as a Sheila-na-Gig, with bulging cheeks, a big grin, open legs and arms pointing to her genitals.

Arrival and information

Bus The station is on Wellington Road.
Tourist office Opposite the bus station (Mon–Fri 9am–5.30/7pm; Easter–Sept also Sat & Sun 10/11am–6/5pm; Oct Sat & Sun 10am–2pm; Ⓣ028/6632 3110, Ⓦwww.fermanagh-online.com) and can help finding B&Bs, most of which are some distance from the town centre.

Accommodation

The Bridges Belmore St Ⓣ028/6634 0110. Situated by the war memorial, this is a modern HINI hostel, complete with onsite restaurant. Dorms £10, rooms ③

Eating and drinking

Blakes of the Hollow 6 Church St ⓣ028/6632 2143. This old pub has been run by the same family since 1887, and continues to pull the crowds. There's a smart bistro on the lower ground floor.

Franco's Queen Elizabeth Rd ⓣ028/6632 4424. Great quality food using local produce in this restaurant with swish, trendy decor. Mains £8–12.

Pat's 1–5 Townhall St ⓣ028/6632 7462. Cozy pub with live music every weekend and good bar food. Mains £5–13.

The Fort Lodge Hotel Forthill St ⓣ028/6632 3275. Live music and DJs at weekends, and good bar food throughout the day and a lunch carvery in their Crannog Lounge. Lunch £6.50.

Moving on

Bus Belfast (8–10 daily; 2hr 20min); Derry (15 daily; 2hr 30min–4hr 30min); Dublin (7 daily; 2hr 20min–3hr).

Italy

HIGHLIGHTS

VENICE: catch a waterbus at night for some utterly romantic views

SIENA: attend the Palio, a frenetic and fiercely partisan horse race

ROME: see the spectacular Colosseum up close

NAPLES: eat pizza in its home town

POMPEII: explore the evocative remains of a city buried by ash

ROUGH COSTS

DAILY BUDGET BASIC €25/with the occasional treat €45

DRINK Wine (€2.50/glass)

FOOD Pizza (€3–5)

HOSTEL/BUDGET HOTEL €18–25/€30–60

TRAVEL Train: Rome–Naples (190km) 2hr, €20; bus: 2hr, €16.

FACT FILE

POPULATION 58.7 million

AREA 301,230 sq km

LANGUAGE Italian

CURRENCY Euro (€)

CAPITAL Rome (population: 2.7 million)

INTERNATIONAL PHONE CODE ⓣ39

Basics

Of all the countries in Europe, Italy is perhaps the hardest to classify. A modern industrialized nation and a harbinger of global style, its designers lead the way with each season's fashions. But it is also a Mediterranean country, with all that that implies. If there is a single national characteristic, it is to embrace life to the full, manifest in the hundreds of local festivals that take place on any given day and in the importance placed on good food. There is also, of course, the country's enormous cultural legacy: Tuscany alone has more classified historical monuments than any country in the world, and every region retains its own relics.

Italy wasn't unified until 1861, a fact that's borne out by the regional nature of the place today. In the northwest, the well-to-do cities of **Turin** and **Milan** epitomize the wealthy, industrial north; further south is **Genoa**, a bustling port with a long seafaring tradition. By far the biggest draw in the north is **Venice** – a unique and beautiful city – though you won't be alone in appreciating it. The centre of the country, specifically **Tuscany**, boasts classic, rolling countryside and the art-packed towns of Florence, Pisa and Siena, while neighbouring **Umbria** has a quieter appeal. **Rome**, the national capital, is a treasure trove of ancient and Renaissance gems. South of here in Campania, **Naples**, a petulant, unforgettable city, is the spiritual heart of the economically undeveloped Italian south, while close by are fine ancient sites and the spectacular **Amalfi Coast**. Puglia, the "heel" of Italy, has underrated pleasures – most notably Lecce, a Baroque gem of a city. **Sicily** is a law unto itself, with attractions ranging from Hellenic remains to the drama of Mount Etna, and the beguiling city of Palermo. **Sardinia**, too, feels far removed from the mainland, especially in its relatively undiscovered interior.

CHRONOLOGY

753 BC Rome founded by Romulus and Remus.
509 BC The city becomes a Republic.
49 BC Julius Caesar successfully wages war against members of the Senate and extends the Roman Empire across Europe.
80 AD Building of the Colosseum.
476 Last Roman Emperor Romulus Augustus overthrown by barbarians.
756 Papal States created after Frankish forces defeat the Lombards.
1173 Building of the Tower of Pisa begins.
1512 Michelangelo completes his frescoes in the Sistine Chapel, as the Italian Renaissance flourishes.
1804 Napoleon declares himself emperor of Italy.
1814 Following Napoleon's defeat, Italy is divided into various states.
1861 Unification of Italian states into a Kingdom by Giuseppe Garibaldi.
1889 Diners everywhere are grateful for the creation of the "Pizza Margherita" in Naples.
1898 First Italian football league established.
1915 Italy joins WWI on the side of the Allies.
1922 Fascist Benito Mussolini becomes Prime Minister.
1929 The Lateran Treaty declares Vatican City an independent state. It is the smallest state in the world.
1940 Italy enters WWII on the side of the Nazis.
1943 Allies capture Sicily and imprison Mussolini. Italy declares war on Germany.
1945 Mussolini is captured and executed by Italian communists.
1946 Republic replaces the monarchy.
1957 The Treaty of Rome establishes the European Economic Community.

2007 Romano Prodi wins a vote of confidence to continue in his role as Prime Minister.

ARRIVAL

The majority of tourists arrive at the **airports** of Rome or Milan, although low-cost European airlines Ryanair (ⓦwww.ryanair.com) and easyJet (ⓦwww.easyjet.com) also offer services to Bari, Bologna, Brindisi, Parma, Perugia, Pisa, Turin and Venice, as well as destinations in Sardinia and Sicily. From North America, national carrier Alitalia (ⓦwww.alitalia.com) runs direct flights to Milan, Rome and Venice, with numerous connecting flights to other cities, although you can invariably find cheaper deals with US airlines such as Delta and American Airlines. The cheapest option, though, can be to fly to London and get a budget flight onward from there.

Train travel from the UK often works out more expensive, but there is a vast choice of routes, mostly arriving in Milan. From elsewhere in Europe, look into TrenItalia's Smart Price fares – you'll need to book at least a week before travel, but the sooner you book, the more likely you are to find a bargain – which offers considerable savings, if you don't mind travelling overnight and foregoing a couchette. You can travel from Paris for €25, Vienna from €29, Prague from €49, Munich from €29 and Ljubljana from just €15; see Ⓦwww.trenitalia.com for details and booking.

Getting to Italy **by bus** can take a soul-destroyingly long time. National Express Eurolines (Ⓦwww.nationalexpress.com) offers cheap fares from London to cities all over Italy from around €70 for a 28-hour trip to Venice. Italian company Gruppo Esposito (Ⓣ081.251.4157, Ⓦwww.clpbus.it) offers services to Rome and cities further south from €80.

Ferries ply routes from Barcelona to Genoa and Civitavecchia outside Rome, from Dubrovnik to Bari, from Malta to Genoa and Catania in Sicily, and from ports in Greece and Croatia to Brindisi and Bari; see Ⓦwww.traghetti.it for further details.

GETTING AROUND

Trains are generally the best way of getting around: tickets are cheap and the rail network extensive, though delays are common. Trains are operated by Italian State Railways (Ferrovie dello Stato or FS; Ⓦwww.ferroviedellostato.it). For most journeys you'll have a choice between Eurostar – the priciest and fastest trains, which require you to reserve a seat – the slower Intercity and the cheap, snail-paced Diretto, Interregionale and Regionale. **InterRail** and **Eurail** passes are valid on the whole FS network, though you'll pay supplements for the fast trains and most long-distance trains. A low-cost offshoot of the state railway, TrenOk (Ⓦwww.trenok.com), runs services between Rome and various provincial towns in the south. Though of little interest in themselves, some of these are just a short bus or train ride from Naples and Bari; if you don't mind taking a roundabout route, you'll save on fares (from €9 one-way). **Tickets** must be validated in the yellow machines at the head of the platform. Call Ⓣ89.20.21, or consult the websites, for train information and on-line tickets.

By bus

Almost everywhere has some kind of bus service, but **schedules** can be sketchy. Buy tickets at *tabacchi* or the bus terminal rather than on board; for longer journeys you can normally buy them in advance direct from the bus company. Major companies which run long-haul services include Marozzi (Rome to the Amalfi Coast, Naples and Brindisi; Ⓦwww.marozzivt.it), SAIS (Rome to Sicily; Ⓦwww.saistrasporti.it) and SITA (Campania, Tuscany and Alpine regions; Ⓦwww.sitabus.it).

By ferry

Italy's network of **ferries** and **hydrofoils** is well developed. Ferries for Sicily and Sardinia depart from Genoa, Civitavecchia, Naples and Fiumicino (near Rome), while smaller islands such as Capri, plus towns in the Bay of Naples and along the Amalfi coast, are served by speedier hydrofoils. Book well **in advance** for the longer routes in high season to find the cheapest fares; for timetables, see Ⓦwww.traghetti.com.

ACCOMMODATION

Most tourist offices have details of hotel rates. Book ahead in the major cities and resorts, especially in summer. **Hotels** in Italy come with a confusing variety of names (*locanda*, *pensione*, *albergo*), but all are star-rated. Rates vary greatly but on average you can expect to pay €60 for a double without private bathroom (*senza bagno*) in a one-star hotel, and a minimum of €80 for a double in a three-star. In very busy places you might have to stay a minimum of three nights.

B&Bs and **agriturismi** (farm-stays) can make a good-value alternative. They are often in spectacular locations and provide excellent Italian home cooking, though you may need a car to get to them: ask for a list from the local tourist office.

There are **hostels** in every major Italian city, charging €18–25 per person for a dorm bed, though for two people travelling together, this isn't much cheaper than a budget hotel room. You can get a full list of HI hostels from the Associazione Italiana Alberghi per la Gioventù (ⓦwww.ostellionline.org). Alternatively, **student accommodation** is a popular budget option in university towns (July and August only), or ask the tourist board about local **case per ferie**, usually religious houses with rooms or beds to let. They can be better value than hostels but often have curfews.

There are plenty of **campsites** and in most cases you pay for location rather than facilities, which can vary enormously. Daily prices are around €7 per person, plus €10 for a tent. See ⓦwww.camping.it for information and booking.

FOOD AND DRINK

There are few places in the world where you can eat and drink as well as in Italy. If you eat only pizza and *panini* (rolls), you'll be missing out on the distinctive **regional cuisines**; don't be afraid to ask what the *piatti tipici* (local dishes) are. Most Italians start their day in a bar, with a cappuccino and a *cornetto* (croissant), a **breakfast** that should cost around €2 if you stand at the counter – or at least double that if you take a seat. At **lunchtime**, bars sell *tramezzini*, sandwiches on white bread, and panini. Another stopgap are *arancini,* fried meat- or cheese-filled rice balls, particularly prevalent in the south. Italian ice cream (*gelato*) is justifiably famous; for the best choice go to a *gelateria*. Markets – to be found in even the smallest of towns – sell fresh, tasty produce for next to nothing, and work out much cheaper than supermarket shopping.

The ultimate **budget option** for sit-down food is pizza. Although trattorias or ristorantes often offer a fixed-price *menu turistico*, it's generally not very good – food is cooked in huge batches to cater for the peak-time tourist droves, with unappetizing results. Traditionally, a trattoria is cheaper than a restaurant, offering *cucina casalinga* (home-style cooking). But in either, pasta dishes go for around €6–9; main fish or meat courses will normally be €9–15. Order vegetables (*contorni*) separately. Afterwards there's fruit (*frutta*) and desserts (*dolci*). As well as the cover charge (*coperto*), service (*servizio*) will often be added, generally about ten percent (if it isn't, it's customary to leave a tip of a couple of euros).

Drink

Bars are less social centres than functional places for a quick coffee or beer. You pay first at the cash desk (*la cassa*), present your receipt (*scontrino*) and give your order. Coffee comes small and black (*espresso*, or just *caffé*), with a dash of milk (*macchiato*) or cream (*con panna*), or white and frothy (*cappuccino*); try a *granita* – cold coffee with crushed ice, usually topped with cream. Tea (*tè*) comes with lemon (*con limone*) unless you ask for milk (*con latte*); it's also served cold (*tè freddo*). A *spremuta* is a fresh fruit juice; crushed-ice fruit *granite* are a refreshing alternative.

Wine is invariably drunk with meals, and is very cheap. Go for the local stuff: ask for *un mezzo* (a half-litre) or *un quarto* (a quarter). Bottles are pricier but still good value; expect to pay around €12 a bottle in a restaurant. The cheapest and most common brands of **beer** (*birra*) are the Italian Peroni and Moretti, or you could choose draught beer (*alla spina*). A generous shot of spirits, or fiery grappa, made from grape pips and stalks, costs from €3. Of the liqueurs, Amaro is a bitter after-dinner drink, Amaretto sweeter with a strong taste of marzipan, and Sambuca a sticky-sweet aniseed concoction. Drinking in pubs is pricey – around €5 for a beer and €6–10 for a cocktail – while drinking in nightclubs can be ruinous, although the entrance fee of €10–15 usually includes one drink.

Most places will be happy to serve you **tap water** (*acqua del rubinetto*), which is perfectly safe to drink. For bottled water, ask for *acqua naturale* (still) or *acqua frizzante* (sparkling).

CULTURE AND ETIQUETTE

Italy remains strongly **family-oriented**, with an emphasis on the traditions and rituals of the Catholic Church, and it is not unusual to find people living with their parents until their early thirties. While the north is cosmopolitan, the south can be rather provincial; women travelling on their own may attract unwanted attention in smaller areas. When entering churches, ensure that your knees and shoulders are covered. In towns and villages all over the country, life stops during the middle of the day for a long lunch.

Tipping is not a big deal in Italy; in restaurants – if a service charge is not included – it's acceptable to reward good service with a couple of euros. In bars, you may see some Italians leave a coin on the counter after finishing their coffee – a convenient way of ridding themselves of small change, but by no means expected of tourists. Likewise, taxi drivers will not expect a tip. Smoking is outlawed in all public places; you can be charged a hefty fine for lighting up.

SPORTS AND OUTDOOR ACTIVITIES

Spectator sports are popular here – Italians are particularly fervent in their passion for **football** (*calcio*), though cycling, motorcycling and motor racing are also high-profile sports. Going to a football match in Italy can be an exhilarating experience. The season runs from the end of August to June; ⓦwww.figc.it for details of forthcoming matches; tickets cost from €18.

Campania, Sardinia and Sicily, with their pristine coastlines and clear waters, provide excellent conditions for **scuba diving** and **snorkelling**, while Rome, Milan, Turin, Venice and, at the other end of the country, Mount Etna in Sicily, are within easy reach of **ski resorts**. The same mountainous terrain is perfectly suited to summertime **hiking**; ask at local tourist offices for maps and itinerary information.

COMMUNICATIONS

Post office opening hours are Monday–Friday 8am–6.30pm, with branches in towns and cities sometimes also open on Saturdays. Stamps can also be bought at *tabacchi* – ask for *posta prioritaria* if you want letters to arrive home before you do. Public **phones** are card-operated; get a phone card (*scheda telefonica*) from *tabacchi* and newsstands for €5/10. For landline calls – local and long-distance – dial all digits, including the area code. International directory enquiries (ⓣ176) are pricey. Most towns have at least one place with Internet access; hourly rates are around €2–5/hour.

ITALY ON THE NET

ⓦ**www.enit.it** Official tourist board site.
ⓦ**www.paginegialle.it** Italian directory of phone numbers.
ⓦ**www.trenitalia.com** Italian rail timetables.

EMERGENCIES

Most of the **crime** you're likely to come across is small-time. You can minimize the risk of this by being discreet, not

Italian

	Italian	Pronunciation
Yes/No	Sì/No	*See/Noh*
Please	Per favore	*Pear fah-vure-ay*
You're welcome	Prego	*Pray-goh*
Thank you	Grazie	*Grraat-see-ay*
Hello/Good day/Hi	Ciao/buongiorno/salve	*Chow/bon jaw-noh/salvay*
Goodbye	Ciao/arrivederci	*Chow/arriva-derchee*
Excuse me	Mi scusi	*Mee scoo-see*
Good	Buono	*Bwo-noh*
Bad	Cattivo	*Cat-ee-voh*
Near	Vicino	*Vih-chee-noh*
Far	Lontano	*Lont-ah-noh*
Today	Oggi	*Ojj-ee*
Yesterday	Ieri	*Ee-air-ee*
Tomorrow	Domani	*Doh-mahn-ee*
How much is....?	Quanto è...?	*Cwan-toe ay?*
What time is it?	Che ore sono?	*Keh orr-ay son-noh*
I don't understand	Non ho capito	*Non oh kapee-toe*
Do you speak English?	Parla Inglese?	*Parr-la inglay-zay?*
One	Uno	*Oo-noh*
Two	Due	*Doo-ay*
Three	Tre	*Tray*
Four	Quattro	*Cwattr-oh*
Five	Cinque	*Chink-way*
Six	Sei	*Say*
Seven	Sette	*Set-tay*
Eight	Otto	*Ot-toe*
Nine	Nove	*Noh-vay*
Ten	Dieci	*Dee-ay-chee*
Getting around		
Ticket	Biglietto	*Bil-yettoh*
Where is..?	Dov'è..?	*Doh-vay?*
Entrance	L'ingresso	*Lingress-oh*
Exit	L'uscita	*Loo-shee-tah*
Platform	Il binario	*Il bin-ah-ree-oh*
Toilet	Il bagno	*Il ban-yo*
Ferry	Il traghetto	*Il trag-ettow*
Bus	L'autobus	*Lout-o-boos*
Plane	L'aereo	*Lah-air-ay-oh*
Train	Il treno	*Il tray-no*
Accommodation		
I would like a...	Vorrei...	*Vorr-ay*
Bed	Letto	*Lett-oh*
Single/double room	Camera singola/doppia	*Cam-errah singolah/doppiah*
Cheap	Economico	*Eck-oh-no-micoh*
Expensive	Caro	*Car-oh*
Open	Aperto	*Apairt-oh*
Closed	Chiuso	*Queue-zoh*
Breakfast	Colazione	*Coll-ats-ioh-nay*
Hotel	L'hotel	*Lott-ell*
Hostel	L'ostello	*Lost-ellow*

flashing anything of value and keeping a firm hand on your camera and bag, particularly on public transport. The police come in many forms: the *Vigili Urbani* deal with traffic offences and the *Carabinieri* with public order and drug control; report thefts to the *Polizia di Stato*. It is worth noting that Italy is currently cracking down on soft drugs offences and treating them as severely as hard drugs.

Pharmacies (*farmacie*) can give advice and dispense prescriptions; there's one open all night in towns and cities (find the address of the nearest on any pharmacy door). For serious ailments, go to the *Pronto Soccorso* (casualty) section of the nearest hospital (*ospedale*).

EMERGENCY NUMBERS

Police ⓣ113; Fire ⓣ115; Ambulance ⓣ118.

INFORMATION AND MAPS

Most towns, major train stations and airports have a tourist office (*ufficio turistico*) which will give out maps for free. If you need something more detailed, Touring Club Italiano produce 1:800,000 and 1:400,000 maps covering north, south and central Italy. Studio FMB has excellent hiking maps covering the north of the country, as does Club Alpino Italiano (ⓦwww.cai.it), available throughout Italy.

MONEY AND BANKS

Italy's currency is the euro (€). Banking hours are Mon–Fri 8.30am–1.30pm & 2.30–3.45pm, and ATMs (*bancomat*) are widespread. The Italian way of life is cash-based, and many smaller restaurants and B&Bs will not accept credit cards. To change cash or travellers' cheques, exchange bureaux tend to give a better rate than the banks.

Under-26s and students are often allowed free entry or reduced rates upon production of a valid student card or proof of age.

OPENING HOURS AND HOLIDAYS

Most shops and businesses open Mon–Sat 8/9am–1pm & 4–7/8pm, though in the north, offices work a 9am–5pm day. Just about everything, with the exception of bars and restaurants, closes on Sunday. Most churches keep shop hours: note that many will not let you in with bare shoulders or wearing short trousers or skirts. Museums traditionally open Tues–Sun 9am–7pm, and are closed on Mon, but some have extended hours. Most archeological sites open daily from 9am until about an hour before sunset.

Many of Italy's inland towns close down almost entirely for the month of August, when Italians head for the coast. Everything closes for national holidays: Jan 1, Jan 6, Easter Monday, April 25, May 1, June 2, Aug 15, Nov 1, Dec 8, Dec 25 & 26.

Rome

Of all Italy's historic cities, **ROME** (Roma) exerts the most fascination. Its sheer weight of history is endlessly compelling, with eras crowding in on each other to a breathtaking degree. Classical features – the Colosseum, the Roman Forum, the spectacular Palatine Hill – stand alongside ancient basilicas containing relics from the early Christian period, while Baroque fountains and churches define the city centre. Swathes of Fascist-era concrete palaces also leave their mark, as well as the occasional modern masterpiece such as Richard Meier's futuristic Ara Pacis. But it's not all history and brickwork: Rome has a vibrant, chaotic life of its own, its crowded streets thronged with traffic, locals, tourists and students.

What to see and do

Rome's city centre is divided neatly into distinct blocks. The **centro storico** (historic centre) occupies a hook of land on the east bank of the River Tiber, bordered to the east by Via del Corso and to the north and south by water. The old Campus Martius of Roman times, it became the heart of the Renaissance city and is now an unruly knot of narrow streets holding some of the best of Rome's classical and Baroque heritage, as well as much of its nightlife.

From here, Rome's central core spreads east, across Via del Corso to the major shopping streets and alleys around the **Spanish Steps** and the main artery of Via Nazionale, and south to the major sites of the **Roman Forum** and **Palatine Hill**. The west bank of the river is home to the **Vatican** and **St Peter's** and, to the south of these, **Trastevere** – even in ancient times a distinct entity from the city proper, and now a hub of the city's nightlife.

The Roman Forum

The best place to start a tour of the city is the Roman Forum (Tues–Sun 9am–1hr before sunset; free), the bustling centre of the ancient city. Following the downfall of the city to various barbarian invaders, the area was left in ruin, its relics quarried for construction in other parts of Rome during medieval and Renaissance times.

Running through the heart of the Forum, the **Via Sacra** was the best-known street of ancient Rome, lined with its most important buildings, such as the Curia in the Forum's northwestern corner – begun in 45 BC, this was the home of the Senate during the Republican period. Next to the Curia is the **Arch of Septimius Severus**, erected in the early third century AD to commemorate the emperor's tenth anniversary in power. The grassy, wide-open scatter of paving and beached columns in front of it was where most of the life of the city took place. In the centre of the Forum is the **House of the Vestal Virgins**, where the six women charged with keeping the sacred flame of Vesta alight lived. On the far side of the site, the towering **Basilica of Maxentius** is probably the Forum's most impressive relic. From the basilica, the Via Sacra climbs to the **Arch of Titus** on a low arm of the Palatine Hill, its reliefs showing the spoils of Jerusalem being carried off by eager Romans.

Palatine Hill

From the Forum, turn right at the Arch of Titus to reach the **Palatine Hill** (Tues–Sun 9am–1hr before sunset; joint ticket with Colosseum €12.50), now a beautiful archeological garden. In the days of the Republic, the Palatine was the most desirable address in Rome (our word "palace" is derived from it). The **Farnese Gardens**, on the right, were laid out by Alessandro Farnese in the mid-sixteenth century. The terrace here looks back over the Forum, while the terrace at the opposite end looks

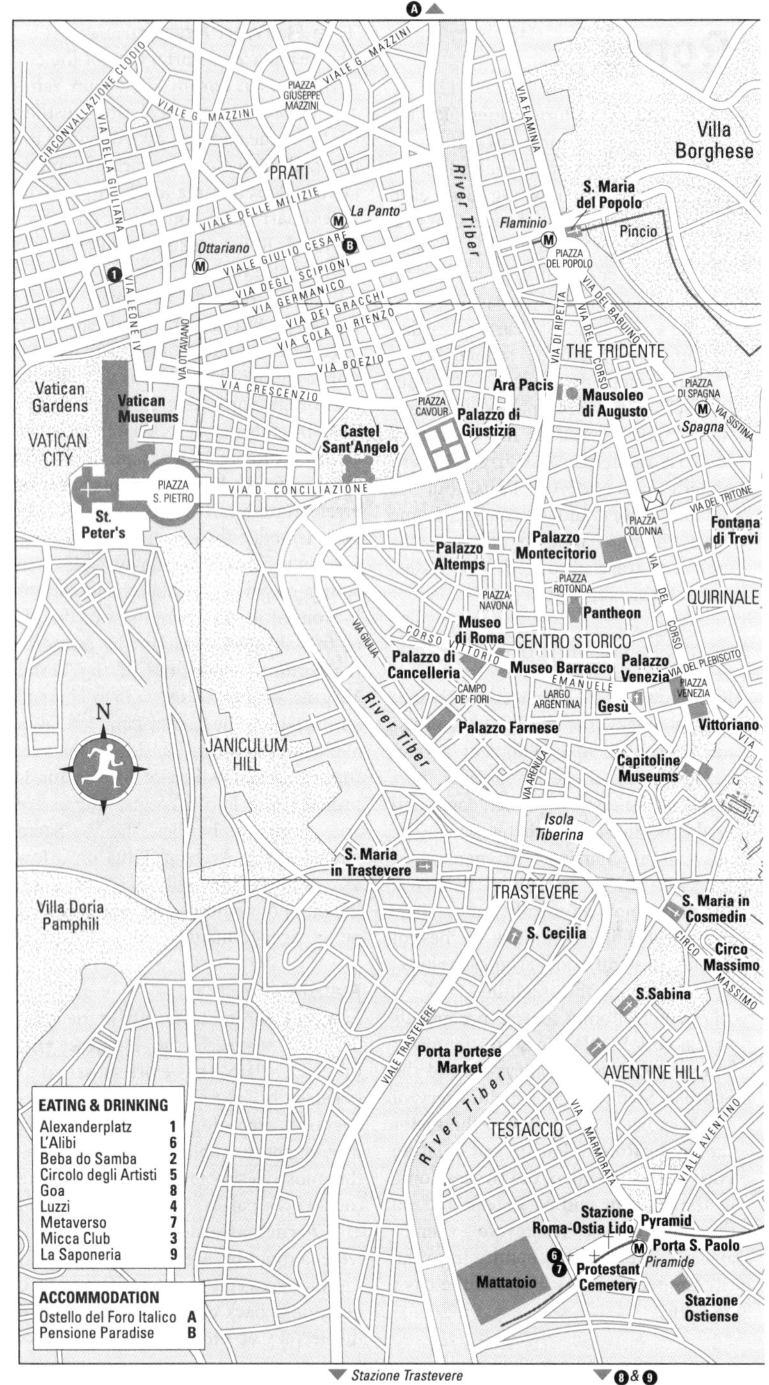

EATING & DRINKING	
Alexanderplatz	1
L'Alibi	6
Beba do Samba	2
Circolo degli Artisti	5
Goa	8
Luzzi	4
Metaverso	7
Micca Club	3
La Saponeria	9

ACCOMMODATION	
Ostello del Foro Italico	A
Pensione Paradise	B

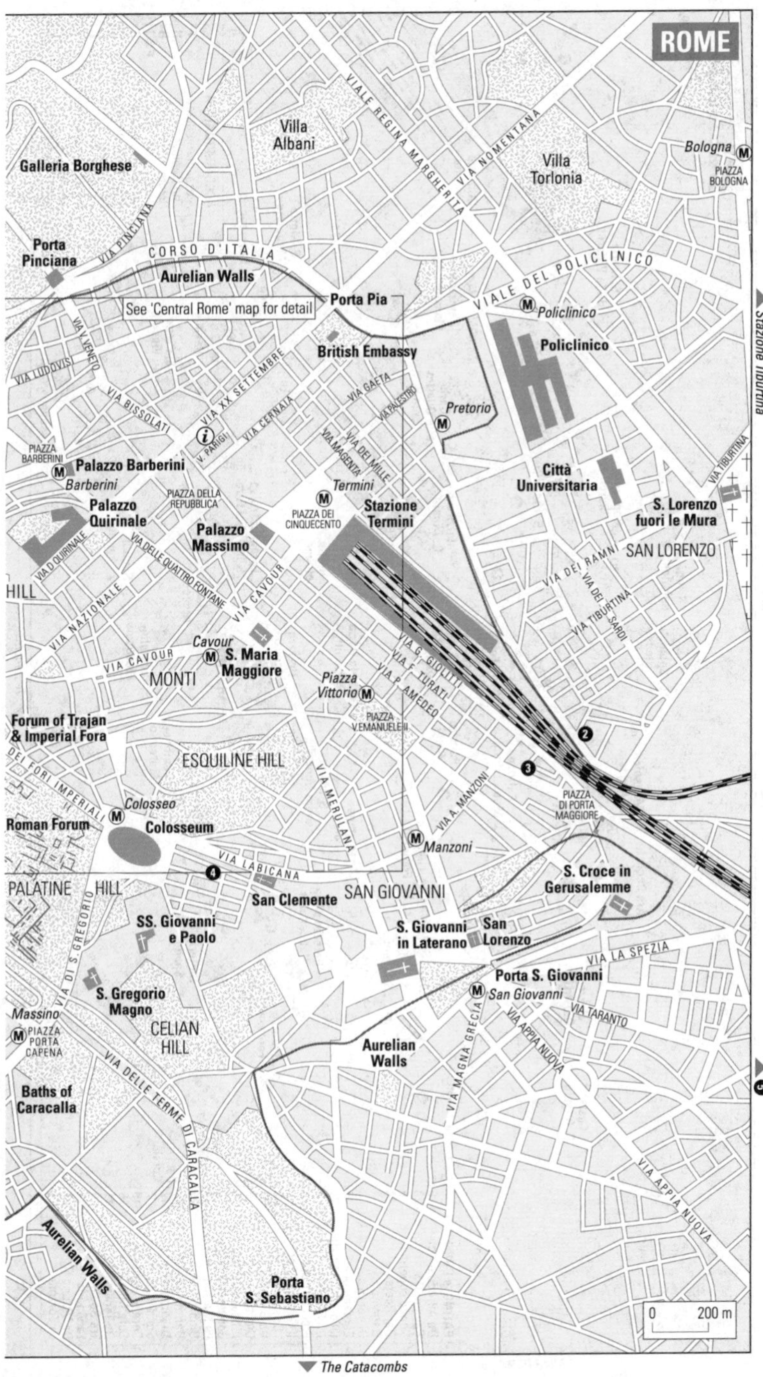
ROME
Villa Albani
Galleria Borghese
Villa Torlonia
Bologna
PIAZZA BOLOGNA
VIALE REGINA MARGHERITA
VIA NOMENTANA
VIA PINCIANA
Porta Pinciana
CORSO D'ITALIA
Aurelian Walls
VIALE DEL POLICLINICO
Policlinico
Porta Pia
See 'Central Rome' map for detail
British Embassy
Stazione Tiburtina
VIA V. VENETO
VIA LUDOVISI
VIA XX SETTEMBRE
VIA BISSOLATI
VIA CERNAIA
VIA GAETA
VIA PALESTRO
Pretorio
PIAZZA BARBERINI
Palazzo Barberini
Barberini
V. PARIGI
VIA DEI MILLE
VIA MAGENTA
Città Universitaria
VIA TIBURTINA
Termini
PIAZZA DELLA REPUBBLICA
Palazzo Quirinale
Stazione Termini
PIAZZA DEI CINQUECENTO
S. Lorenzo fuori le Mura
Palazzo Massimo
SAN LORENZO
VIA D. QUIRINALE
VIA DELLE QUATTRO FONTANE
VIA DEI RAMNI
VIA DEI SARDI
HILL
VIA NAZIONALE
VIA CAVOUR
Cavour
S. Maria Maggiore
MONTI
VIA G. GIOLITTI
VIA F. TURATI
VIA P. AMEDEO
Piazza Vittorio
Forum of Trajan & Imperial Fora
PIAZZA V. EMANUELE II
ESQUILINE HILL
DEI FORI IMPERIALI
VIA MERULANA
VIA A. MANZONI
PIAZZA DI PORTA MAGGIORE
Colosseo
Roman Forum
Colosseum
Manzoni
VIA LABICANA
S. Croce in Gerusalemme
PALATINE HILL
San Clemente
SAN GIOVANNI
SS. Giovanni e Paolo
S. Giovanni in Laterano
San Lorenzo
VIA DI S. GREGORIO
VIA LA SPEZIA
Porta S. Giovanni
S. Gregorio Magno
San Giovanni
Massino
PIAZZA PORTA CAPENA
CELIAN HILL
VIA TARANTO
VIA APPIA NUOVA
Aurelian Walls
VIA MAGNA GRECIA
VIA DELLE TERME DI CARACALLA
Baths of Caracalla
Aurelian Walls
Porta S. Sebastiano
0 200 m
The Catacombs

CENTRAL ROME

EATING & DRINKING	
Da Alfredo e Ada	6
Cavour 313	20
Conad supermarket	4
Dar Poeta	24
Dagnino	1
Di per Di supermarket	3
Enoteca Corsi	15
Il Forno del Ghetto	21
Da Franceso	8
Freni e Frizioni	23
Il Gelato di San Crispino	2
Da Giggetto	22
Giolitti	5
L'Insalata Ricca	16
Jonathan's Angels	9
La Maison	14
Ombre Rosse	25
Bar della Pace	12
Le Piramidi	17
Société Lutèce	7
Sora Margherita	19
Sora Mirella	26
Da Tonino	11
Tre Scalini	10
La Vineria	18
Da Vittorio	27
Lo Zozzone	13

ACCOMMODATION	
Alessandro Palace	F
The Beehive	H
Colors	B
Daphne Inn	E & I
M&J Place Hostel	G
Nostra Signora di Lourdes	D
Ottaviano	A
Pensione Panda	C
Relais Palazzo Taverna	J
Sandy	L
Suore Pie Operaie	K

Piazza del Popolo
Villa Borghese
St Peter's
27
Testaccio
S. Giovanni in Laterano

down on the alleged centre of Rome's ancient beginning – an Iron Age hut, known as the **House of Romulus**, the best-preserved part of a ninth-century village.

Close by, steps lead down to the **Cryptoporticus**, a passage built by Nero to link the Palatine with his palace on the far side of the Colosseum, and decorated along part of its length with Roman stuccowork. A left turn leads to the **House of Livia**, believed to have been the residence of the wife of Augustus, whose courtyard and rooms are decorated with trompe l'oeil marble panels and frescoes.

The Capitoline Hill

Formerly the spiritual and political centre of the Roman Empire, the Capitoline Hill lies behind the Neoclassical Vittoriano monument on traffic-choked Piazza Venezia. Atop the Capitoline is one of Rome's most elegant squares, **Piazza del Campidoglio**, designed by Michelangelo in the 1530s and flanked by the two wings of one of the city's most important museums of ancient art – and the oldest public gallery in the world, dating back to 1471 – the **Capitoline Museums** (Tues–Sun 9am–8pm; €6.50). The Palazzo Nuovo, the museum's left-hand wing, contains some of the best of the city's Roman and Greek sculpture. Highlights of the Palazzo dei Conservatori opposite include various parts of the colossal statue of the Emperor Constantine which once stood in the Forum, and sixteenth-century frescoes of important events in Roman history.

Colosseum

Immediately outside the Forum, the fourth-century **Arch of Constantine,** notable for its magnificent marble reliefs, marks the end of the Via Sacra. Across from here is Rome's most awe-inspiring ancient monument, the **Colosseum** (Tues–Sun 9am–1hr before sunset; joint ticket with Palatine Hill €12.50; buy tickets at the Palatine Hill to bypass the queues). Begun by the Emperor Vespasian in 72 AD, construction was completed by his son Titus about eight years later – an event celebrated with 100 days of games. The arena was about 500m in circumference and could seat 50,000 people; the Romans flocked here for gladiatorial contests and cruel spectacles. Mock sea battles were also staged here – the arena could be flooded in minutes. After the games were outlawed in the fifth century, the Colosseum was pillaged for building material, and is now little more than a magnificent shell. The structure of the place is still easy to see, however, and has served as a model for stadiums around the world ever since.

Domus Aurea

Close by is Nero's **Domus Aurea** (Tues-Fri 10am–4pm; entry by appointment only; call ⓣ06.3996.7700; €4.50), whose entrance is opposite the Colosseum, off Via Labicana. Built by Nero as his private palace, the "Golden House" covered a full square mile, and its extravagant halls were decorated in the most lavish style, though little remains today. Stripped of its marble decor and filled with rubble after Nero's death, when the site was first rediscovered hundreds of years later it was thought to be some sort of mystical cave or grotto.

Campo de' Fiori and the Ghetto

From Piazza Venezia, Via del Plebiscito forges west; take a left turn into the maze of cobbled streets that wind down to pretty **Campo de' Fiori**, one-time heart of the medieval city, now home to a colourful produce market (Mon–Sat 6am–2pm). Surrounded by bars, it's a great spot to watch the *passeggiata* (early-evening stroll).

A short stroll from here, east of Via Arenula, a warren of picturesque narrow streets make up the Ghetto. Rome's

Jews have been present in the city for over 2000 years, making them the oldest Jewish community in Europe. Having moved here from Trastevere in the thirteenth century, the city's Jews were walled off from the rest of the city in 1556, and subsequently suffered centuries of ill-treatment, culminating in the deportations of World War II, when a quarter of the Ghetto's population died in concentration camps. Today, the area has an intimate, back-street feel, and is a great place for a wander – and to sample the delicious Roman-Jewish cuisine.

Trastevere

Across the Tiber from the Ghetto, picturesque **Trastevere**, once the city's shabby bohemian quarter, is now somewhat gentrified, and home to much of the city's most vibrant nightlife and some of its best restaurants. On Sunday morning, the sprawling **Porta Portese** flea market (5am–2pm; bus #H from Termini) stretches down Via Portuense to Trastevere station in a congested medley of antiques, clothing and junk.

The hub of the area is **Piazza di Santa Maria in Trastevere**, and the magnificent twelfth-century church of the same name on the western side of the square. Held to be the first official church in Rome, built on a site where a fountain of oil is said to have sprung on the day of Christ's birth, it is resplendent with thirteenth-century mosaics.

Trastevere's other main sight is tucked away on the area's quieter eastern side: the church of **Santa Cecilia,** built on the site of the second-century home of the patron saint of music. Locked in the hot chamber of her baths for several days, she sang her way through the ordeal, securing her status as the patron saint of music, until her head was hacked half off with an axe.

Pantheon

One of the centro storico's main draws is the **Pantheon** (Mon–Sat 8.30am–7.30pm, Sun 9am–6pm; free) on Piazza della Rotonda, the most complete ancient Roman structure in the city, finished around 125 AD. Inside, the diameter of the dome and height of the building are precisely equal, and the hole in the dome's centre is a full 9m across; there are no visible arches or vaults to hold the whole thing up – instead, they're sunk into the concrete of the walls of the building. The coffered ceiling was covered in solid bronze until the seventeenth century, and the niches were filled with statues of the gods.

Piazza Navona

A ten-minute stroll west of the Pantheon, **Piazza Navona** is one of the city's most appealing squares, and follows the lines of the Emperor Domitian's chariot arena. Pope Innocent X built most of the grandiose palaces that surround it in the seventeenth century and commissioned Renaissance architect Borromini to design the church of **Sant'Agnese in Agone** on the west side. The church supposedly stands on the spot where St Agnes, exposed naked to the public in the stadium, miraculously grew hair to cover herself. Opposite, the **Fontana dei Quattro Fiumi** is by Borromini's archrival, Bernini; each figure represents one of the four great rivers of the world – the Nile, Danube, Ganges and Plate – though only the horse, symbolizing the Danube, was actually carved by Bernini.

The Ara Pacis and around

Walking north along the Lungotevere (riverside drive) from here, you'll arrive at the striking **Ara Pacis** (Tues–Sun 9am–7pm; Ⓦwww.arapacis.it; €6.50). Built in 13 BC to celebrate Augustus's victory over Spain and Gaul, the "altar of peace" is housed in a slick travertine and glass container designed by American architect Richard Meier in 2006. Inside the luminous structure, the altar supports a fragmented frieze showing Augustus, his wife Livia and various children.

Via di Ripetta arrows north from here to **Piazza del Popolo**, all symmetry and grand vistas – although its real attraction is the church of **Santa Maria del Popolo**, which holds some of the best Renaissance art of any Roman church. Two pictures by Caravaggio get most attention – the *Conversion of St Paul* and the *Crucifixion of St Peter*.

Villa Borghese

Leafy **Villa Borghese,** just a few minutes' stroll east of Piazza del Popolo, is a tranquil haven from the noise and chaos of the city. It harbours several fine museums (see Ⓦwww.villaborghese.it for details), not least the **Galleria Borghese** (Tues–Sun 9am–7pm; timed entry every 2hrs; Ⓣ06.32.810, Ⓦwww.galleriaborghese.it; call to book at least a day in advance; €8.50), a dazzling collection of mainly Italian art and sculpture. Highlights include Canova's sculpted marble *Pauline*, the sister of Napoleon portrayed as a reclining Venus, in Room 1; spectacular sculptures by Bernini in rooms 2–4; and the six Caravaggios in Room 8. The picture gallery upstairs contains masterpieces by Antonello da Messina, Raphael, Rubens, Titian and many more.

The Spanish Steps

The area immediately southeast of Piazza del Popolo is historically the artistic quarter of the city, with a distinctly cosmopolitan air. At the centre of the district, long, thin **Piazza di Spagna** features the distinctive boat-shaped Barcaccia fountain, the last work of Bernini's father. The **Spanish Steps** – a venue for international posing – sweep up from the piazza to the sixteenth-century church of **Trinità dei Monti**.

Piazza Barberini and around

From the top of the Spanish Steps, narrow Via Sistina winds down to Piazza Barberini. Bernini's Fontana del Tritone, its muscular Triton held up by four dolphins, dominates the piazza; beyond here, along Via Barberini, **Palazzo Barberini** contains the **Galleria Nazionale d'Arte Antica** (Tues–Sun 8.30am–7.30pm; €5), which displays a rich patchwork of mainly Italian art from the early Renaissance to the late Baroque period; highlights include Filippo Lippi's warmly maternal *Madonna and Child* and Raphael's beguiling *Fornarina*.

West down Via del Tritone, hidden among a web of narrow streets, is one of Rome's more surprising sights – the **Fontana di Trevi**, a deafening gush of water over Baroque statues and rocks built onto the back of a Renaissance palace, which can barely be seen for the crowds.

St Peter's basilica

The **Vatican City**, a tiny territory on the other side of the Tiber, is surrounded by high walls on its far side, but on the near side opens its doors to the rest of the city in the form of Bernini's **Piazza San Pietro**. St Peter's (daily 7am–6/7pm; free) was built to a plan initially conceived at the end of the fifteenth century by Bramante and finished off over a century later by Carlo Maderno, bridging the Renaissance and Baroque eras. The interior is full of Baroque features, although the first thing you see, on the right, is Michelangelo's *Pietà*, completed when he was just 24. On the right-hand side of the nave, the bronze statue of St Peter was cast in the thirteenth century by Arnolfo di Cambio. Bronze was also used in Bernini's imposing 28m-high *baldacchino*, the centrepiece of the sculptor's embellishment of the interior. Bernini's feverish sculpture decorates the apse, too, his *cattedra* enclosing the supposed chair of St Peter in a curvy marble and stucco throne. Under the portico, to the right of the main doors, you can ascend by stairs or lift to the roof, from where there's a steep walk up 320 steps to the dome (daily 8am–5/6pm; €4, €7 with lift), well worth the effort for its glorious views over the city.

The Vatican Museums

A ten-minute walk from the northern side of Piazza San Pietro takes you to the **Vatican Museums** (Mar–Oct Mon–Fri 10am–4.45pm, Sat 10am–2.45pm; Nov–Feb Mon–Sat 10am–1.45pm; last Sun of each month 9am–1.45pm; €13, €8 students under 26; last Sun of the month free) – quite simply the largest, richest museum complex in the world, stuffed with booty from every period of the city's history. If you are pushed for time, start off at the **Stanze di Raffaello**, at the opposite end of the building to the entrance, a set of rooms decorated for Pope Julius II by Raphael among others. Raphael's *School of Athens* fresco depicts his artistic contemporaries as classical figures: Leonardo is Plato and Michelangelo the serious-looking Heraclitus. Other highlights include the **Galleria Chiaramonte**, a superb collection of Roman statues, and the **Galleria delle Carte Geografiche**, with its incredibly precise, richly pigmented maps of Italy.

The **Sistine Chapel**, of course, is the main draw. Built for Pope Sixtus IV in 1481, it serves as the pope's private chapel and hosts the conclaves of cardinals for the election of each new pope. The paintings down each side wall depict scenes from the lives of Moses and Christ by Perugino, Botticelli and Ghirlandaio among others. But it's Michelangelo's ceiling frescoes of the *Creation* that everyone comes to see, executed almost single-handedly over a period of about four years for Pope Julius II. The *Last Judgment*, on the west wall of the chapel, was painted by Michelangelo over twenty years later. The nudity caused controversy from the start, and the pope's zealous successor, Pius IV, insisted that loincloths be added – removed in a recent restoration.

Arrival and information

Air Rome has two airports. Leonardo da Vinci, better known as Fiumicino, handles all scheduled flights; Ciampino is for charter services and low-cost flights. Two train services link Fiumicino to Rome: one to Termini (every 30min until 11.37pm; €9.50), the other to Trastevere, Ostiense and Tiburtina stations (every 15min until 11.27pm; €5). Terravision coach services travel to Termini station 6.30am–6.30pm; €7. From Ciampino, catch a Terravision coach to Via Marsala 7, near Termini station (Ⓦ www.lowcostcoach.com; €8). Alternatively, take the slower Schiaffini bus (10am–10.40pm; every 40min; €1) to Anagnina metro station, then a metro or bus into town.

Train The main **train station** is Termini, meeting-point of the metro lines and city bus routes. Some long-distance services use Stazione Tiburtina, particularly at night. The two stations are connected by metro and bus.

Bus Domestic bus services arrive at the bus terminal outside Stazione Tiburtina.

Tourist office The main tourist office is at Via Parigi 11 (Mon–Sat 9am–7pm; Ⓣ06.488.991). Information is also available from the Tourist Call Centre (daily 9am–6pm; Ⓣ06.8205.9127; Ⓦwww.romaturismo.com). There's a tourist information booth at Fiumicino airport (daily 8am–7pm; Ⓣ06.6595.4471), and green tourist information kiosks near every major sight (daily 9.30am–7.30pm). Enjoy Rome (Mon–Fri 8.30/9am–6.30/7pm, Sat 8.30am–2pm; Via Marghera 8a, Ⓣ06.445.0734, Ⓦwww.enjoyrome.com) is a friendly, independently-run tourist information agency, staffed by English-speakers, which offers maps, advice and a free accommodation-finding service, and organizes walking tours.

Discount passes The Roma Pass (€20 for three days; Ⓦwww.romapass.it) is well worth investing in – it gives you free access to all public transport within the city, as well as free entry to the first two sights you visit, plus many further discounts. Buy the pass from tourist information kiosks or from participating sights.

City transport

Public transport is cheap and reasonably reliable. A day-pass (BIG; €4) or single ticket (BIT; valid for 75min on all public transport, including one trip on the metro; €1) for the metro and bus network can be bought from any newspaper stall or *tabacchi*, from ticket machines in metro stations and on

Piazza dei Cinquecento outside Termini station. Stamp tickets to validate them at the entrance gates to metros and on board buses.
Metro The quickest way to get around, with trains every 3–5min. The city's two metro lines, A and B, meet beneath Termini station. Line B runs 5.30am–11.30pm (Sat till 12.30pm); Line A runs 5.30am–9pm, with shuttle buses replacing the service until 11.30pm.
Bus The bus network is extensive; useful routes include the #40, which passes through the centre en route to the Vatican, and #116, which serves Villa Borghese and the centro storico. Bus references given in this guide all leave from outside Termini station, unless otherwise noted. A network of **night buses** serves most parts of the city, running roughly hourly until about 5.30am. Validate tickets in the machines on board.
Taxi A costly way to get around, with the meter starting at €2.33. Depending on luggage and the time of travel, it should cost €10–15 to get from Termini to the centre. You can hail one in the street, or try the ranks at Termini and Piazza Venezia.

Accommodation

In high season (May–July) Rome is very crowded, so book **accommodation** as far in advance as possible. If you can't, make straight for the tourist office. Many of the city's cheaper hotels are located close to Termini station, but it's pretty insalubrious; pay a bit more to stay in the centre if you can.

Hostels

All of the hostels below offer breakfast (sometimes little more than coffee and cornflakes); none have a curfew.
Alessandro Palace Via Vicenza 42 ⓣ06.446.1958, ⓦwww.hostelalessandro.com. Buzzing hostel, with lively international staff, a kitchen and bar and free Internet. Dorms ❸; private, en-suite doubles ❾
Colors Via Boezio 31 ⓣ06.687.4030, ⓦwww.colorshotel.com. A clean, airy hostel decorated in zingy colours, with friendly, knowledgeable staff and use of kitchen and terrace. Dorms ❷–❸, private rooms ❾
M&J Place Hostel Via Solferino 9 ⓣ06.446.2802, ⓦwww.mejplacehostel.com. Facilities at this hostel are basic, but include kitchen and free Internet access, and it's conveniently located above the *Living Room* nightclub. Dorms ❷, doubles with shared bathroom ❻
Ostello del Foro Italico Viale delle Olimpiadi 61 ⓣ06.323.6267, ⓦwww.hostelbooking.com. Rome's vast, no-frills HI hostel should be a last resort, as it's a fair way out of the centre. Metro Ottaviano, then bus #32. ❷
Ottaviano Dorms are simply furnished and private rooms on the cramped side, but Ottaviano is a good place to meet other travellers, and it's conveniently situated just outside the Vatican walls. ❷
Sandy Via Cavour 136 ⓣ06.488.4585, ⓦwww.sandyhostel.com. Good-value, laid-back hotel/hostel near the Colosseum. ❷

Convents

Some of Rome's convents have private rooms, often in lovely old buildings, at reasonable prices – though restrictions often apply. Those listed below are two of the most central; ask at the tourist office for others.
Nostra Signora di Lourdes Via Sistina 113 ⓣ06.474.5324. Plain convent near the Spanish Steps with singles, doubles for married couples and twins. 10.30pm curfew. ❼
Suore Pie Operaie Via di Torre Argentina 76 ⓣ06.686.1254. Closed Aug. Superbly located and friendly women-only convent, though with an 11pm curfew. Bus #40 from Termini. ❼

Hotels

The Beehive Via Marghera 8 ⓣ06.4470.4553, ⓦwww.the-beehive.com. Funky hotel with designer furnishings and a sunny garden. The spotless rooms all have shared bathrooms; beds in shared apartments (❹) and dorms (❷–❸) are also available. ❾
Daphne Inn Via degli Avignonesi 20, Via di S. Basilio 55 ⓣ06.8745.0087, ⓦwww.daphne-rome.com. Two stylish hotels – one near Via Veneto, the other near the Trevi – run by friendly, English-speaking staff. ❽–❾
Pensione Panda Via della Croce 35 ⓣ06.678.0179, ⓦwww.hotelpanda.it. Well placed near the Spanish Steps, and with clean, neat rooms

TREAT YOURSELF

If you've got your heart set on staying in Rome's centro storico, the **Relais Palazzo Taverna** (Via dei Gabrielli 92 ⓣ06.2039.8064, ⓦwww.relaispalazzotaverna.com; €100–210) is a good bet. This sleek, modern residenza, housed in a fifteenth-century building near Campo de' Fiori, has spacious bedrooms with white-painted wood ceilings and trendy wallpaper.

with wood-beamed ceilings, this hotel is in high demand. No breakfast. ⑨

Pensione Paradise Viale Giulio Cesare 47 ☎06.3600.4331, Ⓦwww.pensioneparadise.com. Rooms are a little cramped and there's no breakfast, but the friendly staff and location near the Vatican are major pluses. ⑥–⑧

Eating

All of Rome's neighbourhoods have at least one **food market** (generally Mon-Sat 7am-2pm); those at Campo de' Fiori and at Piazza Vittorio near Termini have an abundance of stalls selling fresh Italian produce and, in the case of the latter, African fruits and Asian food too. There are plenty of **supermarkets** throughout the centre; two central options are Di per Di (Via Poli 47), near the Trevi Fountain, and Conad, in the mall underneath Termini station.

Snacks, cakes and ice cream

Dagnino Galleria Esedra, Via VE Orlando 75. Closed Sat. A temple to all things sweet and Sicilian, this retro *pasticceria* sells great *cannoli*.

Il Forno del Ghetto Via del Portico d'Ottavia 1. Historic Jewish bakery with marvellous ricotta, and dried-fruit-filled cakes.

Il Gelato di San Crispino Via della Panetteria 42. Closed Tues. Close to the Trevi fountain and selling some of Rome's best ice cream; the fruit flavours – particularly pear and plum – are outstanding.

Giolitti Via degli Uffici del Vicario 40. Closed Mon. A Roman institution, with a choice of seventy ice cream flavours.

Le Piramidi Vicolo del Gallo 11. Closed Mon. Just off Campo de' Fiori, this Middle Eastern takeaway sells tasty falafel and kebabs.

Sora Mirella Lungotevere Anguillara, cnr Ponte Cestio. Closed Oct–Feb. This kiosk selling *grattachecche* – fruity water ices – is inundated with Romans in the sweltering summer months.

Tre Scalini Piazza Navona. Renowned for its remarkable – though expensive – *tartufo* (rich, dark-chocolate) ice cream. Take away to avoid inflated table prices.

Lo Zozzone Via del Teatro Pace 32. Great-value takeaway pizza *bianca* (without tomato) with a range of fillings, just round the corner from Piazza Navona.

Restaurants

Avoid the restaurants next to the main sights, which tend to serve mediocre food at rip-off prices, and head off down the **side streets** instead. The centro storico, Trastevere and Testaccio are full of small, family-run places.

Da Alfredo e Ada Via dei Banchi Nuovi 14. Closed Sat and Sun. Genuine home cooking at great prices, on a picturesque centro storico street. Three courses cost less than €20, including half a litre of wine.

Enoteca Corsi Via del Gesù 87. Lunch only, but hearty dishes in generous portions and good wines, with a well-stocked wine shop next door. Spaghetti €5.

Da Francesco Piazza del Fico 29. Closed Tues lunch. This always-heaving trattoria near Piazza Navona serves great-value pizzas (€6) and classic Roman mains (€8).

Da Giggetto Via del Portico d'Ottavia 21a ☎06.686.1105. Closed Mon. Pricier than most, but its authentic Roman–Jewish cooking is worth it; try the crispy fried artichokes. Mains €14.

L'Insalata Ricca Largo dei Chiavari 85. If you can't face another pizza, this place has over thirty types of salad (€6–8) on the menu – all freshly prepared and served in generous portions.

Luzzi Via Celimontana 1. Closed Wed. This neighbourhood favourite near the Colosseum, with plenty of outdoor tables, is a fun, raucous place to sample an extensive range of pizza and pasta dishes, plus mainly meaty mains (€6–9).

Dar Poeta Vicolo del Bologna 45. One of the best – and cheapest – pizzerias in Rome (try the house special, with courgettes and sausage), so expect to queue. Pizza €5.

Sora Margherita Piazza delle Cinque Scole 30 ☎06.687.4216. A cramped, no-frills trattoria that's big on atmosphere and portions. Opening hours can be erratic; call to check. Mains €8.

Da Tonino Via del Governo Vecchio 18/19. Excellent, unpretentious Roman cooking at low prices; packed at lunch and dinner. Mains €9.

Da Vittorio Via San Cosimato 14a. Closed Sun. Crispy Neapolitan pizza in the heart of Trastevere. Pizza €6.

Drinking and nightlife

The two main areas to go for **a drink** are Trastevere and the centro storico, particularly around Campo de' Fiori. There's a concentration of **clubs** in Testaccio, running the gamut from vast glittering palaces to more down-to-earth student places; the door charge can be anything from €5 to €25. Some of the trendier venues operate a list-only policy; be prepared to talk your way in, or dress up.

Bars

Bar della Pace Via della Pace 3–7. Just off Piazza Navona, the outside tables of this pricey but lovely bar are generally full of Rome's self-consciously beautiful people.

Enoteca Cavour Via Cavour 313. A handy retreat with an easy-going, studenty feel, lots of wine and bottled beers.

Freni e Frizioni Via del Politeama 17. This all-day bar is a popular early-evening hangout, thanks to its generous *aperitivo* buffet and well-priced drinks.

Jonathan's Angels Via della Fossa 18. This colourful bar, an explosion of kitsch decor, serves great cocktails. Bus #40.

Ombre Rosse Piazza Sant'Egidio 12. Open all day, this Trastevere bar is a good place for an early-evening *aperitivo.* Light snacks and newspapers in several languages also available.

Société Lutèce Piazza di Montevecchio 17. Closed Mon. A ten-minute walk from Piazza Navona in a picturesque piazza, this laid-back bar puts on a free *aperitivo* buffet in the evenings.

La Vineria Campo de' Fiori 15. Closed Mon. Historic *vineria* that spills out onto the square during the summer; drink indoors at a third of the price. If it's packed, try the elegant wine bar *Il Nolano,* a couple of doors to the left.

Discos, clubs and venues

Alexanderplatz Via Ostia 9 ⓣ06.3974.2171, ⓦwww.alexanderplatz.it. Rome's foremost jazz club, with an outdoor festival in summer (ⓦwww.villacelimontanajazz.com). Reservations recommended.

L'Alibi Via Monte Testaccio 44. Predominantly – but not exclusively – male venue that's one of Rome's best gay clubs. Downstairs cellar disco and upstairs open-air bar.

Bebo do Samba Via dei Messapi 8 ⓦwww.bebadosamba.it. Closed July & Aug. In the studenty San Lorenzo district, this tiny, candlelit bar has live music nightly – generally world and jazz. Bus #71.

Circolo degli Artisti Via Casilina Vecchia 42 ⓦwww.circoloartisti.it. Closed Mon. Huge bar, disco and garden with live indie-rock; cheap and fun. Bus #412 from Via del Tritone.

Goa Via Libetta 13. Closed Sun–Tues and mid-May to mid-Sept. An ethnic feel, house, techno and trance tunes and high-energy atmosphere. Metro Garbatella.

La Maison Vicolo dei Granari 4 ⓣ06.683.3312. Very glossy disco near Piazza Navona, home to Rome's gilded youth and C-list celebs. Book or queue. Bus #40.

Metaverso Via di Monte Testaccio 38a. Closed Mon–Thurs, Sun & July & Aug. A cheap, down-to-earth club which plays mainly electronica to an alternative crowd.

Micca Club Via Pietro Micca 7a ⓦwww.miccaclub.com. Closed Mon & Tues & June–Aug. DJ sets, live acts and themed club nights in a cool, brick-vaulted space.

La Saponeria Via degli Argonauti 20 ⓦwww.lasaponeria.com. Closed Wed–Sun, mid-May to mid-Sept. A lively Testaccio club playing mainstream pop, hip-hop and R&B. Metro Garbatella.

Culture and festivals

The city's churches host a wide range of **classical music** concerts, many of them free. International names appear at Rome's snail-shell shaped Auditorium in the **northern suburbs** (Viale P. de Coubertin, ⓣ06.808.2058, ⓦwww.auditorium

FESTIVALS

Festival delle Letterature ⓦwww.festivaldelleletterature.it. The floodlit Basilica of Maxentius provides a stunning backdrop to readings by international authors. June.

Fiesta Via Appia Nuova 1245 ⓦwww.fiesta.it. Metro A to Subaugusta, then bus #354 to Ippodromo Capannelle. A festival with a Latin-American flavour based at Rome's racecourse in the southeast of the city. Mid-June to Aug.

Estate Romana ⓦwww.estateromana.it. Events including concerts and cultural happenings – many of them free – in parks and piazzas around town. June–Sept.

La Festa di Noantri Piazza Santa Maria in Trastevere and around. Trastevere's traditional summer festival in honour of the Virgin, with street stalls selling snacks and trinkets, and a grand finale of fireworks. Last two weeks of July.

Enzimi ⓦwww.enzimi.com. A free music and arts festival featuring off-beat performers in unusual locations. Two weeks in mid-Sept.

RomaEuropa Festival ⓦwww.romaeuropa.net. A cutting-edge performing arts festival, generally with some big-name acts, in locations around town. Sept–Nov.

.com), while the **opera scene** is concentrated on the Teatro dell'Opera, Piazza B. Gigli in winter (ⓣ06.4816.0255, ⓦwww.opera.roma.it) and various outdoor venues in summer. **Cinemas** that show films in English include the Nuovo Olimpia (Via in Lucina 16G, off Via del Corso), and the Metropolitan at Via del Corso 7. *RomaC'è,* a comprehensive listings guide (out Wed, €1), contains a short English section.

Shopping

Shops With the exception of the Galleria Alberto Sordi on Via del Corso, there are no malls, and few department stalls. The boutiques around Piazza di Spagna are for big-spenders only, but nearby Via del Corso is lined with shops selling cheap-to-mid-range clothing, books and CDs. Other mainstream outlets can be found along Via Cola di Rienzo near the Vatican, and Via Nazionale, off Piazza dela Repubblica. For one-off boutiques, try the side-streets of the centro storico; Via del Governo Vecchio off Piazza Navona has a string of great vintage stores, and the alleys off Campo de' Fiori harbour independent jewellery and clothing shops. The up-and-coming Monti district near the Colosseum is another haven of hip, independent boutiques.

Markets The sprawling flea market Porta Portese (see p.670) is the city's best-known, but Via Sannio (Mon–Fri 8.30am–1.30pm, Sat 8.30am–6pm; metro San Giovanni) is also a great place to find vintage bargains, as well as designer knock-offs, jewellery and accessories.

Directory

Embassies Australia, Via Antonio Bosio 5 ⓣ06.852.721; Canada, Via Salaria 243 ⓣ06.854.441; New Zealand, Via Zara 28 ⓣ06.441.7171; UK, Via XX Settembre 80 ⓣ06.4220.0001; US, Via V. Veneto 119 ⓣ06.46.741.

Exchange Offices at Termini station operate out of banking hours; also Cambio Rosati, Via Nazionale 186 ⓣ06.488.5498.

Hospitals Ambulance ⓣ118; central hospital: Policlinico Umberto I ⓣ06.49.971; International Medical Center ⓣ06.488.2371.

Internet EasyEverything (Via Barberini 2; daily 8am–2am; €3/hr).

Left luggage At Termini station.

Pharmacies PIRAM, Via Nazionale 228 (24hr), near Termini. Rota posted on pharmacy doors.

Police Emergencies ⓣ113; main police station (*questura*) at Via S. Vitale ⓣ06.4686.

Post office Piazza San Silvestro 19 (Mon–Sat 8am–7pm).

Moving on

Air National carrier Alitalia (ⓦwww.alitalia.com) flies to many Italian cities, including Milan (6 daily; 1hr 10min); Naples (3 daily; 55min), Palermo (6 daily; 1hr 10min) and Venice (3 daily; 1hr). Budget airline Ryanair (ⓦwww.ryanair.com) operates flights to Venice (2 daily; 1hr).

Train Bologna (every 15min; 2hr 40min); Florence (every 15min; 1hr 30min); Milan (hourly; 4hr 30min); Naples (every 30min; 2hr); Paris (5 daily; 13-15hr); Vienna (5 daily; 12-17hr); Zurich (6 daily; 8hr 20min-14hr).

Bus Agrigento (1 daily; 13hr 30min); Amalfi (summer 1–2 daily; 4hr); Lecce (3 daily; 8hr 30min); Palermo (1daily; 12hr 30min); Sorrento (2 daily; 4hr); services run by Marozzi.

Northwest Italy

While the northwest of Italy is many people's first experience of the country, it often represents its least stereotypically "Italian" aspect. **Turin** is the obvious initial stop, the first capital of Italy after the Unification in 1860 and a vibrant city with many reminders of its past. **Milan**, the upbeat capital of **Lombardy**, continues to be taken seriously for its business and fashion credentials, but has an atypically stressful atmosphere. Lombardy's landscape has paid the price for economic success: industry chokes the peripheries of towns, the northern lakes and mountain valleys. Nonetheless, towns such as **Mantua** and **Verona** continue to attract visitors for their literary credentials and evocative architecture and settings. The region of **Liguria** to the south has perhaps the country's most spectacular stretch of coastline. The chief town of the province is the sprawling port of **Genoa**, while southeast, towards **Tuscany**, stretches like the **Cinque Terre** continue to wow travellers with their cliff-top villages and clear blue waters.

TURIN

Following the 2006 Winter Olympics, **TURIN** (Torino) – a virtual Fiat company town and the home of Martini and Lavazza coffee – has emerged resplendent with gracious avenues, opulent palaces and splendid galleries. It's a lively, bustling place with cafés, nightlife and contemporary art to rival any European city.

What to see and do

The grid plan of the Baroque centre makes finding your way around easy. **Via Roma** is the central spine, a grand affair lined with designer shops and ritzy cafés and punctuated by the city's most elegant piazzas, notably **Piazza San Carlo**. Around the corner, the **Museo Egizio** (Tues–Sun 8.30am–7.30pm; Ⓦwww.museoegizio.org; €6.50) holds a superb collection of Egyptian antiquities. A ten-minute walk northwest brings you to the fifteenth-century **Duomo**, home of the Turin Shroud, which is usually kept under wraps. This piece of cloth, imprinted with the image of a man's body, had long been claimed as the shroud in which Christ was wrapped after his crucifixion, although 1989 carbon-dating tests suggested that it was a medieval fake, made between 1260 and 1390.

The **Palazzo Madama**, imposing over **Piazza Castello**, is architecturally stunning, and has a collection of Baroque, Gothic, Renaissance and decorative art on show (Ⓦwww.palazzomadamatorino.it; free). East of Via Roma, the **Mole Antonelliana**, which Turin residents proudly call the Eiffel Tower of Turin, boasts great views over the city from the top of its panoramic lift (Mon–Fri & Sun 9am–8pm, Sat 9am–11pm; €4, €6 including museum). The **Museo Nazionale del Cinema** is on its lower floors (same times as Mole Antonelliana; Ⓦwww.museocinema.it; €4, €6 including lift).

Museums

Turin has a good selection of modern art museums, the best of which is the **GAM** on Via Magenta 31 (Tues–Sun 9am–7pm; Ⓦwww.gamtorino.it; €6), with works from the eighteenth century to the present day by artists such as Giorgio de Chirico and Lucio Fontana. For more contemporary art, the **Castello di Rivoli**, 20km outside Turin (Tues–Sun 10am–5pm; Ⓦwww.castellodirivoli.org; €6.50), is home to the most important collection of postwar art in Italy, with works by Jeff Koons, Carl Andre and Mario Merz. On weekdays, take bus #36 from Piazza Statuto and then walk for twenty minutes; at weekends, there's an (infrequent) direct shuttle bus from Piazza Castello.

Arrival and information

Air Take the train to Turino Dora (€5.50, every 30min). From there bus #52 goes to Porta Nuova. During peak summer months, a train runs straight to Porta Nuova but its timetable is fairly erratic – ask in the station for more information.
Train Turin's main train station is Porta Nuova.
Tourist office The main office is located in the Atrium built for the 2006 Winter Olympics at Piazza Solferino (Mon–Sun 9.30am–7pm; Ⓣ011.535.181, Ⓦwww.turismotorino.org).There is a smaller centre at Porta Nuova train station (Mon–Sat 9.30am–7pm, Sun 9.30am–3pm).
Discount passes The Torino Card (€15/two days, €17/three days) covers travel on all buses, entrance to all museums and discounts on theatre and concert tickets.
Internet Internet Train, Via Carlo Alberto 18, or 28 Via delle Orfane, also has cheap international calls (Internet €2/hr).
Post office Via San Domenico 19.

Accommodation

Many of Turin's budget hotels are in the sleazy area off Via Nizza. The streets opposite Porta Nuova, close to Piazza Carlo Felice, are more expensive but

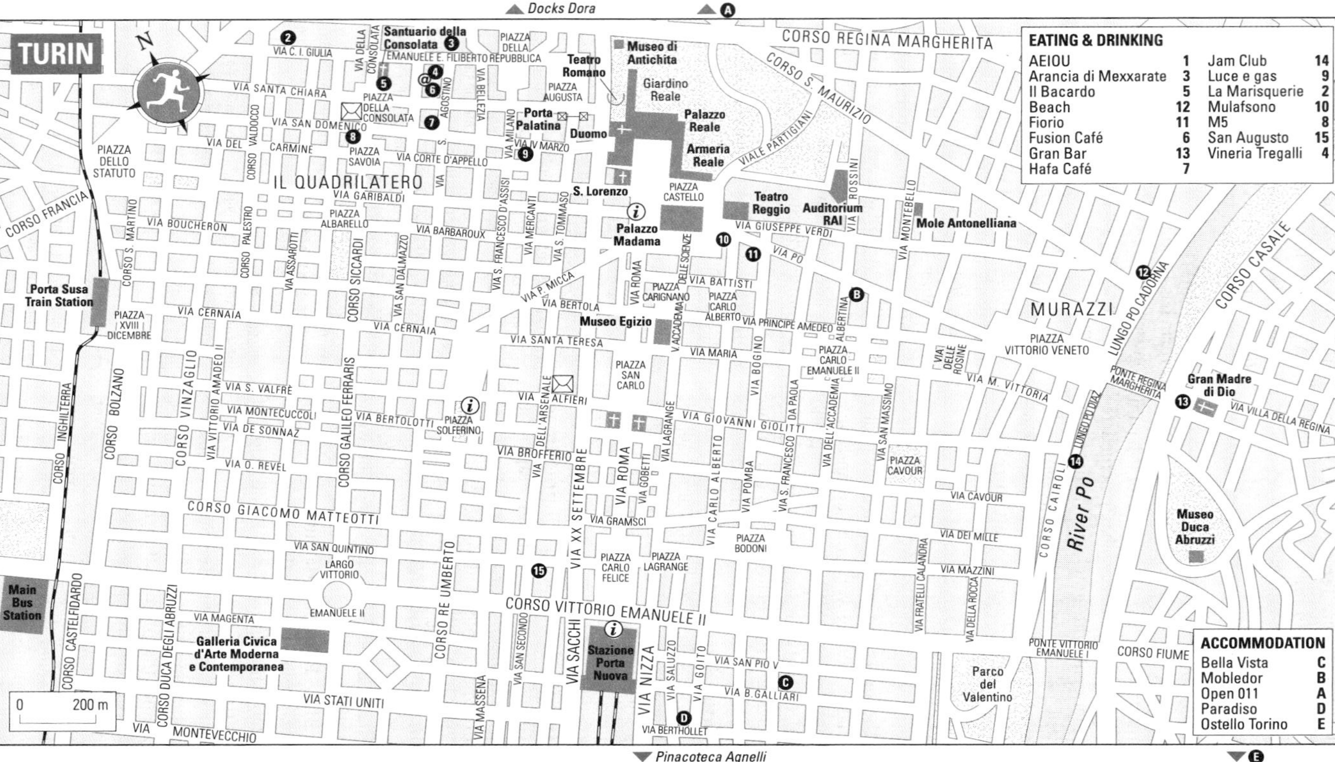
TURIN
EATING & DRINKING
AEIOU 1
Arancia di Mexxarate 3
Il Bacardo 5
Beach 12
Fiorio 11
Fusion Café 6
Gran Bar 13
Hafa Café 7
Jam Club 14
Luce e gas 9
La Marisquerie 2
Mulafsono 10
M5 8
San Augusto 15
Vineria Tregalli 4
ACCOMMODATION
Bella Vista C
Mobledor B
Open 011 A
Paradiso D
Ostello Torino E
Docks Dora
Pinacoteca Agnelli
Santuario della Consolata
Museo di Antichita
Teatro Romano
Giardino Reale
Palazzo Reale
Armeria Reale
Porta Palatina
Duomo
S. Lorenzo
Palazzo Madama
Teatro Reggio
Auditorium RAI
Mole Antonelliana
Museo Egizio
Gran Madre di Dio
Museo Duca Abruzzi
Parco del Valentino
Stazione Porta Nuova
Porta Susa Train Station
Main Bus Station
Galleria Civica d'Arte Moderna e Contemporanea
IL QUADRILATERO
MURAZZI
River Po
CORSO REGINA MARGHERITA
CORSO S. MAURIZIO
VIALE PARTIGIANI
CORSO CASALE
LUNGO PO CADORNA
PONTE REGINA MARGHERITA
VIA VILLA DELLA REGINA
PIAZZA VITTORIO VENETO
LUNGO PO DIAZ
CORSO CAIROLI
PONTE VITTORIO EMANUELE I
CORSO FIUME
CORSO VITTORIO EMANUELE II
CORSO GIACOMO MATTEOTTI
CORSO RE UMBERTO
CORSO GALILEO FERRARIS
CORSO VINZAGLIO
CORSO BOLZANO
CORSO INGHILTERRA
CORSO CASTELFIDARDO
CORSO FRANCIA
CORSO SICCARDI
CORSO PALESTRO
CORSO VALDOCCO
CORSO S. MARTINO
CORSO DUCA DEGLI ABRUZZI
VIA STATI UNITI
VIA MONTEVECCHIO
VIA MAGENTA
LARGO VITTORIO EMANUELE II
VIA SAN QUINTINO
VIA XX SETTEMBRE
VIA ROMA
VIA SACCHI
VIA NIZZA
VIA PO
VIA GIUSEPPE VERDI
VIA GARIBALDI
VIA CERNAIA
PIAZZA CASTELLO
PIAZZA SAN CARLO
PIAZZA CARLO FELICE
PIAZZA LAGRANGE
PIAZZA BODONI
PIAZZA CAVOUR
PIAZZA SOLFERINO
PIAZZA SAVOIA
PIAZZA DELLA CONSOLATA
PIAZZA DELLA REPUBBLICA
PIAZZA AUGUSTA
PIAZZA DELLO STATUTO
PIAZZA XVIII DICEMBRE
PIAZZA ALBARELLO
PIAZZA CARIGNANO
PIAZZA CARLO ALBERTO
PIAZZA CARLO EMANUELE II
0 200 m

more pleasant.
Bella Vista Via Galliari 15 ⓣ011.669.9121. Top floor hotel with big windows, generally populated by polite couples. ❺
Mobledor Via Accademia Albertina 1 ⓣ011.888.445. Small one-star in an excellent location. ❻
Open 011 Corso Venezia ⓣ011.250.535. Welcoming hostel with helpful staff and large, spotless rooms. Take the train from the airport to station Torino Dora, or get bus #46 (Dora stop), #52 (Viba stop) or #10 (the bus, not tram #10) from Porto Nuova station. ❷
Ostello Torino Via Alby 1 ⓣ011.660.2939. Inviting HI hostel with small rooms and Internet access; 30min walk from Porta Nuova or take bus #52. ❷
Paradiso Via Berthollet 3 ⓣ011.669.8678. Clean one-star hotel close to the train station with cheerful proprietors. ❹

Eating

Cafés

Il Bacardo Piazza della Consolata 1. A reasonably-priced restaurant with lovely outdoor seating, famed for its cakes.
Fiorio Via Po 8. The best ice cream in Turin.
Gran Bar Piazza Gran Madre di Dio 2. Cool wine and coffee bar, overlooking the river, with cheerful staff. Also serves delicious casual food. Mains from €5.
Mulafsono Piazza Castello 15. Tiny *fin-de-siècle* café, with wood panelling and cakes served on tiered trays.

Restaurants

La Marisquerie Via Carlo Iulius Giulio 4g ⓣ333.479.0538. Excellent fish at reasonable prices. Mains around €11.
San Augusto Via San Quintino. Famed as the best pizzeria in Turin, with a huge range and outdoor seating. The menu includes delicacies such as flaky pastry with artichokes and *taleggio* cheese fondue, €8.
Vineria Tregalli San Agostino 25. Decent, airy restaurant with huge wine selection. Pasta €8.

> TREAT YOURSELF
>
> **Luce e gas** Via IV Marzo 12, ⓣ011.436.5483, ⓦwww.luceegas.it. Chic restaurant serving fragrant and well-prepared Italian and fusion food, presided over by a giant golden Buddha, with friendly staff. Mains around €18.

Drinking and nightlife

The **liveliest areas**, especially in the summer, are Il Quadrilatero, a few minutes west of Piazza Castello, Via San Quintino, and the Murazzi on the edge of the River Po, where people congregate at outside tables. Beware of pickpockets in this area – on popular nights it is full of police. Student night is Thurs. For what's on, look out for the pamphlet *Zero*, free from bars.

Bars

The standard price for drinks is around €6 for cocktails and €3–5 for beers.
Arancia di Mexxarate Piazza Emmanuelle Filiberto. Buzzy place with tables crammed together outside, invariably packed with gesticulating young Turinese making a lot of noise and having a good time. Serves drinks until 4am.
Fusion Café San Agostino 17. Cocktails and snacks, with outdoor seating and atmospheric lighting.
Hafa Café San Agostino 23. Chilled-out bar with Turkish-style interior and nargila.
M5 Via San Domenico 14–16. Funky and noisy. Features different DJs every night.

Clubs

> **APERITIF TIME**
>
> When you're strapped for cash but want to have a good time, it's worth remembering that between about 6pm and 9pm, most bars either bring you **snacks** or have an aperitif buffet if you buy a drink. These snacks are often substantial enough to fill you up, so you'll be able to save on buying dinner!

AEIOU Via Spanzotti 3 ⓣ011.385.8580. Big warehouse-style club for dancing all night; features rock, Cuban, jam sessions, art and theatre projects. Entrance usually free.
The Beach Arcate Murazzi del Po. One of the coolest clubs in Italy; Tuesday is "Socrates night" featuring music and drinks from a different country each week. Entrance €5. Closes 5am.
Jam Club Arcate Murazzi del Po. An extensive club with a different DJ every night. Free entry for women until 12.30am, otherwise entrance €5; the

busy bar opposite overlooks the river.

Moving on

Train Genoa (every 30min; 1hr 50min); Geneva (every 2hr; 6hr); Milan (every 30min; 1hr 50min); Nice (every 45min; 4hr 45min); Venice (every 90min; 5hr).

MILAN

The dynamo behind the country's economic miracle, **MILAN** (Milano) is the capital of Italy's fashion and design industry, a fast-paced and somewhat unfriendly business city ruled by consumerism and the work ethic. The swanky shops and nightlife are a big draw, but it's a historic place too – the Gothic cathedral has few peers in Italy, while Leonardo da Vinci's iconic fresco of *The Last Supper* is an unmissable treat.

What to see and do

Piazza del Duomo

A good place to start a tour of Milan is **Piazza del Duomo**, the city's historic centre and home to the world's largest Gothic cathedral, the **Duomo**, begun in 1386 and not finished till almost five centuries later. The gloomy interior gives access to the cathedral's fourth-century **baptistery** (Tues–Sun 9.45am–12.45pm & 2–5.45pm; €1.50) and the **cathedral roof** (Tues–Sun 9am–5pm; €5 by elevator, €3.50 on foot), where you are surrounded by a forest of lacy Gothic carving and have superb views of the city. The **Museo del Duomo** (daily 10am–1.15pm & 3–6pm; €6) holds casts of a good many of the three thousand or so statues and gargoyles that spike the cathedral. On the north side of the piazza, the opulent **Galleria Vittorio Emanuele** is a cruciform glass-domed gallery designed in 1865 by Giuseppe Mengoni, who was killed when he fell from the roof a few days before the inaugural ceremony. The Galleria leads through to the world-famous eighteenth-century **La Scala** opera house.

Via Brera

La Scala sets the tone for the city's arty quarter, just to the north, with its fancy galleries and art shops. At its far end, Milan's most prestigious gallery, the awe-inspiring **Pinacoteca di Brera** (Tues–Sun 8.30am–7.30pm; €5), is filled with works looted from the churches and aristocratic collections of French-occupied Italy.

Castello Sforzesco

To the west, the **Castello Sforzesco** rises imperiously from the mayhem of **Foro Buonaparte**, laid out by Napoleon as part of a grand plan for the city. The castle houses the **Museo d'Arte Antica** and **Pinacoteca** (both Tues–Sun 9am–5.30pm; €3) – the former containing Michelangelo's *Rondanini Pietà,* the latter paintings by Vincenzo Foppa, the leading Milanese artist before Leonardo da Vinci.

Santa Maria delle Grazie and the Last Supper

South of the castle, the church of **Santa Maria delle Grazie** is the main attraction. A Gothic pile, partially rebuilt by Bramante (who added the massive dome), it is famous for its fresco of *The Last Supper* by Leonardo da Vinci, which covers one wall of the refectory. Advance booking is essential (call ⓣ02.8942.1146; viewing Tues–Sun 8am–7pm; €8).

Arrival and information

Air Of Milan's two airports, Linate is the closer, 7km from the city centre and connected by the airport bus to Stazione Centrale (every 30min, 6.05am–9.35pm; 20min; €2.50). There are also ordinary city buses (#73; €1) until around midnight from Linate to Piazza San Babila. The other airport, Malpensa, is 50km away towards Lago Maggiore, connected by train to Cadorna station (every

30min; €9) and by bus with Stazione Centrale (until 10.30pm; €5.50).
Train Most international trains pull in at the monumental Stazione Centrale, northeast of the centre on Piazza Duca d'Aosta (metro lines MM2 or MM3).
Bus Buses arrive at and depart from Piazza Castello, in front of the Castello Sforzesco.
Tourist office The main tourist office is at Stazione Centrale (Mon–Sat 9am–6pm, Sun 9am–1pm & 2–5pm; ⓣ02.7252.4301/2/3, ⓦwww.milanoinfotourist.com) and is tricky to find – go up the elevator to the second floor and it's on the right, through a neon-lit archway into what looks like a disused gallery. There's another at Via Marconi 1, off Piazza Duomo (daily 9am–1pm & 2–5pm; same number). Both have the ever-helpful free listings guide, *Milano Mese*, in Italian and English and the *Milan by Night* map, as well as the *Zero* listings guide, which is useful for event details.

City transport

Bus, metro and tram An efficient network of trams, buses and metro (stations denoted below as MM) runs 6am–midnight. There are interconnecting stations so you can change from metro onto overground and back.
Night bus These take over after the other options close, and run until 1am following the train routes, or until about 3am following alternative routes.
Tickets Tickets (normally valid 1hr 15min; €1) can be used for one journey only on the metro or as many bus and tram journeys as you can make in that time; alternatively buy a *blochetto* of ten tickets (€9.20), or a 24hr ticket (€3), valid on metro, tram and buses, from the Centrale or Duomo metro stations.

Accommodation

There are plenty of **one-star hotels**, mostly concentrated in the area around Stazione Centrale, and along Viale Vittorio Veneto and Corso Buenos Aires. When there is an "exposition" on (there are about 25 a year, lasting 2–3 days each) prices rocket.
ABC Hotel Via Molino delle Armi 12 ⓣ02.867.501, ⓦwww.abchotel.it. Amicable hotel with lovely sun terrace and free Internet. ⑦
ACISJF Corso Garibaldi 121 ⓣ02.2900.0164. Hostel run by nuns and open to women under 25 only. Accommodation is in four-bedded rooms. ③
Arno Via Lazzaretto 17 ⓣ02.670.5509. Friendly one-star near the station, run by the helpful Patrizio. Free Internet access; packed from March to July. ⑥
La Cordata Casa Scout Via Burigozzo 11, ⓣ02.5831.4675, ⓔostello@lacordata.it. Well-equipped hostel with kitchen, free Internet and no curfew. ③
Eva Via Lazzaretto 17 ⓣ02.670.6093. Basic one-star hotel near the station, next door to the Arno. ⑦
Kennedy Viale Tunisia 6 ⓣ02.2940.0934, ⓦwww.kennedyhotel.it. Clean, light family-run one-star hotel close to the station. ⑥
Piero Rotta HI Hostel Via Martino Bassi 2 ⓣ02.3926.7095, ⓦwww.ostellionline.org. Though in a red-light district, this huge hostel is comfortable inside. Large beers available for €3, or from the bakery down the road for €1.70. No curfew, check out 10am. Metro QT8 then a 7min walk down Via a Salmoiraghi. ③
Valley Via Soperga 19 ⓣ02.669.2777. Clean, family-run one-star hotel very close to the station. ⑦

Eating

Cafés and food markets

Crota Piemunteisa Piazza Beccaria 10. A vast array of chunky sandwiches for around €4.40.
Grand Italia Via Palermo 5. Cheaper for pizza than La Bruschetta (see below) and just as good.
MAG Ripa di Porta Ticinese 43. Trendy coffee and sandwich bar looking out over the canal.
Princi Via Speronari ⓦwww.princi.it. Chain of bakeries selling fresh pastries and breads by the kilo. The delicious breads are baked in huge stone ovens on-site, and the smell and sheer choice on offer is phenomenal. With standing room around small, trendy tables in the minimalist stone interior. €24 per kg or €1–2 per brioche.

Restaurants

La Bruschetta Piazza Beccaria 12. One of the best-known city-centre pizzerias, though you'll have to wait for a table. Pizza €8.
Al Cantinone Via Agnello 19. Famous old trattoria and bar, with home-made pasta and some choice wines, frequented by city suits at lunchtime. Pastas €5, mains €6.
Circolo del Liberty Via Savona 20. Eccentric, intimate restaurant run by a talkative Neapolitan. Pasta €7.
Cozzeria Via Lodovico Muratori 7. Mussels by the kilo; also does a delicious lemon and *peperoncino* sorbet. Mussels with chips €14.
Slice Café Via Ascanio Sforza 9. Funky bar with leopard-print sofas on the waterfront; 6–9.30pm all you can eat buffet (including pastas, pizzas and salads) with a drink for €7. Beware – after this, prices rise considerably.

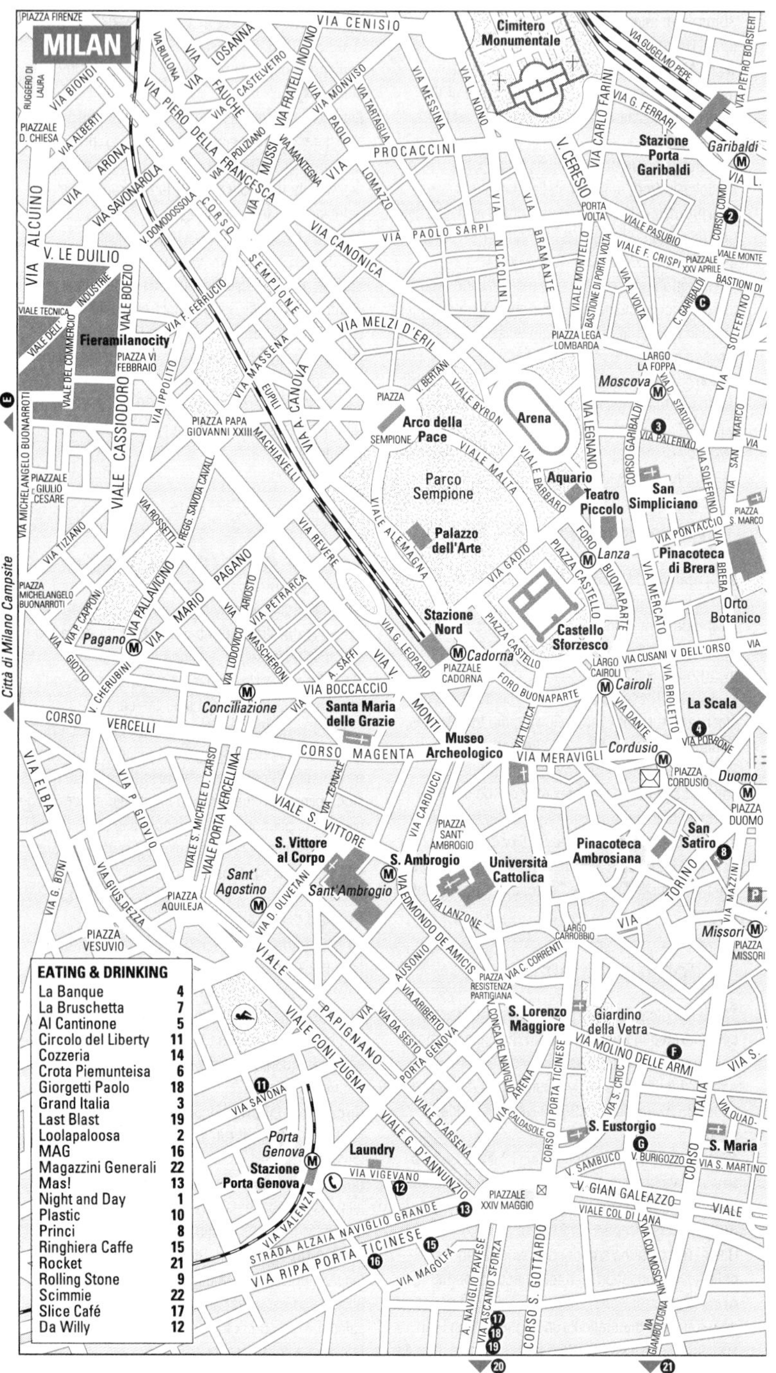
MILAN
Città di Milano Campsite
Cimitero Monumentale
Stazione Porta Garibaldi
Garibaldi
Fieramilanocity
Arco della Pace
Arena
Parco Sempione
Palazzo dell'Arte
Aquario
Teatro Piccolo
San Simpliciano
Pinacoteca di Brera
Orto Botanico
Stazione Nord
Cadorna
Castello Sforzesco
Lanza
Moscova
Cairoli
La Scala
Cordusio
Duomo
Pagano
Conciliazione
Santa Maria delle Grazie
Museo Archeologico
S. Vittore al Corpo
S. Ambrogio
Sant'Ambrogio
Sant' Agostino
Università Cattolica
Pinacoteca Ambrosiana
San Satiro
Missori
S. Lorenzo Maggiore
Giardino della Vetra
S. Eustorgio
S. Maria
Porta Genova
Stazione Porta Genova
Laundry
PIAZZA FIRENZE
VIA CENISIO
VIA PIERO DELLA FRANCESCA
VIA PAOLO SARPI
VIA CANONICA
VIA MELZI D'ERIL
VIALE ALEMAGNA
CORSO VERCELLI
CORSO MAGENTA
VIA MERAVIGLI
VIA BOCCACCIO
VIALE CONI ZUGNA
VIALE D'ARSENA
VIA VIGEVANO
VIA RIPA PORTA TICINESE
ALZAIA NAVIGLIO GRANDE
CORSO DI PORTA TICINESE
CORSO S. GOTTARDO
CORSO ITALIA
VIA TORINO
V. GIAN GALEAZZO
PIAZZALE XXIV MAGGIO
EATING & DRINKING
La Banque 4
La Bruschetta 7
Al Cantinone 5
Circolo del Liberty 11
Cozzeria 14
Crota Piemunteisa 6
Giorgetti Paolo 18
Grand Italia 3
Last Blast 19
Loolapaloosa 2
MAG 16
Magazzini Generali 22
Mas! 13
Night and Day 1
Plastic 10
Princi 8
Ringhiera Caffe 15
Rocket 21
Rolling Stone 9
Scimmie 22
Slice Café 17
Da Willy 12

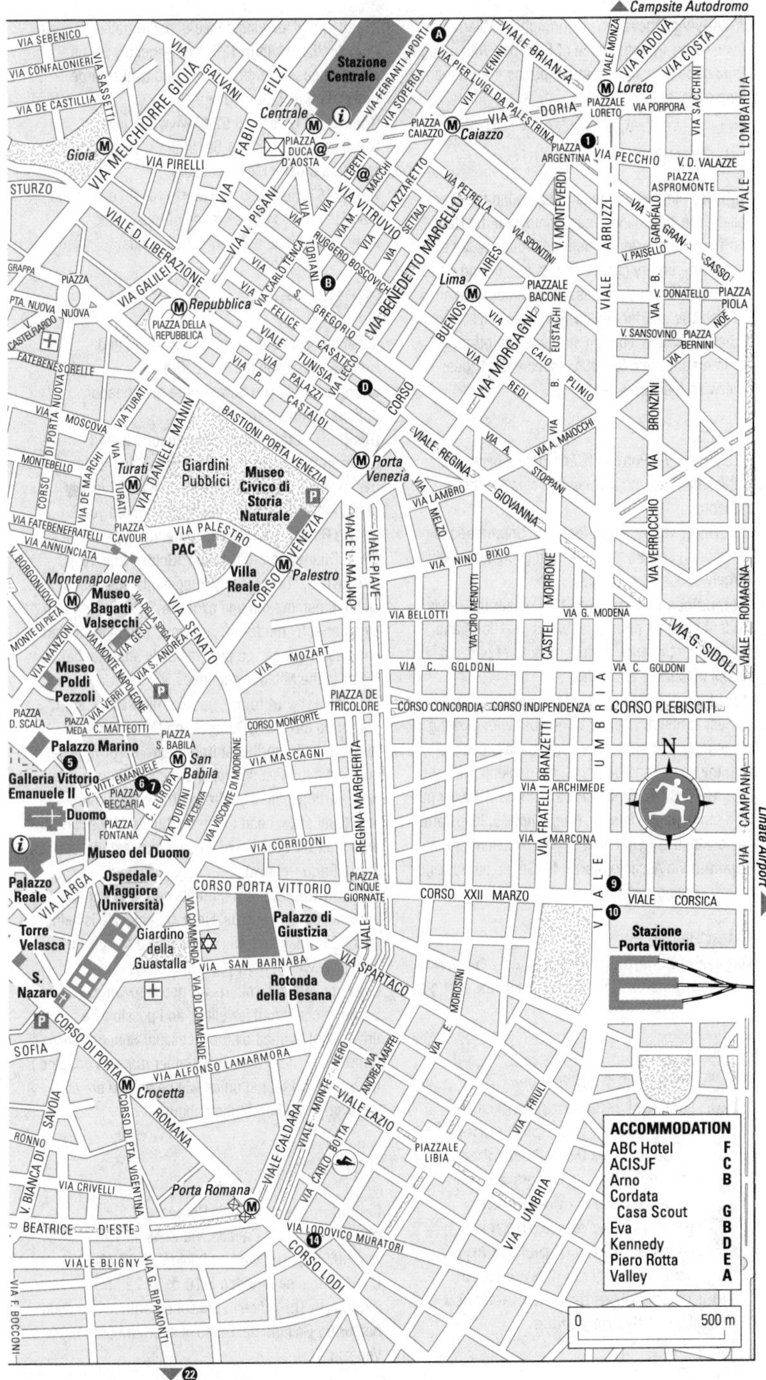
Campsite Autodromo
Stazione Centrale
Centrale
Piazza Duca d'Aosta
Loreto
Piazzale Loreto
Piazza Caiazzo
Caiazzo
Piazza Argentina
Gioia
Repubblica
Piazza della Repubblica
Lima
Piazzale Bacone
Piazza Piola
Piazza Bernini
Piazza Aspromonte
Porta Venezia
Turati
Giardini Pubblici
Museo Civico di Storia Naturale
PAC
Villa Reale
Palestro
Piazza Cavour
Montenapoleone
Museo Bagatti Valsecchi
Museo Poldi Pezzoli
Piazza D. Scala
Piazza Meda
Palazzo Marino
Galleria Vittorio Emanuele II
Piazza S. Babila
San Babila
Piazza Beccaria
Duomo
Piazza Fontana
Museo del Duomo
Palazzo Reale
Ospedale Maggiore (Università)
Torre Velasca
S. Nazaro
Giardino della Guastalla
Palazzo di Giustizia
Rotonda della Besana
Piazza de Tricolore
Piazza Cinque Giornate
Stazione Porta Vittoria
Linate Airport
Crocetta
Porta Romana
Piazzale Libia
Via Melchiorre Gioia
Viale D. Liberazione
Via Vitruvio
Via Benedetto Marcello
Via Morgagni
Corso Buenos Aires
Viale Abruzzi
Viale Regina Giovanna
Bastioni Porta Venezia
Corso Venezia
Via Daniele Manin
Viale Piave
Viale L. Majno
Via Senato
Corso Concordia
Corso Indipendenza
Corso Plebisciti
Viale Umbria
Corso XXII Marzo
Viale Corsica
Corso Porta Vittoria
Via Larga
Corso di Porta Romana
Viale Monte Nero
Viale Lazio
Viale Caldara
Corso Lodi
Via Lodovico Muratori
Viale Bligny
Via G. Ripamonti
Corso di Pta. Vigentina
Via Beatrice d'Este
Corso Monforte
Via Mascagni
Via Corridoni
Via Spartaco
Via Alfonso Lamarmora
ACCOMMODATION
ABC Hotel F
ACISJF C
Arno B
Cordata Casa Scout G
Eva B
Kennedy D
Piero Rotta E
Valley A
0 500 m

Da Willy Via Vigevano 7 or throughout Milan Ⓦwww.dawilly.com. Chain of Pizzerias with a huge range of delicious, gargantuan pizzas from a roaring stone oven, at €6.

Drinking and nightlife

Nightlife centres on the streets around the Brera gallery, the club-filled Corso Como, and the Navigli and Ticinese quarters, clustered around Milan's thirteenth-century canals. Drinks are around €4 for a beer and €7 for cocktails. On summer weekends, the Ticinese quarters fill up with beer stalls, offering a cheaper option. Foreign students can often get free admission to clubs, especially on Tues: otherwise fees are €5–15.

Bars

La Banque Via Porrone 6. Formerly a bank, this fashionable bar and nightspot is close to the cathedral.

Last Blast Via Ascanio Sforza 15. Unpretentious bar serving snacks from €4, with good live music (largely acoustic) every day.

Loolapaloosa Corso Como 15. Popular pub-style student hangout offering aperitifs (5–10pm) and solid tables to dance on to a mixture of pop, old-school favourites and Latin.

Mas! Ripa di P. Ta Ticinese 11 Ⓦwww.mas-milano.it. Fusion restaurant and trendy bar with glowing red interior and outdoor seating, usually packed with the young and beautiful, overlooking the canal.

Ringhiera Caffe Ripa di P. La Ticinese 5. Lively pub with atmospheric interior. Happy hour 5.30–10pm. All cocktails are €5, and it serves excellent crêpes.

Scimmie Via Ascanio Sforza 49. Small, buzzy venue mainly hosting jazz.

Clubs

Magazzini Generali Via Pietrasanta 14 Ⓦwww.magazzinigenerali.it. Huge warehouse attracting a mixed crowd, playing dance and alternative sounds.

Plastic Viale Umbria 120. A gay-friendly venue playing house, electronic, pop and avant-garde music: Friday is Britpop night.

Rocket Via G Pezzotti 52 Ⓦwww.therocket.it. Small and trendy disco-bar in the Ticinese area, a favourite among Milan clubbers.

Rolling Stone Corso XXII Marzo 32. An enormous place that plays a wide range of music, and sometimes hosts big-name rock bands.

TREAT YOURSELF

The season at **La Scala** (Ⓣ02.860.775, Ⓦwww.teatroallascala.org), one of the world's most prestigious opera houses, runs from December to July. Although seats are expensive and can sell out months in advance, there is often a chance of picking up a seat in the gods (from €25) an hour or so before a performance, by heading to the box office.

Shopping

Milan has some of the most expensive and exclusive shops in the world. But if the **window-shopping** gets you down, there are cheaper options around town.

Designer Corso Vittorio Emmanuel, running between Piazza Duomo and Piazza San Babila, has expensive brands, as well as a large variety of high-street names – this is also where you'll find La Rinascente, the monumental department store. Quadrilatero d'Oro (the "Golden Square"), meanwhile, houses every imaginable designer in a cloud of ostentation and expense. Being sneered at by a perfectly made-up, perfumed and high-heeled shop assistant as you peer inside is an essential factor in the Milan experience.

High street and boutiques For high-street stuff, Via Torino (off Piaza Duomo) and Corso Buenos Aires (running northeast from metro Porta Venezia), one of the longest shopping streets in Europe, are well worth a look. If you're interested in a more individual style, head to the boutiques of the Navigli area in the southwest of the city (nearest station metro Porto Genova).

Flea markets Milan's markets can be great for unusual, cut-price finds. Fiera di Senigallia is held every Saturday morning on Viale G. d'Annunzio, along the wharf; here you'll find all types and ages of clothes, furniture, art nouveau lamps, books, records and jewellery, and possibly be driven slightly mad by the incessant Senegalese drumming. There are always other markets popping up, which the tourist office will be able to provide you with more information about.

Directory

Consulates Australia, Via Borgogna 2 Ⓣ02.7770.4217; Canada, Via V. Pisani 19 Ⓣ02.67.581; UK, Via San Paolo 7 Ⓣ02.723.001; US, Via Principe Amedeo 2/10 Ⓣ02.290.351.

Exchange The office in Stazione Centrale is a good bet, or try Galleria del Corso, just off the Corso Venezia.

A DAY TRIP TO LAKE COMO

Trains leave for Como San Giovanni every hour, and take 35min. The lake itself is a 10min walk straight out of the station. You can take a boat trip, or enjoy a stroll around the relaxed, pretty town and surrounding area – maybe looking out for Como's most well-known resident, George Clooney. To take a picnic to the waterside, try Como's well-stocked deli *Casa del Parimgiano* at Via Giuseppe Garibaldi 49.

Hospitals Fatebenefratelli, Corso Porta Nuova 23 ⓣ02.63.631; Ospedale Maggiore Policlinico, Via Francesco Sforza 35 ⓣ02.55.031.
Internet If you're looking for somewhere by the station, try Piazza D'Aosta 14 (Mon–Sat 9am–10pm; €5.60/hr). However, for somewhere cheaper, try the anonymous place two doors down Via Roberto Petit (Mon–Sat 9am–6pm; €3/hr).
Laundry Via Vigevano 20, near Porta Genova; or 7 Corso Plebisciti, near Dateo overground station.
Left luggage Stazione Central (€3/first 3hr). Bags must be under 20kg.
Pharmacy 24hr at Stazione Centrale.
Police Via Montebello ⓣ02.62.261.
Post office Piazza Cordusio 2, or right outside the Stazione, in the middle of Piazza d'Aosta.

Moving on

Air Rome (6 daily; 1hr 10min).
Train Bologna (every 20min; 2hr); Geneva (every 2hr; 4hr 30min); Lyon (4 daily; 7hr); Mantua (every 2hr; 2hr); Rome (hourly; 4hr 30min); Venice (every 30min; 3hr); Vienna (3 daily; 12hr); Zagreb (1 daily; 10hr 15min); Zurich (hourly; 3hr 45min).

MANTUA

Surrounded on three sides by the Mincio river, the tiny city of **MANTUA** (Mantova) lies between the cities of Verona (Verona native Romeo was exiled to Mantua in Shakespeare's tragedy) and Parma. It is undeniably evocative – the birthplace of Vergil and scene of Verdi's *Rigoletto* and with a history of equally operatic plots, most of them perpetrated by the Gonzagas, who ruled the town for three centuries and left two splendid palaces.

What to see and do

The town centres on four interlinking squares. **Piazza Mantegna** is dominated by the **church of Sant'Andrea**; opposite this, sunk below the present level of the busy **Piazza dell'Erbe**, is Mantua's oldest church, the beautiful eleventh-century **Rotonda**, still containing traces of its early medieval frescoes. The dark underpassage beneath the red-brick **Broletto**, the medieval town hall, leads into **Piazza Broletto**, beyond which the sombre **Piazza Sordello** is flanked by the Baroque **Duomo** and the **Palazzo Ducale** (Tues–Sun 8.45am–7.15pm; €6.50, bookings essential on ⓣ041.241.1897), an enormous complex that was once the largest palace in Europe. When it was sacked by the Habsburgs in 1630 eighty carriages were needed to carry the two thousand works of art contained in its five hundred rooms. It now contains works by Mantegna and Rubens and a trompe l'oeil garden. Mantua's other main sight, the extraordinary **Palazzo Te**, on the opposite side of town (Mon 1–6.30pm, Tues–Sun 9am–6.30pm; €10), was designed for Federico Gonzaga and his mistress Isabella Boschetta by Giulio Romano. Its weird and wonderful rooms include the Sala dei Giganti, in which the painted destruction of the giants by the gods appears to come crashing down from above.

Arrival and information

Train The city centre is a 10min walk from the train station down Via Solferino.
Tourist office Around the corner from Sant'Andrea (Mon–Sat 8.30am–12.30pm & 3–6pm, Sun 9.30am–12.30pm; ⓣ0376.328.253, ⓦwww.aptmantova.it).
Internet Rehoboth, Via Bettinelli 21. Mon–Sat 9am– 7pm. €2/hr.

Accommodation

Mantua is sorely lacking in budget accommodation – those who object to staying in three-star hotels are better off staying in Verona or Parma and coming here for the day. The **tourist office** can also provide a list of B&Bs (around ❼).

ABC Piazza Don Leoni 25 ⓣ0376.323.347, ⓦwww.hotelabcmantova.it. Large hotel with an airy breakfast-space and plenty of rooms. ❼

Hotel Apollo Piazza Don Leoni 17 ⓣ0376.328.0207. Pleasant three-star with buffet breakfast, whose friendly staff will regale you with stories about working on the London Underground. ❼

Marago Villanova de Bellis 2 ⓣ0376.370.313, ⓦwww.ristorantemarago.com. Basic but comfortable hotel 3km away in Virgiliana. Take bus #25. ❻

Verde Blu Viale Podgoro 2a ⓣ0376.360.398, ⓦwww.verdeblumantova.com. Charming bed and breakfast with friendly owners, 10min walk from the town centre. ❼

Eating

Cafés and food markets

Chiosco Viola Via Giacomo Matteoti. A cheap snack kiosk with glorified, candlelit and very pleasant outdoor-seating. Paninis €3.

Maison du Chocolat Via Oberdan 8. Serves everything a chocaholic could wish for, including incredible chocolate ice cream in four different sizes.

Punto Supermarket on the corner of Via Battista Spaguoli.

Restaurants

Leoncino Rosso Via Giustiziati 33. Old-fashioned, cosy and laid-back restaurant. Pasta €6.

Osteria delle Erbe Piazza Erbe 16 ⓣ0376.225.880. Not cheap, but with a fantastic location on a gorgeous square, and local specialities such as potato and bean stew and local sausage with polenta. Mains €14.

MOO – BOOST YOUR CALCIUM INTAKE!

La Latteria Fiorina A milk-vending machine, selling milk at €1 per litre (empty bottles are €0.20). Under the bridge by Piazza Sordeli.

Quattrotette da Angelo Vicolo Nazione 4. Open lunchtime daily Mon–Sat, plus evenings Wed–Fri 7–9.30pm. A basic, crowded place (literally, "four tits") that draws a loyal local clientele. Pasta €7.

Drinking and nightlife

Café la Havana Corso Vittorio Emmanuelle 15. Tiny, smoky Cuban bar. Beers €3. Open until 2am.

Libenter Piazza Concordia 18 ⓣ0376.324.064, Trendy, low-lit *osteria* in a beautiful square with DJs and an English-speaking owner. Beer €4.

La Pupitre Viale Gorizia 34, Via Accademia. Great, friendly place for coffees, aperitifs and snacks. Beer €4.

GENOA

GENOA (Genova) has retained its reputation as a tough, cosmopolitan port and combines the beauty of Renaissance palaces with the menace of narrow alleys and dingy corners. It was one of the five Italian maritime republics, and reached the height of its power in the fifteenth and sixteenth centuries. After a long period of economic decline, Genoa is gradually being cleaned up, and the city now offers an interesting mix of ultra-modern architecture and amenities, and old-style streets and eateries.

What to see and do

Genoa spreads outwards from its old town around the port in a confusion of tiny alleyways and old palaces. Its people speak a near-impenetrable dialect – a mixture of Neapolitan, Calabrese and Portuguese.

Palazzo Ducale

From 1384 to 1515, except for brief periods of foreign domination, the doges ruled the city from the ornate, stuccoed **Palazzo Ducale** in Piazza Matteotti (Tues–Sun 10am–7pm; ⓦwww.palazzoducale.genova.it; €4).

Cattedrale di San Lorenzo

Close by, the Gothic **Cattedrale di San Lorenzo** is home to the Renaissance

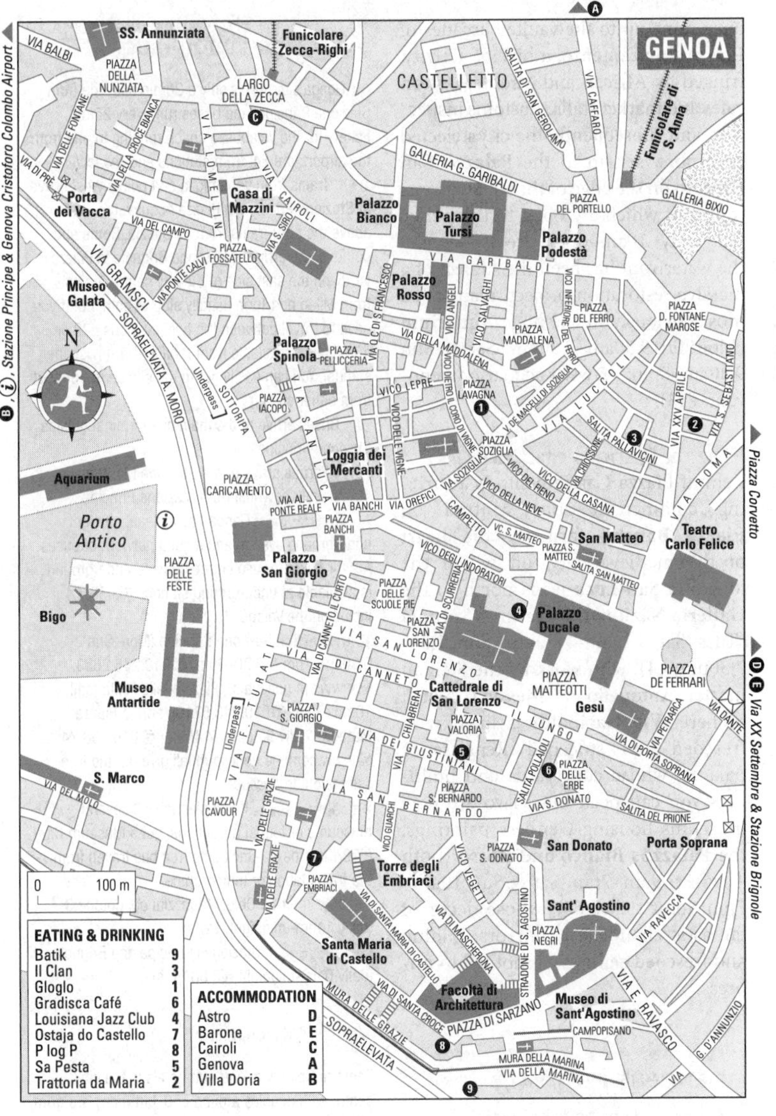

chapel of St John the Baptist, whose remains once rested in the thirteenth-century sarcophagus. After a particularly bad storm, priests carried his casket through the city to placate the sea, and a commemorative procession takes place each June 24 to honour him. His reliquary is in the **treasury** (tours Mon–Sat 9am–noon & 3–6pm; €5.50), along with a polished quartz plate on which, legend says, Salome received his severed head.

The waterfront

Down on the waterfront, ruined by a hideous concrete overpass, the sea once came up to the vaulted arcades of **Piazza Caricamento**, a hive of activity, fringed by African and Middle Eastern cafés and market stalls. Customs inspectors, and subsequently the city's elected governors, set up in the **Palazzo San Giorgio** on the edge of the square, some rooms of which are open to the public (Sat only 10am–6pm; free). Beyond, the waterfront has been the subject of a massive restoration project, manifested most obviously in the huge **Aquarium** (Mon–Fri 9.30am–7.30pm, Sat & Sun 9.30am–8pm; Ⓦwww.acquariodigenova.it; €13).

Piazza Banchi and around

Behind Piazza Caricamento is a thriving commercial zone centred on **Piazza Banchi**, formerly the heart of the medieval city, off which the long **Via San Luca** leads north to the **Galleria Nazionale di Palazzo Spinola** (Tues–Sat 8.30am–7.30pm, Sun 1.30–7.30pm; €4), with work by the Sicilian master Antonello da Messina. North of here, **Via Garibaldi** is lined with frescoed and stuccoed Renaissance palaces, whose courtyards and buildings you can peek into. Two are now museums housing Genoese paintings: the **Palazzos Bianco and Rosso** (both Tues–Fri 9am–7pm, Sat & Sun 10am–7pm; joint ticket €7), whose decor of fantastic chandeliers, mirrors, gilding and frescoed ceilings cannot fail to impress.

GENOESE FESTIVALS

A lively and cosmopolitan city, Genoa holds innumerable festivals with free events throughout the year. The summer is a particularly busy time, with a line-up including the Tango Festival, Film Festival, Tall Ships Races and Mediterranean Music Festival. Dates vary, so check out events at Ⓦwww.comune.genova.it.

Arrival and information

Air Genoa's airport is only a 20min bus-ride from Stazione Principe, and buses run every 25min; tickets for the Volabus, a coach running to and from the airport, are €4, from stations and *tabacchis*.

Train Trains from Ventimiglia and points west arrive at Stazione Principe in Piazza Acquaverde, just above the port; trains from La Spezia, Rome and points south arrive at Stazione Brignole in Piazza Verdi, on the east side of the city centre; trains from Milan and Turin usually stop at both, but if you have to travel between the two, take bus #28 or #33 (tickets available from *tabacchi* or newspaper stands). You can easily get to the city centre on foot from either station.

Bus Buses arrive at the main bus terminal outside Stazione Principe.

Ferry Ferries arrive at the Stazione Marittima, 10min walk downhill from Stazione Principe.

Public transport Genoa has a clean, efficient underground system and a good network of buses. A 24hr ticket for use on the bus and underground is available at underground stations (€3.50, €4 including the Volabus to the airport).

Tourist office Stazione Principe (Mon–Sun 9.30am–1pm & 2.30–6pm; ⓣ010.246.2633, Ⓦwww.apt.genova.it); Piazza delle Feste (daily 10am–7pm; ⓣ010.248.5710); and at Piazza Mateotti (daily 9.30am–7.45pm; ⓣ010.868.7452, Ⓦwww.comune.genova.it): all give out the free listings guide *Passport*.

Discount passes If you plan to visit several museums or tourist attractions, get a Museum Card (€29/three days – including free bus travel) from the train station or tourist office.

Internet Internet Oblo, Magazzini del Cotone 3 (daily 11am–midnight; €2/hr).

Left luggage At Staziones Principe and Brignole (daily 6am–midnight; €3.80/5hrs).

Accommodation

There are plenty of one-star hotels in the city centre with doubles around €50, but many are grim and depressing. **Good areas** to try are the roads bordering the old town, and Piazza Colombo and Via XX Settembre, near Stazione Brignole.

Astro Via XX Settembre 3/21 ⓣ010.481.533. Friendly one-star hotel, clean, if somewhat ramshackle, and very close to Stazione Brignole. ❺

Barone Via XX Settembre 2/23 ⓣ010.587.578. Small hotel with light rooms and welcoming owners, 200m from Stazione Brignole. ❺

Cairoli Via Cairoli 14/4 ⓣ010.246.1454, Ⓦwww.hotelcairoligenova.com. Pleasant, eclectically decorated two-star hotel, handy for the old town and Stazione Principe. Buses #18, #19, #20, #30 or #41 from Stazione Principe. ❽

Genova Passo Costanzi 10 ⓣ010.242.2457. Friendly, clean and well-run HI hostel with great views over the port and Internet access. Take bus #40 or (evening) #640 from Stazione Brignole. From Stazione Principe take bus #35 to Via Napoli and change to bus #40. ❷

Villa Doria Via al Campeggio Villa Doria 15, Pegli ⓣ010.696.9600, ⓦwww.camping.it/liguria/villadoria. Good, leafy campsite 8km from Genoa. It's set in parkland, with its own café, shop and solarium: take a train to Pegli and then bus #93. ❸

Eating

For **cheap lunches**, snacks and picnic ingredients, try the covered *Mercato Orientale*, halfway down Via XX Settembre in the cloisters of an Augustinian monastery. There are a host of restaurants and bars down Via Ravecca, a few hundred metres southeast of the port.

Ostaja do Castello Salita Santa Maria di Castello 32r ⓣ010.246.8980. Open till 1am, closed Sun. Family-run trattoria, offering a fixed menu with two courses and wine €10.

P log P/La Passeggiata Piazza di Santa Croce 21r. A relaxed café, creperie and bar in a bookshop-gallery with views over the port. Espresso €0.80.

Sa Pesta Via Giustiniani 16. Closed Sun and Mon. Well-known for its good local cooking, including *farinata*, a thin chickpea-based pancake, but it closes early. Farinata with sausage €9.

Trattoria da Maria Via Testadoro 14/b, just off Via XXV Aprile. No-nonsense, endearingly chaotic place which serves up simple Ligurian cooking at rock-bottom prices. Pasta €4.50.

Drinking and nightlife

For late-night drinking, head to the bars around Piazza delle Erbe, just south of Palazzo Ducale.

Batik Piazza Sarzano. Oriental-styled disco with classic tunes, free entry and a pretty upstairs chillout room.

Il Clan Salita Pallavicini 16. Trendy bar packed to the rafters with the young and hip. Arrive early to bag one of the loft bed-seats.

Gloglo Piazza Lavagna 19r. Aperitifs come with good snacks at this relaxed place on a typically Italianate square, with washing hanging precariously from the overhead flats. Staff are chatty and drinks are generous.

Gradisca Café Piazza delle Erbe 31r. Closed Sun. Lively bar-restaurant with outdoor seating. Beer €3.

BOAT TRIPS

If you have an extended stay in Genoa, there are a wide range of **boat trips** available, from romantic 45min excursions around the port at night to full-day whale-watching expeditions. There's a kiosk at Via Sottoripa 7/8, ⓣ010.265.712; or check at: ⓦwww.whalewatchliguria.it and ⓦwww.battellierigenova.it.

Louisiana Jazz Club Via S. Sebastiano 36r, ⓦwww.louisianajazzclub.com. Established jazz venue with live music, a bar and a restaurant.

Moving on

Train Bologna (hourly; 3hr 30min); Milan (every 30min; 1hr 30min); Naples (10 daily; 8hr); Pisa (hourly; 2–3hr); Rome (hourly; 5hr 20min).

Ferry Bastia (1 weekly; 9hr); Cagliari (2 weekly in summer; 20hr); Olbia (at least 7 weekly in summer; 13hr); Palermo (6 weekly; 20hr); Porto Torres (7 weekly; 12hr).

THE RIVIERA DI LEVANTE

The stretch of coast east from Genoa, the **RIVIERA DE LEVANTE**, is full of attractive but frenetic resorts populated by the rich and Botoxed. The ports that once survived on navigation, fishing and coral diving have now experienced thirty years of upmarket tourism: the coastline is still wild and beautiful in parts, but the sense of remoteness has gone. All the towns can be reached by train.

Santa Margherita Ligure

Pretty **SANTA MARGHERITA LIGURE** is a small, wealthy resort, with palm trees along its front, a minuscule pebble beach and concrete jetties to swim from. **Accommodation** options include the comfortable and friendly *Annabella*, Via Costasecca 10, just off Piazza Mazzini (ⓣ0185.286.531; ❼); the very welcoming *Nuova Riviera*, Via Belvedere 10, a hotel in Art Nouveau-style with an annexe of cheaper rooms (ⓣ0185.287.403,

ⓦwww.nuovariviera.com; ⓔangelarentals @alice.it; ❽, annexe ❼); and the pleasant *Hotel Conte Verde*, Via Zara 1, a short walk from the sea and with a large garden (ⓣ0185.287.139, ⓦwww.hotelconteverde.it; ❻). For good local **food**, try *Il Faro*, Via Merigliano (closed Tues), or the long-established *Da Pezzi*, at Via Cavour 21 (closed Sat), a canteen-like locals' hangout serving pasta, grills, and takeaway snacks. For a more expensive but extremely tasty meal, try *Oca Bianca*, Via XXV Aprile 21, famed for its succulent grills (ⓣ0185.288.411, daily 7pm–2am). The **tourist office** is on Via XXV Aprile (daily 9.30am–12.30pm & 2/3–5/7.30pm; ⓣ0185.287.485, ⓦwww.apttigullio.liguria.it). **Scooters and bikes** are a fun way of getting around: go to Via XXV Aprile 11 (ⓣ0185.284.420, ⓦwww.gmrent.it).

Rapallo

RAPALLO is a highly developed, though still attractive, resort popular with writers: Ezra Pound wrote the first thirty of his *Cantos* here between 1925 and 1930.

The **tourist office** is at Lungo Vittorio Veneto 7 (Mon–Sat 9.30am–12.30pm & 3 –7.30pm, Sun 9.30am–12.30pm, 4.30–7.30pm; ⓣ0185.230.346). For decent **accommodation**, *Elvezia* at Via Ferraretto 12 is a rambling, friendly place set in a huge garden with good home-cooking (ⓣ018.550.564; ❼). There are a couple of **campsites** – try the large, grassy *Rapallo* at Via San Lazzaro 4 (ⓣ0185.262.018, ⓦwww.campingrapallo.it; bungalow ❻, camping ❸). The most authentic place to eat is the well-priced *Bansin*, at Via Venezia 105 (closed Sun lunch) in the heart of the old town.

Cinque Terre

Further east, the **CINQUE TERRE** (ⓦwww.cinqueterreonline.com) is a series of five beautiful villages perched on tiny cliff-bound inlets. If you're coming from the south, take a train to La Spezia, then a regional train, which stops at each of the villages. Some trains to La Spezia also stop at a couple of the villages, so check the timetable. From the north, take the train to Levanto (the village furthest north), and again, check to see if the train stops at your preferred village, or change to a regional train. You can get round all the villages in a day if you're a fast walker, and the views are well worth it, although the path can get busy at peak seasons. Good shoes are recommended for most of the way, though there is a paved stretch between **Manarola** and **Riomaggiore.** The Cinque Terre Card, available at the tourist office of any of the villages, allows access to the path for €5 a day, or €8 including the train and buses – beware that in bad weather, the paths will be closed. It's also possible to take a hop-on boat that stops at each of the villages hourly, for €12.50 per day. Each of the five villages has a tourist office at its train station, with Internet access and reasonable maps. **Monterosso** is probably the most lively of the villages, though all of them have good restaurants and relaxed bars for an evening drink.

Accommodation tends to be expensive in summer months, at about €120 for a double room, or rental apartments that have to be taken for a week at a time. **Manarola** is the best of the villages for budget accommodation: the warm, clean *Ostello Cinque Terre* on Via Riccobaldi 21 (ⓣ0187.920.215, ⓦwww.hostel5terre.com; ❸) offers gorgeous views, delicious food and chilled-out communal spaces. To get there, head to the top of the town and turn left; it's the green building behind the church. Just down the road from here, at 110 Via Renato Birolli (the main street), *La Cantina dello Zio Bramante* is a small *bruschettieri* and *enoteca* worth a visit just for its delicious anchovy *crostini*.

Northeast Italy

The appeal of **Venice** hardly needs stating: one of Europe's truly unique urban landscapes, it is an unmissable part of any European tour. The region around it, the Veneto, still bears the imprint of Venetian rule and continues to prosper. Gorgeous, vibrant **Verona** plays on its Shakespeare connections and centres on an incredible amphitheatre, while nearby Padua hums with student activity and offers a profusion of artistic and architectural masterpieces. South, between Lombardy and Tuscany, **Emilia-Romagna** is the heartland of northern Italy, a patchwork of ducal territories formerly ruled by a handful of families, whose castles and fortresses remain in well-preserved medieval towns. **Bologna,** the region's capital, has one of the most beautifully preserved city centres in the country, and, thanks to its university, is a hive of young activity. Nearby is **Parma,** a wealthy provincial town worth visiting for its comfortable ambience and paintings by Parmigianino and Correggio. The coast is less interesting but, just south of the Po delta, **Ravenna** boasts probably the finest set of Byzantine mosaics in the world.

VERONA

The magnificent city of **VERONA**, with its Roman sites and streets of pink-hued medieval buildings, stands midway between Milan and Venice at a rail junction for the trans-Alpine line from Innsbruck (Austria). It reached its zenith as an independent city-state in the thirteenth century under the Scaligeri family, who were energetic patrons of the arts; many of Verona's finest buildings date from their rule.

What to see and do

The city centre clusters in a deep bend in the River Adige, and the main sight of its southern reaches is the central hub of **Piazza Bra** and its mighty **Roman Arena** (Mon 1.30–7.15pm, Tues–Sun 8.30am–7.15pm; July & Aug closes 3.30pm; €4). Dating from the first century AD, and originally with seating for some twenty thousand, this is the third-largest surviving Roman amphitheatre in the world, and offers a tremendous panorama from the topmost of the 44 marble tiers.

TREAT YOURSELF

Nowadays the amphitheatre is used as an opera venue for big summer productions. The sight of its stands lit up by the thousands of candles handed out to the audience before the performance begins is one unlikely to be forgotten. The ticket office (Ⓣ045.800.5151, Ⓦwww.arena.it) is outside the arena. Prices begin at €21.

Historical centre

To the north, **Via Mazzini**, a narrow traffic-free street lined with expensive shops, leads to a group of squares, the best of which is the **Piazza dei Signori,** flanked by the medieval **Palazzo degli Scaligeri**. At right angles to this is the fifteenth-century **Loggia del Consiglio**, the former assembly hall of the city council and Verona's outstanding early Renaissance building while, close by, the twelfth-century **Torre dei Lamberti** (same hours as Arena; €3 by elevator, €2 on foot) gives dizzying views of the city. **Juliet's house** is situated in the heart of the old town, at Via Capello 23 (Mon 1.30pm–7.30pm; Tues-Sun 8.30am–7.30pm; €4) – even if you don't want to pay to go inside, you can have a look at the balcony and the thousands of love-notes posted on the walls for free.

Arche Scaligere and the Duomo

Beyond the square, in front of the Romanesque church of **Santa Maria Antica**, the **Arche Scaligere** are the elaborate Gothic funerary monuments of Verona's first family, set in a wrought-iron palisade decorated with ladder motifs, the emblem of the Scaligeri. Verona's **Duomo** (Tues–Sat 10am–5.30pm, Sun 1.30–5.30pm; €5) lies just around the river's bend, a mixture of Romanesque and Gothic styles that houses an *Assumption* by Titian.

Roman theatre

The **Roman theatre**, on the north side of the river, is worth climbing up to for its gorgeous views. In July and August, a Shakespeare festival (in Italian, but it's still great to soak up the atmosphere!) and a jazz festival make use of this amazing venue. Box office ⓣ899.199.057; ⓦwww.geticket.it. Ticket prices start at €8.

Basilica di San Zeno Maggiore

A kilometre or so to the northwest, the **Basilica di San Zeno Maggiore** (Mon–Sat 8.30am–6pm, Sun 1–6pm; €2.50) is one of the most significant Romanesque churches in northern Italy. Its rose window, representing the Wheel of Fortune, dates from the twelfth century, as does the magnificent portal.

Arrival and information

Train The train station is connected with Piazza Bra by bus #11, #12, #13 or #14. Alternatively, it's a simple 20min walk down Corso Porta Nuova.

Tourist office at the train station (Mon–Sat 8am–7pm, Sun 9am–2pm; 3–5pm; ⓣ045.800.0861, ⓦwww.tourism.verona.it), and at Via degli Alpini 9 (Mon–Sat 9am–7pm, Sun 9am–3pm). An excellent map of the city is available at the offices.

Discount passes The Verona Card (€8) covers all Verona's museums and churches and can be purchased at either tourist office.

Exchange Via Cappello 3 (Mon–Sat 9am–8.30pm), or at the station (daily 7.30am–8.30pm).

Internet is available for free at *Square Café* (see opposite) if you buy a drink, or at the Internet Train on Via Roma (Mon–Fri 10am–10pm, Sat & Sun 2–8pm; €3.50/hr).

Left luggage is at the station (daily 7am–11pm; €3.80/5hr). Under 20kg only.

Accommodation

Casa della Giovane Via Pigna 7 ⓣ045.596.880, ⓦwww.casadellagiovane.com. For women under 26 only, this simple, clean hostel is right in the old centre. The curfew is 11pm unless you're going to the opera. Take bus #73 from the station to Piazza Erbe, from where it's a 5min walk. ❷

Al Castello Vicolo Brusco 4, off Corso Cavour ⓣ045.801.5588. Central one-star hotel; most rooms have private bathrooms and TV. ❽

Catullo Via Catullo 1 ⓣ045.800.2786. Friendly one-star hotel just off Via Mazzini. ❼

HI Hostel Via Fontana del Ferro 15 ⓣ045.590.360. Hostel in a frescoed palazzo on the north side of the river, curfew 11.30pm, breakfast included. Bus #72, #73 or #90 from the station. ❷

Eating

Cafés

Snack food and lunches are also available from all the bars listed below. Prices are a fairly standard €3 for paninis and €6 for pastas.

Libreria Gheduzzi Corso S Anastasia 7. Eclectic international bookshop with a café at the back, serving breakfast, lunch and dinner. Coffee €1.50.

Sottoriva 23 Sottoriva 21. Inviting, if misleadingly named, café and bar overlooking the river and up to the Roman theatre. Pizza €5.

Restaurants

Osteria Casa Vino Vicolo Orette 8 ⓣ045.800.4337. Closed Tues. Romantic restaurant down a cosy side-street. Mains €10.

Pero d'Oro Via Ponte Pignolo 25. Restaurant serving inexpensive genuine local dishes. Mains €8.

Via Roma 33 Via Roma 33 ⓣ045.591.917. Super-chic restaurant with atmospheric outdoor tables full of young, well-dressed Veronese. Open until 2am weekends. Mains €11.

Drinking and nightlife

Alter Ego Via Torricelle 9 ⓦwww.alteregoclub.it. Verona's most cutting-edge club is a cab ride from the centre; check the website to see what's on each night.

TREAT YOURSELF

Porta Nuova Café Porto Nuova 48a. Swish bar with a swanky, suede-clad interior with latticed furniture and a spectacular glass waterfall. Cocktails €6. Aperitif buffet from 7–10pm.

Antimo café Via Roma 4. Chilled-out bar in a quiet backstreet. Wine €2.20.

Café Castello Corso Castelvecchio 1B. Intimate, trendy place in the shadow of the *castello*. Wine €2.

Mercedes Café Via Oberdan 19. Friendly, unpretentious central bar with outdoor seating. Wine €2. Open until 4am at weekends.

Square Via Sottoriva 15. A very modern bar oozing urban chic, and strong on cocktails. There's a DJ several evenings a week, magazines galore and free Internet. Beer and wine €3. Open from 6pm, live jazz with a free buffet (when you buy a drink) on Sun.

Moving on

Train Milan (every 30min; 1hr 30min); Padua (every 30min; 55min); Rome (hourly; 5hr); Venice (every 30min; 1hr 30min); Parma (every hour; 2hr 30min).

PADUA

Extensively rebuilt after World War II bomb damage and hemmed in by industrial sprawl, **PADUA** (Padova) is not the most alluring city in northern Italy and while lively during term-time, it can seem rather dull when the students are away. However, it's a particularly ancient city, and makes a good base for seeing Venice (35min away by frequent trains). Donatello and Mantegna both worked here, and in the seventeenth century Galileo researched at the university.

What to see and do

Cappella degli Scrovegni

Just outside the city centre, through a gap in the Renaissance walls off **Corso Garibaldi**, the stunning Giotto frescoes in the lapis-ceilinged **Cappella degli Scrovegni**, affectionately referred to as the "scrawny chapel" for its diminutive size (daily 9am–10pm; appointment only for a 20min slot, book at least 48hr in advance; €12 for joint ticket with Musei Civici; ⓣ049.201.0020, ⓦwww.cappelladegliscrovegni.it), are the main reason for coming to Padua. Commissioned in 1303 by Enrico Scrovegni in atonement for his father's usury, the chapel's walls are covered with breathtakingly detailed and largely well-preserved illustrations of the life of Mary, Jesus and the story of the Passion. It's a bit of a rush to see forty masterpieces in twenty minutes, but well worth it.

Piazza del Santo

In the southwest of the city, down Via Zabarella from the *cappella*, is the starkly impressive Piazza del Santo. The main sight here is Donatello's **Monument to Gattamelata** of 1453, the earliest large bronze sculpture of the Renaissance. On one side of the square, the basilica of San Antonio, or **Il Santo**, was built to house the body of St Anthony; the **Cappella del Tesoro** (daily 9am–12.30pm & 2.30–5pm) houses the saint's tongue and chin in a head-shaped reliquary.

The university

From the basilica, **Via Umberto** leads back towards the university, established in 1221, and older than any other in Italy except Bologna. The main block is the **Palazzo del Bo**, where Galileo taught physics from 1592 to 1610, declaiming from a lectern that is still on show, though the major sight is the sixteenth-century **anatomy theatre** (March–Oct, tours Mon, Wed & Fri at 3.15pm, 4.15pm & 5.15pm, Tues, Thurs & Sat at 9.15am, 10.15am & 11.15am; Nov–Feb tours Mon, Wed & Fri at 3.15pm & 4.15pm, Tues, Thurs and Sat at 10.15am & 11.15am; €5. ⓣ 049.827.3047, booking possible only for groups of ten or more).

The Giardino dell'Arena

Situated in the north of the city and surrounding the *cappella*, this garden (Oct–March 8am–6pm, April–Sept 8am–8pm) is a lush, verdant place to chill out or eat a picnic and has an open-air cinema on summer evenings (ask at the tourist office for details).

Arrival and information

Train Padua train station is at the far end of Corso del Popolo, a few minutes' walk north of the city walls.
Tourist office There is a branch at the station (Mon–Sat 9am–7pm, Sun 9am–noon), but the main office is in Galleria Pedrocchi, just off Via 8 Febbraio (Mon–Sat 9am–1.30pm & 3–7pm; ⓣ049.876.7927, ⓦwww.turismopadova.it).
Discount passes The tourist office sells the 48hr Padova Card (€14), which buys museum access, free bus travel and a parking space.

Accommodation

Dante Via San Polo 5 ⓣ049.876.0408, ⓔhotel.dante@virgilio.it. Clean, old-fashioned rooms a stone's throw from the sights. ❺
Eden Via C. Battisti 255 ⓣ049.650.484, ⓦwww.hoteledenpadova.it. Inviting, easygoing place with colourful walls. Breakfast included. ❼
HI Hostel Via A. Aleardi 30 ⓣ049.875.2219. Unremarkable, with an 11pm curfew. Bus #3, #8, or #18 from the station. ❷
Sporting Center Via Roma 123 ⓣ049.793.400, ⓦwww.sportingcenter.it. Extremely well-equipped, spacious campsite 15km away in Montegrotto Terme, with a reasonable two-star hotel on site. Served by frequent trains (15min). Double ❻, camping ❷

TREAT YOURSELF

Hotel Belludi 37 Via Luca Belludi 37 ⓣ049.665.633, ⓦwww.belludi37.it. Chic, minimalist hotel, all glass angles and swish furnishings. Breakfast is served either in the tiny glass-surround bar, or in your room. The views are great and the staff extremely friendly. Follow directions to St Antony's Basilica to get here; the hotel is just by it, on Via Belludi, which connects the Basilica with the Prato delle Valle. ❽

Eating

Cafés and food markets

For eating on the go, there's a daily fruit market on, unsurprisingly, Piazza della Frutta, or a supermarket, Punto, at Via Incollo Tommaseo (Mon–Sat 9am–6pm).
Bottega del Café Piazza dei Signori 25. Cosy corner-café with speciality teas, coffees and hot chocolates.
Da Emilio Green Point Via Boccalerie 7–9. Takeaway salad bar with amazing fresh fruit and veg. Closed Sun.

Restaurants

Osteria L'Anfora Via dei Soncin 13. *Osteria* with a wine list which attracts locals even at lunchtime; the service is leisurely, but the meal is well worth the wait. *Pasta e fagioli* (Pasta in a bean soup) €8, *stinco* (lamb shank) €14.
Caffe della Piazzetta Via S Martino e Solferino 49. Closed Sun. A laid-back little place in a quiet square serving great organic food. Paninis €5.

Drinking and nightlife

On summer evenings, the bars around Prato della Valle are lively, while Piazza delle Erbe is the place to head for an early evening spritz.
Il Bagatto Via Santa Lucia 79. Modern bar in a backstreet. Wine €2.50, aperitif buffet until 10pm.
Miniera Via S. Francesco 144. A fashionable, dimly-lit late-night spot, largely frequented by students.
Pachuca Via Bernina 18. A club popular with students, a 20min walk behind the train station.

Moving on

Train Bologna (every 30min; 1hr 20min); Milan (every 30min; 2hr 30min); Venice (every 10min; 30min); Verona (every 20min; 1hr).

VENICE

The first-time visitor to **VENICE** (Venezia) arrives with a heavy burden of expectations, most of which won't be disappointed. It is an extraordinarily beautiful city, and the major sights are all they are cracked up to be. The downside is that Venice is expensive and deluged with tourists. Twenty million come here each year, most seduced by the famous motifs – carnival time (see p.702), glass ornaments, singing gondoliers and the fabulously pricey cafés – though others come in search of the quieter quarters of a city that always has the capacity to surprise.

What to see and do

Piazza San Marco

Piazza San Marco is signalled from most parts of the city by the **Campanile** (Oct–March 9.45am–4pm, April–June 9.30am–5pm, July–Sept 9.45am–8pm; €6), which began life as a lighthouse in the ninth century, but is in fact a reconstruction: the original tower collapsed on July 14, 1902. It is the tallest structure in the city, and the view from the top is magnificent, particularly if you manage to make it there at sunset.

Basilica di San Marco

Across the piazza, the **Basilica di San Marco** (March–Oct Mon–Fri 9.45am–4.45pm, Sun 2–4.45pm; April–Sept Mon–Fri 9.45am–5pm, Sun 2–5pm; €1.50) is the most exotic of Europe's cathedrals, modelled on Constantinople's Church of the Twelve Apostles, finished in 1094 and embellished over the succeeding centuries with trophies brought back from abroad. Inside, a steep staircase goes from the church's main door up to the **Museo di San Marco** and the **Loggia dei Cavalli** (March–Oct 9.45am–4.45pm; April–Sept 9.45am–5pm; €3), where you can enjoy fine views of the city and the Gothic carvings along the apex of the facade. However, it's the **Sanctuary,** off the south transept (March–Oct Mon–Fri 9.45am–4.45pm, Sun 1–4.45pm; April–Sept Mon–Fri 9.45am–5pm, Sun 1–5pm; €1.50), that holds the most precious of San Marco's treasures, the **Pala d'Oro**, or golden altar panel, commissioned in 976 in Constantinople. This mind-blowingly intricate explosion of gold, enamel, pearls and gemstones is generally considered to be one of the greatest accomplishments of Byzantine craftsmanship. The **Treasury** (same times; €2) is a similarly dazzling warehouse of chalices, reliquaries and candelabra, while the tenth-century **Icon of the Madonna of Nicopeia** (in the chapel on the east side of the north transept) is the most revered religious image in Venice. Considered by Venetians to be the protector of the city after being brought there from Constantinople by Doge Enrico Dandolo in 1204, she was carried at the head of the Imperial Army in battles.

Palazzo Ducale

The adjacent **Palazzo Ducale** (daily: Nov–March 9am–5pm; April–Oct 9am–7pm; €12 combined ticket with Piazza San Marco museums, €6.50 with student card) was principally the residence of the doge. Like San Marco,

VENICE ORIENTATION

The 118 islands of central Venice are divided into six districts known as *sestieri*, with that of San Marco (enclosed by the lower loop of the Canal Grande) home to most of the essential sights. On the east it's bordered by Castello, to the north by Cannaregio. On the other side of the Canal Grande, the largest of the *sestieri* is Dorsoduro, which stretches from the fashionable quarter at the southern tip of the canal to the docks in the west. Santa Croce roughly follows the curve of the Canal Grande from Piazzale Roma to a point just short of the Rialto, where it joins the smartest of the districts on this bank, San Polo.

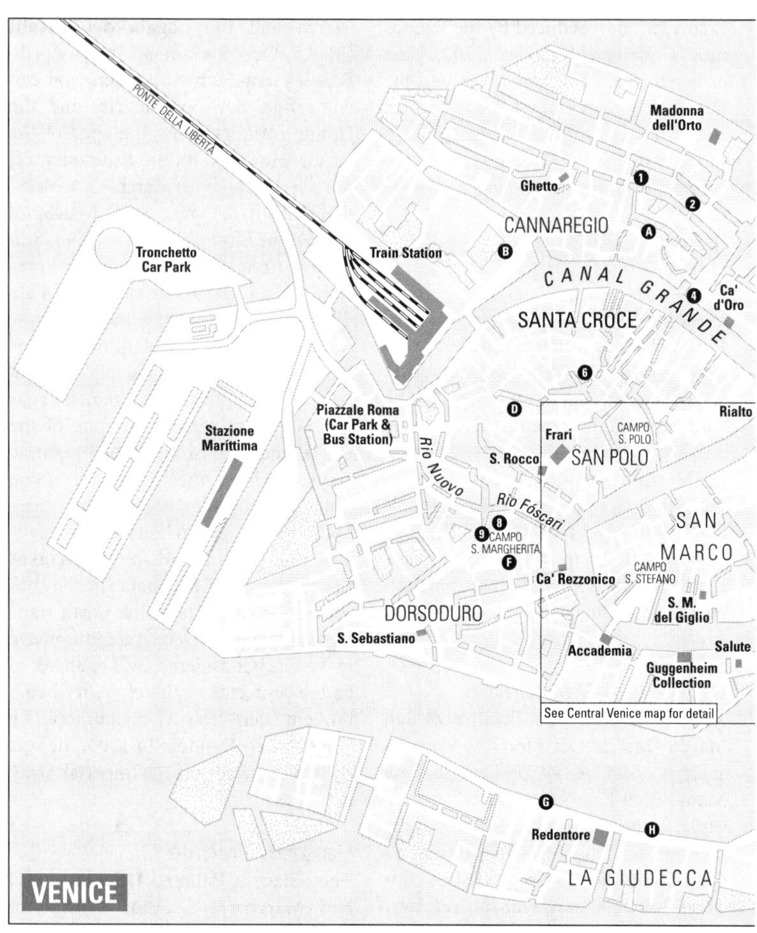

it has been rebuilt many times since its foundation in the first years of the ninth century, but the earliest parts of the current structure date from 1340. As well as fabulous paintings and impressive administrative chambers, the Palazzo contains a maze of prison cells, reached by crossing the world-famous **Ponte dei Sospiri** (Bridge of Sighs).

Guggenheim Collection

In the Dorsoduro area west of San Marco, five minutes' walk from the impressive European art collection in the **Galleria dell'Accademia** (Mon 8.15am–2pm, Tues–Sun 8.15am–7.15pm; €6.50), the unfinished Palazzo Venier dei Leoni is home of the **Guggenheim Collection** (daily except Tues 10am–6pm; €10). Peggy Guggenheim lived here for thirty years until her death in 1979. Her private collection is an eclectic mix of pieces from her favourite modernist artists, with works by Brancusi, De Chirico, Max Ernst and Malevich.

Murano, Burano & Torcello

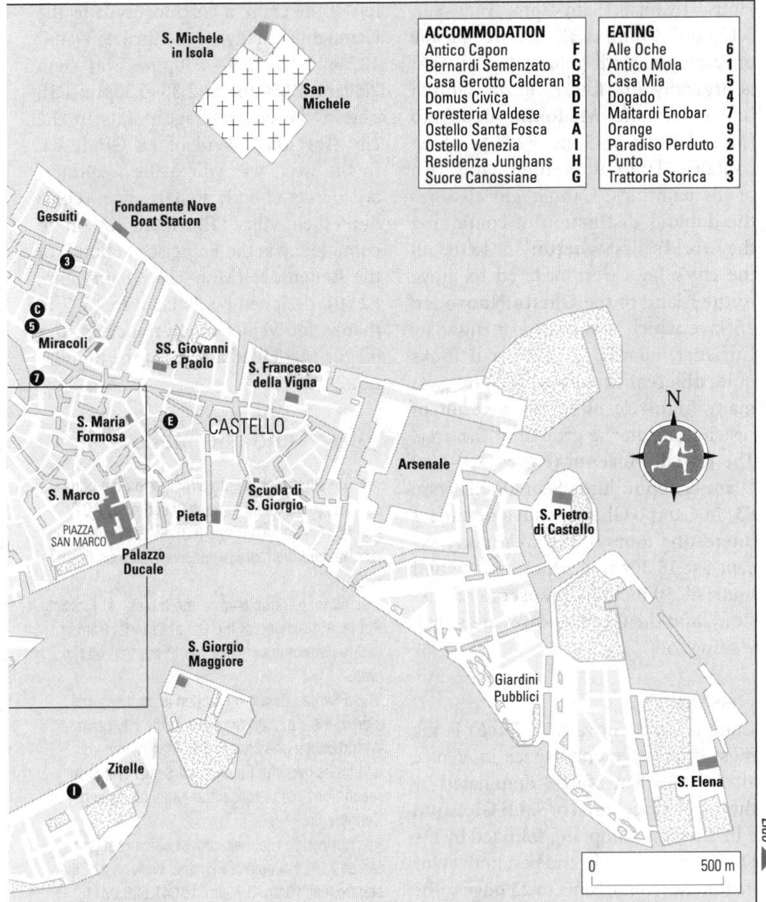

San Polo

On the northeastern edge of **San Polo** is the former trading district of **Rialto**. It still hosts the Rialto market on the far side of the Rialto Bridge, a buzzing, lively affair.

Fifteen minutes' walk west of here is the mountainous brick church **Santa Maria Gloriosa dei Frari** (Mon–Sat 9am–6pm, Sun 1–6pm; €2.50), the main reason people visit San Polo. The collection of artworks there includes a couple of rare paintings by Titian – most notably his radical *Assumption*, painted in 1518. Titian is also buried in the church. At the rear of the Frari is the **Scuola Grande di San Rocco** (daily 9am–7pm; €5.50), home to a cycle of more than fifty major paintings by Tintoretto.

Cannaregio

In the northernmost section of Venice, **Cannaregio**, you can walk from the bustle of the train station to some of the quietest and prettiest parts of the city in a matter of minutes. The district boasts one of the most beautiful *palazzi* in Venice, the **Ca D'Oro**, or Golden

House (Mon 8.15am–2pm, Tues–Sun 8.15am–7.15pm; €5), whose facade once glowed with gold leaf, and what is arguably the finest Gothic church in Venice, the **Madonna dell'Orto** (Mon–Sat 10am–5pm, €2.50), which contains Tintoretto's tomb and two of his paintings. Cannaregio also has the dubious distinction of containing the world's first **ghetto:** in 1516, all the city's Jews were ordered to move to the island of the **Ghetto Nuovo**, an enclave which was sealed at night by Christian guards. Even now it looks quite different to the rest of Venice, its many high-rise buildings a result of restrictions on the growth of the area. The **Jewish Museum** (daily: Oct–May 10am–5.30pm; June–Sept 10am–7pm; €3) in Campo Ghetto Nuovo organizes interesting tours of the area (daily except Sat 10.30am–4.30pm; on the half hour; €8.50 including museum admission), and the Campo's **cafés** are worth visiting too.

Castello

Campo Santi Giovanni e Paolo is the most impressive open space in Venice after Piazza San Marco, dominated by the huge brick church of **Santi Giovanni e Paolo** (San Zanipolo), founded by the Dominicans in 1246 and best known for its funeral monuments to 25 doges. The other essential sight in this area is the **Scuola di San Giorgio degli Schiavoni** (Mon 2.45–6pm, Tues–Sat 9.15am–1pm & 2.45–6pm, Sun 9.15am–1pm; €3), to the east of San Marco, set up by Venice's Slav population in 1451. The building has a superb cycle by Vittore Carpaccio on the ground floor.

Venice's other islands

Immediately south of the Palazzo Ducale, Palladio's church of **San Giorgio Maggiore** stands on the island of the same name and has two pictures by Tintoretto in the chancel – *The Fall of Manna* and *The Last Supper*. On the left of the choir, a corridor leads to the Campanile (daily: Oct–April 9.30am–12.30pm & 2.30–4.30pm, May–Sept 9.30am–12.30pm & 2.30–6.30pm; €3), one of the best vantage points in the city. The long island of **La Giudecca**, to the west, was where the wealthiest aristocrats of early Renaissance Venice built their villas. The main reason to come today is the Franciscan church of the **Redentore** (Mon– Sat 10am–5pm, €2.50), designed by Palladio in 1577 in thanks for Venice's deliverance from a plague that killed a third of the population.

Arrival and information

Air The city's Marco Polo airport is on the edge of the lagoon, linked to the city centre by ACTV bus #5 (€2) and ATVO bus (€3) across Ponte della Libertà, and the more expensive waterbus (from €10).

Bus All road traffic comes into the city at Piazzale Roma, at the head of the Canal Grande, from where waterbus services run to the San Marco area.

Train Santa Lucia train station is on the north side of the canal, to the west of the city centre. Waterbus services run to San Marco, and you can cross over the Ponte degli Scalzi bridge to reach San Polo or follow the canal along to get to Cannaregio.

Tourist office The main tourist office is at San Marco 71/f, a couple of minutes' walk east of the square (daily 9am–3.30pm; ⓣ041.529.8711, ⓦwww.turismovenezia.it). There are also desks at the train station and airport (daily 8am-6.30pm). All three hand out the free English-language listings magazine *Leo* or, for nightlife, the bilingual *Venezia da Vivere*.

Discount passes Tourist offices sell the Museum Pass (€18), which gives entry to most of the main civic museums (it does not include the Accademia or Guggenheim), the Museum Card (€12), which gets you into the Museums of San Marco Square plus a few others, the Chorus Pass (€8), which gives entry to fourteen churches, and the Venezia Card (ⓦwww.venicecard.it; €54/80 for two/seven days), which covers the waterbuses, most museums and most churches.

City transport

Walking is the fastest way of getting around – you can cross the whole city in an hour.

Waterbus Tickets for the waterbus (*vaporetto*) are available from most landing stages. Flat-rate fares are €5 for any one continuous journey including the Canal Grande, or €3.50 excluding it. There are also one-day (€10.50) and three-day (€22) tickets available. Although the waterbuses vary in comfort and can get packed during peak seasons (school holiday times and summer in particular), they're an inexpensive and fun way to see the city and are worth riding on just for the experience.

Gondola The *traghetti* (ferries) that cross the Canal Grande (€0.50 a trip) are a cheap way of getting a ride on a gondola. These old gondolas, stripped of their finery and rowed by two oarsmen, cross from seven piers between the station and the Bacino San Marco (the stretch of water along San Marco), and are indicated by yellow signs along the Grand Canal. Otherwise, the boats are ludicrously expensive, though split between six people they become more affordable: the official tariff is €73 for 50 minutes but you may be quoted up to €100 for 45 minutes and an extra €100 for a singer.

Accommodation

Accommodation is the major expense in Venice and you should always book ahead – you might also consider staying in nearby Padua (30min away by train) or Trieste (2hr away by train). There are **booking offices** (all open daily 9am–8pm) at the station, the Tronchetto, Piazzale Roma, airport and at the *autostrada*'s Venice exit.

Hostels

Domus Civica Calle Campazzo, San Polo 3082 ⓣ041.721.103, ⓦwww.domuscivica.com. Curfew 12.30pm. Basic hostel with small dorms (holding around three people) and free Internet. ❸

Foresteria Valdese Santa Maria Formosa, Castello 5170 ⓣ041.528.6797, ⓦwww.diaconiavaldese.org/venezia. Pleasant hostel in an eighteenth-century palace. Difficult to find – go from Campo Santa Maria Formosa along Calle Lunga, and it's at the foot of the bridge at the far end. ❸

Ostello Santa Fosca S. Maria dei Servi, Cannaregio 2372 ⓣ041.715.775. Student-run hostel in an atmospheric former Servite convent. ❸

Ostello Venezia Fondamenta delle Zitelle, Giudecca 86 ⓣ041.523.8211. The official HI hostel, in a superb location with views of San Marco from the island of Giudecca. Curfew 11pm. Waterbus #82 from the station. Large place, but get there early morning or book. ❷

Residenza Junghans Terzo Ramo della Palada 394, Isola della Giudecca ⓣ041.521.0801, ⓦwww.residenzajunghans.com. Neat, modern student hall of residence. ❼

Suore Canossiane Fondamenta del Ponte Piccolo, Isola della Giudecca 428 ⓣ041.522.2157. Women only, no booking. ❷

Hotels

The low season generally runs from November till the start of carnival, but can vary from place to place. Prices are usually reduced by around twenty percent at this time.

Alex Rio Terra Frari San Polo 2606 ⓣ041.523.1341, ⓦwww.hotelalexinvenice.com. A friendly, recently refurbished one-star hotel. ❼

Antico Capon Campo S. Margherita, Dorsoduro 3004/B ⓣ041.528.5292, ⓦwww.anticocapon.com. Very friendly, family-run place situated on one of the city's most atmospheric squares, in the heart of the student district. Breakfast is at one of the cafés on the square. Prices vary hugely so it's best to book in advance. ❷

Bernardi Semenzato Calle dell'Oca, Cannaregio 4366 ⓣ041.522.7257, ⓦwww.hotelbernardi.com. Good-value two-star place with welcoming and helpful English-speaking owners and some fantastic, opulently decorated rooms. ❼

Caneva Ramo della Fava, Castello 5515 ⓣ041.522.8118. Overlooking the Rio della Fava on the approach to the busy Campo San Bartolomeo, yet very peaceful. ❼

Casa Gerotto Calderan Campo S. Geremia 283, Cannaregio ⓣ041.715.361. Welcoming place not far from the train station. Dorm beds sometimes available. ❼

TREAT YOURSELF

Al Gazzettino C. di Mezzo, San Marco 4971 ⓣ041. 528.6523. Opulent Venetian splendour greets you in this eccentric little hotel, where the rooms are a rich mass of draperies and embossed wallpaper. Double €130. ❾

Eating

Venice is awash with places to eat seafood, and there are also plenty of cheapish **pizzerias** as

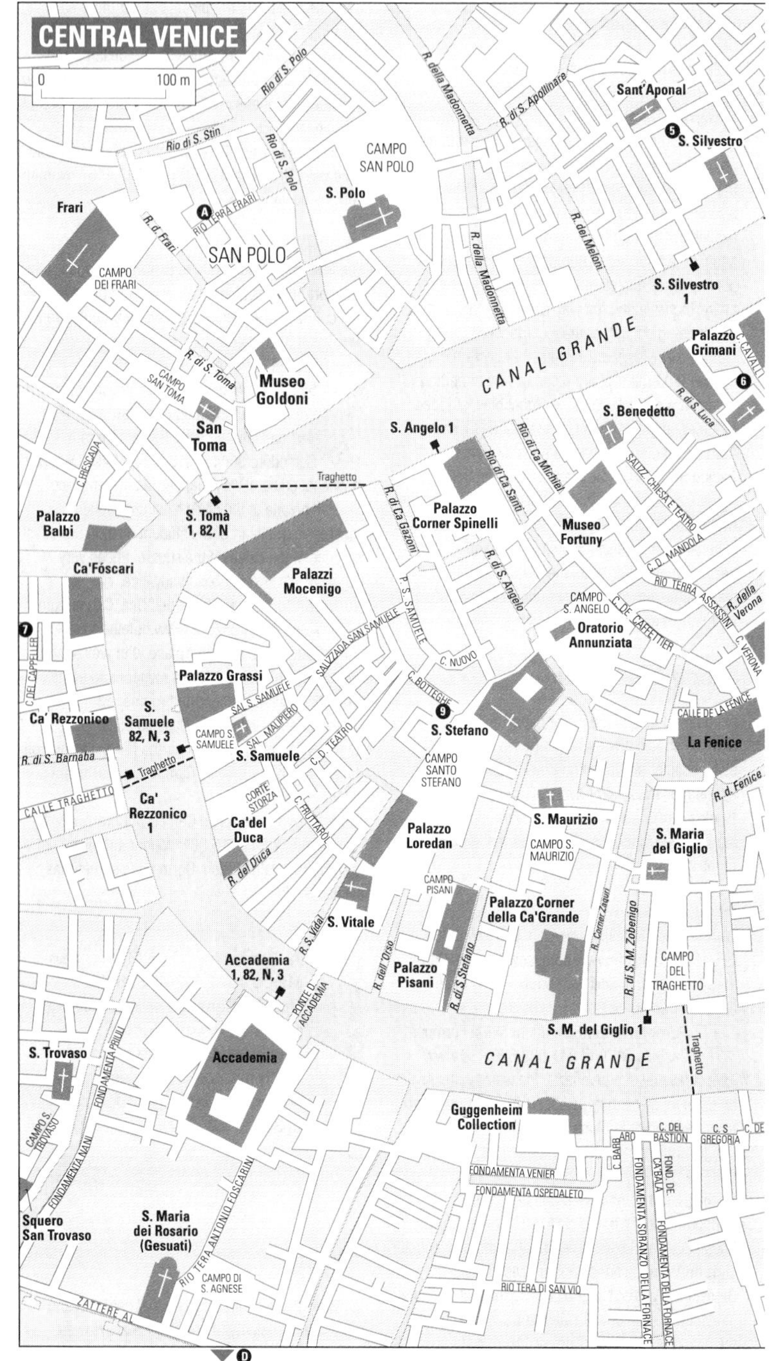
CENTRAL VENICE
0
100 m
Rio di S. Polo
R. della Madonnetta
R. di S. Apollinare
Sant'Aponal
5
S. Silvestro
Rio di S. Stin
Rio di S. Polo
CAMPO SAN POLO
S. Polo
Frari
A
RIO TERRA FRARI
R. d. Frari
SAN POLO
R. della Madonnetta
R. dei Meloni
CAMPO DEI FRARI
S. Silvestro 1
Palazzo Grimani
C. CAVALLI
6
CANAL GRANDE
R. di S. Tomà
CAMPO SAN TOMA
Museo Goldoni
San Toma
S. Angelo 1
S. Benedetto
R. di S. Luca
Rio di Ca Michiel
Rio di Ca Santi
C. TRESCADA
Traghetto
S. Tomà 1, 82, N
R. di Ca Gazoni
Palazzo Corner Spinelli
SALIZZ. CHIESA E TEATRO
Museo Fortuny
Palazzo Balbi
Ca'Foscari
Palazzi Mocenigo
R. di S. Angelo
C. D. MANDOLA
RIO TERRA ASSASSINI
R. della Verona
P. S. SAMUELE
CAMPO S. ANGELO
C. DE CAFFETTIER
Oratorio Annunziata
7
C. DEL CAPPELLER
SALIZZADA SAN SAMUELE
C. NUOVO
C. VERONA
Palazzo Grassi
C. BOTTEGHE
SAL. S. SAMUELE
CALLE DE LA FENICE
Ca' Rezzonico
S. Samuele 82, N, 3
CAMPO S. SAMUELE
SAL. MALIPIERO
9
S. Stefano
La Fenice
R. di S. Barnaba
Traghetto
S. Samuele
C. D. TEATRO
CAMPO SANTO STEFANO
R. d. Fenice
CALLE TRAGHETTO
Ca' Rezzonico 1
CORTE STORZA
C. FRUTTAROL
S. Maurizio
Ca'del Duca
Palazzo Loredan
CAMPO S. MAURIZIO
S. Maria del Giglio
R. del Duca
CAMPO PISANI
Palazzo Corner della Ca'Grande
S. Vitale
R. S. Vidal
R. Corner Zaguri
R. di S. M. Zobenigo
Accademia 1, 82, N, 3
R. dell'Orso
Palazzo Pisani
R. di S. Stefano
CAMPO DEL TRAGHETTO
PONTE D. ACCADEMIA
S. M. del Giglio 1
S. Trovaso
FONDAMENTA PRIULI
Accademia
CANAL GRANDE
Traghetto
Guggenheim Collection
CAMPO S. TROVASO
C. BARBARO
C. DEL BASTION
C. S. GREGORIA
C. DE
FONDAMENTA NANI
FONDAMENTA VENIER
FONDAMENTA OSPEDALETO
FOND. DE CA'BALA
FONDAMENTA SORANZO DELLA FORNACE
FONDAMENTA DELLA FORNACE
Squero San Trovaso
S. Maria dei Rosario (Gesuati)
RIO TERA ANTONIO FOSCARINI
CAMPO DI S. AGNESE
RIO TERA DI SAN VIO
ZATTERE AL
D

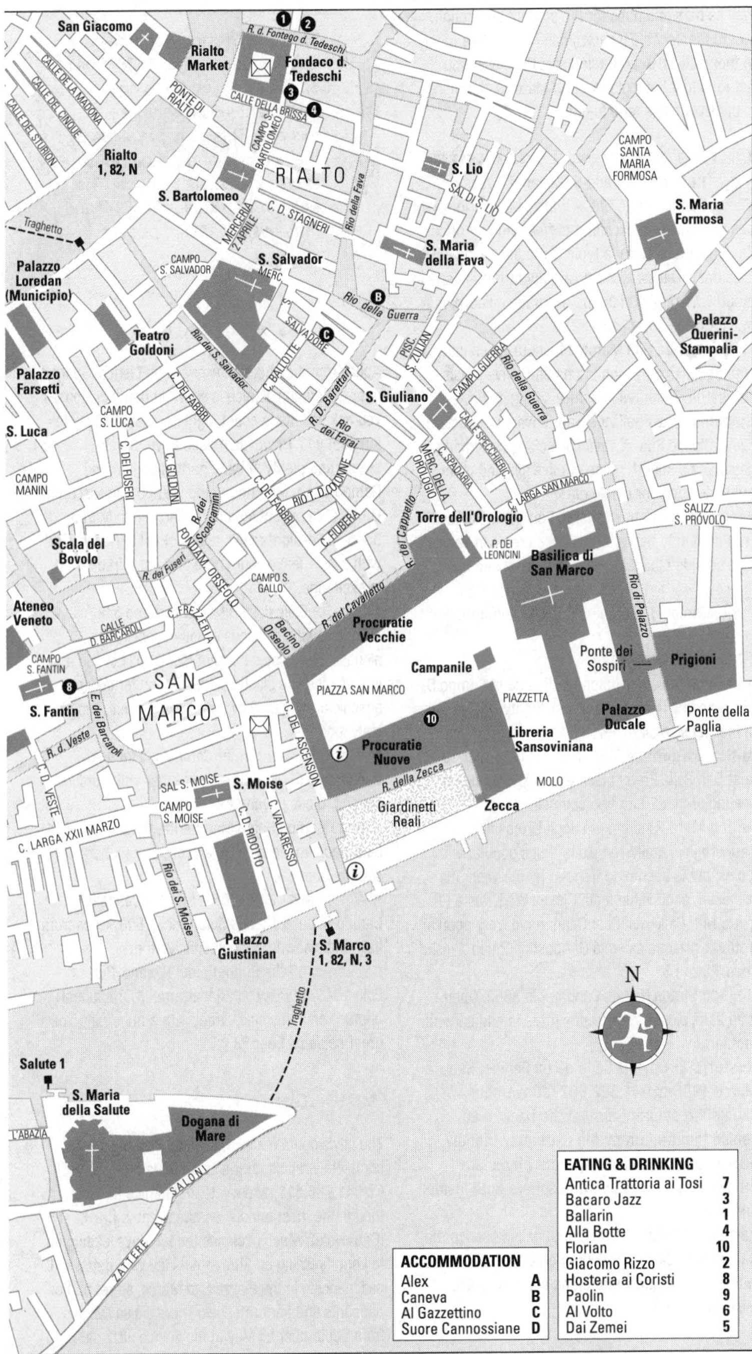
San Giacomo
Rialto Market
Fondaco d. Tedeschi
R. d. Fontego d. Tedeschi
CALLE DELLA BRISSA
CAMPO S. BARTOLOMEO
PONTE DI RIALTO
CALLE DE LA MADONA
CALLE DEL CINQUE
CALLE DEL STURION
Rialto 1, 82, N
RIALTO
S. Bartolomeo
S. Lio
SAL DI S. LIO
CAMPO SANTA MARIA FORMOSA
S. Maria Formosa
Traghetto
MERCERIA 2 APRILE
C. D. STAGNERI
Rio della Fava
S. Maria della Fava
Palazzo Loredan (Municipio)
CAMPO S. SALVADOR
S. Salvador
MERC. S. SALVADOR
Rio della Guerra
Teatro Goldoni
Rio dei S. Salvador
C. BALLOTTE
PISC. S. ZULIAN
Palazzo Querini-Stampalia
Palazzo Farsetti
C. DELFABBRI
R. D. Barettari
S. Giuliano
CAMPO GUERRA
Rio della Guerra
CAMPO S. LUCA
S. Luca
Rio dei Ferai
CALLE SPECCHIERIE
C. SPADARIA
MERC. DELLA OROLOGIO
C. DEI FUSERI
C. GOLDONI
CAMPO MANIN
R. dei Scoacamini
C. DEI FABBRI
RIO T. D. COLONNE
C. FIUBERA
C. LARGA SAN MARCO
R. del Cappello
Torre dell'Orologio
SALIZZ. S. PROVOLO
Scala del Bovolo
FONDAM. ORSEOLO
R. dei Fuseri
P. DEI LEONCINI
Basilica di San Marco
Rio di Palazzo
CAMPO S. GALLO
Ateneo Veneto
C. FREZZERIA
R. del Cavalletto
Procuratie Vecchie
Bacino Orseolo
CALLE D. BARCAROLI
CAMPO S. FANTIN
Campanile
Ponte dei Sospiri
Prigioni
SAN MARCO
PIAZZA SAN MARCO
PIAZZETTA
S. Fantin
E. dei Barcaroli
C. DEL ASCENSION
Palazzo Ducale
Ponte della Paglia
R. d. Veste
Libreria Sansoviniana
Procuratie Nuove
C. D. VESTE
SAL S. MOISE
S. Moise
R. della Zecca
MOLO
CAMPO S. MOISE
C. D. RIDOTTO
C. VALLARESSO
Giardinetti Reali
Zecca
C. LARGA XXII MARZO
Rio dei S. Moise
Palazzo Giustinian
S. Marco 1, 82, N, 3
Traghetto
N
Salute 1
S. Maria della Salute
Dogana di Mare
L'ABAZIA
ZATTERE AL SALONI
ACCOMMODATION
Alex A
Caneva B
Al Gazzettino C
Suore Cannossiane D
EATING & DRINKING
Antica Trattoria ai Tosi 7
Bacaro Jazz 3
Ballarin 1
Alla Botte 4
Florian 10
Giacomo Rizzo 2
Hosteria ai Coristi 8
Paolin 9
Al Volto 6
Dai Zemei 5

well as bars and pubs for the student population, where the *cechetti* (snacks) can constitute a meal in themselves. Bear in mind that the closer you get to tourist hotspots like San Marco's, the more expensive things tend to get.

Cafés and food markets

Ballarin Salizada S Giovanni Grisostomo, Cannaregio 5794. A warm, busy, brightly-lit *pasticcherie* with excellent coffee and low prices; the ideal place to try a typically Italian stand-up breakfast. The *pasticciotti*, a flaky tartlet filled with mouthwateringly thick and aromatic custard, is a must. Coffee and pastry €2.

Florian Piazza San Marco. Museum-piece café with astonishingly high prices and a live music surcharge. Think twice before sitting down.

Giacomo Rizzo Salizada San Giovanni Grisostomo 5778. Closed Sun. A *pastificio* selling handmade pasta and a superb range of olive oils and other products. Ideal for edible gifts.

Paolin Campo Santo Stefano, San Marco. Closed Fri. Reputed to make the best ice cream in Venice, with outside tables in one of the finest settings in the city.

Punto Campo di Margherita 5019B. Supermarket.

Restaurants

Alle Oche Calle del Tintor (south side of Campo S. Giacomo dell'Orio), Cannaregio. Eighty-odd varieties of inexpensive pizza. Pizza €4.

Antica Trattoria ai Tosi Calle del Cappeller 1586, near San Polo. Pretty place with a lovely outdoor seating area. €20 for two courses.

Antico Mola Fondamenta degli Ormesini, Cannaregio. Family-run place that's popular with locals, but is becoming trendier by the year. Still excellent, good value food. Closed Wed. Pasta €8.

Casa Mia Calle dell'Oca, Cannaregio. Very popular trattoria-pizzeria close to St Apostoli Chuch. Closed Tues. Pizza €8.

Dogado Strada Nuova, Cannaregio 3662. Open until 2am, closed Wed.Trendy pizzeria and bar with roof terrace. Pizza €7.

Hosteria ai Coristi Calle de La Fenice, San Marco 1995 ⓣ041.522.6677. Cavernous, candlelit restaurant around the back of La Fenice theatre, run by the extremely friendly Armando. Prices aren't low, but pizzas are affordable (€7) and the atmosphere both inside and out is lovely.

Paradiso Perduto Fondamenta della Misericordia, Cannaregio. Closed Wed. Fronted by a popular bar, with a relaxed atmosphere and occasional live music. Pasta €9.

TREAT YOURSELF

Trattoria Storica Ponte dei Gesuiti, Cannaregio 4858 ⓣ041 528 5266. If you go to one restaurant in Venice, make it this one. This cosy place run by the dynamic and affable Tony serves incredible seafood. The polenta with squid-ink (€14) and *fritta mista* (€12) are perfect.

Drinking and nightlife

Apart from the cheesy *Casanova* on Lista di Spagna near the station, Venice is short on dance action – if you ask Venetians about nightlife, they're likely to laugh at you. However, it does have a lively **artistic scene** and plenty of bars, particularly around Campo Santa Margherita and Campo San Giacomo.

Bacaro Jazz Fontego dei Tedeschi, San Marco 5546. Late-night music and cocktail bar decorated with bras – leave yours here and get a free t-shirt in exchange.

Alle Botte Calle della Bissa, San Marco 5482. *Osteria* serving delicious Venetian specialities, alongside an *enoteca*, where €2.80 will get you a litre of wine in a plastic bottle, perfect for taking on a picnic or for sitting by the side of a canal. And it's tasty too!

Maitardi Enobar Corner Campiello Flaminio, Cannaregio 5600. Relaxed wine-bar with outdoor seating. Glass of wine €2.

Orange Campo Santa Margherita, Dorsoduro 3054. Laid-back, modern bar in a lively, atmospheric square. Beer €3.

Al Volto Calle Cavalli 4081, San Marco, near Campo S. Luca. Closed Sun. Stocks 800 wines from Italy and elsewhere; good snacks, too.

Dai Zemei off the Rughetta del Ravano, San Polo 1045, ⓦwww.ostariadaizemei.it. Traditional *enoteca* on a tiny side-street with a huge range of great *cechetti*. Beer €3.

Entertainment

The city's opera house, La Fenice, has been completely rebuilt after a calamitous fire (ⓣ041.786.511, ⓦwww.teatrolafenice.it), though the most famous annual event is **Carnival** (Carnevale), which occupies the ten days leading up to Lent, finishing on Shrove Tuesday with a masked ball, dancing in the Piazza San Marco, street parties, pageants and performances. There's also live jazz from September till May at the Venice Jazz Club

(Fondamenta del Squero 3102, ⓣ340.150.4985, ⓦwww.venicejazzclub.com). To find out about **concerts and events** going on throughout the city, drop in to Vivaldi (Fontego de Tedeschi, San Bartolomeo 30124 ⓣ041.522.1343, ⓦwww.vivaldistore.com), a classical music shop and ticket office. Alternatively, check out the website ⓦwww.musicinvenice.com. For summertime Shakespeare performances at the Teatro Fondamenta Nuove, see ⓦwww.englishtheatreinvenice.com.

Directory

Exchange Strada Nuova 4194 (daily 9am–6.30pm).
Hospital Ospedale Civili Riunti di Venezia, Campo Santi Giovanni e Paolo (ⓣ041.523.0000).
Internet and International Phone Centre Calle delle Occa, Cannaregio 4426a (Mon–Sat 10am–10.30pm; €3/hr).
Laundry Speedy Wash, Strada Nuovo, Cannaregio 1520, 300m east from station, next to Planet Internet (€6/wash, €3/dry).
Left luggage Train station (daily 6am–midnight; €3.80/5hr).
Pharmacy Campo S Fosca 2233a (ⓣ041.720.600; 24hr).
Police Via Nicoldi 24, Marghera (ⓣ041.271.5511).
Post office Salizada del Fontego dei Tedeschi 5554, by the Rialto Bridge (Mon–Fri 8.30am–2pm, Sat 8.30am–1pm).

Moving on

Air Rome (5 daily; 1hr).
Train Bologna (every 30min; 2hr); Florence (hourly; 3hr); Milan (every 30min; 3hr); Padua (every 10min; 30min); Verona (every 30min; 1hr 30min); Trieste (hourly; 2hr).

BOLOGNA

BOLOGNA is the oldest university town in Europe (the institution dates back to the eleventh century) and teems with students and bookshops. Known for its left-wing politics, "Red Bologna" has long been the Italian Communist Party's spiritual home. It also boasts some of the richest food in Italy, a busy cultural life and a highly convivial café and bar scene.

What to see and do

The compact, colonnaded city centre reputedly has 25km of covered arcades, built to cover the horses brought to Bologna by the first university students, and is still startlingly medieval in plan. Buzzing **Piazza Maggiore** is the obvious place to make for, dominated by the church of **San Petronio**, which was originally intended to have been larger than St Peter's in Rome. You can see models of what the church was supposed to look like in the **museum** (Mon–Sat 9.30am–12.30pm & 2.30–5.30pm; Sun 2.30–5.30pm); otherwise the most intriguing feature is the **astronomical clock** – a long brass meridian line set at an angle across the floor, with a hole left in the roof for the sun to shine through on the right spot. There's an open-air cinema here in the summer – ask at the tourist information office for details.

Archiginnasio

Bologna's university – the **Archiginnasio** – was founded at more or less the same time as the Piazza Maggiore was laid out at the end of the eleventh century, though it didn't get a special building until 1565. The most interesting part is the **Teatro Anatomico** (Mon–Fri 9am–7pm, Sat 9am–1pm; free), the original medical faculty dissection theatre, whose tiers of seats surround a professor's chair, covered with a canopy supported by figures known as *gli spellati* – the skinned ones.

Piazza San Domenico

South, down Via Garibaldi, **Piazza San Domenico** is the site of the church of **San Domenico**, built in 1251 to house the relics of St Dominic. The angel and figures of saints Proculus and Petronius, in the **Arca**, were the work of a very young Michelangelo.

Centro Storico

At Piazza di Porta Ravegnana, the **Torre degli Asinelli** (daily 9am–6pm; €3) and perilously leaning **Torre Garisenda** are together known as the *Due Torri*, the only survivors of hundreds of towers that were scattered across the city during the Middle Ages, when possession of the towers determined the ranks of power within the city. Superstition holds that any student who enters these towers before graduation won't graduate at all.

Santo Stefano

From here, Via San Stefano leads down past a complex of four churches, collectively known as **Santo Stefano**. The striking polygonal church of **San Sepolcro**, reached through the church of **Crocifisso**, is the most interesting: the basin in its courtyard was reputedly used by Pilate to wash his hands after he condemned Christ to death. A doorway leads through to **San Vitale e Agricola**, Bologna's oldest church, built from discarded Roman fragments in the fifth century, while the fourth church, the **Trinita**, lies across the courtyard.

Arrival and information

Air Bologna's airport is northwest of the centre, linked by Airbus (€4.50) to the train station.
Train The train station is on Piazza delle Medaglie d'Oro, at the end of Via dell'Indipendenza.
Tourist office There are information booths at the airport (Mon–Sat 9am–8pm) and the train station (Mon–Sat 8.30am–7.30pm, Sun 9am–1pm; Ⓣ051.659.8751, Ⓦwww.provincia.bologna.it), and a main office at Piazza Maggiore 6 (daily 9am–8pm; Ⓣ051.246.541, Ⓦwww.comune.bologna.it/bolognaturismo for hotel bookings): all provide the free English-language listings magazines *Talkabout* and *Zero*, as well as *2night* for nightlife and *L'Ospite di Bologna* (A Guest of Bologna).
Internet is available for free in the library at Piazza Nettuno 3b; or try *Ital Communication* on Via Caduti Cefalonia 2E, which also has cheap international call booths.

Getting around

Walking is the best way to see Bologna, as the centre is compact and can be walked across in under 30min. Alternatively, you can rent **bikes** at Autorimessa Pincio, Via Independenza 71z (4min walk from the train station; €1.50/hr, €15/day). An underground train system is due to open in 2010.

Accommodation

Trade fairs happen several times a year (though they don't last very long), during which prices usually rise by about thirty percent – consequently, it's best to book ahead.
Albergo Pallone Via del Pallone 4 Ⓣ051.421.0533. Basic but clean place with a hostel feel and friendly staff. Go through the imposing-looking barbed-wire fence to get here. On the bus, stop at Sferisterio at the end of Via del Pallone, 30m from the hotel. ⑦
Camping Hotel and Residence Via Romita 12/4a Ⓣ051.325.016, Ⓦwww.hotelcamping.com. The local campsite, near the exhibition centre, and with a swimming pool. Dorm ③, camping ②
Garisenda Via Rizzoli 9, Galleria del Leone 1 Ⓣ051.224.369, Ⓦwww.albergogarisenda.com. A tiny hotel in the heart of Bologna, with just seven rooms, run by a lovely couple. Enter the covered shopping centre to get here, and go past the McDonalds. ⑦
HI Hostels Due Torri and San Sisto 6km outside the centre, at Via Viadagola 5 and 14 Ⓣ051.501.810; from Via Irnerio take bus #93 till 8pm and 21B after. Popular hostels with 11.30pm curfew. ②
Panorama Via Livraghi 1 Ⓣ051.221.802, Ⓦwww.hotelpanoramabologna.it. A pretty hotel near Piazza Maggiore. ⑦

Eating

Food markets

Condominio dei Via Ugo Bassi Via Ugo Bassi 25. Deli with a wide selection of pasta salads and cured meats. Closed Sundays.
Mercato delle Erbe Via Ugo Bassi 2. The biggest and liveliest of the city's food markets. There's a smaller market on Via Draperie specializing in fruit and sweets.

Restaurants

Broccaindosso Via Broccaindosso 7a. 8.30pm–3am, closed Sun. A legendary restaurant serving as much as you can eat for about €25 – leave room for dessert.
Modo Infoshop Via Mascarella 24b. Cool, laid-back music and bookshop serving organic food and coffees. The smiley staff are happy to help with travel-related queries. Hamburgers €6. Aperitif tapas from 6pm, food served from 7pm.
Quantobasta Via del Fratello 103a Ⓣ051.522.100, Ⓦwww.qbonline.it. Closed Sat lunchtime and Sun.

A tiny place very popular with locals, near the city walls, with a handful of excellent dishes to choose from. Pasta €7.

Drinking

The cheapest and liveliest area is the pub and bar-lined Via Zamboni, where the university students hang out.

College 3 Bar Largho Respighi. Graffitied lounge-style bar serving cheap and cheerful food – the €3.50 menu gets you a pizza and drink or coffee and pasta. Open until 3am.

English Empire 24a Via Zamboni. A lively English-style pub; during happy hour (daily 7–9pm), the aperitif buffet is sufficient to make up dinner. Beer €4. Open till 2am.

Maxim Piazza della Mercanzia 6 ⓦwww.caffemaxim2torri.it. Rowdy, chic and popular bar with good buffet. Beer €4.

Rosa Rose Via D'Azeglio 69. Chilled-out place with half-price drinks at happy hour (7–9.30pm).

Moving on

Train Ferrara (every 30min; 30min); Florence (every 30min; 1hr); Milan (every 30min; 2hr); Ravenna (hourly; 1hr 20min).

PARMA

PARMA, about 80km northwest of Bologna, is about as pleasant a town as you could wish for, with dignified streets, a wide range of good restaurants and an appealing air of provincial affluence. There's also plenty to see, not least the works of two key late-Renaissance artists – Correggio and Parmigianino.

What to see and do

Piazza Garibaldi is the fulcrum of Parma, and its cafés and surrounding alleyways are home to much of the town's nightlife. The mustard-coloured **Palazzo del Governatore** flanks the square, behind which stands the Renaissance church of **Madonna della Steccata**. Inside there are frescoes by a number of sixteenth-century painters, notably Parmigianino. It's also worth visiting the **Duomo**, on Piazza del Duomo in the north-east of the city centre, to see the octagonal **Baptistery** (Mon-Sun 9am–12.30pm & 3–6.30pm; €4), considered to be Benedetto Antelami's finest work, built in 1196. Frescoes by Correggio can be seen in the **Camera di San Paolo** (Tues–Sun 8.30am–1.45pm; €2), in the former Benedictine convent off Via Melloni, a few minutes' walk north.

East of the cathedral square, it's hard to miss Parma's biggest monument, the **Palazzo della Pilotta**, begun for Alessandro Farnese in the sixteenth century and rebuilt after World War II bombing. It now houses the city's main art gallery, the **Galleria Nazionale** (Tues–Sun 8.30am–1.45pm; €6), whose extensive collection includes more works by Correggio and Parmigianino. If you've had enough of all things cultural and fancy checking out some shopping streets, have a stroll down the wide and laid-back **Strada della Republica**.

Arrival and information

Train Parma's train station is a 15min walk from Piazza Garibaldi and all the buses in the city pass through it.

Tourist office Strada Melloni (Mon–Sat 9am–1pm & 2.30–6pm, Sun 9am–1pm; ⓣ0521.218.889, ⓦwww.turismo.comune.parma.it).

Internet Libreria Fiaccadori, Via Duomo 8. €4/hr.

International phone calls Jadom World Communications, Via San Leonardo 4.

Accommodation

Ducale Via Costituente 11 ⓣ0521.281.171, ⓦhttp://digilander.libero.it/bbducale.it/. Pleasant, family-run B&B 10min from the centre of town, with free bike hire. ❼

Foresteria Edison Largo Otto Marzo 9a ⓣ0521.967.088, ⓔsolares@solaresonline.it. An arts foundation with comfortable dorms. To get there take bus #2 from the Teatro Regio to the *capolinea* (the end of the line) and head right – it's round the back of the building opposite the art cinema. ❸

Leon d'Oro Viale A. Fratti 4 ⓣ0521.773.182, ⓦwww.leondoroparma.com. Basic, but clean with a helpful if eccentric owner, who suggests prices are negotiable. ❻

Ostello della Gioventu Via San Leonardo 86 ☎0521.191.7547, Ⓦwww.ostelloparma.it. New and very clean, with big rooms and helpful staff. Take bus #2 or #13 from the train station to Centro Torri (a shopping centre with two prominent towers) – the hostel is opposite, about 50m back up the road. Alternatively, you can walk left out of the station down Via San Leonardo, and be there in 20min. ❷

Eating

Cafés and food markets

Dimeglio Strada XXII Luglio 27c. Supermarket. Closed Sun.

Formaggi & Salumi 65b Strada Garibaldi. Brilliantly stocked-up deli, ideal for a picnic.

Restaurants

La Cantina di Tom Piazza del Carbone 9 ☎0521.030.815. Popular and fashionable place ideal for drinks and snacks. Pizza €4.

Il Gallo D'Oro Borgo Salina 3 (just off Via Farini). Superb unfussy local fare, such as *torta fritta* (small triangles of fried dough served warm with a variety of the cold cuts Parma is known for), at inexpensive prices. Mains €8.

Sorelle Pichi Via Farini 28. Specialising in cured meats; does a particularly spectacular ravioli. Mains €9.

20 Settembre Via XX Settembre ☎0521.385.594, Ⓦwww.ventisettembre.it. Cosy side-street restaurant with live music on Wed. Pasta €7.

Drinking

In the evening, the best place to head to is lively Via Farini, which has a buzzy atmosphere and is full of young people.

Bottiglia Azzura Borgo Felino 63. Charming *enoteca* also serving food.

Centrale del Rum Via Farini 54c ☎0521.533.809. Chilled-out hideaway off the beaten track, serving 218 kinds of rum. Open till 1am. Rum €2.50.

Le Malve Café Via Farini 12b. Vivacious customers overflow into the streets from this popular student hangout. Beers €3.

Tobago P le S Lorenxo 1. Closed Sun. Cool wine bar with a glossy, glassy interior, full of beautiful people.

Tribeca Strada G Mazzini 1. Swish basement cocktail lounge good for a dressy night out.

Entertainment

Free summer concerts are held in the Parco Vero Pellegrini – see the tourist office for details. There's also an annual Verdi festival in May/June (see the tourist office for details), while the Teatro Regio on Via Garibaldi (☎0521.039.300) is renowned for its **opera**. There are open-air films in the summer, usually beginning at 9.30pm ☎0521.218.889 for details.

RAVENNA

RAVENNA's colourful sixth-century mosaics are one of the crowning achievements of Byzantine art – in fact pretty much the only reason for visiting the town, these days a pretty but provincial backwater. The mosaics are the legacy of a quirk of fate 1500 years ago, when Ravenna briefly became capital of the Roman Empire, and can be seen in a day.

What to see and do

Aim for the **basilica of San Vitale**, ten minutes northwest of the centre, completed in 548 AD. Its mosaics, showing scenes from the Old Testament and the life of Christ, are in the apse. On the side walls of the apse are portraits of the Emperor Justinian and his wife Theodora, whose expression gives some hint of her notorious cruelty. Across from the basilica is the tiny **Mausoleo di Galla Placidia**, whose mosaics glow with a deep-blue lustre. Galla Placidia was the daughter, sister, wife and mother of various Roman emperors, and the interior of her fifth-century mausoleum, whose cupola is covered in tiny stars, is breathtaking. Next to San Vitale, the **National Museum of Antiquities** (Tues–Sun 8.30am–7pm; €4) displays a sixth-century statue of Hercules capturing a stag. East of here, on the **Via**

RAVENNA FESTIVAL

In the summer, there's live classical music every night in the atmospheric **Piazza del Popolo**, usually beginning at 9pm. Ⓦwww.ravennafestival.org.

di Roma, is the sixth-century basilica of **Sant'Apollinare Nuovo**, a building lined with colonnades and windows, giving a peaceful, otherworldly atmosphere. Mosaics run the length of the nave, depicting processions of martyrs bearing gifts – the sheer number of martyrs is staggering. Five minutes' walk up Via di Roma, the **Arian Baptistery**, also known as the **Basilica dello Spirito Santo**, has a fine mosaic ceiling.

A **combined ticket** (€9.50) covers most of Ravenna's sights; it's available from any of the participating museums, and is valid for a week. Opening times for all the sights are daily 9am–5pm.

Arrival and information

Train It's only a 5min walk from the train station on Piazza Farini, along Viale Farini and Via A. Diaz, to the central Piazza del Popolo.

Tourist office Via Salara 8/12 (Mon–Sat 8.30am–6pm, Sun 10am–4pm; ⓣ0544.35.404, ⓦwww.turismo.ravenna.it), stocks maps, guides and the *Mega Coolissimo* (ⓦwww.coolissimo.it) booklet, which has details of club nights.

Accommodation

Dante Via Aurelio Nicolodi 12 ⓣ0544.421.164. Large HI hostel 10min walk out of town (turn left out of the station), or take Metrobus Rosso from opposite the station. Curfew 11.30pm. ❷

Locanda del Melarancio Via Mentana 33 ⓣ0544.215.258, ⓦwww.locandadelmelarancio.it. Closed July. A friendly, pretty B&B near Piazza del Popolo, also popular for food and an evening drink. ❺

Eating and drinking

Cabiria Via Mordani 8. Closed Sun. Very welcoming wine bar just off Piazza del Popolo, open till 2am. Beer €4.

Grand Italia Piazza del Popolo 9–10. Trendy central bar and restaurant with seating on the square and a generous "free" buffet during happy hour (6–9pm). Open till 2am. Beer €3.50.

La Rustica Via Alberoni 55 ⓣ0544.218.128. Cosy trattoria serving reasonably priced dishes. Pasta €7.

Moving on

Train to Bologna (every 30min; 90min); Florence (every 45min; 3hr); Pesaro (for Urbino) (hourly; 2hr).

Central Italy

The Italian heartland of **Tuscany** represents the archetypal image of the country, and its walled towns and rolling, vineyard-covered hills are the classic backdrops of Renaissance art. **Florence** is the first port of call, from the Uffizi gallery's masterpieces to the great fresco cycles in the churches. **Siena**, one of the great medieval cities of Europe, is also the scene of Tuscany's one unmissable festival – the Palio – which sees bareback horse riders careering around the cobbled central square, while **Pisa**'s leaning tower, a feat of engineering against gravity, and intricately decorated cathedral justifiably attract hordes of tourists. To the east lies **Umbria** (ⓦwww.umbria2000.it), a beautiful region of rolling hills, woods and valleys; the capital, **Perugia**, is a buzzing and energetic town, while **Assisi** is justifiably famed for its gorgeous setting and extraordinary frescoes by Giotto. Further east still, in the Marche region, is **Urbino**, with its superb Renaissance ducal palace.

FLORENCE

Ever since the nineteenth-century revival of interest in Renaissance art, **FLORENCE** (Firenze) has been a shrine to the beautiful. Its indoor pleasures are incomparable, its chapels, galleries and museums embodying the complex, exhilarating and often elusive spirit of the Renaissance more fully than any other town in the country. The city became the centre of artistic patronage in Italy under the Medici family, who ruled Florence as an independent state

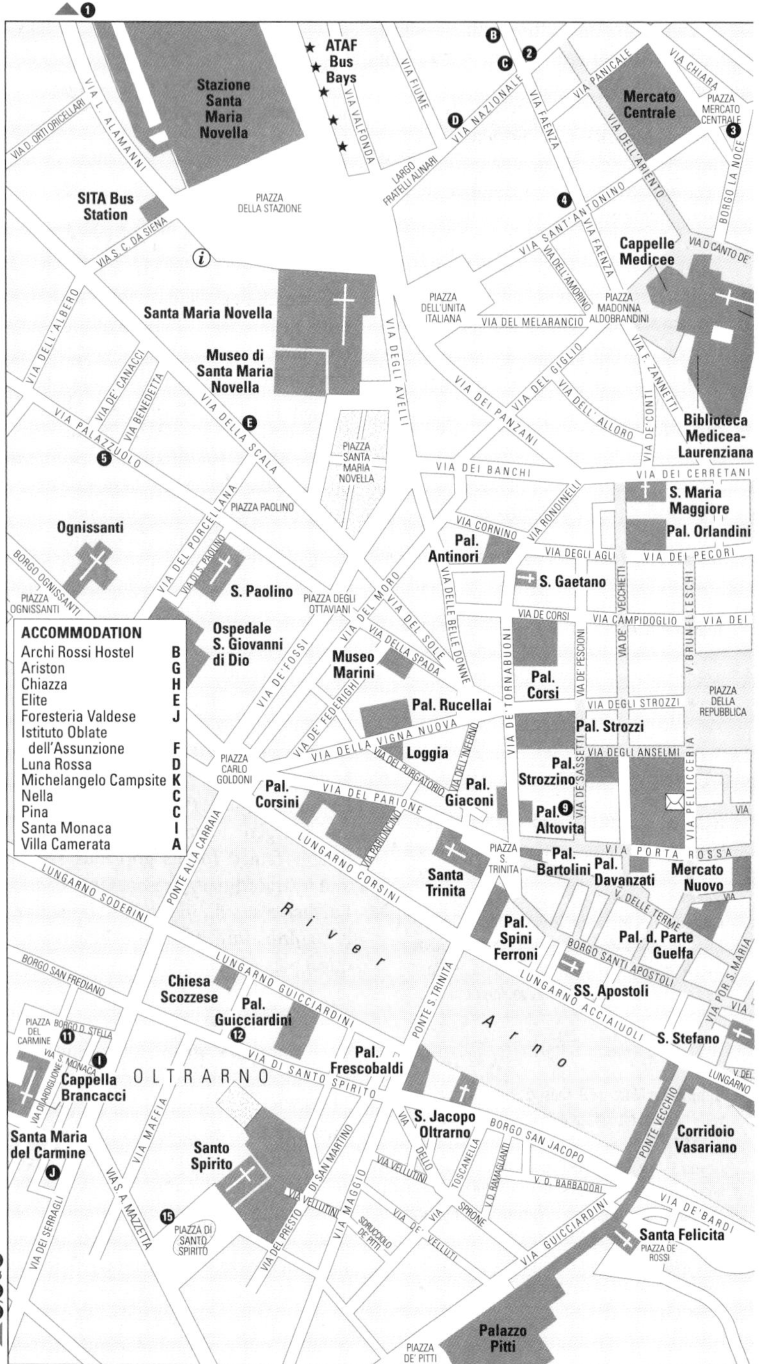
ACCOMMODATION
Archi Rossi Hostel B
Ariston G
Chiazza H
Elite E
Foresteria Valdese J
Istituto Oblate dell'Assunzione F
Luna Rossa D
Michelangelo Campsite K
Nella C
Pina C
Santa Monaca I
Villa Camerata A
ATAF Bus Bays
Stazione Santa Maria Novella
SITA Bus Station
Piazza della Stazione
Mercato Centrale
Piazza Mercato Centrale
Cappelle Medicee
Santa Maria Novella
Museo di Santa Maria Novella
Piazza dell'Unita Italiana
Piazza Madonna Aldobrandini
Biblioteca Medicea-Laurenziana
Piazza Santa Maria Novella
Piazza Paolino
Ognissanti
S. Paolino
Piazza Ognissanti
Ospedale S. Giovanni di Dio
Piazza degli Ottaviani
Museo Marini
S. Maria Maggiore
Pal. Orlandini
Pal. Antinori
S. Gaetano
Pal. Corsi
Piazza della Repubblica
Pal. Rucellai
Pal. Strozzi
Loggia
Piazza Carlo Goldoni
Pal. Corsini
Pal. Giaconi
Pal. Strozzino
Pal. Altovita
Piazza S. Trinita
Santa Trinita
Pal. Bartolini
Pal. Davanzati
Mercato Nuovo
Pal. Spini Ferroni
Pal. d. Parte Guelfa
SS. Apostoli
S. Stefano
River Arno
Chiesa Scozzese
Pal. Guicciardini
Pal. Frescobaldi
Piazza del Carmine
Cappella Brancacci
OLTRARNO
Santa Maria del Carmine
Santo Spirito
Piazza di Santo Spirito
S. Jacopo Oltrarno
Corridoio Vasariano
Santa Felicita
Piazza de' Rossi
Palazzo Pitti
Piazza de' Pitti
Via L. Alamanni
Via d. Orti Oricellari
Via Valfonda
Via Fiume
Via Nazionale
Via Faenza
Via Panicale
Via Chiara
Borgo la Noce
Via dell'Ariento
Largo Fratelli Alinari
Via Sant'Antonino
Via d. Canto de'
Via S. C. da Siena
Via dell'Amorino
Via del Melarancio
Via degli Avelli
Via dell'Albero
Via de' Canacci
Via Benedetta
Via Palazzuolo
Via della Scala
Via dei Panzani
Via del Giglio
Via dell'Alloro
Via F. Zannetti
Via de' Conti
Via dei Banchi
Via dei Cerretani
Via Rondinelli
Via Cornino
Via del Porcellana
Via d. S. Paolino
Borgo Ognissanti
Via degli Agli
Via dei Pecori
Via delle Belle Donne
Via del Moro
Via del Sole
Via della Spada
Via de' Fossi
Via de Corsi
Via Campidoglio
Via de' Vecchietti
Via de' Pescioni
V. Brunelleschi
Via de' Tornabuoni
Via degli Strozzi
Via de' Federighi
Via della Vigna Nuova
Via del Purgatorio
Via dell'Inferno
Via de' Sassetti
Via degli Anselmi
Via Pellicceria
Via del Parione
Via Parioncino
Via Porta Rossa
Ponte alla Carraia
Lungarno Corsini
Lungarno Soderini
V. delle Terme
Borgo Santi Apostoli
Lungarno Acciaiuoli
Via Por S. Maria
Borgo San Frediano
Lungarno Guicciardini
Ponte S. Trinita
Borgo d. Stella
Via S. Monaca
Via d'Ardiglione
Via di Santo Spirito
Via Maffia
Via S. A. Mazzetta
Via dei Serragli
Via del Presto di San Martino
Via Vellutini
Via Maggio
Sdrucciolo de' Pitti
Via dello
Via Toscanella
V. d. Ramaglianti
Via Sprone
Via de' Velluti
Borgo San Jacopo
V. d. Barbadori
Ponte Vecchio
Via de' Bardi
Via Guicciardini
Lungarno
16, 17 & 18

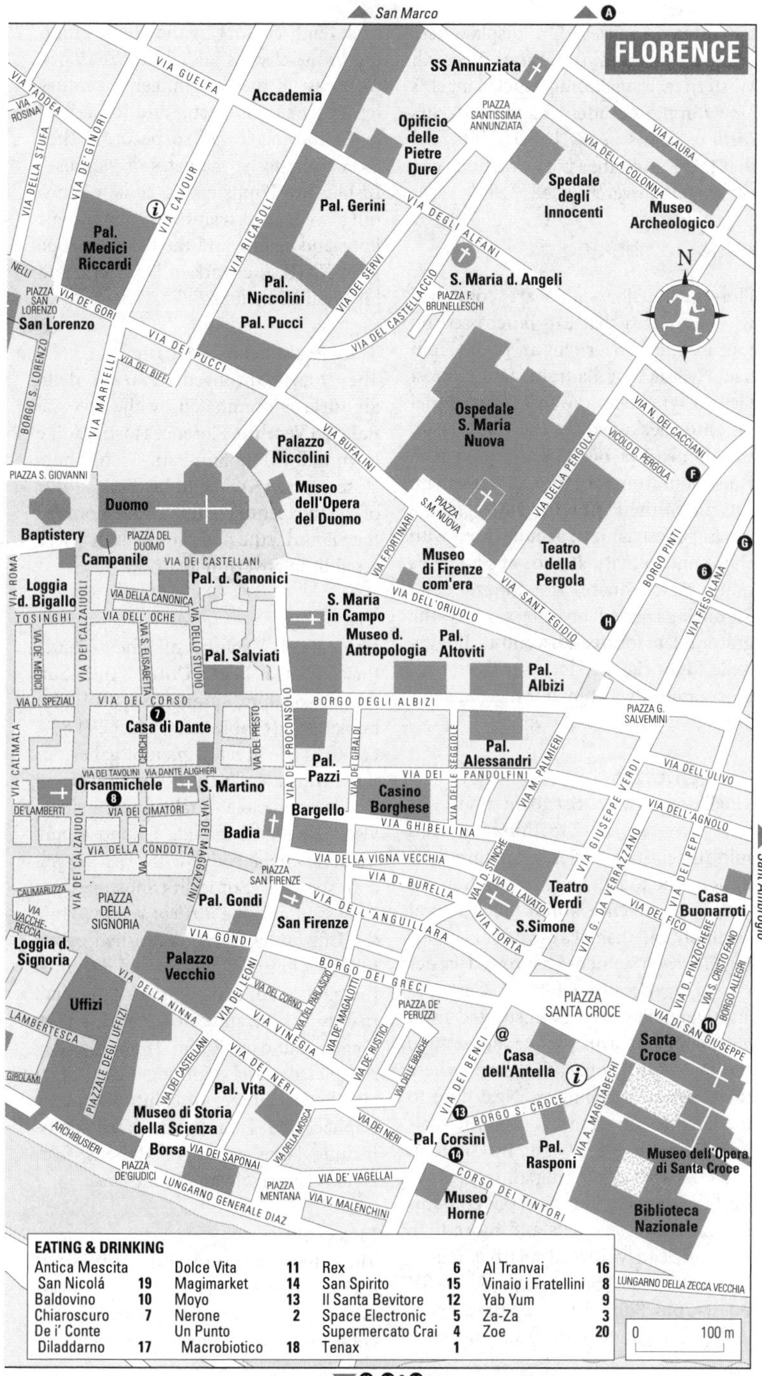

San Marco
A
FLORENCE
SS Annunziata
Accademia
Opificio delle Pietre Dure
PIAZZA SANTISSIMA ANNUNZIATA
VIA GUELFA
VIA TADDEA
VIA ROSINA
VIA DE' GINORI
VIA DELLA STUFA
VIA CAVOUR
VIA RICASOLI
Pal. Gerini
VIA DEGLI ALFANI
VIA LAURA
VIA DELLA COLONNA
Spedale degli Innocenti
Museo Archeologico
Pal. Medici Riccardi
NELLI
PIAZZA SAN LORENZO
VIA DE' GORI
San Lorenzo
Pal. Niccolini
Pal. Pucci
VIA DEI SERVI
VIA DEL CASTELLACCIO
S. Maria d. Angeli
PIAZZA F. BRUNELLESCHI
N
VIA DEI PUCCI
VIA DEI BIFFI
BORGO S. LORENZO
VIA MARTELLI
Ospedale S. Maria Nuova
VIA BUFALINI
Palazzo Niccolini
VIA N. DEI CACCIANI
VICOLO D. PERGOLA
VIA DELLA PERGOLA
F
PIAZZA S. GIOVANNI
Museo dell'Opera del Duomo
Duomo
PIAZZA S.M. NUOVA
Baptistery
PIAZZA DEL DUOMO
Campanile
VIA DEI CASTELLANI
Pal. d. Canonici
VIA F. PORTINARI
Museo di Firenze com'era
Teatro della Pergola
BORGO PINTI
G
6
VIA FIESOLANA
VIA ROMA
Loggia d. Bigallo
VIA DELLA CANONICA
S. Maria in Campo
VIA DELL'ORIUOLO
VIA SANT' EGIDIO
H
TOSINGHI
VIA DELL' OCHE
VIA DE' MEDICI
VIA DEI CALZAIUOLI
VIA S. ELISABETTA
VIA DELLO STUDIO
Pal. Salviati
Museo d. Antropologia
Pal. Altoviti
Pal. Albizi
VIA D. SPEZIALI
VIA DEL CORSO
BORGO DEGLI ALBIZI
7
Casa di Dante
VIA DEL PRESTO
VIA DEL PROCONSOLO
PIAZZA G. SALVEMINI
VIA CALIMALA
VIA DE' GIRALDI
VIA DELLE SEGGIOLE
Pal. Alessandri
VIA M. PALMIERI
CERCHI
Pal. Pazzi
VIA DEI PANDOLFINI
VIA DELL'ULIVO
VIA DEI TAVOLINI
VIA DANTE ALIGHIERI
Orsanmichele
S. Martino
8
Casino Borghese
VIA GIUSEPPE VERDI
VIA DELL'AGNOLO
DE'LAMBERTI
VIA DEI CIMATORI
Bargello
VIA GHIBELLINA
Badia
Sant'Ambrogio
VIA DELLA CONDOTTA
VIA DEI MAGGAZZINI
VIA DELLA VIGNA VECCHIA
VIA D. STINCHE
VIA G. DA VERRAZZANO
VIA DEI PEPI
PIAZZA SAN FIRENZE
VIA D. BURELLA
CALIMARUZZA
PIAZZA DELLA SIGNORIA
Pal. Gondi
VIA DELL'ANGUILLARA
VIA D. LAVATOI
Teatro Verdi
Casa Buonarroti
VIA VACCHERECCIA
San Firenze
VIA TORTA
S.Simone
VIA DEL FICO
Loggia d. Signoria
VIA GONDI
VIA D. PINZOCHERE
VIA S. CRISTO FANO
Palazzo Vecchio
BORGO DEI GRECI
BORGO ALLEGRI
VIA DE' LEONI
VIA DEL CORNO
VIA DEL PARLASCIO
VIA DE' MAGALOTTI
PIAZZA SANTA CROCE
Uffizi
VIA DELLA NINNA
PIAZZA DE' PERUZZI
10
LAMBERTESCA
VIA VINEGIA
VIA DI SAN GIUSEPPE
Santa Croce
VIA DE' RUSTICI
VIA DELLE BRACHE
@
VIA DEI CASTELLANI
Casa dell'Antella
PIAZZALE DEGLI UFFIZI
VIA DEI NERI
VIA DEI BENCI
GIROLAMI
Pal. Vita
VIA A. MAGLIABECHI
BORGO S. CROCE
13
Museo di Storia della Scienza
ARCHIBUSIERI
VIA DELLA MOSCA
VIA DEI NERI
Pal. Corsini
14
Borsa
VIA DEI SAPONAI
Pal. Rasponi
Museo dell'Opera di Santa Croce
PIAZZA DE'GIUDICI
LUNGARNO GENERALE DIAZ
PIAZZA MENTANA
VIA DE' VAGELLAI
VIA V. MALENCHINI
CORSO DEI TINTORI
Museo Horne
Biblioteca Nazionale
EATING & DRINKING
Antica Mescita San Nicolá 19
Baldovino 10
Chiaroscuro 7
De i' Conte Diladdarno 17
Dolce Vita 11
Magimarket 14
Moyo 13
Nerone 2
Un Punto Macrobiotico 18
Rex 6
San Spirito 15
Il Santa Bevitore 12
Space Electronic 5
Supermercato Crai 4
Tenax 1
Al Tranvai 16
Vinaio i Fratellini 8
Yab Yum 9
Za-Za 3
Zoe 20
LUNGARNO DELLA ZECCA VECCHIA
0 100 m
K, 19 & 20

for three centuries. On display here are some of the most famous pieces in Western art, including Michelangelo's *David* in the Accademia and Botticelli's *Birth of Venus* in the Uffizi – but note that these and other big attractions can get seriously overcrowded.

What to see and do

Florence's major sights are contained within an area that can be crossed on foot in a little over half an hour. From Santa Maria Novella train station, most visitors gravitate towards **Piazza del Duomo**, beckoned by the pinnacle of the dome. **Via dei Calzaiuoli**, which runs south from the Duomo, is the main catwalk of the Florentine *passeggiata*, a broad pedestrianized avenue lined with shops and activity. It ends at Florence's other main square, the **Piazza della Signoria**, fringed on one side by the graceful late fourteenth-century **Loggia della Signoria** and dotted with statues, most famously a copy of Michelangelo's *David*.

The Duomo

The **Duomo** (Mon–Sat 10am–5pm) was built between the late thirteenth and mid-fifteenth centuries to an ambitious design. The fourth largest church in the world, its ambience is more that of a great assembly hall than of a devotional building. Its seven stained-glass roundels, designed by Uccello, Ghiberti, Castagno and Donatello, are best inspected from a gallery that forms part of the route to the top of the dome (€6), from where the views are stupendous. Next door to the Duomo stands the **Campanile** (daily 8.30am–7pm; €6) begun by Giotto in 1334. As well as offering an impressive bird's-eye view of Florence, this contains several enormous bells and more than fifty intricately carved marble reliefs. Opposite, the **Baptistery** (Mon–Sat noon–7pm, Sun 8.30am–2pm; €3), generally thought to date from the sixth or seventh century, is the oldest building in the city. Its gilded bronze doors, were cast in the early fifteenth century by Lorenzo Ghiberti, and described by Michelangelo as "so beautiful they are worthy to be the gates of Paradise". Inside, the Baptistery is equally stunning, with a thirteenth-century mosaic floor and ceiling and the tomb of Pope John XXIII, the work of Donatello and his pupil Michelozzo.

The Palazzo Vecchio

The tourist-thronged **Piazza della Signoria** is dominated by the colossal **Palazzo Vecchio**, Florence's fortress-like town hall (Mon–Sun 9am–7pm, Thurs closes 2pm; €6), begun in the last year of the thirteenth century as the home of the Signoria, the highest tier of the city's republican government.

The Uffizi

Immediately south of the piazza, the **Galleria degli Uffizi** (Tues–Sun 8.15am–6.50pm; summer Sat till 10pm; booking advisable on ☎055.294.883; €6.50) is the greatest picture gallery in Italy, with a collection of masterpieces that is impossible to take in on a single visit. Highlights include Filippo Lippi's *Madonna and Child with Two Angels* and some of Botticelli's most famous works, notably the *Birth of Venus*. While the Uffizi doesn't own a finished painting that's entirely by Leonardo da Vinci, there's a celebrated *Annunciation* that's mainly by him, and Michelangelo's *Doni Tondo*, found in Room 18, is his only completed easel painting. The Uffizi also has a number of compositions by Raphael and Titian, while later rooms include large works by Rubens, Van Dyck, Caravaggio and Rembrandt.

Bargello

The **Bargello museum** (Tues–Sat 8.15am–1.50pm; €4) lies just northwest of the Uffizi in Via del Proconsolo. The collection contains numerous works by

Michelangelo, Cellini and Giambologna. Upstairs is Donatello's sexually ambiguous bronze *David*, the first freestanding nude figure since classical times, cast in the early 1430s.

North: San Lorenzo

The church of **San Lorenzo** (daily 10am–5pm; €2.50), north of Piazza del Duomo, has good claim to be the oldest church in Florence. At the top of the left aisle and through the cloisters, the **Biblioteca Medicea-Laurenziana** (Mon–Sat 9am–1.30pm; free) was designed by Michelangelo in 1524; its most startling feature is the vestibule, a room almost filled by a flight of steps resembling a solidified lava flow. Just east of here, the **Accademia** (Tues–Sun 8.15am–6.50pm; €6.50), Europe's first school of drawing, is swamped by people in search of Michelangelo's *David*. Finished in 1504, when the artist was just 29, and carved from a gigantic block of marble, it's an incomparable show of technical bravura.

East: Santa Croce

Down by the river, to the southeast of the centre, the church of **Santa Croce** (Mon–Sat 9.30am–5.30pm, Sun 1–5pm; €4, including museum), begun in 1294, is full of tombstones and commemorative monuments, including Vasari's monument to Michelangelo and, on the opposite side of the church, the tomb of Galileo, built in 1737 when it was finally agreed to give the scientist a Christian burial. Most visitors, however, come to see the dazzling frescoes by Giotto.

South: Oltrarno and beyond

The photogenic thirteenth-century **Ponte Vecchio**, loaded with jewellers' shops overhanging the water, leads from the city centre across the river to the district of **Oltrarno**. Head west, past the relaxed, café-lined square of **Santo Spirito**, to the church of **Santa Maria del Carmine** – an essential visit for the superbly restored frescoes by Masaccio in its **Cappella Brancacci** (Mon & Wed–Sat 10am–5pm, Sun 1–5pm; €4).

Palazzo Pitti

South of Santo Spirito is the massive bulk of the fifteenth-century **Palazzo Pitti.** Nowadays this contains six separate museums, the best of which, the **Galleria Palatina** (Tues–Sun 8.15am–6.50pm; summer Sat till 10pm; €6.50), houses some superb Raphaels and Titians. The rest of the first floor is dominated by the staterooms of the **Appartamenti Monumentali** (included in the Galleria Palatina ticket). The Pitti's enormous formal garden, the delightful **Giardino di Bûboli** (Tues–Sun 8.15am–4.30/7.30pm; €4), is also worth a visit. Beyond here, the multicoloured facade of **San Miniato al Monte** (daily 8am–12.30pm & 2.30–7pm) lures troupes of visitors up the hill. The interior is like no other in the city, and its form has changed little since the mid-eleventh century.

Arrival and information

Air Pisa's international airport is connected by a regular train service (1hr) with Florence's central Santa Maria Novella train station (given on timetables as "Firenze SMN"). Alternatively, the Terravision bus goes to Pisa Airport from outside the train station (1hr; €8). Flights also come into Florence's tiny Peretola airport, 5km out of the city and connected by bus.
Train The main train station is at Piazza Santa Maria Novella, in the northwest of the city centre, 10min walk from the Piazza del Duomo.
Bus The main bus station is located alongside Santa Maria Novella – the SITA buses are a quick, easy way to travel to nearby cities such as Siena and Pisa. ATAF runs the reliable local service.
Tourist office The main tourist office is at Via Cavour 7r, a few hundred metres north of the Duomo (Mon–Sat 8.30am–7pm, Sun 8.30am–2pm; ⓣ055.290.832, ⓦwww.firenzeturismo.it) with a branch opposite the train station.

City transport

Bus If you want to cover a long distance in a hurry, take one of the orange ATAF buses; tickets (€1) are valid for one hour and can be bought from *tabacchi*.

Bike rental Renting a bicycle is a great way to explore the side-streets and enjoy the river views; the council's *Mille e una bici* scheme (€1.50/hr, €8/day) makes it easy – there's a pick-up/drop-off point at the train station, or ask at the tourist office.

Accommodation

Florence's most affordable hotels are close to the station, in particular along and around Via Faenza and the parallel Via Fiume, and along Via della Scala and Piazza Santa Maria Novella; you could also try Via Cavour, north of the Duomo, or the Oltrarno district on the south bank. **Advance booking** is advisable, or try the *Informazioni Turistiche Alberghiere* accommodation office at the train station (daily 8.45am–8pm; ⓣ055.282.893), which can make last-minute reservations for a fee.

Hostels and camping

Archi Rossi Hostel Via Faenza 94r ⓣ055.29.08.04, ⓦwww.hostelarchirossi.com. Lively, arty hostel right by the station with free Internet and a private garden. ❸

Foresteria Valdese Via dei Serragli 49 ⓣ055.212.576, ⓦwww.istitutogould.it/foresteria. A charming hostel in a beautiful old convent, where many of the generously proportioned rooms have en-suite bathrooms and large terraces – book early. ❸

Istituto Oblate dell'Assunzione Via Borgo Pinti 15 ⓣ055.248.0582, ⓔsroblateborgopinti@virgilio.it. Pleasant place not far from the Duomo, run by missionaries. 11.30pm curfew. ❹

Michelangelo Campsite Piazzale Michelangelo, Viale Michelangelo 80 ⓣ055.681.197, ⓦwww.camping.it/toscana/michelangelo. Centrally located campsite with great views and a popular bar. Walking distance from city centre, or take bus #12 or #13. ❷

Santa Monaca Via Santa Monaca 6, Oltrarno ⓣ055.268.338, ⓦwww.ostello.it. Very popular hostel in a converted fifteenth-century convent, with a 1am curfew. ❷

Villa Camerata Viale Righi 2 ⓣ055.601.451. HI hostel in a beautiful park, 30min out of town on bus #17 from the train station, midnight curfew. ❷

Hotels

Ariston Via Fiesolana 40 ⓣ055.247.6980, ⓦwww.hotelaristonfirenze.it. Small, clean hotel in convenient area. ❼

Chiazza Borgo Pinti 5 ⓣ055.248.0363, ⓦwww.chiazzahotel.com. Neat hotel in a quiet but fairly central location with buffet breakfast. ❽

Elite Via della Scala 12 ⓣ055.215.395. Warm and polite two-star hotel near Santa Maria Novella, with some en-suite rooms. ❻

Luna Rossa Via Nazionale 7/3 ⓣ055.230.2185, ⓦwww.marcosplaces.com. Extremely well-equipped place with a relaxed atmosphere, run by the helpful Marco. All rooms have computers with Internet access, and the kitchen has a washing machine which can be used free of charge. ❽

Nella/Pina Via Faenza 69 ⓣ055.265.4346, ⓦwww.hotelnella.net. Two basic, clean hotels under the same friendly owner. ❼

Eating

Cafés and food markets

The best place to find picnic food and snacks is the Mercato Centrale, just east of the train station. Otherwise, try a *vinaio*, a wine cellar/snack bar that serves *crostini* and other snacks.

Antica Mescita San Niccolú Via San Niccolú 60/r. Closed Sun. Delicatessen and *osteria* with an unrivalled cheese and wine selection, plus superb Tuscan soups. Lunch buffet 12.30–2.30pm, €10.

Chiaroscuro Via del Corso 36r. Small, buzzy café and bar with generous aperitif buffet. Coffee €1.50, drink with buffet €8.

Magimarket Corso dei Tintor 18–24. Mon–Sat 8am–9pm, Sun 9am–9pm. Supermarket.

Supermercato Crai Via Faenza 48r. Daily 8am–9pm.

Restaurants

Restaurants in Florence tend to be quite pricey, but most have reasonably priced pizzas and it's possible to eat out cheaply if you're careful what you order.

Al Tranvai Piazza T. Tasso 14/r ⓣ055.225.197. Closed Sun. Good, inexpensive Florentine specialities – arrive early to secure a table. Gnocchi €7.

Baldovino Via San Giuseppe 223 ⓣ055.241.773. Open until 1am, closed Mon. Charming trattoria just off the Piazza San Croce. Pizza €7.

De i'Conte Diladdarno Via de'Serragli 108 ⓣ055.225.001. Closed Sun. Typical Tuscan cuisine at reasonable prices, with a garden at the back. Special deals for students. Main course €8.

Nerone Via Faenza 95 – 97/R ⓣ055.291.217. Friendly pizzeria with stone oven, opulent, funky decor and pavement seating. Pizza €7.

Un Punto Macrobiotico Piazza Tasso 3. Closed Sun. See box, opposite.

Il Santa Bevitore Via di San Spirito 64/66 ⓣ055.211.264. Lovely atmospheric restaurant for a sophisticated evening meal. Pasta €8.

UN PUNTO MACROBIOTICO

These organic vegetarian deli-restaurants can be found throughout Italy and are a great way to have a tasty, cut-price meal. There are two or three macrobiotic set-menus to choose from, at €5 for your first visit, which covers membership, and €2 for subsequent visits.

 **San Spirito** Piazza di Santo Spirito 16r ⓣ055.238.2383. Closed Sun. Lovely buzzy *osteria* in a beautiful square serving simple, delicious food. Pizza €7.

Za-Za Piazza del Mercato Centrale 26r ⓣ055.215.411. A few tables on ground level, and outside in the summer; a bigger canteen below. Pasta €7, grills €14.

Drinking and nightlife

Bars

Mercato Generale, just east of the bus and train station, has some of Florence's cheapest bars. Less cool than the nightlife mentioned below, they are usually packed.

Dolce Vita Piazza del Carmine. 5.30pm–1.30am, closed Sun. Trendy late-night hangout that also stages small-scale art exhibitions.

Vinaio i Fratellini Via dei Cimatori 38. Closed Aug. A typical Florentine *vinaio.*

Moyo Via dei Benci 23r. Chilled-out, atmospheric café and bar with great cocktails, serving food until 5pm and drinks with buffet until 2am. Large beer/cocktail €5.

Rex Via Fiesolana 25r, Santa Croce. Wed–Mon 5pm–2.30am; closed Aug. Good music, a varied clientele, and serves snacks and cocktails.

Zoe Via dei Renail 13/r, Oltrarno ⓣ055243111. Daily 8am–3am. Atmospheric cocktail bar for poseurs, with small-scale painting exhibitions, outdoor seating and snack food during the day. Cocktails €5.

Clubs

Space Electronic Via Palazzuolo 37, ⓦwww.spaceelectronic.com. The favourite cheesy club among young foreigners, open nightly from 10pm.

Tenax Via Pratese 47. Open Fri & Sat from 10pm. The city's biggest club and one of its leading venues for new and established bands, playing an eclectic mix of indie, trance, modern pop and old classics. Bus #29 or #30.

Yab Yum Via de' Sassetti 5r. City-centre club, near the Duomo, playing new dance music. Mon–Sat from 8pm.

Entertainment

For listings information, call in at **Box Office**, Via Alamanni 39 (ⓣ055.210.804), or consult *Firenze Spettacolo* and *Informa Città*. As for festivals, in May the **Maggio Musicale** (ⓦwww.maggiofiorentino.com) features concerts, gigs and other events throughout the city, while the **Festa di San Giovanni** (June 24) sees the city's saint honoured with a massive fireworks display. Free concerts and events take place around Florence throughout the summer – see the tourist office for details. There's a cinema, *Fulgor*, at 22 Via Maso Finguerra.

Shopping

In general, the shopping in Florence is upmarket and fairly expensive, but **markets** and **high street shops** provide some cheaper options. Piazza del Mercato Nuovo, near the Dome, has a market (daily 9am–6.30pm), and Via dei Calzaiuoli is the main shopping street for high street names and department stores. For leather goods, head to the many *pelletterias* around Piazza di San Lorenzo, to the west of the Dome. There's also a market in and around the square (Fri & Sat 9am–7pm), selling clothes and jewellery. If you're feeling flush, Via Por Santa Maria, near the river on the south-west of the Dome, is full of upmarket women's **boutiques** selling clothes, belts and handbags. And of course, there's always the option of window-shopping, in which case you could take in classy Via de' Tornabuoni, running north-south towards the river just southeast of the station, or be dazzled by the gold and silver jewellery on the Ponte Vecchio.

Directory

Consulates UK, Lungarno Corsini 2 ⓣ055.284.133; US, Lungarno Vespucci 38 ⓣ055.239.8276.

Exchange The city is full of ATMs and exchange bureaus; the one at the station is open 8am–7pm daily.

Hospitals Santa Maria Nuova, Piazza Santa Maria Nuova 1 ⓣ055.27.581. English-speaking doctors are on 24hr call at the Tourist Medical Service, Via Lorenzo il Magnifico 59 ⓣ055.475.411.

Internet The cheapest is at Via Fiesolana 10 (daily 9am–midnight; €1.50/hr; contains an international call centre). There are also *Internet Trains* at Via

Guelfa 54/56, Via dell'Oriuolo 40r, and Borgo San Jacopo 30r.
Laundry Wash & Dry (all daily 8am–10pm; €8/load): Via della Scala 52–54r; Via Nazionale 129r; Via del Sole 29r.
Left luggage At the station (daily 6am–midnight; €3.80/5hr). Up to 20kg only.
Pharmacy All-night pharmacy at the train station, Ⓦ www.federfarma.firenze.it.
Police Via Zara 2 Ⓣ 055.49.771.
Post office Via Pellicceria 3 (daily except Sun 8.30am–12.30pm & 3–6pm).

Moving on

Train Bologna (every 30min; 1hr); Genoa (hourly; 3–4hr); Milan (every 30min; 3hr); Naples (every 30min; 4hr); Perugia (hourly; 2hr); Pisa (every 15min; 1hr); Rome (every 30min; 1hr 40min–2hr 30min); Venice (hourly; 2hr 50min); Verona (hourly; 3hr).
Bus Siena (hourly; 1hr 30min).

PISA

There's no escaping the Leaning Tower in **PISA**. The medieval bell tower is one of the world's most familiar images, and yet its beauty still comes as a surprise. It is set in chessboard formation alongside the **Duomo** and **Baptistery** on the manicured grass of the **Campo dei Miracoli**, whose buildings date from the twelfth and thirteenth centuries, when Pisa was one of the great Mediterranean powers. Beyond this pretty square, however, Pisa is somewhat dilapidated, and in the evenings the city takes on an eerie atmosphere.

PISA'S FESTIVALS

Pisa is known for its Gioco del Ponte, held on the last Sunday in June, when teams from the north and south banks of the city stage a series of "battles", including pushing a seven-tonne carriage over the Ponte di Mezzo. But the town's most magical event is the Luminara on June 16, when buildings along the river are festooned with candles to celebrate San Ranieri, the city's patron saint.

What to see and do

Leaning Tower

Perhaps the strangest thing about the **Leaning Tower** (daily 8.30am–8.30pm; €15), begun in 1173, is that it has always tilted; subsidence disrupted the foundations when it had reached just three of its eight storeys. For the next 180 years a succession of architects were brought in to try to correct the tilt, until 1350 when the angle was accepted and the tower completed. Eight centuries after its construction, it was thought to be nearing its limit, and the tower, supported by steel wires, was closed to the public in the 1990s – though it's open for visits once again now that the tilt (and 5m overhang) has been successfully halted.

Duomo

The **Duomo** (Mon–Sat 10am–7.30pm, Sun 1–7.30pm; €2) was begun a century earlier, its facade – with its delicate balance of black and white marble, and tiers of arcades – setting the model for Pisa's highly distinctive brand of Romanesque. The interior continues the use of black and white marble, and with its long arcades of columns has an almost oriental aspect. The third building of the Miracoli ensemble, the circular **Baptistery** (daily 8/9am–4.30/7.30pm; €5), is a slightly bizarre mix of Romanesque and Gothic, embellished with statues (now largely copies) by Giovanni Pisano and his father Nicola. The originals are displayed in the Opera del Duomo museum (March–Sept daily 8am–7.45pm; Oct–Feb daily 9am– 4.45pm; €5) to the east of the Piazza del Duomo.

Camposanto

Along the north side of the Campo is the **Camposanto** (same hours; €5), a cloistered cemetery built towards the end of the thirteenth century. Most of its frescoes were destroyed by Allied bombing in World War II, but two masterpieces survived relatively unscathed in the Cappella Ammanati – a fourteenth-century *Triumph of Death,* and *The Last Judgement*, a ruthless catalogue of horrors painted around the time of the Black Death.

Arrival and information

Train Pisa's train station is south of the centre on Piazza della Stazione, a 10min walk (or bus #3) from Campo dei Miracoli. Take bus LAM Rosso for the 10min journey to the Leaning Tower. From the airport, take the hourly Florence train for the 5min journey.
Tourist office There is one branch to the left of the station (Mon–Fri 9am–7pm, Sat 9am–1.30pm; ⓣ050.42.291, ⓦwww.opapisa.it), and another in the northeast corner of Campo dei Miracoli (Mon–Sat 9am–6pm, Sun 10.30am–4.30pm; ⓣ050.560.464). Both sell a tourist ticket (€10.50) giving admission to most of Pisa's museums, bar the Leaning Tower.
Internet Koinepisa.it at Via dei Mille 2. €3.50/hr.

Accommodation

Campeggio Torre Pendente Viale delle Cascine 86 ⓣ050.561.704, ⓦwww.campingtorrependente.it. Large, well-maintainted campsite 1km west of Campo dei Miracoli, with a restaurant and shop. Closed Nov–March. ❸
HI Hostel Via Pietrasantina 15 ⓣ050.890.622. Take bus #3 from the station or Campo dei Miracoli. ❸
Pensione Helvetia Via G. Boschi 31, off the Piazza Arcivescovado. ⓣ050.553.084. Basic, family-run *pensione* near the Leaning Tower, just behind the *Grand Hotel Duomo* on Via Santa Maria. ❺
La Torre Via C. Battisti 17 ⓣ050.25.220, ⓦwww.hotellatorrepisa.it. A well-equipped pastel place near the station – the rooms without bath or breakfast are the best deal. ❼

Eating

Avoid eating around the tower if you can, as prices here are sky-high for tourists. The best area for restaurants is around the Piazza delle Vettovaglie, and there are fruit markets around Via D. Cavalcaz.
Pizzeria da Cassio Piazza Cavallotti 14. Decent canteen-style hot food. Pizza €5.
Jackson Pollock Piazza Vettovaglie 21, ⓣ050.570.178. Excellent home-cooked food in a charmingly ramshackle setting with friendly owners. Gnocchi with pesto €7.
Caffetteria delle Vettovaglie Piazza delle Vettofaglie 33. Closed Sun. Trendy bar-restaurant with a different menu every day. Mains €8.
Vineria di Piazza Piazza delle Vettovaglie 13. Good soups and decent prices. Soup and fresh bread €6.

Entertainment

Cinema Lumiere Vicolo del Tidi 6 ⓣ050.971.1532, ⓦwww.lumierecinema.it. Shows arthouse and some original language films.
Toscana in Tour Via S. Giuseppe 5 ⓣ333.260.2152, ⓦwww.toscanaintour.it. Rental place with brilliantly ridiculous-looking quadricycles.

Moving on

Train Florence (every 15min; 1hr); Lucca (every 15min; 20min); Siena (hourly; 1hr 45min).
Bus Florence, from Pisa Airport (hourly; 1hr 10min; €8).

SIENA

SIENA, 78km south of Florence, is the perfect antidote to its better-known neighbour. Self-contained and still rural in parts behind excellently-preserved medieval walls, its cityscape is a majestic Gothic attraction that you can roam around and enjoy without venturing into a single museum. It is also a lively university town, so there is no shortage of places to go in the evening. During the Middle Ages, Siena was one of the major cities of Europe – the size of Paris, it controlled most of southern Tuscany and developed a highly sophisticated civic life, with its own written constitution and a quasi-democratic government.

What to see and do

The **Campo** is the centre of Siena in every sense: the main streets lead into it, the Palio takes place around its café-lined perimeter, and it's the natural place to gravitate towards. It's been called the most beautiful square in the world, an assessment that seems pretty fair – taking a picnic onto the stones

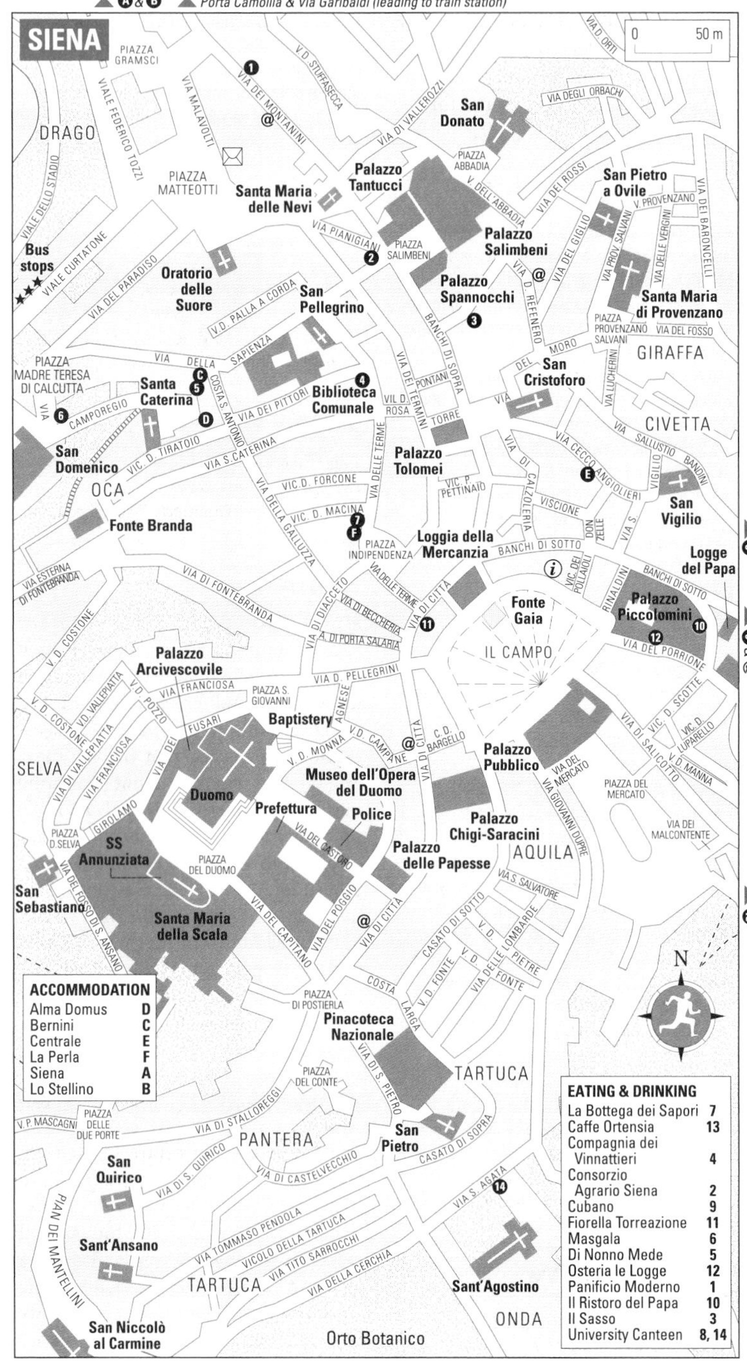
A & B
Porta Camollia & Via Garibaldi (leading to train station)
SIENA
0 50 m
PIAZZA GRAMSCI
DRAGO
VIALE FEDERICO TOZZI
VIA MALAVOLTI
VIA DEI MONTANINI
V. D. STUFFASECCA
VIA DI VALLEROZZI
VIA D. ORTI
VIA DEGLI ORBACHI
San Donato
PIAZZA ABBADIA
PIAZZA MATTEOTTI
Santa Maria delle Nevi
Palazzo Tantucci
V. DELL'ABBADIA
VIA DEI ROSSI
San Pietro a Ovile
V. PROVENZANO
VIA DEI BARONCELLI
VIALE DELLO STADIO
VIA PIANIGIANI
PIAZZA SALIMBENI
Palazzo Salimbeni
VIA DEL GIGLIO
VIA PROV. SALVANI
VIA DELLE VERGINI
Bus stops
VIALE CURTATONE
VIA DEL PARADISO
Oratorio delle Suore
San Pellegrino
V. D. PALLA A CORDA
Palazzo Spannocchi
VIA D. REFENERO
Santa Maria di Provenzano
PIAZZA PROVENZANO SALVANI
VIA DEL FOSSO
BANCHI DI SOPRA
MORO
GIRAFFA
PIAZZA MADRE TERESA DI CALCUTTA
VIA DELLA SAPIENZA
Santa Caterina
COSTA S. ANTONIO
Biblioteca Comunale
VIA DEI TERMINI
PONTANI
San Cristoforo
VIA LUCHERINI
CAMPOREGIO
VIA DEI PITTORI
VIL D. ROSA
TORRE
CIVETTA
San Domenico
VIC. D. TIRATOIO
VIA S. CATERINA
Palazzo Tolomei
VIA DI CALZOLERIA
VIA CECCO ANGIOLIERI
VIA SALLUSTIO BANDINI
OCA
VIC. D. FORCONE
VIA DELLE TERME
VIC. P. PETTINAIO
VISCIONE
DON ZELLE
VIA S. VIGILIO
San Vigilio
VIA DELLA GALLUZZA
VIC. D. MACINA
Fonte Branda
PIAZZA INDIPENDENZA
Loggia della Mercanzia
BANCHI DI SOTTO
Logge del Papa
VIA ESTERNA DI FONTEBRANDA
VIA DI FONTEBRANDA
VIA DI DIACCETO
VIA DI BECCHERIA
VIA DI CITTÀ
VIC. DEI POLLAIOLI
RINALDINI
Fonte Gaia
Palazzo Piccolomini
V. D. COSTONE
A. DI PORTA SALARIA
IL CAMPO
VIA DEL PORRIONE
9 & @
Palazzo Arcivescovile
VIA FRANCIOSA
PIAZZA S. GIOVANNI
VIA D. PELLEGRINI
V. D. COSTONE
VD. VALLEPIATTA
V. D. POZZO
FUSARI
Baptistery
AGNESE
V. D. CAMPANE
C. D. BARGELLO
V. D. MONNA
Palazzo Pubblico
VIA DEL MERCATO
VIA DI SALICOTTO
VIC. D. SCOTTE
VIC. D. LUPARELLO
V. D. MANNA
SELVA
VIA DI VALLEPIATTA
VIA FRANCIOSA
VIA DEI GIROLAMO
Duomo
Museo dell'Opera del Duomo
Prefettura
Police
VIA GIOVANNI DUPRÈ
PIAZZA DEL MERCATO
VIA DEI MALCONTENTE
PIAZZA D. SELVA
SS Annunziata
PIAZZA DEL DUOMO
VIA DEL CASTORO
Palazzo delle Papesse
Palazzo Chigi-Saracini
AQUILA
San Sebastiano
VIA DEL FOSSO DI S. ANSANO
Santa Maria della Scala
VIA DEL CAPITANO
VIA DEL POGGIO
VIA S. SALVATORE
CASATO DI SOTTO
V. D. PIETRE
VIA DELLE LOMBARDE
V. D. FONTE
COSTA LARGA
N
PIAZZA DI POSTIERLA
Pinacoteca Nazionale
VIA DI S. PIETRO
TARTUCA
PIAZZA DEL CONTE
V. P. MASCAGNI
PIAZZA DELLE DUE PORTE
VIA DI STALLOREGGI
PANTERA
San Pietro
CASATO DI SOPRA
San Quirico
VIA DI S. QUIRICO
VIA DI CASTELVECCHIO
VIA S. AGATA
PIAN DEI MANTELLINI
Sant'Ansano
VIA TOMMASO PENDOLA
VICOLO DELLA TARTUCA
VIA TITO SARROCCHI
VIA DELLA CERCHIA
TARTUCA
Sant'Agostino
ONDA
San Niccolò al Carmine
Orto Botanico
ACCOMMODATION
Alma Domus D
Bernini C
Centrale E
La Perla F
Siena A
Lo Stellino B
EATING & DRINKING
La Bottega dei Sapori 7
Caffe Ortensia 13
Compagnia dei Vinnattieri 4
Consorzio Agrario Siena 2
Cubano 9
Fiorella Torreazione 11
Masgala 6
Di Nonno Mede 5
Osteria le Logge 12
Panificio Moderno 1
Il Ristoro del Papa 10
Il Sasso 3
University Canteen 8, 14

THE SIENA PALIO

The **Siena Palio** is the most spectacular festival in Italy, a minute-and-a-half long bareback horse-race around the Campo contested twice a year (July 2 at 7.45pm and Aug 16 at 7pm) between the seventeen ancient wards – or *contrade* – of the city. Even now, a person's *contrada* frequently determines which churches they attend and where they socialize. There's a big build-up, with trials and processions for days before the big event, and traditionally all Sienese return to their *contrada* the night before the race; emotions run too high for rivals to be together, even if they're husband and wife. The Palio itself is a hectic spectacle whose rules haven't been rewritten since the race began – thus supposedly, everything is allowed except to gouge your opponents eyes out. For the best view, you need to have found a position on the inner rail by 2pm and to keep it for the next seven hours. Beware that toilets, shade and refreshments are minimal, the swell of the crowd can be overwhelming, and you won't be able to leave the Campo for at least two hours after the race. If you haven't booked a hotel room, reckon on staying up all night.

to watch the shadows move around the square is a good way to while away an afternoon.

The Palazzo Pubblico

The **Palazzo Pubblico** (daily 10am–5.30/7pm) – with its 107m bell-tower, the **Torre del Mangia** (€6) – occupies virtually the entire south side of the square, and although it's still in use as Siena's town hall, its principal rooms have been converted into a **museum** (€7), frescoed with themes integral to the secular life of the medieval city.

Around the Campo

Between buildings at the top end of the Campo, the fifteenth-century **Loggia di Mercanzia**, built as a dealing room for merchants, marks the intersection of the city centre's principal streets. From here **Via Banchi di Sotto** leads east to the **Palazzo Piccolomini** and on into the workaday quarter of **San Martino**. From the Campo, Via di Città cuts west across the oldest quarter of the city, fronted by some of Siena's finest private *palazzi*. At the end of the street, Via San Pietro leads to the **Pinacoteca Nazionale** (Sun & Mon 8.30am–1.30pm, Tues–Sat 8.30am–7.30pm; €4), a fourteenth-century palace housing a roll-call of Sienese Gothic painting.

The Duomo

Alleys lead north from here to the **Duomo**, completed to virtually its present size around 1215; plans to enlarge it withered with Siena's medieval prosperity. The building is a delight, its style an amazing mix of Romanesque and Gothic, delineated by bands of black and white marble on its facade. Inside, a startling sequence of 56 panels, completed between 1349 and 1547, feature virtually every artist who worked in the city. Midway along the nave, the **Libreria Piccolomini** (daily 9.30am–5/7.30pm; €3), signalled by Pinturicchio's brilliantly coloured fresco of the *Coronation of Pius II*, has superbly vivid frescoes.

Museums

Opposite the Duomo is the complex of **Santa Maria della Scala** (daily 10.30am–5.30pm; €6), the city's hospital for over 800 years and now a vast museum that includes the frescoed Sala del Pellegrinaio (once used as a hospital ward) and, way down in the basement, the dark and spooky **Oratorio di Santa Caterina della Notte** chapel. The **Museo dell'Opera del Duomo** (Mon–Fri 9am–1.30pm; €6), tucked into a corner of the Duomo extension, offers a fine perspective: follow the "Panorama dal Facciatone" signs to steep spiral stairs that climb up to the top of the build-

FESTIVALS

Open-air film festival **Cinema in Fortezza** runs from the end of June until the beginning of August. Screenings of the films, varying from slapstick American comedies and world arthouse to old Italian classics, begin at 9.45pm at the Anfiteatro della Fortezza Medicea (€5). See the advertisements posted around town or check at the tourist office for details. There are also a number of open-air jazz events in the summer: call ⓣ0577.271.401, or check out ⓦwww.sienajazz.it.

ing; the views are sensational but the topmost walkway is narrow and scarily exposed.

Arrival and information

Train The train station is down in the valley 2km northeast of the centre; to get into town, either walk or cross the road from the station and take just about any city bus heading left – they drop off at Piazza Gramsci, about 100m north of Piazza Matteotti.

Bus Buses stop along Viale Curtatone, by the Basilica of San Domenico, and are much faster and more frequent from Florence than the trains (for which change at Empoli). See ⓦwww.sena.it for more information on buses.

Tourist office Piazza del Campo 56 (daily 9am–7pm; ⓣ0577.280.551, ⓦwww.terresiena.it). This has a hotel list and a fairly ineffectual map – you might want to bring your own, though the city quickly becomes easily navigable.

Discount passes If you plan on doing a lot of sight-seeing, the Biglietto Cumulativo includes entrance to most of Siena's museums (€10/16 valid for three/seven days), and can be bought at any of the participating museums.

Exchange Via del Moro 4 (Mon–Sat 10am–5pm).

Internet Internet Siena, Via Montanini 93 (daily 9am–11pm; €2/hr; also has cheap international calls – US, UK, Canada €0.10/min). Or try the Grace of God Internet Centre on Via del Refe Nero 18 (€2/hr).

Pharmacy San Pietro 4 (24hr).

Post office Piazza Matteoti 37. Closed Sun.

Laundry Siena Laundromat, Via di Pantaneto 38 (daily 8am–10pm; €3/wash, €3/dry).

Accommodation

In summer, Siena quickly gets ridiculously booked up; it's worth phoning ahead for accommodation, or **booking rooms** at the Siena Hotels Promotion booth opposite San Domenico (Mon–Sat 9am–8pm; ⓣ0577.288.084, ⓦwww.hotelsiena.com).

Alma Domus Via Camporegio 37 ⓣ0577.44.177. Clean, simple place run by nuns, with a garden and spacious reading room. Some rooms have amazing views over Siena and the Duomo. ❼

Bernini Via della Sapienza 15 ⓣ0577.289.047, ⓦwww.albergobernini.com. Charming and old-fashioned one-star hotel run by a homely family; the views from the huge windows and open air breakfast terrace are breathtaking. Midnight curfew. ❼

Centrale Via Cecco Angiolieri 26 ⓣ0577.280.379, ⓦwww.hotelcentralesiena.com. Superbly located hotel with spacious rooms. ❽

La Perla Via delle Terme 25 ⓣ0577.47.144, ⓦwww.hotellaperlasiena.com. Friendly *pensione* in a very central location, two blocks north of the Campo. ❽

Siena HI Hostel Via Fiorentina 89 ⓣ0577.52.212. A comfortable hostel, 2km northwest of the centre; take bus #10 from the train station or Piazza Gramsci (but from the Piazza make sure you ask the driver if the bus is going there, as the route splits), or bus #15 from Piazza Gramsci. If you're coming from Florence, ask the bus driver to let you off at "Lo Stellino". Midnight curfew. ❷

Lo Stellino Via Fiorentina 95 ⓣ 0577.588.926, ⓦwww.sienaholidays.com. Clean, pretty hotel next to the HI hostel with kitchen facilities and a garden. ❻

Eating

Cafés and food markets

La Bottega dei Sapori Antichi Via delle Terme 39/41. Extravagantly stocked deli run by the friendly Bruno.

Consorzio Agrario Siena Via Pianigiani 7. Closed Sun. Supermarket/deli.

Fiorella Torrefazione Via di Citta 13. Popular stand-up coffee bar with good pastries and refreshing coffee *granitas* made with crushed ice.

Panificio Moderno Via dei Montanini 84. Good bakery for picnic lunches.

Restaurants

Compagnia dei Vinnattieri Via delle Terme 79/Via dei Pittori 1 ⓣ 0577.236.568. Traditional fare served in a majestic basement with occasional live music. Pasta €7.

Di Nonno Mede Via Camporegio 21 ⓣ0577.247.966. Popular pizzeria with stunning views out over the Duomo. Pizza €5.

Il Ristoro del Papa Logge del Papa 1, between Banchi di Sotto and Bia del Porrione ⓣ0577.284.062. Friendly, unpretentious pizzeria and restaurant with outdoor seating area. Pizza €6.

Il Sasso Via dei Rossi 2a ⓣ0577.247.049. Closed Sun. Chic, cosy restaurant down a small side street. Pizza €7.

University Canteen Via S. Agata 1. Open for lunch and dinner daily. Serves decent, cheap food – a complete meal is €7 for non-students and €5 for students. Also at Via S Bandini 47 (lunch only, closed Sat & Sun).

TREAT YOURSELF

Osteria Le Logge Via del Porrione 33. This popular restaurant, sited in an old pharmacy, serves amazing local cuisine. Worth booking in summer. Risotto with truffles €10. Closed Sun.

Drinking and nightlife

The lively bars around the Campo, though a bit pricier than elsewhere, are open until late and drinks come with great snacks early in the evening.

Cubano Via San Martino 31. Lively Cuban-themed place.

Masgala 1 Camporegio. Great cocktails (especially the mojitos) and fantastic views over the Duomo. Beer €4.

Ortensia Via di Pantaneto 95. Student hangout with a friendly hippy owner. Lasagne €4, beer €1.50.

Moving on

Train to Pisa (every 30min; 1hr 50min); Perugia (every 90min; 3hr); Rome (every 70min; 3hr 20min).

Bus to Florence (hourly; 90min); San Gimignano (hourly; 1hr).

SAN GIMIGNANO

SAN GIMIGNANO is one of the best-known villages in Tuscany. Its skyline of towers, framed against classic Tuscan countryside, has justifiably caught the tourist imagination, and in high season this prosperous town is extremely busy. A **combined ticket** (€7.50) covering the town's civic museums is available at any of the participating sites.

The village was a force to be reckoned with in the Middle Ages, with a population of fifteen thousand, twice the present number – hit hard by the Black Death, it never quite recovered. Nowadays you can walk across it in fifteen minutes, and around the walls in an hour. The main entrance gate, facing the bus terminal on the south side of town, is **Porta San Giovanni**, from where **Via San Giovanni** leads to the town's interlocking main squares, **Piazza della Cisterna** and **Piazza del Duomo**. The more austere Piazza Duomo, off to the left, is flanked by the **Collegiata Cathedral** (Mon–Sat 9.30am–5/7.30pm, Sun 1–5pm; €3.50), frescoed with Old and New Testament scenes. The **Palazzo del Popolo**, next door (daily 9.30/10am–5.30/7pm; €5), gives you the chance to climb the **Torre Grossa** (€4.10), the town's highest surviving tower. North from Piazza Duomo, **Via San Matteo** is one of the grandest and best preserved of the city streets, with quiet alleyways running down to the walls. The **Wine Museum** at the Parco della Rocca, is free to enter and you can enjoy a glass of wine while admiring the spectacular view. There are

FOOD AND FILMS

Markets take place in different piazzas every day from 9am to 1pm year round; in summer, there are also brilliantly performed operas in the Piazza del Duomo and an open-air cinema at the Parco di Montestaffoli. Ask at the tourist office for details.

wine-tasting evenings throughout the year (€5, ⓣ0577.941.267 for details).

Arrival and information

Train The nearest train station is Poggibonsi, on the Siena–Empoli line; buses run to San Gimignano every hour (€1.60).
Bus is the best way to get here from Florence (hourly; 1hr 20min) or Siena (hourly; 1hr).
Tourist office Piazza del Duomo (daily 9am–1pm & 2/3–6pm; ⓣ0577.940.008, ⓦwww.sangimignano.com).
Internet Piazza delle Erbe 3. €2/20min.

Accommodation

Accommodation is expensive, and It's advisable to book in advance. **Private rooms** (around €50 for a double) can be arranged through the Associazione Extralberghiere, Piazza della Cisterna 6 (daily 10am–6pm, closed Thurs & Sun 1–2pm; ⓣ0577.943.190) or the Siena Hotels Promotion, Via San Giovanni 125 just inside Porta San Giovanni (Mon, Wed, Fri & Sat 9.30am–12.30pm & 2.30–7pm; Tues & Thurs 2.30–7pm; ⓣ0577.940.809).
Il Boschetto Loc. Santa Lucia 38c ⓣ0577.940.352, ⓦwww.boschettodipiemma.it. Well-equipped campsite 3km downhill in the village of Santa Lucia. ❸
Foresteria del Monastero S Girolamo Via Folgore 30 ⓣ0577.940.573. Clean, somewhat austere, accommodation in a quiet monastery. Booking essential. ❸

Eating and drinking

Taking a **picnic** up to the Parco di Montestaffoli is an excellent way to enjoy the views of the village and surrounding countryside. Try *Gustava Enoteca,* Vai S Matteo 2, an overflowing deli which also has a tiny sit-down area and an amazing range of wines.
La Bettola Del Grillo Via Quercecchio 33 ⓣ0577.907.081. Light, modern restaurant with talkative owners and a chatty atmosphere. Grills €13.
Cum Quibus Via San Martino 17 ⓣ0577.943.199. Closed Tues. Low-key, welcoming place with a small outdoor courtyard and great traditional cuisine. Rabbit ragout pasta €9.
Di Vinorum Piazza Cisterna 30/Via degli Innocenti 5 ⓣ 0577.907.192, ⓦwww.divinorumwinebar.com. Lovely *bruschetteria* built into the town wall with a cool stone interior and leafy garden, with fantastic views over the countryside. Bruschettas €6.
Gelateria di Piazza Piazza Cisterna 1. Many-time ice cream world champions, reputedly asked to stop entering the competitions to give their competitors a chance!

PERUGIA

PERUGIA, the Umbrian capital, is an attractive medieval university town that buzzes with young people of every nationality, many of them students at the *Università per Stranieri* (Foreigners' University). Buitoni, the pasta people, are based here, and it's also where Italy's best-known chocolate, Perugini, is made – though since its takeover by Nestlé, locals favour Vannucci, made by a former Perugini employee.

What to see and do

Perugia hinges on a single street, **Corso Vannucci**, a broad pedestrian thoroughfare, at the far end of which the austere **Piazza Quattro Novembre** is backed by the plain-faced **Duomo San Lorenzo** (daily 8am–noon & 4pm–sunset). In perfect contrast, the lavishly decorated **Collegio di Cambio** (daily 9am–12.30pm & 2.30–5.30pm; €2.60) sits at Corso Vannucci 25. This is the town's medieval money exchange, frescoed by Perugino and said to be the most beautiful bank in the world. The Palazzo dei Priori houses the **Galleria Nazionale di Umbria** (daily 8.30am–7.30pm; closed first Mon of each month; ⓦwww.gallerianazionaleumbria.it; €6.50), one of central Italy's best galleries, whose collection includes statues by Cambio, frescoes by Bonfigli and works by Perugino. The best streets to wander around to get a feel of the old city are around the Duomo. **Via dei Priori** is the most characteristic, its cobbled surface gently winding through the rambling white buildings. This leads down to Agostino di Duccio's colourful **Oratorio di San Bernardino**, whose richly embellished facade is by far the best piece of sculpture in the city. On the southern side of town, along Corso

THE UMBRIA JAZZ FESTIVAL

One of the most prestigious jazz events in Europe, the **Umbria Jazz Festival** has featured stars such as Dizzy Gillespie and Keith Jarrett. It takes place in July and while the main events tend to be in Perugia, there are offshoots – performances and workshops that often make use of stunning churches, courts and open-air spaces – in towns across the region. ⓦwww.umbriajazz.com.

Cavour, the cloisters of the large church of **San Domenico** hold the **Museo Archeologico Nazionale dell'Umbria** (Mon 2.30–7.30pm, Tues–Sun 8.30am–7.30pm; €4), home of one of the most extensive Etruscan collections around.

Arrival and information

Train Trains arrive well away from the centre of Perugia on Piazza Vittorio Veneto; buses #6, #7, #9 and #11 make the 15min journey to Piazza Italia or Piazza Matteotti.

Bus Buses arrive at Piazza Partigiani. Follow the bank of escalators up to Piazza Italia. Spoletina are the biggest bus operators in southeastern Umbria – see ⓦwww.spoletina.com. Buses #1,# 6, #7 or #8 run from the bus terminal to the train station.

Tourist office On Piazza IV Novembre 3 (Mon–Sat 8.30am–1.30pm & 3.30–6.30pm, Sun 9am–1pm; ⓣ075.573.6458, ⓦtourism.comune.perugia.it), and Piazza Matteoti 18 (Mon–Sat 8.30am–1.30pm & 3.30–6.30pm, Sun 9am–1pm; ⓣ075.573.6458). Both provide the invaluable free *Little Blue What to Do* book of information on Perugia.

Internet Coffee Break at Via Danzetta 22 (daily 11am– 1am; €1/hr).

Accommodation

Eden Via C Caporali 9 ⓣ075.572.8102, ⓦwww.hoteleden.perugia.it. A simply decorated two-star in a central location with a nice terrace and breakfast bar. ❼

Ostello Della Gioventu Via Bontempi 13 ⓣ075.572.2880, ⓦwww.ostello.perugia.it. Welcoming hostel two minutes from the Duomo, with a 1am curfew. Closed between 9.30am and 4pm. ❷

Ponte Felcino Via Manicomi 97 ⓣ075.591.3991. A 20min bus ride (#8) from the train station, this is a comfortable, if inconveniently located, HI hostel in a historic building in a park. ❷

Spagnoli Via Cortonese 4 ⓣ075.501.1366. Basic and friendly HI hostel. ❷

Rosalba Via del Circo 7 ⓣ075.572.0626, ⓦwww.hotelrosalba.com. A clean, central hotel. ❼

Eating

Cafés and food markets

Perugia is full of markets and delis friendly to the budget traveller's wallet and stomach.

Antica Salumeria Granieri Amato Green stall on Piazza Matteoti selling sandwiches made from hot roast pork, an Umbrian speciality.

Cacioteka Via Danzetta 1. This generously stocked deli says Giulianos on the front, as the owners haven't changed the sign from the last shop that was there. Closed Sun.

Co-op Piazza Matteoti 15. Daily 9am–8pm. Supermarket.

Fresh Pasta Via Cesare Caparali 3. Closed Sun. Well worth a visit if you're staying at a place with a kitchen, or just to peer at the machinery. Gnocchi €0.75/100g, cappelletti €2/100g.

Mercato Coperto Mon–Sat 9am–1pm. Covered market off Piazza Matteoti, next to the information centre.

Del Soprammuro Piazza Matteoti 24. Excellent *pasticherie* (the coffee is delicious and the pastries are fresh and flaky) with cosy upstairs seating and seats on the piazza, excellent for admiring the surrounding hills and revelling in the *dolce vita*.

Restaurants

Del Gambero Via Baldeschi 17. Closed Mon. Serving Umbrian specialities. Mains €10.

Mediterranea Piazza Piccinino 11/12 ⓣ075.572.1322 The pizza here is so good and so different to any pizza back home that it practically deserves a different name. Get there early as it fills up fast. Pizza €6.

Un Punto Macrobiotico Viale Benedetto Bonfigli. See p.713.

Drinking and nightlife

Frequented by both local and international students, Perugia's **nightlife** is varied and buzzing and unlikely to disappoint. ⓦwww.egeneration.pg.it, effectively Perugia's *Little Blue Book* online, is worth checking out for information on club nights and events.

Cocco pub www.coccopub.com. A stall on Piazza Matteoti where locals buy drinks to sit out on the piazza steps. Belgian beer €3.

Enone Corso Cavour 61 075.572.1950. *Enoteca* and restaurant with huge variety of wines. Every Thurs, food from a different region in Italy is served. As their wines are changed every week, they will sometimes offer discounts if you ask for the leftovers of last week's wine. Glass of wine €3.50.

L'Officina Borgo XX Gingro 56 075.572.1699. Tucked away so you hardly notice it, this modernist *enoteca*'s centerpiece is a glass-walled kitchen, while its walls are lined with dusty bottles. The staff are extremely friendly and the wine is fantastic. Glass of wine €3.

Punto di Vista Viale dell'Indipendenza 2 339.662.0326. Extremely popular bar with a fantastic sunset view. Open until 2.30am. Beer €4.

Moving on

Train Assisi (hourly; 20min); Florence (hourly; 2hr); Rome (hourly; 2hr).

Bus Siena (11am and 9pm, 1hr 30min).

FESTIVALS

As well as its jazz festival, Perugia has a stream of eclectic events throughout the year that are well worth looking up in advance. In mid-October there's a **chocolate festival** that lasts for ten days, while the **Christmas market** is splendid in its scale and opulence. See the tourist office website (tourism.comune.perugia.it) for details.

ASSISI

Thanks to St Francis, Italy's premier saint and founder of the Franciscan order, **ASSISI** is Umbria's best-known town, crammed with people for ten months of the year (Jan and Feb, with their colder weather and lack of religious holidays, are more peaceful). It has a medieval hill-town charm and quietens down in the evening. An earthquake in 1997 caused extensive damage to parts of the town, most notably to the Basilica di San Francesco, but restoration is now complete and the basilica is almost back to its original splendour.

What to see and do

The **Basilica di San Francesco**, at the end of Via San Francesco (daily 8.30am–6pm; www.sanfrancescoassisi.org), houses one of the most overwhelming collections of art outside a gallery anywhere in the world. Begun in 1228, two years after the saint's death, it was financed by donations that flooded in from all over the world. Francis lies under the floor of the Lower Church, in a crypt only brought to light in 1818. The walls have been lavishly frescoed by artists such as Cimabue and Giotto, and the stained glass windows cast a dim light which adds to the majestic atmosphere. The Upper Church, built to a light and airy Gothic plan, is richly decorated too, with dazzling frescoes on the life of St Francis. A short trek up the steep Via di San Rufino leads to the thirteenth-century **Duomo**, which holds the font used to baptize St Francis and St Clare. Close by is the **Basilica di Santa Chiara,** home to the macabre blackened body of Clare herself.

Arrival and information

Train Assisi's train station is 5km south of town, and connected to it by half-hourly buses.

Tourist office Piazza del Comune 12 (Mon–Sat 8am–2pm & 3–6.30pm, Sun 10am–1pm & 2–5pm; www.assisionline.com).

Accommodation

The tourist office can help with private rooms, though do book, especially around Easter.

Albergo Il Duomo Vicolo San Lorenzo 2, 075.812.742. Basic hotel in the heart of town. The reception is at *Hotel San Rufino*, the *Albergo*'s more expensive and less satisfactory partner hotel. 5

Fontemaggio Via Eremo delle Carceri 8 ⓣ075.812.317, ⓦwww.fontemaggio.it. Campsite, hostel, hotel and restaurant with gorgeous views and friendly staff, full of rowdy Italian families and young foreign travellers. 15min walk out of town on the road to the monastery of Eremo delle Carceri. Alternatively, take bus #20 or #34. Dorm ❷, double ❺, camping ❷

New Day Bed and Breakfast Via San Francesco 18 ⓣ075.813.739, ⓦwww.bandbnewdayassisi.it. A tiny, family-run B&B, above a cutesy craft shop. Fantastic breakfast and very helpful owners. ❻

Ostello della Pace Via di Valecchie ⓣ075.816.767, ⓦwww.assisihostel.com. Clean, beautifully located HI hostel, on the hillside just below the town. ❷

Eating

Il Duomo Pizzeria Via Porta Perlici 11 ⓣ075.816.326, ⓦwww.assisiduomo.com. Good, basic stone-oven pizzeria popular with locals. Pizzas €4.

Galleria del Gusto Corso Mazzini 12 ⓦgalleriadelgusto.com. Try a few local wines and some great cured meats and cheeses. Sandwiches €2.50.

La Lanterna Via San Rufino 39 ⓣ075.816.399. Busy, atmospheric restaurant with lively staff and excellent food. Pizza €7.

La Stalla Via Eremo delle Carceri 8 ⓣ075.813.636. The restaurant attached to the *Fontemaggio* (see opposite) is noisy and packed, with good food and great outdoor atmosphere. Pasta €8.

Drinking and nightlife

Caffe Duomo Piazza San Rufino 5. A relaxed place to have a late-night drink. Wine €3.

Magno Vino Trendy bar with a chilled-out ambience, outdoor couches and a great selection of wines. Open until 1am. Glass of wine €3–4.

Moving on

Train Almost all journeys require a change in Foligno. Foligno (30min; hourly); Perugia (30min; hourly).

SPOLETO

SPOLETO is Umbria's most compelling town, with an extremely pretty position, some of Italy's most ancient Romanesque churches and a friendly, relaxed atmosphere. The Lower Town, where you arrive, was badly damaged by World War II bombing, and doesn't hold much of interest, so it's best to take a bus straight to the Upper Town.

What to see and do

There's no single central piazza, but the place to head for is **Piazza della Libertà**, site of a much-restored first-century Roman Theatre, visible at all times, but also visitable more closely in conjunction with the **Museo Archeologico** (Mon–Sun 8.30am–7.30pm; €2). The adjoining **Piazza della Fontana** has more Roman remains, the best of which is the **Arco di Druso**, built to honour the campaign victories of Drusus, son of Tiberius. The homely **Piazza del Mercato**, beyond, is a fine opportunity to take in some streetlife, and from here it's a short walk to the restrained and elegant **Duomo**. Inside, the superlative apse frescoes were painted by the fifteenth-century Florentine artist Fra Lippo Lippi – he died shortly after their completion amid rumours that he was poisoned for seducing the daughter of a local noble family. The **Ponte delle Torri**, a picture-postcard favourite, is an astonishing piece of medieval engineering, best seen as part of a circular walk around the base of the **Rocca** – everyone's idea of a cartoon castle, with towers, crenellations and sheer walls.

Arrival and information

Train Spoleto's train station is 1km north of the town centre – take bus B to Piazza della Libertà, essentially the town centre, from outside the station. Tickets (€0.90) can be bought in the *tabacchi* at the station.

Tourist office Piazza della Libertà (Tues–Sat 9am–1pm & 3–7pm; ⓣ074.347.452).

Accommodation

Camping Monteluco Located behind San Pietro ⓣ0743.220.358. Tiny but extremely pleasant campsite. Closed Oct–March. ❸

Hotel Gattapone, on Via del Ponte 6 (ⓣ0743.223.447, ⓦwww.hotelgattapone.it), stands above the town just behind the castle, with breathtaking views of Monteluco hill and the magnificent Ponte delle Torri bridge. The opulently decorated bar, where breakfast is served in the morning, is completely glass-fronted, so that you feel surrounded by the majestic Umbrian hillscape. The bedrooms also offer panoramic views, and the terrace is gorgeous in the summer. Double €140. ❾

Istituto Bambin Gésu Via S. Angelo 4 (the tiny street opposite no. 73 Via Monteroni) ⓣ074.340.232, ⓦwww.istitutobambingesuspoleto.it. A friendly hostel in a convent with the most beautiful location, surrounded by hills and Umbrian countryside. Book early in summer. Dorms ❷, doubles ❺

Il Panciolle Via del Duomo 3 ⓣ0743.456.77. A well-equipped two-star hotel, central and reasonably priced, with seven rooms. ❻

Eating

There are fruit and vegetable stalls from Mon to Sat at the Piazza del Mercato.

La Barcaccia Piazza Bandiera 3 ⓣ0743.225.082. A friendly restaurant serving traditional food, with a lovely sunlit terrace. Pasta €8.

Forno a Legna Santini 16 Via Deguffo. Daily 7.30am–1.30pm & 5–8pm. Shop with exceptional breads, cheeses and salamis.

Ristoritrovo conte Spoleto Via Porta Fuga 43 ⓣ0743.225.221. Cheap pizza in an atmospheric place with outdoor seating and a grotto out the back. Pizza €4.

Il Tempio del Gusto 11 Via Deguffo ⓣ0743.47121. Typical Umbrian food at good prices, with a nice garden. An American who's been living in Spoleto for years also runs a cookery course here – ⓔinformation@spoletoarts.com for info, or see ⓦwww.spoletoarts.com. Mains €7.

Drinking and nightlife

Osteria dell'Enoteca Via A Saffi 7 ⓣ0743.220.484, ⓦwww.osteriadellenoteca.com. A traditional *enoteca* where you can sample local wines and snacks.

Maz de Paz Via Fontesecca 7. A lively after-hours bar with occasional live music, also serving reasonably priced food. Closed Mon. Pasta €7.

La Portella Bar and Gelateria Via Giro della Rocca. Great for a coffee or evening drink looking out at the incredible scenery – the sunsets are spectacular. Open until 2am. Coffee €1.50, beer €3.

Moving on

Train Most journeys require a change in Foligno. Assisi (direct: 30min; every 1hr 30min); Foligno (20min; 12–18 daily); Pesaro (3hr; every 2hr).

URBINO

URBINO, one of the most prestigious courts in Europe in the fifteenth century, is now a pretty university town, notable for its gorgeous hilltop location and excellent museums, with a contented atmosphere.

What to see and do

In the centre of town, the **Palazzo Ducale** is a fitting monument to Federico da Montefeltro, the fifteenth-century Duke of Urbino whose enthusiastic embrace of Renaissance culture defines the city to this day. It is now home to the **Galleria Nazionale delle Marche** (Mon 8.30am–2pm, Tues–Sun 8.30am–7.15pm; €4). Among the paintings in the Appartamento del Duca are Piero della Francesca's strange *Flagellation*, and the *Ideal City*, a famous perspective painting of a symmetrical and deserted cityscape. The most interesting and best preserved of the *palazzo*'s rooms is Federico's Studiolo, a triumph of illusory perspective. The pleasant jumble of Renaissance and medieval houses making up the rest of Urbino is a welcome antidote to the rarefied atmosphere of the Palazzo Ducale. You can wind down in one of the many bars and trattorias, or take a picnic up to the gardens within the **Fortezza Albornoz,** from where you'll get great views of the town and countryside.

Arrival and information

Bus Urbino is notoriously difficult to reach – the best approach is by bus from Pésaro, about 30km away on the coast (every 30min – last bus around 8pm; 1hr; €2.75). Buses stop in Borgo Mercatale, at the foot of the Palazzo Ducale, which is reached either by lift or by Francesco di Giorgio Martini's spiral staircase.
Tourist office Borgo Mercatale, Rampa Francesco di Giorgio (daily 9am–6pm; ⓣ072.22631, ⓦwww.urbinoculturaturismo.it).

Accommodation

For accommodation, the cheapest options are private rooms – lists are available from the tourist office.
Pensione Fosca Via Raffaello 67 ⓣ0722.329.622. A pleasant family-run place right in the centre with white-washed walls and big windows. ❺
Albergo Italia Corso Garibaldi 32 ⓣ0722.2701, ⓦwww.albergo-italia-urbino.it. This simple three-star hotel is the most convenient choice, and the higher rooms boast excellent views. ❼
Panoramic Via Cardinal Bessarione 20 ⓣ0722.2600. Clean, basic central *pensione*. ❺

Eating

Eating out in Urbino is not cheap. A picnic from one of the delis, or the Margherita Conad supermarket on Via Raffaello 37 (Mon–Sat 7.30am–2pm, 4.30–8pm) provides a cost-effective alternative.
Angeli Borgo Mercenate 21/22. Serves great paninis (€2.50) and snacks.
La Balestra Popular restaurant and pizzeria with reasonably priced dishes. Pizza €8.
Un Punto Macrobiotico Via Pozzo Nuovo 4. See box, p.713.
La Taverna degli Artisti Via Bramante 52. Lovely place with a garden, serving tasty local dishes. Pasta €6.20.

Drinking and nightlife

During term-time Piazza della Repubblica is packed with students.
Bar L'Isola Via dei Veterani 18. A friendly, low-key place with Internet.
El Piquero Via Domenico 1. Often packed student club with different music every night. Beer included in entry, €5.

Moving on

Bus Pésaro (every 30min; 1hr).

Sardinia

Just under 200km from the Italian mainland, **SARDINIA** (Sardegna) is often regarded as the epitome of Mediterranean Europe. Its blue seas, white sands and rolling hills are beautiful and its way of life relaxed. Sardinia also holds fascinating vestiges of the various powers – Roman, Carthaginian, Genoese and Pisan – that have passed through, alongside striking remnants of Sardinia's only significant native culture, known as the Nuraghic civilization, in the the 7000 tower-like *nuraghi* that litter the landscape. The capital, **Cagliari**, is worth exploring for its excellent museums and some of the island's best nightlife. From here, it's only a short trip to the renowned ruined city at **Nora**, and the quieter beaches at **Chia**. The other main ferry port and airport is Olbia, in the north, little more than a transit town for the exclusive resort of the Costa Smeralda. There's a third airport at the bustling package resort of **Alghero** in the northwest.

CAGLIARI

Rising up from its port and crowned by an old citadel squeezed within a protective ring of fortifications, **CAGLIARI** has been Sardinia's capital since at least Roman times and is still the island's biggest town. Nonetheless, its centre is easily explored on foot, with almost all the wandering you will want to do encompassed by the citadel.

What to see and do

The citadel

The most evocative entry to the **citadel** is from the monumental **Bastione San Remy** on Piazza Costituzione (currently going through a restoration process which is expected to be finished in 2009). From here, you can wander off in any direction to enter its intricate

GETTING TO SARDINIA

There are daily **flights** from the Italian mainland to Cagliari, Olbia and Fertilia/Alghero, although these can be tricky to find – and the reasonably priced ones often fly indirect routes. Cheaper but slower, the overnight **ferries** to Cagliari, Arbatax (halfway up the island's eastern coast), Olbia, Golfo degli Aranci (near Olbia) and Porto Torres (on Sardinia's northwestern corner) from mainland Italy (Civitavecchia, Genoa, Livorno, Naples) – as well as from Sicily, Corsica and France – usually take over thirteen hours. In summer, slightly more expensive fast ferries connect Genoa, Piombino, Civitavecchia and Fiumicino to the island. Getting around Sardinia without a car is best done using a mixture of **buses** and **trains**, though connections to some of the more remote areas, though reliable, can be few and far between. Note that Interail/Eurail passes are not valid for the smaller, private rail lines run by Ferrovie della Sardegna (FdS). For up-to-date transport timetables check the back pages of the *Unione Sarda* newspaper, available throughout Sardinia.

maze. The citadel has been altered little since the Middle Ages, though the tidy Romanesque facade on the mainly thirteenth-century **cattedrale** (April–Oct 9am–noon & 5–7pm, Nov–March 9am–12.30pm & 4–6pm; Mass on Sun 9am, 10.30am, noon & 7pm) in Piazza Palazzo is in fact a fake, added in the twentieth century in the old Pisan style.

Piazza dell'Arsenale

At the opposite end of Piazza Palazzo, a road leads into the smaller **Piazza dell'Arsenale,** site of several museums including the **Museo Archeologico Nazionale** (Tues–Sun 9am–8pm; €4), for anyone interested in Sardinia's past. In the same complex, the **Pinacoteca Nazionale** (same hours; €2) features some glowing fifteenth-century altarpieces, while the **Museo delle Cere** (Tues – Sun 9am–1pm & 4–7pm; €1.50) displays a series of beautiful anatomical waxworks executed by Clemente Susini for nineteenth-century medical students.

Towers

Off the piazza stands the **Torre San Pancrazio** (Tues–Sun April–Oct 9am–1pm & 3.30–7.30pm; Nov–March 9am– 4.30pm; €2), from where it's only a short walk to the **Torre dell'Elefante** (hours and price as San Pancrazio), named after the small carving of an elephant on one side; climb to the top for stupendous views over the city and coast.

Anfiteatro Romano

Nearby, Viale Buon Cammino leads to the **Anfiteatro Romano** (Tues–Sat 9.30am–1.30pm, Sun 3.30–5.30pm (Sun 10am–4pm Nov–March); €3.30). Cut out of solid rock in the second century AD, the amphitheatre could hold the city's entire population of twenty thousand.

Beaches

To get to **Poetta Beach**, the unbelievably long stretch connected to Cagliari, take bus #PF or #PQ and, in the summer, #PN, and get off wherever a patch catches your fancy!

Arrival and information

Air The airport sits beside the Stagno di Cagliari, the city's largest lagoon, 15min bus ride west of town.

Boat Cagliari's port lies in the heart of the town, opposite Via Roma.

Tourist office There are tourist offices at the port (Via Roma 145), and opposite the train and bus stations on Piazza Matteotti (April–Sept Mon–Sat 8.30am–7.30pm; Oct–March Mon–Fri 9am–1.30pm & 3–6pm, Sat 9am–2pm; ⓣ070.669.255, ⓦwww.comune.cagliari.it).

Internet Try the bookshop Le Librerie della Costa, Via Roma 63 or *Lamari*, a pleasant café at Via Napoli 43.

Laundry Via Sicilia 20.

Accommodation

Booking is essential in summer. An HI hostel was due to open in 2008: check with the tourist office.

AeR Bundes Jack and **Pensione Vittoria** Via Roma 75 ⓣ070.667.970. Two gems right on the seafront, with original 1930s furnishings and lovely eccentric owners. ❽

Albergo Aurora Salita S. Chiar 19 ⓣ070.658.625. A clean, comfortable hotel in a centre of the city, just off Piazza Yenne. ❻

Palmas Via Sardegna 14 ⓣ070.651.679. Clean one-star hotel. ❺

La Perla Via Sardegna 18 ⓣ070.669.446 Neat, family-run place with doubles and triples. ❺

Eating

Cafés and food markets

Piazza Yenne is full of outdoor cafés and has a great gelateria, *L'Isola del Gelato.*

Antico Forno Via M. Sabotino 9. Good deli with local specialities, including the traditional *su coccoi* bread, which is made from semolina or fine flour and found in different shapes according to the region – here it has spikes!

Le Librerie della Costa il Caffe Largo Carlo Felice 76. Bright, modern café set in a fantastic international bookshop. Closed Sun.

Restaurants

Many of Cagliari's restaurants are clustered around the network of streets surrounding Via Sardegna.

La Damigiana Corso Vittorio Emanuele 115. A simple trattoria with low prices. Mains €7.

Da Fabio Via Sardegna 90. Excellent home-made pasta and friendly, if frazzled, owners. Try the *seadas,* a traditional Sardinian dessert pastry filled with sheep's cheese and honey. Pasta €6.50.

Degli Spiriti Via Canelles 34/San Lorenzo 10. Packed with the young and cool, this trendy restaurant and bar serves great pizzas and cocktails and the views over the city are spectacular. There's a different DJ every night during the summer months. Pizza €7. Open until 3am.

TREAT YOURSELF

La Vecchia Trattoria Via Azuni 55 ⓣ070.652.515. Gorgeous traditional seafood and Sardinian specialities, in an intimate trattoria on a cobbled street. The place to come if you're after romantic ambience and excellent food. Arrive early or book in the summer months. Mains €12.

Drinking and nightlife

Amparias Via Savoia 4, has cheap pizzas, buzzy atmosphere and loud music.

De Candia Via Genovese 12/16. Lounge bar on the bastion with bed-style seating, chill-out tunes and arty photographic projections.

Charlie Via de' Carroz, ⓦwww.gclass.it. Open Fri and Sat only. Lively club a short cab-ride from the city centre, playing pop and retro classics on Friday, and retro and lounge on Saturday.

Karel Via della Università 37. Cool underground bar which serves great-value lunches and is popular with students at night.

Mojito Salita Santa Chiara 25. Tiny, red-draped bar just off Piazza Yenne, with outdoor couches in the summer.

Spazio Newton Via Newton 11. Open Fri and Sat only. Popular disco-bar playing alternative music. For events listings, check the newspaper *L'Unione Sarda.*

Moving on

Train Alghero (4 daily via Sassari; 5hr); Olbia (4 daily; 4hr–4hr 40min).

Bus Barumini for Su Nuraxi (1 daily; 1hr 30min); Chia (hourly; 1hr 15min); Pula (hourly; 50min). For more information on buses in Sardinia, see ⓦwww.arst.sardegna.it.

Ferry Civitavecchia (1 daily; 14hr 30min–16hr 30min); Genoa (mid-July to Aug 2 weekly; 20hr); Livorno (1 weekly; 7hr); Naples (1–2 weekly; 16hr); Palermo (1 weekly; 13hr 30min); Trápani (1 weekly; 11hr). For more information about ferries, there's an office at Via Cugia 1(ⓣ070.342.341, ⓦwww.ferroviesardegna.it).

SU NURAXI

SU NURAXI is the biggest and most famous of the island's ancient stone *nuraghi,* and a good taste of the primitive grandeur of the island's indigenous civilization. The snag is access: the site lies 1km outside **Barumini**, a village 50km north of Cagliari, to which there is only one daily Arst bus (2pm). At Barumini, turn left at the main crossroads and it's a ten-minute walk to Su Nuraxi (daily

9am–4/7pm; obligatory guided tour €4.20). Su Nuraxi is thought to be the oldest Nuraghic complex on the island, dating from around 1500 BC, and may have been a capital city. The central tower once reached 21m (it's now 15m high), and its outer defences and inner chambers are connected by passageways and stairs. To return to Cagliari, get the FdS bus at 6pm from outside *Barumini's* bar (buy tickets in Cagliari) to San Luro train station, for a connection at 7.15pm.

NORA AND AROUND

The charming little town of **PULA**, an hour outside Cagliari, is a great base to explore **Nora** and the stunning southern beaches. *Hotel Quattro Mori*, a basic but clean hotel at Via Cagliari 10, is the cheapest **accommodation** option (Ⓣ070.920.9124; ④) – otherwise, your best bet is to ask at the helpful tourist information centre, located right in the middle of the jolly Piazza del Popolo, the central piazza. The piazza is full of little cafés, one of the best of which is the cheap and cheerful *Mr Jingle's Café* at no. 5, which serves great local pastries flavoured with saffron. Outside of the summer months some establishments may be shut.

Nora Archeological Centre

To get to **NORA** from Pula, take an eight-minute ride on the Follesa bus from Piazza Giovanni XXIII, or follow the signs and walk the pleasant 25 minutes to get there. Nora is the site of an **ancient city** (daily 9am– sunset, Ⓣ070.920.9138) thought to date from the eighth century BC. An administrative, religious and commercial centre for over 1000 years, it was abandonded around the seventh century AD when the Arab invasion forced the inhabitants to retreat inland. The monuments – a theatre, thermal baths (which made use of the natural springs to be found here), a forum, a temple, an aqueduct and noble houses – suggest a sophisticated people, and many of the intricate mosaics decorating the town remain intact.

Laguna di Nora

Next to the archeological centre is the **lagoon** (July & Aug daily 10am–5pm; June & Sept daily 10am–4pm; Ⓣ070.920.9544, Ⓦwww.lagunadinora.it; €8), originally a fish farm and now an environmental park where you can observe nesting birds and local wildlife, paddle around in a **canoe** (€25/3hr, including entry to the lagoon park), or take a **snorkelling** trip to have a look at the Roman remains on the bed of the bay (€25/3hr). Nora beach itself, flanked by the **Torre del Coltellazzo** and the **Torre di Sant Efisio** (which you can climb up for a view over to the mountains of Santa Margherita), is a lovely, family-orientated place for a swim.

Chia and around

For more secluded beaches, take a bus from Pula's Via Lamarmora to **CHIA** (hourly; 25min); Chia beach is a five-minute walk from where the bus terminates. From here, white sands stretch along the west coast for about 4km past turquoise blue waters. The beach offers watersports equipment rental, quiet bays and a pizzeria and a disco, which opens at 1am in season. If you're staying at Pula, you'll need to get a cab back as buses stop at 8.30pm.

ALGHERO

In the northwest of Sardinia, **ALGHERO** is a lively resort with a Catalan flavour. From the **Giardino Pubblico**, the **Porta Terra** is the first of Alghero's seven defensive towers, erected by the prosperous Jewish community before their expulsion in 1492. **Via Roma** runs down from here through the old town's puzzle of lanes to the pedestrianized **Via Carlo Alberto**, which holds most of the bars and shops. Turn right to reach **Piazza Civica,** the old town's main square, at one end of which rises Alghero's mainly sixteenth-century **cattedrale** (guided tours Feb–Sept Mon–Fri 10am–1pm; free). The best excursions are west along the coast, past the long bay of **Porto Conte** to the point of **Capo Caccia**, where the spectacular sheer cliffs are riddled by deep marine caves. The most impressive of these is the *Grotta di Nettuno*, or **Neptune's Grotto** (April–Sept daily 9am–7pm; Oct daily 9am–5pm; Nov– March daily 9am–2pm; €10), a long snaking passage that delves far into the rock and is full of stalagmites and stalactites. The return boat trip from the port costs €11, or take the bus from the Giardino Pubblico to Capo Caccia (June–Sept 3 daily from 9am; Oct–May 1 daily).

Arrival and information

Air The airport is 30min out of town, and served by the AA bus, for which you can buy tickets in any *tabacchi*.

Train Trains arrive 3km north of the centre and are connected to the port by regular local buses.

Bus Long-distance buses arrive in Via Catalogna, on the Giardino Pubblico.

Tourist office Alghero's tourist office is on the corner of the Giardino Pubblico (April–Sept Mon–Sat 8am–8pm, Sun 9am–1pm; Nov–March Mon–Sat 8am–2pm; ⓣ079.979.054, ⓦwww.comune.alghero.ss.it).

Accommodation

Alguer Via Parenzo 79 ⓣ079.930.478. HI hostel located in a fairly distant but tranquil spot 6km along the coast at Fertilia, reachable by hourly local bus from Alghero. ❷

Big Fish Via Togliatti 15 ⓣ079.973.1036, ⓦwww.bigfishalghero.it. Welcoming, eclectically decorated little hotel. ❼

Blue Dolphin Via Marconi 75 ⓣ340.266.2064, ⓦwww.bluedolphinalghero.com. Charming, colourful hotel run by the same family as *Big Fish*. ❼

Lucia Van Alphen Via Sassari 53 ⓣ079.978.218. An inviting family place with a breakfast terrace boasting gorgeous views. ❼

La Mariposa ⓣ079.950.480, ⓦwww.lamariposa.it. Popular, well-equipped campsite 2km north of town, with direct access to the beach. April to mid-Oct. ❸

Eating

Alghero's restaurants are renowned for seafood, at its best in spring and winter. There's also a supermarket, Conad, at Via Mazzini 1a, and a great covered food market on Via Sassari.

Casablanca Via Umberto 76. Good, casual pizzeria. Pizza €4.

La Lepanto Via Carlo Alberto 135 ⓣ079.979.116, ⓦwww.lalepanto-ristorante.it. One of the finest fish restaurants in Alghero. Swordfish gnocchi €13.

Trattoria Maristella Via Kennedy 9. Tasty, reasonably-priced fish restaurant popular with locals. Seafood pasta €8.

Drinking and nightlife

There are a few discos and clubs on Lungomare Dante – they usually open after midnight.

L'Arca Music Bar Lungomare Dante 6. Rowdy bar in a lively area overlooking the port. Free entry, live music every Sat.

L'Ormeggio Banchina Porto. Port-side bar, excellent for a sundown aperitif. Summer months only. Beer €4.

Poco Loco Via Gramsci 8. Pizzeria with live music and bowling. Try a metre-long pizza! (€20, serves 4). Internet available from 5.30pm. Open until 1am.

Moving on

Train Sassari (every 2hr; 40min); Cagliari (4 daily via Sassari; 5hr).

Southern Italy

The Italian **south** or *mezzogiorno* offers quite a different experience to that of the north; indeed, few countries are more tangibly divided into two distinct, often antagonistic, regions. **Naples** is the obvious focus, an utterly compelling city just a couple of hours south of Rome. In the **Bay of Naples**, highlights are the resort of Sorrento and the island of **Capri**, swarmed over by tourists these days but still beautiful enough to be worth your time, while the ancient sites of **Pompeii** and **Herculaneum** are Italy's best-preserved Roman remains. South of Naples,

ARRIVAL BY FERRY: BARI AND BRINDISI

Ferries from Greece and Croatia to **BARI** dock at the Stazione Marittima, next to the old city. From here, it is a short bus ride or 45-minute walk to the tourist office at Piazza Aldo Moro 33a (Mon–Sat 8am–2pm, Tues & Thurs also 3–7.30pm; ⓣ080.524.2361, ⓦwww.pugliaturismo.com/aptbari) and the nearby train station. Ferries from Greece also arrive at **BRINDISI**, 100km southeast of Bari. Most services dock at Costa Morena, though some arrive at the Stazione Marittima on Via del Mare. From Costa Morena there's a minibus (6am–8.30pm; every 15min; free) to the centre; from the Stazione Marittima it's a few minutes' walk to the bottom of Corso Garibaldi, then another twenty minutes on foot, or a short bus ride (every 30min; €0.80) to Brindisi's train station in Piazza Crispi. The tourist office is at Lungomare Regina Margherita 43 (Mon–Fri 9am–1pm, 3.30–7pm; Sat 9am–12.30pm; ⓣ0831.523.072, ⓦwww.pugliaturismo.com/aptbrindisi).

the **Amalfi Coast** is a contender for Europe's most dramatic stretch of coastline. In the far south, **Matera**, jewel of the Basilicata region, harbours ancient cave dwellings dug into a steep ravine. Puglia – the long strip of land that makes up the "heel" of Italy – boasts the Baroque wonders of **Lecce,** and is also useful for ferries to Greece and Croatia.

NAPLES

Wherever else you travel south of Rome, the chances are that you'll wind up in **NAPLES** (Napoli). It's the kind of city people visit with preconceptions, and it rarely disappoints: it is filthy, large and overbearing; it is crime-infested; and it is most definitely like nowhere else in Italy – something the inhabitants will be keener than anyone to tell you. One thing, though, is certain: a couple of days here and you're likely to be as staunch a defender of the place as its most devoted inhabitants.

What to see and do

The area between the vast and busy Piazza Garibaldi, where most buses arrive, and Via Toledo, the main street a mile or so west, makes up the old part of the city – the **centro storico**. Buildings rise high on either side of the narrow, crowded streets; there's little light, and not even much sense of the rest of the city outside. South of here is the busy port, and to the northwest, Naples' finest museums.

The Duomo

From Piazza Garibaldi, Via dei Tribunali cuts through to Via Duomo, where you'll find the tucked-away **Duomo**, a Gothic building from the early thirteenth century dedicated to San Gennaro, the patron saint of the city, martyred in 305 AD. Two phials of his blood miraculously liquefy three times a year – on the first Saturday in May, on September 19 and on December 16. If the blood refuses to liquefy disaster is supposed to befall the city. The first chapel on the right as you walk into the cathedral holds the precious phials and Gennaro's skull. Downstairs, the **Crypt of San Gennaro** is one of the finest examples of Renaissance art in Naples, founded by Cardinal Carafa and holding the tombs of both San Gennaro and Pope Innocent IV.

Spaccanapoli

Across Via Duomo, Via dei Tribunali continues on into **Spaccanapoli**, the heart of the old city and Naples' busiest and architecturally richest quarter. The district's other main drag, running alongside Via dei Tribunali, is Via San Biagio dei Librai; both are a maelstrom of hurrying pedestrians, revving cars and buzzing scooters.

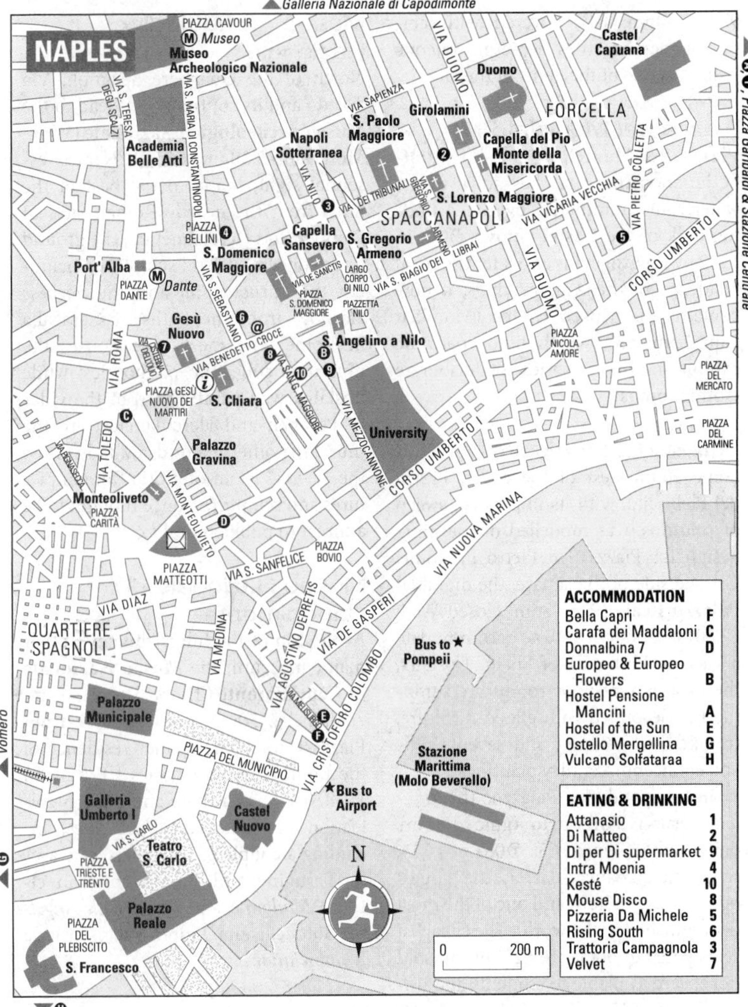

Napoli Sotterranea

West along Via dei Tribunali at Piazza San Gaetano 68 is the city's most important underground site, **Napoli Sotterranea** (Mon–Fri 12–4pm, Sat & Sun 10am–6pm; entry every 2hr by 90min guided tour; ⓦwww.napolisotterranea.org; €9.30), a complex of tunnels and chambers 40m below street level. The labyrinthine passageways – remains of the Greek city of Neapolis – date back to the fourth century BC.

Gesù Nuovo and Santa Chiara

Cut through to Via S. Biagio dei Librai and continue west to the **Gesù Nuovo** church, distinctive for its lava-stone facade, prickled with pyramids that give it an impregnable, prison-like air. Facing the Gesù Nuovo, the church of **Santa Chiara** is quite different, a Provençale-Gothic structure built in 1328 (and rebuilt after World War II). The attached **cloister** (Mon–Sat 9.30am–6.30pm, Sun

9.30–2.30pm; €4), covered with colourful majolica tiles depicting bucolic scenes, is one of the gems of the city.

Piazza del Municipio

Piazza del Municipio is a busy traffic junction that stretches down to the waterfront, dominated by the brooding hulk of the **Castel Nuovo**. Built in 1282 by the Angevins and later the royal residence of the Aragon kings, it now contains the **Museo Civico** (Mon–Sat 9am–7pm; €5), which holds periodic exhibitions in a series of elaborate Gothic rooms.

Piazza del Plebiscito

Some 500m west of the castle, Piazza del Plebiscito, with its impressive sweep of columns, was modelled on Bernini's design for Piazza San Pietro in Rome. On one side of the square, the dignified **Palazzo Reale** (9am–7pm, closed Wed; €7.50) was built in 1602 to accommodate a visit by Philip III of Spain. Upstairs, the palace's first-floor rooms are sumptuously decorated with gilded furniture, trompe-l'oeil ceilings, and seventeenth- and eighteenth-century paintings.

Just beyond the Palazzo, the opulent **Teatro San Carlo** (guided tours daily 9am–5.30pm, €5; ⓣ081.664.545; ⓦwww.teatrosancarlo.it) is the largest opera house in Italy, and one of the most distinguished in the world. The cheapest seats you can book are €25, but unsold tickets are available to students and under-30s for €15 an hour before the performance starts.

Quartiere Spagnoli

West of Via Toledo, the **Quartiere Spagnoli** is one of the most characteristic parts of the city, its narrow streets home to the infamous slum dwellings known as *bassi*. If you're used to big cities, there's no reason not to take a discreet walk around here; don't go at night, however, and take care not to flash valuables.

Museo Archeologico Nazionale

North of the Quartiere Spagnoli, Via Toledo and its continuations lead to the **Museo Archeologico Nazionale** (Wed–Mon 9am–7.30pm; €6.50), Naples' essential sight, home to the best of the finds from the nearby Roman sites of Pompeii and Herculaneum. The ground floor concentrates on sculpture, including the *Farnese Bull* and the *Farnese Hercules* from the Baths of Caracalla in Rome. The mezzanine houses the museum's collection of mosaics, while upstairs, wall paintings from the villas of Pompeii and Herculaneum are the museum's other major draw. Don't miss the "secret" room of erotic Roman pictures and sculptures, once thought to be a threat to public morality.

Museo Nazionale di Capodimonte

At the top of the hill is the city's other major museum, the **Museo Nazionale di Capodimonte** (Thurs–Tues 8.30am–7.30pm; €7.50; buses #24, #R4 from Piazza Dante), the former residence of the Bourbon King Charles III, built in 1738. This has a huge and superb collection of Renaissance paintings, including a couple of Brueghels, canvases by Perugino and Pinturicchio, an elegant *Madonna and Child with Angels* by Botticelli and Lippi's soft, sensitive *Annunciation*.

Vomero

Vomero, the district topping the hill immediately above the old city, can be reached on the Montesanto funicular. A five-minute stroll from the station, the star-shaped fortress of **Castel Sant'Elmo** (Thurs–Tues 8.30am–7.30pm; €3), was built in the fourteenth century. Occupying Naples' highest point, it boasts the best views of the city. The Certosa-Museo di San Martino (same hours; €6, includes entrance to Castel Sant'Elmo), a former Carthusian monastery now converted into a museum, contains an extensive collection of seventeeth- and eighteenth-century Neapolitan painting and sculpture.

Arrival and information

Air Naples' **Capodochino Airport** is northwest of the centre at Viale Ruffo Fulco di Calabria, connected with Piazza Garibaldi by orange bus 3S (6am–11pm; every 10min; journey time 30min; €1). The blue official airport bus Alibus (6.30am–11.30pm; every 20min; €3) runs to the port and to Piazza Garibaldi.
Train Trains arrive at Piazza Garibaldi, the main hub of all transport services.
Bus Most long-distance, inter-regional buses and local buses use Piazza Garibaldi.
Ferry Ferries and hydrofoils dock at Molo Beverello, a short bus ride from the centre.
Tourist information There's tourist information at the train station (Mon–Sat 9am–7pm, Sun 9am–1pm) and airport (daily 9am–7pm), but the **main tourist office** is at Piazza Gesù Nuovo dei Martiri 58 (Mon–Sat 9am–1.30pm & 2.30–6.30pm; ⓣ081.551.2701, ⓦwww.inaples.it). Pick up the free **listings** booklet *Qui Napoli*, handy for events and transport times.
Discount cards If you are around for more than a day, invest in the **Artecard** (from €8; sold in the station, *tabacchis* and museums; ⓦwww.campaniaartecard.it), which is valid on various combinations of transport, including a return trip on the Metro del Mare ferries, along with free museum entrance.

City transport

Tickets Buy tickets – valid on all city transport networks - from *tabacchi*. €1 tickets are valid for 90min, €3 ones for the day; stamp them on board to validate them.
Bus, metro and tram Walking is the best option in the centre, but an extensive bus, metro and tram network is available for the footsore.
Underground metros – indicated by a red M symbol – are fast but, as they only run every 20min or so, it's often quicker to walk. Tram routes #1, #1B and #2B connect Piazza Garibaldi with the city centre.
Funicular Funicular railways, running up to Vomero and the suburbs of Chiaia and Mergellina, are useful for scaling Naples' hills.

Accommodation

Many of the city's cheaper **hotels** are situated around Piazza Garibaldi, within spitting distance of the train station – a convenient but unattractive area. The touts in the station are likely to offer you below-standard accommodation at an inflated price. If you can afford it, shell out a few extra euros to stay in one of the budget hotels in the **centro storico** instead – it's worth booking in advance.

Hostels

Bella Capri Via Melisurgo 4 ⓣ081.552.9494, ⓦwww.bellacapri.it. New hostel right by the port with bright common areas and small, air-conditioned dorms. It's also a hotel, with simple rooms overlooking the bay. Ten percent discount with this book. Dorms ❷, private rooms ❻
Hostel Pensione Mancini Via Mancini 33 ⓣ081.553.6731, ⓦwww.hostelpensionemancini.com. Small, recently redecorated place right across from the station. Ten percent discount with this book. Dorm beds ❷, private rooms ❺–❻
Ostello Mergellina Salita della Grotta 23 ⓣ081.761.2346, ⓔostellonapoli@virgilio.it. Metro or train to Mergellina. HI hostel some way out of the centre with a view of the bay. Dorms ❷, private rooms (bunk beds only) ❹
Hostel of the Sun Via Melisurgo 15 ⓣ081.420.6393, ⓦwww.hostelnapoli.com. Colourful hostel next to the port. The friendly staff are full of advice on how to spend your time in the city and organize nightlife tours and pasta parties. Free Internet. Dorms ❷; ten percent discount on doubles (❻–❼) with this book.

Hotels

Carafa di Maddaloni Via Maddaloni 6 ⓣ081.551.3691, ⓦwww.bb-carafa.com. Elegant rooms in a stunning frescoed palazzo in Spaccanapoli – luxury at a near-budget price. ❼–❾
Donnalbina 7 Via Donnalbina 7 ⓣ081.1956.7817, ⓦwww.donnalbina7.it. The en suites at this boutique-style hotel are surprisingly affordable; €10 discount for stays of two days or more. Free Internet; ❽
Europeo & **Europeo Flowers** Via Mezzocannone 109/c ⓣ081.551.7254. Although slightly cramped, rooms are central and great value. No breakfast. Standard doubles ❹–❽; individually decorated, air-conditioned rooms ❻–❾

Camping

Vulcano Solfatara Via Solfatara 161, Pozzuoli ⓣ081.526.2341, ⓦwww.solfatara.it. Closed Nov–March. Metro to Pozzuoli, then a 10min walk

LIP-SMACKING SNACKS

Pizza is Naples' speciality. It should cost around €3 to take away: the best are *marinara*, with tomato, garlic and oil, or *margherita*, with tomato and mozzarella cheese. The city's **pastries** are also world-famous: hundreds of varieties are sold in *pasticcerie* all over the city, but it's worth seeking out Attanasio (Vico della Ferrovia 1–4; closed Mon), in a tiny alley near the train station, for their hot, sweet ricotta-stuffed *sfogliatella* pastries, a bargain at €1 each.

uphill. This well-equipped campsite, on the edge of a volcanic crater, has a swimming pool, restaurant and Internet access. ❷

Eating

Spaccanapoli is full of small *alimentari* (grocery stores), which will make you up a panini for a few euros, and there's a central **supermarket**, Di per Di, near the university at Via Mezzocannone 99. Colourful produce markets are to be found all over the centre; one of the best (daily 8am–1pm) takes up the streets around Via Pignasecca just north of the Quartiere Spagnoli.

Restaurants and pizzerias

Di Matteo Via Tribunali 94. Closed Sun. Superb for pizza and also offers a deep-fried, ricotta-filled alternative. Pizzas from €2.50.

Pizzeria Da Michele Via Cesare Sersale 1–3. Closed Sun. The best pizza in Naples – enormous, tasty and cheap – served at a historic pizzeria (since 1870). Pizzas from €3.50.

Intra Moenia Piazza Bellini 69–71. A left-wing literary café and publishing house that also offers Internet access. Good for light meals; toasted sandwiches €5, salads €8.

Trattoria Campagnola Via dei Tribunali 47. This lunch-only Spaccanapoli trattoria has been serving up hearty *cucina napoletana* for 60 years. A three-course meal will set you back €12–15.

Drinking and nightlife

Most **discos** and live venues close in July and August and move to the beach; the Neapolitans who remain congregate for a beer in Santa Maria La Nova and Piazza Bellini. The rest of the year, the studenty **bars** and clubs along Via Cisterna dell'Olio, near Via Benedetto Croce on the western edge of Spaccanapoli, are good for a lively night out.

Bars and clubs

Kestè Largo San Giovanni Maggiore 26–27 Ⓦwww.keste.it. A buzzy bar with DJs and live music, popular with students from the nearby university.

Mouse Disco Via San Giovanni Maggiore 45. A small disco playing R&B, pop and house.

Rising South Via S. Sebastiano 19 Ⓣ335.811.7107. Closed mid-May to mid-Sept. The coolest club in Naples, with a velvet Baroque interior and loungey tunes. Call to be put on the list on Thurs, Fri and Sat.

Velvet Via Cisterna dell'Olio 11 Ⓦwww.velvetnapoli.it. Closed Mon and mid-May to Sept. Intimate, buzzing place with arty ambience; the music is generally house and electronica.

Directory

Consulates UK, Via dei Mille 40 Ⓣ081.423.8911; US, Piazza della Repubblica 2 Ⓣ081.583.8111.

Exchange At Stazione Centrale (daily 8am–7.30pm).

Hospital Ambulance Ⓣ118; Cardarelli hospital, Via Cardarelli 9, Vomero Ⓣ081.747.111.

Internet Caffè del Centro Antico (Via B.Croce 15; 7am–9pm; €1.50/30min).

Laundry Bolle Blu, Corso Novara 62–64, near the station (Mon–Sat 8.30am–8pm).

Pharmacy At the train station (24hr).

Police Ⓣ113. Main police station is at Via Medina 75 Ⓣ081.794.1111.

Post office Piazza Matteotti. Mon–Fri 8am–6.30pm, Sat 8am–12.30pm.

Moving on

Air Rome (3 daily; 55min).

Train Lecce (12 daily; 5hr 30min); Palermo (5 daily; 8–11hr); Siracusa (7 daily; 8–10hr).

Ferry Capri (6 daily; 1hr 20min); Palermo (4 daily; 10hr 30min).

Hydrofoil to: Capri (28 daily; 40min); Sorrento (8 daily; 50min).

THE BAY OF NAPLES

For the Romans, the **Bay of Naples** was the land of plenty, a blessed region with a mild climate and gorgeous scenery

TRIPS AROUND THE BAY

Trips around the bay from Naples are straightforward and cheap. The **Circumvesuviana rail system** runs from the station at Piazza Garibaldi around the Bay of Naples as far as Sorrento in about an hour. A more entertaining way to travel is the **Metro del Mare** ferry network from Molo Beverello (summer only; ⓦwww.metrodelmare.com) which goes to Capri, Sorrento and Amalfi, and is probably the cheapest way to get a sea trip.

– and hence a favourite holiday and retirement area for the city's nobility. Of the islands that dot the bay, **Capri** is the best place to visit if you're here for a short time. Sorrento, the brooding presence of **Vesuvius** and the incomparable Roman sites of **Herculaneum** and **Pompeii** are further draws.

Ercolano

The town of **ERCOLANO**, a half-hour hop on the train from Naples on the Circumvesuviana line (€1.70 one-way), is the modern offshoot of the ancient site of **Herculaneum**, which was destroyed by the eruption of Vesuvius on August 2, 79 AD. It's worth stopping here to see the excavations and to get the bus to **Vesuvius**. The tourist office at Via IV Novembre 82 (ⓣ081 788 1243; Mon–Sat 8am–2pm) can help with accommodation, but you're best off avoiding the largely ugly, postwar town itself and making Sorrento or Naples your base instead.

Herculaneum

Situated at the seaward end of Ercolano's main street, **HERCULANEUM** (daily: Apr–Oct 8.30am–5pm, Nov–Mar 8.30am–5pm; ticket office shuts 90min before close; €11; ⓦwww.pompeiisites.org) was a residential town in Roman times, much smaller than Pompeii, and as such it's a more manageable site – less architecturally impressive, but with better-preserved buildings. Because it wasn't a commercial town, there's no central open space, just streets of villas and shops, cut by two very straight main streets. Highlights include the **House of the Mosaic Atrium**, with its mosaic-laid courtyard, the large bath complex and the **Casa del Bel Cortile**, which contains a group of skeletons, poignantly lying in the pose they died in.

Vesuvius

Its most famous eruption, in 79 AD, buried the towns and inhabitants of Pompeii and Herculaneum, and **VESUVIUS** has long dominated the lives of those who live on the Bay of Naples. It's still an active volcano – the only one on mainland Europe – and there have been hundreds of (mostly minor) eruptions over the years. The people who live here fear its reawakening, and with good reason – scientists calculate it should erupt every thirty years or so, and it hasn't done so since 1944. Buses run from Ercolano train station (last bus 3.25pm) to a car park and huddle of souvenir shops and cafés. The walk up to the **crater** from the bus stop takes about half an hour on marked-out paths. At the top (admission €6.50), the crater is a deep, wide, jagged ashtray of red rock emitting the odd plume of smoke. You can walk most of the way around, but take it easy – the fences are old and rickety. See ⓦwww.vesuviopark.it for information on trails around the volcano.

Pompeii

The other Roman town destroyed by Vesuvius, **POMPEII** (daily: April–Oct 8.30am–7.30pm, Nov–March 8.30am–5pm; ticket office closes 90min earlier; €11; ⓣ081.857.5347, ⓦwww.pompeiisites.org) was one of Campania's most important commercial centres. Of a to-

GETTING TO POMPEII

To reach Pompeii from Naples, take the **Circumvesuviana** to Pompeii-Villa dei Misteri (direction Sorrento; journey time 35min); this leaves you right outside the western entrance. It makes most sense to see the site as a day-trip from Naples, but there is an **HI hostel**, *Casa del Pellegrino*, at Via Duca d'Aosta 4 (Ⓣ081.850.8644; ❷), 200m from Pompeii-Santuario station on the Circumvesuviana line, and a large and well-equipped **campsite**, *Zeus*, which also has cheap private rooms (Ⓣ081.861.5320; Ⓦwww.campingzeus.it; camping ❷, private doubles ❺), right outside the Pompeii-Villa dei Misteri station.

tal population of twenty thousand, it's thought that two thousand perished, asphyxiated by the toxic fumes of the volcanic debris, their homes buried under several metres of ash and pumice. The full horror of their death is apparent in plaster casts made from the shapes their bodies left in the volcanic ash – gruesome, writhing figures, some with their hands covering their eyes.

Seeing the site will take you half a day at least. Entering from the Pompeii-Villa dei Misteri side, you come across the **Forum**, a slim open space surrounded by the ruins of some of the town's most important official buildings. North of here lies a small bath complex, and beyond, the **House of the Faun**, its "Ave" (Welcome) mosaic outside beckoning you in to view the atrium and the copy of a tiny bronze dancing faun. A few streets southwest, the recently restored Lupanare was Pompeii's only purpose-built brothel, worth a peek for its racy wall paintings. A short walk from the Porta Ercolano is the **Villa dei Misteri**, the best preserved of all Pompeii's palatial houses. It derives its name from a series of frescoes in one of its larger chambers, depicting the initiation rites of a young woman into the Dionysiac Mysteries, an orgiastic cult transplanted to Italy from Greece in the Republican era.

On the other side of the site, the well-preserved **Grand Theatre** is still used for performances, as is the **Little Theatre** on its far left side. From here, it's a short walk to the **Amphitheatre**, one of Italy's most intact and also its oldest, dating from 80 BC.

SORRENTO

Topping the rocky cliffs close to the end of its peninsula, **SORRENTO** is unashamedly a resort, its inspired location and pleasant climate having drawn foreigners from all over Europe for two hundred years. Nowadays it caters mostly to the package-tour industry, but this bright, lively place is none the worse for it and retains its southern Italian roots. Accommodation and food, though not exactly cheap, are much better value than most of the other resorts along the Amalfi Coast, making it a good base from which to explore the area. Sorrento's centre is **Piazza Tasso**, five minutes from the train station along the busy Corso Italia, the streets around which are pedestrianized for the lively evening *passeggiata*. The town isn't particularly well provided with beaches: most people make do with the rocks and a tiny, crowded strip of sand at **Marina Grande** – fifteen minutes' walk or a short bus ride from Piazza Tasso – or the beaches further along, such as the tiny **Regina Giovanna** at Punta del Capo, again connected by bus from Piazza Tasso, where a natural pool by the ruins of the Roman villa, Pollio Felix, makes a unique place for a swim.

Arrival and information

Train Sorrento train station is the last stop on the Circumvesuviana line from Naples (5.09am–10.42pm; every 30min; €3.20).

Bus Autolinee Curreri coaches from Naples Airport (6 daily; 75min; €6) stop at Via degli Aranci, near the train station; SITA buses (hourly; 6.30am–3am; €3.20) from Amalfi arrive at the station.
Ferry Metro del Mare operates high-season connections from Naples (35–105min; €4.50 one-way) to the port, a short bus ride from the centre.
Tourist office The office in the large yellow Circolo dei Foresteri building at Via de Maio 35, just off Piazza Sant'Antonino (Mon–Sat 8.30am–6.30pm; ⓣ081.807.4033, ⓦwww.sorrentotourism.com) can help with accommodation.

Accommodation

Camping Nube d'Argento Via del Capo 21 ⓣ081.878.1344, ⓦwww.nubedargento.com. Closed Nov–Feb. A 15min walk from Piazza Tasso towards Marina Grande, this campsite has a pool, restaurant and sea views. Campsite ❷, two- to six-person chalets ❼–❾
Casa Astarita Corso Italia 67 ⓣ081.877.4906, ⓦwww.casatarita.com. This beautifully decorated B&B on Sorrento's main street has six spacious, air-conditioned rooms, free Internet and great breakfasts. ❽–❾
Le Sirene Via degli Aranci 160 ⓣ081.807.2925, ⓔinfo@hostellesirene.it. 200m from the station, this hostel is a little cramped, but there's a kitchen, and no curfew. Dorms ❷, private ensuites ❼
Ulisse Via del Mare 22 ⓣ081.877.4753, ⓦwww.ulissedeluxe.com. A bargain a 5min walk from the centre and just 300m from the sea, this "deluxe hostel" has vast, distinctly un-hostelly en suites (no dorms) with a modern, slightly corporate feel. ❹

Eating

There's a Standa **supermarket** at Corso Italia 223, and Ortofrutticola da Armando, near the station at Via degli Aranci 72, makes panini to order.
Da Franco Corso Italia 265 ⓣ081.877.2066. Wooden bench seating is overhung with racks of Parma ham at this no-frills local pizzeria. Pizzas from €5.50.
Mami Camilla Via Cocumella 4 ⓣ081.878.2067, ⓦwww.mamicamilla.com. Call before 6pm to book a four-course dinner with wine at this cookery school for just €15.
Ristorante S. Antonino Via S. Maria delle Grazie 6 ⓣ081.877.1200. Good-value meals served on a shady terrace; pizzas are €6, and a few meaty mains under €10.
Zi'Ntonio Via Luigi de Maio 11 ⓣ081.878.1623. Closed Tues in winter. Family-run trattoria serving up reasonably priced pizza and fish dishes in a wood-beamed, galleon-like dining room.

Drinking and nightlife

In summer, all the **clubbing** action takes place at venues out of Sorrento, along the coast. Promoters distribute tickets from midnight onwards in Piazza Tasso; clubs are a 10min taxi ride from here.
Chaplin's Pub Corso Italia 18. This Irish pub is a bit of a tourist magnet, but it's an appealingly raucous place to sink a skinful, and is open till 3am.
English Inn Corso Italia 55. Not as lively as Chaplin's, this pub is open all day, serves cheap burgers at lunchtimes and has a disco, *The Garden*, on the first floor.
Insolito Corso Italia 38E. A trendy, all-white space open day and night; sleek sister bar *li'ly* (Via Fuorimura 47, ⓦwww.lilysorrento.it) is also a disco.
Photo Via Correale 19–21. This chi-chi bar popular with locals puts on regular photography exhibitions – hence the name – and has an outdoor terrace and occasional DJ sets. Open till 2am.

Moving on

Bus Amalfi (every 40min–1hr; 1hr 30min).
Ferry Capri (4 daily; 25min).
Hydrofoil to: Amalfi (4 daily; 1hr); Capri (23 daily; 20min).

CAPRI

Rising from the sea off the far end of the Sorrentine peninsula, the island of **CAPRI** is the most sought-after destination in the Bay of Naples. During Roman times the emperor Tiberius retreated here to indulge in debauchery; more recently the Blue Grotto and the island's remarkable landscape have drawn tourists in their droves. Capri is a busy and expensive place, but it's easy enough to visit as a day-trip – though in July and August you may prefer to give it a miss rather than fight through the crowds.

What to see and do

Capri town is a very pretty place, with winding alleyways converging on the tiny main square of Piazza Umberto. The Giardini di Augusto give tremendous views of the coast below and the towering jagged cliffs above. Opposite, take the recently-reopened hairpin

GETTING TO CAPRI

There are regular **ferries** and **hydrofoils** to Capri from Naples' Molo Beverello; hydrofoils also operate from the Mergellina jetty a couple of miles north of here, and also from Sorrento and Amalfi. Prices range from €7.60 to €16 one-way; the cheapest deals tend to be from the state-run ferry Caremar and the Metro del Mare.

path, Via Krupp, down to **MARINA PICCOLA**, a huddle of houses and restaurants around a few patches of pebble beach – pleasantly quiet out of season, though in summer it's heaving. You can also reach the ruins of Tiberius' villa, the **Villa Jovis**, from Capri town (daily 9am–1hr before sunset; €2), a steep thirty-minute trek east. The site is among Capri's most exhilarating, with incredible vistas of the bay; get there as soon as it opens to avoid the crush.

The island's other main settlement, **ANACAPRI**, is less picturesque than Capri town, its tacky main square flanked by souvenir shops, but from here a chair-lift (daily: March–Oct 10.30am–6.30pm, Nov–Feb 10.30am–3pm; €7 return) carries you up 596m **Monte Solaro**, the island's highest point. The island's most famous attraction, the **Blue Grotto**, is an hour's trek down Via Lo Pozzo, or take a bus from the main square. At €9.50, with tip expected, it's a bit of a rip-off, with boatmen whisking visitors through the grotto in five minutes flat, but in the evening, you may be able to swim into the cave for free, allowing you to experience the grotto's famed azure iridescence close up; change at the bar next to the entrance.

Arrival and information

Ferry Ferries and hydrofoils dock at Marina Grande, the waterside extension of **Capri town**, which perches on the hill above, connected by funicular.
Tourist office The main one is on Piazza Umberto in Capri town (Mon–Sat: April–Oct 8.30am–8.30pm, Nov–March 9am–1pm, 3.30–6.45pm; Ⓣ081.837.0686; Ⓦwww.capritourism.com.

Accommodation

Bussola di Hermes Via Traversa La Vigna 14, Anacapri t081.838.2010, Ⓦwww.bussolahermes.com. Run by the very helpful Rita, this hotel has some basic private rooms, as well as laundry facilities and Internet; a swimming pool is planned for 2008. Shuttle service from the port. ⑦–⑧
Villa Eva Via La Fabbrica 8 Ⓣ081.837.1549, Ⓦwww.villaeva.com. A trek below Anacapri, *Villa Eva* consists of a series of fantastical villas designed and built by Eva's artist husband, complete with pool and overgrown garden. ⑨
Stella Maris Via Roma 27 Ⓣ081.837.0452. Rooms at this hotel in the heart of Capri are clean and neat, with sea views. ⑨

Eating

Bring a **picnic** to avoid inflated **restaurant** prices, or try one of the island's cheaper options below.
L'Approdo Piazza A. Ferraro 7. The locals come to this restaurant at the end of the harbour for expertly cooked pizza (€6).
Fratelli Capone Via Gradoni Sopramonte 6–8. Closed Wed & Nov–Mar. This *rosticceria* sells tasty, great-value hot and cold food to take away. Roast chicken €7.
Scialapopolo Closed Wed & Nov–Mar. Via Vittorio Emanuele 55. Exceptional ice cream and *granite* have been served from this tiny kiosk since 1952.

THE AMALFI COAST

Occupying the southern side of Sorrento's peninsula, the **Amalfi Coast** is perhaps Europe's most beautiful stretch of coast, its corniche road winding around the towering cliffs. There are no trains; the bus from Sorrento joins the coast road a little west of Positano for the incredible ride east through a handful of villages to Amalfi.

Amalfi

AMALFI has been an established seaside resort since the 1900s, when the British upper classes spent their winters here. In Byzantine times, Amalfi was an independent republic and one of the great naval powers, with a population of some seventy thousand. Vanquished by the Normans in 1131, it was then devastated by an earthquake in 1343. A few remnants of Amalfi's past glories survive, and the town's narrow, high-sided alleyways and tucked-away piazzas make it fun to wander through. The **Duomo** dominates the main piazza, its gaudy facade topped by a glazed-tiled cupola. St Andrew is buried in its crypt, though the most appealing part of the building is the cloister (daily 9am–9pm; €2.50) – oddly Arabic in feel, with its whitewashed arches and palms. Close by in Piazza del Municipio 6, the **Museo Civico** (Mon, Wed, Fri 8.30am–1pm; Tues, Thurs 2.30–5pm; free) displays the *Tavole Amalfitane* – the book of maritime laws which governed the Republic, and the rest of the Mediterranean, until 1570. Beyond these, the focus is the busy seafront, where there's a crowded **beach**.

Arrival and information

Train The nearest major train station is at Salerno, from where there are SITA buses and ferries to Amalfi.
Bus SITA buses from Sorrento and Marozzi buses from Rome (summer only) arrive in Piazza Flavio Gioia, on the tiny waterfront.
Ferry Ferries and hydrofoils from Naples and Sorrento arrive in the tiny harbour.
Tourist office Corso delle Repubbliche Marinare 27 (Mon–Fri 8.30am–1pm, 3–6pm, Sat 8.30am–1pm; ⓣ089.871.107, ⓦwww.amalfitouristoffice.it).

Accommodation

Almost all the **hotels** in Amalfi are expensive; it makes sense to base yourself in a **hostel** in one of the nearby towns, such as Atrani or Positano, a short bus ride from Amalfi.
A' Scalinatella Piazza Umberto I 5–6, Atrani ⓣ089.871.492, ⓦwww.hostelscalinatella.com. SITA bus from Amalfi. This popular hostel-cum-hotel is a 5min walk out of town, near the beach. Dorms ❸, doubles ❼
Beata Solitudo Piazza G. Avitabile 4, Agerola ⓣ081.802.5048, ⓦwww.beatasolitudo.it. Bus to Agerola. This basic hostel 16km north of Amalfi has a small campsite attached. Dorms ❷, campsite ❶

TREAT YOURSELF

Tempted to splash out in one of Amalfi's chi-chi restaurants? **Ristorante Eolo** (Via Comite 3 ⓣ089.871.104, ⓦwww.marinariviera.it) combines gourmet, fusion cuisine with the most spectacular of views as a backdrop; book a window table. At around €40 a head, it's not cheap – but as a one-off gourmet experience, it's well worth the splurge.

Sant'Andrea Via Santolo Camera 1 ⓣ089.871.145. One of the cheaper options in town, this pretty hotel on the central square has views of the Duomo from some rooms. ❽

Eating

You'll find **picnic ingredients** at grocery stores along Via delle Cartiere.
Il Mulino Via delle Cartiere 36 ⓣ089.872.223. A few min walk from the Duomo, this friendly, family-run place does hearty pasta dishes for around €10.
Il Tari Via P.Capuano 9–11 ⓣ089.871.832. Closed Tues. A simple trattoria that's particularly strong on fish dishes; try the grilled mixed fish platter (€12).

Moving on

Bus Ravello (hourly; 30min); Sorrento (4 daily; 1hr).
Ferry Naples (2 daily; 1hr 25min); Sorrento (4 daily; 1hr).

Ravello

The best views of the coast are to be had inland from Amalfi, in **RAVELLO**. For a time an independent republic, nowadays it's little more than a large village. What makes it more than worth the thirty-minute bus ride up from Amalfi's Piazza Flavio Gioia, however, is its unrivalled location, spread across the top of one of the coast's mountains. Buses (roughly hourly; 7am–10pm) drop off just before a road tunnel; walk through this to reach **Piazza del Duomo**. The Duomo (daily 8.30am–1pm, 3–8pm) is an eleventh-century church; ten minutes away, the gardens of the **Villa Cimbrone** (daily 9am–sunset; €5; the villa itself is generally closed to visitors) offer marvellous views over the sea below.

Tourist information is at Via Roma 18 (daily: Mar–Oct, Dec & Jan 9am–8pm, Feb & Nov 9am–2pm; ⓣ089.857.096, ⓦwww.ravellotime.it), which also has the programme for Ravello's famous summer arts festival, held in the Villa Rufolo.

MATERA

Tucked into the instep of Italy in the Basilicata region, **Matera** is one of the south's most fascinating cities. The main point of interest is its *sassi*, rock dwellings dug out of a ravine. During the 1950s and 1960s the residents were forcibly evicted, as the city had degenerated into one huge slum. New blocks were constructed just outside the town to house the population and the *sassi* were left empty, but in 1993 the area was declared a World Heritage Site and has since been slowly repopulated with hotels, restaurants and workshops.

The focus of the Sassi district, a warren of rock streets, is the **chiese rupestri** or rock-hewn churches (all open daily: April–Oct 9am–1pm & 3–7pm, Nov–March 9.30am–1.30pm & 2.30–4.30pm; €2.50 each, or €6 for all). The conical Monte Errone rises in the midst of the Sassi, providing a perch for the most spectacular church, **Madonna de Idris**, with frescoes dating from the fourteenth century. But possibly the most interesting interior is within the **Convincinio S. Antonio**, a complex of four interlinking churches dating from 1200. In 1700, the four churches were converted into cellars – look out for the spouts for red and white wine emerging from what appears to be an altar – then later into houses. For an insight into what life was like for the *sassi*-dwellers, stop by the **Casa Grotta**, just below Madonna de Idris (daily: April–Oct 9.30am–8pm; Nov–March 9.30am–5pm; ⓦwww.casa-grotta.it; €1.50).

Arrival and information

Air Matera is 60km southwest of Bari airport.
Train The train station, on Piazza Matteotti, is served by the private FAL rail line (ⓦwww.fal-srl.it) from Bari.
Bus Direct coach services from Rome (Mon–Sat 1 daily; 5hr 45min; run by Autolinee Liscio, ⓦwww.autolineeliscio.it) stop at the train station.
Tourist office Via Roma trails down from Piazza Matteotti; the tourist office is just off it at Via de Viti de Marco 9 (Mon & Thurs 9am–1pm & 4–6.30pm, Tues, Wed, Fri & Sat 9am–1pm; ⓣ0835.331.983, ⓦwww.aptbasilicata.it).

Accommodation

Antica Locanda San Martino Via San Martino 22 ⓣ0835.256.600, ⓦwww.locandadisanmartino.it. It's worth splashing out on one of the atmospheric new cave **hotels**: this is a cool, fragrant *sassi* conversion 100m from the city centre. ❾
B&B Capriotti Via Gradoni Duomo 25 ⓣ329.619.3757, ⓦcapriotti-bed-breakfast.it. Right in the centre of town, this B&B offers great-value mini-apartments in a sixteenth-century building. ❼
Domus del Barisano Via Lombardi 16 ⓣ333.940.5172, ⓦwww.domusdelbarisano.it. Tucked away in a historic palazzo in the Sassi district, this B&B has four attractive rooms – one with a kitchen, others with balcony or terrace. ❼
Sassi San Giovanni Vecchio 89 ⓣ0835.331.009, ⓦwww.hotelsassi.it. The original cave hotel, in the heart of the Sassi, with individually designed rooms and great views; it also doubles as a hostel. Dorm beds ❷, doubles ❾

Eating and drinking

Caffè del Cavaliere Piazza San Pietro Barisano. Closed Sun & Mon. The place to gather for an evening drink in the atmospheric Sassi district.
La Panca Via Giolitti 39. Closed Mon. There are cheap **restaurants** all over town, but this rowdy pizzeria is one of the most popular; it's a 10min walk from the central Piazza Vittorio Veneto up Via XX Settembre and Via Annunziatella.
Il Terrazzino Vico S. Giuseppe 7. A *sassi* restaurant with great views and a cheap – but far from nasty – tourist menu; try the *orecchiette* pasta with sausage, tomato and mozzarella.

LECCE

LECCE, 40km south of Brindisi port, is often called the "Florence of the south".

These alleys may be well-trodden, but a real sense of discovery still accompanies a visit to the city's vine-enveloped stonework. Carved from a soft sandstone, the buildings are one of the high points in Italian architecture, and very different from the heavy Baroque of Rome. Built for wealthy families, churchmen and merchants during the fifteenth to seventeenth centuries, when Lecce was at the height of its power, these buildings are among the most beautiful examples of the style – some of the most impressive were designed by Giuseppe Zimbalo, known as Lo Zingarello. A short walk from the central Piazza Sant'Oronzo is **Santa Croce** (daily 7am–noon & 5–8pm), the most famous of the Lecce churches, where delicate engravings soften the Baroque outline of the building. Inside, the excess continues with a riot of stars, flowers and foliage covering everything from the top of columns to chapel altarpieces. Next door, the yellow-stone **Palazzo del Governo**, a former Celestine monastery, is another Zingarello building. On **Piazza del Duomo**, a harmonious square surrounded by Baroque *palazzi*, the **Duomo** itself (daily 6.30am–noon & 5–7.30pm, in winter till 6.30pm) is an explosion of Baroque detail.

Arrival and information

Air Lecce is 40km from Brindisi Airport; from here, SITA buses (6 daily; 40min; €5) run to the city centre.
Train The train station is 1km south of the centre on Via Oronze Quarta.
Tourist office Via Vittorio Emanuele 43, near the Duomo (daily 9am–1pm, 4.30–7.30pm; ⓣ0832.248.092, ⓦwww.pugliaturismo.com/aptlecce).

Accommodation

Cappello Via Montegrappa 4 ⓣ0832.308.881, ⓦwww.hotelcappello.it. Basic and rather bland but clean rooms near the station. ❼
Centro Storico B&B Via Vignes 2b ⓣ0832.242.828, ⓦwww.bedandbreakfast.lecce.it. A lovely B&B in a sixteenth-century *palazzo* with beautifully decorated rooms and a sunny rooftop terrace. ❻
Namastè Via Novoli ⓣ0832.329.647, ⓦwww.camping-lecce.it. Bus #26 from Lecce. A small campsite and hostel set in a tranquil pine forest 6km out of Lecce. Camping ❷, mini-apartments with kitchen ❻
Torre Rinalda Campsite Litoranea Salentina 152 ⓣ0832.382.161, ⓦwww.torrerinalda.it. Bus from Porta Napoli. Closed Oct–May. A well-run campsite 15km out of Lecce on the coast, with swimming pool, bar and supermarket. ❸

Eating and drinking

Caffè Letterario Via G. Paladini 46. Open from breakfast till 2am, this café organizes a wealth of arty events, including DJ sets, live music and theatre nights, and is a convivial place for an *aperitivo*.
Il Capriccio Viale Bovio 14. Though pricier than some, this is one of the town's best fish restaurants; try the house speciality, spaghetti with sea urchins (€12).
Osteria degli Angeli Via Cavour 4. Closed Sun in summer & Tues in winter. A reliable central option for a no-frills meal; antipasto and pizza will set you back about €15.
Trattoria Casareccia Via Costadura 9. Closed all day Mon & Sun eve. A popular, old-fashioned trattoria a few streets from the old town serving up inexpensive, Pugliese cooking. Pasta from €7.

Sicily

Perhaps the most captivating of Italy's islands, **SICILY** (Sicilia) feels socially and culturally separate from the rest of Italy. Occupying a strategically vital position, the largest island in the Mediterranean has a history and outlook that has less in common with its modern parent than with its erstwhile rulers – from the Greeks who first settled the east coast, in the eighth century BC, through a bewildering array of Romans, Arabs, Normans, French and Spanish, to the Bourbons, seen off by Garibaldi in 1860. Substantial relics remain, and temples, theatres and churches are scattered across the island.

GETTING TO SICILY

To get to Sicily, you simply take a train from the mainland – they travel across the Straits of Messina on the ferries from Villa San Giovanni and continue on the other side. First stop is Messina, after which services either run west to Palermo (change for Agrigento) or south to Taormina and Siracusa. There are also couchette trains if you are coming overnight from Rome, Naples or further north.

SAIS (Ⓦ www.saistrasporti.it) runs coach services from many Italian cities, including Florence, Rome, Amalfi, Naples and Matera, to Siracusa, Agrigento and Palermo; for Taormina, change buses at Catania. Marozzi (Ⓦ www.marozzivt.it) operates services from Rome, Pisa and Florence to Catania, from where it's an easy change for Palermo and Taormina.

Ferries from Genoa, Livorno, Naples, Rome (Civitavecchia) and Sardinia (Cagiari) dock at Palermo's Stazione Marittima.

The capital, **Palermo**, is a bustling city with an unrivalled display of Norman art and architecture and Baroque churches. The most obvious other target is the chic eastern resort of **Taormina** – to escape the crowds go to the west or south coasts. From Taormina you can skirt around the foothills and even up to the craters of **Mount Etna**, or travel south to the ancient Greek centre of **Siracusa**. To the west, the greatest draw is the grouping of temples at **Agrigento**, the largest concentration of the island's Greek remains.

PALERMO

In its own wide bay beneath the limestone bulk of Monte Pellegrino, **PALERMO** is stupendously sited. Originally a Phoenician, then a Carthaginian colony, this remarkable city was long considered a prize worth capturing, and under Saracen and Norman rule in the ninth to twelfth centuries it became the greatest city in Europe, famed for the wealth of its court and peerless as a centre of learning. Nowadays it's a brash, exciting city, whose unique Baroque and Arab-Norman churches, mosaic work and museums are the equal of anything on the mainland.

What to see and do

Around the Quattro Canti

The heart of the old city is the Baroque **Quattro Canti** crossroads, with **Piazza Pretoria** and its racy fountain just around the corner. In nearby Piazza Bellini, the church of **La Martorana** (Mon–Sat 8am–1pm & 3.30–7pm, Sun 8.30am–1pm) is one of the finest survivors of the medieval city. Its slim twelfth-century campanile and spectacular mosaics make a marked contrast to the adjacent squat chapel of **San Cataldo** (Mon–Fri 9.30am–1pm & 3.30–6pm, Sat & Sun 9.30am–1pm; €1) with its little Saracenic red golfball domes.

Alberghiera

In the district of Alberghiera, a warren of narrow streets to the southwest, you'll find the deconsecrated church of **San Giovanni degli Eremiti** (Via dei Benedettini; Mon–Sat 9am–7pm, Sun 9am–1pm; €4.50), built in 1148 and the most obviously Arabic of the city's Norman relics. A path leads up through citrus trees to the church, which is built on the remains of a mosque and topped with five rosy domes. Behind are its celebrated late thirteenth-century cloisters. From here it's a few paces north to the **Palazzo dei Normanni** (Mon, Tues & Thurs–Sat 8.30am–noon, 2–5pm, Sun 8.30am–12.30pm; entrance on Piazza Indipendenza; €6), the seat of the Sicilian regional parliament. It was originally built by the Saracens and was enlarged considerably by the Normans, under whom it housed the most magnificent of medieval European courts. The beauti-

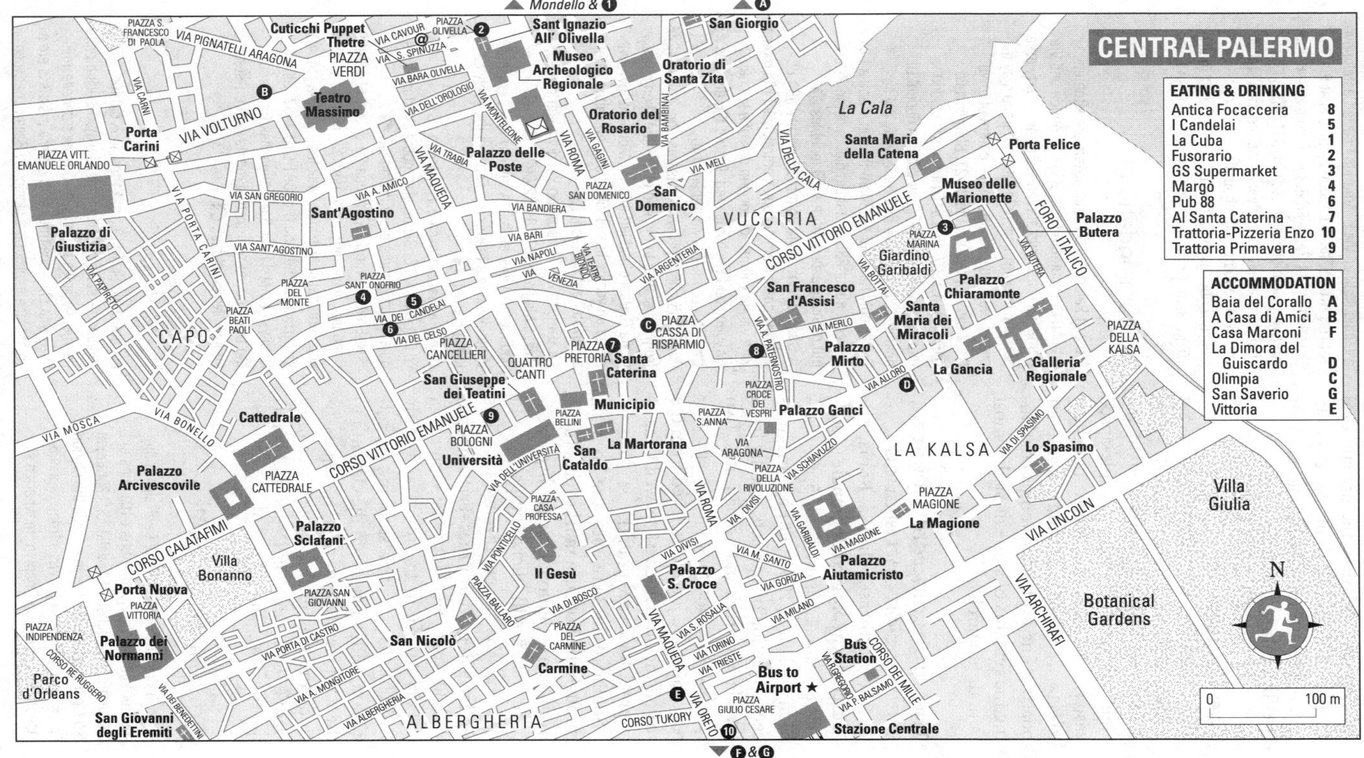
CENTRAL PALERMO
EATING & DRINKING
Antica Focacceria 8
I Candelai 5
La Cuba 1
Fusorario 2
GS Supermarket 3
Margò 4
Pub 88 6
Al Santa Caterina 7
Trattoria-Pizzeria Enzo 10
Trattoria Primavera 9
ACCOMMODATION
Baia del Corallo A
A Casa di Amici B
Casa Marconi F
La Dimora del Guiscardo D
Olimpia C
San Saverio G
Vittoria E
Mondello & 1
A
F & G
Cutichi Puppet Thetre
Sant Ignazio All' Olivella
Museo Archeologico Regionale
San Giorgio
Oratorio di Santa Zita
Oratorio del Rosario
La Cala
Santa Maria della Catena
Porta Felice
Museo delle Marionette
Palazzo Butera
Foro Italico
Teatro Massimo
Piazza Verdi
Porta Carini
Via Volturno
Palazzo delle Poste
San Domenico
Vucciria
Corso Vittorio Emanuele
Sant'Agostino
Palazzo di Giustizia
Capo
Quattro Canti
Santa Caterina
Municipio
San Giuseppe dei Teatini
Cattedrale
Palazzo Arcivescovile
Università
La Martorana
San Cataldo
San Francesco d'Assisi
Giardino Garibaldi
Palazzo Chiaramonte
Santa Maria dei Miracoli
Palazzo Mirto
La Gancia
Galleria Regionale
Palazzo Ganci
La Kalsa
Lo Spasimo
Villa Giulia
La Magione
Palazzo Aiutamicristo
Via Lincoln
Via Archirafi
Botanical Gardens
Palazzo Sclafani
Villa Bonanno
Porta Nuova
Palazzo dei Normanni
Parco d'Orleans
San Giovanni degli Eremiti
Il Gesù
San Nicolò
Carmine
Palazzo S. Croce
Albergheria
Bus to Airport
Bus Station
Stazione Centrale
Corso Tukory
Via Roma
Via Maqueda
N
0 100 m

ful **Cappella Palatina**, the private royal chapel of Roger II (built 1132–1143), is almost entirely covered in glorious twelfth-century mosaics.

The Cattedrale

The Norman **Cattedrale** (Mon–Sat 9.30am–5.30pm, Sun 8am–1.30pm, 4.30–6pm) was much restored in the eighteenth century. Still, the triple-apsed eastern end and the lovely matching towers are all original, and the interior boasts a fine portal and tombs containing the remains of some of Sicily's most famous monarchs.

The Archeological Museum, the Vucciria and around

To the northeast, off Via Roma, the **Museo Archeologico Regionale** (Tues–Fri 8.30am–1.15pm, 3–6.15pm, Sat–Mon 8.30am–1.15pm; €6) is a magnificent collection of artefacts, mainly from the island's Greek and Roman sites. Two cloisters hold anchors, bronze-age pottery, coins and jewels retrieved from the sea off the Sicilian coast, as well as casts of prehistoric cave graffiti.

Southeast of here, be sure to walk through the **Vucciria market** area (daily from 8am) – although not as lively as it once was, it still offers glimpses of old Palermo. You can cut through to Sicily's **Galleria Regionale** (Tues–Fri 9am–1pm & 2.30–7pm, Sat-Mon 9am–1pm; €5), on Via Alloro, in the rough-and-ready La Kalsa district. It's a stunning art collection, with works from the eleventh to the seventeenth centuries. Highlights include the magnificent fifteenth-century fresco *The Triumph of Death*, and paintings by Antonello da Messina.

Arrival and information

Train Trains arrive at Stazione Centrale, at the southern end of Via Roma – bus #101 runs to the centre. Buy tickets (€1; valid for 120min) at *tabacchi* shops or the booth outside the station.
Ferry and hydrofoil Services from Naples dock just off Via Francesco Crispi, from where it's a 10min walk up Via E. Amari to Piazza Castelnuovo.
Tourist office The main tourist office is at Piazza Castelnuovo 34 (Mon–Fri 8.30am–2pm & 3–6pm; Ⓦwww.palermotourism.com; Ⓣ091.583.847). There are smaller branches inside the train station and at the airport (same hours).
Internet Aboriginal Café, Via S. Spinuzza 51 (daily 10am–3am; €3.50/hr; student discount from 8pm).

Accommodation

Most of Palermo's **budget hotels** are situated around the southern ends of Via Maqueda and Via Roma, near the train station – a rather sleazy area at night. It's worth spending a bit more to stay in one of the modern B&Bs in the centre of town.

Baia del Corallo Via Plauto 27, Sferacavallo Ⓣ091.679.7807. Bus #101 from the station to Piazza De Gasperi, then bus #628. A decent HI hostel 12km northwest of the city, by the sea. Buses only run until 10.30pm though – and a taxi will cost about €35 – making nights out in Palermo out of the question. Dorms ❷, doubles ❹

A Casa di Amici Via Volturno 6 Ⓣ091.584.884, Ⓦwww.acasadiamici.com. Central, colourful rooms with vaguely ethnic decor and use of a kitchen, run by young and vivacious staff. Dorms ❸, doubles ❼

Casa Marconi Via Monfenera 140 Ⓣ091.657.0611, Ⓦwww.casamarconi.it. Bus #246 from the station to the end of the line, then cross to Via G. Basile and left into Via Monfenera. A year-round university hostel with basic en suites, Internet and a student canteen. ❻

La Dimora del Guiscardo Via della Vetriera 85, off Piazza Magione Ⓣ328.662.6074, Ⓦwww.ladimoradelguiscardo.it. A friendly and excellent-value place in a restored *palazzo* in the lively La Kalsa district. ❻

Olimpia Piazza Cassa di Risparmio 18 Ⓣ091.616.1276. Clean, airy rooms overlooking a quiet piazza, and a great breakfast. ❹

San Saverio Via G. Di Cristina 39 Ⓣ091.654.7099. Open late July–early Sept. Typically no-frills student accommodation a 10min walk from the station. ❷

Vittoria Via Maqueda 8 Ⓣ091.616.2437. Simple family-run hotel near the station. Ask for one of the three newly-refurbished rooms with en-suite shower. No breakfast. ❹

Eating

For authentic Sicilian **street food**, look out for *friggittorie* – stalls with large metal pans – selling *pane ca' meusa* (spleen in rolls), and *pane e panelle* (rolls filled with chickpea fritters). The city's **markets** are a great place to pick up a picnic; try Ballarò, between

PUPPETRY IN PALERMO

There's a major theatrical and **puppetry** tradition in Sicily, and Palermo has five puppet theatres, with regular performances at *Cuticchio*, Via Bara all'Olivella 95 (performances Sat & Sun 6.30pm; ⓣ091.323.400, ⓦwww.figlidartecuticchio.com). The engaging **Museo Internazionale delle Marionette** (Piazzetta A. Pasqualino 5, Mon–Fri 9am–1pm & 3.30–6.30pm, Sat 9am–1pm; €5) holds the definitive collection of traditional Sicilian puppets – in summer, there are shows (currently Fri 5pm), centring on the swashbuckling exploits of chivalric hero Orlando in his battles against the Saracens.

Piazza Carmine and Piazza Ballarò in the Alberghiera district. There's a GS supermarket in Piazza Marina.

Antica Focacceria Via A. Paternostro 58. A feast of *panelle*, *arancini* (fried rice and meat balls), pizza and tasty sweet *cannoli* will set you back just €6 at this popular backstreet takeaway.

Margò Piazza Sant'Onofrio 3. This cosy neighbourhood restaurant is a good place to try local, fish-based pasta dishes, as well as crispy pizzas (from €7). Closed Mon.

Al Santa Caterina Corso Vittorio Emanuele 254. Filling portions of pizza and pasta. Book one of the tiny balcony tables for a bird's-eye view of Palermo's busiest thoroughfare. Closed Wed. Seafood spaghetti €7.

Trattoria-Pizzeria Enzo Via Maurolico 17/19. Closed Sun. The city's best-value sit-down restaurant, although the location – just over the road from the station – isn't the most attractive. Three-course meals for under €10.

Trattoria Primavera Piazza Bologni 4. Closed Mon. Near the cathedral and with outdoor seating, this trattoria serves great home-style cooking. Meat and fish dishes start at €7.

Drinking and nightlife

In summer, nightlife shifts to the beach resort of **Mondello**, which is full of lively bars, a half-hour bus ride from Palermo (#806 or #833 from Viale della Libertà). The **clubs** around Piazza dell'Unità d'Italia, northwest of central Palermo, are open year-round; entrance €5–15. There are plenty of studenty **bars** in the side streets of the centro storico, especially on Via dei Candelai. For details of what's on, check out listings guide *Lapis Palermo*, available from the tourist office.

I Candelai Via dei Candelai 65. Closed Mon. Some of the hottest live music and DJs in Palermo. Attracts a studenty crowd.

La Cuba Viale Francesco Scaduto, near Piazza dell'Unità d'Italia. This tearoom-restaurant-lounge-bar-club is currently the city's hottest hangout, attracting a trendy clientele to match. Dress up.

Fusorario Piazza Bara all'Olivella 6. This mainstay of the Palermo nightlife scene has a great atmosphere, thanks to a loyal and vibrant student clientele.

Pub 88 Via dei Candelai 88. A perennial centro storico favourite among the city's university students, this is a good place for a drink before heading on elsewhere.

Moving on

You're much better off travelling by **bus** than by **train** in Sicily – buses (services run by SAIS and Interbus) are quicker, taking scenic cross-country routes rather than lumbering round the coast – and ticket prices are similar.

Air Rome (6 daily; 1hr 10min).

Train Taormina (change at Messina; 15 daily; 3hr 45min–5hr 30min); Agrigento (12 daily; 2hr); Siracusa (change at Messina; 10 daily; 5hr 45min–7hr).

Bus Taormina (change at Catania; 9–16 daily; 2hr 40min); Siracusa (2–4 daily; 3hr 15min).

Ferry Naples (4 daily; 8–9hr).

TAORMINA

On Sicily's eastern coast, and dominating two grand sweeping bays, **TAORMINA** is the island's best-known resort. The outstanding remains of its classical theatre, with Mount Etna as an unparalleled backdrop, arrested passing travellers when Taormina was no more than a medieval hill village, and these days it's packed between June and August. It is rather chi-chi, full of designer shops and pricey cafés, but has plenty of charm, its main pedestrianized street, Corso V. Emanuele, lined with fifteenth- to nineteenth-century *palazzi* interspersed with intimate piazzas. The **Teatro Greco** (daily 9am–1hr before sunset; €6) – signposted from just about everywhere – is the only real sight, founded by the Greeks in the third century BC, though most of what's left is a Roman rebuilding from the first century AD, when a deep trench was dug in the orchestra to accommodate the animals and fighters used in gladiatorial contests. These days a summer season of Greek plays (in Italian) is held here.

The closest beach to Taormina is at **MAZZARÓ**, with its much-photographed islet, **Isola Bella**: it's a scenic thirty-minute descent on foot, or use the cable car (summer 8.30am–1.30am; winter 8.30am–10pm; every 15min; €3 return) from Via Pirandello.

Arrival and information

Train The train station, Taormina-Giardini Naxos, is way below town – it's a steep thirty-minute walk up or a short bus ride to the centre (€1.30).
Bus SAIS and Interbus services from Palermo (changing at Catania) stop at the central bus terminal in Via Pirandello.
Tourist office The main office is on Palazzo Corvaja, Piazza Santa Caterina (Mon–Thurs 8.30am–2pm & 4–7pm, Fri 8.30am–2pm; ⓣ0942.23.243, ⓦwww.taormina-ol.it). Also at the train station (same hours).

Accommodation

Camere Il Leone Via Bagnoli Croce 124–126 ⓣ0942.23.878, ⓦwww.camereilleone.it. This friendly B&B has clean, simple rooms, some en suite, some with sea views. Room 3 has a huge panoramic terrace. Doubles ❺–❻, mini-apartments ❽
Casa Grazia Via Lallia Bassia 20 ⓣ0942.24.776, ⓔcasagrazia@libero.it. Open March–Oct. A 5min walk from the Teatro Greco, this family-run hotel has neat rooms, some en suite, all with balcony. The top-floor room, with its private panoramic terrace, must be the town's best bargain at €60. No breakfast. ❺
Taormina's Odyssey Traversa A, Via G.Martino 2, off Via dei Cappuccini ⓣ0942.24.533, ⓦwww.taorminaodyssey.com. A pretty hostel with eight- to ten-person dorms, sea views, a terrace and a kitchen, 10min walk from Porta Messina. Dorms ❷, doubles with shared bath ❺

TREAT YOURSELF

Though just off Taormina's busy Corso, **Villa Schuler** (Piazzetta Bastione ⓣ0942.234.81, ⓦwww.hotelvillaschuler.com; from €124), a lovely, family-run *pensione* set in a beautiful garden, seems a world away. Most rooms have panoramic sea views, and the vistas from the terrace – of a smoking Etna and a dramatic sweep of coast – are second to none.

Villa Schiticchiu Via Nazionale 256 ⓣ349.107.1560, ⓦwww.villaschiticchiu.it. Closed Nov–mid-March. A wonderful family-run B&B below town, a few minutes walk from the cable car. Rooms are spotless and bright and the warm, friendly hosts will welcome you with a cocktail. Ten percent discount with this book. ❾

Eating

Cheap eats are few and far between in Taormina. There's a **mini-market** that can make up panini at Via Bagnoli Croce 68; eat them over the road in the leafy Giardini Pubblici. The *pasticceria* at Corso Umberto 102 sells wonderful Sicilian pastries and ice cream.
Il Baccanale Piazzetta Filea 1 ⓣ0942.624.390. Bustling trattoria with tables spilling out onto the pedestrianized alley outside. Typically Sicilian dishes start at €8.
Rosticceria di Cateno Aucello Via Cappuccini 8. Just up from Porta Messina, this takeaway with a few outdoor tables has a handful of tasty pasta dishes (€4–7), as well as chicken and chips for €6.50.
Vecchia Taormina Vico Ebrei 3 ⓣ0942.24.359. The best of the pizzerias, serving up light, crispy offerings from its wood-fired stove.

Drinking and nightlife

In town, the action takes place in picturesque but posey **Piazza Paladini**, off the Corso. Alternatively, the summer beach-bars and restaurants of nearby **Spisone** are reachable by path from Taormina, from below the cemetery in town, or by bus from Via Pirandello.
Déjà Vu Piazza Garibaldi 2, ⓦwww.dejavucocktailbar.com. An extensive list of cocktails (€8) and a late-night disco make this bar a perennial favourite.

Morgana Scesa Morgana 4. With its sumptuous, candlelit interior and cool lounge music, Morgana attracts Taormina's beautiful people; dress up.
Re di Bastoni Corso Umberto 1. Grab one of the outdoor tables to watch the evening *passeggiata* along Taormina's main drag.
White Bar Piazzetta Garibaldi 6. Closed Nov–March. A trendily minimalist bar, open till 3am, that's popular with Taormina's many gay tourists.

Moving on

Train Palermo (via Messina; 10 daily; 5–9hr); Siracusa (11daily; 2hr 30min)
Bus Etna (Via Catania; hourly; 2hr); Palermo (Via Catania; hourly; 3hr 40min)

MOUNT ETNA

Mount Etna's massive bulk looms over much of the coastal route south of Taormina. If you don't have the time to reach the summit, the **Circumetnea rail service** (around €10 return; InterRail passes not valid) offers a ride around the base from **GIARRE-RIPOSTO**, thirty minutes by train or bus from Taormina; if you make the entire trip to Catania, allow four hours. Catania itself is an attractive enough place, dotted with lava-encrusted relics and splendid Baroque *palazzi*.

At 3323m, Etna is a substantial mountain and the **ascent** is a spectacular trip, worth every effort to make; the fact that it's also one of the world's biggest volcanoes (and still active) only adds to the draw. On **public transport**, you'll need to come via Catania, by bus (daily 8.15am, Mon–Fri also 11.30am; 1hr) from Catania train station up to the huddle of souvenir shops and restaurants at the *Rifugio Sapienza* (Ⓣ095 915 321; Ⓦwww.rifugiosapienza.com; ❺), a cosy, chalet-style hotel which marks the end of the drivable road up the south side of Etna. To get up Etna, you can either take the easy route up (by cable-car and jeep; book through the *Rifugio*; 2hr 30min; €48; see also box on **guided tours** above), or walk (the trip up will take four hours, the return a little less). Take warm clothes, good shoes and glasses to keep the flying grit out of your eyes; you will not be allowed beyond 2900m, marked off by a rope slung across the track. The return bus to Catania leaves at 4.30pm, so if you want to walk all the way you'll have to stay the night in the *Rifugio*. If you're spending the night in Catania, a **tourist office** in the train station can help with accommodation, though if you are travelling alone the cheapest option is the easy-going **hostel**, *Agora*, Piazza Currò 6, near the cathedral (Ⓣ095.723.3010; Ⓦwww.agorahostel.com; dorms ❷, doubles ❺).

> **VISITING THE CRATER**
>
> It's not every day you get to peer into the crater of a volcano; consider booking a specialist tour with an English-speaking vulcanologist. Geo-Etna Explorer (Ⓣ349.6109.957, Ⓦwww.geoetnaexplorer.com) organizes day-long excursions to the lunar-like lava flows from 1983 and 2001, or to the summit craters, from €70 for one person, €55 for two; the company also runs treks and visits to volcanic caves, and provides the necessary outerwear. The same excursion can be booked at dawn or at sunset.

SIRACUSA

Further down Sicily's eastern seaboard, **SIRACUSA** (ancient Syracuse) was first colonized by the Greeks in 733 BC and grew to become their main power base in Sicily. Today, the city boasts some of the best Greek archeological remains anywhere, and also has a strong Baroque character in its old town, squeezed onto the island of **Ortygia**, by the harbour and connected to the new town by two bridges.

What to see and do

Ortygia

At the centre of the island, the most obvious attraction is the **Duomo**, set in a conch-shaped piazza studded with Baroque architecture, and itself incorporating twelve fluted columns from the fifth-century-BC temple that originally stood here. Round the corner at Via Capodieci 16 is the severe thirteenth-century facade of the Galleria Regionale di Palazzo Bellomo (currently closed for restoration), an outstanding collection of medieval art, and paintings by Antonello da Messina.

The Archeological Museum and around

North of the train station, the city is mainly new, though the best of Siracusa's archeological sights are also here. It's a twenty-minute walk, or a short bus ride from Riva della Posta (#1, #3, #12 or #25) to Viale Teocrito, from where you walk east for the **Museo Archeologico Regionale** (Tues & Wed 9am–6pm, Thurs–Sat 9am–11pm, Sun 9am–1pm; €6, €10 joint ticket with Archeological Park), housing a wealth of material from the early Greek colonies; the collection's highlight is a headless marble *Venus*, sculpted rising from the sea. Round the corner, the ruined **Basilica di San Giovanni** has interesting catacombs (Wed–Mon 9am–1pm & 2.30–sunset; €3.50), though the church itself was destroyed by an earthquake in 1693 and never rebuilt.

The Archeological Park

Siracusa's extensive **Parco Archeologico** (Tues-Sun 9am–2hr before sunset; €6, €10 joint ticket with Archeological Museum) is a twenty-minute walk west of the Archeological Museum (bus #10 from Piazza Archimede). Here, the **Ara di Ierone II**, an enormous third-century-BC altar, is the first thing you see, though the main highlight of the park is the **Teatro Greco**, cut out of the rock and looking down towards the sea. Capable of holding around fifteen thousand people, it also hosts a summer season of Greek plays. Nearby, the **Latomia del Paradiso**, a leafy quarry, is best known for the **Orecchio di Dionigi**, an S-shaped cave, 65m long, that Dionysius is supposed to have used as a prison. The last section of the park contains the neglected-looking **Roman amphitheatre**.

A good **day-trip** out of Siracusa is the half-hour train ride to the tumbledown town of **NOTO**, whose deserted station and crumbling suburbs give way to a lovely Baroque town centre that was named a UNESCO World Heritage Site in 2002.

Arrival and information

Train Siracusa's train station is on Via Crispi, a 20min walk from Ortygia.
Bus SAIS buses (Ⓦwww.saistrasporti.it) from Palermo, Amalfi, Pisa, Florence and Genoa stop in Via Trieste, near Riva della Posta.
Tourist office The main tourist office is in the archeological area at Via S. Sebastiano 43 (Mon–Fri 8am–2pm & 3.30–6.30pm, Sat 8am–2pm; Ⓣ0931.481.200, Ⓦwww.apt-siracusa.it).

Accommodation

Abaco Home Via San Paolo 6/10 Ⓣ093.161.982, Ⓦwww.abacohome.it. This B&B, located in the historic centre, has a lovely, tranquil garden and old-fashioned decor. ❼
L'Acanto Via Roma 15 Ⓣ0931.449.304, Ⓦwww.bebsicilia.it. This welcoming place is a find – in the heart of Ortygia, with attractive en suites and a bijou, flower-filled patio. ❼
lolhostel Via F. Crispi 92/96 Ⓣ0931.465.088, Ⓦwww.lolhostel.com. Clean, bright, friendly hostel near the station with four-bed dorms and private rooms. No curfew. Kitchen and Internet access (€3/hr). Dorms ❷, doubles ❼

Eating

L'Ancora Via Perno 7 Ⓣ0931.462.369. Difficult to find – it's by the fish market by the bridge that connects Ortygia to the water – but worth the search, this local trattoria is packed with locals every evening, and serves largely fishy Sicilian fare. Try the delicious *spaghetti con sarde* (with sardines). Pasta from €6.
Castello Fiorentino Via del Crocifisso 6. Ortygia's most popular pizzeria – you may have to queue – serves up superb pizzas with inventive toppings;

try the Bella Donna, with sausage, roast potato and rosemary (€7).

Trattoria Archimede Via Gemmellaro 8. This bustling trattoria just off Via Cavour is inexpensive, good for fish and has a pretty inner garden. Main courses from €10.

Drinking and nightlife

Nightlife centres on the lively Piazzetta San Rocco in Ortygia and the nearby Via delle Vergini and Via Roma.

Enoteca Solaria Via Savoia, Ⓦwww.enotecasolaria.com. This old-fashioned *enoteca* is the place to go to taste some quality Sicilian wines.

Lungolanotte Lungomare Alfeo 21. A popular bar-club overlooking the sea, with DJ sets and occasional live jazz and blues.

Punta del Pero A legendary summer beach bar, served by boats from the harbour in Ortygia (last back around 11pm).

Moving on

Train Agrigento (5 daily; 7hr); Palermo (8 daily; 5–7hr)

Bus Palermo (2–4 daily; 3hr 15min)

AGRIGENTO

Halfway along Sicily's southern coast, **AGRIGENTO** is primarily of interest for the substantial remains of Greek poet Pindar's "most beautiful city of mortals", strung out along a ridge facing the sea a few kilometres below town. The series of Doric temples here, mostly dating from the fifth century BC, are the most evocative of Sicily's remains. They are also the focus of a constant procession of tour buses, so budget accommodation should be booked in advance (though Agrigento could be a day-trip from Palermo). A road winds down from the modern city to the **Valle dei Templi**; buses from the station drop off at a car park between the two separate zones of **archeological remains** (daily 8.30am–7.30pm; €8). The eastern zone is home to the scattered remains of the oldest of the temples, the **Tempio di Ercole**, probably begun in the last decades of the sixth century BC, and the better-preserved **Tempio della Concordia**, dated to around 430 BC, with fine views of the city and sea.

The western zone, back along the path and beyond the car park, is less impressive but still worth wandering around. The mammoth construction that was the **Tempio di Giove**, or Temple of Zeus, the largest Doric temple ever known, was in fact never completed, left in ruins by the Carthaginians and further damaged by earthquakes; the small remnant that is standing is a nineteenth-century reconstruction. Via dei Templi leads back to the town from the car park via the excellent **Museo Nazionale Archeologico** (Wed–Sat 9am–1pm & 2–5.30pm, Sun–Tues 9am–1pm; included in Valle dei Templi ticket) – an extraordinarily rich collection devoted to finds from the city and the surrounding area.

Arrival and information

Train Trains arrive at the edge of the old town, outside which buses #1, #2 and #3 leave for the temples.

Bus SAIS buses from Rome and Naples arrive in Piazzale Roselli, near the train station.

Tourist office in the station (Mon–Fri 8am–2pm & 3–7pm, Sat 8am–2pm; Ⓣ0922.22.780; Ⓦwww.agrigentoweb.it); there's also an information box at the Valle dei Templi site.

Accommodation

Camere a Sud Via Ficani 6 Ⓣ349.6384.424, Ⓦwww.camereasud.it. In an excellent location – a tranquil side street just off Agrigento's main drag – this friendly B&B has bright, spacious rooms and a tiny breakfast terrace where *aperitivi* are served in the summer. ❼

Camping Nettuno Via Le Dune Ⓣ0922.416.269. Bus #2 from outside the station. A basic campsite 5km out of town in the coastal resort of San Leone. ❶

Corte dei Greci Cortile Zeta 3 Ⓣ339.422.0476, Ⓦwww.cortedeigreci.it. This B&B high up in the ancient Arabic quarter has pleasant, airy bedrooms grouped around a central courtyard. ❼

Letto e Latte Via Cannatello 101 Ⓣ0922.651.945, Ⓦwww.lettolatte.it. This tranquil B&B 1km from the Valle dei Templi (the bus stops just outside) has six clean, tastefully furnished en-suite rooms. ❺

Eating

Chez Jean Via Cicerone 2. For the best pizzas in town, head straight for this no-frills pizzeria (pizzas from €5).

La Forchetta Piazza San Francesco 9. Closed Sun. The incredibly cheap but well-prepared mains (€5–8) include a few daily-changing specials. You may have to fight for space with the locals, but it's worth the crush.

Trattoria Caico Via Nettuno. In San Leone near the temples, this is a good-value local trattoria with a decent range of pizzas and pasta dishes (from €8).

Latvia

HIGHLIGHTS

SIGULDA: explore the castle ruins and hiking trails of the gorgeous Gauja Valley

RĪGA: view the exquisite Jugendstil architecture, and party in the lively capital's many bars

LIEPĀJA: stay in a former military prison in Latvia's premier music city

RUNDĀLE PALACE: visit this spectacular Baroque pile – the highlight of southern Latvia

ROUGH COSTS

DAILY budget basic €47/ occasional treat €70

DRINK Aldaris beer €2

FOOD Pork with potatoes and sauerkraut €4

HOSTEL/BUDGET HOTEL €11/€28–35

TRAVEL Bus: Rīga–Liepāja 3hr 30 min–4hr 30min; €6.50; train: Rīga–Liepāja 4hr 45min–6hr; €5.50

FACT FILE

POPULATION 2.3 million

AREA 64,589 sq km

LANGUAGE Latvian; Russian also widely spoken

CURRENCY Lats (Ls)

CAPITAL Rīga (population: 728,000)

INTERNATIONAL PHONE CODE ⓣ371

Basics

The history of Latvia, like that of its neighbour Estonia, is largely one of occupation by foreigners, including the Germans, Poles, Swedish and Russians, ruling the region from the thirteenth century until Latvian independence in 1920. Latvia's autonomy was shortlived, however, and the Soviets annexed the country in 1940. Finally, on August 21, 1991, as the attempted coup against Gorbachev disintegrated in Moscow, Latvia declared its independence for the second time.

Since becoming a member of the European Union in 2004, Latvia has been enjoying impressive economic growth, although the legacy of Soviet occupation, which left the country with a large Russian minority population, means it has entered the new era as a culturally divided country.

The most obvious destination is the capital, **Rīga**, a city of architectural treasures. Places within easy reach of the capital include the palace of **Rundāle**, the resort area of **Jūrmala**, and the scenic **Gauja Valley** with the attractive small towns of Sigulda and **Cēsis**. Latvia also has hundreds of miles of unspoilt coast as well as numerous forests.

CHRONOLOGY

800s AD Vikings seize the areas around present-day Latvia.
1201 German traders found the city of Rīga.
1285 Rīga joins the Hanseatic League, bringing the Baltic region closer economic ties with the rest of Europe.
1330 Rīga Castle (see p.757) is built for the Livonian Knights (it now houses the President of Latvia).
1561 Southern Latvia is conquered by Poland; Catholicism is adopted.
1629 Parts of Latvia are conquered by Sweden.
1793 Latvian land is taken by Russia, following the partition of Poland.
1816 The system of serfdom is abolished.
Late 1800s Cultural and intellectual movements led by the "Young Latvians" increase Latvian national self-consciousness.
1905 Peasant revolt against the rich, land-owning German nobility in Latvia. Brutal repression follows.
1920 Latvia gains independence, despite German and Soviet military attempts to prevent it.
1940 Latvia is taken by the Soviets at the beginning of WWII, as well as by the Germans a year later. Both cause horrendous suffering for Latvians.
1945 By the end of the war Soviets still in control, and Communism rules.
1991 Collapse of the Soviet Union brings about the Latvian restoration of independence.
1999 Vaira Vike-Freiberga, the first female President of Latvia, takes office.
2004 Latvia joins the EU.
2007 After centuries of disputes, Latvia's borders with Russia are set under a treaty signed by both countries.

ARRIVAL

Rīga International Airport (Lidosta Rīga) is served by numerous European airlines, including easyJet, Ryanair, Aer Lingus, Lufthansa, Air France, KLM, Turkish Airlines and Austrian Airlines, as well as Latvia's national carrier **airBaltic** (Ⓦwww.airbaltic.com). You can easily get to the city centre by taking bus #22 or a taxi, which should cost no more than 9Ls.

Options for cross-border **train travel** are fairly limited, with connections to Vilnius, Lithuania, but not to Tallinn, Estonia. Both Eurolines and Ecolines offer frequent **bus services** linking Rīga with Tallinn, Vilnius and St Petersburg, among others. A **ferry service** runs from the Rīga terminal to Stockholm, Sweden, daily and to Lübeck, Germany, four times a week.

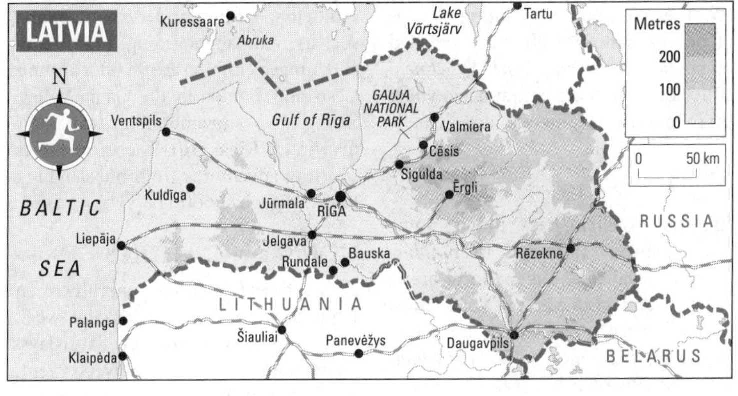

GETTING AROUND

Buy **train** tickets in advance: stations have separate windows for long-distance (*starpilsetu*) and suburban (*pirpilsetu*) trains. Long-distance services are divided into "passenger" (*pasazieru vilciens*) and "fast" (*ātrs*) – both are quite slow but the latter, usually requiring a reservation, stops at fewer places. On timetable boards, look for *atiet* (departure) or *pienāk* (arrival).

Buses are slightly quicker and cheaper than trains but the local services are harder to fathom. Buy long-distance tickets in advance from the ticket counter and opt for an express (*ekspresis*) bus if possible.

Rīga has plentiful and cheap **public transportation. Bicycles** are inexpensive to rent and a good way of getting around the resort areas and small towns.

ACCOMMODATION

Outside Rīga and Jūrmala, **accommodation** is fairly limited. Even in tourist areas, towns will often only have a couple of hotels and a campsite. Budget travellers still have a limited choice but **hostel beds** in the centre of Rīga are easily obtained (check Ⓦwww.hostellinglatvia.com or Ⓦwww.hostels.com). A number of small-sized, good-value **hotels** and **guesthouses** are emerging, but rooms are often in short supply and advance reservations are required in summer. In Rīga and Jūrmala there are agencies offering well-priced **private rooms** of a reasonable standard. There's a handful of decently equipped **campsites** in Rīga, Jūrmala, Sigulda and Cēsis.

FOOD AND DRINK

While meat or fish and potatoes remain the bedrock of Latvian cuisine, Rīga has something to suit every palate, with plenty of international restaurants and vegetarian options. **Eating out**, particularly in the capital's classier joints, is often **expensive**, but there are plenty of self-service fast-food places, offering filling meals for around 3Ls. The numerous supermarkets and markets make **self-catering** a viable option.

Restaurants tend to be open from noon to midnight, with bars keeping similar hours (although some are open past 2am). Cafés typically open at 9 or 10am.

Popular national **starters** include cabbage soup (*kāpostu zupa*), sprats with onions (*sprotes ar sīpoliem*) and *pelēkie zirņi* (mushy peas in pork fat). Slabs of pork garnished with potatoes and sauerkraut constitute the typical **main course**, although freshwater fish (*zivs*) is common too. *Rasols* (cubes of potato, ham and gherkin drenched in cream) is the staple salad. *Pelmeni* (Russian ravioli) are ubiquitous – you'll find them on most menus.

Drinks

Rīga has excellent **bars**, though some are expensive. Imported **beer** (*alus*) is widely available, but the local brews are fine and also cheaper – the most common brands are Aldaris and Cēsu. Worth trying once is *Rīga Melnais Balzāms* (Rīga black balsam), a kind of bitter liqueur (45 percent) made from various roots and herbs.

Coffee (*kafija*) and tea (*tēja*) are usually served black – ask for milk (*piens*) and/or sugar (*cukurs*).

CULTURE AND ETIQUETTE

Latvians are rather reserved and tend to greet each other with solemn handshakes rather than effusive hugs. The distinctive Russian and Latvian communities do not mix much and some resent being mistaken for the other. In the workplace **women** still tend to fill more traditional roles, and the general attitude to women travelling alone tends to be mildly sexist, although women are not likely to encounter harassment. A ten percent **tip** is appropriate for good service in a restaurant.

SPORTS AND ACTIVITIES

Ice hockey is the national sport, and the revered national team plays at the 12,500-seat Arena Rīga (Skanstes 13, ⓣ6738 8200, ⓦwww.arenariga.com). You'll need to book in advance for important games.

Outside Rīga there is plenty of scope for **outdoor pursuits**; a number of beautiful **national parks**, best visited in the summer and home to dozens of protected species, offer extensive hiking and biking trails ripe for exploration. Canoeing, rafting, and extreme *sports* such as mountain boarding, quad biking and bungee jumping are on offer around Cēsis and Sigulda in the Gauja Valley. Skiing and snowmobiling take over in winter. **Rīga Out There** organizes sporting adventures from bobsleighing to clay pigeon shooting.

COMMUNICATIONS

Post offices (*pasts*) are generally open from 8am to 8pm during the week and from 8am to 6pm on Saturdays. *Poste restante* is reasonably efficient. Modern **public phones** are operated with either credit cards or magnetic cards (*telekarte*), which come in 2, 3, 5 and 10Ls denominations, and are sold at post offices and most newsagents. There are plenty of **Internet cafés**, costing around 1Ls/hr in the capital and 60s elsewhere. Free **wi-fi** is available in many cafés, restaurants and youth hostels.

EMERGENCIES

Theft is the biggest hazard. If you're staying in a cheap hotel, don't leave valuables in your room. Muggings and casual violence are not unknown in Rīga; avoid parks and back streets after

LATVIA ON THE NET

ⓦ**www.latviatourism.lv** General portal offering links to all manner of Latvia-related subjects.
ⓦ**www.virtualriga.com** Information on travel, entertainment and accommodation.
ⓦ**www.latviansonline.com** News and features in English.
ⓦ**www.tvnet.lv/en** Welcome to Latvia site with useful links.
ⓦ**www.rigathisweek.lv** Site run by *Riga This Week*, a free listings magazine.
ⓦ**www.latinst.lv** The Latvian Institute's homepage.

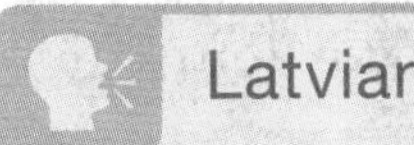

Latvian

In Latvian, the stress always falls on the first syllable of the word. The exception is the word for thank you *(paldies)* which has the stress on the second.

	Latvian	Pronunciation
Yes	*Jā*	Jah
No	*Nē*	Neh
Please	*Lūdzu*	Loodzoo
Thank you	*Paldies*	Paldeeass
Hello/Good day	*Labdien*	Labdeean
Goodbye	*Uz redzēsanos*	Ooz redzehshanwas
Excuse me	*Atvainojiet*	Atvainoyet
Today	*Sodien*	Shwadien
Yesterday	*Vakar*	Vakar
Tomorrow	*Rīt*	Reet
What time is it?	*Cik ir pulkstenis?*	Tsik ir pulkstenis?
Open	*Atvērts*	Atvaerts
Closed	*Slēgts*	Slaegts
Good	*Labs*	Labs
Bad	*Slikts*	Slikts
Do you speak English?	*Vai jūs runājat angliski?*	Vai yoos roonahyat angliski?
I don't understand.	*Es nesaprotu.*	Es nesaprwatoo.
How much is....?	*Cik tas maksā...?*	Tsik tas maksah…?
Cheap	*Lēts*	Laets
Expensive	*Dārgs*	Dahrgs
Student ticket	*Studentu biļeti*	Studentu bilyeti
Boat	*Kuģis*	Kugyis
Bus	*Auto*	Owto
Plane	*Lido*	Lidaw
Train	*Dzelzceļa*	Dzelzcelyuh
Where is the...?	*Kur atrodas…?*	Kur uhtrawduhs...?
Please show me on the map	*Ludzu paradiet man uz kartes*	Loodzu puhrahdeat muhn uz kuhrtes.
Near	*Tuvs*	Tuvs
Far	*Tāls*	Taals
I'd like…	*Es vēlos…*	Es vaalaws…
I'm a vegetarian	*Es esmu veģetārietis/te(m/f)*	Es asmu vejyetahreatis/te
The bill, please	*Lūdzu rēķinu*	Loodzu rehkyinu
Single room	*Vienvietīgu istabu*	Veanveateegu istuhbu
Double room	*Divvietīgu istabu*	Divveateegu istuhbu
Bed	*gulta*	gultuh
Toilet	*Tualete*	Tuuhlete
One	*Viens*	Viens
Two	*Divi*	Divi
Three	*Trīs*	Trees
Four	*Četri*	Chetri
Five	*Pieci*	Pietsi
Six	*Sesi*	Seshi
Seven	*Septiņi*	Septinyi
Eight	*Astoņi*	Astonyi
Nine	*Deviņi*	Devinyi
Ten	*Desmit*	Desmit

dark. **Police** (*policija*), who are unlikely to speak much English, will penalize you if you're caught drinking in public – expect a stiff fine. Strip clubs are notorious for ripping off drunk foreign males.

Pharmacies (*aptieka*) are well-stocked with over-the-counter painkillers, first aid items, sanitary products and the like. In larger cities, they tend to be open from 8am until 7pm. There are 24-hour pharmacies in the capital, where, with some luck, you'll find an English speaker. **Emergency medical care** is free, though if you fall ill, head for home; Latvian medical facilities tend to be run-down.

INFORMATION AND MAPS

Tourist offices run by the Latvian tourist board (Ⓦwww.latviatourism.lv) are located at the centre of most major cities and well-touristed towns. The Kümmerly & Frey 1:1,000,000 **map** of the Baltic States includes Latvia, and has a basic street plan of Rīga. The Falkplan of Rīga includes enlarged sections and public transport routes. Jāņa Sēta (Elizabetes iela 83–85, Rīga) is well-stocked with guides, and publishes its own maps. *Rīga in your Pocket* (1.20Ls, Ⓦwww.inyourpocket.com) is an excellent English-language **listings** guide. *The Baltic Times* weekly (Ⓦwww.baltictimes.com) provides updates on current affairs and events in English while *Rīga This Week* is a detailed up-to-date listings guide.

EMERGENCY NUMBERS

Police Ⓣ02; Ambulance Ⓣ03; Fire Ⓣ01.

MONEY AND BANKS

Latvia's currency is the *lats* (plural *lati*) – normally abbreviated to Ls – which is divided into 100 *santīmi* (s). Coins come in 1, 2, 5, 10, 20 and 50 *santīmi*, and 1 and 2 *lati*, and notes in 5, 10, 20, 50, 100 and 500 *lati*.

STUDENT AND YOUTH DISCOUNTS

ISIC cards will get you a fifty percent **discount** off entry to most museums and attractions, and even some eateries – look for the ISIC sign on doors. HI-affiliated hostels offer discounts for YHA card holders.

Bank (*banka*) **hours** vary, but in Rīga many are open Monday to Friday from 9am to 5pm, and on Saturdays from 10am to 3pm. Outside the capital, many close at 1pm and most are closed on weekends.

Exchanging cash is straightforward, even outside banking hours, as Rīga is full of currency exchange offices *(valktas apmaiņa)*; shop around to get the best rate. ATMs are plentiful nationwide and accept most international cash cards. At the time of writing, €1 was equal to 0.7Ls, $1 to 0.5Ls and £1 to 1Ls.

Major banks such as the Hansa Banka, Rīgas Komercbanka and Unibanka will cash **travellers' cheques** (TravelEx Visa and American Express preferred) and some give advances on **credit cards**. In Rīga the bigger hotels will also cash travellers' cheques. Credit cards are accepted in an increasing number of establishments.

OPENING HOURS AND HOLIDAYS

Shops are usually open weekdays from either 8am or 10am to 6pm or 8pm, and on Saturdays from 10am to 7pm. Some food shops are open until 10pm and are also open on Sundays. In Rīga there are a few 24-hour shops, which sell food and alcohol. Most shops and all banks close on the following **public holidays:** 1 January, Good Friday, Easter Sunday, Easter Monday, May 1, the second Sunday in May, June 23 and 24, November 18, December 25, 26 and 31.

Rīga

RĪGA is the largest, liveliest and most cosmopolitan of the Baltic capitals, with a great selection of accommodation to suit any budget and a wide variety of world cuisine, ranging from cheap Eastern European buffets to the most exquisite sushi. A heady mixture of medieval and contemporary, the city has a good deal to offer architecture and history enthusiasts, with the narrow cobbled streets of Old Rīga and the wide boulevards of New Town ripe for exploration on foot.

Rīga has all the trappings of a modern capital city, with efficient and affordable public transportation, along with excellent shopping to rival that of any Western city. Revellers coming to Rīga to sample its notorious nightlife will not be disappointed – the variety of clubs, bars and live music venues is impressive.

What to see and do

Old Rīga (Vecrīga), centred around Cathedral Square and bisected from east to west by Kaļķu iela, forms the city's nucleus and is home to most of its historic buildings. With its cobbled streets, medieval buildings, narrow lanes and hidden courtyards, it gives the impression of having stepped back in time. To the east, Old Rīga is bordered by Bastejkalns Park, beyond which lies the **New Town** (Milda). Built during rapid urban expansion between 1857 and 1914, its wide boulevards are lined with four- and five-storey apartment buildings, many decorated with extravagant Jugendstil motifs.

Rīga Castle and the Three Brothers

Cathedral Square (Doma laukums) is dominated by the towering red-brick **Rīga Cathedral** (Mon, Tues, Thurs & Sat 9am–6pm, Wed & Fri 9am–5pm, Sun services only; 50s), established in 1211. From Cathedral Square, Pils iela runs down to Castle Square (Pils laukums) and **Rīga Castle** (Rīgas pils), built in 1515 and now home to both the Latvian president and the **Latvian History Museum** (Latvijas vēstures muzejs; Tues–Sun: June–Aug 11am–7pm; Sept–May 11am–5pm; 1Ls), where you'll find an attractive display of iron-age artefacts and peasant life tableaux but little English description. Follow Mazā Pils iela from Pils laukums to see the **Three Brothers** (Trīs brāli), three charming medieval houses, one of which is thought to be the oldest in Latvia.

Swedish Gate and the Powder Tower

Further north on Torņa iela you'll find the seventeenth-century **Swedish Gate** (Zviedru vārti), the sole surviving city gate. At the end of Torņa iela is the **Powder Tower** (Pulvertornis), a vast, fourteenth-century bastion, home to the **Museum Of War** (Wed–Sun 10am–5pm; 50s), a well-presented account of the country's turbulent history.

Bastion Hill and the Guild Hall

Bastion Hill (Bastejkalns) – the park that slopes down to the city canal at

> **THE SINNER'S BELL**
>
> St James's Church (Jēkeba baznīca) on Klostera iela once had a bell that hung under a cupola outside its Gothic spire. Known as "the wretched sinner's bell", it announced upcoming hangings which took place in Rātslaukums (Town Hall Square). It was also rumoured to ring whenever an unfaithful wife passed below. Its incessant chiming so infuriated the townspeople that they had it taken down and thrown in the Daugava River. The bell was never replaced.

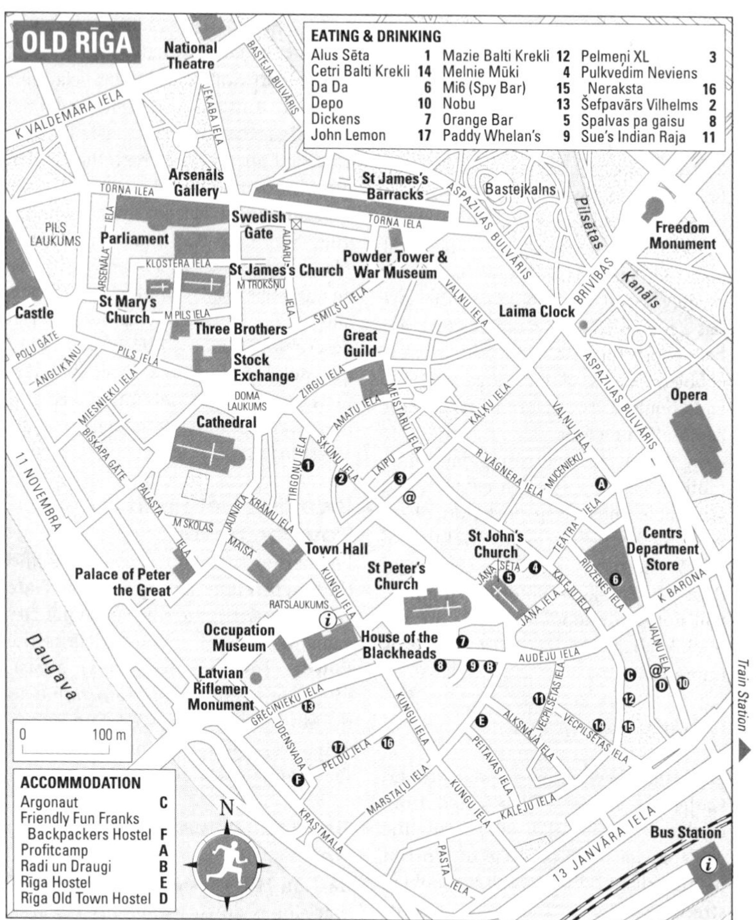

the end of Torna iela – is a reminder of the city's more recent history: on January 20, 1991, four people were killed by Soviet fire during an attempted crackdown on Latvia's independence drive. Stones bearing the victims' names mark where they fell near the Bastejas bulvāris entrance to the park.

From the Powder Tower, Meistaru iela runs down to the fourteenth-century neo-Gothic **Great Guild Hall** (Lielā ģilde) at Amatu 6, the centre of commercial life in Hanseatic Rīga and now housing the **Latvia State Philharmonic** (ⓦwww.music.lv/en).

St Peter's Church

Follow the urban throng west along Kaļķu iela and turn left into Skārņu iela to **St Peter's Church** (Pēter baznīca; Tues–Sun 10am–5.15pm), a large red-brick structure with a graceful three-tiered spire. Climb the tower (2Ls) for panoramic views of the city.

Town Hall Square

From the doors of St Peter's Church, **Rātslaukums** (Town Hall Square) is straight ahead and dominated by the **House of the Blackheads** (Melngalvju nams; Tues–Sun: May–Sept 10am–5pm; Oct–April 11am–5pm; 1.40Ls), a masterpiece of Gothic architecture. Once serving as the boozy headquarters of Rīga's bachelor merchants, and largely destroyed in 1941, it was lovingly reconstructed for the 800th anniversary of Rīga's foundation in 2001. Oozing opulence, with an excellent photo exhibition in the warren-like cellar, it is well worth a visit.

Next door, an imposing concrete structure accommodates the **Occupation Museum of Latvia** (Latvijas okupācijas muzejs; May–Sept daily 11am–5pm; Oct–April Tues–Sun 11am–5pm; donations; ⓦwww.occupationmuseum.lv), a rewarding collection devoted to Latvia's occupation by the Nazis and Soviets.

The Freedom Monument

As you head east out along Kaļķu iela, which becomes Brīvības bulvāris as it enters the **New Town**, the modernist **Freedom Monument** (Brīvības piemineklis) dominates the view, holding aloft three stars symbolizing the three regions of Latvia. Incredibly, the monument survived the Soviet era, and nowadays two soldiers stand guard here in symbolic protection of Latvia's independence.

The Latvian National Museum of Art

Formal Esplanade Park runs north from Brīvības bulvāris. At the far end of the park, the worthwhile **Latvian National Museum of Art** (Valsts mākslas muzejs; Valdemāra iela 10; Mon & Wed–Sun 11am–5pm; Thurs 11am–7pm; 2Ls; ⓦwww.lnmm.lv/en), housed in a grandiose Neoclassical building, displays an impressive array of nineteenth- and twentieth-century Latvian works, as well as changing modern art exhibitions.

Fin-de-Siecle Residences

Rīga is home to some of the most beautiful examples of Art Nouveau architecture in Europe, with over two hundred buildings having survived World War II. Inspired by Austrian and German styles, **Jugendstil architecture** embodies the ideal that "everything useful should be beautiful". Its motifs of mythological creatures and nymphs, which decorate the facades of many of the New Town's apartment buildings, have been described as "music in stone". A stroll along Strēlnieku iela and Alberta iela will take in some fine examples, many in the process of restoration. The beautiful facades of Elizabetes iela 10a and 10b were designed by the Russian-born architect Mikhail Eisenstein, whose own residence at Alberta iela 4 features majestic lions astride the turrets. The nearby **Museum of Janis Rozentāls and Rūdolfs Blaumanis**, at Alberta iela 12, is partially closed for renovation, but it is well worth stopping by if only to view the building's grand interior.

Arrival and information

Air Rīga Airport (Lidosta Rīga, ⓦwww.riga-airport.com) is located about 8km west of the city centre. Bus #22 (every 20 minutes) drops passengers at Strēlnieku laukums, just west of Rātslaukums, and by the train station. A taxi from the airport should cost no more than 9Ls.

Train Rīga's main train station (Centrālā stacija) is just south of Old Rīga on 13 Janvāra iela; it takes about 15mins to walk to Rātslaukums from here. Facilities include ATMs, currency exchange, and an information center.

Bus Rīga's bus station (Autoosta) is five minutes' walk west of the train station along 13 Janvāra iela. To get to Old Rīga, turn left out of the front entrance and use the underpass next to the Coca-Cola Plaza to cross 13 Janvāra iela.

Ferry The ferry terminal (Jūras pasazieru stacija) is to the north of Old Rīga. Trams #5, #7 or #9 run

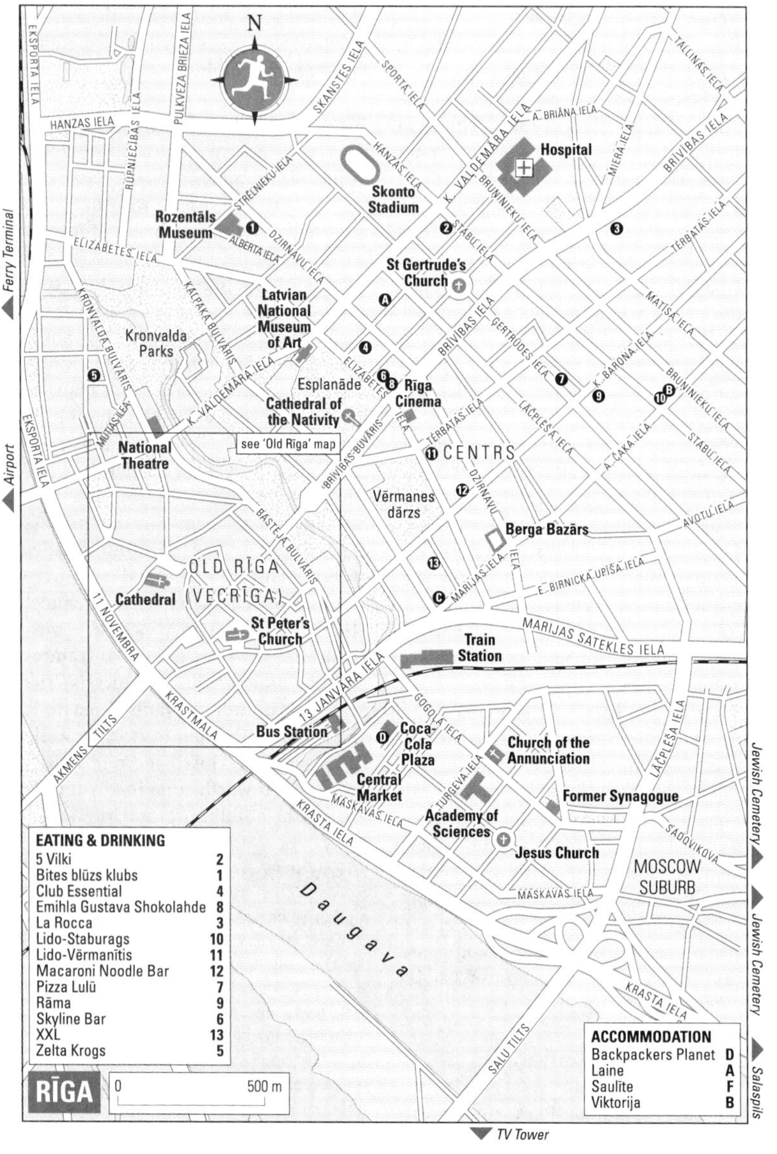

from the stop in front of the terminal on Ausekļa iela to the city centre (two stops).

Tourist office There are tourist offices at the bus station (Mon–Fri 9am–6pm, Sat–Sun 10am–5pm; ⓣ6720 0555), the train station (daily 10am–6:30pm; ⓣ6723 3815), and on Rātslaukums in the centre of the Old Town (daily 10am–7pm; ⓣ6704 4377, ⓦwww.rigatourism.com). They have accommodation lists and also sell the Rīga Card (10/15/20Ls for 24/48/72hr), which gives unlimited use of public transport and museum discounts; check first that it saves money on your particular itinerary.

City transport

Public transport Both Old Rīga and the New Town are easily walkable, and you can reach outlying attractions by frequent and efficient public transport, running between 5:30am and midnight. Buy flat-fare single-journey **tickets** from the conductor for 30s. For bus, tram and trolleybus routes and timetables go to ⓦwww.rigassatiksme.lv.

Taxis During the day, taxis should cost 40s per kilometre; between 10pm and 6am, rates rise to 50s. Watch out for rip-offs or non-functioning meters. Rīga Taxi (ⓣ800 1010) and Bona Taxi (ⓣ800 5050) are generally reliable.

Accommodation

Rīga has a number of youth hostels and extensive budget accommodation, mostly concentrated in the southern half of Old Rīga, with a few options in nearby New Town and by the Central Market. Reserve in advance in summer.

Hostels

Argonaut Kalēju iela 50 ⓣ2614 7214, ⓦwww.argonauthostel.com. Somewhat cramped but clean, with a friendly vibe and central location. Luggage "cages", Internet. Dorms ❷ doubles ❺

Backpackers Planet Negu iela 17 ⓣ6722 6232, ⓦwww.backpackersplanet.lv. Set in a converted Central Market warehouse, this welcoming hostel has spacious dorms, laundry service, Internet, wi-fi, café and bar. ❷

Friendly Fun Franks Backpackers Hostel Novembra krastmala 29 ⓣ6722 0040, ⓦwww.franks.lv. Clean, friendly hostel in Old Rīga with 24-hour bar, kitchen, wi-fi, and Internet. Organizes nights out and trips to the AK-47 shooting range; free beer on arrival. Dorms ❷, doubles ❹

Profitcamp Teatra iela 12 ⓣ6721 6361, ⓦwww.profitcamp.lv. Dorm beds, doubles, triples and quads on offer in a centrally located quiet hostel. Free Internet, cheap laundry service. Dorms ❷, doubles ❺

Riga Hostel Mārstaļu iela 12 ⓣ6722 4520, ⓦwww.riga-hostel.com. Excellent location, bathroom in each dorm, kitchen/common room, Internet. Dorms ❷, doubles ❺

Riga Old Town Hostel Valņu iela 43 ⓣ6722 3406, ⓦwww.rigaoldtownhostel.lv. Clean dorms and doubles, free Internet, wi-fi, bed linen and sauna. Five minutes' walk from bus station. The only hostel with a bar/reception. Dorms ❷, doubles ❸

Hotels

Laine Skolas iela 11 ⓣ6728 8816, ⓦwww.laine.lv. A friendly and comfortable mid-range hotel, ten minutes' walk northeast of Old Rīga, with en-suites and shared facilities. ❸

Radi un Draugi Mārstaļu iela 1/3 ⓣ6728 0200, ⓦwww.draugi.lv. One of the few affordable places in the Old Town, offering cosy en-suites with TV. Very popular, so book well in advance. ❺

Saulīte Merķeļa iela 12 ⓣ6722 8219, ⓦwww.hotel-saulite.lv. Basic but friendly place opposite the train station, with some rooms prone to street noise. More expensive rooms come with modern shower/WC; cheaper ones are unrenovated. ❻

Viktorija Čaka iela 55 ⓣ6701 4111, ⓦwww.hotel-viktorija.lv. Dowdy but comfortable en-suites a short bus ride or brisk walk from the train station. ❹

Camping

Riga City Camping, behind the Ķīpsala exhibition centre at Ķīpsalas iela 8 (late May–mid-Sept only); ⓣ6706 5000, ⓦwww.bt1.lv/camping. This convenient campsite is only 2km northwest of Old Rīga and offers ample tent space. Catch bus #5, #7 or #21 from Valdemāra iela; get off once you've crossed the river. ❶

Eating

Many bars and **cafés** do cheap and filling **food** and there are also plenty of reasonably priced restaurants serving international cuisine.

Cafés and snack bars

Emihla Gustava Shokolahde Marijas iela 13/VI (inside the Berga bazārs arcade). Complete chocolate heaven, from the exquisite truffles to the small cups of rich, flavourful hot chocolate (1.70Ls). Closes 8pm Sun. Other branches at Galeria Centrs and Brīvības iela by *Hotel Reval*.

John Lemon Peldu iela 21. Artsy, welcoming place to while away an afternoon with a coffee (1Ls) or a unique Bob Marley pizza (3Ls).

Lido-Staburags Čaka iela 55. Popular and busy, with traditional Latvian food served amid old-fashioned oak rooms. Mains 3Ls.

Lido-Vērmanītis Elizabetes iela 65. All manner of tasty Baltic meat-and-potato dishes, plus salad and fruit bars on the ground floor, pizza and fast food in the cellar. Mains 3Ls.

Pelmeni XL Kaļķu iela 7. Popular fast-food restaurant on Old Rīga's main street offering six types of *pelmeni* (Russian ravioli) filled with meat or cheese. 72s/200g.

Pizza Lulū Ģertrūdes iela 27. Fashionable little pizzeria with reasonable prices. Medium pizza 3Ls.
Šefpavārs Vilhelms Sķūņu iela 6. Self-service, create-your-own-pancake place near Cathedral Square. 2Ls.

Restaurants

Da Da Audēju iela 16 (Galerija Centrs). Fill up a bowl with fresh meat, seafood, vegetables and noodles, pick a sauce and have it cooked in front of you. 5Ls.
Macaroni Noodle Bar Barona iela 17. Excellent home-made pasta and noodle dishes in this stylish restaurant with minimalist décor. Ten minutes' walk east of Old Town. Mains 4–6Ls.
Mazie Balti Krekli Kalēju iela 54. Relaxing bar-restaurant stuffed with Latvian pop-rock memorabilia. Value for money pork-and-potatoes fare. Mains 3–4Ls.
Melnie Mūki Jāņa sēta 1. High-class international cuisine at affordable prices, with atmospheric medieval interior. Succulent pepper steak 8Ls.
Rāma Barona iela 56. Hare-Krishna-run veggie place in the New Town, catering for vegans, with a tasty range of dirt-cheap Asian dishes. 2Ls.
Sue's Indian Raja Vecpilsētas iela 3. Authentic Indian food in a cosy cellar setting. Huge mains 5–6Ls.
Zelta Krogs Citadeles iela 12. Mixed European-Latvian cuisine in a bright, relaxing spot just north of the Old Town. Plenty of salads, pasta and vegetarian pancakes, all at reasonable prices. Mains 4–5Ls.

Drinking and nightlife

The Old Town offers innumerable opportunities for bar hopping, with a multiplicity of supping venues (many of which serve decent food) filling up with fun-seeking locals seven nights a week.

Bars

5 Vilki (5 Wolves) Stabu iela 6. Watering hole popular with locals with warm decor, reasonably priced drinks and excellent food. Huge portions of chicken wings 3Ls.

> **TREAT YOURSELF**
> The freshest, tastiest **sashimi and sushi** in town attracts a well-heeled crowd to **Nobu**, Grēcinieku iela 28 (☎6735 9746). On weekends you'll need a reservation. Sashimi 1.80–2Ls a piece.

Alus Sēta Tirgoņu iela 6. Sample good, cheap Latvian ales accompanied by the national beer-snack – peas (*zirņi*) sprinkled with bacon bits.
Dickens Grēcinieku iela 11. Brit-pub popular with stag parties boasting a wide range of beers. The cosiest place to watch a match – from American football to the Premier League.
Mi6 (Spy Bar). Kalēju iela 52. The combination of strong cocktails, Bond films, and slightly cheesy decor attracts an arty crowd. Friday funk jam; free entry. Sun–Thurs 5pm–2am, Fri & Sat 5pm–4am.
Orange Bar Jāņa sēta 5. Orange industrial decor, alternative music, a lively young crowd and cheap bar food. Packed on weekends. Sun–Thurs noon–1am, Fri 11am–5am, Sat noon–5am.
Paddy Whelan's Grēcinieku iela 4. Big, lively Irish pub, popular with young locals and expats alike. 18 kinds of beer and cider on tap. Happy hour 5pm–7pm. Sun–Thurs noon–midnight, Fri–Sat noon–3am.
Skyline Bar Elizabetes iela 55. Behold Rīga's splendour from a window seat on the 26th floor of the *Reval Hotel Latvija*. A must.
Spalvas pa gaisu Grēcinieku iela 8. Snazzy and spacious café-bar with loungey corners, loud music and good cocktails. Sun–Tues 11am–midnight, Wed–Thurs 11am–2am, Fri & Sat 11am–5am.

Clubs

Club Essential Skolas iela 2. Plays adventurous music and provides a funky chill-out zone. Dress well. Thurs–Sun 10pm–6am; 3–5Ls.
Depo Vaļņu iela 32. Post-industrial cellar space with alternative DJ nights and live bands. A laid-back café during the day. Mon–Sat until late.
La Rocca Brīvības iela 96. Mingle with the Russians or dance in a cage above the dance floor in Rīga's premier techno club. Cocktails 2Ls. Thurs–Sun 10pm–7am; 3-5Ls.
Pulkvedim Neviens Neraksta Peldu iela 26/28. The hippest club in Rīga: edgy music on two levels and an easygoing, fun-seeking local clientele. Daily until late; 2–3Ls.
XXL Kalniņa iela 4. Gay club and restaurant attracting a mixed, dance-oriented crowd. Good food and wild decor. Daily until 7am; cover charge Tues–Sat 2–5Ls.

Entertainment

Live Music

Bites Blūzs Klubs Dzirnavu iela 34a. Laid-back, unpretentious blues pub festooned with photos of musicians; regular live acts.

Četri Balti Krekli Vecpilsētas iela 12. Large upmarket cellar bar known for its Latvian-only music policy. Regular gigs by domestic rock-pop acts. No trainers.
Opera Aspazijas bulvāris 3 ⓦwww.opera.lv. Opera, ballet and international artists perform here. 5–30Ls, depending on event.

Cinemas

Forum Cinemas (Coca-Cola Plaza) 13 Janvāra iela 8 ⓦwww.forumcinemas.lv. Second-largest cinema in northern Europe with 14 screens. 1.95–3.90Ls.
Riga Cinema Elizabetes iela 61 ⓦwww.cinema-riga.lv. Rīga's oldest cinema, showing foreign films as well as blockbusters. 2.50Ls.

Shopping

Art Nouveau Riga Strēlnieku iela 9. ⓦwww.artnouveauriga.lv. Dedicated entirely to art nouveau merchandise, such as small plaster faces of Rīga's facades. 8am–7pm.
Central Market (Centrālais tirgus) A row of massive 1930s former Zeppelin hangars next to the bus station selling everything from half a cow to fake designer watches.
Dzintara Galerija Torņa iela 4. An extensive collection of amber jewellery and various amber-encrusted items. 10am–8pm.
Food and curio bazaar Elizabetes iela 83/85. Soviet kitsch, freshly-baked bread and organically grown produce. First and third Saturday of the month.

Directory

Bike rental Gandrs, Kalnciema iela 28, ⓣ6761 4775.
Embassies Canada, Baznīcas iela 20/22, ⓣ6781 3945; Ireland, Valdemāra iela 21–632, ⓣ6703 5286; UK, Alunāna iela 5, ⓣ6777 4700; US, Raiņa bulvāris 7, ⓣ6703 6200.
Exchange Marika: Basteja iela 14, Brīvības bulvāris 30, Marijas iela 5, Merķeļa iela 10 (all 24hr).
Hospital Ars, Skolas iela 5, ⓣ6720 1001. Some English-speaking doctors.
Internet access Interneta Planeta Kafe, Vaļņu iela 41 (24hr); Internet Klubs, Kalku iela 10 (24hr).
Left luggage At the bus station (daily 6:30am–11pm), from 20–50s/hour, depending on weight, 20s each additional hour. Lockers at the left-luggage office (Rokas Bagāžas) in the train station basement (50s–1.50Ls per day, 4:30am–midnight).
Pharmacy Vecpilsētas aptieka, Audēju iela 20, ⓣ6721 3340 (24hr).
Post office Brīvības bulvāris 19 (Mon–Fri 7am–10pm, Sat & Sun 8am–8pm).
Tours Rīga Out There, Hospitalu iela 8–49 (ⓣ2938 9450, ⓦwww.out-there.eu), organizes off-the-wall activities, such as paintballing and go-karting, as well as excellent nightlife and sight-seeing tours, all with an English-speaking guide.

Moving on

Train Cēsis (5 daily; 1hr 30min); Liepāja (1 daily; 3hr); Majori, Jūrmala (every 30min; 40min); Moscow, Russia (2 daily; 16hr); St Petersburg, Russia (1 daily; 12hr); Salaspils (at least one hourly; 15 min); Sigulda (5 daily; 1hr); Vilnius, Lithuania (1 every other day – odd dates; 7hr).
Bus Bauska (every 30min; 1hr 10min–1hr 30min); Cēsis (20 daily; 2hr); Kaunas, Lithuania (3 daily; 4hr 30min); Klaipēda, Lithuania (2 daily; 5hr); Liepāja (19 daily, 3hr 30min); Pärnu, Estonia (8 daily; 3hr 30min); Sigulda (hourly; 1hr); Tallinn, Estonia (8 daily; 5hr 30min); Tartu, Estonia (2 daily; 5hr); Vilnius, Lithuania (7 daily; 6hr).

The Rest of Latvia

Latvia has a number of attractions outside Rīga, many of which can be seen in a single day, although for some sights, it's best to allow at least a couple of days for a relaxed visit. Those wishing to combine beach-going with live music can head either to nearby **Jūrmala** or to **Liepāja**, on the west coast of Latvia. Latvia's interior has much to offer nature lovers and history buffs; while Sigulda's and Cēsis's castle ruins can be viewed on a day-trip, **Gauja Valley** is the perfect destination for those who wish to get away from civilization and spend a week or two hiking, camping and canoeing. **Ķemeri National Park**, near Jūrmala, offers numerous nature trails and while it is possible to do a day-trip from Rīga, an overnight stay is required for the night nature tours.

JŪRMALA

A 20-km string of small seaside resorts lining the Baltic coast west of Rīga, **JŪRMALA** was originally favoured by the tsarist nobility and later drew tens of thousands of vacationers from all over the USSR; it continues to be a popular beach resort today. Its wide clean sandy **beach**, backed by dunes and pine woods and dotted with beer tents and climbing frames, seethes with people in summer, especially during the week-long **music festival** in July.

Jomas iela, the pedestrianized main street running east from the station square, teems with holiday-makers and has a number of excellent restaurants and cafés, as well as craft stalls and art exhibitions. A few paths lead to the beach from Jūras iela, north of Jomas iela.

Arrival and Information

Trains Trains leave Rīga's station from platforms 3 and 4 (1.27Ls return). **Majori** is the main stop for Jūrmala, but consult the route map, as the stations are not well signposted.

Tourist office Jomas 42 (June–Aug daily 11am–9pm; Sept–May Mon–Fri 9am–5pm; ⓣ6776 4276, ⓦwww.jurmala.lv). Staff can fix you up with accommodation and provide detailed information on regional excursions (ⓦwww.jurmalatour.lv).

Accommodation

24 Jomas iela 24 ⓣ6776 4401. Cosy en-suite doubles with warm decor in a small, centrally located guesthouse. Doubles ❺

Dzintari Piestātnes iela 6/14, Dzintari ⓣ6775 4196. Clean, sparsely furnished en-suites in a vast former Soviet spa hotel. Rooms ❷–❸

Elina Lienes iela 43 ⓣ6776 1665, ⓦwww.elinahotel.lv. This perpetually popular guesthouse has clean rooms 5 minutes' walk from the beach. Doubles ❺

Kempings Nemo Atbalss iela 1,Vaivari ⓣ6773 2350, ⓦwww.nemo.lv. Campsite in a pleasant middle-of-the-forest location just behind the beach, with clean facilities and a water park on site (2.50Ls). Tents ❶; cabins ❷

Eating and drinking

Café Veranda Jomas iela 58. A good spot for people-watching. Coffee 1Ls. Closes 10pm.

Sue's Asia Jomas iela 74. Busy restaurant serving large portions of excellent Indian, Thai and Chinese cuisine. *Tom yum kuung* is authentically spicy and flavourful (3Ls). Closes midnight.

Sultans Orients Jomas iela 33. Caucasian cuisine in an eclectic setting. Try the *pelmeni* (2.80Ls) and the excellent *shashlik* (4.80Ls). Closes midnight.

Entertainment

Dzintari Concert Hall Turaidas iela 1, Dzintari ⓣ6776 2086, ⓦwww.dzk.lv. This open-air, 2000-capacity concert hall is located near the beach and hosts regular music events in the summer.

Moving on

Train Rīga (at least two hourly; 40min); Ķemeri (at least one hourly, 35min).

ĶEMERI NATIONAL PARK

An extensive preserve west of Jūrmala, **ĶEMERI NATIONAL PARK** is home to a wealth of protected ancient forests and wetlands, with 237 bird species nesting around the fourteen islets of Lake Kaņieris. Traditional fish smoking and canning are still practised in the villages within the national park, and the markets at Ragaciems and Lapmežciems sell freshly smoked eel, salmon and sprats.

To get to the park, take the suburban train from Rīga to the spa town of **Ķemeri** (20 stops, Tukums direction, 1.75Ls), known for its sulphurous springs, where several of the nature trails start. Ķemeri **tourist office** in the Meza Maja (Forest House) at Tūristu 18a (May–Sept: Mon–Fri 9am–6pm, ⓣ6773 0078, ⓦwww.kemeri.gov.lv) has extensive information on hiking, guided tours, bird- and animal-watching excursions, such as the excellent night-time bat tour, as well as accommodation in and around Ķemeri, including numerous camping spots.

SALASPILS

The concentration camp at **SALASPILS**, 22km southeast of Rīga, is where most of Rīga's Jewish population perished during World War II. One hundred thousand people died here, including prisoners of war and Jews from other countries, who were herded into the Rīga Ghetto after most of the indigenous Jewish population had been liquidated. The site is marked by monumental sculptures, with the former locations of the barracks outlined by white stones; look for the offering of toys by the children's barracks.

To get here take a **suburban train** from Rīga central station in the Ogre direction and alight at **Dārziņi** (59s return, at least one train hourly from Rīga) from where a clearly signposted path leads to the clearing, fifteen minutes' walk through the forest. There are no Dārziņi–Rīga trains between 11am and 2pm.

RUNDĀLE PALACE

One of the architectural wonders of Latvia, Baroque **Rundāle Palace** (Rundāles Pils; daily: May, Sept & Oct 10am–6pm; Jun–Aug 10am–7pm; Nov–April 10am–5pm; 3Ls) is 77km south of Rīga. Its 138 rooms were built in two phases during the 1730s and 1760s and designed by **Bartolomeo Rastrelli**, the architect responsible for the Winter Palace in St Petersburg. It was privately owned until 1920 when it fell into disrepair, but has largely been returned to its former glory through meticulous restoration. Each opulent room is decorated in a unique fashion and there are changing art exhibitions both in the palace and outside in the vast landscaped gardens. There are frequent buses from Rīga to **Bauska** (every 30 minutes; 1hr 30min; 1.50Ls); then take a local service to Pilsrundāle (5 buses daily to Bauska; 30 min; 30s). The palace is across the street from the bus stop.

SIGULDA

Dotted with parks and clustered above the southern bank of the River Gauja around 50km northeast of Rīga, **SIGULDA** is Gauja National Park's main centre and a good jumping-off point for exploring the rest of the **Gauja Valley**.

What to see and do

From the train station Raiņa iela runs north into town, passing the bus station. After about 800m a right turn into Baznaca iela brings you to the seven hundred year-old **Sigulda Church** (Siguldas baznīca). Sigulda is home to three castles: Krimulda Castle (Krimuldas pilsdrupas) and Sigulda Castle (Siguldas pilsdrupas), a former stronghold of the German Knights of the Sword, from which you can see Turaida Castle (Turaidas pils), the most impressive of the three.

Turaida Castle

You can reach **Turaida Castle** by bus (for Turaida or Krimulda) from

> **LEARN TO FLY!**
>
> Those wishing to experience the sensation of skydiving without the hassle of parachutes or airplanes can head to **Aerodium** (Tue–Fri 4pm–8pm, Sat–Sun noon–8pm, book online, ⓣ2838 4400, ⓦwww.aerodium.lv; 18Ls for two minutes), 5km outside Sigulda (you'll need to take a taxi). Don the floppy protective gear and experience the intense adrenalin rush of hovering atop an air current created by a giant fan. Beginners fly up to four metres above the fan, while professionals reach heights five times that.

Sigulda bus station. Alternatively, take the cable car (18 daily, 10am–7:30pm, 1.50Ls) across the Gauja River to Krimulda Castle, descend the wooden staircase signposted "Gūtmaņis Cave", then follow the path past the cave. The path turns right before rejoining the main road just short of Turaida itself. Built on the site of an earlier stronghold by the bishop of Rīga in 1214, Turaida Castle was destroyed when lightning hit its gunpowder magazine in the eighteenth century. These days its cellar exhibitions chart the castle's history (Tues–Sun 10am–5/6pm; 2Ls) and it's possible to climb up the main tower.

Information

Tourist office The tourist office is just west of the train and bus stations at Valdemāra 1a (Mon–Fri 8am–7pm, Sat 9am–2pm; ⓣ6797 1335, ⓦwww.sigulda.lv). Staff can book you into **private rooms** and provide information on exploring Gauja Valley. They can also arrange bungee jumping (Fri–Sun from cable car, 20Ls/person) and hot air ballooning (book in advance, ⓣ6761 1614).

Accommodation

Makara Kempings Peldu iela 1 ⓣ6924 4948, ⓦwww.makars.lv. Clean campsite (open May–Sept) in a shady riverside spot northwest and downhill from the town centre. Arranges canoeing and rafting trips. ❶

Melanis Kaķis Pils iela 8 ⓣ6797 0272. Spotless (if somewhat small) rooms with a bar and canteen-style restaurant next door. ❹

Vila Alberta Livkalna iela 10ª ⓣ6797 1060. Inviting guesthouse with own bar offering plush, themed doubles – from New Orleans to the Wild West; more expensive ones have Jacuzzis. Use of sauna and fitness centre costs extra. ❺

Eating and drinking

Kaķu Māja Pils iela 8. The Black Cat café offers large helpings of inexpensive canteen-style food and a tempting cake range. Mains and drink 3Ls.

Mario Pizzeria Pils iela 4b. Next to the bus station, Mario's serves generous portions of soup and very tasty pizza (4Ls).

Trīs Draugi Pils iela 9. Another canteen-style place with a decent selection and large portions of Latvian food. Mains 3Ls.

Moving on

Train Rīga (13 daily, more frequent in the mornings; 1hr 15min).

Bus Rīga (at least once hourly; 1 hr).

GAUJA NATIONAL PARK

Encompassing a diverse range of flora and fauna, **GAUJA NATIONAL PARK** (ⓦwww.gnp.gv.lv) covers over 920 square km of near-pristine forested wilderness, bisected by the 425-km Gauja River. The valley is ideal for exploring by bike, as most of the hiking trails are accessible to cyclists. Numerous "wild" campsites are located along the river's banks, and major campsites in Sigulda, Cēsis and Valmiera, at the north end of the park, arrange overnight canoeing and rafting trips.

CĒSIS

The well-preserved little town of **CĒSIS**, 35km northeast of Sigulda, has a pre-war atmosphere. From the **train** and **bus** stations walk down Raunas iela to **Vienības laukums**, Cēsis's main square. The attractive, somewhat run-down wooden **old town** lies to the south of here, along Rīgas iela. Nearby, on Skolas iela, is the thirteenth-century **St John's Church** (Svēta Jāņa baznīca). East of the square are the remains of **Cēsis Castle** (Cēsu pils; 2 Ls) founded by the Knights of the Sword in 1209, where a toppled statue of Lenin lies anachronistically on the green. Explore the towers' narrow winding staircases with a lantern, peer into the gloom of the dungeon, and peek into the working forge.

Information

Tourist office The helpful staff at the Cēsis tourist office, at Pils 1 (mid-May–early Sept: Mon 9am–6pm, Tue–Fri 9am–8pm, Sat 10am–8pm, Sun 10am–6pm; mid-Sept–early May: Mon–Fri

9am–6pm; ⓣ412 1815, ⓦwww.tourism.cesis.lv) charge 1L to arrange accommodation and also provide information on *cultural events*, such as the Arts Festival (ⓦwww.cesufestivals.lv), and various outdoor activities, such as horse-riding, quad biking, canoeing and cycling. Rent a bicycle opposite the tourist office (10Ls/day).

Accommodation

Kolonna Vienības iela 1 ⓣ412 0122, ⓦwww.hotelkolonna.com. Cēsis's grand hotel has free Internet, decent breakfast and surprisingly good value rooms. ❹–❻

Province Niniera ilea 6 ⓣ412 0122. Friendly small guesthouse with five clean doubles. ❹

Žagarkalns Mūrlejas iela 12 ⓣ2626 6266, ⓦwww.zagarklans.lv. Campsite on the western side of Cēsis by the river. Canoeing trips arranged. ❶

Eating/Drinking

Aroma Cafe Lenču iela 4. Popular cheap and cheerful eatery; many items under 2Ls. Extensive selection of teas for 1L.

Kafejnīca Logi Rigas iela 13. Pizza, soft drinks and large plates of meat, sauerkraut and potatoes (3Ls). Closed Sunday.

Province Niniera iela 6. Inexpensive well-prepared food in the restaurant of the welcoming guesthouse. Try the *shashlik* (3.40Ls).

Moving on

Train Rīga (5 daily, all stopping at Sigulda; 1hr 30min).

Bus Rīga (At least one hourly; 2hrs).

LIEPĀJA

A major trading port with a busy industrial feel, **LIEPĀJA**, 205km west of the capital, is Latvia's third-biggest city after Rīga and Daugavpils. Its streets bear a startling mish-mash of architectural styles, with faded eighteenth- and nineteenth-century facades contrasting with crumbling military installations.

What to see and do

Boasting great nightlife and one of Latvia's best beaches, the city draws visitors from all over Latvia and beyond, many of whom come for the music scene – Liepāja has more musicians per capita than any other Latvian city. The city gets packed out in late July for the Baltic Beach Party (ⓦwww.balticbeachparty.lv), a carnivalesque weekend of fashion shows, live music and sporting events, and again in mid-August for the country's largest rock festival, Liepājas Dzintars.

The centre

The centre of town is south of Tirzniecības Canal and bisected north to south by Lielā iela. Zivju iela branches off to the east of Lielā iela, heading through the city's main shopping area and merging with the small pedestrianized square of **Rožu laukums**. You'll find half-timbered houses and a few old buildings in the side streets to the east.

The park and beach

Walk further south down Liela iela and then head west along Peldu iela to reach the roller-skating paths, outdoor concert halls and beer gardens of lush **Jūrmala Park**. Beyond stretches the long white **beach**, which was cleaned-up after the dismantling of the local Soviet military base.

Karosta

About 3km north of Tirdzniecības Canal and reachable by buses #3, #4, #7 and #8, the suburb of **Karosta** was, during the late-nineteenth century, a naval fortress designed to protect the Tsarist Russian empire and, from the end of World War II until the 1990s, a Soviet submarine base. The wide, semi-abandoned boulevards lined with crumbling remains of military barracks, imposing Tsarist-era buildings and run-down concrete housing blocks are fascinating to explore, especially by bike. Visit the **Karosta community centre**, Atomodas bulvāris 6a (daily 11am–6pm, ⓦwww.karosta.lv) for information on local events and **bike**

rental. The golden-domed **Church of St Nicholas** at Katedrālas 7 stands out like a gem among the ruins. After decades of being used as a gym and warehouse, it is once again a house of worship.

Arrival and information

Bus and train station The stations are in the same building 1500m north of the town centre, but south of Karosta. To get to the centre catch a tram down Rīgas iela, which crosses the Tirdzniecības Canal and becomes Lielā iela, the city centre's main street.

Tourist office The friendly **tourist office,** Rožu laukums 5/6 (Mon–Fri 9am–7pm, Sat 9am–6pm, Sun 10am–3pm; ⓣ6348 0808, ⓦwww.liepaja.lv/turisms), can arrange accommodation and provides free maps.

Accommodation

Fontaine Jūras iela 24 ⓣ6342 0956, ⓦwww.fontaine.lv. This centrally located hotel with a funky red exterior has uniquely decorated rooms (think Elvis, Soviet kitsch) and a curio shop/reception in which to rummage for hidden treasures. ❸

Liepāja Travellers Hostel Republikas iela 25 ⓣ2869 0106, ⓦwww.liepajahostel.lv. Between the beach and the city centre, this friendly hostel offers clean dorms. ❷

Eating and Drinking

Fontaine Delisnack Dzirnavu iela 4. Fast-food joint next to Fontaine Palace, serving up decent burritos, noodles, pizza and burgers at a bargain price (1–3Ls). Open 24 hours.

Kiss Me Lielā iela 13. Espresso bar with red love seats, glass front and a romantic atmosphere. Great coffee for 75s.

Vecais Kapteinis (The Old Captain) Dubelsteina iela 14. Upmarket Latvian cuisine in seafaring-themed brick house; excellent steaks and pasta dishes. 5–6Ls.

PRISONER FOR A NIGHT

For a taste of Soviet-style incarceration, book into **Karosta Prison** (Karosta Scientums, Invalīdu iela 4, ⓣ2636 9470, ⓦwww.karostascietums.lv ❷) and spend the night in a musty cell. Clean bed linen is provided by the prison staff, which is more than the real inmates received, but aside from that, living conditions remain unchanged – you still have to use the same communal washing facilities and squatter toilets. Tours of the imposing red building are also available. Take eastbound bus #4 just south of the bus station to reach the prison.

Entertainment

Big 7 Baznīcas iela 14/16 ⓦwww.big7.lv. Large complex popular with a young crowd. Disco Fri & Sat from 10pm; DJ Chill Out set Thurs–Sat until 6am. Cheap food, pool tables and hookahs also on offer.

Fontaine Palace Dzirnavu iela 4, ⓦwww.fontainepalace.lv. Right by Tirdzniecības Canal, this converted warehouse stages live concerts on weekends, and alternative music nightly, as well as the Fontaine Festival in July. Closes 4am Fri & Sat.

Latvia's 1st Rock Café Stendera iela 18/20, ⓦwww.pablo.lv. One of Liepāja's top spots – four floors of good, cheap food; live music nightly and rooftop beer garden. Closes 4am Fri & Sat.

Moving on

Train Rīga (4 daily; 4hr 30min–5hrs).

Bus Rīga (at least one hourly; 3hr 30min–4hr 30min).

Lithuania

HIGHLIGHTS

PALANGA: Lithuania's premier beach resort; the place to hear live music and party all night

CURONIAN SPIT: a wild, beautiful National Park on the Baltic coast

DEVIL'S MUSEUM, KAUNAS: a fun and quirky collection of devil figures from around the world

GENOCIDE MUSEUM, VILNIUS: a haunting reminder of man's inhumanity

TRAKAI: a fairy-tale medieval castle sitting on its own little island

ROUGH COSTS

DAILY BUDGET basic €35 / occasional treat €50

DRINK Utenos beer €1.50

FOOD Cepelinai (potato and meat parcels) €3

HOSTEL/BUDGET HOTEL €10/€37

TRAVEL Train: Vilnius–Paneriai €0.50; bus: Kaunas–Nida €15

FACT FILE

POPULATION 3.4 million

AREA 65,303 sq km

LANGUAGE Lithuanian; Russian widely spoken

CURRENCY Litas (Lt)

CAPITAL Vilnius (population: 543,000)

INTERNATIONAL PHONE CODE ⓣ370

Basics

Lithuania is a vibrant and quirky country with a bustling capital which is rapidly becoming modernized. You'll find a lively night-life both in Vilnius and on the coast, ample grounds for outdoor pursuits in the as yet unspoiled national parks, and a number of good beaches. Unlike its Baltic neighbours, Lithuania was once a major European power, carving out an extensive east-European empire in the fourteenth century, and more recently, it was the first of the Baltic States to declare its independence on March 11, 1990.

Travel in Lithuania presents no real hardships, and even in well-trodden destinations the volume of visitors is low, leaving you with the feeling that there's still much to discover here. **Vilnius**, with its Baroque old town, is the most architecturally beautiful of the Baltic capitals, while the second city, **Kaunas**, also has an attractive centre and a couple of unique museums, along with a handful of surprisingly good restaurants and bars. The port city of **Klaipēda** is a convenient stopping-off point en route to the resorts of **Neringa**, a unique spit of sand dunes and forest that shields Lithuania from the Baltic Sea, or to **Palanga**, Lithuania's party town which heaves with holidaymakers all summer.

CHRONOLOGY

2000 BC The ancestors of the Lithuanians settle in the Baltic region.
1009 AD First recorded mention of the name Lithuania in the Quedlinburg Annals.
1236 Grand Duke Mindaugas unites Lithuania to ward off German crusaders.
1252 Mindaugas is crowned King of Lithuania.
1386 After an arranged marriage between the King of Lithuania and the Queen of Poland, Lithuania officially converts to Christianity.
1410 The Polish-Lithuanian alliance defeat the Teutonic Knights, increasing their military influence in the Baltic region.
1547 First Lithuanian book, *The Simple Words of Catechism*, is published.
1795 Russia takes control of Lithuania.
1865 Growth of the Lithuanian liberation movement leads to violent repression by the Russians.
1900 Mass Lithuanian emigration across the world to escape Russian repression.
1920 Lithuania gains independence from Russia after heavy fighting.
1939 Lithuania is invaded by Nazi Germany.
1945 During both German and Soviet occupation, thousands of Lithuanian Jews are killed whilst thousands of other Lithuanians are deported.
1990 Following the success of the nationalist "Sajudis" movement, Lithuania is the first Soviet Republic to declare its independence from Moscow.
1991 Lithuanian independence is recognised by the USSR before its collapse.
2004 Lithuania joins the EU; thousands emigrate to work in Western Europe.
2006 Lithuanian government collapses as the Labour Party leave the ruling coalition.

ARRIVAL

Most tourists arrive by **air**; Vilnius airport is served by fourteen European airlines including the national carrier, FlyLAL (Ⓣ252 5555, Ⓦwww.flylal.com) while Kaunas handles Ryanair flights from the UK, Germany and Ireland. Lithuania has good **rail** connections with neighbouring countries, with direct trains arriving in Vilnius from Warsaw, Moscow, St Petersburg, Kaliningrad, and Minsk. Several **bus** companies, including Eurolines provide regular services to Vilnius' central bus station. There are also frequent **ferries** from Kiel, Germany to Klaipeda on Lithuania's Baltic coast. (Ⓣ231 3314, Ⓦwww.krantas.lt).

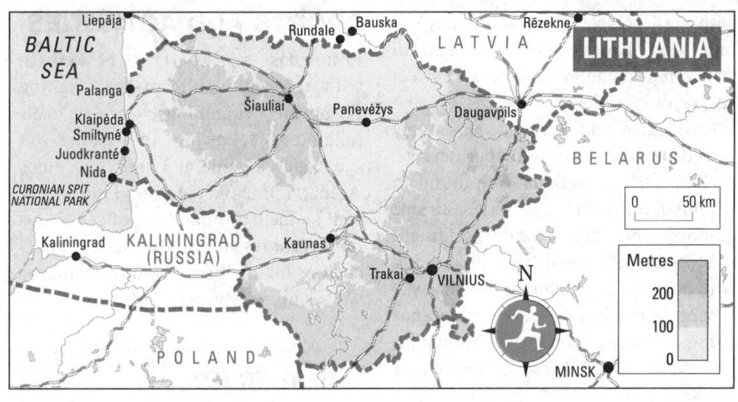

GETTING AROUND

Buses are slightly quicker and slightly more expensive than trains. You should buy **train** tickets in advance – stations have separate windows for long-distance and suburban (*priemiestinis* or *vietinis*) trains. Long-distance services are divided into "passenger" (*keleivinis traukinys*) and "fast" (*greitas*); the latter usually require a reservation. On **timetable boards**, look for *isvyksta* (departure) or *atvyksta* (arrival).

It's best to buy long-distance **bus** tickets in advance, and opt for an express (*ekspresas*), to avoid frequent stops. You can also pay for your ticket on board, although this doesn't guarantee you a seat. Normally **luggage** is taken on board, though large bags may have to go in the luggage compartment. Buses are also useful for travelling to Lithuania's Baltic neighbours.

In Vilnius and Kaunas there is frequent and efficient public transport: buses, trolleybuses and route taxis cover most of the city. Smaller places, such as the Curonian Spit, are best explored by **bicycle**; bike rentals are inexpensive and plentiful.

ACCOMMODATION

The best way to keep **accommodation** costs down is by staying in **private rooms**. The most reliable agency is **Litinterp**, with offices in Vilnius, Kaunas and Klaipėda; the latter can book rooms on the Curonian Spit. Spartan double rooms in Soviet-era **budget hotels** cost as little as 70Lt. Smaller, smarter **mid-range** places charge upwards of 200Lt a double.

There are a few **hostels**, charging 30–35Lt per night. Space is limited and it's best to call in advance; in popular spots like Nida and Palanga, reservations are essential in summer. There are a lot of **campsites** in rural areas, charging around 10Lt per person, 10–15Lt per tent. Weekend retreats to **country houses** (with sauna and meals included, ⓦwww.countryside.lt) are inexpensive and popular with young Lithuanians.

FOOD AND DRINK

Lithuanian **cuisine** is based on traditional **peasant dishes**. Typical **starters** include marinated mushrooms (*marinuoti grybai*), herring (*silkē*) and smoked sausage (*rukyta desra*) along with cold beetroot soup (*saltibarsčiai*). A popular **national dish** is *cepelinai*, or zeppelins – cylindrical potato parcels stuffed with meat, mushrooms or cheese. Others include potato pancakes (*bulviniai blynai*), and *koldūnai* – boiled or fried dumplings with meat or mushroom filling. Popular **beer snacks** include deep-fried sticks of black bread with garlic (*kepta duona*) and smoked pigs' ears. Pancakes (*blynai, blyneliai* or *lietiniai*) come in a plethora of sweet and savoury varieties.

Most cafés and bars do reasonably priced food. Well-stocked supermarkets, such as Iki and Maxima, are found in Vilnius and elsewhere. Many restaurants are open between 11am – midnight daily, with cafes open from 7/8am and with bars closing at 2am at the earliest.

Beer (*alus*) is popular, local brands being Švyturus, Utenos and Kalnapilis, and so is **mead** (*midus*), Lithuania's noble drink. The leading local **firewaters** are Starka, Trejos devynerios and Medžiotojū – invigorating spirits flavoured with herbs. Lively **bars** sprout up daily in Vilnius and Kaunas. Many ape American or Irish models, although there are also plenty of folksy Lithuanian places, while **cafés** (*kavinė*) come in all shapes and sizes. Coffee (*kava*) and tea (*arbata*) are usually served black; ask for milk (*pienas*) and/or sugar (*cukrus*).

CULTURE AND ETIQUETTE

Urban Lithuania is rapidly becoming Westernised, with city dwellers enjoying a thoroughly modern lifestyle. There is a stark difference, however, between the cities and the far poorer rural Lithuania, where traditional culture remains firmly in place and where electronic communication has yet to make inroads. If eating with locals, it is rude to refuse second helpings of food; when toasting someone, always look them in the eye. Always give an odd number of flowers when visiting Lithuanians; even numbers are for the dead. Shaking hands across the threshold is bad luck. Family ties are strong, and extended family gatherings are common. Women tend to fill traditional roles. Only tip in restaurants to reward good service and it suffices to round up the bill by leaving behind spare change; ten percent is fair.

SPORTS AND ACTIVITIES

Lithuania's top sport is **basketball**, with the national team the reigning European champions, and locals religiously following the games on TV. Catch a game at Vilnius's Siemens Arena. Lithuania's **national parks**, as well as the Curonian Spit, offer various opportunities for **outdoor activities** such as hiking, biking and canoeing, as well as more extreme sports.

JUMP TO IT!

Active Holidays Rodunios kelias 8-102, Vilnius ⓣ698 24795, ⓦwww.activeholidays.lt. If you want to try your hand at anything that involves jumping, diving, wheels, raucous nightlife, or even plain old sightseeing, these guys will find it for you and organise transport and an English-speaking guide.

COMMUNICATIONS

In major towns, **post offices** (*pastas*) are open Mon–Fri 8am–6pm & Sat 8am–3pm; in smaller places hours are more restricted. **Stamps** are also available at some kiosks and tourist offices. **Public phones** operate with cards (*telefono kortelė*; 9Lt, 13Lt, 16Lt and 30Lt) which you can purchase at post offices and kiosks. To make a long-distance call, dial ⓣ8 before the area code. When calling Lithuania from abroad, omit

LITHUANIA ON THE NET

ⓦ**www.tourism.lt** National tourist board site with useful information.
ⓦ**www.tourism.vilnius.lt** Vilnius tourist information.
ⓦ**www.search.lt** Lithuanian search engine.
ⓦ**www.muziejai.lt** Portal for Lithuanian museums.
ⓦ**www.lietuva.lt** General information about the country.

the initial 8. For **international calls**, dial ⓣ8, wait for the tone, then dial 10, then the country code as usual. There's a good choice of **internet cafés** in Vilnius and a few in Kaunas; many cafes and restaurants also have **wi-fi**.

EMERGENCIES

You're unlikely to meet trouble in Lithuania; car theft and late-night mugging are the most common crimes. The cash-starved **police** expect to be taken seriously – be polite if you have dealings with them. A few of the younger ones may speak a little English. **Emergency health care** is free but if you get seriously ill, head home.

EMERGENCY NUMBERS

Police ⓣ02; Ambulance ⓣ03; Fire ⓣ01.

INFORMATION & MAPS

Most major towns have **tourist offices** (ⓦwww.tourism.lt), often offering accommodation listings and event calendars in English. The **In Your Pocket** guides to Vilnius, Kaunas and Klaipēda (available from bookshops, newsstands, tourist offices and some hotels; ⓦwww.inyourpocket.com; 5–8Lt) are indispensable sources of practical information. Regional **maps** and detailed street plans of Vilnius are available in bookshops and kiosks.

MONEY AND BANKS

Lithuania's currency is the **Litas** (usually abbreviated to Lt), which is divided into 100 centai. Coins come as 0.01, 0.02, 0.05, 0.10, 0.20, 0.50, 1, 2 and 5Lt, with notes of 10, 20, 50, 100 and 200Lt. The litas is pegged to the euro (€1 = 3.45Lt). **Bank** (*bankas*) opening hours vary, though branches of the Vilniaus Bankas are usually open Mon–Fri 8am–3/4pm. They generally give advances on Visa/MasterCard/AmEx cards and cash travellers' cheques (commission 2–3 percent). Outside banking hours, find an **exchange office** (*valiutos keitykla*). There are plentiful **ATMs** in all major towns as well as the Curonian Spit; **credit cards** are widely accepted.

STUDENT AND YOUTH DISCOUNTS

An ISIC or an IYTC card will get you fifty percent discount on museums and sights, as well as on public transport and some long-distance trains during term-time. A YHA card gets discounts at HI-affiliated youth hostels, while ISIC/IYTC cards are accepted at any hostel.

OPENING HOURS AND PUBLIC HOLIDAYS

Opening hours for **shops** are 9/10am–6/7pm. Outside Vilnius, some places take an hour off for lunch; most usually close on Sun (though some food shops stay open). Most shops and all banks will be closed on the following **public holidays**: Jan 1, Feb 16, March 11, Easter Sun, Easter Mon, May 1, July 6, Aug 15, Nov 1, Dec 25 & 26.

Lithuanian

	Lithuanian	Pronunciation
Yes	*Taip*	Tape
No	*Ne*	Ne
Please	*Prašau*	Prashau
Thank you	*Ačiu*	Achoo
Hello/Good day	*Labas*	Labass
Goodbye	*Viso gero*	Viso gero
Excuse me	*Atsiprašau*	Atsiprashau
Sorry	*Atleiskite*	Ahtlayskita
Where?	*Kur?*	Kur?
Can you show me?	*Galētumēt man parodyti?*	Gahlehtumet mahn pahrawdeeti
Student ticket	*Bilietă studentas*	Bileahtah studantahs
Toilet	*Tualeto*	Tuahlataw
I'd like to try that	*Aš norēčiai išbandyti to*	Ahsh nawrehchow ishbahndeeti taw
I don't eat meat	*Aš nevalgau mēsiško*	Ahsh navahlgow mehsishkaw
Bill	*sǎskaita*	sahskaitah
Good	*Geras*	Gerass
Bad	*Blogas*	Blogass
Near	*Artimas*	Artimass
Far	*Tolimas*	Tolimass
Cheap	*Pigus*	Piguss
Expensive	*Brangus*	Branguss
Open	*Atidarytas*	Atidaritass
Closed	*Uždarytas*	Uzhdaritass
Today	*Siandien*	Shyandyen
Yesterday	*Vakar*	Vakar
Tomorrow	*Rytdiena*	Ritdyena
How much is...?	*Kiek kainuoja ...?*	Kyek kainwoya?
What time is it?	*Kiek valandū?*	Kyek valandoo?
I don't understand	*Nesuprantu*	Nessuprantu
Do you speak English?	*Ar jūs kalbate angliškai?*	Ar yoos kalbate anglishkay?
One	*Vienas*	Vyenass
Two	*Du/dvi*	Du/Dvee
Three	*Trys*	Triss
Four	*Keturi*	Keturee
Five	*Penki*	Penkee
Six	*Šeši*	Sheshee
Seven	*Septyni*	Septinee
Eight	*Aštuoni*	Ashtuonee
Nine	*Devyni*	Devinee
Ten	*Dešimt*	Deshimt

Vilnius

"Narrow cobblestone streets and an orgy of Baroque: almost like a Jesuit city somewhere in the middle of Latin America," wrote the author Czesław Miłosz of prewar **VILNIUS**. Soviet-era satellite suburbs aside, this description still rings true. Despite being the capital of the medieval Lithuanian state, Vilnius was occupied by Poland between the wars, and was inhabited mainly by Poles and Jews, who played such a prominent role in the city's life that it was known as the **"Northern Jerusalem"**. Today, Vilnius is a cosmopolitan place – around twenty percent of its population is **Polish** and another twenty percent is **Russian** – that is relatively compact and easy to get to know.

What to see and do

At the centre of Vilnius, poised between the medieval and nineteenth-century parts of the city, is **Cathedral Square** (Katedros aikstē). To the south of here along Pilies gatvē and Didžioji gatvē is the Old Town, containing perhaps the most impressive concentration of Baroque architecture in northern Europe. West of the square in the New Town is **Gedimino prospektas**, a nineteenth-century boulevard and the focus of the city's commercial and administrative life. The traditionally **Jewish areas** of Vilnius between the Old Town and Gedimino prospektas still retain some sights.

Cathedral Square

Cathedral Square is dominated by the Neoclassical **Cathedral** (Arkikatedros bazilika; daily 7am–7:30pm), originating in the thirteenth century, when a wooden church was built here on the site of a temple dedicated to Perkūnas, the god of thunder. The highlight of the airy, vaulted interior is the opulent **Chapel of St Casimir**, the patron saint of Lithuania. Next to the cathedral on the square is the white **belfry**, once part of the fortifications of the vanished **Lower Castle**. Between the Cathedral and the belfry lies a small coloured tile with *stebuklas* (miracle) written on it, marking the spot from where, in 1989, two million people formed a **human chain** that stretched all the way to Tallinn, Estonia to protest against the Soviet occupation of the Baltic States.

Gediminas Hill and the Upper Castle Museum

Rising behind the cathedral is the tree-clad **Gediminas Hill**, its summit crowned by the red-brick **Gediminas Tower** – one of the city's best-known landmarks – founded by **Grand Duke Gediminas**, the Lithuanian ruler who consolidated the country's independence. According to legend, Gediminas dreamt of an iron wolf howling on a hill overlooking the River Vilnia and was told by a pagan priest to build a castle on the spot. The tower houses the worthwhile **Upper Castle Museum** (Aukstinēs pilies muziejus; May–Sept daily 10am–7pm; Oct–April Tues–Sun 11am–5pm; 4Lt, free on Wed in winter), showing the former extent of the Vilnius fortifications. Take the **funicular** from the courtyard of the **Lithuanian Art Museum** (2Lt).

The Lithuanian National Museum

About 100m north of the cathedral is the **Lithuanian National Museum**, Arsenalo 1 (Lietuvos nacionalinis muziejus; Tues–Sat 10am–5pm; Sun 10am–3pm; 4Lt, free on Wed in winter), covering the history of Lithuania from prehistoric times to 1940 through an interesting collection of artefacts, paintings and photographs, but with mostly Lithuanian and Russian labelling. A little further north on Arsenalo, a separate department houses

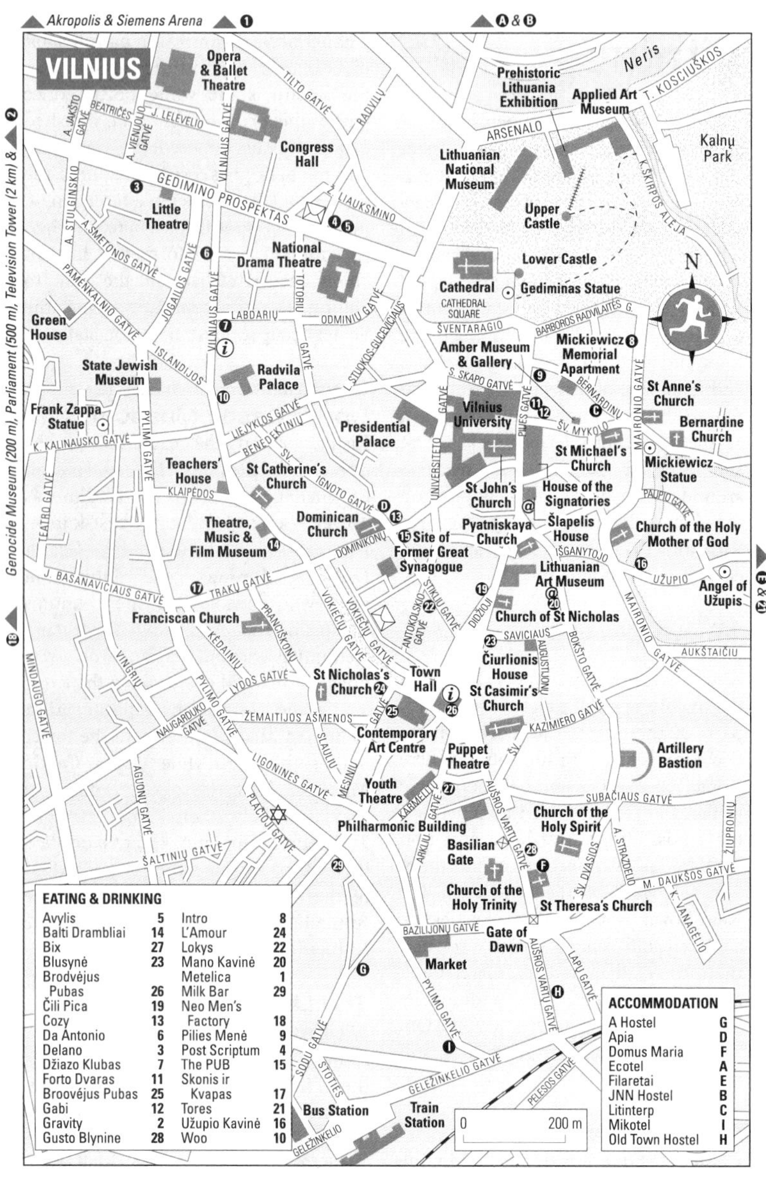

the much snazzier Prehistoric Lithuania **exhibition** (Tues–Sat 10am–5pm, Sun 10am–3pm; 4Lt), displaying flint, iron, bronze and silver artefacts and covering the story of the Lithuanians up to the Middle Ages.

The Old Town

The **Old Town**, just south of Cathedral Square, is a network of narrow, often cobbled streets that forms the Baroque heart of Vilnius, with the pedestrianized **Pilies gatvė** cutting into it from the southeastern corner of the square. To the west of this street is **Vilnius University**, constructed between the sixteenth and eighteenth centuries around nine linked courtyards that extend west to Universiteto gatvē. Within its precincts is the beautiful, ornate Baroque **St John's Church** (Sv Jono baznyčia), founded during the fourteenth century, taken over by the Jesuits in 1561 and given to the university in 1737.

The Presidential Palace and St Anne's Church

The **Presidential Palace**, just west of the university on **Daukanto aikstē**, was originally built during the sixteenth century as a merchant's residence and remodelled into its present Neoclassical form at the end of the eighteenth century. **Napoleon Bonaparte** stayed here briefly during his ill-fated campaign against Russia in 1812. The emperor is said to have been so impressed by **St Anne's Church** (Sv Onos baznyčia; May–Sept Tues–Sun 10am–6pm) on Maironio gatvē, to the east of Pilies gatvē, that he wanted to take it back to Paris on the palm of his hand. Studded with skeletal, finger-like towers, its facade overlaid with intricate brick traceries and fluting, this late-sixteenth-century structure is the finest Gothic building in Vilnius.

Užupis and the Lithuanian Art Museum

Just south of St Anne's a bridge over the river Vilnia forms the border of the self-declared independent republic of **Užupis**, home to a flourishing population of artists, bohemians and yuppies. Stroll up from **Užupio Café** across the bridge to see the psychedelic art gallery with weird and wonderful creations suspended above the river. Some of the buildings are in dire need of repair, but there is a young, up-and-coming feel to the area. West of Užupis, Pilies gatvē becomes Didžioji gatvē as it heads south, with the restored Baroque palace at no. 4 housing the **Lithuanian Art Museum** (Tues–Sat noon–6pm, Sun noon–5pm; 5Lt, free on Wed in winter), with a marvellous collection of sixteenth- to nineteenth-century paintings and sculptures from around the country.

Town Hall Square and around

The colonnaded Neoclassical building at the end of **Town Hall Square** (Rotusēs aikstē) is the **Town Hall**. The **Contemporary Art Centre** (Suolaikinio meno centras or SMC; Tues–Sun 11am–6.30pm; 4Lt, free on Wed in winter) lies behind it, hosting fascinating modern art exhibitions with interactive elements. East of the square, currently undergoing renovation, is the striking **St Casimir's Church** (Sv Kazimiero baznyčia; Mon–Fri 10am–6.30pm, Sun 8am–1.30pm) with a beautiful interior, the oldest Baroque church in the city, dating from 1604. South of here, Didžioji becomes **Aušros Vartū gatvē**, leading to the Baroque seventeenth-century **Church of the Holy Spirit** – Lithuania's main Orthodox church – built in the grounds of a monastery. Inside, the bodies of three fourteenth-century martyred saints are displayed in a glass case, their faces swathed in cloth. The end of the street is marked by the **Gate of Dawn** (Aušros vartū), the sole survivor of the nine city gates. A chapel above the gate houses the *Madonna of the Gates of Dawn*, said to have miraculous powers and revered by Polish Catholics; on Sundays, open-air mass is held. East of Aušros Vartū gatvē on Boksto 20/18 is the seventeenth-century **Artillery Bastion** (Artilerijos bastēja), once part of the city's outer fortification ring and now housing a weapons and armour **museum** (Tues–Sat 10am–5pm, Sun 10am–3pm; 2Lt, free on Wed in winter).

The synagogue and Jewish Museum

Today, the Jewish population of Vilnius numbers only a few thousand and, out

JEWISH VILNIUS

Before World War II Vilnius was one of the most important centres of Jewish life in eastern Europe. The Jews – first invited to settle in 1410 by Grand Duke Vytautas – made up around a third of the city's population, mainly concentrated in the eastern fringes of the Old Town around present-day Vokiečiū gatvē, Zydū gatvē and Antokolskio gatvē. The Great Synagogue was located just off Zydū gatvē, on a site now occupied by a kindergarten. Massacres of the Jewish population began soon after the Germans occupied Vilnius on June 24, 1941, and those who survived the initial killings found themselves herded into two ghettos. The smaller of these ghettos centred around Zydū, Antokolskio, Stikliū and Gaono streets and was liquidated in October 1941, while the larger occupied an area between Pylimo, Vokiečiū, Lydos, Mikalojaus, Karmelitū and Arkliū streets and was liquidated in September 1943. Most of the Jews of Vilnius perished in Paneriai forest on the southwestern edge of the city (see p.781).

of the 96 that once existed, the city has just one surviving **synagogue**, at Pylimo 39 (open for services Mon–Fri & Sun 8am–2pm & 7:30–8pm, Sat 10am–2pm), entrance at Raugyklos 4a. The **Lithuanian State Jewish Museum** (Lietuvos valstybinis Zydū muziejus, Ⓦwww.jmuseum.lt), housed in the **Jewish community offices** at Pylimo 4 (Mon–Thurs 9am–5pm, Fri 9am–4pm; 4Lt, free on Wed in winter) has displays on Jewish partisan resistance, life in the Vilnius ghetto, and an exhibit on Lithuanians who risked their lives to save Jews during the Nazi occupation. The **Green House** (Zalias namas), slightly uphill at Pamenkalnio 12 (Mon–Thurs 9am–5pm, Fri 9am–4pm; 4Lt, ticket valid at all three branches), contains a harrowing display on the fate of Vilnius and Kaunas Jews during World War II, including eyewitness accounts, with some captioning in English. Guided English museum tours can be arranged (25Lt), as well as "history of Jewish Vilnius" tours (Ⓣ5/262 0730).

Frank Zappa statue

Nearby, Kalinausko street is worth a visit to see the bronze head of rocker **Frank Zappa** perched on a column, against a backdrop of street art. Civil servant Saulis Paukstys founded the local Zappa fan club and, in 1992, commissioned the socialist realist sculptor Konstantinas Bogdanas, more accustomed to forging likenesses of Lenin, to create this unique sculpture.

Gedimino prospektas

Gedimino prospektas, running west from Cathedral Square, was the main thoroughfare of nineteenth-century Vilnius, and remains the most important commercial street. **Lukiskiū aikstē**, around 900m west of Cathedral Square, is the former location of the city's Lenin statue, removed after the failed 1991 coup which precipitated the final break-up of the Soviet Union. After the 1863–64 uprising against the Russians, a number of rebels were publicly hanged here, while Gedimino 40, on the southern side of the square, was Lithuania's **KGB headquarters**. The building also served as Gestapo headquarters during the German occupation and more recently the Soviets incarcerated political prisoners in the basement. It's now the excellent **Genocide Museum** (Genocido aukū muziejus; entrance at Aukū 2a; Tues–Sun 10am–4/6pm; 4Lt, no student concession in the summer), with torture cells and the execution courtyard making a grim impression. Well-labelled exhibits on Soviet occupation, deportation and Lithuanian partisan resistance are upstairs; the optional English-language cassette-tape commentary (8Lt) is worthwhile if you want a very detailed prison tour.

Arrival and information

Train and bus The main **train station** is at Geležinkelio 16, with 24hr luggage storage in the basement and 24hr currency exchange, detailed timetables, information office and Maxima supermarket. The main **bus station**, just across the road, has luggage storage, a food kiosk, an information office and an ATM.

Tourist office Branches at Vilniaus 22 (ⓣ5/262 9660, ⓔtic@vilnius.lt; Mon–Fri 9am–6pm), and in the Town Hall at Didžioji 31 (ⓣ5/262 6470; Mon–Fri 9am–6pm, Sat & Sun 10am–4pm) offer advice on accommodation and festivals (ⓦwww.vilniusfestivals.lt); they can also book you private rooms and have a plethora of pamphlets on local attractions. The best source of listings is the excellent *Vilnius in Your Pocket* city guide (ⓦwww.inyourpocket.com), costing 5Lt from newspaper kiosks.

City transport

Public transport Buses and trolleybuses cover most of the city. Tickets cost 1.10Lt from newspaper kiosks or 1.40Lt from the driver; students get fifty percent discount during term-time. Validate your ticket by punching it in the machine on board. Alternatively, hail a minibus at any bus stop in the direction you're going, pay the driver 3Lt and you'll be dropped off at the stop you require.

Taxi Prices are usually reasonable and fares should cost no more than around 3–4Lt per kilometre. Phoning ahead is one way of ensuring a fair rate; try Vilniaus Taksi (ⓣ5/266 6662) or Martono Taksi (ⓣ5/240 0004).

Accommodation

Hostels and private rooms

A Hostel Sodū 17 ⓣ5/213 9994, ⓦwww.ahostel.lt. Clean, bright Japanese-style sleeping cubicles, dorms and VIP rooms. Five minutes' walk from Old Town. Dorms ❶–❷; rooms ❹

Filaretai Filaretū 17 ⓣ5/215 4627. HI-affiliated hostel in the Uzupio district, with large clean dorm rooms and cheap laundry facilities, fifteen minutes' walk east of the Old Town, or bus #34 from the train station. Dorms ❶; rooms ❷

JNN Hostel Konstitucijos 25 ⓣ5/272 2270, ⓦwww.jnn.lt. Take bus #2 from the airport or trolleybus #5 from the train station to Žaliasis Tiltas followed by bus #2 or #46. Spotless en-suite doubles, triples and quads in a concrete building north of the river. 80–190Lt. ❸–❻

Litinterp Bernardinū 7/2 ⓣ5/212 3850, ⓦwww.litinterp.lt. Open Mon–Fri 8.30am–5.30pm, Sat 9.30am–3pm. Private rooms in the Old Town – either with a host family or in the agency's own guest house. Book in advance in summer. ❸–❺

Old Town Hostel Aušros Vartū 20–10 ⓣ5/262 5357, ⓔoldtownhostel@lithuanianhostels.com. Cramped, rowdy, but comfortable HI-affiliated hostel near the train and bus stations with dorms and doubles. Free internet; reservations essential. Dorms ❶; rooms ❸.

Hotels & guesthouses

Domus Maria Aušros Vartū 12 ⓣ5/264 4880, ⓦwww.domusmaria.lt. Central guesthouse in a former monastery. Some of the bright, comfortable rooms look out on the Gate of Dawn. ❺

Ecotel Slucko 8 ⓣ5/210 2700, ⓦwww.ecotel.lt. Minimally furnished but soothing en-suites in a new hotel just north of the river. ❹

Mikotel Pylimo 63 ⓣ5/260 9626, ⓦwww.mikotel.lt. Small hotel a few steps away from the train and bus stations, with pristine, modern en-suites and quirky decor. ❹

Apia Šv Ignoto 12 ⓣ5/212 3426, ⓦwww.apia.lt. Friendly, twelve-room guest house in superb Old Town location. ❻

Eating

There's a fast-growing range of **eateries** in Vilnius offering everything from Lithuanian to Lebanese cuisine. There's little difference between eating and drinking venues: **bars** and **cafés** invariably serve both snacks and meals and often represent better value for money than restaurants. For **self-caterers**, there are a number of well-stocked Maxima supermarkets scattered about.

Cafés and snack bars

Delano Gedimino 24. Huge subterranean self-service cafeteria with large wooden tables and a cheap buffet; salads 3Lt, meat dishes 7Lt, juices 3Lt. Closes at 6pm weekends.

Gabi Šv Mykolo 6. Inexpensive drinks and solid home cooking in a relaxed, non-smoking atmosphere. Mains 15–20Lt.

Gusto Blynine Aušros Vartū 6. Substantial, tasty crepes with every imaginable sweet or savoury filling (5Lt).

Mano Kavinē Bokšto 7. Stylish place in the Old Town with chic, modernist decor, trendy young clientele, free internet in the back, and a wide range of snacks. Speciality teas 10Lt.

Pilies Menē Pilies 8. Flash modern café/bar in a great people-watching location famous for its extensive pancake menu (7Lt).
Post Scriptum Gedimino 7. Popular café serving fresh juices, good cakes and cheap mains (10Lt).
Skonis ir Kvapas Trakū 8. The most beautiful vaulted interior in town. Big pots of tea, excellent coffee, and an affordable range of hot meals. Drinks 7Lt; mains 10–15Lt.
Užupio Kavinē Užupio 2. Relaxed, mildly bohemian place on the eastern fringes of the Old Town, with a lime-tree-shaded outdoor terrace overlooking the Vilnia River. Coffee 5Lt.

Restaurants

Balti Drambliai Vilniaus 41. Vegetarian restaurant with friendly service and an unusual non-smoking policy in the cellar and lively beer garden. Mains 10–15Lt.
Blusynē Saviclaus 5. Small, friendly place, with inventive menu of well-prepared food; fish soup with absinthe 12Lt. Open from 3pm Mon–Wed; 1pm Thurs –Sun.
Čili Pica Didžioji 5. Popular place for inexpensive thin-crust and deep-pan pizzas. Six more branches, one at Gedimino 23, another at the Europa shopping mall. Medium pizza 15–18Lt.
Da Antonio Vilniaus 23. Smart but down-to-earth Italian restaurant, with prompt service and delicious home-made pasta. Pasta dishes 20–28Lt.
Forto Dvaras Pilies 16. An excellent place to try *cepelinai* (zeppelins; 10Lt) or stuffed potato pancakes (8.50Lt). Cheap, tasty and filling.
Freskos Didžioji 31. Imaginative, well-presented modern European cuisine behind the Town Hall. Good-value lunchtime salad buffet 10Lt.
Lokys Stikliū 8/10. Cozy Lithuanian cellar restaurant serving well-cooked game alongside more traditional meat-and-potato favourites. Beaver stew 25Lt; bilberry dumplings 15Lt.
Tores Užupio 40. Good, although not particularly Spanish food in the funky Užupis district. Marvellous views of the old town from the terrace. Mains 20–35Lt.

Drinking and nightlife

Vilnius has a growing club and disco scene worth visiting, though you may have a just as good (and cheaper) time in some of the bars mentioned below.

Bars

Avylis Gedimino 5. Smart and atmospheric brick-clad basement with own beer and good Lithuanian food and snacks. Beer 4Lt; smoked pig's ear 8Lt.
Bix Etmonū 6. Great bar with blood-red walls run by members of legendary post-punk band Bix. Funky décor, loud rock music, karaoke nights and an enjoyable disco in the cellar. Beer 8Lt.
Brodvējus Pubas Mēsiniū 4. Popular drinking/dancing venue with live bands (Thurs–Sun) and DJs, and a full menu of snacks and hot meals including lunchtime specials. Beer 5.50Lt; cover charge 3Lt.
Cozy Dominikonū 10. Indeed a cozy, chilled-out cellar bar; extensive alcohol menu and a bargain 2-course business lunch (12Lt).
The PUB Dominikonū 9. British bar with dark, bookish interior and covered courtyard. Frequent live music, big-screen sport and an extensive food menu. Mains 15–20Lt
Woo Vilniaus 22. Chic urban-style cellar with an Asian theme; DJs play a smooth grooves/alternative set.

Clubs

Gravity Jasinskio 16. Ultra-cool joint offering a mixture of commercial dance and lesser-known music in a former Soviet bomb shelter. Attracts the best big-star DJs. Fri & Sat 10pm–5am.
Intro Maironio 3. Minimally decorated warehouse-style club with a wide-ranging programme of cutting-edge DJ nights. Young crowd (late teens to early 20s). Mon–Thurs, Sun noon–2am; Fri & Sat noon–4am.
L'Amour Vokiečiū 2. Large dance floor, purple and pink lighting, thumping sound system; polished, chic, and popular with hip youth. No cover charge, but drinks are pricey (15Lt).
Metelica Goštauto 12. Trendy place catering to a younger, often Russian crowd. Pop during the week and techno on Sat. Thurs–Sat 10pm–4am.
Milk Bar Pylimo 21. With a range of milky-cocktails, white interior, milk bottle decorations and non-mainstream music, this place attracts an arty crowd. Thurs 9pm–3am, Fri & Sat 10pm–6am.
Neo Men's Factory Ševčenkos 16. Flamboyantly decorated gay bar/club twenty minutes' walk west of the Old Town. Thurs 10pm–4am, Fri & Sat 10pm–7am.

Entertainment

Cinemas

Forum Cinemas Akropolis Ozo 25 Ⓦwww.forumcinemas.lt. Modern, multi-screen cinemas in Vinius's largest shopping mall, showing the latest blockbusters in original language, with subtitles. 15Lt
Skalvija Goštauto 2/15 Ⓦwww.skalvija.lt. Foreign films in this central place by the river.

Live music

Džiazo Klubas (Jazz Club) Vilniaus 22. Brick-lined cellar bar with decent jazz and blues bands at weekends. Also does food. Noon–2am.
Opera & Ballet Theatre Vienuolio 1 ⓣ5/262 0727, ⓦwww.opera.lt. Stunning building featuring well-attended performances by local opera and ballet companies.
Siemens Arena Ozo 14 ⓣ5/1653 Top venue for sports and concerts featuring international stars.
Vilnius Congress Concert Hall Vilniaus 6/14 ⓣ5/261 8828, ⓦwww.lvso.lt. Chamber music, symphonic orchestra performances and ballet.

Shopping

Akropolis Ozo 25. Large shopping complex, featuring an indoor ice rink and the Vichy Aqua Park with water slides and a wave pool (69Lt).
Amber Aušros Vartū 9 ⓦwww.ambergift.lt. An extensive array of amber jewellery and handicrafts.
Linen and Amber Studio Stikliū 3, ⓦwww.lgstudija.lt. Excellent spot for linen and amber goods; very helpful English-speaking staff.
Lino kopos Krokuvos 6, ⓦwww.linokopos.lt. Linen creations by cutting-edge designer Giedrius Šarkauskas. Closed Sun.

Directory

Embassies and consulates Australia, Vilniaus 23 ⓣ5/212 3369; Canada, Jogailos 4 ⓣ5/249 0950; Ireland, Gedimino 1 ⓣ5/262 9460; UK, Antakalnio 2 ⓣ5/246 2900; US, Akmenū 6 ⓣ5/266 5500.
Exchange Parex, outside the station at Geležinkelio 6 (24hr).
Hospital Vilnius University Emergency Hospital, Šiltnamiū 29 ⓣ5/216 9140.
Internet access Bazē, Gedimino 50 (entrance round the corner on Rotundo); Collegium, Pilies 22; Netcafe, Antakalnio 36.
Left luggage Train station: 24hr luggage storage in the basement. Bus station: baggage room open 5:30am–9:45pm.
Pharmacy Gedimino Vaistinē, Gedimino 27 (24hr); only vital essentials available at night.
Police Jogailos 3 ⓣ5/261 6208.
Post office Gedimino prospektas 7 (Mon–Fri 7am–9pm, Sat 9am–4pm).

Moving on

Train Kaunas (16 daily; 1hr 15min–2hr); Klaipēda (3 daily; 5hr); Šeštokai (1 daily; 3hr 30min); Warsaw (3 weekly; 10hr).
Bus Kaunas (every 20–30min; 1hr 30min–2hr); Klaipēda (14 daily; 4hr); Palanga (12 daily, 5hr); Nida (2 daily; 5hr); Rīga (9 daily; 5hr–5hr 30min); Tallinn (2 daily; 11hr 40min); Warsaw (3 daily; 12hr).

PANERIAI

PANERIAI, the site where the Nazis and their Lithuanian accomplices murdered one hundred thousand people during World War II, lies within Vilnius city limits in a **forest** at the edge of a suburb, 10km southwest of the centre. Seventy thousand of those killed at Paneriai were Jews from Vilnius, who were systematically exterminated from the time the Germans arrived in June 1941 until they were driven out by the Soviet army in 1944. To get there, take a **Kaunas-bound train** from Vilnius station (1.30Lt, over twenty daily) and alight at Paneriai (one stop). From the station platform descend onto **Agrastū gatvē**, turn right and follow the road alongside the tracks into the woods for about a kilometre. The entrance to the site is marked by the **Paneriai Memorial** – two stone slabs with Russian and Lithuanian inscriptions commemorating the murdered "Soviet citizens", flanking a central slab with an inscription in Hebrew commemorating "seventy thousand Jewish men, women and children". From the memorial a path leads to the small **Paneriai Museum**, Agrastū 15 (Mon–Wed, 9am–7pm; Sat 9am–5pm; call to check that it's open; ⓣ5/260 2001; donations). Paths lead to the pits in the woods where the Nazis burnt the bodies of their victims and to another eight-metre pit where the bones of the dead were crushed.

TRAKAI

5km west of Vilnius, the little town of **TRAKAI** stretches north along Vytauto gatvē, a mix of concrete Soviet-style buildings merging with the wooden cottages of the Karaim, giving way to medieval beauty across the water. The former capital of the Grand Duchy of Lithuania, Trakai was founded during the fourteenth century and, standing on a peninsula jutting out between two lakes, it's the site of two medieval castles.

What to see and do

To reach the remains of the **Peninsula Castle**, follow Vytauto gatvē from the train and bus stations and turn right down Kēstučio gatvē. Skirting the ruins along the lakeside path, you will see the spectacular **Island Castle** (Salos pilis), one of Lithuania's most famous monuments, reachable by two wooden drawbridges and preceded by rowing-boat rentals (10Lt) and souvenir stalls. Built around 1400AD by Grand Duke Vytautas, under whom Lithuania reached the pinnacle of its power during the fifteenth century, the castle fell into ruin from the seventeenth century until a 1960s restoration returned it to its former glory; (May–Sept 10am–7pm; Oct–April 10am–6pm; 10Lt).

Trakai is home to two hundred Karaim, Lithuania's smallest ethnic minority – a Judaic sect whose ancestors were brought here from the Crimea by Grand Duke Vytautas to serve him as bodyguards. Witness their cultural contribution to Trakai at the **Karaim Ethnographic Exhibition** (22 Karaimū gatvē; Wed–Sun 10am–6pm; 4Lt, half-price with Island castle ticket); or head to the Kenessa, the Karaim prayer house.

You can sample *kibinas* (3.50–6Lt), Trakai's culinary speciality, a mincemeat pasty served up at **cafés** such as *Kibininē*, Karaimū 65, and *Kybynlar*, Karaimū 29. To get to Trakai, take a bus from Vilnius's main bus station (1 hourly, 3Lt) or a train (8 daily; 2.50Lt).

TREAT YOURSELF

Apvalaus Stalo Klubas
Karaimū 53a. This stylish and friendly restaurant offers gourmet cuisine in a picturesque lakeside setting. Sheep's testicles and grilled barbary duck (48Lt) are truly excellent.

The rest of Lithuania

Lithuania is predominantly rural – a gently undulating, densely forested landscape scattered with lakes, and fields dotted with ambling storks in the summer. The major city of **Kaunas**, west of the capital, rivals Vilnius in terms of its historical importance. Further west, the main highlights of the coast are the **Curonian Spit**, whose dramatic dunescapes are reachable by ferry and bus from **Klaipēda**, and **Palanga**, Lithuania's party town where everyone flocks in the summer for a hedonistic good time.

KAUNAS

KAUNAS, 80km west of Vilnius and easily reached by bus or rail, is Lithuania's second city, seen by many Lithuanians as the true heart of their country. It served as provisional **capital** during the interwar period when Vilnius was occupied by Poland, and remains a major commercial and industrial centre.

What to see and do

The most picturesque part of Kaunas is the **Old Town** (Senamiestis), centred around **Town Hall Square** (Rotusēs aikstē), on a spur of land between the Neris and Nemunas rivers. The square is lined with fifteenth- and sixteenth-century merchants' houses in pastel stucco shades, but the overpowering feature is the magnificent **Town Hall**, its

HILL OF CROSSES

Up on a hill, 10km north of the town of Šiauliai, lies the **Mecca of Lithuania**, an ever-growing, poignant collection of over 400,000 crosses and traditional Lithuanian *kolpystulpis* (wooden sculptures of a figure with a little roof). The sight of so many tokens of faith swaying and rattling gently in the wind is truly awe-inspiring and must be seen up close to be fully appreciated. There are many myths surrounding the Hill's origin, but it is commonly thought to have been built to commemorate warriors killed in a great battle. The first crosses appeared in the fourteenth century, being symbolic of both suffering and hope. In pagan times, they were put up as offerings to the gods and sacred fires are believed to have been lit here; in the Soviet era, they were planted by grieving families to commemorate killed and deported loved ones and kept multiplying in spite of repeated bulldozing of the hill by the authorities. Today, crosses have been planted to commemorate the victims of the Twin Towers and other terrorist attacks, to express wishes for world peace or simply to give thanks for a happy event in a person's life. Each cross has a unique story behind it and, for many Lithuanians, the Hill has come to embody the spirit of their country.

To get here, take a train from Vilnius to Šiauliai (5–8 daily; 2hr 45min–3hr 30min) and then take a Riga-bound bus (8 daily; 15min) to the Domantai stop, walking the remaining 2km.

tiered Baroque facade rising to a graceful 53-metre tower.

The Cathedral and castle

Occupying the northeastern shoulder of the square, the red-brick tower of Kaunas' austere **Cathedral** stands at the western end of Vilniaus gatvē. Dating back to the reign of Vytautas the Great, the cathedral was much added to in subsequent centuries. After the plain exterior, the lavish gilt and marble interior comes as a surprise; there are nine altars, though the large, statue-adorned Baroque high altar (1775) steals the limelight. Predating the Cathedral by several centuries is **Kaunas Castle**, whose scant remains survive just northwest of the square. Little more than a restored tower and a couple of sections of wall are left, with temporary art exhibitions inside (5Lt), but in its day the fortification was a major obstacle to the Teutonic Knights.

The New Town

The main thoroughfare of Kaunas' **New Town** is **Laisvēs alēja** (Freedom Avenue), a broad pedestrianized shopping street running east from the Old Town. At the junction with L. Sapiegos the street is enlivened by a bronze statue of **Vytautas the Great**, which faces the **City Garden** where a contemporary memorial composed of horizontal metal shards commemorates the 19-year-old student **Romas Kalanta,** who immolated himself in protest against Soviet rule on May 14, 1972 and whose death sparked anti-Soviet rioting. Towards the eastern end of Laisvēs alēja, the silver-domed **Church of St Michael the Archangel** looms over **Independence Square** (Nepriklausomybēs aikstē). The striking modern building in the northeast corner, with the naked **"Man"** statue in front, is one of the best art galleries in the country, the **Mykolas Zilinskas Art Museum** (Tues–Sun 11am–5pm; closed last Tues of every month; 5Lt), housing a fine collection of Egyptian artefacts, Chinese porcelain and Lithuania's only Rubens.

Unity Square

Kaunas celebrates its role in sustaining Lithuanian national identity on **Unity Square** (Vienybēs aikstē), at the junction of S. Daukanto and K. Donelaičio, a block north of Laisvēs.

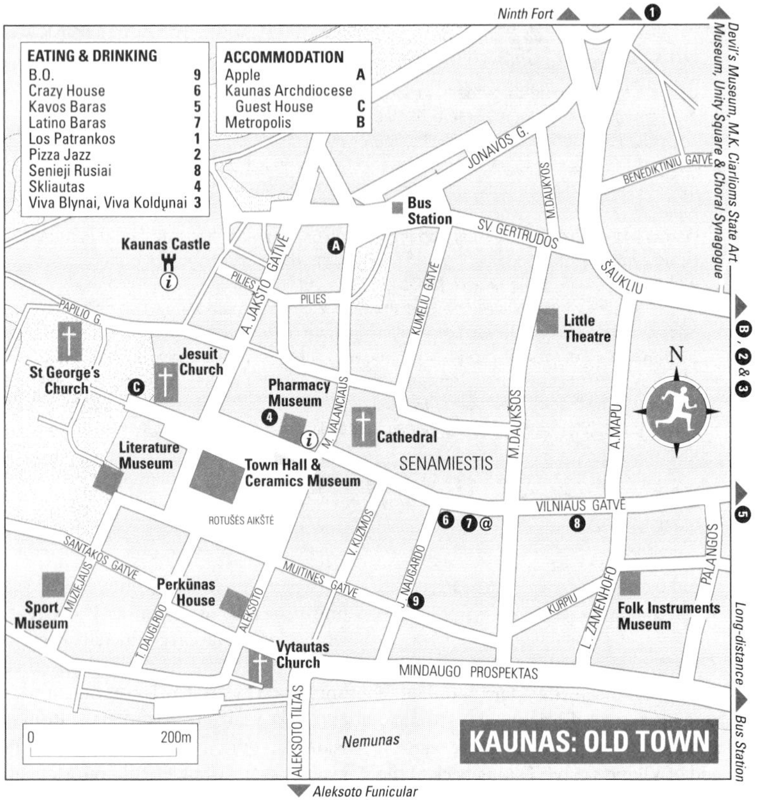

Here a **monument** depicting liberty as a female figure faces an eternal flame flanked by traditional wooden crosses and busts of prominent nineteenth-century Lithuanians.

The museums

Just north of Unity square, Kaunas has two unique art collections. The **A. Zmuidzinavičius Art Museum**, or the **Devil's Museum**, Putvinskio 64 (Tues–Sun 11am–5pm; 5Lt), houses a large and entertaining collection of devil and witch figures put together by the artist Antanas Zmuidzinavičius and donated from around the world. Though most of the images are comic, there's a sinister representation of Hitler and Stalin as devils dancing on a Lithuania composed of skulls. Diagonally opposite, at Putvinskio 55, the dreamy, symbolist paintings of Mikalojus Čiurlionis, Lithuania's cultural hero, are on display in the vast **M. K. Čiurlionis State Art Museum** (same times; 5Lt), along with excellent temporary exhibitions. **Tadas Ivanauskas Zoological Museum**, Laisves 106 (Tues–Sun 11am–7pm; 5Lt), displays every imaginable animal, bird, insect and sea creature stuffed, pinned or pickled.

Jewish Kaunas

Kaunas has experienced its share of historical **anti-Jewish violence**, both during local pogroms and then under the Nazis. During World War II, the city's large Jewish population was all but wiped out; all that remains is the city's sole surviving **synagogue** at Oželkienės 17 in the New Town, which sports a wonderful sky-blue interior (daily services 5:45–6:30pm; Sat 10am–noon) and a **memorial** to the 1,700 children who perished at the **Ninth Fort**. To get there, take any westbound inter-city bus from Kaunas bus station (every 10–30min) and get off at the IX Fortas stop. **Ninth Fort Museum**, Žemaičiū plentas 73 (Mon & Wed–Sun 10am–6pm; 4Lt) is housed in the tsarist-era fortress where the Jews were kept by Nazis while awaiting execution in the killing field beyond; exhibits cover extermination of Jews and deportation of Lithuanians by the Soviets. A massive jagged stone memorial crowns the site. The small and austere former Japanese consulate (Vaižganto 30, 10am–5pm; Sat, Sun 11am–4pm; 3Lt) is now a museum to **Chiune Sugihara**, the consul who saved thousands of Jewish lives during the war by handing out Japanese visas.

Arrival and information

Train and bus Kaunas' train and bus stations are at the southeastern end of the centre, a 15min walk from Laisvės alėja; a 35min walk (or short ride on trolleybus #1, #3, #5 or #7) to the Old Town.
Tourist office Laisvės 36 (Sept–May Mon–Thurs 9am–6pm, Fri 9am–5pm; June–Aug same times plus Sat–Sun 9am–6pm; ⓣ37/323 436, ⓦwww.kaunastic.lt). Provides English-language leaflets, free maps and copies of *Kaunas in Your Pocket* (ⓦwww.inyourpocket.com; 5Lt).
Internet Kavinė Internetas Vilniaus 24 (6Lt/hr).

Accommodation

For accommodation the ever-reliable **Litinterp**, Gedimino 28–7 (ⓣ37/228 718, ⓦwww.litinterp.lt), can sort you out with a room in the centre. ❸–❹
Apple Valančiaus 19 ⓣ37/321 404, ⓦwww.applehotel.lt. Simple but comfy en-suites in the Old Town. Psychedelic reception floor. ❺–❼
Kaunas Archdiocese Guest House Rotuses 21 ⓣ37/322 597, ⓦhttp://kaunas.lcn.lt/sveciunamai. Located centrally between two churches, this charming place has clean doubles and free Internet. ❷–❹
Metropolis just off Laisvės alėja at Daukanto 21 ⓣ37/205 992, ⓦwww.takiojineris.com. Grand Soviet hotel in a great location with inexpensive rooms. A real bargain. ❸–❹

Eating

Cafes and snack bars

Kavos Baras Vilniaus 74. Cheerful prompt service. Good coffees 3–8Lt; tasty breakfast omelettes 8Lt.
Viva Blynai, Viva Koldūnai Laisvės 53. A snazzy self-service buffet specializing in pancakes and *koldūnai* (Lithuanian ravioli). Mains 7–12Lt.

Restaurants

Berneliū Uzeiga Valančiaus 9. Dine on huge portions of meaty Lithuanian staples in an attractive rustic interior. Mains 15–20Lt.
Pizza Jazz Laisvės alėja 68. Delicious thin-crust pizzas to be had here. Medium pizza 15Lt.
Senieji Rusiai Vilniaus 34. Classy subterranean restaurant with inexpensive meat and fish dishes. Mains 16–25Lt.

Drinking and nightlife

Bars

B.O. Muitinės 9. This casual and unpretentious bar is one of the best places to hook up with a young, arty crowd. Closes 3am Fri & Sat.
Crazy House Vilniaus 16. The most entertaining bar in Kaunas, with moving tables, nets dropping from the ceiling, good food and cheap beer (5Lt).
The Skliautas Rotusės 26. Somewhat shabby but friendly bar offering inexpensive drinks and good-value meals. Mains 10–15Lt.

Clubs

Latino Baras Vilniaus 22. Small and bustling, with consistently good Latin music, this club is a great place to mingle and show off your dance moves. Dancing lessons available. Fri & Sat 8pm–4am.
Los Patrankos Savanoriū 124 ⓦwww.lospatrankos.lt. Very popular with students and playing a varied mix of music most nights. Good unpretentious fun. Tues–Thurs 9pm–4am; Fri & Sat 9pm–6am; Sun 1–5pm.

Moving on

Train Klaipėda (2 daily; 3hr 30min); Vilnius (12 daily; 1hr 15min–2hr)
Bus Klaipėda (6 daily; 3hr); Rīga (2 daily; 4hr 30min); Vilnius (every 20–30min; 1hr 30min–2hr); Nida (2 daily; 4hr 30min); Palanga (12 daily; 3hr 45min).

KLAIPĒDA

KLAIPĒDA, Lithuania's third largest city and most important port, lies on the **Baltic coast**, 275km northwest of Vilnius. Though it has a handful of sights, the city is of more interest as a staging post en route to the **Curonian Spit**, or the party town of **Palanga**.

The **tourist office** in Old Town at Turgaus 7 (July–Aug Mon–Fri 9am–7pm, Sat & Sun 10am–4pm; Sept–June Mon–Fri 9am–6pm; ⓣ46/412 186, ⓔtic@one.lt) has cheap internet (2Lt/hour) and stocks *Klaipeda in Your Pocket* (5Lt), a good source of listings information. From Turgaus turn right into Teatro gatvē and then left before the riverside park. The **ferry terminal** lies on the opposite side of Pilies gatvē.

There are several good accommodation options in town. Try *Klaipeda Old Town Hostel*, Butkū Juzēs 7–4 (ⓣ8/685/33104, ⓦwww.lithuanianhostels.org, ⓔguestplace@yahoo.com; ❶), a basic but friendly hostel right next to the bus station. It is a fifteen-minute walk west along S. Daukanto gatvē from the bus or train station to the *Litinterp guest house* at Puodziū 17 (Mon–Fri 8.30am–5.30pm, Sat 9.30am–3pm; ⓣ8/656/18817, ⓦwww.litinterp.lt; ❸–❹) with clean rooms; it can also provide central private rooms (❷).

Good **places to eat** include: *Čili Kaimas*, Manto 17, where you can feast on *cepelinai*, potato pancakes and more in a rustic-themed interior; and *Ararat*, an outstanding Armenian establishment on Liepū 48a, with tender, delicately spiced grilled lamb (25Lt). Head south along Manto gatvē until it becomes Tiltū and turn right.

Moving on

Train Kaunas (2 daily; 3hr 30min); Vilnius (2 daily; 5hr).
Bus Kaunas (13 daily; 3hr); Nida (direct: 2 daily; with transfer in Smiltynē: 8 daily; 50min); Rīga (2 daily; 5hr); Vilnius (13–15 daily; 5hr); Liepaja (3 daily; 2hr 30min); Palanga (19 daily; 45min).
Ferry Smiltynē (every 30 min, 5am–3am; 15min).

PALANGA

25km north of Klaipeda, **PALANGA** is Lithuania's top seaside resort – party central in the summer. From June until the end of August, the non-stop live music and amusement park rides, plus a 10km stretch of beach draw, revellers from all over Lithuania and beyond.

What to see and do

Palanga's biggest attraction is its white sandy **beach**; throughout the summer months it hosts a number of outdoor music events, which tend to last until sunrise. The wooden **pier**, jutting into the sea at the end of Basanavičiaus gatvē, is where families and couples gather to watch the sunset (around 10pm in July), while vendors ply their wares of beer, hotdogs and popcorn up and down its length.

From the beach, head east along pedestrian **Basanavičiaus** with the rest of the human tide past the street musicians, countless eateries, arcade games, amusement park rides and amber stalls. Get fired out of a bungee catapult (45Lt); chill on the pier at sunset; or dance all night at one of the beachside clubs. Music venues are also located on Vytauto gatvē, the main street bisecting Palanga, and on S. Darius ir S. Girēno gatvē, running alongside the Botanical Garden.

If you're interested in cultural attractions, the lush **Botanical Garden** (Botanikos Sodas) houses a fascinating **Amber Museum** (Tues–Sat 10am–8pm, Sun 10am–7pm; 5Lt) with around twenty-five thousand pieces of 'Baltic Gold', many with insects and plants trapped inside. The **Anatanas Mončys House Museum** at S. Daukanto 16 (Tues noon–5pm, Wed–Sun 2–9pm, ⓦwww.muziejal.lt; 3Lt) displays unique sculptures, collages and masks made by the Lithuanian sculptor. Unlike other museums, this one allows visitors to handle all the exhibits due to the sculptor's own obsession with textures and subsequent clause in his will specifying that others can touch his work.

Arrival and information

Arrival The bus station on Kretingos gatvė is a couple of blocks away from Basanavičiaus gatvė, the main tourist street.
Tourist office Kretingos 1 ⓣ460/48811, ⓦwww.palangatic.lt. Open June–Aug Mon–Fri 9am–6pm, Sat & Sun 9am–3pm. Multilingual and helpful staff can book accommodation and provide detailed information both on live music events in Palanga and outdoor pursuits in and around town.

Accommodation

Due to the town's immense summertime popularity, advance bookings are essential. The cheapest option is to haggle with the locals holding up '*Nuomojami kamberiai*' (rooms for rent) signs as the bus enters Palanga, although the quality may vary considerably. Alternatively, the tourist office can assist with finding accommodation.

Hotels & guesthouses

Alanga Nėries gatvė 14 ⓣ460/49215, ⓦwww.alanga.lt. This spotlessly clean hotel offers spacious rooms with balconies, wi-fi and laundry service. ❼
Ema Jurates gatvė 32 ⓣ460/48608, ⓦwww.ema.lt. This brightly painted guesthouse with a cactus out front has cosy modern doubles and a creperie on-site. ❹
Meguva Valanciaus gatvė 1 ⓣ460/48839. Clean basic doubles with shared facilities in this red Soviet block behind the church. ❺

Eating, drinking and nightlife

1925 Basanavičiaus 4. Reliably good crepes and meat dishes in a homey setting. Mains 20Lt.
Čili Basanavičiaus 45. The ubiquitous and ever-popular pizza chain by the pier. Medium pizza 25Lt. Closes 4am Fri & Sat.
Honolulu Night Club Nėries 39. Two-tiered entertainment: lively disco with kitschy décor upstairs (Mon–Thurs & Sun 6pm–3am; Fri & Sat 8pm–6am); and packed nightclub downstairs (daily 10pm–6am).
Kupeta Dariaus ir Girėno 13. Large, raucous and a bit peculiar; order a Kupeta cocktail to make the waiter dance. Lithuanian bands nightly. 9am–midnight.
Laukinių Vakarų Salūnas Basanavičiaus 24a. Packed with a young crowd and offering nightly karaoke, wet t-shirt competitions and the occasional live band. Daily 8pm–7am.
Žuvinė Basanavičiaus 37ª. Fish restaurant with a library feel to it; the generous portions cannot be faulted. Mains 20Lt.

Moving on

Bus Klaipėda (7 daily; 45 min; extra minibuses 8–9pm); Vilnius (12 daily; 7hr).

NERINGA: THE CURONIAN SPIT

NERINGA, or the **Kursiū Nerija,** is the Lithuanian section of the Curonian Spit, a 97-kilometre sliver of land characterized by vast sand dunes and pine forests. Some of the area can be seen as a day-trip from Klaipėda, though it really warrants a stay of several days to soak up the unique atmosphere. **Ferries** from the quayside towards the end of Žvejū gatvė in Klaipėda (1.50Lt return) sail to **Smiltynė** on the northern tip of the spit. From the landing stage, frequent **minibuses** (7.50Lt) run south towards more scenic parts of the spit, stopping at the villages of **Juodkrantė, Pervalka** and **Preila,** and terminating at Nida, 35km south.

Nida

NIDA is the most famous village on the spit – a small fishing community boasting several streets of attractive blue- and brown-painted wooden houses; although in the summertime there are plenty of visitors, it never feels crowded. There are several good **eateries** on Nagliū gatvė and Lotmiskio gatvė, as well as along the waterfront. From the end of Nagliū, a shore path runs to a flight of wooden steps leading up to the top of the **Parnidis dune** south of the village. From the summit you can gaze out across a Saharan sandscape stretching to Russia's **Kaliningrad** province. Retrace the trail along the waterfront to see elaborate **weathervanes** with unique designs – each village has its own. Stop

CYCLING THE SPIT

The best way to explore the Curonian Spit is by **cycling** (bike rental 8Lt/hour, 25Lt/day) along well-marked biking trails that meander through the pine forest. Early morning is a good time to catch sight of elk, wild boar and roe-deer, particularly near **Juodkrantė**, 30km away. Juodkrantė is also home to **Witches' Hill** (Raganos kalnas), a truly entertaining wooden sculpture trail in the woods with wonderfully macabre statues of devils, witches and folk legend heroes – try sliding down the devil's giant tongue. *Vila Flora*, along the waterfront, serves simple yet well-cooked offerings of fresh fish (29Lt) and pancakes (10Lt).

Heading back towards Nida, stop off at the side of the main road to catch a glimpse of the huge **heron and cormorant colony** in the trees. Take a dip in the bracing sea and graze on wild strawberries, blueberries and raspberries in the forest (check samples at the berry market on Lotmiškio gatvė first). But don't forget your mosquito repellent. When passing through **Preila**, look for the *rūkyta žuvis* signs and stop at a traditional smokery for some delicious smoked fish.

by **Nida's History Museum** (Pamario 53; daily 10am–6pm; 2Lt), which traces the village's heritage through photos of crow-eating fishermen and fishing paraphernalia. Also along Pamario is the cemetery with traditional wooden **krikštas** – carved wooden boards instead of headstones – placed upright at the foot of the resting body. Nida's long, luxuriant **beach** stretches along the opposite, western side of the spit, a 30min walk through the forest from the village.

Arrival and information

Bus Buses from the mainland and from Smiltynė stop on Nagliū 18e, Nida's main street. Everything in Nida is within walking distance.

Tourist office Taikos 4 (June–Aug Mon–Sat 10am–8pm; Sun 10am–3pm; Sept–May Mon–Fri 9am–1pm & 2–6pm, Sat 10am–3pm; ⓣ469/523 45, ⓦwww.visitneringa.com). The extremely helpful staff provides info on accommodation and events.

Accommodation

Nida has a few budget **guesthouses**, but as they tend to fill up in the summer, advance reservations are required. **Private rooms** (❷–❸) are available through the tourist office. Litinterp in Klaipėda can book rooms (❸–❹) in advance, for a slightly higher price; a minimum of three nights required.

Jūratė Pamario 3 ⓣ469/52300, ⓦwww.hotel-jurate.lt. Concrete block by the sea with surprisingly bright rooms and helpful staff. Doubles ❻

Kambariū nuoma (rooms to rent) Lotmiškio 7 ⓣ469/52256, ⓦwww.nida.w3.lt, ⓔciciunas@takas.lt. Run by an effusive English-speaking couple, this friendly guesthouse has a pristine kitchen, airy rooms and is just one minute from the sea. ❹

Misko Namas Pamario 11 ⓣ469/52290, ⓦwww.miskonamas.com. Colourful house with private garden and a friendly hostess. Doubles ❸; apartments ❺

Nidos Kempingas 2km southwest of town at Taikos 45a (take Taikos gatvė out of town and follow the signs) ⓣ469/52045, ⓦwww.kempingas.lt. This campsite has clean kitchen and bathroom facilities, ample tent space and swanky self-catering apartments. Tents ❶; rooms ❼; 2- to 6-room apartments ❾

ACTIVITIES AROUND NIDA

Nida offers a wide variety of activities for outdoor enthusiasts and adrenaline junkies alike. Irklakojis (stall by the shore path; ⓣ618 81957, ⓦwww.irklakojis.lt), arranges hiking, biking or canoeing trips in the area. Alternatively, try the exhilarating blokarting (windsurfing on land) on the disused airstrip (60Lt/hour), roll around on a Segway, or go sailing on the lagoon (15Lt/hour; ⓣ6887 81179, ⓦwww.monte.ten.lt).

Eating and drinking

Čili Pica Nagliū 16. Perpetually popular pizza spot by the harbour with large outdoor terrace (June–Aug 9am–3am). Medium pizza 20Lt.

Nidos Prieplauka Nagliū 16. This popular, off-beat bar above Čili Pica has billiards tables, virtual bowling, and tattooed plastic limbs on the walls. Beer 4–6Lt.

Seklyčia Lotmiškio 1. Offers traditional dishes such as *cepelinai* as well as wonderfully fresh fish dishes (40Lt).

Sena Sodyba Nagluī 6. Homely informal place, serving inexpensive Lithuanian dishes. Excellent *Koldunaī* (7Lt) and pancakes (5Lt).

Moving on

Bus From Nida buses go to Klaipēda via Smiltynē(13 daily; 1hr 30min; all stop at Juodkrantē; 3 daily stop at Preila and Pervalka); Vilnius (1 daily; 7hr); Kaunas (2 daily; 4hr 30min); Kaliningrad (2 daily; 1hr 30min).

Morocco

HIGHLIGHTS

CHEFCHAOUEN: beautiful and very friendly little town in the Rif mountains, where the houses look like they're made of blue meringue

MEDINA, FES: an incredible labyrinth of alleys, sights and smells in the world's best-preserved medieval city

DJEMAA EL FNA, MARRAKESH: a spontaneous live circus in a large square in the middle of town, featuring everything from snake charmers to tooth pullers

ESSAOUIRA: arty, laid-back seaside and surfing resort where Jimi Hendrix once played impromptu concerts on the beach

MERZOUGA, SAHARA: camel trek to a berber tent and spend a night under the stars in the world's most famous desert.

ROUGH COSTS

DAILY BUDGET basic €20/ occasional treat €30

FOOD Tagine €2.50

DRINK Pot of mint tea €0.50

HOSTEL/BUDGET HOTEL €5–13

TRAVEL Marrakesh–Casablanca (4hr): €8

FACT FILE

POPULATION 33.7 million

AREA 446,550 sq km

LANGUAGES Arabic, Berber dialects, French

CURRENCY Dirham (dh)

CAPITAL Rabat (population 1.7million)

INTERNATIONAL PHONE CODE ⓣ212

Basics

Just an hour's ferry ride from Spain, Morocco seems very far from Europe, with a deeply traditional Islamic culture. Throughout the country, despite its 44 years of French and Spanish colonial rule, a more distant past constantly makes its presence felt. Travel here is, if not always easy, an intense and rewarding experience.

Berbers, the indigenous population, make up over half of Morocco's population; only around ten percent of Moroccans claim to be "pure" **Arabs**. More telling is the legacy of the **colonial** period: until independence in 1956, the country was divided into Spanish and French zones, the latter building **Villes Nouvelles** (new towns) alongside the long-standing **Medinas** (old towns) in all the country's main cities.

Most visitors' introduction to Morocco is **Tangier** in the north, still shaped by its heyday of "international" port status in the 1950s. To its south, in the Rif mountains, the town of **Chefchaouen** is a small-scale and enjoyably laid-back place, while inland lies the enthralling city of **Fes**, the greatest of the four imperial capitals (the others are Meknes, Rabat and Marrakesh). The sprawl of **Meknes**, with its ancient walls, makes an easy day-trip from Fes.

The power axis of the nation lies on the coast in **Rabat** and **Casablanca**. "Casa" looks a lot like Marseille, while the elegant, orderly capital, Rabat, houses some gems of Moroccan architecture. Further south, **Marrakesh** is an enduring fantasy that won't disappoint. The country's loveliest resort, **Essaouira**, a charming walled seaside town, lies within easy reach of Marrakesh and Casablanca.

CHRONOLOGY

42 AD Romans take control of the coastal regions of Morocco.

600s Arabs conquer Moroccan lands, introducing Islam.

1062 Marrakech is built by the Berber dynasty of Almoravids.

1195 Almoravids replaced by the Almohads, who conquer Southern Spain.

1269 The capital is moved to Fes.

1415 The Portugese capture the Moroccan port of Ceuta.

1492 Influx of Jews who have been expelled from Spain.

1860 Spanish wage war with Morocco, ultimately gaining land in Cueta.

1904 France and Spain divide various areas of influence in Morocco.

1912 Under the terms of the Treaty of Fes, Morocco becomes a French protectorate.

1943 Moroccan Independence Party, Istiqlal, is founded.

1956 Morocco declares independence from France.

1963 First general elections.

1975 Clashes as Morocco forcefully take back land in the Sahara from the Spanish.

2004 Earthquake along the Mediterranean coast kills over five hundred.

2006 Introduction of cheap flights to Marrakesh leads to a noticeable increase in tourism.

2007 Moroccan Government and Polisario Independence Movement remain unable to come to an agreement regarding the disputed land in the Western Sahara..

ARRIVAL

To reach Morocco from Europe you can either fly or take a ferry. The main **airports** are in Casablanca, Fes and Marrakesh, with the latter two being used for budget airlines from UK, Irish and European airports. Ryanair (Ⓦwww.ryanair.com) and easyJet (Ⓦwww.easyjet.com) both sell very cheap online tickets.

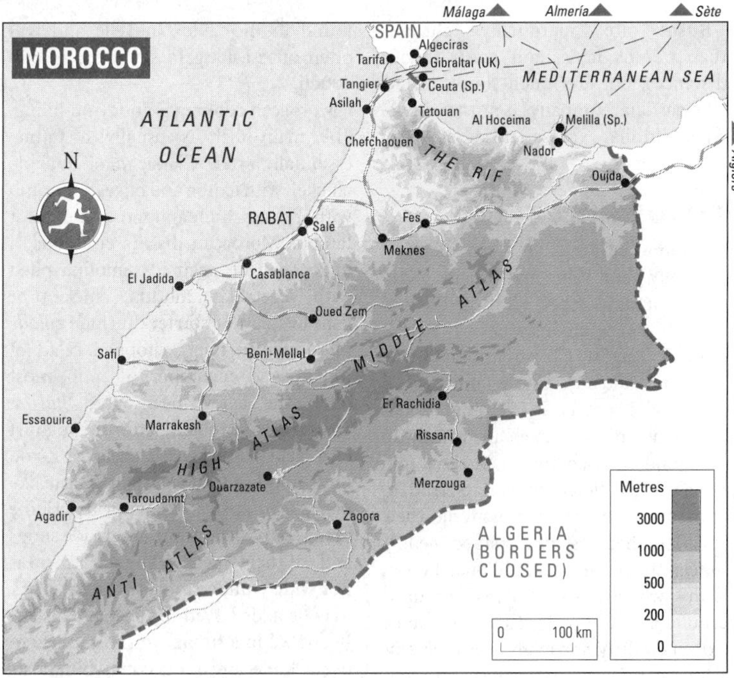

If you decide to take a **boat**, the ports of Ceuta and Tangier are both on the north coast of Morocco and can be reached from France (Sète), Italy (Genoa, 1 per week) and Spain (Algeciras, Tarifa, Malaga). From Ceuta you can catch buses on to Chefchaouen and Tangier. From Tangier you can catch trains and buses to all of the major cities in Morocco. Tickets can be booked online (Ⓦwww.comanav.co.uk, Ⓦwww.euroferrys.com, Ⓦwww.nautasferry.com) or at the ports themselves.

GETTING AROUND

The **train** network is limited, but for travel between the major cities, trains are the best option. Major stations have free timetables, printed by ONCF (Ⓦwww.oncf.org.ma), the national train company. Couchettes (90dh extra) are available on trains from Tangier to Marrakesh (9hr 30min), and are worth the money for extra comfort and security. Only direct trains are listed in this chapter; for connections, consult the ONF website. Any station ticket office will issue a table of direct and connecting services to any other station.

Collective **grands taxis** are usually big Peugeots or Mercedes, plying set routes for a set fare and are much quicker than buses, though the drivers can be reckless. Make clear you only want *une place* (one seat), otherwise drivers may assume you want to charter the whole car. Expect to wait until all six places in the taxi are taken, though you can pay for the extra places if you are in a hurry. Within towns **petits taxis** do short trips, carrying up to three people. They queue in central locations and at stations and can be hailed on streets when they're empty. Payment – usually no more than 15dh – relates to distance travelled.

Buses are marginally cheaper than grands taxis, and cover longer distances, but are much slower. CTM (the national company) is most reliable. An additional express service is run by Supratours.

ACCOMMODATION

Accommodation is inexpensive, generally good value and usually pretty easy to find, although it's more difficult in main cities and resorts in the peak seasons (August, Christmas and Aïd el Kebir in January). Cheap, unclassified hotels and *pensions* (charging about 80–150dh for a double) are mainly to be found in each town's Medina (old town), while hotels with stars tend to concentrate in the Ville Nouvelle (new town). At their best, **unclassified** Medina hotels are beautiful, traditional houses with whitewashed rooms grouped around a central patio. The worst can be extremely dirty, and many have problems with water. Few have en-suite bathrooms, though a *hammam* (public Turkish bath) is usually close at hand. **Classified** hotels' star-ratings are fairly self-explanatory and prices are reasonable. Except in Marrakesh, most hotels do not include breakfast in their room price. HI **hostels** (*auberges de jeunesse*), often bright, breezy and friendly, generally require you to be in by 10pm or 11pm and out by 10am daily. **Campsites** are usually well out of town and tend to charge around 15dh per person plus the same again for your tent.

FOOD AND DRINK

The best budget meals are found at local diners, where *tajines* or roast chicken with chips and salad are usually under 30dh. Even cheaper are sandwiches and *shwarmas*, which cost 10–15dh from street-side vendors, however be careful about ordering *kefta* (minced meat) if you have a weak stomach. Fancier restaurants, definitely worth an occasional splurge, are mostly to be found in the Ville Nouvelle and will often offer a bargain set menu at 60–100dh.

Moroccan cooking is good and filling. The main dish is usually a **tajine**, essentially a stew. Classic *tajines* include chicken with lemon and olives, and lamb with prunes and almonds. The most famous Moroccan dish is **couscous**, a huge bowl of steamed semolina piled with vegetables, mutton, chicken or fish. Restaurant **starters** include *salade marocaine*, a finely chopped salad of tomato and cucumber, or soup, most often the spicy, bean-based *harira*. **Dessert** will probably be fruit, yoghurt or a pastry. Breakfast is cheapest if you buy *msimmen, melaoui* (which taste like pancakes), *harsha* (a heavy gritty griddle bread) or pastries from street-side shops and eat them at cafes. **Vegetarianism** is not widely understood and meat stock may be added even to vegetable dishes. If **invited to a home**, you're unlikely to use a knife and fork; copy your hosts and eat only with your **right hand**.

Drink

The national drink is **thé à la menthe** – green tea with a large bunch of mint and a massive amount of sugar. Coffee (*café* in French; *qahwa* in Arabic) is best in French-style cafés. Moroccans tend to take their coffee with half milk and half coffee (*nus-nus*) in a glass. Many cafés and street stalls sell fresh-squeezed orange juice and **mineral water** is readily available. As an Islamic nation, Morocco gives alcohol a low profile, and it's generally impossible to buy any in the Medinas; however bars can always be found in the Ville Nouvelle. Moroccan **wines**, usually red, can be very drinkable, while the best-value **beer** is Flag Speciale. Most local **bars** are male domains; hotel bars, on the other hand, are more mixed and not much more expensive. The big supermarkets sell alcohol; ask a petit taxi to take you to the nearest Acima, or Marjane.

CULTURE AND ETIQUETTE

Morocco is a Muslim country, and in rural areas particularly, people can be quite **conservative** about dress and displays of affection. It's not the done thing to kiss and cuddle in public, nor even for couples to hold hands. **Dress** is more conservative in rural areas, though even in the cities you can feel uncomfortable in sleeveless tops, short shorts or skirts above the knee. The heat can be oppressive so long, light, loose clothing is best. A shawl allows women to cover up whilst wearing sleeveless tops.

Be sensitive when **taking photographs**, and always ask permission. In certain places, particularly the Djemaa el Fna in Marrakesh, people may demand money from you just for happening to be in a shot you have taken. Also note that it is illegal to photograph anything considered strategic, such as an airport or a police station.

When invited into people's homes, remove footwear before entering the reception rooms. If invited for a meal, take a gift: a box of sweets from a posh patisserie usually goes down well.

It is acceptable (and a good idea) to try bargaining at every opportunity. If you do it with a smile, you can often get surprising reductions.

SHOPPING

You can pick up bargains throughout Morocco, and you will kick yourself if you go home empty handed. However, getting a price you can brag about in the hostel requires a willingness to enter into the spirit of **haggling**. The first price you will be given will often be at least three and up to ten times more than you should pay. Though quality makes a difference, we've included rough prices for some popular goods you could reasonably fit into a backpack. Fixed-price shops in the ville nouvelle also give a good approximation of what you should be paying in the medina.

- Small kilms (coarse rugs) 150–500dh
- Leather bags (cheaper in Fes than Marrakesh) 150–300dh
- Leather baboush 80dh
- Silk scarves 50–100dh
- Jelaba (Traditional Moroccan dress) 80–150dh

SPORTS AND ACTIVITIES

Casablanca and Essaouira cater to **surfers**: the former has better waves while the latter is excellent for **windsurfing**. Tangier and Rabat have decent beaches but with less developed services. Mohammedia, a thirty-minute ride from both Rabat and Casablanca, is a highly recommended destination for avid surfers. Anywhere on the Atlantic coast you should beware of strong undertows.

The Moroccan mountain ranges offer great **hiking** opportunities. Good starting points include: Chefchaouen, in the Rif; Fes and Meknes near the Middle Atlas; and Marrakesh, two hours away from Mount Toubkal – the second highest mountain in Africa. Consult local tourist information offices or hotels for advice and details of the trails.

Horse riding is an expensive but increasingly popular way of seeing Morocco. The High Atlas offer stunning views and are manageable from Marrakesh. *La Roseraie Hotel*, 60 km from Marrakesh, is a popular option for hiring horses to venture into the mountainous countryside. Prices depend on your itinerary but it is not cheap (Ⓦwww.laroseraiehotel.com, Ⓣ024 43 91 28). Camel trekking in the Sahara is a cheaper option; details are given at the end of the chapter.

Football is Morocco's most popular sport. You will see it being played in every conceivable open space. If you start up a game on a beach it won't be long before you are joined by some Moroccans; equally you'll usually be welcome in pick-up games. All the major cities have teams and money is being poured into new stadiums. For fixtures see Ⓦwww.maroc.net/sports/ and for the locations of stadiums see Ⓦwww.maroc-football.com.

COMMUNICATIONS

Post offices (PTT) are open Mon–Thurs 8.30am–12.15pm & 2.30–6.30pm, Fri 8.30–11.30am & 3–6.30pm. Central post offices in large cities will be open longer hours, except in summer and Ramadan. You can also buy **stamps** at postcard shops and sometimes at tobacconists. Always post items at a PTT. International **phone calls** are best made with a phonecard (from post offices and some tobacconists). Alternatively, there are privately run *téléboutiques*, open late. You must dial all nine digits of Moroccan phone numbers. **Internet** access is available pretty much everywhere, and at low rates: 10dh/hr is typical.

EMERGENCIES

Street **robbery** is rare but not unknown, especially in Tangier and Casablanca. Hotels are generally secure for depositing money; campsites less so. There are two main types of **police** – grey-clad gendarmes, with authority outside city limits; and the navy-clad sûreté in towns. There's sometimes a brigade of "tourist police" too. Moroccan **pharmacists** are well trained and dispense a wide range of drugs. In most cities there is a night pharmacy, often at the town hall, and a rota of *pharmacies de garde* which stay open till late and at weekends. You can get a list of English-speaking **doctors** in major cities from consulates. Steer clear of **marijuana** (*kif*) and hashish – it's illegal, and buying it leaves you vulnerable to scams, as well as potentially large fines and prison sentences.

MOROCCO ON THE NET

Ⓦwww.tourisme-marocain.com Moroccan tourist board's website.
Ⓦwww.geocities.com/thetropics/4896/morocco.html A selection of information for visitors.
Ⓦwww.arab.net/morocco Arab.net's Morocco section has pages on history, culture and anything from people to pottery.
Ⓦwww.morocco.com Huge collection of links to sites about every aspect of Morocco.

EMERGENCY NUMBERS

Police – Sûreté Ⓣ19, Gendarmes Ⓣ177, Fire and ambulance Ⓣ15.

INFORMATION AND MAPS

There's a **tourist office** (Délégation du Tourisme) run by the Office National Marocain du Tourisme (**ONMT**) in every major city, and sometimes also a locally funded Syndicat d'Initiative. They stock a limited selection of leaflets and maps, and can put you in touch with official guides. Travel agencies tend to have a fuller range of brochures regarding local activities. There are scores of "**unofficial guides**", some of whom are genuine students, while others are out-and-out hustlers (though these have been clamped down on). If they do find you, be polite but firm. Note that it's illegal to harass tourists. Tourist offices are usually understocked and often can't give away maps; local bookshops and street-side kiosks are a better bet. The most functional are those in the *Rough Guide to Morocco*.

MONEY AND BANKS

The unit of currency is the **dirham** (dh), divided into 100 centimes; in markets, prices may well be in centimes rather than dirhams. There are coins of 10c, 20c, 50c, 1dh, 5dh and 10dh, and notes of 20dh, 50dh, 100dh and 200dh. You can get dirhams in Algeciras (Spain) and Gibraltar, and can usually change foreign notes on arrival at major sea- and airports. It can be difficult to change travellers' cheques anywhere but a bank. For **exchange** purposes, the most useful and efficient chain of banks is the **BMCE** (Banque Marocaine du Commerce Extérieur). Post offices will also change cash. **Travellers' cheques** incur a 10.70dh commission except at the state-run Bank al-Maghrib. Many banks give cash advances on credit cards, which can also be used in tourist

Moroccan Arabic

Moroccan Arabic is the country's official language, with three Berber dialects, but much of the country is bilingual in **French**. For some useful French words and phrases see p.373.

	Moroccan Arabic
Yes	Eyeh
No	La
Please	Afek/Minfadlik
Thank you	Shukran
Hello	Assalam aleikum
Goodbye	Bissalama
Excuse me	Issmahli
Where?	Fayn?
Good	Mezziyen
Bad	Mish Mezziyen
Near (here)	Krayb (min hina)
Far	Baeed
Cheap	Rkhis
Expensive	Ghalee
Open	Mahlul
Closed	Masdud
Today	El Yoom
Yesterday	Imbarih
Tomorrow	Ghedda
How much is....?	Shahal...?
What time is it?	Shahal fisa'a?
I (m) don't understand	Ana mish fahim
I (f) don't understand	Ana mish fahma
Do you (m) speak English?	Takellem ingleezi?
Do you (f) speak English?	Takelma ingleezi?
One	Wahad
Two	Jooj
Three	Tlata
Four	Arba'a
Five	Khamsa
Six	Sitta
Seven	Seba'a
Eight	Temeniya
Nine	Tisaoud
Ten	Ashra

STUDENT AND YOUTH DISCOUNTS

It is always worth pointing out that you are a student when you are bargaining. However, the informality of most transactions means that there are not many established student discounts. There are, however, a few exceptions. ONCF, the train network, has a card for young people that can be purchased for 99dh which gives you fifty percent reductions on sixteen trips. Student cards entitle you to cheaper entry at some museums and other sights, and a small discount on some ferry tickets. They're not worth going out of your way to get, but if you have one you might as well bring it along.

hotels (but not cheap unclassified ones) and the **ATMs** of major banks. Banking hours are: summer Mon–Fri 8am–2pm; winter Mon–Thurs 8.15–11.30am & 2.15–4.30pm, Fri 8.15–11.15am & 2.45–4.45pm. During the holy month of Ramadan, banks open Mon–Fri 9am–2pm. Morocco is inexpensive but poor, and **tips** can make a big difference; it's customary to tip café waiters a dirham or two. At the time of writing, €1 was equal to around 11dh, $1 to 8dh, and £1 to 16dh.

OPENING HOURS AND HOLIDAYS

Shops and stalls in the *souk* (bazaar) areas open roughly 9am–1pm and 3–6pm. Ville Nouvelle shops are also likely to close for lunch, and also once a week, usually Sunday. Islamic **religious holidays** are calculated on the lunar calendar and change each year. In 2008 they fall (approximately) as follows: Dec 20 is **Aïd el Kebir** (when Abraham offered to sacrifice his son for God); Jan 10 is the Muslim New Year; March 20 is **Mouloud** (the birthday of Muhammad); **Ramadan** (when all Muslims fast from sunrise to sunset) falls roughly Sept 1–30. Non-Muslims are not expected to observe Ramadan, but should be sensitive about not breaking the fast in public. The end of Ramadan is celebrated with **Aïd es Seghir** (aka Aïd el Fitr), a two-day holiday. **Secular holidays** are considered less important, with most public services (except banks and offices) operating normally even during the two biggest ones – the Feast of the Throne (July 30), and Independence Day (Nov 18).

Northern Morocco

The northern tip of Morocco contains enough on its own to justify the short ferry ride over from Spain: in three days or so you could check out the delightfully seedy city of **Tangier** and the picturesque, extremely laid-back little mountain town of **Chefchaouen** in the Rif mountains.

> **ARRIVING IN MOROCCO**
>
> From Algeciras (Spain) you can arrive in Morocco either at Tangier or Ceuta. Tangier is the better option as it allows you to connect to all the major transport links, and is itself worth a visit. Ceuta is a dull Spanish enclave with Fnideq, a small but charming Moroccan border town, 3km away. From here you'll have limited transport options.

TANGIER

For the first half of the twentieth century **TANGIER** (Tanja in Arabic; Tanger in French) was an "International City" with its own laws and administration, attracting notoriety through its flamboyant expat community. With independence in 1956, this special status was removed and the expat colony dwindled. Its mixed colonial history and proximity to Spain means that Spanish is a preferred second language. Today Tangier is a grimy but energetic port, mixing modern nightclubs and seedy Moroccan bars with some fine colonial architecture.

What to see and do

The **Grand Socco**, or Zoco Grande – once the main market square (and, since Independence, officially Place du 9 avril 1947) – offers the most straightforward approach to the **Medina**. The arch at the northwest corner opens onto Rue d'Italie, which leads up to the Kasbah. To the right, Rue es Siaghin leads to the atmospheric but seedy **Petit Socco**, or Zoco Chico, the Medina's principal landmark.

The Kasbah

To get to the Kasbah you can take a petit taxi from the Grand Socco or walk from the Petit Socco. Rue des Almohades (aka Rue des Chrétiens) and Rue Ben Raisouli lead to the lower gate. The **Kasbah** (citadel), walled off from the Medina on the highest rise of the coast, has been the palace and administrative quarter since Roman times. The main point of interest is the former Sultanate Palace, or **Dar el Makhzen** (Mon & Wed–Sun 9am–1pm & 3–6pm; 10dh), now converted into a museum, which gives you an excuse to look around, though the exhibits are rather sparse.

Beaches

Tangier's best **beach** is along the Route Malabata (east of the medina, 10–15dh petit taxi from Grand Socco). The beach is long, relatively clean and sandy; the water suffers a bit from being next to a port though it is safe enough for a swim. Unfortunately there are few amenities and no watersports on offer at Tangier's beaches. In late July / August there are vendors selling refreshments, but outside this period it is a good idea to bring enough water and food to last you the day as there are no nearby shops.

Caves of Hercules

Perhaps the area's most popular tourist attraction is the **Caves of Hercules** (Grotte d'Hercule), where the sea has eroded the cave entrance to form the shape of Africa. Grands taxis cost around 100dh from Grand Socco and the journey itself is worth it for the extraordinary views you have of

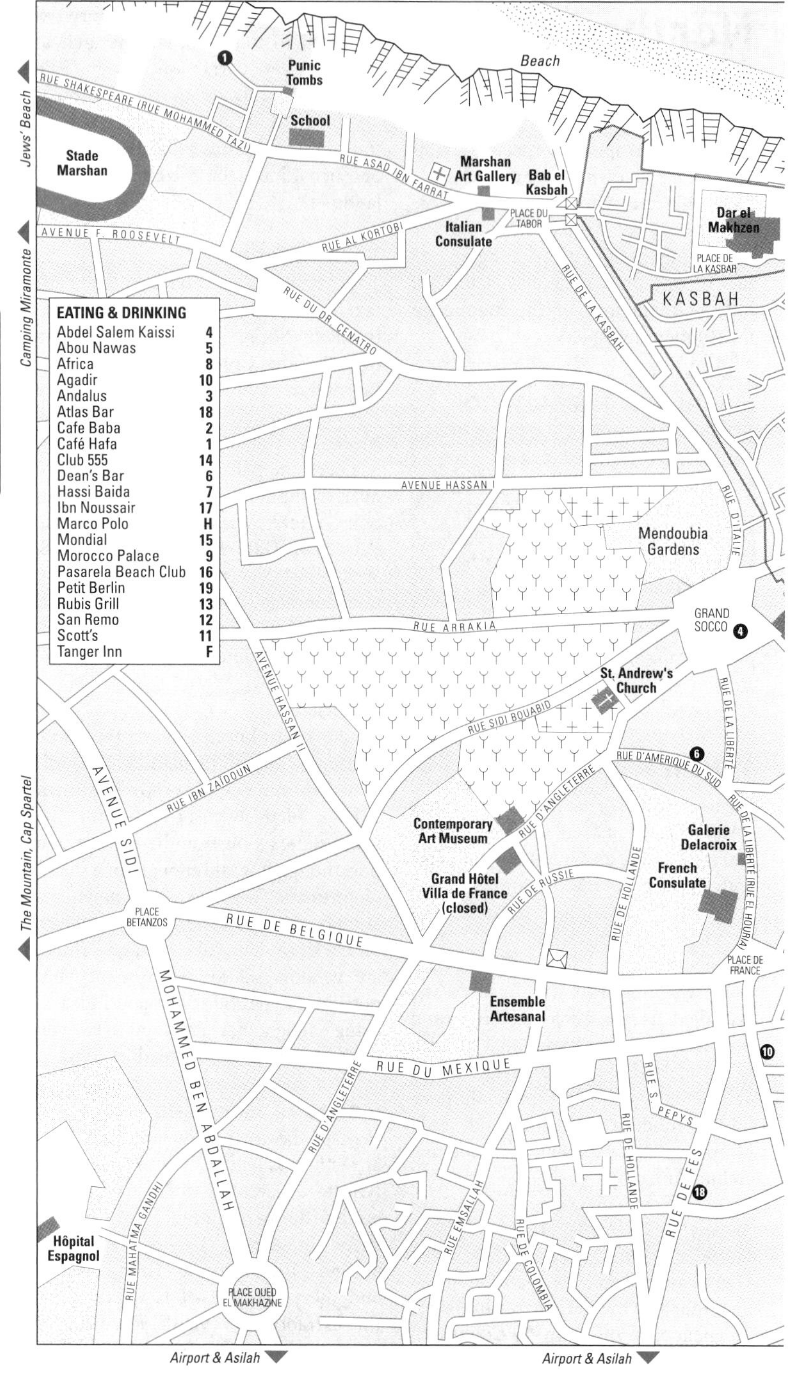
EATING & DRINKING
Abdel Salem Kaissi 4
Abou Nawas 5
Africa 8
Agadir 10
Andalus 3
Atlas Bar 18
Cafe Baba 2
Café Hafa 1
Club 555 14
Dean's Bar 6
Hassi Baida 7
Ibn Noussair 17
Marco Polo H
Mondial 15
Morocco Palace 9
Pasarela Beach Club 16
Petit Berlin 19
Rubis Grill 13
San Remo 12
Scott's 11
Tanger Inn F
Beach
Punic Tombs
School
Stade Marshan
Marshan Art Gallery
Bab el Kasbah
Italian Consulate
Place du Tabor
Dar el Makhzen
Place de la Kasbar
KASBAH
Rue Shakespeare (Rue Mohammed Tazi)
Rue Asad Ibn Farrat
Rue Al Kortobi
Avenue F. Roosevelt
Rue du Dr. Cenatro
Rue de la Kasbah
Avenue Hassan I
Mendoubia Gardens
Rue d'Italie
Rue Arrakia
Grand Socco
St. Andrew's Church
Rue Sidi Bouabid
Avenue Hassan II
Rue de la Liberté
Rue d'Amerique du Sud
Rue Ibn Zaidoun
Avenue Sidi
Rue d'Angleterre
Contemporary Art Museum
Galerie Delacroix
French Consulate
Grand Hôtel Villa de France (closed)
Rue de Russie
Rue de Hollande
Rue de la Liberté (Rue el Houria)
Place Betanzos
Rue de Belgique
Place de France
Ensemble Artesanal
Mohammed Ben Abdallah
Rue du Mexique
Rue S. Pepys
Rue de Fes
Rue Mahatma Gandhi
Rue Emsallah
Rue de Colombia
Hôpital Espagnol
Place Oued El Makhazine
Jews' Beach
Camping Miramonte
The Mountain, Cap Spartel
Airport & Asilah
Airport & Asilah

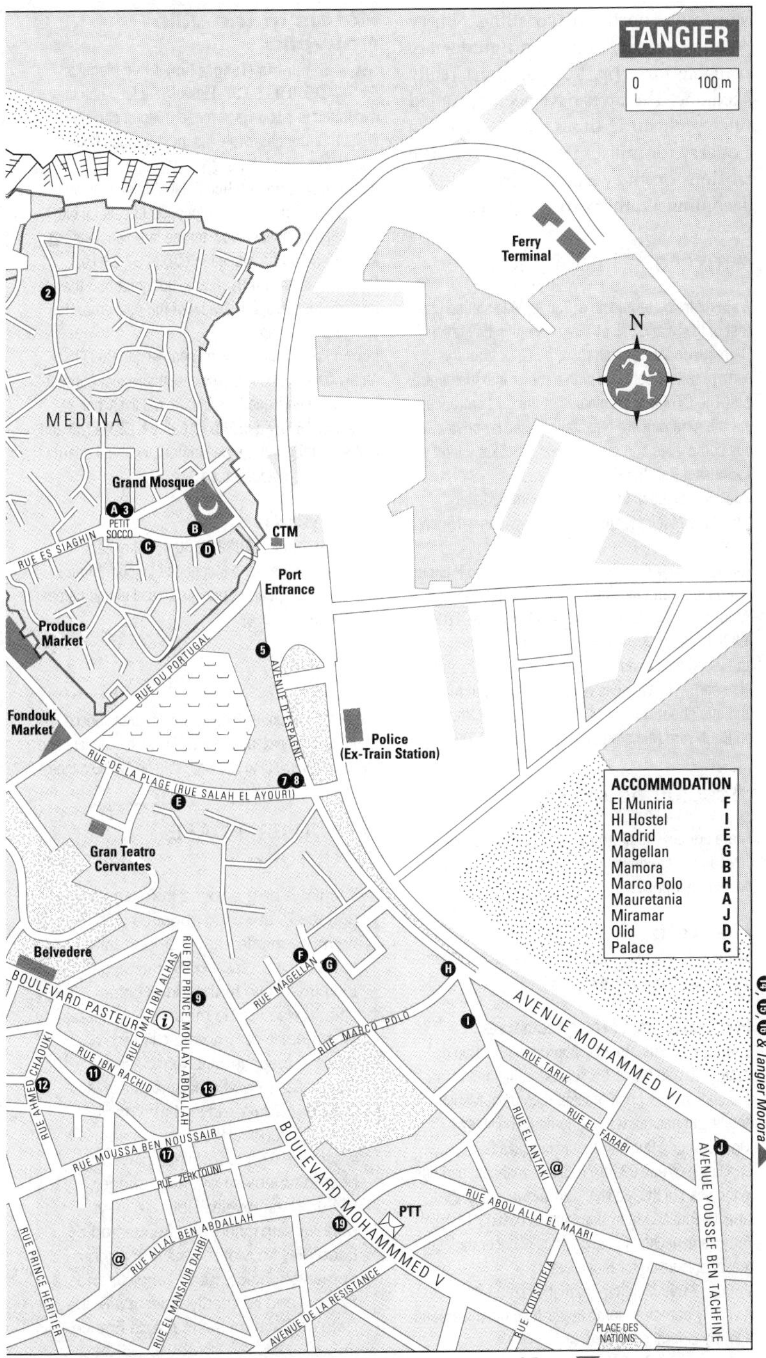
TANGIER
0
100 m
N
Ferry Terminal
MEDINA
Grand Mosque
PETIT SOCCO
RUE ES SIAGHIN
CTM
Port Entrance
Produce Market
RUE DU PORTUGAL
AVENUE D'ESPAGNE
Fondouk Market
Police (Ex-Train Station)
RUE DE LA PLAGE (RUE SALAH EL AYOURI)
Gran Teatro Cervantes
ACCOMMODATION
El Muniria F
HI Hostel I
Madrid E
Magellan G
Mamora B
Marco Polo H
Mauretania A
Miramar J
Olid D
Palace C
Belvedere
BOULEVARD PASTEUR
RUE DU PRINCE MOULAY ABDALLAH
RUE OMAR IBN ALHAS
RUE MAGELLAN
RUE MARCO POLO
AVENUE MOHAMMED VI
RUE TARIK
RUE IBN RACHID
RUE AHMED CHAOUKI
RUE EL FARABI
RUE EL ANTAKI
14, 15, 16 & Tangier Morora
RUE MOUSSA BEN NOUSSAIR
RUE ZERKTOUNI
BOULEVARD MOHAMMED V
AVENUE YOUSSEF BEN TACHFINE
RUE ABOU ALLA EL MAARI
PTT
RUE ALLAL BEN ABDALLAH
RUE PRINCE HERITIER
RUE EL MANSOUR DAHBI
AVENUE DE LA RESISTANCE
RUE YOUSQUEIA
PLACE DES NATIONS
Cap Malabata, Tanger Ville Station, Bus Station, Place de la Ligue, Arabe & Tetouan

Morocco's northern coastline. Entry (9am to sunset) is 5dh and guides are available for a tip, but you don't really need one. The caves have been occupied since prehistoric times, later serving as a quarry for millstones (you can see the erosions on the walls) and in the 1920s becoming a rather exotic brothel.

Arrival and information

Train All trains terminate at Tanger Ville station (2km east of town) and call at Tanger Moghogha station (4km out on the Tetouan road; bus #13 from the port), or take a petit taxi with a meter into the centre.
Bus The CTM bus terminal is at the port entrance, but the gare routière bus station used by private bus companies and grands taxis is 1.5km inland on Av Youssef Ben Tachfine.
Boat Ferries dock at the terminal immediately below the Medina; most hotels are within a 15min walk.
Tourist office The tourist office is at 29 Bd Pasteur, just down from Place de France ⓣ039 94 80 50 (Mon–Thurs 8.30am–noon & 2.30–6.30pm, Fri 8.30–11.30am & 3–6.30pm; sometimes open lunch and weekends in July & Aug). Much more useful is the nearby HIT Voyages which can give you maps and info about Tangier (4 Rue Moussa Ibn Noussair, off Boulevard Mohammed V ⓣ039 93 68 77)

Accommodation

There are dozens of **hotels** and **pensions**, but the city can get crowded in summer, when some places double their prices.

Hostels

HI hostel 8 Rue El Antaki ⓣ039 94 61 27. Clean, friendly and well-run. ❶

Hotels in the Medina

Mamora 19 Rue Mokhtar Ahardane (aka Rue des Postes) ⓣ039 93 41 05. A good-value option in a slightly higher price bracket than most Medina hotels, but has hot water (mornings only). ❶
Mauretania 2 Rue des Almohades (aka Rue des Chrétiens) ⓣ039 93 46 77. Clean, well-kept and right in the heart of the Medina; cold showers only. ❶
Olid 12 Rue Mokhtar Ahardane ⓣ039 93 13 10. Tatty, ramshackle and eccentrically decorated, but reasonable value for money. ❶
Palace 2 Rue Mokhtar Ahardane ⓣ039 93 61 28. A variety of rooms, some better than others, around a lovely central courtyard. ❶

Hotels in the Ville Nouvelle

El Muniria (Tanger Inn) 1 Rue Magellan ⓣ039 93 53 37. Pick of Tangier's hotels, decorated in a laid-back modern Moroccan style. William Burroughs wrote his most famous book, *The Naked Lunch*, here. ❷
Pension Madrid 140 Rue Salah Eddine el Ayoubi ⓣ039 93 16 93. The most popular of several old Spanish townhouses now turned into pensions. ❶
Magellan 16 Rue Magellan ⓣ039 37 23 19. Carpeted, slightly tatty rooms, but quiet and the front rooms have a fine view of the port area. Hot showers 10dh. ❶
Marco Polo corner of Av d'Espagne and Rue El Antaki ⓣ039 94 11 24. A well-established, German-run hotel, with a good restaurant and lively bar. ❷
Miramar 168 Av des FAR ⓣ039 94 17 15. Old and a little shabby, but on the seafront, with quite large rooms and a restaurant. ❷

Campsite

Camping Tingis ⓣ039 32 30 65. 6km east of town, beside the Oued Moghogha lagoon. Often closed for no apparent reason, so call ahead before trekking out there. ❶

Eating

The two main centres for food are the Grand Socco, where you can pick up cheap, filling Moroccan fare and the more diverse (and licensed) strip on Av d'Espagne.

TANGIER'S CAFÉ CULTURE

Tangier is best enjoyed from a café and the Petit Socco abounds with them, each offering the opportunity to lounge and take in the hustle on the street. Two further flung cafés should also not be missed: *Café Hafa* (see map) is cut into the cliff face and looks across the Mediterranean to Spain; *Café Baba* (take the street into the Dar el Makhzen and turn down the right hand fork at Place Amrah where it's signposted) has played host to notables from Mick Jagger to European royalty. Both are very popular with locals and frequented by Ludo playing Moroccans. For a more upmarket choice, go to Tangier's most famous and reputedly oldest cafe, the *Café de Paris* on the Place de France.

Restaurants

Abdel Salem Kaissi Grand Socco. Unmarked restaurant with a 24dh set menu. Sit outside or in a cramped but convivial room above the "kitchen".

Abou Nawas 30 Av. d'Espagne. The fantastic assortment of traditionally prepared Lebanese dishes makes this the pick of Tangier's restaurants. Prices can be negotiated (60–80dh).

Africa 83 Rue Salah Eddine el Ayoubi (aka Rue de la Plage). Good selection of Moroccan dishes, with a 50dh set menu and a drinks licence.

Agadir 21 Rue Prince Héritier Sidi Mohammed, uphill from Place de France. Small and friendly place, serving French and Moroccan dishes, with a good 58dh set menu.

Andalus 7 Rue du Commerce, off the Petit Socco. Small and simple spot in the Medina with excellent, low-priced swordfish steak or fried shrimps (30–40dh).

Hassi Baida 83 Rue Salah Eddine el Ayoubi (aka Rue de la Plage). Bright, tiled restaurant serving fish, couscous and *tajine*, with a 45dh set menu.

Ibn Noussair 37 Rue Moussa Ben Noussair. Immaculate and inexpensive diner with freshly grilled fish, paella, couscous and tasty *tajines* (50dh).

Marco Polo corner of Av d'Espagne and Rue el Antaki. Generous servings at a fair price with snappy service and good views of the bay (80dh).

Petit Berlin 40, Av Mohammed V. *Tajines* at roadside prices but in an upmarket setting, with tapas bar upstairs and happy hour on Friday at 6.30pm (35dh menu).

Rubis Grill 3 Rue Ibn Rochd, off Rue du Prince Moulay Abdallah. Good European-style food, intimate decor and exemplary service (50–80dh).

Drinking and nightlife

Bars

Atlas Bar 30 Rue Prince Heritier, across the road from the *Hôtel Atlas*. Cosy tapas bar open since 1928.

Dean's Bar Rue d'Amérique du Sud. Close to the medina and now popular with Moroccans, this bar had an illustrious artistic clientele in Tangier's heyday, including Francis Bacon and Ian Fleming. A good spot to soak up Tangier's former glories.

Tanger Inn 1 Rue Magellan. An institution since the days of the International Zone, decorated with photos of the Beat Generation authors (Burroughs, Ginsberg and Kerouac) who stayed at the hotel, but quiet midweek off-season.

Clubs

There are a number of big clubs along the seafront. Entrance is usually free for foreigners, and always free for women, but guys may have to pay 100dh.

Club 555 Avenue Mohammed VI ⓣ039 94 41 63 (ⓦhttp://beachclub555.com). A long time favourite with a swimming pool and bustling dance floor, but has a reputation for prostitutes.

Pasarela Beach Club Avenue Mohammed VI ⓣ039 94 52 46. Chic interior with swimming pool, and a friendly policy towards foreigners.

Mondial Avenue Mohammed VI ⓣ063 53 62 88. A recent addition, typical of the classier clubs along the strip.

Directory

American Express Voyages Schwartz, 54 Bd Pasteur ⓣ039 37 48 37.

Consulates UK, Trafalgar House, Rue d'Amérique du Sud ⓣ039 93 69 39 or 40.

Exchange BMCE, 19 Bd Pasteur is the most efficient with a bureau de change and ATM.

Internet Cybercafé Adam, 4 Rue Ibn Rochd (off Bd Pasteur); River-Net, 20 Bd Pasteur (on the corner of Rue du Prince Moulay Abdallah).

Pharmacies There are several English-speaking pharmacies on Place de France and Bd Pasteur.

Post office Main PTT, 33 Bd Mohammed V.

Police The Brigade Touristique are based at the former train station by the port ⓣ039 93 11 29.

Moving on

The overnight train from Tangier to Marrakesh allows you to venture South without losing time. If you want to go east (eg. to Chefchaouen) take a bus.

Bus Casablanca (30 daily; 6hr); Chefchaouen (8 daily; 3hr 30min); Fes (17 daily; 5hr 45min); Fnideq (for Ceuta) (16 daily; 1hr); Marrakesh (6 daily; 10hr); Meknes (12 daily; 7hr); Rabat (30 daily; 5hr); Tetouan (50 daily; 1hr 30min).

Train Casablanca Voyageurs (5 daily; 5hr 15min–6hr 05min); Fes (4 daily; 5hr 10min); Meknes (4 daily; 4hr 10min); Marrakesh (4 daily; 9hr 40min); Rabat (5 daily; 4hr 45min), Rissani (4 daily; 7hr).

Ferry Algeciras, Spain (18–25 daily; 1hr–2hr 30min); Tarifa, Spain (5 daily; 35min); Gibraltar (2 weekly; 1hr 20min), Genoa (1 every 5 days; 48hr), Sète (1 every 4 days; 36hr).

CEUTA/FNIDEQ

Due to the fast ferry, the drab Spanish enclave of **CEUTA** is a popular entry point for travellers coming from Spain. On disembarking you have to catch a taxi or local bus to the Moroccan border. Once across the border there is a huge number of grands taxis that will take you the 3km to the Moroccan town of **FNIDEQ** (3dh). It is advisable to arrive early to leave time for moving on.

Fnideq offers some pleasant **hotels** along the one main road, Mohammad V; *Pension Nador* is the cheapest option whilst *Hotel Fnideq* is far cleaner and more comfortable for a reasonable price. If you're looking for a **restaurant**, try *La Costa*, also on Mohammad V, one of the finest seafood restaurants in Northern Morocco. Rough Guide readers get a twenty percent discount.

Moving on

The **bus station** is signposted at the roundabout where the seafront and Mohammad V meet, marked by a fountain. Buses are infrequent, so it is often quicker and similarly priced to get a grand taxi to Tetouan or Tangier for better connections.

Bus Casablanca (2 daily; 8hr); Meknes (1 daily; 7hr); Marrakesh (1 daily; 11hr); Rabat (2 daily; 7hr); Tangier (6 daily; 1hr); Tetouan (4 daily; 30min).

Ferry Algeciras, mainland Spain (16–20 daily; 35min). Tickets can be booked at the port; it is advisable to arrive an hour early. Times to avoid are at the end of Easter week and the last week of August due to a huge increase in demand. See Ⓦwww.aferry.to for prices, timetables, different companies and to book in advance.

Taxis to Tetouan and Chefchaouen are to be found at the bus station, whilst those for Tangier are picked up behind *La Costa*.

TETOUAN

Coming from Ceuta, you usually need to pick up onward transport at **TETOUAN**, a town with a walled Medina and a reputation for having the worst hustlers in Morocco – but a grand taxi from Fnideq will leave you close enough to Tetouan's bus station to head straight out again. There are regular **buses** to Meknes, Fes and destinations nationwide. For Tangier, Chefchaouen or Ceuta it's easiest to travel by **grand taxi**; those for Fnideq (Ceuta) leave from Boulevard de Mouquaouama, a stone's throw from the bus station, but those for Tangier and Chefchaouen leave from a stand some 2km west, up Boulevard de Mouquaouama to Place Moulay el Mehdi, then west along Av Mohammed V to the end and ask someone. The ONCF office on Av 10 Mai, alongside Place Al Adala, sells **train** tickets that include a shuttle bus to the station at Tnine Sidi Lyamani. If you're stuck in Tetouan, cheap hotels near the bus station include the friendly *Principe*, 20 Av Youssef Ibn Tachfine (Ⓣ066 55 38 20; ❶), on the corner of Boulevard de Mouquaouama midway between the bus station and Place Moulay el Mehdi.

Moving on

Bus Casablanca (26 daily; 6hr); Chefchaouen (26 daily; 2hr); Fnideq (for Ceuta) (17 daily; 1hr); Fes (14 daily; 5hr 20min); Marrakesh (8 daily; 10hr); Meknes (7 daily; 6hr); Rabat (25 daily; 5hr); Tangier (50 daily; 1hr 30min).

CHEFCHAOUEN

Shut in by a fold of the Rif mountains, **CHEFCHAOUEN** (sometimes abbreviated to Chaouen or Xaouen) had, until the arrival of Spanish troops in 1920, been visited by just three Europeans. It's a town of extraordinary light and colour, its whitewash tinted with blue and edged by golden stone walls. *Pensions* are friendly and cheap and a few days here is one of the best introductions to Morocco.

The main entrance to the medina is a tiny arched entrance, Bab el Ain, but the quickest way to negotiate your way to the centre is to get a petit taxi to Place el Makhzen (ask for the Kasbah), where you will find *Hotel Parador*, an expensive hotel, but a good place to pop into for a beer or a swim overlooking the mountains. From here it is only a two-minute walk to **Place Outa el Hammam**. This is where most of the town's evening life takes place, while by day the town's focus is the **Kasbah** (Mon & Wed–Sun 9am–1pm & 3–6pm, Fri 9am–noon; 10dh), a quiet ruin with shady gardens and a small museum, which occupies one side of the square.

Chouen is best enjoyed pottering around the medina and relaxing at coffee shops or on your terrace. For the more adventurous there are **hiking** trails that start from the town. Or you can catch a grand taxi from Place el Makhzen to go to the Oued Laou beach or hike along rivers and waterfalls to God's Bridge (Pont de Dieu) (150dh).

Arrival and information

Arrival Buses and grands taxis drop you outside the town walls.
Tourist office There is no tourist office in Chefchaouen, but your hotel should be able to help with general information.

Accommodation

Hotel Andaluz 1 Rue Sidi Salem ⓣ039 98 60 34. Basic pension just around the corner from *La Castellena* with a central courtyard, friendly staff, terrace (under construction at time of writing) and most importantly a very decent English language book collection. ❶
Camping Azilan ⓣ039 98 69 79. Located up on the hill above town, by the modern *Hôtel Asma*. Chefchaouen's campsite is inexpensive but can be crowded in summer.
Bazar Hicham Place Outa El Hammam ⓣ066 26 79 00, ⓦwww.outahammam.com. Quite simply some of the best accommodation in Morocco. Funkily decorated apartments with a kitchen, showers etc and a great terrace within spitting distance of the Kasbah. Prices start at 400dh (for 4 people). Book ahead. ❷
HI hostel Hay Ouatman No. 4 Goulmima ⓣ066 90 84 42, ⓔarjikamal@yahoo.fr. A very inexpensive but basic and inconveniently located hostel which adjoins the campsite (dorms 20dh, bedding not provided). ❶
Pension La Castellena 4, Sidi Ahmed El Bouhali ⓣ039 98 62 95. Follow the signs at the near end of the Place Outa el Hammam. Cheap and clean with a terrace, laid-back atmosphere and great central seating area. Very popular with travellers. ❶

Eating and drinking

Restaurant Assada on a nameless street just opposite *Hotel Bab el Ain*. Cheap meals (35–40dh) which are highly recommended by both locals and travellers. Very welcoming staff and a terrace that overlooks the medina.
Restaurant el Baraka near *Hotel Andaluz* on Rue Sidi Salem. This is a great little place: a beautiful 150-year-old house, built for a judge, and sensitively, though slightly eccentrically, converted; the food's good, too. Cheap.
Café Restaurant Jibli Place Outta El Hammam. One of several cheap options on the square, serving decent Moroccan food (15dh breakfast, 35dh menu). This is the only one with a well-furnished terrace overlooking the square.

Moving on

It's worth buying tickets a day in advance for Fes and Meknes.
Bus to: Casablanca (5 daily; 9hr); Fes (6 daily; 5hr); Meknes (3 daily; 5hr 30min); Rabat (7 daily; 8hr); Tangier (8 daily; 3hr 30min); Tetouan (26 daily; 2hr).

Central Morocco

Between the mountain ranges of the Rif to the north and the Atlas to the south lie the cities that form Morocco's heart: the great imperial cities of **Meknes** and **Fes**, the modern capital, **Rabat**, and the country's largest city and commercial capital, **Casablanca**.

MEKNES

More than any other Moroccan town, **MEKNES** is associated with a single figure, the Sultan Moulay Ismail, in whose reign (1672–1727) the city went from provincial centre to spectacular capital with over fifty palaces and fifteen miles of exterior walls. Today Meknes is slightly dull, but the medina's palaces and monuments reward a day's exploration, and the ancient sites of Volubilis and Moulay Idriss are nearby.

What to see and do

Place El Hedim

Place El Hedim originally formed the western corner of the Medina, but Moulay Ismail had the houses

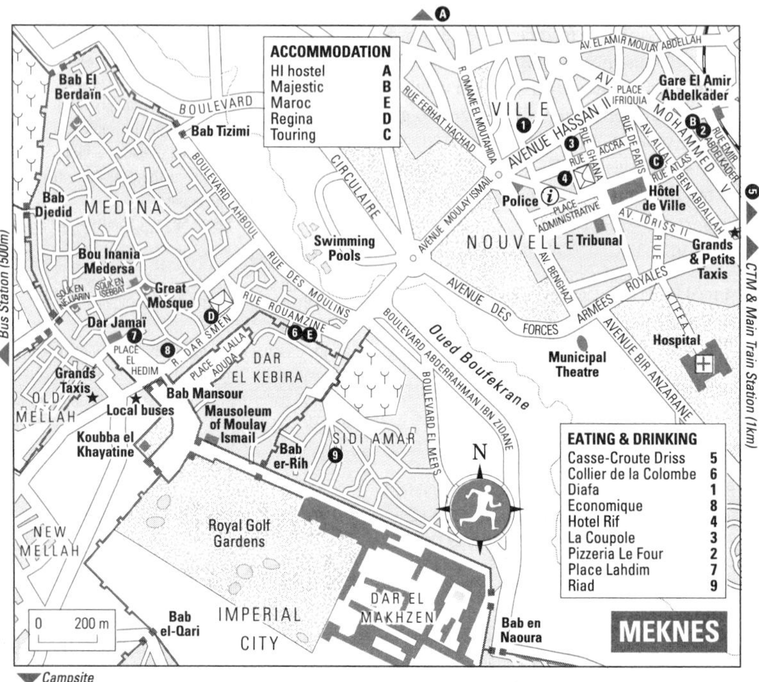

here demolished to provide a grand approach to his palace quarter. The **Dar Jamai** (Mon, Wed, Thurs, Sat & Sun 9am–noon & 3–6.30pm, Fri 9–11.30am & 3–6.30pm; 10dh), at the back of the square, is a great example of a nineteenth-century Moroccan palace, and the museum inside is one of the best in Morocco, with a fantastic display of Middle Atlas carpets. The lane immediately to the left of the Dar Jamai takes you to the Medina's major market street: on your left is **Souk en Nejjarin**, the carpet souk; on your right, leading to the Great Mosque and Bou Inania Medersa, are the fancier goods offered in the **Souk es Sebbat**. The **Bou Inania Medersa** (daily 9am–noon & 3–6.30pm; 10dh), constructed around 1340–50, has an unusual ribbed dome over the entrance hall and from the roof you can look out to the tiled pyramids of the Great Mosque.

The Koubba el Khayatine and Moulay Ismail's Mausoleum

Behind the magnificent **Bab Mansour** (open for occasional exhibitions) is Place Lalla Aouda. Straight ahead bearing left, you come into another open square, on the right of which is the green-tiled dome of the **Koubba el Khayatine**, once a reception hall for ambassadors to the imperial court (daily 9am–noon & 3–6pm; 10dh). Below it, a stairway descends into a vast series of subterranean vaults, known as the **Prison of Christian Slaves**, though it was probably a storehouse or granary. Nearby is the entrance to **Moulay Ismail's Mausoleum** (daily 9am–12.30pm & 3–6.30pm, closed Fri am; 10dh donation expected), where you can approach the sanctuary.

Heri as-Souani and Agdal Basin

Past the mausoleum, a long-walled corridor leads to the **Heri as-Souani**, a series of storerooms and granaries once filled with provisions for siege or drought. From the roof garden café, you can gaze out across much of the Dar el Makhzen (Royal Palace) and the wonderfully still **Agdal Basin**, built as an irrigation reservoir and pleasure lake.

Volubilis and Moulay Idriss

A short grand taxi ride from Meknes (60dh one way, 380dh for half-day excursion) takes you to two of the most important sites in Morocco's history. Volubilis was once the Roman capital of the province; it is still possible to follow the outline of the old city and walk amongst some well-preserved ruins. Moulay Idriss was established by the Prophet's great grandson who is credited with bringing Islam to Morocco. Today, it is a small but bustling town, which Moroccans treat with great respect. It is worth a trip for the views from the top of the town and for an insight into the religious heart of Morocco (particularly true in the festival that takes place in second week of August). However, non-Muslims are barred from visiting the religious shrines of Moulay Idriss for which the town is famous.

Arrival and information

Train Meknes has two train stations, both in the Ville Nouvelle. All trains stop at both stations, but Gare El Amir Abdelkader is more central than Gare de Ville.

Bus and taxi Private buses and most grands taxis arrive west of the Medina by Bab el Khemis; CTM buses arrive at their terminus on Av de Fès, near the Gare de Ville, and some grands taxis from Fes also drop you here.

Tourist office 27 Place Administrative (Mon–Thurs 8.30am–noon & 2.30–6.30pm, Fri 8.30–11.30am & 3–6.30pm; ⓣ035 52 44 26).

Accommodation

Camping Caravaning International (aka Camping Aguedal) ⓣ035 55 53 96. A half-hour walk from Place el Hedim (or a 13dh petit taxi ride), situated opposite the Heri es Souani. Although a little pricey, this is arguably the best campsite in Morocco with good facilities (hot water showers available). The restaurant has menus from 60dh – reservations required.

HI hostel Av Okba Ben Nafi ⓣ035 52 46 98. An easy 1.5km walk northwest of the city centre. Well-maintained and friendly with small dorms and some double rooms around a pleasant courtyard (dorms 45dh with HI card, 50dh without). ❶

Majestic 19 Av Mohammed V, Ville Nouvelle ⓣ035 52 20 35. A good one-star: old, but good-value, comfortable, friendly and handy for El Amir Abdelkader train station. ❷

Maroc 7 Rue Rouamzine, Medina ⓣ035 53 00 75. Pick of the Medina hotels, with plain but decent rooms around a shaded patio garden. ❶

Regina 19 Rue Dar Smen ⓣ035 53 02 80. Best option of several cheap hotels on this street. Has central open area with sofas and terrace overlooking medina. ❶

Touring 34 Av Allal Ben Abdallah, Ville Nouvelle ⓣ035 52 23 51. Central and congenial, with some en-suite rooms. ❶

Eating and drinking

There are good places to **eat** in all price categories in Meknes, and plenty of **bars**, several in Ville Nouvelle hotels, including the 1930s-style bar of the Art Deco *Hôtel Volubilis* at 45 Av des FAR.

Casse-Croute Driss 34 Rue Emir Abdelkader, Ville Nouvelle. Fresh fried fish – cheap and good, but a little bit cramped.

Collier de la Colombe 67 Rue Driba, Medina. Outstanding international cuisine at moderate prices in an ornate early twentieth-century Medina mansion (70dh).

Diafa 12 Rue Badr el Kobra (off Av Hassan II at its western end), Ville Nouvelle. Great home cooking, though not a massive choice, in what looks like a private house in a residential street (50dh).

Economique 123 Rue Dar Smen, opposite Bab Mansour, Medina. A popular café/restaurant serving straight Moroccan food at low prices (30dh).

La Coupole corner of Av Hassan II and Rue Ghana, Ville Nouvelle. Reasonably-priced Moroccan and European food with a bar and nightclub (70dh).

Pizzeria Le Four 1 Rue Atlas, Ville Nouvelle. Decent pizzas, pasta and other Italian dishes,

TREAT YOURSELF

Riad 79 Ksar Chaacha, Medina (follow the green signs from Dar el Kabira) Ⓦwww.riadmeknes.com. A truly memorable experience, this restaurant is situated in the only remaining pavilion of Moulay Ismail's original twelve. The food is local, prepared to a very high standard and served either in a salon or on the terrace. Set menu 150dh. Daily 11am–3pm & 6.30–11pm.

though the interior is a bit on the gloomy side (50dh).

Restaurant Place Lahdim North corner of Place El Hedim. Decent Moroccan food that comes with a great view over the medina (50dh).

Hôtel Rif Rue Omar Ben Chemssi, formerly Rue Accra Ⓣ035 52 25 91, Ⓔhotel_rif@menara.ma. The bar is pleasant, has live music and is not overly expensive and if you want to cool down you can use the pool (80–100dh).

Moving on

Train Casablanca Voyageurs (9 daily; 3hr 30min); Marrakesh (6 daily; 6hr 50min); Fes (10 daily; 50min); Rabat (9 daily; 2hr 30min); Tangier (1 daily; 4hr 15min).

Bus Casablanca (20 daily; 4hr 30min); Chefchaouen (3 daily; 5hr 30min); Fes (approximately half-hourly; 1hr); Marrakesh (6 daily; 9hr); Rabat (approximately half-hourly; 3hr); Rissani (2 daily; 12hr); Tangier (12 daily; 7hr); Tetouan (7 daily; 6hr).

FES (FEZ)

The most ancient of the imperial capitals, **FES** (Fez in English) stimulates the senses and seems to exist somewhere between the Middle Ages and the modern world. Some two hundred thousand of the city's half-million inhabitants (though actual figures are probably much higher than official ones) live in the oldest part of the Medina, **Fes el Bali**, which has a culture and atmosphere quite different from anywhere in mainland Europe.

What to see and do

Getting lost is one of the great joys of the Fes Medina. However, if you want a more informed approach, paper kiosks sell a small green book called 'Fes' that corresponds to tourist trails the government has marked within the Medina by coloured stars. Tour guides also can be employed at the Bab Boujeloud; the official ones wear medallions to identify themselves.

Talaa Kebira

Talaa Kebira, the Medina's main artery, is home to the most brilliant of Fes's monuments, the **Medersa Bou Inania** (daily 8.30am–1pm & 2.30–5.30pm; 10dh), which comes close to perfection in every aspect of its construction, with beautiful carved wood, stucco and *zellij*

FES ORIENTATION

Fes can be difficult to get to grips with orientation-wise. The Medina in Fes is uniquely vast and beautiful, with two distinct parts: the newer section, **Fes el Djedid**, established in the thirteenth century, is mostly taken up by the Royal Palace; the older part, **Fes el Bali**, founded in the eighth century on the River Fes, was populated by refugees from Tunisia on one bank – the **Kairaouine quarter** – and from Spain on the other bank – the **Andalusian quarter**. In practice, almost everything you will want to see is in the Kairaouine quarter. There are several different gates through which you can enter the old city. **Bab Boujeloud** is the most popular and recognizable entry point and is a useful landmark. From here you can turn left at the *Restaurant La Kasbah* to get on to **Talaa Kabira**, the Medina's main thoroughfare. From the north, **Bab el Guissa** offers another port of entry. For **views** of the Medina have a drink at the *Hotel Palais Jamai* (next to Bab Jamai) or *Hotel les Merenides*. An impressive view can also be had from the Arms Museum in the fort above the bus station (Mon & Wed–Sun 8.30am–noon & 2.30–6pm; 10dh).

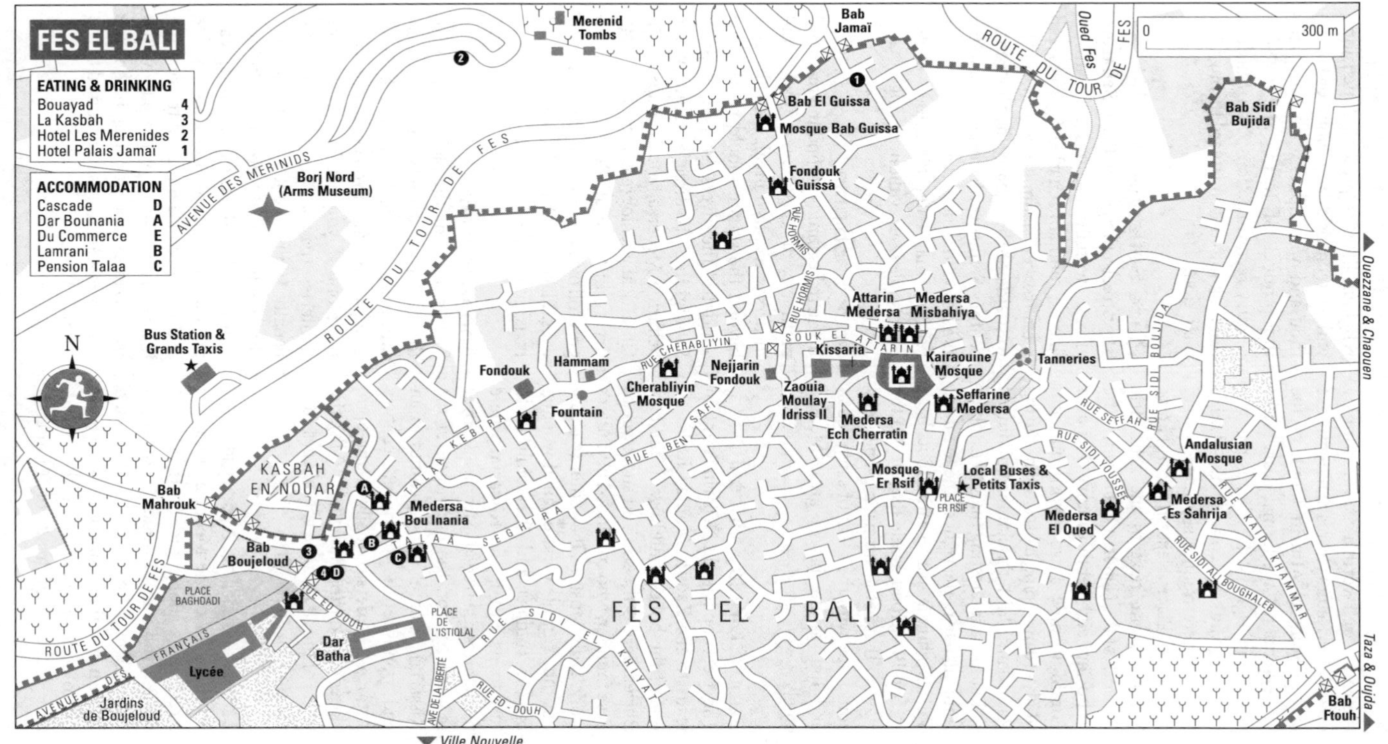

FES EL BALI
EATING & DRINKING
Bouayad 4
La Kasbah 3
Hotel Les Merenides 2
Hotel Palais Jamaï 1
ACCOMMODATION
Cascade D
Dar Bounania A
Du Commerce E
Lamrani B
Pension Talaa C
Merenid Tombs
Bab Jamaï
Bab El Guissa
Mosque Bab Guissa
Fondouk Guissa
Borj Nord (Arms Museum)
Avenue des Merinids
Route du Tour de Fes
Oued Fes
0
300 m
Bab Sidi Bujida
Ouezzane & Chaouen
Taza & Oujda
Bus Station & Grands Taxis
N
Rue Hormis
Attarin Medersa
Medersa Misbahiya
Souk el Attarin
Rue Cherabliyin
Kissaria
Kairaouine Mosque
Tanneries
Rue Sidi Boujida
Fondouk
Hammam
Cherabliyin Mosque
Nejjarin Fondouk
Zaouia Moulay Idriss II
Seffarine Medersa
Medersa Ech Cherratin
Fountain
Rue Seffah
Rue Ben Safi
Talaa Kebira
Mosque Er Rsif
Local Buses & Petits Taxis
Place Er Rsif
Rue Sidi Youssef
Andalusian Mosque
Medersa Es Sahrija
Medersa El Oued
Rue Kaid Khammar
Rue Sidi Ali Boughaleb
Kasbah En Nouar
Bab Mahrouk
Medersa Bou Inania
Talaa Seghira
Bab Boujeloud
Place Baghdadi
Rue ed Douh
Place de l'Istiqlal
Rue Sidi el Khiyat
Fes el Bali
Dar Batha
Français
Lycée
Avenue des Français
Jardins de Boujeloud
Ave de la Liberté
Rue ed-Douh
Bab Ftouh
Ville Nouvelle

tilework – well worth a visit. Continuing down Talâa Kebira you reach the entrance to the **Souk el Attarin** (Souk of the Spice Vendors), the formal heart of the city. To the right, a street leads past the charming **Souk el Henna** – a tree-shaded square where traditional cosmetics are sold – to Place Nejjarin (Carpenters' Square). Here, next to the geometric tilework of the **Nejjarin Fountain**, is the imposing eighteenth-century **Nejjarin Fondouk**, now a woodwork museum (daily 10am–5pm, closes 4pm during Ramadan; 20dh), though the building is rather more interesting than its exhibits. Immediately to the right of the fountain, Talâa Seghira is an alternative route back to Bab Boujeloud, while the alley to the right of that is the aromatic **carpenters' souk**, ripe with the scent of sawn cedar, and top on the list of great Medina smells.

Zaouia Moulay Idriss II

The street opposite the Nejjarin Fountain leads to the **Zaouia Moulay Idriss II**, one of the holiest buildings in the city. Buried here is the son and successor of Fes's founder, who continued his father's work. Only Muslims may enter to check out the *zellij* tilework, original wooden *minbar* (pulpit) and the tomb itself. Just to its east is the **Kissaria**, where fine fabrics are traded. Meanwhile, over to your left (on the other side of the Kissaria), Souk el Attarin comes to an end opposite the fourteenth-century **Attarin Medersa** (daily 9am–6pm; closes 4pm during Ramadan; 10dh), the finest of the city's medieval colleges after the Bou Inania.

The Kairaouine Mosque

To the right of the Medersa, a narrow street runs along the north side of the **Kairaouine Mosque**. Founded in 857 AD by a refugee from Kairouan in Tunisia, the Kairaouine is one of the oldest universities in the world, and the fountainhead of Moroccan religious life. Its present dimensions, with sixteen aisles and room for twenty thousand worshippers, are essentially the product of tenth- and twelfth-century reconstructions. Non-Muslims can look into the courtyard through the main door.

Place Seffarine

The street emerges in **Place Seffarine**, almost wilfully picturesque with its faience fountain, gnarled fig trees and metalworkers hammering away. On the west side of the square, the thirteenth-century **Seffarine Medersa** is still in use as a hostel for students at the Kairaouine (visitors may enter for a look at any reasonable hour without paying).

Souk Sabbighin

If you're beginning to find the medieval prettiness of the central *souks* and *medersas* slightly unreal, then the area beyond the square should provide the antidote. The dyers' market – **Souk Sabbighin** – is directly south of the Seffarine Medersa, and is draped with fantastically coloured yarn and cloth drying in the heat. Below, workers in grey toil over cauldrons of multicoloured dyes. Place er Rsif, nearby, has buses and taxis to the Ville Nouvelle.

The tanneries

The street to the left (north) of the Seffarine Medersa leads to the **tanneries**, constantly visited by tour groups with whom you could discreetly tag along if you get lost. Inside the tanneries (pay a tip to the *gardien*, usually 10dh, to enter), water deluges through holes that were once windows of houses. Hundreds of skins lie spread out on the rooftops, above vats of dye and the pigeon dung used to treat the leather, reminiscent of the pits of hell from Dante's *Inferno*. Straight on, the road eventually leads back round to the Attarin Medersa.

Arrival and information

Train The train station is in the Ville Nouvelle, fifteen minutes' walk north of the hotels around Place Mohammed V. If you prefer to stay in the Medina, take a petit taxi, or walk down to Place de la Résistance (aka La Fiat) and pick up bus #9 to Dar Batha/Place de l'Istiqlal, near the western gate to Fes el Bali, Bab Boujeloud.

Bus The gare routière bus station is just outside the walls near Bab Boujeloud. The terminal for CTM buses is off Rue de l'Atlas, which links the far end of Av Mohammed V with Place de l'Atlas.

Taxi Grands taxis mostly operate from the gare routière; exceptions include those serving Meknes (from the train station).

Tourist office Place de la Résistance (Mon–Thurs 8.30am–noon & 2.30–6.30pm, Fri 8.30–11.30am & 3–6.30pm; ⓣ 035 62 34 60), with a Syndicat d'Initiative on Place Mohammed V (same hours plus Sat 8.30am–noon). Both can tell you about June's seven-day **Festival of World Sacred Music** and the weekend Tadloui (cherry) festival in nearby Sefrou (ⓣ 035 74 05 35, ⓦ www.fesfestival.com).

Accommodation

There's a shortage of hotel space in all categories, so be prepared for higher-than-usual prices; booking ahead is advisable. For atmosphere and character, the Medina is the place to be, though you'll need an easy-going attitude towards size and cleanliness. The less engaging Ville Nouvelle has a wider choice of hotels.

Hostels and camping

Camping Diamant Vert Fôret d'Ain Chkeff ⓣ 035 60 83 67. 6km south of Fes, arrived at by bus#17 from Place Florence in Fes Ville Nouvelle. A relaxed though distant option next door to a leisure complex with great facilities and a night club. ❶

HI hostel 18 Rue Abdeslam Seghrini ⓣ 035 62 40 85. One of Morocco's best hostels – well-kept, friendly and spotlessly clean (dorms 45dh with HI card, 50dh without). ❶

Camping International Route de Sefrou ⓣ 035 61 80 61. Some 4km south of town, this site is pricey for a campsite but has good facilities, including a pool in summer. Take bus #38 from Place de l'Atlas. ❶

Hotels in the Medina

Cascade Just inside Bab Boujeloud, Fes el-Bali ⓣ 035 63 84 42. An old building, with a useful public hammam (bath house) behind. Small rooms, but clean and friendly. The fantastic view from the terrace, where you drink if you bring your own, is the real draw. ❶

Du Commerce Place des Alaouites, Fes el-Djedid, facing the doors of the royal palace ⓣ 035 62 22 31. Still owned by a Jewish family in what was the Jewish quarter; old, but comfortable and friendly, with a lively café at street level. ❶

Dar Bouanania 21 Derb ben Salem (sign posted on Talaa Kebira) ⓣ 035 63 72 82. A riad-lite, with spacious rooms and traditional decor for very reasonable prices. ❷

Lamrani Talâa Seghira, Fes el-Bali ⓣ 035 63 44 11. Friendly with small but spotless rooms, mostly doubles, opposite a hammam. ❶

Pension Talaa 14 Talâa Seghira, Fes el Bali ⓣ 035 63 33 59. A small place and slightly pricier than the other Medina cheapies, but correspondingly more comfortable. ❶

Hotels in the Ville Nouvelle

Amor 31 Rue de l' Arabie Saoudite, formerly Rue du Pakistan ⓣ 035 62 27 24. One block from Av Hassan II, behind the Bank al-Maghrib. Comfortable though sombre rooms with good bathrooms but hot water mornings and evenings only. ❷

Central 50 Bd. Mohammed V ⓣ 035 62 23 33. Clean and well furnished with inviting rooms and good prices – best in the Ville Nouvelle. ❶

Rex 32 Place de l'Atlas ⓣ 035 64 21 33. Small, congenial hotel built in 1910. Clean, pleasant and near the CTM terminal. ❶

Royal 36 Rue es Soudan ⓣ 035 62 46 56. Handy for the train station. All rooms have a shower (some have toilets too), but hot water 7–9am only, and rooms vary in quality so look before you accept. ❶

Eating

Cafés are plentiful in the Ville Nouvelle, with some of the most popular along Av Mohammed es Slaoui and Av Mohammed V. Fes el Bali has two main areas for **budget eating**: around Bab Boujeloud and along Rue Hormis (running from Souk el Attarin towards Bab Guissa), and in the Ville Nouvelle, try the café/restaurants near the municipal market, on the left-hand side of Av Mohammed V as you walk from the post office. Place Al Achabine, just south of Mosque Bab Guissa, is home to several good-quality, cheap Moroccan food stalls.

Fes el Bali

Bouayad inside Bab Boujeloud. Claims to be the oldest restaurant in the medina. Recently refurbished, it serves decent meals at cheap prices (40–60dh) with discounts if you are staying at *Hotel Cascade*.

La Kasbah inside Bab Boujeloud. Two terraces with views over Bab Boujeloud, not to mention great pastilla and delicious *tajines* (the prune and almond meat variety is particularly recommended). 50dh for main and drink.

Ville Nouvelle

Chamonix 5 Rue Moukhtar Soussi, off Av Mohammed V. A reliable restaurant serving Moroccan and European dishes. Attracts a young crowd, and stays open late in summer (50dh).

La Cheminée 6 Rue Chenguit (aka Av Lalla Asma). Small and friendly licensed restaurant with moderate prices (60–80dh).

Chez Vittorio Pizzeria 21 Rue du Nador, nearly opposite *Hôtel Central*. Pizza and pasta; reliable and good value, but not very exciting (50dh).

Marrakech 11 Rue Abes Tazi (between *Hôtel Mounia* and the old CTM terminal). Small, but good and inexpensive, with a limited menu of tasty food (30–40dh).

Roterie les Quatre Coins Rue du Nador. One of four budget eateries at the crossroads that serve mammoth portions of chicken for 20–30dh.

Zagora 5 Av Mohammed V in a small arcade, behind the Derby shoe shop. A pricier option with great food; the upmarket pretensions and the option of a glass of wine are a welcome change from the bustle of the medina (70–100dh).

TREAT YOURSELF

The hotels **Palais Jamaï** (Bab Jamaï) and **Les Merenides** (Borj North, road above Fes el Bali) offer spectacular views across the ancient medina. The hotels themselves are well out of most travellers' price range, but there are few better places to enjoy a sunset with a glass of wine or a beer.

Drinking

While eating options in Fes are plentiful, you have to look a little harder for **bars**. *Eden Chope Bar*, 55 Av Mohammed V, south of Place Mohammed V, with its 1930s mock-classical interior, does good bar snacks, or try the hotel bars.

Directory

Exchange BMCE, Place Mohammed V, Place de l'Atlas and Place Florence (all with ATMs).
Internet Cyber Club, 70 Rue Bou Khessissat, Fes el Djedid; Cyber la Colombe, Av Mohammed V opposite *Hôtel Central*; London Cyber, Place Batha, nearly opposite the #9 bus stop.
Pharmacy Night pharmacy in the *baladiya* (town hall) on Av Moulay Yousef (daily 9.30pm–8.30am).
Police Commissariat Central is on Av Mohammed V behind the post office.
Post office Corner of avenues Mohammed V and Hassan II.

Moving on

Train Casablanca Voyageurs (9 daily; 4hr 15min); Marrakesh (5 daily; 7hr 40min); Meknes (10 daily; 50min); Rabat (9 daily; 3hr 20min); Tangier (1 daily; 5hr 10min).
Bus Casablanca (25 daily; 5hr 30min); Chefchaouen (6 daily; 5hr); Marrakesh (10 daily; 10hr); Meknes (approximately half-hourly; 1hr); Rabat (approximately half-hourly; 4hr); Rissani (4 daily; 8hr); Tangier (17 daily; 5hr 45min); Tetouan (14 daily; 5hr 20min).

RABAT

Often undervalued by tourists, Morocco's capital city hosts a modern political centre (with elegant French architecture), several historical monuments, accessible bars and an ancient Kasbah which overlooks a sandy beach. Though it should not take priority over Fes, Marrakesh or Chefchouen, it is worth a visit if you have the time.

What to see and do

Rabat's compact **Medina** – the whole city until the French arrived in 1912 – is wedged on two sides by the sea and the river, on the others by the twelfth-century Almohad and fifteenth-century Andalusian walls. Laid out in a simple grid, its streets are very easy to navigate.

Kasbah des Oudaïas and around

North lies the **Kasbah des Oudaïas**, a charming and evocative quarter whose principal gateway – Bab el Kasbah or **Oudaïa Gate**, built around 1195 – is one of the most ornate in the Moorish world. Its interior is now used for art exhibitions. Down the steps outside the gate, a lower, horseshoe arch leads directly to **Moulay Ismail's Palace** (daily except Tues 9am–noon & 3–5.30pm; 10dh), which hosts exhibitions on Moroccan art and culture. The adjoining **Andalusian Garden** – one of the most delightful spots in the city – was actually constructed by the French in the last century, though true to Arab Andalusian tradition, with deep, sunken beds of shrubs and flowering annuals.

The Hassan Mosque

The most ambitious of all Almohad buildings, the **Hassan Mosque** (daily 8.30am–6.30pm; free), with its vast minaret, dominates almost every view of the city. Designed by the Almohad ruler Yacoub el Mansour as the centrepiece of the new capital, the mosque seems to have been more or less abandoned at his death in 1199. The minaret, despite its apparent simplicity, is among the most complex of all Almohad structures: each facade is different, with a distinct combination of patterning, yet the whole intricacy of blind arcades and interlacing curves is based on just two formal designs. Facing the tower are the **Mosque and Mausoleum of Mohammed V**, begun on the sultan's death in 1961 and dedicated six years later.

The Archeological Museum and Chellah

On the opposite side of the Ville Nouvelle from the mausoleum is the

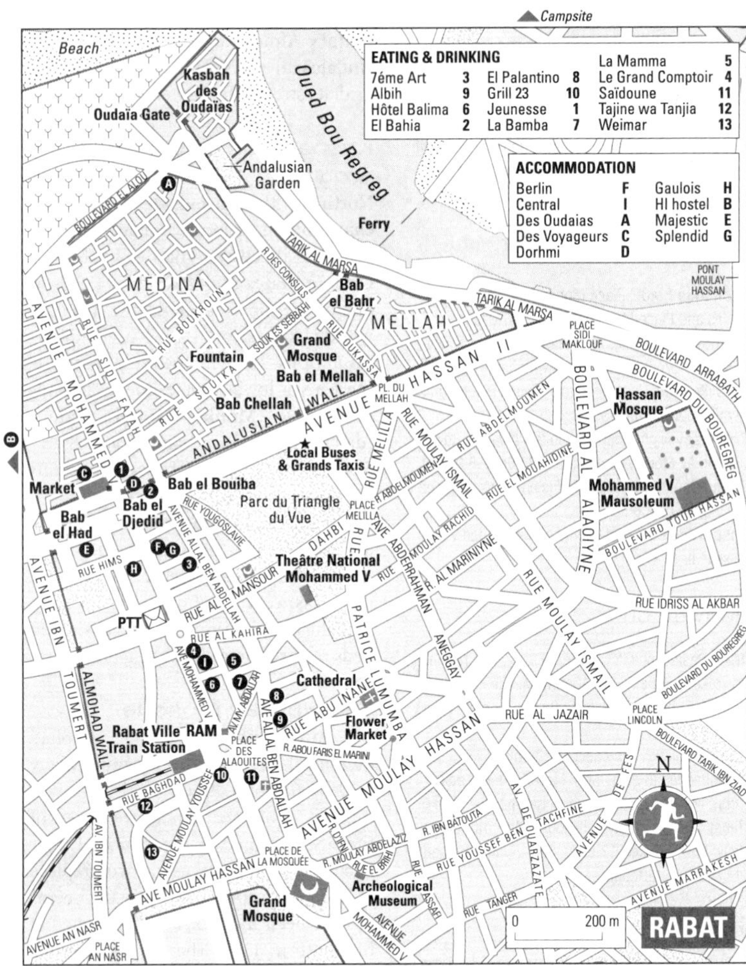

Archeological Museum on Rue Brihi (daily except Tues 8.30am–noon & 2.30–6pm; 10dh), the most important in Morocco. Although small, it has an exceptional collection of Roman-era bronzes, found mainly at Volubilis.

The Chellah

The most beautiful of Moroccan ruins, the royal burial ground, called the **Chellah** (daily 8.30am–6pm; 10dh), is a startling sight as you emerge from the long avenues of the Ville Nouvelle, with its circuit of fourteenth-century walls, legacy of **Abou el Hassan** (1331–51), the greatest of the Merenid rulers. Off to the left of the main gate are the partly excavated ruins of the Roman city that preceded the necropolis. A set of Islamic ruins are further down to the right, situated within a second inner sanctuary, approached along a broad path through half-wild gardens.

Arrival and information

There is no official tourist office in Rabat, but newspaper kiosks sell local tour guidebooks and travel agencies can provide maps and brochures for free.

Train Rabat Ville train station is at the heart of the Ville Nouvelle; do not get off at Rabat Agdal station, 2km from the centre.

Bus The main bus terminal is 3km west of the centre, served by local buses #17, #30 and #41, and by petits taxis. It's easier, if you're arriving by bus from the north, to get off in Salé across the river, and take a grand taxi from there into Rabat.

Taxi Grands taxis for non-local destinations operate from outside the main bus station; those to Casablanca cost only a couple of dirhams more than the bus and leave more or less continuously.

City transport Local bus services radiate from the corner of Rue Nador and Bd Hassan II, where petits taxis and local grands taxis can be found.

Accommodation

Accommodation can fill up in midsummer and during festivals; it's best to phone ahead.

Hostel

HI hostel 43 Rue Marrassa ⓣ037 72 57 69. Just outside the Medina walls north of Bd Hassan II. Closed 10am–noon (30dh per person with HI card, 35dh without). Some double rooms available. ❶

Hotels

Berlin 261 Av Mohammed V ⓣ037 70 34 35. Small hotel with hot showers. Centrally located above the Chinese restaurant *Hong Kong*. ❶

Central 2 Rue Al Basra ⓣ037 70 73 56. Central position near train station and alongside better-known *Hôtel Balima* on Av Mohammed V. A good budget choice and, with 34 rooms, likely to have space. ❶

Des Oudaïas 132 Bv el Alou ⓣ037 26 40 43. The closest hotel to the Kasbah, with comfortable and spacious rooms. The salon downstairs adds character. ❷

Des Voyageurs 8 Souk Semarine, near Bab Djedid ⓣ037 72 37 20. Inexpensive, popular and often full. Clean, airy rooms but no showers. ❶

Dorhmi 313 Av Mohammed V, just inside Bab Djedid ⓣ037 72 38 98. Above *Café Essalem* and Banque Populaire. Well furnished and maintained. ❶

Gaulois 1 Rue Hims (corner of Ave Mohammed V) ⓣ037 72 30 22. Two-star with grand entrance and decent rooms, some en suite. Pricier than other options if the cheap rooms have gone, but can be excellent value-for-money. ❷

Majestic 121 Av Hassan II ⓣ037 72 29 97, ⓦwww.hotel.majestic.ma. Popular and good value, with bright, spotless rooms, some overlooking the Medina. ❷

Splendid 8 Rue Ghazza ⓣ037 72 32 83. Nice place whose best rooms overlook a courtyard, but hot water 10pm–10am only. Café-Restaurant *Ghazza* opposite is good for breakfast. ❷

Campsite

Camping de la Plage ⓣ063 59 36 63. Across the river at Salé. Basic but well-managed, with a shop opposite for supplies.

Eating

Rabat has a wide range of good **restaurants** serving both Moroccan and international dishes. As ever, the cheapest ones are to be found in the **Medina**.

7éme Art Ave Allal Ben Abdallah. Cheap popular and trendy café serving hamburgers, salads and grilled meats in a garden area (30–50dh)

Albih 41 Ave Ben Abdallah. Small, cheap and convenient restaurant, close to train station with a decent Lebanese menu (30–50dh).

El Bahia Bd Hassan II, built into the Andalusian wall, near the junction with Ave Mohammed V. Reasonably priced *tajines*, kebabs and salads, in a pleasant courtyard, upstairs or on the pavement outside, though service can be slow (60dh).

Grill 23 Corner Ave Mohammed V Rue Britlahm. Cheap but delicious shwarma, hamburgers and big salads. Convenient to take out for a train ride, though there is nice seating (30–50dh).

Jeunesse 305 Ave Mohammed V, Medina. One of the city's best budget eateries, with generous portions of couscous, and decent *tajines* (30–40dh).

La Bamba 3 Rue Tanta, behind the *Hôtel Balima*. European and Moroccan dishes, with good-value set menus (80dh European, 100dh Moroccan). Licensed.

La Mamma 6 Rue Tanta, behind the *Hôtel Balima*. Good pizzas and pasta dishes. *La Dolce Vita*, next door, is owned by the same patron and provides luscious Italian-style ice cream for afters (60dh).

Saïdoune in the mall at 467 Ave Mohammed V, opposite the *Hôtel Terminus*. A good Lebanese restaurant run by an Iraqi; licensed, but closed Friday lunchtime.

Tajine wa Tanjia 9 Rue Baghdad. A lovely little place with a wide range of excellent *tajines* and *tanjia* (jugged beef or lamb) for around 60dh.

Weimar 7, Rue Sana'a inside the Goethe Institute. Considered by expats to serve the best food in Rabat, you can choose from a range of pastas, meats and salads accompanied by German wine and beer. Expect to spend around 80dh.

Drinking and nightlife

Avenues Mohammed V and Allal Ben Abdallah have some good cafés, but the best bars are situated in Agdal, a bit of a trek from the centre. Late-night options include a string of disco-bars around Place de Melilla and on Rue Patrice Lumumba.

El Palantino Ave Ben Abdallah. Great, atmospheric Spanish-style bar with happy hour from 7pm. Offers a range of meals, but the tapas are especially good value, filling and very tasty (50–80dh).

Hotel Balima Bar Ave Mohammed V. This bar is convenient and situated on a terrace overlooking the Parliament but it closes at 10pm.

TREAT YOURSELF

Le Grand Comptoir 279 Bd Mohammed V Ⓦwww.legrandcomptoir.ma. A classy brasserie with live music that ranges from jazz to traditional Moroccan. Serves excellent seafood and a decent selection of wines. A meal with wine will end up setting you back 150–200dh.

Directory

Embassies Australia represented by Canada; Canada, 13bis Rue Jaâfar as Sadiq, Agdal Ⓣ037 67 74 00; New Zealand represented by the UK; UK, 28 Av SAR Sidi Mohammed, Souissi Ⓣ037 63 33 33; USA, 2 Av Mohammed el Fassi Ⓣ037 76 22 65. Irish citizens covered by their embassy in Lisbon, but may get emergency help from the UK embassy.

Exchange Along Av Allal Ben Abdallah and Av Mohammed V. BMCE also has a bureau de change in Ville train station.

Internet Student Cyber, 83 Av Hassan II; ETSI Net, 12 Av Prince Moulay Abdallah; Phobos, 113 Bd Hassan II, by *Hôtel Majestic*.

Police Av Tripoli, near the Cathedral. Police post at Bab Djedid.

Post office Halfway down Av Mohammed V.

Moving on

Train Casablanca Voyageurs (14 daily; 1hr); Casablanca Port (half-hourly 6.30am–9pm; 1hr); Fes (9 daily; 3hr 20min); Marrakesh (8 daily; 4hr 25min); Meknes (9 daily; 2hr 30min); Tangier (3 daily; 4hr 40min).

Bus Casablanca (frequent; 1hr 20min); Essaouira (10 daily; 7hr 30min); Fes (approximately half-hourly; 4hr); Marrakesh (hourly; 5hr 30min); Meknes (approximately half-hourly; 3hr); Rissani (2 daily; 10hr); Salé (frequent; 15min); Tangier (30 daily; 5hr).

CASABLANCA

Morocco's main city and economic capital, **CASABLANCA** (or "Casa") is also North Africa's largest port. Casa's Westernized image does not fit with most travellers' stereotype of Morocco but the city offers good food, beaches and decent shopping.

What to see and do

Casablanca's **Medina**, above the port and recently gentrified, is largely the product of the late nineteenth century, when Casa began its modest growth as a commercial centre. Film buffs will be disappointed to learn that Bogart's *Casablanca* wasn't shot here (it was filmed entirely in Hollywood) – the *Bar Casablanca* commemorates it as a gimmick in the luxury *Hyatt Regency* hotel on Place des Nations-Unies.

Grande Mosquée Hassan II

The city's main monument, the **Grande Mosquée Hassan II** (tours daily except Fri 9am, 10am, 11am & 2pm; 120dh, students 60dh), opened in 1993, is the world's second largest mosque after the one in Mecca, with space for one hundred thousand worshippers, and a minaret that soars to a record 200m. Commissioned by the last king, who named it after himself, it cost an estimated £320m/US$500m, raised by not wholly voluntary public subscription. It's a twenty-minute walk northwest from the centre.

The beaches

The **Ain Dab beach**, to the west of Mosque Hassan II, is one of Morocco's best easily accessible beaches. Surf lessons and equipment are readily available along the corniche, which runs alongside the beach (Rusty ⓣ022 79 74 86 and Surf School Marhaba ⓣ023 31 45 16 are local recommendations). **Mohammedia**, 30 km from Casa, is a less crowded option, with better surf. Take the train from Casa Port station for 15dh.

Jewish Museum of Casablanca

Five kilometres south of town, in the suburb of Oasis, the Jewish Museum of Casablanca at 81 Rue Chasseur Jules Gros (Mon–Fri 10am–6pm; 30dh; wheelchair accessible; ⓣ022 99 49 40, ⓦwww.casajewishmuseum.com) is the only Jewish museum in any Muslim country. Many Moroccan Muslims are proud of the fact that Jewish communities have, historically, been protected in Morocco. The museum gives an insight into the disproportionate role that Jews have played in Moroccan life.

Arrival and information

NB Casablanca has been the victim of bombings directed at Western institutions, so it is worth checking your embassy websites for current information.

Air catch a train into Casa Voyageurs from the airport. Grands taxis are extortionately expensive for the 45-minute drive.

Train Some trains stop only at the Gare des Voyageurs (2km southeast of the centre) rather than continuing to the better-situated Gare du Port, between the town centre and the port. Bus #2 runs into town from the Voyageurs; otherwise, it's a twenty-minute walk or a petit taxi ride.

Bus Coming by bus, take the CTM if possible as it drops you downtown on Rue Léon l'Africain, behind *Hôtel Safir* on Av des FAR; other buses arrive at the gare routière (Gare du Habbous) southeast of town on Route des Ouled Ziane.

Taxi Grands taxis from Rabat arrive a block east of the CTM terminal, while those from points south come into a station south of town on the Route de Jadida in Beauséjour.

Tourist office The best information office is located in a kiosk in the corner of Place Mohammed V, whilst another is located next to the Mosquée Hassan II. More established offices are inconveniently located south of the centre at 55 Rue Omar Slaoui (Mon–Thurs 8.30am–noon & 2.30–6.30pm, Fri 8.30–11.30am & 3–6.30pm; ⓣ022 27 11 77). You can also try the Syndicat d'Initiative, 98 Bd Mohammed V, where you can get a tour guide for 450dh (Mon–Fri 8.30am–noon & 3–6.30pm, Sat 8.30am–noon & 3–5pm, Sun 9am–noon; ⓣ022 22 15 24). Further info can be found at ⓦwww.casablanca.ma, a useful site for maps, listings and current attractions.

Accommodation

Hotels are plentiful, though often near capacity, and cheaper rooms in the centre can be hard to find by late afternoon.

Hostel

HI Hostel (Auberge de Jeunesse) 6 Place Ahmed Bidaoui ⓣ022 22 05 57. A friendly, well-maintained place just inside the Medina and signposted from the nearby Gare du Port (45dh per person). ❶

Hotels

Colbert 38 Rue Chaoula ⓣ022 31 42 41 or 022 31 47 11. Huge (103 rooms) well-priced hotel with decent rooms, 3 gardens and 2 terraces. ❶

Du Centre 1 Rue Sidi Belyout, corner of Av des FAR ⓣ022 44 61 80 or 81. A golden oldie, cheered up with a splash of paint and en-suite bathrooms. ❷

Foucauld 52 Rue Araibi Jilali ⓣ022 22 26 66. Great value, with en-suite rooms, near several good café/restaurants. ❶

Mon Rêve 7 Rue Chaouia ⓣ022 31 14 39. Long-standing budget travellers' favourite, though many rooms are at the top of a steep spiral staircase. ❶

Plaza 18 Blvd Felix Houphouët Boigny ⓣ022 29 78 22, ⓔhotel_plaza2000@yahoo.fr. Very central hotel with big rooms, some en suite. ❷

Terminus 184 Blvd Ba Hamad ⓣ022 24 00 25. Handy for the Gare des Voyageurs: clean, decent rooms with hot showers on the corridor. ❶

Touring 87 Rue Allal Ben Abdallah ⓣ022 31 02 16. Refurbished old French hotel that's friendly and excellent value; the best option in an area of cheap hotels. ❶

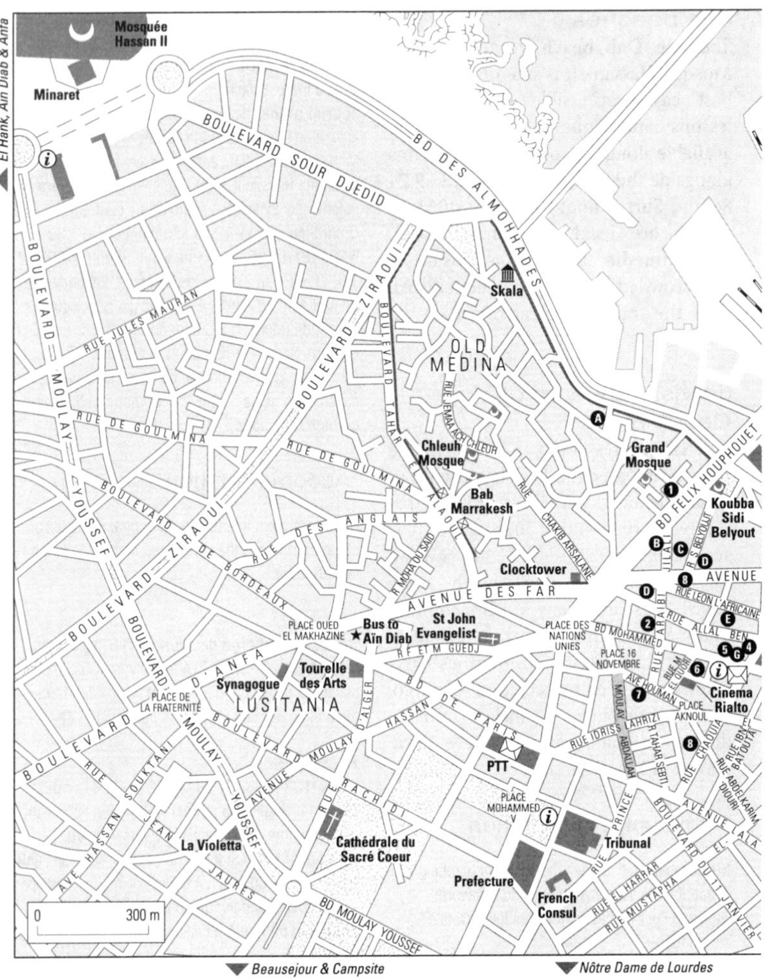

Campsite

Camping Oasis Av Jean Mermoz, Beauséjour ☎022 23 42 57. 4km south of the centre in the suburb of Beauséjour (bus #31 from Place Oued el Makhzine), and a little run-down. ❶

Eating and drinking

Casa has the reputation of being the best place to **eat** in Morocco, and if you can afford the fancier restaurant prices, this is certainly true. For those on a budget, some of the best possibilities lie in the smaller streets off Bd Mohammed V and in the central *marché*, where it is possible to bring fish for the outdoor restaurants to cook for you.

Beverly 6 Av Houmane El Fetwaki. A cheap place to pick up filling food on the go; popular with locals (20–30dh).

La Bodéga 127 Rue Allal Ben Abdallah ☎022 54 18 42, Ⓦwww.bodega.ma. Lively restaurant with a good selection of Spanish cuisine (70–100dh). The atmosphere is enhanced by a downstairs bar and dance floor.

La Tuffe Blanche 57 Tahar Sebti. One of the few remaining Jewish eating places, serving kosher dishes and alcohol for about 50–80dh a head.

Le Buffet 99 Blvd Mohammed V. Quick, bright and popular, with a reasonable 75dh *menu du jour*.

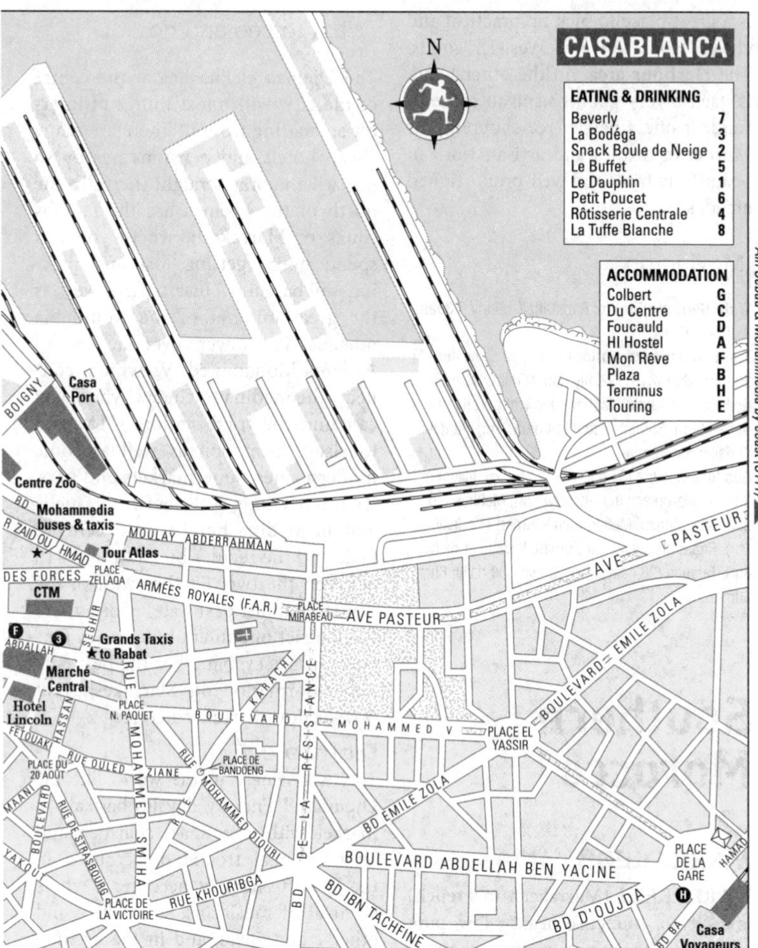

Le Dauphin 115 Blvd Felix Houphouët Boigny ☎022 22 12 00. One of Casa's most famous and popular restaurants, this place deserves its reputation for great seafood in the restaurant and bonhomie in the cramped bar. Worth queuing for; 80–120dh for dinner.

Petit Poucet 86 Blvd Mohammed V. 1920s-Parisian-style restaurant with a reasonably priced menu (50–80dh). Next door there is a much cheaper snack bar – one of the best places in town for serious drinking.

Rôtisserie Centrale 36 Rue Chaouia. Best of a bunch of cheap chicken-on-a-spit joints on this little stretch of road opposite the Marché Central, *Snack Yamine*, next door, is a good cheap fish option.

Snack Boule de Neige 72 Rue Araibi Jilali. Open all hours (except daytime during Ramadan), serving tasty, cheap snacks (30dh).

Shopping

Shopping can be very pleasant in Casablanca. There is an unusually large selection of **high street stores** in the Maarif quarter. While the old medina is a bit down at heel, it has some charm and is a great place to pick up practical and cheap Moroccan and Western goods. The **Harbous** area, on the other hand, is itself a very good reason to come to Casa. It offers hassle-free shopping for Moroccan textiles and artisan work in beautifully fresh and well-proportioned arcades.

Moving on

Train (Port station) to: Rabat (half-hourly 6.30am–8.30pm; 1hr).
Train (Voyageurs station) to: Fes (9 daily; 4hr 20min); Marrakesh (9 daily; 3hr 15min); Meknes (9 daily; 3hr 30min); Mohammed V airport (hourly 6am–10pm; 35min); Rabat (14 daily; 1hr); Tangier (3 daily; 5hr 40min).
Bus to: Essaouira (37 daily; 6hr); Fes (25 daily; 5hr 30min); Marrakesh (half-hourly; 4hr); Meknes (20 daily; 4hr 30min); Mohammed V airport (12 daily; 1hr); Rabat (frequent; 1hr 20min); Rissani (1 daily; 8hr); Tetouan (26 daily; 6hr); Tangier (30 daily; 6hr 30min).

Southern Morocco

MARRAKESH

MARRAKESH (Marrakech in French) is a city of immense beauty, low, pink and tent-like before a great shaft of mountains. It's an immediately exciting place, especially around the vast space of its central square, the **Djemaa el Fna**, the stage for a long-established ritual in which shifting circles of onlookers gather around groups of acrobats, drummers, pipe musicians, dancers, storytellers and comedians. Unlike Fes, for so long its rival as the nation's capital but these days stagnating, Marrakesh's population is growing and it has a thriving industrial area; the city remains the most important market and administrative centre in southern Morocco.

What to see and do

The Djemaa el Fna lies at the centre of the city, with most things of interest emanating from it. There are many cheap hotels and pensions nearby so it is worth going straight there. To the north of the Djemaa are the famous souks of Marrakesh, where you can spend hours getting lost and picking up bargains. Just to the west is the great minaret of the Koutoubia mosque. This towers over the start of Avenue Mohammed V, which connects the medina to Gueliz, where you can find the train station, CTM and tourist information as well as some modern cafes, supermarkets and bars. It's a fairly long walk between Gueliz and the Medina, but there are plenty of taxis and the regular buses #1 and #16 between the two. Further west of the Koutoubia, just past Bab Djedid, there is a district of opulent hotels with fantastic, if pricey, bars. For the best current information on Marrakesh visit Ⓦwww.ilovemarrakech.com.

Djemaa el Fna

There's nowhere in the world like the **Djemaa el Fna**: by day it's basically a market, with a few snake charmers and an occasional troupe of acrobats; in the late afternoon it becomes a whole carnival of musicians, storytellers and other entertainers; and in the evening dozens of stalls set up to dispense hot food to crowds of locals, while the musicians and performers continue. If you get tired of the spectacle, or if things slow down, you can move over to the rooftop terraces of the *Café de France* or the *Restaurant Argana* to gaze at it all from above.

The Koutoubia

The absence of any architectural feature in the Djemaa serves to emphasize the drama of the **Koutoubia Minaret**. Nearly 70m high and visible for miles, it was begun shortly after the Almohad

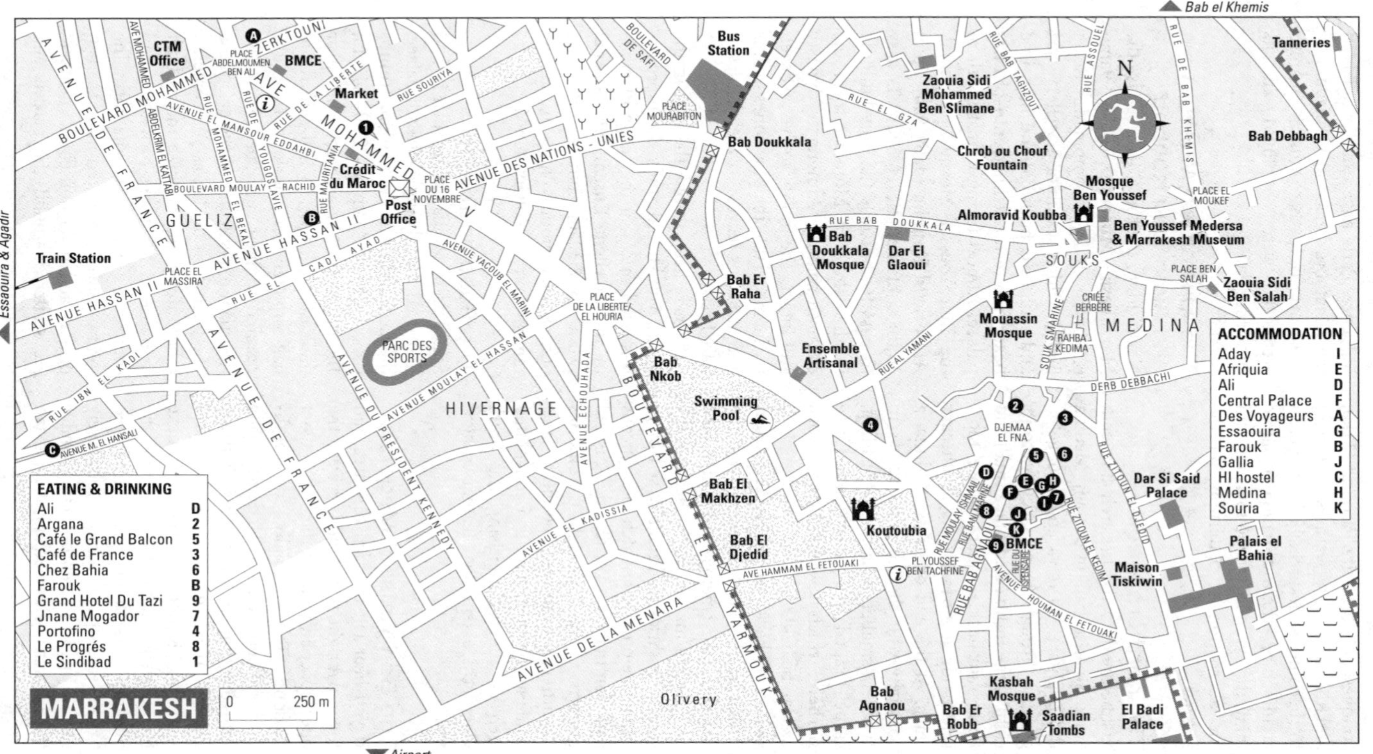
MARRAKESH
EATING & DRINKING
Ali D
Argana 2
Café le Grand Balcon 5
Café de France 3
Chez Bahia 6
Farouk B
Grand Hotel Du Tazi 9
Jnane Mogador 7
Portofino 4
Le Progrés 8
Le Sindibad 1
ACCOMMODATION
Aday I
Afriquia E
Ali D
Central Palace F
Des Voyageurs A
Essaouira G
Farouk B
Gallia J
HI hostel C
Medina H
Souria K
0 250 m
Bab el Khemis
Essaouira & Agadir
Airport
N
CTM Office
BMCE
Market
Crédit du Maroc
Post Office
Train Station
GUELIZ
HIVERNAGE
MEDINA
SOUKS
Olivery
PARC DES SPORTS
Bus Station
Bab Doukkala
Bab Er Raha
Bab Nkob
Swimming Pool
Bab El Makhzen
Bab El Djedid
Bab Agnaou
Bab Er Robb
Kasbah Mosque
Saadian Tombs
El Badi Palace
Maison Tiskiwin
Palais el Bahia
Dar Si Said Palace
Koutoubia
Ensemble Artisanal
Bab Doukkala Mosque
Dar El Glaoui
Mouassin Mosque
Zaouia Sidi Mohammed Ben Slimane
Chrob ou Chouf Fountain
Mosque Ben Youssef
Almoravid Koubba
Ben Youssef Medersa & Marrakesh Museum
Zaouia Sidi Ben Salah
Tanneries
Bab Debbagh
DJEMAA EL FNA
CRIÉE BERBERE
RAHBA KEDIMA
PLACE ABDELMOUMEN BEN ALI
PLACE DU 16 NOVEMBRE
PLACE EL MASSIRA
PLACE DE LA LIBERTE/ EL HOURIA
PLACE MOURABITON
PLACE EL MOUKEF
PLACE BEN SALAH
PL.YOUSSEF BEN TACHFINE
BOULEVARD MOHAMMED V
AVE MOHAMMED V
AVENUE DE FRANCE
BOULEVARD DE FRANCE
AVENUE HASSAN II
AVENUE DES NATIONS - UNIES
AVENUE YACOUB EL MARINI
AVENUE MOULAY EL HASSAN
AVENUE DU PRESIDENT KENNEDY
AVENUE ECHOUHADA
AVENUE EL KADISSIA
AVENUE DE LA MENARA
BOULEVARD EL YARMOUK
BOULEVARD DE SAFI
AVE HAMMAM EL FETOUAKI
AVENUE HOUMAN EL FETOUAKI
AVENUE M. EL HANSALI
RUE IBN EL KADI
RUE EL CADI AYAD
RUE ZERKTOUNI
RUE DE LA LIBERTE
RUE SOURIYA
RUE DE YOUGOSLAVIE
RUE MAURITANIA
RUE MOHAMMED EL BEKAL
AVENUE EL MANSOUR EDDAHBI
BOULEVARD MOULAY RACHID
AVE MOHAMMED ABDELKRIM EL KATTABI
RUE BAB DOUKKALA
RUE EL GZA
RUE BAB TAGHZOUT
RUE ASSOUEL
RUE DE BAB KHEMIS
RUE AL YAMANI
SOUK SMARINE
DERB DEBBACHI
RUE ZITOUN EL DJEDID
RUE ZITOUN EL KEDIM
RUE BAB AGNAOU
RUE MOULAY ISHMAIL
RUE BANI MARINE
RUE DU DISPENSAIRE

conquest of the city, around 1150, and displays many features that were to become widespread in Moroccan architecture – the wide band of ceramic inlay, the pyramid-shaped merlons, and the alternation of patterning on the facades.

The northern Medina

Just before the red ochre arch at its end, Souk Smarine, an important Medina thoroughfare, narrows and you get a glimpse through the passageways to its right of the **Rahba Kedima**, a small and fairly ramshackle square whose most interesting features are its apothecary stalls. At the end of Rahba Kedima, a passageway to the left gives access to another, smaller square – a bustling, carpet-draped area known as la **Criée Berbère**, which is where slave auctions used to be held.

Cutting back to **Souk el Kebir**, which by now has taken over from the Smarine, you emerge at the **kissarias**, the covered markets at the heart of the souks. Kissarias traditionally sell more expensive products, which today means a predominance of Western designs and imports. Off to their right is **Souk des Bijoutiers**, a modest jewellers' lane, while at the north end is a convoluted web of alleys comprising the **Souk Cherratin**, essentially a leatherworkers' market.

The Ben Youssef Medersa

If you bear left through this area and then turn right, you should arrive at the open space in front of the Ben Youssef Mosque. The originally fourteenth-century **Ben Youssef Medersa** (daily 9am–6.30pm; 30dh; combined ticket for this, the Marrakesh Museum and Almoravid Koubba 50dh) – the annexe for students taking courses in the mosque – stands off a side street just to the east. It was almost completely rebuilt in the sixteenth century under the Saadians, with a strong Andalusian influence. Parts have exact parallels in the Alhambra Palace in Granada, and it seems likely that Muslim Spanish architects were employed in its construction.

The Marrakesh Museum and Almoravid Koubba

Next door to the Medersa is the **Marrakesh Museum** (daily 9am–6.30pm; 30dh; combined ticket 50dh) which exhibits jewellery, art and sculpture, both old and new, in a beautifully restored nineteenth-century palace. Almost facing it, just south of the Ben Youssef Mosque, the small **Almoravid Koubba** (daily 9am–6pm; 10dh; combined ticket 50dh) is easy to pass by, but it is the only building in the whole of Morocco from the eleventh-century Almoravid dynasty still intact. The motifs you've just seen in the medersa – the pine cones, palms and acanthus leaves – were all carved here first.

If you're keen to buy the best in the souks, you should study the more-or-less fixed prices of the range of crafts in the excellent **Ensemble Artisanal** (Mon–Sat 8.30am–1pm & 2.30–7pm, Sun 8.30am–noon), just inside the ramparts on Av Mohammed V.

The Saadian Tombs

Sealed up by Moulay Ismail after he had destroyed the adjoining El Badi Palace, the sixteenth-century **Saadian Tombs** (daily 8.30–11.45am & 2.30–5.45pm; 10dh), accessed by a narrow alley near the Kasbah Mosque, lay half-ruined and half-forgotten for centuries but are now restored to their full glory. There are two main mausoleums in the enclosure. The finer is on the left as you come in, a beautiful group of three rooms built to house El Mansour's own tomb and completed within his lifetime. The tombs of over a hundred more Saadian princes and royal household members are scattered around the garden and courtyard, their gravestones likewise brilliantly tiled and often elaborately inscribed.

El Badi Palace

Though substantially in ruins, enough remains of Ahmed el Mansour's **El Badi Palace** (daily 8.30–11.45am & 2.30–5.45pm; 10dh) to suggest that its name – "The Incomparable" – was not entirely immodest. It took a later ruler, Moulay Ismail, over ten years of systematic work to strip the palace of everything movable or of value and, even so, there's a lingering sense of luxury. What you see today is essentially the ceremonial part of the palace complex, planned for the reception of ambassadors. To the rear extends the central court, over 130m long and nearly as wide, and built on a substructure of vaults in order to allow the circulation of water through the pools and gardens. In the southwest corner of the complex is an ancient *minbar* (pulpit) from the Dwiria, or Koutoubia mosque; both mosque and *minbar* have been lovingly restored (admission is an extra 10dh).

Rue Zitoun el Djedid

Heading north from El Badi Palace, **Rue Zitoun el Djedid** leads back to the Djemaa, flanked by various nineteenth-century mansions. Many of these have been converted into carpet shops or tourist restaurants, but one of them has been kept as a museum, the **Palais El Bahia** (Sat–Thurs 8.45–11.45am & 2.45–5.45pm, Fri 8.45–11.30am & 3–5.45pm; 10dh), former residence of a grand vizier. The name of the building means "The Brilliance", an exaggeration perhaps, but it's a beautiful old palace with two lovely patio gardens and some classic painted wooden ceilings. Also on this route is the **Dar Si Said** palace, which houses the **Museum of Moroccan Arts** (daily except Tues 9am–12.15pm & 3–6.15pm; 20dh). A further superb collection of Moroccan and Saharan artefacts is housed in the **Maison Tiskiwin** (daily 9.30am–12.30pm & 3.30–5.30pm; 15dh), which lies between the El Bahia and Dar Si Said palaces at 8 Rue de la Bahia.

Mount Toubkal

Imlil, the setting-off point for trekkers wanting to climb the second highest peak in Africa, is within 2–3 hours' grand taxi drive of Marrakesh (400dh). Most trekkers set out early to mid-morning from Imlil to stay the night at the Toubkal refuge (5–6hr), which gets crowded in summer. It's best to start from here at first light the next morning in order to get the clearest possible panorama from Toubkal's heights (afternoons can be cloudy). The ascent is not difficult if you are fit, but it can be very cold. Trekking maps are available at kiosks both in Marrakesh and Imlil.

Arrival and information

Air The airport, 4km southwest, is served by the erratic bus #19 (every hour) – petits or grands taxis (30–60dh by day, double by night) are a better option.

Train From the train station, by Gueliz, cross the street and take bus #3/#4/#8/#10/#16/#66 or a petit taxi (10–15dh) for Place Foucauld by the Djemaa.

Bus The bus terminal is just outside the northwestern walls of the Medina by Bab Doukkala; from here it's a 20-minute walk to the Djemaa, or take bus #3/#4/#5/#8/#10/#14/#16/#17/#26/#66 (opposite Bab Doukkala), or a petit taxi (8–10dh). CTM buses take you to their office in Gueliz.

Tourist office Place Abdelmoumen Ben Ali (Mon–Thurs 8.30am–noon & 2.30–6.30pm, Fri 8.30–11.30am & 3–6.30pm, also usually Sat 9am–noon & 3–6pm; ⓣ 024 43 62 39) keeps current details of services you might need. There's a branch office at Place Vénus by the Koutoubia (same hours but closed Sat).

Accommodation

The Medina, as ever, has the main concentration of cheap **accommodation** – most places quite pleasant – and, unusually, has a fair number of classified hotels too. Given the attractions of the Djemaa el Fna and the souks, this is the first choice. Booking in advance is advisable. All our recommendations are in the Medina unless stated otherwise.

Hostel

HI hostel Rue El Jahid, Gueliz ⓣ024 44 77 13. Immaculate, refurbished and close to the train station. Closed 9am–2pm. ❶

Hotels

Aday 111 Derb Sidi Bouloukat ⓣ024 44 19 20. A small hotel near the Djemaa; clean, friendly and well-kept. ❶

Afriquia 45 Sidi Bouloukate ⓣ024 442 403. Colourful hotel that's very popular with backpackers; basic rooms and a lively terrace (130dh double). ❶

Ali Rue Moulay Ismail ⓣ024 44 49 79, ⓦwww.hotelali.com. Popular with overlanders and High Atlas trekkers (guides can be found here). Rooms have showers, and there's cheap dorm accommodation (50dh). ❷

Central Palace 59 Sidi Bouloukate ⓣ024 44 02 35. Clean, simple rooms, some of which are stylish and have a/c. Good place to book tours to the Sahara. ❷

Des Voyageurs 40 Bd. Mohammed Zerktouni ⓣ024 44 72 18. Pleasant, old-fashioned hotel, with big, clean rooms and a nice little garden, but hot water mornings only. ❶

Essaouira 3 Derb Sidi Bouloukat ⓣ024 44 38 05, ⓔhotelessaouira@hotmail.com. Well-run, popular cheapie, with laundry service, baggage deposit and rooftop café. ❶

Farouk 66 Av Hassan II, on the corner with Rue Mauretania, Gueliz ⓣ024 43 19 89, ⓔhotelfarouk@hotmail.com. Excellent hotel with en-suite rooms and a popular restaurant, within walking distance of the train station. ❶

Medina 1 Derb Sidi Bouloukat ⓣ024 44 29 97. Clean, friendly and good value, with an English-speaking proprietor and breakfast on the roof terrace. ❶

Souria 17 Rue de la Recette ⓣ072 77 18 47, ⓔlkwika@hotmail.com. Deservedly popular family-run pension, spotless and very homely. ❶

TREAT YOURSELF

Gallia 30 Rue de la Recette ⓣ024 44 59 13 ⓦwww.ilove-marrakesh.com/hotelgallia. Very stylish old French hotel – one of the first in Marrakesh. It is a splurge to stay here, but a real treat. Book ahead. ❷

Eating and drinking

The most atmospheric place to **eat** is the Djemaa el Fna, where foodstalls set up around sunset and serve up everything from *harira* soup and couscous or *tajine* to stewed snails and sheep's heads, all eaten at trestle tables. For tea with a view, the terrace cafés of the *Hôtel CTM* and neighbouring *Café le Grand Balcon* overlook the Djemaa el Fna, as do two relatively reasonable rooftop restaurants: *Argana* and *Hôtel Café de France*. As usual in Morocco, cheap restaurants tend to gather in the Medina, with posher places uptown in Gueliz, along with French-style cafés and virtually all the city's bars.

Café Snack Le Sindbad 216 Av Mohammed V, near the post office, Gueliz. Couscous, *tajine* or *brochettes* at 30–50dh a plate. Open 24hr.

Chez Bahia Riad Zitoun el Kadim, 50m from Djemaa el Fna. Basic café/diner with decent *pastilla*, *tajine*, breakfast and snacks at low prices (main 30dh).

Grand Hotel du Tazi corner of Av El Mouahidine and Rue Bab Agnaou (where the taxis drop you off for the Djemaa). Closest place to the Medina to enjoy a drink. The meals are good but on the pricey side (80–100dh).

Hotel Ali Rue Moulay Ismail. The eat-all-you-like buffet here, served 7–11pm, is justifiably popular and great value at 60dh. There are also lunchtime menus.

Hotel Farouk 66 Av Hassan II, Gueliz. Pizzas or an excellent-value set menu with soup or salad, then couscous, *tajine* or *brochettes*, followed by fruit or home-made yoghurt, for 50dh.

Jnane Mogador Hôtel Derb Sidi Bouloukat by 116 Rue Riad Zitoun el Kedim ⓣ024 42 63 23, ⓦwww.jnanemogador.com. This wonderful riad-style hotel provides a tranquil spot for a decently priced Moroccan meal overlooking the rooftops.

Portofino 279 Av Mohammed V. Some of the best Italian food in Morocco, with chic décor and very professional, friendly service (60–70dh main).

Le Progrès 20 Rue Bani Marine. The best of several decent choices in a street of cheap eateries (30–50dh).

Shopping

Marrakesh is famous for its **souks**, where you can buy goods from all over Morocco. Prices are rarely fixed so before you set out, head to the supposedly fixed price Ensemble Artisanal (Mon–Sat 8.30am–7pm, Sun 8.30am–1pm), on Avenue Mohammed V, midway between the Koutoubia and the ramparts at

Bab Nkob, and get an idea of how much things are worth. It pays to **bargain** hard as the first price you are told can easily be five or ten times the going rate, with the most obscene prices to be found around the edges of the souks.

A lane opposite the *Café de France* on the Djemaa el Fna leads to a stuccowork arch that marks the beginning of the crowded **Souk Smarine**, an important thoroughfare traditionally dominated by **textiles**. At its end the street splits in two. If you take the left-hand fork you will pass a cashpoint, dyers, carpenters and end up at the **slipper** (*babouch*) souk. The right-hand fork leads immediately to Berber **carpet sellers** (on the right), **jewellers** and eventually to the **leather** souk.

Directory

Doctor Dr Abdelmajid Ben Tbib, 171 Av Mohammed V ⓣ 024 43 10 30.
Exchange BMCE has branches with adjoining bureaux de change and ATMs in the Medina (Rue Moulay Ismail, facing Place Foucauld) and Gueliz (114 Av Mohammed V).
Internet Plenty around Djemaa el Fna, including Super Cyber de la Place in an arcade off Rue Bani Marine by the *Hôtel Ichbilia*; Cyber Mohammed Yassine, 36 Rue Bab Aganou.
Mountain trekking guides Ask at the *Hôtel Ali*.
Pharmacy Pharmacie du Progrès, Place Djemaa el Fna at the top of Rue Bab Agnaou; Pharmacie de la Liberté, just off Place de la Liberté (or Houria).
Post office Place du 16 Novembre, midway along Av Mohammed V, and on the Djemaa el Fna.

Moving on

Bus Casablanca (half-hourly 4am–9pm; 4hr); Essaouira (14 daily; 3hr 30min); Fes (10 daily; 10hr); Meknes (6 daily; 9hr); Rabat (hourly; 5hr 30min); Rissani (1 daily; 12hr); Tangier (6 daily; 10hr).
Train Casablanca Voyageurs (9 daily; 3hr 10min); Fes (6 daily; 7hr 35min); Meknes (6 daily; 6hr 45min); Rabat (9 daily; 4hr 15min); Tangier (1 daily; 10hr).

ESSAOUIRA

ESSAOUIRA, the nearest beach resort to Marrakesh, is a lovely eighteenth-century walled seaside town. A favourite with the likes of Frank Zappa and Jimi Hendrix back in the 1960s, its tradition of hippie tourism has created a much more laid-back relationship between local residents and foreign visitors than you'll find in the rest of Morocco. Today Essaouira is a centre for arts and crafts in addition to being the country's top surfing and windsurfing spot.

What to see and do

The ramparts

Essaouira is a great place in which to wander and the **ramparts** are the obvious place to start. Heading north along the lane at the end of Place Prince Moulay el Hassan, you can access the **Skala de la Ville**, the great sea bastion topped by a row of cannons, which runs along the northern cliffs. At the end is the circular **North Bastion**, with panoramic views (closes at sunset). Along the Rue de la Skala, built into the ramparts, are the **wood-carving workshops**, where artisans use thuja, a distinctive local hardwood. You can find another impressive bastion by the harbour, the **Skala du Port** (daily 8.30am–noon & 2.30–6pm; 10dh).

The souks

The town's **souks** spread around and to the south of two arcades, on either side of Rue Mohammed Zerktouni, and up towards the Mellah (former Jewish ghetto), in the northwest corner of the ramparts. Worth particular attention are the **Marché d'Épices** (spice market) and **Souk des Bijoutiers** (jewellers' market).

ORIENTATION

Still largely contained within its ramparts, Essaouira is a simple place to get to grips with. At the northeast end of town is the **Bab Doukkala**; at the southwest is the town's pedestrianized main square, **Place Prince Moulay el Hassan**, and the fishing **harbour**. Between them run two main parallel streets: Av de l'Istiqlal/Av Mohammed Zerktouni and Rue Sidi Mohammed Ben Abdallah.

Art studios and hippie-style clothing shops centre around Place Chefchaouni by the clocktower.

The beaches

The **southern beach** (the northern one is less attractive) extends for miles, past the Oued Ksob riverbed and the ruins of an old fort known as the **Bordj el Berod**, which inspired Hendrix to write *Castles in the Sand*. If you want to do **watersports**, Club Mistral is the closest beachside operator to the Medina, opposite the *Sofitel* hotel ⓣ024 78 39 34, ⓦwww.club-mistral.com. They rent out mainly wind- and kite-surfing gear and offer lessons in both.

Arrival and information

Tourist office Av du Caire (Mon–Fri 9am–noon & 3–6.30pm, June to mid-Sept open Sat same hours; ⓣ024 78 35 32). The well-known *Hotel Sahara* on Ave de L'Istiqlal has some good maps.

Bus The new bus station is about 500m (ten minutes' walk) northeast of Bab Doukkala. Especially at night, it's worth taking a petit taxi (about 5dh) or horse-drawn *calèche* (about 10dh).

Taxi Grands taxis also operate from the bus station, though they will drop arrivals at Bab Doukkala or Place Prince Moulay el Hassan.

Accommodation

Accommodation can be tight over Easter and in summer, when advance booking is recommended. Local residents may approach you with offers of rooms, and Jack's Kiosk (ⓣ024 47 55 38), a newspaper shop on Place Prince Moulay el Hassan, displays ads for apartments.

Hotels

Majestic 40 Rue Laâlouj, opposite the museum ⓣ024 47 49 09. The former French colonial courthouse, with good, clean rooms, though a little cheerless. The terrace is one of the city's highest points. ❶

Sahara Av Okba Ibn Nafia ⓣ024 47 52 92, ⓕ024 47 61 98. Big rooms around a central well, some en suite. ❶

Shahrazed 1 Rue Youssef el Fassi, entrance on Rue du Caire ⓣ024 47 29 77, ⓔhotelshahrazed@yahoo.fr. Comfortable and well-equipped, with spacious rooms, most en suite. ❷

Smara 26 Rue Skala (near the North Bastion) ⓣ024 47 56 55. Cheap and popular hotel, with decent rooms and a stunning view over the town and the Atlantic from its terrace.

Souiri 37 Rue Attarine ⓣ024 47 53 39, ⓔsouiri@menara.ma. Popular, colourful Medina hotel with a range of rooms, the cheaper ones with shared bathroom facilities. ❶

Tafraout 7 Rue Marrakech ⓣ024 47 62 76. Clean and friendly with some en-suite rooms. Hot water mornings and evenings only, but public showers for both sexes right next door. ❶

Campsite

Camping Sidi Magdoul 1km south of town behind the lighthouse ⓣ024 47 21 96. Clean, friendly and well-managed, with hot showers and bungalows, though the ground is rather hard and shade is sparse.

Eating and drinking

For an informal **meal**, you can do no better than eat at the line of grills down at the port. The official prices are on a board as you walk down to the port but haggle to get more for your money. Restaurants can be a bit expensive, but there are plenty of places to pick up cheap sandwiches.

Blue Note Rue Laâlouj ⓣ024 78 53 92. The food is a bit pricey here (80–100dh), but the bar is a great bluesy dive.

Les Chandeliers 14 Rue Laâlouj ⓣ024 47 58 27. A well-established restaurant and wine bar run by a French family and offering both continental and Moroccan options. Cosy bar upstairs; dinner only (70–90dh).

Delices de Mogador 2 Rue Tetouane. Cheap falafel, shwarma and pizzas in a cosy modern Moroccan setting (dishes 30–50dh).

Essalam Place Moulay El Hassan. A cheap set menu, pleasant wooden furnishings and meaty *tajines*.

Snack de la Place 9 Place Prince Moulay El Hassan. If you face the harbour, this sandwich stall is on your left. It offers hot sandwiches at bargain prices (10–20dh).

Moving on

Bus Casablanca (37 daily; 6hr); Rabat (10 daily; 8hr 30min); Marrakesh (14 daily; 3hr 30min).

The Sahara

Though it is a considerable distance from other traveller hotspots, the Sahara is more accessible than it used to be. Even if you only have a few days to spare it's worth making the trip as the desert is a truly unforgettable place. **Excursions** last for several hours or several days and can include camel treks, quad biking and nights in Berber tents. **Tour guides** are easily arranged from the major cities if you ask at tourist information or travel agency offices (fees start around 600dh).

RISSANI

Rissani, a common staging point for Saharan excursions, lies in the southeast of Morocco on the edge of the desert. The town itself holds an important place in Moroccan **history** as the site of the ancient kingdom of Sijilmasa, ruled by Berber dissidents from the eighth to the fourteenth century as the first independent kingdom of the South.

GETTING TO THE DESERT

The DIY approach is to catch a bus to Rissani (you may have to change at Er Rachidia). The CTM station is in the centre of the town – the sign for *Hotel Panorama* is just about visible from the station if you look to your right with your back to the CTM office. The local bus station is just outside the city walls. You can pick up a petit taxi or walk a short distance down the main road. Head towards the archway (you will see the *Hotel Sijilmasa* in front of you) and take the first sharp right to reach the central square. As the journey can take twelve hours you may want to book a hotel in which to recuperate before heading into the desert. Treks tend to set off from Merzouga and Rissani between 3 and 5.30pm in order to catch the sunset.

In the seventeenth century the current Alouite dynasty launched its bid for power from the *zaouia* here. Although many of the monuments to this history have succumbed to erosion, it is still worth following the signposted "circuit touristique" on which you can see several impressive *ksour* (tribal forts) including the Ksar d'Akbar dating from the early nineteenth century. You can rent bikes from the *Hotel Panorama* if you don't fancy doing the tour on foot.

The thrice-weekly **souk** is a major event for the town, bringing Berbers from all over the region (Sunday, Tuesday & Thursday). For **desert treks** try *Hotel Panorama* and *Hotel Sijilmasa*. Budget **accommodation** can be found on the central square, where you'll also find the CTM office and a couple of banks. Both of the aforementioned hotels do decent food (*Sijilmassa* is slightly more expensive), and there are a couple of other inexpensive options around *Panorama*.

Accommodation

Hotel Panorama 6–8 Centre de Rissani ⓣ066 35 18 36. Basic but cheap and friendly hotel with café below on the central square. ❶

Hotel Sijilmasa Place El Massira El Khadra ⓣ035 57 50 42. A comfortable reasonably priced hotel, conveniently next to the grand taxi station, just south of the bus station. ❷

MERZOUGA

If you want to stay closer to the desert, Merzouga is only a short grand taxi ride away from Rissani (from outside *Hotel Sijilmasa*). A very small town, without a cashpoint or many amenities, it is the last stop before the Sahara and the hotels below all offer treks and views across the dunes.

Accommodation

Nasser Palace ⓦwww.nasserpalace.com. One of several plush hotels between Rissani and Merzouga reached by grand taxi (120dh), this is by far the cheapest. It has a swimming pool, well-decorated rooms (some with a/c) and the option of sleeping for less outside. Desert treks start at 150dh. ❷

Le Petit Prince Ⓦwww.hotelpetitprince, Ⓣ062 19 12 18. An inexpensive *auberge* with good rooms and a beautiful view. Conveniently located near the grand taxi station (go through the large arch and follow the sign). ❶

Moving on

Buses from Rissani can be very erratic so it is wise to give yourself more than enough time to get to your next destination.

Bus CTM Fes (daily 10am; 7hr); Meknes (8pm; 8hr).

Local bus Fes (3 daily; 9hr); Meknes (3 daily; 9hr); Rabat (2 daily; 11hr); Marrakesh (1 daily; 11hr); Tangier (1 daily; 15hr); Casablanca (2 daily; 12hr).

The Netherlands

AMSTERDAM: experience canals, coffeeshops and world-famous art

DELFT: enjoy wonderful apple cake in Vermeer's home town

ROTTERDAM: a buzzing port with great nightlife

HOGE VELUWE NATIONAL PARK: cycle through woods to the world's best collection of Van Goghs

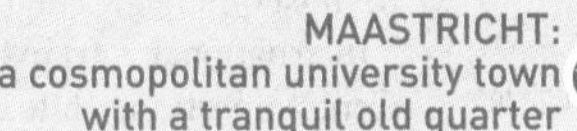

MAASTRICHT: a cosmopolitan university town with a tranquil old quarter

DAILY BUDGET Basic €45/occasional treat €60

DRINK Beer €1.80

FOOD Pancake €7

HOSTEL/BUDGET HOTEL €20–28/€50–65

TRAVEL Train: Amsterdam–Maastricht €27; Bus: Amsterdam–Haarlem €4

FACT FILE

POPULATION 16.5 million

AREA 41,526 sq km

LANGUAGE Dutch

CURRENCY Euro (€)

CAPITAL Amsterdam (population 1 million)

INTERNATIONAL PHONE CODE ⓣ31

Basics

The Netherlands is a country partly reclaimed from the waters of the North Sea, and around half of it lies at or below sea level. Land reclamation has been the dominant motif of its history, resulting in a country of unique images – flat, fertile landscapes punctuated by windmills and church spires; ornately gabled terraces flanking peaceful canals; and mile upon mile of grassy dunes, backing onto stretches of pristine sandy beach.

Most people travel only to atmospheric **Amsterdam**. Nearby is a group of towns known collectively as the **Randstad** (literally "rim town"), including **Haarlem** and **Delft** with their old canal-girded centres, and **Den Haag** (The Hague), a stately city with fine museums and easy beach access. Outside the Randstad, life moves more slowly. To the south, the landscape undulates into heathy moorland, best experienced in the **Hoge Veluwe National Park**. Further south lies the compelling city of **Maastricht**, squeezed between the German and Belgian borders.

CHRONOLOGY

58 BC Julius Caesar conquers the area of the present-day Netherlands.
1275 Amsterdam is founded by Count Floris V of Holland.
1477 The Austrian Habsburgs take control.
1500s Protestant Reformation spreads through the Netherlands, leading to wars against the Catholic Habsburg rulers based in Spain.
1581 Republic of the Netherlands formed, heralding a "Golden Age" of trade and colonial expansion.
1603 The Dutch East India Company establishes its first trading post in Indonesia, an area that it would gradually colonize.
1806 Napoleon annexes the Kingdom of Holland for France.
1813 The French are driven out and the Prince of Orange becomes sovereign of the United Netherlands.
1853 Vincent Van Gogh is born.
1918 The Netherlands remains neutral during WWI.
1920 Dutch airline KLM launches the world's first passenger service.
1940 Nazis invade the Netherlands, forcing the deportation of Jews including Anne Frank's family.
1945 Germans are expelled by Allied forces.
1947 Anne Frank's diary is published.
1975 Cannabis is decriminalized – tourism booms.
1997 Treaty of Amsterdam clears the way for the introduction of a single European currency.
2000 The Netherlands becomes the first European country to legalize euthanasia.
2003 The permanent International Criminal Court is established in The Hague to try war criminals.
2007 Controversial government plans to ban the burqa (Islamic dress for women) in public places gains Cabinet support.

ARRIVAL

Amsterdam's modern Schiphol airport is one of Europe's busiest and is served by over seventy budget airline routes. Trains from here reach central Amsterdam within fifteen minutes and connect the airport to most other cities in the Randstad.

International **trains** terminate at Centraal Station, while international **buses** arrive at Amstel Station, ten minutes south of Centraal Station by metro. The Dutchflyer (Ⓦwww.dutchflyer.co.uk) connects London with Amsterdam Centraal by train and boat, while Stenaline ferries (Ⓦwww.stenaline.co.uk) travel between Harwich and the Hook of Holland. P & O ferries (Ⓦwww.poferries.com) leave from Hull and dock in Rotterdam.

GETTING AROUND

Trains (Ⓦwww.ns.nl) are fast, fares relatively low, and the network comprehensive. Various **passes** cut costs – ask

at a station (passport needed for ID). With any ticket, you're free to stop off en route and continue later that day.

Urban **buses** and **trams** are very efficient. You only need one kind of ticket: a **strippenkaart**. You can buy two- and three-strip *strippenkaarts* from bus drivers, or better-value fifteen-strip (€6.80) or 45-strip (€20.60) *strippenkaarts* in advance from train stations, tobacconists and public transport offices. One *strippenkaart* can be used by any number of people – you just cancel the requisite number of strips per person.

There's a nationwide system of **cycle** paths. You can rent bikes cheaply from main train stations and also from outlets in almost any town and village. Theft is rife: never leave your bike unlocked, and don't leave it on the street overnight – most stations have a storage area. For more information on cycling in the Netherlands, including maps, routes and tips, check out ⓦwww.holland.com/uk.

ACCOMMODATION

Accommodation can be pricey, especially in places like Amsterdam and

Haarlem. Book ahead during the summer and over holiday periods, especially Easter. The cheapest one- or two-star **hotel** double rooms start at around €60; three-star hotel rooms begin around €80. Prices usually include a reasonable breakfast. You can reserve for free through the Netherlands Reservation Centre (Ⓦwww.hotelres.nl), or at tourist offices (for a small charge). There are 30 excellent HI **hostels** nationwide (Ⓦwww.stayokay.com), charging €20–25 per person including breakfast. Larger cities often have independent hostels with similar prices, though standards are sometimes not as reliable. **Private rooms** can usually be arranged through the VVV office (see opposite) in town, and usually cost around €20–25 including breakfast. There are plenty of well-equipped **campsites**: expect to pay around €4 per person, plus €3–5 for a tent. Some sites also have **cabins** for up to four people, for around €35 a night.

FOOD AND DRINK

Dutch **food** tends to be plain but thanks to its colonial history, the Netherlands boasts the best **Indonesian cuisine** outside Indonesia. *Nasi goreng* and *bami goreng* (rice or noodles with meat) are good basic dishes; chicken or beef in peanut sauce (*sateh*) is always available. A *rijsttafel* is rice or noodles served with a huge range of tasty side-dishes.

Breakfast (*ontbijt*) is filling, and usually consists of rolls, cheese, ham, eggs, jam and honey, chocolate spread or peanut butter. **Snacks** include chips – *frites* or *patat* – smothered with mayonnaise, curry, satay or tomato sauce, *kroketten* (bite-size chunks of meat goulash coated in breadcrumbs and deep fried) and *fricandel* (a frankfurter-like sausage). **Fish** specialities sold from street kiosks include salted raw herrings, smoked eel (*gerookte paling*), mackerel in a roll (*broodje makreel*) and mussels. Other common snacks are kebab (*shoarma*) and falafel. Most bars serve sandwiches and rolls (*boterham* and *broodjes* – *stokbrood* if made with baguette) and, in winter, *erwtensoep*, a thick pea soup with smoked sausage, and *uitsmijter*: fried eggs on buttered bread, topped with ham or roast beef. In **restaurants**, stick to the dish of the day (*dagschotel*). Many places have at least one meat-free item, and you'll find veggie restaurants in most towns.

Sampling the Dutch and Belgian **beers** in every region is a real pleasure, often done in a cosy brown café (*bruine kroeg*, named because of the colour of the tobacco-stained walls); the big brands Heineken, Amstel, Oranjeboom and Grolsch are just the tip of the iceberg. A standard, small glass (*een pils*) costs about €1.80; a bigger glass is *een vaasje*. You may also come across *proeflokalen* or tasting houses, small, old-fashioned bars that close around 8pm, and specialize in **jenever**, Dutch gin, drunk straight; *oud* (old) is smooth, *jong* (young) packs more of a punch. **Coffee** is normally good and strong, while **tea** generally comes with lemon. **Chocolate** is also popular, served hot or cold.

DRUGS

Purchases of up to 5g of cannabis, and possession of up to 30g (the legal limit) are tolerated; in practice, many "**coffeeshops**" offer discounted bulk purchases of 50g with impunity. Coffeeshops in city centres –neon-lit dives pumping out mainstream rock, reggae or techno – are worth avoiding. Less touristy districts house more congenial, high-quality outlets. When you walk in, ask to see the **menu**, which lists the different hashes and grasses on offer. Take care with spacecakes (cakes or biscuits baked with hash), mainly because you can never be sure what's in them, and don't ever buy from street dealers. All other narcotics are illegal, and don't even entertain the notion of taking a "souvenir" home with you.

CULTURE AND ETIQUETTE

The Dutch are renowned for their liberal and laidback attitude, so there isn't much in the way of etiquette to observe. Don't be embarrassed about speaking to locals in English – unlike many of their fellow Europeans, the Dutch don't particularly appreciate tourists attempting to speak their language. A ten percent **tip** is generally expected in cafés and restaurants.

SPORTS AND ACTIVITIES

The Netherlands is a nation of **cyclists**, and you won't have any problems finding cycle paths or bikes for rent. With most of the country's major towns sat cheek by jowl in the Randstad, cycling from city to city is very easy. If you're looking for a more rural experience, the island of Texel and the Hoge Veluwe National Park near Arnhem are ideal, with the park even providing free bicycles for visitors. **Football** is also extremely popular, with the season running from September to May and matches held on Sunday at around 2.30pm, with occasional games on Wednesday too. The major teams are PSV Eindhoven, Feyenoord in Rotterdam, and Amsterdam's Ajax.

COMMUNICATIONS

Post offices are open Mon–Fri 9am–5pm, Sat 9am–noon. Post international items in the "Overige" slot. Most **public phones** take phonecards – available from post offices and VVVs (see "Information and maps", right) – or credit cards. The operator is on ⓣ0800/0410 (free). Many cafés and public libraries offer **Internet access**.

EMERGENCIES

If you are wary of pickpockets and badly lit streets at night, you're unlikely to come into contact with the police. **Pharmacies** (*apotheek*) are open Mon–Fri 8.30am–5.30pm; if they are closed there'll be a note of the nearest open pharmacy on the door. Duty **doctors** at the Centrale Doktorsdienst (ⓣ0900/503 2042) offer advice; otherwise head for any hospital (*ziekenhuis*). If you need the emergency services, police, ambulance and fire are all on ⓣ112.

THE NETHERLANDS ON THE NET

ⓦ**www.holland.com** National tourist board.
ⓦ**www.ns.nl** Train information.
ⓦ**www.hotelres.nl** Online hotel bookings.

INFORMATION AND MAPS

VVV tourist offices are usually in town centres or by train stations and have information in English, including maps and accommodation lists; they will also book rooms, again for a small charge. The best general **map** is Kümmerley and Frey's.

MONEY AND BANKS

The Dutch currency is the **euro** (€). **Banking hours** are Mon 1–4/5pm, Tues–Fri 9am–4/5pm; in larger cities some banks also open Thurs 7–9pm and occasionally on Sat mornings. **GWK exchange offices** at train stations open late daily; they change money and travellers' cheques, and give cash

STUDENT AND YOUTH DISCOUNTS

There are small discounts for ISIC card holders in museums and galleries, but no youth discounts; only international trains have a discount for those under 26. If you're staying in the Netherlands for a while and expect to take lots of trains, it might be worth buying the under-26 railcard.

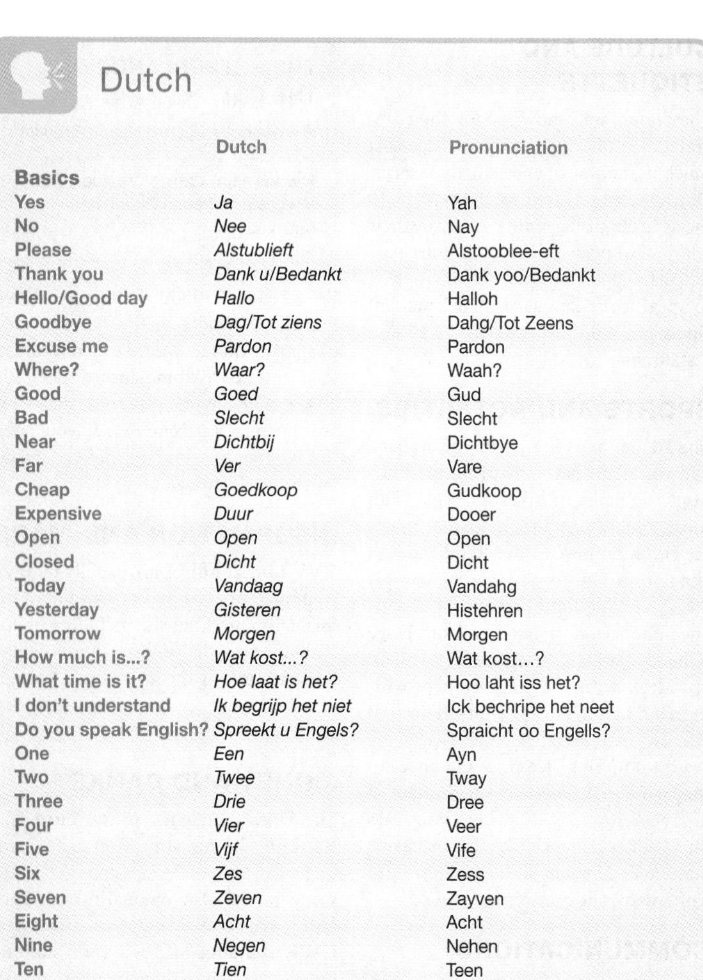

Dutch

	Dutch	Pronunciation
Basics		
Yes	*Ja*	Yah
No	*Nee*	Nay
Please	*Alstublieft*	Alstooblee-eft
Thank you	*Dank u/Bedankt*	Dank yoo/Bedankt
Hello/Good day	*Hallo*	Halloh
Goodbye	*Dag/Tot ziens*	Dahg/Tot Zeens
Excuse me	*Pardon*	Pardon
Where?	*Waar?*	Waah?
Good	*Goed*	Gud
Bad	*Slecht*	Slecht
Near	*Dichtbij*	Dichtbye
Far	*Ver*	Vare
Cheap	*Goedkoop*	Gudkoop
Expensive	*Duur*	Dooer
Open	*Open*	Open
Closed	*Dicht*	Dicht
Today	*Vandaag*	Vandahg
Yesterday	*Gisteren*	Histehren
Tomorrow	*Morgen*	Morgen
How much is...?	*Wat kost...?*	Wat kost…?
What time is it?	*Hoe laat is het?*	Hoo laht iss het?
I don't understand	*Ik begrijp het niet*	Ick bechripe het neet
Do you speak English?	*Spreekt u Engels?*	Spraicht oo Engells?
One	*Een*	Ayn
Two	*Twee*	Tway
Three	*Drie*	Dree
Four	*Vier*	Veer
Five	*Vijf*	Vife
Six	*Zes*	Zess
Seven	*Zeven*	Zayven
Eight	*Acht*	Acht
Nine	*Negen*	Nehen
Ten	*Tien*	Teen

advances. You can also change money at most VVV tourist offices, post offices and bureaux de change, though rates are worse. **ATMs** are widespread. Smaller places (including B&Bs) may not accept cards.

OPENING HOURS AND HOLIDAYS

Many **shops** stay closed on Mon morning, although markets open early. Otherwise, opening hours tend to be 9am–5.30/6pm, with many shops closing late on Thursdays. In major cities, night shops (*avondwinkels*) open 4pm–1/2am. **Museum** times are generally Tues–Sat 10am–5pm, Sun 1–5pm. Shops and banks are closed, and museums adopt Sunday hours, on **public holidays**: Jan 1, Good Fri, Easter Sun & Mon, April 30, May 5, May 13, Whitsun & Mon, Dec 25 & Dec 26.

Amsterdam

AMSTERDAM is a beguiling capital, with a compact mix of the provincial and the cosmopolitan and an enduring appeal for backpackers. For many, its array of world-class museums and galleries – notably the **Rijksmuseum**, **Anne Frank House** and the **Van Gogh Museum** – are reason enough to visit.

Amsterdam started out as a fishing village at the mouth of the River Amstel, and subsequently grew as a trading centre. During the Reformation It took trade away from Antwerp and became a haven for its religious refugees. The city went from strength to strength in the seventeenth century, becoming the centre of a vast trading empire with colonies in Southeast Asia. Amsterdam accommodated its expansion with the cobweb of **canals** that gives the city its distinctive and elegant shape today. By the eighteenth century, Amsterdam was in gentle decline, re-emerging as a fashionable focus for the alternative movements of the 1960s. Despite a backlash in the 1980s, the city still takes a progressive approach to social issues and culture, with a buzz of open-air summer events, intimate clubs and bars, and a relaxed attitude to soft drugs.

What to see and do

Amsterdam's compact centre contains most of the city's leading attractions, but it takes only about forty minutes to stroll from one end to the other. Centraal Station, where you're most likely to arrive, lies on the centre's northern edge, and from here the city fans south in a web of concentric canals, surrounded by expanding suburbs.

At the heart of the city is the **Old Centre**, an oval-shaped area with a jumble of antique streets and beautiful narrow canals. This is the unlikely setting for the infamous **Red Light District**. Forming a ring around it is the first of the major canals, the Singel, followed closely by the Herengracht, Keizersgracht and Prinsengracht. This is the Amsterdam you see in the brochures: still, dreamy canals, crisp reflections of seventeenth-century town houses, cobbled streets, and railings with chained bicycles.

To the south is the city's main square, **Leidseplein**, with the lovely **Vondelpark** nearby. The **Jordaan** to the northwest features mazy streets and narrow canals. To the east is the **Old Jewish Quarter**.

Centraal Station and the Damrak

Amsterdam is a small city, and, although the canal system can be initially confusing, finding your bearings is straightforward. The medieval core boasts the best of the city's bustling streetlife and is home to many shops, bars and restaurants, fanning south from the nineteenth-century **Centraal Station**, one of Amsterdam's most resonant landmarks. From here, the busy thoroughfare **Damrak** marches into the heart of the city, lined with overpriced restaurants and bobbing canal boats, and flanked on the left first by the Modernist stock exchange, the **Beurs** (now a concert hall), and then by the enormous De Bijenkorf department store.

The Red Light District

East of Damrak, the infamous **Red Light District**, stretching across two canals – Oudezijds (abbreviated to O.Z.) Voorburgwal and O.Z. Achterburgwal – is one of the real sights of the city. Treat yourself to the bizarre spectacle of tourists checking out sex toys while pimps and drug addicts huddle nearby. The atmosphere is undeniably sleazy, despite the masses of tourists (including young families) who are evidently not here as serious punters. It's perhaps more fun to visit the place at night, when the seediness is somehow less glaring and the neon-lit window brothels down narrow passageways become strangely scenic.

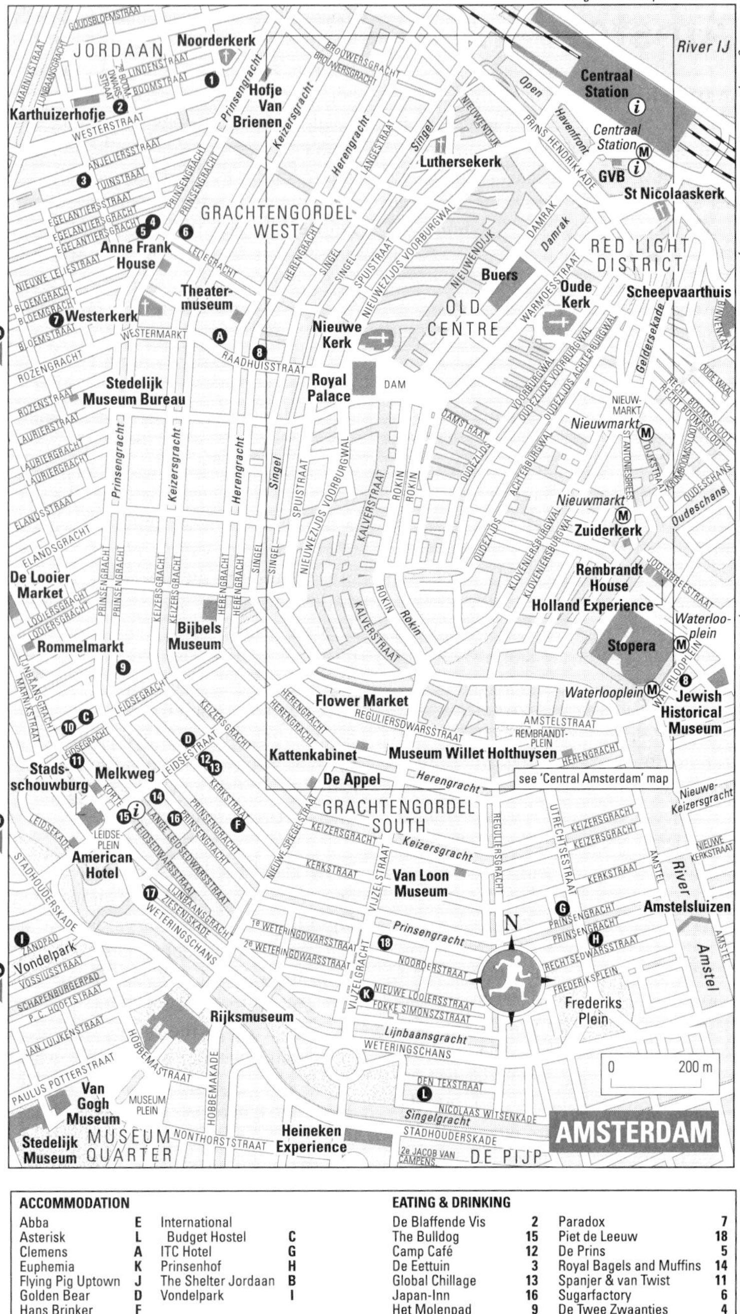

ACCOMMODATION

Abba	E	International Budget Hostel	C
Asterisk	L	ITC Hotel	G
Clemens	A	Prinsenhof	H
Euphemia	K	The Shelter Jordaan	B
Flying Pig Uptown	J	Vondelpark	I
Golden Bear	D		
Hans Brinker	F		

EATING & DRINKING

De Blaffende Vis	2	Paradox	7
The Bulldog	15	Piet de Leeuw	18
Camp Café	12	De Prins	5
De Eettuin	3	Royal Bagels and Muffins	14
Global Chillage	13	Spanjer & van Twist	11
Japan-Inn	16	Sugarfactory	6
Het Molenpad	9	De Twee Zwaantjes	4
Meneer Pannekoek	8	Winkel	1
Paradiso	17	De Zotte Proeflokaal	10

The Oude Kerk

Behind the Beurs, off Warmoesstraat, the precincts of the **Oude Kerk** (Mon–Sat 11am–5pm, Sun 1–5pm; €5; ⓦwww.oudekerk.nl) offer a reverential peace after the excesses of the Red Light District. It's a bare, mostly fourteenth-century church with the memorial tablet of Rembrandt's first wife, Saskia van Uylenburg. Just beyond, Zeedijk leads to the **Nieuwmarkt square**, centred on the turreted **Waag** building, an original part of the city's fortifications. **Kloveniersburgwal**, heading south, was the outer of the three eastern canals of sixteenth-century Amsterdam and boasts, at no. 29, one of the city's most impressive canal houses, built for the Trip family in 1662. Further along on the west side, the Oudemanhuispoort passage is filled with secondhand bookstalls.

The Koninklijk Paleis and Nieuwe Kerk

At the southern end of Damrak, the **Dam** (or Dam square) is the centre of the city, its war memorial serving as a meeting place for tourists. On the western side, the *Koninklijk Paleis* (Royal Palace; open for hour-long guided tours – which must be booked at least a fortnight in advance – and exhibitions) was originally built as the city hall in the mid-seventeenth century. Vying for importance is the adjacent **Nieuwe Kerk** (open for exhibitions only, usually daily 10am–6pm; €10; ⓦwww.nieuwekerk.nl), a fifteenth-century church rebuilt several times.

Rokin and Beginhof

South of Dam square, **Rokin** follows the old course of the Amstel River, lined with grandiose nineteenth-century mansions. Running parallel, Kalverstraat is a monotonous strip of clothes shops, halfway down which, at no. 92, a gateway forms the entrance to the former orphanage that's now the **Amsterdams Historisch Museum** (Mon–Fri 10am–5pm, Sat & Sun 11am–5pm; €7; ⓦwww.ahm.nl), where artefacts, paintings and documents survey the city's development from the thirteenth century. Close by, the **Spui** (pronounced "spow") is a lively corner of town whose mixture of bookshops and packed bars centres on a statue of a young boy known as *'t Lieverdje* (Little Darling).

The Muntplein and Bloemenmarkt

Kalverstraat comes to an end at **Muntplein** and the Munttoren – originally a mint and part of the city walls, topped with a seventeenth-century spire. Across the Singel canal is the fragrant daily **Bloemenmarkt** (Flower Market), while in the other direction Reguliersbreestraat turns towards the loud restaurants of **Rembrandtplein**. To the south is Reguliersgracht, an appealing canal with seven distinctive steep bridges stretching in line from Thorbeckeplein.

Around Leidseplein

Amsterdam's expansion in the seventeenth century was designed around three new canals, **Herengracht**, **Keizersgracht** and **Prinsengracht**, which ring the centre. Development was strictly controlled, resulting in the tall, very narrow residences with decorative gables you see today. The appeal lies in wandering along, taking in the calm tree-lined waterways, while looking into people's windows – Amsterdammers tend not to bother with curtains, a habit which lends the city an open and cosy atmosphere. For shops, bars and restaurants, you're better off exploring the crossing-streets that connect the canals.

From the Spui, trams and pedestrians cross Koningsplein onto Amsterdam's main drag, **Leidsestraat** – a long, slender shopping street that cuts across the main canals. On the corner with Keizersgracht, the designer department store Metz & Co has a top-floor

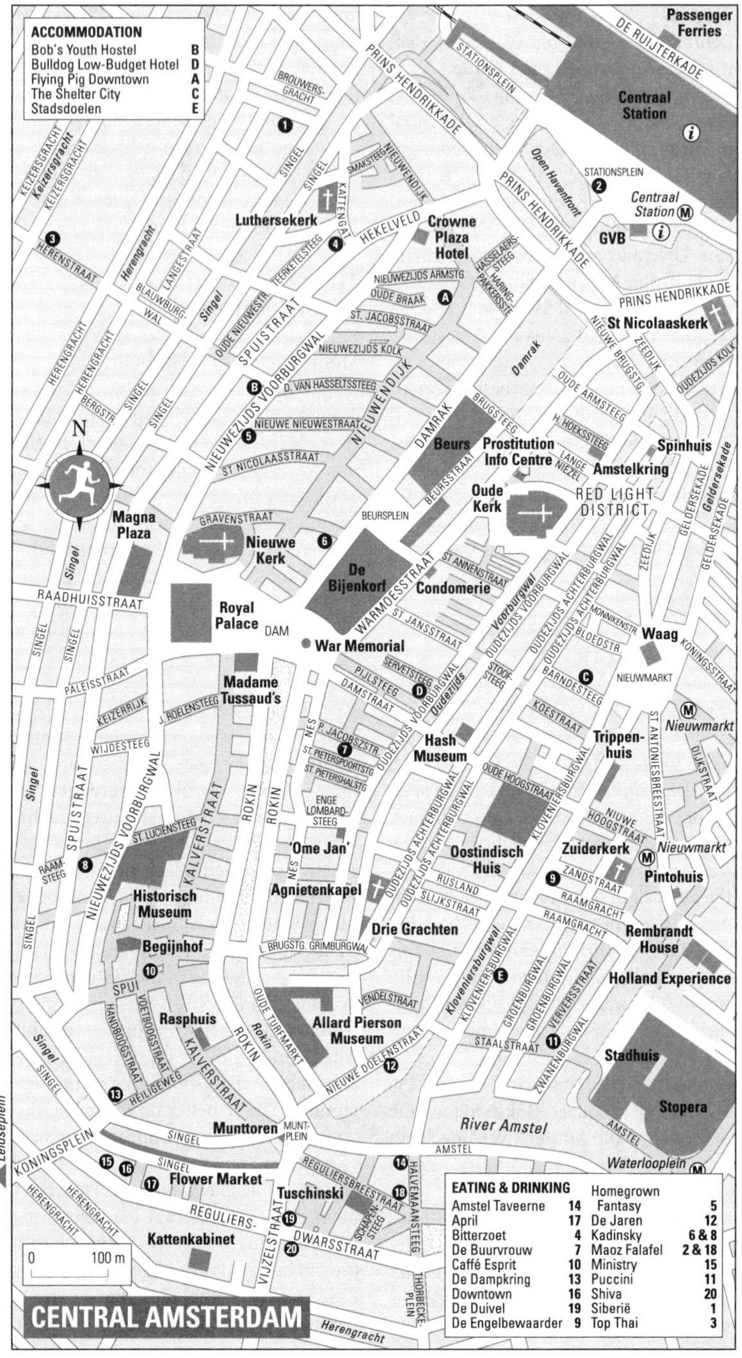
ACCOMMODATION
Bob's Youth Hostel B
Bulldog Low-Budget Hotel D
Flying Pig Downtown A
The Shelter City C
Stadsdoelen E
EATING & DRINKING
Amstel Taveerne 14
April 17
Bitterzoet 4
De Buurvrouw 7
Caffé Esprit 10
De Dampkring 13
Downtown 16
De Duivel 19
De Engelbewaarder 9
Homegrown Fantasy 5
De Jaren 12
Kadinsky 6 & 8
Maoz Falafel 2 & 18
Ministry 15
Puccini 11
Shiva 20
Siberië 1
Top Thai 3
CENTRAL AMSTERDAM
0 100 m
N
Passenger Ferries
DE RUIJTERKADE
Centraal Station
STATIONSPLEIN
Centraal Station
GVB
PRINS HENDRIKKADE
Open Havenfront
BROUWERSGRACHT
SINGEL
KATTENGAT
SMAKSTEEG
NIEUWENDIJK
Luthersekerk
HEKELVELD
Crowne Plaza Hotel
KEIZERSGRACHT
Keizersgracht
HERENSTRAAT
Herengracht
LANGESTRAAT
BLAUWBURGWAL
Singel
TEERKETELSTEEG
OUDE NIEUWESTR.
SPUISTRAAT
NIEUWEZIJDS ARMSTG
OUDE BRAAK
HASSELAERSSTEEG
HARINGPAKKERSSTEEG
ST. JACOBSSTRAAT
NIEUWEZIJDS KOLK
St Nicolaaskerk
Damrak
NIEUWE BRUGSTG
ZEEDIJK
OUDEZIJDS KOLK
HERENGRACHT
BERGSTR.
NIEUWEZIJDS VOORBURGWAL
D. VAN HASSELTSSTEEG
NIEUWE NIEUWESTRAAT
OUDE ARMSTEEG
H. HOEKSSTEEG
BRUGSTEEG
DAMRAK
Beurs
Prostitution Info Centre
LANGE NIEZEL
Amstelkring
Spinhuis
Geldersekade
ST NICOLAASSTRAAT
BEURSSTRAAT
Oude Kerk
RED LIGHT DISTRICT
GELDERSEKADE
Magna Plaza
GRAVENSTRAAT
Nieuwe Kerk
BEURSPLEIN
De Bijenkorf
ST ANNENSTRAAT
Condomerie
Voorburgwal
OUDEZIJDS VOORBURGWAL
OUDEZIJDS ACHTERBURGWAL
RAADHUISSTRAAT
Royal Palace
DAM
WARMOESSTRAAT
ST JANSSTRAAT
MONNIKENSTR.
Waag
BLOEDSTR.
KONINGSSTRAAT
War Memorial
SERVETSTEEG
PIJLSTEEG
DAMSTRAAT
Oudezijds
STOOFSTEEG
BARNDESTEEG
NIEUWMARKT
Madame Tussaud's
PALEISSTRAAT
KEIZERRIJK
J. ROELENSTEEG
KOESTRAAT
Nieuwmarkt
WIJDESTEEG
NES
P. JACOBSZSTR.
ST. PIETERSPOORTSTG
ST. PIETERSHALSTG
Hash Museum
Trippenhuis
ST ANTONIESBREESTRAAT
DIJKSTRAAT
ENGE LOMBARDSTEEG
OUDE HOOGSTRAAT
KLOVENIERSBURGWAL
NIEUWE HOOGSTRAAT
ROKIN
KALVERSTRAAT
ST. LUCIENSTEEG
'Ome Jan'
Oostindisch Huis
Zuiderkerk
Pintohuis
RAAMSTEEG
ZANDSTRAAT
Historisch Museum
Agnietenkapel
RUSLAND
SLIJKSTRAAT
RAAMGRACHT
Drie Grachten
Rembrandt House
Begijnhof
L. BRUGSTG. GRIMBURGWAL
Kloveniersburgwal
GROENBURGWAL
VERVERSSTRAAT
Holland Experience
SPUI
HANDBOOGSTRAAT
VOETBOOGSTRAAT
Rasphuis
VENDELSTRAAT
OUDE TURFMARKT
Allard Pierson Museum
Rokin
STAALSTRAAT
ZWANENBURGWAL
Stadhuis
NIEUWE DOELENSTRAAT
HEILIGEWEG
Stopera
River Amstel
Munttoren
MUNTPLEIN
AMSTEL
Leidseplein
KONINGSPLEIN
Waterlooplein
REGULIERSBREESTRAAT
HALVEMAANSTEEG
Flower Market
Tuschinski
SCHAPENSTEEG
REGULIERS-DWARSSTRAAT
VIJZELSTRAAT
Kattenkabinet
THORBECKEPLEIN
Herengracht

café with one of the best views of the city. Leidsestraat broadens at its southern end into **Leidseplein**, the bustling hub of Amsterdam's nightlife, a cluttered and disorderly open space crisscrossed by tram lines. On the far corner, the **Stadsschouwburg** is the city's prime performance space after the Muziektheater.

The Jordaan and Anne Frank House

Across Prinsengracht to the west, the **Jordaan** is a beguiling area of narrow canals, narrower streets and architecturally varied houses. With some of the city's best bars and restaurants, alternative clothes shops and good outdoor markets, especially those on the square outside the Noorderkerk (which hosts an antique and household goods market on Mondays and a popular farmers' market on Saturdays), it's a wonderful area to wander through, however it is most famous for the **Anne Frank House** (daily: April–Aug 9am–9pm; Sept–March 9am–7pm; closed Yom Kippur; €8; Ⓦwww.annefrank.nl), where the young diarist lived, at Prinsengracht 267. It's deservedly one of the most popular tourist attractions in town, so arrive before 9am (or at the end of the day) and be prepared to queue. Anne, her family and friends went into hiding from the Nazis in 1942, staying in the house for two years until they were betrayed and taken away to labour camps, an experience that only Anne's father survived. The plain, small rooms have been well preserved, and include moving items such as the film star pin-ups on Anne's bedroom wall. The museum also provides plenty of fascinating background on the Holocaust and the experiences of Dutch Jews.

The Westerkerk and Stedelijk Museum

South along Prinsengracht lies the Westerkerk (April–Sept Mon–Fri 11am–3pm; free), with its impressive 85-metre tower (May–Sept Mon–Sat 10am–5pm; €5). Further on, the hottest contemporary artists hold exhibitions at the **Stedelijk Museum**, Rozenstraat 59 (Tues–Sun 11am–5pm; Ⓦwww.smba.nl).

The Vondelpark

Immediately south of Leidseplein begins the **Vondelpark**, the city's most enticing open space, a regular forum for performance arts on summer weekends, when young Amsterdammers flock here to meet friends, laze by the lake and listen to music; in June, July and August there are free concerts every Sunday at 2pm. Southeast of the park is a residential district, with designer shops and delis along chic **P.C. Hooftstraat** and **Van Baerlestraat**, and some of the city's major museums grouped around the grassy wedge of **Museumplein**.

The Rijksmuseum

The **Rijksmuseum**, at Jan Luijkenstraat 1 (daily 9am–6pm, Fri 9am–10pm; €10; Ⓦwww.rijksmuseum.nl), has fine collections of medieval and Renaissance applied art, displays on Dutch history, a fine Asian collection and an array of seventeenth-century Dutch paintings that is among the best in the world. Most people head straight for one of the museum's great treasures, Rembrandt's *The Night Watch*, but there are many other examples of his work, along with portraits by Frans Hals, landscapes by Jan van Goyen and Jacob van Ruisdael, the riotous scenes of Jan Steen and the peaceful interiors of Vermeer and Pieter de Hooch.

The Vincent Van Gogh Museum and Stedelijk Museum

Just southwest is the **Vincent Van Gogh Museum**, at Paulus Potterstraat 7 (Sat–Thurs 10am–6pm, Fri 10am–10pm; €10; Ⓦwww.vangoghmuseum.nl). Long queues can be a problem in high season so arrive early. The collection includes the early years in Holland, continuing to the brighter works he painted after moving to Paris and then Arles, where he produced vivid canvases like *The Yellow House* and the *Sunflowers* series. Along the street, at Paulus Potterstraat 13, the **Stedelijk Museum** of modern art (Ⓦwww.stedelijk.nl) is closed for refurbishment until the end of 2009, though changing exhibitions can be seen in the former post office on Oosterdokskade (daily 10am–6pm; €9), just east of Centraal Station.

The Heineken Experience and De Pijp

Further east along Stadhouderskade from the Rijksmuseum, the rather disappointing **Heineken Experience** at no. 78 (Tues–Sun 10am–6pm, last entry 5pm; €11; Ⓦwww.heinekenexperience.nl) provides an overview of Heineken's history and the brewing process, with a couple of free beers thrown in afterwards. South of here is the neighbourhood known as **De Pijp** (The Pipe) after its long, sombre canyons of brick tenements. This has always been one of the city's closest-knit communities, and one of its liveliest, with numerous inexpensive Surinamese and Turkish restaurants and a cheerful hub in the long slim thoroughfare of **Albert Cuypstraat**, whose food and clothes **market** (Mon–Sat 9.30am–5pm) is the largest in the city.

East of the centre

East of Rembrandtplein across the Amstel, the large, squat **Muziektheater** and **Stadhuis** flank **Waterlooplein**, home to the city's excellent **flea market** (Mon–Sat). Behind, Jodenbreestraat was once the main street of the Jewish quarter (emptied by the Nazis in the 1940s); no. 6 is **Het Rembrandthuis** (Rembrandt House; Mon–Sun 10am–5pm; €8; Ⓦwww.rembrandthuis.nl), which the painter bought at the height of his fame, living here for over twenty years. The interior displays a large number of the artist's engravings and paintings, plus a number of archeological findings from the site

The Jewish Quarter

Across the way, the excellent, award-winning **Joods Historisch Museum** (Jewish Historical Museum; daily 11am–5pm, Thurs 11am–9pm; closed Yom Kippur; €7.50; Ⓦwww.jhm.nl) is cleverly housed in a complex of Ashkenazi synagogues dating from the late seventeenth century and gives an imaginative introduction to Jewish life and beliefs. Photographs and film footage give a vivid impression of Amsterdam's long-gone Jewish ghetto, while interactive pieces successfully demystify Jewish customs.

Down Muiderstraat, the prim **Hortus Botanicus**, at Plantage Middenlaan 2 (Mon–Fri 9am–5pm, Sat & Sun 10am–5pm; €6), is a pocket-sized botanical garden with eight thousand plant species; stop off for a relaxed coffee and cakes in the orangery. The eye-catching Plancius Building at Plantage Kerklaan 61 houses the excellent **Verzetsmuseum** (Dutch Resistance Museum; Tues–Fri 10am–5pm, Sat–Mon 12–5pm; €5.50), where a variety of exhibits depict the ways in which the Dutch people opposed Nazi oppression.

Arrival and information

Air Schiphol airport is connected by train to Centraal Station (every 15min; hourly at night).

Train Centraal Station is the hub of all bus and tram routes and just five minutes' walk from central Dam Square.

Bus International buses arrive at Amstel Station, ten minutes south of Centraal Station by metro.

Tourist office The main VVV is outside Centraal Station, at Stationsplein 10 (daily 8am–9pm; Ⓣ0900/400 4040, Ⓦwww.visitamsterdam.nl); there's another inside the station (Mon–Sat 8am–8pm, Sun 9am–5pm); a smaller kiosk on the Leidseplein corner of Leidsestraat (daily 9.30am–5.30pm); and an office in the airport (daily 7am–10pm). Any of these can sell you an

Amsterdam Card (€33/43/53 for 1/2/3 days), which gives free or reduced entry to major attractions as well as free public transport and selected restaurant discounts. The VVV also has a monthly listings guide, *Day by Day – Amsterdam* (€1.75).

City transport

Public transport The excellent network of trams, buses and the metro (all daily 6/7am–midnight) isn't expensive. The GVB public transport office in front of Centraal Station (Mon–Fri 7am–7/9pm, Sat & Sun 8am–7/9pm; ⓣ0900/8011) has free route maps and an English guide to the *strippenkaart* ticketing system (see "Getting around", p.831). After midnight, night buses take over, running roughly hourly from Centraal Station to most parts of the city.
Cycling Bikes can be rented from Centraal Station or from a number of firms around town (see "Directory", p.844).

Accommodation

In high season it's always worth booking ahead, or you'll find almost everywhere full. If you can't find a room, it's easy enough to travel to another Randstad town by train and use that as an alternative and cheaper base for seeing Amsterdam.

Hostels

Bob's Youth Hostel Nieuwezijds Voorburgwal 92 ⓣ020/623 0063. Lively and smoky, with small dorms, cheap meals and Internet access, this is an old backpackers' favourite. 10min walk southwest from Centraal Station. Dorms ❸, doubles ❼
Bulldog Low-Budget Hotel Oudezijds Voorburgwal 220 ⓣ 020/620 3822, ⓦwww.bulldog.nl. Part of the Bulldog coffeeshop chain, this super-smart hostel has a bar and DVD lounge, dorms with TV and showers, doubles and apartments. Tram #4, #9, #16 or #24 to Dam, then a 3min walk east. Dorms ❸, doubles ❾
Flying Pig Downtown Nieuwendijk 100 ⓣ020/420 6822, ⓦwww.flyingpig.nl. Clean, large establishment run by ex-backpackers, with free kitchen facilities, Internet access, an all-night bar and no curfew; not for faint-hearted non-smokers. Five-minute walk from Centraal Station. There's also the slightly quieter **Flying Pig Uptown** by the Vondelpark at Vossiusstraat 46 (tram #1/#2/#5 to Leidseplein). Both dorms ❸, doubles ❺
Hans Brinker Kerkstraat 136 ⓣ020/622 0687, ⓦwww.hans-brinker.com. Well-established and raucously popular cheapie with a bright café attached. Tram #1/#2/#5 to Prinsengracht. Dorms ❸, doubles ❻
International Budget Hostel Leidsegracht 76 ⓣ020/624 2784, ⓦwww.internationalbudgethostel.com. Excellent, homely budget option on a peaceful little canal in the heart of the city. Tram #1/#2/#5 to Prinsengracht. Dorms ❸, doubles ❼
The Shelter Jordaan Bloemstraat 179 ⓣ020/624 4717, ⓦwww.shelter.nl. Easy-going Christian hostel tucked away in the Jordaan district. No smoking. Single-sex dorms only. Tram #13/#17 to Marnixstraat. Shelter also runs a hostel in the Red Light District, called *Shelter City*, at Barndesteeg 21, with a 2am curfew. Dorms ❷
Stadsdoelen Kloveniersburgwal 97 ⓣ020/624 6832, ⓦwww.stayokay.com. The more accessible of the two HI hostels, with clean semi-private dorms. HI members have priority in high season. Tram #4/#9/#16/#24/#25 to Muntplein. Dorms ❸, doubles ❼
Vondelpark Zandpad 5 ⓣ020/589 8996, ⓦwww.stayokay.com. For facilities, the better of the two HI hostels, this is a huge place with bar, restaurant, TV lounge and kitchen; well located on the edge of the park. Secure lockers and a lift. Tram #1/#2/#5 to Leidseplein, then a brief walk. Dorms ❸, doubles ❽

Hotels

Abba Overtoom 120 ⓣ020/618 3058, ⓦwww.hotel-abba.nl. Conveniently located for the big art museums, Concertgebouw and Leidseplein. All rooms have TVs and those at the back of the hotel are quiet. Breakfast is included. Tram #1 to Constantijn Huygenstraat. ❻
Asterisk Den Texstraat 16 ⓣ020/624 1768, ⓦwww.asteriskhotel.nl. Good-value budget hotel, just across the canal from the Heineken Brewery. Tram #16/#24/#25 to Weteringcircuit. ❽
Clemens Raadhuisstraat 39 ⓣ020/624 6089, ⓦwww.clemenshotel.nl. One of many options on this hotel strip. Clean, neat and good value for money. Ask for a quieter room at the back. Tram #13/#17 to Westermarkt. ❽
Euphemia Fokke Simonszstraat 1 ⓣ020/622 9045, ⓦwww.euphemiahotel.com. A likeable, laid-back atmosphere, and big, basic rooms at reasonable prices, which means it's usually full. Tram #16/#24/#25 to Weteringcircuit. ❾
Prinsenhof Prinsengracht 810 ⓣ020/623 1772, ⓦwww.hotelprinsenhof.com. Only two rooms are en suite, but a hearty breakfast is included and service couldn't be friendlier. ❼

Campsites

Vliegenbos Meeuwenlaan 138 ☎020/636 8855, Ⓦwww.vliegenbos.com. In Amsterdam North, a ten-minute ride on bus #32, #33 or nightbus #361 from Centraal Station. Closed Oct–March. €2 per tent, four-person cabins. ❼

Zeeburg Zuider IJdijk 20 ☎020/694 4430, Ⓦwww.campingzeeburg.nl. Bus #22 to Kramatweg or tram #26 from Centraal Station to IJburg. €5 per tent, two-person cabins. ❹

Eating

Amsterdam has an extensive supply of ethnic restaurants, especially Indonesian and Chinese, as well as *eetcafés* that serve decent, well-priced food in an unpretentious setting.

Cafés

Caffé Esprit Spui 10a. Swish modern café, with wonderful sandwiches and salads. Open 9am–6pm, Thurs until 10pm. Mains €10.

De Jaren Nieuwe Doelenstraat 20–22, near Muntplein. Grand café overlooking the river – one of the best places to peruse the Sunday paper.

Maoz Falafel Leidsestraat 85, near Leidseplein; also Reguliersbreestraat 45 and Muntplein 1. The best street-food in the city – falafel and as much salad as you can eat for €3.90.

Puccini Staalstraat 17–21, near Waterlooplein. Dreamy cakes, pastries and chocolates, all handmade. Sandwiches €9.

Royal Bagels and Muffins Prinsengracht 454, near Leidseplein. Great snack place, with big cups of coffee (half-price refills).

Winkel Noordermarkt 43, opposite the Noorderkerk. Popular local hang-out on Saturday mornings during the farmers' market. Famously delicious apple cake. Mains €12.

Restaurants

De Blaffende Vis Westerstraat 118. Great bar/restaurant in the Jordaan. Popular with students and gets raucous at weekends. Mains €12.

De Eettuin 2e Tuindwarsstraat 10, Jordaan. Hefty portions of Dutch food with DIY salad. Mains €15.

Japan-Inn Leidsekruisstraat 4. Cheap and cheerful Japanese restaurant near the busy Leidseplein. Open until 11.15pm daily. Set menus start at €14.

Meneer Pannekoek Raadhuisstraat 6. Friendly place near the Dam serving excellent pancakes for around €8.

Piet de Leeuw Noorderstraat 11. Superb steakhouse off Vijzelgracht, dating from the 1940s. Good desserts too. Steaks €15.

Shiva Reguliersdwarsstraat 72. Outstanding Indian restaurant, with well-priced, expertly prepared food, and veggie options. Mains €12.

Top Thai Herenstraat 22. Some of the best value authentic Thai food in Amsterdam. Popular, with a friendly atmosphere. Open evenings only. Mains €15.

Drinking and nightlife

Note there is a distinction between bars and so-called **coffeeshops**, where smoking dope is the primary pastime (ask to see "the menu"). You must be 18 or over to enter these, and don't expect alcohol to be served. Most open at 9am and close at 1am (2/3am at weekends). Check out the widely available *Smokers Guide* (€6.50; Ⓦwww.smokersguide.com) for advice on the varieties available, strengths, prices and new places to smoke.

Most **clubs** open around 10pm and close around 4am. Drinks cost around fifty percent more than in a bar, but entry prices are low and there's rarely any kind of door policy.

Bars

De Buurvrouw St Pieterspoortsteeg 29. Dark, noisy bar, just south of Dam Square, with a wildly eclectic crowd.

De Duivel Reguliersdwarsstraat 87. Amsterdam's only hip-hop café, this is an entertaining place to hang out near the Rembrandtplein.

De Engelbewaarder Kloveniersburgwal 59. Relaxed and informal haunt of Amsterdam's bookish types, with live jazz on Sunday afternoons.

Het Molenpad Prinsengracht 653. One of the city's most atmospheric brown cafés, with excellent food. Fills with young professionals after 6pm.

De Prins Prinsengracht 124. Roomy and welcoming *bruine kroeg*, also popular for its great-value food.

Spanjer & van Twist Leliegracht 60. Perfect for laid-back summer afternoons, with chairs overlooking the quietest canal in Jordaan.

De Twee Zwaantjes Prinsengracht 114. Tiny oddball Jordaan bar where locals sing along raucously to accordion music – you'll either love it or hate it.

De Zotte Proeflokaal Raamstraat 29. Belgian hang-out just north of Leidseplein with food, liqueurs and hundreds of different kinds of beers.

Coffeeshops

The Bulldog Leidseplein 15–17 and other central outlets. More like a dodgy club than a coffeeshop,

and certainly not the place for a thoughtful smoke. The dope is reliably good though, if expensive.
De Dampkring Handboogstraat 29. With colourful decor and a refined menu, this coffeeshop is known for its good-quality hash. As a favourite with both tourists and locals, it can get busy.
Global Chillage Kerkstraat 51. Celebrated hippie hang-out with friendly staff.
Homegrown Fantasy Nieuwezijds Voorburgwal 87a. Part of the Dutch Passion seed company, selling the widest range of (mostly Dutch) marijuana in Amsterdam.
Kadinsky Zoutsteeg 9 & Rosmarijnsteeg 9, both in the old centre. Sensational chocolate chip cookies, scrupulously accurate deals and a background of jazz dance.
Paradox 1e Bloemdwarsstraat 2, Jordaan. Satisfies the munchies with outstanding natural food, including spectacular fresh-fruit concoctions. Closes 8pm.
Siberië Brouwersgracht 11. Slightly off the beaten tourist track, very relaxed and very friendly – worth a visit whether you want to smoke or not.

Clubs

Bitterzoet Spuistraat 2 ⓣ020/521 3001, ⓦwww.bitterzoet.com. Club with an eclectic mix of nights, featuring live bands as well as DJs.
Ministry Reguliersdwarsstraat 12. A well-established club near Rembrandtplein which features quality DJs playing speed garage, house and R'n'B to party people. Monday night jam session with the local jazz talent.
Paradiso Weteringschans 6–8. One of the principal venues in the city, which on Fridays hosts an unmissable club night, from midnight onwards. Check listings for one-off events. Near Leidseplein.
Sugarfactory Lijnbaansgracht 238, near Leidseplein, ⓦwww.sugarfactory.nl. Everything from spoken word to cabaret, including straightforward club nights.

Entertainment

Amsterdam is a gathering spot for fringe performances, and buzzes with places offering a wide and inventive range of entertainment. **Cinemas** screen English-language movies, subtitled in Dutch, and rarely show foreign-language films without English subtitles. Check out the lavish Art-Deco interior of the Tuschinski, at Reguliersbreestraat 26, or cult and classic flicks at The Movies, at Haarlemmerdijk 161, and Kriterion, at Roeterstraat 170. Boom Chicago (ⓦwww.boomchicago.nl) is a hugely popular rapid-fire comedy troupe, performing in English at the Leidseplein Theatre most nights. The best source of **listings** information is the *Uitburo*, or AUB, in the Stadsschouwburg Theatre on the corner of Marnixstraat and Leidseplein (daily 10am–6pm, Thurs until 9pm; ⓣ0900/0191). Wednesday's *Het Parool* newspaper has a good entertainment supplement, *Uit en Thuis*.

Rock, jazz and world music venues

Akhnaton Nieuwezijds Kolk 25 ⓣ020/624 3396, ⓦwww.akhnaton.nl. Specializes in African and Latin American music and dance parties.
Café Alto Korte Leidsedwarsstraat 115, near Leidseplein ⓣ020/626 3249, ⓦwww.jazz-cafe-alto.nl. Legendary jazz café-bar, with free live music every night from 10pm until 3am. Big on atmosphere, though not space.
Bimhuis Piet Heinkade 3 ⓣ020/788 2150, ⓦwww.bimhuis.nl. Premier jazz venue. Free impro sessions on Tues from 8pm. First stop on IJ-tram from Centraal Station.
Melkweg Lijnbaansgracht 234a, near Leidseplein ⓣ020/531 8181, ⓦwww.melkweg.nl. Amsterdam's most famous entertainment venue, with a young, hip clientele. Live music from reggae to rock, as well as excellent DJs at the weekend, a monthly film programme, theatre, gallery, bar and restaurant.

Classical music and opera

Beurs van Berlage Damrak 277, city centre. The splendid interior of the former stock exchange hosts a wide selection of music from the Dutch Philharmonic and Dutch Chamber orchestras.
Concertgebouw Concertgebouwplein 2–6 ⓣ020/671 8345, ⓦwww.concertgebouw.nl. Home to the Borodin Quartet. Catch world-renowned orchestras playing amid wonderful acoustics for as little as €15. Summer concerts and free lunchtime performances Wed Sept–May.

Gay Amsterdam

Amsterdam has one of the biggest and best-established **gay scenes** in Europe: attitudes are tolerant and facilities unequalled. The nationwide organization COC, at Rozenstraat 14 (ⓣ020/626 3087, ⓦwww.cocamsterdam.nl), can provide on-the-spot information, and has a café and popular discos. For further advice contact the English-speaking Gay & Lesbian Switchboard (daily 2–10pm; ⓣ020/623 6565, ⓦwww.switchboard.nl) or check ⓦwww.gayamsterdam.com. The gay and lesbian bookshop Vrolijk is just behind Dam square at Paleisstraat 135.

Gay hotels

Golden Bear Kerkstraat 37 ⓣ020/624 4785 ⓦwww.goldenbear.nl. Clean and spacious rooms, not far from the busy Leidseplein. Trams #1, #2 & #5 to Kerkstraat. 8

ITC Hotel Prinsengracht 1051 ⓣ020/623 0230, ⓦwww.itc-hotel.com. Friendly hotel in lovely old house, not far from Rembrandtsplein and main gay areas. Tram #4 to Prinsengracht. 7

Gay cafés and bars

Amstel Taveerne Amstel 54. Perhaps the best-established bar, at its most vivacious in summer when the punters spill out onto the street.

April Reguliersdwarsstraat 37. Large and trendy, with newspapers, coffee and cakes as well as booze.

Camp Café Kerkstraat 45. Agreeable mix of tourists and locals, with tasty dishes on offer.

Downtown Reguliersdwarsstraat 31, off Rembrandtplein. A favourite with visitors. Relaxed and friendly, with inexpensive meals.

Directory

Bike rental Cheapest from main train stations. Also try: Bike City, at Bloemgracht 70 ⓣ020/626 3721; Damstraat Rent-a-Bike at Damstraat 20 ⓣ020/625 5029; or MacBike, at Mr Visserplein 2 ⓣ020/620 0985, Weteringschans 2 ⓣ020/528 76 88 and Stationsplein east ⓣ020/624 8391. All charge around €8 a day, plus €50 deposit with ID.

Bike tours Yellow Bike, at Nieuwezijds Kolk 29 (ⓣ020 620 6940, ⓦwww.yellowbike.nl), organizes three-hour tours around all the main sites as well as "undiscovered Amsterdam", from €19.50 per person.

Embassies and consulates Note that most of the following are in Den Haag, not Amsterdam. Australia, Carnegielaan 4, Den Haag ⓣ070/310 8200; Canada, Sophialaan 7, Den Haag ⓣ070/311 1600; Ireland, Dr Kuyperstraat 9, Den Haag ⓣ070/363 0993; New Zealand, Carnegielaan 10, Den Haag ⓣ070/365 8037; UK, Lange Voorhout 10, Den Haag, ⓣ070/427 0427; US, Museumplein 19, Amsterdam ⓣ020/575 5309.

Exchange GWK in Centraal Station and Leidseplein; Thomas Cook at Dam 23, Damrak 1–5 and Leidseplein 31a; American Express at Damrak 66.

Hospital De Boelelaan 1117 ⓣ020/444 444.

Laundry The Clean Brothers, at Kerkstraat 56 and Jacob van Lennepkade 179.

Left luggage Centraal Station.

Police Elandsgracht 117 ⓣ020/559 9111.

Post office Singel 250 (Mon–Fri 9am–6pm, Thurs until 8pm, Sat 10am–1.30pm).

Moving on

Train Arnhem (for Hoge Veluwe National Park; every 30min; 1hr 10min); Haarlem (every 10min; 15min); Den Haag (every 15min; 50min); Leiden (every 15min; 45min); Maastricht (hourly; 2hr 35min); Rotterdam (every 10min; 1hr); Schiphol airport (every 15min; 20min); Texel (via Den Helder; every 30min; 1hr 10min); Utrecht (every 15min; 30min); Berlin (every 3hr; 6hr 30min); Brussels (hourly; 3hr).

The Randstad

The string of towns known as the **Randstad**, or "rim town", situated amid a typically Dutch landscape of flat fields cut by canals, forms the country's most populated region and still recalls the landscapes painted in the seventeenth-century heyday of the provinces. Much of the area can be visited as day-trips from Amsterdam, but it's easy and more rewarding to make a proper tour. **Haarlem** is worth a look, while to the south, the university centre of **Leiden** makes a pleasant detour before you reach the refined tranquillity of **Den Haag** (The Hague) and the busy urban centre of **Rotterdam**. Nearby **Delft** and **Gouda** repay visits too, the former with one of the best-preserved centres in the region.

HAARLEM

Just over fifteen minutes from Amsterdam by train, **HAARLEM** is a handsome, mid-sized city that sees itself as a cut above its neighbours. It makes a good alternative base for exploring northern Holland, or even Amsterdam itself, especially if you can't find a bed in the city or would rather be somewhere less hectic.

What to see and do

The core of the city is **Grote Markt** and the adjoining Riviervischmarkt, flanked by the gabled, originally fourteenth-century **Stadhuis** and the impressive bulk of the **Grote Kerk** or **Sint Bavokerk** (Mon–Sat 10am–4pm; €2; entrance at no 23). Inside, the mighty Christian Müller organ of 1738 is said to have been played by Handel and Mozart. The town's main attraction is the outstanding **Frans Hals Museum**, at Groot Heiligland 62 (Tues–Sat 11am–5pm, Sun noon–5pm; €7; Ⓦwww.franshalsmuseum.nl), a five-minute stroll from Grote Markt in the Oudemannhuis almshouse. It houses a number of his lifelike seventeenth-century portraits, including the *Civic Guard* series, which established his reputation.

Arrival and information

Train and bus Haarlem train station, connected to Amsterdam and to Leiden by four trains an hour, is on the north side of the city, about ten minutes' walk from the Grote Markt; buses stop right outside.
Tourist office The VVV is attached to the station (April–Sept Mon–Fri 9am–5.30pm, Sat 10am–4pm; Oct–March Mon–Fri 9.30am–5pm, Sat 10am–2pm; Ⓣ0900/616 1600, Ⓦwww.vvvzk.nl).

Accommodation

Amadeus Grote Markt 10 Ⓣ023/532 4530 Ⓦwww.amadeus-hotel.com. Pleasant, if slightly sparse rooms; ask for ones with a view of the Markt. ❽
Carillon Grote Markt 27 Ⓣ023/531 0591, Ⓦwww.hotelcarillon.com. Decent rooms, good bar downstairs, and excellent location on the Markt. ❻
Stayokay Haarlem Jan Gijzenpad 3 Ⓣ023/537 3793, Ⓦwww.stayokay.com. Inconveniently located out of town on a main road, but otherwise this HI hostel is of Stayokay's usual high standard. From the station it's 15min on bus #2, direction Noord. Dorms ❸, doubles ❼

Eating and drinking

Café 1900 Barteljorisstraat 10. Long-standing café serving drinks and light meals in an attractive setting. Snacks €8.

TREAT YOURSELF

Lambermon's Spaarne 96 Ⓣ023/542 7804. Pricey but the best restaurant in town. The *Kooktheater* ("cook-theatre") provides a unique experience and excellent French food. Ten courses are served during the course of the evening, between 6.30pm and 1am, each costing €9.50.

Crackers Junction of Lange Veerstraat and Kleine Houtstraat. Dim, smoky bar with good music and beer by the pint.
In den Uiver Riviervischmarkt 13. Try the home-made beer at this traditional restaurant. Live jazz Thursday and Sunday. Mains €10.
Restaurant La Plume Lange Veerstraat 1 Ⓣ023/531 3202. Popular spot serving traditional Dutch dishes and pastas. Steaks €16.

LEIDEN AND THE BULBFIELDS

The charm of **LEIDEN** lies in the peace and prettiness of its gabled streets and canals, though the town's museums are varied and comprehensive enough to merit a visit.

What to see and do

The most appealing quarter is **Rapenburg**, a peaceful area of narrow pedestrian streets and canals that is home to the country's principal archeological museum, the **Rijksmuseum Van Oudheden** (National Museum of Antiquities; Tues–Fri 10am–5pm, Sat & Sun noon–5pm; €8.50; Ⓦwww.rmo.nl). Outside sits the first-century AD Temple of Teffeh, while inside are more Egyptian artefacts, along with classical Greek and Roman sculptures and exhibits from prehistoric, Roman and medieval times. Across Rapenburg, a network of narrow streets converges on the Gothic **Pieterskerk**. East of here, Breestraat marks the start of a vigorous **market** (Wed & Sat), which sprawls right over the sequence of bridges into

Haarlemmerstraat, the town's major shopping street. Close by, the **Burcht** (daily 10am–10pm; free) is a shell of a fort, whose battlements you can clamber up for views of the town centre. The **Molenmuseum de Valk**, on Molenwerf at 2e Binnenvestgracht 1 (Tues–Sat 10am–5pm, Sun 1–5pm; €2.50), displays the history of windmills.

The bulbfields

Along with Haarlem to the north, Leiden and Delft are the best bases for seeing the Dutch **bulbfields** that flourish here in spring. The view from the train as you travel from Haarlem to Leiden can be sufficient in itself as the line cuts directly through the main growing areas, the fields divided into stark geometric blocks of pure colour. Should you want to get closer, make a bee-line for **LISSE**, home to the **Keukenhof** (mid-March–mid-May daily 8am–7.40pm; €13.50; Ⓦwww.keukenhof.nl), the largest flower gardens in the world. Some six million blooms are on show for their full flowering period, complemented by five thousand square metres of greenhouses. Special buses (#54) run daily to the Keukenhof from Leiden bus station twice an hour.

Arrival and information

Train and bus Leiden's train and bus stations are no more than ten minutes' walk north of the centre.
Tourist office The VVV is a short walk from the stations at Stationsweg 2d (Mon 11am–5.30pm, Tues–Fri 9am–5.30pm, Sat 10am–4.30pm, Sun in high season 11–3pm; Ⓣ0900/222 2333, Ⓦwww.leiden.nl).

Accommodation

Flying Pig Beach Hostel Parallel Boulevard 208 Ⓣ071/362 2533, Ⓦwww.flyingpig.nl. Half an hour's bus ride away from Leiden in the beach town of Noordwijk, this place is the antidote to the bland-but-comfortable hostels found all over the Netherlands and your best bet for visiting Leiden on a budget. The bar is a real traveller hang-out; you could be forgiven for thinking you were in South America. There's a free shuttle from the two Flying Pig hostels in Amsterdam, or take bus #40 or #42 from Leiden to the lighthouse square in Nordwjik. Dorms ③
Nieuw Minerva Boommarkt 23 Ⓣ071/512 6358, Ⓦwww.nieuwminerva.nl. Cosy and central canalside hotel with some interesting themed rooms, including "Delftware" and "Rembrandt". ⑨

Eating and drinking

Barrera Rapenburg 56. Canalside café with big sandwiches for €5.
Jazzcafé The Duke Oude Singel 2. Bar with live jazz most nights.
La Bota Herensteeg 9–11, by the Pieterskerk. Studenty spot serving great-value food and beers. Salad €8.
M'n Broer By the Pieterskerk at Kloksteeg 7. Slightly pricey Dutch menu; open for evening meals only. *Filet mignon* €18.50.

Moving on

Train Amsterdam (every 15min; 45min); Den Haag (every 10min; 15min).

DEN HAAG

With its urbane atmosphere, **DEN HAAG (THE HAGUE)** is different from any other Dutch city. Since the sixteenth century it has been the Netherlands' political capital, though its older buildings are a rather subdued collection with little of Amsterdam's flamboyance. Diplomats and multinational businesses ensure that many of the city's hotels and restaurants are in the expense-account category, and the nightlife is similarly packaged. But among all this, Den Haag does have cheaper and livelier bars and restaurants, as well as some excellent museums.

What to see and do

Right in the centre, the **Binnenhof** is the home of the Dutch parliament and incorporates elements of the town's thirteenth-century castle. The present complex is a rather mundane affair, the small **Hof Vijver** lake mirroring the symmetry of the facade. Inside there's little to see except the **Ridderzaal**, a slender-turreted structure that can be viewed on regular guided tours from the information office at Binnenhof 8a (Mon–Sat 10am–4pm; €5). Immediately east of the Binnenhof, the **Mauritshuis picture gallery** at Korte Vijverberg 8 (Tues–Sat 10am–5pm, Sun 11am–5pm, plus April–Sept Mon 10am–5pm; €9.50; Ⓦwww.mauritshuis.nl), located in a magnificent seventeenth-century mansion, is of more interest, famous for its extensive range of Flemish and Dutch paintings including work by Vermeer, Rubens, Bruegel the Elder and Van Dyck.

Panorama Mesdag and the Gemeente-museum

About fifteen minutes' walk from the Mauritshuis, **Panorama Mesdag** at Zeestraat 65 (Mon–Sat 10am–5pm, Sun noon–5pm; €5; Ⓦwww.panorama-mesdag.com) is an astonishing 360-degree painting of seaside scenes of Scheveningen from the 1880s. North, the **Gemeente-museum**, at Stadhouderslaan 41 (Tues–Sun 11am–5pm; €8.50; bus #4/#14 from Centraal Station), contains superb collections of musical instruments and Islamic ceramics, plus an array of modern art tracing the development of Dutch painting, with the world's largest collection of Mondriaan paintings.

Arrival and information

Train The city has two train stations – Den Haag HS and, about 1km to the north, Den Haag CS. Trains from the UK, France and Belgium stop at the former, which is convenient for cheaper accommodation.

Tourist office The VVV is at Hofweg 1, next to the Binnenhof (Mon–Fri 10am–6pm, Sat 10am–5pm, Sun noon–5pm; Ⓣ0900/340 3505, Ⓦwww.denhaag.com), and has a small stock of private rooms.

Accommodation

Hotel 't Centrum Veenkade 5 Ⓣ070/346 3657, Ⓦwww.hotelhetcentrum.nl. Simple, well-located clean place near the Paleis Noordeinde. Take tram #17 from Centraal Station or Holland Spoor to Noordwal. 7

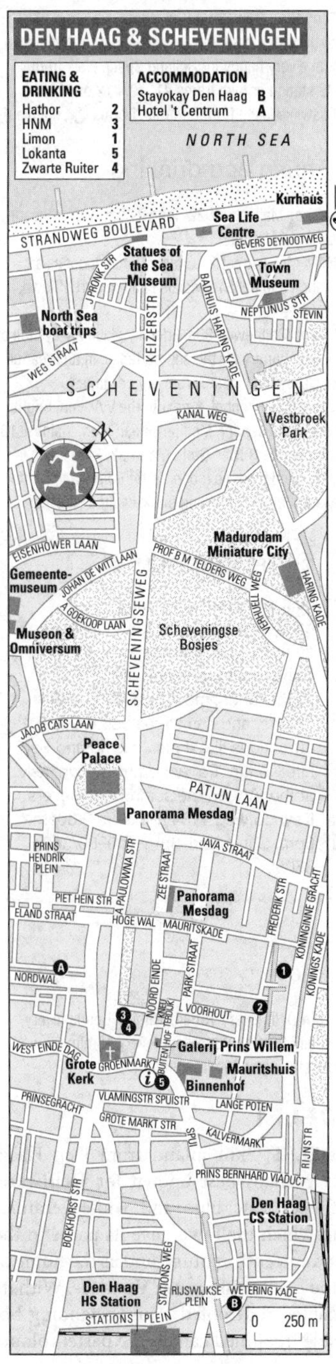

Stayokay Den Haag Scheepmakersstraat 27 ⓣ070/315 7888, ⓦwww.stayokay.com. HI hostel that's very handy for Holland Spoor. Walk from HS station or take trams #1, #9, #12 or #16 to Rijswijkseplein from Centraal. Dorms ❸, double ❼

Eating and drinking

Hathor Maliestraat 22. Touristy bar with pleasant canalside terrace.
HnM Molenstraat 21a. Tasty Dutch, Indonesian, French and Italian specials in a fun part of town. Mains €10.
Limon Denneweg 39a. Friendly place always full of people hungry for the superb tapas, in an area full of classy food joints. From €4 per tapas.
Lokanta Buitenhof 4, next to the VVV. Fun, bright restaurant serving Mediterranean food. Mains €13.
De Zwarte Ruiter Grote Markt 27. Studenty bar with good food; next door is *De Boterwaag* (Grote Markt 8a), an appealing brick-vaulted café-bar.

SCHEVENINGEN

Just 4km from Den Haag and easily accessible by tram (catch #1 from Spui or outside the VVV), **Scheveningen** is one of the Netherlands' most popular beach resorts, and has all the usual side-attractions like a pier, casino and Sea Life Centre. For accommodation, ask at the VVV on the seafront at Gevers Deynootweg 1134 (Mon–Fri 9.30am–6pm, Sun 10am–3pm; ⓣ0900/340 3505).

Moving on

Train Delft (every 15min; 15min); Gouda (every 20min; 20min); Rotterdam (every 15min; 25min); Utrecht (every 20min; 40min).

DELFT

DELFT, 2km inland from Den Haag, is perhaps best known for **Delftware**, the delicate blue and white ceramics to which the town gave its name in the seventeenth century, and as the home of the painter **Johannes Vermeer**. With its gabled red-roofed houses standing beside tree-lined canals, the pastel colours of the pavements, its brickwork and bridges, the town has a faded tranquillity – though one that can suffer beneath the tourist onslaught during summer.

What to see and do

A good starting point is to follow the Historic Walk around the old town with a map from the VVV (€2.20). A fifteen-minute walk south of the centre at Rotterdamsweg 196 is the **Koninklijke Porceleyne Fles**, a factory producing Delftware (daily 9am–5pm; Nov–mid-March closed Sun; €4.50; ⓦwww.royaldelft.com). The **Markt** is also worth exploring for its collection of small speciality art shops and galleries, with the **Nieuwe Kerk** (April–Oct Mon–Sat 9am–6pm, Nov–Mar Mon–Fri 11am–4pm, Sat 10am–5pm; €3, tower €2.50) at one end and the Renaissance **Stadhuis** opposite. William the Silent – leader of the struggle for Dutch independence in the seventeenth century – is buried in this fine old church and you can climb the 370 steps of the tower for spectacular views. West of here, **Wynhaven**, an old canal, leads to Hippolytusbuurt and the Gothic **Oude Kerk** (same hours and ticket as Nieuwe Kerk), perhaps the town's finest building, with an unhealthily leaning tower. Vermeer fans should check out **Vermeercentrum**, Delft's newest attraction (daily: April–Oct Mon–Sat 10am–6pm, Sun 10am–5pm, Nov–March 10am–5pm; €8; ⓦwww.vermeerdelft.nl) at Voldersgracht 1. Although there are no actual Vermeer paintings, only reproductions, the studio space explaining Vermeer's technique is worth a visit.

Arrival and information

Train From Delft's train station, aim for the big steeple you see on exit and it's a ten-minute walk north to the Markt.
Tourist office Delft's VVV, here called TIP, is just north of the Markt at Hippolytusbuurt 4 (Tues–Sat 9/10am–4/6pm, Sun & Mon 10am–4pm; ⓣ015/215 4051; ⓦwww.delft.com).

Accommodation

Delftse Hout Campsite Kortftlaan 5 ⓣ015/213 0040, ⓦwww.delftsehout.com. All kinds of accommodation, from chalets to grass huts and eco-homes. Take bus #64 from the station. Huts ❸
Oosteinde Oosteinde 156 ⓣ015/213 4238. B&B with lovely rooms, right in the centre of Delft. Minimum stay of two nights. ❼
The Soul Inn Williamstraat 55 ⓣ015/215 7246, ⓦwww.soul-inn.nl. Sharply decorated and a great place to stay (though only ten rooms). ❻

Eating and drinking

Cafés and restaurants

Het Stadspannekoeckhuys Oude Delft 113–115. Serves delicious filled pancakes and has a canalside terrace. Closed Mon. Pancakes €7.
Kobus Kuch Beestenmarkt 1. A gem of a café/restaurant – don't miss the famous *appeltart met slagroom* (apple cake with cream) for €2.90.
Uit de Kunst Oude Delft 140, near Oude Kerk. Charming little café decorated with 1940s memorabilia and offering home-made cakes and cheap snacks. Closed Mon–Tues.

Bars and clubs

Bebop Jazz Café Kromstraat 33. Holds jam sessions every other Tuesday.
Locus Publicus Brabantse Turfmarkt 67. Popular local bar, serving a staggering array of beers as well as a good selection of sandwiches.
Speakers Burghwal 45–49. The only club in town; often features live music.

Moving on

Train Amsterdam (every 20min; 1hr); Rotterdam (every 10min; 12min); Utrecht (every 10min; 1hr).

ROTTERDAM

Just south of Delft lies **ROTTERDAM**, at the heart of a maze of rivers and artificial waterways that together form the outlet of the rivers Rijn (Rhine) and Maas (Meuse). After devastating damage during World War II, Rotterdam has grown into a vibrant city dotted with premier cultural attractions and built around Europe's busiest port. Fortunately redevelopment hasn't obliterated the city's earthy character: its grittiness is part of its appeal, as are its boisterous bars and clubs.

What to see and do

You can get a feel for the city by walking from the station (or taking tram #7 from just outside) down to the Museumpark. Here, the enormous **Boijmans Van Beuningen Museum**, at Museumpark 18–20 (Tues–Sun 11am–5pm; €9, free on Wed; ⓦwww.boijmans.nl), has a superb collection of works by Monet, Van Gogh, Picasso, Gauguin and Cézanne, while its earlier canvases include several by Bosch, Bruegel the Elder and Rembrandt. A stroll through the Museumpark brings you to the **Nattuurmuseum Kunsthal** (Tues–Sat 10am–5pm, Sun 11am–5pm; €8.50; ⓦwww.kunsthal.nl) which showcases first-rate exhibitions of contemporary art, photography and design. Also in the park is the **Netherlands Architecture Institute** (same hours as Kunsthal; €8, including entrance to nearby Sonneveld House; ⓦwww.nai.nl), with regularly changing exhibitions focusing on particular architects or areas.

The Maritiem Museum and Museum Het Schielandhuis

Near the Leuvehaven is the entertaining **Maritiem Museum** (Maritime Museum; Tues–Sat 10am–5pm, Sun 11am–5pm; €5; ⓦwww.maritiemmuseum.nl). Another short walk away is **Blaak**, a pocket-sized area that was levelled in World War II, but has since been rebuilt. The architectural highlight is a remarkable series of topsy-turvy, cube-shaped houses, the *kubuswoningen*, completed in 1984. One of them, at No. 70, the **Kijk-Kubus** (Show Cube; daily 11am–5pm; Jan & Feb Sat–Sun 11am-5pm; €2; ⓦwww.kubuswoning.nl), at Overblaak 70, offers somewhat disorientating but compelling tours of the house. Nearby, the Binnenrote **market** (every Tues and Sat) sells fresh cheese, fish and flowers.

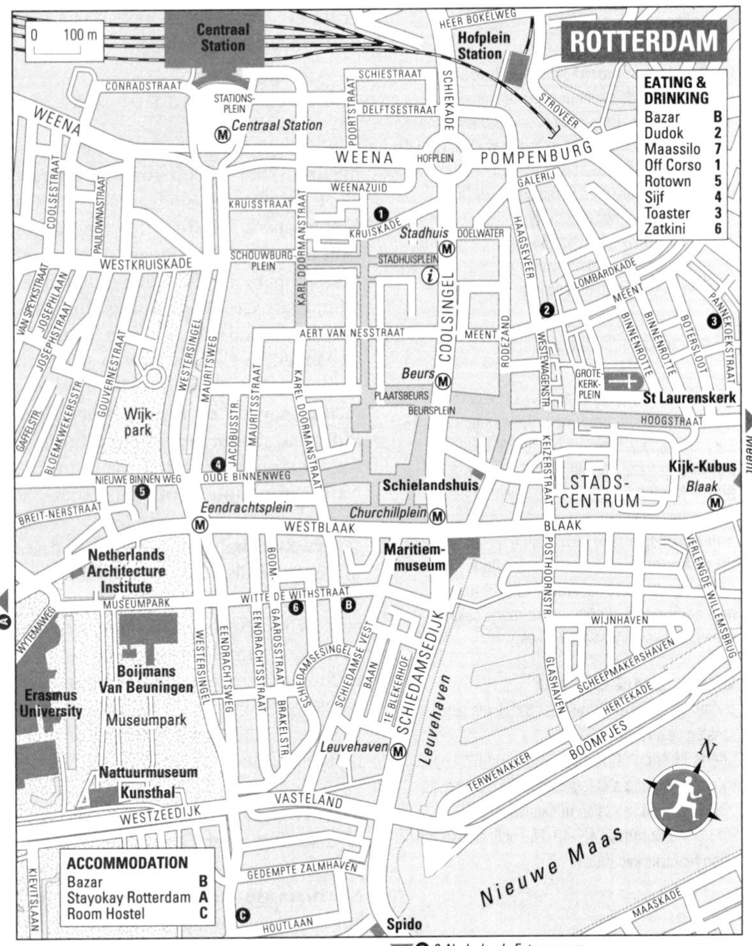

Delfshaven

If little in Rotterdam city centre can exactly be called picturesque, **DELFSHAVEN**, a couple of kilometres southwest of Centraal Station, makes up for it – to get here, catch tram #4 or #8 (direction Schiedam, tram stop Spanjaardstraat), or take the metro. Once the harbour that served Delft, it was from here that the Pilgrim Fathers set sail for the New World in 1620. Most of the buildings lining the district's two narrow canals are eighteenth- and nineteenth-century warehouses. Formerly a *jenever* distillery, the **Museum de Dubbelde Palmboom**, at Voorhaven 12 (Tues–Fri 10am–5pm, Sat & Sun 11am–5pm; €2.70), is now a wide-ranging historical museum.

Arrival and information

Train Rotterdam's large centre is bordered by its main rail terminal, Centraal Station, also the hub of a useful tram and metro system, though best avoided late at night.

Tourist office The main VVV office is a ten-minute walk away at Coolsingel 67 (Mon–Thur

BOAT TRIPS

One of the most fun ways to see the city is from the water. One possibility is to take an exhilarating trip in a **water taxi** from the Leuvehaven (€3.40; water taxis also leave from the Veerhaven but this is a much shorter journey for €2.50) to the splendid *Hotel New York*, which occupies the building where transatlantic cruise liners once docked. Close by is the **Nederlands Fotomuseum**, at Wilhelminakade 332 (Tues-Fri 10am–5pm, Sat-Sun 11am–5pm; €6; ⓦwww.nederlandsfotomuseum.nl), where there's a small permanent exhibition on Rotterdam photography as well as changing exhibitions. From here you can walk back to the centre over the futuristic bridge, the **Erasmusbrug**, an ideal spot for photos. There are also numerous **boat trips** from the Leuvehaven through the harbour (year-round; 1hr 15min; €8.50). In July and August, **day-trips** also run to Dordrecht, Schoonhoven, the nineteen windmills at Kinderdijk, and the Delta Project, from €39–49 per person; contact the VVV or Spido for details (ⓣ010/275 9988, ⓦwww.spido.nl).

9.30am–6pm, Fri 9.30am–9pm, Sat 9.30am–5pm; ⓣ010/414 0000, ⓦwww.vvvrotterdam.nl), where you can pick up free maps and brochures.

Accommmodation

Hostels

Room Hostel Van Vollenhovenstraat 62 ⓣ010/282 7277, ⓦwww.roomrotterdam.nl.Very funky hostel in a better location than the HI option. Extremely helpful staff organize events for guests, and there's a vibrant bar and quieter lounge. From Centraal Station take tram #7 to Westerstraat or tram #8 to Vasteland. Dorms ❷, doubles ❻

Stayokay Rotterdam Rochussenstraat 107–109 ⓣ010/436 5763, ⓦwww.stayokay.com. HI Hostel near the Museumpark. It's big, clean and fairly indistinguishable from the Stayokay chain's other Dutch hostels. Tram #4 or Metro Dijkzigt. Dorms ❸, doubles ❼

TREAT YOURSELF

Bazar Witte de Withstraat 16 ⓣ010/206 5151, ⓦwww.hotelbazar.nl. Superb hotel on one of the hippest streets in the city. Each floor is decorated in the style of a different continent – the rooms are very characterful so choose your favourite from the website (which is unfortunately only in Dutch) when you book. Some have balconies, others hot tubs. The café-restaurant downstairs is one of the best in the city. From the station take tram #5 to Witte de Withstraat or trams #8 or #20 to Churchillplein. ❽

Eating and drinking

The best places for cheap and tasty food are Oude and Nieuwe Binnenweg and Witte de Withstraat.

Cafés and restaurants

Bazar Witte de Withstraat 16. Popular bar/restaurant under the hotel with excellent kebabs and vegetarian food. Mains €11.

Dudok Meent 88. Grand café serving the city's most famous apple cake.

Toaster Pannekoekstraat 38a. Funky snack bar serving almost exclusively toasted sandwiches with surprisingly exotic fillings; save room for a Snickers *tosti* as dessert, and be sure to check out some of the good vintage stores that line the street. Closed Mon. €5.

Bars

Sijf Oude Binnenweg 115 ⓣ010/433 2610. One of the many agreeable bar/restaurants on this stretch, this one in a converted pharmacy.

Zatkini Witte de Withstraat 88. Lively Spanish bar on a great street.

Clubs

Maassilo Maashaven Z.Z. 1-2. Trendy club in a converted grain silo. Open Thurs–Sat. Metro Maashaven.

Off Corso Kruiskade 22 ⓣ010/280 7359. Arty club in an old cinema, specializing in electro and techno. Thurs-Sat. Metro Stadhuis.

Rotown Nieuwe Binnenweg 17–19 ⓣ010/436 2669. Open till 2am. Fun bar with gigs by up-and-coming bands.

Shopping

Rotterdam is famous for **vintage clothing**, and many of the best places are concentrated around Nieuwe Binnenweg: try Sister Moon at 89b, or Episode on nearby Oude Binnenweg at 144a. There are also plenty of **vinyl shops** round here, including Triple Vision (Nieuwe Binnenweg 131b) and Mid-Town Records (Nieuwe Binnenweg 79a).

Moving on

Train Gouda (every 20min; 20min); Utrecht (every 20min; 45min); Amsterdam (every 20min; 1 hour).

GOUDA

A pretty little place some 25km northeast of Rotterdam, **GOUDA** is almost everything you'd expect of a Dutch country town: a ring of quiet canals encircling ancient buildings and old quays.

What to see and do

The town **Markt** is the largest in the Netherlands, a reminder of the town's prominence as a centre of the medieval cloth trade, and later of the manufacture of cheeses and clay pipes. A touristy **cheese market** is held here every Thursday morning from June to August. Slap bang in the middle, the elegant Gothic **Stadhuis** dates from 1450. On the north side is the **Waag**, a tidy seventeenth-century building whose top two floors house a cheese museum (April–Oct Tues–Sun 1–5pm, Thurs 10am–5pm; €2). South, off the Markt, the sixteenth-century **St Janskerk** (April–Oct Mon–Sat 9–5pm, Nov–Mar 10am–4pm; €2.75) is famous for its magnificent stained-glass windows depicting Biblical and secular scenes.

Arrival and information

Train and bus Gouda's train and bus stations are 10 minutes north of the centre.

Tourist office VVV Markt 27 (Mon–Fri 9am–5.30pm, Sat 10am–4pm; June–Aug also Sun noon–3pm; ⓣ 0900/468 32888, ⓦ www.vvvgouda.nl). Can also help arrange private rooms.

Accommodation

B&B Bij Van Briemen Lange Dwarsstraat 21 ⓣ 01825 11 36 7, ⓦ www.bijvanbriemen.nl. Bed and breakfast in very pleasant residential area close to the centre. ❺

De Utrechtsche Dom Geuzenstraat 6 ⓣ 0182/528 833, ⓦ www.hotelgouda.nl. This quiet family hotel is situated right in the centre of town, fifteen minutes' walk from the train station. ❻

Eating and drinking

Café Central Markt 23. A lively bar with an outdoor terrace.

Eetcafé De Beursklok Hoge Gouwe 19. Offers good-quality Dutch food at a reasonable price. Main courses around €15.

Eetcafé Vidocq Koster Gijzensteeg 5. Atmospheric, popular bar off the Markt.

Gewoon Gouds Markt 42. Good salads and pancakes with a view of the Stadhuis. €8 for a salad.

UTRECHT

"I groaned with the idea of living all winter in so shocking a place," wrote Boswell in 1763, and the university town of **UTRECHT**, surrounded by shopping centres and industrial developments, still promises little as you approach. But the centre, with its distinctive sunken canals – whose brick cellar warehouses have been converted into chic cafés and restaurants – is one of the country's most pleasant.

What to see and do

For a place of its size, there's surprisingly little in the way of sights and museums in Utrecht. The focal point is the **Dom Tower**, built between 1321 and 1382, which at over 110m is the highest church tower in the country. A guided tour (May–Sept Mon–Sat 10am–5pm, Sun noon–5pm; €7.50) takes you unnervingly close to the top, from where you can see Rotterdam and Amsterdam on a clear day. Below is the Gothic **Dom Kerk**; only the eastern part of the cathedral remains today after the nave collapsed in 1674, but it's worth peering inside (Mon–Fri 10/11am–4/5pm, Sat 10am–3.30pm, Sun 2–4pm; free) and wandering through the Kloostergang, the fourteenth-century cloisters that link the cathedral to the chapterhouse.

Arrival and information

Train and bus Utrecht's train and bus stations both lead into the Hoog Catharijne shopping centre.
Tourist office The main VVV office is close to the Dom Tower at Domplein 9 (daily 9am–5pm; ⓣ0900/128 8732, ⓦwww.utrecht-city.com).

Accommodation

Hostel B&B Utrecht City Centre Lucas Bolwerk 4 ⓣ031/650434 884, ⓦwww.hostelutrecht.nl. Very decent hostel and much more conveniently located than *Stayokay*, with a lounge plus free Internet and snacks. Buses #3, #4, #11 from Centraal Station to Stadsschouwburg. Dorms ❷, doubles ❼
Stayokay Utrecht-Bunnik Rhijnauwenselaan 14 ⓣ030/656 1277, ⓦwww.stayokay.com. Peaceful, family-orientated HI hostel located a good 5km out of the centre in an old country manor house. Take bus #40 or #41 from the train station to Rhijnauwen. Dorms ❸, doubles ❻
Strowis Boothstraat 8 ⓣ030/238 0280, ⓦwww.strowis.nl. Pleasant guesthouse, a fifteen-minute walk northeast towards Janskerk from Centraal Station or a short ride on bus #3/#4/#8/#11 to the Janskerkhof stop. Dorms ❷, doubles ❻

Eating and drinking

De Oude Muntkelder Oudegracht 112. One of the many cafés on this busy stretch by the canal; serves inexpensive pancakes for around €8.
Stadskasteel Oudaen Oudegracht 99. The oldest house in town, serving beer from its own brewery downstairs. Snack food is served downstairs (€8 for a club sandwich), while upstairs is a more elaborate affair (mains €18).
De Werfkring Oudegracht 123. Offers affordable vegetarian fare, with mains around €11.
De Winkel van Sinkel Oudegracht 158. Bar with regular dance nights and a chill-out room downstairs.

Moving on

Train Arnhem (every 15min; 35min); Amsterdam (every 15min; 30 min); Maastricht (every 30min; 2hr); Rotterdam (every 15min; 40min).

Beyond the Randstad

Outside the Randstad towns, the Netherlands is relatively unknown territory to visitors. To the north, there's superb cycling and hiking to be had through scenic **dune reserves** and delightful villages, with easy access to pristine beaches, while the island of **Texel** offers the country's most complete beach experience, and has plenty of birdlife. The **Hoge Veluwe National Park**, near Arnhem, boasts one of the country's best modern art museums and has cycle paths through a delightful landscape. Further south, in the provinces of North Brabant and Limburg, the landscape slowly fills out, moving into a rougher countryside of farmland and forests and eventually into the hills around **Maastricht**, a city with a vibrant, pan-European feel.

TEXEL

The largest of the islands off the north coast – and the easiest to get to (2hr from Amsterdam) – **TEXEL** (pronounced "tessel") offers diverse and pretty landscapes, and is one of Europe's most important bird-breeding grounds.

What to see and do

Texel's main settlement, **DEN BURG**, makes a convenient base and has bike rental outlets. On the coast 3km southeast of Den Burg is **OUDESCHILD**, home to the **Maritiem en Juttersmuseum** (Beachcombers'

Museum; Tues–Sat 10am–5pm, July & Aug also Mon 10am–5pm, Sun 12–5pm; €5; Ⓦwww.texelsmaritiem.nl), a fascinating collection of marine junk from wrecks. In the opposite direction is **DE KOOG**, with a good sandy beach and the **EcoMare nature centre**, at Ruijslaan 92 (daily 9am–5pm; €8; Ⓦwww.ecomare.nl), a bird and seal sanctuary as well as natural history museum: from here you can visit the **Wad**, the banks of sand and mud to the east of the island, where seals and birds gather.

Arrival and information

Boat Ferries from the town of Den Helder on the mainland depart every hour (€3; coming from Amsterdam, ask for an all-in discounted *Waddenbiljet*).

Tourist office Den Burg's VVV is at Emmalaan 66 (Mon–Fri 9am–6pm, Sat 9am–5pm; Ⓣ0222/314 741, Ⓦwww.texel.net).

Accommodation

Camping's the most popular option here, with good campsites dotted around the island.

Kogerstrand Badweg 33 Ⓣ0222/317 208, Ⓦwww.rsttexel.nl. Campsite set among the beachside dunes in De Koog, the island's busiest resort. Closed Nov–March. ❷

De Koorn Aar Grensweg 388 Ⓣ0222/312 931, Ⓦwww.koorn-aar.nl. Small, well-run place close to Den Burg. Closed Nov–March. ❸

Stayokay Texel Haffelderweg 29 Ⓣ0222/315 441, Ⓦwww.stayokay.com. Brand new HI hostel on the outskirts of Den Burg that's popular with families. There's a big bar and terrace as well as lots of facilities for children including a playground. Dorms ❸, doubles ❼

Eating and drinking

Freya Gravenstraat 4 Ⓣ022/321 686. Be sure to book ahead for Den Burg's best restaurant, which serves a delicious three-course set menu each night for €24.50.

De Pangkoekehuus Kikkertstraat 9, De Cocksdorp. Cosy place serving delicious filled pancakes for around €7.

HOGE VELUWE NATIONAL PARK

Some 70km southeast of Amsterdam, and just north of the town of **Arnhem**, is the huge and scenic **Hoge Veluwe National Park** (daily: April–Aug 8am–8/10pm; Sept–March 9am–6/8pm; €7 park only, or €14 with Kröller-Müller museum; Ⓦwww.hogeveluwe.nl). Formerly the estate of wealthy local couple Anton and Helene Kröller-Müller, it has three entrances – one near the village of **Otterlo** on the northwest perimeter, another near **Hoenderloo** on the northeast edge, and a third to the south at **Rijzenburg**, near the village of Schaarsbergen. The easiest way to get here is by bus #107 from Arnhem's train station, then change at Otterlo to bus #110 which runs direct to the **Bezoekerscentrum** (visitors' centre), which is open daily 9.30am to 5/6pm. Here, you can pick up free white bicycles, by far the best way to explore the park, and visit the terraced café/restaurant, *De Koperen Kop*.

What to see and do

Within the park is the **Museonder** (daily 9.30am–5/6pm), an underground natural history museum, and the **St Hubertus Hunting Lodge** (guided tours only; €2), the former Art Deco home of the Kröller-Müllers. The park's unmissable highlight is the **Kröller-Müller Museum** (Tues–Sun 10am–5pm; €14 including park admission; Ⓦwww.kmm.nl), a superb collection of fine art including nearly three hundred paintings by Van Gogh, plus works by Picasso, Seurat, Léger and Mondriaan. Behind the museum is a lovely and imaginative **sculpture garden** (Tues–Sun 10am–4.30pm; same ticket).

Arrival and information

Train and bus Trains run from Amsterdam to nearby Arnhem, from where you can catch the bus to the park (see above).

Tourist office Arnhem's VVV office is near the station, at Willemsplein 8 (Mon 11am–5.30pm, Tues–Fri 9am–5.30pm, Sat 10am–5pm; ⓣ0900/202 4075; ⓦwww.vvvarnhem.nl).

Accommodation

Hoge Veluwe Campsite ⓣ055/378 2232, ⓦwww.hogeveluwe.nl. Official campsite by the park's northeastern Hoenderloo entrance. Closed Nov–March. ❶

Stayokay Arnhem Diepenbrocklaan 27 ⓣ026/442 0114, ⓦwww.stayokay.com. Set in a no-man's-land north of town, this hostel provides good, cheap accommodation geared towards large groups rather than individuals. Take bus #3 to the Rijnstate hospital, from where it is a five-minute walk. ❸

MAASTRICHT

Squashed between the Belgian and German borders, **MAASTRICHT** is one of the most delightful cities in the Netherlands. A cosmopolitan place, where three languages happily coexist, it's also one of the oldest towns in the country.

What to see and do

The busiest of Maastricht's many squares is **Markt**, at its most crowded during the Wednesday and Friday morning **market**, with the mid-seventeenth-century **Stadhuis** (Mon–Fri 9am–12.30pm & 2–5pm; free) at its centre. Just west, **Vrijthof** is a grander open space flanked by a line of café terraces on one side and on the other by **St Servaaskerk** (daily 10am–4.30pm; €3.50), a tenth-century church. Next door is **St Janskerk** (Easter–Oct Mon–Sat 11am–4pm; free), with its tall fifteenth-century Gothic tower (Mon–Sat 10am–4pm; €1.50). On the other side of the square lies the appealing district of **Stokstraat Kwartier**, with narrow streets winding out to the fast-flowing River Jeker and the **Helpoort** fortress gateway of 1229. Continuing south, the **casemates** in the **Waldeck Park** (guided tours: July–Sept daily 12.30pm and 2pm; Oct–June Sat & Sun 2pm; €4.25) are further evidence of Maastricht's once-impressive fortifications. Fifteen minutes' walk further south is the 110m hill of **St Pietersberg**. Of the two ancient defensive tunnel systems under the hill, the **Zonneberg** is probably the better, situated on the far side of the hill at Casino Slavante (hourly guided tours: July–Sept daily 11am–4pm; €3.75). Just outside the city lies the busy tourist town of **VALKENBURG**, which provides a base for walking the nearby hills and forests.

Bonnefantenmuseum

Across the river is the city's main art gallery, **Bonnefantenmuseum** at Avenue Céramique 250 (ⓣ043/329 0190; Tues-Sun 11am–5pm; €7.50; ⓦwww.bonnefanten.nl). Designed by Aldo Rossi, it's situated in the newest part of Maastricht, **Céramique**, which offers a complete contrast to the feel of the historic city on the east side of the river. The collection ranges from old masters to contemporary artists, but is less of an attraction than the building itself.

Arrival and information

Train and bus The centre of Maastricht is on the west bank of the river. You're likely to arrive, however, on the east bank, in the district known as Wijk, home to the train and bus stations and many of the city's hotels.

Tourist office The central VVV, at Kleine Straat 1, at the end of the main shopping street (Mon–Sat 9am–6pm, Sun 11am–3pm; Nov–March closed Sun; ⓣ043/325 2121, ⓦwww.vvvmaastricht.nl), has copies of a tourist guide with map and a list of private rooms.

Accommodation

Hostel

Stayokay Maastricht Maasboulevard 101 ⓣ043/750 1790, ⓦwww.stayokay.com. Very new HI Hostel in a great location, a few minutes' walk from the town centre. There's a big riverside terrace and it's all done up in a funky retro style, but it can feel utterly soulless. Fifteen-minute walk from the station. Dorms ❸, doubles ❼

Hotels

Botel Maastricht Maasboulevard 95 ⓣ043/321 9023, ⓦwww.botelmaastricht.nl. Moored on the river not far from the Helpoort, this is a fun place – there's a huge difference in cabin size for the same price, so ask for a larger one when you book. ❺

La Cloche Bredestraat 4 ⓣ043/321 2407, ⓦwww.lacloche.com. Pleasant and extremely central hotel with just eight rooms. Check-in is at *Café Cloche*, round the corner at Vrijthof 12. ❽

Campsite

Camping De Bosrand Moerslag 4 ⓣ043/409 1544. Twenty-five minutes south of town on bus #57. Closed Nov–March. ❶

Eating and drinking

Coffeelovers Dominican Sq 1. Part of a chain, but this is a really stylish one in a converted church, and the coffee's great. Perfect if you're exhausted from shopping. Closed Sun.

DeliBelge Tongersestraat 44a. Good snack place if you're in the university quarter. €3 for a sandwich.

Pizzeria Napoli Markt 71. Great pizzas with a twenty-percent student discount. Next door is the town's best *frituur* (chip shop).

Tribunal Tongersestraat 1. Happening brown café that's popular with students.

Zondag Wijckerbrugstraat 42. Great bar near the station in a part of town that's unfairly overlooked by tourists, on the other side of the Maas.

Moving on

Train Amsterdam (hourly; 2hr 35min); Liège (hourly; 30min).

Norway

HIGHLIGHTS

THE LOFOTEN ISLANDS: visit this Arctic archipelago in summer for gorgeous scenery, swimming and fishing

GEIRANGERFJORD: take the Trollstigen highway to this glorious fjord for the quintessential Norwegian experience

GRUNERLØKKA: this former working class district of Oslo is now home to a buzzing collection of bars, clubs and boutique shops

STAVANGER: a little gem of a university town, with great bars and restaurants and sandy, surfable beaches nearby

ROUGH COSTS

DAILY BUDGET Basic €55/occasional treat €75

DRINK Beer €6

FOOD Fish soup €10

HOSTEL/BUDGET HOTEL €25–35/€60–70

TRAVEL Train: Oslo–Bergen (7hr), €25–90

FACT FILE

POPULATION 4 million

AREA 324,220 sq km

LANGUAGE Norwegian

CURRENCY Norwegian kroner (kr)

CAPITAL Oslo (population 500,000)

INTERNATIONAL PHONE CODE ⓣ47

Basics

Norway's extraordinary landscape will lift your heart while high prices squeeze your wallet. The pay-off is the country's mix of likeable, easy-going cities and breathtaking wilderness – during summer, you can hike up a glacier in the morning and thaw out in an urban bar in the evening, watching the sun dip below the horizon for all of half an hour. Deeper into the countryside, you'll find vast stretches of distinctive glacier-formed landscapes. And because of Norway's low population density, it really is possible to travel for hours among all this natural grandeur without seeing a soul.

Beyond **Oslo** – a pretty, increasingly cosmopolitan capital surrounded by mountains and fjords – the major cities of interest are historic **Trondheim**, **Bergen**, on the edge of the fjords, and northern **Tromsø**. Anyone with even a passing fondness for the great outdoors should head to the **western fjords**. Dip into the region from Bergen or **Åndalsnes**, or linger in the region's many waterside towns and villages. Further north, deep in the Arctic Circle, the **Lofoten Islands** are well worth the effort for their calm atmosphere and sheer beauty. To the north of here, the tourist trail focuses on the long journey to **Nordkapp** – the northernmost accessible point in Europe. The route leads through **Finnmark**, one of the last strongholds of the Sami and their herds of reindeer.

CHRONOLOGY

10,000–2,000 BC Seal and reindeer hunting tribes move into present-day Norway.

800–1050 AD Norwegian Vikings become a dominant force in Europe, conducting successful raids across Britain and the Continent.

900 King Harald becomes the first ruler of a united Norway.

1030 The Norwegians adopt Christianity.

1262 Norway increases her empire, forming unions with Greenland and Iceland.

1350 Almost two thirds of the population die during the Black Death.

1396 The Kalmar Union unites Norway with Denmark and Sweden under a single ruler.

1536 Sweden leaves the Kalmar Union, leaving Norway under Danish control.

1814 Norwegian hopes of independence are dashed after Sweden invades and takes control.

1905 Parliament declares independence from Sweden. Haakon VII is crowned the first King of an independent Norway in 525 years.

1913 Norway becomes one of the first countries in the world to give women the vote.

1914 Norway remains neutral during WWI.

1939-1945 Norway initially declares neutrality during WWII but is invaded by the Nazis in 1940. Widespread acts of sabotage take place until liberation in May, 1945.

1960s The discovery of oil and gas in the North Sea leads to greater economic prosperity.

1981 Gro Harlem Brundtland becomes the first female Prime Minister.

2005 Prime Minister Kjell Bodevik is defeated in the general elections, and is replaced by Labour candidate Jens Stolenberg.

2007 Norway is rated as world's most peaceful country in Global Peace Index survey.

ARRIVAL

Norway has dozens of **airports**, but the four busiest are Oslo, Bergen, Trondheim and Stavanger. With typical Norwegian efficiency, all are well connected with local transport, with direct buses or trains to the nearest town centre. The main low-cost carriers are Ryanair (Ⓦwww.ryanair.com), which flies to Haugesund and Oslo, and Norwegian Air Shuttle (Ⓦwww.norwegian.no, Ⓣ21 49 00 15). Norway's long coastline is served by a number of **ferry** companies; the biggest

are DFDS Seaways (ⓦwww.dfds.co.uk, ⓣ (UK) 0871 522 9955) and Color Line (ⓦwww.colorline.com), which ply routes between Newcastle in the UK and Copenhagen in Denmark and the major ports of Stavanger and Bergen. There are frequent international **trains** to Oslo from Stockholm and Gothenburg in Sweden (ⓦwww.nsb.no).

GETTING AROUND

Public transport is very reliable. In the winter (especially in the north), services can be cut back severely, but no part of the country is isolated for long. A synopsis of all the main air, train, bus and ferry services is given in the free *NRI Guide to Transport and Accommodation* brochure, available in advance from the Norwegian Tourist Board; and all local tourist offices have detailed regional public transport timetables. There are four main **train** routes. These link Oslo to Stockholm in the east, to Kristiansand and Stavanger in the southwest, to Bergen in the west and to Trondheim and on to Fauske and Bodø in the north.

InterRail, Eurail and ScanRail (ⓦwww.scanrail.com) **rail passes** are valid in Norway, and also give substantial discounts on some major ferry crossings and certain long-distance bus routes. You'll need to use **buses** principally in the western fjords and the far north. Bus tickets aren't expensive and are usually bought on board; in addition the country's principal bus company, Nor-Way Bussekspress (Ⓦwww.nor-way.no), sells several go-as-you-please passes. Travelling by **ferry** is one of the real pleasures of a trip to Norway. Rates are fixed nationally on a sliding scale, with a ten- to fifteen-minute ride costing 20–30kr for foot passengers. Bus fares include the cost of any ferry journey made en route. Some of the busier ferry routes have a control kiosk, where you pay on arrival, but for the most part a crew member comes round to collect fares either on the quayside or on board. The **Hurtigrute** – "rapid route" (Ⓦwww.norwegiancoastalvoyage.com) boat shuttles up and down the coast, linking Bergen with Kirkenes and stopping off at over thirty ports on the way.

ACCOMMODATION

For budget travellers as well as hikers, climbers and skiers, **hostels** provide the accommodation mainstay; there are about a hundred in total, spread right across the country and run by Norske Vandrerhjem (Ⓦwww.vandrerhjem.no). Prices vary greatly (150–250kr), and bed linen costs extra, although the more expensive hostels nearly always include breakfast in the price of the room. Most places also have a supply of doubles for 400–500kr. HI members get a 15 percent discount. Many HI hostels close 11am–4pm, and there's often an 11pm/midnight curfew; Norway also has a number of excellent independent hostels which are less regimented and with comparable prices.

There are around four hundred official **campsites** listed in the tourist board's free camping brochure (Ⓦwww.camping.no), plenty of them easily reached by public transport. On average expect to pay 80–160kr per night for two people using a tent. Sites also often have **cabins** (*hytter*), usually four-bedded affairs with kitchen facilities and sometimes a bathroom, with prices ranging between 250 and 750kr. You can camp rough in open areas as long as you are at least 150m away from houses or cabins or otherwise have permission from the landowner, and leave no trace. **Hotels** are generally too pricey for travellers on a budget, although summer discounts can net you a double room for as little as 600kr. **Guesthouses** (*pensjonater*) in the more touristy towns are about 550kr a double, and tourist offices in larger towns can often fix you up with a **private room** in someone's house for around 350–400kr a double. In coastal districts, especially the Lofoten Islands, **sjøhus** (literally "sea houses") and **rorbus** (converted fishermen's cabins) can be rented from about 500kr per cabin.

FOOD AND DRINK

Norwegian **food** can be excellent: fish is plentiful, as are reindeer steak and elk. However, eating well on a tight budget can be difficult. Breakfast (*frokost*) – a self-service affair of bread, cheese, eggs, preserves, cold meat and fish, washed down with unlimited tea and coffee – is usually good at hostels, and very good in hotels. If it isn't included in the room rate, reckon on an extra 50–70kr.

Picnic food is the best stand-by during the day, although there are **fast-food** alternatives. The indigenous Norwegian variety, served up at street stalls (*gatekjøkken*), consists mainly of rather unappetizing hot dogs (*varme pølse*), pizza slices and chicken and chips. A much better choice, and often no more expensive, is simply to get a *smørbrød*, a huge open sandwich heaped with a variety of garnishes. The best deals for sit-down food are at **lunchtime** (*lunsj*), when self-service *kafeterias* offer a limited range of daily specials (*dagens rett*) costing 80–100kr. These include a fish or meat dish with vegetables or salad, often a drink, sometimes bread, and occasionally coffee, too. In the larger towns, you'll also find more original cafés called *kaffistovas*, which serve high-quality Norwegian food at quite reasonable prices. **Restaurants**, serving dinner (*middag*), are out of the range of most budgets, but the seafood can be superb. Again, the best deals are at lunchtime, when some restaurants put out a *koldtbord* (the Norwegian *smörgåsbord*), where, for a fixed price (100–200kr), you can eat as much as you like.

Drink

Alcohol prices are among the highest in Europe. Buying from the supermarkets and **Vinmonopolet** (the state–run off-licences) is often the only way you'll afford a tipple: in a bar, **beer** costs around 50kr/500ml. It comes in three strengths: class I is light, class II is what you get in supermarkets and is the most widely served in pubs (what you get when you ask for "a beer"), while class III is the strongest and only available at Vinmonopolet. In the cities, bars stay open until at least 1am; in the smaller towns, they tend to close at around 11pm. Everywhere, look out for *aquavit*, served ice-cold in little glasses; at forty percent proof, it's real headache stuff. Outside bars and restaurants, **wines** and **spirits** can only be purchased from Vinmonopolet. There's generally one in each town, more in the cities; opening hours are usually Mon–Wed 10am–4/5pm, Thurs 10am–5/6pm, Fri 9am–4/6pm, Sat 9am–1/3pm. You have to be eighteen to buy wine and beer, twenty to buy spirits.

CULTURE AND ETIQUETTE

Norwegian people are generally scrupulously polite, helpful and self-deprecating. The famous **Nordic reserve** is apparent, but usually evaporates under the influence of direct friendliness or, failing that, alcohol – which Norwegians consume in large quantities. Despite the oil wealth the country has accrued in recent years, the fact that it spent much of its history under the thumb of foreign rulers might explain why Norway has little of the brashness that usually comes with economic success. This is a robust, pragmatic country where order is favoured over exuberance, and community values are emphasized over individuality. That doesn't mean that Norwegians don't know how to have fun: in cities such as Oslo and Trondheim you'll find a thriving nightlife concentrated in the student areas and former working class districts.

Table manners are conventionally European; there's no need to **tip**, as service staff are usually well paid. Almost everyone speaks excellent English, even in the most isolated towns.

SPORTS AND OUTDOOR ACTIVITIES

Every kind of snow-based sport is represented in Norway, but **skiing** is the national winter pastime and is taken very seriously indeed. To the north of the country, dogsledding and snowmobile trips can help you make the most of the snow, and sailing and kayaking are great ways to enjoy the western fjord region. There are also plentiful hiking and climbing routes, with transport details and maps available from local tourist offices.

Despite the Norwegian national team's rather dismal international performance, **football** is hugely popular and there's always a good turnout to see local teams. The Norway Cup, held every summer, is the biggest youth football tournament in the world and packs out youth hostels and stadiums around the country.

COMMUNICATIONS

Post office opening hours are usually Mon–Fri 8/8.30am–4/5pm, Sat 8/9am–1pm. Stamps are available

NORWAY ON THE NET

Ⓦwww.visitnorway.com Official Norwegian Tourist Board site.
Ⓦwww.odin.dep.no Government site with good information links.

from post offices, snack and newspaper kiosks and some bookstores. Some public phones take coins, but increasingly only accept **phonecards**, available in a variety of denominations from kiosks. There are no area codes. Directory enquiries is ⓣ1881 within Scandinavia, ⓣ1882 international. The international operator is on ⓣ115. Many hotels have **Internet** access, and most libraries offer free access for around 15 mins.

EMERGENCIES

Norway is well-known for its lack of crime, and the Norwegian people are characteristically friendly and helpful. The **police** are amiable and can normally speak English. Most good hotels as well as pharmacies and tourist offices have lists of local **doctors** and dentists. Norway is not in the EU but reciprocal health agreements mean EU citizens get free hospital treatment with an EHIC card. If **pharmacies** (*apotek*) are closed they usually have a rota in the window advising of the nearest pharmacy that is open.

EMERGENCY NUMBERS

Police ⓣ112; Ambulance ⓣ113; Fire ⓣ110.

INFORMATION & MAPS

Every town has a **tourist office**, usually with a stock of free maps and timetables. Many book private rooms and hotel beds, some rent out bikes and change money. During the high season – late June to August – they normally open daily for long hours, while in low season they mostly adopt shop hours; many close down altogether in winter. The *Hallwag* **map** (1:1,000,000) comes with an index, although the *Statens Kartverk* maps, available in Norway at several scales, are best.

MONEY AND BANKS

Norway's currency is the **krone** (kr), divided into 100 øre. Coins are 50 øre, 1kr, 5kr, 10kr and 20kr; notes are 50kr, 100kr, 200kr, 500kr and 1000kr. At the time of writing, €1 is worth 7.66kr; £1 is 11.05kr; and US$1 is 5.42kr.

Banking hours are Mon–Fri 9am–3.30pm, Thurs till 5pm, though many banks close thirty minutes earlier in summer. Most airports and some train stations have exchange offices, open evenings and weekends, and some tourist offices also change money, though at worse rates than banks and post offices. **ATMs** are commonplace even in the smaller towns.

OPENING HOURS AND HOLIDAYS

Opening hours are usually Mon–Wed & Fri 9am–5pm, Thurs 9am–6/8pm, Sat 9am–1/3pm. Almost everything – including supermarkets – is closed on Sunday, the main exceptions being newspaper and snack-food kiosks (*Narvesen*) and takeaway food stalls. Most businesses are closed on **public holidays**: Jan 1, Maundy Thurs, Good Fri, Easter Sun & Mon, May 1, Ascension Day (mid-May), May 17 (Norway's National Day), Whit Sun & Mon, Dec 25 & 26.

NorwegiaN

	Norwegian	Pronunciation
Yes	*Ja*	Ya
No	*Nei*	Nay
Please	*Vaersågod*	Varsaagod
Thank you	*Takk*	Takk
Hello/Good day	*Godmorgen/Goddag*	Godmorgan/Goddag
Goodbye	*Adjø*	Ad-yur
Excuse me	*Unnskyld*	Un-shy-ld
Where?	*Hvor?*	Vor?
Good	*God*	God
Bad	*Dårlig*	Door-lig
Near	*Inaerheten*	Eyenar-he-ten
Far	*Langt borte*	Langt borteh
Cheap	*Billig*	Billig
Expensive	*Dyrt*	Deert
Open	*Åpen*	Or-pen
Closed	*Stengt*	Stengt
Today	*I dag*	Ee-daag
Yesterday	*I går*	Ee-gaar
Tomorrow	*I morgen*	Ee morn
How much is....?	*Hvormyeer...?*	Vorm-yeer?
What time is it?	*Hvor mangeer klokken?*	Vor mang-eer klock-en?
I don't understand	*Jeg forstår ikke*	Yeg forst-aar ik-ke
Do you speak English?	*Snakkerdu engelsk*	Snack-er du eng-elle-sk?
One	*En*	En
Two	*To*	To
Three	*Tre*	Tray
Four	*Fire*	Feer-eh
Five	*Fem*	Fem
Six	*Seks*	Seks
Seven	*Sju*	Shu
Eight	*Åtte*	Or-teh
Nine	*Ni*	Nee
Ten	*Ti*	Tee

Oslo

OSLO is the oldest of the Scandinavian capital cities, founded around 1048 by Harald Hardrada. Several devastating fires and six hundred years later, Oslo upped sticks and shifted west to its present site, abandoning its old name in favour of **Christiania** – after the seventeenth-century Danish king Christian IV responsible for the move. The new city prospered and by the time of the break with Denmark (and then union with Sweden) in 1814, Christiania – indeed Norway as a whole – was clamouring for independence, something it finally achieved in 1905.

Today's city centre is largely the work of the late nineteenth and early twentieth centuries, an era reflected in the wide streets, dignified parks and gardens, solid buildings and long, consciously classical vistas. Its half a million inhabitants have room to spare in a city whose vast boundaries encompass forests, sand and sea.

What to see and do

Oslo is a city that offers all the trappings of metropolitan life within easy reach of both dense forest and sandy beaches. It's also blessed with a clutch of first-rate museums, a lively bar scene and a tempting array of outdoor pursuits, from swimming to skiing. The main street, **Karl Johans gate**, leads west up the slope from Oslo S train station.

Domkirke and Stortinget

The **Domkirke** (Cathedral; daily 10am–5pm; free) is located just off Karl Johans gate but is closed until 2009 for structural renovations. If you arrive after it reopens, the elegant interior, its nave and transepts awash with maroon, green and gold paintwork, is worth a look. From here it's a brief stroll up Karl Johans gate to the **Stortinget**, the parliament building, an imposing chunk of neo-Romanesque architecture that was completed in 1866. In front of the parliament, a narrow park-piazza flanks Karl Johans gate; in summer it teems with promenading city folk, while in winter people flock to its floodlit open-air skating rinks.

Royal Palace

Det Kongelige Slott (Royal Palace) stands right at the top of Karl Johans gate, and the lovely grounds – **Slottsparken** – are open to the public. It was built between 1825 and 1848 by Karl Johan himself, a French general-turned-Swedish-king in charge here during the union between Sweden and Norway. (The current Norwegian royal family was actually imported from England and Denmark in 1905.) Try timing your visit to coincide with the daily changing of the guard (1.30pm) – an eccentric but good-humoured business. During the summer, guided tours of the palace run every 20 minutes (11am–5pm, Mon–Thurs and Sat; 1pm–5pm Fri and Sun, 95kr).

The University and around

Located on Karl Johans Gate, the very grand, nineteenth-century **university buildings** fit well into this monumental end of the city centre. The similarly handsome **Nationaltheatret** (National Theatre) is just opposite. At Universitetsgata 13, you'll find the **Nasjonalgalleriet** (Tues, Wed & Fri 10am–6pm, Thurs 10am–7pm, Sat & Sun 11am–5pm; free; Ⓦwww.nasjonalgalleriet.no), home to Norway's largest and best collection of fine art. Highlights include wonderfully romantic landscapes by Johan Christian Dahl and grim social commentary by sometime Edvard Munch mentor Christian Krohg. A room devoted to Munch features the original version of the famous *Scream*.

City Hall

Heading south from the university buildings, you can't miss the monolithic brickwork of the massive City Hall, the **Rådhus** (daily 9am–4/5pm; free), opened in 1950 to celebrate the city's 900th anniversary. Venture inside to admire some beautiful carved-wood depictions of Norse myths and an enormous hall decorated with a mural by several prominent Norwegian artists – this is where the Peace Prize is awarded.

Folk Museum

The fascinating and slightly spooky **Norsk Folkemuseum**, at Museumsveien 10 (daily mid-May to mid-Sept 10am–6pm, mid-Sept to mid-May 11am–3/4pm, 90kr; ⓦwww.norskfolkemuseum.no), combines indoor collections of medieval clothes, china and silverware with an open-air display of accurately recreated farms, houses and shops from different periods of Norwegian history.

Viking ships

The **Vikingskipshuset** on Langviksvin (Viking Ships Museum, daily May–Sept 9am–6pm, Oct–April 11am–4pm; 40kr; ⓦwww.ukm.uio.no/vikingskipshuset), houses a trio of ninth-century Viking ships, with viewing platforms to let you see inside the hulls. The three oak vessels were retrieved from ritual burial mounds in southern Norway towards the end of the nineteenth century, each embalmed in clay. The star exhibit, the **Oseberg ship**, is thought to have been a pleasure boat for short cruises, and there's more historical fun to be had by gazing at the *Gokstad*, a sturdier ship used for longer voyages, and imagining sailing the open seas in such a basic craft.

Kon-Tiki museet

Down by Bygdøynes pier, the **Kon-Tiki museet** (daily April, May & Sept 10am–5pm, June–Aug 9am–5.30pm, Oct–March 10.30am–4pm; 45kr; ⓦwww.kon-tiki.no) displays the balsawood raft on which Thor Heyerdahl made his now legendary, utterly eccentric 1947 journey across the Pacific to prove the first Polynesian settlers could have sailed from pre-Inca Peru.

Frammuseet

Inside the **Frammuseet,** next to the Bygdøynes dock, (daily Jun–Aug 9am–6pm, Sept–Oct and Mar–May 10am–4pm, Nov–Feb 10am–3pm; 40kr), you can clamber aboard one of Roald Amundsen's ships, the polar vessel *Fram*; this was the ship that carried him to Antarctica in 1912. Complete with most of its original fittings, the interior gives a superb insight into the life and times of these early Polar explorers.

Munch Museum

Out of the centre but without question a major attraction, the **Munch-museet**, Tøyengata 53 (June to Aug daily 10am–6pm, Sept–May Tues–Fri 10am–4pm,

GETTING TO THE BYGDØY PENINSULA

The most enjoyable way to reach the leafy **Bygdøy peninsula**, southwest of the city centre, is by **ferry**. These leave from the Rådhusbrygge (pier 3) behind the Rådhus (late April & Sept every 30min 9am–6.30pm; May–Aug every 15min 8/9am–9.05pm; 22kr in advance/30kr onboard). They stop first at the Dronningen (15min from Rådhusbrygge) and then the Bygdøynes piers (20min).The two most popular attractions – the Viking Ships and Folk museums – are within easy walking distance of the Dronningen pier, the others – the Kon-Tiki, the Maritime and the Fram museums – are beside Bygdøynes. It's a (dull) twenty-minute signposted walk between the two groups of museums. The alternative to the ferry is **bus** #30 (every 15min), which runs all year from Kirkeristen in Dronningens gate. This takes you to the Folk Museum and Viking Ships, and, when the ferry isn't running, to the other three museums as well.

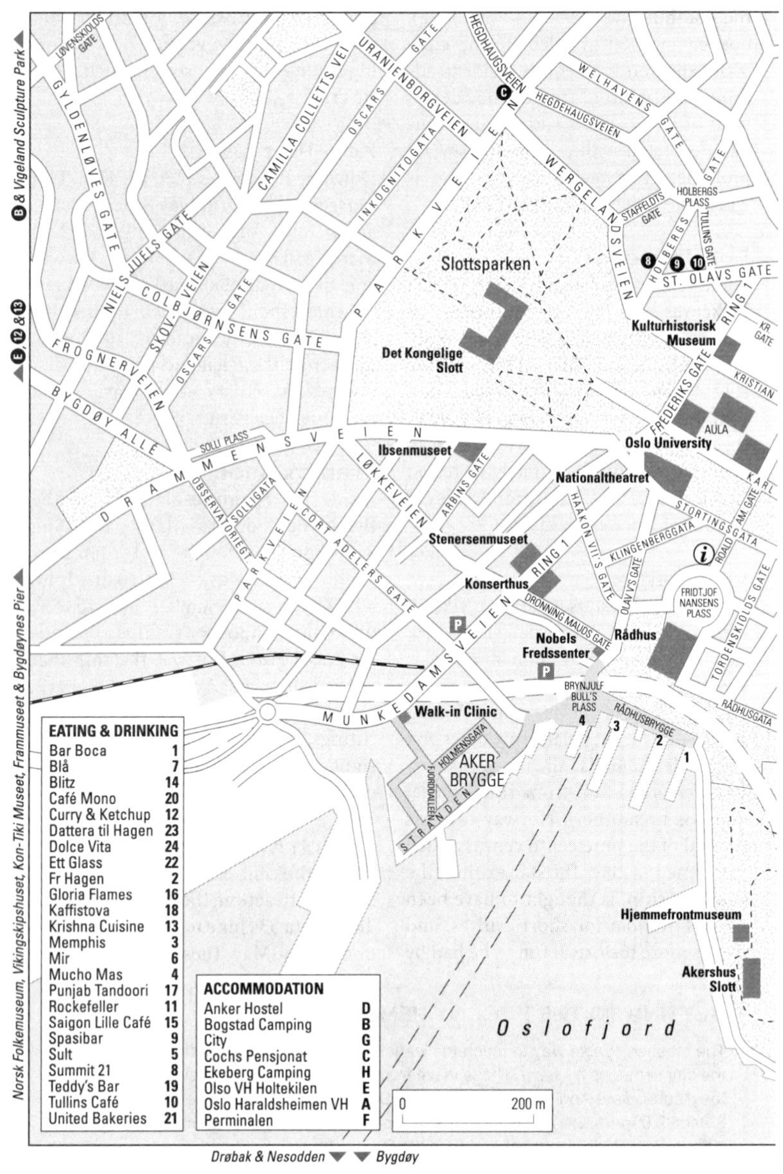

Sat & Sun 11am–5pm, closed Mon; 65kr; Ⓦwww.munch.museum.no), is reachable by T-bane (underground): get off at Tøyen/Munch-museet and it's a signposted five-minute walk. Born in 1863, **Edvard Munch** is Norway's most famous painter. His lithographs and woodcuts – gloom, fog, naked women – are on display here, as well as his early paintings and the great,

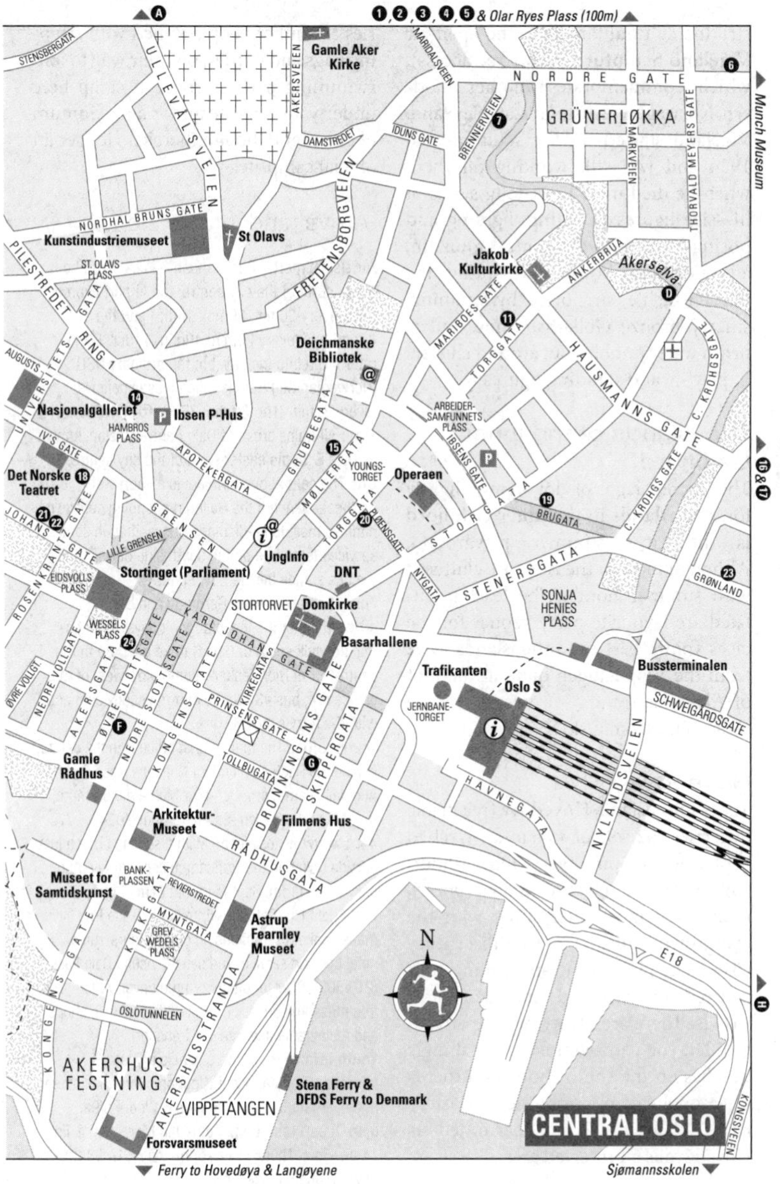

signature works of the 1890s. The museum owns one of two versions of *The Scream*, stolen in 2004 and returned to the museum about two years later in mysterious circumstances.

Vigeland Sculpture Park

On the other side of the city and reachable on tram #12 and #15 from the centre (get off at Vigelandsparken), Frogner Park holds one of Oslo's most striking cultural targets in the open-air **Vigeland Sculpture Park** (free access), which commemorates another modern Norwegian artist, Gustav Vigeland. Vigeland started on the sculptures in 1924 and was still working on them when he died in 1943. A long series of life-size figures frowning, fighting and posing lead up to the central fountain, an enormous bowl representing the burden of life, supported by straining, sinewy bronze Goliaths, while underneath water tumbles out around clusters of playing and standing figures.

The islands of the inner Oslofjord

The archipelago of low-lying, lightly forested **islands** in the **inner Oslofjord** is the city's summer playground. Although most of the islets are cluttered with summer homes, the least populated are favourite party venues for the city's youth. Ferries to the islands leave from the Vippetangen quay, at the foot of Akershusstranda – a twenty-minute walk south from Oslo S.

Hovedøya

The nearest island, **Hovedøya** (reachable by ferries #92, #93 or #94; mid-March to Sept 7.30am–7pm, every 30min–hour; Oct to mid-March three daily; 10min), is also the most interesting, with the overgrown ruins of a twelfth-century Cistercian monastery, and rolling hills covered in farmland and deciduous woods. There are plenty of footpaths to wander, you can swim from the shingle beaches on the south shore, and there's a seasonal café opposite the monastery ruins. Camping is not permitted as Hovedøya is a protected area.

Langøyene

The pick of the other islands is wooded **Langøyene** (ferry #94; June–Aug hourly 9.30am–6.45pm; 30min), the most southerly of the archipelago and the one with the best beaches; at night the ferries are full of people armed with sleeping bags and bottles, on their way to join swimming parties. You can camp here under your own steam for a maxiumum of one night, though there's no longer an official campsite.

Arrival and information

Air Oslo airport – Gardermoen – is located about 50km north of the city centre: the Airport Express train (every 20min; 20min; 160kr) and the SAS Airport bus (every 20min; 40min; 110kr, 170kr return) run into the city, but the ordinary NSB (Norwegian rail) train is much less expensive (every 30min–1hr; 30min; 77kr); ⓣ06400.

Train All trains arrive at Oslo Sentralstasjon, known as Oslo S, at the eastern end of the city centre.

Bus The central bus terminal is a short walk northeast beneath the Galleriet shopping centre: it handles most long–distance buses, though some services terminate on the south side of Oslo S at the bus stands beside Havnegata.

Ferry Car ferries from Germany and Denmark arrive at either the Vippetangen quays, a fifteen-minute walk south of Oslo S (take bus #60 to the centre), or at Hjortneskaia, some 3km west of the city centre; bus #31 to the centre usually connects with the ferry's arrival.

Tourist office The main tourist office is in the centre, behind the Rådhus at Fridtjof Nansens plass 5 (June–Aug daily 9am–7pm; Oct–Mar Mon–Fri 9am–4pm, Apr–May & Sept Mon–Sat 9am–5pm; ⓣ24 14 77 44; ⓦwww.visitoslo.com), with a second branch just outside Oslo S in the Trafikanten centre (May–Aug daily 8am–11pm, Sept Mon–Sat 8am–11pm, Oct–April Mon–Sat 8am–5pm): both issue free city maps, make reservations on guided tours, run a hotel booking service, and sell the useful Oslo Pass (210/300/390kr for one/two/three days), which gives free museum admission, limited discounts in shops and restaurants and free city transport.

Youth information There is also a youth information office, Use It (Ungdoms Informasjonen), at Møllergata 3 (July–Aug Mon & Wed–Fri 9am–6pm, Tues 11am–6pm, Sept–Jun Mon–Wed & Fri 11am–5pm, Thurs 11am–6pm); ⓣ24 14 98 20; ⓦwww.unginfo.oslo.no).

Hiking information The Norwegian hikers' association, Den Norske Turistforening (DNT), has an office in the centre at Storgata 3 (Mon–Wed & Fri 10am–5pm, Thurs 10am–6pm, Sat 10am–2pm; ⓣ40 00 18 68, ⓦwww.turistforeningen.no), where they sell hiking maps and give general advice and information on route planning.

City listings All three information offices provide *Streetwise* – a free budget guide to Oslo – as well as the excellent *Oslo Official Guide* and *What's On in Oslo.*

City transport

Transport information The city transport Trafikanten information office is on Jernbanetorvet, the pedestrianized square outside Oslo S (Mon–Fri 7am–8pm, Sat 8am–6pm; ⓣ177, ⓦwww.trafikanten.no), and supplies a useful free transit map and comprehensive timetable booklet, *Rutebok for Oslo.* Local traffic tickets cost 22kr; a 24-hour travel pass, available from Trafikanten, costs 60kr.
Tram The trams run on eight lines, crossing the centre from east to west.
Bus There are also buses criss-crossing the city; most routes converge at Oslo S and Carl Berners plass.
Underground The Tunnelbanen (T-bane) has six lines, all of which also run along the loop of track circling the centre from Majorstuen in the west to Tøyen in the east.
Ferry Numerous local ferries cross the Oslofjord to the south of the centre, connecting the city with its outlying districts and archipelagos.
Tickets Local transport tickets cost a flat-fare of 20kr; a 24hr-travel pass, available from Trafikanten, costs 60kr.

Accommodation

You're best off staying centrally either around Oslo S or near the western reaches of Karl Johans gate, between the Stortinget and the Nationaltheatret. Always call ahead to check on space. A good budget alternative to the hostels listed below is a private room ❺, booked by the tourist office near Oslo S, though there's often a minimum two-night stay and you should book before 7pm.

Hostels

Anker Hostel Storgata 55 ⓣ22 99 72 00, ⓦwww.ankerhostel.no. Excellent hostel, in a good location between Oslo S and the hip Grunerløkka district. Lively, clean and friendly, with its own bar, laundry and 24-hour reception. Ten minutes' walk from Oslo S or catch tram #11, #12, #13, #15 or #17. Reservations necessary during winter. Dorms ❸, rooms ❻
Oslo Haraldsheim Vandrerhjem Haraldsheimveien 4, Grefsen ⓣ22 22 29 65, ⓦwww.vandrerhjem.no. Best of the HI hostels, 4km northeast of the centre, with about 70 rooms, mostly in four-bed dorms, many en-suite. Take tram #15 or #17 from the bottom of Storgata to the Sinsenkrysset stop, from where it's a signposted five- to ten-minute walk. Advance booking necessary in summer. Dorms ❸, rooms ❻
Oslo Vandrerhjem Holtekilen Micheletsvei 55, 1368 Stabekk. ⓣ67 51 80 40, ⓦwww.vandrerhjem.no. Located 10km west of the city centre, this place has both dorms and one- to four-bedded rooms. Also has kitchen, laundry facilities and restaurant. From Bussterminalen, take bus #151 to the Kveldsroveien bus stop; the hostel is 100m away on the right. Dorms ❸, rooms ❻

Hotels and guest houses

City Skippergaten 19 ⓣ22 41 36 10, ⓦwww.cityhotel.no. This modest but pleasant hotel, a long-time favourite with budget travellers, is located above shops and offices near Oslo S. ❽
Cochs Pensjonat Parkveien 25 ⓣ23 33 24 00, ⓦwww.cochspensjonat.no. Reasonable guesthouse with good deals on triples and quads. Mostly shared bathrooms. Pleasant location to the west of the royal palace. ❼
Perminalen Hotel Øvre Slottsgate 2 ⓣ23 09 30 81, ⓦwww.perminalen.com. Good budget option near the fortress. The majority of the rooms are clean, spacious four-bed dorms with TV and en-suite showers. Dorms ❺, rooms ❽

Campsites

Bogstad Camping Ankeveien 117 ⓣ22 51 08 00, ⓦwww.bogstadcamping.no. Large campsite in a good location by a lake, about 9km from the city centre. Take bus #32 from Oslo S. Camping ❸, four-bed huts ❾
Ekeberg Camping Ekebergveien 65 ⓣ22 19 85 68, ⓦwww.ekebergcamping.no. Family-oriented campsite on a hill to the east of Oslo. Bus #34 or #46 from Oslo S. June–Aug only. ❸

Eating

Those carefully counting the kroner will find it easy to buy bread, fruit and snacks from stalls and shops across the city centre, while fast-food joints offering hamburgers and hot dogs (*pølser*) are legion. For a picnic, buy a bag of freshly cooked, shell-on prawns from one of the fishing boats at the Rådhusbrygge pier, or head to the principal open-air market on Youngstorget (Mon–Sat 7am–2pm), a brief stroll north of the Domkirke along Torggata.
Blitz Café Pilestredet 30C. This alternative cultural centre is a legalised squat in a listed building, and serves vegetarian lunches for a suggested donation of 30kr. Live music three times a month. Closed during summer.
Curry and Ketchup Kirkeveien 51. Fun, quirky little gem of an Indian restaurant, with low prices and huge portions.

Dolce Vita Prinsens gate 22. This Italian café makes and sells the best ice cream in Oslo, along with proper food at decent prices.
Ett Glass Karl Johans gate 33, entrance round the corner on Rosenkrantz gate. Popular, candlelit café/bar. Inexpensive menu focuses on light meals.
Kaffistova Rosenkrantz gate 8. Part of the *Bondeheimen* hotel, this spick-and-span self-service café serves tasty, traditional Norwegian dishes at very fair prices. There's usually a vegetarian option, too.
Krishna Cuisine Kirkeveien 59B. In the middle of busy Majorstukrysset, this is the city's best vegetarian option. Closed Sat & Sun.
Memphis Thorvalds Meyersgate 63. US-themed and good value for money. Menu mainstays are burgers and pasta. Outdoor seating in summer; bar stays open till 3am.
Mucho Mas Thorvalds Meyersgate 36 & Bogstadveien 8. Cute, relaxed bar/restaurant that does a roaring trade in good, reasonably priced Mexican food.
Punjab Tandoori Grønland 24. The best of Grønland's cheap curry restaurants, with main dishes from 65kr.
Saigon Lille Café Møllergate 32c, at end of Bernt Ankersgate. Authentic Vietnamese food at soothingly low prices.
Sult Thorvald Meyersgate 26. Serves innovative dishes using seasonal ingredients, at surprisingly low prices. The attached bar *Tørst* is one of Oslo's most popular spots.
Tullins Café Tullins gate 2. Close to the National Gallery, this fashionable café serves light meals, snacks and coffee in the daytime and turns into a bar at night. Reasonably priced.
United Bakeries Karl Johans gate 37. Traditional, freshly baked Norwegian buns, cakes and doorstep sandwiches at pretty good prices right in the centre of town.

Drinking

Oslo's hippest cafés and bars can be found in the former working-class area of Grünerløkka along Thorvald Meyersgate and Markveien in particular. Downtown Oslo also has a vibrant bar scene, at its most frenetic on summer weekends. The busiest mainstream bars are concentrated in the side streets near the Rådhus and along the Aker Brygge, while other popular places are clustered around Universitetsgata and on Rosenkrantz gate.

TREAT YOURSELF

Summit 21, on the twenty-first floor of the *Radisson SAS Scandinavia* Hotel at Holbergs gate 30, is a swish modern bar boasting glorious, panoramic views over Oslo – including from the men's toilets. Sip a vertiginous margarita (98kr) and admire the skyline.

Bars and pubs

Bar Boca Thorvald Meyers gate 30. Tiny 1950s-retro bar in Grünerløkka, with great cocktails. Get there early.
Dattera til Hagen Grønland 10. A relative of *Fr Hagen* (below), this is a café by day and a lively bar at night, sometimes with a DJ on its small upstairs dance-floor. Check out the beer garden round the back.
Fr Hagen Thorvald Meyersgate 38. Faded grandeur chic: battered upholstery, dark red walls. Open till 3am most nights.
Mir Toftesgate 69. Adorably oddball bar tucked away in a courtyard behind Thorvald Meyersgate, complete with old aeroplane seats and candlelight. Live music three or four nights a week.
Spasibar St Olavs gate 32. Much-praised, arty bar/club in the grounds of the art school. Regular live music, DJ nights and the coolest kids in Oslo.
Teddy's Bar Brugata 3. Genuine 1950s US retro, complete with a Wurlitzer jukebox, at this relaxed bar near Grønland.

Entertainment and nightlife

There are several middle-of-the-road clubs in the centre around Karl Johans gate, but for less mainstream pleasures head to Grønland, Grünerløkka, or the area around Youngs torg. Entry can set you back 50–100kr – though drinks prices are the same as anywhere else in Oslo. Nothing gets going much before 11pm; closing times are generally 3–4am. For entertainment listings check *Natt & Dag*, a monthly Norwegian-language broadsheet available free from cafés, bars and shops.

Clubs and music venues

Blå Brenneriveien 9c Ⓦwww.blx.no. Creative, cultural Grünerløkka nightspot, featuring everything from live jazz and DJ nights to public debates and poetry readings. In summer, there's a pleasant riverside terrace and the food is pretty good too. Open till 3.30am at weekends.
Café Mono Pløensgate 4. Popular bar/club just by Youngs torg. Décor and music are rock-themed, and you can often catch local and international bands here. Open till 3am.

Gloria Flames Grønland 18. An indie kid favourite, with a great roof terrace and frequent live music and DJ nights.
Rockerfeller Music Hall Torggata 16. This former bathhouse is now one of Oslo's major concert venues, hosting well-known and up-and-coming bands – mostly rock or alternative.

Shopping

Fretex Unika Markveien 51. Special branch of the national charity shop, with added cool – the clothes and furniture on sale here are handpicked, and there are some genuine secondhand treasures to be found.
Probat Thorvald Meyersgate 54. Specializes in quirky unisex T-shirts adorned with Norwegian puns. Staff will helpfully translate for you.
Trabant Markeveien 56. Pick up vintage and vintage-inspired fashions at this impeccably cool Grunerløkka boutique.
Tronsmo Kristian Augusts gate 19. Excellent independent bookshop, a cult among Oslo bookworms, with a basement full of comics and graphic novels.

Directory

Embassies and consulates Canada, Wergelandveien 7 ⓣ22 99 53 00; Ireland, Haakon VII's gate 1, 5th Floor ⓣ22 01 72 00; UK, Thomas Heftyes gate 8 ⓣ23 13 27 00; USA, Henrik Ibsens gate 48 ⓣ22 44 85 50.
Exchange The bureau de change in the central post office at Dronningens gate 15 offers decent rates.
Hospital Ullevål Universitetssykhus, Kirkeveien 166 ⓣ22 11 80 80.
Internet Internet access is available free at the city library, Deichmanske Bibliotek, Arne Garborgs Plass 4 (Mon–Fri 10am–6pm, Sat 11am–2pm).
Laundry A Snanvask, Thorvald Meyers gate 18 ⓣ22 37 57 70 (Mon–Fri 10am–8pm, Sat 10am–3pm).
Left Luggage Oslo S (daily 4.30am–1.10am); 20/25/30kr for 24hrs.
Pharmacy Jernbanetorgets Apotek, Jernbanetorget 4b, is a 24hr pharmacy near Oslo S, ⓣ23 35 81 00.
Post office Dronningens gate 15 (Mon–Fri 8am–5pm, Sat 9am–2pm).

Moving on

Train Åndalsnes (2–3 daily; 5hr 30min–6hr 30min); Bergen (4–5 daily; 6hr 30min); Kristiansand (5 daily; 4hr 30 min); Stavanger (3-5 daily; 7hr; 30min); Stockholm (3 daily; 4hr 30min); Trondheim (2–4 daily; 7–10hr); Voss (3–5 daily; 5hr 40min).
Bus Bergen (4–5 daily; 10hr).

Southern Norway

Regular trains run from Olso to the lively harbour towns of **Kristiansand** and **Stavanger** on the south coast. The landscape in this half of the country may not be as dramatic as in the north, but there is still plenty to attract visitors in large numbers, particularly during the summer months. Attractive forests provide ample opportunity for camping and walking, watersports and sailing in particular are popular on the many lakes and beaches, and both towns are fortunate to have a vibrant bar and restaurant scene. Buses run regularly to both Kristiansand and Stavanger, but like the train, the route is inland and you'll need your own transport to explore the smaller coastal villages.

KRISTIANSAND

The appealing town of **KRISTIANSAND** is diverting enough to merit a day or two's stay, with a handful of good museums and a well-preserved neighbourhood of eighteenth-century wooden houses. The neo-Gothic cathedral (Mon–Fri 10am–4pm, Sat 10am–2pm) is right in the middle of town, just beside Wergelands Park, a landscaped square designed by prominent nineteenth-century poet/soldier General Wergeland. The excellent Art Museum (Tue–Fri 11am–4pm, Sat and Sun noon–4pm, closed Mon; 30kr) on Skippergate showcases some interesting modern Norwegian artists – check out the contemporary sculpture gallery on the first floor. Back on the seafront, a walk along the promenade takes in the fantastic fish market (Jun–Aug Mon–Sat 7am–8pm, rest of year Mon–Fri 7am–4pm, Sat 7am–2.30pm) at the southernmost end, the circular fifteenth-century fortress with its row of never-used cannon, and an artificial city beach at the northern end of the walkway. Plunge back into town via Kronprinsensgate for a look at Posebyen, Kristiansand's picturesque old town. Less than 2km north of the town centre, the nature reserve of Baneheia includes some beautiful swimming and fishing spots, forest trails and a healthy wildlife population.

Information

Tourist office The tourist office is currently at Vestre Strandgate 32 but is scheduled to move to a location closer to Markensgate some time in 2008. Opening hours are mid-Jun to mid-Aug Mon-Fri 8.30am–6pm, Sat 10am–6pm, Sun noon–6pm; rest of year Mon-Fri 8.30am–3.30pm. ⓣ38 12 13 14; ⓦwww.sorlandet.com.

Accommodation

123 Hotel Ostre Strandgate 23 ⓣ38 70 15 66, ⓦwww.123-hotel.no. Comfortable, well-equipped hotel with self-service check-in. ❺
Centrum Motel Vestre Strandgate 49 ⓣ38 70 15 65, ⓦwww.motell.no. Drab but serviceable motel beside the train station. ❺

Moving on

Train Oslo (6 daily, 4hr 30 min); Stavanger (7 daily, 3hr).
Bus Bergen (4 daily, 5hr).

STAVANGER

STAVANGER is a breezily charming seaside city that has grown sleek and prosperous as the hub of Norway's oil industry. The presence of a thriving university gives the town a buzz it might otherwise lack, and there's a clutch of excellent bars that wouldn't be out of place in the capital.

What to see and do

The heart-shaped pond, **Breiavatnet**, in the compact town centre is a helpful reference point; the twelfth-century **Norman cathedral** (daily Jun–Aug 11am–7pm, Sept–May 11am–4pm; free) is just north of here and the pretty harbour is visible from the cathedral steps. Boats to **Pulpit Rock** (Preikestolen), the region's most famous attraction, leave regularly from here and connect with a bus service from Tau (timetable and tickets available from the tourist office). The bus deposits you by the *Preikestolen* youth hostel, and from here it's a two-hour hike to the clifftop for a truly breathtaking view. Stavanger's delightful **old town** is just northwest of the cathedral – stroll around the cobbled streets or drop into the entertaining **Norwegian Canning Museum** (Øvre Strandgate 88; daily 11am–4pm; 40kr; ⓣ51 84 27 00), showcasing traditional local industries such as herring canning. Further east along the harbour, the **Oil Museum** (daily Jun–Aug 10am–7pm, rest of year 10am–4/6pm; 80kr; ⓦwww.norskolje.museum.no) is a slick, well-designed space lovingly detailing the history of the oil industry in a series of fascinating interactive exhibits. To the southeast, back in the warren of streets behind the harbour, the **Valberg Tower** is the highest point in the city and has nice if unspectacular views, plus a small museum in the tower itself (Tues–Fri 10am–4/6pm, Sat & Sun 11am–3pm; 20kr). All over Stavanger, look out for the series of **Anthony Gormley sculptures** – austere human figures staring out to sea, placed at regular intervals throughout the city.

Arrival and information

Air The airport, 20km south of the city, is connected to the bus station by regular *flybussen* (Mon–Fri & Sun 5am–9pm, Sat 5am–4pm, every 15–20min; 45min; 75kr).
Train and bus The train and bus stations are next door to each other on Jernbaneveien, facing Breiavatnet.
Ferry International ferries to Britain and Denmark arrive at the town's northernmost quay, by Sandvigå. Cruise ships dock just south of here, on Strandkaien, and domestic ferries to Bergen and nearby towns leave from Jorenholmen on the eastern side of the harbour.

Tourist office The tourist office is opposite the cathedral at Domkirkeplassen 3 (Jun–Aug daily 7am–8pm, Sept–May Mon–Fri 9am–4pm, Sat 9am–2pm; ⓣ51 85 92 00; ⓦwww.regionstavanger.com).

Accommodation

Accommodation is limited and fills up quickly in the summer and during festivals, so it's best to book ahead.

Folken Bed and Breakfast Preikestolen ⓣ97 16 55 51, ⓦwww.folken.no/bedbreak. Ramshackle but likeable temporary dorm in a student union concert venue. Tattered band posters and a distinct smell of stale beer, but it's friendly and cheap and the staff are helpful. Dorms ❸

Preikestolhytta Preikestolen ⓣ97 16 55 51, ⓦwww.preikestolhytta.no. Large, pleasant hostel at the foot of the hiking trail to Pulpit Rock. Gorgeous views and fishing and boating equipment available for hire. The hostel's café/restaurant serves meals for 50–300kr, or cook your own food. Dorms ❸, rooms ❼

Stavanger Bed and Breakfast Vikedalsgate 1A ⓣ51 56 25 00, ⓦwww.stavangerbedandbreakfast.no. No-nonsense B&B close to the town centre. Prices include a cooked breakfast and an evening snack. ❽

Stavanger Camping Mosvangen ⓣ51 53 29 71, ⓦwww.mosvangencamping.no. Campsite by the lake, right next to Stavanger *Youth Hostel* and open slightly longer (May–Oct). Camping ❷, cabins 600kr for up to four people.

Stavanger Youth Hostel Mosvangen Henrik Ibsengate 19 ⓣ51 54 36 36, ⓦwww.vandrerhjem.no. Basic but comfortable summer hostel (mid-Jun to late Aug only) by a lake about 25 minutes' walk from the centre. Get bus #4 and ask for directions. Free internet, breakfast 50kr. Dorms ❸

Eating and drinking

Stavanger has a disproportionate number of good, if expensive, **restaurants**, many of which line the pedestrianised harbour area north of the cathedral. Evening drinking options are plentiful, with some great **bars** on and around Nedre Strandgate and Øvre Holmegate, busy most nights of the week during university termtime.

Akvariet Bar/Folken Ny Olavskleiv 16. The student union café/bar and music venue, open to all. Catch international and local bands or take advantage of the comparatively cheap drinks.

Bøker & Børst Øvre Holmegaten 32. Book-lined, relaxed café/bar on a street of candy-coloured houses. Among other events, there's a Tom Waits cover band here every other Thursday. Gay-friendly.

Cementen Nedre Strandgate 23–25. Friendly, likeable bar overlooking the harbour. Shelves crammed with books and board games make this the best place in town to spend an idle rainy afternoon. DJs at weekends. Open till 3.30am.

Charlottenlund Kongsgaten 45. More affordable than it looks, with light lunches and snacks from 69kr in the daytime. Dinner is pricey, but the lakeside terrace is a nice place to have a beer and watch the ducks.

Checkpoint Charlie Larshertevigsgate 5. Eastern-bloc chic and loud indie music have made this a student favourite. DJs and live music several nights a week.

Food Story Klubbgaten 3. Deli and café with great focaccia sandwiches priced by weight. Main dishes start at 89kr, or buy picnic food and fresh bread to take away.

Gnu Nedre Strand gate 3. Friendly backstreet bar with a jukebox, a giant chandelier, soccer memorabilia, a disused stairlift and band photos on the walls.

Kontoret Skagen 16. One of Stavanger's oldest drinking haunts, this eighteenth-century pub has a good selection of beers.

Sting Valberget 3. This charming café/bar, right opposite the Valberg Tower, serves wine by weight as well as decently priced food. Live music, poetry readings, and jazz in the tiny downstairs club.

Moving on

Train Oslo (5 daily, 8 hr); Kristiansand (7 daily, 3hr).

FROM STAVANGER TO THE BEACH

The 70km of coastline curving south from Stavanger is famous for its sandy beaches, the best in Norway, where surfers congregate over the summer. Buses leave regularly from the town centre and timetables are available at the tourist office. The closest is **Solastranda**, but it's worth making the slightly longer journey to **Viste**, with its sculptural-looking rock formations, or to the surf at **Orre** or **Vaule**. Beware: even in high summer, the water is freezing.

Bus Bergen (8–11 daily, 5 hr 40min); Kristiansand (2–4 daily, 3hr 30min).
Car ferry Bergen (2-6 weekly, 7hr).
Hurtigbåt express boat Bergen (2-4 daily, 4hr).

Bergen and the fjords

The **fjords** are the most familiar and alluring image of Norway – huge clefts in the landscape which occur along the west coast right up to the Russian border, though the most beguiling portion lies between Bergen and Ålesund. **Bergen** is a handy springboard for the fjords, notably the **Flåm valley** and its inspiring mountain railway, which trundles down to the Aurlandsfjord, a tiny arm of the mighty **Sognefjord**, Norway's longest and deepest. North of the Sognefjord, there is the smaller and less stimulating **Nordfjord**, though there's superb compensation in the **Jostedalsbreen** glacier, which nudges the fjord from the east. The tiny S-shaped **Geirangerfjord**, further north again, is magnificent too – narrow, sheer and rugged – while the northernmost **Romsdalsfjord** and its many branches and inlets reach pinnacles of isolation in the **Trollstigen** mountain highway.

BERGEN

BERGEN is the second biggest city in Norway but somehow doesn't feel like it, perhaps because of its air of old-world, well-fed calm. It's one of the rainiest places in rainy Norway, but benefits from a spectacular setting among seven hills and is altogether one of the country's most enjoyable cities. There's plenty to see, from fine old buildings to a series of good museums, and Bergen is also within easy reach of some of Norway's most spectacular scenic attractions, both around the city and further north.

What to see and do

Founded in 1070, the city was the largest and most important town in medieval Norway, a regular residence of the country's kings and queens, and later a Hanseatic port and religious centre, though precious little of that era survives today. Nowadays, the city centre divides into two main parts: the wharf area, **Bryggen**, adjacent to the Bergenhus fortress, once the working centre of the Hanseatic merchants and now the oldest part of Bergen; and the **modern centre**, which stretches inland from the head of the harbour and takes in the best of Bergen's museums, cafés and bars.

Torget and Bryggen

The obvious place to start a visit is **Torget**, an appealing harbourside plaza that's home to a colourful fresh produce and fish market. From here, it's a short stroll round to **Bryggen**, where a string of distinctive wooden buildings line up along the waterfront. These once housed the city's merchants and now hold shops, restaurants and bars. Although none of these structures was actually built by the Hanseatic Germans – most of the originals were destroyed by fire in 1702 – they carefully follow the original building line. Among them, the **Hanseatic Museum** (May & late

FJORD TRANSPORT

By **rail**, you can only reach Bergen and Flåm in the south and Åndalsnes in the north. For everything in between – including most of the Sognefjord, Nordfjord and the Jostedalsbreen glacier – **buses** and **ferries** together comprise a complicated but fully integrated system. It's a good idea to pick up full bus and ferry timetables from any local tourist office whenever you can.

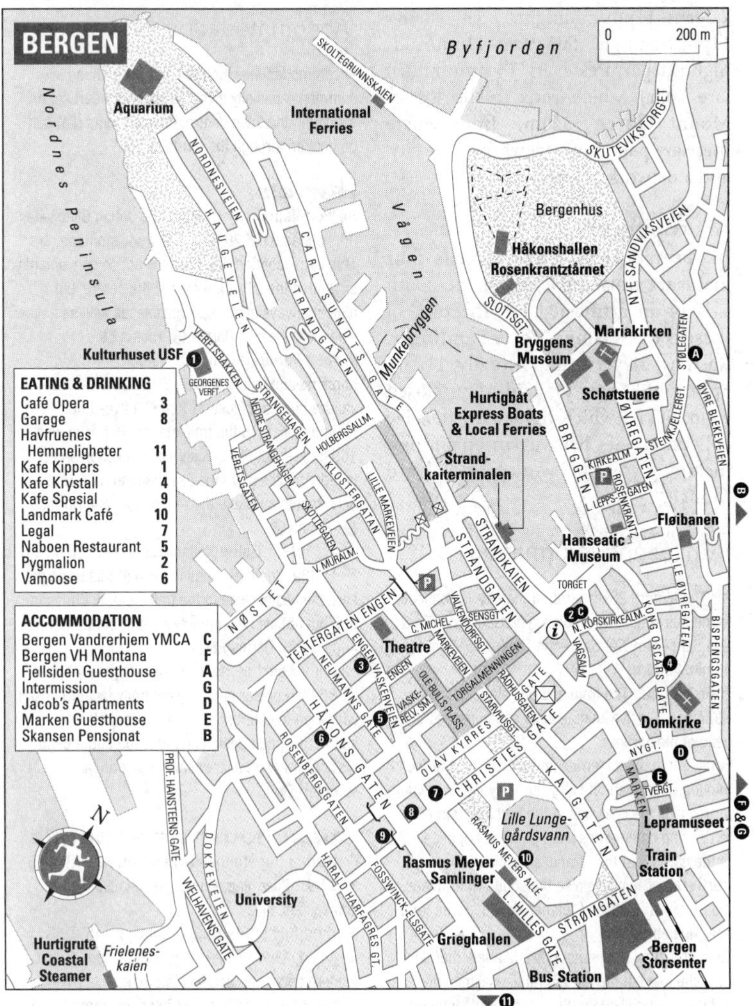

Sept daily 11am–2pm, June–Aug daily 9am–5pm, early Sept daily 10am–3pm, Oct–April Tues–Sat 11am–2pm, Sun noon–5pm; 45kr) is the most diverting, an early eighteenth-century merchant's dwelling kitted out in late-Hansa style.

Bryggens Museum

Also worth visiting is the **Bryggens Museum** (May–Aug daily 10am–5pm, Sept–April Mon–Fri 11am–3pm, Sat noon–3pm, Sun noon–4pm; 40kr), just along the harbourfront, where a series of imaginative exhibitions attempts a complete reassembly of local medieval life – from domestic implements, handicrafts and maritime objects through to trading items.

Mount Fløyen

Nearby you'll find the **Fløibanen**, a dinky funicular railway (Mon–Fri

7.30am–11pm/midnight, Sat 8am–11pm/midnight, Sun 9am–11pm/midnight; departures every 15 min; return fare 70kr), which runs to the top of **Mount Fløyen** (320m), from where there are panoramic views over the city, and a network of forest walks.

Art museums

In the modern centre, Bergen's four main **art museums** are on the south side of an artificial lake. The pick of these is the **Rasmus Meyer Samlinger**, Rasmus Meyers Allé 7 (daily 11am–5pm; mid-Sept to mid-May closed Mon; 50kr), which holds an extensive collection of Norwegian paintings, including several works by Edvard Munch.

Arrival and information

Air The airport, 20km south of the city, is connected to the bus station by regular *flybussen* (Mon–Fri & Sun 5am–9pm, Sat 5am–4pm, every 15–20min; 45min; 75kr).

Train and bus The train and bus stations face Strømgaten, a five-minute walk southeast of the head of the harbour.

Ferry International ferries and cruise ships arrive at Skoltegrunnskaien, the quay just beyond Bergenhus fortress, on the east side of the harbour; domestic ferries and catamarans line up on the opposite side of the harbour at the Strandkaiterminalen.

Hurtigrute The city is also the southern terminus of the Hurtigrute Coastal Steamer, which leaves from near Nøstebryggen.

Tourist office The tourist office is a few metres from the head of the harbour at Vågsallmenning 1 (May–Sept daily 9am–8pm, Oct–April Mon–Sat 9am–4pm; ⓣ55 55 20 00; ⓦwww.visitbergen.com). It issues maps and books private rooms.

Discount passes The tourist office sells the Bergen Card (170kr one day/250kr for two days), which allows travel on all the city's buses and free entrance to, or discounts on, most of the city's sights, including sightseeing trips.

Hiking information The DNT-affiliated Bergen Turlag, Tverrgaten 4–6 (Mon–Wed & Fri 10am–4pm, Thurs 10am–6pm, Sat 10am–2pm; ⓣ55 33 58 10), can advise on hiking trails in the region and sells hiking maps.

Accommodation

Accommodation is plentiful, but book ahead in summer, especially if you've got your heart set on staying in the town centre. Private rooms (❺) can be booked through the tourist office.

Hostels

Bergen Vandrerhjem Montana Johan Blyttsveien 30, Landås ⓣ55 20 80 70, ⓦwww.montana.no. This large, comfortable hostel is not so conveniently located in the hills 4km east of the centre, but almost always has beds available, as well as a nice view over the city. Dorms ❸, rooms ❼

Bergen Vandrerhjem YMCA Nedre Korskirkealmenning 4 ⓣ55 60 60 55, ⓦwww.vandrerhjem.no. Close to Torget, a five- to ten-minute walk from the train station. HI hostel with 160 beds – but fills quickly. Guest kitchen and laundry facilities. Dorms open May to mid-Sept only; rooms available the rest of the year. Dorms ❷, rooms ❺

Intermission Kalfarveien 8 ⓣ55 30 04 00. Cheapest beds in town at this basic but sociable hostel close to the train station. Christian-run, but not overwhelmingly so. Mid-June–mid-August only. Dorms ❷

Jacob's Apartments Kong Oscars gate 44 ⓣ98 23 86 00. Popular and very centrally located hostel with a great café/bar at the front that also serves as the reception desk. Laidback, fun and a good place to meet other travellers. Book ahead in summer. ❸

Guest houses and hotels

Fjellsiden Guesthouse Øvre Blekeveien 16 ⓣ55 32 17 91. Charming, simple guesthouse with a homely feel. ❹

Marken Gjestehus Kong Oscars gate 45 ⓣ55 31 44 04, ⓦwww.marken-gjestehus.com. Bright, modern décor and helpful staff make this 21-room hostel one of Bergen's best accommodation options. Dorms ❸, rooms ❹

Skansen Pensjonat Vestrelidsallmenningen 29 ⓣ55 31 90 80, ⓦwww.skansen-pensjonat.no. Simple but cosy little place in a nineteenth-century stone house just above the Fløibanen terminus, near Torget. Doubles ❼, ❾ for a four-person apartment.

Eating and drinking

Bergen has a good supply of first-rate **restaurants** concentrated in the Bryggen, with local seafood the speciality. Less expensive – and more fashionable – are the city's **café/restaurants**, which often double up as lively **bars**. Several of the best are

BERGEN'S FESTIVALS

In May, the annual **Bergen International Festival** (wwww.festspillene.no) consists of twelve days of music, ballet, folklore and drama, supplemented by **Nattjazz** (Ⓦwww.nattjazz.no), a prestigious international jazz festival. Music festival **Lost Weekend** happens around the first weekend in August, attracting indie bands you've heard of as well as home-grown Norwegian bands.

located to the southwest of Ole Bulls plass, the main pedestrianized square.

Café Opera Engen 24. White wooden building near Ole Bulls plass, bustling with a fashionable crew drinking beer and good coffee. Tasty, filling dishes (from 100kr) including some good veggie options. Crowded club-like venue in the evening.

Garage Christies gate 14. Near-darkness and sticky floors in the club downstairs, friendly bar upstairs. Look out for the unusual door handles – they're trophies handed out in the Norwegian equivalent of the Grammies, donated by musicians.

Havfruenes Hemmeligheter Nygårdsgate 53. Reasonably priced, unfussy fish restaurant – snack on fishcakes or try the sparklingly fresh fish, prepared in traditional Norwegian style.

Kafe Kippers Kulturhuset USF, Georgernes verft. Café/bar in a former herring factory converted into an arts centre, with inexpensive food and a prime seashore location; the terrace is the place to be on sunny summer days.

Kafe Spesial Christies gate 13. Cheap food and quirky décor have made this bar/restaurant popular with students. Menu mainstays are pizza or pasta, from 59kr.

Landmark Café Rasmus Meyers alle 5. Local artists' hang-out named after a Norwegian architect, complete with minimalist décor. Closed on Mondays.

Legal Christies gate 11. Intimate bar done up in fifties and sixties-ish retro. Reasonably priced snacks and it's open late too.

Naboen Restaurant Neumannsgate 20. Excellent meals at manageable prices at this easy-going restaurant, which features Swedish specialities. Mains from 182kr.

TREAT YOURSELF

Prices are high – 595kr a head for a four-course set meal – but dinner at *Kafe Krystall*, an intimate, rather romantic restaurant at Kong Oscars Gate, is widely considered to be the best in Bergen. Food is Norwegian with a Mediterranean twist.

Pygmalion Nedre Korskirkealmening 5. Cosy organic café with art on the walls and a good choice of vegetarian dishes. Main dishes start at around 80kr.

Vamoose Håkons Gatan 27. Alternative bar frequented by students and the like. There's something going on most nights, from Monday jam sessions to a monthly world music night. Curl up in one of the backroom sofas near the tiny stage, or find some elbow room in the retro-chic bar area.

Directory

Exchange The main post office (see below) offers competitive exchange rates for foreign currency and travellers' cheques.

Hospital Haukeland Universitetssykehus, Jonas Liesvei 65.

Internet Free internet at the public library. Bergen Offentilige Bibliotek, Strømgaten 6. Mon 11am–6pm, Tues–Fri 10am–3pm, Sat 10am–3pm, closed Sun.

Laundry Jarlens Vaskoteque, Lille Øvregate 17, near the funicular (Mon, Tues & Fri 10am–6pm, Wed & Thurs 10am–8pm; Sat 10am–3pm).

Left luggage The tourist office has a left-luggage service, 20kr per item.

Pharmacy Apoteket Nordstjernen, at the bus station (Mon–Sat 8am–11pm, Sun 10am–11pm).

Post office Inside Xhibition shopping centre, on the second floor (Mon–Fri 8am–6pm, Sat 9am–3pm).

Moving on

Bus Ålesund (1–2 daily; 10hr); Oslo (express 3 weekly, 9hr; otherwise 1–4 daily, 11hr); Stavanger (3–6 daily, 5hr); Trondheim (2 daily; 14hr); Voss (4 daily; 1hr 45min).

Ferry Balestrand (1–2 daily; 4hr); Flåm (May–Sept only; 1–2 daily; 5hr 30min).

FLÅM VALLEY

If you're short of time, but want to sample a slice of fjord scenery, you can get a taste by taking the train from Bergen, through Voss, to **Myrdal**, where specially built trains squeak down a remarkable branch line that plummets 866m into the **Flåm valley** and the **Aurlandsfjord**. The track took four years to lay and is one of the steepest anywhere in the world, making a wondrously dramatic journey. Pick up transport timetables from the tourist office or at the train station before you set out.

Flåm

The village of **FLÅM**, the train's destination, lies alongside meadows and orchards on the Aurlandsfjord, a matchstick-thin branch of the Sognefjord. Hikers can get off the train at **Berekvam** station, the halfway point, and stroll down from there, or else walk from Flåm to Berekvam and then hop on the train. Flåm is a tiny village that has been touristisfied to within an inch of its life, but out of season – or on summer evenings, when the day-trippers have gone – it can be a pleasantly restful place.

Information

The very busy **tourist office** is at the ferry dock (daily May & Sept 8.30am–4.30pm, June, July & Aug 8.30am–8pm; ⓣ57 63 33 13 or 57 63 21 06), by the train station, and has information on local hikes.

Accommodation and eating

There's not much to Flåm, but if you do decide to stay overnight and try out some of the excellent hiking trails, there's decently priced accommodation at the bucolic *Gjørven Hytter* (ⓣ57 63 21 67; 500–800kr for a four- to eight-person cabin), which provides simple lodgings in cabins nestled in an orchard, 3km from the village, and the excellent *Flåm Camping* (ⓣ57 63 21 21, ⓦwww.flaamcamping.no; May–Sept only), a combined **campsite** and **hostel** (camping ❷, dorms ❷, rooms ❻), 200m from the train station. Everything in Flåm is overpriced, because of the influx of tourists, but the *Torget Café* on the market square is a good option for food and drink.

THE SOGNEFJORD

With the exception of Flåm, the southern shore of the **Sognefjord** remains sparsely populated and relatively inaccessible, whereas the north shore boasts a couple of very appealing resorts.

Balestrand

Top-of-the-list **BALESTRAND** is the prettiest base, a tourist destination since the mid-nineteenth century when it was discovered by European travellers in search of cool, clear air and mountain scenery. Buses (and express boats from Bergen and Flåm) arrive at Balestrand's minuscule harbourfront, near which you'll find the **tourist office** (phone for opening hours ⓣ57 69 12 55). As for somewhere to stay, the comfortable and very appealing *Kringsjå Hotel*, 100m from the tourist office, incorporates the local HI **hostel** (ⓣ57 69 13 03; ⓦwww.vandrerhjem.no; dorms ❸, doubles ❸; late June to mid-Aug only). The beauty of the fjord aside, there are few sights as such to see in Balestrand itself, but several lovely places are within easy striking distance, particularly the delightful village of Fjærland (also known as Mundal), on the Fjærlandsfjord.

Fjærland

The village of **FJÆRLAND** can be reached direct by ferry from Balestrand from May to early September (two daily; 1hr 30min; passengers 175kr; car & driver 370kr), and by bus throughout the rest of the year (change at Sogndal, 2 daily; 1hr). Formerly one of the most isolated spots on the Sognefjord, Fjærland is now connected to the road system, but retains its old-fashioned atmosphere and appearance, with a string of handsome clapboard buildings in a wildly beautiful location. Fjærland is Norway's self-styled book town, packed with little shops selling musty paperbacks, and there are various **literature events** held here in the summer (ⓦwww.booktown.net). Fjærland's other attraction is its proximity to the southern edge of the **Jostedalsbreen glacier**, see opposite.

Information

Tourist office in the centre of the village, about ten minutes' walk from the ferry dock (May to Sept daily 10am–6pm; ⓣ57 69 32 33).

Accommodation

The tourist office can also book private rooms, ❺
Fjaerland Fjordstue Hotell ⓣ57 69 32 00, ⓦwww.fjaerland.no. A well-tended family hotel with traditional, slightly fusty décor. ❾
Bøyum Camping ⓣ57 69 32 52 On the edge of the village, beside the glacier museum. They have four-berth huts (from 550kr per night) as well as dorms ❷, rooms ❾ and space for camping ❷

Jostedalsbreen glacier

The **Jostedalsbreen glacier** is a vast ice plateau that dominates the whole of the inner Nordfjord region. The glacier's 24 arms – or nodules – melt down into the nearby valleys, giving the local rivers and glacial lakes their distinctive blue-green colouring. The glacier is protected within the **Jostedalsbreen Nasjonalpark**, whose guides take organized **glacier walks** (Jun–Sept; from around 300kr) on its various arms, ranging from two-hour excursions to all-day, fully-equipped hikes. One of the many places that takes bookings is the Fjærland tourist office (see opposite). You can also reach an arm of the glacier under your own steam by strolling north from Fjærland on Highway 5; about 10km north of the village, just before the tunnel, a signed side road leads the 200m to the Bøyabreen glacier arm, though you're not allowed to walk on it – viewing only.

The Geirangerfjord

On the north side of the Jostedalsbreen glacier is the **Nordfjord**, but this fjord system doesn't have the scenic lustre of its more famous neighbours and you're much better off pressing on to the S-shaped **Geirangerfjord**, one of the region's smallest and most breathtaking fjords. A convoluted branch of the Storfjord, it cuts deep inland, marked by impressive waterfalls and with a village at either end of its snake-like profile. You can reach the Geirangerfjord in dramatic style by bus from the north or south, but you'd do best to approach from the north if you can. From this direction, the journey begins in Åndalsnes (see below), from where Highway 63 wriggles over the mountains via the wonderful **Trollstigen Highway**, which climbs through some of the country's highest peaks before sweeping down to the tiny Norddalsfjord. From here, it's a quick ferry ride and dramatic journey along the Ørnevegen, the Eagle's Highway, for a first view of the Geirangerfjord and the village that bears its name glinting in the distance. There is little as stunning anywhere in western Norway, and from mid-June to August it can all be seen on a twice-daily bus following this so-called "Golden Route".

ÅNDALSNES

Travelling north from Oslo by train, the line forks at Dombås – the Dovre line continuing northwards over the fells to Trondheim (see p.881), the Rauma line beginning a thrilling, roller-coaster rattle west down through the mountains to the **Isfjord** at Åndalsnes (1hr 30min). Apart from the Aurlandsfjord, an arm of the Sognefjord reached from Bergen, the Isfjord is the only Norwegian fjord accessible by **train**, which explains the number of backpackers wandering its principal town of **ÅNDALSNES**, many people's first – sometimes only – contact with fjord country. Despite a wonderful setting between lofty peaks and looking-glass water, the town is unexciting, but it does make a convenient base for further explorations.

Information

Tourist office at the train station (mid–June to mid–Aug Mon–Fri 9am–6pm, Sat & Sun 11am–6pm; mid–Aug to mid–June, Mon–Fri 8am–3.30pm; ⓣ71 22 16 22; ⓦwww.visitandalsnes.com), has a free and comprehensive guide to local hikes as well as bus, boat and train timetables.

Accommodation

Hostel Åndalsnes has an outstanding HI hostel (ⓣ71 22 13 82, ⓦwww.aandalsnesvandrerhjem.no; dorms ❸, rooms ❽; mid–May to Aug, plus open for advanced bookings the rest of the year), which occupies a group of charming wooden buildings in a rural setting 1.5km away from the town centre, towards Ålesund.
Camping Another very good option is the riverside *Åndalsnes Camping og Motell* (ⓣ71 22 16 29, ⓦwww.andalsnescamp.no) with space for camping ❷, rooms ❹ and cabins (four beds, 450–550kr per night), rowboats and bikes for rent, a 25-minute walk from the train station – take the first left after the river on the road out to the hostel.

Moving on

Train Dombås (2–3 daily; 1hr 30min); Oslo (2–3 daily; 5hr 30min–6hr 30min).
Bus Geiranger (mid–June to late Aug, 2 daily; 3–4hr); Ålesund (3–4 daily; 2hr 20min).

ÅLESUND

At the end of the E136, some 120km west of Åndalsnes, the fishing and ferry port of **ÅLESUND** is immediately – and obviously – different from any other Norwegian town. In 1904, a disastrous fire left ten thousand people homeless and the town centre destroyed. A hectic reconstruction programme saw almost the entire area speedily rebuilt in a style that borrowed heavily from the German Jugendstil (Art Nouveau) movement. Kaiser Wilhelm II, who used to holiday hereabouts, gave assistance, and the architects ended up creating a strange but fetching hybrid of up-to-date foreign influences and folksy local elements, with dragons, faces, flowers and even a decorative pharaoh or two. The finest buildings are concentrated on the main street, **Kongensgate**, and around the slender, central harbour, the **Brosundet**.

Arrival and information

Bus The town's bus station is by the waterfront, a few metres south of the Brosundet.
Tourist office (June–Aug Mon–Fri 8.30am–7pm, Sat 9am–5pm, Sun 11am–5pm; Sept–May Mon–Fri 8am–3pm; ⓣ70 15 76 00, ⓦwww.visitalesund.com).

Accommodation

Brosundent Gjestehus Apotekergata 8 ⓣ70 12 10 00, ⓦwww.brosundet.no. A beautifully converted old wharfside warehouse that reopens in March 2008 after extensive refurbishment. ❾
Thon Hotel Ålesund Kongens gate 27 ⓣ70 12 29 38. Chain hotel with pleasant if anodyne rooms with TV and en-suite bathrooms. ❾
Ålesund Youth Hostel Parkgata 14 ⓣ70 11 58 30, ⓦwww.vandrerhjem.no. Official HI hostel in a creaky but clean old building. Dorms ❸, rooms ❽

Eating

ille Løvenvold Løvenvold gate 2. Striking, red-walled café/bar with retro furniture and cheap sandwiches to soak up the beer. Closed Sundays.
Lyspunktet Kipervik gate 1. Friendly, modern café with big slouchy sofas and unexciting burgers, pasta and sandwiches at low prices.
Metz Notenesgate 1. Busy pub/restaurant overlooking the Brosundet. The menu is formulaic but there's a popular outside terrace for when the weather is fine.
Sjøbua Fiskerestaurant Brunholmgata 1. Expensive but first-rate seafood restaurant, where you can meet your dinner in the lobster tank.

Moving on

Bus Bergen (daily; 10hr); Hellesylt (1–3 daily; 3hr); Stryn (1–3 daily; 4hr); Trondheim (1–3 daily; 8hr).

Northern Norway

The long, thin counties of **Trøndelag** and **Nordland** mark the transition from rural southern to blustery northern Norway. The main town of Trøndelag, appealing **Trondheim**, is easily accessible from Oslo by train, but north of here travelling becomes more of a slog as the distances between places grow ever greater. In **Nordland** things get wilder still, though save the scenery there's little of interest until you reach the steel town of **Mo-i-Rana**. Just north of here lies the **Arctic Circle**, beyond which the land becomes ever more spectacular, not least on the exquisite, mountainous **Lofoten Islands**, whose idyllic fishing villages (and inexpensive accommodation) richly merit a stop. Back on the mainland, **Narvik** is a modern port handling vast quantities of iron ore amid some startling rocky surroundings. Further north still, the provinces of **Tromsø** and **Finnmark** are subtle in their appeal, and the travelling can be hard, with **Tromsø**, a lively urban centre and university town, making the obvious stopping point. As for **Finnmark**, most visitors head straight for **Nordkapp**, from where the Midnight Sun is visible between early May and the end of July.

TRONDHEIM

TRONDHEIM, a loveable and atmospheric city with much of its eighteenth-century centre still intact, has been an important Norwegian power base for centuries, its success guaranteed by the excellence of its harbour and its position at the head of a wide and fertile valley. The early Norse parliament, or **Ting**, met here, and the city was once a major pilgrimage centre. The city centre sits on a small triangle of land, a pocket-sized area where the main sights – bar the marvellous cathedral – have an amiable, low-key quality. Trondheim also possesses a clutch of good restaurants and a string of busy bars.

What to see and do

Domkirke

The colossal **Nidaros Domkirke** – Scandinavia's largest medieval building, gloriously restored following the ravages of the Reformation and several fires – remains the focal point of the city centre (May to mid-Sept Mon–Fri 9am–3/6pm, Sat 9am–2pm, Sun 1–4pm; mid-Sept to April Mon–Fri noon–2.30pm, Sat 11.30am–2pm, Sun 1–3pm; 50kr). Taking Trondheim's former name (Nidaros means "mouth of the River Nid"), the cathedral is dedicated to King Olav, Norway's first Christian ruler, who was killed at the nearby battle of Stiklestad in 1030, and ultimately buried here. Thereafter, it became the traditional burial place of Norwegian royalty and, since 1814, it has also been the place where Norwegian monarchs are crowned. Highlights of the interior are the Gothic choir and the gargoyles on the pointed arches, as well as the striking choir screen and font, both the work of the Norwegian sculptor Gustav Vigeland (1869–1943).

Army and Resistance museum

Behind the Domkirke lies the heavily restored Archbishop's palace, now housing the **Army and Resistance Museum** (same hours as cathedral; free); its most interesting section recalls the German occupation during World War II, dealing honestly with the sensitive issue of collaboration.

Torvet and the Stiftsgården

Near at hand is **Torvet**, the main city square, a spacious open area anchored by a statue of Olav Tryggvason, perched on a stone pillar like some medieval Nelson. The broad and pleasant avenues of Trondheim's centre radiate out from here; they date from the late seventeenth century, when they doubled as fire breaks. They were originally flanked by long rows of wooden buildings, now mostly replaced by uninspiring modern structures, but one conspicuous survivor is the **Stiftsgården** (guided tours hourly, on the hour till 1hr before closing: early June to late Aug, Mon–Sat 10am–3/5pm, Sun noon–5pm; 60kr), the yellow creation just north of Torvet on Munkegata. Built in 1774–78 as the home of a provincial governor, it's now an official royal residence.

Arrival and information

Train and bus The combined bus and train terminal (the Sentralstasjon) is just over the bridge from the town centre, which occupies a small island at the mouth of the River Nid.
Hurtigrute Trondheim is the first major northbound stop of the Bergen-Kirkenes Hurtigrute coastal boat, which docks about 600m behind and to the north of Sentralstasjon.
Tourist office Bang in the middle of town on the main square (mid-May to late Aug, Mon–Fri 8.30am–6/8pm, Sat & Sun 10am–4/6pm; Sept to early May, Mon–Fri 9am–4pm, Sat & Sun 10am–2pm; ⓣ73 80 76 60, ⓦwww.trondheim.no).

Accommodation

The tourist office runs a room reservation service and has a small supply of private rooms, around ❹
Trondheim Youth Hostel Weidermannsvei 41 ⓣ73 87 44 50, ⓦwww.trondheim-vandrerhjem.no. Inconveniently located official hostel, a steep twenty-minute hike east from the centre over the Bakkebru bridge. Dorms ❹, rooms ❼
Trondheim Interrail Centre Elgersetegate 1 ⓣ73 89 95 38, ⓦwww.tirc.no. Fantastic, thrown-together summer hostel in the Trondheim University student union, established and run by local students – a cavernous network of bars, theatres and music venues. Free internet and a great café/bar on the premises. Dorms ❷

Eating and drinking

Bari Munkegata 25. Slick, fashionable bar/restaurant with a good-value lunch menu (light meals from 98kr).
Brukbar Munkegata 26. Lively, eclectically decorated bar frequented by everyone from creative types to local politicians, with a busy schedule of DJ nights.
Café Roman Olav Tryggvasons gate 5. Cheap, semi-fast food in slightly garish but comfy surroundings. Prices for kebabs with rice and salad start at 89kr.
Choco Olav Tryggvasons gate 29 (entry from Nordre gate). Relaxed café with a sizeable local following. Good sandwiches and salads, at average prices.
Den Gode Nabo Øvre Bakklandet 66. Huge selection of international beers and a glorious floating beer garden make this one of Trondheim's best-loved pubs.
Dromedar Nedre Bakklandet 3 & Olav Tryggvasons gate 14. Great coffee, cakes and sandwiches during the week; cheap drinks and tapas on weekend nights.
Persilleriet Erling Skakkes gate 39. Good-value vegetarian lunches in somewhat cramped surroundings.
Pia's Café Elgeseter gate 4. Small but atmospheric bar that showcases local bands several nights a week.

Moving on

Train Bodø (2 daily; 10hr); Dombås (1–4 daily; 2hr 30min); Fauske (2 daily; 9hr 20min); Mo-i-Rana (2–3 daily; 7hr); Oslo (2–4 daily; 7–10hr).
Bus Ålesund (1–3 daily; 8hr); Bergen (2 daily; 14hr); Stryn (2 daily; 7hr 20min).

CROSSING THE ARCTIC CIRCLE

North of Trondheim, it's a long, 730km haul up the coast to the next major place of interest, **Bodø**, which is the main ferry port for the **Lofoten Islands**. The train trip is a rattling good journey with the scenery becoming wilder and bleaker the further north you go. From Trondheim, it takes nine hours to reach Fauske, where the railway reaches its northern limit and turns west for the final 65km dash across to Bodø.

Arctic Circle

On the way you cross the **Arctic Circle**, which, considering the amount of effort it takes to get here, is something of an anticlimax. The bare, bleak landscape – uninhabited for the most part – is undeniably impressive, though rather disfigured by the gleaming **Polarsirkelsenteret** (Arctic Circle Centre; daily: May to early June & Aug 9am–8pm; late June & July 8am–10pm; early Sept 10am–6pm; ⓣ75 12 96 96, ⓦwww.polarsirkelsenteret.no), a giant Arctic-kitsch lampshade of a building plonked by the E6 highway and stuffed with every sort of tourist bauble imaginable, from "Polarsirkelen" certificates to specially stamped postcards.

Mo-i-Rana

If you don't fancy making the long journey between Trondheim and Bodø in one hop, you could stop at **MO-I-RANA**, or simply "Mo", just south of the Arctic Circle – although there's little to specifically draw you here. Formerly a grimy steel town, Mo has recently cleaned itself up and its leafy centre holds a pretty eighteenth-century church with a dinky onion dome. If you need **to stay**, head down Ole Tobias Olsens gate, about 300m from the bus and train stations, to the cheerful *Fammy Hotell*, at no. 4 (ⓣ75 15 19 99; ⓦwww.fammy.no; ❼), opposite the **tourist office** (mid-June to mid-Aug Mon–Fri 9am–8pm, Sat 9am–4pm & Sun 1–7pm; mid-Aug to mid-June Mon–Fri 9am–4pm; ⓣ75 13 92 00, ⓦwww.arctic-circle.no). For the adventurous, there are two great options for **cave-walking** here – one fairly straightforward tour to Grønligrotta (mid-June to mid-Aug, daily 10am–7pm; 90kr), and a more advanced trip into Setergrotta (mid-June to early July, daily tour at 3pm, July to mid-Aug 11.30am and 3pm; 235kr): the tourist office has details of both.

Bodø

BODØ is literally the end of the line: this is where all trains and many long-distance buses terminate. It's also a stop on the **Hurtigrute** coastal boat route and the main port of departure for the Lofoten Islands (see below), with car ferries to Moskenes, Værøy and Røst and Hurtigbåt catamarans to Svolvær. The **bus station** (*Sentrumsterminalen*) at Sjøgata 3 is also home to the **tourist office** (mid-May to Aug Mon–Fri 9am–8pm, Sat 10am–8pm, Sun noon–8pm; Sept to mid-May Mon–Wed & Fri 9am–4pm, Thurs 9am–6pm, Sat 10am–3pm; ⓣ75 54 80 00, ⓦwww.visitbodo.com), which has a small supply of **private rooms** (around ❹). Other budget accommodation options are in short supply – *Bodøsjøen Camping* (ⓣ75 56 36 80; ❷) is about 3km south-east of the town centre, and *Kristiansen Guesthouse* (ⓣ75 52 16 99, ❻), a ten-minute walk from the train station, is fairly basic but as cheap as it gets in the centre of town. A good option for **food** is the traditional and inexpensive *Løvolds Kafé* (Mon–Fri 9am–6pm, Sat 9am–3pm), down by the quay at Tollbugata 9: its Norwegian menu features local ingredients, with a daily special from 85kr. You'll find a younger crowd at *Kafé Kafka*, Sandgata 5b, where the menu includes pasta, burgers and salads.

Moving on

Ferry Svolvær (daily except Sat; 5hr 30min).

THE LOFOTEN ISLANDS

Stretched out in a skeletal curve across the Norwegian Sea, the **Lofoten Islands** are perfect for a simple, uncluttered few days. For somewhere so far north the weather is exceptionally mild, and there's plentiful **accommodation** (ⓦwww.lofoten.info) in *rorbuer*, originally fishermen's shacks, but now more often well-equipped huts sleeping two to six people for around 400kr to 600kr per night, though some of the more deluxe versions can cost

GETTING TO THE ISLANDS

The **Hurtigrute coastal boat** calls at two ports, Stamsund and Svolvær, while the southern Lofoten ferry leaves Bodø for Moskenes, Værøy and Røst. There are also **passenger express catamarans**, which work out slightly cheaper than the Hurtigrute, linking both Bodø and Narvik with Svolvær. By **bus** the main long-distance services from the mainland to the Lofoten are from Bodø to Svolvær via Fauske and from Narvik to Svolvær.

over 1000kr. In addition, the Lofoten Islands have four hostels and plenty of campsites.

Austvågøy

The main town on **Austvågøy**, the largest and northernmost island of the group, is **SVOLVÆR**, a hub of island bus routes. **Passenger ferries** from Bodø (car ferries stop at Moskenes only) dock about 1km west of the town centre, whereas the Hurtigrute docks in the centre, a brief walk from the **bus station** and the busy **tourist office**, where you can pick up island-wide information and bus schedules (late May to mid-June Mon–Fri 9am–4pm & Sat 10am–2pm; mid-June to early Aug Mon–Fri 9am–8pm, Sat 10am–2pm, Sun 4pm–8pm; early Aug to late Aug Mon–Fri 9am–10pm, Sat & Sun 9/10am–8pm; Sept to mid-May Mon–Fri 9am–4pm; ⓣ76 06 98 00, ⓦwww.lofoten.info). One of the most pleasant places **to stay** in Svolvær is the *Svolvær Sjøhus*, by the seashore at the foot of Parkgata (ⓣ76 07 03 36, ⓦwww.svolver-sjohuscamp.no; ❻), five minutes' walk from the square. Alternatively, at the east end of the harbour, a causeway leads out to the slender islet of Svinøya, where accommodation at *Svinøya Rorbuer* (ⓣ76 06 99 30, ⓦwww.svinoya.no) consists of traditional *rorbuer* at 1000kr during the summer (Jun–Aug) and 850kr the rest of the year.

Vestvågøy

It is, however, the next large island to the southwest, **Vestvågøy**, which captivates many travellers, due in no small part to the atmospheric village of **STAMSUND**, whose older buildings are strung along a rocky, fretted seashore. It's the first port of call for the **Hurtigrute coastal boat** as it heads north from Bodø and getting here from Austvågøy is reasonably easy with several **buses** making the trip daily (except Sunday), though you do have to change at Leknes, 16km away to the west.

In Stamsund, the first place to head for is the smashing HI **hostel** (ⓣ76 08 93 34, ⓦwww.vandrerhjem.no; dorms ❷, rooms ❻; closed mid–Oct to Dec); friendly and very informal, it's made up of several cosy *rorbuer* perched over a pint-sized bay, about 1km up the road from the port and 150m from the nearest bus stop – ask the driver to tell you where to get off. **Fishing** around here is first-class: the hostel rents out rowing boats and lines; afterwards, you can cook your catch on the hostel's wood-burning stoves.

Flakstadøya and Moskenesøya

By any standard the next two Lofoten Islands, **Flakstadøya** and **Moskenesøya**, are extraordinarily beautiful. As the Lofoten archipelago tapers towards its southerly conclusion, rearing peaks crimp a sea-shredded coastline studded with a string of fishing villages. Remarkably, the E10 travels along almost all of this dramatic shoreline, by way of tunnels and bridges, to **MOSKENES**, the **ferry port** midway between Bodø and the remote, southernmost bird islands of Værøy and Røst. Some 6km further on, the E10 ends at the tersely named **Å**, one of the Lofoten's most delightful villages, its huddle of old buildings rambling over a foreshore that's wedged in tight between the grey-green mountains and the surging sea. The same family owns the assortment of smart *rorbuer* (❾) that surround the dock, the adjacent **hostel** (dorms ❸, rooms ❼), the bar and the only **restaurant**, where the seafood is very good. All accommodation can be reserved on ⓣ76 09 11 21, ⓦwww.lofoten-rorbu.com). Local **buses** run along the length of the E10 from Leknes to Å four or five times daily from late June to late August, less frequently the rest of the year. Buses don't, however, always coincide with sailings to and from Moskenes, so if you're heading from the Moskenes ferry port to Å, you may have to walk – it's 6km – or take a taxi.

THE NORTHERN LIGHTS

Tromsø's northerly location but relatively mild climate has made it a popular spot from which to view the **Northern Lights**, or Aurora Borealis, which occur here all year round but most frequently between November and April. Caused by solar winds as they hit the Earth's atmosphere, they light up the sky in shimmering waves of blue, yellow and green – a spectacle of celestial proportions.

TROMSØ

Rather preposterously, **TROMSØ** was once known as the "Paris of the North", and the city still likes to think of itself as the capital of northern Norway, with two cathedrals, a clutch of interesting museums and an above-average (and affordable) nightlife, patronized by its high-profile student population. Certainly, as a base for this part of the country, it's hard to beat, set in magnificent landscape – dramatic mountains and craggy shoreline.

What to see and do

In the centre of town, the striking woodwork of the **Domkirke** (Tues–Sat noon–4pm, Sun 10am–2/4pm; 25kr) reflects the town's nineteenth-century prosperity. From the church, it's a short walk north along the harbourfront to the most diverting of the city's museums, the **Polar Museum** (daily: March to mid-June & mid-Aug to Sept 11am–5pm; mid-June to mid-Aug 10am–7pm; Oct–Feb 11am–3pm; Ⓦwww.polarmuseum.no; 50kr), whose varied displays include skeletons retrieved from the permafrost of Svalbard and a detailed section on the polar explorer Roald Amundsen, as well as a bewildering quantity of stuffed animals. On the other side of the water, over the spindly Tromsø Bridge, the white and ultramodern **Arctic Cathedral** (June to mid-Aug Mon–Sat 10am–8pm, Sun 1–8pm; mid-Aug to May daily 4–6pm; all year Sunday service 11am–noon) is spectacular, made up of eleven immense triangular concrete sections representing the eleven Apostles left after the betrayal. Back in the centre, a ten-minute stroll south along the waterfront from the harbour brings you to **Polaria**, Hjalmar Johansengate 12 (daily mid-May to mid-Aug 10am–7pm; mid-Aug to mid-May noon–5pm; 90kr), which combines Polar exhibits and an aquarium – complete with walk-through seal tank – with displays about the region's fragile eco-system.

Arrival and information

Boat The Hurtigrute coastal boat docks in the centre of town at the foot of Kirkegata.

Bus Long-distance buses arrive and leave from the adjacent car park.

Tourist office Kirkegate 2, near the Domkirke (late May–Aug Mon–Fri 8.30am–6pm, Sat & Sun 10am–5pm; Sept to late May Mon–Fri 9am–4pm, Sat 10am–2pm; Ⓣ77 61 00 00; Ⓦwww.destinasjontromso.no).

Accommodation

The tourist office has a small supply of private rooms ❸

ABC Hotell Nord Parkgate 4 Ⓣ77 66 83 00, Ⓦwww.hotellnord.no. Basic but comfortable budget hotel less than 1km from the centre of town. Free wireless and student discounts available. ❻

AMI Hotell Skotegate 1 Ⓣ77 62 10 00, Ⓦwww.amihotel.no. Good-value hotel close to the centre of town, with free wireless, free tea and coffee, and discounts for longer stays and for students. ❻

Fjellheim Sommerhotell Mellanveien 96 Ⓣ77 75 55 60, Ⓦwww.fjellheimsommerhotell.no. Tromsø's cheapest budget option, in a converted school 10 minutes' walk from the centre. Mid-June to mid-Aug only. Dorms ❸, rooms ❻

Tromsø Youth Hostel Åsgårdsveien 9. Elverhøy Ⓣ77 65 76 28, Ⓦwww.vandrerhjem.no. Frugal, no-frills summer hostel some 2km west of the quay; hop on bus #26 from the centre. Late Jun–mid Aug only. Dorms ❸, rooms ❻

Tromsdalen Camping ⓦ77 63 80 37. Pleasant campsite over the bridge on the mainland, about 1800m beyond the Arctic Cathedral. Cabins ❹–❻, camping ❷

Eating

Aunegården Strandtorvet 13. Everything from coffee and cheesecake fresh from the onsite bakery to traditional Norwegian dishes, in a lovely old building.
Il Tabernacolo Storgate 36. Good, filling, reasonably priced pasta at allegedly "the world's northernmost Italian restaurant".
Kaffe å Lars Kirkegate 8. Cute, cosy café with a decent, cheap light lunch menu. The pricey restaurant upstairs is one of Tromsø's best.
Kaffebønner Strandtorget 1 & Stortorget 3. Popular café with lunchtime panini offers and excellent coffee.

Drinking and nightlife

Barometeret Strandtorget 30. Regular live music, DJ nights and student chic at this quirky-cool bar.
Blå Rock Café Strandgate 14. Much-loved bar with a jukebox and a rock'n'roll air.
Jernbanen Strandgate 33. Quirky pub with a railway theme – half the seating is from old trains. Lively at weekends, with an older crowd.
Skarven Strandtorget 13. The place to go for summer drinks late into the polar evening.
Åpen Bar Strandtorget 3. Modern bar serving tapas by day and an eclectic mix of music in its three club rooms by night.

Moving on

Bus Alta (April to late Oct; 1–2 daily; 7hr); Narvik (1–3 daily; 4hr–4hr 40min); Nordkapp (late June to mid-Aug daily except Sat; 14hr).

HONNINGSVÅG

Beyond Tromsø, the northern tip of Norway enjoys no less than two and a half months of permanent daylight on either side of the summer solstice. Here, the bleak and treeless island of **Magerøya** is connected to the northern edge of the mainland by an ambitious combination of tunnels and bridges. The island's only significant settlement is the crusty fishing village of **HONNINGSVÅG**, which makes a steady income from accommodating the hundreds of summertime tourists bent on visiting Nordkapp – the North Cape – just 34km away. *North Cape Guesthouse*, just behind the seafront at Elvebakke 5a, is the best budget option (ⓣ92 82 33 71, ⓦwww.northcapeguesthouse.com, dorms ❸, rooms ❼, summer only). Alternatively, there's *NAF Nordkapp Camping* (ⓣ78 47 33 77; ⓦwww.nordkappcamping.no; late May to mid-Sept; four-bed cabins 550kr, camping ❷), 8km from Honningsvåg on the road to Nordkapp. Long-distance **buses** arrive in the centre of Honningsvåg and there's a limited bus service on to Nordkapp (late June to mid-Aug one–two daily; 50min). When the buses aren't running, the only option is a taxi (about 1000kr return), though the road is closed throughout the winter and often in spring too. For travellers northbound on the **Hurtigrute coastal boat**, a special coach is laid on to get from Honningsvåg to Nordkapp and back within the two-and-a-half-hour stop. For **food** in Honningsvåg, there are a couple of takeaway kiosks along Storgata and a very good seafood restaurant at the *Honningsvåg Brygge Hotel.*

Nordkapp

Whilst the 307m-high cliff known as **NORDKAPP** isn't actually the northernmost point of Europe (that honour belongs to Knivskjellodden, along an 18km signposted track from highway E69), it's officially as far north as you can get. It's a hassle to get here, but there *is* something exhilarating about this bleak, wind-battered promontory. Originally a Sami sacrificial site, it was named by the English explorer Richard Chancellor in 1553. These days the headland is occupied by **Nordkapphallen** (North Cape Hall; daily: early to mid-May & Sept to mid-Oct noon–4pm; mid-May to mid-June noon–1am; mid-June to July 9am–2am; Aug 9am–midnight; mid-Oct to April 12.30–2pm; 195kr for 48hr, including parking), a flashy complex that contains souvenir shops, cafés, restaurants and huge windows from where you can survey the surging ocean below.

Poland

HIGHLIGHTS

SOPOT: enjoy this vast stretch of white sand near Poland's lively summertime resort

A NIGHT OUT IN WARSAW: dance to Western hip-hop amidst the Communist-era buildings and skyscrapers of Poland's capital

AUSCHWITZ-BIRKENAU CAMPS: explore the haunting and sombre Nazi death camps

THE WAWEL, KRAKÓW: the historic seat of Poland's religious and political elite

TATRA MOUNTAINS: hike among jagged alpine peaks, swim in crystal-clear lakes and sample fresh trout in bustling mountain resorts

ROUGH COSTS

DAILY BUDGET Basic €20/ occasional treat €35

DRINK Vodka (50ml shot) €1

FOOD Zurek soup €2–3

HOSTEL/BUDGET HOTEL €8–11/ €27–32

TRAVEL Train: Warsaw–Kraków (390km; 4hr) €12; Bus: (7hr) €15

FACT FILE

POPULATION 38.1 million

AREA 312,685 sq km

LANGUAGE Polish

CURRENCY Zloty (zł/PLN)

CAPITAL Warsaw (population: 1.7 million)

INTERNATIONAL PHONE CODE ⓣ48

Basics

Poland entered the twenty-first century on the cusp of momentous change. After almost two centuries of foreign domination, the nation's return to democracy at the end of the century brought new freedoms and an economic revolution. Adjustments have proven difficult for some, however, and contradictions abound: on highways, you'll find new cars vying for space with tiny, communist-era models and horse-drawn carts. A booming economy has not prevented a flood of emigrants moving westwards since the nation's incorporation into the EU. The role of the Catholic Church, however, is as important as ever, with its presence visible in Baroque buildings, roadside shrines and the many images of the late Pope John Paul II, the former Archbishop of Kraków.

Much of **Warsaw**, the capital, conforms to stereotypes of Eastern European greyness, but its historic centre, beautiful parks and vibrant nightlife are diverting enough. **Kraków**, the ancient royal capital in the south, is the real crowd-puller, rivalling the elegance of Prague and Vienna, while **Gdańsk** on the Baltic Sea offers an insight into Poland's dynamic politics as well as the golden beaches in the nearby resort of **Sopot**. In the west, Germanic influences are apparent in the grand Teutonic castles of **Silesia**, but quintessentially Polish **Poznań** is still revered as the independent heart of the nation. Of the many regions of unspoilt natural beauty, the **Tatra Mountains** on the Slovak border offer exhilarating walking, a unique mountain culture and skiing in the winter.

CHRONOLOGY

966 AD Mieszko I creates the Polish State.
1025 Boleslaw I, Mieazho's son, is crowned the first King of Poland.
1385 The Union of Krewa unites the countries of Poland and Lithuania through an arranged marriage.
1410 United Polish and Lithuanian forces defeat the Teutonic Knights, forcing them to leave Polish land.
1500s The Renaissance sweeps through Poland, giving it significant cultural importance in Europe.
1569 The Lublin Union establishes the Polish-Lithuanian Commonwealth.
1700s The Three Partitions of Poland by Russia, Prussia and Austria.
1863 The January Uprising against Russian authority is brutally repressed.
1918 Independent Polish state created.
1926 Marshal Jozef Pilsudski stages a military coup, marking the failure of democracy.
1939 Poland is invaded by Nazi Germany, beginning WWII.
1945 Soviets drive out the Nazis, and occupy large parts of Poland. By the end of the war more than six million Poles are dead.
1947 Poland becomes a Communist state.
1978 Archbishop of Krakow is elected to become Pope John Paul II.
1980 Workers' uprising at Gdansk, led by Lech Walesa, sweeps through Poland. He forms the Solidarity Party, which becomes an important anti-Communist movement.
1990 Lech Walesa becomes the first popularly elected president of Poland.
2007 The Archbishop of Warsaw resigns over revelations about his co-operation with the secret police during Communist rule.

ARRIVAL

The majority of tourists arrive at Warsaw's **airport**, although Gdańsk, Wrocław, Kraków and Poznań all offer an increasing range of low-cost flights to major Western European destinations. LOT (Ⓦwww.lot.com, Ⓣ0801/703 703), the

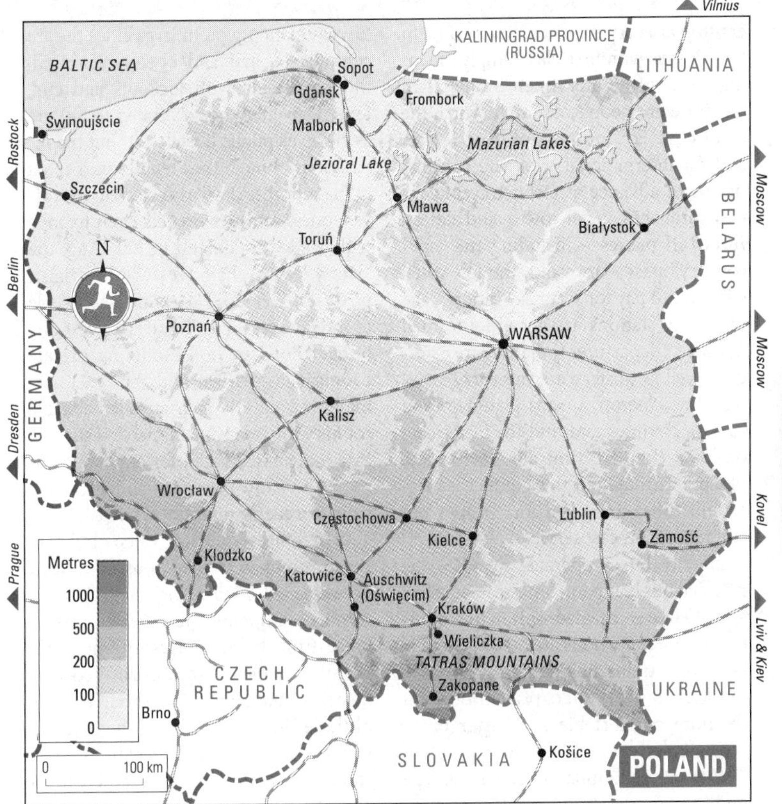

POLAND BASICS

national airline, offers the only non-stop flights to Warsaw from North America.

Poland has fast **rail** connections with all its neighbouring countries. Everyday, several direct trains arrive in both Kraków and Warsaw from Central Europe's backpacker hotspots – Prague, Budapest, Vienna. To the west, Poznań and Wrocław have regular connections to Germany.

Several Polish **bus** companies, including Polski Express (Ⓦwww.polskiexpress.net, Ⓣ022/854 0285) and Eurolines (Ⓦwww.eurolines.pl, Ⓣ032/351 2000) provide services from all major European capitals to Warsaw.

On the southern border, there are daily public buses to the mountain town of Zakopane from the Slovakian resorts of Propad.

On the Baltic Coast, PolFerries (Ⓦwww.polferries.pl, Ⓣ058/343 1887) runs regular ferries to Gdańsk from Nynäshamn in Sweden.

GETTING AROUND

The primary means of transport for budget travellers in Poland is by train, and the PKP **railway** system (Ⓦwww.pkp.pl) runs three main types. Express services (Ekspresowy), particularly IC (intercity) or EC (Eurocity), stop at major cities only, and seat reservations (miejscówka, 10–18zł/€2.50–4.50) are compulsory. "Fast" trains (Pospieszny) are less costly, but not necessarily slower. The cheapest services (Osobowy) are less predictable – some are quick, while others stop at every haystack. Seats come in two classes, with first-class simply meaning a six-seat compartment rather than one for eight people; it's rarely worth the extra cost. For journeys of over 100km and for international trips you can buy tickets in advance at Orbis travel agencies (branches in all towns and cities). **InterRail passes** – including the "one-country" pass - are valid, though you'll still have to pay for seat reservations. The main city stations are generally termed "główny"; departures (odjazdy) are printed on yellow posters; arrivals (przyjazdy) on white; "peron" means platform. You can check times and find the best ticket deals on the PKP timetable (Ⓦrozklad.pkp.pl). Throughout this guide, the prices and times are given for cheaper but still reasonably fast services.

Intercity **buses** operated by PKS, the national bus company, are cheap but slow and often overcrowded; only in the southern mountain regions are buses generally faster than trains. Polski Express (Ⓦwww.polskiexpress.pl) offers pricier journeys in more comfortable and faster buses – particularly out of Warsaw.

With a predominantly flat landscape and accommodation always less than 50km away, Poland is a tempting place for **cyclists**. There are repair shops in many cities and you can take bikes on most trains. Note, however, that Poland is one of Europe's leading nations for road fatalities; beware its combination of poor road surfaces and dangerous driving.

ACCOMMODATION

Private Hostels proliferate in Kraków and Warsaw and are now cropping up in the other cities. They generally offer excellent service, with amenities like Internet access and laundry, for around 50zł/€12.50 per bed. During the Polish summer holidays of July to August, however, it is advisable to book ahead. Even the smallest towns have a **Public Youth Hostel**/"Schroniska Młodzieżowe" which costs around 30zł/€7.50 a head; for a complete list check Ⓦwww.ptsm.org.pl. In large cities they're centrally located and open year-round, though usually with lockouts and curfews. University hostels (open to all) are as cheap as public hostels without the restrictions, though they tend to be located in the suburbs. Similarly priced to the private ones, **summer hostels** open to cope with the extra demand in July–Aug; the "Dizzy Daisy" chain (Ⓦwww.dizzydaisy.pl, Ⓣ012/422/3258) is the most accessible to foreign travellers. There is at least one **budget hotel** or house offering **private rooms** in every town, with 80zł/€21 normally buying you spartan but habitable rooms with communal toilet and shower. Prices increase by half for en-suite bathroom, TV and breakfast, though many have excellent discounts for students. Tourist offices can also often find you cheap rooms in private houses (*kwatera prywatna*; 60–70zł/€16).

Polish **campsites** are often a fair distance from town centres and are only slightly cheaper than a dorm bed in a hostel (20-30zł/€5–7). Though some of these sites, especially in the national parks, have excellent facilities, you should generally expect to find a toilet and little else. For a list of campsites in Poland, check out Ⓦwww.eurocampings.co.uk/en/europe/poland.

FOOD AND DRINK

Poles are passionate about their food, providing meals of feast-like proportions for the most casual visitors. The cuisine is an intriguing mix of European and Eurasian influences and, whilst often wonderfully flavoursome and nutritious, it does live up to its reputation for heaviness. **Polish meals** generally start with soups, the most popular of which are *barszcz*, beetroot broth, and *żurek*, a sour soup of fermented rye. The basis of most main courses is fried or grilled meat, such as *kotlet schabowy* (breaded pork chops). Two inexpensive specialities (5–12zł) you'll find everywhere are *bigos* (sauerkraut stewed with a variety of meats) and *pierogi*, dumplings stuffed with cottage cheese and onion (*ruskie*), meat (*z mięsem*), or cabbage and mushrooms (*z kapustą I grzybami*). The national snack is the *zapiekanki*, a baguette crammed with mushrooms and covered in melted cheese and tomato sauce.

Restaurants are open until 9 or 10pm, later in city centres, and prices are low: in most places outside of Warsaw you can have a two-course meal with a drink for 30zł/€7.50. The cheapest option is the local **milk bar** (*Bar Mleczny*; usually open for breakfast until 5/6pm), which provides fast and filling daytime meals for workers, while cake shops (*Cukierna*) produce sweet pastries that rival any in Central Europe.

Drink

The Poles can't compete with their Czech neighbours when it comes to **beer** (*piwo*), but a range of microbreweries (*browars*) are supplementing the drinkable national brands. Even in Warsaw, you won't pay more than 12zł/€3 for a half litre. Tea (*herbata*) and coffee (*kawa*) are both popular but often come served with lemon rather than milk. But it's **vodka** (*wódka*), ideally served neat and cold, which is the national drink. The best clear variety is Wyborowa, but also try the flavoured types, like Goldwasser in Gdańsk, with its unique golden flakes.

CULTURE AND ETIQUETTE

As a nation in which over seventy-five percent of people are practising Roman Catholics, Poland maintains many conservative religious and social practices, especially in the countryside. Men are often seen as the breadwinner and it is still rare to see women travelling alone at night. Poland's young, urban population tend to be both more relaxed and wilder than their parents; you are likely to encounter some friction between the generations, whether it is booming hip-hop on a walkman causing consternation on a commuter train or young city workers upsetting older peasants as they speed around the countryside in stylish cars. Yet Poles of all ages are also warm, passionate people, fond of handshakes and of lively, informal conversation over a vodka. Table manners follow the Western norm and it is usual to reward good service with a ten percent tip.

THE ART OF POLISH QUEUING

Years of practice during the Cold War era has meant that many Poles have mastered the art of **queue-barging**. Do not be surprised if you get assailed by everything from cheeky excuses – "I'm so late. Can I go first?" – to outright shoving in shops or tourist attractions. Note that many post offices employ a ticket system to organize queues.

SPORTS AND OUTDOOR ACTIVITIES

The most popular **sport** is soccer and the national and top league teams often attract sell-out crowds, but even local village matches or European games shown in the local pub invariably bring many fans. Despite lacking any international stars, the Poles also enjoy tennis and cycling whilst American sports – especially basketball – are also starting to make an impact. For most **hikers**, the highlight of Poland is the Tatra Mountains in the south, though the country's 23 National Parks offer many opportunities for beautiful secluded walks as well as horse-riding. Beach and water sports are centred on Sopot in the North whilst the skiing season (Nov–Feb) brings tourists flocking to the southern mountain resorts like Zakopane.

COMMUNICATIONS

Post offices are identified by the name Poczta, and in larger cities offer poste

POLAND ON THE NET

www.polandtour.org The official tourist website with general details on Poland's major sights and visa information.
www.what-where-when.pl Excellent city guides with the most up-to-date information on accommodation, festivals and places to eat and drink.
www.culture.pl News and essays on Polish cultural events and history.

restante services: anyone addressing mail to you should add "No. 1" after the city's name. Main offices usually open Mon–Sat 8am–8pm; branches close earlier. For public phones you'll need a card (*karta telefoniczna*), available at post offices and RUCH newsagent kiosks. Internet cafes charging 3–6zł/hr are present in all towns.

EMERGENCIES

Poland is a very safe country to travel in, though inevitably thefts from dorms and pick-pocketing do occur. Safely store your valuables whenever possible and, on night trains, lock your compartment when you sleep. Polish **police** (*policja*) are courteous but unlikely to speak English. Medical care can be basic and most foreigners rely on the expensive private medical centres run by Medicover (041/9596, www.medicover.pl).

EMERGENCY NUMBERS

Police 997 (112 with mobile phones); fire service 998; ambulance 999.

INFORMATION & MAPS

Most cities have a tourist office (*informacja turystyczna*), which is generally run by the local municipality though some are merely private agencies selling costly tours. For the best-quality maps (10–15zł), head to bookstores like Empik, which has a branch on most main squares.

MONEY AND BANKS

Currency is the Złoty (zł/PLN), divided into 100 Groszy. Coins come as 1, 2, 5, 10, 20 and 50 groszy, and 1, 2 and 5 złoty; notes as 10, 20, 50, 100 and 200 złoty. **Banks** (usually open Mon–Fri 7.30am–5pm, Sat 7.30am–2pm) and exchange offices (*kantors*) offer similar exchange rates. Major credit cards are widely accepted, and ATMs are common in cities. At the time of writing, €1=3.75zł, US$1=2.70 zł and £1=5.50zł. Euros are not widely accepted, even in Warsaw.

STUDENT AND YOUTH DISCOUNTS

The major cities all have tourist cards (available for one day or longer) that give discounts on transport and at the main sights. Your ISIC card can halve entry prices for museums and city transport, especially in Warsaw, and cut intercity train fares by a third. A Hostelling International card can earn you up to 25 percent off at public hostels.

OPENING HOURS AND HOLIDAYS

Most shops open on weekdays from 10am–6pm, and all but the largest close on Saturday at 2 or 3pm and all day Sunday. RUCH kiosks, selling public transport tickets (*bilety*), open at 6 or 7am. Most museums and historic monuments are closed Monday. Entrance tends to be inexpensive, and is often free one day of the week. Public holidays are: Jan 1, Easter Mon, May 1, May 3, Corpus Christi (May/June), Aug 15, Nov 1, Nov 11, Dec 25 & 26.

Polish Language

Basics

	Polish	Pronunciation
Yes	*Tak*	Tahk
No	*Nie*	Nyeh
Please	*Proszę*	Prosh-eh
Thank you	*Dziękuję*	Djen-ku-yeh
Hello/Good day	*Dzień dobry*	Djen doh-brih
Goodbye	*Do widzenia*	Doh veed-zen-yah
Excuse me/Sorry	*Przepraszam*	Prsheh-prash-ahm
Today	*Dzisiaj*	Djyish-eye
Yesterday	*Wczoraj*	Vchor-eye
Tomorrow	*Jutro*	Yoo-troh
What time is it?	*Która godzina?*	Ktoo-rah go-djee-nah
I don't understand	*Nie rozumiem*	Nyeh roh-zoom-ee-yem
How much is....?	*Ile kosztuje...?*	Ill-eh kosh-too-yeh
Do you speak English?	*Pan/i/mówi po angielsku?*	Pahn/ee/movee poh ahn-gyel-skoo

Getting around

Where is the...?	*Gdzie jest ...?*	G-djeh yest...?
entrance	*Wejscie*	vey-sche
exit	*Wyjscie*	viy-sche
toilet	*Toalety*	To-a-le-ti
hotel	*hotel*	Ho-tel
hostel	*Schronisko/hostel*	Sro-nees-ko
Church	*Kościol*	Kosh-choow
What time does the... leave/arrive?	*O ktorej odehodzi/ przychodzi...?*	O ktoo-rey ot-ho-djee/ pshi-ho-djee
Boat	*lódz*	Woosh
Bus	*autobus*	Aw-tow-boos
Plane	*Samolot*	Sa-moo-lot
Train	*Pociąg*	Po-chonk

Accommodation

I would like a...	*Proprozę o*	Po-pro-she o
Bed	*Lózko*	woosh-ka
Single Room	*Pokoj jednoosobowy*	Po-kooj yed-no-o-so-ba-vi
Double Room	*Pokej lózkiem*	Po-kooj woosh-kyem
Cheap	*Tani*	Tah-nee
Expensive	*Drogi*	Droh-gee
Open	*Otwarty*	Ot-var-tih
Closed	*Zamknięty*	Zahmk-nee-yen-tih
One	*Jeden*	Yed-en
Two	*Dwa*	Dvah
Three	*Trzy*	Trshih
Four	*Cztery*	Chter-ih
Five	*Pięć*	Pyench
Six	*Sześć*	Sheshch
Seven	*Siedem*	Shedem
Eight	*Osiem*	Oshem
Nine	*Dziewięć*	Djyev-yench
Ten	*Dziesięć*	Djyesh-ench

Warsaw

Packed with a bizarre mix of gleaming office buildings and grey, Communist-era apartment blocks, **WARSAW** (Warszawa) often bewilders backpackers on first arrival. Yet if any city rewards exploration, it is the Polish capital. North of the lively centre are stunning Baroque palaces and the meticulously reconstructed Old Town; to the south are two of Central Europe's finest urban parks; and towards the east lie reminders of the rich Jewish heritage extinguished by the Nazis.

Warsaw became the capital in 1596 and initially flourished as one of Europe's most prosperous cities. In 1815, however, Poland's weak international position allowed the Russians to conquer the city and, despite a series of rebellions, it was not until the outbreak of World War I that this control collapsed. Warsaw again became the capital of an independent Poland in 1918, but the German invasion of 1939 ensured that this was to be tragically short-lived. Infuriated by the 1944 Warsaw Uprising, Hitler ordered the total destruction of the city and left 850,000 Varsovians dead and 85 percent of the city in ruins. Rebuilding is an ongoing process.

What to see and do

The main sights are on the western bank of the Wisła (Vistula) river where you'll find the central business and shopping district, Śródmieście, grouped around Centralna station and the nearby Palace of Culture. The more picturesque and tourist-friendly *Old Town* (Stare Miasto) is just to the north.

The Old Town

The title *Old Town* (Stare Miasto) is, in some respects, a misnomer for the historic nucleus of Warsaw. After World War II the beautifully arranged Baroque streets were destroyed, only to be painstakingly reconstructed in the years afterwards. Plac Zamkowy (Castle Square), on the south side of the Old Town, is the obvious place to start a tour.

Royal Castle

On the east side of the square is the thirteenth-century **Royal Castle**, once home of the royal family and seat of the Polish parliament, now the Castle Museum (Tues–Sun 10/11am–4pm; royal apartments 20zł, court rooms 10zł, Sun free). Though a replica, many of the structure's furnishings are originals, having been hidden during the war. After passing the most lavish section of the castle – the Royal Apartments of King Stanisław August – you visit the Lanckoranski Gallery, which contains a fascinating range of aristocratic portraits including two paintings: *Girl in a Picture frame* and *Scholar at his desk* – by Rembrandt.

Cathedral and Old Town Square

On ul. Świętojańska, north of the castle, stands **St John's Cathedral**, the oldest church in Warsaw. A few yards away, the Rynek Starego Miasta (Old Town Square) is one of the most remarkable bits of postwar reconstruction anywhere in Europe. Flattened during the Uprising, its three-storey merchants' houses have been rebuilt in near-flawless imitation of the Baroque originals. It's also home to the Warsaw Historical Museum (Tues & Thurs 11am–6pm, Wed & Fri 10am–3.30pm, Sat & Sun 10.30am–4.30pm; 6zł, free Sun), which has an important section about the resistance to the Nazis and an English-language film (shown Tues–Sat at noon) with poignant footage of both the vibrant, multi-cultural 1930s city and the ruins left in 1945. Crossing the ramparts on the streets heading north brings you to the Rynek Nowego Miasta (New Town Square), the town's commercial hub in the fifteenth century but now a quiet square and a welcome escape from the Old Town's bustle.

Jewish Ghetto

West of the New Town is the former **Ghetto** area, in which an estimated 380,000 Jews – one-third of Warsaw's total population – were crammed from 1939 onwards. By the war's end, the ghetto had been razed to the ground. Around three hundred Jews and just one synagogue, the Nożyk Synagogue at ul. Twarda 6, were left. You can get an idea of what Jewish Warsaw looked like by walking one block east to the miraculously untouched ul. Próżna.

Starting one block north of the synagogue, walk ten minutes west along ul. Grzybowska and then, turning north onto ul. Towarowa, ten minutes more (or take tram #22 from Centralna Station) to ul. Okopowa 49/51 to reach the vast and overgrown Jewish Cemetery (*Cmentarz Zydowski*; Mon–Thurs 10am–5pm, Fri 9am–1pm, Sun 9am–4pm, closed Sat; 4zł), one of the few still in use in Poland.

Warsaw Uprising Museum

Just west of the intersection of ul. Grzybowska and ul. Towarowa is the new **Warsaw Uprising Museum** at ul. Przyokopowa 28 (Mon, Wed, Fri, 8am–6pm; Thurs 8am–8pm; Sat, Sun 10am–6pm; 4zł; tram #22 from Centralna Station to ul. Grzybowska). Set in a century-old brick power station, the museum retells the grim story of how the Varsovians fought and were eventually crushed by the Nazis in 1944 – a struggle that saw the deaths of nearly two hundred thousand Poles and the destruction of most of the city. Special attention is given to the equivocal role played by Soviet troops, who watched passively from the other side of the Vistula as the Nazis defeated the Polish insurgents. Only after the city was a charred ruin did they move across to "liberate" its few remaining inhabitants.

The Royal Way

The road that runs south from Plac Zamkowy to the palace of Wilanów – encompassing the streets of Krakowskie Przedmieście and Nowy Świat – is the old **Royal Way** and is lined with historic buildings. One highlight is the Church of the Nuns of the Visitation, with its columned, statue-topped facade; it's also one of the few buildings in central Warsaw to have come through the War unscathed. Most of the rest of Krakowskie Przedmieście is taken up by University buildings, including several fine Baroque palaces and the Holy Cross Church, wrecked during the Uprising; photographs of the figure of Christ standing among the rubble became poignant emblems of Warsaw's suffering. Sealed inside a column to the left side of the nave there's an urn containing Chopin's heart.

National Museum

South of the university, the main street becomes Nowy Świat (New World), with upmarket shopping and a good selection of cafés. East along al. Jerozolimskie is the **National Museum** (Tues, Wed, Fri–Sun 10am–4pm, Thurs 10am–6pm; 12zł, free Sat), housing an extensive collection of Medieval, Impressionist and Modern art, as well as Christian frescoes from eighth-to thirteenth-century Sudan. Particularly striking is the fourteenth-century sculpture of the Pietá, which is more reminiscent of the modernist distortions in the room nearby than Michaelangelo's famed depiction of the same scene.

Palace of Culture and Science

West of here lies the commercial heart of the city, the Centrum crossroads from which ul. Marszałkowska, the main north-south road, cuts across Al. Jerozolimskie running east-west. Towering over everything is the **Palace of Culture and Science**, a post-World War II gift from Stalin whose vast interior now contains a conference hall, theatres, swimming pools and a casino.

Żoliborz & buses to Truskaw

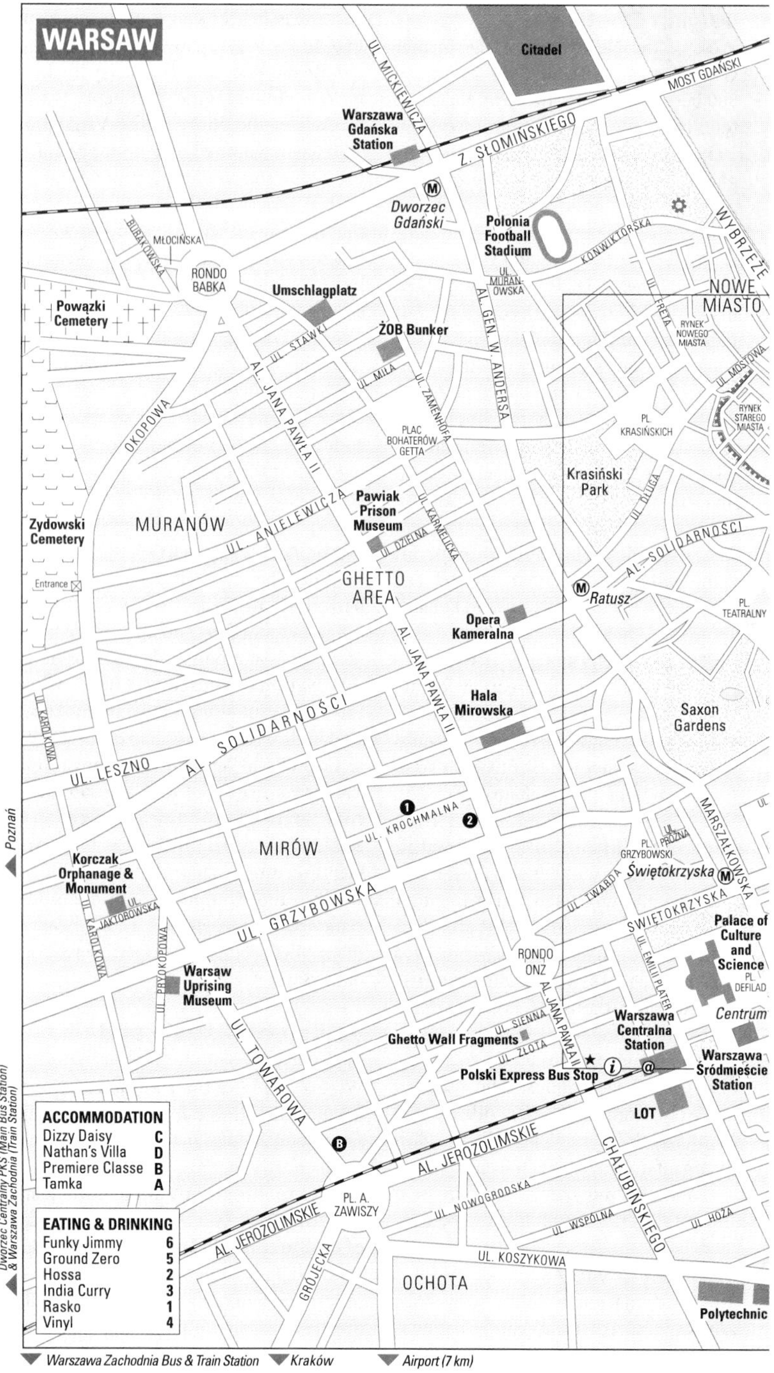

ACCOMMODATION	
Dizzy Daisy	C
Nathan's Villa	D
Premiere Classe	B
Tamka	A

EATING & DRINKING	
Funky Jimmy	6
Ground Zero	5
Hossa	2
India Curry	3
Rasko	1
Vinyl	4

Warszawa Zachodnia Bus & Train Station   Kraków   Airport (7 km)

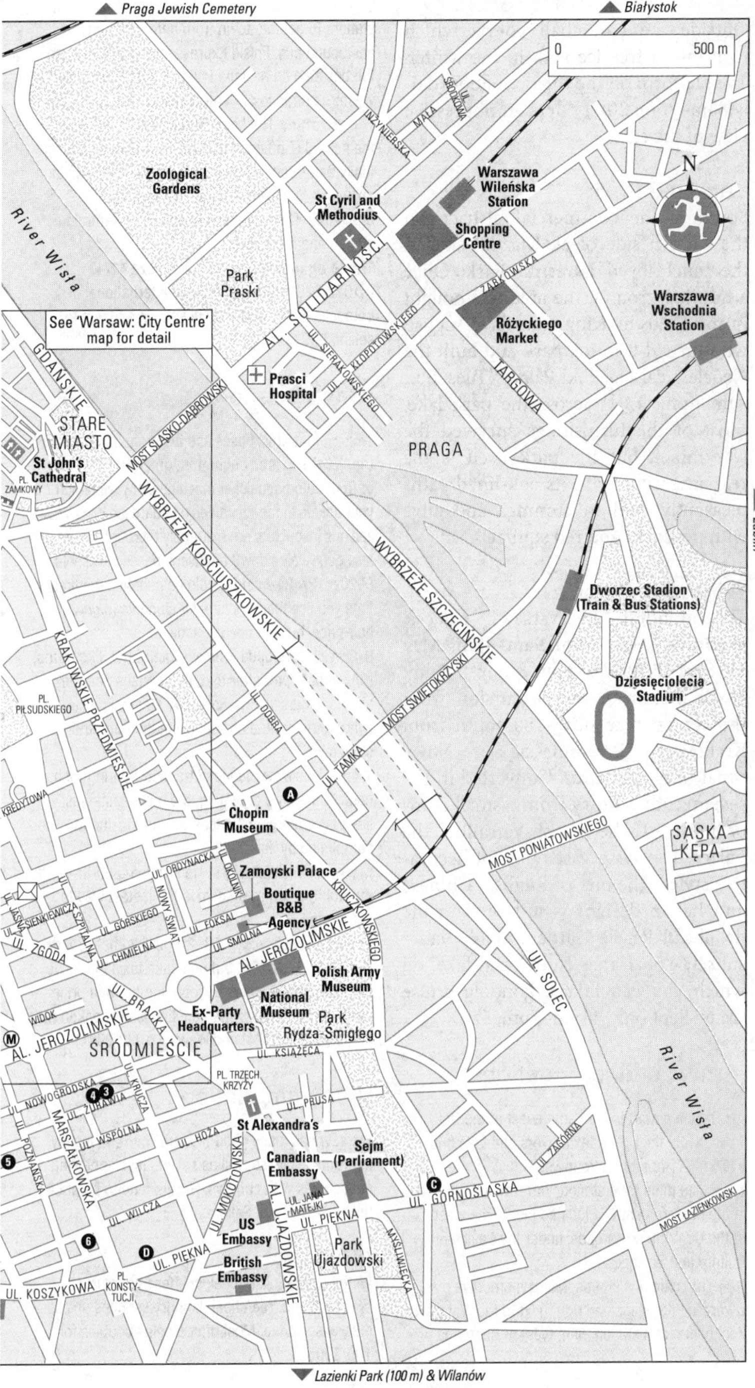

POLAND

WARSAW

Outside are basketball courts which turn into a free ice rink in the winter. The platform on the thirtieth floor (daily 8am–8pm; 20zł) offers an impressive view of the city.

Łazienki Park

South of the commercial district, on the eastern side of al. Ujazdowskie, is the much-loved **Łazienki Park**. Once a hunting ground, the area was bought in the 1760s by King Stanisław August, who turned it into a park and built the Neoclassical Łazienki Palace (Tues–Sun 9am–4pm; 12zł) across the park lake. Most of the furnishings survived the war intact, but the park itself is the real attraction, with its oak-lined paths pleasantly cool in summer and alive with peacocks and red squirrels.

Wilanów Palace

The grandest of Warsaw's palaces, **Wilanów** (Wed–Mon 9am–4pm; May 15–Sept 15, Wed to 6pm & Sun to 7pm; 20zł), makes an easy excursion from the centre: take bus #180 south from Krakowskie Przedmieście or Nowy Świat to its terminus. Converted in the seventeenth century from a small manor house into the "Polish Versailles", the Palace displays a vast range of decorative styles. The mix of English, Chinese and Italian designs is mirrored in the delightful Palace Gardens (daily 9am–sunset; 4.50zł, free Thurs) and lake, on which you can take a gondola cruise (May–Sept only, 11am–7pm; 5zł).

Arrival and information

Air Okęcie airport is 8km southwest of the Old Town: avoid the rip-off taxi drivers and take bus #175 (#611 at night) into town.
Train The main train station, Warszawa Centralna, in the modern centre is located just to the west of the Centrum crossroads, under the Palace of Culture and Science.
Bus The main bus station, Międzynarodowa Dworzec PKS, is located right next to the Warszawa Zachodnia train station, 3km west of Centralna station. To get into town from here catch any eastbound bus. Polski Express intercity buses use the bus stop on al. Jana Pawła II, just outside the western entrance of Centralna train station.
Tourist office The best source of information is the helpful IT office at 39 Krakowskie Przedmieście (daily 9am–8pm; ⓣ022/9431, ⓦwww.warsawtour.pl), which has excellent free city maps and brochures. There are also IT offices at Centralna station and the Airport.
Travel agents STA Travel, ul. Krucza 41/43 (ⓣ022/529 3800) can reserve international or domestic flights and train tickets, in addition to selling ISIC Cards.

City transport

Tickets for trams, buses and the metro (2.40zł single trip; 3.6zł 1hr) are bought from green RUCH kiosks or from automatic ticket machines. Always punch your tickets in the machines on board, as Warsaw's zealous inspectors are extremely thorough. There are also good-value day/3 day/week passes available (7.20zł/12zł/24zł) and should be punched the first time you use them. Tickets for students (*ulgowy*) are half-price, but you need to show ID.
Bus Well-developed if busy system that, like trams, runs until 11pm; after that, night buses operate along ul. Marszałkowska and Al. Jerozolimskie every thirty minutes from beside the main train station.
Trams A quicker means of transport during rush hour. At the time of writing, the main east–west line was undergoing extensive repairs, due for completion by Jan 2008.
Metro A small subway system running north–south through the centre of town is the fastest way to get around.
Taxis Generally cost 1.50–2zł per kilometre, with a minimum fare of 6zł, but only take taxis that have the company name, telephone number and price per kilometre clearly marked. English is spoken at Korpo (ⓣ022/9624) and Wawa (ⓣ022/9644).

Accommodation

Warsaw has many good **private hostels**, mainly in Śródmieście, as well as several less appealing public ones with curfews. **Hotels** tend to be pricier than elsewhere in Poland.

Hostels

All the **hostels** listed below offer free Internet, breakfast and free/cheap laundry services unless otherwise stated. Most offer singles/doubles for 100/200zł.

Dizzy Daisy ul. Gornoslaska 14 ⓣ022/660 6712, ⓦwww.hostel.pl. A clean and friendly summer hostel (with no dorms) near the Łazienki Park; Singles/doubles ❸–❹.

Nathan's Villa ul. Piekna 24/6 ⓣ022/622 2946, ⓦwww.nathansvilla.com. Here you'll find stylish rooms, nice bathrooms and smiling service; Dorms ❷

Oki Doki Pl. Dabrowskiego ⓣ022/826 5112, ⓦwww.okidoki.pl. With an eccentric Communist-era interior and an accompanying bar (0.5lt beer – 6zł), this hostel has by far the liveliest feel of any in town; Dorms ❷

Przy Rynku Rynek Nowago Miasto 4 ⓣ022/831 5033, ⓦwww.cityhostel.net. This small and friendly place has the most affordable rooms in the Stare Miasto; Dorms ❷

Tamka ul. Tamka 30 ⓣ022/826 3095, ⓦwww.tamkahostel.pl. This place has colourful (if basic) dorms and a garden that's handy for a summer barbeque; Dorms ❷

Hotel

Premiere Classe Hotel ul. Towarowa 2 ⓣ022/624 0800, ⓦwww.premiereclasse.com.pl. The city's best budget hotel provides spacious rooms with satellite TV. Breakfast is not included (18zł); Rooms (for up to three people) ❺

Eating

Milk bars

Green Way ul. Szpitalna 6. The locals pack out this fun, inexpensive veggie canteen on most evenings. Mains 8–10zł.

Pod Barbakanem ul. Mostawa 27-9. A popular Milk Bar with wholesome grub that's just outside the Old Town. Mains 4–8zł.

Cafés

Adi ul. Freta 20/24. With artisanal ice cream made fresh every day, Adi is the pick for frozen treats in the Old Town. Cones 1.50zł.

Blikle ul. Nowy Świat 35. Light meals and cakes make this place popular with the refined shopping elite. Mains 30–35zł.

Blikle's Pastry Shop ul. Nowy Świat 35. The mouthwatering array of pastries, cakes and chocolates that you find here is enough to end any thoughts of a wholesome lunch in favour of some sweet treats. Cake slices 3–5zł.

Między Nami ul. Bracka 20. Inauspicious outside (look out for the unmarked grey awnings), but an excellent choice if you want a cultured, light meal, with some innovative vegetarian choices. Mains 20–30zł.

Między Slowami ul. Chimielna 30. Nicely set back in a bright courtyard from the busy street, this is a great chilling spot after a hard day's shopping. Sandwiches 15zł.

Restaurants

India Curry ul. Zurawia 22. The best choice if you're seeking something Oriental is this curry-house, which specializes in Tandoori dishes (30–45zł).

Kompania Piwna ul. Podwale 25. This Bavarian-style restaurant is good value near the Old Town Square. Large beers and huge steaks are the standard fare, but also look out for the tasty, cheap fish dishes. Mains 20–35zł.

Orchidea ul. Szpitalna 1. An inventive mix of affordable Oriental and Polish cuisine coupled with a refined atmosphere makes this a favourite among the city's up-and-coming business crowd. Mains 25–35zł.

Drinking and nightlife

The bar scene in Warsaw has really taken off in the last few years, and the city now genuinely provides a great night out that rivals Prague and needn't blow your budget. The city's festivals enhance the celebratory vibe, especially the Warsaw "Summer Jazz Days" Festival, a series of outdoor concerts held throughout the months of July and August.

Bars

Funky Jimmy ul. Wilcza 35/41. The 70s-style interior lends this place a camp, friendly feel; DJ's perform at weekends. 0.33lt beer 5zł.

Hossa Al. Jana Pawla II 25. Watch the price of your favourite cocktails fluctuate stock-exchange style on the screens behind the bar as you down one after another. Vodka cocktails are generally 10–15zł but no promises.

Irish Pub ul. Miodowa 3. For those seeking a pint of the black stuff and live Irish folk and rock music (8–11pm on most nights). 1lt Guinness 30zł.

Rasko ul. Krochmalna 32A. This small, gay-friendly bar is filled with sofas designed for chilled-out conversation. 0.5lt beer 7zł.

Vinyl ul. Zurawia 22. This is the flashest local spot for a cocktail; as you drink, you can peruse the vinyl records covering the walls. Cocktails 18zł.

Clubs

Ground Zero ul. Wspolna 62. This club draws an enthusiastic if unrefined crowd with its chart dance tunes. 7zł admission. 0.5lt beer 9zł.

Opium ul. Wierzbowa 9/11. The kama sutra wall paintings lend a cosy, oriental feel to this spacious

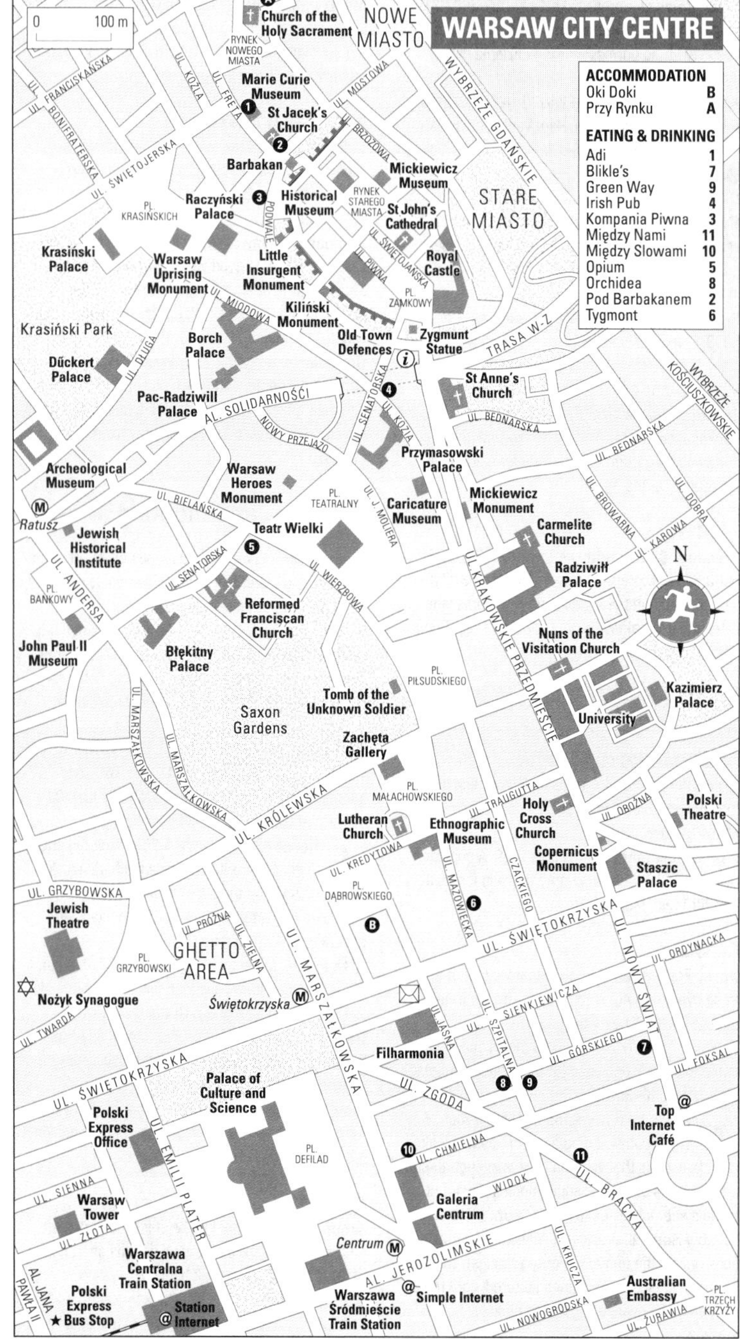

POLAND

WARSAW

two-level club. Tues–Sat, 5pm until the early hours. Cocktails 14–19zł.
Tygmont ul. Mazowiecka 6. The best Jazz club in town, with live bands Mon–Thurs (8–11pm) and Latino dance classes over the weekend from 7.30pm. Look smart as there's a strict dress code.

Entertainment

Cinema

Many films are in English with Polish subtitles, though it's always best to ask regarding the popular Hollywood titles. Tickets range from 15–25zł.
Kinoteka ul. Pl. Defilad 1. Multiplex in the Palace of Culture and Science showing the latest blockbusters.
Kino.Lab ul. Ujazdowskie 6 ⓣ022/628 1271. This small cinema shows a wide range of avant-garde films.

Live Music

Live bands are apt to appear in the city bars without any warning; Tygmont and the Irish Pub are your best bets.
Theatr Wielki Plac Teatralny 1, ⓣ022/826 5019, ⓦwww.teatrwielki.pl. This is worth visiting just for its Neoclassical facade, but it also hosts the best of Poland's National Opera. Check out the website for the latest shows. 20–60zł depending on seats.

Theatre

Teatri Zydowski (Jewish Theatre) Plac Grzybowski, ⓣ022/620 6281, ⓦwww.teatr-zydowski.art.pl. The most striking of Warsaw's several small theatres, specialising in productions (often given in Yiddish) that depict the life of the Jews in Warsaw before the Holocaust. English translations via headphone are available.

Shopping

Malls For the flashest boutiques and department stores, first explore Galeria Centrum (replete with such Western titles as H&M and C&A) opposite the Palace of Culture and Science on ul. Marszałkowska before passing through to the mainly pedestrianized streets of ul. Chimielna and ul. Nowy Świat. Out of town, the Sadyba Best Mall boasts a huge Carrefour Supermarket and a host of clothing stores (including a large Levi's), as well as a cinema and plenty of places to eat. This can be combined with a trip to the Wilanów Palace: just hop on the #180 bus from ul. Krakowskie Przedmięscie or ul. Nowy Świat.
Markets The city authorities are still deciding where to place the famous market that used to reside in the old Stadion Dziesięciolecia (bulldozed for a replacement football Stadium). For a taste of the old market's strange collection of guns, clothes and Christian icons from both East and West, head for the Hala Mirowska market on Jana Paula II (Sat & Sun; get there early for the best deals).

Directory

Embassies and consulates Australia, ul. Nowogrodzka 11, ⓣ022/521 3444, Mon–Fri 8.30am–3pm; Canada, ul. Matejki 1/5, ⓣ022/584 3100, Mon–Fri 10am–4pm; UK, Al. Roz 1, ⓣ022/311 0000, Mon, Tues, Thurs & Fri 8.30am–2pm, Wed 8.30am–noon; USA, ul. Ujazdowskie 29/31, ⓣ022/504 2000, Mon–Fri 8.30am–5pm.
Exchange The Old Town has a host of "kantor" stores willing to exchange foreign cash or travellers' cheques, though you will have to shop around for the best rates. Banks will change your travellers' cheques but they can be slow and rarely offer the best rates. Interchange Poland Ltd at 30 Chimielna (ⓣ022/826 3169; Mon–Sun 8am–11pm) is also a reliable option.
Hospitals The nearest public hospital to the centre is the Prasci, Al. Solidarnosci 67 (ⓣ022/818 5061). In emergencies, many backpackers use the private Med-Centrum, Bednarska 13 (ⓣ022/826 3886; Mon–Fri 8am–6pm).
Internet There is a 24-hour Internet cafe in the Centralna station. Others include Simple, ul. Marszałkowska 99/101 (24hr, 1–4zł per hour); Top Internet Cafe, ul. Nowy Świat 18/20 (Mon–Fri 9am–11pm, Sat–Sun 10am–10pm; 4–7zł).
Laundry Most of the hostels have cheap laundry services available. There are no self-service laundrettes, but Alba (26 ul. Chimelna, ⓣ022/827 4510) does run an expensive washing service (5–10zł per garment).
Left luggage There is a 24hr left luggage room and lockers with storage for up to ten days in the Centralna station.
Pharmacies APTEKA Pharmacy is open 24 hours a day in the Centralna Station, 54 Al. Jerozolimskie. A more central chemist is at ul. Nowy Świat 18/20 (9am–5pm).
Post office ul. Świętokrzyska 31/33 (24hr).

Moving on

Air LOT airlines (ⓦwww.lot.com) has flights to Gdańsk (10 daily; 1hr); Kraków (6 daily; 1hr); Poznań (4 daily; 1hr); Wrocław (8 daily; 1hr).
Train Domestic: Gdańsk (21 daily; 5hr); Kraków (23 daily; 5hr); Poznań (15 daily; 3hr 30min); Toruń (6 daily; 3hr); Wrocław (9 daily; 6hr); Zakopane (5

daily; 8–10hr).

International: Berlin (4 daily; 6hr); Budapest (2 daily; 11hr); Prague (3 daily; 9hr); Vienna (4 daily; 8hr).

Bus PKS (@www.pks.warszawa.pl) runs regular long-distance services to all the major Polish cities from the main terminal.

Northern Poland

Even in a country accustomed to shifting borders, **northern Poland** presents an unusually tortuous historical puzzle. Successively the domain of the crusading Teutonic order, the Hansa merchants and the Prussians, it's only in the last fifty years that the region has become definitively Polish. The conurbation of **Gdańsk**, **Sopot** and **Gdynia**, known as the Tri-City, lines the Baltic coast with its dramatic shipyards and sandy beaches, while highlights inland include the medieval centres of **Malbork** and **Toruń**.

GDAŃSK

Both the starting point of World War II and the setting of the famous strikes against Communist control, **GDAŃSK** has played more than a fleeting role on the world stage. Traces of its past can be seen in the steel skeletons of derelict shipyard cranes and the Hanseatic architecture of the beautifully restored old town. After all the social and political upheavals of the last century this lively city is now busy reinventing itself as a tourist hub.

What to see and do

Entering the city centre is like walking straight through a Hansa merchants' settlement, but its ancient appearance is deceptive: by May 1945, the core of Gdańsk was in ruins, and the present buildings are almost complete reconstructions.

Glowne Miasto

Huge stone gateways guard both entrances to ul. Długa, the main thoroughfare. Start from the sixteenth-century gate at the top, Brama Wyżynna, and you'll soon come across the huge tower of the Town Hall, which houses a **Historical Museum** (Mon 10am–3pm, Tues–Sun 10/11am–6pm; 8zł; free on Mon) with shocking photos of the city's wartime destruction. Past the Town Hall, the street opens onto the wide expanse of ul. Długi Targ, where the ornate façade of Arthur's Court (Mon–Sun 10/11am–4pm; 6zł) stands out in a square filled with fine mansions.

The streets that run parallel are also worth exploring, especially ul. Mariacka, brimming with amber traders, and ul. Chlebnicka, adjacent to **St Mary's Basilica** (Mon–Sat 9am–6pm, Sun 1pm–6pm; 2zł), the largest church in Poland.

The Waterfront and shipyards

At the end of ul. Długi Targ the archways of the Brama Zielona open directly onto the waterfront. Halfway down is the fifteenth-century Gdańsk Crane, the biggest in medieval Europe, which is part of the vast **Central Maritime Museum** (Tues–Sun 10am–4/6pm; 14zł) that spreads out on both banks of the river. Highlights include an exhibition of primitive boats and maritime paintings. Further north loom the cranes of the famous Gdańsk **shipyards**, crucible of the political strife of the 1980s. Poignantly set outside the rusting shipyard gates is the monument to the workers that formed the anti-Communist Solidarity movement, many of whom were killed during the 1970s riots. It was here that frustrated workers began Poland's bloody struggle to topple communism, a story detailed in the shipyard's Roads to Freedom exhibition (set to reopen at press time in the Solidarity offices nearby).

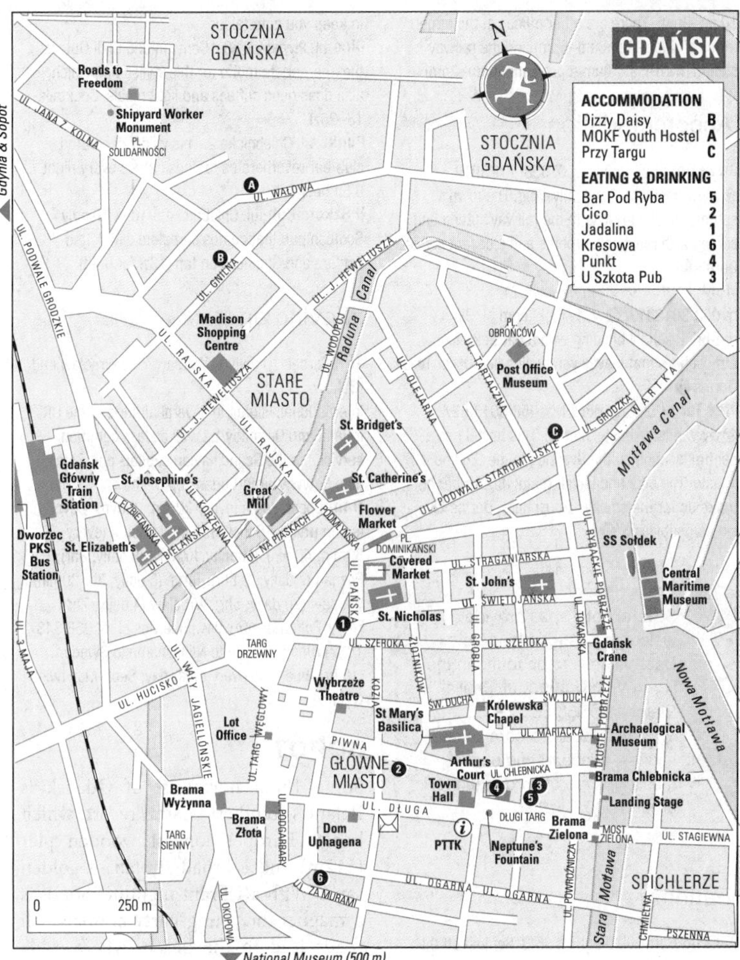

Stara Arzedmiescie

The sole attraction of the city's southern suburb is the **National Museum**, (Tues–Sun 10am–5pm; 10zł) home to a fine collection of Gothic art, the highlight of which is a *Last Judgment* by the Dutch painter Hans Memling.

Arrival and information

Air The Tri-City airport lies 8km out of the city centre. Buses B & #510 (2.40zł) take you to the railway station and Glowne Miasto respectively, leaving around three times an hour. Taxis are 40zł.

Train and bus Make sure to get off at the Główny (Central) Station, which is 15 min walk to the northwest of ul. Długa, at the heart of the Glowne Miasto. The bus station is just across the lines from the railway station, and can be reached by the underground tunnels.

Ferry The ferry terminal is at Gdańsk Nowy Port, 5km to the north. Trams #4,10,14 and 15 run every hour from the nearby tram station to the Glowne Miasto (25min, 2.40zł).

Tourist information Ul. Długa 45 (☎058/3019151, ⓦwww.pttk-gdansk.pl, Mon–Fri 9am–6pm, Sun

10am–6pm). There are other offices at the airport terminal (Mon–Sun 8am–6pm) and the railway station (Mon–Sat 10am–6pm, Sun 10am–2pm).

Accommodation

Dizzy Daisy ul. Gnilna 3, ⓣ058/301 3919, ⓦwww.hostel.pl. Open July–Aug. The town's summer hostel is close to the railway station and comes with reasonable rooms and pleasant service. Dorms ❶

MOKF Youth Hostel ul. Walowa 21 ⓣ058/3012313, ⓦwww.mokf.com.pl. Old red-brick school building with a barracks-like atmosphere that leaves you feeling like Oliver Twist. Dorms ❶

Przy Targu ul. Grodzka 21 ⓣ058/301 5627, ⓦwww.gdanskhostel.com.pl. This hostel has a central location by the riverside in the Glowne Miasto. The bike and kayak rental (8/25zł per hour) make up for the smoky atmosphere. Dorms ❷, single/doubles ❸/❺

> **TREAT YOURSELF**
>
> Several hotel spas provide a welcome post-clubbing detox. Best-value is to be found in the **Hotel Villa Baltica**, ul. Emilia Plater 1 (ⓣ058/555 2800, ⓦwww.villabaltica.com) where saunas, a jacuzzi and exotic massages are offered, each for around 100zł.

Eating

Bar Pod Ryba ul. Dlugi Trg 35/8. Set just off the main street, this canteen provides good-value mains based on baked potatoes with tasty fillings (15–20zł).

Jadalina ul. Panska 69. This popular cellar comes with cheap beer and hearty Polish meals. 0.5lt beer 5.50zł; mains 7–15zł.

Kresowa ul. Ogarna 12. With cuisine from the so-called Lost Territories (*kresy*) to the east of Poland, "Kresowa" has a refined atmosphere and attentive service all for a reasonable price. Don't miss out on the *bigos* based on a traditional sixteenth-century recipe. Mains 20–40zł.

Drinking and nightlife

All the local clubbers prefer the nightlife in Sopot, but there are several bars on Piwna and Chlebnicka to keep you entertained.

Cico ul. Piwna 28/30. "Come in and Chill Out" is the appropriate motto for this stylish bar, which also does good coffees and light meals. Cocktails 18–20zl.

Punkt, ul. Chlebnicka 2. This wildly decorated club/bar reverberates to house tunes every night. 0.5lt beer 6zł.

U Szkota Pub, ul. Chlebnicka 9/10. A friendly Scottish pub that comes complete with kilted waiters and Guinness on tap (13zł for 0.4lt).

Moving on

Air Internal: 10 daily to Warsaw; 5 to Wrocław and Kraków.
International: Flights to several airports in the UK, Ireland and Germany, as well as less common services to the Scandinavian capitals and Rome (see ⓦwww.airport.gdansk.pl).

Train Local: Sopot (every 20min; 25min); Gdynia (same train as Sopot; 35min); Malbork (every 30min; 40min). Intercity: Kraków (8 daily; 8hr); Poznań (7 daily; 4–5hr); Toruń (5 daily; 3hr 30min); Warsaw (20 daily; 5hr); Wrocław (4 daily; 7hr).

Ferry Polferries (ⓦwww.polferries.pl, ⓣ058/343 1887) runs a service to Nynäshamn in Sweden (18 hr, June–Aug every other day; Sept–May twice weekly).

SOPOT

Some 15km northwest of Gdańsk is Poland's trendiest coastal resort, which boasts Europe's longest wooden pier (512m) and a broad stretch of golden sand. With a vibrant nightlife, Sopot is a magnet for young party animals. All roads lead to the beach, where aside from lounging you can meander up the pier (entry 3.80zł) where you'll find boat tours and instructors for water sports operating in summer.

Arrival and information

Train The railway station lies 400m west of the beach and 5 minutes from the busy main street, ul. Monte Cassino.

Tourist office Opposite the train station at ul. Dworcowa 4 (daily 8am–6pm; ⓣ058/550 3783, ⓦwww.sopot.pl/cit). Helps with accommodation, which can be hard to come by in summer.

Internet Cooler Net Cave, ul. Pułaskiego 7a (10am–10pm).

Accommodation

Hufice Sopot Al. Niepodległości 679 ⓣ058/551 0036. It's easiest to jump off at the "Sopot Wyscipi" train stop just before the main station to reach this basic hostel that lies 20min from the beach. You'll need a sleeping bag. Dorms ❷

U Rybaka Guesthouse Pl. Rybakow 16 ⓣ058/551 2302, ⓦwww.urybaka.republika.pl.
Set in a quiet courtyard just 5min from the beach, with several well-furnished singles and doubles with TVs. ❷ per person.

Eating

For best value, avoid ul. Monte Cassino and head for the restaurants around 1km south along the beach.

Bar Przystan Al. Wojska Polskiego 11. This is a touristy but great-value fish restaurant right on the beach. Mains 4–8zł.

Dobra Kuchnia ul. Jagielly 6/1. The best place for reasonably-priced Polish classics in the centre. Mains 10–15zł.

Drinking and nightlife

Aqwarium ul. Monte Cassino 52. Lying behind an eccentric, curved facade, this small dance floor gets packed during the summer season.

Soho ul. Monte Cassino 61. Just down the street from Aqwarium, Soho's colourful interior draws the punters in night and day. Cocktails 12–18zł.

Viva ul. Mamuzski 2.The self-styled "Top Club in the Tri-City" provides chart dance and hip-hop for lots of manic teenage clubbers.

MALBORK

The spectacular fortress of **MALBORK** was built as the headquarters of the Teutonic Order in the fourteenth century and still casts a threatening shadow over what is otherwise a sleepy town. You enter over a moat and through the daunting main gate, before reaching an open courtyard. Brooding above is the **High Castle**, which harbours the centrepiece of the Knights' austere monasticism – the vast **Castle Church** with its faded chivalric paintings. The guided tours (3hr; Tues–Sun: April 15 – Sept 15 9am–7pm, rest of year 9am–3pm; 17.50/30zł) are mandatory, with three daily in English (11am, 1.30pm, 3.30pm). The **railway** and **bus stations** are sited next to each other about ten minutes' walk south of the castle; there are trains every 30min from Gdańsk (40min).

TORUŃ

Originally one of the most beautiful Medieval towns in Central Europe, **Toruń** Hanseatic port was founded by the Teutonic Knights and is still rich with their architectural legacy. Now a friendly university city, with bars and cafés sprinkled throughout the compact streets, it combines nighttime liveliness with its status as a UNESCO World Heritage Site and is set to become European Capital of Culture in 2016.

What to see and do

Highlight of the westerly Old Town is the mansion-lined Rynek and its fourteenth-century Town Hall, now the **Town Museum** (Tues–Sun 10am–4/6pm; 10zł/6zł), with a fine collection of nineteenth-century paintings and intricate wood carvings. South of the Rynek, at ul. Kopernika 15/17, is the **Copernicus Museum** (Tues–Sun 10am–4pm; 10zł), in the brick house where the great man was born, which contains a fascinating model collection of his original instruments. The town's **Planetarium** on ul. Franciszkańska maintains the astrological theme, offering three English language films (daily at 1pm, 3.30pm and 5.30pm) on space exploration. **St John's Cathedral** (Mon–Sat 9am–5.30pm, Sun 2–5.30pm; 2zł/1.50zł), lies at the eastern end of ul. Kopernika, and has a tower offering panoramic views over the city (4zł extra). Further to the northeast lies the **New Town** district, with its opulent commercial residences grouped around the Rynek Nowomiejski.

Arrival and information

Train Toruń Główny, the main railway station, is 2km away south of the river; buses #22 and #27 (every 10min; 1.8zł) both run from outside the station to pl. Rapackiego on the western edge of the Old Town, the first stop after crossing the river.
Bus From the bus station on ul. Dąbrowskiego it is a short walk south to the centre.
Tourist office Rynek Staromiejski 25 ⓣ056/621 0931, ⓦwww.it.torun.pl. Open Mon & Sat 9am–4pm, Tues–Fri 9am–6pm; May–Sept also Sun 9am–1pm.
Internet *Jeremi*, Rynek Staromiejski 33 (10am–11pm).

Accommodation

Dom Turisty PTTK ul. Legionow 24 ⓣ056/622 3855. Simple and clean public hostel; take bus #27 four stops north from the main train station. Dorms ❶
Kopernik ul. Wola Zamkowa 16 ⓣ056/659 7333. This budget hotel offers "student" single/double rooms (open to all) with shared bathroom (❶ per person) and pleasant rooms with TV (❸).
Orange ul. Prosta 19 ⓣ056/652 0033, ⓦwww.hostelorange.pl.The only central hostel with friendly staff and a cosy atmosphere. Dorms ❶, singles/doubles ❷

Eating

Pod Arkadami ul. Rozana 1. Clean, bright Milk Bar with filling soups and potato dishes. Mains 1.50–7zł.
Manekin ul. Wysoka 5. The perfect place for pancake lovers, specializing in innovative meat, veg, and sweet fillings (5–10zł).
Na Plantacji Rynek Staromiejski 23. This central café offers dozens of types of coffee, tea and tasty desserts; don't miss the home-made apple pie. Drinks/desserts 10–15zł.
Oberza ul. Rabianska 9. A cosy restaurant that boasts a farm-house interior and quick, traditional buffet meals. Mains 15zł.

PIERNIKI

You can't leave Toruń without trying the local **pierniki**, or gingerbread, which has been made here since the town was founded. Pierniczek (Zeglarska 25) is a shop offering a mouth-watering if eccentric range.

Drinking and nightlife

Bar Mockba Rynek Staromiejski 22. There's a fun mix of hip-hop and rock in this cellar club on the main square. Cocktails 15–23zł.
Black Rock ul. Zagiarska 9. A rock 'n' roll dive catering for a less touristy crowd. 0.33lt beer 4zł.

Moving on

Train Gdańsk (3 daily; 3hr); Kraków (4 daily; 8hr); Poznań (5 daily; 2hr); Warsaw (10 daily; 3hr); Wrocław (3 daily; 5hr).

Southern Poland

Southern Poland garners more visitors than any other region in the country, and its attractions are clear from a glance at the map. The **Tatra Mountains** that form the border with Slovakia are the most spectacular in the country, snowcapped for much of the year and markedly alpine in feel. The former royal capital of **Kraków** is an architectural gem and the country's intellectual heart. Pope John Paul II was Archbishop here until his election in 1978, but equally important are the city's Jewish roots: before the Holocaust, this was one of Europe's most vibrant Jewish centres. This multi-cultural past echoes in the old district of Kazimierz, and its culmination is starkly enshrined at the death camps of **Auschwitz-Birkenau** 50km west of the city.

KRAKÓW

KRAKÓW was the only major city in Poland to come through World War II essentially undamaged, and its assembly of monuments has since been hailed as one of Europe's most compelling by UNESCO. The city's Old Town (Stare Miasto) swarms with visitors in summer, but retains an atmosphere of fin-de-siècle stateliness, its streets a cavalcade of churches and palaces. A university centre, Kraków has a tangible buzz of arty youthfulness and boasts a dynamic nightlife.

What to see and do

Kraków is bisected by the River Wisła with virtually everything of interest on the north bank. At the heart of the Stare Miasto is the Main Square (Rynek Główny), with the Wawel hill, ancient seat of Poland's kings and Church, and the rejuvenated Kazimierz lying to the south.

The Stare Miasto

The largest square in medieval Europe, the Rynek is now a broad expanse with the vast **Sukiennice** (Cloth Hall) at its centre, ringed by magnificent houses and towering spires. The Sukiennice was rebuilt in the Renaissance and still houses a bustling covered market, with a museum of nineteenth-century Polish art on the upper floor. To its south is the tiny copper-domed **St Adalbert's**, the first church to be founded in Kraków. On the east side is the Gothic **Mariacki Church** (St Mary's; Mon–Sat 11.50am–6pm, Sun 2–6pm; 6zł), the taller of its two towers topped by an amazing ensemble of spires. Inside is the stunning triptych high altar (1477–89), a woodcarving that depicts the Virgin Mary's Quietus among the apostles.

> **THE HEJNAŁ**
>
> Legend has it that during one of the thirteenth-century Tatar raids, a guard watching from the tower of the Mariacki Church saw the invaders approaching and blew his trumpet, only for his alarm to be cut short by an arrow through the throat. Every hour seven local firemen now play the sombre melody (*hejnał*) from the same tower, halting abruptly at the point when the guard is supposed to have been hit.

Czartoryski Palace

A few blocks north of the Rynek on ul. Pijarska is the **Czartoryski Palace**, which, though unimpressive on the outside, houses Kraków's finest art collection (Tues, Thurs & Sun 10am–3.30pm; Weds, Fri & Sat 10am–6pm; 9zł,). Highlights include Rembrandt's brooding *Landscape with Merciful Samaritan* and Leonardo da Vinci's *Lady with an Ermine*, as well as a striking Egyptian exhibition.

The University

West from the Rynek is the university area, whose first element was the fifteenth-century Collegium Maius building, at ul. Jagiellońska 15. Now it's the **University Museum** and is open for guided tours only (☎012/422 0549; Mon, Wed & Fri 10am–3pm; Tues & Thurs 10am–6pm; Sat (free) 10am–2pm; 12zł) – book at least a day in advance. Inside, the ground-floor rooms retain the mathematical and geographical murals once used for the teaching of figures like Copernicus, one of the university's earliest students.

Wawel

For over five hundred years, Wawel Hill was the seat of Poland's monarchy. The original **Cathedral** (Mon–Sat 9am–4pm, Sun 12.30pm–3pm; tombs and bell tower 10zł) was built in 1020, but the present basilica is a fourteenth-century structure, with a crypt that contains the majority of Poland's forty-five monarchs. Their tombs and side chapels are like a directory of European artistic movements, not least the Gothic Holy Cross Chapel and the Renaissance Zygmuntowska chapel. The excellent Cathedral Museum (Tues–Sun, 10am–3pm; 5zł) features a wealth of religious and secular items dating from the thirteenth century, including all manner of coronation robes. Visitor numbers are restricted, so arrive early or book ahead to visit the various sections of **Wawel**

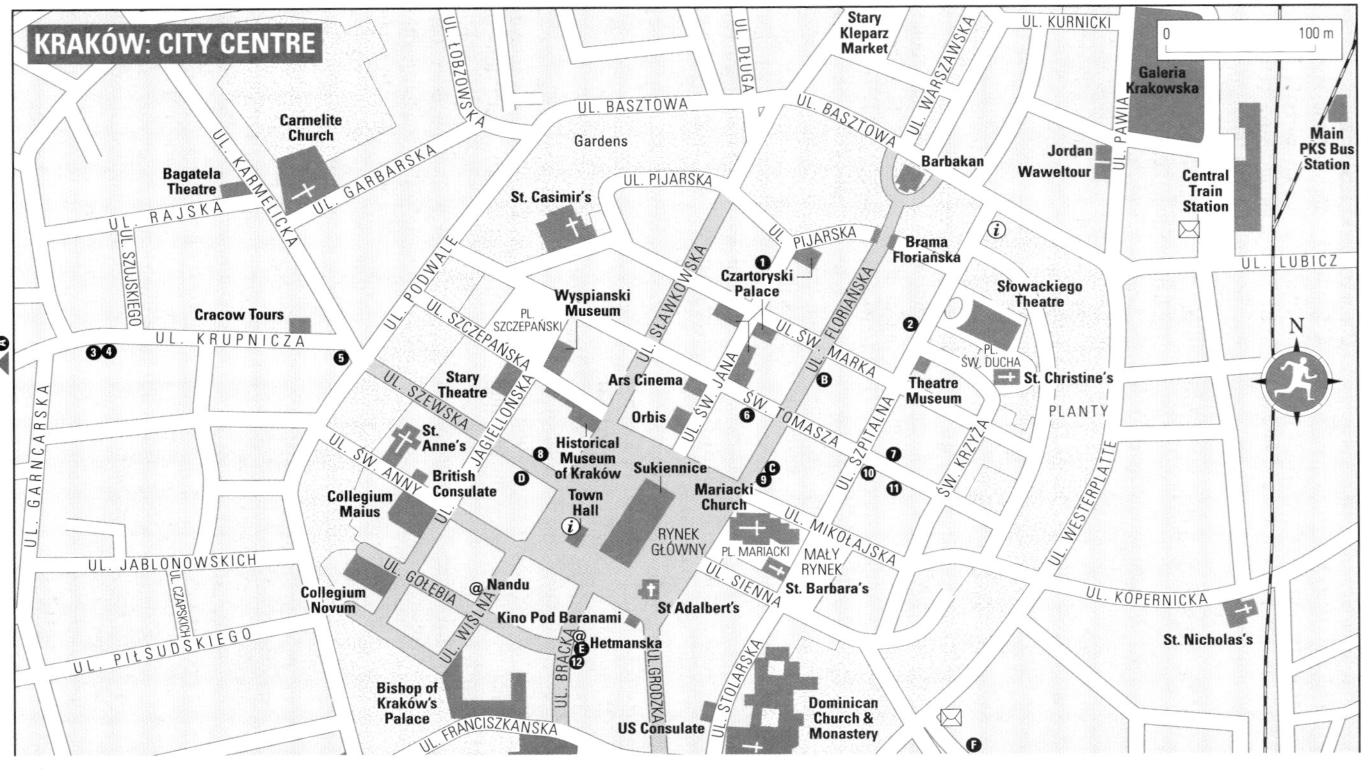
KRAKÓW: CITY CENTRE
0 100 m
N
Stary Kleparz Market
UL. KURNICKI
Galeria Krakowska
UL. PAWIA
Main PKS Bus Station
Central Train Station
Jordan
Waweltour
Barbakan
UL. WARSZAWSKA
UL. BASZTOWA
UL. DŁUGA
UL. ŁOBZOWSKA
Gardens
Carmelite Church
UL. GARBARSKA
UL. KARMELICKA
Bagatela Theatre
UL. RAJSKA
UL. SZUJSKIEGO
UL. PIJARSKA
St. Casimir's
Brama Floriańska
UL. LUBICZ
Słowackiego Theatre
Czartoryski Palace
Wyspianski Museum
PL. SZCZEPAŃSKI
Cracow Tours
UL. KRUPNICZA
UL. PODWALE
UL. SZCZEPAŃSKA
UL. SŁAWKOWSKA
UL. FLORIAŃSKA
UL. ŚW. MARKA
PL. ŚW. DUCHA
St. Christine's
Theatre Museum
PLANTY
Stary Theatre
Ars Cinema
UL. ŚW. JANA
ŚW. TOMASZA
UL. SZPITALNA
ŚW. KRZYŻA
UL. GARNCARSKA
UL. SZEWSKA
St. Anne's
UL. JAGIELLONSKA
Orbis
Historical Museum of Kraków
Sukiennice
Mariacki Church
UL. ŚW. ANNY
British Consulate
Collegium Maius
Town Hall
RYNEK GŁÓWNY
PL. MARIACKI
MAŁY RYNEK
UL. MIKOŁAJSKA
UL. WESTERPLATTE
UL. JABLONOWSKICH
UL. CZAPSKICH
UL. GOŁĘBIA
Nandu
Collegium Novum
Kino Pod Baranami
St Adalbert's
UL. SIENNA
St. Barbara's
UL. KOPERNICKA
St. Nicholas's
UL. PIŁSUDSKIEGO
UL. WIŚLNA
UL. BRACKA
Hetmanska
UL. GRODZKA
UL. STOLARSKA
Bishop of Kraków's Palace
US Consulate
Dominican Church & Monastery
UL. FRANCISZKAŃSKA

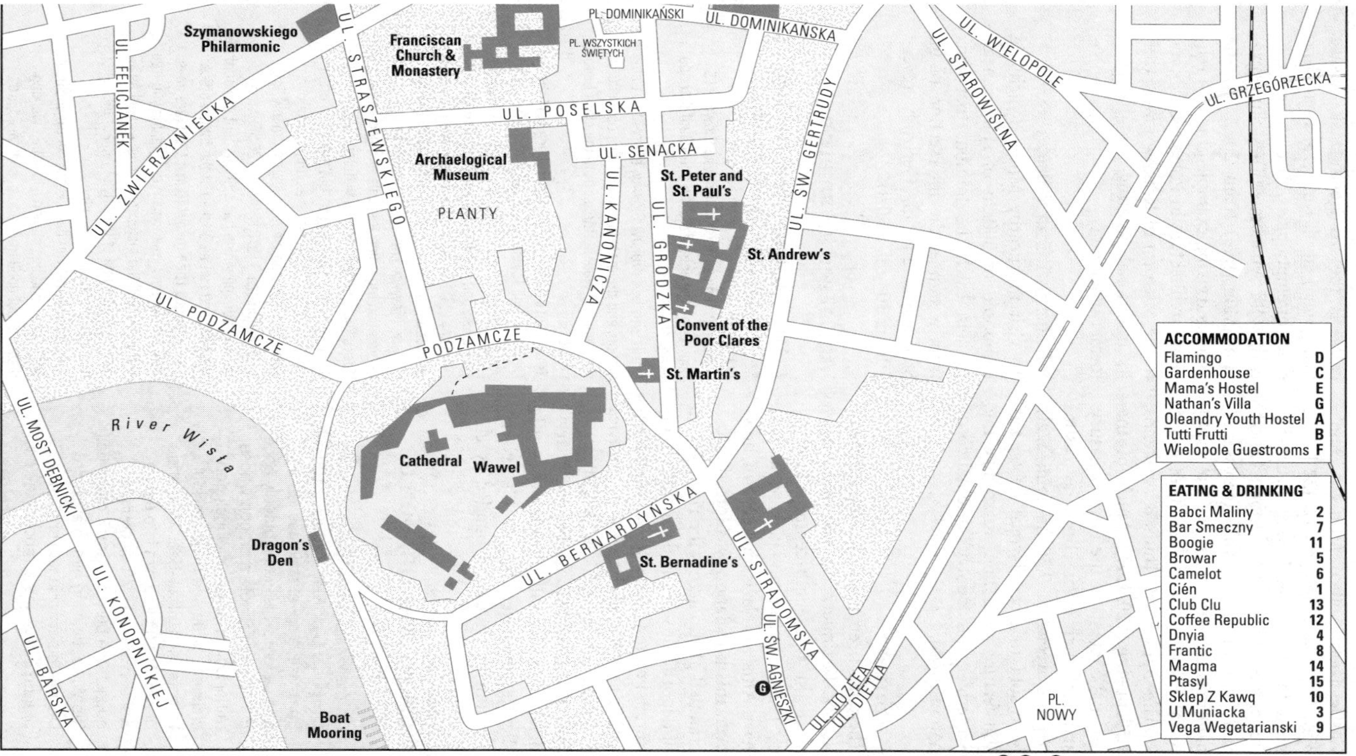
Szymanowskiego Philarmonic
Franciscan Church & Monastery
PL. DOMINIKAŃSKI
PL. WSZYSTKICH ŚWIĘTYCH
UL. DOMINIKAŃSKA
UL. WIELOPOLE
UL. STAROWIŚLNA
UL. GRZEGÓRZECKA
UL. FELICJANEK
UL. ZWIERZYNIECKA
UL. STRASZEWSKIEGO
UL. POSELSKA
UL. SENACKA
Archaelogical Museum
PLANTY
UL. KANONICZA
UL. GRODZKA
St. Peter and St. Paul's
St. Andrew's
UL. ŚW. GERTRUDY
Convent of the Poor Clares
St. Martin's
UL. PODZAMCZE
PODZAMCZE
River Wisła
Cathedral
Wawel
UL. MOST DĘBNICKI
Dragon's Den
UL. BERNARDYŃSKA
St. Bernadine's
UL. STRADOMSKA
UL. ŚW. AGNIESZKI
G
UL. KONOPNICKIEJ
UL. BARSKA
Boat Mooring
UL. JÓZEFA
UL. DIETLA
PL. NOWY
ACCOMMODATION
Flamingo D
Gardenhouse C
Mama's Hostel E
Nathan's Villa G
Oleandry Youth Hostel A
Tutti Frutti B
Wielopole Guestrooms F
EATING & DRINKING
Babci Maliny 2
Bar Smeczny 7
Boogie 11
Browar 5
Camelot 6
Cién 1
Club Clu 13
Coffee Republic 12
Dnyia 4
Frantic 8
Magma 14
Ptasyl 15
Sklep Z Kawq 10
U Muniacka 3
Vega Wegetarianski 9
Kazimierz (250 m) 13, 14 & 15

Castle (ticket office Mon–Sat 9am–3pm, Sun 10am–3pm; ⓣ012/422 1697), including the State Rooms (Tues–Sat 9.30am–3pm, Sun 10am–3pm; 15/8zł, Sun free), furnished with Renaissance paintings and tapestries, and the grand Royal Private Apartments (Tues & Fri 9.30am–5pm; Wed, Thurs & weekends 9.30am–4pm; 20/15zł). Much of the original contents of the Royal Treasury and Armoury (same times as castle, bar the weekend, 9.30am–4pm; 12zł) were sold to pay off royal debts, but still feature some fine works, like the Szczerbiec, the country's original coronation sword.

Kazimierz

There has been a large **Jewish presence** in the Kazimierz district of Kraków since the fourteenth-century, growing by 1939 to accommodate some 65,000 Jews. After the Nazis took control, however, this population was forced into a cramped ghetto across the river. Waves of deportations to the death camps followed, before the ghetto was liquidated in March 1943, ending seven centuries of Jewish life in Kraków. Kazimierz is now a fashionable and bohemian residential district, filled with poignantly silent **synagogues**. Just off Plac Nowy, a colourful square surrounded by chic cafés, is the Synagoga Izaaka (Isaac Synagogue), at ul. Kupa 18, a haunting space of empty pews. At ul. Szeroka 24 is the Old Synagogue (Tues–Sun 9am–5pm, Mon (free) 10am–2pm; 7zł), the oldest surviving example of Jewish religious architecture in Poland and home to the Museum of Kraków Jewry, with its traditional paintings by the area's former inhabitants.

SMOK – THE DRAGON OF KRAKÓW

On the Western side of the hill is the **Dragon's Den** (May–Oct daily 10am–5pm; 3zł), a spiral staircase leading to a cavern. This was reputedly once the home of Smok, a dragon whose rather objectionable diet included children, cattle and unsuccessful knights. Krak, the legendary founder of Kraków, tricked him into eating a sheep stuffed with sulphur; to quench the burning, Smok drank half the Wisła, causing him to explode. Despite his unfortunate end, the dragon is now the symbol of the city.

Wieliczka Salt Mines

To visit the nearby Mines, which are composed of 300km of subterranean tunnels, catch the minibus that runs from a stop at the intersection of ul. Starowilsna and ul. Gertrudy (every 10min; 30 min, 2.50zł).

Arrival and information

Air The Kraków airport is situated 15 km to the west of the city centre. It's easiest to catch the free shuttle bus to the airport's railway station, which has regular trains to Kraków Główny (15 min; 4am–midnight; 4zł). The equivalent taxi ride is 50–60zł.

Train and bus Kraków Główny, the central train station, and the main bus station just opposite, are five minutes' walk northeast from the city's historic centre.

Tourist office The main tourist office is in the Old Town Hall Tower, Rynek Główny 1 (ⓣ012/433 7310). There is also a smaller outlet between the railway station and the Old Town (ul. Szpitalna 25, ⓣ012/432 0062) as well as one in the Kazimierz district (ul. Jozefa 7, ⓣ012/422 0471). Their website (ⓦwww.krakow.pl) provides the latest information regarding festivals and accommodation.

Tours You'll be bombarded with tour offers for the city and surrounding sights, but these are often rushed and cost four times as much as public transport. If you do want a tour, try Cracow Tours at ul. Krupnicza 3 (ⓣ012/430 0726, ⓦwww.cracowtours.pl) which has a 50 percent discount for students and can be booked at the tourist office.

Tourist card The Kraków Tourist Card (2/3 days, 50/65zł; ⓦwww.krakowcard.com) gains you free entrance to all the major museums, as well as discounts at some of the pricier restaurants, shops and tour providers in the city.

City transport Everything in the centre, including the railway and bus stations, is within walking distance but good tram and bus services are also available. Single tickets cost 2.50zł, but you can also buy tickets for an hour (3.10zł) or 1/2/3 days (10.40/18.50/25zł) that will give you a good discount if you are staying in one of the outlying hostels.

Accommodation

The number of hostels has mushroomed in the last few years, but it is still worth booking ahead if you want to stay in the most central spots. All hostels bar the YHA have free Internet, breakfast and cheap laundry services.

Flamingo ul. Szewska 4 ☎012/422 0000, Ⓦwww.flamingo-hostel.com. A clean, colourful place with a lively party crowd. Dorms ❷, singles/doubles ❸

Gardenhouse ul. Florianska 5 ☎012/431 2824, Ⓦwww.gardenhousehostel.com. A hostel made for those seeking a relaxed ambience, with airy dorm rooms and a quiet courtyard just off the Rynek. Dorms ❷, doubles ❹

Mama's Hostel ul. Bracka 4 ☎012/429 5940, Ⓦwww.mamashostel.com.pl. This chilled-out hangout comes with friendly staff and has a great position above the Bracka cafe scene. Bring earplugs for the club downstairs. Dorms ❷

Nathan's Villa Sw. Agnieszki 1 ☎012/422 3545, Ⓦwww.nathansvilla.com. The popular Villa has a bar, cinema and handy location between Stare Miasto and Kazimierz. Dorms ❷

Oleandry Youth Hostel ul. Oleandry 4 ☎012/633 8822. Lying out west by the University, this place is only 15min walk from the centre but comes with a midnight curfew. Dorms ❶

Tutti Frutti ul. Florianska 29 ☎012/428 0028, Ⓦwww.tuttifruttihostel.com. This welcoming hostel does the basics (especially breakfast) very well and also provides guides for guests seeking the best places to go out. Dorms ❷

TREAT YOURSELF

Wielopole Guestrooms, ul. Wielopole 3 ☎012/421 4865. Do you feel like finding somewhere peaceful, away from hostel parties and busy city streets? Try this stylish hotel, which is ideally poised between the Old Town and Kazimierz and where you'll find spacious but cosy apartments, satellite TV and free internet access. Singles/Doubles with breakfast ❺/❽

Eating

Kraków's centre is renowned for its **bars**, **restaurants** and **cafés** which offer much beyond the Polish culinary staples. For best-value head to Kazimierz or the student quarter to the west of the Old Town.

Milk bars

Babci Maliny, ul. Szpitalna 38. This upmarket milk bar has a mountain hut interior and provides suitably wholesome Polish classics. Mains 7–15zł.

Bar Smeczny ul. Tomasza 24. A cheap central canteen that specializes in quick, if unexciting meals. Mains 2–7zł.

Vega Wegatarianski ul. Krupnicza 20. Inexpensive but innovative veggie dishes are on offer here; think tofu, beans and lots of greens. Mains 5–10zł.

Cafés and restaurants

Camelot ul. Tomasza 15. A chic café with western newspapers and excellent desserts, including the best apple pie (8zł) in town.

Coffee Republic ul. Bracka 4. A smart central place that can feed any cravings for Western-style coffee(4–7zł).

Dnyia ul. Krupnicza 20. The city's most stylish student hangout has some delicious smoothies (6zł) and a "fitness menu" (12–17zł) for the diet-conscious.

Magma ul. Szeroka 3. Check out this lively mix of a busy bar scene with a refined menu, including some traditional Jewish options. Mains 15–25zł.

Sklep z kawq: Pozegnanie z Afryka ul. Tomasza 21. Had enough of terrible coffees while on the road? Then head to this fabulously old-fashioned café, which has an array of exotic coffee-bean varieties. Drinks and cakes 5–13zł.

Drinking and nightlife

Bars

Boogie ul. Tomasza 26. The home of many a sophisticated city slicker; there's live jazz on Thursdays. Cocktails 18–30zł.

Browar ul. Podwale 6. A German-style beer hall serving homemade *piwo*, including an intriguing ginger brew. 0.5lt beer 5–7zł.

Ptasyl ul. Szeroka 10/2. This hole in the wall pub is within crawling distance of Kazimierz's clubs and restaurants. 0.5lt beer 3–7zł.

Clubs

Cien ul. Jana 15. House music packs this place out with a lively late-teenage crowd. Cocktails 11–17zł.

Club Clu ul. Szeroka 10/2. Cellar club with chart dance tunes in the heart of Kazimierz. Cocktails 8–17zł.
Frantic ul. Szewska 5. With two dancefloors, there's plenty of space here for grooving to a mix of R'n'B and old school hits. Cocktails 10–20zł.
U Muniacka ul. Florianska 3. The city's best live jazz from 9.30pm every night. 0.33l Beer 5zł.

Entertainment

Cinema

Cinema tickets are 12–15zł throughout the city.
Ars Sw. Jana 6 ☎012/421 4199. Offers the latest blockbusters, though don't expect all of them to be in English.
Kino Pod Baranami Rynek Główny 27 ☎012/423 0768. Offers a range of avant-garde Western, Polish, and Bollywood titles.

KRAKÓW'S FESTIVALS

Hardly a month passes in Kraków without some cultural celebration taking over the streets. Highlights include the Jewish Culture Festival (June/July), which culminates in an open-air concert of international Jewish musicians on ul. Szeroka, and the lively Summer Jazz Festival (July/August).

Shopping

Arts and crafts Touristy Florianska and the boutiques in the Rynek contain a few bargain art dealers amongst the overpriced souvenirs. Kazimierz is filled with reasonably-priced galleries and secondhand shops and, on Sundays, Plac Nowy becomes a colourful flea market of cheap clothes and jewellery.
Clothes and food For a western "mall experience", head for Galleria Krakówska (Mon–Sat 9am–10pm, Sun 10am–9pm), just next to the railway station. It has all the fashionable Western brands that you could wish for, in addition to a large Albert Supermarket.

Directory

Embassies and consulates US Stolarska 9 ☎012/424 5100, ⓦpoland.usembassy.gov; UK Sw. Anny 9 ☎012/421 7030, ⓦwww.britishembassy.gov.uk.
Exchange To avoid the large commission charged at the banks, look around the "Kantor" exchanges that fill the streets around the Rynek for the best rates.
Hospital Krakówski Szpital Specjalistyczny, Pradnicka 80 (☎012/614 2000, ⓦwww.szpitaljp2.krakow.pl).
Internet Cafés are common all over the centre and generally charge 5zł/hour. Two slightly cheaper places are: Nandu, ul. Wiślna 6, 8am–11pm (4zł/hour; 2zł between 8–10am); Hetmanska, ul. Bracka 4 (24hr; 3zł/hour).
Laundry The Stare Miasto has no laundrettes, but Anytime Hostel (ul. Estery 16, ☎012/432 3070, ⓦwww.anytime.com.pl) allows non-guests to use their facilities (5zł per kg).
Left luggage The railway station has a left-luggage depot (6am–10pm, 8zł for 24 hours.)
Pharmacies Euro Apteka, ul. Krowoderska 31 (24hr; ☎012/430 0035).
Post office Ul. Westerplatte 20.

Moving on

Air Kraków's John Paul II International Airport has regular connections to most Western European hubs, as well as Warsaw (6 daily; 1hr).
Train Gdańsk (7 daily; 9hr); Poznań (9 daily; 7hr); Oświęcim/Auschwitz (5 daily, 1hr 30min); Toruń (2 daily; 7hr 30min); Warsaw (22 daily; 2–3hr on Intercity, 4–6hr on others); Wrocław (13 daily; 5hr); Zakopane (13 daily; 4hr).
Bus Oświęcim (15 daily; 1hr 40min) or quicker minibuses (18 daily, 1hr 15min); Zakopane (every 20min; 2.5 hr). Eurolines (ⓦwww.eurolines.pl) runs services to all major European capitals from near the main station at ul. Bosacka 18.

OŚWIĘCIM (AUSCHWITZ-BIRKENAU)

A visit to the Auschwitz camps provides a fascinating, if emotional, day-trip from Kraków. In 1940, **OŚWIĘCIM**, a small town 70km west of Kraków, became the site of the Oświęcim-Brzezinka concentration camp, better known by its German name of **Auschwitz-Birkenau**. Of the many camps built by the Nazis, this was the largest and most horrific: something approaching two million people, 85 percent of them Jews, died here. You can join a tour (4 daily in English at 10am, 11.30am, 1pm, 3pm;

GETTING TO AUSCHWITZ

You can catch one of the regular buses (15 daily; 1hr 40min, 7zł) to the main camp from Kraków's PKS Terminal. There's an hourly shuttle-bus service to the Birkenau section from the car park at Auschwitz from April–October; taxis are also available, otherwise it's a 3km walk.

26zł) but a detailed guidebook (4zł) is just as helpful.

Most of the Auschwitz buildings have been preserved as the **Museum of Martyrdom** (daily: June–Aug 8am–7pm; May & Sept 8am–6pm; Oct & April 8am–5pm; March & Nov to mid-Dec 8am–4pm; mid-Dec to Feb 8am–3pm; free; Ⓦ www.auschwitz-muzeum.oswiecim.pl). The bulk of the camp consists of the prison cell blocks, with the first section dedicated to "exhibits" found in the camp after liberation: rooms full of clothes and suitcases, toothbrushes, glasses, shoes and a gruesome mound of women's hair. Other barracks are given over to national memorials, and the blocks terminate with the gas chambers and the ovens where the bodies were incinerated.

Birkenau

The huge Birkenau camp (same hours) is less visited, though it was here that the majority of executions took place. Birkenau was designed purely as a death camp, and the huge gas chambers at the back of the camp were damaged but not destroyed by the fleeing Nazis in 1945. Victims arrived in closed trains on the platform, where those who were fit to work (around twenty-five percent) were separated from those who were driven straight to the gas chambers. The railway line is still there, just as the Nazis abandoned it. Allow 1–2 hours to fully explore the 175-hectare site.

ZAKOPANE AND THE TATRAS

Some 80km long, with peaks of up to 2500m, **the Tatras** are the most spectacular part of the mountain range extending along Poland's border with Slovakia. The main base for skiing and hiking on the Polish side is the popular resort of **Zakopane**. There are good road and rail links with Kraków, which lies 60km to the north, as well as several mountain resorts across the border in Slovakia.

What to see and do

Skiing here is cheap, with the premier slopes of Kasprowy Wierch just a few minutes out of town, and plenty of places in the centre to rent equipment. **Hikers** may want to avoid the 9km path to the lovely but busy Morskie Oko lake in high season, but there's no shortage of other, more secluded trails. Świat, at ul. Zamoyskiego 12 (Ⓣ018/201 3199, Ⓦwww.swiat.biz.pl), organizes **rafting** tours (with English-speaking guides) on the nearby Dunajec River. Zakopane's **market** at the bottom of ul. Krupówki sells a wide range of traditional local goods, including *oscypek* (smoked sheep's cheese, 7zł) and small woodcarvings (50zł plus). This latter local tradition is intriguingly displayed in the whimsical wooden tombs of the nearby Stary Cementarz (Old Cemetery).

Arrival and information

Train and bus Both stations are a ten-minute walk east of the pedestrianised main street, ul. Krupówki.
Tourist office Just west of the stations at ul. Kościuszki 17 (8am–8pm; Ⓦwww.zakopane.pl). Helpful with accommodation.
Hiking information The Tatra National Park Information Centre, near the park entrance at ul. Chałubińskiego 44 (daily 9am–3pm; Ⓣ018/206 3799), provides good-quality maps and information on routes.
Internet Orion, ul. Krupówki 34a (9am–midnight; 4.50zł/hr).

Accommodation

Finding a place to stay is rarely a problem in Zakopane as, in addition to the hostels, many homeowners in town offer private rooms.

Dom Turisty PTTK ul. Zarowskiego 5 ⓣ018/206 3281. A basic but clean public hostel. Dorms ❶

Goodbye Lenin ul. Chlabowka 44 ⓣ018/2001330, ⓦwww.goodbyelenin.pl. Near the National Park entrance, this hostel has excellent facilities and free transport to the bus station. Dorms ❷

Hotel Fian ul.Chałubińskiego 38 ⓣ018/201 5071, ⓦwww.fian.pl. With a sauna and jacuzzi to ease hiking aches, this place also prides itself on the "gastronomic experience" offered by its resident Polish chef. singles/doubles with satellite TV and breakfast ❸/❹

Stara Polona ul. Nowostarska 59 ⓣ018/206 8902, ⓦwww.starapolana.pl. Warm wood-panelled interior, satellite TV, and friendly service make this hostel excellent value. Dorms ❶

Eating and drinking

Genesis Pl. Niepodleglości 1. The town's lager-and-lasers type club attracts Poland's top DJ's at weekends. 9pm–5am daily; 5zł cover on Fri & Sat.

Mala Szwajcarla ul. Zamoyskiego 11. A refined, quiet Swiss restaurant with delicious fondues for two (30–40zł).

Owczarnia ul. Galicy 4. Giant grilled steaks, *kielbasa* and local trout are the specialities in this lively grill-house. Mains 15–30zł.

Paparazzi ul. Galicy 8. This chic cocktail bar has some leafy outdoor seating and fruity drinks (12–19zł).

Moving on

Train Gdańsk (2 daily; 12hr); Kraków (15 daily; 3–4hr); Poznań (1 daily; 11hr); Toruń (1 daily; 12hr 30min); Warsaw (2 daily; 8hr).

Bus Kraków (every 30min, 6am–8pm; 3hr; better-value than the train) leaves from the PKS Terminal.

To Slovakia There are 2 daily buses to Propad (2hr, 16zł), a Slovakian skiing and hiking centre. In summer, head to Oravice (2 daily; 1 hr, 11zł) and Liprowski Mikulas (2 daily; 1.5 hr, 17zł) both of which have famous aquaparks.

Silesia and Wielkopolska

In Polish it's Śląsk, in Czech Sleszko and in German Schlesien: all three countries have at one time or another claimed **Silesia** as their own, but most of the disputed province now lies within Poland's southwestern region. Silesia's main city, **Wrocław**, is the focus of Poland's new economic dynamism. To the north, the region known as **Wielkopolska** straddles the western border with Germany and also forms the core of the original Polish nation. Its chief interest is supplied by the vibrant and prosperous city of **Poznań**.

WROCŁAW

WROCŁAW (pronounced "vrots-wav") is a city used to rebuilding. Through centuries of regularly changing ownership it was largely dominated by Germans and known as Breslau, but this altered after the war, as thousands of displaced Poles moved to the decimated city. The various influences are reflected in Wrocław's architecture, with its mammoth Germanic churches, Flemish-style mansions and Baroque palaces. The latest rebuilding came after a catastrophic flood in the early 1990s, which left most of the centre underwater. Fortunately, the energy involved in the reconstruction that followed has left the airy Old Town rejuvenated and without the tourist mobs of Kraków.

What to see and do

Wrocław's centre is delineated by the River Odra to the north and the bow-shaped ul. Podwale – the latter following the former city walls, whose moat is now bordered by a shady park.

The Rynek

In the town centre is the vast **Rynek** and the thirteenth-century Town Hall with its magnificently ornate facades.

The hall is now the Historical Museum (Wed–Sun 10/11am–5/6pm; 10zł). In the northwest corner of the Rynek are two curious Baroque houses known as Jaś i Małgosia (Hansel and Gretel), linked by a gateway giving access to St Elizabeth's, the finest of Wrocław's churches. Its ninety-metre tower (Mon–Sat 11am–4pm, Sun 1–4pm; 5zł) is the city's most prominent landmark.

Jewish quarter

Southwest of the Rynek lies the former **Jewish quarter**, whose inhabitants were driven from their tenements during the Third Reich. One of the largest synagogues in Poland, the Synagoga pod Białym Bocianem (Mon–Fri 10am–4pm; 4zł), lies hidden in a courtyard at ul. Włodkowica 9.

The Racławice Panorama and the National Museum

To the east, a rotunda houses Wrocław's best-known sight, the **Panorama of the Battle of Racławice** (Tues–Sun 9am–4pm; shows every 30min but expect queues; 20zł, including entrance to the National Museum). This painting – 120m long and 15m high – was commissioned in 1894 for the centenary of the Russian army's defeat by Tadeusz Kościuszko's militia at Racławice, a village near Kraków. You can visit the nearby National Museum (Wed–Sun 9/10am–4/6pm; 15zł, Thurs free), with its fun and colourful exhibition of twentieth-century Polish installation artists like Jozef Szajna.

University quarter

North of the Rynek is the historic and buzzing **university quarter**, full of bargain eateries and tiny bookshops. At its centre is the huge Collegium Maximum, whose Aula Leopoldina assembly hall, upstairs at Pl. Uniwersytecki 1 (Mon, Tues & Thurs 10.30am–3.30pm, Fri–Sun 11am–5pm; 4zł), is one of the greatest secular interiors of the Baroque age, fusing architecture, painting, sculpture and ornament into one bravura whole.

Wyspa Piasek and Ostrów Tumski

From the Market Hall, the Piaskowy Bridge leads to the island of **Wyspa Piasek** and the fourteenth-century hall church of St Mary of the Sands, with its majestically vaulted ceiling. Two elegant little bridges connect Wyspa Piasek with Ostrów Tumski, the city's ecclesiastical heart. Ul. Katedralny leads past several Baroque palaces to the vast and gloomy Cathedral of St John the Baptist, which was rebuilt after the war: take the lift up the tower (Mon–Sat 10am–5.30pm, Sun 2–4pm; 4zł) for panoramic views of the city.

Arrival and information

Air Take bus #406 to the railway station from the airport (30min, 2zł). The equivalent taxi ride costs more than 50zł.

Train The main train station, Wrocław Główny, faces the broad boulevard of ul. Piłsudskiego, about fifteen minutes' walk south of the Rynek.

Bus The main station is just to the south of the railway station.

Tourist office Rynek 14 (daily: May–Aug 10am–9pm, Sept–April 10am–6pm; ⓣ071/344 3111, ⓦwww.wroclaw.pl). Books accommodation.

Internet Inter Media H@use, ul. Kazimierza Wielkiego 17 (10am–6pm; 3zł/hr).

Accommodation

Hostels

Cinnamon ul. Kazimierza Wielkiego 67 ⓣ071/344 5858, ⓦwww.cinnamonhostel.com. Pleasant, airy rooms and friendly staff make this spice-themed hostel a winner. Dorms ❷

Mleczarnia ul. Wlodkowicva 5 ⓣ071/787 7570, ⓦwww.mleczarniahostel.pl. This is a comfortable, bohemian hangout, situated above a candlelit coffee bar. Dorms ❷; doubles and apartments ❹

Nathan's Villa ul. Swidnicka 13 ⓣ071/344 1095, ⓦwww.nathansvilla.com. This hostel has clean dorms and all the mod cons. Dorms ❷

Stranger ul. Kollataja 16/3 ⓣ071/344 1206, ⓦwww.strangerhostel.com. Close to railway station and with an excellent "media hub"– including Xbox games, 200 DVDs and a giant couch – "Stranger" is also noisy and can get crowded. Dorms ❷

Szkolne Schronisko Mlodziezowe ul. Kollataja

20 ☎071/343 8856. You'll meet with surly service here and there is no internet access or breakfast, but it does have decent dorms and is half the price of the "Stranger" opposite. Dorms ❶

Hotel

Savoy Pl. Koscuiszki 19 ☎071/3403219, Ⓦwww.savoy.wroc.pl. With a TV and bathroom included, these are the best budget hotel rooms in town, though Internet access and breakfast are extra. Singles/doubles ❹

Eating

Milk bars and cafés

Mercers Pl. Solny 20. Upmarket coffee place that also does nice fruit smoothies and salads (all 6–12zł).

Mis ul. Kuznicza 48. A milk bar that provides quick, filling grub for the student crowd. Mains 1–5zł.

Restaurants

Kuchnia Marche ul. Swidnicka 53. The excellent range of international cuisine makes you forget the canteen atmosphere. Mains 4–25zł.

Pod II Strusiem ul. Ruska 61. Set in a rejuvenated former lavatory, this place dishes out some exotic pizza options. Try the "curry" variety. Pizzas 7–20zł.

TREAT YOURSELF

A meal at the renowned **JaDka restaurant** on ul. Rzeznicza 24/5 is never going to be the cheapest (though some classics like *pierogi* come in at only 20zł), but you can be assured of world-class Polish cuisine and excellent service. Make it an evening of high culture by watching some modern international drama at the Teatr Wspolczesny opposite at ul. Rzeznicza 12 (☎071/358 8900).

Drinking and nightlife

Bezsennosc ul. Ruska 51. Just ten minutes away from the Rynek, this graffiti-lined cellar resounds to a fun mix of electronic and reggae tunes. Cocktails 12–17zł.

Daytona Rynek 35-7. The pick of the popular but pricey clubs on the Rynek. Bloody Mary 18zł.

Paparazzi ul. Reznicza 32/3. A favourite with city workers, this bar has a top range of cocktails (15–21zł) and multicultural cuisine, including Argentinian steaks (45zł).

Rej's Pub ul. Kotlarska 32a. This unassuming little student pub has the best-value beer in town at 0.5lt for 3–5zł. noon–1am.

Moving on

Air Wrocław airport (☎071/358 1100, Ⓦwww.airport.wroclaw.pl) currently serves 4 airports in the UK and 3 in Ireland (the normal low-cost-carrier havens) as well as Germany and Italy.

Train Gdańsk (4 daily; 7–8hr); Kraków (14 daily; 5hr); Poznań (2 per hour; 2hr); Toruń (3 daily; 5hr); Warsaw (9 daily; 6hr).

POZNAŃ

Thanks to its position on the Berlin–Warsaw–Moscow rail line, **POZNAŃ** is many visitors' first taste of Poland. Long identified as the cradle of Polish nationhood, today it's an economically dynamic city with stunning architectural diversity. For seven centuries the Stary Rynek, now lined with attractive bars and restaurants, has been the hub of town life.

What to see and do

The sixteenth-century **Town Hall** that dominates the Rynek boasts a striking eastern façade which frames a frieze of notable Polish monarchs. Inside is the **Poznań Historical Museum** (Mon, Tues & Fri 10am–4pm, Wed noon–6pm, Sun 10am–3pm; 5.5zł), worth visiting for the Renaissance Great Hall on the first floor. Many a medieval and Renaissance interior lurks behind the Baroque façades of the houses lining the Stary Rynek. West of here, at al. Marcinkowskiego 9, the excellent **National Museum** (Tues–Sat 9/10am–4/6pm; 10zł, free Sat) houses one of Poland's premier collections of old master paintings. East of the Stary Rynek, a bridge crosses to the quiet holy island of **Ostrów Tumski**, which is towered over by the **Cathedral of SS Peter and Paul**. Most of this cathedral, the country's oldest, was restored to its Gothic shape after wartime devastation. Poland's first two monarchs are buried in the crypt.

Arrival and information

Air Poznań's airport is 7km west of the Stare Miasto (Old Town) and is served by buses #59 & 77 (30min, 3zł) running from the Rondo Kaponiera, just north of the railway station. The ten-minute taxi ride from the airport will cost you 20zł.
Train The main railway station, Poznań Główny, is 2km southwest of the historic quarter; trams # 5 & 9 run from the western exit on ul Glogowska beyond platform 7 to the city centre.
Bus The PKS Terminal is a 15min walk south from the Stary Rynek, at the intersection of ul. Ratajczaka and ul. Krolowej Jadwigi.
Tourist information ul. Ratajczka 44 (Mon–Fri 10am–7pm, Sat 10am–5pm). There is also a handy Provincial Tourist Office on the Stary Rynek at no. 59/60 (open June–Sept & Oct–May: Mon–Fri 9am–5/6pm, Sat 10am–2/4pm).
The Poznań Card (30zł/40zł/45zł for 1/2/3 days), available at the tourist offices. This handy card buys you free trips on the city's buses and trams, free entry into the major museums and discounts at several restaurants.
Public transport Poznań's public transport works on a timed basis; a 10 min (1.30zł) ticket should be adequate for any travel within the centre.

Accommodation

The city's trade fairs, which take place throughout the year (July and August excepted), can cause hotel prices to double, so always book ahead.
Dizzy Daisy Al. Niepodległości 26 ⓣ061/829 3902, ⓦwww.hostel.pl. The town's summer hostel offers dorms with standard facilities and a friendly atmosphere from July to August. Dorms ❶
Frolic Goats ul. Wrocławska 16/6 (entry at ul. Jaskolcza) ⓣ061/852 4411, ⓦwww.frolicgoatshostel.com. This unassuming central hostel (which has no sign) has all the facilities a backpacker could need. Free Internet access and breakfast are included. Dorms ❷
Szkolne no.3, ul. Berwińskiego 2/3 ⓣ061/866 4040. This small public hostel has Spartan rooms and a 10pm curfew. It lies 500m south from the railway station along ul. Glogowska. Dorms ❶

Hotels

Lech Sw. Marcin 74 ⓣ061/853 0151 ⓦwww.hotel-lech.poznan.pl. This reasonably-priced hotel-and-restaurant is in a great location and has some particularly good deals for students. If you carry an ISIC card, you get a half-price deal on the spacious singles/doubles with TV and showers. ❺/❼

Eating and drinking

Milk bars

Pod Kuchcikiem Sw. Marcin 75. This canteen provides classic milk bar grub alongside some nice salads and milkshakes. Mains 1.30–5zł.
Ghiacci Stary Browar (2nd floor), ul. Polwiejska 42. This café is located in an expensive shopping centre that's sure to lighten your wallet, but the sumptuous ice-cream recipes – including an array of "Spaghetti" varieties – make the outlay well worthwhile. Ice creams 18–30zł.
Spaghetti Bar Piccolo ul. Rynkowa 1. The buffet here comprises simple but tasty spaghetti dishes that are hot and ready as you enter. Mains 3–5zł.

Restaurants

Cafe Ptasie Radio, ul. Kosciuszki 74. A favourite with the arty elite, this sophisticated and cosy café provides cheesy pasta dishes and salads. Mains 10–18zł.
Piwnica Murna ul.Murna 3a. The hearty portions of beer and steak served here fit the hunting lodge décor. Mains 15–45zł.

Drinking and nightlife

Brovaria Stary Rynek 73. This bar in the Rynek is predictably pricey, but the home-made *piwo* makes a trip to the bar irresistible. 0.5lt Mulled honey beer 8zł.
Browar Pub Skowdonia Stary Browar (2nd floor), ul. Polwiejska 42. The most exclusive club in town (20zł admission), which attracts the more stylish local clubbers. Cocktails 15–28zł.
Klub Pod Minoga ul. Feliksa Nowowiejskiego 8. This club has karaoke hours every night if you are desperate for a sing-song.
Zamkowa ul. Zamkowa 5. The pick of the central discos, providing a mix of the latest dance and hip-hop tunes to a predominantly tourist crowd. Cocktails 13–18zł.

Moving on

Air Warsaw (8 daily; 1hr). Poznań has international services to 7 UK airports and several others in Germany and France.
Train Gdańsk (4 daily; 5hr); Kraków (8 daily; 7hr); Toruń (6 daily; 2hr 30min); Warsaw (2 every hour; 3–4hr); Wrocląw (2 daily; 3hr).

Portugal

HIGHLIGHTS ✪

PORT WINE LODGES, PORTO: numerous lodges here offer free tours and tastings
THE DOURO RAIL ROUTE: beautifully scenic line along the foot of the steep Douro river valley
QUIEMA DAS FITAS, COIMBRA: join in this university town's renowned end-of-term celebrations in May
ENJOY A NIGHT OUT IN LISBON: check out the Bairro Alto and dance till dawn
THE ALGARVE BEACHES: the Ilha de Tavira has some of the best

ROUGH COSTS

DAILY BUDGET Basic €40/occasional treat €60

DRINK Vinho verde €8 a bottle

FOOD Arroz marisco (rice and seafood stew) €8

HOSTEL/BUDGET HOTEL €15/€20

TRAVEL bus: Porto–Lisbon (314km) 3hr 30min–4hr 30min, €16; train: Lisbon–Faro (297km) 3hr 15min–6hr 30min, €18

FACT FILE

POPULATION 10.6 million

AREA 92,391 sq km

LANGUAGE Portuguese

CURRENCY Euro (€)

CAPITAL Lisbon (population: 564,500)

INTERNATIONAL PHONE CODE ⓣ351

Basics

Portugal has always been influenced by the sea and the Portuguese are very conscious of themselves as a seafaring race; mariners like Vasco da Gama led the way in the exploration of Africa and the Americas, and until thirty years ago Portugal remained a colonial power.

Scenically, the most interesting parts of the country are in the north: the **Minho**, green, damp, and often startling in its rural customs; and the sensational gorge and valley of the **Douro**, followed along its course by the railway, off which antiquated branch lines edge into remote **Trás-os-Montes**. For contemporary interest, spend some time in both **Lisbon** and **Porto**, the two major cities. And if it's monuments you're after, head to the centre of the country – above all, **Coimbra** and **Évora** – which retains a faded grandeur. The coast is virtually continuous beach, and apart from the **Algarve** and a few pockets around Lisbon and Porto, resorts remain low-key. Perhaps the loveliest are along the northern **Costa Verde** or, for isolation, the wild beaches of southern **Alentejo**.

CHRONOLOGY

219 BC The Romans capture the Iberian Peninsula from the Carthaginians, taking the settlement of "Portus Cale" in the process.
711 The Islamic Moors take control of large parts of present-day Portugal.
868 Establishment of the First County of Portugal, within the Kingdom of León.
1095 Crusaders help Portuguese to defeat the Moors.
1139 Afonso I, of the Burgundy dynasty, declares himself King of an independent Portugal.
1386 The Treaty of Windsor, the oldest diplomatic alliance in the world, is signed between England and Portugal securing mutual military support.
1400s Portugal builds up a large empire with colonies across the world including Mozambique, Goa and Brazil.
1580 During a succession crisis, Philip II of Spain invades and crowns himself Philip I of Portugal.
1703 After a trade treaty with England, port wine becomes popular internationally.
1755 An enormous earthquake destroys much of the capital city Lisbon.
1822 Brazil declares independence from Portugal.
1916 Portugal joins WWI on the side of the Allies.
1926 Military coup, led by Antonio de Oliveira Salazar, sweeps control of the country; he remains in power until 1968.
1939 Portugal remains neutral during WWII.
1974 Government overthrown in a near bloodless coup.
1976 First free election are held.
1986 Portugal joins the European Community.
1975 Independence is granted to all Portuguese African colonies.
2007 Mass demonstrations against Portuguese Government's economic reforms.

ARRIVAL

Portugal's three international **airports** are in Faro, Lisbon and Porto. Faro and Lisbon in particular are well-linked to the rest of Europe by the budget airlines, with services to and from Faro increasing during summer. **Bus** is the quickest and most convenient method of overland transport from Spain, particularly if you are arriving from the south of Spain. Common daily routes include Sevilla–Faro, Sevilla–Lisbon and Madrid–Lisbon. **Trains** are less convenient, often involving changes. Madrid–Lisbon via Cáceres (daily) is the main route; another possible route is Badajoz–Lisbon, with a change at Entroncamento (daily, except Sun).

GETTING AROUND

CP (Ⓦwww.cp.pt) operates the **trains**, which are generally reasonably priced, especially suburban services from Porto and Lisbon. Those designated *Regionais* stop at most stations. *Intercidades* are twice as fast and twice as expensive, and must be reserved. The fastest and most luxurious are the *Rápidos* (known as "Alfa"), which speed between Lisbon, Coimbra and Porto. **InterRail passes** are valid, though supplements must be paid on *Intercidades* and *Rápidos*. You can check timetables online or call the information line on ⓣ808 20 82 08. The **bus** network, made up of many regional companies, is more comprehensive and services are often faster, while for long journeys buses can also be cheaper than trains. On a number of major routes (particularly Lisbon–Algarve) express coaches can knock hours off standard multiple-stop bus journeys; Rede Expressos (Ⓦwww.rede-expressos.pt) is the largest bus operator – see website for timetables for most major routes. For 24hr national bus information call ⓣ707 22 33 44. **Cycling** is popular, though there are few facilities and little respect from motorists. In the north and centre of the country the terrain is rather hilly, flattening out south of Lisbon. Bikes can be transported on any *Regional* or *Interregional* train for €1.50–2.50 (free if the bike is dismantled) as long as there is space. Bus companies' policies vary so enquire before travelling.

ACCOMMODATION

In almost any town you should be able to find **accommodation** in a single room for under €25 and a double for under €50. The main budget stand-bys are **pensions**, or *pensões*. A three-star *pensão* is usually about the same price as a one-star **hotel**. Seaside resorts invariably offer cheaper **rooms** (*quartos*) in private houses. Tourist offices have lists. At the higher end of the scale are **pousadas** (Ⓦwww.pousadas.pt). These charge at least four-star hotel prices, and are often converted from old monasteries or castles.

There are over 40 Youth **Hostels** (*Pousadas de Juventude*; Ⓦwww.pousadasjuventude.pt); most stay open all year and some impose a curfew (usually midnight). All require a valid HI card, which can be purchased from the hostelling association in your home country before departure. For details see Ⓦwww.hihostels.com. Alternatively, hostels in Portugal can provide you with a guest card, which must be stamped every night that you stay, for a charge of €2 per stamp. After you receive five stamps, you are a fully paid-up member of Hostelling International. A dormitory bed costs €9–16, depending on season and location; doubles cost €22–45. Breakfast is always included. Portugal has around 200 **campsites**, most small, low-key and attractively located, and all remarkably inexpensive – you'll rarely pay more than €5 a person. You can get a map list from any tourist office, or find details online at Ⓦwww.roteiro-campista.pt. Camping rough is banned; beach areas are especially strict about this.

FOOD AND DRINK

Portuguese **food** is tasty and cheap. Virtually all cafés will serve you a basic meal for under €8, and for a little more you have the run of most of the country's restaurants. **Snacks** include *tosta mistas* (cheese and ham toasties); *prego/bifana* (steak/pork sandwich); *rissóis de carne* (deep-fried meat patties); *pastéis de bacalhau* (codfish cakes); and *sandes* (sandwiches). In **restaurants** you can usually have a substantial meal by ordering a *meia dose* (half portion), or *uma dose* (one portion) between two, as Portuguese portions are famously generous. Most serve an *ementa turística* (set meal), which can be good value, particularly in *pensões* that serve meals, or in the cheaper workers' cafés. It's always worth going for the *prato do dia* (dish of the day), usually the cheapest dish on the menu, and, if you're on the coast, opting for fish and seafood. Typical **dishes** include *sopa de marisco* (shellfish soup); *caldo verde* (finely shredded green kale leaves in broth); and *bacalhau* (dried cod, cooked in myriad different ways). *Caldeirada* is a fish stew cooked with onions and tomatoes, *arroz marisco* a similar stew cooked with seafood and rice. *Cabrito assado* (roast kid) is common in the north of the country, while down south you're sure to see chicken piri-piri (chicken with chilli sauce) on the menu. Regional cheeses are well worth sampling, and **puddings** include *arroz doce* (rice pudding), *salada da fruta* (fresh fruit salad) and *pudím molotoff* (a kind of lightly toasted meringue drenched in caramel sauce). Cakes – *bolos* or *pastéis* – are often at their best in *pastelarias* (patisseries), though you'll also find them in cafés and some *casas de chá* (tearooms). Among the best are custard tarts (*pastéis de nata*).

Drink

Portuguese **wines** (*tinto* for red, *branco* for white) are very inexpensive and of high quality. The fortified port (*vinho do Porto*) and madeira (*vinho da Madeira*) wines are the best known. The light, slightly sparkling **vinhos verdes** are produced in the Minho, and are excellent served chilled. **Brandy** is available in two varieties, Macieiera and Constantino, and like local gin is ridiculously cheap; if you're asking at a bar, always specify "gin nacional", "vodka nacional", etc – it'll save you a fortune. The two most common Portuguese **beers** (*cervejas*) are Sagres and Super Bock.

CULTURE AND ETIQUETTE

Portugal is a **Catholic** country, so it's wise to show respect when visiting churches (bare shoulders should be covered up and short skirts may be frowned upon), and avoid visiting during services, which take place on Sundays and sometimes other days at around 9.30am. It's also a good idea to learn a few basic phrases in **Portuguese** (see p.924); it will certainly endear locals to you if nothing else. In restaurants, it is usual to **tip** five percent to ten percent if you're satisfied with the service.

Lone women travellers should face no problems, but might attract a bit of curiosity from locals.

SPORTS AND OUTDOOR ACTIVITIES

In Portugal, **football** isn't just a sport: it's a national passion. During all major matches, the country goes quiet as people flock to restaurants and bars to watch them on television. The three biggest and most successful football clubs are FC Porto, Sporting Clube de Portugal (based in Lisbon), and Sport Lisboa e Benfica. **Surfing** is also popular; notable areas include Costa da Caparica south of Lisbon, and Lagos in the Algarve. Those seeking something more extreme may be disappointed, as there are few possibilities for **white-water rafting** and **canyoning**; one such company that does offer these activities is Trilhos in Porto (Rua de Belém 94 ⓣ967 014 277, ⓦwww.trilhos.pt). Portugal's **natural parks** and its one **national park**, the Parque Nacional de Peneda-Gerês in the Minho, are a hikers' paradise. More information about the parks can be found at ⓦwww.icn.pt, and tourist offices located near parks can provide maps and other details. Those visiting the Algarve should pick up a copy of the excellent *Trails in the Algarve* booklet, a guide to walking routes in the region, available free from tourist offices.

COMMUNICATIONS

Post offices (*correios*) are normally open Mon–Fri 9am–6pm, Sat 9am–noon. For **poste restante**, look for a counter marked *encomendas*. International **phone calls** can be made direct from any phone booth or post office. Phonecards cost €3, €6 or €9, from post offices, larger newsagents and tobacconists. The operator is on ⓣ118 (domestic), ⓣ098 (international). **Internet** cafés are common (€1.50–3/hr).

EMERGENCIES

Lisbon and the larger tourist areas have seen increases in **petty crime**, such as street theft. Pilfering from dorms is relatively rare, but it's always wise to use the lockers provided or buy a padlock for your luggage. Travel on trains and buses is safe, with thefts a rarity. Portuguese **police** are stationed in most towns, and can be recognized by their dark blue uniform. Lisbon and Porto

PORTUGAL ON THE NET

ⓦwww.min-cultura.pt Ministry of Culture, with an agenda of major events.
ⓦwww.portugal.org Tourist office site, with information and advice.
ⓦwww.portugalvirtual.pt Comprehensive directory listings.
ⓦwww.convida.pt Stylish guides to Lisbon, one neighbourhood at a time.
ⓦwww.algarvenet.com Detailed site dedicated to the Algarve region.

Portuguese

	Portuguese	Pronunciation
Basics		
Yes	*Sim*	Sing
No	*Não*	Now
Please	*Por favor*	Por favor
Thank you	*Obrigado* [said by men]/ *Obrigada* [said by women]	Obrigadoo/obrigada
Hello/Good day	*Olá*	Orla
Goodbye	*Adeus*	Adayoosh
Excuse me	*Desculpe*	Deskulp
Where?	*Onde?*	Ond?
Good	*Bom*	Bom
Bad	*Mau*	Maw
Near	*Perto*	Pertoo
Far	*Longe*	Lonje
Cheap	*Barato*	Baratoo
Expensive	*Caro*	Karoo
Open	*Aberto*	Abertoo
Closed	*Fechado*	Feshardoo
Today	*Hoje*	Oje
Yesterday	*Ontem*	Ontaygn
Tomorrow	*Amanhã*	Amanya
How much is....?	*Quanto é... ?*	Kwantoo eh?
What time is it?	*Que horas são?*	Kay orash sow?
I don't understand	*Não compreendo*	Now compre-ndoo
Do you speak English?	*Fala Inglés?*	Farla inglayz?
One	*Um/Uma*	Oom/ooma
Two	*Dois/Duas*	Doysh/dooash
Three	*Três*	Treysh
Four	*Quatro*	Kwatroo
Five	*Cinco*	Sinkoo
Six	*Seis*	Saysh
Seven	*Sete*	Set
Eight	*Oito*	Oytoo
Nine	*Nove*	Nove
Ten	*Dez*	Desh
Getting around		
Where is the station?	*Onde é a estação?*	Ond e a estasow?
On the left/right	*A esquerda/direita*	A eeshkerdah/deeraitah
A ticket to...	*Um bilhete para...*	Oom beelyet para...
What time is the train/ bus to...?	*A que horas é o comboio/ autocarro para...?*	A kay oras e o convoyo/ autocarro para...
Accommodation		
I would like a room (single/double)	*Queria um quarto individual/casal*	Kereea um kwarto individooal/cazal
May I see the room?	*Posso ver o quarto?*	Posso ver o kwarto?
At the restaurant		
A table for one/two	*Uma mesa para uma pessoa/duas pessoas*	Uma mehzah para ooma pessoa/duash pessoash
I'm a vegetarian	*Sou vegetariano/a*	So vejetarianoh/ah

BASICS PORTUGAL

EMERGENCY NUMBERS

All emergencies ⓣ112.

have separate **tourist police** to deal with issues affecting visitors; their booths are located at Praça dos Restauradores and Rua Clube dos Fenianos 11 respectively. For minor health complaints go to a **pharmacy** (*farmácia*); pharmacists are highly trained and can dispense many drugs without a prescription. Normal open hours are Mon–Fri 9am–1pm & 3–7pm, Sat 9am–1pm. A sign at each one will show the nearest 24hr pharmacy. You can get the address of an English-speaking doctor from a pharmacy or consular office.

INFORMATION & MAPS

You'll find a **tourist office** (*turismo*) in almost every town. Staff can help you find a room, and provide local maps and leaflets. For more comprehensive **maps** try those published by the Automóvel Clube de Portugal, GeoCenter or the Michelin #437.

MONEY AND BANKS

Currency is the euro (€). **Banks** are open Mon–Fri 8.30am–3pm; in Lisbon and in some of the Algarve resorts, exchange offices may open in the evening to change money. ATMs can be found all over and credit cards are widely accepted; travellers' cheques are increasingly difficult to exchange outside tourist hotspots, and commission on them can be high.

OPENING HOURS AND HOLIDAYS

Shop **opening hours** are generally Mon–Fri 9am–12.30/1pm & 2/2.30–6/6.30pm, Sat 9am–12.30/1pm. Larger supermarkets tend to stay open until 8pm, but most are closed on Sunday, with some exceptions in the Algarve. Museums, churches and monuments open from around 10am to 6pm; almost all, however, close on Mondays and at Easter and smaller places often for lunch. The main **public holidays** are: Jan 1, Feb carnival, Good Fri, April 25, May 1, Corpus Christi, June 10, June 13 (Lisbon only), Aug 15, Oct 5, Nov 1, Dec 1, Dec 8, Dec 25.

STUDENT AND YOUTH DISCOUNTS

If you're under 26 it's well worth investing in a Euro 26 card (ⓦwww.euro26.org), which often gives the holder 60 percent off admission costs. Discounts of up to 50 percent for under 25s and students on production of proof of age, a university card or an ISIC card are also very common.

Lisbon

There are few more immediately likeable European capitals than **LISBON** (*Lisboa*). A lively place, it remains in some ways curiously provincial, rooted as much in the 1920s as the 2000s. Wooden trams clank up outrageous gradients, past mosaic pavements, Art Nouveau cafés and the medieval quarter of Alfama, which hangs below the city's São Jorge castle. The city invested heavily for Expo 98 and the 2004 European Football Championships, reclaiming rundown docks and improving communication links, and today it combines an easy-going, human pace and scale, with a vibrant, cosmopolitan identity.

The city has a huge amount of historic interest. The **Great Earthquake** of 1755 (followed by a tidal wave and fire) destroyed most of the grandest buildings, but frantic reconstruction led to many impressive new palaces and churches, as well as the street grid pattern spanning the seven hills of Lisbon. Several buildings from Portugal's golden age survived the quake – notably the Castelo de São Jorge and the Monastery of Jerónimos at Belém. Contemporary sights include the Fundação Calouste Gulbenkian, with its superb collections of ancient and modern art.

What to see and do

Many of Lisbon's major sights, such as the Sé (Cathedral) and the Castelo de São Jorge, are located in the centre's eastern portion, best reached by following Rua de Conceição and its continuations as they wind away from the Baixa towards Alfama. The city centre can be explored on foot, but a quick hop on a **tram** or **elevador** is definitely a less strenuous way of scaling Lisbon's seven hills. Public transport is also necessary to reach outlying sights such as those located in Belém, 6km west of the centre, and the Fundação Calouste Gulbenkian, north of the city's main artery, the Avenida da Liberdade. The Baixa is the city's main shopping district, with more elegant and trendy boutiques located in Chiado and Bairro Alto respectively. Bairro Alto is also the area to head for food, *fado* and fun, as it is home to many of the city's bars and restaurants.

Baixa

The heart of the capital is the lower town – the **Baixa** – Europe's first great example of Neoclassical design and urban planning. It's an imposing quarter of rod-straight streets, some streaming with traffic, but most pedestrianized with mosaic cobbles where buskers and pavement artists ply their trade. **Rossio Square** is the Baixa's northernmost boundary, and is very much a focus for the city, housing some great cafés and the grand Teatro Nacional, built in the 1840s. At the waterfront end of the Baixa lies the city's other main square, the beautiful arcaded Praça do Comércio.

Lisbon Cathedral

A couple of blocks east of the Baixa stands the Sé or **Cathedral** (daily 9am–6pm; free). The oldest church in Lisbon, it was founded in 1147 to commemorate the city's reconquest from the Moors, and occupies the site of the principal mosque of Moorish Lishbuna. Like so many of the country's cathedrals, it is Romanesque and extraordinarily restrained in both size and decoration. It was damaged in the 1755 earthquake, and was extensively restored in the 1930s. You'll need to pay to visit the thirteenth-century cloisters (closed Sun; €1) and the treasury museum (closed Sun; €2.50), including the relics of St Vincent, the patron saint of Lisbon.

Castelo de São Jorge

From the Sé, Rua Augusto Rosa and its continuation, Rua do Limoeiro,

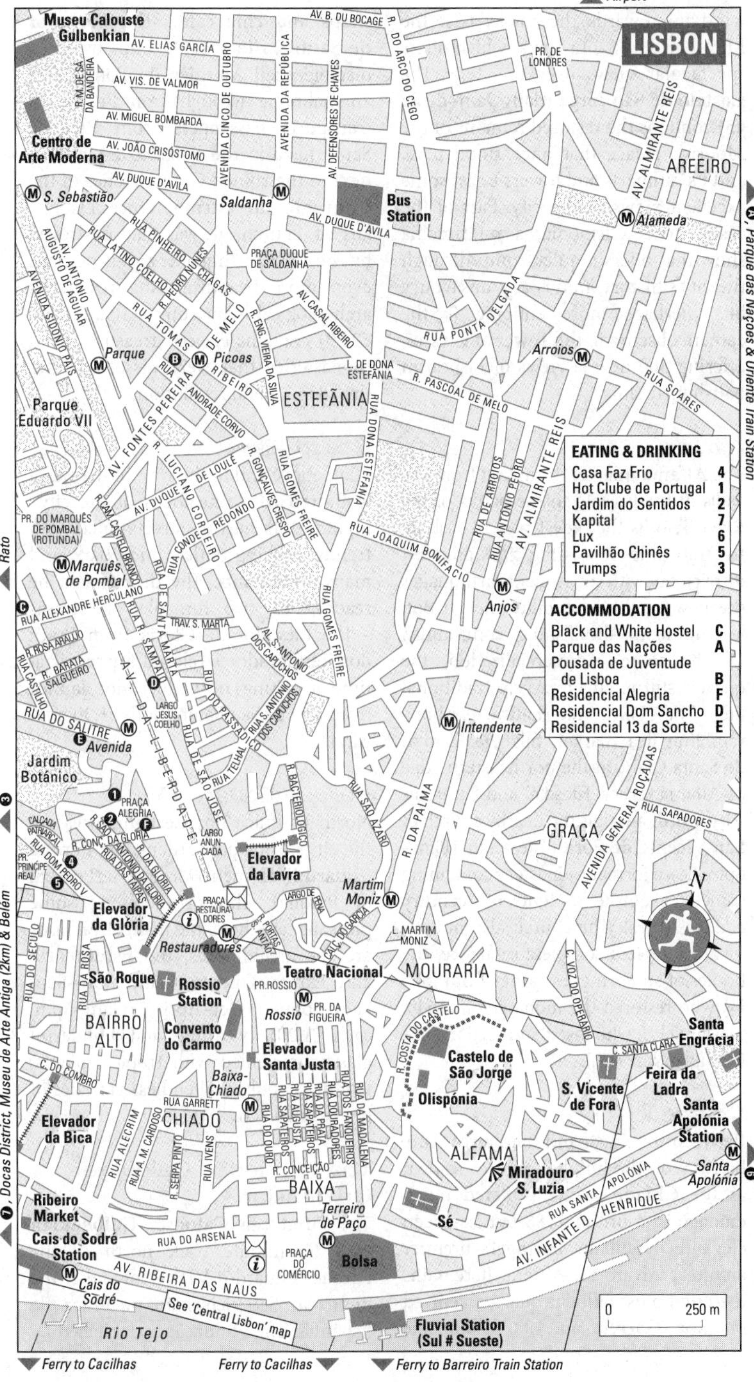
LISBON
Airport
EATING & DRINKING
Casa Faz Frio 4
Hot Clube de Portugal 1
Jardim do Sentidos 2
Kapital 7
Lux 6
Pavilhão Chinês 5
Trumps 3
ACCOMMODATION
Black and White Hostel C
Parque das Nações A
Pousada de Juventude de Lisboa B
Residencial Alegria F
Residencial Dom Sancho D
Residencial 13 da Sorte E
Museu Calouste Gulbenkian
Centro de Arte Moderna
S. Sebastião
Saldanha
Bus Station
Alameda
AREEIRO
ESTEFÂNIA
Arroios
Picoas
Parque
Parque Eduardo VII
Marquês de Pombal
Anjos
Intendente
Avenida
Jardim Botânico
GRAÇA
Elevador da Lavra
Martim Moniz
Elevador da Glória
Restauradores
Teatro Nacional
MOURARIA
São Roque
Rossio Station
Rossio
BAIRRO ALTO
Convento do Carmo
Elevador Santa Justa
Castelo de São Jorge
Olispónia
Santa Engrácia
Feira da Ladra
S. Vicente de Fora
Santa Apolónia Station
Santa Apolónia
Baixa-Chiado
CHIADO
Elevador da Bica
ALFAMA
Miradouro S. Luzia
BAIXA
Terreiro de Paço
Sé
Ribeiro Market
Cais do Sodré Station
Cais do Sodré
Bolsa
Fluvial Station (Sul # Sueste)
Rio Tejo
See 'Central Lisbon' map
0 250 m
A, Parque das Nações & Oriente Train Station
Rato
3
7, Docas District, Museu de Arte Antiga (2km) & Belém
6
Ferry to Cacilhas
Ferry to Cacilhas
Ferry to Barreiro Train Station

wind up towards the castle, past the Miradouro de Santa Luzia, which offers spectacular views over the Tejo. The **Castelo de São Jorge** (daily 9am–dusk; €5) contains the restored remains of the Moorish palace that once stood here, and its ramparts and towers boast some excellent views of the city. Part of the castle hosts Olispónia, a multimedia show that offers a quick romp through the city's history, minus any unsavoury bits. Perhaps more enticing is the camera obscura in the Tower of Ulysses, offering 360 degree views of Lisbon in half-hourly slots.

Alfama

The **Alfama quarter**, tumbling from the walls of the Castelo to the banks of the River Tejo, is the oldest part of Lisbon. In Arab times it was the city's grandest district, but with subsequent earthquakes the new Christian nobility moved out, leaving it to the fishing community. Despite some commercialization, the quarter still retains a largely traditional life. The **Feira da Ladra**, Lisbon's rambling flea market, fills the Campo de Santa Clara, at the northeastern edge of Alfama, every Tuesday and Saturday. Also worth a visit is the nearby church of **São Vicente de Fora** (Tues–Sun 10am–6pm; €4), a former monastery containing some exquisite eighteenth-century *azulejos* (tiles). The church also houses, in more or less complete sequence, the bodies of all Portuguese kings from João IV, who restored the monarchy in 1640, to Manuel II, who lost it and died in exile in England in 1932.

Chiado

Between the Baixa and the Bairro Alto, halfway up the hill, lies an area known as the **Chiado**, which suffered much damage in a fire in 1988 but has been elegantly rebuilt by Portugal's premier architect Álvaro Siza Viera. It remains the city's most affluent quarter, centred on **Rua Garrett** and its fashionable shops and chic cafés. The **Elevador de Santa Justa** (€1.30), built by Eiffel disciple Raul Mésnier de Ponsard, is an elaborate wrought-iron lift which transports passengers from Rua de Santa Justa in the Baixa to a platform next to the ruined Gothic arches of the **Convento do Carmo**. Once Lisbon's largest church, it was half-destroyed by the 1755 earthquake, and is perhaps even more beautiful as a result; its archeological museum (10am–6pm; €2.50) contains eclectic treasures from monasteries that were dissolved after the 1834 Liberal revolution.

Bairro Alto

High above and to the west of the Baixa is **Bairro Alto**, the focus of the city's nightlife. Its narrow streets lined with trendy clothing outlets, *fado* bars, and many restaurants. The district can be reached by two funicular-like trams – the Elevador da Glória from Praça dos Restauradores (closed for repair at time of writing) or the Elevador da Bica from Rua de São Paulo (both €1.30 one-way).

Parque Eduardo VII

North of Praça dos Restauradores are the city's principal gardens, the **Parque Eduardo VII** (metro Marquês de Pombal or Parque). Though there are some pleasant cafés here, the main attractions are the greenhouses, the **Estufa Fria** and **Estufa Quente** (daily May–Sept 9am–6pm; Oct–April 9am–5pm; each €1.20), two huge and wonderful glasshouses filled with tropical plants, flamingo pools, and endless varieties of palms and cacti.

The Fundação Calouste Gulbenkian

The **Fundação Calouste Gulbenkian** is a ten-minute walk north of the Parque Eduardo VII – or take the metro to São Sebastião or Praça de Espanha. The Fundação, established by the oil magnate and prolific collector Calouste Gulbenkian, helps finance various aspects of Portugal's cultural life – including an orchestra, three concert halls and the two art galleries located here. The **Museu Calouste Gulbenkian** (Tues–Sun 10am–6pm; €3, free Sun am) is Portugal's greatest museum, divided into two distinct parts – the first devoted to Egyptian, Greco-Roman, Islamic and Oriental arts, the second to European, including paintings from all the major schools. There's also a stunning room full of Art Nouveau jewellery by René Lalique. Across the gardens, the **Centro de Arte Moderna** (same hours; €3) houses works by all the big names from the twentieth-century Portuguese scene, as well as some top British artists such as Anthony Gormley and David Hockney.

Museu Nacional de Arte Antiga

Lisbon's other top museum is the national art collection, the **Museu Nacional de Arte Antiga** (Tues 2–6pm, Wed–Sun 10am–6pm; €3, free Sun am), situated near the riverfront to the west of the city at Rua das Janelas Verdes 95 (take tram #15 from Praça da Figueira). Its core is formed by fifteenth- and sixteenth-century Portuguese works, the acknowledged masterpiece being Nuno Gonçalves' St Vincent Altarpiece, depicting Lisbon's patron receiving homage from all ranks of its citizens. There are also ceramics, textiles, and furniture from Portugal on display, as well as decorative arts from Asia and Africa.

Belém

Six kilometres west of the centre lies the suburb of **Belém** from where, in 1497, Vasco da Gama set sail for India. Partly funded by a levy on all spices other than pepper, cinnamon and cloves, whose import had become the sole preserve of the Crown, the **Monastery of Jerónimos** (May–Sept 10am–6.30pm; Oct–April 10am–6.30pm; closed Mon; free; cloisters same hours €4.50, free Sun am; tram #15 from Praça da Figueira) was begun in 1502 and is the most ambitious achievement of Manueline architecture. Vaulted throughout and fantastically embellished, the cloister is one of the most original and beautiful pieces of architecture in the country, holding Gothic forms and Renaissance ornamentation in an exuberant balance. Nearby there are a number of museums, of which the **Museu do Design in the Centro Cultural de Belém** (Praça do Império; daily 11am–7pm; €3.50) is the best, featuring design classics from the twentieth century. The turreted **Torre de Belém** (May–Sept 10am–6.30pm; Oct–April 10am–5pm; closed Mon; €3), on the edge of the river around 500m from the monastery, was built during the last five years of Dom Manuel's reign (up to 1520) to guard the entrance to Lisbon's port, and has become symbolic of the Age of Discoveries. Also of interest is the vast concrete **Monument to the Discoveries** (Tues–Sun 9am–5pm; €2;) erected in 1960 to commemorate the 500th anniversary of the death of Henry the Navigator; inside are changing exhibitions on the city's history. A lift takes you to the top for spectacular views.

Parque das Nações and the Oceanarium

Built on reclaimed docklands for Expo '98, the **Parque das Nações** (Park of Nations), 5km east of the centre, has become a popular entertainment park, containing concert venues, theatres, restaurants and a large shopping centre. The Parque occupies a traffic-free riverside zone punctuated by water features and some dazzling modern architecture. The main attraction is the **Oceanário de Lisboa** (daily 10am–7pm; €10.50; metro Oriente station), Europe's second largest oceanarium, an awe-inspiring collection of fish and sea

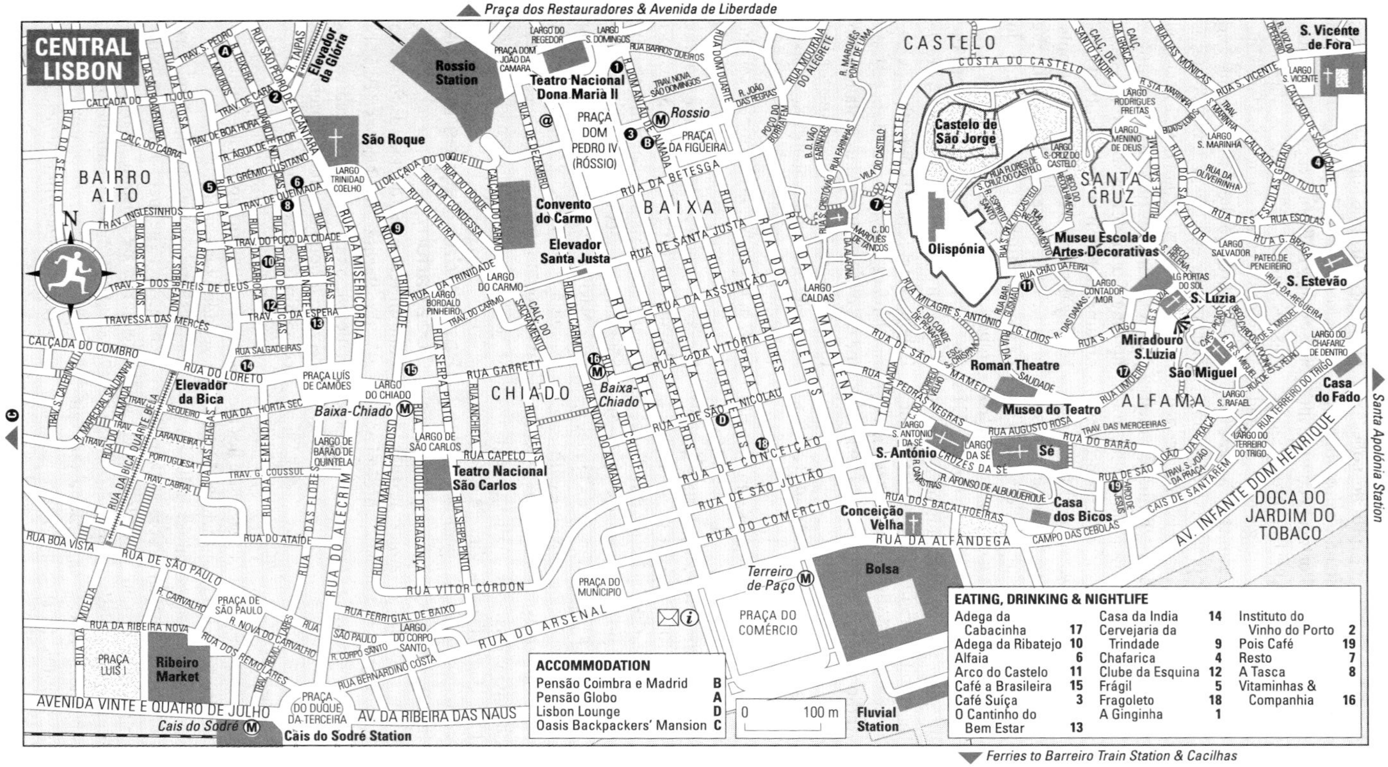

CENTRAL LISBON

Praça dos Restauradores & Avenida de Liberdade

Santa Apolónia Station

Ferries to Barreiro Train Station & Cacilhas

EATING, DRINKING & NIGHTLIFE

Adega da Cabacinha	17
Adega da Ribatejo	10
Alfaia	6
Arco do Castelo	11
Café a Brasileira	15
Café Suíça	3
O Cantinho do Bem Estar	13
Casa da India	14
Cervejaria da Trindade	9
Chafarica	4
Clube da Esquina	12
Frágil	5
Fragoleto	18
A Ginginha	1
Instituto do Vinho do Porto	2
Pois Café	19
Resto	7
A Tasca	8
Vitaminhas & Companhia	16

ACCOMMODATION

Pensão Coimbra e Madrid	B
Pensão Globo	A
Lisbon Lounge	D
Oasis Backpackers' Mansion	C

0 100 m

mammals based around a central tank the size of four Olympic swimming pools. The information kiosk opposite Centro Vasco da Gama supplies maps of the park and sells a discount card (€16.50) valid for all attractions.

Arrival and information

Air From Portela airport, 7km northeast of the centre, the #91 Aerobus (every 20min 7.45am–9pm; takes 20min; €3) runs from outside arrivals to Praça dos Restauradores, Rossio, Praça do Comércio and Cais do Sodré; the ticket is then valid for transport on buses and trams for that day. Local buses #44 and #45 (€1.30) run from the road outside the airport to Rossio and the riverside Cais do Sodré.
Train Trains from northern and central Portugal stop at Santa Apolónia Station, a fifteen-minute walk from Praça do Comércio. Buses #46 and #90 depart from the stop to the left of the station for Rossio Square. Trains from the Algarve terminate at Oriente station, at the end of the red metro line. Local trains from Sintra stop at Sete Rios station next to the Jardim Zoológico metro stop (blue line), and Entre Campos (yellow line).
Bus The main Rede Expressos bus station is next to the Jardim Zoológico metro stop.
Tourist office The main tourist office is the Lisboa Welcome Centre, on the corner of Praça do Comércio and Rua do Arsenal (daily 9am–8pm; Ⓣ 210 312 700, Ⓦ www.visitlisboa.com). There are also Ask Me Lisboa kiosks around the city, including one at the airport (daily 6am–midnight) and one at Santa Apolónia station (Tues–Sat 8am–1pm).
Discount passes The Lisboa Card (€14.85/25.50/31 for 1/2/3 days) is available from all tourist offices, and gives unlimited travel on city transport, entry to 27 attractions, plus discounts. But unless you are planning to do some extremely intensive sightseeing, it doesn't offer great value.

City transport

Metro Lisbon's metro (Ⓦ www.metrolisboa.pt) has four lines, blue (*azul*), green (*verde*), red (*vermelha*), and yellow (*amarela*); tickets cost €0.75/1.05 each (for central/all zones) or €6.65/9.50 for ten. The metro runs between 6.30am and 1am.
Tram and Bus Trams and buses (Ⓦ www.carris.pt) are the most enjoyable way of getting around. Tram #28, which runs from Martim Moniz through the Alfama to Prazeres, has become something of a tourist "must-do". Tickets cost €1.30 when bought on board. Note that Carris, who operate trams, buses and funiculars, do not publish a transport guide; details of all routes can be found at bus stops.
Transport passes The rechargeable Sete Colinas card (€0.50, added to first purchase), available from all metro stations, is the cheapest, most convenient way to get around. A one-day pass costs €3.35, five days costs €13.35, and both allow unlimited travel on buses, trams, metro and elevadores. The cards can also be loaded with single journeys.
Taxi A short taxi journey within the city centre shouldn't cost more than €10, but they can be hard to find at night – if you're leaving a bar or club book one by phone from Rádio Táxis de Lisboa (Ⓣ 218 119 000) or Teletáxis (Ⓣ 218 111 100).

Accommodation

Lisbon has scores of small, cheap **pensions**, most of which are around Rua das Portas de Santo Antão and Rua da Glória. Several good-value, modern **hostels** have also sprung up in recent years. At Easter and in midsummer, availability is stretched: single rooms are sometimes "converted" to doubles and prices are significantly higher. However, during the rest of the year you should have no difficulty finding accommodation, and for maybe a third less than midsummer prices. The addresses below, written as 53-3°, for example, show the street number followed by the floor.

Hostels

Black and White Hostel Rua Alexandre Herculano 39-1°, Liberdade Ⓣ 213 462 212, Ⓦ www.costta.com. Small but stylish hostel with a chilled-out atmosphere and friendly staff. Metro to Marquês de Pombal. Dorms (inc breakfast) ❷
Lisbon Lounge Rua de São Nicolau 41, Baixa Ⓣ 213 462 061, Ⓦ www.lisbonloungehostel.com. Upmarket hostel near Rossio boasting WiFi Internet access and three lounge areas. Dorms ❷, twin ❻
Oasis Backpackers' Mansion Rua de Santa Catarina 24, Chiado Ⓣ 213 478 044, Ⓦ www.oasislisboa.com. Lively, well-equipped hostel with its own bar, located below the Miradouro de Santa Catarina. Laundry and kitchen facilities available. Metro to Baixa-Chiado. Dorms ❷
Pousada de Juventude de Lisboa Hostel Rua Andrade Corvo 46 Ⓣ 213 532 696, Ⓦ www.pousadasjuventude.pt. Well-run hostel with good facilities, located near Parque Eduardo VII. Book well in advance in summer. Metro to Picoas. Dorms €16, twin ❺
Pousada de Juventude do Parque das Nações

Hostel Rua da Moscavide 47, Parque das Nações ⓣ218 920 890. Far from the action, but still lively enough. Reception 8am–midnight. Metro to Oriente. Dorms €13, twin ❹

Pensions and hotels

Pensão Coimbra e Madrid Praça da Figueira 3-3°, Baixa ⓣ213 424 808. Good-value rooms some with en-suite, in a central location. Front-facing rooms can be noisy. ❹

Pensão Globo Rua do Teixeira 37, Bairro Alto ⓣ213 462 279, ⓦwww.pensaoglobo.com. Pleasant pension with clean, well-renovated rooms in a variety of shapes and sizes. ❹–❻

Residencial 13 da Sorte Rua do Salitre 13, Liberdade ⓣ213 539 746, ⓦwww.trezedasorte.no.sapo.pt. "Lucky 13" is a well-located pension with decent en-suite rooms. ❻

Residencial Alegria Praça da Alegria 12 ⓣ213 220 670, ⓦwww.alegrianet.com. Pleasant pension with spacious rooms on a reasonably quiet square between Bairro Alto and Avda. da Liberdade. ❺

Residencial Dom Sancho I Avda. da Liberdade 202 ⓣ213 548 042, ⓦwww.domsancho.com. Smart little hotel with excellent rooms. Often has special offers which are well worth watching out for. Metro to Avenida. ❻

Campsites

Camping Obitur-Guincho Lugar da Areia, Guincho ⓣ214 870 450, ⓦwww.orbitur.pt. A well-located site 12km out of the city in surfer's paradise Guincho, boasting a restaurant, supermarket, and sports facilities. Train from Cais do Sodré to Cascais, then bus to Guincho. ❶

Parque Municipal de Campismo Parque Florestal Monsanto ⓣ217 623 100. Well-equipped main city campsite in a large park 6km west of the centre, complete with pool and shops. The entrance is on Estrada da Circunvalação on the park's west side. Bus #43 from Praça da Figueira. ❶

TREAT YOURSELF

For sports fans, a trip to Portugal wouldn't be complete without watching a **live football match**. Benfica are one of Portugal's most popular and successful teams, and every game at their enormous stadium, the Estádio da Luz, in the Benfica district, 6km northwest of the centre, promises to be exciting and atmospheric. Tickets cost between €20 and €55, and can be purchased at the ground on match days (check ⓦwww.uefa.com for fixtures), in advance online through various agencies, or from ABEP Ticket Agency in Praça dos Restauradores (ⓣ213 475 824). To get to the stadium, take the metro (blue line) to Colégio Militar/Luz.

Eating

Lisbon has some great **cafés and restaurants** serving large portions of food at sensible prices. Seafood is widely available – there's an entire central street, Rua das Portas de Santo Antão, which specializes in it. There are also a considerable number of inexpensive restaurants featuring food from Portugal's former colonies (including Angola, Goa and Macau). Many restaurants are **closed on Sundays**, while on Saturday nights you may need to book for the more popular places. The best **food market** is Mercado da Ribeira, Avda 24 de Julho, Cais do Sodré (Mon–Sat 10am–11pm).

Cafés

Antiga Confeitaria de Belém Rua de Belém 90, Belém. Historic tiled café famous for its delicious custard tarts or *pastéis de nata* (€0.80) – better than all the imitations.

Café a Brasileira Rua Garrett 120, Chiado. The most famous of Rua Garrett's old-style coffee houses, once frequented by Lisbon's literary set.

Café Suíça Praça Dom Pedro IV 96, Baixa. Famous for cakes and pastries, with outdoor seating facing Lisbon's two main squares.

Fragoleto Rua da Prata 74, Baixa. Divine home-made ice cream to take away, prices from €1.20.

Pois Café Rua São João da Praça 93, Baixa. Large, comfortable café with a laid-back vibe. Serves tasty daily specials, which always include a vegetarian option. Closed Mon. Dish of the day €7.50

Vitaminhas & Companhia Avda. Almirante Reis 114, Baixa. Good lunch stop next to Baixa-Chiado metro station, offering a variety of sandwiches, salads and fresh juices. Quiche and salad €6.

Restaurants

Adega da Cabacinha Rua Limoeiro 10. Cavernous traditional restaurant with an excellent value three-course lunch menu for €10.

Arco do Castelo Rua do Chão da Feira 25. Cheerful place by the castle entrance with tempting Goan cooking. Closed Sun. Curry €8.50.

O Cantinho do Bem Estar Rua do Norte 46, Bairro Alto. The service may be erratic, but this tiny place is great value for money – its portions feed two with ease. Cod cakes €12.

Casa da India Rua do Loreto 49, Bairro Alto. Despite the name, the food at this popular, lively restaurant is typically Portuguese. Garlic prawns €9.

Casa Faz Frio Rua Dom Pedro V 96, Bairro Alto. Charmingly traditional restaurant with seating in tiny cubicles. Serves classic Portuguese fare. Salmon €9.

Cervejaria da Trindade Rua Nova da Trindade 20, Bairro Alto. Wonderful, vaulted beer-hall restaurant, the oldest in the city, with a patio garden. Expensive seafood, but other more moderately priced dishes. Steak €14.

Floresta Belém Praça Afonso de Albuquerque 1, Belém. One of the least expensive of the restaurants near the monastery, with outdoor tables. Grilled cod €8.

Jardim do Sentidos Rua da Mãe d'Agua 3. Classy vegetarian restaurant beyond Praça da Alegria with a shady garden and an extensive menu of international dishes. Lasagne €9.

Resto Rua Costa do Castelo 7, Castelo. Two-in-one venue, with tapas and barbecued meat served in a buzzing courtyard, and more expensive international dishes on offer in the upstairs restaurant. Both have excellent river views. Dinner only. Spanish omelette €5.

Drinking and nightlife

The densest concentration of bars and clubs is in **Bairro Alto**. In summer, crowds spill out of bars and into the streets, creating a festive atmosphere. More expensive late-night action can be found in the **Docas** (Docklands) district, just east of the 25 de Abril bridge (train to Alcântara Mar from Cais do Sodré or tram #15). The Doca de Alcântara and the Doca de Santo Amaro (further from the city) host waterfront bars, cafés, and clubs in converted warehouses. Lisbon's **gay scene** centres around Praça do Príncipe Real in the north of Bairro Alto. Clubs don't really get going until at least 2am and tend to stay open till 6am. Admission fees range from €10–20 (usually including a drink), although minimum consumption charges of anything from €10 to €100 are increasingly common.

Bars

Alfaia Travessa da Queimada 18, Bairro Alto. Wine and port bar serving small portions of tapas. Take a seat outside and watch the world go by.

Clube da Esquina Rua da Barroca 30, Bairro Alto. Fashionable little corner bar decorated with old transistor radios – great for people watching.

A Ginginha Largo de São Domingos, Baixa. Small stand-up bar specializing in *ginginha*, a lethal cherry brandy worth sampling at least once.

Instituto do Vinho do Porto Rua de São Pedro de Alcântara 45, Bairro Alto. Over 200 types of port, from €1 a glass. Closed Sun.

Pavilhão Chinês Rua Dom Pedro V 89, Bairro Alto. Famous (and pricey) drinking den decorated with a unique selection of kitsch artefacts.

A Tasca Trav. da Queimada 13–15, Bairro Alto. Cheerful and welcoming tequila bar.

Clubs

Buddha Bar Doca de Santo Amaro. The pick of the docklands nightspots, boasting a roof terrace with views of the 25 de Abril bridge.

Frágil Rua da Atalaia 126, Bairro Alto. Housed in a fine old building, this place is full of poseurs but great fun. Closed Sun.

Kapital Avda. 24 de Julho 68, opposite Santos station. Cool club popular with trendy young Lisboetas.

Lux Doca do Jardim do Tobaco 1100, opposite Santa Apolónia station. The city's best and most fashionable club, hosting top DJs and occasional live bands. Closed Mon.

Trumps Rua da Imprensa Nacional 104b, Rato. The biggest gay venue in Lisbon, with a reasonably relaxed door policy. Closed Mon.

Entertainment

To hear some **fado**, a mournful, romantic singing style somewhere between the blues and flamenco, head for the Bairro Alto, where many restaurants put on *fado* performances. There are always minimum charges for dinner, from €15 upwards. If African music's more your thing, check out the posters around Restauradores. What's-on **listings** can be found in the free *Agenda Cultural*, issued monthly, and available at tourist offices, or in the Friday supplements of the *Independente* or *Diario de Noticias* newspapers.

Fado and live music

Adega do Ribatejo Rua do Diário de Notícias 23, Bairro Alto. Small, atmospheric restaurant with nightly *fado* performances and a reasonable minimum charge. Singers include a couple of professionals, the manager and even one of the cooks. Closed Sun.

Chafarica Calçada de São Vicente 79, Alfama. Long-established Brazilian bar with live music every night. Best after midnight, especially after a few *caipirinhas*.

Hot Clube de Portugal Praça da Alegria 39, off Avda. da Liberdade. Tiny basement jazz club, which hosts local and visiting artists. Closed Mon.

O Senhor Vinho Rua do Meio a Lapa 18, Lapa. Famous club in the diplomatic quarter west of the centre, sporting some of the best *fado* singers in Portugal. Closed Sun.

Paradise Garage Rua João de Oliveira Miguens 38, Alcântara. Big on the club scene, also hosts regular gigs. It's on a side road off Rua da Cruz à Alcântara. Closed Sun–Wed.

Shopping

The trendy **Bairro Alto** shops tend to open from early afternoon until midnight; elsewhere, opening hours are standard.

El Dorado Rua do Norte 23, Bairro Alto. Funky store with a great selection of vintage and new clothes and music.

Mercado da Ribeira Avenida 24 de Julho, Cais do Sodré. The city's main food market, which is also home to a variety of craft stores.

Outra Face da Lua Rua da Assunçao 22, Baixa. Vintage emporium stocking a mishmash of goodies, from clothing to toys. There's also an in-store café.

A Vida Portuguesa Rua Anchieta 11, Baixa. From tiles to sardines, if it's Portuguese, you'll find it here.

Directory

Embassies Australia, Avda. da Liberdade 198–2° ⓣ213 101 500; Canada, Avda. da Liberdade 196–200 ⓣ213 164 600; Ireland, Rua da Imprensa à Estrela 1–4° ⓣ213 929 440; UK, Rua de São Bernardo 33 ⓣ213 924 000; US, Avda. das Forças Armadas ⓣ217 273 300.

Exchange Main bank branches in the Baixa. Exchange office at the airport (24hr) and at Santa Apolónia station (daily 8.30am–3pm).

Hospital British Hospital, Rua Saraiva de Carvalho 46 ⓣ213 955 067.

Internet PT Comunicaçoes, Praça Dom Pedro IV 68, Baixa; Web C@fe, Rua do Diário de Notícias 126, Bairro Alto.

Laundry Lava Neve, Rua de Alegría 37, Bairro Alto (closed Sat pm & all Sun).

Left luggage Available at Oriente and Santa Apolónia stations.

Pharmacy Farmácia Estácio, Rossio Square.

Post office Praça dos Restauradores 58.

Moving on

Train to: Braga (13 daily; 3hr 30min–6hr); Badajoz (6–12 weekly; 5hr); Coimbra (hourly; 2–4hr); Évora (3 daily; 2hr 30min); Faro (6 daily; 3hr 15min–4hr); Madrid (nightly; 10hr 30min); Porto (hourly; 3hr 15 min–4hr); Sintra (every 15min; 45min); Tavira (6 daily; 4hr 30min–5hr); Tomar (hourly; 2hr).

Bus Alcobaça (7 daily; 2hr); Coimbra (hourly; 2hr 20min); Évora (hourly; 1hr 30 min–2hr 30min); Faro (10 daily; 3hr 15 min–4hr 30min); Fátima (hourly; 1hr 30min); Lagos (7–10 daily; 4hr–4hr 30min); Madrid (4 daily; 7hr 30min); Odemira (3 daily; 4hr); Porto (hourly; 3hr 30 min–4hr); Porto Côvo (2–3 daily; 3hr 30min); Sevilla (6 weekly; 7hr); Tomar (2–4 daily; 1hr 45min–2hr); Vila Nova de Milfontes (3–7 daily; 3hr 30min–4hr).

COSTA DA CAPARICA

Half an hour south of Lisbon, dunes stretch along the **COSTA DA CAPARICA**, which the quirks of the River Tejo's currents have largely spared from the pollution that plagues the city. Easily visited as a day-trip from the capital, Costa da Caparica is a thoroughly Portuguese resort, popular with surfers and crammed with restaurants and beach cafés, yet solitude is easy enough to find, thanks to the mini-railway (**transpraia**) that runs along the 8km of dunes in summer. The easiest way to get here is to take bus #153 from Praça de Espanha (every 20min; takes 35min €2.50), although it's perhaps more enjoyable to take a **ferry** from Cais do Sodré to Cacilhas (every 15min; 10min; €0.70) and then pick up the connecting bus to Caparica. Buses stop along Rua dos Pescadores by the beach, which leads to the central Praça da Liberdade, the main square, around which there's a **tourist office** (Mon–Fri 9am–1pm & 2–5.30pm, Sat 9am–1pm; ⓣ212 900 071), market, cinema and banks. There are plenty of decent **restaurants** serving fish and seafood on Rua dos Pescadores, as well as beach **bars** closer to the sand.

SINTRA

Travelling north instead you'll reach the lush wooded heights and royal palaces of **SINTRA.** This cool, hilltop woodland once attracted Moorish lords and the kings of Portugal from Lisbon during the hot summer months, and the place remains one of Portugal's most spectacular attractions.

What to see and do

Sintra can be seen on a day-trip from Lisbon, although you could easily spend several days here. The layout – an amalgamation of three villages – can be confusing, but there are plenty of local buses connecting the sights.

Palácio Nacional

The **Palácio Nacional** (10am–5.30pm, closed Wed; €4, free Sun 10am–2pm), about fifteen minutes' walk from the train station, is an obvious landmark. The palace was probably in existence under the Moors, but takes its present form from the rebuilding commissioned by Dom João I and his successor, Dom Manuel, in the fourteenth and fifteenth centuries. Its style is a fusion of Gothic and the latter king's Manueline additions. The **chapel** and its adjoining chamber – its floor worn by the incessant pacing of the half-mad Afonso VI who was confined here for six years by his brother Pedro I – are well worth seeing, as is the curious Magpies Room, decorated with hundreds of paintings of the birds with the motto "Por Bem" (For the good) in their beaks.

Moorish Castle and Palácio de Pena

Two of Sintra's main sights can be reached on bus #434 – the €4 ticket allows you to get on and off as much as you like. Starting at the train station, the bus stops outside the tourist office before proceeding to the ruined ramparts of the **Moorish Castle** (daily 9.30am–7pm; €3.50), from where the views over the town and surrounding countryside are extraordinary. Further on, the bus stops at both entrances to the immense **Pena Park**, at the top end of which rears the fabulous **Palácio de Pena** (Tues–Sun 10am–6pm; €8, gardens only €4.50), a wild nineteenth-century fantasy of domes, towers and a drawbridge that doesn't draw. The cluttered, kitschy interior has been preserved as left by the royal family on their flight from Portugal in 1910.

Quinta da Regaleira

Back in town, within walking distance of the centre, is another must-see site, the beautiful **Quinta da Regaleira** (daily 10am–8pm; €5, or €10 for guided visits booked in advance on ☎219 106 650). One of Sintra's most elaborate private estates, it lies five minutes' walk west of the Palácio Nacional on the Seteais–Monserrate road. The house and its fantastic gardens were built at the beginning of the twentieth century by an Italian theatrical set designer for one of the richest industrialists in Portugal. The highlight is the **Initiation Well**, inspired by the initiation practices of the Knight Templars and Freemasons. The vast gardens are full of surprising delights, with chapels, follies and fountains at every turn; you could easily spend a few hours here.

Monserrate

Beyond Quinta da Regaleira, the road leads past a series of beautiful private estates to **Monserrate** – about an hour's walk – whose 30-hectare **garden** (daily 9am–6/7pm; €3.50), filled with endless varieties of exotic trees and subtropical shrubs and plants, extends as far as the eye can see.

Arrival and information

Train Trains run regularly to Sintra from Lisbon's Entrecampos and Sete Rios stations (45min; €1.60 one-way).

Tourist office There's one tourist office at the station, and another (daily 9am–7/8pm; ☎219 231 157) just off the central Praça da República, which can help to arrange accommodation.

Accommodation

Sintra boasts some beautiful places to stay, but its popularity keeps prices high. Below are some of the cheaper options.

Dois ao Quadrado Rua João de Deus 68 ⓣ 249 246 160. Sintra's cheapest sleep is this small, rather average hostel near the train station. Dorms ❷, twin ❹

Piela's Avda. Dr Cambournac 1. Pleasant pension in Estefania, above central Sintra. ❻

Vila Marques Rua Sotto Mayor 1. Old-fashioned but attractive and scrupulously clean rooms north of the Palacio Nacional. ❺

Eating

Adega das Caves Rua de Pendora 2. Cheap sandwiches and grilled fare just off the main square. Grilled squid €8.

Casa Piriquita Rua das Padarias 1. Cosy café just south of Praça da República, serving snacks and Sintra's famous *queijadas* (cheesecakes). Sandwiches from €2.50 .

Tasca Mourisca Calçada de San Pedro 28. Tiny traditional restaurant, twenty minutes' walk southwest of the centre. Grilled fish €8.

Central Portugal

The Beiras, Estremadura and Ribatejo regions that comprise the central Portugal region have played crucial roles in each phase of the nation's history – and the monuments are here to prove it. The vast plains of the Beiras are dominated by **Coimbra**, an ancient university town and Portugal's former capital, perched high above the coastal area of the Beira Litoral. Below the Beiras lie Estremadura and Ribatejo, both comparatively small areas of fertile rolling hills, which boast an extraordinary concentration of vivid architecture and engaging towns. **Alcobaça** in Estremadura and **Tomar** in the wine-producing Ribatejo are some of the most striking; both housing famously grand religious monuments, while seaside **Nazaré** offers a relaxing escape from all that culture. Estremadura is also home to the pilgrimage centre of **Fátima**, renowned for its apparent apparitions of the Virgin Mary.

COIMBRA

COIMBRA was Portugal's capital from 1143 to 1255 and ranks behind only Lisbon and Porto in historic importance. Its university, founded in 1290, was the only one in Portugal until the beginning of the twentieth century. For a provincial town it has significant riches, and the many students provide Coimbra with a rather vivacious atmosphere during term-time – especially in May, when they celebrate the end of the academic year with the **Queima das Fitas**, a symbolic tearing or burning of their gowns and faculty ribbons. This is when you're most likely to hear the Coimbra *fado*, distinguished from the Lisbon version by its mournful pace and complex lyrics. During the summer months, the atmosphere is rather more subdued.

What to see and do

Old Coimbra sits on a hill on the right bank of the River Mondego, with the university crowning its summit. The main buildings of the **Old University** (daily: May–Sept 9am–7pm; Oct–April 9am–5pm; €6), dating from the sixteenth century, are set around a courtyard dominated by a Baroque clocktower and a statue of João III. The **chapel** is covered with *azulejos* and intricate decoration, but takes second place to the **Library**, a Baroque fantasy presented to the faculty by João V in the early eighteenth century. A short walk northeast of the Old University, opposite the modern Faculty of Sciences, stands the unprepossessing **Sé Nova** (New Cathedral; Tues–Sat 9.30am–12.30pm & 2–6.30pm; free). Of more interest is the **Sé Velha** (Old Cathedral; Mon–Fri 10am–1pm, Sat 10am–7pm; Cloisters €1), halfway down the hill, a solid and simple construction which is one of Portugal's most important Romanesque buildings. Restraint and simplicity certainly aren't the chief qualities of the flamboyant **Igreja de Santa Cruz** (daily 8.30am–6.30pm; €2.50), at the bottom of the hill on Praça 8 de Maio. In the early sixteenth century, Coimbra was the site of a major sculptural school; the new tombs for Portugal's first kings, Afonso Henriques and Sancho I, and the elaborately carved pulpit, are among its finest works. Other areas of interest include the epicentre of the students' social scene, **Praça da República**, a ten-minute walk from Praça 8 de Maio up Rua Olímpio Nicolau Rui Fernandes and its continuation, and the rambling **Botanic Garden** (Mon–Fri; April–Sept 9am–8pm, Oct–March 9am–5.30pm; €1.50) which sits in the shadow of the sixteenth-century aqueduct to the east of Praça da República.

Arrival and information

Train Intercity trains stop at Coimbra B, 3km north of the city, from where there are frequent connecting services to Coimbra A, in the town centre.

Bus The main bus station is on Avda. Fernão de Magalhães, fifteen minutes' walk from the centre – turn right out of the bus station and head down the main road.

Tourist office The tourist office (Mon–Fri 9.30am–1pm & 2–5.30pm, Sat & Sun 10am–1pm & 2.30–5.30pm; ⓣ 239 488 120, ⓦ www.turismo-centro.pt) is opposite the bridge on Largo da Portagem.

Accommodation

Pousada de Juventude Rua Henrique Seco 14 ⓣ 239 822 955, ⓦ www.pousadasjuventude.pt. Basic but cheap hostel ten minutes north of Praça da República. Buses #7 and #29 from Avda. Emídio Navarro pass close by. Dorms ❷, twin ❸

Residencial Antunes Rua Castro Matoso 8 ⓣ 239 854 720, ⓦ www.residencialantunes.pt.vu. Old-fashioned rooms and free parking in a prime location near the aqueduct. ❺

Residencia Aviz Avda. Fernão de Magalhães 64 ⓣ 239 823 718. A rambling place near the central train station offering decent rooms with and without en-suite (❹). Good value. Double ❸

Residencial Domus Rua Adelino Veiga 62 ⓣ 239 828 584, ⓦ www.residencialdomus.com. Friendly place with clean but faded en-suite rooms. ❹

Eating and drinking

Most of the town's restaurants can be found tucked away in the alleys between **Largo da Portagem** – the place to head for cafés – and **Praça 8 de Maio**.

Adega Paço do Conde Rua Paço do Conde 1. Atmospheric, locally renowned *churrasqueira* serving tasty barbecued meat and fish. Meat and vegetable skewer e5.

Bar Tapas Rua Alexandre Herculano 8. Just off Praça da República, this place specializes in seafood. *Arroz marisco* €8.

Café Tropical Praça da República. A favourite haunt of students, with outdoor tables and cheap drinks. Closed Sun.

Via Latina Rua Almeida Garrett 1. Popular club open Tues to Sat from midnight onwards.

Moving on

Train Lisbon (hourly; 2–3hr); Porto (hourly; 1hr 20min–2hr).

Bus Alcobaça (2 daily; 1hr 30min); Fátima (5 daily; 1hr–1hr 30min); Lisbon (hourly; 2hr 20min); Porto (8–10 daily; 1hr 30min); Tomar (2 daily; 2hr).

ALCOBAÇA

The pretty town of **Alcobaça** is dominated by the vast, beautiful **Mosteiro de Santa Maria de Alcobaça** (daily 9am–5/7pm winter/summer; €4.50). From its foundation in 1147 until its dissolution in 1834, this Cistercian monastery was one of the greatest in the world. Its **church** (free) is one of the largest in Portugal, with a Baroque facade that conceals an interior stripped of most of its later adornments and restored to its original simplicity. The monastery's most precious treasures are the fourteenth-century **tombs** of Dom Pedro and Dona Inês de Castro, sculpted with phenomenal wealth of detail to illustrate the story of Pedro's love for Inês, the daughter of a Galician nobleman. Fearing Spanish influence over the Portuguese throne, Pedro's father, Afonso V, forbade their marriage, which nevertheless took place in secret. Alfonso ordered his daughter-in-law's murder, after which Pedro waited for his succession to the throne in 1357 before exhuming Inês's corpse, and forcing the royal circle to acknowledge her as queen by kissing her decomposing hand. The tombs – inscribed with the motto "Até o Fim do Mundo" (Until the End of the World) – have been placed foot to foot so that on Judgement Day, the lovers may rise and immediately see one another. The monastery's most amazing room is the **kitchen**, featuring a gigantic conical chimney, and a stream tapped from the river to provide Alcobaça's famously gluttonous monks with a constant supply of fresh fish.

Arrival and information

Bus Alcobaça's bus station is five minutes' walk from the monastery in the centre of town, across the bridge.

Tourist office Opposite the monastery on Praça 25 de Abril (daily 10am–1pm & 2/3–6/7pm; ⓣ262 582 377).

Accommodation and eating

Pensão Corações Unidos Rua Frei António Brandão 39 ⓣ262 582 142. Neat, clean pension with modern bathrooms facing the monastery. ❹

Parque de Campismo Avenida Professor Vieira Natividade ⓣ262 582 265. Small municipal site ten minutes north of the bus station. Closed Jan. ❶

Pensão Corações Unidos Rua Frei António Brandão 39. The restaurant below the *pensão*, serves good-value regional cooking.

Ti Fininho Rua Frei António Brandão 34. Offers reasonably priced grilled fish and meats, omelettes, and wine by the jug.

NAZARÉ

A curious combination of fishing village and beach resort, **NAZARÉ** may at first appear to be a victim of its own success as a tourist hotspot. However, upon closer inspection the influx of visitors has done little to damage the town's charm. Womenfolk, often dressed in the local costume of a voluminous knee-length skirt and bright blouse topped with a headscarf, tour the streets advertising rooms for rent and selling handmade crafts and dried fruit, which adds to Nazaré's festive atmosphere. As is its long strip of sand, streaming away from a backdrop of craggy cliffs. Although frequent bus connections with Alcobaça make visiting on a day-trip an easy option, Nazaré offers good-value **accommodation** in the form of private rooms (❸–❹); the tourist office on Avenida da República (July & Aug 9am–9pm; Sept–June 9.30am–1pm & 2–6pm; ⓣ262 561 194) has a list. The village's plentiful **restaurants** dish up great seafood; head to *Cocinha da Nazaré* at Rua da Leiria 17d, a few minutes northeast of the tourist office, for some of the best (grilled squid €6).

FÁTIMA

FÁTIMA is one of the most important centres of pilgrimage in the Catholic world, a status deriving from six **Apparitions of the Virgin Mary**. On May 13, 1917, three children from the village were tending their parents' flock when, in a flash of lightning, they were confronted with "a lady brighter than the sun" sitting in the branches of a tree. The vision returned on the thirteenth day of the next five months, culminating in the so-called Miracle of the Sun on October 13, when a swirling ball of fire cured lifelong illnesses. To commemorate these extraordinary events a vast white **Basilica** and gigantic esplanade have been built, more than capable of holding the crowds of 100,000 who congregate here for the main **pilgrimages** (May 12 & 13; Oct 12 & 13). In the church the tombs of two of the children, who died in the European flu epidemic of 1919–20, are the objects of constant attention. Hospices and convents have sprung up in the shadow of the basilica, and inevitably the fame of Fátima has resulted in its commercialization.

Pensions and restaurants abound, but there's little reason to stay except during the big pilgrimages to witness the midnight processions. Regular **bus services** to Fátima from Tomar make a day-trip possible.

TOMAR

TOMAR is famous for the Convento de Cristo, the spectacular headquarters of the Portuguese branch of the Knights Templar, which overlooks the town from a wooded hill. Riverside Tomar is also an attractive town in its own right – especially during the lively **Festa dos Tabuleiros**, a week of music and dancing, with a procession of women wearing headdresses made of trays stacked high with bread or paper flowers, which is held the first week of July, and has its roots in the practices of Dom Dinis' wife, Dona Isabel.

Built on a simple grid plan, Tomar's centre preserves its traditional charm, with whitewashed cottages lining narrow cobbled streets. West of the central Praça da República is the former Jewish quarter, where at Rua Joaquim Jacinto 73 you'll find an excellently preserved fourteenth-century synagogue, now the **Museu Luso-Hebraicoa Abraham Zacuto** (daily 10am–1pm & 2–6pm; free), one of Portugal's few surviving synagogues. The **Convento de Cristo** (daily June–Sept 9am–6.30pm; Oct–May 9am–5.30pm; €4.50, free Sun am) is set among pleasant gardens with splendid views, a fifteen-minute walk uphill from the town centre. Founded in 1162 by Gualdim Pais, first Master of the Knights Templar, it was the Order's headquarters. At the heart of the complex, surrounded by serene cloisters, is the **Charola**, the high-ceilinged, sixteen-sided temple from which the knights drew their moral conviction. The adjoining two-tiered Principal **Cloister** is one of the purest examples of the Renaissance style in Portugal.

Arrival and information

Bus and train stations are located next to each other on Avenida dos Combatentes de Grande Guerra, ten minutes south of the town centre.
Tourist office At the top of Avenida Dr Cândido Madureira (Mon–Fri 9am–12.30pm & 2–5.30pm).

Accommodation and eating

Residencial União Rua Serpa Pinto 94 ☎ 249 323 161. This is the pick of Tomar's pensions. ❹
Campsite ☎ 249 329 824. Tomar's campsite is a short walk east of Rua Marquês de Pombal. ❶
Restaurante Tabuleiro Rua Serpa Pinto 148. This restaurant offers a changing menu of delicious regional dishes, served in large portions. *Bacalhau a bras* €6.

Northern Portugal

Porto, the country's second largest city, is an attractive and convenient centre from which to begin an exploration of the region. Magnificently set on a rocky cliff astride the River Douro, it is perhaps most famous for the port-producing suburb of **Vila Nova de Gaia**, supplied by vineyards further inland along the river. The **Douro Valley** is traced by a spectacular rail route, with branch lines following valleys north along the River Tâmega to **Amarante** and along the Corgo to **Vila Real** – the main centre for transport connections into the ancient, isolated region of Trás-os-Montes – literally "behind the mountains" – which, more than anywhere else in Portugal, still upholds its traditional customs and farming methods. Its capital, **Bragança**, is guarded by an extraordinary thirteenth-century citadel, and surrounded by farms, its main industry. In the northwest, the **Minho**, considered by many to be the most beautiful part of the country, is a lush wilderness of rolling mountain forests and rugged coastlines (the Costa Verde), with some of the most unspoilt beaches in Europe. A quietly conservative region, its towns have a special charm and beauty, amongst them the religious centre of **Braga**, and the self-proclaimed birthplace of the nation, **Guimarães**, both of which are good bases from which to explore the rest of the Minho.

PORTO

Capital of the north, **PORTO** (sometimes called Oporto in English) is very different from Lisbon - unpretentious and unashamedly commercial, yet extremely welcoming. As the local saying goes: "Coimbra sings; Braga prays; Lisbon shows off; and Porto works." The attraction of the city lies largely in the contrast between the prosperous business core and the earthy charm of its Ribeira area, where the cobbled warren of steep alleys and passages appears to have changed little in centuries.

What to see and do

The waterfront Ribeira district is Porto's historic heart, with narrow, winding alleys so picturesque that the area has been declared a UNESCO World Heritage Site. Boat trips up the Douro, operated by a host of companies, depart regularly from Cais da Ribeira (for around €10), and are a great way of getting your bearings.

Ribeira

Despite being Porto's most touristy quarter, life in the **Ribeira** continues unaffected by visitors, as a wander through its alleyways will soon reveal. The district is also home to many restaurants and bars, as well as the extraordinary **Igreja de São Francisco** on Rua Infante Dom Henrique (9am–5.30/7pm; €3 including museum). Now deconsecrated, its rather plain facade conceals a fabulously opulent, gold-covered interior, refurbished in the eighteenth century. Around the corner on Rua Ferreira Borges is the **Palácio da Bolsa** (Stock Exchange; April–Oct 9am–7pm; Nov–March 9am–1pm & 2pm–6pm; €5), which ceased trading a few years ago and now offers interesting, informative tours every half-hour. The highlight is the ornate Salão Arabe (Arab Room), its Moorish style emulating that of the Alhambra palace in Granada, Spain.

Cordoaria to Mercado de Bolhão

The **Museu Nacional Soares dos Reis** at Rua Dom Manuel II (Tue 2–6pm, Wed–Sun 10am–6pm; €3) lies over to the west, in the area known as Cordoaria. It was the country's first national museum, and contains a formidable selection of eighteenth- and nineteenth-century paintings, as well as the late nineteenth-century sculptures of Soares dos Reis – his *O Desterro (The Exile)* is probably the best-known work in Portugal. East of the museum, superb views of the city are on offer at the **Torre dos Clérigos** (April–July & Sep–Oct 9.30am–1pm & 2–7pm; Aug 10am–1pm & 2–8pm; Nov–March 10am–noon & 2–5pm; €2) attached to the Baroque church of the same name. Downhill from here is the city's biggest boulevard, the transport hub of Avenida dos Aliados, which remains a pleasant place to stop for a coffee in spite of the traffic. To the west lies Sao Bento station, from where bus #500 leaves for the beaches of Foz do Douro. A short walk east of Aliados takes you to the **Mercado de Bolhão** which sells fresh produce every day except Sunday, while the city's main shopping area is located a little further north around Rua Santa Catarina.

Casa da Música

The west of the city is home to some of Portugal's most exciting cultural centres, not to mention some daring architecture. Dominating the Avenida da

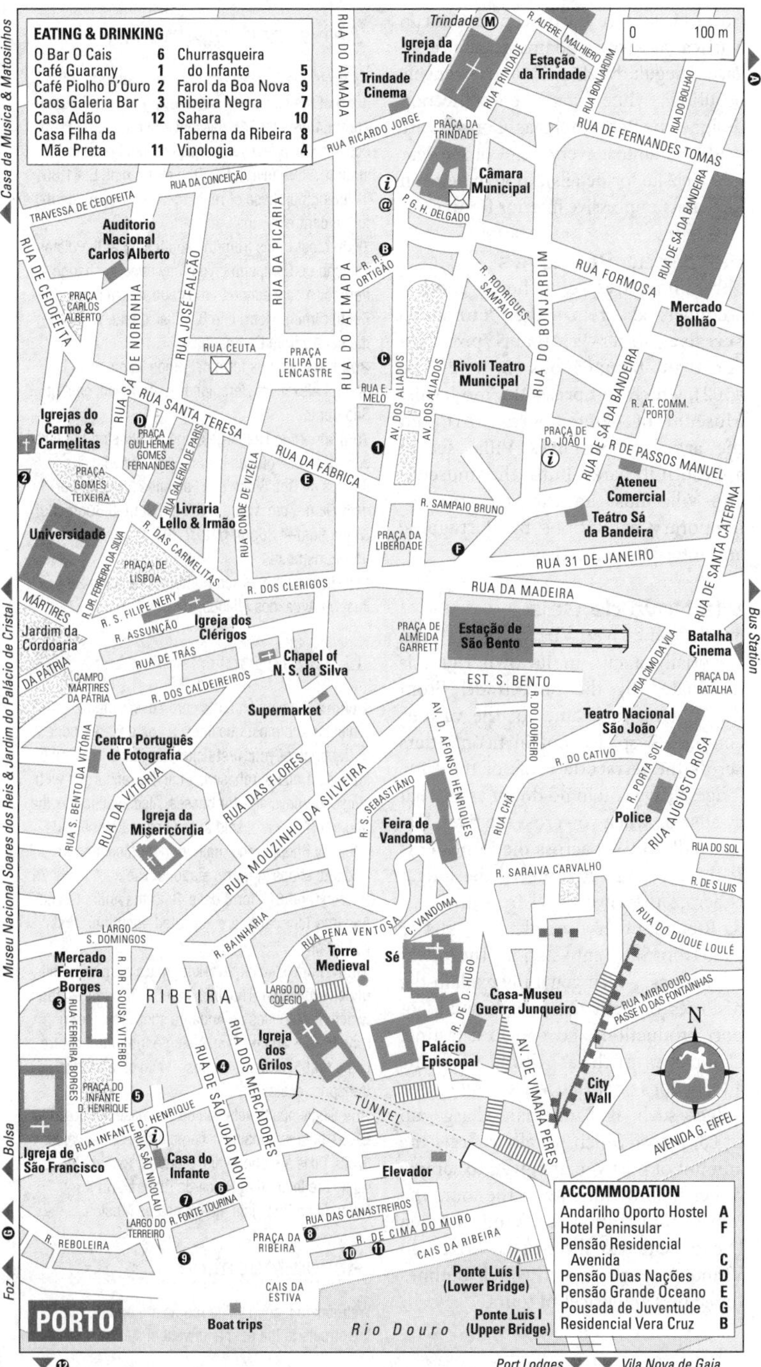

PORTUGAL

NORTHERN PORTUGAL

Boavista, 3km west of the centre, **Casa da Música** (Ⓦwww.casadamusica.com) is a vast, irregularly shaped, and strangely beautiful white concrete confection designed by Rem Koolhaas. Concerts are held here almost every night of the year (see website for details), though you can look at its impressive interior for free.

Fundação Serralves

Three kilometres west of here is another architectural gem, the **Fundação Serralves** (Tues–Fri 10am–7pm, Sat–Sun 10am–8pm; €5; bus #201, #203 or #502), which comprises the modernist Museum of Contemporary Art and the art deco Serralves Villa, set in a beautiful park. Both the museum and villa host an exciting array of temporary exhibitions by Portuguese and international artists.

Vila Nova de Gaia

South of the river, **Vila Nova de Gaia**, essentially a city in its own right, is dominated by the port trade. From the Ribeira, the names of the various companies, spelled out in neon letters across the terracotta roofs of the wine lodges, leave you in no doubt as to what awaits you when you cross the river. You can walk to Gaia across the **Ponte Luís I**: the most direct route to the lodges is across the lower level from the Cais da Ribeira; otherwise, take bus #904 or #905 from São Bento station. The lodges offer **tours**, which generally explain the histories of both the company and of port production, and end in a tasting. Companies such as Croft, Graham's and Taylor's offer free tours, while some lodges such as Sandeman charge up to €3, a cost which usually reflects the amount of port you are given to sample rather than the quality of the tour. The tourist information kiosk on Avenida Diogo Leite has the helpful Caves do Vinho do Porto leaflet, which outlines timetables and prices of tours.

Arrival and information

Air From the Francisco Sá Carneiro airport, 10km north of the city, an Aerobus (every 30min 7.30am–7pm; €4, free for TAP passengers) runs to Avda. dos Aliados, a few yards north of São Bento train station. Alternatively, take the metro (line E, €1.80 including purchase of rechargeable Andante card) to the centre; it runs until 1am.

Train Most trains from the south stop at the distant Estação de Campanhã; you may need to change here for a connection to the central Estação de São Bento (5min). Metro line B will also take you into the centre from Campanhã.

Bus The main bus terminal (Rede-Expressos) is on Rua Alexandre Herculano, a short walk east of São Bento.

Tourist office The largest and most helpful of three central tourist offices is just north of Avda. dos Aliados on Rua Clube dos Fenianos 25 (summer daily 9am–7pm; winter Mon–Fri 9am–5.30pm, Sat & Sun 9am–4.30pm; Ⓣ222 393 472, Ⓦwww.portoturismo.pt).

Internet Onweb, Praça Humberto Delgado 291. Just off Avda. dos Aliados.

City transport

Tickets The new Andante card covers metro, tram, funicular and most bus lines. It costs €0.50, added to the price of your first ticket, available in all metro stations. Once purchased, it can be recharged with single journeys or 24hr passes. Also available is the Andante Tour card, sold at the Loja da Mobilidade (Mobility Shop) in the main tourist office, and at Andante shops in metro stations. The card costs €5 for 24hr and €11 for 3 days. Both the Andante and Andante Tour cards are activated upon their first validation.

Metro Porto's sleek, five-line metro system is still under expansion. The lines meet at Trindade station, which also houses an Andante shop. The metro runs from 6.30am–1am. A single trip in the centre costs €0.85, and a 24hr pass, valid on all forms of transport, costs €3.

Bus Single bus tickets can be purchased onboard for €1.30, but the Andante scheme offers better value.

Taxis Taxis are cheap and plentiful; two useful ranks are located at Praça da Ribeira and the Rotonda da Boa Vista, near Casa da Música.

Accommodation

Well-located, good value rooms are on offer in the streets to the east and west of **Avenida dos**

Aliados. There are also some bargain rooms around lively **Praça da Batalha**.

Hostels

Andarilho Oporto Hostel Rua da Firmeza 364 ☎222 012 073, ⓦwww.andarilhohostel.com. It may not be a bargain, but this hostel offers spacious dorms, a lounge and kitchen, and is a good place to meet other travellers. Metro to Bolhão. Dorms ❷

Pousada de Juventude Rua Paulo Gama 552 ☎226 177 257, ⓦwww.pousadasjuventude.pt. Large, clean and modern, with a great view of the mouth of the Douro. Bus #207 from São Bento or #500 from Casa da Música. Dorms ❷, twin ❹

Pensions and hotels

Hotel Peninsular Rua Sá da Bandeira 21 ☎222 003 012. Offers a wide variety of accommodation at different prices, from small, windowless digs to rooms that border on the luxurious. ❹–❼

Pensão Residencial Avenida Avda. dos Aliados 141 ☎222 009 551, ⓦhttp://planeta.clix.pt/pensaoavenida. Sparklingly clean rooms with smart, modern bathrooms. ❹

Pensão Duas Nações Praça Guilherme Gomes Fernandes 59 ☎222 081 616, ⓦwww.duasnacoes.com.pt. A deservedly popular option, with bright, decently sized rooms, most of which are en suite. ❸

Pensão Grande Oceano Rua da Fábrica 45 ☎222 038 770, ⓦwww.pensaograndeoceano.com. Don't be put off by the faded common areas as the 15 rooms are pleasant and well-maintained, with en-suite bathrooms. One room sleeps up to five. ❸

Residencial Vera Cruz Rua Ramalho Ortigão 14 ☎223 323 396, ⓦwww.residencialveracruz.com. More like a small hotel than a *residencial*, this place is just off Aliados and offers smart, well-kept rooms and a great breakfast. A refurbishment is planned, so prices may increase. ❹

Campsites

Madalena Rua do Cerro ☎227 122 520, ⓦwww.orbitur.com. Located in Gaia, this Orbitur site is well shaded and close to the sea. Take bus #906 from São Bento. ❶

Marisol Rua Alto das Chaquedas 82 ☎227 135 942. Peaceful location south of the river; take bus #906 from São Bento. ❶

Eating

Porto's culinary speciality is *tripas* (tripe), although there are plenty of alternatives on the menu. Its restaurants offer excellent value for money, particularly the **workers' cafés**, which usually offer a set menu for the day. Prime areas are Rua do Almada and Rua de São Bento da Vitória. All places are busy at midday and often close around 7.30pm and all day Sunday. The city has a strong **café culture**, which includes some elegant rivals to the *fin-de-siècle* places in Lisbon.

Cafés and restaurants

Café Guarany Avda. dos Aliados 85-89. Historical café-restaurant with a classy atmosphere and regular live music. Dish of the day €8.50.

Café Piolho D'Ouro Praça de Parada Letão. Near the university, this diner is popular with students and serves cheap food throughout the day before morphing into a packed bar at night. Closed Sun. Squid €6.

Casa Adão Avda. Ramos Pinto 252. On Gaia's riverfront, this restaurant offers tasty Portuguese classics such as grilled sardines, with a dish of the day for just €5. Home-made desserts are also excellent.

Casa Filha da Mãe Preta Arcos do Douro 2–3, Cais da Ribeira. Bustling restaurant with excellent views over the river. Closed Mon. Pork chops €9.

Churrasqueira do Infante Praça Infante Dom Henrique. A wide selection of good-value grilled meat and fish makes this *churrasqueira* a great budget option in the Ribeira. Closed Sun. Grilled hake €6.50.

Farol da Boa Nova Muro dos Bacalheiros 115. A decent choice on the touristy riverfront, with a stylish interior and an extensive wine list. Serves traditional dishes. Cod cakes €8.50.

Praia dos Ingleses Rua da Coronel Raúl Peres, Foz. Restaurant and bar with a large terrace right next to the beach. The food is rather average, but the views are superb. Open until 2am. Bus #500 to Lois. *Francesinha* (meat sandwich in tomato sauce) €8.

Drinking and nightlife

The **Cais da Ribeira** waterfront offers a vibrant scene at night with its lively, late-night bars. Most of the city's big nightclubs are in the outlying **Matosinhos** district or near Foz.

Bars

O Bar O Cais Rua da Fonte Tourina 2. Relaxed bar with a clientele as varied as the soundtrack. Serves a variety of foreign beers, and jugs of cheap sangria.

Caos Galeria Bar Rua de Ferreira Borges 86. Trendy, atmospheric bar offering some late-night action in the centre. Opens at midnight.

Ribeira Negra Rua da Fonte Tourina 66. Lively, inexpensive bar popular with students.
Sahara Cais da Estiva 4. Cosy shisha bar serving a plethora of teas and cocktails.
Taberna da Ribeira Praça da Ribeira. Prime riverside spot with outdoor tables. Closes 2am.
Vinologia Rua de São João 46 Innovative bar offering port-tastings with knowledgeable, friendly staff. Even an expert could learn a lot here.

Clubs

All the clubs below are out of the centre, though you can catch one of the night buses from Aliados or Casa da Música to most if you can't afford a taxi.
Hard Club Cais de Gaia, Vila Nova de Gaia Ⓦ www.hard-club.com. Porto's main venue for international DJs. Check the website for details, as music varies from night to night. Also boasts a cool roof terrace.
Mau Mau Rua do Outeiro 4, Foz. Popular with locals, this club offers a mixture of house and R&B, with occasional guest DJs. Wed–Sat until 4am. Bus #500.
Via Rápida Rua Manuel Pinto de Azevedo 5, Matosinhos. Enormous, fashionable spot with DJs playing house music. Open Fri & Sat midnight until 7am.

Moving on

Train Braga (hourly; 1hr 30min); Coimbra (hourly; 1hr 20min–2hr 30 min); Guimarães (13 daily; 1hr 30min); Lisbon (hourly; 3hr–3hr 30 min); Madrid, Spain (4 daily; 12hr 30 min–14hr 30 min); Vigo, Spain (2 daily; 3hr 30min).
Bus Braga (hourly; 1hr 20min); Bragança (3 daily; 1hr 50min–3hr); Coimbra (8–10 daily; 1hr 30min); Guimarães (12 daily; 2hr); Lisbon (hourly; 3hr 30 min).

BRAGA

Capital of the Minho, **BRAGA** is also Portugal's religious capital – the scene of spectacular **Easter celebrations** with torchlight processions. But it's not all pomp and ceremony; it's also a lively university town, with a compact and pretty historical centre.

What to see and do

Rua Andrade Corvo leads from the train station to the centre, entered via the sixteenth-century Arco da Porta Nova. Just beyond here lies the oldest cathedral in the country, the extraordinary **Sé** (daily 8am–6.30pm; free), which dates back to 1070 and encompasses Gothic, Renaissance and Baroque styles. The most impressive areas of the Sé, the Gothic chapels – most notably the Capela dos Reis (Kings' Chapel), built to house the tombs of Henry of Burgundy and his wife Theresa, the cathedral's founders – may only be visited by guided tour (9am–noon & 2pm–6.30pm; €2 including museum). Near the cathedral is the **Archbishop's Palace** (Mon–Fri 9am–12.30pm & 2–7.30pm; free), a great fortress-like building which now houses university offices and a library. Just behind the Palace lies the lovely Jardim de Santa Bárbara, an oasis of topiary and rose gardens. Braga's main square, the buzzing, café-lined Praça da República, is a short walk northwest of the garden.

Bom Jesus do Monte

Braga's real gem is **Bom Jesus do Monte**, 3km outside the city. Its glorious ornamental stairway is one of Portugal's best-known images. Set on a wooded hillside, high above the city, it's a monumental place of pilgrimage created by Braga's archbishop in the early eighteenth century. The #2 bus runs from in front of the Cristal Farmácia on Avenida da Liberdade in Braga to a car park next to the stairway twice every hour. Turn left out of the car park to ascend the wide, tree-lined staircases and watch Bom Jesus's simple allegory unfold. Each landing holds a small fountain and a chapel containing tableau depictions of the life of Christ, leading up to the Crucifixion scene on the altar of the Neoclassical church which sits atop the staircase. The first fountain symbolizes the Wounds of Christ, the next five the Senses, and the final three represent the Virtues. Beyond the church are wooded gardens, grottoes and a number of hotels and restaurants.

Arrival and information

Train Braga's train station is almost 1km from the centre, down Rua Andrade Corvo.
Bus The bus station, a regional hub, is east of the centre on Avda. General Norton de Matos.
Tourist office (Mon–Fri 9am–6.30pm, Sat & Sun 9am–12.30pm & 2–5.30pm; ⓣ 253 262 550, ⓦ www.cm-braga.pt) is at the corner of Praça da República and Avda. da Liberdade.

Accommodation

Campismo Parque da Ponte ⓣ 253 273 355. Cheap, basic camp site 2km south of central Braga. Bus #9, #15 or #56 from Avda. da Liberdade. ❶
Grande Residencial Avenida Avda. da Liberdade 738–2° ⓣ 253 616 363, ⓔ r.avenida@netcabo.pt. Offers large, air-conditioned rooms, half of which are en suite. ❹
Pousada de Juventude Rua de Santa Margarida 6. ⓣ 253 616 163, ⓦ www.pousadasjuventude.pt. Fairly basic but lively, with 8-bed dorms and en-suite twins. Dorms ❶, twin ❸
Residencial Dora Largo da Senhora a Branca 92–94 ⓣ 253 200 180, ⓦ www.residencialdora.no.sapo.pt. Close to Praça da República, this excellent-value option has 12 sunny en-suite rooms, with breakfast provided by the owners' next-door bakery. ❹

Eating and drinking

A Brasileira Largo Barão de São Marinho. Bustling café with pavement tables serving drinks and light meals. Sandwich €3.
Casa Pimenta Praça Conde de Agrolongo 46 (closed Thurs). Serves reasonably priced, quality Portuguese staples in generous quantities. Grilled sardines €8.
Gosto Superior Praça Mousinho de Albuquerque 29. Northeast of Praça da República, this popular vegetarian restaurant dishes up delicious, cheap daily specials and home-made desserts in a trendy but relaxed environment. Lunch only on Sun. Lunch €5 including drink.

Moving on

Bus Bragança (2 daily; 5hr); Guimarães (every 30min; 30min–1hr); Porto (hourly; 1hr 20min).
Train Lisbon (13 daily; 3hr 30 min–4hr 30min); Porto (hourly; 1hr–1hr 30 min).

GUIMARÃES

The first capital of Portugal, **GUIMARÃES** remains an atmospheric and beautiful university town. The town's chief attraction is the hill-top **castle** (daily 9.30am–12.30pm & 2–5.30pm; free), whose square keep and seven towers are an enduring symbol of the emergent Portuguese nation. Built by the Countess of Mumadona and extended by Henry of Burgundy, it became the stronghold of his son, Afonso Henriques, Portugal's first independent king. Afonso launched the Reconquest from Guimarães, which was replaced by Coimbra as the capital city in 1143. Other key sights include the **Archbishop's Palace** (9.30am–12.30pm & 2–5.30pm; €3, free Sun am) near the castle, a fifteenth-century building which was perfectly restored and used as a presidential residence for Salazar, Portugal's former dictator, and the **Igreja de Nossa Senhora da Oliveira** on Largo da Oliveira (7.15am–noon & 3.30–7.30pm; free), a beautiful convent church founded by Countess Mumadona, in the picturesque medieval centre.

Arrival and information

Bus Guimarães's bus station is fifteen minutes' walk west of town in a vast shopping centre. Follow Avenida Conde de Margaride to reach the town centre.
Train The train station is south of town, connected to the centre by Avenida D. Afonso Henriques.
Tourist office On the corner of Avenida D. Afonso Henriques and Alameda de São Damaso (Mon–Fri 9.30am–6.30pm, Sat 10am–6pm, Sun 10am–1pm; ⓣ 253 412 450, ⓦ www.cm-guimaraes.pt); plus in Praça de Santiago (Mon–Fri 9.30am–6.30pm, Sat 10am–6pm, Sun 10am–1pm; ⓣ 253 518 790).

Accommodation and eating

Cozinha Regional Santiago Praça de Santiago. Lovely little restaurant offering regional specialities at fair prices, set in a pretty square which also houses a number of lively bars.

Pousada de Juventude Hostel Largo da Cidade ⓣ253 421 380, ⓦwww.pousadasjuventude.pt. Stylish new hostel with excellent facilities; definitely the best-value accommodation in town. Dorms ❷, twin ❸

Residencial das Trinas Rua das Trinas 29 ⓣ253 517 358, ⓦwww.residencialtrinas.com. Another good option in the town centre, with pleasant, recently renovated rooms. ❹

THE DOURO RAIL ROUTE

The Douro Valley, a narrow, winding gorge for the majority of its route, offers some of the most spectacular scenery in Portugal. The **DOURO RAIL ROUTE**, which joins the river about 60km inland and then sticks to it across the country, is one of those journeys that needs no justification other than the trip itself.

What to see and do

Porto is a good place to begin a trip, though there are also regular connections along the line as far as Peso da Régua; beyond Régua, there are less frequent connections to Tua and Pocinho, which marks the end of the line. The trip from Porto to Pocinho takes 3hr 15min (€14.90), but the best way to experience the rail route is to take one of the branch lines which lead away from the main track at Livração, Peso da Regua and Tua.

Amarante

At **Livração**, about an hour from Porto, the Tâmega line cuts off for the lovely mountain town of **AMARANTE**. The journey is spectacular, the single-carriage train struggling uphill through pine woods and vineyards, with the river visible like a piece of lapis lazuli far below. Amarante is a pleasant place to stop, with much of its history revolving around the thirteenth-century hermit **Gonçalo**, the Portuguese equivalent of St Valentine, who is credited with founding just about everything in town. Although it has a nice church and unusual modernist museum, the main attraction is the riverside setting, the peaceful atmosphere and relaxed old streets. A good cheap hotel is *Residencial A Raposeira*, Largo António Cândido 53 (ⓣ255 432 221; ❸); for food, try the locally renowned *Adega A Quelha* on Rua de Olivença. The tourist office (July–Sept 9am–7pm; Oct–June 9am–12.30pm & 2–5.30pm) is on Alameda Teixeira de Pascoaes.

Vila Real

Shortly after Livração, the main line finally reaches the Douro and heads upstream to Peso da Régua, the depot through which all port wine must pass on its way to Porto. From here, the narrow-gauge Corgo train line branches off through the mountains destined for **VILA REAL**. The gateway to Trás-os-Montes – and the closest this rural province gets to a city – Vila Real is a lively little spot with an invitingly laid-back atmosphere and some surprisingly sophisticated shopping. It also makes a great base for exploration of the nearby Parque Natural do Alvão, a mountainous park containing an impressive variety of flora and fauna. Also close to Vila Real, reached by bus #1 from Rua Gonçalo Cristóvão, is the Casa de Mateus (March–May & Oct 9am–1pm & 2–6pm; June–Sept 9am–7.30pm; Nov–Feb 10am–1pm & 2–5pm; house & gardens €6.50, gardens only €3.70), instantly recognizable as the house depicted on labels of Mateus Rosé wine. This palatial baroque residence can be visited by guided tour, and is set in a vast formal garden. The best-value accommodation in Vila Real is the charming, well-kept *Residencial Real* (ⓣ259 325 879; ❹), with the bonus of breakfast in the downstairs *pastelaria*. The bulk of the town's restaurants are on Rua Teixeira de Sousa; a good choice for regional specialities is *O Escondidinho* at no. 7 (Roast kid €8). Vila Real's tourist office (June–Sept Mon–Fri 9.30am–7pm, Sat & Sun 9.30am–12.30pm & 2–6pm; Oct–May Mon–Sat 9.30am–12.30pm & 2–6pm) is at Avenida Carvalho Araújo 94.

BRAGANÇA

On a hillock above the small and remote provincial capital of **BRAGANÇA** stands a pristine circle of walls, the extraordinary **Cidadela**, enclosing a medieval village and castle. The **Domus Municipalis** here (Fri–Wed 9am–4.45pm; free), a fifteenth-century pentagonal Romanesque civic building, is the only one of its kind in Europe. Towering above this is what remains of Bragança's **royal castle**, including the Torre de Menagem, which now houses a rather dull **Military Museum** (Fri–Wed 9–11.45am & 2–4.45pm; €1.50, free Sun am). At its side a curious pillory rises from the back of a prehistoric granite pig, or porca, thought to have been a fertility idol of a prehistoric cult. Bragança's central bus station is on Avenida João da Cruz, and operates Rede Expressos and Rodo Norte/Santos buses to Mirando do Douro, Vila Real, and Porto, among other destinations. The modern *Pousada de Juventude* (Ⓣ273 304 600, Ⓦwww.pousadasjuventude.pt; dorm ❷, twin from ❸), 1km west of the centre on Avenida 22 de Maio, is a great place to stay, as is the more central *Residencial Sra da Ribeira* on Travessa da Misericórdia (Ⓣ & Ⓕ273 300 555; ❹). Good dining options include the tasty regional dishes on offer at *Restaurante Poças* at Rua Combatentes de Grande Guerra 200. The tourist office (Mon–Sat 10am–12.30pm & 2–5/6.30pm; Ⓣ273 381 273) is on Avenida Cidade de Zamora, a couple of hundred metres north of the cathedral.

PARQUE NATURAL DO DOURO INTERNACIONAL

South of Bragança, hugging the border with Spain in the east, is the vast and beautiful wilderness of the Parque Natural do Douro Internacional, home to Europe's largest concentration of Egyptian vultures and a huge number of other birds of prey. The best place to base yourself for a visit is the town of **MOGADOURO**, site of the park's headquarters (Rua de Santa Marinha 4) and connected by daily weekday bus from Bragança (1hr 40min). Accommodation is plentiful: try the *Pensão Russo* (Ⓣ279 342 134; ❹), on Rua das Eiras.

Southern Portugal

The huge, sparsely populated plains of the **Alentejo**, southeast of Lisbon, are overwhelmingly agricultural, dominated by vast cork plantations well suited to the low rainfall, sweltering heat and arid soil. This impoverished province is divided into large estates that provide nearly half of the world's cork but only a meagre living for its rural inhabitants. Visitors to the Alentejo often head for **Évora**, the province's dominant and most historic city. But the **Alentejo coast**, the Costa Azul, is a breath of fresh air after the stifling plains of the inland landscape.

With its long, sandy beaches and picturesque rocky coves, the southern coast of the **Algarve** is the most visited region in the country. West of **Faro**, the Algarve's capital, you'll find the classic postcard images of the province – a series of tiny bays and coves, broken up by weird rocky outcrops and fantastic grottoes, at their most exotic around the resort of **Lagos**. To the east of Faro lie the less-developed sandy offshore islets, **the Ilhas** – which front the coastline for some 25 miles – and the lower-key resorts of **Olhão** and **Tavira**. Or head inland where you'll find a more Portuguese way of life at **Silves**, the impressive former capital of the Moors. In summer it is wise to book accommodation in advance, as the Algarve is a popular package holiday destination.

ÉVORA

ÉVORA, a UNESCO World Heritage Site, is one of the most impressive cities in Portugal. The Romans were in occupation for four centuries and the Moors, who settled for just as long, left their stamp in the tangle of narrow alleys that rise steeply among the whitewashed houses. Most of the monuments, however, date from the fourteenth to the sixteenth centuries, when, with royal encouragement, the city was one of the leading centres of Portuguese art and architecture.

What to see and do

The **Templo Romano** in the central square is the best-preserved Roman temple in Portugal, its stark remains consisting of a small platform supporting more than a dozen granite columns with a marble entablature. Next to the temple lies the church of the **Convento dos Lóios**. The convent is now a luxury *pousada*, but the church (Tues–Sun 9.30am–12.30pm & 2–5pm; €3), dedicated to **São João Evangelista**, contains beautiful *azulejos* and an ossuary under the floor. The adjacent palace is the private property of the ducal Cadaval family, though parts of it are sometimes open to visitors for exhibits (usually €2 extra). Nearby, the Romanesque cathedral, or **Sé** (daily 9am–12.30pm & 2–5pm, cloisters and museum €3; museum closed Mon), was begun in 1186, about twenty years after the reconquest of Évora from the Moors. The most memorable sight in town, however, is the **Capela dos Ossos** (daily 9am–1pm & 2.30–5.30pm; €1.50) in the church of **São Francisco**, just south of Praça do Giraldo. A gruesome reminder of mortality, the walls and pillars of this chilling chamber are entirely covered with the bones of more than five thousand monks; an inscription over the door reads, Nós ossos que aqui estamos, Pelos vossos esperamos – "We bones here are waiting for your bones". Just below the church lies a beautiful, shady park with a duck pond and a small café.

Arrival and information

Bus and train Évora's bus and train stations are 1km west of the old town, a twenty-minute walk from the central Praça do Giraldo.
Tourist office Praça do Giraldo (May–Sept Mon–Fri 9am–7pm, Sat & Sun 9.30am–12.30pm & 2–5.30pm; Oct–April 9.30am–12.30pm; ⓣ 266 730 030).

Accommodation

Évora's tourist appeal pushes accommodation prices over the norm. In addition to the places listed below, there are also some attractive *turismo rural* properties in the nearby countryside; the tourist office has details.
Parque de Campismo Estrada de Alcáçovas ⓣ 266 705 190. This well-equipped campsite is 2km out of town on the Alcáçovas road; take the hourly buses #5 and #8 from Praça 1 de Maio. ❶
Pensão O Giraldo Rua dos Mercadores 27 ⓣ 266 705 833. Clean, comfortable rooms; those with en-suite (❻) are more spacious. Prices rise in Aug and Sept. ❹.
Residencial O Alentejo Rua Serpa Pinto 74 ⓣ 266 702 903. Slightly old-fashioned, with pleasant high-ceilinged rooms. ❺
Residencial Policarpo Rua Freiria de Baixo 16 ⓣ 266 702 424, ⓦ www.pensaopolicarpo.com. Beautiful, rambling old place full of rustic charm. Also has rooms sleeping three or four. ❹–❻

Eating and drinking

O Antão Rua João de Deus 5. The place to come for regional specialities such as rabbit. Closed Wed. *Alentejana* €14.
O Aqueducto Rua do Cano 13a. Prize-winning restaurant serving imaginative dishes. Closed Sun eve and all Mon. Daily special €12.
Bar Oficin@ Rua da Moeda 27. Friendly, laid-back bar open until 2am. Closed Sun.
Casa dos Sabores Rua Miguel Bombarda 50. Pleasant café offering inexpensive sandwiches, salads and pastries. Sandwich €2.

THE ALENTEJO COAST

The **ALENTEJO COAST** begins below Lisbon at Troia, stretching southwards to Zambujeira do Mar, and features towns and beaches as inviting as those of the Algarve. Some of the most attractive are pretty Porto Côvo, the bustling resort of Vila Nova de Milfontes, and the small surfers' paradise of Zambujeira do Mar. Admittedly, this stretch of coastline is exposed to the winds and waves of the Atlantic, and the waters are colder, but it's fine for summer swimming and far quieter than the southern coast.

What to see and do

Local bus services and roughly three express buses daily from Lisbon take you within easy range of the whole coastline, stopping at the beaches of Porto Côvo (2hr 30min–3hr), Vila Nova de Milfontes (3hr–3hr 30min), and Zambujeira do Mar (4hr). Accommodation is plentiful in these resorts, especially Vila Nova de Milfontes, but it's wise to book ahead during the summer months. Surfing is popular along the Alentejo coast; first-timers can have lessons at Surf Milfontes in Vila Nova de Milfontes (ⓣ919 922 193, ⓦwww.surfmilfontes.com).

Porto Côvo

Two-and-a-half hours by bus from Lisbon lies the coastal town of **PORTO CÔVO**, a popular Portuguese resort which boasts some beautiful beaches. The sleepy old town is little more than a few cobbled streets, but you won't be stuck for places to stay if you feel the urge to spend a night or two here. Cliff-top paths lead to Praia do Somouqueira, an impressive stretch of golden sand.

There's an attractive campsite (ⓣ269 905 136, ⓔcamping-portocovo@gmail.com; ❶) with its own restaurant and shop just outside town on the road to Vila Nova de Milfontes. A good choice for rooms in town is *Maresia*, at Rua Candido do Silva 57 (ⓣ269 905 449; ❺) above the restaurant of the same name, which serves delicious seafood.

Vila Nova de Milfontes

The larger resort of **VILA NOVA DE MILFONTES** lies south of Porto Côvo on the estuary of the River Mira, whose sandy banks gradually expand and merge into the coastline. This is the most popular resort in the Alentejo, with lines of villas and hotels radiating from the centre of the old village. It's still a pretty place, though, with a handsome little castle and an ancient port, reputed to have harboured Hannibal and his Carthaginians during a storm. Attractive en-suite rooms and a guest kitchen can be found at backpackers' favourite *Casa Amarela* (Rua Dom Luis Castro e Almeida; ⓣ283 996 632, ⓦwww.casaamarelamilfontes.com; ❹), and there are a couple of large **campsites** to the north of town: Parque *de Campismo Milfontes* (ⓣ283 996 140, ⓔparquemilfontes@netc.pt; ❶) and the more modest *Campiférias* (ⓣ283 996 409, ⓔnovafeiras@oninet.pt; ❶). For food, try *Patio das Pizzas* or *A Telha*, both on Rua do Pinhal. Regular buses connect Vila Nova de Milfontes with Porto Côvo (30 mins).

Odemira

The main inland base is **ODEMIRA**, a quiet, unspoilt country town, connected by eight daily buses to Vila Nova de Milfontes. Good-value accommodation is available at *Residencial Rita*, on Estrada da Circunvalação (ⓣ283 322 531; ❹), while *O Tarro*, facing the river south of the bus station, is a pleasant spot for an evening meal.

Zambujeira do Mar

Southwest of Odemira is the tiny village of **ZAMBUJEIRA DO MAR**, where a large cliff provides a dramatic backdrop to the beach, which is prime **surfing** territory. Zambujeira do Mar certainly livens up in summer, with a music festival featuring mostly Portuguese bands held every August, but it's still quieter than Vila Nova de Milfontes. There are only a few small **pensions**, such as the well-run *Mar-e-Sol* (Ⓣ283 961 171; ❺), a few private rooms to rent and a pleasant **campsite** (Ⓣ283 961 172, Ⓦwww.campingzambujeira.com.sapo.pt), about 1km from the cliffs. Restaurants are concentrated around Rua Miramar; *O Martinho* is a decent choice.

There are no direct **transport** connections between Zambujeira and the Algarve; the best way to get here is to take a local bus to Odemira (40min), then get a bus to Faro (2hr). However, these connections can be erratic; check Ⓦwww.rodalentejo.pt for details.

FARO

FARO is the capital of the Algarve, close to the international airport, 6km west of town. Excellent beaches are within easy reach, and thanks to its university there's a laid-back but lively nightlife scene too. While its suburbs may be modern, Faro retains an attractive historic centre south of the marina.

What to see and do

The **Cidade Velha**, or old town, is a semi-walled quarter entered through the eighteenth-century town gate, the **Arco da Vila**. Here you'll find the majestic **Sé** (Mon–Sat 10am–6/7pm; €3 including museum and outdoor bones chapel), which offers superb views – and a home for several nesting storks – from its belltower. The nearby **Museu Municipal** (opening hours vary, check with tourist office; €2) is housed in a sixteenth-century convent on Largo Dom Alfonso III; the most striking exhibit is a third-century Roman mosaic of Neptune and the four winds, unearthed near Faro train station. Faro's most curious sight is the Baroque **Igreja do Carmo** (Mon–Fri 10am–1pm & 3–5pm, Sat 10am–1pm) near the central post office on Largo do Carmo. A door to the right of the altar leads to a macabre **Capela dos Ossos** (€1), its walls decorated with bones disinterred from the adjacent cemetery. The nearby beach (Praia de Faro) can be reached by bus from the Avenida stop opposite the bus station, or by boat from the harbour. Five boats a day also go to the more tranquil Ilha do Farol; the tourist information office has timetables.

Arrival and information

Air Taxis from the airport to the centre cost around €10, or take bus #16 or #14 (up to 24 daily; 7am–9.40pm; €1.20), a twenty-minute journey to town. To get to the airport, catch the bus from the stop opposite the bus station.

Train The train station lies a few minutes beyond the central bus station, up Avda. da República.

Bus The bus station is right in the centre, behind the Hotel Eva, north of the marina.

Tourist office There's one at the airport (daily 8am–11.30pm; Ⓣ289 818 582), though the main office is near the harbour at Rua da Misericórdia 8 (Mon–Fri 9.30am–5.30/7pm, Sat & Sun 9.30am–12.30pm & 2–5.30/7pm; Ⓣ289 803 604, Ⓦwww.rtalgarve.pt).

Accommodation

Pousada de Juventude Rua da Polícia de Segurança Pública 1 Ⓣ289 826 521, Ⓦwww.pousadasjuventude.pt. Basic but friendly hostel east of the centre, some rooms with en suite (❹). Dorms ❷, twin ❸

Pensão São Filipe Rua Infante Dom Henrique 55 Ⓣ289 824 182, Ⓦwww.guesthouse-saofilipe.com. The recently renovated rooms are on the small side, but are immaculately clean. ❺

Residencial Adelaide Rua Cruz dos Mestres 7 Ⓣ289 802 383, Ⓦwww.adelaideresidencial.com. Smart, comfortable air-conditioned rooms. ❺

Residencial Oceano Rua Ivens 21 Ⓣ289 823 349. A pleasant, good-value choice in the town centre. ❹

Eating and drinking

Adega Nova Rua Francisco Barreto 24. Another value-for-money restaurant which is always crammed with locals. Pork chops €6.50.

Café do Coreto Jardim Manuel Bívar. Right next to the marina, this café is open all day serving sandwiches, pizza and drinks. Pizza €7.

Fim do Mundo Rua Vasco da Gama 53. Inexpensive option in the pedestrianized centre. Closed Mon. Roast cod €8

Upa Upa Café Bar Rua Conseilheiro de Bívar 51. Chilled-out spot perfect for a drink before hitting the bars and clubs around nearby Rua do Prior.

Moving on

Train Lagos (7 daily; 1hr 40min); Lisbon (4 daily; 5hr 30min–6hr); Olhão (16 daily; 10min); Silves (7 daily; 1hr–1hr 15min); Tavira (12–17 daily; 35–45min).

Bus Évora (3–5 daily; 4hr–4hr 30min); Huelva (for connections to Sevilla, Spain; 2–4 daily; 3hr 30min); Lagos (8 daily; 2hr 15 min); Lisbon (7–9 daily; 4hr–4hr 30min); Olhão (every 15min–1hr; 20min); Tavira (7–11 daily; 1hr).

LAGOS

The seaside town of **LAGOS** is one of the Algarve's most popular destinations and attracts large numbers of visitors each summer, drawn by its beautiful beaches and lively nightlife. Lagos was also favoured by Henry the Navigator, who used it as a base for African trade. Europe's first slave market was built here in 1441 in the arches of the Customs House, which still stands in the Praça da República near the waterfront.

What to see and do

On the waterfront and to the rear of the town are the remains of Lagos's once impregnable fortifications, devastated by the Great Earthquake. One rare and beautiful church which did survive was the **Igreja de Santo António**; decorated around 1715, its gilt and carved interior is wildly obsessive, every inch filled with a private fantasy of cherubic youths struggling with animals and fish. The church forms part of a visit to the adjacent **Museu Municipal** (Tues–Sun 9.30am–12.30pm & 2–5pm; €2), housing an extraordinarily eclectic collection of artefacts including Roman busts and deformed animal foetuses. Lagos's main attraction, however, is its splendid beaches, the most secluded of which lie below extravagantly eroded cliff faces south of town. **Praia de Dona Ana** is considered the most picturesque, though its crowds make the smaller coves of **Praia do Pinhão**, down a track just opposite the fire station, and **Praia Camilo**, a little further along, more appealing. Over the river east of Lagos is a splendid sweep of sand – **Meia Praia** – where there's space even at the height of summer. Meia Praia is an ideal destination for watersports enthusiasts, as various companies based here offer water-skiing and sailboard lessons, and it's also popular with surfers. Those who like to keep their feet dry might prefer an excursion to the extraordinary rock formations around **Ponta da Piedade**, a headland that can be viewed by boat (around €10) from the harbour.

Arrival and information

Train The train station is across the river, fifteen minutes' walk from the centre via a swing bridge in the marina.

Bus The bus station is slightly closer to the town centre, just off the main Avda. dos Descobrimentos.

Tourist office On Largo Marquês de Pombal in the central pedestrian zone (April & May Mon–Fri 10am–6pm & Sat 10am–2pm; June & Sept Mon–Sat 10am–6pm; July & Aug daily 10am–8pm; ⓣ 282 764 111).

Accommodation

Angela Guesthouse Loteamento da Ameijeira, Rua Teixeira Gomes Bloco AN1-2 ⓣ 962 616 552, ⓔ angelaguesthouse@hotmail.com. Pleasant, comfortable rooms with shared bathroom in a private apartment. ❹

Campismo da Trindade Rossio da Trindade ⓣ 282 763 893. Small, busy campsite close to the sea. To reach it, follow the main road 200m beyond the fort. ❶

Carlos House Hostel Rua Jogo da Bola 8 ⓣ 916 594 225, ⓔ carloshousez@yahoo.com. Popular backpacker hostel offering dorms and private rooms. Dorms ❷, room ❹

Pensão Caravela Rua 25 de Abril 16 ⓣ 282 763 361. Well-kept rooms right in the centre of town. ❺

Pousada de Juventude Rua Lançarote de Freitas 50 ⓣ 282 761 970, ⓦ www.pousadasjuventude.pt.

Busy, well-equipped hostel in a central location; one of the country's best. Dorms ❷, twin from ❹

Eating and drinking

Bon Vivant Rua 25 de Abril 105. Multistorey bar-club with a "tropical" roof terrace.
Casa Rosa Rua do Ferrador 22. Popular with travellers, this café serves good-value international dishes. Chilli con carne €5.
Eddie's Bar Rua 25 de Abril 99. Friendly bar with loud music and cheap drinks.
Mullens Bar Rua Cândido dos Reis 86, Atmospheric bar-restaurant with lively music until 2am.
Néctar Enoteca Rua Silva Lopes 19. Smart wine bar with an extensive tapas menu. Closed Tues. Octopus salad €4.50.
No Patio Rua Lançarote de Freitas 46 ☎282 763 777. Run by a British expat chef, *No Patio* ("on the patio") offers beautifully prepared fusion cuisine at a reasonable price. Thai-style monkfish and prawns €15. Reservations recommended.

Moving on

Train Faro (7 daily; 1hr 40min); Lisbon (4 daily; 5hr 15min); Silves (13 daily; 30–50min).
Bus Faro (5 daily; 2hr 15min); Porto Côvo (1 daily; 3hr) Seville, Spain (4 daily; 5hr30 min); Vila Nova de Milfontes (1 daily; 1hr 45min).

SILVES

SILVES is an inland Algarve town that merits a detour. Capital of the Moorish kings of the al-Gharb (now Algarve), it's still an atmospheric, attractive place that also hosts a lively summer beer festival, held at the end of July and lasting four days. Under the Moors, Silves was a place of grandeur and industry, described in contemporary accounts as being "of shining brightness". In 1189 an army led by Sancho I put an end to this splendour, killing some six thousand Moors in the process. The impressively complete sandstone walls of the Moorish **fortress** (July–Sept 10am–8pm; Oct–May 10am–6pm; €1.50) retain their towers and elaborate communication system, but the inside will remain something of a building site until renovation works are complete. Just below the fortress is Silves' **cathedral** (Mon–Sat 8.30am–6.30pm, Sun between masses only; free), built on the site of the mosque in the thirteenth century. The nearby **Museu de Arqueologia** (Mon–Sat 9am–6pm; €1.50) is an engaging museum that romps through the history of Silves from prehistoric times to the sixteenth century. The **train station**, on the Lagos–Faro line, lies 2km outside the town; there's a connecting bus to the centre. The **tourist office**, at Rua 25 de Abril 26 (Mon–Fri 9.30am–1.30pm & 2.30–6pm; ☎282 442 255), can help you find a **private room**, or try those on offer at *Residencial Ponte Romana*, over the Roman bridge (☎282 443 275; ❸), with the bonus of a decent restaurant below. Other inexpensive **restaurants** cluster round the riverside market building, and on Friday evenings, visit the Fábrica Inglês, where shows are laid on in a former factory packed with cafés and bars.

OLHÃO AND THE ISLANDS

OLHÃO, 8km east of Faro, is the largest fishing port in the Algarve and an excellent base for visiting the local sandbank islands. The pedestrianized centre, close to the seafront, is pretty yet free of tourist hordes, and ensures Olhão retains a blissful traditional charm.

What to see and do

Although Olhão has no sights to speak of, its cafe-strewn centre is well worth a wander, and there's a bustling market on Avenida 5 de Outubro. Olhão's main attraction, however, is its close proximity to and good connections with two of the sandbank islands which comprise the **Ria Formosa Natural Park**. The islands of Armona and Culatra boast some superb, spacious beaches, so expansive that they still feel uncrowded even at the height of summer, within easy reach of Olhão. Ferries to the islands operate year-round, and depart regularly from the jetty to the left of the municipal gardens.

The service to **Armona** (30min; €2.70 return) drops you off at a long strip of holiday chalets and huts that stretches right across the island on either side of the main path. On the ocean side, the beach disappears into the distance and a short walk will take you to totally deserted stretches of sand. Boats to the more distant **Culatra** (30 min; €2.70 return) call first at Praia da Culatra, a vast expanse of sand stretching away from Culatra town. The same service then makes its way to Praia do Farol (1hr; €3.30 return), which is considered to be one of the most beautiful beaches on the sandbank islands. If you head east away from the holiday homes, the beach becomes more deserted, and eventually leads to the peaceful Praia dos Hangares.

Arrival and information

Train and bus The train station is east of Avda. da República northeast of town, while the bus station is nearby, to the west of the Avenida.
Tourist office Largo Sebastião Martins Mestre (May–Sept Mon–Fri 9.30am–7pm; Oct–April Mon–Fri 9.30am–noon & 1–5.30pm ⓣ289 713 936).

Accommodation

Camping Olhão ⓣ289 700 300, ⓦwww.sbsi.pt. Large, well-equipped campsite 2km east of town. In summer a bus runs from near the municipal garden. ❶
Pensão Bela Vista Rua Teófilo Braga 65 ⓣ289 702 538. Offers neat and tidy en-suite rooms with air conditioning. ❺
Pensão Bicuar Rua Vasco da Gama 5 ⓣ289 714 816, ⓦwww.pension-bicuar.net. Friendly guesthouse with a kitchen, roof terrace, and pleasant rooms with shower and sink which sleep up to four. ❹

Eating_

Bela Vista Rua Teófilo Braga 65. Try the excellent local dishes at this restaurant, underneath the Pensão of the same name. Grilled cod €8.
Ria Formosa Avda. 5 de Outubro 14. Popular restaurant with tasty seafood and rice dishes. Arroz *marisco* €8.

TAVIRA

TAVIRA is a good-looking little town made up of cobbled streets, and split into two pretty halves by the river Gilão. The Romans and Moors who once ruled Tavira left behind monuments which enhance its present beauty, but the main tourist attractions, the superb island beaches of the Ilha de Tavira, actually lie offshore. From July to mid-September, boats to the island depart (12 daily; 20min; €1.80 return) from the quayside on Rua do Cais. In addition, year-round boats cross from Quatro Águas (up to 12 daily; 5min; €1 return), 2km east of town. The beach is backed by dunes and stretches west almost as far as Fuzeta, 14km away. Despite increasing development – a small chalet settlement, a campsite, and a handful of bars and restaurants facing the sea – it's still easy to find your own peaceful patch of sand. Back in central Tavira, it's worth wandering up to the remains of the **Moorish castle** (Mon–Fri 8am–5pm, Sat & Sun 10am–7pm; free) perched high above the town, with its walls enclosing a pretty garden that affords splendid views.

Arrival and information

Train The train station is 1km from the centre of town, at the end of Rua da Liberdade.
Bus Buses pull up at the terminal by the river, a two-minute walk from the central square, Praça da República.
Tourist office Rua da Galeria 9 southwest of Praça da República (July & Aug Mon–Fri 9am–7pm, Sept–June Mon–Fri 9.30am–1pm & 2–5.30pm; ⓣ281 322 511).

Accommodation

Camping Tavira Ilha de Tavira ⓣ281 324 455, ⓦwww.campingtavira.com. Busy campsite with a great location on the Ilha de Tavira; follow the path opposite the ferry dock to reach it. Open

April–Sept. ❶

Residencial Imperial Rua Dr José Pires Padinha 24 ⓣ281 322 234. Friendly guesthouse on the nearside of the river, with pleasant, if small, en-suite rooms. ❺

Residencial Lagoas Rua Almirante Cândido dos Reis 24 ⓣ281 322 252. Popular option offering small, clean rooms, some with en suite (❹). Conveniently located above the budget eatery *Bica* over the river. ❸

Residencial Princesa do Gilão Rua Borda d'Agua de Aguiar 10 ⓣ & ⓕ281 325 171. Modern, air-conditioned rooms with an unbeatable location on the far side of the river. ❺

Eating and drinking

Arco Rua Almirante Cândido dos Reis 67. Friendly, laid-back bar on the far side of the river, which attracts both locals and visitors. Closed Mon.

Beira Rio Rua Borda da Àgua de Assêca 44–46. Serves decent pasta, pizza and salads. Spaghetti carbonara €8

Restaurante João Belhi Rua Dr José Pires Padinha 96. Riverside restaurant serving seafood at fairly reasonable prices. Grilled squid €8.

Tavira Romano Praça da República. Bustling café with outdoor tables serving delicious ice cream and cakes.

UBI Rua Vale Caranguejo. Tavira's only club is a warehouse-like space reached by following Rua Almirante Cândido dos Reis to the outskirts of town. Closed Mon in summer, open Fri & Sat only in winter. Closes 6am.

TREAT YOURSELF

A Ver Tavira Calçada da Galeria 13 ⓣ281 381 363. Tavira's finest restaurant is situated next to the castle, with superb views over town from its smart dining room. The menu boasts a delicious fusion of local ingredients and international recipes, and the price is reasonable given the quality of the food and beauty of the setting. Open year-round for lunch and dinner, except in July and August when it's open for dinner only. Vegetable lasagne €11, garlic shrimp with starfruit €17.50.

Romania

HIGHLIGHTS

THE CARPATHIANS: stunning mountain scenery, under two hours from the capital

SIGHIŞOARA: beautiful medieval citadel in the heart of Transylvania, with authentic Dracula connections

MUZEUL ASTRA, SIBIU: a fascinating open-air museum of Romanian village architecture, set in a scenic landscape

BUCHAREST: hectic traffic, Stalinist architecture, pretty residential streets and good dining and nightlife

ROUGH COSTS

DAILY BUDGET Basic €25/occasional treat €35

DRINK Beer €1 (€2 in Bucharest), bottle of Romanian wine €3

FOOD Two-course meal with wine €9

HOSTEL/BUDGET HOTEL €10–13/€12–18

TRAVEL Maxitaxi or Accelerat train about €3 per hour's travel

FACT FILE

POPULATION 22 million

AREA 230,340 sq km

LANGUAGE Romanian

CURRENCY New leu (RON), plural: lei

CAPITAL Bucureşti (Bucharest; population 2 million)

INTERNATIONAL PHONE CODE ⓣ40

Basics

Nowhere in Eastern Europe defies preconceptions quite like Romania. The country suffers from a poor image, but don't be put off – outstanding landscapes, a surprisingly efficient train system, a huge diversity of wildlife and a bizarre mix of cultures and people await you if you seek them out.

Romanians trace their ancestry back to the Romans, and they like to stress their Latin roots, although they have Balkan traits too. They see their future as firmly within the Euro-Atlantic family and were delighted to join NATO and then, on January 1, 2007, the European Union, which is expected to trigger an economic boom.

The capital, **Bucharest**, is perhaps daunting for the first-time visitor – its savage history is only too evident – but parts of this once-beautiful city retain a voyeuristic appeal. More attractive by far, and easily accessible on public transport, is **Transylvania**, a region steeped in history, offering some of the most beautiful mountain scenery in Europe as well as a uniquely multiethnic character. Its chief cities, such as Braşov, Sibiu and Sighişoara, were built by Saxon (German) colonists, and there are also strong Hungarian and Roma (Gypsy) presences here. In the border region of the Banat, also highly multi-ethnic, Timişoara is Romania's most western-looking city and famed as the birthplace of the 1989 revolution.

CHRONOLOGY

513 BC The Dacian tribe inhabit the area of present-day Romania.

106 AD The Roman emperor Trajan conquers the Dacian tribe.

271 Following attacks from the Goths, the Romans withdraw from the area.

1000s Hungary conquers and occupies parts of present-day Romania.

1200s Division of Romanian population into different principalities including Wallachia, Moldavia and Transylvania.

1400s Principalities of Moldavia, Transylvania and Wallachia come under attack from the Turkish Ottomans but manage to maintain their independence.

1448 Vlad "the Impaler" becomes Prince of Wallachia; he is later credited as the inspiration for the character of Dracula.

1700s The Austrian Habsburgs take control of large parts of the Romanian principalities after military successes over the Ottomans.

1862 After battling for independence, Wallachia and Moldavia unite to form Romania. Bucharest is declared the capital.

1878 Romania's claim to independence is formalized by the Treaty of Berlin.

1881 Carol I is named the first King of Romania.

1918 After invasion by the central powers during WWI, Romania is liberated and her borders vastly increased.

1939–1945 Romania sides with Germany at start of WWII, but changes allegiance to the Allies towards the end. Soviets take large parts of Romanian territory.

1947 Soviet influence remains and the Communist Party comes into power in Romania.

1965 Nicolae Ceauşescu becomes Communist Party leader and adopts a foreign-policy stance independent of the Soviets.

1989 Revolution leads to the overthrow of the Communist regime.

2007 Romania joins the European Union.

ARRIVAL

Arriving by **air**, most airlines serve Bucharest's Otopeni (Henri Coanda) airport, but there are half a dozen regional airports (of which Timişoara is the most important), served by Austrian Airlines and a growing number of budget airlines such as Wizzair and Carpatair. An option worth considering for visits to Transylvania is to get a budget flight to Budapest and then travel to Romania by **land**, which is a relatively

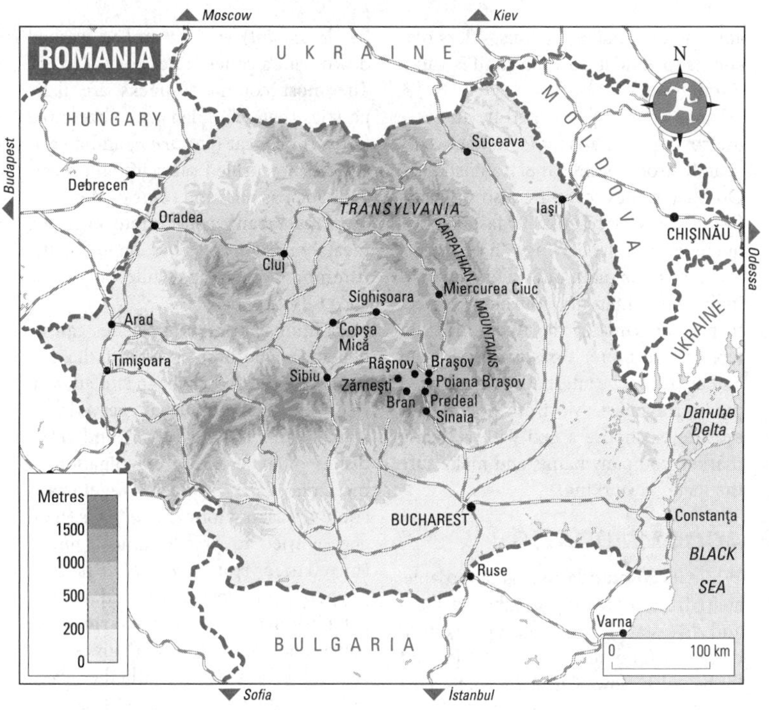

straightforward option, usually crossing from Békéscaba in Hungary to Vârsand in Romania.

Travelling to Romania by **train** is also fairly simple, via Paris, Vienna and Budapest, and there are also through trains from Prague, Belgrade, Sofia and Kiev. This will usually cost as much as flying into the country, but works well as part of a larger Europe-wide trip using either an InterRail pass (for European residents) or a Eurail pass (for non-European residents). Rail Europe (Ⓦwww.raileurope.co.uk), International Rail (Ⓦwww.international-rail.com) and Trainseurope (Ⓦwww.trainseurope.co.uk) all have numerous rail pass and point-to-point ticket options. The international operator **Eurolines** has details on bus journeys to Romania and you can book both one-way and return tickets (with an open-ended option) through them (Ⓦwww.eurolines.co.uk).

GETTING AROUND

InterCity **trains** are the most comfortable; they're followed by Rapid and Accelerat services, which stop more often. Personal trains stop everywhere and are generally grubby and crowded. Some overnight trains have **sleeping carriages** (*vagon de dormit*) and **couchettes** (*cuşet*) for a modest surcharge. Seat reservations are required for all fast trains, and are automatically included with locally purchased tickets. You'll also need a reservation for **international trains** even if you do not require one before entering Romania, so be sure to book a seat before departure or face fines. The best place to **buy tickets** and book seats is at the local Agenţia SNCFR (generally open Mon–Fri 8am–7pm); at the station tickets are slightly cheaper but available only one hour in advance. Wasteels, a Europe-wide youth rail travel agency (Ⓦwww.wasteels.com), available in some major stations, offers discounts for under-26s. InterRail is valid, Eurail is not.

Trains are complemented by an ever-improving rural **bus** (*autobuz*) network, usually from beside the train station. On busy routes there are also **minibus** (*maxitaxi*) services, usually fast and frequent, even if the driving can be manic. Maxitaxis also make quite a few surprisingly long inter-city journeys; expect to pay the same as the Accelerat train fare or a bit more. **Taxis** are very cheap and an attractive alternative to crowded public transport. Most are honest, but be sure to choose a taxi with a clearly marked company name, and make sure the meter is working.

ACCOMMODATION

While **accommodation** is affordable, apart from a growing number of four- and five-star hotels offering Western comforts (and prices), standards tend to be fairly low. Cheaper hotels cost €12–18 per person per night, for a reasonably clean room and shared shower; breakfast is normally an extra €2–3. An alternative is to take a private room (*cazare la persoane particulare*), which will probably be the only option in smaller towns and villages. In season you may come across people offering accommodation at the train or bus station. Expect to pay around €9. Hostels (Ⓦwww.hihostels-romania.ro) are becoming less rare. University towns have student accommodation (*caminul de studenţi*) from late June to August, for around €6 per night. Campsites are usually very basic. Expect to pay around €4.50 per night for tent space, with little more than a tap and dirty loo. Outside national parks, most officials will turn a blind eye if you are discreet about camping wild.

FOOD AND DRINK

Breakfast (*micul dejun*) is typically a light meal, featuring rolls and butter (*chifle cu unt*) and an *omleta* washed down with a coffee (*cafea*) or tea (*ceai*). The most common **snacks** are flaky pastries (*pateuri*) filled with cheese (*cu brânză*) or meat (*cu carne*), and a variety of spicy grilled sausages and meatballs such as *mici* and *chiftele*. Menus in most **restaurants** concentrate on grilled meats, or *friptura*. *Cotlet de porc* is the common pork chop, while *muşchi de vacă* is fillet of beef.

Traditional **Romanian dishes** can be delicious. The best-known of these is *sarmale* – pickled cabbage stuffed with rice, meat and herbs, usually served with sour cream. Stews (*tocană*) and other dishes often feature a combination of meat and dairy products. **Vegetarians** could try asking for *caşcaval pane* (hard cheese fried in breadcrumbs); *ghiveci* (mixed fried veg); *ardei umpluţii* (stuffed peppers); or vegetables and salads. Establishments called **cofetărie** serve coffee and cakes, and sometimes beer and ice cream. Coffee, whether *cafea naturală* (finely ground and cooked Turkish fashion), *filtru* (filtered) or *nes* (instant), is usually drunk black and sweet; ask for it *cu lapte* or *fără zahăr* if you prefer it with milk or without sugar. **Cakes** and **desserts** are sweet and sticky, as throughout the Balkans. Romanians also enjoy pancakes (*clătite*) and pies (*plăcintă*) with various fillings.

DRINK

Evening **drinking** takes place in outdoor beer gardens, *cramas* (beer cellars), restaurants (where boozers often outnumber the diners), and in a growing number of Western-style cafés and bars. Try **ţuică**, a powerful plum brandy taken neat; in rural areas, it is homemade and often twice distilled to yield fearsomely strong *palincă*. Most **beer** (*bere*) is German-style lager. Romania's best **wines** are *Grasa* and *Feteasca Neagră*, and the sweet dessert wines of *Murfatlar*. Expect to pay 30–80 lei for a good-quality bottle.

CULTURE AND ETIQUETTE

Generally speaking, Romanians tend to be very open and friendly people. They will think nothing of striking up a conversation on buses and trains, even if they don't speak much English. Similarly, the Romanian people are for the most part very helpful and will try their best to understand you and to communicate through any language barrier.

When speaking to older people, it is respectful to address them using either *Domnul* (Mr) or *Doamnă* (Mrs), while shaking someone's hand is the most common and familiar way of **greeting** – although bear in mind that a Romanian man may well kiss a woman's hand on introduction. The welcoming attitude of the Romanians may mean you are **invited to someone's home**, if so, it is considered polite to bring a small gift with you, which you should also wrap. A bottle of wine, chocolates or flowers are all considered appropriate – although if you do bring flowers you should ensure an odd number of blooms, as even-numbered bouquets are strictly for funerals.

When **eating out**, etiquette in restaurants is much the same as in the majority of Western countries. Tipping is not necessary, although it will usually be appreciated.

SPORTS AND OUTDOOR ACTIVITIES

Romania's landscape is dominated by the spectacular Carpathian Mountains. A continuation of the Alps, they encircle Transylvania and provide the country with a rocky backbone perfect for activities ranging from hiking and skiing to caving and mountain biking.

Hiking

The main mountain ranges, the Bucegi, the Făgăraş, the Apuseni and the Retezat, provide the best-known destinations for **hiking trips**. There are numerous well-marked trails allowing day trips or longer expeditions, sleeping in a mountain refuge or *cabana* – these are usually very friendly and sociable places, and make good bases for hiking, caving or climbing. All of the trails are marked on the excellent Hartă Turistica maps, which can be found in hiking shops and bookshops in most of the major towns. Some *cabanas* also sell maps or have a map on a wall for you to consult. Spring and summer are the best seasons to explore the mountains and a large number of trails should only be attempted in warmer weather.

Skiing and snowboarding

Romania offers some of Europe's cheapest **skiing** and **snowboarding** between November and April. There are nine major ski and snowboarding resorts in Romania, the most popular of which is Poiana Braşov, near Braşov. Other resorts include Sinaia, Buşteni and Predeal, all on the main road north from Bucharest, Păltiniş near Sibiu, Borşa to the north in Maramureş, and Ceahlău and Durău on the border of Moldavia. Although Borşa is arguably the best resort to head to for

ROMANIA ON THE NET

Ⓦ**www.romaniatourism.com** and Ⓦ**www.romaniatravel.com** Official tourism sites.
Ⓦ**www.ici.ro/romania** General information and news.
Ⓦ**www.inyourpocket.com** Online guide to Bucharest.
Ⓦ**http://leosuteu.rdsor.ro** Hiking information and links.
Ⓦ**www.eco-romania.ro** Association of ecotourism operators.

Romanian

	Romanian	Pronunciation
Yes	*Da*	Da
No	*Nu*	Noo
Please	*Vă rog*	Ve rog
Thank you	*Mulțumesc*	Mult-sumesk
Hello/Good day	*Salut/bună ziua*	Saloot/boona zhewa
Goodbye	*La revedere*	La re-ve-dairy
Excuse me	*Permiteți-mi*	Per-mi-tets-may
Where?	*Unde?*	Oun-day?
Good	*Bun/bine*	Boon/Bee-ne
Bad	*Rău*	Rau
Near	*Apropriat*	A-prope-reeat
Far	*Departe*	D'par-tay
Cheap	*Ieftin*	Yeftin
Expensive	*Scump*	Scoomp
Open	*Închis*	Un-keez
Closed	*Deschis*	Des-keez
Today	*Azi*	Az
Yesterday	*Ieri*	Ee-airy
Tomorrow	*Mâine*	Mwee-ne
How much is...?	*Cât costa...?*	Cuut costa?
What time is it?	*Ce ora este?*	Che ora est?
I don't understand	*Nu înțeleg*	Noo unts-eledge
Do you speak English?	*Vorbiți Englezeste?*	Vor-beetz eng-lay-zeste?
One	*Un, una*	Oon, oona
Two	*Doi, doua*	Doy, doo-a
Three	*Trei*	Tray
Four	*Patru*	Pat-ru
Five	*Cinci*	Chinch
Six	*Şase*	Shass-er
Seven	*Şapte*	Shap-tay
Eight	*Opt*	Opt
Nine	*Nouă*	No-ar
Ten	*Zece*	Zay-chay

absolute beginners, the larger resorts all have a number of easy and medium pistes and one or more black run.

COMMUNICATIONS

Post offices (*poşta*) in major cities are open Mon–Fri 8am–7pm, Sat 8am–1pm; in smaller places they may close an hour or two earlier. You can **phone** from the orange cardphones or post offices. Phonecards (10 or 15 lei – get the latter for international calls) are available from post offices and news kiosks. Rates are lower from 11pm to 7am. **Internet** access is available in most towns; it's cheap, though not fast.

EMERGENCIES

Watch for pickpockets in crowded buses and trams. Do not believe anyone claiming to be a policeman and asking to see your passport and/or the contents of your wallet. Make sure you have health

EMERGENCY NUMBER

In all emergencies call ⓣ112.

insurance. Bucharest's central emergency **hospital** is up to western standards, while Medicover, Calea Plevnei 96 (☎021/310 4410), also offers western-standard care, with English-speaking doctors. **Pharmacies** (*farmacie*) are usually well stocked and open Mon–Sat 9am–6pm.

INFORMATION AND MAPS

Local authorities are now obliged to have **tourist information centres**, but you're best off going to privately run **tourist agencies**, many of which have English-speaking staff. Most bookshops and street vendors have up-to-date maps (*harta*), though it's best to buy them at home.

MONEY AND BANKS

Romania's currency is the new (or 'heavy') **leu** (plural lei, international code RON), introduced in 2005; if you're told that something costs a hundred thousand lei, for instance, you should knock off four zeroes to get the actual price. Hotels, rental agencies and other services quote prices in euros. There are plenty of **ATMs** in towns. **Changing money** is best done at private exchange offices (*casa de schimb*). Travellers' cheques are seldom accepted, a hassle to change, and have high commission rates. Never change money on the streets. **Credit cards** are generally accepted at hotels and upmarket shops. At the time of writing 1 leu = €0.30, €1 = 3.35 lei.

OPENING HOURS AND HOLIDAYS

Shop **opening hours** are Mon–Fri 9am–6pm, Sat 9am–1pm, with many food shops open until 10pm (or even 24hr) including weekends. Museums and castles also open roughly 9am–6pm (though most are closed on Mon or Tues); **admission charges** are minimal hence we've not quoted them in the Guide unless they are above the norm. National holidays are: Jan 1 and 2, Easter Monday, May 1, Dec 1, Dec 25 and 26.

Bucharest

Arriving in **BUCHAREST** (Bucureşti), most tourists want to leave as quickly as possible, but to do so would mean missing the heart of Romania. Bucharest does have its charm and elegance – it's just that it does need digging for. Among the ruptured roads and disintegrating buildings you'll find leafy squares, shaded parks and dressed-up young Romanians adding a touch of glamour to the surroundings. What's more, it's a dynamic city, changing faster than any other in Romania as new office towers sprout and new shops and bars appear all over. Even so, old residential areas with beautiful, if crumbling, eclectic architecture survive and show what the city was like in a bygone era. Head south of the centre into the Centru Civic and you'll come across unfinished projects from Ceauşescu's reign, such as the abandoned cultural centre known to locals as "Hiroshima". Seeing the true scale of what a dictatorship can do is something you won't forget and reason enough to spend a day or two in the capital.

What to see and do

The heart of the city lies to the north of the Dâmboviţa river, between two north-south avenues; it's a jumble of modern hotels, ancient Orthodox churches, and decaying apartment blocks, relieved by some attractive parks. Freezing in winter and hot and dusty in the summer, the northern outskirts are cooled by woodlands and a girdle of lakes.

Piaţa Revoluţiei

Most inner-city sights are within walking distance of Calea Victoriei, an avenue of vivid contrasts, scattered with vestiges of *ancien régime* elegance interspersed with apartment blocks, glass and steel facades and cake shops. Fulcrum of the avenue is **Piaţa Revoluţiei**, created during the 1930s on Carol II's orders to ensure a field of fire around the Royal Palace.

On the north side of the square is the **Athénée Palace Hotel** (now a Hilton), famous for its role as an "intelligence factory" from the 1930s until the 1980s, with its bugged rooms, tapped phones and informer prostitutes. To its east are the grand **Romanian Atheneum**, the city's main concert hall, and the **University Library**, torched, allegedly by the Securitate, in the confusion of the 1989 revolution, but since rebuilt and reopened.

To the southeast of the square is the former Communist Party HQ, now the **Senate**, where Nicolae Ceauşescu made his last speech from a low balcony on December 21. His speech drowned out by booing, the dictator's disbelief was broadcast to the nation just before the TV screens went blank. He and his wife Elena fled by helicopter from the roof, but were captured and executed on Christmas Day.

The Royal Palace

The **Royal Palace**, on the western side of Piaţa Revoluţiei, now contains the excellent **National Art Museum** (Wed–Sun 10/11am–6/7pm; Ⓦwww.art.museum.ro; €3, free on first Wed of month) with fantastic works by El Greco, Rembrandt, Brueghel and the great modern Romanian sculptor Brâncuşi, plus a huge and marvellous collection of medieval and modern Romanian art.

The Creţulescu Church and Cişmigiu Park

Standing opposite the Senate, the restored eighteenth-century **Creţulescu Church** fronts a tangle of streets wending west towards **Cişmigiu Park**, Bucharest's oldest, containing a boating lake, playgrounds, summer terrace cafés and animated chess players.

The historic centre

At the southern end of B-dul Brătianu is Bucharest's **historic centre**: a maze of dusty cobblestone streets with decrepit houses and tiny shops, centred on the pedestrianized Strada Lipscani, where a lively **Gypsy street market** (Mon–Sat 8am–4pm), sells Turkish jeans, pirated cassettes and all manner of other goodies. The whole area is currently in the midst of a major EU-funded renovation project, urgently necessary to save what's left, even if it causes the area to lose some of its authenticity.

The Stavropoleos Church

Just south of Strada Lipscani stands the small **Stavropoleos Church**; built in the 1720s, it has gorgeous, almost arabesque, patterns decorating its facade, and an elegant columned portico.

The Old Court and around

Even further south of the centre, just beyond the Stavropoleos Church, are the modest remains of the **Curtea Veche** (Old Court; daily 10am–4pm), Vlad the Impaler's fifteenth-century citadel. Dating from 1559, the adjacent Old Court Church is Bucharest's oldest church. Inside the large white building opposite the church you'll find the lush courtyard of the **Hanul lui Manuc Inn**, now home to a hotel and an overpriced restaurant. The inn's southern wall forms one side of Piața Unirii, which is where the old Bucharest makes way for the new.

The Centru Civic

The infamous **Centru Civic** was Ceauşescu's pet urban project. After an earthquake in 1977 damaged much of the city, Ceauşescu took the opportunity to remodel the entire southern portion of central Bucharest as a monument to Communism. By the early 1980s bulldozers had moved in to clear the way for the Victory of Socialism Boulevard (now Bulevardul Unirii), taking with them thousands of architecturally significant houses, churches and monuments. Now colossal apartment blocks line Bulevardul Unirii, at 4km long and 120m wide slightly larger – intentionally so – than the Champs-Elysées on which it was modelled. The eastern end of the boulevard is now a banking district, while the other end is dominated by the Palatul Parlamentului (Parliament Palace).

The Palatul Parlamentului

The **Palatul Parlamentului** (Parliament Palace) is supposedly the second-largest administration building in the world. Started in 1984 – but still not complete despite the toil of 100,000 workers – the building contains 1100 rooms and a nuclear shelter, and now houses the Romanian Parliament and a conference centre. Guided tours in English (daily 10am–4pm; €6 plus €10 for the use of cameras) start at the entrance in the centre of its north side (to the right as you face the building).

Piața Universității

You're bound to pass through busy **Piața Universității**, overshadowed by the Hotel Intercontinental on B-dul Carol I. This is where students pitched their post-revolution City of Peace encampment, which was violently overrun, together with the illusion of true democracy, by the miners that President Iliescu had called in to "restore order" in June 1990. The miners returned to Bucharest in 1991, this time in protest against the government rather than to protect it.

The National Theatre and Bucharest University

Just to the east of Piața Universității rises Elena Ceauşescu's **Teatrul National** (National Theatre), resembling an Islamicized reworking of the Colosseum. Across the boulevard, **Bucharest University** is surrounded

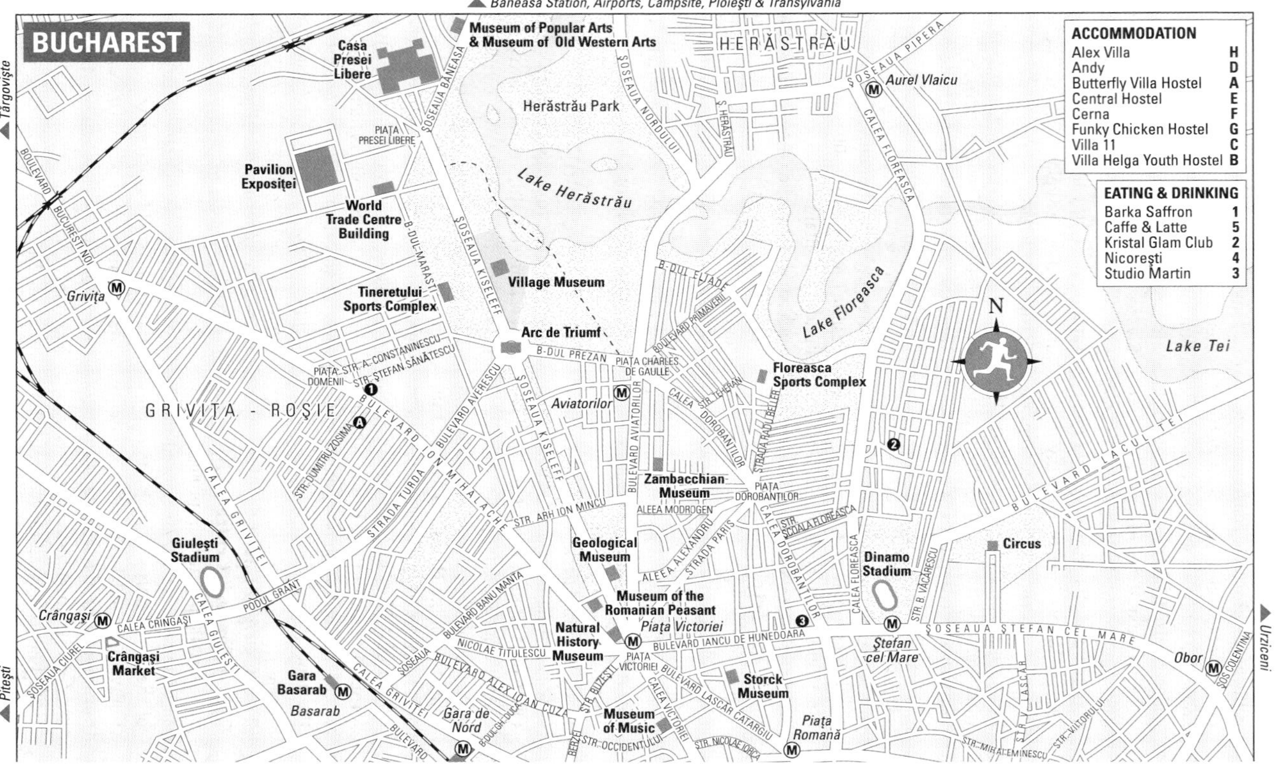
Băneasa Station, Airports, Campsite, Ploieşti & Transylvania
BUCHAREST
ACCOMMODATION
Alex Villa H
Andy D
Butterfly Villa Hostel A
Central Hostel E
Cerna F
Funky Chicken Hostel G
Villa 11 C
Villa Helga Youth Hostel B
EATING & DRINKING
Barka Saffron 1
Caffe & Latte 5
Kristal Glam Club 2
Nicoreşti 4
Studio Martin 3
Museum of Popular Arts & Museum of Old Western Arts
Casa Presei Libere
HERĂSTRĂU
Herăstrău Park
Lake Herăstrău
Aurel Vlaicu
Pavilion Expoziţiei
World Trade Centre Building
Village Museum
Tineretului Sports Complex
Arc de Triumf
Lake Floreasca
Floreasca Sports Complex
Lake Tei
N
Griviţa
GRIVIŢA - ROŞIE
Aviatorilor
Zambacchian Museum
Circus
Giuleşti Stadium
Geological Museum
Dinamo Stadium
Museum of the Romanian Peasant
Piaţa Victoriei
Natural History Museum
Crângaşi
Crângaşi Market
Gara Basarab
Basarab
Gara de Nord
Museum of Music
Storck Museum
Ştefan cel Mare
Obor
Piaţa Romană
Târgovişte
Piteşti
Urziceni
ŞOSEAUA KISELEFF
ŞOSEAUA BĂNEASA
ŞOSEAUA NORDULUI
CALEA FLOREASCA
ŞOSEAUA PIPERA
B-DUL PREZAN
PIAŢA CHARLES DE GAULLE
BULEVARD AVIATORILOR
CALEA DOROBANŢILOR
PIAŢA DOROBANŢILOR
BULEVARD LACUL TEI
ŞOSEAUA ŞTEFAN CEL MARE
CALEA GRIVIŢEI
CALEA GIULEŞTI
CALEA CRINGAŞI
PODUL GRANT
BULEVARD ION MIHALACHE
STRADA TURDA
BULEVARD AVERESCU
STR. ARH ION MINCU
BULEVARD IANCU DE HUNEDOARA
BULEVARD LASCĂR CATARGIU
CALEA VICTORIEI
BULEVARD BANU MANTA
BULEVARD ALEX IOAN CUZA
NICOLAE TITULESCU
B-DUL MARASTI
PIAŢA PRESEI LIBERE
BOULEVARD BUCUREŞTI NOI
STR. DUMITRU ZOSIMA
PIAŢA DOMENII
STR. A. CONSTANTINESCU
STR. ŞTEFAN SĂNĂTESCU
B-DUL ELADE
BULEVARD PRIMAVERII
STRADA RADU BELLER
STRADA PARIS
ALEEA ALEXANDRU
ALEEA MODROGEN
STR. ŞCOALA FLOREASCA
STR. B VĂCĂRESCU
STR. MIHAI EMINESCU
STR. VITORULUI
STR. V. LASCĂR
STR. OCCIDENTULUI
STR. NICOLAE IORGA
STR. BUZEŞTI
BERZEI
ŞOSEAUA CIUREL
ŞOS COLENTINA
Ş. HERĂSTRĂU

BUCHAREST

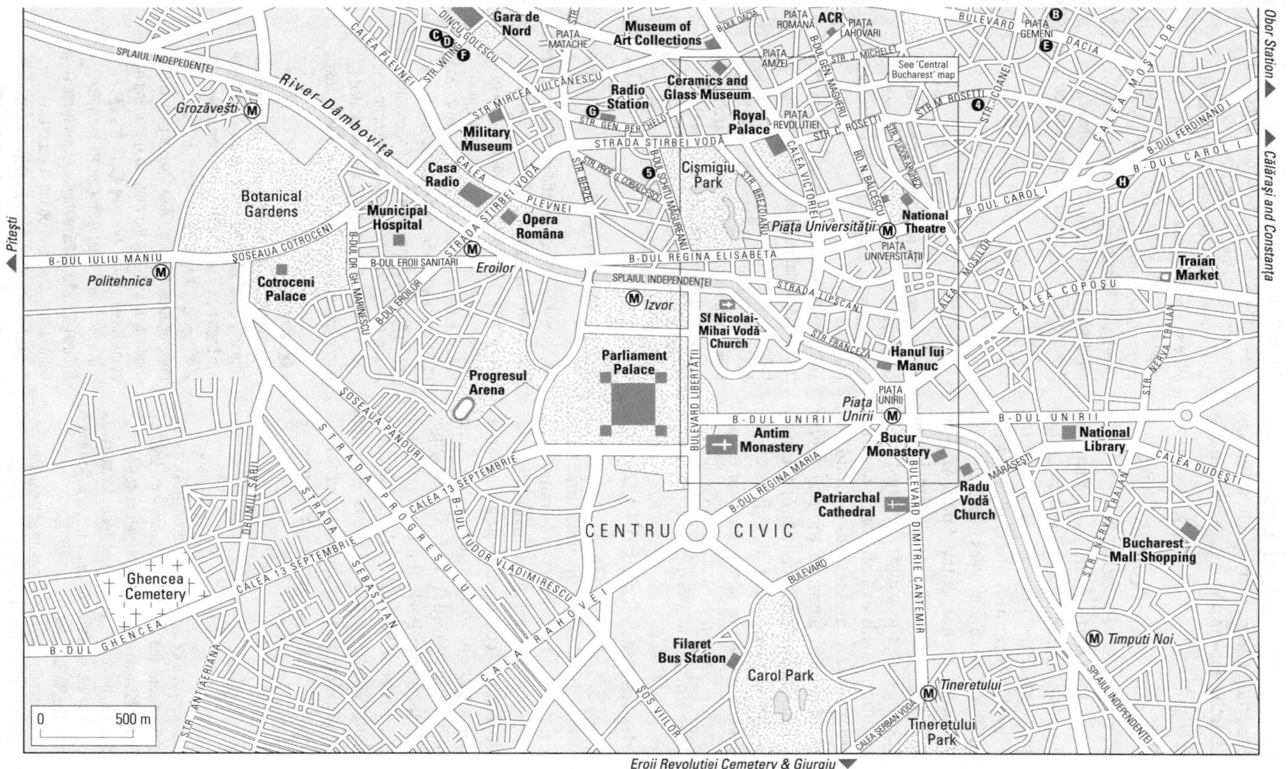
Obor Station
Călăraşi and Constanţa
Piteşti
Eroii Revoluţiei Cemetery & Giurgiu
Traian Market
National Library
Bucharest Mall-Shopping
Timpuri Noi
Radu Vodă Church
Bucur Monastery
Tineretului
Tineretului Park
Patriarchal Cathedral
Carol Park
Filaret Bus Station
Antim Monastery
Piaţa Unirii
Hanul lui Manuc
National Theatre
Piaţa Universităţii
Sf Nicolai-Mihai Vodă Church
Parliament Palace
Izvor
CENTRU CIVIC
Progresul Arena
Cişmigiu Park
Royal Palace
Ceramics and Glass Museum
Museum of Art Collections
Radio Station
ACR
Gara de Nord
Military Museum
Opera Româna
Casa Radio
Eroilor
Municipal Hospital
Botanical Gardens
Cotroceni Palace
Grozăveşti
Politehnica
Ghencea Cemetery
River Dâmboviţa
See 'Central Bucharest' map
B-DUL UNIRII
BULEVARD DIMITRIE CANTEMIR
BULEVARD LIBERTĂŢII
B-DUL REGINA ELISABETA
CALEA VICTORIEI
B-DUL CAROL I
CALEA MOŞILOR
CALEA DUDEŞTI
STR. NERVA TRAIAN
SPLAIUL INDEPENDENŢEI
B-DUL REGINA MARIA
CALEA 13 SEPTEMBRIE
B-DUL TUDOR VLADIMIRESCU
STRADA PROGRESULUI
STRADA SEBASTIAN
CALEA RAHOVEI
ŞOS VIILOR
DRUMUL SĂRII
STR. ANTIAERIANA
B-DUL GHENCEA
B-DUL IULIU MANIU
ŞOSEAUA COTROCENI
B-DUL DR. GH. MARINESCU
B-DUL EROII SANITARI
B-DUL EROILOR
ŞOSEAUA PANDURI
CALEA PLEVNEI
STRADA ŞTIRBEI VODĂ
B-DUL GEN. MAGHERU
BD. N. BALCESCU
STRADA LIPSCANI
STR. FRANCEZĂ
STR. BREZOIANU
B-DUL SCHITU MĂGUREANU
CALEA ŞERBAN VODĂ
CALEA COPOŞU
B-DUL DACIA
BULEVARD DACIA
PIAŢA ROMANĂ
PIAŢA LAHOVARI
PIAŢA AMZEI
PIAŢA REVOLUŢIEI
PIAŢA MATACHE
PIAŢA GEMENI
PIAŢA UNIVERSITĂŢII
PIAŢA UNIRII
B-DUL FERDINAND I
STR. C. ROSETTI
STR. TUDOR ARGHEZI
STR. J. MICHELET
STR. M. ROSETTI
STR. COANEI
DINCU GOLESCU
STR. MIRCEA VULCĂNESCU
STR. GEN. BERTHELOT
STR. BERZEI
MĂRĂŞEŞTI
0
500 m

by students, snack stands and book vendors. The bulbous domes of the Students' Church, originally a Russian church, appear through a gap in the grand buildings to its south.

The Museum of the Romanian Peasant

Stretching north from Piața Victoriei, Şoseaua Kiseleff leads into the more pleasant, leafy suburbs. At no. 3, the **Muzeul Țăranului Român** (Museum of the Romanian Peasant; Tues–Sun 10am–6pm, last entry 5pm; Ⓦwww.itcnet.ro/mtr) is a must-see, giving an insight into the country's varied rural traditions, with exhibits on everything from costume and textiles to wood and glass painted icons; to the rear there's a beautiful wooden church of the type found in Maramureş, as well as an excellent souvenir shop. The somewhat worthy Natural History and Geological Museums are adjacent.

Herăstrău Park and the Village Museum

Just to the north of the museums, traffic heading for the airport and Transylvania swings around a familiar-looking Arc de Triumf, commemorating Romania's participation on the side of the Allied victors in World War I. To the right, in **Herăstrău Park**, the city's largest, is the **Muzeul Satului** (Village Museum; daily 9am–6pm), a fabulous ensemble of wooden houses, churches, windmills and other structures from various regions of the country.

Arrival and information

Air Henri Coandâ airport is at Otopeni, 16km north of the centre; the only reliable taxis are marked FlyTaxi (outside International Arrivals or Ⓣ9440/1), charging a fixed €8; alternatively, head for the #783 bus stop just outside – buy your two-ride ticket (€2) from the RATB kiosk.
Train Virtually all trains terminate at the much-improved Gara de Nord, from where it's a thirty-minute walk into the centre, or a short ride on the metro (change lines at Piața Victoriei to reach Piața Universității).
Taxis (see below) can be found outside the main entrance beyond the Wasteels ticket office.
Tourist information Bucharest has no tourist office so you should pick up a copy of the excellent, English-language city guide *Bucharest in Your Pocket* (Ⓦwww.inyourpocket.com; €2), with essential reviews of accommodation, restaurants, nightlife and sights; buy it at Gara de Nord's Wasteels office, the airport kiosk or from hotels and bookstores.

City transport

Public transport, although crowded, is efficient and very cheap. The most useful lines of the metro system are the M2 (north-south) and M3 (a near-circle). There's also an array of trams, buses and trolleybuses.
Tickets must be bought from kiosks located near the bus stops, and validated in the machine on board.
Taxi After 11.30pm, you'll have to depend on taxis, which remain incredibly cheap, at about €0.20/km; the most reputable companies are Cristaxi (Ⓣ9461), Cobalcescu (Ⓣ9451) or Meridian (Ⓣ9444) – make sure the meter is running.

Accommodation

Bucharest has a handful of budget **hotels** to choose from, as well as a growing number of **private apartments**, which are often better and more spacious than hotel rooms – try Relax Comfort Suites, at B-dul Nicolae Bălcescu 22 (Ⓣ021/311 0210, Ⓦwww.relaxcomfort-suites.ro or Ⓦwww.bucharest-accommodation.ro) or Professional Reality (Ⓣ021/232 4006, Ⓦwww.accommodation.com.ro), both of which have centrally located rooms and apartments from around €40 per day.

Hostels

Alex Villa Str Avram Iancu 5 Ⓣ021/312 1653. Formerly *Elvis' Villa*, this bright and lively HI hostel has been newly refurbished, with rooms sleeping 2–8 people. Take trolleybus #85 from Piața Universității east to the Calea Moşilor stop, and continue on foot past the roundabout, turning right at the Greek church. Doubles ❷, dorms ❶
Funky Chicken Hostel Str Gen. Berthelot 63 Ⓣ0040 /21 312 1425, Ⓔfunkychickenhostel@hotmail.com. Claims to be the cheapest in Bucharest with all beds a guaranteed €8. It offers free cigarettes to all guests but no breakfast or Internet. No reservations, but guaranteed

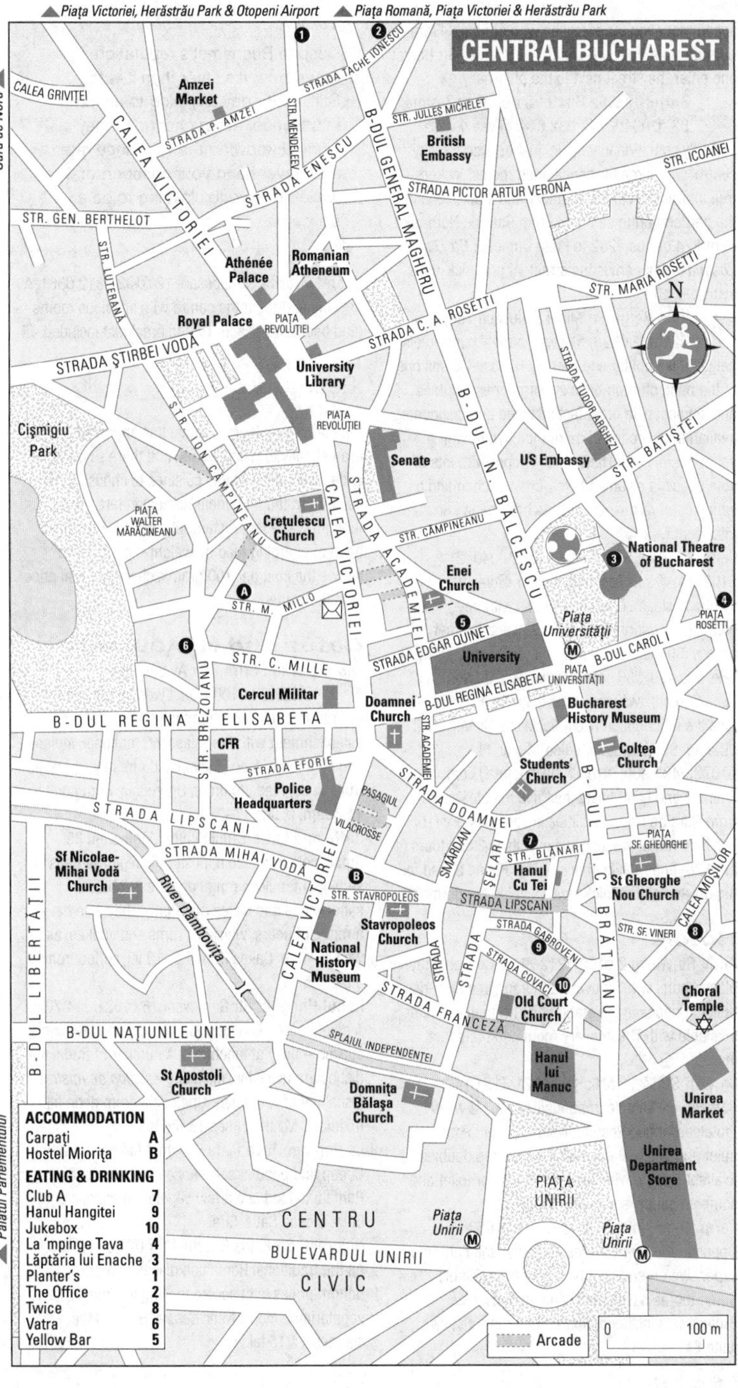
CENTRAL BUCHAREST
Piaţa Victoriei, Herăstrău Park & Otopeni Airport
Piaţa Romană, Piaţa Victoriei & Herăstrău Park
Gara de Nord
Palatul Parlamentului
Amzei Market
British Embassy
Athénée Palace
Romanian Atheneum
Royal Palace
University Library
Cişmigiu Park
Senate
US Embassy
Creţulescu Church
National Theatre of Bucharest
Enei Church
Piaţa Universităţii
University
Cercul Militar
Doamnei Church
Bucharest History Museum
CFR
Colţea Church
Students' Church
Police Headquarters
Sf Nicolae-Mihai Vodă Church
Hanul Cu Tei
St Gheorghe Nou Church
Stavropoleos Church
National History Museum
Choral Temple
Old Court Church
St Apostoli Church
Hanul lui Manuc
Domniţa Bălaşa Church
Unirea Market
Unirea Department Store
PIAŢA UNIRII
CENTRU CIVIC
Piaţa Unirii
BULEVARDUL UNIRII
ACCOMMODATION
Carpaţi A
Hostel Mioriţa B
EATING & DRINKING
Club A 7
Hanul Hangitei 9
Jukebox 10
La 'mpinge Tava 4
Lăptăria lui Enache 3
Planter's 1
The Office 2
Twice 8
Vatra 6
Yellow Bar 5
Arcade
0 100 m

accommodation for everyone who turns up. From Gara de Nord, follow B-dul Golescu, cross Str Berzei and enter the street next to the pharmacy. ❶

Butterfly Villa Hostel Str Dumitru Zosima 82 ⓣ0040/ 747 032 644, ⓦwww.villa-butterfly.com. Friendly hostel just outside the city centre, with large air-conditioned rooms, lockers, free Internet, breakfast, laundry and a barbecue in the garden during summer. From Gara de Nord take tram #24 or bus #282 to Piaţa Domenii; *Str Dumitru Zosima* is just across the street. Airport pick-up is available. ❷

Villa Helga Str Mihai Eminescu 184, ⓣ004/ 021 212 0828, ⓦwww.rotravel.com/hotels/helga. This popular and friendly HI hostel is still one of the best, offering beds in dormitories, doubles and singles, with breakfast included and discounts available for groups of more than five or with a youth hostel card. There is a TV room with lots of sofa space, a clean and well-fitted kitchen and a sunny courtyard where guests have been known to pitch tents. ❷–❸

Central Hostel Str Salcamilor 2, ⓣ0040/ 21 6102214, ⓔinfo@centralhostel.ro, ⓦwww.centralhostel.ro. Clean and simple with free breakfast, laundry (€15 per 4 kilos) and Internet access (50 minutes for free, after that one hour €1.5) Take bus #79, #86 or #133 from Gara de Nord to Piaţa Gemeni, two stops after Piaţa Romană; then take the first right off B-dul Dacia into Str Viitorului. ❷

Villa 11 Str Institutul Medico-Militar 11 ⓣ0722/495 900, ⓔvila11bb@hotmail.com. Friendly and quiet hostel just five minutes' walk from Gara de Nord. Facilities include laundry (10 lei), bike rental (45 lei per day), city walking tours (4 hrs €20) and mobile phone rental. Phone ahead for airport and station pick-ups. Doubles ❹, dorms ❷

Hotels

Andy Str Witing 2 ⓣ021/212 7154. Conveniently placed hotel with its own restaurant, in a high-rise building opposite the station. Fairly small en suites available with TVs in every room and breakfast included. ❽–❾

Carpăti Str Matei Millo 16 ⓣ021/315 0140, ⓔrezervari@hotelcarpatibucuresti.ro, ⓦwww.hotelcarpatibucuresti.ro. Near Cişmigiu Park, quiet and with helpful staff. Singles and doubles available, some with shared showers or toilet and some en suites, some with TV. ❹–❽

Cerna B-dul Golescu 29 ⓣ021/311 0535. Opposite the *Andy*; rooms are clean and light; more expensive en-suite doubles are also available. Some rooms have small concrete balconies. Breakfast is included. Shared bathroom ❸, en suite ❻

Despite Bucharest's reputation for **scams**, it's safer than it was. Still, never pay anything to anyone in advance, never change money without knowing the exchange rate, and never hand your passport or wallet to anyone claiming to be a policeman.

Hostel Mioriţa Str Lipscani 12 ⓣ021/312 0361. A new place right in the centre with spacious rooms (and beds), with cable TV and breakfast included. ❺

Eating

Bucharest's restaurant scene has improved dramatically in recent years, and there's now a wide selection of ethnic cuisines to choose from aside from the traditional Romanian fare. Beware, though, that a few restaurants still have the nasty habit of charging food by weight – if the menu shows the cost per 100 grams, check the real price with the waiter.

Cafés and restaurants

Barka Saffron Str Av Sănătescu 1 ⓣ021/224 1004. Just west of the Arc de Triumf, a relaxed, charmingly decorated establishment with first-class international, Indian and vegetarian food. They also do freshly squeezed fruit juices, made to order. Open daily from noon to 11.30pm. Mains 11–26 lei.

Caffe and Latte B-dul Schitu Măgureanu 35. Small, colourful café opposite Cişmigiu Gardens serving a fabulous range of coffees, shakes, sandwiches and cakes (to 10pm). They also have a range of beers, whiskies, rums and vodkas, as well as wine. Cakes from 4.5–10 lei, coffee from 6.5–14.5 lei.

Hanul Hangiţei Str Gabroveni 16 ⓣ021/314 7046. A neighbourhood restaurant serving good Romanian cuisine – busy at lunchtime. A number of traditional dishes are available, including *escalop de mistreţ* (escalope of wild boar). Open daily from noon till midnight. Main courses 16–26 lei.

La 'mpinge Tava Piaţa Rosetti 4 (on B-dul Carol I). Cheap and popular self-service restaurant serving Romanian food and a few vegetarian options until 6pm. Closed Sat & Sun.

Nicoreşti Str Maria Rosetti 40 ⓣ021/211 2480. All the traditional Romanian dishes at rock-bottom prices with accompanying live music. Few vegetarian options. Near *Central Hostel*. Main courses 14/15 lei.

Vatra Str Brezoianu 23. Very central, very affordable, with great Romanian dishes such as *ciorba*.

Drinking and nightlife

In the historic centre the area around Strada Gabroveni attracts many new bars and crowds, while, in summer, the clubs and restaurants around Herăstrău Lake are popular. The weekly Romanian-language *Şapte Seri* magazine, found free at bars, has events and cinema listings.

Bars

Jukebox Str Sepcari 22. Opposite Hanul lui Manuc, this raucous cellar bar has nightly live music and karaoke sessions. Daily 7pm–5am.
Lăptăria lui Enache 4th floor of the National Theatre, Piaţa Universităţii. One of Bucharest's most popular bars, with live music in winter, and free films on the rooftop terrace in summer. Entrance near the *Intercontinental* hotel near the *Café Deko* sign. Daily noon–2am (Fri & Sat to 4am).
Planter's Club Str Mendeleev 8. Immensely popular bar-cum-club with a small dance floor and pricey drinks. Daily 10am–7am.
Yellow Bar Str E. Quinet 10, near Piaţa Universităţii. Trendy cellar-lounge bar with comfortable sofas and lots of beautiful people. Mon–Fri 10am–2am, Sat & Sun 6pm–5am.

Clubs

Club A Str Blănari 14. Catering to a studenty crowd, this good-time party place is the city's most established club. Mon–Wed 10pm–5am, Thurs 9pm–5am, Fri 9pm–5am, Sat 9pm–6am, Sun 9pm–5am.
Kristal Glam Str. J.S. Bach 2. The only real choice for serious clubbers, this imposing, all-action club regularly plays host to some of Europe's star DJs (Seb Fontaine and Steve Mac, to name but two). Thurs–Sun 10pm–5am.
Studio Martin B-dul Iancu de Hunedoara 61, near Piaţa Victoriei. Brings in the ravers with its international guest DJs (playing techno and house) and gay-friendly atmosphere. Fri & Sat 10pm–5am, closed Sun–Thurs.
The Office Str Tache Ionescu 2. Fashionable club, with a hip crowd and great music, but pricey and posy. Thurs–Sat 9.30pm–5am, Sun 10pm–2am, closed Mon–Wed.
Twice Str Sf. Vineri 4. Banging techno tunes at Bucharest's biggest club; heaving and very popular. Wed–Sat 9pm–5am.

Shopping

Unirea department store Piaţa Unirii 1, open Mon–Sat 9am–9pm, Sun 9am–3pm. Imposingly large but a good place to find familar names, labels and all modern conveniences.
Bucuresti Mall Calea Vitan 55–59, open daily 10am–10pm. As above.
World Trade Centre Building B-dul Expoziţiei 2, open daily 8am–8pm. Also houses the World Trade Plaza.
Hanul cu Tei bazaar Conveniently located between Str. Lipscani 63–65 and Str. Blănari 5. Open daily selling Romanian antiques and souvenirs.
Târgul Vitan flea market On Calea Vitan, Sundays only.
Unirii Market Just behind the Unirea department store, with trinkets, souvenirs and fresh foods. Open daily.

Directory

Embassies and consulates Australia, B-dul Unirii 74, 5th floor ⓣ021/320 9802; Canada, Str N. Iorga 36 ⓣ021/307 5000; UK, Str J. Michelet 24 ⓣ021/312 0303; US, Str T. Arghezi 7–9 ⓣ021/210 4042.
Exchange There are plenty of ATMs, as well as exchange counters, most of which are open until late in the evening. Changing travellers' cheques is relatively painless; among the quickest and most efficient places is the Bank Austria Creditanstalt on Piaţa Revoluţiei, and the BCR at B-dul Regina Elisabeta 5.
Gay and lesbian For information, contact Accept, Str Lirei 10 ⓣ021/252 1637, ⓦwww.accept-romania.ro.
Hospital Spitalul Clinic de Urgenţa, Calea Floreasca 8 ⓣ021/230 0106. Medicover, Calea Plevnei 96 ⓣ021/310 4410.
Internet *Brit Café*, Calea Dorobanţilor 14; *PC-Net Café*, Calea Victoriei 136 and B-dul Regina Elisabeta 25.
Laundry Immaculate Cleaners, Str. Polonă 76 (Mon–Fri 9am–10pm, Sat 9am–4pm; ⓣ021/211 4413); Nufărul, Calea Moşilor 276 (Mon–Fri 7am–8pm, Sat 9am–1pm; ⓣ021/210 1441); Nuf Nuf, Calea Şerban Vodă 76–78 (ⓣ021/335 0168).
Left luggage *Bagaj de mână* (roughly €1.50; open 24hr) at the Gara de Nord, opposite platforms 4 and 5.
Pharmacy There is at least one 24hr pharmacy in each sector of the city. Sensiblu have a number of pharmacies throughout Bucharest, including central outlets at Calea Dorobanţilor 65, Str. G. Enescu 36–40, B-dul Titulescu 39–49, B-dul Bălcescu

7 (there's a good optician here, too), and in the Unirea department store. Helpnet pharmacy has 24hr outlets at B-dul Ion Mihalache 92 and B-dul Unirii 24.

Post office Str M. Millo 10 (Mon–Fri 7.30am–8pm).

Moving on

Train Braşov (every 45–60min; 2hr 30min–4hr 45min); Sibiu (5 daily; 4hr 45min–5hr 50min); Sighişoara (10 daily; 4hr–7hr 30min); Timişoara (6 daily; 7hr 30min–10hr 30min).

Bus Braşov (every 30min; 2hr 45min); Sibiu (3 daily; 4hr 30min).

Transylvania

From Bucharest, trains carve their way north through the spectacular **Carpathian mountain range** into the heart of **Transylvania**. The Carpathians offer Europe's cheapest skiing in winter and wonderful hiking during the summer (see p.959), along with caves, alpine meadows, dense forests sheltering bears, and lowland valleys with quaint villages. The population is a mix of Romanians, Magyars, Germans, Gypsies and others, thanks to centuries of migration and colonization. The Trianon Treaty of 1920 placed Transylvania within the Romanian state, but the character of many towns still reflects past patterns of settlement. Most striking are the former seats of Saxon power with their defensive towers and fortified churches. Sighişoara is the most picturesque but could be the Saxons' cenotaph: they have left their houses and churches but their living culture has evaporated, as it threatens to do in Braşov and Sibiu.

BRAŞOV

With an eye for trade and invasion routes, the medieval Saxons sited their largest settlements near Transylvania's mountain passes. **BRAŞOV**, which they called Kronstadt, grew prosperous as a result, and Saxon dominance lasted until the Communist government brought thousands of Moldavian villagers to work in the new factories. As a result, there are two parts to Braşov: the Gothic and Baroque centre beneath Mount Tâmpa, which looks great, and the surrounding sprawl of flats, which doesn't. The central square, surrounded by restored merchants' houses, is now the heart of a buzzing city with many fine new bars and restaurants.

What to see and do

Buses from the station will leave you near the central square, Piaţa Sfatului, overshadowed by the Gothic pinnacles of the city's most famous landmark, the **Black Church** (Mon–Sat 10am–5pm),

THE FORTIFIED CHURCHES OF TRANSYLVANIA

Transylvania's Saxon legacy is clearly apparent in the fortified churches erected throughout the region's villages following the migration of the Saxons to Romania under King Géza II in 1150. There are over a hundred fortified churches scattered across rural Transylvania, and seven have been listed as UNESCO World Heritage Sites. The Mioritics Association, in conjuction with UNESCO, is dedicated to preserving the fortified churches and developing tourism around them (ⓣ021/260 0113/ +40 788301830, ⓔcontact@mioritics.ro, ⓦwww.fortified-churches.com). Despite this, most are not well known and there is little information supplied on them. However, most are accessible with their original gate-key, which is usually kept by one of the elder villagers for safekeeping. Simply ask in the village for the key-holder, who should be able to open up the church and show you around. It is normal to pay them a small amount (usually about 5 lei) for their trouble.

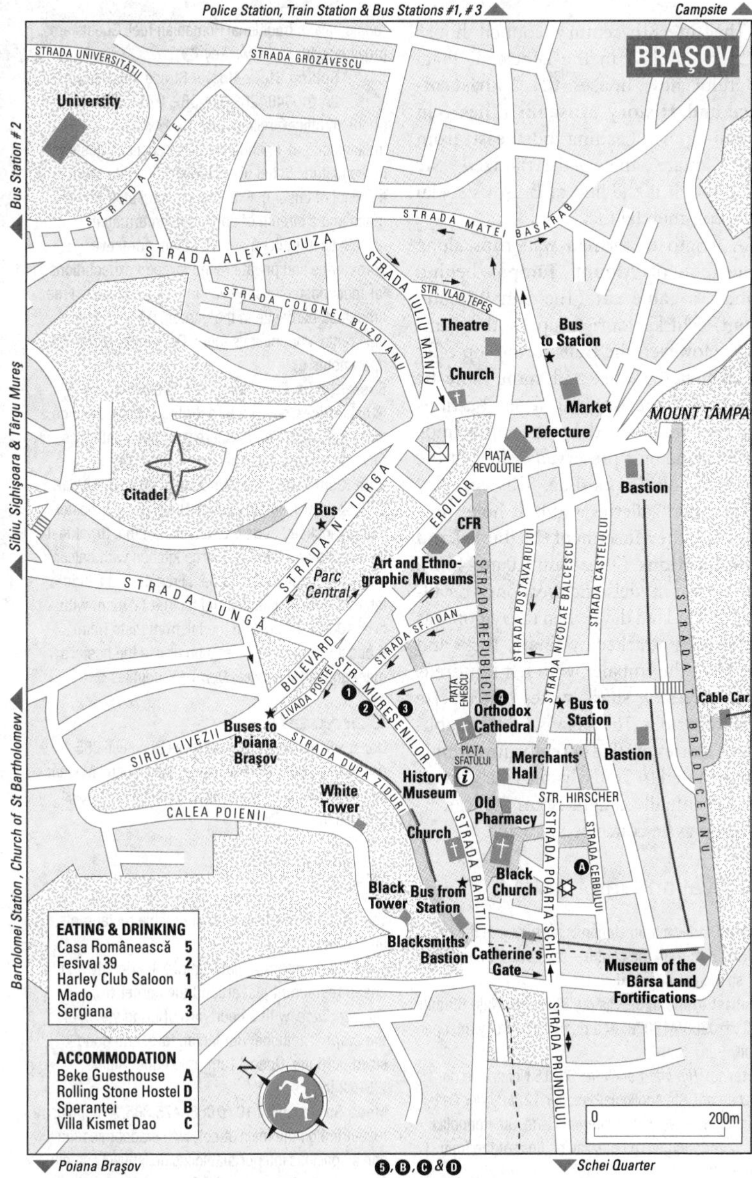

which stab upwards like a series of daggers. An endearingly monstrous hall-church that took almost a century to complete (1383–1477), it is so called for its soot-blackened walls, the result of being torched by the Austrian army in 1689. Inside, by contrast, the church is startlingly white, with Oriental carpets creating splashes of colour along the walls of the nave. In summer (June–Sept Tues, Thurs & Sat at 6pm), the church's 4000-pipe organ is used for concerts.

The fifteenth-century council house (Casa Sfatului) in the centre of Piăta Sfatului now houses the **Tourist office** and **History Museum** (Tues–Sun 10am–5pm). Leading northeast from the square the pedestrianized **Str Republicii** is the hub of Braşov's social and commercial life.

A length of fortress wall runs along the foot of **Mount Tâmpa**, behind which a **cable car** (Tue–Sun 9.30am–9pm) whisks tourists up to the summit. However, the trails to the top offer a challenging walk and some fantastic views. Of the original seven bastions (towers maintained by the city's trade guilds) the best preserved is that of the weavers, on Str Coşbuc. This complex of wooden galleries and bolt-holes now contains the **Museum of the Bârsa Land Fortifications** (Tues–Sun 10am–4pm). Inside are models and weaponry recalling the bad old days when the region was repeatedly attacked by Tatars, Turks and by Vlad the Impaler, who left hundreds of captives on sharp stakes to terrorize the townsfolk. The Saxons' widely publicized stories of Vlad's cruelty unwittingly contributed to Transylvania's dark image and eventually caught Bram Stoker's attention as he conceived *Dracula*.

Arrival and information

Train Braşov's train station is northeast of the old town, 2km from the centre – take bus #4 into town or spend €1 on a taxi.
Tourist office in the History Museum, Piața Sfatului 30 (ⓣ0268/419078, ⓔturism@brasovcity.ro), open daily 9am–5pm.
Internet *Hip Internet C@fe*, Str. 15 Noiembrie no. 1; *Cybercafé*, Str. Apollonia Hirscher 12; *Internet Café*, Str. Michael Weiss 11; *Internet Caffé*, Str. Republicii 41 (24hr); and on the mezzanine floor of the train station.
Listings The Romanian-language magazine *Zile şi Nopți*, free at bars, lists events.

Accommodation

Beke Guesthouse Str Cerbului 32 ⓣ0723/461 888. Cosy and quiet guesthouse, and the spotless rooms have a traditional Romanian feel. Guests are provided with their own key. ❷
Rolling Stone Hostel Strada Piatra Mare 2A ⓣ0040/ 268 311 962, 0744 816970 (mob), ⓔoffice@rollingstone.ro, ⓦwww.rollingstone.ro. Friendly and very sociable hostel in the historic Schei district (near the Piața Unirii terminal of bus #4). Extremely helpful staff provide maps and a stream of up-to-date information as well as a drink on arrival. Clean, attractive dormitories and private rooms exceed expectations for most hostels – one even includes a jacuzzi. Free breakfast, barbecue in the garden, WiFi, car and bike rental and minibus tours. Dorms ❷, rooms ❸, apartments ❹
Speranței Str Piatra Mare 101 ⓣ0268/472 415, ⓔcshospice@hospice.bv.astral.ro. A quiet hospice close to *Rolling Stone*, where your payment helps towards treatment for cancer victims. ❷
Villa Kismet Dao Str Democrației 2B ⓣ0268/514 295, ⓦwww.kismetdao.com. Busy, popular hostel with no lockout, curfew or checkout time. Breakfast is included and there is a large kitchen with balcony and a barbecue in the garden. Free perks include Internet access, laundry and a large TV room with over 100 DVDs. Just up the hill from Piața Unirii – bus #4 from the train station or use the hostel's meet and greet service. Dorm ❷, doubles ❹

Campsite

Dârste Southeast of town at Calea Bucureşti 285 ⓣ0268/315 863, ⓔcamp.dirste@deltanet.ro. Modern campsire with cabins as well as tent-space; it's best reached by taxi. ❶

Eating

The old town is dotted with affordable restaurants and cafés.
Casa Românească Piața Unirii 13. Friendly and cheap restaurant just around the corner from *Rolling Stone*, with a courtyard offering views of the *piața*. Traditional Romanian fare, and good-sized portions. Open 11am–midnight. Mains 7.5–22 lei.
Mado Str Republicii 10 ⓣ068/ 475 385. A popular restaurant on the main street, with outdoor seating and a spacious interior that looks deceptively small from outside. A variety of foods available, including traditional Romanian dishes and also some Turkish specialities. There is also a wide selection of Romanian wines, including the hearty and spicy hot wine favoured in rural Transylvania during winter. Home-made cakes and large portions make this a good choice for the centre of town. Mains 10–16 lei. Coffee 4 lei.

Sergiana Str Mureşenilor 22 ⓣ0268/419 775. Serves good Romanian food in the atmospheric cellars. Open 11am–midnight. Mains 9–21 lei.

Drinking

A great place to drink is *Festival 39*, Str Mureşenilor 23, which is full of the strangest things – from badly stuffed animals and fake plastic trophies to a Cuban barman. A few doors up the street, *Harley Club Saloon* at no. 13 has more seating and bar food.

Moving on

Train Bucharest (every 45–60min; 2hr 30min–4hr 45min); Sibiu (8 daily; 2hr 15min–3hr 55min); Sighişoara (15 daily; 1hr 40min–3hr); Timişoara (1 daily; 8hr 45min).
Bus Bran (every 30min 7am–6pm Mon–Fri, hourly Sat/Sun; 45min); Zărneşti (hourly Mon–Fri, 8 Sat, 2 Sun; 1hr).

BRAN

Cosy little **BRAN**, 28km southwest of Braşov, is situated at the foot of the stunning Bucegi Mountains. Despite what you may hear, its **castle** (Tues–Sun 9am–5pm) has only tenuous associations with Dracula – aka Vlad the Impaler, who may have attacked it in 1460. Hyperbole is forgivable, though, as Bran really does look like a vampire-count's residence. The castle was built in 1377 by the Saxons of Braşov to safeguard what used to be the main route into Wallachia, and it rises in tiers of towers and ramparts from amongst the woods, against a glorious mountain background. A warren of stairs, nooks and chambers around a small courtyard, the interior is filled with elaborately carved four-poster beds, throne-like chairs and portraits of grim-faced boyars.

Buses to Bran and Zărneşti leave at least hourly (less often at weekends) from bus station #2, 3km north of central Braşov at the end of Str Lungă; take bus #12 from the centre or bus #10 from the train station, and get off opposite the stadium. There's no shortage of **private rooms** in Bran; *Ovi-Tours*, Str Bologa 16 (ⓣ0268/236 666; ❷), have some clean and rustic-style rooms or can help book one elsewhere.

Moving on

Bus Braşov (every 30min 7am–6pm Mon–Fri, hourly Sat/Sun; 45min); Zărneşti (9 daily; 30min).

RÂŞNOV AND ZĂRNEŞTI

For a more authentic experience than Bran, jump off the Braşov bus in nearby **RÂŞNOV**, where the hilltop fortress and the views are stunning. North of Bran is **ZĂRNEŞTI**, a small, cosy town that is the perfect jump-off point for trips into the Făgăraş Mountains. You can also stay at *Pensiunea Mosorel*, Str Dr Senchea 162 (ⓣ/ⓕ0268/222 774, ⓔgeorge@ecoland-ro.com; ❷).

For a near-medieval mountain escape, spend a night at *Cabana Montana* (ⓣ0744/801 094; ❷), in the picturesque hamlet of **MAGURĂ**, on the flanks of the Piatra Craiului Mountains just south of Zărneşti. Be sure to phone ahead and they'll pick you up from Zărneşti's bus station.

SIGHIŞOARA

A forbidding silhouette of battlements and needle spires looms over the citadel of **SIGHIŞOARA**, perched on a hill overlooking the Târnave Mare valley; it seems fitting that this was the birthplace of Vlad Ţepeş, the man known to posterity as **Dracula**. Look out for the Medieval Arts and the Inter-ethnic Cultural **festivals** held annually in July and August, when Sighişoara may be overrun by thousands of beer-swillers.

What to see and do

The route from the train station to the centre passes the **Romanian Orthodox Cathedral**, its gleaming white, multifaceted facade a striking contrast to the dark interior. Across the **Târnave Mare** river, the **citadel** dominates the

WOLF AND BEAR TRACKING IN THE CARPATHIANS

Romania has the largest **wolf** and **brown bear** populations in Europe, and if you fancy finding out more about them or observing their trails and markings, you can contact *Transylvanian Wolf* (Ⓣ0744/319 708, Ⓔdan_marin_zarnesti@yahoo.co.uk), an organization that offers guided walks (€70 for up to 5 people, €15 for each extra person) tracking wolves, bears, red deer and lynx under the eagle-eye of Dan Marin, an experienced tracker who has been voted one of the top three guides in the world by readers of *Wanderlust* magazine and who works closely with conservation organizations and the new Piatra Craiului National Park. In winter this also offers the chance to see some spectacular snow-covered landscapes, and is combined with sleigh rides and cross-country skiing, along with up-to-date and authoritative information and presentations. If you really want to treat yourself, you can also stay in the Marins' spectacular family guesthouse (Str. I. Metianu nr. 108, Zărneşti, Jud. Braşov, ❹), where you will receive home-cooked traditional and regional food, made using local produce and fresh herbs, every day, with all meals (breakfast, dinner and a lunch-pack) included in the price of your room.

town from a hill whose slopes support a jumble of ancient houses. Steps lead up from the lower town's main square, Piaţa Hermann Oberth, to the main gateway, above which rises the mighty **clock tower**. This was built in the fourteenth century when Sighişoara became a free town controlled by craft guilds – each of which had to finance the construction of a bastion and defend it in wartime. Sighişoara grew rich on the proceeds of trade with Moldavia and Wallachia, as attested by the regalia and strongboxes in the tower's **museum** (daily 9am–3.30/6.30pm). The ticket also gives access to the seventeenth-century **torture chamber** and the **Museum of Armaments** next door with its small and poorly presented Dracula Exhibition. In 1431 or thereabouts, the child later known as Dracula was born at Str Muzeului 6 near the clock tower. At the time his father – Vlad Dracul – was commander of the mountain passes into Wallachia, but the younger Vlad's privileged childhood ended eight years later, when he and his brother Radu were sent to Anatolia as hostages to the Turks. There Vlad observed the Turks' use of terror, which he would later turn against them, earning the nickname of "The Impaler". Nowadays, Vlad's birthplace is a mediocre tourist restaurant.

Arrival and information

Train Sighişoara's train station is on the northern edge of town, on Str Libertăţii.
Tourist office There's tourist information at the *International Café*, Piaţa Cetăţii 8.

Accommodation

Backpackers are met at the station by runners for the town's many excellent private rooms; perhaps the best are with the Faur family in the citadel at Str Cojocarilor 1 (Ⓣ0744/119 211).

Hostels

Burg Hostel Str Bastionului 4–6 Ⓣ0040/ 265 77 84 89, Ⓔburghostel@ibz.ro / info@ibz.ro Ⓦwww.ibz.ro. Centrally located with clean dorm rooms, doubles, and triples. There is a bar in the cellar and Internet access (3.5 lei per hour). Breakfast isn't included, but there is a good value restaurant in the hostel courtyard. Dorms ❶, doubles ❷, with private bath ❸

Nathan's Villa Str Libertăţii 8 Ⓣ0040/ 265 77 2546, Ⓔsighisoara@nathansvilla.com, Ⓦwww.nathansvilla.com/sighisoara.html. Friendly, popular hostel with no curfew and no checkout time. Bright, airy dorms, all with ten beds, and one private double. Other perks include free breakfast, laundry and local information. Dorms ❶, double with private bath ❸

Hotels

Casa cu Cerb Str Şcolii 1 Ⓣ0265/774 625, Ⓦwww.casacucerb.ro. A good choice for romantics, as the bathtubs fit two and the most expensive rooms have four-poster double beds. The contents of the minibar are also included in the price (but breakfast isn't). 5

Casa Wagner Piaţa Cetăţii 7 ⓣ0265/506 014, ⓦwww.casa-wagner.com. Very large, comfortable rooms in a carefully restored building with beautiful antique furniture – most of which is of Romanian origin – and views of the *piaţa*. Breakfast is included. 5

Steaua Str 1 Decembrie 12 ⓣ0265/771 000. Cheaper hotel, upgraded but still reminiscent of the communist era. Rooms are a little run down and the en suites have showers in the sink. 3

Eating and drinking

Casa cu Cerb Str Şcolii 1 ⓣ0265/774 625, ⓦwww.casacucerb.ro. In the hotel of the same name on Piaţa Cetăţii, with a sunny and pleasant outdoor seating area. One of the best restaurants in the citadel, with good breakfasts and light meals and more expensive dinners. Open 9am–10pm every day. Mains from 11 to 31 lei.

International Café Piaţa Cetăţii 8. A cosy café serving delicious and filling home-made sandwiches and cakes, and just about the only quiche in Transylvania. Open 8am–9pm in summer and 10am–6pm in winter, daily except Sunday. Sandwiches 6 lei, quiche 7 lei, coffee 5 lei.

Rustica Str 1 Decembrie 1918 no. 5. Fairly good Romanian food in nice surroundings and a popular bar at night. Good breakfast menu. Mains 15 lei.

La Strada Str Morii 7. Good pizzas and outdoor seating. Open Sun–Thur 10am–midnight, Fri–Sat 10am–1am. Mains 8–15 lei.

The Music Pub In the basement of the Burg Hostel, with some live rock/pop music, mainly weekend evenings.

Moving on

Train Braşov (15 daily; 1hr 45min–2hr 45min); Bucharest (9 daily; 4hr 15min–5hr); Sibiu (change at Copşa Mică or Mediaş; 6 daily; 2hr 5min–2hr 45min).

SIBIU

The narrow streets and old gabled houses of **SIBIU**'s older quarters seem to have come straight off the page of a fairytale. Like Braşov, Sibiu was founded by Germans invited by Hungary's King Géza II to colonize strategic regions of Transylvania in 1143. Its inhabitants dominated trade in Transylvania and Wallachia, but their citadels were no protection against the tide of history, which eroded their influence after the eighteenth century. Within the last decades almost the entire Saxon community has left Romania. Sibiu still has stronger and more lucrative links with Germany than any Transylvanian town, and its stint as **European Capital of Culture** in 2007 has left its buildings handsomely refurbished.

What to see and do

Cross the square from the train station and follow Str Gen. Magheru to **Piaţa Mare**. On its western side stands the **Muzeul Brukenthal** (Tues–Sun 9am–5pm), one of the finest in Romania with an evocative collection of works by Transylvanian painters. The city's **Muzeul de Istorie** (History Museum; Tues–Sun 9am–5pm) is nearby in the impressive Old City Hall. On the north side of Piaţa Mare, the huge Catholic church stands next to the **Council Tower** (daily 10am–6pm), which offers fine views to the Carpathians. Just beyond, on Piaţa Huet, the **Evangelical Cathedral** (9am–6pm, Sun from 10am) is a massive hall-church raised during the fourteenth and fifteenth centuries. You can climb the tower (Mon–Sat noon–4pm). The crypt, entered from outside, contains impressive tombstones of local notables as well as of Mihnea the Bad, the Impaler's son, stabbed to death outside here in 1510.

Set aside most of a day to explore Sibiu's wonderful open-air **Muzeul Astra** (Tues–Sun 9am–5pm) on Calea Răşinari, south of the centre; take trolleybus #1 to the end of the line. Set against a mountain backdrop, the museum offers a fantastic insight into rural life, with authentically furnished wooden houses, churches and mills; there's also a traditional inn serving local food and drink.

Arrival and information

Train and bus Sibiu's train and bus stations are next to each other on Piața 1 Decembrie 1918, 400m northeast of the main square.
Tourist office Sibiu's tourist office, inside the Schiller bookstore on Piața Mare (Ⓣ0269/211 110, Ⓦwww.sibiu.ro/en), also sells maps and hands out the *Sibiu Live* and *Şapte Seri* listings magazines.

Accommodation

Hostels

Evangelisches Pfarrhaus Piața Huet 1 Ⓣ0269/211 203. Next to the cathedral, the Lutheran parish house (8am–3pm, or call in advance so a key can be left for you) has a hostel with simple rooms sleeping two to four. ❷
Old Town Hostel Piața Mică 26 Ⓣ0269/216 445, Ⓔcontact@hostelsibiu.ro Ⓦwww.hostelsibiu.ro. Located above a historic pharmacy in a 450-year-old building, the hostel has three large, airy dormitories – the biggest of which also has a TV. There is no breakfast, but there is a pleasant, well-equipped kitchen that you can use all day plus free tea and coffee. Internet access is free, and the hostel can also arrange bike hire (35 lei per day) and does laundry (€2 for 5kg). ❷

Hotels

Ela Str Nouă 43 Ⓣ0269/215 197. A friendly family-run hotel, with a pleasant garden, eight spotless en-suite rooms and guest kitchen. Breakfast is extra (15 lei). From the train station take Strada 9 Mai, turn right onto Str Rebreanu, then first left onto Str Nouă. ❹–❻
Podul Minciunilor Str Azilului 1 Ⓣ0269/217 259. A small family-run guesthouse, with five doubles and one triple. No breakfast or Internet, but will do laundry on request (15 lei). ❺–❻.

Campsite

Just outside of Sibu, in the village of Sălişte, you can find the fantastic **Pensiune and Camping Sălişteanca**, at Str. Băii 13, Sălişte, Ⓣ0269/553121, Ⓔjulian_parau@yahoo.com, Ⓦwww.salisteanca.com. A good choice in the summer, when Sibiu's guesthouses and hostels are packed, this campsite is also a lovely place to stay in its own right, with a riverside site, clean, large, modern facilities and 24-hour hot showers, as well as CE electricity plugs for caravans. There are also a few large en-suite rooms available, beautifully furnished in traditional Transylvanian style, if you don't fancy roughing it outside. ❸–❹
It costs €2.50 per person to stay at the campsite and €1.50 per tent or €3 per caravan (€4 for camper vans). Breakfast is avilable for 10 lei and home-made dinner is available in the pensiune on request.

Eating

Crama Sibiu Vechi Str Ilarian 3 Ⓦwww.sibiuvechi.ro. This cellar restaurant decorated in very local style is the best place for something typically Romanian, complete with live folk music and traditionally dressed staff. They also have cheap wine on tap. Mains 9–26 lei.
Mara Str Bălcescu 21 Ⓦwww.restaurantmara.go.ro. Excellent local food is served up here, and they have a large selection of wines, including Romanian varieties. Open daily 10am–midnight. Mains 11–38 lei.
La Turn Piața Mare 1. With a good central location next to the Council Tower and a range of grilled and barbecued dishes. Open 10.30am–11pm, mains 11–36 lei.

Drinking

Sibiu is quiet after 9pm; however, there are a few options if you want to stay out later.
Art Café Str Filarmonicii 2. In the cellars of an atmospheric building, this stays open from 8am until 2am or later. Drinks are cheap and there are occasional jazz gigs.
The Chill Out Club Piața Mică 23. Playing mostly house music, this holds out till 6am.

Moving on

Train Braşov (8 daily; 2hr 10min–3hr 50min); Bucharest (2 daily; 5hr 25min); Sighişoara (change at Copşa Mică or Mediaş; 5 daily; 2hr 15min–3hr); Timişoara (3 daily; 5hr 10min–6hr).

TIMIŞOARA

The engaging city of **TIMIŞOARA**, 250km west of Sibiu near the Serbian border and the rail junction at Arad, was the capital of the Banat region until the Turks conquered it in 1552; they ruled until 1716 when they were ousted by the Habsburgs. Nowadays this is Romania's most westward-oriented city, its good location and multilingual inhabitants attracting much foreign investment. The city's fame abroad rests on its crucial role in the overthrow of the Ceauşescu regime. A Calvinist minister, Lászlo Tökes, stood up for the rights of the Hungarian community, and when the police came to evict him on December 16, 1989, his parishioners barred their way. The riots that ensued inspired the people of Bucharest to follow, so that Timişoara sees itself as the guardian of the revolution.

What to see and do

Approaching from the train station, you'll enter the centre at the attractive pedestrianized Piața Victoriei, with fountains and flowerbeds strewn along its length. Its focal point is the huge **Romanian Orthodox Cathedral**, completed in 1946 with a blend of neo-Byzantine and Moldavian architectural elements. At the opposite end, the unattractive Opera House stands near the **castle** which now houses the stuffy and very missable Museum of the Banat. Antique trams trundle past the Baroque **Town Hall** on the central Piața Libertății, while two blocks north the vast Piața Unirii is dominated by the monumental **Roman Catholic and Serbian Orthodox cathedrals**. Built between 1736 and 1773, the former (to the east) is a fine example of Viennese Baroque; the latter is roughly contemporaneous and almost as impressive. In 1868, the municipality demolished most of the redundant citadel, leaving two bastions to the east and west of Piața Unirii. The eastern one is occupied by an **Ethnographic Museum** (Tues–Sun 10am–5pm; entrance at Str Popa Șapcă 4). Varied folk costumes, painted glass icons and furnished rooms illustrate the region's ethnic diversity effectively, but in an anodyne fashion – for example, there's no mention of the thousands of Serbs deported in 1951 when the Party fell out with Tito's neighbouring Yugoslavia.

Arrival and information

Train Timişoara Nord train station is a fifteen-minute walk west of the centre along B-dul Republicii.

Tourist office The small tourist office (Mon–Sat 10am–8pm, Sun 10am–2pm; ⊕0256/437 973), hidden away in the Bazaar courtyard (opposite the Bega shopping centre) on B-dul Revoluției, has basic maps and copies of the free English-language listings magazine *Timişoara What Where When*.

Internet There's cheap Internet access at Savoya 22, south of Piața Unirii.

Accommodation

Hotel

Hotel Nord B-dul Gen, Dragalina 47 ⊕0256/497 504, ⓔreceptie@hotelnord.ro. The hotel is conveniently located opposite the train station, but can get a bit noisy outside at night. Inside it is bright and clean with single, double and triple en-suite rooms. Breakfast is included. ❸–❻

Campsite

The well-kept **campsite**, 4km west of town on Aleea Pădurea Verde (⊕0256/208 925), also has huts sleeping two to four people. Take trolleybus #11 from the train station or centre.

Eating

Club XXI Piața Victoriei 2. Serves large, hearty meals, including some traditional dishes from the Banat region. Open daily 10am–midnight. Mains 14/15 lei.

Harold's Aleea Studenților 17. Simple, understated and surprisingly classy restaurant, with a wide selection of international and vegetarian options, including the large 'Harold's Vegetarian Plate' – to share for 45 lei. Open daily 11.30am–midnight. Most main courses cost about 17 lei, spaghetti 11–15 lei, Chinese dishes 18–28 lei.

Stil Very useful 24hr supermarket on Str Mărăşeşti (at Str Lazăr), a short walk northwest of Piața Libertății.

Drinking and nightlife

Party animals should head for the canalside bars behind the cathedral such as the *Bănăteana* (Parcul Justiției 1), or the *Terasa Boss* (Str. V. Pârvan 1). Find out what's going on in the weekly *Şapte Seri* listings magazine, found free at most bars.

Baroque Piața Unirii 14. At the southeastern corner of the square, this lives up to its name, with wrought iron tables and chairs outside and a decadently large array of teas, coffees, milkshakes and hot-chocolate – both alcoholic and non-alcoholic. Breakfasts for 11–13 lei, hot drinks from 4 lei – as much as 11 lei for more extravagant or alcoholic varieties. Open 8am–1am.

Club 3 Piața Victoriei 7. In the Cinema Timiş, this has good jazz, often live. Open 6pm–3am.

Java Coffee House Str Rodnei 6. Open 24 hours a day (in theory), this dark bar on the southeastern corner of Piața Unirii is a good place for a coffee or something stronger. Drinks range from the classic to the more inventive, including their "ice cream chocolate coffee". Drinks 3.50–13 lei.

Piranha Cocktail Bar Str Savoya 5. A popular drinking den with a range of professionally made cocktails and truly eye-catching surroundings, complete with fish tanks, live lizards and snakes. It is open around the clock (in theory) but is also pleasant for morning coffee.

Moving on

Train Braşov (1 daily; 9hr); Bucharest (6 daily; 7hr 30min–8hr 45min); Sibiu (3 daily; 5hr 5min–6hr 30min).

Russia

HIGHLIGHTS

THE HERMITAGE, ST PETERSBURG: defines the heart of the city architecturally, intellectually and historically

KUNSTKAMMER, ST PETERSBURG: don't miss Peter the Great's eighteenth-century collection of curiosities

THE KREMLIN, MOSCOW: a complex of political, architectural and artistic associations

BANYA: purge your pores in style at Moscow's Sandunovskiy baths

VODKA: knock back a shot of Russia's "little water" in its natural habitat

ROUGH COSTS

DAILY BUDGET basic €45/with the occasional treat €70

DRINK beer (pivo) €2

FOOD pancake (blini) €1

HOSTEL/BUDGET HOTEL €20/ €35

TRAVEL train: Moscow–St Petersburg (7–9 hours), €20

FACT FILE

POPULATION 143 million

AREA 131,900 sq km (including six thousand islands)

LANGUAGE Russian

CURRENCY Ruble

CAPITAL Moscow (population 10.4 million)

INTERNATIONAL PHONE CODE ⓣ7

Basics

European Russia stretches from the borders of Belarus and Ukraine to the Ural mountains, over 1000km east of Moscow; even without the rest of the vast Russian Federation, it constitutes by far the largest country in Europe. Although visas are obligatory and accommodation often has to be booked in advance, independent travel is increasing every year. Moscow and St Petersburg are connected to the rest of Europe by fast trains and buses.

Moscow, the capital, is chaotic – not an obviously beautiful city. But its hectic splendour reflects Russia's fascinating history: from the Kremlin with its Tsarist palaces and orthodox churches, through the relics of the Communist years, to the massive building projects which have given the city a radical face-lift since the 1990s. By contrast, **St Petersburg**, Russia's second city, is Europe at its most gracious, an attempt by the eighteenth-century tsar Peter the Great to emulate the best of Western European elegance in what was then a far-flung outpost. Its position in the delta of the River Neva is unparalleled, giving it endless watery vistas. With its delicately coloured, low-roofed palaces barely seeming to break the join between water and sky, St Petersburg preserves a unity of style which Moscow lacks. Visible – often ostentatious – but uneven wealth creation in both cities has made them twin figureheads for Russia's recent high-speed renaissance.

CHRONOLOGY

862 AD A Scandinavian warrior, Rurik, founds the state of "Russ".

989 Grand Duke Vladimir I adopts Orthodox Christianity.

1552 Ivan the Terrible conquers the Tatars and builds the famous domed St. Basil's Cathedral in Red Square, Moscow.

1613 Michael Romanov is elected as Tsar of Russia, ushering in 300 years of Romanov rule.

1725 Peter the Great builds the new capital of St Petersburg after defeating Sweden in the Great Northern War.

1751 First recorded reference to "vodka" is made in a decree made by Empress Elizabeth.

1812 Napoleon invades Russia but is defeated.

1869 Tolstoy writes "War and Peace".

1892 Tchaikovsky composes the famous ballet, "The Nutcracker".

1905 Revolution leads to the masses gaining both a constitution and a parliament.

1914 Russia enters WWI on behalf of the Allies.

1917 The October Revolution witnesses the Communist Bolsheviks, led by Lenin, overthrowing the monarchy and government.

1924 Joseph Stalin takes control of the Soviet Union.

1941 The Nazis invade Russian territory; after intense fighting and victory at Stalingrad, the Red Army repel the Germans from Russia.

1961 Yuri Gagarin becomes the first human to travel into space aboard the *Vostok*.

1962 The Cuban Missile Crisis heightens tensions with the US during the Cold War.

1991 The Soviet Union collapses; many former Soviet countries declare independence. Boris Yeltsin is elected President.

1999 Yeltsin resigns and is replaced by Vladimir Putin.

2007 Russian relations with the US deteriorate over their plans to install anti-missile launchers around Russia's borders.

ARRIVAL

Most international travellers arriving by plane start in Moscow, at either **Sheremetyevo Airport**, connected to Rechnoy Vokzal metro station by bus no.851 or minibus 48, or **Domodedovo**, connected to Domodedovskaya metro station by bus no. 405 or minibuses. Train travellers, meanwhile, will pull into one of four Moscow **train sta-**

tions: Rizhskiy station (from Riga), Leningradskiy station (from Tallinn), Belorusskiy station (from Minsk, Warsaw, Prague, or Berlin), or Kievskiy station (from Kiev, Odessa, or Sofia). Train stations in both Moscow and St Petersburg are well connected to the **metro**; all Moscow's "vokzals" link to a stop on the (brown) circle line. European train routes into St Petersburg include arrivals from Helsinki (three daily) and one daily from Riga, Warsaw, Kiev, Vilnius, Tallinn, Berlin, Minsk and Odessa. The most convenient way to come to St Petersburg for travellers coming from the Baltic States may be by **bus**; the city bus station in the southeast of the city receives six daily buses from Tallinn, two from Riga and two from Helsinki. Ferries into St Petersburg from Helsinki and Tallinn arrive at the Vasilyevskiy island Ferry Terminal.

GETTING AROUND

The network of **trains** and buses is extensive and largely efficient. Up to twenty trains a day in each direction connect the two main cities. **Express trains** such as the Aurora and the Er-200 whisk passengers from one city to the other in under five hours in the early evening, but cheapest, and most atmospheric, are **overnight trains**, a quintessential Russian experience, which take around eight hours. Trains are generally safe, reliable and cheap (from approx. R700 one way in a four-person compartment or coupé). Buy **tickets** in advance from Leningradskiy station in Moscow or Moskovskiy station in St

ACCOMMODATION AND VISA CONTACTS

Ⓦ www.infinity.ru Reliable travel company offering visa service.
Ⓦ www.ostwest.com Mainly St Petersburg accommodation, including B&B; visa support.
Ⓦ www.russianembassy.net Russian embassies and consulates near you.
Ⓦ www.scottstours.co.uk One-stop shop visa service, handy for travellers combining Russia with Ukraine, Belarus, the Baltics or Central Asia.
Ⓦ www.trans-siberian.co.uk The Russia Experience organises trips to Moscow and St Petersburg and across the world's largest country on board the iconic train. Personalized trip packages available.
Ⓦ www.visatorussia.com Outstanding visa service.
Ⓦ www.visitrussia.org.uk Russian national tourist office in the UK

Petersburg. **City transport** in Moscow and St Petersburg centres on the punctual metro; overground transport includes **buses**, **trams**, **trolleybuses** and **minibuses** (**marshrútki**). Official **taxis** can be very expensive; unofficial taxis are not necessarily safe. **Bike** hire in St Petersburg furnishes a pleasant way to see the city's quieter outer corners. Cycle around Moscow at your peril.

ACCOMMODATION AND VISAS

Hostels tend to be safer, cleaner, and more pleasant than cheap **hotels**, many of which have "economy" rooms unaltered since Soviet times, and the hostel market in Moscow and St Petersburg is fast expanding. The standard **rate** is around R700–880 a night; aim to reserve three to four weeks in advance. **Booking ahead** by phone or with Ⓦ www.hostelbookers.com or Ⓦ www.hostelworld.com will guarantee you a bed for the night (and, in some cases, a small discount). Anyone travelling on a **tourist visa** to Russia must (nominally) have accommodation arranged before arrival. If you book a hostel in advance you can request **visa support** before you go. Hostels may provide invitations valid for a longer stay even if you spend only one night there. If you haven't yet decided where to stay when you get your visa, tourist agents in your home country are often prepared to arrange visa "**invitations**" in which they state that you will be staying at a randomly selected hotel. There is no obligation to actually do so once in Russia. If you book your hostel on arrival, request visa assistance – hostels can direct you to a visa registration agency. Note that it's important to **register your visa** within three working days of your arrival. On arrival you fill out an immigration card: you will be given back the bottom half which you must keep and present on departure.

FOOD AND DRINK

Moscow and St Petersburg are bursting at the seams with cafés and restaurants covering everything from budget blow-outs to *elitni* extravagance. Japanese is the cuisine du jour, so sushi abounds, but traditional Russian fare is still at the heart of many locals' everyday diets. **National dishes** worth tasting include *borshch* (beetroot soup), *shchi* (cabbage soup) and *pirogi* (small pies stuffed with potato, cabbage or *tvorog*, a kind of cream cheese. Try these and more at one of the *stolovaya* (canteen)-style restaurants loved by ordinary Russians, such as *Moo-Moo*. *Blini*, available from street stalls such as *Teremok* and *Russkoe Blini*, are also often the cheapest items on a café's menu. They subdivide into *blinchiki*, wrap-around pancakes stuffed with meat or berries, and flat pancakes, best served with honey, condensed milk, sour cream (*smetana*) or red caviar (*chorniy ikra*). In summer, Russians go mad for *morozhenoe*, ice cream at a fraction of the western price. For calorific suicide, opt for a *sirok* bar – a yoghurty sour-cream wodge encased in chocolate.

Vodka (*vódka*) is, of course, the national drink, knocked back in one gulp after chilling and chased with a bite on black bread or salted cucumber. **Beer** (*pivo*) is essential in summer (many Russians drink on their way to work); try Baltika, rated in strength from 3 to 9, Stariy Melnik or Nevskoe. Soviet champagne (*sovyetskoe shampanskoe*) is a unique treat, sickly-sweet to those accustomed to the French variety, but dirt-cheap; more refined palates may prefer excellent semi-sweet Georgian **wines** (Khvanchkara was Stalin's favourite). For cheap eating, you could do a lot worse than to stock up at a *produkti* (product store), scattered across both cities, though concentrated in the suburbs. These sell the full range of Russian dairy delights (try sour milk, *kefir*), salami sausages and (a relief) fresh fruit and veg. Traditionally, breakfast is eaten at 8am and "dinner" at 3pm; evening meals out tend to be eaten around 9pm.

CULTURE AND ETIQUETTE

Quirks of Russian social life include the practice of asking people on the metro if they are getting off at the next stop ("*vwee viyhoditye?*") just reply "da" (yes) or get out of the way. **Tipping** is in vogue only at high-end eating and drinking establishments, and five to ten percent should cover it. In **churches**, women should cover their head and shoulders, and men in shorts may be refused entry; you'll also notice that Russians avoid turning their back to the iconostasis which screens the altar.

SPORTS AND ACTIVITIES

Spectator sports centre on **football**, with Moscow's biggest teams Dinamo (Leningradskiy prospect 36 ⓣ095/612 7172, ⓦwww.fcdynamo.ru; Dinamo metro) and Spartak (Spartak stadium, 3rd Grazhdanskaya ul. 47a ⓣ095/105 0562, ⓦwww.spartak.com; Preobrazhenskaya ploshchad metro), while Petersburgers support Zenit (Petrovskiy stadium, 2nd Petrovskiy island ⓦwww.fc-zenit.ru; Sportivnaya metro).

Get involved in winter fun with skating, sledging or skiing. **Skating rinks** include Moscow's year-round cov-

READING RUSSIAN

Below are some common Cyrillic signs you are likely to encounter.

Вход	*khod*	entrance
Выход	*víykhod*	exit
Выход в город	*víykhod v górod*	way out to the town
открыт	*otkréet*	open
закрыт	*zakréet*	closed
перерыв	*pereréev*	break (in service, for tea/technical repairs)
туалет	*tooalyét*	toilet
мужчины, or M	*moózhshini*	men's (gents')
женщины, or Z	*zhénshini*	women's (ladies')
на ремонт	*na remónt*	under repair (usually for a building)
На себя	*na sebyá*	pull (for a door; lit. towards yourself)
От себя	*at cebyá*	push (for a door; lit. away from yourself)

ered rink at Gorky Park, Krymskiy Val ul. 9, Park Kultury metro, and Iskra at Selskokhozyaytvennaya ul. 26, Botanichesky Sad metro. **Sledging** in Moscow benefits from good verticals on the Sparrow Hills (Vorobyovye gory; Universitet metro), where you can overlook Moscow State University, the largest of the "seven sisters", the city's collection of 1950s Stalinist-Gothic skyscrapers. **Ski** venues, meanwhile, include Novo-Peredelkino (Proektiruemy prospect 9635/1; Yugo-Zapadnaya metro) and Kurkino (Landyshevaya ul., Planernaya metro). Summer or winter, **swim** in the open air at Chayka, Tuchaninov per. 1/3, Park Kultury metro or Luzhniki Luzhnetskaya nab. 24, Vorobyevy Gory metro. Year-round, pedalling enthusiasts can see St Petersburg with a **bike tour** (Skatprokat Rent a Bike, Goncharnaya ul. 7, Pl. Vosstaniya metro) or **walking tour** (Peter's Walking Tours, through International Youth Hostel, Ⓦwww.peterswalk.com, R450 for 4–5 hours).

COMMUNICATIONS

Most **post offices** are open Mon–Sat 8am–7pm. St Petersburg alone has four hundred of them, and blue post boxes are affixed to walls across both cities. However, local snail-mail is slow and not particularly reliable, so for urgent letters use **express companies** such as WestPost, which lets you obtain a Finnish post PO address, then receive your post in Russia as poste restante, or DHL. **Internet cafés** are abundant and cheap; most hostels offer Internet access on a limited number of screens for free or for R1 per minute. For **international calls** get a pre-paid international phone card such as the Zebra Telecom card or MTU-Net card, usable from any phone. Ask at a bank or telecoms kiosk for a *telefonnaya karta*. Alternatively, Ⓦwww.waytorussia.net lets you buy a card pin online which you use to make instant international calls. Non-Russian **mobiles** work on roaming via local providers, but you'll pay an arm and a leg for the pleasure. Get a local SIM card, or stick to SMS.

EMERGENCY NUMBERS

Police Ⓣ02; ambulance Ⓣ03; fire Ⓣ01
911 rescue service: Ⓣ095/937 9911
Metro lost and found: Ⓣ095/622 2085

EMERGENCIES

You really won't be bothered by the so-called Russian "mafia", but beware of **petty crime**, particularly pickpockets. Don't leave valuables in your hotel room, and lock the door before going to sleep. Be aware that undesirable characters tend to cluster around metro stations and train stations. The **police** (*militsia*) wear blue-grey uniforms; report a robbery to them. High-street **pharmacies** (*aptéka*) offer many familiar medicines over the counter. Foreigners tend to rely for treatment on expensive **private clinics**, so travel insurance is essential. St Petersburg **water** contains the giardia parasite, which can cause severe diarrhoea – metranidazol is the cure, but it's better to avoid drinking tap water in either city (in Moscow largely for the sake of your tastebuds).

INFORMATION & MAPS

Tourist offices are few and far between. Moscow's official tourist office (Gostiniy Dvor, Ilyinka ulitsa 4) has some English-language bumph, mostly on excursions out of town. Much better is St Petersburg's Tourist Information Office (**Sadovaya ulitsa 14, Nevskiy prospekt metro**); pick up the excellent *In Your Pocket* guide and a bite-size Yellow Pages. Hostel and hotel receptions carry leaflets and maps, and you can get up-to-date bar, restaurant and entertainment listings and reviews from **English-language papers**. The *Moscow Times* and the more ponderously pro-Kremlin *Moscow News* are well-estab-

Russian

English	Russian	Pronunciation
Yes	да	Da
No	нет	Nyet
Please	пожалуйста	Pazháaloosta
Thank you	спасибо	Spaséeba
Hello/Good day	здравствуйтеюдо	Zdrávstweetye
Goodbye	свидания	Da svidáaneya
Excuse me	извините	Izvinéetye
Sorry	простите	Prostitye
Where?	где?	Gdye…?
Good	хороший	Khoróshee
Bad	плохой	Plokhóy
Near	близко	Bléezki
Far	далеко	Dalyekó
Cheap	дешево	Deshóvee
Expensive	дорогой	Daragóy
Open	открыто	Otkryt
Closed	закрыто	Zakryt
Today	сегодня	Sevódnya
Yesterday	вчера	Vcherá
Tomorrow	завтра	Závtra
How much is....?	сколько стоит?	Skóllka stówit?
What time is it?	Который час?	Katóree chass?
I don't understand	я не понима/	Ya ne ponimáyou
Do you speak English?	вы говорите по-английски?	Vwee gavoréetye
Where are the toilets?	где туалеты?	Gdye zdyes tualyét?
My name is....	меня зовет	Menyá zavóot….
What is your name?	как вас зовет?	Kak vas zavóot?
I don't speak Russian	я не говор/ по-ресски	Ya nye gavaryóo pa-róosski.
One student ticket	один студенческий билет	Adéen stoodyéncheski bilyét
How much is the cheapest ticket?	сколько стоит самы дешевы билет?	Skolko stowit sammiy dyoshoviy bilyet?
Can I have....	мо;но?	Mózhna
Please give me	дайте (мне), пожалуйста	Dáyetye pazháloosta
Tea	чай	Chay
Beer	пиво	Péeva
Juice	сок	Sok
I am a vegetarian	я вегетарианец	Ya vegetariyánets
The bill, please	сч=т по;алейста	Shchyot, pazháloosta
One bed	одна кровать	Adéen kravát
Breakfast	завтрак	Závtrak
One	один	Adéen
Two	два	Dva
Three	три	Tree
Four	четыре	Chetéeri
Five	пять	Pyat
Six	iесть	Shest
Seven	семь	Syeem
Eight	восемь	Vósyem
Nine	девять	Dáyvyat
Ten	десять	Dáysyat

RUSSIA ON THE NET

Ⓦ**www.go-magazine.ru** The *Moscow Times* online guide to the capital.
Ⓦ**www.sptimesrussia.com** English-language newspaper on the Net, with useful tourist information and current listings.
Ⓦ**www.moscowcity.com** Official Moscow city guide.
Ⓦ**www.city-guide.spb.ru** Official St Petersburg city guide.
Ⓦ**www.yell.ru/msk** and Ⓦ**www.yell.ru/spb**. Yellow Pages comprehensive listings.
Ⓦ**www.waytorussia.com**. Outstanding, detailed practical advice.

lished; *Element* is directed at young city-dwellers (Ⓦwww.elementmoscow.ru), and there's also tongue-in-cheek expat mag *The Exile* (Ⓦwww.exile.ru) and *Where Moscow* magazine (Ⓦwww.wheremoscow.spn.ru). Maps in English are cheap and readily available at bookstores such as Moskva (Tverskaya ul. 8/7, Moscow) and Biblio-Globus (Myasnitskaya ul. 6/3, Moscow).

MONEY AND BANKS

Russia's currency is the **ruble**, divided into 100 kopeks. There are coins of 1, 5, 10, 20 and 50 kopeks and 1, 2 and 5 rubles, and notes of 5, 10, 50, 100, 500 and 1000 rubles. Everything is paid for in rubles, although some hostels make a habit of citing prices in either euros or dollars. At the time of writing €1=R35. **Change money** only in an official bank or currency exchange. Most **exchange offices** are open Mon–Sat 10am–8pm or later, and **ATMs** are plentiful. In general, prices in both cities range from "new Russian" prices (Moscow was recently named the most expensive city in the world) down to what the average Russian salary will cover, making many shops, bars, and cafés highly affordable for the budget-conscious traveller.

STUDENT AND YOUTH DISCOUNTS

"Foreigner prices" at museums and galleries are often steeper than for Russian citizens, although the differential is less acute than in Soviet times. The prices given here are all directed at foreigners, but most museums offer tickets for foreign **students** which cost half or two-thirds of the full price. An ISIC card is your best bet, though other student cards often work too. Ask for *adeen studyencheskiy bilyet* in your most authentic tones. It's worth knowing that St Petersburg's fabulous Hermitage is completely free to students.

OPENING HOURS AND HOLIDAYS

Most **shops** are open Mon–Sat 8am–7pm or later; Sunday hours are slightly shorter. **Museums** tend to open 9am–5pm, with last ticket sales an hour before closing time, and they are invariably closed one day a week, with one day a month aside as "cleaning day". **Churches** are accessible from 8am until the end of evening service. **Clubs** open late – many until 6am – or don't close at all, morphing into early-morning cafés. Russian **public holidays** fall on Jan 1, Jan 6 & 7, Jan 19, Feb 23 (Defender of the Motherland Day), March 8 (Women's Day), May 1 & 2 (Labour Day), May 9 (Victory Day), June 12 (Russia Day), and Nov 4 (Day of Popular Unity).

Moscow

MOSCOW (Москва) is all things to all people. To Westerners, the city may look European, but its unruly spirit is never far beneath the surface. To Muscovites, Moscow is both a "Mother City" and a "big village", a tumultuous community with an underlying collective instinct that surfaces in times of trouble. Moscow has been imbued with a sense of its own destiny since the fourteenth century, when the principality of **Muscovy** led the struggle against the Mongol-Tatars who had reduced the Kievan state to ruins. In the fifteenth and sixteenth centuries under **Ivan the Great** and **Ivan the Terrible** Moscow's realm reached from the White Sea to the Caspian. After the fall of Constantinople to the Turks in 1453, Moscow assumed Byzantium's suzerainty over the entire Orthodox world. Despite the changes wrought by **Peter the Great** – not least the **transfer of the capital** to St Petersburg – Moscow kept its mystique and bided its time until the **Communists** elevated it once more to most-favoured city status. In the 1990s, after the **fall of Communism**, Muscovites largely gave themselves over to "wild capitalism", and **major building programmes** lifted the face of the city radically.

What to see and do

Moscow's general **layout** is easily grasped – a series of concentric circles and radial lines emanating from Red Square and the Kremlin – and the centre is compact enough to explore on foot. Moscow's sights can also be mapped as strata of its history: the old Muscovy that Russians are eager to show; the now retro-chic Soviet-era sites such as VDHKh, Lenin's Mausoleum, and the Sculpture Park; and the exclusive restaurants and shopping malls that mark out the new Russia.

Red Square

Every visitor to Moscow is irresistibly drawn to **Red Square**, the historic and spiritual heart of the city. The name (*Krasnaya ploshchad*) has nothing to do with Communism, deriving from *krasniy*, the old Russian word for beautiful. The Lenin Mausoleum squats beneath the ramparts of the Kremlin and, facing it, sprawls **GUM** – what was during Soviet times the State Department Store – built in 1890–93, and now devoted to costly fashion outlets.

The Lenin Mausoleum and Kremlin wall

In post–Communist Russia, the **Lenin Mausoleum,** which houses Vladimir Ilyich Ulianov's embalmed corpse (Tues–Sun 10am–1pm; free) can be seen as either an awkward reminder of the old days or a cherished relic. The Mausoleum itself is a stylish piece of architecture in granite, black labradorite and red porphyry. Descend past stony-faced guards into the dimly-lit chasm where the leader's body lies. Stopping for any length of time or giggling will

TREAT YOURSELF

Get the city grit out of your skin at the exquisitely elaborate ✪ **Sandunovskiy baths**, patronized by Muscovites since 1896. Join Russian businessmen in the *banya*, a wooden hut heated with a furnace where you are invited to sweat out impurities, get beaten energetically with bunches of birch twigs, and finally be immersed in ice-cold water. Respite/anaesthesia comes from the obligatory follow-up: beer with dried fish. Men's and women's baths are separate, with the women's section more like a modern spa. A two-hour session starts from R700. Neglinnaya ul. 14/ 3–7; Teatralnaya metro, Ⓦ www.sanduny.ru.

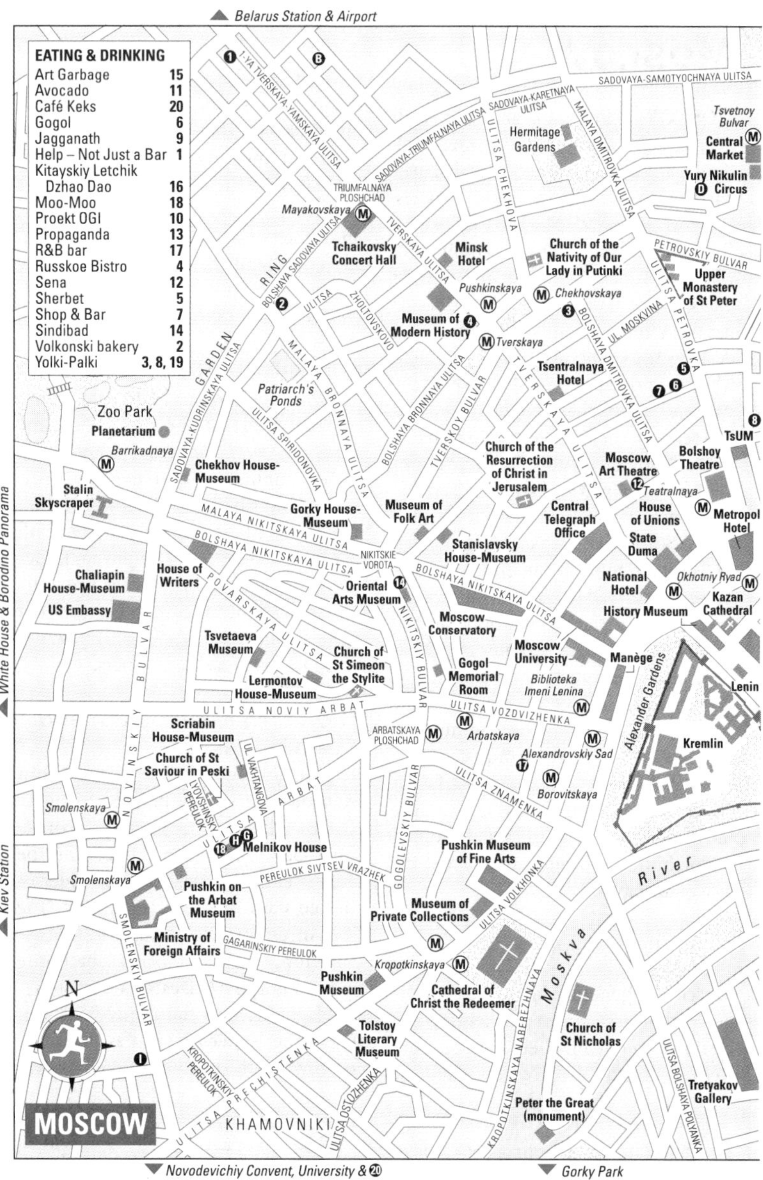

earn you stern rebukes. Behind the Mausoleum, the **Kremlin wall** – 19m high and 6.5m thick – contains a **mass grave** of Bolsheviks who perished during the battle for Moscow in 1917. The ashes of an array of **luminaries**, including writer Maxim Gorky and the first man in space, Yuri Gagarin, are here too. Beyond lie the graves of a select group of **Soviet leaders**, each with his own bust: Stalin still gets the most flowers laid down.

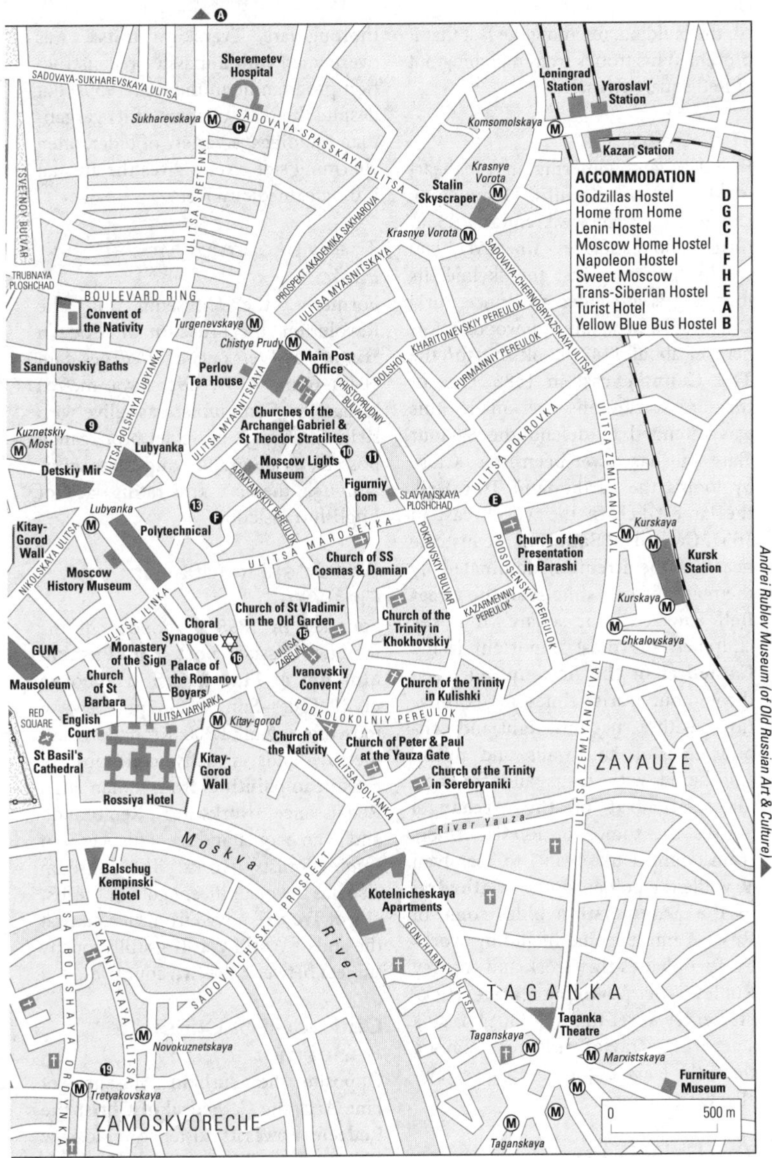

St Basil's Cathedral

No description can do justice to **St Basil's Cathedral** (11am–7pm, closed Tues and first Mon of month; R100), silhouetted against the skyline where Red Square slopes down towards the Moskva River. Commissioned by Ivan the Terrible to celebrate his capture of the Tatar stronghold of Kazan in 1552, its name commemorates St Basil the Blessed, a "holy fool" who foretold the fire that swept Moscow in 1547. Stalin longed to demolish the building, resenting the fact that it prevented his troops from marching out of Red Square en masse.

The Kremlin

Brooding and glittering in the heart of Moscow, the **Kremlin** (10am–5pm, closed Thurs; Ⓦwww.kreml.ru; R350) thrills and tantalizes whenever you see its towers against the skyline. Its founding is attributed to Prince Yuriy Dolgorukiy, who built a wooden fort here in about 1147. Look out for the **Tsar Cannon**, cast in 1586. One of the largest cannons ever made, this was intended to defend the Saviour Gate, but has never been fired. Close by looms the earthbound **Tsar Bell**, the largest bell in the world, cast in 1655. **Cathedral Square** is the historic heart of the Kremlin, dominated by the magnificent, white **Ivan the Great Bell Tower.** Of the square's four key churches, the most important is the **Cathedral of the Assumption**, used throughout tsarist times for coronations, with a spacious, light and echoing interior and walls and pillars smothered with icons and frescoes. The **Cathedral of the Archangel** houses the tombs of Russia's rulers from Grand Duke Ivan I to Tsar Ivan V, while the golden-domed **Cathedral of the Annunciation** hides some of Russia's finest icons, including works by Theophanes the Greek and Andrey Rublev. The **Armoury Palace** (ticketed entry at set times; R350) boasts a staggering array of treasures – among them the tsars' coronation robes, jewellery, and armour.

The Beliy Gorod

The **Beliy Gorod** (White Town) is the historic name of the residential district that encircled the Kremlin. Multi-domed churches cluster around **Kitay-Gorod**: this was the very heart of the city during the sixteenth century. Its main seventeenth-century thoroughfare, **Tverskaya ulitsa**, was overhauled with a massive reconstruction programme in the mid-1930s, but despite the scale of some of its gargantuan buildings, a variety of older, often charming side streets gives the area an intimate, medieval feel.

The Museum of Modern History

Formerly the Museum of the Revolution, the **Museum of Modern History** at Tverskaya ul. 21 (Tues–Sun 10am–6pm; R150; Tverskaya metro) brings the Communist past alive with striking displays of Soviet propaganda posters, photographs and state gifts, although there's a frustrating lack of English translation.

The Pushkin Museum of Fine Arts

Founded in 1898 in honour of the famous Russian poet, the **Pushkin Museum of Fine Arts** at Volkhonka ul. 12 (Tues–Sun 10am–7pm; Ⓦwww.museum.ru/gmii; R300; Kropotkinskaya metro) holds a hefty collection of **European painting**, from Italian High Renaissance works to Rembrandt, and an outstanding display of Impressionists' works. The museum also has the magnificent gold of the lost city of **Troy**, removed from Germany at the end of World War II – still a touchy subject between the two countries.

Cathedral of Christ the Redeemer

Opposite the Pushkin Museum of Fine Arts, the **Cathedral of Christ the Redeemer** owes its existence to Moscow Mayor Yury Mikhaylovich Luzhkov who began rebuilding it in 1994. The vast original structure had been blown up by the Soviet government in 1934 and a swimming pool built on the site, and this strident, even garish building became a symbol of Moscow's (and Russia's) post-Communist revival.

House-museums in the Zemlyanoy Gorod

Separated from the Beliy Gorod by the tree-lined "boulevard ring", **Zemlyanoy Gorod** epitomizes gentrified Moscow, where Neoclassical and Art Nouveau mansions abound. Admirers of Bulgakov, Chekhov, Lermontov, Gorky and Pushkin will find their former homes preserved as museums.

Anton Chekhov lived at Sadovaya-Kudrinskaya ul. 6, in what is now the **Chekhov House-Museum** (Thurs, Sat & Sun 11am–5pm, Wed & Fri 2–7pm; R100), while **Maxim Gorky's House-Museum** on the corner of Povarskaya ulitsa and ulitsa Spiridonovka (Wed–Sun 11am–8pm; closed last Thurs of month; free), is worth seeing purely for its delectable Art Nouveau decor, raspberry ice-cream pink both inside and out.

Patriarch's Ponds

Mikhail Bulgakov's magical realist masterpiece *The Master and Margarita* is indelibly associated with this spot between Malaya Bronnaya ulitsa and Bolshaya Sadovaya ulitsa (Mayakovskaya metro). The heavy overhanging canopy and steep drop to the water still evoke something of the novel's atmosphere of impending disaster. A plaque at Bolshaya Sadovaya ul. 10 attests that Mikhail Bulgakov lived here from 1921 to 1924.

The Borodino Panorama Museum

The **Borodino Panorama Museum** at Kutuzovskiy pr. 38 (10am–5pm; closed Fri & last Tues of month; ⓦwww.1812panorama.ru; R50) holds an immense painting of the **Battle of Borodino**, fought against Napoleon in 1812. The panorama is 115m long and 15m high, with three thousand figures. Napoleon won the battle, but lost the war.

Novodevichiy Convent

A cluster of shining domes above a fortified rampart proclaims the presence of the lovely **Novodevichiy Convent** (daily 8am–7pm for worship; museum 10am–5pm; closed Tues & first Mon of month; R150; Metro Sportivnaya). At its heart stands the white Cathedral of the Virgin of Smolensk. In its venerable **Cemetery** (daily 10am–6pm) lie numerous famous writers, musicians and artists, including Gogol, Chekhov, Stanislavsky, Bulgakov and Shostakovich. Krushchev is also here – he died out of office and was denied burial in the Kremlin wall.

The Tretyakov Gallery

Founded in 1892 by the financier Pavel Tretyakov, the **Tretyakov Gallery** at Lavrushinskiy pereulok (Tues–Sun 10am–7.30pm; ⓦwww.tretyakov.ru/english; R250; Metro Tretyakovskaya) displays an outstanding collection of pre-Revolutionary Russian art. Russian icons are magnificently displayed, and the exhibition continues through to the late nineteenth century, with one vast room filled with the nightmarish, fantastical works of Mikhail Vrubel. For those in danger of icon overload, the twentieth-century and contemporary art at the New Tretyakov (see below) is essential viewing.

The New Tretyakov Gallery

Opposite the entrance to Gorky Park, at Krymskiy val 10, the **New Tretyakov Gallery** (Tues–Sun 10am–7.30pm; R100; Park Kultury metro) takes a breakneck gallop through twentieth-century Russian art, from the neo-primitivist visionaries of the turn of the century through recently rediscovered photographs of the Thirties to the 1980s "second wave" avant-garde. Full and illuminating commentary in English is a bonus. While in the area, drop into the **Sculpture Park** (inside Gorky Park, 10am–5pm; R100) where displaced Communist-era statues of one-time popular heroes lie disconsolately.

VDNKh

Untrammelled Soviet triumphalism gets an airing at the Exhibition of Economic Achievements, or **VDNKh** (Prospekt Mira, VDNKh/Prospekt Mira metro). Glance at the permanent trade-fair-cum-shopping-centre housed in the grandiose Stalinist architecture of the All-Union Agricultural Exhibition of 1939, then gape at one of the most hubristic Soviet monuments ever built, the **Space Obelisk**, which bears witness to Soviet designs on the stratosphere. A rocket blasts nearly 100m into the sky on a stylized plume of energy clad in shining titanium. It was unveiled in 1964, three years after Gagarin orbited the earth.

Arrival and information

Air Planes from Western Europe arrive either at Sheremetevo, Terminal 2 or Domodedovo. Avoid taxi drivers and take a bus or minibus (*marshrutka*) or official bus to the metro (bus 851 runs to Rechnoy Vokzal for Sheremetevo, costing just R20, or minibus 48 from Rechnoy Vokzal; bus 405 to Domodedovskaya metro for Domodedovo costs around R35). The Aeroexpress train also runs from Paveletsky rail terminal to Domodedovo, costing R150.

Train All stations are well connected to the centre of town via the metro.

Arrivals to Belorusskiy station from Belarus, Lithuania, Poland or Western Europe. From Vilnius, two trains daily (around 15 hours). From Prague, one daily (around 32 hours). From Warsaw, one daily (around 16 hours). From Berlin, one daily (around 27 hours).

Arrivals to Kievskiy station: from Kiev, eight trains daily (around 10 hours); from Odessa, five daily (25 hours), and from Sofia, one daily between July and September (around 55 hours).

Arrivals to Leningradskiy station: if coming from St Petersburg, around 14 trains daily (4.5–10 hours), two daily from Tallinn, and one daily from Helsinki.

Arrivals at Rizhskiy station: from Riga, in Latvia, two daily (around 16 hours).

Bus Ecolines buses from Germany and the Baltic States terminate at Aerovokzal on Leningradskoe shosse. Eurolines buses run from European destinations including Berlin, Riga, Tallinn, Helsinki and Minsk to both St Petersburg and Moscow.

Ferry/Boat Northern River Boat-Station, Leningradskoye shosse 51, Rechnoy Vokzal metro, Ⓣ095/457 4050; Southern River Boat-Station, Andropova prospect 11/2, Kolomenskaya metro Ⓣ095/118 0811.

Tourist office, 4 Ilyinka Street, Gostiny Dvor, Ⓣ095/232 5657, Ⓦwww.moscowcity-ru.

Good guides include the official Moscow guide from the information office and the Moscow Multilingual Guide, available at Ⓦwww.streetbystreet.ru.

City transport

Metro With its Soviet mosaics, murals and statuary, and stained glass, Moscow's Metro is deservedly world-famous. Look out for the bronze statues at Ploshchad Revolutsii and stained glass at Novoslodobskaya. The metro runs from 5.30am to 1am daily. Stations are marked with a large "M". You can travel any distance and change lines as many times as you like for the cost of one ride (R15). Buy a card for 10 or 20 journeys (ask at the *kassa* for 'dyéssiyet/dvátset póezdok').

Trams and trolleybuses Often the best way to tackle a big road like a section of Tverskaya ulitsa or the Garden Ring. Trolleybus stops have blue-and-white signs. Most routes operate from 5am to 1am; fares cost R10.

Buses Bus stops are marked with yellow signs and single tickets (around R12) or batches of ten are available from the driver.

Minibuses *Marshrutkas* are cheap (around R15 a journey). They wait to fill up with passengers, then take the route advertised on the side. You can ask to get out at any point. Pay the driver on board.

Taxis In theory, you can hitch a ride with non-accredited taxis, but women especially should be careful. Official taxis come in all shapes and sizes and can be viciously expensive.

Accommodation

Hotels are mostly astronomically priced or perilously decrepit, making Moscow's growing number of **hostels**, generally, a better bet.

Hostels

Godzillas Hostel Bolshoi Karetniy 6, flat 5 (first floor); Tsvetnoy Bulvar/Tverskaya metro. Ⓣ095/699 4223, Ⓦwww.godzillashostel.com. Relaxed, popular hostel with fresh decor, lots of Moscow information to hand, and charming, helpful staff; dorms ❸, doubles ❺

Home from Home Stariy Arbat 49, entrance 2, flat 2, Smolenskaya metro, Ⓣ095/229 8018, Ⓦwww.

home-fromhome.com. Cosy, welcoming hostel in sterling, central location. Dorms ❸, doubles ❻

Lenin Hostel Bolshaya Sukharevskaya Square 16/18, flat 5, entrance 1, on 4th floor, Sukharevsky metro, ⓣ 095/241 1446 (same ownership as *Sweet Moscow*). Opened in summer 2007 and situated right on the garden ring, with staggeringly cool interiors, *Lenin* looks set to be a backpackers' hot spot. Dorms ❸, doubles ❼

Moscow Home Hostel 2nd Nepalimosky pereulok, 1/12, Park Kultury metro; ⓣ 095/109 4228, ⓦ www.moshostel.com. Stylish and clean hostel in a lovely part of town. 24-hour check in. Accepts credit cards. Dorms ❸, doubles ❼

Napoleon Hostel Maly Zaloutinskiy pereulok 2, 4th floor, Kitay-Gorod metro, ⓣ 095/628 6695, ⓦ www.napoleonhostel.ru. Fun, friendly hostel in the best possible location for sampling Moscow nightlife. DVD/widescreen TV; beers for 30 rubles during happy hour, 6pm–8pm. Dorms ❸

Sweet Moscow. Stariy Arbat 51, flat 31, 8th floor, Smolenskaya metro, ⓣ 095/241 1446, ⓦ www.sweetmoscow.com. Trendily kitted out, youth-focused hostel, even if the communal area is a trifle cramped. Dorms ❷

Trans-Siberian Hostel: Barashevsky pereulok 12, Kurskaya metro, ⓣ 095/916 2030, ⓦ www.transsiberianhostel.com. Slightly shoddy, but clean and full of character, with pet cat attached. Dorms ❸, doubles ❺

Yellow Blue Bus Hostel: 4th Tverskaya-Yamskaya ul. 5, flat 8. Mayakovskaya metro. ⓣ 095/250 1364. Not quite central and less of an "international" feel than rivals, but friendly with all mod cons. Dorms ❷, double ❼

Hotels

Turist Selskokhozyaystvennaya ul. 17/2, Botanichesky Sad metro. ⓣ 095/980 7391, ⓦ www.hotelturist.com. A clean, personable place located in a green corner of Moscow. Economy doubles ❼

Eating

For true economy when eating out, go for "**canteens**", a café/restaurant format favoured by locals where you compile a tray of dishes smorgasbord-style. Many are no-frills filling stations rather than places to while away an afternoon, but perfectly pleasant. Alternatively, many small **restaurants** offer business lunches for around R150.

Canteens

Moo-Moo ul. Arbat 45/24; Smolenskaya metro or ul Myanitskaya 14. Just point at what you want: it's all laid out for you. Pork shashlik R140.

Russkoe Bistro Tverskaya ul. 16, Pushkingskaya metro and branches. Super-cheap snack-size pies and pancakes from chain popular with locals. Grab a quick *pirog* for R25.

Sena 1st Kamergerski Pereulok 6, off Tverskaya, Teatralnaya metro. Central and cheap. Assemble your selection of simple Russian food. Beers from under R70.

Yolki-Palki Neglinnaya 8/10; Bolshaya Dmitrovka ul. 23/8; Klimentovskiy per. 14/1, and branches. Russian/Ukrainian/Mongolian food at rock-bottom prices, even if the interior design is a tad tacky. Russian salads, grills, and *blini* (R140).

Cafés

Jagganath Kuznetskiy Most ul. 11, Kuznetskiy Most metro. This veggie café-cum-health food store is an unlikely but much-loved Moscow institution. Curries, light cakes and fresh salads delight the hearts of those tiring of unrelenting carbs and dairy. Miniscule prices, and ethical without being too earnest. Internet points. *Pirogi* from R30; home-made ginger beer, R20.

Volkonskiy bakery Bolshaya Sadovaya ul. 2/46, Mayakovskaya metro. Sit nursing a hot chocolate on a chilly day or pick up teatime goodies to go. Cakes from R40.

Restaurants

Avocado Chistoprudniy bulvar 12/2; Chistye Prudy metro. Upmarket, non-smoking vegetarian restaurant with business lunch for just R150.

Sherbet Stretenka ul. 32; Teatralnaya metro. Wildly popular lunch spot with generous Uzbek dishes. Scented hookahs enliven the ambience. *Plov* (spiced rice with lamb, onion and carrot), R200.

Sindibad Nikitskiy bulvar 14; Arbatskaya metro. Small Lebanese café with suspect decor but good Middle Eastern/Greek dishes. *Sejok* (spiced lamb with Arabian bread) R310.

Drinking

Moscow's famous **nightlife** is marred by the practice of "face control", excluding plebs from *elitni* clubs. Those venues listed here are largely accessible.

Bars

Café Keks ul. Timura Frunze 11; Park Kultury metro. Open 24 hours Fri and Sat. Keks fuses elegance and affordability, with cosy-chic fabric upholstering and cocktails from R140.

TREAT YOURSELF

Nurse a mojito and soak up the nouveau glow at the very knowingly fabulous new **Denis Simachyov Boutique & Bar**, 12/2 Stoleshnikov pereulok, Teatralnaya metro. Cocktails from R200. The store sells everything from cosmonaut helmets to designer clothes by Denis himself.

Gogol Stoleshnikov pereulok 11; Kuznetskiy Most metro. Stylish 24-hour bar-club-cafe with *fin-de-siècle* decor, al fresco dining in summer and a free ice-rink in the yard in winter. The wryly titled "Soviet menu" is excellent value, and cocktails are R140–250.
Help – Not Just A Bar 1-aya Tverskaya Yamskaya ultisa, 27/1, Belorusskaya metro. Masculine, pubbish bar with deals including 2-for-1s after midnight and free desserts on Wednesdays. Shots R100.
Proekt OGI Potapovsky pereulok 8/12. Chistye Prudy metro. Hip club, bar and restaurant which, once found, wins lifetime devotees. Look out for the weight of edible items in grams on the menu. Cocktails start from just R70; *blini* with condensed milk costs R35.
R&B bar Starovagankovskiy per. 19/2l; Biblioteka im. Lenina metro. Central live-music bar with exuberant atmosphere and capacious courtyard. Beers from R70.

Clubs

Art Garbage Starosadskiy per. 5/6; Kitay-gorod metro. Ⓦwww.art-garbage.ru. Civilized club which combines a disco, contemporary art gallery and live concert venue. Cocktails from R180.
Kitayskiy Letchik Dzhao Dao Lubyanskiy proezd 25/1; Kitay-Gorod metro, Ⓦwww.jao-da.ru. Avoid the Chinese restaurant upstairs and descend to the artfully scuffed-up basement, host to outstanding bands. Beers from R70–90.
Propaganda Bolshoy Zlatoustinskiy per. 7; Kitay-Gorod metro. Flirt with the risk of face control at this perennially popular club. Drum 'n' bass nights on Fridays. If you'd rather not know if your face passes muster, go early for drinks or dinner. 2 for 1 after midnight Mon–Wed.

Entertainment

Theatre, **classical music** and **ballet** all have superb vintages in Russia, and can be surprisingly cheap, provided you ask for the cheapest ticket available (*samiy deshoviy bilyet*). The showmanship at Russia's **circuses** is impressive, too, if you can hack the animal acts.

Circus

Grand Moscow State Circus Vernadskovo prospect 7; Ⓣ095/930 0272, Ⓦwww.bolshoicircus.ru; Universitet metro.
Nikulin Moscow Circus Tsvetnoy bul. 13 Ⓣ095/625 8970; Tsvetnoy Bulvar metro.

Cinema

Dome Cinema 18/1 Olimpiyskiy pr. Ⓣ095/931 9873; Prospekt Mira/Kievskaya metro. English-language films.

Music

B2 Bolshaya Sadovaya ul. 8/1; Mayakovskaya metro. A consistent performer on the live music scene. Men pay R300 after 10pm Fri/Sat.
Tchaikovsky concert hall, Triumfalnaya ploshad 4/31, Mayakovskaya metro; Ⓣ095/232 5353, Ⓦwww.meloman.ru. Pick a night when Russian music heads the bill and admire the view; the hall is festooned with red stars. Tickets start at just R100.

Theatre

Bolshoy Theatre Teatralnaya pl. 1 Ⓣ095/250 7317, Ⓦwww.bolshoi.ru; Teatralnaya metro. Simply the world's most famous ballet.
Sovremennik Theatre Chistopurdny bulvar, 19a, Chisti Prudi metro; Ⓣ095/628 77 49, Ⓦwww.sovremennik.ru. Critically acclaimed productions of classics and contemporary writing.

Shopping

Get hold of Soviet paraphernalia and memorabilia including coins, medals, uniforms and postcards at the **Museum of Modern History** shop, from R50. **Kristall** (Pokrovka ul. 19) does a great selection of vodkas, from Yuri Dolgoruki costing R450 to Kristallnaya for R115. **Stalls inside churches** Worth a browse for small icons, delicate chains and crosses, or "holy" honey, from around R40.

Directory

Embassies Australia: 13 Kropotkinskiy pereulok, metro Park Kultury Ⓣ095/956 6070; UK: 10 Smolenskaya nab., metro Smolenskaya Ⓣ095/956 7200; Canada: 23 Starokonuyushenniy pereulok, metro Kropotkinskaya Ⓣ095/105 6000; USA: 19 Novinskiy bulvar, metro Smolenskaya

Ⓣ095/728 5000; New Zealand: 44 Povarskaya ul., metro Barrikadnaya, Ⓣ095/956 3579; Ireland: Grokholskiy per. 5 Ⓣ095/937 5911.
Internet *Cafemax*, ul. Pyatnitskaya 25/1, Novokuznetskaya metro; Netcity, Kamergersky per. 5/6, Teatralnaya metro; IMAGE.RU, Novoslodbodskaya ul. 16a, Novoslobodskaya metro; Time Online, Okhotni Ryad shopping centre basement level to the right of the escalators, Okhotni Ryad metro.
Laundry California Cleaners, Maliy Gnezdnikovskiy per. 12.
Left luggage Most train stations have lockers and/or a 24hr left-luggage office.
Medical European Medical Center, Spiridonovskiy per. 1 Ⓣ095/933 6655, Ⓦwww.emcmos.ru; International SOS Clinic, 31 Grokholskiy per. 10th floor Ⓣ095/937 5760, Ⓦwww.internationalsos.com. Both recognized by international insurance companies.
Pharmacy Stariy Arbat, Arbatskaya ul. 25; Multifarma, Turistkaya ul. 27; 24hr pharmacy at pr. Mira 71.
Post office Central Telegraph Office, Tverskaya ul. 7; Main Post Office, Myasnitskaya ul. 26/2, 9am–6pm. Express postal services via Westpost Ⓣ095/234 9038, Ⓦwww.westpost.ru; Courier Service, Bolshaya Sadovaya 10; Mayakovskaya metro Ⓣ095/209 1735. DHL: 1st Tverskaya Yamskaya ul. 11, Belorusskaya metro.

Moving on

Train Berlin (1 daily; 25hr 30min); Budapest (1 daily; 37hr); Cologne (1 daily; 34hr); Helsinki (1 daily; 12hr 30min); Prague (1 daily; 33hr); Riga (2 daily; 15hr 30min); St Petersburg (frequent; 4hr 30min–8hr); Sofia (1 daily; 56hr); Tallinn (1 daily; 15hr); Warsaw (2 daily; 18hr).
Bus Riga (2 daily; 20hr); St Petersburg (1 daily; 13hr); Tallinn (1 daily; 18hr 30min).

St Petersburg

ST PETERSBURG (Санкт-Петербург), Petrograd, Leningrad and St Petersburg again – the city's succession of names mirrors Russia's turbulent history. Founded in 1703 by **Peter the Great** as a "window on the West", St Petersburg was for two centuries the capital of the tsarist empire, synonymous with magnificence and excess. In 1917, it became the cradle of the **Revolution** that overthrew the monarchy and brought the Bolsheviks to power. As **Leningrad** it epitomized the Soviet Union's heroic sacrifices in World War II, withstanding nine hundred days of Nazi siege. In 1991 – the year the USSR collapsed – the change of name back to St Petersburg symbolized the end of an era. Today, St Petersburg, after being buffed up for the 2003 tricentenary celebrations, is a self-assured and future-focused city. The most celebrated **time to visit** is during the midsummer White Nights (mid-June to mid-July), when darkness never falls, but autumn and winter bathe the city in wonderful light, too. From May to October all bridges across the Neva are raised from 2–5am – a beautiful sight, if inconvenient when on the wrong side of the water.

What to see and do

St Petersburg's centre lies on the south bank of the River Neva, with the curving River Fontanka marking its southern boundary. The area within the Fontanka is riven by a series of avenues fanning out from the golden spire of the Admiralty, on the Neva's south bank. Many of the city's top sights are located on and around **Nevskiy prospekt**, the well-to-do main avenue where Petersburgers promenade. Across the Neva is **Vasilevskiy Island**, with the Strelka at its eastern tip, and the Petrograd Side, home to the **Peter and Paul Fortress**. Beyond the River Fontanka lie **Smolniy**, where the Bolsheviks fomented revolution in 1917, and the peaceful **Alexander Nevsky Monastery**. Although Petersburgers favour the formal public spaces of the Summer Garden, a stroll around the pedestrian-friendly streets branching off the northeastern side of Liteyniy prospect or behind **Kazan Cathedral** is a study in tranquillity.

Nevskiy Prospekt

Stretching from the Alexander Nevskiy Monastery to Palace Square and the

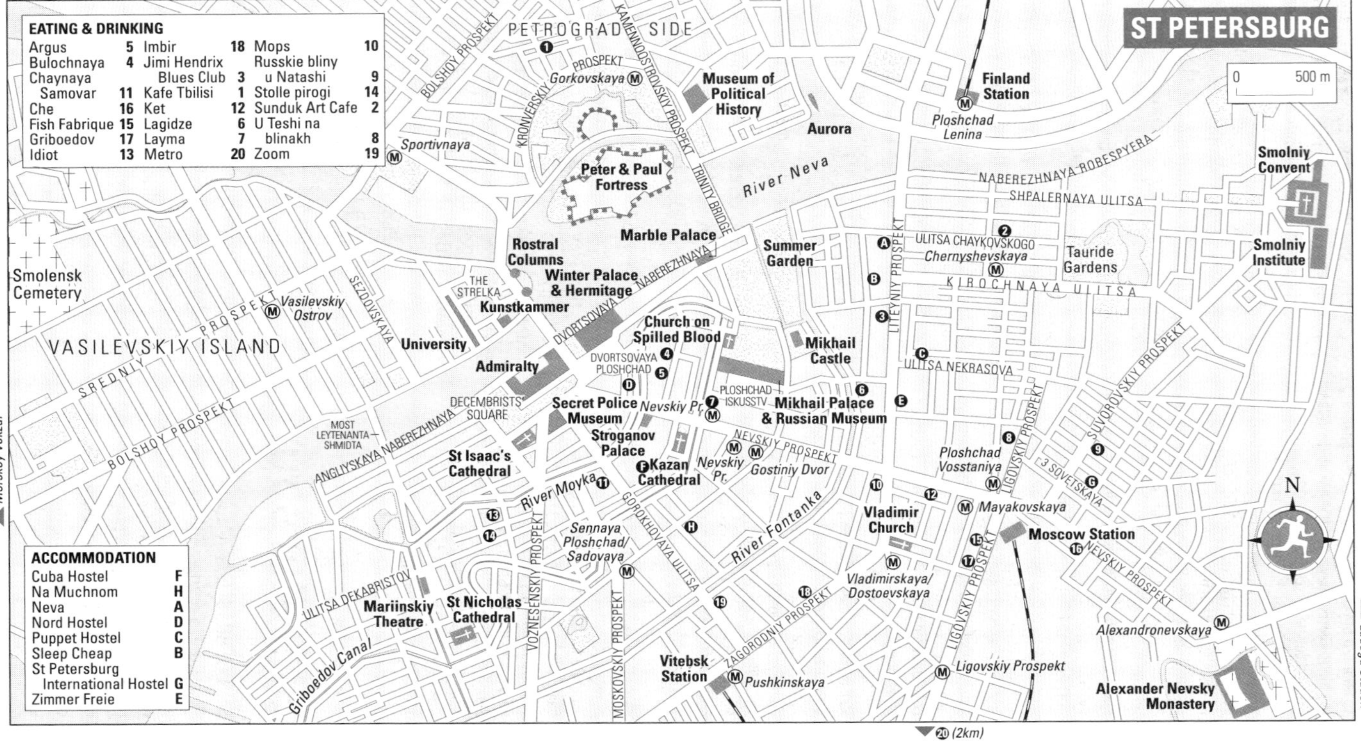
ST PETERSBURG
0 500 m
EATING & DRINKING
Argus 5
Bulochnaya 4
Chaynaya Samovar 11
Che 16
Fish Fabrique 15
Griboedov 17
Idiot 13
Imbir 18
Jimi Hendrix Blues Club 3
Kafe Tbilisi 1
Ket 12
Lagidze 6
Layma 7
Metro 20
Mops 10
Russkie bliny u Natashi 9
Stolle pirogi 14
Sunduk Art Cafe 2
U Teshi na blinakh 8
Zoom 19
ACCOMMODATION
Cuba Hostel F
Na Muchnom H
Neva A
Nord Hostel D
Puppet Hostel C
Sleep Cheap B
St Petersburg International Hostel G
Zimmer Freie E
PETROGRAD SIDE
VASILEVSKIY ISLAND
Smolensk Cemetery
Peter & Paul Fortress
Museum of Political History
Aurora
Finland Station
Ploshchad Lenina
Smolniy Convent
Smolniy Institute
Tauride Gardens
Summer Garden
Marble Palace
Rostral Columns
Winter Palace & Hermitage
Kunstkammer
University
Admiralty
Church on Spilled Blood
Mikhail Castle
Mikhail Palace & Russian Museum
Secret Police Museum
Stroganov Palace
Kazan Cathedral
St Isaac's Cathedral
Mariinskiy Theatre
St Nicholas Cathedral
Vladimir Church
Moscow Station
Vitebsk Station
Alexander Nevsky Monastery
River Neva
River Moyka
River Fontanka
Griboedov Canal
THE STRELKA
DECEMBRISTS' SQUARE
DVORTSOVAYA PLOSHCHAD
PLOSHCHAD ISKUSSTV
MOST LEYTENANTA SHMIDTA
BOLSHOY PROSPEKT
SREDNIY PROSPEKT
SEZDOVSKAYA
KRONVERSKIY PROSPEKT
KAMENNOOSTROVSKIY PROSPEKT
TRINITY BRIDGE
DVORTSOVAYA NABEREZHNAYA
ANGLIYSKAYA NABEREZHNAYA
NABEREZHNAYA ROBESPYERA
SHPALERNAYA ULITSA
ULITSA CHAYKOVSKOGO
KIROCHNAYA ULITSA
LITEYNIY PROSPEKT
ULITSA NEKRASOVA
NEVSKIY PROSPEKT
LIGOVSKIY PROSPEKT
SUVOROVSKIY PROSPEKT
3 SOVETSKAYA
GOROKHOVAYA ULITSA
VOZNESENSKIY PROSPEKT
MOSKOVSKIY PROSPEKT
ZAGORODNIY PROSPEKT
ULITSA DEKABRISTOV
Gorkovskaya
Sportivnaya
Vasilevskiy Ostrov
Chernyshevskaya
Nevskiy Pr.
Gostiniy Dvor
Ploshchad Vosstaniya
Mayakovskaya
Sennaya Ploshchad/ Sadovaya
Vladimirskaya/ Dostoevskaya
Pushkinskaya
Ligovskiy Prospekt
Alexandronevskaya
Morskoy Vokzal
Ladoga Station
20 (2km)
N

Hermitage, **Nevskiy prospekt** has been the backbone and heart of the city for the last three centuries. Built on an epic scale during the reign of Peter the Great, it showcases every style of architecture from eighteenth-century Baroque to 1950s Stalinist Classicism.

The Winter Palace

The two-hundred-metre long Baroque **Winter Palace** at the westernmost end of Nevskiy prospekt is the city's largest, most opulent palace. As loaded with history as it is with gilt and stucco, the palace was the official residence of the tsars, their court and 1500 servants. The main building was finished in 1762 and later new buildings were added to the east: the Small and Large Hermitages were added by Catherine the Great, while the New Hermitage was launched as Russia's first public art museum in 1852.

The Hermitage

Of awesome size and scope, the **Hermitage** collection (Tues–Sat 10.30am–6pm, Sun 10.30am–5pm; Ⓦwww.hermitagemuseum.org; R350; free to students and to all on first Thurs of every month) embraces some three million objects, from ancient Scythian gold to Cubism, making it one of the world's greatest museums. After the state rooms and the Gold Collection, the most universally popular section covers modern European art from the nineteenth and twentieth centuries, with an array of works by Picasso, Gauguin, Van Gogh, Rodin, Monet and Renoir.

Kazan Cathedral

Curving **Kazan Cathedral** (10am–6pm, free entry; Nevskiy prospekt metro), built between 1801 and 1811, was modelled on St Peter's in the Vatican and is unique in die-straight St Petersburg. The cathedral was built to house a venerated icon, Our Lady of Kazan, reputed to have appeared miraculously overnight in Kazan in 1579, and later transferred to St Petersburg, where it resided until its disappearance in 1904. In Soviet times the cathedral housed the Museum of Religion and Atheism, but today it offers a refreshing contrast to many other St Petersburg churches by being filled not with tourists but with worshippers.

The Church on Spilled Blood

The multicoloured, onion-domed **Church on Spilled Blood** at 26 Kanala Groboedova embankment (11am–7pm, closed Wed; R300) was begun in 1882 in memory of Tsar Alexander II, assassinated on the site by student radicals a year earlier. In pseudo-traditional Russian style, it is one of St Petersburg's most striking landmarks, quite unlike the dominant Neoclassical architecture. Inside, it is stuffed full of thousands of metres of mosaics.

The Russian Museum

The Mikhail Palace is the main building of the **Russian Museum** (4 Inzhenernaya Ulitsa; Mon 10am–5pm, Wed–Sun 10am–6pm; Ⓣ812/595 4248, Ⓦwww.rusmuseum.ru; R350). Its collection of Russian art, the world's finest, ranges from fourteenth-century icons to the avant-garde movements of the early twentieth century. Most interesting is Russian art's coming of age in the late nineteenth century, with Vasnetsov's epic historic-mythical paeans to Old Russia, Ilya Repin's socially conscious realism, and Kuindzui's superlative studies of light on landscape.

The Summer Garden

Most popular of all St Petersburg's public gardens is the **Summer Garden** on Kutuzov Embankment, commissioned by Peter the Great in 1704 and rebuilt by Catherine the Great in the informal English style that survives today (daily 8/11am–6/10pm). Also charming are Mikhail Garden behind the Russian Museum (daily 10am–8/10pm) and

Marsovo pole (the Field of Mars) on the other side of the River Moyka where a flame burns for the fallen of the Revolution and civil war (1917–21).

The Admiralty and Decembrists' Square

The **Admiralty** perched at the western end of Nevskiy prospekt, its central tower culminating in a slender spire, is a magnificent expression of naval triumphalism. Founded in 1704 as a fortified shipyard, it extends 407m along the waterfront from Palace Square to **Decembrists' Square**, named after a group of reformist officers who, in December 1825, marched three thousand soldiers into the square in a doomed attempt to proclaim a constitutional monarchy. Today, Decembrists' Square is dominated by the Bronze Horseman, Falconet's 1778 statue of Peter the Great and the city's unofficial symbol.

St Isaac's Cathedral

Looming above Decembrists' square, **St Isaac's Cathedral** (11am–7pm, colonnade till 4.30pm, closed Wed; ⓦwww.cathedral.ru; R300, colonnade R150; Nevskiy prospekt metro) is one of the glories of St Petersburg's skyline, its gilded dome the third largest in Europe. The opulent interior is equally impressive, decorated with fourteen kinds of marble. The cathedral's height (101.5m) and rooftop statues are best appreciated by climbing the 262 steps to the outside colonnade.

The Peter and Paul Fortress

Across the Neva from the Winter Palace, on little Zayachiy island, stands the **Peter and Paul Fortress**, built to secure Russia's hold on the Neva delta. The Fortress (8am–10pm; free) shelters a cathedral as well as rotating exhibitions in the Engineers' House and Commandant's House. The Dutch-style Peter and Paul Cathedral (10am–7pm, closed Wed; ⓦwww.spbmuseum.ru; R150/R70 students), completed in 1733, remained the tallest structure in the city until the 1960s. Sited around the nave are the tombs of **Romanov monarchs** from Peter the Great onwards, excluding Peter II, Ivan VI and Nicholas II. Nicholas and his family, whose bones were discovered in a mineshaft in the Urals in 1989, are in a chapel of their own to one side. Their burial here in 1998 was highly controversial, reopening old debates about the restoration of the throne to the Romanov line.

The Kunstkammer

Not to be missed is the **Kunstkammer** at Universitetskaya nab. 3, Vasilevsky island (11am–6pm, closed Mon and last Tues of month; ⓦwww.kunstkamera.ru; R200; Vasileosrovskaya metro), Russia's oldest public museum, founded by Peter the Great in 1714. Its name (meaning "art chamber" in German) dignified Peter's fascination for curiosities and freaks: he offered rewards for "human monsters" and unknown animals, which were preserved in vinegar or vodka. The result is a grisly but strangely compelling exhibition, with excellent commentary on all exhibits.

Museum of Political History

The rigorous and lively **Museum of Political History** at Kuibysheva ulitsa 2/4 (10am–6pm except Thurs; ⓦwww.polithistory.ru; free entry on public holidays; R150; Gorkovskaya metro) gives in-depth insights into Soviet-era political and social life, displaying children's textbooks reworked to demonize the *kulaks* (moneyed peasants), appalling photographic evidence of Stalin's purges, and film footage recalling how Western culture enthralled Soviet youngsters in the 1960s and 1970s. Helpful attendants can provide booklets with comprehensive English-language translations.

Secret Police Museum

This intriguing exhibition on the **History of the Political Police** (10am–6pm Mon–Fri; R100; Admiralteysky prospect

6, metro Nevskiy Prospect) at an annexe of the Museum of Political History includes previously classified police reports on individuals suspected of subversive activity from the dying days of the late Tsarist regime to the present. Look out for Okhrana (Tsarist secret police) reports on Lenin from 1909, photos of undercover KGB officers at meetings between US/USSR presidents, and painfully recent testimony from Russian federal agents operating in Grozny, Chechnya. Limited English translations are available from solicitous attendants.

Smolniy Cathedral and Institute

Smolniy Cathedral (3/1 Rastrelli Square, Chernyshevskaya metro; 10am–8pm except Wed; R200), a peerless ice-blue Rastrelli Baroque creation, is the focal point of the Smolniy district. The neighbouring **Smolniy Institute** (pl. Proletarskoy diktaturi 3) is now the Headquarters of St Petersburg's Governor, but was built in 1806–08 to house the Institute for Young Noblewomen; then Lenin ran the Revolution of 1917 from here, and changed the course of history. The man himself still stands in front of the building, and as you enter the Institute's grounds, look out for the now-familiar Communist slogan: "Workers of the World, Unite!" (Пролетарии всех стран, соединяйтесь!)

Alexander Nevsky Monastery

At the eastern end of Nevskiy prospekt lies the **Alexander Nevsky Monastery** (10am–8pm; free; Aleksandra Nevskogo metro), founded in 1713 by Peter the Great and one of only four monasteries in the Russian Empire with the rank of *lavra*, the highest in Orthodox monasticism. The contemplative atmosphere of the St Trinity cathedral is best experienced during services, at 10am and 5pm. Fill out a prayer slip to have your loved ones included in the monks' prayers. Two famous **cemeteries** lie in the monastery grounds: the "Necropolis for Masters of the Arts", where Dostoyevsky, Rimsky-Korsakov, Tchaikovsky and Glinka lie, and directly opposite the Lazarus Cemetery, the oldest in the city. Tickets are required for entry to both (summer 9.30am–8.30pm; winter 10am–7pm, closed Thurs; R140/R70 students).

Arrival and information

Air International flights arrive at Pulkovo Airport, Terminal 2. Avoid the waiting taxis and take a bus (#13, #113 or #213) or a commercial minibus, both departing around every 15 minutes, to the end of the metro line (Moskovskaya), or get the Pulkovo Express Bus, which runs 24/7, to Pushkinskaya metro.

Train Three trains daily from Helsinki bring you to Ladoga Station (Ladozhskiy vokzal), on Zhanevskiy prospekt 73, at Ladozhskaya metro.

Trains from Berlin (one daily), Prague (one a day Mon & Wed–Sat), Riga (one daily) and Vilnius (one daily) terminate at Vitebsk Station (Vitebskiy vokzal), at Pushkinskaya metro. Trains from Moscow (around twenty daily) draw into Moscow Station, at Ploshchad Vosstaniya metro.

Bus Eurolines operates buses from the Baltic States which arrive at St Petersburg's Baltiyskiy station at Obvodnogo kanal 120, Baltiskaya metro. Daily buses include services from Minsk (15hr), from Berlin (38hr), from Riga (8hr), and Helsinki (8hr), and several from Tallinn (7hr). At the city bus station at Obvodnovo kanal 36, fifteen minutes' walk from Ligovskiy Prospekt metro, arrivals include six buses daily from Tallinn, two daily from Helsinki and one daily from Riga; some of the same buses pass through here and the Baltiyskiy terminal. See timetables at Ⓦ www.eurolines.eu.

Ferry In the summer months (ie when the ice melts) there are ferries from Tallinn, Helsinki and Rostock in Germany, operated by Silja Line (Ⓦ www.silja.com) and Estonian operators Tallink (Ⓦ www.tallink.ee). They arrive at the Morskoy vokzal, Prospect Morskoy Slavy 1, Vasilieostrovskaya metro, at the western end of Vasilevskiy Island (bus or minibus to the centre).

Tourist office The tourist information centre at Sadovaya ul. 14/52 (Nevskiy prospekt metro, Ⓣ 812/310 8262, Ⓦ www.ctic.spb.ru) has a wealth of material in English. For listings and events, pick up the quarterly freebie *Where St Petersburg*, the Friday *St Petersburg Times* and the monthly *Pulse* from hotels and shops.

City transport

Metro The St Petersburg metro, the deepest in the world, runs from 5.30am to midnight. Small numbers of journeys (R15 a journey) are sold using chips, which you feed into ticket machines. For 10 or more rides, buy a plastic card.
Buses and trolleybuses Often the best way to tackle a big road like Nevskiy prospekt, overground transport is more useful in the city centre than the metro. Buy tickets from the driver on embarking.
Minibuses in the form of *marshrutkas* (yellow in St Petersburg) are cheap (around R15–20 a journey) and cheerful. The K-147 goes from Moskovskiy vokzal right to the upper end of Nevskiy prospekt.
Boat One of the best ways to see the city is by boat (May–Oct) – either a private motorboat from any bridge on Nevskiy prospekt (from R1800/hr per boat), or a large tour boat by the Anichkov Bridge (R250 rubles per person). AngloTourismo offer English-guided tours from their pier on Fontanka 64, by Lomonosova Bridge; ⓣ921/989 47 22.

Accommodation

Hostels

Cuba Hostel Kazanskaya ul. 5, 4th floor, Nevskiy prospekt metro ⓣ812/921 7115, ⓦwww.cubahostel.ru. Lively, vibrantly decorated hostel in an excellent location behind Kazan Cathedral. Free tea, coffee, pasta and rice in the kitchen, plus free Internet. Bikes to rent from R150 for 2 hours. Mixed dorms; dorms, depending on size ❸–❹
Na Muchnom Sadovaya ul. 25/4, Gostiniy Dvor metro ⓣ812/310 0412, ⓦwww.namuchnom.ru. Large, impersonal hotel-style dorm at the heart of Dostoyevskian St Petersburg. Very central, if hectic, location, and no kitchen, though there is a "canteen". Dorms ❸, doubles ❼
Nord Hostel Bolshaya Morskaya ul. 10 ⓣ812/571 0342, ⓦwww.nordhostel.com; Gostiniy dvor metro. Nothing could be more central, although the kitchen/communal area closes at 10pm. Breakfast with paté and yogurt included. Dorms ❸
Puppet Hostel Nekrasova ul. 12 ⓣ812/272 5401, ⓦwww.hostel-puppet.ru; Mayakovskaya metro. Affiliated to the International Youth Hostel, this is a professional if slightly subdued outfit. No kitchen, and the parrot may strain your nerves. Dorms ❷, doubles ❺
St Petersburg International Hostel 3-ya Sovetskaya ul. 28 ⓣ812/329 8018, ⓦwww.ryh.ru; Pl. Vosstaniya metro. Popular, with spacious dorms and doubles, so book well ahead. Continental breakfast with attendant babushkas' bullying is an integral part of the experience. Dorms ❸, doubles ❹
Sleep Cheap Mokhovaya ul. 18–32 ⓣ812/115 1304, ⓦwww.sleepcheap.spb.ru; Chernyshevskaya metro. With just 16 beds, this clean and friendly little hostel is five minutes from the Summer Garden. Dorms ❷
Zimmer Freie Liteyniy pr. 46, flat 23 ⓣ812/973 3757, ⓦwww.zimmer.ru; Mayakovskaya metro. Cosy communal area, separate men's and women's dorms, and a fridge in every room. 6-bed dorm ❸; double ❺

Hotels

Neva Chaykovskogo ul. 17 ⓣ812/ 278-0504, ⓦwww.nevahotel.spb.ru; Chernyshevskaya metro. Spotless, charming little hotel in an atmospheric old building. Choose between unrefurbished Soviet-era rooms or the more impersonal newly renovated suites. Prices may rise as renovations continue but at present cheapest doubles ❼

Eating

Cafés

Avoid big-name coffee shops on Nevskiy and go for the more intimate café/restaurants that offer a better feel for local life. Canteen-style restaurants, in particular, are cheap.
Bulochnaya Bolshaya Konyushennaya 15; Nevskiy prospekt metro. An authentic Russian experience, unglamorous but eminently satisfying. Delicious pies and cakes, attentive service, decent coffee and 50ml shots of berry liqueurs for an alluring R17 make this an essential mid-afternoon fuelling point. The name just means "bakery", so don't confuse it with lesser variants. Slab of cheesecake R41, jellies R12.
Chaynaya Samovar Gorochovaya ul. 27; Sadovaya metro. Ubercheap and palatable pancakes, pies and salads. *Blini* from R16.
Lagidze Belinskovo ul. 3; Chernyshevskaya metro. Just off the Fontanka, this unassuming place offers Russian and Caucasian lunch food. *Khachapuri* R120.
Layma nab. kanala Griboedova 16; Gostiniy Dvor/ Nevskiy Prospekt metro. Fast-food canteen near the Church on Spilled Blood. Open 24hr. Fish cutlets R70, salads R50.
Russkie bliny u Natashi 5-ya Sovetskaya ul. 24. Pig out on the city's most outstanding pancakes at the cheapest known prices. *Blini* with red caviar R80.
Stolle pirogi ul. Dekabristov 19. Quality pies in chic environs. Buy a section of a thick plait or decorated square of pie; specialities include seasonal berries and salmon. Pies from R45.
U Teshi na blinakh Ligovskiy pr. 31, Ploshchad Vosstaniya metro; also 16 Sitninckaya ul., 33 Sadovaya ul. Fast, filling food at this chain restaurant. *Blini* from R30.

Restaurants

Idiot nab. reki Moyki 82, Sadovaya metro. Unchallenging vegetarian underground restaurant teeming with foreigners. Free vodka shot on arrival. Farmers' cheesecakes with honey, R170.

Imbir Zagorodniy pr. 15. Mixture of traditional Russian and Japanese dishes at moderate prices in polished surroundings. Honeyed lighting is a bonus. Seafood salad R190.

Kafe Tbilisi Sitninskaya ul. 10, Gorkovskaya metro. Delicate Georgian cuisine and to-die-for Armenian pomegranate wine in this St Petersburg institution; the live singing conjures Caucasian heat. Dainty meat dishes from R260.

Ket Stremyannaya ul. 22; Mayakovskaya metro. Rich, varied Georgian food in an atmospheric, dark-wooded room. *Khinkali* (Georgian *pelmeni*) from R250.

Drinking

Bars

Argus Bolshaya Konyushennaya ul. 15; Nevskiy prospekt metro. Noisy, central, British-style bar, with its own small brewery. Bar snacks e.g. grilled cheese, R125.

Che Poltavskaya ul. 3; Moskovskiy Vokzal metro. This cocktail-focused bar/café fancies itself something rotten, but it's open 24 hours and has great bands on late. Wallet shock is a real risk, though, with mojitos costing R275.

Sunduk Art Cafe Furshtatskaya ul. 42; Chernyshevskaya metro. Great food and cocktails, by a boulevard, with outdoor veranda; live jazz most evenings from 8.30pm to 11pm, at R100 cover charge. Cocktails from R170.

Zoom Gorokhovaya ul. 22; Sadovaya metro. Sleek spot for literati offering veggie dishes such as marrows with sour cream, R80.

Clubs

Fish Fabrique Ligovskiy pr. 53; Mayakovskovo metro. This grungy place, which once launched Petersburg's hippest bands, is now a slackers' haven at the heart of the city's famous artists' colony. Rich honey beer (*medovúkha*) at R90.

Griboedov Voronezhskaya ul. 2a; Ligovskiy Prospekt metro. Cool, if self-conscious, club in a former bomb shelter. 5pm–6am; DJs start midnight. Beers from R70.

Jimi Hendrix Blues Club Liteyniy pr. 33; Chernyshevskaya metro. Good food and an engaged audience in tiny subterranean hideaway. 11am–1am. Beers from R40 and cocktails from R140.

Metro Ligovskiy pr. 174; Ligovskiy Prospekt metro. It's big, it's loud, it's tacky, but this three-floor club is not that expensive, and everyone keeps coming back for pop, electronic and disco. Entry R210.

TREAT YOURSELF

Mops Rubinsteina ul. 12 ⓣ812/572 3834, ⓦwww.mopscafe.ru; Dostoevskaya metro. This Thai restaurant-cum-cocktail bar embodies moneyed Petersburg's flawless, if studied, chic. Secure a seat on the summer veranda if you can. Mains start from R260, but if nothing else, permit yourself a cocktail: the delicate flavours and scrupulous service ethos make a half-hour here a real treat. The toilets are also luxurious enough to be worth lingering in.

Entertainment

Beware: theatres tend to close for the summer until mid-September. For details of what's on, check the listings papers (see "Arrival").

Classical, opera and ballet

Mariinskiy (formerly Kirov) Theatre Teatralnaya pl. 1 ⓣ812/114 5264, ⓦwww.mariinsky.ru. Prices €8–120. Performances at 7pm, matinees at noon.

Philharmonia Mikhaylovskaya ul. 2 ⓣ812/110 4290; Nevskiy Prospekt metro. Draws international classical musicians as well as Russia's best. Performances at 7pm.

Live music

JFC Jazz Club Shpalernaya ul. 33; Chernyshevskaya metro. The city's most exciting jazz programme, tucked away in a courtyard. Music 7pm–10.30pm. Admission R140.

Shopping

Shop for Russian speciality foods at **Kuznechniy market** (3 Kuznechniy Pereulok, Vladimirskaya metro), which has mouth-watering displays of sweets and cakes, fresh mushrooms and salted cucumbers, stonking sausage counters and plaited cheese rinds. Open 8am to 8pm daily.

Directory

Consulates UK, pl. Proletarskoy diktatury 5 ⓣ812/320 3200; US, Furshtadtskaya ul. 15

Ⓣ812/331 2600; Canada, Malodetskoselskiy pr. 32 Ⓣ812/325 8448; Australia: Italyanskaya ul. 1 Ⓣ812/325 7333.
Internet access Quo Vadis, Nevskiy prospect 76, 9am–11pm, Mayakovskaya metro; *Cafemax at the Hermitage*, in the Rastrelli Gallery, 10.30am–6pm; *Cafemax*, Nevskiy prospect 90/92, Mayakovskaya metro, open 24hr; Free Time, Lomonosova ul. 2, open 24hr, Nevskiy Prospekt metro.
Left luggage Main stations have lockers and/or a 24hr left-luggage office.
Laundry May, Reki Moiky 42, Nevskiy prospect metro; 11am–7pm.
Medical International Clinic, Dostoevskovo ul. 19/21 Ⓣ812/336 3333, Ⓦwww.icspb.com; Euromed, Suvorovskiy pr. 60 Ⓣ812/327 0301, Ⓦwww.euromed.ru; American Medical Clinic, reki Moyki nab. 78 Ⓣ812/740 2090, Ⓦwww.amclinic.ru
Pharmacy Petropharm, at Nevskiy pr. 22 (24hr). Other branches at nos. 50, 66 & 83.
Post office Main post office at Pochtamskaya ul. 9, Nevskiy prospect metro. Open 24hr.
Express letter post: Westpost, Nevskiy pr. 86 Ⓣ812/327 3092, Ⓦwww.westpost.ru. DHL: Nevskiy pr. 10 Ⓣ812/326 6400, Ⓦwww.dhl.ru.

Moving on

Train Moscow (3 express trains, 4 hrs 30min to 5 hrs, and around 17 others, between 7 and 9hr); Helsinki (3 daily; 6hr); Riga (1 daily; 8 hr); Tallinn (1 daily; 5hr 30min); Vilnius (1 every 2 days; 12 hr).
Bus Tallinn (7 daily; 8hr 30min); Tartu, Estonia (1 daily; 8hr 30min).
Ferry (May–Sept) Helsinki (14hr); Tallinn (13hr); Rostock, Germany (37hr).

DAY-TRIPS FROM ST PETERSBURG

The Imperial palaces of **Peterhof** and **Tsarskoe Selo**, half an hour to an hour outside the city, are both splendid. Although entering the palaces is increasingly expensive, you can slip away from the crowds into the surrounding parks, a joy in themselves. As you leave St Petersburg on the bus, look out for the awe-inspiring war monument to Leningrad's WWII sacrifice, and Lenin in demagogic pose near Finland Station.

The Peterhof

Most visitors with time for just one day-trip opt for **Peterhof** (10.30am–6pm, closed Mon; Ⓦwww.peterhof.ru; palace R420, Lower Park R280), 29km west of St Petersburg, famed for the marvellous fountains and impressive cascades at the Great Palace. Travel by hydrofoil in summer (R170 each way) from outside the Winter Palace or take one of the frequent minibuses from Avtovo metro station (R25). Small trains also run from Baltiyskiy station in the capital to Noviy Peterhof station.

Tsarskoe Selo and the Pavlovsk

Tsarskoe Selo (also known as **Pushkin**, for the "Russian Shakespeare" who was schooled at the neighbouring Lyceum school), 17km southeast of St Petersburg, centres on the **Catherine Palace** (10am–5pm, closed Tues; R600, park R175/R80 students). The vulgar blue-and-white Baroque structure built by Catherine the Great is surrounded by a richly landscaped park, filled with fancies like "creaking" bridges, a Chinese village and a wide lake to dip your feet in on a hot day. Scottish architect Charles Cameron's supremely elegant Neoclassical Gallery stretches high above the park. The famous Amber Room in the Catherine Palace, stolen by the Germans during World War II and subsequently "mislaid", was recreated in time for St Petersburg's 300th anniversary in 2003; but visitors with an eye on their wallet will get ample rewards by just paying the R175 to enter the park and get luxuriously lost.

To **get to** Pushkin, take one of the frequent minibuses (R28) from outside Moskovskaya metro station; 286, 299, 342, and 545 service the route. The same minibuses will take you on to the more intimate, humbler Great Palace at **Pavlovsk** (10am–5pm, closed Fri; Ⓦwww.pavlovskmuseum.ru; palace R380, park R100).

Serbia

HIGHLIGHTS

NOVI SAD AND FRUŠKA GORA: cosmopolitan, laid-back city on the Danube close to lovely wooded hills

BELGRADE NIGHTLIFE: congenial cafés, bars and clubs

KALEMEGDAN FORTRESS, BELGRADE: this dramatically sited fortification has been subjected to more than a hundred invasions

STUDENICA MONASTERY: the finest of Serbia's fresco-laden, medieval monastic churches

ROUGH COSTS

DAILY BUDGET basic 2000din/with the occasional treat 3500din

DRINK Pivo 100din (half litre)

FOOD Pljeskavica 100–200din

HOSTEL/BUDGET HOTEL €13/€35

TRAVEL Belgrade-Novi Sad (74km) 480din by bus; Belgrade-Niš (235km) 580din by bus.

FACT FILE

POPULATION 10 million

AREA 88,361 sq km

LANGUAGE Serbian

CURRENCY Dinar

CAPITAL Belgrade

INTERNATIONAL PHONE CODE ⓣ381

Basics

For centuries under the thrall of Turkish rule, Serbia only attained independence in 1878, before becoming the hub of the short-lived Kingdom of Serbs, Croats and Slovenes, and then, after World War II, the modern Yugoslav state. Sanctions imposed following the onset of war in Bosnia in 1992 crippled the economy, while a decade of ruinous Milošević rule culminated in NATO air strikes in 1999, and a popular uprising against the Serbian president a year later. While the country continues to struggle with enormous economic and political problems, tourists are, at last, beginning to discover its unexpected delights. Indeed, though many of Serbia's physical sights are steeped in its violent history, the country's busy streets and café-bars – and the passion and warmth of the locals – hint at a more promising future.

Serbia's capital, **Belgrade**, is the quintessential Balkan city, a noisy, vigorous place, whose nightlife is fast gaining a reputation as being amongst the most exciting in eastern Europe. Northwest of here, on the iron-flat Vojvodina plain, is the charming city of **Novi Sad**, close to the Fruška Gora hills, which offer fine walking and the chance to visit several historic monasteries. Serbia's most revered **monastic churches**, however, are located deep in the mountainous tract of land south of Belgrade – namely Žiča, Studenica and Sopoćani. Southeast of here the industrial city of **Niš**, birthplace of Constantine the Great, holds a handful of curious sights worth visiting en route to Bulgaria.

CHRONOLOGY

168 BC The Romans defeat the Illyrian tribe and establish their rule of the area of present-day Serbia.
630 AD Serbs settle in the region.
1166 Stefan Nemanja, leader of the Serbs, declares independence from Byzantine rule.
1219 The Serbian Orthodox Church is established.
1389 The Ottomans defeat the Serbians in the Battle of Kosovo, ushering in four centuries of direct rule.
1882 Serbia once again becomes a kingdom.
1913 The Ottomans lose their remaining authority in Serbia during the Balkan wars.
1918 Following World War I the Kingdom of Serbs, Croats and Slovenes is formed.
1929 The Kingdom is renamed Yugoslavia.
1945 Following fighting during World War II, Serbia is absorbed into Socialist Yugoslavia.
1989 Slobodan Milosevic, a Serbian communist, becomes President of Serbia.
1992 Serbia enters a bloody war with the Croats and Bosnian Muslims. Although fighting stops three years later, many problems remain unresolved.
1998 Serbia launches a violent campaign against ethnic minorities in Kosovo, costing thousands of lives. The war ends a year later after international intervention.
2000 Mass protests lead to the resignation of Milosevic.
2003 Serbian Prime Minister, Zoran Djindjic, is assassinated in Belgrade.
2006 Milosevic dies in prison, awaiting trial at the International Criminal Court on charges of genocide.
2006 Montenegro peacefully gains independence from Serbia.

ARRIVAL

As a landlocked country at the heart of the Balkans, Serbia has many points of entry on both road and rail networks. The southeastern city of Niš is a transport hub for trains and buses heading to and from Bulgaria and Macedonia,

while in the north, Novi Sad lies on the main routes leading to Hungary and Croatia. This accessibility also comes in useful for air passengers: UK budget airlines do not yet fly direct to Serbia (though British Airways does on most days), but the transfer by road or rail from nearby destinations is relatively painless, and cheaper than taking a connecting flight in central Europe.

GETTING AROUND

Years of little or no investment has left the public transport system in a rather dilapidated state, though it just about does the job. Ask any local and they will tell you to use the **buses**, which are for the most part faster and more reliable than trains, with regular services fanning out from Belgrade to all parts of the country (see ⓦwww.lasta.co.yu).

Bus stations are generally crowded and chaotic, but negotiable with a bit of patience. Keep hold of the coin handed back with your ticket – you need it to pass through to the forecourt. Heavy baggage will incur a fee of up to 40din.

If you do travel by **train** (Ⓦwww.serbianrailways.com), be sure to avoid the *putnički* (slow) variety. Though generally unnecessary, it's probably wise to make a reservation for international journeys, particularly to Bar on the Montenegrin coast in summer. InterRail and Eurail tickets are valid.

If time is a factor, then **renting a car** might be necessary to see some of the more rural sights. There are many international and local companies in Belgrade – ask at the tourist office. When driving, beware of poor lighting on country roads, particularly in the hilly region south of Belgrade.

ACCOMMODATION

Accommodation is neither as varied nor cheap as you might expect, and many places look in serious need of a paint job. Bog-standard doubles at two-star **hotels** start at around €35, with refurbished three-star rooms more like €70. Thankfully, the **hostel scene** has finally taken off in a big way, especially in Belgrade, where new places are opening at a phenomenal rate. A dorm generally costs around €10–18. **Campsites** remain relatively sparse, and of those that do exist most are fairly rudimentary.

FOOD AND DRINK

In common with other Balkan countries, Serbian **cuisine** is overwhelmingly dominated by meat, and many dishes manifest Turkish or Hungarian influences. **Breakfast** *(doručak)* typically comprises a coffee, roll and cheese or salami, while also popular is *burek*, a greasy, flaky pastry filled with cheese (*sa sirom*) or meat (*sa mesom*). *Burek* is also served as a **street snack**, as are the ubiquitous *čevapčići* (rissoles of spiced minced meat served with onion), *pljeskavica* (oversized hamburger) and (*pancakes*). You will find these on just about every **restaurant** (*restoran*) menu, alongside other characteristic Serbian dishes such as the typical starter, *čorba* (a thick meat or fish soup), and **main dishes** such as *pasulj (*a thick bean soup spotted with pieces of bacon or sausage), *podvarak* (roast meat in sauerkraut), *kolenica* (leg of suckling pig), and the gut-busting *karađorđe vasnicla*, a breaded veal cutlet, rolled and stuffed with cheese. A popular accompaniment to all these dishes is *pogača*, a large bread cake. Typical **desserts** include *strudla* (strudel), *krofna* (plain, jam or chocolate doughnut), and *baklava*, a sweet Turkish pastry smothered with syrup.

Pizzerias aside, **vegetarians** will have a fairly tough time of it, though dishes worth trying are *srpska salata* (salad with tomato, onion and hot peppers), *šopska salata* (similar but topped with grated soft cheese), *gibanica* (layered cheese pie) and *zeljanica* (cheese pie with spinach).

Drinking

Few Serbs get by without a strong cup of **coffee** (*kafa*) to kick-start the day, traditionally served Turkish-style (black, thick and with the grinds at the bottom), though you can ask for milk (*mleko*). **Fruit juice** (*voćni sok*) comes in various guises, such as *gusti* (thick), a natural, dense pulp. The best domestic **beers** (*pivo*) are actually those brewed in Montenegro, such as Nikšićko, which comes in both light and dark varieties, while the best **wines**, such as the red Vranac, also hail from Montenegro. *Spricer* (white wine with soda or sparkling mineral water) is a refreshing alternative on hot summer days. Above all, though, Serbia is renowned for its *rakija*, a ferociously powerful brandy served neat, the most common of

SERBIA ON THE NET

Ⓦ **www.serbia-tourism.org** Official tourist board site.

Ⓦ **www.beograd.org.yu** Detailed information on sights and events in the capital.

Ⓦ **www.novisadtourism.org.yu** Useful site on Serbia's second city.

which is the plum variety, *šlijvovica*. Another popular drink is *pelinkovac*, a bittersweet aperitif-type liqueur.

CULTURE AND ETIQUETTE

A relative dearth of international visitors – particularly from the West – since the break-up of Yugoslavia means that Serbs will often go out of their way to welcome their guests.

The vast majority of locals belong to the **Serbian Orthodox Church**, which still dictates local customs and etiquette to a large degree. This is most overtly evident in and around the many churches, where respect should be shown in both manner and clothing (no short skirts or shorts). The younger generation is **increasingly liberal** – nowhere more so than in Belgrade's raucous nightclubs – though the gay and lesbian scene remains relatively underground.

Tipping at restaurants is generally uncommon, not least because many places already add a small service charge.

SPORTS AND OUTDOOR ACTIVITIES

While organized sporting activities remain thin on the ground, Serbia's wide **rural expanses** offer plenty of opportunities for excursions, either by bike or on foot. The Fruska Gora national park (Ⓦwww.npfruskagora.co.yu) is a prime example of this, with hiking maps available from most bookshops in nearby Novi Sad.

As for **spectator sports**, the locals are passionate about their football, and watching a match involving Belgrade rivals Red Star (Ⓦwww.fc-redstar.net) or FK Partizan (Ⓦwww.partizan.co.yu) – against each other, preferably – is a spectacle in itself.

COMMUNICATIONS

Most **post offices** (*pošta*) are open Mon–Fri 8am–7pm, Sat 8am–3pm. **Stamps** (*markice*) can also be bought at newsstands. Public **phones** use cards (*Halo kartice*), currently valued at 200, 300 and 500din and available from post offices, kiosks and tobacconists. It's usually easier to make long-distance and international calls at a post office, where you're assigned a cabin and given the bill afterwards. **Internet** access is fairly widespread; expect to pay around 100din/hr.

EMERGENCIES

The crime rate, even in Belgrade, is low by European standards, though the usual precautions apply. The **police** (*policija*) are generally easygoing and may speak some basic English. Routine checks on identity cards and documents are not uncommon, so always carry your passport or a photocopy.

Pharmacies (*apoteka*) tend to follow shop hours, and a rota system covers night-time and weekend opening; details are posted in the window of each pharmacy. Opening hours are generally Mon–Fri 8am–8pm, Sat 8am–3pm. If the pharmacy can't help, they will direct you to a hospital (*bolnica*).

EMERGENCY NUMBERS

Police ⓣ92; Ambulance ⓣ94; Fire ⓣ93.

Serbian

Serbia uses the **Cyrillic alphabet**, and with most street signs, train and bus timetables – and the occasional menu – having no Roman translation, things can get confusing. Some hostels are beginning to produce maps with both alphabets, which should help matters. However, a decent level of English is spoken in most places, so just ask.

	Serbian	Pronunciation
Yes	*Da*	Da
No	*Ne*	Ne
Thank you	*Hvala*	Hvala
Hello/Good day	*Zdravo/Dobar Dan*	Zdravo/Dobar Dan
Goodbye	*Doviđenja*	Doveejenya
Excuse me	*Izvinite*	Eezveeneete
Where?	*Gde?*	Gede?
Good	*Dobro*	Dobro
Bad	*Loše*	Loshe
Near	*Blizu*	Bleezoo
Far	*Daleko*	Daaleko
Cheap	*Jeftino*	Yefteeno
Expensive	*Skupo*	Skoopo
Open	*Otvoreno*	Otvoreno
Closed	*Zatvoreno*	Zatvoreno
Today	*Danas*	Danas
Yesterday	*Juće*	Yooche
Tomorrow	*Sutra*	Sootra
How much is....?	*Koliko Košta...?*	Koleeko Koshta...?
What time is it?	*Koliko je sati?*	Koleeko ye satee?
I don't understand	*Ne razumem*	Ne razoomem
Do you speak English?	*Da li pricate engleski?*	Da lee Preechate engleskee?
One	*Jedan*	Yedan
Two	*Dva*	Dva
Three	*Tri*	Tree
Four	*Četiri*	Cheteeree
Five	*Pet*	Pet
Six	*Šest*	Shest
Seven	*Sedam*	Sedam
Eight	*Osam*	Osam
Nine	*Devet*	Devet
Ten	*Deset*	Deset

INFORMATION AND MAPS

Most towns and resorts have a **tourist information office** (*turističke informacije*), whose staff invariably speak excellent English. Although they do not book rooms they can advise on local accommodation. Freytag & Berndt publishes a good 1:300,000 country **map**.

MONEY AND BANKS

The currency is the **dinar** (usually abbreviated to din), comprising coins of 1, 2, 5, 10 and 20 dinar (and also 50 para coins – 100 para equals 1 dinar), and notes of 10, 20, 50, 100, 200, 1000 and 5000 dinar. Exchange **rates** are currently around 80din to the euro, 120din to the pound, and 60din to the US dollar.

STUDENT AND YOUTH DISCOUNTS

Euro26 cards are valid in Serbia (Ⓦwww.euro26.org.yu; 900din). Balkan Flexipass rail tickets are also valid.

Accommodation prices are sometimes quoted in euros, which is by far the easiest foreign currency to change. The best place to change money is at one of the many **exchange offices** (*menjačnica*), or at a bank (*banka*), which are generally open Mon–Fri 8am–7pm and Sat 8am–3pm. **ATMs** are everywhere in urban areas and **credit cards** are accepted in most hotels and restaurants.

OPENING HOURS AND HOLIDAYS

Most **shops** open Mon–Fri 8am–7/8pm (sometimes with a break for lunch), and Sat 8am–2pm. In downtown Belgrade, shops sometimes stay open even later. Museum times vary, but most are usually closed on Monday. All shops and banks are closed on **public holidays**: Jan 1, 2 & 7, Feb 15, and May 1 & 2. The Orthodox Church celebrates Easter between one and five weeks later than the other churches.

Belgrade

By no stretch of the imagination can **BELGRADE** (Beograd) be described as one of Europe's most attractive cities. Nor can it boast world-class museums, galleries or architecture. Yet the raw vigour of its streets, the warmth and humour of its citizens, and a bar and club scene unmatched anywhere else in the Balkans, will ensure that a day or two spent here will be one of the unexpected high points on any European itinerary.

Occupying a strategic point on the junction of the **Danube** and **Sava rivers**, Belgrade was the property of a warlike succession of Celts, Romans, Huns and Avars until the Turks wrenched it from the Hungarians in 1521. The city has since been repeatedly burned, sacked and bombed, including heavy shelling during World War II which razed much of it, and in 1999, when it withstood more than two months of NATO air strikes.

What to see and do

The city's chief attraction is the **Kalemegdan Fortress**, which sweeps around a wooden bluff overlooking the wayward swerve of the Danube. Just outside the park boundary is the **Old City**, whose dense lattice of streets conceals Belgrade's most interesting sights. South of here is Belgrade's central square, **Trg Republike**, and the old Bohemian quarter of **Skadarlija**, beyond which lie several more worthwhile sites, including one of the world's largest Orthodox churches. For something a bit more relaxing head west across the Sava to the village-like suburb of **Zemun**, or further south still towards the island of **Ada Ciganija**, the city's prime recreational spot.

Kalemegdan Fortress

Splendidly sited on an exposed nub of land overlooking the confluence of the mighty Sava and Danube rivers is **Kalemegdan Park**, dominated by the substantial remains of the **Kalemegdan Fortress**. Originally built by the Celts, expanded upon by the Romans, and rebuilt in the Middle Ages, most of what remains is the result of a short-lived Austrian occupation in the early part of the eighteenth century, before the Ottomans handed it over to Serbia. Some of the subterranean passageways are occasionally used for art exhibitions, while, appropriately enough, the fortress also houses a **Military Museum** (Tues–Sun 10am–5pm; 100din), containing an array of ferocious-looking weaponry. The park, frequented by walkers, joggers and elderly gentlemen participating in impromptu games of chess, is a lovely place to stroll around.

The Orthodox Cathedral

Exiting the park and crossing Pariska, you'll find yourself in the oldest part of the city. At Kralja Petra 7 is the **Orthodox Cathedral**, a rather stark Neoclassical edifice built in 1840 featuring a fine Baroque tower and a beautiful iconostasis. Built around the same time is the oddly titled **"?" café** (see p.1015), whose name was originally a temporary solution to a row with church leaders who objected to its then name, the *Café at the Cathedral.*

Konak of Princess Ljubica and museums

Just around the corner, at Sime Markovića 8, is the **Konak of Princess Ljubica** (Mon–Fri 10am–5pm, Sat & Sun 9am–4pm; 150din), the one-time residence of Princess Ljubica Obrenović, wife of Miloš. Restored in the 1970s, the interior of this early eighteenth-century house reflects the style and opulence of the upper classes at that time, each room sporting an intriguing blend of Turkish and Oriental flourishes in the form of carpets, period furniture, objets d'art and paintings.

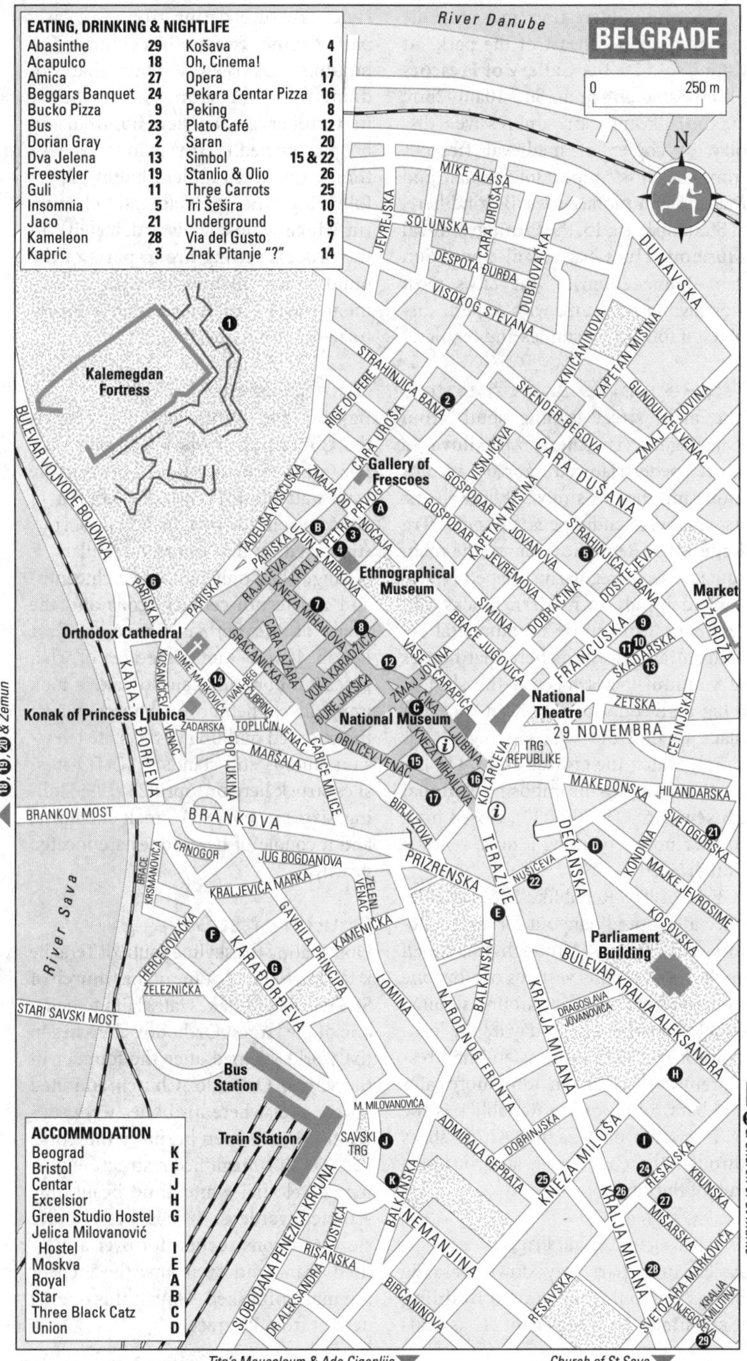
BELGRADE
0 250 m
N
EATING, DRINKING & NIGHTLIFE
Abasinthe 29
Acapulco 18
Amica 27
Beggars Banquet 24
Bucko Pizza 9
Bus 23
Dorian Gray 2
Dva Jelena 13
Freestyler 19
Guli 11
Insomnia 5
Jaco 21
Kameleon 28
Kapric 3
Košava 4
Oh, Cinema! 1
Opera 17
Pekara Centar Pizza 16
Peking 8
Plato Café 12
Šaran 20
Simbol 15 & 22
Stanlio & Olio 26
Three Carrots 25
Tri Šešira 10
Underground 6
Via del Gusto 7
Znak Pitanje "?" 14
ACCOMMODATION
Beograd K
Bristol F
Centar J
Excelsior H
Green Studio Hostel G
Jelica Milovanović Hostel I
Moskva E
Royal A
Star B
Three Black Catz C
Union D
River Danube
River Sava
Kalemegdan Fortress
Gallery of Frescoes
Ethnographical Museum
Orthodox Cathedral
Konak of Princess Ljubica
National Museum
National Theatre
Market
Parliament Building
Bus Station
Train Station
TRG REPUBLIKE
SAVSKI TRG
18, 19, 20 & Zemun
23 & Church of St Marko
Tito's Mausoleum & Ada Ciganlija
Church of St Sava

Two more interesting museums lie a short walk southeast of the park. At Cara Uroša 20, the **Gallery of Frescoes** (Tues–Sat 10am–5pm, Sun 10am–2pm; 100din) keeps an impressive display of copies of medieval frescoes from the most important Serbian and Macedonian monasteries. Beyond here, at Studentski trg 13, the **Ethnographical Museum** (Tues–Sat 10am–5pm, Sun 9am–2pm; 120din) is the city's most worthwhile museum, with superb displays of folk art, costumes and textiles.

Trg Republike and around

The main street leading south from Kalemegdan is **Kneza Mihailova**, a slick, pedestrianized *korzo* accommodating the city's most stylish shops. Its southern end opens up onto **Trg Republike** (Republic Square), the main square, an irregularly shaped space flanked by glassy modern blocks and remnants from more monumental architectural times. It is here that hordes of youthful locals meet at the start of a big night out, making it an excellent place to find out what's going on, or simply watch the crowds go by. On the north side stands the imposing **National Museum** (☎111330-6000), closed until further notice pending a huge renovation project.

East of Trg Republike is **Skadarlija**, once a favoured hangout for artists, actors and writers. Although this small enclave still retains vestiges of a bygone Bohemian era – centred around sloping, cobbled **Skadarska** – today it's the location for the city's most established restaurants, as well as a handful more cafés and bars. South of Trg Republike is the wide swathe of **Terazije**, which slices through the commercial and business hub of the city.

Parliament Building

A left turn part way down Terazije brings you to the **Parliament Building** (Skupština), an inelegant Classical-style structure dating from the early part of the twentieth century. The building has seen its fair share of drama over the years, most recently in October 2000 when hundreds of people crashed their way in to retrieve thousands of fraudulent ballot papers following the presidential election (in which Milošević was defeated), in the process setting fire to parts of the building and making off with various mementoes – most of which were returned upon request.

Church of St Marko

Beyond the Parliament Building is the **Church of St Marko**, a solid neo-Byzantine structure built between the wars and modelled on the church of Gračanica in Kosovo. Its hollow shrine, supported by four enormous pillars, is distinguished only by some eighteenth- and nineteenth-century icons and the tomb of the Serbian Emperor, Czar Dušan. If you want some idea of what precision bombing can do, take a look immediately behind the church, where the wrecked building of the state television studios still stands – NATO missiles struck here on April 23, 1999, killing sixteen people. A small memorial and a couple of headstones are located nearby.

Church of St Sava

Dominating the skyline south of Terazije is the huge gilded dome of the **Church of St Sava**, which stakes fair claim to being one of the largest Orthodox churches in the world. Named after the founder of the Serbian Orthodox Church, and sited on the spot where his bones were supposed to have been burnt by the Turks in 1594, this magnificent structure glistens a celestial white amid beautifully sculpted gardens. It has been under stop-start construction for over a hundred years, and even now the interior remains unfinished, though this doesn't detract from its grace.

Tito's Mausoleum

One other site worth making the effort to get to is **Tito's Mausoleum** (Tues–Sun; free), located around 1.5km south of the centre on Bulevar Mira (bus #40 or #41 from Kneza Miloša). Also known as Kuca cvece (House of Flowers), the great man's tombstone stands in a large, dignified hall bordered by flowers and watched over by a stern-faced guard. Nearby, you'll find a fun museum exhibiting the various gifts presented to Tito by foreign dignitaries, including a mildly terrifying Bolivian witch doctor's costume.

Zemun

For a peaceful escape from the city centre, head across the Sava river to the suburb of **Zemun**, an attractive jumble of low-slung houses, narrow winding streets and market squares. Zemun's main sights are centred around the hilly waterside district of Gardoš, which holds the remnants of a Gothic-style fortress, and the Baroque **Nikolajevska Church**, the city's oldest Orthodox church, featuring a beautiful iconostasis. At night, locals gravitate toward the riverbank for its collection of superb fish restaurants and swanky floating bars. To get here take bus #15 or #84 from Zeleni Venac, or bus #83 from outside the train station. Either way, alight on Glavna, the main street.

Ada Cignalija

During the summer, Belgraders flock to **Ada Ciganlija** (Gypsy Island), a long wooded strip stretching along the bank of the Sava just south of the centre. Aside from its sandy beaches (including a naturist area at the southern end), cafés and restaurants, there are opportunities aplenty to partake in various sporting activities such as sailing on the artificial lake or, for the more adventurous, bungee jumping from a crane. To get here, take bus #53 or #56 from Zeleni Venac.

Arrival and information

Air Belgrade's airport is 18km northwest of the city in Surčin, and connected to the city by regular Yugoslav airlines (JAT) buses (hourly 7am–10pm; 160din), which drop off at the train station and Trg Slavija, and bus #72 (5.15am–midnight; 60din), which terminates at the Zeleni Venac market. A taxi should cost no more than 1000din.

Train and bus The main train (železnička stanica) and bus (autobuska stanica) stations are located adjacent to each other on Savski trg and Železnička respectively, just fifteen minutes' walk southwest of the centre.

Tourist office The city's main tourist information centre is located in the subway under Terazije – the entrance is on the corner of Kneza Mihailova near the Albanija building (Mon–Fri 9am–8pm, Sat 9am–5pm, Sun 10am–4pm; Ⓣ11/635-622, Ⓦwww.tob.co.yu), with a further office at the train station (Mon–Fri 9am–8pm, Sat 9am–5pm). Both can provide city maps and a copy of the free listings magazine *This Month in Belgrade.*

City transport

Public transport An efficient, if chaotic and overcrowded, system of buses, trolleybuses and trams operates throughout the city (Ⓦwww.gsp.co.yu).

Tickets can be bought from a kiosk or newsstand (30din) or on the vehicle itself (40din) – either way, tickets must be validated in the machine on board.

Night buses operate between midnight and 4am (65din).

Accommodation

Many of Belgrade's hostels are unofficial, ramshackle operations, though in some ways this adds to the laid-back, welcoming environment that the friendly hosts tend to generate. The scene is changing rapidly, so it's always worth asking around.

Hostels

Green Studio Karađorđeva 69/42 Ⓣ11/263-3626, Ⓔgreenhostelstudio@gmail.com. A new hostel with spotless, a/c rooms, close to the bus station. ❷

Jelica Milovanović Krunska 8 Ⓣ11/330-4809, Ⓦwww.hostel-jelica.info. Massive capacity at this student hostel means you'll always be able to stay in one of the basic dorm rooms; open mid-June to Aug. ❷

Star Cara Uroša 6/2 ⓣ11/262-9826, ⓦwww.star-hostel.com. Small but excellent place, with tidy rooms, good kitchen and Internet facilities and extremely personable staff. ❷

Three Black Catz Čika Ljubina 7/49 ⓣ11/262-9826, ⓔjogurt@sezampro.yu. Fairly cramped and at the top of a grimy stairwell, but it remains one of the friendliest places going. ❷

Hotels

Beograd Balkanska 52 ⓣ11/264-5199, ⓕ11/264-5361. A short walk uphill from the train station, this dull place has bog-standard, but clean, rooms. ❺

Bristol Karađorđeva 50 ⓣ11/268-8400 or 11/303-7161. Grimy brown hulk right next to the bus station, with a no-frills approach; the cleanest rooms are on the third floor. ❹

Centar Savski trg 7 ⓣ11/264-6598. This relic is as grubby as it gets, but it is the cheapest hotel going, and opposite the train station. ❸

Excelsior Kneza Miloša 5 ⓣ11/323-1381, ⓦwww.hotelexcelsior.co.yu. Fairly unkempt exterior, but this place has tidy rooms with interesting period furniture, and offers good value for the price. ❹

Royal Kralja Petra 56 ⓣ11/263-4222, ⓦwww.hotelroyal.co.yu. This well-located place has decent a/c rooms and a 24hr lobby bar. One of the cheapest three-star options. ❺

Union Kosovska 1 ⓣ11/324-8022 or 11/322-4480. The best, and most expensive of the city's lower-end hotels, with spacious, tidy and decently furnished rooms. ❼

TREAT YOURSELF

Moskva Hotel Balkanska 1 ⓣ11/268-6255, ⓦwww.hotelmoskva.co.yu. A striking Art Nouveau landmark, this hotel exudes history and extravagance; it's miles ahead of the competition, but at a hefty cost – doubles are 10,440din. ❾

Camping

Dunav Cara Dušana 49 ⓣ11/199-072. Located some 12km from the centre, in Zemun (bus #704 or #706 from Zeleni Venac market), with a handful of bungalows. ❶

Eating

Belgrade's restaurant scene is evolving fast, and there are an increasing number of ethnic restaurants hitting town. For those seeking the most authentic Serbian eating experience, head to the area around Skadarska.

Fast food, self-service and snack bars

Amica Mišarska 7. Terrific range of sweet and savoury pancakes at this bright and funky café, whose pool table is a rare bonus.

Bucko Pizza Francuska 18. Perennially busy hole-in-the-wall pizza place – perfect on the way home from a club.

Jaco Svetogorska 29. Pleasant corner café with inexpensive toasted sandwiches and salads (no food on weekends).

Pekara Centar Pizza Kolarčeva 10. Huge range of pastries and pizzas at this bustling bakery just off Trg Republike.

Stanlio & Olio Kralja Milana 47. Cheeky place near Slavija, with cheap fast-food bites to go.

Restaurants

Dva Jelena Skadarska 32. One of several quality places serving local food on this street, but this attractive place also offers vegetarian alternatives. Mains 600–750din.

Guli Skadarska 13. The clean, red-brick interior creates a cosy environment to eat tasty oven-baked pizzas. Pizza 500din.

Kapric Kralja Petra 44. The best Italian food in town – including gnocchi and risotto – at this florally decorated pasta place. Good veggie options; dishes around 400din.

Košava Kralja Petra 36. Homely little trattoria on two levels with simple decor and great pizzas. Pizza 400din.

Opera Obilićev venac 30. Neat mid-range outfit offering a mix of Serbian and Italian food in classy surroundings. Mains 750din.

TREAT YOURSELF

Šaran Kej oslobođenja 53. Absolutely delightful fish restaurant in Zemun, with fresh and exotic choices, fine local wines and live music. Ideal for a romantic evening. Fish 1000–1500din.

Peking Vuka Karadžića 2. The city's first Chinese restaurant boasts a long list of standard dishes. Mains 600–750din.
Tri Šešira Skadarska 29. "Three Hats" offers big, juicy portions of local grilled meats, with a lovely tree-shaded courtyard. Mains 550din.
Via del Gusto Knez Mihailova 48. Delicious Mediterranean food, and a great location to soak up the city's buzzing atmosphere. Pizza 450din.
Znak Pitanje "?" Kralja Petra 6. Built in 1832, the city's oldest restaurant is a characterful peasant-style inn (with low wooden tables and stools) that serves solid Serbian fare.

Drinking and nightlife

Belgraders like to party hard, and the city's **nightlife** is currently amongst the most varied and exciting in Eastern Europe, much to the surprise of many a visitor. There are a staggering number of places to drink and dance, with particularly heavy concentrations along Strahinjića bana, Obilićev venac and Njegoševa. Hugely popular amongst Belgraders during the summer months are the many river rafts (*splavovi*), variously housing restaurants, bars and discos. Most are concentrated on the bank of the Danube behind the *Hotel Jugoslavija* – a conspicuous block on the main road towards Zemun – and along the Sava around the Brankov Bridge. Be sure to pace yourself; most of Belgrade's nightspots are open until around 3–4am (and beyond).

Cafés and bars

Abasinthe Kralja Milutina 33. Candle-topped tables, good drinks and attractive waiting staff keep the youthful, beautiful crowd happy.
Dorian Gray Strahinjića Bana. Classy cocktail bar with atmospheric terrace on one of the city's most gentrified streets.
Insomnia Strahinjića Bana 66. Cool brown-leather sofas and big windows make this trendy hangout an ideal spot for people-watching.
Kameleon Njegoševa 10. Daring – or foolish – types can try the nine-spirit "Tsunami" at this roadside cocktail bar.
Plato Café Akademski Plato 1. Comfy outdoor deckchairs and smooth live jazz music make this a perfect chill-out nightspot.
Simbol Nušićeva 4 & Obilićev venac 27. Busy, Roman-themed café – with two branches – that more than suffices for a coffee, beer or glass of wine.
Three Carrots Kneza Miloša 16. The city's token Irish pub isn't a bad place at all, with tasty beers on tap and simple pub food available.

Clubs and live music

Acapulco Bulevar Nikole Tesla bb. If you want to experience a night of Serbia's infamous Turbo-folk (an excruciating hybrid of electronic pop and Balkan folk music), then this rocking raft behind the *Hotel Jugoslavija* is the place to come.
Beggars Banquet Resavska 24. So named after the Stones' album, this barn-like venue has regular live rock music.
Bus Aberdareva 1. As the name implies, this place is in a red double-decker bus, across from the bombed-out TV studios, and has regular DJ nights, with discounted prices on Tuesday.
Freestyler Brodarska (River Sava). One of a string of banging raft clubs near Brankov most; others include *Sound* and *Exile*. All are style-conscious and relatively pricey, but this is the place to go for some serious clubbing.
Oh, Cinema! Kalemegdan Terasa (during summer) and Gračanička 18 (during winter). Both these venues – one an atmospheric indoor hall, the other an outdoor terrace – are popular party places with frequent live music, and remain open until dawn on summer weekends.
Underground Pariska 1. Well established on the local club scene, *Underground* is a warren of vast rooms under the fortress accommodating thumping house and techno tunes alongside chill-out areas.

Entertainment

Tickets for events at all the venues below can be bought from the Bilet Servis ticket agency at Trg Republike 5, inside the IPS shop (Mon–Fri 9am–8pm, Sat 9am–3pm). Tickets at the cinema on Trg Nikole Pašića cost just 200-250din.
National Theatre Trg Republike Ⓦ www.narodnopozoriste.co.yu. The centre for much of Belgrade's rich cultural life. Tickets for theatre (100–600din) and opera/ballet (100–800din) can be purchased from the box office inside the theatre (10am–2pm & 5pm till performance).
Belgrade Philharmonia At the Kolarčev Concert Hall, Studentski trg 5. Box office 10am–2pm & 2.30–7.30pm; tickets 200–500din.
The Dom Omladine Youth Cultural Centre Makedonska 22 Ⓦ www.domomladine.org. Often has a good cross-section of Serbian and international music as well as films and multimedia events.

Shopping

Kneza Mihailova is littered with familiar high street brands, with prices only marginally lower than western Europe. At the far end of Skadarska throbs the open-air market, Bajlonova Pijace (off Džordža; summer daily 6am–9pm), a dense collection of stalls selling everything from fresh food to kitchen utensils, all at bargain prices.

Directory

Embassies and consulates Australia, Čika Ljubina 13 ⓣ11/624-655; Canada, Kneza Miloša 13 ⓣ11/306-3000; Ireland ⓣ11/302-9600; New Zealand ⓣ11/428-2208; UK, Resavska 46 ⓣ11/264-5055; US, Kneza Miloša 50 ⓣ11/361-9344.
Exchange At the train station and all along Knesa Mihailova (most are open until 10pm).
Hospital Pasterova 2 ⓣ11/361-8444.
Internet Dom Omladine (Youth Centre), Makedonska 22; Plato Plus, Vasina 19.
Laundry Resavska 34 ⓣ11/323-9098. Mon–Sat 8am–10pm, Sun 8am–2pm; 250din.
Left luggage (*prtljag*). At train station (around 200din p/day).
Pharmacy Kralja Milana 9 (ⓣ11/324-0533) and Nemanjina 2 (ⓣ11/264-3170) – both 24hr.
Police Savski trg 2 ⓣ11/645-764.
Post office Zmaj Jovina 17. Mon–Sat 8am–7pm.

Moving on

Train Kraljevo (2 daily; 4hr); Ljubljana (4 daily; 10hr); Niš (10 daily; 4hr); Novi Sad (10 daily; 1hr 30min); Skopje (2 daily; 8hr 30min); Ušče (2 daily; 5hr); Zagreb (5 daily; 7hr).
Bus Kraljevo (every 60–90min; 2hr); Niš (hourly; 3hr); Novi Pazar (every 60–90min; 3hr); Novi Sad (every 20–40min; 1hr 20min).

Northern Serbia

North of Belgrade towards the Hungarian border is the Vojvodina, a flat, fertile and largely featureless plain that contains the country's most disparate mix of peoples, including a large Hungarian minority. The region's main draw is **Novi Sad**, a friendly, graceful city that makes for an easy and enjoyable day-trip from the capital. It's also an excellent base for forays into **Fruška Gora**, a series of gently undulating hills to the south, peppered with ancient Orthodox monasteries.

NOVI SAD

The cosmopolitan city of **NOVI SAD**, some 75km northwest of Belgrade on the main road and rail routes towards Budapest, is Serbia's most appealing urban centre, with much to show for its centuries of Austro-Hungarian rule. The imperious Petrovaradin fortress looks over the city from across the Danube, and in summer plays host to thousands of international revellers during the four-day Exit festival.

What to see and do

The city developed in tandem with the huge **Petrovaradin Fortress** on the Danube's south bank. There had been fortifications here since Roman times, but the fortress took its present shape in the eighteenth century when the Austrians turned it into a barrier against Turkish expansionism. In the event, no assault was ever made on the fortress and it eventually became a jail, its most celebrated inmate being a young Tito, briefly imprisoned for propagating socialist ideas. Visitors can see around 1km of the vast underground chambers (daily 9am–6pm; 100din), or stroll along the fortress walls and take in the splendid views of the town and surrounding countryside.

Across the river, the hub of the city is **Trg Slobode** (Freedom Square), a spacious square with an ostentatious town hall on one side and the neo-Gothic, brick-clad **Catholic Church of the Virgin Mary** on the other. Running east from here is the bustling Zmaj Jovina which, together with the adjoining Laze Telečkog and Dunavska, forms the town's pedestrianized centre for shopping, dining and drinking. At the bottom end of Dunavska, at no. 35, is the excellent **Museum of Vojvodina** (Tues–

THE EXIT FESTIVAL

For four days at the beginning of July each year the grounds of **Petrovaradin Fortress** play host to the **Exit Noise Festival** (Ⓦwww.exitfest.org), now established as the premier music event in southeastern Europe, attracting some of the biggest names in rock, hip-hop and techno.

Fri 9am–2pm & 6pm–10pm, Sat 9am–2pm; 100din), located in two buildings, the first displaying a comprehensive archeological and ethnographical exhibition, and the second detailing Serbian involvement in both world wars.

Sun lovers should head for the **Štrand** (May–Sept; 30din), a tidy expanse of sandy beach and extensive lawns on the Danube's north bank, opposite the fortress. The beachy atmosphere is enhanced by the plethora of cafés, bars and kiosks dotted along the front.

Arrival and information

Train and bus The adjacent bus and train stations are 1km north of the centre on Bulevar Jaše Tomića. The easiest way into town is to take one of the regular buses #4 or #11 (30din) from the train station forecourt, jumping off on when you see the cathedral spire. Walking takes about fifteen minutes: head straight down Bulevar Oslobođenja and turn left into Jevrejska.

Tourist office The helpful tourist information centre is at Mihaila Pupina 9 (Mon–Fri 8.30am–8pm, Sat 8.30am–1:30pm; Ⓣ21/421-811, Ⓦwww.novisadtourism.org.yu), the town's main thoroughfare.

Accommodation

Brankovo Kolo Episkopa Visariona 3 Ⓣ21/622-160, Ⓦwww.hostelns.com. Large HI-affiliated student hostel two blocks north of the Vojvodina Museum, with decent shared facilities; July & Aug only. ❷

Downtown Hostel Laze Telečkog 10 Ⓣ64/192-0342, Ⓦwww.hostelnovisad.com. Centrally located with comfortable, wooden-floored rooms, and a laid-back vibe typical of the city. ❷

Fontana Nikole Pašićeva 27 Ⓣ21/662-1777, Ⓔfontana@eunet.yu. Turn left at the end of Zmaj Jovina to find this place, with good-value private rooms and a fabulous courtyard restaurant. ❹

Hotel Mediteraneo Ilije Ognjanovića 10 Ⓣ21/427-135, Ⓦwww.hotel-mediteraneo.co.yu. Modern almost to the point of futuristic, this bright hotel punches way above its two-star rating, and is a stone's throw from the main square. ❼

Hotel Vojvodina Trg Svobode Ⓣ21/622-2122. The oldest hotel in the region is beginning to look its age, but its rooms are snug enough, and the location is unbeatable. ❻

Hotel Zenit Zmaj Jovina 8 Ⓣ21/662-1444, Ⓦwww.hotelzenit.co.yu. An excellent – if pricey – hotel, with smart, colourful rooms, tucked away from the main street (Zmaj Jovina). ❼

Eating

Alla Lanterna Dunavska 27. Dine on delicious pasta at this romantic Italian restaurant, with candlelit outdoor tables overlooking Dunavska park. Pasta 450din.

Arhiv Ilije Ognjanovića 16. Cosy, narrow place boasting a classy menu with national and international dishes. Just behind Hotel Zenit. Mains 500–600din.

Europa Dunavska 6. Serves a wide choice of ice cream flavours and cakes for next to nothing.

Drinking

The pedestrian zone east of Trg Svobode is littered with café-bars, most of which have outdoor areas in summer. Zmaj Jovina is perfect for a quiet drink, while the narrow Laze Telečkog is packed with a young and boisterous crowd.

Jelisavetin Bastion Petrovaradinska tvrđava Ⓦwww.bastion.co.yu. Innovative multi-roomed nightclub set in underground chambers within the fortress complex. International DJs draw big crowds and make the drinks relatively expensive.

Lazino Tele Laze Telečkog 16. Lively pub spread over two floors, with a good selection of cheap draught beer.

Moving on

Train Belgrade (10 daily; 1hr 30min); Budapest (2 daily; 6 hours).

Bus Belgrade (hourly; 1hr 15min).

AROUND NOVI SAD

Shadowing the city to the south are the low rolling hills of the **Fruška Gora**

(Holy Mountain), a densely wooded region of farms, orchards and vineyards carved up by a well-worn nexus of simple hiking trails. Moreover, the Fruška Gora shelter some seventeen monasteries, the most interesting of which lie in fairly close proximity to each other on the southeastern rim of the hills. Just off the main road before the village of Irig, about 15km south of Novi Sad, is **Hopovo**, the largest and most Byzantine in style, frescoed with seventeenth-century works of an unknown monk-artist from Mount Athos. Not far from Hopovo are two monastic churches dating from the sixteenth century, **Krušedol** and **Vrdnik**; the latter one once held the relics of the heroic Serbian leader Tsar Lazar, though only part of his collar bone still remains.

Without wheels, visiting the monasteries is a tricky business. Using public transport your best bet to take bus #61 or #62 from the Novi Sad bus station to **Sremski Karlovci** (20min; 65din), a quaint, sleepy town on the eastern fringes of the national park. On the main square, Branko Radičević, you'll find the tourist office (Mon–Fri 8:30am–4pm, Sat 10am–5pm, Sun 11am–5pm; ⓣ02/188-3855, ⓦwww.karlovci.co.yu), which, with some advance warning, can organize group sightseeing tours of the main monasteries (1200din) or at least arrange for a driver (around 2000din for 3hr).

Southern Serbia

South of Belgrade, the landscape becomes increasingly more appealing, the green rolling heartland of its central hills and mountains the setting for a sprinkling of fine sights. Chief amongst these are Serbia's revered medieval monasteries, the best possible illustration of an age that Serbs, even today, look back on with pride. Three of the most important are **Žiča**, **Studenica** and **Sopoćani**, all of which belong to the so-called Raška School, a style dating from the foundation of the Serbian state in the late twelfth century and which are distinguished by some fine Romanesque architecture and monumental frescoes. Elsewhere, the region's main city, **Niš**, conveniently straddles major road and rail routes to Bulgaria and Macedonia further south, and has a few worthy sights in its own right.

ŽIČA, STUDENICA AND SOPOĆANI MONASTERIES

In the hilly stretch from the industrial town of Kraljevo (itself some 170km south of Belgrade), south to the Muslim-influenced Novi Pazar lies some of Serbia's most impressive monasteries. **Žiča**, just 4km southeast of Kraljevo is a proud, brightly coloured thirteenth-century creation of St Sava – Serbia's patron saint. The church itself has been heavily restored over the years, though the frescoes remain in a rather parlous state.

Set unobtrusively against the wild, roaming slopes some 12km from the village of **Ušće** is **Studenica**, the first and greatest of the Serbian monasteries. Established at the end of the twelfth century by Stefan Nemanja, the complex comprises three churches (there were nine at one time) enclosed within an oval paddock. The largest and most important of these is the church of **Sv Bogdorica** (Church of Our Lady), whose paintings represent the first flowering of Serbian fresco painting, manifest in such pieces as the remarkably well-preserved *Crucifixion* on the west wall of the nave. The inner sanctum also holds the marble tomb of Stefan Nemanja. Either side of Sv Bogdorica is the much smaller,

VISITING THE MONASTERIES

While **Žiča** is easily accessible by bus from Kraljevo (every 30–45min; 35din), if you want to see more than one of the famous monasteries in one day, the unreliable rural buses mean you'll probably need a car. For this you can try Autotehna in Kraljevo (Karađorđeva 12/1; ⓣ36/319-944, ⓦwww.autotehna.com), or one of the many agencies in Niš or Belgrade. Prices should start at around €40–50 p/day. If you have more time, you could try public buses. Some buses ply the Kraljevo–Novi Pazar route, passing through the small town of **Ušće**. From here, there are 2–3 daily buses to Studenica (though few locals seem to agree on timings).

fourteenth-century Kraljeva Crkva (King's Church) and the Church of Sv Nikola (Church of St Nicholas), both of which contain impressive frescoes, such as *Three Marys at Christ's Grave* in the latter. There's an adjoining **guesthouse**, which has accommodation in multi-bed dorms (ⓣ36/836-050; ❷).

Around 16km from Novi Pazar, **Sopoćani**, a thirteenth-century construction that was left ruined by invading Turks until restoration in the 1920s, holds arguably some of Serbia's finest frescoes.

NIŠ

NIŠ, 235km southeast of Belgrade, is a gritty industrial city whose hard-nosed edge is unlikely to win over new arrivals. However, its location on the country's main road and rail arteries makes it a useful stopover point on the way to Bulgaria and Macedonia, while a collection of intriguing sights and a typically Serbian vibe means it has more to offer than first meets the eye.

What to see and do

The city's centrepiece is its main square, **Trg Kralja Milana**, which sits across the Nišava River from **Niš Fortress**. Built on the site of a Roman fortress, the current fortifications date from the beginning of the eighteenth century. The most interesting parts are the well-preserved Istanbul Gate (now the entrance), and the Mosque of Bali Beg, an arsenal converted to a modern art gallery. Most people, though, come here for a quiet stroll, or to relax at the bars and cafés crammed inside the courtyard. Niš's other sights are equally steeped in military history, including the grisly **Ćele Kula** (Tower of Skulls; Mon–Sat 9am–4pm, Sun 10am–2pm; 100din), east of the centre on Brače Taskoviča (bus #24). Surrounded by the Turkish army on nearby Čegar Hill in 1809, Stevan Sinđelić and his men chose death before dishonour and ignited their gunpowder supplies, blowing to pieces most of the Turks, and all of the Serbians. As a statement of Turkish sovereignty, the Pasha ordered around a thousand Serbian heads to be stuffed and mounted on the tower; around sixty still remain. No less morbid is the World War II **Crveni Krst (Red Cross) concentration camp** (daily 9am–6pm; 100din) tucked away anonymously 500m northwest of the bus station on Bulevar 12 Februar. The well-preserved remains – barbed-wire fences and watchtowers included – give the impression of a place recently abandoned, adding to the eerie ambience. Inside the building itself is a sombre memorial to the former inmates – partisans, communists, gypsies and Jews; most chilling is a set of paintings by local schoolchildren depicting in bright colours a bloody escape attempt on February 12, 1942, when fifty prisoners were machine-gunned against the walls.

Arrival and information

Bus The bus station is located just to the west of the citadel on Bulevar Februar 12.

Train The train station is 2km west of town on Dimitrija Tucovica.

Tourist office You can get useful information and maps from the tourist office at Voždova Karađorđa 7 (Mon–Fri 7.30am–7pm, Sat 9am–1pm; ⓣ18/523-118, ⓦwww.nistourism.org.yu).

Accommodation

Hotel Ambasador Trg Kralja Milana ⓣ18/501-800, ⓦwww.srbijaturist.com. An unsightly high-rise, but the clean rooms are reasonably priced considering its perfect location on the main square. ⑤

Hostel Niš Dobrička 3a ⓣ18/513-703, ⓦwww.hostelnis.com. Make this your first port of call if staying in Niš. A small but fantastic new hostel, with a spotless 12-bed dorm, one double, and extremely friendly owners. Well signposted, it's just a few minutes' walk west from the fortress entrance. ②

Eating and drinking

For the best selection of bars and live music, head to the cobbled Kazandžijsko Sokače (Tinker's alley), five minutes' walk south of trg Kralja Milana opposite the giant Kalča shopping centre.

Fabio's Cara Dušana (junction with Prvomajska, 500m east of Sokače). Laughably conspicuous on account of its gratuitous chic decor, but the appetizing cocktails are still cheap.

Hamam Tvrđava bb. Just inside the fort entrance, offering a good range of grills and fish. Mains 400din.

Reka Kej Kola Sroskih Sestara. This chilled-out riverside café opposite the fortress pumps out dance tunes to a trendy crowd until 4am on weekends.

Sinđelić Nikole Pašica 25 (100m west from the Kalča centre). Feast on huge portions of meaty local specialities in a leafy courtyard – a must if dining out. Mains 500–700din.

Moving on

Train Belgrade (7 daily; 4–5hr); Kraljevo (3 daily; 3hr 45min).

Bus Belgrade (hourly; 3hr); Kraljevo (6 daily; 3hr); Skopje (6 daily; 5-6hr); Sofia (2 daily; 2hr 30min).

Slovakia

HIGHLIGHTS

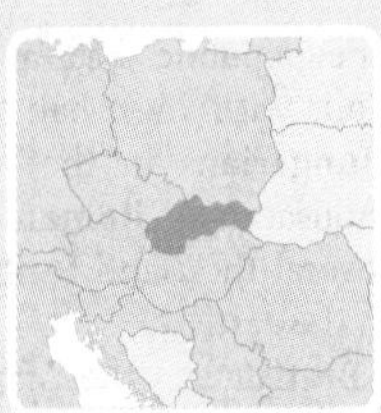

HIGH TATRAS: admire the majesty of Slovakia's highest peaks

LEVOČA: explore the crumbling backstreets of this beautiful walled town

KOŠICE: join Slovakia's second city as it gradually comes to life

BRATISLAVA: indulge in the capital's fantastic gastroculture

DANUBE: cruise between Europe's closest capitals

ROUGH COSTS

DAILY BUDGET Basic €25/ occasional treat €30

DRINK Beer €1.40

FOOD Potato dumplings €3

HOSTEL/BUDGET HOTEL €10/20

TRAVEL Train Banská Štiavnice–Poprad (247km) €9

FACT FILE

POPULATION 5.4 million

AREA 49,037 sq km

LANGUAGE Slovak

CURRENCY Slovak koruna (SKK)

CAPITAL Bratislava (population: 45,0000)

INTERNATIONAL PHONE CODE ⓣ421

Basics

Slovakia consists of the long, narrow strip of land that stretches from the fertile plains of the Danube basin up to the peaks of the High Tatras, Europe's most exhilarating mountain range outside the Alps.

The republic has a diverse population, with over half a million ethnic **Hungarians** in the south, as well as thousands of **Romanies** (Gypsies) and several thousand **Ruthenians** (Rusyns) in the east.

Bratislava, the capital, has been beautifully restored in the last decade and is a rewarding, lively place to visit. **Poprad** provides the transport hub for **the High Tatras**, and is also the starting point for exploring the intriguing medieval towns of the **Spiš** region. Further east still, **Prešov** is the cultural centre of the Ruthenian minority; while **Košice**, Slovakia's vibrant second city, boasts a fine Gothic cathedral, ethnic diversity and a lively independence from much of the rest of the country.

CHRONOLOGY

450 BC Celts inhabit the area known as present-day Slovakia.
623 Samo becomes King of the Slavs after defeating the Avarians near Bratislava.
828 First Christian Church consecrated in Slovakia.
862 First Slavic alphabet written in Greater Moravia by apostles Cyril and Methodius of the Byzantine empire.
997 The Nitrian Principality, or present-day Slovakia, is absorbed into the Hungarian Empire.
1241 Mongol invasion of Slovakia results in heavy losses.
1526 Defeat in the Battle of the Mohacs leads the Habsburgs to move their capital to Bratislava.
1800s Growth in Slovak nationalism.
1895 Czech and Slovak peoples partake in mutual co-operation against their Hungarian oppressors.
1913 Slovak Štefan Banič invents the parachute.
1918 The independent republic of Czechoslovakia is announced upon the defeat of Austria-Hungary in WWI.
1939 Germany takes the Sudetenland in Czechoslovakia, before occupying the rest of the country.
1945 Slovak National Uprising against German occupation is successful, but thousands of Slovakian Jews have already been sent to concentration camps.
1948 The Communist Party comes into power in Czechoslovakia.
1991 The collapse of Soviet Communism leads the way for political independence in Czechoslovakia.
1993 Slovakia gains full independence after Czechoslovakia splits peacefully.
2004 Slovakia joins NATO and the EU.
2007 Slovakian troops withdraw from Iraq.

ARRIVAL

Most international visitors will fly into Bratislava **airport**, linked to the main train station by bus #61; taxis into town should not cost more than 500SKK. There is also an **international airport** in Košice, which receives flights from Prague, Vienna, Bratislava, Poprad, London and Dublin. It's approximately 6km south of the town, and a taxi to Košice is around 30SKK.

By train

Slovakia has good rail connections with Austria, Hungary, Poland and the Czech Republic. Most trains from these countries terminate in Bratislava, but trains from Budapest, Krakov and Prague also run to Košice. The capital's **train station**, Bratislava-Hlavná stanica, is about a kilometre north of the city centre. From the **tram** terminus below you can hop on tram #13 into town: buy a ticket from one of the machines outside the train station before boarding.

By bus

Buses from Europe run frequently to Bratislava, and usually arrive at Mylnske

Nivy in the Old Town. Coachline Bratislava runs an International network of bus connections to Bratislava and is managed by two companies, SkyEurope Airlines Ⓦwww1.skyeurope.com/en and Eurolines Ⓦwww.eurolines.sk.

By hydrofoil

You can also take the **hydrofoil** from Budapest or Vienna to Bratislava. These arrive at Razusovo Nabrezie Embankment or Fajnorova Nabrezie Embankment, in the heart of the city.

GETTING AROUND

Train services are slow, but some journeys are worth it for the scenery alone. Slovak Railways (Železnice Slovenskej republiky or ŽSR) runs fast *rýchlik* trains that stop at major towns; the *osobný vlak*, or local train, stops everywhere. You can buy **tickets** (*lístok*) for domestic journeys at the station (*stanica*) before or on the day of departure. Supplements are payable on all EuroCity (EC) trains, and occasionally for InterCity (IC) and Express (Ex) trains. ŽSR runs reasonably priced sleepers (*lužkový vozeń*) and couchettes (*ležadlový vozeń*) – book in advance, no later than six hours before departure. InterRail is valid; **Eurail** requires supplements. Search train timetables online at Ⓦwww.zsr.sk.

Buses (*autobus*) are quicker and cover a more extensive network. The state bus company is Slovenská automobilová doprava or SAD. Buy your **ticket** from the driver. Book in advance if you're travelling at the weekend or early in the morning on one of the main routes.

Although much of Slovakia is mountainous and therefore not an ideal option for cyclists, the countryside around Bratislava has easy and well-maintained bike paths which run into Austria and Hungary. More demanding rides can take you into the Little Carpathians. Most trains allow bikes.

ACCOMMODATION

Arrange **accommodation** as far in advance as possible. While the old state hotels and spa complexes are slowly being refurbished, their rooms are usually box-like and overpriced; the new **hotels and pensions** that have opened up are often better value for money. **Private rooms** are a good option in many towns – keep your eyes peeled for *Zimmer frei* or *Priváty* signs or book through the local tourist information office. Prices start at around €8 per person per night.

There is no real network of **hostels,** though a few are affiliated to HI and others come under CKM, the student travel agency (Ⓦwww.ckm.sk). Bratislava has a few private hostels offering varying degrees of discomfort. Elsewhere, CKM or local tourist offices can give information on cheap **student accommodation** in the university towns during July and August. In the High Tatras, you can find a fair number of chalet-style **refuges** (*chata*) scattered about the hillsides. Some are practically hotels and cost around €15/bed, while simpler, more isolated wooden shelters cost much less. **Campsites** are plentiful, and many feature simple **bungalows** (*chata* again), often available for upwards of €7.50/bed.

FOOD AND DRINK

Slovak **food** is no-nonsense, filling fare; traces of Hungarian, Polish and Ukrainian influences can be found in different regions. Most menus start with **soup** (*polievka*). Main courses are usually pork, beef or chicken, but trout and carp are often featured somewhere on the menu. Main courses are served with potatoes (*zemiaky*) – fresh salads or green vegetables are still a rarity in local restaurants. Typical **desserts** include apple or cottage-cheese strudel, and *palačinky* (cold pancakes) filled with chocolate, fruit and cream.

A classic mid-morning **snack** at the *bufet* (stand-up canteen) is **párek**, a hot frankfurter dipped in mustard or horseradish and served inside a white roll. *Bryndzové halušky* is the national dish – dumplings with a thick sheep's cheese sauce and crumbled, grilled bacon – but Hungarian goulash is also very popular, as are **langoše** – deep-fried dough smothered in a variety of toppings.

In outlying regions **closing time** will still be 9 or 10pm, the bigger cities have restaurants open till 11pm or later. The **cake shop** (*cukráreň*) is an important part of social life, particularly on Sunday mornings when it's often the only place that's open in town. Whatever the season, Slovaks love their daily fix of **ice cream** (*zmrzlina*), available at *cukráreň* or dispensed from little window kiosks in the sides of buildings.

Drink

Coffee (*káva*) is drunk black – espresso-style in the big cities, but sometimes simply hot water poured over grounds (described rather hopefully as "Turkish" or *turecká*).

Vineyards in the south of Slovakia produce some pretty good white **wines** – one of the most distinctive is the sweet wine, Tokaj. The most famous local firewaters are *slivovice*, a plum **brandy** available just about everywhere, and *borovička*, made with juniper berries. Slovaks love draught **beer**, but the *pivnica* (beer hall), where most heavy drinking goes on, is still less common in Slovakia than in the Czech Republic. Slovaks tend to head instead for restaurants or wine bars (*vináreň*), which usually have slightly later opening hours and often double as nightclubs.

CULTURE AND ETIQUETTE

Tipping is mostly done by handing money over directly, rather than leaving money on the table, although this is changing. Ten percent is usual, depending on the establishment: you may want to tip twenty percent for smarter places.

If you travel on **trains**, you will find that politeness is valued when sharing a carriage. At the very least, people usually say, *Dobrý deň* (hello) when they enter a carriage and *Dovidenia* (goodbye) when they leave.

SPORTS AND OUTDOOR ACTIVITIES

Slovakia is fanatical about **ice hockey**, which you can see live on screens in bars across the Republic – or you can go to games in stadiums from September to April (@www.hcslovan.sk). Tickets cost between 80–200SKK and can be bought from the arena on match days. Bratislava is due to host the ice hockey world cup in 2011.

Naturally, there's plenty of **hiking**, **skiing** and **mountaineering** to be done in the High Tatras (@www.tatry.sk) and caving in the Slovak Karst in East Slovakia (@www.saske.sk/cave).

COMMUNICATIONS

Most **post offices** (*pošta*) open Mon–Fri 8am–5pm. You can also buy stamps (*známky*) from some tobacconists (*tabák*) and street kiosks. Poste restante is available in major towns; write Pošta 1 (the main office), followed by the name of the town. Cheap local calls can be made from any **phone**, but for international calls it's best to use a card phone; buy a card (*telefonná karta*) from a tobacconist or post office. Internet cafés have appeared in the larger towns; expect to pay 50–100SK/hr.

SLOVAKIA ON THE NET

@www.slovakspectator.sk English-language weekly, with news and listings.
@www.tatry.sk Excellent guide to the High Tatras, with plenty of travel and accommodation info.
@www.sacr.sk Tourist board site, with basic but useful information.

EMERGENCIES

The **state police** (*polícia*) wear khaki-green uniforms, and the local municipal or *mestská polícia* wear a variety of outfits. Theft from cars and hotel rooms is your biggest worry, though pickpocketing is also common in the larger towns. You should carry your passport with you at all times, though you're most unlikely to get stopped. Minor ailments can be easily dealt with by the **pharmacist** (*lekáreň*), but language is likely to be a problem. If the pharmacy can't help, they'll direct you to a **hospital** (*nemocnica*).

EMERGENCY NUMBERS

Police ⓣ158; Ambulance ⓣ155; Fire ⓣ150.

INFORMATION & MAPS

Just about every town has some kind of **tourist office** (*informačné centrum*), most with English speakers. In summer they're generally open Mon–Fri 9am–6pm, Sat & Sun 9am–2pm; in winter they tend to close an hour earlier and all day Sun (sometimes also Sat). **Maps** are available from bookshops and some hotels (a town plan is *plán mesta or orientačná mapa*). The VKÚ's excellent 1:50,000 series details hiking paths.

MONEY AND BANKS

Currency is the **Slovak crown** or *Slovenská koruna* (SKK), which is divided into 100 heller or *halér* (h). Coins are 10h, 20h, 50h, 1SKK, 2SKK, 5SKK and 10SKK; notes are 20, 50, 100, 200, 500 and 1000SKK. The crown is not fully convertible, which means you can't buy any currency until you arrive. **Credit** and **debit cards** are accepted in

STUDENT AND YOUTH DISCOUNTS

To get up to fifty percent off entry into some attractions you will need an ISIC card, as many places will not accept individual university cards.

Slovak

	Slovak	Pronunciation
Yes	*Áno*	Uh-no
No	*Nie*	Nyeh
Please	*Prosím*	Pro-seem
Thank you	*D'akujem vam*	Dya-koo-yem vam
Hello/Good day	*Dobrý deń/Ahoj*	Dob-rie den[y]/a-hoy
Goodbye	*Dovidenia*	Do-vid-en-ya
Excuse me	*Prepáčte*	Pre-patch-teh
Where	*Kde*	Gde
Good	*Dobrý*	Dob-rie
Bad	*Zle*	Zleh
Near	*Blízko*	Bli-sko
Far	*D'aleko*	D[y]a-lek-o
Cheap	*Lacný*	Lats-nie
Expensive	*Drahý*	Dra-hie
Open	*Otvorený*	Ot-vor-eh-nie
Closed	*Zatvorený*	Zat-vor-eh-nie
Today	*Dnes*	Dnes
Yesterday	*Včera*	Ftch-er-a
Tomorrow	*Zajtra*	Zuyt-ra
How much is....?	*Kol'ko stát'...?*	Kol-ko stat[y]
What time is it?	*Kol'ko je hodín?*	Kol-ko ye hod-in
I don't understand	*Nerozumiem*	Ne-ro-zoom-yem
Do you speak English?	*Hovoríte po Anglicky?*	Hov-or-i-te po ang-lits-ky
One	*Jeden*	Yed-en
Two	*Dva*	Dva
Three	*Tri*	Tri
Four	*Štyri*	Shtir-i
Five	*Pät'*	Pyat[y]
Six	*Šest'*	Shest[y]
Seven	*Sedem*	Sed-em
Eight	*Osem*	Oss-em
Nine	*Devät'*	Dev-yat[y]
Ten	*Desat'*	Dess-at[y]
Getting around		
Where...?	*Kde...?*	Gudeh
Entrance	*Vchod*	FHod
Exit	*Východ*	VeeHot
Ticket	*Lístok*	Leestok
Hotel	*Hotel*	Hotel
Toilet	*Záchod*	ZaHod
Square	*Námestie*	Nahmestee
Station	*Stanica*	Stani-tza
Accommodation		
Do you have a...?	*Máte...?*	Ma-te...?
Single room	*jednopostel'ovú izbu?*	yed-no-pos-tye-lyo-voo iz-bu?
Two-bed room	*dvojpostel'ovú izbu*	dvoy-pos-tye-lyo-voo iz-bu
Open	*Otvorené*	Otvor-en-air
Closed	*Zatvorené*	Zatvor-en-air
Cheap	*Lacné*	Luhts-nair

most upmarket hotels and restaurants and some shops, and there are plenty of **ATMs** in all the larger towns. **Exchange offices** (*zmenáren*) can be found in all major hotels, travel agencies and department stores. At time of writing, €1=33.5SKK, $1=23.5SKK and £1= 48SKK.

OPENING HOURS AND HOLIDAYS

Opening hours for shops are Mon–Fri 9am–6pm, Sat 8am–noon, with some shops and most supermarkets staying open later. In large towns, supermarkets and out-of-town hypermarkets also open on Sunday. Smaller shops take an hour or so for lunch between noon and 2pm.

The basic opening hours for **castles** and **monasteries** are Tues–Sun 9am–5pm. Out of the season, hours are often restricted to weekends and holidays. Most castles are closed in winter. When visiting a sight, always ask for an *anglický* text, an often unintentionally hilarious English résumé. **Museums** are usually open Tues–Sun year-round, though most close early in winter. **Admission** rarely costs more than 100SKK – hence we've only quoted prices greater than this. **Public holidays** include Jan 1, Jan 6, Good Fri, Easter Mon, May 1, May 8, July 5, Aug 29, Sept 1, Sept 15, Nov 1, Dec 24, 25 and 26.

Bratislava

While parts of Bratislava exhibit the concrete looks of the average East European metropolis, the streets of the old town are glutted with sophisticated gastro-culture, and the large student population makes for a lively after-dark atmosphere, ensuring that the capital is a veritable playground for the backpacker. The city's cosmopolitanism is enhanced by its enticing proximity to Vienna (only 60km apart, the two cities are the world's closest capitals) and Budapest, but Bratislava's engaging melange of old and new makes it a worthwhile destination in its own right.

What to see and do

The **Staré Mesto** – where you'll spend most of your time – lies on the north side of the Danube; on the rocky hill to the west is the well-known landmark, the **castle**. Northeast of the old town are the residential blocks of **nove mesto**, which give way to sprawling suburbs.

Michalská veža

Opposite the mass of the **Kostol trinitárov**, one of the city's finest churches, a footbridge crosses a small section of what used to be a moat towards the city's last remaining double gateway. The tower above the gateway's second arch, the **Michalská veža** (Tues–Fri 9.30/10am–4.30/5pm, Sat & Sun 11am–6pm), provides an impressive entrance to the old town and is now a weapons museum – worth visiting if only for the view from the top.

Baroque palaces

Michalská and Ventúrska, which run into each other, are lined with some of Bratislava's finest **Baroque palaces**, alongside the university library – so there are usually plenty of students milling about amongst the shoppers. The palaces of the Austro-Hungarian aristocracy continue into Panská, starting with the **Pálffy Palace**, at Panská 19, now an art gallery.

Old town

A little northeast of here are the adjoining main squares of the **old town** – Hlavné námestie and Františkánske námestie – on the east side of which is the **Old Town Hall**, a lively hotchpotch of Gothic, Renaissance and nineteenth-century styles containing the main **City Museum** (Tues–Fri 10am–5pm, Sat & Sun 11am–6pm), which features a medieval torture exhibition in the basement dungeons. Up Františkánska from Františkánska námestie, you'll find the Counter-Reformation **Jesuit Church** and the **Mirbach Palace** (Tues–Sun 11am–6pm), one of the best preserved of Bratislava's Rococo buildings. The permanent collection of Baroque and Rococo art isn't up to much but there are good temporary exhibitions.

QUIRKY BRATISLAVA

Bratislava is full of little idiosyncrasies, such as the **Dancing Bells**: on a scruffy piece of lawn on Hurbanovo naméstie you can find a small square on the ground divided into nine metal panels. Jumping up and down on these sets tiny bells ringing.

There are also various amusing **statues** scattered throughout the old town: **Čumil**, peeking out from a manhole, is an old favourite, as is the cheerful statue of Ignac Lamar, both often accompanied by copycat street performers. During the summer, there's the opportunity to play **giant chess** on Hviezdoslavovo námestie.

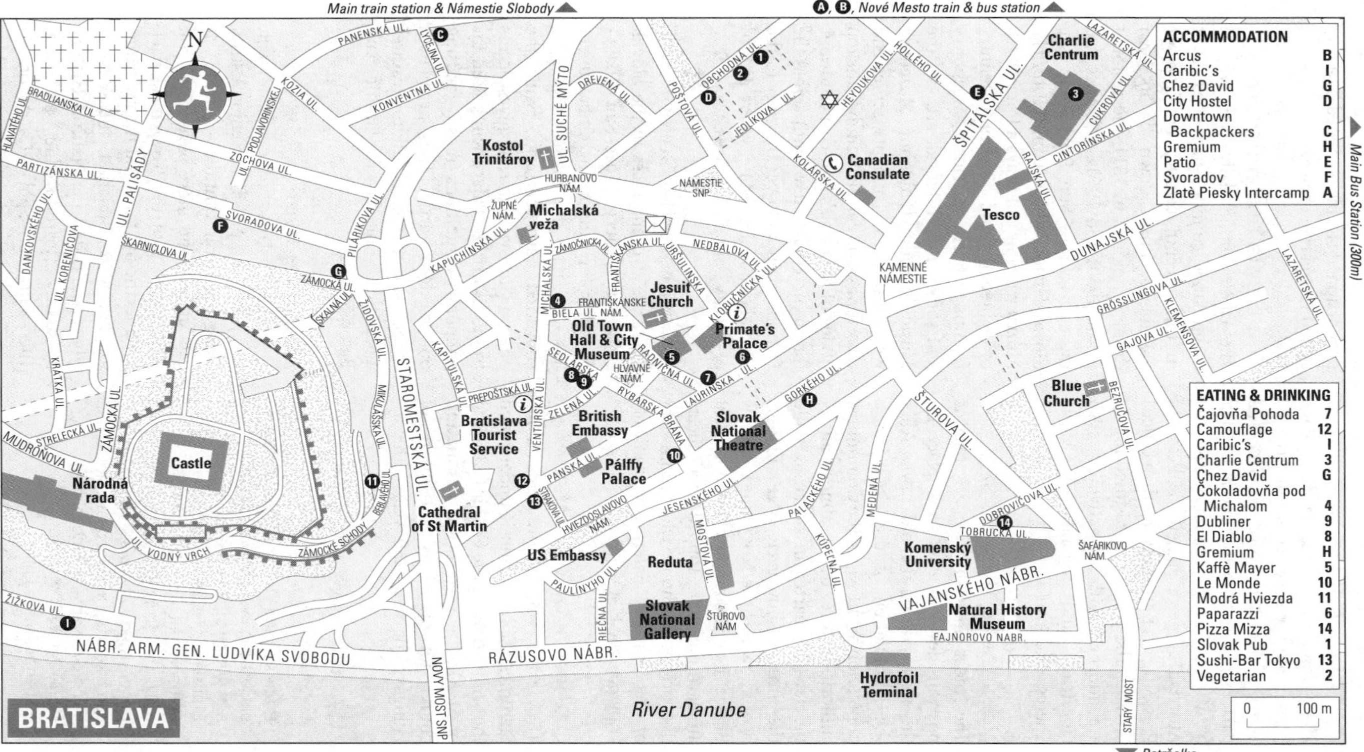
BRATISLAVA
Main train station & Námestie Slobody
A, B, Nové Mesto train & bus station
Main Bus Station (300m)
Petržalka
ACCOMMODATION
Arcus B
Caribic's I
Chez David G
City Hostel D
Downtown Backpackers C
Gremium H
Patio E
Svoradov F
Zlatè Piesky Intercamp A
EATING & DRINKING
Čajovňa Pohoda 7
Camouflage 12
Caribic's I
Charlie Centrum 3
Chez David G
Čokoladovňa pod Michalom 4
Dubliner 9
El Diablo 8
Gremium H
Kaffè Mayer 5
Le Monde 10
Modrá Hviezda 11
Paparazzi 6
Pizza Mizza 14
Slovak Pub 1
Sushi-Bar Tokyo 13
Vegetarian 2
0 100 m
N
Charlie Centrum
Canadian Consulate
Tesco
Kostol Trinitárov
Michalská veža
Jesuit Church
Primate's Palace
Old Town Hall & City Museum
Bratislava Tourist Service
British Embassy
Pálffy Palace
Slovak National Theatre
Blue Church
Cathedral of St Martin
US Embassy
Reduta
Slovak National Gallery
Komenský University
Natural History Museum
Hydrofoil Terminal
Castle
Národná rada
River Danube
Kamenné Námestie
Hurbanovo Nám.
Župné Nám.
Námestie SNP
Františkánske Nám.
Hlavné Nám.
Hviezdoslavovo Nám.
Šafárikovo Nám.
Štúrovo Nám.
Panenská Ul.
Lycejná Ul.
Kozia Ul.
Konventná Ul.
Podjavorinskej Ul.
Bradlianska Ul.
Hlavatého Ul.
Partizánska Ul.
Zochova Ul.
Ul. Palisády
Svoradova Ul.
Škarniclova Ul.
Dankovského Ul.
Ul. Koreničova
Kratka Ul.
Strelecká Ul.
Mudroňova Ul.
Zámocká Ul.
Ul. Vodný Vrch
Zámocké Schody
Žižkova Ul.
Nábr. Arm. Gen. Ludvíka Svobodu
Rázusovo Nábr.
Nový Most SNP
Staromestská Ul.
Židovská Ul.
Mikulášska Ul.
Beblavého Ul.
Skalná Ul.
Pilárikova Ul.
Kapuchínska Ul.
Kapitulská Ul.
Prepoštská Ul.
Ventúrska Ul.
Michalská Ul.
Biela Ul.
Zámočnícka Ul.
Františkánska Ul.
Uršulínska Ul.
Nedbalova Ul.
Klobučnícka Ul.
Sedlárska Ul.
Radničná Ul.
Laurinská Ul.
Zelená Ul.
Rybárska Brána
Panská Ul.
Strakova Ul.
Gorkého Ul.
Jesenského Ul.
Paulínyho Ul.
Riečna Ul.
Mostová Ul.
Palackého Ul.
Medená Ul.
Kúpeľná Ul.
Štúrova Ul.
Dobrovičova Ul.
Tobrucká Ul.
Vajanského Nábr.
Fajnorovo Nábr.
Starý Most
Bezručova Ul.
Gajova Ul.
Grösslingova Ul.
Klemensova Ul.
Lazaretská Ul.
Dunajská Ul.
Rajská Ul.
Špitálska Ul.
Cintorínska Ul.
Cukrová Ul.
Hollého Ul.
Heydukova Ul.
Kolárska Ul.
Jedlíkova Ul.
Obchodná Ul.
Poštová Ul.
Drevená Ul.
Ul. Suché Mýto

Primate's Palace

The Neoclassical **Primate's Palace** (Primacálny palác) Tues–Sun 10am–5pm) is definitely worth a visit. The palace's main claim to fame is its Hall of Mirrors, where Napoleon and the Austrian emperor signed the Peace of Pressburg (as Bratislava was then called) in 1805. The beautifully restored rooms are adorned with attractive "English tapestries" and portraits of Maria Theresa and Josef II.

Nový most (Most SNP)

The most insensitive of Bratislava's postwar developments took place on the west side of the old town. After the annihilation of the city's Jewish population by the Nazis, the Communist authorities tore down almost all of the Jewish quarter in order to build the brutal showpiece **SNP Bridge**, now known as the **Nový most** or New Bridge. Its one support column leans at an alarming angle, topped by a saucer-like, pricey penthouse café reminiscent of the *Starship Enterprise*, ironically known as the UFO.

Cathedral of St Martin

The traffic which now tears along Staromestská has seriously undermined the foundations of the Gothic Cathedral of St Martin, used as the **coronation church** for the kings and queens of Hungary for over 250 years. The ill-proportioned steeple is topped by a tiny gilded Hungarian crown.

TRIPS ALONG THE DANUBE

Bratislava and Vienna are the world's closest capitals, and you can take a **hydrofoil** trip between them from Bratislava's Razusovo Nabrezie Embankment (up to 3 departures daily; 1hr 15min; €15–27; Ⓦwww.twincityliner). Otherwise, you can take a trip to Budapest from Fajnorova Nabrezie Embankment (April–Oct; €79; Ⓦwww.mahartpassnave.hu).

The castle and museums

The **castle** (*hrad*; daily 9am–6/8pm) is an unwelcoming giant box built in the fifteenth century by Emperor Sigismund, burnt down by its own drunken soldiers in 1811 and restored in the 1950s and 1960s. It houses two museums (Tues–Sun 9am–5pm): the **Slovak Historical Museum** (Historické Múzeum), which displays a hotchpotch of eighteenth- and nineteenth-century furniture, portraits, clocks, weaponry and some modern Slovak art, and the Music Museum (Hudobné Múzeum), with local folk instruments, scores and recordings. You can also climb to the top of one of the castle's four corner towers, for an incredible **view** south across the Danube plain and over the river to the Petržalka housing estate, where a third of the city's population lives.

Slovak National Gallery

There are two entrances to the **Slovak National Gallery** (Tues–Sun 10am–5.30pm): the one on the embankment lets you into the main building, a converted naval barracks, while the one on Stúrovo námestie gives access to the **Esterházy Palace** wing, used for temporary exhibitions (mostly focusing on modern art). The permanent collection in the main building features a rundown of Slovak Gothic and Baroque art.

Along the river

Despite the fast road on the embankment, it is just about possible to enjoy a stroll along the **River Danube** – (*Dunaj*). It gets quieter and more pleasant as you walk away from the Nový most back towards the old town and the moorings for ferries to Budapest and Vienna, where you'll find the **Natural History Museum** (Prírodovedné Múzeum; Tues–Sun 9am–5pm). Carry on to

Safárikovo námestie, and up Bezručova to Ödön Lechner's concrete, sky-coloured Art Nouveau **Blue Church** (Modrý Kostolík), a lost monument to this once-Hungarian city, abandoned in the Slovak capital and dedicated to St Elizabeth, the city's one and only famous saint, born here in 1207.

Arrival and information

Train The main **train station,** Bratislava-Hlavná stanica, is walking distance – 1km north – of the centre.
Trams Trams are the best option for late-night arrivals at the main train station: from the tram terminus just down the steps from the main train station exit, you can hop on tram #13 into town (tickets from the platform machines). Some trains, particularly those heading for west Slovakia, pass through Bratislava Nové Mesto station, 4km northeast of the centre, which is linked to town by tram #6.
Buses The main bus station is Bratislava autobusová stanica, on Mlynské nivy, fifteen minutes' walk east of the centre. Trolleybuses #206 and #208 serve the centre, Hodžovo námestie.
Tourist office BKIS, at Klobucnícká 2 (June–Sept Mon–Fri 8.30am–7pm, Sat 9am–5pm, Sun 9.30am–4pm; Oct–May Mon–Fri 8.30am–6pm, Sat 9am–2pm; ⓣ02/5443 3715, ⓦwww.bkis.sk, ⓦwww.bratislava.sk). There's another smaller office in the main train station.
Discount card The Bratislava City Card is available from BKIS Tourist Information Offices: it's available for up to three days (costing up to €15) and gets you a twenty percent discount on a variety of tours and attractions, as well as free transport.

City transport

Walking is the only way to see the mainly pedestrianized Staré Mesto (old town).
Trams Outside the old town, trams are the easiest way to travel: a day pass costs 90SKK, and you can buy tickets from the Bratislava Transport (Obchodna 14, ⓦwww.dpb.sk), and at the booth to the left of the train station's main exit, for multiple days. Buy tickets from machines and newsagents for trams valid for 10 min/14SKK; 30min/18SKK; 1hr/22SKK. You also need a half-fare ticket for any bulky luggage.
Buses The bus network (run by the Bratislva Transport) serves the town both sides of the river; trams and trolleybuses only run north of the river.
Bikes You can hire bikes (ⓦwww.bratislava.info/trips/bike) but there are no special bike paths in Bratislava's streets, and motorists can be erratic.

Accommodation

Hotels are more expensive than anywhere else in the country, making hostels and **private rooms** the most popular options for budget travellers. You can book centrally located rooms through the tourist office (50SKK fee). Bratislava's various **student hostels** are open only in summer.

Hostels

City Hostel Obchodná 38 ⓣ02/5263 6041, ⓦwww.cityhostel.sk. Modern, well-located and ideal for backpackers. All rooms have en-suite facilities. ❻
Downtown Backpacker's Panenská 31, ⓣ02/5464 1191, ⓦwww.backpackers.sk. Friendly HI-affiliated place on the edge of the old town, with 24hr Internet access. Open all year. Dorms ❷; doubles ❸
Patio Špitálska 35 ⓣ02/5292 5797, ⓦwww.patiohostel.com. Five minutes' walk from the city centre, this refurbished hostel has 24hr reception, a laundry and Internet access. Open all year. Dorms ❷; doubles ❸
Svoradov Svoradova 13 ⓣ02/5441 1908. Centrally located student hostel, just two blocks north of the castle. No curfew, open beginning of June to late August. ❷

Hotels and pensions

Arcus Moskovská 5 ⓣ02/5557 2522, ⓦwww.hotelarcus.sk. Small, personal pension within walking distance of the old town; double ❽
Caribic's Žižkova 1a ⓣ02/5441 8334, ⓦwww.caribics.com. Pleasant rooms in an old

TREAT YOURSELF

If you're planning to spend all your energy on mountain activities, you might want to pamper yourself by staying in the plush **Grand Hotel** (Starý Smokovec 062 01 ⓣ52/4780 000, ⓦwww.grandhotel.sk). With stylish decor evoking the elegance of the first half of the twentieth century and a lovely coffee bar, it's a great place to recharge and relax. Rooms are equally luxurious. Doubles ❾ fisherman's lodge and pretty good value given its proximity to the old town, though rather noisy thanks to passing trams. Excellent restaurant downstairs. 6

Chez David Zamocká 13 ⓣ02/5441 3824, ⓦwww.chezdavid.sk. Centrally located, with helpful staff and a kosher Jewish restaurant attached. 8

Gremium Gorkého 11 ⓣ02/5413 1026. Decent, relatively inexpensive option in the old town. Clean, with extremely basic en-suite bathrooms, plus a café and sports bar on the bottom two floors. 3

Campsites

Zlaté Piesky Intercamp ⓣ02/4425 7373, ⓦwww.intercamp.sk. 8km northeast of the city centre. Take tram #2 from the main train station or #4 from town. Swimming lake with lifeguard services. Tent camping May to mid-Oct. 1

Eating

Bratislava boasts an excellent selection of restaurants and cafés to suit all tastes, and prices are generally fairly low.

Trznica Market at Námestie SNP 25 is an excellent indoor market, selling local herbs, fruits and vegetables – perfect for a healthy snack.

Cafés

Čajovňa Pohoda Radnicá 1. Hip teahouse with a huge range of herbal teas served in kitsch teapots and cups.

Čokoladovňa pod Michalom Michalská 6. Small, dark café near the Michalská veža, with all kinds of indulgent hot and ice chocolate on offer. Iced chocolate 79SKK.

Kaffé Mayer Hlavné námestie 4. A resurrected century-old café that emulates its Viennese-style ancestor. Opulently decked out and much loved by the "Kaffee-und-Kuchen" crowd. Latte 71SKK.

Restaurants

Caribic's Žižkova 1 ⓣ02/5441 8334. Known also as *Rybársky cech*. Excellent fish restaurant on the ground floor of the hotel (see p.1031) by the waterfront below the castle: pricey but worth it. Reservations recommended if you're going in the evening. Mains 300–1100SKK.

Chez David Zamocká 13. Classy kosher restaurant serving fresh, beautifully prepared Jewish cuisine. Mains 97–397SKK.

Modrá Hviezda Beblavého 14. Intimate cellar in the side of the castle serving traditional Pressburg (Bratislava) cuisine. Mains 145–520SKK.

Pizza Mizza Tobrucká 5. This place has a cute little terrace and a huge selection of pizzas. Pizza sticks 89SKK; mains 99–359SKK.

Sushi-Bar Tokyo Straková 2. Japanese and Thai specialities and Japanese drinks. Mains 120–290SKK.

Vegetarian Obchodná 58. Self-service vegetarian restaurant with traditional Slovak and International cuisine. Closed on weekends. Mains 70–90SKK.

Drinking and nightlife

There are few purely dance clubs, but you'll find plenty of late-opening pubs and bars helping to fill the gap.

Bars and clubs

Charlie Centrum Špitálska 4. Bratislava's longest-serving nightspot, with a multiscreen art-house cinema and a late-night bar/club in the basement.

GASTRO-BRATISLAVA

Bratislava is famous for its cosmopolitan gourmet culture, and you can find most cuisines represented at a variety of prices, all prepared with a good deal of pride and imagination. If you are going to spend a bit more than usual, this is the place to do it. Here's our pick of the best:

Camouflage, at Ventúrska 1 (ⓣ02/2092 2711) is a pricey but excellent restaurant with original pictures by Andy Warhol from the "Camouflage" series. Not only is the restaurant incredibly chic – the toilets alone are a work of art – but the food is phenomenal: the duck, for example, is succulent and juicy and comes with delicious couscous. The service is also impeccable. Mains are 500–600SKK.

Le Monde, at Rybárska Brána 8, Hviezdoslavovo námestie (ⓣ02 5441 5411) is another fantastic restaurant providing a beautifully stylish dining experience. The best seats are upstairs on the terrace, which affords great views of the city. Attentive service, perfectly executed mains and lovingly presented desserts. Mains 295-955SKK.

Dubliner Sedlárska 6. Very popular, stereotypical Irish bar – complete with cobbled floor – with live sports events on screens and occasional live music

El Diablo Sedlárska 4. Mexican-themed bar with lively late nights at weekends.

Gremium Gorkého 11. Busy sports bar, with a big screen, betting shop and a gallery area, along with a café upstairs.

Paparazzi Laurinská 1. Impeccably stylish cocktail bar complete with cool, black and white pictures of iconic bon vivants and a perfectly executed cocktail menu.

Slovak Pub Obchodná 62. The place to be. This large pub manages to be popular with both backpackers and local students.

Entertainment

Opera and ballet Slovak National Theatre, Historical Building: Hviezdoslavovo námestie. Tickets can be obtained here one hour before the performance (entrance from Jenesenského street) and cost 100–500SKK.; otherwise, use the cash desk in the new building, Pribinova 17 (ⓦwww.snd.sk).

Classical music The Reduta concert hall, Hviezdoslavovo námestie is home to the Slovak Philharmonic Orchestra. See ⓦwww.filharm.sk.

Cinema The Istropolis complex on Trnavské myto, Vajorská 100 (tram #2 from the station; tram #4 or #6 from the centre). Shows a range of current films. See ⓦwww.istropoliscinemacenter.sk.

Shopping

Michalská and Ventúrska are good places for general souvenir shopping; there are also plenty of souvenir stalls lining the main square.

Aupark Shopping Centre Einsteinova 18. Big shopping centre in the new town to suit most practical needs.

In Vivo Michalská 11; Panská 13. Cool and quirky home accessories.

Directory

Embassies and consulates Australia Ventúrská 10, ⓣ02/5443 2985; Canada Mostová 2 ⓣ02/5920 4031; UK Panská 16 ⓣ02/5441 9632; USA Hviedoslavovo námestie 5, ⓣ02/ 5443 3338.

Festivals The prestigious Bratislava Music Festival (ⓦwww.hc.sk), is held in October. If you're visiting in summer, don't miss the Summer Culture Festival (ⓦwww.bkis.sk), which has a range of (often free) events.

Hospital Policlinic Ruzinov on Ruzinova Street 10 (trams # 8, 9, 14).

Internet MEGAiNET, Klariská 5; 1SKK/minute.

Laundry Vydavatelstvo Perfekt Karpatska 7.

Left luggage Train stations daily 5.30am–midnight; bus station Mon–Fri 6am–10pm, Sat & Sun 6am–6pm.

Listings The tourist office (see above) stocks *Kam do mesta* (free) and the English-language *What's on Bratislava & Slovakia* (40SKK). The weekly *Slovak Spectator*, available from kiosks and hotels, has news and some listings.

Pharmacy Lekaren u Archaniela Gabriela, Obchodná 12.

Post office POFIS Námestie Slobody 27.

Moving on

Train Poprad-Tatry (7 daily; 4hr 12min–5hr); Košice (10 daily; 5hr 20min–7hr 10min).

Bus Poprad-Tatry (every 15min; 5hr 35min–7hr 45min) Košice (every 5–30 min; 6hr 50min–8hr).

Slovakia's mountain regions

The great virtue of Slovakia is its **mountains**, particularly the **High Tatras**, which, in their short span, reach Alpine heights and have an austere, stunning beauty. By far the country's most popular destination, they are, in fact, the least typical of Slovakia's mountains – predominantly densely forested, round-topped limestone ranges. In the heart of the mountains lie **small towns** originally settled by German miners in the thirteenth century, and still redolent of those times. Rail lines, where they exist, make for some of the most scenic **train journeys** in the country.

BANSKÁ ŠTIAVNICA

Set in picturesque country, the UNESCO-protected town of Banská Štiavnica is a previously German mining town, now faded into economic insignificance and content to slumber in the shadow of its former glory. The dwindling population gives the old town a distinctly isolated feel. Its sloping streets possess an almost ghostly air, haunted in the evenings by the town's small, but vocal, young population.

What to see and do

The principal sights are in the historic core of the town, whose nucleus is the main square, Námestie sv Trojice. There, you'll find the burgher houses, museum and gallery, with the old castle nearby to the west.

Námestie sv Trojice

In the main square is the red marble **Holy Trinity Column** and some pretty burgher houses; check out number 6, at Berggericht, which houses a diverse mineral collection. There is also the **Jozef Kollar Gallery** (Mon–Fri, 8am–5pm, last entry 2pm) at number 12, which focuses on the local twentieth-century Slovak painter: there are interesting temporary exhibitions of modern Slovak art and permanent collections of Gothic through to Baroque art.

The Old Castle

Starý zámok, the **Old Castle** (daily 9am–5pm May–Oct; Nov–April, Mon–Fri 8am–4pm). Begun in the thirteenth century, this rather austere castle currently houses sparse exhibits of **Baroque sculptures** and medieval blacksmiths' work. There are fine views of the town and the surrounding countryside from the church.

Klopačker

"**Clapper Tower**", up on Sládkoviča, houses a wooden clapper that stems from the tradition of raising miners out of bed at 5am. The klopačer itself dates from the seventeenth century, and it's definitely worth a visit here to get a sense of the town's *raison d'être*.

Arrival and information

Train and bus Both stations are at the bottom of a steep hill leading to the old town.
Tourist office Námestie sv Trojice 3, ⓣ045/694 9653, ⓦwww.banskastiavnica.sk. May–Sept 8am–5.30pm; Oct–April Mon–Fri 8am–4pm, Sat 8am–2pm.

Accommodation

Penzion Tomino Akademicá 9 ⓣ045/692 1307, ⓦwww.penziontomino.sk. Excellent price for its central location, and small, cheerful rooms. ❷
Salamander J Palárika 1 ⓣ045/691 39 92 ⓦwww.hotelsalamander.sk. Modern, spacious rooms with a restaurant below. ❹

Eating and drinking

Art Café Akademicá 2. Cool local hang-out; really more of a bar than a café, with a large selection of wines and occasional live music.
Jazz Café Kammerhofská. Cosy café with funky decor; great for coffee and cakes.
U Mateja Akademicá 4. Friendly restaurant with a good veggie selection. Mains 62–218SKK.

Moving on

Train Banska Bystrica (every 2hr; 1hr 10min–1hr 20min); Bratislava (every 2hrs; 3hr 30min–4hr 20min); Poprad (every 2hr; 4–6hr).
Bus Banska Bystrica (every 30min; 1hr 10min–1hr 25min); Bratislava (every 30min–1hr 30min; 3hr 30min–4hrs 15mins); Poprad (every 1hr–1hr 30min; 3hr 30min–4hr 10min).

THE HIGH TATRAS

Rising like a giant granite reef above the patchwork Poprad plain, the **High Tatras** are the main reason for venturing this far into Slovakia. Even after all the tourist-board hype, they are still an inspirational sight. A wilderness, however, they are not; all summer, visitors are shoulder to shoulder in the necklace of resorts that sit at the foot of the mountains – and in winter, skiers take over. Sadly, a huge storm in 2004 uprooted much of the pine forest here, but, once you're surrounded by bare primeval scree slopes and icy blue tarns, nothing can take away the exhilaration or the breathtaking views.

To make the most of your visit, use **Poprad** as the transport hub, but try to go straight on to one of the mountain resorts. The best base in the mountains is the scattered settlement of **Stary Smokovec**.

Arrival and Information

Train The mainline train station for the Tatras is Poprad-Tatry in Poprad. From there, cute, red tram-like trains (TEZ; hourly; 35 min to Stary Smokovec; 10SKK) trundle across the fields, linking Poprad with the string of resorts and spas halfway up the Tatras within the Tatra National Park.

Tourist office At the western end of námestie sv Egidia (Mon–Fri 9am–5pm, Sat 9am–noon; July & Aug Mon–Fri 8am–6pm, Sat 9am–1pm, Sun 1–4pm; ⓣ052/16 186, ⓦwww.poprad.sk).

Accommodation

The tourist office at Stary Smokovec – in the modern white building about 100m to your left as you face the *Grand Hotel* – can help with accommodation (Mon–Fri 8/9am–4/5pm; in summer also Sat & Sun 8am–2pm; ⓣ052/442 34 40, ⓦwww.tatry.sk).

Eurocamp FICC just south of Tatranská Lomnica ⓣ052/446 77413, ⓦwww.eurocamp-ficc.sk. Bungalows with hot showers, and a restaurant and café on site. The campsite has its own train station: either take the ordinary train from Poprad-Tatry via Studený Potok or the TEZ, changing at Starý Smokovec and Tatranská Lomnica. ❶

Hotel Atrium Novy Smokovec 42 ⓣ52 442 2342-4, ⓦwww.atriumhotel.sk. Distinctively circular in shape, this hotel offers rooms with wonderful views of the Tatras. ❻

Hotel Smokovec Starý Smokovec 25 ⓣ52 442 5191-3, ⓦwww.hotelsmokovec.sk. This hotel has bright, inviting rooms and its own well-equipped fitness centre. ❹

Activities

Climbing To climb here, you have to be a member of a recognized climbing club with a

HIKING IN THE TATRAS

Any illusions of wilderness are vanquished for most people as they set off on trails behind Starý Smokovec among a herd of other hikers. If not, being overtaken by the ground cable car or an ice cream van in the first few minutes will probably do it. Take heart, though, because a hike in the Tatras invariably culminates in spectacular scenery.

Hiking is best from July to September, when the views are wonderfully clear. Many paths are open year-round, though high-level paths, above the mountain huts, are open mid-June to October only.

The most straightforward and rewarding climb from Starý Smokovec is to follow the blue-marked path that leads from behind the *Grand* to the summit of Slavkovský štít (2452m), a return journey of nine hours. Alternatively, a narrow-gauge funicular, starting from behind the *Grand* (daily 7.30am–7pm, closed May & Nov), climbs 250m to Hrebienok chatty.

Don't go without the green 1:25 000 Vysoké Tatry hiking map (available from the tourist office); walking boots; water; food; and waterproofs. For daily weather reports and more information on hiking go to the Horská služba (mountain rescue), just uphill from Starý Smokovec station, ⓣ052/442 28 20, ⓦwww.hzs.sk.

Cable car

If you don't have the time or inclination to hike, you can still enjoy fabulous views by taking a series of **cable cars** (daily 8.30am–3.50/5.50pm; book at least two or three days in advance; closed May & Nov) from Tatranská Lomnica to the summit of Lomnický štít (2632m), the Tatras' second-highest peak.

valid membership card or you must hire a guide. The latter can be done from the Spolok horských vodcov, ⓣ052/442 20 66, ⓦwww.tatraguide.sk.
Skiing The ski season runs from December to March and there are plenty of places in Starý Smokovec to rent equipment. Štrbské Pleso hosts the national and international skiing events, ⓦwww.parksnow.sk.

Moving On

Train Košice (hourly; 1hr 7min–1hr 55min).
Bus Levoča (twice hourly; 15–45min); Spišské Podhradie (hourly; 25min–1hr 10min); Prešov (hourly; 1hr 05min–2hr).

East Slovakia

Stretching from the High Tatras east to the Ukrainian border, the landscape of **East Slovakia** is decidedly different from the rest of the country. Ethnically, this is probably the most diverse region in the country, with different groups coexisting even within a single valley. The majority of the country's Romanies live here, mostly on the edge of Slovak villages, in shantytowns of almost medieval squalor. In the ribbon-villages of the north and east, the Rusyn minority struggle to preserve their culture and religion, while along the southern border there are large numbers of Hungarians. After spending time in the rural backwaters, you will find cosmopolitan **Košice** a **lively return to city life.**

The land that stretches northeast up the Poprad Valley to the Polish border and east along the River Hornád towards Prešov is known as the **Spiš** region, for centuries a semi-autonomous province within the Hungarian kingdom. Worth a visit for the architectural remnants of the Renaissance, the region's tourist growth reflects interest in its ethnic diversity and a wealthy cultural heritage.

LEVOČA

Some 25km east of Poprad, across a broad sweep of undulating Spiš countryside, the ravishingly beautiful walled town of **LEVOČA**, set on a slight incline, has a wonderfully medieval look.

What to see and do

Inside the walls of the historic town, the crumbling streets lead up to Námestie Majstra Pavla, the main square and heart of the town. Here, you'll find many of the town's attractions and restaurants. The backstreets are easy and fascinating to explore, set out on a grid system, with most streets leading to the city walls.

To the north is the square's least distinguished but most important building, the **municipal weigh-house**; a law of 1321 obliged every merchant passing through the region to hole up at Levoča for fourteen days, pay various taxes and allow the locals first refusal on their goods.

SV Jakub

The Catholic church of **SV Jakub** (Mon 11/11.30am–4/5pm, Tues–Sat 8.30/9am–4/5pm, Sun 1–4/5pm; Nov–Easter closed Sun & Mon) is crammed with **religious art**, the star attraction being the magnificent sixteenth-century wooden altarpiece by Master Pavol of Levoča – at 18.6m, reputedly the tallest of its kind in the world. The church can be visited only with a guide, and tours (every 30min, hourly in winter) leave from the ticket office opposite the main entrance. A small **museum** (daily 9am–5pm) dedicated to Master Pavol stands opposite the church on the eastern side of the square.

Town hall

South of the church is the **town hall** (daily 8/9am–4/5pm), built in a sturdy Renaissance style. On the first floor, there's a museum on the Spiš region, and some fine examples of Spiš handicrafts on the top floor.

SPIŠSKÉ HRAD

It's easy to see why **Spišské hrad** (May–Oct daily 9am–6pm) finds its way into almost every tourist brochure. This pile of chalk-white ruins, strung out on a bleak hill, is irresistibly photogenic and the demanding climb to the top is rewarded by the stunning panorama of the Spiš countryside. From Levoča, buses to **Spišské Podhradie** leave up to every half-hour, and the journey takes 25min.

Alternatively, explore Spis* countryside on **horseback**: contact Penzíon Podzámok, ⓣ053/4541 755, ⓦwww.penzionpodzamok.sk for further details.

Lutheran Church

The last building in the centre of the square is the oddly squat Lutheran church, built in an uncompromisingly Neoclassical style: you may want to visit for comparison with the more lavish Catholic Church to get a sense of the difference in ethos between the two denominations.

Arrival and information

Bus The bus station is a ten-minute walk southeast of the old town. If you're coming from the east get off one stop earlier at the Košice gate.
Tourist office Located in the northwest corner of the main square (May–Sept Mon–Fri 10am–4.30pm, Sat & Sun 9.30am–1.30pm; Oct–April Mon–Fri 9am–4.30pm, Sat 9am–noon; ⓣ053/451 37 63, ⓦwww.levoca.sk).

Accommodation

There is an abundance of private rooms, which the tourist office (see above) can help organize.
Hotel Barbakan Košická 15 ⓣ053/451 43 10, ⓦwww.barbakan.sk. Friendly and tasteful hotel with an atmospheric restaurant; doubles ❺
Hotel U Leva Námestie Majstra Pavla 25 ⓣ053/450 23 11, ⓦwww.uleva.sk. A welcoming, well-cared-for hotel with a lovely restaurant attached (see below). Rooms are modern and comfortable and staff are friendly and tirelessly accommodating. ❻
Penzión pri Košickej bráne Košická 16 ⓣ053/469 79 13, ⓦwww.penzionkosicka.sk. A cheaper, adequate option. ❸

Campsite

Kováčova vila Campsite 3km north of Levoča. Fishing and watersports facilities available. ❶

Eating

Pizzeria Vetrová 4. Popular with locals, this no-nonsense restaurant has a decent selection of pizzas, 110–160SKK.
Restaurant U Leva Námestie Majstra Pavla 25. Accomplished, well-presented food, with a large selection of fish and meat dishes, at great prices. Mains 87–195SKK.

Moving on

Bus Spišské Podhradie (every 5–30min; 10–30min); Prešov (every 25min; 50min–1hr 55 min).

PREŠOV

Capital of the Slovak Šariš region and a cultural centre for the Rusyn (Ruthenian) minority, **PREŠOV** has the lively student population to thank for its youthful, vibrant feel.

What to see and do

Most attractions lie along the main square, where you'll find a good selection of restaurants. Hlavná is the main street, which runs along the square, a twenty-minute walk north from the main bus and train stations.

Greek Catholic Cathedral

At the tip of Hlavná ulica, a main square flanked by creamy eighteenth-century facades, is the **Catholic Cathedral**, dedicated to John the Baptist and decked out in grand Rococo style.

Town Hall and Rákóziho Dom

The unsuitably small balcony of the **Town hall** is historically significant: it was where Béla Kun's Hungarian Red Army declared the short-lived Slovak Socialist Republic in 1919.

Situated in the dogtooth-gabled **Rákócziho dom** at no. 86 (Tues 9am–6pm, Wed–Fri 9am–5pm, Sun 1–6pm), is a museum offering a thorough account of the history of the town and the Šariš region.

Catholic and Protestant Churches

The Catholic and Protestant churches vie with each other at the widest point of the square: the fourteenth-century Catholic church of **sv Mikuláš** has the edge, not least for its modern Moravian stained-glass windows and its sumptuous Baroque altarpiece. Behind sv Mikulás is the much plainer **Lutheran church**, built in the mid-seventeenth century.

Arrival and information

Train and bus The bus and train stations are opposite each other about 1km south of the main square; buses and trolleybuses into town stop at Na Hlavnej.
Tourist office Hlavná 67, 100m from the town hall (Mon–Fri 9am–6pm, Sat 9am–1pm; ⓣ051/773 11 13, ⓦwww.presov.sk).
Internet *Film Café* at Hlavná 121.

Accommodation

Pension Antonio Jarková 22 ⓣ051/772 32 25, ⓦwww.antoniopension.sk. Idiosyncratic little pension in the historic centre. ❹

Penzion Adam Jarková 16 ⓣ051/758 17 89, ⓦwww.penzionadam.sk. Delightfully friendly pension, with two apartments, and fourteen well-equipped rooms. Doubles ❺; apartments ❼

Eating and nightlife

On warm summer evenings, Hlavná street literally buzzes with people dining alfresco.
Carpe diem Hlavná 95. One of Prešov's more hip bar/restaurants, with average cocktails. Mains 165–650SKK; cocktails 50–140SKK.
Chevalier Hlavná 69. Ideal for winter eating in the cosy, medieval-style vaulted cellar, or sit outside in summer. Mains 18–84SKK.
Staré Mexico Jarková 16. Themed pub with occasional live music.

Moving on

Train Košice (daily; 1hr).
Bus Košice (up to 7 daily; 30–55min); Levoča (daily; 1–2hrs).

KOŠICE

KOŠICE is a candidate for the 2013 European Capital of Culture, and preparation for this has really put a spring in its step. The city has a number of worthwhile museums and what is arguably Slovakia's finest cathedral. Just 21km north of the Hungarian border, Košice also acts as a magnet for the Hungarian community – to whom the city is known as Kassa – and the underemployed Romanies of the surrounding region, lending it a diversity and vibrancy absent from small-town Slovakia.

What to see and do

Hlavné Námestie is the main square and the nucleus of city life. The singing fountain by the state theatre in its centre is a popular spot for meeting, people-watching and generally cooling off on hot summer days. The square is lined with attractions, restaurants and quirky activities such as giant chess in the summer and, currently, competitions for participation in Košice's 2013 Capital of Culture bid.

Cathedral of St Elizabeth

This fine **Gothic Cathedral is dedicated to St Elizabeth** of Hungary; there are scenes from her life on the right-hand side of the altar; its charcoal-coloured stone was recently sandblasted back to the original honeyed hue. Begun in 1378, it's an unusual building from the outside, with striped roof tiles and two contorted towers – one of them serves as a vantage point (Mon–Fri 9.30am–4.30pm, Sat 9am–1.30pm). On the busy north side of the cathedral is the fourteenth-century **Urbanova veža**, the town tower, standing on its own set of mini-arcades.

Mikuluš Prison

This is a macabre attraction (Tues–Sat 9am–5pm, Sun 9am–1pm), east off the square down Univerzitna, whose original dimly lit dungeons and claustrophobic cells transport you into its history as the **city prison** and torture chamber. More thought-provoking than frightening, it contains exhibits of torture instruments and musky underground chambers.

East Slovak Museum

At the northern tip of the main square, námestie Maratónu mieru is flanked to the east and west by the bulky nineteenth-century **East Slovak Museum** (Tues–Sat 9am–5pm, Sun 9am–1pm), filled with medieval and Baroque religious art. It's worth visiting to see the portraits of Maria Theresa and Josef II – two of the most influential people in Slovakia's history – and to gain a sense of the evolution of the use of materials in religious art from the Gothic to the Baroque period. There is also a small but informative room dedicated to **Eastern Slovak Ethnography**.

Arrival and information

Train and bus The train and bus stations are opposite each other. Walk west through the Municipal Park towards the old town; it's a 10min walk.

Tourist office Hlavná 59 (Mon–Fri 9am–6pm, Sat 8am–1pm; ⓣ055/6258888, ⓦwww.kosice.sk). It has Internet access.

Internet At the tourist office (see above).

Listings *Best in Košice* is a free booklet available from the Tourist Information Office and has listings for hotels, restaurants, nightlife and attractions.

Accommodation

Hostels

The tourist office can help with finding rooms and sorting out accommodation in student hostels in the summer holidays.

Student Hostel Podhradová 11 ⓣ055/633 34 37. Cheap and basic hostel, but clean. July–Aug only. ❶

Domov Mládeže Medická 2 ⓣ055/643 56 88, ⓦwww.dmmed.kecom.sk. Outside of the city centre, *Domov Mládeže* is a big block of a hostel, with very basic, but comfortable rooms. ❶

Hotels

Centrum Južná trieda 2a, ⓣ055/678 31 01, ⓦwww.hotel-centrum.sk. Big and ugly on the outside, but with adequate rooms, this is a five-minute walk south of the main square, on the way to the train and bus stations. ❺

Penzion Slovakia Orlia 6, ⓣ055/728 98 20, ⓦwww.penzionslovakia.sk. Centrally located and very friendly; each room is devoted to a different Slovakian town. ❺

Campsite

A T C Salaš Barca ⓣ055/623 33 97. Thirty pitches over two hectares with a swimming pool. Open May–Oct. ❶

Eating

Ajvega Orlia 10. A popular vegetarian place with a summer terrace, serving soya versions of standard Slovak dishes and fresh juices. Mains 65–99SKK.

Kleopatra Pizza Bar Hlavná 24. Irrepressibly upbeat with outdoor tables in summer overlooking the gardens to the south of the cathedral. Pizzas 68–170SKK.

Sedliacky dvor Biela 3. Decorated in the style of an old country cottage, this restaurant serves up hearty traditional cuisine to match. Mains 150–250SKK.

Slavia *Hotel Slavia*, Hlavná 63. Coffee or cocktails in a stylish Art Nouveau setting.

Drinking and nightlife

Košice's nightlife largely takes place in the main square and surrounding streets.

Cosmopolitan Cocktail Bar Kováčska 9. One of the city's more hip bars, with genuine energy and an international ethos.

Jazz Club Kováčska 39. Cosy ambience, often with live jazz and other live music.

Music Pub Diesel Hlavná 92. Irish themed pub serving Guinness and an array of Czech beers; at its liveliest on Friday nights.

Moving on

Train Prešov (11 daily; 40min); Bratislava (daily; 5–9hr).
Bus Poprad (every 1–2hr; 2hr 15min–2hr 45min); Prešov (every 10–20min; 30–55min).

Slovenia

HIGHLIGHTS

PTUJ: Slovenia's oldest settlement is also the most endearing

LAKE BOHINJ: pearl of Slovenian lakes

KOBARID MUSEUM, SOČA VALLEY: immensely beautiful valley, compelling museum

OLD TOWN LJUBLJANA: stunning architecture, a hilltop castle and leafy riverside cafés

ŠKOCJAN CAVES: magnificent underground canyon

PIRAN: historic coastal town strewn with gorgeous Venetian Gothic architecture and pretty squares

ROUGH COSTS

DAILY BUDGET Basic €30/with the occasional treat €50

DRINK Pivo (beer) €2.50 for half a litre

FOOD Pizzas €5–7

HOSTEL/BUDGET HOTEL €10–20/€60–80

TRAVEL Ljubljana–Maribor (130km) €9 by train; Ljubljana–Bled (65km) €7 by bus

FACT FILE

POPULATION 2 million

AREA 20,273 sq km

LANGUAGE Slovenian

CURRENCY Euro (€)

CAPITAL Ljubljana

INTERNATIONAL PHONE CODE ⓣ386

Basics

Stable, prosperous and welcoming, Slovenia is a charming and comfortable place to travel, with an array of spectacular sights. The country managed to avoid much of the strife that plagued other nations during the messy disintegration of the Yugoslav Republic, and has integrated quickly with western Europe, joining the euro zone at the start of 2007. Administered by German-speaking overlords until 1918, Slovenes absorbed the culture of their rulers while managing to retain a strong sense of ethnic identity through their Slavic language.

Slovenia's sophisticated capital, **Ljubljana**, is easily the best of the cities, manageably small and cluttered with Baroque and Habsburg buildings. Elsewhere, the Julian Alps provide stunning mountain scenery, most accessible at **Lake Bled** and **Lake Bohinj**, and most memorable along the **Soča Valley**. Further south are spectacular caves, including those at **Postojna** and **Škocjan**, while the short stretch of Slovenian coast is punctuated by two starkly different towns: **Piran** and **Portorož**. In the eastern, wine-making reaches, **Ptuj** is Slovenia's oldest and most well-preserved town, while the country's second city, **Maribor**, is a worthwhile stopover point on the way to Austria.

CHRONOLOGY

181 BC The Romans conquer the area of present day Slovenia.
550 AD Slavs begin to inhabit the area.
600s The first Slovenian state, the Duchy of Carantania, is established.
745 The Frankish Empire takes over Carantania, and converts the Slavs to Christianity.
1335 The Habsburgs take control of Slovenian regions through marriage.
1550 First book is published in the Slovenian language.
1867 Slovenia is brought under the direct control of Austria.
Late 1800s Growth of Slovenian nationalism.
1918 Following the collapse of the Austro-Hungarian Empire after WWI, Slovenia is incorporated into the Kingdom of the Serbs, Croats and Slovenes.
1929 The Kingdom is renamed Yugoslavia.
1945 After being occupied by the Germans during WWII, a liberation force led by Slovenian General Tito incorporates Slovenia into the Republic of Socialist Yugoslavia.
1950s The industrialisation of Slovenia leads to rapid economic development.
1980 General Tito dies; disintegration of Yugoslavia begins.
1990 Slovenians vote for independence in a referendum.
1991 Slovenia declares its independence from Socialist Yugoslavia, leading to a ten-day war with the Yugoslav army. The Slovenians win.
2003 The oldest wooden wheel in the world, thought to be 5000 years old, is discovered in Slovenia.
2004 Slovenia joins NATO as well as the EU.
2007 Slovenia is the first former communist state to adopt the European single currency.

ARRIVAL

Direct **flights** to Slovenia from the UK are increasing in number, with low-cost carrier easyJet (Ⓦwww.easyjet.com) flying daily to Ljubljana, and Ryanair (Ⓦwww.ryanair.com) operating a new London Stansted–Maribor route three times a week. Otherwise, Slovenia's location – wedged between Austria, Croatia, Hungary and Italy – makes it easily approachable by **road** or **rail**; Ljubljana is well connected by bus and train with major cities in all four countries. Access to the Slovene coast is also straightforward: buses arrive daily from Trieste (Italy) and Pula (Croatia), and you can also enter the country via a ferry from Venice.

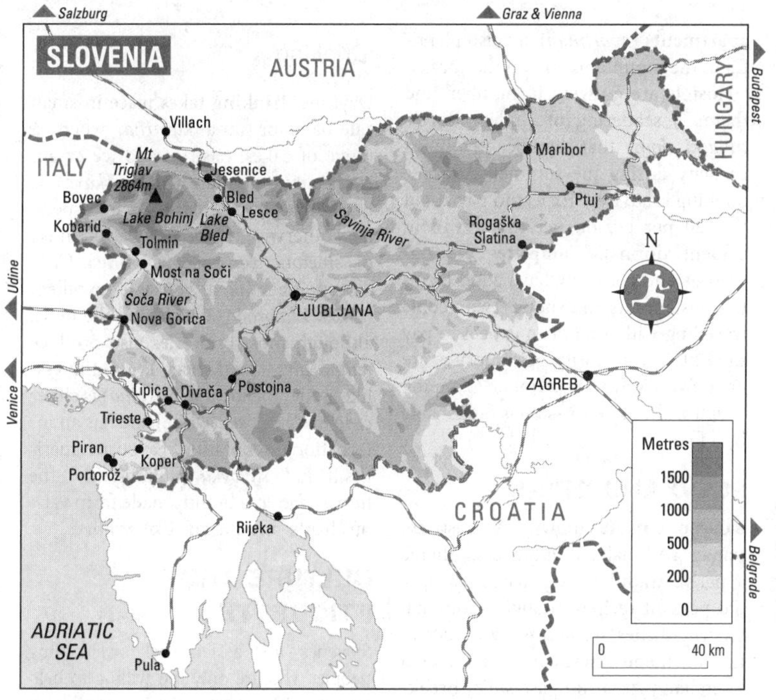

GETTING AROUND

Slovene Railways (Slovenske železnice; ⓦwww.slo-zeleznice.si) is smooth and efficient. **Trains** (*vlaki*) are divided into slow (*LP*), and Intercity (IC) express trains, as well as the fast Inter City Slovenia trains (ICS) between Ljubljana and Maribor. Reservations (*rezervacije*) are obligatory, but free, on ICS trains, and there is a €5 booking fee for international trains to Italy. Most timetables have English notes; "departures" is *odhodi*, "arrivals" is *prihodi*. Eurail and InterRail passes are valid. Some weekend return journeys qualify for a 30 percent discount – ask at the ticket office.

The **bus** network consists of an array of local companies offering a reliable service. Towns such as Ljubljana, Maribor and Koper have big bus stations, where you can buy your tickets in advance – recommended if you're travelling between Ljubljana and the coast in high season. Elsewhere, simply pay the driver or conductor. You'll be charged extra for cumbersome items of baggage.

All public transport services are significantly reduced on Sundays.

ACCOMMODATION

Accommodation is universally clean and good quality. In the capital, expect to pay from €50 for a double at a two-star **hotel**, from €75 for three stars. Family-run **pensions** in rural areas, especially the mountains, offer the same facilities as hotels but usually at a lower price. **Private rooms** (*zasebne sobe*) are available throughout Slovenia, with bookings often made by the local tourist office or travel agents like Kompas. Rooms are pretty good value at about €30–40 for a double, although stays of three nights or less are invariably subject to a harsh surcharge of up to fifty percent in peak season. Self-catering apartments (*apartmaji*) are also plentiful in the mountains and on the coast.

Hostels are growing in number, and there's a scattering of student dorms (*dijaški dom*) that significantly boost capacity during the summer. Advance booking is advised. Expect to pay about €17–20 per person per night (€10 in student dorms). **Campsites** are numerous and generally have good facilities, restaurants and shops. Two people travelling with a tent can expect to pay €15–20. The majority of campsites are open from May to September. Camping rough without permission is punishable by a fine.

FOOD AND DRINK

Slovene **cuisine** draws on Austrian, Italian and Balkan influences. There's a native tradition, too, based on age-old peasant recipes, though traditional Slovene dishes are becoming harder to find on menus increasingly dominated by Italian pizzas and pastas. For **breakfast** and **snacks**, *okrepčevalnice* (snack bars) and street kiosks dole out *burek*, a flaky pastry filled with cheese (*sirov burek*) or meat (*burek z mesom*). Sausages come in various forms, most commonly *kranjska klobasa* (big spicy sausages). **Menus** in a *restavracija* (restaurant) or *gostilna* (inn) will invariably include roast meats (*pečenka*) and schnitzels (*zrezek*). Goulash (*golaž*) is also common. Two traditional dishes are *žlikrofi*, ravioli filled with potato, onion and bacon; and *žganci*, once the staple diet of rural Slovenes, a buckwheat or maize porridge often served with sauerkraut. Few local dishes are suitable for **vegetarians**, though international restaurants will usually offer something veggie. On the coast you'll find plenty of fish (*riba*), mussels (*žkoljke*) and squid (*kalamari*). Typical **desserts** include strudel filled with apple or rhubarb; *žtruklji*, dumplings with fruit filling; and *prekmurska gibanica*, a delicious local cheesecake.

Drinking

Daytime **drinking** takes place in small café-bars, or in a *kavarna*, where a range of cakes, pastries and ice cream is usually on offer. **Coffee** (*kava*) is generally served black unless specified otherwise – ask for *mleko* (milk) or *smetana* (cream), as is **tea** (*čaj*). Slovene **beer** (*pivo*) is usually excellent (*Laško Zlatorog* is considered the best), although most breweries also produce *temno pivo* ("dark beer"), a Guinness-like stout. The local **wine** (*vino*) is either *črno* (red) or *belo* (white) and has an international reputation. Favourite aperitifs include *slivovka* (plum brandy), the fiery *sadjevec*, a brandy made from various fruits, and the gin-like *brinovec*.

CULTURE AND ETIQUETTE

Slovenes are a laid-back, welcoming people, who are only too willing to help tourists. The predominant religion is Catholicism, and respectful attire (no sleeveless tops or above-the-knee skirts) should be worn inside churches and around religious sites. Tipping is generally not required, though always welcome.

SPORTS AND OUTDOOR ACTIVITIES

Slovenia's dramatic and varied landscape provides ample opportunities for any number of sporting activities, be it **hiking**, **cycling** and **rafting** in summer, or **skiing** in winter. Most places cater well for the adventure-seeking visitor, especially in the mountains, with healthy competition generally keeping prices fair. Local tourist offices will have comprehensive information on activities and sporting agencies in the town. For more information see boxes on p.1054 and p.1057.

COMMUNICATIONS

Most **post offices** (*pošta*) are open Mon–Fri 8am–6/7pm and Sat 8am–noon.

Slovene

	Slovene	Pronunciation
Yes	*Ja*	Ya
No	*Ne*	Ne
Please	*Prosim*	Proseem
Thank you	*Hvala*	Huala
Hello/Good day	*Živijo/dober dan*	Jeeveeyo/dober dan
Goodbye	*Nasvidenje*	Nasveedenye
Excuse me	*Oprostite*	Oprosteete
Where?	*Kje?*	Kye
Good	*Dobro*	Dobro
Bad	*Slabo*	Slabo
Near	*Blizu*	Bleezoo
Far	*Dalеč*	Daalech
Cheap	*Poceni*	Potzenee
Expensive	*Drago*	Drago
Open	*Odprto*	Odpurto
Closed	*Zaprto*	Zapurto
Today	*Danes*	Danes
Yesterday	*Včeraj*	Ucheray
Tomorrow	*Jutri*	Yutree
How much is....?	*Koliko stane...?*	Koleeko stane...?
What time is it?	*Koliko je ura?*	Koleeko ye oora?
I don't understand	*Ne razumem*	Ne razoomem
Do you speak English?	*Ali govorite angleško?*	Alee govoreete angleshko?
One	*Ena*	Ena
Two	*Dve*	Dve
Three	*Tri*	Tree
Four	*Štiri*	Shteeree
Five	*Pet*	Pet
Six	*Šest*	Shest
Seven	*Sedem*	Sedem
Eight	*Osem*	Osem
Nine	*Devet*	Devet
Ten	*Deset*	Deset

Stamps (*znamke*) can also be bought at newsstands. Public **phones** use cards (*telekartice*; €3, €4, €7, €14.5), available from post offices, kiosks and tobacconists. Make long-distance and international calls at a post office, where you're assigned to a cabin and given the bill afterwards. **Internet** access is now fairly widespread – expect to pay around €2–4/hr.

EMERGENCIES

The **police** (*policija*) are generally easy-going and likely to speak some English. **Pharmacies** (*lekarna*) follow shop hours, and a rota system covers night-time opening; details are in the window of each pharmacy.

EMERGENCY NUMBERS

Police ☎113; Ambulance & Fire ☎112.

INFORMATION AND MAPS

Most towns and resorts have a **tourist information office**, some of which rent private rooms. A very high standard of English is spoken pretty much eve-

SLOVENIA ON THE NET

www.bled.si Useful site to Slovenia's most popular destinations.
www.slovenia.info Official tourist board site.
www.ljubljana.si Detailed information on sights and events in the capital.
www.burger.si Superb interactive maps and panoramic photos.

rywhere. Freytag & Berndt publishes a good 1:300,000 **country map**, while the Slovene Alpine Association's excellent **hiking maps** (www.pzs.si) are widely available in bookshops.

MONEY AND BANKS

Slovenia adopted the euro in January 2007. **Banks** (*banka*) generally open Mon–Fri 8.30am–12.30pm & 2–5pm, Sat 8.30am–11am/noon. You can also change money in tourist offices, post offices, travel agencies and exchange bureaux (*menjalnica*). **Credit cards** are accepted in a large number of hotels and restaurants, and **ATMs** are widespread.

OPENING HOURS AND HOLIDAYS

Most **shops** open Mon–Fri 8am–7pm and Sat 8am–1pm; an increasing number open on Sun. Museum times vary, but many close on Mondays. All shops and banks are closed on the following **public holidays**: Jan 1 & 2, Feb 8, Easter Mon, April 27, May 1 & 2, June 25, Aug 15, Oct 31, Nov 1, Dec 25 & 26.

STUDENT & YOUTH DISCOUNTS

The EURO<26 card (€8.35) is valid in Slovenia, and can be used to get discounts on many attractions. You can also purchase the affiliated SŽ-EURO<26 (€17; from most train stations) to get an additional 30 percent off train fares within Slovenia, and 25 percent off international rail travel.

Ljubljana

The Slovene capital **LJUBLJANA** curls under its castle-topped hill, an old centre marooned in the shapeless modernity that stretches out across the plain, a vital and fast-growing capital. The city's sights are only part of the picture; first and foremost Ljubljana is a place to meet people and to get involved in the nightlife – the buildings just provide the backdrop.

What to see and do

Ljubljana's main point of reference is **Slovenska cesta**, a busy north–south thoroughfare that slices the city down the middle. Most of the sights are within easy walking distance of here, with the **Old Town** straddling the River Ljubljanica to the south and east and the nineteenth-century quarter to the west, where the principal museums and galleries are.

The Old Town

From the bus and train stations head south down Miklošičeva for ten minutes and you'll reach **Prešernov trg**, the hub around which everything in Ljubljana's delightful **Old Town** revolves. Overlooking the bustling square and the River Ljubljanica, the Baroque seventeenth-century **Church of the Annunciation** (daily 9am–noon & 3–7pm), blushes a sandy red; it's worth a look inside for Francesco Robba's marble high-altar, richly adorned with spiral columns and plastic figurines. Robba, an Italian architect and sculptor, was brought in to remodel the city in its eighteenth-century heyday. His best piece, a beautifully sculpted **fountain** that symbolizes the meeting of the rivers Sava, Krka and Ljubljanica, lies across the river, in front of the town hall on Mestni trg. To get there cross the elegant **Tromostovje** (Triple Bridge), one of many innovative creations by Jože Plečnik in Ljubljana, his birthplace. A local darling, Plečnik made his mark on the city between the two world wars with his classically inspired designs, and in doing so brought Ljubljana into Europe's architectural elite.

St Nicholas' Cathedral and the market

A little east of Mestni trg, on Ciril-Metodov trg, **St Nicholas' Cathedral** (daily 6am–noon & 3–6pm; free) is the most sumptuous and overblown of Ljubljana's Baroque statements. Smothered with fabulous frescoes, this is the best preserved of the city's ecclesiastical buildings. Along the riverside, you can't fail to miss Plečnik's **colonnaded market** (closed Sun). Just beyond the market, also take a look at the beautiful **Dragon Bridge**, each corner pylon topped with spitting dragons – the city's symbol.

The Castle

Opposite the market, Študentovska winds up the thickly wooded hillside to the **Castle** (daily 9/10am–9/10pm), originally a twelfth-century construction whose present appearance dates from the sixteenth century, following an earthquake in 1511. Within the castle, the **Virtual Museum** (daily 9/10am–6/10pm; €3.30 including entrance to clock tower) presents the development of the city in the form of an enlightening 3D visual presentation. Climb the **clock tower** for a superlative view of the Old Town below and the magnificent Kamniške Alps to the north. A **funicular railway** (€2 return) provides an easier way up and down the castle hill.

South of Prešernov trg

Back on the western side of the river, further south on Slovenska cesta, the park-like expanse of Kongresni trg slopes away from the early eighteenth-

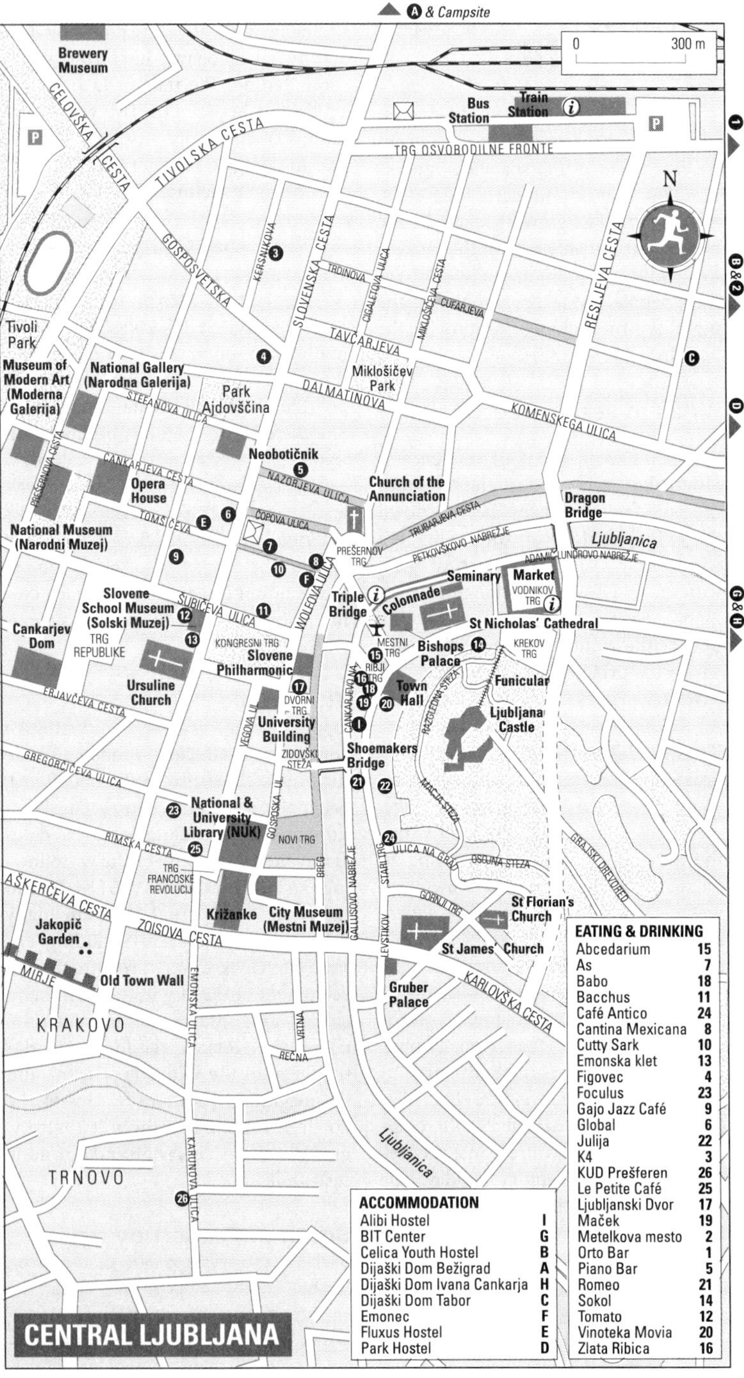
CENTRAL LJUBLJANA
A & Campsite
0 300 m
Museum of Modern History
Brewery Museum
Bus Station
Train Station
TRG OSVOBODILNE FRONTE
Tivoli Park
Museum of Modern Art (Moderna Galerija)
National Gallery (Narodna Galerija)
Park Ajdovščina
Miklošičev Park
Neobotičnik
Opera House
Church of the Annunciation
Dragon Bridge
Ljubljanica
National Museum (Narodni Muzej)
PREŠERNOV TRG
Seminary
Market
VODNIKOV TRG
Triple Bridge
Colonnade
St Nicholas' Cathedral
Slovene School Museum (Solski Muzej)
Cankarjev Dom
TRG REPUBLIKE
KONGRESNI TRG
Slovene Philharmonic
MESTNI TRG
Bishops Palace
KREKOV TRG
RIBJI TRG
Town Hall
Funicular
Ursuline Church
DVORNI TRG
University Building
Ljubljana Castle
ZIDOVSKI STEZA
Shoemakers Bridge
National & University Library (NUK)
NOVI TRG
TRG FRANCOSKE REVOLUCIJ
Križanke
City Museum (Mestni Muzej)
St Florian's Church
St James' Church
Jakopič Garden
Old Town Wall
Gruber Palace
KRAKOVO
TRNOVO
CELOVŠKA CESTA
TIVOLSKA CESTA
GOSPOSVETSKA
KERSNIKOVA
SLOVENSKA CESTA
TRDINOVA
CIGALETOVA ULICA
MIKLOŠIČEVA CESTA
ČUFARJEVA
RESLJEVA CESTA
TAVČARJEVA
DALMATINOVA
KOMENSKEGA ULICA
ŠTEFANOVA ULICA
PREŠERNOVA CESTA
CANKARJEVA CESTA
NAZORJEVA ULICA
TOMŠIČEVA
ČOPOVA ULICA
TRUBARJEVA CESTA
PETKOVŠKOVO NABREŽJE
ADAMIČ-LUNDROVO NABREŽJE
WOLFOVA ULICA
ŠUBIČEVA ULICA
ERJAVČEVA CESTA
VEGOVA UL
CANKARJEVO NABREŽJE
GREGORČIČEVA ULICA
GOSPOSKA UL
REBER
ŠTREKLJEVA STEZA
MACJA STEZA
RIMSKA CESTA
BREG
GALLUSOVO NABREŽJE
STARI TRG
ULICA NA GRAD
OSOJNA STEZA
GRAJSKI DREVORED
GORNJI TRG
AŠKERČEVA CESTA
ZOISOVA CESTA
LEVSTIKOV
KARLOVŠKA CESTA
MIRJE
EMONSKA ULICA
VRTNA
REČNA
KARUNOVA ULICA
EATING & DRINKING
Abcedarium 15
As 7
Babo 18
Bacchus 11
Café Antico 24
Cantina Mexicana 8
Cutty Sark 10
Emonska klet 13
Figovec 4
Foculus 23
Gajo Jazz Café 9
Global 6
Julija 22
K4 3
KUD Prešferen 26
Le Petite Café 25
Ljubljanski Dvor 17
Maček 19
Metelkova mesto 2
Orto Bar 1
Piano Bar 5
Romeo 21
Sokol 14
Tomato 12
Vinoteka Movia 20
Zlata Ribica 16
ACCOMMODATION
Alibi Hostel I
BIT Center G
Celica Youth Hostel B
Dijaški Dom Bežigrad A
Dijaški Dom Ivana Cankarja H
Dijaški Dom Tabor C
Emonec F
Fluxus Hostel E
Park Hostel D

SLOVENIA
LJUBLJANA

century **Ursuline Church**, whose looming Baroque coffee-cake exterior is one of the city's most impressive. Vegova Ulica leads south from Kongresni trg towards Trg francoske revolucije, passing on the way the chequered pink, green and grey brickwork of the **National University Library**, arguably Plečnik's greatest work. The **Illyrian Monument** on Trg francoske revolucije was erected in 1930 in belated recognition of Napoleon's short-lived attempt to create a fiefdom of the same name centred on Ljubljana. Virtually next door is the seventeenth-century monastery complex of **Križanke**: originally the seat of a thirteenth-century order of Teutonic Knights, its delightful courtyard was restored to form a permanent venue for the Summer Festival.

Museums west of Slovenska

The town's cultural quarter boasts a neat collection of museums and galleries. The grand **National Museum** (Tues–Sun 10am–6pm, Thurs till 8pm; €5; Ⓦwww.narmuz-lj.si), at Muzejska 1, features a comprehensive archeological display and interesting temporary exhibitions. The building also houses the **Natural History Museum** (same hours and ticket), notable for having the only complete mammoth skeleton found in Europe. **The National Gallery** at Prešernova cesta 24 (Tues–Sun 10am–6pm; €4.20, free after 2pm Sat; Ⓦwww.ng-slo.si) is housed in the former Narodni Dom, built in the 1890s to accommodate Slovene cultural institutions in defiance of the Habsburgs. The gallery is rich in local medieval Gothic work, although most visitors gravitate towards the halls devoted to the Slovene Impressionists, and in particular the outstanding works by Ivan Grohar and Rihard Jakopič. Diagonally across from here the **Museum of Modern Art** at Cankarjeva cesta 15 (Tues–Sun 10am–6pm; Ⓦwww.mg-lj.si; closed for renovation until 2008) flaunts the more experimental styles of the twentieth century.

Tivoli Park

Beyond the galleries lies **Tivoli Park**, an expanse of lawns and tree-lined walkways backed by dense woodland, perfect for a short ramble. A villa above the centre contains the most enjoyable of Ljubljana's museums, the **Museum of Modern History** (Tues–Sun 10am–6pm; €3.50; Ⓦwww.muzej-nz.si) with dioramas, video screens and period music combining to produce an evocative journey through Slovenia's conflict-riddled twentieth-century history, including both world wars and the struggle for independence in 1991.

Arrival, information and city transport

Air Brnik airport is 23km north of the city, and connected by hourly buses (40min; €4). Taxis should cost around €35-40; ask for a meter.
Train and bus The stations are located side-by-side on Trg Osvobodilne fronte, a short walk north of the centre.
Tourist office The Slovenian Tourist Information Centre (STIC) is at Krekov trg 10 (daily 8am–7/9pm; Ⓣ01/306-4575), with the main Ljubljana Tourist Information Office (TIC) in the Old Town on Adamič Lundrovo Nabrežje 2, next to the Triple Bridge (daily 8am–7/9pm; Ⓣ01/306-1215, Ⓦwww.ljubljana.si); there's another branch at the train station (daily 8/10am–7/10pm; Ⓣ01/433-9475).
Discount passes If you're staying for a few days, the Ljubljana Tourist Card (€12.50), available from all the above tourist offices, entitles you to three days' unlimited travel on the city's public bus network, and discounted entrance fees to selected museums, galleries and restaurants.
City transport Ljubljana's buses are cheap and frequent; you pay on the bus – put your money in a box next to the driver (€1.25 per journey) – or buy tokens (*žetoni*; €0.80) in advance from post offices and most newspaper kiosks.
Bikes Cycling offers a simple yet delightful way to see the city on warmer days; rent them from the STIC for €5/day.
Walking Tours The Ljubljana tourist office organizes a range of pleasant walking tours (April–Sept; €7.50) around the Old Town.

Accommodation

Most budget accommodation fills up quickly, so early reservations are advised. Student residences are only available in July and August.

Hostels

Alibi Cankarjevo Nabrežje 27 ⓣ01/251-1244, ⓦwww.alibi.si. Large, youthful place right in the heart of the old town, with graffiti art on the walls and large communal spaces. ❷

Celica Youth Hostel Metelkova 9 ⓣ01/430-1890, ⓦwww.hostelcelica.com. Brilliantly original hostel in a refurbished former military prison, with two/three-bed "cells" and dorms. ❷–❸.

Dijaški Dom Bežigrad Kardeljeva ploščad 28, ⓣ01/534-2867, ⓦwww.hostel-ddb.si. Passable student dorms and doubles, set in a park 2km north of centre off Dunajska cesta. Buses #6, #8 or #21 from Slovenska cesta (alight at Merkator stop). ❶–❷.

Dijaški Dom Ivana Cankarja Poljanska cesta 26, ⓣ01/474-8600, ⓦwww.dic.si. A ten-minute walk east of Krekov trg, this is the city's cheapest option. Basic student dorms and a self-service breakfast for just €3 extra. ❷

Dijaški Dom Tabor Vidovdanska 7 ⓣ01/234-8840, ⓔddtaborlj@guest.arnes.si. Busy student hostel, with adequate rooms and very helpful staff. ❷

Fluxus Hostel Tomšičeva 4 ⓣ01/251-5760, ⓦwww.fluxus-hostel.com. Clean, bright and spacious hostel with a more homely feel than most. ❸

Park Tabor 9 ⓣ01/300-2500, ⓦwww.hotelpark.si. Sharing facilities with a hotel of the same name (❽), the drab exterior of this high-rise belies its smart rooms and modern facilities. ❷

Hotels

BIT Center Litijska 57 ⓣ01/548-0055, ⓦwww.bit-center.net. Modern, functional rooms in this sports centre 2km east of the centre. Dorm beds also available (❷) and guests get a 50 percent discount on sporting facilities. Buses #5, #9 and #13. ❺

Emonec Wolfova 12 ⓣ01/200-1520, ⓦwww.hotel-emonec.com. In the heart of town, this trendy hotel has immaculate, minimalist rooms, and beautifully designed bathrooms. ❼

Campsite

Ježica Dunajska 270 ⓣ01/568-3913, ⓦwww.ljubljanaresort.si. Pleasant site 5km north of the centre, which also has a few bungalows. Buses #6 or #8 from Slovenska cesta. ❷

Eating

Ljubljana's Old Town boasts a tight concentration of restaurants, most of which offer excellent value for money. The best choice for snacks are the many kiosks and stands near the stations and scattered elsewhere throughout town, selling *burek*, hot dogs and the local *gorenjska* sausages. There's a lively food market on Vodnikov trg. On summer evenings the cafés and bars of Ljubljana's Old Town spill out onto the streets, and a wander along the riverbanks will yield one enticing place after another.

Cafés

Babo Krojaška 4, just off Cankarjevo Nabrežje. Detox with a delicious fruit smoothie at this organic café.

Café Antico Stari trg 27. Lovely Old Town hangout with a pleasantly dated ambience, offering a decent range of coffee, wine and draught beer.

Le Petite Café Trg francoske revolucije 4. Wonderful place, ideal for a coffee and croissant during the day or a glass of wine in the evening.

Tomato Šubičeva ulica 2. Snazzy, post-modern diner café, serving cheap sandwiches and snacks.

Restaurants

Abcedarium Ribji trg 2. Located within Ljubljana's oldest house, this modern place offers a good range of local food and cracking breakfasts.

Cantina Mexicana Knafljev prehod. On a lively alleyway between Slovenska cesta and Wolfova ulica, this colourful place serves Mexican standards and fancy cocktails. Fajitas €10.

Emonska klet Plečnikov trg 1. The food at this capacious cellar (formerly the halls of the Ursuline convent) is often secondary to live music and a cracking bar. Just off Slovenska cesta. Mains €8.

Figovec Gosposvetska 1. Charmingly rustic restaurant specializing in horseflesh steaks and traditional Slovene standards. More expensive than most, but with good reason. €15.

Foculus Gregorčičeva 3. Warm colours and leaf prints create an autumnal backdrop to the cheap pizza and salad options. €5–7

Julija Stari trg 9. First-rate place with a simple Mediterranean menu and a lovely Old Town location. €8–10.

Ljubljanski Dvor Dvorni trg 1. Best thin-crust pizzas in town at this fast and furious place, which also has a great terrace overlooking the Ljubljanica.

Romeo Stari trg 6. Standing obediently opposite *Julija*, this stylish place serves up Mexican bites until late. €9

Sokol Ciril Metodov trg 18. Busy and atmospheric inn-style place, serving hearty, inexpensive portions of traditional Slovene food. Local meat dishes €9–14

Zlata Ribica Cankarjevo Nabrežje 5. With a great outdoor dining area, this modest fish restaurant by the River Ljubljanica is delightful. Mains €10.

Drinking and nightlife

The informative free English-language magazine *Ljubljana Life* (Ⓦ www.ljubljanalife.com), available from the tourist offices, contains bar and club listings.

Bars

Cutty Sark Knafljev prehod 1. "Old-world" pub, with draught beers and a raucous atmosphere, which also offers snack-size pizzas for €2.

Maček Krojaška 5. Hip riverside café with large outdoor terrace; great place to watch the Old Town go by.

Vinoteka Movia Mestni trg 1. Cosy little bar that's the best place in town to sample some of Slovenia's exceptional wines.

Clubs and discos

As Čopova 5. Resident DJs turn the cellar below this upmarket restaurant into a bouncing dance floor on weekends.

Bacchus Kongresni trg 3. Stylish, three-in-one restaurant, lounge bar and club.

Gajo Jazz Club Beethovnova 8. Suitably refined and atmospheric venue for the genre, with quality live offerings.

Global Slovenska cesta (top of the Nama department store). Take a glass elevator up to this fashionable rooftop disco with excellent views of the Old Town.

K4 Kersnikova 4. Stalwart of Ljubljana's alternative scene, offering varied music, and at least one gay night a week.

KUD Prešeren Karunova 14. Superb gig venue that also hosts regular literary events, workshops and art exhibitions.

Metelkova mesto Metelkova cesta. Ljubljana's alternative cultural Mecca, consisting of a cosmopolitan cluster of clubs and bars, is located in the former army barracks next to the *Celica* youth hostel.

Orto Bar Grabloviševa 1. Loud and groovy bar-cum-club east of the train station with pumping disco tunes and frequent live-rock evenings.

Piano Bar Nazorjeva ul 6. Brand-new cocktail bar, with classy decor and themed party nights.

Entertainment

The free monthly *Where To?* pamphlet, available from tourist offices, has complete listings.

Cankarjev Dom Prešernova cesta 10, Ⓣ 01/241-7300. This bulky building is the city's cultural headquarters, hosting major orchestral and theatrical events, as well as folk and jazz concerts. Ticket office Mon–Fri 11am–1pm & 3–8pm, Sat 11am–1pm and 1hr before performance.

International Summer Festival Ⓣ 01/241-6026, Ⓦ www.festival-lj.si, July to mid-Sept. Features orchestral concerts at major venues.

National Opera and Ballet Theatre Župančičeva 1 Ⓣ 01/241-1740, Ⓦ www.opera.si. The impressive nineteenth-century neo-Renaissance building stages contemporary and classical works. Ticket office Mon–Fri 2–5pm, Sat 6–7pm and 1hr before performance.

Shopping

BTC City Šmartinska 152. Massive shopping centre on the northeastern fringes of the capital. Buses #2, #7 and #12.

Flea Market Cankarjevo Nabrežje. Local handicraft stalls along the eastern riverbank (Sun 8am–1pm).

Kod & Kam Trg Francoske revolucije 4. Best place to go for maps, including specialist hiking and sailing prints.

Directory

Embassies and consulates Australia, Trg republike 3 Ⓣ 01/425-4252; Canada, Dunajska 22 Ⓣ 01/430-3570; UK, Trg republike 3 Ⓣ 01/200-3910; US, Prešernova 31 Ⓣ 01/200-5500.

Exchange At the train station and *Menjalnica* on Pogaršarjev trg.

Hospital Bohoričeva 4 Ⓣ 01/232-3060

Internet Cybercafe Xplorer, Petkovškovo Nabrežje 23 (Mon–Fri 10am–10pm, Sat & Sun 2–10pm); Cyber Café, Slovenska 10 (Mon–Thurs 7am–11pm, Fri 7am–midnight, Sat 11am–midnight); Slovenian Tourist Information Centre, Krekov trg 10 (daily 8am–7/9pm).

Laundry Chemo-express, Wolfova 12 (Mon–Fri 7am–6pm; Ⓣ 01/251-4404).

Left luggage At the train station (€2/day).

Pharmacy Prisojne 7 Ⓣ 01/230-6230 (24hr).

Post office Slovenska 32 and Trg Osvobodilne fronte 5.

Moving on

Train Divača (hourly; 1hr 30min); Koper (5 daily; 2hr 30min); Maribor (hourly; 1hr 45min–2hr 30min); Postojna (hourly; 1hr); Ptuj (2 daily; 2hr 30min).
Bus Bled (hourly; 1hr 15min); Bohinj (hourly; 2hr); Bovec (4 daily; 4hr 15min); Divača (8 daily; 1hr 30min); Kobarid (3 daily; 3hr 30min); Koper (8 daily; 2hr); Maribor (7 daily; 3hr 45min); Piran (8 daily; 2hr 40min); Portorož (8 daily; 2hr 30 min); Postojna (hourly; 1hr).

Southwest Slovenia

Emphatically not to be missed while you're in Ljubljana is a visit to either the **Postojna** or **Škocjan caves** – both spectacular, and both easily manageable either as a day-trip from the capital or en route south to Slovene Istria, to Croatia or to Italy. More low-key trips than the caves are **Lipica**, where the celebrated white Lipizzaner horses are bred, or **Predjama Castle**, near Postojna, an atmospherically sombre castle craftily etched into the karst landscape. On the small stretch of Adriatic coastline are a number of charismatic towns, heavily influenced by a legacy of Venetian rule. Of these, the neighbouring **Piran** and **Portorož**, Slovenia's answer to Venice and Vegas, combine fishing-village charm with brash modernity in an effective holiday double act.

POSTOJNA

POSTOJNA is on the main rail route south, 65km from Ljubljana, but as the walk to the caves is shorter from the bus stop, most people opt for this mode of transport. Once in the town, signs direct you to the **caves** (May–Sept daily 9am–6pm; Oct-April daily 10am–4am; tours every 1–2hr; €18; Ⓦwww.turizem-kras.si). Inside, a railway whizzes you through a host of preliminary systems before the guided 1.5km walking tour starts. The vast and fantastic jungles of rock formations are quite breathtaking, while the 40m high "concert hall" makes for a suitably climactic finale. Consider wearing a jacket: at a roughly constant 8°C, the air inside the caves is decidedly chilly. A good bet for **sleeping** in Postojna are private rooms arranged by Kompas, Titov trg 2a (Mon–Fri 8am–7pm, Sat 9am–1pm; Ⓣ05/721-1480, Ⓦwww.kompas-postojna.si; ❹). The only other cheap options are the basic student dorms at *Hostel Proteus* (Ⓣ05/726-1336; ❷) in Postojne town, or the *Pivka* **campsite** (Ⓣ05/726-5382, Ⓦwww.venus-trade.si; ❶), 4km beyond the cave entrance en route to Predjama Castle, which also has four-person bungalows (❼).

PREDJAMA CASTLE

Well-signposted 7km northwest of the caves, but not served by public transport, is **Predjama Castle** (daily 9/10am–4/7pm; €7). Pushed up high against a cave entrance in the midst of the dramatic karst landscape, this sixteenth-century castle is an impressive sight and affords excellent views of the surrounding countryside. Its damp and rather melancholy interior is less rewarding, though there are a few interesting exhibits from this and an earlier castle that stood nearby. There are **guided tours** of the cave below the castle (May–Sept daily 11am, 1pm, 3pm & 5pm; €7).

LIPICA

Located 7km west of the drab railway-junction town of Divača, **LIPICA** gave its name to the **Lipizzaner** horses associated with Vienna's Spanish Riding School. The marvellous creatures are the product of fastidious breeding that can be dated back to 1580, when the Austrian Archduke Charles established the farm in order to add Spanish and Arab blood to the Lipizzaner strain that was first used by the Romans for chariot races. Hourly tours are given round the **stud farm** (Tues–Sun 9/10am–3/6pm; €9; ⓦwww.lipica.org), and the horses give the elegant displays for which they're famous (April Fri & Sun 3pm; May–Oct Tues, Fri & Sun 3pm; €16). You can stay the night by the farm at the *Maestoso* (ⓣ05/739-1580; ❼); it's not cheap but provides a useful base for local horse-riding and golf facilities.

ŠKOCJAN CAVES

Much less visited (but arguably more enchanting) than Postojna, the **ŠKOCJAN CAVES** are a stunning system of echoing chambers, secret passages and collapsed valleys carved out by the Reka River, which begins its journey some 50km south near the Croatian border. Daily **tours** (June–Sept hourly; Oct–May 2–3 daily; €11; ⓦwww.park-skocjanske-jame.si) take you through several stalactite-infested chambers and halls, before you reach the breathtaking **Murmuring Cave**, reputedly the world's largest subterranean canyon. If you need to stay, try the *Pension Risnik* (ⓣ05/763-0008; ❸), 200m up from the train station in Divača.

PORTOROŽ

Easily reached by bus from the train terminus in Koper, **PORTOROŽ** ("Port of Roses") sprawls at the end of a long, tapering peninsula that projects like a lizard's tail north into the Adriatic. Known since the end of the nineteenth century for its mild climate and the health-inducing properties of its salty mud baths, the resort is now a vibrant strip of high-rise hotels, glitzy casinos and beaches. There's not a great deal of culture here, though the town's modernity and buzzing nightlife are unrivalled on this stretch of the coast. The **tourist office** (daily: July & Aug 9am–9pm; Sept–June 10am–5pm; ⓣ05/674-2220, ⓦwww.portoroz.si) is on the main coastal strip, Obala Maršala Tita, just down from the bus terminal. Tourist Service Portorož (ⓣ05/674-0360), near the bus station, offers good-value private rooms (❸–❹), or there's the three-star *Camp Lucija* (ⓣ05/690-6000 ❷; April–Sept) just beyond the Marina to the south of Portorož.

GETTING TO LIPICA AND ŠKOCJAN

A new shuttle bus service operates from **Divača train station**, making it fairly easy to visit these two attractions. Four departures daily (split between morning and afternoon) are designed to coincide with train arrivals, and are free with valid train tickets to Divača. Ask at the Slovenia tourist office in Ljubljana for timetable information. At the time of writing, the last shuttle for Divača leaves Škocjan Caves at 15:47 and Lipica farm at 16:20.

TREAT YOURSELF

Exploit Portorož's historical reputation as a healing centre to the full with a trip to the extravagant **Terme & Wellness Palace**, Obala 33 (ⓣ05/692-9001, ⓦwww.lifeclass.net). Four hours in the 1000-square-metre sauna park (daily 2–9pm) – complete with ice cave – costs €17–20, while an exhaustive selection of pricey spa treatments is listed on the website.

PIRAN

PIRAN, at the tip of the peninsula, 4km from Portorož's bus station, couldn't be more different. Its web of arched alleys, tightly packed ranks of houses and little Italianate squares is simply delightful. The centre, 200m around the harbour from the bus station, is **Tartinijev trg**, named after the eighteenth-century Italian violinist and composer Giuseppe Tartini, who was born in a house on the square and is commemorated by a weather-beaten bronze statue in the centre. With its striking oval-shape, it's one of the loveliest squares on this coast, fringed by a mix of Venetian palaces and a grand-looking Austrian town hall. Across the harbour, in the Gabrielli Palace, the **Maritime Museum** (Tues–Sun 9am–noon & 3/6–6/9pm; €3.50) houses a collection of fine model ships. From the square's eastern edge, follow Rozmanova ulica all the way up to the barn-like Baroque **Church of Sv Jurij**, crowning a commanding spot on the far side of Piran's peninsula.

Arrival and information

Bus The primitive station is on Cankarjevo nabrežje, a five-minute seafront walk from the main square, Tartinijev trg.
Tourist office Tartinijev trg ⓣ05/673-0220. July & Aug daily 9am–1.30pm & 3–9pm; Sept–June Mon–Fri 9am–5pm & Sat 10am–2pm.

Accommodation

Private rooms can be booked through Maona, at Cankarjevo nabrežje 7, between the bus station and the square (ⓣ05/673-4520, ⓦwww.maona.si; ❹–❺).
Alibi Hostel Bonifacijeva 14 & Trubarjeva 60 ⓣ03/136-3666, ⓦwww.alibi.si. Two old houses, one offering modern 4-bed dorms with private bathroom and kitchenette, the other tasteful en-suite doubles; reservations essential. ❷–❸
Fiesa Camping Fiesa 57b ⓣ05/674-6230. Decent site 1km away, past the church. ❷
Hostel Val Gregorčičeva 38a ⓣ05/673-2555, ⓦwww.hostel-val.com. Friendly, well-run place, with excellent facilities and a delightful restaurant ❸

Eating and drinking

Though a pleasant drinking spot, things quieten down fairly early in Piran. For a big night out, head over to Portorož, where the beachside discos stay often open until dawn.
Batana Kidričevo Nabrežje. A stylish pizzeria with pleasant terrace. Pizza €8.
Café Teater St Jenkova 1. Sophisticated cocktail bar overlooking the harbour.
Da Noi Prešernovo Nabrežje. Popular, cellar-like bar on the seafront, which is open later than most.
Riva Gregorčičeva 35. One of the more romantic seafront restaurants, serving tasty meat and fish dishes €10.

Moving on

Bus to: Ljubljana (7–10 daily; 2hr 40min); Portorož (every 20min; 10min); Trieste (Mon-Sat 5 daily; 1hr).

Northwest Slovenia

Within easy reach of Ljubljana are the stunning mountain lakes of **Bled** and **Bohinj**. The magnificent **Soča valley**, on the western side of the Slovene Alps, is much less touristy, although small towns like **Kobarid** and **Bovec** make excellent bases for hiking and adventure sports.

BLED

There's no denying that the lake resort of **BLED** has all the right ingredients for a memorable visit – a placid mirror lake with a romantic island, a medieval cliff-top castle and a backdrop of snow-capped mountains. In summer, the lake forms the setting for a whole host of water sports – including major rowing contests – and in winter the surface becomes a giant fairy-tale skating rink.

HIKING MAPS

If you're interested in serious **hiking**, good maps are essential: your best bets are the 1:50,000 *Triglav National Park*, the 1:25,000 *Mount Triglav* and the 1:25,000 *Bled and environs* – all published by the Slovene Alpine Association. Pick them up in Ljubljana bookshops or from the tourist offices in Bled and Ribčev Laz.

What to see and do

During the day a constant relay of stretched gondolas leaves from below the *Park Hotel*, the *Pension Mlino*, and the bathing resort below the castle, ferrying tourists back and forth to Bled's picturesque **island**. With an early start (and by renting your own rowing boat from *Mlino*) you can beat them to it. Crowning the island, the Baroque **Church of Sv Marika Božja** is the last in a line of churches on a spot that's long held religious significance: under the present building, below the north chapel, are remains of a pre-Roman temple. From the north shore a couple of crooked paths run uphill to **Bled Castle** (daily 8am–5/8pm; €6), originally an eleventh-century fortification but whose present appearance dates from the seventeenth; the museum, containing local artefacts, is pretty dull, but the lovely courtyard affords views across the lake and towards the Alps that verge on the divine.

Vintgar Gorge

The main attraction in the outlying hills is the **Vintgar Gorge** (mid-April to Oct daily 8am–8pm; €4), 4km north of town, an impressive defile accessed via a series of wooden walkways and bridges suspended from the rock face. To get there, take one of the morning buses to the village of Zasip, climb to the hilltop chapel of **Sv Katarina** and pick up a path through the forest to the gorge entrance.

Arrival and information

Train Trains from Ljubljana stop at Bled-Lesce, 4km southeast of Bled itself and connected to the town by regular buses.
Bus The bus station is a five-minute walk northeast of the lake on Grajska cesta.
Tourist office Cesta svobode 10, opposite the *Park Hotel* ⓣ 04/574-1122, ⓦ www.bled.si. July & Aug daily 8am–9pm; Sept–June Mon–Sat 8am–5/8pm, Sun 9am–5pm.

Accommodation

Private rooms are available through Kompas in the shopping centre at Ljubljanska 4 (ⓣ 04/572-7501, ⓦ www.kompas-bled.si; ❹–❻).
Bled campsite Kidričeva 10 ⓣ 04/575-2000, ⓦ www.camping-bled.com. Beautifully located amid the pines at the western end of the lake, this family-friendly campsite features first-rate facilities. ❷
Bledec hostel Grajska 17 ⓣ 04/574-5250, ⓦ www.mlino.si. Clean, homely rooms and close proximity to lake makes this a great-value option. ❷
Pension Mlino Cesta svobode 45 ⓣ 04/574-1404, ⓦ www.mlino.si. This delightful lakeside pension boasts great views of Bled castle and also decent rooms and an excellent restaurant. ❼

Eating and drinking

The best places for **eating** are in the hillside area between Bled's bus station and castle, though most pensions on the lake's perimeter offer reliable fare.
Gostilna Pri Planincu Grajska 8. Serves up solid Slovene home cooking. Mains €9.
Jasmin Cesta svobode. Next door to the tourist office, this sophisticated café has a decent range of specialist teas, cakes and cocktails for after dark.
Union Ljubljanska 9. This complex, near the bus station, contains an excellent terraced restaurant and late-night bar. Mains €10.

LAKE BOHINJ

From Bled hourly buses make the 25km trip through the verdant, mist-laden Sava Bohinjka Valley to **LAKE BOHINJ**. In appearance and character Lake Bohinj is utterly different from Bled: the lake crooks a narrow finger under the wild mountains, woods slope gently down to the water, and a lazy stillness hangs over all.

Ribčev Laz

RIBČEV LAZ (often referred to as Jezero on bus timetables), at the eastern end of the lake, is where most facilities are based, as well as the intriguing **Church of Sv Janez** (July & Aug daily 9am–noon & 5–8pm), whose extraordinary frescoes date back to the fourteenth century. **Walking trails** lead round both

GETTING TO THE LAKES

Buses are the easiest way to get to the lakes (hourly from Ljubljana; 1hr 15min to Bled, 2hr to Bohinj; €7–9). Direct **train** access to the region is via the main northbound line from Ljubljana (hourly; 40min–1hr; €4), which calls at Bled-Lesce. Trains on the Jesenice-Nova Gorica branch call at both Bled Jezero and Bohinjska Bistrica (7 daily; €1.50). An old-fashioned steam train also sporadically plies the same route, providing a wonderful scenic option as it chugs steadily through the mountains towards Italy (check Ⓦwww.slo-zeleznice.si; €10).

sides of the lake, or north onto the eastern shoulders of the Triglav range. One route leads north from Stara Fužina into the Voje valley, passing through the dramatic **Mostnica Gorge**, a popular local beauty spot.

Ukanc, Mount Vogel and the Valley of the Seven Lakes

About 5km from Ribčev Laz at the western end of the lake is the hamlet of **UKANC** (sometimes referred to as Zlatorog), where there's a **cable car** (daily 7am–6pm, every 30min; closed Nov; €10 return), which whizzes you up to the summit of **Mount Vogel** (1540m) in no time – if the Alps look dramatic from the lakeside, from Vogel's summit they're breathtaking. Ukanc is also the starting point for a 45-minute walk north to the photogenic **Savica Waterfalls** (April–Oct 8am–8pm; €2). From here, the serious hiking can commence, either as a day-trip to the **Valley of the Seven Lakes** – an area strewn with eerie boulders and hardy firs – or as an expedition to scale Mount Triglav itself (see below).

CLIMBING MOUNT TRIGLAV

Inexperienced hikers should seek advice before attempting this climb. The hike to the summit (Slovenia's tallest peak at 2863m) and back takes two to three days, so at least one night in a mountain hut, and can be daunting, particularly if weather conditions deteriorate. The tourist office in Ribčev Laz will supply details of hiking paths, distances and available huts.

Information

Tourist information centre Ribčev Laz 48 ⓣ04/574-6010, Ⓦwww.bohinj.si. The excellent centre is 50m from the lake, next to the Mercator supermarket. July & Aug daily 8am–8pm; Sept–June Mon–Sat 8am–6pm, Sun 9am–3pm.

Accommodation

The tourist office offers a plentiful choice of private rooms (❷) and apartments (❺) around Ribčev Laz and in the idyllic villages of Stara Fužina and Studor, 1km and 2.5km north respectively.

Danica Triglavska 60 ⓣ04/572-1702, Ⓦwww.camp-danica.si. 5km from the lake, in Bohinjska Bistrica, this large campsite has good sporting facilities. ❷

Zlatorog Ukanc 2 ⓣ04/572-3482. Pleasant campsite on the western tip of the lake, which is a good base for trips up the mountains. ❶–❷

Eating and drinking

Center Of the smattering of standard pizzerias by the lake at Ribčev Laz, the rustic *Center*, next to the tourist office, is better than most. Pizza €5–7

Grill Promenade This cabin, on the street outside *Hotel Jezero*, has cheap meaty takeaways.

Maxzaxmesiter A welcoming outdoor bar across the road from *Grill Promenade*.

THE SOČA VALLEY

On the other, less touristy side of the mountains from Bohinj, the River Soča slices through the western spur of the Julian Alps, running parallel with the Italian border. During World War I, the Soča marked the front line between the Italian and Austro-Hungarian armies;

GETTING TO THE SOČA VALLEY

Four buses a day travel from Ljubljana, reaching Kobarid in about 3hr. Approaching the Soča valley from the Bled-Bohinj area involves catching one of ten daily trains from Bohinjska Bistrica to **Most na Soči** (40min; €2), where five buses daily run onwards up the valley. Getting here from the coast is an arduous task: from Koper, several bus changes are required to reach Kobarid, and expect a journey of 5–7hr.

now memorial chapels and abandoned fortifications are nestled incongruously amidst awesome Alpine scenery. The valley is also a major centre for activity-based tourism, with the foaming, emerald river itself providing the ideal venue for **rafting** and **kayaking** throughout the spring and summer. The main tourist centres are **Kobarid** and **Bovec**, both small towns boasting a range of walking possibilities. The 1:50,000 *Zgornje Posočje* **map** covers trails in the region: it's best to pick it up in Ljubljana if you can, as local shops can easily run out of stock.

Kobarid

It was at the little Alpine town of **KOBARID** that German and Austrian troops finally broke through Italian lines in 1917, almost knocking Italy out of World War I in the process. Ernest Hemingway, then a volunteer ambulance driver on the Italian side, took part in the chaotic retreat that followed, an experience that resurfaced in his novel *A Farewell to Arms*. The **Kobarid museum**, Gregorčičeva 10 (Mon–Fri 9/10am–5/6pm, Sat & Sun 9am–6/7pm; €4; Ⓦwww.kobariski-muzej.si), presents a thoughtful account of the 29 months of fighting in the region through a gripping collection of photographs, maps and mementoes. Just down from the museum, on Kobarid's main square, a processional way leads up to a three-tiered **Italian War Memorial**, opened by Benito Mussolini in 1938, from where you can enjoy views of the surrounding Alps. This also marks the start of the Kobarid historical trail, a five-kilometre loop where remote woodland paths are punctuated by forgotten wartime landmarks. At the trail's farthest point from town bubbles the **Kozjak waterfall** (40min walk), less impressive for its height than for the cavern-like space that it has carved out of the surrounding rock.

The **tourist office**, Trg Svobode 16 (daily 9am–8pm; Ⓣ05/380-0490, Ⓦwww.lto-sotocje.si), can find **private rooms** (❷) in Kobarid and surrounding villages, and there are two well-equipped **campsites**: the *Koren* (Ⓣ05/389-1311, Ⓦwww.kamp-koren.si; ❶); and the *Lazar* (Ⓣ05/388-5333, Ⓦwww.lazar-sp.si; ❶) – located on opposite banks of the River Soča, 500m out of town near the trail. Pizzerias offer the best-value **food**; try *Fedrig*, in town on Volaričeva 11, or *Gostišče Jazbec*, 1km south of town in Irdsko.

ADVENTURE SPORTS

In Kobarid the main **rafting** company is X-Point (Ⓣ05/388-5308, Ⓦwww.xpoint.si), just north of Trg svobode at Stresova 1; they also organize a range of other outdoor activities. Expect to pay around €35 for a rafting trip.

In Bovec, you'll find a string of companies offering similarly priced activities, both on and off the river. Popular outfits include Bovec Rafting Team (Ⓣ05/388-6128, Ⓦwww.bovec-rafting-team.com), located in a small hut just a few minutes' walk from the main square, and Soča Rafting (Ⓣ05/389-6200, Ⓦwww.socarafting.si), opposite the tourist office at Trg Golobarskih zrtev 14.

Moving on

Bus to: Bovec (5 daily; 40min); Ljubljana (3–4 daily; 4hr); Nova Gorica (3 daily; 1hr 15min).

Bovec

Some 25km up the valley from Kobarid, the village of **BOVEC** straggles between imperious mountain ridges. Thanks to its status as a winter ski resort, it has a greater range of accommodation options and sporting agencies than Kobarid, and as a result, a more vibrant atmosphere. The quickest route into the mountains from here is provided by the **gondola** that departs on the hour 1km south of the village (June–Sept 8am–3pm; €11.50 return), which ascends to the pasture-cloaked Mount Kanin over to the west.

The **tourist office** is just around the corner from the bus stop at Trg golobarskih žrtev 8 (July & Aug daily 8:30am–8:30pm; Sept–June Mon–Fri 9am–5pm, Sat & Sun 9am–noon; ⓣ05/389-6444, ⓦwww.bovec.si), and can help with renting **private rooms** (❷–❸). Alternatively, try Go tours, at Trg golobarskih žrtev 50 (ⓣ05/389-6366, ⓦwww.gotourbovec.com). The nearest **campsite** is *Polovnik*, Ledina 8 (ⓣ05/388-6069); follow the road north out of the village and it's signed to the right after 500m. The best place to **eat** around the main square is *Stari Kovai*, at Rupa 3, with a long list of inexpensive pizzas alongside the usual schnitzels. Most revellers head to the *Pink Panther* club on weekends, about 500m up the hill on the road leading from the main square.

Eastern Slovenia

The lush landscapes to the east of Ljubljana – where many of the country's most reputable vineyards are concentrated – have generally been less explored by travellers. But as host to Slovenia's second city, **Maribor**, and oldest settlement, **Ptuj**, which lie on the main routes to Austria and Hungary respectively, the region can reward the passing visitor with its rich historical heritage, traditional culture and passion for fine wine.

MARIBOR

Located 130km northeast of Ljubljana, **MARIBOR** is perched snugly on the Drava river between hillside vineyards and the Pohorje mountain range. Though beset by war and occupation, the old town's beautiful architecture preserves myriad historical and cultural influences.

What to see and do

Maribor's main attractions are condensed in a pedestrianized centre, a ten-minute walk west along Partizanska cesta from the main train and bus stations. Along this route, the imposing, late nineteenth-century red-bricked **St Mary's Franciscan church** (daily 6am–noon & 3–7:45pm) catches the eye first. The church looms over Trg Svobode, with **Maribor castle**, which houses the regional museum, opposite (ⓣ02/228-3551, ⓦwww.pmuzej-mb.si; closed for maintenance until further notice). Nearby you can foray into the labyrinth of underground catacombs that make up the **Vinag Wine Cellar** (Tues–Fri 9am–7pm, Sat 8am–1pm; ⓣ02/220-8114, ⓦwww.vinag.si), stopping to sample some of the acclaimed vintages. On the western fringe of the pedestrianized zone sits the photogenic **Slomškov trg**, a serene, leafy opening surrounded by a few landmarks, including the university building and **National Theatre** (ⓣ02/250-6100). Opposite the university, and mimicking its distinct yellow colour, is the sixteenth-century gothic **Cathedral Church**, with a bell

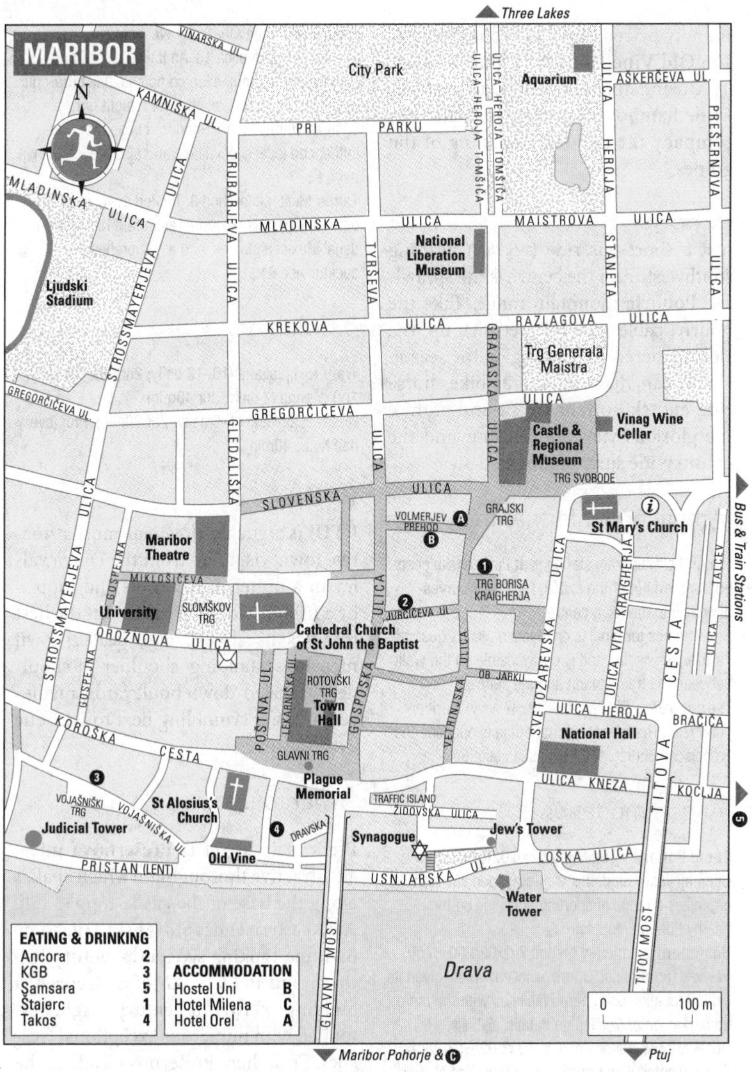

tower that offers fantastic views to the edges of the city and beyond (daily 8am–6pm; free). South of Slomškov, another charming square, **Glavni trg**, epitomizes the hopscotch architectural styles of the city. Its centrepiece is the mournful **Plague Memorial**, erected after the deadly disease wiped out around a fifth of the town's population in the seventeenth century.

Lent

Between Glavni and the river, the streets become narrow and uneven, as you enter the oldest part of town, **Lent**. It is here that world's oldest productive vine, a protected national monument, grows majestically outside the **Old Vine House** (Tues–Sun 10am–6pm; free). Inside, a small exhibition complements the range of top-quality, reasonably priced vintages from the area. The Old Vine House is a blur of activity during the summer Lent festival, while flamboyant celebrations also accompany the annual harvesting of the grapes.

Pohorje

Just a short bus ride (#6; €1) heading southwest from the centre is the sprawling **Pohorje** mountain range. Take the hourly cable car (€7 return) up the slope, where – depending on the season – you can hike, mountain bike, horse ride and ski, or simply sit and admire the glorious views of Maribor and the countryside surrounding it.

Arrival and information

Train The main train station is at Partizanska cesta 50; turn left out of the exit and the road curves directly into the town centre.

Bus The bus terminal is on Mlinska ulica 1 (just off Partizanska cesta), and is easily visible on the walk between the train station and the centre.

Tourist office ⓣ02/234-6611, ⓦwww.mariborpohorje.si. The friendly tourist office is opposite the Franciscan church at Partizanska cesta 6a .

Accommodation

Camp Pohorje Pot k Mlinu 57 ⓣ02/614-0950. Open all year round, this well-equipped site also organizes a range of sporting activities on the nearby Pohorje Mountain. ❷

Hostel Uni Volkmerjev prehod 7 ⓣ02/250-6700, ⓦwww.termemb.si. Offers excellent value, given its central location and shared facilities with the more upmarket *Hotel Orel* (same details; ❽). ❺

Hotel Milena Pohorska ulica 49 ⓣ02/613-2808, ⓦwww.hotelmilena-garni.com. At the foot of Pohorje Mountain, this place has a cosy, peaceful feel to it. ❻

Eating and drinking

The best bars are located in Lent, on the banks of the Drava.

Ancora Jurčičeva 7. This popular place offers decent and affordable Mediterranean dishes. Mains €8–10

KGB Vojašniški trg 5. One of two rowdy student dives (*KMŠ* is the other) just west of Lent.

Samsara Loška ulica 13. An Italian restaurant, cocktail bar and nightclub combined, this ultra-chic complex has all the facilities for a night out.

Štajerc Vetrinjska 30. Good for cheap, German-influenced local specialities, and also brews its own beer. €5–7

Takos Mesarski prehod 3. Tucked away on a narrow alley, this colourful restaurant has all the usual Mexican staples, and a comprehensive cocktail list. €10

Moving on

Train to: Ljubljana (10–12 daily; 2hr); Ptuj (8 daily; 1hr); Vienna (2 daily; 3hr 40min).

Bus to: Ljubljana (4–5 daily; 2hr 30min); Ptuj (every half hour; 40min).

PTUJ

PTUJ is arguably Slovenia's most attractive town, rising up from the Drava valley in a flutter of red roofs and topped by a friendly-looking castle. But the best thing is its streets, with scaled-down mansions standing shoulder-to-shoulder on scaled-down boulevards, medieval fantasies crumbling next to Baroque extravagances.

What to see and do

Ptuj's main street is **Prešernova ulica**, an attractive thoroughfare which snakes along the base of the castle-topped hill. At its eastern end is **Slovenski Trg**, home to a fine-looking sixteenth-century bell tower and the **Church of St George**, a building of twelfth-century origin festooned with numerous exceptional frescoes. From here Prešernova leads to the **Archeological Museum** (mid-April to Dec daily 10am–5pm), housed in what was once a Dominican monastery, gutted in the eighteenth century and now hung with spidery decoration, and worth a look for the carvings and statuary around its likeably dishevelled cloisters. At either end of Prešernova, cobbled paths wind up to the **castle.** There's been a fortification of sorts here for as long as there's been a town, since Ptuj was the only bridging point across the Drava for miles around, holding the defences against the tribes of the north. An agglomeration of styles from the fourteenth to the eighteenth centuries, the castle was home to a succession of noble families, the most prominent of which were the Herbersteins, Austro-Slovene aristocrats who made their fortune in the Habsburg Empire's wars against the Turks. The castle **museum** (daily 9am–5/6pm; July & Aug Sat & Sun till 8pm; €4) contains uninspiring collections of period furniture, tapestries and paintings, though the colourful exhibition on the *Kurenti*, an extravagant and unusual Shrovetide (late Feb/early March) carnival that celebrates the rite of spring, is entertaining.

Arrival and information

Train and bus Both stations are located within a few hundred metres of each on Osojnikova cesta, five minutes' walk northeast of town. On arrival, head down the main road to its junction with ul Heroja Lacka: a right turn here lands you straight in the centre.

Tourist office Slovenski trg 5 ⓣ02/779-6011, ⓦwww.ptuj-tourism.si (Mon–Fri 8am–6pm, Sat-Sun 9am–1pm). The Centre for Free Time Activities (CID), near the bus station at Osojnikova 9 (Mon–Fri 9am–6pm, Sat 10am–1pm; ⓣ02/780-5540, ⓦwww.cid.si), can also provide friendly assistance.

Accommodation

Eva Jadranska ulica 20 ⓣ02/771-2441, ⓦwww.bikeek.si. Relatively cramped rooms, but modern facilities and a spacious communal area make this place very good value. Reception is in an adjacent bike shop. ❷

Kurent Osojnikova cesta 9 ⓣ02/771-0814, ⓔyhptuj@csod.si. Tidy, four-bed rooms with private bathrooms in this youth hostel, which is superbly managed by the CID. ❷

Terme Ptuj Pot v Toplice ⓣ02/749-4580, ⓦwww.terme-ptuj.si. Across the river, some 2km west of town, guests at this fabulous campsite can also use the Thermal Park pools and saunas. ❷; Four-person cottages available (❽).

TREAT YOURSELF

Mitra Prešernova ulica 6 ⓣ02/787-7455, ⓦwww.hotel-mitra.si. The place to stay if your budget allows, with a beautifully furnished interior and large, comfortable rooms. The makeshift outdoor theatre on the roof terrace is a delightful touch. ❼

Eating and drinking

Amadeus Prešernova 36. Enjoy a hearty Slovene dish in the restaurant, or just a freshly-squeezed lemonade at the attached café. Meat dishes €8–10.

Bo Café Slovenski Trg 7. Quaint tea shop on main square with a variety of herbal varieties.

Café Evropa Mestni trg. The liveliest venue for a drink, by day or night.

Perutnina Ptuj Novi trg 2. A cheap and cheerful place, with buffet option for lunch (€8).

Ribič Dravska ulica 9. The exceptional seafood at this riverside eatery justifies the slightly higher price tag. Fish €10.

Moving on

Trains to: Budapest (2 daily; 6hr 15min); Llubljana (2 daily; 2hr 30min); Maribor (7 daily; 1hr)

Buses to: Maribor (every half hour; 40min).

Spain

HIGHLIGHTS

MUSEO GUGGENHEIM, BILBAO: the building is as big an attraction as the art it houses

SAN SEBASTIÁN: stunning beaches and mouth-watering cuisine - the perfect pit stop

SANTIAGO DE COMPOSTELA: the end-point of Europe's most famous pilgrim trail

BARCELONA: perhaps Europe's most alluring city

PLAZA MAYOR, SALAMANCA: the finest square in a beautiful university city

MADRID: world-class museums and legendary nightlife

ALHAMBRA, GRANADA: evocative Moorish palace atop this charming Andalucian city

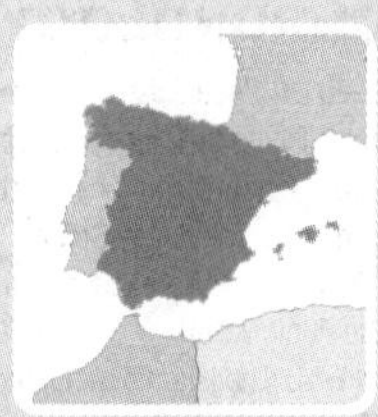

ROUGH COSTS

DAILY BUDGET Basic €30/with the occasional treat €50

DRINK €1.20–2 per caña (small beer)

FOOD Three-course menú del día €8

HOSTEL/BUDGET HOTEL €7–19/€16–35

TRAVEL Madrid–Barcelona (505km): bus €26–37, train €38–65

FACT FILE

POPULATION 41 million

AREA 504,030 sq km

LANGUAGE Spanish

CURRENCY Euro (€)

CAPITAL Madrid

INTERNATIONAL PHONE CODE ⓣ34

Basics

Spain might appear from the brochures to be no more than a clichéd whirl of bullfights and crowded beaches, castles and cathedrals. Travel for any length of time, however, and the sheer variety of this huge country cannot fail to impress. The separate kingdoms that made up the original Spanish nation remain very much in evidence, in a diversity of language, culture and traditions.

Of the regions, **Catalonia** (Catalunya) in the northeast is vibrant and go-ahead; **Galicia** in the northwest a verdant rural idyll; the **Basque country** around Bilbao a remarkable contrast between post-industrial depression and unbridled optimism; and **Castile** and the **south** still, somehow, quintessentially "Spanish". There are definite highlights: the three great cities of **Barcelona, Madrid** and **Seville**; the Moorish monuments of **Andalucía** in the south and the Christian ones of **Old Casile** in the west; beachlife on the islands of **Ibiza** or on the more deserted strands around **Cádiz**; and, for some of the best trekking in Europe, the **Pyrenees**.

CHRONOLOGY

1000 BC Phoenicians colonize the Iberian Peninsula, establishing the cities of Cádiz and Málaga.

400s BC Carthaginians exert power over large parts of present-day Spain.

200s BC The Romans capture "Hispania" during the Punic Wars.

711 AD The Islamic Moors conquer Spain, and Moorish culture flourishes.

1085 With the capture of Toledo, Spanish Christians begin to diminish the influence of the Moors in Spain.

1480 The Spanish Inquisition persecutes non-Christians, leading to mass conversions of Jews.

1492 Christopher Columbus discovers lands in the Americas for the Spanish Crown.

1605 The world's first "novel", *Don Quixote* by Cervantes, is published.

1714 The British capture Gibraltar.

1800s Spanish colonies in the Americas gain their independence.

1931 Surrealist artist Salvador Dali completes his most famous painting, *The Persistence of Memory*.

1936 The Spanish Civil War breaks out as Nationalist forces led by General Franco defeat Republican forces.

1939 Spain remains neutral at the outbreak of World War II.

1975 Franco dies and is replaced by King Juan Carlos.

1977 First free elections are held in almost four decades.

2004 Bombs detonated on busy Madrid trains leave 191 people dead. An Islamic group takes responsibility.

2007 The government's struggle with Basque separatists, ETA, continues as the group end their ceasefire.

ARRIVAL

Getting to Spain should be straightforward, as transportation links are already very good and constantly improving. The quickest – and cheapest – way is on one of the budget-airline **flights** (try Iberia subsidiary Clickair as well as easyJet and Ryanair). All the major airlines serve Barcelona and Madrid airports, both of which are well connected to their respective cities by bus and metro, and are ideal bases from which to start backpacking around the country. **Trains** from France serve San Sebastían (from Biarritz), Barcelona (from Toulouse and Perpignan) and Girona (from Perpignan); while **trains** from Portugal run from Lisbon to Caceres (and Madrid) and from Porto to Santiago de Compostela. **Ferries** also arrive in Bilbao and Santander from the UK, but crossings take at least 24 hours and can be pricey in the peak summer months.

GETTING AROUND

Spain's public transport is backpacker friendly, offering safe and efficient travel options. Whilst trains are good for short hops, buses are often more comfortable – and cheaper – for longer journeys.

By train

RENFE (Ⓦwww.renfe.es) operates **trains**, with three types of service: *Cercanías* (red) are local commuter trains that service major cities; *Regionales* (orange) run between cities, and are equivalent to buses in **speed** and cost – *Regional Exprés* and *Delta* trains cover longer distances; and *Largo recorrido* express trains (grey) come as – in ascending order of luxury – *Diurno*, *Intercity* (*IC*), *Estrella* (*), *Talgo*, *Talgo Pendular*, *Talgo 200* (*T200*) and *Trenhotel*. Anything above *Intercity* can cost twice as much as standard second class. There are also private high-speed trains such as the sleek and efficient *AVE* (Madrid–Zaragoza and Madrid–Seville), *Alaris* (Madrid–Valencia), *Altaria* (Madrid–Alicante) and *Euromed* (Barcelona–Alicante). A good way to avoid queuing at the station is to buy tickets from travel agents that display the RENFE sign – they can also make seat reservations (€3, the same as at the station), which are obligatory on *Largo recorrido* trains. **InterRail** and **Eurail** passes are valid on all RENFE trains and also on *Euromed*; additional supplements are charged on the fastest trains. Book well in advance, especially at weekends and holidays. If you're travelling only around Spain, there's no reason to buy rail passes, as train fares are quite cheap.

By bus

For longer journeys around Spain, **buses** are more comfortable than trains and save more time and pennies – Alsa (Ⓦwww.alsa.es), Auto Res (Ⓦwww.auto-res.net) and Continental Auto (Ⓦwww.continetal-auto.es) are the best companies, covering a lot of the country between them.

ACCOMMODATION

Simple, reasonably priced rooms (*habitaciones*) or beds (*camas*) are widely available in rural Spain, advertised in private houses or above bars, often with the phrase "*camas y comidas*" ("beds and meals"). In most towns, you'll be able to get a double for around €35, a single for €20 or so. Prices in popular areas drop in low season – tourist offices always have lists of places to stay, but often miss these cheaper deals.

Hotels and hostels

Hotels go by various names. Budget travellers are best sticking to *casas de huéspedes* (*CH*) and *pensiones* (*P*) – simple accommodation that doesn't usually provide breakfast. Slightly more expensive, but far more common, are *hostales* (marked *Hs*) and *hostal-residencias* (*HsR*), categorized from one to three stars. HI **hostels** (*albergues juveniles*; Ⓦwww.reaj.com) are rarely very practical. In most of the country, few stay open all year and in towns and cities they can be inconveniently located, suffer from curfews and are often block-reserved by school groups. At €12–25 per person (HI card required), usually including breakfast, they are rarely cheaper than sharing a double room in a *pensión*. On the other hand, Madrid and Barcelona have a growing network of centrally located **backpacker hostels** with good facilities, no curfew, and the prospect of meeting like-minded travellers. Beds are €17–23, and membership is not required: check Ⓦwww.hostelspain.com for lists of budget hotels and hostels.

Casas rurales and camping

Nationwide, **agroturismo** and **casa rural** programmes offer excellent cheap accommodation in rural areas. Tourist offices have full lists. There are hundreds of **campsites**, mostly on the coast, charging about €4 per person plus the same for a tent. The National Tourist Board has the free *Mapa de Campings* and the complete *Guía de Campings* (€6); or see Ⓦwww.vayacamping.net. **Camping rough** is not a good idea; you can be fined for camping near a tourist beach or campsite.

FOOD AND DRINK

Bars and cafés are best for **breakfast**, which can consist of a brioche/croissant, *churros con chocolate* – long tubular doughnuts with thick drinking chocolate – *tostadas* (toast) served *con aceite* (with oil) or *con mantequilla y mermelada* (butter and jam), or *tortilla* (omelette). **Coffee** and **pastries** are available at the many excellent *pastelerías* and *confiterías*, while *bocadillos* (sandwiches filled with sliced meats, cheese or *tortilla*), are available everywhere. *Tabernas, tascas, bodegas, cervecerías* and bars all serve **tapas** or *pinchos*: mini portions of meat, fish, *tortilla* or salad for €1.30–3 a plate. Their big brothers, **raciones** (€4–10), make a sufficient meal in themselves. Good value two- or three-course main meals (*cubierto, menú del día* or *menú de la casa*) with wine are served at **comedores** or **cafeterías** (€7–10). *Cafeterías* serve rather bland *platos combinados* such as egg and fries or *calamares* and salad, with bread and a drink included (€5–8). At a **restaurant**, the cheapest full meal plus wine costs €7–10. **Fish** and **seafood** are fresh and excellent, particularly regional specialities such as Galician fish stews (*zarzuelas*) and Valencian paellas (which may also contain meat). Restaurants serving exclusively fish and seafood are called **marisquerías**. The big cities, notably Madrid, Barcelona and Valencia, are fab for **vegetarians**, with scores of veggie restaurants, plus fusion cuisine and Asian specialities widely available.

Drink

Wine, either *tinto* (red), *blanco* (white) or *rosado/clarete* (rosé), is usually very good. The best red is Rioja, and Catalonia produces the best whites, especially Penedès or Peralada; alternatively, try the refreshing Galician Albariño or the more economical Ribeiro. Vino de Jerez, Andalucian **sherry**, is served chilled and either *fino/jerez seco* (dry), *amontillado* (medium), or *oloroso/jerez dulce* (sweet). *Cerveza*, lager-type **beer**, is more expensive than wine but also good. **Sangría**, a wine-and-fruit punch, and **sidra**, a dry farmhouse cider most typical in the Basque Country, are worth sampling. Spaniards often take a *copa* of liqueur with their coffee; the best are *anís* (like Pernod) or *coñac*, local vanilla-flavoured brandy. There are cheaper Spanish equivalents (*nacional*) of most spirits. **Coffee** is invariably espresso, unless you specify *cortado* (with a drop of milk), *con leche* (a more generous dollop) or *americano* (weaker black coffee). **Tea** is drunk black. If you want milk, ask afterwards: ordering *té con leche* might get you a glass of milk with a teabag floating on top. Herbal teas, such as *tila* (lime blossom), *menta* (mint) and *manzanilla* (camomile), are very good.

CULTURE AND ETIQUETTE

The main cultural difference between Spain and other northern European countries is its **daily schedule.** Lunch is usually eaten from 2pm and dinner from 8pm. The stereotype that Spain "shuts down" for a siesta in between isn't true in the largest Spanish cities, where a lot of shops, tourist offices and restaurants stay open all day. However, in smaller towns and especially villages, don't expect much to be open between the hours of 2 and 5pm.

In terms of **tipping**, ten percent in restaurants is the norm, although not everyone does tip – and nor do all waiters expect it. When paying by credit/debit card in shops, you will always need photo ID, so make sure you carry some with you at all times.

SPORTS AND ACTIVITIES

Lapped by the warm, calm waters of the Mediterranean, the beaches in the south are the best for **swimming**; while the north coast is ideal for watersports such as **windsurfing** and **surfing**: Playa de Zurriola in San Sebastián is a popular choice, as is Santander's Sardinero beach. The latter is good for beginner surfers, as the waves in La Concha bay aren't too rough; check out Ⓦwww.escueladesurfsardinero.com for more details on the surf school there. At the other end of the spectrum, the Aragonese Pyrenees, Picos de Europa and the Sierra Nevada, in Andalucía, are excellent in winter for **skiing** and equally good for **hiking** in summer.

Spectator sports

For those who prefer to watch from the sidelines, Spain has some great sporting events for spectators. A match at Real Madrid's Estadio Santiago Bernabéu is a must for any **football** fan (tickets €15–72; Ⓣ913 984 300, Ⓦwww.realmadrid.es), as is a game at the Camp Nou, FC Barcelona's 100,000-seater stadium (tickets €18–162; Ⓣ902 189 900, Ⓦwww.fcbarcelona.com). Catch the two teams playing each other and you'll witness an unforgettable atmosphere – if you're lucky enough to get hold of a ticket. For something a bit different, the Basque **jai alai** (or *pelota vasca*) is a fast-paced game where teams volley a ball within a three-walled court using wicker *cestas* – match details can be found Ⓦwww.fipv.net.

Another activity to witness from the safety of the sidelines is the **bull runnings** (or *encierros),* the most famous of which take place every July in the city of Pamplona during the Fiesta de San Fermín (see p.1103). Every morning between the seventh and the fourteenth of the month, man and bull run together along the narrow city streets in an electrifying, unmissable spectacle.

COMMUNICATIONS

Post offices (*correos*) open Monday to Friday 8.30am to 2pm, Saturday 9am– to noon; big branches in cities open until 8pm. **Stamps** are also sold at tobacconists (*estancos*). Poste restante should be addressed to "*Lista de Correos*", followed by the name of the town and province. You can make international calls from almost any public **phone**. The various discount cards for domestic and overseas calls are the cheapest way to pay (available from tobacconists, newspaper kiosks and Internet cafés and in €5 or €6 denominations). Most phone boxes accept coins as well as cards. The operator is on ⓣ1003 domestic, ⓣ025 international. Within Spain, dial all nine digits. **Internet** access is widely available.

Many smaller villages are accessible only by **bus**, almost always leaving from the capital of their province. Service varies in quality, but buses are often faster than trains and prices pretty standard at around €6 per 100km. Services are drastically reduced on Sundays and holidays.

EMERGENCIES

The paramilitary **Guardia Civil** (green uniforms and kepis) still police some rural areas, borders and most highways. In cities, you'll find the **Policía Nacional** (talk to them if you get robbed) and the **Policía Municipal** (traffic police), and there's a **Patrulla Rural** in some outlying areas. Petty theft can be particularly bad in some cities and during fiestas; use common sense and keep an eye (and an arm) on your things at all times. For minor **health** complaints, go to a pharmacy (*farmacia*), which you'll find in almost any town. In more serious cases, head to *Urgencias* at the nearest **hospital**, or get the address of an English-speaking doctor from the nearest consulate, *farmacia*, local police or tourist office.

INFORMATION & MAPS

The **Spanish National Tourist Office** (*Información* or *Oficina de turismo*) has a branch in virtually every major town, giving away maps and accommodation lists. There are also provincial or municipal *Turismos*. Both types are usually open Monday to Friday 9/10am to 1pm and 4pm to 7/8pm, Saturday 9am to 1/2pm. Good touring and city **maps** are published by Editorial Telstar (ⓦwww.distrimapas-telstar.es) and Editorial Almax (ⓦwww.almax-editores.com). Serious **trekkers** should look for topographical maps issued by Editorial Alpina (ⓦwww.editorialalpina.com), or the Mapas Excursionistas produced by the Institut Cartogràfic de Catalunya (ⓦwww.icc.es), which covers the Pyrenees in five sheets.

EMERGENCY NUMBERS

All emergencies ⓣ112; ambulance ⓣ061.

MONEY AND BANKS

Currency is the euro (€). **Banks** and *cajas de ahorro* have branches in all but the smallest towns, open Monday to Friday 8.30am to 2pm, also Saturday in low season. You can usually change cash at larger hotels (bad rates, but low commission), at travel agents, and at most El Corte Inglés department stores. In tourist areas, you'll also find **casas de cambio**, with more convenient hours, but worse exchange rates. **ATMs** are widespread.

OPENING HOURS, HOLIDAYS AND FESTIVALS

In general, shops are **open** Monday to Saturday 9am to 8pm and are closed

SPAIN ON THE NET

ⓦwww.tourspain.co.uk Comprehensive website of the Spanish tourist board.
ⓦwww.spain.info Information on almost every aspect of Spain.
ⓦwww.guiadelocio.com Nationwide restaurant and entertainment listings, updated weekly (in Spanish only).
ⓦwww.gospain.org Useful links directory.

Spanish

	Spanish	Pronunciation
Yes	*Si*	See
No	*No*	Noh
Please	*Por favor*	Por fabor
Thank you	*Gracias*	Grath-yass
Hello/Good day	*Hola*	Ola
Goodbye	*Adiós*	Ad-yoss
Excuse me	*Con permiso*	Con pairmeeso
Sorry (strong)	*Lo siento*	Loh see-en-toh
Sorry (mild)	*Perdón*	Pear-don
Where?	*Donde?*	Donday?
Good	*Bueno*	Bwayn
Bad	*Malo*	Mal
Near	*Próximo*	Prox-eemo
Far	*Lejos*	Layhoss
Cheap	*Barato*	Bar-ato
Expensive	*Caro*	Caro
Open	*Abierto*	Ab-yairto
Closed	*Cerrado*	Thairrado
Today	*Hoy*	Oy
Yesterday	*Ayer*	A-yair
Tomorrow	*Mañana*	Man-yana
How much is....?	*Cuánto cuesta?*	Kwanto kwesta?
What time is it?	*Tiene la hora?*	Tee-eynay-la ora?
Where is...?	*Dónde está...?*	Don-des-ta?
How do I reach...?	*Cómo llego a...?*	Com-oh-yeg-oh-a?
I don't understand	*No entiendo*	No ent-yendo
I would like....	*Quisiera...*	Ki-si-air-a
Do you speak English?	*Habla ingles?*	Abla een-glayss?
One	*Un/Uno*	Oon/Oona
Two	*Dos*	Doss
Three	*Tres*	Tress
Four	*Cuatro*	Kwatro
Five	*Cinco*	Theenko
Six	*Seis*	Say-eess
Seven	*Siete*	See-ettay
Eight	*Ocho*	O-cho
Nine	*Nueve*	Nwaybay
Ten	*Diez*	D-yeth

(or open for less time) on Sundays. Most towns take a **siesta** between 1pm and 4pm, although some shops in cities such as Madrid and Barcelona will stay open all day. Shops and banks are closed on the following public holidays: 1st and 6th January, the week before Easter Monday, 1st May, 15th August, 12th October, 1st November, 6th, 8th and 24th December. In addition to these dates, each town and city will celebrate their own annual **fiesta** in honour of their patron saint – check the town/regional tourist offices for festival dates. Local communities put an extraordinary amount of effort into their fiestas; if you're in town when one is on, make sure you don't miss what are pretty much without exception vibrant, cultural experiences.

Madrid

MADRID became Spain's capital thanks to its geography; when Philip II moved the seat of government here in 1561, his aim was to create a symbol of Spanish unification and centralization. However, the city has few natural advantages – it is 300km from the sea on a 650-metre-high plateau, freezing in winter, baking in summer – and it was only the determination of successive rulers to promote a strong central capital that ensured its success. Today, Madrid's streets are a beguiling mix of old and new, with narrow, atmospheric alleys and wide, open boulevards. It is also home to some of Spain's best artworks, from the Museo del Prado's world-renowned classical collection, to the impressive modern works at the Reina Sofía. Galleries and sights aside, much of Madrid's charm comes from immersing yourself in the daily life of the city: hanging out in the traditional cafés and *chocolaterías* or the summer *terrazas*, packing the lanes of the Sunday Rastro flea market, or playing very hard and very late in a thousand bars, clubs, and discos.

What to see and do

Central **Puerta del Sol**, with its bustling crowds and traffic, is as good a place as any to start. This is officially the centre of the nation: a stone slab in the pavement outside the main building on the south side marks **Kilómetro Zero**, from where six of Spain's *Rutas Nacionales* (National Routes) begin. The city's emblem, a statue of a bear pawing a *madroño* bush, lies on the north side. To the west, c/Arenal heads directly towards the Teatro Real and Palacio Real, but there's more of interest along **c/Mayor**, one of Madrid's oldest thoroughfares, which runs southwest through the heart of the medieval city and ends close to the Palacio Real.

Plaza Mayor

Walking down c/Mayor from the Puerta del Sol, it's easy to miss altogether the **Plaza Mayor**, the most important architectural and historical landmark in Madrid. This almost perfectly preserved, extremely beautiful, seventeenth-century arcaded square, set back from the street, was planned by Philip II and Juan Herrera as the public meeting place of the new capital: *autos-da-fé* (trials of faith) were held by the Inquisition here, kings were crowned, festivals and demonstrations staged, bulls fought and gossip spread. The more important of these events would be watched by royalty from the frescoed **Casa Panadería**, named after the bakery that it replaced. Along with its popular but pricey cafés, the plaza still performs several public functions today: in summer, it's an outdoor theatre and music stage; in autumn, a book fair; and just before Christmas it becomes a bazaar for festive decorations and religious regalia.

Plaza de la Villa

About two-thirds of the way along c/Mayor is the **Plaza de la Villa**, almost a casebook of Spanish architectural development. The oldest survivor here is the **Torre de los Lujanes**, a fifteenth-century building in Mudéjar style; next in age is the **Casa de Cisneros**, built by a nephew of Cardinal Cisneros in sixteenth-century Plateresque style; and to complete the picture is the **Ayuntamiento** (free tours in Spanish only, Mon at 5pm), begun in the seventeenth century, but later remodelled in Baroque mode. Baroque is taken a stage further around the corner on c/San Justo, where the church of **San Miguel** shows the unbridled imagination of its eighteenth-century Italian architects.

Palacio Real

From Calle Mayor, turn right into Calle San Nicolás and follow it to the end until you reach the **Teatro Real** (Ⓦwww.teatro-real.com) or Royal Opera House, which is separated from the Palacio Real by the newly renovated **Plaza de Oriente**. The chief attraction of the area is the grandiose **Palacio Real**, or Royal Palace (Mon–Sat 9.30am–5/6pm, Sun 9am–3pm; €8, excellent student discounts, free Wed to EU citizens; Metro Ópera). Built after the earlier Muslim Alcázar burned down on Christmas Day 1734, this was the principal royal residence until Alfonso XIII went into exile in 1931. The present royal family inhabits a more modest residence on the western outskirts of the city, using the Palacio Real only on state occasions. The building scores high on statistics: it claims more rooms than any other European palace; a **library** with one of the biggest collections of books, manuscripts, maps and musical scores in the world; an **armoury** with an unrivalled and often bizarre collection of weapons dating back to the fifteenth century; and an original **pharmacy**, a curious mixture of alchemist's den and early laboratory. Take your time to contemplate the extraordinary opulence of the place: acres of Flemish and Spanish tapestries, endless Rococo decoration, bejewelled clocks and pompous portraits of the monarchs. In the **Sala del Trono** (Throne Room), there's a magnificent frescoed ceiling by Tiepolo representing the glory of Spain – an extraordinary achievement for an artist by then in his seventies.

The Gran Vía

North from the palace, c/Bailén runs into the Plaza de España, longtime home of the tallest skyscrapers in the city. From here join **Gran Vía**; once the capital's major thoroughfare, it effectively divides the old city to the south from the newer parts. Permanently crowded with shoppers and sightseers, the street is appropriately named, with splendidly quirky Art Nouveau and Art Deco facades fronting its banks, offices and apartments, and huge posters on the cinemas. At its far end, by the magnificent cylindrical **Edificio Metropolis**, it joins with c/Alcalá on the approach to Plaza de Cibeles. Just across the junction is the majestic old **Círculo de las Bellas Artes**, a contemporary art space with a trendy café/bar (€1 entry).

On an entirely different plane, the **Monasterio de las Descalzas Reales** (Tues–Thurs & Sat 10.30am–12.45pm & 4–5.45pm, Fri 10.30am–12.45pm, Sun 11am–1.45pm; €5), one of the hidden treasures of the city, lies just south of Gran Vía, off the Plaza de Callao. It's a beautiful, tranquil locale, contrasting with the frenzied commercialism all around. A whistle-stop guided tour in Spanish is available.

Museo del Prado

South across the Paseo del Prado from the Círculo de la Bellas Artes lies Madrid's **Museo del Prado** (Tues–Sun 9am–8pm, ticket office shuts 30min before closing; €6, EU students under 25 free; free Sun; Ⓣ913 795 299, Ⓦwww.museoprado.es; Metro Atocha), which has been one of Europe's key art galleries ever since it opened in 1819. It houses over three thousand paintings in all, including the world's finest collections of Goya, Velázquez, Rubens and Bosch. Pick up a leaflet at the entrance to find your way around. The central downstairs gallery houses the **early Spanish collection**, and a dazzling array of portraits and religious paintings by El Greco, among them his mystic and hallucinatory *Crucifixion* and *Adoration of the Shepherds*. Beyond this are the Prado's **Italian** treasures: superb Titian portraits of Charles V and Philip II, as well as works by Tintoretto, Bassano,

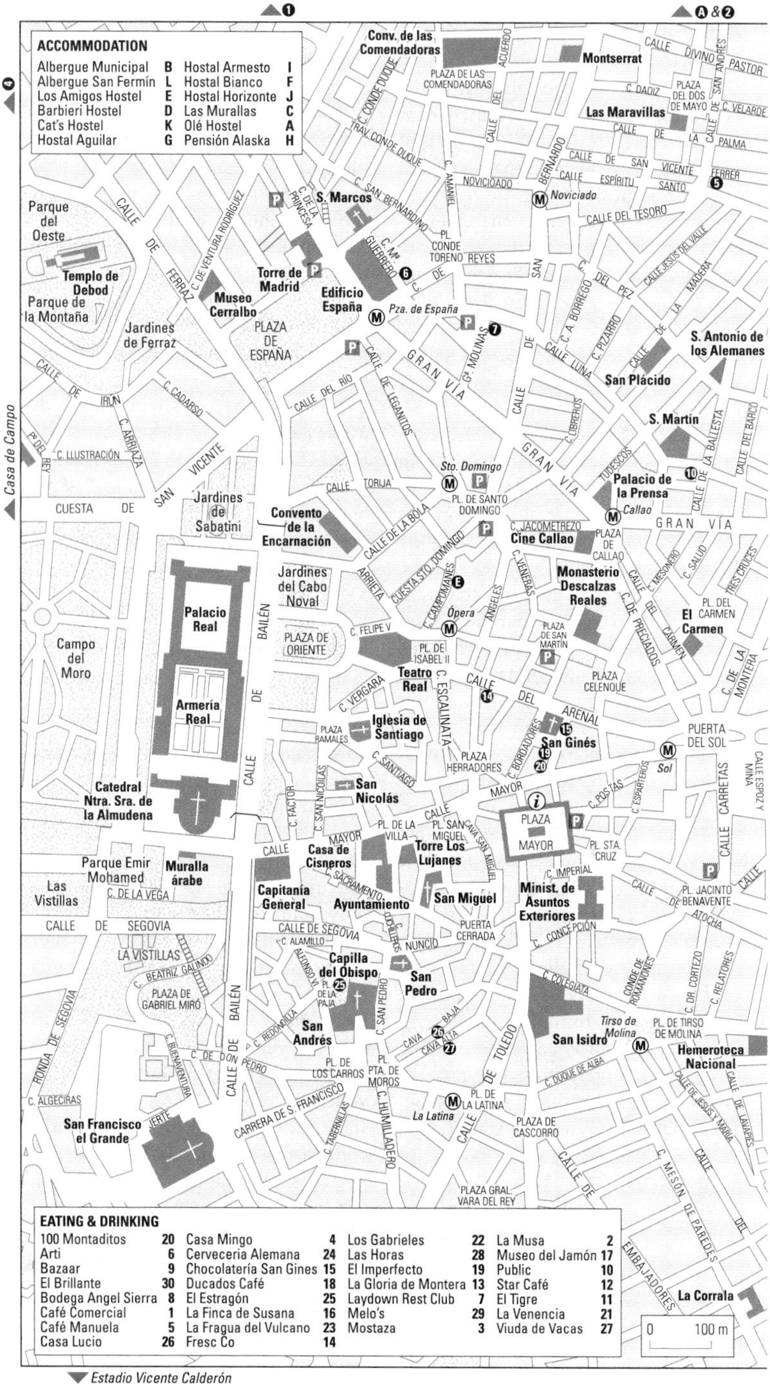

ACCOMMODATION

Albergue Municipal	B	Hostal Armesto	I
Albergue San Fermín	L	Hostal Bianco	F
Los Amigos Hostel	E	Hostal Horizonte	J
Barbieri Hostel	D	Las Murallas	C
Cat's Hostel	K	Olé Hostel	A
Hostal Aguilar	G	Pensión Alaska	H

Conv. de las Comendadoras
Montserrat
Las Maravillas
S. Marcos
Parque del Oeste
Templo de Debod
Parque de la Montaña
Torre de Madrid
Museo Cerralbo
Edificio España
Jardines de Ferraz
PLAZA DE ESPAÑA
S. Antonio de los Alemanes
San Plácido
S. Martín
Palacio de la Prensa
Casa de Campo
Jardines de Sabatini
Convento de la Encarnación
Cine Callao
Monasterio Descalzas Reales
Jardines del Cabo Noval
Palacio Real
PLAZA DE ORIENTE
El Carmen
Campo del Moro
Armería Real
Teatro Real
Iglesia de Santiago
San Ginés
PUERTA DEL SOL
San Nicolás
Catedral Ntra. Sra. de la Almudena
Casa de Cisneros
Torre Los Lujanes
PLAZA MAYOR
Parque Emir Mohamed
Muralla árabe
Las Vistillas
Capitanía General
Ayuntamiento
San Miguel
Minist. de Asuntos Exteriores
Capilla del Obispo
San Pedro
San Andrés
San Isidro
Hemeroteca Nacional
San Francisco el Grande
La Latina
La Corrala
GRAN VÍA
Estadio Vicente Calderón

EATING & DRINKING

100 Montaditos	20	Casa Mingo	4	Los Gabrieles	22	La Musa	2
Arti	6	Cerveceria Alemana	24	Las Horas	28	Museo del Jamón	17
Bazaar	9	Chocolatería San Gines	15	El Imperfecto	19	Public	10
El Brillante	30	Ducados Café	18	La Gloria de Montera	13	Star Café	12
Bodega Angel Sierra	8	El Estragón	25	Laydown Rest Club	7	El Tigre	11
Café Comercial	1	La Finca de Susana	16	Melo's	29	La Venencia	21
Café Manuela	5	La Fragua del Vulcano	23	Mostaza	3	Viuda de Vacas	27
Casa Lucio	26	Fresc Co	14				

0 100 m

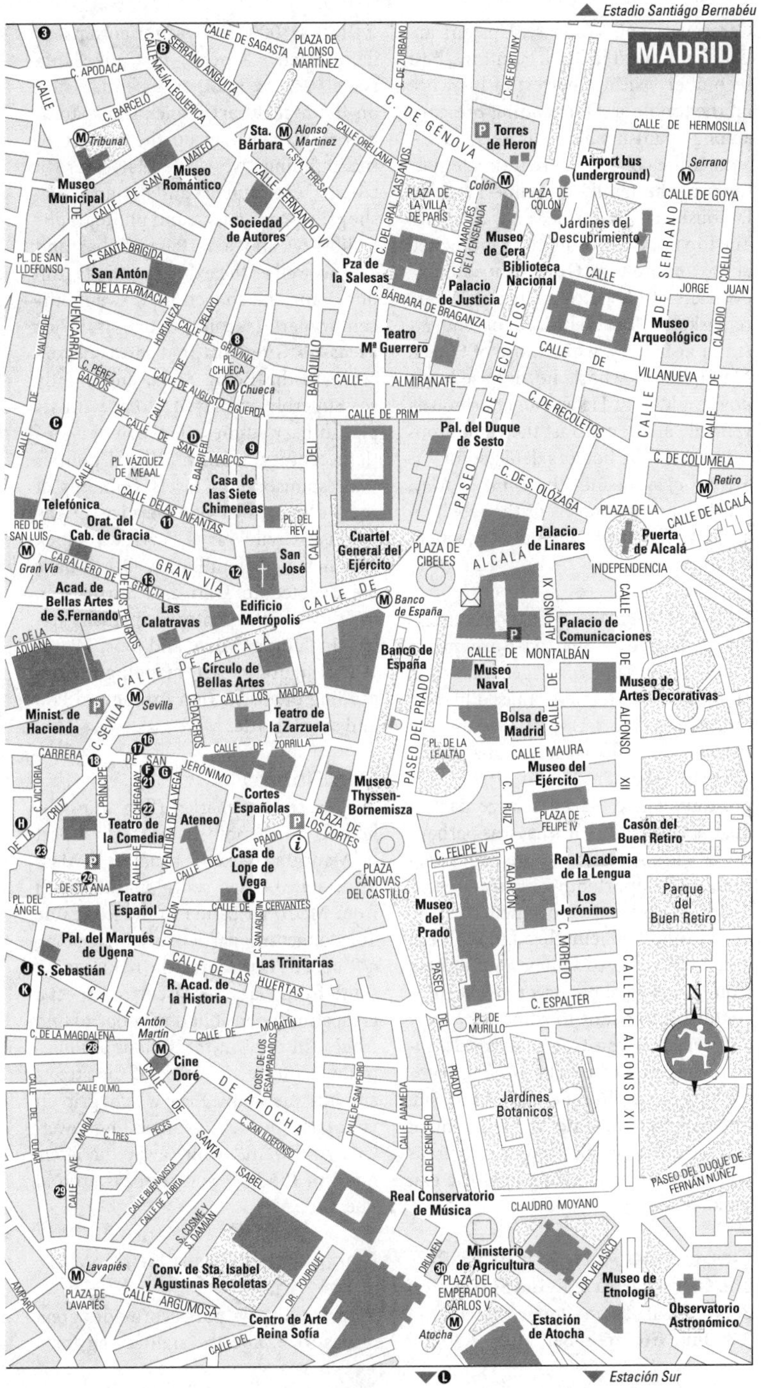
Estadio Santiágo Bernabéu
MADRID
Calle de Sagasta
Plaza de Alonso Martínez
C. de Zurbano
C. de Fortuny
C. Serrano Anguita
Calle Mejía Lequerica
C. Apodaca
C. Barceló
C. de Génova
Calle de Hermosilla
Torres de Heron
Sta. Bárbara
Alonso Martínez
Calle Orellana
C. Sta. Teresa
Tribunal
Calle de San Mateo
Museo Municipal
Museo Romántico
Calle Fernando VI
Calle Gral Castaños
Plaza de la Villa de París
C. del Marqués de la Ensenada
Colón
Plaza de Colón
Airport bus (underground)
Serrano
Calle de Goya
Jardines del Descubrimiento
Sociedad de Autores
Museo de Cera
Biblioteca Nacional
Serrano
Coello
Pl. de San Ildefonso
C. Santa Brígida
San Antón
C. de la Farmacia
Pza de la Salesas
C. Bárbara de Braganza
Palacio de Justicia
Calle Jorge Juan
Fuencarral
Valverde
Hortaleza
Calle de Pelayo
Calle de Gravina
Teatro Mª Guerrero
Recoletos
Museo Arqueológico
Claudio
Pl. Chueca
Chueca
C. Pérez Galdós
Calle de Augusto Figueroa
Barquillo
Calle Almiranate
Calle de Villanueva
C. de Recoletos
Calle de Prim
Pal. del Duque de Sesto
Calle de San Marcos
Barbieri
Pl. Vázquez de Mella
Deli
Paseo de Recoletos
C. de Columela
Retiro
Casa de las Siete Chimeneas
C. de S. Olózaga
Telefónica
Calle de las Infantas
Pl. del Rey
Red de San Luis
Orat. del Cab. de Gracia
Cuartel General del Ejército
Palacio de Linares
Plaza de la Independencia
Puerta de Alcalá
Calle de Alcalá
Gran Vía
Caballero de Gracia
V. de los Peligros
San José
Plaza de Cibeles
Alcalá
Acad. de Bellas Artes de S.Fernando
Las Calatravas
Edificio Metrópolis
Calle de Alcalá
Banco de España
Alfonso XI
Palacio de Comunicaciones
C. de la Aduana
Círculo de Bellas Artes
Calle de Montalbán
Museo Naval
Museo de Artes Decorativas
Minist. de Hacienda
Sevilla
C. Sevilla
Calle Los Madrazo
Cedaceros
Teatro de la Zarzuela
Paseo del Prado
Bolsa de Madrid
Calle de Alfonso XII
Carrera de San Jerónimo
Calle de Zorrilla
Pl. de la Lealtad
Calle Maura
Museo del Ejército
C. Victoria
C. Príncipe
Echegaray
Ventura de la Vega
Museo Thyssen-Bornemisza
Cortes Españolas
Plaza de los Cortes
C. Ruiz de Alarcón
Plaza de Felipe IV
Casón del Buen Retiro
Cruz
Teatro de la Comedia
Ateneo
Prado
Casa de Lope de Vega
C. Felipe IV
Real Academia de la Lengua
Pl. de Sta Ana
Plaza Cánovas del Castillo
Teatro Español
Calle de Cervantes
Pl. del Ángel
Museo del Prado
Los Jerónimos
Parque del Buen Retiro
C. de León
C. San Agustín
Pal. del Marqués de Ugena
C. Moreto
S. Sebastián
Calle de las Huertas
Las Trinitarias
R. Acad. de la Historia
Paseo del Prado
C. Espalter
Calle de Alfonso XII
Antón Martín
C. de la Magdalena
Calle de Moratín
Pl. de Murillo
Cost. de los Desamparados
Calle Olmo
Cine Doré
Calle de Atocha
Calle de San Pedro
Calle Alameda
Jardines Botanicos
Calle del Olivar
Ave María
C. Tres Peces
C. San Ildefonso
Calle de Santa Isabel
C. del Cenicero
Paseo del Duque de Fernán Núñez
Calle Buenavista
Calle de Zurita
Real Conservatorio de Música
Claudio Moyano
S. Cosme y S. Damián
Dr. Fourquet
Drumen
Ministerio de Agricultura
Lavapiés
Conv. de Sta. Isabel y Agustinas Recoletas
Plaza del Emperador Carlos V
C. Dr. Velasco
Museo de Etnología
Observatorio Astronómico
Amparo
Plaza de Lavapiés
Calle Argumosa
Centro de Arte Reina Sofía
Atocha
Estación de Atocha
Calle del
Estación Sur
SPAIN
MADRID

Caravaggio and Veronese. Upstairs are Goya's unmissable Black Paintings, best seen after visiting the rest of his work on the top floor. Outstanding presence among Spanish painters is Velázquez – among the collection are intimate portraits of the family of Felipe IV, most famously his masterpiece *Las Meninas*. The top floor of the building is devoted almost entirely to **Goya**, whose many portraits of his patron, Charles IV, are remarkable for their lack of any attempt at flattery, while those of Queen María Luisa, whom he despised, are downright ugly. He was an enormously versatile artist: contrast the voluptuous *Majas* with the horrors depicted in *The Second of May* and *The Third of May*, on-the-spot portrayals of the rebellion against Napoleon and the subsequent reprisals.

Museo Thyssen-Bornemisza

The **Museo Thyssen-Bornemisza** (Tues–Sun 10am–7pm; general ticket €6; ⓣ913 690 151, ⓦwww.museothyssen.org; Metro Atocha) occupies the old Palacio de Villahermosa, diagonally opposite the Prado. In 1993, this prestigious site played a large part in Spain's acquisition of what was perhaps the world's greatest private art collection, with important works from every major period and movement – from Duccio and Holbein, through El Greco and Caravaggio, to Schiele and Rothko; from a strong showing of nineteenth-century Americans to some very early and very late Van Goghs; and side-by-side hangings of parallel Cubist studies by Picasso, Braque and Mondrian. There's a **bar and café** in the basement and re-entry is allowed, so long as you get your hand stamped at the exit desk.

Centro de Arte Reina Sofía

The **Centro de Arte Reina Sofía** (Mon & Wed–Sat 10am–9pm, Sun 10am–2.30pm; €6, free Sat after 2.30pm; ⓣ917 741 000, ⓦwww.museoreinasofia.es; Metro Atocha) in Calle Santa Isabel, 52, is another essential stop on the Madrid art scene. Transparent lifts shuttle visitors up the outside of the building, whose levels feature a cinema; excellent art and design bookshops; a print, music and photographic library; and a restaurant, bar and café, as well as the exhibition halls (top floor) and the collection of twentieth-century art (second floor). It is for **Picasso's Guernica** that most visitors come to the Reina Sofía, and rightly so. Superbly displayed along with its preliminary studies, this icon of twentieth-century Spanish art and politics – a response to the fascist bombing of the Basque town of Guernica in the Spanish Civil War – carries a shock that defies all familiarity. Other halls are devoted to **Dalí** and Surrealism, early-twentieth-century Spanish artists including **Miró** and post-World War II figurative art, mapping the beginning of abstraction through to Pop and avant-garde.

The Rastro

The **Rastro** flea market (Sun and public hols 10am–3pm) is as much a part of Madrid's weekend ritual as a Mass or a *paseo*. The stalls sprawl south from Metro La Latina to the Ronda de Toledo, getting particularly busy along c/Ribera de Curtidores, the road leading south from Plaza de Cascorro. Expect a great atmosphere, but don't hope to find fabulous bargains; the serious antiques trade has mostly moved off the streets and into the shops. Keep a tight grip on your bags, pockets, cameras and jewellery. Afterwards, while away the afternoon in the bars and *terrazas* around Puerta de Moros.

Parque del Buen Retiro and other parks

Madrid's many parks provide great places to escape the sightseeing for a few hours. The most central and most popular is the **Parque del Buen Retiro** (Metro Retiro) behind the Prado, a stunning mix of formal gardens and wilder spaces. You can jog, row a boat, picnic, have your fortune told and, above all, promenade. The atmosphere on Sunday afternoons makes visiting a must, as half of Madrid turns up for a *paseo*, whilst listening to groups of musicians enjoying impromptu jamming sessions around the Alfonso XVI statue by the lake. You can also visit the newly built "Hill of the Absents" – a mound constructed in memory of those who died in the Madrid bombing of 2004. Travelling art exhibitions are frequently housed in the beautiful **Palacio de Velázquez** and the nearby **Palacio de Cristal** (times and prices vary according to exhibition). Although charming by day, Retiro is best avoided at night. The nearby **Jardines Botánicos** (daily 10am–sunset; €2; Metro Atocha), whose entrance faces the southern end of the Prado, are also delightful. The **Parque del Oeste** on the city's western edge (Metro Ventura Rodríguez; access via c/Luisa Fernanda) is worth visiting for its spectacular views around sunset; it also boasts a genuine Egyptian temple (Tues–Fri 10am–2pm & 6–8pm, Sat & Sun 10am–1pm & 4–8pm; free).

Arrival and information

Plane Barajas airport is 16km out of town and connected with the central Nuevos Ministerios metro station (12min) by line #8. Alternatively, bus #200 leaves terminals 1 and 2 (6am–11.30pm; weekdays every 10min; weekends & public hols every 20min; €1) for the Avenida de America interchange, where you can get the metro into the centre. A taxi into town should cost no more than €25 – check the driver's meter is switched on.

Train Trains from the north and Portugal arrive at the Estación de Chamartín, in the north of the city but connected to the centre – and all major city locations – via metro line #10. Estación de Atocha serves the south, east and west of Spain. Local trains use the Estación de Príncipe Pío, also known as Estación del Norte, which, despite the name, lies towards the western edge of the city.

Bus Terminals are scattered throughout the city, but the largest – used by all international services – is the Estación del Sur (Metro Méndez Alvaro) on c/Méndez Alvaro, south of Estación de Atocha.

Tourist office The main municipal tourist office is at Plaza Mayor 27 (Mon–Sat 10am–8pm, Sun 10am–3pm; ⓣ915 881 636, ⓦwww.esmadrid.com) and offers free Internet. Branches at Duque de Medinaceli 2, near Plaza de las Cortes (Mon–Fri 8am–8pm, Sat 9am–1pm; ⓣ914 294 951), and at the airport (daily 8am–8pm; ⓣ913 058 656).

City transport

Public transport The centre is comfortably walkable, but Madrid also has an efficient **metro system** that runs from 6am until 1.30am (flat fare €1; €6.40 for a ten-journey ticket, valid on buses, too). The urban **bus** network is more comprehensive but more complicated – the transport information stand in Plaza de Cibeles is more reliable than the quickly outdated handouts. Buses run from 6am to 11.30pm, but there are also several night-bus lines in the centre, from Plaza de Cibeles and Puerta del Sol (midnight–5am; every 15min). For a taxi, call ⓣ914 475 180, 914 055 500 or 914 459 008.

Tour bus Hop-on hop-off Madrid Vision tour buses stop at all the major sights (€15.30/20 for 1/2 days).

Accommodation

The cheapest **accommodation** is around Estación de Atocha, though places closest to the station are rather grim and the area can feel threatening at night. A better option is to head up c/Atocha towards Puerta del Sol, to the streets surrounding the buzzing, pedestrianized Plaza Santa Ana. Other promising areas include Gran Vía and up noisy c/Fuencarral towards Chueca and Malsaña. The price at all hostels listed below includes breakfast.

Hostels

Albergue Municipal c/Mejia Lequerica 21 ⓣ915 939 688, ⓦwww.ajmadrid.es. This new government-run hostel is a gem. The stylish decor mixes ultra-modern furnishings and graffiti murals. Facilities include a gym, free unlimited Internet, games room and laundry. Breakfast buffet, sheets and lockers included in the price. Metro

Alonso Martínez or Tribunal, bus #21. Dorms under 26s ❷, over 26s ❸

Albergue San Fermín Ava Fueros 36 ⓣ917 929 897, ⓦwww.san-fermin.org. HI hostel with colourful dorms and great facilities. Bus#123 from Metro Legazpi or #85/86/59 from Atocha Station. Dorms ❷

Barbieri Hostel c/Barbieri 15 ⓣ915 310 258, ⓦwww.barbierihostel.com. Basic, mixed-dorm accommodation in youthful, hip Chueca. Kitchen, communal TV room, and films for rent. Metro Chueca. Dorms ❷

Cat's Hostel c/Cañizares 6 ⓣ913 692 807, ⓦwww.catshostel.com. Huge backpackers' haven in converted eighteenth-century palace with beautiful central patio. Rooms are a bit cramped but the building buzzes with life. Good underground bar plus free Internet. Metro Antón Martín. Dorms ❷, doubles ❸

Los Amigos Hostel Campomanes 6-4° ⓣ915 471 707, ⓦwww.losamigoshostel.com. Friendly hostel with kitchen and Internet, on a quiet street near the Palacio Real. Very popular, booking ahead advisable. Metro Opera. Separate branch at c/Arenal, 26-4° ⓣ915 592 472. Dorms ❷, doubles ❺

Olé Hostel c/Manuela Malasaña 23-1° ⓣ914 465 165, ⓦwww.olehostel.com. Right in the centre of Madrid's trendiest nightlife, this dorm accommodation has all the standard facilities you'll need, from Internet to laundry and kitchen. Metro Bilbao/San Bernardo. Dorms ❷

Hotels

Hostal Aguilar c/San Jerónimo 32-2° ⓣ914 295 926, ⓦwww.hostalaguilar.com. One of several sound choices in an old building packed with possibilities. Good central location. Metro Sevilla/Sol. ❻

Hostal Armesto c/San Agustin 6 ⓣ914 290 940, ⓦwww.hostalarmesto.com. Small, very pleasant *hostal*, well positioned for the Santa Ana area and art galleries. Metro Antón Martín. ❻

Hostal Bianco c/Echegary 5-1° ⓣ913 691 332, ⓦwww.hostalbianco.com. Spotless, air-con rooms. Excellent rates for a central location. Metro Sevilla/Sol. ❺

Hostal Horizonte c/Atocha 28 ⓣ913 690 996, ⓦwww.hostalhorizonte.com. Well-maintained and characterful rooms near the Plaza Santa Ana, though can be noisy. Metro Antón Martín. ❹

Las Murallas c/Fuencarral 23-4° ⓣ915 321 063, ⓦwww.hostalmurallas.com. Accommodation with private bathrooms and balconies overlooking one of Madrid's best shopping streets. Metro Gran Vía. ❹

Pensión Alaska c/Espoz y Mina 7-4° ⓣ915 211 845, ⓦwww.hostalalaska.com. Clean, safe accommodation 1min from Plaza Mayor. English-speaking, polite owners. Metro Sol. ❺

Eating

Madrid has an incredible variety of **restaurants**; best of all, it's easy to dine out on a tight budget. In summer, all areas of the city have **pavement café/bars**, where you can sip coffee by day and drink pretty much all night. Check out, too, the numerous tantalizing **chocolate shops**, such as the recommended Chocolatería San Gines, at Pasadizo de San Ginés 5.

Cafés and tapas

100 Montaditos c/Mayor 22. This chain is popular country-wide due, as the name implies, to its 100 sandwiches, at just €1.10 a pop. Good for a quick snack: simply fill in a menu form, pay at the counter and wait for your food. Metro Sol.

Arti Maestro Guerrero 4, just off Plaza España. Decent place for a light breakfast – cheap food and good music make it a popular spot for students and backpackers. Metro Plaza de España.

Café Comercial Glorieta de Bilbao. Supposedly the oldest meeting place in Madrid. Linger over coffee, *coñac* or cakes. Metro Bilbao.

Ducados Cafe Pl de las Canalejas 3. Young, funky bar/café, serving good salads and pizza, as well as decent cocktails. A popular spot for the first drink of the night.

El Brillante Glorieta del Emperador Carlos V 8. Renowned for its squid *bocadillos* and super-efficient staff. Metro Atocha.

El Tigre c/de las Infantas 30. A must. This great bar is deservedly popular; if you're willing to elbow your way through the crowds, it is the best in the capital for free tapas – every *caña* (€1.50) comes with a heaped plate. Metro Gran Vía.

Melo's c/Ave María 44. Excellent-value Galician place serving huge portions. A Lavapiés institution.

Museo del Jamón c/San Jerónimo 6, Puerta del Sol end. Extraordinary place where hundreds of hams hang from the ceiling, and even the *cañas* (€1.10) come with a free tapa. The best breakfast deals in town. Numerous other branches.

Restaurants

Casa Mingo Paseo de la Florida 34. Cheap and cheerful, with three things on the menu: chicken, cider and salad. Take-away also available. Metro Príncipe Pío. Daily 11am–midnight.

El Estragón Pl de la Paja 10 ⓣ913 658 982. Terracotta tiles, gingham tablecloths and attractive views – this three-storey vegetarian restaurant is a cosy place to eat. Economical *menú del día*, and Internet access. Metro La Latina.

Fresc Co c/Las Fuentes 12. All-you-can-eat buffet for under €10 at this popular chain restaurant. Metro Ópera.

La Gloria de Montera Caballero de Gracia 10. Top-quality Mediterranean food at bargain prices. Understandably popular, so arrive at 1pm for lunch or 8.30pm for dinner – or be prepared to queue (there's no advance booking). Metro Gran Vía. Managed by the same owners are: **La Finca de Susana** c/Arlaban 4 (Metro Sevilla); **Bazaar** c/Libertad 21 (Metro Chueca); and **Public** c/Desengaño 11 (Metro Callao). All match *La Gloria's* quality and value – and extreme popularity.

La Musa c/Manuela Malasaña, 18 ⓣ914 487 558. Always heaving with a young clientele, the food here is sensational. Try the *bombas* (stuffed potatoes) or the enormous meat kebab that hangs above your table from a nifty contraption. Metro Bilbao.

Mostaza c/Fuencarral 102. For a cheap satisfying meal, this place is great for burgers (€3) and sandwiches (€2.50–5). Metro Bilbao.

Viuda de Vacas c/Cava Alta 23. Good-value no-frills Castilian restaurant in an area packed with great bars. Main courses from €10. Metro La Latina.

Drinking and nightlife

Most **bars** in Madrid only really get going around 10.30pm. You won't find many locals downing pints with the aim of getting drunk; the drinking culture is very laid-back and alcohol is often enjoyed with a free tapa. Madrid parties late, with clubs open from 1am until well beyond dawn. For diving in and out of **clubs**, as Madrileños like to do, the student area of Malsaña, focused on Plaza del Dos de Mayo, holds most promise. Gay-area Chueca and multi-cultural Lavapiés/Anton Martín also have a buzzing nightlife.

Bars

Bodega Ángel Sierra c/Gravina 11. Great old bar right on Plaza Chueca, just the place for an apéritif. Open noon–1.30/2.30am. Metro Chueca.

Café Manuela c/San Vincent Ferrer 29. Beautiful decor and a large selection of board games. Good for coffee or jugs of fruity sangria. Open 7pm–2am; closed Aug. Metro Tribunal.

Cervecería Alemána Plaza Santa Ana 6. One of Hemingway's favourite haunts and consequently full of Americans; good traditional atmosphere none the less. Pricey but worth it. Open 10.30am–12.30/2am; closed Aug. Metro Antón Martín/Sol.

El Imperfecto c/Coloreros 5. Excellent bar for cocktails – sip on their great mojitos whilst admiring the topsy-turvy interior, including chairs nailed to the walls. There's also an outdoor seating area. Metro Sol.

La Fragua de Vulcano Nuñez del Arce. In the northwest corner of Plaza Santa Ana, this great bar is known for its free king prawn tapas.

Las Horas c/de la Magdalena 32. Surreal decor with equally crazy prices. Beers half-price (€0.60) on Thurs eve (9pm–1am). Metro Tirso de Molina.

Star Café c/Marqués de Valdeiglesias 5. Hip, happening gay/mixed bar. Funky grooves in the basement at weekends. Closed Sun. Metro Banco de España.

La Venencia c/Echegaray 7. Marvellous old wooden bar, serving sherry only and the most basic of tapas – cheese and pressed tuna. A must. Metro Sevilla.

Los Gabrieles c/Echegaray 17. One of the most spectacular tiled bars in Madrid, with fabulous nineteenth-century drinking scenes on the ceramic tiles, including a great version of Velázquez's *Los Borrachos* (*The Drunkards*). Metro Sevilla.

TREAT YOURSELF

Madrid's culinary scene is extensive, with many restaurants begging to be tried. Get dressed-up and loosen the purse strings at **Laydown Rest Club** (Plaza Mostenses 9 ⓣ915 487 937, ⓦwww.laydown.es; Metro Plaza de España). No tables and chairs here – kick your shoes off, climb onto one of the large white beds and enjoy a meal in this chilled-out, so-trendy-it-hurts joint. Their Sunday brunch deals are particularly good and the website is worth checking for live music evenings and special offers. If you fancy a more traditional evening, splash out at **Casa Lucio** (Cava Baja 35; Metro La Latina), a prestigious restaurant, popular with celebrities and politicians, where you can eat like a king. The food is authentic, traditional and home made, and a set lunch costs around €20.

Clubs

Cool Ballroom c/Isabel La Católica 6. Disco and house dominate the dance floor. Entry price varies depending on event. Metro Santo Domingo.
Kapital c/Atocha 125. A biggie, worth mentioning simply for the seven levels of different dance floors. The €15 admission includes one drink, but don't buy any extras unless you want your wallet severely dented. No trainers. Metro Atocha.
La Vía Láctea c/Velarde 18. Hot-spot of the post-Franco *movida.* 1980s memorabilia covers the walls and the music playlist is pop-rock. Excellent ambience. Daily until 3am. Free entry. Metro Tribunal/Bilbao.
Low Plaza Mostenses 11. This large indie/electro/rock club attracts an alternative crowd and famous DJs. Entry price varies. Metro Plaza España.
Macumba Above Estación Chamartín. Weekend favourite for hardcore clubbers, where the likes of Ministry of Sound hit the decks until 9am. Entry price varies. Metro Chamartín.
Mondo Sala Stella, c/Arlabán 7. Trendy electro club, open Thurs and Sat from 1am. Entry €12. Metro Sevilla.
Ohm Pl del Callao 4. Perennially popular mixed/gay night. Metro Callao.
Palacio de Gaviria c/de Arenal 9 Ⓦwww.palaciogaviria.com. Classic eighteenth-century palace converted into a club. Hosts special nights for foreign-exchange students. Daily from 11pm. Entry Mon–Thurs & Sun €10, Fri & Sat €15. Metro Sol.
Pasapoga Gran Vía 37. This elegant theatre was a dance hall venue in the 1950s. It now hosts everything from mixed/gay to Oriental nights. Entry €12. Metro Callao.
Tupperware Corredora Alta de San Pueblo 26. This club is fun through-and-through, from its über-kitsch decor to its eclectic playlist. Free entry. Open until 3.30am daily. Metro Tribunal.

Entertainment

Big **rock concerts** are usually held at Palacio Vistalegre, Utebo 1 (Metro Oporto), and La Peineta stadium, Avenida Arcentales (Metro Las Musas). **Flamenco** can be heard at its best in the summer, especially at the Cumbre Flamenco, a week of free concerts – held in a metro station – in September (Ⓦwww.cumbreflamenca.es). What's-on **listings** are detailed in free English-language monthly *InMadrid* (available from most hostels and Irish pubs), *esMADRID* magazine (tourist offices), *Guía del Ocio*, *El País*, and *Metropoli*, which comes free with *El Mundo* on a Friday. In July and August, the city council sponsors a **Veranos de la Villa** programme of concerts and free cinema in some attractive outside venues.

Cinema

Alphaville and **Renoir** c/Martín de los Héroes 14 and 12. English-speaking films remain un-dubbed, and Renoir offers student discounts. Metro Plaza de España.
Círculo de Bellas Artes c/del Marqués de Casa Riera. Shows arty film-cycles, tickets usually €4. Metro Banco de España.
Filmoteca c/Santa Isabel 3. Offers a bargain (€2) programme of classic films, a pleasant bar and, in summer, an outdoor cine-terraza.
Ideal Yelmo Cineplex c/del Doctor Cortezo 6. Multi-screen complex, showing all the latest titles in original-language versions.
Institute for the British Council c/Miguel Ángel 1 Ⓦwww.britishcouncil.es. Sometimes holds cultural events in English. Metro Alonso Martínez.

Bullfights

Plaza de Toros (Las Ventas). Hosts some of the year's most prestigious events, especially during the May/June San Isidro festivities. Also a concert venue. Tickets for all but the biggest events are available at the box office (Ⓣ913 562 200, Ⓦwww.las-ventas.com). Metro Ventas.

Live music

Arena c/Princesa 1 Ⓦwww.salarena.com. Top DJs and big-name bands play at this club. Metro Plaza de España.
Café Central Plaza del Angel 10. One of the best places in Europe to hear live jazz. Open from noon for drinks, with music nightly from 10.30pm. Metro Sol.
Gruta 77 c/Nicolas Morales, s/n & c/Cucillo 6. Cool foreign indie bands often play here. Metro Oporto.
La Boca del Lobo c/Echegaray 11 Ⓦwww.labocadellobo.com. Good gig venue with a reputation for showcasing new acts of varied music genres. Metro Sevilla.
Moby Dick c/Avda. de Brasil 5. Popular nautically themed venue attracting foreign bands. Excellent dance floor. Metro Santiago Bernabéu.
Siroco c/San Dimas 3. Late-night music venue with bands playing everything from pop and rock to hip-hop, jazz and funk. Metro San Bernardo.

Flamenco

Candela c/Olmo 2. Legendary bar frequented by musicians, with occasional performances. Open daily 10.30pm–2.30am. Metro Tirso de Molino.
Cardamomo c/Echegaray 15. This flamenco bar attracts a young crowd and on some week-nights

puts on a live flamenco jamming session that's not to be missed. Free entry. Open daily 9pm–3.30am. Metro Sevilla.
Casa Patas c/Cañizares 10. Classic Flamenco club with bar and restaurant. Best nights Thurs & Fri. Entrance €12, or €25–30 with dinner. Metro Antón Martín.

Shopping

Madrid's shopping scene can be divided into four main sections: alternative, designer, high street and traditional Spanish handicrafts.
Alternative shops Chueca and also c/Fuencarral and c/Hortaleza (off Gran Vía). There are several great places here to find that quirky something that no one will have back home, but particularly worth visiting – if only for its unique clientele – is Mercado de Fuencarral, c/Fuencarral 45 (Mon–Sat 10am–9pm), a three-storey mall with over forty shops and stalls selling outlandish clothes, accessories and more.
Designers All the big-names that will probably blow your budget span several streets of the Salamanca district, principally Paseo Castellana, c/Goya, c/Velázquez and c/Serrano.
High street For friendlier prices, shop for popular names on Gran Vía and the streets radiating from Sol.
Traditional handicrafts The area from Plaza Mayor to Puerta de Toledo is filled with shops selling everything from religious icons to embroidered shawls – great for browsing and picking up the odd authentic souvenir, but often quite expensive.

Directory

Bookshops Fnac c/Preciados 28 (Metro Callao) has an English section. J&J Books and Coffee, c/Espiritú Santo 47 (Metro Noviciado) does secondhand books. Petra's International Bookshop c/Campomanes 13 (Metro Ópera) lets you swap your old books for other secondhands.
Embassies Australia, Plaza Descubridor Diego de Ordás 3 ⓣ913 536 600; Canada, Nuñez de Balboa 35 ⓣ914 233 250; Ireland, Paseo de la Castellana 46 ⓣ914 364 093; New Zealand, Plaza de la Lealtad 2 ⓣ915 234 003; UK, c/Fernando el Santo 16 ⓣ917 008 200; US, c/Serrano 75 ⓣ915 872 200.
Exchange Large branches of most major banks on c/Alcalá and Gran Vía. Round-the-clock currency exchange at the airport; Banco Central is best for AmEx travellers' cheques.
Hospitals La Paz del Insalud, Paseo de la Castellana 261 ⓣ917 277 000 (Metro Begoña); Hospital de Madrid, Plaza Conde del Valle de Suchil 16 ⓣ914 476 600 (Metro Quevedo or San Bernardo).
Laundry Ondablu, c/León 3, also has Internet (Metro Antón Martín); Onda Luna c/Estrella 10 (Metro Gran Vía); c/Cervantes 1 (Metro Anton Martín); c/Pelayo 44 (Metro Chueca).
Left Luggage Estación de Atocha has lockers open daily 6am–10pm. Lost property at Plaza de Legazpi 7 ⓣ915 884 348.
Pharmacies Farmacia Atocha, c/Atocha 114 ⓣ915 273 415; Farmacia Lopez Vicente, Gran Vía 26 ⓣ915 213 148; Farmacia c/Mayor 59 ⓣ915 592 395 (24hr). All have a list of night pharmacies posted outside.
Post office Palacio de Comunicaciones, Plaza de Cibeles.
Taxi ⓣ913 712 131 or 913 713 711.

Moving on

Train Algeciras (2 daily; 5hr 30min); Alicante (6–7 daily; 3hr 45min–4hr); Barcelona (9–10 daily; 4hr 45min–9hr 30min); Bilbao (1–2 daily; 6hr–9hr 30min); Cáceres (5–6 daily; 3hr 25min–5hr); Cádiz (2 daily; 5hr); Córdoba (at least 21 daily; 1hr 40min–2hr); Granada (2 daily; 4hr 30min); León (8–9 daily; 4–6hr); Málaga (6 daily; 4hr); Mérida (4–5 daily; 4hr 20min–6hr 50min); Oviedo (2–3 daily; 5hr 45min–7hr 50min); Pamplona (3–4 daily; 3hr 30min); Salamanca (7 daily; 2hr 30min); San Sebastián (3 daily; 5hr 15min–8hr); Santiago de Compostela (3 daily; 8–9hr); Segovia (7–9 daily; 2hr); Seville (12–19 daily; 2hr 30min–3hr 30min); Toledo (9–11 daily; 30min); Valencia (10–14 daily; 3hr 30min–5hr 30min); Zaragoza (10–18 daily; 1hr 45min–3hr 30min).
Bus Algeciras (4 daily; 8hr 30min); Alicante (8 daily; 5hr); Barcelona (at least 19 daily; 7hr 30min); Bilbao (11 daily; 4hr 45min); Cáceres (7–10 daily; 3hr 30min–4hr); Cádiz (6 daily; 7hr); Córdoba (6 daily; 4hr 30min); El Escorial (hourly; 1hr); Granada (6–9 daily; 6hr); León (11 daily; 4hr); Málaga (7 daily; 7hr); Mérida (9 daily; 4hr–4hr 40min); Oviedo (12 daily; 5hr 30min); Pamplona (4 daily; 6hr); Salamanca (24 daily; 2hr 30min–3hr 15min); San Sebastián (8–9 daily; 6hr 30min); Santander (8 daily; 6hr); Santiago de Compostela (6 daily; 8–9hr); Segovia (10am–11pm every 30min; 1hr 30min); Seville (11 daily; 6–8hr); Toledo (6.30am–10pm every 30min; 1hr 15min); Valencia (14 daily; 4hr); Zaragoza (at least 19 daily; 3hr 45min– 4hr 30min).

Day-trips from Madrid

Surrounding the capital are some of Spain's most fascinating cities, all an easy day-trip from Madrid or a convenient stop-off on the main routes out. From **Toledo** you can turn south to Andalucía or strike west towards Extremadura. To the northwest the roads lead past **El Escorial**, from where a bus runs to Franco's tomb at **El Valle de los Caídos**, and through the dramatic scenery of the Sierra de Guadarrama to **Segovia**.

TOLEDO

Capital of medieval Spain until 1560, UNESCO World Heritage site **TOLEDO** remains the seat of the Catholic primate and a city redolent of past glories. Set in a desolate landscape, it rests on a rocky mound isolated on three sides by a looping gorge of the Río Tajo (Tagus). Every available inch of this outcrop has been built on: houses, synagogues, churches and mosques are heaped upon one another in a haphazard spiral, which the dark, somewhat claustrophobic cobbled lanes infiltrate as best they can. To see the city at its finest, lose yourself in the back streets or stay the night; by 6pm, the tour buses have all gone home.

What to see and do

The **Catedral** is at the core of the city (daily 10.30am–noon & 4–7pm, free; museum Mon–Sat 10am–6.30pm, Sun 2–6.30pm, €6). This Gothic construction took almost three centuries to complete (1227–1493) and is bursting with treasures from numerous great artists. The Sacristía and New Museums are home to the most opulent paintings, most notably by El Greco (who settled in Toledo around 1577). The Choir's two-tiered carved wooden stalls (closed Sun am) are at the heart of the building, with the Capilla Mayor's huge altarpiece directly opposite. Behind is the Baroque *Transparente*, with marble cherubs and clouds, especially magnificent when the sun reaches through the strategically placed opening in the roof above.

The Alcázar and around

Toledo is dominated by the imposing **Alcázar** (closed for restoration until at least 2008), east of the cathedral. In 1936, during the Civil War, six hundred barricaded Nationalists held out against relentless Republican attack for over two months until finally relieved by one of Franco's armies. Franco's regime completely rebuilt the fortress as a monument to the endurance and glory of its defenders. An excellent collection of El Grecos can be seen to the north of here in the **Museo de Santa Cruz** (Mon–Sat 10am–6pm, Sun 10am–2pm; free). Also worth a visit is the **Museo de los Concilios y de la Cultura Visigótica** (Tues–Sat 10am–2pm & 4–6.30pm, Sun 10am–2pm; €0.60, free Sat pm and Sun am), in the Mudéjar church of **San Román**, a short way northwest of the cathedral; the building, a delightful combination of Moorish and Christian elements, perhaps even outshines the Visigothic artefacts within. However, El Greco's masterpiece, *The Burial of the Count of Orgaz*, is housed in an annexe to the nearby fourteenth-century church of **Santo Tomé** (daily 10am–7pm; €1.90), whose tower is one of the finest examples of Mudejar architecture in Toledo.

The Judería

From Santo Tomé, c/de San Juan de Dios leads down to the old Jewish Quarter, the **Judería** and, on c/Reyes Católicos, the **Sinagoga del Tránsito**, built along Moorish lines by Samuel Levi in 1366 (Tues–Sat 10am–2pm & 4–9pm, Sun 10am–2pm; €2.40). The only other surviving synagogue, **Santa María la Blanca** (daily 10am–6.45pm;

€1.90), is a short way down the same street, though it looks more like a mosque. If you leave the city by the **Puerta del Cambrón**, you can follow the Paseo de Recaredo northeast along a stretch of Moorish walls to the **Hospital de Tavera** (10am–1.30pm & 3–5.30pm; €4), a Renaissance palace with beautiful twin patios. Heading back to town, pass through the main city gate, the **Puerta Nueva de Bisagra**, from where you can climb a series of stepped alleyways to the tiny **Mezquita Cristo de la Luz** (daily 10am–7pm; €1.90). Built in 999, the mosque is one of the oldest Moorish monuments surviving in Spain.

Arrival and information

Train Super-fast *Avant* trains run regularly from Estación de Atocha in Madrid (€9) and cut the journey time to just 30min (last train back to Madrid at 9.25pm). Book weekend tickets in advance. From Toledo's train station east of town, it's a beautiful (but uphill) 20min walk to the central Plaza Zocódover (bus #5 or #6; €0.85).

Bus The bus station is on Avenida de Castilla la Mancha in the modern part of the city, a 10min walk north of Plaza Zocódover via c/Armas. Buses depart from Madrid's Estación del Sur (€4), with the last bus back to the capital leaving Toledo at 10.30pm (Sun 11.30pm).

Tour bus Spanish-speaking tour starts at the train station and ends at the cathedral. Departs 10am, 11am and 1pm (10am & 11.30am weekends), for €10 per person.

Tourist office The main tourist office is in Plaza Ayuntamiento (daily 10.30am–2.30pm & 4.30–7pm, closed Mon pm; ⓣ925 254 030, ⓦwww.turismocastillalamancha.com), with branches at Puerta de Bisagra (daily 9am–7pm; ⓣ925 220 843) and the Zococentre, Sillería 14 (daily 10am–2pm & 3–6pm; ⓣ925 220 300).

Accommmodation

Camping El Greco c/Cordonerias 6 ⓣ925 220 090, ⓦwww.campingelgreco.es. Out on the road to Puebla de Montalban, this site has good views of the city and a large communal *terraza*. Extra charge to use pool. ❶, 4-person bungalow ❾

Pensión Castilla c/Recoletos 6 ⓣ925 256 318. Located on a winding, pedestrianized street, this establishment offers comfortable, clean rooms with high-beamed ceilings. Small discount on doubles for HI cardholders. ❸

Pensión Nuncio Viejo c/Nuncio Viejo 19-3° ⓣ925 228 178/617 415 410. Rooms can be cramped but the friendly owner and top location (just down from the cathedral) make up for it. ❹

Pensión Segovia c/Recoletos no.2 ⓣ925 211 124. Just around the corner from *Castilla*, with cheaper rates and shared bathrooms. ❷

Pensión Virgen de la Estrella/Arrabal Real de Arrabal 18 ⓣ925 253 134. Local family owns several rooms scattered along this and neighbouring streets. Check-in at restaurant *La Estrella* on c/Airosas, 1. All rooms have TV and balcony. ❸

Eating and drinking

El Ambigú c/Tendillas 8. Cheap and cheerful bar-cum-restaurant. The €9.80 lunchtime menu offers a massive range of filling dishes. Any drink from the bar plus "tapa of the day" costs a mere €1.80. Open daily from 2pm.

Carnicería Rafa c/Tendillas, opposite *El Ambigú*. This meat deli makes filling sandwiches for €1.

Dar Al-chal Teteria For something different, this Moorish bar next to the Santa La Maria synagogue is full of character and serves a wide selection of aromatic teas.

El Trébol Santa Fe 15. Good quality, reasonably priced tapas. Famed for its delicious *bombas* (potatoes stuffed with minced meat).

El Zoco Plaza Barrio Rey 7. Just off the touristy Plaza de Zocódover, *El Zoco* offers better value than the restaurants on its neighbouring square. Set menus from €10. Serves the local speciality, *perdiz* (partridge).

EL ESCORIAL

Fifty kilometres northwest of Madrid, nestled in the foothills of the Sierra de Guadarrama are **SAN LORENZO DEL ESCORIAL** and the monastery of **El Escorial** (April–Sept 10am–6.30pm, last entry 5.30pm; Oct–March Tues–Sun 10am–6pm, last entry 4.30pm; €8, with 1hr guided tour €11; excellent student discounts, free on Wed for EU citizens; ⓣ918 905 904/905). The city grew around this enormous building – a piece of architecture that splits opinions. Whatever your view, there's no disputing its popularity – for fewer crowds,

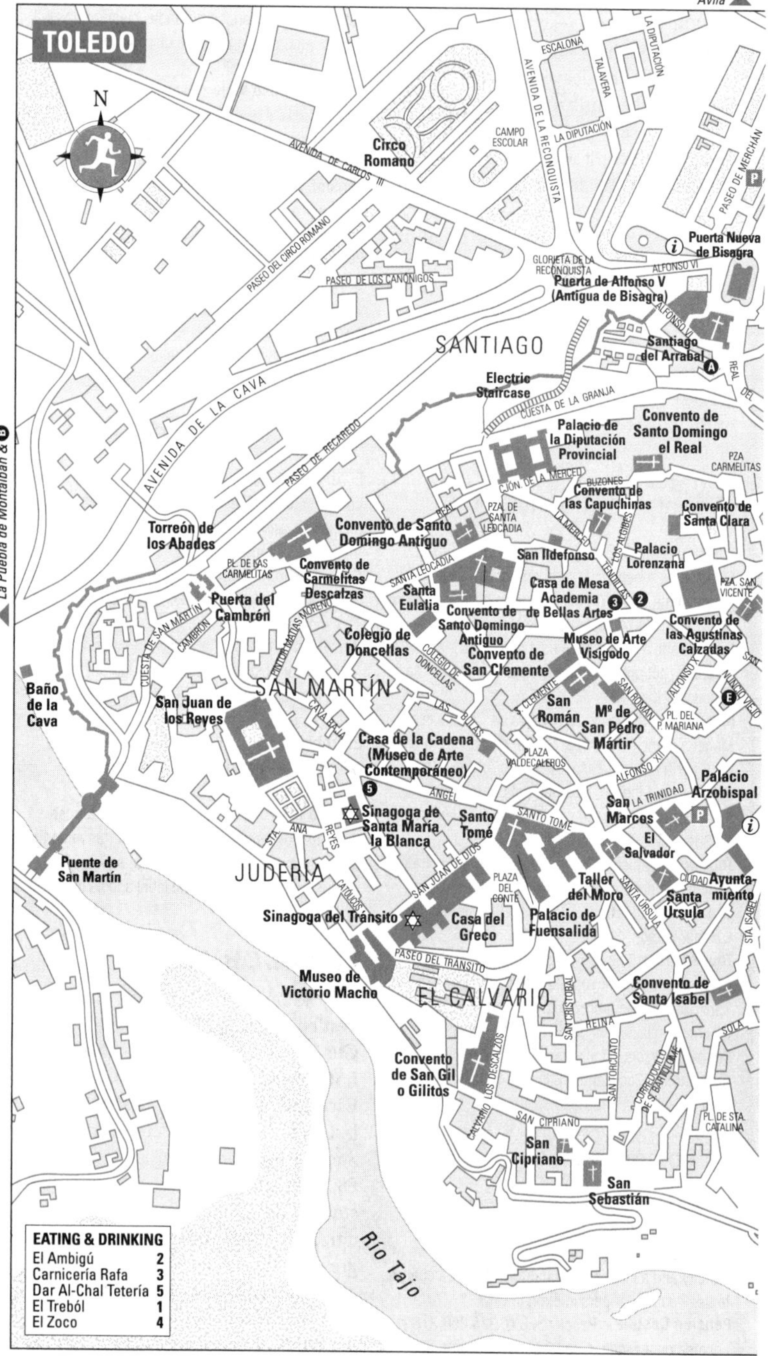
TOLEDO
N
Ávila
Circo Romano
Puerta Nueva de Bisagra
Puerta de Alfonso V (Antigua de Bisagra)
SANTIAGO
Santiago del Arrabal
Electric Staircase
Palacio de la Diputación Provincial
Convento de Santo Domingo el Real
Convento de las Capuchinas
Convento de Santa Clara
Torreón de los Abades
Convento de Santo Domingo Antiguo
San Ildefonso
Palacio Lorenzana
Convento de Carmelitas Descalzas
Santa Eulalia
Casa de Mesa Academia de Bellas Artes
Puerta del Cambrón
Convento de Santo Domingo Antiguo
Convento de las Agustinas Calzadas
Colegio de Doncellas
Convento de San Clemente
Museo de Arte Visigodo
Baño de la Cava
San Juan de los Reyes
SAN MARTÍN
San Román
Mº de San Pedro Mártir
Casa de la Cadena (Museo de Arte Contemporáneo)
Palacio Arzobispal
Sinagoga de Santa María la Blanca
Santo Tomé
San Marcos
El Salvador
Puente de San Martín
JUDERÍA
Taller del Moro
Ayuntamiento
Santa Úrsula
Sinagoga del Tránsito
Casa del Greco
Palacio de Fuensalida
Museo de Victorio Macho
EL CALVARIO
Convento de Santa Isabel
Convento de San Gil o Gilitos
San Cipriano
San Sebastián
Río Tajo
La Puebla de Montalbán & B
EATING & DRINKING
El Ambigú 2
Carnicería Rafa 3
Dar Al-Chal Tetería 5
El Treból 1
El Zoco 4

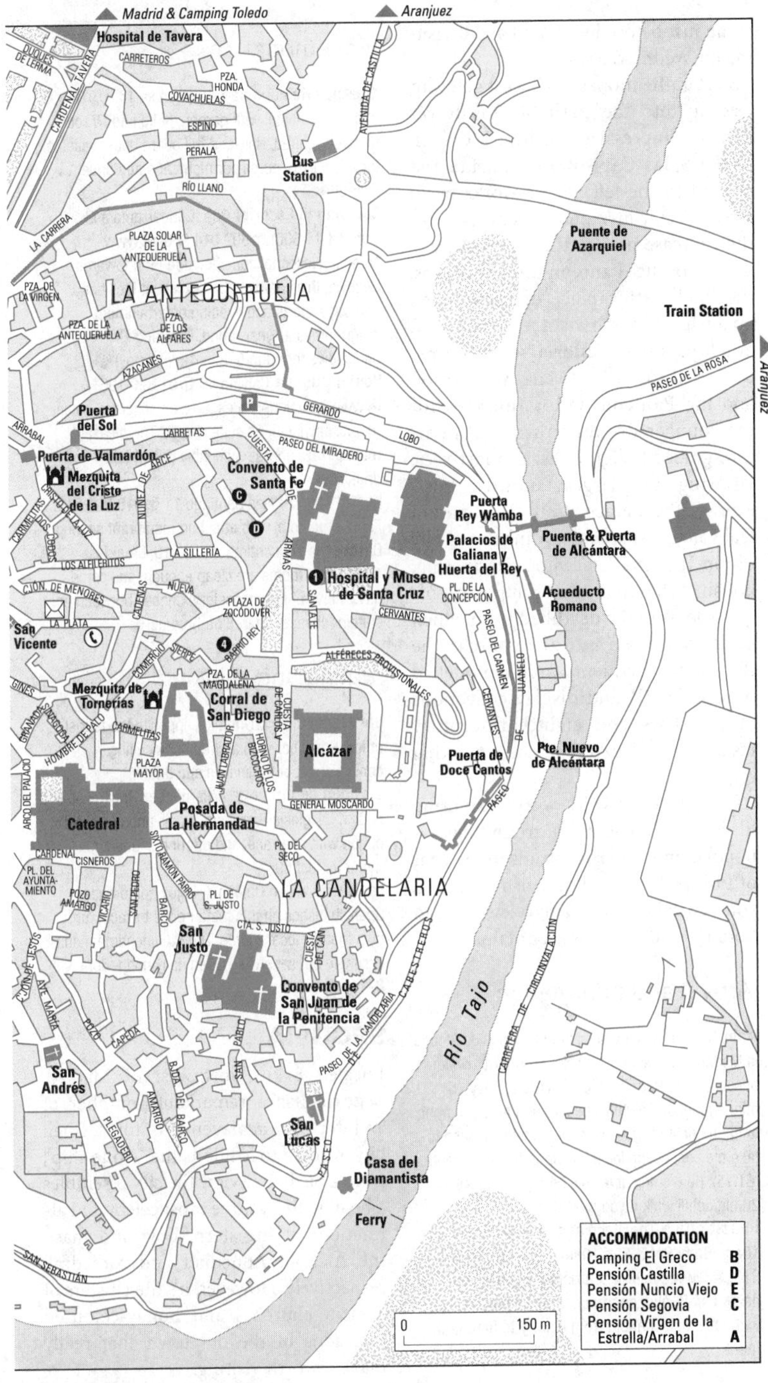

Madrid & Camping Toledo
Aranjuez
Hospital de Tavera
Bus Station
Puente de Azarquiel
Train Station
LA ANTEQUERUELA
Puerta del Sol
Puerta de Valmardón
Mezquita del Cristo de la Luz
Convento de Santa Fe
Puerta Rey Wamba
Palacios de Galiana y Huerta del Rey
Puente & Puerta de Alcántara
Hospital y Museo de Santa Cruz
Acueducto Romano
San Vicente
Mezquita de Tornerías
Corral de San Diego
Alcázar
Puerta de Doce Cantos
Pte. Nuevo de Alcántara
Catedral
Posada de la Hermandad
LA CANDELARIA
San Justo
Convento de San Juan de la Penitencia
Río Tajo
San Andrés
San Lucas
Casa del Diamantista
Ferry
ACCOMMODATION
Camping El Greco B
Pensión Castilla D
Pensión Nuncio Viejo E
Pensión Segovia C
Pensión Virgen de la Estrella/Arrabal A
0 150 m

come just before lunch and avoid visiting on Wednesdays.

Start at the monastery's west gateway, leading into the **Patio de los Reyes** and the impressive Basilica. Move on to the **Salas Capitulares**, outside and around to the left, to see works by El Greco, Velázquez and Ribera. Nearby, the staircase next to the Sacristía leads down to the **Panteón de los Reyes**, the final resting place of virtually all Spanish monarchs since Charles V. You'll pass the **Prudería**, where corpses are left to rot for twenty years prior, and the **Panteón de los Infantes**, for the younger Royal corpses – all interesting, albeit slightly eerie, must-sees. Drawing the largest crowds, however, is the **Palace** itself. The spartan Habsburg Apartments inhabited by Philip II remain the most fascinating, housing the chair that supported his gouty leg and the deathbed from which he looked down into the church. The Bourbon Apartments were remodelled by Charles III and display collections of tapestries and eighteenth-century fashion (€3.60 extra, advance booking required).

If time permits, it's worth exploring El Escorial's natural surroundings. A popular and easy route leads to the **Seat of Philip II**, a large boulder from which you can take in amazing views of San Lorenzo and Abantos mountain.

Arrival and information

Train Trains run every hour from Estación de Atocha in Madrid to El Escorial (1hr; €5.50 return), while buses leaving from the Moncloa area (every 15 min; 50min) are slightly cheaper and take you right to the monastery. If arriving by train, you'll need to take the connecting local bus up to the town centre (€1.15). Be warned, it leaves promptly and it's a 20min uphill walk if you miss it.

Tourist office The office at c/Grimaldi 2 (Mon–Fri 10am–6pm, Sat & Sun 10am–7pm; ⓣ918 905 313, ⓦwww.sanlorenzoturismo.org) has very helpful staff, plus an attached exhibition space with local information, from history to flora and fauna.

Accomodation

Albergue Residencia c/Residencia 14 ⓣ918 905 924. Large hostel with garden, patio and TV room. HI card required. Half-and full board both available for a few extra euros per night. 25s and under ❶, over 25s ❷

Camping El Escorial Ctra. Guadarrama a El Escorial (M-600) ⓣ902 014 900, ⓦwww.campingelescorial.com. Located 5km towards Segovia, this campsite has excellent facilities and busy sports and evening entertainment programmes all year round. Camping ❶, bungalows for up to 5 (min 4-night stay) ❾

Hostal Cristina Calvirio 45 ⓣ91 890 1961, ⓦwww.hostalcristina.es. Sixteen spacious, clean rooms, each with en suite and TV. The pleasant main *terraza* offers reasonably priced tapas and drinks. ❻

Hostal Vasco Plaza Santiago 11 ⓣ918 901 619. Family-run hotel with attached restaurant serving Basque food (lunchtime menu €10, breakfast €4.50). The rooms are clean enough, and some have views of the monastery. Choose between en suite or cheaper shared bathrooms. ❹

Eating and drinking

Bar Monasterio c/Grimaldi, opposite the tourist office. Small bar with arched brick ceiling. A convenient spot for snacks and drinks.

El Fogón de Domingo c/Hernández Briz 9. Located behind La Iglesia Parroquia, this is another cheap option with a terrace, and offering a lunchtime menu for just €9.

La Oficina c/San Quintín 4. Enjoy homemade Spanish dishes on this restaurant's terrace, run by a friendly local couple. The €8 lunchtime menu is simple but satisfying. Open daily noon–5pm & 8–11pm.

SEGOVIA

Located 87km northwest of Madrid, **Segovia** has a remarkable number of architectural achievements for a small city. Known to locals as the "stone ship", from a bird's-eye view the city resembles a boat, with its three most celebrated attractions at the stern, bow and mast: the Alcázar, Aqueduct and cathedral, respectively. However, it's the clusters of ancient churches and honey-coloured mansions of the old town that really make it worth visiting.

What to see and do

The **cathedral** (daily 9.30am–6.30pm; €2, free on Sun mornings but no museum access; ⓣ921 462 205) was the last major Gothic building constructed in Spain and it takes that style to its logical extreme, with pinnacles and flying buttresses tacked on at every conceivable point. The treasures are almost all confined to the **museum**, which opens off the cloisters.

The Alcázar and Aqueduct

Beside the cathedral, c/Daoiz leads on to a small park in front of the **Alcázar** (daily 10am–7pm; €4, third Tues of every month, free; tower access €2; ⓣ921 460 759, ⓦwww.alcazardesegovia.com). This extraordinary castle with narrow towers and turrets looks like something out of Disneyland. And indeed, it isn't entirely authentic – after the fifteenth-century original was destroyed by fire in 1862, an imitation model was built in its place. The city's other main attraction is the **Aqueduct**, a grand structure that dominates the Plaza del Azoguejo, stretching over 800m and towering 30m high. And as if these dimensions weren't impressive enough, the entire structure stands up without a drop of mortar. No one knows exactly when it was built, but it was probably around the end of the first century AD under the emperor Trajan.

Vera Cruz and around

Segovia is an excellent city for walking, with some fine views and beautiful churches to be enjoyed just outside the boundaries. For the most interesting interior, visit **Vera Cruz** (Dec–Oct Tues–Sun 10.30am–1.30pm & 3.30–7pm; €1.75; ⓣ921 431 475), a remarkable twelve-sided building in the valley facing the Alcázar, erected by the Knights Templar in the early thirteenth century. Climb the tower for a highly photogenic vista of the city. While you're over here you could also visit the prodigiously walled **Convento de los Carmelitas** (daily 4–8pm, also Tues–Sun 10am–1.30pm; free; ⓣ921 431 349) and the ramshackle fifteenth-century **Monasterio del Parral** (Tues–Sun 10am–2pm, Wed–Sun also 4–7pm; free; ⓣ921 431 298).

Arrival and information

Train and bus *Cercanía* trains run to Segovia from Madrid's Estación de Atocha or Chamartín every two hours, or there's a bus from Madrid's bus station on Paseo de Florida, near Príncipe Pío. The train station is a 15min walk out of town – turn right out of the station and follow the left-hand fork, or take any bus (every 30min) marked "Puente Hierro/Estación Renfe" to the central Plaza Mayor.
Tourist office The main tourist office is at Plaza del Azoguejo 1 (daily 9am–8pm; ⓣ921 466 070, ⓦwww.turismodesegovia.com), with the local branch at Plaza Mayor 10 (Mon–Thurs & Sun 9am–8pm, Fri & Sat 9am–9pm; ⓣ921 460 334).
Internet Internetcaf.és, Teodosio el Grande 10 (daily 9am–11pm).

Accommodation

Camping Acueducto Avda. D.Juan de Borbón 49 ⓣ921 425 000, ⓦwww.campingacueducto.com. Clean site with standard facilities, including swimming pool, bar and shop. Closed Oct–March. Camping ❶, bungalows ❺
Hostal Aragón Plaza Mayor 4 ⓣ921 460 914. This simple, family-run *hostal* is hidden between two restaurants on the main square. Rooms are slightly weathered but spacious – and the location can't be beat. Shared bathrooms ❷
Hospedaje El Gato Plaza del Salvador 10 ⓣ921 423 244, ⓦwww.infosegovia.com/alojamiento/elgato. *Pensión* prices for hotel-standard facilities. All rooms have hairdryers, iron, satellite TV and air-con – not forgetting views of the Aqueduct. Supplementary breakfast for a bargain €1.80. ❹

Eating and drinking

Eating out in Segovia is expensive. The local delicacies – *cochinillo asado* (suckling pig) and *judiones de La Granja* (a rich broad bean stew) – are well worth sampling, but are pricey and not often found on a set menu for under €20. The best budget option is to visit the central supermarket (Plaza Dr Laguna 4) and picnic in one of the city's green spaces.

La Cueva de San Esteban Plaza San Esteban. Highly recommended tavern with chunky wooden tables and a brilliant atmosphere. Perfect for sharing big plates of tasty tapas. Open daily 11am–midnight.

Restaurante San Miguel c/Infanta Isabel 6. The lively bar serves cheap tapas while the restaurant out back offers €9–18 menus. Generous portions served at both.

Restaurante Muñoz c/Ochoa Ondátegui 19. A traditional-style restaurant serving good Castilian fare. Offers a bargain set-menu with *cochinillo* for €16.

Bar Santana Infanta Isabel 18. A good venue for live music.

Extremadura

The harsh environment of **Extremadura**, west of Madrid, was the cradle of the *conquistadores*. Remote before and forgotten since, the area enjoyed a brief golden age when the heroes returned with their gold to live in a flourish of splendour. **Cáceres** preserves an entire town built with *conquistador* wealth, the streets crowded with the ornate mansions of returning empire builders. An even more ancient past becomes tangible in the wonders of **Mérida**, the most completely preserved Roman city in Spain. Generally, the province attracts fewer tourists in June and July, as temperatures get unbearably hot.

CÁCERES

Old **CÁCERES**, 295km southwest of Madrid, was largely built on the proceeds of American exploration and is home to the University of Extremadura. The Ciudad Monumental is great for a wander, with its contrast of immaculate historical buildings and colourful modern-art sculptures. Don't forget to look up here – the sky is buzzing with storks that reside in huge rooftop nests. Almost every building in the central **Plaza Mayor** is magnificent, featuring ancient walls pierced by the low **Arco de la Estrella**, the **Torre del Bujaco** – whose foundations date back to Roman times – and the **Torre del Horno**, one of the best-preserved Moorish mud-brick structures in Spain. Another highlight, through the Estrella gate, is the **Casa de Toledo-Montezuma** to which a follower of Cortés brought back one of the New World's more exotic prizes – a daughter of the Aztec emperor as his bride. On the Plaza de las Veletas is the **Museo Provincial** (Tues–Sat 9am–2.30pm & 5–8.15pm, Sun 10.15am–2.30pm; EU citizens free, non-EU €1.20 or free on Sun; ⓣ927 010 877, ⓦwww.museosextremadura.com/caceres), whose highlight is the cistern of the original Moorish Alcázar, with rooms of wonderful horseshoe arches.

Arrival and information

Train and bus Cáceres' train and bus stations face each other across the Carretera Sevilla, some way out of town; bus #1 runs every 15min to Plaza de San Juan (€0.75), a square near the centre, with signs leading on towards the Plaza Mayor.

Tourist office The main tourist office is at Plaza Mayor 10 (Mon–Fri 8am–3pm, Sat & Sun 10am–2pm; ⓣ927 010 834, ⓦwww.turismoextremadura.com); there's another on c/Ancha (Tues–Sun 10am–2pm & 4.30–8.30pm; ⓣ927 247 172). For arts and entertainment listings, pick up *La Guía Ocio.*

Accommodation

Albergue Las Veletas c/Margallo 36 ⓣ927 211 210. Completely refurbished in July 2007, all dorms have modern furnishings and air-con. Spotless bathrooms and very friendly staff. Breakfast for an additional €2.50. ❷

Pensión Carretero Plaza Mayor 22 ⓣ927 247 482. Enjoys a brilliant location, but rooms are distinctly no-frills – some even lack a window. ❷

Los Naranjos Alfonso IX 12 ⓣ24 35 08. A safe bet, with clean, comfortable, en-suite rooms and just a few streets from the Plaza Mayor. ❺

Cáceres Camping Ctra. N-630km ⓣ927 233 100, ⓦwww.campingcaceres.com. Located 4km from the historical centre, this site is open all year round and offers excellent facilities (including a swimming pool and Wi-Fi) for dirt-cheap rates. Camping ❶, 2-person studio ❸, 4-person bungalow ❻

Eating and drinking

Café Adarve c/Sánchez Garrido 4 ⓣ927 244 874. This café-restaurant prides itself on efficient service and, oddly, its prawn tapas. Food is cheap, filling and home-made. Set menus (€7.50–9) are served between 1.30pm and 3.30pm.

Mesón El Encinar Plaza Mayor 6 ⓣ927 248 531. Great ambience, probably the most popular *terraza* on the main square. Good tapas from €1.20 and *platos combinados* starting at €10.

Moanin c/Duque. Just off Plaza Mayor, this funky bar attracts a young clientele. Come here for a cheap breakfast deal or evening drinks.

La Traviata c/Sergio Sánchez 8. Extremely popular with the young crowd, this bar is full of character. Enjoy a cocktail on a lamp-lit table outside or venture inside for monthly art exhibitions and DJ sessions. Open daily 4pm–3am.

TREAT YOURSELF

The streets of Cáceres are blisteringly hot during the summer months, and the Arab baths at **El Aljibe de Cáceres** on c/Peña (ⓣ927 223 256, ⓦwww.hammamcaceres.com) are the perfect remedy with the traditional warm, hot, then cold pools. Sessions last up to an hour and a half and cost €15 (student discounts available). Reservations are essential.

MÉRIDA

MÉRIDA, 70km south of Cáceres, contains one of Europe's most remarkable concentrations of Roman monuments. With the aid of a map and a little imagination, it's not hard to reconstruct the Roman city within the not-especially-attractive modern town. A **combined ticket** (€10) gives access to all the sites (daily 9.30am–1.45pm & 5–7.15pm). The **Teatro Romano and Anfiteatro** were presents to the city from Marcus Agrippa in around 15BC. The stage is in a particularly good state of repair, and in July and August it's the scene for a season of classical plays (tickets from €9). In its day, the adjacent amphitheatre could accommodate up to fifteen thousand people – almost half Mérida's population today. Also worth seeing is the magnificent **Puente Romano**, the Roman bridge across the islet-strewn Guadiana – sixty arches long, and defended by an enormous, plain Moorish **Alcazaba.** By the theatre's entrance, you'll find the vast, red-brick bulk of the **Museo Nacional de Arte Romano** (Tues–Sat 10am–2pm & 4–9pm, Sun 10am–2pm; €2.40, free for EU citizens on Sat pm & Sun; ⓣ924 311 690, ⓦwww.mnar.es). This high-ceiling building does full justice to its superior collection, including portrait statues of Augustus, Tiberius and Drusus, and some glorious mosaics.

Arrival and information

Train The train station is a short walk along from the Santa Eulalia church on Avenida de Extremadura. Follow c/Cardero towards the city centre and municipal tourist office.

Bus The bus station is on Avenida de la Libertad, on the opposite side of the river to the city centre. Catch bus # 4 or 6 over the Lusitania bridge. Eight buses run here daily from Estacíon Conde de Casal in Madrid, three daily from Cáceres.

Tourist office The town's tourist office is at the entrance to the Teatro Romano on Paseo José Saenz de Burnaga (Mon–Fri 9am–1.45pm & 4–7.15pm, Sat & Sun 9.30am–2pm; ⓣ924 009 730, ⓦwww.turismoextremadura.com). Municipal information is at c/Santa Eulalia 64 (daily 9.30am–2pm & 5–8pm; ⓣ924 330 722). Pick up Extremadura's monthly entertainment listings guide, *Guíate,* with some pages in English.

Accommodation

Hostal Bueno c/Calvario 9 ⓣ924 302 977. Shares owners with *Salud*, but this *hostal* is slightly cheaper and a little less polished. ❸

Hostal Nueva España Avda. Extremadura 6 ⓣ924 313 356. Clean, spacious rooms with TV and private bath, just a short walk from the train station. ❹

Hostal Salud c/Vespasiano 41 ⓣ924 31 22 59, ⓔhsalud@blunet.com. En-suite rooms equipped with TV, some with air-con. ❹

Camping Mérida Ctra. Madrid-Lisboa ⓣ924 303 453, ⓕ924 300 398. Open all year round, with pool and restaurant. ❶

Eating and drinking

Via Flavia Plaza del Rastro 9. The location of this bar is great. Enjoy tapas on the terrace whilst taking in views of the sixteenth-century Plaza de España and the Alcazaba.

La Despensa del Castúo c/José Ramón Mélida 48. On the road leading to the amphitheatre, this shop/bar/restaurant is the most popular in a line of eating establishments. *Jamón* is the speciality here, with legs hanging from the ceiling and the largest ham menu known to man. Most tapas are €1, so order a few – when you want more, alert the waiter with the buzzer on your table.

Old Castile

The foundations of modern Spain were laid in the kingdom of **Castile**, west and north of Madrid. A land of frontier fortresses – the *castillos* from which it takes its name – it became the most powerful and centralizing force of the Reconquest. The monarchs of this triumphant and expansionist age were enthusiastic patrons of the arts, endowing their cities with superlative monuments above which, quite literally, tower the great Gothic cathedrals of **Salamanca** and **León**.

SALAMANCA

SALAMANCA is probably the most graceful city in Spain, home to what was once one of the most prestigious universities in the world. It's a small place, but with many golden sandstone monuments and the best Plaza Mayor in the country. As if that weren't enough, Salamanca's student population ensure their town is lively at night during term time.

What to see and do

A postcard-worthy overview of Salamanca is easy to attain: go to the extreme south of the city and cross its oldest surviving monument, the much-restored, four-hundred-metre-long **Puente Romano** (Roman Bridge). To explore Salamanca from close-up make for the grand **Plaza Mayor**, its bare central expanse enclosed by a four-storey building decorated with iron balconies and medallion portraits. Nowhere is the Churrigueresque variation of Baroque so refined as here, the restrained elegance of the designs heightened by the changing strength and angle of the sun. From the south side, Rúa Mayor leads to the celebrated fifteenth-century **Casa de las Conchas**, or House of Shells (Mon–Fri 9am–9pm, Sat & Sun 9am–2pm & 5–8pm; free), so called because its facades are decorated with rows of carved scallop shells, symbol of the pilgrimage to Santiago.

Patio de las Escuelas Menores

From the Casa de las Conchas, c/ Libreros leads to the **Patio de Las Escuelas Menores** and the Renaissance entrance to the **Universidad** (Mon–Sat 9.30am–1.30pm & 4–7.30pm, Sun 10am–1.30pm; €4, free Mon morning). The ultimate achievement of Plateresque art, this reflects the tremendous reputation of Salamanca in the early sixteenth century, when it was one of Europe's greatest universities. See if you can spot the legendary "*rana de suerte*" (lucky frog) on its intricately sculpted facade.

The cathedrals

As a further declaration of Salamanca's standing, the Gothic **Catedral Nueva** (daily 9am–8pm; free) was begun in 1512, and acted as a buttress for the Old Cathedral, which was in danger of collapsing. Joaquín Churriguera and his brother Alberto, two architects from a prodigiously creative family, both worked here – the former on the choir stalls, the latter on the dome. Entry to the **Catedral Vieja** (daily 10am–7.30pm; €4) is through the first chapel on the right. Tiny by comparison and a stylistic hotch-potch of Romanesque and Gothic, its most striking feature is the huge fifteenth-century retable.

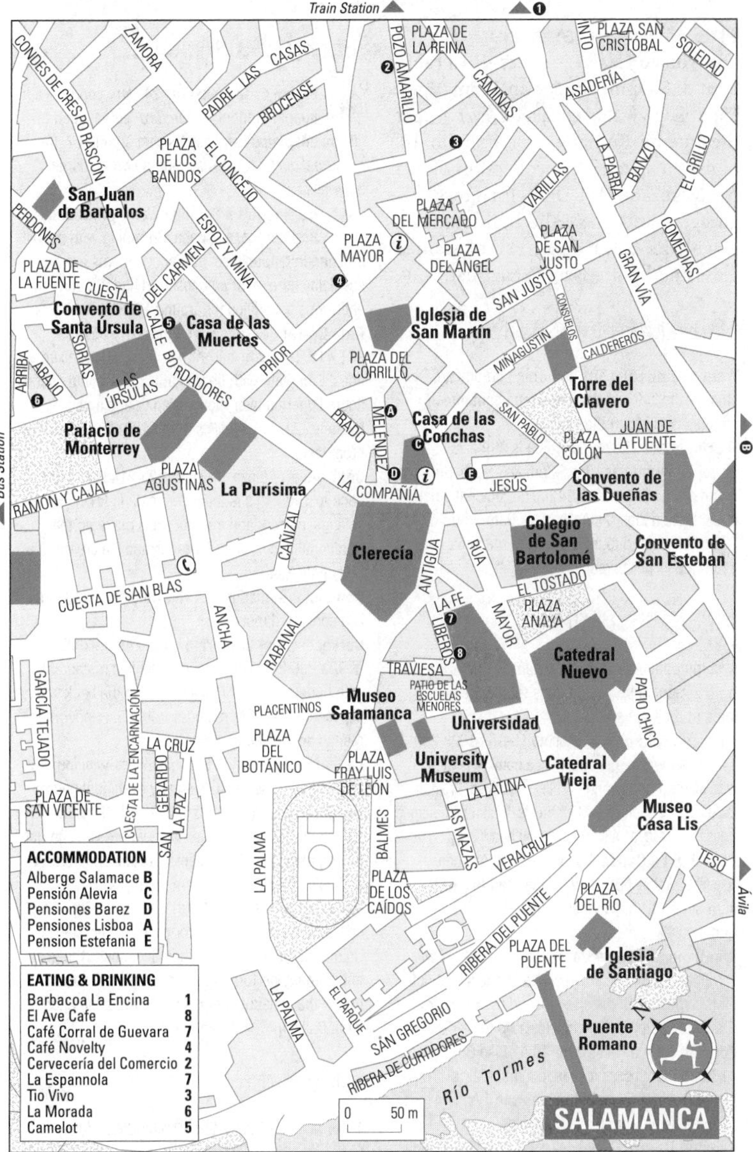

The conventsThe **Convento de San Esteban** (daily 10am–2pm & 4–8pm, closed Sun pm and Mon & Tues am; €2) is a short walk down c/Tostado from the Plaza de Anaya at the side of the Catedral Nueva. Although the cloisters here are magnificent, they're even more beautiful at the **Convento de las Dueñas** (Mon–Sat 11am–12.45pm & 4.30–6.45pm; €1.50). Built on an irregular pentagonal plan, its upper-storey capitals are wildly carved with writhing demons and human skulls.

The Museo Casa Lis

The **Museo Casa Lis** (Tues–Fri 11am–2pm & 5–9pm, Sat & Sun 11am–9pm; €3; Ⓦwww.museocasalis.org) near the Puente Romano, at c/Expolio 14, houses a spectacular collection of Art Nouveau and Art Deco furniture, ornaments and glass; the building itself – with its extravagant use of stained glass and light – is an extra treat.

Arrival and information

Train and bus The bus and train stations are on opposite sides of the city, each about fifteen minutes' walk from the centre.

Tourist office The tourist office is at Plaza Mayor 27 (Mon–Sat 10am–2pm & 5–8pm, Sun 10am–2pm; Ⓣ923 218 342). The regional office is in the Casa de las Conchas (daily 9am–9pm; Ⓣ923 268 571). Guided tours leave from the latter daily at 11am, €6–7 per person.

Accommodation

Accommodation is especially hard to find at **fiesta time** in September, when touts tend to be out in force at the train station.

Albergue Salamanca c/Escoto 13-15 Ⓣ923 269 141, Ⓦwww.alberguesalamanca.com. HI hostel with six-bed dorms and excellent facilities. Provides lockers for valuables and all meals. Walkable distance from Plaza Mayor, also reached by bus #2. ❷

Camping La Capea Aldeaseca de la Armuña Ⓣ&Ⓕ923 251 066. Just off the road to Zamora, 4km out of the city and surrounded by woodlands. Camping ❶

Don Quijote In Cabrerizos Ⓣ923 209 052, Ⓦwww.campingdonquijote.com. Riverside campsite about 5km to the east of the city, reached by bus #2 from Gran Vía. Camping ❶, bungalows ❼

Pensión Alevia Rúa Mayor 20-1 Piso B Ⓣ659 413 736. Spotless, excellent condition for a *pensión*, with private bathrooms and TVs. Two minutes' walk from Plaza Mayor. ❹

Pensión Barez c/Meléndez 19-1 Ⓣ923 217 495. Rooms are a little weathered and bathrooms are shared, but it's popular with travellers due to its cheap rates. ❸

Pensión Estefanía c/Jesús 3-5 Ⓣ923 217 372/620 909 072. Great-value accommodation in the centre, with very friendly staff. ❸

Pensión Lisboa c/Meléndez 1 Ⓣ923 214 333. Along the road from Barez. Basic accommodation, some rooms with private showers. ❸

Eating and drinking

El Ave Café c/Libreros 24. Very popular with hungry students, "*The Bird*" serves food to fill you up: *platos combinados* cost around €7, the *menú del día* €11. Eye-catching artwork adorns the walls.

Barbacoa La Encina c/Van Dyck 9, 5min north of Plaza España. Brimming with people and understandably so. Barbecued meats are the speciality here, with *pinchos* from under a euro and enormous bocadillos for around €3. Fill your boots.

Café Corral de Guevara c/Libreros 44 Ⓣ923 271 416. This café-bar attracts a crowd of mixed ages. Complete with board games, you could spend hours lingering over their coffee or apple San Miguels. Large *bocadillos* from €2.50 and bargain breakfasts.

Café Novelty Plaza Mayor Ⓣ923 214 956. Dating back to 1905, this is the oldest café in town. High ceilings, mirrors and iron figurines make up the traditional decor. Good for tapas and ice cream. Daily until 2am.

Camelot c/Bordadores 3. This medieval-style club is a converted monastery.

Cervecería del Comercio c/Pozo Amarillo 23 Ⓣ923 260 280. Very inviting Castilian restaurant with huge mosaic of Plaza Mayor on the back wall. Set menus €10–15, *raciones* from €5. Handwritten menus add a nice touch.

La Española Gran Via 51. This award-winning cocktail bar must feature on any evening itinerary.

La Morada c/Arriba 13 Ⓣ645 210 119. Young crowds gather at this "litre bar", where you can get five tapas plus a litre of beer or *calimocho* (red wine and coke) for €6. Daily 11am–late.

Tio Vivo c/Clavel 3–5. Worth visiting just for its eccentric interior with merry-go-round horses. Unique furnishings aside, their live music, theatre and comedy performances are also a big attraction. Check the schedule at Ⓦwww.tiovivosalamanca.com. Daily 4pm–4.30am.

Moving on

Train Madrid (7 daily, 2hr 30min); Bilbao (daily; 6hr).

Bus Mérida (5 daily; 4hr 30min); Seville (5 daily; 8hr); Madrid (16 daily; 2hr 30min); Santiago de Compostela (twice daily; 7hr); León (twice daily; 3hr).

LEÓN

The old *barrio* of **LEÓN** is steeped in history: in 914, as the Reconquest edged its way south from Asturias, the city became the Christian capital, and along with its territories it grew so rapidly that by 1035 the county of Castile had matured into a fully fledged kingdom. For the next two centuries, León and Castile jointly spearheaded the war against the Moors, but by the thirteenth century Castile's power had eclipsed that of even her mother territory. History aside, León also has an attractive and enjoyable modern quarter.

What to see and do

León's **Catedral** (daily 8.30am–1.30pm & 4–8pm) dates from the city's final years of greatness. It is said to be a miracle that it's still standing: it has the largest proportion of glass to stone of any Gothic cathedral. The kaleidoscopic stained-glass windows present one of the most magical and harmonious spectacles in Spain, and the colours used – reds, golds and yellows – could only be Spanish; the bewildering sensation of refracting light was further enhanced by the addition last century of a glass screen, allowing a clear view up to the altar. The west facade, dominated by a massive rose window, is also magnificent.

Real Colegiata de San Isidoro

The city's other great attraction is the **Real Colegiata de San Isidoro**, in the Plaza de San Isidoro, just a few minutes' walk west from the Catedral. It houses the bodies of the early kings of Castile and León. Ferdinand I, who united the two kingdoms in 1037, commissioned the complex as a shrine for the bones of St Isidore, which lie in a reliquary on the high altar, and a mausoleum for himself and his successors. The **pantheon** (Mon–Sat 10am–1.30pm & 4–6.30pm, Sun 10am–1.30pm; €3, free Thurs pm), a pair of small crypt-like chambers, is in front of the west facade. One of the earliest Romanesque buildings in Spain (1054–63), it was decorated towards the end of the twelfth century with some of the most imaginative and impressive paintings of Romanesque art.

Monasterio de San Marcos

Also worth seeing is the opulent **Monasterio de San Marcos** in the Plaza de San Marcos, located far west of the city's old pedestrianised quarter, by the Río Bernesga (daily 10am–2pm & 4–8pm). Built in 1168 for the Knights of Santiago, one of several chivalric orders founded in the twelfth century both to protect pilgrims on their way to Santiago de Compostela and to lead the Reconquest. Today, it operates as a hotel, but the church's sacristy houses a small **museum** (Tues–Sat 10am–2pm & 4–8pm, Sun 10am–2pm; €1.20) of priceless exhibits, housed in a room separated from the hotel lobby by a thick pane of glass.

Arrival and information

Train and bus The train and bus stations are both just south of the river: the former at the end of Avenida de Palencia, the bridge across into town, and the latter on Paseo Ingeniero Saenz de Miera – from here, turn left onto the Paseo to reach the bridge. From the roundabout, just across the river at Glorieta Guzmán El Bueno, you can see straight down Avenida de Ordoño II and across the Plaza de Santo Domingo to the cathedral. Alternatively, catch bus #7 to the centre (€1).

Tourist office Plaza de la Regla 3 (summer daily 9am–8pm; rest of year Mon–Fri 9am–2pm & 5–7pm, Sat & Sun 10am–2pm & 5–8pm; ⓣ987 237 082, ⓦwww.turismocastillayleon.com).

Accommodation

Albergue de León c/Campos Góticos 3 ⓣ987 081 832, ⓔalberguemunicipal@aytoleon.com or alberguedeleon@hotmail.com. Located by the bullring, about twenty minutes' walk from the cathedral. Rooms are spick and span with excellent facilities including mini-fridge and TV. Free Internet until 11pm. Max stay 3 nights. Dorms ❶

Pensión Berta Plaza Mayor 8-2° ⓣ987 257 039. Very basic accommodation, but the central location and cheap rates can't be beat. ❷

Pensión Blanca c/Villafranca 2-2° ⓣ987 251 991/678 660 224, ⓦwww.pymesleon.com/pensionblanca. Immaculate, inviting rooms, and welcoming staff. Cheery bedspreads, kitchen access, laundry and Internet make this *pensión* a comfortable home from home. Breakfast included. ❹

Pensión La Torre c/La Torre 3 ⓣ987 225 594. Rooms are excellent-quality and spacious. Private bathrooms, laundry service and free Internet. Slightly more expensive than *Blanca*. ❹

Eating and drinking

Free **tapas** is the name of the game in León, particularly in the Barrio Humedor around Plaza San Martín. To get more for your money, ask for a *corto* of beer, wine, shandy (*corto con limón)* or fizzy orange (*butano*). These are small, cost around €0.60 and still come with a plate of free food.

Albany Plaza Real (corner of c/Ancha). Great place for cakes, coffees and people-watching.

El Llar Plaza San Martín 9 ⓣ987 354 287. Authentic Leónese bar with dark wood interior and terracotta walls. The blue-cheese potatoes – free with every drink – are brilliant.

Latino Plaza San Martín 8. Light, airy mirrored bar. The fish is particularly superb, but the king prawns taste even better as they're complimentary with every drink.

Pizzería La Competencia c/Conde Rebolledo 17 ⓣ987 849 477. Good pizzas, pastas and salads. Your bill won't amount to more than €10 here.

Rebote Plaza San Martín 10. *Cortos* are €0.90 and come with free *croquetas*.

Directory

Laundry c/La Paloma and c/Lucas de Tuy.

Pharmacy Avenida Ordoño, just off Plaza Santo Domingo is 24hr.

Post Office Avenida Independencia, on the corner with Paseo San Francisco.

Shopping Ever-popular fashion company Inditex was founded in León, and almost every shop on c/Alcázar de Toledo belongs to the company (Zara, Pull & Bear, Massimo Dutti and Bershka to name but a few).

Moving on

Train to: Barcelona (3 daily; 10hr–11hr 40min); Bilbao (daily; 5hr); Madrid (7 daily; 4hr–6hr 20min); Oviedo (7 daily; 2hr); San Sebastián (daily; 5hr); Santiago de Compostela (daily; 6hr).

Bus Santander (7 daily; 5–6hr); Bilbao (1–2 daily excluding Sat, 4hr–5hr 30 min); San Sebastián (6 weekly; 6hr 40min); Barcelona (3 daily; 10hr 15min); Madrid (5 daily; 3hr 30min).

The north coast

Spain's **north coast** veers wildly from the typical conception of the country, with a rocky, indented coastline full of cove beaches and fjord-like *rías*. It's an immensely beautiful region – mountainous, green and thickly forested, with frequent rains often shrouding the countryside in a fine mist. In the east, butting against France, is **Euskadi**, or the País Vasco – the **Basque Country** – which, despite some of the heaviest industrialization on the peninsula, remains remarkably unspoiled. **San Sebastián** is the big seaside attraction, a major resort with superb but crowded beaches, but there are any number of lesser-known, equally attractive coastal villages all the way to **Bilbao** and beyond. Note that the Basque language, Euskera, bears almost no relation to Spanish (we've given the alternative Basque names where popularly used) – it's perhaps the most obvious sign of Spain's strongest separatist movement. To the west lies **Cantabria**, centred on the port of **Santander**, with more good beaches and superb trekking in the mountains of the **Picos de Europa**. In the far west, **Galicia** is green and lush but, despite its fertile appearance, has a history of famine and poverty. This province also treasures its independence, and Gallego is still spoken by around 85 percent of the population. For travellers, the obvious highlight here is **Santiago de Compostela**, the greatest goal for pilgrims in medieval Europe.

FEVE RAIL LINE

If you're not in a great hurry, you may want to make use of the independent **FEVE rail line** (☎902 100 818, Ⓦwww.feve.es; rail passes not valid). The 650-kilometre rail line begins at Bilbao and follows the coast west, with inland branches to Oviedo and León, all the way to El Ferrol in Galicia. Despite recent major repairs and upgrading, it's still slow but it's cheap and a terrific journey, skirting beaches, crossing rivers and snaking through a succession of limestone gorges.

BILBAO

Although traditionally an industrial city, **BILBAO** (Bilbo) has given itself a makeover and is now a priority destination on any Spanish tour. And no surprise: a state-of-the-art metro (designed by Britain's Lord Foster) links the city's widespread attractions; the breathtaking Museo Guggenheim by Frank Gehry – along with Jeff Koons' puppy sculpture in flowers – is a major draw; the airport and one of the many dramatic river bridges are Calatrava-designed; and there are various bids to further develop the riverfront with university buildings and public parks. The city's vibrant, friendly atmosphere, elegant green spaces and some of the best cafés, restaurants and bars in Euskadi, combine to make Bilbao an appealing destination. From the first Saturday after August 15, the whole city goes totally wild during the annual bullfighting extravaganza, **La Semana Grande**, with scores of open-air bars, live music and impromptu dancing.

What to see and do

The **Casco Viejo**, the old quarter on the east bank of the river, is focused on the beautiful **Teatro Arriaga**, the elegantly arcaded **Plaza Nueva**, the fourteenth-century Gothic **Catedral de Santiago** (Tues–Sat 10am–1.30pm & 4pm–7pm, Sun 10.30am–1.30pm; free), and the interesting **Museo Vasco** on Plaza Miguel Unamuno 4 (Tues–Sat 11am–5pm, Sun 11am–2pm; ☎944 155 423, Ⓦwww.euskal-museoa.org; €3). However, it is along the Río Nervión that a whole number of exciting new buildings have appeared.

Museo Guggenheim

A good route leads from the Casco Viejo down the river past the Campo Volantín footbridge and the more imposing Puente Zubizuri to the sensual, billowing titanium curves of the **Museo Guggenheim** (daily 10am–8pm; Sept–June closed Mon; €12.50, ticket office shuts 30min before closing; Ⓦwww.guggenheim-bilbao.es), described as "the greatest building of our time" by architect Philip Johnson. The building and exterior sculptures are arguably more of an attraction than most of the art inside: the permanent collection, which includes works by Kandinsky, Klee, Mondrian, Picasso, Chagall and Warhol, to name a few, is housed in traditional galleries; temporary exhibitions and individual artists' collections are displayed in the huge sculpted spaces nearer the river.

Museo de Bellas Artes

Further along from the Guggenheim, on the edge of the Parque de Doña Casilda de Hurriza, is the **Museo de Bellas Artes** (Tues–Sat 10am–8pm, Sun 10am–2pm; €5.50, combined ticket with the Guggenheim €12, free on Weds; ☎944 396 060, Ⓦwww.museobilbao.com), which houses works by Goya and El Greco and some fine temporary exhibitions.

Arrival and information

Train, bus, ferry and plane The FEVE and RENFE train stations are located just over the river from the Casco Viejo, while most buses arrive some

way out of the centre at Estación Termibús in San Mamés – from here to the centre is a 20min walk. Alternatively, catch the metro (€1.25 single, €3 day pass) or, for better views, the swish overground tram (also known as tranvía/Euskotran, €1.10 single, €3 day pass). Make sure you validate your ticket in the platform's machine before boarding the tram, or you could face a hefty fine. From the airport (ⓣ902 404 704), the Bikaibus runs to Plaza Moyua in the centre (daily 6.15am–midnight; every 30min; €1). Ferries come here from Portsmouth – check with companies for specifics (P&O ⓣ944 234 477; Acciona Trasmediterránea ⓣ902 454 645).
City transport The "Bilbaocard" is good value if you're planning on covering the city in a short space of time, as it can be used on all transport systems in the city (€6 for 1 day, €10 for 2, €12 for 3). It also provides discounts on some museums – check at the tourist office for details. For a healthier option, the council offers free bike hire; Arriaga tourist office is a popular pick-up/drop-off point, but there are several others around the city (ⓣ645 006 635).
Tourist office c/Plaza Ensanche 11 (Mon–Fri 9am–2pm & 4–7.30pm; ⓣ944 795 760, ⓦwww.bilbao.net), with branches in the basement of the theatre at Plaza Arriaga 1 (Mon–Fri 9am–2pm & 4–7.30pm, Sat 9.30am–2pm & 5–7.30pm and Sun 9.30am–2pm), outside the Guggenheim (July & Aug 10am–7pm, Sun 10am–3pm; Sept–June Tues–Sat 11am–7pm, Sun 11am–2pm) and the airport (daily 7.30am–11pm). All provide a good listings guide called *Bilbao*. There's also a central reservations system (ⓣ902 877 298, ⓦwww.bilbaoreservas.com) for all bookings, from rooms to restaurants.
Internet Laser, c/Sendaja 31.

Accommodation

In summer and at weekends, booking ahead is advisable.
Albergue Bilbao Ctra. Basurto-Kastrexana Errep 70 ⓣ944 270 054, ⓔalbergue.bilbao.net. Ten minutes from the city centre, connected by #58 and 80 bus, this eight-storey building has a TV room, Internet and laundry. HI card required, dorms and doubles. ❷
Pensión de la Fuente c/Sombrerería 2-2º ⓣ944 169 989. Good-value *pensión* in a beautiful renovated building. Communal sitting area, and laundry service for €6.
Pensión Mendez c/Santa María 13-4° ⓣ944 160 364, ⓦwww.pensionmendez.com. Very busy accommodation, all rooms usually full. The friendly owner provides city maps for travellers. Attractive rooms, all with balcony. Be warned, the *pensión* is on the fourth floor – and there's no lift. ❹
Pensión Serantes c/Somera 14-2° ⓣ944 151 557. Owned by friendly people, the *Serantes* enjoys a great location. The hall is painted fluorescent, but the rooms themselves are spacious and tranquil. ❹
Pensión Zubia c/Amistad 5-1º ⓣ944 248 566. Fresh, clean accommodation in a nice building. All rooms have colourful bedspreads, wooden floors and TV. ❹
Residencia Manoli c/Libertad 2-4º ⓣ944 155 636, ⓦwww.pensionmanoli.com. Don't let the slightly musty interior put you off, the rooms are clean enough. All come with bathroom, balcony and Wi-Fi. ❸

Eating and drinking

Gatz c/Sta Maria 10 ⓣ944 154 861. Lively bar known for its award-winning "fusion" tapas. Sample the creative *pinchos* (Basque tapas) for €1.60 a pop and wash down with *txakoli* (Basque wine) for €1.40. There's also a dining area for sit-down meals.
Rio-Oja c/Perro 4. Highly-recommended Basque restaurant, specializing in grilled meats and stews. Portions are very filling and good value.
Taberna Madariaga c/Somera 43 ⓣ944 162 360. A popular choice, serving less-experimental tapas than *Gatz* and *Zuga*. Sandwiches and prawn kebabs are the staple foods here and cost €1.20 each.
Zuga c/Cueva Goiko-Lau ⓣ944 150 321. Tucked in the corner of Plaza Nueva, serving imaginative pinchos at €1.60 each and tasty mussels for €3. The bar itself is small, but its many customers spill out onto the square and eat *pinchos* from the barrels outside.

Directory

Consulate UK, Alameda Urquijo 2-8° ⓣ944 157 600.
Currency Exchange Available in all main bank branches (general opening hours are Mon–Sat 8.30am–2pm). Bureau de change in the basement of El Corte Inglés, Gran Vía 7-9.
First aid clinic Alameda Urquijo 65 ⓣ944 434 792.
Hospital Santa Maria, Ctra. Santa Maria 41 ⓣ944 006 900.
Internet Laser, c/Sendaja 31.
Lost Property Luis Briñas 14 ⓣ944 204 981.
Pharmacy Farmacia Zaballa, Gran Vía 56 (daily 9am–10pm; ⓣ944 411 796).
Post Office Alameda Urquijo 19 ⓣ902 197 197.

Moving on

Train León (daily; 4hr 40min); Madrid (1–2 daily; 5hr 10min–8hr 30min); San Sebastián (6–7 daily; 2hr 30min).
Bus San Sebastián (1–2 hourly; 1hr 10min); Santiago de Compostela (3 daily; 11–12hr); Santander (21 daily; 1hr 30min).

SAN SEBASTIÁN

The undisputed queen of Basque resorts, **SAN SEBASTIÁN** (Donostia), just an hour by road from Bilbao, has excellent beaches and is acknowledged by Spaniards as an unrivalled gastronomic centre. Along with Santander, San Sebastian has always been a fashionable place to escape the heat of the southern summers, and in July and August it's packed with well-to-do-families. Its summer **festivals** include annual rowing races between the villages along the coast, and an International Jazz Festival (late July; ⓦwww.jazzaldia.com), that attracts top performers to play in different locations around town.

What to see and do

San Sebastián is beautifully situated around the deep, still bay of **La Concha**. The **Parte Vieja** (old quarter) sits on the eastern promontory, while newer development has spread inland along the banks of the River Urumea and around the edge of the bay to the foot of Monte Igüeldo.

Parte Vieja

The **Parte Vieja**'s cramped and noisy streets are where crowds congregate in the evenings to wander among the small bars and shops or sample the shellfish from the traders down by the fishing harbour. Here, too, are the town's chief sights: the gaudy Baroque facade of the church of **Santa María**, and the more elegantly restrained sixteenth-century **San Vicente**. The centre of the old town is the Plaza de la Constitución, known locally as "*La Consti*"; the numbers on the balconies of the buildings around the square refer to the days when it was used as a bullring. Just behind San Vicente, the excellent **Museo de San Telmo** (July & Aug Tues–Sat 9.30am-8.30pm, Sun 10.30am–2pm; Sept–June Tues–Sat 10.30am–1.30pm & 4–7.30pm Sun 10.30am–2pm; free) is a fascinating jumble of Basque folklore, funerary relics and assorted artworks. Behind this, **Monte Urgull** is criss-crossed by winding footpaths to the top. From the mammoth figure of Christ on its summit, there are great views out to sea and back across the bay to town.

Monte Igüeldo and La Concha

Still better views across the bay can be had from the top of **Monte Igüeldo**; take bus #16 or walk around the coastline to its base, from where a **funicular** (daily: July–Sept 10am–10pm; Oct–March 11am–8pm; April–June 10am–9pm closed Wed in winter; €2.10 return) will carry you to the summit, the home of a funfair (pay per ride, from €1.50 each). **La Concha** beach is the most central and most celebrated, a wide crescent of yellow sand stretching round the inlet from the town. Out in La Concha bay is a small island, **Isla de Santa Clara**, which makes a good spot for picnics; a boat leaves from the Paseo Mollaberria (June–Sept 10am–8.30pm; every 30min; €3.40).

Ondaretta

Ondaretta, considered the best beach in San Sebastián for swimming, is found beyond the rocky outcrop that supports the **Palacio Miramar** (gardens open 9am–sunset; free), once a summer home of Spain's royal family. Its facilities are good (showers €0.80, towels €0.90 and lockers €1.20) but the atmosphere here is more staid – it's known as La Diplomática for the number of Madrid's "best" families who holiday here. Far less crowded, and popular with surfers, **Playa de Zurriola** and the adjacent **Playa de Gros** have breakwaters to shield them from dangerous currents. Should you tire of sun and antiquity, head for the sparkling conference and cultural centre, the **Palacio Kursaal** (guided tours Mon–Fri 1.30pm, Sat & Sun 11.30am, 12.30pm & 1.30pm; €3) on Avenida de Zurriola. Designed by Rafael Moneo, and set on the banks of the River Urumea by Playa de Zurriola, the building consists of two translucent glass cubes not dissimilar to Japanese lanterns – an elegant sight at night.

Arrival and information

Train The mainline train station is across the River Urumea on Paseo de Francia, although local lines to Hendaye and Bilbao (rail passes not valid) have their terminus on c/Easo.

Bus National buses arrive at Plaza Pío XII, twenty minutes' walk or a bus journey (#28) from the Parte Vieja. The terminal isn't very user-friendly – some *taquillas* close at lunch and there are no luggage lockers. Buy tickets from the appropriate *taquilla* along Paseo de Bizkaia or Avda. de Sancho El Sabio at least 30min before boarding.

Tourist office c/Reina Regente 3 (June–Sept Mon–Sat 9am–8pm, Sun 10am–2pm & 3.30–7pm; Sept–June Mon–Sat 9am–1.30pm & 3.30–7pm, Sun 10am–2pm; ⓣ943 481 166, ⓦwww.sansebastianturismo.com). Also has an online reservations service at ⓦwww.paisvasco.com/centralreservas.

Listings guide The detailed *Donostiaisia* is in Spanish, available at tourist offices.

Internet Locutorio Puerto, c/Puerto 14; Cibernetworld, c/Aldamar 3; and Zarr@net, c/San Lorenzo 6 are open till late.

Accommodation

Pensión Amaiur c/31° de Agosto 44 ⓣ943 429 654, ⓦwww.pensionamaiur.com. Incredible attention to detail marks out the *Amaiur*: the charming young owners have thought of everything, from lending beach towels to organizing book-exchanges between travellers. All rooms – especially the kitchens – are well equipped and incredibly stylish. Internet access. ❺

Pensión Larrea c/Narrica 21-1° ⓣ943 422 694, ⓦwww.pensionlarrea.com. The owner, Amparo, is probably the friendliest person you'll meet on your travels. The rooms are also excellent, and bathrooms have powerful, spacious showers. Every room has balcony, soundproof windows and Wi-Fi access. ❺

Pensión San Vicente c/San Vincente 7-3° ⓣ943 422 977. Not as slick as *Amaiur* or *Larrea*, but the owners are gregarious, rooms are clean and rates are cheaper. Laundry service for €8. ❹

La Sirena Hostel Paseo de Igüeldo 25 ⓣ943 310 268, ⓦwww.donostialbergues.org. The cheapest accommodation option by far. Just 200m from Ondarreta beach in a building with a Swiss cottage-style facade. HI card required. Dorms ❷

TREAT YOURSELF

San Sebastián's amazing gastronomic scene is understandably pricey, but worth a one-off splurge. **Kaskazuri** at Paseo de Salamanca 14 (ⓣ943 420 894) is a great restaurant that will tantalize your tastebuds without hurting your wallet as much as other places – set-menus are priced €15–20. Get a table on the second floor to overlook stunning sea views.

Eating and drinking

Bidebide c/31° de Agosto. New in July 2007, this restaurant is looking to impress. Minimalist, sleek furnishings, chill-out music and great food that isn't as expensive as you'd expect. Burgers from €4.40, salads from €5.80 and *platos combinados* from €7.10.

La Cuchara de San Telmo c/31° de Agosto 28. If you don't like the way most bars leave *pinchos* sitting out all day, you'll love this place. They cook the food fresh in front of you, and each mini-dish is perfectly turned out.

Nightlife

Etxekalte c/Mari Kalea 11. Overlooking the port and beach, a young clientele grooves to jazz, urban soul and hip-hop. Free entry.

Tas-Tas c/Fermín Calbetón 35. Very popular with backpackers, so expect drink promotions, imported beers and cheesy music. Free entry. Open daily until 3am.

Zibbibio's Plaza Sarriegi 8. Also draws the international crowd. This mini-club plays dance music, serves good sangria and has happy hours and themed nights. Free entry.

Directory

Laundry c/Iparragirre 6 ⓣ943 293 150.
Pharmacy The one on c/Legazpi 7 (ⓣ943 424 826) is open 24hr.
Post Office c/Urdaneta 7 ⓣ902 197 197.

Moving on

Train Bilbao (6–7 daily; 2hr 30min); Madrid (3 daily; 6hr 30min–9hr); Pamplona (2–3 daily; 1hr 45min); Salamanca (2 daily; 6–7hr); Valencia (weekly; 11hr); Zaragoza (2–3 daily; 4–5hr).
Bus Bilbao (1–2 hourly; 1hr 10min); Madrid (8–9 daily; 6hr 30min); Pamplona (13 daily; 2hr).

SANTANDER

Long a favourite summer resort of Madrileños, **SANTANDER** has an elegant, reserved, almost French feel. Some people find it a clean, restful base for a short stay; for others, it is dull and snobbish. On a brief visit, the balance is tipped in its favour by its excellent beaches and the sheer style of its setting.

What to see and do

The narrow **Bahía de Santander** is dramatic, with the city and port on one side, in clear view of open countryside, and high mountains on the other; it's a great first view of Spain if you're arriving on the ferry from England. Santander was severely damaged by fire in 1941 and what's left of the city divides into two parts: the **town and port**, clumsily reconstructed on the old grid around a mundane cathedral; and the beach suburb of **El Sardinero**, a twenty-minute walk (or bus #7 or #9; €1) from the centre. There are few real sights to distract you, and it's for the glorious beaches that most people come. The first of these, **Playa de la Magdalena**, begins on the near side of the wooded headland of the same name. This beautiful yellow strand, sheltered by cliffs and flanked by a summer windsurfing school, is deservedly popular. If you find these beaches too crowded, head for **Somo** (which has a surf school, boards to rent and a summer campsite) or **Pedreña**; jump on a *lancha*, a cheap taxi-ferry (every 15min; €3.70 return) from the central Puerto Chico dock.

Arrival and information

Ferry Ferries from Plymouth dock in the middle of the Bahía de Santander, right opposite the Jardines de Pereda and the tourist office (see ⓦwww.brittany-ferries.co.uk for more information).
Train and bus The RENFE and FEVE train and bus stations are centrally located, side by side near the waterfront at Plaza de las Estaciones.
Bike hire The local council offers free bike hire – check the tourist office for details.
Tourist office There are two tourist offices: the best is in the Jardines de la Pereda (July–Sept daily 9am–9pm; Oct–June Mon–Fri 9.30am–1.30pm & 4–7pm, Sat 9.30am–1.30pm; ⓣ942 203 000).

Accommmodation

El Albaicin c/Francisco Palazuelos 21–23 ⓣ942 217 753. This summer-only hostel is a school the rest of the year. Up a steep hill, but views from rooms are breathtaking. Breakfast and Internet included. Dorms ❷
Los Caracoles c/Marina 1-1°. Basic rooms in the commercial centre. Tucked away on a tiny street off c/Medina. ❹
Pensión Luisito Avda. de los Castros 11 ⓣ942 271 971. A sound option just minutes away from El Sardinero beach, with a very welcoming owner. All rooms have views overlooking the pleasant front lawn or the neighbour's vegetable garden. Closed Oct–June. ❺
Pension Soledad Avda. de los Castros 17 ⓣ942 270 936. Also in a great location for El Sardinero beach, and worth checking out if the *Luisito* is full. ❺

Eating and drinking

California Café c/Casimiro Sainz. Cheap, hearty meals are served in this friendly bar.
Canela Plaza de Cañadío. For drinking, this bar is a good choice on a buzzing square. Live music Tues.
Casa José c/Mocejón. One of the cheaper options in the fish-restaurant district (*barrio pesquero).* Set menu €7.50. Closed Tues.
La Rana Verde c/Daoiz y Velarde 30 ⓣ942 222 402. Very popular, and famed for its *patatas bravas.* Literally hundreds of frog-figurines adorn the walls.

El Solecito c/Bonifaz 19 ⓣ942 360 633. Fun decor, and excellent pizzas at bargain prices.

Directory

Consulate UK, Paseo de Pereda, 27 ⓣ942 220 000.
Currency exchange Banco Santander, Avenida Calvo Sotelo, 19, across from the post office.

Moving on

Ferry Plymouth, UK (twice weekly; 20hr 30min).
Train Madrid (3 daily; 5hr 35min–8hr 30min).
Bus Pamplona (3 daily; 3hr 45min); Bilbao (19 daily; 1hr 45min); Santiago de Compostela (2-3 daily; 8hr–10hr 10 min).

PARQUE NACIONAL PICOS DE EUROPA

The **Picos de Europa** offer some of the finest hiking, canoeing and other mountain activities in Spain. The densely forested national park boasts two glacial lakes, a series of peaks over 2400m high, and wildlife including otters and bears. From Santander, about 80km to the east, the park is reached by car by passing through San Vicente de la Barquera, Unquera and Cares; alternative access is from Oviedo in the south, a spectacular drive of 80km along winding, narrow roads. **CANGAS DE ONÍS**, a major gateway to the park, has a helpful **tourist office** (June–Sept daily 10am–10pm; Oct–May Mon–Sat 10am–2pm & 4–7pm; ⓣ985 848 005, ⓦwww.picosdeeuropa.com) and **accommodation**, at *Hospedaje Torreón* (ⓣ985 848 211, ⓦwww.galeon.com/pensiontorreon; ❺). There's also a private hostel, *Albergue La Posada del Monasterio* (ⓣ985 848 553, ⓦwww.posadadelmonasterio.com), offering dorms (€15) and private rooms (❹), in an atmospheric old monastery in La Vega-Villanueva, 2km northwest of Cangas de Onís; the management organizes canoeing, hiking and other activities in the park. Alternatively, you can stay at **COVADONGA** in the park at the *Hospedería del Peregrino* (ⓣ985 846 047; ❹).

SANTIAGO DE COMPOSTELA

SANTIAGO DE COMPOSTELA, built in a warm golden granite, is one of the most beautiful of all Spanish cities and has been declared a national monument. Its size is manageable and the streets are almost wholly pedestrianized. The **pilgrimage to Santiago** (see box opposite) captured the imagination of medieval Christian Europe on an unprecedented scale, peaking at half a million pilgrims each year during the eleventh and twelfth centuries. People of all social backgrounds came to visit the supposed shrine of St James the Apostle (Santiago to the Spanish), making this the third-holiest site in Christendom, after Jerusalem and Rome. Once host to kings and all manner of society, Santiago is by no means a dead city now – it's the seat of Galicia's regional government, and houses a great contemporary art gallery and a large student population.

What to see and do

All roads lead to the **cathedral** (daily 7.30am–9pm, visits allowed outside Mass), whose sheer grandeur you first appreciate upon venturing into Praza do Obradoiro. The fantastic granite pyramid (adorned with statues of St James) was built in the mid-eighteenth century by an obscure Santiago-born architect, Fernando Casas y Novoa. Just inside this facade is the building's original west front: the **Pórtico de Gloria**. So many millions have pressed their fingers into the roots of its sacred Tree of Jesse that five deep holes have been worn into the solid marble. Behind, the **High Altar** symbolizes the spiritual climax of the pilgrimage. Visitors climb steps behind the altar, embrace the *Most Sacred Image of Santiago*, kiss his bejewelled cape, and receive a Latin certificate called a Compostela – a procedure that's seven centuries old. The elaborate pulley system in front of the altar is for

THE CAMINO DE SANTIAGO

The most famous Christian pilgrimage in the world, the **Camino de Santiago** – or Way of St James – traces routes through France and Spain to Santiago de Compostela. If you're travelling in this part of the world, you will doubtless see many pilgrims, identified – mainly to each other – by the coquille St Jacques, a large effigy of a scallop shell, that they wear attached to their backpack. "Santiago de Compostela" comes from the Latin meaning "St James of the Field of Stars"; it's named after a peasant who had a vision in a field of stars near where the town now lies; soon after, the Catholic Church miraculously discovered that the disciple James had been buried in that very spot. There are those that scoff at the notion that James was ever in Spain, never mind buried here; some see it as an early church PR exercise to garner some enthusiasm against the Moors. Whether you believe or not, the reality is that millions do – if not in the legend, at least in the physical and mental challenge of a pilgrimage on foot. Should you be interested in walking, cycling or taking the train, check Ⓦwww.xacobeo.es.

moving the immense incense-burner – **El Botafumeiro** – which, operated by eight priests, is swung in a vast ceiling-to-ceiling arc across the transept. It is stunning to watch, but takes place only during certain festival services – check with the tourist office. You can also visit the treasury, archeological museum, cloisters and crypt (Mon–Sat 10.30am–2pm & 4–8pm; closed Aug; €5).

San Martín Pinario monastery and around

The enormous Benedictine **San Martín Pinario monastery** stands close to the cathedral, the vast altarpiece in its church depicting its patron riding alongside St James. Nearby is the **Convento de San Francisco**, reputedly founded by the saint himself during his pilgrimage to Santiago. In the north of the city are Baroque **Convento de Santa Clara**, with a unique curving facade, and a little southwards, **Convento de Santo Domingo de Bonaval**. This last is perhaps the most interesting of the buildings, featuring a magnificent seventeenth-century triple stairway, each spiral leading to a different storey of a single tower. The adjacent **Museo do Pobo Gallego** is a fascinating museum of Galician culture (Tues–Sat 10am–2pm & 4–8pm, Sun 11am–2pm; free). Just next door is the **Centro Galego de Arte Contemporánea** (Tues–Sun 11am–8pm; free; Ⓣ981 546 629, Ⓦwww.cgac.org), a beautiful gallery designed by Portuguese architect Álvaro Siza and host to changing exhibition cycles.

Arrival and information

Train, bus and plane The train station is a walkable distance south of the plaza along Rúa do Horreo. Arriving at Santiago bus station, you're 1km or so north of the town centre; bus #5 runs every 20 to 30min to Praza Galicia at the city's southern edge. The airport, 12 km northeast of town (Ⓣ981 547 501, Ⓦwww.aena.es), is linked to the centre by hourly buses (€1.55).

Tourist office Rúa do Vilar 63 (daily: Semana Santa and June 9am–9pm; rest of year 9am–2pm & 4–7pm; Ⓣ981 555 129, Ⓦww.santiagoturismo.com). Has a central accommodation booking system (Ⓣ902 190 160, Ⓦwww.santiagoreservas.com) and a branch at the airport. Spanish guided tours leave from Plaza de Platerías daily at noon (April to mid-Oct also at 6pm) for €8 per person.

Listings guide *Culturall* is very comprehensive. Available at tourist offices.

Internet Cibernova, Rúa Nova 50.

Accommodation

You should have no difficulty finding inexpensive **accommodation**, but note that *pensiones* here are often called *hospedajes*.

Campsite As Cancelas Rúa do 25 de Xulio 35, Ⓣ981 580 266, Ⓦwww.campingascancelas.com. 2.5km north of the cathedral; take city bus #4 or #6. Located in a tranquil green zone, this

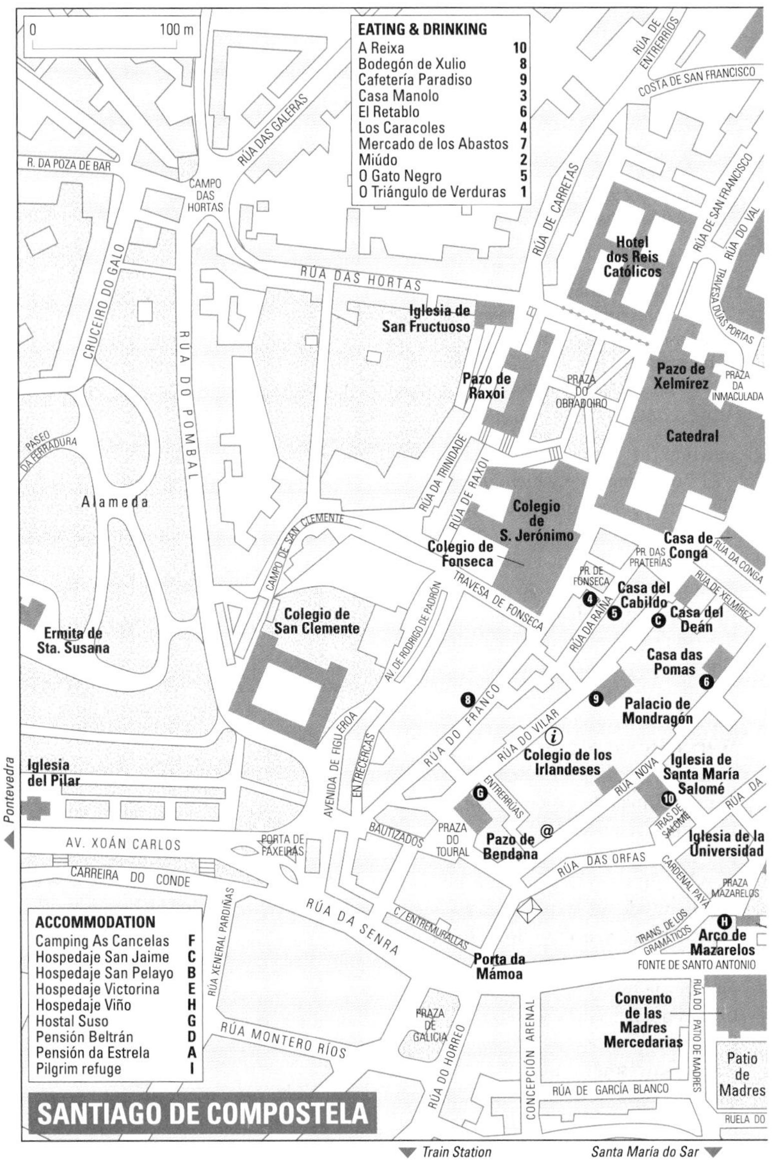

camping offers good facilities, including an outdoor swimming pool. There is also currency exchange and medical services on-site. 1, bungalow 7

Hospedaje San Jaime Rúa do Vilar 12-2° ☎981 583 134. Welcoming accommodation for friendly prices. Some of the homelier rooms have balconies decorated with plants. Free bicycle storage. 3

Hospedaje San Pelayo c/San Paio 2 ☎981 565 016. Basic-standard *pensión* rooms with a couple of extras thrown in: free laundry service and kitchen access. Just 3min from the cathedral. 4

Hospedaje Victorina c/Virxe da Cerca 9 ☎981

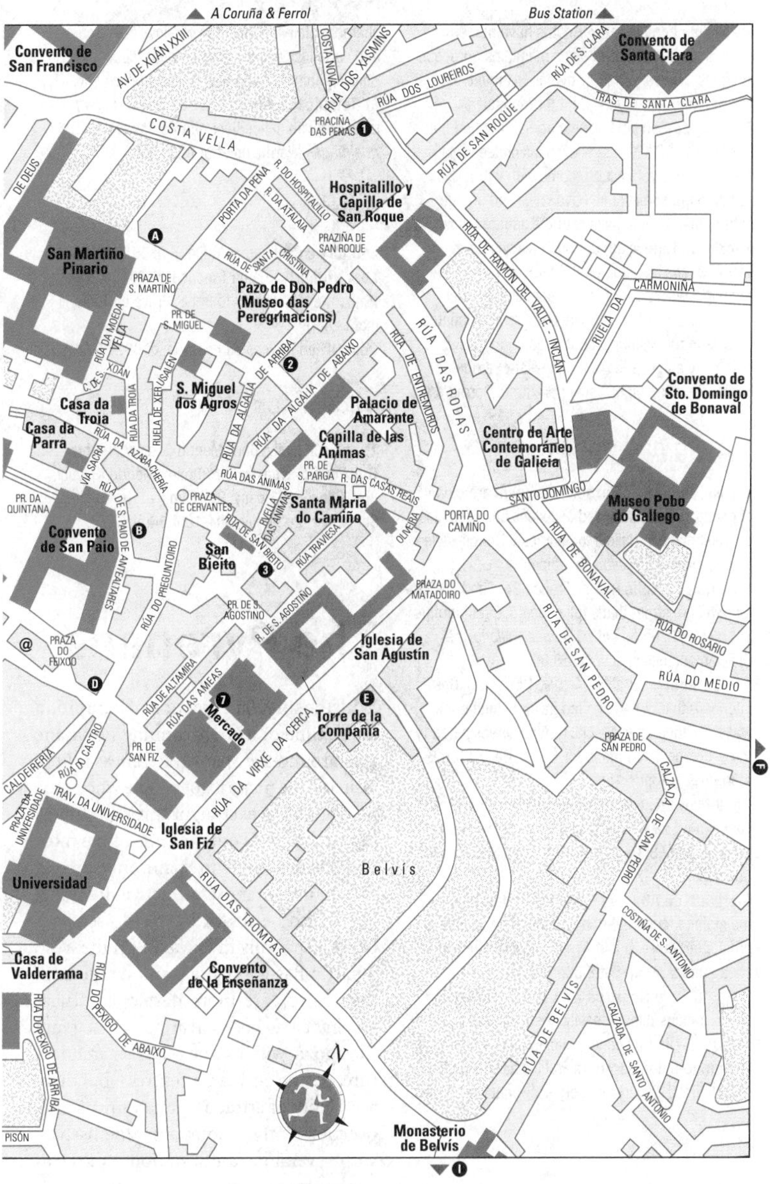

565 342. Simple accommodation and shared bathrooms. On a main road opposite the market. ❸

Hostal Suso Rúa do Vilar 65 ☎ 981 583 134. Clean, modern rooms with new bathrooms. The café below does a great breakfast – *churros* costs just €0.80. ❹

Hospedaje Viño Praza de Mazarelos 7 ☎ 981 585 185. Located next to the only existing entrance of the old city wall. Basic rooms, no sink, but some have balcony. ❸

Pensión Beltrán c/Preguntoiro 36-2° ☎ 981 582 225. Beautiful *pensión*, set in an old converted palace with stunning views and at absolute bargain rates. Rooms have modern furnishings but the large *salón* maintains gorgeous antiques. The very friendly owner will make you feel at home. Open July–Sept for tourists. ❸

Pensión da Estrela Plazuela de San Martin Pinario 5-2º ⓣ981 576 924, ⓦwww.pensiondaestrela.com. Spotless yet inviting rooms with warm-coloured bedspreads. All have Wi-Fi and private bathrooms. Stunning views of the square below. ❺

Pilgrim Refuge Avda. Quiroga Palacios 2a ⓣ981 589 200. *The* last stop on the famous *Camino de Santiago*, where pilgrims traditionally take their final, well-deserved rest. The large refuge, located outside of the historical centre, has great views of the city and overlooks the pleasant Parque de Belvís. Only one night's stay permitted. Dorms ❶

Eating and drinking

Thanks, perhaps, to the students, there are plenty of cheap **restaurants** and excellent **bars**; it's also the best place in Galicia to hear local Breton-style **music**, played on *gaitas* (bagpipes).

Bodegón de Xulio Rúa do Franco 24. Good choice for fish on a street that's full of seafood restaurants. Set menu €9, portion of *pulpo a la Gallego*, the Galician octopus speciality, €8.80.

Los Caracoles c/Raíña 14 ⓣ981 561 498. Cosy interior with low-hanging lamps and stone brick walls. Try their snail speciality. Also serves a hearty three-course lunch menu for €9.80. Daily 11am–4.30pm & 7.30pm–1am.

Casa Manolo Praza de Cervantes ⓣ981 582 950. Looks more expensive than it actually is – the set menu is just €8. Daily 1–4pm & 8–11.30pm, closed Sun eve.

Mercado de Abastos Plaza de Abastos. Well-maintained food market built around an attractive granite structure. Quality fresh, local produce at cheap prices. Mon–Sat 8.30am–2pm.

O Gato Negro c/Raíña. Very basic decor means this bar easily goes unmissed. It shouldn't – its traditional Galician food is first class.

O Triángulo das Verduras Praciña das Penas 2 ⓣ981 576 212. Very good organic vegetarian dishes.

Nightlife

A Reixa Tras de Salomé 3. Maroon bar with funky lighting and a chilled-out vibe. The huge CD collection behind the bar means an eclectic play list. Can get quite smoky.

Cafetería Paradiso Rúa do Vilar 29. This gorgeous green-tiled, mirrored bar is a good place to start the night. Free tapas with each €1.50 drink.

Miúdo c/Truques 3 ⓣ617 082 447. Bar with character: fairy lights in the window, board games and darts inside. Serves *queimadas* (spectacular Galician flaming cocktails). Occasional live music.

El Retablo Rúa Nova 13 ⓣ981 564 851. Very large bar with dance floor and €5 *copas* – and *queimadas*. Warms up after midnight.

Directory

Laundry c/Santiago de Chile, 7 ⓣ981 599 954.
Lost property Rúa da Trindade ⓣ 981 543 027.
Pharmacy Cantón do Toural 1; Praza do Toural 11 (both 24hr).
Post Office Travesa de Fonseca, ⓣ902 197 197.

Moving on

Train León (daily; 6hr); Madrid (2 daily; 8–9hr).
Bus Porto (4 weekly; 2hr 30min); Madrid (6 daily; 8hr), Bilbao (2–3 daily; 9hr 15min–11hr 15min); Santander (2–3 daily; 8hr–10hr 10min).

The Pyrenees

With the singular exception of **Pamplona** at the time of its bull-running fiesta, the area around the Spanish Pyrenees is little visited – the majority of people who come here at all travel straight through. In doing so they miss out on some of the most wonderful scenery in Spain, and some of the country's most attractive trekking. You'll also be struck by the slower pace of life, especially in **Navarra** (in the west, a partly Basque region) and **Aragón** (in the centre). are more developed. There are few cities here - Pamplona itself and **Zaragoza**, with its fine Moorish architecture, are the only large centres - but there are plenty of attractive small towns and, of course, the mountains themselves, with several beautiful **national parks** as a focus for exploration.

PAMPLONA

PAMPLONA (Iruña) has been the capital of Navarra since the ninth century, and long before that was a powerful fortress town defending the northern

SAN FERMÍN: THE RUNNING OF THE BULLS

From midday on July 6 until midnight on July 14, Pamplona gives itself up to the riotous non-stop celebration of the **Fiestas de San Fermín**. The centre of the festivities is the **encierro**, or running of the bulls – in which the animals decisively have the upper hand. Six bulls are released each day at 8am to run from their corral near the Plaza San Domingo to the bullring. In front, around and occasionally under them scramble the hundreds of locals and tourists who are foolish or drunk enough to test their daring against the horns. It was Hemingway's *The Sun Also Rises* that really put this on the map, and the area in front of the Plaza de Toros has been renamed Plaza Hemingway by a grateful council. To watch the *encierro* it's essential to arrive early – crowds form an hour before it starts. The best vantage points are near the start or on the wall leading into the bullring. The event has two parts: first the bull runnings; and then bullocks with padded horns are let loose on the crowd in the bullring. If you watch the actual running, you won't be able to get into the bullring, so go on two separate mornings to see both. At midnight on July 14, there's a mournful candlelit procession, the **Pobre De Mi**, at which the festivities are officially wound up for another year. See the official website Ⓦwww.sanfermin.com for more details.

approaches to Spain. Even now it has something of the appearance of a garrison city, with its hefty walls and elaborate pentagonal citadel.

What to see and do

The compact and lively streets of the old town offer plenty to look at: the elaborately restored **cathedral** with its magnificent cloister and interesting **Museo Diocesano** (June–Sept 10am–7pm; Oct–May Mon–Sat 10am–1.30pm & 4–7pm; €3); the colossal **city walls** and **citadel**; the display of regional archeology, history and art in the **Museo de Navarra** (Tues–Sat 9.30am–2pm & 5–7pm, Sun 11am–2pm; €2, free Sat pm & all Sun; Ⓦwww.cfnavarra.es/cultura/museo), and much more – but most visitors come here for just one thing: the thrilling week of the Fiestas de San Fermín (see box above).

Arrival and information

Train and bus The train station is 2.5km from the old part of town, but bus #9 runs every 15min to the end of Paseo de Sarasate, a few minutes' walk from the central Plaza del Castillo – there is a RENFE ticket office at c/Estella 8. The bus station is on c/Conde Oliveto in front of the citadel.

Tourist office c/Eslava 1, on Plaza San Francisco (Mon–Fri 9am–8pm, Sat 10am–8pm, Sun 10am–2pm; Ⓣ848 420 420, Ⓦwww.navarra.es). Also offers a free Bluetooth information service. Pick up pocket-sized monthly *El Bolo Feroz* for detailed events listings.

Internet c/San Antón 30.

Accommodation

Rooms are in short supply during summer, and at fiesta time you've virtually no chance of a place without booking. Most hotels double their prices during San Fermín, so you're better off staying nearby (San Sebastián is a viable option) and travelling to Pamplona to enjoy the night-long festivities and early morning running of the bulls. If you end up **sleeping rough**, remember that there is safety in numbers – head for one of the many parks such as Vuelta del Castillo or Media Luna and bring a sleeping bag, as the nights are cool. For a hot shower or bath, there are public baths at c/Eslava 9bis (Tues–Sat 8.30am–8pm, Sun 9am–1pm; shower €1, towel and soap €0.80). All prices below are high season, outside of fiesta time.

Ezcaba Camping Ⓣ948 330 315, Ⓦwww.campingezcaba.com. Located 7km out of town, on the road to France, reached by bus #7. Fills several days before the fiesta. ❶

Fonda La Montañesa c/San Gregorio 2 Ⓣ948 224 380. Simple, spacious rooms, some with balcony overlooking the street. Guests can use the washing machine for free. ❸

Pensión Escaray Lozano c/Nueva 24-1° Ⓣ948 227 825, Ⓔjescaray@pnte.cfnavarra.es. Good enough rooms with wooden floors and high ceilings in a recently renovated building. ❹

Pensión Eslava Don't let the building's peeling facade put you off, the rooms inside (albeit weathered) are clean enough with bright tartan bedspreads. ❹

Pensión Otano, c/San Nicolás 5, ⓣ948 227 036/948 225 095, ⓦwww.casaotano.com. This bar-cum-*pensión* is in a great location and the rooms are comfortable. Free parking 50m away. ❹

Eating and drinking

Pamplona has a number of great little **restaurants**, but the cheapest food is available at the Caprabo **supermarket** (daily 9am–9pm), inside the **Mercado de Santo Domingo**, the town's main food market (Tues–Sat 9.30am–2pm & 5–7pm), worth a browse in its own right.

Bar Ona c/San Gregorio 2 ⓣ948 226 910. This small establishment is bursting with character, from the pop-art pieces to the "quote of the day" on the blackboard. The food menu is fun, varied and cheap. Beers from €1.70 and large *copas* are €5. Mon–Sat 11am–4am, closed Mon in winter.

Dom Lluis c/San Nicolás 1. Good selection of Castilian dishes, and the €12 set menu has a lot of choice.

Erburu c/San Lorenzo 19. Something of a local institution, this bar serves €4–5 sandwiches during the day, and on weekends is open until 3am for dancing and drinks.

Lazaro Taberna Avenida Baja Navarra 8. An elegant spot for breakfast or coffee and cake.

Sarasate c/San Nicolás 19. An excellent vegetarian restaurant that could convert even the most committed carnivores. All dishes are creative and can be washed down with organic wine or one of the many teas on offer. The €10 set menu comes with a bottle of wine. Daily 1–4pm, also open Fri & Sat eve from 8pm.

Moving on

Train Madrid (4 daily; 3hr 30min); San Sebastián (3 daily; 1hr 40min–2hr 10min).

Bus Jaca (twice daily; 1hr 40min); Madrid (6–10 daily; 4hr); Santander (twice daily; 3hr 30min); San Sebastián (10 daily; 1hr).

ZARAGOZA

ZARAGOZA is the capital of Aragón, and easily its largest and liveliest city, with over half the province's one million people and the majority of its industry. There are some excellent bars and restaurants tucked in among its remarkable monuments, and it's also a handy transport centre, with good connections into the Pyrenees and east towards Barcelona.

What to see and do

Try and be here for **Semana Santa** – the week before Easter – for the spectacular street processions. Zaragoza's highlight is the city's only surviving legacy from Moorish times. From the tenth to the eleventh century this was the centre of an independent dynasty, the Beni Kasim, and their palace, the **Aljafería** (Mon–Wed & Sat 10am–2pm & 4.30–8pm, Fri 4.30–8pm, Sun 10am–2pm; ⓣ976 289 683/684, ⓦwww.cortesaragon.es; €3), surrounded by a moat and gardens, was built in the heyday of their rule in the mid-eleventh century, and thus predates the Alhambra in Granada as well as Seville's Alcázar. From the original design, the foremost relic is a tiny and beautiful mosque adjacent to the ticket office. Further on is an intricately decorated court, the **Patio de Santa Isabella**. Crossing from here, the **Grand Staircase** (added in 1492) leads to a succession of rooms remarkable chiefly for their carved ceilings.

Basilica de Nuestra Señora del Pilar

The most imposing of the city's churches, majestically fronting the Río Ebro, is the **Basilica de Nuestra Señora del Pilar** (daily 5.45am–9.30pm), one of Zaragoza's two cathedrals. It takes its name from the column that the Virgin is said to have brought from Jerusalem during her lifetime to found the first Marian chapel in Christendom. Topped

EXPO' ZARAGOZA 2008

From June 14 to September 14, 2008, Zaragoza will host the spectacular **International Exposition**. Based around the theme of water, eight architectural masterpieces have been constructed just north of the **River Ebro**, including a **Water Tower** and **Aquarium**. These will house exhibitions and over 3400 performances during the event. If you're planning on visiting Zaragoza during this period, you'll need to book **tickets** (and accommodation) as soon as possible (day-passes from €27); don't worry if you're not, as the innovative structures will remain after the Expo' has been and gone. For more information, visit Ⓦwww.expozaragoza2008.es.

by a diminutive image of the Virgin, the pillar forms the centrepiece of the Holy Chapel and is the focal point for pilgrims, who line up to kiss an exposed section encased in a silver sheath.

San Salvador and the Museo Camón Aznar

In terms of beauty, the basilica can't compare with the nearby Gothic-Mudéjar old cathedral, **San Salvador**, or **La Seo** (summer Tues–Fri 10am–7pm, Sat & Sun 10am–1pm & 2–7pm; winter: Tues–Fri 10am–2pm & 4–6pm, Sat & Sun 10am–1pm & 4–6pm; Oct–June closed Sun; €2), at the far end of the pigeon-thronged Plaza del Pilar. Just south of the cathedral, at c/Espoz y Mina 23, lies the wonderful **Museo Camón Aznar** (Tues–Fri 9am–2.15pm & 6–9pm, Sat 10am–2pm & 6–9pm, Sun 11am–2pm; €1), housed in a sixteenth-century building and an absolute must for Goya fans.

Roman remains

The city has recently been bringing to light its Roman past in several underground excavations: the **Forum** and **river port** (just off the Plaza del Pilar), and the **Roman Baths** (all Tues–Sat 10am–2pm & 5–8pm, Sun 10am–2pm; €2) and the **amphitheatre** in c/Verónica (Tues-Sat 10am–9pm, Sun 10am–2pm; €3.25). You can visit all of them with a combined ticket (€6). Following the semicircle of c/Coso and c/Cesar Augusto, the **Roman walls** are steadily being excavated; the best place to view them is at c/Echegaray at the junction with c/Coso, where remains of towers and ramparts can be seen.

Arrival and information

Train and bus Zaragoza's stunning modern station, Intermodal Delicias, serves all train and bus destinations. It's on Avda Navarra, about a 30min walk from the centre and connected by bus #51 (every 10min).

Tourist office The main tourist office is in Plaza del Pilar (daily 10am–9pm; Ⓣ976 393 537, Ⓦwww.zaragozaturismo.es). The square outside has free Internet – both as Wi-Fi and on a couple of interactive screens. There's also tourist information at Torreón de la Zuda (Mon–Sat 10am–2pm & 4.30pm–8pm, Sun 10am–2pm; Ⓣ976 201 200).

Accommodation

La Asturiana c/San Vicente de Paul 30 Ⓣ976 291 784. Simple, no-frills accommodation. All rooms have a sink and views of the street below. ④

Pensión Iglesias c/Verónica 14-2° Ⓣ&Ⓕ976 293 161. Excellent, spotless rooms, each with TV and sink/shower behind attractive glass partitions. Many rooms overlook the Roman amphitheatre. ③

Pensión La Peña c/Cinegio 3-1° Ⓣ976 299 089. Rooms have old furnishings and some are windowless, but the location is unbeatable. ③

Pensión Miramar c/Capitán Casado 17 Ⓣ976 443 342. Basic accommodation close to Estación de Portillo. All rooms have TV and either shower or bath. ④

Eating and drinking

There is a great variety of **restaurants** in Zaragoza but those on a self-catering budget can try

Zaragoza's main fresh-food market, **Mercado Central**, on c/Caesar Agosto (daily until 2pm).
Bodegas Almau c/Estébanes 10. Fill your boots during happy hour (daily 7–8pm) when sixty items are just €0.60 each – including beer, wine and tapas.
Café Tertulia Actual c/don Jaime I 28. Probably one of the only restaurants in Spain that doesn't charge extra for service on the *terraza*. Great lunchtime menu for €9.50, and art exhibitions inside. Also open until late for drinks.
El Clavel c/Jordan de Urries 8. A gem of a restaurant with friendly staff and delicious food. Try the local speciality, lamb *madeja* (€4.90). The ham and cheese *tostada clavelita* is also good.
Fantoba c/don Jaime I 21. A beautiful bakery dating back to 1856 and specializing in Aragonese *dulces*. Each sugary treat is small but perfectly turned out. Pay by weight.
Gran Café Zaragonozo c/Coso 35. A lively place for drinks throughout the afternoons and evenings. Quirky decor, from barbers' chairs to transparent flooring.
Lai Lai c/Don Jaime 34 ⓣ976 200 651. If you fancy a break from Spanish cuisine, this elaborately decorated Chinese restaurant (complete with fountain) provides a good four-course lunch (€7.35).
La Tasquilla de Pedro c/Cinegio 3. Great for cheap tapas and beers (all €1.50 a pop). The owner is friendly, and the lively walls crammed with knick-knacks will keep you entertained for hours.

Moving on

Train Barcelona (14–16 daily; 3–6hr); Bilbao (twice daily; 4hr 55min–7hr 40min); Canfranc (2 daily; 3hr 30min); Jaca (3 daily; 3hr 10min); Madrid (13 daily; 1hr 45min–4hr 30min); Pamplona (4–5 daily; 2hr).
Bus Barcelona (15–25 daily; 3hr 30min–5hr); Madrid (19 daily; 3hr 30min); Pamplona (7–8 daily; 2hr–2hr 45min).

JACA

Heading towards the Pyrenees from Zaragoza, **JACA** is Aragon's northernmost significant town and a principal base for exploring the Aragonese Pyrenees.

What to see and do

A magnificent **cathedral** (daily 11.30am–1.30pm & 4–8pm), the first in Spain to be built in the Romanesque style, dominates the town centre from its position at the northern edge of the old quarter. It remains impressive despite much internal remodelling over the centuries, and there's a powerful added attraction in its **Museo Diocesano** (currently closed due to works). The shady cloisters are home to a collection of beautiful Romanesque and Gothic religious sculpture and frescoes, gathered from village churches in the area and from higher up in the Pyrenees. As well as being a popular Pyrenean ski resort (800m), Jaca is primarily an army town, with recruits attending the local mountain-warfare academy. The military connection is nothing new: the **Ciudadela**, a sixteenth-century fort built to the stellar ground plan in vogue at the time, still offers good views of surrounding peaks. You can visit parts of the interior on a guided tour only (Tues–Sun 11am–2pm & 5–8pm; €10 includes entrance to its Museo de Miniaturas Militares) though, frankly, the exterior is far more compelling.

Arrival and information

Train and bus Arriving in Jaca by train, you'll find yourself 1km or so north of centre; an urban shuttle bus takes you to the bus station on Avda. Jacetania, 200m northwest of the cathedral.
Tourist office Plaza San Pedro 11-13, next to the cathedral (July–Aug Mon–Sat 9am–9pm, Sun 9am–3pm; rest of year Mon–Sat 9am–1.30pm & 4.30–7.30pm; ⓣ974 360 098, ⓦwww.aytojaca.es).

Accommodation

Jaca's accommodation prices are pushed up by the ski- and cross-border trade, and reservations are advisable in August and during winter. All the budget options are in the northern half of the old town.
Albergue Escuela Pías Avda.Perimetral ⓣ974 360 536. Located next to the ice-rink, this *albergue* has a swimming pool, table-tennis room and football pitch. HI card required. Dorms ❷, doubles ❸
Hostal Paris Plaza de San Pedro 5 ⓣ974 361 010, ⓦwww.jaca.com/hostalparis. A good, quiet option with clean rooms. ❹

Pena Oroel Camping 3km down the Sabiñanigo road, ☎974 360 215. Open Easter and summer only, this campsite is also quite basic, but a good base for exploring the surrounding Pyrenees. ❶

Victoria Camping Avd. de la Victoria 34 ☎974 357 008, Ⓦwww.campingvictoria.es. Located 1.5km west of town on the road to Pamplona, this campsite is a pleasant place to stay, albeit quite basic. On-site restaurant and bar. ❶, doubles ❸

Eating and drinking

El Arco c/San Nicolas 4. A good option for vegetarians, with daily set menus and a large range of fruit juices. Also open for breakfast. Closed Sun in the off-season.

Mesón Corbacho c/Ramiro Primero 2. With stone-effect walls, beamed ceilings and tiled floors, the interior has a welcoming feel. Offers decent set menus of traditional Spanish dishes.

PARQUE NACIONAL DE ORDESA

For summertime walking, there's no better destination than the **Parque Nacional de Ordesa**, focused on a vast, trough-like valley flanked by imposingly striated limestone palisades. The bus from Jaca (Mon–Sat 10.15am) reaches **Sabiñánigo** in time to connect with the 11am service (also July & Aug Mon–Sat at 6.30pm; Sept–June Fri & Sun at 5.30pm) to **Torla**, the best base for the park. Approaching Sabiñánigo by bus or train from Zaragoza, you'll need departures before 8.30am and 7.15am respectively to make the 11am connection. Note that bus services between Torla and Sabiñánigo are very limited, so plan your journey well. At Torla, a regular shuttle bus takes you to and from the park (the park is not accessible by car) but trekkers should opt instead for the lovely trail (1hr 30min) on the far side of the river, well marked as the GR15.2. Further **treks** can be as gentle or as strenuous as you like, the most popular outing being an all-day trip to the **Circo de Soaso** waterfalls. For detailed information on the park, contact either Torla's tourist office (summer only Mon–Fri 10am–1pm & 6–8pm, Sat & Sun 9.30am–1.30pm & 5–8.30pm; ☎974 486 184) or the park's **Centro de Visitantes**, 3km north of the Puente de los Navarros (☎974 486 472, Ⓦwww.ordesa.net).

Accommodation

Torla itself, a formerly sleepy, stone-built village, has been overwhelmed in its contemporary role as gateway to the park, though older corners are still visually attractive. Reserve well in advance for **accommodation** in July and August; even the three campsites, *San Antón* (☎974 486 063), *Río Ara* (☎974 486 248), and *Ordesa* (☎974 486 146), strung out between 1km and 3km north, often fill up.

Refugio Lucien Briet In the village centre ☎974 486 221, Ⓦwww.ordesa.net/refugio-lucienbriet. Simple *refugio* in the middle of Torla, offering good-value meals. Dorms ❶, doubles ❹

Refugio L'Atalaya In the village centre ☎974 486 022, Ⓦwww.ordesa.net/refugioatalaya. Similar set-up to the *Lucien Briet*, this 21-place also does food for a decent price. ❶

Catalonia

With its own language, culture and, to a degree, government, **Catalonia** (Cataluña in Castilian Spanish, Catalunya in Catalan) has a unique identity. **Barcelona**, the capital, is very much the main event, one of the most vibrant and exciting cities in Europe. Inland, the monastery of **Montserrat**, Catalonia's premier "sight", is perched on one of the most unusual rock formations in Spain. The coast immediately either side of Barcelona is rather plain, with the exception of the Modernist buildings and gay nightlife of **Sitges**, a thirty-minute train ride southwest. Further north, the rugged **Costa Brava** is slowly shedding its erstwhile unfortunate touristy image and boasts the best beaches in the region. Since the use of the Catalan language is so widespread, we've used Catalan spellings, with Castilian equivalents in parentheses. **Hostels** can be booked online or by a central reservations phone service (ⓣ934 838 363, ⓦwww.tujuca.com).

THE COSTA BRAVA

Stretching for 145km from the French border to the town of Blanes, the **Costa Brava** (Rugged Coast) boasts wooded coves, high cliffs, pretty beaches and deep blue water. Struggling under its image as the first developed package-tour coast in Spain, it is very determinedly reinventing itself by revitalizing its local essence and shifting away from mass tourism. Broadly, the coast is split into three areas: the southern tip, clustered around brash **Lloret de Mar**, and popular with raucous holiday-makers; the stylish, but expensive, central area between **Palamós** and **Pals**; and the more rugged northern part, dominated by the spectacular **Cap de Creus** headland and park, and the bohemian town of **Cadaqués.** Inland are the twin hubs of **Girona**, the beautiful medieval capital of the region, and **Figueres**, Dalí's birthplace and home to his outrageous **museum**. **Buses** in the region are almost all operated by SARFA (ⓣ972 364 295), with an office in every town. To visit the smaller, and more picturesque coves, a car or bike is useful, or you could walk the fabulous Camí de Ronda necklace of footpaths running along the coastline.

Figueres

The northernmost parts of the Costa Brava are reached via **FIGUERES**, a provincial Catalan town with a lively *rambla* and plenty of cheap food and accommodation. The place would pass almost unnoticed, however, were it not for the most visited museum in Spain after El Prado, the surreal **Museu Dalí** (Jan–Feb & Nov–Dec daily 10.30am–5.45pm; March–June & Oct 9.30am–5.45pm; July–Sept 9am–7.45pm; €10; ⓣ972 677 500, ⓦwww.salvador-dali.org). Born in Figueres, Dalí also died here and is now buried in a stone sarcophagus inside the museum, which contains a range of his work and will appeal to everyone's innate love of fantasy, absurdity and participation.

To make your way into the centre of town, simply follow the "Museu Dalí" signs from the **train station**. The **tourist office** (July–Sept Mon–Sat 9am–8pm, Sun 10am–3pm; Oct–June 9am–2pm & 3–7pm; ⓣ972 503 155, ⓦwww.figueresciutat.com) is in front of the post office building by the Plaça del Sol, and runs English-language guided walks of the town in summer. For a comfortable **room**, try *Pensió Isabel II*, c/Isabel II 16 (ⓣ972 504 735; ④), or *Pensión San Mar*, c/Rec Arnau 31 (ⓣ972 509 813, ⓦwww.hostalsanmar.com; ③). *Hostal Androl* (ⓣ972 675 496, ⓦwww.androl.internet-park.net; ⑤) offers some more expensive rooms but also has year-round camping (③ for 2 people, including a tent) and a restaurant/bar. There's a gaggle of cheap tourist **restaurants** in the narrow streets around the Museu Dalí and some nice, but pricier, pavement cafés lining the *rambla*.

TREAT YOURSELF

Every July and August, the **Festival Castell de Peralada** (ⓦwww.festivalperalada.com) attracts internationally acclaimed musicians and artists, to perform within the gardens of this medieval castle just outside of Figueres. Tickets cost €25–35.

Moving on

Bus Barcelona (3–6 daily; 2hr 15min); Cadaqués (7 daily; 1hr); L'Escala (6 daily; 45min); Palafrugell (4 daily; 1hr 30min).
Train Barcelona (every 30min; 2hr); Cerbère (10 daily; 30min); Girona (every 30min; 30min); Madrid (daily; 11hr); Montpellier (3–6 daily; 2hr 15min); Portbou (10 daily; 30min).

Cadaqués

The beautiful fishing village of **CADAQUÉS**, an hour by regular SARFA bus from Figueres, was the artist's home from 1930 until his death, and has attracted an arty crowd ever since. The stunning **Casa-Museu Dalí** (mid-June to mid-Sept daily 9.30am–9pm; mid-Sept to Jan & mid-March to mid-June 10.30am–6pm (last entry 50min before close); €10; booking required ⓣ972 251 015), the museum set up in his jumble of a home, lies 1km northeast in the tiny Portlligat cove and offers an enthralling glimpse into his private life. Cadaqués itself is a whitewashed village with tiny beaches and narrow cobbled streets straddling a hill topped by an imposing church. **Accommodation** is expensive; the cheapest options can be found at the *Pensión Marina* (ⓣ972 159 091; ❹) and at *Hostal Vehi* (ⓣ972 258 470; ❺). Alternatively, there is a campsite on Avda. Salvador Dalí (ⓣ972 258 126; ❷), which also has a pool open during July and August. For a **drink** or a **meal**, the areas around c/Miguel Rosset and below the church are the liveliest. If you fancy visiting some of the surrounding coast, hire a bike or scooter from Rent@bit on Avda. Caritat Serinyana (scooter €45/day; bike €20/day).

Girona

GIRONA, 37km south of Figueres, is one of Spain's loveliest unsung cities, with alleyways winding around its compact old town, the **Barri Vell**, through the atmospheric streets of **El Call**, the beautifully preserved medieval Jewish quarter. Fought over every century since the Romans first set foot here, and dominated by its towering **cathedral** (daily: April–Oct 10am–8pm; Nov–March 10am–7pm; €4, free Sun; services Sat from 4.30pm, Sun 10am–2pm, at which time only part of the cathedral can be visited) Girona's eclectic past is tangible in its **medieval walls**, which provide a great afternoon's walk. The **tourist office** on the *rambla* (Mon–Fri 8am–8pm, Sat 8am–2pm & 4–8pm, Sun 9am–2pm; ⓣ972 226 575, ⓦwww.ajuntament.gi/turisme) dispenses maps, and there's also an information stand at the train station. Good, central **accommodation** can be found at the HI hostel *Alberg Ceverí de Girona*, c/dels Ciutadans 9 (reservations on ⓣ934 838 363; ❷); beware, though, that in summer it is likely to be packed with groups of screaming school children. Another option slightly further out is *Pensión Massó*, Plaça Sant Pere 12 (ⓣ972 207 175; ❸). The *rambla* is fine for a relaxing **drink**, but it's best to go into the Barri Vell or the area around Plaça Independència for more interesting places to **eat** at night – try *La Lliberria* at c/Ciutadans 15, serving up tasty meals, with live music every Friday, and **Internet** access.

EMPÚRIES

The fascinating ancient Greek and Roman ruin of **Empúries** (June–Sept 10am–8pm; Oct–May 10am–6pm; €2.40; ⓦwww.mac.es), one of the most important archeological sites in Spain, makes an interesting day-trip from Girona. To get there, take the bus to L'Escala (2–3 daily; 1hr) from where it's a two-kilometre walk to the ruins.

Moving on

Bus Barcelona (3–7 daily; 2hr 15min); Cadaqués (2–3 daily; 1hr 50min).
Train Barcelona (every 30min; 1hr 30min); Figueres (every 30min; 30min); Madrid (1 daily; 10hr 45min).

BARCELONA

BARCELONA, the self-confident and progressive capital of Catalonia, is a tremendous place to be. A thriving port and the most prosperous commercial centre in Spain, it has a sophistication and cultural dynamism way ahead of the rest of the country. But Barcelona has also evolved an individual and ec-

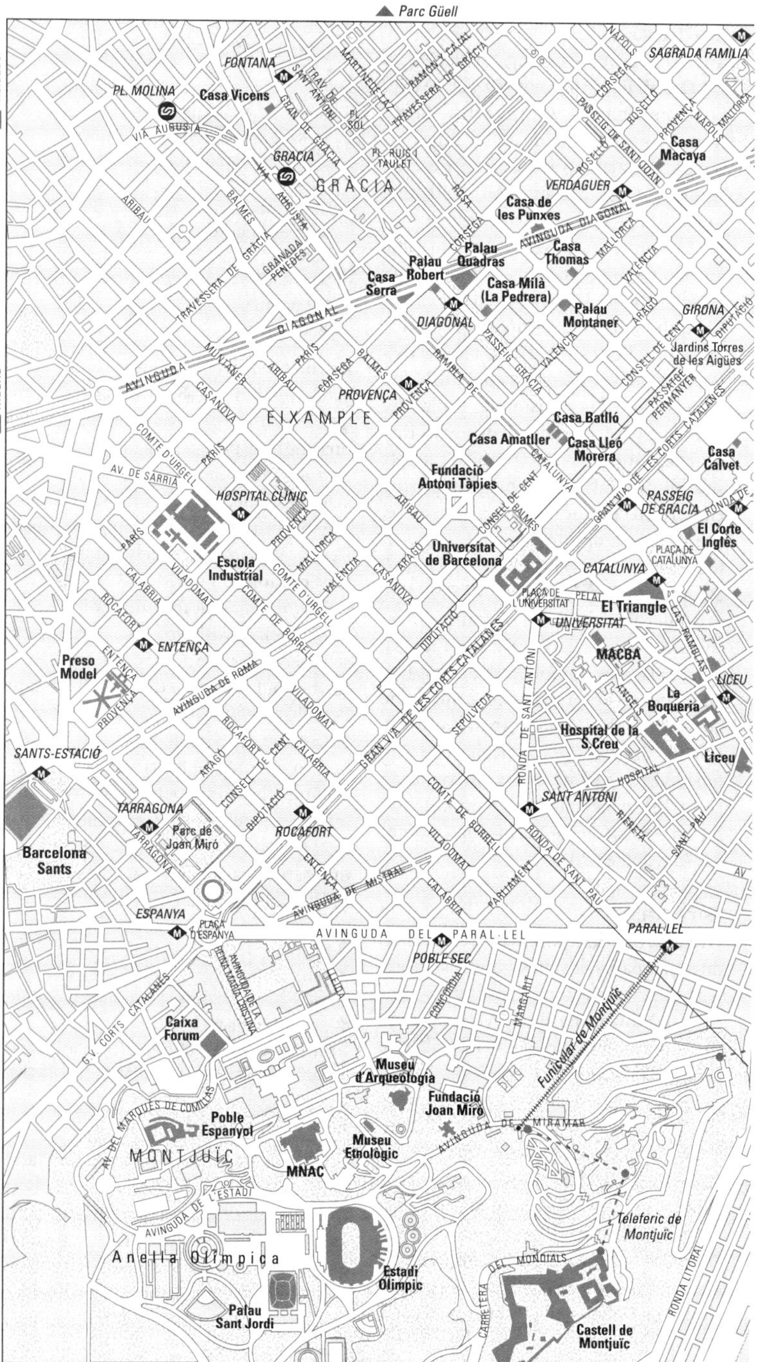

Parc Güell
Tibidabo
Madrid
Airport
FONTANA
PL. MOLINA
Casa Vicens
GRACIA
GRÀCIA
SAGRADA FAMILIA
Casa Macaya
VERDAGUER
Casa de les Punxes
Palau Quadras
Casa Thomas
Palau Robert
Casa Serra
Casa Milà (La Pedrera)
DIAGONAL
Palau Montaner
GIRONA
Jardins Torres de les Aigües
PROVENÇA
EIXAMPLE
Casa Batlló
Casa Amatller
Casa Lleó Morera
Casa Calvet
Fundació Antoni Tàpies
HOSPITAL CLÍNIC
PASSEIG DE GRÀCIA
El Corte Inglés
PLAÇA DE CATALUNYA
Universitat de Barcelona
Escola Industrial
CATALUNYA
PLAÇA DE L'UNIVERSITAT
UNIVERSITAT
El Triangle
MACBA
ENTENÇA
Preso Model
LICEU
La Boqueria
Hospital de la S.Creu
Liceu
SANTS-ESTACIÓ
SANT ANTONI
TARRAGONA
Parc de Joan Miró
ROCAFORT
Barcelona Sants
ESPANYA
PLAÇA D'ESPANYA
AVINGUDA DEL PARAL·LEL
PARAL·LEL
POBLE SEC
Funicular de Montjuïc
Caixa Forum
Museu d'Arqueologia
Fundació Joan Miró
Poble Espanyol
MONTJUÏC
Museu Etnològic
MNAC
AVINGUDA DE MIRAMAR
Telefèric de Montjuïc
Anella Olímpica
Estadi Olímpic
Palau Sant Jordi
Castell de Montjuïc
RONDA LITORAL

CATALONIA SPAIN

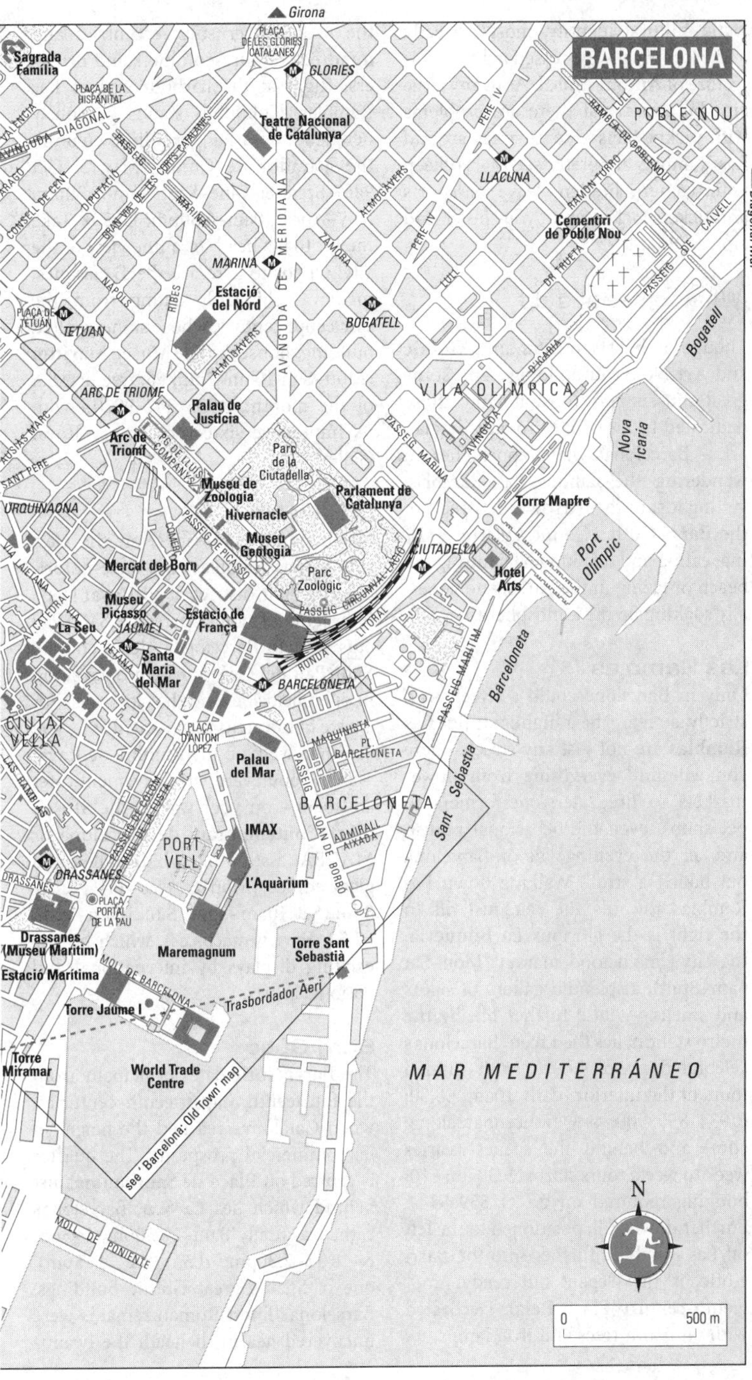

SPAIN

CATALONIA

lectic cultural identity, most perfectly and eccentrically expressed in the architecture of **Antoni Gaudí.** As in any large city, be aware that there are problems with pickpockets – some areas around Las Ramblas are pretty seedy – so keep your camera hidden, leave passports and tickets locked up in your hotel, and zip bags up.

What to see and do

Though it boasts outstanding **Gothic** and **Art Nouveau** buildings, and some great museums – most notably those dedicated to Picasso, Miró and Catalan art – Barcelona's main appeal lies in wandering the famous Las Ramblas; getting lost in the narrow side streets of the **Barri Gòtic** (Gothic Quarter); rising, eating and drinking late; hitting the beach or lazing in the parks; and generally soaking up the atmosphere.

Las Ramblas

Only in Barcelona could a street – or, strictly, streets – be a highlight. But **Las Ramblas** are not just any street – here you will find everything from flower markets to fire eaters, performers to pet shops, even the occasional nudist, and, in the evening, all of Barcelona out taking a stroll. Walking down Las Ramblas towards the sea, just off to the right is the glorious **La Boqueria**, the city's main food market (Mon–Sat 6am–8pm), a splendid gallery of sights and smells. A little further on, by the metro station, lies the **Liceu**, Barcelona's celebrated opera house, with guided tours of the interior (daily 10am; €8.50; ⓣ934 859 900, ⓦwww.liceubarcelona.com) and behind the scenes (varies week to week; tours start at 9.30am; €10; booking required on ⓣ934 859 914). Further down still, positioned to the left off Las Ramblas, further into the Barri Gòtic, is the elegant but seedy nineteenth-century **Plaça Reial**. Decorated with tall palm trees and iron lamps, it's the haunt of crusties, eccentrics and hundreds of alfresco diners and drinkers. Right at the harbour end of Las Ramblas, Columbus stands perilously perched atop a tall, grandiose column, the **Mirador de Colón** (May & Oct 9am–8pm & June–Sept 9am–8.30pm; Nov–April 10am–6.30pm; €2.30). Take the lift to his head for a fine view of the city. Opposite here are the **Drassanes**, medieval shipyards dating from the thirteenth century, whose stone-vaulted buildings house the fine **Museu Marítim** (Mon–Sun 10am–7pm; €6; free first Sat of the month; ⓣ933 342 9920), with its impressive sixteenth-century Royal Galley.

El Raval

North of the Drassanes, on the west side of Las Ramblas, the once-notorious red-light district of **El Raval** has a few sights of note. Carrer de Sant Pau cuts west to Barcelona's oldest church, **Sant Pau del Camp**, which once stood in open fields beyond the city walls. For a taste of the area's regenerated side, you can then walk up the **Rambla de Raval** – a new boulevard with pavement cafés and bars – on your way to the **Museu d'Art Contemporani de Barcelona** or MACBA, a stunning white-walled and glass edifice (Mon & Wed–Fri 11am–8pm, Sat 10am–8pm, Sun 10am–3pm; €7.50; ⓦwww.macba.es), which houses exciting displays by international and national artists.

Barri Gòtic

The **Barri Gòtic** dates principally from the fourteenth and fifteenth centuries, when Catalunya reached the height of its commercial prosperity. The quarter is centred on **Plaça de Sant Jaume**, just behind which lies **La Seu**, Barcelona's cathedral (daily 8am–12.30pm, 1–5pm & 5.15–7.30pm; €5, free 1–5pm), one of Spain's great Gothic buildings. Barcelona's finest Roman remains were uncovered nearby, beneath the beautiful **Plaça del Rei**, and now form part of the **Museu d'Història de la Ciutat** (April–Sept Tues–Sat 10am–8pm, Sun 10am–3pm; Oct–March Tues–Sat 10am–2pm & 4pm–7pm, Sun 10am–3pm; €5, students €3.50). You'll also be able to see the interiors of the Plaça del Rei's finest buildings – including the famous **Saló del Tinell**, on whose steps Ferdinand and Isabella stood to receive Columbus on his triumphant return from his famous voyage of 1492. Behind the *plaça*, the **Museu Frederic Marés** (Tues–Sat 10am–7pm, Sun 10am–3pm; €3; ⓦwww.museumares.bcn.cat) consists of a fascinating personal collection of social and historical oddities gathered over fifty years of travel, and has a lovely, shaded café in its grounds.

La Ribera and Parc de la Ciutadella

Heading east from Plaça de Sant Jaume, you cross Vía Laietana into **La Ribera** and reach the **Carrer de Montcada**, crowded with beautifully restored old buildings. One of these houses the **Museu Picasso** (Tues–Sun 10am–8pm; €6.50; ⓦwww.museupicasso.bcn.es), one of the world's most important collections of Picasso's work, providing a unique opportunity to trace the artist's development from his early paintings as a young boy in Barcelona to the major works of later years. Continue down the street and at its end you'll find yourself opposite the stunning basilica of **Santa María del Mar** (daily 9am–1.30pm & 4.30–8pm; Sun choral Mass at 12.30pm) built on what was the seashore in the fourteenth century. The elongated square leading from the church to the old Mercat del Born is the **Passeig del Born**, heart of the trendy **El Born** neighbourhood, a pleasant area for wandering, and home to the city's best nightlife. A few minutes' walk from here is the green and peaceful **Parc de la Ciutadella,** whose attractions include the meeting place of the Catalan parliament, a lake, Gaudí's monumental fountain and the interesting city **zoo** (daily 10am–5pm; €14.95; ⓦwww.zoobarcelona.com).

Port Vell, Barceloneta and Port Olímpic

The whole **Port Vell** area has been revitalized, notably by the **Maremàgnum** complex, and is now a pleasant, attractive place with an upmarket shopping mall, an overpriced aquarium, cinema, IMAX theatre and a multitude of bars and pricey restaurants. The other side of the port, past the marina, the **Barceloneta** district, in contrast, is one of the few remaining *barris* harbouring genuine local Catalan life: here, you'll find cleaned-up **beaches**, and the city's most famous **seafood** restaurants. A cable car, the **Trasbordador Aeri**, runs from the tip of Barceloneta to Montjuïc (daily: Jan, Feb & mid-Oct to Dec 10.30am–5.45pm; March to mid-June & mid-Sept to mid-Oct 10.45am–7pm, mid-June to mid-Sept 11am–8pm; €9 one-way, €12.50 return). Walk 1km east along the beach promenade and you'll find **Port Olímpic** with its myriad bars and restaurants. At night, the tables are stacked up, dance floors emerge and the area hosts one of the city's most vibrant bar and club scenes.

Sagrada Família

Barcelona offers – above all through the work of **Antoni Gaudí** (1852–1926) – some of the most fantastic and exciting modern architecture to be found anywhere in the world. Without doubt his most famous creation is the incomplete **Temple Expiatori de la Sagrada Família** (April–Sept 9am–8pm; Oct–March 9am–6pm; €8; ⓦwww.sagradafamilia.org; metro Sagrada Família), in the northeastern sector of the Eixample. With construction still ongoing, the interior is a giant building site, but it's fascinating to watch Gaudí's last-known plans being slowly realized. The size alone is startling, with eight spires rising to over 100m. For Gaudí, these were metaphors for the Twelve Apostles; he planned to build four more above the main facade and to add a 180-metre tower topped with a gallery over the transept, itself to be surrounded by four smaller towers symbolizing the Evangelists. Take the lift, or climb up one of the towers, and you can enjoy a dizzy view down over the whole complex and clamber still further round the walls and into the towers. The tourist office issues a handy leaflet describing all Gaudí's works, with a map of their locations.

Parc Güell

In the north of the city, **Parc Güell** (daily 10am–8pm; free; ⓣ934 132 400) is Gaudí's most ambitious project after the Sagrada Família – and shouldn't be missed. This almost hallucinatory experience, with giant decorative lizards and a vast Hall of Columns, contains a small **museum** (daily 10am–8pm; €3) with some of the furniture Gaudí designed. To get here, take the metro to Vallcarça or Lesseps (15min walk from either) or bus #24 from Plaça de Catalunya to the eastern side gate.

Montjuïc

The hill of **Montjuïc** has yet more varied attractions: half a dozen museums, gardens, the "Spanish Village", Olympic arena, a superbly sited castle, and spectacular views of the sprawling city below. The most obvious approach is to take the metro to **Plaça d'Espanya** and walk from there up the imposing Avda. de la Reina María Cristina. If you'd rather start with the castle, take the **Funicular de Montjuïc** (daily 9am–10pm; every 10min; €2.20 return), which runs from Paral.lel metro station to the start of the **Telefèric de Montjuïc** (daily: April, May & Oct 10am–7pm; June–Sept 10am–9pm, Nov–March 10am–6pm; €5.50, €7.50 return), which in turn leads to the **Castell de Montjuïc** (April–May daily 10am–2pm; June–Aug daily 10am–8pm; Sept–March Sat & Sun 10am–2pm; ⓣ932 892 830). This eighteenth-century fortress offers magnificent views across the city, has an outdoor café within its ramparts, a mediocre military museum (€2.50), and a panoramic pathway into the surrounding woods. The alternative option to reach Montjuïc is to take bus #50 from Plaça Universitat along Gran Vía to Montjuïc.

MNAC and the Fundació Joan Miró

Although Montjuïc is a hill, a kind city planner had the forethought to install a series of escalators to take visitors up the majority of the way to the **Palau Nacional**, without breaking into a sweat. This imposing peach-coloured building is home to one of Spain's great museums, the **Museu Nacional d'Art de Catalunya** or **MNAC** (Tues–Sat 10am–7pm, Sun 10am–2.30pm; €8.50, free first Sun of month; ⓦwww.mnac.es). Its enormous bounty includes a Romanesque collection that is the best of its kind in the world: 35 rooms of eleventh- and twelfth-century frescoes, meticulously removed from a series of small Pyrenean churches and beautifully displayed. There is also a substantial number of Gothic, Baroque and Renaissance works. Nearby, to the east, is the **Fundació Joan Miró** (Tues–Sat 10am–8pm, Thurs till 9.30pm, Sun closes 2.30pm; €7.50; ⓦwww.bcn.fjmiro.es), the most adventurous of Barcelona's art museums, devoted to one of the greatest Catalan artists. The beautiful white building houses a permanent collection of paintings, graphics, tapestries and sculptures donated by Miró himself and covering the period from 1914 to 1978.

Estadi Olimpic and the Poble Espanyol

By partly retracing your steps and following signs, the road leads from the

DAY-TRIP: MONTSERRAT

The weird and bulbous mountains of **Montserrat**, 60km northwest of Barcelona, make for an interesting day-trip out of the city. As well as some short hikes (1-3hr) through the national park's unusual rock formations, the main attraction is the Benedictine monastery, home to an unusual twelfth-century black carving of the Virgin Mary (*La Morenata*) and the oldest boys' choir in Europe (Mon–Sat recitals 1pm & 7.10pm, Sun noon). To get here, take the train from Plaça Espanya (every hour at 36min past) to Monserrat Aeri (for the cable car), or to Monistrol de Monserrat (for the rack railway to the town).

Fundació Joan Miró to what was the principal **Olympic arena** in 1992 and various other Olympic sights. The Olympic Stadium itself, the **Estadi Olimpic** (daily 10am–8pm; free), built originally for the 1929 Exhibition, was completely refitted to accommodate the 1992 opening and closing ceremonies. Heading downhill and to the west brings you to the **Poble Espanyol** or "Spanish Village" (Mon 9am–8pm, Tues–Thurs 9am–2am, Fri & Sat 9am–4am, Sun 9am–midnight; €7.50; Ⓦwww.poble-espanyol.com), consisting of replicas of famous or characteristic buildings from all over Spain, and with a lively club scene at night.

Arrival and information

Air The airport is linked by train to the main train station, Barcelona Sants (daily 6am–10.45pm, every 30min; €2.50), from where you can take the metro to the city centre (line #3 to Liceu for Las Ramblas). Some trains from the airport also run on to Plaça de Catalunya, a more direct way of reaching the Barri Gòtic. The Airbus (5.30am–1am, every 8min; €3.90) runs to Plaça d'Espanya, Gran Vía de les Corts Catalanes and Plaça de Catalunya. A taxi to the centre will cost around €22.

Train Barcelona Sants (metro Sants) is the city's main train station, for national and some international arrivals – many national buses also stop here. Estació de França (metro Barceloneta), near Parc de la Ciutadella, is the terminal for long-distance Spanish and European express and intercity trains.

Bus The main bus terminal is the Estació del Nord (three blocks north of Parc de la Ciutadella; metro Arc de Triomf).

Ferry Balearics ferries dock at the Estació Marítima (metro Drassanes) at the bottom of Las Ramblas.

Tourist office Plaça de Catalunya (daily 8am–8pm; Ⓣ932 853 834, Ⓦwww.barcelonaturisme.com; metro Catalunya).

City transport

The quickest way of getting around is by **metro** (Mon–Thurs & Sun 5am–midnight, Fri til 2am, all night Sat) as **bus** routes (5am–10.30pm, plus night-bus network) are far more complicated – though every bus stop does display a comprehensive route map. There's more information on Ⓦwww.tmb.net, or pick up a free **transport map** at TMB customer service centres at Barcelona Sants or Universitat and Diagonal metro stations.

Tickets and diuscount cards There's a flat fare on both metro and buses (€1.25), but it's cheaper to buy a ten-ride *targeta* (called a "T10") for €6.90, available at any metro station, which covers the metro, buses and some regional train lines. Similarly, there are daily passes that offer unlimited travel (T-Dia; €5.25 for 1 day up to €20.80 for 5 days), or the Barcelona Card, available from any tourist office (€24 for 2 days up to €36 for 5 days), covering transport to/from the airport, all city transport, plus discounts at museums, shops and restaurants. The Art Ticket (€20) gains you free entry to seven of the city's main art galleries. Note that student ticket prices in museums and galleries are often only available to those who are both a student and under 25.

Bus Turístic Links 27 of Barcelona's major sights, at which you can hop off and on at your leisure (€19 for 1 day; €23 for 2 days); tickets are available at tourist offices or on the bus itself.

Taxis Black and yellow taxis are plentiful and very useful late at night. There's a minimum charge of €1.15, €1.30 after 10pm and at weekends, with an average cross-town journey costing €6–7.

Accommodation

Accommodation in Barcelona is among the most expensive in Spain, and in summer you'll be hard pushed to find a hostel bed for under €20, or a

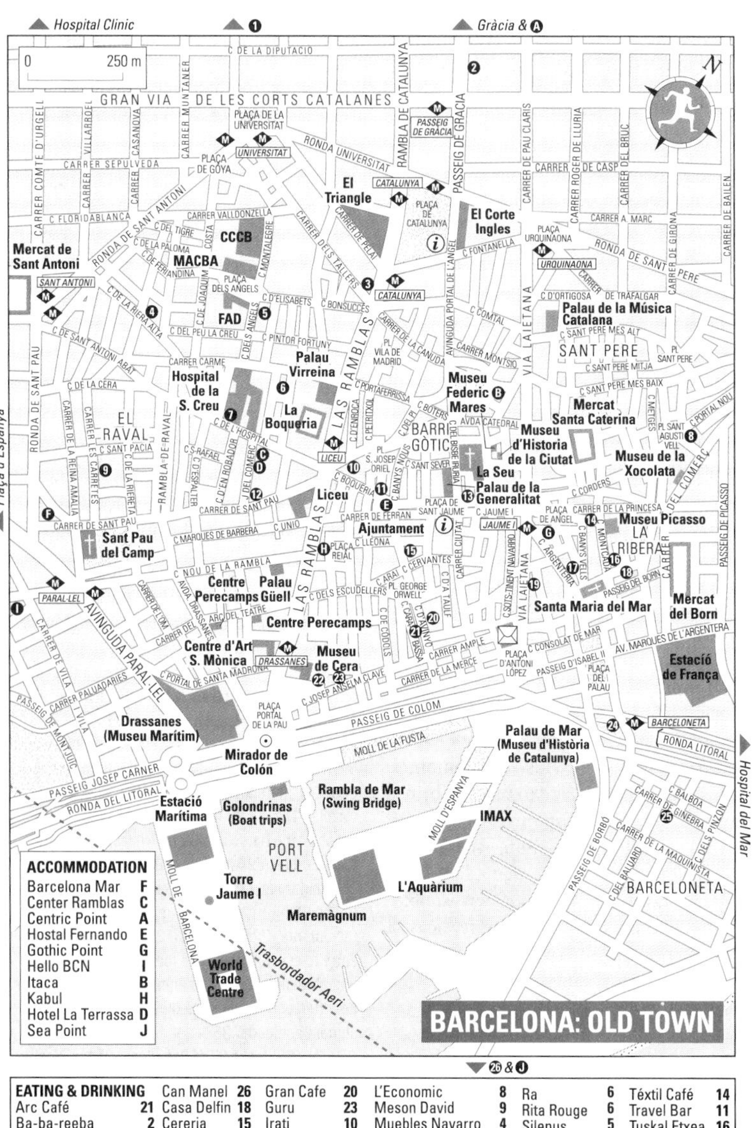

EATING & DRINKING											
Arc Café	21	Can Manel	26	Gran Cafe	20	L'Economic	8	Ra	6	Téxtil Café	14
Ba-ba-reeba	2	Casa Delfin	18	Guru	23	Meson David	9	Rita Rouge	6	Travel Bar	11
Boada	3	Cereria	15	Irati	10	Muebles Navarro	4	Silenus	5	Tuskal Etxea	16
Bosc de las Fades	22	Fira	1	Jai-Ca	25	Organic	12	Taller de Tapas	17	Vaso de Oro	24
		Gelaaati!	13	Juicy Jones	7	Ovni	19				

double room for under €50. You're also strongly advised to **book ahead**, at least for the first couple of nights. Most of the cheapest accommodation is to be found in the side streets off and around Las Ramblas, particularly in the **Barri Gòtic** between Las Ramblas and Plaça de Sant Jaume, in the area bordered by c/Escudellers and c/de la Boqueria. **El Raval**, on the other side of Las Ramblas, also has some cheap choices, especially around c/Junta del Comerç, though this neighbourhood has a slightly edgier feel at night. The tourist office at Plaça de Catalunya can help find rooms (though not hostel space), or you can use **Barcelona Online** (ⓣ933 437 993, ⓦwww.barcelona-online.es) or the online hostel and budget-hotel **reservation service** www.hostelbarcelona.com. For **longer stays**, the English-run Barcelona Home Search (mobile ⓣ605 609 707, ⓦwww.barcelonahomesearch.com) rents out well-maintained **apartments** in various city-centre locations. There are hundreds of **campsites** on the coast in either direction, but none less than 11km from the city. Note that none of the hostels below have curfews unless otherwise stated

Hostels

Albergue Verge de Montserrat Pg. Mare de Déu del Coll 41–51, Horta ⓣ932 105 151, ⓦwww.tujuca.com. A lovely HI mansion hostel with gardens and views, around 30min from the centre. Five-night maximum stay. Metro Vallcarça. ❸

Barcelona Mar c/Sant Pau 80, El Raval ⓣ933 248 530, ⓦwww.youthostel-barcelona.com. Large, fun hostel with mixed dorms and Internet, close to MACBA and the Raval nightlife. Metro Paral.lel /Drassanes. ❸

Center Ramblas c/Hospital 63, El Raval ⓣ934 124 069, ⓦwww.center-ramblas.com. Popular HI hostel, just off Las Ramblas, with a bar and laundry. Friendly, but the decor's a bit grim. Metro Liceu. ❸

Centric Point c/Passeig de Gràcia 33, Eixample ⓣ932 156 538, ⓦwww.centricpointhostel.com. A beautiful, old mansion-conversion in the smart Passeig de Gracia. All rooms have en-suite bathrooms. Free Internet. Metro Passeig de Gracia. ❷

Gothic Point c/Vigatans 5–9, La Ribera ⓣ932 687 808, ⓦwww.gothicpoint.com. Excellent location, featuring a sunny patio with deckchairs, plus bike rental and organized social events. Metro Jaume I. ❸

Hello BCN c/Lafont 8-10 ⓣ934 428 392, ⓦwww.hellobcnhostel.com. A busy new hostel 10min from Las Ramblas. Crowded dorms but great atmosphere; also has gym, kitchen, free Internet and bar. Metro Paral.lel. ❸

Itaca c/Ripoll 21, Barri Gòtic ⓣ933 019 751, ⓦwww.itacahostel.com. Funky little hostel near La Seu, with spacious mixed dorms (women-only dorm also available), plus plenty of communal spaces and a kitchen. Metro Jaume I. Curfew 4–7am. ❸

Kabul Pl. Reial 17, Barri Gòtic ⓣ933 185 190, ⓦwww.kabul.es. Very popular – thanks to the great location – with big dorms and a party atmosphere. ❸

Sea Point Pl. del Mar 1–4, Barceloneta ⓣ932 247 075, ⓦwww.seapointhostel.com. Beachfront accommodation with en-suite dorms, and café looking right out onto the boardwalk. Metro Barceloneta. ❸

Hotels

Hostal Fernando c/de Ferran 31, Barri Gòtic ⓣ933 017 993, ⓦwww.hfernando.com. Well-kept rooms in the *hostal*, plus top-floor dorm accommodation. Metro Liceu. Dorms ❷, rooms ❻

Hotel La Terrassa c/Junta del Comerç 11, El Raval ⓣ933 025 174, ⓦwww.laterrassa-barcelona.com. Good-value favourite, incorporating part of an Augustine monastery and with a pleasant terrace. No dorms. Metro Liceu. ❻

Eating

Barcelona is a reasonably **expensive** place to eat out. Awash as it is with trendy new restaurants, the best bet for a cheap meal is to take advantage of the lunchtime *menú del día* many of these places offer. For picnics, head for **La Boqueria** market off Las Ramblas, or stop in at one of the many bakeries. Tapas is another option, and there are hundreds of excellent bars in the old town, although these can end up being costly, depending on the portion size.

TREAT YOURSELF

The uber-smart, minimalist Michelin-starred restaurant **Alkimia** (c/Indústria 79, ⓣ932 076 115) is the perfect place to mingle with chic locals. A range of its Catalan-inspired cuisine can be sampled on its excellent tasting menu for €52. It's best to book in advance, and the restaurant is closed for three weeks in August.

Cafés

Cereria Bxda. de Sant Miquel 3, Barri Gòtic. So laid-back it's horizontal – a literary café with good cakes and daily specials. Metro Jaume I.

Téxtil Café c/Montcada 12, La Ribera. In the atmospheric medieval courtyard of the textile museum, with braziers in winter. Closed Mon. Metro Jaume I.

Tapas bars

Ba-ba-reeba Pg. de Gràcia 28, Eixample. Delicious range of tapas, all at reasonable prices (€3.25–8.35). Open until 1.30am. Metro Passeig. de Gràcia.

Euskal Etxea Pl. Montcada 1–3, La Ribera. Specializing in mouthwatering *pintxos* (Basque tapas) for around €5. Closed Mon. Metro Jaume I.

Irati c/Cardenal de Casanyes 17. Excellent tapas bar and restaurant, serving new-wave Basque cuisine. Metro Liceu.

Jai-Ca c/Ginebra 13, Barceloneta. Small, atmospheric cornerside bar with some of the best tapas (€5–10) in town. Closed Mon. Metro Barceloneta.

Taller de Tapas c/de l'Argenteria. One of several city-centre branches of this popular chain of tapas bars/restaurants offering simple, quality food in elegant, relaxed surroundings. Tapas €3–12. Highly recommended. Metro Jaume I.

Vaso de Oro c/de Balboa. A tiny but lively bar, packed with locals and oozing noise and character. Excellent tapas, at around €3.50. Closed Sept. Metro Barceloneta.

Restaurants

Arc Café c/Carabassa 19, Barri Gòtic. Students, travellers and artists all hang out in this old-town brasserie-bar. Mains €8. Popular Thai food nights on Thurs and Fri. Metro Drassanes.

Can Manel Pg. Joan de Borbó 60, Barceloneta. Probably the best-value place by the harbour, though the weekday €8.25 *menú del día* features disappointingly little seafood. Metro Barceloneta.

Casa Delfin Pg. del Born 36, La Ribera. Paper-tablecloth bar-restaurant that packs in the locals. Cheap and cheerful €10 *menú del día,* three courses including bread and wine. Mon–Sat 6am–6pm. Metro Barceloneta.

Gelaaati! c/Llibreteria 7, Ⓦwww.gelaaati.es. Homemade Italian ice creams, in an array of delicious – and sometimes unusual – flavours. Try the chilli or avocado varieties for something a bit different. Metro Jaume I.

Gran Cafe c/Avinyó, 9, Barri Gòtic. Elegant Barcelona institution offering exceptional service and good Catalan/French food (mains €14). Closed Mon. Metro Jaume I.

Juicy Jones c/Hospital 74, El Raval Ⓣ934 439 082. The only vegan restaurant in town, with bright, funky murals and an extraordinary range of fruit juices and blends. Three courses €8.50. Daily noon–midnight. Metro Liceu.

L'Economic Pl. Sant Agustí Vell 13, La Ribera Ⓣ933 196 494. The beautiful tiled dining room is the backdrop for one of the city's bargains – an excellent three-course lunch for under €8, wine included. Closed weekends. Metro Jaume I.

Meson David c/Carrates 63, Ⓣ934 415 934. Lively, bustling, family-run Galician restaurant, with mains from around €7. Tues–Sun 1pm–2am & 8pm–midnight. Metro Paral.lel.

Organic c/Junta de Comerc 11. Funky organic vegetarian restaurant with a hippy vibe, serving tasty meals (main course and salad €7.50). Also includes an apothecary's shop of teas and herbs. Metro Liceu.

Ovni c/Via Laietana 32. Stylish, fantastic-value vegetarian restaurant serving all-you-can eat buffet for €6.60 or €7.95 at weekends. Free Internet access for 30min. Metro Jaume I.

Ra Pl. Gardunya 34. Trendy bar/restaurant behind La Boqueria, serving an excellent €10.99 three-course lunch menu. Metro Liceu.

Rita Rouge Pl. Gardunya 33, El Raval Ⓣ934 813 686. Chic new restaurant with outside tables and a *menú del día* for €10. Metro Liceu.

Silenus c/Angels 8, El Raval. Just round the corner from the MACBA and with a decidedly hip clientele, this billowing white space serves delicious food. Come for lunch, though, and you can eat for just €12.50. Metro Liceu.

Drinking and nightlife

Barcelona's **nightlife** is some of Europe's most exciting, though it's not cheap – in the most exclusive places, even a beer costs roughly ten times as much as in the neighbourhood bar next door. Nevertheless, many clubs give a free drink on entry. The hi-tech theme palaces are concentrated mainly in the Eixample, especially around c/Ganduxer, Avda. Diagonal and Vía Augusta. Laid-back and/or alternative places can be found in the streets of El Raval, while the waterfront Port Olímpic area is a more mainstream summer-night playground. Music **bars** close at 3am, the clubs at 4 or 5am, though later at weekends. For listings, buy the weekly *Guía del Ocio* from any newsstand (Ⓦwww.guiadelociobcn.com). The thriving gay scene in Barcelona (Ⓦwww.gaybarcelona.net), is prevalent in the so-called Gaixample, a few square blocks northwest of the main university: SexTienda, at c/Rauric 11 (near Plaça Reial), supplies free maps of gay Barcelona with a list of bars, clubs and contacts.

BARCELONA BEATS

If electronica is your thing, make sure you're in town for **Sonar** (Ⓦwww.sonar.es), an internationally recognized multimedia art and progressive music festival, held every June in Barcelona. Day tickets cost €28, whilst a three-day, two-night pass will set you back €140.

Bars

Boada c/de Tallers 1. A popular old-fashioned cocktail bar just off Las Ramblas, with barmen in black tie. Tues–Sun noon–midnight. Metro Liceu.
Bosc de las Fades Pasaje de la Blanca 7. Means "Fairies' Wood" in Catalan, and reflecting this theme throughout. A popular place, though difficult to find tucked away, as it is, behind the Museu de Cera.
Fira c/Provença 171, Eixample. Only in Barcelona – fairground rides and circus paraphernalia adorn this long-standing theme bar. Tues–Sat from 11pm. Metro Provença.
Guru c/Josep Anselm Clavé 19. A chic yet unpretentious lounge-bar boasting a fabulous cocktail menu. Try the Lolita; a blend of fresh strawberries, passion fruit and liqueur. Drinks promotions. Metro Drassanes.
Muebles Navarro c/Riera Alta 4–6, El Raval. Converted furniture store with big, comfy sofas and big, strong drinks. Popular with a gay crowd. Tues–Sun from 6pm. Metro Sant Antoni.
Travel Bar c/Boqueria 27, Barri Gòtic. Popular backpackers' dive: one-stop shop for cheap food, Internet access, fun city tours and general chilling out. Metro Liceu.

Clubs

Moog c/Arc del Teatre 3, El Raval. Techno temple with regular appearances from top UK and Euro DJs. Best on Wed & Sun. Cover charge €8. Metro Drassanes.
Sala Apolo/Club Nitsa c/Nou de la Rambla 113, Poble Sec. Regular live gigs by biggish names and burgeoning stars from the worlds of alternative rock, electronica and techno – *Nitsa* club night rules the roost at weekends. Metro Paral.lel.
Jamboree Pl. Reial 17, Barri Gotic. Very international crowd, dancing to hip-hop or funky jazz. Cover charge €9. Metro Liceu.
Catwalk Club Ramon Trias Fargas 2–4, Port Olímpic. One of the biggest clubs in Barcelona, underneath two large hotels. Guest DJs have included Eric Morillo, Steve Angelli and many more. Cover charge €15. Metro Ciutadella.
Razzmatazz Club c/Amogàvers 122. Something for everyone, with five different rooms each dedicated to a different genre: pop, rock and electro amongst others. Cover charge €12. Metro Marina.

Shopping

Barcelona is fast gaining a reputation for great **shopping**, and it's easy to see why. All the big names of the fashion industry can be found along the smart Passeig de Gràcia, but if this breaks your budget, the oceanic shopping centre **Maremagnum** has many high-street brands located under one roof. For a more unique purchase, the crooked passages of La Ribera and El Born, south of the Barri Gòtic, are home to dozens of little **boutiques**, whilst in Raval, numerous funky **vintage** shops lie along the Carrer de la Riera Baixa. There are also a number of excellent speciality **food** retailers in the city, and chocolate shops lie scattered throughout the Ciutat Vella.
Bijou Brigitte c/Argenteria 6. Good-value semi-precious jewellery and other fun accessories. Closed Sun.
La Base c/Carme 27. Assorted hippy garments and bits and bobs, including bandanas, skirts and so on. Next door – but part of the same shop – stocks cool T-shirts and mainstream clothing. Mon–Sat 11am–2.30pm & 5.30–9pm.
La Botifarrería de Santa María c/Santa María 4. Sells fabulous speciality hams, cheeses and their famous *botifarras* (sausages).
Cannibal 0607 c/Carme. A wide range of trendy men's and women's informal clothes. Also a small jewellery section. Mon–Sat 11am–9pm.
Como Agua de Mayo c/Argenteria 43. Beautiful, albeit expensive, boutique in La Ribera, stocking women's clothing. Silks and natural fibres predominate. Closed Sun.
Natura c/Avinyó 22. One of an Asian-inspired chain, selling objects for the home, and a variety of cotton clothing and scarves. Daily 11am–9pm.
Papabubble c/Ample 28. Sweet-smelling candy store, where you can watch confectionery taking shape before your eyes. Closed Aug.
Produit National Brut c/Avinyó. Vintage and customized clothes for men and women, plus retro sunglasses. Daily 11am–9pm.
Xocoa c/Princesa 10. *Chocolatier* selling handmade chocolates and funky chocolate bars sealed in retro-style wrapping. Mon–Fri 10.30am–8.45pm, Sun 11am–3pm & 4–7.45pm.

Directory

Consulates Australia, Gran Vía Carles III 98, Les Corts ⓣ933 309 496; Canada, c/Elisenda de Pinós 10, Sàrria ⓣ932 042 700; Ireland, Gran Vía Carles III 94, Les Corts ⓣ934 915 021; New Zealand, Trav. de Gràcia 64, Gràcia ⓣ932 090 399; UK, Avda. Diagonal 477, Eixample ⓣ934 199 044; US, Passeig de la Reina Elisenda 23, Sàrria ⓣ932 802 227.
Exchange Most banks are located in Pl. de Catalunya and Pg. de Gràcia. ATMs and money exchange available at the airport; Barcelona Sants; the tourist office at Pl. Catalunya; and at *casas de cambio* throughout the centre.

Hospitals 24hr accident and emergency centres at: Centre Perecamps, Avda. Drassanes 13, El Raval ⓣ934 410 600; Hospital Clinic, c/Villarroel 170, Eixample ⓣ932 275 400; Hospital del Mar, Pg. Marítim 25, Vila Olímpica ⓣ932 483 000.
Internet access Ciberopcion, Gran Via de les Corts Catalanes 602, Eixample; easyEverything, Ronda de l'Universitat, Eixample, and Ramblas 31; Internet Gallery Café, Barra de Ferro 3.
Laundry Lavomatic, Pl. Joaquim Xirau, Barri Gòtic, and c/Consolat del Mar 43, La Ribera.
Left luggage Lockers at all the stations; €3–4.50 per day.
Lost property ⓣ934 023 161.
Pharmacies At least one *farmacía* (marked with a green cross) in each neighbourhood is open 24hr – look in the window of any pharmacy for addresses.
Police Guardia Urbana (City Police), Ramblas 43 ⓣ933 441 300; open 24hr.
Post office Correus, Pl. Antoni López (Mon–Sat 8.30am–9.30pm, Sun 8.30am–2.30pm).

Moving on

Train Bilbao (2 daily; 9hr–10hr 20min); Girona (hourly; 1hr 15min–1hr 30min); Tarragona (every 30min; 1hr); Valencia (14 daily; 3–5hr); Zaragoza (15 daily; 3hr 40min–4hr 30min).
Bus Alicante (7 daily; 8hr); Madrid (7–15 daily; 7hr 30min); Valencia (14–17 daily; 4–5hr); the Vall d'Aran (daily; 6hr 30min); Zaragoza (15–25 daily; 3hr 30min–5hr).
Ferry Ibiza (7 weekly; 4hr 30min–9hr); Palma (2–4 daily; 8hr 30min).

The Balearic islands

The four chief **Balearic islands** – Ibiza, Formentera, Mallorca and Menorca – maintain a character distinct from the mainland and from each other. **Ibiza**, firmly established among Europe's hippest resorts, has an intense, outrageous street life and a floating summer population that includes clubbers, fashion victims and gay visitors from every corner of Europe, and beyond. Tiny neighbouring **Formentera** is relatively undeveloped and tranquil by comparison, with miles of breathtaking sandy beaches bathed by waters turquoise enough to rival the Caribbean. **Mallorca**, the largest of the Balearics, still battles with its image as a mass-market tourism destination, though in reality you'll find all the clichés crammed into the sprawling resorts along the Bay of Palma. Away from these there are soaring pine-forested mountains, traditional villages, lively fishing ports, some beautiful coves and the Balearics' one real city, **Palma**. The farthest island from the mainland, Menorca, is a quiet family-orientated holiday destination; for those short of time, a visit to the other three islands is more worthwhile.

Getting there

Ferries from mainland Spain (and Marseille) and inter-island connections are overpriced considering the distances involved: the cheapest mainland ferry connections are from Denia (south of Valencia), costing from €50 one-way to Mallorca or Ibiza. The ferry timetables vary hugely from winter to summer. Times listed here are a guide, but for more up-to-date information see ⓦwww.iscomarferrys.com, ⓦwww.trasmediterranea.com or ⓦwww.balearia.com; bear in mind, though, that special **flight** deals mean it can be cheaper to fly. **Prices** on all the Balearic islands are considerably above the mainland, and from mid-June to mid-September budget **rooms** are in extremely short supply, so book in advance.

IBIZA

IBIZA (Eivissa in Catalan) is an island of excess. Internationally heralded as one of the world's top clubbing destinations, each summer Europe's best DJs play at its clubs, attracting a host of young people looking to party 24/7. Yet it also has a quieter side, with beautiful beaches and

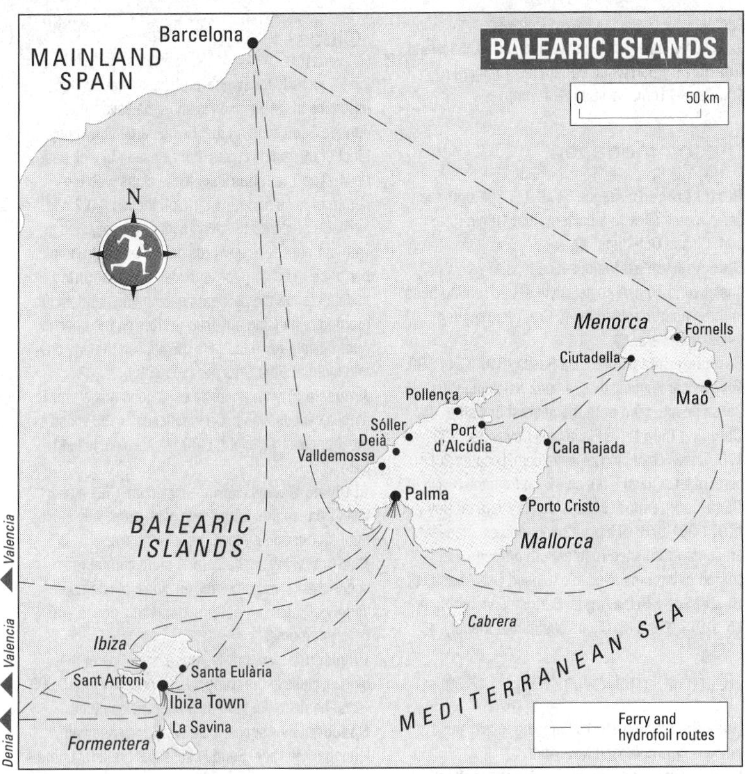

a bohemian vibe; a legacy from the 1960s when the island was a hippy hang-out.

What to see and do

In physical as well as atmospheric terms, **IBIZA TOWN** is the most attractive place on the island. Set around a dazzling natural harbour, it's one of the Mediterranean's most cosmopolitan small capitals. The old city walls enclose the ancient quarter of **Dalt Vila**, whilst the port area is a maze of small, whitewashed houses, market stalls and expensive boutiques specializing in boho regalia. Most **beaches** are easily accessible from the town – the best include Las Salinas, a long strip of sand surrounded by forests (bus #11; hourly 9.30am–7.30pm; €1.35), and Cala Bassa, a cove on the easterly side of the island 20km northeast of Ibiza Town and roughly 9km west of the town of Sant Antoni; take bus #3 from Ibiza Town to Sant Antoni (every 30min 7am–11.30pm; €1.35), then bus #7 (every 1–2hr 9.30am–6.30pm; €1.35) from Sant Antoni to Cala Bassa. For celebrity spotting, head to the tiny Platja de Benirràs, near San Miguel, a favourite of the Euro jet-set.

Arrival and information

Air The airport is 6km out of town; there's a regular bus (daily 7.30am–11pm; €1.85), or you can take a taxi (€16).

Tourist office Opposite the ferry building, at c/Antoni Riquer 2 (May–Oct Mon–Fri 8am–8pm, Sat 9.30am–7.30pm; Nov–April Mon–Fri 8am–3pm, Sat 9.30am–1pm; ⓣ971 301 900, ⓔoitport@cief.es).

Alternatively, check out Ⓦwww.ibiza-spotlight.com for excellent up-to-date information about the island.
Internet Try Surf@net, c/Riambau 4 (Mon–Fri 10.30am–11pm, Sat–Sun 3–11pm).

Accommodation

Hostal Aragon c/Aragon 54 Ⓣ971 306 060. Clean, basic rooms all with a balcony, just 10min from the port. Closed Oct–June. ❼
Blue Apartments Various locations Ⓦwww.hostelworld.com. A hostel-style set up renting beds in three apartments in town. Great for meeting fellow travellers. ❸
Camping Cala Bassa Cala Bassa Ⓣ971 344 599, Ⓦwww.campingcalabassa.com. Adjoining Cala Bassa beach, 50m from the nearest bus stop. ❶
Camping Cala Nova Platja Cala Nova Ⓣ971 331 776, Ⓦwww.campingcalanova.com. Located 20km north of Ibiza Town – but only 50m from the beach. ❶
Casa de Huéspedes Vara de Rey Vara de Rey 7 Ⓣ971 301 376, Ⓔhibiza@wanadoo.es. Pleasant, artistically furnished rooms. Both en-suite and shared bathrooms available. Closed Oct–March. ❽
Hostal Sol y Brisa Avgda. Bartomeu Vicent Ramon 15 Ⓣ971 310 818. Clean, cheap and friendly. ❻

Eating and drinking

Base Bar c/Garijo 15–16 Pumping music and a raucous crowd. Closed Nov–April.
Bom Profit Pl. del Parque 5. Excellent seafood restaurant with a loyal clientele, with mains around €10. Kitchen closes at 10pm. Closed Sun and Jan.
C'an Costa c/Creu 19. A popular local restaurant serving typical Spanish fare (mains €6). Mon–Sat 1–3.15pm & 8–11.30pm. Closed Oct–March.
Can Bar Pou c/Lluis Tur i Palau 19. Affordable, popular bar on the waterfront.
Comida San Juan c/Arturo Mari Ribas 5 Ⓣ971 311 603. Small atmospheric place, with a great menu. Arrive early to avoid queuing. Closed Sun and Feb.
Lo Cura c/Antonio Mari Ribas 4 Ⓦwww.lo-cura.com. Tiny little bar near the port, with cheap drinks and DJ.
Rock Bar c/Garijo 14. One of the cheaper portside bars, attracting many English-speakers. A good place to meet fellow partygoers.
Sunset Café Pl. del Parque 9. Despite the name, this is really a funky bar on the popular Plaza del Parque.

Clubs

Ibiza's globally renowned **club** scene needs little introduction. The season is short, however (mid-June to Sept), with August being particularly busy. Most of the main venues don't close until well past dawn. The **Discobus** links these clubs with the centre of town and runs through the night (€2 one-way). Be prepared to spend a lot of money, though, with entrance fees upwards of €35 and astronomical bar prices. Look out for touts selling **discounted** tickets around the port bars each night, and for club promoters handing out **free invites** on the beaches. Alternatively, head to Playa d'Embossa to party day and night at *Bora Bora* bar (free entry).
Amnesia Ⓦwww.amnesia.es. A good mix of music across various nights. On Wednesdays, the island's most popular gay night, La Troya Asesina, is held here.
El Divino Ⓦwww.eldivino-ibiza.com. Only a short walk from central Ibiza Town, with great views over the harbour and a mix of popular music.
Pacha Ⓦwww.pacha.com. A more commercial scene than some other Ibizan clubs, playing a variety of music – but predominantly house – in different rooms.
Privilege Ⓦwww.privilegeibiza.com. One of the biggest clubs in the world, with a capacity for 10,000 – and home to the famous Manumission night.
Space Ⓦwww.space-ibiza.es. Day-venue with legendary terrace. Sunday sessions are a favourite.

Gay bars and clubs

Ibiza has one of the best **gay scenes** in Europe (Ⓦwww.gayibiza.net), with the action centred on one wild street: the c/Verge "village" in the port. Another cluster of bars can be found just off this street, on c/d'Alfonso XII. In addition, many mainstream Ibizan clubs hold a weekly gay night.
Angelo c/Alfonso XII 11. Another trendy bar, tucked away below *Soap*. May–Oct daily 10pm–3.30am; Nov–April Thurs–Sat 11pm–4am.
Anfora c/San Carlos 7, Dalt Vila Ⓦwww.disco-anfora.com. Ibiza's only dedicated gay club (men only). Closed mid-Oct to April.
Soap c/Santa Lucia 23-21 Ⓦwww.soap-ibiza.com. One of the most popular gay bars in town, with minimalist interior. Daily 10am–4pm. Closed Oct–April.

Moving on

Ferry Barcelona (7 weekly; 4hr 30min–9hr); Formentera (6–9 daily; 30min–1hr); Palma (2–4 daily; 2–4hr); Valencia (1–6 weekly; 3–9hr)

FORMENTERA

For a complete contrast with Ibiza's hedonism, **FORMENTERA** makes for a relaxing, although expensive, day-trip. Just three nautical miles south of its neighbour and the smallest of the inhabited islands, its uncrowded **beaches** are a haven for anyone seeking escape, with little in the way of sophistication.

What to see and do

The whitewashed capital, **SANT FRANCESC**, is 2km from the harbour at La Savina, along a narrow road that continues on to the easternmost point at La Mola. Along it, or just off it, are almost all of the island's settlements, including the village of **Sant Ferran**, and the small resort of **Es Pujols**. The best **beaches** are the stunning white sands of **Platja Illetes** on the slim spur of land that stretches out to the north of La Savina, and **Platja de Migjorn**, a five-kilometre strip of sand occupying most of southern Formentera and broken only by the occasional bar or hotel – it's popular with nude sunbathers.

Arrival and information

Ferry Boats from Ibiza (€21–35 return) dock at the tiny harbour of **La Savina**, where you can rent mopeds or bicycles – a great way of getting around.
Tourist office The island's main **tourist office** is by the quay (Ⓣ971 322 057; daily 9.30am–3pm & 5–7pm; closed Sun am).

Accommodation

Camping is illegal, but there are a few reasonably priced places to stay on the island.
Hostal La Sabina Avda. Mediterranea 22-40, La Savina Ⓣ971 322 279, Ⓔhostallasavina@terra.es. Stylish hotel near the port, with a terrace backing onto a tranquil lagoon speckled with yachts. ❽
Hostal-Residencia Illes Pitiuses Avda. Joan Castelló Guasch 48, Sant Ferran Ⓣ971 328 740, Ⓦwww.illespitiuses.com. Friendly hotel 2.5km from the beach at Es Pujols. ❾
Pensión Bon Sol c/Major 84–76, Sant Ferran Ⓣ971 328 882, Ⓔfelixbonsol@terra.es. Clean, simply furnished rooms with balconies. ❻

Eating and drinking

Blue Bar Fantastic chilled-out bar-restaurant at the end of a dirt track on Platja de Migjorn. Follow signposts off the main Sant Ferran–La Mola road. Daily noon–4pm & 6pm–midnight.
Fonda Pepe c/Major 51, Sant Ferran. Hippy favourite and something of a local institution. Mains €12.
Sa Garrafa c/Major 21, Sant Ferran. Lounge bar and restaurant with attractive terrace and lots of good veggie options (mains €9).

MALLORCA

MALLORCA has a split identity. As one of Europe's most popular tourist resorts it pulls in around three million tourists a year, and there are sections of its coast where the concrete curtain of high-rise hotels and shopping centres is continuous. But the spread of development is limited to the **Bay of Palma**, a forty-kilometre strip flanking the island's capital. To the north and east, things are very different – not only are there good cove **beaches** and wonderful rural hotels, but there's a startling variety and physical beauty to the land itself, which makes the island many people's favourite of the Balearics.

What to see and do

At first sight, the island's capital, **PALMA** can seem tacky, but it has a historic city centre filled with quaint streets and stylish boutiques, and in summer the port bristles with hundreds of yacht masts, and the local fishermen mend their nets by the harbour. The main sight, however, is the **cathedral** (April–May & Oct Mon–Fri 10am–5.15pm, Sat 10am–2.15pm; June–Sept Mon–Fri 10am–6.30pm, Sat

PALMA–SÓLLER TRAIN RIDE

Although it may sound a little touristy, the **train ride from Palma to Sóller** (7 daily; €9 one-way) is definitely worth the trip. Built in 1911 to carry fruit to Palma, the line rattles and rolls in wooden carriages through the dusty outskirts of the capital before a cross-country climb up mountain passes and through tunnels, passing almond groves, unruffled lakes and craggy peaks topping a thousand metres. From Sóller, you can then take the tram on to Port Sóller (every 30min; €6 return), a little coastal town with plenty of character and a small, sandy cove for bathing.

10am–2.15pm; Nov–March Mon–Fri 10am–3.15pm, Sat 10am–2.15pm; €4), which was built in recognition of the Christian Reconquest of Mallorca, and later worked on by Gaudí. Nearby, within the old "Portela" quarter, are the **arab baths** (April–Nov 9am–8pm; Dec–March 9am–6pm; €1.50), whilst up the hill overlooking the bay lies the **Castell Bellver** (April–Sept Mon–Sat 8am–8.15pm, Sun 10am–7pm; Oct–March Mon–Sat 8am–7.15pm, Sun 10am–5pm; €2), offering spectacular views from its highpoint over the city.

The best beaches are on the east coast of the island and around its southernmost point. Mon Dragó is a lovely spot set in a nature reserve, in the southeast of Mallorca, accessible by bus L501 from Palma to Portopetro (5 daily; in summer, it goes on directly to the beach) and from there, the little "train" (really just a motorized wagon pulling carriages), which goes along the coast. Alternatively, head to Colonia de Sant Jordi (bus L502; 3–7 daily; €5.45), where the coast forms a number of long, sandy beaches, particularly fine ones including Es Trenc and Sa Rapita.

Arrival and information

Air Palma airport, 8km east of the city, is served by bus #1 (every 15min; €1.85) to the Passeig Mallorca.
Boat The large ferry port is 3.5km west of the city centre, connected to Palma by bus #1.
Tourist office Plaça de la Reina 2 (Mon–Fri 9am–8pm, Sat 9am–2pm; ⓣ971 712 216, ⓦwww.visitbalears.com).
Internet Head to the Correus on Constitucio, just off Passeig de Born.

Accommodation

The best areas to look for **accommodation** are around the Passeig Mallorca, on c/Apuntadores or c/Sant Feliu running west from Passeig d'es Born. There are no official **campsites** on the island.

Albergue Playa de Palma c/Costa Brava 13, El Arenal ⓣ971 260 892. Slightly outside of Palma, and often booked by school groups. Take bus #15 from Plaça d' Espanya or Plaça de la Reina. ❷

Hostal Apuntadores c/Apuntadores 8 ⓣ971 713 491, ⓦwww.palma-hostales.com. Very central little hotel offering dorm accommodation, and with a great terrace overlooking the harbour. Dorms ❸, rooms ❺

Hostal Terramar Pl. Mediterraneo 8 ⓣ971 739 931, ⓦwww.palma-hostales.com. Behind Paseo Maritimo, a converted house maintaining its homely feel. Popular with yacht crews. ❷

TREAT YOURSELF

If you're fed up with searching for enough space to spread out a tea towel, let alone a beach towel, ditch the packed beaches and make tracks to **Purobeach** (Cala Estancia ⓣ971 744 744, ⓦwww.purobeach.com), a private, luxury pool, bar and restaurant by Cala Estancia beach, run by *Puro* hotel in Palma. For €40 you can expect five-star treatment and poolside service, and, after sunset, live DJs playing chilled tunes for you to sip your cocktails to. It's best to arrive early to ensure a sunbed. To get here from Palma, take bus #52 (daily 11am–2am).

Eating and drinking

Bar Dia c/Apuntadores 18. Cheap and delicious, specializing in tapas (€3–5).
El Pilon c/Cifre 4. Bags of local atmosphere and great tapas, in a tiny alley just off Passeig d'es Born. Tapas €6.
Vecchio Giovani c/Sant Joan 3. A good-value option for lunch; three-course *menú del día* plus drink comes in at €10.

Clubs

Levels Avda. Gabriel Roca 42. Waterfront venue with guest DJs from Ibiza and the UK. Cover charge €15.
Tito's Placa Gomila 3. Hardy perennial of the Palma scene. Cover charge €18.

Moving on

Ferry Barcelona (5 daily; 4–7hr); Ibiza (5–6 daily; 2–4hr); Valencia (6 weekly; 8hr).

Valencia and Murcia

Much of the coast around **Valencia** and further south on the **Costa Blanca** has been insensitively overdeveloped, suffering from mass package-tourism and its associated ills. Nevertheless, the stretch between Jávea and Altea has escaped the worst excesses – but you will need your own vehicle to reach many of its beautiful beaches. The cities, however – vibrant Valencia and relaxed **Alicante** – are much more accessible, and are worth a stop for anyone travelling down the east coast.

VALENCIA

Although hosting the America's Cup in 2007 has encouraged the growth of many new restaurants and bars, **VALENCIA** still remains a distant second cousin to the other big Spanish cities. There is little of specific local interest, although it does have some good museums, a reasonable beach, and, of course, its famous festivals: the world-famous Las Fallas and La Tomatina, held in nearby **Buñol**.

What to see and do

The most interesting area for wandering is undoubtedly the maze-like **Barrio del Carmen**, with its arty, underground atmosphere. Stretching north of the Mercado Central up to the riverbed of the Río Turia, it's full of historic buildings being renovated and stylish cafés opening up next to crumbling townhouses.

Palacio del Marqués de Dos Aguas

The Palacio del Marqués de Dos Aguas, a short walk north of the train station, is an excellent example of traditional Valencian architecture and definitely worth a visit. Hipólito Rovira, who designed its amazing alabaster doorway, died insane in 1740, which should come as no surprise to anyone who's seen it. Inside is the **Museo Nacional de Cerámica** (Tues–Sat 10am–2pm & 4–8pm, Sun 10am–2pm; €2.40, free Sat pm & Sun), with a vast collection of ceramics from all over Spain.

Plaza Patriarca, Plaza de la Reina and the Mercado Central

Nearby, in the **Plaza Patriarca**, is the Neoclassical former university, with beautiful cloisters (hosts to a series of classical concerts in July), plus a small, but interesting, **art museum** (Tues–Sat 10am–1pm & 4pm–8pm, Sun 10am–2pm; €1.20). From here, up c/de la Paz, is the **Plaza de la Reina**, home to the impressive thirteenth-century **Catedral**, whose bell-tower, the **Miguelete** (Mon–Fri 10am–6pm, Sat–Sun 2pm–6.30pm; €1.20), gives stun-

ning city views. Just southwest of the cathedral lies the enormous **Mercado Central**, a huge iron and glass structure housing over one thousand stalls selling local fruit, vegetables and seafood until 2pm (closed Sun).

The museums

Art lovers will find **IVAM**, the modern art museum at c/Guillém de Castro 118 (June–Sept 10am–10pm; Oct–May Tues–Sun 10am–8pm; €2, free Sun; ⓣ963 863 000, ⓦwww.ivam.es), a treat, but the real highlight of the city's musuems is the **Ciudad de las Artes y las Ciencias** (City of Arts and Sciences; daily 10am–8pm, closes midnight in summer; €30.50 for two-day pass; ⓣ902 100 031, ⓦwww.cac.es). Sitting in a huge landscaped park that was built in the old riverbed of the Río Turia, this breathtaking collection of futuristic concrete, steel and glass architecture comprises five main buildings, four of which were designed by local architect Santiago Calatrava. The complex includes an eyeball-shaped IMAX **cinema**, a vast **science museum**, a huge **oceanographic park** (with beluga whales, sharks and turtles) and a dramatic pistachio nut-shaped **arts centre**.

Arrival and information

Train and bus Valencia's train station is centrally located: cross the busy c/Xátiva ring road and up Avda. Marqués de Sotelo for the Plaza del Ayuntamiento, continuing north for the Barrio del Carmen. The bus station is further out, to the northwest, on the far bank of the Río Turia riverbed; take local bus #8, the metro to Turia, or allow thirty minutes if you walk.
Boat Bus #19 connects the Balearic Ferry Terminal with the central Plaza del Ayuntamiento.
Tourist office There are offices of the regional tourist board (Ⓦwww.turisvalencia.es) at c/Paz 48 (Mon–Fri 9am–8pm, Sat 10am–8pm, Sun 10am–2pm; Ⓣ963 986 422), and at Plaza de la Reina 19 (Mon–Sat 9am–7pm, Sun 10am–2pm; Ⓣ963 153 931): both hand out the free English-language listings guides *24-7 Valencia* and *Hello Valencia*.
Discount Cards The Valencia Tourist Card (€7/12/15 for 1/2/3 days) gives you free travel on buses and metro and discounts in some museums, shops and restaurants. Available at tourist offices.

Accommodation

Although prices given here are for high season, note that many hostels put prices up even further for the **Las Fallas** festival.
Hôme c/La Lonja 4 Ⓣ963 916 229, Ⓦwww.likeathome.net. One of three *Hôme* hostels in the city. Comfortable, relaxed and in great central location. Metro Xátiva. ❷
Hosteleria del Pilar Plaza del Mercado 19 Ⓣ963 916 600. Small, basic *pensión* near the Mercado Central. Metro Xátiva. ❷
Indigo c/Guillem de Castro 64 Ⓣ963 153 988, Ⓦwww.indigohostel.com. A bit further out than some other hostels, but with a laid-back atmosphere and free Internet, tea and coffee. Metro Angel Guimerá. ❷
Purple Nest Hostel Plaza Tetuan 5 Ⓣ963 532 561, Ⓦwww.purplenesthostel.com. Younger sibling of the Red Nest Hostel, similar in style but often not as busy. Metro Alameda. ❷
Red Nest Hostel c/La Paz 36 Ⓣ963 427 168, Ⓦwww.rednesthostel.com. Bright, fun decor and lots of communal space, with pool table and table football. Metro Colón. ❷

Eating

The quality of Valencia's **restaurants** has improved in recent years, with a new wave of trendy places opening across the city. There are plenty of decent options near the Mercado Central and in the Barrio del Carmen but avoid touristy places too near the plazas de la Reina and de la Virgen.
Al Pan, Queso c/Serranos 19. A Brazilian café offering tapas-style snacks and exotic fruit juices. Menú del día €5.50. Mon–Fri 9am–midnight, Sat–Sun 10am–midnight.
Kokura Automatic Sushi c/Cabrito 3. Very reasonably priced sushi and some good menu offers, including eight pieces of sushi plus a drink for €7.
Pepita Pulgarcita c/Cavalleros 19 Ⓣ963 914 608. Tapas (€4.50) and light meals are available in this stylish, yet unpretentious restaurant.
El Rall c/Turidores 2 Ⓣ963 922 090. Specializes in rice dishes, including the famous Valencian paella (€11). Daily 1.30pm–3.30pm & 8.30pm–11.30pm.

Drinking and nightlife

Valencia can seem dead at night, but only because the action is widely dispersed. The best of the city-centre **nightlife** is in the Barrio del Carmen (c/Caballeros, c/Quart and c/Alta). For **salsa**, head to the bars on c/Juan Llorens. The best **gay bars and clubs** are in and around c/Quart.
L'Aplec c/Mar 29. Groovy, alternative bar with pool table and dartboard in back room. Tues–Sat 7pm–3am.
La Claca c/San Vicente Martir 3. A fine spot to mingle with the locals, and it has live DJs every night.
Le Club c/Alameda 15. A real mix of everything; rock, indie, pop, etc.
Latex Avda Constitución 29. Popular nightclub with electronica and house DJs playing on two floors.
The Lounge c/Estamineria Vieja 2 Ⓦwww.theloungecafebar.com. Trendy, café-bar, with free Internet access, and Happy Hour Mon–Thurs 8–10pm. Mon–Sun 4pm–1.30am.
Picadilly c/Embajador Vich 8, Ⓔinfo@groovelives.com. One of the most original and eclectic clubs in town. Free before 2am. €12 with a free drink. Daily 1am–7.30am.
Radio City c/Santa Teresa 19 Ⓦwww.

FESTIVALS

The famous **Las Fallas** is held annually on March 19, when over seven hundred papier-mache caricatures are burnt amidst a riot of fireworks in a tribute to St Joseph, the patron saint of carpenters. Summer heralds a host of festivals in and around Valencia: you can rock-on at the **Festival Internacional de Benicassim** (Ⓦwww.fiberfib.com), a four-day music festival in the beach town of Benicassim, between Barcelona and Valencia, featuring well-known indie, pop and electronic acts; or indulge in some childhood fantasies at **La Tomatina** (www.latomatina.es), essentially an enormous public tomato fight that takes place on the last Wednesday in August, in the tiny town of Buñol, one hour to the west of the city.

radiocityvalencia.com. Starts the night as a popular bar and finishes as a disco. A young clientele. Free entry.

Directory

Consulates UK, c/Colon 22, Valencia ⓣ963 520 710, or Plaza Calvo Sotelo 1–2, Alicante ⓣ965 216 022; US, c/Romagosa 1, Valencia ⓣ963 516 973.
Exchange Main branches of banks are around Pl. del Ayuntamiento or along c/Játiva 24. Outside banking hours, try Caja de Ahorros, c/Játiva 14, to the left as you come out of the train station.
Hospital Avda. Cid, at the Tres Cruces junction ⓣ963 862 900.
Internet ONO, c/San Vicente Mártir 22; Ahmed Internet, c/Pie de la Cruz.
Laundry The L@undry Stop, c/Baja 17 (daily 8am–10pm).
Left luggage At the bus station (€3.50/24hr)
Pharmacies Farmacia Baviera, c/Don Juan de Austria (ⓣ963 512 459; 24hr)
Police Gran Vía Ramón y Cajal 40 (ⓣ963 539 539).
Post office c/San Vicente Mártir 23.

Moving on

Train Barcelona (17 daily; 3hr); Granada (twice daily; 9hr); Madrid (10 daily; 3–6hr).
Bus Alicante (hourly; 4hr); Barcelona (14–17 daily; 4–5hr); Denia (8 daily; 1hr 45min); Madrid (13 daily; 4hr); Seville (3 daily; 11hr).
Ferry Ibiza (1–6 weekly; 3–7hr); Palma (6–13 weekly; 9hr).

ALICANTE

ALICANTE is a living, thoroughly Spanish city, despite its proximity to a strip of package-holiday resorts. With good beaches nearby, lively nightlife and plenty of cheap hotels and restaurants, it makes a pleasant stop. Wide esplanades give the town an elegant air, and around the Plaza de Luceros and along the seafront *paseo* you can relax beneath palm trees at terrace cafés. If you can, time your visit to coincide with the **Hogueres fiesta** of processions, fire and fireworks, which culminates in an orgy of burning on the night of June 23/24. The towering fortress **Castillo de Santa Bárbara** (April–Sept 10am–8pm; Oct–March 9am–7pm €2.40 for the lift), on the bare rock behind the town beach, is Alicante's only real "sight", with pleasant park areas and a tremendous view from the top. Access it from Playa Postiguet via a tunnel, then a lift shaft cut straight up through the rock. For the best local **beaches**, head for **Playa San Juan**, ten minutes from the town, on the tram towards Costa Blanca (hourly).

Arrival and information

Air The airport is 12km south of town. Buses (Line C6, 6.30am–10.20pm; every 40min) stop opposite the bus station on c/Portugal.
Train The main train station is on Avda. Salamanca, but trains on the private FGV line to Benidorm and Denia leave from the small station at the far end of the Playa Postiguet.
Tourist office Avda. Rambla Méndez Nuñez 23 (Mon–Sat 9am–8pm, Sun 10am–2pm; ⓣ965 200 000; ⓦwww.alicanteturismo.com. There are also offices inside the train and bus stations, and at the airport.

Accommodation

Outside July and August, you shouldn't have too much trouble finding **accommodation**, with the bulk of the options concentrated at the lower end of the old town, above the Esplanada de España – especially on c/San Fernando, c/Jorge Juan and c/Castaño.
Albergue Juvenil La Florida Avda. de Orihuela 59 ⓣ965 113 044 or 902 225 552 (reservations). Pretty institutional HI hostel, also used as student residences during term-time. ❶
Camping Costa Blanca c/Convento 193, El Campello ⓣ965 630 670, ⓦwww.campingcostablanca.com. In a small town, Campello, 10km to the north of Alicante, and close to the beach. Easily accessible by tram or bus (Línea 21). ❶
Camping La Marina ⓣ965 419 200, ⓦwww.campinglamarina.com. Some 29km south of town, and 500m from the beach, with lots of facilities, including a pool and tennis courts. ❶
Hostal San Fernando c/San Fernando 34 ⓣ965 213 656. A marginally more expensive option but clean and comfortable. ❺
Hostal Santa Lucia Avda. Doctor Gadea 6 ⓣ965 218 735. Central hotel with a slightly shabby air. ❹
Hostal Ventura c/San Fernando 10 ⓣ965 208 337. Fifth-floor hotel with tidy, en-suite rooms but rather small bathrooms. ❺

Eating and drinking

TriBeCa c/Alberola Romero 3. Self-styled American bar serving €5 hamburgers and the like. Open evenings only.
Casa Dimas Portico de Ansaldo 2. Tucked away down a side street, serving large selection of cheap tapas and *raciones* for between €3 and €9.

Moving on

Train Barcelona (8 daily; 5–6hr); Madrid (8 daily; 3hr 30min–4hr); Valencia (10 daily; 2hr).
Bus Barcelona (11 daily; 8hr); Granada (3–7 daily; 5hr); Madrid (8 daily; 6hr); Málaga (7 daily; 8hr); Valencia (hourly; 4hr).

Andalucía

The southern region of **Andalucía** is likely to both meet and defy your preconceptions of Spain. Everywhere there is evidence of this passionate, parched country at its most exuberant: it is the home of **flamenco** and the **bullfight**, tradition and fierce pride. But it's also much more than the cliché. Evidence of the **Moors'** sophistication remains visible to this day in **Córdoba**, in **Seville** and, particularly, in **Granada's Alhambra**. On the coast you could despair – extending to either side of **Málaga** is the **Costa del Sol**, Europe's most developed resort area, with its beaches hidden behind a remorseless curtain of concrete. But there is life beyond the Costa del Sol, especially the beaches of the **Costa de la Luz.** Here, **Tarifa** sits on the most southerly tip of Europe, its exposed position drawing swarms of windsurfers. Andalucía is also where Europe stops and Africa begins: in places, the mountains of that great continent appear almost close enough to touch; in reality, they are just an hour away by ferry.

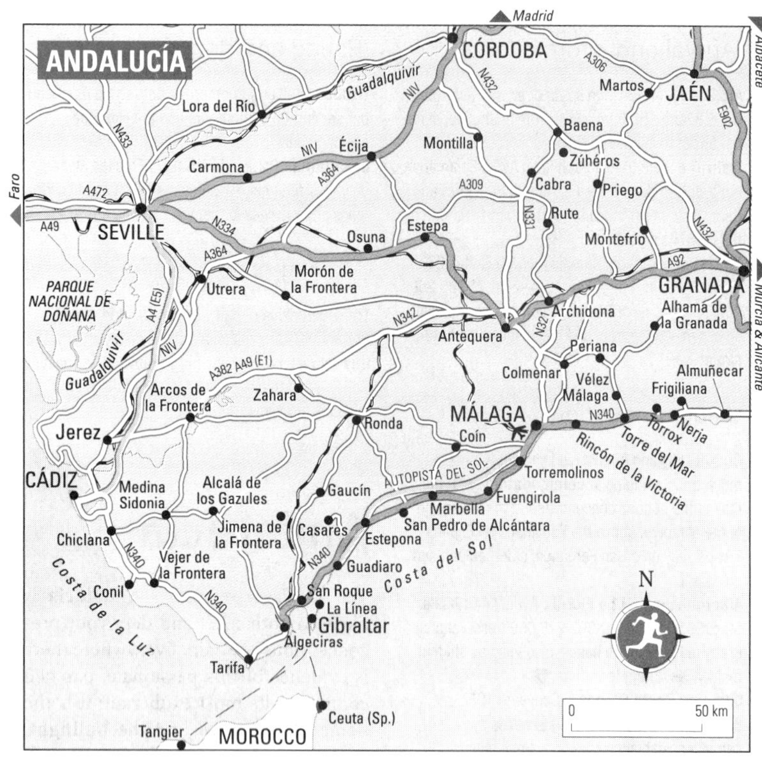

GRANADA

If you see only one town in Spain, it should be **GRANADA**, with its wonderful backdrop of the **Sierra Nevada**. For here stands Spain's most visited monument, the **Alhambra** – the spectacular and serene climax of Moorish art in Spain. Granada was established as an independent kingdom in 1238 by **Ibn Ahmar**, a prince of the Arab Nasrid tribe, who had been driven south from Zaragoza. The Moors of Granada maintained their autonomy for two and a half centuries, but by 1490 only the city itself remained in Muslim hands. **Boabdil**, the last Moorish king, appealed in vain for help from his fellow Muslims in Morocco, Egypt and Turkey, and in the following year Ferdinand and Isabella marched on Granada with an army said to total 150,000 troops. For seven months, through the winter of 1491, they laid siege to the city. On January 2, 1492, Boabdil surrendered, and with the fall of Granada the Christian Reconquest of Spain was complete.

What to see and do

The main attraction of the town is without doubt the Alhambra, the stunning Moorish palace complex set up on a vantage point overlooking the city. However, Granada's centre has some fine architecture of its own, including the cathedral and the royal mausoleum, the Capilla Real. To the northeast of the town centre, and on an adjacent hill to the Alhambra, lies the Albaicín, offering the opportunity to wander through atmospheric cobbled streets and white-

A hot tip is to buy a **bono turístico Granada** (tourist voucher; €24.50) from the tourist office, which lets you jump the lengthy queues and gets you into a range of museums and sights throughout the city, as well as allowing ten bus trips.

washed houses with Moorish touches still in evidence. In fact, Granada retains much of its North African legacy, from the *teterías* offering shisha and sweet pastries to the Arabic doorways of its houses. Although the Nasrid dynasty may have left five hundred years ago, its presence is still felt.

The Alhambra: the Alcazaba and the Palacios Nazaries

The standard approach to the **Alhambra** is along the Cuesta de Gomérez, the road that climbs uphill from Plaza Nueva, either on foot or by taking the Alhambrabus from Plaza Nueva (every 10min; €0.85). Ideally, you should start your visit with the earliest, most ruined, part of the fortress – the **Alcazaba**. It was the hue to this building that led to the complex's name, since "al-Hamra" means "red" in Arabic. At the summit is the **Torre de la Vela**, named after a huge bell on its turret, from where there's a fine overview of the whole area. The buildings in the **Palacios Nazaries** show a brilliant use of light and space with ornamental stucco decoration, in rhythmic repetitions of supreme beauty. Arabic inscriptions feature prominently: some are poetic eulogies of the buildings and rulers, but most are taken from the Koran. The sultans used the **Palacio del Mexuar**, the first series of rooms, for business and judicial purposes. In the **Serallo**, beyond, they received distinguished guests: here is the royal throne room, known as the **Hall of the Ambassadors**, the largest room of the palace. The last section, the **Harem**, formed their private living quarters. These are the most beautiful rooms of the palace, and include the **Patio de los Leones**, which has become the archetypal image of Granada.

The Alhambra: the Palacio de Carlos V and the Generalife

Next to the Palacios Nazaries, the **Palacio de Carlos V**, an ostentatious, but distinguished piece of Renaissance architecture, was built by its namesake Charles V, the grandson of Ferdinand and Isabella, by demolishing a wing of the Palacios Nazaries. From here, a short walk takes you to the **Generalife,** the gardens and summer palace of the sultans. Paradise is described in the Koran as a shaded, leafy garden refreshed by running water where the "fortunate ones" may take their rest under tall canopies. It is an image that perfectly describes the Generalife, whose name means "Garden of the Architect".

ALHAMBRA PRACTICALITIES

Tickets to the Alhambra (daily: March–Oct 8.30am–8pm; Nov–Feb 8.30am–6pm; €10) are limited, so buy in advance by phone (Ⓣ902 888 001; lines open 8am–midnight; credit cards only; €1 booking fee); or online (Ⓦwww.alhambra-tickets.es). If there are no tickets available, get to the ticket office for 7am on the day you want to visit and queue up for the limited tickets that are sold on the day. Tickets are timed for the **Palacios Nazaries**; you are given a 30min slot to make your way around, make sure not to miss it.

The Albaicín

From just below the entrance to the Generalife, the **Cuesta del Rey Chico** winds down towards the River Darro and the old Arab quarter of the **Albaicín**, where you'll find the marvel-

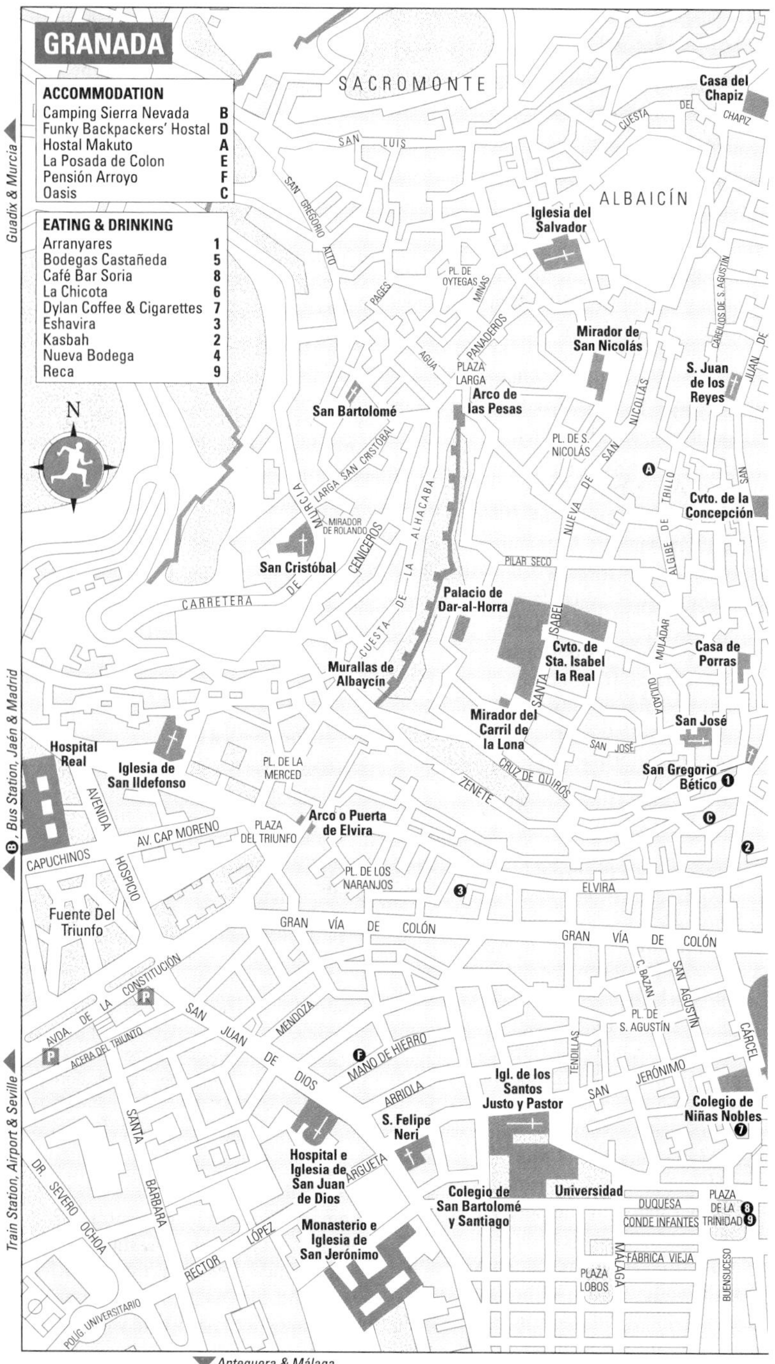

SPAIN

ANDALUCÍA

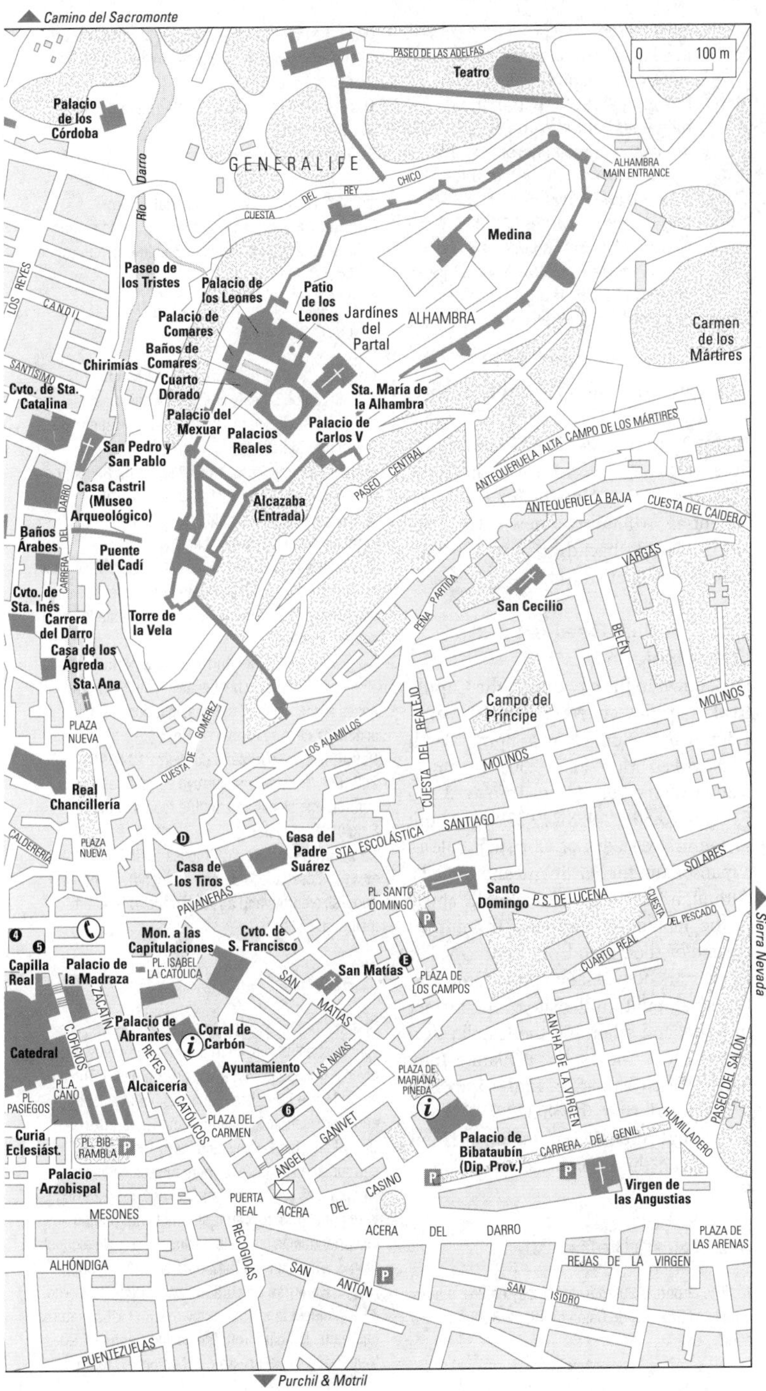

Camino del Sacromonte
PASEO DE LAS ADELFAS
Teatro
0 100 m
Palacio de los Córdoba
GENERALIFE
Río Darro
CUESTA DEL REY CHICO
ALHAMBRA MAIN ENTRANCE
Medina
Paseo de los Tristes
Palacio de los Leones
Patio de los Leones
Jardínes del Partal
ALHAMBRA
Carmen de los Mártires
Palacio de Comares
Baños de Comares
Chirimías
Cuarto Dorado
Palacio del Mexuar
Palacios Reales
Sta. María de la Alhambra
Palacio de Carlos V
Cvto. de Sta. Catalina
San Pedro y San Pablo
Casa Castril (Museo Arqueológico)
Alcazaba (Entrada)
PASEO CENTRAL
ANTEQUERUELA ALTA CAMPO DE LOS MÁRTIRES
ANTEQUERUELA BAJA
CUESTA DEL CAIDERO
Baños Árabes
Puente del Cadí
Cvto. de Sta. Inés
Carrera del Darro
Torre de la Vela
PEÑA PARTIDA
VARGAS
San Cecilio
BELÉN
Casa de los Agreda
Sta. Ana
PLAZA NUEVA
Campo del Príncipe
MOLINOS
LOS ALAMILLOS
CUESTA DE GOMÉREZ
CUESTA DEL REALEJO
Real Chancillería
CALDERERÍA
SANTIAGO
Casa del Padre Suárez
STA. ESCOLÁSTICA
SOLARES
Casa de los Tiros
PAVANERAS
PL. SANTO DOMINGO
Santo Domingo
P.S. DE LUCENA
CUESTA DEL PESCADO
Sierra Nevada
Mon. a las Capitulaciones
Cvto. de S. Francisco
CUARTO REAL
Capilla Real
Palacio de la Madraza
PL. ISABEL LA CATÓLICA
San Matías
PLAZA DE LOS CAMPOS
SAN MATÍAS
ZACATÍN
Palacio de Abrantes
Corral de Carbón
ANCHA DE LA VIRGEN
C. OFICIOS
Catedral
Ayuntamiento
LAS NAVAS
PLAZA DE MARIANA PINEDA
PASEO DEL SALÓN
REYES CATÓLICOS
Alcaicería
PL.A. CANO
PL. PASIEGOS
PLAZA DEL CARMEN
GANIVET
HUMILLADERO
Curia Eclesiást.
PL. BIB-RAMBLA
Palacio de Bibataubín (Dip. Prov.)
CARRERA DEL GENIL
ANGEL
Palacio Arzobispal
Virgen de las Angustias
PUERTA REAL
ACERA DEL CASINO
MESONES
ACERA DEL DARRO
PLAZA DE LAS ARENAS
RECOGIDAS
REJAS DE LA VIRGEN
ALHÓNDIGA
SAN ANTÓN
SAN ISIDRO
PUENTEZUELAS
Purchil & Motril

SPAIN ANDALUCÍA

TREAT YOURSELF

In summer, Granada can be an extremely hot and sticky place, but you can escape from the heat – and at the same time immerse yourself (literally) in the city's Moorish culture – at the **Aljibe Banos Arabes** (c/San Miguel Alta 41 ⓣ958 522 867, ⓦwww.aljibesanmiguel.es), plush, modern Arab baths. €24 will buy you entry to the baths, a massage and aromatherapy.

lous eleventh-century **Baños Árabes**, at Carrera del Darro 31 (Tues–Sat 10am–2pm; free; ⓣ958 027 800). From here, you can wind your way up to the **Mirador de San Nicolás** for the quintessential Alhambra view, with the Sierra Nevada backdrop – it's particularly stunning at sunset.

The Capilla Real and the Catedral

Back down in the city centre, the **Capilla Real** (April-Oct Mon-Sat 10.45am–1.30pm & 4–8pm, Sun 4–8pm; March & Nov-Feb Mon-Sat 10.30am–1pm & 3.30–6.30pm, Sun 11am–1pm & 3.30–6.30pm; €3.50 ⓣ958 229 239) was built in the first decades of Christian rule as a mausoleum for Ferdinand and Isabella. Although their tombs are simple, above is the fabulously elaborate monument erected by their grandson, Charles V. For all its stark Renaissance bulk, Granada's **Catedral,** built on the site of the former mosque, and adjoining the Capilla Real (April-Oct Mon-Sat 9.30am—4pm; Nov—March Mon-Sat 11am—5pm; Sun 2.30-6pm all year; ⓣ958 222 959), has a simple but imposing grandeur. It is entered from the door beside the Capilla Real.

Arrival and information

Air The airport is 20km from the city centre; a bus runs in to Gran Vía de Colón (6.40am–8.25pm, hourly; €3).

Train The train station is 1km out of town on Avda. de Andaluces, and is connected to the centre by buses #8, #4 and #11.

Bus From the bus station, on Carretera de Jaén, bus #3 runs into town.

Tourist office Plaza Mariana Pineda 10 (Mon–Fri 9am–8pm, Sat 10am–7pm, Sun 10am–3pm; ⓣ958 247 128, ⓦwww.granadatur.com).

Internet There are several **Internet** cafés around c/Santa Escolástica, including Net Internet, Plaza de los Girones 3.

Accommodation

Camping Sierra Nevada Avda. de Madrid 107 ⓣ958 150 062. Leafy campsite within easy walking distance of the train station. Closed mid-Oct to mid-March. ❶

Funky Backpackers' Hostal c/Cuesta Roderigo del Campo 13 ⓣ958 221 462, ⓔfunky@alternativeacc.com. Bright, colourful hostel with great rooftop terrace and bar. ❷

Hostal Makuto c/Tiña 18 ⓣ958 805 876, ⓦwww.makutoguesthouse.com. Hostel up in the Albaicín, with a hippy vibe and hammocks available in small courtyard. ❷

Oasis Placeta Correo Viejo 3 ⓣ958 215 848, ⓦwww.hosteloasis.com. Fantastic hostel hidden just off c/Elvira, in a converted sixteenth-century Arabic house. ❷

Pensión Arroyo c/Mano de Hierro 18 ⓣ958 203 828, ⓦwww.hostalarroyo.com. Clean and comfortable single and double rooms with a/c. Singles ❷, doubles ❹

La Posada de Colon c/Cruellas ⓣ958 229 843, ⓦwww.posadadecolon.com. A friendly place with good-size dorms and a roof terrace. Breakfast included. ❷

Eating

Granada has some good, cheap **restaurants**, but your best bet is to head to a **tapas** bar where you are given a free tapas with every drink ordered. The area around Calle Elvira has numerous bars, restaurants, and Moroccan-style teashops known as **teterías**. Or try Plaza Bib-Rambla and Plaza Trinidad, and the surrounding streets for a more relaxed setting.

Arranyares c/Cuesta Marañas 4 ⓣ958 228 401. Very popular Moroccan restaurant with photos of celebrity guests on walls. Mains €4–10. No alcohol. Mon & Wed–Sun 1.30–4.30pm & 7.30–11.30pm.

Bodegas Castañeda c/Almireceros 1. The oldest tapas bar in town, with rustic features and hams hanging from the ceiling. Tapas €1.90–2.90. Daily 11.30am–5pm & 7.30pm–1.30am.

Café Bar Soria Plaza Trinidad 4 ⓣ958 263 024. A typical tapas bar, but not much atmosphere. Bought tapas cost around €4. Daily 7am–2am.
La Chicota c/Navas 20 ⓣ958 220 349. Popular with an international crowd and serving only *raciones*. Daily 7am–1am.
Kasbah Calderia Nueva 4 ⓣ958 227 936. Specializing in Moroccan fare, eaten in an atmospheric Arabic-themed setting. Mains €10. Daily noon–1.30am.
Nueva Bodega c/Cetti Merién 3 ⓣ958 225 934. Good-value, no-frills tapas just off c/Elvira. *Menú del día* €9.65. Daily noon-midnight.

Drinking and nightlife

Nightlife is focused on c/Elvira, with its large number of bars. Another good area for drinking is around the university, on c/Gran Capitán and c/Pedro Antonio de Alarcón. In term-time, students also gather in **pubs** near the bus station around the Campo del Príncipe, a square on the southern slopes of the Alhambra.
Dylan Coffee & Cigarettes Plaza Romanilla. Chic bar with fake chandeliers and a clientele of *pijo* Spaniards. Daily 4pm–2am.
Eshavira, c/Postigo de la Cinca 2. Atmospheric little bar, and the best place in town to see live flamenco. Mon–Thurs & Sun 9.30pm–3am, Fri & Sat 9.30pm–4am.
Granada 10 Carcel Baja 10 ⓦwww.granada10.com. A cinema during the daytime, a popular student nightclub – playing commercial music – in the evening.
Reca c/Alhondiga. Smart little bar with outside seating on Plaza Trinidad. Mon–Thurs 10am–2am, Fri & Sat 10am–3am.
Sala Principe Campo de Principe ⓣ958 228 088, ⓦwww.salaprincipe.com. A favourite club for upmarket Spaniards in Realejo.

Moving on

Train Madrid (3 daily; 5hr); Málaga (7 daily; 1hr 50min); Seville (4 daily; 3hr); Valencia (4 daily; 7hr–8hr).
Bus Alicante (3–11 daily; 5hr); Cádiz (4 daily; 6hr); Córdoba (7 daily; 3hr); Madrid (6–9 daily; 6hr); Málaga (14 daily; 1hr 45min); Seville (7–9 daily; 3hr 30min–4hr 30min); Valencia (3 daily; 7hr).

CÓRDOBA

Now a minor provincial capital, **CÓRDOBA** was once the largest city of Roman Spain, and for three centuries the heart of the great medieval caliphate of the Moors. It's an engaging, atmospheric city, easily explored, and with excellent transport connections to Seville and Granada.

What to see and do

For visitors, Córdoba's main attraction comes down to a single building: **La Mezquita** – the grandest and most beautiful mosque ever constructed by the Moors. This stands right in the centre of the city, surrounded by the labyrinthine Jewish and Moorish quarters, and is a building of extraordinary mystical and aesthetic power.

La Mezquita

Córdoba's domination of Moorish Spain began thirty years after the conquest, in 756 AD, when the city was placed under **Abd ar-Rahman I**, who established control over all but the north of Spain. It was he who began the building of the Great Mosque – in Spanish, **La Mezquita** (Mon–Sat 10am–7pm, Sun am for worship & 2–7pm; €8; ⓣ957 470 512) – which is approached through the **Patio de los Naranjos,** a classic Islamic court preserving both its orange trees and fountains for ritual purification before prayer. Inside, a thicket of nearly a thousand twin-layered red and white pillars combine to mesmeric effect, the harmony culminating only at the foot of the beautiful **Mihrab** (prayer niche).

La Judería and around

North of La Mezquita lies **La Judería**, Córdoba's old Jewish quarter, a fascinating network of lanes that are more atmospheric and less commercialized than Seville's. Near the heart of the quarter, at c/Maimonides 18, is a tiny **synagogue** (Tues–Sat 9.30am–2pm & 3.30–5.30pm, Sun 9.30am–1.30pm; €0.30, free for EU citizens; ⓣ957 202 928), one of only three in Spain that survived the Jewish expulsion of

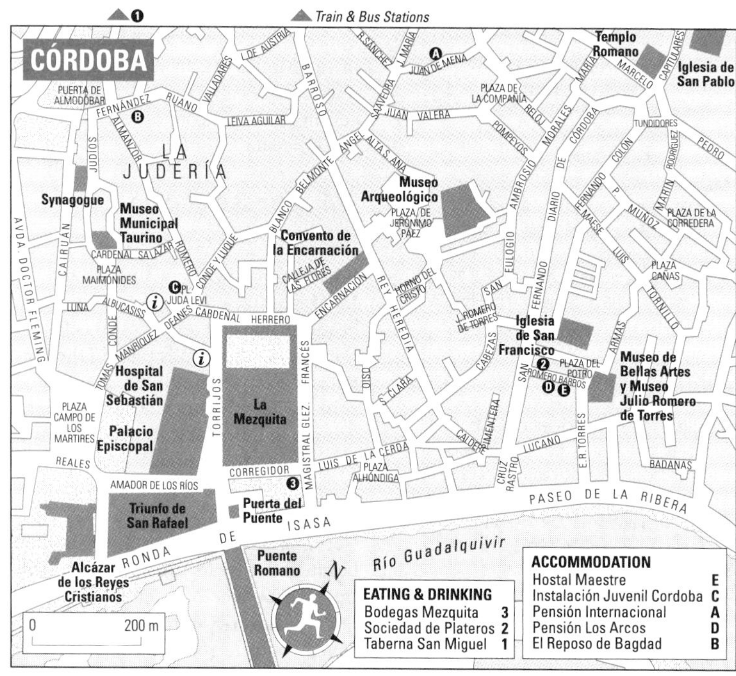

1492. East of La Judería, the **Museo Arqueológico** (Tues 2.30–8.30pm, Wed–Sat 9am–8.30pm, Sun 9am–2.30pm; €1.50, free for EU citizens; ⓣ957 355 517) occupies a small Renaissance mansion in which Roman foundations have been incorporated into an imaginative display. Northeast of here, you can watch craftsmen at work in the **Museo Regina**, on Plaza Luís Venegas (Mon, Tues & Wed–Sun 10am–2pm & 6.30–9pm; €3; ⓣ957 496 889), which is devoted to the history of jewellery.

Arrival and information

Bus and Train The bus and train stations are 1km northwest of the old town, opposite each other. Bus #3 goes to La Judería, whilst #4 heads slightly further north to Plaza Tendillas.

Tourist office Palacio de Congresos y Exposiciones, c/Torrijos 10 (Mon–Fri 9am–8pm, Sat 10am–7pm, Sun 10am–2pm; ⓣ957 355 179, ⓦwww.ayuncordoba.es).

Internet Tele-Click! c/Eduardo Dato 9 (Mon–Fri 10am–3pm & 5.30–10.30pm, Sat–Sun noon–11pm).

Accommodation

Camping El Brillante Avda del Brillante ⓣ957 403 836, ⓦwww.campingelbrillante.com. Campsite 2km north on the road to Villaviciosa, with a pool. Take bus #10 or #11 from the train or bus station. ❶

Hostal Maestre c/Romero Barros 16 ⓣ957 475 395. Clean but slightly dingy rooms, all en suite and with their own TV. ❸

Instalación Juvenil Córdoba Plaza Juda Levi ⓣ957 355 040 or 902 510 000 (reservations), ⓔcordoba.itj@juntadeandalucia.es. The town's only HI youth hostel, very centrally located. ❷

Pensión Internacional c/Juan de Mena 14 ⓣ957 478 349. Cheap and simple accommodation just north of La Judería. ❸

Pensión Los Arcos c/Rameros Barros 14 ⓣ957 485 643, ⓔhostallosarcos@yahoo.es. Good-value en-suite rooms, some with their own small roof terrace. ❷

El Reposo de Bagdad c/Fernandez Ruano 11 ⓣ957 202 854. A charming hotel set in a traditional house, with its own Moroccan *tetería* and shisha pipes. ❹

Eating and drinking

Avoid the touristy places around La Mezquita, and you'll find **bars** and **restaurants** are reasonably priced. Loads of alternatives can be found in La Judería and in the old quarters off to the east, above Paseo de la Ribera. Look out for the **Córdoban delicacies** of *almorejo, berenjenas a la miel* (aubergines with honey soup), and *pastel cordobés* (a delectable sticky pastry). Montilla and Moriles wines, resembling dry sherries, are also from the region.

Bodegas Mezquita c/Corregidor Luis de la Cerda 73. Fairly smart restaurant with gourmet shop attached. Extensive tapas selection (€2.50–3.15).

Sociedad de Plateros c/San Francisco 6. Popular with the locals and tourists alike, serving inexpensive tapas and *raciones*. Mains €8–10.

Taberna San Miguel Pl. San Miguel 1. A Córdoba institution, with a room devoted to bullfighting history. Serves local wines. Closed Sun and August.

Moving on

Train Madrid (every 30min; 1hr 40min–4hr 30min); Málaga (8–10 daily; 2hr 10min–3hr 30min); Seville (20 daily; 1hr–1hr 30min).

Bus Granada (7 daily; 3hr); Madrid (6 daily; 4hr 30min); Málaga (7 daily; 3hr–3hr 30min); Seville (10 daily; 2hr 30min).

SEVILLE

SEVILLE (Sevilla) is the great city of the Spanish south, intensely hot in summer and with an abiding reputation for exuberance and intensity. It has three important monuments – the **Giralda** tower, the **Catedral** and the **Alcázar** – and an illustrious history, but it's the living self of this city of Carmen, Don Juan and Figaro that remains the great attraction. It is expressed on a phenomenally grand scale at the city's two great festivals: **Semana Santa**, during the week before Easter, and the **Feria de Abril**, which lasts a week at the end of the month. Seville is also Spain's second most important centre for **bullfighting** after Madrid. While it has an upbeat modern dimension to its buildings and infrastructure, the soul of the city still lies in its historic latticework of narrow streets, patios and plazas, where minarets jostle for space among cupolas and palms.

What to see and do

Seville was one of the earliest Moorish conquests (in 712 AD) and, as part of the Caliphate of Córdoba, became the second city of al-Andalus. When the caliphate broke up in the early eleventh century it was the most powerful of the independent states to emerge and, under the Almohad dynasty, became the capital of the last real Moorish empire in Spain from 1170 until 1212. The Almohads rebuilt the **Alcázar**, enlarged the principal mosque and erected a new and brilliant minaret – the **Giralda.** Today, they occupy the southern corner of the popular *barrio* of Santa Cruz, a haven of restaurants and bars. To the west of this, the city centre lies in a curve of the Rio Guadalquivir, on its eastern bank. Across the riverbed, immediately opposite the *barrio* of El Arenal, is the charming neighbourhood of Triana.

La Giralda

Topped with four copper spheres, **La Giralda** (Mon–Sat 9.30am–4pm, Sun 2.30–6pm; €7.50, including entrance to the Catedral, free Sun; ⓣ945 214 971) still dominates the skyline today and you can ascend the minaret for a remarkable view of the city. The Giralda was so venerated by the Moors that they wanted to destroy it before the Christian conquest of the city. Instead, in 1402 it became the bell tower of the **Catedral** (same hours as La Giralda; ⓦwww.catedralsevilla.org), the world's largest Gothic church, and third largest cathedral. Its centre is dominated by a vast retable composed of 45 carved biblical scenes, making up the largest altarpiece in the world.

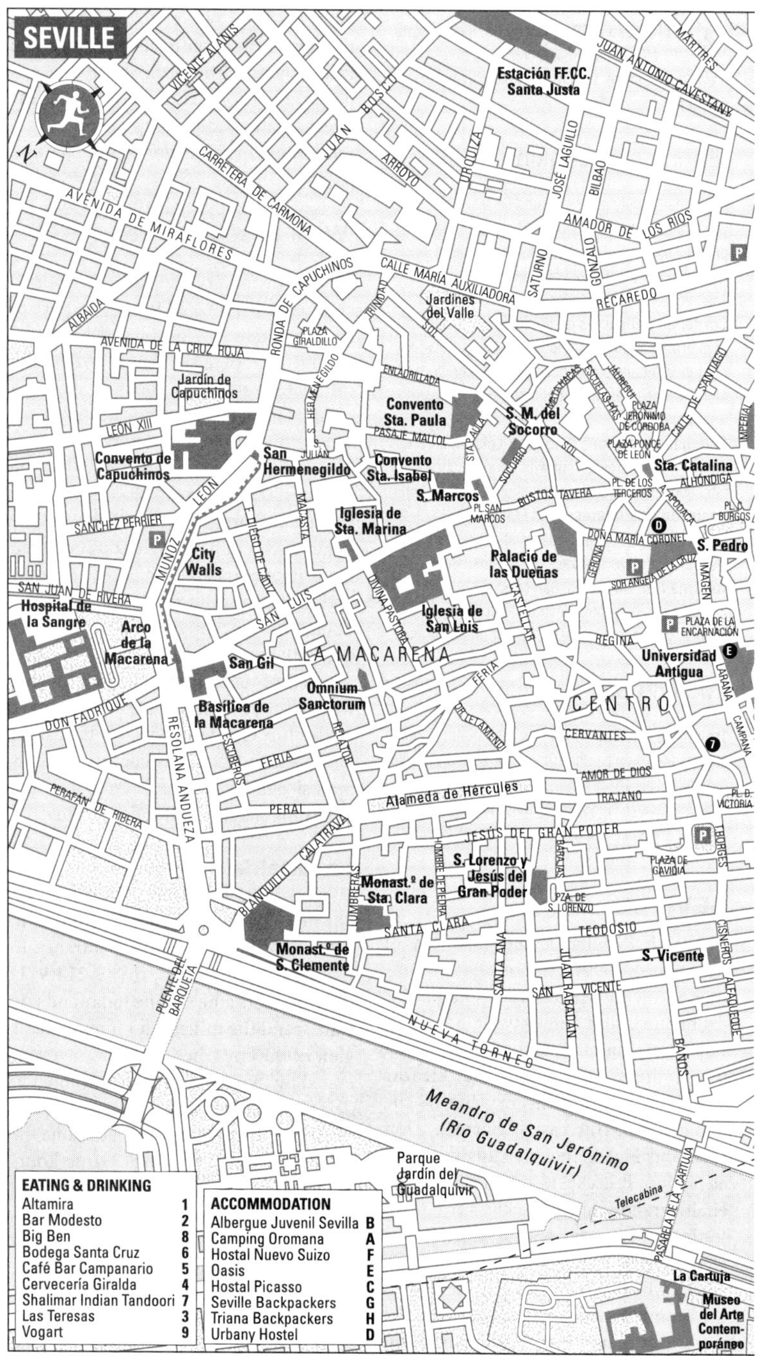
SEVILLE
N
Estación FF.CC. Santa Justa
Jardines del Valle
Jardín de Capuchinos
Convento de Capuchinos
San Hermenegildo
Convento Sta. Paula
S. M. del Socorro
Convento Sta. Isabel
S. Marcos
Iglesia de Sta. Marina
Sta. Catalina
S. Pedro
City Walls
Palacio de las Dueñas
Hospital de la Sangre
Arco de la Macarena
Iglesia de San Luis
Universidad Antigua
San Gil
LA MACARENA
Basílica de la Macarena
Omnium Sanctorum
CENTRO
S. Lorenzo y Jesús del Gran Poder
Monast.º de Sta. Clara
Monast.º de S. Clemente
S. Vicente
Alameda de Hércules
Meandro de San Jerónimo (Río Guadalquivir)
Parque Jardín del Guadalquivir
Telecabina
La Cartuja
Museo del Arte Contemporáneo
EATING & DRINKING
Altamira 1
Bar Modesto 2
Big Ben 8
Bodega Santa Cruz 6
Café Bar Campanario 5
Cervecería Giralda 4
Shalimar Indian Tandoori 7
Las Teresas 3
Vogart 9
ACCOMMODATION
Albergue Juvenil Sevilla B
Camping Oromana A
Hostal Nuevo Suizo F
Oasis E
Hostal Picasso C
Seville Backpackers G
Triana Backpackers H
Urbany Hostel D

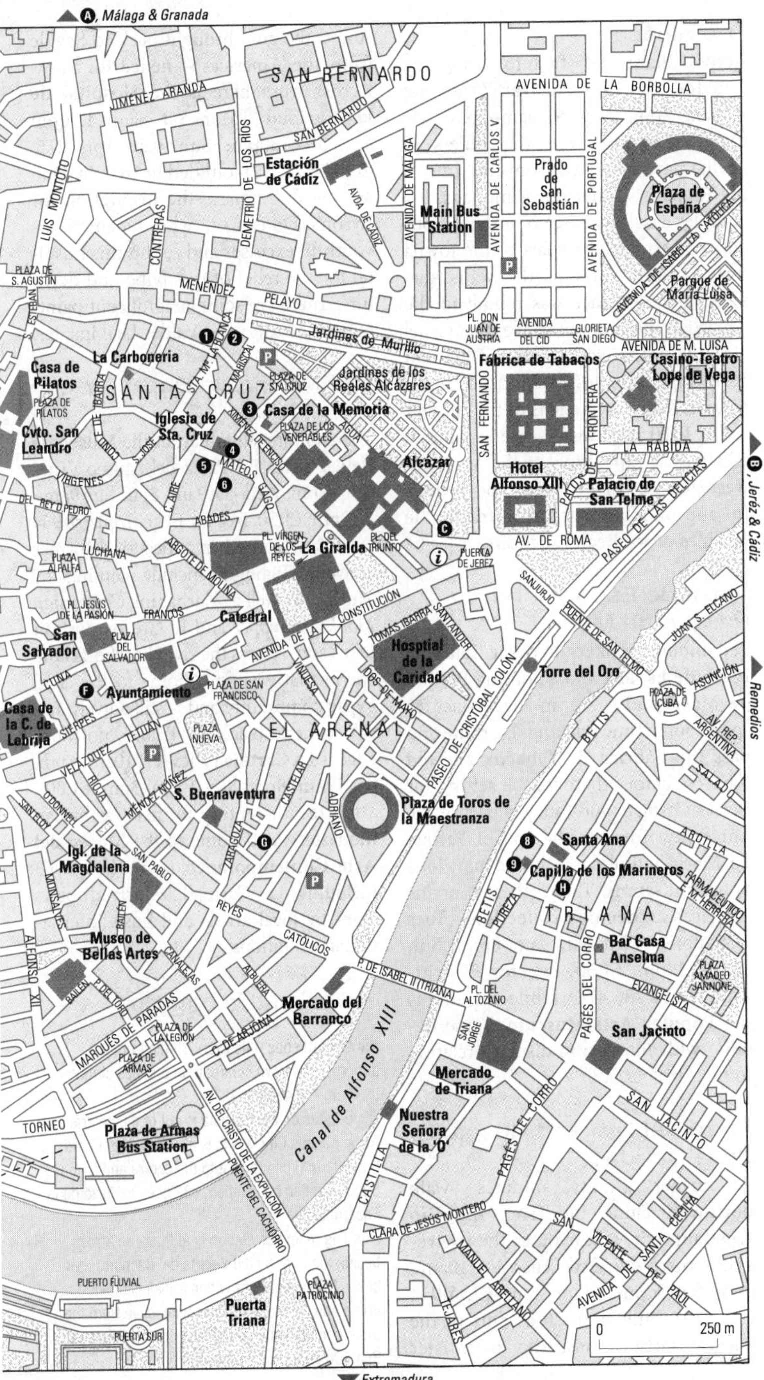

SPAIN

ANDALUCÍA

The Alcázar

Across Plaza del Triunfo from the Catedral lies the **Alcázar** (Tues–Sat 9.30am–7pm, Sun 9.30am–5pm; €7; ☎954 502323), a site that rulers of Seville have occupied from the time of the Romans. Under the Almohads, the complex was turned into an enormous citadel, forming the heart of the town's fortifications. Parts of the walls survive, but the palace was rebuilt in the Christian period by Pedro the Cruel (1350–69). His works, some of the best surviving examples of Mudéjar architecture, form the nucleus of the Alcázar today. Later additions include a wing in which early expeditions to the Americas were planned. Don't miss the beautiful and rambling Alcázar **gardens**, the Jardines de los Reales Alcázares.

Plaza de España and Parque de María Luisa

Ten minutes' walk south of the Catedral, **Plaza de España** and adjoining **Parque de María Luisa** are an ideal place to spend some time relaxing. En route you pass the **Fábrica de Tabacos**, the old tobacco factory that was the setting for Bizet's *Carmen*, and today is part of the university. Towards the end of Parque de María Luisa, some grand pavilions house **museums**. The furthest contains the city's **archeology collections** (Tues 2.30–8pm, Wed–Sat 9am–8pm, Sun 9am–2.30pm; €1.50, free for EU citizens; ☎954 786 474), while opposite is the **Popular Arts Museum** (same details) with interesting displays relating to the April *feria*.

Torre del Oro and Hospital de la Caridad

A further twenty minutes' walk northwest along the river, the **Río Guadalquivir**, takes you to the twelve-sided **Torre del Oro** (Tues–Fri 10am–2pm, Sat & Sun 11am–2pm; €2; ☎954 222 419), built in 1220 as part of the Alcázar fortifications. The tower later stored the gold brought back to Seville from the Americas – hence its name. Across from here is the **Hospital de la Caridad** (Mon–Sat 9am–1.30pm & 3.30–7.30pm, Sun 9am–1pm; €5; ☎954 223 232) founded in 1676 by Don Miguel de Manara, the inspiration for Byron's Don Juan, who repented his youthful excesses and set up this hospital for the relief of the dying and destitute. There are some magnificent paintings by Murillo and Valdés Leal inside.

The Museo de Bellas Artes and Triana

There's more superb art at the **Museo de Bellas Artes** on Plaza del Museo (Tues 2.30–8pm, Wed–Sat 9am–8pm, Sun 9am–2.30pm; €1.50, free for EU citizens; ☎954 786 482), housed in a beautiful former convent. Highlights include paintings by Murillo, as well as Zurbarán's *Carthusian Monks at Supper* and El Greco's portrait of his son. Across the river lies the **Triana** *barrio* that was once home to the city's gypsy community and is still a lively and atmospheric place. At Triana's northern edge is **La Cartuja** (Tues–Fri 10am–8pm, Sat 11am–8pm, Sun 10am–3pm; €1.80), a fourteenth-century former Carthusian monastery, and home to the **Museo del Arte Contemporáneo** (same hours; €3 including La Cartuja), which displays work by local artists and hosts international exhibitions.

Arrival and information

Air A shuttle bus runs every 30min from the airport to the town centre, train and bus stations (5.45am–12.45am; €2).

Train Estación Santa Justa is out of the centre, on Avda. Kansas City, which is also the airport road; bus #C1 (€1) connects it to the centre and to the San Sebastián bus station, #32 goes to Plaza de la Encarnación.

Bus The main bus station is at Plaza de Armas, beside the river by the Puente del Cachorro, but buses for destinations within Andalucía (plus Barcelona, Alicante and Valencia) leave from the more central terminal at Plaza de San Sebastián. Bus #C4 connects the two terminals.

Tourist office The main tourist offices are at Plaza San Francisco 19 (Mon–Fri 8am–8pm; ⓣ954 595 288, ⓦwww.turismo.sevilla.org) and Avda. de la Constitución 21 (Mon–Fri 9am–7.30pm, Sat 10am–2pm & 3–7pm, Sun 10am–2pm; ⓣ954 221 404, ⓦwww.andalucia.org).

Accommodation

The most attractive – and pricey – area to stay is the maze-like **Barrio Santa Cruz**, near the Catedral. Cheaper options can be found in c/Farnesio, on the periphery of the *barrio*, or slightly further out beyond Plaza Nueva, towards the river and the Plaza de Armas bus station. During **Easter Week and the Feria de April**, prices double, and you'll need to book six months in advance.

Camping Oromana Camino del Maestre ⓣ955 683 257, ⓦwww.campingoromana.com. Campsite 15km away from town, connected by regular buses. ❶

Hostal Nuevo Suizo c/Azofaifo 7 ⓣ954 229 147, ⓦwww.nuevosuizo.com. More like a hotel than a hostel, with free international phone calls and a lovely terrace. ❷

Hostal Picasso Avda. de la Constitución ⓣ954 210 864. Central hostel, with free Internet. All dorms are en suite. ❷

Oasis Plaza Encarnación 29 ⓣ954 293 777, ⓦwww.hosteloasis.com. Fantastic hostel, with helpful staff and a rooftop swimming pool. ❷

Seville Backpackers c/Santas Patronas 31 ⓣ954 222 132. Stylish hostel with very comfortable beds and pillows. ❷

Triana Backpackers c/Roderigo de Triana 69 ⓣ954 459 960. Friendly place, with lots of events organized. ❷

Urbany Hostel c/Doña Maria Coronel 12 ⓣ954 227 949, ⓦwww.sevillaurbany.com. Funky, bright hostel, just south of Plaza Encarnación. ❷

Eating

Seville is packed with lively bars and restaurants, but it can be expensive, particularly in the **Barrio Santa Cruz**. Another area to try are the streets around **Plaza Nueva**.

Altamira c/Santa Maria la Blanca 4. Fairly expensive but wide range of Spanish and international dishes available. Mains €12.

Bar Modesto c/Cano y Cueto 5. A slightly more expensive option, but with a great selection of seafood dishes (around €12).

Bodega Santa Cruz c/Rodrigo Caro 1. Popular bar serving cheap tapas (€1.70–2). Try the *pringá*, a meaty sandwich and local speciality.

Café Bar Campanario c/Mateos Gago 8. Delicious-smelling café serving tapas and other light meals. Mains €5.

Cervecería Giralda c/Mateos Gago 1. Fairly expensive bistrot-like tapas bar, serving a good variety of seafood, with mains from €12.

Shalimar Indian Tandoori c/Javier Lasso de la Vega 9. The only Indian restaurant in town, offering tasty food at reasonable prices (mains €8). Closed Wed.

Las Teresas c/Santa Teresa 2. Atmospheric tapas bar (portions around €2) with bullfighting paraphernalia adorning the walls. Mon-Fri 10am–4pm & 6pm–midnight, Sat & Sun 11am–4pm & 7pm–1am.

Drinking and nightlife

There are bars all over Seville, but the **Alfalfa** area, north of the Catedral, is particularly lively at night. The other main area for nightlife, popular with tourists, is just across the river in **Triana**, on the waterfront c/Betis.

Big Ben c/Betis 54. Friendly bar with cheap drinks – beer and shots for €1.

Göa Club Avda. Garcia Morato. One of the chicest clubs in town, Asian inspired with an outdoor terrace. Daily 11pm–late.

Terraza Alfonso Paseo de las Delicias ⓣ954 233 735. Club in the middle of Parque de Maria Luisa, playing commercial and dance music. Daily 7pm-late.

Vogart c/Betis 40. Trendy waterfront bar with drinks deals and cocktails for €4–6.

Flamenco

Flamenco – or more accurately **Sevillanas** – music and dance can be seen at dozens of places in the city, though many are tacky and expensive. To avoid this, head to one of the following bars where flamenco takes place spontaneously, or go to c/Rodrigo de Triana, the home of a handful of flamenco academies, to check out the students in action.

TREAT YOURSELF

Unleash your latin passion at the **Museo del Baile Flamenco** (c/Manuel Rojas Marcos 3 ⓣ954 340 311, ⓦwww.museoflamenco.com). It offers one-week intensive flamenco courses for €330, which, though pricey, is a quite inimitable experience.

Bar Casa Anselma c/Pages del Carro 49. Free flamenco in a traditional atmosphere. Arrive after 11.30pm to see the dancing.
La Carbonería c/Levías 18. A bar well-known for its free flamenco concerts – but it can be quite touristy.
Casa de la Memoria c/Ximenez de Enciso 28 ⓣ954 560 670, ⓦwww.casadelamemoria.es. Daily performances at this cultural centre, at 7.30pm/9pm/10.30pm depending on season. €13.

Bullfighting

The season starts with the Feria de Abril and continues until October, with most *corridas* held on Sun evenings. Tickets from the **Plaza de Toros de la Maestranza**, Paseo de Colón 12 (ⓣ954 501 382), which also houses a museum, from as little as €10.

Directory

Consulates Australia, Federico Rubio 14 ⓣ954 220 971; Ireland, Plaza de Santa Cruz 6 ⓣ954 216 361; US, Plaza Nueva 8 ⓣ954 218751.
Exchange Banks and *cambios* can be found around the tourist office on Avda. de la Constitución.
Hospital Hospital Virgen del Rocío, Avda. Manuel Siurot ⓣ955 012 000. Also, emergency clinic just behind the Alcázar, at corner of Menendez Pelayo and Avda. de Cádiz.
Internet Correos Avda. de la Constitución 32 (Mon–Fri 8.30am–10pm, Sat 9.30am–10pm, Sun noon–10pm).
Laundry c/Castelar 2.
Left luggage At the train station (24hr; €4.50 for a big bag).
Pharmacies Throughout the town centre; check the notice in the window for the pharmacy open in the locality after hours.
Police Plaza de la Gavidia (ⓣ954 228 840).
Post office Avda. de la Constitución 32.

Moving on

Train Cádiz (15 daily; 2hr); Córdoba (every 20–30min; 40min); Madrid (every 30min; 2hr 30min); Málaga (9 daily; 2hr 30min).
Bus Cádiz (11 daily; 1hr 45min–2hr); Córdoba (10 daily; 2hr 30min); Granada (7–9 daily; 3hr 30min–4hr 30min); Madrid (11 daily; 6–8hr); Málaga (12 daily; 3hr).

CÁDIZ

CÁDIZ is among the oldest settlements in Spain and has long been one of the country's principal ports. Its heyday was the eighteenth century, when it enjoyed a virtual monopoly on the Spanish-American trade in gold and silver. Central Cádiz, built on a peninsula island, remains much as it must have looked in those days, with its grand open squares, narrow alleyways and high, turreted houses. It's also the spiritual home of flamenco, and you get a sense of that to this day; the city, crumbling from the effect of sea air on soft limestone, has a tremendous atmosphere – slightly seedy, definitely in decline, but still full of mystique. Cádiz's big party time is its annual **carnival**, normally held in February and early March; expect frenzied celebrations, masked processions and satirical digs at the local big shots.

What to see and do

With its blind alleys, back streets and cafés, Cádiz is fascinating to wander around. To understand the city's layout, climb the **Torre Tavira**, Marqués del Real Tesoro 10 (daily 10am–8pm; €4; ⓦwww.torretavira.com), tallest of the 160 lookout towers in the city, with an excellent camera obscura, a device that uses mirrors to project a live image of the city onto a flat surface in the tower. Some specific sites to check out are the huge sea-facing **Catedral Nueva** (Tues–Fri 10am–8pm, Sat 10am–2pm, Sun 11am–1pm; €4, free Tues–Fri 7–8pm & Sun) – an unusually successful blend of High Baroque and Neoclassical styles, decorated entirely in stone. The oval, eighteenth-century chapel of **Santa Cueva,** c/Rosario (Tues–Fri 10am–1pm & 4.30–8pm, Sat & Sun 10am–1pm; €0.50), has eight magnificent arches decorated with frescoes by Goya.

Arrival and information

Train The train station is on the periphery of the old town, close to the Plaza de San Juan de Dios, the busiest of the squares.

Bus Arriving by bus, you'll be dropped a few blocks north of the Plaza de San Juan de Dios, along the waterfront.
Tourist office Plaza de San Juan de Dios 11 (Mon–Fri 9am–8pm, Sat–Sun 10am–2pm; ⓣ956 241 001).

Accommodation

Casa Caracol c/Suárez de Salazar 4 ⓣ956 261 166. Hostel with a chilled-out, hippy vibe. You can even sleep in hammocks on the roof for €10. Dorms ❷
Hostal Colón c/Marqués de Cádiz 6 ⓣ956 285 351. Pleasant hotel offering homely rooms and a rooftop terrace with view of the cathedral. ❼
Pensión España c/Marqués de Cádiz 9 ⓣ956 285 500. Attractive *pensión* set in a lovely old house, offering comfortable rooms with or without bathrooms. ❺
Pensión Fantoni c/Flamenco 5 ⓣ956 282 704, ⓦwww.hostalfantoni.net. Small hotel with simple rooms Centrally located, and just around the corner from *Pensión España*. ❺

Eating and drinking

For a **drink**, head to the area surrounding the cathedral where there are lots of quirky bars.
El Aljibe c/Plocia 25. Pleasant restaurant with plenty of tapas (€1.50–4) on offer.

Moving on

Bus to: Seville (11 daily; 2hr); Granada (5 daily; 5hr–5hr 30min).

TARIFA

If there is one thing that defines **TARIFA**, it is the wind. This is the most southerly point in mainland Europe, and in the summer the prevailing, massively powerful, levant has made it one of the world's most popular **wind- and kite-surfing** destinations. The elements aside, there's a good feel to the place – with its funky, laid-back atmosphere and maze of narrow streets. Africa feels very close, too, with the Rif Mountains clearly visible – and easily accessible, via the ferry that runs to Tangier in Morocco.

What to see and do

The ten-kilometre white, sandy **beaches, Playa de los Lances** and **Playa Valdevaqueros**, are the places to head for wind- and kite-surfing, whilst just to the east of town are the dramatic rocky coves of **La Caleta**. If you're keen to try kite-surfing or other aquatic sports, you can book a course or rent equipment from a number of outfitters on c/Batalla del Salado, including Art of Kiting (ⓣ605 031 880, ⓦwww.artofkiting.com). Most charge similar prices, and a four-hour taster course in kite-surfing costs €90. Alternatively, you can go on a **whale-watching trip** – try Whale Watch, Avda. de la Constitución 6 (ⓣ956 627 013, ⓦwww.whalewatchtarifa.net; €27) – to see the local population of pilot whales and dolphins; in July and August, killer whales can also be seen.

Arrival and information

Bus Buses drop off passengers at the stop on the main road, Batalla del Salado: walk straight down the road to get to the town centre.
Tourist office Paseo de la Alameda (Mon–Fri 10.30am–2pm; ⓣ956 680 993, ⓦwww.tarifaweb.com).

Accommodation

In the summer, finding **accommodation** can be tricky, making it advisable to book in advance. There are a few **campsites** near the main windsurfing beaches: *Tarifa* (ⓣ956 684 778), *Paloma* (ⓣ956 684 203) and *Torre de la Peña* (ⓣ956 684 903), all of which have their own pools.
Hostal Africa c/María Antonia Toledo 12 ⓣ956 680 220, ⓔhostal_africa@hotmail.com. Hotel set in a refurbished house in the old town, with a fantastic view across to North Africa from its large roof terrace. ❺
Melting Pot Hostel c/Turriano Gracil 5 ⓣ956 682 906, ⓔhostelthemeltingpottarifa@hotmail.com. The only hostel in town, crammed with an assortment of backpackers and beach bums. ❷
Pensión Facundo c/Batalla del Salado 40 & 47 ⓣ956 684 298. Cheap and cheerful hotel, with very inexpensive rooms outside high season. ❸

Eating and drinking

Almedina c/Almedina 3 ⓣ629 617 520. An Arabic-themed restaurant (mains €6) set in one of the old town gateways. Live flamenco on Thurs. Daily 11am–3am.
Bamboo c/Paseo Alameda 2 ⓣ956 627 304. Bob Marley music, deep sofas and fantastic smoothies and juices. Turns into a hip bar after dark. Daily 10am-2am.
Bossa Puerta de Jerez. Offers breakfasts until 2pm and has a very long Happy Hour (5–9pm) with cocktails for €2.90. Daily 10am–2pm & 5pm–3am.
Chilimosa c/Peso 6 ⓣ956 685 092. Fabulous vegetarian restaurant serving up healthy food with an Eastern twist. Mains €5. Also offers takeaways. Daily 12.30–3.30pm & 7–11pm.
Raices c/Melo 3. One of the cheapest bars in town, with draught beers costing only €1. Mon–Thurs 10.30pm–2am, Fri–Sun 10.30pm–3am.

Moving on

Ferry Tangier, Morocco (summer 4 daily; winter 5 weekly; 30–45min; €31 one-way).
Bus Cádiz (7 daily; 1–2hr); La Línea de la Concepción (7 daily; 1hr 30min–2hr);

MÁLAGA

MÁLAGA is the second city of the south after Seville, and also one of the poorest. It's the main city on the Costa del Sol, the richest and fastest-growing resort area in the Mediterranean, yet while the clusters of high-rises look pretty grim as you approach, the historic centre has plenty of charm. Around the old fishing villages of El Palo and Pedregalejo, to the east of the centre, are a series of small **beaches** and a promenade lined with some of the best fish and **seafood restaurants** in the province. Overlooking the town and port are the Moorish citadels of the **Alcazaba** (Tues–Sun 8.30am–8pm; €1.95), where the lengthy excavation of a **Roman amphitheatre** continues, and the **Gibralfaro castle** (April–Oct daily 9am–7.45pm; Nov–March daily 9am–5.45pm; €1.95), just fifteen minutes' walk from the train or bus stations, and visible from most central points. Málaga's most famous native son, born here in 1881, is honoured in the new **Museo Picasso**, on c/San Agustín (Tues–Thurs & Sun 10am–8pm, Fri & Sat 10am–9pm; €6), which displays works spanning Picasso's entire career, from his earliest sketches to some of his last paintings created shortly before his death in 1973.

Arrival and information

Air Málaga Airport is the hub of the south – hundreds of charter flights arrive here every week, which means that it's often possible to get an absurdly cheap ticket from London. From the airport, catch the electric train (every 30min) to the main train station, or continue another stop to Málaga Centro: Alameda for the city centre. The airport bus (#19) leaves every 20–30min to the centre, via the bus station.
Train and bus Buses #3 and #4 connect the main train station to the centre, while #4 and #12 leave from the bus station to the town centre.
Tourist office Plaza de la Marina (Mon–Fri 9am–7pm, Sat & Sun 10am–7pm; ⓣ952 122 020, ⓦwww.malagaturismo.com).

Accommodation

Instalación Juvenil Málaga Plaza Pio XII 6 ⓣ51 308 170 or 902 510 000 (reservations). Cheap but pretty institutional HI *hostal*, with characterless dorms. ❶
The Melting Pot Paseo de Salvador Rueda 9 ⓣ952 600 571, ⓔhostelthemeltingpot@hotmail.com. A stone's throw from the beach, and easily accessible from the town centre, with bar and terrace. ❷
Picasso's Corner c/San Juan de Letrán 9 ⓣ952 212 287, ⓦwww.picassoscorner.com. Helpful hostel with lots of useful information and spacious dorms. ❷

Eating and drinking

Málaga's **cuisine** – fried fish and sweet Málaga wine – can be enjoyed at a vast choice of **tapas bars and restaurants**. You'll find plenty of them in the area between Plaza de la Merced and Plaza de los Mártires, which is buzzing till late at the weekend.
Flor de Lis Plaza de la Merced 18 ⓣ952 214 453. Healthy food on offer, and a great *menú del día* for only €8.20.

Mesón Lo Güeno c/Marín Garcia 9 ⓣ952 223 048. Over 75 different tapas (€2–4) to choose from in this little rustic bar. 12.30–4.30pm & 8pm–12.30am.

Moving on

Train Córdoba (8–10 daily; 2hr 10min–3hr 30min); Madrid (5–8 daily; 4–7hr); Seville (6 daily; 3hr).
Bus Algeciras (10 daily; 3hr); Córdoba (2–5 daily; 3hr–3hr 30min); Granada (14 daily; 2hr); Ronda (18 daily; 2hr 45min–3hr); Seville (2 daily; 3hr).

RONDA

Andalucía is dotted with small, brilliantly whitewashed villages known as **pueblos blancos** (white towns), most often straggling up hillsides towards a castle or towered church. The most spectacular lie in a roughly triangular area between Málaga, Algeciras and Seville, at the centre of which is the startling town of **RONDA.**

What to see and do

Built on an isolated ridge of the sierra, and ringed by dark, angular mountains, Ronda is split in two by a gaping river **gorge** with a sheer drop, spanned by an eighteenth-century arched bridge. The town is full of character despite the steady flow of day-trippers from the coast, and forms two halves: the larger modern part and the tiny old quarter on the other side of the gorge. Most sights of interest are in the latter area, including the distinctive **Baños Árabes** (daily 10am–7pm, Sat 10am–1.45pm & 3–6pm, Sun 10am–3pm; €2; ⓣ656 950 937) and the delightful, tiled garden of the **Casa Don Bosco** (daily 9am–2pm & 2.30–6.30pm; €1.20; ⓣ952 871 653) at Calle San Juan de Lefran 20. Behind the town church is the **Palacio de Mondragón** (Mon–Fri 10am–7pm, Sat 10am–1.45pm & 3–6pm, Sun 10am–3pm; €2; ⓣ952 878 450), probably once the palace of the Moorish kings and now home to the **Museo Municipal** (same hours, included in the price). The principal gate of the town, through which the Christian conquerors passed, stands beside the **Alcázar**, destroyed by the French in 1809. In the modern Mercadillo quarter are the **bullring** (daily 10am–8pm; €6 including museum; ⓣ952 874 132, ⓦwww.rmcr.org) – one of the most prestigious in Spain – and the **Jardín de la Mina**, which ascends the gorge in a series of stepped terraces offering superb views of the river, new bridge and the remarkable stairway of the **Casa del Rey Moro** (daily 10am–7pm; €4; ⓣ952 187 200), an early eighteenth-century mansion built on Moorish foundations, on the opposite side of the gorge.

Arrival and information

Bus The bus station is 500m north of the town centre, from where it's an easy walk to the old quarter.
Tourist office Opposite the entrance to the bullring at Plaza de Toros (Mon–Fri 10am–7pm, Sat & Sun 10.15am–2pm & 3.30–6.30pm; ⓣ952 187 119, ⓦwww.turismoderonda.es).

Accommodation

Camping El Sur ⓣ952 875 939, ⓦwww.campingelsur.com. Campsite with pool and restaurant located 1.5km down the Algeciras road. ❶
Hostal Biarritz c/Almendras 7 ⓣ952 872 910. Clean but no-frills *hostal*, with shared bathrooms. ❷
Hotel Colon c/Pozo 1 ⓣ952 870 218, ⓦwww.hcolon.es. Small hotel with café downstairs, and smart, pleasant rooms. ❹
Hotel Morales c/Sevilla 51 ⓣ952 871 538. Clean, tidy rooms, all with air-con and TV. ❹
Pensión La Purísima c/Sevilla 10 ⓣ952 871 050. Run by a friendly couple, with basic rooms, though some are spacious. ❸
Pensión Ronda Sol c/Almendras 11 ⓣ952 874 497. The sister hotel to *Biarritz*, and located next door. Cheap and cheerful. ❷

Eating and drinking

In addition to the restaurants below, it's worth browsing the local produce on offer at Queso y Jamon, Plaza de Espana 1 (daily 10am–8pm), an excellent **gourmet shop** that sells fine hams, *chorizo* and cheeses.

Bar Restaurante Brillante c/Sevilla 29. Cheap little bar serving food, with a *menú del día* including three courses plus a drink for only €7. Daily 7am–midnight.

Churrería Alba c/Espinel 44 ⓣ952 190 953. Serves up the classic Spanish dish *churros* (a deep-fried dough) *y chocolate* for only €3, plus juices and other snacks. Daily 8am–3pm.

Hotel Don Miguel Plaza de España 4 ⓣ952 871 090, ⓦwww.dmiguel.com. Expensive food but worth having a drink on the terrace to admire the amazing views of the gorge. Daily 12.30–4pm & 8–11pm.

Restaurante Pizzeria Michelangelo c/Lorenzo Borrego 5 ⓣ952 873 683. Standard Italian pizzeria serving pasta and pizzas for around €6. Mon, Tues & Thurs–Sun noon–4pm & 8pm–midnight.

Moving on

Bus Granada (twice daily; 3hr 30min); Málaga (hourly; 3hr 30min); Seville (3–5 daily; 2hr 45min)
Train Córdoba (twice daily; 1hr 45min); Málaga (daily; 1hr 50min).

ALGECIRAS

The main reason to visit **ALGECIRAS**, a bus ride along the coast from Cádiz, is for the **ferry to Tangier, Morocco**, though the old town has some pleasant plazas and parks. The best place to buy tickets is at the **port**, directly from the ferry companies, as many travel agents will only offer tickets from their client companies – though wait till Tangier before buying any Moroccan currency. Either way, it's worth dropping by *The Lighthouse* on Avda. Villa Nueva (Mon–Fri 9.30am–5pm), a helpful one-stop shop for backpackers, offering free advice on travel to Morocco, free luggage storage and, in its cheap café, a selection of guidebooks to peruse. The number of people passing through Algeciras guarantees plenty of inexpensive **rooms**. Try the family-run *Pensión Tetuan* at Duque de Almodóvar 9 (ⓣ956 652 854; ❷), or the economic *Hostal La Plata* c/ Cayetano del Toro 29 (ⓣ956 662 152; ❷), just around the corner. If you have trouble finding space, check the list in the **tourist office** near the port on Avda. Villa Nueva (Mon–Fri 9am–8pm; ⓣ956 784 131). For a **meal**, head to the first floor of the *Hotel Al-Mar* on Avda. de la Marina ⓣ956 654 661; Mon—Fri 1–4pm), where you can eat as much as you like for €6.

Moving on

Ferry Tangier, Morocco (every 30min; 1hr–2hr 30min; €37.50 one-way).
Train Madrid (2 daily; 6hr); Ronda (5 daily; 1hr 40min); Granada (3 daily; 4hr).
Bus Córdoba (2 daily; 6hr); Granada (6 daily; 3hr 45min–5hr 30min); Málaga (every 30min; 1hr 45min–3hr).

GIBRALTAR

Long-coveted for its strategic position at the entrance to the Mediterranean, the British territory of **GIBRALTAR**, at the southern tip of Spain, has been the source of tension between the two countries for nearly three hundred years since it was ceded to **Britain** under the Treaty of Utrecht. It is now a small slice of Britain perched next to the Spanish mainland, complete with red post-boxes, chippies and, of course, the pound. Despite having British currency, its **tax-free status** makes it an excellent place to stock up on alcohol, cigarettes and cheap electronic equipment. Make sure though, that you pay in pounds sterling for your purchases as, although euros are accepted, the exchange rate offered is normally poor.

What to see and do

The town is dominated by a huge limestone rock, the famous **Rock of Gibraltar,** which is the area's main attraction, and was thought, in antiquity, to be a pillar of Hercules. It is best accessed by the cable car running from Red Sands Road (daily 9.30am–7.15pm, £8 one-way), which drops visitors at the top of the rock. From here, there are spectacular views of the coastline, and the distant African continent. Following signs from the cable-car exit will lead you to the **nature reserve** (daily 9.30am–7.15pm; £8) on the Rock, which includes the cavernous **St Michael's Cave**, the **Great Siege Tunnels**, constructed in 1782–3, and – the home of the peninsula's famous simian residents– the **Apes' Den**.

To **get to Gibraltar**, simply walk across the border from La Línea de la Concepción, and from there follow Winston Churchill Avenue into town (10min). For more information on the area, head to the bilingual **tourist Office** on Casemates Square (Mon–Fri 9am–5.30pm, Sat 10am–3pm, Sun 10am–1pm; ⓣ350 450 00), where there are also a large number of cafes and **restaurants**. Gibraltar makes a good day-trip, which is probably why it has only six **hotels**, but if you do decide to stay, the cheapest accommodation can be found at *Cannon Hotel 9* on Cannon Lane (ⓣ350 517 11; ❻).

Moving on

Bus La Línea de la Concepción to: Algeciras (every 30–45min; 40min); Málaga (4 daily; 2hr 30min); Seville (4 daily; 5hr).

Sweden

HIGHLIGHTS

THE ICE HOTEL, KIRUNA: visit this icy confection of a building, remade every year

INLANDSBANAN: whistle past virgin forest and crystal-clear streams en route to Lapland

STOCKHOLM: wander the atmospheric streets of the well-preserved medieval centre

GOTLAND: join the summer revellers at this lively holiday isle

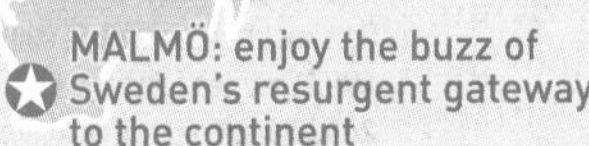

MALMÖ: enjoy the buzz of Sweden's resurgent gateway to the continent

ROUGH COSTS

DAILY BUDGET Basic €35/occasional treat €50

DRINK Schnapps (€5)

FOOD Tunnbrodsrulle (Swedish kebab) €4

HOSTEL/BUDGET HOTEL €19–25/€50–64

TRAVEL Train: Stockholm–Gothenburg (471km) €76

FACT FILE

POPULATION 9 million

AREA 449,964 sq km

LANGUAGE Swedish

CURRENCY Swedish krona (kr)

CAPITAL Stockholm (population: 800,000)

INTERNATIONAL PHONE CODE ⓣ46

Basics

Sweden combines stylish, sophisticated cities and a vast wilderness of coniferous forests and crystal-clear mountain lakes. Quality of life is high, almost everyone speaks fluent English, and the atmosphere of order and contentment is infectious. You could easily spend a week or two enjoying the beauty of the countryside, but it would be a shame to miss the cultural pleasures of its urban hubs.

Sweden is one of the world's biggest exporters of **music** and a hothouse for new brands, and the cities and big towns are where it shows. The west coast has a host of historic ports – **Gothenburg**, **Helsingborg** and **Malmö**, linked by bridge to Copenhagen – but it is **Stockholm**, the capital, that is the country's supreme attraction, a bundle of islands housing monumental architecture, fine museums and the country's most active nightlife. The two university towns, **Lund** and **Uppsala**, demand a visit too, as does the buzzing holiday island of Gotland, off the southeast coast. Moving northwards, the picturesque **Dalarna** region is steeped in cultural heritage, while **Östersund**, attractively sited on a lake, makes a good place to pause before hitting the far north. Press on further north via the famed Inlandsbanen railway into the Arctic Circle to discover the attractions of **Kiruna** and its world-famous ice hotel. Here you'll find the country of tourist brochures: great swathes of forest, inexhaustible lakes (some 96,000 of them) and some of the best wilderness hiking in Europe.

CHRONOLOGY

98 AD Tacitus refers to a Scandinavian tribe known as the "Suiones".

800s The Swedish Vikings become a powerful force in Europe over the following few centuries.

1397 The Kalmar Union unites Sweden with Denmark and Norway through a marriage arrangement.

1520 Hundreds of nobles are killed by Danish forces during the "Stockholm Massacre". A counter-attack is led by Swede Gustav Vasa.

1523 Gustav is crowned King Gustav I and leads the Protestant Reformation of Sweden.

1536 Sweden leaves the Kalmar Union, asserting independence.

1721 Sweden is defeated by a coalition led by Russia in the Great Northern War, ending the success of the Swedish Empire.

1814 Sweden invades and conquers Norway.

1901 First Nobel Prize held, as part of the will of Swedish inventor Alfred Nobel.

1905 Sweden peacefully concedes Norwegian independence.

1914 Sweden remains neutral during WWI.

1939 Sweden declares neutrality during WWII, and is one of only five countries to maintain it.

1943 The first IKEA store is opened by founder Ingvar Kamprad.

1974 ABBA top the charts after winning the Eurovision Song Contest with "Waterloo".

1975 Constitutional reforms make the role of monarchy solely ceremonial.

1986 Prime Minister Olof Palme is assassinated in Stockholm; the crime is still unresolved.

1995 Sweden joins the EU.

2003 Sweden decides against the adoption of the euro.

ARRIVAL

Most travellers arrive at one of Stockholm's three main international **airports**. The biggest and most convenient, Arlanda, is served by most big international airlines, including national carrier SAS (Ⓦwww.sas.se). Ryanair operates flights from various major European cities into Skavsta and Västerås airports, though both are a long way from the city; it's also possible to fly into Gothenburg and Malmö with Ryanair.

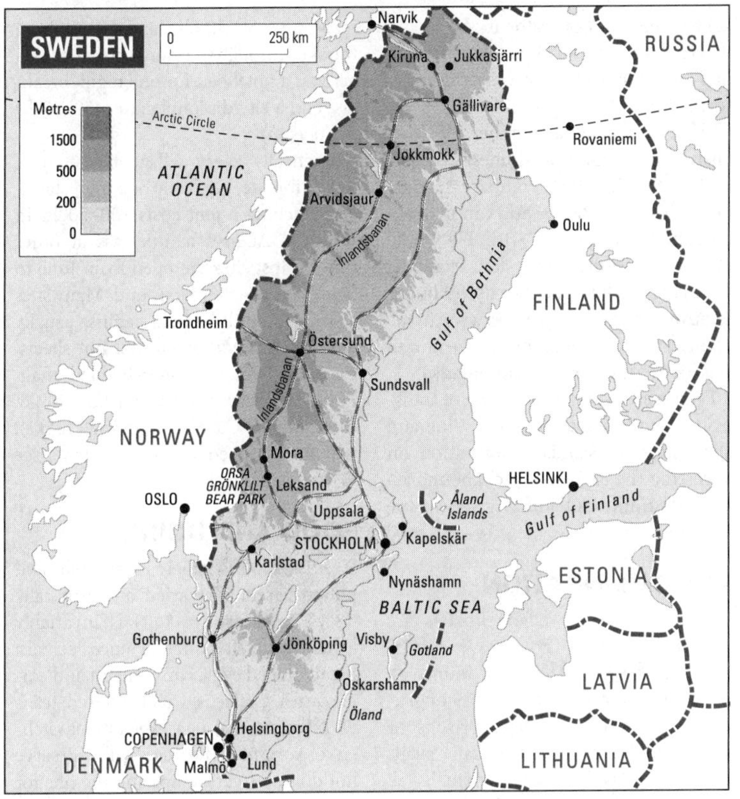

International **trains** arrive in Stockholm and Gothenburg from Norway, Denmark and Germany; in the north, Kiruna is the first stop in Sweden for visitors arriving from northern Norway.

International **ferry routes** include: Stockholm–Tallin (Estonia), Stockholm–Helsinki and Turku (Finland); Helsingborg–Helsingør (Denmark) and Oslo (Norway); Gothenburg–Kiel (Germany) and Newcastle (Britain).

GETTING AROUND

The best way to explore Sweden is by train. **Swedish State Railways'** extensive network (SJ; Ⓦwww.sj.se) runs as far north as Östersund and, on the east coast, Sundsvall. The famous **Inlandsbanan** line (Ⓦwww.inlandsbanan.se), which travels through central and northern Sweden, is privately run and only operates from mid-June to September (see p.1174). A third company, **Connex**, runs services from Gothenburg and Stockholm to the north and on into Norway. **InterRail** and **Eurail** are valid on all trains, as is the **ScanRail** pass (see p.35).

Buses cost around half as much as trains, though are also a slower way to travel. The main national companies are Swebus Express (Ⓦwww.swebusexpress.se) – ISIC cardholders get a twenty-percent discount on travel – and Säfflebussen (Ⓦwww.safflebussen.se). Ybuss (Ⓦwww.ybuss.

se) are the main operator in the north, where the rail network is less extensive and thus bus routes become the main form of public transport.

There are now a number of **low-cost airlines** running domestic routes within Sweden that compare favourably with the railways. You can fly from Stockholm to Kiruna with FlyNordic (ⓦwww.flynordic.com), for example, for as little as 800kr. Other useful budget airlines include FlyMe (ⓦwww.flyme.com) and, for Gothenburg–Stockholm flights, Sterling (ⓦwww.sterling.dk).

Ferries are an essential mode of transport given Sweden's long coastline and thousands of islands. Information on accessing the islands of Stockholm's archipelago and Gotland is given in the chapter.

ACCOMMODATION

The majority of Sweden's **hostels** are operated by STF (ⓦwww.svenskaturistforeningen.se). They are found all over the country, often in incongruous surroundings, such as prisons or ships. Double rooms are usually available as well as dorms, and virtually all hostels have self-catering kitchens and serve a buffet breakfast. Prices are low (120–200kr for a bed), but you have to pay extra for sheets and breakfast (usually 50–60kr extra each), so if you're on a tight budget it's worth bringing a sleeping bag and seeking out cheaper breakfasts elsewhere. Non-HI members pay around 50kr extra per night. There are also many non-STF hostels, mostly run by SVIF (ⓦwww.svif.se). In larger towns you can book a **private room** through the tourist office for about the same as a hostel bed.

Hotels come cheaper than you might think, especially in Stockholm and the bigger towns during the summer; when they slash their rates breakfast is always included in the price. At weekends, and during the weeks between mid-June and mid-August, package deals are available in Malmö, Stockholm and Gothenburg (booked through the tourist board) which get you a hotel bed for one night, breakfast and a city discount card (450–550kr per person).

Practically every village has at least one **campsite**, generally of a high standard. Pitching a tent costs 100–200kr in July and August, a little less at other times. Most sites are open from June to September, some year-round. Many sites also have bunk-bedded cabins, usually with kitchen equipment but not sheets, for 500–700kr for a four-bedded affair. For a list of campsites, and how to get the Camping Card Scandinavia (125kr), which you need to pitch a tent, see ⓦwww.camping.se.

FOOD AND DRINK

Swedish **food** is largely meat-, fish- and potato-based; it's varied and generally tasty. **Breakfast** (*frukost*) is invariably a help-yourself buffet of juice, cereals, bread, boiled eggs, jams, salami and coffee or tea. Coffee is usually filtered; tea is DIY. For **snacks**, a *gatukök* (street kitchen) or *korvstånd* (hot-dog stall) will serve hot dogs, burgers, chips and the like for around 40kr. Coffee shops always display a range of freshly baked pastries (coffee and cake for 40–60kr), and also serve *smörgåsar* – open sandwiches piled high with toppings (30–60kr) – and usually a good range of salads.

Lunch (*lunch*; served 11am–2pm) is the main meal of the day for many Swedes. Restaurants tend to be great value at lunchtime, with most places offering a set meal (*dagens rätt*) of a main dish with bread and salad at 65–75kr. Specialities include northern Swedish delicacies, such as reindeer, elk and pickled herring in many different guises. More expensive is the **smörgåsbord** (150–200kr) offered by some hotels and restaurants, from which you help yourself to unlimited portions of herring, smoked and fresh salmon, hot and cold meats, potatoes, salad, cheese and fruit. Otherwise meals in restaurants, especially at **dinner** (*middag*), can be expensive: 200–250kr for two courses, plus drinks. Better value are pizzerias and Chinese restaurants. Note that Swedes tend to eat early, tucking into dinner from around 6pm.

Drinking

Bars and pubs close around midnight, a little later in Malmö, Gothenburg and Stockholm. Although the costs have come down in recent years, Sweden remains one of the most expensive places in Europe to **drink**: you'll pay 40–55kr for half a litre of lager-type **beer** – a *stor stark* (literally, "big strong") – in a bar. Unless you specify, it will be *starköl*, the strongest beer, or the slightly weaker *mellanöl*; *folköl* is the cheaper and weaker brew; cheapest (around half the price) is *lättöl*, a concoction that is virtually non-alcoholic. With the exception of the latter, the only outlets where you can buy alcohol outside of bars and restaurants are the government-run **Systembolaget** (known informally as System) shops, where alcohol costs around a third of what you'll pay in a bar. There are at least one or two branches in even the smallest towns. A glass of **wine** in a bar or restaurant costs around 50–60kr, while you can buy a whole bottle for a little more at Systembolaget.

CULTURE AND ETIQUETTE

To generalize, you could say that Swedes are a mix of apparent contradictions: fiercely patriotic yet outward-looking and globally minded, confident yet self-deprecating, orderly yet creative. Throughout the country you'll find the small ritual of *fika* – a verb that means something like "to have a coffee and a bun and a chat with a friend or two" – is a common pastime, along with singalongs and complaining about winter. **Traditional festivities** like Midsummer's Day and Easter inspire enormous enthusiasm among Swedes of all ages, and on holidays young and old alike head for the countryside to celebrate. The vast majority of Swedes speak some **English** and most speak it with disarming fluency, so Anglophone travellers will have no problem striking up conversations.

SPORTS AND OUTDOOR ACTIVITIES

Skiing and **snowboarding** are hugely popular and the winter Olympics is followed avidly here, with Swedish athletes invariably returning home with a handful of medals. The best ski resorts are in Åre, Kittelfjäll, Riksgränsen and Ramundberget. In summer, everyone flocks to Sweden's exquisite, unpolluted lakes and to Stockholm's archipelago for **swimming**, **sailing** and – off the coast of Gotland in particular – even **surfing**. Sweden is a fantastic place for **hiking**, with some of Europe's most unspoilt wildernesses to explore. The most trekked path is the 500-kilometre Kungsleden (King's Trail), which is easily accessible and punctuated by cabins and mountain lodges.

SWEDEN ON THE NET

Ⓦ **www.cityguide.se** Up-to-date guide to events and entertainment in the main Swedish cities.

Ⓦ **www.visit-sweden.com** The largest single source of information in English on Sweden, its provinces, nature, culture and society.

Ⓦ **www.stockholmtown.com** Everything you ever wanted to know about the Swedish capital.

Ⓦ **www.svenskaturistforeningen.se** Tips and ideas on where to visit in Sweden, courtesy of STF (the Swedish Youth Hostel Association).

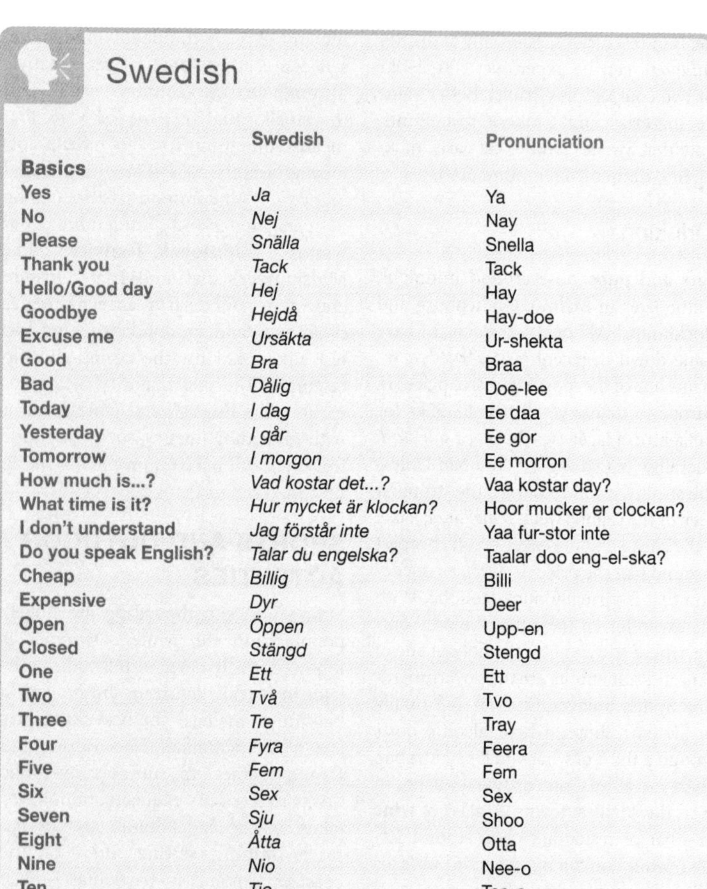

Swedish

	Swedish	Pronunciation
Basics		
Yes	*Ja*	Ya
No	*Nej*	Nay
Please	*Snälla*	Snella
Thank you	*Tack*	Tack
Hello/Good day	*Hej*	Hay
Goodbye	*Hejdå*	Hay-doe
Excuse me	*Ursäkta*	Ur-shekta
Good	*Bra*	Braa
Bad	*Dålig*	Doe-lee
Today	*I dag*	Ee daa
Yesterday	*I går*	Ee gor
Tomorrow	*I morgon*	Ee morron
How much is...?	*Vad kostar det...?*	Vaa kostar day?
What time is it?	*Hur mycket är klockan?*	Hoor mucker er clockan?
I don't understand	*Jag förstår inte*	Yaa fur-stor inte
Do you speak English?	*Talar du engelska?*	Taalar doo eng-el-ska?
Cheap	*Billig*	Billi
Expensive	*Dyr*	Deer
Open	*Öppen*	Upp-en
Closed	*Stängd*	Stengd
One	*Ett*	Ett
Two	*Två*	Tvo
Three	*Tre*	Tray
Four	*Fyra*	Feera
Five	*Fem*	Fem
Six	*Sex*	Sex
Seven	*Sju*	Shoo
Eight	*Åtta*	Otta
Nine	*Nio*	Nee-o
Ten	*Tio*	Tee-o

COMMUNICATIONS

Post office services can now be found in supermarkets, newsagents, tobacconists and hotels. **Public phones** take either cash or cards (*telefonkort*), available from newsagents and kiosks. You can also use credit cards in payphones marked "CCC". Directory enquiries is on ⓣ118 118 (domestic), ⓣ118 119 (international). **Internet** cafés are surprisingly rare, though you should find at least one in the larger towns (40–60kr/hr). Access is free in local libraries.

EMERGENCY NUMBERS

All emergencies ⓣ112.

EMERGENCIES

The **police** are courteous and fluent in English. In case of health problems go to a **hospital** with your passport, where for a maximum of around 500kr you'll receive treatment; if you have to stay it costs an extra 85kr per day. Urgent treatment is free for anyone with a European Health Insurance Card (EHIC; see p.50). **Pharmacies** (*Apoteket*), which have a distinctive green-and-white shopfront,

STUDENT AND YOUTH DISCOUNTS

The main cities all have **tourist cards** or passes, which offer either free or discounted entry to museums, unlimited use of local transport (often including ferries), and sometimes other goodies, such as discounts in cafés and restaurants. An **ISIC card** can halve the price of museums, and attract variable discounts on some accommodation, shops and restaurants.

operate shop opening hours; larger towns operate a rota system, with the address of the nearest late-opener posted on each pharmacy's door. Stockholm has a 24-hour pharmacy (see p.1162).

INFORMATION AND MAPS

Almost all towns have a **tourist office**, giving out maps and timetables; they are also usually able to book private rooms, rent out bikes and change money. The best **map** is the Motormännens *Sveriges Atlas*.

MONEY AND BANKS

Currency is the **krona** (abbreviated to kr; plural: kronor), made up of 100 öre. There are coins of 50 öre, 1kr, 5kr and 10kr, and notes of 20kr, 50kr, 100kr, 500kr, 1000kr and 10,000kr. At the time of writing €1 was worth 9kr, US$1 was 6.5kr, and £1 was 13kr. **Banks** are open Monday to Friday 9.30am–3pm, and on Thursday also 4–5.30pm. Outside these hours you can **change money** at airports and ferry terminals, as well as at Forex offices, which usually offer the best rates (minimum 30kr commission). **ATMs** are plentiful and **credit cards** are accepted just about everywhere.

OPENING HOURS AND HOLIDAYS

Shops open Monday to Friday 9am–6pm, and on Saturday from 9am to 1/4pm. Some larger stores stay open until 8/10pm, and may open on Sunday (noon–4pm). Banks, offices and shops close on **public holidays** (Jan 1, Jan 6, Good Fri, Easter Sun & Mon, May 1, Ascension, Whit Sun & Mon, June 20 & 21, Nov 1, Dec 24–26 & 31). They may also close early the preceding day.

Stockholm

Built on fourteen islands, **STOCKHOLM** is blessed with post-card-pretty views, especially in its old town. With the air of a grand European capital on a small, Scandinavian scale, it's a vibrant and instantly likeable city, boasting a thriving café culture, some excellent museums and a great night-life.

Stockholm was a natural site for the fortifications, erected in 1255, that grew into the current city. In the seventeenth century it became the centre of the Swedish trading empire that covered present-day Scandinavia and beyond. Following the waning of Swedish power it only rose to prominence again in the nineteenth century when industrialization took off.

What to see and do

The best way to get around the city is to walk. Just a 200-metre walk south from the Central Station across Vasabron Bridge is Stockholm's old town, Gamla Stan, which is made up of three islands – Riddarholmen, Staden and Helgeandsholmen. The main commercial district, **Norrmalm**, is located east of the station, with most of the activity along Klarabergsgatan, Sveavägen and Hamngatan. South of Gamla Stan is **Södermalm**, packed with bars and clubs, while to the east of the city centre is peaceful **Djurgården**, with a brace of fine museums.

However, one of the city's main attractions lies next door to the station right at the water's edge: the **Stadshuset** at Hantverkargatan 1 (guided tours daily 10am & noon; June–Sept also 2pm; 60kr; T-bana: T-Centralen). Climbing its gently tapering 106-metre-high red-brick **tower** (May–Sept daily 10am–4pm; 20kr) will give you the best fix on the city's layout.

Kungliga Slottet

Over the bridge from Norrmalm on Helgeandsholmen lies Stockholm's most distinctive monumental building, the **Kungliga Slottet** (Royal Palace; T-Gamla Stan), a beautiful Renaissance successor to Stockholm's original castle. Finished in 1760, it's a striking achievement, outside sombre, inside a magnificent Baroque and Rococo swirl. The **apartments** (mid-May to mid-Sept daily 10am–4/5pm; mid-Sept to mid-May Tues–Sun noon–3pm; 90kr) are a dazzling collection of regal furniture and tapestries; the **Treasury** (same times as apartments; 90kr) displays ranks of regalia, including jewel-studded crowns and a sword belonging to Gustav Vasa. Also worth catching is the **Livrustkammaren** (Royal Armoury; June–Aug daily 10am–5pm; Sept–May Tues, Weds & Fri–Sun 11am–5pm, Thurs 11am–8pm; 50kr), which displays suits of armour, costumes and horse-drawn coaches from the sixteenth century onwards.

Gamla Stan

Beyond the palace lies Gamla Stan proper, a clutter of seventeenth- and eighteenth-century Renaissance buildings, hairline medieval alleys and tall, dark houses whose intricate doorways still bear the arms of the wealthy merchants who once dwelled within.

The first major building is the **Storkyrkan** (daily 9am–4/6pm; 25kr, free in winter), consecrated in 1306 and technically Stockholm's cathedral – the monarchs of Sweden are married and crowned here. The Baroque interior is marvellous, with an animated fifteenth-century sculpture of *St George and the Dragon*, the royal pews – more like golden billowing thrones – and a monumental black and silver altarpiece.

Stortorget, Gamla Stan's main square, is handsomely proportioned and crowded with eighteenth-century buildings. The surrounding narrow streets house a succession of arts and craft shops, restaurants and discreet fast-food outlets, clogged (in the summer) by buskers and evening strollers. The excellent Nobel Museum on Stortorget (daily 10am–5/8pm; 60kr) showcases the work and milieu of various Nobel prize-winners.

Head right from Stortorget until you get to the handsome Baroque **Riddarhuset** (Mon–Fri 10.30am–12.30pm; 40kr), which was formerly used by the Swedish aristocracy as a parliament. From here it's a matter of seconds across the bridge onto Riddarholmen, and to **Riddarholms Kyrkan** (mid-May to Sept daily 10am–4/5pm; 30kr), originally a Franciscan monastery and long the burial place of Swedish royalty.

The National Art Museum and Skeppsholmen

Off Gamla Stan's eastern reaches on the way to the island of **Skeppsholmen**, you'll find the **National Art Museum** on Strömkajen (Tues–Sun 11am–5/8pm; 80kr; T-Kungsträdgården), an impressive collection of applied art: beds slept in by kings, cabinets used by queens, plus Art Nouveau coffee pots and vases and examples of Swedish furniture design. Upstairs there is a plethora of European sculpture, mesmerizing sixteenth- and seventeenth-century Russian Orthodox icons, and a quality selection of paintings.

Skeppsholmen's **Moderna Muséet** (Tues–Sun 10am–6/8pm; free), one of the better modern art collections in Europe, has a comprehensive selection of works by some of the twentieth century's leading artists including Dalí, Warhol and Matisse. In summer, there's a great café with outdoor seating.

Norrmalm and Östermalm

Modern Stockholm lies immediately north of Gamla Stan. It's split into two distinct sections: the central **Norrmalm** and the classier, residential streets of **Östermalm** to the east – though there's not much apart from a couple of specialist museums to draw you here.

On the waterfront, at the foot of Norrbro, is **Gustav Adolfs Torg**, more a traffic island than a square, with the eighteenth-century **Opera House** its proudest and most notable building. It was at a masked ball here in 1792 that King Gustav III was shot; you'll find Gustav's ball costume, as well as the assassin's pistols and mask, displayed in the Livrustskammaren in the Royal Palace. Norrmalm's eastern boundary is marked by **Kungsträdgården**, the most fashionable and central of the city's numerous parks.

On the opposite side of Norrmalm in Östermalm is the **Historiska Muséet** (May–Sept daily 10am–5pm, Oct–April Tues, Weds, Fri & Sat 11am–5pm, Thurs 11am–8pm; 60kr; T-Karlaplan). Ground-floor highlights include a Stone Age household and a mass of Viking weapons, coins and boats, while upstairs there's an evocative collection of medieval church art and architecture.

Södermalm and Långholmen

Stockholm's hippest island has to be **Södermalm**, just south of Gamla Stan. Head south from the traffic hub of Slussen along Götgatan, past Medborgarplatsen, lined with shops and bars, to arrive at the central district of **SoFo** (South of Folkungagatan), which bristles with cool bars, clubs and boutiques. To the west of Södermalm, **Hornstull** is SoFo's quieter cousin, with a cluster of bars and restaurants along Hornsgatan and around Bergsundstrand. It's a short walk from here to the lovely, uninhabited island of **Långholmen**, perfect for picnics or summertime swimming in the surprisingly clean water.

Djurgården

A former royal hunting ground, **Djurgården** is the nearest large expanse of park to the city centre and home to several interesting museums. You could walk to the park from Central Station, but it's quite a hike: it's quicker to take a bus or ferry instead. Bus #44 makes the journey from Karlaplan, while the #47 and #69 run from Nybroplan. Ferries leave in summer from Nybroplan, and all year round from Slussen.

The palatial **Nordiska Muséet** (daily 10/11am–4/5pm; 60kr) showcases Swedish cultural history in an accessible fashion, with a particularly interesting Sámi section. Close by, the **Vasa Muséet** (daily 10am–5/7/8pm; 80kr, 50kr on Wed late Aug–early June) is an essential stop, displaying a famous Swedish design disaster: the top-heavy *Vasa* warship, which sank in Stockholm harbour just twenty minutes into its maiden voyage in 1628. Preserved in mud, the ship was raised in 1961, along with 12,000 objects. Films and videos explain the social and political life of the period – all

> **TREAT YOURSELF**
>
> Stockholm is one of the few cities in Europe where you can ride in a **hot-air balloon** directly over the city centre. The price you pay for this once-in-a-lifetime experience is steep at around 1995kr per person, but if you're looking to blow the budget, this is a spectacular way to do it. To find out more, call ⓣ08/645 77 00, check ⓦwww.farochflyg.se or contact the tourist office.

with excellent English notes and regular English-language guided tours.

Arrival and information

Air Both Skavsta and Västerås airports, each 100km from the capital, are connected by bus (both 130kr single; 199kr return; 1hr 20min) to the Cityterminalen. From the main airport, Arlanda, buses (95kr single; 175kr return) and trains (220kr single; 47 percent discount with ISIC card) run frequently into the city arriving at the Cityterminalen and Central Station respectively.

Train By train, you arrive at Central Station, a cavernous structure on Vasagatan in Norrmalm. All branches of the Tunnelbana, Stockholm's metro, meet at T-Centralen, the station directly below Central Station.

Bus Cityterminalen, adjacent to Central Station, handles all bus services, both domestic and international.

Ferry Viking Line ferries arrive at Tegelvikshamnen in Södermalm, in the south of the city. The terminal is a thirty-minute walk from the centre, or connected by bus to the transport interchange Slussen and then by Tunnelbana to T-Centralen. The Silja Line terminal is in the northeastern reaches of the city, a short walk from Gärdet or Ropsten Tunnelbana stations.

Tourist office The useful tourist office is at Hamngatan 27 in Norrmalm (Mon–Fri 9am–7pm, Sat 10–5pm, Sun 10am–4pm; ⓣ08/508 28 508, ⓦwww.stockholmtown.com). It sells the Stockholm Card (290/420/540kr for 24/48/72 hours), which gives unlimited use of city transport (except direct airport buses), free museum entry and boat tours.

City transport

Tickets Buses and trains (both T-bana – underground – and local) are operated by Storstockholms Lokaltrafik (SL; ⓦwww.sl.se). One hour of travel on the T-bana and buses costs 26kr – buy tickets in advance from Pressbyrån stores. If you're going to travel around the city a lot, it's worth getting a Stockholm Card (see above). Another option is to buy a strip of twenty transferable SL ticket coupons (*Rabattkuponger*, 160kr); you'll need two coupons for any single journey in the centre by bus or T-bana.

Metro The Tunnelbana (T-bana) is the quickest way to get about. There are three main lines.

Bus There are four main "blue bus" lines that run across the city centre, numbered #1 to #4; numerous other lines serve suburban destinations. Buy tickets before you board.

Ferry Ferries link some of the central islands and are a useful way of getting to Djurgården (see p.1159). Individual tickets are relatively expensive but the Stockholm Card is valid.

Taxi You can hail taxis in the street, or book on ⓣ08/15 00 00. A daytime trip across the city centre costs 170–200kr; women get a 5–10 percent discount at weekends.

Accommodation

There's plenty of accommodation, but booking in advance is always a good idea. The cheapest choices on the whole lie north of Cityterminalen, in the streets west of Adolf Fredriks Kyrka, but there are some good alternatives on Södermalm. **Hotellcentralen**, a booking service on the lower level of Central Station (daily 8/9am–4/6/8pm; ⓣ08/508 28 508, ⓦwww.stockholmtown.com), charges a fee of 60kr per room, 25kr for a hostel if you go in person, but is free online. Hotelltjänst, Nybrogatan 44 (ⓣ08/10 44 37, ⓦwww.hotelltjanst.com), can fix you up with a double **private room**, with prices from 700kr.

Hostels

Af Chapman Flaggmansvägen 8, Skeppsholmen ⓣ08/463 22 66, ⓦwww.stfchapman.com. Official hostel on an atmospheric sailing ship moored at Skeppsholmen. Without a reservation, the chances of a bed in summer are negligible. Dorms ❷, rooms ❼

City Backpackers Upplandsgatan 2A, Norra Bantorget ⓣ08/20 69 20, ⓦwww.citybackpackers.se. Fun, sociable non-STF hostel with four-bed rooms and cheaper eight-bed dorms. Free pasta and free Internet. Dorms ❸, rooms ❻–❼

City Lodge Klara Norra Kyrkogatan 15 ⓣ08/22 6630, ⓦwww.citylodge.se. There's free Internet and no curfew at this very pleasant, central hostel. Dorms ❸, rooms ❼

Långholmen Kronohäktet, Långholmen ⓣ08/720 85 00, ⓦwww.langholmen.com. Stockholm's grandest official hostel is located within an old prison on Långholmen island. Spend the night in a converted cell: there are ordinary doubles in summer as well as dorms. To reach it take the T-bana to Hornstull, turn left and follow the signs. Dorms ❸, rooms ❼

M/S Rygerfjord Söder Mälarstrand-Kajplats 12 ⓣ08/84 08 30, ⓦwww.rygerfjord.se. Comfortable hostel-ship moored on Södermalm close to Slussen T-bana station. Book ahead to be sure of a bed. Dorms ❸

Zinkensdamm Zinkens väg 20, Södermalm ⓣ08/616 81 00, ⓦwww.zinkensdamm.com. Huge official hostel, nicely situated in the midst of children's playgrounds and allotments, with kitchen facilities. Zinkensdamm or Hornstull T-bana. Dorms ❸, rooms ❼

Hotels and pensions

Pensionat Oden Kammakargatan 62, Hornsgatan 66b & Odengatan 38 ⓣ08/796 96 00, ⓦwww.pensionat.nu. All three branches of this mini-chain have light, airy rooms and a good location close to bars and shops. ❽

Tre små rum Högbergsgatan 81 ⓣ08/641 23 71, ⓦwww.tresmarum.se. Bright, modern rooms (none en suite) in the heart of Södermalm. Also offers bike hire to help you zip around the city. Mariatorget T-bana. ❽

Campsites

Ängby Blackebergsvägen 25 ⓣ08/37 04 20, ⓦwww.angbycamping.se. Pretty, well-organized site west of the city on Lake Mälaren and near the beach. T-bana to Ängbyplan, then a 300-metre walk. Open all year. ❷

Bredäng Stora Sällskapets Väg ⓣ08/97 70 71, ⓦwww.bredangcamping.se. Pricey place with a hostel and restaurant on site, 10km southwest of the centre by Lake Mälaren. Take T-bana to Bredäng from where it's a 700m walk. April–Oct only. Camping ❸, dorms ❷, rooms ❻

Östermalms Citycamping Fiskartorpsvägen 2 ⓣ08/10 29 03. Surrounded by woodland, this is Stockholm's most centrally located campsite, at the Östermalm sports ground. Late June to late Aug only. ❷

Eating

Norrmalm, Gamla Stan and Södermalm are the three best areas to find decent places to eat. The Hötorgshallen in Hötorget is a cheap and varied indoor **market**, awash with small cafés and ethnic snacks. Outside is an excellent daily fruit and veg market too.

Cafés

Art Café Västerlånggatan 60, Gamla Stan. A seventeenth-century arty cellar-café serving sandwiches, good coffee and cakes.

Café Rival Mariatorget 1–3. It's a boutique hotel, it's a bar, it's a café – and the café, with its quirky decor and views over the leafy square outside, is one of the nicest in Stockholm. Plus the owner is a former member of ABBA.

Cosmic Café Wollmar Yxkullsgatan 5B, Södermalm, opposite Mariatorget T-bana. A tiny, fun, wholefood vegetarian café with good-value salads, pastas and great fresh fruit milkshakes.

Mocco Kungholmensgatan 16, Rådhuset. Modishly decorated, airy café serving huge sandwiches and health-conscious salads.

Muggen Götgatan 28. Lively café/bar, good for snuggling up with a hot chocolate in winter or people-watching over lunch in summer.

String Café Nytorgsgatan 38, Södermalm. Laid-back retro café. Like the furniture? You can buy it. Good coffee, plus muffins, brownies and the like.

Vetakatten Kungsgatan 55. Elegant 1920s coffee house with glorious cakes, pastries and sandwiches and bags of old-world charm.

Restaurants

Creperie Fyra Knop Svartensgatan 4, Södermalm. Good-value crêpes are served in this dark, evocative restaurant which is fashionably tatty and plays the likes of Leonard Cohen.

Frapino Långholmsgatan 3, Hornstull. Fantastic pick'n'mix salads and good-value lunch deals.

Hermitage Stora Nygatan 11, Gamla Stan. Excellent vegetarian place with delicious fresh salads and breads as well as filling main courses.

Lasse i Parken Högalidsgatan 56, Södermalm. Beautiful café/restaurant in an eighteenth-century house with a pleasant garden. Hornstull T-bana.

Pontus by the Sea Skeppsbrokajen Tullhus 2. Loungy, decadent-looking bar/restaurant in a converted customs house, with a great lunch buffet and a glorious outdoor terrace area in summer. T-bana Slussen.

Drinking and nightlife

Many places that serve food during the day offer entertainment in the evening. As well as the weekend, Wednesday is an active night, and there will be queues at the more popular nightlife haunts. Live music venues charge 60–100kr admission.

Bars and pubs

Bar Nada Åsögatan 140. Discreetly hip Söder hang-out. They serve cheap, tapas-type snacks to soak up the drink.

Carmen Tjärhovsgatan 14. Amiably skuzzy SoFo bar with cheap beer.

East Stureplan 13, Östermalmstorg. Lively, busy bar/restaurant with a heated outdoor area, always packed at weekends when DJs play late into the night.

Indigo Götgatan 19. Small, gorgeously decorated bar frequented by indie kids, who just love the background music.

Marie Laveau Hornsgatan 66, Zinkensdamm. Chic bar/club, always busy at weekends, with a rota of DJ nights. Pricey food is available.

Söderkallaren Tjärhovsgatan 12, Södermalm. Great atmosphere, gloriously cheap drinks and winning music. Quintessentially Söder.

Live music and clubs

Berns Berzelii Park, Kungsträdgården, ⓦwww.berns.se. DJs and live music. The stunning decor here is a mix of nineteenth-century Baroque and the very latest Nordic designs. T-Bana Kungsträdgården.

Debaser Karl Johans Torg 1, ⓦwww.debaser.nu. One of Stockholm's best-known live music and DJ venues, attracting great local and international bands. T-bana Slussen/Gamla Stan.

Fredsgatan 12 Fredsgatan 12 ⓦwww.fredsgatan12.com. There's a posh restaurant at this address, but more importantly it's host during the summer to an excellent club where the young and well dressed gather to dance and drink on the crowded terrace.

Mosebacke Etablisement Mosebacke Torg 3 ⓦwww.mosebacke.se. *Etablisement* is a music and theatre venue featuring big international acts as well as local heroes. The sprawling terrace is one of the best places in town to hang out in summer, with barbecues and live music. T-bana Slussen.

StureCompagniet Sturegatan 4 ⓦwww.sturecompagniet.se. Terrific light show with house and techno sounds blaring on three floors of bars. T-bana Östermalmstorg.

Gay Stockholm

The city's main **gay centre**, RFSL, Sveavägen 57 (ⓣ08/50 16 29 50; T-bana Rådmansgatan), has information about the ever-changing bar and club scene in Stockholm and throughout the rest of the country.

Lino Södra Riddarholmshamnen 19, Riddarholmen ⓦwww.linoclub.com. Currently the hippest spot playing house and eighties/nineties hits. Sat till 3am.

Patricia Stadsgårdshamnen, Slussen ⓦwww.patricia.st. Drag shows, dancing and comedy on what was the Queen Mother's royal yacht. Also an excellent restaurant on the upper deck. Gay on Sun only. Slussen T-bana.

Side Track Wollmar Yxkullsgatan 7, Södermalm. Söder bar popular with leather and denim boys, though everyone is welcome.

Shopping

IKEA Modulvägen 1, Skärholmen. The Swedish design behemoth's flagship store. There's an hourly free bus service from Regeringsgatan.

Judits Hornsgatan 75. Truly fantastic second-hand clothes emporium with a wealth of great shoes and accessories at affordable prices. The menswear equivalent is just up the road.

Perry Come On! Bergsundstand 32, Hornstull. Small but perfectly formed collection of own-brand men's and women's wear.

Sound Pollution Stora Nygatan 16, Gamla Stan. Well-known Stockholm record shop, heavy on the heavy metal. A good place to pick up flyers for upcoming gigs.

Weekdays Götgatan 21. Stocks local jeans brand Cheap Monday and other designer items. On-site tailors can make adjustments for you.

Directory

Embassies Australia, Sergels Torg 12 ⓣ08/613 29 00; Canada, Tegelbacken 4 ⓣ08/453 30 00; Ireland, Östermalmsgatan 97 ⓣ08/661 80 05; UK, Skarpögatan 6–8 ⓣ08/671 30 00; US, Dag Hammarskjöldsväg 31 ⓣ08/783 53 00.

Hospital Medical Care Information ⓣ08/672 24 00.

Internet Funcity, Sveavägen 17; Laser Dome, Sveavägen 108; Matrix, Hötorget; Sidewalk Express, Central Station; The Plays, Slöjdgatan 2–4.

Laundry Tvättsmaten, Västmangatan 61 ⓣ08/34 64 80.

Left luggage Lockers in Central Station.

Pharmacy C.W. Scheele, Klarabergsgatan 64 ⓣ08/454 81 30 (24hr).

Post office There's no central post office, but you can send packages from Posten counters in branches of Åhlens and ICA.

Moving on

Train Copenhagen (5 daily; 5hr); Gothenburg (hourly; 3hr); Helsingborg (hourly, change at Lund;

5hr); Kiruna (2 daily; 17hr); Lund (hourly; 4hr 40min); Malmö (hourly; 4hr 30min); Mora (2 daily; 4hr); Oslo (2 daily; 6hr); Östersund (5 daily; 6hr); Uppsala (every 30min; 40min).
Ferry Helsinki (Helsingsfors), Finland (2 daily; 15hr); Tallinn, Estonia (3–4 weekly; 15hr); Turku (Åbo), Finland (4 daily; 13hr).

Around Stockholm

The pine-clad islands of Stockholm's **archipelago** make for a peaceful escape from the city. Or head to the charming, historic town of **Uppsala**, a short train ride away.

THE STOCKHOLM ARCHIPELAGO

For 80km east of the capital stretches the **Stockholm archipelago**, made up of 24,000 islands, most of which are little more than lumps of rock rising up from the sea. In summer, the area bristles with tourists, day-trippers, sailing boats and locals making use of their summer homes. If you're sticking around for a while, invest in a Båtluffakortet (300kr), a **pass** which entitles you to five days of unlimited transport around the islands; it's available at the tourist office, where you can also pick up a boat timetable. Or if time is short, take a **tour** (from 130kr; details available from the tourist office). Boats leave from Strömkajen near Slussen and run by Waxholmbolaget (ⓣ08/614 64 50, ⓦwww.waxholmsbolaget.se).

Vaxholm

Just 45km from Stockholm, **VAXHOLM** is one of the most accessible of the archipelago resorts; luckily it's also one of the prettiest. Approached from the water, the town is a charming, villagey cluster of red-roofed houses. You'll find the oldest buildings in the **North Harbour** area, some of which date back to the mid-seventeenth century, but the key architectural attraction is the **Vaxholm Fortress**, an imposing citadel that was in use as recently as World War II.

Vaxholm is actually reachable by car but it's worth taking the scenic **ferry** route instead (1hr). The **tourist office** is in the quaint Rådhuset (ⓣ08/541 314 80). It's a short journey back to Stockholm, but if you decide to **stay** overnight on the island there's a peaceful HI hostel (ⓣ08/541 750 60; dorms ❷) at Per Brahesväg 1, about 3km from the harbour.

Sandhamn

Two hours by boat from Stockholm, **SANDHAMN** is ringed with sandy beaches, the most popular of which is **Trouville**. If you're unlucky with the weather, the volunteer-run **Sandhamn Museum** (June–Aug daily 10am–5pm; free) is a good place to while away an hour examining fishing equipment and items confiscated from 1920s bootleggers; the eighteenth-century customs house is also worth a look. Otherwise, there's not much to do here but swim, sail, eat and drink – in summertime Sandhamn caters for all those needs very well.

Sandhamn can be visited in a day, but if you want to stay longer, opt for the **youth hostel** at Gammalgården (STF; ⓣ070/10 73 015; ❸), which has sixteen beds in a traditional red wooden house. Booking ahead is essential in high season.

UPPSALA

Forty minutes' train ride north of Stockholm, **UPPSALA** is regarded as the historical and religious centre of Sweden. Close to Arlanda airport, it's a tranquil alternative to the capital, with a delightful river-cut centre, not to mention an active student-geared nightlife.

What to see and do

The picturesque medieval town is a ten-minute walk from the train station. To reach the ancient settlement of **Gamla Uppsala**, about 5km north of town, take bus #2, #24 or #54, each of which run frequently from Kungsgatan.

The medieval town

At the centre of the medieval town is the truly beautiful **Domkyrkan** (daily 8am–6pm; free), Scandinavia's largest cathedral. It was consecrated in 1435, damaged in the fire of 1702 (which destroyed three-quarters of the city) and subsequently restored in the nineteenth century. Poke around and you'll find the tombs of Reformation rebel monarch Gustav Vasa and his son Johan III, and that of the great botanist Carl von Linné.

Opposite the cathedral, and very much worth a visit, is the **Gustavianum** (10/11am–4pm; 40kr), built in 1625 as part of the university and much touted for its atmospheric, beautifully reconstructed anatomical theatre. The same building houses small collections of Egyptian, Classical and Nordic antiquities and the **Uppsala University Museum**, which contains the Augsburg Art Cabinet, a monumentally kitsch monstrosity presented to Gustav II Adolf.

The **castle** (June–Aug English guided tours at 1pm & 3pm; 60kr) is worth a visit, although the 1702 fire did away with all but one side and two towers of this opulent palace.

Gamla Uppsala

At Gamla Uppsala, three huge **barrows**, atmospheric royal burial mounds dating back to the sixth century, mark the original site of Uppsala. This was a pagan settlement and a place of ancient sacrificial rites: every ninth year a festival demanded the death of nine men, hanged from a nearby tree until their corpses rotted. The pagan temple where this took place is marked by the Christian **Gamla Uppsala Kyrka** (daily 9am–4/6pm), built when the Swedish kings first took baptism in the new faith.

The worthwhile **Gamla Uppsala Museum** (Feb–April & Sept–Nov Wed, Sat & Sun noon–3pm; May–Aug daily 11am–5pm; 50kr) explains the origin of local myths from Roman times and Uppsala's era of greatness.

Arrival and information

Arrival Uppsala's train and bus stations are beside each other, not far from the tourist office.
Information The tourist office, at Fyris Torg 8 (Mon–Fri 10am–6pm, Sat 10am–3pm; mid-June to mid-Aug also Sun noon–4pm; ⓣ018/727 48 00, ⓦwww.uppland.nu), provides an English map and handout.

Accommodation

STF Uppsala Vadraren Hostel Vattholmavägen 16C ⓣ018/10 43 00, ⓔinfo@vandraren.com. Summer only and slightly further out than *Uppsala Vandrarhem City*. Dorms ❸
Uppsala Vandrarhem City Hostel St Persgatan 16 ⓣ018/24 20 08, ⓦwww.uppsalavandrarhem.se. Great value and central. Dorms ❷; rooms ❸

Eating and drinking

Cupido Inside Forum Gallerian, Forumtorget. Enormous, fresh takeaway salads with a huge choice of ingredients. A bargain.
Joel's Östra Ågatan 58. Authentically decorated 1950s retro café just by the river, serving US-style pancakes alongside coffee, sandwiches and more substantial dishes.
Ofvandahls Sysslomansgatan 5. Appealingly fusty and old-fashioned café, like a grandmotherly parlour, with cheap coffee, cakes and light lunches.
Svenssons Tavernan Sysslomansgatan 14. An Uppsala classic, and the best restaurant in town for Swedish traditional fare.

Moving on

Train Mora (2 daily; 2hr 15min), Östersund (3 daily; 4hr 30min); Stockholm (every 30min; 40min).

Southern Sweden

Southern Sweden is a nest of coastal provinces, extensive lake and forest regions, gracefully ageing cities and superb beaches. Much of the area, especially the southwest coast, is the target of Swedish holidaymakers, with a wealth of campsites and cycle tracks, yet it retains a sense of space and tranquillity; there are also some historical and cultural high points. The grandest coastal city is charming **Gothenburg**, well deserving exploration. South of here, **Helsingborg**, a stone's throw from Denmark, and **Malmö**, still sixteenth-century at its core, are both worth a day or two. **Lund**, a medieval cathedral and university town, lies conveniently between the two. The attractions of southeastern Sweden are generally less well known than the cities of the southwest; one exception is the attractive island of **Gotland**, whose beaches and bars are awash with visitors over the summer.

GOTHENBURG

Sweden's second city, **GOTHENBURG** (Göteborg) has an air of continental cosmopolitanism and a culture and nightlife scene to rival the capital. Beyond the industrial gloom of its shipyards, it's an attractive and relaxed place with broad avenues and an elegant canal system, designed in the seventeenth century by the Dutch for whom this was an important mercantile centre.

What to see and do

Most of Gothenburg's key sights are within strolling distance of each other, and the city's appealing bars and cafés allow for pleasant stop-offs along the way.

Old Gothenburg

The area defined by the central canal represents what's left of old Gothenburg, centring on **Gustav Adolfs Torg**, a windswept square flanked by the nineteenth-century **Börshuset** (Exchange Building), and the fine **Rådhus**, originally built in 1672. Around the corner, the **Kronhuset**, off Kronhusgatan, is a typical seventeenth-century Dutch construction. The cobbled courtyard outside is flanked by the mid-eighteenth-century **Kronhusbodarna** (Mon–Fri 11am–4pm, Sat 11am–2pm), now transformed into craft shops selling sweets and souvenirs. The **Stadsmuseum**, Norra Hamngatan 12 (daily 10am–5/8pm; closed Mon Sept–April; 40kr), is worth a visit for its rich collection of archeological, cultural and industrial exhibits.

Maritima Centrum and the Opera House

The **Maritima Centrum** (March–Oct daily 10am–4/6pm; 75kr) allows you to clamber aboard a destroyer and submarine moored at the quayside. It's worth coming down here just to look at the shipyards beyond, like a rusting Meccano set put into sharp perspective by the striking **Opera House** (daily noon–6pm), a graceful and imaginative ship-like structure.

Nya Elfsborg Fortress

Great views of the harbour and surrounding area can be had from the excursion boats that run from Lilla Bommen to the **Nya Elfsborg Fortress** (mid-May to Aug

TREAT YOURSELF

The modern, oddly beautiful **Gothenburg Opera House**, designed by Jan Izikowitz, is best experienced as a member of the audience, where you can appreciate the technical and acoustic whiz that has gone into the building. There's an eclectic schedule of contemporary and traditional ballet, opera and musicals; tickets start at 95kr for gallery seats (Ⓣ031/13 13 00 for tickets or check Ⓦwww.opera.se).

daily 9.30am–4.20pm; 110kr, including guided tour of fortress), a seventeenth-century island defence guarding the harbour entrance, whose surviving buildings have been turned into a museum and café.

Avenyn

South of the medieval centre, Kungsportsavenyn is Gothenburg's showiest thoroughfare. Known simply as **Avenyn**, this wide strip was once flanked by private houses fronted by gardens and is now lined with overpriced yet popular pavement restaurants and brasseries. About halfway down, the excellent **Röhsska Museum of Arts and Crafts** at Vasagatan 37–39 (daily except Mon 11am/noon–5pm, Tues till 8pm; 40kr) houses a vast collection of textiles, furniture and *objets d'art*, with an emphasis on Swedish design.

At the top end of Avenyn, **Götaplatsen** is the modern cultural centre of Gothenburg, home to a concert hall, theatre and **Art Museum** (daily except Mon 11am–5/6pm; Wed till 9pm; 40kr, free for under-20s). The enormous collections of the last include a good selection of Impressionist paintings, Pop Art and – most impressively – superb Swedish work in the Furstenburg galleries on the sixth floor.

Haga, Linnégatan and Liseberg

Just a few minutes' walk west of Avenyn, the old working-class district of **Haga** is now a picturesque area of gentrified chic with plenty of daytime cafés and boutiques. A few steps further, **Linnégatan** is a more charismatic and cosmopolitan version of Avenyn, with the most diverse places to eat, drink and stroll.

Five minutes' walk southeast of Götaplatsen, on the edge of the centre, is **Liseberg**, a surprisingly attractive amusement park (late April to early Oct; opening times vary; Åkpass 280kr for unlimited rides all day; Ⓦwww.liseberg.com) with some high-profile rides and acres of gardens, restaurants and fast food.

Arrival and information

Air Ryanair flights arrive at Gothenburg City airport, 17km north of the city; bus departures for Central Station are synchronized with flight arrivals (30min; 50kr). All other airlines arrive at Landvetter airport, 25km east (buses leave for the city every 15–20min; 75kr).
Train Trains arrive at Central Station on Drottningtorget, a five-minute walk from Gustav Adolfs Torg.
Bus Buses from all destinations use the Nils Ericsonsplatsen bus terminal, which adjoins Central Station.
Ferry Stena Line ferries from Frederikshavn in Denmark and Kiel in Germany dock within twenty minutes' walk of the centre. Trams #3 and #9 run past to the centre.
Information Gothenburg has two tourist offices: a kiosk (Mon–Fri 10am–6pm, Sat 10am–5pm, Sun noon–5pm) in Nordstan, the shopping centre next to Central Station, and a main office on the canal front at Kungsportsplatsen 2 (June–Aug daily 9.30am–6/8pm; rest of year Mon–Sat 9.30am–2/5pm; Ⓣ031/61 25 00, Ⓦwww.goteborg.com).
Discount passes The tourist office sells the Gothenburg Pass (225/310kr for 24/48hr), giving unlimited bus and tram travel, free or half-price museum entry and concessions including a free boat trip to Elfsborg Fortress and fifty-percent discount on a day-trip to Frederikshavn in Denmark.
Internet Gameonline, Magasinsgatan 26, and Game Net, at Viktoriagatan 22.

Accommodation

The tourist office's **Gothenburg Package** (from 530kr/person) gets you a room in a central hotel, with breakfast and a free Gothenburg Pass – book a minimum of four days ahead. The tourist office can also book **private rooms** (❷).

Göteborgs Vandrarhem Mölndalsvägen 23, Ⓦwww.goteborgsvandrarhem.se. This brisk, well-equipped hostel is one of Gothenburg's most central; take tram #4, direction towards Mölndal (stop: Getebergsäng). Dorms ❸; rooms ❻
Kärralund Camping Liseberg Olbergsgatan. Ⓦwww.liseberg.se. Busy site 4km from the centre, with all amenities, plus a youth hostel (dorms only) on site. From the city centre, hop on tram #5 to Welandergatan (direction: Torp). Tents ❷; dorms ❸
Kvibergs Kvibergsvägen 5 Ⓣ031/43 50 55, Ⓦwww.vandrarhem.com. Pleasant hostel with rooms only (no dorms), housed in an old barracks building and close to Gothenburg's largest weekend flea market – take tram #6, #7 or #11 to Kviberg (10min). ❺
Slottskogen Vegagatan 21 Ⓣ031/42 65 20, Ⓦwww.sov.nu. Well-appointed and sociable hostel in a lively part of town. Two minutes' walk from Linnégatan; take tram #1 or #6 to Olivedalsgatan. Dorms ❷; rooms ❻
Stigbergsliden Stigbergsliden 10 Ⓣ031/24 16 20, Ⓦwww.hostel-gothenburg.com. Comfortable hostel in a charming old house, close to Linné and the Stena ferry terminal. Tram lines #3, #9 and #11 from the city centre. Dorms ❷; rooms ❻

Eating

Casa Nostra Vegagatan 50. Buzzy trattoria serving Italian food at very reasonable prices.
Cyrano Prinsgatan 7. An authentic Provençal bistro that also does great-value pizza, this is a cracking local restaurant with a convivial atmosphere.
Junggrens Café Avenyn 37. This old-school, traditional café has been a Göteborg favourite for years, and the prices are surprisingly low for this part of town.
Konditori Kringlan Haga Nygatan 13. Filling lunches and a dazzling array of buns and pastries are served at this lovely, laid-back café.
Solrosen Kaponjärgatan 4. Classic vegetarian restaurant in Haga district that turns into a lively drinking venue at night.
Tintin Café Engelbrektsgatan 22, off Avenyn. This 24-hour, Tintin-themed café/restaurant is popular among students and late-night drinkers. A fun experience at 4am on a Saturday.

Drinking and nightlife

Jazzå Andra Långgatan 4b Ⓣ031/14 16 90. Newly renovated, jazz-flavoured bar with live music several nights a week.

Nefertiti Hvitfeldtsplatsen 6 Ⓦ www.nefertiti.se. The best place to see live jazz and world music, with impressive acts visiting from overseas as well as local bands.
Publik Andra Långgatan 20. Stripped-down decor and an underground feel. There's live music and poetry readings on occasion, plus the kitchen turns out some good, cheap dishes.
Pusterviksbaren Järntorgsgatan 14. Currently Gothenburg's hippest bar/club, with live music or DJs most nights and a friendly, unpretentious feel.

Moving on

Train Copenhagen (10 daily; 4hr); Helsingborg (10 daily; 2hr 40min); Lund (10 daily; 3hr 15min); Malmö (10 daily; 3hr 30min); Oslo (2 daily; 4hr); Stockholm (hourly; 3hr 30min–5hr).
Ferry Frederikshavn, Denmark (4–8 daily; 3hr 15min); Kiel, Germany (1 daily; 14hr).

HELSINGBORG

At **HELSINGBORG** only a narrow sound separates Sweden from Denmark; indeed, Helsingborg was Danish for most of the Middle Ages, with its castle controlling the southern regions of what is now Sweden. Fought over for centuries, the Swedes finally took it back for good in 1710, after which the battered town lay abandoned for almost two hundred years. Only in the nineteenth century, when the harbour was expanded and the railway constructed, did Helsingborg find new prosperity. Today, the dramatically redeveloped harbour area has breathed new life into this likeable, relaxed town.

What to see and do

Directly south of the North Harbour café-bars, the strikingly designed **Henry Dunker Cultural House** (daily except Mon 10am–5pm, till 8pm on Thurs; 70kr), Kungsgatan 11, named after the city's foremost industrialist benefactor, aims to provide a full vision of Helsingborg's history. East from Hamntorget and the harbours, the massive, neo-Gothic **Rådhus** marks the bottom of **Stortorget**, the long thin square sloping up to the lower battlements of what's left of Helsingborg's castle, the **kärnan** or keep (June–Aug daily 11am–7pm; Sept–May daily except Mon 9/11am–3/4pm; 20kr), a fourteenth-century brick tower, the only survivor from the original fortress. The views from the top are worth the entrance fee although you don't miss much from the lower (free) battlements. Off Stortorget, along **Norra Storgatan** are Helsingborg's oldest buildings, attractive seventeenth- and eighteenth-century merchants' houses with quiet courtyards.

Arrival and information

Arrival Apart from the HH Ferries passenger ferry from Helsingør (Denmark), which pulls up across an arm of the docks, and the Acelink ferries, which arrive on Hamntorget, all ferries, trains and buses arrive at Knutpunkten, the harbourside central terminal.
Tourist office It's just a couple of minutes' walk from the central terminal to the tourist office inside the town hall at the corner of Stortorget and Järnvägsgatan (Mon–Fri 9/10am–6/8pm, Sat 9/10am–2/5pm; mid-June to Aug also Sun 10am–3pm; Ⓣ 042/10 43 50, Ⓦ www.helsingborg.se), which has free city maps and masses of brochures.

Accommodation

Helsingsborg Vandrarhem Cheap, central and very comfortable youth hostel. Dorms ❷ (May–July only); rooms ❺
Miatorps Vandrarhem Planteringsvägen 69-71 Ⓣ 042/13 11 30, Ⓦ www.stfvandrarhem.helsingborg.nu. Inconveniently located but clean and pleasant hostel. Get bus #1 from the centre. Dorms ❸; rooms ❺
Råå Camping Kustgatan, Råå Vallar Ⓣ 042/10 76 80, Ⓦ www.camping.se. Pretty waterfront site 5km south of Helsingborg. Take bus #1 from outside the Rådhus. ❸
Villa Thalassa Drottninggatan Ⓣ 042/38 06 60, Ⓦ www.villathalassa.com. Bright, welcoming hostel 4km from town; take bus #219. Dorms ❸; rooms ❻

Eating

Café Annorledes Södra Storgatan 15. The loopily traditional decor includes mannequins dressed in vintage clothes. Coffee, cakes and sandwiches at low prices.

Ebbas Fik Bruksgatan 20. Meticulously authentic 1950s/60s retro café, decked out in genuine memorabilia. Decent light lunches, snacks and good coffee.

K & Co Nedre Långvinkelsgatan 5. Gorgeous wallpaper and even better salads, sandwiches and coffee, made with professional dedication.

Papadam Bruksgatan 10. Centrally located Indian restaurant with a good selection of balti and biriyani dishes.

Drinking and nightlife

Bara Vara Nedre Långvinkelsgatan 15. Great decor, fun atmosphere and a good selection of cocktails too. Open summer only Thurs–Sat only.

Tempel Bruksgatan 2. Busy, upmarket DJ bar with late-night opening and a dressy crowd at weekends.

The Tivoli Hamntorget 11. By day, it's a café/restaurant; by night, this is where you'll get the best in Swedish and international dance and indie music, plus live bands.

Moving on

Train Gothenburg (10 daily; 2hr); Lund (hourly; 40min); Malmö (hourly; 45min).

Ferry Helsingør, Denmark (3 hourly; 25min).

LUND

Forty minutes by train south of Helsingborg and fifteen minutes from Malmö, **LUND** is a beautiful university town. Its picturesque medieval centre has a unique buzz when the students are around.

What to see and do

Lund's weather-beaten **Domkyrkan** (Mon–Fri 8am–6pm, Sat & Sun 9.30am–5/6pm; free), consecrated in 1145, is considered by many to be Scandinavia's finest medieval building. Its plain interior culminates in a delicate, semicircular apse with a gleaming fifteenth-century altarpiece and a mosaic of Christ surrounded by angels – although what draws most attention is a fourteenth-century astronomical clock, revealing an ecclesiastical Punch and Judy show (daily Mon–Sat noon & 3pm, Sun 1pm & 3pm).

Outside the cathedral, **Kyrkogatan**, lined with staunch, solid, nineteenth-century civic buildings, leads into the main square, **Stortorget**, off which **Kattesund** is home to a glassed-in set of excavated medieval walls. Adjacent at Kattesund 6 is the **Drottens Museum** (Mon–Fri 9am–4pm, Sat 10am–2pm, Sun noon–4pm; 30kr), the remains of a medieval church in the basement of another modern building, but the real interest is in the powerful atmosphere of the old streets behind the Domkyrkan. In this web of streets, **Kulturen** (mid-April to Sept daily 11am–5pm; Oct to mid-April daily except Mon noon–4pm; 50kr) is a village in itself of indoor and open-air collections of southern Swedish art, silverware, ceramics and musical instruments. Finish off your meanderings with a visit to the **Botaniska Trädgård** (daily 6am–8pm; free) just beyond, an extensive botanical garden.

Arrival and information

Train Trains arrive on the western edge of town, an easy walk from the centre.

Tourist office Opposite the Domkyrkan at Kyrkogatan 11, and well signposted from the train station (June–Aug Mon–Fri 10am–6pm, Sat & Sun 10am–2pm; Sept–May Mon–Fri 10am–5pm; May & Sept also Sat 10am–2pm; ⓣ046/35 50 40, ⓦwww.lund.se).

Internet is available at the city library, St Petri Kyrkogata 6.

Accommodation

Lund makes an appealing alternative stopover to Malmö or Helsingborg. The tourist office can book **private rooms** (❸, plus a 50kr booking fee).

Tåget Vävaregatan 22 ⓣ046/14 28 20, ⓦwww.trainhostel.com. This unusual HI hostel packs you into three-tiered sleeping compartments of six 1940s carriages parked on a branch line behind the train station; turn right and follow the signs. Dorms ❸

Eating

Café Ariman Kungsgatan 2. Student café/bar with a shabby, left-wing coffee-house appeal and good, cheap food. Open late at weekends.

Coffee Point Skomakergatan 5. Agreeable, cosy café serving coffee, cakes and cheap light lunches.
Conditori Lundagård Kyrkogatan 17. The classic student café, in traditional Swedish style. Tasty cakes and coffee.
Tegnérs Sandgatan 2. Classy restaurant next to the student union that serves really fine food at surprisingly reasonable prices.

Drinking and nightlife

The best of Lund's nightlife is confined to university clubs and hang-outs – if you want to experience this side of the city, you'll have to find a friendly student.
Basilika Stora Södergatan 13. Popular club with some excellent indie, electro and hip hop nights. Minimum age 22.
Herkules Bar/Stortorget Stortorget 1. DJ bar and a café/restaurant rolled into one. Attractively furnished interior and pleasant outdoor seating in summer.

Moving on

Train Gothenburg (10 daily; 2hr 40min); Helsingborg (hourly; 40min); Malmö (4 daily; 15min).

MALMÖ

The startlingly pretty city of MALMÖ has been the centre of a tug-of-war between Sweden and Denmark for much of its history, and in many ways is as Danish as it is Swedish. It's a handsome place, with a cobbled medieval core that has a lived-in, workaday feel, worlds apart from the staid quality of many other Swedish town centres. With the construction of **Øresund Link**, a sensational seventeen-kilometre-long road and rail bridge, and an influx of immigrants from Europe and beyond, Malmö really has become the Swedish gateway from continental Europe. With that it is enjoying an economic revival.

What to see and do

The city's canals, parks and largely pedestrianized streets and squares make it a great place to stroll around. Most of the city's sights are squeezed into the compact centre, bounded on all sides by the canal. South of the old centre is the bohemian district of Möllevångstorget, where you'll find many of the best places to eat and drink.

Stortorget

Most of the medieval centre was taken apart in the early sixteenth century to make way for **Stortorget**, a vast market square. It's as impressive today as it must have been when it first appeared, flanked on one side by the **Rådhus**, built in 1546 and covered with statuary and spiky accoutrements; there are tours of the well-preserved interior (check with the tourist office for times).

Södergatan, Malmö's main pedestrianized shopping street, runs south from here towards the canal. Behind the Rådhus stands the **St Petri Kyrka** (daily 10am–6pm; free), a fine Gothic church with an impressively decorative pulpit and a four-tiered altarpiece.

Lilla Torg

A late-sixteenth-century spin-off from Stortorget, **Lilla Torg** is everyone's favourite part of the city – indeed, it's been voted the most popular square in Sweden. Lined with cafés and restaurants, it's usually pretty crowded. The southern side of the square is formed by a row of mid-nineteenth-century brick and timber warehouses; the shops around here sell books, antiques and gifts, though the best place to call into is the nearby **Saluhallen**, an excellent indoor market.

Malmöhus

A ten-minute walk west of Lilla Torg lies the **Malmöhus** (daily 10am/noon–4pm; 40kr), a low fortified castle defended by a wide moat, two circular keeps and grassy ramparts. Built by Danish king Christian III in 1536, the castle was later used for a time as a prison, but it now houses the **Malmö Museums**, a network of exhibitions on everything from geology to photography – and an aquarium, too. The pleasant grounds, the **Kungsparken**, are peppered with small lakes and an old windmill.

The Turning Torso

Follow the road round about 1.5km to the northern end of the city and you'll arrive at Malmö's most recent high-profile acquisition, the **Turning Torso** – a white skyscraper wrapped around itself. Completed in 2005, the 190-metre structure is Scandinavia's tallest building. The Turning Torso Gallery next door shows a short film on the tower and its architect, Santiago Calatreva.

Arrival and information

Air Malmö Sturup airport is 30km southeast of the city; buses to the centre are timed to coincide with flights (45min; 95kr).
Train All rail traffic arrives at Central Station, including the local Pågatåg services that run from Helsingborg and Lund (rail passes are valid). The train station also has showers (20kr) and beds (5.30am–11pm; 25kr/hour).
Bus The main bus terminal is outside Central Station, in Centralplan.
Tourist office Inside the station (Mon–Fri 9am–5/6/7pm, Sat 9/10am–2/3/5pm; May–Sept also Sun 10am–3/5pm; ⓣ040/34 12 00, ⓦwww.malmo.se/turist). They sell the Malmo Card (see below).
Discount passes The Malmö Card (130kr/160kr/190kr for one/two/three days) gives free museum entry, free travel on city buses, free car parking in public places, a free sightseeing tour by bus and ten percent off the airport bus.
Internet Surfer's Paradise, Amiralsgatan 14, or Cyber Space, Engelbrektsgatan 13a.

Accommodation

Bosses Gästvåningar Södra Förstadsgatan 110b ⓣ040/32 62 50, ⓦwww.bosses.se. A comfortable B&B, twenty-minutes' walk south from the station or bus #15 or #20 to Södervärn.
Malmö City Hostel Rönngatan 1 ⓣ040/611 62 20. Bright, comfortable and well-equipped STF hostel 1km south of the centre in a great location for nightlife and shops. Dorms ❷; rooms ❺
Malmö STF Vandrarhem Backavägen 18 ⓣ040/822 20. The city's second STF hostel is rather more inconveniently located, about 4km from the centre of town – take bus #21 from Central Station. Dorms ❸; rooms ❻
Sibbarps Camping Strandgatan 101 ⓣ040/15 51 65. Idyllic waterside campsite not far from the Øresund Link. Bus #12B from Central Station. ❸

Eating

Bageri Café Saluhallen, off Lilla Torg. Stop off here at lunchtime to buy filled baguettes and bagels.
Café Siesta Hjorttackegatan 1, off Lilla Torg. A fun café serving filling if pricey sandwiches and home-made apple cake.
Di Penco Roskildevägen 3, 1km southwest of the centre. Excellent, authentic fresh pasta and fantastic desserts are dished up at this homely Italian restaurant.
Krua Thai Möllevångstorget 12–14. Unlicensed Thai restaurant – the food is good and the portions are big; prices start at around 60kr.
Red Dog Södra Förstadsgatan 84a. Cheap and cheerful, studenty café with sandwiches from 35kr and wireless Internet.
Solde Regemensgatan 2, along the canal just south of the old centre. Cute, playfully decorated café where the staff are pretty serious about their coffee.

Drinking and nightlife

Debaser Norra Parkgatan 2 ⓦwww.debaser.nu. The Malmö branch of this popular Stockholm club/venue opened in 2007. Live music, DJ nights, dancing and drinking until late into the night.
Mello Yello Lilla Torg 1. The best of Lilla Torg's many bar/restaurants, though there's not so much to choose between them.
Mrs Brown Storgatan 26 ⓣ040/97 22 50. Beautifully designed bar/restaurant with expensive cocktails and even more expensive food.
Möllan Bergsgatan 37. Somewhere halfway between a pub and a bar, with outdoor seating and good, reasonably priced food.
Wonk Amiralsgatan 20 ⓦwww.wonk.se. Popular and unforgettably named gay club (Sat only).

Moving on

Train Copenhagen (4 daily; 35min); Gothenburg (10 daily; 2hr 45min); Helsingborg (at least hourly; 50min); Lund (at least hourly; 15min); Oslo (1 daily; 8hr)

GOTLAND: VISBY

Ninety kilometres off the east coast lies the island of **Gotland**, packed with historical intrigue, lined with great beaches, and one of Sweden's most popular summer spots. The island's quaint, cobbled main town, **VISBY** has been buffeted around by history, passing through German, Danish, Russian and Swedish rule, and enjoying time in the limelight as a trading centre as far back as 900 AD. These days, it's settled into a rather more sedate role as a tourist destination and summer playground for everyone from urban surfers to cottage-owning grandparents. Bustling and vibrant in the summer, when the surrounding beaches come into their own, and darkly atmospheric during the long winter, Visby is definitely worth a visit.

What to see and do

Visby is dominated by its ten ruined churches and ringed by a partially preserved, 3.4-kilometre medieval wall. The **tourist office** is close to the ferry terminal – pick up a map here to help you navigate the historic town's warren of cobbled alleyways and squares.

The fragmented walls of **St Hans** on **St Hansgatan** are your first glimpse of Visby's old churches – a photogenic ruin with an outdoor café in summer. Just west of here, the **Art Museum** at St Hansgatan 21 (daily 11am/noon–5pm; closed Mon Oct–May; 50kr) includes a selection of paintings by nineteenth-century Canadian artist William Blair Bruce, who lived and worked in Gotland. Practically next door, the **Gotlands Fornsal** (May to mid-Sept daily 10am–5pm, mid-Sept to April daily except Mon noon–4pm; 75kr) is an attractive museum with exhibitions on the history of the island, including archeological finds from the Viking era.

Back on St Hansgatan, it's a short walk to **Stora Torget**, Visby's picturesque, café-lined main square; it's dominated by the impressive St Katarina ruin. Close by, thirteenth-century **St Maria Cathedral** (daily 8am–6.30/9pm; free) has a glorious medieval interior. The stained-glass windows are modern, but just as impressive as the rest of the building.

Arrival and information

Air The airport is 5km north of Visby. An infrequent bus service runs into the centre of town; taxis should cost 120–150kr.

Bus The main bus terminal is beyond the town wall to the southeast, on Kung Magnus väg.

Ferry Ferries arrive at the harbour just by Skeppsbron.

Tourist office Skeppsbron 4–6, near the ferry terminal (mid-June to mid-Aug daily 8am–7pm, mid-Aug to mid-June Mon–Fri 8am–5pm, Sat & Sun 10am–4pm; ⓣ0498/20 17 00, ⓦwww.gotland.info).

Internet Gamecenter, Hamngatan 4.

Accommodation

Kanonen Hostel Langsväg 2 ⓣ0498/29 96 90. Basic but useful hostel in an activity centre, complete with a bowling alley. ❸

Visby Prison Hostel Skeppsbron 1 ⓣ0498/20 50 60, ⓦwww.gotland.net/visbyfangelse. Striking but shabby youth hostel in a converted prison, with laundry and kitchen facilities. The dorms face onto a courtyard and the showers are just across – not great in bad weather. Dorms ❸; rooms ❼

Visby STF Youth Hostel Alléskolan, Faltgatan 30 ⓣ0498/26 98 42. Well-equipped summer hostel with kitchen, laundry and TV (late June to early Aug only). Dorms ❷; rooms ❹

Visby Strandby & Snäcks Camping Holiday houses and a pleasant campsite just beside Snäckviken beach, about 4km from the town centre. ❷

Eating and drinking

Café Vinegar Hästgatan 3. This stylish café/bar is popular with locals, perhaps because its modern decor is a respite from Visby's olde-worlde charm.

Effes Ådelsgatan 2. A cross between a mildly hippy-dippy restaurant – serving a bountiful lunch buffet – and an atmospheric bar, with DJs and live music. The building is ancient – it's attached to the town wall and used to be a prison.

Köpmannen Il Walters plats 7. Light, airy restaurant with reasonably priced seasonal specials and good, cheap pizzas.

GETTING TO GOTLAND

Visby is accessible by **ferry** from the mainland ports of **Nynäshamn**, a one-hour train ride south of Stockholm, and **Oskarhamn**, five hours by train from Gothenburg. Both crossings take around three hours and are run by Destination Gotland (☎0771/22 33 00, Ⓦwww.destinationgotland.se). For the cheapest fares (one-way tickets start at 180kr for students or 236kr for non-students), book 21 days in advance; regular fares cost around 25 percent more.

Two **airlines**, Gotlandsflyg (Ⓦwww.gotlandsflyg.se) and Skyways (Ⓦwww.skyways.se) fly to Gotland, with services all year round from Stockholm (Bromma, Arlanda and Skavsta airports) and summer flights from Gothenburg and cities as far afield as Oslo and Helsinki. The cheapest single fares start at 289kr.

Munkkallaren Stora Torget. This Visby nightlife stalwart is an eccentric complex of twelve rooms with a thrown-together feel. The options here range from the lovably eccentric *Vinyl Bar* to a traditional restaurant.

Strykjärnet Wallersplats 3. Tiny, monochrome creperie with an emphasis on organic and local ingredients. Sweet and savoury crepes, with main courses coming in at around 100kr. Closed Mon.

Central Sweden

The rural Sweden of most visitors' imaginations begins in the central provinces: vast tracts of forest, peaceful lakes and log cabins. On the eastern side, Sweden's coast forms one edge of the Gulf of Bothnia, with its jumble of erstwhile fishing towns and squeaky-clean contemporary urban planning. To the west, folklorish **Dalarna** province is the most picturesque region, with sweeping green countryside and inhabitants who maintain a cultural heritage (echoed in contemporary handicrafts and traditions) that goes back to the Middle Ages. This is the place to spend midsummer, particularly Midsummer's Night (June 21) when the whole region erupts in celebration. The **Inlandsbanan**, the great Inland Railway, cuts right through this area from Lake Siljan through the modern lakeside town of **Östersund** and above into the Arctic Circle.

DALARNA

The **Dalarna** region is the spiritual home of the little red cottage and holds a special, misty-eyed place in the Swedish heart. It's especially appealing in summer and spring, when its sparkling lakes and rolling hills are postcard-pretty. **Lake Siljan**, at the heart of the province, is the major draw, its gentle surroundings, traditions and local handicrafts weaving a subtle spell.

Leksand

At the southern tip of Lake Siljan, **LEKSAND** is perhaps the most popular and traditional of the Dalarna villages and certainly worth making the effort to reach at midsummer. This is a big deal all over Sweden, but a particularly big deal here, when the festivals recall age-old maypole dances, the celebrations culminating in the **church boat races**, an aquatic procession of decorated longboats which the locals once rowed to church every Sunday.

The **tourist office** in the train station building (Mon–Fri 10am–5/7pm, Sat 10am–2/5pm; ☎0247/79 61 30, Ⓦwww.siljan.se) has lots of information on the area, as does the **hostel** (☎0247/152 50; ❷) at Parkgattu 6, 2km south of the centre at Parkgården.

Mora

If you've only got time to see part of the lake, **MORA** is as good a place as any, and a starting point for the Inlandsbanan rail route (see overleaf). At the northwestern corner of Lake Siljan, the little town is a showcase for the work of Anders Zorn, the Swedish painter who lived in Mora and whose work is exhibited in the **Zorn Museum**, Vasagatan 36 (mid-May to mid-Sept Mon–Sat 9am–5pm, Sun 11am–5pm; rest of year Mon–Sat noon–5pm; 60kr), along with his small but well-chosen personal collection. Zorn's oils reflect a passion for Dalarna's pastoral lifestyle, but it's his earlier watercolours of southern Europe and North Africa that really stand out.

Mora's **tourist office** (Mon–Fri 10am–5pm, Sat 10am–2pm, closed Sun; ⓣ0250/59 20 20, ⓦwww.siljan.se) is at the train station, and the central HI **hostel** is at Fredsgatan 6 (ⓣ0250/381 96, ⓔinfo@maalkullann.se; ❷).

THE INLANDSBANAN

The **Inlandsbanen** (Inland Railway), which cuts a route through 1300km of Sweden's best-looking scenery, ranks amongst the most enthralling of European train journeys. The quaint, toy-like line, which turned 100 in 2007, links central Sweden with Gällivare in the north, a two-day trip if attempted without a break.

The railway (ⓣ0771/53 53 53, ⓦwww.inlandsbanan.se) operates between mid-June and mid-September only. InterRail pass holders under the age of 26 travel for free. With a ScanRail Pass there is a 25-percent discount off an Inland Railway Card (otherwise 1395kr), which offers unlimited travel on the line for fourteen days. The full second-class fare from Östersund to Gällivare is 762kr, plus an optional 50kr seat reservation.

Orsa

The Inlandsbanan, having begun in Mora (see p.1173), makes its first stop at **ORSA**, fifteen minutes up the line, where the nearby **Grönklitt Bear Park** (mid-May to mid-Sept daily 10am–3/6pm; 140kr) provides the best chance to see the bears that roam the countryside. The STF **hostel** at the park (ⓣ0250/462 00; ❹) has good facilities.

Östersund

The Inlandsbanan's halfway point is marked by **ÖSTERSUND**. It's a very provincial but welcoming town, and the **Storsjön** (Great Lake) gives it a holiday atmosphere unusual this far north. The lake is also alleged to be the home of a Loch Ness-style monster and its child.

The main thing to do in town is to visit **Jamtli** (11am–5pm; closed Mon Sept–May; 90kr), an impressive, partly open-air **museum**, fifteen minutes' walk north from the centre along Rådhusgatan. There are some gripping displays, housed in a sleek if very gloomy series of exhibition rooms, along with some rather twee re-creations of traditional village life, complete with costumed guides. The museum's key exhibits are the ninth-century **Överhogdal tapestries**, whose simple handwoven patterns of horses, dogs and other beasts are quite breathtaking.

From the **harbour** you can take the bridge over the lake to the rather idyllic **Frösön** island, site of the original Viking settlement here.

Arrival and information

Train It's a five-minute walk north into the centre from Ostersund Central train station.

Bus The main bus station is on Gustavs III Torg, off Rådhusgatan.

Tourist office Rådhusgatan 44 (Mon–Fri 9am–5pm; June–Aug until 7/8pm and also Sat & Sun 10am–3/7pm; ⓣ063/14 40 01, ⓦwww.turist.ostersund.se).They sell the Östersundskortet, valid for three days (June–Aug; 270kr), giving free access to the town's sights, free bike rental and other discounts.

Internet There's free Internet in the municipal library on Rådhusgatan, opposite the bus station.

Accommodation

Fornborgen Youth Hostel Fornborgensvägen 15 ⓣ063/341 30, ⓔmicke2@algonet.se. Spacious, likeable STF hostel on the island of Frösön. Dorms ❷, rooms ❹

Frösö Camping ⓣ063/432 54. The most picturesque of Östersund's campsites. June–early Aug only; bus #3 or #4 from the centre. ❶

Jamtli Hostel ⓣ063/12 20 60, ⓔvandrarhemmet@jamtli.com. Quaint, appealing hostel in the grounds of Jamtli museum. Booking ahead is essential in summer. ❷

Eating and drinking

Captain Cook Hamngatan 9. Wood-panelled drinking haunt and restaurant – mains around 100kr – with a jumble of memorabilia on the walls. Live music on Wed.

News Samuel Permansgatan 9. Possibly Östersund's nicest hang-out, this breezy, attractively designed bar serves decent food and fills up at the weekend with a young crowd.

Wedermarks Café Prästgatan 27. Popular, congenial, traditional café with a cosy downstairs lunch bar and an elegant upstairs seating area.

Moving on

Train Stockholm (5 daily; 6hr); Uppsala (3 daily; 4hr 30min).

Northern Sweden

The long wedge of land that comprises **northern Sweden** – Swedish Lapland – is the wildest, strangest part of the country, worlds away from the busy and cosmopolitan south. The Inlandsbanan continues as far up as Gällivare, making for a stunning train journey through a mostly unpopulated region of lakes and forests – watch out for reindeer beside the track. The Sámi reindeer herders who were once the sole inhabitants here are still in evidence in the settlement at **Arvidsjaur**, and in **Jokkmokk**, where a handful of museums are dedicated to preserving their rather fragile cultural heritage. Many visitors to the far north will be heading straight for **Kiruna**, close to which the justly celebrated **Icehotel** makes for a fascinating if chilly sight, or even a once-in-a-lifetime stay if you're feeling rich.

ARVIDSJAUR

Deep in Lapland, 1000km from Stockholm, **ARVIDSJAUR** contains Sweden's oldest surviving Sámi village, **Lappstaden,** dating from the late eighteenth century. Today's huddle of houses was once the centre of a great winter market. They were not meant to be permanent homes, but rather a meeting place during festivals, and the last weekend in August is still taken up by a great celebratory shindig.

There's a cosy private **hostel,** *Lappugglans Turistviste,* at Västra Skolgatan 9 (ⓣ0960/124 13), ⓔlappugglan@hem.utfors.se, ❷), and *Camp Gielas* (ⓣ0960/55 600; ❷), beside one of the lakes 1km south of the station, which has cabins from 670kr. The **tourist office** (Mon–Fri 8.30am–noon & 1–4.30pm; June to mid-Aug daily 9.30am–6pm; ⓣ0960/175 00; ⓦwww.polcirkeln.nu) is at Östra Skolgatan 18c.

JOKKMOKK

Three and a half hours north of Arvidsjaur, the Inlandsbanan finally crosses the **Arctic Circle**, signalled by a bout of whistle-blowing as the train pulls up. Painted white rocks curve away over the hilly ground, a crude but popular representation of the Circle. Seven kilometres on, in the midst of remote, densely forested, marshy country, **JOKKMOKK** is a welcome oasis.

Once wintertime Sámi quarters, the town is today a renowned handicraft centre, with a Sámi educational college keeping the language and culture alive. The **Ájtte Museum** (Mon–Fri 9/10–4/6pm, Sat & Sun 9am/noon–4/6pm; Oct–April closed Sat; 50kr) on Kyrkgatan is the place to see some of the intricate work. Have a glance, too, at the so-called **Lapp Kyrka**, enclosed by a wide wooden fence, in which corpses were interred during winter, waiting for the thaw when the Sámi could go out and dig graves.

The great **winter market** still survives, now nearly 400 years old, held on the first Thursday, Friday and Saturday of each February. It's the best and busiest time to be in Jokkmokk, and staying means booking accommodation a good six months in advance. A smaller, less traditional autumn fair at the end of August is an easier option.

The **tourist office** is at Stortorget 4 (mid-June to mid-Aug daily 9am–6pm; mid-Aug to mid-June Mon–Fri 8.30am–4pm; ⓣ0971/222 50, ⓦwww.turism.jokkmokk.se). In summer there should be no problem getting a place at the friendly HI **hostel** at Åsgatan 20 (ⓣ0971/559 77; ❷); just follow the signs from the station. Jokkmokk has two **campsites:** *Jokkmokk Camping Centre* is 3km east on route 97, and *Skabram Stugby Camping* is 3km west on route 747.

KIRUNA

If you're arriving by train from Norway, the dourly industrial town of **KIRUNA**, 145km north of the Arctic Circle, may well be your first stop. Kiruna has lately achieved modest international fame after it was announced that portions of the town would have to be moved 4km northwest, to avoid them collapsing into the ever-expanding **iron ore mine** beneath. Residents have taken this news in their stride, as the mine has always been the reason for Kiruna's existence – it's now the biggest of its kind in the world.

What to see and do

The whittled-down mountain of **Kiirunavaara** that crowns the **mine** still dominates the town. Guided tours of the mine (daily 11am & 3pm; book at the tourist office; 200kr), run by LKAB, the mining company, are truly fascinating and slightly spooky.

Another unusual day-trip from Kiruna is to **Esrange**, a civilian space centre that launches and monitors satellites (tours in English Tues & Thurs 9.15am; book at the tourist office; 390kr). Anyone who had even the most passing childhood interest in astronauts and spaceships will enjoy this glimpse into a genuine scientific workplace.

Arrival and information

Air Kiruna airport is 9km from the city. An airport bus runs during the summer; otherwise take a shared taxi (125kr/person).

Train The train station is at the western edge of town, on Bangårdsvägen. It's a ten-minute uphill walk into the centre from here.

Bus The bus station is at the top of Skolgatan.

Tourist office Right in the town centre, on the main square at Lars Janssonsgatan 17 (Mon–Fri 8.30am–5/6/8pm; Sat till 3/6pm; open Sun till 5pm mid-June to mid-Aug; ⓣ0980/188 80, ⓦwww.lappland.se).

Accommodation

Camp Ripan Campingvägen 5 ⓣ0980/630 00, ⓦwww.ripan.se. Boisterous family-oriented campsite with an on-site restaurant and swimming pool. You can even hire an igloo for the night (❾). Camping ❷; cabins ❾

Kiruna Youth Hostel Bergmästaregatan 7 ⓣ0980/171 95, ⓦwww.logimaklaren.se. Sociable and well-equipped STF hostel just round the corner from the bus station, with TV, sauna and kitchen facilities. Dorms ❷, rooms ❺

Yellow House Hantverkaregatan 25 ⓣ0980/137 50, ⓦwww.yellowhouse.nu. Popular independent hostel across not one but two yellow houses. Advance booking recommended. Dorms ❷, rooms ❺

Eating and drinking

Momma's Steakhouse Lars Janssonsgatan 15. Rowdy bar/restaurant in the *Scandic Hotel* with live music on Wed. Drinks are pricier than you'd expect.

O'Leary's Föreningsgatan 11. This uninspiring chain pub/restaurant is one of the liveliest nightlife choices in Kiruna, with friendly staff and a good if greasy food menu.

Safari Attractive, cosy café serving buns, coffee and sandwiches, near the bus station. Outdoor terrace in summer. Closed Sun.

Moving on

Train Narvik (Norway; 2 daily; 3hr); Stockholm (2 daily; 17hr).

THE ICEHOTEL AND JUKKASJÄRVI

Seventeen kilometres east of Kiruna, in the small village of **JUKKASJÄRVI**, the **Icehotel** (early Dec to mid-April; ⓣ0980/66 800, ⓦwww.icehotel.com; ❾) has achieved near-legendary status. Made from locally cut ice and designed by a different architect every year, the hotel is a fairytale fantasy.

Guests spend just one night in the sub-zero temperatures within the ice structure (around –5°C, compared with –20°C to –30°C outside), before retreating to conventional rooms. The overnight stay should be a perilous affair, but the hotel manages to strike the right balance between survival measures – you sleep on reindeer skins in sleeping bags used by the Swedish army – and creature comforts, and many guests even report an excellent night's sleep.

Just up the road from the hotel at Marknadsvägen 11, the **Sami Museum** (June–Aug, 10am–6pm; 90kr) is also well worth a visit. Enthusiastic Sami guides will show you around reconstructed Sami housing, and there's a reindeer enclosure where you can get close enough to feed and pet these odd-looking beasts.

Bus 501 makes the twenty-minute journey from Kiruna to Jukkasjärvi.

Switzerland

HIGHLIGHTS

ZÜRICH: trendy bars, cutting-edge clubs and a beautiful medieval old town

LAUSANNE: lively and extremely hilly town in a beautiful setting on Lake Geneva

JUNGFRAU REGION: chocolate-box mountain views plus unlimited skiing and adventure sports

WORLD'S HIGHEST BUNGEE JUMP: a death-defying 220m off the Verzasca Dam

THE MATTERHORN: towering, world-famous mountain peak, with guaranteed skiing and snowboarding year-round

ROUGH COSTS

DAILY BUDGET basic €45/ occasional treat €70

DRINK BEER €2.50

FOOD FONDUE €13.20

HOSTEL/BUDGET HOTEL €18/ €66

TRAVEL Geneva–Zürich (2hr 45min) €46; Luzern–Interlaken Ost (1hr 50min) €17.50

FACT FILE

POPULATION 7.4 million

AREA 41,293 sq km

LANGUAGE German, French, Italian, Romansch

CURRENCY Swiss Franc (Fr.)

CAPITAL Bern (population: 128, 041)

INTERNATIONAL PHONE CODE ⓣ41

Basics

All the quaint stereotypes are true – cheese, chocolate, clocks, obsessive punctuality – but there's much more to Switzerland than this. The major cities are cosmopolitan and vibrant; transport links are excellent; and the scenery will take your breath away. Switzerland is diverse and multilingual – almost everyone speaks some English along with at least one of the official languages (German, French, Italian, and, in the south-east, Romansh).

The most visited Alpine area is the picturesque **Bernese Oberland**, but the loftiest Alps are further south, where the Toblerone-peaked **Matterhorn** looms above **Zermatt**. In the southeast, forested mountain slopes surround chic **St Moritz**. Of the northern German-speaking cities, **Zürich** has tons of sightseeing and nightlife and provides easy access to the tiny principality of **Liechtenstein** on the Rhine. **Basel** and the capital **Bern** are quieter, each with an attractive historic core, while **Luzern** lies in an appealing setting of lakes and mountains. In the French-speaking west, the cities of **Lake Geneva** – notably **Geneva** and **Lausanne** – make up the heart of Suisse-Romande. South of the Alps, sunny, Italian-speaking Ticino can seem a world apart, particularly the palm-fringed lakeside resorts of **Lugano** and **Locarno**.

CHRONOLOGY

800–58 BC The Helvetian Celtic tribe inhabit the area of present day Switzerland.
58 BC Julius Caesar conquers the Helvetians.
1291 AD Three valleys unite against Habsburg rule with some success; they form the basis of the Swiss Confederation.
1388 The Swiss Confederation defeats the Habsburgs.
1536 Protestant Reformation in Switzerland led by Calvin.
1719 Liechtenstein becomes an independent principality of the Holy Roman Empire.
1803 The Swiss start to produce chocolate.
1864 Red Cross founded in Geneva.
1866 Liechtenstein gains full independence.
1914 Switzerland remains neutral during WWI.
1920 The League of Nations headquarters are based in Geneva.
1921 Liechtenstein adopts Swiss currency.
1939–1945 Switzerland remains neutral during WWII. Neutrality tainted by the acceptance of Nazi plunder by Swiss banks.
1959 A political agreement known as the "magic formula" is established between four parties in order to share power.
1971 Swiss women are among the last in Europe to gain the vote.
1993 Liechtenstein elects Europe's youngest leader, Mario Frick, at the tender age of 28.
1998 Swiss banks agree to pay $1.25 billion in compensation to Holocaust survivors and families.
2006 Referendum backs plan to make Swiss asylum laws the toughest in Europe. Liechtenstein re-measures its borders discovering it has grown in size by 123 acres.
2007 Swiss tennis number one, Roger Federer enters the record books having won twelve Grand Slam titles.

ARRIVAL

Switzerland's main **airports** are Geneva International Airport (Ⓦwww.gva.ch) and Zürich Airport (Ⓦwww.zurich-airport.com). Of the no-frills budget airlines, Easyjet, based in the UK, flies to Geneva and Basel, whilst Air Berlin flies into Zürich. Travelling to Switzerland from the continent, it's most likely you'll arrive by **train**. Geneva is the terminus for trains from Toulouse, Lyon and the south of France. Services from Paris also arrive at Lausanne and Bern. Travelling via Strasbourg, or heading

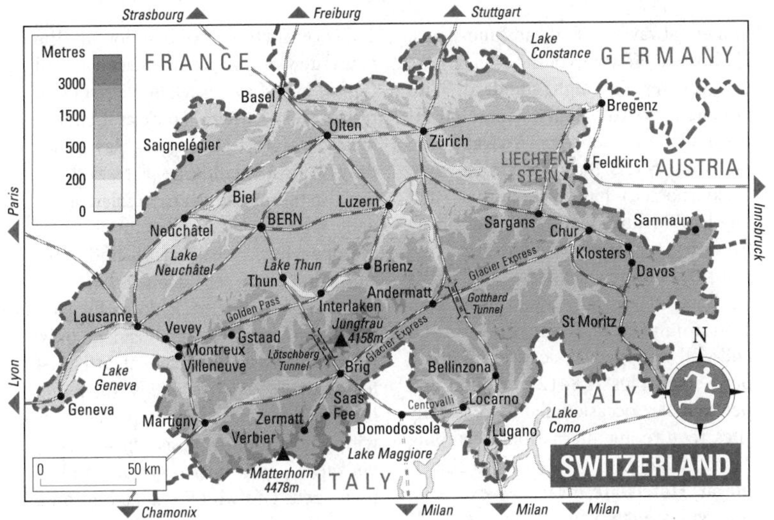

south from Germany, you're most likely to arrive at one of Basel's international stations. Zürich is the major rail hub for services arriving from Austria and Eastern Europe; overnight trains from both Prague and Vienna terminate here; there's also a direct line from Milan. Undoubtedly the most scenic way to cross the border is by **ferry**; crossing the beautiful Lake Maggiore, from one of the Italian resorts such as Stresa, to arrive in Locarno. Similarly, boats arrive in the far north-east of Switzerland from the German side of Lake Constance.

GETTING AROUND

Public transport is comprehensive. Main stations keep a public copy of the national timetable, which covers all rail, bus, boat and cable-car services. Travelling by **train** is comfortable, hassle-free and extremely scenic, with many mountain routes an attraction in their own right. The main network, run by SBB-CFF-FFS, covers much of the country, but many routes, especially Alpine lines, are operated by smaller companies. **Buses** take over where train track runs out – generally yellow postbuses, which depart from train-station forecourts. InterRail and Eurail are valid on SBB and most smaller lines, but the discounts they bring are patchy on boats, cable cars and mountain railways (specified in the text as "**IR**" for InterRail and "**ER**" for Eurail). Postbuses are free with all Swiss passes (specified as "**SP**") – although Alpine routes command a Fr.8–15 supplement, along with seat reservation – but not to Eurail and InterRail pass-holders. Most lake **ferries** run only in summer (June–Sept), and duplicate routes which can be covered more cheaply and quickly by rail.

ACCOMMODATION

Accommodation isn't as expensive as you might think, and is nearly always excellent. Tourist offices can often book rooms for free in their area; they often have a display-board (with a courtesy phone) on the street or at the train station, giving details of every hotel. When you check in, ask for a **guest card**, which can give substantial discounts on local attractions and transport. A **hostel** (Jugendherberge; Auberge de Jeunesse; Albergo/Ostello per la Gioventù) represents great value for money (always book ahead June–Sept). **HI hostels** (Ⓦwww.youthhostel.ch) are of a universally high standard, with doubles as well as small dorms. Non-HI members pay Fr.6 extra. A rival group known as **Swiss Backpackers** (Ⓦwww.backpacker.ch) has lively hostels that are less institutional, often in prime town-centre locations and priced to compete; they're specified in the text as **SB hostels**. Typically a bed in a dorm costs around Fr.30. **Campsites** are clean and well equipped. Prices are about Fr.8 per person plus Fr.8–12 per pitch and per vehicle, occasionally more. Many sites require an international camping carnet. Camping outside official sites is illegal. **Hotels** are invariably excellent, but will stretch your budget; shared-bath doubles start around Fr.90 (average Fr.110), en suites around Fr.135.

FOOD AND DRINK

Eating out in Switzerland can punch a hole in your wallet. Burgers, pizza slices, kebabs and falafel are universal **snack** standbys, as are pork *bratwürste* sausages. Dairy products find their way into most Swiss dishes. Cheese **fondue** – a pot of wine-laced molten cheese into which you dip cubes of bread or potato – is the national dish. It's usually priced as a two-person (or more) meal, or as an all-you-can-eat deal (*fondue à discrétion* or *à gogo*). Another speciality is **raclette** – piquant molten cheese spread on a plate and scooped up with bread or potato. A Swiss-German staple is **rösti**, grated potatoes topped with cheese, chopped ham or a fried egg. Almost everywhere offers vegetarian alternatives. **Cafés** and **restaurants** usually serve meals at set times (noon–2pm & 6–10pm), with only snacks available in between. To get the best value, make lunch your main meal, and always opt for the dish of the day (*Tagesmenu*, *Tagesteller*, *Tageshit*; *plat/assiette du jour*; *piatto del giorno*) – substantial nosh for Fr.16.50 or less. The same meal in the evening, or choosing *à la carte* anytime, can cost double. The main **department stores**, *Manor* and *Globus* both have excellent **self-service** restaurants, where pick-and-choose meals are great value: you pay about Fr.7/13 for a small/large plate, with no limit on the quantity of fresh salad or hot daily special you can pile onto it. Cafés are open from breakfast till midnight/1am and often sell alcohol; bars and pubs tend to open their doors for late-afternoon and evening business only. **Beers** are invariably excellent, at Fr.3–4 for a glass (*e'Schtange, une pression, una birra*). Even the simplest places have wine, most affordably as *Offene Wein, vin ouvert, vino aperto* – a handful of house reds and whites chalked up on a board (small glass Fr.4–5).

CULTURE AND ETIQUETTE

It's not customary to **tip;** restaurant prices are calculated to include service. If you're impressed by the service you could copy the locals and round up your bill to the nearest franc.

SPORTS AND ACTIVITIES

Spectacular Alpine scenery and an excellent transport infrastructure combine to make Switzerland one of Europe's top destinations for **skiing**, **hiking** and **climbing**. For skiers and snowboarders, the choice of prestigious resorts is overwhelming. **Verbier** is renowned for its challenging on and off-piste skiing, as is **Zermatt**. The quaint picturesque resorts of the Jungfrau region – **Grindelwald**, **Mürren** and **Wengen** – cater better for intermediates; whilst those of the Graubünden – **Davos**, **Klosters** and **St Moritz** are magnets for the rich and famous. **Lift passes** vary in price between resorts – typically you should expect to pay Fr.55–65 for a day pass or Fr.265 upwards for six days. Glaciers at Saas Fee and Zermatt stay open for **summer skiing** (Fr.64 for a

ADVENTURE SPORTS IN SWITZERLAND

With its landscape of mountains, glaciers, deep gorges and fast-flowing rivers, Switzerland is ideal territory for **adventure sports**. Dozens of companies, based in all the main resorts, offer activities through the summer, such as **canyoning** (Fr.110/half-day), **river-rafting** (Fr.110/half-day), **bungee-jumping** (Fr.85 from 100m; Fr.230 from 180m), **zorbing** (where you're strapped inside a giant plastic sphere and rolled down a mountainside; Fr.50), **house-running** (where you hook a rope round yourself and run full-tilt down the side of a tall building; Fr.75), and **flying fox** (where you glide down a vertical cliff on a rope; Fr.80). **Hang-gliding** (Fr.180), **paragliding** (Fr.150) and **skydiving** from 4000m (Fr.400) can all be done alone or in tandem with an instructor. Tourist offices and Ⓦwww.myswitzerland.com have full details.

day lift pass at both). **Hiking** is a major summer sport in Switzerland and with over 65,000km of marked trails, most revealing stunning Alpine vistas, it's not hard to see why. The **Jungfrau** region is particularly popular as a base for hiking; whilst proximity to the **Matterhorn** makes Zermatt popular with hikers, as well as more serious climbers. **Hiking trails** are clearly signed in yellow; more challenging mountain trails in red and white. Ask at the local tourist office for further information or consult Ⓦwww.myswitzerland.com for routes and tips.

COMMUNICATIONS

Main **post offices** tend to open Mon–Fri 7.30am–noon & 1.30–6.30pm, Sat 8–11am. Most **public phones** take phonecards (*taxcards*), available from post offices and news kiosks, as well as credit cards; some take Swiss and euro coins. Kiosks also sell good-value discount cards for calling internationally. The expensive **operator** is on Ⓣ111 (domestic) or Ⓣ1141 (international). **Internet access** is widespread, at cafés (Fr.4–12/hr) or free at many hotels and hostels.

EMERGENCIES

Swiss **police** – who may not speak English – are courteous enough. You'll have to pay **hospital** (*Spital, hôpital, ospedale*) bills up-front and claim expenses back later. Every district has one local **pharmacy** (*Apotheke, pharmacie, farmacia*) open outside normal hours; each pharmacy has a sign telling you where the nearest open one is.

EMERGENCY NUMBERS

Police Ⓣ117; fire Ⓣ118; ambulance Ⓣ144.

INFORMATION & MAPS

All towns have a **tourist office** (*Verkehrsverein* or *Tourismus*; *Office du Tourisme*; *Ente Turistico*), invariably located near the train station and always extremely useful. Most staff speak English, but **opening hours** in smaller towns allow for a long lunch and can be limited at weekends and in the off-season. All have accommodation

SWITZERLAND AND LIECHTENSTEIN ON THE NET

Ⓦ**www.myswitzerland.com** Tourist office site – vast, detailed and authoritative.
Ⓦ**www.postbus.ch** Details of the postbus network, including Alpine routes.
Ⓦ**www.museums.ch** Information on museums nationwide.
Ⓦ**www.swissinfo.org** News database in English, with good links.
Ⓦ**www.tourismus.li** The Liechtenstein tourist board.

STUDENT AND YOUTH DISCOUNTS

If you have an ISIC card, you can take advantage of student discounts at almost all **museums** and galleries (sometimes admission is discounted by as much as fifty percent). Although there is no student discount available for cable-car tickets, during the winter season, many resorts do offer a youth-discount on **lift passes** for under 20s.

and transport lists, and **maps**. *Swiss Backpacker News* (Ⓦwww.backpacker.ch) is an excellent free paper, widely available. Ⓦwww.swisstopo.ch has 1:50,000 and 1:25,000 walkers' maps.

MONEY AND BANKS

Both countries use the **Swiss franc** (CHF or Fr.), divided into 100 Rappen (Rp), centimes or centisimi (c). There are coins of 5c, 10c, 20c, 50c, Fr.1, Fr.2 and Fr.5, and notes of Fr.10, Fr.20, Fr.50, Fr.100, Fr.200 and Fr.1000. Train stations are the best places for **changing money**. **Banks** usually open Mon–Fri 8.30am–4.30pm; some in cities and resorts also open Sat 9am–4pm. **Post offices** give a similar exchange rate to banks, and **ATMs** are everywhere. Many shops and services, especially in tourist hubs, accept euros. At the time of writing, €1 was roughly equal to Fr.1.63, US$1 to Fr.1.20 and £1 to Fr.2.39.

OPENING HOURS AND HOLIDAYS

Shop hours are Mon–Fri 9am–6.30pm, Sat 8.30am–4pm, sometimes with a lunch-break and earlier closing in smaller towns. **Museums** and attractions generally close on Mon. Almost everything is closed on **public holidays**: Jan 1, Good Fri & Easter Mon, Ascension Day, Whit Mon, Dec 25 & 26. In Switzerland, shops and banks close for all or part of the national holiday (Aug 1) and on a range of local holidays. Liechtenstein keeps May 1 as a public holiday, and Aug 15 as the national holiday.

LANGUAGE

Almost everyone you meet will be able to converse in English, though a word or two of the local lingo never goes amiss. **French** (see p.373) is used in the western third of the country. From roughly Bern eastwards, **German** (see p.460) will be understood, although people actually speak **Swiss German**, an entirely different language where the standard greeting is *Grüezi* (sometimes *Grüss Gott*) and every town has its own unique dialect. The southern Ticino region is **Italian**-speaking (see p.663), while **Romansh**, a direct descendant of Latin, survives in the Alpine valleys around St Moritz.

Lake Geneva

French-speaking Switzerland, or Suisse Romande, occupies the western third of the country, comprising the shores of **Lake Geneva** (Lac Léman) and the hills and lakes leading north almost to Basel. The ambience here is thoroughly Gallic: historical animosity between Geneva and France has nowadays given way to a yearning on the part of most francophone Swiss to abandon their bumpkin compatriots in the east and embrace the EU. **Geneva**, at the south-western tip of the lake, was once a haven for free thinkers from all over Europe; now it's a city of diplomats and big business. Halfway around the lake, **Lausanne** is full of young people; it's a cultured, energetic town acclaimed as the skateboarding capital of Europe. Further east, the shore features vineyards and opulent villas – **Montreux** is particularly chic – and the stunning medieval **Château de Chillon**, which drew Byron and the Romantic poets. Mont Blanc, western Europe's highest mountain (4807m), is visible from Geneva city centre, while Montreux and neighbouring **Vevey** have breathtaking views across the water to the French Alps. On a sunny day, the train ride around the beautiful northern shore is memorably scenic, but the lake's excellent boat service (IR no discount; ER & SP free; Ⓦwww.cgn.ch) helps bring home the full grandeur of the setting.

GENEVA

The Puritanism of **GENEVA** (Genève) is inextricably linked with the city's struggle for independence. Long ruled by the dukes of Savoy, sixteenth-century Genevans saw the Reformation as a useful aid in their struggle to rid themselves of Savoyard influence. By the time the city's independence was won in 1602, its religious zeal had painted it as the "Protestant Rome". Geneva remained outside the Swiss Confederation until 1815 (the Catholic cantons opposed its entry), and acquired a reputation for joylessness which it still struggles to shake off.

Today, it's a wealthy, working city, sharply focused on its prominent role in international diplomacy and big business.

What to see and do

Jet d'Eau and the Old Town

On the Rive Gauche, beyond the ornamental flowerbeds of the Jardin Anglais, erupts the roaring 140-metre-high plume of Geneva's trademark **Jet d'Eau.** Nearby is the main thoroughfare of the Old Town, the cobbled, steeply ascending Grande Rue. Here, among the secondhand bookshops and galleries, you'll find the atmospheric seventeenth-century **Hôtel de Ville** and the arcaded armoury, backed by a lovely terrace with the longest wooden bench in the world (126m). A block away is the huge late-Romanesque **Cathédrale**

ORIENTATION

Orientation centres on the Rhône, which flows from the lake west into France. The **Rive Gauche**, on the south bank, takes in a grid of waterfront streets which comprise the main shopping and business districts and the adjacent high ground of the Old Town. Further south lies **Carouge**, characterized by artisans' shops and picturesque Italianate architecture. Behind the grand hotels lining the northern **Rive Droite** waterfront is the main station and the cosmopolitan (and in places sleazy) **Les Pâquis** district, filled with cheap restaurants. Further north are the offices of the dozens of international organizations headquartered in Geneva, including the UN.

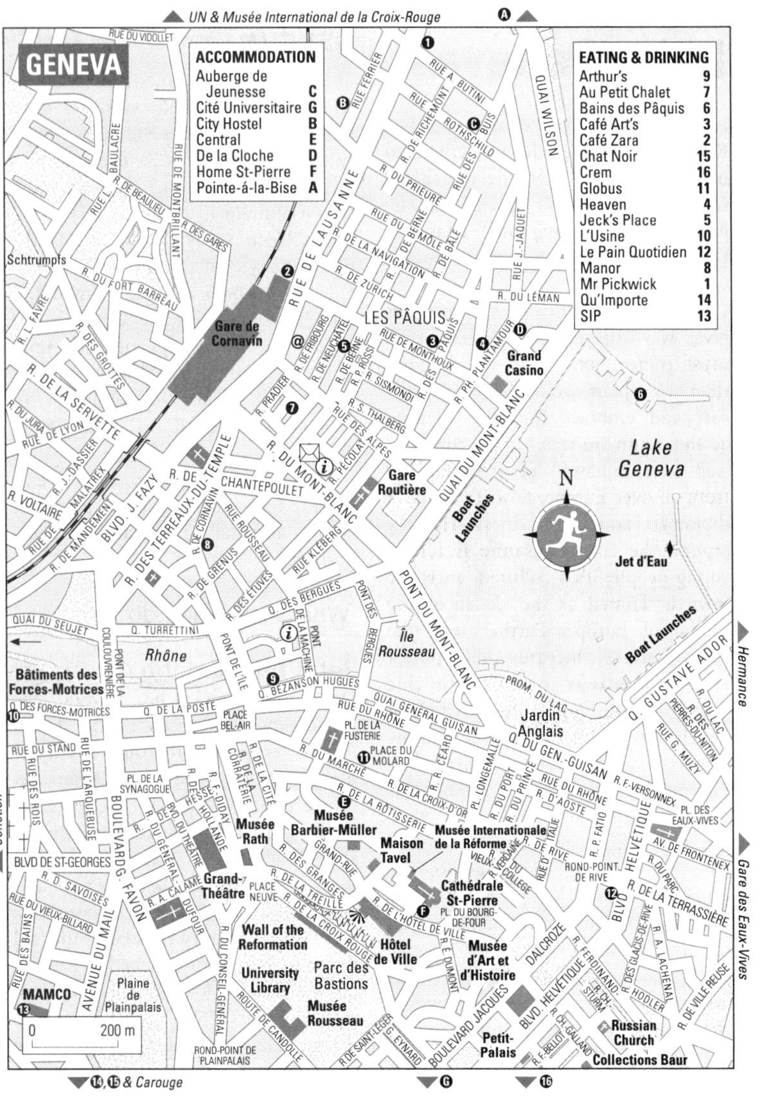

St-Pierre (Mon–Sat 9.30am–5/6.30pm, Sun 12am–6.30pm; free), with an incongruous eighteenth-century portal and a plain, soaring interior. Tucked behind the Cathedral, the excellent **Musée Internationale de la Réforme** (Tues–Sun 10am–5pm; Fr.10; Ⓦwww.musee-reforme.ch), housed in the eighteenth century Maison Mallet, documents Geneva's contribution to the Reformation. Round the corner is the hub of the Old Town, **Place du Bourg-de-Four**, a picturesque split-level square perched on the hillside and ringed by cafés. Alleys wind down from here to the university park and its austere **Wall of the Reformation** (1909–17) alongside busy Place Neuve.

The Museé d'Art et d'Histoire

A stroll east of the Old Town is the gigantic **Musée d'Art et d'Histoire**, 2 Rue Charles Galland (Tues–Sun 10am–5pm, Ⓦmah.ville-ge.ch; free). The fine-art collection includes pieces by Rodin, Renoir and Modigliani; the highlight, however, is Konrad Witz's famous altarpiece, made for the cathedral in 1444, showing Christ and the fishermen transposed onto Lake Geneva. The basement holds a massive archeological collection, including Egyptian mummies and Greek and Roman statuary. Nearby is the **Collections Baur**, 8 Rue Munier-Romilly (Tues–Sun 2–6pm, till 8pm Wed; Ⓦcollections-baur.ch; Fr.5), the country's premier collection of East Asian art.

MAMCO

Make time, if possible, for **MAMCO**, a top-quality museum of modern and contemporary art housed in a spacious factory west of the Old Town at 10 Rue des Vieux-Grenadiers (Tues–Fri noon–6pm, Wed till 9pm, Sat & Sun 11am–6pm; first Sunday of month free; Fr.8; Ⓦwww.mamco.ch).

Museé International de la Croix-Rouge

About 1km north of the station is the thought-provoking **Musée International de la Croix-Rouge** (Mon & Wed–Sun 10am–5pm; Fr.10; Ⓦwww.micr.ch; bus #8 or #F to Appia), which documents the origins and achievements of the Red Cross through carefully chosen audiovisual material. Quietly dramatic exhibits – such as the 34 footprints in a tiny cell-space where a delegate found seventeen people crammed together – leave a powerful impression.

Palais des Nations

Across the road, stands the imposing UN complex (tram #13 or 15 to Nations). Guided tours of the **Palais des Nations** (April–Oct 10am–noon & 2–4pm, July & Aug 10am–5pm; Fr.10; passport required; Ⓦwww.unog.org) start in the new wing and take you through to the original Palais des Nations, built to house the League of Nations between 1929 and 1936; the highlight is the Council Chamber, with allegorical ceiling murals by José-Maria Sert. Don't expect to see debates in session though; the tour is didactic in tone, aiming to enlighten visitors as to the workings and structure of the UN.

Carouge

Twenty minutes south of the centre by tram #12 or #13 lies the late-Baroque suburb of **Carouge**, built by the king of Sardinia in the eighteenth century as a separate town. Its low Italianate houses and leafy streets are now largely occupied by fashion designers and small galleries, and the area's reputation as an outpost of tolerance and hedonism lives on in its numerous cafés and music bars.

Arrival and information

Air From the airport, 5km northwest, trains and bus #10 run into the city.
Train The main station, Gare de Cornavin, lies at the head of Rue du Mont-Blanc in the city centre. Expresses from Paris, Lyon and Grenoble arrive in a separate French section (passport control), while local French trains from Annecy/Chamonix terminate at Gare des Eaux-Vives on the east side of town (tram #12 or #16 into the centre).
Bus The international bus station (Gare Routière) is on Place Dorcière in the centre.
Ferry Boats dock at several central quays.
Tourist office in the main post office at 18 Rue du Mont-Blanc (Mon–Sun 9/10am–6pm, Sept to mid-June closed Sun; Ⓣ022 909 70 00, Ⓦwww.genevatourism.ch). Staff will reserve rooms for a Fr.5 fee. There's also a desk within the municipality's information office, on the Pont de la Machine (Mon noon–6pm, Tues–Fri 9am–6pm, Sat 10am–5pm; Ⓣ022 41820 00, Ⓦwww.ville-ge.ch). Both have stacks of material in English, including information on budget accommodation options.

Accommodation

Make sure you pick up a **Geneva transport card** when you check in – this entitles you to free public transport for the duration of your stay.

Hostels

Auberge de Jeunesse (HI) 30 Rue Rothschild ⓣ022 732 62 60, ⓦwww.youthhostel.ch & ⓦwww.yh-geneva.ch. Big, bustling, well-maintained 330-bed hostel in a central location. Bus #1 to Wilson. Dorms ❷, doubles ❺

Cité Universitaire 46 Av Miremont ⓣ022 839 22 22, ⓦwww.unige.ch/cite-uni. Huge place 3km south (bus #3), with dorms available July–Sept. Plenty of cut-price singles, doubles and studios year-round. Breakfast extra. Dorms ❷, rooms ❺

City Hostel (SB) 2 Rue Ferrier ⓣ022 901 15 00, ⓦwww.cityhostel.ch. Friendly 100-bed backpacker place near the HI hostel; an excellent budget option. Each corridor shares a kitchen. No breakfast. Three- or four-bed dorms ❷, two-bed dorms ❸, doubles ❻

Home St-Pierre 4 Cour St-Pierre ⓣ022 310 37 07, ⓦwww.homestpierre.ch. In the heart of the Old Town opposite the cathedral, with two dorms plus single and double rooms (all women-only), a large kitchen, roof terrace and wireless. Pay extra for breakfast. Dorms ❷, rooms ❹

Hotels

Central 2 Rue de la Rôtisserie ⓣ022 818 81 00, ⓦwww.hotelcentral.ch. Quiet, good-value top-floor rooms just below the Old Town, all with balcony. ❻

De la Cloche 6 Rue de la Cloche ⓣ022 732 94 81, ⓦwww.geneva-hotel.ch/cloche. Eight characterful, high-ceilinged rooms in a quiet area of the Pâquis 50m from the lake. Regularly full. ❼

Campsite

Pointe-à-la-Bise ⓣ022 752 12 96, ⓦwww.tcs.ch. Good-quality site 7km northeast in Vésanaz; bus #E. April–Sept. ❷

Eating

Cafés and snack options

Bains des Pâquis 30 Quai du Mont-Blanc. Popular café-bar attached to the lakefront swimming area. Summer only. *Plat du jour* Fr.12.

Globus 48 Rue du Rhone. Deli section of the department store, with counters selling a wide range of international food (noodles, tapas, sushi) to take-way or eat-in. Open till 10pm. Closed Sunday.

Manor 6 Rue Cornavin. Supermarket on the ground floor of this department store, with a deli counter selling good take-away panini and ciabattas (Fr.6.50).

Restaurants

Au Petit Chalet 6 Rue Chaponnière/17 Rue de Berne. Unpretentious place for Swiss fondues and rösti (Fr.18); also serves good pizzas for Fr.21. Closed Mon.

Café Zara 25 Rue de Lausanne. Simple little Eritrean/Ethiopian café-restaurant near the station. Daily menu from Fr 15. Closed Mon.

Jeck's Place 14 Rue de Neuchâtel. Friendly Singaporean and Thai restaurant with a good-value lunch menu (Fr.14–19). Closed Sat lunch and Sun lunch.

Le Pain Quotidien 21 Boulevard Helvétique. Homely café with delicious pastries (Fr.2.50), a wide selection of newspapers and a lavish weekend brunch menu (Fr. 25–32).

TREAT YOURSELF

Heaven 25 Rue Plantamour, ⓦwww.heavenlounge.ch. Stylish, yet relaxed restaurant/lounge-bar on a quiet Pâquis backstreet. Mediterranean-influenced menu and excellent deserts: *plat du jour* Fr. 19; lunch-time mains Fr. 24, rising in the evening to Fr.26–33.

Drinking and nightlife

Bars

Arthur's 79 Rue du Rhône, ⓦwww.arthurs.ch. Sophisticated lounge- bar on the quai-side of the Rive Gauche; you pay for the view.

Café Art's 17 Rue des Pâquis. Café-bar with eclectic décor and a bohemian feel.

Chat Noir 13 Rue Vautier, Carouge ⓦwww.chatnoir.ch. Bar and cellar venue with live music (anything from folk to metal). Wed–Sat until 4am.

Mr Pickwick 80 Rue de Lausanne. Homely English pub with TV football. Open until 2am.

Qu'Importe 1 Rue Ancienne, Carouge, ⓦwww.quimporte.ch. Relaxed wine-bar with outdoor sofas. Tram# 13 to Anciennes. Closed Mon.

Clubs

crem 10 Boulevard Helvétique, ⓦwww.lacrem.ch. One of Geneva's trendiest bar-clubs, where DJs spin music till 5am (Thurs–Sat).

SIP 10 Rue des Vieux Grenadiers, ⓦwww.lasip.ch. Former factory with modern, hip interior and wide-

ranging programme; open Thurs–Sat till 4/5am.
L'Usine 4 Place des Volontaires, Ⓦwww.usine.ch. Converted factory hosting a plethora of arts and live –music events. Zoo run club nights (hiphop, breakbeat, electronica) here for urban 'night animals'; Ⓦwww.lezoo.ch

Entertainment

Cinema During July and August films are screened by the lake-side on the Quai Gustave-Ador; Fr. 17; Ⓦorangecinema.ch

Shopping

Designer stores The Rue du Rhône and the Rive Gauche is lined with the glass-fronted facades of expensive jewelers and big -name designers.
Carouge A better bet for more affordable and whimsical shopping; it's crammed with cute boutiques and hosts a colourful market (Wed & Sat).
Flea market (Wed & Sat) At Plainpalais near Geneva's old town.
Globus 48 Rue du Rhône. One of Geneva's largest department stores.
Off the Shelf 15 Bd Georges Favon (upstairs), Ⓦwww.offtheshelf.ch. Friendly English bookshop, stocking an impressive selection of novels, non-fiction and travel guides.

Directory

Consulates Australia, 2 Chemin des Fins Ⓣ022 799 91 00; Canada, 5 Ave de l'Ariana Ⓣ022 919 92 00; New Zealand, 2 Chemin des Fins Ⓣ022 929 03 50; UK, 37 Rue de Vermont Ⓣ022 918 24 00; USA, 7 Rue Versonnex Ⓣ022 840 51 60. Embassies are in Bern.
Exchange at the train station (Mon–Sat 7am–7.40pm, Sun 9.15am–5.50pm).
Hospital Hôpital Cantonal, 24 Rue Micheli-du-Crest Ⓣ022 372 33 11.
Left luggage at the train station (4.30am–12.45pm; Fr.4/7).
Laundry Lavseul, 29 Rue de Monthoux.
Post office 18 Rue du Mont-Blanc.
Internet Charly's Checkpoint, 7 Rue de Fribourg (Mon–Sat 9am–12am, Sunday 1am–11pm).
Pharmacy Amavita, at the train station.

Moving on

Train Barcelona (1 daily; 9hr 30min); Basel (hourly; 2hr 45min); Bern (every 30min; 1hr 45min); Lausanne (every 15min; 35min); Lyon (10 daily; 1hr 40min); Montreux (every 30min; 1hr 10min); Vevey (every 30min; 1hr 5min); Zürich (every 30min–1hr; 2hr 45min).
Ferry (May–Sept) Lausanne (2 daily; 3hr 30min); Venice (1 daily; 6hr 35min); Vevey (2 daily; 4hr 30min).

LAUSANNE

Geneva's neighbour **LAUSANNE** is attractive, vibrant and well aware of how to have a good time. It's tiered above the lake on a succession of south-facing terraces, with the Old Town at the top, the train station and commercial districts in the middle, and the one-time fishing village of Ouchy, now prime territory for waterfront café-lounging and strolling, at the bottom. The hills are incredibly steep; copy the locals and catch a bus into the Joret forests above the city, and then blade or **skateboard** your way down to **Ouchy**: aficionados have been clocked doing 90kph through the streets. Switzerland's biggest university makes this a lively, fun city to visit. For chilled-out bars, head for the converted warehouses of the trendy Flon district.

What to see and do

The Cathedral and around

From Place de la Palud the medieval Escaliers du Marché lead up to the **Cathedral** (daily 8am–7pm), a fine

ORIENTATION

To get to the central **Place St-François** from the train station, walk up the steep **Rue du Petit-Chêne**, or take the metro to **Flon**; from the metro platforms, lifts shuttle you up to the level of the giant Grand Pont, between **Place Bel-Air** on the left and St François on the right. From here, Rue St-François drops down into the valley and up the other side to the cobbled **Place de la Palud**, an ancient, fountained square flanked by the arcades of the Renaissance town hall.

Romanesque-Gothic jumble. Opposite, in the former bishop's palace, is the **Musée Historique** (Tues–Sun 11am–5/6pm, also Mon Jul & Aug; Ⓦwww.lausanne.ch/mhl; Fr.8). Lausanne suffered from many medieval fires, and is the last city in Europe to keep alive the tradition of the **nightwatch**: every night, on the hour (10pm–2am), a sonorous-voiced civil servant calls out from the cathedral tower "C'est le guet; il a sonné l'heure" ("This is the nightwatch; the hour has struck").

Collection de l'Art Brut

Ten minutes' walk northwest of Riponne on Ave Vinet (or bus #2 or #3 to Jomini) is the outstanding **Collection de l'Art Brut**, 11 Ave des Bergières (Tues–Sun 11am–6pm; July & Aug also Mon 11am–6pm; Fr.10; Ⓦwww.artbrut.ch). This unique gallery is devoted to "outsider art", the creative output of ordinary people with no artistic training at all – often loners, psychotics or the criminally insane. It's utterly absorbing.

Ouchy, the Olympic Museum and Museé de l'Elysée

Ouchy's waterfront hosts regular free music events all summer, and people come down here to do a spot of café sunbathing or blade-cruising (rent blades or skates from beside Ouchy metro). In a park on the waterfront sits Lausanne's **Olympic Museum** (daily 9am–6pm; Oct–April closed Mon; Ⓦwww.olympic.org; Fr.15), a vacuous place that trumpets the Olympic ideal through snippets of archive footage, stirring music and Cathy Freeman's old running shoes. Bypass it for the **Musée de l'Elysée**, an excellent museum of photography in the same park (Tues–Sun 11am–6pm; Fr.5; free on first Sat of month).

LAUSANNE FESTIVALS

Lausanne's big party is the **Festival de la Cité** in early July (Ⓦwww.festivaldelacite.ch), featuring music, dance and drama on several open-air stages in the old town. Also check out July's big-name **Paleo Rock Festival** in nearby Nyon (Ⓦwww.paleo.ch).

Arrival and information

Boats from Lake Geneva arrive on the quayside at Ouchy.

Train Lausanne's train station is below the old town; from Place de la Gare, head up Rue du Petit-Chêne.

Tourist office Lausanne has two tourist offices (Ⓣ021 613 73 92, Ⓦwww.lausanne-tourisme.ch): one in the train station (daily 9am–7pm), the other beside Ouchy metro station (daily 9am–8pm; Oct–March closes 6pm; Ⓣ 021 013 73 01).

Accommodation

Hostels

Jeunotel (HI) 36 Chemin du Bois-de-Vaux Ⓣ021 626 02 22, Ⓦwww.youthhostel.ch. Huge place beside Vidy campsite with four-bed dorms and rooms, plus cheap meals on request (Fr.13.40). Dorms ❸, doubles ❻

Lausanne Guest House (SB) 4 Epinettes Ⓣ021 601 80 00, Ⓦwww.lausanne-guesthouse.ch. Friendly, no-smoking hostel with lake views, four-bedded dorms and rooms. Dorms ❸, rooms ❻

Hotels and pensions

Pension Bienvenue 2 Rue du Simplon Ⓣ021 616 29 86, Ⓦwww.pension-bienvenue.ch. Respectable women-only guesthouse behind the station. ❺

Old Inn 11 Av de la Gare Ⓣ021 323 62 21, Ⓦ www.oldinn.ch. Quiet, spartan little pension with 11 twin bed rooms and a shared kitchen. ❽

Du Raisin 19 Place de la Palud Ⓣ021 312 27 56. Seven plain rooms above an old café in the heart of the Old Town. ❽

Campsite

Camping Vidy Ⓣ021 622 50 00, Ⓦwww.campinglausannevidy.ch. Bus #1 to Maladière and walk 5min ahead to this decent lakeside campsite with restaurant and supermarket. Bungalows available to rent (❹). Tents ❷

Eating

Au Couscous 2 Rue Enning ⓦwww.au-couscous.ch. North African restaurant with tajine (from Fr.27), couscous dishes (Fr.33–38) and mezze (Fr.30–37). Closed Sat & Sun lunchtimes.

La Bossette 4 Pl du Nord. Friendly local café on a patch of green beneath the château, serving speciality beers plus excellent food (from Fr.20).

Café de l'Évêché 4 Rue Curtat. Haunt of talkative students and local old-timers, just below the cathedral, with pleasant garden terrace at the rear and mains under Fr.20.

Laxmi 5 Escaliers du Marché. Indian/veggie restaurant. All-you-can-eat buffet lunches are Fr.19 (Fr.16 for vegetarian dishes); evening mains cost little more. Closed Mon lunch & Sun.

Ma Jong 3 Escaliers du Grand-Pont. Snack place just down from Manora, serving Japanese, Thai and wok-fried meals for Fr.15. Closed Sun.

Manora 17 Pl St-François. Branch of the self-service cafeteria chain; wide range of hot and cold food for Fr.13 or under.

Café Romand Pl St-François (under *Le Dynasty*). Bustling, heartwarming place with cosy alcoves for beer, coffee or heavy Swiss fare. Mains Fr.17–27. Closed Sun.

Drinking and nightlife

Bars

Au Château 1 Pl du Tunnel. Bar with funky music and flavourful home-brewed beers.

Bleu Lézard 10 Rue Enning, ⓦwww.bluelezard.ch. Fashionable, lively café-bar with regular live music sets downstairs.

Nomade Place de L'Europe 9, ⓦwww.restaurantnomade.ch. Relaxed wine and tapas bar on the edge of the Flon. Closed Sun.

Clubs

D! Pl Centrale. Happening basement club playing house and drum 'n' bass. Thurs–Sat.

Le Loft 1 Escaliers Bel-Air. Bar and club with a mixed programme, including popular electro nights. Free entry for women before midnight. Weds–Sat.

MAD (Moulin à Danse) 23 Rue de Genève, ⓦwww.mad.ch. Cutting-edge dance club with adjoining theatre, art galleries and alternative-style café; hub of the trendy Flon district. Attracts well-known DJs.

VO Le Music Club 11 Pl du Tunnel. Unpretentious café-bar and live venue with regular DJ nights.

Moving on

Train Basel (every 30min; 2hr 10min); Bern (every 30min; 1hr 10min); Geneva (every 15min; 35min); Montreux (every 15min; 20min); Vevey (every 15min; 15min); Zürich (every 30min; 2hr 10min).

Ferry (May–Sept) Geneva (3 daily; 3hr 30min); Montreux (5 daily; 1hr 30min); Vevey (5 daily; 1hr).

VEVEY

East of Lausanne, trains meander through steep vineyards to **VEVEY**, a small market town looking over the French Alps. It holds a Street Artists' Festival in late August: jugglers, acrobats and mime artists performing on the lakeside (ⓦwww.artistesderue.ch). Vevey's charm centres on the huge Grande Place, a few minutes' walk southeast of the station – known also as **Place du Marché** and packed with market stalls (Tues & Sat) – and the narrow streets which lead off into the old town to the east. The excellent fine-art museum, **Musée Jenisch** on Rue de la Gare (Tues–Sun 11am–5.30pm; Fr.12), puts on high-quality exhibitions drawing on its extensive graphic collections (it has one of Europe's largest collections of Rembrandt lithographs). East of Place du Marché is a statue of Charlie Chaplin, "The Tramp", who moved to Vevey from the US in the 1950s to escape McCarthyism. To head on to Montreux and Chillon, ditch the train in favour of bus #1 (direction Villeneuve), which plies the coast road every 10min. If you have time, walk the floral lakeside path.

Arrival and information

Train From the train station, it's a 5min walk to the Grand Place and the lake.

Tourist office in the pillared Grenette building on Grande-Place (June–Sept Mon–Fri 9am–6pm & Sat 8.30am–1.30pm; Oct–May Mon–Fri 8.30am–12.30pm & 1.30pm–6pm, Sat 8.30am–12.30pm). Vevey and Montreux tourist offices have the same information (ⓣ0848 868 484, ⓦwww.montreux-vevey.com). Be sure to get a 'Riviera card' when checking in at your hostel or hotel; this entitles you to free public transport during your stay, in addition to discounts at local museums.

Accommodation

Riviera Lodge 5 Grande-Place ⓣ021 923 80 40, ⓦwww.rivieralodge.ch. Excellent hostel near the lake with 8-bed dorms, large shared kitchen and modern chill-out areas. Dorms ❷, rooms ❻
Les Négociants 27 Rue du Conseil ⓣ021 922 70 11, ⓦwww.hotelnegociants.ch. Simple, cosy rooms with TV and en-suite bathrooms. ❽
La Pichette campsite ⓣ021 921 09 97 (April–Sept); lakeside campsite 2km west of Vevey. ❶

Eating and drinking

Manora St Antoine mall, opposite the train station (second floor). Large branch of the self-service chain, serving inexpensive hot and cold dishes for Fr.13 and under.
Le National 25 Rue du Torrent. Busy café-bar-restaurant with a large garden terrace and colourful modern interior. Set lunch menu Fr.17; there are several salad and veggie options.
Les Négociants 27 Rue du Conseil. Hotel brasserie serving good Swiss fare. Rösti Fr.21.

Moving on

Train Geneva (every 30min; 1hr); Lausanne (every 15min; 15min); Montreux (3 hourly; 5min).
Bus #1 to Montreux (every 10 min).

MONTREUX

MONTREUX, 6km east of Vevey, is a snooty place, full of money; it's not particularly exciting, except during the annual **jazz festival** (see box). The town is protected from chill northerly winds by a wall of mountains and so basks in its own microclimate, boasting lakeside palm trees and exotic flowers. The zigzagging streets of the old quarter above the train station provide more interest than the Grand-Rue below (head 100m left out of the station and cut down the stairs between buildings), although you should make time for the statue of one-time resident **Freddie Mercury** silently serenading the swans on the lakefront.

Montreux's **tourist office** is beside the ferry landing-stage, by the Grand Rue (June–Sept daily 9am–noon; Oct–May Mon–Fri 9am–12.30pm & 1.30–6pm). **Accommodation** fills up quickly during the festival; book in advance. There's an *HI hostel* at 8 Passage de l'Auberge, beside Territet station 1500m east of Montreux (ⓣ021 963 49 34, ⓦwww.youthhostel.ch; dorms ❸, doubles ❻). Another budget option is the family-run *Pension Wilhelm* 13-15 Rue du Marché (ⓣ 021 963 14 31. ⓔhotel.wilhelm@span.ch; ❼); rooms are basic, but central. During the festival, the lake-front is crammed with a plethora of stalls, bars and snack stands. Otherwise, *Brasserie des Alpes*, 23 Avenue des Alpes, is an unassuming backstreet **café** with affordable pizzas (Fr.17).

MONTREUX JAZZ FESTIVAL

The town livens up during its star-studded **Montreux Jazz Festival** (ⓦwww.montreuxjazz.com), held in early July. The festival's been running for over 40 years, and although it's pulled in the likes of Miles Davies and Ray Charles in the past, 'jazz' is now something of a misnomer; these days the festival features big-name acts from all walks of popular music. Check online for tickets (Fr.50–150) or just join the street parties and free entertainment around the lake.

Moving on

Train Geneva (every 30min; 1hr 10min); Interlaken (every 30min; 2hr 45min – change at Zweisimmen & Spiez); Lausanne (every 15min; 20min); Vevey (3 hourly; 5min).

CHÂTEAU DE CHILLON

The highlight of a journey around Lake Geneva is the spectacular thirteenth-century **Château de Chillon** (daily 9/10am–5/6pm; Fr.12; ⓦwww.chillon.ch), one of the best-preserved medieval castles in Europe. It's a 45-minute walk east from Montreux, or a short hop on bus #1. Your first glimpse of the castle, jutting out into the water and framed by craggy mountains, is simply unforgettable. On entering you receive a pamphlet, which directs you to the atmospheric stone dungeons, where François Bonivard, a Genevan priest, was imprisoned from 1530 to 1536; the story captured the imagination of Lord Byron, who composed his poem *The Prisoner of Chillon* after a sailing trip here with Shelley in 1816. Byron's signature, scratched on the dungeon's third pillar, probably isn't genuine. Upstairs you'll find grand knights' halls, lavish bedchambers and dreamy views of the lake.

The Swiss heartland

The Mittelland – the populated countryside between Lake Geneva and Zürich, flanked by the Jura range to the north and the high Alps to the south – is a region of gentle hills, lakes and some high peaks. There's a wealth of cultural and historical interest in the German-speaking cities of **Basel**, **Luzern** and the federal capital, **Bern**. Wherever you base yourself, the mountains are never more than a couple of hours away by train.

BASEL (BÂLE)

Situated on the Rhine, where Switzerland, France and Germany touch noses, **BASEL** (Bâle in French) is a logical staging post en-route north. Despite its pan-European location, the city has gained a reputation for insularity. Certainly, Basel feels like a working city; it's neither as picturesque as Bern or Luzern, nor as vibrant as Zürich. Yet it's a wealthy place and thanks to longstanding patronage of the arts boasts a smattering of first-rate museums and galleries, in addition to some superb contemporary architecture. It's also holds a massive three-day **carnival** in February (Ⓦwww.fasnacht.ch), beginning at 4am on the Monday after Mardi Gras.

What to see and do

The River Rhine curves through the centre of Basel, flowing from east to north. On the south/west bank (1km north of the main station) is the historic Old Town, which is centred on the hectic, higgledy-piggledy main square **Barfüsserplatz**. Across the river, on the north bank lies **Kleinbasel**; historically scorned by the city's prosperous merchants as a working class quarter. Look out for the Lällekönig bust facing towards the **Mittlere Brücke**, sticking out its tongue at the Kleinbaslers. Nowadays, the steps down to the Rhine are a popular place to sit and catch the sun.

Historisches Museum

The city's cultural pre-eminence in the fifteenth and sixteenth centuries is amply demonstrated in the **Barfüsserkirche**, now home to the **Historisches Museum** (Mon & Wed–Sun 10am–5pm; Fr.7); don't miss the sumptuous medieval tapestries, hidden behind protective blinds.

The Münster

Sixteenth-century lanes lead up behind the Historisches Museum to Basel's cathedral, the **Münster** (daily 10/11am–4/4.30/5pm). Inside, in the north aisle, is the tomb of the Renaissance humanist Erasmus, and behind the church is the Pfalz terrace, a fine spot for a picnic. From Barfüsserplatz, shop-lined Gerbergasse and Freiestrasse run north to Marktplatz, dominated by the elaborate scarlet facade of the sixteenth-century **Rathaus**.

Kunstmuseum and Museum für Gegenwarstkunst

Back at Barfüsserplatz, Steinenberg climbs east to meet St Alban-Graben. Here, at no. 16, you'll find Basel's **Kunstmuseum** (Tues–Sun 10am–5pm; Fr.7, or joint ticket Fr.12 includes entry to Museum für Gegenwartskunst; free on 1st Sun of month), which has a dazzling array of twentieth-century art, in addition to an outstanding medieval collection, including a large number of works by the Holbein family. Set in a tranquil spot down by the river, the **Museum für Gegenwartskunst** (Tues–Sun 11am–5pm, Wed until 7pm; joint admission with Kunstmuseum), contains installations by Frank Stella and Joseph Beuys.

Museum Jean Tinguely

A walk away on the north bank, in Solitude Park, is the beautifully designed **Museum Jean Tinguely** (Wed–Sun 11am–7pm; Fr.10; Ⓦwww.tinguely.ch), dedicated to one of Switzerland's best-loved artists. Tinguely used scrap metal, plastic and bits of everyday junk to create room-sized Monty-Pythonesque machines that – with the touch of a foot-button – judder into life, clanking and squeaking. Sculptures veer between the grotesque and the comical.

Fondation Beyeler

Basel's finest gallery – **Fondation Beyeler** (daily 10am–6pm, Wed until 8pm; Fr.12/8; tram #6; Ⓦwww.beyeler.com) is out in the suburbs; but it's certainly worth the trip. Sympathetically designed by Renzo Piano, architect of Paris' Pompidou Centre, the gallery contains a small but exceptionally high-quality collection, featuring some of the most impressive works by Picasso, Giacometti, Rothko, Rodin, Bacon, Miró and others. Sink into a huge white sofa opposite a giant Monet, to indulge in dreamy contemplation of the waterlilies in front of you and the watery gardens outside.

Arrival and information

Train Basel has two train stations straddling three countries. Basel SBB is the main one, most of it in Switzerland; at one end, past passport control, is a section in French territory entitled Bâle SNCF which handles trains from Paris and Strasbourg. Trams #8 and #11 shuttle to Barfüsserplatz. Some trains from Germany terminate at Basel Badischer Bahnhof (Basel Bad. for short), in a German enclave on the north side of the river (passport control), from where tram #6 runs to Barfüsserplatz.

Tourist office in a side entrance of the Stadt Casino on Barfüsserplatz (Mon–Fri 8.30am–6.30pm, Sat 10am–5pm, Sun 10am–4pm; Ⓣ061 268 68 68, Ⓦwww.baseltourismus.ch), with a branch office inside the main SBB train station (Mon–Fri 8.30am–6.30pm, Sat 9am–5pm & Sun 9am–4pm). A full list of Basel's museums and galleries is available here. If you stay overnight you're entitled to a Mobility Card, giving free city transport; pick it up from your hotel at check-in.

The Basel Card (Fr.20/27/35 for 24/48/72 hours) gives free museum entry, free city tours, plus discounts at restaurants, bars and clubs.

Accommodation

Hostels

Basel Backpack (SB) Dornacherstr. 192 Ⓣ061 333 00 37, Ⓦwww.baselbackpack.ch. Good hostel in a funky renovated factory/arts complex behind the station. Colour-coded dorms, bar, kitchen and industrial-style bathrooms. Tram #15 or #16 to Tell Platz. Dorms ❷, rooms ❼

Jugendherberge City (HI) Pfeffingerstr. 8 Ⓣ061 365 99 60, Ⓦwww.youthhostel.ch/basel. Comfortable hostel on a quiet street behind the station, with Internet and garden area. 4-bed rooms ❸, doubles ❺

Jugendherberge St Alban (HI) St Alban-Kirchrain 10 Ⓣ061 272 05 72, Ⓦwww.youthhostel.ch. Quiet

TREAT YOURSELF

Au Violon Im Lohnhof 4 Ⓣ061 269 87 11, Ⓦwww.au-violon.com. Comfortable, stylish old town hotel (a converted former prison), next to St Leohard Church. There are fourteen converted "cell rooms" (all ensutie) or you can opt for the grandeur of a former "polics office" with great views. ❾ hostel on the river. Due to close for renovation after Euro 2008. Dorms ❷, doubles ❻

Hotels

Hecht am Rhein Rheingasse 8 ⓣ061 691 22 20. Friendly, unfussy, small hotel with budget doubles. ❽

Eating

Manora Greifengasse. Excellent-value self-service hot meals, salads and snacks for Fr.13 or under.
Mr Wong Steinenvorstadt 3. Popular Asian fast-food joint just off Barfüsserplatz with noodle dishes from Fr.11.
Pfalz Münsterberg 11. Small café with fresh juices and a salad buffet; eat in or take-away (pay for the weight of your plate). Closed Sat & Sun.
Parterre Klybeckstr. 1. Lively Kleinbasel hangout, with busy outside terrace and a creative, vegetarian-friendly menu; mains Fr. 22–34. Closed Sun.
Zum Roten Engel Andreasplatz. Busy liitle café in a dinky cobbled square, attracting a studenty clientele.

Drinking and nightlife

Bars

Eo Ipso Dornachstr. 192. Trendy, spacious industrial bar in a buzzing factory complex behind the train station.
Fischerstube Rheingasse 45. Atmospheric Kleinbasel beerhall with a hearty, older clientele.

Nightclubs and live music

Atlantis Klosterberg 10, ⓦwww.atlan-tis.ch Club-bar with regular music and dance; club nights Fri and Sat till 4am.
Bird's Eye Kohlenberg 20, ⓦwww.birdseye.ch. Basel's main jazz venue. Entrance prices vary, but generally hover around Fr.10. Open Tues–Sat from 9pm.
Kaserne Klybeckstr. 1b, ⓦwww.kaserne-basel.ch. Alternative hangout with varied live-music, theatre and dance programme. Mutates on Tues into Basel's premier gay/lesbian meeting-point.

Moving on

Train Geneva (hourly; 2hr 45min); Interlaken Ost (every 30min; 2hr 10min); Lausanne (every 30min; 2hr 5min); Lugano (every 2 hours; 3hr 50min); Luzern (hourly; 1hr 10min); Zürich (2 hourly; 1hr).

LUZERN (LUCERNE)

An hour south of Basel and Zürich is beautiful **LUZERN** (Lucerne), offering captivating mountain views, lake cruises and a picturesque medieval quarter. The giant Mount Pilatus rears up behind the town, which is split by the River Reuss, flowing rapidly out of the northwestern end of the oddly shaped **Vierwaldstättersee** ("Lake of the Four Forest Cantons" or plain Lake Luzern). Altdorf, just around the lake, was where **William Tell** shot the apple from his son's head. Luzern also boasts a lively café culture and a raucous **carnival**, ending on Ash Wednesday. A six-day round of drinking, dancing and partying, it's considered the biggest and best in Switzerland.

What to see and do

Pilatusstrasse and around

From the train station – located on the waterfront, alongside the **KKL**, a stunning concert hall with a giant roof that seems to float unsupported – busy Pilatusstrasse storms southwest away from the river. About 100m along is the **Sammlung Rosengart gallery** (daily 10/11am–5/6pm; Fr.15) with a superb collection of twentieth-century art. The ground floor is devoted to Picasso, the basement to Paul Klee, and the upper floor to Chagall, Monet, Renoir and others.

The Old Town

The alleyways of the old town span both riverbanks, linked by the fourteenth-century **Kapellbrücke**, a covered wooden bridge angled around the squat mid-river **Wasserturm**. After a disastrous fire in 1993, it was reconstructed and the medieval paintings fixed to its roof-beams replaced by facsimiles.

The Löwenplatz and around

Northeast of the Old Town is **Löwenplatz**, dominated by the absorbing **Bourbaki Panorama** (daily 9am–6pm; Fr.8), a 110m-by-10m circular mural, depicting the flight of General Bourbaki's 87,000 strong army into Switzerland during the Franco-Prussian War. Just off the square is the **Löwendenkmal**, a dying lion hewn out of a cliff-face to commemorate 700 Swiss mercenaries killed by French revolutionaries in 1792.

The Verkehrshaus

A pleasant 2km stroll east along the lakeside (or bus #6 or #8), lies the **Verkehrshaus**, Lidostrasse 5 (daily 10am–5/6pm; Fr.24 or Fr.32 including IMAX cinema; Ⓦwww.verkehrshaus.ch). Inadequately translated as "Transport Museum", this vast complex contains original space capsules, railway locomotives, cable cars and a planetarium. An incongruous highlight is the museum dedicated to whimsical contemporary Swiss artist **Hans Erni** (daily 10am–5/6pm; Fr.12 without Verkehrshaus; Ⓦwww.hansernimuseum.ch).

Lake Luzern

You shouldn't leave Luzern without taking a trip on the **lake** (ferry routings at Ⓦwww.lakelucerne.ch; ER & SP free, IR half-price; tourist info at Ⓦwww.lakeluzern.ch), Switzerland's most beautiful and dramatic by far, the thickly wooded slopes rising sheer from the water. Of the lakeside towns, **VITZNAU** (1hr from Luzern) is the base-station of the oldest rack-railway in the world, serving the majestic **Mount Rigi** (SP, IR & ER fifty percent discount; Ⓦwww.rigi.ch)

Arrival and information

Train and tourist office Luzern's train station is on the south bank, with the tourist office on platform 3 (Mon–Fri 8.30am–5.30/7pm, Sat & Sun 9am–5/7pm; Winter closed Sun afternoon; Ⓣ041 227 17 17, Ⓦwww.luzern.org).

Accommodation

Hostels

Backpackers Lucerne (SB) Alpenquai 42 Ⓣ041 360 04 20, Ⓦwww.backpackerslucerne.ch. Friendly hostel in a quiet spot near the lake with dorms, twins and doubles. Take bus #6/7/8 to Weinbergli, then cut left. Dorms ❷, rooms ❺

HI Hostel Sedelstr. 12 Ⓣ041 420 88 00, Ⓦwww.youthhostel.ch. Modern, serviceable hostel, located 1km northwest of town by Lake Rotsee. Less convenient than the SB place. Take bus #18 to Jugendherberge. Dorms ❸, rooms ❻

Hotels

Tourist Hotel St Karliquai 12 Ⓣ041 410 24 74, Ⓦwww.touristhotel.ch. Functional, central budget option with dorms (❸) and doubles (❼).

TREAT YOURSELF

Schlüssel Franziskanerplatz 12 Ⓣ041 210 10 61. Quaint hotel, full of character; built on the old city wall. Charming doubles, some with views over pretty Franzikanerplatz. ❾

Camping

Camping International Lido Lidostrasse 19 Ⓣ041 370 21 46, Ⓦwww.camping-international.ch. Good campsite 5-min walk from the Verkehrshaus (bus #6 or #8), with caravan and bungalows available to rent, plus some cheap dorm beds. Tents and dorms ❷

Eating

Cafés and restaurants

Hofgarten Stadthofstr. 14. Good, fresh vegetarian mains for around Fr.20 in this courtyard restaurant.

Hug Mühlenplatz. Popular local café chain, with excellent pastries and set breakfast menus from Fr.9

KKL World Café Europlatz 1. Modern café in the KKL concert-hall, serving daily hot specials with a global twist for Fr.16.50.

Manora Weggisgasse 11. Branch of the cheap self-service chain, with a large roof-top terrace. Closed Sun.

Drinking and nightlife

Jazz Kantine Grabenstr. 8 ⓦwww.jsl.ch/kantine.htm. Old -town bar near Luzern's music school, with DJs and live bands downstairs.
Schüür Tribschenstr. 1 ⓦwww.schuur.ch. Happening DJ bar and club with a wide-ranging programme of live music acts. Open till 4am Fri and Sat.

Moving on

Train Basel (hourly; 1hr 10min); Bern (every 30min; 1hr 20min); Interlaken Ost (hourly; 1hr 50min); Lugano (every 2 hours; 2hr 45min); Zürich (every 30min; 45min).
Ferry (May–Sept) Alpnachstad (6 daily; 1hr 40min); Flüelen (8 daily; 2hr 50min); Kehrsiten (hourly; 35min); Vitznau (hourly; 1hr).

ENGELBERG

Only one hour from Luzern by train, the picturesque Alpine resort of ENGELBERG is popular with day-trippers. Signposted from the station is a four-stage cable car serving the snowbound summit of **Mount Titlis** (3239m), the highest point in Central Switzerland (ⓦwww.titlis.ch), which hosts snowsports all summer long. ER, IR and SP bring discounts on the eyepopping trip up and down, and there are countless offers and all-in rental deals for mountain-bikes, scooters, DevilBikes and snowboarders to take advantage of. Engelberg also has a range of adventure sports on offer. The main operator *Outventure* (ⓣ041 611 14 41, ⓦwww.outventure.ch) organises canyoning, bungee-jumping and more, bookable direct or through hostels.

BERN

Of all Swiss cities, BERN is the most immediately charming. Crammed onto a steep-sided peninsula in a crook of the fast-flowing River Aare, the city's quiet, cobbled lanes, lined with sandstone arcaded buildings, have changed little in five hundred years. It's sometimes hard to remember that this quiet, attractive town of just 130,000 people is the nation's capital.

ORIENTATION

Bern's compact old centre is best explored from the focal east–west **Spitalgasse**. As it leads away from the Bahnhofplatz, Spitalgasse becomes **Marktgasse**, Kramgasse and then Gerechtigkeitsgasse, before taking you across the river Aare to **the Bärengraben** (or bear pits). Many of the Bern's larger museums are clustered around Helvetiaplatz, on the south bank of the river, across the Kirchenfeldbrücke.

What to see and do

The Old Town and the Münster

Marktgasse, lined with attractive seventeenth and eighteenth century buildings and arcaded shops, leads you past a number of historic landmarks, such as the sixteenth century Zytglogge; a distinctively top-heavy clock tower, converted from a medieval town gate. To the left in Kornhausplatz, the most notorious of Bern's fountains, the horrific Kindlifresserbrunnen, depicts an ogre devouring a baby. Münstergasse, one block south, takes you to the fifteenth-century Gothic **Münster** (Tues–Sat 10am–4/5pm, Sun 11.30am–5pm), noted for the magnificently gilded high-relief *Last Judgement* above the main entrance. Its 254-stepped tower (closes 30min earlier; Fr.4), the tallest in Switzerland, offers terrific views.

The Bärengraben

At the eastern end of the centre, the Nydeggbrücke crosses the river to the **Bärengraben** (open access), Bern's famed bear-pits, which have housed generations of morose shaggies since the early sixteenth century. Legend has it that the town's founder Berchtold V of Zähringen named Bern after killing one of the beasts during a hunt. The current layout is due to be overhauled in 2009, becoming the centrepiece of a much larger park-like enclosure.

The Kunstmuseum

Bern's **Kunstmuseum**, near the station at Hodlerstrasse 8–12 (Tues 10am–9pm, Wed–Sun 10am–5pm; Fr.7), is especially strong on twentieth-century art, with works by Matisse, Kandinsky, Braque and Picasso.

The Historisches Museum and around

The vast **Historisches Museum** (Tues–Sun 10am–5pm, Wed until 8pm; Fr.13), on Helvetiaplatz, south of the river, is home to the superb **Einstein Museum** (same hours, Fr.18), which documents the physicist's eventful family life and his chequered early career. Exhibits include examples of the young Einstein's schoolwork, complete with scathing marginalia. The multi-media presentation of his theory of relativity is engaging; accessible even to those whose maths homework suffered a similar fate. Across the road, the displays at the **Alpines Museum** (Mon 2–5.30pm, Tues–Sun 10am–5.30pm; Fr.9) explore mountain culture.

Zentrum Paul Klee

East of the centre at Ostring, the **Paul Klee Centre** (Tues–Sun 10am–5pm, Thurs until 9pm; Fr.16; Ⓦwww.zpk.ch; bus #12) has the world's largest collection of works by the artist, who spent much of his life in Bern. The building is a stunning, triple-arched design by the star Italian architect Renzo Piano.

Arrival and information

Train The station is to the west of the old town; the main entrance is on Bahnhofplatz.
Tourist office in the train station (June–Sept Mon–Sun 9am–8.30pm; Oct–May Mon–Sat 9am–6.30pm & Sun 10am–5pm; Ⓣ031 328 12 12, Ⓦwww.berninfo.com), with a branch at the Bärengraben (June–Sept daily 9am–6pm; shorter hours in winter; Nov–Feb Fri–Sun 11am–6pm only). Both can sell you the **Bern Card** (Fr.20/31/38 for 24/48/72 hours), which entitles you to free public transport and discounts.

City Transport

Bern's old town is compact and can easily be covered on foot.
Bikes can be rented for free from "Bern rollt" on Hirschengraben, near the station (daily 7.30am–9.30pm; Ⓦ www.bernrollt.ch). Rental is free, but you need photo ID and Fr.20 deposit and must return bikes the same day.
Bus #12 runs from the train station, through the old town to the Bärengraben and then to the Zentrum Paul Klee.

Accommodation

Hostels

Bern Backpackers/Hotel Glocke (SB) Rathausgasse 75 Ⓣ031 311 37 71, Ⓦwww.bernbackpackers.com. Very central hostel (if consequently a little noisy) with a large common room and kitchen area. Dorms ❷, rooms ❻
HI Hostel Weihergasse 4 Ⓣ031 311 63 16, Ⓦwww.youthhostel.ch/bern. Good hostel in a quiet location beside the river, just below the Bundeshaus. Breakfast included. Dorms ❸, doubles ❻
Landhaus (SB) Altenbergstr. 4 Ⓣ031 331 41 66, Ⓦwww.landhausbern.ch. Excellent hostel in an old house near the Bärengraben. Full of character, with wonky wooden floors and a lively downstairs bar. Dorms have neat 2-bed cubicles. Dorms ❸, doubles ❼

Campsite

Eichholz campsite Strandweg 49 Ⓣ031 961 26 02, Ⓦwww.campingeichholz.ch; take tram #9 to Wabern. Good-value campsite. April–Sept. ❷

Eating and drinking

Altes Tramdepot Gr Muristalden 6, Ⓦwww.altestramdepot.ch. Microbrewery with attractive beer-garden next to the Bärengraben. The restaurant here serves Swiss cuisine; daily lunch special Fr.16.50.
Le Lötschberg Zeughaugasse 16, Ⓦwww.loetschberg-aoc.ch. Friendly wine bar and deli

serving a range of cheese platters and substantial salads for Fr.9–15. Closed Sun.

Café des Pyrénées Kornhausplatz. Jovial café-bar, serving snacks and pasta dishes (Fr.13). Closed Sun.

Sous Le Pont Neubrückstrasse 8, Ⓦwww.souslepont.ch. Café-bar in the Reitschule, a dilapidated arts centre beside the train tracks on Bollwerk. Tues–Fri 11.30am–2.30pm & 6pm–midnight, Fri 11.30am–2.30pm & 7pm–2am, Sat 7pm– 2am.

Tibits Bahnhofplatz 10, Ⓦwww.tibits.ch. Excellent, trendy self-service place, with a great selection of salads and hot dishes. You pay for the weight of your plate.

Nightlife and live music

Bern hosts a huge open-air rock event (Ⓦwww.gurtenfestival.ch) in July.

Reitschule Neubrückstrasse 8, Ⓦwww.reitschule.ch. Grungy arts-squat at the heart of the alternative clubbing scene.

Dampfzentrale Marzilistr. 47. Ⓣ031 310 05 40, Ⓦwww.dampfenzentrale.ch. Bern's premier venue for live music, hosting a range of acts.

Shopping

Waisenhausplatz market sells everything from crafts to clothes and CDs (May–Oct, Tues 8am–7pm & Sat 8am–5pm). There's a **produce market** in Bärenplatz (Tues & Sat 7am–noon), and on the first Saturday of each month, Munsterplattform hosts a **craft market**.

Directory

Embassies Australia, embassy in Berlin Ⓣ004930/880 0880, consulate in Geneva Ⓣ022 799 91 00; Canada, Kirchenfeldstr. 88, Bern Ⓣ031 357 32 00; Ireland, Kirchenfeldstr. 68, Bern Ⓣ031 352 14 42; New Zealand, embassy in Berlin Ⓣ004930/20 6210, consulate in Geneva Ⓣ022 929 03 50; UK, Thunstr. 50, Bern Ⓣ031 359 77 00; USA, Jubiläumstr. 93, Bern Ⓣ031 357 70 11.

Hospital Inselspital, Freiburgstr. Ⓣ031 632 24 64.

Internet weblane.ch, Gerechtikeitstrasse, 58. Self-service Internet (Mon–Sun 10am–9.30pm; Fr.5 for 30 min).

Laundry Jet Wash, Dammweg 43.

Left Luggage in the station (6am–midnight; Fr.5/6/8).

Pharmacy Bahnhof Apotheke, in the station.

Post office Schanzenstr., behind the station.

Moving on

Train Basel (every 30min; 55min); Geneva (every 30min; 1hr 45min); Interlaken Ost (every 30min; 55min); Lausanne (every 30min; 1hr 10min); Luzern (every 30min; 1hr 20min); Zürich (every 30min; 1hr–1hr 25min).

The Swiss Alps

South of Bern and Luzern, and east of Montreux, lies the grand Alpine heart of Switzerland, a massively impressive region of classic Swiss scenery – high peaks, sheer valleys and cool lakes – that makes for great summer hiking and world-class winter sports. The Bernese Oberland, centred on the **Jungfrau Region**, is the most accessible and touristed area, but beyond this first great wall of peaks is another even more daunting range in which the **Matterhorn**, marking the Italian border, is star attraction. The wild summits and remote valleys in the southeastern corner of Switzerland shelter the world-famous mountain resort of **St Moritz**.

Note that very little happens in the mountains in the **off-seasons** (April, May, Oct & Nov); shops and hotels may be shut at these times, cable cars closed for renovations, and smaller resorts virtually deserted.

THE JUNGFRAU REGION

The spectacular **Jungfrau Region** is named after a grand triple-peaked ridge – the Eiger, Mönch and Jungfrau – which crests 4000m. Endlessly touted hereabouts is the rack-railway excursion up to the **Jungfraujoch**, the highest train station in Europe at 3454m ("Top of Europe"). The cable-car ride up the **Schilthorn** (2970m) gets second billing, but is in fact quicker, cheaper, offers a more scenic ride up, and has better

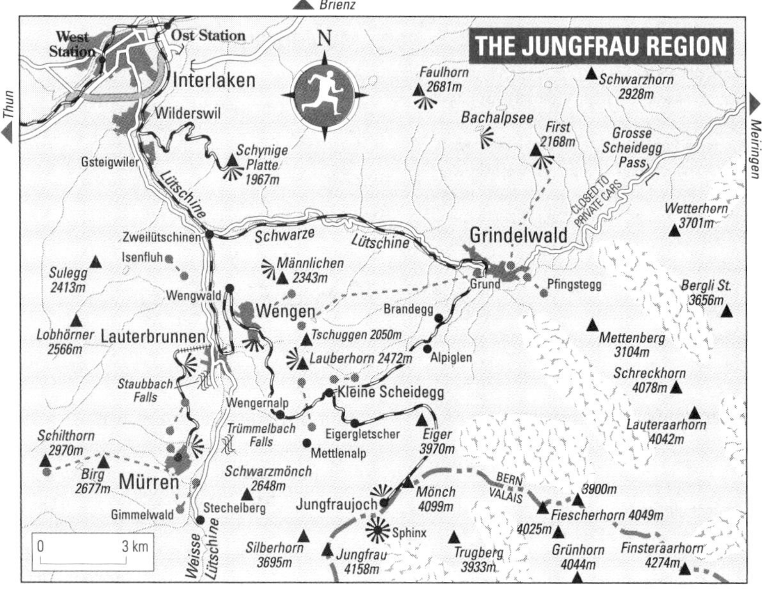

views from the top: don't be misled. A round-trip from Interlaken takes six hours to the Jungfraujoch, four hours to the Schilthorn (both including an hour at the summit). Setting off on the first train of the day (6.30am) brings discounts on both routes. The most beautiful part of the region's countryside is the **Lauterbrunnen valley**, overlooked by the resort of **Mürren**, which provides an excellent base for winter skiing and summer hiking, as does **Grindelwald**, in its own valley slightly east. **Interlaken** is the main transport hub for the region, but the sheer volume of tourist traffic passing through the town can make it a less-than-restful place to stay.

INTERLAKEN

INTERLAKEN is centred on its long main street, Höheweg, which is lined with cafés and hotels and has a train station at each end, though the best way to arrive is by boat. The town lies on a neck of land between two of Switzerland's most attractive lakes, and it exists chiefly to amuse the trippers passing through on their way to the mountains. Interlaken Ost station is the mainline terminus and the departure

TO THE JUNGFRAUJOCH

Switzerland's most popular **mountain railway** trundles south from Interlaken before coiling up across mountain pastures, and tunnelling clean through the Eiger to emerge at the **Jungfraujoch** (3454m), an icy, windswept col just beneath the Jungfrau summit. Touted relentlessly as the "Top of Europe" – the journey is scenic in parts, but very long (2hr 20min from Interlaken) and prohibitively expensive; it's only worthwhile on a clear day, when you gain spectacular **panoramic views** from the Sphinx Terrace (3571m) to Germany's Black Forest in one direction and across a gleaming wasteland to the Italian Alps in the other. Don't forget your sunglasses.

> **TREAT YOURSELF**
>
> Interlaken is a real hub for extreme sports; paragliders spiral above the town, dominating the sky-line. If you decide to splash out on an adventure, **Alpin Raft** (Hauptsrasse 7, ⓣ033 823 41 00, ⓦwww.alpinraft.ch) is the local market leader, arranging everything from tandem skydiving (Fr.380) to canyon jumping (Fr.129), and bookable direct or at hostels.

point for trains into the mountains (see p.1073); coming from Luzern, you could get out at Brienz and do the last stretch to Interlaken Ost by boat. Trains from the Bern/Zürich direction pass first through Interlaken West (docking point for boats from Thun).

Arrival and information

Train Interlaken has two train stations; Interlaken West and Interlaken Ost. Interlaken West is located near to Bahnhofstrasse, which becomes the main street Höheweg, at the far eastern end of which is Interlaken Ost station.

Tourist office Beneath the town's tallest building at Höheweg 37 (Mon–Fri 8am–6pm & Sat 8am–noon; July & Aug also Sat 8am–5pm & Sun 10am–noon & 5–7pm; shorter hours in winter; ⓣ033 826 53 00, ⓦwww.interlaken.ch).

Accommodation

Accommodation fills up quickly in the high seasons; it really is essential to **book ahead**. There are hotel lists and courtesy phones at both stations.

Hostels

Balmer's Herberge (SB) Hauptstr. 23-33, ⓣ033 822 19 61, ⓦwww.balmers.com. Sociable hostel fifteen minutes south of town with beer-garden and DJ bar; the hub of Interlaken's lively backpacker scene. Dorms ❷, rooms ❺

Backpackers Villa Sonnenhof (SB) Alpenstr. 16 ⓣ033 826 71 71, ⓦwww.villa.ch. Excellent hostel; quieter than Balmers, but well-equipped and friendly. Pay Fr.5 extra for a room with a balcony and stunning mountain view. Dorms ❸, doubles ❻

Happy Inn (SB) Rosenstr. 17 ⓣ033 822 32 25, ⓦwww.happy-inn.com. Reasonable back-up option if Balmers and Sonnehof are full. Dorms ❷, rooms ❺

HI Hostel Aareweg 21 in Bönigen (ⓣ033 822 43 53, ⓦwww.youthhostel.ch. 2km east from Interlaken, near lake Brienz (take bus #1). Dorms ❷

Campsite

River Lodge behind Interlaken Ost station ⓣ0338224424, ⓦwww.riverlodge.ch. Convenient location on the river, just a short walk from town. You can pitch a tent or stay in a bungalow. Tents ❷, dorms ❹, private bungalows ❻

Eating

Budget and snack options

Coop opposite Interlaken Ost. Large supermarket for picnic ingredients.

Migros opposite West station. Cheap self-service staples. Closed Sun.

Restaurants

El Azteca Jungfraustr. 30. Friendly Mexican restaurant, with a tasty but rather pricey menu. Enchiladas Fr.22/28.

PizPaz Centralstr. Large place, serving reasonably priced pizza (Fr.16.50) and pasta (from Fr.14.40). Closed Mon.

Tamil Asian Shop/Restaurant Uniongasse, 1. Tiny south Indian restaurant tucked away on a side-street. Eat-in or take-out for Fr.10.90.

Drinking and nightlife

Most backpackers congregate at one of busier hostel bars; **Balmer's** is most popular and has cheap beer; **Funny Farm** Haupstrasse is a maverick hostel attracting party-goers; and **Happy Inn** has a lively downstairs bar.

Positiv Einfach Centralstr. 11. A hip music bar; a change from the backpacker scene.

Moving on

Train (Interlaken Ost) to: Bern (every 30min; 55min); Grindelwald (every 30min; 35min); Jungfraujoch (every 30min; 2hr 20min – change at Grindelwald or Lauterbrunnen, then Kleine Scheidegg); Lauterbrunnen (every 30min; 20min); Luzern (hourly; 1hr 55min); Zürich (every 2hr; 2hr 5min).

LAUTERBRUNNEN

It's hard to overstate just how stunning the **Lauterbrunnen valley** is. An immense U-shaped cleft with bluffs on either side rising 1000m sheer, doused by some 72 waterfalls, it is utterly spectacular. The **Staubbach falls** – highest in Switzerland at nearly 300m – tumble just beyond the village of **LAUTERBRUNNEN** at the valley entrance, whose train station (served by trains from Interlaken Ost) is opposite both the funicular station for Mürren and the **tourist office** (Mon–Fri 9am–6pm; June–Sept also Sat & Sun 9am–6pm; ⓣ033 856 85 68, ⓦwww.lauterbrunnen.ch). **Accommodation** is down by the tracks at the cosy *SB Valley Hostel* (ⓣ033 855 20 08, ⓦwww.valleyhostel.ch; dorms ❷, doubles ❺) or up at the excellent *Mountain Hostel* in Gimmelwald (see below).

From Lauterbrunnen, it's a scenic half-hour walk, or an hourly postbus, 3km up the valley to the spectacular **Trümmelbach falls** (April–Nov daily 8.30/9am–5/6pm; Fr.11), a series of thunderous waterfalls – the runoff from the mountain glaciers – which have carved corkscrew channels into the valley walls. The postbus continues 1.5km to **STECHELBERG** at the end of the road, starting point for the **cable-car ride** up to Gimmelwald, Mürren and the Schilthorn; the huge base station complex is 1km before the hamlet.

MÜRREN AND UP TO THE SCHILTHORN

The cable car from Stechelberg leaps the valley's west wall to reach the quiet hamlet of **GIMMELWALD**, a little-visited spot with the superb self-catering *Mountain Hostel* (ⓣ 033 855 17, ⓦwww.mountainhostel.com; ❷). Further up is the car-free village of **MÜRREN**. It's worth the journey for the views: from here, the valley floor is 800m straight down, and the panorama of snowy peaks filling the sky is dazzling. Mürren is also accessible from Lauterbrunnen on the BLM Bergbahn, comprising a steep funicular to Grütschalp (Fr.7.80/15.60) and a spectacular little cliff-edge train from there (IR no discount; ER twenty-five percent discount; SP free). It's easy to do a round-trip by cable-car and train. The cable car continues from Mürren on a breathtaking ride (20min) up to the 2970m summit of the **Schilthorn** (ⓦwww.schilthorn.ch), where you can enjoy exceptional panoramic views and sip cocktails in the revolving *Piz Gloria* summit restaurant. Schilthornbahn prices, compared to the Jungfraujoch ride, are a **bargain**. From Stechelberg to the top is Fr.89 round-trip, from Mürren Fr.69.40 (IR no discount; ER twenty-five percent discount; SP free to Mürren, then fifty percent off). Going up before 8.40am or after 3.10pm knocks the ticket price down to Fr.67.

GRINDELWALD

Valley-floor trains from Interlaken Ost also run to the more popular holiday centre of **GRINDELWALD**, nestling under the craggy trio of the Wetterhorn, Mettenberg and Eiger. Numerous trails around **Pfingstegg** and especially **First** – both at the end of gondola lines from Grindelwald – provide excellent hiking. The **tourist office** (daily 8/9am–noon & 1.30–5/6pm; shorter hours in April & Nov; ⓣ033 854 12 12, ⓦwww.grindelwald.com) is 200m east of the station, and shares a building with the **Bergsteigerzentrum** (Mountaineering Centre; ⓣ033 854 12 80, ⓦwww.gomountain.ch), which offers bungee jumps, canyon leaps and guided ascents. **Tandem Flights** (ⓦwww.paragliding-grindelwald.ch) arranges accompanied paragliding jumps from Fr.200. A steep fifteen-minute walk will get you to Terrassenweg, a quiet lane running above the village, where there's an excellent *HI hostel* (ⓣ033 853 10 09, ⓦwww.youthhostel.ch; dorms ❷, doubles ❺) and the friendly

Naturfreundehaus (☎033 853 13 33; dorms ❷, rooms ❺). The well-run *SB Mountain Hostel* (☎033 853 3838, Ⓦwww.mountainhostel.ch; dorms ❸, rooms ❻) is on the valley floor beside Grindelwald-Grund station (Trains from Grindelwald pass through Grund on their way up to Kleine Scheidegg). You can **camp** at *Aspen* (☎033 854 40 00, Ⓦwww.hotel-aspen.ch; March–Oct; ❷).

Mountain transport

Trains There are two routes to the top of the Jungfrau from Interlaken, travelling either via Lauterbrunnen or Grindelwald. All trains terminate at the spectacularly located hamlet of Kleine Scheidegg, where you must change for the final pull to Jungfraujoch; the popular practice is to go up one way and down the other.

Fares and tickets The adult round-trip fare from Interlaken to the Jungfraujoch is a budget-crunching Fr.176 (IR no discount; ER Fr. 133.80; SP Fr.108) – but the discounted "Good Morning ticket", valid if you travel up on the first or second trains of the day (which start from Interlaken Ost at 6.30am & 7.20am) is Fr.158 from Interlaken, Fr. 133 from Lauterbrunnen and Fr.134 from Grindelwald.

Walking Hiking some sections, up or down, is perfectly feasible in summer, and can help save a great deal on train tickets. Excellent transport networks and vista-rich footpaths linking all stations mean that with a hiking map and timetable you can see and do a great deal in a day.

ZERMATT AND THE MATTERHORN

The shark's-tooth **Matterhorn** (4478m) is the most famous of Switzerland's mountains – no other natural or human structure in the whole country is so immediately recognizable. In most people's minds, the Matterhorn stands for Switzerland like the Eiffel Tower stands for France. One reason it's so famous is that it stands alone, its impossibly pointy shape sticking up from an otherwise uncrowded horizon above **ZERMATT** village; another is that the quintessential Swiss chocolate, Toblerone, was modelled on it.

What to see and do

Zermatt's main street is thronged year-round with an odd mixture of professional climbers, tour-groups, backpackers and fur-clad socialites. No cars are allowed in the village; electric minibuses ferry people between the train station at the northern end of the village and the cable-car terminus 1km south. Opposite the station, GGB Gornergrat-Bahn trains (ER twenty-five percent discount, IR half-price, SP free) climb above the village, giving spectacular Matterhorn views (sit on the right). They take you all the way up to the **Gornergrat**, a vantage point with a magnificent Alpine panorama including Switzerland's highest peak, the **Dufourspitze** (4634m). In summer, GGB trains leave Zermatt once-weekly at dawn to arrive in time for a breathtaking Alpine sunrise. At the south end of Zermatt village a cable car heads up via Furi to the **Schwarzsee** (2583m), the most popular point from which to view the peak and, in summer, the trailhead for a zigzag walk (2hr) to the *Berghaus Matterhorn* inn (3260m), right below the mountain. All of Zermatt's cable cars and trains bring you to trailheads and spectacular views, while lifts to **Trockener Steg** give access to 21km of ski runs and a snowboard half-pipe that are open all summer long (day-pass Fr.64).

Arrival and information

Train The only way to reach Zermatt is on the spectacular narrow-gauge MGB train line (ER no discount, IR half-price, SP free; Ⓦwww.mgbahn.ch). Coming from Bern, Zürich or Milan change at Brig (Briga in Italian); coming from Geneva, Lausanne or Paris change at Visp. The most celebrated way to arrive is on the long east–west St Moritz-to-Zermatt Glacier Express, a day-long journey by panoramic train (reserve at any train station; ER twenty-five percent discount, SP free; IR half-price; Ⓦwww.glacierexpress.ch).

Tourist office (Mon–Sat 8.30am–6pm; June–Sept & Dec–April also Sun 9.30am–noon & 4–6pm;

☎027 966 81 00, Ⓦwww.zermatt.ch) near the station; there's a hotel list courtesy phone here.
Alpin centre Bahnhofstrasse, 58 (daily 8.30am–noon & 3–7pm, ☎027 966 24 60; Ⓦwww.zermatt.ch/alpincenter) runs canyoning, heli-skiing, snowshoeing and guided climbs (from Fr.296).
Ski and Snowboard School in the Alpin Centre (Mon–Fri 8am–noon & 3am–7pm, Sat & Sun 5am–9pm; ☎ 027 966 24 64).

Accommodation

Matterhorn Hostel (SB) Schulmattstrasse ☎027 968 19 19, Ⓦwww.matterhornhostel.com. Friendly staff, but rather cramped and in need of a re-vamp. Dorms ❸, doubles ❻
Zermatt Youth Hostel Winkelmatten, Staldenweg 5 ☎027 967 23 20, Ⓦwww.youthhostel.ch. Excellent hostel on the east side of the village. Half-board only. Dorms ❸, doubles ❺
Hotel Tannenhof to the east of the Kirchplatz ☎0279673188, Ⓦwww.tannenhof.zermatt.info. Good-value hotel, popular with climbers. Cosy doubles, available with or without a private bathroom. ❼
Matterhorn campsite Bahnhofstrasse ☎027 967 39 21, Ⓔmatterhorn@campings.ch. Very close to the village; just north of the train station. June–Sept. ❷

Eating and drinking.

Brown Cow Bahnhofstr., in the Hotel Post. Busy pub, serving reasonably priced snacks; sandwiches (Fr.9), salads (Fr.9–15.50) and burgers (Fr.12).
Whymper-Stube Bahnhofstr., ☎027 967 22 96, Ⓦwww.whypmer-stube.ch. Renowned for its fondues (Fr.23) and traditional Swiss fare.
North Wall Steinmattstr. Lively British-run bar across the river.
Papperla Pub Steinmattstr. 34, Ⓦwww.paperlapub.ch. Zermatt's busiest après-ski spot.

Moving on

Train Brig (hourly; 1hr 20min); Visp (hourly; 1hr 10min); St Moritz (1–2 daily; 7hr 50min)

ST MORITZ

If you're drawn to **ST MORITZ** by a desire to mingle with the wealthy and well-connected, you won't be disappointed. Sitting in the wild and beautiful Engadine Valley, this is a town of glass-fronted designer stores, impervious dark sunglasses and permanent suntans. For a century or more, it's been the prime winter retreat of social high-flyers, minor European royalty and the international jet set, who've sparked the arrival of Vuitton, Cartier and Armani amidst this stunningly romantic setting of forest, lake and mountains. When the tourist office trumpets St Moritz's "champagne climate", they don't necessarily mean the sparkling sunshine (although there's an amazing 322 days of that a year, on average).

What to see and do

The town spans two villages, **St Moritz-Bad** on the lake and **St Moritz-Dorf** on the hillside 2km above, linked by the main Via dal Bagn. Dorf is the upmarket one, while Bad – site of a Roman spa – is more down-to-earth. The area boasts legendary bob and toboggan courses, including the death-defying 1.2km **Cresta Run** (end-Dec to Feb; Fr.500 for 5 rides; men only, no women allowed; Ⓦwww.cresta-run.com). You can rent wooden sleds for the famous winter **Preda–Bergün toboggan run** (Mon–Sun 10.10am–4.45pm; one ride Fr.12; day ticket Fr.33; Ⓦwww.berguen.ch), starting from Preda train station and taking a zigzag 5km course down through the scenic Albula valley to Bergün, where trains cart you back to the beginning. The course is floodlit at night (Tues–Sun 6.45–11.30pm).

Arrival and information

Train and tourist office Via Serlas winds up from the train station below Dorf to a central square, from where the tourist office is 100m east at Via Maistra 12 (Mon–Sat 9am–6.30pm, Sun 4–6pm; April–June, Oct & Nov Sat closes noon, closed Sun; ☎081 837 33 33, Ⓦwww.stmoritz.ch).

Accommodation

Hostels

HI Hostel Stille Via Surpunt 60 ⓣ081 833 39 69, ⓦwww.youthhostel.ch. Well-equipped, modern hostel, twenty minutes walk around the lake from the station. Half-board only. Dorms ❹, doubles ❼

Hotels

Hotel Bellaval Via Grevas 55 ⓣ081 833 32 45, ⓦwww.bellaval-stmoritz.ch. Simple rooms near the train station; pay extra for a balcony facing the lake. ❾

Stille Sports Hotel ⓣ081 833 69 48, ⓦwww.hotelstille.ch. Spartan rooms near to the HI hostel. Geared towards athletes and groups. ❼

Campsite

Olympiaschanze campsite Stadtstrasse 30 ⓣ081 833 40 90. Located in a pleasant spot, just 10min walk from St. Moritz–Bad (June–Sept). ❷

Eating and drinking

Coop Via del Bagn/ Via Grevas. Enormous supermarket on the road down to Bad. With scenery this stunning and restaurants this expensive, you'll probably want to picnic.

Boccalino Via dal Bagn 6. Affordable pizzeria; prices start at Fr.10 for a Margharita.

Bobby's Pub Via dal Bagn 52. Attracts crowds during the winter season.

Moving on

Train Chur (hourly; 2 hr) – change for Zürich.

Bus Lugano (mid-June to mid-Oct daily, other times 3 weekly; 3hr 45min).

ZÜRICH

Not so long ago, **ZÜRICH** was famed for being the cleanest, most icily efficient city in Europe: apocryphal stories abound of tourists embarking on efforts to find a cigarette butt or food wrapper discarded on the streets – and drawing a blank every time. But there's a lot more to Zürich these days than its obsessive cleanliness: this most beautiful of cities, astride a river and turned towards a crystal-clear lake and distant snowy peaks, has plenty to recommend it, not least bars and clubs as hip and varied as those in more celebrated European cities. The steep, cobbled alleys of the Old Town are great to wander around, with an engaging café culture and a wealth of nightlife. You could easily spend days here.

ORIENTATION

Flowing north from the Zürichsee, the River Limmat bisects the city's historic centre. On the right bank is the **Niederdorf** district; on the left, the train station and Zürich's main shopping streets. To the north-west of the centre, the city's former industrial quarter, known as 'Züri-West' has become home to many of the city's trendiest clubs.

What to see and do

Across the River Limmat from the station, the narrow lanes of the medieval **Niederdorf** district stretch south, quiet during the day and bustling after dark. The waterfront is lined with fine Baroque *Zunfthäuser* (guildhalls), arcaded lower storeys fronting the quayside, their extravagantly decorated dining-rooms now mostly upmarket restaurants. One block in is **Niederdorfstrasse**, initially tacky, but offering plenty of opportunities to explore atmospheric cobbled side-alleys and secluded courtyards: Lenin lived at Spiegelgasse 14 in 1917 (pre-Revolution), while a café at Spiegelgasse 1 once housed the Cabaret Voltaire, birthplace of the Dada art movement. Just south is Zürich's trademark **Grossmünster** (Great Minster; Mon–Sat 9am–5pm & Sun 12.30–5.30pm), where Huldrych Zwingli, father of Swiss Protestantism, began preaching the Reformation in 1519. Its exterior is largely fifteenth-century, while its twin towers were topped with distinctive octagonal domes in the seventeenth century. The interior is austere apart from the intensely coloured choir windows

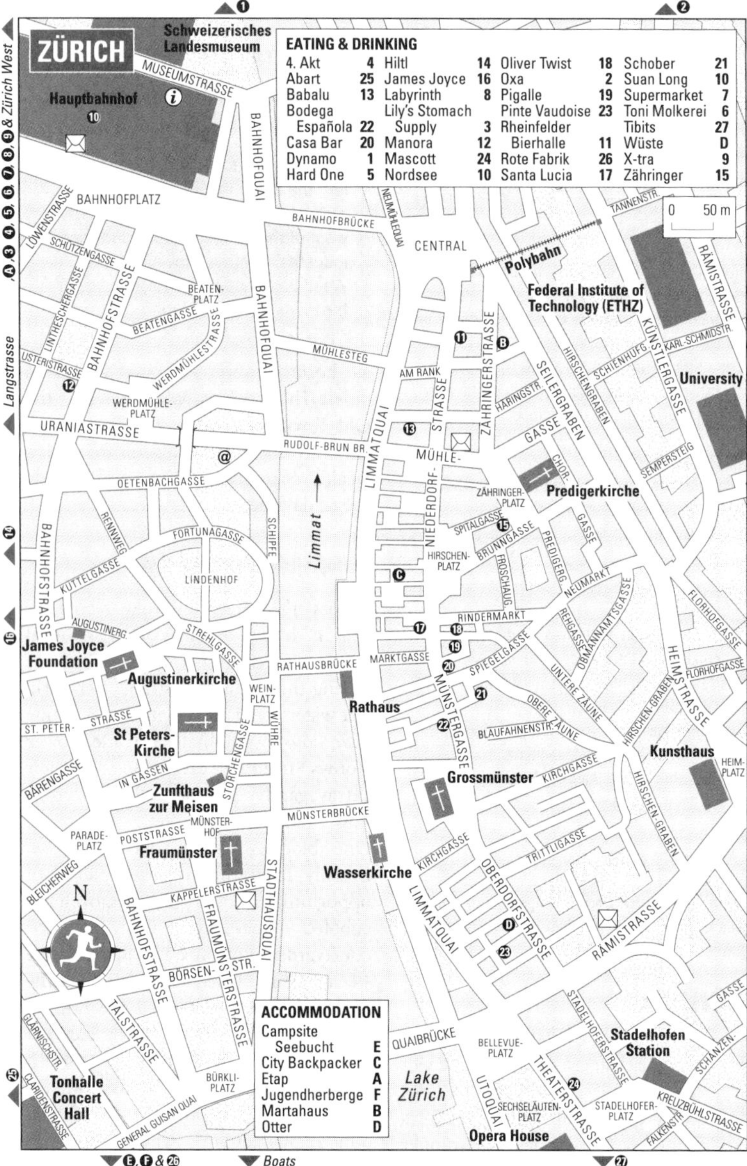

(1933) by Augusto Giacometti and the Romanesque crypt which contains an oversized fifteenth-century statue of Charlemagne, popularly associated with the foundation of the church in the ninth century. A door, to the right on exiting, gives into the atmospheric **cloister**.

The Kunsthaus

Switzerland's best gallery, the **Kunsthaus** (Tues–Thurs 10am–9pm, Fri–Sun

10am–5pm; Fr.12; more for temporary exhibits; Ⓦwww.kunsthaus.ch) is up the hill from the church via several alleys. Some fascinating late-Gothic paintings are fleshed out by a roomful of Venetian masters and fine Flemish pieces. The collection of twentieth-century art is stunning: works by Miró, Dalí and De Chirico head a wonderful Surrealist overview; Picasso, Chagall, Klee and Kandinsky all have rooms to themselves; there are two of Monet's most beautiful waterlily canvases, plenty of Warhols, an array of Giacometti's sculpture, and the largest Munch collection outside Norway.

West of the centre

The **west bank** is the main commercial district, while further west of the centre are the coolest hangouts and the best streetlife. Tram #2 or #3 to Bezirksgebäude will deliver you to relaxed **Helvetiaplatz**, from where funky **Langstrasse** heads north – lowlife bars rubbing shoulders with avant-garde galleries, the smells of kebabs and pizza mixing with the pungent aroma of marijuana. This fascinating street is a mingle of styles and cultures – Swiss-German blending with French-African, Turkish, Balkan, East Asian and Latin American.

Bahnhofstrasse and Paradeplatz

Leading south from the station, **Bahnhofstrasse** is one of the most prestigious shopping streets in Europe. This is the gateway into the modern city, and is where all of Zürich strolls, to browse at the inexpensive department stores that crowd the first third of the street, or to sign away Fr.25,000 on a Rolex watch or a Vuitton bag at the understated super-chic boutiques further south. Two-thirds of the way down is **Paradeplatz**, a tram-packed little square offering some of the best people-watching in the city.

Lindenhof and St Peters-Kirche

The narrow lanes between Bahnhofstrasse and the river lead up to the Lindenhof, site of a Roman fortress and customs post. James Joyce wrote Ulysses in Zürich (1915–19), and the **Joyce Foundation**, nearby at Augustinergasse 9 (Tues–Thurs 2–6pm; free), can point you to his various hangouts, and his grave. Steps away is **St Peters-Kirche** (Mon–Fri 8am–6pm & Sat 8am–4pm), renowned for its enormous sixteenth-century clock face – the largest in Europe. Immediately south rises the slender-spired Gothic **Fraumünster** (Mon–Sat 10am–4/6pm; also Sun 11.30am–6pm in summer), which began life as a convent in the ninth century; its spectacular stained glass by Marc Chagall is unmissable.

Arrival and information

Air Zurich's airport (Flughafen) lies 11km northeast of the city centre. Frequent trains leave for the city station.

Train Zürich's main station, the giant Hauptbahnhof (HB), is served by trains from all over Europe. The building extends three storeys below ground, taking in a shopping mall, supermarket and some good eateries; the main concourse is the haunt of pickpockets and bag-snatchers, so keep your valuables safe.

Bus The international bus station is 50m north on Sihlquai.

Tourist office on the station concourse (Mon–Sat 8/8.30am–7/8.30pm, Sun 8.30/9am–6.30pm; Ⓣ044 215 40 00, Ⓦwww.zuerich.com) will book rooms for free, and sells the **Zürich Card** (Fr.17/34 one/three days), which entitles you to free rides on public transport and free entry to museums.

City transport

Bike rental Free (with photo-ID & Fr.20 deposit) from Velogate, next to platform 18 of the station (daily May–Oct 7.30am–9.30pm).

Tram and bus Although most sites can be covered on foot, the tram and bus system is easy to use (Ⓦwww.vbz.ch), with all tickets valid on trams, buses, some boats and local "S-Bahn" city trains.

Tickets Buy tickets from machines at every stop: choose between the green button (24hr; Fr.7.80); blue button (1hr; Fr.3.90); or yellow button (short one-way hop; Fr.2.40). You'll need a multizone ticket to get to or from the airport.
Taxis Alpha Taxi ⓣ 044 777 77 77; Züritaxi ⓣ 044 222 22 22.

Accommodation

Hostels

City Backpacker (SB) Niederdorfstr. 5 ⓣ 044 251 90 15, ⓦ www.city-backpacker.ch. Good atmosphere and central location, plus free kitchen use, laundry and Internet (though a Fr.20 key deposit). Can be a little cramped when full. No check-in after 10pm. Dorms (exc. breakfast) ❸, rooms ❻
Jugendherberge (HI) Mutschellenstr. 114 ⓣ 043 399 78 00, ⓦ www.youthhostel.ch. Rather institutional hostel, out in a southwestern suburb. Tram #7 (direction Wollishofen) to Morgental, then walk 5min. Breakfast included. 4-bed dorms ❸, rooms ❽

Hotels

Etap Technoparkstr. 2 ⓣ 044 276 20 00, ⓦ www.etaphotel.com. Generic, functional hotel out west in the old industrial quarter, behind the trendy Schiffbau arts centre. ❻
Martahaus Zähringerstr. 36 ⓣ 044 251 45 50, ⓦ www.martahaus.ch. Clean Old Town budget hotel with cabin-dorms and doubles, plus a café, Internet and laundry. Dorms ❸, doubles ❻

Campsite

Seebucht Seestr. 559 ⓣ 044 482 16 12, ⓦ www.camping-zurich.ch. Well-serviced site on the lakeside, 2km south of the centre. Bus #161 or #165 from Bürkliplatz to Stadtgrenze. Closed Oct–April. ❷

TREAT YOURSELF

Otter Oberdorfstr. 7 ⓣ 044 251 22 07, ⓦ www.wueste.ch. Friendly, quirky Old Town hotel. Rooms are decorated thematically and there's also a dreamy top-floor apartment. Breakfast included; bathrooms are shared. Pay more for a balcony room with stunning views of the Old Town. ❽

Eating

A wander through the Niederdorf district will turn up dozens of eating options – falafel, sausage, noodle and french-fry stands, plus beer halls serving daily specials for about Fr.13.

Snack options

Manora 5th floor of Manor store, Bahnhofstr. 75. Good, varied self-service fare for under Fr.13.
Nordsee Train station concourse. Good-value fish dishes (Fr.13) and snacks (Fr.7.50) to eat in or take away.
Suan Long Train station lower level. Cheap, filling stir-fries – meat and veggie from Fr.9.50.

Cafés and restaurants

Bodega Española Münstergasse 15. Atmospheric tapas bar and paella restaurant. Tapas from Fr.10.
Hiltl Sihlstr. 28, ⓦ www.hiltl.ch. Top-quality vegetarian buffet, with budget prices for takeaway. Daily specials Fr.16.50. Mutates into a trendy cocktail bar at night.
Lily's Stomach Supply Langstr. 197. Bustling pan-Asian noodle-bar, serving enormous bowls of noodles and wok-dishes from Fr.15. Eat-in or take-out.
Pinte Vaudoise in *Hotel Villette*, Kruggasse 4. Traditional place serving what some say is the best fondue in Zürich (Fr.25.50). Closed Sat in summer & Sun.
Santa Lucia Marktgasse 21. Popular local chain, serving wide selection of good-value pasta and pizza from Fr.17. Open late.
Schober Napfgasse 4. Frilly confectionary shop and café with hot-chocolate and cakes to die for.
Tibits Seefeldstr. 2, beside the Opera House. Chic café with excellent self-service veggie food; pay for the weight of your plate. Daily till midnight.
Zähringer Zähringerplatz 11. Co-operative-run café-bar with an alternative-minded clientele and a simple, substantial daily menu (Fr.20).

Drinking and nightlife

Supplementing its lively music venues, Zürich's **club scene** has skyrocketed recently, and you'll find dance floors heaving. The hip quarter around Langstrasse, west of the centre, is full of DJ bars, and the industrial quarter to the northwest is where the best clubs hide themselves. August sees the **Street Parade** (ⓦ www.street-parade.ch), a hedonistic weekend of techno street-dancing. *ZüriTipp* (ⓦ www.zueritipp.ch) magazine has listings and is available at the tourist office.

Bars

4. Akt Heinrichstrasse 22. Lively Züri-west bar, packed with a young crowd.
Babalu Schmidgasse 6. Tiny, chic DJ-bar on an Old Town sidestreet.
Casa Bar Münstergasse 20. Live jazz and blues nightly in the Old Town.
Hard One Hardstrasse 260. Stylish, dimly-lit fifth-floor lounge bar with a spectacular view over the industrial quarter.
James Joyce Pelikanstr. 8. Original nineteenth-century interior, transported piece by piece from Dublin. Closed Sat from 7pm & all Sun.
Oliver Twist Rindermarkt 6. Homely English pub on an Old Town lane with British and Irish beers.
Pigalle Marktgasse 14. Legendary little bar filled with the elegantly wasted. Open till 4am Fri and Sat.
Rheinfelder Bierhalle Niederdorfstr. 76. Best of the hearty beerhalls. Closed Sun.
Wüste In Hotel Otter, Oberdorfstr. 7. Mellow, relaxed bar near the Grossmünster. Open till 2am at the weekend.

Clubs

Abart Manessestr. 170, ⓦwww.abart.ch. Regular choice of local and foreign bands.
Dynamo Wasserwerkstr. 21. Alternative, punkish bands and dance nights.
Labyrinth Pfingstweidstr. 70. Hard house at this mixed gay/straight venue.
Mascott Theaterstrasse 10, ⓦwww.mascotte.ch. Most popular of the Old town clubs. Renowned for its Tuesday rock/metal 'Karaoke from Hell' night.
Oxa Andreasstr. 70. Techno and house; famed after-hours parties (Sun 5am–noon).
Rote Fabrik Seestr. 395 ⓦ www.rotefabrick.ch. Alternative bands, big-name DJs, cheap food and a great riverside bar.
Supermarket Geroldstrasse 17, ⓦwww.supermarket.li. Popular Züri-West club, attracting international DJs Thurs–Sat.
Toni Molkerei Förrlibuckstr. 109. Eclectic dance club in a vast industrial space.
X-tra Limmatstr. 118, ⓦwww.x-tra.ch. Spacious modern bar, with popular upstairs DJ club.

Shopping

Bahnhofstrasse is the place to find designer and high street stores.
Niederdorfstrasse is crammed with grungy indie boutiques (particularly shoe shops).
Kirchgasse has a high concentration of second-hand bookshops, antiques shops and galleries.
Flea market Bürkliplatz (May–Oct Sat 8am–4pm).
Jelmoli Seidengasse 1. Zürich's largest department store.
Travel Book Shop Rindermarkt 20. Good selection of maps and travel guides. Closed Sun and Mon am.
Schober Napfgasse 4. Good option for chocolate.

Directory

Consulates Ireland, Claridenstr. 25 ⓣ044 289 25 15; UK, Hegibachstr. 47 ⓣ044 383 65 60; USA, Dufourstr. 101 ⓣ044 422 25 66. Embassies are in Bern.
Exchange/bank UBS Bahnhofstrasse 45 (Mon–Fri 8.15am–4.15pm); or try the station.
Hospital Permanence Medical Centre, Bahnhofplatz 15 ⓣ044 215 44 44.
Internet Urania, Uraniastrasse 3 (Mon–Sat 7/8am–11pm & Sun 10am–10pm).
Laundry Mühlegasse 11, Niederdorf.
Left luggage in the station
Pharmacy Bellevue, Theaterstrasse 14 (24hr) ⓣ044 266 62 22.
Post office Kasernenstrasse, beside the station.

Moving on

Train Basel (2 hourly; 1hr); Bern (every 30min; 1hr–1hr 25min); Geneva (every 30min–1hr; 2hr 45min); Innsbruck (5 daily; 3hr 20min); Interlaken Ost (every 2hr; 2hr 5min); Lausanne (every 30min; 2hr 10min); Lugano (hourly; 3hr); Luzern (every 30min; 45min); Milan (hourly ; 4hr 25min); Prague (1 daily; 13hr); Sargans (every 30min; 1hr); St Moritz (hourly; 3hr 20min – change at Chur); Vienna (3 daily; 9hr).

THE RHINE FALLS

A great fine-weather excursion from Zürich is the half-day trip north to the **Rhine falls** (ⓦwww.rhinefalls.com), Europe's largest waterfalls, which tumble 3km west of **SCHAFFHAUSEN**. They are magnificent, not so much for their height (a mere 23m) as for their impressive breadth (150m) and the sheer drama of the place, with spray rising in a cloud of rainbows above the forested banks. The turreted castle **Schloss Laufen** on the south bank completes the spectacle. Be here on August 1, Switzerland's national day, for a famous fireworks display. Damp steps lead down from the castle souvenir shop to platforms at the water's edge (Fr.1), where the falls roar inches from your nose. In summer, the best views are from daredevil boats, which scurry about in the spray (Fr.6.50–11). Take a **train** from Zürich either to Winterthur – from where hourly trains serve Schloss Laufen's own little station (April–Oct only) – or to Schaffhausen, from where you can walk (20min) or take bus #1 or #6 to Neuhausen Zentrum, 5min from the falls.

Ticino

The Italian-speaking region of **Ticino** (*Tessin* in German and French) occupies the balmy, lake-laced southern foothills of the Alps. It's radically different from the rest of Switzerland in almost every way: culture, food, architecture, attitude and driving style owe more to Milan than Zürich. Switzerland has controlled the area since the early 1500s, when it defeated the Duke of Milan's army. The main attractions are the beautiful lakeside resorts of **Locarno** and **Lugano**, where mountain scenery merges with the subtropical flora encouraged by the warm climate.

Unless you approach from Italy, there's only one train line in – through the 16km **Gotthard Tunnel**. The track's spiralling contortions on the approach climb are famous: trains pass the onion-domed church at Wassen three times, first far above you, then on a level, and finally far below, before entering the subalpine tunnel.

LOCARNO

Mainline trains speed south to Lugano and Milan, while a branch line heads west from Bellinzona to **LOCARNO**, a characterful old town on a broad sweeping bay in **Lake Maggiore**, its piazzas overlooked by subtropical gardens of palm trees, camellias and bougainvillea. It can get overrun with the rich and wannabe-famous on summer weekends yet manages to retain its sun-drenched cool.

LOCARNO INTERNATIONAL FILM FESTIVAL

Early August's Locarno International Film Festival (Ⓦwww.pardo.ch) is stealing a march on Cannes for star-appeal; catch nightly offerings on Europe's largest movie screen, set up in Piazza Grande.

What to see and do

The focus of town is **Piazza Grande**, just off the lakefront, where on warm summer nights exquisitely groomed locals parade to and fro. The Renaissance Old Town is ranged on gently rising ground behind the piazza: wandering through the alleys with an ice cream is the best way to blend in with Locarno life.

The church of **Madonna del Sasso** (daily 6.30am–6.45pm) is an impressive ochre vision floating above the town on a wooded crag, consecrated in 1487. The walk up (or down) through a wooded ravine and past decaying shrines is glorious; or take the funicular (Fr.6.60 return) from just west of the station to Ticino's greatest photo-op, looking down on the church and lake.

From the top station, an ear-poppingly steep cable car climbs to **Cardada**, set amidst fragrant pine woods, with walking routes and a spectacular, silent chairlift whisking you up to **Cimetta**, where the restaurant terrace offers a view you won't forget in a hurry.

A short bus-ride east of Locarno is **Valle Verzasca**, where deathwish freaks can re-enact the opening scene of the James Bond film *Goldeneye*, by **bungee-jumping** a world-record 220m off the Verzasca Dam (April–Oct daily; Fr.255; book on ⓣ091 780 7800, ⓦwww.trekking.ch) – in June, July & August, you can jump by moonlight; see the website.

Arrival and information

Train Locarno's train station is 150m northeast of Piazza Grande.
Boat The landing-stage is between the train station and Piazza Grande; summer boats run to nearby Swiss lakeside resorts such as Ascona, and south to Italian ones such as Stresa (on the main line to Milan).
Tourist office in the Casino complex opposite the landing-stage (Mon–Fri 9am–6pm; April–Oct also Sat 10am–6pm, Sun 10am–1.30pm & 2.30–5pm; ⓣ091 791 00 91, ⓦwww.maggiore.ch).

Accommodation

Città Vecchia Via Torretta 13, ⓣ091 751 45 54, ⓦwww.cittavecchia.ch; March–Oct. Basic pension with peculiar bathroom arrangements and large dorms. Very central though. Dorms ❸, doubles ❻
HI hostel 'Palagiovani' Via Varenna 18 ⓣ091 756 15 00, ⓦwww.youthhostel.ch; bus #31/36 to Cinque Vie. Friendly hostel 10 minutes walk from the centre of town with four- or six-bed dorms (❸) and doubles (❻).
Delta campsite ⓣ091 751 60 81, ⓦwww.campingdelta.com; March–Oct. Expensive but well-equipped campsite 20min walk south along the lakeshore (just past the lido). Possibility of paying extra for a lake-side pitch. ❺

Eating and drinking

Cantina Canetti Little place just off the Piazza Grande with plain local cooking (from Fr.14) and live accordion on weekend nights.
Casa del Popolo Piazetta del Corporazioni. Busy, inexpensive pizzeria in a small square. Pizzas from Fr.15.
Manora Branch of the self-service chain by the train-station, with a wide-range of good, cheap meals for Fr.13 or under. Open late and Sun.

Moving on

Train Zürich (hourly; 3hr 10min); Basel (every 2hr; 4hr 10min); Bellinzona – change for Lugano (every 30min; 25min).

LUGANO

With its cluster of piazzas and tree-lined promenades, **LUGANO** is the most alluring of Ticino's lake resorts, less touristic than Locarno but with, if anything, double the chic.

What to see and do

The centre of town is **Piazza della Riforma**, a huge café-lined square just by the exceptionally beautiful **Lago di Lugano**. Through the maze of steep lanes northwest of Riforma, Via Cattedrale dog-legs up to **Cattedrale San Lorenzo**, characterized by a fine Renaissance portal, fragments of interior frescoes and spectacular views from its terrace. Also from Riforma, narrow Via Nassa – home of big-name designer boutiques – heads southwest to the medieval church of **Santa Maria degli Angioli**, containing a stunning wall-sized fresco of the Crucifixion. A little further south is the **Museo d'Arte Moderna**, Riva Caccia 5 (Tues–Fri 10am–noon & 2–6pm, Sat & Sun 11am–6pm; entry varies), with world-class exhibitions; a little further still is the modestly named district of **Paradiso**, from where a funicular rises to **San Salvatore**, a rugged rock pinnacle offering fine views of the lake and surrounding countryside.

The best of the lake is behind (south of) San Salvatore on the Ceresio peninsula, accessed by boats or postbuses. Here you'll find tiny **Montagnola**, where the writer Hermann Hesse lived for 43 years; his first house, **Casa Camuzzi**, is now a small museum (Tues–Sun 10am–6.30pm; Nov–Feb Sat & Sun only 10am–5.30pm; Fr.6), with an excellent 45-minute English film on Hesse's life in Ticino. Jewel of the lake is **Morcote** on the southern tip of the peninsula; tranquil stepped lanes lead up to its photogenic church of **Santa Maria del Sasso**, and several walks explore the woods, including a trail back to San Salvatore (2hr 30min).

Arrival and information

Train Lugano's train station overlooks the town from the west, linked to the centre by a short funicular or by steps down to Via Cattedrale.
Tourist office Palazzo Civico, off Riforma (Mon–Fri 9am–5/7pm; April–Oct also Sat 9am–6pm, Sun 10am–6pm; ⓣ091 913 32 32, ⓦwww.lugano-tourism.ch); boats around the lake (IR & ER no discount, SP free) depart from directly opposite.

Accommodation

HI hostel Via Cantonale 13, Savosa; bus #5 to Crocifisso from the stop 200m left out of the train station ⓣ091 966 27 28, ⓦwww.youthhostel.ch (March–Oct). Excellent, quiet hostel with a large garden area and swimming pool. Dorms ❷, doubles ❺
Hostel Montarina (SB) Via Montarina 1 ⓣ091 966 72 72, ⓦwww.montarina.com. More central (just behind the train station) with large dorms and a swimming pool. Dorms ❷, rooms ❼
La Piodella campsite ⓣ091 994 77 88, ⓦwww.campingtcs.ch. One of several lakeside campsites in Agno, further west round the lake. Take the train from the FLP station (direction Ponte Tresa). ❸

Eating and drinking

Etnic Quartiere Maghetti. Relaxed café-bar, serving beer, cocktails and Mediterranean-style snacks; salads Fr.17.
La Tinèra off Via dei Gorini, behind Riforma. Good place for pasta and tasty Ticinese chicken stews (Fr.16). Closed Sun.
Manora Piazza Cioccaro. Inexpensive self-service staples for under Fr13. There's an outside terrace at this branch.

Moving on

Train Luzern (every 2hr; 2hr 45min); Zürich (hourly; 3hr).
Bus St Moritz (mid-June to mid-Oct daily, otherwise 3 weekly; 3hr 45min); book at the train station.

Liechtenstein

Only slightly larger than Manhattan island, **Liechtenstein** is the world's sixth-smallest country. It's an unassuming place squashed between Switzerland and Austria, ruled over by His Serene Highness Prince Hans Adam II, and has made a mint from nursing some Fr.90 billion in its numbered bank accounts. The main reason to visit is the novelty value – at less than two hours from Zürich, you can see the whole country in a day. Swiss francs are legal tender, but the phone system is separate (country code ⓣ423).

VADUZ

From Sargans train station on the Zürich–Chur line, regular bus #1 shuttles over the Rhine (no border controls) in half-an-hour to the capital **VADUZ**, a tiny town bulging with glass-plated **banks** and squadrons of aimless visitors. Central hub is the post office, where all buses stop, midway between the two parallel main streets, Äulestrasse and pedestrianized Städtle. Facing it is the sleek **Kunstmuseum** (Tues–Sun 10am–5pm, Thurs till 8pm; Fr.8), displaying temporary art exhibitions, some of which draw on the private collection inherited – and added to – by the prince. Perched on the forested hillside above is the prince's restored sixteenth-century **castle** (no public access).

Postbuses from Vaduz serve all points in Liechtenstein – if you have time to spare, catch bus #10 to the mountain resort of **MALBUN**, at 1602m. Buses also serve Feldkirch just across the border in Austria (passport needed), from where trains run on to Bregenz, Innsbruck and Vienna.

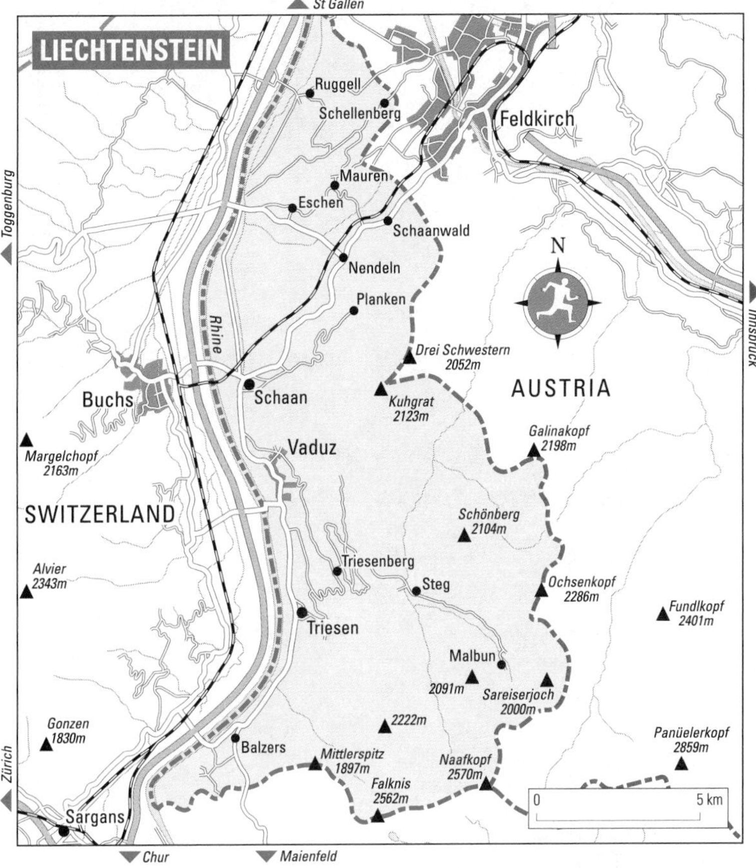

Arrival and information

Arrival Buses from Sargans stop on Vaduz's main street, by the post office.

Tourist office Städtle 37 (daily 9am–noon & 1.30–5pm; Nov–April closed Sat & Sun; ⓣ 239 63 00, Ⓦ www.tourismus.li), will bang a stamp into your passport as a memento (Fr.2).

Accommodation

HI hostel Schaan-Vaduz Untere Rüttigasse 6 ⓣ 232 50 22 (March–Oct). Quiet rural location, looking out over fields and mountains. 5min walk from the Mühleholz bus stop in Schaan (2km north of Vaduz). Dorms ❷, doubles ❻

Mittagsspitze campsite ⓣ 392 36 77, Ⓦ www.campingtriesen.li. Tranquil campsite with swimming pool, 5km south in the countryside near Triesen. ❷

Eating and drinking

Café Wolf Städtle 29. Pavement café with daily 2-course set lunch menu (Swiss/ Italian fare) for Fr.18/22.

Pizza Bar Potenza Herrengasse 9. Tiny bar serving up crispy thin-crust pizzas (from Fr.12.50) to bankers, locals and tourists.

Moving on

Bus Malbun (hourly; 30min).

Turkey

HIGHLIGHTS

COVERED BAZAAR, İSTANBUL: the world's largest covered market with over 3000 stalls

CAPPADOCIA: a lunar landscape, complete with eerie caves and underground cities

EPHESUS: one of the world's best-preserved ancient cities

ANTALYA: enjoy an operetta in the atmospheric open air theatre of Aspendos

KAŞ: a great base for beaches, ancient sites, and adventure sports

ROUGH COSTS

DAILY BUDGET basic €22/with the occasional treat €35

DRINK €3

FOOD Kebab with side order €6

HOSTEL/BUDGET HOTEL €8 /€13–22

TRAVEL Bus: Ankara-Nevşehir (250km) €13

FACT FILE

POPULATION 72 million

AREA 780,580 sq km

LANGUAGE Turkish

CURRENCY New Turkish lira (YTL)

CAPITAL Ankara (population 4.3 million)

INTERNATIONAL PHONE CODE ⓣ90

Basics

Turkey has multiple identities. Poised uneasily between East and West, mosques coexist with churches, and Roman remnants crumble alongside ancient Hittite sites. The country is politically secular, though the majority of its people are Muslim, and is an immensely rewarding place to travel, not least because of the people, whose reputation for friendliness and hospitality is richly deserved.

Much of the country's delights are inexpensive pleasures. Whether it's indulging in tasty *börek* pastries, catching your own food with local fishermen or dancing in back-street bars, there are plenty of activities to consume your time but not your budget. Although extravagant options for recreation and accommodation abound, these are not completely out of the budget traveller's reach and a bit of skilful bartering usually ensures incredible value for money.

Most visitors begin their trip in **İstanbul**; a heady mix between European shopping districts, Ottoman architecture and Anatolian cultural influences. Moving south, small country towns are swathed in olive groves, while the area is littered with ancient sites, including **Assos**, **Pergamon** and **Ephesus**. Beyond the functional city of **İzmir**, the Aegean coast is Turkey at its most developed, with large numbers drawn to hedonistic party resorts such as **Bodrum** and **Marmaris**. Beyond here, the aptly named **Turquoise Coast** is home to resorts infamous for fabulous water and adventure sports facilities such as **Fethiye** and **Kaş**. Inland from here is the spectacular **Cappadocia**, with its famous rock churches, subterranean cities and landscape studded with cave dwellings. Further north, **Ankara**, Turkey's capital, is a planned city whose contrived Western feel gives some indication of the priorities of the modern Turkish Republic.

CHRONOLOGY

1250 BC According to Homer's *Iliad* Troy is cleverly taken by the Greeks who sneak into the city in a wooden horse.

334 BC Alexander the Great marches through Anatolia, present-day Turkey.

129 BC Romans conquer Anatolia.

47 AD St Paul brings Christianity to Anatolia.

330 Emperor Constantine, founds Constantinople, calling it the new Rome and founding the Byzantine Empire.

1288 The Islamic Ottoman Empire starts to expand across present-day Turkey.

1526 The Ottomans defeat the Habsburgs gaining large areas of Europe.

1832 Following heavy fighting, the Greeks gain independence from Ottoman Turkey.

1918 The Ottomans enter WWI on the side of the Germans and are defeated by the Allies.

1923 After the Turkish war of Independence, Turkey is declared a Republic led by President Kemal Atatürk.

1928 The Turkish constitution declares Turkey to be a secular state.

1945 Turkey remains neutral during WWII, lending nominal assistance to the Nazis whilst outwardly supporting the Allies.

1960 Army takes power in a coup that encounters minimal resistance, dismissing the ruling Democrat Party and hanging its leaders.

1980 Once more the army overthrows government and takes control. Governance is given back to civilians a couple of years later.

1993 Tansu Cillar becomes Turkey's first female Prime Minister.

2005 Talks about Turkish accession to the EU are held, but a decision remains elusive.

2007 Tensions rise between secularists and Islamists over whether Turkey should remain a secular state.

ARRIVAL AND VISAS

Tourist visas (25YTL) are required for individuals from most countries and can be obtained upon arrival. These commonly last for three months and enable visitors to travel between Turkey and neighbouring countries. French, German and New Zealand nationals can enter Turkey without a visa and stay up to three months. Contact your local Turkish embassy (see p.49) for more information.

The most common point of arrival is İstanbul with overland travellers arriving at the *otogar* (**bus station**) or Sirkeci **train station** located near the pier in Eminönü. International **air arrivals** fly into İstanbul's Atatürk airport, where connecting flights can be caught to other popular destinations such as İzmir and Ankara. Travellers intent on spending the majority of their trip on Turkey's Turquoise Coast will find Antalya's international airport a good bet for moving on to any one of the region's many resorts. If you're travelling to Turkey **by sea** you're likely to arrive at either Kuşadasi or Marmaris where ferries connect Turkey with the Greek islands.

GETTING AROUND

The **train** system, run by TCDD (ⓦwww.tcdd.gov.tr) is limited. The most useful services are the expresses between İstanbul and Ankara, and other long-distance links to main provincial cities such as Edirne, Konya, Denizli and İzmir. Cheap sleeper cabins are available on overnight services. Reservations are only necessary at weekends or on national holidays. An ISIC card gets a 20 percent discount. InterRail passes are valid, Eurail aren't.

Long-distance **buses** are a more reliable way of getting around. Most routes are covered by several competing firms, which all have ticket booths at the bus station (*otogar* or *terminal*) from which they operate, as well as an office in the town centre. Fares vary only slightly between companies: expect to pay about 10YTL/100km. For short hops you're most likely to use a **dolmuş**, a car or minibus that follows a set route, picking up and dropping off along the way. Sometimes the destination will be posted on a sign at the kerbside, and sometimes within the *dolmuş* itself, though you'll generally have to ask. Fares are very low.

Nearly all **ferries** are run by Türkiye Denizcilik Işletmesi (TDI), who operate everything from inner-city shuttles and inter-island lines to international routes. Overnight services are popular, and you should buy tickets in advance through authorized TDI agents. A third-class double cabin from İstanbul to İzmir costs about 90YTL per person. Students get a thirty percent discount with an ISIC card.

ACCOMMODATION

Finding **accommodation** is generally no problem, except in high season at the busier coastal resorts and in the larger towns. A double room in a one-star **hotel** costs 20–45YTL in season depending on the location, with breakfast sometimes included. Basic ungraded hotels or **pansiyons** (pensions) may offer spartan rooms, with or without bathroom, for as low as 15YTL. A new type of "bijou" hotel/pension, often in historic buildings, offers high levels of comfort, sometimes at surprisingly reasonable prices. There's also a well-established network of **backpacker hotels**. Most rooms tend to be sparse but clean, at 7–20YTL for a dorm bed, 25–50YTL for an en-suite double. Most resort-based places **close in winter**, so it's wise to call ahead or check with the local tourist office. **Campsites** are common only on the coast and in national parks; tourist offices stock a map of them all. Per-person charges run from 3.50–20YTL, plus 5–7YTL per tent. Campsites often rent out tents or provide chalet accommodation for 20–40YTL.

FOOD AND DRINK

At its finest, Turkish **food** is one of the world's great cuisines, yet prices are on the whole affordable. **Breakfast** (*kahvaltı*) served at hotels and *pansiyons* is usually a buffet (approximately 5YTL), offering bread with butter, cheese, jam, honey, olives and tea or coffee. Many workers start the morning with a *börek* (1.50YTL) or a *poça*, pastries filled with meat, cheese or potato that are sold at a tiny **büfe** (stall/café) or at street carts. Others make do with a simple *simit* (sesame-seed bread ring). **Snack** vendors hawk *lahmacun*, small "pizzas" with meat-based toppings, and, in coastal cities, *midye tava* (deep-fried mussels). Another option is *pide*, or Turkish pizza – flat bread with various toppings.

Meat dishes in **restaurants** (*lokanta*) include several variations on the kebab (*kebap*). Fish and seafood are good, if usually pricey, and sold normally by weight. **Mezes** – an extensive array of cold appetizers – come in all shapes and sizes, the most common being *dolma* (peppers or vine leaves stuffed with rice), *patlícan salata* (aubergine in tomato sauce), and *acılı* (a mixture of tomato paste, onion, chilli and parsley), which along with *sebze turlu* (vegetable stew), and *nohut* (chickpeas) are the few dishes available for vegetarians. Most budget restaurants are alcohol-free; some places marked *içk ili* (licensed) may be more expensive.

For **dessert**, there's every imaginable concoction at a *pastane* (sweet-shop): best are the honey-soaked *baklava*, and a variety of milk puddings, most commonly *sütlaç*. Other sweets include *aşure* (Noah's pudding), a sort of rosewater jelly laced with pulses, raisins and nuts: and *lokum* or Turkish delight.

NARGILES

Any visitor to Turkey will soon observe the nation's love affair with smoking. Smoke-free zones in restaurants and other public places are virtually nonexistent. Instead, a variety of bars exist specialising in **nargile** (waterpipe) smoking. Nargiles use special flavoured tobacco with varieties ranging from chocolate to strawberry. In touristy cafés smoking a nargile can cost about 13YTL compared with 7YTL in a local's joint. There's no real etiquette as such – people tend to share nargiles but change the mouth piece when it comes to their turn to smoke.

Drinks

Tea (*çay*) is the national drink, with sugar on the side but no milk. **Turkish coffee** (*kahve*) is served in tiny cups. Instant coffee is losing ground to fresh filter coffee in trendier cafés. **Fruit juices** (*meyva suyu*) can be excellent but are usually sweetened. Mineral water, either still (*su*) or fizzy (*maden suyu*), is found on the table in most restaurants. You'll also come across *ayran*, watered-down yoghurt, which makes a refreshing drink. The main locally brewed brands of **beer** (*bira*) are Efes Pilsen and Tuborg; imported beers are available, but at a horrendous mark-up. The national aperitif is anis-flavoured **rakí** – a strong spirit consisting of forty-five percent alcohol. It's usually topped up with water and enjoyed with mezes or a **nargile** (see above).

CULTURE AND ETIQUETTE

Turkey's unspoken codes of conduct can catch the first-time visitor off guard. Away from the main cities you should **dress modestly** and avoid shorts and revealing attire – this is particularly important the further east you travel. If you are a female traveller, it is essential to wear a headscarf or shawl if you plan on visiting a **mosque**. Be aware that the area surrounding a mosque, as well as the mosque itself, is regarded with a great deal of respect and nearby restaurants commonly do not serve alcohol.

In almost every sphere of social interaction, **tea drinking** plays an important role. You'll notice shop salesmen commonly invite you to peruse their goods over tea. It's even drunk during the sweltering summer months, the logic being that the hot liquid helps equalize the body's temperature.

Although interaction between Turkish men and women is quite formalized, **single female travellers** may experience some harassment. A common approach is being stopped to answer a quick question. Be aware that a quick question is never a quick question and you could find yourself embroiled in a desperate attempt to solicit your phone number or arrange a dinner date. Note also that while many young Turkish women visit bars and clubs few of them go out unaccompanied at night and you should observe this rule away from tourist areas.

TURKEY ON THE NET

- ⓦ **www.about-turkey.com** Tourist information.
- ⓦ **www.hitit.co.uk** Alternative tourism.
- ⓦ **www.goturkey.com** Countrywide info.
- ⓦ **www.istanbulcityguide.com** Good city listings.
- ⓦ **www.mymerhaba.com** Information site aimed at ex-pats.
- ⓦ **www.turkishdailynews.com** Main local English newspaper.

HAGGLING

Shopping in Turkey requires more than just money. In bazaars, market stalls and independent shops, shoppers are expected to engage in a lively **haggling** session. The art of securing a good deal is an acquired skill, but adopting a friendly, understated approach usually results in a fair price. Avoid displaying too much enthusiasm over your desired item and if the price quoted sounds expensive, inform the shopkeeper that you would like to shop around for a better deal. If you don't receive a lower quote, don't be afraid to walk away – remember the orignal price quoted can be three times the price of the item's actual value.

SPORTS AND ACTIVITIES

Most tour operators in the established resorts have information about both summer and winter adventure sports. For **scuba-diving**, check out Ⓦwww.meddiving.com, while for **skiing** see Ⓦwww.guidetoturkey.com/ski_centers/. Undoubtedly the most popular sport enjoyed by locals is **football**, with Galatasaray and Beşiktaş being a couple of the nation's favourite teams. Major stadiums for national games include 19 Mayıs stadium, located in Ankara. To view forthcoming games and buy tickets, visit Ⓦwww.biletix.com.

COMMUNICATIONS

Most **post offices (PTT)** open Mon–Sat 8.30am–5.30pm, with main branches opening till 7/8pm and on Sun. Use the *yurtdışı* (overseas) slot on postboxes. **Phone calls** can be made from Turk Telecom booths and the PTT. Post offices and kiosks sell phonecards (30, 60 and 100 units) and also have metered phones. Some payphones accept credit cards. Numerous private **phone shops** (*Köntürlü* telefon) offer metered calls at dubious, unofficial rates. The international operator is on Ⓣ115. There are **Internet cafés** in most towns, charging 1.50YTL–3.50YTL/hr.

INFORMATION AND MAPS

Most towns of any size have a **tourist office** (*Turizm Danışma Bürosu*) generally open Mon–Fri 8.30am–12.30pm & 1.30–5.30pm. Staff may not speak English, but they often have good brochures and maps, and should be able to help you with accommodation. The best **maps** are by Geo Centre/RV ("Turkey West" and "Turkey East"). City tourist offices normally stock reasonable street plans.

MONEY AND BANKS

Currency is the **new Turkish lira** (YTL), divided into 100 kuruş. There are coins of 1, 5, 10, 25, 50 kuruş, and 1YTL, and notes of 1, 5, 10, 20, 50, 100YTL. Exchange rates for foreign currency are always better inside Turkey. Many pensions and hotels, particularly in the popular destinations, also quote prices in euros, and you can usually pay in either euros or Turkish lira. The current **exchange rate** is 2.50YTL to £1; 1.25YTL to US$1; and 1.75YTL to €1.

STUDENT AND YOUTH DISCOUNTS

Finding places that consistently offer **student discounts** in Turkey is a task in itself. Despite the presence of a large student population in many of the major cities, few shops or bars offer student discounts. Nevertheless, an ISIC card can get you a small discount on bus travel with some of the major firms such as Kamil Koç, Pamukkale, Uludag and Varan. It's also worth asking about student discounts before you book into a hotel, as many may be willing to offer a discount but reluctant to publicise the fact.

Turkish

	Turkish	Pronunciation
Yes	*Evet*	Evet
No	*Hayır/yok*	Hi-uhr/yok
Please	*Lütfen*	Lewtfen
Thank you	*Teskküler/mersi/sağol*	Teshekkewrler/sa-ol
Hello/Good day	*Merhaba*	Merhabuh
Goodbye	*Hosça kalın*	Hosh-cha kaluhn
Excuse me	*Pardon*	Pardon
Where?	*Nerede?*	Neredeh?
Good	*Iyi*	Eeyee
Bad	*Kötü*	Kurtew
Near	*Yakın*	Yakuhn
Far	*Uzak*	Oozak
Cheap	*Ucuz*	Oojooz
Expensive	*Pahalı*	Pahaluh
Open	*Açık*	Achuhk
Closed	*Kapalı*	Kapaluh
Today	*Bugün*	Boogewn
Yesterday	*Dün*	Dewn
Tomorrow	*Yarın*	Yaruhn
How much is...?	*Ne kadar...?*	Ne kadar...?
What time is it?	*Saatiniz var mı?*	Saatiniz var muh?
I don't understand	*Anlamıyorum*	Anlamuh-yoroom
Do you speak English?	*Ingilizce biliyor musunuz?*	Eengeeleezjeh beeleeyor moosoonooz
Sorry	*Özür dilerim*	Erzer delereem
Do you have...?	*Var mı…?*	Va mur...?
I would like...	*Istiyorum*	Ee-stee-yo-rum
What is your name?	*Adınız ne?*	A-denurz nay?
Can you stop here?	*Ineçek var?*	Inner-jek va?
I'd like the bill	*Hesabı Istiyorum*	*hes-ab ee-stee-yo-rum*
One	*Bir*	Bir
Two	*Iki*	Iki
Three	*Uç*	Ewch
Four	*Dört*	Durt
Five	*Beş*	Besh
Six	*Altı*	Altuh
Seven	*Yedi*	Yedi
Eight	*Sekiz*	Sekiz
Nine	*Dokuz*	Dokuz
Ten	*On*	On

Banks open Mon–Fri 8.30am–noon & 1.30–5pm; some, notably Garanti Bankasi, are open at lunchtimes and on Sat. Most charge a commission of about 6YTL for travellers' cheques. Some of the **exchange booths** run by banks in coastal resorts, airports and ferry docks charge a small commission. Private exchange offices have competitive rates and no commission. Almost all banks have **ATMs**. Post offices in sizeable towns also sometimes change cash and cheques, for a one-percent commission.

OPENING HOURS AND HOLIDAYS

Shops are generally open Mon–Sat 9am–7/8pm, and possibly Sun, depending on the owner. The two **religious holidays** are Kurban Bayram (the Feast of the Sacrifice), which falls on December 7–11 in 2008 and the Şeker Bayram (Sugar Holiday), which marks the end of the Muslim fasting month of Ramadan (Oct 11–14, 2008). If either falls midweek, the government may choose to extend the holiday period to as much as nine days, announcing this only a couple of weeks beforehand. In big resorts, museums generally stay open but in smaller towns they may close. Many shops and restaurants also close as their owners return to their home towns for the holiday. Banks and public offices are also closed on the **secular holidays**: Jan 1, April 23, May 19, Aug 30, Oct 29.

EMERGENCIES

Street **crime** is uncommon and theft is rare, apart from passport theft and the odd case of phone-snatching in İstanbul. The authorities usually treat tourists with courtesy, and all **police** wear dark blue uniforms with baseball caps, with their division – *trafik*, *narkotik*, etc – clearly marked. In rural areas, you'll find the camouflage-clad **Jandarma**, a division of the regular army. For minor health complaints, head for the nearest **pharmacy** (*eczane*). Night-duty pharmacists are known as *nöbetçi*; the current rota is posted in every pharmacy's front window. For more serious ailments, go to a **hospital** (*klinik*) – either public (*Devlet Hastane* or *SSK Hastanesi*), or the much higher-quality and cleaner private (*Özel Hastane*).

EMERGENCY NUMBERS

Police ☎155; Ambulance ☎112; Fire ☎110.

İstanbul

Arriving in **İSTANBUL** can result in sensory overload: back streets teem with traders pushing handcarts and porters carrying burdens twice their size, the smell of grilled food from roadside vendors lingers in the air whilst the inescapable sales patter of hawkers fills the streets. Yet this is merely one aspect of modern İstanbul. With its trendy bars and pavement cafes, a distinctly Continental influence also pervades throughout.

İstanbul is the only city in the world to have played capital to consecutive Christian and Islamic empires, and retains features of both. Named **Byzantium** after the Greek Colonists Byzas, the city was an important trading centre. In the fourth century it was renamed Constantinople when Constantine chose it as the new capital of the **Roman Empire**. The city later became an independent empire, adopting the Greek language and Christianity as its religion. The region gradually became ruled by the Islamic Ottomans and in 1453 the city was captured by the Ottoman Conqueror Mehmet. By the nineteenth century, the glory days of Ottoman domination were over. After the War of Independence, the territorial boundaries of modern day Turkey were set and the country's leader, Atatürk, created a new capital in Ankara.

What to see and do

The city is divided in two by the **Bosphorus,** a stretch of water which runs between the Black Sea and the Sea of Marmara, dividing Europe from Asia. At right angles to it, the inlet of the **Golden Horn** cuts the European side in two. It is this European section where most visitors spend their time; wandering around the cobbled streets

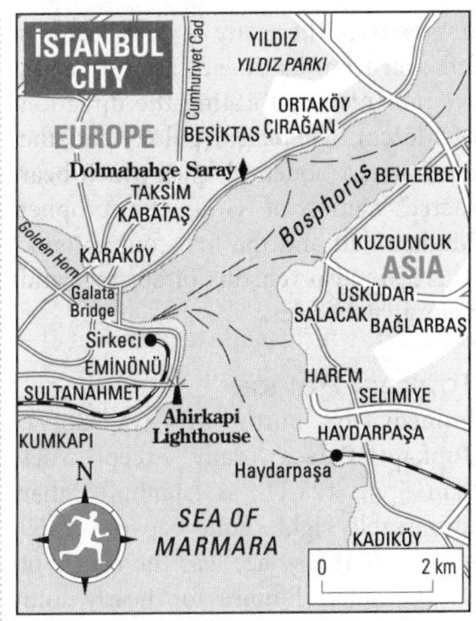

and tourist sites in **Sultanahmet** or exploring the fast paced district of **Beyoğlu**. Sandwiched between the two is **Eminönü** and the old Levantine area of Galata, now **Karaköy**, home to one of the city's most famous landmarks, the Galata Tower. An exploration on foot of each of these areas can easily be done. Navigation between and beyond these areas, however, requires the use of public transport. The handy **akbil** travel pass (6YTL – must be credited with money) provides travellers with a marginal discount on travel and enables you to hop on and off the metro, tram and bus to your heart's content.

Aya Sofya

The former Byzantine cathedral of **Aya Sofya** (Tues–Sun 9.15am–4.30/6pm; 15YTL), readily visible thanks to its massive domed structure, is perhaps the single most compelling sight in the city. Commissioned in the sixth century by the Emperor Justinian, it was converted to a mosque in 1453, after which the minarets were added; it's been a museum since 1934. For centuries this was the largest enclosed space in the world, and the interior – filled with shafts of light from the high windows around the dome – is still profoundly impressive. There are a few features left over from its time as a mosque – a *mihrab* (niche indicating the direction of Mecca), a *mimber* (pulpit) and the enormous wooden plaques which bear sacred names of God, the prophet Muhammad and the first four caliphs. There are also remains of abstract and figurative mosaics.

Topkapı Palace

Immediately north of Aya Sofya, **Topkapı Palace** (daily except Tues 9am–5pm; 12YTL) is İstanbul's other unmissable sight. Built between 1459 and 1465, the palace was the centre of the Ottoman Empire for nearly four centuries. The ticket office is in the first courtyard, followed by the beautifully restored Divan, containing the Imperial Council Hall in the second courtyard. Around the corner is the **Harem**, well worth the obligatory guided tour (9am–noon & 1–4pm, every 30min; 10YTL; buy your ticket at least 15min in advance). The only men once allowed in here were eunuchs and the imperial guardsmen, who were only employed at certain hours and even then blinkered. Back in the main body of the palace, in the third courtyard, the **throne room** was where the sultan awaited the outcome of sessions of the Divan. Nearby, the **Pavilion of the Conqueror** (9am–5pm; 10YTL) houses the Topkapı treasury, where you can see such famous items as the Topkapı Dagger, and the Spoonmaker's Diamond, the fifth largest in the world. The fourth courtyard consists of gardens graced with various pavilions, including the **circumcision room** and the sumptuously decorated **Mecidiye Köşkü**, which commands the best view of any of the Topkapı pavilions.

The Blue Mosque

With its six minarets, the Sultanahmet Camii, or **Blue Mosque** (daily 9am–7pm; closed prayer times), is instantly recognizable; inside, its four "elephant foot" pillars obscure parts of the building and dwarf the dome they support. It's the 20,000-odd blue tiles inside that lend the mosque its name – fine examples of late sixteenth-century Iznık ware, they include flower and tree panels as well as more abstract designs. Outside the precinct wall is the **Tomb of Sultan Ahmet** (daily 8.30am–5pm), where the sultan is buried along with his wife and three of his sons. Behind the mosque is the **Vakıf Carpet Museum** (Tues–Sat 9am–4pm; free), which houses antique carpets and kilims from all over Turkey.

The Archeological Museum and around

Just west of Topakı, Gülhane Parkı, once the palace gardens, now houses three museums all covered by one ticket (10YTL). In the **Archeological Museum** (Tues–Sun 9am–5pm) is a superb collection of sarcophagi, sculptures and other remains of past civilizations. The adjacent **Çinili Köşk** is the oldest secular building in İstanbul, now a Museum of Ceramics (Tues–Sun 9.30am–5pm) housing a select collection of Iznık ware and Selçuk tiles. Nearby, the **Museum of the Ancient** (Wed-Sun 9:30am–5pm) contains a small but dazzling collection of Anatolian, Egyptian and Mesopotamian artefacts.

THE CALL OF THE MOSQUE

A quintessential sound of any Turkish city is the **call of the mosque**. This song-like chant is blasted out of loudspeakers and can be heard from miles around. The sound can take some getting used to – especially since morning prayers can be heard as early as 4am. The call is in Arabic and states that God is great, that there is no God but Allah and requests that listeners come together for prayer.

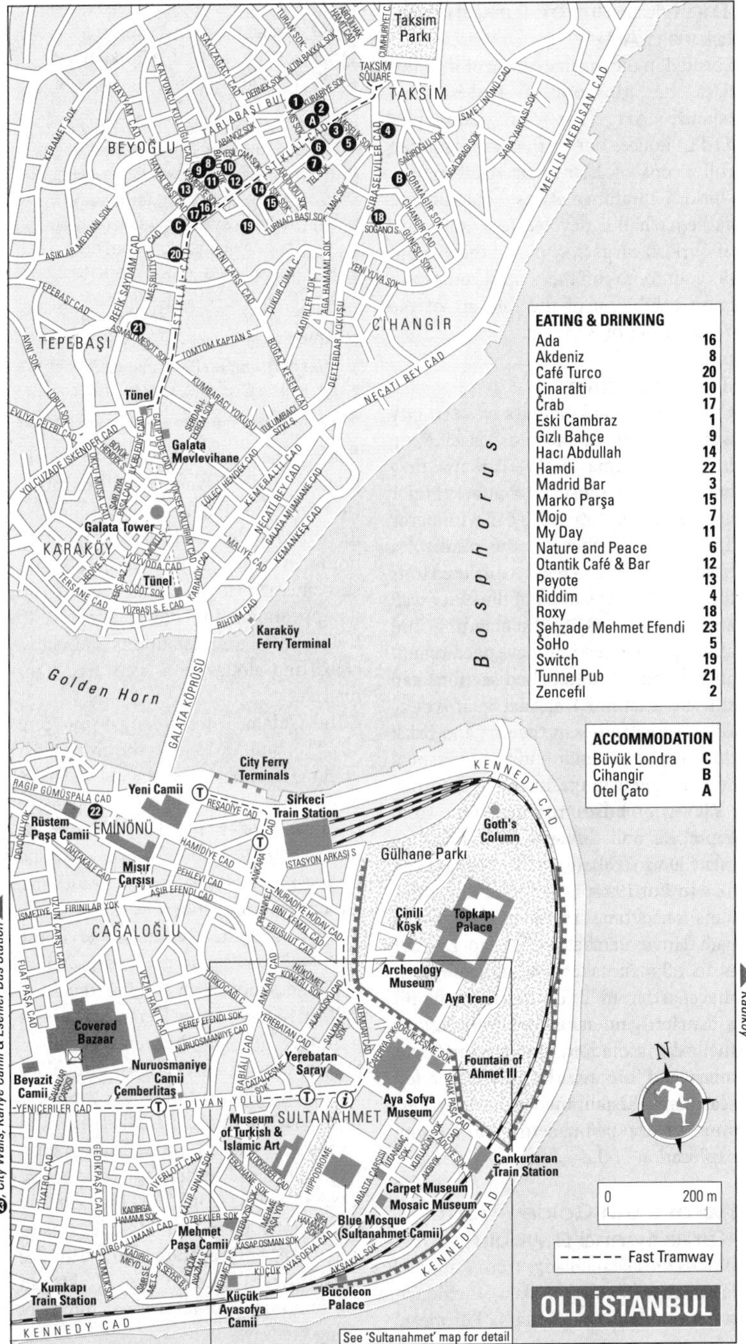

TURKEY

İSTANBUL

The Museum of Turkish and Islamic Art

Located in the former palace of Ibrahim Paşa, the **Museum of Turkish and Islamic Art** (Tues–Sun 9am–5pm; 4YTL) houses one of the best exhibited collections of Islamic artefacts in the world. Ibrahim Paşa's magnificent audience hall is devoted to a collection of Turkish carpets, while on the ground floor, in rooms off the central courtyard, is an exhibition of the folk art of the Yörük tribes of Anatolia.

The city walls

Over 6km long, İstanbul's western **city walls** are among the most fascinating Byzantine remains in Turkey; they barred the peninsula to attackers for 800 years. First raised by the Emperor Theodosius II, they are the result of a hasty rebuilding to repel Attila the Hun's forces in 447 AD. Most of the outer wall and its 96 towers are still standing, and although long sections have been rebuilt and closed off, untouched sections can still be examined in detail if you're willing to clamber in the dirt and brick dust. Do pay attention to your personal security here, especially in the evening.

Plenty of **buses** run this way from Eminönü and Sultanahmet, including bus #80 to Yedikule, #84 to Topkapı and #86 to Edirnekapı, while the tram line runs west from Aksaray to the Topkapı gate. However, the best way to get here is to take the scenic train ride along the coast from Eminönü to Yediküle, a district lying at the southern end of the walls in the attractive former Greek quarter of Samatya. This also has a few reasonable restaurants and cafés where you can stop before setting off on your exploration of the walls.

Across the Golden Horn: Karaköy and Beyoulu

Across the Galata Bridge from Eminönü is **Karaköy** (formerly Galata). Previously functioning as the capital's "European" quarter, the district was home to Jewish, Greek and Armenian minorities. In the 1960s the area began to lose its cosmopolitan flavour, becoming home to brothels, pick-up joints and sex cinemas. It has since cleaned up its appearance and now plays host to trendy café-bars, restaurants and clubs, coexisting alongside a seedy red-light district.

The **Galata Tower** (daily 9am–7pm; 10YTL), built in 1348, is the area's most obvious landmark; its viewing galleries, café and ridiculously expensive restaurant offer the best panoramas of the city. Up towards Istiklâl Caddesi, Beyoulu's main boulevard, an unassuming doorway leads to the courtyard of the **Galata Mevlevihane** (9am–4.30pm, closed Wed; 2YTL), a former monastery and ceremonial hall of the Whirling Dervishes, a sect founded in the thirteenth century. Staged dervish ceremonies take place most Sundays throughout the year (information on ⓣ0212/245 4141), and also at the Sirkeci Central Train Station Exhibition Hall (every Sun, Wed & Fri; ⓣ0212/485 8834; 30YTL). The best way to continue along Istiklâl Caddesi is to hop on the antique tram which trundles for 1km or so to Taksim Square, taking in the sumptuous *fin-de-siècle* architecture along the way.

TREAT YOURSELF

Rather than just a simple dip in the tub, a visit to a **Turkish bath** (*hamam*) consists of a session in a steam room, followed by an exfoliation, soap down and massage session with a professional masseuse. Most people spend two to three hours in a *hamam*, so watch out for tourist imitations that only allot an hour for the whole process. The reputed best for cleanliness and quality is Galatasaray Hamami (50YTL) with separate sections for men and women (Turnacibasi Sok 24, Istiklal Cad ⓣ0212/249 4342).

The Covered Bazaar

Off the main street of Divan Yolu lies the district of Beyazıt, centred on the **Kapalı Çarşı** or Covered Bazaar (Mon–Sat 8.30am–6.30/7.30pm; Beyazıt tram stop), a huge web of passageways housing over 4000 shops. It has long since spilled out of the covered area, sprawling into the streets that lead down to the Golden Horn. There are carpet shops everywhere catering for all budgets, shops selling leather goods around Kurkçular Kapı and Perdahçılar Caddesi, and gold jewellery on Kuyumcular Caddesi. Don't forget to haggle (see box, p.1220). When you need a break, the *Fes Café* on Halıcilar Caddesi is a comfortable spot to gloat over your booty.

Arrival and information

Air İstanbul's airport is 24km west of the city. Buses run to Taksim Square northeast of Beyoğlu (7YTL). Taxis taking the direct route along the seafront road (Sahil Yolu) cost 25YTL; make sure they use the meter. This is a better bet than trusting a shuttle bus tout at the airport – prices are usually double the price of a taxi. The airport metro runs to the city centre at Aksaray, but for Sultanahmet it's best to change onto the tramway at Zeytinburnu; this entire journey costs around 2YTL.

Train Trains from Europe terminate at Sirkeci station, linked to Sultanahmet by a short tram ride; trains from Asia terminate at Haydarpaşa station on the east bank of the Bosphorus, from where you can get a ferry to Eminönü and a tram from there to Sultanahmet.

Bus From İstanbul's bus station at Esenler, 15km northwest, the better bus companies run courtesy minibuses to various points in the city, although if you're heading for Sultanahmet it's often quicker to take the metro (actually an express tramway; 1.30YTL). Some buses also stop at the Harem bus station on the Asian side, from where there are regular *dolmuşes* to Haydarpaşa station. Taxis to Sultanahmet cost approximately 15YTL. Watch out for drivers who offer their services near to the departure area. These are usually unlicensed and do not operate a meter.

Tourist office The most central office (although not particularly helpful) is in Sultanahmet, near the Hippodrome on Divanyolu Cad (daily 9am–5pm; ⓣ0212/518 8754). Smaller branches can be found at the airport (24hr), the Hilton Hotel (ⓣ0212/233 0592) and the two train stations.

City transport

Bus Two bus services operate on the same city routes, either the private Halk Otobus service (pay conductor on entry; 1.30YTL) or the more common municipality buses (marked IETT), for which you have to buy tickets (1.30YTL) in advance from bus stations, newspaper kiosks or fast-food booths; some longer routes, usually served by double-deckers, require two advance tickets (look for the sign *iki bilet geçerlidir*). There are route maps at main bus stops.

Tram The European side has two tram lines, one running from Kabataş through Sultanahmet to Topkapı and outlying suburbs, the other running along Istiklâl Caddesi from Beyoğlu to Taksim using an antique tram; buy tokens (*jetons*; 1.30YTL) from a booth before you enter the platform.

Train There's also a municipal train network running along the Marmara shore – west from Sirkeci station on the European side, and east from Haydarpaşa on the Asian (allow at least an hour to get to the Asian station from the centre). On the European side you buy a token (1.30YTL) to let you through the turnstile onto the platform, while on the Asian side you buy a ticket (same price).

Dolmuş There are also *dolmuşes* which have their point of departure and destination displayed somewhere about the windscreen.

Boat Ferries run between Eminönü and Karaköy on the European side, and Üsküdar, Kadiköy and Haydarpaşa in Asia; buy your ticket (1.30YTL) from the dockside kiosks. There are also sightseeing hop-on-and-off boats which cruise the Bosphorus. These leave from the Boğaz Iskelesi terminal near the Eminönü tram stop and stop at either Anadolu Hisarı or Anadolu Kavağı. The trip on a government run boat costs between 6 and 10YTL, whereas private boat tours can cost up to 45YTL (includng hotel pick and guided tour). The cruise takes approximately 1hr 45min each way and the last return boat from Anadolu Kavağı in summer is at 5pm, after which you must resort to a bus or *dolmuş*.

Accommodation

Some of the city's best small hotels and **pansiyons** are situated in Sultanahmet, particularly around Yerebatan Caddesi and the back streets between the Blue Mosque and the sea. Taksim is also a convenient base, and comes into its own at night as a centre of cultural and culinary activity; take

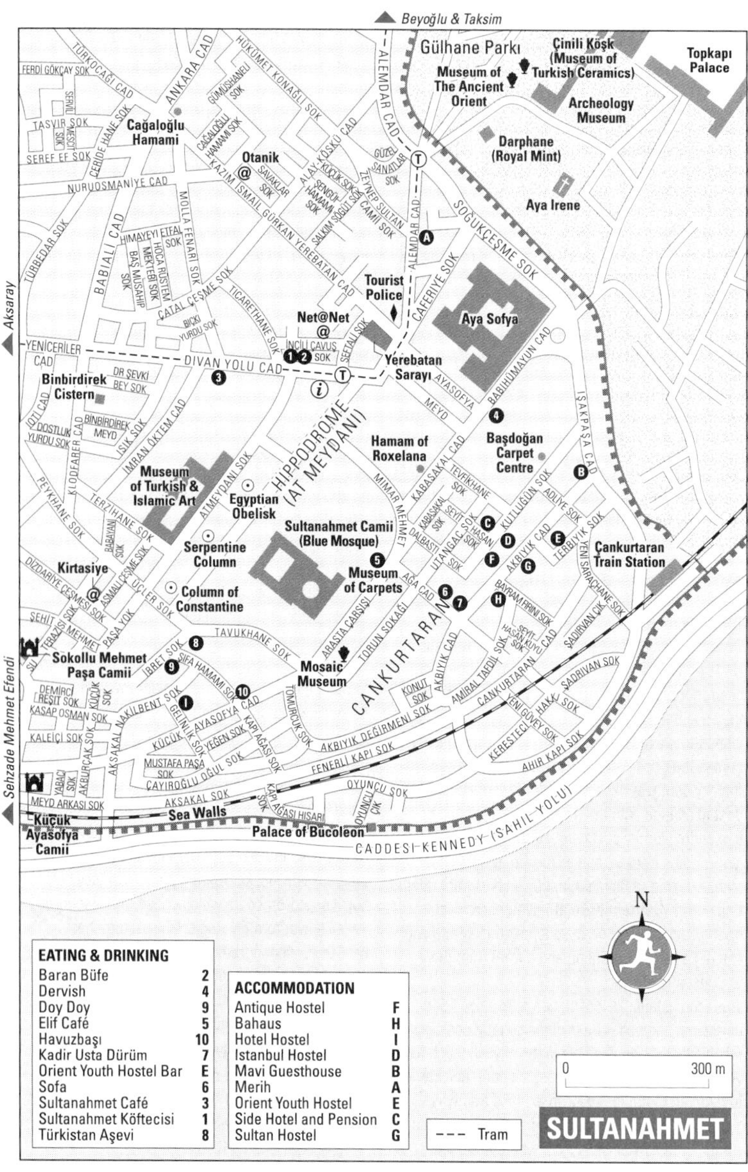

bus #T4 from Sultanahmet, which runs via Karaköy. From Eminönü and Aksaray, many buses pass through either Karaköy or Taksim, or both. Most **hotels** include breakfast in the price and some offer air-con, cable TV and free Internet access.

Sultanahmet

Antique Hostel Kutlugün Sok 51 ⓣ0212/638 1637, ⓦwww.antiquehostel.com. Quiet, comfortable hotel with large, traditionally furnished rooms; TV, en-suite and air-con rooms available. Dorms ❷, rooms ❸

Bahaus Akbıyık Cad, Bayramfırın Sok 11-13 ⓣ0212/638 6534. Cosy and intimate hostel and hotel with a vibrant backpacker vibe. Prices include breakfast; Internet access available. Dorms ❶, doubles ❹

Hotel Hostel Sultanahmet Mah Şifa Hamamı Sok 30 ⓣ0212/638 4562, ⓦwww.yunusemrehotel.com. Basic dorm rooms with en suites. Rooms in the upstairs hotel are fresh and clean but not worth their price tag – try bargaining. Dorms ❷, doubles ❺–❻

Istanbul Hostel Kutlugün Sok 35 ⓣ0212/516 9380, ⓦwww.istanbulhostel.net. Friendly long-running hostel, with Internet access, terrace, bar and competent travel agency. Ground-floor rooms are noisy. Dorms ❶, doubles ❸

Mavi Guesthouse Ishak Paşa Cad, Kutlugün Sok 3 ⓣ0212/516 5878, ⓦwww.maviguesthouse.com. Backpacker-friendly place with dorms and rooftop beds. Dorms ❶, doubles ❷

Merih Alemdar Cad 20 ⓣ0212/526 9708, ⓔmerihotel@superonline.com. Friendly hotel with dorms and a few dingy doubles, just down from Aya Sofya; front rooms can be noisy. Dorms ❶, doubles ❸

Orient International Youth Hostel Akbıyık Cad 13 ⓣ0212/518 0789. Clean and simple rooms, Internet access, an excellent roof bar and in-house entertainment such as belly dancing. Dorms ❶, rooms ❸

Side Hotel and Pansiyon Utangaç Sok 20 ⓣ0212/517 2282, ⓦwww.sidehotel.com. Good value hotel where guests are treated like family. Tastefully decorated single rooms to apartment suites; excellent sea views from the terrace. ❷–❽

Sultan Hostel Akbıyık Cad 21 ⓣ0212/516 9260. Large, well-run, popular backpackers' joint with friendly and helpful staff, Internet access and a lively street-side bar and roof terrace – the nearby rooms are noisy. Dorms ❶, rooms ❷

Beyoğlu and Taksim

Büyük Londra Oteli Meşrutiyet Cad 117, Tepebaşi ⓣ0212/249 1025. Century-old Italian-built hotel, full of character, with spacious, well-furnished rooms. Bargaining could halve the price. ❺

Cihangir Arslanyataği Sok 33, Taksim ⓣ0212/251 5317, ⓦwww.cihangirhotel.com. Smart hotel on quiet back street with a/c rooms, some with balconies enjoying outstanding Bosphorus views. ❼

Otel Çato İstiklal Cad, Bekar Sok 3 ⓣ0212/245 2579. Nice bright entrance but the rest of the building is in need of renovation. Decent sized rooms with small en suites. Twenty-five percent student discount. ❷–❹

Eating

Sultanahmet has some decent **restaurants**, although the principal concentrations are in Beyoğlu and Taksim. The Balık Pazar, particularly, behind the Çiçek Pasajı (off Istiklâl Cad), is a great area for *mezes*, kebabs and fish, while Çiçek Pasajı itself offers similar fare but is overpriced and touristy. **Snacks** include *kokoreç* (skeins of sheep's innards) sold from street stalls and delicious corn on the cob sold everywhere.

Cafés

Ada Istiklal Cad 158-A, Beyoğlu. A café with an adjoining bookshop. Relaxed atmosphere and good selection of treats ranging from toasted sandwiches to pasta and cheesecake. Pasta 8–10YTL.

Elif Café Mimar Mehmet Ağa Cad 14, 34400 Arasta Çarşı. Outdoor café located in the centre of the Arasta Bazaar. Tables are adorned with traditional tablecloths and there's live music at night. Sandwiches 5–7YTL. Soft drink 3YTL.

Dervish Café & Restaurant Kabasakal Sok 1-2. Slightly touristy but great for simple good quality food. Toasted sandwiches 2.50–3.50YTL. Salads 5–10YTL.

Otantik Café & Bar Istiklal Cad Balo Sok 1. A much needed haven from the busy streets below. Renowned for its rakí tables (a selection of *mezes* and bread served with the spirit raki). Mains 8–12YTL.

Sofa Café Restaurant Mimar Mehmet Ağa Cad. Stylish little café that transforms into a winebar restaurant at night. Mainly Western dishes and good vegetarian options. Mains 9YTL.

Sultanahmet Café & Restaurant Divan Yolu

CATCH YOUR OWN DINNER

Join the local fishermen on the Galata Bridge and try catching your dinner. Fishing rods and tackle can be rented on the bridge (20–55YTL). After you've caught something, wander down to the end of the bridge near the Eminönü tram stop where fresh fish sandwiches are cooked and sold. Simply write down the phrase, "Ben balığımı kendim pisirebiligrmiyim?" (Can I cook my fish here?), and present it to one of the local fishermen. Most should be willing to help for a price.

Cad 25/A. Friendly café where Turkish lunchtime specials are laid out buffet style. Mains 8YTL.

Street snacks

Kadir Usta Dürüm Corner of Akbıyık Cad and Mimar Mehmet Ağa Cad. Night-time street vendor with miniature stool seating area. Serves huge kebabs wrapped in fresh tortillas. Open from 8.30pm–1am; kebabs 3YTL.

Restaurants

Baran Büfe Divan Yolu Cad 7. Good spot to watch the world go by whilst enjoying some cheap tasty eats such as *lahmacun* or a nargile. Open 24hr. Mains 8YTL.

Doy Doy Şifa Hamamı Sok 13. Large restaurant with a great roof terrace and cushioned nargile smoking area. Excellent value huge meals of local food topped with baskets full of *pide* (flat bread). No alcohol. Mains 6YTL.

Hacı Abdullah Sakızağcı Cad 17. A local legend – stunning home cooking at reasonable prices. No alcohol. Mains 13YTL.

Hamdi Tahmis Cad Kalçın Sok 17 ⓣ0212/528 0390. Third-floor restaurant next to the spice bazaar with great views over the Golden Horn. Fresh *mezes* and *köfte* are all served to a high standard. Highly popular, reservations advised. Mains 10–14YTL.

Havuzbaşı Küçükayasofya Mah, Nakilbent Sok 2. Outdoor restaurant with low cushioned seating, traditional music and whirling dervish shows at night. Good for *gözleme*. Mains 8–16YTL.

Marko Paşa Sark Sadri Alışık Sok 8. Cosy, traditional restaurant where old Turkish women sit perched in the window making *gözleme* (3–4.50YTL). Great value.

Nature and Peace Büyükparmakkapı Sok 21, Istiklâl Cad. Vegetarian place three blocks from Taksim, offering lentil *köfte* and other veggie dishes. Mains 8YTL

Şehzade Mehmet Efendi Şehzade Camii, Şehzadebaşı Cad. Wonderfully atmospheric restaurant located in the *medrese* of the Şehzade mosque. Excellent *pides*, kebabs and stews. Mains 10–19YTL.

Sultanahmet Köftecisi Divan Yolu Cad 12/a, Sultanahmet. Busy, basic restaurant; good for tasty traditional Turkish dishes. Mains 7–9YTL.

Türkistan Aşevi Tavukhane Sok 36, Sultanahmet. A restored Ottoman house restaurant serving set three-course meals of Turkish dishes. Live music at night. Mains 13YTL.

Zencefıl Kurabiye Sok 3. Two branches opposite each other, serving cheap Turkish and vegetarian dishes. Popular with expats. Mains 8YTL.

Drinking and nightlife

Western-style **bars** and **clubs** – invariably trendy and expensive – have all but taken over the city, with **house** being the current music of choice (most kick off around midnight). Backpackers, especially Antipodeans, tend to gather in the bars on Akbıyık Caddesi in Sultanahmet.

Bars

Akdeniz Nevizade Sok 25, Beyoğlu. Rambling, multistorey student bar, playing rock music and serving cheap drinks.

Eski Cambraz Mıs Sok 32, Beyoğlu. Small, cosy bar on two floors. Mixed pop music played at levels conducive to conversation. Free entrance weekdays; weekend 20YTL and two free drinks.

Café Turco Istiklal Cad, Saka Salim Çıkmazı 1. Passageway café bar with more action outside than inside in the summer. Good vibe with live acoustic music.

Çinaralti Istiklal Cad Balo Sok 14. Trendy bar with a lively outdoor dance floor pumping out headache-inducing techno music.

Crab Istiklal Cad 107/2, Beyoğlu. Small and smokey Turkish rock bar; live music from local musicians.

Gızlı Bahçe Nevizade Sok 27, Istiklâl Cad, Beyoğlu. Cutting-edge dance music in a dilapidated Ottoman town-house bar. Mixed trendy crowd, and a deliciously illicit atmosphere.

Madrid Bar Ipek Sok 20, Beyoğlu. Cheap bar popular with students and impecunious expats alike.

My Day Balo Sok 18, Beyoğlu. Small, modern, trendy bar with samba music on Thursday nights.

Tunnel Pub Asmalı Mescit Mah, General Yazgan Sok 6, Beyoğlu. Abuzz with students till late even on a week night.

Clubs

Mojo Büyükparmakkapı Sok, Istiklâl Cad, Beyoğlu. Trendy basement dive with live bands most nights. Closes 4am.

Peyote Sahne Sok 24, Beyoğlu. Small, modern club playing deep/hard house to a trendy crowd.

Riddim Sıraselviler cad 69/1 Taksim. Large club with quirky layout and flat-screen TVs playing music videos. R'n'B music downstairs.

Roxy Arslanyatağı Sok 113, Siraselviler Cad, Taksim. DJs and regular live bands in a pricey, professional-oriented bar/disco.

SoHo Meşelik Sok 14, Beyoğlu. The current hard-house dance club to be seen in with inflated bar prices to match. Good DJs. Very popular at weekends.

Switch Muammer Karaca Çıkmazı, Istiklal Cad, Taksim. Underground dance club with local and foreign DJs.

Shopping

Bazaars

Arasta Bazaar Mimar Mehmet Ağa Cad 14, Sultanahmet. Good for handmade crafts and carpets.

Mısır Çarşısı (Egyptian Spice Bazaar) Everything from spices to jewellery, natural apple tea and aphrodisiacs including chewy sweet-like blocks of Viagra.

Clothes

TREAT YOURSELF

The sleek and contemporary **Erdem Kıramer Akademi** (İstiklal Cad. No.469, ⓣ0212 252 4498, ⓦwww.erdemkiramer.com) salon offers free hair cuts to anyone who is willing to embrace a new look. An English-speaking stylist will give you a consultation before an Akademi trainee transforms your coiffure. Book in advance.

Eymen Halcilik Arasta Çarşışı 107, Sultanahmet. Handmade traditional clothing for both men and women.

Ünal Istiklal Cad 328. Eclectic mix of colourful traditional clothing made from rich textiles.

Topshop Istiklal Cad. The Turkish branch of the British women's fashion store. Prices are marginally cheaper.

Bookshops

Galeri Kayseri Bookshop Divan Yolu Cad 11, Sultanahmet. English bookshop with a wide selection of travel literature.

Robinson Crusoe Kitabevi Istiklal Cad 195A (389). A good selection of maps as well as books including other titles from the Rough Guides series.

Souvenirs

Mevlana Alibaba Alemdar Cad 14, Sultanahmet. A small basement shop selling nargiles, carpets, antique daggers and other memorabilia.

Entertainment

Atatürk Cultural Centre Taksim Square, Beyoğlu. Concert and exhibition venue. Principal centre for events during the International Music Festival (June-July).

Emek Cinema Yeşilçam Sok 5, İstiklâl Cad. Popular cinema regularly screening international releases. One of the International Film Festival (April) venues. Student discount available.

Nardis Jazz Club Galata Kulesi Sok. Small, dimly lit jazz club where music rather than conversation takes centre stage. Performances by international artists during the Istanbul Jazz Festival (July).

Directory

Consulates Australia, Tepecik Yolu 58, Etiler ⓣ0212/257 7050; Ireland, Cumhuriyet Cad 26a, Elmadağ ⓣ0212/246 6025; New Zealand, Yeşil Çimen Cad 75, Ihlamur ⓣ0212/258 8722; UK, Meşrutiyet Cad 34, Tepebaşı, Beyoğlu ⓣ0212/334 6400; US, Kaplicalar Mevkii Sok 2, Istinye ⓣ0212/335 9000.

Hospitals American Hospital, Güzelbahçe Sok 20, Nişantaşı ⓣ0212/231 4050; International Hospital, İstanbul Cad 82, Yeşilköy ⓣ0212/663 3000.

Internet *Internet Café*, 2nd floor, Incili Çavuş Sok 31, Divan Yolu; *Blue Internet Café*, Yerbatan Cad 54; Seycom, Divan Yolu Cad 54/4, Sultanahmet.

Laundry Amfora, Binbirdirek Mah. Peykhane Cad 53/1; Pop up Laundry, Divan Yolu Cad Işık Sok 10/B-1, Sultanahmet ⓣ0212/458 1997.

Left luggage Sirkeci and Haydarpaşa train stations.

Police Tourist Police, Yerebatan Cad, Sultanahmet ⓣ0212/527 4503.

Post office Yeni Posthane Cad, Sirkeci.

Telephone International Cheap Call, Dr Eminpaşa Sok 2, Divan Yolu Cad, Sultanahmet.

Travel agents Road Runner Travel Agency (Alemdar Cad 2/B, Sultanahmet ⓦwww.roadrunnertravel.net) creates packages to suit even the tiniest of budgets. Fez Bus (Akbıyık Cad 15, Sultanahmet ⓦwww.feztravel.com) runs a hop-on-and-off bus system aimed at travellers who wish to visit several destinations in western Turkey. Passes cost from 275YTL and tours can be booked for an additional fee.

Moving on

Train Ankara (6 daily; 8–9hr 30min); Edirne (1 daily; 6hr 30min); Denizli (1 daily; 14hr 30min); İzmir (1 daily; 11hr); Konya (1 daily; 14hr); Budapest, Hungary (26hr); Sofia, Bulgaria (15hr).

Bus/domuş Alanya (hourly; 14hr); Antalya (4 daily; 12hr); Bodrum (5 daily; 12hr); Bursa (hourly; 5hr); Çanakkale (hourly; 5hr 30min); Datça (1 daily; 17hr); Denizli (hourly; 15hr); Edirne (hourly; 3hr); Fethiye (hourly; 15hr); İzmir (hourly; 10hr); Iznik (Orhangazi; hourly; 5hr); Göreme (5 daily; 12hr

30min); Kuşadası (3 daily; 11hr); Marmaris (4 daily; 13hr); Nevşehir (3 daily; 12hr); Ürgüp (5 daily; 12hr 30min); Kaş (2 daily; 12hr); Konya (7 daily; 11hr); Sofia, Bulgaria (12hr).
Ferry Yalova (for Bursa or Iznık, 8daily; 1hr 30min).

Around the Sea of Marmara

Despite their proximity to İstanbul, the shores and hinterland of the **Sea of Marmara** are relatively neglected by foreign travellers – but there are good reasons to come: not least the border town of **Edirne** which was once the Ottoman capital, while nearby **Bursa**, the first Ottoman capital, has some of the finest monuments in the Balkans. Many visitors also stop off at the extensive World War I battlefields and cemeteries of the **Gelibolu peninsula** (Gallipoli), using either the port of **Eceabat** as a base, or, more commonly, **Çanakkale** – from where it's also easy to visit the ruins of ancient Troy.

EDIRNE

EDIRNE boasts an impressive number of elegant monuments and makes for an easily digestible introduction to Turkey. Bordering both Greece and Bulgaria, it's a small sleepy town where few of the locals speak English, so don't be afraid to whip out your phrasebook. The city springs to life for the week-long **oil wrestling festival** of Kırkpınar (end of June).

What to see and do

You can see the sights on foot in a day. The best starting point is the **Eski Camii** bang in the centre, the oldest mosque in town, begun in 1403. Just across the way, the **Bedesten** was Edirne's first covered market, though the plastic goods it now touts are no match for the building itself. Nearby, the **Semiz Ali Paşa Çarşısı** is the other main bazaar, while a short way north of here is the beautiful **Üç Şerefeli Camii**, dating from 1447; its name means "three-balconied", derived from the presence of three galleries for the muezzin on the tallest of the four idiosyncratic minarets.

The Selimiye and Museum of Turkish and Islamic Arts

A little way east, the masterly **Selimiye Camii** was designed by Minar Sinan. Its four slender minarets, among the tallest in the world, also have three balconies; the interior is most impressive, its dome planned to surpass that of Aya Sofya in İstanbul. Next door, the **Museum of Turkish and Islamic Arts** (Tues–Sun 8.30am–noon & 1–5.30pm; 1YTL) houses assorted wooden, ceramic and martial knick-knacks from the province.

The Archeological Museum

The main **Archeological Museum** (Tues–Sun 8.30am-noon & 1–5.30pm; 1YTL), just northeast of the mosque, contains an assortment of Greco-Roman fragments, some Neolithic finds and an ethnographic section that focuses on local crafts.

Arrival and information

Bus The bus station is 9km southeast of the centre. Upon arrival, walk through the terminal to the car park on the other side. Here you'll find *dolmuşes* which go to the centre of town (0.50YTL). Get off either near the main shopping area or near the mosque.
Train The train station is 1km further in the same direction as the bus station.
Tourist office There are two tourist offices (both daily 8.30am–5.30pm; ⓣ0284/213 9208), both on Talat Paşa Caddesi, the main one about 500m west towards the Gazi Mihal bridge at no. 76a, and a helpful annexe up near Hürriyet Meydanı by the traffic signals.
Internet *Eska Internet Café*, Ilk Kapalıhan Cad 5.

Accommodation

Efe Hotel Maarif Cad 13 ⓣ0284/213 6080. ⓦwww.efehotel.com. Smart, immaculate hotel with large rooms. ❺

Rüştem Paşa Kervanseray Iki Kapılı Han Cad ⓣ0284/225 2195, ⓔek.saray@netone.com. Reasonable rooms in a restored Ottoman *karavanserai* though bargaining is recommended. ❸

Şaban Açikgöz Çilingirler Cad 9 ⓣ0284/213 0313. Comfortable and clean with air conditioning.

Saray ⓣ0284/212 1457, ⓦwww.edirnesarayhotel.com. Best of the cheapies with TVs in each room. ❷

Eating and drinking

Ak Piliç Saraçlar Cad 14. Good selection of local food including chicken dishes such as *tavuk sote*. Mains 12YTL.

Seckin Patisserie Hükümet Cad 9. Small and inviting patisserie with an overwhelming selection of naughty delights. Cakes 2.50YTL.

Urfa Gaziantep Saraçlar Cad 84. Excellent value – great *lahmacun* and *şiş* kebab. Kebab 11YTL.

Moving on

Bus/dolmuş Çanakkale (4 daily; 4hr 30min); İstanbul (hourly; 3hr) Plovdiv (7hr)

CROSSING TO BULGARIA

Edirne is a popular base for travellers crossing the border into Bulgaria. Regular buses leave from Edirne to Plovdiv and tickets cost 30–35YTL. If visiting Edirne for the day, bring your **passport** along even if you don't intend to cross the border. When departing, officials at the bus station may ask to see your passport in order to verify that you haven't crossed over the border from Bulgaria illegally.

ÇANAKKALE

Although celebrated for its setting on the Dardanelles, **ÇANAKKALE** has little to detain you. However, it is a popular base for visiting the Gelibolu (Gallipoli) sites and the sparse ruins of Troy. Almost everything of interest in town – park, naval museum (daily 8am–noon & 1–5pm; 2YTL) and archeological museum (daily 8am–noon & 1–5.30pm; 3.50YTL) – is within walking distance of the **ferry docks**, close to the start of the main Demircioğlu Caddesi.

Arrival and information

Bus The bus station is out on the coastal highway, Atatürk Caddesi, a fifteen-minute walk from the waterfront; if you're arriving on the bus from İstanbul, get off at the ferry rather than going out to the bus station.

Ferry Four ferries a day run between Çanakkale and Eceabat. Tickets can be bought at the ferry terminal for 1.50YTL. Buy your ticket with small change as ticket officers are often reluctant to change large denominations of cash.

Tourist office Beside the ferry docks (daily 8am–noon & 1–5/8pm; ⓣ0286/217 1187). You can pick up a free map of the Gallipoli battlefields here.

Accommodation

Except for a crowded couple of weeks during the Çanakkale/Troy Festival (mid-Aug), or on ANZAC Day (April 25), when the town is inundated with Antipodeans, you'll have little trouble finding budget **accommodation**.

Anzac House Cumhuriyet Meydanı 61 ⓣ0286/213 5969, ⓦwww.anzachouse.com. Clean, good-sized rooms, no air conditioning but fans provided if asked for; shared bathrooms with cubicle showers; Internet access and good Gallipoli tours. ❸

Çanakkale Hotel Cumhuriyet Meydanı Dibek Sok 1 ⓣ0286/214 0906, ⓦwww.canakhotel.com. Pristine hotel styled to suit mature or business trip type clientele. Large rooms with en suites, satellite TVs and minibar. ❸

Efes Hotel Fetvahane Sok 15 ⓣ0286/217 3256 Friendly, homely and excellent value. ❷

Yellow Rose Yeni Sok 5 ⓣ0286/217 3343, ⓦwww.yellowrose.4mg.com. Clean and bright rooms topped off with clashing bedspreads. Dorms ❶, doubles ❷

Eating and drinking

Depo Fetvahane Sokak. Hotspot bar with pumping bass lines.

Doyum Cumhuriyet Meydani 13 ⓣ0286/217 1866. Popular with the locals with hardly a tourist in sight. Great for kebabs and other Turkish dishes but a disappointing drinks selection. Mains 8YTL.

Jest Bar Café Small streetside café with outdoor seating offering simple, inexpensive snack food. Juice 4YTL, mains 6YTL.

Lodos Nara Cad 1. Good for dance music and regular live sets.

Maydos Yali Caddesi 12. Elegant restaurant serving a wide variety of Turkish and international cuisine. Great harbour views but service can be slow. Mains 14YTL.

Moving on

Bus Istanbul (5hr), İzmir (6hr), Selçuk (7hr)
Ferry Eceabat (30min).

THE GELIBOLU (GALLIPOLI) PENINSULA

Though endowed with splendid scenery and beaches, the slender **Gelibolu (Gallipoli) peninsula**, which forms the northwest side of the Dardanelles, is known chiefly for its grim military history. In April 1915 it was the site of a plan, devised by Winston Churchill, to land Allied troops, many of them Australian and New Zealand units, with a view to putting Turkey out of the war. It failed miserably, with massive casualties. Nevertheless, this was the first time Australians and New Zealanders had seen action under their own commanders; the date of the first landings, April 25, is celebrated as **ANZAC Day**.

What to see and do

The World War I battlefields and Allied cemeteries are by turns moving and numbing in the sheer multiplicity of graves, memorials and obelisks. However, it's difficult now to imagine the bare desolation of 1915 given the lush landscape of much of the area. The first stop on most tours is the **Kabatepe Orientation Centre and Museum** (daily 8am–6pm; 2YTL), beyond which are the **Beach**, **Shrapnel Valley** and **Shell Green** cemeteries, followed by **Anzac Cove** and **Arıburnu**, site of the ANZAC landing. Beyond Arıburnu, a left fork leads towards the beaches and salt lake at **Cape Suvla**, today renamed Kemikli Burnu; most tourists bear right for Büyük Anafartalar village and **Çonkbayırı Hill**, where there's a massive New Zealand memorial and a Turkish memorial detailing Atatürk's words and deeds. Working your way back down towards the orientation centre, you pass **The Nek**, **Walker's Ridge** and **Quinn's Post**, where the trenches of the opposing forces lay within a few metres of each other: the modern road corresponds to no-man's-land. From here the perilous supply line ran down-valley to the present location of **Beach Cemetery**.

> **BATTLEFIELD TOURS**
>
> Various local companies offer **battlefield tours** (around 50YTL per person, including lunch). The best include those operated by the *Eceabat Hotel* (Ⓣ0286/814 3121, Ⓦwww.anzacgallipolitours.com) and the Hassle Free Travel Agency in Çanakkale (Cumhuriyet Meydani 61, Ⓣ0286/213 5969). However, for groups, renting a car and doing it yourself would work out cheaper.

Moving on

Bus Selçuk (7hr 30min), İzmir (6hr 30min).
Ferries Lapseki (15 daily; 20min).

TROY

Although not the most spectacular archeological site in Turkey, **TROY** (Truva) is probably the most celebrated, thanks to its key role in Homer's *Iliad*. The ruins of the ancient city, just west of the main road around 20km south of Çanakkale, are on a much smaller scale than other sites, consisting mainly of defensive walls, a small theatre and the remains of a temple. Some come away disappointed, but it's worth remembering that the settlement dates back to the late Bronze Age, making Troy far older than most other classical cities. Çanakkale is the most sensible base: take one of the frequent *dolmuşes* (2YTL), rather than forking out 35YTL to join an organized tour. The *dolmuşes* leave every hour from the parked area under the bridge near the jetty. Returning from the site, however, requires a bit of patience. Although *dolmüses* should return every hour from Troy, this timetable is used pretty loosely – you may find yourself waiting for about two hours for a *dolmuş* on your way back. At the site (daily 8am–5/7pm; 12YTL) entrance, a road leads to a giant wooden horse. Just beyond is the ruined city itself, a craggy outcrop overlooking the plain, which stretches about 8km to the sea. It's a fantastic view, and despite the sparseness of the remains, as you stand on what's left of the ramparts and look out across the plain, it's not too difficult to imagine a besieging army camped out below.

BURSA

Draped along the leafy lower slopes of Uludağ, which towers more than 2000m above, **BURSA** – first capital of the Ottoman Empire and the burial place of several sultans – does more justice to its setting than any other Turkish city besides İstanbul. Gathered here are some of the finest early Ottoman monuments in Turkey, in a tidy and appealing city centre, though traffic congestion can make getting around a daunting experience.

What to see and do

Flanked by the busy Atatürk Caddesi, the compact **Koza Parkı**, with its fountains, benches and cafés, is the real heart of Bursa. On the far side looms the fourteenth-century **Ulu Camii**, whose interior is dominated by a huge *şadırvan* pool for ritual ablutions. Close by is Bursa's covered market, the **Bedesten**, given over to the sale of jewellery and precious metals, and the **Koza Hanı**, flanking the park, still entirely occupied by silk and brocade merchants. Across the river to the east, the **Yeşil Camii** (daily 8am–8.30pm) is easily the most spectacular of Bursa's imperial mosques. The nearby hexagonal **Yeşil Türbe** (daily 8am–noon & 1–7pm) contains the sarcophagus of Çelebi Mehmet I and assorted offspring. The immediate environs of the mosque are a busy tangle of cafés and souvenir shops.

Museum of Turkish and Islamic Art

The *medrese,* the largest surviving dependency of the mosque, now houses Bursa's recently renovated **Museum of Turkish and Islamic Art** (Tues–Sun 8.30am–noon & 1–5.30pm; 2YTL), with Çanakkale ceramics, glass items and a mock-up of an Ottoman circumcision chamber. West of the centre, the **Hisar** ("citadel") district was Bursa's original nucleus. Narrow lanes wind up past dilapidated Ottoman houses, while walkways clinging to the rock face offer fabulous views. The best-preserved dwellings are a little way west in medieval **Muradiye**, where the **Muradiye Külliyesi** mosque and

THE EVIL EYE

Take a short stroll around any Turkish town and it won't be long until you spot one of the ubiquitous **evil eye symbols**. This circular blue and white emblem with a dot in the middle is a good luck charm designed to ward off evil spirits. As well as being proudly displayed in homes and businesses, the symbol is also printed on pendants, bracelets and broaches.

medrese complex was begun in 1424. This is the last imperial foundation in Bursa, although it's most famous for its tombs, set in lovingly tended gardens. Out beyond the Kültür Parkı, the **Yeni Kaplıca** (daily 9am–11pm; 10YTL) are the nearest of Bursa's baths, a faded reminder of the days when the town was patronized as a spa.

Arrival and information

Bus Bursa's bus terminal is 5km north on the main road to İstanbul, from where bus #38 (every 15min) runs to Koza Parkı.
Tourist office Corner of Koza Parkı (Mon–Fri 8.30am–5.30pm; ⓣ0224/220 1848).

Accommodation

Çeşmeli Heykel Gümüşçeken Cad 6 ⓣ0224/224 1512. Comfortable en-suite rooms with all the added extras you could possibly want including a minibar. Ask for one of the upper rooms with great views. ❹
Demirci Otel Hammamlar Cad 33 ⓣ0224/236 5104. Unpretentious and well-run hotel with its own *hamam*. ❷
Gunes Ineby Cad 75 ⓣ0224/224 1404. Cheap, clean and friendly. ❷
Hotel Dikmen Maksem Cad 78 ⓣ0224/224 1840. Cable TV in all rooms. Clean with hospitable staff. ❹
Hotel Efehan Heykel Gümüşçeken Cad 34 ⓣ0224/225 2260. ⓦwww.efehan.com.tr. Welcoming hotel with a retro-glam feel full of simple and spacious rooms with TVs. ❷

Eating and drinking

Arap Şükrü Sakarya Cad 6. Great for fish and other Turkish cuisine. Reasonably priced. Mains 15YTL.
Çiçek Izgara Belediye Cad 15. Elegant restaurant with a decent take on Ottoman dishes. Mains 8YTL.
İskender A great choice for trying Bursa's speciality, the *İskender kebap* (13YTL).
Piccolo Sakarya Cad 16. Reasonably priced contemporary bar.

Moving on

Bus Çanakkale (hourly; 5hr); İstanbul (hourly; 5hr); İznik (2 hours).

The Aegean coast

The **Aegean coast** is, in many ways, Turkey's most enticing destination, home to some of the best of its Classical antiquities and the most appealing resorts. Tiny **Assos** with its ancient ruins is one of the gems of the coast. **Bergama**, 70km to the southeast, makes a charming place to stop for a few days. Further south, the city of **İzmir** serves as a base for day-trips to adjacent sights and beaches. Visitors continuing south will be spoilt for sightseeing choices as the territory is rich in Classical, Hellenistic and Roman ruins, notably **Ephesus** and the remains inland at **Hierapolis** – sitting atop the famous pools and mineral formations of **Pamukkale**. The coast itself is better down south, too, and although the larger resorts, including **Kuşadası** and **Marmaris**, have been marred by the developers, **Bodrum** still has a certain charm.

ASSOS

ASSOS, 70km south of Çanakkale, is a tiny stone village built on a hill around the ruins of the ancient town of the same name, founded in the sixth century BC and once home to Aristotle. The old-town ruins (daily 8.30am–5/7pm; 5YTL) are for the most part blissfully quiet; the **Temple of Athena** has had its Doric columns re-erected, and there are breathtaking views from here to the Greek island of Lésvos. The only transport is a **minibus** from Ayvacik, 25km to the north, which passes through both the upper village of Assos and its twin settlement downhill around the fishing harbour; it runs according to demand, so out of season and at off-peak times you may have a long wait.

Before Assos, beside an antique bridge is the popular and immaculate *Old Bridge House* (ⓣ0286/721 7426;

dorms ❷, rooms ❸), with cabins set in landscaped gardens. **Pansiyons** in the upper village are all in restored stone houses and include the delightful *Timur Pansiyon*, just below the entrance to the ruins (☎0286/721 7449, Ⓦwww.hitit.co.uk/timur; rooms ❷–❸) with excellent views. Further along the shore to the east, are several small **campsites** including *Çakır* (☎0286/721 7048).

BERGAMA

BERGAMA is the site of the Hellenistic – and later Roman – city of Pergamon, ruled for several centuries by a powerful local dynasty. Excavations were completed here in 1886, but unfortunately much of what was found has since been carted off to Germany. However, the acropolis of Eumenes II remains a major attraction, and there are a host of lesser sights and an old quarter of ramshackle charm that deserve a day or two.

What to see and do

The old town lies at the foot of the acropolis, about ten minutes' walk from the bus station. Its foremost attraction is the **Kızıl Avlu** (daily 8.30am–5.30pm; 5YTL), a huge edifice on the river not far from the acropolis, originally built as a temple to the Egyptian god Osiris and converted to a basilica by the early Christians, when it was one of the Seven Churches of Asia Minor addressed by St John in the Book of Revelation. South along the main street is the **Archaeological Museum** (Tues–Sun 8.30am–6pm; 4YTL), which has a large collection of locally unearthed booty, including busts of Zeus and Socrates and a model of the Zeus altar. Bergama has a particularly good **hamam**, the *Haci Hekim*, Bankalar Cad 32 (from 8YTL).

Pergamon

Pergamon, the ancient city of kings, is set on top of a rocky bluff towering over modern Bergama. Taking a short cut through the old town still means an uphill walk of around half an hour. By taxi, the ride costs €6 or more; a taxi-tour around all Bergama's sights costs about 25YTL but is only recommended if you are pushed for time. The first attraction on the **acropolis** (daily 9am–5/7pm; 10YTL) is the huge horseshoe-shaped **Altar of Zeus**, built during the reign of Eumenes II to commemorate his father's victory over the Gauls. North of the Zeus altar lie the sparse remains of a **Temple of Athena**, above which loom the restored columns of the **Temple of Trajan**, where the deified Roman emperor and his successor Hadrian were revered in the imperial era. From the Temple of Athena a narrow staircase leads down to the theatre, the most spectacular part of the ruined acropolis, capable of seating ten thousand spectators, and a **Temple of Dionysos**, just off-stage to the northwest.

Arrival and information

Bus Bergama's bus station is on the main road, 500m from the town centre, and within fifteen minutes' walk of most accommodation.
Tourist office (daily 8.30am–noon & 1–5.30pm; ☎0232/633 1862) is on the main street, Zafer Mah, İzmir Cad 54, a short stroll away from the Archeological Museum.

Accommodation

Böblingen Askeplion Cad 2 ☎0232/633 2153. Good value doubles with shower. ❷
Efsane Ataturk Bul 82 ☎0232/633 6350. Large hotel with an abundance of dated rooms with 1970s decor. This is made up for by the hotel's pool and restaurant serving simple Turkish meals. ❷
Manolya Tanpinar Sok 11 ☎0232/633 1763. Modern rooms with TV and a/c. ❷

Eating and drinking

Arzu Pide Istiklal Meydanı 10. Huge *pides* (flat breads) and Turkish pizzas are baked in traditional brick ovens, resulting in a delicious home-baked taste. Mains 8YTL.

Pala Mescit Karacac 4. Good for staple Turkish dishes. Renowned for its delicious *köfte* (9YTL).
Pergamon Bankalar Cad 5. The hottest bar in town, housed in an old mansion, with live music at weekends.
Sağlam 3 Cumhuriyet Meydani 29. An extensive menu of Turkish classics, with specialities being lamb dishes and *goulash*. Mains 12YTL.

İZMIR

İZMIR – ancient Smyrna – is home to nearly three million people. Mostly burned down in the Turkish–Greek war of 1922, İzmir has been built pretty much from scratch and is nowadays booming, cosmopolitan and relentlessly modern. Its hot climate is offset by its location, straddling a fifty-kilometre-long gulf fed by several streams and flanked by mountains on all sides. Orientation can be confusing – many streets are unmarked – but most points of interest lie near each other and walking is the most enjoyable way of exploring.

What to see and do

İzmir cannot be said to have a single centre, although **Konak**, the busy park, city bus terminal and shopping centre on the waterfront, is where visitors spend most time. It's marked by the ornate **Saat Kulesi** (clock tower), the city's official symbol, and the **Konak Camii**, distinguished by its facade of enamelled tiles. Head north and you'll reach the Kūltur Parkı, a large park with regular outdoor entertainment particularly in the summer. Continue in the same direction and you'll soon reach the district of Alsançak – the hub of evening entertainment with al fresco bars and restaurants.

Archeological Museum

Southwest of the Konak Camii is İzmir's **Archeological Museum** (Tues–Sun 8.30am–5.30pm; 4YTL). The collection consists of finds from all over İzmir province, including some stunning marble statues and sarcophagi.

Kemeraltı

Immediately east of Konak is Kemeraltı, İzmir's **bazaar**. The main drag, Anafartalar Caddesi, is lined with clothing, jewellery and shoe shops; Fevzipaşa Bulvarı and the alleys just south are strong on leather garments. Worth seeking out is the covered bazaar area, Kızlarağası Hanı, on 871 Sok. Inside you'll find everything from jewellery to nargiles and carpet shops. If you're musically inclined, you may want to invest in a small *darbuka* (a traditional carved copper drum that makes a great sound) which can be bought from any of the several music shops inside.

Kadifekale

A symbol of İzmir's historic past, the castle ruins of **Kadifekale** (always open; free) provide great views of İzmir's metropolitan expanse. The site is somewhat neglected but a trek up the hill is well worth it not just for the views but also to watch Kurdish women weave carpets in the open air and to browse their array of textile products for sale. To get to the castle, take a red-and-white city bus #33 from Konak and get off shortly after you see the national flag flying from the top of the hill. Buses back to Konak can be caught from the bus shelter at the corner of the road approaching the castle.

TREAT YOURSELF

A small leap across the water from Konak, the fashionable district of **Karşiyaka** is a great place to explore. After taking a ferry from Konak (1.25YTL), wander round the sleek and contemporary shops on Kemalpaşa Caddesi and then explore the rest of the area by **horse-drawn carriage**. Carriages leave from the jetty and a 45-minute ride costs 20YTL, although this could be cheaper depending on your bargaining skills.

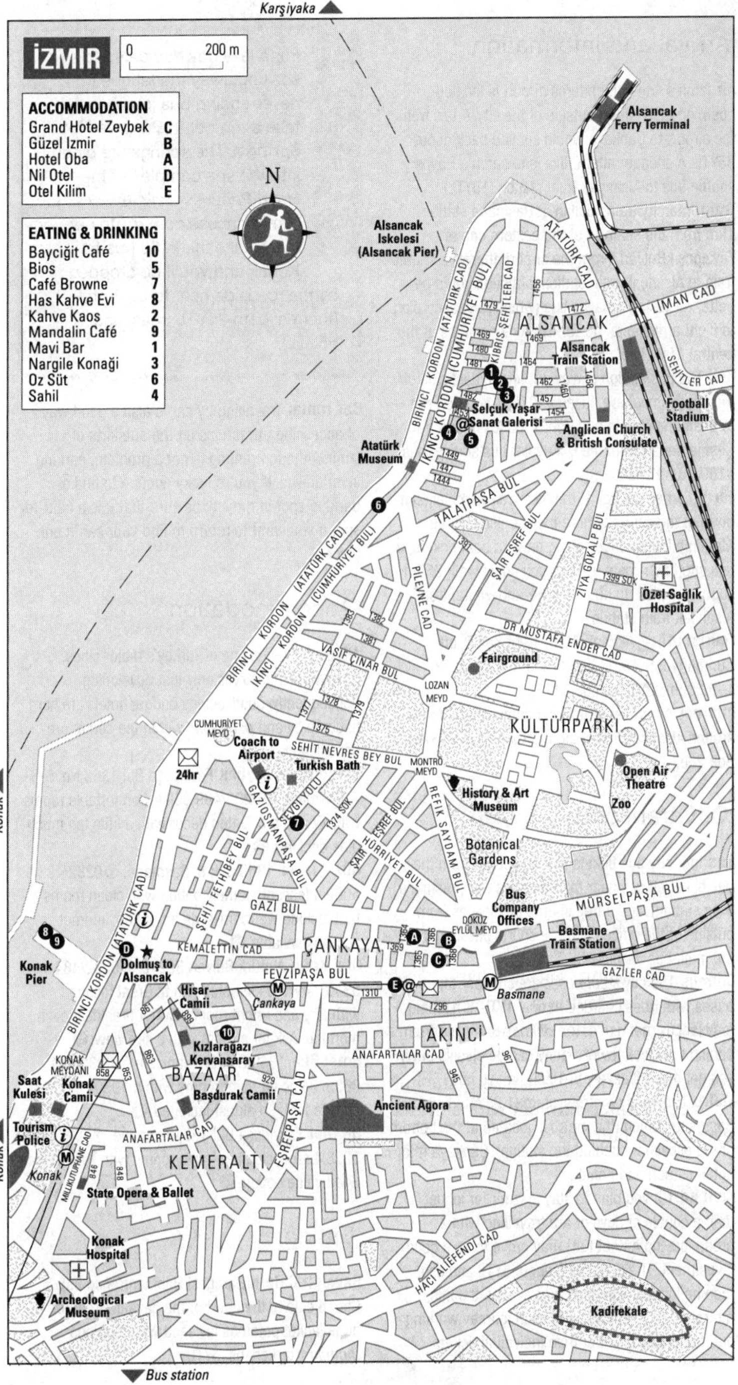

İZMIR
0 200 m
ACCOMMODATION
Grand Hotel Zeybek C
Güzel Izmir B
Hotel Oba A
Nil Otel D
Otel Kilim E
EATING & DRINKING
Bayciğit Café 10
Bios 5
Café Browne 7
Has Kahve Evi 8
Kahve Kaos 2
Mandalin Café 9
Mavi Bar 1
Nargile Konaği 3
Oz Süt 6
Sahil 4
Karşiyaka
Alsancak Ferry Terminal
Alsancak Iskelesi (Alsancak Pier)
ALSANCAK
Alsancak Train Station
Selçuk Yaşar Sanat Galerisi
Atatürk Museum
Anglican Church & British Consulate
Football Stadium
Özel Sağlık Hospital
Fairground
KÜLTÜRPARKI
Open Air Theatre
Zoo
History & Art Museum
Botanical Gardens
Coach to Airport
Turkish Bath
24hr
Bus Company Offices
Basmane Train Station
Basmane
ÇANKAYA
Çankaya
Dolmuş to Alsancak
Hisar Camii
Konak Pier
Kızlarağazı Kervansaray
BAZAAR
Başdurak Camii
AKINCI
Ancient Agora
Saat Kulesi
Konak Camii
Tourism Police
Konak
KEMERALTI
State Opera & Ballet
Konak Hospital
Archeological Museum
Kadifekale
Bus station

Arrival and information

Air İzmir's Adnan Menderes airport is located approximately 15km outside of the city. A taxi from the airport to Çankaya would set you back about 35YTL. A cheaper alternative is to catch a Havaş shuttle bus to Alsançak train station (10YTL).
Train Intercity trains pull in at Basmane station, 1km from the seafront at the eastern end of Fevzipaşa Bulvarı. From the airport, there's a shuttle train to Alsançak train station, although you'd be better off taking a Havaş bus (which runs according to flight arrivals) to the Turkish Airlines office at the central *Efes Hotel*.
Bus The bus station is way out on the east side of the city, from where buses #50, #51 and #54 run to Basmane station and Konak. Buses to and from Çeşme depart from the Uçkuyular bus station: bus #169 from Konak.
Ferry Ferries anchor at the Alsançak terminal, 2km north of the centre, where there's also a Turkish Maritime Lines office selling onward boat tickets; a taxi into town costs 9YTL or you could walk 250m south and pick up bus #2 (blue-and-white) from Alsançak train station.
Tourist office Akdeniz Mah, 1344 Sok 2, off Cumhuriyet Bulvari (daily 8.30am–noon & 1–5.30pm; ⓣ0232/483 5117).
Internet A number of Internet cafés can be found around Alsançak, including *Internet House*, 1378 Sok 26b.

City transport

Bus Intercity bus tickets can be bought from the bus ticket offices near the Basmane Gar (Basmane train station), and a free shuttle bus leaves from outside of the offices and transports passengers to the main bus terminal.
Dolmuş The city's *dolmuşes* are cheaper than buses with rides charged at only 1YTL. If heading to Alsançak, get one of the *dolmuşes* leaving from behind the clock tower – they can be elusive but if you get one it'll save you 10YTL in taxi fare.
Metro The handy metro system (1.25YTL) links Basmane station (the metro is located at the bottom of the escalators behind the station), Çankaya (the hotel district) and Konak.
Kent Kart If you plan to stay in İzmir for longer than a couple of days or are travelling with a group, buying a Kent Kart may prove to be a good investment. The card costs about 5YTL and can then be loaded with cash for travel on the bus, metro or ferry network with each journey working out marginally cheaper than individual tickets.

TREAT YOURSELF

For a lazy day dedicated to soaking away the fatigue from never-ending bus journeys, take a trip out to **Balçova Hot Springs**. The springs are piped into the spa complex of the *Hotel Princess İzmir* (ⓦwww.izmirprincess.com.tr). To get there, take the #169 bus from Konak and you'll be dropped by the roadside near to the hotel (thermal bath 25YTL, massage 55YTL).

Car rental Travelling by car is also a good way of accessing attractions on the outskirts of İzmir. Although renting is not a problem, parking invariably is. If you're lucky enough to find a parking spot in the city be sure that it is a paid-for spot if you want to return to find your car in one piece.

Accommodation

Although İzmir is one of Turkey's major cities, its tourism industry is only just developing. Consequently, good-quality budget hotels are hard to come by and *pansiyons* within the centre are nonexistent.
Grand Hotel Zeybek Fevzipaşa Bul 1368 No. 5-6-7, Basmane ⓣ0232/489 6694. Comfortable rooms with TV and a/c. Dated decor with a little too much pine decking. ❸
Güzel İzmir 1368 Sok 8, Basmane. ⓣ0232/483 5069. Pleasant, homely option with clean rooms that include wetroom-style en-suites. Internet access available. ❷
Otel Kilim Atatürk Bulvarı 35210 ⓣ0232/484 5340, ⓦwww.kilimotel.com.tr. Great location with airy and bright rooms. Buffet breakfast each morning. Ask for a room with a sea view. ❻
Hotel Oba 1369 Sok 27, Çankaya ⓣ0232/441 9605. Basic en-suite rooms with a 1950s' nursing college feel. Breakfast included. ❷
Nil Otel Fevzipaşa Bul 155, Basmane. ⓣ0232/483 5228. Large, clean en-suite rooms with TV and a/c. Good value option. ❷

Eating

Bayciğit Café Kizlarağasi Hani (entrance 33). Cheap café in the heart of the bazaar. Great for huge jacket potatoes lavished with toppings (*kumpirs*) or kebabs. 5YTL.

Café Browne 1379 Sok. Delicious soups and veggie dishes, snacks and main courses. Omelette 3.50YTL. Kebab 10YTL.
Has Kahve Evi Atatürk Cad, Konak. Starbucks style café serving calorie-filled goodies, frappés and lattes. Cakes 6YTL
Mandalin Café Atatürk Cad, Konak. Coastal views, great milkshakes and food for all palates ranging from a Turkish take on pasta to well-presented, traditional Ottoman dishes. Mains 12YTL.
Oz Süt Atatürk Cad 180. Excellent continental coffee and cakes. Cheese cake 4.50YTL.

Drinking

Bios Gazi Kadınlar Sokağı 18, 1453 Sokak, Alsançak. Rock club bar with a lively dance floor packed with young ravers.
Kahve Kaos 1482 Sok, no. 20/35220, Alsançak. Classy café/bar with a garden courtyard. Busy at weekends.
Mavi Bar Cumhuriyet Bulvari 206, Alsançak. Funk rock bar in a converted warehouse attracting a diverse, fashionable crowd.
Nargile Konaği 1482 Sok, Alsançak. Outdoor lounge-bar with a chilled-out hippy vibe. Perfect for late-night nargile smoking.
Sahil Gazi Kadınlar Sok. Open-air hang-out open late for backgammon, tea or nargiles. No alcohol.

Entertainment

Bostanlı Karşıyaka Açıkhava Tiyatrosu Saat Taşer Tiyatrosu, İzmir. Large concert hall hosting regular pop concerts in Konak Pier. Open daily from 10.30am–9.30pm.
Cinebonus Konak Pier, İzmir. Cinema with recent Hollywood releases. Student discount available.
Halkapınar Spor Salonu İzmir Large sports stadium. For forthcoming games see ⓦ www.biletix.com or visit the Biletix ticket office.
State Opera and Ballet Milli Kütüphane Cad, Konak ⓣ 0232/484 3692. A diverse programme of concerts ranging from classical to jazz and pop.

Moving on

Train Selçuk (7 daily; 1hr).
Bus/domuş Ankara (every 30min; 8hr); Bergama (hourly; 2hr); Bodrum (hourly; 4hr); Bursa (6 daily; 7hr); Çanakkale (4 daily; 5hr); Datça (hourly; 7hr); Denizli (hourly; 4hr); Fethiye (12–18 daily; 7hr); Konya (1 daily; 8hr); Kuşadası (every 30min; 1hr 40min); Marmaris (hourly; 5hr); Nevşehir (1 daily; 12hr); Selçuk (every 40min; 1hr).

KUŞADASI

KUŞADASI is Turkey's most bloated resort, a brash coastal playground that extends along several kilometres of seafront. In just three decades its population has swelled from 6000 to around 50,000. Unfortunately, the town is many people's introduction to the country: ferry services link it with the Greek island of Sámos, while the resort is a port of call for Aegean cruise ships, which disgorge vast numbers in summer.

What to see and do

Liman Caddesi runs from the ferry port up to Atatürk Bulvarı, the main harbour esplanade, from which pedestrianized Barbaros Hayrettin Bulvarı ascends the hill. To the left of here, the **Kale** district, huddled inside the town walls, is the oldest and most appealing part of town, with a mosque and some fine traditional houses. Kuşadası's most famous beach, **Kadınlar Denizi**, 3km southwest of town, is a popular strand, usually too crowded for its own good in season. **Güvercin island**, closer to the centre, is mostly landscaped terraces dotted with tea gardens and snack bars. For the closest sandy beach, head 500m further south, just before **Yılancı Burnu**, or alternatively try **Tusan** beach, 7km north of town, served by all Kuşadası–Selçuk *dolmuşes*, as well as more frequent ones labelled *Şehir Içi*. Much the best beach in the area is **Pamucak**, at the mouth of the Kücük Menderes River, 15km north, an exposed 4km stretch of sand that is as yet little developed; in season it's served by regular *dolmuşes* from both Kuşadası and Selçuk.

Arrival and information

Bus The combined *dolmuş* and long-distance bus station is about 2km out, past the end of Kahramanlar Caddesi on the ring road to Söke, while the *dolmuş* stop is closer to the centre on Adnan Menderes Bulvarı.

Tourist office (Mon–Fri 8am–6pm; summer also Sat & Sun; ⓣ0256/614 1103) is right by the ferry port.
Internet Available at m@ilhouse, opposite the Kale Camii on Barbarosh Bul.

Accommodation

Golden Bed Aslanlar Cad, Uğurlu Çıkmazı 4. ⓣ0256/614 8708, ⓦwww.kusadasihotels.com/goldenbed. Characterful, good value en-suite rooms. ❷–❸
Sammy's Palace Kıbriş Cad 14 ⓣ0256/612 2588, ⓦwww.sammystravel.com. Lively hotel with helpful staff and tour information. ❸
Sezgin Hotel Aslanlar Cad 68. ⓣ0256/614 4225, ⓦwww.sezginhotel.com. Comfortable en-suite rooms and a swimming pool. ❷–❸
Stella Hostel Bezirgan Sok 44, ⓣ0256/614 1632, ⓦwww.stellahostel.com. Presentable en-suite rooms with private balconies and a roof bar. Dorms ❶, doubles ❷

Eating and drinking

Alize Karagöz Sok 7. Popular bar with young locals; live music after dark.
Avlu Cephane Sok 15/A. Serves a wide range of kebabs, stews, steamed vegetables and *mezes* in an outdoor courtyard. Mains 7YTL.
Öz Urfa Cephane Sok. Excellent-value *lahmacun* (Turkish pizza; 3YTL) and *pide*. Mains 10YTL.

Moving on

Bus/dolmuş Pamukkale (12 daily; 3hr 30min); Selçuk (20 min); Bodrum (3 daily; 3hr); Fethiye (4hr).

FERRIES TO GREECE

Every day in high season a morning and evening **ferry** leaves from Kuşadası to the Greek island of **Sámos** (42YTL single, 50YTL day return, 85YTL open return). Diana on Kıbrıs Cad (ⓣ0256/614 3859) runs up to two boats daily in summer. From Sámos, a popular follow-on destination is the party island **Íos** (see p.563). Tickets from Sámos to Ios can be bought from ITSA travel agents located near the pier.

SELÇUK

SELÇUK has been catapulted into the limelight of premier-league tourism by its proximity to the ruins of Ephesus. The flavour of tourism here, though, is different from that at nearby Kuşadası, its location and ecclesiastical connections making it a haven for a disparate mix of backpackers and pilgrims from every corner of the globe, with Pamucak beach easily accessible by a short *dolmuş* ride.

What to see and do

Ayasoluk hill (daily 8.30am–5.30pm; 4YTL), the traditional burial place of St John the Evangelist, who died here around 100 AD, boasts the remains of a basilica built by Justinian that was one of the largest Byzantine churches in existence; various colonnades and walls have been re-erected, giving a hint of the building's magnificence. The tomb of the evangelist is marked by a slab at the former site of the altar; beside the nave is the baptistry, where religious tourists pose in the act of dunking their heads for the camera. Just behind the tourist office, the Efes **Archeological Museum** (Tues–Sun 8.30am–5.30pm; 4YTL) has galleries of finds from Ephesus, while beyond the museum, 600m along the road towards Ephesus, are the scanty remains of the **Artemision** or sanctuary of Artemis. This massive Hellenistic structure was considered one of the Seven Wonders of the Ancient World, though this is hard to believe today. Some 9km southwest of Selçuk lies **Meryemana** (daily dawn–dusk; 10YTL), a tiny Greek chapel (Mass, summer daily 7.15am, Sun also 10.30am) where some Orthodox theologians believe the Virgin Mary passed her last years, having travelled to the region with St John the Evangelist. Evidence of Mary's residence is somewhat circumstantial but that doesn't stop coach tours to Ephesus making the detour.

Arrival and information

Train and bus At the base of the castle hill in town, a pedestrian precinct leads east to the train station. Following the main highway a bit further south brings you to the bus and *dolmuş* terminal.
Tourist office opposite the bus terminal (daily 8.30am–noon & 1–5.30pm; winter closed Sat & Sun; ⓣ0232/892 6945).
Internet Cheap Internet facilities are at NetHouse, Sieburg Cad 4b.

Accommodation

ANZ Guesthouse 1064 Sok 12 ⓣ0232/892 6050, ⓦwww.anzguesthouse.com. Popular backpacker choice with Internet access and bike hire available. Dorms ❶, doubles ❹
Homeros Pansiyon Atatürk Mah Asmalı Sok 17 ⓣ0232/892 3995, ⓦwww.homerospension.com. Incredibly friendly and homely *pansiyon*. Wonderfully unique rooms with the quirkiness of a grandma's house crammed with local textiles. Breakfast included. ❷
Jimmy's Place Atatürk Mah, 1016 Sok 19 ⓣ0232/892 7558, ⓦwww.jimmysplaceephesus.com. Spotlessly clean and immaculate rooms. Dorms, standard rooms and deluxe suites finished to an unrivalled standard. Friendly staff plus Internet access, satellite TV and a swimming pool. Unbeatable value. Dorms ❶, doubles ❹
Paris Hotel Atatürk Mah, 1019 Sok 6 ⓣ0232/892 4487. Welcoming hotel where both travellers and staff congregate in the evenings on the outside terrace. Clean and basic rooms, Internet access and tour information available. ❷

Eating and drinking

Amazon Anton Kallinger Cad 22. Classy bistro café-bar with outdoor and indoor seating. Menu includes soups to pasta dishes, and a good selection of dishes aimed to suit western palates. Mains 12YTL.
Okumuzlar Pide 1006 Sokak. Simple, inexpensive restaurant popular with the locals. Mains 8YTL.
Natural Pastanesi 1005 Sok 13/b. Serves a wide selection of cakes, pastries and other sweet temptations. Cakes 4YTL.

EPHESUS

With the exception of Pompeii, **EPHESUS** (Efes in Turkish) is the largest and best-preserved ancient city around the Mediterranean. Not surprisingly, the ruins are busy in summer, although with a little planning it's possible to tour the site in relative peace. Certainly, it's a place you should not miss. You'll need at least three partly shady hours, and a water bottle.

Originally situated close to a temple devoted to the goddess Artemis, Ephesus' location by a fine harbour was the secret of its success in ancient times, eventually making it the wealthy capital of Roman Asia, ornamented with magnificent public buildings. During the Byzantine era the city went into decline, owing to the abandoning of Artemis worship, Arab raids and (worst of all) the final silting up of the harbour, leading the population to move to the nearby hill crowned by the tomb and church of St John, future nucleus of the town of Selçuk.

What to see and do

Approaching from Kuşadası, get the *dolmuş* to drop you at the *Tusan Motel* junction, 1km from the gate. From Selçuk, it's a 3km walk. In the centre of the **site** (daily 8am–6pm; 15YTL) is the **Arcadian Way**, which was once lined with hundreds of shops and illuminated at night. The nearby **theatre** has been partly restored to allow its use for open-air concerts and occasional summer festivals; it's worth the climb to the top for the views over the surrounding countryside. **Marble Street** passes the main **agora**, and a **Temple of Serapis** where the city's Egyptian merchants would have worshipped. About halfway along is a footprint, a female head and a heart etched into the rock – an alleged signpost for a brothel. Across the intersection looms the elegant **Library of Celsus**, erected by the consul Gaius Julius Aquila between 110 and 135 AD as a memorial to his father, Celsus Polemaeanus. Just uphill, a Byzantine fountain looks across the Street of the Curetes to the **public latrines**, a favourite with visitors. Continuing along, you'll come to the **Temple of Hadrian**, behind which sprawl the **Baths of Scholastica**, named after a fifth-century Byzantine woman whose headless statue adorns the entrance. The tour finally ends at the craft stalls located near the exit. There are some potential bargains to be found here, so it's worth bringing some extra money (or your credit card).

BODRUM

In the eyes of its devotees, **BODRUM** – ancient Halicarnassos – with its whitewashed houses and subtropical gardens, is the most attractive Turkish resort, a quality outfit in comparison to its upstart Aegean rivals. And it is a pleasant town in most senses, despite having no real beach, although development has proceeded apace over the last couple of decades.

What to see and do

The centrepiece is the **Castle of St Peter** (Tues–Sun 8.30am–noon & 1–5.30pm; 10YTL), built by the Knights of St John over a Selçuk fortress between 1437 and 1522. Inside, the various towers house a **Museum of Underwater Archeology**, which includes coin and jewellery rooms, Classical and Hellenistic statuary, and Byzantine relics retrieved from two wrecks. The **Carian Princess Hall** (Tues–Fri 10am–noon & 2–4pm; 4YTL extra) displays the skeleton and sarcophagus of a fourth-century BC noblewoman unearthed in 1989. There is also the **Glass Wreck Hall** (Tues–Fri 10am–noon & 2–4pm; 4YTL extra) containing the wreck and cargo of an ancient Byzantine ship, which sank near Marmaris. Immediately north of the castle lies the **bazaar**, from where you can stroll up Türkkuyusu Caddesi to the **Mausoleum** (daily 8am–5pm; 4YTL), the burial place of Mausolus, ruler of Halicarnassos and the origin of the word mausoleum.

Arrival and information

Bus The bus station is 500m up Cevat Şakir Caddesi, which divides the town roughly in two.
Ferry Ferries dock at the jetty west of the castle.
Tourist office close to the jetty on Iskele Meydanı (Mon–Fri 8.30am–5.30pm; summer also Sat & Sun).
Internet Hakim's Internet on Atatürk Caddesi.

Accommodation

Bahçeli Ağar Aile Neyzen Tevfik Cad 1402, Sok 4 ⓣ0252/316 1648. Family-run pension where rooms and guests are well looked after. A quiet escape from the densely packed tourist establishments. ❷
Bodrum Backpackers Atatürk Cad 31b ⓣ0252/316 1564 ⓦwww.bodrumbackpackers.net. Lively and friendly backpackers' hotel regularly hosting both budget travellers and the English party crowd. Great for amenities such as Internet access and laundry services. Dorms ❶, rooms ❷
Dönen Türkkuyusu Cad 21 ⓣ0252/316 4017. Clean rooms with a homely touch. ❸
Sevin Türkkuyusu Cad 5 ⓣ0252/316 7682 ⓦwww.sevinpension.com. Small, well-run hotel with staff who are keen to help despite limited English. The shady garden area and restaurant provide a pleasant, low-key option for dinner. ❸

Eating and drinking

Café del Mar Cumhuriyet Cad 170. Café-bar with a small club upstairs playing hard house.
Gemibaşi Firkayten Sok, Neyzen Tevfik. Perfect for simple meat or fish dishes. *Mezes* 5YTL, fish 25–30YTL.
Nazik Ana Eski Hukumet Sok 7. Traditional Turkish cuisine in a vine-covered restaurant. *Manti* 5YTL, mains 8YTL.
Roka Cumhuriyet Cad 100. Upmarket rooftop bar with great views.
Secret Garden Sanat Okullu Cad 1019 Sok. Picturesque, walled courtyard garden restaurant. Pricey but good for a romantic splurge. Mains 40YTL.

Moving on

Bus/dolmuş Fethiye (6 daily; 4hr 30min); İzmir (hourly; 4hr); Kaş (3 daily; 6hr); Kuşadası (3 daily; 3hr); Marmaris (14 daily; 3hr 15min); Selçuk (hourly; 3hr).
Domestic ferry Datça (April–Oct 3 daily; 1hr 30min).

International ferry Bodrum Ferryboat Association (☎0252/316 0882) runs ferries to Kos (40YTL one way, 75YTL open return), as well as domestic services to Datça, while Bodrum Express Lines (☎0252/316 1087) handles hydrofoils to Kos (40YTL one way), Rhodes (75YTL one way, 85YTL day return, 170YTL open return) and domestic services to Marmaris. There's a port tax (17YTL), payable on arrival in Greece if you're not returning the same day.

MARMARIS

MARMARIS rivals Kuşadası as the largest and most developed Aegean resort – there is little left of the sleepy fishing village that it was a mere two decades ago. Instead, the town is now a clubbers' paradise – ideal for fans of 18-24 package holidays. Its huge marina and proximity to Dalaman airport mean that tourists pour in more or less nonstop during the warmer months. Ulusal Egemenlik Bulvarı cuts Marmaris in half, and the maze of narrow streets east of it is home to most things of interest. The **Kaleiçi** district, the warren of streets at the base of the tiny castle, offers a pleasant wander, and the **castle museum** (Tues–Sun 8am–noon & 1–5.30pm; 2YTL) has a worthwhile archaeology and ethnography collection.

Arrival and information

Bus 2km east of the centre on the Muğla road, pick up a *dolmuş* to take you into town. Many of the bus companies also offer a free transfer minibus to the centre.

Ferry and tourist office The dock abuts Iskele Meydanı, on one side of which stands the helpful tourist office (Mon–Fri 8.30am–noon & 1–5/7pm; summer also Sat & Sun).

Boat tours Marmaris's harbour is awash with boats offering day trips around nearby bays. Most excursions include a trip to the fish farm on Paradise Island and shopping and swimming near Turunç village. Buy your ticket the day before (15YTL) and you'll be picked up for free from your hotel.

Accommodation

The majority of **budget hotels** are located in and around the streets off Atatürk Cad, close to the harbour. The slightly more upmarket hotels such as *Hotel Oasis* are dotted along the road heading west out of the centre of town.

Çubuk Otel Atatürk Cad Konti Sok 1. ☎0252/412 6774. Clean en-suite rooms with a small terrace, TV and air conditioning. Good budget option. ❷

Hotel Oasis Kemal Seufettin Elgin Bulvarı 73. Tastefully furnished en-suite rooms with satellite TV and air conditioning. Good-sized outdoor swimming pool. ❸

Pansiyon Nadir Kemerati Mahalesi ☎0252/412 1167. Grim and grimy box-sized rooms with no air conditioning and unhelpful staff. The cheapest for a reason. ❷

Yeşim Atatürk Cad 60, Sok 3 ☎0252/412 3001. Friendly hotel with large but dated rooms. Roadside rooms are noisy. ❷

Eating and drinking

Marmaris's collection of **bars and clubs** are primarily located behind the bazaar, five minutes away from the harbour. Bar street (Barlar Sok) is the principal thoroughfare and is easy to locate due to its huge crowds and thumping bass lines.

Bar Celona Tepe Mah 193. Quaint outdoor bar, ideal for escaping the noise of Bar Street.

Castle Café & Bar Tepe Mah 37 Sok no.53. Ideal location for panoramic views of Marmaris.

Çorba Restaurant Café Servisimiz 7/24, Saat Açıkıtır. A perfect perch for people watching whilst indulging in some tasty *lahmacun* or pasta. *Lahmacun* 3.50YTL, mains 10YTL.

Davy Jones's Locker Barlar Sok (Bar Street). Funky live music rock bar attracting an older crowd than the other Bar Street joints.

TREAT YOURSELF

Start the day with a **traditional Turkish breakfast.** A favourite with locals for Sunday morning brunch is the *Tepe Restaurant* at Siteler Mah, 212 Sok – great for panoramic views of the Aegean coastline (brunch 7.50YTL).

Özlem Restaurant Kemaraltı Mah Atatürk Cad 4/A no.99. Good-value but touristy restaurant which serves a selection of English food such as roast beef and Yorkshire pudding in addition to fast food and a small selection of Turkish dishes. Evening entertainment each night. Mains 8YTL.

Moving on

Bus Bodrum (3hr); Fethiye (3hr); Kaş (6hr); Nevşehir (14hr).
International ferries Rhodes (daily 9am & 4.30pm in high season, weekly in winter). Tickets cost 75YTL or 120YTL for an open return and must be booked a day before travel. Agents include Yeşil Marmaris, Barbaros Cad 13 (ⓣ0252/412 2290), and Engin Turizm, 3rd floor, G. Mustafa Cad 16 (ⓣ0252/412 6944).

PAMUKKALE

The rock formations of **PAMUKKALE** (literally "Cotton Castle"), 140km northeast of Marmaris, are the most-visited attraction in this part of Turkey, a series of white terraces saturated with dissolved calcium bicarbonate, bubbling up from the feet of the Çal Dağı Mountains beyond. As the water surges over the edge of the plateau and cools, carbon dioxide is given off and calcium carbonate precipitated as hard chalk or travertine. The spring emerges in what was once the ancient city of Hierapolis, the ruins of which would merit a stop even if they weren't coupled with the natural phenomenon. The **travertine terraces** (daily 24hr; 5YTL) are deservedly the first item on most visitors' agendas, but you should bear in mind the fragility of this natural phenomenon. Nowadays most of the pools are very shallow and closed off, with tourists confined to walking on specially marked routes, though this is, thankfully, having a positive effect, as the travertines slowly return to their former pristine whiteness, enhanced by night-time **illumination** (8–11pm). Up on the plateau is what is spuriously billed as the **sacred pool** (daily 8am–8pm; €5YTL) of the ancients, open for bathing in the 35°C mineral water. Although the therapeutic properties of this crowded swimming pool may be questionable, bring along a swimsuit as a dip in the water on a hot day is rejuvenation in itself.

Hierapolis

The archaeological zone of **HIERAPOLIS** lies behind the Pamukkale terraces and is admissible by the same entrance fee. Its main features include a **Temple of Apollo** and the infamous, albeit inconspicuous, plutonium cavern. Within the cave brews a toxic mixture of sulphur dioxide and carbon dioxide. The site has been firmly sealed off following the death of two German tourists. There's also a restored **Roman theatre** dating from the second century AD, with most of the stage buildings and their elaborate reliefs intact. Arguably the most interesting part of the city, though, is the **colonnaded street** which once extended for almost 1km, terminating in monumental portals a few paces outside the walls – of which only the most northerly, a triple arch, still stands. At the summit of the terraces next to the tourist office is the small **museum** (Tues–Sun 9am–12.30pm & 1.30–5.30pm; 2.50YTL), home to a disappointing collection of sarcophagi and masonry fragments.

The Mediterranean coast

The first stretch of Turkey's **Mediterranean coast**, dominated by the Akdağ and Bey mountain ranges of the Taurus chain and known as the "**Turquoise Coast**", is its most popular, famed for its pine-studded shore, minor ruins and beautiful scenery. Most of this is connected by Highway 400, which winds precipitously above the sea from Marmaris to Antalya. In the west, **Fethiye**, along with the nearby lagoon of **Ölüdeniz**, give good access to the pick of the region's Lycian ruins, such as **Xanthos**. The scenery becomes increasingly spectacular as you head towards the site of **Olympos**, and **Kaş**, which offers great scuba-diving, before reaching the port and major city of **Antalya**.

FETHIYE AND AROUND

FETHIYE is well sited for access to some of the region's ancient sites, many of which date from the time when this area was the independent kingdom of Lycia. The best beaches, around the Ölüdeniz lagoon, are now much too crowded for comfort, but Fethiye is still a market town and has been able to spread to accommodate increased tourist traffic.

What to see and do

Fethiye itself occupies the site of the Lycian city of **Telmessos**, little of which remains other than the impressive ancient theatre, which was only unearthed in 1992, and a number of Lycian rock tombs on the hillside above the bus station. You can also visit the remains of the medieval fortress, on the hillside behind the harbour area of town. In the centre of town, off Atatürk Caddesi, the small **museum** (Tues–Sun 8.30am–5.30pm; 4YTL) has some fascinating exhibits from local sites and a good ethnographic section.

Kaya Köyü

One of the most dramatic sights in the area is the ghost village of **KAYA KÖYÜ** (Levissi), 7km out of town, served by *dolmuşes* from the old bus station. The village was abandoned in 1923, when its Anatolian-Greek population was relocated, and all you see now is a hillside covered with more than two thousand ruined cottages and an attractive basilica. **Ölüdeniz** is about two hours on foot from Kaya Köyü – through the village, over the hill and down to the lagoon – or a *dolmuş* ride from Fethiye. The warm waters of this lagoon make for pleasant swimming, if you don't mind paying the small entrance fee, although the crowds can reach saturation level in high season – in which case the nearby beaches of Belceğiz and Kidrak are better bets. Ölüdeniz is also the starting point for the **Lycian Way** trekking route, which starts from near the *Montana Holiday Village* on the Fethiye–Ölüdeniz road and winds along the coast almost as far as Antalya.

Letoön and Xanthos

East of Fethiye lies the heartland of **ancient Lycia**, home to a number of important archeological sites. The closest is the **LETOÖN**, accessible by *dolmuş* from Fethiye to Kumluova, the site lying 4km off the main highway. The Letoön (daily 7am–7.30pm; 4YTL) was the official sanctuary of the Lycian Federation, and the extensive remains bear witness to its importance. On the other side of the valley, the remains of the hilltop city of **XANTHOS** are perhaps the most fascinating of the Lycian sites. Buses between Fethiye and Patara drop you off in Kanak, from where it's a ten-minute walk up to the **ruins** (daily 7am–7.30pm; 4YTL). West of the car park are the acropolis, agora and a Roman theatre, beside which are two Lycian tombs and a **sarcophagus** standing on a pillar tomb.

Arrival and information

Bus Fethiye's bus station is 2km east of the centre; *dolmuşes* to and from Ölüdeniz, Çalış Beach and Kaya Köyü use the old station, east of the central market.

Tourist office Close to the theatre, near the harbour at Iskele Meydanı 1 (daily 8.30am–5.30/7.30pm; ⓣ0252/612 1527).

Tours Bigbackpackers Yachting, Zafer Cad 1 (ⓣ0242/612 7834, ⓦwww.guletcruiseturkey.com), can organize four-day boat trips in a traditional Turkish *gulet* from Fethiye to Olympos (Demre) for around €150 per person.

Internet The cheapest Internet access is at Trend, Kayaiş Hani 6.

Accommodation

Ferah Pension Orta Yol 21 ⓣ0252/614 2816, ⓦwww.ferahpension.com. Highly organized, family run pension with good facilities and stunning views. Dorms ❶, doubles ❸

Ideal Pension Zafer Cad 1 ⓣ0252/614 1981, ⓦwww.idealpension.net. Popular with backpackers, great terrace and Internet access. Dorms ❶, doubles ❷

Irem Fevzi Çakmak Cad 45 ⓣ0252/614 3985. Clean doubles with sea views. ❸

V-Go's Hotel 2. Karagozler Ordu Cad 66 ⓣ0252/612 2113. Large, modern hotel with clean, newly refurbished rooms, Internet access and a swimming pool. ❸

Eating and drinking

The town's main roads, Atatürk Cad and Cumhuriyet Cad, are minutes away from the harbour and are surrounded by most of the town's amenities, bars and restaurants.

Café Oley Cumhuriyet Cad. Quality food and great milkshakes at reasonable prices. Mains 7YTL.

4 Corners Eski Camii, Atatürk Caddesi. Stylish yachting-themed bar. Buzzing till late.

Meğri Likya Sok. Satisfying meals and excellent *pide* (4YTL).

Ottoman Dance Bar Paspartu Sokak. Trendy and popular bar in an Ottoman house.

Moving on

Bus/dolmuş Kaş (hourly; 4hr); Marmaris (every 30min; 3hr); Patara (10 daily; 1hr 30min).

KAŞ

KAŞ sprang to prominence after about 1850, when it established itself as a Greek fishing and timber port. It is beautifully located, nestled in a small curving bay below rocky cliffs – the name itself means "eyebrow" or "something curved". But what was once a sleepy fishing village is fast becoming an adventure-sports centre for backpackers, with nightlife to match, and provides a handy base for paragliding, mountain biking and some of the cheapest and best **scuba-diving** in Turkey.

Many of the *pansiyons* listed (right) can organize such activities, or try one of the numerous operators in town, such as the professionally run Bougainville (ⓣ0242/836 3737, ⓦwww.bougainville-turkey.com) or Sun Diving (ⓣ0242/836 2637).

Scattered around the streets and to the west are the remains of ancient **Antiphellos**, one of the few Lycian cities to bear a Greek name, small in number but nevertheless impressive. Five hundred metres west of town lies an almost complete Hellenistic theatre, behind which is a unique Doric tomb named *Kesme Mezar*, again almost completely intact. Kaş is also well situated for the nearby ruins of **Kekova** and **Patara**.

> **Paragliding** is perfect for thrill seekers or those craving a novel way of viewing the landscape. Flights last approximately 20 minutes, cost €100/175YTL and can be booked either through your *pansiyon* or the Naturablue office on Likya Cad 1/A (ⓦwww.naturablue.com). If you're a paragliding novice you'll fly in tandem with an instructor – so all you need to do is hold on.

Arrival and information

Bus All buses and *dolmuşes* arrive at the small bus station just north of the town at the top of Elmalı Caddesi.

Tourist office in the town square at Cumhuriyet Maydanı 5 (April–Oct Mon–Fri 8.30am–7pm, Sat & Sun 10am–7pm; ⓣ0242/836 1238).

Internet Reliable places include NetHouse and Magicom on Çukurbaulı Caddesi.

Accommodation

Most **pansiyons** are located in the streets close to the bus station, particularly around Recep Bilgin Cad and immediately beyond.

Ani Recep Bilgin Cad 12 ⓣ0242/836 1791. ⓦwww.motelani.com. Welcoming atmosphere with a social terrace eating area. Basic rooms but there is potential to negotiate the price. Dorms ❶, doubles ❷

Ateş Yeni Cami Sok 3 ⓣ0242/836 1393. Backpacker favourite, good breakfasts and an attached quality hotel. Dorms ❷, doubles ❷–❸

Otel Nur Kücük Çakıl Plajı 07580 ⓣ0242/836 1328. Fresh, well-equipped rooms. Small but exposed swimming pool. Minutes from the beach. ❹

Santosa Pension Recep Bilgin Cad 4 ⓣ0242/836 1714. Family-run pension with great views from the communal rooftop. Bright and pleasant rooms. ❶–❷

Eating and drinking

Bar Celona Uzunçarşı Gürsoy Sok 2/a. A good choice for late evening drinks.

Kaş Genç Spor Çay Bahçesi Cumhuriyet Mey. Soguk Çeşme Karşisı. Relaxed tea gardens serving great value light food. Toasted sandwich 1.25YTL.

Li Lokma Hükümet Cad 2. A charming restaurant in a postcard location overlooking the harbour. Authentic Turkish cuisine is beautifully presented and delightfully morish whilst prices are surprisingly low. Mains 9YTL.

Mavi Cumhuriyet Medanı. Ever-popular bar with local party animals. Busy even on weeknights.

Midtown Café Bar Ilkokul Sok. New York-style outdoor café with a Turkish twist. Great for cheap treats like garlic chips. Mains 7YTL.

OLYMPOS AND ÇIRALI

There's another Lycian site, **OLYMPOS**, 50km before Antalya, located on a beautiful sandy bay and the banks of a largely dry river. It's an idyllic location with a small village that is now firmly on the backpacker circuit. The site itself (2.50YTL when someone is manning the ticket office) features some recently excavated tombs, the walls of a Byzantine church and a theatre, most of whose seats have gone. On the north side of the river are more striking ruins, including a well-preserved marble temple entrance. Beyond is a Byzantine bath house, with mosaic floors, and a Byzantine canal which would have carried water to the heart of the city. A pleasant 1.5km walk away is the holiday village of **Çıralı.** About an hour's well-marked stroll above the village's citrus groves flickers the dramatic **Chimaera** (open 24hr; 2.50YTL), a series of eternal flames issuing from cracks in the bare rock. The fire has been burning since antiquity, and inspired the Lycians to worship the god Hephaestos (or Vulcan to the Romans). The mountain was associated with a fire-breathing monster, also known as the Chimaera, with a lion's head, a goat's rear and a snake for a tail.

Arrival and information

Bus Catch any Kaş–Antalya bus to the minibus stop on the main highway, 8km up from the shore; in season there are hourly minibuses from there to Olympos. There are also one or two minibuses a day from Antalya to Çıralı in season.

Money Note that there are no banks or ATMs in Olympos or Çıralı, so make sure you have enough cash before arriving. Many of the *pansiyons* can accept card payment for accommodation.

Accommodation

With few road names around Olympos it's best to ask at the bus station ticket office for directions or arrange pick-ups.

Olympos

Bayram's ⓣ0242/892 1243, ⓦwww.bayrams.com. Accommodation ranges from bungalow shacks to tree-house dormitory rooms. Excellent facilities include laundry service and Internet access. Dorms ❷, bungalows ❸–❹

Kadir's ⓣ0242/892 1250, ⓦwww.olympostreehouse.com. Good facilities including an al fresco nightclub. Dorms ❷, bungalows ❷

Şaban ⓣ0242/892 1265, ⓦwww.sabanpansion.com. Treehouse style *pansyion* with excellent home-made food and a friendly, relaxed atmosphere. ❷–❸

Çıralı

Bariş Pansiyon Çıralı Cad ⓣ0212/825 7080. Best of the budget options. Set around a pretty garden; near to the beach. ❸

Eating and drinking

There are a handful of pleasant beach **restaurants** including *Yavuz* and *Olympos*, or for excellent lunchtime *gözleme* try *Pehlivan*, close to the ticket office. *Orange*, nestled amongst the rocks in a small side valley, is the best of the three **bars** in the area.

ANTALYA

ANTALYA is blessed with an ideal climate and a stunning setting, and, despite the grim appearance of its concrete sprawl, it's an agreeable place – although the main area of interest for visitors is confined to the relatively small old quarter; its beaches don't rate much consideration. A short bus ride away are the charming **Düden falls** where tourists and locals flock on hot summer days. Antalya's principal attraction, however, is situated on the outskirts of the city – **Aspendos**, the city's Roman theatre which still holds live performances.

What to see and do

Antalya is dominated by the **Yivli Minare** or "Fluted Minaret", erected in the thirteenth century. Downhill from here is the **old harbour**, recently restored and site of the evening promenade. North is the bazaar, while south, beyond the Saat Kalesi (clock tower), lies **Kaleiçi** or the old town, with every house now a carpet shop, café or *pansiyon*. On the far side, on Atatürk Caddesi, the triple-arched **Hadrian's Gate** recalls a visit by the emperor in 130 AD; while Hesapçı Sokak leads south past the **Kesik Minare** to a number of tea gardens.

The Antalya Museum

The one thing you shouldn't miss is the **Antalya Museum** (Tues–Sun 9am–6.30pm; 15YTL), one of the top five archeological collections in the country; it's on the western edge of town at the far end of Kenan Evren Bulvarı, easily reachable by a tram that departs from the clock tower in Kaleiçi. Highlights include an array of Bronze Age urn burials, second-century statuary, an adjoining sarcophagus wing, and a number of mosaics, not to mention an ethnography section with ceramics, household implements, weapons and embroidery.

Düden falls

A small but nonetheless enchanting waterfall, **Düden falls** attracts a large amount of visitors. The upper falls provide the best visual spectacle and are situated in the midst of a park. There is even a precarious walkway carved out to enable visitors to walk behind the falls. Try finishing the day by spreading out a picnic on one of the many picnic tables dotted around the site or by enjoying a *gözleme* (a bread-like pancake snack filled with potatoes, meat, cheese or some other treat) or an ice cream from the nearby tea gardens. To get to the falls from Kaleiçi, get a number 14 bus from the *dolmuş otogar* (2YTL). Ask the driver for Düden falls and you'll be dropped near the entrance. The journey should take approximately twenty-five minutes.

Arrival and information

Air The airport is 12km northeast; Havaş buses into town depart from the domestic terminal, five-minutes' walk from the international terminal, while city-centre-bound *dolmuşes* pass nearby.

TREAT YOURSELF

An opportunity to attend an evening performance at **Aspendos Theatre** should not be missed. Tickets cost in the region of 50YTL and forthcoming performances can be viewed and booked at ⓦwww.biletix.com.

Getting to Aspendos can be an arduous task, but it can be done. Catch a bus from Antalya's main terminal heading to Serik (6YTL) and inform the ticket office that you wish to get off near Aspendos. The bus will stop two kilometres away from the site and from here you will need a taxi. It may a good idea to arrange this second leg of the journey through the tourist office. Remember that Aspendos is an old, open-air theatre, so bring along anything you may need for comfortable viewing.

Bus Antalya's main bus station is 8km north of town, although regular *dolmuşes* and city buses run from here to a terminal at the top of Kazım Özalp Caddesi (still known by its old name of Sarampol), which runs for just under 1km down to the clock tower on the fringe of the old town.
Ferry About 5km west of the centre is the ferry dock, connected to the centre by *dolmuş*.
Tourist office A fifteen-minute walk west from the clock tower on Cumhuriyet Cad (daily 8am–6/7pm; ⓣ0242/241 1747).
Travel agents There are several travel agents around the city specializing in tours in and around Antalya. This is a great way of seeing some of the key sites in the area if you don't have the patience to rely on public transport. Check out Nirvana Travel at Barboros Mh Hesapcı Sok no. 3 (ⓦwww.nirvanatour.com).
Internet *Moonlight Café* on 1291 Sok opposite Hadrian's Gate, has cheap, fast Internet access.

City transport

Bus Buses and *dolmuşes* can be caught throughout the city but many buses (including #14 to Düden falls) depart from the car park area off Ali Çetinkaya Caddesi.
Tram The tram runs through Kaleiçi and starts from Zerdalilik and ends its route at the Museum. Tickets can be bought at the turnstile booths.

Accommodation

Most **budget accommodation** can be found in the area sandwiched between Hadrian's Gate and the back of the bazaar.
Blue Sea Garden Hotel Kılçarslan Mah Hesapçı 65 ⓣ0242/248 8213, ⓦwww.blueseagarden.com. Modern, bright rooms accented with a rose on each bed. Most guests spend lazy days in the hotel's garden which has a pool and a small restaurant area. ❸
Konukzade Konağı Kılıçarslan Mah Hıdırlık Sok ⓣ0242/244 7456. Cosy, small hotel with basic rooms and a small courtyard restaurant. Good for animal lovers as chickens, dogs and cats roam around its courtyard entrance. ❷
Sabah Pansiyon Hesapçı Sok 60a ⓣ0242/247 5345, ⓦwww.sabahpansiyon.8m.com. Laid-back backpackers' haunt with simple and clean rooms. Dorms ❶, doubles ❷
White Garden Kaleiçi Kılıçaslan Hesapçı Geçidi ⓣ0242/241 9115. Charming, Continental-style pension; immaculate rooms with large en suites. Buffet Turkish breakfasts from fresh local produce. Excellent value. ❷

Eating and drinking

Most **bars** and **clubs** in Antalya do not start to get busy until after midnight – so be prepared to party till the crack of dawn.
Akdeniz Çiçek Pasaje Uzun Çarşı 24–26, Kaleiçi. Three-level bar with live Turkish music inducing regular sessions of impromptu dancing.
Aynali Café Restaurant Hearty meals with good portions. Next to the harbour. Mains 8YTL.
Gaziantep Ismet Paşa Cad 3. Excellent warm *pides* and meat dishes. Mains 12YTL.
Liman Café Tophane Çay Bahçesı. Decked out with traditional textiles and cushioned seating. Inexpensive drinks and light food. *Gözleme* 5YTL.
Olympos 100 Yıl Bul. Trance-music club packed with well-dressed locals. Check out Nirvana Travel for transport and drinks coupon packages.

Moving on

Bus/dolmuş Antakya (3 daily; 12hr); Denizli (6 daily; 5hr 30min); Fethiye, by inland route (6 daily; 4hr); İstanbul (4 daily; 12hr); İzmir (6 daily; 9hr 30min); Kaş (6 daily; 5hr); Konya (6 daily; 5hr 30min); Sıde (3 hourly; 1hr 15min); Nevşehir (1 daily; 11hr); Olympos (every 30min; 2hr 30min).

Central Turkey

When the first Turkish nomads arrived in **Anatolia** during the tenth and eleventh centuries, the landscape must have been strongly reminiscent of their Central Asian homeland. Today, the landscape's charm lies in its juxtaposition of contrasts: rolling vistas surround burgeoning metropolises and vast solitary expanses skirt around bustling village communities. Eddying back and forth between these two different faces of the region is easily possible from wherever you're based. The south-central part of the country draws more visitors, not least for **Cappadocia** in the far east of the region, where water and wind have created a land of fantastic forms from the soft tufa rock, including forests of cones, table mountains and canyon-like valleys. Further south still, **Konya** is best known as the birthplace of the mystical **Sufi** sect and is a good place to stop over between Cappadocia and the coast.

ANKARA

Modern **ANKARA** is really two cities, a double identity that is due to the breakneck pace at which it has developed since being declared capital of the Turkish Republic in 1923. Until then Ankara – known as Angora – had been a small provincial city, famous chiefly for the production of soft goat's wool. This city still exists, in and around the old citadel that was the site of the original settlement. The other Ankara is the modern metropolis that has grown up around a carefully planned attempt to create a seat of government worthy of a modern, Western-looking state.

What to see and do

The city is bisected north–south by **Atatürk Bulvarı**, and everything you need is in easy reach of this broad and busy street. At the northern end, **Ulus Meydanı**, a large square and an important traffic intersection marked by a huge equestrian Atatürk statue, is the best jumping-off point for the old part of the city – a village of narrow cobbled streets and ramshackle wooden houses centring on the **Hisar**, Ankara's old fortress and citadel. To the south, the modern shopping district of **Kızılay** sees Turkish students congregate on its streets and aspiring authors sell and sign their books on street corners. At night, the area is awash with evening entertainment, bars and restaurants which is also mirrored in the neighbouring districts of **Kavaklidere** and **Çankaya**.

The Museum of Anatolian Civilizations

Located in Ulus, at the end of Kadife Sokak, is the **Museum of Anatolian Civilizations** (Tues–Sun 9am–5.30pm; 10YTL) which boasts an incomparable collection of archeological objects housed in a restored Ottoman *bedesten*, or covered market. Hittite carving and relief work form the most compelling section of the museum, mostly taken from Carchemish, near the present Syrian border. There are also Neolithic finds from Çatal Höyük, the site of one of Anatolia's oldest settlements and widely regarded as the world's first "city".

Hisar

A steep walk up Hisarparkı Cad brings you to the **Hisar**, a small citadel amidst the old city walls. Most of what can be seen today dates from Byzantine times, with substantial Selçuk and Ottoman additions. Inside the confines, follow the steps leading up the hill and look out for the flag flying in the distance and you'll soon reach Ak Kale, a castle ruin which provides a perfect perch for viewing Ankara from above. A walk around the rest of the Hisar will let you amble in and out of the narrow alleys that intersect the ramshackle houses. Continue to head south and you'll find the twelfth-century mosque, **Alâeddin Camii**, along with a series of touristy souvenir stalls selling handmade carpet bags, jewellery and crockery.

Roman Ankara

What's left of Roman Ankara lies north of Ulus Meydanı. First stop is the Column of Julian on Hükümet Meydanı, shaped somewhat like a giant doner kebab. Close by are the ruins of the Temple of Augustus and Rome built in honour of Augustus around 20 BC. Northeast of here are the remains of Ankara's **Roman baths** (daily 8.30am–12.30pm & 1.30–5.30pm; 2YTL). Only the foundation stones that supported the heating and service areas remain; nevertheless, a walk around the site will enable you to imagine their former grandeur.

Parliament & Çankaya Köşku

South of the districts of Kızılay and Kocatepe lie Turkey's parliament building, a strip of embassies, and the **Presidential Palace** (Çankaya Köşku; guided tours Sun 1.30–5pm; free). This includes Atatürk's Ankara residence, whose grounds are home to the Çankaya Atatürk Museum (same times and ticket).

Arrival and information

Air Ankara's Esenboğa airport is 33km north of town. Havaş buses (7YTL) meet incoming Turkish Airlines flights; a taxi will set you back 50YTL.
Train The train station is at the corner of Talat Paşa Caddesi and Cumhuriyet Bulvarı, from where frequent buses run to Kızılay and Ulus.
Bus The bus station lies 5km to the southwest; some companies run service minibuses to the centre, otherwise take a *dolmuş* or the Ankaray rapid transit system (2.50YTL) to Kızılay and change onto the metro (same ticket) for Ulus, where most of the budget hotels are located.
Tourist office There's an incredibly helpful tourist office across from the train station at Gazi Mustafa Kemal Bulvarı 121, just outside Maletepe station on the Ankaray (Mon–Fri 9am–5pm, Sat & Sun 10am–5pm; winter closed Sun; ⓣ0312/231 5572).

City transport

Bus As well as displaying numbers, buses in Ankara also display the names of their destinations, so it's easy to work out which one to catch. For buses heading from Ulus to Çankaya, try catching #413, #228 or the GOP although a multitude of other buses also head in this direction. Buy bus tickets in advance from kiosks next to the main bus stops (it's a good idea to stock up, as some areas have no kiosks). Tickets cost 1.30YTL and should be inserted into the machine next to the driver. However, on some buses you can buy your ticket on board from the conductor. Most buses stop running between 12 and 1am.
Metro/Ankaray The metro runs from Batıkent in the northwest and splits at Kızılay where the metro becomes the Ankaray (light railway). The Ankaray heads to either Aşti (where the bus station is based) or Dikimevi in the east. Tickets (1.30YTL one way) can be bought from the ticket offices inside the station. In the summer, the metro stops running at midnight and in the winter it terminates at 11pm.

Accommodation

Most of the **cheaper hotels** are in the streets east of Atatürk Bulvarı between Ulus and Opera Meydanı; there are a few more upmarket places north of Ulus, on and around Çankırı Caddesi, and further options banded along Gazi Mustafa Kemal Bulvarı in Maltepe and on Atatürk Bulvarı south of Kızılay, with prices increasing as you move south.
Devran Sanayi Cad, Tavus Sok 8, Ulus ⓣ0312/311 0485. Best value of the cheaper choices with bright, clean en-suite rooms with TV. ❷
Güleryüz Sanayı Cad 37, Ulus ⓣ0312/310 4910. Dated 1970s decor, rooms with TV and en suites of questionable cleanliness. ❸
Hisar Hisarpark Cad 6, Ulus ⓣ0312/311 9889. Small hotel with no elevator. Rooms lack en-suites but contain awkwardly placed shower cubicles inside. ❷
Kale Anafartalar Cad, Alataş Sok 13, Ulus ⓣ0312/311 3393. Slightly dark, basic en-suite rooms with TV. Breakfast included. ❺
Mithat Itfaiye Meydanı, Tavus Sok 2, Ulus ⓣ0312/311 5410, ⓦwww.otelmithat.com.tr. Professionally run, offering singles and doubles with bathrooms, TV, breakfast and plenty of hot water. ❷–❹

Eating

Standard *pide* and kebab places can be found on just about every street in Ankara and there's an abundance of good sweet and **cake shops**. Ulus, particularly along Çankırı Caddesi, is the place to look for cheap lunchtime venues, although most **night-time eating and drinking** takes place in the modern centre around Kızılay, where Sakarya, Selanik and Bayindir *sokaks* harbour a range of possibilities. Or try south in the well-heeled district of Kavaklıdere, particularly Tunali Hilmi and Bestekar *sokaks*. Further south still is upmarket Çankaye.

Cafés

Cemilzâde Ankara Kalesi, Kapidaği Sok 1/A. Converted cabin café in the city walls of the Hisar. Good for weekend breakfasts, *gözlemes* and kebabs. Breakfast 9YTL.
Kiler Inkilap Mah Anafartalar Cad 5-3, Ulus. (Inside Şehir Çarşisi). Diner-style café with bargain meals. Most expensive dish is 7YTL. Pizza 5YTL.

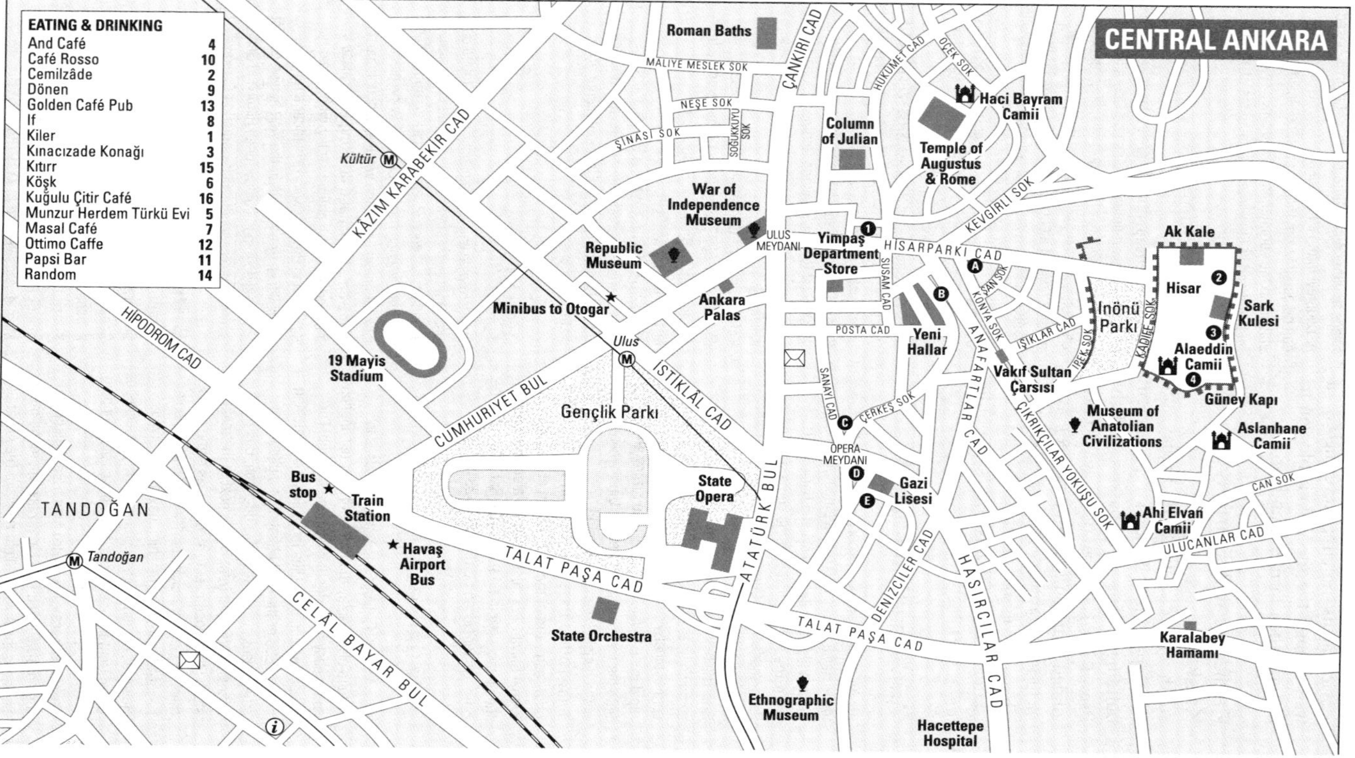
CENTRAL ANKARA
EATING & DRINKING
And Café 4
Café Rosso 10
Cemilzâde 2
Dönen 9
Golden Café Pub 13
If 8
Kiler 1
Kınacızade Konağı 3
Kıtırr 15
Köşk 6
Kuğulu Çitir Café 16
Munzur Herdem Türkü Evi 5
Masal Café 7
Ottimo Caffe 12
Papsi Bar 11
Random 14
Roman Baths
Çankırı Cad
Maliye Meslek Sok
Neşe Sok
Şinası Sok
Soğukkuyu Sok
Hükümet Cad
Oçek Sok
Haci Bayram Camii
Column of Julian
Temple of Augustus & Rome
Kevgirli Sok
Kültür
Kâzım Karabekir Cad
War of Independence Museum
Ulus Meydanı
Yimpaş Department Store
Hisarparkı Cad
Ak Kale
Hisar
Sark Kulesi
Republic Museum
Ankara Palas
Susam Cad
San Sok
Konya Sok
Işıklar Cad
İnönü Parkı
Kadife Sok
İpek Sok
Alaeddin Camii
Güney Kapı
Minibus to Otogar
Posta Cad
Yeni Hallar
Vakıf Sultan Çarsısı
Hipodrom Cad
Ulus
19 Mayis Stadium
İstiklâl Cad
Anafartlar Cad
Sanayi Cad
Çerkeş Sok
Cumhuriyet Bul
Gençlik Parkı
Çıkrıkçılar Yokuşu Sok
Museum of Anatolian Civilizations
Aslanhane Camii
Opera Meydanı
Bus stop
Train Station
State Opera
Gazi Lisesi
Can Sok
Tandoğan
Atatürk Bul
Ahi Elvan Camii
Ulucanlar Cad
Havaş Airport Bus
Talat Paşa Cad
Denizciler Cad
Hasırcılar Cad
Celâl Bayar Bul
State Orchestra
Karalabey Hamamı
Ethnographic Museum
Hacettepe Hospital

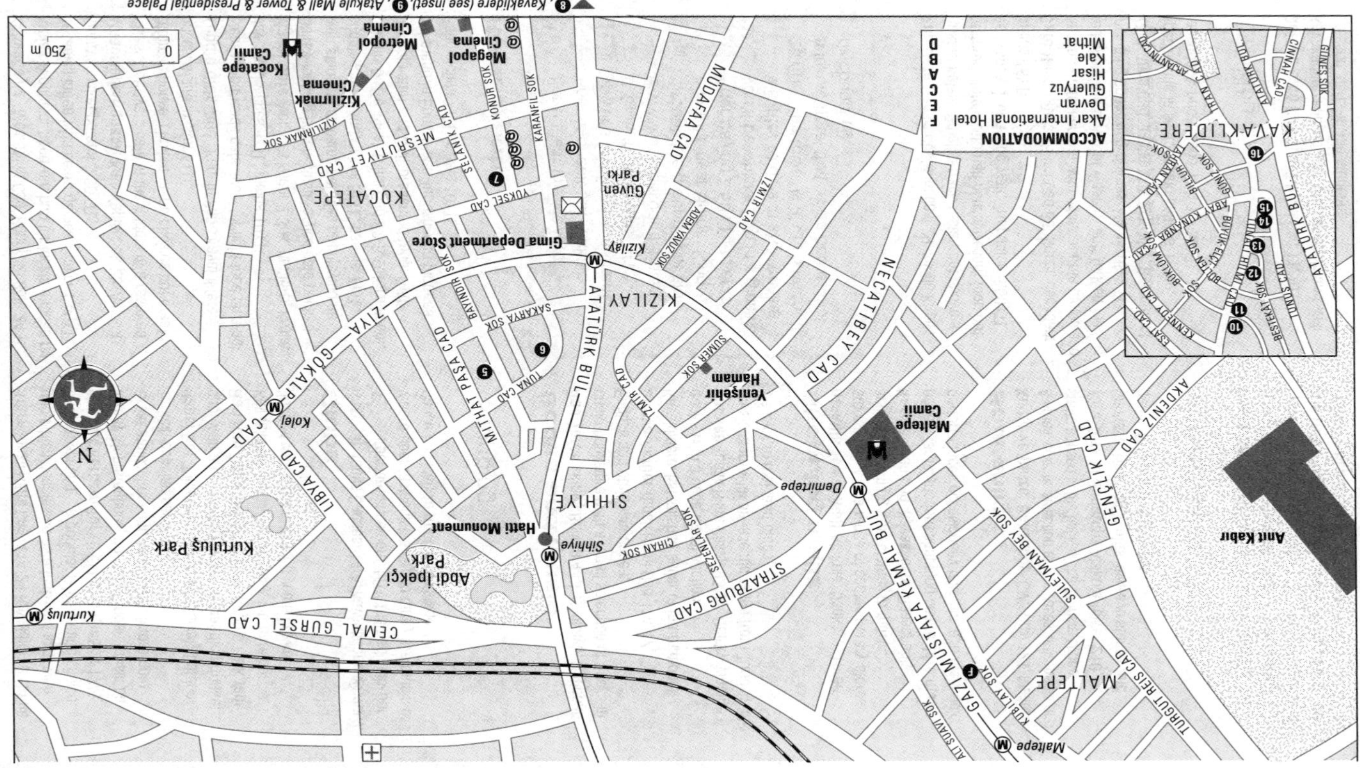
8, Kavaklidere (see inset), 9, Atakule Mall & Tower & Presidential Palace
ACCOMMODATION
Akar International Hotel F
Devran E
Güleryüz C
Hisar A
Kale B
Mithat D
0
250 m
N
Kocatepe Camii
Kizilirmak Cinema
Metropol Cinema
Megapol Cinema
KOCATEPE
MESRUTIYET CAD
KIZILIRMAK SOK
SELANIK CAD
KONUR SOK
KARANFIL SOK
YÜKSEL CAD
Güven Parkı
MUDAFAA CAD
Gima Department Store
Kizilay
KIZILAY
ADEM YAVUZ SOK
IZMIR CAD
NECATIBEY CAD
ZIYA GÖKALP CAD
Kolej
BAYINDIR SOK
SAKARYA SOK
TUNA CAD
MITHAT PAŞA CAD
ATATÜRK BUL
SUMER SOK
Yenişehir Hamam
Maltepe Camii
LIBYA CAD
Kurtuluş Park
Hatti Monument
SIHHIYE
Sihhiye
Demirtepe
Abdi İpekçi Park
CIHAN SOK
SEZENLAR SOK
STRAZBURG CAD
Kurtuluş
CEMAL GÜRSEL CAD
GAZI MUSTAFA KEMAL BUL
SULEYMAN BEY SOK
GENÇLIK CAD
AKDENIZ CAD
Anıt Kabir
MALTEPE
TURGUT REIS CAD
KUBILAY SOK
ALI SUAVI SOK
Maltepe
KAVAKLIDERE
ATATÜRK BUL
CINNAH CAD
GÜNEŞ SOK
IRAN CAD
ARJANTIN CAD
BILLUR SOK
GÜNIZ SOK
ABAY KUNANBAY CAD
BÜYUK ELÇI SOK
BÜKLÜM SOK
BÜLTEN SOK
TUNALI HILMI CAD
TUNUS CAD
BESTEKÂR SOK
KENNEDY CAD
ESAT CAD

Kahvedeyiz Meşrutiyet Cad, Konur (2) Sok, 24/B, Kızılay. A popular hang-out hub for locals enticed by its tables laden with board games. Panini 1.50YTL, *kumpir* (jacket potato) 3.50YTL.
Kınacızade Konağı Kale Kapısı Sok 28, Ankara Kalesi. Courtyard café in the middle of a restored Ottoman house. Limited menu choices but great prices. *Manti* (pasta) 4YTL.
Kuğulu Çitir Café Kuğulu Park, Kavaklidere. Pleasant parkside café. Ideal for light food on a hot day. Sandwiches 4YTL, mains 10YTL.
Masal Café Alopaket Konur 2 Sok, no.36/B, Kızılay. Quirky-looking beach-shack-styled café packed with students smoking nargiles or enjoying its simple food. Sandwiches 5YTL, nargile 7YTL.
Ottimo Caffe Tunalı Hilmi Cad 82-B/9, Kavalıdere. Amiable staff and well-presented food. Fold-out menu in English and Turkish with pictures. Sandwiches 7YTL, mains 10YTL.

Restaurants

TREAT YOURSELF

For unbeatable views of Ankara check out Atakule Tower's revolving restaurant, **Dönen** (Ⓣ0312/440 7412, Ⓦwww.atakule.com). Enter through the ground floor side entrance near Burger King. After paying 2.50YTL to enter, you'll be whisked up in a glass elevator to dine in style (mains 25YTL). The tower is also home to a luxury hotel that offers occasional discounts (❼–❽)

And Café Demirfırka Mahallesi 29, İçkale Kapısı, Ankara Kalesi. Small terrace restaurant above a restored stately Ottoman house. Decent food but be prepared for a long wait. Fruit Juice 5.50YTL, mains 15YTL.
Café Rosso Tunalı Hilmi Cad 66. Small, decadent restaurant decked out with white marble tables and red chandeliers. Mix of Western and Turkish food including appetizing *dolmas*. Mains 16–25YTL.
Kösk Tuna Cad, Inkılap Sok 2, Kızılay. Restaurant specializing in seafood and kebabs. Fresh, reasonably priced food. Fish 15–30YTL.

Drinking

Golden Café Pub Tunalı Hilmi Cad 112/D, Kavaklıdere. Packed with professionals and well dressed, darts-loving students.
Kıtırr Tunalı Hilmi Cad, 114/24 Kavaklıdere. Small pub which doubles up as a fast-food joint with outdoor seating – a popular late evening choice.
Munzur Herdem Türkü Evi Bayındır Sok 17/5, Kızılay. Unpretentious, no-frills Turkish music bar. Great atmosphere and music with impromptu Turkish dancing sessions.
Papsi Bar Tunalı Hilmi Cad 68/C. Lively outdoor spot with an accordion player serenading drinkers.
Random Tunalı Hilmi Cad 114, Kuğulu Park Yanı, Kavaklıdere (below *Kıtırr*). Busy, intimate bar flooded with a good-looking youth crowd.

Clubs

If Tunus Caddesi 14/A, Kavaklıdere. Ⓦwww.ifperformance.com. MTV-themed club-bar where über fashionistas bop to funky live music or dance manickly in front of the stage.

Shopping

Books and music

Ada Turan Güneş Bulvarı 44B, Çankaya. National chain bookstore with a small selection of books in English and other languages.
Dünya Aktüel Tunalı Hilmi Cad 114/17, Kavaklıdere. Established seller of international books with a good travel section.
Shades Tunalı Hilmi Pasaji 95/37. Quirky, vintage music store with an eclectic range from Turkish folk classics to rock and blues.

Shopping malls

Atakule Tower Mall Atakule, Çankaya. Three-storey mall with a range of contemporary stores selling everything from clothes to music.
Karum Iran Cad, Kavaklıdere. Reasonably priced, large, modern shopping centre. Live music performances occasionally take place in the week.

Souvenirs

Kültür ve Turizm Bakanlığı GMK Bulv 121, Maltepe. A small, eclectic selection of fine vases, ornaments and crafts housed in the back of the Tourism Office.
Yöre Türk El Sanatları Atakule Tower 210, Çankaya. Handmade gifts, evil-eye stones and gems. Prices are negotiable.

Entertainment

Opera House Ankara's citizens are proud of the Opera House at Opera Meydanı, which is great value: admission is usually 17YTL or under for lively and well-attended performances of works such as *Madame Butterfly* and *La Bohème*.

19 Mayis Stadyumu Gazi Mustafa Kemal Bulvarı. Large sports stadium hosting an array of matches and home to Gençlerbirliği, Ankaragücü and Ankaraspor football teams. See ⓦ www.biletix.com for tickets.
Anadolu Gösteri Kongre Merkezi Türkocağl Cad Balgat. Large performance hall for theatre or music concerts. See ⓦ www.biletix.com for tickets.

Directory

Embassies Australia, Nenehatun Cad 83, Gaziosmanpaşa ⓣ 0312/459 9500; Canada, Cinnah Cad 58, Çankaya ⓣ 0312/409 2700; New Zealand, Iran Cad 13/4, Kavaklıdere ⓣ 0312/467 9054; UK, Şehit Ersan Cad 46a, Çankaya ⓣ 0312/468 6230; US, Atatürk Bul 110, Kavaklıdere ⓣ 0312/455 5555.
Hamam Karacabey Hamami, Talat Paşa Bul 101 (men 6am–11pm; women 7am–7pm; from 15YTL).
Hospital Hacettepe University Medical Faculty, west of Hasırcılar Sok, Sıhhıye ⓣ 0312/305 5000.
Internet *Intek Internet Café*, Karanfil Sok 47a, Kızılay; *Internet Café*, next to PTT, Maltepe.
Left luggage At the bus and train stations.
Post office Merkez Postahane, on Atatürk Bulvarı, Ulus.

Moving on

Train İzmir (2 daily; 10hr).
Bus/dolmuş Antalya (12 daily; 10hr); Bodrum (10 daily; 10hr); Bursa (hourly; 7hr); Fethiye (2 daily; 12hr); İstanbul (every 30min; 7hr); İzmir (hourly; 8hr); Konya (14 daily; 3hr 30min); Marmaris (14 daily; 13hr); Nevşehir (12 daily; 4hr 30min).

CAPPADOCIA

A land created by the complex interaction of natural and human forces over vast spans of time, **CAPPADOCIA**, around 150km southeast of Ankara, is initially a disturbing place, the great expanses of bizarrely eroded volcanic rock giving an impression of barrenness. It is in fact an exceedingly fertile region, and one whose weird formations of soft, dusty rock have been adapted over centuries by many cultures, from Hittites to later Christians hiding away from Arab marauders. The region is over 15,000 square miles and encompasses dozens of small towns dotted around its unearthly-looking domain. Popular with both budget travellers and high spenders, Cappadocia scores highly on value for money thanks to the wide selection of competitively priced accommodation, restaurants and activities on offer. The small town of Göreme is the favourite base for most visitors, and the town has its own bus station which links to the region's central bus terminal in Nevşehir and intercity buses.

GÖREME

The small town of **GÖREME** is the best known of the few remaining Cappadocian villages whose rock-cut houses and fairy chimneys are still inhabited. In the last few years these ancient living quarters have slowly been destroyed by development, which has led to a "Save Göreme" campaign. However, it is still possible to get away from what is now essentially a holiday village, and the tufa landscapes are just a short stroll away.

What to see and do

There are two churches in the hills above the village, the **Durmuş kadir kilisesi**, clearly visible across the vineyard next to a cave-house with rock-cut steps, and the double-domed **Karşıbucak yusuf koç kilisesi**, which houses frescoes in very good condition. About 2km outside the village, the **Göreme Open-Air Museum** (daily 8am–5/6pm; 12YTL) is the site of over thirty other churches, mainly dating from the ninth to the end of the eleventh century and containing some of the best of all the frescoes in Cappadocia. The best-preserved church is the **Tokalı kilise** (5YTL extra), located away from the others on the opposite side of the road, about 50m back towards the village. It's in fact two churches, both frescoed: an old church, dating from 920 AD, and a new church, whose frescoes represent some of the finest examples of tenth-century Byzantine art. The most famous of the churches in the main complex are the **Elmalı kilise**, the **Karanlık kilise**, whose frescoes have

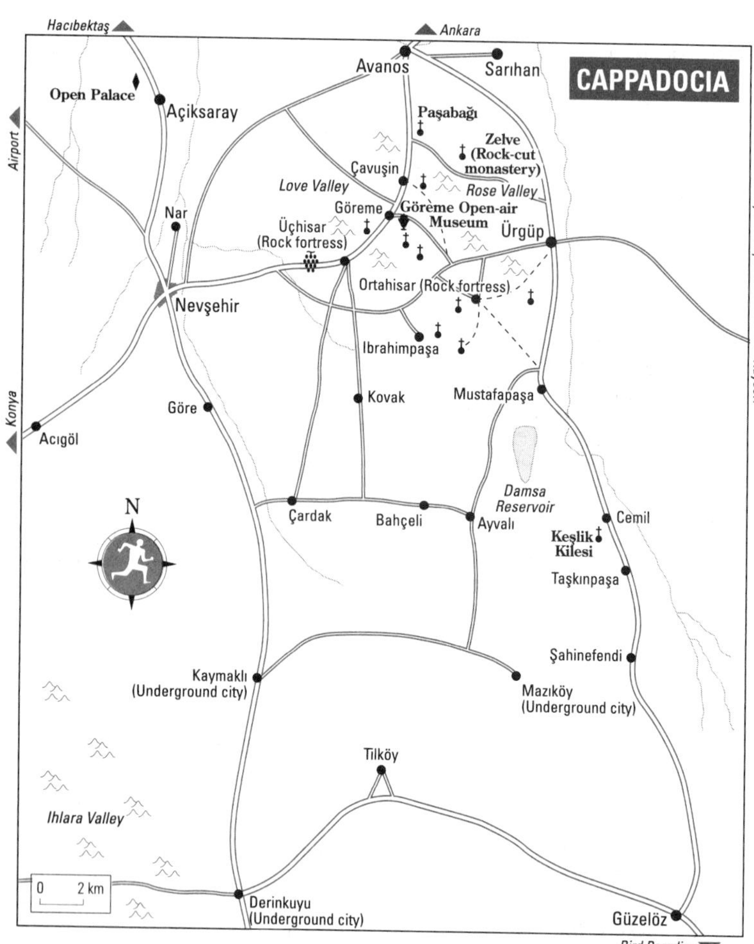

recently been restored, and the **Carıklı kilise** – all eleventh-century churches heavily influenced by Byzantine forms and painted with superb skill. Look, too, at the church of **St Barbara**, named after the depiction of the saint on the north wall.

Arrival and information

Bus When buying your bus ticket to Göreme be sure to check the end destination. Direct services arrive at the Göreme bus station, located in front of Müze Cad, in the centre of town. However, some firms will drop you off in Nevşehir, from where you'll have to continue by local bus or *dolmuş* (the last of which leaves Nevşehir at about 6pm).

Tourist office (daily 5am–9pm) in the bus station has a useful accommodation list and maps of the local area.

Tours There are various travel agencies based in Göreme which offer tours of Cappadocia. Nomad Travel (☎0384/271 2767) and Otuken Travel (Gaferli Mah Müze Cad 24/b) run tours of both the north (to areas such as Avanos, Çavuşin and Zelve) and the south of the region (50YTL). This is a great way to visit areas which are difficult to access via public transport such as Ihlara Valley. Tours can also be booked through most hotels and pensions.

Accommodation

Cave hotels are the most popular form of accommodation in Göreme, and great budget options are dotted around the area close to the bus

TREAT YOURSELF

For a breathtaking perspective on Cappadocia's geological wonderland you could splash out on a **hot-air-balloon ride**: Göreme Balloons (Ⓣ0384/341 5662, Ⓦwww.goremeballoons.com) has offices in Göreme and Ürgüp and fly every morning between April and November. Classic flights last 1 hour and 45 minutes (€210) and budget flights last 45 minutes (€150). Try to book well in advance as flights are occasionally cancelled due to poor weather.

station and further out on the road leading south out of town. Some of them can be tricky to find but the accommodation office at the bus station will arrange free pick-ups.

Backpacker's Cave Hostel Ⓣ0384/271 2258. Slightly dank and dark cave rooms but with quirky layouts. Wide selection of budget rooms. Dorms ❶, doubles ❷

Köse Pansion Ⓣ0384/271 2294. Large, homely *pansiyon* with swimming pool. Dorm rooms are comfortable with a maximum of four to a room. Breakfast extra. Dorms ❶, doubles ❶–❷

Panoramic Ⓣ0384/271 2040, Ⓦwww.panoramiccave.com. Located at the top of the valley near to the peaks of the fairy chimneys, this cave hotel has commanding views from its terrace. Cave rooms are large and creatively decorated with local textiles. Dorms ❶, doubles ❷

Shoestring Ⓣ0384/271 2450, Ⓦwww.shoestringcave.com. Spacious rooms fitted with plush, top-quality en suites. Comfortable dorm rooms, top floor swimming pool and helpful staff. Dorms ❶, doubles ❷

Eating and drinking

Several restaurants and bars can be found on Müze Cad, located behind the bus station.

Alaturca Müze Caddesi Ⓦwww.alaturcagoreme.com. Fine-dining restaurant ideal for an evening treat. Staff are attentive and recommend the delicious grilled meat dishes, crêpes or soup. Mains 20YTL.

Café Meeting Point Müze Cad 34. Snug and intimate café open till late. Serves drinks, light food and nargiles. Toasted sandwich 5YTL.

Flintstones Bar Müze Caddesi. Local hub for low-key nocturnal entertainment.

Hazan Türkü Evi Müze Yolu Üzeri. Live Turkish music in a classic, tavern-style bar.

Mercan Restaurant Ⓣ0384/271 2476. Family-run restaurant where portions are generously heaped onto the plate. Chef specials vary each day but highlights include *köfte* and juicy kebabs. Mains 7YTL.

Pacha Bar Müze Caddesi. Cheesy music bar but a good atmosphere for mingling with locals and tourists alike.

Moving on

Bus/dolmuş Ankara (6 hr); Konya (4 daily; 3hr).

DERINKUYU AND KAYMAKLI

Among the most extraordinary phenomena of the Cappadocia region are the remains of a number of **underground settlements**, some of them large enough to have accommodated up to 30,000 people. The cities are thought to date back to Hittite times, though the complexes were later enlarged by Christian communities, who added missionary schools, churches and wine cellars. A total of forty such settlements have been discovered, and the most thoroughly excavated is **DERINKUYU** (daily 8am–5.30pm; 10YTL), 29km from Nevşehir and accessible by *dolmuş*. The city is well lit, and the original ventilation system still functions remarkably well, though some of the passages are small and cramped. The excavated area (only a quarter of the total) consists of eight floors and includes stables, wine presses and a dining hall or schoolroom with two long, rock-cut tables, plus living quarters, churches, armouries, a cruciform church, meeting hall and dungeon. Some 10km north of Derinkuyu is **KAYMAKLI** (daily 8am–5.30pm; 10YTL), where only five of its underground levels have been excavated to date. The layout is very similar to Derinkuyu, with networks of streets and small living spaces leading off into underground plazas with various functions, the more obvious of which are stables, smoke-blackened kitchens, storage spaces and wine presses.

KONYA

Roughly midway between Antalya and Nevşehir, **KONYA** is a place of pilgrimage for the Muslim world – the home of Celalledin Rumi or the **Mevlâna** ("Our Master"), the mystic who founded the Mevlevî or **Whirling Dervish** sect, and the centre of **Sufic** mystical practice and teaching. It was also a capital during the Selçuk era, many of the buildings from which are still standing, along with examples of their highly distinctive crafts and applied arts, now on display in Konya's museums.

What to see and do

The Mevlâna Museum

The **Mevlâna** Museum (daily 10am–5pm; 4YTL) is housed in the first lodge (*tekke*) of the Mevlevî dervish sect, at the eastern end of Mevlâna Bulvarı, easily recognizable by its distinctive fluted turquoise dome. The main building of the museum holds the mausoleum containing the tombs of the Mevlâna, his father and other notables – as with mosques, shoes must be left at the door, women must cover their heads, and whether you're male or female, if you're wearing shorts you'll be given a skirt-like garment to cover your legs. You can take photographs of the mausoleum, but remember to be respectful; it is an extremely holy site. The original *semahane* (ceremonial hall) exhibits some of the musical instruments of the first dervishes, the original illuminated poetical work of the Mevlâna, and a 500-year-old silk carpet from Selçuk Persia that is supposedly the finest ever woven. In the adjoining room, a casket containing hairs from the beard of the Prophet Muhammad is displayed alongside illuminated medieval Korans.

Karatay Tile Museum

Built by Emir Celaleddin Karatay in the thirteenth century, the interior of the **Karatay Tile Museum** (Atatürk Cad, Mon-Sat 8.30am-12pm & 1.30-5.30pm; 2YTL) is equally as fascinating as the ceramics on show. The beautifully decorated domed central ceiling and ornamental green tiles are reminiscent of the interior of a mosque and are testament to the building's original use as a centre for Islamic studies.

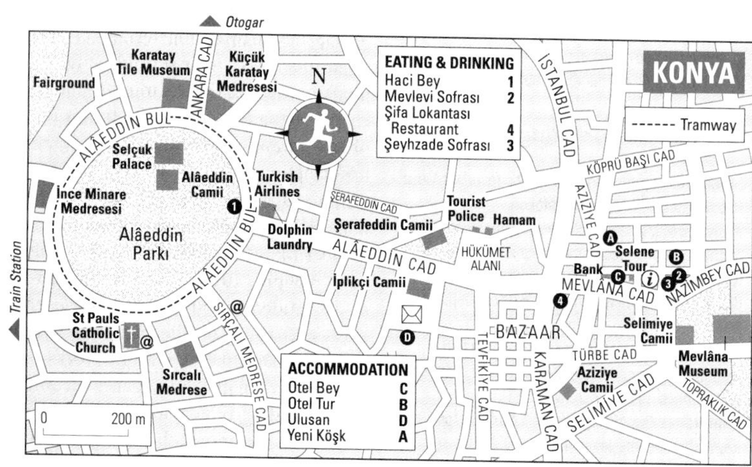

WHIRLING DERVISH CEREMONY

This meditational ceremony, where worshippers spin around to draw closer to God, is held at the Mevlâna Cultural Centre close to the museum. The ceremony is free and takes place every Saturday night. Tickets can be booked through most hotels or the tourist information office. Alternatively, Selene Travel Agency organizes private viewings of the ceremony from June to August. Performances take place on Monday, Wednesday and Friday at 8.30pm and cost 25YTL.

Arrival and information

Bus Konya's bus station is 10km out of town, from where the Konak *dolmuş* and tramway connects with the town centre; the train station is 2km out of the centre at the far end of Istasyon Caddesi, connected to the centre by regular *dolmuşes*.
Tourist office Mevlâna Cad 21 (Mon–Fri 8am–5.30pm; ⓣ0332/351 1074).
Travel agent The city's only travel agent is Selene Tours (Avanbey Sok 22 ⓣ02332/353 6745, ⓦwww.selene.com.tr) which specializes in trips to Beyşehir, known for its natural beauty and Hittite monuments, and "village life" tours enabling you to experience life and work in a traditional village.
Internet Internet cafés can be found on Mimar Muzaffer Cad near to St Paul's Catholic church and at the corner next to Sirçali Medresse Cad.

Accommodation

Otel Tur Esarizade Sok 13 ⓣ0332/351 9825. Quiet YMCA-style hotel. Rooms with TV. Breakfast extra. ❷–❸
Ulusan Kurşuncular Sok 4 ⓣ0332/351 5004. Spotlessly clean – by far the best out of the budget options. Free Internet access and breakfast included. ❷
Yeni Köşk Kadılar Sok 28 ⓣ0332/352 0671. Reasonably large en-suite rooms but the decor is in need of an update. ❸–❹

Eating and drinking

Konya has a rather pious atmosphere with a limited selection of restaurants and no reputable bars or pubs. The nightlife scene is underground and few women venture out at night alone.
Haci Bey Alâeddin Camii, Alâeddin Cad. Pleasant park café. A family favourite for sundaes and ice creams. Mains 7YTL.
Mevlevi Sofrası Nazimbey Cad no1/A. Great choice for enjoying tasty kebabs, *Et Sote* (lamb with vegetables) and salads whilst admiring the impressive views of the museum garden. A photo menu in Turkish and English is available. Mains 7YTL.
Şifa Lokantası Mevlâna Cad 29. Diner with a buffet of *dolmas* and stewed and baked meat dishes served with an abundance of rice and *pides*. Mains 7–12YTL.
Şeyhzade Sofrası Mevlâna Cad. Traditional restaurant with views over the square and the mosque from the terrace. Mains 10YTL.

Moving on

Bus/dolmuş Antalya (6hr); Nevşehir (4hr).

KILISTRA

Situated 45km outside of Konya, the ancient city of **KILISTRA** has an important place in early Christian history. Acknowledged as a site visited by St Paul during his tour of Anatolia, its environs still retain evidence of an early Christian community with small chapels embedded deep within the rock and hidden cave dwellings all testament to their furtive existence. Unfortunately, the site is much neglected, without a walkway or information plaque in sight. Also, the surrounding terrain is laden with thistles, so wear sensible shoes. As no buses travel the 45-minute journey from Konya to Kilistra, the trip is only worth taking with a group. The tourist information office in Konya can arrange round-trip taxi rides to the site for 70YTL. Alternatively, a car can be hired from VIP car rental (ⓣ0332/237 0827) for the same price. Drive south of Konya on the Hatunsaray Road for 34km and then turn onto the Asphalt Road and 15km later you will reach the site.

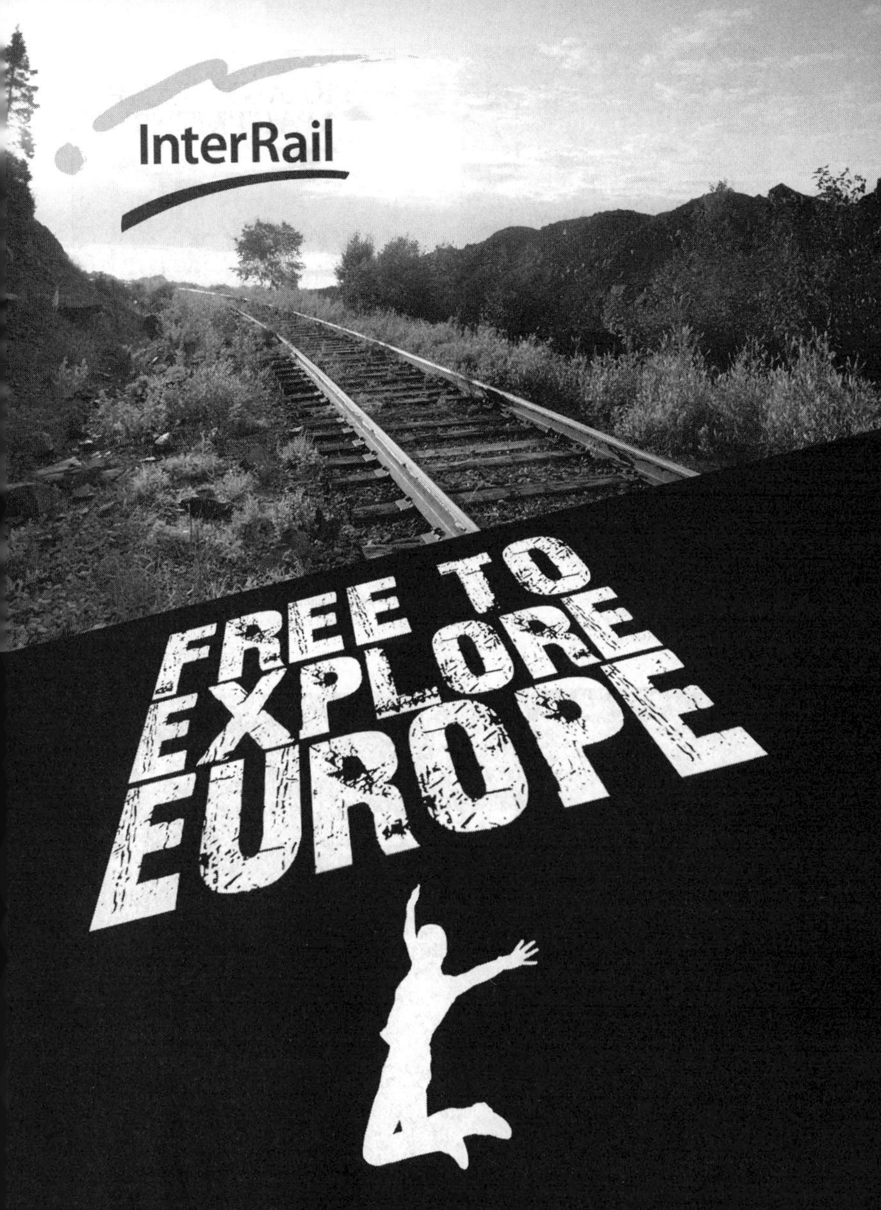
InterRail
FREE TO
EXPLORE
EUROPE

Small print and

Index

A Rough Guide to Rough Guides

Published in 1982, the first Rough Guide – to Greece – was a student scheme that became a publishing phenomenon. Mark Ellingham, a recent graduate in English from Bristol University, had been travelling in Greece the previous summer and couldn't find the right guidebook. With a small group of friends he wrote his own guide, combining a highly contemporary, journalistic style with a thoroughly practical approach to travellers' needs.

The immediate success of the book spawned a series that rapidly covered dozens of destinations. And, in addition to impecunious backpackers, Rough Guides soon acquired a much broader and older readership that relished the guides' wit and inquisitiveness as much as their enthusiastic, critical approach and value-for-money ethos.

These days, Rough Guides include recommendations from shoestring to luxury and cover more than 200 destinations around the globe, including almost every country in the Americas and Europe, more than half of Africa and most of Asia and Australasia. Our ever-growing team of authors and photographers is spread all over the world, particularly in Europe, the USA and Australia.

In the early 1990s, Rough Guides branched out of travel, with the publication of Rough Guides to World Music, Classical Music and the Internet. All three have become benchmark titles in their fields, spearheading the publication of a wide range of books under the Rough Guide name.

Including the travel series, Rough Guides now number more than 350 titles, covering: phrasebooks, waterproof maps, music guides from Opera to Heavy Metal, reference works as diverse as Conspiracy Theories and Shakespeare, and popular culture books from iPods to Poker. Rough Guides also produce a series of more than 120 World Music CDs in partnership with World Music Network.

Visit www.roughguides.com to see our latest publications.

Rough Guide travel images are available for commercial licensing at www.roughguidespictures.com

Rough Guide credits

Text editor: Andy Turner
Layout: Dan May
Cartography: Maxine Repath, Katie Lloyd-Jones, Ed Wright
Picture editor: Sarah Cummins
Production: Rebecca Short
Proofreading: Stewart Wild, Wendy Smith, Karen Parker
Cover design: Chloë Roberts
Editorial: **London** Claire Saunders, Ruth Blackmore, Alison Murchie, Karoline Densley, Andy Turner, Keith Drew, Edward Aves, Alice Park, Lucy White, Jo Kirby, James Smart, Natasha Foges, Róisín Cameron, Emma Traynor, Emma Gibbs, Kathryn Lane, Christina Valhouli, Joe Staines, Peter Buckley, Matthew Milton, Tracy Hopkins, Ruth Tidball; **New York** Andrew Rosenberg, Steven Horak, AnneLise Sorensen, April Isaacs, Ella Steim, Anna Owens, Sean Mahoney; **Delhi** Madhavi Singh, Karen D'Souza
Design & Pictures: **London** Scott Stickland, Dan May, Diana Jarvis, Mark Thomas, Chloë Roberts, Nicole Newman, Sarah Cummins, Emily Taylor; **Delhi** Umesh Aggarwal, Ajay Verma, Jessica Subramanian, Ankur Guha, Pradeep Thapliyal, Sachin Tanwar, Anita Singh, Nikhil Agarwal
Production: Rebecca Short, Vicky Baldwin
Cartography: **London** Maxine Repath, Ed Wright, Katie Lloyd-Jones; **Delhi** Jai Prakash Mishra, Rajesh Chhibber, Ashutosh Bharti, Rajesh Mishra, Animesh Pathak, Jasbir Sandhu, Karobi Gogoi, Amod Singh, Alakananda Bhattacharya, Swati Handoo
Online: Narender Kumar, Rakesh Kumar, Amit Verma, Rahul Kumar, Ganesh Sharma, Debojit Borah, Saurabh Sati
Marketing & Publicity: **London** Liz Statham, Niki Hanmer, Louise Maher, Jess Carter, Vanessa Godden, Vivienne Watton, Anna Paynton, Rachel Sprackett; **New York** Geoff Colquitt, Megan Kennedy, Katy Ball; **Delhi** Ragini Govind
Manager India: Punita Singh
Reference Director: Andrew Lockett
Publishing Coordinator: Helen Phillips
Publishing Director: Martin Dunford
Commercial Manager: Gino Magnotta
Managing Director: John Duhigg

Publishing information

This first edition published March 2008 by
Rough Guides Ltd,
80 Strand, London WC2R 0RL
345 Hudson St, 4th Floor,
New York, NY 10014, USA
14 Local Shopping Centre, Panchsheel Park,
New Delhi 110017, India
Distributed by the Penguin Group
Penguin Books Ltd,
80 Strand, London WC2R 0RL
Penguin Group (USA)
375 Hudson Street, NY 10014, USA
Penguin Group (Australia)
250 Camberwell Road, Camberwell,
Victoria 3124, Australia
Penguin Books Canada Ltd,
10 Alcorn Avenue, Toronto, Ontario,
Canada M4V 1E4
Penguin Group (NZ)
67 Apollo Drive, Mairangi Bay, Auckland 1310,
New Zealand
Cover concept by Peter Dyer.

Typeset in Minion, DIN and Helvetica to an original design by Henry Iles, Diana Jarvis and Dan May

Printed in Italy by LegoPrint S.p.A

1280pp includes index

A catalogue record for this book is available from the British Library

ISBN: 978-1-84353-994-0

The publishers and authors have done their best to ensure the accuracy and currency of all the information in **The Rough Guide to Europe on a Budget**, however, they can accept no responsibility for any loss, injury, or inconvenience sustained by any traveller as a result of information or advice contained in the guide.

1 3 5 7 9 8 6 4 2

Help us update

We've gone to a lot of effort to ensure that the 1st edition of **The Rough Guide to Europe on a Budget** is accurate and up to date. However, things change – places get "discovered", opening hours are notoriously fickle, restaurants and rooms raise prices or lower standards. If you feel we've got it wrong or left something out, we'd like to know, and if you can remember the address, the price, the hours, the phone number, so much the better.

Please send your comments with the subject line "**Rough Guide to Europe on a Budget Update**" to ⓔmail@roughguides.com. We'll credit all contributions and send a copy of the next edition (or any other Rough Guide if you prefer) for the very best emails.

Have your questions answered and tell others about your trip at ⓦcommunity.roughguides.com

Acknowledgements

Thanks to all the writers who updated this edition: Sophie Barling (Ireland), Tim Burford (Romania), Lucy Cowan (Spain), Ella Davies (Switzerland & Lichtenstein), Donald Eastwood (France), Sarah Eno (Basics), Chris Fitzgerald (Morocco), Natasha Foges (Italy), Hannah Forbes Black (Finland, Norway & Sweden), Anya Goldstein (Germany), Alex Gladwell (Britain), Victoria Hall (Bulgaria and Romania), Olivia Humphreys (Belgium & Luxembourg and The Netherlands), Mike Kielty (Poland), Anna Khmelnitski (Estonia, Latvia and Lithuania), Sophie Middlemiss (Russia), Victoria Noble (Andorra and Spain), Jane Orton (Czech Republic and Slovakia), Alex Larman (France), Emily Paine (Italy), Mark Rogers (Serbia and Slovenia), Mark Rushmore (Chronologies), Rmishka Singh (Croatia and Hungary), Kate Tolley (Greece), Andy Turner (Denmark), Kate Turner (Portugal), Ann-Marie Weaver (Turkey) and Matt Willis (Bulgaria).

Thanks also to Sarah Eno, Dan May, Jo Kirby, AnneLise Sorensen, Andrew Rosenberg, Kate Berens, Maxine Repath, Ed Wright, Katie-Lloyd Jones, Sarah Cummins and, last but not least, the London editorial team.

Photo credits

All photos © Rough Guides except the following:

Introduction

Woman canoeing in the Nord Fjord Region, Norway © Corbis
Parc Güell, Barcelona © Image State/Jupiter Images
St Pancras Station © Michael Walter/Troika
European Union flags © M.Llorden/Getty

Art and culture

The Creation of Adam by Michelangelo, Sistine Chapel, Rome © Jim Zuckerman/Corbis
The Hermitage, St Petersburg © Roland Weihrauch/dpa/Corbis
Interior of Aya Sofya, Istanbul © Atlantide Phototravel/Corbis
Production of Coriolanus at the Globe Theatre, London © Robbie Jack/Corbis
Main market square, Krakow © David Norton Photography/Alamy

Sports and activities

Naked man, Finland © Silvia Otte/Photonica/ Getty
High Tatra Mountains, Slovakia © John Warburton-Lee Photography/Alamy
Sailing, Kos © Nicholas Pitt/Alamy
Hot air balloon over Cappodocia © Ross Pictures/Jupiter images
Snowboarder, French Alps © Suzy Bennett/Alamy
Horse riding © Digital Rail Road
Whitewater rafting on the River Soca, Slovenia © James Osmond/Alamy

Festivals and events

Dancers on beach, Ibiza © Everynight Images/ Alamy
St Patricks Day © Andrew Fox/Alamy
Exit festival © Mihaela Ninic/Alamy
Running of the Bulls during the Fiesta de San Fermín © Denis Doyle/Getty
Glastonbury Festival © Timothy Allen/Axiom

Index

Map entries are in colour

A

Aachen 497
Aalborg 326
Aarhus .... *see Århus*
Aberdeen 216
Abergavenny 194
Aberystwyth 195
Aegean islands, northeastern 570
Agrigento 749
airlines
in Australia & NZ 33
in Britain 30
in Ireland 32
in North America 29
Ajaccio 446
Alcobaça 937
Alentejo coast 949
Ålesund 880
Algarve, The 947–954
Algeciras 1146
Alghero 728
Alhambra, The 1131
Alicante 1128
Alps (France) 435–438
Alps (Slovenia) 1057
Alps (Switzerland) .. 1199–1210
Alsace 402
Amalfi Coast 738
Amarante 946
Ambleside 183
Amsterdam 835–844
Amsterdam 836
Amsterdam: central 838
Anatolia 1251
Åndalsnes 879
Andalucía 1129–1147
Andalucía 1130
ANDORRA 57–72
Andorra 59
Andorra la Vella 64–65
Andorra la Vella 63–66
Anglesey 197
Ankara 1252–1257
Ankara 1254–1255
Antalya 1250
Antwerp 118–121
Antwerp 119
Aquitaine 408–413
Aran islands 641
Arctic Circle (Finland) ... 366
Arctic Circle (Norway) ... 882
Arctic Circle (Sweden) 1175
Ardennes 128
Areópoli 550
Arhéa Kórinthos 544
Århus 322–326
Århus 323
Arinsal 67
Arles 434
Arnhem 854
Arvidsjaur 1175
Assisi 722
Assos 1236
Athens 535–543
Athens 536–537
Auschwitz-Birkenau 912
AUSTRIA 73–102
Austria 75
Austvågøy 884
Avebury 162
Avignon 431–434
Avignon 432
Aya Sofya 1223

B

Bacharach 499
Bad Ischl 96
Badacsony 603
Baden-Baden 508
Bakken 317
Bâle .... *see Basel*
Balearic islands .. 1120–1124
Balearic islands 1121
Balestrand 878
Ballinskelligs 636
banks 52
Banská Štiavnica 1034
Bansko 230–235
Barcelona 1109–1120
Barcelona 1110–1111
Barcelona: Old Town . 1116
Barèges 417
Basel 1193–1195
Basque country 1092
Bastia 448
Bath 162
Bavaria 512–526
Bayeux 392
Bayonne 419
Beaune 401
Belfast 646–651
Belfast 647
BELGIUM 103–130
Belgium 105
Belgium's Provincial and Linguistic borders 109
Belgrade 1010–1016
Belgrade 1011
Berchtesgaden 525
Bergama 1237
Bergen 874–877
Bergen 875
Berlin 461–473
Berlin: Central 462–463
Berlin: Kreuzberg & Friedrichshain 470
Berlin: Mitte & Prenzlauerberg 468
Bern 1197–1199
Betws-y-Coed 196
Biarritz 417–419
Bilbao 1093
Bingen 499
Black Forest 507–510
Black Sea (Bulgaria) 239–242
Blaenau Ffestiniog 196
Bled 1054
Blue Mosque 1224
Bodensee (Austria) 101
Bodensee (Germany) 512
Bodø 883
Bodrum 1244
Bohemia 284–295
Bologna 703–705
Bom Jesus 944
Bonifacio 452
Bonn 496
Bordeaux 409
Bordeaux 409
Boulogne 390
Bovec 1058
Bowness 182
Braĉ 262
Braga 944
Bragança 947
Bran 973
Braşov 970–973
Braşov 971
Bratislava 1028–1033
Bratislava 1029
Brecon Beacons 193
Bregenz 101
Brighton 157
Brighton 156–157

INDEX

Bristol 163–165
BRITAIN 131–216
Britain 133
Brittany 394–397
Brno 295–298
Brno 296
Bruges 123–126
Bruges 124
Brugge *see Bruges*
Brussels 111–118
Brussels 112–113
Bruxelles *see Brussels*
Bucharest 962–970
Bucharest 964–965
Bucharest: central 967
Bucureşti *see Bucharest*
Budapest 592–601
Budapest 593
BULGARIA 217–242
Bulgaria 219
Bulgarian phrases 223
bulls, running of the (Pamplona) 1103
bureaux de change 52
Burgas 240
Burgundy 400–402
Burgundy vineyards 401
Bursa 1235
bus travel
- from Britain 31
- in Europe 38

C

České Budějovice 289
Český Krumlov 290
Cáceres 1086
Cadaqués 1109
Cádiz 1142
Caernarfon 197
Cágliari 725–727
Calvi 449
Camargue 435
Cambridge 174–177
Cambridge 175
camping 40
Çanakkale 1233
Canillo 70
cannabis 832
Cannes 441
Canterbury 155
Caparica 934
Cape Sounion 543
Cappadocia 1257
Cappadocia 1258
Cápri 737
Carcassonne 423
Cardiff 191–193
Cardiff 192
Carnac 395
carnivals 42
Casablanca 816–820
Casablanca 818–819
Cashel 630
Cashel, Rock of 630
Catalonia 1107–1120
Catalan phrases 62
Cēsis 766
cell phones 53
Ceuta 803
Chamonix 437
Champagne 391
Chartres 389
Chefchaouen 804
Chepstow 193
Chillon 1192
Çıralı 1249
Cinque Terre 690
Clermont-Ferrand 426
climate 8–9
climate change 30
clothes sizes 53
Cognac 408
Coimbra 936
Coleraine 651
collect calls 53
Cologne 491–496
Cologne 492
Coniston 183
contraceptives 50
Conwy 187
Copenhagen 308–317
Copenhagen 310–311
Córdoba 1135
Córdoba 1136
Corfu 574
Corinth 544
Cork 631–634
Cork 633
Cornwall 166–168
Corsica 446
Corsica 447
Corte 450
Costa Blanca 1125
Costa Brava 1108
costs 46
Côte d'Azur 438–446
Couchsurfing 40
Crete 577–583
Crete 578
Crickhowell 194
crime 46
CROATIA 243–272
Croatia 245
Croatian phrases 249
culture and etiquette 44
Curonian Spit 787
customs 50
Cyclades 558–566
Czech phrases 273
CZECH REPUBLIC 273–300
Czech Republic 275

D

Dalarna 1173
Dalí, Salvador 1108
Dalmatian Coast 258–271
Danish phrases 307
Danube river (Austria) 87
Danube river (Hungary) 600
Dartmoor 166
D-Day 393
Delft 848
Delos 561
Delphi 552
Den Haag 846–848
Den Haag 847
DENMARK 301–328
Denmark 303
Derinkuyu 1259
Derry 652–654
Derwent Water 183
Devenish island 654
dialling codes 53
Dieppe 392
Dingle 636
disabled travellers 56
Disneyland Paris 389
Dodecanese islands 566–570
Donegal 645
Doolin 638
Dordogne 408
Douro valley 946
Dover 154
Dracula, Count 973
Dragør 308
Dresden 477–481
Dresden 478
drugs 47
Dublin 620–627
Dublin 622
Dubrovnik 268–271
Dubrovnik 269
Dunquin 638
Durham 187–188
Dutch phrases 834

INDEX

E

Eden Project 166
Edinburgh 198–204
Edinburgh 200–201
Edirne 1232
Efes 1243
Eger 607
Eisenach 477
El Escorial 1081
El Serrat 69
electric current 47
Elgol 213
email 51
embassies 48
Encamp 69
Engelberg 1197
ENGLAND 138–190
Ennis 638
Enniskillen 654
Ephesus 1243
Epidaurus 546
Ercolano 735
Esbjerg 322
Essaouira 825
ESTONIA 329–348
Estonia 331
Estonian phrases 334
Etna 747
Eurail passes 36
euro 9, 52
European Health Insurance card 50
European Union 9
Évora 948
Extremadura 1086

F

Faro 950
Fátima 938
ferries
- from Britain 31
- from Ireland 31
- in Europe 38

Fes 808–809
Fes El Bali 809
Fes Ville Nouvelle 811
festivals 14, 42
Fethiye 1247
Fez *see Fes*
Fiesta of San Fermín 1103
Figueres 1108
FINLAND 349–352
Finland 351
Finnish phrases 354
Firenze *see Florence*
Fishguard 195
Fjærland 878
fjords (Norway) 874
Flakstadøya 884
Flåm 877
Flemish 109
flights
- from Australia 33
- from Britain 30
- from Canada 29
- from Ireland 32
- from NZ 33
- from the US 29

Florence 707–622
Florence 708–709
Fnideq 803
Formentera 1122
Fort William 215
FRANCE 369–452
France 371
Frankfurt 501
Frankfurt 502
Frederikshavn 322
Freiburg im Breisgau 509
French phrases 373
Funen 320–321
Füssen 524

G

Gallipoli 1234
Galway 639–641
Galway 640
Gamla Uppsala 1164
Garmisch-Partenkirchen 524
Gavernie 417
gay travellers 50
Gdańsk 902
Gdańsk 903
Geirangerfjord 879
Geliboli peninsula 1234
Geneva 1185–1189
Geneva 1186
Genoa 686–689
Genoa 687
Genova *see Genoa*
Gent *see Ghent*
German phrases 460
GERMANY 453–526
Germany 455
Ghent 121–123
Ghent 122
Giant's Causeway 651
Gibraltar 1146
Girona 1109
Giverny 389
Glasgow 204–209
Glasgow 206–207
Glastonbury 165
Glencolmcille 646
Golden Horn 1226
Golfe de Porto 448
Göreme 1257–1259
Gorge of Samariá 582
Górtys 580
Goslar 490
Gothenburg 1165–1168
Gothenburg 1166
Gotland 1171
Gouda 852
Granada 1130–1135
Granada 1132–1133
Graz 89–92
Graz 90
Great Plain (Hungary) 609
GREECE 527–584
Greece 529
Greek ferries 530
Greek phrases 533
Grenoble 435
Grindelwald 1202
Guaja National Park 766
Guimarães 945

H

Haarlem 844
Hadrian's Wall 190
Hague, The *see Den Haag*
Hallstatt 96
Hamburg 482–486
Hamburg 484
Haniá 582
Hannover 488–490
Harlech 195
health issues 50
Heidelberg 505
Heidelberg 506
Helsingborg 1168
Helsingør 317
Helsinki 356–361
Helsinki 357
Herculaneum 735
Hersónissos 580
Hévíz 603
HI hostels 39
Hierapolis 1246
High Tatras 1034
Hoge Veluwe 854
Hohenschwangau 524
Holyhead 195
Honningsvåg 886
hostels 39
hotels 40

INDEX

Humlebæk 317
Hungarian phrases 590
HUNGARY 585–612
Hungary 587
Hvar 263–265

I

İstanbul 1223–1231
İstanbul: City 1223
İstanbul: Old 1225
İstanbul: Sultanahmet.. 1228
İzmir 1238–1241
İzmir 1239
Ibiza 1120–1122
Ice Hotel (Sweden) 1177
Igoumenítsa 552
Inari 367
Inisheer 643
Inishmaan 642
Inishmore 642
Inlandsbanan, The 1174
Innsbruck 97–101
Innsbruck 98
insurance 51
Interlaken 1200
Internet 51
InterRail passes 34
Inverness 214
Ioánnina 554
Iona 212
Ionian islands 574
Íos 563
Iráklion 578
IRELAND 613–656
Ireland 615
Irish phrases 619
Istria 255–258
Italian phrases 663
ITALY 657–750
Italy 659
itineraries 17–25

J

Jaca 1106
Jezero 1055
Jokkmokk 1175
Jostedalsbreen 879
Jūrmala 764
Jungfrau Region 1199
Jungfrau Region 1200
Jutland 322–328

K

Kalambáka 553
Kardhamýli 550
Karlovy Vary 293
Kaş 1248
Kaunas 782–785
Kaunas 784
Kaya Köyü 1247
Kaymaklı 1259
Kecskemét 609
Kefalloniá 575
Kemeri National Park ... 764
Kérkyra .... *see Corfu*
Keswick 183
Keszthely 602
Keukenhof 846
Kilistra 1261
Kilkenny 629
Killarney 634
Kiruna 1176
Klaipėda 786
Knossós 579
Kobarid 1057
København .... *see Copenhagen*
Koblenz 499
Köln .... *see Cologne*
Konstanz 512
Konya 1260
Konya 1260
Koprivshtitsa 236–237
Korčula 266–268
Kós 568
Košice 1038–1040
Kraków 906–912
Kraków 908–909
Kristiansand 871
Kuopio 365
Kuşadası 1241
Kutná Hora 294

L

La Massana 67
La Roche-en-Ardennes 128
La Rochelle 407
Lagos 951
Lahemaa National Park.. 343
Lake Balaton 601
Lake Bohinj 1055
Lake Constance .... *see Bodensee*
Lake District (UK).. 181–184
Lake District: central ... 182
Lake Geneva 1185
Lake Luzern 1196
Land's End 167
Languedoc 420
Lapland 366
LATVIA 751–768
Latvia 753
Latvian phrases 755
Lausanne 1189
Lauterbrunnen 1202
Le Puy 427
Lecce 740
left luggage 51
Leiden 845
Leipzig 474
León 1090
lesbian travellers 50
Lésvos 571
Letoön 1247
Levoča 1036
LIECHTENSTEIN 1212
Liechtenstein 1213
Liepāja 767
Lille 390
Limerick 628
Linz 88
Lipica 1052
Lisboa .... *see Lisbon*
Lisbon 926–934
Lisbon 927
Lisbon: central 930
Lisse 846
LITHUANIA 769–790
Lithuania 771
Lithuanian phrases 774
Liverpool 179–181
Ljubljana 1047–1050
Ljubljana 1048
Llanberis 196
Locarno 1210
Loch Lomond 211
Loch Ness 215
Lofoten islands 883
Loire Valley 397–400
London 138–154
London 140–141
London: West End 148–149
Londonderry .... *see Derry*
Lourdes 417
Lübeck 486
Lucerne .... *see Luzern*
Lugano 1211
Lund 1169
LUXEMBOURG ... 128–130
Luxembourg 105
Luxembourg City 128–130
Luxembourg City 129
Luzern 1195–1197
Lycian Way 1247

INDEX

Lyon 428–431
Lyon 429

M

Maastricht 855–856
Madrid 1072–1073
Madrid 1070–1079
mail 52
Mainz 498
Málaga 1144
Malbork 905
Malbun 1212
Mália 580
Mallorca 1123–1125
Malmö 1170
Manchester 177–179
Máni peninsula 549
Mantova *see Mantua*
Mantua 685
maps 52
Mariánské Lázně 292
Maribor 1058
Maribor 1059
Marmaris 1245
Marrakesh 820–825
Marrakesh 821
Marseille 438
Marseille 439
Massif Central 426
Matera 740
Matterhorn 1203
media 41
Meissen 482
Meknes 805–704
Meknes 806
Melk 87
Mérida 1087
Meritxell 69
Merzouga 827
Metéora 553
Métsovo 554
Milan 680–685
Milan 682–683
Mittenwald 525
mobile phones 53
Mogadouro 947
Mo-i-Rana 883
Monaco 445
Monemvasiá 548
Mont Blanc 437
Mont St-Michel 392
Monte Carlo 445
Montpellier 422
Montreux 1192
Moravia 295–299
Moroccan Arabic phrases 797
MOROCCO 791–828
Morocco 793
Moscow 987–994
Moscow 988–989
Moskenes 884
Moskenesøya 884
Moskva *see Moscow*
Mount Etna 747
Mount Olympus (Greece) 558
Mull 212
München *see Munich*
Munich 518–523
Munich 519
music festivals 14, 42
Mýkonos 559–561
Mýkonos Town 560
Mycenae 545
Mykínes 545
Mystra 547

N

Náfplio 546
Namur 127
Nancy 402
Nantes 396
Naples 730–734
Naples 731
Napoli *see Naples*
Náxos 562
Nazaré 938
Neringa 787
Nesebâr 241
NETHERLANDS 829–856
Netherlands 831
Neuschwanstein 524
Newcastle-upon-Tyne 188–190
Newcastle-upon-Tyne 188
Newquay 168
newspapers 41
Nice 442–445
Nice 443
Nida 787
Nîmes 421
Niś 1019
Nordkapp 886
Normandy 392–394
Northern Lights (Norway) 885
NORWAY 857–886
Norway 859
Norwegian phrases 863
Novi Sad 1016
Nuremberg 515–517
Nuremberg 516
Nürnberg ... *see Nuremberg*

O

Odemira 949
Odense 320–321
Okehampton 166
Olhão 952
Olomouc 298
Olympia (Greece) 550
Olympos (Turkey) 1249
Olympus, Mt (Greece) 558
Oporto *see Porto*
Ordesa 1107
Ordino 67
Orléans 399
Orsa 1174
Oświęcim 912
Oslo 864–871
Oslo 866–867
Östersund 1174
Oulu 366
Oxford 169–173
Oxford 170–171

P

Padova *see Padua*
Padstow 168
Padua 693
Pal 67
Palanga 786
Palermo 742–745
Palermo 743
Palio, The 717
Palma 1123
Pamplona 1102–1104
Pamukkale 1246
Paneriai 781
Paris 376–389
Paris 378–379
Paris: central 382–383
Parma 705
Pärnu 345
Páros 562
Pas de la Casa 71
Pátmos 569
Pátra 543
Pécs 606
Peloponnese 543–551
Pembroke 194
pensions 40

INDEX

Penzance 166
Périgueux 412
Perpignan 425
Perugia 720
Phaestos 580
phones 52–54
Picos de Europa 1098
Pilsen *(see Plzeň)*
Piran 1053
Pisa 714–715
Plakiás 582
Plovdiv 232–235
Plovdiv 233
Plzeň 291
Poitiers 405
POLAND 887–918
Poland 889
police 47
Polish phrases 893
Pompeii 735
Porto Côvo 949
Porto 940–945
Porto 941
Portorož 1053
Portree 213
Portstewart 652
PORTUGAL 919–954
Portugal 921
Portuguese phrases 924
Porvoo 361
post 52
Postojna 1052
Potsdam 473
Poznań 916
Prague 280–289
Prague 280–281
Praha *see Prague*
Predjama Castle 1052
Prešov 1037
prices 46
Provence 428–435
Ptuj 1060
Pula 255
Pyrenees (France) 414–417
Pyrenees (Spain) 1102

Q

Quiberon 396
Quimper 395

R

Rabat 813–816
Rabat 814
radio 41
rail passes 34
Ramadan 43
Randstad 844–853
Rapallo 690
Râşnov 973
Ravello 739
Ravenna 706
Regensburg 517
Reims 391
Réthymnon 581
Rhine falls 1209
Rhine Gorge 498
Rhodes 566–568
Rhodes Town 567
Rīga 757–763
Rīga 760
Rīga: old 758
Ribčev Laz 1055
Rijeka 255
Rila 230
Ring of Kerry 635
Rissani 827
Riviera di Levante 689
Rock of Cashel 630
ROMANIA 955–978
Romania 957
Romanian phrases 960
Rome 665–676
Rome 666–667
Rome: central 668
Ronda 1145
Roskilde 318
Rosslare Harbour 628
Rostock 487
Rothenburg ob der Tauber 514
Rotterdam 849–852
Rotterdam 850
Rouen 393
Roussillon 420
Rovaniemi 366
Rovinj 257–258
Royal Shakespeare Company (RSC) 173
Rügen 488
Rundāle Palace 765
RUSSIA 979–1002
Russia 981
Russian phrases 985

S

Škocjan Caves 1053
Saaremaa 344
safety 46
Sahara 827
Salamanca 1088–1090
Salamanca 1089
Salaspils 765
Salisbury 161
Salzburg 92–95
Salzburg 93
Salzkammergut 95
Samarian Gorge 582
Sámos 570
San Gimignano 719
San Sebastián 1095–1097
Sandhamn 1163
Santander 1097
Santiago de Compostela 1098–1102
Santiago de Compostela 1100–1101
Santoríni 565
Sardinia 725–729
Saumur 398
Savonlinna 364
Schaffhausen 1209
Scheveningen 847
Schilthorn 1202
Schwangau 524
SCOTLAND 197–216
Scottish Highlands 215
Segovia 1084
Selçuk 1242
SERBIA 1003–1020
Serbia 1005
Serbian phrases 1008
Seville 1137–1142
Seville 1138–1139
sexual harassment 56
shoe sizes 53
shopping 54
Sibiu 975
Sicily 741–750
Siena 715–719
Siena 716
Sífnos 559
Sighişoara 973
Sigulda 765
Silves 952
Sintra 934
Siófok 601
Siracusa 747–749
Sitía 580
Skagen 327
Skópelos 572
Skýros 573

Skye.............................213
Slea Head......................637
Slieve League...............645
Sligo 644
Slovak phrases...........1027
SLOVAKIA........1021–1040
Slovakia.....................1023
Slovene phrases.........1045
SLOVENIA 1041–1062
Slovenia 1043
smoking..........................44
Snowdonia...................196
Soča valley 1056
Sofia....................224–229
Sofia 226
Sognefjord 878
Soldeu 70
Sopocani 1018
Sopot............................904
Sopron 604–606
Sorrento.......................736
Sozopol 241
SPAIN..............1063–1148
Spain 1065
Spanish phrases.........1069
Spárti 547
Spiš region 1036
Spišské hrad..............1037
Split.....................260–262
Spoleto 723
Sporades islands..........572
St Andrews...................210
St Ives..........................167
St Moritz....................1204
St Petersburg....994–1002
St Petersburg..............996
St Wolfgang 95
Staffa 213
Starý Smokovec.........1035
Stavanger 872
Stirling 209
St-Malo........................394
Stockholm.......1156–1162
Stockholm........1156–1157
Stonehenge 161
Stoúpa 550
Strasbourg 403
Strasbourg...................404
Stratford-upon-Avon 173
Studenica 1018
student discounts...........56
study........................44–46
Stuttgart 510
Su Nuraxi.....................727
Svolvær 884
SWEDEN..........1149–1178
Sweden 1151
Swedish phrases........1154
Swiss German 1184
SWITZERLAND..1179–1214
Switzerland 1181
Sýros 559
Szeged 610
Szentendre 600

T

Tallinn..................335–343
Tallinn 336–337
Tampere.......................363
Tangier................799–803
Tangier 800–801
Taormina......................745
Tarifa 1143
Tartu............................347
Tatra mountains
(Poland).....................913
Tatra mountains
(Slovakia) 1035
Tavira 953
Teelin Bay 645
TEFL 45
telephones...............52–54
temperatures 8–9
Tetouan........................804
Texel 853
The Hague.. *see Den Haag*
Thessaloníki........555–557
Thessaloníki................556
Thíra..............*see Santoríni*
Ticino 1210–1212
time zones 55
Timişoara............976–978
Tintern Abbey 193
tipping 44
Tirol....................*(see Tyrol)*
Tobermory 212
Toledo 1080–1083
Toledo 1082–1083
Tomar..........................939
Topkapı Palace..........1224
Torino...................*see Turin*
Torla...........................1107
Toruń...........................905
Toulouse 414–417
Toulouse......................415
tourist information 54
Tours 397
train passes 34
train travel.......................7
Eurail 35
from Britain 31
from Ireland.......................32
in Europe.................. 7, 34–38
InterRail 34
Trakai 781
Transylvania 970–978
Trás-os-Montes 946
travel insurance 51
travellers with disabilities..56
travellers' cheques 52
Triberg..........................509
Trier.............................499
Tromsø.........................885
Trondheim....................881
Trossachs 211
Troy............................1234
Turin 677–680
Turin 678
TURKEY...........1215–1262
Turkey........................1217
Turkish phrases 1221
Turku....................361–363
Turquoise Coast..1246–1251
Tuscany 707
TV 41
Tyrol 97

U

Ukanc 1056
Uppsala 1163
Urbino..........................724
Utrecht........................852

V

Vaduz.........................1212
Valencia 1125–1128
Valencia.....................1126
Valentia Island 636
Valkenburg...................855
Varna 239
Vatican.................671–672
Vaxholm.....................1163
Veliko Târnovo 237–239
Venezia ....*see Venice*
Venice 694–703
Venice..................696–697
Venice: central 700–701
Vergina.........................557
Verona.................691–693
Versailles......................389
Vestvågøy 884
Vesuvius 735
Vevey 1191
Vézère Valley................412
Vienna 79–87
Vienna 80–81
Vila Nova de Milfontes..949
Vila Real.......................946
Vilnius 775–781

INDEX

Vilnius....776
Vis....265
visas....47
Vitznau....1196

W

WALES....190–197
Warsaw....894–901
Warsaw....896–897
Warsaw: central....900
Waterville....636
weather....8–9
Weimar....475
Westport....643
Wexford....627
White island....654
Wien....*see Vienna*
Winchester....159
Windermere....182
women travellers....56
work....44–46
Wrocław....914–916
Würzburg....513

X

Xanthos....1247

Y

Yíthio....549
York....184–187
York....185
youth discounts....56
youth hostels....39

Z

Žiča....1018
Zărneşti....973
Zadar....258
Zagreb....250–255
Zagreb....251
Zakopane....913
Zákynthos....577
Zambujeira do Mar....949
Zaragoza....1104
Zermatt....1203
Zürich....1205–1209
Zürich....1206

INDEX

NOTES

Map symbols

maps are listed in the full index using coloured text

International boundary
Province boundary
Railway
Funicular
Cable car/lift
Motorway
Tolled motorway
Road
Pedestrianized street
Steps
Path
Ferry route
Waterway
Wall
Mountains
Peak
Rocks
Ruins
Waterfall
Fountain
Viewpoint
Lighthouse
Point of interest
Museum
Stately house
Tower
Castle
Monument
Church (region)

Synagogue
Mosque
Hospital
Post office
Information office
Telephone office
Internet access
Transport stop
Metro station
RER station
S-Bahn
Tram stop
U-Bahn
London Underground Station
Parking
Gate
Swimming pool
Statue
Airport
Building
Church (town)
Stadium
Park
Christian cemetery
Muslim cemetery
Jewish cemetery
Beach
Glacier
Forest